DOCUMENTS SUPPLEMENT TO
INTERNATIONAL ENVIRONMENTAL LAW AND WORLD ORDER
A PROBLEM–ORIENTED COURSEBOOK

Third Edition

■ ■ ■

By

Jonathan C. Carlson
Professor of Law
Victor and Carol Alvarez Fellow in Law
Director of Environmental Policy Research Program
The University of Iowa

Sir Geoffrey W.R. Palmer, P.C., K.C.M.G., A.C.
Barrister
Distinguished Fellow Victoria University of Wellington
Faculty of Law and Centre for Public Law

Burns H. Weston
Bessie Dutton Murray Distinguished Professor of Law Emeritus
Senior Scholar, UI Center for Human Rights
The University of Iowa

AMERICAN CASEBOOK SERIES®

WEST®
A Thomson Reuters business

Mat #40743606

COPYRIGHT © 1994 WEST PUBLISHING CO.
COPYRIGHT © 1999 By WEST GROUP
© 2012 Thomson Reuters
 610 Opperman Drive
 St. Paul, MN 55123
 1–800–313–9378
Printed in the United States of America

ISBN: 978–0–314–19402–2

PREFACE

This collection, like its predecessors, has been assembled to serve primarily as a documentary supplement to our coursebook *International Environmental Law and World Order—A Problem–Oriented Coursebook* (3rd ed., Thomson Reuters, 2011). Therefore, a fair number of the instruments contained in these pages (*e.g.*, Johannesburg Plan of Implementation), particularly if they are not principally environmental instruments (*e.g.*, the Helsinki Final Act, the GATT, etc.), are not reprinted in full and contain only those provisions that are pertinent to our pedagogical purposes. On the other hand, we have included as much as possible of significant environmental treaties, often including preambles and annexes. We believe that exposure of students to the complete text of these treaties is important even if only a few treaty provisions are directly pertinent to the legal issues raised in the Coursebook's problems.

In general, we have tried to be as thorough in our coverage as space would allow. To persons outside the classroom who are engaged in research or otherwise working in the international environmental law field—international civil servants and diplomats, governmental officials, non-governmental (citizen action) organizations, practicing lawyers, and others—we thus recommend this volume as a convenient quick and easy general reference.

As may be quickly ascertained from the Table of Contents, the majority of the instruments that follow are organized around the same themes to which our coursebook is dedicated, namely, the conceptually divisible components of our otherwise indivisible global environment: the atmosphere, the hydrosphere, the lithosphere, and the biosphere. The remainder—the "constitutive/organic" and the "miscellaneous"—reflect the truism that international environmental law, while clearly deserving of distinctive treatment in its own right, is nonetheless an interdependent function of the larger world order of which it is a part.

Three additional features merit special mention.

First, to help demonstrate the timing and evolution of international environmental law, we present the instruments that give partial expression to its existence in each topical area in chronological order.

Second, in Section 8, we have summarized and excerpted the leading international adjudicative and arbitral decisions in this field, several of which pre-date World War II. There are a handful of cases that are widely regarded as having helped lay the foundations of the emerging, modern-day customary international law of global environmental protection (e.g. the *Trail Smelter Arbitration,* the *Lac Lanoux Arbitration,* and the *Nuclear Test Cases*). To those cases we have added recent decisions that show the continuing development of international environmental law and that will certainly shape its future (e.g. the *Case Concerning the Gabciko-vo–Nagymaros Project,* the *Case Concerning Pulp Mills on the River Uruguay,* and the *Iron Rhine Railway Arbitration*). We have also dipped more deeply into the past than in prior editions and have reproduced material from two pre-World War I international arbitrations dealing with the exploitation of living resources in the marine environment: the *Bering Sea Fur Seals Arbitration* and the *North Atlantic Fisheries Case.* These arbitrations are interesting and instructive in their own right, and they demonstrate that some of the most important principles of modern international environmental law were invoked by advocates and arbitrators many decades before the adoption of the Stockholm Declaration.

Third, in the Appendix, we have detailed the status, usually as of at least January 1, 2011, of the instruments contained in this volume.[1] In so doing, we have sought to contribute to the knowledge that is needed to assess the extent to which, if at all, any given instrument "counts as law."

Each of these features, we believe, adds significantly to the utility of this volume both within and beyond the classroom.

Finally, while not wanting to imply in any way any dissatisfaction with those who have helped us and to whom we extend our sincere thanks in the Acknowledgments, we recognize that there always is room for improvement. Accordingly, we will welcome any and all suggestions for improvements should our effort warrant future editions.

JONATHAN C. CARLSON
Iowa City, Iowa

SIR GEOFFREY W.R. PALMER
Wellington, New Zealand

BURNS H. WESTON
Stockholm, Sweden
Keene, New York
Iowa City, Iowa

October 2011

---

1. Anyone seeking to know the status of these or other environmentally pertinent instruments beginning after 1 January 2011 is encouraged to consult Burns Weston & Jonathan Carlson eds., *International Law and World Order: Basic Documents* (1994–), available on the internet beginning in late 2011 at Martinus Nijhoff Online, http://nijhoffonline.nl/subject?id= ILWO.

ACKNOWLEDGMENTS

Inasmuch as this *Supplement of Basic Documents to International Environmental Law and World Order* builds upon two prior editions, we continue to remain indebted to those who helped so graciously to assist in the preparation of the first and second editions. Their names are recorded therein and we thank them again.

This third edition would not have been possible without the able assistance of Professor Carlson's research assistants at The University of Iowa: Samuel Perlmutter and Yangyu Wang. We also wish to express our sincere appreciation and gratitude to Mary E. Sleichter, who put many hours of effort toward all aspects of this endeavor.

J.C.C.

G.W.R.P.

B.H.W.

October 2011

TABLE OF ABBREVIATIONS

The following abbreviations are used in the headnotes and footnotes to the instruments included in this documentary supplement.

A	United Nations General Assembly; IMO Assembly
Add.	Addendum
A.J.I.L.	American Journal of International Law
Alb.	Albania
Arg	Argentina
AMR/SCM	Document of the Session of the Special Consultative Meeting on Antarctic Mineral Resources
App.	Appendix
Art.,	Arts. Article, Articles
Aust.	Australia
ATSCM	Special Consultative Meeting of Antarctic Treaty Parties
Belg	Belgium
B.Y.B.I.L.	British Yearbook of International Law
Can.	Canada
CBD	Convention on Biological Diversity
C/E, CE	Council of Europe
CONF, Conf	Conference
COP	Conference of the Parties
CP	Contracting Parties
Corr.	Corrigendum
Doc., Doc	Document
E	United Nations Economic and Social Council
EC	European Community
E.C.E., ECE	Economic Commission for Europe
EEC	European Economic Community
EU	European Union
FAO	Food and Agriculture Organisation of the United Nations
FCCC	Framework Convention on Climate Change
Fr.	France
G.A., GA	United Nations General Assembly
G.A.O.R., GAOR	General Assembly Official Records
G.A.T.T., GATT	General Agreement on Tariffs and Trade
G.B., GB	Great Britain
GEF	Global Environment Facility
Hung.	Hungary
I.A.E.A., IAEA	International Atomic Energy Agency
IAEA INFCIRC	International Atomic Energy Agency Information Circular
IAEA Leg. Ser.	International Atomic Energy Agency Legal Series
IBRD	International Bank for Reconstruction and Development
I.C.J., ICJ	Reports of Judgments, Advisory Opinions and Orders of the International Court of Justice
I.L.A., ILA	International Law Association, Reports of Annual Conferences of the International Law Association

I.L.C., ILC	International Law Commission
I.L.M., ILM	International Legal Materials
I.L.R.	International Law Reports
I.M.C.O., IMCO	Inter–Governmental Maritime Consultative Organisation
I.M.O., IMO	International Maritime Organisation
Ire	Ireland
Leg. Legal,	Legislation
Mtg.	Meeting
MARPOL	International Convention for the Prevention of Pollution from Ships
MSC	Marine Safety Committee
MTN	Multilateral Trade Negotiations
Neth	Netherlands
N.Z., NZ	New Zealand
No.	Number
N.R.J.	Natural Resources Journal
O.A.S. Off. Rec.	Organisation of American States Official Records
O.A.S.T.S.	Organisation of American States Treaty Series
O.A.U., OAU	Organisation of African Unity
OEA/Ser.	Organizacion Estados Americanos Series (Organisation of American States Series)
O.E.C.D., OECD	Organisation for Economic Co-operation and Development
Off.	Official
O.J.E.C., OJEC	Official Journal of the European Communities
O.J.E.U., OJEU	Official Journal of the European Union
P.C.I.J.	Permanent Court of International Justice: Reports Pt., pt. Part
Proceed, A.S.I.L.	Proceedings of the American Society of International Law
RES, Res.	Resolution
Rev.	Revision, Revised
S	United Nations Security Council
S.	Treaty Doc Senate Treaty Document (United States)
Ser.	Series
Sess.	Session
Slovk.	Slovakia
Stat. U.S.	Statutes at Large
Supp.	Supplement
T.I.A.S. U.S.	Treaties and Other International Acts Series
TNC	Trade Negotiations Committee
TS	Treaty Series (U.S. Department of State)
U.K., UK	United Kingdom
U.N., UN	United Nations
UNCED	United Nations Conference on Environment and Development
UNDP	United Nations Development Programme
U.N.E.P., UNEP	United Nations Environment Programme
UNESCO	United Nations Economic and Social Council
U.N.G.A., UNGA	United Nations General Assembly
U.N. GAOR	United Nations General Assembly Official Record
U.N.J.Y.B.	United Nations Juridical Yearbook
U.N.R.I.A.A.	United Nations Reports of International Arbitral Awards
UNSC	United Nations Security Council

U.N.T.S., UNTS	United Nations Treaty Series
U.N.Y.B., UNYB	Yearbook of the United Nations
Urug	Uruguay
U.S., US	United States
U.S.C.	United States Code
U.S.T., UST	U.S. Treaties
	Weston & Carlson International Law and World Order: Basic Documents (Burns H. Weston & Jonathan C. Carlson ed., 5 vols, 1994—)*
WCED	World Commission on Environment and Development
WL	Westlaw
W.T.O., WTO	World Trade Organization
Y.B.I.L.C.	Yearbook of the International Law Commission
Y.B.U.N.	Yearbook of the United Nations

---

* This collection of documents was published in hard copy by Transnational Publishers, Inc. until 2006 and by Martinus Nijhoff Publishers from 2007–2010. Beginning in late 2011, the collection will be available on the internet at Martinus Nijhoff Online, http://nijhoffonline.nl/subject?id= ILWO. The document alpha-numeric reference system in the online version differs frequently from the hardcopy version. Alpha-numeric references to Weston and Carlson in the present volume are to the online version of the collection for Titles I–III and to the hardcopy version for Titles IV and V. Titles IV and V are being revised for on-line production as of this writing.

TABLE OF CONTENTS

DOCUMENTS SUPPLEMENT TO
INTERNATIONAL ENVIRONMENTAL LAW AND WORLD ORDER
A PROBLEM–ORIENTED COURSEBOOK

Third Edition

PART 1.   CONSTITUTIVE/ORGANIC

A.   GENERAL

1.1   CONSTITUTION OF THE UNITED STATES OF AMERICA. *Arts. I, II, III, V & Amendment X*

ARTICLE I

* * *

SECTION 8.   The Congress shall have Power To lay and collect Taxes, Duties, Imposts and Excises, to pay the Debts and provide for the common Defence and general Welfare of the United States; but all Duties, Imposts and Excises shall be uniform throughout the United States;

To borrow Money on the credit of the United States;

To regulate Commerce with foreign Nations, and among the several States, and with the Indian Tribes;

To establish an uniform Rule of Naturalization, and uniform Laws on the subject of Bankruptcies throughout the United States;

To coin Money, regulate the Value thereof, and of foreign Coin, and fix the Standard of Weights and Measures;

To provide for the Punishment of counterfeiting the Securities and current Coin of the United States;

To establish Post Offices and post Roads;

To promote the Progress of Science and useful Arts, by securing for limited Times to Authors and Inventors the exclusive Right to their respective Writings and Discoveries;

To constitute Tribunals inferior to the supreme Court;

To define and punish Piracies and Felonies committed on the high Seas, and Offences against the Law of Nations;

To declare War, grant Letters of Marque and Reprisal, and make Rules concerning Captures on Land and Water;

To raise and support Armies, but no Appropriation of Money to that Use shall be for a longer Term than two Years;

To provide and maintain a Navy;

To make Rules for the Government and Regulation of the land and naval Forces;

To provide for calling forth the Militia to execute the Laws of the Union, suppress Insurrections and repel Invasions;

To provide for organizing, arming, and disciplining, the Militia, and for governing such Part of them as may be employed in the Service of the United States, reserving to the States respectively, the Appointment of the Officers, and the Authority of training the Militia according to the discipline prescribed by Congress;

To exercise exclusive Legislation in all Cases whatsoever, over such District (not exceeding ten Miles square) as may, by Cession of particular States, and the Acceptance of Congress, become the Seat of the Government of the United States, and to exercise like Authority over all Places purchased by the Consent of the Legislature of

1

the State in which the Same shall be, for the Erection of Forts, Magazines, Arsenals, dock-Yards, and other needful Buildings;—And

To make all Laws which shall be necessary and proper for carrying into Execution the foregoing Powers, and all other Powers vested by this Constitution in the Government of the United States, or in any Department or Officer thereof.

SECTION 9.   The Migration or Importation of such Persons as any of the States now existing shall think proper to admit, shall not be prohibited by the Congress prior to the Year one thousand eight hundred and eight, but a Tax or duty may be imposed on such Importation, not exceeding ten dollars for each Person.

The Privilege of the Writ of Habeas Corpus shall not be suspended, unless when in Cases of Rebellion or Invasion the public Safety may require it.

No Bill of Attainder or ex post facto Law shall be passed.

No Capitation, or other direct, Tax shall be laid, unless in Proportion to the Census or Enumeration herein before directed to be taken.

No Tax or Duty shall be laid on Articles exported from any State.

No Preference shall be given by any Regulation of Commerce or Revenue to the Ports of one State over those of another; nor shall Vessels bound to, or from, one State, be obliged to enter, clear or pay Duties in another.

No Money shall be drawn from the Treasury, but in Consequence of Appropriations made by Law; and a regular Statement and Account of the Receipts and Expenditures of all public Money shall be published from time to time.

No Title of Nobility shall be granted by the United States: And no Person holding any Office of Profit or Trust under them, shall, without the Consent of the Congress, accept of any present, Emolument, Office, or Title, of any kind whatever, from any King, Prince or foreign State.

SECTION 10.   No State shall enter into any Treaty, Alliance, or Confederation; grant Letters of Marque and Reprisal; coin Money; emit Bills of Credit; make any Thing but gold and silver Coin a Tender in Payment of Debts; pass any Bill of Attainder, ex post facto Law, or Law impairing the Obligation of Contracts, or grant any Title of Nobility.

No State shall, without the Consent of the Congress, lay any Imposts or Duties on Imports or Exports, except what may be absolutely necessary for executing its inspection Laws: and the net Produce of all Duties and Imposts, laid by any State on Imports or Exports, shall be for the Use of the Treasury of the United States; and all such Laws shall be subject to the Revision and Control of the Congress.

No State shall, without the Consent of Congress, lay any Duty of Tonnage, keep Troops, or Ships of War in time of Peace, enter into any Agreement or Compact with another State, or with a foreign Power, or engage in War, unless actually invaded, or in such imminent Danger as will not admit of delay.

ARTICLE II

SECTION 1.   The executive Power shall be vested in a President of the United States of America. He shall hold his Office during the Term of four Years[.]

* * *

SECTION 2.   The President shall be Commander in Chief of the Army and Navy of the United States, and of the Militia of the several States, when called into the actual Service of the United States; he may require the Opinion, in writing, of the principal Officer in each of the executive Departments, upon any Subject relating to the Duties of their respective Offices, and he shall have Power to grant Reprieves and Pardons for Offences against the United States, except in Cases of Impeachment.

He shall have Power, by and with the Advice and Consent of the Senate, to make Treaties, provided two thirds of the Senators present concur; and he shall nominate, and by and with the Advice and Consent of the Senate, shall appoint Ambassadors, other public Ministers and Consuls, Judges of the supreme Court, and all other Officers of the United States, whose Appointments are not herein otherwise provided for, and which shall be established by Law: but the Congress may by Law vest the Appointment of such inferior Officers, as they think proper, in the President alone, in the Courts of Law, or in the Heads of Departments.

The President shall have Power to fill up all Vacancies that may happen during the Recess of the Senate, by granting Commissions which shall expire at the End of their next Session.

SECTION 3.   He shall * * * receive Ambassadors and other public Ministers.

* * *

ARTICLE III

SECTION 1.   The judicial Power of the United States, shall be vested in one supreme Court, and in such inferior Courts as the Congress may from time to time ordain and establish. * * *

SECTION 2.   The judicial Power shall extend to all Cases, in Law and Equity, arising under this Constitution, the Laws of the United States, and Treaties made, or which shall be made, under their Authority;—to all Cases affecting Ambassadors, other public ministers and Consuls;—to all Cases of admiralty and maritime Jurisdiction;—to Controversies to which the United States shall be a Party;—to Controversies between two or more States;—between a State and Citizens of another State;—between Citizens of different States;—between Citizens of the same State claiming Lands under Grants of different States, and between a State, or the Citizens thereof, and foreign States, Citizens or Subjects.

In all Cases affecting Ambassadors, other public Ministers and Consuls, and those in which a State shall be Party, the supreme Court shall have original Jurisdiction. In all the other Cases before mentioned, the supreme Court shall have appellate Jurisdiction, both as to Law and Fact, with such Exceptions, and under such Regulations as the Congress shall make.

* * *

SECTION 3.   Treason against the United States, shall consist only in levying War against them, or in adhering to their Enemies, giving them Aid and Comfort. No Person shall be convicted of Treason unless on the Testimony of two Witnesses to the same overt Act, or on Confession in open Court.

The Congress shall have Power to declare the Punishment of Treason, but no Attainder of Treason shall work Corruption of Blood, or Forfeiture except during the Life of the Person attainted.

* * *

ARTICLE VI

This Constitution, and the Laws of the United States which shall be made in Pursuance thereof; and all Treaties made, or which shall be made, under the Authority of the United States, shall be the supreme Law of the Land; and the Judges in every

State shall be bound thereby, any Thing in the Constitution or Laws of any State to the Contrary notwithstanding.

* * *

AMENDMENT X

The powers not delegated to the United States by the Constitution, nor prohibited by it to the States, are reserved to the States respectively, or to the people.

* * *

1.2 CHARTER OF THE UNITED NATIONS (as Amended). Concluded at San Francisco, 26 June 1945. Entered into force, 24 October 1945. 1 UNTS XVI, 1976 YBUN 1043, 59 Stat 1031, TS No 993, *reprinted in* 1 Weston & Carlson I.A.1

WE THE PEOPLES OF THE UNITED NATIONS DETERMINED

to save succeeding generations from the scourge of war, which twice in our life-time has brought untold sorrow to mankind, and

to reaffirm faith in fundamental human rights, in the dignity and worth of the human person, in the equal rights of men and women and of nations large and small, and

to establish conditions under which justice and respect for the obligations arising from treaties and other sources of international law can be maintained, and

to promote social progress and better standards of life in larger freedom,

AND FOR THESE ENDS

to practice tolerance and live together in peace with one another as good neighbours, and

to unite our strength to maintain international peace and security, and

to ensure, by the acceptance of principles and the institution of methods, that armed force shall not be used, save in the common interest, and

to employ international machinery for the promotion of the economic and social advancement of all peoples,

HAVE RESOLVED TO COMBINE OUR EFFORTS
TO ACCOMPLISH THESE AIMS

Accordingly, our respective Governments, through representatives assembled in the city of San Francisco, who have exhibited their full powers found to be in good and due form, have agreed to the present Charter of the United Nations and do hereby establish an international organization to be known as the United Nations.

CHAPTER I.   PURPOSES AND PRINCIPLES

Article 1

The Purposes of the United Nations are:

1.   To maintain international peace and security, and to that end: to take effective collective measures for the prevention and removal of threats to the peace, and for the suppression of acts of aggression or other breaches of the peace, and to bring about by peaceful means, and in conformity with the principles of justice and international law, adjustment or settlement of international disputes or situations which might lead to a breach of the peace;

2.   To develop friendly relations among nations based on respect for the principle of equal rights and self-determination of peoples, and to take other appropriate measures to strengthen universal peace;

3.   To achieve international co-operation in solving international problems of an economic, social, cultural, or humanitarian character, and in promoting and encouraging respect for human rights and for fundamental freedoms for all without distinction as to race, sex, language, or religion; and

4.   To be a centre for harmonizing the actions of nations in the attainment of these common ends.

Article 2

The Organization and its Members, in pursuit of the Purposes stated in Article 1, shall act in accordance with the following Principles.

1. The Organization is based on the principle of the sovereign equality of all its Members.

2. All Members, in order to ensure to all of them the rights and benefits resulting from membership, shall fulfil in good faith the obligations assumed by them in accordance with the present Charter.

3. All Members shall settle their international disputes by peaceful means in such a manner that international peace and security, and justice, are not endangered.

4. All Members shall refrain in their international relations from the threat or use of force against the territorial integrity or political independence of any state, or in any other manner inconsistent with the Purposes of the United Nations.

5. All Members shall give the United Nations every assistance in any action it takes in accordance with the present Charter, and shall refrain from giving assistance to any state against which the United Nations is taking preventive or enforcement action.

6. The Organization shall ensure that states which are not Members of the United Nations act in accordance with these Principles so far as may be necessary for the maintenance of international peace and security.

7. Nothing contained in the present Charter shall authorize the United Nations to intervene in matters which are essentially within the domestic jurisdiction of any state or shall require the Members to submit such matters to settlement under the present Charter; but this principle shall not prejudice the application of enforcement measures under Chapter VII.

CHAPTER II. MEMBERSHIP

Article 3

The original Members of the United Nations shall be the states which, having participated in the United Nations Conference on International Organization at San Francisco, or having previously signed the Declaration by United Nations of 1 January 1942, sign the present Charter and ratify it in accordance with Article 110.

Article 4

1. Membership in the United Nations is open to all other peace-loving states which accept the obligations contained in the present Charter and, in the judgment of the Organization, are able and willing to carry out these obligations.

2. The admission of any such state to membership in the United Nations will be effected by a decision of the General Assembly upon the recommendation of the Security Council.

Article 5

A Member of the United Nations against which preventive or enforcement action has been taken by the Security Council may be suspended from the exercise of the rights and privileges of membership by the General Assembly upon the recommendation of the Security Council. The exercise of these rights and privileges may be restored by the Security Council.

Article 6

A Member of the United Nations which has persistently violated the Principles contained in the present Charter may be expelled from the Organization by the General Assembly upon the recommendation of the Security Council.

CHAPTER III. ORGANS

Article 7

1. There are established as the principal organs of the United Nations: a General Assembly, a Security Council, an Economic and Social Council, a Trusteeship Council, an International Court of Justice, and a Secretariat.

2. Such subsidiary organs as may be found necessary may be established in accordance with the present Charter.

Article 8

The United Nations shall place no restrictions on the eligibility of men and women to participate in any capacity and under conditions of equality in its principal and subsidiary organs.

CHAPTER IV. THE GENERAL ASSEMBLY

Composition

Article 9

1. The General Assembly shall consist of all the Members of the United Nations.

2. Each Member shall have not more than five representatives in the General Assembly.

Function and powers

Article 10

The General Assembly may discuss any questions or any matters within the scope of the present Charter or relating to the powers and functions of any organs provided for in the present Charter, and, except as provided in Article 12, may make recommendations to the Members of the United Nations or to the Security Council or to both on any such questions or matters.

Article 11

1. The General Assembly may consider the general principles of co-operation in the maintenance of international peace and security, including the principles governing disarmament and the regulation of armaments, and may make recommendations with regard to such principles to the Members or to the Security Council or to both.

2. The General Assembly may discuss any questions relating to the maintenance of international peace and security brought before it by any Member of the United Nations, or by the Security Council, or by a state which is not a Member of the United Nations in accordance with Article 35, paragraph 2, and, except as provided in Article 12, may make recommendations with regard to any such questions to the state or states concerned or to the Security Council or to both. Any such question on which action is necessary shall be referred to the Security Council by the General Assembly either before or after discussion.

3. The General Assembly may call the attention of the Security Council to situations which are likely to endanger international peace and security.

4. The powers of the General Assembly set forth in this Article shall not limit the general scope of Article 10.

Article 12

1. While the Security Council is exercising in respect of any dispute or situation the functions assigned to it in the present Charter, the General Assembly shall not

make any recommendation with regard to that dispute or situation unless the Security Council so requests.

2.   The Secretary–General, with the consent of the Security Council, shall notify the General Assembly at each session of any matters relative to the maintenance of international peace and security which are being dealt with by the Security Council and shall similarly notify the General Assembly, or the Members of the United Nations if the General Assembly is not in session, immediately the Security Council ceases to deal with such matters.

Article 13

1.   The General Assembly shall initiate studies and make recommendations for the purpose of:

a.   Promoting international co-operation in the political field and encouraging the progressive development of international law and its codification;

b.   Promoting international co-operation in the economic, social, cultural, educational, and health fields, and assisting in the realization of human rights and fundamental freedoms for all without distinction as to race, sex, language, or religion.

2.   The further responsibilities, functions and powers of the General Assembly with respect to matters mentioned in paragraph 1(b) above are set forth in Chapters IX and X.

Article 14

Subject to the provisions of Article 12, the General Assembly may recommend measures for the peaceful adjustment of any situation, regardless of origin, which it deems likely to impair the general welfare or friendly relations among nations, including situations resulting from a violation of the provisions of the present Charter setting forth the Purposes and Principles of the United Nations.

Article 15

1.   The General Assembly shall receive and consider annual and special reports from the Security Council; these reports shall include an account of the measures that the Security Council has decided upon or taken to maintain international peace and security.

2.   The General Assembly shall receive and consider reports from the other organs of the United Nations.

Article 16

The General Assembly shall perform such functions with respect to the international trusteeship system as are assigned to it under Chapters XII and XIII, including the approval of the trusteeship agreements for areas not designated as strategic.

Article 17

1.   The General Assembly shall consider and approve the budget of the Organization.

2.   The expenses of the Organization shall be borne by the Members as apportioned by the General Assembly.

3.   The General Assembly shall consider and approve any financial and budgetary arrangements with specialized agencies referred to in Article 57 and shall examine the administrative budgets of such specialized agencies with a view to making recommendations to the agencies concerned.

Voting

Article 18

1.   Each member of the General Assembly shall have one vote.

2.   Decisions of the General Assembly on important questions shall be made by a two-thirds majority of the members present and voting. These questions shall include: recommendations with respect to the maintenance of international peace and security, the election of the non-permanent members of the Security Council, the election of members of the Economic and Social Council, the election of the members of the Trusteeship Council in accordance with paragraph 1(c) of Article 86, the admission of new Members to the United Nations, the suspension of the rights and privileges of membership, the expulsion of Members, questions relating to the operation of the trusteeship system, and budgetary questions.

3.   Decisions on other questions, including the determination of additional categories of questions to be decided by a two-thirds majority, shall be made by a majority of the members present and voting.

Article 19

A Member of the United Nations which is in arrears in the payment of its financial contributions to the Organization shall have no vote in the General Assembly if the amount of its arrears equals or exceeds the amount of the contributions due from it for the preceding two full years. The General Assembly may, nevertheless, permit such a member to vote if it is satisfied that the failure to pay is due to conditions beyond the control of the Member.

Procedure

Article 20

The General Assembly shall meet in regular annual sessions and in such special sessions as occasion may require. Special sessions shall be convoked by the Secretary–General at the request of the Security Council or of a majority of the Members of the United Nations.

Article 21

The General Assembly shall adopt its own rules of procedure. It shall elect its President for each session.

Article 22

The General Assembly may establish such subsidiary organs as it deems necessary for the performance of its functions.

CHAPTER V.   THE SECURITY COUNCIL

Composition

Article 23[a]

1.   The Security Council shall consist of fifteen Members of the United Nations. The Republic of China, France, the Union of Soviet Socialist Republics, the United Kingdom of Great Britain and Northern Ireland, and the United States of America shall be permanent members of the Security Council. The General Assembly shall elect ten other Members of the United Nations to be non-permanent members of the Security Council, due regard being specially paid, in the first instance to contribution of Members of the United Nations to the maintenance of international peace and

a.   Amended text of Article 23, which entered into force on 31 August 1965.

security and to the other purposes of the Organization, and also to equitable geographical distribution.

2. The non-permanent members of the Security Council shall be elected for a term of two years. In the first election of the non-permanent members after the increase of the membership of the Security Council from eleven to fifteen, two of the four additional members shall be chosen for a term of one year. A retiring member shall not be eligible for immediate re-election.

3. Each member of the Security Council shall have one representative.

Functions and powers

Article 24

1. In order to ensure prompt and effective action by the United Nations, its Members confer on the Security Council primary responsibility for the maintenance of international peace and security, and agree that in carrying out its duties under this responsibility the Security Council acts on their behalf.

2. In discharging these duties the Security Council shall act in accordance with the Purposes and Principles of the United Nations. The specific powers granted to the Security Council for the discharge of these duties are laid down in Chapters VI, VII, VIII, and XII.

3. The Security Council shall submit annual and, when necessary, special reports to the General Assembly for its consideration.

Article 25

The members of the United Nations agree to accept and carry out the decisions of the Security Council in accordance with the present Charter.

Article 26

In order to promote the establishment and maintenance of international peace and security with the least diversion for armaments of the world's human and economic resources, the Security Council shall be responsible for formulating, with the assistance of the Military Staff Committee referred to in Article 47, plans to be submitted to the Members of the United Nations for the establishment of a system for the regulation of armaments.

Voting

Article 27[b]

1. Each member of the Security Council shall have one vote.

2. Decisions of the Security Council on procedural matters shall be made by an affirmative vote of nine members.

3. Decisions of the Security Council on all other matters shall be made by an affirmative vote of nine members including the concurring votes of the permanent members; provided that, in decisions under Chapter VI, and under paragraph 3 of Article 52, a party to a dispute shall abstain from voting.

Procedure

Article 28

1. The Security Council shall be so organized as to be able to function continuously. Each member of the Security Council shall for this purpose be represented at all times at the seat of the Organization.

b. Amended text of Article 27, which entered into force on 31 August 1965.

2. The Security Council shall hold periodic meetings at which each of its members may, if it so desires, be represented by a member of the government or by some other specially designated representative.

3. The Security Council may hold meetings at such places other than the seat of the Organization as in its judgment will best facilitate its work.

Article 29

The Security Council may establish such subsidiary organs as it deems necessary for the performance of its functions.

Article 30

The Security Council shall adopt its own rules of procedure, including the method of selecting its President.

Article 31

Any Member of the United Nations which is not a member of the Security Council may participate, without vote, in the discussion of any question brought before the Security Council whenever the latter considers that the interests of that Member are specially affected.

Article 32

Any Member of the United Nations which is not a member of the Security Council or any state which is not a Member of the United Nations, if it is a party to a dispute under consideration by the Security Council, shall be invited to participate, without vote, in the discussion relating to the dispute. The Security Council shall lay down such conditions as it deems just for the participation of a state which is not a Member of the United Nations.

CHAPTER VI. PACIFIC SETTLEMENT OF DISPUTES

Article 33

1. The parties to any dispute, the continuance of which is likely to endanger the maintenance of international peace and security, shall, first of all, seek a solution by negotiation, enquiry, mediation, conciliation, arbitration, judicial settlement, resort to regional agencies or arrangements, or other peaceful means of their own choice.

2. The Security Council shall, when it deems necessary, call upon the parties to settle their dispute by such means.

Article 34

The Security Council may investigate any dispute, or any situation which might lead to international friction or give rise to a dispute, in order to determine whether the continuance of the dispute or situation is likely to endanger the maintenance of international peace and security.

Article 35

1. Any Member of the United Nations may bring any dispute, or any situation of the nature referred to in Article 34, to the attention of the Security Council or of the General Assembly.

2. A state which is not a Member of the United Nations may bring to the attention of the Security Council or of the General Assembly any dispute to which it is a party if it accepts in advance, for the purposes of the dispute, the obligations of pacific settlement provided in the present Charter.

3.   The proceedings of the General Assembly in respect of matters brought to its attention under this Article will be subject to the provisions of Articles 11 and 12.

Article 36

1.   The Security Council may, at any stage of a dispute of the nature referred to in Article 33 or of a situation of like nature, recommend appropriate procedures or methods of adjustment.

2.   The Security Council should take into consideration any procedures for the settlement of the dispute which have already been adopted by the parties.

3.   In making recommendations under this Article the Security Council should also take into consideration that legal disputes should as a general rule be referred by the parties to the International Court of Justice in accordance with the provisions of the Statute of the Court.

Article 37

1.   Should the parties to a dispute of the nature referred to in Article 33 fail to settle it by the means indicated in that Article, they shall refer it to the Security Council.

2.   If the Security Council deems that the continuance of the dispute is in fact likely to endanger the maintenance of international peace and security, it shall decide whether to take action under Article 36 or to recommend such terms of settlement as it may consider appropriate.

Article 38

Without prejudice to the provisions of Articles 33 to 37, the Security Council may, if all the parties to any dispute so request, make recommendations to the parties with a view to a pacific settlement of the dispute.

CHAPTER VII.   ACTION WITH RESPECT TO THREATS TO THE PEACE, BREACHES OF THE PEACE, AND ACTS OF AGGRESSION

Article 39

The Security Council shall determine the existence of any threat to the peace, breach of the peace, or act of aggression and shall make recommendations, or decide what measures shall be taken in accordance with Articles 41 and 42, to maintain or restore international peace and security.

Article 40

In order to prevent an aggravation of the situation, the Security Council may, before making the recommendations or deciding upon the measures provided for in Article 39, call upon the parties concerned to comply with such provisional measures as it deems necessary or desirable. Such provisional measures shall be without prejudice to the rights, claims, or position of the parties concerned. The Security Council shall duly take account of failure to comply with such provisional measures.

Article 41

The Security Council may decide what measures not involving the use of armed force are to be employed to give effect to its decisions, and it may call upon the Members of the United Nations to apply such measures. These may include complete or partial interruption of economic relations and of rail, sea, air, postal, telegraphic, radio, and other means of communication, and the severance of diplomatic relations.

Article 42

Should the Security Council consider that measures provided for in Article 41 would be inadequate or have proved to be inadequate, it may take such action by air, sea, or land forces as may be necessary to maintain or restore international peace and security. Such action may include demonstrations, blockade, and other operations by air, sea, or land forces of Members of the United Nations.

Article 43

1. All Members of the United Nations, in order to contribute to the maintenance of international peace and security, undertake to make available to the Security Council, on its call and in accordance with a special agreement or agreements, armed forces, assistance, and facilities, including rights of passage, necessary for the purpose of maintaining international peace and security.

2. Such agreement or agreements shall govern the numbers and types of forces, their degree of readiness and general location, and the nature of the facilities and assistance to be provided.

3. The agreement or agreements shall be negotiated as soon as possible on the initiative of the Security Council. They shall be concluded between the Security Council and Members or between the Security Council and groups of members and shall be subject to ratification by the signatory states in accordance with their respective constitutional processes.

Article 44

When the Security Council has decided to use force it shall, before calling upon a Member not represented on it to provide armed forces in fulfilment of the obligations assumed under Article 43, invite that Member, if the Member so desires, to participate in the decisions of the Security Council concerning the employment of contingents of that Member's armed forces.

Article 45

In order to enable the United Nations to take urgent military measures, Members shall hold immediately available national air-force contingents for combined international enforcement action. The strength and degree of readiness of these continents and plans for their combined action shall be determined, within the limits laid down in the special agreement or agreements referred to in Article 43, by the Security Council with the assistance of the Military Staff Committee.

Article 46

Plans for the application of armed force shall be made by the Security Council with the assistance of the Military Staff Committee.

Article 47

1. There shall be established a Military Staff Committee to advise and assist the Security Council on all questions relating to the Security Council's military requirements for the maintenance of international peace and security, the employment and command of forces placed at its disposal, the regulation of armaments, and possible disarmament.

2. The Military Staff Committee shall consist of the Chiefs of Staff of the permanent members of the Security Council or their representatives. Any Member of the United Nations not permanently represented on the Committee shall be invited by the Committee to be associated with it when the efficient discharge of the Committee's responsibilities requires the participation of that Member in its work.

3. The Military Staff Committee shall be responsible under the Security Council for the strategic direction of any armed forces placed at the disposal of the Security Council. Questions relating to the command of such forces shall be worked out subsequently.

4. The Military Staff Committee, with the authorization of the Security Council and after consultation with appropriate regional agencies, may establish regional subcommittees.

Article 48

1. The action required to carry out the decisions of the Security Council for the maintenance of international peace and security shall be taken by all the Members of the United Nations or by some of them, as the Security Council may determine.

2. Such decisions shall be carried out by the Members of the United Nations directly and through their action in the appropriate international agencies of which they are members.

Article 49

The Members of the United Nations shall join in affording mutual assistance in carrying out the measures decided upon by the Security Council.

Article 50

If preventive or enforcement measures against any state are taken by the Security Council, any other state, whether a Member of the United Nations or not, which finds itself confronted with special economic problems arising from the carrying out of those measures shall have the right to consult the Security Council with regard to a solution of those problems.

Article 51

Nothing in the present Charter shall impair the inherent right of individual or collective self-defence if an armed attack occurs against a Member of the United Nations, until the Security Council has taken measures necessary to maintain international peace and security. Measures taken by Members in the exercise of this right of self-defence shall be immediately reported to the Security Council and shall not in any way affect the authority and responsibility of the Security Council under the present Charter to take at any time such action as it deems necessary in order to maintain or restore international peace and security.

Chapter VIII. REGIONAL ARRANGEMENTS

Article 52

1. Nothing in the present Charter precludes the existence of regional arrangements or agencies for dealing with such matters relating to the maintenance of international peace and security as are appropriate for regional action, provided that such arrangements or agencies and their activities are consistent with the Purposes and Principles of the United Nations.

2. The Members of the United Nations entering into such arrangements or constituting such agencies shall make every effort to achieve pacific settlement of local disputes through such regional arrangements or by such regional agencies before referring them to the Security Council.

3. The Security Council shall encourage the development of pacific settlement of local disputes through such regional arrangements or by such regional agencies either on the initiative of the states concerned or by reference from the Security Council.

4. This Article in no way impairs the application of Articles 34 and 35.

Article 53

1. The Security Council shall, where appropriate, utilize such regional arrangements or agencies for enforcement action under its authority. But no enforcement action shall be taken under regional arrangements or by regional agencies without the authorization of the Security Council, with the exception of measures against any enemy state, as defined in paragraph 2 of this Article, provided for pursuant to Article 107 or in regional arrangements directed against renewal of aggressive policy on the part of any such state, until such time as the Organization may, on request of the Governments concerned, be charged with the responsibility for preventing further aggression by such a state.

2. The term enemy state as used in paragraph 1 of this Article applies to any state which during the Second World War has been an enemy of any signatory of the present Charter.

Article 54

The Security Council shall at all times be kept fully informed of activities undertaken or in contemplation under regional arrangements or by regional agencies for the maintenance of international peace and security.

CHAPTER IX. INTERNATIONAL ECONOMIC AND SOCIAL CO–OPERATION

Article 55

With a view to the creation of conditions of stability and well-being which are necessary for peaceful and friendly relations among nations based on respect for the principle of equal rights and self-determination of peoples, the United Nations shall promote:

    a. higher standards of living, full employment, and conditions of economic and social progress and development.

    b. solutions of international economic, social, health, and related problems; and international cultural and educational co-operation; and

    c. universal respect for, and observance of, human rights and fundamental freedoms for all without distinction as to race, sex, language, or religion.

Article 56

All Members pledge themselves to take joint and separate action in co-operation with the Organization for the achievement of the purposes set forth in Article 55.

Article 57

1. The various specialized agencies, established by intergovernmental agreement and having wide international responsibilities, as defined in their basic instruments, in economic, social, cultural, educational, health, and related fields, shall be brought into relationship with the United Nations in accordance with the provisions of Article 63.

2. Such agencies thus brought into relationship with the United Nations are hereinafter referred to as specialized agencies.

Article 58

The Organization shall make recommendations for the co-ordination of the policies and activities of the specialized agencies.

Article 59

The Organization shall, where appropriate, initiate negotiations among the states concerned for the creation of any new specialized agencies required for the accomplishment of the purposes set forth in Article 55.

Article 60

Responsibility for the discharge of functions of the Organization set forth in this Chapter shall be vested in the General Assembly and, under the authority of the General Assembly, in the Economic and Social Council, which shall have for this purpose the powers set forth in Chapter X.

Chapter X.   THE ECONOMIC AND SOCIAL COUNCIL

Composition

Article 61[c]

1.   The Economic and Social Council shall consist of fifty-four Members of the United Nations elected by the General Assembly.

2.   Subject to the provisions of paragraph 3, eighteen members of the Economic and Social Council shall be elected each year for a term of three years. A retiring member shall be eligible for immediate re-election.

3.   At the first election after the increase in the membership of the Economic and Social Council from twenty-seven to fifty-four members, in addition to the members elected in place of the nine members whose terms of office expires at the end of that year, twenty-seven additional members shall be elected. Of these twenty-seven additional members, the term of office of nine members so elected shall expire at the end of one year, and of nine other members at the end of two years, in accordance with arrangements made by the General Assembly.

4.   Each member of the Economic and Social Council shall have one representative.

Functions and powers

Article 62

1.   The Economic and Social Council may make or initiate studies and reports with respect to international economic, social, cultural, educational, health, and related matters and may make recommendations with respect to any such matters of the General Assembly, to the Members of the United Nations, and to the specialized agencies concerned.

2.   It may make recommendations for the purpose of promoting respect for, and observance of, human rights and fundamental freedoms for all.

3.   It may prepare draft conventions for submission to the General Assembly, with respect to matters falling within its competence.

4.   It may call, in accordance with the rules prescribed by the United Nations, international conferences on matters falling within its competence.

Article 63

1.   The Economic and Social Council may enter into agreements with any of the agencies referred to in Article 57, defining the terms on which the agency concerned shall be brought into relationship with the United Nations. Such agreements shall be subject to approval by the General Assembly.

2.   It may co-ordinate the activities of the specialized agencies through consultation with and recommendations to such agencies and through recommendations to the General Assembly and to the Members of the United Nations.

c.   Amended text of Article 61, which entered into force on 24 September 1973.

Article 64

1.   The Economic and Social Council may take appropriate steps to obtain regular reports from the specialized agencies. It may make arrangements with the Members of the United Nations and with the specialized agencies to obtain reports on the steps taken to give effect to its own recommendations and to recommendations on matters falling within its competence made by the General Assembly.

2.   It may communicate its observations on these reports to the General Assembly.

Article 65

The Economic and Social Council may furnish information to the Security Council and shall assist the Security Council upon its request.

Article 66

1.   The Economic and Social Council shall perform such functions as fall within its competence in connexion with the carrying out of the recommendations of the General Assembly.

2.   It may, with the approval of the General Assembly, perform services at the request of Members of the United Nations and at the request of specialized agencies.

3.   It shall perform such other functions as are specified elsewhere in the present Charter or as may be assigned to it by the General Assembly.

Voting

Article 67

1.   Each member of the Economic and Social Council shall have one vote.

2.   Decisions of the Economic and Social Council shall be made by a majority of the members present and voting.

Procedure

Article 68

The Economic and Social Council shall set up commissions in economic and social fields and for the promotion of human rights, and such other commissions as may be required for the performance of its functions.

Article 69

The Economic and Social Council shall invite any Member of the United Nations to participate, without vote, in its deliberations on any matter of particular concern to that Member.

Article 70

The Economic and Social Council may make arrangements for representatives of the specialized agencies to participate, without vote, in its deliberations and in those of the commissions established by it, and for its representatives to participate in the deliberations of the specialized agencies.

Article 71

The Economic and Social Council may make suitable arrangements for consultation with non-governmental organizations which are concerned with matters within its competence. Such arrangements may be made with international organizations and, where appropriate, with national organizations after consultation with the Member of the United Nations concerned.

Article 72

1. The Economic and Social Council shall adopt its own rules of procedure, including the method of selecting its President.

2. The Economic and Social Council shall meet as required in accordance with its rules, which shall include provision for the convening of meetings on the request of a majority of its members.

CHAPTER XI.   DECLARATION REGARDING NON–SELF–GOVERNING TERRITORIES

Article 73

Members of the United Nations which have or assume responsibilities for the administration of territories whose peoples have not yet attained a full measure of self-government recognize the principle that the interests of the inhabitants of these territories are paramount, and accept as a sacred trust the obligation to promote to the utmost, within the system of international peace and security established by the present Charter, the well-being of the inhabitants of these territories, and, to this end:

a. to ensure, with due respect for the culture of the peoples concerned, their political, economic, social, and educational advancement, their just treatment, and their protection against abuses;

b. to develop self-government, to take due account of the political aspirations of the peoples, and to assist them in the progressive development of their free political institutions, according to the particular circumstances of each territory and its peoples and their varying stages of advancement;

c. to further international peace and security;

d. to promote constructive measures of development, to encourage research, and to cooperate with one another and, when and where appropriate, with specialized international bodies with a view to the practical achievement of the social, economic, and scientific purposes set forth in this Article; and

e. to transmit regularly to the Secretary–General for information purposes, subject to such limitation as security and constitutional considerations may require, statistical and other information of a technical nature relating to economic, social, and educational conditions in the territories for which they are respectively responsible other than those territories to which Chapters XII and XIII apply.

Article 74

Members of the United Nations also agree that their policy in respect of the territories to which this Chapter applies, no less than in respect of their metropolitan areas, must be based on the general principle of good-neighbourliness, due account being taken of the interests and well-being of the rest of the world, in social, economic, and commercial matters.

CHAPTER XII.   INTERNATIONAL TRUSTEESHIP SYSTEM

Article 75

The United Nations shall establish under its authority an international trustee-ship system for the administration and supervision of such territories as may be placed thereunder by subsequent individual agreements. These territories are hereinafter referred to as trust territories.

Article 76

The basic objectives of the trusteeship system, in accordance with the Purposes of the United Nations laid down in Article 1 of the present Charter, shall be:

a. to further international peace and security;

b. to promote the political, economic, social, and educational advancement of the inhabitants of the trust territories, and their progressive development towards self-government or independence as may be appropriate to the particular circumstances of each territory and its peoples and the freely expressed wishes of the peoples concerned, and as may be provided by the terms of each trusteeship agreement;

c. to encourage respect for human rights and for fundamental freedoms for all without distinction as to race, sex, language, or religion, and to encourage recognition of the interdependence of the peoples of the world; and

d. to ensure equal treatment in social, economic, and commercial matters for all Members of the United nations and their nationals, and also equal treatment for the latter in the administration of justice, without prejudice to the attainment of the foregoing objectives and subject to the provisions of Article 80.

Article 77

1. The trusteeship system shall apply to such territories in the following categories as may be placed thereunder by means of trusteeship agreements:

a. territories now held under mandate;

b. territories which may be detached from enemy states as a result of the Second World War; and

c. territories voluntarily placed under the system by states responsible for their administration.

2. It will be a matter for subsequent agreement as to which territories in the foregoing categories will be brought under the trusteeship system and upon what terms.

Article 78

The trusteeship system shall not apply to territories which have become Members of the United Nations, relationship among which shall be based on respect for the principle of sovereign equality.

Article 79

The terms of trusteeship for each territory to be placed under the trusteeship system, including any alteration or amendment, shall be agreed upon by the states directly concerned, including the mandatory power in the case of territories held under mandate by a Member of the United Nations, and shall be approved as provided for in Articles 83 and 85.

Article 80

1. Except as may be agreed upon in individual trusteeship agreements, made under Articles 77, 79, and 81, placing each territory under the trusteeship system, and until such agreements have been concluded, nothing in this Chapter shall be construed in or of itself to alter in any manner the rights whatsoever of any states or any peoples or the terms of existing international instruments to which Members of the United Nations may respectively be parties.

2. Paragraph 1 of this Article shall not be interpreted as giving grounds for delay or postponement of the negotiation and conclusion of agreements for placing mandated and other territories under the trusteeship system as provided for in Article 77.

Article 81

The trusteeship agreement shall in each case include the terms under which the trust territory will be administered and designate the authority which will exercise the administration of the trust territory. Such authority, hereinafter called the administering authority, may be one or more states or the organization itself.

Article 82

There may be designated, in any trusteeship agreement, a strategic area or areas which may include part or all of the trust territory to which the agreement applies, without prejudice to any special agreement or agreements made under Article 43.

Article 83

1. All functions of the United Nations relating to strategic areas, including the approval of the terms of the trusteeship agreements and of their alterations or amendment, shall be exercised by the Security Council.

2. The basic objectives set forth in Article 76 shall be applicable to the people of each strategic area.

3. The Security Council shall, subject to the provisions of the trusteeship agreements and without prejudice to security considerations, avail itself of the assistance of the Trusteeship Council to perform those functions of the United Nations under the trusteeship system relating to political, economic, social, and educational matters in the strategic areas.

Article 84

It shall be the duty of the administering authority to ensure that the trust territory shall play its part in the maintenance of international peace and security. To this end the administering authority may make use of volunteer forces, facilities, and assistance from the trust territory in carrying out the obligations towards the Security Council undertaken in this regard by the administering authority, as well as for local defence and the maintenance of law and order within the trust territory.

Article 85

1. The functions of the United Nations with regard to trusteeship agreements for all areas not designated as strategic, including the approval of the terms of the trusteeship agreements and of their alteration or amendment, shall be exercised by the General Assembly.

2. The Trusteeship Council, operating under the authority of the General Assembly, shall assist the General Assembly in carrying out these functions.

CHAPTER XIII.   THE TRUSTEESHIP COUNCIL

Composition

Article 86

1. The Trusteeship Council shall consist of the following Members of the United Nations:

a. those Members administering trust territories;

b. such of those Members mentioned by name in Article 23 as are not administering trust territories; and

c. as many other Members elected for three-year terms by the General Assembly as may be necessary to ensure that the total number of members of the Trusteeship

Council is equally divided between those Members of the United Nations which administer trust territories and those which do not.

2. Each member of the Trusteeship Council shall designate one specially qualified person to represent it therein.

Functions and powers

Article 87

The General Assembly and, under its authority, the Trusteeship Council, in carrying out their functions, may:

    a.   consider reports submitted by the administering authority;

    b.   accept petitions and examine them in consultation with the administering authority;

    c.   provide for periodic visits to the respective trust territories at times agreed upon with the administering authority; and

    d.   take these and other actions in conformity with the terms of the trusteeship agreements.

Article 88

The Trusteeship Council shall formulate a questionnaire on the political, economic, social, and educational advancement of the inhabitants of each trust territory, and the administering authority for each trust territory within the competence of the General Assembly shall make an annual report to the General Assembly upon the basis of such questionnaire.

Voting

Article 89

1. Each member of the Trusteeship Council shall have one vote.

2. Decisions of the Trusteeship Council shall be made by a majority of the members present and voting.

Procedure

Article 90

1. The Trusteeship Council shall adopt its own rules of procedure, including the method of selecting its President.

2. The Trusteeship Council shall meet as required in accordance with its rules, which shall include provision for the convening of meetings on the request of a majority of its members.

Article 91

The Trusteeship Council shall, when appropriate, avail itself of the assistance of the Economic and Social Council and of the specialized agencies in regard to matters with which they are respectively concerned.

CHAPTER XIV. THE INTERNATIONAL COURT OF JUSTICE

Article 92

The International Court of Justice shall be principle judicial organ of the United Nations. It shall function in accordance with the annexed Statute, which is based upon the Statute of the Permanent Court of International Justice and forms an integral part of the present Charter.

Article 93

1.   All Members of the United Nations are ipso facto parties to the Statute of the International Court of Justice.

2.   A state which is not a Member of the United Nations may become a party to the Statute of the International Court of Justice on conditions to be determined in each case by the General Assembly upon the recommendation of the Security Council.

Article 94

1.   Each Member of the United Nations undertakes to comply with the decision of the International Court of Justice in any case to which it is a party.

2.   If any party to a case fails to perform the obligations incumbent upon it under a judgment rendered by the Court, the other party may have recourse to the Security Council, which may, if it deems necessary, make recommendations or decide upon measures to be taken to give effect to the judgment.

Article 95

Nothing in the present Charter shall prevent members of the United Nations from entrusting the solution of their differences to other tribunals by virtue of agreements already in existence or which may be concluded in the future.

Article 96

1.   The General Assembly or the Security Council may request the International Court of Justice to give an advisory opinion on any legal question.

2.   Other organs of the United Nations and specialized agencies, which may at any time be so authorized by the General Assembly, may also request advisory opinions of the Court on legal questions arising within the scope of their activities.

CHAPTER XV.   THE SECRETARIAT

Article 97

The Secretariat shall comprise a Secretary–General and such staff as the Organization may require. The Secretary–General shall be appointed by the General Assembly upon the recommendation of the Security Council. He shall be the chief administrative officer of the Organization.

Article 98

The Secretary–General shall act in that capacity in all meetings of the General Assembly, of the Security Council, of the Economic and Social Council, and of the Trusteeship Council, and shall perform such other functions as are entrusted to him by these organs. The Secretary–General shall make an annual report to the General Assembly on the work of the Organization.

Article 99

The Secretary–General may bring to the attention of the Security Council any matter which in his opinion may threaten the maintenance of international peace and security.

Article 100

1.   In the performance of their duties the Secretary–General and the staff shall not seek or receive instructions from any government or from any other authority external to the Organization. They shall refrain from any action which might reflect on their position as international officials responsible only to the Organization.

2. Each Member of the United Nations undertakes to respect the exclusively international character of the responsibilities of the Secretary–General and the staff and not to seek to influence them in the discharge of their responsibilities.

Article 101

1. The staff shall be appointed by the Secretary–General under regulations established by the General Assembly.

2. Appropriate staffs shall be permanently assigned to the Economic and Social Council, the Trusteeship Council, and, as required, to other organs of the United Nations. These staffs shall form a part of the Secretariat.

3. The paramount consideration in the employment of the staff and in the determination of the conditions of service shall be the necessity of securing the highest standards of efficiency, competence, and integrity. Due regard shall be paid to the importance of recruiting the staff on as wide a geographical basis as possible.

Chapter XVI. MISCELLANEOUS PROVISIONS

Article 102

1. Every treaty and every international agreement entered into by any Member of the United Nations after the present Charter comes into force shall as soon as possible be registered with the Secretariat and published by it.

2. No party to any such treaty or international agreement which has not been registered in accordance with the provisions of paragraph 1 of this Article may invoke that treaty or agreement before an organ of the United Nations.

Article 103

In the event of a conflict between the obligations of the Members of the United Nations under the present Charter and their obligations under any other international agreement, their obligations under the present Charter shall prevail.

Article 104

The Organization shall enjoy in the territory of each of its Members such legal capacity as may be necessary for the exercise of its functions and the fulfilment of its purposes.

Article 105

1. The Organization shall enjoy in the territory of each of its Members such privileges and immunities as are necessary for the fulfilment of its purposes.

2. Representatives of the Members of the United Nations and officials of the Organization shall similarly enjoy such privileges and immunities as are necessary for the independent exercise of their functions in connexion with the Organization.

3. The General Assembly may make recommendations with a view to determining the details of the application of paragraphs 1 and 2 of this Article or may propose conventions to the Members of the United Nations for this purpose.

Chapter XVII. TRANSITIONAL SECURITY ARRANGEMENTS

Article 106

Pending the coming into force of such special agreements referred to in Article 43 as in the opinion of the Security Council enable it to begin the exercise of its responsibilities under Article 42, the parties to the Four–Nation Declaration, signed at Moscow, 30 October 1943, and France, shall, in accordance with the provisions of paragraph 5 of that Declaration, consult with one another and as occasion requires with other Members of the United Nations with a view to such joint action on behalf of the Organization as may be necessary for the purpose of maintaining international peace and security.

Article 107

Nothing in the present Charter shall invalidate or preclude action, in relation to any state which during the Second World War has been an enemy of any signatory to the present Charter, taken or authorized as a result of that war by the Governments having responsibility for such action.

CHAPTER XVIII.   AMENDMENTS

Article 108

Amendments to the present Charter shall come into force for all Members of the United Nations when they have been adopted by a vote of two thirds of the members of the General Assembly and ratified in accordance with their respective constitutional processes by two thirds of the Members of the United Nations, including all the permanent members of the Security Council.

Article 109[d]

1.   A General Conference of the Members of the United Nations for the purpose of reviewing the present Charter may be held at a date and place to be fixed by a two-thirds vote of the members of the General Assembly and by a vote of any nine members of the Security Council. Each Member of the United Nations shall have one vote in the conference.

2.   Any alteration of the present Charter recommended by a two-thirds vote of the conference shall take effect when ratified in accordance with their respective constitutional processes by two thirds of the Members of the United Nations including all the permanent members of the Security Council.

3.   If such a conference has not been held before the tenth annual session of the General Assembly following the coming into force of the present Charter, the proposal to call such a conference shall be placed on the agenda of that session of the General Assembly, and the conference shall be held if so decided by a majority vote of the members of the General Assembly and by a vote of any seven members of the Security Council.

CHAPTER XIX.   RATIFICATION AND SIGNATURE

Article 110

1.   The present Charter shall be ratified by the signatory states in accordance with their respective constitutional processes.

2.   The ratifications shall be deposited with the Government of the United States of America, which shall notify all the signatory states of each deposit as well as the Secretary–General of the Organization when he has been appointed.

3.   The present Charter shall come into force upon the deposit of ratifications by the Republic of China, France, the Union of Soviet Socialist Republics, the United Kingdom of Great Britain and Northern Ireland, and the United States of America, and by a majority of the other signatory states. A protocol of the ratifications deposited shall thereupon be drawn up by the Government of the United States of America which shall communicate copies thereof to all the signatory states.

d.   Amended text of Article 109, which entered into force on 12 June 1968.

4.   The states signatory to the present Charter which ratify it after it has come into force will become original Members of the United Nations on the date of the deposit of their respective ratifications.

Article 111

The present Charter, of which the Chinese, French, Russian, English, and Spanish texts are equally authentic, shall remain deposited in the archives of the Government of the United States of America. Duly certified copies thereof shall be transmitted by that Government to the Governments of the other signatory states.

1.3 STATUTE OF THE INTERNATIONAL COURT OF JUSTICE. **Concluded at San Francisco, 26 June 1945. Entered into force, 24 October 1945. 1976 YBUN 1052, 59 Stat 1031, TS No 993,** *reprinted in* **1 Weston & Carlson I.A.2**

Article 1

THE INTERNATIONAL COURT OF JUSTICE established by the Charter of the United Nations as the principal judicial organ of the United Nations shall be constituted and shall function in accordance with the provisions of the present Statute.

CHAPTER I. ORGANIZATION OF THE COURT

Article 2

The Court shall be composed of a body of independent judges, elected regardless of their nationality from among persons of high moral character, who possess the qualifications required in their respective countries for appointment to the highest judicial offices, or are jurisconsults of recognized competence in international law.

Article 3

1. The Court shall consist of fifteen members, no two of whom may be nationals of the same state.

2. A person who for the purposes of membership in the Court could be regarded as a national of more than one state shall be deemed to be a national of the one in which he ordinary exercises civil and political rights.

Article 4

1. The members of the Court shall be elected by the General Assembly and by the Security Council from a list of persons nominated by the national groups in the Permanent Court of Arbitration, in accordance with the following provisions.

2. In the case of Members of the United Nations not represented in the Permanent Court of Arbitration, candidates shall be nominated by national groups appointed for this purpose by their governments under the same conditions as those prescribed for members of the Permanent Court of Arbitration by Article 44 of the Convention of the Hague of 1907 for the pacific settlement of international disputes.

3. The conditions under which a state which is a party to the present Statute but is not a Member of the United Nations may participate in electing the members of the Court shall, in the absence of a special agreement, be laid down by the General Assembly upon recommendation of the Security Council.

Article 5

1. At least three months before the date of the election, the Secretary–General of the United Nations shall address a written request to the members of the Permanent Court of Arbitration belonging to the states which are parties to the present Statute, and to the members of the national groups appointed under Article 4, paragraph 2, inviting them to undertake, within a given time, by national groups, the nomination of persons in a position to accept the duties of a member of the Court.

2. No group may nominate more than four persons, not more than two of whom shall be of their own nationality. In no case may the number of candidates nominated by a group be more than double the number of seats to be filled.

Article 6

Before making these nominations, each national group is recommended to consult its highest court of justice, its legal faculties and schools of law, and its national academies and national sections of international academies devoted to the study of law.

Article 7

1. The Secretary–General shall prepare a list in alphabetical order of all the persons thus nominated. Save as provided in Article 12, paragraph 2, these shall be the only persons eligible.

2. The Secretary–General shall submit this list to the General Assembly and to the Security Council.

Article 8

The General Assembly and the Security Council shall proceed independently of one another to elect the members of the Court.

Article 9

At every election, the electors shall bear in mind not only that the persons to be elected should individually possess the qualifications required, but also that in the body as a whole the representation of the main forms of civilization and of the principal legal systems of the world should be assured.

Article 10

1. Those candidates who obtain an absolute majority of votes in the General Assembly and in the Security Council shall be considered as elected.

2. Any vote of the Security Council, whether for the election of judges or for the appointment of members of the conference envisaged in Article 12, shall be taken without any distinction between permanent and non-permanent members of the Security Council.

3. In the event of more than one national of the same state obtaining an absolute majority of the votes both of the General Assembly and of the Security Council, the eldest of these only shall be considered as elected.

Article 11

If, after the first meeting held for the purpose of the election, one or more seats remain to be filled, a second and, if necessary, a third meeting shall take place.

Article 12

1. If, after the third meeting, one or more seats still remain unfilled, a joint conference consisting of six members, three appointed by the General Assembly and three by the Security Council, may be formed at any time at the request of either the General Assembly or the Security Council, for the purpose of choosing by the vote of an absolute majority one name for each seat still vacant, to submit to the General Assembly and the Security Council for their respective acceptance.

2. If the joint conference is unanimously agreed upon any person who fulfils the required conditions, he may be included in its list, even though he was not included in the list of nominations referred to in Article 7.

3. If the joint conference is satisfied that it will not be successful in procuring an election, those members of the Court who have already been elected shall, within a period to be fixed by the Security Council, proceed to fill the vacant seats by selection from among those candidates who have obtained votes either in the General Assembly or in the Security Council.

4. In the event of an equality of votes among the judges, the eldest judge shall have a casting vote.

Article 13

1.   The members of the Court shall be elected for nine years and may be re-elected; provided, however, that of the judges elected at the first election, the terms of five judges shall expire at the end of three years and the terms of five more judges shall expire at the end of six years.

2.   The judges whose terms are to expire at the end of the above-mentioned initial periods of three and six years shall be chosen by lot to be drawn by the Secretary–General immediately after the first election has been completed.

3.   The members of the Court shall continue to discharge their duties until their places have been filled. Though replaced, they shall finish any cases which they may have begun.

4.   In the case of the resignation of a member of the Court, the resignation shall be addressed to the President of the Court for transmission to the Secretary–General. This last notification makes the place vacant.

Article 14

Vacancies shall be filled by the same methods as that laid down for the first election, subject to the following provision: the Secretary–General shall, within one month of the occurrence of the vacancy, proceed to issue the invitations provided for in Article 5, and the date of the election shall be fixed by the Security Council.

Article 15

A member of the Court elected to replace a member whose term of office has not expired shall hold office for the remainder of his predecessor's term.

Article 16

1.   No member of the Court may exercise any political or administrative function, or engage in any other occupation of a professional nature.

2.   Any doubt on this point shall be settled by the decision of the Court.

Article 17

1.   No member of the Court may act as agent, counsel, or advocate in any case.

2.   No member may participate in the decision of any case in which he has previously taken part as agent, counsel, or advocate for one of the parties, or as a member of a national or international court, or of a commission of enquiry, or in any other capacity.

3.   Any doubt on this point shall be settled by the decision of the Court.

Article 18

1.   No member of the Court can be dismissed unless, in the unanimous opinion of the other members, he has ceased to fulfil the required conditions.

2.   Formal notification thereof shall be made to the Secretary–General by the Registrar.

3.   This notification makes the place vacant.

Article 19

The members of the Court, when engaged on the business of the Court, shall enjoy diplomatic privileges and immunities.

Article 20

Every member of the Court shall, before taking up his duties, make a solemn declaration in open court that he will exercise his powers impartially and conscientiously.

Article 21

1. The Court shall elect its President and Vice–President for three years; they may be re-elected.

2. The Court shall appoint its Registrar and may provide for the appointment of such other officers as may be necessary.

Article 22

1. The seat of the Court shall be established at The Hague. This, however, shall not prevent the Court from sitting and exercising its functions elsewhere whenever the Court considers it desirable.

2. The President and the Registrar shall reside at the seat of the Court.

Article 23

1. The Court shall remain permanently in session, except during the judicial vacations, the dates and duration which shall be fixed by the Court.

2. Members of the Court are entitled to periodic leave, the dates and duration of which shall be fixed by the Court, having in mind the distance between The Hague and the home of each judge.

3. Members of the Court shall be bound, unless they are on leave or prevented from attending by illness or other serious reasons duly explained to the President, to hold themselves permanently at the disposal of the Court.

Article 24

1. If, for some special reason, a member of the Court considers that he should not take part in the decision of a particular case, he shall so inform the President.

2. If the President considers that for some special reason one of the members of the Court should not sit in a particular case, he shall give him notice accordingly.

3. If in any such case the member of the Court and the President disagree, the matter shall be settled by the decision of the Court.

Article 25

1. The full Court shall sit except when it is expressly provided otherwise in the present Statute.

2. Subject to the condition that the number of judges available to constitute the Court is not thereby reduced below eleven, the Rules of the Court may provide for allowing one or more judges, according to circumstances and in rotation, to be dispensed from sitting.

3. A quorum of nine judges shall suffice to constitute the Court.

Article 26

1. The Court may from time to time form one or more chambers, composed of three or more judges as the Court may determine, for dealing with particular categories of cases; for example, labour cases and cases relating to transit and communications.

2. The Court may at any time form a chamber for dealing with a particular case. The number of judges to constitute such a chamber shall be determined by the Court with the approval of the parties.

3. Cases shall be heard and determined by the chambers provided for in this Article if the parties so request.

Article 27

A judgment given by any of the chambers provided for in Articles 26 and 29 shall be considered as rendered by the Court.

Article 28

The chambers provided for in Articles 26 and 29 may, with the consent of the parties, sit and exercise their functions elsewhere than at The Hague.

Article 29

With a view to the speedy dispatch of business, the Court shall form annually a chamber composed of five judges which, at the request of the parties, may hear and determine cases by summary procedure. In addition, two judges shall be selected for the purpose of replacing judges who find it impossible to sit.

Article 30

1. The Court shall frame rules for carrying out its functions. In particular, it shall lay down rules of procedure.

2. The Rules of the Court may provide for assessors to sit with the Court or with any of its chambers, without the right to vote.

Article 31

1. Judges of the nationality of each of the parties shall retain their right to sit in the case before the Court.

2. If the Court includes upon the Bench a judge of the nationality of one of the parties, any other party may choose a person to sit as judge. Such person shall be chosen preferably from among those persons who have been nominated as candidates as provided in Articles 4 and 5.

3. If the Court includes upon the Bench no judge of the nationality of the parties, each of these parties may proceed to choose a judge as provided in paragraph 2 of this Article.

4. The provisions of this Article shall apply to the case of Articles 26 and 29. In such cases, the President shall request one or, if necessary, two of the members of the Court forming the chamber to give place to the members of the Court of the nationality of the parties concerned, and, failing such, or if they are unable to be present, to the judges specially chosen by the parties.

5. Should there be several parties in the same interest, they shall, for the purpose of the preceding provisions, be reckoned as one party only. Any doubt upon this point shall be settled by the decision of the Court.

6. Judges chosen as laid down in paragraphs 2, 3, and 4 of this Article shall fulfil the conditions required by Articles 2, 17 (paragraph 2), 20, and 24 of the present Statute. They shall take part in the decision on terms of complete equality with their colleagues.

Article 32

1. Each member of the Court shall receive an annual salary.

2. The President shall receive a special annual allowance.

3. The Vice–President shall receive a special allowance for every day on which he acts as President.

4. The judges chosen under Article 31, other than members of the Court, shall receive compensation for each day on which they exercise their functions.

5. These salaries, allowances, and compensation shall be fixed by the General Assembly. They may not be decreased during the term of office.

6. The salary of the Registrar shall be fixed by the General Assembly on the proposal of the Court.

7. Regulations made by the General Assembly shall fix the conditions under which retirement pensions may be given to members of the Court and to the Registrar, and the conditions under which members of the Court and the Registrar shall have their travelling expenses refunded.

8. The above salaries, allowances, and compensation shall be free of all taxation.

Article 33

The expenses of the Court shall be borne by the United Nations in such a manner as shall be decided by the General Assembly.

Chapter II. COMPETENCE OF THE COURT

Article 34

1. Only states may be parties in cases before the Court.

2. The Court, subject to and in conformity with its Rules, may request of public international organizations information relevant to cases before it, and shall receive such information presented by such organizations on their own initiative.

3. Whenever the construction of the constituent instrument of a public international organization or of an international convention adopted thereunder is in question in a case before the Court, the Registrar shall so notify the public international organization concerned and shall communicate to it copies of all the written proceedings.

Article 35

1. The Court shall be open to the states parties to the present Statute.

2. The conditions under which the Court shall be open to other states shall, subject to the special provisions contained in treaties in force, be laid down by the Secretary Council, but in no case shall such conditions place the parties in a position of inequality before the Court.

3. When a state which is not a Member of the United Nations is a party to a case, the Court shall fix the amount which that party is to contribute towards the expenses of the Court. This provision shall not apply it such state is bearing a share of the expenses of the Court.

Article 36

1. The jurisdiction of the Court comprises all cases which the parties refer to it and all matters specially provided for in the Charter of the United Nations or in treaties and conventions in force.

2. The states parties to the present Statute may at any time declare that they recognize as compulsory *ipso facto* and without special agreement, in relation to any other state accepting the same obligation, the jurisdiction of the Court in all legal disputes concerning:

  a. the interpretation of a treaty;

  b. any question of international law;

  c. the existence of any fact which, if established, would constitute a breach of an international obligation;

  d. the nature or extent of the reparation to be made for the breach of an international obligation.

 3. The declarations referred to above may be made unconditionally or on condition of reciprocity on the part of several or certain states, or for a certain time.

 4. Such declarations shall be deposited with the Secretary–General of the United Nations, who shall transmit copies thereof to the parties to the Statute and to the Registrar of the Court.

 5. Declarations made under Article 36 of the Statute of the Permanent Court of International Justice and which are still in force shall be deemed, as between the parties to the present Statute, to be acceptances of the compulsory jurisdiction of the International Court of Justice for the period which they still have to run and in accordance with their terms.

 6. In the event of a dispute as to whether the Court has jurisdiction, the matter shall be settled by the decision of the Court.

Article 37

Wherever a treaty or convention in force provides for reference of a matter to a tribunal to have been instituted by the League of Nations, or to the Permanent Court of International Justice, the matter shall, as between the parties to the present Statute, be referred to the International Court of Justice.

Article 38

 1. The Court, whose function is to decide in accordance with international law such disputes as are submitted to it, shall apply:

  a. international conventions, whether general or particular, establishing rules expressly recognized by the contesting states;

  b. international custom, as evidence of a general practice accepted as law;

  c. the general principles of law recognized by civilized nations;

  d. subject to the provisions of Article 59, judicial decisions and the teachings of the most highly qualified publicists of the various nations, as subsidiary means for the determination of rules of law.

 2. This provision shall not prejudice the power of the Court to decide a case *ex aequo et bono,* if the parties agree thereto.

CHAPTER III. PROCEDURE

Article 39

 1. The official languages of the Court shall be French and English. If the parties agree that the case shall be conducted in French, the judgment shall be delivered in French. If the parties agree that the case shall be conducted in English, the judgment shall be delivered in English.

 2. In the absence of an agreement as to which language shall be employed, each party may, in the pleadings, use the language which it prefers; the decision of the Court shall be given in French and English. In this case the Court shall at the same time determine which of the two texts shall be considered as authoritative.

3. The Court shall, at the request of any party, authorize a language other than French or English to be used by that party.

Article 40

1. Cases are brought before the Court, as the case may be, either by the notification of the special agreement or by a written application addressed to the Registrar. In either case the subject of the dispute and the parties shall be indicated.

2. The Registrar shall forthwith communicate the application to all concerned.

3. He shall also notify the Members of the United Nations through the Secretary–General, and also any other states entitled to appear before the Court.

Article 41

1. The Court shall have the power to indicate, if it considers that circumstances so require, any provisional measures which ought to be taken to preserve the respective rights of either party.

2. Pending the final decision, notice of the measures suggested shall forthwith be given to the parties and to the Security Council.

Article 42

1. The parties shall be represented by agents.

2. They may have the assistance of counsel or advocates before the Court.

3. The agents, counsel, and advocates of parties before the Court shall enjoy the privileges and immunities necessary to the independent exercise of their duties.

Article 43

1. The procedure shall consist of two parts: written and oral.

2. The written proceedings shall consist of the communication to the Court and to the parties of memorials, counter-memorials and, if necessary, replies; also all papers and documents in support.

3. These communications shall be made through the Registrar, in the order and within the time fixed by the Court.

4. A certified copy of every document produced by one party shall be communicated to the other party.

5. The oral proceedings shall consist of the hearing by the Court of witnesses, experts, agents, counsel, and advocates.

Article 44

1. For the service of all notices upon persons other than the agents, counsel, and advocates, the Court shall apply direct to the government of the state upon whose territory the notice has to be served.

2. The same provision shall apply whenever steps are to be taken to procure evidence on the spot.

Article 45

The hearing shall be under the control of the President or, if he is unable to preside, of the Vice–President; if neither is able to preside, the senior judge present shall preside.

Article 46

The hearing in Court shall be public, unless the Court shall decide otherwise, or unless the parties demand that the public be not admitted.

Article 47

1. Minutes shall be made at each hearing and signed by the Registrar and the President.

2. These minutes alone shall be authentic.

Article 48

The Court shall make orders for the conduct of the case, shall decide the form and time in which each party must conclude its arguments, and make all arrangements connected with the taking of evidence.

Article 49

The Court may, even before the hearing begins, call upon the agents to produce any document or to supply any explanations. Formal note shall be taken of any refusal.

Article 50

The Court may, at any time, entrust any individual, body, bureau, commission, or other organization that it may select, with the task of carrying out an enquiry or giving an expert opinion.

Article 51

During the hearing any relevant questions are to be put to the witnesses and experts under the conditions laid down by the Court in the rules of procedure referred to in Article 30.

Article 52

After the Court has received the proofs and evidence within the time specified for the purpose, it may refuse to accept any further oral or written evidence that one party may desire to present unless the other side consents.

Article 53

1. Whenever one of the parties does not appear before the Court, or fails to defend its case, the other party may call upon the Court to decide in favour of its claim.

2. The Court must, before doing so, satisfy itself, not only that it has jurisdiction in accordance with Articles 36 and 37, but also that the claim is well founded in fact and law.

Article 54

1. When, subject to the control of the Court, the agents, counsel, and advocates have completed their presentation of the case, the President shall declare the hearing closed.

2. The Court shall withdraw to consider the judgment.

3. The deliberation of the Court shall take place in private and remain secret.

Article 55

1. All questions shall be decided by a majority of the judges present.

2. In the event of an equality of votes, the President or the judge who acts in his place shall have a casting vote.

Article 56

1. The judgment shall state the reasons on which it is based.

2. It shall contain the names of the judges who have taken part in the decision.

Article 57

If the judgment does not represent in whole or in part the unanimous opinion of the judges, any judge shall be entitled to deliver a separate opinion.

Article 58

The judgment shall be signed by the President and by the Registrar. It shall be read in open court, due notice having been given to the agents.

Article 59

The decision of the Court has no binding force except between the parties and in respect of that particular case.

Article 60

The judgment is final and without appeal. In the event of dispute as to the meaning or scope of the judgment, the Court shall construe it upon the request of any party.

Article 61

1. An application for revision of a judgment may be made only when it is based upon the discovery of some fact of such a nature as to be a decisive factor, which fact was, when the judgment was given, unknown to the Court and also to the party claiming revision, always provided that such ignorance was not due to negligence.

2. The proceedings for revision shall be opened by a judgment of the Court expressly recording the existence of the new fact, recognizing that it has such a character as to lay the case open to revision, and declaring the application admissible on this ground.

3. The Court may require previous compliance with the terms of the judgment before it admits proceedings in revision.

4. The application for revision must be made at latest within six months of the discovery of the new fact.

5. No application for revision may be made after the lapse of ten years from the date of the judgment.

Article 62

1. Should a state consider that it has an interest of a legal nature which may be affected by the decision in the case, it may submit a request to the Court to be permitted to intervene.

2. It shall be for the Court to decide upon this request.

Article 63

1. Whenever the construction of a convention to which states other than those concerned in the case are parties is in question, the Registrar shall notify all such states forthwith.

2. Every state so notified has the right to intervene in the proceedings; but if it uses this right, the construction given by the judgement will be equally binding upon it.

Article 64

Unless otherwise decided by the Court, each party shall bear its own costs.

Chapter IV. ADVISORY OPINIONS

Article 65

1. The Court may give an advisory opinion on any legal question at the request of whatever body may be authorized by or in accordance with the Charter of the United Nations to make such a request.

2. Questions upon which the advisory opinion of the Court is asked shall be laid before the Court by means of a written request containing an exact statement of the question upon which an opinion is required, and accompanied by all documents likely to throw light upon the question.

Article 66

1. The Registrar shall forthwith give notice of the request for an advisory opinion to all states entitled to appear before the Court.

2. The Registrar shall also, by means of a special and direct communication, notify any state entitled to appear before the Court or international organization considered by the Court, or, should it not be sitting, by the President, as likely to be able to furnish information on the question, that the Court will be prepared to receive, within a time limit to be fixed by the President, written statements, or to hear, at a public sitting to be held for the purpose, oral statements relating to the question.

3. Should any such state entitled to appear before the Court have failed to receive the special communication referred to in paragraph 2 of this Article, such state may express a desire to submit a written statement or to be heard; and the Court will decide.

4. States and organizations having presented written or oral statements or both shall be permitted to comment on the statements made by other states or organizations in the form, to the extent, and within the time limits which the Court, or, should it not be sitting, the President, shall decide in each particular case. Accordingly, the Registrar shall in due time communicate any such written statements to states and organizations having submitted similar statements.

Article 67

The Court shall deliver its advisory opinions in open court, notice having been given to the Secretary–General and to the representatives of Members of the United Nations, of other states and of international organizations immediately concerned.

Article 68

In the exercise of its advisory functions the Court shall further be guided by the provisions of the present Statute which apply in contentious cases to the extent to which it recognizes them to be applicable.

Chapter V. AMENDMENT

Article 69

Amendments to the present Statute shall be effected by the same procedure as is provided by the Charter of the United Nations for amendments to that Charter, subject however to any provisions which the General Assembly upon recommendation of the Security Council may adopt concerning the participation of states which are parties to the present Statute but are not Members of the United Nations.

Article 70

The Court shall have power to propose such amendments to the present Statute as it may deem necessary, through written communications to the Secretary–General, for consideration in conformity with the provisions of Article 69.

1.4 STATUTE OF THE INTERNATIONAL ATOMIC ENERGY AGENCY (IAEA) (as Amended). **Concluded at New York, 26 October 1956. Entered into force, 29 July 1957. 276 UNTS 3, TIAS No 3873, 8 TS No 1093; 471 UNTS 334, TIAS No 5284, 14 TS No 135; TIAS No 7668, 24 TS No 1637;** *reprinted in* 5 **Weston & Carlson V.A.3:** *Arts. I, II, III, XI, XII*

Art. I. *Establishment of the agency*

The parties hereto establish an International Atomic Energy Agency (hereinafter referred to as "the Agency") upon the terms and conditions hereinafter set forth.

Art. II. *Objectives*

The agency shall seek to accelerate and enlarge the contribution of atomic energy to peace, health and prosperity throughout the world. It shall ensure, so far as it is able, that assistance provided by it or at its request or under its supervision or control is not used in such a way as to further any military purpose.

Art. III. *Functions*

(A) The agency is authorized:

1. To encourage and assist research on, and development and practical application, of atomic energy for peaceful uses throughout the world; and, if requested to do so, to act as an intermediary for the purposes of securing the performance of services or the supplying of materials, equipment, or facilities by one member of the agency for another; and to perform any operation or service useful in research on, or development or practical application of, atomic energy for peaceful purposes;

2. To make provision, in accordance with this statute, for materials, services, equipment, and facilities to meet the needs of research on, and development and practical application of, atomic energy for peaceful purposes, including the production of electric power, with due consideration for the needs of the under-developed areas of the world;

3. To foster the exchange of scientific and technical information on peaceful uses of atomic energy;

4. To encourage the exchange and training of scientists and experts in the field of peaceful uses of atomic energy;

5. To establish and administer safeguards designed to ensure that special fissionable and other materials, services, equipment, facilities and information made available by the agency or at its request or under its supervision or control are not used in such a way as to further any military purpose; and to apply safeguards, at the request of the parties, to any bilateral or multilateral arrangement, or, at the request of a state, to any of that state's activities in the field of atomic energy;

6. To establish or adopt, in consultation and, where appropriate, in collaboration with the competent organs of the United Nations and with the specialized agencies concerned, standards of safety for protection of health and minimization of danger to life and property (including such standards for labor conditions), and to provide for the application of these standards to its own operations as well as to the operations making use of materials, services, equipment, facilities and information made available by the agency or at its request or under its control or supervision; and to provide for the application of these standards, at the request of the parties, to operations under any bilateral or multilateral arrangement, or, at the request of a state, to any of that state's activities in the field of atomic energy;

7. To acquire or establish any facilities, plant and equipment useful in carrying out its authorized functions, whenever the facilities, plant and equipment otherwise available to it in the area concerned are inadequate or available only on terms it deems unsatisfactory.

(B) In carrying out its functions, the agency shall:

1. Conduct its activities in accordance with the purposes and principles of the United Nations to promote peace and international cooperation, and in conformity with policies of the United Nations furthering the establishment of safeguarded world-wide disarmament and in conformity with any international agreements entered into pursuant to such policies;

2. Establish control over the use of special fissionable materials received by the agency, in order to ensure that these materials are used only for peaceful purposes;

3. Allocate its resources in such a manner as to secure efficient utilization and the greatest possible general benefit in all areas of the world, bearing in mind the special needs of the underdeveloped areas of the world;

4. Submit reports on its activities annually to the General Assembly of the United Nations and, when appropriate, to the Security Council: if in connection with the activities of the agency there should arise questions that are within the competence of the Security Council, the agency shall notify the Security Council, as the organ bearing the main responsibility for the maintenance of international peace and security, and may also take the measures open to it under this statute, including those provided in paragraph C of Article XII;

5. Submit reports to the Economic and Social Council and other organs of the United Nations on matters within the competence of these organs.

(C) In carrying out its functions, the agency shall not make assistance to members subject to any political, economic, military, or other conditions incompatible with the provisions of this statute.

(D) Subject to the provisions of this statute and to the terms of agreements concluded between a state or a group of states and the agency which shall be in accordance with the provisions of the statute, the activities of the agency shall be carried out with due observance of the sovereign rights of states.

* * *

Art. XI. *Agency projects*

(A) Any member or group of members of the agency desiring to set up any project for research on, or development or practical application of, atomic energy for peaceful purposes may request the assistance of the agency in securing special fissionable and other materials, services, equipment and facilities necessary for this purpose. Any such request shall be accompanied by an explanation of the purpose and extent of the project and shall be considered by the Board of Governors.

(B) Upon request, the agency may also assist any member or group of members to make arrangements to secure necessary financing from outside sources to carry out such projects. In extending this assistance, the agency will not be required to provide any guarantees or to assume any financial responsibilities for the project.

(C) The agency may arrange for the supplying of any materials, services, equipment, and facilities necessary for the project by one or more members or may itself undertake to provide any or all of these directly, taking into consideration the wishes of the member or members making the request.

(D) For the purpose of considering the request, the agency may send into the territory of the member or group of members making the request a person or persons qualified to examine the project. For this purpose the agency may, with the approval of the member or group of members making the request, use members of its own staff or employ suitably qualified nationals of any member.

(E) Before approving a project under this Article, the Board of Governors shall give due consideration to:

1. The usefulness of the project, including its scientific and technical feasibility;

2. The adequacy of plans, funds, and technical personnel to assure the effective execution of the project;

3. The adequacy of proposed health and safety standards for handling and storing materials and for operating facilities;

4. The inability of the member or group of members making the request to secure the necessary finances, materials, facilities, equipment, and services;

5. The equitable distribution of materials and other resources available to the agency;

6. The special needs of the under-developed areas of the world; and

7. Such other matters as may be relevant.

(F) Upon approving a project, the agency shall enter into an agreement with the member or group of members submitting the project, which agreement shall:

1. Provide for allocation to the project of any required special fissionable or other materials;

2. Provide for transfer of special fissionable materials from their then place of custody, whether the materials be in custody of the agency or of the member making them available for use in agency projects, to the member or group of members submitting the project, under conditions which ensure the safety of any shipment required and meet applicable health and safety standards;

3. Set forth the terms and conditions, including charges, on which any materials, services, equipment and facilities are to be provided by the agency itself, and, if any such materials, services, equipment and facilities are to be provided by a member, the terms and conditions as arranged for by the member or group of members submitting the project and the supplying member;

4. Include undertakings by the member or group of members submitting the project (*a*) that the assistance provided shall not be used in such a way as to further any military purpose; and (*b*) that the project shall be subject to the safeguards provided for in Article XII, the relevant safeguards being specified in the agreement;

5. Make appropriate provision regarding the rights and interests of the agency and the member or members concerned in any inventions or discoveries, or any patents therein, arising from the project;

6. Make appropriate provision regarding settlement of disputes;

7. Include such other provisions as may be appropriate.

(G) The provisions of this Article shall also apply where appropriate to a request for materials, services, facilities, or equipment in connection with an existing project.

Art. XII. *Agency safeguards*

(A) With respect to any agency project or other arrangement where the agency is requested by the parties concerned to apply safeguards, the agency shall have the following rights and responsibilities to the extent relevant to the project or arrangement:

1. To examine the design of specialized equipment and facilities, including nuclear reactors, and to approve it only from the viewpoint of assuring that it will not further any military purpose, that it complies with applicable health and safety standards, and that it will permit effective application of the safeguards provided for in this Article;

2. To require the observance of any health and safety measures prescribed by the agency;

3. To require the maintenance and production of operating records to assist in ensuring accountability for source and special fissionable materials used or produced in the project or arrangement;

4. To call for and receive progress reports;

5. To approve the means to be used for the chemical processing of irradiated materials solely to ensure that this chemical processing will not lend itself to diversion of materials for military purposes and will comply with applicable health and safety standards; to require that special fissionable materials recovered or produced as a by-product be used for peaceful purposes under continuing agency safeguards for research or in reactors, existing or under construction, specified by the member or members concerned; and to require deposit with the agency of any excess of any special fissionable materials recovered or produced as a by-product over what is needed for the above stated uses in order to prevent stock-piling of these materials, provided that thereafter at the request of the member or members concerned special fissionable materials so deposited with the agency shall be returned promptly to the member or members concerned for use under the same provisions as stated above;

6. To send into the territory of the recipient state or states inspectors, designated by the agency after consultation with the state or states concerned, who shall have access at all times to all places and data and to any person who by reason of his occupation deals with materials, equipment, or facilities which are required by this statute to be safeguarded, as necessary to account for source and special fissionable materials supplied and fissionable products and to determine whether there is compliance with the undertaking against use in furtherance of any military purpose referred to in sub-Paragraph F–4 of Article XI, with the health and safety measures referred to in sub-Paragraph A–2 of this Article, and with any other conditions prescribed in the agreement between the agency and the state or states concerned. Inspectors designated by the agency shall be accompanied by representatives of the authorities of the state concerned, if that state so requests, provided that the inspectors shall not thereby be delayed or otherwise impeded in the exercise of their functions;

7. In the event of non-compliance and failure by the recipient state or states to take requested corrective steps within a reasonable time, to suspend or terminate assistance and withdraw any materials and equipment made available by the agency or a member in furtherance of the project.

(B) The agency shall, as necessary, establish a staff of inspectors. The staff of inspectors shall have the responsibility of examining all operations conducted by the agency itself to determine whether the agency is complying with the health and safety measures prescribed by it for application to projects subject to its approval, supervision or control, and whether the agency is taking adequate measures to prevent the source and special fissionable materials in its custody or used or produced in its own operations from being used in furtherance of any military purpose. The agency shall take remedial action forthwith to correct any non-compliance or failure to take adequate measures.

(C) The staff of inspectors shall also have the responsibility of obtaining and verifying the accounting referred to in sub-Paragraph A–6 of this Article and of determining whether there is compliance with the undertaking referred to in sub-Paragraph F–4 in Article XI, with the measures referred to in sub-Paragraph A–2 of this Article, and with all other conditions of the project prescribed in the agreement between the agency and the state or states concerned. The inspectors shall report any non-compliance to the director general who shall thereupon transmit the report to the board of governors. The board shall call upon the recipient state or states to remedy forthwith any non-compliance which it finds to have occurred. The board shall report the non-compliance to all members and to the Security Council and General Assembly of the United Nations. In the event of failure of the recipient state or states to take fully corrective action within a reasonable time, the board may take one or both of the following measures: direct curtailment or suspension of assistance being provided by the agency or by a member, and call for the return of materials and equipment made available to the recipient member or group of members. The agency may also, in accordance with Article XIV, suspend any non-complying member from the exercise of the privileges and rights of membership.

1.5 EUROPEAN UNION: CONSOLIDATED VERSIONS OF THE TREATY ON EUROPEAN UNION AND THE TREATY ON THE FUNCTIONING OF THE EUROPEAN UNION. Treaty of Rome, concluded at Rome, 25 March 1957 and entered into force, 1 January 1958. Amended by the Treaty on European Union, concluded at Maastricht, 7 Feb 1992, and entered into force, 1 November 1993; the Treaty of Amsterdam, concluded at Amsterdam, 2 October 1997 and entered into force, 1 May 1999; the Treaty of Nice, concluded at Nice, 26 February 2001, entered into force, 1 February 2003; and the Treaty of Lisbon, concluded at Lisbon, 13 December 2007 and entered into force, 1 December 2009. *Reprinted in consolidated form at* OJEU 2010/C 83/01.

Consolidated Version of the Treaty on European Union
Articles 1, 3, 4, 13, 14, 15, 16, 17, 19, & 21

TITLE I

COMMON PROVISIONS

Article 1 (ex Article 1 TEU)

By this Treaty, the HIGH CONTRACTING PARTIES establish among themselves a EUROPEAN UNION, hereinafter called 'the Union', on which the Member States confer competences to attain objectives they have in common.

This Treaty marks a new stage in the process of creating an ever closer union among the peoples of Europe, in which decisions are taken as openly as possible and as closely as possible to the citizen.

The Union shall be founded on the present Treaty and on the Treaty on the Functioning of the European Union (hereinafter referred to as 'the Treaties'). Those two Treaties shall have the same legal value. The Union shall replace and succeed the European Community.

* * *

Article 3 (ex Article 2 TEU)

1. The Union's aim is to promote peace, its values and the well-being of its peoples.

2. The Union shall offer its citizens an area of freedom, security and justice without internal frontiers, in which the free movement of persons is ensured in conjunction with appropriate measures with respect to external border controls, asylum, immigration and the prevention and combating of crime.

3. The Union shall establish an internal market. It shall work for the sustainable development of Europe based on balanced economic growth and price stability, a highly competitive social market economy, aiming at full employment and social progress, and a high level of protection and improvement of the quality of the environment. It shall promote scientific and technological advance.

It shall combat social exclusion and discrimination, and shall promote social justice and protection, equality between women and men, solidarity between generations and protection of the rights of the child.

It shall promote economic, social and territorial cohesion, and solidarity among Member States.

It shall respect its rich cultural and linguistic diversity, and shall ensure that Europe's cultural heritage is safeguarded and enhanced.

4. The Union shall establish an economic and monetary union whose currency is the euro.

5.   In its relations with the wider world, the Union shall uphold and promote its values and interests and contribute to the protection of its citizens. It shall contribute to peace, security, the sustainable development of the Earth, solidarity and mutual respect among peoples, free and fair trade, eradication of poverty and the protection of human rights, in particular the rights of the child, as well as to the strict observance and the development of international law, including respect for the principles of the United Nations Charter.

6.   The Union shall pursue its objectives by appropriate means commensurate with the competences which are conferred upon it in the Treaties.

Article 4

1.   In accordance with Article 5, competences not conferred upon the Union in the Treaties remain with the Member States.

2.   The Union shall respect the equality of Member States before the Treaties as well as their national identities, inherent in their fundamental structures, political and constitutional, inclusive of regional and local self-government. It shall respect their essential State functions, including ensuring the territorial integrity of the State, maintaining law and order and safeguarding national security. In particular, national security remains the sole responsibility of each Member State.

3.   Pursuant to the principle of sincere cooperation, the Union and the Member States shall, in full mutual respect, assist each other in carrying out tasks which flow from the Treaties.

The Member States shall take any appropriate measure, general or particular, to ensure fulfilment of the obligations arising out of the Treaties or resulting from the acts of the institutions of the Union.

The Member States shall facilitate the achievement of the Union's tasks and refrain from any measure which could jeopardise the attainment of the Union's objectives.

* * *

TITLE III

PROVISIONS ON THE INSTITUTIONS

Article 13

1.   The Union shall have an institutional framework which shall aim to promote its values, advance its objectives, serve its interests, those of its citizens and those of the Member States, and ensure the consistency, effectiveness and continuity of its policies and actions.

The Union's institutions shall be:

— the European Parliament,

— the European Council,

— the Council,

— the European Commission (hereinafter referred to as 'the Commission'),

— the Court of Justice of the European Union,

— the European Central Bank,

— the Court of Auditors.

2.   Each institution shall act within the limits of the powers conferred on it in the Treaties, and in conformity with the procedures, conditions and objectives set out in them. The institutions shall practice mutual sincere cooperation.

3. The provisions relating to the European Central Bank and the Court of Auditors and detailed provisions on the other institutions are set out in the Treaty on the Functioning of the European Union.

4. The European Parliament, the Council and the Commission shall be assisted by an Economic and Social Committee and a Committee of the Regions acting in an advisory capacity.

Article 14

1. The European Parliament shall, jointly with the Council, exercise legislative and budgetary functions. It shall exercise functions of political control and consultation as laid down in the Treaties. It shall elect the President of the Commission.

* * *

Article 15

1. The European Council shall provide the Union with the necessary impetus for its development and shall define the general political directions and priorities thereof. It shall not exercise legislative functions.

2. The European Council shall consist of the Heads of State or Government of the Member States, together with its President and the President of the Commission. The High Representative of the Union for Foreign Affairs and Security Policy shall take part in its work.

* * *

Article 16

1. The Council shall, jointly with the European Parliament, exercise legislative and budgetary functions. It shall carry out policy-making and coordinating functions as laid down in the Treaties.

* * *

Article 17

1. The Commission shall promote the general interest of the Union and take appropriate initiatives to that end. It shall ensure the application of the Treaties, and of measures adopted by the institutions pursuant to them. It shall oversee the application of Union law under the control of the Court of Justice of the European Union. It shall execute the budget and manage programmes. It shall exercise coordinating, executive and management functions, as laid down in the Treaties. With the exception of the common foreign and security policy, and other cases provided for in the Treaties, it shall ensure the Union's external representation. It shall initiate the Union's annual and multiannual programming with a view to achieving interinstitutional agreements.

2. Union legislative acts may only be adopted on the basis of a Commission proposal, except where the Treaties provide otherwise. Other acts shall be adopted on the basis of a Commission proposal where the Treaties so provide.

* * *

Article 19

1. The Court of Justice of the European Union shall include the Court of Justice, the General Court and specialised courts. It shall ensure that in the interpretation and application of the Treaties the law is observed.

Member States shall provide remedies sufficient to ensure effective legal protection in the fields covered by Union law.

2. The Court of Justice shall consist of one judge from each Member State. It shall be assisted by Advocates–General.

The General Court shall include at least one judge per Member State.

The Judges and the Advocates–General of the Court of Justice and the Judges of the General Court shall be chosen from persons whose independence is beyond doubt and who satisfy the conditions set out in Articles 253 and 254 of the Treaty on the Functioning of the European Union. They shall be appointed by common accord of the governments of the Member States for six years. Retiring Judges and Advocates–General may be reappointed.

3. The Court of Justice of the European Union shall, in accordance with the Treaties:

(a) rule on actions brought by a Member State, an institution or a natural or legal person;

(b) give preliminary rulings, at the request of courts or tribunals of the Member States, on the interpretation of Union law or the validity of acts adopted by the institutions;

(c) rule in other cases provided for in the Treaties.

* * *

TITLE V

GENERAL PROVISIONS ON THE UNION'S EXTERNAL ACTION
AND SPECIFIC PROVISIONS ON THE COMMON FOREIGN
AND SECURITY POLICY

CHAPTER 1

GENERAL PROVISIONS ON THE UNION'S EXTERNAL ACTION

Article 21

1. The Union's action on the international scene shall be guided by the principles which have inspired its own creation, development and enlargement, and which it seeks to advance in the wider world: democracy, the rule of law, the universality and indivisibility of human rights and fundamental freedoms, respect for human dignity, the principles of equality and solidarity, and respect for the principles of the United Nations Charter and international law.

The Union shall seek to develop relations and build partnerships with third countries, and international, regional or global organisations which share the principles referred to in the first subparagraph. It shall promote multilateral solutions to common problems, in particular in the framework of the United Nations.

2. The Union shall define and pursue common policies and actions, and shall work for a high degree of cooperation in all fields of international relations, in order to:

(a) safeguard its values, fundamental interests, security, independence and integrity;

(b) consolidate and support democracy, the rule of law, human rights and the principles of international law;

(c) preserve peace, prevent conflicts and strengthen international security, in accordance with the purposes and principles of the United Nations Charter, with the principles of the Helsinki Final Act and with the aims of the Charter of Paris, including those relating to external borders;

(d) foster the sustainable economic, social and environmental development of developing countries, with the primary aim of eradicating poverty;

(e) encourage the integration of all countries into the world economy, including through the progressive abolition of restrictions on international trade;

(f) help develop international measures to preserve and improve the quality of the environment and the sustainable management of global natural resources, in order to ensure sustainable development;

(g) assist populations, countries and regions confronting natural or man-made disasters; and

(h) promote an international system based on stronger multilateral cooperation and good global governance.

* * *

Consolidated Version of the Treaty on the Functioning of the European Union
Articles 1, 3, 4, 11, 191, 192, 193, 251, 252, 258, 259, 260, 265, 266, 267, 288, 289

PART ONE

PRINCIPLES

Article 1

1. This Treaty organises the functioning of the Union and determines the areas of, delimitation of, and arrangements for exercising its competences.

2. This Treaty and the Treaty on European Union constitute the Treaties on which the Union is founded. These two Treaties, which have the same legal value, shall be referred to as 'the Treaties'.

TITLE I

CATEGORIES AND AREAS OF UNION COMPETENCE

* * *

Article 3

1. The Union shall have exclusive competence in the following areas:

(a) customs union;

(b) the establishing of the competition rules necessary for the functioning of the internal market;

(c) monetary policy for the Member States whose currency is the euro;

(d) the conservation of marine biological resources under the common fisheries policy;

(e) common commercial policy.

2. The Union shall also have exclusive competence for the conclusion of an international agreement when its conclusion is provided for in a legislative act of the Union or is necessary to enable the Union to exercise its internal competence, or in so far as its conclusion may affect common rules or alter their scope.

Article 4

1. The Union shall share competence with the Member States where the Treaties confer on it a competence which does not relate to the areas referred to in Articles 3 and 6.

2.   Shared competence between the Union and the Member States applies in the following principal areas:

(a) internal market;

(b) social policy, for the aspects defined in this Treaty;

(c) economic, social and territorial cohesion;

(d) agriculture and fisheries, excluding the conservation of marine biological resources;

(e) environment;

(f) consumer protection;

(g) transport;

(h) trans-European networks;

(i) energy;

(j) area of freedom, security and justice;

(k) common safety concerns in public health matters, for the aspects defined in this Treaty.

3.   In the areas of research, technological development and space, the Union shall have competence to carry out activities, in particular to define and implement programmes; however, the exercise of that competence shall not result in Member States being prevented from exercising theirs.

4.   In the areas of development cooperation and humanitarian aid, the Union shall have competence to carry out activities and conduct a common policy; however, the exercise of that competence shall not result in Member States being prevented from exercising theirs.

* * *

TITLE II

PROVISIONS HAVING GENERAL APPLICATION

* * *

Article 11 (ex Article 6 TEC)

Environmental protection requirements must be integrated into the definition and implementation of the Union's policies and activities, in particular with a view to promoting sustainable development.

* * *

PART THREE

UNION POLICIES AND INTERNAL ACTIONS

* * *

TITLE XX

ENVIRONMENT

Article 191 (ex Article 174 TEC)

1.   Union policy on the environment shall contribute to pursuit of the following objectives:

— preserving, protecting and improving the quality of the environment,

— protecting human health,

— prudent and rational utilisation of natural resources,

— promoting measures at international level to deal with regional or worldwide environmental problems, and in particular combating climate change.

2.   Union policy on the environment shall aim at a high level of protection taking into account the diversity of situations in the various regions of the Union. It shall be based on the precautionary principle and on the principles that preventive action should be taken, that environmental damage should as a priority be rectified at source and that the polluter should pay.

In this context, harmonisation measures answering environmental protection requirements shall include, where appropriate, a safeguard clause allowing Member States to take provisional measures, for non-economic environmental reasons, subject to a procedure of inspection by the Union.

3.   In preparing its policy on the environment, the Union shall take account of:

— available scientific and technical data,

— environmental conditions in the various regions of the Union,

— the potential benefits and costs of action or lack of action,

— the economic and social development of the Union as a whole and the balanced development of its regions.

4.   Within their respective spheres of competence, the Union and the Member States shall cooperate with third countries and with the competent international organisations. The arrangements for Union cooperation may be the subject of agreements between the Union and the third parties concerned.

The previous subparagraph shall be without prejudice to Member States' competence to negotiate in international bodies and to conclude international agreements.

Article 192 (ex Article 175 TEC)

1.   The European Parliament and the Council, acting in accordance with the ordinary legislative procedure and after consulting the Economic and Social Committee and the Committee of the Regions, shall decide what action is to be taken by the Union in order to achieve the objectives referred to in Article 191.

2.   By way of derogation from the decision-making procedure provided for in paragraph 1 and without prejudice to Article 114, the Council acting unanimously in accordance with a special legislative procedure and after consulting the European Parliament, the Economic and Social Committee and the Committee of the Regions, shall adopt:

(a) provisions primarily of a fiscal nature;

(b) measures affecting:

— town and country planning,

— quantitative management of water resources or affecting, directly or indirectly, the availability of those resources,

— land use, with the exception of waste management;

(c) measures significantly affecting a Member State's choice between different energy sources and the general structure of its energy supply.

The Council, acting unanimously on a proposal from the Commission and after consulting the European Parliament, the Economic and Social Committee and the Committee of the Regions, may make the ordinary legislative procedure applicable to the matters referred to in the first subparagraph.

3.   General action programmes setting out priority objectives to be attained shall be adopted by the European Parliament and the Council, acting in accordance with the ordinary legislative procedure and after consulting the Economic and Social Committee and the Committee of the Regions.

The measures necessary for the implementation of these programmes shall be adopted under the terms of paragraph 1 or 2, as the case may be.

4.   Without prejudice to certain measures adopted by the Union, the Member States shall finance and implement the environment policy.

5.   Without prejudice to the principle that the polluter should pay, if a measure based on the provisions of paragraph 1 involves costs deemed disproportionate for the public authorities of a Member State, such measure shall lay down appropriate provisions in the form of:

— temporary derogations, and/or

— financial support from the Cohesion Fund set up pursuant to Article 177.

Article 193 (ex Article 176 TEC)

The protective measures adopted pursuant to Article 192 shall not prevent any Member State from maintaining or introducing more stringent protective measures. Such measures must be compatible with the Treaties. They shall be notified to the Commission.

* * *

PART SIX
INSTITUTIONAL AND FINANCIAL PROVISIONS
TITLE I
INSTITUTIONAL PROVISIONS
CHAPTER 1
THE INSTITUTIONS

* * *

SECTION 5
THE COURT OF JUSTICE OF THE EUROPEAN UNION

Article 251 (ex Article 221 TEC)

The Court of Justice shall sit in chambers or in a Grand Chamber, in accordance with the rules laid down for that purpose in the Statute of the Court of Justice of the European Union.

When provided for in the Statute, the Court of Justice may also sit as a full Court.

Article 252 (ex Article 222 TEC)

The Court of Justice shall be assisted by eight Advocates–General. Should the Court of Justice so request, the Council, acting unanimously, may increase the number of Advocates–General.

It shall be the duty of the Advocate–General, acting with complete impartiality and independence, to make, in open court, reasoned submissions on cases which, in accordance with the Statute of the Court of Justice of the European Union, require his involvement.

* * *

Article 258 (ex Article 226 TEC)

If the Commission considers that a Member State has failed to fulfil an obligation under the Treaties, it shall deliver a reasoned opinion on the matter after giving the State concerned the opportunity to submit its observations.

If the State concerned does not comply with the opinion within the period laid down by the Commission, the latter may bring the matter before the Court of Justice of the European Union.

Article 259 (ex Article 227 TEC)

A Member State which considers that another Member State has failed to fulfil an obligation under the Treaties may bring the matter before the Court of Justice of the European Union.

Before a Member State brings an action against another Member State for an alleged infringement of an obligation under the Treaties, it shall bring the matter before the Commission.

The Commission shall deliver a reasoned opinion after each of the States concerned has been given the opportunity to submit its own case and its observations on the other party's case both orally and in writing.

If the Commission has not delivered an opinion within three months of the date on which the matter was brought before it, the absence of such opinion shall not prevent the matter from being brought before the Court.

Article 260 (ex Article 228 TEC)

1. If the Court of Justice of the European Union finds that a Member State has failed to fulfil an obligation under the Treaties, the State shall be required to take the necessary measures to comply with the judgment of the Court.

2. If the Commission considers that the Member State concerned has not taken the necessary measures to comply with the judgment of the Court, it may bring the case before the Court after giving that State the opportunity to submit its observations. It shall specify the amount of the lump sum or penalty payment to be paid by the Member State concerned which it considers appropriate in the circumstances.

If the Court finds that the Member State concerned has not complied with its judgment it may impose a lump sum or penalty payment on it.

This procedure shall be without prejudice to Article 259.

3. When the Commission brings a case before the Court pursuant to Article 258 on the grounds that the Member State concerned has failed to fulfil its obligation to notify measures transposing a directive adopted under a legislative procedure, it may, when it deems appropriate, specify the amount of the lump sum or penalty payment to be paid by the Member State concerned which it considers appropriate in the circumstances.

If the Court finds that there is an infringement it may impose a lump sum or penalty payment on the Member State concerned not exceeding the amount specified by the Commission. The payment obligation shall take effect on the date set by the Court in its judgment.

* * *

Article 265 (ex Article 232 TEC)

Should the European Parliament, the European Council, the Council, the Commission or the European Central Bank, in infringement of the Treaties, fail to act, the Member States and the other institutions of the Union may bring an action before the

Court of Justice of the European Union to have the infringement established. This Article shall apply, under the same conditions, to bodies, offices and agencies of the Union which fail to act.

The action shall be admissible only if the institution, body, office or agency concerned has first been called upon to act. If, within two months of being so called upon, the institution, body, office or agency concerned has not defined its position, the action may be brought within a further period of two months.

Any natural or legal person may, under the conditions laid down in the preceding paragraphs, complain to the Court that an institution, body, office or agency of the Union has failed to address to that person any act other than a recommendation or an opinion.

Article 266 (ex Article 233 TEC)

The institution whose act has been declared void or whose failure to act has been declared contrary to the Treaties shall be required to take the necessary measures to comply with the judgment of the Court of Justice of the European Union.

This obligation shall not affect any obligation which may result from the application of the second paragraph of Article 340.

Article 267 (ex Article 234 TEC)

The Court of Justice of the European Union shall have jurisdiction to give preliminary rulings concerning:

(a) the interpretation of the Treaties;

(b) the validity and interpretation of acts of the institutions, bodies, offices or agencies of the Union;

Where such a question is raised before any court or tribunal of a Member State, that court or tribunal may, if it considers that a decision on the question is necessary to enable it to give judgment, request the Court to give a ruling thereon.

Where any such question is raised in a case pending before a court or tribunal of a Member State against whose decisions there is no judicial remedy under national law, that court or tribunal shall bring the matter before the Court.

If such a question is raised in a case pending before a court or tribunal of a Member State with regard to a person in custody, the Court of Justice of the European Union shall act with the minimum of delay.

* * *

CHAPTER 2

LEGAL ACTS OF THE UNION, ADOPTION PROCEDURES AND OTHER PROVISIONS

SECTION 1

THE LEGAL ACTS OF THE UNION

Article 288 (ex Article 249 TEC)

To exercise the Union's competences, the institutions shall adopt regulations, directives, decisions, recommendations and opinions.

A regulation shall have general application. It shall be binding in its entirety and directly applicable in all Member States.

A directive shall be binding, as to the result to be achieved, upon each Member State to which it is addressed, but shall leave to the national authorities the choice of form and methods.

A decision shall be binding in its entirety. A decision which specifies those to whom it is addressed shall be binding only on them.

Recommendations and opinions shall have no binding force.

Article 289

1. The ordinary legislative procedure shall consist in the joint adoption by the European Parliament and the Council of a regulation, directive or decision on a proposal from the Commission. This procedure is defined in Article 294.

2. In the specific cases provided for by the Treaties, the adoption of a regulation, directive or decision by the European Parliament with the participation of the Council, or by the latter with the participation of the European Parliament, shall constitute a special legislative procedure.

* * *

1.6 DECLARATION ON THE INADMISSIBILITY OF INTERVENTION IN THE DOMESTIC AFFAIRS OF STATES AND THE PROTECTION OF THEIR INDEPENDENCE AND SOVEREIGNTY. **Adopted by the U.N. General Assembly, 21 December 1965. GA Res 2131, UN GAOR, 20th Sess, Supp No 14, at 11, UN Doc A/6014 (1966);** *reprinted in* **5 ILM 374 & 1 Weston & Carlson I.D.5a**

The General Assembly . . . solemnly declares:

1. No State has the right to intervene, directly or indirectly, for any reason whatever, in the internal or external affairs of any other State. Consequently, armed intervention and all other forms of interference or attempted threats against the personality of the State or against its political, economic and cultural elements, are condemned.

2. No State may use or encourage the use of economic, political or any other type of measures to coerce another State in order to obtain from it the subordination of the exercise of its sovereign rights or to secure from it advantages of any kind. Also, no State shall organize, assist, foment, Finance, incite or tolerate subversive, terrorist or armed activities directed towards the violent overthrow of the regime of another State, or interfere in civil strife in another State.

3. The use of force to deprive peoples of their national identity constitutes a violation of their inalienable rights and of the principle of non-intervention.

4. The strict observance of these obligations is an essential condition to ensure that nations live together in peace with one another, since the practice of any form of intervention not only violates the spirit and letter of the Charter of the United Nations but also leads to the creation of situations which threaten international peace and security.

5. Every State has an inalienable right to choose its political, economic, social and cultural systems, without interference in any form by another State.

6. All States shall respect the right of self-determination and independence of peoples and nations, to be freely exercised without any foreign pressure, and with absolute respect for human rights and fundamental freedoms. Consequently, all States shall contribute to the complete elimination of racial discrimination and colonialism in all its forms and manifestations.

7. For the purpose of the present Declaration, the term "State" covers both individual States and groups of States.

8. Nothing in this Declaration shall be construed as affecting in any manner the relevant provisions of the Charter of the United Nations relating to the maintenance of international peace and security, in particular those contained in Chapters VI, VII and VIII.

1.7 Vienna Convention on the Law of Treaties (With Annex). Concluded at Vienna, 23 May 1969. Entered into force, 27 January 1988. 1155 UNTS 331; *reprinted in* 1 Weston & Carlson I.E.1

The States Parties to the present Convention,

Considering the fundamental role of treaties in the history of international relations,

Recognizing the ever-increasing importance of treaties as a source of international law and as a means of developing peaceful co-operation among nations, whatever their constitutional and social systems,

Noting that the principles of free consent and of good faith and the *pacta sunt servanda* rule are universally recognized,

Affirming that disputes concerning treaties, like other international disputes, should be settled by peaceful means and in conformity with the principles of justice and international law,

Recalling the determination of the peoples of the United Nations to establish conditions under which justice and respect for the obligations arising from treaties can be maintained,

Having in mind the principles of international law embodied in the Charter of the United Nations, such as the principles of the equal rights and self-determination of peoples, of the sovereign equality and independence of all States, of noninterference in the domestic affairs of States, of the prohibition of the threat or use of force and of universal respect for, and observance of, human rights and fundamental freedoms for all,

Believing that the codification and progressive development of the law of treaties achieved in the present Convention will promote the purposes of the United Nations set forth in the Charter, namely, the maintenance of international peace and security, the development of friendly relations and the achievement of co-operation among nations,

Affirming that the rules of customary international law will continue to govern questions not regulated by the provisions of the present Convention,

Have agreed as follows:

PART I. INTRODUCTION

Article 1. Scope of the Present Convention

The present Convention applies to treaties between States

Article 2. Use of Terms

1. For the purposes of the present Convention:

(*a*) "Treaty" means an international agreement concluded between States in written form and governed by international law, whether embodied in a single instrument or in two or more related instruments and whatever its particular designation;

(*b*) "Ratification", "acceptance", "approval" and "accession" means in each case the international act so named whereby a State establishes on the international plane its consent to be bound by a treaty;

(*c*) "Full powers" means a document emanating from the competent authority of a State designating a person or persons to represent the State for negotiating, adopting or authenticating the text of a treaty, for expressing the consent of the State to be bound by a treaty, or for accomplishing any other act with respect to a treaty;

(*d*) "Reservation" means a unilateral statement, however phrased or named, made by a State, when signing, ratifying, accepting, approving or acceding to a treaty, whereby it purports to exclude or to modify the legal effect of certain provisions of the treaty in their application to that State;

(*e*) "Negotiating State" means a State which took part in the drawing up and adoption of the text of the treaty;

(*f*) "Contracting State" means a State which has consented to be bound by the treaty, whether or not the treaty has entered into force;

(*g*) "Party" means a State which has consented to be bound by the treaty and for which the treaty is in force;

(*h*) "Third State" means a State not a party to the treaty;

(*i*) "International organization" means an intergovernmental organization.

2. The provisions of paragraph 1 regarding the use of terms in the present Convention are without prejudice to the use of those terms or to the meanings which may be given to them in the internal law of any State.

Article 3. INTERNATIONAL AGREEMENTS NOT WITHIN THE SCOPE OF THE PRESENT CONVENTION

The fact that the present Convention does not apply to international agreements concluded between States and other subjects of international law or between such other subjects of international law, or to international agreements not in written form, shall not affect:

(*a*) The legal force of such agreements;

(*b*) The application to them of any of the rules set forth in the present Convention to which they would be subject under international law independently of the Convention;

(*c*) The application of the Convention to the relations of States as between themselves under international agreements to which other subjects of international law are also parties.

Article 4. NON-RETROACTIVITY OF THE PRESENT CONVENTION

Without prejudice to the application of any rules set forth in the present Convention to which treaties would be subject under international law independently of the Convention, the Convention applies only to treaties which are concluded by States after the entry into force of the present Convention with regard to such States.

Article 5. TREATIES CONSTITUTING INTERNATIONAL ORGANIZATIONS AND TREATIES ADOPTED WITHIN AN INTERNATIONAL ORGANIZATION

The present Convention applies to any treaty which is the constituent instrument of an international organization and to any treaty adopted within an international organization without prejudice to any relevant rules of the organizations.

PART II. CONCLUSION AND ENTRY INTO FORCE OF TREATIES

SECTION 1. CONCLUSION OF TREATIES

Article 6. CAPACITY OF STATES TO CONCLUDE TREATIES

Every State possesses capacity to conclude treaties.

Article 7. FULL POWERS

1. A person is considered as representing a State for the purpose of adopting or authenticating the text of a treaty or for the purpose of expressing the consent of the State to be bound by a treaty if:

(*a*) He produces appropriate full powers; or

(*b*) It appears from the practice of the States concerned or from other circumstances that their intention was to consider that person as representing the State for such purposes and to dispense with full powers.

2. In virtue of their functions and without having to produce full powers, the following are considered as representing their State:

(*a*) Heads of State, Heads of Government and Ministers for Foreign Affairs, for the purpose of performing all acts relating to the conclusion of a treaty;

(*b*) Heads of diplomatic missions, for the purpose of adopting the text of a treaty between the accrediting State and the State to which they are accredited;

(*c*) Representatives accredited by States to an international conference or to an international organization or one of its organs, for the purpose of adopting the text of a treaty in that conference, organization or organ.

Article 8. SUBSEQUENT CONFIRMATION OF AN ACT PERFORMED WITHOUT AUTHORIZATION

An act relating to the conclusion of a treaty performed by a person who cannot be considered under Article 7 as authorized to represent a State for that purpose is without legal effect unless afterwards confirmed by that State.

Article 9. ADOPTION OF THE TEXT

1. The adoption of the text of a treaty takes place by the consent of all the States participating in its drawing up except as provided in paragraph 2.

2. The adoption of the text of a treaty at an international conference takes place by the vote of two thirds of the States present and voting, unless by the same majority they shall decide to apply a different rule.

Article 10. AUTHENTICATION OF THE TEXT

The text of a treaty is established as authentic and definitive:

(*a*) By such procedure as may be provided for in the text or agreed upon by the States participating in its drawing up; or

(*b*) Failing such procedure, by the signature, signature ad referendum or initialling by the representatives of those States of the text of the treaty or of the Final Act of a conference incorporating the text.

Article 11. MEANS OF EXPRESSING CONSENT TO BE BOUND BY A TREATY

The consent of a State to be bound by a treaty may be expressed by signature, exchange of instruments constituting a treaty, ratification, acceptance, approval or accession, or by any other means if so agreed.

Article 12. CONSENT TO BE BOUND BY A TREATY EXPRESSED BY SIGNATURE

1. The consent of a State to be bound by a treaty is expressed by the signature of its representative when:

(*a*) The treaty provides that signature shall have that effect;

(*b*) It is otherwise established that the negotiating States were agreed that signature should have that effect; or

(c) The intention of the state to give that effect to the signature appears from the full powers of its representative or was expressed during the negotiation.

2. For the purposes of paragraph 1:

(a) The initialling of a text constitutes a signature of the treaty when it is established that the negotiating States so agreed;

(b) The signature *ad referendum* of a treaty by a representative, if confirmed by his State, constitutes a full signature of the treaty.

Article 13. CONSENT TO BE BOUND BY A TREATY EXPRESSED BY
AN EXCHANGE OF INSTRUMENTS CONSTITUTING A TREATY

The consent of States to be bound by a treaty constituted by instruments exchanged between them is expressed by that exchange when:

(a) The instruments provide that their exchange shall have that effect; or

(b) It is otherwise established that those States were agreed that the exchange of instruments shall have that effect.

Article 14. CONSENT TO BE BOUND BY A TREATY EXPRESSED
BY RATIFICATION, ACCEPTANCE OR APPROVAL

1. The consent of a State to be bound by a treaty is expressed by ratification when:

(a) The treaty provides for such consent to be expressed by means of ratification;

(b) It is otherwise established that the negotiating States were agreed that ratification should be required;

(c) The representative of the State has signed the treaty subject to ratification; or

(d) The intention of the State to sign the treaty subject to ratification appears from the full powers of its representative or was expressed during the negotiation.

2. The consent of a State to be bound by a treaty is expressed by acceptance or approval under conditions similar to those which apply to ratification.

Article 15. CONSENT TO BE BOUND BY A TREATY EXPRESSED BY ACCESSION

The consent of a State to be bound by a treaty is expressed by accession when:

(a) The treaty provides that such consent may be expressed by that State by means of accession;

(b) It is otherwise established that the negotiating States were agreed that such consent may be expressed by that State by means of accession; or

(c) All the parties have subsequently agreed that such consent may be expressed by that State by means of accession.

Article 16. EXCHANGE OR DEPOSIT OF INSTRUMENTS OF
RATIFICATION, ACCEPTANCE, APPROVAL OR ACCESSION

Unless the treaty otherwise provides, instruments of ratification, acceptance, approval or accession establish the consent of a State to be bound by a treaty upon:

(a) Their exchange between the contracting States;

(b) Their deposit with the depositary; or

(c) Their notification to the contracting States or to the depositary, if so agreed.

Article 17. Consent to be Bound by Part of a
Treaty and Choice of Differing Provisions

1. Without prejudice to Articles 19 to 23, the consent of a State to be bound by part of a treaty is effective only if the treaty so permits or the other contracting States so agree.

2. The consent of a State to be bound by a treaty which permits a choice between differing provisions is effective only if it is made clear to which of the provisions the consent relates.

Article 18. Obligation not to Defeat the Object and
Purpose of a Treaty Prior to its Entry into Force

A State is obliged to refrain from acts which would defeat the object and purpose of a treaty when:

(*a*) It has signed the treaty or has exchanged instruments constituting the treaty subject to ratification, acceptance or approval, until it shall have made its intention clear not to become a party to the treaty; or

(*b*) It has expressed its consent to be bound by the treaty, pending the entry into force of the treaty and provided that such entry into force is not unduly delayed.

Section 2. Reservations

Article 19. Formulation of Reservations

A State may, when signing, ratifying, accepting, approving or acceding to a treaty, formulate a reservation unless:

(*a*) The reservation is prohibited by the treaty;

(*b*) The treaty provides that only specified reservations, which do not include the reservation in question, may be made; or

(*c*) In cases not falling under sub-paragraphs (*a*) and (*b*), the reservation is incompatible with the object and purpose of the treaty.

Article 20. Acceptance of and Objection to Reservations

1. A reservation expressly authorized by a treaty does not require any subsequent acceptance by the other contracting States unless the treaty so provides.

2. When it appears from the limited number of the negotiating States and the object and purpose of a treaty that the application of the treaty in its entirety between all the parties is an essential condition of the consent of each one to be bound by the treaty, a reservation requires acceptance by all the parties;

3. When a treaty is a constituent instrument of an international organization and unless it otherwise provides, a reservation requires the acceptance of the competent organ of that organization.

4. In cases not falling under the preceding paragraphs and unless the treaty otherwise provides:

(*a*) Acceptance by another contracting State of a reservation constitutes the reserving State a party to the treaty in relation to that other State if or when the treaty is in force for those States;

(*b*) An objection by another contracting State to a reservation does not preclude the entry into force of the treaty as between the objecting and reserving States unless a contrary intention is definitely expressed by the objecting State;

(*c*) An act expressing a State's consent to be bound by the treaty and containing a reservation is effective as soon as at least one other contracting State has accepted the reservation.

5. For the purposes of paragraphs 2 and 4 and unless the treaty otherwise provides, a reservation is considered to have been accepted by a State if it shall have raised no objection to the reservation by the end of a period of twelve months after it was notified of the reservation or by the date on which it expressed its consent to be bound by the treaty, whichever is later.

Article 21. Legal Effects of Reservations and of Objections to Reservations

1. A reservation established with regard to another party in accordance with Articles 19, 20 and 23:

(*a*) Modifies for the reserving State in its relations with that other party the provisions of the treaty to which the reservation relates to the extent of the reservation; and

(*b*) Modifies those provisions to the same extent for that other party in its relations with the reserving State.

2. The reservation does not modify the provisions of the treaty for the other parties to the treaty *inter se.*

3. When a State objecting to a reservation has not opposed the entry into force of the treaty between itself and the reserving State, the provisions to which the reservation relates do not apply as between the two States to the extent of the reservation.

Article 22. Withdrawal of Reservations and of Objections to Reservations

1. Unless the treaty otherwise provides, a reservation may be withdrawn at any time and the consent of a State which has accepted the reservation is not required for its withdrawal.

2. Unless the treaty otherwise provides, an objection to a reservation may be withdrawn at any time.

3. Unless the treaty otherwise provides, or it is otherwise agreed:

(*a*) The withdrawal of a reservation becomes operative in relation to another contracting State only when notice of it has been received by that State;

(*b*) The withdrawal of an objection to a reservation becomes operative only when notice of it has been received by the State which formulated the reservation.

Article 23. Procedure Regarding Reservations

1. A reservation, an express acceptance of a reservation and an objection to a reservation must be formulated in writing and communicated to the contracting States and other States entitled to become parties to the treaty.

2. If formulated when signing the treaty subject to ratification, acceptance or approval, a reservation must be formally confirmed by the reserving State when expressing its consent to be bound by the treaty. In such a case the reservation shall be considered as having been made on the date of its confirmation.

3. An express acceptance of, or an objection to, a reservation made previously to confirmation of the reservation does not itself require confirmation.

4. The withdrawal of a reservation or of an objection to a reservation must be formulated in writing.

Section 3. Entry into Force Provisional Application of Treaties

Article 24. Entry into Force

1. A treaty enters into force in such manner and upon such date as it may provide or as the negotiating States may agree.

2. Failing any such provision or agreement, a treaty enters into force as soon as consent to be bound by the treaty has been established for all the negotiating States.

3. When the consent of a State to be bound by a treaty is established on a date after the treaty has come into force, the treaty enters into force for that State on that date, unless the treaty otherwise provides.

4. The provisions of a treaty regulating the authentication of its text, the establishment of the consent of States to be bound by the treaty, the manner or date of its entry into force, reservations, the functions of the depositary and other matters arising necessarily before the entry into force of the treaty apply from the time of the adoption of its text.

Article 25. PROVISIONAL APPLICATION

1. A treaty or a part of a treaty is applied provisionally pending its entry into force if:

(*a*) The treaty itself so provides; or

(*b*) The negotiating States have in some other manner so agreed.

2. Unless the treaty between provides or the negotiating States have otherwise agreed, the provisional application of a treaty or a part of a treaty with respect to a State shall be terminated if that State notifies the other States between which the treaty is being applied provisionally of its intention not to become a party to the treaty.

PART III. OBSERVANCE, APPLICATION AND INTERPRETATION OF TREATIES

SECTION 1. OBSERVANCE OF TREATIES

Article 26. "PACTA SUNT SERVANDA"

Every treaty in force is binding upon the parties to it and must be performed by them in good faith.

Article 27. INTERNAL LAW AND OBSERVANCE OF TREATIES

A party may not invoke the provisions of its internal law as justification for its failure to perform a treaty. This rule is without prejudice to Article 46.

SECTION 2. APPLICATION OF TREATIES

Article 28. NON-RETROACTIVITY OF TREATIES

Unless a different intention appears from the treaty or is otherwise established, its provisions do not bind a party in relation to any act or fact which took place or any situation which ceased to exist before the date of the entry into force of the treaty with respect to that party.

Article 29. TERRITORIAL SCOPE OF TREATIES

Unless a different intention appears from the treaty or is otherwise established, a treaty is binding upon each party in respect of its entire territory.

Article 30. APPLICATION OF SUCCESSIVE TREATIES RELATING TO THE SAME SUBJECT-MATTER

1. Subject to Article 103 of the Charter of the United Nations, the rights and obligations of States parties to successive treaties relating to the same subject-matter shall be determined in accordance with the following paragraphs.

2. When a treaty specifies that it is subject to, or that it is not to be considered as incompatible with, an earlier or later treaty, the provisions of that other treaty prevail.

3. When all the parties to the earlier treaty are parties also to the later treaty but the earlier treaty is not terminated or suspended in operation under Article 59, the earlier treaty applies only to the extent that its provisions are compatible with those of the later treaty.

4. When the parties to the later treaty do not include all the parties to the earlier one:

(*a*) As between States parties to both treaties the same rule applies as in paragraph 3;

(*b*) As between a State party to both treaties and a State party to only one of the treaties, the treaty to which both States are parties governs their mutual rights and obligations.

5. Paragraph 4 is without prejudice to Article 41, or to any question of the termination or suspension of the operation of a treaty under Article 60 or to any question of responsibility which may arise for a State from the conclusion or application of a treaty the provisions of which are incompatible with its obligations towards another State under another treaty.

SECTION 3.   INTERPRETATION OF TREATIES

Article 31.   GENERAL RULE OF INTERPRETATION

1. A treaty shall be interpreted in good faith in accordance with the ordinary meaning to be given to the terms of the treaty in their context and in the light of its object and purpose.

2. The context for the purpose of the interpretation of a treaty shall comprise, in addition to the text, including its preamble and annexes:

(*a*) Any agreement relating to the treaty which was made between all the parties in connexion with the conclusion of the treaty;

(*b*) Any instrument which was made by one or more parties in connexion with the conclusion of the treaty and accepted by the other parties as an instrument related to the treaty.

3. There shall be taken into account, together with the context:

(*a*) Any subsequent agreement between the parties regarding the interpretation of the treaty or the application of its provisions;

(*b*) Any subsequent practice in the application of the treaty which establishes the agreement of the parties regarding its interpretation;

(*c*) Any relevant rules of international law applicable in the relations between the parties.

4. A special meaning shall be given to a term if it is established that the parties so intended.

Article 32.   SUPPLEMENTARY MEANS OF INTERPRETATION

Recourse may be had to supplementary means of interpretation, including the preparatory work of the treaty and the circumstances of its conclusion, in order to confirm the meaning resulting from the application of Article 31, or to determine the meaning when the interpretation according to Article 31:

(*a*) Leaves the meaning ambiguous or obscure; or

(*b*) Leads to a result which is manifestly absurd or unreasonable.

Article 33. INTERPRETATION OF TREATIES AUTHENTICATED IN TWO OR MORE LANGUAGES

1. When a treaty has been authenticated in two or more languages, the text is equally authoritative in each language, unless the treaty provides or the parties agree that, in case of divergence, a particular text shall prevail.

2. A version of the treaty in a language other than one of those in which the text was authenticated shall be considered an authentic text only if the treaty so provides or the parties so agree.

3. The terms of the treaty are presumed to have the same meaning in each authentic text.

4. Except where a particular text prevails in accordance with paragraph 1, when a comparison of the authentic texts discloses a difference of meaning which the application of Articles 31 and 32 does not remove, the meaning which best reconciles the texts, having regard to the object and purpose of the treaty, shall be adopted.

SECTION 4. TREATIES AND THIRD STATES

Article 34. GENERAL RULE REGARDING THIRD STATES

A treaty does not create either obligations or rights for a third State without its consent.

Article 35. TREATIES PROVIDING FOR OBLIGATIONS FOR THIRD STATES

An obligation arises for a third State from a provision of a treaty if the parties to the treaty intend the provision to be the means of establishing the obligation and the third State expressly accepts that obligation in writing.

Article 36. TREATIES PROVIDING FOR RIGHTS FOR THIRD STATES

1. A right arises for a third State from a provision of a treaty if the parties to the treaty intend the provision to accord that right either to the third State, or to a group of States to which it belongs, or to all States, and the third State assents thereto. Its assent shall be presumed so long as the contrary is not indicated, unless the treaty otherwise provides.

2. A State exercising a right in accordance with paragraph 1 shall comply with the conditions for its exercise provided for in the treaty or established in conformity with the treaty.

Article 37. REVOCATION OR MODIFICATION OF OBLIGATIONS OR RIGHTS OF THIRD STATES

1. When an obligation has arisen for a third State in conformity with Article 35, the obligation may be revoked or modified only with the consent of the parties to the treaty and of the third State, unless it is established that they had otherwise agreed.

2. When a right has arisen for a third State in conformity with Article 36, the right may not be revoked or modified by the parties if it is established that the right was intended not to be revocable or subject to modification without the consent of the third State.

Article 38. RULES IN A TREATY BECOMING BINDING ON THIRD STATES THROUGH INTERNATIONAL CUSTOM

Nothing in Articles 34 to 37 precludes a rule set forth in a treaty from becoming binding upon a third State as a customary rule of international law, recognized as such.

PART IV. AMENDMENT AND MODIFICATION OF TREATIES

Article 39. General Rule Regarding the Amendment of Treaties

A treaty may be amended by agreement between the parties. The rules laid down in Part II apply to such an agreement except in so far as the treaty may otherwise provide.

Article 40. Amendment of Multilateral Treaties

1.   Unless the treaty otherwise provides, the amendment of multilateral treaties shall be governed by the following paragraphs.

2.   Any proposal to amend a multilateral treaty as between all the parties must be notified to all the contracting States, each one of which shall have the right to take part in:

(*a*) The decision as to the action to be taken in regard to such proposal;

(*b*) The negotiation and conclusion of any agreement for the amendment of the treaty.

3.   Every State entitled to become a party to the treaty shall also be entitled to become a party to the treaty as amended.

4.   The amending agreement does not bind any State already a party to the treaty which does not become a party to the amending agreement; Article 30, paragraph 4(b), applies in relation to such State.

5.   Any State which becomes a party to the treaty after the entry into force of the amending agreement shall, failing an expression of a different intention by that State:

(*a*) be considered as a party to the treaty as amended; and

(*b*) be considered as a party to the unamended treaty in relation to any party to the treaty not bound by the amending agreement.

Article 41. Agreements to Modify Multilateral Treaties
Between Certain of the Parties Only

1.   Two or more of the parties to a multilateral treaty may conclude an agreement to modify the treaty as between themselves alone if:

(*a*) The possibility of such a modification is provided for by the treaty; or

(*b*) The modification in question is not prohibited by the treaty and:

(i) Does not affect the enjoyment by the other parties of their rights under the treaty or the performance of their obligations;

(ii) Does not relate to a provision, derogation from which is incompatible with the effective execution of the object and purpose of the treaty as a whole.

2.   Unless in a case falling under paragraph 1(a) the treaty otherwise provides, the parties in question shall notify the other parties of their intention to conclude the agreement and of the modification to the treaty for which it provides.

PART V. INVALIDITY, TERMINATION AND SUSPENSION
OF THE OPERATION OF TREATIES

Section 1. General Provisions

Article 42. Validity and Continuance in Force of Treaties

1.   The validity of a treaty or of the consent of a State to be bound by a treaty may be impeached only through the application of the present Convention.

2.   The termination of a treaty, its denunciation or the withdrawal of a party, may take place only as a result of the application of the provisions of the treaty or of

the present Convention. The same rule applies to suspension of the operation of a treaty.

Article 43. OBLIGATIONS IMPOSED BY INTERNATIONAL LAW INDEPENDENTLY OF A TREATY

The invalidity, termination or denunciation of a treaty, the withdrawal of a party from it, or the suspension of its operation, as a result of the application of the present Convention or of the provisions of the treaty, shall not in any way impair the duty of any State to fulfil any obligation embodied in the treaty to which it would be subject under international law independently of the treaty.

Article 44. SEPARABILITY OF TREATY PROVISIONS

1. A right of a party, provided for in a treaty or arising under Article 56, to denounce, withdraw from or suspend the operation of the treaty may be exercised only with respect to the whole treaty unless the treaty otherwise provides or the parties otherwise agree.

2. A ground for invalidating, terminating, withdrawing from or suspending the operation of a treaty recognized in the present Convention may be invoked only with respect to the whole treaty except as provided in the following paragraphs or in Article 60.

3. If the ground relates solely to particular clauses, it may be invoked only with respect to those clauses where:

(*a*) The said clauses are separable from the remainder of the treaty with regard to their application;

(*b*) It appears from the treaty or is otherwise established that acceptance of those clauses was not an essential basis of the consent of the other party or parties to be bound by the treaty as a whole; and

(*c*) Continued performance of the remainder of the treaty would not be unjust.

4. In cases falling under Articles 49 and 50 the State entitled to invoke the fraud or corruption may do so with respect either to the whole treaty or, subject to paragraph 3, to the particular clauses alone.

5. In cases falling under Articles 51, 52 and 53, no separation of the provisions of the treaty is permitted.

Article 45. LOSS OF A RIGHT TO INVOKE A GROUND FOR INVALIDATING, TERMINATING, WITHDRAWING FROM OR SUSPENDING THE OPERATION OF A TREATY

A State may no longer invoke a ground for invalidating, terminating, withdrawing from or suspending the operation of a treaty under Articles 46 to 50 or Articles 60 and 62 if, after becoming aware of the facts:

(*a*) It shall have expressly agreed that the treaty is valid or remains in force or continues in operation, as the case may be; or

(*b*) It must by reason of its conduct be considered as having acquiesced in the validity of the treaty or in its maintenance in force or in operation, as the case may be.

SECTION 2. INVALIDITY OF TREATIES

Article 46. PROVISIONS OF INTERNAL LAW REGARDING COMPETENCE TO CONCLUDE TREATIES

1. A State may not invoke the fact that its consent to be bound by a treaty has been expressed in violation of a provision of its internal law regarding competence to conclude treaties as invalidating its consent unless that violation was manifest and concerned a rule of its internal law of fundamental importance.

2. A violation is manifest if it would be objectively evident to any State conducting itself in the matter in accordance with normal practice and in good faith.

Article 47. SPECIFIC RESTRICTIONS ON AUTHORITY TO EXPRESS THE CONSENT OF A STATE

If the authority of a representative to express the consent of a State to be bound by a particular treaty has been made subject to a specific restriction, his omission to observe the restriction may not be invoked as invalidating the consent expressed by him unless the restriction was notified to the other negotiating States prior to his expressing such consent.

Article 48. ERROR

1. A State may invoke an error in a treaty as invalidating its consent to be bound by the treaty if the error relates to a fact or situation which was assumed by that State to exist at the time when the treaty was concluded and formed an essential basis of its consent to be bound by the treaty.

2. Paragraph 1 shall not apply if the State in question contributed by its own conduct to the error or if the circumstances were such as to put that State on notice of a possible error.

3. An error relating only to the wording of the text of a treaty does not affect its validity; Article 79 then applies.

Article 49. FRAUD

If a State has been induced to conclude a treaty by the fraudulent conduct of another negotiating State, the State may invoke the fraud as invalidating its consent to be bound by the treaty.

Article 50. CORRUPTION OF A REPRESENTATIVE OF A STATE

If the expression of a State's consent to be bound by a treaty has been procured through the corruption of its representative directly or indirectly by another negotiating State, the State may invoke such corruption as invalidating its consent to be bound by the treaty

Article 51. COERCION OF A REPRESENTATIVE OF A STATE

The expression of a State's consent to be bound by a treaty which has been procured by the coercion of its representative through acts or threats directed against him shall be without any legal effect.

Article 52. COERCION OF A STATE BY THE THREAT OR USE OF FORCE

A treaty is void if its conclusion has been procured by the threat or use of force in violation of the principles of international law embodied in the Charter of the United Nations.

Article 53. TREATIES CONFLICTING WITH A PEREMPTORY NORM
OF GENERAL INTERNATIONAL LAW ("JUS COGENS")

A treaty is void if, at the time of its conclusion, it conflicts with a peremptory norm of general international law. For the purposes of the present Convention, a peremptory norm of general international law is a norm accepted and recognized by the international community of States as a whole as a norm from which no derogation is permitted and which can be modified only by a subsequent norm of general international law having the same character.

SECTION 3. TERMINATION AND SUSPENSION OF THE OPERATION OF TREATIES

Article 54. TERMINATION OF OR WITHDRAWAL FROM A TREATY
UNDER ITS PROVISIONS OR BY CONSENT OF THE PARTIES

The termination of a treaty or the withdrawal of a party may take place:

(*a*) In conformity with the provisions of the treaty; or

(*b*) At any time by consent of all the parties after consultation with the other contracting States.

Article 55. REDUCTION OF THE PARTIES TO A MULTILATERAL TREATY
BELOW THE NUMBER NECESSARY FOR ITS ENTRY INTO FORCE

Unless the treaty otherwise provides a multilateral treaty does not terminate by reason only of the fact that the number of the parties falls below the number necessary for its entry into force.

Article 56. DENUNCIATION OF OR WITHDRAWAL FROM A TREATY CONTAINING NO
PROVISION REGARDING TERMINATION, DENUNCIATION OR WITHDRAWAL

1. A treaty which contains no provision regarding its termination and which does not provide for denunciation or withdrawal is not subject to denunciation or withdrawal unless:

(*a*) It is established that the parties intended to admit the possibility of denunciation or withdrawal; or

(*b*) A right of denunciation or withdrawal may be implied by the nature of the treaty.

2. A party shall give no less than twelve months' notice of its intention to denounce or withdraw from a treaty under paragraph 1.

Article 57. SUSPENSION OF THE OPERATION OF A TREATY
UNDER ITS PROVISIONS OR BY CONSENT OF THE PARTIES

The operation of a treaty in regard to all the parties or to a particular party may be suspended:

(*a*) In conformity with the provisions of the treaty; or

(*b*) At any time by consent of all the parties after consultation with the other contracting States.

Article 58. SUSPENSION OF THE OPERATION OF A MULTILATERAL TREATY
BY AGREEMENT BETWEEN CERTAIN OF THE PARTIES ONLY

1. Two or more parties to a multilateral treaty may conclude an agreement to suspend the operation of provisions of the treaty, temporarily and as between themselves alone, if:

(*a*) The possibility of such a suspension is provided for by the treaty; or

(*b*) The suspension in question is not prohibited by the treaty and:

(i) Does not affect the enjoyment by the other parties of their rights under the treaty or the performance of their obligations;

(ii) Is not incompatible with the object and purpose of the treaty.

2. Unless in a case falling under paragraph 1(*a*) the treaty otherwise provides, the parties in question shall notify the other parties of their intention to conclude the agreement and of those provisions of the treaty the operation of which they intend to suspend.

Article 59. TERMINATION OR SUSPENSION OF THE OPERATION OF
A TREATY IMPLIED BY CONCLUSION OF A LATER TREATY

1. A treaty shall be considered as terminated if all the parties to it conclude a later treaty relating to the same subject-matter and:

(*a*) It appears from the later treaty or is otherwise established that the parties intended that the matter should be governed by that treaty; or

(*b*) The provisions of the later treaty are so far incompatible with those of the earlier one that the two treaties are not capable of being applied at the same time.

2.   The earlier treaty shall be considered as only suspended in operation if it appears from the later treaty or is otherwise established that such was the intention of the parties.

Article 60.   Termination or Suspension of the Operation
of a Treaty as a Consequence of its Breach

1.   A material breach of a bilateral treaty by one of the parties entitles the other to invoke the breach as a ground for terminating the treaty or suspending its operation in whole or in part.

2.   A material breach of a multilateral treaty by one of the parties entitles:

(*a*) The other parties by unanimous agreement to suspend the operation of the treaty in whole or in part or to terminate it either:

(i) In the relations between themselves and the defaulting State, or

(ii) As between all the parties;

(*b*) A party specially affected by the breach to invoke it as a ground for suspending the operation of the treaty in whole or in part in the relations between itself and the defaulting State;

(*c*) Any party other than the defaulting State to invoke the breach as a ground for suspending the operation of the treaty in whole or in part with respect to itself if the treaty is of such a character that a material breach of its provisions by one party radically changes the position of every party with respect to the further performance of its obligations under the treaty.

3.   A material breach of a treaty, for the purposes of this Article, consists in:

(*a*) A repudiation of the treaty not sanctioned by the present Convention; or

(*b*) The violation of a provision essential to the accomplishment of the object or purpose of the treaty.

4.   The foregoing paragraphs are without prejudice to any provision in the treaty applicable in the event of a breach.

5.   Paragraphs 1 to 3 do not apply to provisions relating to the protection of the human person contained in treaties of a humanitarian character, in particular to provisions prohibiting any form of reprisals against persons protected by such treaties.

Article 61.   Supervening Impossibility of Performance

1.   A party may invoke the impossibility of performing a treaty as a ground for terminating or withdrawing from it if the impossibility results from the permanent disappearance or destruction of an object indispensable for the execution of the treaty. If the impossibility is temporary, it may be invoked only as a ground for suspending the operation of the treaty.

2.   Impossibility of performance may not be invoked by a party as a ground for terminating, withdrawing from or suspending the operation of a treaty if the impossibility is the result of a breach by that party either of an obligation under the treaty or of any other international obligation owed to any other party to the treaty.

Article 62.   Fundamental Change of Circumstances

1. A fundamental change of circumstances which has occurred with regard to those existing at the time of the conclusion of a treaty, and which was not foreseen by the parties, may not be invoked as a ground for terminating or withdrawing from the treaty unless:

(*a*) The existence of those circumstances constituted an essential basis of the consent of the parties to be bound by the treaty; and

(*b*) The effect of the change is radically to transform the extent of obligations still to be performed under the treaty.

2. A fundamental change of circumstances may not be invoked as a ground for terminating or withdrawing from a treaty:

(*a*) If the treaty establishes a boundary; or

(*b*) If the fundamental change is the result of a breach by the party invoking it either of an obligation under the treaty or of any other international obligation owed to any other party to the treaty.

3. If, under the foregoing paragraphs, a party may invoke a fundamental change of circumstances as a ground for terminating or withdrawing from a treaty it may also invoke the change as a ground for suspending the operation of the treaty.

Article 63.   Severance of Diplomatic or Consular Relations

The severance of diplomatic or consular relations between parties to a treaty does not affect the legal relations established between them by the treaty except in so far as the existence of diplomatic or consular relations is indispensable for the application of the treaty.

Article 64.   Emergence of a New Peremptory Norm of
General International Law ("JUS COGENS")

If a new peremptory norm of general international law emerges, any existing treaty which is in conflict with that norm becomes void and terminates.

Section 4.   Procedure

Article 65.   Procedure to be Followed with Respect to Invalidity, Termination, Withdrawal from or Suspension of the Operation of a Treaty

1. A party which, under the provisions of the present Convention, invokes either a defect in its consent to be bound by a treaty or a ground for impeaching the validity of a treaty, terminating it, withdrawing from it or suspending its operation, must notify the other parties of its claim. The notification shall indicate the measure proposed to be taken with respect to the treaty and the reasons therefore.

2. If, after the expiry of a period which, except in cases of special urgency, shall not be less than three months after the receipt of the notification, no party has raised any objection, the party making the notification may carry out in the manner provided in Article 67 the measure which it has proposed.

3. If, however, objection has been raised by any other party, the parties shall seek a solution through the means indicated in Article 33 of the Charter of the United Nations.

4. Nothing in the foregoing paragraphs shall affect the rights or obligations of the parties under any provisions in force binding the parties with regard to the settlement of disputes.

5. Without prejudice to Article 45, the fact that a State has not previously made the notification prescribed in paragraph 1 shall not prevent it from making such

notification in answer to another party claiming performance of the treaty or alleging its violation.

Article 66. PROCEDURES FOR JUDICIAL SETTLEMENT, ARBITRATION AND CONCILIATION

If, under paragraph 3 of Article 65, no solution has been reached within a period of twelve months following the date on which the objection was raised, the following procedures shall be followed:

(*a*) Any one of the parties to a dispute concerning the application or the interpretation of Articles 53 to 64 may, by a written application, submit it to the International Court of Justice for a decision unless the parties by common consent agree to submit the dispute to arbitration;

(*b*) Any one of the parties to a dispute concerning the application or the interpretation of any of the other Articles in Part V of the present Convention may set in motion the procedure specified in the Annex to the Convention by submitting a request to that effect to the Secretary–General of the United Nations.

Article 67. INSTRUMENTS FOR DECLARING INVALID, TERMINATING, WITHDRAWING
FROM OR SUSPENDING THE OPERATION OF A TREATY

1.   The notification provided for under Article 65, paragraph 1 must be made in writing.

2.   Any act declaring invalid, terminating, withdrawing from or suspending the operation of a treaty pursuant to the provisions of the treaty or of paragraphs 2 or 3 of Article 65 shall be carried out through an instrument communicated to the other parties. If the instrument is not signed by the Head of State, Head of Government or Minister for Foreign Affair, the representative of the State communicating it may be called upon to produce full powers.

Article 68. REVOCATION OF NOTIFICATIONS AND INSTRUMENTS
PROVIDED FOR IN ARTICLES 65 AND 67

A notification or instrument provided for in Articles 65 or 67 may be revoked at any time before it takes effect.

SECTION 5.   CONSEQUENCES OF THE INVALIDITY, TERMINATION
OR SUSPENSION OF THE OPERATION OF A TREATY

Article 69. CONSEQUENCES OF THE INVALIDITY OF A TREATY

1.   A treaty the invalidity of which is established under the present Convention is void. The provisions of a void treaty have no legal force.

2.   If acts have nevertheless been performed in reliance on such a treaty:

(*a*) Each party may require any other party to establish as far as possible in their mutual relations the position that would have existed if the acts had not been performed;

(*b*) Acts performed in good faith before the invalidity was invoked are not rendered unlawful by reason only of the invalidity of the treaty.

3.   In cases falling under Articles 49, 50, 51 or 52, paragraph 2 does not apply with respect to the party to which the fraud, the act of corruption or the coercion is imputable.

4.   In the case of the invalidity of a particular State's consent to be bound by a multilateral treaty, the foregoing rules apply in the relations between that State and the parties to the treaty.

Article 70. Consequences of the Termination of a Treaty

1. Unless the treaty otherwise provides or the parties otherwise agree, the termination of a treaty under its provisions or in accordance with the present Convention:

(*a*) Releases the parties from any obligation further to perform the treaty;

(*b*) Does not affect any right, obligation or legal situation of the parties created through the execution of the treaty prior to its termination.

2. If a State denounces or withdraws from a multilateral treaty, paragraph 1 applies in the relations between that State and each of the other parties to the treaty from the date when such denunciation or withdrawal takes effect.

Article 71. Consequences of the Invalidity of a Treaty which Conflicts with a Peremptory Norm of General International Law

1. In the case of a treaty which is void under Article 53 the parties shall:

(*a*) Eliminate as far as possible the consequences of any act performed in reliance on any provision which conflicts with the peremptory norm of general international law; and

(*b*) Bring their mutual relations into conformity with the peremptory norm of general international law.

2. In the case of a treaty which becomes void and terminates under Article 64, the termination of the treaty:

(*a*) Releases the parties from any obligation further to perform the treaty;

(*b*) Does not affect any right, obligation or legal situation of the parties created through the execution of the treaty prior to its termination, provided that those rights, obligations or situations may thereafter be maintained only to the extent that their maintenance is not in itself in conflict with the new peremptory norm of general international law.

Article 72. Consequences of the Suspension of the Operation of a Treaty

1. Unless the treaty otherwise provides or the parties otherwise agree, the suspension of the operation of a treaty under its provisions or in accordance with the present Convention:

(*a*) Releases the parties between which the operation of the treaty is suspended from the obligation to perform the treaty in mutual relations during the period of the suspension;

(*b*) Does not otherwise affect the legal relations between the parties established by the treaty.

2. During the period of the suspension the parties shall refrain from acts tending to obstruct the resumption of the operation of the treaty.

PART VI. MISCELLANEOUS PROVISIONS

Article 73. Cases of State Succession, State Responsibility and Outbreak of Hostilities

The provisions of the present Convention shall not prejudge any question that may arise in regard to a treaty from a succession of States or from the international responsibility of a State or from the outbreak of hostilities between States.

Article 74. DIPLOMATIC AND CONSULAR RELATIONS AND THE CONCLUSION OF TREATIES

The severance or absence of diplomatic or consular relations between two or more States does not prevent the conclusion of treaties between those States. The conclusion of a treaty does not in itself affect the situation in regard to diplomatic or consular relations.

Article 75. CASE OF AN AGGRESSOR STATE

The provisions of the present Convention are without prejudice to any obligation in relation to a treaty which may arise for an aggressor State in consequence of measures taken in conformity with the Charter of the United Nations with reference to that State's aggression.

PART VII. DEPOSITARIES, NOTIFICATIONS, CORRECTIONS AND REGISTRATION

Article 76. DEPOSITARIES OF TREATIES

1. The designation of the depositary of a treaty may be made by the negotiating States, either in the treaty itself or in some other manner. The depositary may be one or more States, an international organization or the chief administrative officer of the organization.

2. The functions of the depositary of a treaty are international in character and the depositary is under an obligation to act impartially in their performance. In particular, the fact that a treaty has not entered into force between certain of the parties or that a difference has appeared between a State and a depositary with regard to the performance of the latter's functions shall not affect that obligation.

Article 77. FUNCTIONS OF DEPOSITARIES

1. The functions of a depositary, unless otherwise provided in the treaty or agreed by the contracting States, comprise in particular:

(a) Keeping custody of the original text of the treaty and of any full powers delivered to the depositary;

(b) Preparing certified copies of the original text and preparing any further text of the treaty in such additional languages as may be required by the treaty and transmitting them to the parties and to the States entitled to become parties to the treaty;

(c) Receiving any signatures to the treaty and receiving and keeping custody of any instruments, notifications and communications relating to it;

(d) Examining whether the signature or any instrument, notification or communication relating to the treaty is in due and proper form and, if need be, bringing the matter to the attention of the State in question;

(e) Informing the parties and the States entitled to become parties to the treaty of acts, notifications and communications relating to the treaty;

(f) Informing the States entitled to become parties to the treaty when the number of signatures or of instruments of ratification, acceptance, approval or accession required for the entry into force of the treaty has been received or deposited;

(g) Registering the treaty with the Secretariat of the United Nations;

(h) Performing the functions specified in other provisions of the present Convention.

2. In the event of any difference appearing between a State and the depositary as to the performance of the latter's functions, the depositary shall bring the question to

the attention of the signatory States and the contracting States or, where appropriate, of the competent organ of the international organization concerned.

Article 78. NOTIFICATIONS AND COMMUNICATIONS

Except as the treaty or the present Convention otherwise provides, any notification or communication to be made by any State under the present Convention shall:

(*a*) If there is no depositary, be transmitted direct to the States for which it is intended, or if there is a depositary, to the latter;

(*b*) Be considered as having been made by the State in question only upon its receipt by the State to which it was transmitted or, as the case may be, upon its receipt by the depositary;

(*c*) If transmitted to a depositary, be considered as received by the State for which it was intended only when the latter State has been informed by the depositary in accordance with Article 77, paragraph 1(e).

Article 79. CORRECTION OF ERRORS IN TEXTS OR IN CERTIFIED COPIES OF TREATIES

1. Where, after the authentication of the text of a treaty, the signatory States and the contracting States are agreed that it contains an error, the error shall, unless they decide upon some other means of correction, be corrected:

(*a*) By having the appropriate correction made in the text and causing the correction to be initialled by duly authorized representatives;

(*b*) By executing or exchanging an instrument or instruments setting out the correction which it has been agreed to make; or

(*c*) By executing a corrected text of the whole treaty by the same procedure as in the case of the original text.

2. Where the treaty is one for which there is a depositary, the latter shall notify the signatory States and the contracting States of the error and of the proposal to correct it and shall specify an appropriate time-limit within which objection to the proposed correction may be raised. If, on the expiry of the time-limit:

(*a*) No objection has been raised, the depositary shall make and initial the correction in the text and shall execute a *process-verbal* of the rectification of the text and communicate a copy of it to the parties and to the States entitled to become parties to the treaty;

(*b*) An objection has been raised, the depositary shall communicate the objection to the signatory States and to the contracting States.

3. The rules in paragraphs 1 and 2 apply also where the text has been authenticated in two or more languages and it appears that there is a lack of concordance which the signatory States and the contracting States agree should be corrected.

4. The corrected text replaces the defective text *ab initio,* unless the signatory States and the contracting States otherwise decide.

5. The correction of the text of a treaty that has been registered shall be notified to the Secretariat of the United Nations.

6. Where an error is discovered in a certified copy of a treaty, the depositary shall execute a *process-verbal* specifying the rectification and communicate a copy of it to the signatory States and to the contracting States.

Article 80. REGISTRATION AND PUBLICATION OF TREATIES

1. Treaties shall, after their entry into force, be transmitted to the Secretariat of the United Nations for registration or filing and recording, as the case may be, and for publication.

2. The designation of a depositary shall constitute authorization for it to perform the acts specified in the preceding paragraph.

PART VIII.   FINAL PROVISIONS

Article 81.   SIGNATURE

The present Convention shall be open for signature by all States Members of the United Nations or of any of the specialized agencies or of the International Atomic Energy Agency or parties to the Statute of the International Court of Justice, and by any other State invited by the General Assembly of the United Nations to become a party to the Convention, as follows: until 30 November 1969, at the Federal Ministry for Foreign Affairs of the Republic of Austria, and subsequently, until 30 April 1970, at United Nations Headquarters, New York.

Article 82.   RATIFICATION

The present Convention is subject to ratification. The instruments of ratification shall be deposited with the Secretary–General of the United Nations.

Article 83.   ACCESSION

The present Convention shall remain open for accession by any State belonging to any of the categories mentioned in Article 81. The instruments of accession shall be deposited with the Secretary–General of the United Nations.

Article 84.   ENTRY INTO FORCE

1. The present Convention shall enter into force on the thirtieth day following the date of deposit of the thirty-fifth instrument of ratification or accession.

2. For each State ratifying or acceding to the Convention after the deposit of the thirty-fifth instrument of ratification or accession, the Convention shall enter into force on the thirtieth day after deposit by such State of its instrument of ratification or accession.

Article 85.   AUTHENTIC TEXTS

The original of the present Convention, of which the Chinese, English, French, Russian and Spanish texts are equally authentic, shall be deposited with the Secretary–General of the United Nations.

ANNEX

1. A list of conciliators consisting of qualified jurists shall be drawn up and maintained by the Secretary–General of the United Nations. To this end, every State which is a Member of the United Nations or a party to the present Convention shall be invited to nominate two conciliators, and the names of the persons so nominated shall constitute the list. The term of a conciliator, including that of any conciliator nominated to fill a casual vacancy, shall be five years and may be renewed. A conciliator whose term expires shall continue to fulfil any function for which he shall have been chosen under the following paragraph.

2. When a request has been made to the Secretary–General under Article 66, the Secretary–General shall bring the dispute before a conciliation commission constituted as follows:

The State or States constituting one of the parties to the dispute shall appoint:

(*a*) One conciliator of the nationality of that State or of one of those States, who may or may not be chosen from the list referred to in paragraph 1; and (*b*) One conciliator not of the nationality of that State or of any of those States, who shall be chosen from the list.

The State or States constituting the other party to the dispute shall appoint two conciliators in the same way. The four conciliators chosen by the parties shall be appointed within sixty days following the date on which the Secretary–General receives the request.

The four conciliators shall, within sixty days following the date of the last of their own appointments, appoint a fifth conciliator chosen from the list, who shall be chairman.

If the appointment of the chairman or of any of the other conciliators has not been made within the period prescribed above for such appointment, it shall be made by the Secretary–General within sixty days following the expiry of that period. The appointment of the chairman may be made by the Secretary–General either from the list or from the membership of the International Law Commission. Any of the periods within which appointments must be made may be extended by agreement between the parties to the dispute.

Any vacancy shall be filled in the manner prescribed for the initial appointment.

3. The Conciliation Commission shall decide its own procedure. The Commission, with the consent of the parties to the dispute, may invite any party to the treaty to submit to it its views orally or in writing. Decisions and recommendations of the Commission shall be made by a majority vote of the five members.

4. The Commission may draw the attention of the parties to the dispute to any measures which might facilitate an amicable settlement.

5. The Commission shall hear the parties, examine the claims and objections, and make proposals to the parties with a view to reaching an amicable settlement of the dispute.

1.8 DECLARATION ON PRINCIPLES OF INTERNATIONAL LAW CONCERNING FRIENDLY RELATIONS AND CO-OPERATION AMONG STATES IN ACCORDANCE WITH THE CHARTER OF THE UNITED NATIONS. Adopted by the U.N. General Assembly, 24 October 1970. GA Res 2625, UN GAOR, 25th Sess, Supp No 28, at 121, UN Doc A/8028 (1971); *reprinted in* 9 ILM 1292 (1970) & 1 Weston & Carlson I.D.7

THE GENERAL ASSEMBLY,

Reaffirming in the terms of the Charter that the maintenance of international peace and security and the development of friendly relations and co-operation between nations are among the fundamental purposes of the United Nations,

Recalling that the peoples of the United Nations are determined to practise tolerance and live together in peace with one another as good neighbours,

Bearing in mind the importance of maintaining and strengthening international peace and founded upon freedom, equality, justice and respect for fundamental human rights and of developing friendly relations among nations irrespective of their political, economic and social systems or the levels of their development,

Bearing in mind also the paramount importance of the Charter of the United Nations in the promotion of the rule of law among nations,

Considering that the faithful observance of the principles of international law concerning friendly relations and co-operation among States, and fulfilment in good faith of the obligation assumed by States, in accordance with the Charter, is of the greatest importance for the maintenance of international peace and security, and for the implementation of the other purposes of the United Nations,

Noting that the great political, economic and social changes and scientific progress which have taken place in the world since the adoption of the Charter of the United Nations give increased importance to these principles and to the need for their more effective application in the conduct of States wherever carried on,

Recalling the established principle that outer space, including the Moon and other celestial bodies, is not subject to national appropriation by claim of sovereignty by means of use or occupation or by any other means, and mindful of the fact that consideration is being given in the United Nations to the question of establishing other appropriate provisions similarly inspired,

Convinced that the strict observance by States of the obligation not to intervene in the affairs of any other State is an essential condition to ensure that nations live together in peace with one another since the practice of any form of intervention not only violates the spirit and letter of the Charter of the United Nations but also leads to the creation of situations which threaten international peace and security,

Recalling the duty of States to refrain in their international relations from military, political, economic or any other form of coercion aimed against the political independence or territorial integrity of any State,

Considering it essential that all States shall refrain in their international relations from the threat or use of force against the territorial integrity or political independence of any State, or in any other manner inconsistent with the purposes of the United Nations,

Considering it equally essential that all States shall settle their international disputes by peaceful means in accordance with the Charter,

Reaffirming, in accordance with the Charter, the basic importance of sovereign equality and stressing that the purposes of the United Nations can be implemented only if States enjoy sovereign equality and comply fully with the requirements of this principle in their international relations,

Convinced that the subjection of peoples to alien subjugation, domination and exploitation constitutes a major obstacle to the promotion of international peace and security,

Convinced that the principle of equal rights and self-determination of peoples constitutes a significant contribution to contemporary international law, and that its effective application is of paramount importance for the promotion of friendly relations among States, based on respect for the principle of sovereign equality,

Convinced in consequence that any attempt aimed at the partial or total disruption of the national unity and territorial integrity of a State or country or at its political independence is incompatible with the purposes and principles of the Charter,

Considering the provisions of the Charter as a whole and taking into account the role of relevant resolutions adopted by the competent organs of the United Nations relating to the content of the principles,

Considering that the progressive development and codification of the following principles:

(a) The principle that States shall refrain in their international relations from the threat or use of force against the territorial integrity or political independence of any State, or in any other manner inconsistent with the purposes of the United Nations,

(b) The principle that States shall settle their international disputes by peaceful means in such a manner that international peace and security and justice are not endangered,

(c) The duty not to intervene in matters within the domestic jurisdiction of any State, in accordance with the Charter,

(d) The duty of States to co-operate with one another in accordance with the Charter,

(e) The principle of equal rights and self-determination of peoples,

(f) The principle of sovereign equality of States,

(g) The principle that States shall fulfil in good faith the obligations assumed by them in accordance with the Charter, so as to secure their more effective application within the international community would promote the realization of the purposes of the United Nations,

Having considered the principles of international law relating to friendly relations and cooperation among States,

1. *Solemnly proclaims* the following principles:

The principle that States shall refrain in their international relations from the threat or use of force against the territorial integrity or political independence of any State, or in any other manner inconsistent with the purposes of the United Nations,

Every State has the duty to refrain in its international relations from the threat or use of force against the territorial integrity or political independence of any State, or in any other manner inconsistent with the purposes of the United Nations. Such a threat or use of force constitutes a violation of international law and the Charter of the United Nations and shall never be employed as a means of settling international issues.

A war of aggression constitutes a crime against the peace, for which there is responsibility under international law.

In accordance with the purposes and principles of the United Nations, States have the duty to refrain from propaganda for wars of aggression.

Every State has the duty to refrain from the threat or use of force to violate the existing international boundaries of another State or as a means of solving international disputes, including territorial disputes and problems concerning frontiers of States.

Every State likewise has the duty to refrain from the threat or use of force to violate international lines of demarcation, such as armistice lines, established by or pursuant to an international agreement to which it is a party or which it is otherwise bound to respect. Nothing in the foregoing shall be construed as prejudicing the positions of the parties concerned with regard to the status and effects of such lines under their special regimes or as affecting their temporary character.

States have a duty to refrain from acts of reprisal involving the use of force.

Every State has the duty to refrain from any forcible action which deprives peoples referred to in the elaboration of the principle of equal rights and self-determination of their right to self-determination and freedom and independence.

Every State has the duty to refrain from organizing or encouraging the organization of irregular forces or armed bands, including mercenaries, for incursion into the territory of another state.

Every State has the duty to refrain from organizing, instigating, assisting or participating in acts of civil strife or terrorist acts in another State or acquiescing in organized activities within its territory directed towards the commission of such acts, when the acts referred to in the present paragraph involve a threat or use of force.

The territory of a State shall not be the object of military occupation resulting from the use of force in contravention of the provisions of the Charter. The territory of a State shall not be the object of acquisition by another State resulting from the threat or use of force. No territorial acquisition resulting from the threat or use of force shall be recognized as legal. Nothing in the foregoing shall be construed as affecting:

(*a*) Provisions of the Charter or any international agreement prior to the Charter regime and valid under international law; or

(*b*) The powers of the Security Council under the Charter.

All States shall pursue in good faith negotiations for the early conclusion of a universal treaty on general and complete disarmament under effective international control and strive to adopt appropriate measures to reduce international tensions and strengthen confidence among States.

All States shall comply in good faith with their obligations under the generally recognized principles and rules of international law with respect to the maintenance of international peace and security, and shall endeavour to make the United Nations security system based upon the Charter more effective.

Nothing in the foregoing paragraphs shall be construed as enlarging or diminishing in any way the scope of the provisions of the Charter concerning cases in which the use of force is lawful.

The principle that States shall settle their international disputes by peaceful means in such a manner that international peace and security and justice are not endangered

Every State shall settle its international disputes with other States by peaceful means, in such a manner that international peace and security, and justice, are not endangered.

States shall accordingly seek early and just settlement of their international disputes by negotiation, inquiry, mediation, conciliation, arbitration, judicial settlement, resort to regional agencies or arrangements or other peaceful means of their choice. In seeking such a settlement, the parties shall agree upon such peaceful means as may be appropriate to the circumstances and nature of the dispute.

The parties to a dispute have the duty, in the event of failure to reach a solution by any one of the above peaceful means, to continue to seek a settlement of the dispute by other peaceful means agreed upon by them.

States parties to an international dispute, as well as other States, shall refrain from any action which may aggravate the situation so as to endanger the maintenance of international peace and security, and shall act in accordance with the purposes and principles of the United Nations.

International disputes shall be settled on the basis of the sovereign equality of States and in accordance with the principle of free choice of means. Recourse to, or acceptance of, a settlement procedure freely agreed to by States with regard to existing or future disputes to which they are parties shall not be regarded as incompatible with sovereign equality.

Nothing in the foregoing paragraphs prejudices or derogates from the applicable provisions of the Charter, in particular those relating to the pacific settlement of international disputes.

The principle concerning the duty not to intervene in matters within the domestic jurisdiction of any State, in accordance with the Charter

No State or group of States has the right to intervene, directly or indirectly, for any reason whatever, in the internal or external affairs of any other State. Consequently, armed intervention and all other forms of interference or attempted threats against the personality of the State or against its political, economic and cultural elements, are in violation of international law.

No State may use or encourage the use of economic, political or any other type of measures to coerce another State in order to obtain from it the subordination of the exercise of its sovereign rights and to secure from it advantages of any kind. Also, no State shall organize, assist, foment, finance, incite or tolerate subversive, terrorist or armed activities directed towards the violent overthrow of the regime of another State, or interfere in civil strife in another State.

The use of force to deprive peoples of their national identity constitutes a violation of their inalienable rights and of the principle of non-intervention.

Every State has an inalienable right to choose its political, economic, social and cultural systems, without interference in any form by another State.

Nothing in the foregoing paragraphs shall be construed as affecting the relevant provisions of the Charter relating to the maintenance of international peace and security.

The duty of States to co-operate with one another in accordance with the Charter

States have the duty to co-operate with one another, irrespective of the differences in their political, economic and social systems, in the various spheres of international relations, in order to maintain international peace and security and to promote international economic stability and progress, the general welfare of nations and international co-operation free from discrimination based on such differences.

To this end:

(a) States shall co-operate with other States in the maintenance of international peace and security;

(b) States shall co-operate in the promotion of universal respect for and observance of human rights and financial freedoms for all, and in the elimination of all forms of racial discrimination and all forms of religious intolerance;

(c) States shall conduct their international relations in the economic, social, cultural, technical and trade fields in accordance with the principles of sovereign equality and non-intervention;

(d) States Members of the United Nations have the duty to take joint and separate action in co-operation with the United Nations in accordance with the relevant provisions of the Charter.

States should co-operate in the economic, social and cultural fields as well as in the field of science and technology and for the promotion of international cultural and educational progress. States should co-operate in the promotion of economic growth throughout the world, especially that of the developing countries.

The principle of equal rights and self-determination of peoples

By virtue of the principle of equal rights and self-determination of peoples enshrined in the Charter, all peoples have the right freely to determine, without external interference, their political status and to pursue their economic, social and cultural development, and every State has the duty to respect this right in accordance with the provisions of the Charter.

Every State has the duty to promote, through joint and separate action, the realization of the principle of equal rights and self-determination of peoples, in accordance with the provisions of the Charter, and to render assistance to the United Nations in carrying out the responsibilities entrusted to it by the Charter regarding the implementation of the principle in order:

(*a*) To promote friendly relations and co-operation among States; and

(*b*) To bring a speedy end to colonialism, having due regard to the freely expressed will of the peoples concerned;

and bearing in mind that subjection of peoples to alien subjugation, domination and exploitation constitutes a violation of the principle, as well as a denial of fundamental human rights, and is contrary to the Charter of the United Nations.

Every State has the duty to promote through joint and separate action universal respect for and observance of human rights and fundamental freedoms in accordance with the Charter.

The establishment of a sovereign and independent State, the free association or integration with an independent State or the emergence into any other political status freely determined by a people constitute modes of implementing the right of self-determination by that peoples.

Every State has the duty to refrain from any forcible action which deprives peoples referred to above in the elaboration of the present principle of their right to self-determination and freedom and independence. In their actions against and resistance to such forcible action in pursuit of the exercise of their right to self-determination such peoples are entitled to seek and to receive support in accordance with the purposes and principles of the Charter of the United Nations.

The territory of a colony or other non-self-governing territory has, under the Charter of the United Nations, a status separate and distinct from the territory of the State administering it; and status separate and distinct from the territory of the State administering it; and such separate and distinct status under the Charter shall exist until the people of the colony or non-self-governing territory have exercised their right of self-determination in accordance with the Charter, and particularly its purposes and principles.

Nothing in the foregoing paragraphs shall be construed as authorizing or encouraging any action which would dismember or impair, totally or in part, the territorial integrity or political unity of sovereign and independent States conducting themselves in compliance with the principle of equal rights and self-determination of peoples as described above and thus possessed of a government representing the whole people belonging to the territory without distinction as to race, creed or colour.

Every State shall refrain from any action aimed at the partial or total disruption of the national unity and territorial integrity of any State or country.

The principle of sovereign equality of States

All States enjoy sovereign equality. They have equal right and duties and are equal members of the international community, notwithstanding differences of an economic, social, political or other nature.

In particular, sovereign equality includes the following elements:

(*a*) States are juridically equal;

(*b*) Each State enjoys the rights inherent in full sovereignty;

(*c*) Each State has the duty to respect the personality of other States;

(*d*) The territorial integrity and political independence of the State are inviolable;

(*e*) Each State has the right freely to choose and develop its political, social, economic and cultural systems;

(*f*) Each State has the duty to comply fully and in good faith with its international obligations and to live in peace with other States.

The principle that States shall fulfil in good faith the obligations assumed by them in accordance with the Charter

Every State has the duty to fulfil in good faith the obligations assumed by it in accordance with the Charter of the United Nations.

Every State has the duty to fulfil in good faith its obligations under the generally recognized principles and rules of international law.

Every State has the duty to fulfil in good faith its obligations under international agreements valid under the generally recognized principles and rules of international law.

Where obligations arising under international agreements are in conflict with the obligations of Members of the United Nations under the Charter of the United Nations, the obligations under the Charter shall prevail.

General part

2. *Declares* that:

In their interpretation and application the above principles are interrelated and each principle should be construed in the context of the other principles,

Nothing in this Declaration shall be construed as prejudicing in any manner the provisions of the Charter or the rights and duties of Member States under the Charter or the rights of peoples under the Charter taking into account the elaboration of these rights in this Declaration,

3. *Declares further* that:

The principles of the Charter which are embodied in this Declaration constitute basic principles of international law, and consequently appeals to all States to be guided by these principles in their international conduct and to develop their mutual relations on the basis of their strict observance.

1.9 ARTICLES ON THE RESPONSIBILITY OF STATES FOR INTERNATIONALLY WRONGFUL ACTS. **Adopted by the International Law Commission, 9 August 2001.** *Report of the International Law Commission on the Work of its Fifty-third Session.* **UN GAOR, 56th Sess, Supp No 10, at 43–58, UN Doc A/56/10 and Corr 1 (2001);** *reprinted in* **I Weston & Carlson I.G.4**

PART ONE
THE INTERNATIONALLY WRONGFUL ACT OF A STATE

Chapter I. General principles

Article 1

Responsibility of a State for its internationally wrongful acts

Every internationally wrongful act of a State entails the international responsibility of that State.

Article 2

Elements of an internationally wrongful act of a State

There is an internationally wrongful act of a State when conduct consisting of an action or omission:

(a) Is attributable to the State under international law; and

(b) Constitutes a breach of an international obligation of the State.

Article 3

Characterization of an act of a State as internationally wrongful

The characterization of an act of a State as internationally wrongful is governed by international law. Such characterization is not affected by the characterization of the same act as lawful by internal law.

Chapter II. Attribution of conduct to a State

Article 4

Conduct of organs of a State

1. The conduct of any State organ shall be considered an act of that State under international law, whether the organ exercises legislative, executive, judicial or any other functions, whatever position it holds in the organization of the State, and whatever its character as an organ of the central government or of a territorial unit of the State.

2. An organ includes any person or entity which has that status in accordance with the internal law of the State.

Article 5

Conduct of persons or entities exercising elements of governmental authority

The conduct of a person or entity which is not an organ of the State under article 4 but which is empowered by the law of that State to exercise elements of the governmental authority shall be considered an act of the State under international law, provided the person or entity is acting in that capacity in the particular instance.

Article 6

Conduct of organs placed at the disposal of a State by another State

The conduct of an organ placed at the disposal of a State by another State shall be considered an act of the former State under international law if the organ is acting in the exercise of elements of the governmental authority of the State at whose disposal it is placed.

Article 7

Excess of authority or contravention of instructions

The conduct of an organ of a State or of a person or entity empowered to exercise elements of the governmental authority shall be considered an act of the State under international law if the organ, person or entity acts in that capacity, even if it exceeds its authority or contravenes instructions.

Article 8

Conduct directed or controlled by a State

The conduct of a person or group of persons shall be considered an act of a State under international law if the person or group of persons is in fact acting on the instructions of, or under the direction or control of, that State in carrying out the conduct.

Article 9

Conduct carried out in the absence or default of the official authorities

The conduct of a person or group of persons shall be considered an act of a State under international law if the person or group of persons is in fact exercising elements of the governmental authority in the absence or default of the official authorities and in circumstances such as to call for the exercise of those elements of authority.

Article 10

Conduct of an insurrectional or other movement

1. The conduct of an insurrectional movement which becomes the new government of a State shall be considered an act of that State under international law.

2. The conduct of a movement, insurrectional or other, which succeeds in establishing a new State in part of the territory of a pre-existing State or in a territory under its administration shall be considered an act of the new State under international al law.

3. This article is without prejudice to the attribution to a State of any conduct, however related to that of the movement concerned, which is to be considered an act of that State by virtue of articles 4 to 9.

Article 11

Conduct acknowledged and adopted by a State as its own

Conduct which is not attributable to a State under the preceding articles shall nevertheless be considered an act of that State under international law if and to the extent that the State acknowledges and adopts the conduct in question as its own.

Chapter III. Breach of an international obligation

Article 12

Existence of a breach of an international obligation

There is a breach of an international obligation by a State when an act of that State is not in conformity with what is required of it by that obligation, regardless of its origin or character.

Article 13

International obligation in force for a State

An act of a State does not constitute a breach of an international obligation unless the State is bound by the obligation in question at the time the act occurs.

Article 14

Extension in time of the breach of an international obligation

1. The breach of an international obligation by an act of a State not having a continuing character occurs at the moment when the act is performed, even if its effects continue.

2. The breach of an international obligation by an act of a State having a continuing character extends over the entire period during which the act continues and remains not in conformity with the international obligation.

3. The breach of an international obligation requiring a State to prevent a given event occurs when the event occurs and extends over the entire period during which the event continues and remains not in conformity with that obligation.

Article 15

Breach consisting of a composite act

1. The breach of an international obligation by a State through a series of actions or omissions defined in aggregate as wrongful, occurs when the action or omission occurs which, taken with the other actions or omissions, is sufficient to constitute the wrongful act.

2. In such a case, the breach extends over the entire period starting with the first of the actions or omissions of the series and lasts for as long as these actions or omissions are repeated and remain not in conformity with the international obligation.

Chapter IV. Responsibility of a State in connection with the act of another State

Article 16

Aid or assistance in the commission of an internationally wrongful act

A State which aids or assists another State in the commission of an internationally wrongful act by the latter is internationally responsible for doing so if:

(a) That State does so with knowledge of the circumstances of the internationally wrongful act; and

(b) The act would be internationally wrongful if committed by that State.

Article 17

Direction and control exercised over the commission of an internationally wrongful act

A State which directs and controls another State in the commission of an internationally wrongful act by the latter is internationally responsible for that act if:

(a) That State does so with knowledge of the circumstances of the internationally wrongful act; and

(b) The act would be internationally wrongful if committed by that State.

Article 18

Coercion of another State

A State which coerces another State to commit an act is internationally responsible for that act if:

(a) The act would, but for the coercion, be an internationally wrongful act of the coerced State; and

(b) The coercing State does so with knowledge of the circumstances of the act.

Article 19
Effect of this chapter

This chapter is without prejudice to the international responsibility, under other provisions of these articles, of the State which commits the act in question, or of any other State.

Chapter V. Circumstances precluding wrongfulness

Article 20
Consent

Valid consent by a State to the commission of a given act by another State precludes the wrongfulness of that act in relation to the former State to the extent that the act remains within the limits of that consent.

Article 21
Self-defence

The wrongfulness of an act of a State is precluded if the act constitutes a lawful measure of self-defence taken in conformity with the Charter of the United Nations.

Article 22
Countermeasures in respect of an internationally wrongful act

The wrongfulness of an act of a State not in conformity with an international obligation towards another State is precluded if and to the extent that the act constitutes a countermeasure taken against the latter State in accordance with chapter II of Part Three.

Article 23
Force majeure

1.   The wrongfulness of an act of a State not in conformity with an international obligation of that State is precluded if the act is due to *force majeure*, that is the occurrence of an irresistible force or of an unforeseen event, beyond the control of the State, making it materially impossible in the circumstances to perform the obligation.

2.   Paragraph 1 does not apply if:

(a) The situation of *force majeure* is due, either alone or in combination with other factors, to the conduct of the State invoking it; or

(b) The State has assumed the risk of that situation occurring.

Article 24
Distress

1.   The wrongfulness of an act of a State not in conformity with an international obligation of that State is precluded if the author of the act in question has no other reasonable way, in a situation of distress, of saving the author's life or the lives of other persons entrusted to the author's care.

2.   Paragraph 1 does not apply if:

(a) The situation of distress is due, either alone or in combination with other factors, to the conduct of the State invoking it; or

(b) The act in question is likely to create a comparable or greater peril.

Article 25
Necessity

1.   Necessity may not be invoked by a State as a ground for precluding the wrongfulness of an act not in conformity with an international obligation of that State unless the act:

(a) Is the only way for the State to safeguard an essential interest against a grave and imminent peril; and

(b) Does not seriously impair an essential interest of the State or States towards which the obligation exists, or of the international community as a whole.

2. In any case, necessity may not be invoked by a State as a ground for precluding wrongfulness if:

(a) The international obligation in question excludes the possibility of invoking necessity; or

(b) The State has contributed to the situation of necessity.

Article 26
Compliance with peremptory norms

Nothing in this chapter precludes the wrongfulness of any act of a State which is not in conformity with an obligation arising under a peremptory norm of general international law.

Article 27
Consequences of invoking a circumstance precluding wrongfulness

The invocation of a circumstance precluding wrongfulness in accordance with this chapter is without prejudice to:

(a) Compliance with the obligation in question, if and to the extent that the circumstance precluding wrongfulness no longer exists;

(b) The question of compensation for any material loss caused by the act in question.

PART TWO
CONTENT OF THE INTERNATIONAL RESPONSIBILITY OF A STATE
Chapter I. General principles

Article 28
Legal consequences of an internationally wrongful act

The international responsibility of a State which is entailed by an internationally wrongful act in accordance with the provisions of Part One involves legal consequences as set out in this Part.

Article 29
Continued duty of performance

The legal consequences of an internationally wrongful act under this Part do not affect the continued duty of the responsible State to perform the obligation breached.

Article 30
Cessation and non-repetition

The State responsible for the internationally wrongful act is under an obligation:

(a) To cease that act, if it is continuing;

(b) To offer appropriate assurances and guarantees of non-repetition, if circumstances so require.

Article 31
Reparation

1. The responsible State is under an obligation to make full reparation for the injury caused by the internationally wrongful act.

2. Injury includes any damage, whether material or moral, caused by the internationally wrongful act of a State.

Article 32
Irrelevance of internal law

The responsible State may not rely on the provisions of its internal law as justification for failure to comply with its obligations under this Part.

Article 33
Scope of international obligations set out in this Part

1. The obligations of the responsible State set out in this Part may be owed to another State, to several States, or to the international community as a whole, depending in particular on the character and content of the international obligation and on the circumstances of the breach.

2. This Part is without prejudice to any right, arising from the international responsibility of a State, which may accrue directly to any person or entity other than a State.

Chapter II. Reparation for injury

Article 34
Forms of reparation

Full reparation for the injury caused by the internationally wrongful act shall take the form of restitution, compensation and satisfaction, either singly or in combination, in accordance with the provisions of this chapter.

Article 35
Restitution

A State responsible for an internationally wrongful act is under an obligation to make restitution, that is, to re-establish the situation which existed before the wrongful act was committed, provided and to the extent that restitution:

(a) Is not materially impossible;

(b) Does not involve a burden out of all proportion to the benefit deriving from restitution instead of compensation.

Article 36
Compensation

1. The State responsible for an internationally wrongful act is under an obligation to compensate for the damage caused thereby, insofar as such damage is not made good by restitution.

2. The compensation shall cover any financially assessable damage including loss of profits insofar as it is established.

Article 37
Satisfaction

1. The State responsible for an internationally wrongful act is under an obligation to give satisfaction for the injury caused by that act insofar as it cannot be made good by restitution or compensation.

2. Satisfaction may consist in an acknowledgement of the breach, an expression of regret, a formal apology or another appropriate modality.

3. Satisfaction shall not be out of proportion to the injury and may not take a form humiliating to the responsible State.

Article 38
Interest

1. Interest on any principal sum due under this chapter shall be payable when necessary in order to ensure full reparation. The interest rate and mode of calculation shall be set so as to achieve that result.

2. Interest runs from the date when the principal sum should have been paid until the date the obligation to pay is fulfilled.

Article 39
Contribution to the injury

In the determination of reparation, account shall be taken of the contribution to the injury by wilful or negligent action or omission of the injured State or any person or entity in relation to whom reparation is sought.

Chapter III. Serious breaches of obligations under peremptory norms of general international law

Article 40
Application of this chapter

1. This chapter applies to the international responsibility which is entailed by a serious breach by a State of an obligation arising under a peremptory norm of general international law.

2. A breach of such an obligation is serious if it involves a gross or systematic failure by the responsible State to fulfil the obligation.

Article 41
Particular consequences of a serious breach of an obligation under this chapter

1. States shall cooperate to bring to an end through lawful means any serious breach within the meaning of article 40.

2. No State shall recognize as lawful a situation created by a serious breach within the meaning of article 40, nor render aid or assistance in maintaining that situation.

3. This article is without prejudice to the other consequences referred to in this Part and to such further consequences that a breach to which this chapter applies may entail under international law.

PART THREE
THE IMPLEMENTATION OF THE INTERNATIONAL RESPONSIBILITY OF A STATE

Chapter I. Invocation of the responsibility of a State

Article 42
Invocation of responsibility by an injured State

A State is entitled as an injured State to invoke the responsibility of another State if the obligation breached is owed to:

(a) That State individually; or

(b) A group of States including that State, or the international community as a whole, and the breach of the obligation:

(i) Specially affects that State; or

(ii) Is of such a character as radically to change the position of all the other States to which the obligation is owed with respect to the further performance of the obligation.

Article 43
Notice of claim by an injured State

1.   An injured State which invokes the responsibility of another State shall give notice of its claim to that State.

2.   The injured State may specify in particular:

(a) The conduct that the responsible State should take in order to cease the wrongful act, if it is continuing;

(b) What form reparation should take in accordance with the provisions of Part Two.

Article 44
Admissibility of claims

The responsibility of a State may not be invoked if:

(a) The claim is not brought in accordance with any applicable rule relating to the nationality of claims;

(b) The claim is one to which the rule of exhaustion of local remedies applies and any available and effective local remedy has not been exhausted.

Article 45
Loss of the right to invoke responsibility

The responsibility of a State may not be invoked if:

(a) The injured State has validly waived the claim;

(b) The injured State is to be considered as having, by reason of its conduct, validly acquiesced in the lapse of the claim.

Article 46
Plurality of injured States

Where several States are injured by the same internationally wrongful act, each injured State may separately invoke the responsibility of the State which has committed the internationally wrongful act.

Article 47
Plurality of responsible States

1.   Where several States are responsible for the same internationally wrongful act, the responsibility of each State may be invoked in relation to that act.

2.   Paragraph 1:

(a) Does not permit any injured State to recover, by way of compensation, more than the damage it has suffered;

(b) Is without prejudice to any right of recourse against the other responsible States.

Article 48
Invocation of responsibility by a State other than an injured State

1.   Any State other than an injured State is entitled to invoke the responsibility of another State in accordance with paragraph 2 if:

(a) The obligation breached is owed to a group of States including that State, and is established for the protection of a collective interest of the group; or

(b) The obligation breached is owed to the international community as a whole.

2.   Any State entitled to invoke responsibility under paragraph 1 may claim from the responsible State:

(a) Cessation of the internationally wrongful act, and assurances and guarantees of non-repetition in accordance with article 30; and

(b) Performance of the obligation of reparation in accordance with the preceding articles, in the interest of the injured State or of the beneficiaries of the obligation breached.

3.   The requirements for the invocation of responsibility by an injured State under articles 43, 44 and 45 apply to an invocation of responsibility by a State entitled to do so under paragraph 1.

Chapter II.   Countermeasures

Article 49
Object and limits of countermeasures

1.   An injured State may only take countermeasures against a State which is responsible for an internationally wrongful act in order to induce that State to comply with its obligations under Part Two.

2.   Countermeasures are limited to the non-performance for the time being of international obligations of the State taking the measures towards the responsible State.

3.   Countermeasures shall, as far as possible, be taken in such a way as to permit the resumption of performance of the obligations in question.

Article 50
Obligations not affected by countermeasures

1.   Countermeasures shall not affect:

(a) The obligation to refrain from the threat or use of force as embodied in the Charter of the United Nations;

(b) Obligations for the protection of fundamental human rights;

(c) Obligations of a humanitarian character prohibiting reprisals;

(d) Other obligations under peremptory norms of general international law.

2.   A State taking countermeasures is not relieved from fulfilling its obligations:

(a) Under any dispute settlement procedure applicable between it and the responsible State;

(b) To respect the inviolability of diplomatic or consular agents, premises, archives and documents.

Article 51
Proportionality

Countermeasures must be commensurate with the injury suffered, taking into account the gravity of the internationally wrongful act and the rights in question.

Article 52
Conditions relating to resort to countermeasures

1.   Before taking countermeasures, an injured State shall:

(a) Call on the responsible State, in accordance with article 43, to fulfil its obligations under Part Two;

(b) Notify the responsible State of any decision to take countermeasures and offer to negotiate with that State.

2. Notwithstanding paragraph 1 (b), the injured State may take such urgent countermeasures as are necessary to preserve its rights.

3. Countermeasures may not be taken, and if already taken must be suspended without undue delay if:

(a) The internationally wrongful act has ceased; and

(b) The dispute is pending before a court or tribunal which has the authority to make decisions binding on the parties.

4. Paragraph 3 does not apply if the responsible State fails to implement the dispute settlement procedures in good faith.

Article 53
Termination of countermeasures

Countermeasures shall be terminated as soon as the responsible State has complied with its obligations under Part Two in relation to the internationally wrongful act.

Article 54
Measures taken by States other than an injured State

This chapter does not prejudice the right of any State, entitled under article 48, paragraph 1 to invoke the responsibility of another State, to take lawful measures against that State to ensure cessation of the breach and reparation in the interest of the injured State or of the beneficiaries of the obligation breached.

PART FOUR
GENERAL PROVISIONS

Article 55
Lex specialis

These articles do not apply where and to the extent that the conditions for the existence of an internationally wrongful act or the content or implementation of the international responsibility of a State are governed by special rules of international law.

Article 56
Questions of State responsibility not regulated by these articles

The applicable rules of international law continue to govern questions concerning the responsibility of a State for an internationally wrongful act to the extent that they are not regulated by these articles.

Article 57
Responsibility of an international organization

These articles are without prejudice to any question of the responsibility under international law of an international organization, or of any State for the conduct of an international organization.

Article 58
Individual responsibility

These articles are without prejudice to any question of the individual responsibility under international law of any person acting on behalf of a State.

Article 59
Charter of the United Nations

These articles are without prejudice to the Charter of the United Nations.

1.10 GUIDING PRINCIPLES APPLICABLE TO UNILATERAL DECLARATIONS OF STATES CAPABLE OF CREATING LEGAL OBLIGATIONS. **Adopted by the International Law Commission, 4 August 2006.** *Report of the International Law Commission on the Work of its Fifty-eight Session.* **UN GAOR, 61st Sess., Supp. No. 10, at 367–689, UN Doc A/61/10 (2006)**

The International Law Commission,

Noting that States may find themselves bound by their unilateral behaviour on the international plane,

Noting that behaviours capable of legally binding States may take the form of formal declarations or mere informal conduct including, in certain situations, silence, on which other States may reasonably rely,

Noting also that the question whether a unilateral behaviour by the State binds it in a given situation depends on the circumstances of the case,

Noting also that in practice, it is often difficult to establish whether the legal effects stemming from the unilateral behaviour of a State are the consequence of the intent that it has expressed or depend on the expectations that its conduct has raised among other subjects of international law,

Adopts the following Guiding Principles which relate only to unilateral acts *stricto sensu*, i.e. those taking the form of formal declarations formulated by a State with the intent to produce obligations under international law,

1. Declarations publicly made and manifesting the will to be bound may have the effect of creating legal obligations. When the conditions for this are met, the binding character of such declarations is based on good faith; States concerned may then take them into consideration and rely on them; such States are entitled to require that such obligations be respected;

2. Any State possesses capacity to undertake legal obligations through unilateral declarations;

3. To determine the legal effects of such declarations, it is necessary to take account of their content, of all the factual circumstances in which they were made, and of the reactions to which they gave rise;

4. A unilateral declaration binds the State internationally only if it is made by an authority vested with the power to do so. By virtue of their functions, heads of State, heads of Government and ministers for foreign affairs are competent to formulate such declarations. Other persons representing the State in specified areas may be authorized to bind it, through their declarations, in areas falling within their competence;

5. Unilateral declarations may be formulated orally or in writing;

6. Unilateral declarations may be addressed to the international community as a whole, to one or several States or to other entities;

7. A unilateral declaration entails obligations for the formulating State only if it is stated in clear and specific terms. In the case of doubt as to the scope of the obligations resulting from such a declaration, such obligations must be interpreted in a restrictive manner. In interpreting the content of such obligations, weight shall be given first and foremost to the text of the declaration, together with the context and the circumstances in which it was formulated;

8. A unilateral declaration which is in conflict with a peremptory norm of general international law is void;

9. No obligation may result for other States from the unilateral declaration of a State. However, the other State or States concerned may incur obligations in relation to such a unilateral declaration to the extent that they clearly accepted such a declaration;

10. A unilateral declaration that has created legal obligations for the State making the declaration cannot be revoked arbitrarily. In assessing whether a revocation would be arbitrary, consideration should be given to:

(i) Any specific terms of the declaration relating to revocation;

(ii) The extent to which those to whom the obligations are owed have relied on such obligations;

(iii) The extent to which there has been a fundamental change in the circumstances.

B.   ENVIRONMENTAL

1.11   RESOLUTION ON PERMANENT SOVEREIGNTY OVER NATURAL RESOURCES. Adopted by the U.N. General Assembly, 14 December 1962. GA Res 1803, UN GAOR, 17th Sess, Supp No 17, at 15, UN Doc A/5217 (1963), 16 UNYB 503; *reprinted in* **2 ILM 223 (1963) & 5 Weston & Carlson V.B.1**

The General Assembly,

Recalling its resolutions 523(VI) of 12 January 1952 and 626(VII) of 21 December 1952,

Bearing in mind its resolution 1314(XIII) of 12 December 1958, by which it established the Commission on Permanent Sovereignty over Natural Resources and instructed it to conduct a full survey of the status of permanent sovereignty over natural wealth and resources as a basic constituent of the right to self-determination, with recommendations, where necessary, for its strengthening, and decided further that, in the conduct of the full survey of the status of the permanent sovereignty of peoples and nations over their natural wealth and resources, due regard should be paid to the rights and duties of States under international law and to the importance of encouraging international co-operation in the economic development of developing countries,

Bearing in mind its resolution 1515(XV) of 15 December 1960, in which it recommended that the sovereign right of every State to dispose of its wealth and its natural resources should be respected,

Considering that any measure in this respect must be based on the recognition of the inalienable right of all States freely to dispose of their natural wealth and resources in accordance with their national interests, and on respect for the economic independence of States,

Considering that nothing in paragraph 4 below in any way prejudices the position of any Member State on any aspect of the question of the rights and obligations of successor States and Governments in respect of property acquired before the accession to complete sovereignty of countries formerly under colonial rule,

Noting that the subject of succession of States and Governments is being examined as a matter of priority by the International Law Commission,

Considering that it is desirable to promote international co-operation for the economic development of developing countries, and that economic and financial agreements between the developed and the developing countries must be based on the principles of equality and of the right of peoples and nations to self-determination,

Considering that the provision of economic and technical assistance, loans and increased foreign investment must not be subject to conditions which conflict with the interests of the recipient State,

Considering the benefits to be derived from exchanges of technical and scientific information likely to promote the development and use of such resources and wealth, and the important part which the United Nations and other international organizations are called upon to play in that connexion,

Attaching particular importance to the question of promoting the economic development of developing countries and securing their economic independence,

Noting that the creation and strengthening of the inalienable sovereignty of States over their natural wealth and resources reinforces their economic independence,

Desiring that there should be further consideration by the United Nations of the subject of permanent sovereignty over natural resources in the spirit of international co-operation in the field of economic development, particularly that of the developing countries,

I

Declares that:

1.   The right of peoples and nations to permanent sovereignty over their natural wealth and resources must be exercised in the interest of their national development and of the well-being of the people of the State concerned.

2.   The exploration, development and disposition of such resources, as well as the import of the foreign capital required for these purposes, should be in conformity with the rules and conditions which the peoples and nations freely consider to be necessary or desirable with regard to the authorization, restriction or prohibition of such activities.

3.   In cases where authorization is granted, the capital imported and the earnings on that capital shall be governed by the terms thereof, by the national legislation in force, and by international law. The profits derived must be shared in the proportions freely agreed upon, in each case, between the investors and the recipient State, due care being taken to ensure that there is no impairment, for any reason, of that State's sovereignty over its natural wealth and resources.

4.   Nationalization, expropriation or requisitioning shall be based on grounds or reasons of public utility, security or the national interest which are recognized as overriding purely individual or private interests, both domestic and foreign. In such cases the owner shall be paid appropriate compensation, in accordance with the rules in force in the State taking such measures in the exercise of its sovereignty and in accordance with international law. In any case where the question of compensation gives rise to a controversy, the national jurisdiction of the State taking such measures shall be exhausted. However, upon agreement by sovereign States and other parties concerned, settlement of the dispute should be made through arbitration or international adjudication.

5.   The free and beneficial exercise of the sovereignty of peoples and nations over their natural resources must be furthered by the mutual respect of States based on their sovereign equality.

6.   International co-operation for the economic development of developing countries, whether in the form of public or private capital investments, exchange of goods and services, technical assistance, or exchange of scientific information, shall be such as to further their independent national development and shall be based upon respect for their sovereignty over their natural wealth and resources.

7.   Violation of the rights of peoples and nations to sovereignty over their natural wealth and resources is contrary to the spirit and principles of the Charter of the United Nations and hinders the development of international co-operation and the maintenance of peace.

8.   Foreign investment agreements freely entered into by or between sovereign States shall be observed in good faith: States and international organizations shall strictly and conscientiously respect the sovereignty of peoples and nations over their natural wealth and resources in accordance with the Charter and the principles set forth in the present resolution.

II

Welcomes the decision of the International Law Commission to speed up its work on the codification of the topic of responsibility of States for the consideration of the General Assembly;

III

Requests the Secretary–General to continue the study of the various aspects of permanent sovereignty over natural resources, taking into account the desire of Member States to ensure the protection of their sovereign rights while encouraging international co-operation in the field of economic development, and to report to the Economic and Social Council and to the General Assembly, if possible at its eighteenth session.

1.12 STOCKHOLM DECLARATION OF THE UNITED NATIONS CONFERENCE ON THE HUMAN ENVIRONMENT. **Adopted by the UN Conference on the Human Environment at Stockholm, 16 June 1972.** *Report of the UN Conference on the Human Environment, Stockholm, 5–16 June 1972,* **UN Doc A/CONF.48/14/Rev. 1 at 3 (1973), UN Doc A/CONF.48/14 at 2–65, and Corr 1 (1972);** *reprinted in* **11 ILM 1416 (1972) & 5 Weston & Carlson V.B.3**

THE UNITED NATIONS CONFERENCE ON THE HUMAN ENVIRONMENT.

HAVING MET at Stockholm from 5 to 16 June 1972.

HAVING CONSIDERED the need for a common outlook and for common principles to inspire and guide the peoples of the world in the preservation and enhancement of the human environment.

I

PROCLAIMS THAT:

1. Man is both creature and moulder of his environment, which gives him physical sustenance and affords him the opportunity for intellectual, moral, social and spiritual growth. In the long and tortuous evolution of the human race on this planet a stage has been reached when, through the rapid acceleration of science and technology, man has acquired the power to transform his environment in countless ways and on an unprecedented scale. Both aspects of man's environment, the natural and the man-made, are essential to his well-being and to the enjoyment of basic human rights—even the right to life itself.

2. The protection and improvement of the human environment is a major issue which affects the well-being of peoples and economic development throughout the world; it is the urgent desire of the peoples of the whole world and the duty of all Governments.

3. Man has constantly to sum up experience and go on discovering, inventing, creating and advancing. In our time, man's capability to transform his surroundings, if used wisely, can bring to all peoples the benefits of development and the opportunity to enhance the quality of life. Wrongly or heedlessly applied, the same power can do incalculable harm to human beings and the human environment. We see around us growing evidence of man-made harm in many regions of the earth: dangerous levels of pollution in water, air, earth and living beings; major and undesirable disturbances to the ecological balance of the biosphere; destruction and depletion of irreplaceable resources; and gross deficiencies harmful to the physical, mental and social health of man, in the man-made environment, particularly in the living and working environment.

4. In the developing countries most of the environmental problems are caused by under-development. Millions continue to live far below the minimum levels required for a decent human existence, deprived of adequate food and clothing, shelter and education, health and sanitation. Therefore, the developing countries must direct their efforts to development, bearing in mind their priorities and the need to safeguard and improve the environment. For the same purpose, the industrialized countries should make efforts to reduce the gap between themselves and the developing countries. In the industrialized countries, environmental problems are generally related to industrialization and technological development.

5. The natural growth of population continuously presents problems on the preservation of the environment, and adequate policies and measures should be adopted, as appropriate, to face these problems. Of all things in the world, people are the most precious. It is the people that propel social progress, create social wealth, develop science and technology and, through their hard work, continuously transform

the human environment. Along with social progress and the advance of production, science and technology, the capability of man to improve the environment increases with each passing day.

6. A point has been reached in history when we must shape our actions throughout the world with a more prudent care for their environmental consequences. Through ignorance or indifference we can do massive and irreversible harm to the earthly environment on which our life and well-being depend. Conversely, through fuller knowledge and wiser action, we can achieve for ourselves and our posterity a better life in an environment more in keeping with human needs and hopes. There are broad vistas for the enhancement of environmental quality and the creation of a good life. What is needed is an enthusiastic but calm state of mind and intense but orderly work. For the purpose of attaining freedom in the world of nature, man must use knowledge to build, in collaboration with nature, a better environment. To defend and improve the human environment for present and future generations has become an imperative goal for mankind—a goal to be pursued together with, and in harmony with, the established and fundamental goals of peace and of world-wide economic and social development.

7. To achieve this environmental goal will demand the acceptance of responsibility by citizens and communities and by enterprises and institutions at every level, all sharing equitably in common efforts. Individuals in all walks of life as well as organizations in many fields, by their values and the sum of their actions, will shape the world environment of the future. Local and national governments will bear the greatest burden for large-scale environmental policy and action within their jurisdictions. International co-operation is also needed in order to raise resources to support the developing countries in carrying out their responsibilities in this field. A growing class of environmental problems, because they are regional or global in extent or because they affect the common international realm, will require extensive co-operation among nations and action by international organizations in the common interest. The Conference calls upon Governments and peoples to exert common efforts for the preservation and improvement of the human environment, for the benefit of all the people and for their posterity.

II

Principles

STATES THE COMMON CONVICTION THAT:

Principle 1

Man has the fundamental right to freedom, equality and adequate conditions of life, in an environment of a quality that permits a life of dignity and well-being, and he bears a solemn responsibility to protect and improve the environment for present and future generations. In this respect, policies promoting or perpetuating apartheid, racial segregation, discrimination, colonial and other forms of oppression and foreign domination stand condemned and must be eliminated.

Principle 2

The natural resources of the earth including the air, water, land, flora and fauna and especially representative samples of natural ecosystems must be safeguarded for the benefit of present and future generations through careful planning or management, as appropriate.

Principle 3

The capacity of the earth to produce vital renewable resources must be maintained and, wherever practicable, restored or improved.

Principle 4

Man has a special responsibility to safeguard and wisely manage the heritage of wildlife and its habitat which are now gravely imperilled by a combination of adverse factors. Nature conservation including wildlife must therefore receive importance in planning for economic development.

Principle 5

The non-renewable resources of the earth must be employed in such a way as to guard against the danger of their future exhaustion and to ensure that benefits from such employment are shared by all mankind.

Principle 6

The discharge of toxic substances or of other substances and the release of heat, in such quantities or concentrations as to exceed the capacity of the environment to render them harmless, must be halted in order to ensure that serious or irreversible damage is not inflicted upon ecosystems. The just struggle of the peoples of all countries against pollution should be supported.

Principle 7

States shall take all possible steps to prevent pollution of the seas by substances that are liable to create hazards to human health, to harm living resources and marine life, to damage amenities or to interfere with other legitimate uses of the sea.

Principle 8

Economic and social development is essential for ensuring a favourable living and working environment for man and for creating conditions on earth that are necessary for the improvement of the quality of life.

Principle 9

Environmental deficiencies generated by the conditions of underdevelopment and natural disasters pose grave problems and can best be remedied by accelerated development through the transfer of substantial quantities of financial and technological assistance as a supplement to the domestic effort of the developing countries and such timely assistance as may be required.

Principle 10

For the developing countries, stability of prices and adequate earnings for primary commodities and raw material are essential to environmental management since economic factors as well as ecological processes must be taken into account.

Principle 11

The environmental policies of all States should enhance and not adversely affect the present or future development potential of developing countries, nor should they hamper the attainment of better living conditions for all, and appropriate steps should be taken by States and international organizations with a view to reaching agreement on meeting the possible national and international economic consequences resulting from the application of environmental measures.

Principle 12

Resources should be made available to preserve and improve the environment, taking into account the circumstances and particular requirements of developing countries and any costs which may emanate from their incorporating environmental safeguards into their development planning and the need for making available to them, upon their request, additional international technical and financial assistance for this purpose.

Principle 13

In order to achieve a more rational management of resources and thus to improve the environment, State should adopt an integrated and coordinated approach to their development planning so as to ensure that development is compatible with the need to protect and improve the human environment for the benefit for their population.

Principle 14

Rational planning constitutes an essential tool for reconciling any conflict between the needs of development and the need to protect and improve the environment.

Principle 15

Planning must be applied to human settlements and urbanization with a view to avoiding adverse effects on the environment and obtaining maximum social, economic and environmental benefits for all. In this respect projects which are designed for colonialist and racist domination must be abandoned.

Principle 16

Demographic policies, which are without prejudice to basic human rights and which are deemed appropriate by Governments concerned, should be applied in those regions where the rate of population growth or excessive population concentrations are likely to have adverse effects on the environment or development, or where low population density may prevent improvement of the human environment and impede development.

Principle 17

Appropriate national institutions must be entrusted with the task of planning, managing or controlling the environmental resources of States with the view to enhancing environmental quality.

Principle 18

Science and technology, as part of their contribution to economic and social development, must be applied to the identification, avoidance and control of environmental risks and the solution of environmental problems and for the common good of mankind.

Principle 19

Education in environmental matters, for the younger generation as well as adults, giving due consideration to the underprivileged, is essential in order to broaden the basis for an enlightened opinion and responsible conduct by individuals, enterprises and communities in protecting and improving the environment in its full human dimension. It is also essential that mass media of communications avoid contributing to the deterioration of the environment, but, on the contrary, disseminate information of an educational nature, on the need to protect and improve the environment in order to enable man to develop in every respect.

Principle 20

Scientific research and development in the context of environmental problems, both national and multinational, must be promoted in all countries, especially the developing countries. In this connection, the free flow of up-to-date scientific information and transfer of experience must be supported and assisted, to facilitate the solution of environmental problems; environmental technologies should be made available to developing countries on terms which would encourage their wide dissemination without constituting an economic burden on the developing countries.

Principle 21

States have, in accordance with the Charter of the United Nations and the principles of international law, the sovereign right to exploit their own resources pursuant to their own environmental policies, and the responsibility to ensure that activities within their jurisdiction or control do not cause damage to the environment of other States or of areas beyond the limits of national jurisdiction.

Principle 22

States shall co-operate to develop further the international law regarding liability and compensation for the victims of pollution and other environmental damage caused by activities within the jurisdiction or control of such States to areas beyond their jurisdiction.

Principle 23

Without prejudice to such criteria as may be agreed upon by the international community, or to standards which will have to be determined nationally, it will be essential in all cases to consider the systems of values prevailing in each country, and the extent of the applicability of standards which are valid for the most advanced countries but which may be inappropriate and of unwarranted social cost for the developing countries.

Principle 24

International matters concerning the protection and improvement of the environment should be handled in a co-operative spirit by all countries, big or small, on an equal footing. Co-operation through multilateral or bilateral arrangements or other appropriate means is essential to effectively control, prevent, reduce and eliminate adverse environmental effects resulting from activities conducted in all spheres, in such a way that due account is taken of the sovereignty and interests of all States.

Principle 25

States shall ensure that international organizations play a coordinated, efficient and dynamic role for the protection and improvement of the environment.

Principle 26

Man and his environment must be spared the effects of nuclear weapons and all other means of mass destruction. States must strive to reach prompt agreement, in the relevant international organs, on the elimination and complete destruction of such weapons.

1.13   RESOLUTION ON THE INSTITUTIONAL AND FINANCIAL ARRANGEMENT FOR INTERNATIONAL ENVIRONMENT COOPERATION (ESTABLISHING THE UNITED NATIONS ENVIRONMENT PROGRAM, UNEP). **Adopted by the U.N. General Assembly, 15 December 1972. GA Res 2997, UN GAOR, 27th Sess, Supp 30, at 42, UN Doc A/8370 (1973);** *reprinted in* **13 ILM 234 (1974) & 5 Weston & Carlson V.A.4**

I

Governing Council of the United Nations Environment Programme

1. *Decides* to establish a Governing–Council of the United Nations Environment Programme, composed of fifty-eight members elected by the General Assembly for three-year terms on the following basis:

(*a*) Sixteen seats for African States;

(*b*) Thirteen seats for Asian States;

(*c*) Six seats for Eastern European States;

(*d*) Ten seats for Latin American States;

(*e*) Thirteen seats for Western European and other States;

2. *Decides* that the Governing Council shall have the following main functions and responsibilities:

(*a*) To promote international co-operation in the field of the environment and to recommend, as appropriate, policies to this end;

(*b*) To provide general policy guidance for the direction and co-ordination of environmental programmes within the United Nations system;

(*c*) To receive and review the periodic reports of the Executive Director, referred to in section II, paragraph 2, below, on the implementation of environmental programmes within the United Nations system;

(*d*) To keep under review the world environmental situation in order to ensure that emerging environmental problems of wide international significance receive appropriate and adequate consideration by Governments;

(*e*) To promote the contribution of the relevant international scientific and other professional communities to the acquisition, assessment and exchange of environmental knowledge and information and, as appropriate, to the technical aspects of the formulation and implementation of environmental programmes within the United Nations system;

(*f*) To maintain under continuing review the impact of national and international environmental policies and measures on developing countries, as well as the problem of additional costs that may be incurred by developing countries in the implementation of environmental programmes and projects, and to ensure that such programmes and projects shall be compatible with the development plans and priorities of those countries;

(*g*) To review and approve annually the programme of utilization of resources of the Environment Fund referred to in section III below;

3. *Decides* that the Governing Council shall report annually to the General Assembly through the Economic and Social Council, which will transmit to the Assembly such comments on the report as it may deem necessary, particularly with regard to questions of co-ordination and to the relationship of environmental policies and programmes within the United Nations system to over-all economic and social policies and priorities;

II

Environment secretariat

1. *Decides* that a small secretariat shall be established in the United Nations to serve as a focal point for environmental action and co-ordination within the United Nations system in such a way as to ensure a high degree of effective management;

2. *Decides* that the environment secretariat shall be headed by the Executive Director of the United Nations Environment Programme, who shall be elected by the General Assembly on the nomination of the Secretary–General for a term of four years and who shall be entrusted, *inter alia,* with the following responsibilities:

(*a*) To provide substantive support to the Governing Council of the United Nations Environment Programme;

(*b*) To co-ordinate, under the guidance of the Governing Council, environmental programmes within the United Nations system to keep their implementation under review and to assess their effectiveness;

(*c*) To advise, as appropriate and under the guidance of the Governing Council, intergovernmental bodies of the United Nations system on the formulation and implementation of environmental programmes;

(*d*) To secure the effective co-operation of, and contribution from, the relevant scientific and other professional communities in all parts of the world;

(*e*) To provide, at the request of all parties concerned, advisory services for the promotion of international co-operation in the field of the environment;

(*f*) To submit to the Governing Council, on his own initiative or upon request, proposals embodying medium-range and long-range planning for United Nations programmes in the field of the environment;

(*g*) To bring to the attention of the Governing Council any matter which he deems to require consideration by it;

(*h*) To administer, under the authority and policy guidance of the Governing Council, the Environment Fund referred to in section III below;

(*i*) To report on environmental matters to the Governing Council;

(*j*) To perform such other functions as may be entrusted to him by the Governing Council;

3. *Decides* that the costs of servicing the Governing Council and providing the small secretariat referred to in paragraph 1 above shall be borne by the regular budget of the United Nations and that operational programme costs, programme support and administrative costs of the Environment Fund established under section III below shall be borne by the Fund;

III

Environment Fund

1. *Decides* that, in order to provide for additional financing for environmental programmes, a voluntary fund shall be established, with effect from 1 January 1973, in accordance with existing United Nations financial procedures;

2. *Decides* that, in order to enable the Governing Council of the United Nations Environment Programme to fulfil its policy-guidance role for the direction and co-ordination of environmental activities, the Environment Fund shall finance wholly or partly the costs of the new environmental initiatives undertaken within the United Nations system—which will include the initiatives envisaged in the Action Plan for the Human Environment adopted by the United Nations Conference on the Human Environment, with particular attention to integrated projects, and such other environ-

mental activities as may be decided upon by the Governing Council—and that the Governing Council shall review these initiatives with a view to taking appropriate decisions as to their continued financing;

3. *Decides* that the Environment Fund shall be used for financing such programmes of general interest as regional and global monitoring, assessment and data-collecting systems, including, as appropriate, costs for national counterparts; the improvement of environmental quality management; environmental research; information exchange and dissemination; public education and training; assistance for national, regional and global environmental institutions; the promotion of environmental research and studies for the development of industrial and other technologies best suited to a policy of economic growth compatible with adequate environmental safeguards; and such other programmes as the Governing Council may decide upon, and that in the implementation of such programmes due account should be taken of the special needs of the developing countries;

4. *Decides* that, in order to ensure that the development priorities of developing countries shall not be adversely affected, adequate measures shall be taken to provide additional financial resources on terms compatible with the economic situation of the recipient developing country, and that, to this end, the Executive Director, in co-operation with competent organizations, shall keep this problem under continuing review;

5. *Decides* that the Environment Fund, in pursuance of the objectives stated in paragraphs 2 and 3 above, shall be directed to the need for effective co-ordination in the implementation of international environmental programmes of the organizations in the United Nations system and other international organizations;

6. *Decides* that, in the implementation of programmes to be financed by the Environment Fund, organizations outside the United Nations system, particularly those in the countries and regions concerned, shall also be utilized as appropriate, in accordance with the procedures established by the Governing Council, and that such organizations are invited to support the United Nations environmental programmes by complementary initiatives and contributions;

7. *Decides* that the Governing Council shall formulate such general procedures as are necessary to govern the operations of the Environment Fund.

IV

Environment Co-ordination Board

1. *Decides* that, in order to provide for the most efficient co-ordination of United Nations environmental programmes, an Environment Co-ordination Board, under the chairmanship of the Executive Director, shall be established under the auspices and within the framework of the Administrative Committee on Co-ordination;

2. *Further decides* that the Environment Co-ordination Board shall meet periodically for the purpose of ensuring co-operation and co-ordination among all bodies concerned in the implementation of environmental programmes and that it shall report annually to the Governing Council of the United Nations Environment Programme;

3. *Invites* the organizations of the United Nations system to adopt the measures that may be required to undertake concerted and coordinated programmes with regard to international environmental problems, taking into account existing procedures for prior consultation, particularly on programme and budgetary matters;

4. *Invites* the regional economic commissions and the United Nations Economic and Social Office at Beirut, in co-operation where necessary with other appropriate regional bodies, to intensify further their efforts directed towards contributing to the

implementation of environmental programmes in view of the particular need for the rapid development of regional co-operation in this field;

5. *Also invites* other intergovernmental and those non-governmental organizations that have an interest in the field of the environment to lend their full support and collaboration to the United Nations with a view to achieving the largest possible degree of co-operation and co-ordination;

6. *Calls upon* Governments to ensure that appropriate national institutions shall be entrusted with the task of the co-ordination of environmental action, both national and international;

7. *Decides* to review as appropriate, at its thirty-first session, the above institutional arrangements, bearing in mind, *inter alia,* the responsibilities of the Economic and Social Council under the Charter of the United Nations.

1.14 RESOLUTION ON CO-OPERATION IN THE FIELD OF THE ENVIRONMENT CONCERNING NATURAL RESOURCES SHARED BY TWO OR MORE STATES. **Adopted by the U.N. General Assembly, 13 December 1973. GA Res 3129, UN GAOR, 28th Sess, Supp No 30, at 48, UN Doc A/RES/3129 (1973);** *reprinted in* **13 ILM 232 (1974) & 5 Weston & Carlson V.B.5**

The General Assembly,

Reaffirming principles 21, 22 and 24 of the Declaration of the United Nations Conference on the Human Environment, held at Stockholm from 5 to 16 June 1972,

Recalling its resolutions 2995 (XXVII), 2996 (XXVII) and 2997 (XXVII) of 15 December 1972 relating to co-operation between States in the field of the environment, to international responsibility of States in regard to the environment and to the establishment of the Governing Council of the United Nations Environment Programme, respectively,

Reaffirming the duty of the international community to adopt measures to protect and improve the environment, and particularly the need for continuous international collaboration to that end,

Convinced of the need to pursue, in the field of the environment, the elaboration of international norms conducive to the achievement of those purposes,

Taking note with satisfaction of the important Economic Declaration adopted by the Fourth Conference of Heads of State or Government of Non–Aligned Countries, held at Algiers from 5 to 9 September 1973,

Conscious of the importance and urgency of safeguarding the conservation and exploitation of the natural resources shared by two or more States, by means of an effective system of co-operation, as indicated in the above-mentioned Economic Declaration of Algiers,

1. *Considers* that it is necessary to ensure effective co-operation between countries through the establishment of adequate international standards for the conservation and harmonious exploitation of natural resources common to two or more States in the context of the normal relations existing between them;

2. *Considers further* that co-operation between countries sharing such natural resources and interested in their exploitation must be developed on the basis of a system of information and prior consultation within the framework of the normal relations existing between them;

3. *Requests* the Governing Council of the United Nations Environment Programme, in keeping with its function of promoting international co-operation according to the mandate conferred upon it by the General Assembly, to take duly into account the preceding paragraphs and to report on measures adopted for their implementation;

4. *Urges* Member States, within the framework of their mutual relations, to take fully into account the provisions of the present resolution.

1.15 RESOLUTION ON PERMANENT SOVEREIGNTY OVER NATURAL RESOURCES. **Adopted by the U.N. General Assembly, 17 December 1973. GA Res 3171, UN GAOR, 28th Sess, Supp No 30, at 52, UN Doc A/9030 (1974);** *reprinted in* **13 ILM 238 (1974) & 5 Weston & Carlson V.B.6**

The General Assembly,

Reiterating that the inalienable right of each State to the full exercise of national sovereignty over its natural resources has been repeatedly recognized by the international community in numerous resolutions of various organs of the United Nations,

Reiterating also that an intrinsic condition of the exercise of the sovereignty of every State is that it be exercised fully and effectively over all the natural resources of the State, whether found on land or in the sea,

Reaffirming the inviolable principle that every country has the right to adopt the economic and social system which it deems most favourable to its development,

Recalling its resolutions 1803 (XVII) of 14 December 1962, 2158 (XXI) of 25 November 1966, 2386 (XXIII) of 19 November 1968, 2625 (XXV) of 24 October 1970, 2692 (XXV) of 11 December 1970 and 3016 (XXVII) of 18 December 1972, and Security Council resolution 330 (1973) of 21 March 1973, which relate to permanent sovereignty over natural resources,

Recalling, in particular, the Declaration on Principles of International Law concerning Friendly Relations and Co-operation among States in accordance with the Charter of the United Nations, which proclaims that no State may use or encourage the use of economic, political or any other type of measures to coerce another State in order to obtain from it the subordination of the exercise of its sovereign rights and to secure from it advantages of any kind,

Considering that the full exercise by each State of sovereignty over its natural resources is an essential condition for achieving the objectives and targets of the Second United Nations Development Decade, and that this exercise requires that action by States aimed at achieving a better utilization and use of those resources must cover all stages, from exploration to marketing,

Taking note of section VII of the Economic Declaration adopted by the Fourth Conference of Heads of State or Government of Non–Aligned Countries, held at Algiers from 5 to 9 September 1973,

Taking note also of the report of the Secretary–General on permanent sovereignty over natural resources,

1. *Strongly reaffirms* the inalienable rights of States to permanent sovereignty over all their natural resources, on land within their international boundaries as well as those in the sea-bed and the subsoil thereof within their national jurisdiction and in the superjacent waters;

2. *Supports resolutely* the efforts of the developing countries and of the peoples of the territories under colonial and racial domination and foreign occupation in their struggle to regain effective control over their natural resources;

3. *Affirms* that the application of the principle of nationalization carried out by States, as an expression of their sovereignty in order to safeguard their natural resources, implies that each State is entitled to determine the amount of possible compensation and the mode of payment, and that any disputes which might arise should be settled in accordance with the national legislation of each State carrying out such measures;

4. *Deplores* acts of States which use force, armed aggression, economic coercion or any other illegal or improper means in resolving disputes concerning the exercise of the sovereign rights mentioned in paragraphs 1 to 3 above;

5. *Re-emphasizes* that actions, measures or legislative regulations by States aimed at coercing, directly or indirectly, other States or peoples engaged in the reorganization of their internal structure or in the exercise of their sovereign rights over their natural resources, both on land and in their coastal waters, are in violation of the Charter of the United Nations and of the Declaration contained in General Assembly resolution 2625 (XXV) and contradict the targets, objectives and policy measures of the International Development Strategy for the Second United Nations Development Decade, and that to persist therein could constitute a threat to international peace and security;

6. *Emphasizes* the duty of all States to refrain in their international relations from military, political, economic or any other form of coercion aimed against the territorial integrity of any State and the exercise of its national jurisdiction;

7. *Recognizes* that, as stressed in Economic and Social Council resolution 1737 (LIV) of 4 May 1973, one of the most effective ways in which the developing countries can protect their natural resources is to establish, promote or strengthen machinery for co-operation among them which has as its main purpose to concert pricing policies, to improve conditions of access to markets, to co-ordinate production policies and, thus, to guarantee the full exercise of sovereignty by developing countries over their natural resources;

8. *Requests* the Economic and Social Council, at its fifty-sixth session, to consider the report of the Secretary–General mentioned in the last preambular paragraph above and requests the Secretary–General to prepare a supplement to that report, in the light of the discussions that are to take place at the fifty-sixth session of the Council and of any other relevant developments, and to submit that supplementary report to the General Assembly at its twenty-ninth session.

1.16 FINAL ACT OF THE CONFERENCE ON SECURITY AND CO-OPERATION IN EUROPE. **Adopted by the Conference on Security and Co-operation in Europe at Helsinki, 1 August 1975.** *Reprinted in* **14 ILM 1292 (1975) & 1 Weston & Carlson I.D.9:** *Co-operation in the Field of Economics, of Science and Technology and of the Environment*

* * *

Motivated by the political will, in the interest of peoples, to improve and intensify their relations and to contribute in Europe to peace, security, justice and co-operation as well as to rapprochement among themselves and with the other States of the world,

Determined, in consequence, to give full effect to the results of the Conference and to assure, among their States and throughout Europe, the benefits deriving from those results and thus to broaden, deepen and make continuing and lasting the process of detente.

The High Representatives of the participating States have solemnly adopted the following:

* * *

CO–OPERATION IN THE FIELD OF ECONOMICS, OF SCIENCE AND TECHNOLOGY AND OF THE ENVIRONMENT

The participating States,

Convinced that their efforts to develop co-operation in the fields of trade, industry, science and technology, the environment and other areas of economic activity contribute to the reinforcement of peace and security in Europe and in the world as a whole,

Recognizing that co-operation in these fields would promote economic and social progress and the improvement of the conditions of life,

Aware of the diversity of their economic and social systems,

Reaffirming their will to intensify such co-operation between one another, irrespective of their systems,

Recognizing that such co-operation, with due regard for the different levels of economic development, can be developed, on the basis of equality and mutual satisfaction of the partners, and of reciprocity permitting, as a whole, an equitable distribution of advantages and obligations of comparable scale, with respect for bilateral and multilateral agreements,

Taking into account the interests of the developing countries throughout the world, including those among the participating countries as long as they are developing from the economic point of view; reaffirming their will to co-operate for the achievement of the aims and objectives established by the appropriate bodies of the United Nations in the pertinent documents concerning development, it being understood that each participating State maintains the positions it has taken on them; giving special attention to the least developed countries,

Convinced that the growing world-wide, economic interdependence calls for increasing common and effective efforts towards the solution of major world economic problems such as food, energy, commodities, monetary and financial problems, and therefore emphasizes the need for promoting stable and equitable international economic relations, thus contributing to the continuous and diversified economic development of all countries,

Having taken into account the work already undertaken by relevant international organizations and wishing to take advantage of the possibilities offered by these organizations, in particular by the United Nations Economic Commission for Europe, for giving effect to the provisions of the final documents of the Conference,

Considering that the guidelines and concrete recommendations contained in the following texts are aimed at promoting further development of their mutual economic relations, and convinced that their co-operation in this field should take place in full respect for the principles guiding relations among participating States as set forth in the relevant document,

Have adopted the following:

* * *

5. Environment

The participating States,

Affirming that the protection and improvement of the environment, as well as the protection of nature and the rational utilization of its resources in the interests of present and future generations, is one of the tasks of major importance to the well-being of peoples and the economic development of all countries and the many environmental problems, particularly in Europe, can be solved effectively only through close international co-operation,

Acknowledging that each of the participating States, in accordance with the principles of international law, ought to ensure, in a spirit of co-operation, that activities carried out on its territory do not cause degradation of the environment in another State or in areas lying beyond the limits of national jurisdiction,

Considering that the success of any environmental policy presupposes that all population groups and social forces, aware of their responsibilities, help to protect and improve the environment, which necessitates continued and thorough educative action, particularly with regard to youth,

Affirming that experience has shown that economic development and technological progress must be compatible with the protection of the environment and the preservation of historical and cultural values; that damage to the environment is best avoided by preventive measures; and that the ecological balance must be preserved in the exploitation and management of natural resources,

Aims of co-operation

Agree to the following aims of co-operation, in particular:

— to study, with a view to their solution, those environmental problems which, by their nature, are of a multilateral, bilateral, regional or sub-regional dimension; as well as to encourage the development of an interdisciplinary approach to environmental problems;

— to increase the effectiveness of national and international measures for the protection of the environment, by the comparison and, if appropriate, the harmonization of methods of gathering and analyzing facts, by improving the knowledge of pollution phenomena and rational utilization of natural resources, by the exchange of information, by the harmonization of definitions and the adoption, as far as possible, of a common terminology in the field of the environment;

— to take the necessary measures to bring environmental policies closer together and, where appropriate and possible, to harmonize them;

— to encourage, where possible and appropriate, national and international efforts by their interested organizations, enterprises and firms in the development, production and improvement of equipment designed for monitoring, protecting and enhancing the environment.

Fields of co-operation

To attain these aims, the participating States will make use of every suitable opportunity to co-operate in the field of environment and, in particular, within the areas described below as examples:

Control of air pollution

Desulphurization of fossil fuels and exhaust gases; pollution control of heavy metals, pArticles, aerosols, nitrogen oxides, in particular those emitted by transport, power stations, and other industrial plants; systems and methods of observation and control of air pollution and its effects, including long-range transport of air pollutants;

Water pollution control and fresh water utilization

Prevention and control of water pollution, in particular of transboundary rivers and international lakes; techniques for the improvement of the quality of water and further development of ways and means for industrial and municipal sewage effluent purification; methods of assessment of fresh water resources and the improvement of their utilization, in particular by developing methods of production which are less polluting and lead to less consumption of fresh water;

Protection of the marine environment

Protection of the marine environment of participating States, and especially the Mediterranean Sea, from pollutants emanating from land-based sources and those from ships and other vessels, notably the harmful substances listed in Annexes I and II to the London Convention on the Prevention of Marine Pollution by the Dumping of Wastes and Other Matters; problems of maintaining marine ecological balances and food chains, in particular such problems as may arise from the exploration and exploitation of biological and mineral resources of the seas and the seabed;

Land utilization and soils

Problems associated with more effective use of lands, including land amelioration, reclamation and recultivation; control of soil pollution, water and air erosion, as well as other forms of soil degradation; maintaining and increasing the productivity of soils with due regard for the possible negative effects of the application of chemical fertilizers and pesticides;

Nature conservation and nature reserves

Protection of nature and nature reserves; conservation and maintenance of existing genetic resources, especially rare animal and plant species; conservation of natural ecological systems; establishment of nature reserves and other protected landscapes and areas, including their use for research, tourism, recreation and other purposes;

Improvement of environmental conditions in areas of human settlement

Environmental conditions associated with transport, housing, working areas, urban development and planning, water supply and sewage disposal systems; assessment of harmful effects of noise, and noise control methods; collection, treatment and utilization of wastes, including the recovery and recycling of materials; research on substitutes for non-biodegradable substances;

Fundamental research, monitoring, forecasting and assessment of environmental changes

Study of changes in climate, landscapes and ecological balances under the impact of both natural factors and human activities; forecasting of possible genetic changes in flora and fauna as a result of environmental pollution; harmonization of statistical data, development of scientific concepts and systems of monitoring networks, standardized methods of observation, measurement and assessment of changes in the biosphere; assessment of the effects of environmental pollution levels and degradation of the environment upon human health; study and development of criteria and standards for various environmental pollutants and regulation regarding production and use of various products;

Legal and administrative measures

Legal and administrative measures for the protection of the environment including procedures for establishing environmental impact assessments.

Forms and methods of co-operation

The participating States declare that problems relating to the protection and improvement of the environment will be solved on both a bilateral and multilateral, including regional and sub-regional, basis, making full use of existing patterns and forms of co-operation. They will develop co-operation in the field of the environment in particular by taking into consideration the Stockholm Declaration on the Human Environment, relevant resolutions of the United Nations General Assembly and the United Nations Economic Commission for Europe Prague symposium on environmental problems.

The participating States are resolved that co-operation in the field of the environment will be implemented in particular through:

— exchanges of scientific and technical information, documentation and research results, including information on the means of determining the possible effects on the environment of technical and economic activities;

— organization of conferences, symposia and meetings of experts;

— exchanges of scientists, specialists and trainees;

— joint preparation and implementation of programmes and projects for the study and solution of various problems of environmental protection;

— harmonization, where appropriate and necessary, of environmental protection standards and norms, in particular with the object of avoiding possible difficulties in trade which may arise from efforts to resolve ecological problems of production processes and which relate to the achievement of certain environmental qualities in manufactured products:

— consultations on various aspects of environmental protection, as agreed upon among countries concerned, especially in connection with problems which could have international consequences.

The participating States will further develop such co-operation by:

— promoting the progressive development, codification and implementation of international law as one means of preserving and enhancing the human environment, including principles and practices, as accepted by them, relating to pollution and other environmental damage caused by activities within the jurisdiction or control of their States affecting other countries and regions;

— supporting and promoting the implementation of relevant international Conventions to which they are parties, in particular those designed to prevent and combat marine and fresh water pollution, recommending States to ratify Conventions which have already been signed, as well as considering possibilities of accepting other appropriate Conventions to which they are not parties at present;

— advocating the inclusion, where appropriate and possible, of the various areas of co-operation into the programmes of work of the United Nations Economic Commission for Europe, supporting such co-operation within the framework of the Commission and of the United Nations Environment Programme, and taking into account the work of other competent international organizations of which they are members;

— making wider use in all types of co-operation, of information already available for national and international sources, including internationally agreed criteria, and utilizing the possibilities and capabilities of various competent international organizations.

The participating States agree on the following recommendations on specific measures:

— to develop through international co-operation an extensive programme for the monitoring and evaluation of the long-range transport of air pollutants, starting with sulphur dioxide and with possible extension to other pollutants, and to this end to take into account basic elements of a co-operation programme which were identified by the experts who met in Oslo in December 1974 at the invitation of the Norwegian Institute of Air Research;

— to advocate that within the framework of the United Nations Economic Commission for Europe a study be carried out of procedures and relevant experience relating to the activities of Governments in developing the capabilities of their countries to predict adequately environmental consequences of economic activities and technological development.

1.17   DRAFT PRINCIPLES OF CONDUCT IN THE FIELD OF THE ENVIRONMENT FOR GUIDANCE OF STATES IN THE CONSERVATION AND HARMONIOUS UTILIZATION OF NATURAL RESOURCES SHARED BY TWO OR MORE STATES. Approved by the UN Environment Programme Governing Council, 19 May 1978. UN Doc UNEP/IG12/2 (1978); *reprinted in* 17 ILM 1097 (1978) & 5 Weston & Carlson V.B.8

Principle 1

It is necessary for States to co-operate in the field of the environment concerning the conservation and harmonious utilization of natural resources shared by two or more States. Accordingly, it is necessary that consistent with the concept of equitable utilization of shared natural resources, States co-operate with a view to controlling, preventing, reducing or eliminating adverse environmental effects which may result from the utilization of such resources. Such co-operation is to take place on an equal footing and taking into account the sovereignty, rights and interests of the States concerned.

Principle 2

In order to ensure effective international co-operation in the field of the environment concerning the conservation and harmonious utilization of natural resources shared by two or more States, States sharing such natural resources should endeavor to conclude bilateral or multilateral agreements between or among themselves in order to secure specific regulation of their conduct in this respect, applying as necessary the present principles in a legally binding manner or should endeavor to enter into other arrangements, as appropriate, for this purpose. In entering into such agreements or arrangements, States should consider the establishment of institutional structures, such as joint international commissions, for consultations on environmental problems relating to the protection and use of shared natural resources.

Principle 3

1.   States have, in accordance with the Charter of the United Nations and the principles of international law, the sovereign right to exploit their own resources pursuant to their own environmental policies, and the responsibility to ensure that activities within their jurisdiction or control do not cause damage to the environment of other States or of areas beyond the limits of national jurisdiction.

2.   The principles set forth in paragraph 1, as well as the other principles contained in this document, apply to shared natural resources.

3.   Accordingly, it is necessary for each State to avoid to the maximum extent possible and to reduce to the minimum extent possible the adverse environmental effects beyond its jurisdiction of the utilization of a shared natural resource so as to protect the environment, in particular when such utilization might:

   (*a*) cause damage to the environment which could have repercussions on the utilization of the resource by another sharing State;

   (*b*) threaten the conservation of a shared renewable resource;

   (*c*) endanger the health of the population of another State.

Without prejudice to the generality of the above principle, it should be interpreted, taking into account, where appropriate, the practical capabilities of States sharing the natural resource.

Principle 4

States should make environmental assessments before engaging in any activity with respect to a shared natural resource which may create a risk of significantly[a] affecting the environment of another State or States sharing that resource.

Principle 5

States sharing a natural resource should, to the extent practicable, exchange information and engage in consultations on a regular basis on its environmental aspects.

Principle 6

1. It is necessary for every State sharing a natural resource with one or more other States:

(*a*) to notify in advance the other State or States of the pertinent details of plans to initiate, or make a change in, the conservation or utilization of the resource which can reasonably be expected to affect significantly the environment in the territory of the other State or States; and

(*b*) upon request of the other State or States, to enter into consultations concerning the above-mentioned plans; and

(*c*) to provide, upon request to that effect by the other State or States, specific additional pertinent information concerning such plans; and

(*d*) if there has been no advance notification as envisaged in sub-paragraph (a) above, to enter into consultations about such plans upon request of the other State or States.

2. In cases where the transmission of certain information is prevented by national legislation or international conventions, the State or States withholding such information shall nevertheless, on the basis, in particular, of the principle of good faith and in the spirit of good neighbourliness, co-operate with the other interested State or States with the aim of finding a satisfactory solution.

Principle 7

Exchange of information, notification, consultations and other forms of co-operation regarding shared natural resources are carried out on the basis of the principle of good faith and in the spirit of good neighbourliness and in such a way as to avoid any unreasonable delays either in the forms of co-operation or in carrying out development or conservation projects.

Principle 8

When it would be useful to clarify environmental problems relating to a shared natural resource, States should engage in joint scientific studies and assessments, with a view to facilitating the finding of appropriate and satisfactory solutions to such problems on the basis of agreed data.

Principle 9

1. States have a duty urgently to inform other States which may be affected:

(*a*) Of any emergency situation arising from the utilization of a shared natural resource which might cause sudden harmful effects on their environment;

(*b*) Of any sudden grave natural events related to a shared natural resource which may affect the environment of such States.

2. States should also, when appropriate, inform the competent international organizations of any such situation or event.

---

a. See "Definition" following Principle 15.

3.   States concerned should co-operate, in particular by means of agreed contingency plans, when appropriate, and mutual assistance, in order to avert grave situations, and to eliminate, reduce or correct, as far as possible, the effects of such situations or events.

Principle 10

States sharing a natural resource should, when appropriate, consider the possibility of jointly seeking the services of any competent international organization in clarifying the environmental problems relating to the conservation or utilization of such natural resource.

Principle 11

1.   The relevant provisions of the Charter of the United Nations and of the Declaration of Principles of International Law concerning Friendly Relations and Co-operation among States in accordance with the Charter of the United Nations apply to the settlement of environmental disputes arising out of the conservation or utilization of shared natural resources.

2.   In case negotiations or other non-binding means have failed to settle a dispute within a reasonable time, it is necessary for States to submit the dispute to an appropriate settlement procedure which is mutually agreed by them, preferably in advance. The procedure should be speedy, effective and binding.

3.   It is necessary for the States parties to such a dispute to refrain from any action which may aggravate the situation with respect to the environment to the extent of creating an obstacle to the amicable settlement of the dispute.

Principle 12

1.   States are responsible for the fulfillment of their international obligations in the field of the environment concerning the conservation and utilization of shared natural resources. They are subject to liability in accordance with applicable international law for environmental damage resulting from violations of these obligations caused to areas beyond their jurisdiction.

2.   States should co-operate to develop further international law regarding liability and compensation for the victims of environmental damage arising out of the utilization of a shared natural resource and caused to areas beyond their jurisdiction.

Principle 13

It is necessary for States, when considering, under their domestic environmental policy, the permissibility of domestic activities, to take into account the potential adverse environmental effects arising out of the utilization of shared natural resources, without discrimination as to whether the effects would occur within their jurisdiction or outside it.

Principle 14

States should endeavour, in accordance with their legal systems and, where appropriate, on a basis agreed by them, to provide persons in other States who have been or may be adversely affected by environmental damage resulting from the utilization of shared natural resources with equivalent access to and treatment in the same administrative and judicial proceedings, and make available to them the same remedies as are available to persons within their own jurisdictions who have been or may be similarly affected.

Principle 15

The present principles should be interpreted and applied in such a way as to enhance and not to affect adversely development and the interests of all countries, and in particular of the developing countries.

DEFINITION

In the present text, the expression "significantly affect" refers to any appreciable effects on a shared natural resource and excludes "*de minimis*" effects.

1.18   RESOLUTION ON HISTORICAL RESPONSIBILITY OF STATES FOR THE PRESERVATION OF NATURE FOR PRESENT AND FUTURE GENERATIONS. **Adopted by the U.N. General Assembly, 30 October 1980. GA Res 35/48, UN GAOR, 35th Sess, Supp No 48, at 15, UN Doc A/35/48 (1981);** *reprinted in* **5 Weston & Carlson V.B.9**

The General Assembly,

Having considered the item entitled "Historical responsibility of States for the preservation of nature for present and future generations",

Conscious of the disastrous consequences which a war involving the use of nuclear weapons and other weapons of mass destruction would have on man and his environment,

Noting that the continuation of the arms race, including the testing of various types of weapons, especially nuclear weapons, and the accumulation of toxic chemicals are adversely affecting the human environment and damaging the vegetable and animal world,

Bearing in mind that the arms race is diverting material and intellectual resources from the solution of the urgent problems of preserving nature,

Attaching great importance to the development of planned, constructive international co-operation in solving the problems of preserving nature,

Recognizing that the prospects for solving problems so universal as the preservation of nature are closely linked to the strengthening and development of international detente and the creation of conditions which would banish war from the life of mankind,

Noting with satisfaction the drafting and signature in recent years of a number of international agreements designed to preserve the environment,

Determined to preserve nature as a prerequisite for the normal life of man,

1. *Proclaims* the historical responsibility of States for the preservation of nature for present and future generations;

2. *Draws the attention* of States to the fact that the continuing arms race has pernicious effects on the environment and reduces the prospects for the necessary international co-operation in preserving nature on our planet;

3. *Calls upon* States, in the interests of present and future generations, to demonstrate due concern and take the measures, including legislative measures, necessary for preserving nature, and also to promote international co-operation in this field;

4. *Requests* the Secretary–General, with the co-operation of the United Nations Environment Programme, to prepare a report on the pernicious effects of the arms race on nature and to seek the views of States on possible measures to be taken at the international level for the preservation of nature;

5. *Decides* to include in the provisional agenda of its thirty-sixth session an item entitled "Historical responsibility of States for the preservation of nature for present and future generations: report of the Secretary–General".

1.19   ILA RULES ON INTERNATIONAL LAW APPLICABLE TO TRANSFRONTIER POLLUTION. Adopted at Montreal, 4 September 1982. 60 ILA 158 (1983); *reprinted in* 5 Weston & Carlson V.B.10

Article 1 (Applicability)

The following rules of international law concerning transfrontier pollution are applicable except as may be otherwise provided by convention, agreement or binding custom among the States concerned.

Article 2 (Definition)

(1) "Pollution" means any introduction by man, directly or indirectly, of substance or energy into the environment resulting in deleterious effects of such a nature as to endanger human health, harm living resources, ecosystems and material property and impair amenities or interfere with other legitimate uses of the environment.

(2) "Transfrontier pollution" means pollution of which the physical origin is wholly or in part situated within the territory of one State and which has deleterious effects in the territory of another State.

Article 3 (Prevention and Abatement)

(1) Without prejudice to the operation of the rules relating to the reasonable and equitable utilisation of shared natural resources States are in their legitimate activities under an obligation to prevent, abate and control transfrontier pollution to such an extent that no substantial injury is caused in the territory of another State.

(2) Furthermore States shall limit new and increased transfrontier pollution to the lowest level that may be reached by measures practicable and reasonable under the circumstances.

(3) States should endeavour to reduce existing transfrontier pollution, below the requirements of paragraph 1 of this Article, to the lowest level that may be reached by measures practicable and reasonable under the circumstances.

Article 4 (Highly Dangerous Substances)

Notwithstanding the provisions in Article 3 States shall refrain from causing transfrontier pollution by discharging into the environment substances generally considered as being highly dangerous to human health. If such substances are already being discharged, States shall eliminate the polluting discharge within a reasonable time.

Article 5 (Prior Notice)

(1) States planning to carry out activities which might entail a significant risk of transfrontier pollution shall give early notice to States likely to be affected. In particular they shall on their own initiative or upon request of the potentially affected States, communicate such pertinent information as will permit the recipient to make an assessment of the probable effects of the planned activities.

(2) In order to appraise whether a planned activity implies a significant risk of transfrontier pollution, States should make environmental assessment before carrying out such activities.

Article 6 (Consultations)

(1) Upon request of a potentially affected State, the State furnishing the information should enter into consultations on transfrontier pollution problems connected with the planned activities and pursue such consultations in good faith and over a reasonable period of time.

(2) States are under an obligation to enter into consultations whenever transfrontier pollution problems arise in connection with the equitable utilization of a shared natural resource as envisaged in Art. 5.

Article 7 (Emergency Situations)

When as a result of an emergency situation or of other circumstances activities already carried out in the territory of a State cause or might cause a sudden increase in the existing level of transfrontier pollution the State of origin is under a duty:

(a) to promptly warn the affected or potentially affected States;

(b) to provide them with such pertinent information as will enable them to minimize the transfrontier pollution damage;

(c) to inform them of the steps taken to abate the cause of the increased transfrontier pollution level.

1.20 WORLD CHARTER FOR NATURE. **Adopted by the U.N. General Assembly, 28 October 1982. GA Res 37/7 (Annex), UN GAOR, 37th Sess, Supp No 51, at 17, UN Doc A/37/51;** *reprinted in* **22 ILM 455 (1983) & 5 Weston & Carlson V.B.11**

The General Assembly,

Reaffirming the fundamental purposes of the United Nations, in particular the maintenance of international peace and security, the development of friendly relations among nations and the achievement of international cooperation in solving international problems of an economic, social, cultural, technical, intellectual or humanitarian character,

Aware that:

(*a*) Mankind is a part of nature and life depends on the uninterrupted functioning of natural systems which ensure the supply of energy and nutrients,

(*b*) Civilization is rooted in nature, which has shaped human culture and influenced all artistic and scientific achievement, and living in harmony with nature gives man the best opportunities for the development of his creativity, and for rest and recreation,

Convinced that:

(*a*) Every form of life is unique, warranting respect regardless of its worth to man, and, to accord other organisms such recognition, man must be guided by a moral code of action,

(*b*) Man can alter nature and exhaust natural resources by his action or its consequences and, therefore, must fully recognize the urgency of maintaining the stability and quality of nature and of conserving natural resources,

Persuaded that:

(*a*) Lasting benefits from nature depend upon the maintenance of essential ecological processes and life support systems, and upon the diversity of life forms, which are jeopardized through excessive exploitation and habitat destruction by man,

(*b*) The degradation of natural systems owing to excessive consumption and misuse of natural resources, as well as to failure to establish an appropriate economic order among peoples and among States, leads to the breakdown of the economic, social and political framework of civilization,

(*c*) Competition for scarce resources creates conflicts, whereas the conservation of nature and natural resources contributes to justice and the maintenance of peace and cannot be achieved until mankind learns to live in peace and to forsake war and armaments,

Reaffirming that man must acquire the knowledge to maintain and enhance his ability to use natural resources in a manner which ensures the preservation of the species and ecosystems for the benefit of present and future generations,

Firmly convinced of the need for appropriate measures, at the national and international, individual and collective, and private and public levels, to protect nature and promote international co-operation in this field,

Adopts, to these ends, the present World Charter for Nature, which proclaims the following principles of conservation by which all human conduct affecting nature is to be guided and judged.

I. General Principles

1. Nature shall be respected and its essential processes shall not be impaired.

2. The genetic viability on the earth shall not be compromised; the population levels of all life forms, wild and domesticated, must be at least sufficient for their survival, and to this end necessary habitats shall be safeguarded.

3. All areas of the earth, both land and sea, shall be subject to these principles of conservation; special protection shall be given to unique areas, to representative samples of all the different types of ecosystems and to the habitats of rare or endangered species.

4. Ecosystems and organisms, as well as the land, marine and atmospheric resources that are utilized by man, shall be managed to achieve and maintain optimum sustainable productivity, but not in such a way as to endanger the integrity of those other ecosystems or species with which they coexist.

5. Nature shall be secured against degradation caused by warfare or other hostile activities.

II. Functions

6. In the decision-making process it shall be recognized that man's needs can be met only by ensuring the proper functioning of natural systems and by respecting the principles set forth in the present Charter.

7. In the planning and implementation of social and economic development activities, due account shall be taken of the fact that the conservation of nature is an integral part of those activities.

8. In formulating long-term plans for economic development, population growth and the improvement of standards of living, due account shall be taken of the long-term capacity of natural systems to ensure the subsistence and settlement of the populations concerned, recognizing that this capacity may be enhanced through science and technology.

9. The allocation of areas of the earth to various uses shall be planned, and due account shall be taken of the physical constraints, the biological productivity and diversity and the natural beauty of the areas concerned.

10. Natural resources shall not be wasted, but used with a restraint appropriate to the principles set forth in the present Charter, in accordance with the following rules:

(a) Living resources shall not be utilized in excess of their natural capacity for regeneration;

(b) The productivity of soils shall be maintained or enhanced through measures which safeguard their long-term fertility and the process of organic decomposition, and prevent erosion and all other forms of degradation;

(c) Resources, including water, which are not consumed as they are used shall be reused or recycled;

(d) Non-renewable resources which are consumed as they are used shall be exploited with restraint, taking into account their abundance, the rational possibilities of converting them for consumption, and the compatibility of their exploitation with the functioning of natural systems.

11. Activities which might have an impact on nature shall be controlled, and the best available technologies that minimize significant risks to nature or other adverse effects shall be used; in particular:

(a) Activities which are likely to cause irreversible damage to nature shall be avoided;

(b) Activities which are likely to pose a significant risk to nature shall be preceded by an exhaustive examination; their proponents shall demonstrate that expected benefits outweigh potential damage to nature, and where potential adverse effects are not fully understood, the activities should not proceed.

(c) Activities which may disturb nature shall be preceded by assessment of their consequences, and environmental impact studies of development projects shall be conducted sufficiently in advance, and if they are to be undertaken, such activities shall be planned and carried out so as to minimize potential adverse effects;

(d) Agriculture, grazing, forestry and fisheries practices shall be adapted to the natural characteristics and constraints of given areas;

(e) Areas degraded by human activities shall be rehabilitated for purposes in accord with their natural potential and compatible with the well-being of affected populations.

12. Discharge of pollutants into natural systems shall be avoided and:

(a) Where this is not feasible, such pollutants shall be treated at the source, using the best practicable means available;

(b) Special precautions shall be taken to prevent discharge of radioactive or toxic wastes.

13. Measures intended to prevent, control or limit natural disasters, infestations and diseases shall be specifically directed to the causes of these scourges and shall avoid adverse side-effects on nature.

III. Implementation

14. The principles set forth in the present Charter shall be reflected in the law and practice of each State, as well as at the international level.

15. Knowledge of nature shall be broadly disseminated by all possible means, particularly by ecological education as an integral part of general education.

16. All planning shall include, among its essential elements, the formulation of strategies for the conservation of nature, the establishment of inventories of ecosystems and assessments of the effects on nature of proposed policies and activities; all of these elements shall be disclosed to the public by appropriate means in time to permit effective consultation and participation.

17. Funds, programmes and administrative structures necessary to achieve the objective of the conservation of nature shall be provided.

18. Constant efforts shall be made to increase knowledge of nature by scientific research and to disseminate such knowledge unimpeded by restrictions of any kind.

19. The status of natural processes, ecosystems and species shall be closely monitored to enable early detection of degradation or threat, ensure timely intervention and facilitate the evaluation of conservation policies and methods.

20. Military activities damaging to nature shall be avoided.

21. States and, to the extent they are able, other public authorities, international organizations, individuals, groups and corporations shall:

(a) Co-operate in the task of conserving nature through common activities and other relevant actions, including information exchange and consultations;

(b) Establish standards for products and manufacturing processes that may have adverse effects on nature, as well as agreed methodologies for assessing these effects;

(c) Implement the applicable international legal provisions for the conservation of nature and the protection of the environment;

(*d*) Ensure that activities within their jurisdictions or control do not cause damage to the natural systems located within other States or in the areas beyond the limits of national jurisdiction;

(*e*) Safeguard and conserve nature in areas beyond national jurisdiction.

22. Taking fully into account the sovereignty of States over their natural resources, each State shall give effect to the provisions of the present Charter through its competent organs and in co-operation with other States.

23. All persons, in accordance with their national legislation, shall have the opportunity to participate, individually or with others, in the formulation of decisions of direct concern to their environment, and shall have access to means of redress when their environment has suffered damage or degradation.

24. Each person has a duty to act in accordance with the provisions of the present Charter; acting individually, in association with others or through participation in the political process, each person shall strive to ensure that the objectives and requirements of the present Charter are met.

1.21   Legal Principles for Environmental Protection and Sustainable Development. **Adopted by the Experts Group on Environmental Law of the World Commission on Environment and Development (WCED), 18–20 June 1986. UN Doc WCED/86/23/Add. 1 (1986);** *reprinted in* 5 **Weston & Carlson V.B.12**

USE OF TERMS

For the purposes of the present text:

(a) "use of a natural resource" means any human conduct, which, directly or indirectly, takes advantage of the benefits of a natural resource in the form of preservation, exploitation, consumption or otherwise of the natural resource, in so far as it does not result in an environmental interference as defined in Paragraph (f);

(b) "interference with the use of a natural resource" means any impairment, directly or indirectly, by man of the use of a natural resource in so far as it does not constitute an environmental interference as defined in Paragraph (f);

(c) "transboundary natural resource" means a natural resource which physically crosses the boundary between an area under the national jurisdiction of a State and an area under the national jurisdiction of another State or an area beyond the limits of national jurisdiction to the extent that its use in an area under the national jurisdiction of one State may affect its use in an area under the national jurisdiction of another State or in an area beyond the limits of national jurisdiction or vice versa;

(d) "transboundary interference with the use of a transboundary natural resource" means an interference with the use of a natural resource of which the physical origin is wholly or in part located outside the area under national jurisdiction of a State or outside the area beyond the limits of national jurisdiction in which the use takes place;

(e) "international natural resource" means a natural resource physically within an area beyond the limits of national jurisdiction to the extent that the origin and effects of any impairment of the use of the natural resource remain within the area beyond the limits of national jurisdiction;

(f) "environmental interference" means any impairment of human health, living resources, ecosystems, material property, amenities or other legitimate uses of a natural resource or the environment caused, directly or indirectly, by man through polluting substances, ionizing radiation, noise, explosions, vibration or other forms of energy, plants, animals, diseases, flooding, sand-drift or other similar means;

(g) "transboundary environmental interference" means an environmental interference of which the physical origin is wholly or in part located either outside the area under national jurisdiction of a State in which the effects caused by the interference occur, or outside the area beyond the limits of national jurisdiction in which the effects caused by the interference occur;

(h) "international environmental interference" means an environmental interference of which the physical origin and the effects are located within an area beyond the limits of national jurisdiction;

(i) "conservation" means the management of human use of a natural resource or the environment in such a manner that it may yield the greatest sustainable benefit to present generations while maintaining its potential to meet the needs and aspirations of future generations. It embraces preservation, maintenance, sustainable utilization, restoration and enhancement of a natural resource or the environment.

GENERAL PRINCIPLES CONCERNING NATURAL RESOURCES AND ENVIRONMENTAL INTERFERENCES

Article 1

Fundamental human right

All human beings have the fundamental right to an environment adequate for their health and well-being.

Article 2

Conservation for present and future generations

States shall ensure that the environment and natural resources are conserved and used for the benefit of present and future generations.

Article 3

Ecosystems, related ecological processes, biological diversity, and sustainability

States shall:

(a) maintain ecosystems and related ecological processes essential for the functioning of the biosphere in all its diversity, in particular those important for food production, health and other aspects of human survival and sustainable development;

(b) maintain maximum biological diversity by ensuring the survival and promoting the conservation in their natural habitat of all species of fauna and flora, in particular those which are rare, endemic or endangered;

(c) observe in the exploitation of living natural resources and ecosystems, the principle of optimum sustainable yield.

Article 4

Environmental standards and monitoring

States shall:

(a) establish specific environmental standards, in particular environmental quality standards, emission standards, technological standards and product standards aimed at preventing or abating interferences with natural resources or the environment;

(b) establish systems for the collection and dissemination of data and regular observation of natural resources and the environment in order to permit adequate planning of the use of natural resources and the environment, to permit early detection of interferences with natural resources or the environment and ensure timely intervention, and to facilitate the evaluation of conservation policies and methods.

Article 5

Assessment of planned activities

States planning to carry out or permit activities which may significantly affect a natural resource or the environment shall make or require an assessment of their effects before carrying out or permitting the planned activities.

Article 6

Timely information, access and due process

States shall inform all persons in a timely manner of activities which may significantly affect their use of a natural resource or their environment and shall grant the concerned persons access to and due process in administrative and judicial proceedings.

Article 7

Planning and implementation of development activities

1. States shall ensure that the conservation of natural resources and the environment is treated as an integral part of the planning and implementation of development activities. Particular attention shall be paid to environmental problems arising in developing countries and to the need to incorporate environmental considerations in all development assistance programmes.

2. States shall make available to other States, and especially to developing countries, upon their request and under agreed terms scientific and technical information and expertise, results of research programmes, training opportunities and specialized equipment and facilities which are needed by such other States to promote rational use of natural resources, and the environment or to prevent or abate interference with natural resources or the environment, in particular in cases of environmental emergencies.

Article 8

General obligation to co-operate

States shall co-operate in good faith with other States or through competent international organizations in the implementation of the provisions of the preceding Articles.

PRINCIPLES SPECIFICALLY CONCERNING TRANSBOUNDARY NATURAL RESOURCES AND ENVIRONMENTAL INTERFERENCES

Article 9

Reasonable and equitable use of transboundary natural resources

States shall use transboundary natural resources in a reasonable and equitable manner.

Article 10

Prevention and abatement of a transboundary environmental interference

States shall, without prejudice to the principles laid down in Articles 11 and 12, prevent or abate any transboundary environmental interference or a significant risk thereof which causes substantial harm—i.e. harm which is not minor or insignificant.

Article 11

Liability for transboundary environmental interferences resulting from lawful activities

1. If one or more activities create a significant risk of substantial harm as a result of a transboundary environmental interference, and if the overall technical and socio-economic cost or loss of benefits involved in preventing or reducing such risk far exceeds in the long run the advantage which such prevention or reduction would entail, the State which carried out or permitted the activities shall ensure that compensation is provided should substantial harm occur in an area under national jurisdiction of another State or in an area beyond the limits of national jurisdiction.

2. A State shall ensure that compensation is provided for substantial harm caused by transboundary environmental interferences resulting from activities carried

out or permitted by that State notwithstanding that the activities were not initially known to cause such interferences.

Article 12

Transboundary environmental interferences involving substantial harm far less than cost of prevention

1. If a State is planning to carry out or permit an activity which will entail a transboundary environmental interference causing harm which is substantial but far less than the overall technical and socio-economic cost or loss of benefits involved in preventing or reducing such interference, such State shall enter into negotiations with the affected State on the equitable conditions, both technical and financial, under which the activity could be carried out.

2. In the event of a failure to reach a solution on the basis of equitable principles within a period of 18 months after the beginning of the negotiations or within any other period of time agreed upon by the States concerned, the dispute shall at the request of any of the States concerned, and under the conditions set forth in Paragraphs 3 and 4 of Article 22, be submitted to conciliation or thereafter to arbitration or judicial settlement in order to reach a solution on the basis of equitable principles.

Article 13

Non-discrimination between domestic and transboundary environmental interferences

Without prejudice to the principles laid down in Articles 10, 11 and 12 when calling for a more stringent approach, States shall, when considering under their domestic policy or law the permissibility of an environmental interference or a significant risk thereof, take into account the detrimental effects which are or may be caused by the environmental interference without discrimination as to whether the effects would occur inside or outside the area under their national jurisdiction.

Article 14

General obligation to co-operate on transboundary environmental problems

1. States shall co-operate in good faith with the other States concerned in maintaining or attaining for each of them a reasonable and equitable use of a transboundary natural resource or in preventing or abating a transboundary environmental interference or significant risk thereof.

2. The co-operation shall, as much as possible, be aimed at arriving at an optimal use of the transboundary natural resource or at maximizing the effectiveness of measures to prevent or abate a transboundary environmental interference.

Article 15

Exchange of information

States shall provide the other States concerned upon their request and in a timely manner with all relevant and reasonably available data concerning a transboundary natural resource, including the uses made of such a resource and transboundary interferences with them, or concerning a transboundary environmental interference.

Article 16

Prior notice of planned activities, environmental impact assessments

1. States planning to carry out or permit activities which may entail a transboundary interference or a significant risk thereof with the reasonable and equitable use of

a transboundary natural resource or which may entail a transboundary environmental interference or a significant risk thereof causing substantial harm in an area under national jurisdiction of another State or in an area beyond the limits of national jurisdiction shall give timely notice to the States concerned. In particular, they shall on their own initiative or upon request of the other States concerned provide such relevant information as will permit those other States to make an assessment of the probable effects of the planned activities.

2. When a State has reasonable grounds for believing that planned activities may have the effects referred to in Paragraph 1, it shall make an assessment of those effects before carrying out or permitting the planned activities.

Article 17

Consultations

Consultations shall be held in good faith, upon request, at an early stage between, on the one hand, States whose reasonable and equitable use of a transboundary natural resource is or may be affected by a transboundary interference or whose environmental interests are or may be affected by a transboundary environmental interference and, on the other hand, States in whose area under national jurisdiction or under whose jurisdiction such a transboundary interference originates or may originate in connection with activities carried on or contemplated therein or thereunder.

Article 18

Co-operative arrangements for environmental assessment and protection

In order to maintain or attain a reasonable and equitable use of a transboundary natural resource or to prevent or abate transboundary environmental interferences or significant risks thereof the States concerned shall, inter alia:

(a) establish co-ordinated or unified systems for the collection and dissemination of data relating to the transboundary natural resource or for regular observation of transboundary environmental interferences;

(b) co-ordinate and, where appropriate, jointly undertake scientific or technical studies to that effect;

(c) establish by common agreement specific environmental standards, in particular environmental quality standards and emission standards;

(d) jointly establish or resort to an institutional mechanism or other appropriate arrangement.

Article 19

Emergency situations

1. In the case of an emergency situation or other change of circumstances suddenly giving rise to a transboundary interference or a significant risk thereof with the reasonable and equitable use of a transboundary natural resource or to a transboundary environmental interference or a significant risk thereof, causing substantial harm in an area under national jurisdiction of another State or in an area beyond the limits of national jurisdiction, the State in whose area under national jurisdiction or under whose jurisdiction the interference originates shall promptly warn the other States concerned, provide them with such pertinent information as will enable them to minimize the transboundary environmental interference, inform them of steps taken to abate the cause of the transboundary environmental interference, and co-operate with those States in order to prevent or minimize the harmful effects of such an emergency situation or other change of circumstances.

2. States shall develop contingency plans in order to prevent or minimize the harmful effects of an emergency situation or other change of circumstances referred to in Paragraph 1.

Article 20

Non-intergovernmental proceedings

States shall provide remedies for persons who have been or may be detrimentally affected by a transboundary interference with their use of a transboundary natural resource or by a transboundary environmental interference. In particular, States of origin shall grant those persons equal access as well as due process and equal treatment in the same administrative and judicial proceedings as are available to persons within their own jurisdiction who have been or may be similarly affected.

Article 21

1. A State is responsible under international law for a breach of an international obligation relating to the use of a natural resource or the prevention or abatement of an environmental interference.

2. In particular, it shall:

(a) cease the internationally wrongful act;

(b) as far as possible, re-establish the situation which would have existed if the internationally wrongful act had not taken place;

(c) provide compensation for the harm which results from the internationally wrongful act;

(d) where appropriate, give satisfaction for the internationally wrongful act.

PEACEFUL SETTLEMENT OF DISPUTES

Article 22

1. States, when they cannot avoid international disputes concerning the use of a natural resource or concerning an environmental interference in accordance with the preceding Articles, shall settle such disputes by peaceful means in such a manner that international peace and security, and justice, are not endangered.

2. States shall accordingly seek a settlement of such disputes by negotiation, good offices, enquiry, mediation, conciliation, arbitration, judicial settlement, resort to appropriate bodies or arrangements, whether global or regional, or by any other peaceful means of their own choice.

3. In the event of a failure to reach a solution by another non-binding peaceful means within a period of 18 months after the dispute has arisen or within any other period of time agreed upon by the States concerned, the dispute shall be submitted to conciliation at the request of any of the States concerned, unless it is agreed to proceed with an already agreed peaceful means or to submit the dispute to another binding or non-binding means of peaceful settlement.

4. In the event that the conciliation envisaged in Paragraph 3, or any other non-binding means of peaceful settlement resorted to in lieu thereof, does not lead to a solution of the dispute, the dispute shall be submitted to arbitration or judicial settlement at the request of any of the States concerned, unless it is agreed to submit the dispute to another means of peaceful settlement.

1.22 Restatement (Third) of the Foreign Relations Law of the United States. Adopted by the American Law Institute, 14 May 1987: §§ 601–604 (with comments)

§ 601. State Obligations with Respect to Environment of Other States and the Common Environment

(1) A state is obligated to take such measures as may be necessary, to the extent practicable under the circumstances, to ensure that activities within its jurisdiction or control

(a) conform to generally accepted international rules and standards for the prevention, reduction, and control of injury to the environment of another state or of areas beyond the limits of national jurisdiction; and

(b) are conducted so as not to cause significant injury to the environment of another state or of areas beyond the limits of national jurisdiction.

(2) A state is responsible to all other states

(a) for any violation of its obligations under Subsection (1)(a), and

(b) for any significant injury, resulting from such violation, to the environment of areas beyond the limits of national jurisdiction.

(3) A state is responsible for any significant injury, resulting from a violation of its obligations under Subsection (1), to the environment of another state or to its property, or to persons or property within that state's territory or under its jurisdiction or control.

Comment:

a. Application of general principles of state responsibility. This Part applies to environmental questions the general principles of international law relating to the responsibility of states for injury to another state or its property or to persons within its territory or their property, or for injury to interests common to all states. A state is responsible under Subsections (2) and (3) for breach of any of its obligations under Subsection (1). It is responsible under Subsection (2) to all states, and any state may request that it abate a threat of pollution and make arrangements to prevent future violations. Under Subsection (3), it is responsible to an injured state for any significant injury and is required to make reparation for the injury. The conditions of responsibility and the remedies available may differ with the circumstances and with the interests affected. See Comment *d* and § 602; see also the general principles in § 711 and §§ 901–902.

b. "Generally accepted international rules and standards." This phrase is adopted from the law of the sea; see § 502, Comment *c*. The obligation under Subsection (1)(a) refers to both general rules of customary international law (see, *e.g.,* the *Trail Smelter* case, Reporters' Note 1) and those derived from international conventions, and from standards adopted by international organizations pursuant to such conventions, that deal with a specific subject, such as oil pollution or radioactive wastes. See Reporters' Notes 3–7 and § 603, Reporters' Notes 4 and 5; see also § 102, Comments *f* and *g,* and § 103, Comment *c*. A state is also obligated to comply with an environmental rule or standard that has been accepted by both it and an injured state, even if that rule or standard has not been generally accepted.

Where an international rule or standard has been violated, any state can object to the violation; where a state has been injured in consequence of such violation, it is entitled to damages or other appropriate relief from the responsible state; where there is a threat of injury, the threatened state, or any state acting on behalf of threatened common interests, is entitled to have the dangerous activity terminated. See § 602.

c. *"Activities within its jurisdiction" and "significant injury."* An activity is considered to be within a state's jurisdiction under this section if the state may exercise jurisdiction to prescribe law with respect to that activity under §§ 402–403. The phrase "activities within its jurisdiction or control" includes activities in a state's territory, on the coastal waters that are under its jurisdiction, Part V, as well as activities on ships flying its flag or on installations on the high seas operating under its authority. See § 502(1)(b) and Comment *c* thereto, § 514, Comment *i* and § 521, Comment *c*. International law does not address internal pollution, but a state is responsible under this section if pollution within its jurisdiction causes significant injuries beyond its borders. "Significant injury" is not defined but references to "significant" impact on the environment are common in both international law and United States law. The word "significant" excludes minor incidents causing minimal damage. In special circumstances, the significance of injury to another state is balanced against the importance of the activity to the state causing the injury. See Reporters' Note 3.

d. *Conditions of responsibility.* A state is responsible under Subsections (2) and (3) for both its own activities and those of individuals or private or public corporations under its jurisdiction. The state may be responsible, for instance, for not enacting necessary legislation, for not enforcing its laws against persons acting in its territory or against its vessels, or for not preventing or terminating an illegal activity, or for not punishing the person responsible for it. In the case of ships flying its flags, a state is responsible for injury due to the state's own defaults under Subsection (1) but is not responsible for injury due to fault of the operators of the ship. In both cases, a state is responsible only if it has not taken "such measures as may be necessary" to comply with applicable international standards and to avoid causing injury outside its territory, as required by Subsection (1). In general, the applicable international rules and standards do not hold a state responsible when it has taken the necessary and practicable measures; some international agreements provide also for responsibility regardless of fault in case of a discharge of highly dangerous (radioactive, toxic, etc.) substances, or an abnormally dangerous activity (*e.g.,* launching of space satellites). See also the principles applicable to weather modification, Comment *f*. In all cases, however, some defenses may be available to the state; *e.g.,* that it had acted pursuant to a binding decision of the Security Council of the United Nations, or that injury was due to the failure of the injured state to exercise reasonable care to avoid the threatened harm. Compare Restatement, Second, Torts §§ 519, 520, and 524. A state is not responsible for injury due to a natural disaster such as an eruption of a volcano, unless such disaster was triggered or aggravated by a human act, such as nuclear explosion in a volcano's vicinity. But a state is responsible if after a natural disaster has occurred it does not take necessary and practicable steps to prevent or reduce injury to other states.

Under Subsections (2)(b) and (3), responsibility of a state for a significant injury entails payment of appropriate damages if the complaining state proves the existence of a causal link between an activity within the jurisdiction of the responsible state and the injury to the complaining state. Determination of responsibility raises special difficulties in cases of long-range pollution where the link between multiple activities in some distant states and the pollution in the injured state might be difficult to prove. Where more than one state contributes to the pollution causing significant injury, the liability will be apportioned among the states, taking into account, where appropriate, the contribution to the injury of the injured state itself.

A state is responsible under this section for environmental harm proximately caused by activity under its own jurisdiction, not for activity by another state. For instance, a state is not responsible under this section merely because it encourages activities in another state, such as plant eradication programs, that inflict environmental injury in that state or in a third state. Similarly, if a group of states imposes economic sanctions on state A depriving it of oil supplies and requiring state A to use coal, which results in an increase in air pollution in state B, the boycotting states are not responsible under principles of international environmental law for injury resulting to state B.

Although there has been no authoritative consideration of the issue, international environmental law has apparently not extended responsibility beyond the state directly responsible for the activities causing injury, under principles analogous to "product liability" which apply in some national legal systems. Thus, under this section, state A is responsible for a radioactive emission from a nuclear reactor operated in its territory that causes injury to state B, but there is no recognized responsibility to B by state C in which the defective reactor was manufactured or from which it was sold to state A. There may, however, be such responsibility pursuant to an international agreement between state A and state C, and in special circumstances under general principles of state responsibility. See, *e.g.*, §§ 207, 711, and 901. Also, there may be liability by the manufacturer or seller of the defective reactor, whether it is a state or a private person, under principles of national law applicable to the transaction. Compare, for example, Restatement, Second, Torts §§ 388–408.

Under this section, a state is obligated to take all necessary precautionary measures where an activity is contemplated that poses a substantial risk of a significant transfrontier environmental injury; if the activity has already taken place, the state is obligated to take all necessary measures to prevent or reduce pollution beyond its borders. Similarly, where a violation of international environmental rules and standards has already occurred, the violating state is obligated to take promptly all necessary preventive or remedial measures, even if no injury has yet taken place.

For the remedies for breach of obligations under this section, see § 602.

e. Obligation to notify and consult. Under Subsection 1(a), a state has an obligation to warn another state promptly of any situation that may cause significant pollution damage in that state. A state has also an obligation to consult with another state if a proposed activity within its jurisdiction or control poses a substantial risk of significant injury to the environment of the other state, but it need not permit such consultations to delay the proposed activity unduly.

f. Weather modification. Weather modification programs are normally used either to prevent injuries to the environment (*e.g.*, by a storm) or to obtain some benefit (*e.g.*, by causing rain during a drought). A state's weather modification programs have sometimes caused injury to another state, *e.g.*, by bringing it excessive rain or by depriving it of rain, or, by changing the direction of a storm, causing injury to that state's ships at sea, to its shore, or to the marine environment. Under international law, a state engaged in weather modification activities is responsible for any significant injuries if causation can be proved, even if the injury was neither intended nor due to negligence, and even if the state took all necessary measures to prevent or reduce injury. Compare the rule as to abnormally dangerous activities, Comment *d*.

* * *

§ 602. Remedies for Violation of Environmental Obligations

(1) A state responsible to another state for violation of § 601 is subject to general interstate remedies (§ 902) to prevent, reduce, or terminate the activity threatening or causing the violation, and to pay reparation for injury caused.

(2) Where pollution originating in a state has caused significant injury to persons outside that state, or has created a significant risk of such injury,

the state of origin is obligated to accord to the person injured or exposed to such risk access to the same judicial or administrative remedies as are available in similar circumstances to persons within the state.

Comment:

a. International law remedies. The remedies referred to in Subsection (1) usually begin with a protest against the violation, accompanied by a demand that the offending state terminate the violation, desist from further violations, and make reparation for past violations. If the matter is not resolved by diplomatic negotiations, the aggrieved state may resort to agreed third-party procedures, such as conciliation, mediation, arbitration, or adjudication. Some neighboring states have established international joint commissions to deal with transboundary problems, including pollution, but usually such commissions can only make recommendations. Strictly limited and reasonable measures of "self help" may be permitted in special circumstances. See § 905. Remedies under international law are to the injured state; whether that state is obligated to pay any reparation received over to any injured person in its territory is a matter of its domestic law. See § 902, Comments *i* and *l*.

Remedies under this section are available for injury to a state's environmental interests within its territory as well as to interests beyond its territory, such as injury to its fishing interests on the high seas; it may pursue remedies, not only for injury to state interests but also to those of its political subdivisions or of its inhabitants or nationals. A state may also pursue appropriate remedies for injury to the common interest in the global commons, such as the high seas.

Even where reparations for past injuries are not appropriate or feasible, a state may demand that violations be discontinued.

b. Local remedies. A state responsible for transfrontier pollution can fulfill its obligation to inhabitants of other states who suffered injuries by giving them access to its tribunals for adjudication of their claims. If such local remedies are available, the person who suffered injuries must exhaust these remedies before the state of which he is a national can bring an international claim on his behalf under Subsection (1). See § 703, Comment *d*; § 713, Comments *b* and *f*; § 902, Comment *k*. The two states, however, may agree at any time to settle the claim or include it in a lump-sum settlement. See § 902, Comment *i*.

Subsection (2) applies the principle of non-discrimination against foreign nationals (§ 711, Comment *f*). This principle requires that a state in which pollution originates avoid discrimination in the enforcement of applicable international rules and standards, as well as give to foreign victims the benefit of its own rules and standards for the protection of the environment, even if they are stricter than the international rules or standards. Subsection (2) applies the principle of nondiscrimination also to remedies. A state must provide the same procedures, and apply the same substantive law and the same measures of compensation, to persons outside its territory as are available to persons injured within its territory. Thus, a state applying the "polluter-pays" principle should apply it to all pollution originating within the state, whether it causes injury at home or abroad. If a state applies the principle of strict liability, a victim of transfrontier pollution will be entitled to the benefit of that principle. On the other hand, if the state makes liability conditional on fault or negligence, the foreign victim can be required to meet that condition even if in the place of injury fault or negligence is not a necessary element for liability. Similarly, if a state's law imposes an obligation to reduce pollution to the lowest level that is attainable by the application of the most advanced technology that is economically feasible, this requirement applies equally to pollution at home and abroad.

When environmental injury in one state results from private activity in another state, a remedy may sometimes be available in the courts of the victim state, or even of a third state, and if the victim has received satisfaction by such a remedy the interstate remedy would abate.

c. Availability of private remedies under state law. Under the law of many states, pollution damage is considered a local tort; suit for damages lies only in the state where the injury occurred, not in the state where the pollution originated. If personal jurisdiction over the person responsible for the pollution can be obtained in the state where the injury occurred, a suit for compensation or for an injunction would lie, but such suit might not be possible if the alleged polluter has no business or property in that state. Even if a suit there is brought under a long-arm statute and results in a default judgment, the judgment might not be enforceable in the polluter's home state. See § 421(2)(j) and § 481, Reporters' Note 4.

* * *

§ 603. State Responsibility for Marine Pollution

(1) A state is obligated

(a) to adopt laws and regulations to prevent, reduce, and control any significant pollution of the marine environment that are no less effective than generally accepted international rules and standards; and

(b) to ensure compliance with the laws and regulations adopted pursuant to clause (a) by ships flying its flag, and, in case of a violation, to impose adequate penalties on the owner or captain of the ship.

(2) A state is obligated to take, individually and jointly with other states, such measures as may be necessary, to the extent practicable under the circumstances, to prevent, reduce, and control pollution causing or threatening to cause significant injury to the marine environment.

Source Note:

This section is based on Articles 194, 207–12, 217, and 220 of the 1982 Convention on the Law of the Sea.

Comment:

a. State responsibility for marine pollution. This section applies the principles of § 601 to marine pollution. In fulfilling their obligations under this section, states must use "the best practicable means at their disposal and in accordance with their capabilities," and must "endeavour to harmonize their policies in this connection." LOS Convention, Article 194(1). In taking measures to prevent, reduce, or control pollution, states are obligated to implement any pertinent international rules and standards, and to refrain from unjustifiable interference with activities carried out by other states in exercise of their rights and in pursuance of their duties in conformity with international law. Articles 194(4) and 213–22.

The measures to be taken must "minimize to the fullest possible extent" the release of toxic, harmful, or noxious substances from land-based sources (such as rivers, estuaries, pipelines, and sewers), from or through the atmosphere, or by dumping of waste. Articles 194(3), 207, 210, and 212. In order to limit pollution from ships, all states must take measures for preventing accidents and dealing with emergencies, ensuring the safety of operations at sea, and preventing harmful discharges, whether intentional or unintentional. Navigational routing systems should also be designed to minimize the danger of accidents. Articles 194(3)(b) and 211(1). For the obligations of flag states, see Comment *b*; for the obligations of states engaged in sea-bed mining, see Comment *c*.

Under the principles of § 601(2) and (3), a state is responsible for injuries caused by pollution resulting from a violation of its obligations under this section to a coast or coastal waters of another state or to the marine areas beyond the limits of national jurisdiction, *i.e.*, areas of the sea not included in internal waters, the territorial sea, or the exclusive economic zone of a state, or in the archipelagic waters of an archipelagic state. See Article 86. State responsibility extends to injuries such as those caused by pollution, *e.g.*, by: toxic or noxious substances flowing down-river into the sea and moving into the coastal waters of a neighboring state; sewage drifting from the coastal waters of one state to the coast of another state; toxic or noxious substances dumped, or garbage or fuel discharged, by ships flying the flag of one state and landing on the coast of another state; or oil spills, mineral tailings, or other discharges from installations for exploration and exploitation of oil or polymetallic nodules that contaminate the high seas or are moved by currents to the waters or coast of another state.

b. Obligations of flag state. The flag state has the primary obligation to ensure that its ships respect generally accepted international anti-pollution rules and standards established through the competent international organization or general diplomatic conference, and that they comply with the state's laws and regulations implementing such rules and standards. A flag state is obligated to prohibit its ships from sailing unless they have complied with such international rules and standards, and have also met standards set by the state's own laws, especially those relating to design, construction, equipment, and manning of ships; to require its ships to carry on board certificates of compliance with the international rules; and to inspect its ships periodically to verify that their condition conforms to the certificates they carry. Other states must accept the certificates issued by the flag state as evidence of the condition of the ship, unless there are clear grounds for believing that the condition of the ship does not correspond substantially to the certificates. Article 217(1)–(3).

The flag state is obligated to provide for penalties for pollution by its vessels adequate in severity to discourage violations. Article 217(8). For further enforcement obligations of the flag state, see § 604, Comment *c*.

c. Obligations of sea-bed mining states. States are obligated to adopt laws, regulations, and other measures for preventing, reducing, and controlling pollution of the marine environment arising from or in connection with their exploration and exploitation of the sea-bed and subsoil, or from artificial islands, installations, and structures under their jurisdiction that are operating in the marine environment. Such laws, regulations, and measures must be no less effective than international rules, standards, and recommended practices and procedures. Articles 194(3)(c) and (d) and 208.

d. Protection of fragile ecosystems. States are obligated to take measures necessary to protect and preserve rare or fragile ecosystems, and the habitat of depleted, threatened, or endangered species and other forms of marine life. Where the area to be protected forms part of a state's exclusive economic zone, the competent international organization may authorize that state to implement special international rules and standards applicable to such zones. Articles 194(5) and 211(6).

A coastal state also has the right to adopt and enforce nondiscriminatory laws and regulations for the prevention, reduction, and control of marine pollution from vessels in ice-covered areas within the limits of its exclusive economic zone, where particularly severe climatic conditions and the presence of ice for most of the year create obstructions or exceptional hazards to navigation, and where pollution of the marine environment could cause major harm to, or irreversible disturbance of, the ecological balance. The coastal state is obligated to base such laws and regulations on the best available scientific evidence and to have due regard to navigation. Article 234.

e. Obligation to notify. When a state becomes aware that the marine environment has been injured or is in imminent danger of being injured, it is obligated immediately to notify other states likely to be affected by such injuries as well as the competent global or regional international organization. Article 198.

f. Joint action in emergencies. States in an area affected by a maritime pollution disaster are obligated to cooperate in eliminating the effects of pollution and in preventing or minimizing injury. To be able to deal better with such emergencies, neighboring states are obligated to develop and be ready to put into operation contingency plans for responding to pollution incidents affecting the marine environment in their vicinity. Article 199.

g. Pollution by aircraft. States are responsible under this section for pollution of the marine environment by aircraft of their registry, *e.g.,* by noxious emissions. States are obligated to adopt laws and regulations to prevent, reduce, and control such pollution, taking into account internationally agreed rules, standards, and recommended practices and procedures adopted by the International Civil Aviation Organization, but must not prejudice thereby the safety of air navigation. Article 212.

* * *

§ 604. Remedies for Marine Pollution

(1) A state responsible to another state for a violation of the principles of § 603 is subject to general interstate remedies (§ 902) to prevent, reduce, or terminate the activity threatening or causing pollution, and to pay reparation for injury caused.

(2) A state is obligated to ensure that a remedy is available, in accordance with its legal system, to provide prompt and adequate compensation or other relief for an injury to private interests caused by pollution of the marine environment resulting from a violation of § 603.

(3) In addition to remedies that may be available to it under Subsection (1):

(a) a coastal state may detain, and institute proceedings against, a foreign ship:

(i) navigating in its territorial sea, for a violation therein of antipollution laws that the coastal state adopted in accordance with applicable international rules and standards; or

(ii) navigating in its territorial sea or its exclusive economic zone, for a violation in that zone of applicable international antipollution rules and standards that resulted in a discharge causing or threatening a major injury to the coastal state;

(b) a port state may institute proceedings against a foreign ship that has voluntarily come into that state's port,

(i) for a violation of the port state's antipollution laws adopted in accordance with applicable international rules and standards, if the violation had occurred in the port state's territorial sea or exclusive economic zone; or

(ii) for a discharge in violation of applicable international antipollution rules and standards that had occurred beyond the limits of national jurisdiction of any state; and

(c) a port state is obligated to investigate, as far as practicable, whether a foreign ship that has voluntarily come into that state's port was responsible for a discharge in violation of applicable international antipollution rules and standards,

(i) at the request of another state, where the discharge was alleged to have occurred in waters subject to that state's jurisdiction, or to have caused or threatened damage to that state; or

(ii) at the request of the flag state, irrespective of where the violation was alleged to have occurred.

Source Note:

This section is based on Articles 211, 217–18, 220, and 228 of the 1982 Convention on the Law of the Sea.

Comment:

a. Ordinary remedies between states. Subsection (1) states that ordinary international remedies are available for violations of obligations under § 603 as for violations of other obligations under international environmental law (§ 602), or of international obligations generally (§ 902). A state is responsible for a violation of international antipollution rules and standards, resulting from an act or omission by state officials or public vessels, or by ships, aircraft, platforms, or other structures at sea, or by natural or juridical persons, that are under the state's jurisdiction.

Interstate remedies may include claims for reparation for injury to the state or its political subdivisions, or injury to its nationals or inhabitants when they are not afforded reparation by domestic remedy in the offending state. See Subsection (2) and Comment *b*. The obligations of states in respect of the common environment are *erga omnes* and any state may pursue remedies for violations that inflict significant injury on that environment (for instance, to obtain termination of the wrongful conduct). See also Comment *c*.

b. Remedies for private injury. Under Subsection (2), when a natural or juridical person for whose acts a state is responsible under § 601 has caused injury to interests of a private person who is not the state's own national or resident, the state must provide to the injured person access to domestic remedies so that prompt and adequate compensation or preventive or injunctive relief may be obtained. See LOS Convention, Article 235. Where the injury results from a violation by a private ship or installation, the owner is presumably liable under domestic law, and the responsibility of the state is invoked only where adequate reparation is not obtained from the person responsible by domestic remedies. If complex patterns of ownership and agency make it difficult to determine who was legally liable under domestic law for the violation causing the injury, the state is responsible for ensuring that the injured person is compensated.

c. Enforcement by flag states. In addition to the remedies set forth in Comments *a* and *b,* if a ship has committed a violation of applicable international rules and standards, the flag state is obligated to investigate immediately and to institute appropriate proceedings, irrespective of the place of the violation or injury. See LOS Convention, Article 217. The state that is the victim of a violation by a ship (or, in case of pollution of the common environment, any state) may complain to the flag state and request that the guilty persons be punished and be enjoined from further pollution (see Articles 217(6) and 235); if dissatisfied with action taken by the flag state, it may invoke against the flag state the remedies available under international law. Subsection (1) and Comment *a*. In addition, if the flag state has repeatedly disregarded its obligations to enforce effectively the applicable international rules and standards in respect of violations committed by its ships, a port state where proceedings against a ship have been instituted under Subsection (3)(b) or (c) may continue such proceedings and impose penalties, regardless of a request of the flag state that the proceedings be transferred to it. See Comment *e*; LOS Convention, Article 228(1).

d. Enforcement by coastal states. The authority of the coastal state to bring proceedings against an offending foreign vessel (Subsection 3(a)) varies according to where the vessel is located and where the violation occurred. The coastal state has jurisdiction to prescribe, adjudicate, and enforce with respect to acts of pollution committed in its ports. The coastal state can also institute proceedings against a ship voluntarily in port, or against its crew, for a violation of its laws that occurred within its territorial sea or exclusive economic zone, provided that its laws were adopted in accordance with applicable international rules and standards. An offshore terminal is assimilated to a port for these purposes. LOS Convention, Article 220(1).

Where there are clear grounds for believing that a foreign ship, while passing through the territorial sea of the coastal state, violated laws and regulations of that state adopted in accordance with applicable international rules and standards, the coastal state may, subject to certain procedural safeguards (see Article 226), undertake physical inspection of the vessel in the territorial sea in order to ascertain the facts relating to the violation. Where evidence so warrants, the coastal state may institute proceedings against the ship, in accordance with its laws, and may detain the ship pending such proceedings. Article 220(2); see also Articles 19(2)(h), 21(1)(f), and 27.

When a violation of applicable international antipollution rules and standards is committed in the exclusive economic zone of the coastal state, and the ship is still in the zone or in the territorial sea of the coastal state, that state can take various steps, depending on the gravity of the violation. Where there are clear grounds for believing that a violation has occurred, the coastal state may require the ship to identify itself and its port of registry, indicate its last and its next port of call, and provide other relevant information needed to establish whether a violation has occurred. When there are clear grounds for believing that the violation resulted in "a substantial discharge causing or threatening significant pollution of the marine environment," and the ship either refuses to give information or the information supplied is manifestly at variance with the facts, the coastal state is entitled to proceed with a physical inspection. Only if there is "clear objective evidence" that the ship committed the violation and that the discharge is causing or threatens to cause "major damage to the coastline or related interests of the coastal state, or to any resources of its territorial sea or exclusive economic zone," is that state entitled to institute proceedings in accordance with its laws, and to detain the ship. Article 220(3)–(6).

To ensure that a ship is not unduly detained, appropriate procedures must be established, either through the competent international organization or by special agreement, for bonding or other appropriate financial security. If the ship makes the necessary arrangements, the coastal state is obligated to allow the vessel to proceed. Only monetary penalties may be imposed, unless the violation was committed in the territorial sea and the act of pollution was willful and serious, in which case the vessel may be confiscated and the person responsible may be tried and punished. Articles 220(7) and 230.

The principle of sovereign immunity protects warships, warplanes, and other government ships and aircraft on noncommercial service against coastal state proceedings, but the flag state is obligated to ensure that such ships or aircraft act in a manner consistent, as far as is reasonable and practicable, with applicable international rules and standards. Article 236.

e. Enforcement by port states. The jurisdiction of the port state with respect to a foreign ship voluntarily in its port or offshore terminal includes authority for the state to investigate and, where the evidence warrants, to institute proceedings with respect to any discharge from that ship that occurred on the high seas. The port state may also institute proceedings if an unlawful discharge outside its coastal waters caused or is likely to cause pollution within those waters. If the discharge occurred in the coastal waters of another state, the port state is obligated to institute proceedings, as far as practicable, when requested by that state. In addition, under Subsection (3)(c), the port state is obligated to conduct an investigation, as far as practicable, when so requested by the flag state, or by a state damaged or threatened by the discharge. LOS Convention, Article 218(1)–(4).

The records of the investigation carried out by a port state must be transmitted to the state that asked for the investigation if it so requests. The state in whose coastal waters the violation took place, but not the state where the injury occurred, is entitled to have the proceedings transferred to it. Once the records, the evidence, and the bonds (or other financial security) are transmitted to the requesting state, the proceedings in the port state must be suspended. Article 218(4).

The flag state is entitled to have penal proceedings against its ship in a foreign state suspended as soon as the flag state has itself instituted proceedings against the ship. However, the state that has instituted the proceedings need not suspend them (1) if the violation was committed in its territorial sea; (2) if the coastal state suffered major damage; or (3) if the flag state "has repeatedly disregarded its obligations to enforce effectively the applicable international rules and standards in respect of violations committed by its vessels." A proceeding that is suspended is to be terminated upon completion of proceedings in the flag state. Article 228(1). If the coastal state is dissatisfied with the action taken by the flag state after the case has been transferred, it may protest both to the flag state and to the competent international organization; and if the lack of enforcement recurs, the coastal state may refuse to suspend proceedings on a future occasion.

f. Liability for wrongful enforcement measures. If a state has taken measures against a foreign ship that were unlawful or exceeded those reasonably required in the light of available information, it is obligated to pay the flag state for any injury or loss attributable to such measures. It must provide for recourse in its courts for private actions in respect of such injury or loss. LOS Convention, Article 232.

1.23   DECLARATION OF THE HAGUE. **Concluded at The Hague, 11 March 1989. UN Doc A/44/340–E/1989/120 (Annex) (1989);** *reprinted in* **28 ILM 1308 (1989) & 5 Weston & Carlson V.E.13**

The right to live is the right from which all other rights stem. Guaranteeing this right is the paramount duty of those in charge of all States throughout the world.

Today, the very conditions of life on our planet are threatened by the severe attacks to which the earth's atmosphere is subjected.

Authoritative scientific studies have shown the existence and scope of considerable dangers linked in particular to the warming of the atmosphere and to the deterioration of the ozone layer. The latter has already led to action, under the 1985 Vienna Convention for the Protection of the Ozone Layer and the 1987 Montreal Protocol, while the former is being addressed by the Intergovernmental Panel on Climatic Change established by UNEP and WMO, which has just begun its work. In addition the UN General Assembly adopted Resolution 43/53 on the Protection of the Global Climate in 1988, recognizing climate change as a common concern of mankind.

According to present scientific knowledge, the consequences of these phenomena may well jeopardize ecological systems as well as the most vital interests of mankind at large.

Because the problem is planet-wide in scope, solutions can only be devised on a global level. Because of the nature of the dangers involved, remedies to be sought involve not only the fundamental duty to preserve the ecosystem, but also the right to live in dignity in a viable global environment, and the consequent duty of the community of nations vis-à-vis present and future generations to do all that can be done to preserve the quality of the atmosphere.

Therefore we consider that, faced with a problem the solution to which has three salient features, namely that it is vital, urgent and global, we are in a situation that calls not only for implementation of existing principles but also for a new approach, through the development of new principles of international law including new and more effective decision-making and enforcement mechanisms.

What is needed here are regulatory, supportive and adjustment measures that take into account the participation and potential contribution of countries which have reached different levels of development. Most of the emissions that affect the atmosphere at present originate in the industrialized nations. And it is in these same nations that the room for change is greatest, and these nations are also those which have the greatest resources to deal with this problem effectively.

The international community and especially the industrialized nations have special obligations to assist developing countries which will be very negatively affected by changes in the atmosphere although the responsibility of many of them for the process may only be marginal today.

Financial institutions and development agencies, be they international or domestic, must coordinate their activities in order to promote sustainable development.

Without prejudice to the international obligations of each State, the signatories acknowledge and will promote the following principles:

    (*a*) The principle of developing, within the framework of the United Nations, new institutional authority, either by strengthening existing institutions or by creating a new institution, which, in the context of the preservation of the earth's atmosphere, shall be responsible for combating any further global warming of the atmosphere and shall involve such decision-making procedures as may be effective even if, on occasion, unanimous agreement has not been achieved;

    (*b*) The principle that this institutional authority undertake or commission the necessary studies, be granted appropriate information upon request, ensure the circulation and exchange of scientific and technological information—including facilitation of access to the technology needed—, develop instruments and define standards to enhance or guarantee the protection of the atmosphere and monitor compliance herewith;

(c) The principle of appropriate measures to promote the effective implementation of and compliance with the decisions of the new institutional authority, decisions which will be subject to control by the International Court of Justice;

(d) The principle that countries to which decisions taken to protect the atmosphere shall prove to be an abnormal or special burden, in view, inter alia, of the level of their development and actual responsibility for the deterioration of the atmosphere, shall receive fair and equitable assistance to compensate them for bearing such burden. To this end mechanisms will have to be developed;

(e) The negotiation of the necessary legal instruments to provide an effective and coherent foundation, institutionally and financially, for the aforementioned principles.

The Heads of State and Government or their representatives, who have expressed their endorsement of this Declaration by placing their signatures under it, stress their resolve to promote the principles thus defined by:

— furthering the development of their initiative within the United Nations and in close coordination and collaboration with existing agencies set up under the auspices of the United Nations;

— inviting all States of the world and the international organisations competent in this field to join in developing, taking into account studies by the IPCC, the framework conventions and other legal instruments necessary to establish institutional authority and to implement the other principles stated above to protect the atmosphere and to counter climate change, particularly global warming;

— urging all States of the world and the international organisations competent in this field to sign and ratify conventions relating to the protection of nature and the environment;

— calling upon all States of the world to endorse the present declaration.

The original of this Declaration, drawn up in French and English, will be transmitted to the Government of the Kingdom of the Netherlands, which will retain it in its archives. Each of the participating States will receive from the Government of the Kingdom of the Netherlands a true copy of this Declaration.

The Prime Minister of the Netherlands is requested to transmit the text of this Declaration, which is not eligible for registration under Article 102 of the Charter of the United Nations, to all members of the United Nations.

1.24 THE LANGKAWI DECLARATION ON ENVIRONMENT. **Adopted by the Commonwealth Heads of Government at Langkawi (Malaysia), 21 October 1989.** *Reprinted in* **5 AJIL 589 (1990) & 5 Weston & Carlson V.C.9**

We, the Heads of Government of the Commonwealth, representing a quarter of the world's population and a broad cross-section of global interests, are deeply concerned at the serious deterioration in the environment and the threat this poses to the well-being of present and future generations. Any delay in taking action to halt this progressive deterioration will result in permanent and irreversible damage.

2. The current threat to the environment, which is a common concern of all mankind, stems essentially from past neglect in managing the natural environment and resources. The environment has been degraded by decades of industrial and other forms of pollution, including unsafe disposal of toxic wastes, the burning of fossil fuels, nuclear testing and non-sustainable practices in agriculture, fishery and forestry.

3. The main environment problems facing the world are the greenhouse effect (which may lead to severe climatic changes that could induce floods, droughts and rising sea levels), the depletion of the ozone layer, acid rain, marine pollution, land degradation and the extinction of numerous animal and plant species. Some developing countries also face distinct environmental problems arising from poverty and population pressure. In addition, some islands and low-lying areas of other countries, are threatened by the prospect of rising sea level.

4. Many environmental problems transcend national boundaries and interests, necessitating a co-ordinated global effort. This is particularly true in areas outside national jurisdiction, and where there is transboundary pollution on land and in the oceans, atmosphere and outer space.

5. The need to protect the environment should be viewed in a balanced perspective and due emphasis be accorded to promoting economic growth and sustainable development, including eradication of poverty, meeting basic needs, and enhancing the quality of life. The responsibility for ensuring a better environment should be equitably shared and the ability of developing countries to respond be taken into account.

6. To achieve sustainable development, economic growth is a compelling necessity. Sustainable development implies the incorporation of environmental concerns into economic planning and policies. Environmental concerns should not be used to introduce a new form of conditionality in aid and development financing, nor as a pretext for creating unjustified barriers to trade.

7. The success of global and national environmental programmes requires mutually reinforcing strategies and the participation and commitment of all levels of society—government, individuals and organisations, industry and the scientific community.

8. Recognising that our shared environment binds all countries to a common future, we, the Heads of Government of the Commonwealth, resolved to act collectively and individually, commit ourselves to the following programme of action:

— advance policies and programmes which help achieve sustainable development, including the development of new and better techniques in integrating the environmental dimension in economic decision-making;

— strengthen and support the development of international funding mechanisms and appropriate decision-making procedures to respond to environmental protection needs which will include assisting developing countries to obtain access to and transfer of needed environmental technologies and which should take account of proposals for an international environment fund/Planet Protection Fund;

— support the work of the UNEP/WMO Intergovernmental Panel on Climate Change (IPCC);

— call for the early conclusion of an international convention to protect and conserve the global climate and, in this context, applaud the efforts of member governments to advance the negotiation of a framework convention under UN auspices;

— support the findings and recommendations of the Commonwealth Expert Group's Report on Climate Change as a basis for achievable action to develop strategies for adapting to climate change and for reducing greenhouse gas emissions, as well as making an important contribution to the work of the IPCC;

— support measures to improve energy conservation and energy efficiency;

— promote the reduction and eventual phase-out of substances depleting the ozone layer;

— promote afforestation and agricultural practices in developed and developing countries to arrest the increase in atmospheric carbon dioxide and halt the deterioration of land and water resources;

— strengthen efforts by developing countries in sustainable forest management and their manufacture and export of higher value-added forest products and, in this regard, support the activities of the International Tropical Timber Organisation and the Food and Agriculture Organisation's Tropical Forestry Action Plan, as well as take note of the recommendations of the 13th Commonwealth Forestry Conference;

— support activities related to the conservation of biological diversity and genetic resources, including the conservation of significant areas of virgin forest and other protected natural habitats;

— support low-lying and island countries in their efforts to protect themselves and their vulnerable natural marine ecosystems from the effects of sea level rise;

— discourage and restrict non-sustainable fishing practices and seek to ban tangle net and pelagic drift net fishing;

— support efforts to prevent marine pollution including curbing ocean dumping of toxic wastes;

— strengthen international action to ensure the safe management and disposal of hazardous wastes and to reduce transboundary movements, particularly to prevent dumping in developing countries;

— participate in relevant international agreements relating to the environment and promote new and innovated instruments which will attract widespread support for protecting the global environment; and

— strengthen national, regional and international institutions responsible for environmental protection as well as the promotion of active programmes on environmental education to heighten public awareness and support.

9.   We, the Heads of Government of the Commonwealth, resolve to take immediate and positive actions on the basis of the above programme. In this regard, we pledge our full support for the convening of the 1992 UN Conference on Environment and Development.

10.   We call on the international community to join us in the endeavour.

1.25   RESOLUTION ON THE NEED TO ENSURE A HEALTHY ENVIRONMENT FOR THE WELL-BEING OF INDIVIDUALS. **Adopted by the U.N. General Assembly, 14 December 1990. GA Res 45/94, UN GAOR, 45th Sess, Supp No 14, at 178, UN Doc A/Res/45/94 (1990)**

The General Assembly,

Recalling that, in accordance with the provisions of the Universal Declaration of Human Rights and the International Covenant on Economic, Social and Cultural Rights, everyone has the right to an adequate standard of living for his or her own health and well-being and that of his or her family and to the continuous improvement of living conditions,

Recognizing the need to promote universal respect for, and observance of, human rights and fundamental freedoms in all their aspects,

Considering that a better and healthier environment can help contribute to the full enjoyment of human rights by all,

Reaffirming that in accordance with the Declaration of the United Nations Conference on the Human Environment, men and women have the fundamental right to freedom, equality and adequate conditions of life in an environment of a quality that permits a life of dignity and well-being, and that they bear a solemn responsibility to protect and improve the environment for present and future generations,

Bearing in mind the fact that increasing environmental degradation could endanger the very basis of life,

Bearing in mind also that the economic growth and development of the developing countries are essential in order to address the problems of the degradation and protection of the environment,

Emphasizing the increasing role of the United Nations in addressing global environmental problems,

Recalling that the United Nations Conference on Environment and Development, to be held in Brazil in 1992, will elaborate strategies and measures to halt and reverse the effects of environmental degradation in the context of strengthened national and international efforts to promote sustainable and environmentally sound development in all countries,

Stressing the importance for all countries to take effective actions for the protection and enhancement of the environment in accordance with their respective capacities and responsibilities and taking into account the specific needs of developing countries and that, as the major sources of pollution, the developed countries have the main responsibility for taking appropriate measures urgently,

Welcoming Commission on Human Rights resolution 1990/41 of 6 March 1990 and Sub–Commission on Prevention of Discrimination and Protection of Minorities resolution 1990/7 of 30 August 1990, in which they decided to study the problems of the environment and its relation to human rights,

1.   Recognizes that all individuals are entitled to live in an environment adequate for their health and well-being;

2.   Calls upon Member States and intergovernmental and non-governmental organizations dealing with environmental questions to enhance their efforts towards ensuring a better and healthier environment;

3.   Encourages the Commission on Human Rights, with the assistance of its Sub–Commission on Prevention of Discrimination and Protection of Minorities, to continue studying the problems of the environment and its relation to human rights, with a

view to submitting to the Preparatory Committee of the United Nations Conference on Environment and Development, through the Economic and Social Council, a report on the progress made on the matter;

4. Believes that appropriate organs of the United Nations, within their respective competences, should pursue active efforts in seeking to promote a better and healthier environment.

1.26 Convention on Environmental Impact Assessment in a Transboundary Context[a]. **Adopted at Espoo (Finland), 25 February 1991. Entered into force, 10 September 1997. 1989 UNTS 309.** *Reprinted in* **30 ILM 800 (1991) & 5 Weston & Carlson V.B.15**

The Parties to this Convention,

Aware of the interrelationship between economic activities and their environmental consequences,

Affirming the need to ensure environmentally sound and sustainable development,

Determined to enhance international co-operation in assessing environmental impact, in particular in a transboundary context,

Mindful of the need and importance to develop anticipatory policies and of preventing, mitigating and monitoring significant adverse environmental impact in general and more specifically in a transboundary context,

Recalling the relevant provisions of the Charter of the United Nations, the Declaration of the Stockholm Conference on the Human Environment, the Final Act of the Conference on Security and Co-operation in Europe (CSCE) and the Concluding Documents of the Madrid and Vienna Meetings of Representatives of the Participating States of the CSCE,

Commending the ongoing activities of States to ensure that, through their national legal and administrative provisions and their national policies, environmental impact assessment is carried out,

Conscious of the need to give explicit consideration to environmental factors at an early stage in the decision-making process by applying environmental impact assessment, at all appropriate administrative levels, as a necessary tool to improve the quality of information presented to decision makers so that environmentally sound decisions can be made paying careful attention to minimizing significant adverse impact, particularly in a transboundary context,

Mindful of the efforts of international organizations to promote the use of environmental impact assessment both at the national and international levels, and taking into account work on environmental impact assessment carried out under the auspices of the United Nations Economic Commission for Europe, in particular results achieved by the Seminar on Environmental Impact Assessment (September 1987, Warsaw, Poland) as well as noting the Goals and Principles on environmental impact assessment adopted by the Governing Council of the United Nations Environment Programme, and the Ministerial Declaration on Sustainable Development (May 1990, Bergen, Norway),

Have agreed as follows:

Article 1. Definitions

For the purposes of this Convention;

(i) "Parties" means, unless the text otherwise indicates, the Contracting Parties to this Convention;

(ii) "Party of origin" means the Contracting Party or Parties to this Convention under whose jurisdiction a proposed activity is envisaged to take place;

(iii) "Affected Party" means the Contracting Party or Parties to this Convention likely to be affected by the transboundary impact of a proposed activity;

(iv) "Concerned Parties" means the Party of origin and the affected Party of an environmental impact assessment pursuant to this Convention;

a. *See also* Basic Document 1.39.

(v) "Proposed activity" means any activity or any major change to an activity subject to a decision of a competent authority in accordance with an applicable national procedure;

(vi) "Environmental impact assessment" means a national procedure for evaluating the likely impact of a proposed activity on the environment;

(vii) "Impact" means any effect caused by a proposed activity on the environment including human health and safety, flora, fauna, soil, air, water, climate, landscape and historical monuments or other physical structures or the interaction among these factors; it also includes effects on cultural heritage or socio-economic conditions resulting from alterations to those factors;

(viii) "Transboundary impact" means any impact, not exclusively of a global nature, within an area under the jurisdiction of a Party caused by a proposed activity the physical origin of which is situated wholly or in part within the area under the jurisdiction of another Party;

(ix) "Competent authority" means the national authority or authorities designated by a Party as responsible for performing the tasks covered by this Convention and/or the authority or authorities entrusted by a Party with decision-making powers regarding a proposed activity;

(x) "The Public" means one or more natural or legal persons *and, in accordance with national legislation or practice, their associations, organizations or groups.*[b]

Article 2.   *General Provisions*

1.   The Parties shall, either individually or jointly, take all appropriate and effective measures to prevent, reduce and control significant adverse transboundary environmental impact from proposed activities.

2.   Each Party shall take the necessary legal, administrative or other measures to implement the provisions of this Convention, including, with respect to proposed activities listed in Appendix I that are likely to cause significant adverse transboundary impact, the establishment of an environmental impact assessment procedure that permits public participation and preparation of the environmental impact assessment documentation described in Appendix II.

3.   The Party of origin shall ensure that in accordance with the provisions of this Convention an environmental impact assessment is undertaken prior to a decision to authorize or undertake a proposed activity listed in Appendix I that is likely to cause a significant adverse transboundary impact.

4.   The Party of origin shall, consistent with the provisions of this Convention, ensure that affected Parties are notified of a proposed activity listed in Appendix I that is likely to cause a significant adverse transboundary impact.

5.   Concerned Parties shall, at the initiative of any such Party, enter into discussions on whether one or more proposed activities not listed in Appendix I is or are likely to cause a significant adverse transboundary impact and thus should be treated as if it or they were so listed. Where those Parties so agree, the activity or activities shall be thus treated. General guidance for identifying criteria to determine significant adverse impact is set forth in Appendix III.

6.   The Party of origin shall provide, in accordance with the provisions of this Convention, an opportunity to the public in the areas likely to be affected to participate in relevant environmental impact assessment procedures regarding pro-

b.   As amended (italicized language) on 27   as of this writing.
February 2001. The amendment is not in force

posed activities and shall ensure that the opportunity provided to the public of the affected Party is equivalent to that provided to the public of the Party of origin.

7. Environmental impact assessments as required by this Convention shall, as a minimum requirement, be undertaken at the project level of the proposed activity. To the extent appropriate, the Parties shall endeavour to apply the principles of environmental impact assessment to policies, plans and programmes.

8. The provisions of this Convention shall not affect the right of Parties to implement national laws, regulations, administrative provisions or accepted legal practices protecting information the supply of which would be prejudicial to industrial and commercial secrecy or national security.

9. The provisions of this Convention shall not affect the right of particular Parties to implement, by bilateral or multilateral agreement where appropriate, more stringent measures than those of this Convention.

10. The provisions of this Convention shall not prejudice any obligations of the Parties under international law with regard to activities having or likely to have a transboundary impact.

11. If the Party of origin intends to carry out a procedure for the purposes of determining the content of the environmental impact assessment documentation, the affected Party should to the extent appropriate be given the opportunity to participate in this procedure.[c]

Article 3. Notification

1. For a proposed activity listed in Appendix I that is likely to cause a significant adverse transboundary impact, the Party of origin shall, for the purposes of ensuring adequate and effective consultations under Article 5, notify any Party which it considers may be an affected Party as early as possible and no later than when informing its own public about that proposed activity.

2. This notification shall contain, *inter alia:*

(a) Information on the proposed activity, including any available information on its possible transboundary impact;

(b) The nature of the possible decision; and

(c) An indication of a reasonable time within which a response under paragraph 3 of this Article is required, taking into account the nature of the proposed activity;

and may include the information set out in paragraph 5 of this Article.

3. The affected Party shall respond to the Party of origin within the time specified in the notification, acknowledging receipt of the notification, and shall indicate whether it intends to participate in the environmental impact assessment procedure.

4. If the affected Party indicates that it does not intend to participate in the environmental impact assessment procedure, or if it does not respond within the time specified in the notification, the provisions in paragraphs 5, 6, 7 and 8 of this Article and in Articles 4 to 7 will not apply. In such circumstances the right of a Party of origin to determine whether to carry out an environmental impact assessment on the basis of its national law and practice is not prejudiced.

5. Upon receipt of a response from the affected Party indicating its desire to participate in the environmental impact assessment procedure, the Party of origin shall, if it has not already done so, provide to the affected Party:

c. As amended (italicized language) on 4   of this writing.
June 2004. The amendment is not in force as

(a) Relevant information regarding the environmental impact assessment procedure, including an indication of the time schedule for transmittal of comments; and

(b) Relevant information on the proposed activity and its possible significant adverse transboundary impact.

6.   An affected Party shall, at the request of the Party of origin, provide the latter with reasonably obtainable information relating to the potentially affected environment under the jurisdiction of the affected Party, where such information is necessary for the preparation of the environmental impact assessment documentation. The information shall be furnished promptly and, as appropriate, through a joint body where one exists.

7.   When a Party considers that it would be affected by a significant adverse transboundary impact of a proposed activity listed in Appendix I, and when no notification has taken place in accordance with paragraph 1 of this Article, the concerned Parties shall, at the request of the affected Party, exchange sufficient information for the purposes of holding discussions on whether there is likely to be a significant adverse transboundary impact. If those Parties agree that there is likely to be a significant adverse transboundary impact, the provisions of this Convention shall apply accordingly. If those Parties cannot agree whether there is likely to be a significant adverse transboundary impact, any such Party may submit that question to an inquiry commission in accordance with the provisions of Appendix IV to advise on the likelihood of significant adverse transboundary impact, unless they agree on another method of settling this question.

8.   The concerned Parties shall ensure that the public of the affected Party in the areas likely to be affected be informed of, and be provided with possibilities for making comments or objections on the proposed activity, and for the transmittal of these comments or objections to the competent authority of the Party of origin, either directly to this authority or, where appropriate, through the Party of origin.

Article 4.   Preparation of the Environmental Impact Assessment Documentation

1.   The environmental impact assessment documentation to be submitted to the competent authority of the Party of origin shall contain, at a minimum, the information described in Appendix II.

2.   The Party of origin shall furnish the affected Party, as appropriate through a joint body where one exists, with the environmental impact assessment documentation. The concerned Parties shall arrange for distribution of the documentation to the authorities and the public of the affected Party in the areas likely to be affected and for the submission of comments to the competent authority of the Party of origin, either directly to this authority or, where appropriate, through the Party of origin within a reasonable time before the final decision is taken on the proposed activity.

Article 5.   Consultations on the Basis of the Environmental Impact Assessment Documentation

The Party of origin shall, after completion of the environmental impact assessment documentation, without undue delay enter into consultations with the affected Party concerning, *inter alia,* the potential transboundary impact of the proposed activity and measures to reduce or eliminate its impact. Consultations may relate to:

(a) Possible alternatives to the proposed activity, including the no-action alternative and possible measures to mitigate significant adverse transboundary impact and to monitor the effects of such measures at the expense of the Party of origin;

(b) Other forms of possible mutual assistance in reducing any significant adverse transboundary impact of the proposed activity; and

(c) Any other appropriate matters relating to the proposed activity.

The Parties shall agree, at the commencement of such consultations, on a reasonable time-frame for the duration of the consultation period. Any such consultations may be conducted through an appropriate joint body, where one exists.

Article 6. Final Decision

1. The Parties shall ensure that, in the final decision on the proposed activity, due account is taken of the outcome of the environmental impact assessment, including the environmental impact assessment documentation, as well as the comments thereon received pursuant to Article 3, paragraph 8 and Article 4, paragraph 2, and the outcome of the consultations as referred to in Article 5.

2. The Party of origin shall provide to the affected Party the final decision on the proposed activity along with the reasons and considerations on which it was based.

3. If additional information on the significant transboundary impact of a proposed activity, which was not available at the time a decision was made with respect to that activity and which could have materially affected the decision, becomes available to a concerned Party before work on that activity commences, that Party shall immediately inform the other concerned Party or Parties. If one of the concerned Parties so requests, consultations shall be held as to whether the decision needs to be revised.

Article 7. Post–Project Analysis

1. The concerned Parties, at the request of any such Party, shall determine whether, and if so to what extent, a post-project analysis shall be carried out, taking into account the likely significant adverse transboundary impact of the activity for which an environmental impact assessment has been undertaken pursuant to this Convention. Any post-project analysis undertaken shall include, in particular, the surveillance of the activity and the determination of any adverse transboundary impact. Such surveillance and determination may be undertaken with a view to achieving the objectives listed in Appendix V.

2. When, as a result of post-project analysis, the Party of origin or the affected Party has reasonable grounds for concluding that there is a significant adverse transboundary impact or factors have been discovered which may result in such an impact, it shall immediately inform the other Party. The concerned Parties shall then consult on necessary measures to reduce or eliminate the impact.

Article 8. Bilateral and Multilateral Co-operation

The Parties may continue existing or enter into new bilateral or multilateral agreements or other arrangements in order to implement their obligations under this Convention *and under any of its protocols to which they are a Party*[d]. Such agreements or other arrangements may be based on the elements listed in Appendix VI.

Article 9. Research Programmes

* * *

d. As amended (italicized language) on 4 June 2004. The amendment is not in force as of this writing.

Article 10.   Status of the Appendices

The Appendices attached to this Convention form an integral part of the Convention.

Article 11.   Meeting of Parties

* * *

Article 12.   Right to vote

* * *

Article 13.   Secretariat

The Executive Secretary of the Economic Commission for Europe shall carry out the following secretariat functions: . . .

* * *

Article 14.   Amendments to the Convention

* * *

Article 15.   Settlement of Disputes

1.   If a dispute arises between two or more Parties about the interpretation or application of this Convention, they shall seek a solution by negotiation or by any other method of dispute settlement acceptable to the parties to the dispute.

2.   When signing, ratifying, accepting, approving or acceding to this Convention, or at any time thereafter, a Party may declare in writing to the Depositary that for a dispute not resolved in accordance with paragraph 1 of this Article, it accepts one or both of the following means of dispute settlement as compulsory in relation to any Party accepting the same obligation:

(a) Submission of the dispute to the International Court of Justice;

(b) Arbitration in accordance with the procedure set out in Appendix VII.

3.   If the parties to the dispute have accepted both means of dispute settlement referred to in paragraph 2 of this Article, the dispute may be submitted only to the International Court of Justice, unless the parties agree otherwise.

Article 16.   Signature

* * *

Article 17.   Ratification, Acceptance, Approval and Accession

* * *

Article 18.   Entry into Force

* * *

Article 19.   Withdrawal

* * *

Article 20.   Authentic Texts

* * *

APPENDICES

APPENDIX I[e]

LIST OF ACTIVITIES

1. Crude oil refineries (excluding undertakings manufacturing only lubricants from crude oil) and installations for the gasification and liquefaction of 500 tonnes or more of coal or bituminous shale per day.

2. Thermal power stations and other combustion installations with a heat output of 300 megawatts or more and nuclear power stations and other nuclear reactors (except research installations for the production and conversion of fissionable and fertile materials, whose maximum power does not exceed 1 kilowatt continuous thermal load).

3. Installations solely designed for the production or enrichment of nuclear fuels, for the reprocessing of irradiated nuclear fuels or for the storage, disposal and processing of radioactive waste.

4. Major installations for the initial smelting of cast-iron and steel and for the production of non-ferrous metals.

5. Installations for the extraction of asbestos and for the processing and transformation of asbestos and products containing asbestos: for asbestos-cement products, with an annual production of more than 20,000 tonnes finished product; for friction material, with an annual production of more than 50 tonnes finished product; and for other asbestos utilization of more than 200 tonnes per year.

6. Integrated chemical installations.

7. Construction of motorways, express roads[1] and lines for long-distance railway traffic and of airports with a basic runway length of 2,100 metres or more.

8. Large-diameter oil and gas pipelines.

9. Trading ports and also inland waterways and ports for inland-waterway traffic which permit the passage of vessels of over 1,350 tonnes.

10. Waste-disposal installations for the incineration, chemical treatment or land-fill of toxic and dangerous wastes.

11. Large dams and reservoirs.

12. Groundwater abstraction activities in cases where the annual volume of water to be abstracted amounts to 10 million cubic metres or more.

13. Pulp and paper manufacturing of 200 air-dried metric tonnes or more per day.

14. Major mining, on-site extraction and processing of metal ores or coal.

15. Offshore hydrocarbon production.

e. On 4 June 2004, the parties to the Convention adopted an amended Appendix I. The amendment is not in force as of this writing, and the text reproduced here is the original unamended text of Appendix I.

1. For the purposes of this Convention:

— "Motorway" means a road specially designed and built for motor traffic, which does not serve properties bordering on it, and which:

(a) Is provided, except at special points or temporarily, with separate carriageways for the two directions of traffic, separated from each other by a dividing strip not intended for traffic or, exceptionally, by other means;

(b) Does not cross at level with any road, railway or tramway track, or footpath; and

(c) Is specially sign-posted as a motorway.

— "Express road" means a road reserved for motor traffic accessible only from interchanges or controlled junctions and on which, in particular, stopping and parking are prohibited on the running carriageway(s).

16. Major storage facilities for petroleum, petrochemical and chemical products.

17. Deforestation of large areas.

APPENDIX II
CONTENT OF THE ENVIRONMENTAL IMPACT ASSESSMENT DOCUMENTATION

* * *

APPENDIX III
GENERAL CRITERIA TO ASSIST IN THE DETERMINATION OF THE ENVIRONMENTAL SIGNIFICANCE OF ACTIVITIES NOT LISTED IN APPENDIX I

1. In considering proposed activities to which Article 2, paragraph 5, applies, the concerned Parties may consider whether the activity is likely to have a significant adverse transboundary impact in particular by virtue of one or more of the following criteria:

(a) Size: proposed activities which are large for the type of the activity;

(b) Location: proposed activities which are located in or close to an area of special environmental sensitivity or importance (such as wetlands designated under the Ramsar Convention, national parks, nature reserves, sites of special scientific interest, or sites of archaeological, cultural or historical importance); also, proposed activities in locations where the characteristics of proposed development would be likely to have significant effects on the population;

(c) Effects: proposed activities with particularly complex and potentially adverse effects, including those giving rise to serious effects on humans or on valued species or organisms, those which threaten the existing or potential use of an affected area and those causing additional loading which cannot be sustained by the carrying capacity of the environment.

2. The concerned Parties shall consider for this purpose proposed activities which are located close to an international frontier as well as more remote proposed activities which could give rise to significant transboundary effects far removed from the site of development.

APPENDIX IV
INQUIRY PROCEDURE

* * *

APPENDIX V
POST–PROJECT ANALYSIS

* * *

APPENDIX VI
ELEMENTS FOR BILATERAL AND MULTILATERAL CO–OPERATION

* * *

APPENDIX VII
ARBITRATION

* * *

1.27 RIO DECLARATION ON ENVIRONMENT AND DEVELOPMENT. Adopted by the U.N. Conference on Environment and Development (UNCED) at Rio de Janeiro, 13 June 1992. UN Doc A/CONF.151/26 (vol. I) (1992); *reprinted in* 31 ILM 874 (1992) & 5 Weston & Carlson V.B.16

The United Nations Conference on Environment and Development,

Having met at Rio de Janeiro from 3 to 14 June 1992,

Reaffirming the Declaration of the United Nations Conference on the Human Environment, adopted at Stockholm on 16 June 1972, and seeking to build upon it,

With the goal of establishing a new and equitable global partnership through the creation of new levels of cooperation among States, key sectors of societies and people,

Working towards international agreements which respect the interests of all and protect the integrity of the global environmental and developmental system,

Recognizing the integral and interdependent nature of the Earth, our home,

Proclaims that:

Principle 1

Human beings are at the centre of concerns for sustainable development. They are entitled to a healthy and productive life in harmony with nature.

Principle 2

States have, in accordance with the Charter of the United Nations and the principles of international law, the sovereign right to exploit their own resources pursuant to their own environmental and developmental policies, and the responsibility to ensure that activities within their jurisdiction or control do not cause damage to the environment of other States or of areas beyond the limits of national jurisdiction.

Principle 3

The right to development must be fulfilled so as to equitably meet developmental and environmental needs of present and future generations.

Principle 4

In order to achieve sustainable development, environmental protection shall constitute an integral part of the development process and cannot be considered in isolation from it.

Principle 5

All States and all people shall cooperate in the essential task of eradicating poverty as an indispensable requirement for sustainable development, in order to decrease the disparities in standards of living and better meet the needs of the majority of the people of the world.

Principle 6

The special situation and needs of developing countries, particularly the least developed and those most environmentally vulnerable, shall be given special priority. International actions in the field of environment and development should also address the interests and needs of all countries.

Principle 7

States shall cooperate in a spirit of global partnership to conserve, protect and restore the health and integrity of the Earth's ecosystem. In view of the different contributions to global environmental degradation, States have common but differentiated responsibilities. The developed countries acknowledge the responsibility that they bear in the international pursuit of sustainable development in view of the pressures their societies place on the global environment and of the technologies and financial resources they command.

Principle 8

To achieve sustainable development and a higher quality of life for all people, States should reduce and eliminate unsustainable patterns of production and consumption and promote appropriate demographic policies.

Principle 9

States should cooperate to strengthen endogenous capacity-building for sustainable development by improving scientific understanding through exchanges of scientific and technological knowledge, and by enhancing the development, adaptation, diffusion and transfer of technologies, including new and innovative technologies.

Principle 10

Environmental issues are best handled with the participation of all concerned citizens, at the relevant level. At the national level, each individual shall have appropriate access to information concerning the environment that is held by public authorities, including information on hazardous materials and activities in their communities, and the opportunity to participate in decision-making processes. States shall facilitate and encourage public awareness and participation by making information widely available. Effective access to judicial and administrative proceedings, including redress and remedy, shall be provided.

Principle 11

States shall enact effective environmental legislation. Environmental standards, management objectives and priorities should reflect the environmental and developmental context to which they apply. Standards applied by some countries may be inappropriate and of unwarranted economic and social cost to other countries, in particular developing countries.

Principle 12

States should cooperate to promote a supportive and open international economic system that would lead to economic growth and sustainable development in all countries, to better address the problems of environmental degradation. Trade policy measures for environmental purposes should not constitute a means of arbitrary or unjustifiable discrimination or a disguised restriction on international trade. Unilateral actions to deal with environmental challenges outside the jurisdiction of the importing country should be avoided. Environmental measures addressing transboundary or global environmental problems should, as far as possible, be based on an international consensus.

Principle 13

States shall develop national law regarding liability and compensation for the victims of pollution and other environmental damage. States shall also cooperate in an expeditious and more determined manner to develop further international law regarding liability and compensation for adverse effects of environmental damage caused by activities within their jurisdiction or control to areas beyond their jurisdiction.

Principle 14

States should effectively cooperate to discourage or prevent the relocation and transfer to other States of any activities and substances that cause severe environmental degradation or are found to be harmful to human health.

Principle 15

In order to protect the environment, the precautionary approach shall be widely applied by States according to their capabilities. Where there are threats of serious or irreversible damage, lack of full scientific certainty shall not be used as a reason for postponing cost-effective measures to prevent environmental degradation.

Principle 16

National authorities should endeavor to promote the internalization of environmental costs and the use of economic instruments, taking into account the approach that the polluter should, in principle, bear the cost of pollution, with due regard to the public interest and without distorting international trade and investment.

Principle 17

Environmental impact assessment, as a national instrument, shall be undertaken for proposed activities that are likely to have a significant adverse impact on the environment and are subject to a decision of a competent national authority.

Principle 18

States shall immediately notify other States of any natural disasters or other emergencies that are likely to produce sudden harmful effects on the environment of those States. Every effort shall be made by the international community to help States so afflicted.

Principle 19

States shall provide prior and timely notification and relevant information to potentially affected States on activities that may have a significant adverse transboundary environmental effect and shall consult with those States at an early stage and in good faith.

Principle 20

Women have a vital role in environmental management and development. Their full participation is therefore essential to achieve sustainable development.

Principle 21

The creativity, ideals and courage of the youth of the world should be mobilized to forge a global partnership in order to achieve sustainable development and ensure a better future for all.

Principle 22

Indigenous people and their communities and other local communities have a vital role in environmental management and development because of their knowledge and traditional practices. States should recognize and duly support their identity, culture and interests and enable their effective participation in the achievement of sustainable development.

Principle 23

The environment and natural resources of people under oppression, domination and occupation shall be protected.

Principle 24

Warfare is inherently destructive of sustainable development. States shall therefore respect international law providing protection for the environment in times of armed conflict and cooperate in its further development, as necessary.

Principle 25

Peace, development and environmental protection are interdependent and indivisible.

Principle 26

States shall resolve all their environmental disputes peacefully and by appropriate means in accordance with the Charter of the United Nations.

Principle 27

States and people shall cooperate in good faith and in a spirit of partnership in the fulfilment of the principles embodied in this Declaration and in the further development of international law in the field of sustainable development.

1.28 AGENDA **21. Approved by the U.N. Conference on Environment and Development (UNCED) at Rio de Janeiro, 13 June 1992. UN Doc A/CONF. 151/26 (vols. I, II, & III) (1992);** *reprinted in* **5 Weston V.B.17:** *Table of Contents & Chs. 5, 15, 17, 20, 33, 38.*

Agenda 21 was adopted by the U.N. Conference on Environment and Development (UNCED) at Rio de Janeiro, 13 June 1992. The complete text is too lengthy for publication in this volume. The following table of contents provides a summary of its provisions. The full text may be found in the above-cited source.

* * *

Chapter 5

DEMOGRAPHIC DYNAMICS AND SUSTAINABILITY

5.1.   This chapter contains the following programme areas:

(a) Developing and disseminating knowledge concerning the links between demographic trends and factors and sustainable development;

(b) Formulating integrated national policies for environment and development, taking into account demographic trends and factors;

(c) Implementing integrated, environment and development programmes at the local level, taking into account demographic trends and factors.

PROGRAMME AREAS

A.   *Developing and disseminating knowledge concerning the links between demographic trends and factors and sustainable development*

Basis for action

5.2.   Demographic trends and factors and sustainable development have a synergistic relationship.

5.3.   The growth of world population and production combined with unsustainable consumption patterns places increasingly severe stress on the life-supporting capacities of our planet. These interactive processes affect the use of land, water, air, energy and other resources. Rapidly growing cities, unless well-managed, face major environmental problems. The increase in both the number and size of cities calls for greater attention to issues of local government and municipal management. The human dimensions are key elements to consider in this intricate set of relationships and they should be adequately taken into consideration in comprehensive policies for sustainable development. Such policies should address the linkages of demographic trends and factors, resource use, appropriate technology dissemination, and development. Population policy should also recognize the role played by human beings in environmental and development concerns. There is a need to increase awareness of this issue among decision makers at all levels and to provide both better information on which to base national and international policies and a framework against which to interpret this information.

5.4.   There is a need to develop strategies to mitigate both the adverse impact on the environment of human activities and the adverse impact of environmental change on human populations. The world's population is expected to exceed 8 billion by the year 2020. Sixty per cent of the world's population already live in coastal areas, while 65 per cent of cities with populations above 2.5 million are located along the world coasts; several of them are already at or below the present sea level.

Objectives

5.5.   The following objectives should be achieved as soon as practicable:

(a) To incorporate demographic trends and factors in the global analysis of environment and development issues;

(b) To develop a better understanding of the relationships among demographic dynamics, technology, cultural behaviour, natural resources and life support systems;

(c) To assess human vulnerability in ecologically sensitive areas and centres of population to determine the priorities for action at all levels, taking full account of community defined needs.

Activities

Research on the interaction between demographic trends and factors and sustainable development

* * *

B. *Formulating integrated national policies for environment and development, taking into account demographic trends and factors*

Basis for action

5.16.　Existing plans for sustainable development have generally recognized demographic trends and factors as elements that have a critical influence on consumption patterns, production, lifestyles and long-term sustainability. But in future, more attention will have to be given to these issues in general policy formulation and the design of development plans. To do this, all countries will have to improve their own capacities to assess the environment and development implications of their demographic trends and factors. They will also need to formulate and implement policies and action programmes where appropriate. Policies should be designed to address the consequences of population growth built into population momentum, while at the same time incorporating measures to bring about demographic transition. They should combine environmental concerns and population issues within a holistic view of development whose primary goals include the alleviation of poverty; secure livelihoods; good health; quality of life; improvement of the status and income of women and their access to schooling and professional training, as well as fulfilment of their personal aspirations; and empowerment of individuals and communities. Recognizing that large increases in the size and number of cities will occur in developing countries under any likely population scenario, greater attention should be given to preparing for the needs, in particular of women and children, for improved municipal management and local government.

Objective

5.17.　Full integration of population concerns into national planning, policy and decision-making processes should continue. Population policies and programmes should be considered, with full recognition of women's rights.

Activities

5.18.　Governments and other relevant actors could, *inter alia,* undertake the following activities, with appropriate assistance from aid agencies, and report on their status of implementation to the International Conference on Population and Development to be held in 1994, especially to its committee on population and environment.

(a) *Assessing the implications of national demographic trends and factors*

5.19.　The relationships between demographic trends and factors and environmental change and between environmental degradation and the components of demographic change should be analysed.

5.20.　Research should be conducted on how environmental factors interact with socio-economic factors as a cause of migration.

5.21.　Vulnerable population groups (such as rural landless workers, ethnic minorities, refugees, migrants, displaced people, women heads of household) whose changes in demographic structure may have specific impacts on sustainable development should be identified.

5.22. An assessment should be made of the implications of the age structure of the population on resource demand and dependency burdens, ranging from educational expenses for the young to health care and support for the elderly, and on household income generation.

5.23. An assessment should also be made of national population carrying capacity in the context of satisfaction of human needs and sustainable development, and special attention should be given to critical resources, such as water and land, and environmental factors, such as ecosystem health and biodiversity.

5.24. The impact of national demographic trends and factors on the traditional livelihoods of indigenous groups and local communities, including changes in traditional land use because of internal population pressures, should be studied.

(b) *Building and strengthening a national information base*

* * *

(c) *Incorporating demographic features into policies and plans*

* * *

5.31. National population policy goals and programmes that are consistent with national environment and development plans for sustainability and in keeping with the freedom, dignity and personally held values of individuals should be established and implemented.

* * *

Means of implementation

(a) *Financing and cost evaluation*

5.36. The Conference secretariat has estimated the average total annual cost (1993–2000) of implementing the activities of this programme to be about $90 million from the international community on grant or concessional terms. These are indicative and order-of-magnitude estimates only and have not been reviewed by Governments. Actual costs and financial terms, including any that are non-concessional, will depend upon, *inter alia,* the specific strategies and programmes Governments decide upon for implementation.

* * *

C. *Implementing integrated environment and development programmes at the local level, taking into account demographic trends and factors*

Basis for action

5.42. Population programmes are more effective when implemented together with appropriate cross-sectoral policies. To attain sustainability at the local level, a new framework is needed that integrates demographic trends and factors with such factors as ecosystem health, technology and human settlements, and with socio-economic structures and access to resources. Population programmes should be consistent with socio-economic and environmental planning. Integrated sustainable development programmes should closely correlate action on demographic trends and factors with resource management activities and development goals that meet the needs of the people concerned.

Objective

5.43. Population programmes should be implemented along with natural resource management and development programmes at the local level that will ensure sustainable use of natural resources, improve the quality of life of the people and enhance environmental quality.

Activities

5.44. Governments and local communities, including community-based women's organizations and national non-governmental organizations, consistent with national plans, objectives, strategies and priorities, could, *inter alia*, undertake the activities set out below with the assistance and cooperation of international organizations, as appropriate. Governments could share their experience in the implementation of Agenda 21 at the International Conference on Population and Development, to be held in 1994, especially its committee on population and environment.

(a) *Developing a framework for action*

* * *

(b) *Supporting programmes that promote changes in demographic trends and factors towards sustainability*

5.49. Reproductive health programmes and services, should, as appropriate, be developed and enhanced to reduce maternal and infant mortality from all causes and enable women and men to fulfil their personal aspirations in terms of family size, in a way in keeping with their freedom and dignity and personally held values.

5.50. Governments should take active steps to implement, as a matter of urgency, in accordance with country-specific conditions and legal systems, measures to ensure that women and men have the same right to decide freely and responsibly on the number and spacing of their children, to have access to the information, education and means, as appropriate, to enable them to exercise this right in keeping with their freedom, dignity and personally held values taking into account ethical and cultural considerations.

5.51. Governments should take active steps to implement programmes to establish and strengthen preventive and curative health facilities that include women-centred, women-managed, safe and effective reproductive health care and affordable, accessible services, as appropriate, for the responsible planning of family size, in keeping with freedom, dignity and personally held values and taking into account ethical and cultural considerations. Programmes should focus on providing comprehensive health care, including pre-natal care, education and information on health and responsible parenthood and should provide the opportunity for all women to breast-feed fully, at least during the first four months post-partum. Programmes should fully support women's productive and reproductive roles and well being, with special attention to the need for providing equal and improved health care for all children and the need to reduce the risk of maternal and child mortality and sickness.

5.52. Consistent with national priorities, culturally based information and education programmes that transmit reproductive health messages to men and women that are easily understood should be developed.

(c) *Creating appropriate institutional conditions*

5.53. Constituencies and institutional conditions to facilitate the implementation of demographic activities should, as appropriate, be fostered. This requires support and commitment from political, indigenous, religious and traditional authorities, the private sector and the national scientific community. In developing these appropriate institutional conditions, countries should closely involve established national machinery for women.

5.54. Population assistance should be coordinated with bilateral and multilateral donors to ensure that population needs and requirements of all developing countries are addressed, fully respecting the overall coordinating responsibility and the choice and strategies of the recipient countries.

* * *

Means of implementation

(a) *Financing and cost evaluation*

5.57. The Conference secretariat has estimated the average total annual cost (1993–2000) of implementing the activities of this programme to be about $7 billion, including about $3.5 billion from the international community on grant or concessional terms. These are indicative and order-of-magnitude estimates only and have not been reviewed by Governments. Actual costs and financial terms, including any that are non-concessional, will depend upon, *inter alia,* the specific strategies and programmes Governments decide upon for implementation.

* * *

Chapter 17

PROTECTION OF THE OCEANS, ALL KINDS OF SEAS, INCLUDING ENCLOSED AND SEMI–ENCLOSED AREAS, AND COASTAL AREAS AND THE PROTEC-TION, RATIONAL USE AND DEVELOPMENT OF THEIR LIVING RE-SOURCES

INTRODUCTION

17.1. The marine environment—including the oceans and all seas and adjacent coastal areas—forms an integrated whole that is an essential component of the global life-support system and a positive asset that presents opportunities for sustainable development. International law, as reflected in the provisions of the United Nations Convention on the Law of the Sea, referred to in this chapter of Agenda 21, sets forth rights and obligations of States and provides the international basis upon which to pursue the protection and sustainable development of the marine and coastal environ-ment and its resources. This requires new approaches to marine and coastal area management and development at the national, subregional, regional and global levels, approaches that are integrated in content and are precautionary and anticipatory in ambit, as reflected in the following programme areas:

(a) Integrated management and sustainable development of coastal areas, includ-ing exclusive economic zones;

(b) Marine environmental protection;

(c) Sustainable use and conservation of marine living resources of the high seas;

(d) Sustainable use and conservation of marine living resources under national jurisdiction;

(e) Addressing critical uncertainties for the management of the marine environ-ment and climate change;

(f) Strengthening international, including regional, cooperation and coordination;

(g) Sustainable development of small islands.

17.2. The implementation by developing countries of the activities set forth below shall be commensurate with their individual technological and financial capaci-ties and priorities in allocating resources for development needs and ultimately depends on the technology transfer and financial resources required and made avail-able to them.

PROGRAMME AREAS

A. *Integrated management and sustainable development of coastal and marine areas, including exclusive economic zones*

Basis for action

17.3. The coastal area contains diverse and productive habitats important for human settlements, development and local subsistence. More than half the world's population lives within 60 km of the shoreline, and this could rise to three quarters by the year 2020. Many of the world's poor are crowded in coastal areas. Coastal resources are vital for many local communities and indigenous people. The exclusive economic zone (EEZ) is also an important marine area where the States manage the development and conservation of natural resources for the benefit of their people. For small island States or countries, these are the areas most available for development activities.

17.4. Despite national, subregional, regional and global efforts, current approaches to the management of marine and coastal resources have not always proved capable of achieving sustainable development, and coastal resources and the coastal environment are being rapidly degraded and eroded in many parts of the world.

Objectives

17.5. Coastal States commit themselves to integrated management and sustainable development of coastal areas and the marine environment under their national jurisdiction. To this end, it is necessary to, *inter alia:*

(a) Provide for an integrated policy and decision-making process, including all involved sectors, to promote compatibility and a balance of uses;

(b) Identify existing and projected uses of coastal areas and their interactions;

(c) Concentrate on well-defined issues concerning coastal management;

(d) Apply preventive and precautionary approaches in project planning and implementation, including prior assessment and systematic observation of the impacts of major projects;

(e) Promote the development and application of methods, such as national resource and environmental accounting, that reflect changes in value resulting from uses of coastal and marine areas, including pollution, marine erosion, loss of resources and habitat destruction;

(f) Provide access, as far as possible, for concerned individuals, groups and organizations to relevant information and opportunities for consultation and participation in planning and decision-making at appropriate levels.

Activities

(a) *Management-related activities*

17.6. Each coastal State should consider establishing, or where necessary, strengthening, appropriate coordinating mechanisms (such as a high-level policy planning body) for integrated management and sustainable development of coastal and marine areas and their resources, at both the local and national levels....

* * *

17.7. Coastal States, with the support of international organizations, upon request, should undertake measures to maintain biological diversity and productivity of marine species and habitats under national jurisdiction. *Inter alia,* these measures might include: surveys of marine biodiversity, inventories of endangered species and critical coastal and marine habitats; establishment and management of protected areas; and support of scientific research and dissemination of its results.

(b) *Data and information*

17.8. Coastal States, where necessary, should improve their capacity to collect, analyse, assess and use information for sustainable use of resources, including environmental impacts of activities affecting the coastal and marine areas....

* * *

(c) *International and regional cooperation and coordination*

17.10. The role of international cooperation and coordination on a bilateral basis and, where applicable, within a subregional, interregional, regional or global framework, is to support and supplement national efforts of coastal States to promote integrated management and sustainable development of coastal and marine areas.

* * *

B. *Marine environmental protection*

Basis for action

17.18. Degradation of the marine environment can result from a wide range of sources. Land-based sources contribute 70 per cent of marine pollution, while maritime transport and dumping-at-sea activities contribute 10 per cent each. The contaminants that pose the greatest threat to the marine environment are, in variable order of importance and depending on differing national or regional situations, sewage, nutrients, synthetic organic compounds, sediments, litter and plastics, metals, radionucleides, oil/hydrocarbons and polycyclic aromatic hydrocarbons (PAHs). Many of the polluting substances originating from land-based sources are of particular concern to the marine environment since they exhibit at the same time toxicity, persistence and bioaccumulation in the food chain. There is currently no global scheme to address marine pollution from land-based sources.

17.19. Degradation of the marine environment can also result from a wide range of activities on land. Human settlements, land use, construction of coastal infrastructure, agriculture, forestry, urban development, tourism and industry can affect the marine environment. Coastal erosion and siltation are of particular concern.

17.20. Marine pollution is also caused by shipping and sea-based activities. Approximately 600,000 tons of oil enter the oceans each year as a result of normal shipping operations, accidents and illegal discharges. With respect to offshore oil and gas activities, currently machinery space discharges are regulated internationally and six regional conventions to control platform discharges have been under consideration. The nature and extent of environmental impacts from offshore oil exploration and production activities generally account for a very small proportion of marine pollution.

17.21. A precautionary and anticipatory rather than a reactive approach is necessary to prevent the degradation of the marine environment. This requires, *inter alia,* the adoption of precautionary measures, environmental impact assessments, clean production techniques, recycling, waste audits and minimization, construction and/or improvement of sewage treatment facilities, quality management criteria for the proper handling of hazardous substances, and a comprehensive approach to damaging impacts from air, land and water. Any management framework must include the improvement of coastal human settlements and the integrated management and development of coastal areas.

Objectives

17.22. States, in accordance with the provisions of the United Nations Convention on the Law of the Sea on protection and preservation of the marine environment, commit themselves, in accordance with their policies, priorities and resources, to prevent, reduce and control degradation of the marine environment so as to maintain and improve its life-support and productive capacities. To this end, it is necessary to:

(a) Apply preventive, precautionary and anticipatory approaches so as to avoid degradation of the marine environment, as well as to reduce the risk of long-term or irreversible adverse effects upon it;

(b) Ensure prior assessment of activities that may have significant adverse impacts upon the marine environment;

(c) Integrate protection of the marine environment into relevant general environmental, social and economic development policies;

(d) Develop economic incentives, where appropriate, to apply clean technologies and other means consistent with the internalization of environmental costs, such as the polluter pays principle, so as to avoid degradation of the marine environment;

(e) Improve the living standards of coastal populations, particularly in developing countries, so as to contribute to reducing the degradation of the coastal and marine environment.

17.23. States agree that provision of additional financial resources, through appropriate international mechanisms, as well as access to cleaner technologies and relevant research, would be necessary to support action by developing countries to implement this commitment.

Activities

(a) *Management-related activities*

Prevention, reduction and control of degradation of the marine environment from land-based activities

17.24. In carrying out their commitment to deal with degradation of the marine environment from land-based activities, States should take action at the national level and, where appropriate, at the regional and subregional levels, in concert with action to implement programme area A, and should take account of the Montreal Guidelines for the Protection of the Marine Environment from Land–Based Sources.

* * *

17.27. As concerns sewage, priority actions to be considered by States may include:

(a) Incorporating sewage concerns when formulating or reviewing coastal development plans, including human settlement plans;

(b) Building and maintaining sewage treatment facilities in accordance with national policies and capacities and international cooperation available;

(c) Locating coastal outfalls so as to maintain an acceptable level of environmental quality and to avoid exposing shell fisheries, water intakes and bathing areas to pathogens;

(d) Promoting environmentally sound co-treatments of domestic and compatible industrial effluents, with the introduction, where practicable, of controls on the entry of effluents that are not compatible with the system;

(e) Promoting primary treatment of municipal sewage discharged to rivers, estuaries and the sea, or other solutions appropriate to specific sites;

(f) Establishing and improving local, national, subregional and regional, as necessary, regulatory and monitoring programmes to control effluent discharge, using minimum sewage effluent guidelines and water quality criteria and giving due consideration to the characteristics of receiving bodies and the volume and type of pollutants.

17.28. As concerns other sources of pollution, priority actions to be considered by States may include:

(a) Establishing or improving, as necessary, regulatory and monitoring programmes to control effluent discharges and emissions, including the development and application of control and recycling technologies;

(b) Promoting risk and environmental impact assessments to help ensure an acceptable level of environmental quality;

(c) Promoting assessment and cooperation at the regional level, where appropriate, with respect to the input of point source pollutants from new installations;

(d) Eliminating the emission or discharge of organohalogen compounds that threaten to accumulate to dangerous levels in the marine environment;

(e) Reducing the emission or discharge of other synthetic organic compounds that threaten to accumulate to dangerous levels in the marine environment;

(f) Promoting controls over anthropogenic inputs of nitrogen and phosphorus that enter coastal waters where such problems as eutrophication threaten the marine environment or its resources;

(g) Cooperating with developing countries, through financial and technological support, to maximize the best practicable control and reduction of substances and wastes that are toxic, persistent or liable to bio-accumulate and to establish environmentally sound land-based waste disposal alternatives to sea dumping;

(h) Cooperating in the development and implementation of environmentally sound land-use techniques and practices to reduce run-off to water-courses and estuaries which would cause pollution or degradation of the marine environment;

(i) Promoting the use of environmentally less harmful pesticides and fertilizers and alternative methods for pest control, and considering the prohibition of those found to be environmentally unsound;

(j) Adopting new initiatives at national, subregional and regional levels for controlling the input of non-point source pollutants, which require broad changes in sewage and waste management, agricultural practices, mining, construction and transportation.

17.29. As concerns physical destruction of coastal and marine areas causing degradation of the marine environment, priority actions should include control and prevention of coastal erosion and siltation due to anthropogenic factors related to, *inter alia,* land-use and construction techniques and practices. Watershed management practices should be promoted so as to prevent, control and reduce degradation of the marine environment.

Prevention, reduction and control of degradation of the marine environment from sea-based activities

17.30. States, acting individually, bilaterally, regionally or multilaterally and within the framework of IMO and other relevant international organizations, whether subregional, regional or global, as appropriate, should assess the need for additional measures to address degradation of the marine environment:

(a) From shipping, by:

(i) Supporting wider ratification and implementation of relevant shipping conventions and protocols;

(ii) Facilitating the processes in (i), providing support to individual States upon request to help them overcome the obstacles identified by them;

(iii) Cooperating in monitoring marine pollution from ships, especially from illegal discharges (e.g., aerial surveillance), and enforcing MARPOL discharge, provisions more rigorously;

(iv) Assessing the state of pollution caused by ships in particularly sensitive areas identified by IMO and taking action to implement applicable measures, where necessary, within such areas to ensure compliance with generally accepted international regulations;

(v) Taking action to ensure respect of areas designated by coastal States, within their exclusive economic zones, consistent with international law, in order to protect and preserve rare or fragile ecosystems, such as coral reefs and mangroves;

(vi) Considering the adoption of appropriate rules on ballast water discharge to prevent the spread of non-indigenous organisms;

(vii) Promoting navigational safety by adequate charting of coasts and ship-routing, as appropriate;

(viii) Assessing the need for stricter international regulations to further reduce the risk of accidents and pollution from cargo ships (including bulk carriers);

(ix) Encouraging IMO and IAEA to work together to complete consideration of a code on the carriage of irradiated nuclear fuel in flasks on board ships;

(x) Revising and updating the IMO Code of Safety for Nuclear Merchant Ships and considering how best to implement a revised code;

(xi) Supporting the ongoing activity within IMO regarding development of appropriate measures for reducing air pollution from ships;

(xii) Supporting the ongoing activity within IMO regarding the development of an international regime governing the transportation of hazardous and noxious substances carried by ships and further considering whether the compensation funds similar to the ones established under the Fund Convention would be appropriate in respect of pollution damage caused by substances other than oil;

(b) From dumping, by:

(i) Supporting wider ratification, implementation and participation in relevant Conventions on dumping at sea, including early conclusion of a future strategy for the London Dumping Convention;

(ii) Encouraging the London Dumping Convention parties to take appropriate steps to stop ocean dumping and incineration of hazardous substances;

(c) From offshore oil and gas platforms, by assessing existing regulatory measures to address discharges, emissions and safety and assessing the need for additional measures;

(d) From ports, by facilitating establishment of port reception facilities for the collection of oily and chemical residues and garbage from ships, especially in MARPOL special areas, and promoting the establishment of smaller scale facilities in marinas and fishing harbours.

17.31. IMO and as appropriate, other competent United Nations organizations, when requested by the States concerned, should assess, where appropriate, the state of marine pollution in areas of congested shipping, such as heavily used international straits, with a view to ensuring compliance with generally accepted international regulations, particularly those related to illegal discharges from ships, in accordance with the provisions of Part III of the United Nations Convention on the Law of the Sea.

17.32. States should take measures to reduce water pollution caused by organotin compounds used in anti-fouling paints.

17.33. States should consider ratifying the Convention on Oil Pollution Preparedness, Response and Cooperation, which addresses, *inter alia,* the development of contingency plans on the national and international level, as appropriate, including provision of oil-spill response material and training of personnel, including its possible extension to chemical spill response.

17.34. States should intensify international cooperation to strengthen or establish, where necessary, regional oil/chemical-spill response centres and/or, as appropriate, mechanisms in cooperation with relevant subregional, regional or global intergovernmental organizations and, where appropriate, industry-based organizations.

* * *

C. *Sustainable use and conservation of marine living resources of the high seas*

Basis for action

17.44. Over the last decade, fisheries on the high seas have considerably expanded and currently represent approximately 5 per cent of total world landings. The provisions of the United Nations Convention on the Law of the Sea on the marine living resources of the high seas sets forth rights and obligations of States with respect to conservation and utilization of those resources.

17.45. However, management of high seas fisheries, including the adoption, monitoring and enforcement of effective conservation measures, is inadequate in many areas and some resources are overutilized. There are problems of unregulated fishing, overcapitalization, excessive fleet size, vessel reflagging to escape controls, insufficiently selective gear, unreliable databases and lack of sufficient cooperation between States. Action by States whose nationals and vessels fish on the high seas, as well as cooperation at the bilateral, subregional, regional and global levels, is essential particularly for highly migratory species and straddling stocks. Such action and cooperation should address inadequacies in fishing practices, as well as in biological knowledge, fisheries statistics and improvement of systems for handling data. Emphasis should also be on multi-species management and other approaches that take into account the relationships among species, especially in addressing depleted species, but also in identifying the potential of underutilized or unutilized populations.

Objectives

17.46. States commit themselves to the conservation and sustainable use of marine living resources on the high seas. To this end, it is necessary to:

(a) Develop and increase the potential of marine living resources to meet human nutritional needs, as well as social, economic and development goals;

(b) Maintain or restore populations of marine species at levels that can produce the maximum sustainable yield as qualified by relevant environmental and economic factors, taking into consideration relationships among species;

(c) Promote the development and use of selective fishing gear and practices that minimize waste in the catch of target species and minimize by-catch of non-target species;

(d) Ensure effective monitoring and enforcement with respect to fishing activities;

(e) Protect and restore endangered marine species;

(f) Preserve habitats and other ecologically sensitive areas;

(g) Promote scientific research with respect to the marine living resources in the high seas.

17.47. Nothing in paragraph 17.46 above restricts the right of a State or the competence of an international organization, as appropriate, to prohibit, limit or regulate the exploitation of marine mammals on the high seas more strictly than provided for in that paragraph. States shall cooperate with a view to the conservation of marine mammals and, in the case of cetaceans, shall in particular work through the appropriate international organizations for their conservation, management and study.

17.48. The ability of developing countries to fulfil the above objectives is dependent upon their capabilities, including the financial, scientific and technological means at their disposal. Adequate financial, scientific and technological cooperation should be provided to support action by them to implement these objectives.

Activities

A) Management-related Activities

17.49 States should take effective action, including bilateral and multilateral cooperation, where appropriate at the subregional, regional and global levels, to ensure that high seas fisheries are managed in accordance with the provisions of the United Nations Convention on the Law of the Sea. In particular, they should:

(a) Give full effect to these provisions with regard to fisheries populations whose ranges lie both within and beyond exclusive economic zones (straddling stocks);

(b) Give full effect to these provisions with regard to highly migratory species;

(c) Negotiate, where appropriate, international agreements for the effective management and conservation of fishery stocks;

(d) Define and identify appropriate management units;

* * *

17.51. States should ensure that fishing activities by vessels flying their flags on the high seas take place in a manner so as to minimize incidental catches.

17.52. States should take effective action consistent with international law to monitor and control fishing activities by vessels flying their flags on the high seas to ensure compliance with applicable conservation and management rules, including full, detailed, accurate and timely reporting of catches and effort.

* * *

17.55. States should fully implement General Assembly resolution 46/215 on large-scale pelagic drift-net fishing.

* * *

C) INTERNATIONAL AND REGIONAL COOPERATION AND COORDINATION

17.58. States, through bilateral and multilateral cooperation and within the framework of subregional and regional fisheries bodies, as appropriate, and with the support of other international intergovernmental agencies, should assess high seas resource potentials and develop profiles of all stocks (target and non-target).

17.59. States should, where and as appropriate, ensure adequate coordination and cooperation in enclosed and semi-enclosed seas and between subregional, regional and global intergovernmental fisheries bodies.

17.60. Effective cooperation within existing subregional, regional or global fisheries bodies should be encouraged. Where such organizations do not exist, States should, as appropriate, cooperate to establish such organizations.

17.61. States with an interest in a high seas fishery regulated by an existing subregional and/or regional high seas fisheries organization of which they are not members should be encouraged to join that organization, where appropriate.

* * *

Chapter 20

ENVIRONMENTALLY SOUND MANAGEMENT OF HAZARDOUS WASTES, INCLUDING PREVENTION OF ILLEGAL INTERNATIONAL TRAFFIC IN HAZARDOUS WASTES

INTRODUCTION

20.1. Effective control of the generation, storage, treatment, recycling and reuse, transport, recovery and disposal of hazardous wastes is of paramount importance for proper health, environmental protection and natural resource management, and sustainable development. This will require the active cooperation and participation of the international community, Governments and industry. Industry, as referred to in this paper, shall include large industrial enterprises, including transnational corporations and domestic industry.

20.2. Prevention of the generation of hazardous wastes and the rehabilitation of contaminated sites are the key elements, and both require knowledge, experienced people, facilities, financial resources and technical and scientific capacities.

20.3. The activities outlined in the present chapter are very closely related to, and have implications for, many of the programme areas described in other chapters, so that an overall integrated approach to hazardous waste management is necessary.

20.4. There is international concern that part of the international movement of hazardous wastes is being carried out in contravention of existing national legislation and international instruments to the detriment of the environment and public health of all countries, particularly developing countries.

20.5. In section I of resolution 44/226 of 22 December 1989, the General Assembly requested each regional commission, within existing resources, to contribute to the prevention of the illegal traffic in toxic and dangerous products and wastes by monitoring and making regional assessments of that illegal traffic and its environmental and health implications. The Assembly also requested the regional commissions to interact among themselves and cooperate with the United Nations Environment Programme (UNEP), with a view to maintaining efficient and coordinated monitoring and assessment of the illegal traffic in toxic and dangerous products and wastes.

Overall objective

20.6. Within the framework of integrated life-cycle management, the overall objective is to prevent to the extent possible, and minimize, the generation of hazardous wastes, as well as to manage those wastes in such a way that they do not cause harm to health and the environment.

Overall targets

20.7. The overall targets are:

(a) Preventing or minimizing the generation of hazardous wastes as part of an overall integrated cleaner production approach; eliminating or reducing to a minimum transboundary movements of hazardous wastes, consistent with the environmentally sound and efficient management of those wastes; and ensuring that environmentally sound hazardous waste management options are pursued to the maximum extent possible within the country of origin (the self-sufficiency principle). The transboundary movements that take place should be on environmental and economic grounds and based upon agreements between the States concerned;

(b) Ratification of the Basel Convention on the Control of Transboundary Movements of Hazardous Wastes and their Disposal and the expeditious elaboration of related protocols, such as the protocol on liability and compensation, mechanisms and guidelines to facilitate the implementation of the Basel Convention;

(c) Ratification and full implementation by the countries concerned of the Bamako Convention on the Ban on the Import into Africa and the Control of Transboundary Movement of Hazardous Wastes within Africa and the expeditious elaboration of a protocol on liability and compensation;

(d) Elimination of the export of hazardous wastes to countries that, individually or through international agreements, prohibits the import of such wastes, such as, the contracting parties to the Bamako Convention, the fourth Lomé Convention or other relevant conventions, where such prohibition is provided for.

20.8.   The following programme areas are included in this chapter:

(a) Promoting the prevention and minimization of hazardous waste;

(b) Promoting and strengthening institutional capacities in hazardous waste management;

(c) Promoting and strengthening international cooperation in the management of transboundary movements of hazardous wastes;

(d) Preventing illegal international traffic in hazardous wastes.

PROGRAMME AREAS

A.   *Promoting the prevention and minimization of hazardous waste*

Basis for action

20.9.   Human health and environmental quality are undergoing continuous degradation by the increasing amount of hazardous wastes being produced. There are increasing direct and indirect costs to society and to individual citizens in connection with the generation, handling and disposal of such wastes. It is therefore crucial to enhance knowledge and information on the economics of prevention and management of hazardous wastes, including the impact in relation to the employment and environmental benefits, in order to ensure that the necessary capital investment is made available in development programmes through economic incentives. One of the first priorities in hazardous waste management is minimization, as part of a broader approach to changing industrial processes and consumer patterns through pollution prevention and cleaner production strategies.

20.10.   Among the most important factors in these strategies is the recovery of hazardous wastes and their transformation into useful material. Technology application, modification and development of new low-waste technologies are therefore currently a central focus of hazardous waste minimization.

Objectives

20.11.   The objectives of this programme area are:

(a) To reduce the generation of hazardous wastes, to the extent feasible, as part of an integrated cleaner production approach;

(b) To optimize the use of materials by utilizing, where practicable and environmentally sound, the residues from production processes;

(c) To enhance knowledge and information on the economics of prevention and management of hazardous wastes.

20.12. To achieve those objectives, and thereby reduce the impact and cost of industrial development, countries that can afford to adopt the requisite technologies without detriment to their development should establish policies that include:

(a) Integration of cleaner production approaches and hazardous waste minimization in all planning, and the adoption of specific goals;

(b) Promotion of the use of regulatory and market mechanisms;

(c) Establishment of an intermediate goal for the stabilization of the quantity of hazardous waste generated;

(d) Establishment of long-term programmes and policies including targets where appropriate for reducing the amount of hazardous waste produced per unit of manufacture;

(e) Achievement of a qualitative improvement of waste streams, mainly through activities aimed at reducing their hazardous characteristics;

(f) Facilitation of the establishment of cost-effective policies and approaches to hazardous waste prevention and management, taking into consideration the state of development of each country.

Activities

(a) *Management-related activities*

* * *

(k) Governments should establish regulations that lay down the ultimate responsibility of industries for environmentally sound disposal of the hazardous wastes their activities generate.

(b) *Data and information*

20.14. The following activities should be undertaken:

* * *

(f) Governments should encourage industries to be transparent in their operations and provide relevant information to the communities that might be affected by the generation, management and disposal of hazardous wastes.

(c) *International and regional cooperation and coordination*

20.15. International/regional cooperation should encourage the ratification by States of the Basel and Bamako Conventions and promote the implementation of those Conventions. Regional cooperation will be necessary for the development of similar conventions in regions other than Africa, if so required. In addition there is a need for effective coordination of international regional and national policies and instruments. Another activity proposed is cooperating in monitoring the effects of the management of hazardous wastes.

* * *

B. *Promoting and strengthening institutional capacities in hazardous waste management*

Basis for action

20.20. Many countries lack the national capacity to handle and manage hazardous wastes. This is primarily due to inadequate infrastructure, deficiencies in regulatory frameworks, insufficient education and training programmes and lack of coordination between the different ministries and institutions involved in various aspects of waste management. In addition, there is a lack of knowledge about environmental contamination and pollution and the associated health risk from the exposure of populations, especially women and children, and ecosystems to hazardous wastes; assessment of risks; and the characteristics of wastes. Steps need to be taken immediately to identify populations at high risk and to take remedial measures, where necessary. One of the main priorities in ensuring environmentally sound management of hazardous wastes is to provide awareness, education and training programmes covering all levels of society. There is also a need to undertake research programmes to understand the nature of hazardous wastes, to identify their potential environmental effects and to develop technologies to safely handle those wastes. Finally, there is a need to strengthen the capacities of institutions that are responsible for the management of hazardous wastes.

Objectives

20.21.   The objectives in this programme area are:

(a) To adopt appropriate coordinating, legislative and regulatory measures at the national level for the environmentally sound management of hazardous wastes, including the implementation of international and regional conventions;

(b) To establish public awareness and information programmes on hazardous waste issues and to ensure that basic education and training programmes are provided for industry and government workers in all countries;

(c) To establish comprehensive research programmes on hazardous wastes in countries;

(d) To strengthen service industries to enable them to handle hazardous wastes, and to build up international networking;

(e) To develop endogenous capacities in all developing countries to educate and train staff at all levels in environmentally sound hazardous waste handling and monitoring and in environmentally sound management;

(f) To promote human exposure assessment with respect to hazardous waste sites and identify the remedial measures required;

(g) To facilitate the assessment of impacts and risks of hazardous wastes on human health and the environment by establishing appropriate procedures, methodologies, criteria and/or effluent-related guidelines and standards;

(h) To improve knowledge regarding the effects of hazardous wastes on human health and the environment;

(i) To make information available to Governments and to the general public on the effects of hazardous wastes, including infectious wastes, on human health and the environment.

* * *

C.   *Promoting and strengthening international cooperation in the management of transboundary movements of hazardous wastes*

Basis for action

20.32.   In order to promote and strengthen international cooperation in the management, including control and monitoring, of transboundary movements of hazardous wastes, a precautionary approach should be applied. There is a need to harmonize the procedures and criteria used in various international and legal instruments. There is also a need to develop or harmonize existing criteria for identifying wastes dangerous to the environment and to build monitoring capacities.

Objectives

20.33. The objectives of this programme area are:

(a) To facilitate and strengthen international cooperation in the environmentally sound management of hazardous wastes, including control and monitoring of transboundary movements of such wastes, including wastes for recovery, by using internationally adopted criteria to identify and classify hazardous wastes and to harmonize relevant international legal instruments;

(b) To adopt a ban on or prohibit, as appropriate, the export of hazardous wastes to countries that do not have the capacity to deal with those wastes in an environmentally sound way or that have banned the import of such wastes;

(c) To promote the development of control procedures for the transboundary movement of hazardous wastes destined for recovery operations under the Basel Convention that encourage environmentally and economically sound recycling options.

Activities

(a) *Management-related activities*

Strengthening and harmonizing criteria and regulations

20.34. Governments, according to their capacities and available resources and with the cooperation of [the] United Nations and other relevant organizations, as appropriate, should:

(a) Incorporate the notification procedure called for in the Basel Convention and relevant regional conventions, as well as in their annexes, into national legislation;

(b) Formulate, where appropriate, regional agreements such as the Bamako Convention regulating the transboundary movement of hazardous wastes;

(c) Help promote the compatibility and complementarity of such regional agreements with international conventions and protocols;

(d) Strengthen national and regional capacities and capabilities to monitor and control the transboundary movement of hazardous wastes;

(e) Promote the development of clear criteria and guidelines, within the framework of the Basel Convention and regional conventions, as appropriate, for environmentally and economically sound operation in resource recovery, recycling reclamation, direct use or alternative uses and for determination of acceptable recovery practices, including recovery levels where feasible and appropriate, with a view to preventing abuses and false presentation in the above operations;

(f) Consider setting up, at national and regional levels, as appropriate, systems for monitoring and surveillance of the transboundary movements of hazardous wastes;

(g) Develop guidelines for the assessment of environmentally sound treatment of hazardous wastes;

(h) Develop guidelines for the identification of hazardous wastes at the national level, taking into account existing internationally—and, where appropriate, regionally—agreed criteria and prepare a list of hazard profiles for the hazardous wastes listed in national legislation;

(i) Develop and use appropriate methods for testing, characterizing and classifying hazardous wastes and adopt or adapt safety standards and principles for managing hazardous wastes in an environmentally sound way.

Implementing existing agreements

20.35. Governments are urged to ratify the Basel Convention and the Bamako Convention, as applicable, and to pursue the expeditious elaboration of related protocols, such as protocols on liability and compensation, and of mechanisms and guidelines to facilitate the implementation of the Conventions.

Means of implementation

(a) *Financing and cost evaluation*

20.36. Because this programme area covers a relatively new field of operation and because of the lack so far of adequate studies on costing of activities under this programme, no cost estimate is available at present. However, the costs for some of the activities related to capacity-building that are presented under this programme could be considered to have been covered under the costing of programme area B above.

20.37. The interim secretariat for the Basel Convention should undertake studies in order to arrive at a reasonable cost estimate for activities to be undertaken initially until the year 2000.

(b) *Capacity-building*

20.38. Governments, according to their capacities and available resources and with the cooperation of [the] United Nations and other relevant organizations, as appropriate, should:

(a) Elaborate or adopt policies for the environmentally sound management of hazardous wastes, taking into account existing international instruments;

(b) Make recommendations to the appropriate forums or establish or adapt norms, including the equitable implementation of the polluter pays principle, and regulatory measures to comply with obligations and principles of the Basel Convention, the Bamako Convention and other relevant existing or future agreements, including protocols, as appropriate, for setting appropriate rules and procedures in the field of liability and compensation for damage resulting from the transboundary movement and disposal of hazardous wastes;

(c) Implement policies for the implementation of a ban or prohibition, as appropriate, of exports of hazardous wastes to countries that do not have the capacity to deal with those wastes in an environmentally sound way or that have banned the import of such wastes;

(d) Study, in the context of the Basel Convention and relevant regional conventions, the feasibility of providing temporary financial assistance in the case of an emergency situation, in order to minimize damage from accidents arising from transboundary movements of hazardous wastes or during the disposal of those wastes.

D. *Preventing illegal international traffic in hazardous wastes*

Basis for action

20.39. The prevention of illegal traffic in hazardous wastes will benefit the environment and public health in all countries, particularly developing countries. It will also help to make the Basel Convention and regional international instruments, such as the Bamako Convention and the fourth Lomé Convention, more effective by promoting compliance with the controls established in those agreements. Article IX of the Basel Convention specifically addresses the issue of illegal shipments of hazardous wastes. Illegal traffic of hazardous wastes may cause serious threats to human health and the environment and impose a special and abnormal burden on the countries that receive such shipments.

20.40. Effective prevention requires action through effective monitoring and the enforcement and imposition of appropriate penalties.

Objectives

20.41. The objectives of this programme area are:

(a) To reinforce national capacities to detect and halt any illegal attempt to introduce hazardous wastes into the territory of any State in contravention of national legislation and relevant international legal instruments;

(b) To assist all countries, particularly developing countries, in obtaining all appropriate information concerning illegal traffic in hazardous wastes;

(c) To cooperate, within the framework of the Basel Convention, in assisting countries that suffer the consequences of illegal traffic.

Activities

(a) *Management-related activities*

20.42. Governments, according to their capacities and available resources and with the cooperation of the United Nations and other relevant organizations, as appropriate, should:

(a) Adopt, where necessary, and implement legislation to prevent the illegal import and export of hazardous wastes;

(b) Develop appropriate national enforcement programmes to monitor compliance with such legislation, detect and deter violations through appropriate penalties and give special attention to those who are known to have conducted illegal traffic in hazardous wastes and to hazardous wastes that are particularly susceptible to illegal traffic.

(b) *Data and information*

20.43. Governments should develop as appropriate, an information network and alert system to assist in detecting illegal traffic in hazardous wastes. Local communities and others could be involved in the operation of such a network and system.

20.44. Governments should cooperate in the exchange of information on illegal transboundary movements of hazardous wastes and should make such information available to appropriate United Nations bodies such as UNEP and the regional commissions.

(c) *International and regional cooperation*

20.45. The regional commissions, in cooperation with and relying upon expert support and advice from UNEP and other relevant bodies of the United Nations system, taking full account of the Basel Convention, shall continue to monitor and assess the illegal traffic in hazardous wastes, including its environmental, economic and health implications, on a continuing basis, drawing upon the results and experience gained in the joint UNEP/ESCAP preliminary assessment of illegal traffic.

20.46. Countries and international organizations, as appropriate, should cooperate to strengthen the institutional and regulatory capacities, in particular of developing countries, in order to prevent the illegal import and export of hazardous wastes.

* * *

SECTION IV. MEANS OF IMPLEMENTATION

Chapter 33

FINANCIAL RESOURCES AND MECHANISMS

INTRODUCTION

33.1. The General Assembly, in resolution 44/228 of 22 December 1989, *inter alia,* decided that the United Nations Conference on Environment and Development should:

Identify ways and means of providing new and additional financial resources, particularly to developing countries, for environmentally sound development programmes and projects in accordance with national development objectives, priorities and plans and to consider ways of effectively monitoring the provision of such new and additional financial resources, particularly to developing countries, so as to enable the international community to take further appropriate action on the basis of accurate and reliable data;

Identify ways and means of providing additional financial resources for measures directed towards solving major environmental problems of global concern and especially of supporting those countries, in particular developing countries, for which the implementation of such measures would entail a special or abnormal burden, owing, in particular, to their lack of financial resources, expertise or technical capacity;

Consider various funding mechanisms, including voluntary ones, and examine the possibility of a special international fund and other innovative approaches, with a view to ensuring, on a favourable basis, the most effective and expeditious transfer of environmentally sound technologies to developing countries;

Quantify the financial requirements for the successful implementation of Conference decisions and recommendations and identify possible sources, including innovative ones, of additional resources.

33.2.   This chapter deals with the financing of the implementation of Agenda 21, which reflects a global consensus integrating environmental considerations into an accelerated development process. For each of the other chapters, the secretariat of the Conference has provided indicative estimates of the total costs of implementation for developing countries and the requirements for grant or other concessional financing needed from the international community. These reflect the need for a substantially increased effort, both by countries themselves and by the international community.

BASIS FOR ACTION

33.3.   Economic growth, social development and poverty eradication are the first and overriding priorities in developing countries and are themselves essential to meeting national and global sustainability objectives. In the light of the global benefits to be realized by the implementation of Agenda 21 as a whole, the provision to developing countries of effective means, *inter alia,* financial resources and technology, without which it will be difficult for them to fully implement their commitments, will serve the common interests of developed and developing countries and of humankind in general, including future generations.

33.4.   The cost of inaction could outweigh the financial costs of implementing Agenda 21. Inaction will narrow the choices of future generations.

33.5.   For dealing with environmental issues, special efforts will be required. Global and local environmental issues are interrelated. The United Nations Framework Convention on Climate Change and the Convention on Biological Diversity address two of the most important global issues.

33.6.   Economic conditions, both domestic and international, that encourage free trade and access to markets will help make economic growth and environmental protection mutually supportive for all countries, particularly for developing countries and countries undergoing the process of transition to a market economy (see chapter 2 for a fuller discussion of these issues).

* * *

33.10.   The implementation of the huge sustainable development programmes of Agenda 21 will require the provision to developing countries of substantial new and additional financial resources. Grant or concessional financing should be provided according to sound and equitable criteria and indicators. The progressive implementation of Agenda 21 should be matched by the provision of such necessary financial resources. The initial phase will be accelerated by substantial early commitments of concessional funding.

OBJECTIVES

33.11. The objectives are as follows:

(a) To establish measures concerning financial resources and mechanisms for the implementation of Agenda 21;

(b) To provide new and additional financial resources that are both adequate and predictable;

(c) To seek full use and continuing qualitative improvement of funding mechanisms to be utilized for the implementation of Agenda 21.

ACTIVITIES

33.12. Fundamentally, the activities of this chapter are related to the implementation of all the other chapters of Agenda 21.

MEANS OF IMPLEMENTATION

33.13. In general, the financing for the implementation of Agenda 21 will come from a country's own public and private sectors. For developing countries, particularly the least developed countries, ODA [Official Development Assistance] is a main source of external funding, and substantial new and additional funding for sustainable development and implementation of Agenda 21 will be required. Developed countries reaffirm their commitments to reach the accepted United Nations target of 0.7 per cent of GNP for ODA and, to the extent that they have not yet achieved that target, agree to augment their aid programmes in order to reach that target as soon as possible and to ensure prompt and effective implementation of Agenda 21. Some countries have agreed to reach the target by the year 2000. It was decided that the Commission on Sustainable Development would regularly review and monitor progress towards this target. This review process should systematically combine the monitoring of the implementation of Agenda 21 with a review of the financial resources available. Those countries that have already reached the target are to be commended and encouraged to continue to contribute to the common effort to make available the substantial additional resources that have to be mobilized. Other developed countries, in line with their support for reform efforts in developing countries, agree to make their best efforts to increase their level of ODA. In this context, the importance of equitable burden-sharing among developed countries is recognized. Other countries, including those undergoing the process of transition to a market economy, may voluntarily augment the contributions of the developed countries.

33.14. Funding for Agenda 21 and other outcomes of the Conference should be provided in a way that maximizes the availability of new and additional resources and uses all available funding sources and mechanisms. These include, among others:

(a) The multilateral development banks and funds:

(i) *The International Development Association (IDA)*. Among the various issues and options that IDA deputies will examine in connection with the forthcoming tenth replenishment of IDA, the statement made by the President of the World Bank at the United Nations Conference on Environment and Development should be given special consideration in order to help the poorest countries meet their sustainable development objectives as contained in Agenda 21;

(ii) *Regional and subregional development banks.* The regional and subregional development banks and funds should play an increased and more effective role in providing resources on concessional or other favourable terms needed to implement Agenda 21;

(iii) *The Global Environment Facility,* managed jointly by the World Bank, UNDP and UNEP, whose additional grant and concessional funding is designed to achieve global environmental benefits, should cover the agreed incremental costs of relevant activities under Agenda 21, in particular for developing countries. Therefore, it should be restructured so as to, *inter alia:*

Encourage universal participation;

Have sufficient flexibility to expand its scope and coverage to relevant programme areas of Agenda 21, with global environmental benefits, as agreed;

Ensure a governance that is transparent and democratic in nature, including in terms of decision-making and operations, by guaranteeing a balanced and equitable representation of the interests of developing countries and giving due weight to the funding efforts of donor countries;

Ensure new and additional financial resources on grant and concessional terms, in particular to developing countries;

Ensure predictability in the flow of funds by contributions from developed countries, taking into account the importance of equitable burden-sharing;

Ensure access to and disbursement of the funds under mutually agreed criteria without introducing new forms of conditionality;

(b) *The relevant specialized agencies, other United Nations bodies and other international organizations,* which have designated roles to play in supporting national Governments in implementing Agenda 21;

(c) *Multilateral institutions for capacity-building and technical cooperation.* Necessary financial resources should be provided to UNDP to use its network of field offices and its broad mandate and experience in the field of technical cooperation for facilitating capacity-building at the country level, making full use of the expertise of the specialized agencies and other United Nations bodies within their respective areas of competence, in particular UNEP and including the multilateral and regional development banks;

(d) *Bilateral assistance programmes.* These programmes will need to be strengthened in order to promote sustainable development;

(e) *Debt relief.* It is important to achieve durable solutions to the debt problems of low-and middle-income developing countries in order to provide them with the needed means for sustainable development. Measures to address the continuing debt problems of low- and middle-income countries should be kept under review. All creditors in the Paris Club should promptly implement the agreement of December 1991 to provide debt relief for the poorest heavily indebted countries pursuing structural adjustment; debt relief measures should be kept under review so as to address the continuing difficulties of those countries;

(f) *Private funding.* Voluntary contributions through non-governmental channels, which have been running at about 10 per cent of ODA, might be increased.

33.15. *Investment.* Mobilization of higher levels of foreign direct investment and technology transfers should be encouraged through national policies that promote investment and through joint ventures and other modalities.

33.16. *Innovative financing.* New ways of generating new public and private financial resources should be explored, in particular:

(a) Various forms of debt relief, apart from official or Paris Club debt, including greater use of debt swaps;

(b) The use of economic and fiscal incentives and mechanisms;

(c) The feasibility of tradeable permits;

(d) New schemes for fund-raising and voluntary contributions through private channels, including non-governmental organizations;

(e) The reallocation of resources at present committed to military purposes.

33.17. A supportive international and domestic economic climate conducive to sustained economic growth and development is important, particularly for developing countries, in order to achieve sustainability.

33.18. The secretariat of the Conference has estimated the average annual costs (1993–2000) of implementing in developing countries the activities in Agenda 21 to be over $600 billion, including about $125 billion on grant or concessional terms from the international community. These are indicative and order-of-magnitude estimates only, and have not been reviewed by Governments. Actual costs will depend upon, *inter alia,* the specific strategies and programmes Governments decide upon for implementation.

33.19. Developed countries and others in a position to do so should make initial financial commitments to give effect to the decisions of the Conference. They should report on such plans and commitments to the United Nations General Assembly at its forty-seventh session, in 1992.

33.20. Developing countries should also begin to draw up national plans for sustainable development to give effect to the decisions of the Conference.

33.21. Review and monitoring of the financing of Agenda 21 is essential. Questions related to the effective follow-up of the Conference are discussed in chapter 38 (International institutional arrangements). It will be important to review on a regular basis the adequacy of funding and mechanisms, including efforts to reach agreed objectives of the present chapter, including targets where applicable.

Chapter 38

INSTITUTIONAL STRUCTURE

A) General Assembly

38.9. The General Assembly, as the highest intergovernmental mechanism, is the principal policy-making and appraisal organ on matters relating to the follow-up of the Conference. The Assembly would organize a regular review of the implementation of Agenda 21. In fulfilling this task, the Assembly could consider the timing, format and organizational aspects of such a review. In particular, the Assembly could consider holding a special session not later than 1997 for the overall review and appraisal of Agenda 21, with adequate preparations at a high level.

B) Economic and Social Council

38.10. The Economic and Social Council, in the context of its role under the Charter *vis-à-vis* the General Assembly and the ongoing restructuring and revitalization of the United Nations in the economic, social and related fields, would assist the General Assembly by overseeing system-wide coordination in the implementation of Agenda 21 and making recommendations in this regard. In addition, the Council would undertake the task of directing system-wide coordination and integration of environmental and developmental aspects of United Nations policies and programmes and would make appropriate recommendations to the General Assembly, specialized agencies concerned and Member States. Appropriate steps should be taken to obtain regular reports from specialized agencies on their plans and programmes related to the implementation of Agenda 21, pursuant to Article 64 of the Charter of the United Nations. The Economic and Social Council should organize a periodic review of the work of the Commission on Sustainable Development envisaged in paragraph 38.11, as well as of system-wide activities to integrate environment and development, making full use of its high-level and coordination segments.

C) Commission on Sustainable Development

38.11.   In order to ensure the effective follow-up of the Conference, as well as to enhance international cooperation and rationalize the intergovernmental decisionmaking capacity for the integration of environment and development issues and to examine the progress in the implementation of Agenda 21 at the national, regional and international levels, a high-level Commission on Sustainable Development should be established in accordance with Article 68 of the Charter of the United Nations. This Commission would report to the Economic and Social Council in the context of the Council's role under the Charter *vis-à-vis* the General Assembly. It would consist of representatives of States elected as members with due regard to equitable geographical distribution. Representatives of non-member States of the Commission would have observer status. The Commission should provide for the active involvement of organs, programmes and organizations of the United Nations system, international financial institutions and other relevant intergovernmental organizations, and encourage the participation of non-governmental organizations, including industry and the business and scientific communities. The first meeting of the Commission should be convened no later than 1993. The Commission should be supported by the secretariat envisaged in paragraph 38.19. Meanwhile the Secretary–General of the United Nations is requested to ensure adequate interim administrative secretariat arrangements.

38.12.   The General Assembly, at its forty-seventh session, should determine specific organizational modalities for the work of this Commission, such as its membership, its relationship with other intergovernmental United Nations bodies dealing with matters related to environment and development, and the frequency, duration and venue of its meetings. These modalities should take into account the ongoing process of revitalization and restructuring of the work of the United Nations in the economic, social and related fields, in particular measures recommended by the General Assembly in resolutions 45/264 of 13 May 1991 and 46/235 of 13 April 1992 and other relevant Assembly resolutions. In this respect, the Secretary–General of the United Nations, with the assistance of the Secretary–General of the United Nations Conference on Environment and Development, is requested to prepare for the Assembly a report with appropriate recommendations and proposals.

38.13.   The Commission on Sustainable Development should have the following functions:

(a) To monitor progress in the implementation of Agenda 21 and activities related to the integration of environmental and developmental goals throughout the United Nations system through analysis and evaluation of reports from all relevant organs, organizations, programmes and institutions of the United Nations system dealing with various issues of environment and development, including those related to finance;

(b) To consider information provided by Governments, including, for example, information in the form of periodic communications or national reports regarding the activities they undertake to implement Agenda 21, the problems they face, such as problems related to financial resources and technology transfer, and other environment and development issues they find relevant;

(c) To review the progress in the implementation of the commitments contained in Agenda 21, including those related to provision of financial resources and transfer of technology;

(d) To receive and analyse relevant input from competent non-governmental organizations, including the scientific and private sectors, in the context of the overall implementation of Agenda 21;

(e) To enhance the dialogue, within the framework of the United Nations, with non-governmental organizations and the independent sector, as well as other entities outside the United Nations system;

(f) To consider, where appropriate, information regarding the progress made in the implementation of environmental conventions, which could be made available by the relevant Conferences of Parties;

(g) To provide appropriate recommendations to the General Assembly through the Economic and Social Council on the basis of an integrated consideration of the reports and issues related to the implementation of Agenda 21;

(h) To consider, at an appropriate time, the results of the review to be conducted expeditiously by the Secretary–General of all recommendations of the Conference for capacity-building programmes, information networks, task forces and other mechanisms to support the integration of environment and development at regional and subregional levels.

38.14. Within the intergovernmental framework, consideration should be given to allowing non-governmental organizations, including those related to major groups, particularly women's groups, committed to the implementation of Agenda 21 to have relevant information available to them, including information, reports and other data produced within the United Nations system.

D) The Secretary–General

38.15. Strong and effective leadership on the part of the Secretary–General is crucial, since he/she would be the focal point of the institutional arrangements within the United Nations system for the successful follow-up to the Conference and for the implementation of Agenda 21.

* * *

H) Organs, Programmes and Organizations of the United Nations System

38.20. In the follow-up to the Conference, in particular the implementation of Agenda 21, all relevant organs, programmes and organizations of the United Nations system will have an important role within their respective areas of expertise and mandates in supporting and supplementing national efforts. Coordination and mutual complementarity of their efforts to promote integration of environment and development can be enhanced by encouraging countries to maintain consistent positions in the various governing bodies.

1) United Nations Environment Programme

38.21. In the follow-up to the Conference, there will be a need for an enhanced and strengthened role for UNEP and its Governing Council. The Governing Council should, within its mandate, continue to play its role with regard to policy guidance and coordination in the field of the environment, taking into account the development perspective.

38.22. Priority areas on which UNEP should concentrate include the following:

(a) Strengthening its catalytic role in stimulating and promoting environmental activities and considerations throughout the United Nations system;

(b) Promoting international cooperation in the field of environment and recommending, as appropriate, policies to this end;

(c) Developing and promoting the use of such techniques as natural resource accounting and environmental economics;

(d) Environmental monitoring and assessment, through both improved participation by the United Nations system agencies in the Earthwatch programme and expanded relations with private scientific and non-governmental research institutes; and strengthening and making operational its early-warning function;

(e) Coordination and promotion of relevant scientific research with a view to providing a consolidated basis for decision-making;

(f) Dissemination of environmental information and data to Governments and to organs, programmes and organizations of the United Nations system;

(g) Raising general awareness and action in the area of environmental protection through collaboration with the general public, non-governmental entities and intergovernmental institutions;

(h) Further development of international environmental law, in particular conventions and guidelines, promotion of its implementation, and coordinating functions arising from an increasing number of international legal agreements, *inter alia,* the functioning of the secretariats of the conventions, taking into account the need for the most efficient use of resources, including possible co-location of secretariats established in the future;

(i) Further development and promotion of the widest possible use of environmental impact assessments, including activities carried out under the auspices of specialized agencies of the United Nations system, and in connection with every significant economic development project or activity;

(j) Facilitation of information exchange on environmentally sound technologies, including legal aspects, and provision of training;

(k) Promotion of subregional and regional cooperation and support to relevant initiatives and programmes for environmental protection, including playing a major contributing and coordinating role in the regional mechanisms in the field of environment identified for the follow-up to the Conference;

(l) Provision of technical, legal and institutional advice to Governments, upon request, in establishing and enhancing their national legal and institutional frameworks, in particular, in cooperation with UNDP capacity-building efforts;

(m) Support to Governments, upon request, and development agencies and organs in the integration of environmental aspects into their development policies and programmes, in particular through provision of environmental, technical and policy advice during programme formulation and implementation;

(n) Further developing assessment and assistance in cases of environmental emergencies.

38.23. In order to perform all of these functions, while retaining its role as the principal body within the United Nations system in the field of environment and taking into account the development aspects of environmental questions, UNEP would require access to greater expertise and provision of adequate financial resources and it would require closer cooperation and collaboration with development organs and other relevant organs of the United Nations system. Furthermore, the regional offices of UNEP should be strengthened without weakening its headquarters in Nairobi, and UNEP should take steps to reinforce and intensify its liaison and interaction with UNDP and the World Bank.

2) United Nations Development Programme

38.24. UNDP, like UNEP, also has a crucial role in the follow-up to the United Nations Conference on Environment and Development. Through its network of field offices it would foster the United Nations system's collective thrust in support of the implementation of Agenda 21, at the country, regional, interregional and global levels, drawing on the expertise of the specialized agencies and other United Nations organizations and bodies involved in operational activities. The role of the resident representative/resident coordinator of UNDP needs to be strengthened in order to coordinate the field-level activities of the United Nations operational activities.

38.25. Its role should include the following:

(a) Acting as the lead agency in organizing United Nations system efforts towards capacity-building at the local, national and regional levels;

(b) Mobilizing donor resources on behalf of Governments for capacity-building in recipient countries and, where appropriate, through the use of the UNDP donor round-table mechanisms;

(c) Strengthening its own programmes in support of follow-up to the Conference without prejudice to the fifth programming cycle;

(d) Assisting recipient countries, upon request, in the establishment and strengthening of national coordination mechanisms and networks related to activities for the follow-up to the Conference;

(e) Assisting recipient countries, upon request, in coordinating the mobilization of domestic financial resources;

(f) Promoting and strengthening the role and involvement of women, youth and other major groups in recipient countries in the implementation of Agenda 21.

3) United Nations Conference on Trade and Development

38.26. UNCTAD should play an important role in the implementation of Agenda 21 as extended at its eighth session, taking into account the importance of the interrelationships between development, international trade and the environment and in accordance with its mandate in the area of sustainable development.

* * *

1.29 Resolution on Institutional Arrangement to Follow up the United Nations Conference on Environment and Development. **Adopted by the U.N. General Assembly, 22 December 1992. UN Doc A/47/191;** *reprinted in* **32 ILM 238 (1993) & 5 Weston & Carlson V.A.7**

The General Assembly,

Welcoming the adoption by the United Nations Conference on Environment and Development of Agenda 21, in particular chapter 38, entitled "International institutional arrangements", which contains a set of important recommendations on institutional arrangements to follow up the Conference,

Stressing the overall objective of the integration of environment and development issues at the national, subregional, regional and international levels, including the United Nations system institutional arrangements, and the specific objectives recommended by the Conference in paragraph 38.8 of Agenda 21,

Taking note of the report of the Secretary–General, prepared with the assistance of the Secretary–General of the United Nations Conference on Environment and Development, on institutional arrangements to follow up the Conference, as well as the recommendations and proposals contained therein,

1. *Endorses* the recommendations on international institutional arrangements to follow up the United Nations Conference on Environment and Development as contained in chapter 38 of Agenda 21, particularly those on the establishment of a high-level Commission on Sustainable Development;

Commission on Sustainable Development

2. *Requests* the Economic and Social Council, at its organizational session for 1993, to set up a high-level Commission on Sustainable Development as a functional commission of the Council in accordance with Article 68 of the Charter of the United Nations in order to ensure the effective follow-up of the Conference, as well as to enhance international cooperation and rationalize the intergovernmental decision-making capacity for the integration of environment and development issues and to examine the progress of the implementation of Agenda 21 at the national, regional and international levels, fully guided by the principles of the Rio Declaration on Environment and Development and all other aspects of the Conference, in order to achieve sustainable development in all countries;

3. *Recommends* that the Commission shall have the following functions, as agreed in paragraphs 38.13, 33.13 and 33.21 of Agenda 21:

(a) To monitor progress in the implementation of Agenda 21 and activities related to the integration of environmental and developmental goals throughout the United Nations system through analysis and evaluation of reports from all relevant organs, organizations, programmes and institutions of the United Nations system dealing with various issues of environment and development, including those related to finance;

(b) To consider information provided by Governments, including, for example, in the form of periodic communications or national reports regarding the activities they undertake to implement Agenda 21, the problems they face, such as problems related to financial resources and technology transfer, and other environment and development issues they find relevant;

(c) To review the progress in the implementation of the commitments contained in Agenda 21, including those related to the provision of financial resources and transfer of technology;

(d) To review and monitor regularly progress towards the United Nations target of 0.7 per cent of the gross national product of developed countries for official development assistance. This review process should systematically combine the monitoring of the implementation of Agenda 21 with the review of financial resources available;

(e) To review on a regular basis the adequacy of funding and mechanisms, including efforts to reach agreed objectives of chapter 33 of Agenda 21, including targets where applicable;

(f) To receive and analyse relevant input from competent non-governmental organizations, including the scientific and the private sector, in the context of the overall implementation of Agenda 21;

(g) To enhance the dialogue, within the framework of the United Nations, with non-governmental organizations and the independent sector, as well as other entities outside the United Nations system;

(h) To consider, where appropriate, information regarding the progress made in the implementation of environmental conventions, which could be made available by the relevant Conferences of Parties;

(i) To provide appropriate recommendations to the General Assembly, through the Economic and Social Council, on the basis of an integrated consideration of the reports and issues related to the implementation of Agenda 21;

(j) To consider, at an appropriate time, the results of the review to be conducted expeditiously by the Secretary–General of all recommendations of the Conference for capacity-building programmes, information networks, task forces and other mechanisms to support the integration of environment and development at regional and subregional levels;

4. *Also recommends* that the Commission shall:

(a) Promote the incorporation of the principles of the Rio Declaration on Environment and Development in the implementation of Agenda 21;

(b) Promote the incorporation of the Non-legally Binding Authoritative Statement of Principles for a Global Consensus on the Management, Conservation and Sustainable Development of All Types of Forests in the implementation of Agenda 21, in particular in the context of the review of the implementation of chapter 11 thereof;

(c) Keep under review the implementation of Agenda 21, recognizing that it is a dynamic programme that could evolve over time, taking into account the agreement to review Agenda 21 in 1997, and make recommendations, as appropriate, on the need for new cooperative arrangements related to sustainable development to the Economic and Social Council and, through it, to the General Assembly;

5. *Decides* that the Commission, in the fulfilment of its functions, will also:

(a) Monitor progress in promoting, facilitating and financing, as appropriate, the access to and the transfer of environmentally sound technologies and corresponding know-how, in particular to developing countries, on favourable terms, including on concessional and preferential terms, as mutually agreed, taking into account the need to protect intellectual property rights as well as the special needs of developing countries for the implementation of Agenda 21;

(b) Consider issues related to the provision of financial resources from all available funding sources and mechanisms, as contained in paragraphs 33.13 to 33.16 of Agenda 21;

6. *Recommends* that the Commission consist of representatives of 53 States elected by the Economic and Social Council from among the Member States of the United Nations and its specialized agencies for three-year terms, with due regard to equitable geographical distribution. The regional allocation of seats could be the same as in the Commission on Science and Technology for Development, as decided in Economic and Social Council decision 1992/222 of 29 May 1992. Representation should

be at a high level, including ministerial participation. Other Member States of the United Nations and its specialized agencies, as well as other observers of the United Nations, may participate in the Commission in the capacity of observer, in accordance with established practice;

7. *Also recommends* that the Commission should:

(a) Provide for representatives of various parts of the United Nations system and other intergovernmental organizations, including international financial institutions, the General Agreement on Tariffs and Trade, regional development banks, subregional financial institutions, relevant regional and subregional economic and technical cooperation organizations and regional economic integration organizations, to assist and advise the Commission in the performance of its functions within their respective areas of expertise and mandates, and participate actively in its deliberations; and provide for the European Economic Community, within its areas of competence, to participate—as will be appropriately defined in the rules of procedure of the Commission on Sustainable Development—fully, without the right to vote;

(b) Provide for non-governmental organizations, including those related to major groups as well as industry and the scientific and business communities, to participate effectively in its work and contribute within their areas of competence to its deliberations;

8. *Requests* the Secretary–General, in the light of paragraph 7 above, to submit, for the consideration of the the Economic and Social Council at its organizational session for 1993, his proposals on the rules of procedure of the Commission, including those related to participation of relevant intergovernmental and non-governmental organizations, as recommended by the United Nations Conference on Environment and Development, taking into account the following:

(a) The procedures, while ensuring the intergovernmental nature of the Commission, should allow its members to benefit from the expertise and competence of relevant intergovernmental and non-governmental organizations;

(b) The procedures should permit relevant intergovernmental organizations inside and outside the United Nations system, including multilateral financial institutions, to appoint special representatives to the Commission;

(c) The rules of procedure of the Economic and Social Council and the rules of procedure of its functional commissions;

(d) The rules of procedure of the United Nations Conference on Environment and Development;

(e) Decisions 1/1 and 2/1 of the Preparatory Committee for the United Nations Conference on Environment and Development;

(f) Paragraphs 38.11 and 38.44 of Agenda 21;

9. *Recommends* that the Commission on Sustainable Development shall meet once a year for a period of two to three weeks. The first substantive session of the Commission will be held in New York in 1993, without prejudice to the venue of its future sessions;

10. *Requests* the Committee on Conferences to consider the need for readjusting the calendar of meetings in order to take account of the interrelationship between the work of the Commission and the work of other relevant United Nations intergovernmental subsidiary organs, in order to ensure timely reporting to the Economic and Social Council;

11. *Recommends* that in 1993, as a transitional measure, the Commission hold a short organizational session in New York. At that session, the Commission will elect the Bureau of the Commission, consisting of a chairperson, three vice-chairpersons and

a rapporteur, coming from each of the regional groups, decide on the agenda of its first substantive session and consider all other organizational issues as may be necessary. The agenda of the organizational session of the Commission shall be decided on by the Economic and Social Council at its organizational session of 1993;

12. *Also recommends* that the Commission, at its first substantive session, adopt a multi-year thematic programme of its work that will provide a framework to assess progress achieved in the implementation of Agenda 21 and ensure an integrated approach to all of its environment and development components as well as linkages between sectoral and cross-sectoral issues. This programme could be of clusters that would integrate in an effective manner related sectoral and cross-sectoral components of Agenda 21 in such a way as to allow the Commission to review the progress of the implementation of the entire Agenda 21 by 1997. This programme of work could be adjusted, as the need may arise, at the future sessions of the Commission;

13. *Requests* the Secretary–General to submit his proposals for such a programme of work during the organizational session of the Commission;

14. *Recommends* that in order to carry out its functions and implement its work programme effectively the Commission consider organizing its work on the following lines:

(a) Financial resources, mechanisms, transfer of technology, capacity-building and other cross-sectoral issues;

(b) Review of implementation of Agenda 21 at the international level, as well as at the regional and national levels, including the means of implementation, in accordance with paragraph 12 above and the functions of the Commission, taking into account, where appropriate, information regarding the progress in the implementation of relevant environmental conventions;

(c) A high-level meeting, with ministerial participation, to have an integrated overview of the implementation of Agenda 21, to consider emerging policy issues and to provide necessary political impetus to the implementation of decisions of the United Nations Conference on Environment and Development and commitments contained therein.

Review and consideration of implementation of Agenda 21 should be in an integrated manner;

15. *Requests* the Secretary–General to provide for each session of the Commission, in accordance with the programme of work mentioned in paragraph 12 above and in accordance with its organizational modalities, analytical reports containing information on relevant activities to implement Agenda 21, progress achieved and emerging issues to be addressed;

16. *Also requests* the Secretary–General to prepare, for the first substantive session of the Commission, reports containing information and proposals, as appropriate, on the following issues:

(a) Initial financial commitments, financial flows and arrangements to give effect to the decisions of the Conference from all available funding sources and mechanisms;

(b) Progress achieved in facilitating and promoting transfer of environmentally sound technologies, cooperation and capacity-building;

(c) Progress in the incorporation of recommendations of the United Nations Conference on Environment and Development in the activities of international organizations and measures undertaken by the Administrative Committee on Coordination to ensure that sustainable development principles are incorporated into programmes and processes within the United Nations system;

(d) Ways in which, upon request, the United Nations system and bilateral donors are assisting countries, particularly developing countries, in the preparation of national reports and national Agenda 21 action plans;

(e) Urgent and major emerging issues that may be addressed in the course of the high-level meeting;

17. *Decides* that organizational modalities for the Commission should be reviewed in the context of the overall review and appraisal of Agenda 21 during the special session of the General Assembly and adjusted, as may be required, to improve its effectiveness;

Relationship with other United Nations intergovernmental bodies

18. *Recommends* that the Commission, in discharging its functions, submit its consolidated recommendations to the Economic and Social Council and, through it, to the General Assembly, to be considered by the Council and the Assembly in accordance with their respective responsibilities as defined in the Charter of the United Nations and the relevant provisions of paragraphs 38.9 and 38.10 of Agenda 21;

19. *Also recommends* that the Commission actively interact with other intergovernmental United Nations bodies dealing with matters related to environment and development;

20. *Emphasizes* that the ongoing restructuring and revitalization of the United Nations in the economic, social and related fields should take into account the organizational modalities for the Commission on Sustainable Development, with a view to optimizing the work of the Commission and other intergovernmental United Nations bodies dealing with matters related to environment and development;

Coordination within the United Nations system

21. *Requests* all United Nations specialized agencies and related organizations of the United Nations system to strengthen and adjust their activities, programmes and medium-term plans, as appropriate, in line with Agenda 21, in particular regarding projects for promoting sustainable development, in accordance with paragraph 38.28 of Agenda 21, and make their reports on steps they have taken to give effect to this recommendation available to the Commission on Sustainable Development and the Economic and Social Council in 1993 or, at the latest, in 1994, in accordance with Article 64 of the Charter of the United Nations;

22. *Invites* all relevant governing bodies to ensure that the tasks assigned to them are carried out effectively, including the elaboration and publication on a regular basis of reports on the activities of the organs, programmes and organizations for which they are responsible, and that continuous reviews are undertaken of their policies, programmes, budgets and activities;

23. *Invites* the World Bank and other international, regional and subregional financial and development institutions, including the Global Environment Facility, to submit regularly to the Commission on Sustainable Development reports containing information on their experience, activities and plans to implement Agenda 21;

24. *Requests* the Secretary–General to submit to the Commission on Sustainable Development, at its substantive session of 1993, recommendations and proposals for improving coordination of programmes related to development data that exist within the United Nations system, taking into account provisions of paragraph 40.13 of Agenda 21, *inter alia,* regarding "Development Watch";

United Nations Environment Programme, United Nations Development Programme, United Nations Conference on Trade and Development and United Nations Sudano–Sahelian Office

25. *Requests* the Governing Councils of the United Nations Environment Programme, the United Nations Development Programme and the Trade and Develop-

ment Board to examine the relevant provisions of chapter 38 of Agenda 21 at their next sessions and submit reports on their specific plans to implement Agenda 21 to the General Assembly at its forty-eighth session, through the Commission on Sustainable Development and the Economic and Social Council;

26. *Takes note* of the work of the United Nations Centre on Urgent Environmental Assistance, established by the Governing Council of the United Nations Environment Programme on an experimental basis, and invites the Governing Council to report to the General Assembly at its forty-eighth session on the experience gained within the Centre;

Regional commissions

27. *Requests* United Nations regional commissions to examine the relevant provisions of chapter 38 of Agenda 21 at their next sessions and submit reports on their specific plans to implement Agenda 21;

28. *Requests* the Economic and Social Council to decide on the arrangements required so that the reports of regional commissions with the conclusions related to such a review be made available to the Commission on Sustainable Development in 1993, or at the latest in 1994;

High-level Advisory Board

29. *Endorses* the view of the Secretary–General that the High-level Advisory Board should consist of eminent persons broadly representative of all regions of the world, with recognized expertise on the broad spectrum of issues to be dealt with by the Commission on Sustainable Development, drawn from relevant scientific disciplines, industry, finance and other major non-governmental constituencies, as well as various disciplines related to environment and development, and that due account should also be given to gender balance;

30. *Decides* that the main task of this Board is to give broad consideration to issues related to implementation of Agenda 21, taking into account the thematic multi-year programme of work of the Commission on Sustainable Development, and provide expert advice in that regard to the Secretary–General and, through him to the Commission, the Economic and Social Council and the General Assembly;

31. *Takes note* of the views of the Secretary–General regarding the functions of the Board and of the Committee for Development Planning, and requests the Secretary–General to submit appropriate proposals to the Economic and Social Council at its organizational session for 1993, including the possibility of organizing expert rosters;

Secretariat support arrangements

32. *Takes note* of the decision of the Secretary–General to establish at the Under–Secretary–General level a new Department for Policy Coordination and Sustainable Development and in this context calls upon the Secretary–General to establish a clearly identifiable, highly qualified and competent secretariat support structure to provide support for the Commission on Sustainable Development, the Inter–Agency Committee on Sustainable Development and the High–Level Advisory Board, taking into account gender balance at all levels, the paramount importance of securing the highest standards of efficiency, competence and integrity, and the importance of recruiting the staff on as wide a geographical basis as possible in accordance with Articles 8 and 101 of the Charter of the United Nations and the following criteria:

(a) It should draw on the expertise gained and the working methods and organizational structures developed during the preparatory process for the United Nations Conference on Environment and Development;

(b) It should work closely with United Nations and other expert bodies in the field of sustainable development and should cooperate closely and cooperatively with the economic and social entities of the Secretariat and the secretariats of relevant organs, organizations and bodies of the United Nations system, including the secretariats of international financial institutions, and it should provide for effective liaison with relevant non-governmental organizations, including those related to major groups, in particular non-governmental organizations from developing countries;

(c) The secretariat, which will be located in New York, should ensure easy access to all countries to its services; effective interaction with secretariats of other international organizations, financial institutions and relevant conventions whose secretariats have been established definitely or on an interim basis and should have a relevant office at Geneva to establish close links with activities related to follow-up of legal instruments, signed at or mandated by the United Nations Conference on Environment and Development, and to liaise with agencies in the fields of environment and development. The secretariat should also have a liaison office at Nairobi, on the basis of arrangements of the United Nations Conference on Environment and Development;

(d) It should be headed by a high-level official designated by the Secretary–General to work closely and directly with him and with assured access to him, as well as with the heads of relevant organizations of the United Nations system, including the multilateral financial and trade organizations, dealing with the implementation of Agenda 21;

(e) It should be funded from the United Nations regular budget and depend to the maximum extent possible upon existing budgetary resources;

(f) It should be supplemented or reinforced, as appropriate, by secondments from other relevant bodies and agencies of the United Nations system, especially the United Nations Environment Programme, the United Nations Development Programme and the World Bank, taking into account the need to ensure that the work programmes of those organizations are not negatively affected, and national Governments, as well as by appropriate specialists on limited-term contracts from outside the United Nations in such areas as may be required;

(g) It should take into account relevant resolutions and decisions of the General Assembly and the Economic and Social Council regarding women in the United Nations Secretariat;

(h) Sustainable development should be integrated and coordinated with other economic, social and environmental activities of the Secretariat. Organizational decisions should be consistent with consensus resolutions in the context of the restructuring and revitalization of the United Nations in the economic, social and related fields;

33. *Requests* the Secretary–General to make the necessary interim secretariat arrangements to ensure adequate preparations and support for the first session of the Commission on Sustainable Development and the work of the Inter–Agency Committee on Sustainable Development;

34. *Also requests* the Secretary–General to report to the General Assembly at its forty-eighth session on the implementation of the present resolution.

1.30 Instrument for the Establishment of the Restructured Global Environment Facility (as amended, but Without annexes). **Concluded at Geneva, 16 May 1994. Adopted by the Implementing Agencies of the GEF, 13 May 1994 (UNDP), 24 May 1994 (IBRD), and 18 June 1994 (UNEP).** *Reprinted in* **33 ILM 1273 & 5 Weston & Carlson V.A.8**

I. BASIC PROVISIONS

Restructuring and Purpose of GEF

1. The restructured GEF shall be established in accordance with the present Instrument. This Instrument, having been accepted by representatives of the States participating in the GEF at their meeting in Geneva, Switzerland, from March 14 to 16, 1994, shall be adopted by the Implementing Agencies in accordance with their respective rules and procedural requirements.

2. The GEF shall operate, on the basis of collaboration and partnership among the Implementing Agencies, as a mechanism for international cooperation for the purpose of providing new and additional grant and concessional funding to meet the agreed incremental costs of measures to achieve agreed global environmental benefits in the following focal areas:

(a) biological diversity;

(b) climate change;

(c) international waters;

(d) land degradation, primarily desertification and deforestation;

(e) ozone layer depletion; and

(f) persistent organic pollutants.

3. The agreed incremental costs of activities to achieve global environmental benefits concerning chemicals management as they relate to the above focal areas shall be eligible for funding. The agreed incremental costs of other relevant activities under Agenda 21 that may be agreed by the Council shall also be eligible for funding insofar as they achieve global environmental benefits by protecting the global environment in the focal areas.

4. The GEF shall ensure the cost-effectiveness of its activities in addressing the targeted global environmental issues, shall fund programs and projects which are country-driven and based on national priorities designed to support sustainable development and shall maintain sufficient flexibility to respond to changing circumstances in order to achieve its purposes.

5. The GEF operational policies shall be determined by the Council in accordance with paragraph 20(f) and with respect to GEF-financed projects shall provide for full disclosure of all non-confidential information, and consultation with, and participation as appropriate of, major groups and local communities throughout the project cycle.

6. In partial fulfillment of its purposes, the GEF shall, on an interim basis, operate the financial mechanism for the implementation of the United Nations Framework Convention on Climate Change and shall be, on an interim basis, the institutional structure which carries out the operation of the financial mechanism for the implementation of the Convention on Biological Diversity, in accordance with such cooperative arrangements or agreements as may be made pursuant to paragraphs 27 and 31. The GEF shall be available to continue to serve for the purposes of the financial mechanisms for the implementation of those conventions if it is requested to do so by their Conferences of the Parties. The GEF shall also be available to serve as an entity entrusted with the operation of the financial mechanism of the Stockholm Convention on Persistent Organic Pollutants. In such respects, the GEF shall function under the guidance of, and be accountable to, the Conferences of the Parties which

shall decide on policies, program priorities and eligibility criteria for the purposes of the conventions. The GEF shall also be available to meet the agreed full costs of activities under Article 12, paragraph 1, of the United Nations Framework Convention on Climate Change.

Participation

7. Any State member of the United Nations or of any of its specialized agencies may become a Participant in the GEF by depositing with the Secretariat an instrument of participation substantially in the form set out in Annex A. In the case of a State contributing to the GEF Trust Fund, an instrument of commitment shall be deemed to serve as an instrument of participation. Any Participant may withdraw from the GEF by depositing with the Secretariat an instrument of termination of participation substantially in the form set out in Annex A.

Establishment of GEF Trust Fund

8. The new GEF Trust Fund shall be established, and the World Bank shall be invited to serve as the Trustee of the Fund. The GEF Trust Fund shall consist of the contributions received in accordance with the present Instrument, the balance of funds transferred from the GET pursuant to paragraph 32, and any other assets and receipts of the Fund. In serving as the Trustee of the Fund, the World Bank shall serve in a fiduciary and administrative capacity, and shall be bound by its Articles of Agreement, by-laws, rules and decisions, as specified in Annex B.

Eligibility

9. GEF funding shall be made available for activities within the focal areas defined in paragraphs 2 and 3 of this Instrument in accordance with the following eligibility criteria:

(a) GEF grants that are made available within the framework of the financial mechanisms of the conventions referred to in paragraph 6 shall be in conformity with the eligibility criteria decided by the Conference of the Parties of each convention, as provided under the arrangements or agreements referred to in paragraph 27.

(b) All other GEF grants shall be made available to eligible recipient countries and, where appropriate, for other activities promoting the purposes of the Facility in accordance with this paragraph and any additional eligibility criteria determined by the Council. A country shall be an eligible recipient of GEF grants if it is eligible to borrow from the World Bank (IBRD and/or IDA) or if it is an eligible recipient of UNDP technical assistance through its country Indicative Planning Figure (IPF). GEF grants for activities within a focal area addressed by a convention referred to in paragraph 6 but outside the framework of the financial mechanism of the convention, shall only be made available to eligible recipient countries that are party to the convention concerned.

(c) GEF concessional financing in a form other than grants that is made available within the framework of the financial mechanism of the conventions referred to in paragraph 6 shall be in conformity with eligibility criteria decided by the Conference of the Parties of each convention, as provided under the arrangements or agreements referred to in paragraph 27. GEF concessional financing in a form other than grants may also be made available outside those frameworks on terms to be determined by the Council.

II.   CONTRIBUTIONS AND OTHER FINANCIAL PROVISIONS FOR REPLENISHMENT

10. Contributions to the GEF Trust Fund for the first replenishment period shall be made to the Trustee by Contributing Participants in accordance with the financial

provisions for replenishment as specified in Annex C. The Trustee's responsibility for mobilization of resources pursuant to paragraph 20(e) of this Instrument and paragraph 4(a) of Annex B shall be initiated for subsequent replenishments at the request of the Council.

III. GOVERNANCE AND STRUCTURE

11. The GEF shall have an Assembly, a Council and a Secretariat. In accordance with paragraph 24, a Scientific and Technical Advisory Panel (STAP) shall provide appropriate advice.

12. The Implementing Agencies shall establish a process for their collaboration in accordance with an interagency agreement to be concluded on the basis of the principles set forth in Annex D.

Assembly

13. The Assembly shall consist of Representatives of all Participants. The Assembly shall meet once every three years. Each Participant may appoint one Representative and one Alternate to the Assembly in such manner as it may determine. Each Representative and each Alternate shall serve until replaced. The Assembly shall elect its Chairperson from among the Representatives.

14. The Assembly shall:

(a) review the general policies of the Facility;

(b) review and evaluate the operation of the Facility on the basis of reports submitted by the Council;

(c) keep under review the membership of the Facility; and

(d) consider, for approval by consensus, amendments to the present Instrument on the basis of recommendations by the Council.

Council

15. The Council shall be responsible for developing, adopting and evaluating the operational policies and programs for GEF-financed activities, in conformity with the present Instrument and fully taking into account reviews carried out by the Assembly. Where the GEF serves for the purposes of the financial mechanisms of the conventions referred to in paragraph 6, the Council shall act in conformity with the policies, program priorities and eligibility criteria decided by the Conference of the Parties for the purposes of the convention concerned.

16. The Council shall consist of 32 Members, representing constituency groupings formulated and distributed taking into account the need for balanced and equitable representation of all Participants and giving due weight to the funding efforts of all donors. There shall be 16 Members from developing countries, 14 Members from developed countries and 2 Members from the countries of central and eastern Europe and the former Soviet Union, in accordance with Annex E. There shall be an equal number of Alternate Members. The Member and Alternate representing a constituency shall be appointed by the Participants in each constituency. Unless the constituency decides otherwise, each Member of the Council and each Alternate shall serve for three years or until a new Member is appointed by the constituency, whichever comes first. A Member or Alternate may be reappointed by the constituency. Members and Alternates shall serve without compensation. The Alternate Member shall have full power to act for the absent Member.

17. The Council shall meet semi-annually or as frequently as necessary to enable it to discharge its responsibilities. The Council shall meet at the seat of the Secretariat

unless the Council decides otherwise. Two-thirds of the Members of the Council shall constitute a quorum.

18. At each meeting, the Council shall elect a Chairperson from among its Members for the duration of that meeting. The elected Chairperson shall conduct deliberations of the Council at that meeting on issues related to Council responsibilities listed in paragraphs 20(b), (g), (i), (j) and (k). The position of elected Chairperson shall alternate from one meeting to another between recipient and non-recipient Council Members. The Chief Executive Officer of the Facility (CEO) shall conduct deliberations of the Council on issues related to Council responsibilities listed in paragraphs 20(c), (e), (f) and (h). The elected Chairperson and the CEO shall jointly conduct deliberations of the Council on issues related to paragraph 20(a).

19. Costs of Council meetings, including travel and subsistence of Council Members from developing countries, in particular the Least Developed Countries, shall be disbursed from the administrative budget of the Secretariat as necessary.

20. The Council shall:

(a) keep under review the operation of the Facility with respect to its purposes, scope and objectives;

(b) ensure that GEF policies, programs, operational strategies and projects are monitored and evaluated on a regular basis;

(c) review and approve the work program referred to in paragraph 29, monitor and evaluate progress in the implementation of the work program and provide related guidance to the Secretariat, the Implementing Agencies and the other bodies referred to in paragraph 28, recognizing that the Implementing Agencies will retain responsibility for the further preparation of individual projects approved in the work program;

(d) arrange for Council Members to receive final project documents and within four weeks transmit to the CEO any concerns they may have prior to the CEO endorsing a project document for final approval by the Implementing Agency;

(e) direct the utilization of GEF funds, review the availability of resources from the GEF Trust Fund and cooperate with the Trustee to mobilize financial resources;

(f) approve and periodically review operational modalities for the Facility, including operational strategies and directives for project selection, means to facilitate arrangements for project preparation and execution by organizations and entities referred to in paragraph 28, additional eligibility and other financing criteria in accordance with paragraphs 9(b) and 9(c) respectively, procedural steps to be included in the project cycle, and the mandate, composition and role of STAP;

(g) act as the focal point for the purpose of relations with the Conferences of the Parties to the conventions referred to in paragraph 6, including consideration, approval and review of the arrangements or agreements with such Conferences, receipt of guidance and recommendations from them and compliance with requirements under these arrangements or agreements for reporting to them;

(h) in accordance with paragraphs 26 and 27, ensure that GEF-financed activities relating to the conventions referred to in paragraph 6 conform with the policies, program priorities and eligibility criteria decided by the Conference of the Parties for the purposes of the convention concerned;

(i) appoint the CEO in accordance with paragraph 21, oversee the work of the Secretariat, and assign specific tasks and responsibilities to the Secretariat;

(j) review and approve the administrative budget of the GEF and arrange for periodic financial and performance audits of the Secretariat and the Implementing Agencies with regard to activities undertaken for the Facility;

(k) in accordance with paragraph 31, approve an annual report and keep the UN Commission on Sustainable Development apprised of its activities; and

(*l*) exercise such other operational functions as may be appropriate to fulfill the purposes of the Facility.

Secretariat

21. The GEF Secretariat shall service and report to the Assembly and the Council. The Secretariat, which shall be headed by the CEO/Chairperson of the Facility, shall be supported administratively by the World Bank and shall operate in a functionally independent and effective manner. The CEO shall be appointed to serve for three years on a full time basis by the Council on the joint recommendation of the Implementing Agencies. Such recommendation shall be made after consultation with the Council. The CEO may be reappointed by the Council. The CEO may be removed by the Council only for cause. The staff of the Secretariat shall include staff members seconded from the Implementing Agencies as well as individuals hired competitively on an as needed basis by one of the Implementing Agencies. The CEO shall be responsible for the organization, appointment and dismissal of Secretariat staff. The CEO shall be accountable for the performance of the Secretariat functions to the Council. The Secretariat shall, on behalf of the Council, exercise the following functions:

(a) implement effectively the decisions of the Assembly and the Council;

(b) coordinate the formulation and oversee the implementation of program activities pursuant to the joint work program, ensuring liaison with other bodies as required, particularly in the context of the cooperative arrangements or agreements referred to in paragraph 27;

(c) in consultation with the Implementing Agencies, ensure the implementation of the operational policies adopted by the Council through the preparation of common guidelines on the project cycle. Such guidelines shall address project identification and development, including the proper and adequate review of project and work program proposals, consultation with and participation of local communities and other interested parties, monitoring of project implementation and evaluation of project results;

(d) review and report to the Council on the adequacy of arrangements made by the Implementing Agencies in accordance with the guidelines referred to in paragraph (c) above, and if warranted, recommend to the Council and the Implementing Agencies additional arrangements for project preparation and execution under paragraphs 20(f) and 28;

(e) chair interagency group meetings to ensure the effective execution of the Council's decisions and to facilitate coordination and collaboration among the Implementing Agencies;

(f) coordinate with the Secretariats of other relevant international bodies, in particular the Secretariats of the conventions referred to in paragraph 6, the Secretariats of the Montreal Protocol on Substances that Deplete the Ozone Layer and its Multilateral Fund and the United Nations Convention to Combat Desertification in Countries Experiencing Serious Drought and/or Desertification, Particularly in Africa;

(g) report to the Assembly, the Council and other institutions as directed by the Council;

(h) provide the Trustee with all relevant information to enable it to carry out its responsibilities; and

(i) perform any other functions assigned to the Secretariat by the Council.

Implementing Agencies

22. The Implementing Agencies of the GEF shall be UNDP, UNEP, and the World Bank. The Implementing Agencies shall be accountable to the Council for their GEF-financed activities, including the preparation and cost-effectiveness of GEF projects, and for the implementation of the operational policies, strategies and decisions of the Council within their respective areas of competence and in accordance with an interagency agreement to be concluded on the basis of the principles of cooperation set forth in Annex D to the present Instrument. The Implementing Agencies shall cooperate with the Participants, the Secretariat, parties receiving assistance under the GEF, and other interested parties, including local communities and non-governmental organizations, to promote the purposes of the Facility.

23. The CEO shall periodically convene meetings with the heads of the Implementing Agencies to promote interagency collaboration and communication, and to review operational policy issues regarding the implementation of GEF-financed activities. The CEO shall transmit their conclusions and recommendations to the Council for its consideration.

Scientific and Technical Advisory Panel (STAP)

24. UNEP shall establish, in consultation with UNDP and the World Bank and on the basis of guidelines and criteria established by the Council, the Scientific and Technical Advisory Panel (STAP) as an advisory body to the Facility. UNEP shall provide the STAP's Secretariat and shall operate as the liaison between the Facility and the STAP.

IV. PRINCIPLES OF DECISION–MAKING

25. (a) Procedure

The Assembly and the Council shall each adopt by consensus regulations as may be necessary or appropriate to perform their respective functions transparently; in particular, they shall determine any aspect of their respective procedures, including the admission of observers and, in the case of the Council, provision for executive sessions.

(b) Consensus

Decisions of the Assembly and the Council shall be taken by consensus. In the case of the Council if, in the consideration of any matter of substance, all practicable efforts by the Council and its Chairperson have been made and no consensus appears attainable, any Member of the Council may require a formal vote.

(c) Formal Vote

(i) Unless otherwise provided in this Instrument, decisions requiring a formal vote by the Council shall be taken by a double weighted majority; that is, an affirmative vote representing both a 60 percent majority of the total number of Participants and a 60 percent majority of the total contributions.

(ii) Each Member of the Council shall cast the votes of the Participant or Participants he/she represents. A Member of the Council appointed by a group of Participants may cast separately the votes of each Participant in the constituency he/she represents.

(iii) For the purpose of voting power, total contributions shall consist of the actual cumulative contributions made to the GEF Trust Fund as specified in Annex C (Attachment 1) and in subsequent replenishments of the GEF Trust Fund, contributions made to the GET, and the grant equivalent of co-financing and parallel financing made under the GEF pilot program, or agreed with the Trustee, until the effective date of the GEF Trust Fund. Until the effective date of the GEF Trust

Fund, advance contributions made under paragraph 7(c) of Annex C shall be deemed to be contributions to the GET.

V. RELATIONSHIP AND COOPERATION WITH CONVENTIONS

26.   The Council shall ensure the effective operation of the GEF as a source of funding activities under the conventions referred to in paragraph 6. The use of the GEF resources for purposes of such conventions shall be in conformity with the policies, program priorities and eligibility criteria decided by the Conference of the Parties of each of those conventions.

27.   The Council shall consider and approve cooperative arrangements or agreements with the Conferences of the Parties to the conventions referred to in paragraph 6, including reciprocal arrangements for representation in meetings. Such arrangements or agreements shall be in conformity with the relevant provisions of the convention concerned regarding its financial mechanism and shall include procedures for determining jointly the aggregate GEF funding requirements for the purpose of the convention. With regard to each convention referred to in paragraph 6, until the first meeting of its Conference of the Parties, the Council shall consult the convention's interim body.

VI. COOPERATION WITH OTHER BODIES

28.   The Secretariat and the Implementing Agencies under the guidance of the Council shall cooperate with other international organizations to promote achievement of the purposes of the GEF. The Implementing Agencies may make arrangements for GEF project preparation and execution by multilateral development banks, specialized agencies and programs of the United Nations, other international organizations, bilateral development agencies, national institutions, non-governmental organizations, private sector entities and academic institutions, taking into account their comparative advantages in efficient and cost-effective project execution. Such arrangements shall be made in accordance with national priorities. Pursuant to paragraph 20(f), the Council may request the Secretariat to make similar arrangements in accordance with national priorities. In the event of disagreements among the Implementing Agencies or between an Implementing Agency and any entity concerning project preparation or execution, an Implementing Agency or any entity referred to in this paragraph may request the Secretariat to seek to resolve such disagreements.

VII. OPERATIONAL MODALITIES

29.   The Secretariat shall coordinate the preparation of and determine the content of a joint work program for the GEF among the Implementing Agencies, including an indication of the financial resources required for the program, for approval by the Council. The work program shall be prepared in accordance with paragraph 4 and in cooperation with eligible recipients and any executing agency referred to in paragraph 28.

30.   GEF projects shall be subject to endorsement by the CEO before final project approval. If at least four Council Members request that a project be reviewed at a Council meeting because in their view the project is not consistent with the Instrument or GEF policies and procedures, the CEO shall submit the project document to the next Council meeting, and shall only endorse the project for final approval by the Implementing Agency if the Council finds that the project is consistent with the Instrument and GEF policies and procedures.

VIII. REPORTING

31.   The Council shall approve an annual report on the activities of the GEF. The report shall be prepared by the Secretariat and circulated to all Participants. It shall

contain information on the activities carried out under the GEF, including a list of project ideas submitted for consideration and a review of the project activities funded by the Facility and their outcomes. The report shall contain all the information necessary to meet the principles of accountability and transparency that shall characterize the Facility as well as the requirements arising from the reporting arrangements agreed with each Conference of the Parties to the conventions referred to in paragraph 6. The report shall be conveyed to each of these Conferences of the Parties, the United Nations Commission on Sustainable Development and any other international organization deemed appropriate by the Council.

IX. TRANSITIONAL AND FINAL PROVISIONS
Termination of the GET

32. The World Bank shall be invited to terminate the existing Global Environment Trust Fund (GET) on the effective date of the establishment of the new GEF Trust Fund, and any funds, receipts, assets and liabilities held in the GET upon termination, including the administration of any cofinancing by the Trustee in accordance with the provisions of Resolution No. 91–5 of the Executive Directors of the World Bank, shall be transferred to the new GEF Trust Fund. Pending the termination of the GET under this provision, projects financed from the GET resources shall continue to be processed and approved subject to the rules and procedures applicable to the GET.

Interim Period

33. The Council may, pursuant to the provisions of this Instrument, be convened during the period from the adoption of this Instrument and its annexes by the Implementing Agencies until the effective date of the establishment of the new GEF Trust Fund: (a) to appoint, by consensus, the CEO in order to enable him/her to assume the work of the Secretariat; and (b) to prepare the Council's rules of procedure and the operational modalities for the Facility. The first meeting of the Council shall be organized by the secretariat of the GEF pilot program. Administrative expenses during this interim period shall be covered by the existing GET.

Amendment and Termination

34. Amendment or termination of the present Instrument may be approved by consensus by the Assembly upon the recommendation of the Council, after taking into account the views of the Implementing Agencies and the Trustee, and shall become effective after adoption by the Implementing Agencies and the Trustee in accordance with their respective rules and procedural requirements. This paragraph shall apply to the amendment of any annex to this Instrument unless the annex concerned provides otherwise.

35. The Trustee may at any time terminate its role as trustee in accordance with paragraph 14 of Annex B, and an Implementing Agency may at any time terminate its role as implementing agency, after consultation with the other Implementing Agencies and after giving the Council six months' notice in writing.

1.31 NAIROBI DECLARATION AND GOVERNING COUNCIL DECISION ON THE ROLE, MANDATE AND GOVERNANCE OF THE UNITED NATIONS ENVIRONMENT PROGRAMME. **Adopted by the Governing Council of the United Nations Environmental Programme, 7 February 1997. UN Doc GC19/1/1997 (1997)**

A. Nairobi Declaration on the Role and Mandate of the United Nations Environmental Programme

We, the ministers and heads of delegation attending the nineteenth session of the Governing Council of the United Nations Environment Programme, held in Nairobi from 27 January to 7 February 1997,

Recalling the goal of the Rio Declaration on Environment and Development, which is to establish a new and equitable global partnership through the creation of new levels of cooperation among States, key sectors of society and people,

Reiterating our commitment to the implementation of the Rio Declaration, Agenda 21, and the Non-legally Binding Authoritative Statement of Principles for a Global Consensus on the Management, Conservation and Sustainable Development of All Types of Forests, adopted by the United Nations Conference on Environment and Development, as well as other environmental conventions agreed upon in the Rio process,

Recognizing the progress made in the implementation of the Rio agreements,

Deeply concerned, nevertheless, at the continuing deterioration of the global environment, including the worsening trends in environmental pollution and the degradation of natural resources, as reflected in the Global Environment Outlook report of the United Nations Environment Programme,

Aware of the rapid changes currently taking place in the world and the increasing complexity and fragmentation of the institutional responses to them, as well as the far-reaching significance of the concept of sustainable development which encompasses economic, social and environmental dimensions, supported by capacity-building, transfer of technology and financial resources to developing countries, in particular least developed countries,

Convinced that a strong, effective and revitalized United Nations Environment Programme is essential to assist the international community in its efforts to reverse environmentally unsustainable trends,

Aware that the special session of the General Assembly for the purpose of an overall review and appraisal of the implementation of Agenda 21 offers a unique opportunity to review and appraise the follow-up to the United Nations Conference on Environment and Development and to confirm the revitalized role of the United Nations Environment Programme,

Determined to assist the General Assembly in this important task, and guided by the principles agreed in the Rio Declaration on Environment and Development,

Declare:

1. That the United Nations Environment Programme has been and should continue to be the principal United Nations body in the field of the environment and that we, the ministers of the environment and heads of delegation attending the nineteenth session of the Governing Council, are determined to play a stronger role in the implementation of the goals and objectives of the United Nations Environment Programme;

2. That the role of the United Nations Environment Programme is to be the leading global environmental authority that sets the global environmental agenda, that promotes the coherent implementation of the environmental dimension of sustainable

development within the United Nations system and that serves as an authoritative advocate for the global environment;

3. That to this end, we reaffirm the continuing relevance of the mandate of the United Nations Environment Programme deriving from General Assembly resolution 2997 (XXVII) of 15 December 1972 and further elaborated by Agenda 21. The core elements of the focused mandate of the revitalized United Nations Environment Programme should be the following:

(a) To analyse the state of the global environment and assess global and regional environmental trends, provide policy advice, early warning information on environmental threats, and to catalyse and promote international cooperation and action, based on the best scientific and technical capabilities available;

(b) To further the development of its international environmental law aiming at sustainable development, including the development of coherent interlinkages among existing international environmental conventions;

(c) To advance the implementation of agreed international norms and policies, to monitor and foster compliance with environmental principles and international agreements and stimulate cooperative action to respond to emerging environmental challenges;

(d) To strengthen its role in the coordination of environmental activities in the United Nations system in the field of the environment, as well as its role as an Implementing Agency of the Global Environment Facility, based on its comparative advantage and scientific and technical expertise;

(e) To promote greater awareness and facilitate effective cooperation among all sectors of society and actors involved in the implementation of the international environmental agenda, and to serve as an effective link between the scientific community and policy makers at the national and international levels;

(f) To provide policy and advisory services in key areas of institution-building to Governments and other relevant institutions;

4. That, for the effective discharge of its focused mandate and to ensure the implementation of the global environmental agenda, we have decided to improve the governance structure of United Nations Environment Programme. In doing so, we have been guided by the following considerations:

(a) The United Nations Environment Programme should serve as the world forum for the ministers and the highest-level government officials in charge of environmental matters in the policy and decision-making processes of the United Nations Environment Programme;

(b) Regionalization and decentralization should be strengthened through the increased involvement and participation of regional ministerial and other relevant forums in the United Nations Environment Programme process, complementary to the central coordinating role of the Programme's headquarters in Nairobi;

(c) The participation of major groups should be increased;

(d) A cost-effective and politically influential intersessional mechanism should be designed;

5. That, in order to operationalize its mandate, the revitalized United Nations Environment Programme needs adequate, stable and predictable financial resources and, in this regard, we recognize the interrelationship between excellence, relevance and cost-effectiveness in programme delivery, confidence in the organization and a consequent increase in the competitive ability of the Programme to attract funding;

6. That ways must be sought to assure financial stability for the implementation of the global environmental agenda. In this regard, the predictability and early

notification of expected contributions to the Environment Fund would facilitate an effective planning and programming process;

7. That we reaffirm the central importance of the Environment Fund as the principal source of financing for the implementation of the programme of the United Nations Environment Programme;

8. That we are convinced that the expeditious implementation of our decisions and the principles contained in this Declaration, adopted in the year of the twenty-fifth anniversary of the founding of the United Nations Environment Programme, will revitalize and strengthen the organization and place it at the forefront of international efforts to protect the global environment for present and future generations and in the pursuit of sustainable development;

9. That we request the President of the Governing Council to present this Declaration to the high-level segment of the fifth session of the Commission on Sustainable Development and to the special session of the General Assembly for the purpose of an overall review and appraisal of the implementation of Agenda 21.

B. *Governance of the United Nations Environment Programme*

The Governing Council,

Recalling United Nations General Assembly resolution 2997 (XXVII) of 15 December 1972 on institutional and financial arrangements for international environmental cooperation, including the mandate of the Governing Council of the United Nations Environment Programme,

Recalling also its decision 18/2 of 26 May 1995 on the review of the governing structures of the United Nations Environment Programme,

Reaffirming the importance for the United Nations Environment Programme to continue to be the leading global environmental authority that sets the global environmental agenda, and to promote the coherent implementation of the environmental dimension of sustainable development within the United Nations system,

Conscious of the need to improve the governance of the United Nations Environment Programme to enable it to fulfil its mandate as strengthened by chapter 38 of Agenda 21, and further enhanced by the Nairobi Declaration on the Role and Mandate of the United Nations Environment Programme adopted by the Governing Council in its decision 19/1 A of 7 February 1997,

Emphasizing the importance of democratic, efficient, transparent and representative governing structures of the United Nations Environment Programme, with a complementary, specific and distinct role and mandate for each of their components,

Recognizing the need for properly mandated subsidiary bodies that can act during the inter-sessional period for and on behalf of the Governing Council within their respective mandates and the framework of the decisions adopted by the Council,

Recognizing also the need to ensure adequate and predictable funding for the United Nations Environment Programme,

Decides

1. To establish a High-level Committee of Ministers and Officials as a subsidiary organ of the Governing Council, with the following mandate:

    (a) To consider the international environmental agenda and to make reform and policy recommendations to the Governing Council;

    (b) To provide guidance and advice to the Executive Director on emerging environmental issues between sessions of the Governing Council to enable the United Nations Environment Progamme to make a timely response;

(c) To enhance the collaboration and cooperation of the United Nations Environment Programme with other relevant multilateral bodies as well as with the environmental conventions and their secretariats;

(d) To support the Executive Director in mobilizing adequate and predictable financial resources for the United Nations Environment Programme for the implementation of the global environmental agenda approved by the Governing Council;

2. That the High-level Committee of Ministers and Officials shall consist of 36 members, elected by the Governing Council from among Members of the United Nations and members of its specialized agencies, for a period of two years, taking into account the principle of equitable regional representation as reflected in the composition of the Governing Council. The President of the Governing Council and the Chairman of the Committee of Permanent Representatives shall be invited to attend the meetings. No member State shall serve on the Committee for more than two consecutive terms;

3. That the European Community and other regional intergovernmental economic organizations may attend the meetings of the Committee;

4. That the High-level Committee of Ministers and Officials shall elect from amongst its members a Chairperson, three Vice–Chairpersons and a Rapporteur;

5. That the High-level Committee of Ministers and Officials shall meet at least once a year in Nairobi. Meetings of the Committee may be convened elsewhere by its Chairperson, in consultation with its Bureau, in connection with major international environmental meetings;

6. That the report of the meetings of the High-level Committee of Ministers and Officials shall be made immediately available to all members of the United Nations Environment Programme;

7. That, with a view to strengthening the Committee of Permanent Representatives, as a subsidiary organ of the Governing Council, it shall have henceforth the following mandate:

(a) Within the policy and budgetary framework provided by the Governing Council, to review, monitor and assess the implementation of decisions of the Council on administrative, budgetary and programme matters;

(b) To review the draft programme of work and budget during their preparation by the secretariat;

(c) To review reports requested of the secretariat by the Governing Council on the effectiveness, efficiency and transparency of the functions and work of the secretariat and to make recommendations thereon to the Governing Council;

(d) To prepare draft decisions for consideration by the Governing Council based on inputs from the secretariat and on the results of the functions specified above;

8. That the Committee of Permanent Representatives shall consist of the representatives of all States Members of the United Nations and members of its specialized agencies, and the European Community, accredited to the United Nations Environment Programme, whether based in Nairobi or outside;

9. That the Committee of Permanent Representatives shall elect a Bureau composed of a Chairperson, three Vice–Chairpersons and a Rapporteur, for a period of two years, taking into account the principles of rotation and equitable geographical representation;

10. That the Committee of Permanent Representatives shall hold four regular meetings a year. Extraordinary meetings may be also convened by its Chairperson,

after consultation with the other members of the Bureau or at the request of at least five members of the Committee. The Committee of Permanent Representatives may establish subcommittees, working groups and task forces as deemed appropriate to carry out its mandate;

11. That the High-level Committee of Ministers and Officials and the Committee of Permanent Representatives shall be accountable to the Governing Council and will submit reports on their work at each session of the Governing Council;

12. That, save as otherwise provided in this decision, the rules of procedure of the Governing Council, including rule 63 shall apply, mutatis mutandis, to the High-level Committee of Ministers and Officials until it adopts its own rules of procedure. The proceedings of the Committee of Permanent Representatives will be conducted in English;

13. That the secretariat shall provide documentation and information related to the meetings of the High-level Committee of Ministers and Officials and the Committee of Permanent Representatives, four weeks in advance of the meeting in question;

14. That an appropriate budget shall be allocated by the Governing Council for these two subsidiary organs. The financial implications of the present decision shall not be borne by the Environment Fund and should be within the financial provisions currently available for meetings of the Governing Council;

15. To invite Members of the United Nations and members of its specialized agencies to consider providing financial assistance to facilitate the participation of developing countries and in particular the least developed among them, as well as countries with economies in transition, and to establish a trust fund to this end;

16. That this governance structure shall be reviewed by the Governing Council at its twenty-first session, with a view to assessing its effectiveness taking into account any relevant results of the reform process of the United Nations system.

1.32 RESOLUTION ON RESPONSIBILITY AND LIABILITY UNDER INTERNATIONAL LAW FOR ENVIRONMENTAL DAMAGE. **Adopted by the Institute of International Law, at Strasbourg, 4 September 1997.**

The Institute of International Law,

Recalling the "Declaration on a Programme of Action on the Protection of the Global Environment" adopted at the 65th Session of the Institute in Basle;

Mindful of the increasing activities that entail risks of environmental damage with transboundary and global impacts;

Taking into account the evolving principles and criteria governing State responsibility, responsibility for harm alone and civil liability for environmental damage under both international and national law;

Noting in particular Principle 21 of the Stockholm Declaration and Principle 2 of the Rio Declaration on the responsibility of States to ensure that activities within their jurisdiction or control do not cause damage to the environment of other States or of areas beyond the limits of national jurisdiction;

Realizing that both responsibility and liability have in addition to the traditional role of ensuring restoration and compensation that of enhancing prevention of environmental damage;

Seeking to identify, harmonize and to the necessary extent develop the principles of international law applicable to responsibility and liability in the context of environmental damage;

Desiring to make useful recommendations for the negotiation and management of regimes on responsibility and liability for environmental damage established under international conventions in furtherance of the objectives of adequate environmental protection (environmental regimes);

Realizing that international environmental law is developing significant new links with the concepts of intergenerational equity, the precautionary approach, sustainable development, environmental security and with human rights law, as well as with the principle of shared but differentiated responsibility, thereby also influencing the issues relating to responsibility and liability;

Adopts this Resolution:

Basic Distinction on Responsibility and Liability

Article 1

The breach of an obligation of environmental protection established under international law engages responsibility of the State (international responsibility), entailing as a consequence the obligation to reestablish the original position or to pay compensation.

The latter obligation may also arise from a rule of international law providing for strict responsibility on the basis of harm or injury alone, particularly in case of ultrahazardous activities (responsibility for harm alone).

Civil liability of operators can be engaged under domestic law or the governing rules of international law regardless of the lawfulness of the activity concerned if it results in environmental damage.

The foregoing is without prejudice to the question of criminal responsibility of natural or juridical persons.

Article 2

Without precluding the application of rules of general international law, environmental regimes should include specific rules on responsibility and liability in order to ensure their effectiveness in terms of both encouraging prevention and providing for restoration and compensation. The object and purpose of each regime should be taken into account in establishing the extent of such rules.

International Responsibility

Article 3

The principles of international law governing international responsibility also apply to obligations relating to environmental protection.

When due diligence is utilized as a test for engaging responsibility it is appropriate that it be measured in accordance with objective standards relating to the conduct to be expected from a good government and detached from subjectivity. Generally accepted international rules and standards further provide an objective measurement for the due diligence test.

Responsibility for Harm Alone

Article 4

The rules of international law may also provide for the engagement of strict responsibility of the State on the basis of harm or injury alone. This type of responsibility is most appropriate in case of ultra-hazardous activities, and activities entailing risk or having other similar characteristics.

Failure of the State to enact appropriate rules and controls in accordance with environmental regimes, even if not amounting as such to a breach of an obligation, may result in its responsibility if harm ensues as a consequence, including damage caused by operators within its jurisdiction or control.

The use of methods facilitating the proof required to substantiate a claim for environmental damage should be considered under such regimes.

Civil Liability

Article 5

While fault-based, strict and absolute standards of civil liability are provided for under national legislation, environmental regimes should prefer the strict liability of operators as the normal standard applicable under such regimes, thereby relying on the objective fact of harm and also allowing for the appropriate exceptions and limits to liability. This is without prejudice to the role of harmonization of national laws and the application in this context of the standards generally prevailing under such national legislation.

Article 6

Environmental regimes should normally assign primary liability to operators. States engaged in activities qua operators are governed by this rule.

This is without prejudice to the questions relating to international responsibility which may be incurred for failure of the State to comply with the obligation to establish and implement civil liability mechanisms under national law, including insurance schemes, compensation funds and other remedies and safeguards, as provided for under such regimes.

An operator fully complying with applicable domestic rules and standards and government controls may be exempted from liability in case of environmental damage under environmental regimes. In such case the rules set out above on international responsibility and responsibility for harm alone may apply.

Article 7

A causal nexus between the activity undertaken and the ensuing damage shall normally be required under environmental regimes. This is without prejudice to the establishment of presumptions of causality relating to hazardous activities or cumulative damage or long-standing damages not attributable to a single entity but to a sector or type of activity.

Article 8

Subsidiary State liability, contributions by the State to international funds and other forms of State participation in compensation schemes should be considered under environmental regimes as a back-up system of liability in case that the operator who is primarily liable is unable to pay the required compensation. This does not prejudice the question of the State obtaining reimbursement from operators under its domestic law.

Limits to Responsibility for Harm Alone and Civil Liability

Article 9

In accordance with the evolving rules of international law it is appropriate for environmental regimes to permit for reasonable limits to the amount of compensation resulting from responsibility for harm alone and civil liability, bearing in mind both the objective of achieving effective environmental protection and ensuring adequate reparation of damage and the need to avoid discouragement of investments. Limits so established should be periodically reviewed.

Insurance

Article 10

States should ensure that operators have adequate financial capacity to pay possible compensation resulting from liability and are required to make arrangements for adequate insurance and other financial security, taking into account the requirements of their respective domestic laws. Where insurance coverage is not available or is inadequate, the establishment of national insurance funds for this purpose should be considered. Foreseeability of damage in general terms of risk should not affect the availability of insurance.

Apportionment of Liability

Article 11

Apportionment of liability under environmental regimes should include all entities that legitimately may be required to participate in the payment of compensation so as to ensure full reparation of damage. To this end, in addition to primary and subsidiary liability, forms of several and joint liability should also be considered particularly in the light of the operations of major international consortia.

Such regimes should also provide for product liability to the extent applicable so as to reach the entity ultimately liable for pollution or other forms of environmental damage.

Collective Reparation

Article 12

Should the source of environmental damage be unidentified or compensation be unavailable from the entity liable or other back-up sources, environmental regimes should ensure that the damage does not remain uncompensated and may consider the intervention of special compensation funds or other mechanisms of collective reparation, or the establishment of such mechanisms where necessary.

Entities engaged in activities likely to produce environmental damage of the kind envisaged under a given regime may be required to contribute to a special fund or another mechanism of collective reparation established under such regime.

Preventive Mechanisms Associated with Responsibility and Liability

Article 13

Environmental regimes should consider the appropriate connections between the preventive function of responsibility and liability and other preventive mechanisms such as notification and consultation, regular exchange of information and the increased utilization of environmental impact assessments. The implications of the precautionary principle, the "polluter pays" principle and the principle of common but differentiated responsibility in the context of responsibility and liability should also be considered under such regimes.

Response Action

Article 14

Environmental regimes should provide for additional mechanisms which ensure that operators shall undertake timely and effective response action, including preparation of the necessary contingency plans and appropriate restoration measures directed to prevent further damage and to control, reduce and eliminate damage already caused.

Response action and restoration should be undertaken also to the extent necessary by States, technical bodies established under such regimes, and by private entities other than the operator in case of emergency.

Article 15

The failure to comply with the obligations on response action and restoration should engage civil liability of operators, the operation of back-up liability mechanisms and possible international responsibility. Compliance with the obligations should not preclude responsibility for harm alone or civil liability for the ensuring damage except to the extent that it has eliminated or significantly reduced such damage.

Article 16

States and other entities undertaking response action and restoration are entitled to be reimbursed by the entity liable for the costs incurred as a consequence of the discharge of these obligations. While claims for these costs can be made independently of responsibility for harm alone or civil liability, they may also be consolidated with other claims for compensation for environmental damage.

Activities Engaging Responsibility for Harm Alone or Strict Civil Liability

Article 17

Environmental regimes should define such environmentally hazardous activities that may engage responsibility for harm alone or strict civil liability, taking into account the nature of the risk involved and the financial implications of such definition.

Specific sectors of activity, lists of dangerous substances and activities, or activities undertaken in special sensitive areas may be included in this definition.

Article 18

If more than one liability regime applies to a given activity, the regime prepared later in time should provide criteria to establish an order of priority. The standard most favorable to the environment or for the compensation of the victim should be adopted for this purpose.

Degree of Damage

Article 19

Environmental regimes should provide for the reparation and compensation of damage in all circumstances involving the breach of an obligation. In the case of a regime providing for responsibility for harm alone, the threshold above which damage must be compensated must be clearly established.

Article 20

The submission of a given proposed activity to environmental impact assessment under environmental regimes does not in itself exempt from responsibility for harm alone or civil liability if the assessed impact exceeds the limit judged acceptable. An environmental impact assessment may require that a specific guarantee be given for adequate compensation should the case arise.

Exemptions from Responsibility and Civil Liability

Article 21

Exemptions from international responsibility are governed by the principles and rules of international law. Environmental regimes may provide for exemptions from responsibility for harm alone or civil liability, as the case may be, to the extent compatible with their objectives. The mere unforeseeable character of an impact should not be accepted in itself as an exemption.

Article 22

Without prejudice to the rules of international law governing armed conflicts, such an event as well as terrorism and a natural disaster of an irresistible character and other similar situations normally provided for under civil liability conventions may be considered as acceptable exemptions in environmental regimes, subject to the principle that no one can benefit from his or her own wrongful act.

Intentional or grossly negligent acts or omissions of a third party shall also normally be an acceptable exemption, but the third party should in such case be fully liable for the damage.

Damage resulting from humanitarian activities may be exempted from liability if the circumstances so warrant.

Compensation and Reparation of Damage

Article 23

Environmental regimes should provide for the reparation of damage to the environment as such separately from or in addition to the reparation of damage relating to death, personal injury or loss of property or economic value. The specific type of damage envisaged shall depend on the purpose and nature of the regime.

Article 24

Environmental regimes should provide for a broad concept of reparation, including cessation of the activity concerned, restitution, compensation and, if necessary, satisfaction. Compensation under such regimes should include amounts covering both economic loss and the costs of environmental reinstatement and rehabilitation. In this context, equitable assessment and other criteria developed under international conventions and by the decisions of tribunals should also be considered.

Article 25

The fact that environmental damage is irreparable or unquantifiable shall not result in exemption from compensation. An entity which causes environmental damage of an irreparable nature must not end up in a possibly more favorable condition that other entities causing damage that allows for quantification.

Where damage is irreparable for physical, technical or economic reasons, additional criteria should be made available for the assessment of damage. Impairment of use, aesthetic and other non-use values, domestic or international guidelines, intergenerational equity, and generally equitable assessment should be considered as alternative criteria for establishing a measure of compensation.

Full reparation of environmental damage should not result in the assessment of excessive, exemplary or punitive damages.

Access to Dispute Prevention and Remedies

Article 26

Access by States, international organizations and individuals to mechanisms facilitating compliance with environmental regimes, with particular reference to consultations, negotiations and other dispute prevention arrangements, should be provided for under such regimes.

In the event of preventive mechanisms being unsuccessful, expeditious access to remedies, as well as submission of claims relating to environmental damage, should also be provided for.

Article 27

Environmental regimes should make flexible arrangements to facilitate the standing of claimants, with particular reference to claims concerning the environment per se and damages to areas beyond the limits of national jurisdiction. This is without prejudice to the requirement of a direct legal interest of the affected or potentially affected party to make an environmental claim under international law.

Article 28

Environmental regimes should identify entities that would be entitled to make claims and receive compensation in the absence of a direct legal interest if appropriate. Institutions established under such regimes, including ombudsmen and funds, might be empowered to this end. A High Commissioner for the Environment might also be envisaged to act on behalf or in the interests of the international community.

Article 29

Dispute prevention might also be facilitated by the participation of qualified States and entities in the planning process of major projects of another State in the context of mechanisms of international cooperation. Domestic and regional environmental impact assessment should also be required for activities likely to have transboundary effects or affect areas beyond the limits of national jurisdiction.

Remedies Available to Interested Entities and Persons for Domestic and Transnational Claims

Article 30

Environmental regimes should provide for equal access on a non-discriminatory basis to domestic courts and remedies by national and foreign entities and by all other interested persons.

Article 31

Environmental regimes should provide for the waiver of State immunity from legal process in appropriate claims. Arbitral awards and other decisions rendered by international tribunals under such regimes should have the same force as national decisions at the domestic level.

In cases having multinational aspects, environmental regimes should take into consideration existing rules on jurisdiction and choice of law and, if necessary, provide for such rules.

1.33   Convention on Access to Information, Public Participation in Decision-Making and Access to Justice in Environmental Matters (With annexes).[a] Concluded at Aarhus (Denmark), 25 June 1998. Entered into force, 30 October 2001. 2161 UNTS 447; *reprinted in* 38 ILM 517 (1999) & 5 Weston & Carlson V.B.18

The Parties to this Convention,

Recalling principle 1 of the Stockholm Declaration on the Human Environment,

Recalling also principle 10 of the Rio Declaration on Environment and Development,

Recalling further General Assembly resolutions 37/7 of 28 October 1982 on the World Charter for Nature and 45/94 of 14 December 1990 on the need to ensure a healthy environment for the well-being of individuals,

Recalling the European Charter on Environment and Health adopted at the First European Conference on Environment and Health of the World Health Organization in Frankfurt-am-Main, Germany, on 8 December 1989,

Affirming the need to protect, preserve and improve the state of the environment and to ensure sustainable and environmentally sound development,

Recognizing that adequate protection of the environment is essential to human well-being and the enjoyment of basic human rights, including the right to life itself,

Recognizing also that every person has the right to live in an environment adequate to his or her health and well-being, and the duty, both individually and in association with others, to protect and improve the environment for the benefit of present and future generations,

Considering that, to be able to assert this right and observe this duty, citizens must have access to information, be entitled to participate in decision-making and have access to justice in environmental matters, and acknowledging in this regard that citizens may need assistance in order to exercise their rights,

Recognizing that, in the field of the environment, improved access to information and public participation in decision-making enhance the quality and the implementation of decisions, contribute to public awareness of environmental issues, give the public the opportunity to express its concerns and enable public authorities to take due account of such concerns,

Aiming thereby to further the accountability of and transparency in decision-making and to strengthen public support for decisions on the environment,

Recognizing the desirability of transparency in all branches of government and inviting legislative bodies to implement the principles of this Convention in their proceedings,

Recognizing also that the public needs to be aware of the procedures for participation in environmental decision-making, have free access to them and know how to use them,

Recognizing further the importance of the respective roles that individual citizens, non-governmental organizations and the private sector can play in environmental protection,

Desiring to promote environmental education to further the understanding of the environment and sustainable development and to encourage widespread public awareness of, and participation in, decisions affecting the environment and sustainable development,

a.   *See also* Basic Document 1.40.

Noting, in this context, the importance of making use of the media and of electronic or other, future forms of communication,

Recognizing the importance of fully integrating environmental considerations in governmental decision-making and the consequent need for public authorities to be in possession of accurate, comprehensive and up-to-date environmental information,

Acknowledging that public authorities hold environmental information in the public interest,

Concerned that effective judicial mechanisms should be accessible to the public, including organizations, so that its legitimate interests are protected and the law is enforced,

Noting the importance of adequate product information being provided to consumers to enable them to make informed environmental choices,

Recognizing the concern of the public about the deliberate release of genetically modified organisms into the environment and the need for increased transparency and greater public participation in decision-making in this field,

Convinced that the implementation of this Convention will contribute to strengthening democracy in the region of the United Nations Economic Commission for Europe (ECE),

Conscious of the role played in this respect by ECE and recalling, inter alia, the ECE Guidelines on Access to Environmental Information and Public Participation in Environmental Decision-making endorsed in the Ministerial Declaration adopted at the Third Ministerial Conference "Environment for Europe" in Sofia, Bulgaria, on 25 October 1995,

Bearing in mind the relevant provisions in the Convention on Environmental Impact Assessment in a Transboundary Context, done at Espoo, Finland, on 25 February 1991, and the Convention on the Transboundary Effects of Industrial Accidents and the Convention on the Protection and Use of Transboundary Watercourses and International Lakes, both done at Helsinki on 17 March 1992, and other regional conventions,

Conscious that the adoption of this Convention will have contributed to the further strengthening of the "Environment for Europe" process and to the results of the Fourth Ministerial Conference in Aarhus, Denmark, in June 1998,

Have agreed as follows:

Article 1—Objective

In order to contribute to the protection of the right of every person of present and future generations to live in an environment adequate to his or her health and well-being, each Party shall guarantee the rights of access to information, public participation in decision-making, and access to justice in environmental matters in accordance with the provisions of this Convention.

Article 2—Definitions

For the purposes of this Convention,

1. "Party" means, unless the text otherwise indicates, a Contracting Party to this Convention;

2. "Public authority" means:

(a) Government at national, regional and other level;

(b) Natural or legal persons performing public administrative functions under national law, including specific duties, activities or services in relation to the environment;

(c) Any other natural or legal persons having public responsibilities or functions, or providing public services, in relation to the environment, under the control of a body or person falling within subparagraphs (a) or (b) above;

(d) The institutions of any regional economic integration organization referred to in article 17 which is a Party to this Convention.

This definition does not include bodies or institutions acting in a judicial or legislative capacity;

3. "Environmental information" means any information in written, visual, aural, electronic or any other material form on:

(a) The state of elements of the environment, such as air and atmosphere, water, soil, land, landscape and natural sites, biological diversity and its components, including genetically modified organisms, and the interaction among these elements;

(b) Factors, such as substances, energy, noise and radiation, and activities or measures, including administrative measures, environmental agreements, policies, legislation, plans and programmes, affecting or likely to affect the elements of the environment within the scope of subparagraph (a) above, and cost-benefit and other economic analyses and assumptions used in environmental decision-making;

(c) The state of human health and safety, conditions of human life, cultural sites and built structures, inasmuch as they are or may be affected by the state of the elements of the environment or, through these elements, by the factors, activities or measures referred to in subparagraph (b) above;

4. "The public" means one or more natural or legal persons, and, in accordance with national legislation or practice, their associations, organizations or groups;

5. "The public concerned" means the public affected or likely to be affected by, or having an interest in, the environmental decision-making; for the purposes of this definition, non-governmental organizations promoting environmental protection and meeting any requirements under national law shall be deemed to have an interest.

Article 3—General Provisions

1. Each Party shall take the necessary legislative, regulatory and other measures, including measures to achieve compatibility between the provisions implementing the information, public participation and access-to-justice provisions in this Convention, as well as proper enforcement measures, to establish and maintain a clear, transparent and consistent framework to implement the provisions of this Convention.

2. Each Party shall endeavour to ensure that officials and authorities assist and provide guidance to the public in seeking access to information, in facilitating participation in decision-making and in seeking access to justice in environmental matters.

3. Each Party shall promote environmental education and environmental awareness among the public, especially on how to obtain access to information, to participate in decision-making and to obtain access to justice in environmental matters.

4. Each Party shall provide for appropriate recognition of and support to associations, organizations or groups promoting environmental protection and ensure that its national legal system is consistent with this obligation.

5. The provisions of this Convention shall not affect the right of a Party to maintain or introduce measures providing for broader access to information, more extensive public participation in decision-making and wider access to justice in environmental matters than required by this Convention.

6. This Convention shall not require any derogation from existing rights of access to information, public participation in decision-making and access to justice in environmental matters.

7. Each Party shall promote the application of the principles of this Convention in international environmental decision-making processes and within the framework of international organizations in matters relating to the environment.

8. Each Party shall ensure that persons exercising their rights in conformity with the provisions of this Convention shall not be penalized, persecuted or harassed in any way for their involvement. This provision shall not affect the powers of national courts to award reasonable costs in judicial proceedings.

9. Within the scope of the relevant provisions of this Convention, the public shall have access to information, have the possibility to participate in decision-making and have access to justice in environmental matters without discrimination as to citizenship, nationality or domicile and, in the case of a legal person, without discrimination as to where it has its registered seat or an effective centre of its activities.

Article 4—Access to Environmental Information

1. Each Party shall ensure that, subject to the following paragraphs of this article, public authorities, in response to a request for environmental information, make such information available to the public, within the framework of national legislation, including, where requested and subject to subparagraph (b) below, copies of the actual documentation containing or comprising such information:

(a) Without an interest having to be stated;

(b) In the form requested unless:

(i) It is reasonable for the public authority to make it available in another form, in which case reasons shall be given for making it available in that form; or

(ii) The information is already publicly available in another form.

2. The environmental information referred to in paragraph 1 above shall be made available as soon as possible and at the latest within one month after the request has been submitted, unless the volume and the complexity of the information justify an extension of this period up to two months after the request. The applicant shall be informed of any extension and of the reasons justifying it.

3. A request for environmental information may be refused if:

(a) The public authority to which the request is addressed does not hold the environmental information requested;

(b) The request is manifestly unreasonable or formulated in too general a manner; or

(c) The request concerns material in the course of completion or concerns internal communications of public authorities where such an exemption is provided for in national law or customary practice, taking into account the public interest served by disclosure.

4. A request for environmental information may be refused if the disclosure would adversely affect:

(a) The confidentiality of the proceedings of public authorities, where such confidentiality is provided for under national law;

(b) International relations, national defence or public security;

(c) The course of justice, the ability of a person to receive a fair trial or the ability of a public authority to conduct an enquiry of a criminal or disciplinary nature;

(d) The confidentiality of commercial and industrial information, where such confidentiality is protected by law in order to protect a legitimate economic interest.

Within this framework, information on emissions which is relevant for the protection of the environment shall be disclosed;

(e) Intellectual property rights;

(f) The confidentiality of personal data and/or files relating to a natural person where that person has not consented to the disclosure of the information to the public, where such confidentiality is provided for in national law;

(g) The interests of a third party which has supplied the information requested without that party being under or capable of being put under a legal obligation to do so, and where that party does not consent to the release of the material; or

(h) The environment to which the information relates, such as the breeding sites of rare species.

The aforementioned grounds for refusal shall be interpreted in a restrictive way, taking into account the public interest served by disclosure and taking into account whether the information requested relates to emissions into the environment.

5. Where a public authority does not hold the environmental information requested, this public authority shall, as promptly as possible, inform the applicant of the public authority to which it believes it is possible to apply for the information requested or transfer the request to that authority and inform the applicant accordingly.

6. Each Party shall ensure that, if information exempted from disclosure under paragraphs 3 (c) and 4 above can be separated out without prejudice to the confidentiality of the information exempted, public authorities make available the remainder of the environmental information that has been requested.

7. A refusal of a request shall be in writing if the request was in writing or the applicant so requests. A refusal shall state the reasons for the refusal and give information on access to the review procedure provided for in accordance with article 9. The refusal shall be made as soon as possible and at the latest within one month, unless the complexity of the information justifies an extension of this period up to two months after the request. The applicant shall be informed of any extension and of the reasons justifying it.

8. Each Party may allow its public authorities to make a charge for supplying information, but such charge shall not exceed a reasonable amount. Public authorities intending to make such a charge for supplying information shall make available to applicants a schedule of charges which may be levied, indicating the circumstances in which they may be levied or waived and when the supply of information is conditional on the advance payment of such a charge.

Article 5—Collection and Dissemination of Environmental Information

1. Each Party shall ensure that:

(a) Public authorities possess and update environmental information which is relevant to their functions;

(b) Mandatory systems are established so that there is an adequate flow of information to public authorities about proposed and existing activities which may significantly affect the environment;

(c) In the event of any imminent threat to human health or the environment, whether caused by human activities or due to natural causes, all information which could enable the public to take measures to prevent or mitigate harm arising from the threat and is held by a public authority is disseminated immediately and without delay to members of the public who may be affected.

2. Each Party shall ensure that, within the framework of national legislation, the way in which public authorities make environmental information available to the public is transparent and that environmental information is effectively accessible, inter alia, by:

(a) Providing sufficient information to the public about the type and scope of environmental information held by the relevant public authorities, the basic terms and conditions under which such information is made available and accessible, and the process by which it can be obtained;

(b) Establishing and maintaining practical arrangements, such as:

(i) Publicly accessible lists, registers or files;

(ii) Requiring officials to support the public in seeking access to information under this Convention; and

(iii) The identification of points of contact; and

(c) Providing access to the environmental information contained in lists, registers or files as referred to in subparagraph (b) (i) above free of charge.

3. Each Party shall ensure that environmental information progressively becomes available in electronic databases which are easily accessible to the public through public telecommunications networks. Information accessible in this form should include:

(a) Reports on the state of the environment, as referred to in paragraph 4 below;

(b) Texts of legislation on or relating to the environment;

(c) As appropriate, policies, plans and programmes on or relating to the environment, and environmental agreements; and

(d) Other information, to the extent that the availability of such information in this form would facilitate the application of national law implementing this Convention,

provided that such information is already available in electronic form.

4. Each Party shall, at regular intervals not exceeding three or four years, publish and disseminate a national report on the state of the environment, including information on the quality of the environment and information on pressures on the environment.

5. Each Party shall take measures within the framework of its legislation for the purpose of disseminating, inter alia:

(a) Legislation and policy documents such as documents on strategies, policies, programmes and action plans relating to the environment, and progress reports on their implementation, prepared at various levels of government;

(b) International treaties, conventions and agreements on environmental issues; and

(c) Other significant international documents on environmental issues, as appropriate.

6. Each Party shall encourage operators whose activities have a significant impact on the environment to inform the public regularly of the environmental impact of their activities and products, where appropriate within the framework of voluntary eco-labelling or eco-auditing schemes or by other means.

7. Each Party shall:

(a) Publish the facts and analyses of facts which it considers relevant and important in framing major environmental policy proposals;

(b) Publish, or otherwise make accessible, available explanatory material on its dealings with the public in matters falling within the scope of this Convention; and

(c) Provide in an appropriate form information on the performance of public functions or the provision of public services relating to the environment by government at all levels.

8. Each Party shall develop mechanisms with a view to ensuring that sufficient product information is made available to the public in a manner which enables consumers to make informed environmental choices.

9. Each Party shall take steps to establish progressively, taking into account international processes where appropriate, a coherent, nationwide system of pollution inventories or registers on a structured, computerized and publicly accessible database compiled through standardized reporting. Such a system may include inputs, releases and transfers of a specified range of substances and products, including water, energy and resource use, from a specified range of activities to environmental media and to on-site and off-site treatment and disposal sites.

10. Nothing in this article may prejudice the right of Parties to refuse to disclose certain environmental information in accordance with article 4, paragraphs 3 and 4.

Article 6—Public Participation in Decisions on Specific Activities

1. Each Party:

(a) Shall apply the provisions of this article with respect to decisions on whether to permit proposed activities listed in annex I;

(b) Shall, in accordance with its national law, also apply the provisions of this article to decisions on proposed activities not listed in annex I which may have a significant effect on the environment. To this end, Parties shall determine whether such a proposed activity is subject to these provisions; and

(c) May decide, on a case-by-case basis if so provided under national law, not to apply the provisions of this article to proposed activities serving national defence purposes, if that Party deems that such application would have an adverse effect on these purposes.

2. The public concerned shall be informed, either by public notice or individually as appropriate, early in an environmental decision-making procedure, and in an adequate, timely and effective manner, inter alia, of:

(a) The proposed activity and the application on which a decision will be taken;

(b) The nature of possible decisions or the draft decision;

(c) The public authority responsible for making the decision;

(d) The envisaged procedure, including, as and when this information can be provided:

    (i) The commencement of the procedure;

    (ii) The opportunities for the public to participate;

    (iii) The time and venue of any envisaged public hearing;

    (iv) An indication of the public authority from which relevant information can be obtained and where the relevant information has been deposited for examination by the public;

    (v) An indication of the relevant public authority or any other official body to which comments or questions can be submitted and of the time schedule for transmittal of comments or questions; and

(vi) An indication of what environmental information relevant to the proposed activity is available; and

(e) The fact that the activity is subject to a national or transboundary environmental impact assessment procedure.

3. The public participation procedures shall include reasonable time-frames for the different phases, allowing sufficient time for informing the public in accordance with paragraph 2 above and for the public to prepare and participate effectively during the environmental decision-making.

4. Each Party shall provide for early public participation, when all options are open and effective public participation can take place.

5. Each Party should, where appropriate, encourage prospective applicants to identify the public concerned, to enter into discussions, and to provide information regarding the objectives of their application before applying for a permit.

6. Each Party shall require the competent public authorities to give the public concerned access for examination, upon request where so required under national law, free of charge and as soon as it becomes available, to all information relevant to the decision-making referred to in this article that is available at the time of the public participation procedure, without prejudice to the right of Parties to refuse to disclose certain information in accordance with article 4, paragraphs 3 and 4. The relevant information shall include at least, and without prejudice to the provisions of article 4:

(a) A description of the site and the physical and technical characteristics of the proposed activity, including an estimate of the expected residues and emissions;

(b) A description of the significant effects of the proposed activity on the environment;

(c) A description of the measures envisaged to prevent and/or reduce the effects, including emissions;

(d) A non-technical summary of the above;

(e) An outline of the main alternatives studied by the applicant; and

(f) In accordance with national legislation, the main reports and advice issued to the public authority at the time when the public concerned shall be informed in accordance with paragraph 2 above.

7. Procedures for public participation shall allow the public to submit, in writing or, as appropriate, at a public hearing or enquiry with the applicant, any comments, information, analyses or opinions that it considers relevant to the proposed activity.

8. Each Party shall ensure that in the decision due account is taken of the outcome of the public participation.

9. Each Party shall ensure that, when the decision has been taken by the public authority, the public is promptly informed of the decision in accordance with the appropriate procedures. Each Party shall make accessible to the public the text of the decision along with the reasons and considerations on which the decision is based.

10. Each Party shall ensure that, when a public authority reconsiders or updates the operating conditions for an activity referred to in paragraph 1, the provisions of paragraphs 2 to 9 of this article are applied mutatis mutandis, and where appropriate.

11. Each Party shall, within the framework of its national law, apply, to the extent feasible and appropriate, provisions of this article to decisions on whether to permit the deliberate release of genetically modified organisms into the environment.

Article 7—Public Participation Concerning Plans, Programmes
and Policies Relating to the Environment

Each Party shall make appropriate practical and/or other provisions for the public to participate during the preparation of plans and programmes relating to the environment, within a transparent and fair framework, having provided the necessary information to the public. Within this framework, article 6, paragraphs 3, 4 and 8, shall be applied. The public which may participate shall be identified by the relevant public authority, taking into account the objectives of this Convention. To the extent appropriate, each Party shall endeavour to provide opportunities for public participation in the preparation of policies relating to the environment.

Article 8—Public Participation During the Preparation of Executive Regulations
and/or Generally Applicable Legally Binding Normative Instruments

Each Party shall strive to promote effective public participation at an appropriate stage, and while options are still open, during the preparation by public authorities of executive regulations and other generally applicable legally binding rules that may have a significant effect on the environment. To this end, the following steps should be taken:

(a) Time-frames sufficient for effective participation should be fixed;

(b) Draft rules should be published or otherwise made publicly available; and

(c) The public should be given the opportunity to comment, directly or through representative consultative bodies.

The result of the public participation shall be taken into account as far as possible.

Article 9—Access to Justice

1. Each Party shall, within the framework of its national legislation, ensure that any person who considers that his or her request for information under article 4 has been ignored, wrongfully refused, whether in part or in full, inadequately answered, or otherwise not dealt with in accordance with the provisions of that article, has access to a review procedure before a court of law or another independent and impartial body established by law.

In the circumstances where a Party provides for such a review by a court of law, it shall ensure that such a person also has access to an expeditious procedure established by law that is free of charge or inexpensive for reconsideration by a public authority or review by an independent and impartial body other than a court of law.

Final decisions under this paragraph 1 shall be binding on the public authority holding the information. Reasons shall be stated in writing, at least where access to information is refused under this paragraph.

2. Each Party shall, within the framework of its national legislation, ensure that members of the public concerned

(a) Having a sufficient interest or, alternatively,

(b) Maintaining impairment of a right, where the administrative procedural law of a Party requires this as a precondition,

have access to a review procedure before a court of law and/or another independent and impartial body established by law, to challenge the substantive and procedural legality of any decision, act or omission subject to the provisions of article 6 and, where so provided for under national law and without prejudice to paragraph 3 below, of other relevant provisions of this Convention.

What constitutes a sufficient interest and impairment of a right shall be determined in accordance with the requirements of national law and consistently with the objective of giving the public concerned wide access to justice within the scope of this Convention. To this end, the interest of any non-governmental organization meeting the requirements referred to in article 2, paragraph 5, shall be deemed sufficient for the purpose of subparagraph (a) above. Such organizations shall also be deemed to have rights capable of being impaired for the purpose of subparagraph (b) above.

The provisions of this paragraph 2 shall not exclude the possibility of a preliminary review procedure before an administrative authority and shall not affect the requirement of exhaustion of administrative review procedures prior to recourse to judicial review procedures, where such a requirement exists under national law.

3. In addition and without prejudice to the review procedures referred to in paragraphs 1 and 2 above, each Party shall ensure that, where they meet the criteria, if any, laid down in its national law, members of the public have access to administrative or judicial procedures to challenge acts and omissions by private persons and public authorities which contravene provisions of its national law relating to the environment.

4. In addition and without prejudice to paragraph 1 above, the procedures referred to in paragraphs 1, 2 and 3 above shall provide adequate and effective remedies, including injunctive relief as appropriate, and be fair, equitable, timely and not prohibitively expensive. Decisions under this article shall be given or recorded in writing. Decisions of courts, and whenever possible of other bodies, shall be publicly accessible.

5. In order to further the effectiveness of the provisions of this article, each Party shall ensure that information is provided to the public on access to administrative and judicial review procedures and shall consider the establishment of appropriate assistance mechanisms to remove or reduce financial and other barriers to access to justice.

Article 10—Meeting of the Parties

1. The first meeting of the Parties shall be convened no later than one year after the date of the entry into force of this Convention. Thereafter, an ordinary meeting of the Parties shall be held at least once every two years, unless otherwise decided by the Parties, or at the written request of any Party, provided that, within six months of the request being communicated to all Parties by the Executive Secretary of the Economic Commission for Europe, the said request is supported by at least one third of the Parties.

* * *

Article 11—Right to Vote

1. Except as provided for in paragraph 2 below, each Party to this Convention shall have one vote.

2. Regional economic integration organizations, in matters within their competence, shall exercise their right to vote with a number of votes equal to the number of their member States which are Parties to this Convention. Such organizations shall not exercise their right to vote if their member States exercise theirs, and vice versa.

Article 12—Secretariat

The Executive Secretary of the Economic Commission for Europe shall carry out the following secretariat functions:

(a) The convening and preparing of meetings of the Parties;

(b) The transmission to the Parties of reports and other information received in accordance with the provisions of this Convention; and

(c) Such other functions as may be determined by the Parties.

Article 13—Annexes

The annexes to this Convention shall constitute an integral part thereof.

Article 14—Amendments to the Convention

* * *

Article 15—Review of Compliance

The Meeting of the Parties shall establish, on a consensus basis, optional arrangements of a non-confrontational, non-judicial and consultative nature for reviewing compliance with the provisions of this Convention. These arrangements shall allow for appropriate public involvement and may include the option of considering communications from members of the public on matters related to this Convention.

Article 16—Settlement of Disputes

1.   If a dispute arises between two or more Parties about the interpretation or application of this Convention, they shall seek a solution by negotiation or by any other means of dispute settlement acceptable to the parties to the dispute.

2.   When signing, ratifying, accepting, approving or acceding to this Convention, or at any time thereafter, a Party may declare in writing to the Depositary that, for a dispute not resolved in accordance with paragraph 1 above, it accepts one or both of the following means of dispute settlement as compulsory in relation to any Party accepting the same obligation:

(a) Submission of the dispute to the International Court of Justice;

(b) Arbitration in accordance with the procedure set out in annex II.

3.   If the parties to the dispute have accepted both means of dispute settlement referred to in paragraph 2 above, the dispute may be submitted only to the International Court of Justice, unless the parties agree otherwise.

Article 17—Signature

* * *

Article 18—Depositary

* * *

Article 19—Ratification, Acceptance, Approval and Accession

* * *

Article 20—Entry into Force

* * *

Article 21—Withdrawal

* * *

Article 22—Authentic Texts

* * *

ANNEX I

LIST OF ACTIVITIES REFERRED TO IN ARTICLE 6, PARAGRAPH 1 (a)

1. Energy sector:

● Mineral oil and gas refineries;

● Installations for gasification and liquefaction;

● Thermal power stations and other combustion installations with a heat input of 50 megawatts (MW) or more;

* * *

8. (a) Construction of lines for long-distance railway traffic and of airports[1] with a basic runway length of 2,100 m or more;

(b) Construction of motorways and express roads;[2]

(c) Construction of a new road of four or more lanes, or realignment and/or widening of an existing road of two lanes or less so as to provide four or more lanes, where such new road, or realigned and/or widened section of road, would be 10 km or more in a continuous length.

9. (a) Inland waterways and ports for inland-waterway traffic which permit the passage of vessels of over 1,350 tons;

(b) Trading ports, piers for loading and unloading connected to land and outside ports (excluding ferry piers) which can take vessels of over 1,350 tons.

* * *

20. Any activity not covered by paragraphs 1–19 above where public participation is provided for under an environmental impact assessment procedure in accordance with national legislation.

* * *

22. Any change to or extension of activities, where such a change or extension in itself meets the criteria/thresholds set out in this annex, shall be subject to article 6, paragraph 1 (a) of this Convention. Any other change or extension of activities shall be subject to article 6, paragraph 1 (b) of this Convention.

ANNEX II

ARBITRATION

* * *

1. For the purposes of this Convention, "airport" means an airport which complies with the definition in the 1944 Chicago Convention setting up the International Civil Aviation Organization (Annex 14).

2. For the purposes of this Convention, "express road" means a road which complies with the definition in the European Agreement on Main International Traffic Arteries of 15 November 1975.

1.34　THE EARTH CHARTER. Adopted at The Hague by the Earth Charter Commission, 29 June 2000. Available from the Earth Charter Commission at <www.earthcharter.org>. *Reprinted in* **5 Weston & Carlson V.K.2a**

Preamble

We stand at a critical moment in Earth's history, a time when humanity must choose its future. As the world becomes increasingly interdependent and fragile, the future at once holds great peril and great promise. To move forward we must recognize that in the midst of a magnificent diversity of cultures and life forms we are one human family and one Earth community with a common destiny. We must join together to bring forth a sustainable global society founded on respect for nature, universal human rights, economic justice, and a culture of peace. Towards this end, it is imperative that we, the peoples of Earth, declare our responsibility to one another, to the greater community of life, and to future generations.

Earth, Our Home

Humanity is part of a vast evolving universe. Earth, our home, is alive with a unique community of life. The forces of nature make existence a demanding and uncertain adventure, but Earth has provided the conditions essential to life's evolution. The resilience of the community of life and the well-being of humanity depend upon preserving a healthy biosphere with all its ecological systems, a rich variety of plants and animals, fertile soils, pure waters, and clean air. The global environment with its finite resources is a common concern of all peoples. The protection of Earth's vitality, diversity, and beauty is a sacred trust.

The Global Situation

The dominant patterns of production and consumption are causing environmental devastation, the depletion of resources, and a massive extinction of species. Communities are being undermined. The benefits of development are not shared equitably and the gap between rich and poor is widening. Injustice, poverty, ignorance, and violent conflict are widespread and the cause of great suffering. An unprecedented rise in human population has overburdened ecological and social systems. The foundations of global security are threatened. These trends are perilous—but not inevitable.

The Challenges Ahead

The choice is ours: form a global partnership to care for Earth and one another or risk the destruction of ourselves and the diversity of life. Fundamental changes are needed in our values, institutions, and ways of living. We must realize that when basic needs have been met, human development is primarily about being more, not having more. We have the knowledge and technology to provide for all and to reduce our impacts on the environment. The emergence of a global civil society is creating new opportunities to build a democratic and humane world. Our environmental, economic, political, social, and spiritual challenges are interconnected, and together we can forge inclusive solutions.

Universal Responsibility

To realize these aspirations, we must decide to live with a sense of universal responsibility, identifying ourselves with the whole Earth community as well as our local communities. We are at once citizens of different nations and of one world in which the local and global are linked. Everyone shares responsibility for the present and future well-being of the human family and the larger living world. The spirit of human solidarity and kinship with all life is strengthened when we live with reverence for the mystery of being, gratitude for the gift of life, and humility regarding the human place in nature.

We urgently need a shared vision of basic values to provide an ethical foundation for the emerging world community. Therefore, together in hope we affirm the following interdependent principles for a sustainable way of life as a common standard by which the conduct of all individuals, organizations, businesses, governments, and transnational institutions is to be guided and assessed.

PRINCIPLES

I. RESPECT AND CARE FOR THE COMMUNITY OF LIFE

1. Respect Earth and life in all its diversity.

a. Recognize that all beings are interdependent and every form of life has value regardless of its worth to human beings.

b. Affirm faith in the inherent dignity of all human beings and in the intellectual, artistic, ethical, and spiritual potential of humanity.

2. Care for the community of life with understanding, compassion, and love.

a. Accept that with the right to own, manage, and use natural resources comes the duty to prevent environmental harm and to protect the rights of people.

b. Affirm that with increased freedom, knowledge, and power comes increased responsibility to promote the common good.

3. Build democratic societies that are just, participatory, sustainable, and peaceful.

a. Ensure that communities at all levels guarantee human rights and fundamental freedoms and provide everyone an opportunity to realize his or her full potential.

b. Promote social and economic justice, enabling all to achieve a secure and meaningful livelihood that is ecologically responsible.

4. Secure Earth's bounty and beauty for present and future generations.

a. Recognize that the freedom of action of each generation is qualified by the needs of future generations.

b. Transmit to future generations values, traditions, and institutions that support the long-term flourishing of Earth's human and ecological communities.

In order to fulfill these four broad commitments, it is necessary to:

II. ECOLOGICAL INTEGRITY

5. Protect and restore the integrity of Earth's ecological systems, with special concern for biological diversity and the natural processes that sustain life.

a. Adopt at all levels sustainable development plans and regulations that make environmental conservation and rehabilitation integral to all development initiatives.

b. Establish and safeguard viable nature and biosphere reserves, including wild lands and marine areas, to protect Earth's life support systems, maintain biodiversity, and preserve our natural heritage.

c. Promote the recovery of endangered species and ecosystems.

d. Control and eradicate non-native or genetically modified organisms harmful to native species and the environment, and prevent introduction of such harmful organisms.

e. Manage the use of renewable resources such as water, soil, forest products, and marine life in ways that do not exceed rates of regeneration and that protect the health of ecosystems.

f. Manage the extraction and use of non-renewable resources such as minerals and fossil fuels in ways that minimize depletion and cause no serious environmental damage.

6. Prevent harm as the best method of environmental protection and, when knowledge is limited, apply a precautionary approach.

a. Take action to avoid the possibility of serious or irreversible environmental harm even when scientific knowledge is incomplete or inconclusive.

b. Place the burden of proof on those who argue that a proposed activity will not cause significant harm, and make the responsible parties liable for environmental harm.

c. Ensure that decision making addresses the cumulative, long-term, indirect, long distance, and global consequences of human activities.

d. Prevent pollution of any part of the environment and allow no build-up of radioactive, toxic, or other hazardous substances.

e. Avoid military activities damaging to the environment.

7. Adopt patterns of production, consumption, and reproduction that safeguard Earth's regenerative capacities, human rights, and community well-being.

a. Reduce, reuse, and recycle the materials used in production and consumption systems, and ensure that residual waste can be assimilated by ecological systems.

b. Act with restraint and efficiency when using energy, and rely increasingly on renewable energy sources such as solar and wind.

c. Promote the development, adoption, and equitable transfer of environmentally sound technologies.

d. Internalize the full environmental and social costs of goods and services in the selling price, and enable consumers to identify products that meet the highest social and environmental standards.

e. Ensure universal access to health care that fosters reproductive health and responsible reproduction.

f. Adopt lifestyles that emphasize the quality of life and material sufficiency in a finite world.

8. Advance the study of ecological sustainability and promote the open exchange and wide application of the knowledge acquired.

a. Support international scientific and technical cooperation on sustainability, with special attention to the needs of developing nations.

b. Recognize and preserve the traditional knowledge and spiritual wisdom in all cultures that contribute to environmental protection and human well-being.

c. Ensure that information of vital importance to human health and environmental protection, including genetic information, remains available in the public domain.

III. SOCIAL AND ECONOMIC JUSTICE

9. Eradicate poverty as an ethical, social, and environmental imperative.

a. Guarantee the right to potable water, clean air, food security, uncontaminated soil, shelter, and safe sanitation, allocating the national and international resources required.

b. Empower every human being with the education and resources to secure a sustainable livelihood, and provide social security and safety nets for those who are unable to support themselves.

c. Recognize the ignored, protect the vulnerable, serve those who suffer, and enable them to develop their capacities and to pursue their aspirations.

10. *Ensure that economic activities and institutions at all levels promote human development in an equitable and sustainable manner.*

a. Promote the equitable distribution of wealth within nations and among nations.

b. Enhance the intellectual, financial, technical, and social resources of developing nations, and relieve them of onerous international debt.

c. Ensure that all trade supports sustainable resource use, environmental protection, and progressive labor standards.

d. Require multinational corporations and international financial organizations to act transparently in the public good, and hold them accountable for the consequences of their activities.

11. *Affirm gender equality and equity as prerequisites to sustainable development and ensure universal access to education, health care, and economic opportunity.*

a. Secure the human rights of women and girls and end all violence against them.

b. Promote the active participation of women in all aspects of economic, political, civil, social, and cultural life as full and equal partners, decision makers, leaders, and beneficiaries.

c. Strengthen families and ensure the safety and loving nurture of all family members.

12. *Uphold the right of all, without discrimination, to a natural and social environment supportive of human dignity, bodily health, and spiritual well-being, with special attention to the rights of indigenous peoples and minorities.*

a. Eliminate discrimination in all its forms, such as that based on race, color, sex, sexual orientation, religion, language, and national, ethnic or social origin.

b. Affirm the right of indigenous peoples to their spirituality, knowledge, lands and resources and to their related practice of sustainable livelihoods.

c. Honor and support the young people of our communities, enabling them to fulfill their essential role in creating sustainable societies.

d. Protect and restore outstanding places of cultural and spiritual significance.

IV. DEMOCRACY, NONVIOLENCE, AND PEACE

13. *Strengthen democratic institutions at all levels, and provide transparency and accountability in governance, inclusive participation in decision making, and access to justice.*

a. Uphold the right of everyone to receive clear and timely information on environmental matters and all development plans and activities which are likely to affect them or in which they have an interest.

b. Support local, regional and global civil society, and promote the meaningful participation of all interested individuals and organizations in decision making.

c. Protect the rights to freedom of opinion, expression, peaceful assembly, association, and dissent.

d. Institute effective and efficient access to administrative and independent judicial procedures, including remedies and redress for environmental harm and the threat of such harm.

e. Eliminate corruption in all public and private institutions.

f. Strengthen local communities, enabling them to care for their environments, and assign environmental responsibilities to the levels of government where they can be carried out most effectively.

14. Integrate into formal education and life-long learning the knowledge, values, and skills needed for a sustainable way of life.

a. Provide all, especially children and youth, with educational opportunities that empower them to contribute actively to sustainable development.

b. Promote the contribution of the arts and humanities as well as the sciences in sustainability education.

c. Enhance the role of the mass media in raising awareness of ecological and social challenges.

d. Recognize the importance of moral and spiritual education for sustainable living.

15. Treat all living beings with respect and consideration.

a. Prevent cruelty to animals kept in human societies and protect them from suffering.

b. Protect wild animals from methods of hunting, trapping, and fishing that cause extreme, prolonged, or avoidable suffering.

c. Avoid or eliminate to the full extent possible the taking or destruction of non-targeted species.

16. Promote a culture of tolerance, nonviolence, and peace.

a. Encourage and support mutual understanding, solidarity, and cooperation among all peoples and within and among nations.

b. Implement comprehensive strategies to prevent violent conflict and use collaborative problem solving to manage and resolve environmental conflicts and other disputes.

c. Demilitarize national security systems to the level of a non-provocative defense posture, and convert military resources to peaceful purposes, including ecological restoration.

d. Eliminate nuclear, biological, and toxic weapons and other weapons of mass destruction.

e. Ensure that the use of orbital and outer space supports environmental protection and peace.

f. Recognize that peace is the wholeness created by right relationships with oneself, other persons, other cultures, other life, Earth, and the larger whole of which all are a part.

The Way Forward

As never before in history, common destiny beckons us to seek a new beginning. Such renewal is the promise of these Earth Charter principles. To fulfill this promise, we must commit ourselves to adopt and promote the values and objectives of the Charter.

This requires a change of mind and heart. It requires a new sense of global interdependence and universal responsibility. We must imaginatively develop and apply the vision of a sustainable way of life locally, nationally, regionally, and globally. Our cultural diversity is a precious heritage and different cultures will find their own distinctive ways to realize the vision. We must deepen and expand the global dialogue that generated the Earth Charter, for we have much to learn from the ongoing collaborative search for truth and wisdom.

Life often involves tensions between important values. This can mean difficult choices. However, we must find ways to harmonize diversity with unity, the exercise of freedom with the common good, short-term objectives with long-term goals. Every individual, family, organization, and community has a vital role to play. The arts, sciences, religions, educational institutions, media, businesses, nongovernmental organizations, and governments are all called to offer creative leadership. The partnership of government, civil society, and business is essential for effective governance.

In order to build a sustainable global community, the nations of the world must renew their commitment to the United Nations, fulfill their obligations under existing international agreements, and support the implementation of Earth Charter principles with an international legally binding instrument on environment and development.

Let ours be a time remembered for the awakening of a new reverence for life, the firm resolve to achieve sustainability, the quickening of the struggle for justice and peace, and the joyful celebration of life.

1.35   Unites Nations Millennium Declaration. **Adopted by the U.N. General Assembly, 8 December 2000. GA Res 55/2, UN GAOR, 55th Sess, Supp No 49, vol I, UN Doc A/Res/55/2 (2000)**

I.   Values and principles

1.   We, heads of State and Government, have gathered at United Nations headquarters in New York from 6 to 8 September 2000, at the dawn of a new millennium, to reaffirm our faith in the Organization and its Charter as indispensable foundations of a more peaceful, prosperous and just world.

2.   We recognize that, in addition to our separate responsibilities to our individual societies, we have a collective responsibility to uphold the principles of human dignity, equality and equity at the global level. As leaders we have a duty therefore to all the world's people, especially the most vulnerable and, in particular, the children of the world, to whom the future belongs.

3.   We reaffirm our commitment to the purposes and principles of the Charter of the United Nations, which have proved timeless and universal. Indeed, their relevance and capacity to inspire have increased, as nations and peoples have become increasingly interconnected and interdependent.

4.   We are determined to establish a just and lasting peace all over the world in accordance with the purposes and principles of the Charter. We rededicate ourselves to support all efforts to uphold the sovereign equality of all States, respect for their territorial integrity and political independence, resolution of disputes by peaceful means and in conformity with the principles of justice and international law, the right to self-determination of peoples which remain under colonial domination and foreign occupation, non-interference in the internal affairs of States, respect for human rights and fundamental freedoms, respect for the equal rights of all without distinction as to race, sex, language or religion and international cooperation in solving international problems of an economic, social, cultural or humanitarian character.

5.   We believe that the central challenge we face today is to ensure that globalization becomes a positive force for all the world's people. For while globalization offers great opportunities, at present its benefits are very unevenly shared, while its costs are unevenly distributed. We recognize that developing countries and countries with economies in transition face special difficulties in responding to this central challenge. Thus, only through broad and sustained efforts to create a shared future, based upon our common humanity in all its diversity, can globalization be made fully inclusive and equitable. These efforts must include policies and measures, at the global level, which correspond to the needs of developing countries and economies in transition and are formulated and implemented with their effective participation.

6.   We consider certain fundamental values to be essential to international relations in the twenty-first century. These include:

- **Freedom.** Men and women have the right to live their lives and raise their children in dignity, free from hunger and from the fear of violence, oppression or injustice. Democratic and participatory governance based on the will of the people best assures these rights.

- **Equality.** No individual and no nation must be denied the opportunity to benefit from development. The equal rights and opportunities of women and men must be assured.

- **Solidarity.** Global challenges must be managed in a way that distributes the costs and burdens fairly in accordance with basic principles of equity and social justice. Those who suffer or who benefit least deserve help from those who benefit most.

- **Tolerance.** Human beings must respect one other, in all their diversity of belief, culture and language. Differences within and between societies should be neither feared nor repressed, but cherished as a precious asset of humanity. A culture of peace and dialogue among all civilizations should be actively promoted.

- **Respect for nature.** Prudence must be shown in the management of all living species and natural resources, in accordance with the precepts of sustainable development. Only in this way can the immeasurable riches provided to us by nature be preserved and passed on to our descendants. The current unsustainable patterns of production and consumption must be changed in the interest of our future welfare and that of our descendants.

- **Shared responsibility.** Responsibility for managing worldwide economic and social development, as well as threats to international peace and security, must be shared among the nations of the world and should be exercised multilaterally. As the most universal and most representative organization in the world, the United Nations must play the central role.

7. In order to translate these shared values into actions, we have identified key objectives to which we assign special significance.

II. Peace, security and disarmament

8. We will spare no effort to free our peoples from the scourge of war, whether within or between States, which has claimed more than 5 million lives in the past decade. We will also seek to eliminate the dangers posed by weapons of mass destruction.

9. We resolve therefore:

- To strengthen respect for the rule of law in international as in national affairs and, in particular, to ensure compliance by Member States with the decisions of the International Court of Justice, in compliance with the Charter of the United Nations, in cases to which they are parties.

- To make the United Nations more effective in maintaining peace and security by giving it the resources and tools it needs for conflict prevention, peaceful resolution of disputes, peacekeeping, post-conflict peace-building and reconstruction. In this context, we take note of the report of the Panel on United Nations Peace Operations and request the General Assembly to consider its recommendations expeditiously.

- To strengthen cooperation between the United Nations and regional organizations, in accordance with the provisions of Chapter VIII of the Charter.

- To ensure the implementation, by States Parties, of treaties in areas such as arms control and disarmament and of international humanitarian law and human rights law, and call upon all States to consider signing and ratifying the Rome Statute of the International Criminal Court.

- To take concerted action against international terrorism, and to accede as soon as possible to all the relevant international conventions.

- To redouble our efforts to implement our commitment to counter the world drug problem.

- To intensify our efforts to fight transnational crime in all its dimensions, including trafficking as well as smuggling in human beings and money laundering.

- To minimize the adverse effects of United Nations economic sanctions on innocent populations, to subject such sanctions regimes to regular reviews and to eliminate the adverse effects of sanctions on third parties.

- To strive for the elimination of weapons of mass destruction, particularly nuclear weapons, and to keep all options open for achieving this aim, including the possibility of convening an international conference to identify ways of eliminating nuclear dangers.

• To take concerted action to end illicit traffic in small arms and light weapons, especially by making arms transfers more transparent and supporting regional disarmament measures, taking account of all the recommendations of the forthcoming United Nations Conference on Illicit Trade in Small Arms and Light Weapons.

• To call on all States to consider acceding to the Convention on the Prohibition of the Use, Stockpiling, Production and Transfer of Anti-personnel Mines and on Their Destruction, as well as the amended mines protocol to the Convention on conventional weapons.

10. We urge Member States to observe the Olympic Truce, individually and collectively, now and in the future, and to support the International Olympic Committee in its efforts to promote peace and human understanding through sport and the Olympic Ideal.

III. Development and poverty eradication

11. We will spare no effort to free our fellow men, women and children from the abject and dehumanizing conditions of extreme poverty, to which more than a billion of them are currently subjected. We are committed to making the right to development a reality for everyone and to freeing the entire human race from want.

12. We resolve therefore to create an environment—at the national and global levels alike—which is conducive to development and to the elimination of poverty.

13. Success in meeting these objectives depends, *inter alia*, on good governance within each country. It also depends on good governance at the international level and on transparency in the financial, monetary and trading systems. We are committed to an open, equitable, rule-based, predictable and non-discriminatory multilateral trading and financial system.

14. We are concerned about the obstacles developing countries face in mobilizing the resources needed to finance their sustained development. We will therefore make every effort to ensure the success of the High-level International and Intergovernmental Event on Financing for Development, to be held in 2001.

15. We also undertake to address the special needs of the least developed countries. In this context, we welcome the Third United Nations Conference on the Least Developed Countries to be held in May 2001 and will endeavour to ensure its success. We call on the industrialized countries:

• To adopt, preferably by the time of that Conference, a policy of duty-and quota-free access for essentially all exports from the least developed countries;

• To implement the enhanced programme of debt relief for the heavily indebted poor countries without further delay and to agree to cancel all official bilateral debts of those countries in return for their making demonstrable commitments to poverty reduction; and

• To grant more generous development assistance, especially to countries that are genuinely making an effort to apply their resources to poverty reduction.

16. We are also determined to deal comprehensively and effectively with the debt problems of low-and middle-income developing countries, through various national and international measures designed to make their debt sustainable in the long term.

17. We also resolve to address the special needs of small island developing States, by implementing the Barbados Programme of Action and the outcome of the twenty-second special session of the General Assembly rapidly and in full. We urge the international community to ensure that, in the development of a vulnerability index, the special needs of small island developing States are taken into account.

18. We recognize the special needs and problems of the landlocked developing countries, and urge both bilateral and multilateral donors to increase financial and technical assistance to this group of countries to meet their special development needs and to help them overcome the impediments of geography by improving their transit transport systems.

19. We resolve further:

• To halve, by the year 2015, the proportion of the world's people whose income is less than one dollar a day and the proportion of people who suffer from hunger and, by the same date, to halve the proportion of people who are unable to reach or to afford safe drinking water.

• To ensure that, by the same date, children everywhere, boys and girls alike, will be able to complete a full course of primary schooling and that girls and boys will have equal access to all levels of education.

• By the same date, to have reduced maternal mortality by three quarters, and under-five child mortality by two thirds, of their current rates.

• To have, by then, halted, and begun to reverse, the spread of HIV/AIDS, the scourge of malaria and other major diseases that afflict humanity.

• To provide special assistance to children orphaned by HIV/AIDS.

• By 2020, to have achieved a significant improvement in the lives of at least 100 million slum dwellers as proposed in the "Cities Without Slums" initiative.

20. We also resolve:

• To promote gender equality and the empowerment of women as effective ways to combat poverty, hunger and disease and to stimulate development that is truly sustainable.

• To develop and implement strategies that give young people everywhere a real chance to find decent and productive work.

• To encourage the pharmaceutical industry to make essential drugs more widely available and affordable by all who need them in developing countries.

• To develop strong partnerships with the private sector and with civil society organizations in pursuit of development and poverty eradication.

• To ensure that the benefits of new technologies, especially information and communication technologies, in conformity with recommendations contained in the ECOSOC 2000 Ministerial Declaration, are available to all.

IV. Protecting our common environment

21. We must spare no effort to free all of humanity, and above all our children and grandchildren, from the threat of living on a planet irredeemably spoilt by human activities, and whose resources would no longer be sufficient for their needs.

22. We reaffirm our support for the principles of sustainable development, including those set out in Agenda 21, agreed upon at the United Nations Conference on Environment and Development.

23. We resolve therefore to adopt in all our environmental actions a new ethic of conservation and stewardship and, as first steps, we resolve:

• To make every effort to ensure the entry into force of the Kyoto Protocol, preferably by the tenth anniversary of the United Nations Conference on Environment and Development in 2002, and to embark on the required reduction in emissions of greenhouse gases.

• To intensify our collective efforts for the management, conservation and sustainable development of all types of forests.

• To press for the full implementation of the Convention on Biological Diversity and the Convention to Combat Desertification in those Countries Experiencing Serious Drought and/or Desertification, particularly in Africa.

• To stop the unsustainable exploitation of water resources by developing water management strategies at the regional, national and local levels, which promote both equitable access and adequate supplies.

• To intensify cooperation to reduce the number and effects of natural and man-made disasters.

• To ensure free access to information on the human genome sequence.

V. Human rights, democracy and good governance

24. We will spare no effort to promote democracy and strengthen the rule of law, as well as respect for all internationally recognized human rights and fundamental freedoms, including the right to development.

25. We resolve therefore:

• To respect fully and uphold the Universal Declaration of Human Rights.

• To strive for the full protection and promotion in all our countries of civil, political, economic, social and cultural rights for all.

• To strengthen the capacity of all our countries to implement the principles and practices of democracy and respect for human rights, including minority rights.

• To combat all forms of violence against women and to implement the Convention on the Elimination of All Forms of Discrimination against Women.

• To take measures to ensure respect for and protection of the human rights of migrants, migrant workers and their families, to eliminate the increasing acts of racism and xenophobia in many societies and to promote greater harmony and tolerance in all societies.

• To work collectively for more inclusive political processes, allowing genuine participation by all citizens in all our countries.

• To ensure the freedom of the media to perform their essential role and the right of the public to have access to information.

VI. Protecting the vulnerable

26. We will spare no effort to ensure that children and all civilian populations that suffer disproportionately the consequences of natural disasters, genocide, armed conflicts and other humanitarian emergencies are given every assistance and protection so that they can resume normal life as soon as possible.

We resolve therefore:

• To expand and strengthen the protection of civilians in complex emergencies, in conformity with international humanitarian law.

• To strengthen international cooperation, including burden sharing in, and the coordination of humanitarian assistance to, countries hosting refugees and to help all refugees and displaced persons to return voluntarily to their homes, in safety and dignity and to be smoothly reintegrated into their societies.

• To encourage the ratification and full implementation of the Convention on the Rights of the Child and its optional protocols on the involvement of children in armed conflict and on the sale of children, child prostitution and child pornography.

VII. Meeting the special needs of Africa

27. We will support the consolidation of democracy in Africa and assist Africans in their struggle for lasting peace, poverty eradication and sustainable development, thereby bringing Africa into the mainstream of the world economy.

28. We resolve therefore:

• To give full support to the political and institutional structures of emerging democracies in Africa.

• To encourage and sustain regional and subregional mechanisms for preventing conflict and promoting political stability, and to ensure a reliable flow of resources for peacekeeping operations on the continent.

• To take special measures to address the challenges of poverty eradication and sustainable development in Africa, including debt cancellation, improved market access, enhanced Official Development Assistance and increased flows of Foreign Direct Investment, as well as transfers of technology.

• To help Africa build up its capacity to tackle the spread of the HIV/AIDS pandemic and other infectious diseases.

VIII. Strengthening the United Nations

29. We will spare no effort to make the United Nations a more effective instrument for pursuing all of these priorities: the fight for development for all the peoples of the world, the fight against poverty, ignorance and disease; the fight against injustice; the fight against violence, terror and crime; and the fight against the degradation and destruction of our common home.

30. We resolve therefore:

• To reaffirm the central position of the General Assembly as the chief deliberative, policy-making and representative organ of the United Nations, and to enable it to play that role effectively.

• To intensify our efforts to achieve a comprehensive reform of the Security Council in all its aspects.

• To strengthen further the Economic and Social Council, building on its recent achievements, to help it fulfill the role ascribed to it in the Charter.

• To strengthen the International Court of Justice, in order to ensure justice and the rule of law in international affairs.

• To encourage regular consultations and coordination among the principal organs of the United Nations in pursuit of their functions.

• To ensure that the Organization is provided on a timely and predictable basis with the resources it needs to carry out its mandates.

• To urge the Secretariat to make the best use of those resources, in accordance with clear rules and procedures agreed by the General Assembly, in the interests of all Member States, by adopting the best management practices and technologies available and by concentrating on those tasks that reflect the agreed priorities of Member States.

• To promote adherence to the Convention on the Safety of United Nations and Associated Personnel.

• To ensure greater policy coherence and better cooperation between the United Nations, its agencies, the Bretton Woods Institutions and the World Trade Organization, as well as other multilateral bodies, with a view to achieving a fully coordinated approach to the problems of peace and development.

• To strengthen further cooperation between the United Nations and national parliaments through their world organization, the Inter–Parliamentary Union, in various fields, including peace and security, economic and social development, international law and human rights and democracy and gender issues.

• To give greater opportunities to the private sector, non-governmental organizations and civil society, in general, to contribute to the realization of the Organization's goals and programmes.

31.   We request the General Assembly to review on a regular basis the progress made in implementing the provisions of this Declaration, and ask the Secretary-General to issue periodic reports for consideration by the General Assembly and as a basis for further action.

32.   We solemnly reaffirm, on this historic occasion, that the United Nations is the indispensable common house of the entire human family, through which we will seek to realize our universal aspirations for peace, cooperation and development. We therefore pledge our unstinting support for these common objectives and our determination to achieve them.

1.36 Draft Preamble and Draft Articles on Prevention of Transboundary Harm From Hazardous Activities. **Adopted by the International Law Commission, 11 May 2001.** *Report of the International Law Commission on the Work of its Fifty-third Session.* **UN GAOR, 56th Sess, Supp No 10, at 370–376, UN Doc A/56/10 and Corr 1 (2001);** *reprinted in* **5 Weston & Carlson V.J.17**

The States Parties,

Having in mind Article 13, paragraph 1 (a) of the Charter of the United Nations, which provides that the General Assembly shall initiate studies and make recommendations for the purpose of encouraging the progressive development of international law and its codification,

Bearing in mind the principle of permanent sovereignty of States over the natural resources within their territory or otherwise under their jurisdiction or control,

Bearing also in mind that the freedom of States to carry on or permit activities in their territory or otherwise under their jurisdiction or control is not unlimited,

Recalling the Rio Declaration on Environment and Development of 13 June 1992,

Recognizing the importance of promoting international cooperation,

Have agreed as follows:

Article 1 Scope

The present articles apply to activities not prohibited by international law which involve a risk of causing significant transboundary harm through their physical consequences.

Article 2 Use of terms

For the purposes of the present articles:

(a) *Risk of causing significant transboundary harm* includes risks taking the form of a high probability of causing significant transboundary harm and a low probability of causing disastrous transboundary harm;

(b) *Harm* means harm caused to persons, property or the environment;

(c) *Transboundary harm* means harm caused in the territory of or in other places under the jurisdiction or control of a State other than the State of origin, whether or not the States concerned share a common border;

(d) *State of origin* means the State in the territory or otherwise under the jurisdiction or control of which the activities referred to in article 1 are planned or are carried out;

(e) *State likely to be affected* means the State or States in the territory of which there is the risk of significant transboundary harm or which have jurisdiction or control over any other place where there is such a risk;

(f) *States concerned* means the State of origin and the State likely to be affected.

Article 3 Prevention

The State of origin shall take all appropriate measures to prevent significant transboundary harm or at any event to minimize the risk thereof.

Article 4 Cooperation

States concerned shall cooperate in good faith and, as necessary, seek the assistance of one or more competent international organizations in preventing significant transboundary harm or at any event in minimizing the risk thereof.

Article 5 Implementation

States concerned shall take the necessary legislative, administrative or other action including the establishment of suitable monitoring mechanisms to implement the provisions of the present articles.

Article 6 Authorization

1. The State of origin shall require its prior authorization for:

(a) Any activity within the scope of the present articles carried out in its territory or otherwise under its jurisdiction or control;

(b) Any major change in an activity referred to in subparagraph (a);

(c) Any plan to change an activity which may transform it into one falling within the scope of the present articles.

2. The requirement of authorization established by a State shall be made applicable in respect of all pre-existing activities within the scope of the present articles. Authorizations already issued by the State for pre-existing activities shall be reviewed in order to comply with the present articles.

3. In case of a failure to conform to the terms of the authorization, the State of origin shall take such actions as appropriate, including where necessary terminating the authorization.

Article 7 Assessment of risk

Any decision in respect of the authorization of an activity within the scope of the present articles shall, in particular, be based on an assessment of the possible transboundary harm caused by that activity, including any environmental impact assessment.

Article 8 Notification and information

1. If the assessment referred to in article 7 indicates a risk of causing significant transboundary harm, the State of origin shall provide the State likely to be affected with timely notification of the risk and the assessment and shall transmit to it the available technical and all other relevant information on which the assessment is based.

2. The State of origin shall not take any decision on authorization of the activity pending the receipt, within a period not exceeding six months, of the response from the State likely to be affected.

Article 9 Consultations on preventive measures

1. The States concerned shall enter into consultations, at the request of any of them, with a view to achieving acceptable solutions regarding measures to be adopted in order to prevent significant transboundary harm or at any event to minimize the risk thereof. The States concerned shall agree, at the commencement of such consultations, on a reasonable time-frame for the consultations.

2. The States concerned shall seek solutions based on an equitable balance of interests in the light of article 10.

3. If the consultations referred to in paragraph 1 fail to produce an agreed solution, the State of origin shall nevertheless take into account the interests of the State likely to be affected in case it decides to authorize the activity to be pursued, without prejudice to the rights of any State likely to be affected.

Article 10 Factors involved in an equitable balance of interests

In order to achieve an equitable balance of interests as referred to in paragraph 2 of article 9, the States concerned shall take into account all relevant factors and circumstances, including:

(a) The degree of risk of significant transboundary harm and of the availability of means of preventing such harm, or minimizing the risk thereof or repairing the harm;

(b) The importance of the activity, taking into account its overall advantages of a social, economic and technical character for the State of origin in relation to the potential harm for the State likely to be affected;

(c) The risk of significant harm to the environment and the availability of means of preventing such harm, or minimizing the risk thereof or restoring the environment;

(d) The degree to which the State of origin and, as appropriate, the State likely to be affected are prepared to contribute to the costs of prevention;

(e) The economic viability of the activity in relation to the costs of prevention and to the possibility of carrying out the activity elsewhere or by other means or replacing it with an alternative activity;

(f) The standards of prevention which the State likely to be affected applies to the same or comparable activities and the standards applied in comparable regional or international practice.

Article 11 Procedures in the absence of notification

1. If a State has reasonable grounds to believe that an activity planned or carried out in the State of origin may involve a risk of causing significant transboundary harm to it, it may request the State of origin to apply the provision of article 8. The request shall be accompanied by a documented explanation setting forth its grounds.

2. In the event that the State of origin nevertheless finds that it is not under an obligation to provide a notification under article 8, it shall so inform the requesting State within a reasonable time, providing a documented explanation setting forth the reasons for such finding. If this finding does not satisfy that State, at its request, the two States shall promptly enter into consultations in the manner indicated in article 9.

3. During the course of the consultations, the State of origin shall, if so requested by the other State, arrange to introduce appropriate and feasible measures to minimize the risk and, where appropriate, to suspend the activity in question for a reasonable period.

Article 12 Exchange of information

While the activity is being carried out, the States concerned shall exchange in a timely manner all available information concerning that activity relevant to preventing significant transboundary harm or at any event minimizing the risk thereof. Such an exchange of information shall continue until such time as the States concerned consider it appropriate even after the activity is terminated.

Article 13 Information to the public

States concerned shall, by such means as are appropriate, provide the public likely to be affected by an activity within the scope of the present articles with relevant information relating to that activity, the risk involved and the harm which might result and ascertain their views.

Article 14 National security and industrial secrets

Data and information vital to the national security of the State of origin or to the protection of industrial secrets or concerning intellectual property may be withheld, but the State of origin shall cooperate in good faith with the State likely to be affected in providing as much information as possible under the circumstances.

Article 15 Non-discrimination

Unless the States concerned have agreed otherwise for the protection of the interests of persons, natural or juridical, who may be or are exposed to the risk of significant transboundary harm as a result of an activity within the scope of the present articles, a State shall not discriminate on the basis of nationality or residence or place where the injury might occur, in granting to such persons, in accordance with its legal system, access to judicial or other procedures to seek protection or other appropriate redress.

Article 16 Emergency preparedness

The State of origin shall develop contingency plans for responding to emergencies, in cooperation, where appropriate, with the State likely to be affected and competent international organizations.

Article 17 Notification of an emergency

The State of origin shall, without delay and by the most expeditious means, at its disposal, notify the State likely to be affected of an emergency concerning an activity within the scope of the present articles and provide it with all relevant and available information.

Article 18 Relationship to other rules of international law

The present articles are without prejudice to any obligation incurred by States under relevant treaties or rules of customary international law.

Article 19 Settlement of disputes

1. Any dispute concerning the interpretation or application of the present articles shall be settled expeditiously through peaceful means of settlement chosen by mutual agreement of the parties to the dispute, including negotiations, mediation, conciliation, arbitration or judicial settlement.

2. Failing an agreement on the means for the peaceful settlement of the dispute within a period of six months, the parties to the dispute shall, at the request of any of them, have recourse to the establishment of an impartial fact-finding commission.

3. The Fact-finding Commission shall be composed of one member nominated by each party to the dispute and in addition a member not having the nationality of any of the parties to the dispute chosen by the nominated members who shall serve as Chairperson.

4. If more than one State is involved on one side of the dispute and those States do not agree on a common member of the Commission and each of them nominates a member, the other party to the dispute has the right to nominate an equal number of members of the Commission.

5. If the members nominated by the parties to the dispute are unable to agree on a Chairperson within three months of the request for the establishment of the Commission, any party to the dispute may request the Secretary–General of the United Nations to appoint the Chairperson who shall not have the nationality of any of the parties to the dispute. If one of the parties to the dispute fails to nominate a member within three months of the initial request pursuant to paragraph 2, any other party to the dispute may request the Secretary–General of the United Nations to appoint a person who shall not have the nationality of any of the parties to the dispute. The person so appointed shall constitute a single-member Commission.

6. The Commission shall adopt its report by a majority vote, unless it is a single-member Commission, and shall submit that report to the parties to the dispute setting forth its findings and recommendations, which the parties to the dispute shall consider in good faith.

1.37 JOHANNESBURG DECLARATION ON SUSTAINABLE DEVELOPMENT. **Adopted by the World Summit on Sustainable Development at Johannesburg, 4 September 2002. UN Doc A/CONF.199/20 at 1 (2002)**

From our origins to the future

1. We, the representatives of the peoples of the world, assembled at the World Summit on Sustainable Development in Johannesburg, South Africa, from 2 to 4 September 2002, reaffirm our commitment to sustainable development.

2. We commit ourselves to building a humane, equitable and caring global society, cognizant of the need for human dignity for all.

3. At the beginning of this Summit, the children of the world spoke to us in a simple yet clear voice that the future belongs to them, and accordingly challenged all of us to ensure that through our actions they will inherit a world free of the indignity and indecency occasioned by poverty, environmental degradation and patterns of unsustainable development.

4. As part of our response to these children, who represent our collective future, all of us, coming from every corner of the world, informed by different life experiences, are united and moved by a deeply felt sense that we urgently need to create a new and brighter world of hope.

5. Accordingly, we assume a collective responsibility to advance and strengthen the interdependent and mutually reinforcing pillars of sustainable development— economic development, social development and environmental protection—at the local, national, regional and global levels.

6. From this continent, the cradle of humanity, we declare, through the Plan of Implementation of the World Summit on Sustainable Development and the present Declaration, our responsibility to one another, to the greater community of life and to our children.

7. Recognizing that humankind is at a crossroads, we have united in a common resolve to make a determined effort to respond positively to the need to produce a practical and visible plan to bring about poverty eradication and human development.

From Stockholm to Rio de Janeiro to Johannesburg

8. Thirty years ago, in Stockholm, we agreed on the urgent need to respond to the problem of environmental deterioration. Ten years ago, at the United Nations Conference on Environment and Development, held in Rio de Janeiro, we agreed that the protection of the environment and social and economic development are fundamental to sustainable development, based on the Rio Principles. To achieve such development, we adopted the global programme entitled Agenda 2l3 and the Rio Declaration on Environment and Development, to which we reaffirm our commitment. The Rio Conference was a significant milestone that set a new agenda for sustainable development.

9. Between Rio and Johannesburg, the world's nations have met in several major conferences under the auspices of the United Nations, including the International Conference on Financing for Development, as well as the Doha Ministerial Conference. These conferences defined for the world a comprehensive vision for the future of humanity.

10. At the Johannesburg Summit, we have achieved much in bringing together a rich tapestry of peoples and views in a constructive search for a common path towards a world that respects and implements the vision of sustainable development. The Johannesburg Summit has also confirmed that significant progress has been made towards achieving a global consensus and partnership among all the people of our planet.

The challenges we face

11. We recognize that poverty eradication, changing consumption and production patterns and protecting and managing the natural resource base for economic and social development are overarching objectives of and essential requirements for sustainable development.

12. The deep fault line that divides human society between the rich and the poor and the ever-increasing gap between the developed and developing worlds pose a major threat to global prosperity, security and stability.

13. The global environment continues to suffer. Loss of biodiversity continues, fish stocks continue to be depleted, desertification claims more and more fertile land, the adverse effects of climate change are already evident, natural disasters are more frequent and more devastating, and developing countries more vulnerable, and air, water and marine pollution continue to rob millions of a decent life.

14. Globalization has added a new dimension to these challenges. The rapid integration of markets, mobility of capital and significant increases in investment flows around the world have opened new challenges and opportunities for the pursuit of sustainable development. But the benefits and costs of globalization are unevenly distributed, with developing countries facing special difficulties in meeting this challenge.

15. We risk the entrenchment of these global disparities and unless we act in a manner that fundamentally changes their lives the poor of the world may lose confidence in their representatives and the democratic systems to which we remain committed, seeing their representatives as nothing more than sounding brass or tinkling cymbals.

Our commitment to sustainable development

16. We are determined to ensure that our rich diversity, which is our collective strength, will be used for constructive partnership for change and for the achievement of the common goal of sustainable development.

17. Recognizing the importance of building human solidarity, we urge the promotion of dialogue and cooperation among the world's civilizations and peoples, irrespective of race, disabilities, religion, language, culture or tradition.

18. We welcome the focus of the Johannesburg Summit on the indivisibility of human dignity and are resolved, through decisions on targets, timetables and partnerships, to speedily increase access to such basic requirements as clean water, sanitation, adequate shelter, energy, health care, food security and the protection of biodiversity. At the same time, we will work together to help one another gain access to financial resources, benefit from the opening of markets, ensure capacity-building, use modern technology to bring about development and make sure that there is technology transfer, human resource development, education and training to banish underdevelopment forever.

19. We reaffirm our pledge to place particular focus on, and give priority attention to, the fight against the worldwide conditions that pose severe threats to the sustainable development of our people, which include: chronic hunger; malnutrition; foreign occupation; armed conflict; illicit drug problems; organized crime; corruption; natural disasters; illicit arms trafficking; trafficking in persons; terrorism; intolerance and incitement to racial, ethnic, religious and other hatreds; xenophobia; and endemic, communicable and chronic diseases, in particular HIV/AIDS, malaria and tuberculosis.

20. We are committed to ensuring that women's empowerment, emancipation and gender equality are integrated in all the activities encompassed within Agenda 21, the Millennium development goals and the Plan of Implementation of the Summit.

21. We recognize the reality that global society has the means and is endowed with the resources to address the challenges of poverty eradication and sustainable development confronting all humanity. Together, we will take extra steps to ensure that these available resources are used to the benefit of humanity.

22. In this regard, to contribute to the achievement of our development goals and targets, we urge developed countries that have not done so to make concrete efforts reach the internationally agreed levels of official development assistance.

23. We welcome and support the emergence of stronger regional groupings and alliances, such as the New Partnership for Africa's Development, to promote regional cooperation, improved international cooperation and sustainable development.

24. We shall continue to pay special attention to the developmental needs of small island developing States and the least developed countries.

25. We reaffirm the vital role of the indigenous peoples in sustainable development.

26. We recognize that sustainable development requires a long-term perspective and broad-based participation in policy formulation, decision-making and implementation at all levels. As social partners, we will continue to work for stable partnerships with all major groups, respecting the independent, important roles of each of them.

27. We agree that in pursuit of its legitimate activities the private sector, including both large and small companies, has a duty to contribute to the evolution of equitable and sustainable communities and societies.

28. We also agree to provide assistance to increase income-generating employment opportunities, taking into account the Declaration on Fundamental Principles and Rights at Work of the International Labour Organization.

29. We agree that there is a need for private sector corporations to enforce corporate accountability, which should take place within a transparent and stable regulatory environment.

30. We undertake to strengthen and improve governance at all levels for the effective implementation of Agenda 21, the Millennium development goals and the Plan of Implementation of the Summit.

Multilateralism is the future

31. To achieve our goals of sustainable development, we need more effective, democratic and accountable international and multilateral institutions.

32. We reaffirm our commitment to the principles and purposes of the Charter of the United Nations and international law, as well as to the strengthening of multilateralism. We support the leadership role of the United Nations as the most universal and representative organization in the world, which is best placed to promote sustainable development.

33. We further commit ourselves to monitor progress at regular intervals towards the achievement of our sustainable development goals and objectives.

Making it happen!

34. We are in agreement that this must be an inclusive process, involving all the major groups and Governments that participated in the historic Johannesburg Summit.

35. We commit ourselves to act together, united by a common determination to save our planet, promote human development and achieve universal prosperity and peace.

36. We commit ourselves to the Plan of Implementation of the World Summit on Sustainable Development and to expediting the achievement of the time-bound, socio-economic and environmental targets contained therein.

37. From the African continent, the cradle of humankind, we solemnly pledge to the peoples of the world and the generations that will surely inherit this Earth that we are determined to ensure that our collective hope for sustainable development is realized.

1.38   Plan of Implementation of the World Summit on Sustainable Development. **Adopted by the World Summit on Sustainable Development, 4 September 2002. UN Doc A/CONF.199/20 at 7 (2002):** *Table of Contents & Chs. I, III, IV, X & XI.*

Contents

I. Introduction

1.   The United Nations Conference on Environment and Development, held in Rio de Janeiro in 1992, provided the fundamental principles and the programme of action for achieving sustainable development. We strongly reaffirm our commitment to the Rio principles, the full implementation of Agenda 21 and the Programme for the Further Implementation of Agenda 21. We also commit ourselves to achieving the internationally agreed development goals, including those contained in the United

Nations Millennium Declaration and in the outcomes of the major United Nations conferences and international agreements since 1992.

2. The present plan of implementation will further build on the achievements made since the United Nations Conference on Environment and Development and expedite the realization of the remaining goals. To this end, we commit ourselves to undertaking concrete actions and measures at all levels and to enhancing international cooperation, taking into account the Rio principles, including, inter alia, the principle of common but differentiated responsibilities as set out in principle 7 of the Rio Declaration on Environment and Development. These efforts will also promote the integration of the three components of sustainable development—economic development, social development and environmental protection—as interdependent and mutually reinforcing pillars. Poverty eradication, changing unsustainable patterns of production and consumption and protecting and man aging the natural resource base of economic and social development are overarching objectives of, and essential requirements for, sustainable development.

3. We recognize that the implementation of the outcomes of the Summit should benefit all, particularly women, youth, children and vulnerable groups. Furthermore, the implementation should involve all relevant actors through partnerships, especially between Governments of the North and South, on the one hand, and between Governments and major groups, on th e other, to achieve the widely shared goals of sustainable development. As reflected in the Monterrey Consensus, such partnerships are key to pursuing sustainable development in a globalizing world.

4. Good governance within each country and at the international level is essential for sustainable development. At the domestic level, sound environmental, social and economic policies, democratic institutions responsive to the needs of the people, the rule of law, anti-corruption measures, gender equality and an enabling environment for investment are the basis for sustainable development. As a result of globalization, external factors have become critical in determining the success or failure of developing countries in their national efforts. The gap between developed and developing countries points to the continued need for a dynamic and enabling international economic environment supportive of international cooperation, particularly in the areas of finance, technology transfer, debt and trade and full and effective participation of developing countries in global decision-making, if the momentum for global progress towards sustainable development is to be maintained and increased.

5. Peace, security, stability and respect for human rights and fundamental freedoms, including the right to development, as well as respect for cultural diversity, are essential for achieving sustainable development and ensuring that sustainable development benefits all.

6. We acknowledge the importance of ethics for sustainable development and, therefore, emphasize the need to consider ethics in the implementation of Agenda 21.

* * *

III. Changing unsustainable patterns of consumption and production

14. Fundamental changes in the way societies produce and consume are indispensable for achieving global sustainable development. All countries should promote sustainable consumption and production patterns, with the developed countries taking the lead and with all countries benefiting from the process, taking into account the Rio principles, including, inter alia, the principle of common but differentiated responsibilities as set out in principle 7 of the Rio Declaration on Environment and Development. Governments, relevant international organizations, the private sector and all major groups should play an active role in changing unsustainable consumption and production patterns. This would include the actions at all levels set out below.

15. Encourage and promote the development of a 10–year framework of programmes in support of regional and national initiatives to accelerate the shift towards sustainable consumption and production to promote social and economic development within the carrying capacity of ecosystems by addressing and, where appropriate, delinking economic growth and environmental degradation through improving efficiency and sustainability in the us e of resources and production processes and reducing resource degradation, pollution and waste. All countries should take action, with developed countries taking the lead, taking into account the development needs and capabilities of developing countries, through mobilization, from all sources, of financial and technical assistance and capacity-building for developing countries. This would require actions at all levels to:

(a) Identify specific activities, tools, policies, measures and monitoring and assessment mechanisms, including, where appropriate, life-cycle analysis and national indicators for measuring progress, bearing in mind that standards applied by some countries may be inappropriate and of unwarranted economic and social cost to other countries, in particular developing countries;

(b) Adopt and implement policies and measures aimed at promoting sustainable patterns of production and consumption, applying, inter alia, the polluter-pays principle described in principle 16 of the Rio Declaration on Environment and Development;

(c) Develop production and consumption policies to improve the products and services provided, while reducing environmental and health impacts, using, where appropriate, science-based approaches, such as life-cycle analysis;

(d) Develop awareness-raising programmes on the importance of sustainable production and consumption patterns, particularly among youth and the relevant segments in all countries, especially in developed countries, through, inter alia, education, public and consumer information, advertising and other media, taking into account local, national and regional cultural values;

(e) Develop and adopt, where appropriate, on a voluntary basis, effective, transparent, verifiable, non-misleading and non-discriminatory consumer information tools to provide information relating to sustainable consumption and production, including human health and safety aspects. These tools should not be used as disguised trade barriers;

(f) Increase eco-efficiency, with financial support from all sources, where mutually agreed, for capacity-building, technology transfer and exchange of technology with developing countries and countries with economies in transition, in cooperation with relevant international organizations.

* * *

22. Prevent and minimize waste and maximize reuse, recycling and use of environmentally friendly alternative materials, with the participation of government authorities and all stakeholders, in order to minimize adverse effects on the environment and improve resource efficiency, with financial, technical and other assistance for developing countries. This would include actions at all levels to:

(a) Develop waste management systems, with the highest priority placed on waste prevention and minimization, reuse and recycling, and environmentally sound disposal facilities, including technology to recapture the energy contained in waste, and encourage small-scale waste—recycling initiatives that support urban and rural waste management and provide income-generating opportunities, with international support for developing countries;

(b) Promote waste prevention and minimization by encouraging production of reusable consumer goods and biodegradable products and developing the infrastructure required.

* * *

23. Renew the commitment, as advanced in Agenda 21, to sound management of chemicals throughout their life cycle and of hazardous wastes for sustainable development as well as for the protection of human health and the environment, inter alia, aiming to achieve, by 2020, that chemicals are used and produced in ways that lead to the minimization of significant adverse effects on human health and the environment, using transparent science-based risk assessment procedures and science-based risk management procedures, taking into account the precautionary approach, as set out in principle 15 of the Rio Declaration on Environment and Development, and support developing countries in strengthening their capacity for the sound management of chemicals and hazardous wastes by providing technical and financial assistance. This would include actions at all levels to:

(a) Promote the ratification and implementation of relevant international instruments on chemicals and hazardous waste, including the Rotterdam Convention on Prior Informed Consent Procedures for Certain Hazardous Chemicals and Pesticides in International Trade 10 so that it can enter into force by 2003 and the Stockholm Convention on Persistent Organic Pollutants so that it can enter into force by 2004, and encourage and improve coordination as well as supporting developing countries in their implementation;

(b) Further develop a strategic approach to international chemicals management based on the Bahia Declaration and Priorities for Action beyond 2000 of the Intergovernmental Forum on Chemical Safety by 2005, and urge that the United Nations Environment Programme, the Intergovernmental Forum, other international organizations dealing with chemical management and other relevant international organizations and actors closely cooperate in this regard, as appropriate;

(c) Encourage countries to implement the new globally harmonized system for the classification and labelling of chemicals as soon as possible with a view to having the system fully operational by 2008;

(d) Encourage partnerships to promote activities aimed at enhancing environmentally sound management of chemicals and hazardous wastes, implementing multilateral environmental agreements, raising awareness of issues relating to chemicals and hazardous waste and encouraging the collection and use of additional scientific data;

(e) Promote efforts to prevent international illegal trafficking of hazardous chemicals and hazardous wastes and to prevent damage resulting from the transboundary movement and disposal of hazardous wastes in a manner consistent with obligations under relevant international instruments, such as the Basel Convention on the Control of Transboundary Movements of Hazardous Wastes and Their Disposal;

(f) Encourage development of coherent and integrated information on chemicals, such as through national pollutant release and transfer registers;

(g) Promote reduction of the risks posed by heavy metals that are harmful to human health and the environment, including through a review of relevant studies, such as th e United Nations Environment Programme global assessment of mercury and its compounds.

* * *

IV. Protecting and managing the natural resource base of economic and social development

* * *

30. Oceans, seas, islands and coastal areas form an integrated and essential component of the Earth's ecosystem and are critical for global food security and for sustaining economic prosperity and the well-being of many national economies, particularly in developing countries. Ensuring the sustainable development of the oceans

requires effective coordination and cooperation, including at the global and regional levels, between relevant bodies, and actions at all levels to:

(a) Invite States to ratify or accede to and implement the United Nations Convention on the Law of the Sea of 1982, which provides the overall legal framework for ocean activities;

(b) Promote the implementation of chapter 17 of Agenda 21, which provides the programme of action for achieving the sustainable development of oceans, coastal areas and seas through its programme areas of integrated management and sustainable development of coastal areas, including exclusive economic zones; marine environmental protection; sustainable use and conservation of marine living resources; addressing critical uncertainties for the management of the marine environment and climate change; strengthening international, including regional, cooperation and coordination; and sustainable development of small islands;

(c) Establish an effective, transparent and regular inter-agency coordination mechanism on ocean and coastal issues within the United Nations system;

(d) Encourage the application by 2010 of the ecosystem approach, noting the Reykjavik Declaration on Responsible Fisheries in the Marine Ecosystem and decision V/6 of the Conference of Parties to the Convention on Biological Diversity;

(e) Promote integrated, multidisciplinary and multisectoral coastal and ocean management at the national level and encourage and assist coastal States in developing ocean policies and mechanisms on integrated coastal management;

(f) Strengthen regional cooperation and coordination between the relevant regional organizations and programmes, the regional seas programmes of the United Nations Environment Programme, regional fisheries management organizations and other regional science, health and development organizations;

(g) Assist developing countries in coordinating policies and programmes at the regional and subregional levels aimed at the conservation and sustainable management of fishery resources and implement integrated coastal area management plans, including through the promotion of sustainable coastal and small-scale fishing activities and, where appropriate, the development of related infrastructure;

(h) Take note of the work of the open-ended informal consultative process established by the United Nations General Assembly in its resolution 54/33 in order to facilitate the annual review by the Assembly of developments in ocean affairs and the upcoming review of its effectiveness and utility to be held at its fifty-seventh session under the terms of the above-mentioned resolution.

31. To achieve sustainable fisheries, the following actions are required at all levels:

(a) Maintain or restore stocks to levels that can produce the maximum sustainable yield with the aim of achieving these goals for depleted stocks on an urgent basis and where possible not later than 2015;

(b) Ratify or accede to and effectively implement the relevant United Nations and, where appropriate, associated regional fisheries agreements or arrangements, noting in particular the Agreement for the Implementation of the Provisions of the United Nations Convention on the Law of the Sea of 10 December 1982 relating to the Conservation and Management of Straddling Fish Stocks and Highly Migratory Fish Stocks and the 1993 Agreement to Promote Compliance with International Conservation and Management Measures by Fishing Vessels on the High Seas;

(c) Implement the 1995 Code of Conduct for Responsible Fisheries, taking note of the special requirements of developing countries as noted in its article 5, and the relevant international plans of action and technical guidelines of the Food and Agriculture Organization of the United Nations;

(d) Urgently develop and implement national and, where appropriate, regional plans of action, to put into effect the international plans of action of the Food and Agriculture Organization of the United Nations, in particular the International Plan of Action for the Management of Fishing Capacity by 2005 and the International Plan of Action to Prevent, Deter and Eliminate Illegal, Unreported and Unregulated Fishing by 2004. Establish effective monitoring, reporting and enforcement, and control of fishing vessels, including by flag States, to further the International Plan of Action to Prevent, Deter and Eliminate Illegal, Unreported and Unregulated Fishing;

(e) Encourage relevant regional fisheries management organizations and arrangements to give due consideration to the rights, duties and interests of coastal States and the special requirements of developing States when addressing the issue of the allocation of share of fishery resources for straddling stocks and highly migratory fish stocks, mindful of the provisions of the United Nations Convention on the Law of the Sea and the Agreement for the Implementation of the Provisions of the United Nations Convention on the Law of the Sea of 10 December 1982 relating to the Conservation and Management of Straddling Fish Stocks and Highly Migratory Fish Stocks, on the high seas and within exclusive economic zones;

(f) Eliminate subsidies that contribute to illegal, unreported and unregulated fishing and to over-capacity, while completing the efforts undertaken at the World Trade Organization to clarify and improve its disciplines on fisheries subsidies, taking into account the importance of this sector to developing countries;

(g) Strengthen donor coordination and partnerships between international financial institutions, bilateral agencies and other relevant stakeholders to enable developing countries, in particular the least developed countries and small island developing States and countries with economies in transition, to develop their national, regional and subregional capacities for infrastructure and integrated management and the sustainable use of fisheries;

(h) Support the sustainable development of aquaculture, including small-scale aquaculture, given its growing importance for food security and economic development.

* * *

34. Enhance maritime safety and protection of the marine environment from pollution by actions at all levels to:

(a) Invite States to ratify or accede to and implement the conventions and protocols and other relevant instruments of the International Maritime Organization relating to the enhancement of maritime safety and protection of the marine environment from marine pollution and environmental damage caused by ships, including the use of toxic anti-fouling paints, and urge the International Maritime Organization (IMO) to consider stronger mechanisms to secure the implementation of IMO instruments by flag States;

(b) Accelerate the development of measures to address invasive alien species in ballast water. Urge the International Maritime Organization to finalize its draft International Convention on the Control and Management of Ships' Ballast Water and Sediments.

* * *

38. Change in the Earth's climate and its adverse effects are a common concern of humankind. We remain deeply concerned that all countries, particularly developing countries, including the least developed countries and small island developing States, face increased risks of negative impacts of climate change and recognize that, in this context, the problems of poverty, land degradation, access to water and food and human health remain at the centre of global attention. The United Nations Framework Convention on Climate Change is the key instrument for addressing climate

change, a global concern, and we reaffirm our commitment to achieving its ultimate objective of stabilization of greenhouse gas concentrations in the atmosphere at a level that would prevent dangerous anthropogenic interference with the climate system, within a time frame sufficient to allow ecosystems to adapt naturally to climate change, to ensure that food production is not threatened and to enable economic development to proceed in a sustainable manner, in accordance with our common but differentiated responsibilities and respective capabilities. Recalling the United Nations Millennium Declaration, in which heads of State and Government resolved to make every effort to ensure the en try into force of the Kyoto Protocol to the United Nations Framework Convention on Climate Change, preferably by the tenth anniversary of the United Nations Conference on Environment and Development in 2002, and to embark on the required reduction of emissions of greenhouse gases, States that have ratified the Kyoto Protocol strongly urge States that have not already done so to ratify it in a timely manner. Actions at all levels are required to:

(a) Meet all the commitments and obligations under the United Nations Framework Convention on Climate Change;

(b) Work cooperatively towards achieving the objectives of the Convention;

(c) Provide technical and financial assistance and capacity-building to developing countries and countries with economies in transition in accordance with commitments under the Convention, including the Marrakesh Accords;

(d) Build and enhance scientific and technological capabilities, inter alia, through continuing support to the Intergovernmental Panel on Climate Change for the exchange of scientific data and information especially in developing countries;

(e) Develop and transfer technological solutions;

(f) Develop and disseminate innovative technologies in regard to key sectors of development, particularly energy, and of investment in this regard, including through private sector involvement, market-oriented approaches, and supportive public policies and international cooperation;

(g) Promote the systematic observation of the Earth's atmosphere, land and oceans by improving monitoring stations, increasing the use of satellites and appropriate integration of these observations to produce high-quality data that could be disseminated for the use of all countries, in particular developing countries;

(h) Enhance the implementation of national, regional and international strategies to monitor the Earth's atmosphere, land and oceans, including, as appropriate, strategies for integrated global observations, inter alia, with the cooperation of relevant international organizations, especially the specialized agencies, in cooperation with the Convention;

(i) Support initiatives to assess the consequences of climate change, such as the Arctic Council initiative, including the environmental, economic and social impacts on local and indigenous communities.

* * *

41. Strengthen the implementation of the United Nations Convention to Combat Desertification in Those Countries Experiencing Serious Drought and/or Desertification, particularly in Africa, to address causes of desertification and land degradation in order to maintain and restore land, and to address poverty resulting from land degradation. This would include actions at all levels to:

(a) Mobilize adequate and predictable financial resources, transfer of technologies and capacity-building at all levels;

(b) Formulate national action programmes to ensure timely and effective implementation of the Convention and its related projects, with the support of the international community, including through decentralized projects at the local level;

(c) Encourage the United Nations Framework Convention on Climate Change, the Convention on Biological Diversity and the Convention to Combat Desertification to continue exploring and enhancing synergies, with due regard to their respective mandates, in the elaboration and implementation of plans and strategies under the respective Conventions;

(d) Integrate measures to prevent and combat desertification as well as to mitigate the effects of drought through relevant policies and programmes, such as land, water and forest management, agriculture, rural development, early warning systems, environment, energy, natural resources, health and education, and poverty eradication and sustainable development strategies;

(e) Provide affordable local access to information to improve monitoring and early warning related to desertification and drought;

(f) Call on the Second Assembly of the Global Environment Facility (GEF) to take action on the recommendations of the GEF Council concerning the designation of land degradation (desertification and deforestation) as a focal area of GEF as a means of GEF support for the successful implementation of the Convention to Combat Desertification; and consequently, consider making GEF a financial mechanism of the Convention, taking into account the prerogatives and decisions of the Conference of the Parties to the Convention, while recognizing the complementary roles of GEF and the Global Mechanism of the Convention in providing and mobilizing resources for the elaboration and implementation of action programmes;

(g) Improve the sustainability of grassland resources through strengthening management and law enforcement and providing financial and technical support by the international community to developing countries.

* * *

X. Means of implementation

81. The implementation of Agenda 21 and the achievement of the internationally agreed development goals, including those contained in the Millennium Declaration as well as in the present plan of action, require a substantially increased effort, both by countries themselves and by the rest of the international community, based on the recognition that each country has primary responsibility for its own development and that the role of national policies and development strategies cannot be overemphasized, taking fully into account the Rio principles, including, in particular, the principle of common but differentiated responsibilities, which states:

"States shall cooperate in a spirit of global partnership to conserve, protect and restore the health and integrity of the Earth's ecosystem. In view of the different contributions to global environmental degradation, States have common but differentiated responsibilities. The developed countries acknowledge the responsibility that they bear in the international pursuit of sustainable development in view of the pressures their societies place on the global environment and of the technologies and financial resources they command."

The internationally agreed development goals, including those contained in the Millennium Declaration and Agenda 21, as well as in the present plan of action, will require significant increases in the flow of financial resources as elaborated in the Monterrey Consensus, including through new and additional financial resources, in particular to developing countries, to support the implementation of national policies and programmes developed by them, improved trade opportunities, access to and transfer of environmentally sound technologies on a concessional or preferential basis, as mutually agreed, education and awareness-raising, capacity-building and information for decision-making and scientific capabilities within the agreed time frame required to meet these goals and initiatives. Progress to this end will require that the international community implement the outcomes of major United Nations conferences, such as the programmes of action adopted at the Third United Nations Conference on the Least Developed Countries 39 and the Global Conference on the Sustainable Development of Small Island Developing States, and relevant international agreements since 1992, particularly those of the International Conference on Financing for Development and the Fourth Ministerial Conference of the World Trade Organization, including building on them as part of a process of achieving sustainable development.

* * *

XI. Institutional framework for sustainable development

* * *

A. Objectives

139. Measures to strengthen institutional arrangements on sustainable development, at all levels, should be taken within the framework of Agenda 21, 45 build on developments since the United Nations Conference on Environment and Development and lead to the achievement of, inter alia, the following objectives:

(a) Strengthening commitments to sustainable development;

(b) Integration of the economic, social and environmental dimensions of sustainable development in a balanced manner;

(c) Strengthening of the implementation of Agenda 21, including through the mobilization of financial and technological resources, as well as capacity-building programmes, particularly for developing countries;

(d) Strengthening coherence, coordination and monitoring;

(e) Promoting the rule of law and strengthening of governmental institutions;

(f) Increasing effectiveness and efficiency through limiting overlap and duplication of activities of international organizations, within and outside the United Nations system, based on their mandates and comparative advantages;

(g) Enhancing participation and effective involvement of civil society and other relevant stakeholders in the implementation of Agenda 21, as well as promoting transparency and broad public participation;

(h) Strengthening capacities for sustainable development at all levels, including the local level, in particular those of developing countries;

(i) Strengthening international cooperation aimed at reinforcing the implementation of Agenda 21 and the outcomes of the Summit.

B. Strengthening the institutional framework for sustainable development at the international level

140. The international community should:

* * *

(d) Fully implement the outcomes of the decision on international environmental governance adopted by the Governing Council of the United Nations Environment Programme at its seventh special session 46 and invite the General Assembly at its fifty-seventh session to consider the important but complex issue of establishing universal membership for the Governing Council/Global Ministerial Environment Forum;

* * *

D. Role of the Economic and Social Council

144. Pursuant to the relevant provisions of the Charter of the United Nations, the provisions of Agenda 21 regarding the Economic and Social Council and General Assembly resolutions 48/162 and 50/227, which reaffirmed the Council as the central mechanism for the coordination of the United Nations system and its specialized agencies and supervision of subsidiary bodies, in particular its functional commissions, and to promote the implementation of Agenda 21 by strengthening system-wide coordination, the Council should:

(a) Increase its role in overseeing system-wide coordination and the balanced integration of economic, social and environmental aspects of United Nations policies and programmes aimed at promoting sustainable development;

(b) Organize periodic consideration of sustainable development themes in regard to the implementation of Agenda 21, including the means of implementation. Recommendations in regard to such themes could be made by the Commission on Sustainable Development;

(c) Make full use of its high-level, coordination, operational activities and the general segments to effectively take into account all relevant aspects of the work of the United Nations on sustainable development. In this context, the Council should encourage the active participation of major groups in its high-level segment and the work of its relevant functional commissions, in accordance with the respective rules of procedure;

(d) Promote greater coordination, complementarity, effectiveness and efficiency of activities of its functional commissions and other subsidiary bodies that are relevant to the implementation of Agenda 21;

(e) Terminate the work of the Committee on Energy and Natural Resources for Development and transfer its work to the Commission on Sustainable Development;

(f) Ensure that there is a close link between the role of the Council in the follow-up to the Summit and its role in the follow-up to the Monterrey Consensus, in a sustained and coordinated manner. To that end, the Council should explore ways to develop arrangements relating to its meetings with the Bretton Woods institutions and the World Trade Organization, as set out in the Monterrey Consensus;

(g) Intensify its efforts to ensure that gender mainstreaming is an integral part of its activities concerning the coordinated implementation of Agenda 21.

E. Role and function of the Commission on Sustainable Development

145. The Commission on Sustainable Development should continue to be the high-level commission on sustainable development within the United Nations system and serve as a forum for consideration of issues related to integration of the three dimensions of sustainable development. Although the role, functions and mandate of the Commission as set out in relevant parts of Agenda 21 and adopted in General Assembly resolution 47/191 continue to be relevant, the Commission needs to be strengthened, taking into account the role of relevant institutions and organizations. An enhanced role of the Commission should include reviewing and monitoring progress in the implementation of Agenda 21 and fostering coherence of implementation, initiatives and partnerships.

* * *

1.39 PROTOCOL ON STRATEGIC ENVIRONMENTAL ASSESSMENT TO THE CONVENTION ON ENVIRONMENTAL IMPACT ASSESSMENT IN A TRANSBOUNDARY CONTEXT (WITH ANNEXES I–V)[a]. Adopted at Kiev, 21 May 2003. Entered into force, 11 July 2010. UN Doc ECE/MP.EIA/2003/2; *reprinted in* 5 Weston & Carlson V.B.19

Article 1
Objective

The objective of this Protocol is to provide for a high level of protection of the environment, including health, by:

(a) Ensuring that environmental, including health, considerations are thoroughly taken into account in the development of plans and programmes;

(b) Contributing to the consideration of environmental, including health, concerns in the preparation of policies and legislation;

(c) Establishing clear, transparent and effective procedures for strategic environmental assessment;

(d) Providing for public participation in strategic environmental assessment; and

(e) Integrating by these means environmental, including health, concerns into measures and instruments designed to further sustainable development.

Article 2
Definitions

For the purposes of this Protocol,

1. "Convention" means the Convention on Environmental Impact Assessment in a Transboundary Context.

2. "Party" means, unless the text indicates otherwise, a Contracting Party to this Protocol.

3. "Party of origin" means a Party or Parties to this Protocol within whose jurisdiction the preparation of a plan or programme is envisaged.

4. "Affected Party" means a Party or Parties to this Protocol likely to be affected by the transboundary environmental, including health, effects of a plan or programme.

5. "Plans and programmes" means plans and programmes and any modifications to them that are:

(a) Required by legislative, regulatory or administrative provisions; and

(b) Subject to preparation and/or adoption by an authority or prepared by an authority for adoption, through a formal procedure, by a parliament or a government.

6. "Strategic environmental assessment" means the evaluation of the likely environmental, including health, effects, which comprises the determination of the scope of an environmental report and its preparation, the carrying out of public participation and consultations, and the taking into account of the environmental report and the results of the public participation and consultations in a plan or programme.

7. "Environmental, including health, effect" means any effect on the environment, including human health, flora, fauna, biodiversity, soil, climate, air, water, landscape, natural sites, material assets, cultural heritage and the interaction among these factors.

8. "The public" means one or more natural or legal persons and, in accordance with national legislation or practice, their associations, organizations or groups.

a. *See also* Basic Document 1.26.

Article 3
General Provisions

1. Each Party shall take the necessary legislative, regulatory and other appropriate measures to implement the provisions of this Protocol within a clear, transparent framework.

2. Each Party shall endeavour to ensure that officials and authorities assist and provide guidance to the public in matters covered by this Protocol.

3. Each Party shall provide for appropriate recognition of and support to associations, organizations or groups promoting environmental, including health, protection in the context of this Protocol.

4. The provisions of this Protocol shall not affect the right of a Party to maintain or introduce additional measures in relation to issues covered by this Protocol.

5. Each Party shall promote the objectives of this Protocol in relevant international decision-making processes and within the framework of relevant international organizations.

6. Each Party shall ensure that persons exercising their rights in conformity with the provisions of this Protocol shall not be penalized, persecuted or harassed in any way for their involvement. This provision shall not affect the powers of national courts to award reasonable costs in judicial proceedings.

7. Within the scope of the relevant provisions of this Protocol, the public shall be able to exercise its rights without discrimination as to citizenship, nationality or domicile and, in the case of a legal person, without discrimination as to where it has its registered seat or an effective centre of its activities.

Article 4
Field of Application Concerning Plans and Programmes

1. Each Party shall ensure that a strategic environmental assessment is carried out for plans and programmes referred to in paragraphs 2, 3 and 4 which are likely to have significant environmental, including health, effects.

2. A strategic environmental assessment shall be carried out for plans and programmes which are prepared for agriculture, forestry, fisheries, energy, industry including mining, transport, regional development, waste management, water management, telecommunications, tourism, town and country planning or land use, and which set the framework for future development consent for projects listed in annex I and any other project listed in annex II that requires an environmental impact assessment under national legislation.

3. For plans and programmes other than those subject to paragraph 2 which set the framework for future development consent of projects, a strategic environmental assessment shall be carried out where a Party so determines according to article 5, paragraph 1.

4. For plans and programmes referred to in paragraph 2 which determine the use of small areas at local level and for minor modifications to plans and programmes referred to in paragraph 2, a strategic environmental assessment shall be carried out only where a Party so determines according to article 5, paragraph 1.

5. The following plans and programmes are not subject to this Protocol:

(a) Plans and programmes whose sole purpose is to serve national defence or civil emergencies;

(b) Financial or budget plans and programmes.

Article 5
Screening

* * *

Article 6
Scoping

* * *

Article 7
Environmental Report

1.   For plans and programmes subject to strategic environmental assessment, each Party shall ensure that an environmental report is prepared.

2.   The environmental report shall, in accordance with the determination under article 6, identify, describe and evaluate the likely significant environmental, including health, effects of implementing the plan or programme and its reasonable alternatives. The report shall contain such information specified in annex IV as may reasonably be required, taking into account:

(a) Current knowledge and methods of assessment;

(b) The contents and the level of detail of the plan or programme and its stage in the decision-making process;

(c) The interests of the public; and

(d) The information needs of the decision-making body.

3.   Each Party shall ensure that environmental reports are of sufficient quality to meet the requirements of this Protocol.

Article 8
Public Participation

1.   Each Party shall ensure early, timely and effective opportunities for public participation, when all options are open, in the strategic environmental assessment of plans and programmes.

2.   Each Party, using electronic media or other appropriate means, shall ensure the timely public availability of the draft plan or programme and the environmental report.

3.   Each Party shall ensure that the public concerned, including relevant non-governmental organizations, is identified for the purposes of paragraphs 1 and 4.

4.   Each Party shall ensure that the public referred to in paragraph 3 has the opportunity to express its opinion on the draft plan or programme and the environmental report within a reasonable time frame.

5.   Each Party shall ensure that the detailed arrangements for informing the public and consulting the public concerned are determined and made publicly available. For this purpose, each Party shall take into account to the extent appropriate the elements listed in annex V.

Article 9
Consultation with Environmental and Health Authorities

* * *

Article 10
Transboundary Consultations

1. Where a Party of origin considers that the implementation of a plan or programme is likely to have significant transboundary environmental, including health, effects or where a Party likely to be significantly affected so requests, the Party of origin shall as early as possible before the adoption of the plan or programme notify the affected Party.

2. This notification shall contain, inter alia:

(a) The draft plan or programme and the environmental report including information on its possible transboundary environmental, including health, effects; and

(b) Information regarding the decision-making procedure, including an indication of a reasonable time schedule for the transmission of comments.

3. The affected Party shall, within the time specified in the notification, indicate to the Party of origin whether it wishes to enter into consultations before the adoption of the plan or programme and, if it so indicates, the Parties concerned shall enter into consultations concerning the likely transboundary environmental, including health, effects of implementing the plan or programme and the measures envisaged to prevent, reduce or mitigate adverse effects.

4. Where such consultations take place, the Parties concerned shall agree on detailed arrangements to ensure that the public concerned and the authorities referred to in article 9, paragraph 1, in the affected Party are informed and given an opportunity to forward their opinion on the draft plan or programme and the environmental report within a reasonable time frame.

Article 11
Decision

1. Each Party shall ensure that when a plan or programme is adopted due account is taken of:

(a) The conclusions of the environmental report;

(b) The measures to prevent, reduce or mitigate the adverse effects identified in the environmental report; and

(c) The comments received in accordance with articles 8 to 10.

2. Each Party shall ensure that, when a plan or programme is adopted, the public, the authorities referred to in article 9, paragraph 1, and the Parties consulted according to article 10 are informed, and that the plan or programme is made available to them together with a statement summarizing how the environmental, including health, considerations have been integrated into it, how the comments received in accordance with articles 8 to 10 have been taken into account and the reasons for adopting it in the light of the reasonable alternatives considered.

Article 12
Monitoring

* * *

Article 13
Policies and Legislation

* * *

Article 14
The Meeting of the Parties to the Convention Serving as the Meeting of the Parties to the Protocol

* * *

Article 15
Relationship to Other International Agreements

The relevant provisions of this Protocol shall apply without prejudice to the UNECE Conventions on Environmental Impact Assessment in a Transboundary Context and on Access to Information, Public Participation in Decision-making and Access to Justice in Environmental Matters.

Article 16
Right to Vote

* * *

Article 17
Secretariat

The secretariat established by article 13 of the Convention shall serve as the secretariat of this Protocol and article 13, paragraphs (a) to (c), of the Convention on the functions of the secretariat shall apply mutatis mutandis to this Protocol.

Article 18
Annexes

The annexes to this Protocol shall constitute an integral part thereof.

Article 19
Amendments to the Protocol

* * *

Article 20
Settlement of Disputes

The provisions on the settlement of disputes of article 15 of the Convention shall apply mutatis mutandis to this Protocol.

Article 21
Signature

* * *

Article 22
Depositary

* * *

Article 23
Ratification, Acceptance, Approval and Accession

* * *

Article 24
Entry into Force

* * *

Article 25
Withdrawal

* * *

Article 26
Authentic Texts

* * *

Annex I
List of projects as referred to in article 4, paragraph 2

1. Crude oil refineries (excluding undertakings manufacturing only lubricants from crude oil) and installations for the gasification and liquefaction of 500 metric tons or more of coal or bituminous shale per day.

2. Thermal power stations and other combustion installations with a heat output of 300 megawatts or more and nuclear power stations and other nuclear reactors (except research installations for the production and conversion of fissionable and fertile materials, whose maximum power does not exceed 1 kilowatt continuous thermal load).

3. Installations solely designed for the production or enrichment of nuclear fuels, for the reprocessing of irradiated nuclear fuels or for the storage, disposal and processing of radioactive waste.

* * *

7. Construction of motorways, express roads and lines for long-distance railway traffic and of airports with a basic runway length of 2,100 metres or more.

8. Large-diameter oil and gas pipelines.

9. Trading ports and also inland waterways and ports for inland-waterway traffic which permit the passage of vessels of over 1,350 metric tons.

* * *

11. Large dams and reservoirs.

12. Groundwater abstraction activities in cases where the annual volume of water to be abstracted amounts to 10 million cubic metres or more.

* * *

Annex II
Any other projects referred to in article 4, paragraph 2

1. Projects for the restructuring of rural land holdings.

2. Projects for the use of uncultivated land or seminatural areas for intensive agricultural purposes.

3. Water management projects for agriculture, including irrigation and land drainage projects.

* * *

Annex III
Criteria for determining of the likely significant environmental, including health, effects referred to in article 5, paragraph 1

* * *

<u>Annex IV</u>
Information referred to in article 7, paragraph 2

* * *

<u>Annex V</u>
Information referred to in article 8, paragraph 5

* * *

1.40   Protocol on Pollutant Release and Transfer Registers (Without Annexes).[a] **Adopted at Kiev, 21 May 2003. Entered into force, 8 October 2009. UN Doc MP.PP/2003/1;** *reprinted in* **5 Weston & Carlson V.B.20**

The Parties to this Protocol,

Recalling article 5, paragraph 9, and article 10, paragraph 2, of the 1998 Convention on Access to Information, Public Participation in Decision-making and Access to Justice in Environmental Matters (the Aarhus Convention),

Recognizing that pollutant release and transfer registers provide an important mechanism to increase corporate accountability, reduce pollution and promote sustainable development, as stated in the Lucca Declaration adopted at the first meeting of the Parties to the Aarhus Convention,

* * *

Wishing to provide a mechanism contributing to the ability of every person of present and future generations to live in an environment adequate to his or her health and well-being, by ensuring the development of publicly accessible environmental information systems,

* * *

Convinced of the value of pollutant release and transfer registers as a cost-effective tool for encouraging improvements in environmental performance, for providing public access to information on pollutants released into and transferred in and through communities, and for use by Governments in tracking trends, demonstrating progress in pollution reduction, monitoring compliance with certain international agreements, setting priorities and evaluating progress achieved through environmental policies and programmes,

* * *

Have agreed as follows:

Article 1
Objective

The objective of this Protocol is to enhance public access to information through the establishment of coherent, integrated, nationwide pollutant release and transfer registers (PRTRs) in accordance with the provisions of this Protocol, which could facilitate public participation in environmental decision-making as well as contribute to the prevention and reduction of pollution of the environment.

Article 2
Definitions

For the purposes of this Protocol,

1. "Party" means, unless the text indicates otherwise, a State or a regional economic integration organization referred to in article 24 which has consented to be bound by this Protocol and for which the Protocol is in force;

2. "Convention" means the Convention on Access to Information, Public Participation in Decision-making and Access to Justice in Environmental Matters, done at Aarhus, Denmark, on 25 June 1998;

a.   *See also* Basic Document 1.33.

3. "The public" means one or more natural or legal persons, and, in accordance with national legislation or practice, their associations, organizations or groups;

* * *

Article 3
General Provisions

1. Each Party shall take the necessary legislative, regulatory and other measures, and appropriate enforcement measures, to implement the provisions of this Protocol.

2. The provisions of this Protocol shall not affect the right of a Party to maintain or introduce a more extensive or more publicly accessible pollutant release and transfer register than required by this Protocol.

* * *

Article 4
Core Elements of a Pollutant Release and Transfer Register System

In accordance with this Protocol, each Party shall establish and maintain a publicly accessible national pollutant release and transfer register that:

(a) Is facility-specific with respect to reporting on point sources;

(b) Accommodates reporting on diffuse sources;

(c) Is pollutant-specific or waste-specific, as appropriate;

(d) Is multimedia, distinguishing among releases to air, land and water;

(e) Includes information on transfers;

(f) Is based on mandatory reporting on a periodic basis;

(g) Includes standardized and timely data, a limited number of standardized reporting thresholds and limited provisions, if any, for confidentiality;

(h) Is coherent and designed to be user-friendly and publicly accessible, including in electronic form;

(i) Allows for public participation in its development and modification; and

(j) Is a structured, computerized database or several linked databases maintained by the competent authority.

Article 5
Design and Structure

* * *

Article 6
Scope of the Register

* * *

Article 7
Reporting Requirements

1. Each Party shall either:

(a) Require the owner or the operator of each individual facility within its jurisdiction that undertakes one or more of the activities specified in annex I above the applicable capacity threshold specified in annex I, column 1, and:

(i) Releases any pollutant specified in annex II in quantities exceeding the applicable thresholds specified in annex II, column 1;

(ii) Transfers off-site any pollutant specified in annex II in quantities exceeding the applicable threshold specified in annex II, column 2, where the Party has opted for pollutant-specific reporting of transfers pursuant to paragraph 5 (d);

(iii) Transfers off-site hazardous waste exceeding 2 tons per year or other waste exceeding 2,000 tons per year, where the Party has opted for waste-specific reporting of transfers pursuant to paragraph 5 (d); or

(iv) Transfers off-site any pollutant specified in annex II in waste water destined for waste-water treatment in quantities exceeding the applicable threshold specified in annex II, column 1b;

to undertake the obligation imposed on that owner or operator pursuant to paragraph 2; or

(b) Require the owner or the operator of each individual facility within its jurisdiction that undertakes one or more of the activities specified in annex I at or above the employee threshold specified in annex I, column 2, and manufactures, processes or uses any pollutant specified in annex II in quantities exceeding the applicable threshold specified in annex II, column 3, to undertake the obligation imposed on that owner or operator pursuant to paragraph 2.

2. Each Party shall require the owner or operator of a facility referred to in paragraph 1 to submit the information specified in paragraphs 5 and 6, and in accordance with the requirements therein, with respect to those pollutants and wastes for which thresholds were exceeded.

3. In order to achieve the objective of this Protocol, a Party may decide with respect to a particular pollutant to apply either a release threshold or a manufacture, process or use threshold, provided that this increases the relevant information on releases or transfers available in its register.

4. Each Party shall ensure that its competent authority collects, or shall designate one or more public authorities or competent bodies to collect, the information on releases of pollutants from diffuse sources specified in paragraphs 7 and 8, for inclusion in its register.

5. Each Party shall require the owners or operators of the facilities required to report under paragraph 2 to complete and submit to its competent authority, the following information on a facility-specific basis:

(a) The name, street address, geographical location and the activity or activities of the reporting facility, and the name of the owner or operator, and, as appropriate, company;

(b) The name and numerical identifier of each pollutant required to be reported pursuant to paragraph 2;

(c) The amount of each pollutant required to be reported pursuant to paragraph 2 released from the facility to the environment in the reporting year, both in aggregate and according to whether the release is to air, to water or to land, including by underground injection;

(d) Either:

(i) The amount of each pollutant required to be reported pursuant to paragraph 2 that is transferred off-site in the reporting year, distinguishing between the amounts transferred for disposal and for recovery, and the name and address of the facility receiving the transfer; or

(ii) The amount of waste required to be reported pursuant to paragraph 2 transferred off-site in the reporting year, distinguishing between hazardous waste and other waste, for any operations of recovery or disposal, indicating respectively with 'R' or 'D' whether the waste is destined for recovery or disposal pursuant to annex III and, for transboundary movements of hazardous waste, the name and address of the recoverer or disposer of the waste and the actual recovery or disposal site receiving the transfer;

(e) The amount of each pollutant in waste water required to be reported pursuant to paragraph 2 transferred off-site in the reporting year; and

(f) The type of methodology used to derive the information referred to in subparagraphs (c) to (e), according to article 9, paragraph 2, indicating whether the information is based on measurement, calculation or estimation.

6. The information referred to in paragraph 5 (c) to (e) shall include information on releases and transfers resulting from routine activities and from extraordinary events.

7. Each Party shall present on its register, in an adequate spatial disaggregation, the information on releases of pollutants from diffuse sources for which that Party determines that data are being collected by the relevant authorities and can be practicably included. Where the Party determines that no such data exist, it shall take measures to initiate reporting on releases of relevant pollutants from one or more diffuse sources in accordance with its national priorities.

8. The information referred to in paragraph 7 shall include information on the type of methodology used to derive the information.

Article 8
Reporting Cycle

* * *

Article 9
Data Collection and Record-keeping

* * *

Article 10
Quality Assessment

* * *

Article 11
Public Access to Information

1. Each Party shall ensure public access to information contained in its pollutant release and transfer register, without an interest having to be stated, and according to the provisions of this Protocol, primarily by ensuring that its register provides for direct electronic access through public telecommunications networks.

2. Where the information contained in its register is not easily publicly accessible by direct electronic means, each Party shall ensure that its competent authority upon request provides that information by any other effective means, as soon as possible and at the latest within one month after the request has been submitted.

3. Subject to paragraph 4, each Party shall ensure that access to information contained in its register is free of charge.

4. Each Party may allow its competent authority to make a charge for reproducing and mailing the specific information referred to in paragraph 2, but such charge shall not exceed a reasonable amount.

5. Where the information contained in its register is not easily publicly accessible by direct electronic means, each Party shall facilitate electronic access to its register in

publicly accessible locations, for example in public libraries, offices of local authorities or other appropriate places.

Article 12
Confidentiality

1. Each Party may authorize the competent authority to keep information held on the register confidential where public disclosure of that information would adversely affect:

(a) International relations, national defence or public security;

(b) The course of justice, the ability of a person to receive a fair trial or the ability of a public authority to conduct an enquiry of a criminal or disciplinary nature;

(c) The confidentiality of commercial and industrial information, where such confidentiality is protected by law in order to protect a legitimate economic interest;

(d) Intellectual property rights; or

(e) The confidentiality of personal data and/or files relating to a natural person if that person has not consented to the disclosure of the information to the public, where such confidentiality is provided for in national law.

The aforementioned grounds for confidentiality shall be interpreted in a restrictive way, taking into account the public interest served by disclosure and whether the information relates to releases into the environment.

2. Within the framework of paragraph 1 (c), any information on releases which is relevant for the protection of the environment shall be considered for disclosure according to national law.

3. Whenever information is kept confidential according to paragraph 1, the register shall indicate what type of information has been withheld, through, for example, providing generic chemical information if possible, and for what reason it has been withheld.

Article 13
Public Participation in the Development of National Pollutant Release and Transfer Registers

* * *

Article 14
Access to Justice

1. Each Party shall, within the framework of its national legislation, ensure that any person who considers that his or her request for information under article 11, paragraph 2, has been ignored, wrongfully refused, whether in part or in full, inadequately answered, or otherwise not dealt with in accordance with the provisions of that paragraph has access to a review procedure before a court of law or another independent and impartial body established by law.

2. The requirements in paragraph 1 are without prejudice to the respective rights and obligations of Parties under existing treaties applicable between them dealing with the subject matter of this article.

Article 15
Capacity-building

* * *

Article 16
International Cooperation

* * *

Article 17
Meeting of the Parties

* * *

Article 18
Right to Vote

* * *

Article 19
Annexes

Annexes to this Protocol shall form an integral part thereof and, unless expressly provided otherwise, a reference to this Protocol constitutes at the same time a reference to any annexes thereto.

Article 20
Amendments

* * *

Article 21
Secretariat

* * *

Article 22
Review of Compliance

At its first session, the Meeting of the Parties shall by consensus establish cooperative procedures and institutional arrangements of a non-judicial, non-adversarial and consultative nature to assess and promote compliance with the provisions of this Protocol and to address cases of non-compliance. In establishing these procedures and arrangements, the Meeting of the Parties shall consider, inter alia, whether to allow for information to be received from members of the public on matters related to this Protocol.

Article 23
Settlement of Disputes

1.   If a dispute arises between two or more Parties about the interpretation or application of this Protocol, they shall seek a solution by negotiation or by any other peaceful means of dispute settlement acceptable to the parties to the dispute.

2.   When signing, ratifying, accepting, approving or acceding to this Protocol, or at any time thereafter, a State may declare in writing to the Depositary that, for a dispute not resolved in accordance with paragraph 1, it accepts one or both of the following means of dispute settlement as compulsory in relation to any Party accepting the same obligation:

(a) Submission of the dispute to the International Court of Justice;

(b) Arbitration in accordance with the procedure set out in annex IV.

A regional economic integration organization may make a declaration with like effect in relation to arbitration in accordance with the procedures referred to in subparagraph (b).

3.   If the parties to the dispute have accepted both means of dispute settlement referred to in paragraph 2, the dispute may be submitted only to the International Court of Justice, unless the parties to the dispute agree otherwise.

Article 24
Signature

* * *

Article 25
Depositary

* * *

Article 26
Ratification, Acceptance, Approval and Accession

* * *

Article 27
Entry into Force

* * *

Article 28
Reservations

No reservations may be made to this Protocol.

Article 29
Withdrawal

* * *

Article 30
Authentic Texts

* * *

1.41 WORLD BANK OPERATIONAL POLICIES 4.00, 4.01, and 4.10. World Bank
       Operations Manual (March 2005)

Operational Policy 4.00 & Table A (sections A, B & E) Piloting the Use of Borrower Systems to Address Environmental and Social Safeguard Issues in Bank–Supported Projects

1. The Bank's[1] environmental and social ("safeguard") policies[2] are designed to avoid, mitigate, or minimize adverse environmental and social impacts of projects supported by the Bank. The Bank encourages its borrowing member countries to adopt and implement systems[3] that meet these objectives while ensuring that development resources are used transparently and efficiently to achieve desired outcomes. To encourage the development and effective application of such systems and thereby focus on building borrower capacity beyond individual project settings, the Bank is piloting the use of borrower systems in Bank-supported projects. The key objective of the pilot program is to improve overall understanding of implementation issues related to greater use of country systems.

2. **Equivalence and Acceptability**. The Bank considers a borrower's environmental and social safeguard system to be equivalent to the Bank's if the borrower's system is designed to achieve the objectives and adhere to the applicable operational principles set out in Table A1. Since equivalence is determined on a policy-by-policy basis, the Bank may conclude that the borrower's system is equivalent to the Bank's in specific environmental or social safeguard areas in particular pilot projects, and not in other such areas. Before deciding on the use of borrower systems, the Bank also assesses the acceptability of the borrower's implementation practices, track record, and capacity.

* * *

5. **Bank Responsibility**. The Bank is responsible for determining the equivalence and acceptability of borrower systems, and for appraising and supervising pilot projects that use these systems. The Bank carries out its responsibility, including supervision of borrower implementation practices, track record, and capacity, in a manner proportional to potential impacts and risks. The Bank may explore with the borrower (and, as appropriate, third-parties) the feasibility of arrangements to strengthen ownership and country capacity to implement specific operational principles in Table A1.Without limitation to its responsibility under this paragraph, the Bank may also explore with the borrower (and, as appropriate, third-parties) the feasibility of establishing alternative monitoring arrangements for overseeing the implementation of the project.

* * *

1. "Bank" includes IBRD and IDA; "loan" includes IDA credit and IDA grant; and "borrower" includes grant recipient.

2. The Bank's environmental and social safeguards policies and procedures are: OP/BP 4.01, Environmental Assessment; OP/BP 4.04, Natural Habitats; OP 4.09, Pest Management; OP/BP 4.10, Indigenous Peoples; OP/BP 4.11,Physical Cultural Resources; OP/BP 4.12, Involuntary Resettlement; OP 4.36, Forests; and OP/BP 4.37, Safety of Dams.

3. When used in this policy statement "country systems" means a country's legal and institutional framework, consisting of its national, subnational, or sectoral implementing institutions and applicable laws, regulations, rules, and procedures.

Table A1
Environmental and Social Safeguard Policies—Policy Objectives and
Operational Principles

Objectives	*Operational Principles*
A. Environmental Assessment	
To help ensure the environmental and social soundness and sustainability of investment projects.	1. Use a screening process for each proposed project, as early as possible, to determine the appropriate extent and type of environmental assessment (EA) so that appropriate studies are undertaken proportional to potential risks and to direct, and, as relevant, indirect, cumulative, and associated impacts. Use sectoral or regional environmental assessment when appropriate.
To support integration of environmental and social aspects of projects into the decision making process.	2. Assess potential impacts of the proposed project on physical, biological, socio-economic and physical cultural resources, including transboundary and global concerns, and potential impacts on human health and safety.
	3. Assess the adequacy of the applicable legal and institutional framework, including applicable international environmental agreements, and confirm that they provide that the cooperating government does not finance project activities that would contravene such international obligations.
	4. Provide for assessment of feasible investment, technical, and siting alternatives, including the "no action" alternative, potential impacts, feasibility of mitigating these impacts, their capital and recurrent costs, their suitability under local conditions, and their institutional, training and monitoring requirements associated with them.
	5. Where applicable to the type of project being supported, normally apply the Pollution Prevention and Abatement Handbook (PPAH). Justify deviations when alternatives to measures set forth in the PPAH are selected.
	6. Prevent and, where not possible to prevent, at least minimize, or compensate for adverse project impacts and enhance positive impacts through environmental management and planning that includes the proposed mitigation measures, monitoring, institutional capacity development and training measures, an implementation schedule, and cost estimates.
	7. Involve stakeholders, including project-affected groups and local nongovernmental organizations, as early as possible, in the preparation process and ensure that their views and concerns are made known to decision makers and taken into account. Continue consultations throughout project implementation as necessary to address EA-related issues that affect them.
	8. Use independent expertise in the preparation of EA where appropriate. Use independent advisory panels during preparation and implementation of projects that are highly risky or contentious or that involve serious and multidimensional environmental and/or social concerns.

Objectives	Operational Principles
	9. Provide measures to link the environmental assessment process and findings with studies of economic, financial, institutional, social and technical analyses of a proposed project.
	10. Provide for application of the principles in this Table to subprojects under investment and financial intermediary activities.
	11. Disclose draft EA in a timely manner, before appraisal formally begins, in an accessible place and in a form and language understandable to key stakeholders.

Objectives	Operational Principles
B. Natural Habitats	
To promote environmentally sustainable development by supporting the protection, conservation, maintenance, and rehabilitation of natural habitats and their functions.	1. Use a precautionary approach to natural resources management to ensure opportunities for environmentally sustainable development. Determine if project benefits substantially outweigh potential environmental costs.
	2. Avoid significant conversion or degradation of critical natural habitats, including those habitats that are (a) legally protected, (b) officially proposed for protection, (c) identified by authoritative sources for their high conservation value, or (d) recognized as protected by traditional local communities.
	3. Where projects adversely affect non-critical natural habitats, proceed only if viable alternatives are not available, and if appropriate conservation and mitigation measures, including those required to maintain ecological services they provide, are in place. Include also mitigation measures that minimize habitat loss and establish and maintain an ecologically similar protected area.
	4. Whenever feasible, give preference to siting projects on lands already converted.
	5. Consult key stakeholders, including local nongovernmental organizations and local communities, and involve such people in design, implementation, monitoring, and evaluation of projects, including mitigation planning.
	6. Provide for the use of appropriate expertise for the design and implementation of mitigation and monitoring plans.
	7. Disclose draft mitigation plan in a timely manner, before appraisal formally begins, in an accessible place and in a form and language understandable to key stakeholders.

Objectives	Operational Principles
E. Indigenous Peoples	
To design and implement projects in a way that fosters full respect for Indigenous Peoples' dignity, human rights, and cultural uniqueness and so that they: (a) receive culturally compatible so-	1. Screen early to determine whether Indigenous Peoples are present in, or have collective attachment to, the project area. Indigenous Peoples are identified as possessing the following characteristics in varying degrees: selfidentification and recognition of this identity by others;

Objectives	*Operational Principles*
cial and economic benefits; and (b) do not suffer adverse effects during the development process.	collective attachment to geographically distinct habitats or ancestral territories and to the natural resources in these habitats and territories; presence of distinct customary cultural, economic, social or political institutions; and indigenous language.
	2. Undertake free, prior and informed consultation with affected Indigenous Peoples to ascertain their broad community support for projects affecting them and to solicit their participation: (a) in designing, implementing, and monitoring measures to avoid adverse impacts, or, when avoidance is not feasible, to minimize, mitigate, or compensate for such effects; and (b) in tailoring benefits in a culturally appropriate manner.
	3. Undertake social assessment or use similar methods to assess potential project impacts, both positive and adverse, on Indigenous Peoples. Give full consideration to options preferred by the affected Indigenous Peoples in the provision of benefits and design of mitigation measures. Identify social and economic benefits for Indigenous Peoples that are culturally appropriate, and gender and inter-generationally inclusive and develop measures to avoid, minimize and/or mitigate adverse impacts on Indigenous Peoples.
	4. Where restriction of access of Indigenous Peoples to parks and protected areas is not avoidable, ensure that the affected Indigenous Peoples' communities participate in the design, implementation, monitoring and evaluation of management plans for such parks and protected areas and share equitably in benefits from the parks and protected areas.
	5. Put in place an action plan for the legal recognition of customary rights to lands and territories, when the project involves: (a) activities that are contingent on establishing legally recognized rights to lands and territories that Indigenous Peoples traditionally owned, or customarily used or occupied; or (b) the acquisition of such lands.
	6. Do not undertake commercial development of cultural resources or knowledge of Indigenous Peoples without obtaining their prior agreement to such development.
	7. Prepare an Indigenous Peoples Plan that is based on the social assessment and draws on indigenous knowledge, in consultation with the affected Indigenous Peoples' communities and using qualified professionals. Normally, this plan would include a framework for continued consultation with the affected communities during project implementation; specify measures to ensure that Indigenous Peoples receive culturally appropriate benefits, and identify measures to avoid, minimize, mitigate or compensate for any

Objectives	*Operational Principles*
	adverse effects; and include grievance procedures, monitoring and evaluation arrangements, and the budget for implementing the planned measures.
	8. Disclose the draft Indigenous Peoples Plan, including documentation of the consultation process, in a timely manner before appraisal formally begins, in an accessible place and in a form and language that are understandable to key stakeholders.
	9. Monitor implementation of the Indigenous Peoples Plan, using experienced social scientists.

Operational Policy 4.01
Environmental Assessment

1.   The Bank requires environmental assessment (EA) of projects proposed for Bank financing to help ensure that they are environmentally sound and sustainable, and thus to improve decision making.

2.   EA is a process whose breadth, depth, and type of analysis depend on the nature, scale, and potential environmental impact of the proposed project. EA evaluates a project's potential environmental risks and impacts in its area of influence; examines project alternatives; identifies ways of improving project selection, siting, planning, design, and implementation by preventing, minimizing, mitigating, or compensating for adverse environmental impacts and enhancing positive impacts; and includes the process of mitigating and managing adverse environmental impacts throughout project implementation. The Bank favors preventive measures over mitigatory or compensatory measures, whenever feasible.

3.   EA takes into account the natural environment (air, water, and land); human health and safety; social aspects (involuntary resettlement, indigenous peoples, and physical cultural resources); and transboundary and global environmental aspects.[4] EA considers natural and social aspects in an integrated way. It also takes into account the variations in project and country conditions; the findings of country environmental studies; national environmental action plans; the country's overall policy framework, national legislation, and institutional capabilities related to the environment and social aspects; and obligations of the country, pertaining to project activities, under relevant international environmental treaties and agreements. The Bank does not finance project activities that would contravene such country obligations, as identified during the EA. EA is initiated as early as possible in project processing and is integrated closely with the economic, financial, institutional, social, and technical analyses of a proposed project.

4.   The borrower is responsible for carrying out the EA. For Category A projects, the borrower retains independent EA experts not affiliated with the project to carry out the EA.[5] For Category A projects that are highly risky or contentious or that involve serious and multidimensional environmental concerns, the borrower should

---

4.   Global environmental issues include climate change, ozone-depleting substances, pollution of international waters, and adverse impacts on biodiversity

5.   EA is closely integrated with the project's economic, financial, institutional, social, and technical analyses to ensure that (a) environmental considerations are given adequate weight in project selection, siting, and design decisions; and (b) EA does not delay project processing. However, the borrower ensures that when individuals or entities are engaged to carry out EA activities, any conflict of interest is avoided. For example, when an independent EA is required, it is not carried out by the consultants hired to prepare the engineering design.

normally also engage an advisory panel of independent, internationally recognized environmental specialists to advise on all aspects of the project relevant to the EA.[6] The role of the advisory panel depends on the degree to which project preparation has progressed, and on the extent and quality of any EA work completed, at the time the Bank begins to consider the project.

5. The Bank advises the borrower on the Bank's EA requirements. The Bank reviews the findings and recommendations of the EA to determine whether they provide an adequate basis for processing the project for Bank financing. When the borrower has completed or partially completed EA work prior to the Bank's involvement in a project, the Bank reviews the EA to ensure its consistency with this policy. The Bank may, if appropriate, require additional EA work, including public consultation and disclosure.

* * *

EA Instruments

7. Depending on the project, a range of instruments can be used to satisfy the Bank's EA requirement: environmental impact assessment (EIA), regional or sectoral EA, strategic environmental and social assessment (SESA), environmental audit, hazard or risk assessment, environmental management plan (EMP) and environmental and social management framework (ESMF). EA applies one or more of these instruments, or elements of them, as appropriate. When the project is likely to have sectoral or regional impacts, sectoral or regional EA is required.

Environmental Screening

8. The Bank undertakes environmental screening of each proposed project to determine the appropriate extent and type of EA. The Bank classifies the proposed project into one of four categories, depending on the type, location, sensitivity, and scale of the project and the nature and magnitude of its potential environmental impacts.

(a) *Category A*: A proposed project is classified as Category A if it is likely to have significant adverse environmental impacts that are sensitive,[7] diverse, or unprecedented. These impacts may affect an area broader than the sites or facilities subject to physical works. EA for a Category A project examines the project's potential negative and positive environmental impacts, compares them with those of feasible alternatives (including the "without project" situation), and recommends any measures needed to prevent, minimize, mitigate, or compensate for adverse impacts and improve environmental performance. For a Category A project, the borrower is responsible for preparing a report, normally an EIA (or a suitably comprehensive regional or sectoral EA) that includes, as necessary, elements of the other instruments referred to in para. 7.

(b) *Category B*: A proposed project is classified as Category B if its potential adverse environmental impacts on human populations or environmentally important areas—including wetlands, forests, grasslands, and other natural habitats—are less adverse than those of Category A projects. These impacts are site-specific; few if any of

---

6. The panel (which is different from the dam safety panel required under OP/BP 4.37, *Safety of Dams*) advises the borrower specifically on the following aspects: (a) the terms of reference for the EA, (b) key issues and methods for preparing the EA, (c) recommendations and findings of the EA, (d) implementation of the EA's recommendations, and (e) development of environmental management capacity.

7. A potential impact is considered "sensitive" if it may be irreversible (e.g., lead to loss of a major natural habitat) or raise issues covered by OP 4.04, *Natural Habitats*; OP/BP 4.10, *Indigenous Peoples*; OP/BP 4.11, *Physical Cultural Resources* or OP 4.12, *Involuntary Resettlement*.

them are irreversible; and in most cases mitigatory measures can be designed more readily than for Category A projects. The scope of EA for a Category B project may vary from project to project, but it is narrower than that of Category A EA. Like Category A EA, it examines the project's potential negative and positive environmental impacts and recommends any measures needed to prevent, minimize, mitigate, or compensate for adverse impacts and improve environmental performance. The findings and results of Category B EA are described in the project documentation (Project Appraisal Document and Project Information Document).[8]

(c) *Category C*: A proposed project is classified as Category C if it is likely to have minimal or no adverse environmental impacts. Beyond screening, no further EA action is required for a Category C project.

(d) *Category FI*: A proposed project is classified as Category FI if it involves investment of Bank funds through a financial intermediary, in subprojects that may result in adverse environmental impacts.

* * *

Public Consultation

14.   For all Category A and B projects proposed for IBRD or IDA financing, during the EA process, the borrower consults project-affected groups and local nongovernmental organizations (NGOs) about the project's environmental aspects and takes their views into account. The borrower initiates such consultations as early as possible. For Category A projects, the borrower consults these groups at least twice: (a) shortly after environmental screening and before the terms of reference for the EA are finalized; and (b) once a draft EA report is prepared. In addition, the borrower consults with such groups throughout project implementation as necessary to address EA-related issues that affect them.[9]

* * *

Operational Policy 4.10
Indigenous Peoples

1.   This policy contributes to the Bank's mission of poverty reduction and sustainable development by ensuring that the development process fully respects the dignity, human rights, economies, and cultures of Indigenous Peoples. For all projects that are proposed for Bank financing and affect Indigenous Peoples,[10] the Bank requires the borrower to engage in a process of free, prior, and informed consultation.[11]

8.   When the screening process determines, or national legislation requires, that any of the environmental issues identified warrant special attention, the findings and results of Category B EA may be set out in a separate report. Depending on the type of project and the nature and magnitude of the impacts, this report may include, for example, a limited environmental impact assessment, an environmental mitigation or management plan, an environmental audit, or a hazard assessment. For Category B projects that are not in environmentally sensitive areas and that present well-defined and well-understood issues of narrow scope, the Bank may accept alternative approaches for meeting EA requirements: for example, environmentally sound design criteria, siting criteria, or pollution standards for small-scale industrial plants or rural works; environmentally sound siting criteria, construction standards,

or inspection procedures for housing projects; or environmentally sound operating procedures for road rehabilitation projects.

9.   For projects with major social components, consultations are also required by other Bank policies—for example, OP/BP 4.10, *Indigenous Peoples*, and OP/BP 4.12, *Involuntary Resettlement*.

10.   This policy applies to all components of the project that affect Indigenous Peoples, regardless of the source of financing.

11.   Free, prior, and informed consultation with the affected Indigenous Peoples' communities refers to a culturally appropriate and collective decisionmaking process subsequent to meaningful and good faith consultation and informed participation regarding the preparation and implementation of the project. It does

The Bank provides project financing only where free, prior, and informed consultation results in broad community support to the project by the affected Indigenous Peoples.[12] Such Bank-financed projects include measures to (a) avoid potentially adverse effects on the Indigenous Peoples' communities; or (b) when avoidance is not feasible, minimize, mitigate, or compensate for such effects. Bank-financed projects are also designed to ensure that the Indigenous Peoples receive social and economic benefits that are culturally appropriate and gender and intergenerationally inclusive.

2. The Bank recognizes that the identities and cultures of Indigenous Peoples are inextricably linked to the lands on which they live and the natural resources on which they depend. These distinct circumstances expose Indigenous Peoples to different types of risks and levels of impacts from development projects, including loss of identity, culture, and customary livelihoods, as well as exposure to disease. Gender and intergenerational issues among Indigenous Peoples also are complex. As social groups with identities that are often distinct from dominant groups in their national societies, Indigenous Peoples are frequently among the most marginalized and vulnerable segments of the population. As a result, their economic, social, and legal status often limits their capacity to defend their interests in and rights to lands, territories, and other productive resources, and/or restricts their ability to participate in and benefit from development. At the same time, the Bank recognizes that Indigenous Peoples play a vital role in sustainable development and that their rights are increasingly being addressed under both domestic and international law.

3. *Identification.* Because of the varied and changing contexts in which Indigenous Peoples live and because there is no universally accepted definition of "Indigenous Peoples," this policy does not define the term. Indigenous Peoples may be referred to in different countries by such terms as "indigenous ethnic minorities," "aboriginals," "hill tribes," "minority nationalities," "scheduled tribes," or "tribal groups."

4. For purposes of this policy, the term "Indigenous Peoples" is used in a generic sense to refer to a distinct, vulnerable, social and cultural group[13] possessing the following characteristics in varying degrees:

(a) self-identification as members of a distinct indigenous cultural group and recognition of this identity by others;

(b) collective attachment to geographically distinct habitats or ancestral territories in the project area and to the natural resources in these habitats and territories[14]

(c) customary cultural, economic, social, or political institutions that are separate from those of the dominant society and culture; and

(d) an indigenous language, often different from the official language of the country or region.

A group that has lost "collective attachment to geographically distinct habitats or ancestral territories in the project area"; (paragraph 4 (b)) because of forced severance remains eligible for coverage under this policy.[15] Ascertaining whether a particular

---

not constitute a veto right for individuals or groups (see paragraph 10).

12. For details on "broad community support to the project by the affected Indigenous Peoples," see paragraph 11.

13. The policy does not set an *a priori* minimum numerical threshold since groups of Indigenous Peoples may be very small in number and their size may make them more vulnerable.

14. "Collective attachment" means that for generations there has been a physical presence in and economic ties to lands and territories traditionally owned, or customarily used or occupied, by the group concerned, including areas that hold special significance for it, such as sacred sites. "Collective attachment" also refers to the attachment of transhumant/nomadic groups to the territory they use on a seasonal or cyclical basis.

15. "Forced severance" refers to loss of collective attachment to geographically distinct habitats or ancestral territories occurring within the concerned group members' lifetime be-group is considered as "Indigenous Peoples" for the purpose of this policy may require a technical judgment (see paragraph 8).

5. *Use of Country Systems.* The Bank may decide to use a country's systems to address environmental and social safeguard issues in a Bank-financed project that affects Indigenous Peoples. This decision is made in accordance with the requirements of the applicable Bank policy on country systems.[16]

Project Preparation

6. A project proposed for Bank financing that affects Indigenous Peoples requires:

(a) screening by the Bank to identify whether Indigenous Peoples are present in, or have collective attachment to, the project area (see paragraph 8);

(b) a social assessment by the borrower (see paragraph 9 and Annex A);

(c) a process of free, prior, and informed consultation with the affected Indigenous Peoples' communities at each stage of the project, and particularly during project preparation, to fully identify their views and ascertain their broad community support for the project (see paragraphs 10 and 11);

(d) the preparation of an Indigenous Peoples Plan (see paragraph 12 and Annex B) or an Indigenous Peoples Planning Framework (see paragraph 13 and Annex C); and

(e) disclosure of the draft Indigenous Peoples Plan or draft Indigenous Peoples Planning Framework (see paragraph 15).

7. The level of detail necessary to meet the requirements specified in paragraph 6 (b), (c), and (d) is proportional to the complexity of the proposed project and commensurate with the nature and scale of the proposed project's potential effects on the Indigenous Peoples, whether adverse or positive.

Screening

8. Early in project preparation, the Bank undertakes a screening to determine whether Indigenous Peoples (see paragraph 4) are present in, or have collective attachment to, the project area.[17] In conducting this screening, the Bank seeks the technical judgment of qualified social scientists with expertise on the social and cultural groups in the project area. The Bank also consults the Indigenous Peoples concerned and the borrower. The Bank may follow the borrower's framework for identification of Indigenous Peoples during project screening, when that framework is consistent with this policy.

Social Assessment

9. *Analysis.* If, based on the screening, the Bank concludes that Indigenous Peoples are present in, or have collective attachment to, the project area, the borrower

cause of conflict, government resettlement programs, dispossession from their lands, natural calamities, or incorporation of such territories into an urban area. For purposes of this policy, "urban area" normally means a city or a large town, and takes into account all of the following characteristics, no single one of which is definitive: (a) the legal designation of the area as urban under domestic law; (b) high population density; and (c) high proportion of nonagricultural economic activities relative to agricultural activities.

16. The currently applicable Bank policy is OP/BP 4.00, *Piloting the Use of Borrower Sys-* *tems to Address Environmental and Social Safeguard Issues in Bank–Supported Projects.* Applicable only to pilot projects using borrower systems, the policy includes requirements that such systems be designed to meet the policy objectives and adhere to the operational principles related to Indigenous Peoples identified in OP 4.00 (see Table A1).

17. The screening may be carried out independently or as part of a project environmental assessment (see OP 4.01, *Environmental Assessment*, paragraphs 3, 8).

undertakes a social assessment to evaluate the project's potential positive and adverse effects on the Indigenous Peoples, and to examine project alternatives where adverse effects may be significant. The breadth, depth, and type of analysis in the social assessment are proportional to the nature and scale of the proposed project's potential effects on the Indigenous Peoples, whether such effects are positive or adverse (see Annex A for details). To carry out the social assessment, the borrower engages social scientists whose qualifications, experience, and terms of reference are acceptable to the Bank.

10. *Consultation and Participation.* Where the project affects Indigenous Peoples, the borrower engages in free, prior, and informed consultation with them. To ensure such consultation, the borrower:

(a) establishes an appropriate gender and intergenerationally inclusive framework that provides opportunities for consultation at each stage of project preparation and implementation among the borrower, the affected Indigenous Peoples' communities, the Indigenous Peoples Organizations (IPOs) if any, and other local civil society organizations (CSOs) identified by the affected Indigenous Peoples' communities;

(b) uses consultation methods[18] appropriate to the social and cultural values of the affected Indigenous Peoples' communities and their local conditions and, in designing these methods, gives special attention to the concerns of Indigenous women, youth, and children and their access to development opportunities and benefits; and

(c) provides the affected Indigenous Peoples' communities with all relevant information about the project (including an assessment of potential adverse effects of the project on the affected Indigenous Peoples' communities) in a culturally appropriate manner at each stage of project preparation and implementation.

11. In deciding whether to proceed with the project, the borrower ascertains, on the basis of the social assessment (see paragraph 9) and the free, prior, and informed consultation (see paragraph 10), whether the affected Indigenous Peoples' communities provide their broad support to the project. Where there is such support, the borrower prepares a detailed report that documents:

(a) the findings of the social assessment;

(b) the process of free, prior, and informed consultation with the affected Indigenous Peoples' communities;

(c) additional measures, including project design modification, that may be required to address adverse effects on the Indigenous Peoples and to provide them with culturally appropriate project benefits;

(d) recommendations for free, prior, and informed consultation with and participation by Indigenous Peoples' communities during project implementation, monitoring, and evaluation; and

(e) any formal agreements reached with Indigenous Peoples' communities and/or the IPOs.

The Bank reviews the process and the outcome of the consultation carried out by the borrower to satisfy itself that the affected Indigenous Peoples' communities have provided their broad support to the project. The Bank pays particular attention to the social assessment and to the record and outcome of the free, prior, and informed consultation with the affected Indigenous Peoples' communities as a basis for ascertaining whether there is such support. The Bank does not proceed further with project processing if it is unable to ascertain that such support exists.

---

18. Such consultation methods (including using indigenous languages, allowing time for consensus building, and selecting appropriate venues) facilitate the articulation by Indigenous Peoples of their views and preferences. *The Indigenous Peoples Guidebook* (forthcoming) will provide good practice guidance on this and other matters.

Indigenous Peoples Plan/Planning Framework

12. *Indigenous Peoples Plan.* On the basis of the social assessment and in consultation with the affected Indigenous Peoples' communities, the borrower prepares an Indigenous Peoples Plan (IPP) that sets out the measures through which the borrower will ensure that (a) Indigenous Peoples affected by the project receive culturally appropriate social and economic benefits; and (b) when potential adverse effects on Indigenous Peoples are identified, those adverse effects are avoided, minimized, mitigated, or compensated for (see Annex B for details). The IPP is prepared in a flexible and pragmatic manner,[19] and its level of detail varies depending on the specific project and the nature of effects to be addressed. The borrower integrates the IPP into the project design. When Indigenous Peoples are the sole or the overwhelming majority of direct project beneficiaries, the elements of an IPP should be included in the overall project design, and a separate IPP is not required. In such cases, the Project Appraisal Document (PAD) includes a brief summary of how the project complies with the policy, in particular the IPP requirements.

13. *Indigenous Peoples Planning Framework.* Some projects involve the preparation and implementation of annual investment programs or multiple subprojects.[20] In such cases, and when the Bank's screening indicates that Indigenous Peoples are likely to be present in, or have collective attachment to, the project area, but their presence or collective attachment cannot be determined until the programs or subprojects are identified, the borrower prepares an Indigenous Peoples Planning Framework (IPPF). The IPPF provides for the screening and review of these programs or subprojects in a manner consistent with this policy (see Annex C for details). The borrower integrates the IPPF into the project design.

14. *Preparation of Program and Subproject IPPs.* If the screening of an individual program or subproject identified in the IPPF indicates that Indigenous Peoples are present in, or have collective attachment to, the area of the program or subproject, the borrower ensures that, before the individual program or subproject is implemented, a social assessment is carried out and an IPP is prepared in accordance with the requirements of this policy. The borrower provides each IPP to the Bank for review before the respective program or subproject is considered eligible for Bank financing.[21]

Disclosure

15. The borrower makes the social assessment report and draft IPP/IPPF available to the affected Indigenous Peoples' communities in an appropriate form, manner, and language.[22] Before project appraisal, the borrower sends the social assessment and draft IPP/IPPF to the Bank for review. Once the Bank accepts the documents as providing an adequate basis for project appraisal, the Bank makes them available to the public in accordance with The World Bank Policy on Disclosure of Information, and the borrower makes them available to the affected Indigenous Peoples' communities in the same manner as the earlier draft documents.

19. When non-Indigenous Peoples live in the same area with Indigenous Peoples, the IPP should attempt to avoid creating unnecessary inequities for other poor and marginal social groups.

20. Such projects include community-driven development projects, social funds, sector investment operations, and financial intermediary loans.

21. If the Bank considers the IPPF to be adequate for the purpose, however, the Bank may agree with the borrower that prior Bank review of the IPP is not needed. In such case, the Bank reviews the IPP and its implementa-

tion as part of supervision (see OP 13.05, *Project Supervision*)

22. The social assessment and IPP require wide dissemination among the affected Indigenous Peoples' communities using culturally appropriate methods and locations. In the case of an IPPF, the document is disseminated using IPOs at the appropriate national, regional, or local levels to reach Indigenous Peoples who are likely to be affected by the project. Where IPOs do not exist, the document may be disseminated using other CSOs as appropriate.

Special Considerations

Lands and Related Natural Resources

16. Indigenous Peoples are closely tied to land, forests, water, wildlife, and other natural resources, and therefore special considerations apply if the project affects such ties. In this situation, when carrying out the social assessment and preparing the IPP/IPPF, the borrower pays particular attention to:

(a) the customary rights[23] of the Indigenous Peoples, both individual and collective, pertaining to lands or territories that they traditionally owned, or customarily used or occupied, and where access to natural resources is vital to the sustainability of their cultures and livelihoods;

(b) the need to protect such lands and resources against illegal intrusion or encroachment;

(c) the cultural and spiritual values that the Indigenous Peoples attribute to such lands and resources; and

(d) Indigenous Peoples' natural resources management practices and the long-term sustainability of such practices.

17. If the project involves (a) activities that are contingent on establishing legally recognized rights to lands and territories that Indigenous Peoples have traditionally owned or customarily used or occupied (such as land titling projects), or (b) the acquisition of such lands, the IPP sets forth an action plan for the legal recognition of such ownership, occupation, or usage. Normally, the action plan is carried out before project implementation; in some cases, however, the action plan may need to be carried out concurrently with the project itself. Such legal recognition may take the following forms:

(a) full legal recognition of existing customary land tenure systems of Indigenous Peoples; or

(b) conversion of customary usage rights to communal and/or individual ownership rights.

If neither option is possible under domestic law, the IPP includes measures for legal recognition of perpetual or long-term renewable custodial or use rights.

* * *

---

23. "Customary rights" to lands and resources refers to patterns of long-standing community land and resource usage in accordance with Indigenous Peoples' customary laws, values, customs, and traditions, including seasonal or cyclical use, rather than formal legal title to land and resources issued by the State.

1.42 ILC DRAFT PRINCIPLES ON THE ALLOCATION OF LOSS IN THE CASE OF TRANSBOUN-DARY HARM ARISING OUT OF HAZARDOUS ACTIVITIES. Adopted by the International Law Commission, 8 Aug 2006. *Report of the International Law Commission on the Work of its Fifty-eighth Session.* **UN GAOR, 61th Sess, Supp No 10, at 106, UN Doc A/61/10 (2006);** *reprinted in* **5 Weston & Carlson V.J.19**

Principle 1
Scope of application

The present draft principles apply to transboundary damage caused by hazardous activities not prohibited by international law.

Principle 2
Use of terms

For the purposes of the present draft principles:

(a) "damage" means significant damage caused to persons, property or the environment;and includes:

(i) loss of life or personal injury;

(ii) loss of, or damage to, property, including property which forms part of the cultural heritage;

(iii) loss or damage by impairment of the environment;

(iv) the costs of reasonable measures of reinstatement of the property, or environment, including natural resources;

(v) the costs of reasonable response measures;

(b) "environment" includes natural resources, both abiotic and biotic, such as air, water, soil, fauna and flora and the interaction between the same factors, and the characteristic aspects of the landscape;

(c) "hazardous activity" means an activity which involves a risk of causing significant harm;

(d) "State of origin" means the State in the territory or otherwise under the jurisdiction or control of which the hazardous activity is carried out;

(e) "transboundary damage" means damage caused to persons, property or the environment in the territory or in other places under the jurisdiction or control of a State other than the State of origin;

(f) "victim" means any natural or legal person or State that suffers damage;

(g) "operator" means any person in command or control of the activity at the time the incident causing transboundary damage occurs.

Principle 3
Purposes

The purposes of the present draft principles are:

(a) to ensure prompt and adequate compensation to victims of transboundary damage; and

(b) to preserve and protect the environment in the event of transboundary damage, especially with respect to mitigation of damage to the environment and its restoration or reinstatement.

Principle 4
Prompt and adequate compensation

1. Each State should take all necessary measures to ensure that prompt and adequate compensation is available for victims of transboundary damage caused by hazardous activities located within its territory or otherwise under its jurisdiction or control.

2. These measures should include the imposition of liability on the operator or, where appropriate, other person or entity. Such liability should not require proof of fault. Any conditions, limitations or exceptions to such liability shall be consistent with draft principle 3.

3. These measures should also include the requirement on the operator or, where appropriate, other person or entity, to establish and maintain financial security such as insurance, bonds or other financial guarantees to cover claims of compensation.

4. In appropriate cases, these measures should include the requirement for the establishment of industry-wide funds at the national level.

5. In the event that the measures under the preceding paragraphs are insufficient to provide adequate compensation, the State of origin should also ensure that additional financial resources are made available.

Principle 5
Response measures

Upon the occurrence of an incident involving a hazardous activity which results or is likely to result in transboundary damage:

(a) the State of origin shall promptly notify all States affected or likely to be affected of the incident and the possible effects of the transboundary damage;

(b) the State of origin, with the appropriate involvement of the operator, shall ensure that appropriate response measures are taken and should, for this purpose, rely upon the best available scientific data and technology;

(c) the State of origin, as appropriate, should also consult with and seek the cooperation of all States affected or likely to be affected to mitigate the effects of transboundary damage and if possible eliminate them;

(d) the States affected or likely to be affected by the transboundary damage shall take all feasible measures to mitigate and if possible to eliminate the effects of such damage;

(e) the States concerned should, where appropriate, seek the assistance of competent international organizations and other States on mutually acceptable terms and conditions.

Principle 6
International and domestic remedies

1. States shall provide their domestic judicial and administrative bodies with the necessary jurisdiction and competence and ensure that these bodies have prompt, adequate and effective remedies available in the event of transboundary damage caused by hazardous activities located within their territory or otherwise under their jurisdiction or control.

2. Victims of transboundary damage should have access to remedies in the State of origin that are no less prompt, adequate and effective than those available to victims that suffer damage, from the same incident, within the territory of that State.

3. Paragraphs 1 and 2 are without prejudice to the right of the victims to seek remedies other than those available in the State of origin.

4. States may provide for recourse to international claims settlement procedures that are expeditious and involve minimal expenses.

5. States should guarantee appropriate access to information relevant for the pursuance of remedies, including claims for compensation.

Principle 7
Development of specific international regimes

1. Where, in respect of particular categories of hazardous activities, specific global, regional or bilateral agreements would provide effective arrangements concerning compensation, response measures and international and domestic remedies, all efforts should be made to conclude such specific agreements.

2. Such agreements should, as appropriate, include arrangements for industry and/or State funds to provide supplementary compensation in the event that the financial resources of the operator, including financial security measures, are insufficient to cover the damage suffered as a result of an incident. Any such funds may be designed to supplement or replace national industry-based funds.

Principle 8
Implementation

1. Each State should adopt the necessary legislative, regulatory and administrative measures to implement the present draft principles.

2. The present draft principles and the measures adopted to implement them shall be applied without any discrimination such as that based on nationality, domicile or residence.

3. States should cooperate with each other to implement the present draft principles.

1.43 DRAFT UN GENERAL ASSEMBLY DECLARATION ON THE ECOLOGICAL RIGHTS AND RESPONSIBILITIES OF PRESENT AND FUTURE GENERATIONS. *In* **Burns H. Weston & Tracy Bach, Recalibrating the Law of Humans with the Laws of Nature: Climate Change, Human Rights, and Intergenerational Justice 87 (Recommendation No. 13A abstract) (Climate Legacy Initiative, 2008), also available online in Appendix B at http://www.vermontlaw.edu/Academics/Environmental_Law_Center/Institutes_and_ Initiatives/Climate_Legacy_Initiative/Publications.htm (accessed Sept. 9, 2011)**

The General Assembly,

Bearing in mind that the fundamental rights of the human family are the foundation of freedom, justice, and peace in the world,

Recognizing that the human family consists of past, present, and future generations linked together, past to present and present to future, in an unending partnership of shared responsibility for one another and for the earth-space environment upon which life on Earth depends;

Concerned, however, that the fate of the human family is increasingly threatened by serious and potentially irreversible damage to the earth's atmosphere, biosphere, hydrosphere, and lithosphere as a consequence of global warming and other manifestations of climate change;

Conscious of the assessment reports of the Intergovernmental Panel on Climate Change (IPCC) which state clearly that climate change and its attendant threats (sea level rises, changed precipitation patterns, heightened extreme-weather frequency and intensity, reduced stream flows due to glacial retreat, species extinctions, increased disease vector ranges) are the consequence largely of human activity at this time in history,

Conscious also that the fundamental rights of the human family to water, food, health, livelihood, habitat, culture, self-determination, and life itself are at major risk if climate change is left unabated and its harms are therefore allowed to grow in breadth and severity, especially for the disenfranchised, the poor, the geophysically vulnerable, and those future members of the human family who, if without representation among the present generations from who they descend, are without capacity to avoid or mitigate the predicted harms,

Mindful of the goals and targets of the 2000 United Nations Millennium Declaration in which the signatory Heads of State and Government resolve to "spare no effort to free all of humanity, and above all our children and grandchildren, from the threat of living on a planet irredeemably spoilt by human activities, and whose resources would no longer be sufficient for their needs,"

Recalling that environmental responsibilities on the part of present generations towards future generations have been proclaimed or referred to previously in the 1972 Convention for the Protection of the World Cultural and Natural Heritage, the 1972 Stockholm Declaration of the United Nations Conference on the Human Environment, the 1982

World Charter for Nature, the 1982 Rio Declaration on Environment and Development and its companion Agenda 21: Programme of Action for Sustainable Development, the 1992 United Nations Framework Convention on Climate Change and its 1997 Kyoto Protocol, the 1992 Convention on Biological Diversity, the 1997 UNESCO Declaration on the Responsibilities of the Present Generation Towards Future Generations, the 2002 Johannesburg Declaration on Sustainable Development, and the United Nations General Assembly resolutions relating to "the protection of global climate for present and future generations of mankind" adopted since 1988,

Convinced that the foregoing and other provisions of international law reflect a growing consensus that future generations have a legal as well as moral right to be treated with ecological respect by present generations,

Stressing that full respect for the human rights of future generations in general and their ecological rights in particular constitute an essential element of humane democratic governance of the whole human family,

Bearing in mind that the fate of future generations of the human family depends greatly on decisions and actions taken today, and that present-day problems, including poverty, technological and material underdevelopment, unemployment, exclusion, and discrimination as well as threats to the environment, must be solved in the interests of both present and future generations,

Asserting the need to affirm an ecological right for present and future generations that can facilitate the human family's perpetuity and well-being,

Resolved to strengthen at all levels of governance the development of laws that protect the ecological rights of present and future generations,

Solemnly adopts the following Universal Declaration on the Ecological Rights and Responsibilities of Present and Future Generations.

Article 1

1. Present and future generations have an inalienable right to live in a clean, healthy, ecologically balanced, and sustainable environment within, across, and beyond national boundaries. This right is universal, indivisible, and interdependent with other human rights.

2. Ecosystem integrity and quality are the foundations of this right. The right therefore presupposes a life of dignity for all. It includes:

a. freedom from activities that cause serious or irreversible damage to the atmosphere, the biosphere, the hydrosphere, or the lithosphere;

b. freedom from pollution, the dispersal of dangerous substances and hazardous wastes, and other environmental threats to the rights of present and future generations to water, food, health, livelihood, habitat, culture, and life itself; and

c. freedom to belong to a clean, healthy, ecologically balanced, and sustainable community, including its ecological stability and respect for its cultural self-determination.

3. The right of present and future generations to live in a clean, healthy, ecologically balanced, and sustainable environment recognizes that future generations are entitled to diversity of resources comparable to that enjoyed by previous generations, to a quality of the planet comparable or better than that enjoyed by previous generations, and to equitable rights of access to these environmental legacies from past generations.

Article 2

1. Present generations have the duty to promote and protect the right of future generations to live in a clean, healthy, ecologically balanced, and sustainable environment. At a minimum, it is their duty to pass on to all who succeed them an environment unimpaired by any degradation or depletion that compromises the ability of future generations to secure their rights and needs.

2. This duty requires that all members of present generations, individually or in association with others, shall not unduly restrict the ecological options available to future generations in solving their problems and satisfying their needs, shall maintain if not improve the quality of planet Earth so that it is passed on to future generations in no worse condition than received from previous generations, and shall conserve for

future generations equitable rights of access to the environmental legacies of past generations.

3. The duty requires also that all members of present generations, individually or in association with others, spare no effort to prevent pollution, the dispersal of dangerous substances and hazardous wastes, and other environmental threats to the rights of future as well as present generations to water, food, health, livelihood, habitat, culture, and life itself.

Article 3

In fulfillment of the duty to promote and protect the right of future generations to live in a clean, healthy, ecologically balanced, and sustainable environment, local municipalities, national bodies, intergovernmental organizations, ecological commons communities, and other juridically competent representatives of present generations shall:

1. adopt administrative, legislative, judicial, and other measures necessary to implement effectively the right defined in this Universal Declaration;

2. take precautionary measures to anticipate, prevent, or mitigate serious or irreversible damage to the environment, and to this end not use lack of full scientific certainty as a reason to postpone such measures; and

3. cooperate with other States, competent intergovernmental organizations, and appropriate members of civil society in respect of areas beyond national jurisdiction.

Article 4

When facing the difficult challenge of allocating limited resources between present and future generations, it shall be accepted principle that acts of the present generation shall not impinge upon the fundamental human rights and needs of the poorest or otherwise most vulnerable individual and group members of future generations, including their ecological rights. Likewise, the fundamental human rights and needs of the poor and otherwise vulnerable among present generations, including their ecological rights, shall not be sacrificed for the benefit of future generations.

Article 5

Present generations shall strive to save succeeding generations from the scourge of war and its ecological consequences. In so doing, they shall take steps towards peace, security, and respect for human rights, fundamental freedoms, and the rule of law. The burden of ecological and other damage from armed conflicts shall not be borne by future generations.

Article 6

In fulfillment of this Universal Declaration, the United Nations and all regional organizations shall use their good offices to establish an Office of Legal Guardian for Future Generations charged with responsibility to safeguard the ecological rights and interests of future generations. The Office of Legal Guardian shall be headed by a jurist of high moral character and recognized competence in human rights law and policy, environmental law and science, and guardianship or functionally equivalent administration. It also shall be granted legal standing before the Human Rights Council and all other relevant intergovernmental bodies, both treaty and non-treaty, on all matters pertinent to the right of future generations to a clean, healthy, ecologically balanced, and sustainable environment.

Article 7

Everyone in every generation is entitled to all the rights and freedoms set forth in this Declaration, without distinction of any kind, such as race, colour, sex, language, religion, political or other opinion, national or social origin, property, birth or other status, including the international status of the territory in which a person lives, be it independent, trust, non-self-governing, or under any other limitation of full sovereignty.

Article 8

Local municipalities, national bodies, intergovernmental and nongovernmental organizations, public and private business enterprises, and individuals shall spare no effort in promoting, in particular through legislation and in general through education, training, and information, respect for the provisions set forth in this Declaration, and encourage by all appropriate means their full recognition and effective application.

PART 2. ATMOSPHERE/SPACE

A. AIR POLLUTION

2.1 CONVENTION ON LONG-RANGE TRANSBOUNDARY AIR POLLUTION (LRTAP) (Without Protocols).[a] Concluded at Geneva, 13 November 1979. Entered into force, 16 March 1983. 1302 UNTS 217, TIAS No 10541; *reprinted in* 18 ILM 1442 (1979) & 5 Weston & Carlson V.E.3

The Parties to the present Convention,

Determined to promote relations and co-operation in the field of environmental protection,

Aware of the significance of the activities of the United Nations Economic Commission for Europe in strengthening such relations and co-operation, particularly in the field of air pollution including long-range transport of air pollutants,

Recognizing the contribution of the Economic Commission for Europe to the multilateral implementation of the pertinent provisions of the Final Act of the Conference on Security and Co-operation in Europe,

Cognizant of the references in the chapter on environment of the Final Act of the Conference on Security and Co-operation in Europe calling for co-operation to control air pollution and its effects, including long-range transport of air pollutants, and to the development through international co-operation of an extensive programme for the monitoring and evaluation of long-range transport of air pollutants, starting with sulphur dioxide and with possible extension to other pollutants,

Considering the pertinent provisions of the Declaration of the United Nations Conference on the Human Environment, and in particular principle 21, which expresses the common conviction that States have, in accordance with the Charter of the United Nations and the principles of international law, the sovereign right to exploit their own resources pursuant to their own environmental policies, and the responsibility to ensure that activities within their jurisdiction or control do not cause damage to the environment of other States or of areas beyond the limits of natural jurisdiction,

Recognizing the existence of possible adverse effects, in the short and long term, of air pollution including transboundary air pollution,

Concerned that a rise in the level of emissions of air pollutants within the region as forecast may increase such adverse effects,

---

a. Eight protocols to the Convention have been adopted and entered into force. The Gothenburg Protocol to Abate Acidification, Eutrophication and Ground-level Ozone is reproduced in this volume. *See* Basic Document 2.5. The other protocols, not reproduced here, are the Protocol on Long–Term Financing of the Co-operative Programme for Monitoring and Evaluation of the Long–Range Transmission of Air Pollutants in Europe (EMEP)(28 Sep 84/28 Jan 88), 1491 UNTS 167, 5 Weston & Carlson V.E.4; Protocol on the Reduction of Sulphur Emissions or Their Transboundary Fluxes by at Least 30 percent (8 Jul 85/2 Sep 87), 1480 UNTS 215, 5 Weston & Carlson V.E.6; Proto-col Concerning the Control of Nitrogen Oxides or their Transboundary Fluxes (31 Oct 88/14 Feb 91), 1593 UNTS 287, 5 Weston & Carlson V.E.10; Protocol Concerning the Control of Emissions of Volatile Organic Compounds or Their Transboundary Fluxes (18 Nov 1991/29 Sep 1997), 2001 UNTS 187, 5 Weston & Carlson V.E.18; Protocol on Further Reduction of Sulphur Emissions (14 Jun 1994/5 Aug 1998), 2030 UNTS 122, 5 Weston & Carlson V.E.20a; Protocol on Persistent Organic Pollutants (24 Jun 1998/23 Oct 1998), 2230 UNTS 79, 5 Weston & Carlson V.E.20e; Protocol on Heavy Metals (24 Jun 1998/29 Dec 2003), 2237 UNTS 4, 5 Weston & Carlson V.E.20f.

Recognizing the need to study the implications of the long-range transport of air pollutants and the need to seek solutions for the problems identified,

Affirming their willingness to reinforce active international co-operation to develop appropriate national policies and by means of exchange of information, consultation, research and monitoring, to co-ordinate national action for combating air pollution including long-range transboundary air pollution,

Have agreed as follows:

DEFINITIONS

Article 1

For the purposes of the present Convention:

(a) *"air pollution"* means the introduction by man, directly or indirectly, of substances or energy into the air resulting in deleterious effects of such a nature as to endanger human health, harm living resources and ecosystems and material property and impair or interfere with amenities and other legitimate uses of the environment, and "air pollutants" shall be construed accordingly;

(b) *"long-range transboundary air pollution"* means air pollution whose physical origin is situated wholly or in part within the area under the national jurisdiction of one State and which has adverse effects in the area under the jurisdiction of another State at such a distance that it is not generally possible to distinguish the contribution of individual emission sources or groups of sources.

FUNDAMENTAL PRINCIPLES

Article 2

The Contracting Parties, taking due account of the facts and problems involved, are determined to protect man and his environment against air pollution and shall endeavour to limit and, as far as possible, gradually reduce and prevent air pollution including long-range transboundary air pollution.

Article 3

The Contracting Parties, within the framework of the present Convention, shall by means of exchanges of information, consultation, research and monitoring, develop without undue delay policies and strategies which shall serve as a means of combating the discharge of air pollutants, taking into account efforts already made at national and international levels.

Article 4

The Contracting Parties shall exchange information on and review their policies, scientific activities and technical measures aimed at combating, as far as possible, the discharge of air pollutants which may have adverse effects, thereby contributing to the reduction of air pollution including long-range transboundary air pollution.

Article 5

Consultations shall be held, upon request, at an early stage between, on the one hand, Contracting Parties which are actually affected by or exposed to a significant risk of long-range transboundary air pollution and, on the other hand, Contracting Parties within which and subject to whose jurisdiction a significant contribution to long-range transboundary air pollution originates, or could originate, in connexion with activities carried on or contemplated therein.

AIR QUALITY MANAGEMENT

Article 6

Taking into account articles 2 to 5, the ongoing research, exchange of information and monitoring and the results thereof, the cost and effectiveness of local and other remedies and, in order to combat air pollution, in particular that originating from new or rebuilt installations, each Contracting Party undertakes to develop the best policies and strategies including air quality management systems and, as part of them, control measures compatible with balanced development, in particular by using the best available technology which is economically feasible and low-and non-waste technology.

RESEARCH AND DEVELOPMENT

Article 7

The Contracting Parties, as appropriate to their needs, shall initiate and co-operate in the conduct of research into and/or development of:

(a) existing and proposed technologies for reducing emissions of sulphur compounds and other major air pollutants, including technical and economic feasibility, and environmental consequences;

(b) instrumentation and other techniques for monitoring and measuring emission rates and ambient concentrations of air pollutants;

(c) improved models for a better understanding of the transmission of long-range transboundary air pollutants;

(d) the effects of sulphur compounds and other major air pollutants on human health and the environment, including agriculture, forestry, materials, aquatic and other natural ecosystems and visibility, with a view to establishing a scientific basis for dose/effect relationships designed to protect the environment;

(e) the economic, social and environmental assessment of alternative measures for attaining environmental objectives including the reduction of long-range transboundary air pollution;

(f) education and training programmes related to the environmental aspects of pollution by sulphur compounds and other major air pollutants.

EXCHANGE OF INFORMATION

Article 8

The Contracting Parties, within the framework of the Executive Body referred to in article 10 and bilaterally, shall, in their common interests, exchange available information on:

(a) data on emissions at periods of time to be agreed upon, of agreed air pollutants, starting with sulphur dioxide, coming from grid-units of agreed size; or on the fluxes of agreed air pollutants, starting with sulphur dioxide, across national borders, at distances and at periods of time to be agreed upon;

(b) major changes in national policies and in general industrial development, and their potential impact, which would be likely to cause significant changes in long-range transboundary air pollution;

(c) control technologies for reducing air pollution relevant to long-range transboundary air pollution;

(d) the projected cost of the emission control of sulphur compounds and other major air pollutants on a national scale;

(e) meteorological and physico-chemical data relating to the processes during transmission;

(f) physico-chemical and biological data relating to the effects of long-range transboundary air pollution and the extent of the damage which these data indicate can be attributed to long-range transboundary air pollution;

(g) national, subregional and regional policies and strategies for the control of sulphur compounds and other major air pollutants.

IMPLEMENTATION AND FURTHER DEVELOPMENT OF THE CO–OPERATIVE PROGRAMME FOR THE MONITORING AND EVALUATION OF THE LONG–RANGE TRANSMISSION OF AIR POLLUTANTS IN EUROPE

Article 9

The Contracting Parties stress the need for the implementation of the existing "Co-operative programme for the monitoring and evaluation of the long-range transmission of air pollutants in Europe" (hereinafter referred to as EMEP) and, with regard to the further development of this programme, agree to emphasize:

(a) the desirability of Contracting Parties joining in and fully implementing EMEP which, as a first step, is based on the monitoring of sulphur dioxide and related substances;

(b) the need to use comparable or standardized procedures for monitoring whenever possible;

(c) the desirability of basing the monitoring programme on the framework of both national and international programmes. The establishment of monitoring stations and the collection of data shall be carried out under the national jurisdiction of the country in which the monitoring stations are located;

(d) the desirability of establishing a framework for a co-operative environmental monitoring programme, based on and taking into account present and future national, subregional, regional and other international programmes;

(e) the need to exchange data on emissions at periods of time to be agreed upon, of agreed air pollutants, starting with sulphur dioxide, coming from grid-units of agreed size; or on the fluxes of agreed air pollutants, starting with sulphur dioxide, across national borders, at distances and at periods of time to be agreed upon. The method, including the model, used to determine the fluxes, as well as the method, including the model, used to determine the transmission of air pollutants based on the emissions per grid-unit, shall be made available and periodically reviewed, in order to improve the methods and the models;

(f) their willingness to continue the exchange and periodic updating of national data on total emissions of agreed air pollutants, starting with sulphur dioxide;

(g) the need to provide meteorological and physico-chemical data relating to processes during transmission;

(h) the need to monitor chemical components in other media such as water, soil and vegetation, as well as a similar monitoring programme to record effects on health and environment;

(i) the desirability of extending the national EMEP networks to make them operational for control and surveillance purposes.

EXECUTIVE BODY

Article 10

1. The representatives of the Contracting Parties shall, within the framework of the Senior Advisers to ECE Governments on Environmental Problems, constitute the Executive Body of the present Convention, and shall meet at least annually in that capacity.

2. The Executive Body shall:

(a) review the implementation of the present Convention;

(b) establish, as appropriate, working groups to consider matters related to the implementation and development of the present Convention and to this end to prepare appropriate studies and other documentation and to submit recommendations to be considered by the Executive Body;

(c) fulfil such other functions as may be appropriate under the provisions of the present Convention.

3. The Executive Body shall utilize the Steering Body for the EMEP to play an integral part in the operation of the present Convention, in particular with regard to data collection and scientific co-operation.

4. The Executive Body, in discharging its functions, shall, when it deems appropriate, also make use of information from other relevant international organizations.

SECRETARIAT

Article 11

The Executive Secretary of the Economic Commission for Europe shall carry out, for the Executive Body, the following secretariat functions:

(a) to convene and prepare the meetings of the Executive Body;

(b) to transmit to the Contracting Parties reports and other information received in accordance with the provisions of the present Convention;

(c) to discharge the functions assigned by the Executive Body.

AMENDMENTS TO THE CONVENTION

Article 12

1. Any Contracting Party may propose amendments to the present Convention.

2. The text of proposed amendments shall be submitted in writing to the Executive Secretary of the Economic Commission for Europe, who shall communicate them to all Contracting Parties. The Executive Body shall discuss proposed amendments at its next annual meeting provided that such proposals have been circulated by the Executive Secretary of the Economic Commission for Europe to the Contracting Parties at least ninety days in advance.

3. An amendment to the present Convention shall be adopted by consensus of the representatives of the Contracting Parties, and shall enter into force for the Contracting Parties which have accepted it on the ninetieth day after the date on which two-thirds of the Contracting Parties have deposited their instruments of acceptance with the depositary. Thereafter, the amendment shall enter into force for any other Contracting Party on the ninetieth day after the date on which that Contracting Party deposits its instrument of acceptance of the amendment.

SETTLEMENT OF DISPUTES

Article 13

If a dispute arises between two or more Contracting Parties to the present Convention as to the interpretation or application of the Convention, they shall seek a solution by negotiation or by any other method of dispute settlement acceptable to the parties to the dispute.

SIGNATURE

Article 14

1. The present Convention shall be open for signature at the United Nations Office at Geneva from 13 to 16 November 1979 on the occasion of the High-level Meeting within the framework of the Economic Commission for Europe on the Protection of the Environment, by the member States of the Economic Commission for Europe as well as States having consultative status with the Economic Commission for Europe, pursuant to paragraph 8 of Economic and Social Council resolution 36 (IV) of 28 March 1947, and by regional economic integration organizations, constituted by sovereign States members of the Economic Commission for Europe, which have competence in respect of the negotiation, conclusion and application of international agreements in matters covered by the present Convention.

2. In matters within their competence, such regional economic integration organizations shall, on their own behalf, exercise the rights and fulfil the responsibilities which the present Convention attributes to their member States. In such cases, the member States of these organizations shall not be entitled to exercise such rights individually.

RATIFICATION, ACCEPTANCE, APPROVAL AND ACCESSION

Article 15

1. The present Convention shall be subject to ratification, acceptance or approval.

2. The present Convention shall be open for accession as from 17 November 1979 by the States and organizations referred to in article 14, paragraph 1.

3. The instruments of ratification, acceptance, approval or accession shall be deposited with the Secretary–General of the United Nations, who will perform the functions of the depositary.

ENTRY INTO FORCE

Article 16

1. The present Convention shall enter into force on the ninetieth day after the date of deposit of the twenty-fourth instrument of ratification, acceptance, approval or accession.

2. For each Contracting Party which ratifies, accepts or approves the present Convention or accedes thereto after the deposit of the twenty-fourth instrument of ratification, acceptance, approval or accession, the Convention shall enter into force on the ninetieth day after the date of deposit by such Contracting Party of its instrument of ratification, acceptance, approval or accession.

WITHDRAWAL

Article 17

At any time after five years from the date on which the present Convention has come into force with respect to a Contracting Party, that Contracting Party may withdraw from the Convention by giving written notification to the depositary. Any such withdrawal shall take effect on the ninetieth day after the date of its receipt by the depositary.

AUTHENTIC TEXTS

Article 18

The original of the present Convention, of which the English, French and Russian texts are equally authentic, shall be deposited with the Secretary–General of the United Nations.

2.2 MEMORANDUM OF INTENT BETWEEN CANADA AND THE UNITED STATES CONCERNING TRANSBOUNDARY AIR POLLUTION (**Without Annex**). **Concluded at Washington, 5 August 1980. Entered into force, 5 August 1980. 32 UST 2521, TIAS No 9856;** *reprinted in* **20 ILM 690 (1981)**

The Government of the United States of America and the Government of Canada,

Share a concern about actual and potential damage resulting from transboundary air pollution, (which is the short and long range transport of air pollutants between their countries), including the already serious problem of acid rain;

Recognize this is an important and urgent bilateral problem as it involves the flow of air pollutants in both directions across the international boundary, especially the long range transport of air pollutants;

Share also a common determination to combat transboundary air pollution in keeping with their existing international rights, obligations, commitments and cooperative practices, including those set forth in the 1909 Boundary Waters Treaty, the 1972 Stockholm Declaration on the Human Environment, the 1978 Great Lakes Water Quality Agreement, and the 1979 ECE Convention on Long Range Transboundary Air Pollution;

Undertook in July 1979 to develop a bilateral cooperative agreement on air quality which would deal effectively with transboundary air pollution;

Are resolved as a matter of priority both to improve scientific understanding of the long range transport of air pollutants and its effects and to develop and implement policies, practices and technologies to combat its impact;

Are resolved to protect the environment in harmony with measures to meet energy needs and other national objectives;

Note scientific findings which indicate that continued pollutant loadings will result in extensive acidification in geologically sensitive areas during the coming years, and that increased pollutant loadings will accelerate this process;

Are concerned that environmental stress could be increased if action is not taken to reduce transboundary air pollution;

Are convinced that the best means to protect the environment from the effects of transboundary air pollution is through the achievement of necessary reductions in pollutant loadings;

Are convinced also that this common problem requires cooperative action by both countries;

Intend to increase bilateral cooperative action to deal effectively with transboundary air pollution, including acid rain.

In particular, the Government of the United States of America and the Government of Canada *intend*:

1. to develop a bilateral agreement which will reflect and further the development of effective domestic control programs and other measures to combat transboundary air pollution;

2. to facilitate the conclusion of such an agreement as soon as possible; and,

3. pending conclusion of such an agreement, to take interim actions available under current authority to combat transboundary air pollution.

The specific undertakings of both Governments at this time are outlined below.

INTERIM ACTIONS

1. Transboundary Air Pollution Agreement

Further to their Joint Statement of July 26, 1979, and subsequent bilateral discussions, both Governments shall take all necessary steps forthwith:

(a) to establish a United States/Canada Coordinating Committee which will undertake preparatory discussions immediately and commence formal negotiations no later than June 1, 1981, of a cooperative agreement on transboundary air pollution; and

(b) to provide the necessary resources for the Committee to carry out its work, including the working group structure as set forth in the Annex. Members will be appointed to the work groups by each Government as soon as possible.

2. Control Measures

To combat transboundary air pollution both Governments shall:

(a) develop domestic air pollution control policies and strategies, and as necessary and appropriate, seek legislative or other support to give effect to them;

(b) promote vigorous enforcement of existing laws and regulations as they require limitation of emissions from new, substantially modified and existing facilities in a way which is responsive to the problems of transboundary air pollution; and

(c) share information and consult on actions being taken pursuant to (a) and (b) above.

3. Notification and Consultation

Both Governments shall continue and expand their long-standing practice of advance notification and consultation on proposed actions involving a significant risk or potential risk of causing or increasing transboundary air pollution, including:

(a) proposed major industrial development or other actions which may cause significant increases in transboundary air pollution; and

(b) proposed changes of policy, regulations or practices which may significantly affect transboundary air pollution.

4. Scientific Information, Research and Development

In order to improve understanding of their common problem and to increase their capability for controlling transboundary air pollution both Governments shall:

(a) exchange information generated in research programs being undertaken in both countries on the atmospheric aspects of the transport of air pollutants and on their effects on aquatic and terrestrial ecosystems and on human health and property;

(b) maintain and further develop a coordinated program for monitoring and evaluation of the impacts of transboundary air pollution, including the maintenance of a United States/Canada sampling network and exchange of data on current and projected emissions of major air pollutants; and

(c) continue to exchange information on research to develop improved technologies for reducing emissions of major air pollutants of concern.

The Memorandum of Intent will become effective on signature and will remain in effect until revised by mutual agreement.

2.3   Mexico–United States Agreement to Co-operate in the Solution of Environmental Problems in the Border Area **(Without Annexes). Concluded at La Paz (Mexico), 14 August 1983. Entered into force, 16 February 1984.** *Reprinted in* **22 ILM 1025 (1983)**

Whereas, the Governments of Mexico and the United States share many environmental problems related to large and expanding urban populations, substantial industrial activity, and a common border between the two countries; and both countries possess many areas of natural and man-made scenic and recreational value; and

Whereas, the Subsecretariat for Environmental Improvement of Mexico (SMA) and the Environmental Protection Agency (EPA) of the United States share a concern for protecting and improving the human and natural environments of their respective nations, and a common interest in the cause of global as well as common border environmental protection and improvement; and

Whereas, the Governments of Mexico and the U.S. have pledged increased cooperation through the Consultative Mechanism set up by the two Presidents to include environmental cooperation;

It is Hereby AGREED that:

1. The SMA and EPA will initiate a cooperative effort to resolve environmental problems of mutual concern in border areas as well as any environmental protection matter through exchanges of information and personnel, and the establishment of parallel projects which the two parties consider appropriate to adopt.

2. The SMA and EPA will accomplish parallel activities, while allowing for the possibility that, at any given time, through special agreement, joint actions tending to resolve specific problems, may be conducted.

3. SMA and EPA senior officials will meet annually, unless they mutually agree otherwise, to discuss overall policies, programs and problems which are of common concern. The annual meeting will be held, alternately in each country, at a mutually agreeable time and site.

4. Experts designated by SMA and EPA will meet periodically or as necessary to review technical issues and plan parallel projects, including pollution abatement and control, regulations, quality assurance, research, and monitoring, that are of common interest or concern to both Mexico and the United States. An annual meeting of designated experts will be held at a site mutually agreed to by both parties and may coincide with the U.S./Mexico Border Health Association annual meetings or with other meetings. The SMA and EPA experts may make policy recommendations for consideration by the respective heads of SMA and EPA.

5. The meetings of the SMA and EPA representatives will not be limited to consideration of border problems alone but may include discussions of all areas of environmental protection and enhancement. It is understood that the Water Treaty of 1944 between the two Governments entrusted the solution of border sanitation problems to the International Boundary and Water Commission.

6. Each Party will name one person to act as coordinator to facilitate exchanges of information and other cooperation under this Memorandum of Understanding. The coordinators will establish procedures and details for the meetings of the senior officials as well as experts, including the time, place and agenda.

7. The coordinators may invite representatives of federal, state and local government agencies, international organizations, members of private organizations or other private citizens to participate in meetings, conferences, and other parallel activities as deemed appropriate.

8. Parallel activities may be conducted when approved by appropriate authorities of the respective governments and may include but will not be limited to the following:

— Development of pollution abatement and control programs directed toward specific pollution problems affecting either or both countries along the border.

— Development of an early warning system to alert the two Governments to potential environmental problems.

— Review and consultation regarding national environmental policies and strategies of Mexico and the United States.

— Development of data gathering, processing and mechanisms for the exchanges of information of common interest.

9.   The coordinators will be responsible for the general management of programs, workshops, projects and activities undertaken pursuant to this Memorandum of Understanding. This includes definition of each program, workshop or project as to scope, priority, and completion schedules. The coordinators may delegate work on a special problem area to a special subcommittee which shall examine the problem in detail and make recommendations to the Governments through the SMA and EPA, respectively.

10.   Unless otherwise agreed, each Party will bear the cost of its participation, including personnel costs, in activities undertaken pursuant to this Memorandum of Understanding.

11.   Work under this Memorandum of Understanding is subject to the availability of funds and other resources to each Party, and to the laws and regulations of Mexico and the United States.

12.   Results of work accomplished under this Memorandum of Understanding will be fully available to both parties and either Party may release information in its possession to the public on 10 days notice to the other Party.

13.   This Memorandum of Understanding will enter into force when signed by both Parties and approved by the two Governments through an exchange of notes. The Memorandum of Understanding will remain in force indefinitely until either Party notifies the other of its intent to terminate the agreement, with 90 days notification.

2.4   Convention on the Transboundary Effects of Industrial Accidents (With Annexes). Done at Helsinki, 17 March 1992. Entered into force, 19 April 2000. 2105 UNTS 457; *reprinted in* 31 ILM 1330 (1992) & 5 Weston & Carlson V.I.14a

The Parties to this Convention,

Mindful of the special importance, in the interest of present and future generations, of protecting human beings and the environment against the effects of industrial accidents,

Recognizing the importance and urgency of preventing serious adverse effects of industrial accidents on human beings and the environment, and of promoting all measures that stimulate the rational, economic and efficient use of preventive, preparedness and response measures to enable environmentally sound and sustainable economic development,

Taking into account the fact that the effects of industrial accidents may make themselves felt across borders, and require cooperation among States,

Affirming the need to promote active international cooperation among the States concerned before, during and after an accident, to enhance appropriate policies and to reinforce and coordinate action at all appropriate levels for promoting the prevention of, preparedness for and response to the transboundary effects of industrial accidents,

Noting the importance and usefulness of bilateral and multilateral arrangements for the prevention of, preparedness for and response to the effects of industrial accidents,

Conscious of the role played in this respect by the United Nations Economic Commission for Europe (ECE) and recalling, inter alia, the ECE Code of Conduct on Accidental Pollution of Transboundary Inland Waters and the Convention on Environmental Impact Assessment in a Transboundary Context,

Having regard to the relevant provisions of the Final Act of the Conference on Security and Cooperation in Europe (CSCE), the Concluding Document of the Vienna Meeting of Representatives of the Participating States of the CSCE, and the outcome of the Sofia Meeting on the Protection of the Environment of the CSCE, as well as to pertinent activities and mechanisms in the United Nations Environment Programme (UNEP), in particular the APELL programme, in the International Labour Organisation (ILO), in particular the Code of Practice on the Prevention of Major Industrial Accidents, and in other relevant international organizations,

Considering the pertinent provisions of the Declaration of the United Nations Conference on the Human Environment, and in particular principle 21, according to which States have, in accordance with the Charter of the United Nations and the principles of international law, the sovereign right to exploit their own resources pursuant to their own environmental policies, and the responsibility to ensure that activities within their jurisdiction or control do not cause damage to the environment of other States or of areas beyond the limits of national jurisdiction,

Taking account of the polluter-pays principle as a general principle of international environmental law,

Underlining the principles of international law and custom, in particular the principles of good-neighbourliness, reciprocity, non-discrimination and good faith,

Have agreed as follows:

Article 1
Definitions

For the purposes of this Convention,

(a) "Industrial accident" means an event resulting from an uncontrolled development in the course of any activity involving hazardous substances either:

(i) In an installation, for example during manufacture, use, storage, handling, or disposal; or

(ii) During transportation in so far as it is covered by paragraph 2(d) of Article 2;

(b) "Hazardous activity" means any activity in which one or more hazardous substances are present or may be present in quantities at or in excess of the threshold quantities listed in Annex I hereto, and which is capable of causing transboundary effects;

(c) "Effects" means any direct or indirect, immediate or delayed adverse consequences caused by an industrial accident on, inter alia:

(i) Human beings, flora and fauna;

(ii) Soil, water, air and landscape;

(iii) The interaction between the factors in (i) and (ii);

(iv) Material assets and cultural heritage, including historical monuments;

(d) "Transboundary effects" means serious effects within the jurisdiction of a Party as a result of an industrial accident occurring within the jurisdiction of another Party;

(e) "Operator" means any natural or legal person, including public authorities, in charge of an activity, e.g. supervising, planning to carry out or carrying out an activity;

(f) "Party" means, unless the text otherwise indicates, a Contracting Party to this Convention;

(g) "Party of origin" means any Party or Parties under whose jurisdiction an industrial accident occurs or is capable of occurring;

(h) "Affected Party" means any Party or Parties affected or capable of being affected by transboundary effects of an industrial accident;

(i) "Parties concerned" means any Party of origin and any affected Party;

(j) "The public" means one or more natural or legal persons.

Article 2
Scope

1. This Convention shall apply to the prevention of, preparedness for and response to industrial accidents capable of causing transboundary effects, including the effects of such accidents caused by natural disasters, and to international cooperation concerning mutual assistance, research and development, exchange of information and exchange of technology in the area of prevention of, preparedness for and response to industrial accidents.

2. This Convention shall not apply to:

(a) Nuclear accidents or radiological emergencies;

(b) Accidents at military installations;

(c) Dam failures, with the exception of the effects of industrial accidents caused by such failures;

(d) Land-based transport accidents with the exception of:

(i) Emergency response to such accidents;

(ii) Transportation on the site of the hazardous activity;

(e) Accidental release of genetically modified organisms;

(f) Accidents caused by activities in the marine environment, including seabed exploration or exploitation;

(g) Spills of oil or other harmful substances at sea.

Article 3
General Provisions

1. The Parties shall, taking into account efforts already made at national and international levels, take appropriate measures and cooperate within the framework of this Convention, to protect human beings and the environment against industrial accidents by preventing such accidents as far as possible, by reducing their frequency and severity and by mitigating their effects. To this end, preventive, preparedness and response measures, including restoration measures, shall be applied.

2. The Parties shall, by means of exchange of information, consultation and other cooperative measures and without undue delay, develop and implement policies and strategies for reducing the risks of industrial accidents and improving preventive, preparedness and response measures, including restoration measures, taking into account, in order to avoid unnecessary duplication, efforts already made at national and international levels.

3. The Parties shall ensure that the operator is obliged to take all measures necessary for the safe performance of the hazardous activity and for the prevention of industrial accidents.

4. To implement the provisions of this Convention, the Parties shall take appropriate legislative, regulatory, administrative and financial measures for the prevention of, preparedness for and response to industrial accidents.

5. The provisions of this Convention shall not prejudice any obligations of the Parties under international law with regard to industrial accidents and hazardous activities.

Article 4
Identification, Consultation and Advice

1. For the purpose of undertaking preventive measures and setting up preparedness measures, the Party of origin shall take measures, as appropriate, to identify hazardous activities within its jurisdiction and to ensure that affected Parties are notified of any such proposed or existing activity.

2. Parties concerned shall, at the initiative of any such Party, enter into discussions on the identification of those hazardous activities that are, reasonably, capable of causing transboundary effects. If the Parties concerned do not agree on whether an activity is such a hazardous activity, any such Party may, unless the Parties concerned agree on another method of resolving the question, submit that question to an inquiry commission in accordance with the provisions of Annex II hereto for advice,

3. The Parties shall, with respect to proposed or existing hazardous activities, apply the procedures set out in Annex III hereto.

4. When a hazardous activity is subject to an environmental impact assessment in accordance with the Convention on Environmental Impact Assessment in a Transboundary Context and that assessment includes an evaluation of the transboundary effects of industrial accidents from the hazardous activity which is performed in conformity with the terms of this Convention, the final decision taken for the purposes of the Convention on Environmental Impact Assessment in a Transboundary Context shall fulfil the relevant requirements of this Convention.

Article 5
Voluntary Extension

Parties concerned should, at the initiative of any of them, enter into discussions on whether to treat an activity not covered by Annex I as a hazardous activity. Upon mutual agreement, they may use an advisory mechanism of their choice, or an inquiry commission in accordance with Annex II, to advise them. Where the Parties concerned so agree, this Convention, or any part thereof, shall apply to the activity in question as if it were a hazardous activity.

Article 6
Prevention

1. The Parties shall take appropriate measures for the prevention of industrial accidents, including measures to induce action by operators to reduce the risk of industrial accidents. Such measures may include, but are not limited to those referred to in Annex IV hereto.

2. With regard to any hazardous activity, the Party of origin shall require the operator to demonstrate the safe performance of the hazardous activity by the provision of information such as basic details of the process, including but not limited to, analysis and evaluation as detailed in Annex V hereto.

Article 7
Decision-making on Siting

Within the framework of its legal system, the Party of origin shall, with the objective of minimizing the risk to the population and the environment of all affected Parties, seek the establishment of policies on the siting of new hazardous activities and on significant modifications to existing hazardous activities. Within the framework of their legal systems, the affected Parties shall seek the establishment of policies on significant developments in areas which could be affected by transboundary effects of an industrial accident arising out of a hazardous activity so as to minimize the risks involved. In elaborating and establishing these policies, the Parties should consider the matters set out in Annex V, paragraph 2, subparagraphs (1) to (8), and Annex VI hereto.

Article 8
Emergency Preparedness

1. The Parties shall take appropriate measures to establish and maintain adequate emergency preparedness to respond to industrial accidents. The Parties shall ensure that preparedness measures are taken to mitigate transboundary effects of such accidents, on-site duties being undertaken by operators. These measures may include, but are not limited to those referred to in Annex VII hereto. In particular, the Parties concerned shall inform each other of their contingency plans.

2. The Party of origin shall ensure for hazardous activities the preparation and implementation of on-site contingency plans, including suitable measures for response and other measures to prevent and minimize transboundary effects. The Party of origin shall provide to the other Parties concerned the elements it has for the elaboration of contingency plans.

3. Each Party shall ensure for hazardous activities the preparation and implementation of off-site contingency plans covering measures to be taken within its territory to prevent and minimize transboundary effects. In preparing these plans, account shall be taken of the conclusions of analysis and evaluation, in particular the matters set out in Annex V, paragraph 2, subparagraphs (1) to (5). Parties concerned shall endeavour to make such plans compatible. Where appropriate, joint off-site

contingency plans shall be drawn up in order to facilitate the adoption of adequate response measures.

4. Contingency plans should be reviewed regularly, or when circumstances so require, taking into account the experience gained in dealing with actual emergencies.

Article 9
Information To, and Participation of the Public

1. The Parties shall ensure that adequate information is given to the public in the areas capable of being affected by an industrial accident arising out of a hazardous activity. This information shall be transmitted through such channels as the Parties deem appropriate, shall include the elements contained in Annex VIII hereto and should take into account matters set out in Annex V, paragraph 2, subparagraphs (1) to (4) and (9).

2. The Party of origin shall, in accordance with the provisions of this Convention and whenever possible and appropriate, give the public in the areas capable of being affected an opportunity to participate in relevant procedures with the aim of making known its views and concerns on prevention and preparedness measures, and shall ensure that the opportunity given to the public of the affected Party is equivalent to that given to the public of the Party of origin.

3. The Parties shall, in accordance with their legal systems and, if desired, on a reciprocal basis provide natural or legal persons who are being or are capable of being adversely affected by the transboundary effects of an industrial accident in the territory of a Party, with access to, and treatment in the relevant administrative and judicial proceedings, including the possibilities of starting a legal action and appealing a decision affecting their rights, equivalent to those available to persons within their own jurisdiction.

Article 10
Industrial Accident Notification Systems

1. The Parties shall, with the aim of obtaining and transmitting industrial accident notifications containing information needed to counteract transboundary effects, provide for the establishment and operation of compatible and efficient industrial accident notification systems at appropriate levels.

2. In the event of an industrial accident, or imminent threat thereof, which causes or is capable of causing transboundary effects, the Party of origin shall ensure that affected Parties are, without delay, notified at appropriate levels through the industrial accident notification systems. Such notification shall include the elements contained in Annex IX hereto.

3. The Parties concerned shall ensure that, in the event of an industrial accident or imminent threat thereof, the contingency plans prepared in accordance with Article 8 are activated as soon as possible and to the extent appropriate to the circumstances.

Article 11
Response

1. The Parties shall ensure that, in the event of an industrial accident, or imminent threat thereof, adequate response measures are taken, as soon as possible and using the most efficient practices, to contain and minimize effects.

2. In the event of an industrial accident, or imminent threat thereof, which causes or is capable of causing transboundary effects, the Parties concerned shall ensure that the effects are assessed—where appropriate, jointly for the purpose of taking adequate response measures. The Parties concerned shall endeavour to coordinate their response measures.

Article 12
Mutual Assistance

1.   If a Party needs assistance in the event of an industrial accident, it may ask for assistance from other Parties, indicating the scope and type of assistance required. A Party to whom a request for assistance is directed shall promptly decide and inform the requesting Party whether it is in a position to render the assistance required and indicate the scope and terms of the assistance that might be rendered.

2.   The Parties concerned shall cooperate to facilitate the prompt provision of assistance agreed to under paragraph 1 of this Article, including, where appropriate, action to minimize the consequences and effects of the industrial accident, and to provide general assistance. Where Parties do not have bilateral or multilateral agreements which cover their arrangements for providing mutual assistance, the assistance shall be rendered in accordance with Annex X hereto, unless the Parties agree otherwise.

Article 13
Responsibility and Liability

The Parties shall support appropriate international efforts to elaborate rules, criteria and procedures in the field of responsibility and liability.

Article 14
Research and Development

The Parties shall, as appropriate, initiate and cooperate in the conduct of research into, and in the development of methods and technologies for the prevention of, preparedness for and response to industrial accidents. For these purposes, the Parties shall encourage and actively promote scientific and technological cooperation, including research into less hazardous processes aimed at limiting accident hazards and preventing and limiting the consequences of industrial accidents.

Article 15
Exchange of Information

The Parties shall, at the multilateral or bilateral level, exchange reasonably obtainable information, including the elements contained in Annex XI hereto.

Article 16
Exchange of Technology

1.   The Parties shall, consistent with their laws, regulations and practices, facilitate the exchange of technology for the prevention of, preparedness for and response to the effects of industrial accidents, particularly through the promotion of:

(a) Exchange of available technology on various financial bases;

(b) Direct industrial contacts and cooperation;

(c) Exchange of information and experience;

(d) Provision of technical assistance.

2.   In promoting the activities specified in paragraph 1, subpararagraphs (a) to (d) of this Article, the Parties shall create favourable conditions by facilitating contacts and cooperation among appropriate organizations and individuals in both the private and the public sectors that are capable of providing technology, design and engineering services, equipment or finance.

Article 17
Competent Authorities and Points of Contact

1. Each Party shall designate or establish one or more competent authorities for the purposes of this Convention.

2. Without prejudice to other arrangements at the bilateral or multilateral level, each Party shall designate or establish one point of contact for the purpose of industrial accident notifications pursuant to Article 10, and one point of contact for the purpose of mutual assistance pursuant to Article 12. These points of contact should preferably be the same.

3. Each Party shall, within three months of the date of entry into force of this Convention for that Party, inform the other Parties, through the secretariat referred to in Article 20, which body or bodies it has designated as its point(s) of contact and as its competent authority or authorities.

4. Each Party shall, within one month of the date of decision, inform the other Parties, through the secretariat, of any changes regarding the designation(s) it has made under paragraph 3 of this Article.

5. Each Party shall keep its point of contact and industrial accident notification systems pursuant to Article 10 operational at all times.

6. Each Party shall keep its point of contact and the authorities responsible for making and receiving requests for, and accepting offers of assistance pursuant to Article 12 operational at all times.

Article 18
Conference of the Parties

1. The representatives of the Parties shall constitute the Conference of the Parties of this Convention and hold their meetings on a regular basis. The first meeting of the Conference of the Parties shall be convened not later than one year after the date of the entry into force of this Convention. Thereafter, a meeting of the Conference of the Parties shall be held at least once a year or at the written request of any Party, provided that, within six months of the request being communicated to them by the secretariat, it is supported by at least one third of the Parties.

2. The Conference of the Parties shall:

(a) Review the implementation of this Convention;

(b) Carry out advisory functions aimed at strengthening the ability of Parties to prevent, prepare for and respond to the transboundary effects of industrial accidents, and at facilitating the provision of technical assistance and advice at the request of Parties faced with industrial accidents;

(c) Establish, as appropriate, working groups and other appropriate mechanisms to consider matters related to the implementation and development of this Convention and, to this end, to prepare appropriate studies and other documentation and submit recommendations for consideration by the Conference of the Parties;

(d) Fulfil such other functions as may be appropriate under the provisions of this Convention;

(e) At its first meeting, consider and, by consensus, adopt rules of procedure for its meetings.

3. The Conference of the Parties, in discharging its functions, shall, when it deems appropriate, also cooperate with other relevant international organizations.

4. The Conference of the Parties shall, at its first meeting, establish a programme of work, in particular with regard to the items contained in Annex XII hereto. The Conference of the Parties shall also decide on the method of work, including the

use of national centres and cooperation with relevant international organizations and the establishment of a system with a view to facilitating the implementation of this Convention, in particular for mutual assistance in the event of an industrial accident, and building upon pertinent existing activities within relevant international organizations. As part of the programme of work, the Conference of the Parties shall review existing national, regional and international centres, and other bodies and programmes aimed at coordinating information and efforts in the prevention of, preparedness for and response to industrial accidents, with a view to determining what additional international institutions or centres may be needed to carry out the tasks listed in Annex XII.

5.   The Conference of the Parties shall, at its first meeting, commence consideration of procedures to create more favourable conditions for the exchange of technology for the prevention of, preparedness for and response to the effects of industrial accidents.

6.   The Conference of the Parties shall adopt guidelines and criteria to facilitate the identification of hazardous activities for the purposes of this Convention.

Article 19
Right to Vote

1.   Except as provided for in paragraph 2 of this Article, each Party to this Convention shall have one vote.

2.   Regional economic integration organizations as defined in Article 27 shall, in matters within their competence, exercise their right to vote with a number of votes equal to the number of their member States which are Parties to this Convention. Such organizations shall not exercise their right to vote if their member States exercise theirs, and vice versa.

Article 20
Secretariat

The Executive Secretary of the Economic Commission for Europe shall carry out the following secretariat functions:

(a) Convene and prepare meetings of the Parties;

(b) Transmit to the Parties reports and other information received in accordance with the provisions of this Convention;

(c) Such other functions as may be determined by the Parties.

Article 21
Settlement of Disputes

1.   If a dispute arises between two or more Parties about the interpretation or application of this Convention, they shall seek a solution by negotiation or by any other method of dispute settlement acceptable to the parties to the dispute.

2.   When signing, ratifying, accepting, approving or acceding to this Convention, or at any time thereafter, a Party may declare in writing to the Depositary that, for a dispute not resolved in accordance with paragraph 1 of this Article, it accepts one or both of the following means of dispute settlement as compulsory in relation to any Party accepting the same obligation:

(a) Submission of the dispute to the International Court of Justice;

(b) Arbitration in accordance with the procedure set out in Annex XIII hereto.

3.   If the parties to the dispute have accepted both means of dispute settlement referred to in paragraph 2 of this Article, the dispute may be submitted only to the International Court of Justice, unless the parties to the dispute agree otherwise.

Article 22
Limitations on the Supply of Information

1. The provisions of this Convention shall not affect the rights or the obligations of Parties in accordance with their national laws, regulations, administrative provisions or accepted legal practices and applicable international regulations to protect information related to personal data, industrial and commercial secrecy, including intellectual property, or national security.

2. If a Party nevertheless decides to supply such protected information to another Party, the Party receiving such protected information shall respect the confidentiality of the information received and the conditions under which it is supplied, and shall only use that information for the purposes for which it was supplied.

Article 23
Implementation

The Parties shall report periodically on the implementation of this Convention.

Article 24
Bilateral and Multilateral Agreements

1. The Parties may, in order to implement their obligations under this Convention, continue existing or enter into new bilateral or multilateral agreements or other arrangements.

2. The provisions of this Convention shall not affect the right of Parties to take, by bilateral or multilateral agreement where appropriate, more stringent measures than those required by this Convention.

Article 25
Status of Annexes

The Annexes to this Convention form an integral part of the Convention.

Article 26
Amendments to the Convention

1. Any Party may propose amendments to this Convention.

2. The text of any proposed amendment to this Convention shall be submitted in writing to the Executive Secretary of the Economic Commission for Europe, who shall circulate it to all Parties. The Conference of the Parties shall discuss proposed amendments at its next annual meeting, provided that such proposals have been circulated to the Parties by the Executive Secretary of the Economic Commission for Europe at least ninety days in advance.

3. For amendments to this Convention—other than those to Annex I, for which the procedure is described in paragraph 4 of this Article:

(a) Amendments shall be adopted by consensus of the Parties present at the meeting and shall be submitted by the Depositary to all Parties for ratification, acceptance or approval;

(b) Instruments of ratification, acceptance or approval of amendments shall be deposited with the Depositary. Amendments adopted in accordance with this Article shall enter into force for Parties that have accepted them on the ninetieth day following the day of receipt by the Depositary of the sixteenth instrument of ratification, acceptance or approval;

(c) Thereafter, amendments shall enter into force for any other Party on the ninetieth day after that Party deposits its instruments of ratification, acceptance or approval of the amendments.

4. For amendments to Annex I:

(a) The Parties shall make every effort to reach agreement by consensus. If all efforts at consensus have been exhausted and no agreement reached, the amendments shall, as a last resort, be adopted by a nine-tenths majority vote of the Parties present and voting at the meeting. If adopted by the Conference of the Parties, the amendments shall be communicated to the Parties and recommended for approval;

(b) On the expiry of twelve months from the date of their communication by the Executive Secretary of the Economic Commission for Europe, the amendments to Annex I shall become effective for those Parties to this Convention which have not submitted a notification in accordance with the provisions of paragraph 4(c) of this Article, provided that at least sixteen Parties have not submitted such a notification;

(c) Any Party that is unable to approve an amendment to Annex I of this Convention shall so notify the Executive Secretary of the Economic Commission for Europe in writing within twelve months from the date of the communication of the adoption. The Executive Secretary shall without delay notify all Parties of any such notification received. A Party may at any time substitute an acceptance for its previous notification and the amendment to Annex I shall thereupon enter into force for that Party.

(d) For the purpose of this paragraph "Parties present and voting" means Parties present and casting an affirmative or negative vote.

Article 27
Signature

This Convention shall be open for signature at Helsinki from 17 to 18 March 1992 inclusive, and thereafter at United Nations Headquarters in New York until 18 September 1992, by States members of the Economic Commission for Europe, as well as States having consultative status with the Economic Commission for Europe pursuant to paragraph 8 of Economic and Social Council resolution 36 (IV) of 28 March 1947, and by regional economic integration organizations constituted by sovereign States members of the Economic Commission for Europe to which their member States have transferred competence in respect of matters governed by this Convention, including the competence to enter into treaties in respect of these matters.

Article 28
Depositary

The Secretary–General of the United Nations shall act as the Depositary of this Convention.

Article 29
Ratification, Acceptance, Approval and Accession

1. This Convention shall be subject to ratification, acceptance or approval by the signatory States and regional economic integration organizations referred to in Article 27.

2. This Convention shall be open for accession by the States and organizations referred to in Article 27.

3. Any organization referred to in Article 27 which becomes Party to this Convention without any of its member States being a Party shall be bound by all the obligations under this Convention. In the case of such organizations, one or more of whose member States is a Party to this Convention, the organization and its member

States shall decide on their respective responsibilities for the performance of their obligations under this Convention. In such cases, the organization and the member States shall not be entitled to exercise rights under this Convention concurrently.

4. In their instruments of ratification, acceptance, approval or accession, the regional economic integration organizations referred to in Article 27 shall declare the extent of their competence with respect to the matters governed by this Convention. These organizations shall also inform the Depositary of any substantial modification to the extent of their competence.

Article 30
Entry into Force

1. This Convention shall enter into force on the ninetieth day after the date of deposit of the sixteenth instrument of ratification, acceptance, approval or accession.

2. For the purposes of paragraph 1 of this Article, any instrument deposited by an organization referred to in Article 27 shall not be counted as additional to those deposited by States members of such an organization.

3. For each State or organization referred to in Article 27 which ratifies, accepts or approves this Convention or accedes thereto after the deposit of the sixteenth instrument of ratification, acceptance, approval or accession, this Convention shall enter into force on the ninetieth day after the date of deposit by such State or organization of its instrument of ratification, acceptance, approval or accession.

Article 31
Withdrawal

1. At any time after three years from the date on which this Convention has come into force with respect to a Party, that Party may withdraw from this Convention by giving written notification to the Depositary. Any such withdrawal shall take effect on the ninetieth day after the date of the receipt of the notification by the Depositary.

2. Any such withdrawal shall not affect the application of Article 4 to an activity in respect of which a notification has been made pursuant to Article 4, paragraph 1, or a request for discussions has been made pursuant to Article 4, paragraph 2.

Article 32
Authentic Texts

The original of this Convention, of which the English, French and Russian texts are equally authentic, shall be deposited with the Secretary–General of the United Nations.

IN WITNESS WHEREOF the undersigned, being duly authorized thereto, have signed this Convention.

DONE at Helsinki, this seventeenth day of March one thousand nine hundred and ninety-two.

ANNEX I
HAZARDOUS SUBSTANCES FOR THE PURPOSES OF DEFINING HAZARDOUS ACTIVITIES

The quantities set out below relate to each activity or group of activities. Where a range of quantities is given in Part I, the threshold quantities are the maximum quantities given in each range. Five years after the entry into force of this Convention, the lowest quantity given in each range shall become the threshold quantity, unless amended.

Where a substance or preparation named in Part II also falls within a category in Part I, the threshold quantity set out in Part II shall be used.

For the identification of hazardous activities, Parties shall take into consideration the foreseeable possibility of aggravation of the hazards involved and the quantities of the hazardous substances and their proximity, whether under the charge of one or more operators.

PART I.   Categories of substances and preparations
not specifically named in Part II

Category	Threshold Quantity (Tonnes)
1. Flammable gases . . . including LPG	200
2. Highly flammable liquids	50,000
3. Very toxic	20
4. Toxic	500–200
5. Oxidizing	500–200
6. Explosive	200–50
7. Flammable liquids (handled under special conditions of pressure and temperature)	200
8. Dangerous for the environment	200

FLAMMABLE GASES: substances which in the gaseous state at normal pressure and mixed with air become flammable and the boiling point of which at normal pressure is 20° C or below;

HIGHLY FLAMMABLE LIQUIDS: substances which have a flash point lower than 21° C and the boiling point of which at normal pressure is above 20° C;

VERY TOXIC: substances . . . owing to their physical and chemical properties, are capable of creating industrial accident hazards.

OXIDIZING: substances which give rise to highly exothermic reaction when in contact with other substances, particularly flammable substances.

EXPLOSIVE: substances which may explode under the effect of flame or which are more sensitive to shocks or friction than dinitrobenzene.

FLAMMABLE LIQUIDS: substances which have a flash point lower than 55° C and which remain liquid under pressure, where particular processing conditions, such as high pressure and high temperature, may create industrial accident hazards.

DANGEROUS FOR THE ENVIRONMENT: substances showing the values for acute toxicity to the aquatic environment. . . .

PART II.   Named substances

Substance	Threshold Quantity (Tonnes)
1. Ammonia	500
2 a. Ammonium nitrate	2,500
2 b. Ammonium nitrate in the form of fertilizers	10,000
3. Acrylonitrile	200
4. Chlorine	25
5. Ethylene oxide	50
6. Hydrogen cyanide	20
7. Hydrogen fluoride	50

8.	Hydrogen sulphide	50
9.	Sulphur dioxide	250
10.	Sulphur trioxide	75
11.	Lead alkyls	50
12.	Phosgene	0.75
13.	Methyl isocyanate	0.15

[Text of Annexes II—XXIII is omitted]

ANNEX II
INQUIRY COMMISSION PROCEDURE PURSUANT TO ARTICLES 4 AND 5

ANNEX III
PROCEDURES PURSUANT TO ARTICLE 4

ANNEX IV
PREVENTIVE MEASURES PURSUANT TO ARTICLE 6

ANNEX V
ANALYSIS AND EVALUATION

ANNEX VI
DECISION–MAKING ON SITING PURSUANT TO ARTICLE 7

ANNEX VII
EMERGENCY PREPAREDNESS MEASURES PURSUANT TO ARTICLE 8

ANNEX VIII
INFORMATION TO THE PUBLIC PURSUANT TO ARTICLE 9

ANNEX IX
INDUSTRIAL ACCIDENT NOTIFICATION SYSTEMS PURSUANT TO ARTICLE 10

ANNEX X
MUTUAL ASSISTANCE PURSUANT TO ARTICLE 12

ANNEX XI
EXCHANGE OF INFORMATION PURSUANT TO ARTICLE 15

ANNEX XII
TASKS FOR MUTUAL ASSISTANCE PURSUANT TO ARTICLE 18, PARAGRAPH 4

ANNEX XIII
ARBITRATION

2.5 Protocol to the 1979 Convention on Long–Range Transboundary Air Pollution to Abate Acidification, Eutrophication and Ground–Level Ozone. Concluded at Gothenburg (Sweden), 30 November 1999. Entered into force 17 May 2005. UN Doc E/EB.AIR/1999/1. *Reprinted in 5 Weston & Carlson V.E.20g*

The Parties,

Determined to implement the Convention on Long-range Transboundary Air Pollution,

Aware that nitrogen oxides, sulphur, volatile organic compounds and reduced nitrogen compounds have been associated with adverse effects on human health and the environment,

Concerned that critical loads of acidification, critical loads of nutrient nitrogen and critical levels of ozone for human health and vegetation are still exceeded in many areas of the United Nations Economic Commission for Europe's region,

Concerned also that emitted nitrogen oxides, sulphur and volatile organic compounds, as well as secondary pollutants such as ozone and the reaction products of ammonia, are transported in the atmosphere over long distances and may have adverse transboundary effects,

Recognizing that emissions from Parties within the United Nations Economic Commission for Europe's region contribute to air pollution on the hemispheric and global scales, and recognizing the potential for transport between continents and the need for further study with regard to that potential,

Recognizing also that Canada and the United States of America are bilaterally negotiating reductions of emissions of nitrogen oxides and volatile organic compounds to address the transboundary ozone effect,

Recognizing furthermore that Canada will undertake further reductions of emissions of sulphur by 2010 through the implementation of the Canada-wide Acid Rain Strategy for Post–2000, and that the United States is committed to the implementation of a nitrogen oxides reduction programme in the eastern United States and to the reduction in emissions necessary to meet its national ambient air quality standards for particulate matter,

Resolved to apply a multi-effect, multi-pollutant approach to preventing or minimizing the exceedances of critical loads and levels,

Taking into account the emissions from certain existing activities and installations responsible for present air pollution levels and the development of future activities and installations,

Aware that techniques and management practices are available to reduce emissions of these substances,

Resolved to take measures to anticipate, prevent or minimize emissions of these substances, taking into account the application of the precautionary approach as set forth in principle 15 of the Rio Declaration on Environment and Development,

Reaffirming that States have, in accordance with the Charter of the United Nations and the principles of international law, the sovereign right to exploit their own resources pursuant to their own environmental and developmental policies, and the responsibility to ensure that activities within their jurisdiction or control do not cause damage to the environment of other States or of areas beyond the limits of national jurisdiction,

Conscious of the need for a cost-effective regional approach to combating air pollution that takes account of the variations in effects and abatement costs between countries,

Noting the important contribution of the private and non-governmental sectors to knowledge of the effects associated with these substances and available abatement techniques, and their role in assisting in the reduction of emissions to the atmosphere,

Bearing in mind that measures taken to reduce emissions of sulphur, nitrogen oxides, ammonia and volatile organic compounds should not constitute a means of arbitrary or unjustifiable discrimination or a disguised restriction on international competition and trade,

Taking into consideration best available scientific and technical knowledge and data on emissions, atmospheric processes and effects on human health and the environment of these substances, as well as on abatement costs, and acknowledging the need to improve this knowledge and to continue scientific and technical coopera- tion to further understanding of these issues,

Noting that under the Protocol concerning the Control of Emissions of Nitrogen Oxides or their Transboundary Fluxes, adopted at Sofia on 31 October 1988, and the Protocol concerning the Control of Emissions of Volatile Organic Compounds or their Transboundary Fluxes, adopted at Geneva on 18 November 1991, there is already provision to control emissions of nitrogen oxides and volatile organic compounds, and that the technical annexes to both those Protocols already contain technical guidance for reducing these emissions,

Noting also that under the Protocol on Further Reduction of Sulphur Emissions, adopted at Oslo on 14 June 1994, there is already provision to reduce sulphur emissions in order to contribute to the abatement of acid deposition by diminishing the exceedances of critical sulphur depositions, which have been derived from critical loads of acidity according to the contribution of oxidized sulphur compounds to the total acid deposition in 1990,

Noting furthermore that this Protocol is the first agreement under the Convention to deal specifically with reduced nitrogen compounds,

Bearing in mind that reducing the emissions of these substances may provide additional benefits for the control of other pollutants, including in particular trans- boundary secondary particulate aerosols, which contribute to human health effects associated with exposure to airborne particulates,

Bearing in mind also the need to avoid, in so far as possible, taking measures for the achievement of the objectives of this Protocol that aggravate other health and environment-related problems,

Noting that measures taken to reduce the emissions of nitrogen oxides and ammonia should involve consideration of the full biogeochemical nitrogen cycle and, so far as possible, not increase emissions of reactive nitrogen including nitrous oxide which could aggravate other nitrogen-related problems,

Aware that methane and carbon monoxide emitted by human activities contribute, in the presence of nitrogen oxides and volatile organic compounds, to the formation of tropospheric ozone, and

Aware also of the commitments that Parties have assumed under the United Nations Framework Convention on Climate Change,

Have agreed as follows:

Article 1

Definitions

For the purposes of the present Protocol,

1. "Convention" means the Convention on Long-range Transboundary Air Pollu- tion, adopted at Geneva on 13 November 1979;

2. "EMEP" means the Cooperative Programme for Monitoring and Evaluation of Long-range Transmission of Air Pollutants in Europe;

3. "Executive Body" means the Executive Body for the Convention constituted under article 10, paragraph 1, of the Convention;

4. "Commission" means the United Nations Economic Commission for Europe;

5. "Parties" means, unless the context otherwise requires, the Parties to the present Protocol;

6. "Geographical scope of EMEP" means the area defined in article 1, paragraph 4, of the Protocol to the 1979 Convention on Long-range Transboundary Air Pollution on Long-term Financing of the Cooperative Programme for Monitoring and Evaluation of the Long-range Transmission of Air Pollutants in Europe (EMEP), adopted at Geneva on 28 September 1984;

7. "Emission" means the release of a substance from a point or diffuse source into the atmosphere;

8. "Nitrogen oxides" means nitric oxide and nitrogen dioxide, expressed as nitrogen dioxide (NO_2);

9. "Reduced nitrogen compounds" means ammonia and its reaction products;

10. "Sulphur" means all sulphur compounds, expressed as sulphur dioxide (SO_2);

11. "Volatile organic compounds", or "VOCs", means, unless otherwise specified, all organic compounds of an anthropogenic nature, other than methane, that are capable of producing photochemical oxidants by reaction with nitrogen oxides in the presence of sunlight;

12. "Critical load" means a quantitative estimate of an exposure to one or more pollutants below which significant harmful effects on specified sensitive elements of the environment do not occur, according to present knowledge;

13. "Critical levels" means concentrations of pollutants in the atmosphere above which direct adverse effects on receptors, such as human beings, plants, ecosystems or materials, may occur, according to present knowledge;

14. "Pollutant emissions management area", or "PEMA", means an area designated in annex III under the conditions laid down in article 3, paragraph 9;

15. "Stationary source" means any fixed building, structure, facility, installation or equipment that emits or may emit sulphur, nitrogen oxides, volatile organic compounds or ammonia directly or indirectly into the atmosphere;

16. "New stationary source" means any stationary source of which the construction or substantial modification is commenced after the expiry of one year from the date of entry into force of the present Protocol. It shall be a matter for the competent national authorities to decide whether a modification is substantial or not, taking into account such factors as the environmental benefits of the modification.

Article 2

Objective

The objective of the present Protocol is to control and reduce emissions of sulphur, nitrogen oxides, ammonia and volatile organic compounds that are caused by anthropogenic activities and are likely to cause adverse effects on human health, natural ecosystems, materials and crops, due to acidification, eutrophication or ground-level ozone as a result of long-range transboundary atmospheric transport, and to ensure, as far as possible, that in the long term and in a stepwise approach, taking into account advances in scientific knowledge, atmospheric depositions or concentrations do not exceed:

(a) For Parties within the geographical scope of EMEP and Canada, the critical loads of acidity, as described in annex I ;

(b) For Parties within the geographical scope of EMEP, the critical loads of nutrient nitrogen, as described in annex I; and

(c) For ozone:

>(i) For Parties within the geographical scope of EMEP, the critical levels of ozone, as given in annex I ;

>(ii) For Canada, the Canada-wide Standard for ozone; and

>(iii) For the United States of America, the National Ambient Air Quality Standard for ozone.

Article 3
Basic Obligations

1. Each Party having an emission ceiling in any table in annex II shall reduce and maintain the reduction in its annual emissions in accordance with that ceiling and the timescales specified in that annex. Each Party shall, as a minimum, control its annual emissions of polluting compounds in accordance with the obligations in annex II.

2. Each Party shall apply the limit values specified in annexes IV, V and VI to each new stationary source within a stationary source category as identified in those annexes, no later than the timescales specified in annex VII. As an alternative, a Party may apply different emission reduction strategies that achieve equivalent overall emission levels for all source categories together.

3. Each Party shall, in so far as it is technically and economically feasible and taking into consideration the costs and advantages, apply the limit values specified in annexes IV, V and VI to each existing stationary source within a stationary source category as identified in those annexes, no later than the timescales specified in annex VII. As an alternative, a Party may apply different emission reduction strategies that achieve equivalent overall emission levels for all source categories together or, for Parties outside the geographical scope of EMEP, that are necessary to achieve national or regional goals for acidification abatement and to meet national air quality standards.

4. Limit values for new and existing boilers and process heaters with a rated thermal input exceeding 50 MWth and new heavy-duty vehicles shall be evaluated by the Parties at a session of the Executive Body with a view to amending annexes IV, V and VIII no later than two years after the date of entry into force of the present Protocol.

5. Each Party shall apply the limit values for the fuels and new mobile sources identified in annex VIII, no later than the timescales specified in annex VII.

6. Each Party should apply best available techniques to mobile sources and to each new or existing stationary source, taking into account guidance documents I to V adopted by the Executive Body at its seventeenth session (decision 1999/1) and any amendments thereto.

7. Each Party shall take appropriate measures based, *inter alia*, on scientific and economic criteria to reduce emissions of volatile organic compounds associated with the use of products not included in annex VI or VIII. The Parties shall, no later than at the second session of the Executive Body after the entry into force of the present Protocol, consider with a view to adopting an annex on products, including criteria for the selection of such products, limit values for the volatile organic compound content of products not included in annex VI or VIII, as well as timescales for the application of the limit values.

8.   Each Party shall, subject to paragraph 10:

(a) Apply, as a minimum, the ammonia control measures specified in annex IX; and

(b) Apply, where it considers it appropriate, best available techniques for preventing and reducing ammonia emissions, as listed in guidance document V adopted by the Executive Body at its seventeenth session (decision 1999/1) and any amendments thereto.

9.   Paragraph 10 shall apply to any Party:

(a) Whose total land area is greater than 2 million square kilometres;

(b) Whose annual emissions of sulphur, nitrogen oxides, ammonia and/or volatile organic compounds contributing to acidification, eutrophication or ozone formation in areas under the jurisdiction of one or more other Parties originate predominantly from within an area under its jurisdiction that is listed as a PEMA in annex III, and which has presented documentation in accordance with subparagraph (c) to this effect;

(c) Which has submitted upon signature, ratification, acceptance or approval of, or accession to, the present Protocol a description of the geographical scope of one or more PEMAs for one or more pollutants, with supporting documentation, for inclusion in annex III; and

(d) Which has specified upon signature, ratification, acceptance or approval of, or accession to, the present Protocol its intention to act in accordance with this paragraph.

10.   A Party to which this paragraph applies shall:

(a) If within the geographical scope of EMEP, be required to comply with the provisions of this article and annex II only within the relevant PEMA for each pollutant for which a PEMA within its jurisdiction is included in annex III; or

(b) If not within the geographical scope of EMEP, be required to comply with the provisions of paragraphs 1, 2, 3, 5, 6 and 7 and annex II, only within the relevant PEMA for each pollutant (nitrogen oxides, sulphur and/or volatile organic compounds) for which a PEMA within its jurisdiction is included in annex III, and shall not be required to comply with paragraph 8 anywhere within its jurisdiction.

11.   Canada and the United States of America shall, upon their ratification, acceptance or approval of, or accession to, the present Protocol, submit to the Executive Body their respective emission reduction commitments with respect to sulphur, nitrogen oxides and volatile organic compounds for automatic incorporation into annex II.

12.   The Parties shall, subject to the outcome of the first review provided for under article 10, paragraph 2, and no later than one year after completion of that review, commence negotiations on further obligations to reduce emissions.

Article 4
Exchange of Information and Technology

1.   Each Party shall, in a manner consistent with its laws, regulations and practices and in accordance with its obligations in the present Protocol, create favourable conditions to facilitate the exchange of information, technologies and techniques, with the aim of reducing emissions of sulphur, nitrogen oxides, ammonia and volatile organic compounds by promoting *inter alia*:

(a) The development and updating of databases on best available techniques, including those that increase energy efficiency, low-emission burners and good environmental practice in agriculture;

(b) The exchange of information and experience in the development of less polluting transport systems;

(c) Direct industrial contacts and cooperation, including joint ventures; and

(d) The provision of technical assistance.

2. In promoting the activities specified in paragraph 1, each Party shall create favourable conditions for the facilitation of contacts and cooperation among appropriate organizations and individuals in the private and public sectors that are capable of providing technology, design and engineering services, equipment or finance.

Article 5
Public Awareness

1. Each Party shall, in a manner consistent with its laws, regulations and practices, promote the provision of information to the general public, including information on:

(a) National annual emissions of sulphur, nitrogen oxides, ammonia and volatile organic compounds and progress towards compliance with the national emission ceilings or other obligations referred to in article 3;

(b) Depositions and concentrations of the relevant pollutants and, where applicable, these depositions and concentrations in relation to critical loads and levels referred to in article 2;

(c) Levels of tropospheric ozone; and

(d) Strategies and measures applied or to be applied to reduce air pollution problems dealt with in the present Protocol and set out in article 6.

2. Furthermore, each Party may make information widely available to the public with a view to minimizing emissions, including information on:

(a) Less polluting fuels, renewable energy and energy efficiency, including their use in transport;

(b) Volatile organic compounds in products, including labelling;

(c) Management options for wastes containing volatile organic compounds that are generated by the public;

(d) Good agricultural practices to reduce emissions of ammonia;

(e) Health and environmental effects associated with the pollutants covered by the present Protocol; and

(f) Steps which individuals and industries may take to help reduce emissions of the pollutants covered by the present Protocol.

Article 6
Strategies, Policies, Programmes, Measures and Information

1. Each Party shall, as necessary and on the basis of sound scientific and economic criteria, in order to facilitate the implementation of its obligations under article 3:

(a) Adopt supporting strategies, policies and programmes without undue delay after the present Protocol enters into force for it;

(b) Apply measures to control and reduce its emissions of sulphur, nitrogen oxides, ammonia and volatile organic compounds;

(c) Apply measures to encourage the increase of energy efficiency and the use of renewable energy;

(d) Apply measures to decrease the use of polluting fuels;

(e) Develop and introduce less polluting transport systems and promote traffic management systems to reduce overall emissions from road traffic;

(f) Apply measures to encourage the development and introduction of low-polluting processes and products, taking into account guidance documents I to V adopted by the Executive Body at its seventeenth session (decision 1999/1) and any amendments thereto;

(g) Encourage the implementation of management programmes to reduce emissions, including voluntary programmes, and the use of economic instruments, taking into account guidance document VI adopted by the Executive Body at its seventeenth session (decision 1999/1) and any amendments thereto;

(h) Implement and further elaborate policies and measures in accordance with its national circumstances, such as the progressive reduction or phasing-out of market imperfections, fiscal incentives, tax and duty exemptions and subsidies in all sectors that emit sulphur, nitrogen oxides, ammonia and volatile organic compounds which run counter to the objective of the Protocol, and apply market instruments; and

(i) Apply measures, where cost-effective, to reduce emissions from waste products containing volatile organic compounds.

2. Each Party shall collect and maintain information on:

(a) Actual levels of emissions of sulphur, nitrogen compounds and volatile organic compounds, and of ambient concentrations and depositions of these compounds and ozone, taking into account, for those Parties within the geographical scope of EMEP, the work plan of EMEP; and

(b) The effects of ambient concentrations and of the deposition of sulphur, nitrogen compounds, volatile organic compounds and ozone on human health, terrestrial and aquatic ecosystems and materials.

3. Any Party may take more stringent measures than those required by the present Protocol.

Article 7
Reporting

1. Subject to its laws and regulations and in accordance with its obligations under the present Protocol:

(a) Each Party shall report, through the Executive Secretary of the Commission, to the Executive Body, on a periodic basis as determined by the Parties at a session of the Executive Body, information on the measures that it has taken to implement the present Protocol. Moreover:

    (i) Where a Party applies different emission reduction strategies under article 3, paragraphs 2 and 3, it shall document the strategies applied and its compliance with the requirements of those paragraphs;

    (ii) Where a Party judges certain limit values, as specified in accordance with article 3, paragraph 3, not to be technically and economically feasible, taking into consideration the costs and advantages, it shall report and justify this;

(b) Each Party within the geographical scope of EMEP shall report, through the Executive Secretary of the Commission, to EMEP, on a periodic basis to be determined by the Steering Body of EMEP and approved by the Parties at a session of the Executive Body, the following information:

    (i) Levels of emissions of sulphur, nitrogen oxides, ammonia and volatile organic compounds using, as a minimum, the methodologies and the temporal and spatial resolution specified by the Steering Body of EMEP;

(ii) Levels of emissions of each substance in the reference year (1990) using the same methodologies and temporal and spatial resolution;

(iii) Data on projected emissions and current reduction plans; and

(iv) Where it deems it appropriate, any exceptional circumstances justifying emissions that are temporarily higher than the ceilings established for it for one or more pollutants; and

(c) Parties in areas outside the geographical scope of EMEP shall make available information similar to that specified in subparagraph (b), if requested to do so by the Executive Body.

2. The information to be reported in accordance with paragraph 1 (a) shall be in conformity with a decision regarding format and content to be adopted by the Parties at a session of the Executive Body. The terms of this decision shall be reviewed as necessary to identify any additional elements regarding the format or the content of the information that is to be included in the reports.

3. In good time before each annual session of the Executive Body, EMEP shall provide information on:

(a) Ambient concentrations and depositions of sulphur and nitrogen compounds as well as, where available, ambient concentrations of volatile organic compounds and ozone; and

(b) Calculations of sulphur and oxidized and reduced nitrogen budgets and relevant information on the long-range transport of ozone and its precursors.

Parties in areas outside the geographical scope of EMEP shall make available similar information if requested to do so by the Executive Body.

4. The Executive Body shall, in accordance with article 10, paragraph 2 (b), of the Convention, arrange for the preparation of information on the effects of depositions of sulphur and nitrogen compounds and concentrations of ozone.

5. The Parties shall, at sessions of the Executive Body, arrange for the preparation, at regular intervals, of revised information on calculated and internationally optimized allocations of emission reductions for the States within the geographical scope of EMEP, using integrated assessment models, including atmospheric transport models, with a view to reducing further, for the purposes of article 3, paragraph 1, the difference between actual depositions of sulphur and nitrogen compounds and critical load values as well as the difference between actual ozone concentrations and the critical levels of ozone specified in annex I, or such alternative assessment methods as approved by the Parties at a session of the Executive Body.

Article 8
Research, Development and Monitoring

The Parties shall encourage research, development, monitoring and cooperation related to:

(a) The international harmonization of methods for the calculation and assessment of the adverse effects associated with the substances addressed by the present Protocol for use in establishing critical loads and critical levels and, as appropriate, the elaboration of procedures for such harmonization;

(b) The improvement of emission databases, in particular those on ammonia and volatile organic compounds;

(c) The improvement of monitoring techniques and systems and of the modelling of transport, concentrations and depositions of sulphur, nitrogen compounds and volatile organic compounds, as well as of the formation of ozone and secondary particulate matter;

(d) The improvement of the scientific understanding of the long-term fate of emissions and their impact on the hemispheric background concentrations of sulphur, nitrogen, volatile organic compounds, ozone and particulate matter, focusing, in particular, on the chemistry of the free troposphere and the potential for intercontinental flow of pollutants;

(e) The further elaboration of an overall strategy to reduce the adverse effects of acidification, eutrophication and photochemical pollution, including synergisms and combined effects;

(f) Strategies for the further reduction of emissions of sulphur, nitrogen oxides, ammonia and volatile organic compounds based on critical loads and critical levels as well as on technical developments, and the improvement of integrated assessment modelling to calculate internationally optimized allocations of emission reductions taking into account the need to avoid excessive costs for any Party. Special emphasis should be given to emissions from agriculture and transport;

(g) The identification of trends over time and the scientific understanding of the wider effects of sulphur, nitrogen and volatile organic compounds and photochemical pollution on human health, including their contribution to concentrations of particulate matter, the environment, in particular acidification and eutrophication, and materials, especially historic and cultural monuments, taking into account the relationship between sulphur oxides, nitrogen oxides, ammonia, volatile organic compounds and tropospheric ozone;

(h) Emission abatement technologies, and technologies and techniques to improve energy efficiency, energy conservation and the use of renewable energy;

(i) The efficacy of ammonia control techniques for farms and their impact on local and regional deposition;

(j) The management of transport demand and the development and promotion of less polluting modes of transport;

(k) The quantification and, where possible, economic evaluation of benefits for the environment and human health resulting from the reduction of emissions of sulphur, nitrogen oxides, ammonia and volatile organic compounds; and

(*l*) The development of tools for making the methods and results of this work widely applicable and available.

Article 9
Compliance

Compliance by each Party with its obligations under the present Protocol shall be reviewed regularly. The Implementation Committee established by decision 1997/2 of the Executive Body at its fifteenth session shall carry out such reviews and report to the Parties at a session of the Executive Body in accordance with the terms of the annex to that decision, including any amendments thereto.

Article 10
Reviews by the Parties at Sessions of the Executive Body

1. The Parties shall, at sessions of the Executive Body, pursuant to article 10, paragraph 2 (a), of the Convention, review the information supplied by the Parties, EMEP and subsidiary bodies of the Executive Body, the data on the effects of concentrations and depositions of sulphur and nitrogen compounds and of photochemical pollution as well as the reports of the Implementation Committee referred to in article 9 above.

2. (a) The Parties shall, at sessions of the Executive Body, keep under review the obligations set out in the present Protocol, including:

(i) Their obligations in relation to their calculated and internationally optimized allocations of emission reductions referred to in article 7, paragraph 5, above; and

(ii) The adequacy of the obligations and the progress made towards the achievement of the objective of the present Protocol;

(b) Reviews shall take into account the best available scientific information on the effects of acidification, eutrophication and photochemical pollution, including assessments of all relevant health effects, critical levels and loads, the development and refinement of integrated assessment models, technological developments, changing economic conditions, progress made on the databases on emissions and abatement techniques, especially related to ammonia and volatile organic compounds, and the fulfilment of the obligations on emission levels;

(c) The procedures, methods and timing for such reviews shall be specified by the Parties at a session of the Executive Body. The first such review shall commence no later than one year after the present Protocol enters into force.

Article 11
Settlement of Disputes

1. In the event of a dispute between any two or more Parties concerning the interpretation or application of the present Protocol, the parties concerned shall seek a settlement of the dispute through negotiation or any other peaceful means of their own choice. The parties to the dispute shall inform the Executive Body of their dispute.

2. When ratifying, accepting, approving or acceding to the present Protocol, or at any time thereafter, a Party which is not a regional economic integration organization may declare in a written instrument submitted to the Depositary that, in respect of any dispute concerning the interpretation or application of the Protocol, it recognizes one or both of the following means of dispute settlement as compulsory *ipso facto* and without special agreement, in relation to any Party accepting the same obligation:

(a) Submission of the dispute to the International Court of Justice;

(b) Arbitration in accordance with procedures to be adopted by the Parties at a session of the Executive Body, as soon as practicable, in an annex on arbitration.

A Party which is a regional economic integration organization may make a declaration with like effect in relation to arbitration in accordance with the procedures referred to in subparagraph (b).

3. A declaration made under paragraph 2 shall remain in force until it expires in accordance with its terms or until three months after written notice of its revocation has been deposited with the Depositary.

4. A new declaration, a notice of revocation or the expiry of a declaration shall not in any way affect proceedings pending before the International Court of Justice or the arbitral tribunal, unless the parties to the dispute agree otherwise.

5. Except in a case where the parties to a dispute have accepted the same means of dispute settlement under paragraph 2, if after twelve months following notification by one party to another that a dispute exists between them, the parties concerned have not been able to settle their dispute through the means mentioned in paragraph 1, the dispute shall be submitted, at the request of any of the parties to the dispute, to conciliation.

6. For the purpose of paragraph 5, a conciliation commission shall be created. The commission shall be composed of an equal number of members appointed by each party concerned or, where parties in conciliation share the same interest, by the group sharing that interest, and a chairperson chosen jointly by the members so appointed.

The commission shall render a recommendatory award, which the parties to the dispute shall consider in good faith.

Article 12
Annexes

The annexes to the present Protocol shall form an integral part of the Protocol.

Article 13
Amendments and Adjustments

1. Any Party may propose amendments to the present Protocol. Any Party to the Convention may propose an adjustment to annex II to the present Protocol to add to it its name, together with emission levels, emission ceilings and percentage emission reductions.

2. Proposed amendments and adjustments shall be submitted in writing to the Executive Secretary of the Commission, who shall communicate them to all Parties. The Parties shall discuss the proposed amendments and adjustments at the next session of the Executive Body, provided that those proposals have been circulated by the Executive Secretary to the Parties at least ninety days in advance.

3. Amendments to the present Protocol, including amendments to annexes II to IX, shall be adopted by consensus of the Parties present at a session of the Executive Body, and shall enter into force for the Parties which have accepted them on the ninetieth day after the date on which two thirds of the Parties have deposited with the Depositary their instruments of acceptance thereof. Amendments shall enter into force for any other Party on the ninetieth day after the date on which that Party has deposited its instrument of acceptance thereof.

4. Amendments to the annexes to the present Protocol, other than to the annexes referred to in paragraph 3, shall be adopted by consensus of the Parties present at a session of the Executive Body. On the expiry of ninety days from the date of its communication to all Parties by the Executive Secretary of the Commission, an amendment to any such annex shall become effective for those Parties which have not submitted to the Depositary a notification in accordance with the provisions of paragraph 5, provided that at least sixteen Parties have not submitted such a notification.

5. Any Party that is unable to approve an amendment to an annex, other than to an annex referred to in paragraph 3, shall so notify the Depositary in writing within ninety days from the date of the communication of its adoption. The Depositary shall without delay notify all Parties of any such notification received. A Party may at any time substitute an acceptance for its previous notification and, upon deposit of an instrument of acceptance with the Depositary, the amendment to such an annex shall become effective for that Party.

6. Adjustments to annex II shall be adopted by consensus of the Parties present at a session of the Executive Body and shall become effective for all Parties to the present Protocol on the ninetieth day following the date on which the Executive Secretary of the Commission notifies those Parties in writing of the adoption of the adjustment.

Article 14
Signature

1. The present Protocol shall be open for signature at Gothenburg (Sweden) on 30 November and 1 December 1999, then at United Nations Headquarters in New York until 30 May 2000, by States members of the Commission as well as States having consultative status with the Commission, pursuant to paragraph 8 of Economic and Social Council resolution 36 (IV) of 28 March 1947, and by regional economic integration organizations, constituted by sovereign States members of the Commission,

which have competence in respect of the negotiation, conclusion and application of international agreements in matters covered by the Protocol, provided that the States and organizations concerned are Parties to the Convention and are listed in annex II.

2. In matters within their competence, such regional economic integration organizations shall, on their own behalf, exercise the rights and fulfil the responsibilities which the present Protocol attributes to their member States. In such cases, the member States of these organizations shall not be entitled to exercise such rights individually.

Article 15
Ratification, Acceptance, Approval and Accession

1. The present Protocol shall be subject to ratification, acceptance or approval by Signatories.

2. The present Protocol shall be open for accession as from 31 May 2000 by the States and organizations that meet the requirements of article 14, paragraph 1.

3. The instruments of ratification, acceptance, approval or accession shall be deposited with the Depositary.

Article 16
Depositary

The Secretary–General of the United Nations shall be the Depositary.

Article 17
Entry into Force

1. The present Protocol shall enter into force on the ninetieth day following the date on which the sixteenth instrument of ratification, acceptance, approval or accession has been deposited with the Depositary.

2. For each State and organization that meets the requirements of article 14, paragraph 1, which ratifies, accepts or approves the present Protocol or accedes thereto after the deposit of the sixteenth instrument of ratification, acceptance, approval or accession, the Protocol shall enter into force on the ninetieth day following the date of deposit by such Party of its instrument of ratification, acceptance, approval or accession.

Article 18
Withdrawal

At any time after five years from the date on which the present Protocol has come into force with respect to a Party, that Party may withdraw from it by giving written notification to the Depositary. Any such withdrawal shall take effect on the ninetieth day following the date of its receipt by the Depositary, or on such later date as may be specified in the notification of the withdrawal.

Article 19
Authentic Texts

The original of the present Protocol, of which the English, French and Russian texts are equally authentic, shall be deposited with the Secretary–General of the United Nations.

Annex I

CRITICAL LOADS AND LEVELS

I. CRITICAL LOADS OF ACIDITY

A. For Parties within the geographical scope of EMEP

1. Critical loads (as defined in article 1) of acidity for ecosystems are determined in accordance with the Convention's *Manual on methodologies and criteria for map-*

ping critical levels/loads and geographical areas where they are exceeded. They are the maximum amount of acidifying deposition an ecosystem can tolerate in the long term without being damaged. Critical loads of acidity in terms of nitrogen take account of within-ecosystem nitrogen removal processes (e.g. uptake by plants). Critical loads of acidity in terms of sulphur do not. A combined sulphur and nitrogen critical load of acidity considers nitrogen only when the nitrogen deposition is greater than the ecosystem nitrogen removal processes. All critical loads reported by Parties are summarized for use in the integrated assessment modelling employed to provide guidance for setting the emission ceilings in annex II.

B. For Parties in North America

2. For eastern Canada, critical sulphur plus nitrogen loads for forested ecosystems have been determined with scientific methodologies and criteria (1997 Canadian Acid Rain Assessment) similar to those in the Convention's *Manual on methodologies and criteria for mapping critical levels/loads and geographical areas where they are exceeded*. Eastern Canada critical load values (as defined in article 1) of acidity are for sulphate in precipitation expressed in kg/ha/year. Alberta in western Canada, where deposition levels are currently below the environmental limits, has adopted the generic critical load classification systems used for soils in Europe for potential acidity. Potential acidity is defined by subtracting the total (both wet and dry) deposition of base cations from that of sulphur and nitrogen. In addition to critical loads for potential acidity, Alberta has established target and monitoring loads for managing acidifying emissions.

3. For the United States of America, the effects of acidification are evaluated through an assessment of the sensitivity of ecosystems, the total loading within ecosystems of acidifying compounds, and the uncertainty associated with nitrogen removal processes within ecosystems.

4. These loads and effects are used in integrated assessment modelling and provide guidance for setting the emission ceilings and/or reductions for Canada and the United States of America in annex II.

II. CRITICAL LOADS OF NUTRIENT NITROGEN

For Parties within the geographical scope of EMEP

5. Critical loads (as defined in article 1) of nutrient nitrogen (eutrophication) for ecosystems are determined in accordance with the Convention's *Manual on methodologies and criteria for mapping critical levels/loads and geographical areas where they are exceeded*. They are the maximum amount of eutrophying nitrogen deposition an ecosystem can tolerate in the long term without being damaged. All critical loads reported by Parties are summarized for use in the integrated assessment modelling employed to provide guidance for setting the emission ceilings in annex II.

III. CRITICAL LEVELS OF OZONE

A. For Parties within the geographical scope of EMEP

6. Critical levels (as defined in article 1) of ozone are determined to protect plants in accordance with the Convention's *Manual on methodologies and criteria for mapping critical levels/loads and geographical areas where they are exceeded*. They are expressed as a cumulative exposure over a threshold ozone concentration of 40 ppb (parts per billion by volume). This exposure index is referred to as AOT40 (accumulated exposure over a threshold of 40 ppb). The AOT40 is calculated as the sum of the differences between the hourly concentration (in ppb) and 40 ppb for each hour when the concentration exceeds 40 ppb.

7. The long-term critical level of ozone for crops of an AOT40 of 3000 ppb.hours for May–July (used as a typical growing season) and for daylight hours was used to define areas at risk where the critical level is exceeded. A specific reduction of exceedances was targeted in the integrated assessment modelling undertaken for the present Protocol to provide guidance for setting the emission ceilings in annex II. The long-term critical level of ozone for crops is considered also to protect other plants such as trees and natural vegetation. Further scientific work is under way to develop a more differentiated interpretation of exceedances of critical levels of ozone for vegetation.

8. A critical level of ozone for human health is represented by the WHO Air Quality Guideline level for ozone of 120 μg/m3 as an 8–hour average. In collaboration with the World Health Organization's Regional Office for Europe (WHO/EURO), a critical level expressed as an AOT60 (accumulated exposure over a threshold of 60 ppb), i.e. 120 μg/m3, calculated over one year, was adopted as a surrogate for the WHO Air Quality Guideline for the purpose of integrated assessment modelling. This was used to define areas at risk where the critical level is exceeded. A specific reduction of these exceedances was targeted in the integrated assessment modelling undertaken for the present Protocol to provide guidance for setting the emission ceilings in annex II.

B. For Parties in North America

9. For Canada, critical levels of ozone are determined to protect human health and the environment and are used to establish a Canada-wide Standard for ozone. The emission ceilings in annex II are defined according to the ambition level required to achieve the Canada-wide Standard for ozone.

10. For the United States of America, critical levels of ozone are determined to protect public health with an adequate margin of safety, to protect public welfare from any known or expected adverse effects, and are used to establish a national ambient air quality standard. Integrated assessment modelling and the air quality standard are used in providing guidance for setting the emission ceilings and/or reductions for the United States of America in annex II.

Annex II

EMISSION CEILINGS

The emission ceilings listed in the tables below relate to the provisions of article 3, paragraphs 1 and 10, of the present Protocol. The 1980 and 1990 emission levels and the percentage emission reductions listed are given for information purposes only.

Table 1. Emission ceilings for sulphur (thousands of tonnes of SO$_2$ per year)

	Emission levels		Emission ceilings for 2010		Percentage emission reductions for 2010 (base year 1990)
Party	1980	1990			
Armenia	141		73	73	0%
Austria	400		91	39	–57%
Belarus	740		637	480	–25%
Belgium	828		372	106	–72%
Bulgaria	2050		2008	856	–57%
Canada national a/	4643		3236		
PEMA (SOMA)	3135		1873		
Croatia	150		180	70	–61%

Czech Republic	2257	1876	283	–85%
Denmark	450	182	55	–70%
Finland	584	260	116	–55%
France	3208	1269	400	–68%
Germany	7514	5313	550	–90%
Greece	400	509	546	7%
Hungary	1633	1010	550	–46%
Ireland	222	178	42	–76%
Italy	3757	1651	500	–70%
Latvia	-	119	107	–10%
Liechtenstein	0.39	0.15	0.11	–27%
Lithuania	311	222	145	–35%
Luxembourg	24	15	4	–73%
Netherlands	490	202	50	–75%
Norway	137	53	22	–58%
Poland	4100	3210	1397	–56%
Portugal	266	362	170	–53%
Republic of Moldova	308	265	135	–49%
Romania	1055	1311	918	–30%
Russian Federation b/	7161	4460		
PEMA	1062	1133	635	–44%
Slovakia	780	543	110	–80%
Slovenia	235	194	27	–86%
Spain b/	2959	2182	774	–65%
Sweden	491	119	67	–44%
Switzerland	116	43	26	–40%
Ukraine	3849	2782	1457	–48%
United Kingdom	4863	3731	625	–83%
United States of America c/				
European Community	26456	16436	4059	–75%

a/ Upon ratification, acceptance or approval of, or accession to, the present Protocol, Canada shall submit an emission ceiling for sulphur, either at a national level or for its PEMA, and will endeavour to provide a ceiling for 2010. The PEMA for sulphur will be the sulphur oxides management area (SOMA) that was designated pursuant to annex III to the Protocol on Further Reduction of Sulphur Emissions adopted at Oslo on 14 June 1994 as the South-east Canada SOMA. This is an area of 1 million km_2 which includes all the territory of the provinces of Prince Edward Island, Nova Scotia and New Brunswick, all the territory of the province of Quebec south of a straight line between Havre–St. Pierre on the north coast of the Gulf of Saint Lawrence and the point where the Quebec–Ontario boundary intersects the James Bay coastline, and all the territory of the province of Ontario south of a straight line between the point where the Ontario–Quebec boundary intersects the James Bay coastline and Nipigon River near the north shore of Lake Superior.

b/ Figures apply to the European part within the EMEP area.

c/ Upon ratification, acceptance or approval of, or accession to, the present Protocol, the United States of America shall provide for inclusion in this annex: (a) specific emission reduction measures applicable to mobile and stationary sources of sulphur to be applied either nationally or within a PEMA if it has submitted a PEMA for sulphur for inclusion in annex III; (b) a value for total estimated sulphur emission levels for 1990, either national or for the PEMA; (c) an indicative value for total sulphur emission levels for 2010, either national or for the PEMA; and (d) associated estimates of the percentage reduction in sulphur emissions. Item (b) will be included in the table and items (a), (c) and (d) will be included in a footnote to the table.

Table 2. Emission ceilings for nitrogen oxides
(thousands of tonnes of NO_2 per year)

Party	Emission levels 1990	Emission ceilings for 2010	Percentage emission reductions for 2010 (base year 1990)
Armenia	46	46	0%
Austria	194	107	−45%
Belarus	285	255	−11%
Belgium	339	181	−47%
Bulgaria	361	266	−26%
Canada a1/	2104		
Croatia	87	87	0%
Czech Republic	742	286	−61%
Denmark	282	127	−55%
Finland	300	170	−43%
France	1882	860	−54%
Germany	2693	1081	−60%
Greece	343	344	0%
Hungary	238	198	−17%
Ireland	115	65	−43%
Italy	1938	1000	−48%
Latvia	93	84	−10%
Liechtenstein	0.63	0.37	−41%
Lithuania	158	110	−30%
Luxembourg	23	11	−52%
Netherlands	580	266	−54%
Norway	218	156	−28%
Poland	1280	879	−31%
Portugal	348	260	−25%
Republic of Moldova	100	90	−10%
Romania	546	437	−20%
Russian Federation b1/	3600		
PEMA	360	265	−26%
Slovakia	225	130	−42%
Slovenia	62	45	−27%
Spain b1/	1113	847	−24%
Sweden	338	148	−56%
Switzerland	166	79	−52%
Ukraine	1888	1222	−35%
United Kingdom	2673	1181	−56%

Party	Emission levels 1990	Emission ceilings for 2010	Percentage emission reductions for 2010 (base year 1990)
United States of America c1/			
European Community	13161	6671	−49%

a1/ Upon ratification, acceptance or approval of, or accession to, the present Protocol, Canada shall submit 1990 emission levels and 2010 emission ceilings for nitrogen oxides, either at a national level or for its PEMA for nitrogen oxides, if it has submitted one.

b1/ Figures apply to the European part within the EMEP area.

c1/ Upon ratification, acceptance or approval of, or accession to, the present Protocol, the United States of America shall provide for inclusion in this annex: (a) specific emission reduction measures applicable to mobile and stationary sources of nitrogen oxides to be applied either nationally or within a PEMA if it has submitted a PEMA for nitrogen oxides for inclusion in annex III; (b) a value for total estimated nitrogen oxide emission levels for 1990, either national or for the PEMA; (c) an indicative value for total nitrogen oxide emission levels for 2010, either national or for the PEMA; and (d) associated estimates of the percentage reduction in nitrogen oxide emissions. Item (b) will be included in the table and items (a), (c) and (d) will be included in a footnote to the table.

Table 3.   Emission ceilings for ammonia (thousands of tonnes of NH_3 per year)

Party	Emission levels 1990	Emission ceilings for 2010	Percentage emission reductions for 2010 (base year 1990)
Armenia	25	25	0%
Austria	81	66	−19%
Belarus	219	158	−28%
Belgium	107	74	−31%
Bulgaria	144	108	−25%
Croatia	37	30	−19%
Czech Republic	156	101	−35%
Denmark	122	69	−43%
Finland	35	31	−11%
France	814	780	−4%
Germany	764	550	−28%
Greece	80	73	−9%
Hungary	124	90	−27%
Ireland	126	116	−8%
Italy	466	419	−10%
Latvia	44	44	0%
Liechtenstein	0.15	0.15	0%
Lithuania	84	84	0%
Luxembourg	7	7	0%
Netherlands	226	128	−43%
Norway	23	23	0%
Poland	508	468	−8%
Portugal	98	108	10%

Party	Emission levels 1990	Emission ceilings for 2010	Percentage emission reductions for 2010 (base year 1990)
Republic of Moldova	49	42	–14%
Romania	300	210	–30%
Russian Federation a2/	1191		
PEMA	61	49	–20%
Slovakia	62	39	–37%
Slovenia	24	20	–17%
Spain a2/	351	353	1%
Sweden	61	57	–7%
Switzerland	72	63	–13%
Ukraine	729	592	–19%
United Kingdom	333	297	–11%
European Community	3671	3129	–15%

a2/ Figures apply to the European part within the EMEP area.

Table 4.   Emission ceilings for volatile organic compounds
(thousands of tonnes of VOC per year)

Party	Emission levels 1990	Emission ceilings for 2010	Percentage emission reductions for 2010 (base year 1990)
Armenia	81	81	0%
Austria	351	159	–55%
Belarus	533	309	–42%
Belgium	324	144	–56%
Bulgaria	217	185	–15%
Canada a3/	2880		
Croatia	105	90	–14%
Czech Republic	435	220	–49%
Denmark	178	85	–52%
Finland	209	130	–38%
France	2957	1100	–63%
Germany	3195	995	–69%
Greece	373	261	–30%
Hungary	205	137	–33%
Ireland	197	55	–72%
Italy	2213	1159	–48%
Latvia	152	136	–11%
Liechtenstein	1.56	0.86	–45%
Lithuania	103	92	–11%
Luxembourg	20	9	–55%
Netherlands	502	191	–62%
Norway	310	195	–37%
Poland	831	800	–4%
Portugal	640	202	–68%

Party	Emission levels 1990	Emission ceilings for 2010	Percentage emission reductions for 2010 (base year 1990)
Republic of Moldova	157	100	–36%
Romania	616	523	–15%
Russian Federation b3/	3566		
PEMA	203	165	–19%
Slovakia	149	140	–6%
Slovenia	42	40	–5%
Spain b3/	1094	669	–39%
Sweden	526	241	–54%
Switzerland	292	144	–51%
Ukraine	1369	797	–42%
United Kingdom	2555	1200	–53%
United States of America c3/			
European Community	15353	6600	–57

a3/ Upon ratification, acceptance or approval of, or accession to, the present Protocol, Canada shall submit 1990 emission levels and 2010 emission ceilings for volatile organic compounds, either at a national level or for its PEMA for volatile organic compounds, if it has submitted one.

b3/ Figures apply to the European part within the EMEP area.

c3/ Upon ratification, acceptance or approval of, or accession to, the present Protocol, the United States of America shall provide for inclusion in this annex: (a) specific emission reduction measures applicable to mobile and stationary sources of volatile organic compounds to be applied either nationally or within a PEMA if it has submitted a PEMA for volatile organic compounds for inclusion in annex III; (b) a value for total estimated volatile organic compound emission levels for 1990, either national or for the PEMA; (c) an indicative value for total volatile organic compound emission levels for 2010, either national or for the PEMA; and (d) associated estimates of the percentage reduction in volatile organic compound emissions. Item (b) will be included in the table and items (a), (c) and (d) will be included in a footnote to the table.

Annex III

DESIGNATED POLLUTANT EMISSIONS MANAGEMENT AREA (PEMA)

The following PEMA is listed for the purpose of the present Protocol:

Russian Federation PEMA

This is the area of Murmansk oblast, the Republic of Karelia, Leningrad oblast (including St. Petersburg), Pskov oblast, Novgorod oblast and Kaliningrad oblast. The boundary of the PEMA coincides with the State and administrative boundaries of these constituent entities of the Russian Federation.

<u>Annex IV</u>

LIMIT VALUES FOR EMISSIONS OF SULPHUR FROM STATIONARY SOURCES

1. Section A applies to Parties other than Canada and the United States of America, section B applies to Canada and section C applies to the United States of America.

* * *

<u>Annex V</u>

LIMIT VALUES FOR EMISSIONS OF NITROGEN OXIDES FROM STATIONARY SOURCES

1. Section A applies to Parties other than Canada and the United States of America, section B applies to Canada and section C applies to the United States of America.

* * *

<u>Annex VI</u>

LIMIT VALUES FOR EMISSIONS OF VOLATILE ORGANIC COMPOUNDS FROM STATIONARY SOURCES

1. Section A applies to Parties other than Canada and the United States of America, section B applies to Canada and section C applies to the United States of America.

* * *

<u>Annex VII</u>

TIME SCALES UNDER ARTICLE 3

1. The timescales for the application of the limit values referred to in article 3, paragraphs 2 and 3, shall be:

(a) For new stationary sources, one year after the date of entry into force of the present Protocol for the Party in question; and

(b) For existing stationary sources:

(i) In the case of a Party that is not a country with an economy in transition, one year after the date of entry into force of the present Protocol or 31 December 2007, whichever is the later; and

(ii) In the case of a Party that is a country with an economy in transition, eight years after the entry into force of the present Protocol.

2. The timescales for the application of the limit values for fuels and new mobile sources referred to in article 3, paragraph 5, and the limit values for gas oil referred to in annex IV, table 2, shall be:

(i) In the case of a Party that is not a country with an economy in transition, the date of entry into force of the present Protocol or the dates associated with the measures specified in annex VIII and with the limit values specified in annex IV, table 2, whichever is the later; and

(ii) In the case of a Party that is a country with an economy in transition, five years after the date of entry into force of the present Protocol or five years after the dates associated with the measures specified in annex VIII and with the limit values in annex IV, table 2, whichever is the later.

This timescale shall not apply to a Party to the present Protocol to the extent that that Party is subject to a shorter timescale with regard to gas oil under the Protocol on Further Reduction of Sulphur Emissions.

3. For the purpose of the present annex, "a country with an economy in transition" means a Party that has made with its instrument of ratification, acceptance, approval or accession a declaration that it wishes to be treated as a country with an economy in transition for the purposes of paragraphs 1 and/or 2 of this annex.

<u>Annex VIII</u>

LIMIT VALUES FOR FUELS AND NEW MOBILE SOURCES

* * *

<u>Annex IX</u>

MEASURES FOR THE CONTROL OF EMISSIONS OF
AMMONIA FROM AGRICULTURAL SOURCES

* * *

2.6 DIRECTIVE 2001/81/EC ON NATIONAL EMISSION CEILINGS FOR CERTAIN ATMO-SPHERIC POLLUTANTS. Adopted by the European Parliament and the Council of the European Union, 23 October 2001. Entered into force, 27 November 2001. OJEC L 309/22

THE EUROPEAN PARLIAMENT AND THE COUNCIL OF THE EUROPEAN UNION,

* * *

Acting in accordance with the procedure laid down in Article 251 of the Treaty, in the light of the joint text approved by the Conciliation Committee on 2 August 2001,

Whereas:

(1) The general approach and strategy of the Fifth Environmental Action Programme was approved by the Resolution of 1 February 1993 of the Council and the Representatives of the Governments of the Member States meeting within the Council on a Community programme of policy and action in relation to the environment and sustainable development and it sets as objectives that critical loads and levels for acidification in the Community are not to be exceeded. The programme requires that all people should be effectively protected against health risks from air pollution and that permitted levels of pollution should take account of the protection of the environment. The programme also requires that guideline values from the World Health Organisation (WHO) should become mandatory at Community level.

(2) The Member States have signed the Gothenburg Protocol of 1 December 1999 to the United Nations Economic Commission for Europe (UNECE) Convention on long-range transboundary air pollution to abate acidification, eutrophication and ground-level ozone.

(3) Decision No 2179/98/EC of the European Parliament and of the Council of 24 September 1998 on the review of the European Community programme of policy and action in relation to the environment and sustainable development Towards sustainability specified that particular attention should be given to developing and implementing a strategy with the goal of ensuring that critical loads, in relation to exposure to acidifying, eutrophying and photochemical air pollutants, are not exceeded.

(4) Council Directive 92/72/EEC of 21 September 1992 on air pollution by ozone requires the Commission to submit to the Council a report on the evaluation of photochemical pollution in the Community, accompanied by any proposals the Commission deems appropriate on the control of air pollution by ground-level ozone and, if necessary, on reducing emissions of ozone precursors.

(5) Significant areas of the Community are exposed to depositions of acidifying and eutrophying substances at levels which have adverse effects on the environment. The WHO guideline values for the protection of human health and vegetation from photochemical pollution are substantially exceeded in all Member States.

(6) The exceedance of critical loads should therefore be gradually eliminated and guideline levels respected.

(7) At present it is not technically feasible to meet the long-term objectives of eliminating the adverse effects of acidification and reducing exposure to ground-level ozone of man and the environment to the guideline values established by the WHO. It is therefore necessary to provide for interim environmental objectives for acidification and ground-level ozone pollution, on which the necessary measures to reduce such pollution are to be based.

(8) Interim environmental objectives and the measures to meet them should take account of technical feasibility and the associated costs and benefits. Such measures should ensure that any action taken is cost-effective for the Community as a whole and

should take account of the need to avoid excessive costs for any individual Member State.

(9) Transboundary pollution contributes to acidification, soil eutrophication and ground-level ozone formation, the abatement of which requires coordinated Community action.

(10) Reducing emissions of the pollutants causing acidification and exposure to ground-level ozone will also reduce soil eutrophication.

(11) A set of national ceilings for each Member State for emissions of sulphur dioxide, nitrogen oxides, volatile organic compounds and ammonia is a cost-effective way of meeting interim environmental objectives. Such emission ceilings will allow the Community and the Member States flexibility in determining how to comply with them.

(12) Member States should be responsible for implementing measures to comply with national emission ceilings. It will be necessary to evaluate progress towards compliance with the emission ceilings. National programmes for the reduction of emissions should therefore be drawn up and reported on to the Commission and should include information on the measures adopted or envisaged to comply with the emission ceilings.

(13) In accordance with the principle of subsidiarity as set out in Article 5 of the Treaty and taking account, in particular, of the precautionary principle, the objective of this Directive, namely limitation of emissions of acidifying and eutrophying pollutants and ozone precursors, cannot be sufficiently achieved by the Member States because of the transboundary nature of the pollution and can therefore be better achieved by the Community; in accordance with the principle of proportionality this Directive does not go beyond what is necessary to achieve that purpose.

(14) There should be a timely review of the progress made by Member States towards the emission ceilings, as well as a review of the extent to which implementing the ceilings is likely to meet interim environmental objectives, for the Community as a whole. Such review should consider also scientific and technical progress, developments in Community legislation and emission reductions outside the Community with special regard to progress made inter alia by the accession candidate countries. In that review, the Commission should undertake a further examination of the costs and benefits of the emission ceilings, including their cost-effectiveness, marginal costs and benefits and socio-economic impact and any impact on competitiveness. The review should also consider the limitations on the scope of this Directive.

(15) The Commission should for this purpose prepare a report to the European Parliament and the Council and, if it considers it necessary, propose appropriate amendments to this Directive taking account of the effects of any relevant Community legislation inter alia setting emission limits and product standards for relevant sources of emissions and international regulations concerning ship and aircraft emissions.

(16) Sea transport is a significant contributor to emissions of sulphur dioxide and nitrogen oxides and also to concentrations and depositions of air pollutants in the Community. Such emissions should therefore be reduced. Article 7(3) of Council Directive 1999/32/EC of 26 April 1999 relating to a reduction in the sulphur content of certain liquid fuels and amending Directive 93/12/EEC requires the Commission to consider which measures could be taken to reduce the contribution to acidification of the combustion of marine fuels other than those specified in Article 2(3) of that Directive.

(17) Member States should seek to ratify Annex VI to the International Convention for the Prevention of Pollution from Ships (MARPOL) as soon as possible.

(18) Owing to the transboundary nature of acidification and ozone pollution, the Commission should continue to examine further the need to develop harmonised

Community measures, without prejudice to Article 18 of Council Directive 96/61/EC of 24 September 1996 concerning integrated pollution prevention and control, with the aim of avoiding distortion of competition, and taking into account the balance between benefits and cost of action.

(19) The provisions of this Directive should apply without prejudice to the Community legislation regulating emissions of those pollutants from specific sources and to the provisions of Council Directive 96/61/EC in relation to emission limit values and use of best available techniques.

(20) Emission inventories are necessary to monitor progress towards compliance with the emission ceilings and must be calculated in accordance with internationally agreed methodology and reported on regularly to the Commission and the European Environment Agency (EEA).

(21) Member States should lay down rules on penalties applicable to infringements of the provisions of this Directive and ensure that they are implemented. The penalties should be effective, proportionate and dissuasive.

(22) The measures necessary for the implementation of this Directive should be adopted in accordance with Council Decision 1999/468/EC of 28 June 1999 laying down the procedures for the exercise of implementing powers conferred on the Commission.

(23) The Commission and Members States should cooperate internationally with a view to achieving the objectives of this Directive,

HAVE ADOPTED THIS DIRECTIVE:

Article 1   Objective

The aim of this Directive is to limit emissions of acidifying and eutrophying pollutants and ozone precursors in order to improve the protection in the Community of the environment and human health against risks of adverse effects from acidification, soil eutrophication and ground-level ozone and to move towards the long-term objectives of not exceeding critical levels and loads and of effective protection of all people against recognised health risks from air pollution by establishing national emission ceilings, taking the years 2010 and 2020 as benchmarks, and by means of successive reviews as set out in Articles 4 and 10.

Article 2   Scope

This Directive covers emissions in the territory of the Member States and their exclusive economic zones from all sources of the pollutants referred to in Article 4 which arise as a result of human activities.

It does not cover:

(a) emissions from international maritime traffic;

(b) aircraft emissions beyond the landing and take-off cycle;

(c) for Spain, emissions in the Canary Islands;

(d) for France, emissions in the overseas departments;

(e) for Portugal, emissions in Madeira and the Azores.

Article 3   Definitions

For the purposes of this Directive:

(a) 'AOT 40' means the sum of the difference between hourly concentrations of ground-level ozone greater than 80 μg/m3 (= 40 ppb) and 80 μg/m^3 during daylight hours accumulated from May to July each year;

(b) 'AOT 60' means the sum of the difference between hourly concentrations of ground-level ozone greater than 120 $\mu g/m^3$ (=60 ppb) and 120 $\mu g/m^3$ accumulated throughout the year;

(c) 'critical load' means a quantitative estimate of an exposure to one or more pollutants below which significant adverse effects on specified sensitive elements of the environment do not occur, according to present knowledge;

(d) critical level means the concentration of pollutants in the atmosphere above which direct adverse effects on receptors, such as human beings, plants, ecosystems or materials, may occur, according to present knowledge;

(e) 'emission' means the release of a substance from a point or diffuse source into the atmosphere;

(f) 'grid cell' means a square 150 km x 150 km, which is the resolution used when mapping critical loads on a European scale, and also when monitoring emissions and depositions of air pollutants under the Cooperative Programme for Monitoring and Evaluation of the long-range Transmission of Air Pollutants in Europe (EMEP);

(g) 'landing and take-off cycle' means a cycle represented by the following time in each operating mode: approach 4,0 minutes; taxi/ground idle 26,0 minutes, take-off 0,7 minutes; climb 2,2 minutes;

(h) 'national emission ceiling' means the maximum amount of a substance expressed in kilotonnes, which may be emitted from a Member State in a calendar year;

(i) 'nitrogen oxides' and 'NO_x' mean nitric oxide and nitrogen dioxide, expressed as nitrogen dioxide;

(j) 'ground-level ozone' means ozone in the lowermost part of the troposphere;

(k) 'volatile organic compounds' and 'VOC' mean all organic compounds arising from human activities, other than methane, which are capable of producing photochemical oxidants by reactions with nitrogen oxides in the presence of sunlight.

Article 4   National emission ceilings

1.   By the year 2010 at the latest, Member States shall limit their annual national emissions of the pollutants sulphur dioxide (SO_2), nitrogen oxides (NO_x), volatile organic compounds (VOC) and ammonia (NH_3) to amounts not greater than the emission ceilings laid down in Annex I, taking into account any modifications made by Community measures adopted following the reports referred to in Article 9.

2.   Member States shall ensure that the emission ceilings laid down in Annex I are not exceeded in any year after 2010.

Article 5   Interim environmental objectives

The national emission ceilings in Annex I shall have as their purpose to meet broadly the following interim environmental objectives, for the Community as a whole, by 2010:

(a) *Acidification*

The areas where critical loads are exceeded shall be reduced by at least 50% (in each grid cell) compared with the 1990 situation.

(b) *Health-related ground-level ozone exposure*

The ground-level ozone load above the critical level for human health (AOT60=0) shall be reduced by two-thirds in all grid cells compared with the 1990 situation. In addition, the ground-level ozone load shall not exceed an absolute limit of 2,9 ppm.h in any grid cell.

(c) *Vegetation-related ground-level ozone exposure*

The ground-level ozone load above the critical level for crops and semi-natural vegetation (AOT40=3 ppm.h) shall be reduced by one-third in all grid cells compared with the 1990 situation. In addition, the ground-level ozone load shall not exceed an absolute limit of 10 ppm.h, expressed as an exceedance of the critical level of 3 ppm.h in any grid cell.

Article 6   National programmes

1. Member States shall, by 1 October 2002 at the latest, draw up programmes for the progressive reduction of national emissions of the pollutants referred to in Article 4 with the aim of complying at least with the national emission ceilings laid down in Annex I by 2010 at the latest.

2. The national programmes shall include information on adopted and envisaged policies and measures and quantified estimates of the effect of these policies and measures on emissions of the pollutants in 2010. Anticipated significant changes in the geographical distribution of national emissions shall be indicated.

3. Member States shall update and revise the national programmes as necessary by 1 October 2006.

4. Member States shall make available to the public and to appropriate organisations such as environmental organisations the programmes drawn up in accordance with paragraphs 1, 2 and 3. Information made available to the public and to organisations under this paragraph shall be clear, comprehensible and easily accessible.

Article 7   Emission inventories and projections

1. Member States shall prepare and annually update national emission inventories and emission projections for 2010 for the pollutants referred to in Article 4.

2. Member States shall establish their emission inventories and projections using the methodologies specified in Annex III.

3. The Commission, assisted by the European Environment Agency, shall, in cooperation with the Member States and on the basis of the information provided by them, establish inventories and projections of the pollutants referred to in Article 4. The inventories and projections shall be made publicly available.

4. Any updating of the methodologies to be used in accordance with Annex III, shall be made in accordance with the procedure set out in Article 13(2).

Article 8   Reports by the Member States

1. Member States shall each year, by 31 December at the latest, report their national emission inventories and their emission projections for 2010 established in accordance with Article 7 to the Commission and the European Environment Agency. They shall report their final emission inventories for the previous year but one and their provisional emission inventories for the previous year. Emission projections shall include information to enable a quantitative understanding of the key socioeconomic assumptions used in their preparation.

2. Member States shall, by 31 December 2002 at the latest, inform the Commission of the programmes drawn up in accordance with Article 6(1) and (2).

Member States shall, by 31 December 2006 at the latest, inform the Commission of the updated programmes drawn up in accordance with Article 6(3).

3. The Commission shall forward the national programmes received to the other Member States within one month of their reception.

4. The Commission shall, in accordance with the procedure set out in Article 13(2), establish provisions to ensure consistent and transparent reporting of national programmes.

Article 9   Reports by the Commission

1. In 2004 and 2008 the Commission shall report to the European Parliament and the Council on progress on the implementation of the national emission ceilings laid down in Annex I and on the extent to which the interim environmental objectives set out in Article 5 are likely to be met by 2010 and on the extent to which the long-term objectives set out in Article 1 could be met by 2020. The reports shall include an economic assessment, including cost-effectiveness, benefits, an assessment of marginal costs and benefits and the socioeconomic impact of the implementation of the national emission ceilings on particular Member States and sectors. They shall also include a review of the limitations of the scope of this Directive as defined in Article 2 and an evaluation of the extent to which further emission reductions might be necessary in order to meet the interim environmental objectives set out in Article 5. They shall take into account the reports made by Member States pursuant to Article 8(1) and (2), as well as, *inter alia*:

(a) any new Community legislation which may have been adopted setting emission limits and product standards for relevant sources of emissions;

(b) developments of best available techniques in the framework of the exchange of information under Article 16 of Directive 96/61/EC;

(c) emission reduction objectives for 2008 for emissions of sulphur dioxide and nitrogen oxides from existing large combustion plants, reported by Member States pursuant to Directive 2001/80/EC of the European Parliament and of the Council of 23 October 2001 on the limitation of emissions of certain pollutants into the air from large combustion plants;

(d) emission reductions and reduction commitments by third countries, with particular focus on measures to be taken in the accession candidate countries, and the possibility for further emission reductions in regions in the vicinity of the Community;

(e) any new Community legislation and any international regulations concerning ship and aircraft emissions;

(f) the development of transport and any further action to control transport emissions;

(g) developments in the field of agriculture, new livestock projections and improvements in emission reduction methods in the agricultural sector;

(h) any major changes in the energy supply market within a Member State and new forecasts reflecting the actions taken by Member States to comply with their international obligations in relation to climate change;

(i) assessment of the current and projected exceedances of critical loads and the WHO s guideline values for ground-level ozone;

(j) the possibility of identification of a proposed interim objective for reducing soil eutrophication;

(k) new technical and scientific data including an assessment of the uncertainties in:

   (i) national emission inventories;

   (ii) input reference data;

   (iii) knowledge of the transboundary transport and deposition of pollutants;

   (iv) critical loads and levels;

   (v) the model used;

and an assessment of the resulting uncertainty in the national emission ceilings required to meet the interim environmental objectives mentioned in Article 5.

(*l*) whether there is a need to avoid excessive costs for any individual Member State;

(m) a comparison of model calculations with observations of acidification, eutrophication and ground-level ozone with a view to improving models;

(n) the possible use, where appropriate, of relevant economic instruments.

2. In 2012 the Commission shall report to the European Parliament and the Council on compliance with the ceilings in Annex I and on progress in relation to the interim environmental objectives in Article 5 and the long-term objectives set out in Article 1. Its report shall take account of the reports made by Member States pursuant to Article 8(1) and (2) as well as the matters listed in points (a) to (n) of paragraph 1.

Article 10   Review

1. The reports referred to in Article 9 shall take into account the factors listed in Article 9(1). In the light of these factors, of progress towards attaining the emission ceilings by the year 2010, of scientific and technical progress, and of the situation regarding progress towards attaining the interim objectives of this Directive and the long-term objectives of no exceedance of critical loads and levels and of WHO air quality guidelines for ozone, the Commission shall carry out a review of this Directive in preparation for each report.

2. In the review to be completed in 2004 an evaluation will be carried out of the indicative emission ceilings for the Community as a whole set out in Annex II. The evaluation of these indicative ceilings shall be a factor for consideration during analysis of further cost-effective actions that might be taken in order to reduce emissions of all relevant pollutants, with the aim of attaining the interim environmental objectives set out in Article 5, for the Community as a whole by 2010.

3. All reviews shall include a further investigation of the estimated costs and benefits of national emission ceilings, computed with state-of-the-art models and making use of the best available data to achieve the least possible uncertainty and taking also into account progress in the enlargement of the European Union, and of the merits of alternative methodologies, in the light of the factors listed in Article 9.

4. Without prejudice to Article 18 of Directive 96/61/EC, with the aim of avoiding distortion of competition, and taking into account the balance between benefits and costs of action, the Commission shall examine further the need to develop harmonised Community measures, for the most relevant economic sectors and products contributing to acidification, eutrophication and formation of ground-level ozone.

5. The reports referred to in Article 9 will, if appropriate, be accompanied by proposals for:

(a) modifications of the national ceilings in Annex I with the aim of meeting the interim environmental objectives of Article 5 and/or for modifications to those interim environmental objectives;

(b) possible further emission reductions with the aim of meeting, preferably by 2020, the long-term objectives of this Directive;

(c) measures to ensure compliance with the ceilings.

Article 11   Cooperation with third countries

To promote the achievement of the objective set out in Article 1, the Commission and Member States, as appropriate, shall, without prejudice to Article 300 of the Treaty, pursue bilateral and multilateral cooperation with third countries and relevant international organisations such as the United Nations Economic Commission for Europe (UNECE), the International Maritime Organization (IMO) and the International Civil Aviation Organization (ICAO), including through the exchange of information, concerning technical and scientific research and development and with the aim of improving the basis for the facilitation of emission reductions.

Article 12   Reports concerning ship and aircraft emission

1.   By the end of 2002 the Commission shall report to the European Parliament and Council on the extent to which emissions from international maritime traffic contribute to acidification, eutrophication and the formation of ground-level ozone within the Community.

2.   By the end of 2004 the Commission shall report to the European Parliament and Council on the extent to which emissions from aircraft beyond the landing and take-off cycle contribute to acidification, eutrophication and the formation of ground-level ozone within the Community.

3.   Each report shall specify a programme of actions which could be taken at international and Community level as appropriate to reduce emissions from the sector concerned, as a basis for further consideration by the European Parliament and Council.

Article 13   Committee

1.   The Commission shall be assisted by the Committee set up by Article 12 of Directive 96/62/EC, hereinafter referred to as 'the Committee'.

2.   Where reference is made to this paragraph, Articles 4 and 7 of Decision 1999/468/EC shall apply, having regard to the provisions of Article 8 thereof.

The period referred to in Article 4(3) of Decision 1999/468/EC shall be set at three months.

3.   The Committee shall adopt its rules of procedure.

Article 14   Penalties

Member States shall determine the penalties applicable to breaches of the national provisions adopted pursuant to this Directive. The penalties shall be effective, proportionate and dissuasive.

Article 15   Transposition

1.   Member States shall bring into force the laws, regulations and administrative provisions necessary to comply with this Directive before 27 November 2002. They shall forthwith inform the Commission thereof.

When Member States adopt those provisions, they shall contain a reference to this Directive or be accompanied by such reference on the occasion of their official publication. Member States shall determine how such reference is to be made.

2.   Member States shall communicate to the Commission the text of the main provisions of national law, which they adopt in the field covered by this Directive.

Article 16   Entry into force

This Directive shall enter into force on the day of its publication in the *Official Journal of the European Communities.*

Article 17   Addressees

This Directive is addressed to the Member States.

* * *

Annex I

**National emission ceilings for SO_2, NO_x, VOC
and NH_3, to be attained by 2010[1]**

Country	SO_2 Kilotonnes	NO_x Kilotonnes	VOC Kilotonnes	NH_3 Kilotonnes
Austria	39	103	159	66
Belgium	99	176	139	74
Denmark	55	127	85	69
Finland	110	170	130	31
France	375	810	1050	780
Germany	520	1051	995	550
Greece	523	344	261	73
Ireland	42	65	55	116
Italy	475	990	1159	419
Luxembourg	4	11	9	7
Netherlands	50	260	185	128
Portugal	160	250	180	90
Spain	746	847	662	353
Sweden	67	148	241	57
UK	585	1167	1200	297
EC 15	**3850**	**6519**	**6510**	**3110**

Annex II

Emission ceilings for SO_2, NO_x and VOC (thousand tonnes)

	SO_2 Kilotonnes	NO_x Kilotonnes	VOC Kilotonnes
EC 15	3634	5923	5581

These emission ceilings are designed with the aim of attaining the interim environmental objectives set out in Article 5 for the Community as a whole by 2010.

Annex III

Methodologies for emission inventories and projections

Member States shall establish emission inventories and projections using the methodologies agreed upon by the Convention on Long-range Transboundary Air Pollution and are requested to use the joint EMEP/CORINAIR[2](') guidebook in preparing these inventories and projections.

1. These national emission ceilings are designed with the aim of broadly meeting the interim environmental objectives set out in Article 5. Meeting those objectives is expected to result in a reduction of soil eutrophication to such an extent that the Community area with depositions of nutrient nitrogen in excess of the critical loads will be reduced by about 30% compared with the situation in 1990.

2. Air emissions inventory of the European Environment Agency.

2.7 DIRECTIVE 2008/50/EC OF 21 MAY 2008 ON AMBIENT AIR QUALITY AND CLEANER AIR FOR EUROPE. Adopted by the European Parliament and the Council of the European Union, 21 May 2008. Entered into force, 11 June 2008. OJEU L 151/1

THE EUROPEAN PARLIAMENT AND THE COUNCIL OF THE EUROPEAN UNION,

Having regard to the Treaty establishing the European Community, and in particular Article 175 thereof,

* * *

Acting in accordance with the procedure laid down in Article 251 of the Treaty,

Whereas:

(1) The Sixth Community Environment Action Programme adopted by Decision No 1600/2002/EC of the European Parliament and of the Council of 22 July 2002 establishes the need to reduce pollution to levels which minimise harmful effects on human health, paying particular attention to sensitive populations, and the environment as a whole, to improve the monitoring and assessment of air quality including the deposition of pollutants and to provide information to the public.

(2) In order to protect human health and the environment as a whole, it is particularly important to combat emissions of pollutants at source and to identify and implement the most effective emission reduction measures at local, national and Community level. Therefore, emissions of harmful air pollutants should be avoided, prevented or reduced and appropriate objectives set for ambient air quality taking into account relevant World Health Organisation standards, guidelines and programmes.

(3) Council Directive 96/62/EC of 27 September 1996 on ambient air quality assessment and management, Council Directive 1999/30/EC of 22 April 1999 relating to limit values for sulphur dioxide, nitrogen dioxide and oxides of nitrogen, particulate matter and lead in ambient air, Directive 2000/69/EC of the European Parliament and of the Council of 16 November 2000 relating to limit values for benzene and carbon monoxide in ambient air, Directive 2002/3/EC of the European Parliament and of the Council of 12 February 2002 relating to ozone in ambient air (8) and Council Decision 97/101/EC of 27 January 1997 establishing a reciprocal exchange of information and data from networks and individual stations measuring ambient air pollution within the Member States need to be substantially revised in order to incorporate the latest health and scientific developments and the experience of the Member States. In the interests of clarity, simplification and administrative efficiency it is therefore appropriate that those five acts be replaced by a single Directive and, where appropriate, by implementing measures.

(4) Once sufficient experience has been gained in relation to the implementation of Directive 2004/107/EC of the European Parliament and of the Council of 15 December 2004 relating to arsenic, cadmium, mercury, nickel and polycyclic aromatic hydrocarbons in ambient air consideration may be given to the possibility of merging its provisions with those of this Directive.

(5) A common approach to the assessment of ambient air quality should be followed according to common assessment criteria. When assessing ambient air quality, account should be taken of the size of populations and ecosystems exposed to air pollution. It is therefore appropriate to classify the territory of each Member State into zones or agglomerations reflecting the population density.

(6) Where possible modelling techniques should be applied to enable point data to be interpreted in terms of geographical distribution of concentration. This could serve as a basis for calculating the collective exposure of the population living in the area.

(7) In order to ensure that the information collected on air pollution is sufficiently representative and comparable across the Community, it is important that standardised measurement techniques and common criteria for the number and location of measuring stations are used for the assessment of ambient air quality. Techniques other than measurements can be used to assess ambient air quality and it is therefore necessary to define criteria for the use and required accuracy of such techniques.

(8) Detailed measurements of fine particulate matter at rural background locations should be made in order to understand better the impacts of this pollutant and to develop appropriate policies. Such measurements should be made in a manner consistent with those of the cooperative programme for monitoring and evaluation of the long range transmission of air pollutants in Europe (EMEP) set up under the 1979 Convention on Long-range Transboundary Air Pollution approved by Council Decision 81/462/EEC of 11 June 1981.

(9) Air quality status should be maintained where it is already good, or improved. Where the objectives for ambient air quality laid down in this Directive are not met, Member States should take action in order to comply with the limit values and critical levels, and where possible, to attain the target values and long-term objectives.

(10) The risk posed by air pollution to vegetation and natural ecosystems is most important in places away from urban areas. The assessment of such risks and the compliance with critical levels for the protection of vegetation should therefore focus on places away from built-up areas.

(11) Fine particulate matter ($PM_{2,5}$) is responsible for significant negative impacts on human health. Further, there is as yet no identifiable threshold below which $PM_{2,5}$ would not pose a risk. As such, this pollutant should not be regulated in the same way as other air pollutants. The approach should aim at a general reduction of concentrations in the urban background to ensure that large sections of the population benefit from improved air quality. However, to ensure a minimum degree of health protection everywhere, that approach should be combined with a limit value, which is to be preceded in a first stage by a target value.

(12) The existing target values and long-term objectives of ensuring effective protection against harmful effects on human health and vegetation and ecosystems from exposure to ozone should remain unchanged. An alert threshold and an information threshold for ozone should be set for the protection of the general population and sensitive sections, respectively, from brief exposures to elevated ozone concentrations. Those thresholds should trigger the dissemination of information to the public on the risks of exposure and the implementation, if appropriate, of short-term measures to reduce ozone levels where the alert threshold is exceeded.

(13) Ozone is a transboundary pollutant formed in the atmosphere from the emission of primary pollutants addressed by Directive 2001/81/EC of the European Parliament and of the Council of 23 October 2001 on national emission ceilings for certain atmospheric pollutants. Progress towards the air quality targets and long term objectives for ozone set in this Directive should be determined by the targets and emission ceilings provided for in Directive 2001/81/EC and, if appropriate, by implementing air quality plans as provided for in this Directive.

(14) Fixed measurements should be mandatory in zones and agglomerations where the long-term objectives for ozone or the assessment thresholds for other pollutants are exceeded. Information from fixed measurements may be supplemented by modelling techniques and/or indicative measurements to enable point data to be interpreted in terms of geographical distribution of concentrations. The use of supplementary techniques of assessment should also allow for reduction of the required minimum number of fixed sampling points.

(15) Contributions from natural sources can be assessed but cannot be controlled. Therefore, where natural contributions to pollutants in ambient air can be determined with sufficient certainty, and where exceedances are due in whole or in part to these natural contributions, these may, under the conditions laid down in this Directive, be subtracted when assessing compliance with air quality limit values. Contributions to exceedances of particulate matter PM10 limit values attributable to winter-sanding or -salting of roads may also be subtracted when assessing compliance with air quality limit values provided that reasonable measures have been taken to lower concentrations.

(16) For zones and agglomerations where conditions are particularly difficult, it should be possible to postpone the deadline for compliance with the air quality limit values in cases where, notwithstanding the implementation of appropriate pollution abatement measures, acute compliance problems exist in specific zones and agglomerations. Any postponement for a given zone or agglomeration should be accompanied by a comprehensive plan to be assessed by the Commission to ensure compliance by the revised deadline. The availability of necessary Community measures reflecting the chosen ambition level in the Thematic Strategy on air pollution to reduce emissions at source will be important for an effective emission reduction by the time frame established in this Directive for compliance with the limit values and should be taken into account when assessing requests to postpone deadlines for compliance.

(17) The necessary Community measures to reduce emissions at source, in particular measures to improve the effectiveness of Community legislation on industrial emissions, to limit the exhaust emissions of engines installed in heavy duty vehicles, to further reduce the Member States' permitted national emissions of key pollutants and the emissions associated with refuelling of petrol cars at service stations, and to address the sulphur content of fuels including marine fuels should be duly examined as a priority by all institutions involved.

(18) Air quality plans should be developed for zones and agglomerations within which concentrations of pollutants in ambient air exceed the relevant air quality target values or limit values, plus any temporary margins of tolerance, where applicable. Air pollutants are emitted from many different sources and activities. To ensure coherence between different policies, such air quality plans should where feasible be consistent, and integrated with plans and programmes prepared pursuant to Directive 2001/80/EC of the European Parliament and of the Council of 23 October 2001 on the limitation of emissions of certain pollutants into the air from large combustion plants, Directive 2001/81/EC, and Directive 2002/49/EC of the European Parliament and of the Council of 25 June 2002 relating to the assessment and management of environmental noise. Full account will also be taken of the ambient air quality objectives provided for in this Directive, where permits are granted for industrial activities pursuant to Directive 2008/1/EC of the European Parliament and of the Council of 15 January 2008 concerning integrated pollution prevention and control.

(19) Action plans should be drawn up indicating the measures to be taken in the short term where there is a risk of an exceedance of one or more alert thresholds in order to reduce that risk and to limit its duration. When the risk applies to one or more limit values or target values, Member States may, where appropriate, draw up such short-term action plans. In respect of ozone, such short-term action plans should take into account the provisions of Commission Decision 2004/279/EC of 19 March 2004 concerning guidance for implementation of Directive 2002/3/EC of the European Parliament and of the Council relating to ozone in ambient air.

(20) Member States should consult with one another if, following significant pollution originating in another Member State, the level of a pollutant exceeds, or is likely to exceed, the relevant air quality objectives plus the margin of tolerance where applicable or, as the case may be, the alert threshold. The transboundary nature of

specific pollutants, such as ozone and particulate matter, may require coordination between neighbouring Member States in drawing up and implementing air quality plans and short-term action plans and in informing the public. Where appropriate, Member States should pursue cooperation with third countries, with particular emphasis on the early involvement of candidate countries.

(21) It is necessary for the Member States and the Commission to collect, exchange and disseminate air quality information in order to understand better the impacts of air pollution and develop appropriate policies. Up-to-date information on concentrations of all regulated pollutants in ambient air should also be readily available to the public.

(22) In order to facilitate the handling and comparison of air quality information, data should be made available to the Commission in a standardised form.

(23) It is necessary to adapt procedures for data provision, assessment and reporting of air quality to enable electronic means and the Internet to be used as the main tools to make information available, and so that such procedures are compatible with Directive 2007/2/EC of the European Parliament and the Council of 14 March 2007 establishing an infrastructure for spatial information in the European Community (INSPIRE).

(24) It is appropriate to provide for the possibility of adapting the criteria and techniques used for the assessment of the ambient air quality to scientific and technical progress and adapting thereto the information to be provided.

(25) Since the objectives of this Directive cannot be sufficiently achieved by the Member States by reason of the transboundary nature of air pollutants and can therefore be better achieved at Community level, the Community may adopt measures, in accordance with the principle of subsidiarity as set out in Article 5 of the Treaty. In accordance with the principle of proportionality, as set out in that Article, this Directive does not go beyond what is necessary in order to achieve those objectives.

(26) Member States should lay down rules on penalties applicable to infringements of the provisions of this Directive and ensure that they are implemented. The penalties should be effective, proportionate and dissuasive.

(27) Certain provisions of the acts repealed by this Directive should remain in force in order to ensure the continuance of existing air quality limits for nitrogen dioxide until they are replaced from 1 January 2010, the continuance of air quality reporting provisions until new implementing measures are adopted, and the continuance of obligations relating to the preliminary assessments of air quality required under Directive 2004/107/EC.

(28) The obligation to transpose this Directive into national law should be confined to those provisions which represent a substantive change as compared with the earlier Directives.

(29) In accordance with point 34 of the Interinstitutional Agreement on better lawmaking, Member States are encouraged to draw up, for themselves and in the interest of the Community, their own tables illustrating, as far as possible, the correlation between the Directive and the transposition measures, and to make them public.

(30) This Directive respects the fundamental rights and observes the principles recognised in particular by the Charter of Fundamental Rights of the European Union. In particular, this Directive seeks to promote the integration into the policies of the Union of a high level of environmental protection and the improvement of the quality of the environment in accordance with the principle of sustainable development as laid down in Article 37 of the Charter of Fundamental Rights of the European Union.

(31) The measures necessary for the implementation of this Directive should be adopted in accordance with Council Decision 1999/468/EC of 28 June 1999 laying down the procedures for the exercise of implementing powers conferred on the Commission.

(32) The Commission should be empowered to amend Annexes I to VI, Annexes VIII to X and Annex XV. Since those measures are of general scope and are designed to amend non-essential elements of this Directive, they must be adopted in accordance with the regulatory procedure with scrutiny provided for in Article 5a of Decision 1999/468/EC.

(33) The transposition clause requires Member States to ensure that the necessary urban background measurements are in place well in time to define the Average Exposure Indicator, in order to guarantee that the requirements related to the assessment of the National Exposure Reduction Target and to the calculation of the Average Exposure Indicator are met,

HAVE ADOPTED THIS DIRECTIVE:

CHAPTER I
GENERAL PROVISIONS

Article 1   Subject matter

This Directive lays down measures aimed at the following:

1.   defining and establishing objectives for ambient air quality designed to avoid, prevent or reduce harmful effects on human health and the environment as a whole;

2.   assessing the ambient air quality in Member States on the basis of common methods and criteria;

3.   obtaining information on ambient air quality in order to help combat air pollution and nuisance and to monitor long-term trends and improvements resulting from national and Community measures;

4.   ensuring that such information on ambient air quality is made available to the public;

5.   maintaining air quality where it is good and improving it in other cases;

6.   promoting increased cooperation between the Member States in reducing air pollution.

Article 2   Definitions

For the purposes of this Directive:

1.   'ambient air' shall mean outdoor air in the troposphere, excluding workplaces as defined by Directive 89/654/EEC where provisions concerning health and safety at work apply and to which members of the public do not have regular access;

2.   'pollutant' shall mean any substance present in ambient air and likely to have harmful effects on human health and/or the environment as a whole;

3.   'level' shall mean the concentration of a pollutant in ambient air or the deposition thereof on surfaces in a given time;

4.   'assessment' shall mean any method used to measure, calculate, predict or estimate levels;

5.   'limit value' shall mean a level fixed on the basis of scientific knowledge, with the aim of avoiding, preventing or reducing harmful effects on human health and/or the environment as a whole, to be attained within a given period and not to be exceeded once attained;

6. 'critical level' shall mean a level fixed on the basis of scientific knowledge, above which direct adverse effects may occur on some receptors, such as trees, other plants or natural ecosystems but not on humans;

7. 'margin of tolerance' shall mean the percentage of the limit value by which that value may be exceeded subject to the conditions laid down in this Directive;

8. 'air quality plans' shall mean plans that set out measures in order to attain the limit values or target values;

9. 'target value' shall mean a level fixed with the aim of avoiding, preventing or reducing harmful effects on human health and/or the environment as a whole, to be attained where possible over a given period;

10. 'alert threshold' shall mean a level beyond which there is a risk to human health from brief exposure for the population as a whole and at which immediate steps are to be taken by the Member States;

11. 'information threshold' shall mean a level beyond which there is a risk to human health from brief exposure for particularly sensitive sections of the population and for which immediate and appropriate information is necessary;

12. 'upper assessment threshold' shall mean a level below which a combination of fixed measurements and modelling techniques and/or indicative measurements may be used to assess ambient air quality;

13. 'lower assessment threshold' shall mean a level below which modelling or objective-estimation techniques alone may be used to assess ambient air quality;

14. 'long-term objective' shall mean a level to be attained in the long term, save where not achievable through proportionate measures, with the aim of providing effective protection of human health and the environment;

15. 'contributions from natural sources' shall mean emissions of pollutants not caused directly or indirectly by human activities, including natural events such as volcanic eruptions, seismic activities, geothermal activities, wild-land fires, high-wind events, sea sprays or the atmospheric re-suspension or transport of natural particles from dry regions;

16. 'zone' shall mean part of the territory of a Member State, as delimited by that Member State for the purposes of air quality assessment and management;

17. 'agglomeration' shall mean a zone that is a conurbation with a population in excess of 250 000 inhabitants or, where the population is 250 000 inhabitants or less, with a given population density per km^2 to be established by the Member States;

18. 'PM_{10}' shall mean particulate matter which passes through a size-selective inlet as defined in the reference method for the sampling and measurement of PM_{10}, EN 12341, with a 50% efficiency cut-off at 10 μm aerodynamic diameter;

19. '$PM_{2,5}$' shall mean particulate matter which passes through a size-selective inlet as defined in the reference method for the sampling and measurement of $PM_{2,5}$, EN 14907, with a 50% efficiency cut-off at 2,5 μm aerodynamic diameter;

20. 'average exposure indicator' shall mean an average level determined on the basis of measurements at urban background locations throughout the territory of a Member State and which reflects population exposure. It is used to calculate the national exposure reduction target and the exposure concentration obligation;

21. 'exposure concentration obligation' shall mean a level fixed on the basis of the average exposure indicator with the aim of reducing harmful effects on human health, to be attained over a given period;

22. 'national exposure reduction target' shall mean a percentage reduction of the average exposure of the population of a Member State set for the reference year with

the aim of reducing harmful effects on human health, to be attained where possible over a given period;

23. 'urban background locations' shall mean places in urban areas where levels are representative of the exposure of the general urban population;

24. 'oxides of nitrogen' shall mean the sum of the volume mixing ratio (ppbv) of nitrogen monoxide (nitric oxide) and nitrogen dioxide expressed in units of mass concentration of nitrogen dioxide (μg/m^3);

25. 'fixed measurements' shall mean measurements taken at fixed sites, either continuously or by random sampling, to determine the levels in accordance with the relevant data quality objectives;

26. 'indicative measurements' shall mean measurements which meet data quality objectives that are less strict than those required for fixed measurements;

27. 'volatile organic compounds' (VOC) shall mean organic compounds from anthropogenic and biogenic sources, other than methane, that are capable of producing photochemical oxidants by reactions with nitrogen oxides in the presence of sunlight;

28. 'ozone precursor substances' means substances which contribute to the formation of ground-level ozone, some of which are listed in Annex X.

Article 3   Responsibilities

Member States shall designate at the appropriate levels the competent authorities and bodies responsible for the following:

(a) assessment of ambient air quality;

(b) approval of measurement systems (methods, equipment, networks and laboratories);

(c) ensuring the accuracy of measurements;

(d) analysis of assessment methods;

(e) coordination on their territory if Community-wide quality assurance programmes are being organised by the Commission;

(f) cooperation with the other Member States and the Commission.

Where relevant, the competent authorities and bodies shall comply with Section C of Annex I.

Article 4
Establishment of zones and agglomerations

Member States shall establish zones and agglomerations throughout their territory. Air quality assessment and air quality management shall be carried out in all zones and agglomerations.

CHAPTER II
ASSESSMENT OF AMBIENT AIR QUALITY

SECTION 1

Assessment of ambient air quality in relation to sulphur dioxide, nitrogen dioxide and oxides of nitrogen, particulate matter, lead, benzene and carbon monoxide

Article 5   Assessment regime

1. The upper and lower assessment thresholds specified in Section A of Annex II shall apply to sulphur dioxide, nitrogen dioxide and oxides of nitrogen, particulate matter (PM$_{10}$ and PM$_{2,5}$), lead, benzene and carbon monoxide.

Each zone and agglomeration shall be classified in relation to those assessment thresholds.

2. The classification referred to in paragraph 1 shall be reviewed at least every five years in accordance with the procedure laid down in Section B of Annex II.

However, classifications shall be reviewed more frequently in the event of significant changes in activities relevant to the ambient concentrations of sulphur dioxide, nitrogen dioxide or, where relevant, oxides of nitrogen, particulate matter (PM_{10}, $PM2,5$), lead, benzene or carbon monoxide.

Article 6   Assessment criteria

1. Member States shall assess ambient air quality with respect to the pollutants referred to in Article 5 in all their zones and agglomerations, in accordance with the criteria laid down in paragraphs 2, 3 and 4 of this Article and in accordance with the criteria laid down in Annex III.

2. In all zones and agglomerations where the level of pollutants referred to in paragraph 1 exceeds the upper assessment threshold established for those pollutants, fixed measurements shall be used to assess the ambient air quality. Those fixed measurements may be supplemented by modelling techniques and/or indicative measurements to provide adequate information on the spatial distribution of the ambient air quality.

3. In all zones and agglomerations where the level of pollutants referred to in paragraph 1 is below the upper assessment threshold established for those pollutants, a combination of fixed measurements and modelling techniques and/or indicative measurements may be used to assess the ambient air quality.

4. In all zones and agglomerations where the level of pollutants referred to in paragraph 1 is below the lower assessment threshold established for those pollutants, modelling techniques or objective-estimation techniques or both shall be sufficient for the assessment of the ambient air quality.

5. In addition to the assessments referred to in paragraphs 2, 3 and 4, measurements shall be made, at rural background locations away from significant sources of air pollution, for the purposes of providing, as a minimum, information on the total mass concentration and the chemical speciation concentrations of fine particulate matter ($PM_{2,5}$) on an annual average basis and shall be conducted using the following criteria:

(a) one sampling point shall be installed every 100 000 km^2;

(b) each Member State shall set up at least one measuring station or may, by agreement with adjoining Member States, set up one or several common measuring stations, covering the relevant neighbouring zones, to achieve the necessary spatial resolution;

(c) where appropriate, monitoring shall be coordinated with the monitoring strategy and measurement programme of the Cooperative Programme for Monitoring and Evaluation of the Long-range Transmission of Air Pollutants in Europe (EMEP);

(d) Sections A and C of Annex I shall apply in relation to the data quality objectives for mass concentration measurements of particulate matter and Annex IV shall apply in its entirety.

Member States shall inform the Commission of the measurement methods used in the measurement of the chemical composition of fine particulate matter ($PM_{2,5}$).

Article 7   Sampling points

1. The location of sampling points for the measurement of sulphur dioxide, nitrogen dioxide and oxides of nitrogen, particulate matter (PM_{10}, $PM_{2,5}$), lead, benzene

and carbon monoxide in ambient air shall be determined using the criteria listed in Annex III.

2. In each zone or agglomeration where fixed measurements are the sole source of information for assessing air quality, the number of sampling points for each relevant pollutant shall not be less than the minimum number of sampling points specified in Section A of Annex V.

3. For zones and agglomerations within which information from fixed measurement sampling points is supplemented by information from modelling and/or indicative measurement, the total number of sampling points specified in Section A of Annex V may be reduced by up to 50%, provided that the following conditions are met:

(a) the supplementary methods provide sufficient information for the assessment of air quality with regard to limit values or alert thresholds, as well as adequate information for the public;

(b) the number of sampling points to be installed and the spatial resolution of other techniques are sufficient for the concentration of the relevant pollutant to be established in accordance with the data quality objectives specified in Section A of Annex I and enable assessment results to meet the criteria specified in Section B of Annex I.

The results of modelling and/or indicative measurement shall be taken into account for the assessment of air quality with respect to the limit values.

4. The application in Member States of the criteria for selecting sampling points shall be monitored by the Commission so as to facilitate the harmonised application of those criteria through-out the European Union.

Article 8   Reference measurement methods

1. Member States shall apply the reference measurement methods and criteria specified in Section A and Section C of Annex VI.

2. Other measurement methods may be used subject to the conditions set out in Section B of Annex VI.

SECTION 2

Assessment of ambient air quality in relation to ozone

Article 9   Assessment criteria

1. Where, in a zone or agglomeration, concentrations of ozone have exceeded the long-term objectives specified in Section C of Annex VII during any of the previous five years of measurement, fixed measurements shall be taken.

2. Where fewer than five years' data are available, Member States may, for the purposes of determining whether the long-term objectives referred to in paragraph 1 have been exceeded during those five years, combine the results from measurement campaigns of short duration carried out when and where levels are likely to be at their highest, with the results obtained from emission inventories and modelling.

Article 10   Sampling points

1. The siting of sampling points for the measurement of ozone shall be determined using the criteria set out in Annex VIII.

2. The sampling points for fixed measurements of ozone in each zone or agglomeration within which measurement is the sole source of information for assessing air quality shall not be less than the minimum number of sampling points specified in Section A of Annex IX.

3. For zones and agglomerations within which information from sampling points for fixed measurements is supplemented by information from modelling and/or indicative measurements, the number of sampling points specified in Section A of Annex IX may be reduced provided that the following conditions are met:

(a) the supplementary methods provide sufficient information for the assessment of air quality with regard to target values, long-term objectives, information and alert thresholds;

(b) the number of sampling points to be installed and the spatial resolution of other techniques are sufficient for the concentration of ozone to be established in accordance with the data quality objectives specified in Section A of Annex I and enable assessment results to meet the criteria specified in Section B of Annex I;

(c) the number of sampling points in each zone or agglomeration amounts to at least one sampling point per two million inhabitants or one sampling point per 50 000 km², whichever produces the greater number of sampling points, but must not be less than one sampling point in each zone or agglomeration;

(d) nitrogen dioxide is measured at all remaining sampling points except at rural background stations as referred to in Section A of Annex VIII.

The results of modelling and/or indicative measurement shall be taken into account for the assessment of air quality with respect to the target values.

4. Nitrogen dioxide shall be measured at a minimum of 50% of the ozone sampling points required under Section A of Annex IX. That measurement shall be continuous except at rural background stations, as referred to in Section A of Annex VIII, where other measurement methods may be used.

5. In zones and agglomerations where, during each of the previous five years of measurement, concentrations are below the long-term objectives, the number of sampling points for fixed measurements shall be determined in accordance with Section B of Annex IX.

6. Each Member State shall ensure that at least one sampling point is installed and operated in its territory to supply data on concentrations of the ozone precursor substances listed in Annex X. Each Member State shall choose the number and siting of the stations at which ozone precursor substances are to be measured, taking into account the objectives and methods laid down in Annex X.

Article 11   Reference measurement methods

1. Member States shall apply the reference method for measurement of ozone, set out in point 8 of Section A of Annex VI. Other measuring methods may be used subject to the conditions set out in Section B of Annex VI.

2. Each Member State shall inform the Commission of the methods it uses to sample and measure VOC, as listed in Annex X.

CHAPTER III
AMBIENT AIR QUALITY MANAGEMENT

Article 12   Requirements where levels are lower than the limit values

In zones and agglomerations where the levels of sulphur dioxide, nitrogen dioxide, PM_{10}, $PM_{2,5}$, lead, benzene and carbon monoxide in ambient air are below the respective limit values specified in Annexes XI and XIV, Member States shall maintain the levels of those pollutants below the limit values and shall endeavour to preserve the best ambient air quality, compatible with sustainable development.

Article 13   Limit values and alert thresholds for the protection of human health

1.   Member States shall ensure that, throughout their zones and agglomerations, levels of sulphur dioxide, PM_{10}, lead, and carbon monoxide in ambient air do not exceed the limit values laid down in Annex XI.

In respect of nitrogen dioxide and benzene, the limit values specified in Annex XI may not be exceeded from the dates specified therein.

Compliance with these requirements shall be assessed in accordance with Annex III.

The margins of tolerance laid down in Annex XI shall apply in accordance with Article 22(3) and Article 23(1).

2.   The alert thresholds for concentrations of sulphur dioxide and nitrogen dioxide in ambient air shall be those laid down in Section A of Annex XII.

Article 14   Critical levels

1.   Member States shall ensure compliance with the critical levels specified in Annex XIII as assessed in accordance with Section A of Annex III.

2.   Where fixed measurements are the sole source of information for assessing air quality, the number of sampling points shall not be less than the minimum number specified in Section C of Annex V. Where that information is supplemented by indicative measurements or modelling, the minimum number of sampling points may be reduced by up to 50% so long as the assessed concentrations of the relevant pollutant can be established in accordance with the data quality objectives specified in Section A of Annex I.

*Article 15   National $PM_{2,5}$ exposure reduction
target for the protection of human health*

1.   Member States shall take all necessary measures not entailing disproportionate costs to reduce exposure to $PM_{2,5}$ with a view to attaining the national exposure reduction target laid down in Section B of Annex XIV by the year specified therein.

2.   Member States shall ensure that the average exposure indicator for the year 2015 established in accordance with Section A of Annex XIV does not exceed the exposure concentration obligation laid down in Section C of that Annex.

3.   The average exposure indicator for $PM_{2,5}$ shall be assessed in accordance with Section A of Annex XIV.

4.   Each Member State shall, in accordance with Annex III, ensure that the distribution and the number of sampling points on which the average exposure indicator for $PM_{2,5}$ is based reflect the general population exposure adequately. The number of sampling points shall be no less than that determined by application of Section B of Annex V.

Article 16 $PM_{2,5}$ target value and limit value for the protection of human health

1.   Member States shall take all necessary measures not entailing disproportionate costs to ensure that concentrations of $PM_{2,5}$ in ambient air do not exceed the target value laid down in Section D of Annex XIV as from the date specified therein.

2.   Member States shall ensure that concentrations of $PM_{2,5}$ in ambient air do not exceed the limit value laid down in Section E of Annex XIV throughout their zones and agglomerations as from the date specified therein. Compliance with this requirement shall be assessed in accordance with Annex III.

3.   The margin of tolerance laid down in Section E of Annex XIV shall apply in accordance with Article 23(1).

Article 17

Requirements in zones and agglomerations where ozone concentrations exceed the target values and long-term objectives

1. Member States shall take all necessary measures not entailing disproportionate costs to ensure that the target values and long-term objectives are attained.

2. For zones and agglomerations in which a target value is exceeded, Member States shall ensure that the programme prepared pursuant to Article 6 of Directive 2001/81/EC and, if appropriate, an air quality plan is implemented in order to attain the target values, save where not achievable through measures not entailing disproportionate costs, as from the date specified in Section B of Annex VII to this Directive.

3. For zones and agglomerations in which the levels of ozone in ambient air are higher than the long-term objectives but below, or equal to, the target values, Member States shall prepare and implement cost-effective measures with the aim of achieving the long-term objectives. Those measures shall, at least, be consistent with all the air quality plans and the programme referred to in paragraph 2.

Article 18

Requirements in zones and agglomerations where ozone concentrations meet the long-term objectives

In zones and agglomerations in which ozone levels meet the long-term objectives, Member States shall, in so far as factors including the transboundary nature of ozone pollution and meteorological conditions permit, maintain those levels below the long-term objectives and shall preserve through proportionate measures the best ambient air quality compatible with sustainable development and a high level of environmental and human health protection.

Article 19

Measures required in the event of information or alert thresholds being exceeded

Where the information threshold specified in Annex XII or any of the alert thresholds laid down therein is exceeded, Member States shall take the necessary steps to inform the public by means of radio, television, newspapers or the Internet.

Member States shall also forward to the Commission, on a provisional basis, information concerning the levels recorded and the duration of the periods during which the alert threshold or information threshold was exceeded.

Article 20   Contributions from natural sources

1. Member States shall transmit to the Commission, for a given year, lists of zones and agglomerations where exceedances of limit values for a given pollutant are attributable to natural sources. Member States shall provide information on concentrations and sources and the evidence demonstrating that the exceedances are attributable to natural sources.

2. Where the Commission has been informed of an exceedance attributable to natural sources in accordance with paragraph 1, that exceedance shall not be considered as an exceedance for the purposes of this Directive.

3. The Commission shall by 11 June 2010 publish guidelines for demonstration and subtraction of exceedances attributable to natural sources.

Article 21

Exceedances attributable to winter-sanding or -salting of roads

1. Member States may designate zones or agglomerations or equal to, the target values, Member States shall prepare and within which limit values for PM_{10} are exceeded in ambient air due to the re-suspension of or -salting of roads.

2.   Member States shall send the Commission lists of any such zones or agglomerations together with information on concentrations and sources of PM_{10} therein.

3.   When informing the Commission in accordance with Article 27, Member States shall provide the necessary evidence to demonstrate that any exceedances are due to re-suspended particulates and that reasonable measures have been taken to lower the concentrations.

4.   Without prejudice to Article 20, in the case of zones and agglomerations referred to in paragraph 1 of this Article, Member States need to establish the air quality plan provided for in Article 23 only in so far as exceedances are attributable to PM_{10} sources other than winter-sanding or -salting of roads.

5.   The Commission shall by 11 June 2010 publish guidelines for determination of contributions from the re-suspension of particulates following winter-sanding or -salting of roads.

Article 22
Postponement of attainment deadlines and exemption from the obligation to apply certain limit values

1.   Where, in a given zone or agglomeration, conformity with the limit values for nitrogen dioxide or benzene cannot be achieved by the deadlines specified in Annex XI, a Member State may postpone those deadlines by a maximum of five years for that particular zone or agglomeration, on condition that an air quality plan is established in accordance with Article 23 for the zone or agglomeration to which the postponement would apply; such air quality plan shall be supplemented by the information listed in Section B of Annex XV related to the pollutants concerned and shall demonstrate how conformity will be achieved with the limit values before the new deadline.

2.   Where, in a given zone or agglomeration, conformity with the limit values for PM_{10} as specified in Annex XI cannot be achieved because of site-specific dispersion characteristics, adverse climatic conditions or transboundary contributions, a Member State shall be exempt from the obligation to apply those limit values until 11 June 2011 provided that the conditions laid down in paragraph 1 are fulfilled and that the Member State shows that all appropriate measures have been taken at national, regional and local level to meet the deadlines.

3.   Where a Member State applies paragraphs 1 or 2, it shall ensure that the limit value for each pollutant is not exceeded by more than the maximum margin of tolerance specified in Annex XI for each of the pollutants concerned.

4.   Member States shall notify the Commission where, in their view, paragraphs 1 or 2 are applicable, and shall communicate the air quality plan referred to in paragraph 1 including all relevant information necessary for the Commission to assess whether or not the relevant conditions are satisfied. In its assessment, the Commission shall take into account estimated effects on ambient air quality in the Member States, at present and in the future, of measures that have been taken by the Member States as well as estimated effects on ambient air quality of current Community measures and planned Community measures to be proposed by the Commission.

Where the Commission has raised no objections within nine months of receipt of that notification, the relevant conditions for the application of paragraphs 1 or 2 shall be deemed to be satisfied.

If objections are raised, the Commission may require Member States to adjust or provide new air quality plans.

CHAPTER IV
PLANS

Article 23   *Air quality plans*

1.   Where, in given zones or agglomerations, the levels of pollutants in ambient air exceed any limit value or target value, plus any relevant margin of tolerance in

each case, Member States shall ensure that air quality plans are established for those zones and agglomerations in order to achieve the related limit value or target value specified in Annexes XI and XIV.

In the event of exceedances of those limit values for which the attainment deadline is already expired, the air quality plans shall set out appropriate measures, so that the exceedance period can be kept as short as possible. The air quality plans may additionally include specific measures aiming at the protection of sensitive population groups, including children.

Those air quality plans shall incorporate at least the information listed in Section A of Annex XV and may include measures pursuant to Article 24. Those plans shall be communicated to the Commission without delay, but no later than two years after the end of the year the first exceedance was observed.

Where air quality plans must be prepared or implemented in respect of several pollutants, Member States shall, where appropriate, prepare and implement integrated air quality plans covering all pollutants concerned.

2. Member States shall, to the extent feasible, ensure consistency with other plans required under Directive 2001/80/EC, Directive 2001/81/EC or Directive 2002/49/EC in order to achieve the relevant environmental objectives.

Article 24   Short-term action plans

1. Where, in a given zone or agglomeration, there is a risk that the levels of pollutants will exceed one or more of the alert thresholds specified in Annex XII, Member States shall draw up action plans indicating the measures to be taken in the short term in order to reduce the risk or duration of such an exceedance. Where this risk applies to one or more limit values or target values specified in Annexes VII, XI and XIV, Member States may, where appropriate, draw up such short-term action plans.

However, where there is a risk that the alert threshold for ozone specified in Section B of Annex XII will be exceeded, Member States shall only draw up such short-term action plans when in their opinion there is a significant potential, taking into account national geographical, meteorological and economic conditions, to reduce the risk, duration or severity of such an exceedance. When drawing up such a short-term action plan Member States shall take account of Decision 2004/279/EC.

2. The short-term action plans referred to in paragraph 1 may, depending on the individual case, provide for effective measures to control and, where necessary, suspend activities which contribute to the risk of the respective limit values or target values or alert threshold being exceeded. Those action plans may include measures in relation to motor-vehicle traffic, construction works, ships at berth, and the use of industrial plants or products and domestic heating. Specific actions aiming at the protection of sensitive population groups, including children, may also be considered in the framework of those plans.

3. When Member States have drawn up a short-term action plan, they shall make available to the public and to appropriate organisations such as environmental organisations, consumer organisations, organisations representing the interests of sensitive population groups, other relevant health-care bodies and the relevant industrial federations both the results of their investigations on the feasibility and the content of specific short-term action plans as well as information on the implementation of these plans.

4. For the first time before 11 June 2010 and at regular intervals thereafter, the Commission shall publish examples of best practices for the drawing-up of short-term action plans, including examples of best practices for the protection of sensitive population groups, including children.

Article 25   Transboundary air pollution

1.   Where any alert threshold, limit value or target value plus any relevant margin of tolerance or long-term objective is exceeded due to significant transboundary transport of air pollutants or their precursors, the Member States concerned shall cooperate and, where appropriate, draw up joint activities, such as the preparation of joint or coordinated air quality plans pursuant to Article 23 in order to remove such exceedances through the application of appropriate but proportionate measures.

2.   The Commission shall be invited to be present and to assist in any cooperation referred to in paragraph 1. Where appropriate, the Commission shall, taking into account the reports established pursuant to Article 9 of Directive 2001/81/EC, consider whether further action should be taken at Community level in order to reduce precursor emissions responsible for transboundary pollution.

3.   Member States shall, if appropriate pursuant to Article 24, prepare and implement joint short-term action plans covering neighbouring zones in other Member States. Member States shall ensure that neighbouring zones in other Member States which have developed short-term action plans receive all appropriate information.

4.   Where the information threshold or alert thresholds are exceeded in zones or agglomerations close to national borders, information shall be provided as soon as possible to the competent authorities in the neighbouring Member States concerned. That information shall also be made available to the public.

5.   In drawing up plans as provided for in paragraphs 1 and 3 and in informing the public as referred to in paragraph 4, Member States shall, where appropriate, endeavour to pursue cooperation with third countries, and in particular with candidate countries.

CHAPTER V
INFORMATION AND REPORTING

Article 26   Public information

1.   Member States shall ensure that the public as well as appropriate organisations such as environmental organisations, consumer organisations, organisations representing the interests of sensitive populations, other relevant health-care bodies and the relevant industrial federations are informed, adequately and in good time, of the following:

(a) ambient air quality in accordance with Annex XVI;

(b) any postponement decisions pursuant to Article 22(1);

(c) any exemptions pursuant to Article 22(2);

(d) air quality plans as provided for in Article 22(1) and Article 23 and programmes referred to in Article 17(2).

The information shall be made available free of charge by means of any easily accessible media including the Internet or any other appropriate means of telecommunication, and shall take into account the provisions laid down in Directive 2007/2/EC.

2.   Member States shall make available to the public annual reports for all pollutants covered by this Directive.

Those reports shall summarise the levels exceeding limit values, target values, long-term objectives, information thresholds and alert thresholds, for the relevant averaging periods. That information shall be combined with a summary assessment of the effects of those exceedances. The reports may include, where appropriate, further information and assessments on forest protection as well as information on other pollutants for which monitoring provisions are specified in this Directive, such as, inter alia, selected non-regulated ozone precursor substances as listed in Section B of Annex X.

3. Member States shall inform the public of the competent authority or body designated in relation to the tasks referred to in Article 3.

Article 27   Transmission of information and reporting

1. Member States shall ensure that information on ambient air quality is made available to the Commission within the required timescale as determined by the implementing measures referred to in Article 28(2).

2. In any event, for the specific purpose of assessing compliance with the limit values and critical levels and the attainment of target values, such information shall be made available to the Commission no later than nine months after the end of each year and shall include:

(a) the changes made in that year to the list and delimitation of zones and agglomerations established under Article 4;

(b) the list of zones and agglomerations in which the levels of one or more pollutants are higher than the limit values plus the margin of tolerance where applicable or higher than target values or critical levels; and for these zones and agglomerations:

(i) levels assessed and, if relevant, the dates and periods when such levels were observed;

(ii) if appropriate, an assessment on contributions from natural sources and from re-suspension of particulates following winter-sanding or -salting of roads to the levels assessed, as declared to the Commission under Articles 20 and 21.

3. Paragraphs 1 and 2 shall apply to information collected as from the beginning of the second calendar year after the entry into force of the implementing measures referred to in Article 28(2).

Article 28   Implementing measures

1. Measures designed to amend the non-essential elements of this Directive, namely Annexes I to VI, Annexes VIII to X and Annex XV, shall be adopted in accordance with the regulatory procedure with scrutiny referred to in Article 29(3).

However, the amendments may not have the effect of directly or indirectly modifying either of the following:

(a) the limit values, exposure reduction targets, critical levels, target values, information or alert thresholds or long-term objectives specified in Annex VII and Annexes XI to XIV;

(b) the dates for compliance with any of the parameters referred to in point (a).

2. The Commission shall, in accordance with the regulatory procedure referred to in Article 29(2), determine the additional information to be made available by Member States pursuant to Article 27 as well as the timescales in which such information is to be communicated.

The Commission shall also identify ways of streamlining the way data are reported and the reciprocal exchange of information and data from networks and individual stations measuring ambient air pollution within the Member States, in accordance with the regulatory procedure referred to in Article 29(2).

3. The Commission shall draw up guidelines for the agreements on setting up common measuring stations as referred to in Article 6(5).

4. The Commission shall publish guidance on the demonstration of equivalence referred to in Section B of Annex VI.

CHAPTER VI
COMMITTEE, TRANSITIONAL AND FINAL PROVISIONS

Article 29 Committee

1. The Commission shall be assisted by a committee, 'the Ambient Air Quality Committee'.

2. Where reference is made to this paragraph, Articles 5 and 7 of Decision 1999/468/EC shall apply, having regard to the provisions of Article 8 thereof.

The period laid down in Article 5(6) of Decision 1999/468/EC shall be set at three months.

3. Where reference is made to this paragraph, Article 5a(1) to (4) and Article 7 of Decision 1999/468/EC shall apply, having regard to the provisions of Article 8 thereof.

Article 30 Penalties

Member States shall lay down the rules on penalties applicable to infringements of the national provisions adopted pursuant to this Directive and shall take all measures necessary to ensure that they are implemented. The penalties provided for must be effective, proportionate and dissuasive.

Article 31 Repeal and transitional provisions

1. Directives 96/62/EC, 1999/30/EC, 2000/69/EC and 2002/3/EC shall be repealed as from 11 June 2010, without prejudice to the obligations on the Member States relating to time-limits for transposition or application of those Directives.

However, from 11 June 2008, the following shall apply:

(a) in Directive 96/62/EC, paragraph 1 of Article 12 shall be replaced by the following:

'1. The detailed arrangements for forwarding the information to be provided under Article 11 shall be adopted in accordance with the procedure referred to in paragraph 3.';

(b) in Directive 1999/30/EC, Article 7(7), footnote 1 in point I of Annex VIII and point VI of Annex IX shall be deleted;

(c) in Directive 2000/69/EC, Article 5(7) and point III in Annex VII shall be deleted;

(d) in Directive 2002/3/EC, Article 9(5) and point II of Annex VIII shall be deleted.

2. Notwithstanding the first subparagraph of paragraph 1, the following Articles shall remain in force:

(a) Article 5 of Directive 96/62/EC until 31 December 2010;

(b) Article 11(1) of Directive 96/62/EC and Article 10(1), (2) and (3) of Directive 2002/3/EC until the end of the second calendar year following the entry into force of the implementing measures referred to in Article 28(2) of this Directive;

(c) Article 9(3) and (4) of Directive 1999/30/EC until 31 December 2009.

3. References made to the repealed Directives shall be construed as being made to this Directive and should be read in accordance with the correlation table in Annex XVII.

4. Decision 97/101/EC shall be repealed with effect from the end of the second calendar year following the entry into force of the implementing measures referred to in Article 28(2) of this Directive.

However, the third, fourth and fifth indents of Article 7 of Decision 97/101/EC shall be deleted with effect from 11 June 2008.

Article 32   Review

1. In 2013 the Commission shall review the provisions related to $PM_{2,5}$ and, as appropriate, other pollutants, and shall present a proposal to the European Parliament and the Council.

As regards $PM_{2,5}$, the review shall be undertaken with a view to establishing a legally binding national exposure reduction obligation in order to replace the national exposure reduction target and to review the exposure concentration obligation laid down in Article 15, taking into account, *inter alia*, the following elements:

— latest scientific information from WHO and other relevant organisations,

— air quality situations and reduction potentials in the Member States,

— the revision of Directive 2001/81/EC,

— progress made in implementing Community reduction measures for air pollutants,

2. The Commission shall take into account the feasibility of adopting a more ambitious limit value for $PM_{2,5}$, shall review the indicative limit value of the second stage for $PM_{2,5}$ and consider confirming or altering that value.

3. As part of the review, the Commission shall also prepare a report on the experience and on the necessity of monitoring of PM_{10} and $PM_{2,5}$, taking into account technical progress in automatic measuring techniques. If appropriate, new reference methods for the measurement of PM_{10} and $PM_{2,5}$ shall be proposed.

Article 33   Transposition

1. Member States shall bring into force the laws, regulations and administrative provisions necessary to comply with this Directive before 11 June 2010. They shall forthwith communicate to the Commission the text of those measures.

When Member States adopt these measures, they shall contain a reference to this Directive or shall be accompanied by such reference on the occasion of their official publication. The methods of making such reference shall be laid down by Member States.

2. However, Member States shall ensure that a sufficient number of urban background measurement stations of $PM_{2,5}$ necessary for the calculation of the Average Exposure Indicator, in accordance with Section B of Annex V, is established at the latest by 1 January 2009, in order to comply with the time frame and the conditions indicated in Section A of Annex XIV.

3. Member States shall communicate to the Commission the text of the main provisions of national law which they adopt in the field covered by this Directive.

Article 34   Entry into force

This Directive shall enter into force on the day of its publication in the Official Journal of the European Union.

Article 35   Addressees

This Directive is addressed to the Member States.

* * *

ANNEX I
DATA QUALITY OBJECTIVES

* * *

ANNEX II
Determination of requirements for assessment of concentrations of sulphur dioxide, nitrogen dioxide and oxides of nitrogen, particulate matter (PM$_{10}$ and PM$_{2,5}$), lead, benzene and carbon monoxide in ambient air within a zone or agglomeration

A. Upper and lower assessment thresholds

The following upper and lower assessment thresholds will apply:

1. Sulphur dioxide

	Health protection	Vegetation protection
Upper assessment threshold	60% of 24–hour limit value (75 µg/m^3, not to be exceeded more than 3 times in any calendar year)	60% of winter critical level (12 µg/m^3)
Lower assessment threshold	40% of 24–hour limit value (50 µg/m^3, not to be exceeded more than three times in any calendar year)	40% of winter critical level (8 µg/m^3)

2. Nitrogen dioxide and oxides of nitrogen

	Hourly limit value for the protection of human health (NO$_2$)	Annual limit value for the protection of human health (NO$_2$)	Annual critical level for the protection of vegetation and natural ecosystems (NO$_x$)
Upper assessment threshold	70% of limit value (140 µg/m^3, not to be exceeded more than 18 times in any calendar year)	80% of limit value (32 µg/m^3)	80% of critical level (24 µg/m^3)
Lower assessment threshold	50% of limit value (100 µg/m^3, not to be exceeded more than 18 times in any calendar year) Annual limit value for the protection of human health (NO$_2$)	65% of limit value (26 µg/m^3)	65% of critical level (19,5 µg/m^3)

3. Particulate matter (PM$_{10}$/ PM$_{2,5}$)

	24–hour average PM$_{10}$	Annual average PM$_{10}$	Annual average PM$_{2,5}$(1)
Upper assessment threshold	70% of limit value (35 µg/m^3, not to be exceeded more than 35 times in any calendar year)	70% of limit value (28 µg/m^3)	70% of limit value (17 µg/m^3)
Lower assessment threshold	50% of limit value (25 µg/m^3, not to be exceeded more	50% of limit value (20 µg/m^3)	50% of limit value (12 µg/m^3)

	than 35 times in any calendar year)		

(1) The upper assessment threshold and the lower assessment threshold for $PM_{2,5}$ do not apply to the measurements to assess compliance with the $PM_{2,5}$ exposure reduction target for the protection of human health.

4. Lead

	Annual Average
Upper assessment threshold	70% of limit value (0,35 μg/m³)
Lower assessment threshold	50% of limit value (0,25 μg/m³)

5. Benzene

	Annual average
Upper assessment threshold	70% of limit value (3,5 μg/m³)
Lower assessment threshold	40% of limit value (2 μg/m³)

6. Carbon monoxide

	Eight-hour average
Upper assessment threshold	70% of limit value (7 mg/m³)
Lower assessment threshold	50% of limit value (5 mg/m³)

B. Determination of exceedances of upper and lower assessment thresholds

Exceedances of upper and lower assessment thresholds shall be determined on the basis of concentrations during the previous five years where sufficient data are available. An assessment threshold shall be deemed to have been exceeded if it has been exceeded during at least three separate years out of those previous five years.

Where fewer than five years' data are available, Member States may combine measurement campaigns of short duration during the period of the year and at locations likely to be typical of the highest pollution levels with results obtained from information from emission inventories and modelling to determine exceedances of the upper and lower assessment thresholds.

ANNEX III
Assessment of ambient air quality and location of sampling points for the measurement of sulphur dioxide, nitrogen dioxide and oxides of nitrogen, particulate matter (PM_{10} and $PM_{2,5}$), lead, benzene and carbon monoxide in ambient air

* * *

ANNEX IV
MEASUREMENTS AT RURAL BACKGROUND LOCATIONS IRRESPECTIVE OF CONCENTRATION

A. Objectives

The main objectives of such measurements are to ensure that adequate information is made available on levels in the background. This information is essential to judge the enhanced levels in more polluted areas (such as urban background, industry related locations, traffic related locations), assess the possible contribution from long-range transport of air pollutants, support source apportionment analysis and for the understanding of specific pollutants such as particulate matter. It is also essential for the increased use of modelling also in urban areas.

* * *

ANNEX V
Criteria for determining minimum numbers of sampling points for fixed measurement of concentrations of sulphur dioxide, nitrogen dioxide and oxides of nitrogen, particulate matter (PM$_{10}$, PM$_{2,5}$), lead, benzene and carbon monoxide in ambient air

* * *

ANNEX VI
Reference methods for assessment of concentrations of sulphur dioxide, nitrogen dioxide and oxides of nitrogen, particulate matter (PM$_{10}$ and PM$_{2,5}$), lead, benzene, carbon monoxide, and ozone

* * *

ANNEX VII
OZONE TARGET VALUES AND LONG–TERM OBJECTIVES

A. Definitions and criteria

1. Definitions

AOT40 (expressed in (μg/m^3) $\bullet$ hours) means the sum of the difference between hourly concentrations greater than 80 μg/m^3 (= 40 parts per billion) and 80 μg/m3 over a given period using only the one-hour values measured between 8.00 and 20.00 Central European Time (CET) each day.

2. Criteria

The following criteria shall be used for checking validity when aggregating data and calculating statistical parameters:

Parameter	Required proportion of valid data
One hour values	75% (i.e. 45 minutes)
Eight hours values	75% of values (i.e. six hours)
Maximum daily 8 hours mean from hourly running 8 hours	75% of the hourly running eight hours averages (i.e. 18 eight-hourly averages per day)
AOT40	90% of the one hour values over the time period defined for calculating the AOT40 value (1)
Annual mean	75% of the one hour values over summer (April to September) and 75% over winter (January to March, October to December) seasons separately
Number of exceedances and maximum values per month	90% of the daily maximum eight hours mean values (27 available daily values per month)
	90% of the one hour values between 8.00 and 20.00 CET
Number of exceedances and maximum values per year	five out of six months over the summer season (April to September)

(1) In cases where all possible measured data are not available, the following factor shall be used to calculate AOT40 values:

$$\text{AOT40}_{\text{estimate}} = \text{AOT40}_{\text{measured}} \times \frac{\text{total possible number of hours (*)}}{\text{number of measured hourly values}}$$

(*) being the number of hours within the time period of AOT40 definition, (i.e. 08:00 to 20:00 CET from 1 May to 31 July each year, for vegetation protection and from 1 April to 30 September each year for forest protection).

B. Target values

Objective	Averaging period	Target value	Date by which target value should be met (1)
Protection of human health	Maximum daily eight-hour mean (2)	120 µg/m³ not to be exceeded on more than 25 days per calendar year averaged over three years (3)	1.1.2010
Protection of vegetation	May to July	AOT40 (calculated from 1 h values) 18 000 µg/m³ • h averaged over five years (3)	1.1.2010

(1) Compliance with target values will be assessed as of this date. That is, 2010 will be the first year the data for which is used in calculating compliance over the following three or five years, as appropriate.

(2) The maximum daily eight-hour mean concentration shall be selected by examining eight-hour running averages, calculated from hourly data and updated each hour. Each eight-hour average so calculated shall be assigned to the day on which it ends. i.e. the first calculation period for any one day will be the period from 17:00 on the previous day to 01:00 on that day; the last calculation period for any one day will be the period from 16:00 to 24:00 on the day.

(3) If the three or five year averages cannot be determined on the basis of a full and consecutive set of annual data, the minimum annual data required for checking compliance with the target values will be as follows:

— for the target value for the protection of human health: valid data for one year,
— for the target value for the protection of vegetation: valid data for three years.

C. Long-term objectives

Objective	Averaging period	Longterm objective	Date by which the longterm objective should be met
Protection of human health	Maximum daily eight-hour mean within a calendar year	120 µg/m³	not defined
Protection of vegetation	May to July	AOT40 (calculated from 1 h values) 6 000 µg/m³ • h	not defined

ANNEX VIII
Criteria for classifying and locating sampling points for assessments of ozone concentrations

* * *

ANNEX IX
Criteria for determining the minimum number of sampling points for fixed measurement of concentrations of ozone

* * *

ANNEX X
MEASUREMENTS OF OZONE PRECURSOR SUBSTANCES

A. Objectives

The main objectives of such measurements are to analyse any trend in ozone precursors, to check the efficiency of emission reduction strategies, to check the consistency of emission inventories and to help attribute emission sources to observed pollution concentrations.

An additional aim is to support the understanding of ozone formation and precursor dispersion processes, as well as the application of photochemical models.

B. Substances

Measurement of ozone precursor substances shall include at least nitrogen oxides (NO and NO2), and appropriate volatile organic compounds (VOC). A list of volatile organic compounds recommended for measurement is given below:

	1–Butene	Isoprene	Ethyl benzene
Ethane	Trans–2–Butene	n-Hexane	m + p-Xylene
Ethylene	cis–2–Butene	i-Hexane	o-Xylene
Acetylene	1,3–Butadiene	n-Heptane	1,2,4–Trimethyle-benzene
Propane	n-Pentane	n-Octane	1,2,3–Trimethyle-benzene
Propene	i-Pentane	i-Octane	1,3,5–Trimethyle-benzene
n-Butane	1–Pentene	Benzene	Formaldehyde
i-Butane	2–Pentene	Toluene	Total non-methane hydrocarbons

C. Siting

Measurements shall be taken in particular in urban or suburban areas at any monitoring site set up in accordance with the requirements of this Directive and considered appropriate with regard to the monitoring objectives referred to in Section A.

ANNEX XI
LIMIT VALUES FOR THE PROTECTION OF HUMAN HEALTH

A. Criteria

Without prejudice to Annex I, the following criteria shall be used for checking validity when aggregating data and calculating statistical parameters:

Parameter	Required proportion of valid data
One hour values	75% (i.e. 45 minutes)
Eight hours values	75% of values (i.e. 6 hours)
Maximum daily 8–hour mean	75% of the hourly running eight hour averages (i.e. 18 eight hour averages per day)
24–hour values	75% of the hourly averages (i.e. at least 18 hour values)
Annual mean	90% (1) of the one hour values or (if not available) 24–hour values over the year
(1) The requirements for the calculation of annual mean do not include losses of data due to the regular calibration or the normal maintenance of the instrumentation.	

B. Limit values

Averaging Period	Limit value	Margin of Tolerance	Date by which limit value is to be met
Sulphur dioxide			
One hour	350 μg/m³, not to be exceeded more than 24 times a calendar year	150 μg/m³ (43%)	—(1)
One day	125 μg/m³, not to be exceeded more than 3 times a calendar year	None	—(1)
Nitrogen dioxide			
One hour	200 μg/m³, not to be exceeded more than 18 times a calendar year	50% on 19 July 1999, decreasing on 1 January 2001 and every 12 months thereafter by equal annual percentages to reach 0% by 1 January 2010	1 January 2010
Calendar year	40 μg/m³	50% on 19 July 1999, decreasing on 1 January 2001 and every 12 months thereafter by equal annual percentages to reach 0% by 1 January 2010	1 January 2010
Benzene			
Calendar year	5 μg/m³	5 μg/m³ (100%) on 13 December 2000, decreasing on 1 January 2006 and every 12 months thereafter by 1 μg/m³ to reach 0% by 1 January 2010	1 January 2010

Carbon monoxide			
maximum daily eight hour mean (2)	10 mg/m^3	60%	—(1)
Lead			
Calendar year	$0,5 \text{ μg/m}^3$ (3)	100%	—(3)
PM_{10}			
One day	50 μg/m^3, not to be exceeded more than 35 times a calendar year	50%	—(1)
Calendar year	40 μg/m^3	20%	—(1)

(1) Already in force since 1 January 2005

(2) The maximum daily eight hour mean concentration will be selected by examining eight hour running averages, calculated from hourly data and updated each hour. Each eight hour average so calculated will be assigned to the day on which it ends i.e. the first calculation period for any one day will be the period from 17:00 on the previous day to 01:00 on that day; the last calculation period for any one day will be the period from 16:00 to 24:00 on that day.

(3) Already in force since 1 January 2005. Limit value to be met only by 1 January 2010 in the immediate vicinity of the specific industrial sources situated on sites contaminated by decades of industrial activities. In such cases, the limit value until 1 January 2010 will be $1,0 \text{ μg/m}^3$. The area in which higher limit values apply must not extend further than 1 000 m from such specific sources

ANNEX XII
INFORMATION AND ALERT THRESHOLDS

* * *

ANNEX XIII
CRITICAL LEVELS FOR THE PROTECTION OF VEGETATION

Averaging period	Critical level	Margin of tolerance
Sulphur dioxide		
Calendar year and winter (1 October to 31 March)	20 μg/m^3	None
Oxides of nitrogen		
Calendar year	$30 \text{ μg/m}^3 \text{ NO}_x$	None

ANNEX XIV
NATIONAL EXPOSURE REDUCTION TARGET, TARGET VALUE AND LIMIT VALUE FOR $PM_{2,5}$

A. Average exposure indicator

The Average Exposure Indicator expressed in μg/m^3 (AEI) shall be based upon measurements in urban background locations in zones and agglomerations throughout the territory of a Member State. It should be assessed as a three-calendar year running annual mean concentration averaged over all sampling points established pursuant to Section B of Annex V. The AEI for the reference year 2010 shall be the mean concentration of the years 2008, 2009 and 2010.

However, where data are not available for 2008, Member States may use the mean concentration of the years 2009 and 2010 or the mean concentration of the years 2009, 2010 and 2011. Member States making use of these possibilities shall communicate their decisions to the Commission by 11 September 2008.

The AEI for the year 2020 shall be the three-year running mean concentration averaged over all those sampling points for the years 2018, 2019 and 2020. The AEI is used for the examination whether the national exposure reduction target is met.

The AEI for the year 2015 shall be the three-year running mean concentration averaged over all those sampling points for the years 2013, 2014 and 2015. The AEI is used for the examination whether the exposure concentration obligation is met.

B. National exposure reduction target

Exposure reduction target relative to the AEI in 2010		Year by which the exposure reduction target should be met
Initial concentration in µg/m³	Reduction target in percent	2020
< 8,5 = 8,50	0%	
> 8,5—< 13	10%	
= 13—< 18	15%	
= 18—< 22	20%	
≥ 22	All appropriate measures to achieve 18 µg/m³	

Where the AEI in the reference year is 8,5 µg/m³ or less the exposure reduction target shall be zero. The reduction target shall be zero also in cases where the AEI reaches the level of 8,5 µg/m³ at any point of time during the period from 2010 to 2020 and is maintained at or below that level.

C. Exposure concentration obligation

Exposure concentration obligation	Year by which the obligation value is to be met
20 µg/m³	2015

D. Target value

Averaging period	Target value	Date by which target value should be met
Calendar year	25 µg/m³	1 January 2010

E. Limit value

Averaging period	Limit value	Margin of tolerance	Date by which limit value is to be met
STAGE 1			
Calendar year	25 µg/m³	20% on 11 June 2008, decreasing on the next 1 January and every 12 months thereafter by equal annual percentages to reach 0 %By 1 January 2015	1 January 2015
STAGE 2 (1)			

Calendar year	20 μg/m³		1 January 2020

(1) Stage 2—indicative limit value to be reviewed by the Commission in 2013 in the light of further information on health and environmental effects, technical feasibility and experience of the target value in Member States.

ANNEX XV
Information to be included in the local, regional or national air quality plans for improvement in ambient air quality

* * *

ANNEX XVI
PUBLIC INFORMATION

1. Member States shall ensure that up-to-date information on ambient concentrations of the pollutants covered by this Directive is routinely made available to the public.

2. Ambient concentrations provided shall be presented as average values according to the appropriate averaging period as laid down in Annex VII and Annexes XI to XIV. The information shall at least indicate any levels exceeding air quality objectives including limit values, target values, alert thresholds, information thresholds or long term objectives of the regulated pollutant. It shall also provide a short assessment in relation to the air quality objectives and appropriate information regarding effects on health, or, where appropriate, vegetation.

3. Information on ambient concentrations of sulphur dioxide, nitrogen dioxide, particulate matter (at least PM_{10}), ozone and carbon monoxide shall be updated on at least a daily basis, and, wherever practicable, information shall be updated on an hourly basis. Information on ambient concentrations of lead and benzene, presented as an average value for the last 12 months, shall be updated on a three-monthly basis, and on a monthly basis, wherever practicable.

4. Member States shall ensure that timely information about actual or predicted exceedances of alert thresholds, and any information threshold is provided to the public. Details supplied shall include at least the following information:

(a) information on observed exceedance(s):

— location or area of the exceedance,

— type of threshold exceeded (information or alert),

— start time and duration of the exceedance,

— highest one hour concentration and in addition highest eight hour mean concentration in the case of ozone;

(b) forecast for the following afternoon/day(s):

— geographical area of expected exceedances of information and/or alert threshold,

— expected changes in pollution (improvement, stabilisation or deterioration), together with the reasons for those changes;

(c) information on the type of population concerned, possible health effects and recommended behaviour:

— information on population groups at risk,

— description of likely symptoms,

— recommended precautions to be taken by the population concerned,

— where to find further information;

(d) information on preventive action to reduce pollution and/or exposure to it: indication of main source sectors; recommendations for action to reduce emissions;

(e) in the case of predicted exceedances, Member State shall take steps to ensure that such details are supplied to the extent practicable.

ANNEX XVII
CORRELATION TABLE

* * *

B. Climate Change

2.8 United Nations Framework Convention on Climate Change (Without Annexes I & II). Concluded at Rio de Janeiro, 9 May 1992. Entered into force, 21 March 1994. 1771 UNTS 107. *Reprinted in* 31 ILM 849 (1992) & 5 Weston & Carlson V.E.19

The Parties to this Convention,

Acknowledging that change in the Earth's climate and its adverse effects are a common concern of humankind,

Concerned that human activities have been substantially increasing the atmospheric concentrations of greenhouse gases, that these increases enhance the natural greenhouse effect, and that this will result on average in an additional warming of the Earth's surface and atmosphere and may adversely affect natural ecosystems and humankind,

Noting that the largest share of historical and current global emissions of greenhouse gases has originated in developed countries, that per capita emissions in developing countries are still relatively low and that the share of global emissions originating in developing countries will grow to meet their social and development needs,

Aware of the role and importance in terrestrial and marine ecosystems of sinks and reservoirs of greenhouse gases,

Noting that there are many uncertainties in predictions of climate change, particularly with regard to the timing, magnitude and regional patterns thereof,

Acknowledging that the global nature of climate change calls for the widest possible cooperation by all countries and their participation in an effective and appropriate international response, in accordance with their common but differentiated responsibilities and respective capabilities and their social and economic conditions,

Recalling the pertinent provisions of the Declaration of the United Nations Conference on the Human Environment, adopted at Stockholm on 16 June 1972,

Recalling also that States have, in accordance with the Charter of the United Nations and the principles of international law, the sovereign right to exploit their own resources pursuant to their own environmental and developmental policies, and the responsibility to ensure that activities within their jurisdiction or control do not cause damage to the environment of other States or of areas beyond the limits of national jurisdiction,

Reaffirming the principle of sovereignty of States in international cooperation to address climate change,

Recognizing that States should enact effective environmental legislation, that environmental standards, management objectives and priorities should reflect the environmental and developmental context to which they apply, and that standards applied by some countries may be inappropriate and of unwarranted economic and social cost to other countries, in particular developing countries,

Recalling the provisions of General Assembly resolution 44/228 of 22 December 1989 on the United Nations Conference on Environment and Development, and resolutions 43/53 of 6 December 1988, 44/207 of 22 December 1989, 45/212 of 21 December 1990 and 46/169 of 19 December 1991 on protection of global climate for present and future generations of mankind,

Recalling also the provisions of General Assembly resolution 44/206 of 22 December 1989 on the possible adverse effects of sealevel rise on islands and coastal areas, particularly low-lying coastal areas and the pertinent provisions of General Assembly resolution 44/172 of 19 December 1989 on the implementation of the Plan of Action to Combat Desertification,

Recalling further the Vienna Convention for the Protection of the Ozone Layer, 1985, and the Montreal Protocol on Substances that Deplete the Ozone Layer, 1987, as adjusted and amended on 29 June 1990,

Noting the Ministerial Declaration of the Second World Climate Conference adopted on 7 November 1990,

Conscious of the valuable analytical work being conducted by many States on climate change and of the important contributions of the World Meteorological Organization, the United Nations Environment Programme and other organs, organizations and bodies of the United Nations system, as well as other international and intergovernmental bodies, to the exchange of results of scientific research and the coordination of research,

Recognizing that steps required to understand and address climate change will be environmentally, socially and economically most effective if they are based on relevant scientific, technical and economic considerations and continually re-evaluated in the light of new findings in these areas,

Recognizing that various actions to address climate change can be justified economically in their own right and can also help in solving other environmental problems,

Recognizing also the need for developed countries to take immediate action in a flexible manner on the basis of clear priorities, as a first step towards comprehensive response strategies at the global, national and, where agreed, regional levels that take into account all greenhouse gases, with due consideration of their relative contributions to the enhancement of the greenhouse effect,

Recognizing further that low-lying and other small island countries, countries with low-lying coastal, arid and semi-arid areas or areas liable to floods, drought and desertification, and developing countries with fragile mountainous ecosystems are particularly vulnerable to the adverse effects of climate change,

Recognizing the special difficulties of those countries, especially developing countries, whose economies are particularly dependent on fossil fuel production, use and exportation, as a consequence of action taken on limiting greenhouse gas emissions,

Affirming that responses to climate change should be coordinated with social and economic development in an integrated manner with a view to avoiding adverse impacts on the latter, taking into full account the legitimate priority needs of developing countries for the achievement of sustained economic growth and the eradication of poverty,

Recognizing that all countries, especially developing countries, need access to resources required to achieve sustainable social and economic development and that, in order for developing countries to progress towards that goal, their energy consumption will need to grow taking into account the possibilities for achieving greater energy efficiency and for controlling greenhouse gas emissions in general, including through the application of new technologies on terms which make such an application economically and socially beneficial,

Determined to protect the climate system for present and future generations,

Have agreed as follows:

ARTICLE 1
DEFINITIONS

For the purposes of this Convention:

1. "Adverse effects of climate change" means changes in the physical environment or biota resulting from climate change which have significant deleterious effects on the composition, resilience or productivity of natural and managed ecosystems or on the operation of socio-economic systems or on human health and welfare.

2. "Climate change" means a change of climate which is attributed directly or indirectly to human activity that alters the composition of the global atmosphere and which is in addition to natural climate variability observed over comparable time periods.

3. "Climate system" means the totality of the atmosphere, hydrosphere, biosphere and geosphere and their interactions.

4. "Emissions" means the release of greenhouse gases and/or their precursors into the atmosphere over a specified area and period of time.

5. "Greenhouse gases" means those gaseous constituents of the atmosphere, both natural and anthropogenic, that absorb and re-emit infrared radiation.

6. "Regional economic integration organization" means an organization constituted by sovereign States of a given region which has competence in respect of matters governed by this Convention or its protocols and has been duly authorized, in accordance with its internal procedures, to sign, ratify, accept, approve or accede to the instruments concerned.

7. "Reservoir" means a component or components of the climate system where a greenhouse gas or a precursor of a greenhouse gas is stored.

8. "Sink" means any process, activity or mechanism which removes a greenhouse gas, an aerosol or a precursor of a greenhouse gas from the atmosphere.

9. "Source" means any process or activity which releases a greenhouse gas, an aerosol or a precursor of a greenhouse gas into the atmosphere.

ARTICLE 2
OBJECTIVE

The ultimate objective of this Convention and any related legal instruments that the Conference of the Parties may adopt is to achieve, in accordance with the relevant provisions of the Convention, stabilization of greenhouse gas concentrations in the atmosphere at a level that would prevent dangerous anthropogenic interference with the climate system. Such a level should be achieved within a time-frame sufficient to allow ecosystems to adapt naturally to climate change, to ensure that food production is not threatened and to enable economic development to proceed in a sustainable manner.

ARTICLE 3
PRINCIPLES

In their actions to achieve the objective of the Convention and to implement its provisions, the Parties shall be guided, *inter alia,* by the following:

1. The Parties should protect the climate system for the benefit of present and future generations of humankind, on the basis of equity and in accordance with their common but differentiated responsibilities and respective capabilities. Accordingly, the developed country Parties should take the lead in combating climate change and the adverse effects thereof.

2. The specific needs and special circumstances of developing country Parties, especially those that are particularly vulnerable to the adverse effects of climate change, and of those Parties, especially developing country Parties, that would have to bear a disproportionate or abnormal burden under the Convention, should be given full consideration.

3. The Parties should take precautionary measures to anticipate, prevent or minimize the causes of climate change and mitigate its adverse effects. Where there are threats of serious or irreversible damage, lack of full scientific certainty should not be used as a reason for postponing such measures, taking into account that policies and measures to deal with climate change should be cost-effective so as to ensure global benefits at the lowest possible cost. To achieve this, such policies and measures should take into account different socio-economic contexts, be comprehensive, cover all relevant sources, sinks and reservoirs of greenhouse gases and adaptation, and comprise all economic sectors. Efforts to address climate change may be carried out cooperatively by interested Parties.

4. The Parties have a right to, and should, promote sustainable development. Policies and measures to protect the climate system against human-induced change should be appropriate for the specific conditions of each Party and should be integrated with national development programmes, taking into account that economic development is essential for adopting measures to address climate change.

5. The Parties should cooperate to promote a supportive and open international economic system that would lead to sustainable economic growth and development in all Parties, particularly developing country Parties, thus enabling them better to address the problems of climate change. Measures taken to combat climate change, including unilateral ones, should not constitute a means of arbitrary or unjustifiable discrimination or a disguised restriction on international trade.

ARTICLE 4
COMMITMENTS

1. All Parties, taking into account their common but differentiated responsibilities and their specific national and regional development priorities, objectives and circumstances, shall:

(a) Develop, periodically update, publish and make available to the Conference of the Parties, in accordance with Article 12, national inventories of anthropogenic emissions by sources and removals by sinks of all greenhouse gases not controlled by the Montreal Protocol, using comparable methodologies to be agreed upon by the Conference of the Parties;

(b) Formulate, implement, publish and regularly update national and, where appropriate, regional programmes containing measures to mitigate climate change by addressing anthropogenic emissions by sources and removals by sinks of all greenhouse gases not controlled by the Montreal Protocol, and measures to facilitate adequate adaptation to climate change;

(c) Promote and cooperate in the development, application and diffusion, including transfer, of technologies, practices and processes that control, reduce or prevent anthropogenic emissions of greenhouse gases not controlled by the Montreal Protocol in all relevant sectors, including the energy, transport, industry, agriculture, forestry and waste management sectors;

(d) Promote sustainable management, and promote and cooperate in the conservation and enhancement, as appropriate, of sinks and reservoirs of all greenhouse gases not controlled by the Montreal Protocol, including biomass, forests and oceans as well as other terrestrial, coastal and marine ecosystems;

(e) Cooperate in preparing for adaptation to the impacts of climate change; develop and elaborate appropriate and integrated plans for coastal zone management, water resources and agriculture, and for the protection and rehabilitation of areas, particularly in Africa, affected by drought and desertification, as well as floods;

(f) Take climate change considerations into account, to the extent feasible, in their relevant social, economic and environmental policies and actions, and employ appropriate methods, for example impact assessments, formulated and determined nationally, with a view to minimizing adverse effects on the economy, on public health and on the quality of the environment, of projects or measures undertaken by them to mitigate or adapt to climate change;

(g) Promote and cooperate in scientific, technological, technical, socio-economic and other research, systematic observation and development of data archives related to the climate system and intended to further the understanding and to reduce or eliminate the remaining uncertainties regarding the causes, effects, magnitude and timing of climate change and the economic and social consequences of various response strategies;

(h) Promote and cooperate in the full, open and prompt exchange of relevant scientific, technological, technical, socio-economic and legal information related to the climate system and climate change, and to the economic and social consequences of various response strategies;

(i) Promote and cooperate in education, training and public awareness related to climate change and encourage the widest participation in this process, including that of non-governmental organizations; and

(j) Communicate to the Conference of the Parties information related to implementation, in accordance with Article 12.

2. The developed country Parties and other Parties included in annex I commit themselves specifically as provided for in the following:

(a) Each of these Parties shall adopt national policies and take corresponding measures on the mitigation of climate change, by limiting its anthropogenic emissions of greenhouse gases and protecting and enhancing its greenhouse gas sinks and reservoirs. These policies and measures will demonstrate that developed countries are taking the lead in modifying longer-term trends in anthropogenic emissions consistent with the objective of the Convention, recognizing that the return by the end of the present decade to earlier levels of anthropogenic emissions of carbon dioxide and other greenhouse gases not controlled by the Montreal Protocol would contribute to such modification, and taking into account the differences in these Parties' starting points and approaches, economic structures and resource bases, the need to maintain strong and sustainable economic growth, available technologies and other individual circumstances, as well as the need for equitable and appropriate contributions by each of these Parties to the global effort regarding that objective. These Parties may implement such policies and measures jointly with other Parties and may assist other Parties in contributing to the achievement of the objective of the Convention and, in particular, that of this subparagraph;

(b) In order to promote progress to this end, each of these Parties shall communicate, within six months of the entry into force of the Convention for it and periodically thereafter, and in accordance with Article 12, detailed information on its policies and measures referred to in subparagraph (a) above, as well as on its resulting projected anthropogenic emissions by sources and removals by sinks of greenhouse gases not controlled by the Montreal Protocol for the period referred to in subparagraph (a), with the aim of returning individually or jointly to their 1990 levels these anthropogenic emissions of carbon dioxide and other greenhouse gases not controlled by the Montreal Protocol. This information will be reviewed by the Conference of the Parties, at its first session and periodically thereafter, in accordance with Article 7;

(c) Calculations of emissions by sources and removals by sinks of greenhouse gases for the purposes of subparagraph (b) above should take into account the best available scientific knowledge, including the effective capacity of sinks and the respective contributions of such gases to climate change. The Conference of the Parties shall consider and agree on methodologies for these calculations at its first session and review them regularly thereafter;

(d) The Conference of the Parties shall, at its first session, review the adequacy of subparagraphs (a) and (b) above. Such review shall be carried out in the light of the best available scientific information and assessment on climate change and its impacts, as well as relevant technical, social and economic information. Based on this review, the Conference of the Parties shall take appropriate action, which may include the adoption of amendments to the commitments in subparagraphs (a) and (b) above. The Conference of the Parties, at its first session, shall also take decisions regarding criteria for joint implementation as indicated in subparagraph (a) above. A second review of subparagraphs (a) and (b) shall take place not later than 31 December 1998, and thereafter at regular intervals determined by the Conference of the Parties, until the objective of the Convention is met;

(e) Each of these Parties shall:

(i) coordinate as appropriate with other such Parties, relevant economic and administrative instruments developed to achieve the objective of the Convention; and

(ii) identify and periodically review its own policies and practices which encourage activities that lead to greater levels of anthropogenic emissions of greenhouse gases not controlled by the Montreal Protocol than would otherwise occur;

(f) The Conference of the Parties shall review, not later than 31 December 1998, available information with a view to taking decisions regarding such amendments to the lists in annexes I and II as may be appropriate, with the approval of the Party concerned;

(g) Any Party not included in annex I may, in its instrument of ratification, acceptance, approval or accession, or at any time thereafter, notify the Depositary that it intends to be bound by subparagraphs (a) and (b) above. The Depositary shall inform the other signatories and Parties of any such notification.

3. The developed country Parties and other developed Parties included in annex II shall provide new and additional financial resources to meet the agreed full costs incurred by developing country Parties in complying with their obligations under Article 12, paragraph 1. They shall also provide such financial resources, including for the transfer of technology, needed by the developing country Parties to meet the agreed full incremental costs of implementing measures that are covered by paragraph 1 of this Article and that are agreed between a developing country Party and the international entity or entities referred to in Article 11, in accordance with that Article. The implementation of these commitments shall take into account the need for adequacy and predictability in the flow of funds and the importance of appropriate burden sharing among the developed country Parties.

4. The developed country Parties and other developed Parties included in annex II shall also assist the developing country Parties that are particularly vulnerable to the adverse effects of climate change in meeting costs of adaptation to those adverse effects.

5. The developed country Parties and other developed Parties included in annex II shall take all practicable steps to promote, facilitate and finance, as appropriate, the transfer of, or access to, environmentally sound technologies and know-how to other Parties, particularly developing country Parties, to enable them to implement the provisions of the Convention. In this process, the developed country Parties shall support the development and enhancement of endogenous capacities and technologies of developing country Parties. Other Parties and organizations in a position to do so may also assist in facilitating the transfer of such technologies.

6. In the implementation of their commitments under paragraph 2 above, a certain degree of flexibility shall be allowed by the Conference of the Parties to the Parties included in annex I undergoing the process of transition to a market economy, in order to enhance the ability of these Parties to address climate change, including with regard to the historical level of anthropogenic emissions of greenhouse gases not controlled by the Montreal Protocol chosen as a reference.

7. The extent to which developing country Parties will effectively implement their commitments under the Convention will depend on the effective implementation by developed country Parties of their commitments under the Convention related to financial resources and transfer of technology and will take fully into account that economic and social development and poverty eradication are the first and overriding priorities of the developing country Parties.

8. In the implementation of the commitments in this Article, the Parties shall give full consideration to what actions are necessary under the Convention, including actions related to funding, insurance and the transfer of technology, to meet the specific needs and concerns of developing country Parties arising from the adverse effects of climate change and/or the impact of the implementation of response measures, especially on:

(a) Small island countries;

(b) Countries with low-lying coastal areas;

(c) Countries with arid and semi-arid areas, forested areas and areas liable to forest decay;

(d) Countries with areas prone to natural disasters;

(e) Countries with areas liable to drought and desertification;

(f) Countries with areas of high urban atmospheric pollution;

(g) Countries with areas with fragile ecosystems, including mountainous ecosystems;

(h) Countries whose economies are highly dependent on income generated from the production, processing and export, and/or on consumption of fossil fuels and associated energy-intensive products; and

(i) Land-locked and transit countries.

Further, the Conference of the Parties may take actions, as appropriate, with respect to this paragraph.

9. The Parties shall take full account of the specific needs and special situations of the least developed countries in their actions with regard to funding and transfer of technology.

10. The Parties shall, in accordance with Article 10, take into consideration in the implementation of the commitments of the Convention the situation of Parties, particularly developing country Parties, with economies that are vulnerable to the adverse effects of the implementation of measures to respond to climate change. This applies notably to Parties with economies that are highly dependent on income generated from the production, processing and export, and/or consumption of fossil fuels and associated energy-intensive products and/or the use of fossil fuels for which such Parties have serious difficulties in switching to alternatives.

ARTICLE 5
RESEARCH AND SYSTEMATIC OBSERVATION

In carrying out their commitments under Article 4, paragraph 1(g), the Parties shall:

(a) Support and further develop, as appropriate, international and intergovernmental programmes and networks or organizations aimed at defining, conducting, assessing and financing research, data collection and systematic observation, taking into account the need to minimize duplication of effort;

(b) Support international and intergovernmental efforts to strengthen systematic observation and national scientific and technical research capacities and capabilities, particularly in developing countries, and to promote access to, and the exchange of, data and analyses thereof obtained from areas beyond national jurisdiction; and

(c) Take into account the particular concerns and needs of developing countries and cooperate in improving their endogenous capacities and capabilities to participate in the efforts referred to in subparagraphs (a) and (b) above.

ARTICLE 6
EDUCATION, TRAINING AND PUBLIC AWARENESS

In carrying out their commitments under Article 4, paragraph 1(i), the Parties shall:

(a) Promote and facilitate at the national and, as appropriate, subregional and regional levels, and in accordance with national laws and regulations, and within their respective capacities:

(i) the development and implementation of educational and public awareness programmes on climate change and its effects;

(ii) public access to information on climate change and its effects;

(iii) public participation in addressing climate change and its effects and developing adequate responses; and

(iv) training of scientific, technical and managerial personnel.

(b) Cooperate in and promote, at the international level, and, where appropriate, using existing bodies:

(i) the development and exchange of educational and public awareness material on climate change and its effects; and

(ii) the development and implementation of education and training programmes, including the strengthening of national institutions and the exchange or secondment of personnel to train experts in this field, in particular for developing countries.

ARTICLE 7
CONFERENCE OF THE PARTIES

1. A Conference of the Parties is hereby established.

2. The Conference of the Parties, as the supreme body of this Convention, shall keep under regular review the implementation of the Convention and any related legal instruments that the Conference of the Parties may adopt, and shall make, within its mandate, the decisions necessary to promote the effective implementation of the Convention. To this end, it shall:

(a) Periodically examine the obligations of the Parties and the institutional arrangements under the Convention, in the light of the objective of the Convention, the experience gained in its implementation and the evolution of scientific and technological knowledge;

(b) Promote and facilitate the exchange of information on measures adopted by the Parties to address climate change and its effects, taking into account the differing circumstances, responsibilities and capabilities of the Parties and their respective commitments under the Convention;

(c) Facilitate, at the request of two or more Parties, the coordination of measures adopted by them to address climate change and its effects, taking into account the differing circumstances, responsibilities and capabilities of the Parties and their respective commitments under the Convention;

(d) Promote and guide, in accordance with the objective and provisions of the Convention, the development and periodic refinement of comparable methodologies, to be agreed on by the Conference of the Parties, *inter alia,* for preparing inventories of greenhouse gas emissions by sources and removals by sinks, and for evaluating the effectiveness of measures to limit the emissions and enhance the removals of these gases;

(e) Assess, on the basis of all information made available to it in accordance with the provisions of the Convention, the implementation of the Convention by the Parties, the overall effects of the measures taken pursuant to the Convention, in particular environmental, economic and social effects as well as their cumulative impacts and the extent to which progress towards the objective of the Convention is being achieved;

(f) Consider and adopt regular reports on the implementation of the Convention and ensure their publication;

(g) Make recommendations on any matters necessary for the implementation of the Convention;

(h) Seek to mobilize financial resources in accordance with Article 4, paragraphs 3, 4 and 5, and Article 11;

(i) Establish such subsidiary bodies as are deemed necessary for the implementation of the Convention;

(j) Review reports submitted by its subsidiary bodies and provide guidance to them;

(k) Agree upon and adopt, by consensus, rules of procedure and financial rules for itself and for any subsidiary bodies;

(*l*) Seek and utilize, where appropriate, the services and cooperation of, and information provided by, competent international organizations and intergovernmental and non-governmental bodies; and

(m) Exercise such other functions as are required for the achievement of the objective of the Convention as well as all other functions assigned to it under the Convention.

3.   The Conference of the Parties shall, at its first session, adopt its own rules of procedure as well as those of the subsidiary bodies established by the Convention, which shall include decision-making procedures for matters not already covered by decision-making procedures stipulated in the Convention. Such procedures may include specified majorities required for the adoption of particular decisions.

4.   The first session of the Conference of the Parties shall be convened by the interim secretariat referred to in Article 21 and shall take place not later than one year after the date of entry into force of the Convention. Thereafter, ordinary sessions of the Conference of the Parties shall be held every year unless otherwise decided by the Conference of the Parties.

5.   Extraordinary sessions of the Conference of the Parties shall be held at such other times as may be deemed necessary by the Conference, or at the written request of any Party, provided that, within six months of the request being communicated to the Parties by the secretariat, it is supported by at least one-third of the Parties.

6.   The United Nations, its specialized agencies and the International Atomic Energy Agency, as well as any State member thereof or observers thereto not Party to the Convention, may be represented at sessions of the Conference of the Parties as

observers. Any body or agency, whether national or international, governmental or non-governmental, which is qualified in matters covered by the Convention, and which has informed the secretariat of its wish to be represented at a session of the Conference of the Parties as an observer, may be so admitted unless at least one-third of the Parties present object. The admission and participation of observers shall be subject to the rules of procedure adopted by the Conference of the Parties.

ARTICLE 8
SECRETARIAT

1. A secretariat is hereby established.

2. The functions of the secretariat shall be:

(a) To make arrangements for sessions of the Conference of the Parties and its subsidiary bodies established under the Convention and to provide them with services as required;

(b) To compile and transmit reports submitted to it;

(c) To facilitate assistance to the Parties, particularly developing country Parties, on request, in the compilation and communication of information required in accordance with the provisions of the Convention;

(d) To prepare reports on its activities and present them to the Conference of the Parties;

(e) To ensure the necessary coordination with the secretariats of other relevant international bodies;

(f) To enter, under the overall guidance of the Conference of the Parties, into such administrative and contractual arrangements as may be required for the effective discharge of its functions; and

(g) To perform the other secretariat functions specified in the Convention and in any of its protocols and such other functions as may be determined by the Conference of the Parties.

3. The Conference of the Parties, at its first session, shall designate a permanent secretariat and make arrangements for its functioning.

ARTICLE 9
SUBSIDIARY BODY FOR SCIENTIFIC AND TECHNOLOGICAL ADVICE

1. A subsidiary body for scientific and technological advice is hereby established to provide the Conference of the Parties and, as appropriate, its other subsidiary bodies with timely information and advice on scientific and technological matters relating to the Convention. This body shall be open to participation by all Parties and shall be multidisciplinary. It shall comprise government representatives competent in the relevant field of expertise. It shall report regularly to the Conference of the Parties on all aspects of its work.

2. Under the guidance of the Conference of the Parties, and drawing upon existing competent international bodies, this body shall:

(a) Provide assessments of the state of scientific knowledge relating to climate change and its effects;

(b) Prepare scientific assessments on the effects of measures taken in the implementation of the Convention;

(c) Identify innovative, efficient and state-of-the-art technologies and know-how and advise on the ways and means of promoting development and/or transferring such technologies;

(d) Provide advice on scientific programmes, international cooperation in research and development related to climate change, as well as on ways and means of supporting endogenous capacity-building in developing countries; and

(e) Respond to scientific, technological and methodological questions that the Conference of the Parties and its subsidiary bodies may put to the body.

3.　The functions and terms of reference of this body may be further elaborated by the Conference of the Parties.

ARTICLE 10
SUBSIDIARY BODY FOR IMPLEMENTATION

1.　A subsidiary body for implementation is hereby established to assist the Conference of the Parties in the assessment and review of the effective implementation of the Convention. This body shall be open to participation by all Parties and comprise government representatives who are experts on matters related to climate change. It shall report regularly to the Conference of the Parties on all aspects of its work.

2.　Under the guidance of the Conference of the Parties, this body shall:

(a) Consider the information communicated in accordance with Article 12, paragraph 1, to assess the overall aggregated effect of the steps taken by the Parties in the light of the latest scientific assessments concerning climate change;

(b) Consider the information communicated in accordance with Article 12, paragraph 2, in order to assist the Conference of the Parties in carrying out the reviews required by Article 4, paragraph 2(d); and

(c) Assist the Conference of the Parties, as appropriate, in the preparation and implementation of its decisions.

ARTICLE 11
FINANCIAL MECHANISM

1.　A mechanism for the provision of financial resources on a grant or concessional basis, including for the transfer of technology, is hereby defined. It shall function under the guidance of and be accountable to the Conference of the Parties, which shall decide on its policies, programme priorities and eligibility criteria related to this Convention. Its operation shall be entrusted to one or more existing international entities.

2.　The financial mechanism shall have an equitable and balanced representation of all Parties within a transparent system of governance.

3.　The Conference of the Parties and the entity or entities entrusted with the operation of the financial mechanism shall agree upon arrangements to give effect to the above paragraphs, which shall include the following:

(a) Modalities to ensure that the funded projects to address climate change are in conformity with the policies, programme priorities and eligibility criteria established by the Conference of the Parties;

(b) Modalities by which a particular funding decision may be reconsidered in light of these policies, programme priorities and eligibility criteria;

(c) Provision by the entity or entities of regular reports to the Conference of the Parties on its funding operations, which is consistent with the requirement for accountability set out in paragraph 1 above; and

(d) Determination in a predictable and identifiable manner of the amount of funding necessary and available for the implementation of this Convention and the conditions under which that amount shall be periodically reviewed.

4.   The Conference of the Parties shall make arrangements to implement the above-mentioned provisions at its first session, reviewing and taking into account the interim arrangements referred to in Article 21, paragraph 3, and shall decide whether these interim arrangements shall be maintained. Within four years thereafter, the Conference of the Parties shall review the financial mechanism and take appropriate measures.

5.   The developed country Parties may also provide and developing country Parties avail themselves of, financial resources related to the implementation of the Convention through bilateral, regional and other multilateral channels.

ARTICLE 12
COMMUNICATION OF INFORMATION RELATED TO IMPLEMENTATION

1.   In accordance with Article 4, paragraph 1, each Party shall communicate to the Conference of the Parties, through the secretariat, the following elements of information:

(a) A national inventory of anthropogenic emissions by sources and removals by sinks of all greenhouse gases not controlled by the Montreal Protocol, to the extent its capacities permit, using comparable methodologies to be promoted and agreed upon by the Conference of the Parties;

(b) A general description of steps taken or envisaged by the Party to implement the Convention; and

(c) Any other information that the Party considers relevant to the achievement of the objective of the Convention and suitable for inclusion in its communication, including, if feasible, material relevant for calculations of global emission trends.

2.   Each developed country Party and each other Party included in annex I shall incorporate in its communication the following elements of information:

(a) A detailed description of the policies and measures that it has adopted to implement its commitment under Article 4, paragraphs 2(a) and 2(b); and

(b) A specific estimate of the effects that the policies and measures referred to in subparagraph (a) immediately above will have on anthropogenic emissions by its sources and removals by its sinks of greenhouse gases during the period referred to in Article 4, paragraph 2(a).

3.   In addition, each developed country Party and each other developed Party included in annex II shall incorporate details of measures taken in accordance with Article 4, paragraphs 3, 4 and 5.

4.   Developing country Parties may, on a voluntary basis, propose projects for financing, including specific technologies, materials, equipment, techniques or practices that would be needed to implement such projects, along with, if possible, an estimate of all incremental costs, of the reductions of emissions and increments of removals of greenhouse gases, as well as an estimate of the consequent benefits.

5.   Each developed country Party and each other Party included in annex I shall make its initial communication within six months of the entry into force of the Convention for that Party. Each Party not so listed shall make its initial communication within three years of the entry into force of the Convention for that Party, or of the availability of financial resources in accordance with Article 4, paragraph 3. Parties that are least developed countries may make their initial communication at their discretion. The frequency of subsequent communications by all Parties shall be determined by the Conference of the Parties, taking into account the differentiated timetable set by this paragraph.

6.   Information communicated by Parties under this Article shall be transmitted by the secretariat as soon as possible to the Conference of the Parties and to any

subsidiary bodies concerned. If necessary, the procedures for the communication of information may be further considered by the Conference of the Parties.

7.   From its first session, the Conference of the Parties shall arrange for the provision to developing country Parties of technical and financial support, on request, in compiling and communicating information under this Article, as well as in identifying the technical and financial needs associated with proposed projects and response measures under Article 4. Such support may be provided by other Parties, by competent international organizations and by the secretariat, as appropriate.

8.   Any group of Parties may, subject to guidelines adopted by the Conference of the Parties, and to prior notification to the Conference of the Parties, make a joint communication in fulfilment of their obligations under this Article, provided that such a communication includes information on the fulfilment by each of these Parties of its individual obligations under the Convention.

9.   Information received by the secretariat that is designated by a Party as confidential, in accordance with criteria to be established by the Conference of the Parties, shall be aggregated by the secretariat to protect its confidentiality before being made available to any of the bodies involved in the communication and review of information.

10.   Subject to paragraph 9 above, and without prejudice to the ability of any Party to make public its communication at any time, the secretariat shall make communications by Parties under this Article publicly available at the time they are submitted to the Conference of the Parties.

ARTICLE 13
RESOLUTION OF QUESTIONS REGARDING IMPLEMENTATION

The Conference of the Parties shall, at its first session, consider the establishment of a multilateral consultative process, available to Parties on their request, for the resolution of questions regarding the implementation of the Convention.

ARTICLE 14
SETTLEMENT OF DISPUTES

1.   In the event of a dispute between any two or more Parties concerning the interpretation or application of the Convention, the Parties concerned shall seek a settlement of the dispute through negotiation or any other peaceful means of their own choice.

2.   When ratifying, accepting, approving or acceding to the Convention, or at any time thereafter, a Party which is not a regional economic integration organization may declare in a written instrument submitted to the Depositary that, in respect of any dispute concerning the interpretation or application of the Convention, it recognizes as compulsory *ipso facto* and without special agreement, in relation to any Party accepting the same obligation:

(a) Submission of the dispute to the International Court of Justice, and/or

(b) Arbitration in accordance with procedures to be adopted by the Conference of the Parties as soon as practicable, in an annex on arbitration.

A Party which is a regional economic integration organization may make a declaration with like effect in relation to arbitration in accordance with the procedures referred to in subparagraph (b) above.

3.   A declaration made under paragraph 2 above shall remain in force until it expires in accordance with its terms or until three months after written notice of its revocation has been deposited with the Depositary.

4. A new declaration, a notice of revocation or the expiry of a declaration shall not in any way affect proceedings pending before the International Court of Justice or the arbitral tribunal, unless the parties to the dispute otherwise agree.

5. Subject to the operation of paragraph 2 above, if after twelve months following notification by one Party to another that a dispute exists between them, the Parties concerned have not been able to settle their dispute through the means mentioned in paragraph 1 above, the dispute shall be submitted, at the request of any of the parties to the dispute, to conciliation.

6. A conciliation commission shall be created upon the request of one of the parties to the dispute. The commission shall be composed of an equal number of members appointed by each party concerned and a chairman chosen jointly by the members appointed by each party. The commission shall render a recommendatory award, which the parties shall consider in good faith.

7. Additional procedures relating to conciliation shall be adopted by the Conference of the Parties, as soon as practicable, in an annex on conciliation.

8. The provisions of this Article shall apply to any related legal instrument which the Conference of the Parties may adopt, unless the instrument provides otherwise.

ARTICLE 15
AMENDMENTS TO THE CONVENTION

1. Any Party may propose amendments to the Convention.

2. Amendments to the Convention shall be adopted at an ordinary session of the Conference of the Parties. The text of any proposed amendment to the Convention shall be communicated to the Parties by the secretariat at least six months before the meeting at which it is proposed for adoption. The secretariat shall also communicate proposed amendments to the signatories to the Convention and, for information, to the Depositary.

3. The Parties shall make every effort to reach agreement on any proposed amendment to the Convention by consensus. If all efforts at consensus have been exhausted, and no agreement reached, the amendment shall as a last resort be adopted by a three-fourths majority vote of the Parties present and voting at the meeting. The adopted amendment shall be communicated by the secretariat to the Depositary, who shall circulate it to all Parties for their acceptance.

4. Instruments of acceptance in respect of an amendment shall be deposited with the Depositary. An amendment adopted in accordance with paragraph 3 above shall enter into force for those Parties having accepted it on the ninetieth day after the date of receipt by the Depositary of an instrument of acceptance by at least three-fourths of the Parties to the Convention.

5. The amendment shall enter into force for any other Party on the ninetieth day after the date on which that Party deposits with the Depositary its instrument of acceptance of the said amendment.

6. For the purposes of this Article, "Parties present and voting" means Parties present and casting an affirmative or negative vote.

ARTICLE 16
ADOPTION AND AMENDMENT OF ANNEXES TO THE CONVENTION

1. Annexes to the Convention shall form an integral part thereof and, unless otherwise expressly provided, a reference to the Convention constitutes at the same time a reference to any annexes thereto. Without prejudice to the provisions of Article 14, paragraphs 2(b) and 7, such annexes shall be restricted to lists, forms and any

other material of a descriptive nature that is of a scientific, technical, procedural or administrative character.

2. Annexes to the Convention shall be proposed and adopted in accordance with the procedure set forth in Article 15, paragraphs 2, 3, and 4.

3. An annex that has been adopted in accordance with paragraph 2 above shall enter into force for all Parties to the Convention six months after the date of the communication by the Depositary to such Parties of the adoption of the annex, except for those Parties that have notified the Depositary, in writing, within that period of their non-acceptance of the annex. The annex shall enter into force for Parties which withdraw their notification of non-acceptance on the ninetieth day after the date on which withdrawal of such notification has been received by the Depositary.

4. The proposal, adoption and entry into force of amendments to annexes to the Convention shall be subject to the same procedure as that for the proposal, adoption and entry into force of annexes to the Convention in accordance with paragraphs 2 and 3 above.

5. If the adoption of an annex or an amendment to an annex involves an amendment to the Convention, that annex or amendment to an annex shall not enter into force until such time as the amendment to the Convention enters into force.

ARTICLE 17
PROTOCOLS

1. The Conference of the Parties may, at any ordinary session, adopt protocols to the Convention.

2. The text of any proposed protocol shall be communicated to the Parties by the secretariat at least six months before such a session.

3. The requirements for the entry into force of any protocol shall be established by that instrument.

4. Only Parties to the Convention may be Parties to a protocol.

5. Decisions under any protocol shall be taken only by the Parties to the protocol concerned.

ARTICLE 18
RIGHT TO VOTE

1. Each Party to the Convention shall have one vote, except as provided for in paragraph 2 below.

2. Regional economic integration organizations, in matters within their competence, shall exercise their right to vote with a number of votes equal to the number of their member States that are Parties to the Convention. Such an organization shall not exercise its right to vote if any of its member States exercises its right, and vice versa.

ARTICLE 19
DEPOSITARY

The Secretary–General of the United Nations shall be the Depositary of the Convention and of protocols adopted in accordance with Article 17.

ARTICLE 20
SIGNATURE

This Convention shall be open for signature by States Members of the United Nations or of any of its specialized agencies or that are Parties to the Statute of the International Court of Justice and by regional economic integration organizations at

Rio de Janeiro, during the United Nations Conference on Environment and Development, and thereafter at United Nations Headquarters in New York from 20 June 1992 to 19 June 1993.

ARTICLE 21
INTERIM ARRANGEMENTS

1. The secretariat functions referred to in Article 8 will be carried out on an interim basis by the secretariat established by the General Assembly of the United Nations in its resolution 45/212 of 21 December 1990, until the completion of the first session of the Conference of the Parties.

2. The head of the interim secretariat referred to in paragraph 1 above will cooperate closely with the Intergovernmental Panel on Climate Change to ensure that the Panel can respond to the need for objective scientific and technical advice. Other relevant scientific bodies could also be consulted.

3. The Global Environment Facility of the United Nations Development Programme, the United Nations Environment Programme and the International Bank for Reconstruction and Development shall be the international entity entrusted with the operation of the financial mechanism referred to in Article 11 on an interim basis. In this connection, the Global Environment Facility should be appropriately restructured and its membership made universal to enable it to fulfil the requirements of Article 11.

ARTICLE 22
RATIFICATION, ACCEPTANCE, APPROVAL OR ACCESSION

1. The Convention shall be subject to ratification, acceptance, approval or accession by States and by regional economic integration organizations. It shall be open for accession from the day after the date on which the Convention is closed for signature. Instruments of ratification, acceptance, approval or accession shall be deposited with the Depositary.

2. Any regional economic integration organization which becomes a Party to the Convention without any of its member States being a Party shall be bound by all the obligations under the Convention. In the case of such organizations, one or more of whose member States is a Party to the Convention, the organization and its member States shall decide on their respective responsibilities for the performance of their obligations under the Convention. In such cases, the organization and the member States shall not be entitled to exercise rights under the Convention concurrently.

3. In their instruments of ratification, acceptance, approval or accession, regional economic integration organizations shall declare the extent of their competence with respect to the matters governed by the Convention. These organizations shall also inform the Depositary, who shall in turn inform the Parties, of any substantial modification in the extent of their competence.

ARTICLE 23
ENTRY INTO FORCE

1. The Convention shall enter into force on the ninetieth day after the date of deposit of the fiftieth instrument of ratification, acceptance, approval or accession.

2. For each State or regional economic integration organization that ratifies, accepts or approves the Convention or accedes thereto after the deposit of the fiftieth instrument of ratification, acceptance, approval or accession, the Convention shall enter into force on the ninetieth day after the date of deposit by such State or regional economic integration organization of its instrument of ratification, acceptance, approval or accession.

3.   For the purposes of paragraphs 1 and 2 above, any instrument deposited by a regional economic integration organization shall not be counted as additional to those deposited by States members of the organization.

ARTICLE 24
RESERVATIONS

No reservations may be made to the Convention.

ARTICLE 25
WITHDRAWAL

1.   At any time after three years from the date on which the Convention has entered into force for a Party, that Party may withdraw from the Convention by giving written notification to the Depositary.

2.   Any such withdrawal shall take effect upon expiry of one year from the date of receipt by the Depositary of the notification of withdrawal, or on such later date as may be specified in the notification of withdrawal.

3.   Any Party that withdraws from the Convention shall be considered as also having withdrawn from any protocol to which it is a Party.

ARTICLE 26
AUTHENTIC TEXTS

The original of this Convention, of which the Arabic, Chinese, English, French, Russian and Spanish texts are equally authentic, shall be deposited with the Secretary–General of the United Nations.

2.9 KYOTO PROTOCOL TO THE UNITED NATIONS FRAMEWORK CONVENTION ON CLIMATE CHANGE. **Done at Kyoto, Japan, 10 December 1997. Entered into force, 16 February 2005. 2303 UNTS 148;** *reprinted in* **37 ILM 32 (1998) & 5 Weston & Carlson V.E.20d**

The Parties to this Protocol,

Being Parties to the United Nations Framework Convention on Climate Change, hereinafter referred to as "the Convention",

In pursuit of the ultimate objective of the Convention as stated in its Article 2,

Recalling the provisions of the Convention,

Being guided by Article 3 of the Convention,

Pursuant to the Berlin Mandate adopted by decision 1/CP.1 of the Conference of the Parties to the Convention at its first session,

Have agreed as follows:

Article 1

For the purposes of this Protocol, the definitions contained in Article 1 of the Convention shall apply. In addition:

1. "Conference of the Parties" means the Conference of the Parties to the Convention.

2. "Convention" means the United Nations Framework Convention on Climate Change, adopted in New York on 9 May 1992.

3. "Intergovernmental Panel on Climate Change" means the Intergovernmental Panel on Climate Change established in 1988 jointly by the World Meteorological Organization and the United Nations Environment Programme.

4. "Montreal Protocol" means the Montreal Protocol on Substances that Deplete the Ozone Layer, adopted in Montreal on 16 September 1987 and as subsequently adjusted and amended.

5. "Parties present and voting" means Parties present and casting an affirmative or negative vote.

6. "Party" means, unless the context otherwise indicates, a Party to this Protocol.

7. "Party included in Annex I" means a Party included in Annex I to the Convention, as may be amended, or a Party which has made a notification under Article 4, paragraph 2(g), of the Convention.

Article 2

1. Each Party included in Annex I in achieving its quantified emission limitation and reduction commitments under Article 3, in order to promote sustainable development, shall:

(a) Implement and/or further elaborate policies and measures in accordance with its national circumstances, such as:

(i) Enhancement of energy efficiency in relevant sectors of the national economy;

(ii) Protection and enhancement of sinks and reservoirs of greenhouse gases not controlled by the Montreal Protocol, taking into account its commitments under relevant international environmental agreements; promotion of sustainable forest management practices, afforestation and—reforestation;

(iii) Promotion of sustainable forms of agriculture in light of climate change considerations;

(iv) Promotion, research, development and increased use of new and renewable forms of energy, of carbon dioxide sequestration technologies and of advanced and innovative environmentally sound technologies;

(v) Progressive reduction or phasing out of market imperfections, fiscal incentives, tax and duty exemptions and subsidies in all greenhouse gas emitting sectors that run counter to the objective of the Convention and apply market instruments;

(vi) Encouragement of appropriate reforms in relevant sectors aimed at promoting policies and measures which limit or reduce emissions of greenhouse gases not controlled by the Montreal Protocol;

(vii) Measures to limit and/or reduce emissions of greenhouse gases not controlled by the Montreal Protocol in the transport sector;

(viii) Limitation and/or reduction of methane through recovery and use in waste management, as well as in the production, transport and distribution of energy;

(b) Cooperate with other such Parties to enhance the individual and combined effectiveness of their policies and measures adopted under this Article, pursuant to Article 4, paragraph 2(e)(i), of the Convention. To this end, these Parties shall take steps to share their experience and exchange information on such policies and measures, including developing ways of improving their comparability, transparency and effectiveness. The Conference of the Parties serving as the meeting of the Parties to this Protocol shall, at its first session or as soon as practicable thereafter, consider ways to facilitate such cooperation, taking into account all relevant information.

2. The Parties included in Annex I shall pursue limitation or reduction of emissions of greenhouse gases not controlled by the Montreal Protocol from aviation and marine bunker fuels, working through the International Civil Aviation Organization and the International Maritime Organization, respectively.

3. The Parties included in Annex I shall strive to implement policies and measures under this Article in such a way as to minimize adverse effects, including the adverse effects of climate change, effects on international trade, and social, environmental and economic impacts on other Parties, especially developing country Parties and in particular those identified in Article 4, paragraphs 8 and 9 of the Convention, taking into account Article 3 of the Convention. The Conference of the Parties serving as the meeting of the Parties to this Protocol may take further action, as appropriate, to promote the implementation of the provisions of this paragraph.

4. The Conference of the Parties serving as the meeting of the Parties to this Protocol, if it decides that it would be beneficial to coordinate any of the policies and measures in paragraph 1(a) above, taking into account different national circumstances and potential effects, shall consider ways and means to elaborate the coordination of such policies and measures.

Article 3

1. The Parties included in Annex I shall, individually or jointly, ensure that their aggregate anthropogenic carbon dioxide equivalent emissions of the greenhouse gases listed in Annex A do not exceed their assigned amounts, calculated pursuant to their quantified emission limitation and reduction commitments inscribed in Annex B and in accordance with the provisions of this Article, with a view to reducing their overall emissions of such gases by at least 5 per cent below 1990 levels in the commitment period 2008 to 2012.

2. Each Party included in Annex I shall, by 2005, have made demonstrable progress in achieving its commitments under this Protocol.

3. The net changes in greenhouse gas emissions from sources and removals by sinks resulting from direct human-induced land use change and forestry activities, limited to afforestation, reforestation, and deforestation since 1990, measured as verifiable changes in stocks in each commitment period shall be used to meet the commitments in this Article of each Party included in Annex I. The greenhouse gas emissions from sources and removals by sinks associated with those activities shall be reported in a transparent and verifiable manner and reviewed in accordance with Articles 7 and 8.

4. Prior to the first session of the Conference of the Parties serving as the meeting of the Parties to this Protocol, each Party included in Annex I shall provide for consideration by the Subsidiary Body for Scientific and Technological Advice data to establish its level of carbon stocks in 1990 and to enable an estimate to be made of its changes in carbon stocks in subsequent years. The Conference of the Parties serving as the meeting of the Parties to this Protocol shall, at its first session or as soon as practicable thereafter, decide upon modalities, rules and guidelines as to how and which additional human-induced activities related to changes in greenhouse gas emissions and removals in the agricultural soil and land use change and forestry categories, shall be added to, or subtracted from, the assigned amount for Parties included in Annex I, taking into account uncertainties, transparency in reporting, verifiability, the methodological work of the Intergovernmental Panel on Climate Change, the advice provided by the Subsidiary Body for Scientific and Technological Advice in accordance with Article 5 and the decisions of the Conference of the Parties. Such a decision shall apply in the second and subsequent commitment periods. A Party may choose to apply such a decision on these additional human-induced activities for its first commitment period, provided that these activities have taken place since 1990.

5. The Parties included in Annex I undergoing the process of transition to a market economy whose base year or period was established pursuant to decision 9/CP.2 of the Conference of the Parties at its second session, shall use that base year or period for the implementation of their commitments under this Article. Any other Party included in Annex I undergoing the process of transition to a market economy which has not yet submitted its first national communication under Article 12 of the Convention may also notify the Conference of the Parties serving as the meeting of the Parties to this Protocol that it intends to use a historical base year or period other than 1990 for the implementation of its commitments under this Article. The Conference of the Parties serving as the meeting of the Parties to this Protocol shall decide on the acceptance of such notification.

6. Taking into account Article 4, paragraph 6, of the Convention, in the implementation of their commitments under this Protocol other than those in this Article, a certain degree of flexibility shall be allowed by the Conference of the Parties serving as the meeting of the Parties to this Protocol to the Parties included in Annex I undergoing the process of transition to a market economy.

7. In the first quantified emission limitation and reduction commitment period, from 2008 to 2012, the assigned amount for each Party included in Annex I shall be equal to the percentage inscribed for it in Annex B of its aggregate anthropogenic carbon dioxide equivalent emissions of the greenhouse gases listed in Annex A in 1990, or the base year or period determined in accordance with paragraph 5 above, multiplied by five. Those Parties included in Annex I for whom land use change and forestry constituted a net source of greenhouse gas emissions in 1990 shall include in their 1990 emissions base year or period the aggregate anthropogenic carbon dioxide equivalent emissions minus removals in 1990 from land use change for the purposes of calculating their assigned amount.

8.   Any Party included in Annex I may use 1995 as its base year for hydrofluorocarbons, perfluorocarbons and sulphur hexafluoride, for the purposes of the calculation
referred to in paragraph 7 above.

9.   Commitments for subsequent periods for Parties included in Annex I shall be
established in amendments to Annex B to this Protocol, which shall be adopted in
accordance with the provisions of Article 20, paragraph 7. The Conference of the
Parties serving as the meeting of the Parties to this Protocol shall initiate the
consideration of such commitments at least seven years before the end of the first
commitment period mentioned in paragraph 7 above.

10.   Any emission reduction units, or any part of an assigned amount, which a
Party acquires from another Party in accordance with the provisions of Article 6 and of
Article 16 bis shall be added to the assigned amount for that Party.

11.   Any emission reduction units, or any part of an assigned amount, which a
Party transfers to another Party in accordance with the provisions of Article 6 and of
Article 16 bis shall be subtracted from the assigned amount for that Party.

12.   Any certified emission reductions which a Party acquires from another Party
in accordance with the provisions of Article 12 shall be added to the assigned amount
for that Party.

13.   If the emissions of a Party included in Annex I during a commitment period
are less than its assigned amount under this Article, this difference shall, on request of
that Party, be added to the assigned amount for that Party for subsequent commitment periods.

14.   Each Party included in Annex I shall strive to implement the commitments
mentioned in paragraph 1 above in such a way as to minimize adverse social,
environmental and economic impacts on developing country Parties, particularly those
identified in Article 4, paragraphs 8 and 9, of the Convention. In line with relevant
decisions of the Conference of the Parties on the implementation of those paragraphs,
the Conference of the Parties serving as the meeting of the Parties to this Protocol
shall, at its first session, consider what actions are necessary to minimize the adverse
effects of climate change and/or the impacts of response measures on Parties referred
to in those paragraphs. Among the issues to be considered shall be the establishment
of funding, insurance and transfer of technology.

Article 4

1.   Any Parties included in Annex I that have agreed to jointly fulfil their
commitments under Article 3 shall be deemed to have met those commitments
provided that their total combined aggregate anthropogenic carbon dioxide equivalent
emissions of the greenhouse gases listed in Annex A do not exceed their assigned
amounts calculated pursuant to their quantified emission limitation and reduction
commitments inscribed in Annex B and in accordance with the provisions of Article 3.
The respective emission level allocated to each of the Parties to the agreement shall be
set out in that agreement.

2.   The Parties to any such agreement shall notify the secretariat of the terms of
the agreement on the date of deposit of their instruments of ratification, acceptance,
approval or accession. The secretariat shall in turn inform the Parties and signatories
to the Convention of the terms of the agreement.

3.   The agreement shall remain in operation for the duration of the commitment
period specified in Article 3, paragraph 7.

4.   If Parties acting jointly do so in the framework of, and together with, a
regional economic integration organization, any alteration in the composition of the
organization after adoption of this Protocol shall not affect existing commitments
under this Protocol. Any alteration in the composition of the organization shall only

apply for the purposes of those commitments under Article 3 that are adopted subsequent to that revision.

5. In the event of failure by the Parties to such an agreement to achieve their total combined level of emission reductions, each Party to such an agreement shall be responsible for its own level of emissions set out in the agreement.

6. If Parties acting jointly do so in the framework of, and together with, a regional economic integration organization which is itself a Party to this Protocol, each member State of that regional economic integration organization individually, and together with the regional economic integration organization acting in accordance with Article 23, shall, in the event of failure to achieve the total combined level of emission reductions, be responsible for its level of emissions as notified in accordance with this Article.

Article 5

1. Each Party included in Annex I shall have in place, no later than one year prior to the start of the first commitment period, a national system for the estimation of anthropogenic emissions by sources and removals by sinks of all greenhouse gases not controlled by the Montreal Protocol. Guidelines for such national systems, which shall incorporate the methodologies specified in paragraph 2 below, shall be decided upon by the Conference of the Parties serving as the meeting of the Parties to this Protocol at its first session.

2. Methodologies for estimating anthropogenic emissions by sources and removals by sinks of all greenhouse gases not controlled by the Montreal Protocol shall be those accepted by the Intergovernmental Panel on Climate Change and agreed upon by the Conference of the Parties at its third session. Where such methodologies are not used, appropriate adjustments shall be applied according to methodologies agreed upon by the Conference of the Parties serving as the meeting of the Parties to this Protocol at its first session. Based on the work of, inter alia, the Intergovernmental Panel on Climate Change and advice provided by the Subsidiary Body for Scientific and Technological Advice, the Conference of the Parties serving as the meeting of the Parties to this Protocol shall regularly review and, as appropriate, revise such methodologies and adjustments, taking fully into account any relevant decisions by the Conference of the Parties. Any revision to methodologies or adjustments shall be used only for the purposes of ascertaining compliance with commitments under Article 3 in respect of any commitment period adopted subsequent to that revision.

3. The global warming potentials used to calculate the carbon dioxide equivalence of anthropogenic emissions by sources and removals by sinks of greenhouse gases not controlled by the Montreal Protocol listed in Annex A shall be those accepted by the Intergovernmental Panel on Climate Change and agreed upon by the Conference of the Parties at its third session. Based on the work of, inter alia, the Intergovernmental Panel on Climate Change and advice provided by the Subsidiary Body for Scientific and Technological Advice, the Conference of the Parties serving as the meeting of the Parties to this Protocol shall regularly review and, as appropriate, revise the global warming potential of each such greenhouse gas, taking fully into account any relevant decisions by the Conference of the Parties. Any revision to a global warming potential shall apply only to those commitments under Article 3 in respect of any commitment period adopted subsequent to that revision.

Article 6

1. For the purpose of meeting its commitments under Article 3, any Party included in Annex I may transfer to, or acquire from, any other such Party emission reduction units resulting from projects aimed at reducing anthropogenic emissions by

sources or enhancing anthropogenic removals by sinks of greenhouse gases in any sector of the economy, provided that:

(a) Any such project has the approval of the Parties involved;

(b) Any such project provides a reduction in emissions by sources, or an enhancement of removals by sinks, that is additional to any that would otherwise occur;

(c) It does not acquire any emission reduction units if it is not in compliance with its obligations under Articles 5 and 7; and

(d) The acquisition of emission reduction units shall be supplemental to domestic actions for the purposes of meeting commitments under Article 3.

2. The Conference of the Parties serving as the meeting of the Parties to this Protocol may, at its first session or as soon as practicable thereafter, further elaborate guidelines for the implementation of this Article, including for verification and reporting.

3. A Party included in Annex I may authorize legal entities to participate, under its responsibility, in actions leading to the generation, transfer or acquisition under this Article of emission reduction units.

4. If a question of implementation by a Party included in Annex I of the requirements referred to in this paragraph is identified in accordance with the relevant provisions of Article 8, transfers and acquisitions of emission reduction units may continue to be made after the question has been identified, provided that any such units may not be used by a Party to meet its commitments under Article 3 until any issue of compliance is resolved.

Article 7

1. Each Party included in Annex I shall incorporate in its annual inventory of anthropogenic emissions by sources and removals by sinks of greenhouse gases not controlled by the Montreal Protocol, submitted in accordance with the relevant decisions of the Conference of the Parties, the necessary supplementary information for the purposes of ensuring compliance with Article 3, to be determined in accordance with paragraph 4 below.

2. Each Party included in Annex I shall incorporate in its national communication, submitted under Article 12 of the Convention, the supplementary information necessary to demonstrate compliance with its commitments under this Protocol, to be determined in accordance with paragraph 4 below.

3. Each Party included in Annex I shall submit the information required under paragraph 1 above annually, beginning with the first inventory due under the Convention for the first year of the commitment period after this Protocol has entered into force for it. Each such Party shall submit the information required under paragraph 2 above as part of the first national communication due under the Convention after this Protocol has entered into force for it and after the adoption of guidelines as provided for in paragraph 4 below. The frequency of subsequent submission of information required under this Article shall be determined by the Conference of the Parties serving as the meeting of the Parties to this Protocol, taking into account any timetable for the submission of national communications decided upon by the Conference of the Parties.

4. The Conference of the Parties serving as the meeting of the Parties to this Protocol shall adopt at its first session, and review periodically thereafter, guidelines for the preparation of the information required under this Article, taking into account guidelines for the preparation of national communications by Parties included in Annex I adopted by the Conference of the Parties. The Conference of the Parties

serving as the meeting of the Parties to this Protocol shall also, prior to the first commitment period, decide upon modalities for the accounting of assigned amounts.

Article 8

1. The information submitted under Article 7 by each Party included in Annex I shall be reviewed by expert review teams pursuant to the relevant decisions of the Conference of the Parties and in accordance with guidelines adopted for this purpose by the Conference of the Parties serving as the meeting of the Parties to this Protocol under paragraph 4 below. The information submitted under Article 7, paragraph 1, by each Party included in Annex I shall be reviewed as part of the annual compilation and accounting of emissions inventories and assigned amounts. Additionally, the information submitted under Article 7, paragraph 2, by each Party included in Annex I shall be reviewed as part of the review of communications.

2. Expert review teams shall be coordinated by the secretariat and shall be composed of experts selected from those nominated by Parties to the Convention and, as appropriate, by intergovernmental organizations, in accordance with guidance provided for this purpose by the Conference of the Parties.

3. The review process shall provide a thorough and comprehensive technical assessment of all aspects of the implementation by a Party of this Protocol. The expert review teams shall prepare a report to the Conference of the Parties serving as the meeting of the Parties to this Protocol, assessing the implementation of the commitments of the Party and identifying any potential problems in, and factors influencing, the fulfilment of commitments. Such reports shall be circulated by the secretariat to all Parties to the Convention. The secretariat shall list those questions of implementation indicated in such reports for further consideration by the Conference of the Parties serving as the meeting of the Parties to this Protocol.

4. The Conference of the Parties serving as the meeting of the Parties to this Protocol shall adopt at its first session, and review periodically thereafter, guidelines for the review of implementation by expert review teams taking into account the relevant decisions of the Conference of the Parties.

5. The Conference of the Parties serving as the meeting of the Parties to this Protocol shall, with the assistance of the Subsidiary Body for Implementation and, as appropriate, the Subsidiary Body for Scientific and Technological Advice, consider:

(a) The information submitted by the Parties under Article 7 and the reports of the expert reviews thereon conducted under this Article; and

(b) Those questions of implementation listed by the secretariat under paragraph 3 above, as well as any questions raised by Parties.

6. Pursuant to its consideration of the information referred to in paragraph 5 above, the Conference of the Parties serving as the meeting of the Parties to this Protocol shall take decisions on any matter required for the implementation of this Protocol.

Article 9

1. The Conference of the Parties serving as the meeting of the Parties to this Protocol shall periodically review this Protocol in the light of the best available scientific information and assessments on climate change and its impacts, as well as relevant technical, social and economic information. Such reviews shall be coordinated with pertinent reviews under the Convention, in particular those required by Article 4, paragraph 2(d), and Article 7, paragraph 2(a), of the Convention. Based on these reviews, the Conference of the Parties serving as the meeting of the Parties to this Protocol shall take appropriate action.

2.   The first review shall take place at the second session of the Conference of the Parties serving as the meeting of the Parties to this Protocol. Further reviews shall take place at regular intervals and in a timely manner.

Article 10

All Parties, taking into account their common but differentiated responsibilities and their specific national and regional development priorities, objectives and circumstances, without introducing any new commitments for Parties not included in Annex I, but reaffirming existing commitments in Article 4, paragraph 1, of the Convention, and continuing to advance the implementation of these commitments in order to achieve sustainable development, taking into account Article 4, paragraphs 3, 5 and 7, of the Convention, shall:

(a) Formulate, where relevant and to the extent possible, cost-effective national, and where appropriate regional programmes to improve the quality of local emission factors, activity data and/or models which reflect the socio-economic conditions of each Party for the preparation and periodic updating of national inventories of anthropogenic emissions by sources and removals by sinks of all greenhouse gases not controlled by the Montreal Protocol, using comparable methodologies to be agreed upon by the Conference of the Parties, and consistent with the guidelines for national communications adopted by the Conference of the Parties;

(b) Formulate, implement, publish and regularly update national and, where appropriate, regional programmes containing measures to mitigate climate change and measures to facilitate adequate adaptation to climate change:

(i) Such programmes would, inter alia, concern the energy, transport and industry sectors as well as agriculture, forestry and waste management. Furthermore, adaptation technologies and methods for improving spatial planning would improve adaptation to climate change; and

(ii) Parties included in Annex I shall submit information on action under this Protocol, including national programmes, according to the guidelines laid down in Article 8; and other Parties shall seek to include in their national communications, as appropriate, information on programmes which contain measures that the Party believes contribute to addressing climate change and its adverse impacts, including the abatement of increase in greenhouse gas emissions, and enhancement of and removals by sinks, capacity building and adaptation measures.

(c) Cooperate in the promotion of effective modalities for the development, application and diffusion of, and take all practicable steps to promote, facilitate and finance, as appropriate, the transfer of, or access to, environmentally sound technologies, know-how, practices and processes pertinent to climate change, in particular to developing countries, including the formulation of policies and programmes for the effective transfer of environmentally sound technologies that are publicly owned or in the public domain and the creation of an enabling environment for the private sector, to promote and enhance access to, and transfer of, environmentally sound technologies;

(d) Cooperate in scientific and technical research and promote the maintenance and the development of systematic observation systems and development of data archives to reduce uncertainties related to the climate system, the adverse impacts of climate change and the economic and social consequences of various response strategies, and promote the development and strengthening of endogenous capacities and capabilities to participate in international and intergovernmental efforts, programmes and networks on research and systematic observation, taking into account Article 5 of the Convention;

(e) Cooperate in and promote at the international level, and, where appropriate, using existing bodies, the development and implementation of education and training programmes, including the strengthening of national capacity building, in particular human and institutional capacities and the exchange or secondment of personnel to train experts in this field, in particular for developing countries, and facilitate at the national level public awareness and public access to information on climate change. Suitable modalities should be developed to implement these activities through the relevant bodies of the Convention taking into account Article 6 of the Convention;

(f) Include in their national communications information on programmes and activities undertaken pursuant to this Article in accordance with relevant decisions of the Conference of the Parties; and

(g) Give full consideration, in implementing the commitments in this Article, to Article 4, paragraph 8, of the Convention.

Article 11

1. In the implementation of Article 10, Parties shall take into account the provisions of Article 4, paragraphs 4, 5, 7, 8 and 9 of the Convention.

2. In the context of the implementation of Article 4, paragraph 1, of the Convention, in accordance with the provisions of Article 4, paragraph 3, and Article 11 of the Convention, and through the operating entity or entities of the financial mechanism of the Convention, the developed country Parties and other developed Parties included in Annex II to the Convention shall:

(a) Provide new and additional financial resources to meet the agreed full costs incurred by developing country Parties in advancing the implementation of existing commitments under Article 4, paragraph 1(a), of the Convention that are covered in Article 10, subparagraph (a); and

(b) Also provide such financial resources, including for the transfer of technology, needed by the developing country Parties to meet the agreed full incremental costs of advancing the implementation of existing commitments in Article 4, paragraph 1, of the Convention that are covered by Article 10 and that are agreed between a developing country Party and the international entity or entities referred to in Article 11 of the Convention, in accordance with that Article.

The implementation of these existing commitments shall take into account the need for adequacy and predictability in the flow of funds and the importance of appropriate burden sharing among developed country Parties. The guidance to the financial mechanism of the Convention in relevant decisions of the Conference of the Parties, including those agreed before the adoption of this Protocol, shall apply mutatis mutandis to the provisions of this paragraph.

3. The developed country Parties and other developed Parties in Annex II to the Convention may also provide, and developing country Parties avail themselves of, financial resources for the implementation of Article 10, through bilateral, regional and other multilateral channels.

Article 12

1. A clean development mechanism is hereby defined.

2. The purpose of the clean development mechanism shall be to assist Parties not included in Annex I in achieving sustainable development and in contributing to the ultimate objective of the Convention, and to assist Parties included in Annex I in achieving compliance with their quantified emission limitation and reduction commitments under Article 3.

3. Under the clean development mechanism:

(a) Parties not included in Annex I will benefit from project activities resulting in certified emission reductions; and

(b) Parties included in Annex I may use the certified emission reductions accruing from such project activities to contribute to compliance with part of their quantified emission limitation and reduction commitments under Article 3, as determined by the Conference of the Parties serving as the meeting of the Parties to this Protocol.

4. The clean development mechanism shall be subject to the authority and guidance of the Conference of the Parties serving as the meeting of the Parties to this Protocol and be supervised by an executive board of the clean development mechanism.

5. Emission reductions resulting from each project activity shall be certified by operational entities to be designated by the Conference of the Parties serving as the meeting of the Parties to this Protocol, on the basis of:

(a) Voluntary participation approved by each Party involved;

(b) Real, measurable, and long-term benefits related to the mitigation of climate change; and

(c) Reductions in emissions that are additional to any that would occur in the absence of the certified project activity.

6. The clean development mechanism shall assist in arranging funding of certified project activities as necessary.

7. The Conference of the Parties serving as the meeting of the Parties to this Protocol shall, at its first session, elaborate modalities and procedures with the objective of ensuring transparency, efficiency and accountability through independent auditing and verification of project activities.

8. The Conference of the Parties serving as the meeting of the Parties to this Protocol shall ensure that a share of the proceeds from certified project activities is used to cover administrative expenses as well as to assist developing country Parties that are particularly vulnerable to the adverse effects of climate change to meet the costs of adaptation.

9. Participation under the clean development mechanism, including in activities mentioned in paragraph 3(a) above and acquisition of certified emission reductions, may involve private and/or public entities, and is to be subject to whatever guidance may be provided by the executive board of the clean development mechanism.

10. Certified emission reductions obtained during the period from the year 2000 up to the beginning of the first commitment period can be used to assist in achieving compliance in the first commitment period.

Article 13

1. The Conference of the Parties, the supreme body of the Convention, shall serve as the meeting of the Parties to this Protocol.

2. Parties to the Convention that are not Parties to this Protocol may participate as observers in the proceedings of any session of the Conference of the Parties serving as the meeting of the Parties to this Protocol. When the Conference of the Parties serves as the meeting of the Parties to this Protocol, decisions under this Protocol shall be taken only by those that are Parties to it.

3. When the Conference of the Parties serves as the meeting of the Parties to this Protocol, any member of the Bureau of the Conference of the Parties representing a Party to the Convention but, at that time, not a Party to this Protocol, shall be substituted by an additional member to be elected by and from amongst the Parties to this Protocol.

4. The Conference of the Parties serving as the meeting of the Parties to this Protocol shall keep under regular review the implementation of this Protocol and shall make, within its mandate, the decisions necessary to promote its effective implementation. It shall perform the functions assigned to it by this Protocol and shall:

(a) Assess, on the basis of all information made available to it in accordance with the provisions of this Protocol, the implementation of this Protocol by the Parties, the overall effects of the measures taken pursuant to this Protocol, in particular environmental, economic and social effects as well as their cumulative impacts and the extent to which progress towards the objective of the Convention is being achieved;

(b) Periodically examine the obligations of the Parties under this Protocol, giving due consideration to any reviews required by Article 4, paragraph 2(d), and Article 7, paragraph 2, of the Convention, in the light of the objective of the Convention, the experience gained in its implementation and the evolution of scientific and technological knowledge, and in this respect consider and adopt regular reports on the implementation of this Protocol;

(c) Promote and facilitate the exchange of information on measures adopted by the Parties to address climate change and its effects, taking into account the differing circumstances, responsibilities and capabilities of the Parties and their respective commitments under this Protocol;

(d) Facilitate, at the request of two or more Parties, the coordination of measures adopted by them to address climate change and its effects, taking into account the differing circumstances, responsibilities and capabilities of the Parties and their respective commitments under this Protocol;

(e) Promote and guide, in accordance with the objective of the Convention and the provisions of this Protocol, and taking fully into account the relevant decisions by the Conference of the Parties, the development and periodic refinement of comparable methodologies for the effective implementation of this Protocol, to be agreed on by the Conference of the Parties serving as the meeting of the Parties to this Protocol;

(f) Make recommendations on any matters necessary for the implementation of this Protocol;

(g) Seek to mobilize additional financial resources in accordance with Article 11, paragraph 2;

(h) Establish such subsidiary bodies as are deemed necessary for the implementation of this Protocol;

(i) Seek and utilize, where appropriate, the services and cooperation of, and information provided by, competent international organizations and intergovernmental and non-governmental bodies; and

(j) Exercise such other functions as may be required for the implementation of this Protocol, and consider any assignment resulting from a decision by the Conference of the Parties.

5. The rules of procedure of the Conference of the Parties and financial procedures of the Convention shall be applied mutatis mutandis under this Protocol, except as may be otherwise decided by consensus by the Conference of the Parties serving as the meeting of the Parties to this Protocol.

6. The first session of the Conference of the Parties serving as the meeting of the Parties to this Protocol shall be convened by the secretariat in conjunction with the first session of the Conference of the Parties that is scheduled after the date of the entry into force of this Protocol. Subsequent ordinary sessions of the Conference of the Parties serving as the meeting of the Parties to this Protocol shall be held every year and in conjunction with ordinary sessions of the Conference of the Parties unless

otherwise decided by the Conference of the Parties serving as the meeting of the Parties to this Protocol.

7.   Extraordinary sessions of the Conference of the Parties serving as the meeting of the Parties to this Protocol shall be held at such other times as may be deemed necessary by the Conference of the Parties serving as the meeting of the Parties to this Protocol, or at the written request of any Party, provided that, within six months of the request being communicated to the Parties by the secretariat, it is supported by at least one third of the Parties.

8.   The United Nations, its specialized agencies and the International Atomic Energy Agency, as well as any State member thereof or observers thereto not party to the Convention, may be represented at sessions of the Conference of the Parties serving as the meeting of the Parties to this Protocol as observers. Any body or agency, whether national or international, governmental or non-governmental, which is qualified in matters covered by this Protocol and which has informed the secretariat of its wish to be represented at a session of the Conference of the Parties serving as the meeting of the Parties to this Protocol as an observer, may be so admitted unless at least one third of the Parties present object. The admission and participation of observers shall be subject to the rules of procedure, as referred to in paragraph 5 above.

Article 14

1.   The secretariat established by Article 8 of the Convention shall serve as the secretariat of this Protocol.

2.   Article 8, paragraph 2, of the Convention on the functions of the secretariat, and Article 8, paragraph 3, of the Convention on arrangements made for the functioning of the secretariat, shall apply mutatis mutandis to this Protocol. The secretariat shall, in addition, exercise the functions assigned to it under this Protocol.

Article 15

1.   The Subsidiary Body for Scientific and Technological Advice and the Subsidiary Body for Implementation established by Articles 9 and 10 of the Convention shall serve as, respectively, the Subsidiary Body for Scientific and Technological Advice and the Subsidiary Body for Implementation of this Protocol. The provisions relating to the functioning of these two bodies under the Convention shall apply mutatis mutandis to this Protocol. Sessions of the meetings of the Subsidiary Body for Scientific and Technological Advice and the Subsidiary Body for Implementation of this Protocol shall be held in conjunction with the meetings of, respectively, the Subsidiary Body for Scientific and Technological Advice and the Subsidiary Body for Implementation of the Convention.

2.   Parties to the Convention that are not Parties to this Protocol may participate as observers in the proceedings of any session of the subsidiary bodies. When the subsidiary bodies serve as the subsidiary bodies of this Protocol, decisions under this Protocol shall be taken only by the Parties to this Protocol.

3.   When the subsidiary bodies established by Articles 9 and 10 of the Convention exercise their functions with regard to matters concerning this Protocol, any member of the Bureaux of those subsidiary bodies representing a Party to the Convention but, at that time, not a party to this Protocol, shall be substituted by an additional member to be elected by and from amongst the Parties to this Protocol.

Article 16

The Conference of the Parties serving as the meeting of the Parties to this Protocol shall, as soon as practicable, consider the application to this Protocol of, and modify as appropriate, the multilateral consultative process referred to in Article 13 of the Convention, in the light of any relevant decisions that may be taken by the Conference of the Parties. Any multilateral consultative process that may be applied to this Protocol shall operate without prejudice to the procedures and mechanisms established in accordance with Article 17.

Article 17

The Conference of the Parties shall define the relevant principles, modalities, rules and guidelines, in particular for verification, reporting and accountability for emissions trading. The Parties included in Annex B may participate in emissions trading for the purposes of fulfilling their commitments under Article 3 of this Protocol. Any such trading shall be supplemental to domestic actions for the purpose of meeting quantified emission limitation and reduction commitments under that Article.

Article 18

The Conference of the Parties serving as the meeting of the Parties to this Protocol shall, at its first session, approve appropriate and effective procedures and mechanisms to determine and to address cases of non-compliance with the provisions of this Protocol, including through the development of an indicative list of consequences, taking into account the cause, type, degree and frequency of non-compliance. Any procedures and mechanisms under this Article entailing binding consequences shall be adopted by means of an amendment to this Protocol.

Article 19

The provisions of Article 14 of the Convention on settlement of disputes shall apply mutatis mutandis to this Protocol.

Article 20

1. Any Party may propose amendments to this Protocol.

2. Amendments to this Protocol shall be adopted at an ordinary session of the Conference of the Parties serving as the meeting of the Parties to this Protocol. The text of any proposed amendment to this Protocol shall be communicated to the Parties by the secretariat at least six months before the meeting at which it is proposed for adoption. The secretariat shall also communicate the text of any proposed amendments to the Parties and signatories to the Convention and, for information, to the Depositary.

3. The Parties shall make every effort to reach agreement on any proposed amendment to this Protocol by consensus. If all efforts at consensus have been exhausted, and no agreement reached, the amendment shall as a last resort be adopted by a three-fourths majority vote of the Parties present and voting at the meeting. The adopted amendment shall be communicated by the secretariat to the Depositary, who shall circulate it to all Parties for their acceptance.

4. Instruments of acceptance in respect of an amendment shall be deposited with the Depositary. An amendment adopted in accordance with paragraph 3 above shall enter into force for those Parties having accepted it on the ninetieth day after the date of receipt by the Depositary of an instrument of acceptance by at least three fourths of the Parties to this Protocol.

5. The amendment shall enter into force for any other Party on the ninetieth day after the date on which that Party deposits with the Depositary its instrument of acceptance of the said amendment.

Article 21

1. Annexes to this Protocol shall form an integral part thereof and, unless otherwise expressly provided, a reference to this Protocol constitutes at the same time

a reference to any annexes thereto. Any annexes adopted after the entry into force of this Protocol shall be restricted to lists, forms and any other material of a descriptive nature that is of a scientific, technical, procedural or administrative character.

2.   Any Party may make proposals for an annex to this Protocol and may propose amendments to annexes to this Protocol.

3.   Annexes to this Protocol and amendments to annexes to this Protocol shall be adopted at an ordinary session of the Conference of the Parties serving as the meeting of the Parties to this Protocol. The text of any proposed annex or amendment to an annex shall be communicated to the Parties by the secretariat at least six months before the meeting at which it is proposed for adoption. The secretariat shall also communicate the text of any proposed annex or amendment to an annex to the Parties and signatories to the Convention and, for information, to the Depositary.

4.   The Parties shall make every effort to reach agreement on any proposed annex or amendment to an annex by consensus. If all efforts at consensus have been exhausted, and no agreement reached, the annex or amendment to an annex shall as a last resort be adopted by a three-fourths majority vote of the Parties present and voting at the meeting. The adopted annex or amendment to an annex shall be communicated by the secretariat to the Depositary, who shall circulate it to all Parties for their acceptance.

5.   An annex, other than Annex A or B, that has been adopted or amended in accordance with paragraphs 3 and 4 above shall enter into force for all Parties to this Protocol six months after the date of the communication by the Depositary to such Parties of the adoption or amendment of the annex, except for those Parties that have notified the Depositary in writing within that period of their non-acceptance of the annex or amendment to the annex. The annex or amendment to an annex shall enter into force for Parties which withdraw their notification of non-acceptance on the ninetieth day after the date on which withdrawal of such notification has been received by the Depositary.

6.   If the adoption of an annex or an amendment to an annex involves an amendment to this Protocol, that annex or amendment to an annex shall not enter into force until such time as the amendment to this Protocol enters into force.

7.   Amendments to Annexes A and B to this Protocol shall be adopted and enter into force in accordance with the procedure set out in Article 19, provided that any amendments to Annex B shall be adopted only with the written consent of the Party concerned.

Article 22

1.   Each Party shall have one vote, except as provided for in paragraph 2 below.

2.   Regional economic integration organizations, in matters within their competence, shall exercise their right to vote with a number of votes equal to the number of their member States which are Parties to this Protocol. Such an organization shall not exercise its right to vote if any of its member States exercises its right, and vice versa.

Article 23

The Secretary–General of the United Nations shall be the Depositary of this Protocol.

Article 24

1.   This Protocol shall be open for signature and subject to ratification, acceptance or approval by States and regional economic integration organizations which are Parties to the Convention. It shall be open for signature at United Nations Headquarters in New York from 16 March 1998 to 15 March 1999. This Protocol shall be open

for accession from the day after the date on which it is closed for signature. Instruments of ratification, acceptance, approval or accession shall be deposited with the Depositary.

2. Any regional economic integration organization which becomes a Party to this Protocol without any of its member States being a Party shall be bound by all the obligations under this Protocol. In the case of such organizations, one or more of whose member States is a Party to this Protocol, the organization and its member States shall decide on their respective responsibilities for the performance of their obligations under this Protocol. In such cases, the organization and the member States shall not be entitled to exercise rights under this Protocol concurrently.

3. In their instruments of ratification, acceptance, approval or accession, regional economic integration organizations shall declare the extent of their competence with respect to the matters governed by this Protocol. These organizations shall also inform the Depositary, who shall in turn inform the Parties, of any substantial modification in the extent of their competence.

Article 25

1. This Protocol shall enter into force on the ninetieth day after the date on which not less than 55 Parties to the Convention, incorporating Parties included in Annex I which accounted in total for at least 55 per cent of the total carbon dioxide emissions for 1990 of the Parties included in Annex I, have deposited their instruments of ratification, acceptance, approval or accession.

2. For the purposes of this Article, "the total carbon dioxide emissions for 1990 of the Parties included in Annex I" means the amount communicated on or before the date of adoption of this Protocol by the Parties included in Annex I in their first national communications submitted in accordance with Article 12 of the Convention.

3. For each State or regional economic integration organization that ratifies, accepts or approves this Protocol or accedes thereto after the conditions set out in paragraph 1 above for the entry into force have been fulfilled, this Protocol shall enter into force on the ninetieth day following the date of deposit of its instrument of ratification, acceptance, approval or accession.

4. For the purposes of this Article, any instrument deposited by a regional economic integration organization shall not be counted as additional to those deposited by States members of the organization.

Article 26

No reservations may be made to this Protocol.

Article 27

1. At any time after three years from the date on which this Protocol has entered into force for a Party, that Party may withdraw from this Protocol by giving written notification to the Depositary.

2. Any such withdrawal shall take effect upon expiry of one year from the date of receipt by the Depositary of the notification of withdrawal, or on such later date as may be specified in the notification of withdrawal.

3. Any Party that withdraws from the Convention shall be considered as also having withdrawn from this Protocol.

Article 28

The original of this Protocol, of which the Arabic, Chinese, English, French, Russian and Spanish texts are equally authentic, shall be deposited with the Secretary–General of the United Nations.

Done at Kyoto this tenth day of December one thousand nine hundred and ninety-seven.

Annex A

Greenhouse gases

Carbon dioxide (CO sub2)
Methane (CH sub4)
Nitrous oxide (N sub2 O)
Hydrofluorocarbons (HFCs)
Perfluorocarbons (PFCs)
Sulphur hexafluoride (SF sub6)

Sectors/source categories

Energy

Fuel combustion
Energy industries
Manufacturing industries and construction
Transport
Other sectors
Other
Fugitive emissions from fuels
Solid fuels
Oil and natural gas
Other

Industrial processes

Mineral products

Chemical industry
Metal production
Other production
Production of halocarbons and sulphur hexafluoride
Consumption of halocarbons and sulphur hexafluoride
Other

Solvent and other product use

Agriculture

Enteric fermentation
Manure management
Rice cultivation
Agricultural soils
Prescribed burning of savannas
Field burning of agricultural residues
Other

Waste

Solid waste disposal on land
Wastewater handling
Waste incineration
Other

Annex B[b]

Party	Quantified emission limitation or reduction commitment (percentage of base year or period)
Australia	108
Austria	92
Belgium	92
Bulgaria	92
Canada	94
Croatia	95
Czech Republic	92
Denmark	92
Estonia	92
European Community	92
Finland	92
France	92
Germany	92
Greece	92
Hungary	94
Iceland	110
Ireland	92
Italy	92
Japan	94
Latvia	92
Liechtenstein	92
Lithuania	92
Luxembourg	92
Monaco	92
Netherlands	92
New Zealand	100
Norway	101
Poland	94
Portugal	92
Romania	92
Russian Federation	100
Slovakia	92
Slovenia	92
Spain	92
Sweden	92

b. An amendment to Annex B was adopted at the Second Meeting of the Parties to the Montreal Protocol in Nairobi on 17 November 2006. The amendment is not yet in force and is not reflected here.

Switzerland	92	United States of America	93
Ukraine	100		
United Kingdom	92		

2.10 MALÉ DECLARATION ON THE HUMAN DIMENSION OF GLOBAL CLIMATE CHANGE. **Adopted at the Conference of the Alliance of Small Island States on Preparing for Bali and Beyond: The Human Dimension of Global Climate Change, at Malé, Republic of Maldives, on 14 November 2007**

We the representatives of the Small Island Developing States having met in Male' from 13 to 14 November 2007,

Aware that the environment provides the infrastructure for human civilization and that life depends on the uninterrupted functioning of natural systems;

Accepting the conclusions of the WMO/UNEP Intergovernmental Panel on Climate Change (IPCC) including, *inter alia*, that climate change is unequivocal and accelerating, and that mitigation of emissions and adaptation to climate change impacts is physically and economically feasible if urgent action is taken;

Persuaded that the impacts of climate change pose the most immediate, fundamental and far-reaching threat to the environment, individuals and communities around the planet, and that these impacts have been observed to be intensifying in frequency and magnitude;

Emphasizing that small island, low-lying coastal, and atoll states are particularly vulnerable to even small changes to the global climate and are already adversely affected by alterations in ecosystems, changes in precipitation, rising sea-levels and increased incidence of natural disasters;

Convinced that immediate and effective action to mitigate and adapt to climate change presents the greatest opportunity to preserve the prospects for future prosperity, and that further delay risks irreparable harm and jeopardizes sustainable development;

Reaffirming the United Nations Charter and the Universal Declaration of Human Rights;

Recalling the relevant provisions of declarations, resolutions and programmes of action adopted by major United Nations conferences, summits and special sessions and their follow-up meetings, in particular the Declaration of the United Nations Conference on the Human Environment of 1972 (Stockholm Declaration), the 1992 Rio Declaration on Environment and Development and Agenda 21, and the 2002 Johannesburg Declaration on Sustainable Development and Plan of Implementation of the World Summit on Sustainable Development;

Noting that the fundamental right to an environment capable of supporting human society and the full enjoyment of human rights is recognized, in varying formulations, in the constitutions of over one hundred states and directly or indirectly in several international instruments;

Recognizing the leadership of the Alliance of Small Island States in promoting and organizing international responses to climate change for the benefit of their citizens and humanity through *inter alia* the Male' Declaration on Sea Level Rises, the Barbados Programme of Action, and the Mauritius Strategy;

Acknowledging the United Nations Framework Convention on Climate Change(UNFCCC) and its Kyoto Protocol as important initial multilateral efforts to address climate change through global legal instruments, and the primacy of the United Nations process as the means to address climate change;

Anticipating the publication of the United Nations Development Programme's(UNDP) Human Development Report and the meeting of Commonwealth Heads of Government in Uganda, both of which will emphasise the human aspects of sustainable development;

Concerned that climate change has clear and immediate implications for the full enjoyment of human rights including *inter alia* the right to life, the right to take part in cultural life, the right to use and enjoy property, the right to an adequate standard of living, the right to food, and the right to the highest attainable standard of physical and mental health;

Do solemnly request:

1. The international community to commit in Bali to a formal process that will ensure a post–2012 consensus to protect people, planet and prosperity by taking urgent action to stabilize the global climate and ensure that temperature rises fall well below 2°C above pre-industrial averages, and that greenhouse gas concentrations are less than 450ppm, consistent with the principles of common but differentiated responsibilities.

2. The members of AOSIS in New York to consider including the human dimension of global climate change as one of the agenda items for the meeting of AOSIS Ministers in Bali, and to explore possible alternatives for advancing this initiative in Bali in order to stress the moral and ethical imperatives for action;.

3. The Conference of the Parties of the United Nations Framework Convention on Climate Change, with the help of the Secretariat, under article 7.2(*l*), to seek the cooperation of the Office of the United Nations High Commissioner for Human Rights and the United Nations Human Rights Council in assessing the human rights implications of climate change.

4. The Office of the United Nations High Commissioner for Human Rights to conduct a detailed study into the effects of climate change on the full enjoyment of human rights, which includes relevant conclusions and recommendations thereon, to be submitted prior to the tenth session of the Human Rights Council.

5. The United Nations Human Rights Council to convene, in March 2009, a debate on human rights and climate change.

Committed to an inclusive process that puts people, their prosperity, homes, survival and rights at the centre of the climate change debate, other AOSIS members not present in Male' are invited to endorse this Declaration.

2.11 COPENHAGEN ACCORD. **Adopted 18 December 2009. Report of the UNFCCC Conference of the Parties on its 15th Sess., 7 to 19 December 2009; FCCC/CP/2009/11/Add.1 at 5 (2010)**

The Heads of State, Heads of Government, Ministers, and other heads of the following delegations present at the United Nations Climate Change Conference 2009 in Copenhagen:1Albania, Algeria, Armenia, Australia, Austria, Bahamas, Bangladesh, Belarus, Belgium, Benin, Bhutan, Bosnia and Herzegovina, Botswana, Brazil, Bulgaria, Burkina Faso, Cambodia, Canada, Central African Republic, Chile, China, Colombia, Congo, Costa Rica, Côte d'Ivoire, Croatia, Cyprus, Czech Republic, Democratic Republic of the Congo, Denmark, Djibouti, Eritrea, Estonia, Ethiopia, European Union, Fiji, Finland, France, Gabon, Georgia, Germany, Ghana, Greece, Guatemala, Guinea, Guyana, Hungary, Iceland, India, Indonesia, Ireland, Israel, Italy, Japan, Jordan, Kazakhstan, Kiribati, Lao People's Democratic Republic, Latvia, Lesotho, Liechtenstein, Lithuania, Luxembourg, Madagascar, Malawi, Maldives, Mali, Malta, Marshall Islands, Mauritania, Mexico, Monaco, Mongolia, Montenegro, Morocco, Namibia, Nepal, Netherlands, New Zealand, Norway, Palau, Panama, Papua New Guinea, Peru, Poland, Portugal, Republic of Korea, Republic of Moldova, Romania, Russian Federation, Rwanda, Samoa, San Marino, Senegal, Serbia, Sierra Leone, Singapore, Slovakia, Slovenia, South Africa, Spain, Swaziland, Sweden, Switzerland, the former Yugoslav Republic of Macedonia, Tonga, Trinidad and Tobago, Tunisia, United Arab Emirates, United Kingdom of Great Britain and Northern Ireland, United Republic of Tanzania, United States of America, Uruguay and Zambia,

In pursuit of the ultimate objective of the Convention as stated in its Article 2,

Being guided by the principles and provisions of the Convention,

Noting the results of work done by the two Ad hoc Working Groups,

Endorsing decision 1/CP.15 on the Ad hoc Working Group on Long-term Cooperative Action and decision 1/CMP.5 that requests the Ad hoc Working Group on Further Commitments of Annex I Parties under the Kyoto Protocol to continue its work,

Have agreed on this Copenhagen Accord which is operational immediately.

1.   We underline that climate change is one of the greatest challenges of our time. We emphasise our strong political will to urgently combat climate change in accordance with the principle of common but differentiated responsibilities and respective capabilities. To achieve the ultimate objective of the Convention to stabilize greenhouse gas concentration in the atmosphere at a level that would prevent dangerous anthropogenic interference with the climate system, we shall, recognizing the scientific view that the increase in global temperature should be below 2 degrees Celsius, on the basis of equity and in the context of sustainable development, enhance our long-term cooperative action to combat climate change. We recognize the critical impacts of climate change and the potential impacts of response measures on countries particularly vulnerable to its adverse effects and stress the need to establish a comprehensive adaptation programme including international support.

2.   We agree that deep cuts in global emissions are required according to science, and as documented by the IPCC Fourth Assessment Report with a view to reduce global emissions so as to hold the increase in global temperature below 2 degrees Celsius, and take action to meet this objective consistent with science and on the basis of equity. We should cooperate in achieving the peaking of global and national emissions as soon as possible, recognizing that the time frame for peaking will be longer in developing countries and bearing in mind that social and economic development and poverty eradication are the first and overriding priorities of developing countries and that a low-emission development strategy is indispensable to sustainable development.

3. Adaptation to the adverse effects of climate change and the potential impacts of response measures is a challenge faced by all countries. Enhanced action and international cooperation on adaptation is urgently required to ensure the implementation of the Convention by enabling and supporting the implementation of adaptation actions aimed at reducing vulnerability and building resilience in developing countries, especially in those that are particularly vulnerable, especially least developed countries, small island developing States and Africa. We agree that developed countries shall provide adequate, predictable and sustainable financial resources, technology and capacity-building to support the implementation of adaptation action in developing countries.

4. Annex I Parties commit to implement individually or jointly the quantified economywide emissions targets for 2020, to be submitted in the format given in Appendix I by Annex I Parties to the secretariat by 31 January 2010 for compilation in an INF document. Annex I Parties that are Party to the Kyoto Protocol will thereby further strengthen the emissions reductions initiated by the Kyoto Protocol. Delivery of reductions and financing by developed countries will be measured, reported and verified in accordance with existing and any further guidelines adopted by the Conference of the Parties, and will ensure that accounting of such targets and finance is rigorous, robust and transparent.

5. Non–Annex I Parties to the Convention will implement mitigation actions, including those to be submitted to the secretariat by non-Annex I Parties in the format given in Appendix II by 31 January 2010, for compilation in an INF document, consistent with Article 4.1 and Article 4.7 and in the context of sustainable development. Least developed countries and small island developing States may undertake actions voluntarily and on the basis of support. Mitigation actions subsequently taken and envisaged by Non–Annex I Parties, including national inventory reports, shall be communicated through national communications consistent with Article 12.1(b) every two years on the basis of guidelines to be adopted by the Conference of the Parties. Those mitigation actions in national communications or otherwise communicated to the Secretariat will be added to the list in appendix II. Mitigation actions taken by Non–Annex I Parties will be subject to their domestic measurement, reporting and verification the result of which will be reported through their national communications every two years. Non–Annex I Parties will communicate information on the implementation of their actions through National Communications, with provisions for international consultations and analysis under clearly defined guidelines that will ensure that national sovereignty is respected. Nationally appropriate mitigation actions seeking international support will be recorded in a registry along with relevant technology, finance and capacity building support. Those actions supported will be added to the list in appendix II. These supported nationally appropriate mitigation actions will be subject to international measurement, reporting and verification in accordance with guidelines adopted by the Conference of the Parties.

6. We recognize the crucial role of reducing emission from deforestation and forest degradation and the need to enhance removals of greenhouse gas emission by forests and agree on the need to provide positive incentives to such actions through the immediate establishment of a mechanism including REDD-plus, to enable the mobilization of financial resources from developed countries.

7. We decide to pursue various approaches, including opportunities to use markets, to enhance the cost-effectiveness of, and to promote mitigation actions. Developing countries, especially those with low emitting economies should be provided incentives to continue to develop on a low emission pathway.

8. Scaled up, new and additional, predictable and adequate funding as well as improved access shall be provided to developing countries, in accordance with the relevant provisions of the Convention, to enable and support enhanced action on

mitigation, including substantial finance to reduce emissions from deforestation and forest degradation (REDD-plus), adaptation, technology development and transfer and capacity-building, for enhanced implementation of the Convention. The collective commitment by developed countries is to provide new and additional resources, including forestry and investments through international institutions, approaching USD 30 billion for the period 2010–2012 with balanced allocation between adaptation and mitigation. Funding for adaptation will be prioritized for the most vulnerable developing countries, such as the least developed countries, small island developing States and Africa. In the context of meaningful mitigation actions and transparency on implementation, developed countries commit to a goal of mobilizing jointly USD 100 billion dollars a year by 2020 to address the needs of developing countries. This funding will come from a wide variety of sources, public and private, bilateral and multilateral, including alternative sources of finance. New multilateral funding for adaptation will be delivered through effective and efficient fund arrangements, with a governance structure providing for equal representation of developed and developing countries. A significant portion of such funding should flow through the Copenhagen Green Climate Fund.

9. To this end, a High Level Panel will be established under the guidance of and accountable to the Conference of the Parties to study the contribution of the potential sources of revenue, including alternative sources of finance, towards meeting this goal.

10. We decide that the Copenhagen Green Climate Fund shall be established as an operating entity of the financial mechanism of the Convention to support projects, programme, policies and other activities in developing countries related to mitigation including REDD-plus, adaptation, capacitybuilding, technology development and transfer.

11. In order to enhance action on development and transfer of technology we decide to establish a Technology Mechanism to accelerate technology development and transfer in support of action on adaptation and mitigation that will be guided by a country-driven approach and be based on national circumstances and priorities.

12. We call for an assessment of the implementation of this Accord to be completed by 2015, including in light of the Convention's ultimate objective. This would include consideration of strengthening the long-term goal referencing various matters presented by the science, including in relation to temperature rises of 1.5 degrees Celsius.

C. Ozone Depletion

2.12 Vienna Convention for the Protection of the Ozone Layer (With Annexes I & II).[c] Concluded at Vienna, 22 March 1985. Entered into force, 22 September 1988. 1513 UNTS 293; *reprinted in* 26 ILM 1529 (1987) & 5 Weston & Carlson V.E.5

Article 1
Definitions

For the purposes of this Convention:

1. 'The ozone layer' means the layer of atmospheric ozone above the planetary boundary layer.

2. 'Adverse effects' means changes in the physical environment or biota, including changes in climate, which have significant deleterious effects on human health or on the composition, resilience and productivity of natural and managed ecosystems, or on materials useful to mankind.

3. 'Alternative technologies or equipment' means technologies or equipment the use of which makes it possible to reduce or effectively eliminate emissions of substances which have or are likely to have adverse effects on the ozone layer.

4. 'Alternative substances' means substances which reduce, eliminate or avoid adverse effects on the ozone layer.

5. 'Parties' means, unless the text otherwise indicates, Parties to this Convention.

6. 'Regional economic integration organization' means an organization constituted by sovereign States of a given region which has competence in respect of matters governed by this Convention or its protocols and has been duly authorized, in accordance with its internal procedures, to sign, ratify, accept, approve or accede to the instruments concerned.

7. 'Protocols' means protocols to this Convention.

Article 2
General Obligations

1. The Parties shall take appropriate measures in accordance with the provisions of this Convention and of those protocols in force to which they are party to protect human health and the environment against adverse effects resulting or likely to result from human activities which modify or are likely to modify the ozone layer.

2. To this end the Parties shall, in accordance with the means at their disposal and their capabilities:

(a) Co-operate by means of systematic observations, research and information exchange in order to better understand and assess the effects of human activities on the ozone layer and the effects on human health and the environment from modification of the ozone layer;

(b) Adopt appropriate legislative or administrative measures and co-operate in harmonizing appropriate policies to control, limit, reduce or prevent human activities under their jurisdiction or control should it be found that these activities have or are likely to have adverse effects resulting from modification or likely modification of the ozone layer;

c. *See also* Basic Document 2.13, *infra*.

(c) Co-operate in the formulation of agreed measures, procedures and standards for the implementation of this Convention, with a view to the adoption of protocols and annexes;

(d) Co-operate with competent international bodies to implement effectively this Convention and protocols to which they are party.

3.   The provisions of this Convention shall in no way affect the right of Parties to adopt, in accordance with international law, domestic measures additional to those referred to in paragraphs 1 and 2 above, nor shall they affect additional domestic measures already taken by a Party, provided that these measures are not incompatible with their obligations under this Convention.

4.   The application of this article shall be based on relevant scientific and technical considerations.

Article 3
Research and Systematic Observations

1.   The Parties undertake, as appropriate, to initiate and co-operate in, directly or through competent international bodies, the conduct of research and scientific assessments on:

(a) The physical and chemical processes that may affect the ozone layer;

(b) The human health and other biological effects deriving from any modifications of the ozone layer, particularly those resulting from changes in ultra-violet solar radiation having biological effects (UV–B);

(c) Climatic effects deriving from any modifications of the ozone layer;

(d) Effects deriving from any modifications of the ozone layer and any consequent change in UV–B radiation on natural and synthetic materials useful to mankind;

(e) Substances, practices, processes and activities that may affect the ozone layer, and their cumulative effects;

(f) Alternative substances and technologies;

(g) Related socio-economic matters;

and as further elaborated in annexes I and II.

2.   The Parties undertake to promote or establish, as appropriate, directly or through competent international bodies and taking fully into account national legislation and relevant ongoing activities at both the national and international levels, joint or complementary programmes for systematic observation of the state of the ozone layer and other relevant parameters, as elaborated in annex I.

3.   The Parties undertake to co-operate, directly or through competent international bodies, in ensuring the collection, validation and transmission of research and observational data through appropriate world data centres in a regular and timely fashion.

Article 4
Co-operation in the Legal, Scientific and Technical Fields

1.   The Parties shall facilitate and encourage the exchange of scientific, technical, socio-economic, commercial and legal information relevant to this Convention as further elaborated in annex II. Such information shall be supplied to bodies agreed upon by the Parties. Any such body receiving information regarded as confidential by the supplying Party shall ensure that such information is not disclosed and shall aggregate it to protect its confidentiality before it is made available to all Parties.

2.   The Parties shall co-operate, consistent with their national laws, regulations and practices and taking into account in particular the needs of the developing

countries, in promoting, directly or through competent international bodies, the development and transfer of technology and knowledge. Such co-operation shall be carried out particularly through:

(a) Facilitation of the acquisition of alternative technologies by other Parties;

(b) Provision of information on alternative technologies and equipment, and supply of special manuals or guides to them;

(c) The supply of necessary equipment and facilities for research and systematic observations;

(d) Appropriate training of scientific and technical personnel.

Article 5
Transmission of Information

The Parties shall transmit, through the secretariat, to the Conference of the Parties established under article 6 information on the measures adopted by them in implementation of this Convention and of protocols to which they are party in such form and at such intervals as the meetings of the parties to the relevant instruments may determine.

Article 6
Conference of the Parties

1. A Conference of the Parties is hereby established. The first meeting of the Conference of the Parties shall be convened by the secretariat designated on an interim basis under article 7 not later than one year after entry into force of this Convention. Thereafter, ordinary meetings of the Conference of the Parties shall be held at regular intervals to be determined by the Conference at its first meeting.

2. Extraordinary meetings of the Conference of the Parties shall be held at such other times as may be deemed necessary by the Conference, or at the written request of any Party, provided that, within six months of the request being communicated to them by the secretariat, it is supported by at least one third of the Parties.

3. The Conference of the Parties shall by consensus agree upon and adopt rules of procedure and financial rules for itself and for any subsidiary bodies it may establish, as well as financial provisions governing the functioning of the secretariat.

4. The Conference of the Parties shall keep under continuous review the implementation of this Convention, and, in addition, shall:

(a) Establish the form and the intervals for transmitting the information to be submitted in accordance with article 5 and consider such information as well as reports submitted by any subsidiary body;

(b) Review the scientific information on the ozone layer, on its possible modification and on possible effects of any such modification;

(c) Promote, in accordance with article 2, the harmonization of appropriate policies, strategies and measures for minimizing the release of substances causing or likely to cause modification of the ozone layer, and make recommendations on any other measures relating to this Convention;

(d) Adopt, in accordance with articles 3 and 4, programmes for research, systematic observations, scientific and technological co-operation, the exchange of information and the transfer of technology and knowledge;

(e) Consider and adopt, as required, in accordance with articles 9 and 10, amendments to this Convention and its annexes;

(f) Consider amendments to any protocol, as well as to any annexes thereto, and, if so decided, recommend their adoption to the parties to the protocol concerned;

(g) Consider and adopt, as required, in accordance with article 10, additional annexes to this Convention;

(h) Consider and adopt, as required, protocols in accordance with article 8;

(i) Establish such subsidiary bodies as are deemed necessary for the implementation of this Convention;

(j) Seek, where appropriate, the services of competent international bodies and scientific committees, in particular the World Meteorological Organization and the World Health Organization, as well as the Co-ordinating Committee on the Ozone Layer, in scientific research, systematic observations and other activities pertinent to the objectives of this Convention, and make use as appropriate of information from these bodies and committees;

(k) Consider and undertake any additional action that may be required for the achievement of the purposes of this Convention.

5.   The United Nations, its specialized agencies and the International Atomic Energy Agency, as well as any State not party to this Convention, may be represented at meetings of the Conference of the Parties by observers. Any body or agency, whether national or international, governmental or non-governmental, qualified in fields relating to the protection of the ozone layer which has informed the secretariat of its wish to be represented at a meeting of the Conference of the Parties as an observer may be admitted unless at least one-third of the Parties present object. The admission and participation of observers shall be subject to the rules of procedure adopted by the Conference of the Parties.

Article 7
Secretariat

1.   The functions of the secretariat shall be:

(a) To arrange for and service meetings provided for in articles 6, 8, 9 and 10;

(b) To prepare and transmit reports based upon information received in accordance with articles 4 and 5, as well as upon information derived from meetings of subsidiary bodies established under article 6;

(c) To perform the functions assigned to it by any protocol;

(d) To prepare reports on its activities carried out in implementation of its functions under this Convention and present them to the Conference of the Parties;

(e) To ensure the necessary co-ordination with other relevant international bodies, and in particular to enter into such administrative and contractual arrangements as may be required for the effective discharge of its functions;

(f) To perform such other functions as may be determined by the Conference of the Parties.

2.   The secretariat functions will be carried out on an interim basis by the United Nations Environment Programme until the completion of the first ordinary meeting of the Conference of the Parties held pursuant to article 6. At its first ordinary meeting, the Conference of the Parties shall designate the secretariat from amongst those existing competent international organizations which have signified their willingness to carry out the secretariat functions under this Convention.

Article 8
Adoption of Protocols

1.   The Conference of the Parties may at a meeting adopt protocols pursuant to article 2.

2. The text of any proposed protocol shall be communicated to the Parties by the secretariat at least six months before such a meeting.

Article 9
Amendment of the Convention or Protocols

1. Any Party may propose amendments to this Convention or to any protocol. Such amendments shall take due account, *inter alia,* of relevant scientific and technical considerations.

2. Amendments to this Convention shall be adopted at a meeting of the Conference of the Parties. Amendments to any protocol shall be adopted at a meeting of the Parties to the protocol in question. The text of any proposed amendment to this Convention or to any protocol, except as may otherwise be provided in such protocol, shall be communicated to the Parties by the secretariat at least six months before the meeting at which it is proposed for adoption. The secretariat shall also communicate proposed amendments to the signatories to this Convention for information.

3. The Parties shall make every effort to reach agreement on any proposed amendment to this Convention by consensus. If all efforts at consensus have been exhausted, and no agreement reached, the amendment shall as a last resort be adopted by a three-fourths majority vote of the Parties present and voting at the meeting, and shall be submitted by the Depositary to all Parties for ratification, approval or acceptance.

4. The procedure mentioned in paragraph 3 above shall apply to amendments to any protocol, except that a two-thirds majority of the parties to that protocol present and voting at the meeting shall suffice for their adoption.

5. Ratification, approval or acceptance of amendments shall be notified to the Depositary in writing. Amendments adopted in accordance with paragraph 3 or 4 above shall enter into force between parties having accepted them on the ninetieth day after the receipt by the Depositary of notification of their ratification, approval or acceptance by at least three-fourths of the Parties to this Convention or by at least two-thirds of the parties to the protocol concerned, except as may otherwise be provided in such protocol. Thereafter the amendments shall enter into force for any other Party on the ninetieth day after that Party deposits its instrument of ratification, approval or acceptance of the amendments.

6. For the purposes of this article, "Parties present and voting" means Parties present and casting an affirmative or negative vote.

Article 10
Adoption and Amendment of Annexes

1. The annexes to this Convention or to any protocol shall form an integral part of this Convention or of such protocol, as the case may be, and, unless expressly provided otherwise, a reference to this Convention or its protocols constitutes at the same time a reference to any annexes thereto. Such annexes shall be restricted to scientific, technical and administrative matters.

2. Except as may be otherwise provided in any protocol with respect to its annexes, the following procedure shall apply to the proposal, adoption and entry into force of additional annexes to this Convention or of annexes to a protocol:

(a) Annexes to this Convention shall be proposed and adopted according to the procedure laid down in article 9, paragraphs 2 and 3, while annexes to any protocol shall be proposed and adopted according to the procedure laid down in article 9, paragraphs 2 and 4;

(b) Any party that is unable to approve an additional annex to this Convention or an annex to any protocol to which it is party shall so notify the Depositary, in writing, within six months from the date of the communication of the adoption by the Depositary. The Depositary shall without delay notify all Parties of any such notification received. A Party may at any time substitute an acceptance for a previous declaration of objection and the annexes shall thereupon enter into force for that Party;

(c) On the expiry of six months from the date of the circulation of the communication by the Depositary, the annex shall become effective for all Parties to this Convention or to any protocol concerned which have not submitted a notification in accordance with the provision of subparagraph (b) above.

3. The proposal, adoption and entry into force of amendments to annexes to this Convention or to any protocol shall be subject to the same procedure as for the proposal, adoption and entry into force of annexes to the Convention or annexes to a protocol. Annexes and amendments thereto shall take due account, *inter alia,* of relevant scientific and technical considerations.

4. If an additional annex or an amendment to an annex involves an amendment to this Convention or to any protocol, the additional annex or amended annex shall not enter into force until such time as the amendment to this Convention or to the protocol concerned enters into force.

Article 11
Settlement of Disputes

1. In the event of a dispute between Parties concerning the interpretation or application of this Convention, the parties concerned shall seek solution by negotiation.

2. If the parties concerned cannot reach agreement by negotiation, they may jointly seek the good offices of, or request mediation by, a third party.

3. When ratifying, accepting, approving or acceding to this Convention, or at any time thereafter, a State or regional economic integration organization may declare in writing to the Depositary that for a dispute not resolved in accordance with paragraph 1 or paragraph 2 above, it accepts one or both of the following means of dispute settlement as compulsory:

(a) Arbitration in accordance with procedures to be adopted by the Conference of the Parties at its first ordinary meeting;

(b) Submission of the dispute to the International Court of Justice.

4. If the parties have not, in accordance with paragraph 3 above, accepted the same or any procedure, the dispute shall be submitted to conciliation in accordance with paragraph 5 below unless the parties otherwise agree.

5. A conciliation commission shall be created upon the request of one of the parties to the dispute. The commission shall be composed of an equal number of members appointed by each party concerned and a chairman chosen jointly by the members appointed by each party. The commission shall render a final and recommendatory award, which the parties shall consider in good faith.

6. The provisions of this article shall apply with respect to any protocol except as otherwise provided in the protocol concerned.

Article 12
Signature

This Convention shall be open for signature by States and by regional economic integration organizations at the Federal Ministry for Foreign Affairs of the Republic of Austria in Vienna from 22 March 1985 to 21 September 1985, and at United Nations Headquarters in New York from 22 September 1985 to 21 March 1986.

Article 13
Ratification, Acceptance or Approval

1.   This Convention and any protocol shall be subject to ratification, acceptance or approval by States and by regional economic integration organizations. Instruments of ratification, acceptance or approval shall be deposited with the Depositary.

2.   Any organization referred to in paragraph 1 above which becomes a Party to this Convention or any protocol without any of its member States being a Party shall be bound by all the obligations under the Convention or the protocol, as the case may be. In the case of such organizations, one or more of whose member States is a Party to the Convention or relevant protocol, the organization and its member States shall decide on their respective responsibilities for the performance of their obligation under the Convention or protocol, as the case may be. In such cases, the organization and the member States shall not be entitled to exercise rights under the Convention or relevant protocol concurrently.

3.   In their instruments of ratification, acceptance or approval, the organizations referred to in paragraph 1 above shall declare the extent of their competence with respect to the matters governed by the Convention or the relevant protocol. These organizations shall also inform the Depositary of any substantial modification in the extent of their competence.

Article 14
Accession

1.   This Convention and any protocol shall be open for accession by States and by regional economic integration organizations from the date on which the Convention or the protocol concerned is closed for signature. The instruments of accession shall be deposited with the Depositary.

2.   In their instruments of accession, the organizations referred to in paragraph 1 above shall declare the extent of their competence with respect to the matters governed by the Convention or the relevant protocol. These organizations shall also inform the Depositary of any substantial modification in the extent of their competence.

3.   The provisions of article 13, paragraph 2, shall apply to regional economic integration organizations which accede to this Convention or any protocol.

Article 15
Right to Vote

1.   Each Party to this Convention or to any protocol shall have one vote.

2.   Except as provided for in paragraph 1 above, regional economic integration organizations, in matters within their competence, shall exercise their right to vote with a number of votes equal to the number of their member States which are Parties to the Convention or the relevant protocol. Such organizations shall not exercise their right to vote if their member States exercise theirs, and vice versa.

Article 16
Relationship between the Convention and its Protocols

1.   A State or a regional economic integration organization may not become a party to a protocol unless it is, or becomes at the same time, a Party to the Convention.

2.   Decisions concerning any protocol shall be taken only by the parties to the protocol concerned.

Article 17
Entry into Force

1.   This Convention shall enter into force on the ninetieth day after the date of deposit of the twentieth instrument of ratification, acceptance, approval or accession.

2.   Any protocol, except as otherwise provided in such protocol, shall enter into force on the ninetieth day after the date of deposit of the eleventh instrument of ratification, acceptance or approval of such protocol or accession thereto.

3.   For each Party which ratifies, accepts or approves this Convention or accedes thereto after the deposit of the twentieth instrument of ratification, acceptance, approval or accession, it shall enter into force on the ninetieth day after the date of deposit by such Party of its instrument of ratification, acceptance, approval or accession.

4.   Any protocol, except as otherwise provided in such protocol, shall enter into force for a party that ratifies, accepts or approves that protocol or accedes thereto after its entry into force pursuant to paragraph 2 above, on the ninetieth day after the date on which that party deposits its instrument of ratification, acceptance, approval or accession, or on the date on which the Convention enters into force for that Party, whichever shall be the later.

5.   For the purposes of paragraphs 1 and 2 above, any instrument deposited by a regional economic integration organization shall not be counted as additional to those deposited by member States of such organization.

Article 18
Reservations

No reservations may be made to this Convention.

Article 19
Withdrawal

1.   At any time after four years from the date on which this Convention has entered into force for a Party, that Party may withdraw from the Convention by giving written notification to the Depositary.

2.   Except as may be provided in any protocol, at any time after four years from the date on which such protocol has entered into force for a party, that party may withdraw from the protocol by giving written notification to the Depositary.

3.   Any such withdrawal shall take effect upon expiry of one year after the date of its receipt by the Depositary, or on such later date as may be specified in the notification of the withdrawal.

4.   Any Party which withdraws from this Convention shall be considered as also having withdrawn from any protocol to which it is party.

Article 20
Depositary

1.   The Secretary–General of the United Nations shall assume the functions of Depositary of this Convention and any protocols.

2.   The Depositary shall inform the Parties, in particular, of:

(a) The signature of this Convention and of any protocol, and the deposit of instruments of ratification, acceptance, approval or accession in accordance with articles 13 and 14;

(b) The date on which the Convention and any protocol will come into force in accordance with article 17;

(c) Notifications of withdrawal made in accordance with article 19;

(d) Amendments adopted with respect to the Convention and any protocol, their acceptance by the parties and their date of entry into force in accordance with article 9;

(e) All communications relating to the adoption and approval of annexes and to the amendment of annexes in accordance with article 10;

(f) Notifications by regional economic integration organizations of the extent of their competence with respect to matters governed by this Convention and any protocols, and of any modifications thereof;

(g) Declarations made in accordance with article 11, paragraph 3.

Article 21
Authentic Texts

The original of this Convention, of which the Arabic, Chinese, English, French, Russian and Spanish texts are equally authentic, shall be deposited with the Secretary–General of the United Nations.

Annex I
Research and Systematic Observations

1.   The Parties to the Convention recognize that the major scientific issues are:

(a) Modification of the ozone layer which would result in a change in the amount of solar ultra-violet radiation having biological effects (UV–B) that reaches the Earth's surface and the potential consequences for human health, for organisms, ecosystems and materials useful to mankind;

(b) Modification of the vertical distribution of ozone, which could change the temperature structure of the atmosphere and the potential consequences for weather and climate.

2.   The Parties to the Convention, in accordance with article 3, shall co-operate in conducting research and systematic observations and in formulating recommendations for future research and observation in such areas as:

(a) *Research into the physics and chemistry of the atmosphere*

(i) Comprehensive theoretical models: further development of models which consider the interaction between radiative, dynamic and chemical processes; studies of the simultaneous effects of various man-made and naturally occurring species upon atmospheric ozone; interpretation of satellite and non-satellite measurement data sets; evaluation of trends in atmospheric and geophysical parameters, and the development of methods for attributing changes in these parameters to specific causes;

(ii) Laboratory studies of: rate coefficients, absorption cross-sections and mechanisms of tropospheric and stratospheric chemical and photochemical processes; spectroscopic data to support field measurements in all relevant spectral regions;

(iii) Field measurements: the concentration and fluxes of key source gases of both natural and anthropogenic origin; atmospheric dynamics studies; simultaneous measurements of photochemically-related species down to the planetary boundary layer, using *in situ* and remote sensing instruments; intercomparison of different sensors, including co-ordinated correlative measurements for satellite instrumentation; three-dimensional fields of key atmospheric trace constituents, solar spectral flux and meteorological parameters;

(iv) Instrument development, including satellite and non-satellite sensors for atmospheric trace constituents, solar flux and meteorological parameters;

(b) *Research into health, biological and photodegradation effects*

(i) The relationship between human exposure to visible and ultra-violet solar radiation and (a) the development of both non-melanoma and melanoma skin cancer and (b) the effects on the immunological system;

(ii) Effects of UV–B radiation, including the wavelength dependence, upon (a) agricultural crops, forests and other terrestial ecosystems and (b) the aquatic food web and fisheries, as well as possible inhibition of oxygen production by marine phytoplankton;

(iii) The mechanisms by which UV–B radiation acts on biological materials, species and ecosystems, including: the relationship between dose, dose rate, and response; photorepair, adaptation, and protection;

(iv) Studies of biological action spectra and the spectral response using polychromatic radiation in order to include possible interactions of the various wavelength regions;

(v) The influence of UV–B radiation on: the sensitivities and activities of biological species important to the biospheric balance; primary processes such as photosynthesis and biosynthesis;

(vi) The influence of UV–B radiation on the photodegradation of pollutants, agricultural chemicals and other materials;

(c) *Research on effects on climate*

(i) Theoretical and observational studies of the radiative effects of ozone and other trace species and the impact on climate parameters, such as land and ocean surface temperatures, precipitation patterns, the exchange between the troposphere and stratosphere;

(ii) The investigation of the effects of such climate impacts on various aspects of human activity;

(d) *Systematic observations on:*

(i) The status of the ozone layer (i.e. the spatial and temporal variability of the total column content and vertical distribution) by making the Global Ozone Observing System, based on the integration of satellite and ground-based systems, fully operational;

(ii) The tropospheric and stratospheric concentrations of source gases for the HO_x, NO_x, $C10_x$ and carbon families;

(iii) The temperature from the ground to the mesosphere, utilizing both ground-based and satellite systems;

(iv) Wavelength-resolved solar flux reaching, and thermal radiation leaving, the Earth's atmosphere, utilizing satellite measurements;

(v) Wavelength-resolved solar flux reaching the Earth's surface in the ultra-violet range having biological effects (UV–B);

(vi) Aerosol properties and distribution from the ground to the mesosphere, utilizing ground-based, airborne and satellite systems;

(vii) Climatically important variables by the maintenance of programmes of high-quality meteorological surface measurements;

(viii) Trace species, temperatures, solar flux and aerosols utilizing improved methods for analysing global data.

3. The Parties to the Convention shall co-operate, taking into account the particular needs of the developing countries, in promoting the appropriate scientific and technical training required to participate in the research and systematic observations outlined in this annex. Particular emphasis should be given to the intercalibra-

tion of observational instrumentation and methods with a view to generating comparable or standardized scientific data sets.

4. The following chemical substances of natural and anthropogenic origin, not listed in order of priority, are thought to have the potential to modify the chemical and physical properties of the ozone layer.

(a) Carbon substances

(i) *Carbon monoxide (CO)*

Carbon monoxide has significant natural and anthropogenic sources, and is thought to play a major direct role in tropospheric photochemistry, and an indirect role in stratospheric photochemistry.

(ii) *Carbon dioxide (CO_2)*

Carbon dioxide has significant natural and anthropogenic sources, and affects stratospheric ozone by influencing the thermal structure of the atmosphere.

(iii) *Methane (CH_4)*

Methane has both natural and anthropogenic sources, and affects both tropospheric and stratospheric ozone.

(iv) *Non-methane hydrocarbon species*

Non-methane hydrocarbon species, which consist of a large number of chemical substances, have both natural and anthropogenic sources, and play a direct role in tropospheric photochemistry and an indirect role in stratospheric photochemistry.

(b) Nitrogen substances

(i) *Nitrous oxide (N_2O)*

The dominant sources of N_2O are natural, but anthropogenic contributions are becoming increasingly important. Nitrous oxide is the primary source of stratospheric NO_x, which play a vital role in controlling the abundance of stratospheric ozone.

(ii) *Nitrogen oxides (NO_x)*

Ground-level sources of NO_x play a major direct role only in tropospheric photochemical processes and an indirect role in stratospheric photochemistry, whereas injection of NO_x close to the tropopause may lead directly to a change in upper tropospheric and stratospheric ozone.

(c) Chlorine substances

(i) *Fully halogenated alkanes, e.g. CCl_4, $CFCl_3$ (CFC–11), CF_2Cl_2 (CFC–12), $C_2F_3Cl_3$ (CFC–113), $C_2F_4Cl_2$ (CFC–114)*

Fully halogenated alkanes are anthropogenic and act as a source of $C10_x$, which plays a vital role in ozone photochemistry, especially in the 30–50 km altitude region.

(ii) *Partially halogenated alkanes, e.g. CH_3Cl, CHF_2Cl (CFC–22), CH_3CCl_3, $CHFCl_2$ (CFC–21)*

The sources of CH_3Cl are natural, whereas the other partially halogenated alkanes mentioned above are anthropogenic in origin. These gases also act as a source of stratospheric $C10_x$.

(d) Bromine substances

Fully halogenated alkanes, e.g. CF_3Br

These gases are anthropogenic and act as a source of BrO_x, which behaves in a manner similar to ClO_x.

(e) Hydrogen substances

(i) *Hydrogen (H_2)*

Hydrogen, the source of which is natural and anthropogenic, plays a minor role in stratospheric photochemistry.

(ii) *Water (H₂O)*

Water, the source of which is natural, plays a vital role in both tropospheric and stratospheric photochemistry. Local sources of water vapour in the stratosphere include the oxidation of methane and, to a lesser extent, of hydrogen.

Annex II
Information Exchange

1. The Parties to the Convention recognize that the collection and sharing of information is an important means of implementing the objectives of this Convention and of assuring that any actions that may be taken are appropriate and equitable. Therefore, Parties shall exchange scientific, technical, socio-economic, business, commercial and legal information.

2. The Parties to the Convention, in deciding what information is to be collected and exchanged, should take into account the usefulness of the information and the costs of obtaining it. The Parties further recognize that co-operation under this annex has to be consistent with national laws, regulations and practices regarding patents, trade secrets, and protection of confidential and proprietary information.

3. *Scientific information*

This includes information on:

(a) Planned and ongoing research, both governmental and private, to facilitate the co-ordination of research programmes so as to make the most effective use of available national and international resources;

(b) The emission data needed for research;

(c) Scientific results published in peer-reviewed literature on the understanding of the physics and chemistry of the Earth's atmosphere and of its susceptibility to change, in particular on the state of the ozone layer and effects on human health, environment and climate which would result from changes on all time-scales in either the total column content or the vertical distribution of ozone;

(d) The assessment of research results and the recommendations for future research.

4. *Technical information*

This includes information on:

(a) The availability and cost of chemical substitutes and of alternative technologies to reduce the emissions of ozone-modifying substances and related planned and ongoing research;

(b) The limitations and any risks involved in using chemical or other substitutes and alternative technologies.

5. *Socio-economic and commercial information on the substances referred to in annex I*

This includes information on:

(a) Production and production capacity;

(b) Use and use patterns;

(c) Imports/exports;

(d) The costs, risks and benefits of human activities which may indirectly modify the ozone layer and of the impacts of regulatory actions taken or being considered to control these activities.

6. *Legal information*

This includes information on:

(a) National laws, administrative measures and legal research relevant to the protection of the ozone layer;

(b) International agreements, including bilateral agreements, relevant to the protection of the ozone layer;

(c) Methods and terms of licensing and availability of patents relevant to the protection of the ozone layer.

2.13 MONTREAL PROTOCOL ON SUBSTANCES THAT DEPLETE THE OZONE LAYER (As Amended and Adjusted). Adopted on 16 September 1987. Entered into force, 1 January 1989. 1522 UNTS 3. *Reprinted in* 26 ILM 1550 (1987) & 5 Weston & Carlson V.E.9.[d]

Preamble

The Parties to this Protocol,

Being Parties to the Vienna Convention for the Protection of the Ozone Layer,

Mindful of their obligation under that Convention to take appropriate measures to protect human health and the environment against adverse effects resulting or likely to result from human activities which modify or are likely to modify the ozone layer,

Recognizing that world-wide emissions of certain substances can significantly deplete and otherwise modify the ozone layer in a manner that is likely to result in adverse effects on human health and the environment,

Conscious of the potential climatic effects of emissions of these substances,

Aware that measures taken to protect the ozone layer from depletion should be based on relevant scientific knowledge, taking into account technical and economic considerations,

Determined to protect the ozone layer by taking precautionary measures to control equitably total global emissions of substances that deplete it, with the ultimate objective of their elimination on the basis of developments in scientific knowledge, taking into account technical and economic considerations and bearing in mind the developmental needs of developing countries,

Acknowledging that special provision is required to meet the needs of developing countries, including the provision of additional financial resources and access to relevant technologies, bearing in mind that the magnitude of funds necessary is predictable, and the funds can be expected to make a substantial difference in the world's ability to address the scientifically established problem of ozone depletion and its harmful effects,

Noting the precautionary measures for controlling emissions of certain chlorofluorocarbons that have already been taken at national and regional levels,

Considering the importance of promoting international co-operation in the research, development and transfer of alternative technologies relating to the control and reduction of emissions of substances that deplete the ozone layer, bearing in mind in particular the needs of developing countries,

HAVE AGREED AS FOLLOWS:

ARTICLE 1.   DEFINITIONS

For the purposes of this Protocol:

1.   "Convention" means the Vienna Convention for the Protection of the Ozone Layer, adopted on 22 March 1985.

2.   "Parties" means, unless the text otherwise indicates, Parties to this Protocol.

3.   "Secretariat" means the Secretariat of the Convention.

4.   "Controlled substance" means a substance in Annex A, Annex B, Annex C or Annex E to this Protocol, whether existing alone or in a mixture. It includes the isomers of any such substance, except as specified in the relevant Annex, but excludes

---

d. Details concerning amendments to the Protocol are as follows: London Amendment (29 Jun 1990/10 Aug 1992), 1598 UNTS 469; Copenhagen Amendment (25 Nov 1992/14 Jun 1994), 1785 UNTS 517; Montreal Amendment (17 Sep 1997/10 Nov 1999), UN Doc UNEP/OzL.Pro.9/12; Beijing Amendment (3 Dec 1999/24 Feb 2002), 2173 UNTS 183.

any controlled substance or mixture which is in a manufactured product other than a container used for the transportation or storage of that substance.

5. "Production" means the amount of controlled substances produced, minus the amount destroyed by technologies to be approved by the Parties and minus the amount entirely used as feedstock in the manufacture of other chemicals. The amount recycled and reused is not to be considered as "production".

6. "Consumption" means production plus imports minus exports of controlled substances.

7. "Calculated levels" of production, imports, exports and consumption means levels determined in accordance with Article 3.

8. "Industrial rationalization" means the transfer of all or a portion of the calculated level of production of one Party to another, for the purpose of achieving economic efficiencies or responding to anticipated shortfalls in supply as a result of plant closures.

ARTICLE 2. CONTROL MEASURES

1. Incorporated in Article 2A.

2. Replaced by Article 2B.

3. Replaced by Article 2A.

4. Replaced by Article 2A.

5. Any Party may, for one or more control periods, transfer to another Party any portion of its calculated level of production set out in Articles 2A to 2F, and Article 2H, provided that the total combined calculated levels of production of the Parties concerned for any group of controlled substances do not exceed the production limits set out in those Articles for that group. Such transfer of production shall be notified to the Secretariat by each of the Parties concerned, stating the terms of such transfer and the period for which it is to apply.

5 *bis*. Any Party not operating under paragraph 1 of Article 5 may, for one or more control periods, transfer to another such Party any portion of its calculated level of consumption set out in Article 2F, provided that the calculated level of consumption of controlled substances in Group I of Annex A of the Party transferring the portion of its calculated level of consumption did not exceed 0.25 kilograms per capita in 1989 and that the total combined calculated levels of consumption of the Parties concerned do not exceed the consumption limits set out in Article 2F. Such transfer of consumption shall be notified to the Secretariat by each of the Parties concerned, stating the terms of such transfer and the period for which it is to apply.

6. Any Party not operating under Article 5, that has facilities for the production of Annex A or Annex B controlled substances under construction, or contracted for, prior to 16 September 1987, and provided for in national legislation prior to 1 January 1987, may add the production from such facilities to its 1986 production of such substances for the purposes of determining its calculated level of production for 1986, provided that such facilities are completed by 31 December 1990 and that such production does not raise that Party's annual calculated level of consumption of the controlled substances above 0.5 kilograms per capita.

7. Any transfer of production pursuant to paragraph 5 or any addition of production pursuant to paragraph 6 shall be notified to the Secretariat, no later than the time of the transfer or addition.

8. (a) Any Parties which are Member States of a regional economic integration organization as defined in Article 1 (6) of the Convention may agree that they shall jointly fulfil their obligations respecting consumption under this Article and Articles

2A to 2I provided that their total combined calculated level of consumption does not exceed the levels required by this Article and Articles 2A to 2I.

(b) The Parties to any such agreement shall inform the Secretariat of the terms of the agreement before the date of the reduction in consumption with which the agreement is concerned.

(c) Such agreement will become operative only if all Member States of the regional economic integration organization and the organization concerned are Parties to the Protocol and have notified the Secretariat of their manner of implementation.

9. (a) Based on the assessments made pursuant to Article 6, the Parties may decide whether:

(i) Adjustments to the ozone depleting potentials specified in Annex A, Annex B, Annex C and/or Annex E should be made and, if so, what the adjustments should be; and

(ii) Further adjustments and reductions of production or consumption of the controlled substances should be undertaken and, if so, what the scope, amount and timing of any such adjustments and reductions should be;

(b) Proposals for such adjustments shall be communicated to the Parties by the Secretariat at least six months before the meeting of the Parties at which they are proposed for adoption;

(c) In taking such decisions, the Parties shall make every effort to reach agreement by consensus. If all efforts at consensus have been exhausted, and no agreement reached, such decisions shall, as a last resort, be adopted by a two-thirds majority vote of the Parties present and voting representing a majority of the Parties operating under Paragraph 1 of Article 5 present and voting and a majority of the Parties not so operating present and voting;

(d) The decisions, which shall be binding on all Parties, shall forthwith be communicated to the Parties by the Depositary. Unless otherwise provided in the decisions, they shall enter into force on the [expiration] of six months from the date of the circulation of the communication by the Depositary.

10. Based on the assessments made pursuant to Article 6 of this Protocol and in accordance with the procedure set out in Article 9 of the Convention, the Parties may decide:

(a) whether any substances, and if so which, should be added to or removed from any annex to this Protocol, and

(b) the mechanism, scope and timing of the control measures that should apply to those substances;

11. Notwithstanding the provisions contained in this Article and Articles 2A to 2I Parties may take more stringent measures than those required by this Article and Articles 2A to 2I.

ARTICLE 2A. CFCs

1. Each Party shall ensure that for the twelve-month period commencing on the first day of the seventh month following the date of entry into force of this Protocol, and in each twelve-month period thereafter, its calculated level of consumption of the controlled substances in Group I of Annex A does not exceed its calculated level of consumption in 1986. By the end of the same period, each Party producing one or more of these substances shall ensure that its calculated level of production of the substances does not exceed its calculated level of production in 1986, except that such level may have increased by no more than ten per cent based on the 1986 level. Such increase shall be permitted only so as to satisfy the basic domestic needs of the Parties

operating under Article 5 and for the purposes of industrial rationalization between Parties.

2.   Each Party shall ensure that for the period from 1 July 1991 to 31 December 1992 its calculated levels of consumption and production of the controlled substances in Group I of Annex A do not exceed 150 [percent] of its calculated levels of production and consumption of those substances in 1986; with effect from 1 January 1993, the twelve-month control period for these controlled substances shall run from 1 January to 31 December each year.

3.   Each Party shall ensure that for the twelve-month period commencing on 1 January 1994, and in each twelve-month period thereafter, its calculated level of consumption of the controlled substances in Group I of Annex A does not exceed, annually, twenty-five per cent of its calculated level of consumption in 1986. Each Party producing one or more of these substances shall, for the same periods, ensure that its calculated level of production of the substances does not exceed, annually, twenty-five [percent] of its calculated level of production in 1986. However, in order to satisfy the basic domestic needs of the Parties operating under paragraph 1 of Article 5, its calculated level of production may exceed that limit by up to ten per cent of its calculated level of production in 1986.

4.   Each Party shall ensure that for the twelve-month period commencing on 1 January 1996, and in each twelve-month period thereafter, its calculated level of consumption of the controlled substances in Group I of Annex A does not exceed zero. Each Party producing one or more of these substances shall, for the same periods, ensure that its calculated level of production of the substances does not exceed zero. However, in order to satisfy the basic domestic needs of the Parties operating under paragraph 1 of Article 5, its calculated level of production may exceed that limit by up to fifteen per cent of its calculated level of production in 1986. This paragraph will apply save to the extent that the Parties decide to permit the level of production or consumption that is necessary to satisfy uses agreed by them to be essential.

5.   Each Party shall ensure that for the twelve-month period commencing on 1 January 2003 and in each twelve-month period thereafter, its calculated level of production of the controlled substances in Group I of Annex A for the basic domestic needs of the Parties operating under paragraph 1 of Article 5 does not exceed eighty per cent of the annual average of its production of those substances for basic domestic needs for the period 1995 to 1997 inclusive.

6.   Each Party shall ensure that for the twelve-month period commencing on 1 January 2005 and in each twelve-month period thereafter, its calculated level of production of the controlled substances in Group I of Annex A for the basic domestic needs of the Parties operating under paragraph 1 of Article 5 does not exceed fifty per cent of the annual average of its production of those substances for basic domestic needs for the period 1995 to 1997 inclusive.

7.   Each Party shall ensure that for the twelve-month period commencing on 1 January 2007 and in each twelve-month period thereafter, its calculated level of production of the controlled substances in Group I of Annex A for the basic domestic needs of the Parties operating under paragraph 1 of Article 5 does not exceed fifteen per cent of the annual average of its production of those substances for basic domestic needs for the period 1995 to 1997 inclusive.

8.   Each Party shall ensure that for the twelve-month period commencing on 1 January 2010 and in each twelve-month period thereafter, its calculated level of production of the controlled substances in Group I of Annex A for the basic domestic needs of the Parties operating under paragraph 1 of Article 5 does not exceed zero.

9.   For the purposes of calculating basic domestic needs under paragraphs 4 to 8 of this Article, the calculation of the annual average of production by a Party includes

any production entitlements that it has transferred in accordance with paragraph 5 of Article 2, and excludes any production entitlements that it has acquired in accordance with paragraph 5 of Article 2.

ARTICLE 2B. HALONS

1. Each Party shall ensure that for the twelve-month period commencing on 1 January 1992, and in each twelve-month period thereafter, its calculated level of consumption of the controlled substances in Group II of Annex A does not exceed, annually, its calculated level of consumption in 1986. Each Party producing one or more of these substances shall, for the same periods, ensure that its calculated level of production of the substances does not exceed, annually, its calculated level of production in 1986. However, in order to satisfy the basic domestic needs of the Parties operating under paragraph 1 of Article 5, its calculated level of production may exceed that limit by up to ten per cent of its calculated level of production in 1986.

2. Each Party shall ensure that for the twelve-month period commencing on 1 January 1994, and in each twelve-month period thereafter, its calculated level of consumption of the controlled substances in Group II of Annex A does not exceed zero. Each Party producing one or more of these substances shall, for the same periods, ensure that its calculated level of production of the substances does not exceed zero. However, in order to satisfy the basic domestic needs of the Parties operating under paragraph 1 of Article 5, its calculated level of production may exceed that limit by up to fifteen per cent of its calculated level of production in 1986. This paragraph will apply save to the extent that the Parties decide to permit the level of production or consumption that is necessary to satisfy uses agreed by them to be essential.

3. Each Party shall ensure that for the twelve-month period commencing on 1 January 2005 and in each twelve-month period thereafter, its calculated level of production of the controlled substances in Group II of Annex A for the basic domestic needs of the Parties operating under paragraph 1 of Article 5 does not exceed fifty per cent of the annual average of its production of those substances for basic domestic needs for the period 1995 to 1997 inclusive.

4. Each Party shall ensure that for the twelve-month period commencing on 1 January 2010 and in each twelve-month period thereafter, its calculated level of production of the controlled substances in Group II of Annex A for the basic domestic needs of the Parties operating under paragraph 1 of Article 5 does not exceed zero.

ARTICLE 2C. OTHER FULLY HALOGENATED CFCs

1. Each Party shall ensure that for the twelve-month period commencing on 1 January 1993, its calculated level of consumption of the controlled substances in Group I of Annex B does not exceed, annually, eighty per cent of its calculated level of consumption in 1989. Each Party producing one or more of these substances shall, for the same period, ensure that its calculated level of production of the substances does not exceed, annually, eighty [percent] of its calculated level of production in 1989. However, in order to satisfy the basic domestic needs of the Parties operating under paragraph 1 of Article 5, its calculated level of production may exceed that limit by up to ten [percent] of its calculated level of production in 1989.

2. Each Party shall ensure that for the twelve-month period commencing on 1 January 1994, and in each twelve-month period thereafter, its calculated level of consumption of the controlled substances in Group I of Annex B does not exceed, annually, twenty-five per cent of its calculated level of consumption in 1989. Each Party producing one or more of these substances shall, for the same periods, ensure that its calculated level of production of the substances does not exceed, annually, twenty-five [percent] of its calculated level of production in 1989. However, in order to satisfy the basic domestic needs of the Parties operating under paragraph 1 of Article

5, its calculated level of production may exceed that limit by up to ten [percent] of its calculated level of production in 1989.

3.   Each Party shall ensure that for the twelve-month period commencing on 1 January 1996, and in each twelve-month period thereafter, its calculated level of consumption of the controlled substances in Group I of Annex B does not exceed zero. Each Party producing one or more of these substances shall, for the same periods, ensure that its calculated level of production of the substances does not exceed zero. However, in order to satisfy the basic domestic needs of the Parties operating under paragraph 1 of Article 5, its calculated level of production may exceed that limit by up to fifteen per cent of its calculated level of production in 1989. This paragraph will apply save to the extent that the Parties decide to permit the level of production or consumption that is necessary to satisfy uses agreed by them to be essential.

4.   Each Party shall ensure that for the twelve-month period commencing on 1 January 2007 and in each twelve-month period thereafter, its calculated level of production of the controlled substances in Group I of Annex B for the basic domestic needs of the Parties operating under paragraph 1 of Article 5 does not exceed fifteen per cent of the annual average of its production of those substances for basic domestic needs for the period 1998 to 2000 inclusive.

5.   Each Party shall ensure that for the twelve-month period commencing on 1 January 2010 and in each twelve-month period thereafter, its calculated level of production of the controlled substances in Group I of Annex B for the basic domestic needs of the Parties operating under paragraph 1 of Article 5 does not exceed zero.

ARTICLE 2D.   CARBON TETRACHLORIDE

1.   Each Party shall ensure that for the twelve-month period commencing on 1 January 1995, its calculated level of consumption of the controlled substance in Group II of Annex B does not exceed, annually, fifteen [percent] of its calculated level of consumption in 1989. Each Party producing the substance shall, for the same period, ensure that its calculated level of production of the substance does not exceed, annually, fifteen [percent] of its calculated level of production in 1989. However, in order to satisfy the basic domestic needs of the Parties operating under paragraph 1 of Article 5, its calculated level of production may exceed that limit by up to ten per cent of its calculated level of production in 1989.

2.   Each Party shall ensure that for the twelve-month period commencing on 1 January 1996, and in each twelve-month period thereafter, its calculated level of consumption of the controlled substance in Group II of Annex B does not exceed zero. Each Party producing the substance shall, for the same periods, ensure that its calculated level of production of the substance does not exceed zero. However, in order to satisfy the basic domestic needs of the Parties operating under paragraph 1 of Article 5, its calculated level of production may exceed that limit by up to fifteen [percent] of its calculated level of production in 1989. This paragraph will apply save to the extent that the Parties decide to permit the level of production or consumption that is necessary to satisfy uses agreed by them to be essential.

ARTICLE 2E.   1,1,1–TRICHLOROETHANE (METHYL CHLOROFORM)

1.   Each Party shall ensure that for the twelve-month period commencing on 1 January 1993, its calculated level of consumption of the controlled substance in Group III of Annex B does not exceed, annually, its calculated level of consumption in 1989. Each Party producing the substance shall, for the same period, ensure that its calculated level of production of the substance does not exceed, annually, its calculated level of production in 1989. However, in order to satisfy the basic domestic needs of the Parties operating under paragraph 1 of Article 5, its calculated level of production may exceed that limit by up to ten [percent] of its calculated level of production in 1989.

2. Each Party shall ensure that for the twelve-month period commencing on 1 January 1994, and in each twelve-month period thereafter, its calculated level of consumption of the controlled substance in Group III of Annex B does not exceed, annually, fifty [percent] of its calculated level of consumption in 1989. Each Party producing the substance shall, for the same periods, ensure that its calculated level of production of the substance does not exceed, annually, fifty [percent] of its calculated level of production in 1989. However, in order to satisfy the basic domestic needs of the Parties operating under paragraph 1 of Article 5, its calculated level of production may exceed that limit by up to ten [percent] of its calculated level of production in 1989.

3. Each Party shall ensure that for the twelve-month period commencing on 1 January 1996, and in each twelve-month period thereafter, its calculated level of consumption of the controlled substance in Group III of Annex B does not exceed zero. Each Party producing the substance shall, for the same periods, ensure that its calculated level of production of the substance does not exceed zero. However, in order to satisfy the basic domestic needs of the Parties operating under paragraph 1 of Article 5, its calculated level of production may exceed that limit by up to fifteen [percent] of its calculated level of production for 1989. This paragraph will apply save to the extent that the Parties decide to permit the level of production or consumption that is necessary to satisfy uses agreed by them to be essential.

ARTICLE 2F.   HYDROCHLOROFLOUROCARBONS

1. Each Party shall ensure that for the twelve-month period commencing on 1 January 1996, and in each twelve-month period thereafter, its calculated level of consumption of the controlled substances in Group I of Annex C does not exceed, annually, the sum of:

(a) Two point eight [percent] of its calculated level of consumption in 1989 of the controlled substances in Group I of Annex A; and

(b) Its calculated level of consumption in 1989 of the controlled substances in Group I of Annex C.

2. Each Party shall ensure that for the twelve month period commencing on 1 January 2004, and in each twelve-month period thereafter, its calculated level of consumption of the controlled substances in Group I of Annex C does not exceed, annually, sixty-five per cent of the sum referred to in paragraph 1 of this Article.

3. Each Party shall ensure that for the twelve-month period commencing on 1 January 2010, and in each twelve-month period thereafter, its calculated level of consumption of the controlled substances in Group I of Annex C does not exceed, annually, thirty-five per cent of the sum referred to in paragraph 1 of this Article.

4. Each Party shall ensure that for the twelve-month period commencing on 1 January 2015, and in each twelve-month period thereafter, its calculated level of consumption of the controlled substances in Group I of Annex C does not exceed, annually, ten per cent of the sum referred to in paragraph 1 of this Article.

5. Each Party shall ensure that for the twelve-month period commencing on 1 January 2020, and in each twelve-month period thereafter, its calculated level of consumption of the controlled substances in Group I of Annex C does not exceed, annually, zero point five per cent of the sum referred to in paragraph 1 of this Article. Such consumption shall, however, be restricted to the servicing of refrigeration and air conditioning equipment existing at that date.

6. Each Party shall ensure that for the twelve-month period commencing on 1 January 2030, and in each twelve-month period thereafter, its calculated level of consumption of the controlled substances in Group I of Annex C does not exceed zero.

7. As of 1 January 1996, each Party shall [endeavor] to ensure that:

(a) The use of controlled substances in Group I of Annex C is limited to those applications where other more environmentally suitable alternative substances or technologies are not available;

(b) The use of controlled substances in Group I of Annex C is not outside the areas of application currently met by controlled substances in Annexes A, B and C, except in rare cases for the protection of human life or human health; and

(c) Controlled substances in Group I of Annex C are selected for use in a manner that minimizes ozone depletion, in addition to meeting other environmental, safety and economic considerations.

8. Each Party producing one or more of these substances shall ensure that for the twelve-month period commencing on 1 January 2004, and in each twelve-month period thereafter, its calculated level of production of the controlled substances in Group I of Annex C does not exceed, annually, the average of:

(a) The sum of its calculated level of consumption in 1989 of the controlled substances in Group I of Annex C and two point eight per cent of its calculated level of consumption in 1989 of the controlled substances in Group I of Annex A; and

(b) The sum of its calculated level of production in 1989 of the controlled substances in Group I of Annex C and two point eight per cent of its calculated level of production in 1989 of the controlled substances in Group I of Annex A.

However, in order to satisfy the basic domestic needs of the Parties operating under paragraph 1 of Article 5, its calculated level of production may exceed that limit by up to fifteen per cent of its calculated level of production of the controlled substances in Group I of Annex C as defined above.

ARTICLE 2G.   HYDROBROMOFLOUROCARBONS

Each Party shall ensure that for the twelve-month period commencing on 1 January 1996, and in each twelve-month period thereafter, its calculated level of consumption of the controlled substances in Group II of Annex C does not exceed zero. Each Party producing the substances shall, for the same periods, ensure that its calculated level of production of the substances does not exceed zero. This paragraph will apply save to the extent that the Parties decide to permit the level of production or consumption that is necessary to satisfy uses agreed by them to be essential.

ARTICLE 2H.   METHYL BROMIDE

1. Each Party shall ensure that for the twelve-month period commencing on 1 January 1995, and in each twelve-month period thereafter, its calculated level of consumption of the controlled substance in Annex E does not exceed, annually, its calculated level of consumption in 1991. Each Party producing the substance shall, for the same period, ensure that its calculated level of production of the substance does not exceed, annually, its calculated level of production in 1991. However, in order to satisfy the basic domestic needs of the Parties operating under paragraph 1 of Article 5, its calculated level of production may exceed that limit by up to ten per cent of its calculated level of production in 1991.

2. Each Party shall ensure that for the twelve-month period commencing on 1 January 1999, and in the twelve-month period thereafter, its calculated level of consumption of the controlled substance in Annex E does not exceed, annually, seventy-five [percent] of its calculated level of consumption in 1991. Each Party producing the substance shall, for the same periods, ensure that its calculated level of production of the substance does not exceed, annually, seventy-five [percent] of its calculated level of production in 1991. However, in order to satisfy the basic domestic needs of the Parties operating under paragraph 1 of Article 5, its calculated level of

production may exceed that limit by up to ten [percent] of its calculated level of production in 1991.

3.   Each Party shall ensure that for the twelve-month period commencing on 1 January 2001, and in the twelve-month period thereafter, its calculated level of consumption of the controlled substance in Annex E does not exceed, annually, fifty percent of its calculated level of consumption in 1991. Each Party producing the substance shall, for the same periods, ensure that its calculated level of production of the substance does not exceed, annually, fifty [percent] of its calculated level of production in 1991. However, in order to satisfy the basic domestic needs of the Parties operating under paragraph 1 of Article 5, its calculated level of production may exceed that limit by up to ten [percent] of its calculated level of production in 1991.

4.   Each Party shall ensure that for the twelve-month period commencing on 1 January 2003, and in the twelve-month period thereafter, its calculated level of consumption of the controlled substance in Annex E does not exceed, annually, thirty [percent] of its calculated level of consumption in 1991. Each Party producing the substance shall, for the same periods, ensure that its calculated level of production of the substance does not exceed, annually, thirty [percent] of its calculated level of production in 1991. However, in order to satisfy the basic domestic needs of the Parties operating under paragraph 1 of Article 5, its calculated level of production may exceed that limit by up to ten [percent] of its calculated level of production in 1991.

5.   Each Party shall ensure that for the twelve-month period commencing on 1 January 2005, and in each twelve-month period thereafter, its calculated level of consumption of the controlled substance in Annex E does not exceed zero. Each Party producing the substance shall, for the same periods, ensure that its calculated level of production of the substance does not exceed zero. However, in order to satisfy the basic domestic needs of the Parties operating under paragraph 1 of Article 5, its calculated level of production may, until 1 January 2002 exceed that limit by up to fifteen per cent of its calculated level of production in 1991; thereafter, it may exceed that limit by a quantity equal to the annual average of its production of the controlled substance in Annex E for basic domestic needs for the period 1995 to 1998 inclusive. This paragraph will apply save to the extent that the Parties decide to permit the level of production or consumption that is necessary to satisfy uses agreed by them to be critical uses.

5 *bis*. Each Party shall ensure that for the twelve-month period commencing on 1 January 2005 and in each twelve-month period thereafter, its calculated level of production of the controlled substance in Annex E for the basic domestic needs of the Parties operating under paragraph 1 of Article 5 does not exceed eighty per cent of the annual average of its production of the substance for basic domestic needs for the period 1995 to 1998 inclusive.

5 *ter*. Each Party shall ensure that for the twelve-month period commencing on 1 January 2015 and in each twelve-month period thereafter, its calculated level of production of the controlled substance in Annex E for the basic domestic needs of the Parties operating under paragraph 1 of Article 5 does not exceed zero.

6.   The calculated levels of consumption and production under this Article shall not include the amounts used by the Party for quarantine and pre-shipment applications.

ARTICLE 2I: BROMOCHLOROMETHANE

Each Party shall ensure that for the twelve-month period commencing on 1 January 2002, and in each twelve-month period thereafter, its calculated level of consumption and production of the controlled substance in Group III of Annex C does not exceed zero. This paragraph will apply save to the extent that the Parties decide to permit the level of production or consumption that is necessary to satisfy uses agreed by them to be essential.

ARTICLE 3. CALCULATION OF CONTROL LEVELS

For the purposes of Articles 2, 2A to 2I and 5, each Party shall, for each group of substances in Annex A, Annex B, Annex C or Annex E determine its calculated levels of:

(a) Production by:

(i) multiplying its annual production of each controlled substance by the ozone depleting potential specified in respect if it [is] in Annex A, Annex B, Annex C or Annex E;

(ii) adding together, for each such Group, the resulting figures;

(b) Imports and exports, respectively, by following, mutatis mutandis, the procedure set out in subparagraph (a); and

(c) Consumption by adding together its calculated levels of production and imports and subtracting its calculated level of exports as determined in accordance with subparagraphs (a) and (b). However, beginning on 1 January 1993, any export of controlled substances to non-Parties shall not be subtracted in calculating the consumption level of the exporting Party.

ARTICLE 4. CONTROL OF TRADE WITH NON–PARTIES

1. As of 1 January 1990, each party shall ban the import of the controlled substances in Annex A from any State not party to this Protocol.

1 *bis*. Within one year of the date of the entry into force of this paragraph, each Party shall ban the import of the controlled substances in Annex B from any State not party to this Protocol.

1 *ter*. Within one year of the date of entry into force of this paragraph, each Party shall ban the import of any controlled substances in Group II of Annex C from any State not party to this Protocol.

1 *qua*. Within one year of the date of entry into force of this paragraph, each Party shall ban the import of the controlled substance in Annex E from any State not party to this Protocol.

1 *quin*. As of 1 January 2004, each Party shall ban the import of the controlled substances in Group I of Annex C from any State not party to this Protocol.

1 *sex*. Within one year of the date of entry into force of this paragraph, each Party shall ban the import of the controlled substance in Group III of Annex C from any State not party to this Protocol.

2. As of 1 January 1993, each Party shall ban the export of any controlled substances in Annex A to any State not party to this Protocol.

2 *bis*. Commencing one year after the date of entry into force of this paragraph, each Party shall ban the export of any controlled substances in Annex B to any State not party to this Protocol.

2 *ter*. Commencing one year after the date of entry into force of this paragraph, each Party shall ban the export of any controlled substances in Group II of Annex C to any State not party to this Protocol.

2 *qua*. Within one year of the date of entry into force of this paragraph, each Party shall ban the export of the controlled substance in Annex E to any State not party to this Protocol.

2 *quin*. As of 1 January 2004, each Party shall ban the export of the controlled substances in Group I of Annex C to any State not party to this Protocol.

2 *sex*. Within one year of the date of entry into force of this paragraph, each Party shall ban the export of the controlled substance in Group III of Annex C to any State not party to this Protocol.

3. By 1 January 1992, the Parties shall, following the procedures in Article 10 of the Convention, elaborate in an annex a list of products containing controlled substances in Annex A. Parties that have not objected to the annex in accordance with those procedures shall ban, within one year of the annex having become effective, the import of those products from any State not party to this Protocol.

3 *bis*. Within three years of the date of the entry into force of this paragraph, the Parties shall, following the procedures in Article 10 of the Convention, elaborate in an annex a list of products containing controlled substances in Annex B. Parties that have not objected to the annex in accordance with those procedures shall ban, within one year of the annex having become effective, the import of those products from any State not party to this Protocol.

3 *ter*. Within three years of the date of entry into force of this paragraph, the Parties shall, following the procedures in Article10 of the Convention, elaborate in an annex a list of products containing controlled substances in Group II of Annex C. Parties that have not objected to the annex in accordance with those procedures shall ban, within one year of the annex having become effective, the import of those products from any State not party to this Protocol.

4. By 1 January 1994, the Parties shall determine the feasibility of banning or restricting, from States not party to this Protocol, the import of products produced with, but not containing, controlled substances in Annex A. If determined feasible, the Parties shall, following the procedures in Article 10 of the Convention, elaborate in an annex a list of such products. Parties that have not objected to the annex in accordance with those procedures shall ban, within one year of the annex having become effective, the import of those products from any State not party to this Protocol.

4 *bis*. Within five years of the date of the entry into force of this paragraph, the Parties shall determine the feasibility of banning or restricting, from States not party to this Protocol, the import of products produced with, but not containing, controlled substances in Annex B. If determined feasible, the Parties shall, following the procedures in Article 10 of the Convention, elaborate in an annex a list of such products. Parties that have not objected to the annex in accordance with those procedures shall ban or restrict, within one year of the annex having become effective, the import of those products from any State not party to this Protocol.

4 *ter*. Within five years of the date of entry into force of this paragraph, the Parties shall determine the feasibility of banning or restricting, from States not party to this Protocol, the import of products produced with, but not containing, controlled substances in Group II of Annex C. If determined feasible, the Parties shall, following the procedures in Article 10 of the Convention, elaborate in an annex a list of such products. Parties that have not objected to the annex in accordance with those procedures shall ban or restrict, within one year of the annex having become effective, the import of those products from any State not party to this Protocol.

5. Each Party undertakes to the fullest practicable extent to discourage the export to any State not party to this Protocol of technology for producing and for utilizing controlled substances in Annexes A, B, C and E.

6. Each Party shall refrain from providing new subsidies, aid, credits, guarantees or insurance programmes for the export to States not party to this Protocol of products, equipment, plants or technology that would facilitate the production of controlled substances in Annexes A, B, C and E.

7. Paragraphs 5 and 6 shall not apply to products, equipment, plants or technology that improve the containment, recovery, recycling or destruction of controlled

substances, promote the development of alternative substances, or otherwise contribute to the reduction of emissions of controlled substances in Annexes A, B, C and E.

8. Notwithstanding the provisions of this Article, imports and exports referred to in paragraphs 1 to 4 *ter* of this Article may be permitted from, or to, any State not party to this Protocol, if that State is determined, by a meeting of the Parties, to be in full compliance with Article 2, Articles 2A to 2I and this Article, and have submitted data to that effect as specified in Article 7.

9. For the purposes of this Article, the term "State not party to this Protocol" shall include, with respect to a particular controlled substance, a State or regional economic integration organization that has not agreed to be bound by the control measures in effect for that substance.

10. By 1 January 1996, the Parties shall consider whether to amend this Protocol in order to extend the measures in this Article to trade in controlled substances in Group I of Annex C and in Annex E with States not party to the Protocol.

ARTICLE 4A. CONTROL OF TRADE WITH PARTIES

1. Where, after the phase-out date applicable to it for a controlled substance, a Party is unable, despite having taken all practicable steps to comply with its obligation under the Protocol, to cease production of that substance for domestic consumption, other than for uses agreed by the Parties to be essential, it shall ban the export of used, recycled and reclaimed quantities of that substance, other than for the purpose of destruction.

2. Paragraph 1 of this Article shall apply without prejudice to the operation of Article 11 of the Convention and then on-compliance procedure developed under Article 8 of the Protocol.

ARTICLE 4B. LICENSING

1. Each Party shall, by 1 January 2000 or within three months of the date of entry into force of this Article for it, whichever is the later, establish and implement a system for licensing the import and export of new, used, recycled and reclaimed controlled substances in Annexes A, B, C and E.

2. Notwithstanding paragraph 1 of this Article, any Party operating under paragraph 1 of Article 5 which decides it is not in a position to establish and implement a system for licensing the import and export of controlled substances in Annexes C and E, may delay taking those actions until 1 January 2005 and 1 January 2002, respectively.

3. Each Party shall, within three months of the date of introducing its licensing system, report to the Secretariat on the establishment and operation of that system.

4. The Secretariat shall periodically prepare and circulate to all Parties a list of the Parties that have reported to it on their licensing systems and shall forward this information to the Implementation Committee for consideration and appropriate recommendations to the Parties.

ARTICLE 5. SPECIAL SITUATION OF DEVELOPING COUNTRIES

1. Any Party that is a developing country and whose annual calculated level of consumption of the controlled substances in Annex A is less than 0.3 kilograms per capita on the date of the entry into force of the Protocol for it, or any time thereafter until 1 January 1999, shall, in order to meet its basic domestic needs, be entitled to delay for ten years its compliance with the control measures set out in Articles 2A to 2E, provided that any further amendments to the adjustments or Amendment adopted at the Second Meeting of the Parties in London, 29 June 1990, shall apply to the

Parties operating under this paragraph after the review provided for in paragraph 8 of this Article has taken place and shall be based on the conclusions of that review.

1 *bis*. The Parties shall, taking into account the review referred to in paragraph 8 of this Article, the assessments made pursuant to Article 6 and any other relevant information, decide by 1 January 1996, through the procedure set forth in paragraph 9 of Article 2:

(a) With respect to paragraphs 1 to 6 of Article 2F, what base year, initial levels, control schedules and phase-out date for consumption of the controlled substances in Group I of Annex C will apply to Parties operating under paragraph 1 of this Article;

(b) With respect to Article 2G, what phase-out date for production and consumption of the controlled substances in Group II of Annex C will apply to Parties operating under paragraph 1 of this Article; and

(c) With respect to Article 2H, what base year, initial levels and control schedules for consumption and production of the controlled substance in Annex E will apply to Parties operating under paragraph 1 of this Article.

2. However, any Party operating under paragraph 1 of this Article shall exceed neither an annual calculated level of consumption of the controlled substances in Annex A of 0.3 kilograms per capita nor an annual calculated level of consumption of controlled substances of Annex B of 0.2 kilograms per capita.

3. When implementing the control measures set out in Articles 2A to 2E, any Party operating under paragraph 1 of this Article shall be entitled to use:

(a) For controlled substances under Annex A, either the average of its annual calculated level of consumption for the period 1995 to 1997 inclusive or a calculated level of consumption of 0.3 kilograms per capita, whichever is the lower, as the basis for determining its compliance with the control measures relating to consumption.

(b) For controlled substances under Annex B, the average of its annual calculated level of consumption for the period 1998 to 2000 inclusive or a calculated level of consumption of 0.2 kilograms per capita, whichever is the lower, as the basis for determining its compliance with the control measures relating to consumption.

(c) For controlled substances under Annex A, either the average of its annual calculated level of production for the period 1995 to 1997 inclusive or a calculated level of production of 0.3 kilograms per capita, whichever is the lower, as the basis for determining its compliance with the control measures relating to production.

(d) For controlled substances under Annex B, either the average of its annual calculated level of production for the period 1998 to 2000 inclusive or a calculated level of production of 0.2 kilograms per capita, whichever is the lower, as the basis for determining its compliance with the control measures relating to production.

4. If a Party operating under paragraph 1 of this Article, at any time before the control measures obligations in Articles 2A to 2I become applicable to it, finds itself unable to obtain an adequate supply of controlled substances, it may notify this to the Secretariat. The Secretariat shall forthwith transmit a copy of such notification to the Parties, which shall consider the matter at their next Meeting, and decide upon appropriate action to be taken.

5. Developing the capacity to fulfil the obligations of the Parties operating under paragraph 1 of this Article to comply with the control measures set out in Articles 2A to 2E and Article 2I, and any control measures in Articles 2F to 2H that are decided pursuant to paragraph 1 *bis* of this Article, and their implementation by those same Parties will depend upon the effective implementation of the financial co-operation as provided by Article 10 and the transfer of technology as provided by Article 10A.

6. Any Party operating under paragraph 1 of this Article may, at any time, notify the Secretariat in writing that, having taken all practicable steps it is unable to implement any or all of the obligations laid down in Articles 2A to 2E and Article 2I, or any or all obligations in Articles 2F to 2H that are decided pursuant to paragraph 1 bis of this Article, due to the inadequate implementation of Articles 10 and 10A. The Secretariat shall forthwith transmit a copy of the notification to the Parties, which shall consider the matter at their next Meeting, giving due recognition to paragraph 5 of this Article and shall decide upon appropriate action to be taken.

7. During the period between notification and the Meeting of the Parties at which the appropriate action referred to in paragraph 6 above is to be decided, or for a further period if the Meeting of the Parties so decides, the non-compliance procedures referred to in Article 8 shall not be invoked against the notifying Party.

8. A Meeting of the Parties shall review, not later than 1995, the situation of the Parties operating under paragraph 1 of this Article, including the effective implementation of financial co-operation and transfer of technology to them, and adopt such revisions that may be deemed necessary regarding the schedule of control measures applicable to those Parties.

8 *bis*. Based on the conclusions of the review referred to in paragraph 8 above:

(a) With respect to the controlled substances in Annex A, a Party operating under paragraph 1 of this Article shall, in order to meet its basic domestic needs, be entitled to delay for ten years its compliance with the control measures adopted by the Second Meeting of the Parties in London, 29 June 1990, and reference by the Protocol to Articles 2A and 2B shall be read accordingly;

(b) With respect to the controlled substances in Annex B, a Party operating under paragraph 1 of this Article shall, in order to meet its basic domestic needs, be entitled to delay for ten years its compliance with the control measures adopted by the Second Meeting of the Parties in London, 29 June 1990, and reference by the Protocol to Articles 2C to 2E shall be read accordingly.

8 *ter*. Pursuant to paragraph 1 *bis* above:

(a) Each Party operating under paragraph 1 of this Article shall ensure that for the twelve-month period commencing on 1 January 2016, and in each twelve-month period thereafter, its calculated level of consumption of the controlled substances in Group I of Annex C does not exceed, annually, its calculated level of consumption in 2015. As of 1 January 2016 each Party operating under paragraph 1 of this Article shall comply with the control measures set out in paragraph 8 of Article 2F and, as the basis for its compliance with these control measures, it shall use the average of its calculated levels of production and consumption in 2015;

(b) Each Party operating under paragraph 1 of this Article shall ensure that for the twelve-month period commencing on 1 January 2040, and in each twelve-month period thereafter, its calculated level of consumption of the controlled substances in Group I of Annex C does not exceed zero;

(c) Each Party operating under paragraph 1 of this Article shall comply with Article 2G;

(d) With regard to the controlled substance contained in Annex E:

(i) As of 1 January 2002 each Party operating under paragraph 1 of this Article shall comply with the control measures set out in paragraph 1 of Article 2H and, as the basis for its compliance with these control measures, it shall use the average of its annual calculated level of consumption and production, respectively, for the period of 1995 to 1998 inclusive;

(ii) Each Party operating under paragraph 1 of this Article shall ensure that for the twelve-month period commencing on 1 January 2005, and in each twelve-month period thereafter, its calculated levels of consumption and production of the controlled substance in Annex E do not exceed, annually, eighty [percent] of the average of its annual calculated levels of consumption and production, respectively, for the period of 1995 to 1998 inclusive;

(iii) Each Party operating under paragraph 1 of this Article shall ensure that for the twelve-month period commencing on 1 January 2015 and in each twelve-month period thereafter, its calculated levels of consumption and production of the controlled substance in Annex E do not exceed zero. This paragraph will apply save to the extent that the Parties decide to permit the level of production or consumption that is necessary to satisfy uses agreed by them to be critical uses;

(iv) The calculated levels of consumption and production under this subparagraph shall not include the amounts used by the Party for quarantine and pre-shipment applications.

9.   Decisions of the Parties referred to in paragraph 4, 6 and 7 of this Article shall be taken according to the same procedure applied to decision-making under Article 10.

ARTICLE 6.   ASSESSMENT AND REVIEW OF CONTROL MEASURES

Beginning in 1990, and at least every four years thereafter, the Parties shall assess the control measures provided for in Article 2 and Articles 2A to 2I on the basis of available scientific, environmental, technical and economic information. At least one year before each assessment, the Parties shall convene appropriate panels of experts qualified in the fields mentioned and determine the composition and terms of reference of any such panels. Within one year of being convened, the panels will report their conclusions, through the Secretariat, to the Parties.

ARTICLE 7.   REPORTING OF DATA

1.   Each Party shall provide to the Secretariat, within three months of becoming a Party, statistical data on its production, imports and exports of each of the controlled substances in Annex A for the year 1986, or the best possible estimates of such data where actual data are not available.

2.   Each Party shall provide to the Secretariat statistical data on its production, imports and exports of each of the controlled substances

— in Annexes B and Groups I and II of Annex C, for the year 1989;

— in Annex E, for the year 1991,

or the best possible estimates of such data where actual data are not available, not later than three months after the date when the provisions set out in the Protocol with regard to the substances in Annexes B, C and E respectively enter into force for that Party.

3.   Each Party shall provide to the Secretariat statistical data on its annual production (as defined in paragraph 5 of Article 1) of each of the controlled substances listed in Annexes A, B, C and E and, separately, for each substance,

— Amounts used for feedstocks,

— Amounts destroyed by technologies approved by the Parties, and

— Imports from and exports to Parties and non-Parties respectively,

for the year during which provisions concerning the substances in Annexes A, B, C and E respectively entered into force for that Party and for each year thereafter. Each Party shall provide to the Secretariat statistical data on the annual amount of the controlled substance listed in Annex E used for quarantine and pre-shipment applications. Data shall be forwarded not later than nine months after the end of the year to which the data relate.

3 *bis*. Each Party shall provide to the Secretariat separate statistical data of its annual imports and exports of each of the controlled substances listed in Group II of Annex A and Group I of Annex C that have been recycled.

4. For Parties operating under the provisions of paragraph 8 (a) of Article 2, the requirements in paragraphs 1, 2, 3 and 3 *bis* of this Article in respect of statistical data on imports and exports shall be satisfied if the regional economic integration organization concerned provides data on imports and exports between the organization and States that are not members of that organization.

ARTICLE 8. NON–COMPLIANCE

The Parties, at their first meeting, shall consider and approve procedures and institutional mechanisms for determining non-compliance with the provisions of this Protocol and for treatment of Parties found to be in non-compliance.

ARTICLE 9. RESEARCH, DEVELOPMENT, PUBLIC AWARENESS AND EXCHANGE OF INFORMATION

1. The Parties shall co-operate, consistent with their national laws, regulations and practices and taking into account in particular the needs of developing countries, in promoting, directly or through competent international bodies, research, development and exchange of information on:

(a) best technologies for improving the containment, recovery, recycling, or destruction of controlled substances or otherwise reducing their emissions;

(b) possible alternatives to controlled substances, to products containing such substances, and to products manufactured with them; and

(c) costs and benefits of relevant control strategies.

2. The Parties, individually, jointly or through competent international bodies, shall co-operate in promoting public awareness of the environmental effects of the emissions of controlled substances and other substances that deplete the ozone layer.

3. Within two years of the entry into force of this Protocol and every two years thereafter, each Party shall submit to the Secretariat a summary of the activities it has conducted pursuant to this Article.

ARTICLE 10. FINANCIAL MECHANISM

1. The Parties shall establish a mechanism for the purposes of providing financial and technical co-operation, including the transfer of technologies, to Parties operating under paragraph 1 of Article 5 of this Protocol to enable their compliance with the control measures set out in Articles 2A to 2E and Article 2I, and any control measures in Articles 2F to 2H that are decided pursuant to paragraph 1 *bis* of Article 5 of the Protocol. The mechanism, contributions to which shall be additional to other financial transfers to Parties operating under that paragraph, shall meet all agreed incremental costs of such Parties in order to enable their compliance with the control measures of the Protocol. An indicative list of the categories of incremental costs shall be decided by the meeting of the Parties.

2. The mechanism established under paragraph 1 shall include a Multilateral Fund. It may also include other means of multilateral, regional and bilateral co-operation.

3. The Multilateral Fund shall:

(a) Meet, on a grant or concessional basis as appropriate, and according to criteria to be decided upon by the Parties, the agreed incremental costs;

(b) Finance clearing-house functions to:

(i) Assist Parties operating under paragraph 1 of Article 5, through country specific studies and other technical co-operation, to identify their needs for co-operation;

(ii) Facilitate technical co-operation to meet these identified needs;

(iii) Distribute, as provided for in Article 9, information and relevant materials, and hold workshops, training sessions, and other related activities, for the benefit of Parties that are developing countries; and

(iv) Facilitate and monitor other multilateral, regional and bilateral co-operation available to Parties that are developing countries;

(c) Finance the secretarial services of the Multilateral Fund and related support costs.

4. The Multilateral Fund shall operate under the authority of the Parties who shall decide on its overall policies.

5. The Parties shall establish an Executive Committee to develop and monitor the implementation of specific operational policies, guidelines and administrative arrangements, including the disbursement of resources, for the purpose of achieving the objectives of the Multilateral Fund. The Executive Committee shall discharge its tasks and responsibilities, specified in its terms of reference as agreed by the Parties, with the co-operation and assistance of the International Bank for Reconstruction and Development (World Bank), the United Nations Environment Programme, the United Nations Development Programme or other appropriate agencies depending on their respective areas of expertise. The members of the Executive Committee, which shall be selected on the basis of a balanced representation of the Parties operating under paragraph 1 of Article 5 and of the Parties not so operating, shall be endorsed by the Parties.

6. The Multilateral Fund shall be financed by contributions from Parties not operating under paragraph 1 of Article 5 in convertible currency or, in certain circumstances, in kind and/or in national currency, on the basis of the United Nations scale of assessments. Contributions by other Parties shall be encouraged. Bilateral and, in particular cases agreed by a decision of the Parties, regional co-operation may, up to a percentage and consistent with any criteria to be specified by decision of the Parties, be considered as a contribution to the Multilateral Fund, provided that such co-operation, as a minimum:

(a) Strictly relates to compliance with the provisions of this Protocol;

(b) Provides additional resources; and

(c) Meets agreed incremental costs.

7. The Parties shall decide upon the programme budget of the Multilateral Fund for each fiscal period and upon the percentage of contributions of the individual Parties thereto.

8. Resources under the Multilateral Fund shall be disbursed with the concurrence of the beneficiary Party.

9. Decisions by the Parties under this Article shall be taken by consensus whenever possible. If all efforts at consensus have been exhausted and no agreement reached, decisions shall be adopted by a two-thirds majority vote of the Parties present and voting, representing a majority of the Parties operating under paragraph 1 of Article 5 present and voting and a majority of the Parties not so operating present and voting.

10. The financial mechanism set out in this Article is without prejudice to any future arrangements that may be developed with respect to other environmental issues.

ARTICLE 10A. TRANSFER OF TECHNOLOGY

Each Party shall take every practicable step, consistent with the programmes supported by the financial mechanism, to ensure:

(a) that the best available, environmentally safe substitutes and related technologies are expeditiously transferred to Parties operating under paragraph 1 of Article 5; and

(b) that the transfers referred to in subparagraph (a) occur under fair and most favourable conditions.

ARTICLE 11. MEETINGS OF THE PARTIES

1. The Parties shall hold meetings at regular intervals. The Secretariat shall convene the first meeting of the Parties not later than one year after the date of the entry into force of this Protocol and in conjunction with a meeting of the Conference of the Parties to the Convention, if a meeting of the latter is scheduled within that period.

2. Subsequent ordinary meetings of the parties shall be held, unless the Parties otherwise decide, in conjunction with meetings of the Conference of the Parties to the Convention. Extraordinary meetings of the Parties shall be held at such other times as may be deemed necessary by a meeting of the Parties, or at the written request of any Party, provided that within six months of such a request being communicated to them by the Secretariat, it is supported by at least one third of the Parties.

3. The Parties, at their first meeting, shall:

(a) adopt by consensus rules of procedure for their meetings;

(b) adopt by consensus the financial rules referred to in paragraph 2 of Article 13;

(c) establish the panels and determine the terms of reference referred to in Article 6;

(d) consider and approve the procedures and institutional mechanisms specified in Article 8; and

(e) begin preparation of work plans pursuant to paragraph 3 of Article 10. [The Article 10 in question is that of the original Protocol adopted in 1987.]

4. The functions of the meetings of the Parties shall be to:

(a) review the implementation of this Protocol;

(b) decide on any adjustments or reductions referred to in paragraph 9 of Article 2;

(c) decide on any addition to, insertion in or removal from any annex of substances and on related control measures in accordance with paragraph 10 of Article 2;

(d) establish, where necessary, guidelines or procedures for reporting of information as provided for in Article 7 and paragraph 3 of Article 9;

(e) review requests for technical assistance submitted pursuant to paragraph 2 of Article 10;

(f) review reports prepared by the secretariat pursuant to subparagraph (c) of Article 12;

(g) assess, in accordance with Article 6, the control measures;

(h) consider and adopt, as required, proposals for amendment of this Protocol or any annex and for any new annex;

(i) consider and adopt the budget for implementing this Protocol; and

(j) consider and undertake any additional action that may be required for the achievement of the purposes of this Protocol.

5.   The United Nations, its specialized agencies and the International Atomic Energy Agency, as well as any State not party to this Protocol, may be represented at meetings of the Parties as observers. Any body or agency, whether national or international, governmental or non-governmental, qualified in fields relating to the protection of the ozone layer which has informed the secretariat of its wish to be represented at a meeting of the Parties as an observer may be admitted unless at least one third of the Parties present object. The admission and participation of observers shall be subject to the rules of procedure adopted by the Parties.

ARTICLE 12.   SECRETARIAT

For the purposes of this Protocol, the Secretariat shall:

(a) arrange for and service meetings of the Parties as provided for in Article 11;

(b) receive and make available, upon request by a Party, data provided pursuant to Article 7;

(c) prepare and distribute regularly to the Parties reports based on information received pursuant to Articles 7 and 9;

(d) notify the Parties of any request for technical assistance received pursuant to Article 10 so as to facilitate the provision of such assistance;

(e) encourage non-Parties to attend the meetings of the Parties as observers and to act in accordance with the provisions of this Protocol;

(f) provide, as appropriate, the information and requests referred to in subparagraphs (c) and (d) to such non-party observers; and

(g) perform such other functions for the achievement of the purposes of this Protocol as may be assigned to it by the Parties.

ARTICLE 13.   FINANCIAL PROVISIONS

1.   The funds required for the operation of this Protocol, including those for the functioning of the Secretariat related to this Protocol, shall be charged exclusively against contributions from the Parties.

2.   The Parties, at their first meeting, shall adopt by consensus financial rules for the operation of this Protocol.

ARTICLE 14.   RELATIONSHIP OF THIS PROTOCOL TO THE CONVENTION

Except as otherwise provided in this Protocol, the provisions of the Convention relating to its protocols shall apply to this Protocol.

ARTICLE 15.   SIGNATURE

This Protocol shall be open for signature by States and by regional economic integration organizations in Montreal on 16 September 1987, in Ottawa from 17 September 1987 to 16 January 1988, and at United Nations Headquarters in New York from 17 January 1988 to 15 September 1988.

ARTICLE 16.   ENTRY INTO FORCE

1.   This Protocol shall enter into force on 1 January 1989, provided that at least eleven instruments of ratification, acceptance, approval of the Protocol or accession thereto have been deposited by States or regional economic integration organizations representing at least two-thirds of 1986 estimated global consumption of the controlled substances, and the provisions of paragraph 1 of Article 17 of the Convention have been fulfilled. In the event that these conditions have not been fulfilled by that date,

the Protocol shall enter into force on the ninetieth day following the date on which the conditions have been fulfilled.

2. For the purposes of paragraph 1, any such instrument deposited by a regional economic integration organization shall not be counted as additional to those deposited by member States of such organization.

3. After the entry into force of this Protocol, any State or regional economic integration organization shall become a Party to it on the ninetieth day following the date of deposit of its instrument of ratification, acceptance, approval or accession.

ARTICLE 17. PARTIES JOINING AFTER ENTRY INTO FORCE

Subject to Article 5, any State or regional economic integration organization which becomes a Party to this Protocol after the date of its entry into force, shall fulfil forthwith the sum of the obligations under Article 2, as well as under Articles 2A to 2I and Article 4, that apply at that date to the States and regional economic integration organizations that became Parties on the date the Protocol entered into force.

ARTICLE 18. RESERVATIONS

No reservations may be made to this Protocol.

ARTICLE 19. WITHDRAWAL

Any Party may withdraw from this Protocol by giving written notification to the Depositary at any time after four years of assuming the obligations specified in paragraph 1 of Article 2A. Any such withdrawal shall take effect upon expiry of one year after the date of its receipt by the Depositary, or on such later date as may be specified in the notification of the withdrawal.

ARTICLE 20. AUTHENTIC TEXTS

The original of this Protocol, of which the Arabic, Chinese, English, French, Russian and Spanish texts are equally authentic, shall be deposited with the Secretary–General of the United Nations.

In Witness Whereof the Undersigned, Being Duly Authorized to That Effect, Have Signed this Protocol Done at Montreal this Sixteenth Day of September, One Thousand Nine Hundred and Eighty Seven.

ANNEX A
CONTROLLED SUBSTANCES

Group	Substance	Ozone depleting Potential*
Group I		
$CFCl_3$	(CFC–11)	1.0
CF_2Cl_2	(CFC–12)	1.0
$C_2F_3Cl_3$	(CFC–113)	0.8
$C_2F_4Cl_2$	(CFC–114)	1.0
C_2F_5Cl	(CFC–115)	0.6
Group II		
CF_2BrCl	(halon–1211)	3.0
CF_3Br	(halon–1301)	10.0
$C_2F_4Br_2$	(halon–2402)	6.0

* These ozone depleting potentials are estimates based on existing knowledge and will be reviewed and revised periodically.

ANNEX B
CONTROLLED SUBSTANCES

Group	Substance	Ozone–Depleting Potential
Group I		
CF3Cl	(CFC–13)	1.0
C2FCl5	(CFC–111)	1.0
C2F2Cl4	(CFC–112)	1.0
C3FCl7	(CFC–211)	1.0
C3F2Cl6	(CFC–212)	1.0
C3F3Cl5	(CFC–213)	1.0
C3F4Cl4	(CFC–214)	1.0
C3F5Cl3	(CFC–215)	1.0
C3F6Cl2	(CFC–216)	1.0
C3F7Cl	(CFC–217)	1.0

Group II
Ccl4   carbon tetrachloride   1.1

Group III
C2H3Cl3*   1,1,1–trichloroethane*   (methyl chloroform) 0.1
* This formula does not refer to 1,1,2–trichloroethane.

ANNEX C
CONTROLLED SUBSTANCES

Group	Substance	Number of isomers	Ozone–Depleting Potential*
Group I			
CHFCl2	(HCFC–21)**	1	0.04
CHF2Cl	(HCFC–22)**	1	0.055
CH2FCl	(HCFC–31)	1	0.02
C2HFCl4	(HCFC–121)	2	0.01–0.04
C2HF2Cl3	(HCFC–122)	3	0.02–0.08
C2HF3Cl2	(HCFC–123)	3	0.02–0.06
CHCl2CF3	(HCFC–123)**-		0.02
C2HF4Cl	(HCFC–124)	2	0.02–0.04
CHFClCF3	(HCFC–124)**-		0.022
C2H2FCl3	(HCFC–131)	3	0.007–0.05
C2H2F2Cl2	(HCFC–132)	4	0.008–0.05
C2H2F3Cl	(HCFC–133)	3	0.02–0.06
C2H3FCl2	(HCFC–141)	3	0.005–0.07
CH3CFCl2	(HCFC–141b)**-		0.11
C2H3F2Cl	(HCFC–142)	3	0.008–0.07
CH3CF2Cl	(HCFC–142b)**-		0.065
C2H4FCl	(HCFC–151)	2	0.003–0.005
C3HFCl6	(HCFC–221)	5	0.015–0.07
C3HF2Cl5	(HCFC–222)	9	0.01–0.09
C3HF3Cl4	(HCFC–223)	12	0.01–0.08
C3HF4Cl3	(HCFC–224)	12	0.01–0.09
C3HF5Cl2	(HCFC–225)	9	0.02–0.07
CF3CF2CHCl2	(HCFC–225ca)**-		0.025
CF2ClCF2CHClF	(HCFC–225cb)**-		0.033
C3HF6Cl	(HCFC–226)	5	0.02–0.10
C3H2FCl5	(HCFC–231)	9	0.05–0.09
C3H2F2Cl4	(HCFC–232)	16	0.008–0.10
C3H2F3Cl3	(HCFC–233)	18	0.007–0.23
C3H2F4Cl2	(HCFC–234)	16	0.01–0.28

Group	Substance	Number of isomers	Ozone–Depleting Potential*
C3H2F5Cl	(HCFC–235)	9	0.03–0.52
C3H3FCl4	(HCFC–241)	12	0.004–0.09
C3H3F2Cl3	(HCFC–242)	18	0.005–0.13
C3H3F3Cl2	(HCFC–243)	18	0.007–0.12
C3H3F4Cl	(HCFC–244)	12	0.009–B0.14
C3H4FCl3	(HCFC–251)	12	0.001–0.01
C3H4F2Cl2	(HCFC–252)	16	0.005–0.04
C3H4F3Cl	(HCFC–253)	12	0.003–0.03
C3H5FCl2	(HCFC–261)	9	0.002–0.02
C3H5F2Cl	(HCFC–262)	9	0.002–0.02
C3H6FCl	(HCFC–271)	5	0.001–0.03

Group II

CHF Br2		1	1.00
CHF2Br	(HBFC–22B1)	1	0.74
CH2FBr		1	0.73
C2HFBr4		2	0.3–0.8
C2HF2Br3		3	0.5–1.8
C2HF3Br2		3	0.4–1.6
C2HF4Br		2	0.7–1.2
C2H2FBr3		3	0.1–1.1
C2H2F2Br2		4	0.2–1.5
C2H2F3Br		3	0.7–1.6
C2H3FBr2		3	0.1–1.7
C2H3F2Br		3	0.2–1.1
C2H4FBr		2	0.07–0.1
C3HFBr6		5	0.3–1.5
C3HF2Br5		9	0.2–1.9
C3HF3Br4		12	0.3–1.8
C3HF4Br3		12	0.5–2.2
C3HF5Br2		9	0.9–2.0
C3HF6Br		5	0.7–3.3
C3H2FBr5		9	0.1–1.9
C3H2F2Br4		16	0.2–2.1
C3H2F3Br3		18	0.2–5.6
C3H2F4Br2		16	0.3–7.5
C3H2F5Br		8	0.9–1.4
C3H3FBr4		12	0.08–1.9
C3H3F2Br3		18	0.1–3.1
C3H3F3Br2		18	0.1–2.5
C3H3F4Br		12	0.3–4.4
C3H4FBr3		12	0.03–0.3
C3H4F2Br2		16	0.1–1.0
C3H4F3Br		12	0.07–0.8
C3H5FBr2		9	0.04–0.4
C3H5F2Br		9	.07–0.8
C3H6FBr		5	0.02–0.7

Group III

CH2BrCl	bromochloromethane	1	0.12

* Where a range of ODPs is indicated, the highest value in that range shall be used for the purposes of the Protocol. The ODPs listed as a single value have been determined from calculations based on laboratory measurements. Those listed as a range are based on estimates and are less certain. The range pertains to an isomeric group. The upper value is the estimate of the ODP of the isomer with the highest ODP, and the lower value is the estimate of the ODP of the isomer with the lowest ODP.

** Identifies the most commercially viable substances with ODP values listed against them to be used for the purposes of the Protocol.

ANNEX D*:
A LIST OF PRODUCTS** CONTAINING CONTROLLED SUBSTANCES SPECI-
FIED IN ANNEX A

Products	Customs code number
1. Automobile and truck air conditioning units (whether incorporated in vehicles or not)	_____
2. Domestic and commercial refrigeration and air conditioning/heat pump equipment***	_____
e.g.	
Refrigerators	_____
Freezers	_____
Dehumidifiers	_____
Water coolers	_____
Ice machines	_____
Air conditioning and heat pump units	_____
3. Aerosol products, except medical aerosols	_____
4. Portable fire extinguisher	_____
5. Insulation boards, panels and pipe covers	_____
6. Pre-polymers	_____

* This Annex was adopted by the Third Meeting of the Parties in Nairobi, 21 June 1991 as required by paragraph 3 of Article 4 of the Protocol.

** Though not when transported in consignments of personal or household effects or in similar non-commercial situations normally exempted from customs attention.

*** When containing controlled substances in Annex A as a refrigerant and/or in insulating material of the product.

ANNEX E
CONTROLLED SUBSTANCE

Group	Substance	Ozone–Depleting Potential
Group I		
CH3Br	methyl bromide	0.6

D. NUCLEAR

2.14 CONVENTION ON THIRD PARTY LIABILITY IN THE FIELD OF NUCLEAR ENERGY (As Amended Through 1964). Concluded at Paris, 29 July 1960. Entered into force, 1 April 1968. 956 UNTS 251; *reprinted in* 5 Weston & Carlson V.J.1

THE GOVERNMENTS of the Federal Republic of Germany, the Republic of Austria, the Kingdom of Belgium, the Kingdom of Denmark, Spain, the French Republic, the Kingdom of Greece, the Italian Republic, the Grand Duchy of Luxembourg, the Kingdom of Norway, the Kingdom of the Netherlands, the Portuguese Republic, the United Kingdom of Great Britain and Northern Ireland, the Kingdom of Sweden, the Swiss Confederation and the Turkish Republic;

CONSIDERING that the OECD Nuclear Energy Agency, established within the framework of the Organisation for Economic Co-operation and Development (hereinafter referred to as the "Organisation"), is charged with encouraging the elaboration and harmonization of legislation relating to nuclear energy in participating countries, in particular with regard to third party liability and insurance against atomic risks;

DESIROUS of ensuring adequate and equitable compensation for persons who suffer damage caused by nuclear incidents whilst taking the necessary steps to ensure that the development of the production and uses of nuclear energy for peaceful purposes is not thereby hindered;

CONVINCED of the need for unifying the basic rules applying in the various countries to the liability incurred for such damage, whilst leaving these countries free to take, on a national basis, any additional measures which they deem appropriate;

Article 1

(*a*) For the purposes of this Convention:

(i) "A nuclear incident" means any occurrence or succession of occurrences having the same origin which causes damage, provided that such occurrence or succession of occurrences, or any of the damage caused, arises out of or results either from the radioactive properties, or a combination of radioactive properties with toxic, explosive, or other hazardous properties of nuclear fuel or radioactive products or waste or with any of them, or from ionizing radiations emitted by any other source of radiation inside a nuclear installation.

(ii) "Nuclear installation" means reactors other than those comprised in any means of transport; factories for the manufacture or processing of nuclear substances; factories for the separation of isotopes of nuclear fuel; factories for the reprocessing of irradiated nuclear fuel; facilities for the storage of nuclear substances other than storage incidental to the carriage of such substances; and such other installations in which there are nuclear fuel or radioactive products or waste as the Steering Committee for Nuclear Energy of the Organisation (hereinafter referred to as the "Steering Committee") shall from time to time determine; any Contracting Party may determine that two or more nuclear installations of one operator which are located on the same site shall, together with any other premises on that site where radioactive material is held, be treated as a single nuclear installation.

(iii) "Nuclear fuel" means fissionable material in the form of uranium metal, alloy, or chemical compound (including natural uranium), plutonium metal, alloy, or chemical compound, and such other fissionable material as the Steering Committee shall from time to time determine.

(iv) "Radioactive products or waste" means any radioactive material produced in or made radioactive by exposure to the radiation incidental to the process of producing or utilizing nuclear fuel, but does not include (1) nuclear fuel, or (2) radioisotopes outside a nuclear installation which have reached the final stage of fabrication so as to be usable for any industrial, commercial, agricultural, medical, scientific or educational purpose.

(v) "Nuclear substances" means nuclear fuel (other than natural uranium and other than depleted uranium) and radioactive products or waste.

(vi) "Operator" in relation to a nuclear installation means the person designated or recognized by the competent public authority as the operator of that installation.

(b) The Steering Committee may, if in its view the small extent of the risks involved so warrants, exclude any nuclear installation, nuclear fuel, or nuclear substances from the application of this Convention.

Article 2

This Convention does not apply to nuclear incidents occurring in the territory of non-Contracting States or to damage suffered in such territory, unless otherwise provided by the legislation of the Contracting Party in whose territory the nuclear installation of the operator liable is situated, and except in regard to rights referred to in article 6(e).

Article 3

(a) The operator of a nuclear installation shall be liable, in accordance with this Convention, for:

(i) damage to or loss of life of any person; and

(ii) damage to or loss of any property other than

1. the nuclear installation itself and any other nuclear installation, including a nuclear installation under construction, on the site where that installation is located; and

2. any property on that same site which is used or to be used in connection with any such installation, upon proof that such damage or loss (hereinafter referred to as "damage") was caused by a nuclear incident in such installation or involving nuclear substances coming from such installation, except as otherwise provided for in Article 4.

(b) Where the damage or loss is caused jointly by a nuclear incident and by an incident other than a nuclear incident, that part of the damage or loss which is caused by such other incident shall, to the extent that it is not reasonably separable from the damage or loss caused by the nuclear incident, be considered to be damage caused by the nuclear incident. Where the damage or loss is caused jointly by a nuclear incident and by an emission of ionizing radiation not covered by this Convention, nothing in this Convention shall limit or otherwise affect the liability of any person in connection with that emission of ionizing radiation.

Article 4

In the case of carriage of nuclear substances, including storage incidental thereto, without prejudice to article 2:

(a) The operator of a nuclear installation shall be liable, in accordance with this Convention, for damage upon proof that it was caused by a nuclear incident outside that installation and involving nuclear substances in the course of carriage therefrom, only if the incident occurs:

(i) before liability with regard to nuclear incidents involving the nuclear substances has been assumed, pursuant to the express terms of a contract in writing, by the operator of another nuclear installation;

(ii) in the absence of such express terms, before the operator of another nuclear installation has taken charge of the nuclear substances; or

(iii) where the nuclear substances are intended to be used in a reactor comprised in a means of transport, before the person duly authorized to operate that reactor has taken charge of the nuclear substances; but

(iv) where the nuclear substances have been sent to a person within the territory of a non-Contracting State, before they have been unloaded from the means of transport by which they have arrived in the territory of that non-Contracting State.

(*b*) The operator of a nuclear installation shall be liable, in accordance with this Convention, for damage upon proof that it was caused by a nuclear incident outside that installation and involving nuclear substances in the course of carriage thereto, only if the incident occurs:

(i) after liability with regard to nuclear incidents involving the nuclear substances has been assumed by him, pursuant to the express terms of a contract in writing, from the operator of another nuclear installation;

(ii) in the absence of such express terms, after he has taken charge of the nuclear substances; or

(iii) after he has taken charge of the nuclear substances from a person operating a reactor comprised in a means of transport; but

(iv) where the nuclear substances have, with the written consent of the operator, been sent from a person within the territory of a non-Contracting State, after they have been loaded on the means of transport by which they are to be carried from the territory of that State.

(*c*) The operator liable in accordance with this Convention shall provide the carrier with a certificate issued by or on behalf of the insurer or other financial guarantor furnishing the security required pursuant to Article 10. However, a Contracting Party may exclude this obligation in relation to carriage which takes place wholly within its own territory. The certificate shall state the name and address of that operator and the amount, type and duration of the security, and these statements may not be disputed by the person by whom or on whose behalf the certificate was issued. The certificate shall also indicate the nuclear substances and the carriage in respect of which the security applies and shall include a statement by the competent public authority that the person named is an operator within the meaning of this Convention.

(*d*) A Contracting Party may provide by legislation that, under such terms as may be contained therein and upon fulfilment of the requirements of article 10(*a*), a carrier may, at his request and with the consent of an operator of a nuclear installation situated in its territory, by decision of the competent public authority, be liable in accordance with this Convention in place of that operator. In such case for all the purposes of this Convention the carrier shall be considered, in respect of nuclear incidents occurring in the course of carriage of nuclear substances, as an operator of a nuclear installation on the territory of the Contracting Party whose legislation so provides.

Article 5

(*a*) If the nuclear fuel or radioactive products or waste involved in a nuclear incident have been in more than one nuclear installation and are in a nuclear installation at the time damage is caused, no operator of any nuclear installation in which they have previously been shall be liable for the damage.

(*b*) Where, however, damage is caused by a nuclear incident occurring in a nuclear installation and involving only nuclear substances stored therein incidentally to their carriage, the operator of the nuclear installation shall not be liable where another operator or person is liable pursuant to article 4.

(*c*) If the nuclear fuel or radioactive products or waste involved in a nuclear incident have been in more than one nuclear installation and are not in a nuclear installation at the time damage is caused, no operator other than the operator of the last nuclear installation in which they were before the damage was caused or an operator who has subsequently taken them in charge, or has assumed liability therefor pursuant to the express terms of a contract in writing shall be liable for the damage.

(*d*) If damage gives rise to liability of more than one operator in accordance with this Convention, the liability of these operators shall be joint and several: provided that where such liability arises as a result of damage caused by a nuclear incident involving nuclear substances in the course of carriage in one and the same means of transport, or, in the case of storage incidental to the carriage, in one and the same nuclear installation, the maximum total amount for which such operators shall be liable shall be the highest amount established with respect to any of them pursuant to article 7 and provided that in no case shall any one operator be required, in respect of a nuclear incident, to pay more than the amount established with respect to him pursuant to article 7.

Article 6

(*a*) The right to compensation for damage caused by a nuclear incident may be exercised only against an operator liable for the damage in accordance with this Convention, or, if a direct right of action against the insurer or other financial guarantor furnishing the security required pursuant to article 10 is given by national law, against the insurer or other financial guarantor.

(*b*) Except as otherwise provided in this article, no other person shall be liable for damage caused by a nuclear incident, but this provision shall not affect the application of any international agreement in the field of transport in force or open for signature, ratification or accession at the date of this Convention.

(*c*)(i) Nothing in this Convention shall affect the liability:

1. of any individual for damage caused by a nuclear incident for which the operator, by virtue of article 3(*a*)(ii)(1) and (2) or Article 9, is not liable under this Convention and which results from an act or omission of that individual done with intent to cause damage;

2. of a person duly authorized to operate a reactor comprised in a means of transport for damage caused by a nuclear incident when an operator is not liable for such damage pursuant to article 4(*a*)(iii) or (*b*)(iii).

(ii) The operator shall incur no liability outside this Convention for damage caused by a nuclear incident.

(*d*) Any person who has paid compensation in respect of damage caused by a nuclear incident under any international agreement referred to in paragraph (*b*) of this article or under any legislation of a non-Contracting State shall, up to the amount which he has paid, acquire by subrogation the rights under this Convention of the person suffering damage whom he has so compensated.

(*e*) Any person who has his principal place of business in the territory of a Contracting Party or who is the servant of such a person and who has paid compensation in respect of damage caused by a nuclear incident occurring in the territory of a non-Contracting State or in respect of damage suffered in such territory shall, up to the amount which he has paid, acquire the rights which the person so compensated would have had against the operator but for the provisions of article 2.

(*f*) The operator shall have a right of recourse only:

(i) if the damage caused by a nuclear incident results from an act or omission done with intent to cause damage, against the individual acting or omitting to act with such intent;

(ii) if and to the extent that it is so provided expressly by contract.

(*g*) If the operator has a right of recourse to any extent pursuant to paragraph (*f*) of this article against any person, that person shall not, to that extent, have a right against the operator under paragraphs (*d*) or (*e*) of this article.

(*h*) Where provisions of national or public health insurance, social security, workmen's compensation or occupational disease compensation systems include compensation for damage caused by a nuclear incident, rights of beneficiaries of such systems and rights of recourse by virtue of such systems shall be determined by the law of the Contracting Party or by the regulations of the inter-Governmental organization which has established such systems.

Article 7

(*a*) The aggregate of compensation required to be paid in respect of damage caused by a nuclear incident shall not exceed the maximum liability established in accordance with this article.

(*b*) The maximum liability of the operator in respect of damage caused by a nuclear incident shall be 15,000,000 Special Drawing Rights as defined by the International Monetary Fund and used by it for its own operations and transactions (hereinafter referred to as "Special Drawing Rights"). However,

(i) any Contracting Party, taking into account the possibilities for the operator of obtaining the insurance or other financial security required pursuant to Article 10, may establish by legislation a greater or lesser amount;

(ii) any Contracting Party, having regard to the nature of the nuclear installation or the nuclear substances involved and to the likely consequences of an incident originating therefrom, may establish a lower amount;

provided that in no event shall any amounts so established be less than 5,000,000 Special Drawing Rights. The sums mentioned above may be converted into national currency in round figures.

(*c*) Compensation for damage caused to the means of transport on which the nuclear substances involved were at the time of the nuclear incident shall not have the effect of reducing the liability of the operator in respect of other damage to an amount less than either 5,000,000 Special Drawing Rights, or any higher amount established by the legislation of a Contracting Party.

(*d*) The amount of liability of operators of nuclear installations in the territory of a Contracting Party established in accordance with paragraph (*b*) of this article as well as the provisions of any legislation of a Contracting Party pursuant to paragraph (*c*) of this article shall apply to the liability of such operators wherever the nuclear incident occurs.

(*e*) A Contracting Party may subject the transit of nuclear substances through its territory to the condition that the maximum amount of liability of the foreign operator concerned be increased, if it considers that such amount does not adequately cover the risks of a nuclear incident in the course of the transit: provided that the maximum amount thus increased shall not exceed the maximum amount of liability of operators of nuclear installations situated in its territory.

(*f*) The provisions of paragraph (*e*) of this article shall not apply:

(i) to carriage by sea where, under international law, there is a right of entry in cases of urgent distress into the ports of such Contracting Party or a right of innocent passage through its territory; or

(ii) to carriage by air where, by agreement or under international law there is a right to fly over or land on the territory of such Contracting Party.

(*g*) Any interest and costs awarded by a court in actions for compensation under this Convention shall not be considered to be compensation for the purposes of this Convention and shall be payable by the operator in addition to any sum for which he is liable in accordance with this article.

Article 8

(*a*) The right of compensation under this Convention shall be extinguished if an action is not brought within ten years from the date of the nuclear incident. National legislation may, however, establish a period longer than ten years if measures have been taken by the Contracting Party in whose territory the nuclear installation of the operator liable is situated to cover the liability of that operator in respect of any actions for compensation begun after the expiry of the period of ten years and during such longer period: provided that such extension of the extinction period shall in no case affect the right of compensation under this Convention of any person who has brought an action in respect of loss of life or personal injury against the operator before the expiry of the period of ten years.

(*b*) In the case of damage caused by a nuclear incident involving nuclear fuel or radioactive products or waste which, at the time of the incident have been stolen, lost, jettisoned or abandoned and have not yet been recovered, the period established pursuant to paragraph (*a*) of this article shall be computed from the date of that nuclear incident, but the period shall in no case exceed twenty years from the date of the theft, loss, jettison or abandonment.

(*c*) National legislation may establish a period of not less than two years for the extinction of the right or as a period of limitation either from the date at which the person suffering damage has knowledge or from the date at which he ought reasonably to have known of both the damage and the operator liable: provided that the period established pursuant to paragraphs (*a*) and (*b*) of this article shall not be exceeded.

(*d*) Where the provisions of article 13(*c*)(ii) are applicable, the right of compensation shall not, however, be extinguished if, within the time provided for in paragraphs (*a*), (*b*) and (*c*) of this Article.

(i) prior to the determination by the Tribunal referred to in article 17, an action has been brought before any of the courts from which the Tribunal can choose; if the Tribunal determines that the competent court is a court other than that before which such action has already been brought, it may fix a date by which such action has to be brought before the competent court so determined; or

(ii) a request has been made to a Contracting Party concerned to initiate a determination by the Tribunal of the competent court pursuant to article 13(*c*)(ii) and an action is brought subsequent to such determination within such time as may be fixed by the Tribunal.

(*e*) Unless national law provides to the contrary, any person suffering damage caused by a nuclear incident who has brought an action for compensation within the period provided for in this article may amend his claim in respect of any aggravation of the damage after the expiry of such period provided that final judgment has not been entered by the competent court.

Article 9

The operator shall not be liable for damage caused by a nuclear incident directly due to an act of armed conflict, hostilities, civil war, insurrection or, except in so far as the legislation of the Contracting Party in whose territory his nuclear installation is situated may provide to the contrary, a grave natural disaster of an exceptional character.

Article 10

(*a*) To cover the liability under this Convention, the operator shall be required to have and maintain insurance or other financial security of the amount established pursuant to article 7 and of such type and terms as the competent public authority shall specify.

(*b*) No insurer or other financial guarantor shall suspend or cancel the insurance or other financial security provided for in paragraph (*a*) of this article without giving notice in writing of at least two months to the competent public authority or in so far as such insurance or other financial security relates to the carriage of nuclear substances, during the period of the carriage in question.

(*c*) The sums provided as insurance, reinsurance, or other financial security may be drawn upon only for compensation for damage caused by a nuclear incident.

Article 11

The nature, form and extent of the compensation, within the limits of this Convention, as well as the equitable distribution thereof, shall be governed by national law.

Article 12

Compensation payable under this Convention, insurance and reinsurance premiums, sums provided as insurance, reinsurance, or other financial security required pursuant to article 10, and interest and costs referred to in article 7(*g*), shall be freely transferable between the monetary areas of the Contracting Parties.

Article 13

(*a*) Except as otherwise provided in this article, jurisdiction over actions under articles 3, 4, 6(*a*) and 6(*e*) shall lie only with the courts of the Contracting Party in whose territory the nuclear incident occurred.

(*b*) Where a nuclear incident occurs outside the territory of the Contracting Parties, or where the place of the nuclear incident cannot be determined with certainty, jurisdiction over such actions shall lie with the courts of the Contracting Party in whose territory the nuclear installation of the operator liable is situated.

(*c*) Where jurisdiction would lie with the courts of more than one Contracting Party by virtue of paragraphs (*a*) or (*b*) of this article, jurisdiction shall lie,

(i) if the nuclear incident occurred partly outside the territory of any Contracting Party and partly in the territory of a single Contracting Party, with the courts of that Contracting Party; and

(ii) in any other case, with the courts of the Contracting Party determined, at the request of a Contracting Party concerned, by the Tribunal referred to in article 17 as being the most closely related to the case in question.

(*d*) Judgments entered by the competent court under this article after trial, or by default, shall, when they have become enforceable under the law applied by that court, become enforceable in the territory of any of the other Contracting Parties as soon as the formalities required by the Contracting Party concerned have been complied with.

The merits of the case shall not be the subject of further proceedings. The foregoing provisions shall not apply to interim judgements.

(*e*) If an action is brought against a Contracting Party under this Convention, such Contracting Party may not, except in respect of measures of execution, invoke any jurisdictional immunities before the court competent in accordance with this article.

Article 14

(*a*) This Convention shall be applied without any discrimination based upon nationality, domicile, or residence.

(*b*) "National law" and "national legislation" mean the national law or the national legislation of the court having jurisdiction under this Convention over claims arising out of a nuclear incident, and that law or legislation shall apply to all matters both substantive and procedural not specifically governed by this Convention.

(*c*) That law and legislation shall be applied without any discrimination based upon nationality, domicile, or residence.

Article 15

(*a*) Any Contracting Party may take such measures as it deems necessary to provide for an increase in the amount of compensation specified in this Convention.

(*b*) In so far as compensation for damage involves public funds and is in excess of the 5,000,000 Special Drawing Rights referred to in Article 7, any such measure in whatever form may be applied under conditions which may derogate from the provisions of this Convention.

Article 16

Decisions taken by the Steering Committee under article 1(*a*)(ii), 1(*a*)(iii) and 1(*b*) shall be adopted by mutual agreement of the members representing the Contracting Parties.

Article 17

Any dispute arising between two or more Contracting Parties concerning the interpretation or application of this Convention shall be examined by the Steering Committee and in the absence of friendly settlement shall, upon the request of a Contracting Party concerned, be submitted to the Tribunal established by the Convention of 20th December, 1957, on the Establishment of a Security Control in the Field of Nuclear Energy.

Article 18

(*a*) Reservations to one or more of the provisions of this Convention may be made at any time prior to ratification of or accession to this Convention or prior to the time of notification under article 23 in respect of any territory or territories mentioned in the notification, and shall be admissible only if the terms of these reservations have been expressly accepted by the signatories.

(*b*) Such acceptance shall not be required from a signatory which has not itself ratified this Convention within a period of twelve months after the date of notification to it of such reservation by the Secretary–General of the Organisation in accordance with article 24.

(*c*) Any reservation admitted in accordance with this article may be withdrawn at any time by notification addressed to the Secretary–General of the Organisation.

Article 19

(a) This Convention shall be ratified. Instruments of ratification shall be deposited with the Secretary–General of the Organisation.

(b) This Convention shall come into force upon the deposit of instruments of ratification by not less than five of the signatories. For each Signatory ratifying thereafter, this Convention shall come into force upon the deposit of its instrument of ratification.

Article 20

Amendments to this Convention shall be adopted by mutual agreement of all the Contracting Parties. They shall come into force when ratified or confirmed by two-thirds of the Contracting Parties. For each Contracting Party ratifying or confirming thereafter, they shall come into force at the date of such ratification or confirmation.

Article 21

(a) The Government of any Member or Associate country of the Organisation which is not a signatory to this Convention may accede thereto by notification addressed to the Secretary–General of the Organisation.

(b) The Government of any other country which is not a signatory to this Convention may accede thereto by notification addressed to the Secretary–General of the Organisation and with the unanimous assent of the Contracting Parties. Such accession shall take effect from the date of such assent.

Article 22

(a) This Convention shall remain in effect for a period of ten years as from the date of its coming into force. Any Contracting Party may, by giving twelve months' notice to the Secretary–General of the Organisation, terminate the application of this Convention to itself at the end of the period of ten years.

(b) This Convention shall, after the period of ten years, remain in force for a period of five years for such Contracting Parties as have not terminated its application in accordance with paragraph *(a)* of this article, and thereafter for successive periods of five years for such Contracting Parties as have not terminated its application at the end of one of such periods of five years by giving twelve months' notice to that effect to the Secretary–General of the Organisation.

(c) A conference shall be convened by the Secretary–General of the Organisation in order to consider revisions to this Convention after a period of five years as from the date of its coming into force or, at any other time, at the request of a Contracting Party, within six months from the date of such request.

Article 23

(a) This Convention shall apply to the metropolitan territories of the Contracting Parties.

(b) Any signatory or Contracting Party may, at the time of signature or ratification of or accession to this Convention or at any later time, notify the Secretary–General of the Organisation that this Convention shall apply to those of its territories, including the territories for whose international relations it is responsible, to which this Convention is not applicable in accordance with paragraph *(a)* of this article and which are mentioned in the notification. Any such notification may in respect of any territory or territories mentioned therein be withdrawn by giving twelve months' notice to that effect to the Secretary–General of the Organisation.

(c) Any territories of a Contracting Party, including the territories for whose international relations it is responsible, to which this Convention does not apply shall

be regarded for the purposes of this Convention as being a territory of a non-Contracting State.

Article 24

The Secretary–General of the Organisation shall give notice to all Signatories and acceding Governments of the receipt of any instrument of ratification, accession, withdrawal, notification under article 23, and decisions of the Steering Committee under article 1*(a)* (ii), 1*(a)* (iii) and 1*(b)*. He shall also notify them of the date on which this Convention comes into force, the text of any amendment thereto and of the date on which such amendment comes into force, and any reservation made in accordance with article 18.

2.15   Convention Supplementary to the 1960 Convention on Third Party Liability in the Field of Nuclear Energy **(With Annex and as Amended Through 1964). Concluded at Brussels, 31 January 1963. Entered into force, 4 December 1974. 1041 UNTS 350;** *reprinted in* **2 ILM 685 (1963) & 5 Weston & Carlson V.J.2**

Article 1

The system instituted by this Convention is supplementary to that of the Paris Convention, shall be subject to the provisions of the Paris Convention, and shall be applied in accordance with the following Articles.

Article 2

(a) The system of this Convention shall apply to damage caused by nuclear incidents, other than those occurring entirely in the territory of a State which is not a Party to this Convention:

(i) for which an operator of a nuclear installation, used for peaceful purposes, situated in the territory of a Contracting Party to this Convention (hereinafter referred to as a "Contracting Party"), and which appears on the list established and kept up to date in accordance with the terms of Article 13, is liable under the Paris Convention, and

(ii) suffered

(1) in the territory of a Contracting Party; or

(2) on or over the high seas on board a ship or aircraft registered in the territory of a Contracting Party; or

(3) on or over the high seas by a national of a Contracting Party, provided that, in the case of damage to a ship or an aircraft, the ship or aircraft is registered in the territory of a Contracting Party;

provided that the courts of a Contracting Party have jurisdiction pursuant to the Paris Convention.

(b) Any Signatory or acceding Government may, at the time of signature of or accession to this Convention or on the deposit of its instrument of ratification, declare that, for the purposes of the application of paragraph (a)(ii)(3) of this Article, individuals or certain categories thereof, considered under its law as having their habitual residence in its territory, are assimilated to its own nationals.

(c) In this Article, the expression "a national of a Contracting Party" shall include a Contracting Party or any of its constituent sub-divisions, or a partnership, or any public or private body whether corporate or not established in the territory of a Contracting Party.

Article 3

(a) Under the conditions established by this Convention, the Contracting Parties undertake that compensation in respect of the damage referred to in Article 2 shall be provided up to the amount of 300 million Special Drawing Rights per incident.

(b) Such compensation shall be provided:

(i) up to an amount of at least 5 million Special Drawing Rights, out of funds provided by insurance or other financial security, such amount to be established by the legislation of the Contracting Party in whose territory the nuclear installation of the operator liable is situated;

(ii) between this amount and 175 million Special Drawing Rights, out of public funds to be made available by the Contracting Party in whose territory the nuclear installation of the operator liable is situated;

(iii) between 175 million and 300 million Special Drawing Rights, out of public funds to be made available by the Contracting Parties according to the formula for contributions specified in Article 12.

(c) For this purpose, each Contracting Party shall either:

(i) establish the maximum liability of the operator, pursuant to Article 7 of the Paris Convention, at 300 million Special Drawing Rights, and provide that such liability shall be covered by all the funds referred to in paragraph (b) of this Article; or

(ii) establish the maximum liability of the operator at an amount at least equal to that established pursuant to paragraph (b)(i) of this Article and provide that, in excess of such amount and up to 300 million Special Drawing Rights, the public funds referred to in paragraph (b)(ii) and (iii) of this Article shall be made available by some means other than as cover for the liability of the operator, provided that the rules of substance and procedure laid down in this Convention are not thereby affected.

(d) The obligation of the operator to pay compensation, interest or costs out of public funds made available pursuant to paragraphs (b)(ii) and (iii), and (f) of this Article shall only be enforceable against the operator as and when such funds are in fact made available.

(e) The Contracting Parties, in carrying out this Convention, undertake not to make use of the right provided for in Article 15(b) of the Paris Convention to apply special conditions:

(i) in respect of compensation for damage provided out of the funds referred to in paragraph (b)(i) of this Article;

(ii) other than those laid down in this Convention in respect of compensation for damage provided out of the public funds referred to in paragraph (b)(ii) and (iii) of this Article.

(f) The interest and costs referred to in Article 7(g) of the Paris Convention are payable in addition to the amounts referred to in paragraph (b) of this Article and shall be borne in so far as they are awarded in respect of compensation payable out of the funds referred to in:

(i) paragraph (b)(i) of this Article, by the operator liable;

(ii) paragraph (b)(ii) of this Article, by the Contracting Party in whose territory the nuclear installation of that operator is situated;

(iii) paragraph (b)(iii) of this Article, by the Contracting Parties together.

(g) For the purposes of this Convention, "Special Drawing Right" means the Special Drawing Right as it is defined by the International Monetary Fund. The amounts mentioned in this Convention shall be converted into the national currency of a Contracting Party in accordance with the value of that currency at the date of the incident, unless another date is fixed for a given incident by agreement between the Contracting Parties. The equivalent in Special Drawings Rights of the national currency of a Contracting Party shall be calculated in accordance with the method of valuation applied at the date in question by the International Monetary Fund for its own operations and transactions.

Article 4

(a) If a nuclear incident causes damage which gives rise to liability of more than one operator, the aggregate liability provided for in Article 5(d) of the Paris Convention shall not, to the extent that public funds have to be made available pursuant to Article 3(b)(ii) and (iii), exceed 300 million Special Drawing Rights.

(b) The total amount of the public funds made available pursuant to Article 3 (b)(ii) and (iii) shall not, in such event, exceed the difference between 300 million Special Drawing Rights and the sum of the amounts established with respect to such operators pursuant to Article 3(b)(i) or, in the case of an operator whose nuclear installation is situated in the territory of a State which is not a Party to this Convention, the amount established pursuant to Article 7 of the Paris Convention. If more than one Contracting Party is required to make available public funds pursuant to Article 3(b)(ii), such funds shall be made available by them in proportion to the number of nuclear installations situated in their respective territories, which are involved in the nuclear incident and of which the operators are liable.

Article 5

(a) Where the operator liable has a right of recourse pursuant to Article 6(f) of the Paris Convention, the Contracting Party in whose territory the nuclear installation of that operator is situated shall take such legislative measures as are necessary to enable both that Contracting Party and the other Contracting Parties to benefit from this recourse to the extent that public funds have been made available pursuant to Article 3(b)(ii) and (iii), and (f).

(b) Such legislation may provide for the recovery of public funds made available pursuant to Article 3(b)(ii) and (iii), and (f) from such operator if the damage results from fault on his part.

Article 6

In calculating the public funds to be made available pursuant to this Convention, account shall be taken only of those rights to compensation exercised within ten years from the date of the nuclear incident. In the case of damage caused by a nuclear incident involving nuclear fuel or radioactive products or waste which, at the time of the incident have been stolen, lost, jettisoned, or abandoned and have not yet been recovered such period shall not in any case exceed twenty years from the date of the theft, loss, jettison or abandonment. It shall also be extended in the cases and under the conditions laid down in Article 8(d) of the Paris Convention. Amendments made to claims after the expiry of this period, under the conditions laid down in Article 8(e) of the Paris Convention, shall also be taken into account.

Article 7

Where a Contracting Party makes use of the right provided for in Article 8(c) of the Paris Convention, the period which it establishes shall be a period of prescription of three years either from the date at which the person suffering damage has knowledge or from the date at which he ought reasonably to have known of both the damage and the operator liable.

Article 8

Any person who is entitled to benefit from the provisions of this Convention shall have the right to full compensation in accordance with national law for damage suffered, provided that, where the amount of damage exceeds or is likely to exceed:

(i) 300 million Special Drawing Rights; or

(ii) if there is aggregate liability under Article 5(d) of the Paris Convention and a higher sum results therefrom, such higher sum;

any Contracting Party may establish equitable criteria for apportionment. Such criteria shall be applied whatever the origin of the funds and, subject to the provisions of Article 2, without discrimination based on the nationality, domicile or residence of the person suffering the damage.

Article 9

(a) The system of disbursements by which the public funds required under Article 3(b)(ii) and (iii), and (f) are to be made available shall be that of the Contracting Party whose courts have jurisdiction.

(b) Each Contracting Party shall ensure that persons suffering damage may enforce their rights to compensation without having to bring separate proceedings according to the origin of the funds provided for such compensation.

(c) No Contracting Party shall be required to make available the public funds referred to in Article 3(b)(ii) and (iii) so long as any of the funds referred to in Article 3(b)(i) remain available.

Article 10

(a) The Contracting Party whose courts have jurisdiction shall be required to inform the other Contracting Parties of a nuclear incident and its circumstances as soon as it appears that the damage caused by such incident exceeds, or is likely to exceed, 175 million Special Drawing Rights. The Contracting Parties shall without delay make all the necessary arrangements to settle the procedure for their relations in this connection.

(b) Only the Contracting Party whose courts have jurisdiction shall be entitled to request the other Contracting Parties to make available the public funds required under Article 3(b)(iii) and (f) and shall have exclusive competence to disburse such funds.

(c) Such Contracting Party shall, when the occasion arises, exercise the right of recourse provided for in Article 5 on behalf of the other Contracting Parties who have made available public funds pursuant to Article 3(b)(iii) and (f).

(d) Settlements effected in respect of the payment of compensation out of the public funds referred to in Article 8(b)(ii) and (iii) in accordance with the conditions established by national legislation shall be recognized by the other Contracting Parties, and judgements entered by the competent courts in respect of such compensation shall become enforceable in the territory of the other Contracting Parties in accordance with the provisions of Article 13(d) of the Paris Convention.

Article 11

(a) If the courts having jurisdiction are those of a Contracting Party other than the Contracting Party in whose territory the nuclear installation of the operator liable is situated, the public funds required under Article 3(b)(ii) and (f) shall be made available by the first-named Contracting Party. The Contracting Party in whose territory the nuclear installation of the operator liable is situated shall reimburse to the other Contracting Party the sums paid. These two Contracting Parties shall agree on the procedure for reimbursement.

(b) In adopting all legislative, regulatory or administrative provisions, after the nuclear incident has occurred, concerning the nature, form and extent of the compensation, the procedure for making available the public funds required under Article 3(b)(ii) and, if necessary, the criteria for the apportionment of such funds, the Contracting Party whose courts have jurisdiction shall consult the Contracting Party in whose territory the nuclear installation of the operator liable is situated. It shall further take all measures necessary to enable the latter to intervene in proceedings and to participate in any settlement concerning compensation.

Article 12

(a) The formula for contributions according to which the Contracting Parties shall make available the public funds referred to in Article 3(b)(iii) shall be determined as follows:

(i) as to 50%, on the basis of the ratio between the gross national product at current prices of each Contracting Party and the total of the gross national products at current prices of all Contracting Parties as shown by the official statistics published by the Organisation for Economic Co-operation and Development for the year preceding the year in which the nuclear incident occurs;

(ii) as to 50%, on the basis of the ratio between the thermal power of the reactors situated in the territory of each Contracting Party and the total thermal power of the reactors situated in the territories of all the Contracting Parties. This calculation shall be made on the basis of the thermal power of the reactors shown at the date of the nuclear incident in the list referred to in Article 2(a)(i): provided that a reactor shall only be taken into consideration for the purposes of this calculation as from the date when it first reaches criticality.

(b) For the purposes of this Convention, "thermal power" means

(i) before the issue of a final operating licence, the planned thermal power;

(ii) after the issue of such licence, the thermal power authorized by the competent national authorities.

Article 13

(a) Each Contracting Party shall ensure that all nuclear installations used for peaceful purposes situated in its territory, and falling within the definition in Article 1 of the Paris Convention, appear in the list referred to in Article 2(a)(i).

(b) For this purpose, each Signatory or acceding Government shall, on the deposit of its instrument of ratification or accession, communicate to the Belgian Government full particulars of such installations.

(c) Such particulars shall indicate:

(i) in the case of all installations not yet completed, the expected date on which the risk of a nuclear incident will exist;

(ii) and further, in the case of reactors, the expected date on which they will first reach criticality, and also their thermal power.

(d) Each Contracting Party shall also communicate to the Belgian Government the exact date of the existence of the risk of a nuclear incident and, in the case of reactors, the date on which they first reached criticality.

(e) Each Contracting Party shall also communicate to the Belgian Government all modifications to be made to the list. Where such modifications include the addition of a nuclear installation, the communication must be made at least three months before the expected date on which the risk of a nuclear incident will exist.

(f) If a Contracting Party is of the opinion that the particulars, or any modification to be made to the list, communicated by another Contracting Party do not comply with the provisions of Article 2(a)(i) and of this Article, it may raise objections thereto only by addressing them to the Belgian Government within three months from the date on which it has received notice pursuant to paragraph (h) of this Article.

(g) If a Contracting Party is of the opinion that a communication required in accordance with this Article has not been made within the time prescribed in this Article, it may raise objections only by addressing them to the Belgian Government within three months from the date on which it knew of the facts which, in its opinion, ought to have been communicated.

(h) The Belgian Government shall give notice as soon as possible to each Contracting Party of the communications and objections which it has received pursuant to this Article.

(i) The list referred to in Article 2(a)(i) shall consist of all the particulars and modifications referred to in paragraphs (b), (c), (d) and (e) of this Article, it being understood that objections submitted pursuant to paragraphs (f) and (g) of this Article shall have effect retrospective to the date on which they were raised, if they are sustained.

(j) The Belgian Government shall supply any Contracting Party on demand with an up-to-date statement of the nuclear installations covered by this Convention and the details supplied in respect of them pursuant to this Article.

Article 14

(a) Except insofar as this Convention otherwise provides, each Contracting Party may exercise the powers vested in it by virtue of the Paris Convention, and any provisions made thereunder may be invoked against the other Contracting Parties in order that the public funds referred to in Article 3(b)(ii) and (iii) be made available.

(b) Any such provisions made by a Contracting Party pursuant to Articles 2 and 9 of the Paris Convention as a result of which the public funds referred to in Article 3(b)(ii) and (iii) are required to be made available may not be invoked against any other Contracting Party unless it has consented thereto.

(c) Nothing in this Convention shall prevent a Contracting Party from making provisions outside the scope of the Paris Convention and of this Convention, provided that such provisions shall not involve any further obligation on the part of the other Contracting Parties insofar as their public funds are concerned.

Article 15

(a) Any Contracting Party may conclude an agreement with a State which is not a Party to this Convention concerning compensation out of public funds for damage caused by a nuclear incident.

(b) To the extent that the conditions for payment of compensation under any such agreement are not more favourable than those which result from the measures adopted by the Contracting Party concerned for the application of the Paris Convention and of this Convention, the amount of damage caused by a nuclear incident covered by this Convention and for which compensation is payable by virtue of such an agreement may be taken into consideration, where the proviso to Article 8 applies, in calculating the total amount of damage caused by that incident.

(c) The provisions of paragraphs (a) and (b) of this Article shall in no case affect the obligations under Article 3(b)(ii) and (iii) of those Contracting Parties which have not given their consent to such agreement.

(d) Any Contracting Party intending to conclude such an agreement shall notify the other Contracting Parties of its intention. Agreements concluded shall be notified to the Belgian Government.

Article 16

(a) The Contracting Parties shall consult each other upon all problems of common interest raised by the application of this Convention and of the Paris Convention, especially Articles 20 and 22(c) of the latter Convention.

(b) They shall consult each other on the desirability of revising this Convention after a period of five years from the date of its coming into force, and at any other time upon the request of a Contracting Party.

Article 17

Any dispute arising between two or more Contracting Parties concerning the interpretation or application of this Convention shall, upon the request of a Contracting Party concerned, be submitted to the European Nuclear Energy Tribunal established by the Convention of 20th December 1957 on the Establishment of a Security Control in the Field of Nuclear Energy.

Article 18

(a) Reservations to one or more of the provisions of this Convention may be made at any time prior to ratification of this Convention if the terms of these reservations have been expressly accepted by all Signatories or, at the time of accession or of the application of the provisions of Articles 21 and 24, if the terms of these reservations have been expressly accepted by all Signatories and acceding Governments.

(b) Such acceptance shall not be required from a Signatory which has not itself ratified this Convention within a period of twelve months after the date of notification to it of such reservation by the Belgian Government in accordance with Article 25.

(c) Any reservation accepted in accordance with the provisions of paragraph (a) of this Article may be withdrawn at any time by notification addressed to the Belgian Government.

Article 19

No State may become or continue to be a Contracting Party to this Convention unless it is a Contracting Party to the Paris Convention.

Article 20

(a) The Annex to this Convention shall form an integral part thereof.

(b) This Convention shall be ratified. Instruments of ratification shall be deposited with the Belgian Government.

(c) This Convention shall come into force three months after the deposit of the sixth instrument of ratification.

(d) For each Signatory ratifying this Convention after the deposit of the sixth instrument of ratification, it shall come into force three months after the date of the deposit of its instrument of ratification.

Article 21

Amendments to this Convention shall be adopted by agreement among all the Contracting Parties. They shall come into force on the date when all Contracting Parties have ratified or confirmed them.

Article 22

(a) After the coming into force of this Convention, any Contracting Party to the Paris Convention which has not signed this Convention may request accession to this Convention by notification addressed to the Belgian Government.

(b) Such accession shall require the unanimous assent of the Contracting Parties.

(c) Once such assent has been given, the Contracting Party to the Paris Convention requesting accession shall deposit its instrument of accession with the Belgian Government.

(d) The accession shall take effect three months from the date of deposit of the instrument of accession.

Article 23

(a) This Convention shall remain in force until the expiry of the Paris Convention.

(b) Any Contracting Party may, by giving twelve months' notice to the Belgian Government, terminate the application of this Convention to itself after the end of the period of ten years specified in Article 22(a) of the Paris Convention. Within six months after receipt of such notice, any other Contracting Party may, by notice to the Belgian Government, terminate the application of this Convention to itself as from the date when it ceases to have effect in respect of the Contracting Party which first gave notice.

(c) The expiry of this Convention or the withdrawal of a Contracting Party shall not terminate the obligations assumed by each Contracting Party under this Convention to pay compensation for damage caused by nuclear incidents occurring before the date of such expiry or withdrawal.

(d) The Contracting Parties shall, in good time, consult each other on what measures should be taken after the expiry of this Convention or the withdrawal of one or more of the Contracting Parties, to provide compensation comparable to that accorded by this Convention for damage caused by nuclear incidents occurring after the date of such expiry or withdrawal and for which the operator of a nuclear installation in operation before such date within the territories of the Contracting Parties is liable.

Article 24

(a) This Convention shall apply to the metropolitan territories of the Contracting Parties.

(b) Any Contracting Party desiring the application of this Convention to one or more of the territories in respect of which, pursuant to Article 23 of the Paris Convention, it has given notification of application of that Convention, shall address a request to the Belgian Government.

(c) The application of this Convention to any such territory shall require the unanimous assent of the Contracting Parties.

(d) Once such assent has been given, the Contracting Party concerned shall address to the Belgian Government a notification which shall take effect as from the date of its receipt.

(e) Such notification may, as regards any territory mentioned therein, be withdrawn by the Contracting Party which has made it by giving twelve months' notice to that effect to the Belgian Government.

(f) If the Paris Convention ceases to apply to any such territory, this Convention shall also cease to apply thereto.

Article 25

The Belgian Government shall notify all Signatories and acceding Governments of the receipt of any instrument of ratification, accession or withdrawal, and shall also notify them of the date on which this Convention comes into force, the text of any amendment thereto and the date on which such amendment comes into force, any reservations made in accordance with Article 18, and all notifications which it has received.

ANNEX

THE GOVERNMENTS OF THE CONTRACTING PARTIES declare that compensation for damage caused by a nuclear incident not covered by the Supplementary Convention solely by reason of the fact that the relevant nuclear installation, on account of its utilization, is not on the list referred to in Article 2 of the Supplementary Convention, (including the case where such installation is considered by one or more but not all of the Governments to be outside the Paris Convention):

— shall be provided without discrimination among the nationals of the Contracting Parties to the Supplementary Convention; and

— shall not be limited to less than 300 million Special Drawing Rights.

In addition, if they have not already done so, they shall endeavor to make the rules for compensation of persons suffering damage caused by such incidents as similar as possible to those established in respect of nuclear incidents occurring in connection with nuclear installations covered by the Supplementary Convention.

2.16 IAEA Convention on Early Notification of a Nuclear Accident. Concluded at Vienna and New York, 26 September 1986. Entered into force, 27 October 1986. 1439 UNTS 275; *reprinted in* 25 ILM 1369 (1986) & 5 Weston & Carlson V.I.2

Article 1
Scope of application

1. This Convention shall apply in the event of any accident involving facilities or activities of a State Party or of persons or legal entities under its jurisdiction or control, referred to in paragraph 2 below, from which a release of radioactive material occurs or is likely to occur and which has resulted or may result in an international transboundary release that could be of radiological safety significance for another State.

2. The facilities and activities referred to in paragraph 1 are the following:

(a) any nuclear reactor wherever located;

(b) any nuclear fuel cycle facility;

(c) any radioactive waste management facility;

(d) the transport and storage of nuclear fuels or radioactive wastes;

(e) the manufacture, use, storage, disposal and transport of radioisotopes for agricultural, industrial, medical and related scientific and research purposes; and

(f) the use of radioisotopes for power generation in space objects.

Article 2
Notification and information

In the event of an accident specified in article 1 (hereinafter referred to as a "nuclear accident"), the State Party referred to in that article shall:

(a) forthwith notify, directly or through the International Atomic Energy Agency (hereinafter referred to as the "Agency"), those States which are or may be physically affected as specified in article 1 and the Agency of the nuclear accident, its nature, the time of its occurrence and its exact location where appropriate; and

(b) promptly provide the States referred to in sub-paragraph (a), directly or through the Agency, and the Agency with such available information relevant to minimizing the radiological consequences in those States, as specified in article 5.

Article 3
Other Nuclear Accidents

With a view to minimizing the radiological consequences, States Parties may notify in the event of nuclear accidents other than those specified in article 1.

Article 4
Functions of the Agency

The Agency shall:

(a) forthwith inform States Parties, Member States, other States which are or may be physically affected as specified in article 1 and relevant international intergovernmental organizations (hereinafter referred to as "international organizations") of a notification received pursuant to sub-paragraph (a) of article 2; and

(b) promptly provide any State Party, Member State or relevant international organization, upon request, with the information received pursuant to sub-paragraph (b) of article 2.

Article 5
Information to be provided

1.   The information to be provided pursuant to sub-paragraph (b) of article 2 shall comprise the following data as then available to the notifying State Party:

(a) the time, exact location where appropriate, and the nature of the nuclear accident;

(b) the facility or activity involved;

(c) the assumed or established cause and the foreseeable development of the nuclear accident relevant to the transboundary release of the radioactive materials;

(d) the general characteristics of the radioactive release, including, as far as is practicable and appropriate, the nature, probable physical and chemical form and the quantity, composition and effective height of the radioactive release;

(e) information on current and forecast meteorological and hydrological conditions, necessary for forecasting the transboundary release of the radioactive materials;

(f) the results of environmental monitoring relevant to the transboundary release of the radioactive materials;

(g) the off-site protective measures taken or planned;

(h) the predicted behaviour over time of the radioactive release.

2.   Such information shall be supplemented at appropriate intervals by further relevant information on the development of the emergency situation, including its foreseeable or actual termination.

3.   Information received pursuant to sub-paragraph (b) of article 2 may be used without restriction, except when such information is provided in confidence by the notifying State Party.

Article 6
Consultations

A State Party providing information pursuant to sub-paragraph (b) of article 2 shall, as far as is reasonably practicable, respond promptly to a request for further information or consultations sought by an affected State Party with a view to minimizing the radiological consequences in that State.

Article 7
Competent authorities and points of contact

1.   Each State Party shall make known to the Agency and to other States Parties, directly or through the Agency, its competent authorities and point of contact responsible for issuing and receiving the notification and information referred to in article 2. Such points of contact and a focal point within the Agency shall be available continuously.

2.   Each State Party shall promptly inform the Agency of any changes that may occur in the information referred to in paragraph 1.

3.   The Agency shall maintain an up-to-date list of such national authorities and points of contact as well as points of contact of relevant international organizations and shall provide it to States Parties and Member States and to relevant international organizations.

Article 8
Assistance to States Parties

The Agency shall, in accordance with its Statute and upon a request of a State Party which does not have nuclear activities itself and borders on a State having an active nuclear programme but not Party, conduct investigations into the feasibility and establishment of an appropriate radiation monitoring system in order to facilitate the achievement of the objectives of this Convention.

Article 9
Bilateral and multilateral arrangements

In furtherance of their mutual interests, States Parties may consider, where deemed appropriate, the conclusion of bilateral or multilateral arrangements relating to the subject matter of this Convention.

Article 10
Relationship to other international agreements

This Convention shall not affect the reciprocal rights and obligations of States Parties under existing international agreements which relate to the matters covered by this Convention, or under future international agreements concluded in accordance with the object and purpose of this Convention.

Article 11
Settlement of disputes

1.   In the event of a dispute between States Parties, or between a State Party and the Agency, concerning the interpretation or application of this Convention, the parties to the dispute shall consult with a view to the settlement of the dispute by negotiation or by any other peaceful means of settling disputes acceptable to them.

2.   If a dispute of this character between States Parties cannot be settled within one year from the request for consultation pursuant to paragraph 1, it shall, at the request of any party to such dispute, be submitted to arbitration or referred to the International Court of Justice for decision. Where a dispute is submitted to arbitration, if, within six months from the date of the request, the parties to the dispute are unable to agree on the organization of the arbitration, a party may request the President of the International Court of Justice or the Secretary–General of the United Nations to appoint one or more arbitrators. In cases of conflicting requests by the parties to the dispute, the request to the Secretary–General of the United Nations shall have priority.

3.   When signing, ratifying, accepting, approving or acceding to this Convention, a State may declare that it does not consider itself bound by either or both of the dispute settlement procedures provided for in paragraph 2. The other States Parties shall not be bound by a dispute settlement procedure provided for in paragraph 2 with respect to a State Party for which such a declaration is in force.

4.   A State Party which has made a declaration in accordance with paragraph 3 may at any time withdraw it by notification to the depositary.

Article 12
Entry into force

1.   This Convention shall be open for signature by all States and Namibia, represented by the United Nations Council for Namibia, at the headquarters of the International Atomic Energy Agency in Vienna and at the headquarters of the United Nations in New York, from 26 September 1986 and 6 October 1986 respectively, until its entry into force or for twelve months, whichever period is longer.

2.   A State and Namibia, represented by the United Nations Council for Namibia, may express its consent to be bound by this Convention either by signature, or by deposit of an instrument of ratification, acceptance or approval following signature made subject to ratification, acceptance or approval, or by deposit of an instrument of

accession. The instruments of ratification, acceptance, approval or accession shall be deposited with the depositary.

3. This Convention shall enter into force thirty days after consent to be bound has been expressed by three States.

4. For each State expressing consent to be bound by this Convention after its entry into force, this Convention shall enter into force for that State thirty days after the date of expression of consent.

5. (a) This Convention shall be open for accession, as provided for in this article, by international organizations and regional integration organizations constituted by sovereign States, which have competence in respect of the negotiation, conclusion and application of international agreements in matters covered by this Convention.

(b) In matters within their competence such organizations shall, on their own behalf, exercise the rights and fulfil the obligations which this Convention attributes to States Parties.

(c) When depositing its instrument of accession, such an organization shall communicate to the depositary a declaration indicating the extent of its competence in respect of matters covered by this Convention.

(d) Such an organization shall not hold any vote additional to those of its Member States.

Article 13
Provisional application

A State may, upon signature or at any later date before this Convention enters into force for it, declare that it will apply this Convention provisionally.

Article 14
Amendments

1. A State Party may propose amendments to this Convention. The proposed amendment shall be submitted to the depositary who shall circulate it immediately to all other States Parties.

2. If a majority of the States Parties request the depositary to convene a conference to consider the proposed amendments, the depositary shall invite all States Parties to attend such a conference to begin not sooner than thirty days after the invitations are issued. Any amendment adopted at the conference by a two-thirds majority of all States Parties shall be laid down in a protocol which is open to signature in Vienna and New York by all States Parties.

3. The protocol shall enter into force thirty days after consent to be bound has been expressed by three States. For each State expressing consent to be bound by the protocol after its entry into force, the protocol shall enter into force for that State thirty days after the date of expression of consent.

Article 15
Denunciation

1. A State Party may denounce this Convention by written notification to the depositary.

2. Denunciation shall take effect one year following the date on which the notification is received by the depositary.

Article 16
Depositary

1. The Director General of the Agency shall be the depositary of this Convention.

2. The Director General of the Agency shall promptly notify States Parties and all other States of:

(a) each signature of this Convention or any protocol of amendment;

(b) each deposit of an instrument of ratification, acceptance, approval or accession concerning this Convention or any protocol of amendment;

(c) any declaration or withdrawal thereof in accordance with article 11;

(d) any declaration of provisional application of this Convention in accordance with article 13;

(e) the entry into force of this Convention and of any amendment thereto; and

(f) any denunciation made under article 15.

Article 17
Authentic texts and certified copies

The original of this Convention, of which the Arabic, Chinese, English, French, Russian and Spanish texts are equally authentic, shall be deposited with the Director General of the International Atomic Energy Agency who shall send certified copies to States Parties and all other States.

* * *

2.17 IAEA Convention on Assistance in the Case of a Nuclear Accident or Radiological Emergency. Concluded at Vienna and New York, 26 September 1986. Entered into force, 26 February 1987. 1457 UNTS 133; *reprinted in* 25 ILM 1377 (1986) & 5 Weston & Carlson V.I.3

Article 1
General provisions

1. The States Parties shall cooperate between themselves and with the International Atomic Energy Agency (hereinafter referred to as the "Agency") in accordance with the provisions of this Convention to facilitate prompt assistance in the event of a nuclear accident or radiological emergency to minimize its consequences and to protect life, property and the environment from the effects of radioactive releases.

2. To facilitate such cooperation States Parties may agree on bilateral or multilateral arrangements or, where appropriate, a combination of these, for preventing or minimizing injury and damage which may result in the event of a nuclear accident or radiological emergency.

3. The States Parties request the Agency, acting within the framework of its Statute, to use its best endeavours in accordance with the provisions of this Convention to promote, facilitate and support the cooperation between States Parties provided for in this Convention.

Article 2
Provision of assistance

1. If a State Party needs assistance in the event of a nuclear accident or radiological emergency, whether or not such accident or emergency originates within its territory, jurisdiction or control, it may call for such assistance from any other State Party, directly or through the Agency, and from the Agency, or, where appropriate, from other international intergovernmental organizations (hereinafter referred to as "international organizations").

2. A State Party requesting assistance shall specify the scope and type of assistance required and, where practicable, provide the assisting party with such information as may be necessary for that party to determine the extent to which it is able to meet the request. In the event that it is not practicable for the requesting State Party to specify the scope and type of assistance required, the requesting State Party and the assisting party shall, in consultation, decide upon the scope and type of assistance required.

3. Each State Party to which a request for such assistance is directed shall promptly decide and notify the requesting State Party, directly or through the Agency, whether it is in a position to render the assistance requested, and the scope and terms of the assistance that might be rendered.

4. States Parties shall, within the limits of their capabilities, identify and notify the Agency of experts, equipment and materials which could be made available for the provision of assistance to other States Parties in the event of a nuclear accident or radiological emergency as well as the terms, especially financial, under which such assistance could be provided.

5. Any State Party may request assistance relating to medical treatment or temporary relocation into the territory of another State Party of people involved in a nuclear accident or radiological emergency.

6. The Agency shall respond, in accordance with its Statute and as provided for in this Convention, to a requesting State Party's or a Member State's request for assistance in the event of a nuclear accident or radiological emergency by:

(a) making available appropriate resources allocated for this purpose;

(b) transmitting promptly the request to other States and international organizations which, according to the Agency's information, may possess the necessary resources; and

(c) if so requested by the requesting State, co-ordinating the assistance at the international level which may thus become available.

Article 3
Direction and control of assistance

Unless otherwise agreed:

(a) the overall direction, control, co-ordination and supervision of the assistance shall be the responsibility within its territory of the requesting State. The assisting party should, where the assistance involves personnel, designate in consultation with the requesting State, the person who should be in charge of and retain immediate operational supervision over the personnel and the equipment provided by it. The designated person should exercise such supervision in cooperation with the appropriate authorities of the requesting State;

(b) the requesting State shall provide, to the extent of its capabilities, local facilities and services for the proper and effective administration of the assistance. It shall also ensure the protection of personnel, equipment and materials brought into its territory by or on behalf of the assisting party for such purpose;

(c) ownership of equipment and materials provided by either party during the periods of assistance shall be unaffected, and their return shall be ensured;

(d) a State Party providing assistance in response to a request under paragraph 5 of article 2 shall co-ordinate that assistance within its territory.

Article 4
Competent authorities and points of contact

1.   Each State Party shall make known to the Agency and to other States Parties, directly or through the Agency, its competent authorities and point of contact authorized to make and receive requests for and to accept offers of assistance. Such points of contact and a focal point within the Agency shall be available continuously.

2.   Each State Party shall promptly inform the Agency of any changes that may occur in the information referred to in paragraph 1.

3.   The Agency shall regularly and expeditiously provide to States Parties, Member States and relevant international organizations the information referred to in paragraphs 1 and 2.

Article 5
Functions of the Agency

The States Parties request the Agency, in accordance with paragraph 3 of article 1 and without prejudice to other provisions of this Convention, to:

(a) collect and disseminate to States Parties and Member States information concerning:

(i) experts, equipment and materials which could be made available in the event of nuclear accidents or radiological emergencies;

(ii) methodologies, techniques and available results of research relating to response to nuclear accidents or radiological emergencies;

(b) assist a State Party or a Member State when requested in any of the following or other appropriate matters:

(i) preparing both emergency plans in the case of nuclear accidents and radiological emergencies and the appropriate legislation;

(ii) developing appropriate training programs for personnel to deal with nuclear accidents and radiological emergencies;

(iii) transmitting requests for assistance and relevant information in the event of a nuclear accident or radiological emergency;

(iv) developing appropriate radiation monitoring programmes, procedures and standards;

(v) conducting investigations into the feasibility of establishing appropriate radiation monitoring systems;

(c) make available to a State Party or a Member State requesting assistance in the event of a nuclear accident or radiological emergency appropriate resources allocated for the purpose of conducting an initial assessment of the accident or emergency;

(d) offer its good offices to the States Parties and Member States in the event of a nuclear accident or radiological emergency;

(e) establish and maintain liaison with relevant international organizations for the purposes of obtaining and exchanging relevant information and data, and make a list of such organizations available to States Parties, Member States and the aforementioned organizations.

Article 6
Confidentiality and public statements

1. The requesting State and the assisting party shall protect the confidentiality of any confidential information that becomes available to either of them in connection with the assistance in the event of a nuclear accident or radiological emergency. Such information shall be used exclusively for the purpose of the assistance agreed upon.

2. The assisting party shall make every effort to coordinate with the requesting State before releasing information to the public on the assistance provided in connection with a nuclear accident or radiological emergency.

Article 7
Reimbursement of costs

1. An assisting party may offer assistance without costs to the requesting State. When considering whether to offer assistance on such a basis, the assisting party shall take into account:

(a) the nature of the nuclear accident or radiological emergency;

(b) the place of origin of the nuclear accident or radiological emergency;

(c) the needs of developing countries;

(d) the particular needs of countries without nuclear facilities; and

(e) any other relevant factors.

2. When assistance is provided wholly or partly on a reimbursement basis, the requesting State shall reimburse the assisting party for the costs incurred for the services rendered by persons or organizations acting on its behalf, and for all expenses in connection with the assistance to the extent that such expenses are not directly defrayed by the requesting State. Unless otherwise agreed, reimbursement shall be provided promptly after the assisting party has presented its request for reimbursement to the requesting State, and in respect of costs other than local costs, shall be freely transferrable.

3.   Notwithstanding paragraph 2, the assisting party may at any time waive, or agree to the postponement of, the reimbursement in whole or in part. In considering such waiver or postponement, assisting parties shall give due consideration to the needs of developing countries.

Article 8
Privileges, immunities and facilities

1.   The requesting State shall afford to personnel of the assisting party and personnel acting on its behalf the necessary privileges, immunities and facilities for the performance of their assistance functions.

2.   The requesting State shall afford the following privileges and immunities to personnel of the assisting party or personnel acting on its behalf who have been duly notified to and accepted by the requesting State:

(a) immunity from arrest, detention and legal process, including criminal, civil and administrative jurisdiction, of the requesting State, in respect of acts or omissions in the performance of their duties; and

(b) exemption from taxation, duties or other charges, except those which are normally incorporated in the price of goods or paid for services rendered, in respect of the performance of their assistance functions.

3.   The requesting State shall:

(a) afford the assisting party exemption from taxation, duties or other charges on the equipment and property brought into the territory of the requesting State by the assisting party for the purpose of the assistance; and

(b) provide immunity from seizure, attachment or requisition of such equipment and property.

4.   The requesting State shall ensure the return of such equipment and property. If requested by the assisting party, the requesting State shall arrange, to the extent it is able to do so, for the necessary decontamination of recoverable equipment involved in the assistance before its return.

5.   The requesting State shall facilitate the entry into, stay in and departure from its national territory of personnel notified pursuant to paragraph 2 and of equipment and property involved in the assistance.

6.   Nothing in this article shall require the requesting State to provide its nationals or permanent residents with the privileges and immunities provided for in the foregoing paragraphs.

7.   Without prejudice to the privileges and immunities, all beneficiaries enjoying such privileges and immunities under this article have a duty to respect the laws and regulations of the requesting State. They shall also have the duty not to interfere in the domestic affairs of the requesting State.

8.   Nothing in this article shall prejudice rights and obligations with respect to privileges and immunities afforded pursuant to other international agreements or the rules of customary international law.

9.   When signing, ratifying, accepting, approving or acceding to this Convention, a State may declare that it does not consider itself bound in whole or in part by paragraphs 2 and 3.

10.   A State Party which has made a declaration in accordance with paragraph 9 may at any time withdraw it by notification to the depositary.

Article 9
Transit of personnel, equipment and property

Each State Party shall, at the request of the requesting State or the assisting party, seek to facilitate the transit through its territory of duly notified personnel, equipment and property involved in the assistance to and from the requesting State.

Article 10
Claims and compensation

1.   The States Parties shall closely cooperate in order to facilitate the settlement of legal proceedings and claims under this article.

2.   Unless otherwise agreed, a requesting State shall in respect of death or of injury to persons, damage to or loss of property, or damage to the environment caused within its territory or other area under its jurisdiction or control in the course of providing the assistance requested:

(a) not bring any legal proceedings against the assisting party or persons or other legal entities acting on its behalf;

(b) assume responsibility for dealing with legal proceedings and claims brought by third parties against the assisting party or against persons or other legal entities acting on its behalf;

(c) hold the assisting party or persons or other legal entities acting on its behalf harmless in respect of legal proceedings and claims referred to in sub-paragraph (b); and

(d) compensate the assisting party or persons or other legal entities acting on its behalf for:

(i) death of or injury to personnel of the assisting party or persons acting on its behalf;

(ii) loss of or damage to non-consumable equipment or materials related to the assistance;

except in cases of wilful misconduct by the individuals who caused the death, injury, loss or damage.

3.   This article shall not prevent compensation or indemnity available under any applicable international agreement or national law of any State.

4.   Nothing in this article shall require the requesting State to apply paragraph 2 in whole or in part to its nationals or permanent residents.

5.   When signing, ratifying, accepting, approving or acceding to this Convention, a State may declare:

(a) that it does not consider itself bound in whole or in part by paragraph 2;

(b) that it will not apply paragraph 2 in whole or in part in cases of gross negligence by the individuals who caused the death, injury, loss or damage.

6.   A State Party which has made a declaration in accordance with paragraph 5 may at any time withdraw it by notification to the depositary.

Article 11
Termination of assistance

The requesting State or the assisting party may at any time, after appropriate consultations and by notification in writing, request the termination of assistance received or provided under this Convention. Once such a request has been made, the parties involved shall consult with each other to make arrangements for the proper conclusion of the assistance.

Article 12
Relationship to other international agreements

This Convention shall not affect the reciprocal rights and obligations of States Parties under existing international agreements which relate to the matters covered by this Convention, or under future international agreements concluded in accordance with the object and purpose of this Convention.

Article 13
Settlement of disputes

1.   In the event of a dispute between States Parties, or between a State Party and the Agency, concerning the interpretation or application of this Convention, the parties to the dispute shall consult with a view to the settlement of the dispute by negotiation or by any other peaceful means of settling disputes acceptable to them.

2.   If a dispute of this character between States Parties cannot be settled within one year from the request for consultation pursuant to paragraph 1, it shall, at the request of any party to such dispute, be submitted to arbitration or referred to the International Court of Justice for decision. Where a dispute is submitted to arbitration, if, within six months from the date of the request, the parties to the dispute are unable to agree on the organization of the arbitration, a party may request the President of the International Court of Justice or the Secretary–General of the United Nations to appoint one or more arbitrators. In cases of conflicting requests by the parties to the dispute, the request to the Secretary–General of the United Nations shall have priority.

3.   When signing, ratifying, accepting, approving or acceding to this Convention, a State may declare that it does not consider itself bound by either or both of the dispute settlement procedures provided for in paragraph 2. The other States Parties shall not be bound by a dispute settlement procedure provided for in paragraph 2 with respect to a State Party for which such a declaration is in force.

4.   A State Party which has made a declaration in accordance with paragraph 3 may at any time withdraw it by notification to the depositary.

Article 14
Entry into force

1.   This Convention shall be open for signature by all States and Namibia, represented by the United Nations Council for Namibia, at the Headquarters of the International Atomic Energy Agency in Vienna and at the Headquarters of the United Nations in New York, from 26 September 1986 and 6 October 1986 respectively, until its entry into force or for twelve months, whichever period is longer.

2.   A State and Namibia, represented by the United Nations Council for Namibia, may express its consent to be bound by this Convention either by signature, or by deposit of an instrument of ratification, acceptance or approval following signature made subject to ratification, acceptance or approval, or by deposit of an instrument of accession. The instruments of ratification, acceptance, approval or accession shall be deposited with the depositary.

3.   This Convention shall enter into force thirty days after consent to be bound has been expressed by three States.

4.   For each State expressing consent to be bound by this Convention after its entry into force, this Convention shall enter into force for that State thirty days after the date of expression of consent.

5.   (a) This Convention shall be open for accession, as provided for in this article, by international organizations and regional integration organizations constituted by

sovereign States, which have competence in respect of the negotiation, conclusion and application of international agreements in matters covered by this Convention.

(b) In matters within their competence such organizations shall, on their own behalf, exercise the rights and fulfil the obligations which this Convention attributes to States Parties.

(c) When depositing its instrument of accession, such an organization shall communicate to the depositary a declaration indicating the extent of its competence in respect of matters covered by this Convention.

(d) Such an organization shall not hold any vote additional to those of its Member States.

Article 15
Provisional application

A State may, upon signature or at any later date before this Convention enters into force for it, declare that it will apply this Convention provisionally.

Article 16
Amendments

1. A State Party may propose amendments to this Convention. The proposed amendment shall be submitted to the depositary who shall circulate it immediately to all other States Parties.

2. If a majority of the States Parties request the depositary to convene a conference to consider the proposed amendments, the depositary shall invite all States Parties to attend such a conference to begin not sooner than thirty days after the invitations are issued. Any amendment adopted at the conference by a two-thirds majority of all States Parties shall be laid down in a protocol which is open to signature in Vienna and New York by all States Parties.

3. The protocol shall enter into force thirty days after consent to be bound has been expressed by three States. For each State expressing consent to be bound by the protocol after its entry into force, the protocol shall enter into force for that State thirty days after the date of expression of consent.

Article 17
Denunciation

1. A State Party may denounce this Convention by written notification to the depositary.

2. Denunciation shall take effect one year following the date on which the notification is received by the depositary.

Article 18
Depositary

1. The Director General of the Agency shall be the depositary of this Convention.

2. The Director General of the Agency shall promptly notify States Parties and all other States of:

(a) each signature of this Convention or any protocol of amendment;

(b) each deposit of an instrument of ratification, acceptance, approval or accession concerning this Convention or any protocol of amendment;

(c) any declaration or withdrawal thereof in accordance with articles 8, 10 and 13;

(d) any declaration of provisional application of this Convention in accordance with article 15;

(e) the entry into force of this Convention and of any amendment thereto; and

(f) any denunciation made under article 17.

Article 19
Authentic texts and certified copies

The original of this Convention, of which the Arabic, Chinese, English, French, Russian and Spanish texts are equally authentic, shall be deposited with the Director General of the International Atomic Energy Agency who shall send certified copies to States Parties and all other States.

2.18 CONVENTION ON NUCLEAR SAFETY. Adopted on 17 June 1994. Entered into force, 24 October 1996. 1963 UNTS 293; *reprinted in* 33 ILM 1514 (1994) & 5 Weston & Carlson V.I.6a

THE CONTRACTING PARTIES

(i) Aware of the importance to the international community of ensuring that the use of nuclear energy is safe, well regulated and environmentally sound;

(ii) Reaffirming the necessity of continuing to promote a high level of nuclear safety worldwide;

(iii) Reaffirming that responsibility for nuclear safety rests with the State having jurisdiction over a nuclear installation;

(iv) Desiring to promote an effective nuclear safety culture;

(v) Aware that accidents at nuclear installations have the potential for transboundary impacts;

(vi) Keeping in mind the Convention on the Physical Protection of Nuclear Material (1979), the Convention on Early Notification of a Nuclear Accident (1986), and the Convention on Assistance in the Case of a Nuclear Accident or Radiological Emergency (1986);

(vii) Affirming the importance of international co-operation for the enhancement of nuclear safety through existing bilateral and multilateral mechanisms and the establishment of this incentive Convention;

(viii) Recognizing that this Convention entails a commitment to the application of fundamental safety principles for nuclear installations rather than of detailed safety standards and that there are internationally formulated safety guidelines which are updated from time to time and so can provide guidance on contemporary means of achieving a high level of safety;

(ix) Affirming the need to begin promptly the development of an international convention on the safety of radioactive waste management as soon as the ongoing process to develop waste management safety fundamentals has resulted in broad international agreement;

(x) Recognizing the usefulness of further technical work in connection with the safety of other parts of the nuclear fuel cycle, and that this work may, in time, facilitate the development of current or future international instruments;

HAVE AGREED as follows:

CHAPTER 1. OBJECTIVES, DEFINITIONS AND SCOPE OF APPLICATION

ARTICLE 1. OBJECTIVES

The objectives of this Convention are:

(i) to achieve and maintain a high level of nuclear safety worldwide through the enhancement of national measures and international co-operation including, where appropriate, safety-related technical co-operation;

(ii) to establish and maintain effective defences in nuclear installations against potential radiological hazards in order to protect individuals, society and the environment from harmful effects of ionizing radiation from such installations;

(iii) to prevent accidents with radiological consequences and to mitigate such consequences should they occur.

ARTICLE 2. DEFINITIONS

For the purpose of this Convention:

(i) "nuclear installation" means for each Contracting Party any land-based civil nuclear power plant under its jurisdiction including such storage, handling and treatment facilities for radioactive materials as are on the same site and are directly related to the operation of the nuclear power plant. Such a plant ceases to be a nuclear installation when all nuclear fuel elements have been removed permanently from the reactor core and have been stored safely in accordance with approved procedures, and a decommissioning programme has been agreed to by the regulatory body.

(ii) "regulatory body" means for each Contracting Party any body or bodies given the legal authority by that Contracting Party to grant licences and to regulate the siting, design, construction, commissioning, operation or decommissioning of nuclear installations.

(iii) "licence" means any authorization granted by the regulatory body to the applicant to have the responsibility for the siting, design, construction, commissioning, operation or decommissioning of a nuclear installation.

ARTICLE 3. SCOPE OF APPLICATION

This Convention shall apply to the safety of nuclear installations.

CHAPTER 2. OBLIGATIONS

(a) General Provisions

ARTICLE 4. IMPLEMENTING MEASURES

Each Contracting Party shall take, within the framework of its national law, the legislative, regulatory and administrative measures and other steps necessary for implementing its obligations under this Convention.

ARTICLE 5. REPORTING

Each Contracting Party shall submit for review, prior to each meeting referred to in Article 20, a report on the measures it has taken to implement each of the obligations of this Convention.

ARTICLE 6. EXISTING NUCLEAR INSTALLATIONS

Each Contracting Party shall take the appropriate steps to ensure that the safety of nuclear installations existing at the time the Convention enters into force for that Contracting Party is reviewed as soon as possible. When necessary in the context of this Convention, the Contracting Party shall ensure that all reasonably practicable improvements are made as a matter of urgency to upgrade the safety of the nuclear installation. If such upgrading cannot be achieved, plans should be implemented to shut down the nuclear installation as soon as practically possible. The timing of the shut-down may take into account the whole energy context and possible alternatives as well as the social, environmental and economic impact.

(b) Legislation and regulation

ARTICLE 7. LEGISLATIVE AND REGULATORY FRAMEWORK

1. Each Contracting Party shall establish and maintain a legislative and regulatory framework to govern the safety of nuclear installations.

2. The legislative and regulatory framework shall provide for:

(i) the establishment of applicable national safety requirements and regulations;

(ii) a system of licensing with regard to nuclear installations and the prohibition of the operation of a nuclear installation without a licence;

(iii) a system of regulatory inspection and assessment of nuclear installations to ascertain compliance with applicable regulations and the terms of licences;

(iv) the enforcement of applicable regulations and of the terms of licences, including suspension, modification or revocation.

ARTICLE 8.   REGULATORY BODY

1.   Each Contracting Party shall establish or designate a regulatory body entrusted with the implementation of the legislative and regulatory framework referred to in Article 7, and provided with adequate authority, competence and financial and human resources to fulfil its assigned responsibilities.

2.   Each Contracting Party shall take the appropriate steps to ensure an effective separation between the functions of the regulatory body and those of any other body or organization concerned with the promotion or utilization of nuclear energy.

ARTICLE 9.   RESPONSIBILITY OF THE LICENCE HOLDER

Each Contracting Party shall ensure that prime responsibility for the safety of a nuclear installation rests with the holder of the relevant licence and shall take the appropriate steps to ensure that each such licence holder meets its responsibility.

(c) *General Safety Considerations*

ARTICLE 10.   PRIORITY TO SAFETY

Each Contracting Party shall take the appropriate steps to ensure that all organizations engaged in activities directly related to nuclear installations shall establish policies that give due priority to nuclear safety.

ARTICLE 11.   FINANCIAL AND HUMAN RESOURCES

1.   Each Contracting Party shall take the appropriate steps to ensure that adequate financial resources are available to support the safety of each nuclear installation throughout its life.

2.   Each Contracting Party shall take the appropriate steps to ensure that sufficient numbers of qualified staff with appropriate education, training and retraining are available for all safety-related activities in or for each nuclear installation, throughout its life.

ARTICLE 12.   HUMAN FACTORS

Each Contracting Party shall take the appropriate steps to ensure that the capabilities and limitations of human performance are taken into account throughout the life of a nuclear installation.

ARTICLE 13.   QUALITY ASSURANCE

Each Contracting Party shall take the appropriate steps to ensure that quality assurance programmes are established and implemented with a view to providing confidence that specified requirements for all activities important to nuclear safety are satisfied throughout the life of a nuclear installation.

ARTICLE 14.   ASSESSMENT AND VERIFICATION OF SAFETY

Each Contracting Party shall take the appropriate steps to ensure that:

(i) comprehensive and systematic safety assessments are carried out before the construction and commissioning of a nuclear installation and throughout its life. Such assessments shall be well documented, subsequently updated in the light of operating experience and significant new safety information, and reviewed under the authority of the regulatory body;

(ii) verification by analysis, surveillance, testing and inspection is carried out to ensure that the physical state and the operation of a nuclear installation continue to be in accordance with its design, applicable national safety requirements, and operational limits and conditions.

ARTICLE 15.   RADIATION PROTECTION

Each Contracting Party shall take the appropriate steps to ensure that in all operational states the radiation exposure to the workers and the public caused by a nuclear installation shall be kept as low as reasonably achievable and that no individual shall be exposed to radiation doses which exceed prescribed national dose limits.

ARTICLE 16.   EMERGENCY PREPAREDNESS

1.   Each Contracting Party shall take the appropriate steps to ensure that there are on-site and off-site emergency plans that are routinely tested for nuclear installations and cover the activities to be carried out in the event of an emergency. For any new nuclear installation, such plans shall be prepared and tested before it commences operation above a low power level agreed by the regulatory body.

2.   Each Contracting Party shall take the appropriate steps to ensure that, insofar as they are likely to be affected by a radiological emergency, its own population and the competent authorities of the States in the vicinity of the nuclear installation are provided with appropriate information for emergency planning and response.

3.   Contracting Parties which do not have a nuclear installation on their territory, insofar as they are likely to be affected in the event of a radiological emergency at a nuclear installation in the vicinity, shall take the appropriate steps for the preparation and testing of emergency plans for their territory that cover the activities to be carried out in the event of such an emergency.

(d) Safety of Installations

ARTICLE 17.   SITING

Each Contracting Party shall take the appropriate steps to ensure that appropriate procedures are established and implemented:

(i) for evaluating all relevant site-related factors likely to affect the safety of a nuclear installation for its projected lifetime;

(ii) for evaluating the likely safety impact of a proposed nuclear installation on individuals, society and the environment;

(iii) for re-evaluating as necessary all relevant factors referred to in sub-paragraphs (i) and (ii) so as to ensure the continued safety acceptability of the nuclear installation;

(iv) for consulting Contracting Parties in the vicinity of a proposed nuclear installation, insofar as they are likely to be affected by that installation and, upon request providing the necessary information to such Contracting Parties, in order to enable them to evaluate and make their own assessment of the likely safety impact on their own territory of the nuclear installation.

ARTICLE 18.   DESIGN AND CONSTRUCTION

Each Contracting Party shall take the appropriate steps to ensure that:

(i) the design and construction of a nuclear installation provides for several reliable levels and methods of protection (defense in depth) against the release of radioactive materials, with a view to preventing the occurrence of accidents and to mitigating their radiological consequences should they occur;

(ii) the technologies incorporated in the design and construction of a nuclear installation are proven by experience or qualified by testing or analysis;

(iii) the design of a nuclear installation allows for reliable, stable and easily manageable operation, with specific consideration of human factors and the man-machine interface.

ARTICLE 19.   OPERATION

Each Contracting Party shall take the appropriate steps to ensure that:

(i) the initial authorization to operate a nuclear installation is based upon an appropriate safety analysis and a commissioning programme demonstrating that the installation, as constructed, is consistent with design and safety requirements;

(ii) operational limits and conditions derived from the safety analysis, tests and operational experience are defined and revised as necessary for identifying safe boundaries for operation;

(iii) operation, maintenance, inspection and testing of a nuclear installation are conducted in accordance with approved procedures;

(iv) procedures are established for responding to anticipated operational occurrences and to accidents;

(v) necessary engineering and technical support in all safety-related fields is available throughout the lifetime of a nuclear installation;

(vi) incidents significant to safety are reported in a timely manner by the holder of the relevant licence to the regulatory body;

(vii) programmes to collect and analyse operating experience are established, the results obtained and the conclusions drawn are acted upon and that existing mechanisms are used to share important experience with international bodies and with other operating organizations and regulatory bodies;

(viii) the generation of radioactive waste resulting from the operation of a nuclear installation is kept to the minimum practicable for the process concerned, both in activity and in volume, and any necessary treatment and storage of spent fuel and waste directly related to the operation and on the same site as that of the nuclear installation take into consideration conditioning and disposal.

CHAPTER 3.   MEETINGS OF THE CONTRACTING PARTIES

ARTICLE 20.   REVIEW MEETINGS

1. The Contracting Parties shall hold meetings (hereinafter referred to as "review meetings") for the purpose of reviewing the reports submitted pursuant to Article 5 in accordance with the procedures adopted under Article 22.

2. Subject to the provisions of Article 24 sub-groups comprised of representatives of Contracting Parties may be established and may function during the review meetings as deemed necessary for the purpose of reviewing specific subjects contained in the reports.

3. Each Contracting Party shall have a reasonable opportunity to discuss the reports submitted by other Contracting Parties and to seek clarification of such reports.

ARTICLE 21. TIMETABLE

1. A preparatory meeting of the Contracting Parties shall be held not later than six months after the date of entry into force of this Convention.

2. At this preparatory meeting, the Contracting Parties shall determine the date for the first review meeting. This review meeting shall be held as soon as possible, but not later than thirty months after the date of entry into force of this Convention.

3. At each review meeting, the Contracting Parties shall determine the date for the next such meeting. The interval between review meetings shall not exceed three years.

ARTICLE 22. PROCEDURAL ARRANGEMENTS

1. At the preparatory meeting held pursuant to Article 21 the Contracting Parties shall prepare and adopt by consensus Rules of Procedure and Financial Rules. The Contracting Parties shall establish in particular and in accordance with the Rules of Procedure:

(i) guidelines regarding the form and structure of the reports to be submitted pursuant to Article 5;

(ii) a date for the submission of such reports;

(iii) the process for reviewing such reports.

2. At review meetings the Contracting Parties may, if necessary, review the arrangements established pursuant to sub-paragraphs (i)–(iii) above, and adopt revisions by consensus unless otherwise provided for in the Rules of Procedure. They may also amend the Rules of Procedure and the Financial Rules, by consensus.

ARTICLE 23. EXTRAORDINARY MEETINGS

An extraordinary meeting of the Contracting Parties shall be held:

(i) if so agreed by a majority of the Contracting Parties present and voting at a meeting, abstentions being considered as voting; or

(ii) at the written request of a Contracting Party, within six months of this request having been communicated to the Contracting Parties and notification having been received by the secretariat referred to in Article 28, that the request has been supported by a majority of the Contracting Parties.

ARTICLE 24. ATTENDANCE

1. Each Contracting Party shall attend meetings of the Contracting Parties and be represented at such meetings by one delegate, and by such alternates, experts and advisers as it deems necessary.

2. The Contracting Parties may invite, by consensus, any intergovernmental organization which is competent in respect of matters governed by this Convention to attend, as an observer, any meeting, or specific sessions thereof. Observers shall be required to accept in writing, and in advance, the provisions of Article 27.

ARTICLE 25. SUMMARY REPORTS

The Contracting Parties shall adopt, by consensus, and make available to the public a document addressing issues discussed and conclusions reached during a meeting.

ARTICLE 26. LANGUAGES

1. The languages of meetings of the Contracting Parties shall be Arabic, Chinese, English, French, Russian and Spanish unless otherwise provided in the Rules of Procedure.

2. Reports submitted pursuant to Article 5 shall be prepared in the national language of the submitting Contracting Party or in a single designated language to be agreed in the Rules of Procedure. Should the report be submitted in a national language other than the designated language, a translation of the report into the designated language shall be provided by the Contracting Party.

3. Notwithstanding the provisions of paragraph 2, if compensated, the secretariat will assume the translation into the designated language of reports submitted in any other language of the meeting.

ARTICLE 27. CONFIDENTIALITY

1. The provisions of this Convention shall not affect the rights and obligations of the Contracting Parties under their law to protect information from disclosure. For the purposes of this Article, "information" includes, inter alia, (i) personal data; (ii) information protected by intellectual property rights or by industrial or commercial confidentiality; and (iii) information relating to national security or to the physical protection of nuclear materials or nuclear installations.

2. When, in the context of this Convention, a Contracting Party provides information identified by it as protected as described in paragraph 1, such information shall be used only for the purposes for which it has been provided and its confidentiality shall be respected.

3. The content of the debates during the reviewing of the reports by the Contracting Parties at each meeting shall be confidential.

ARTICLE 28. SECRETARIAT

1. The International Atomic Energy Agency, (hereinafter referred to as the "Agency") shall provide the secretariat for the meetings of the Contracting Parties.

2. The secretariat shall:

(i) convene, prepare and service the meetings of the Contracting Parties;

(ii) transmit to the Contracting Parties information received or prepared in accordance with the provisions of this Convention.

The costs incurred by the Agency in carrying out the functions referred to in subparagraphs i) and (ii) above shall be borne by the Agency as part of its regular budget.

3. The Contracting Parties may, by consensus, request the Agency to provide other services in support of meetings of the Contracting Parties. The Agency may provide such services if they can be undertaken within its programme and regular budget. Should this not be possible, the Agency may provide such services if voluntary funding is provided from another source.

CHAPTER 4. FINAL CLAUSES AND OTHER PROVISIONS

ARTICLE 29. RESOLUTION OF DISAGREEMENTS

In the event of a disagreement between two or more Contracting Parties concerning the interpretation or application of this Convention, the Contracting Parties shall consult within the framework of a meeting of the Contracting Parties with a view to resolving the disagreement.

ARTICLE 30. SIGNATURE, RATIFICATION, ACCEPTANCE, APPROVAL, ACCESSION

1. This Convention shall be open for signature by all States at the Headquarters of the Agency in Vienna from 20 September 1994 until its entry into force.

2. This Convention is subject to ratification, acceptance or approval by the signatory States.

3. After its entry into force, this Convention shall be open for accession by all States.

4. (i) This Convention shall be open for signature or accession by regional organizations of an integration or other nature, provided that any such organization is constituted by sovereign States and has competence in respect of the negotiation, conclusion and application of international agreements in matters covered by this Convention.

(ii) In matters within their competence, such organizations shall, on their own behalf, exercise the rights and fulfil the responsibilities which this Convention attributes to States Parties.

(iii) When becoming party to this Convention, such an organization shall communicate to the Depositary referred to in Article 34, a declaration indicating which States are members thereof, which articles of this Convention apply to it, and the extent of its competence in the field covered by those articles.

(iv) Such an organization shall not hold any vote additional to those of its Member States.

5. Instruments of ratification, acceptance, approval or accession shall be deposited with the Depositary.

ARTICLE 31. ENTRY INTO FORCE

1. This Convention shall enter into force on the ninetieth day after the date of deposit with the Depositary of the twenty-second instrument of ratification, acceptance or approval, including the instruments of seventeen States, each having at least one nuclear installation which has achieved criticality in a reactor core.

2. For each State or regional organization of an integration or other nature which ratifies, accepts, approves or accedes to this Convention after the date of deposit of the last instrument required to satisfy the conditions set forth in paragraph 1, this Convention shall enter into force on the ninetieth day after the date of deposit with the Depositary of the appropriate instrument by such a State or organization.

ARTICLE 32. AMENDMENTS TO THE CONVENTION

1. Any Contracting Party may propose an amendment to this Convention. Proposed amendments shall be considered at a review meeting or an extraordinary meeting.

2. The text of any proposed amendment and the reasons for it shall be provided to the Depositary who shall communicate the proposal to the Contracting Parties promptly and at least ninety days before the meeting for which it is submitted for consideration. Any comments received on such a proposal shall be circulated by the Depositary to the Contracting Parties.

3. The Contracting Parties shall decide after consideration of the proposed amendment whether to adopt it by consensus, or, in the absence of consensus, to submit it to a Diplomatic Conference. A decision to submit a proposed amendment to a Diplomatic Conference shall require a two-thirds majority vote of the Contracting Parties present and voting at the meeting, provided that at least one half of the Contracting Parties are present at the time of voting. Abstentions shall be considered as voting.

4. The Diplomatic Conference to consider and adopt amendments to this Convention shall be convened by the Depositary and held no later than one year after the appropriate decision taken in accordance with paragraph 3 of this Article. The

Diplomatic Conference shall make every effort to ensure amendments are adopted by consensus. Should this not be possible, amendments shall be adopted with a two-thirds majority of all Contracting Parties.

5. Amendments to this Convention adopted pursuant to paragraphs 3 and 4 above shall be subject to ratification, acceptance, approval, or confirmation by the Contracting Parties and shall enter into force for those Contracting Parties which have ratified, accepted, approved or confirmed them on the ninetieth day after the receipt by the Depositary of the relevant instruments by at least three fourths of the Contracting Parties. For a Contracting Party which subsequently ratifies, accepts, approves or confirms the said amendments, the amendments will enter into force on the ninetieth day after that Contracting Party has deposited its relevant instrument.

ARTICLE 33. DENUNCIATION

1. Any Contracting Party may denounce this Convention by written notification to the Depositary.

2. Denunciation shall take effect one year following the date of the receipt of the notification by the Depositary, or on such later date as may be specified in the notification.

ARTICLE 34. DEPOSITARY

1. The Director General of the Agency shall be the Depositary of this Convention.

2. The Depositary shall inform the Contracting Parties of:

(i) the signature of this Convention and of the deposit of instruments of ratification, acceptance, approval or accession, in accordance with Article 30;

(ii) the date on which the Convention enters into force, in accordance with Article 31;

(iii) the notifications of denunciation of the Convention and the date thereof, made in accordance with Article 33;

(iv) the proposed amendments to this Convention submitted by Contracting Parties, the amendments adopted by the relevant Diplomatic Conference or by the meeting of the Contracting Parties, and the date of entry into force of the said amendments, in accordance with Article 32.

ARTICLE 35. AUTHENTIC TEXTS

The original of this Convention of which the Arabic, Chinese, English, French, Russian and Spanish texts are equally authentic, shall be deposited with the Depositary, who shall send certified copies thereof to the Contracting Parties.

2.19 VIENNA CONVENTION ON CIVIL LIABILITY FOR NUCLEAR DAMAGE (AS AMENDED BY THE 1997 PROTOCOL). **Concluded on 21 May 1963; entered into force, 12 November 1977. Amending Protocol adopted, 12 September 1997; entered into force, 4 October 2003. 1063 UNTS 265, IAEA INFCIRC 500 (1996)(original);** *reprinted in* **27 ILM 727 (1963) & 5 Weston & Carlson V.J.3. Protocol** *reprinted in* **36 ILM 1462 (1997) & 5 Weston & Carlson V.J.13**

The Contracting Parties,

Having recognized the desirability of establishing some minimum standards to provide financial protection against damage resulting from certain peaceful uses of nuclear energy,

Believing that a convention on civil liability for nuclear damage would also contribute to the development of friendly relations among nations, irrespective of their differing constitutional and social systems,

Have decided to conclude a convention for such purposes, and thereto have agreed as follows—

ARTICLE I

1. For the purposes of this Convention—

(a) "Person" means any individual, partnership, any private or public body whether corporate or not, any international organization enjoying legal personality under the law of the Installation State, and any State or any of its constituent sub-divisions.

(b) "National of a Contracting Party" includes a Contracting Party or any of its constituent sub-divisions, a partnership, or any private or public body whether corporate or not established within the territory of a Contracting Party.

(c) "Operator", in relation to a nuclear installation, means the person designated or recognized by the Installation State as the operator of that installation.

(d) "Installation State", in relation to a nuclear installation, means the Contracting Party within whose territory that installation is situated or, if it is not situated within the territory of any State, the Contracting Party by which or under the authority of which the nuclear installation is operated.

(e) "Law of the competent court" means the law of the court having jurisdiction under this Convention, including any rules of such law relating to conflict of laws.

(f) "Nuclear fuel" means any material which is capable of producing energy by a self-sustaining chain process of nuclear fission.

(g) "Radioactive products or waste" means any radioactive material produced in, or any material made radioactive by exposure to the radiation incidental to, the production or utilization of nuclear fuel, but does not include radioisotopes which have reached the final stage of fabrication so as to be usable for any scientific, medical, agricultural, commercial or industrial purpose.

(h) "Nuclear material" means—

(i) nuclear fuel, other than natural uranium and depleted uranium, capable of producing energy by a self-sustaining chain process of nuclear fission outside a nuclear reactor, either alone or in combination with some other material; and

(ii) radioactive products or waste.

(i) "Nuclear reactor" means any structure containing nuclear fuel in such an arrangement that a self-sustaining chain process of nuclear fission can occur therein without an additional source of neutrons.

(j) "Nuclear installation" means—

(i) any nuclear reactor other than one with which a means of sea or air transport is equipped for use as a source of power, whether for propulsion thereof or for any other purpose;

(ii) any factory using nuclear fuel for the production of nuclear material, or any factory for the processing of nuclear material, including any factory for the re-processing of irradiated nuclear fuel;

(iii) any facility where nuclear material is stored other than storage incidental to the carriage of such material; provided that the Installation State may determine that several nuclear installations of one operator which are located at the same site shall be considered as a single nuclear installation, and

(iv) such other installations in which there are nuclear fuel or radioactive products or waste as the Board of Governors of the International Atomic Energy Agency shall from time to time determine.

(k) "Nuclear Damage" means—

(i) loss of life or personal injury;

(ii) loss of or damage to property;

and each of the following to the extent determined by the law of the competent court—

(iii) economic loss arising from loss or damage referred to in sub-paragraph (i) or (ii), insofar as not included in those sub-paragraphs, if incurred by a person entitled to claim in respect of such loss or damage;

(iv) the costs of measures of reinstatement of impaired environment, unless such impairment is insignificant, if such measures are actually taken or to be taken, and insofar as not included in sub-paragraph (ii);

(v) loss of income deriving from an economic interest in any use or enjoyment of the environment, incurred as a result of a significant impairment of that environment, and insofar as not included in sub-paragraph (ii);

(vi) the costs of preventive measures, and further loss or damage caused by such measures;

(vii) any other economic loss, other than any caused by the impairment of the environment, if permitted by the general law on civil liability of the competent court, in the case of subparagraphs (i) to (v) and (vii) above, to the extent that the loss or damage arises out of or results from ionizing radiation emitted by any source of radiation inside a nuclear installation, or emitted from nuclear fuel or radioactive products or waste in, or of nuclear material coming from, originating in, or sent to, a nuclear installation, whether so arising from the radioactive properties of such matter, or from a combination of radioactive properties with toxic, explosive or other hazardous properties of such matter.

(*l*) "Nuclear incident" means any occurrence or series of occurrences having the same origin which causes nuclear damage or, but only with respect to preventive measures, creates a grave and imminent threat of causing such damage.

(m) "Measures of reinstatement" means any reasonable measures which have been approved by the competent authorities of the State where the measures were taken, and which aim to reinstate or restore damaged or destroyed components of the environment, or to introduce, where reasonable, the equivalent of these components into the environment. The law of the State where the damage is suffered shall determine who is entitled to take such measures.

(n) "Preventive measures" means any reasonable measures taken by any person after a nuclear incident has occurred to prevent or minimize damage referred to in sub-paragraphs (k)(i) to (v) or (vii), subject to any approval of the competent authorities required by the law of the State where the measures were taken.

(o) "Reasonable measures" means measures which are found under the law of the competent court to be appropriate and proportionate having regard to all the circumstances, for example—

(i) the nature and extent of the damage incurred or, in the case of preventive measures, the nature and extent of the risk of such damage;

(ii) the extent to which, at the time they are taken, such measures are likely to be effective; and

(iii) relevant scientific and technical expertise.

(p) "Special Drawing Right", hereinafter referred to as SDR, means the unit of account defined by the International Monetary Fund and used by it for its own operations and transactions.

2. An Installation State may, if the small extent of the risks involved so warrants, exclude any nuclear installation or small quantities of nuclear material from the application of this Convention, provided that—

(a) with respect to nuclear installations, criteria for such exclusion have been established by the Board of Governors of the International Atomic Energy Agency and any exclusion by an Installation State satisfies such criteria; and

(b) with respect to small quantities of nuclear material, maximum limits for the exclusion of such quantities have been established by the Board of Governors of the International Atomic Energy Agency and any exclusion by an Installation State is within such established limits.

The criteria for the exclusion of nuclear installations and the maximum limits for the exclusion of small quantities of nuclear material shall be reviewed periodically by the Board of Governors.

ARTICLE I A

1. This Convention shall apply to nuclear damage wherever suffered.

2. However, the legislation of the Installation State may exclude from the application of this Convention damage suffered—

(a) in the territory of a non-Contracting State; or

(b) in any maritime zones established by a non-Contracting State in accordance with the international law of the sea.

3. An exclusion pursuant to paragraph 2 of this Article may apply only in respect of a non-Contracting State which at the time of the incident—

(a) has a nuclear installation in its territory or in any maritime zones established by it in accordance with the international law of the sea; and

(b) does not afford equivalent reciprocal benefits.

4. Any exclusion pursuant to paragraph 2 of this Article shall not affect the rights referred to in sub-paragraph (a) of paragraph 2 of Article IX and any exclusion pursuant to paragraph 2(b) of this Article shall not extend to damage on board or to a ship or an aircraft.

ARTICLE I B

This Convention shall not apply to nuclear installations used for non-peaceful purposes.

ARTICLE II

1. The operator of a nuclear installation shall be liable for nuclear damage upon proof that such damage has been caused by a nuclear incident—

(a) in his nuclear installation; or

(b) involving nuclear material coming from or originating in his nuclear installation, and occurring—

(i) before liability with regard to nuclear incidents involving the nuclear material has been assumed, pursuant to the express terms of a contract in writing, by the operator of another nuclear installation;

(ii) in the absence of such express terms, before the operator of another nuclear installation has taken charge of the nuclear material; or

(iii) where the nuclear material is intended to be used in a nuclear reactor with which a means of transport is equipped for use as a source of power, whether for propulsion thereof or for any other purpose, before the person duly authorized to operate such reactor has taken charge of the nuclear material; but

(iv) where the nuclear material has been sent to a person within the territory of a non-Contracting State, before it has been unloaded from the means of transport by which it has arrived in the territory of that non-Contracting State;

(c) involving nuclear material sent to his nuclear installation, and occurring—

(i) after liability with regard to nuclear incidents involving the nuclear material has been assumed by him, pursuant to the express terms of a contract in writing, from the operator of another nuclear installation;

(ii) in the absence of such express terms, after he has taken charge of the nuclear material; or

(iii) after he has taken charge of the nuclear material from a person operating a nuclear reactor with which a means of transport is equipped for use as a source of power, whether for propulsion thereof or for any other purpose; but

(iv) where the nuclear material has, with the written consent of the operator, been sent from a person within the territory of a non-Contracting State, only after it has been loaded on the means of transport by which it is to be carried from the territory of that State; provided that, if nuclear damage is caused by a nuclear incident occurring in a nuclear installation and involving nuclear material stored therein incidentally to the carriage of such material, the provisions of sub-paragraph (a) of this paragraph shall not apply where another operator or person is solely liable pursuant to the provisions of sub-paragraph (b) or (c) of this paragraph.

2. The Installation State may provide by legislation that, in accordance with such terms as may be specified therein, a carrier of nuclear material or a person handling radioactive waste may, at his request and with the consent of the operator concerned, be designated or recognized as operator in the place of that operator in respect of such nuclear material or radioactive waste respectively. In this case such carrier or such person shall be considered, for all the purposes of this Convention, as an operator of a nuclear installation situated within the territory of that State.

3.   (a) Where nuclear damage engages the liability of more than one operator, the operators involved shall, in so far as the damage attributable to each operator is not reasonably separable, be jointly and severally liable. The Installation State may limit the amount of public funds made available per incident to the difference, if any, between the amounts hereby established and the amount established pursuant to paragraph 1 of Article V.

(b) Where a nuclear incident occurs in the course of carriage of nuclear material, either in one and the same means of transport, or, in the case of storage incidental to the carriage, in one and the same nuclear installation, and causes nuclear damage which engages the liability of more than one operator, the total liability shall not exceed the highest amount applicable with respect to any one of them pursuant to Article V.

(c) In neither of the cases referred to in sub-paragraphs (a) and (b) of this paragraph shall the liability of any one operator exceed the amount applicable with respect to him pursuant to Article V.

4.   Subject to the provisions of paragraph 3 of this Article, where several nuclear installations of one and the same operator are involved in one nuclear incident, such operator shall be liable in respect of each nuclear installation involved up to the amount applicable with respect to him pursuant to Article V. The Installation State may limit the amount of public funds made available as provided for in sub-paragraph (a) of paragraph 3 of this Article.

5.   Except as otherwise provided in this Convention, no person other than the operator shall be liable for nuclear damage. This, however, shall not affect the application of any international convention in the field of transport in force or open for signature, ratification or accession at the date on which this Convention is opened for signature.

6.   No person shall be liable for any loss or damage which is not nuclear damage pursuant to sub-paragraph (k) of paragraph 1 of Article I but which could have been determined as such pursuant to the provisions of that sub-paragraph. could have been included as such pursuant to sub-paragraph (k) (ii) of that paragraph.

7.   Direct action shall lie against the person furnishing financial security pursuant to Article VII, if the law of the competent court so provides.

ARTICLE III

The operator liable in accordance with this Convention shall provide the carrier with a certificate issued by or on behalf of the insurer or other financial guarantor furnishing the financial security required pursuant to Article VII. However, the Installation State may exclude this obligation in relation to carriage which takes place wholly within its own territory. The certificate shall state the name and address of that operator and the amount, type and duration of the security, and these statements may not be disputed by the person by whom or on whose behalf the certificate was issued. The certificate shall also indicate the nuclear material in respect of which the security applies and shall include a statement by the competent public authority of the Installation State that the person named is an operator within the meaning of this Convention.

ARTICLE IV

1.   The liability of the operator for nuclear damage under this Convention shall be absolute.

2.   If the operator proves that the nuclear damage resulted wholly or partly either from the gross negligence of the person suffering the damage or from an act or omission of such person done with intent to cause damage, the competent court may, if

its law so provides, relieve the operator wholly or partly from his obligation to pay compensation in respect of the damage suffered by such person.

3. No liability under this Convention shall attach to an operator if he proves that the nuclear damage is directly due to an act of armed conflict, hostilities, civil war or insurrection.

4. Whenever both nuclear damage and damage other than nuclear damage have been caused by a nuclear incident or jointly by a nuclear incident and one or more other occurrences, such other damage shall, to the extent that it is not reasonably separable from the nuclear damage, be deemed, for the purposes of this Convention, to be nuclear damage caused by that nuclear incident. Where, however, damage is caused jointly by a nuclear incident covered by this Convention and by an emission of ionizing radiation not covered by it, nothing in this Convention shall limit or otherwise affect the liability, either as regards any person suffering nuclear damage or by way of recourse or contribution, of any person who may be held liable in connection with that emission of ionizing radiation.

5. The operator shall not be liable under this Convention for nuclear damage—

(a) to the nuclear installation itself and any other nuclear installation, including a nuclear installation under construction, on the site where that installation is located; and

(b) to any property on that same site which is used or to be used in connection with any such installation.

6. Compensation for damage caused to the means of transport upon which the nuclear material involved was at the time of the nuclear incident shall not have the effect of reducing the liability of the operator in respect of other damage to an amount less than either 150 million SDRs, or any higher amount established by the legislation of a Contracting Party, or an amount established pursuant to sub-paragraph (c) of paragraph 1 of Article V.

7. Nothing in this Convention shall affect the liability of any individual for nuclear damage for which the operator, by virtue of paragraph 3 or 5 of this Article, is not liable under this Convention and which that individual caused by an act or omission done with intent to cause damage.

ARTICLE V

1. The liability of the operator may be limited by the Installation State for any one nuclear incident, either—

(a) to not less than 300 million SDRs; or

(b) to not less than 150 million SDRs provided that in excess of that amount and up to at least 300 million SDRs public funds shall be made available by that State to compensate nuclear damage; or

(c) for a maximum of 15 years from the date of entry into force of this Protocol, to a transitional amount of not less than 100 million SDRs in respect of a nuclear incident occurring within that period. An amount lower than 100 million SDRs may be established, provided that public funds shall be made available by that State to compensate nuclear damage between that lesser amount and 100 million SDRs.

2. Notwithstanding paragraph 1 of this Article, the Installation State, having regard to the nature of the nuclear installation or the nuclear substances involved and to the likely consequences of an incident originating therefrom, may establish a lower amount of liability of the operator, provided that in no event shall any amount so established be less than 5 million SDRs, and provided that the Installation State ensures that public funds shall be made available up to the amount established pursuant to paragraph 1.

3. The amounts established by the Installation State of the liable operator in accordance with paragraphs 1 and 2 of this Article and paragraph 6 of Article IV shall apply wherever the nuclear incident occurs.

ARTICLE V A

1. Interest and costs awarded by a court in actions for compensation of nuclear damage shall be payable in addition to the amounts referred to in Article V.

2. The amounts mentioned in Article V and paragraph 6 of Article IV may be converted into national currency in round figures.

ARTICLE V B

Each Contracting Party shall ensure that persons suffering damage may enforce their rights to compensation without having to bring separate proceedings according to the origin of the funds provided for such compensation.

ARTICLE V C

1. If the courts having jurisdiction are those of a Contracting Party other than the Installation State, the public funds required under sub-paragraphs (b) and (c) of paragraph 1 of Article V and under paragraph 1 of Article VII, as well as interest and costs awarded by a court, may be made available by the first-named Contracting Party. The Installation State shall reimburse to the other Contracting Party any such sums paid. These two Contracting Parties shall agree on the procedure for reimbursement.

2. If the courts having jurisdiction are those of a Contracting Party other than the Installation State, the Contracting Party whose courts have jurisdiction shall take all measures necessary to enable the Installation State to intervene in proceedings and to participate in any settlement concerning compensation.

ARTICLE V D

1. A meeting of the Contracting Parties shall be convened by the Director General of the International Atomic Energy Agency to amend the limits of liability referred to in Article V if one-third of the Contracting Parties express a desire to that effect.

2. Amendments shall be adopted by a two-thirds majority of the Contracting Parties present and voting, provided that at least one-half of the Contracting Parties shall be present at the time of the voting.

3. When acting on a proposal to amend the limits, the meeting of the Contracting Parties shall take into account, inter alia, the risk of damage resulting from a nuclear incident, changes in the monetary values, and the capacity of the insurance market.

4. (a) Any amendment adopted in accordance with paragraph 2 of this Article shall be notified by the Director General of the IAEA to all Contracting Parties for acceptance. The amendment shall be considered accepted at the end of a period of 18 months after it has been notified provided that at least one-third of the Contracting Parties at the time of the adoption of the amendment by the meeting have communicated to the Director General of the IAEA that they accept the amendment. An amendment accepted in accordance with this paragraph shall enter into force 12 months after its acceptance for those Contracting Parties which have accepted it.

(b) If, within a period of 18 months from the date of notification for acceptance, an amendment has not been accepted in accordance with sub-paragraph (a), the amendment shall be considered rejected.

5. For each Contracting Party accepting an amendment after it has been accepted but not entered into force or after its entry into force in accordance with paragraph

4 of this Article, the amendment shall enter into force 12 months after its acceptance by that Contracting Party.

6. A State which becomes a Party to this Convention after the entry into force of an amendment in accordance with paragraph 4 of this Article shall, failing an expression of a different intention by that State—

(a) be considered as a Party to this Convention as so amended; and

(b) be considered as a Party to the unamended Convention in relation to any State Party not bound by the amendment.

ARTICLE VI

1. (a) Rights of compensation under this Convention shall be extinguished if an action is not brought within—

> (i) with respect to loss of life and personal injury, thirty years from the date of the nuclear incident;

> (ii) with respect to other damage, ten years from the date of the nuclear incident.

(b) If, however, under the law of the Installation State, the liability of the operator is covered by insurance or other financial security including State funds for a longer period, the law of the competent court may provide that rights of compensation against the operator shall only be extinguished after such a longer period which shall not exceed the period for which his liability is so covered under the law of the Installation State.

(c) Actions for compensation with respect to loss of life and personal injury or, pursuant to an extension under sub-paragraph (b) of this paragraph with respect to other damage, which are brought after a period of ten years from the date of the nuclear incident shall in no case affect the rights of compensation under this Convention of any person who has brought an action against the operator before the expiry of that period.

2. (Deleted—1997)

3. Rights of compensation under the Convention shall be subject to prescription or extinction, as provided by the law of the competent court, if an action is not brought within three years from the date on which the person suffering damage had knowledge or ought reasonably to have had knowledge of the damage and of the operator liable for the damage, provided that the periods established pursuant to sub-paragraphs (a) and (b) of paragraph 1 of this Article shall not be exceeded.

4. Unless the law of the competent court otherwise provides, any person who claims to have suffered nuclear damage and who has brought an action for compensation within the period applicable pursuant to this Article may amend his claim to take into account any aggravation of the damage, even after the expiry of that period, provided that final judgment has not been entered.

5. Where jurisdiction is to be determined pursuant to sub-paragraph (b) of paragraph 3 of Article XI and a request has been made within the period applicable pursuant to this Article to any one of the Contracting Parties empowered so to determine, but the time remaining after such determination is less than six months, the period within which an action may be brought shall be six months, reckoned from the date of such determination.

ARTICLE VII

1. (a) The operator shall be required to maintain insurance or other financial security covering his liability for nuclear damage in such amount, of such type and in such terms as the Installation State shall specify. The Installation State shall ensure

the payment of claims for compensation for nuclear damage which have been established against the operator by providing the necessary funds to the extent that the yield of insurance or other financial security is inadequate to satisfy such claims, but not in excess of the limit, if any, established pursuant to Article V. Where the liability of the operator is unlimited, the Installation State may establish a limit of the financial security of the operator liable, provided that such limit is not lower than 300 million SDRs. The Installation State shall ensure the payment of claims for compensation for nuclear damage which have been established against the operator to the extent that the yield of the financial security is inadequate to satisfy such claims, but not in excess of the amount of the financial security to be provided under this paragraph.

(b) Notwithstanding sub-paragraph (a) of this paragraph, where the liability of the operator is unlimited, the Installation State, having regard to the nature of the nuclear installation or the nuclear substances involved and to the likely consequences of an incident originating therefrom, may establish a lower amount of financial security of the operator, provided that in no event shall any amount so established be less than 5 million SDRs, and provided that the Installation State ensures the payment of claims for compensation for nuclear damage which have been established against the operator by providing necessary funds to the extent that the yield of insurance or other financial security is inadequate to satisfy such claims, and up to the limit provided pursuant to sub-paragraph (a) of this paragraph.

2. Nothing in paragraph 1 of this Article or sub-paragraphs (b) and (c) of paragraph 1 of Article V shall require a Contracting Party or any of its constituent sub-divisions, such as States or Republics, to maintain insurance or other financial security to cover their liability as operators.

3. The funds provided by insurance, by other financial security or by the Installation State pursuant to paragraph 1 of this Article or sub-paragraphs (b) and (c) of paragraph 1 of Article V shall be exclusively available for compensation due under this Convention.

4. No insurer or other financial guarantor shall suspend or cancel the insurance or other financial security provided pursuant to paragraph 1 of this Article or sub-paragraphs (b) and (c) of paragraph 1 of Article V without giving notice in writing of at least two months to the competent public authority or, in so far as such insurance or other financial security relates to the carriage of nuclear material, during the period of the carriage in question.

ARTICLE VIII

1. Subject to the provisions of this Convention, the nature, form and extent of the compensation, as well as the equitable distribution thereof, shall be governed by the law of the competent court.

2. Subject to application of the rule of sub-paragraph (c) of paragraph 1 of Article VI, where in respect of claims brought against the operator the damage to be compensated under this Convention exceeds, or is likely to exceed, the maximum amount made available pursuant to paragraph 1 of Article V, priority in the distribution of the compensation shall be given to claims in respect of loss of life or personal injury.

ARTICLE IX

1. Where provisions of national or public health insurance, social insurance, social security, workmen's compensation or occupational disease compensation systems include compensation for nuclear damage, rights of beneficiaries of such systems to obtain compensation under this Convention and rights of recourse by virtue of such systems against the operator liable shall be determined, subject to the provisions of this Convention, by the law of the Contracting Party in which such systems have been

established, or by the regulations of the intergovernmental organization which has established such systems.

2. (a) If a person who is a national of a Contracting Party, other than the operator, has paid compensation for nuclear damage under an international convention or under the law of a non-Contracting State, such person shall, up to the amount which he has paid, acquire by subrogation the rights under this Convention of the person so compensated. No rights shall be so acquired by any person to the extent that the operator has a right of recourse against such person under this Convention.

(b) Nothing in this Convention shall preclude an operator who has paid compensation for nuclear damage out of funds other than those provided pursuant to paragraph 1 of Article VII from recovering from the person providing financial security pursuant to that paragraph or from the Installation State, up to the amount he has paid, the sum which the person so compensated would have obtained under this Convention.

ARTICLE X

The operator shall have a right of recourse only—

(a) if this is expressly provided for by a contract in writing; or

(b) if the nuclear incident results from an act or omission done with intent to cause damage, against the individual who has acted or omitted to act with such intent. The right of recourse provided for under this Article may also be extended to benefit the Installation State insofar as it has provided public funds pursuant to this Convention.

ARTICLE XI

1. Except as otherwise provided in this Article, jurisdiction over actions under Article II shall lie only with the courts of the Contracting Party within whose territory the nuclear incident occurred.

1bis. Where a nuclear incident occurs within the area of the exclusive economic zone of a Contracting Party or, if such a zone has not been established, in an area not exceeding the limits of an exclusive economic zone, were one to be established, jurisdiction over actions concerning nuclear damage from that nuclear incident shall, for the purposes of this Convention, lie only with the courts of that Party. The preceding sentence shall apply if that Contracting Party has notified the Depositary of such area prior to the nuclear incident. Nothing in this paragraph shall be interpreted as permitting the exercise of jurisdiction in a manner which is contrary of the international law of the sea, including the United Nations Convention on the Law of the Sea.

2. Where a nuclear incident does not occur within the territory of any Contracting Party, or within an area notified pursuant to paragraph 1bis, or where the place of the nuclear incident cannot be determined with certainty, jurisdiction over such actions shall lie with the courts of the Installation State of the operator liable.

3. Where under paragraph 1, 1bis or 2 of this Article, jurisdiction would lie with the courts of more than one Contracting Party, jurisdiction shall lie—

(a) if the nuclear incident occurred partly outside the territory of any Contracting Party, and partly within the territory of a single Contracting Party, with the courts of the latter; and

(b) in any other case, with the courts of that Contracting Party which is determined by agreement between the Contracting Parties whose courts would be competent under paragraph 1 or 2 of this Article.

4. The Contracting Party whose courts have jurisdiction shall ensure that only one of its courts shall have jurisdiction in relation to any one nuclear incident.

ARTICLE XI A

The Contracting Party whose courts have jurisdiction shall ensure that in relation to actions for compensation of nuclear damage—

(a) any State may bring an action on behalf of persons who have suffered nuclear damage, who are nationals of that State or have their domicile or residence in its territory, and who have consented thereto; and

(b) any person may bring an action to enforce rights under this Convention acquired by subrogation or assignment.

ARTICLE XII

1. A judgment that is no longer subject to ordinary forms of review entered by a court of a Contracting Party having jurisdiction shall be recognized, except—

(a) where the judgment was obtained by fraud;

(b) where the party against whom the judgment was pronounced was not given a fair opportunity to present his case; or

(c) where the judgment is contrary to the public policy of the Contracting Party within the territory of which recognition is sought, or is not in accord with fundamental standards of justice.

2. A judgment which is recognized under paragraph 1 of this Article shall, upon being presented for enforcement in accordance with the formalities required by the law of the Contracting Party where enforcement is sought, be enforceable as if it were a judgment of a court of that Contracting Party. The merits of a claim on which the judgment has been given shall not be subject to further proceedings.

ARTICLE XIII

1. This Convention and the national law applicable thereunder shall be applied without any discrimination based upon nationality, domicile or residence.

2. Notwithstanding paragraph 1 of this Article, insofar as compensation for nuclear damage is in excess of 150 million SDRs, the legislation of the Installation State may derogate from the provisions of this Convention with respect to nuclear damage suffered in the territory, or in any maritime zone established in accordance with the international law of the sea, of another State which at the time of the incident, has a nuclear installation in such territory, to the extent that it does not afford reciprocal benefits of an equivalent amount.

ARTICLE XIV

Except in respect of measures of execution, jurisdictional immunities under rules of national or international law shall not be invoked in actions under this Convention before the courts competent pursuant to Article XI.

ARTICLE XV

The Contracting Parties shall take appropriate measures to ensure that compensation for nuclear damage, interest and costs awarded by a court in connection therewith, insurance and reinsurance premiums and funds provided by insurance, reinsurance or other financial security, or funds provided by the Installation State, pursuant to this Convention, shall be freely transferable into the currency of the Contracting Party within whose territory the damage is suffered, and of the Contracting Party within whose territory the claimant is habitually resident, and, as regards insurance or reinsurance premiums and payments, into the currencies specified in the insurance or reinsurance contract.

ARTICLE XVI

No person shall be entitled to recover compensation under this Convention to the extent that he has recovered compensation in respect of the same nuclear damage under another international convention on civil liability in the field of nuclear energy.

ARTICLE XVII

This Convention shall not, as between the parties to them, affect the application of any international agreements or international conventions on civil liability in the field of nuclear energy in force, or open for signature, ratification or accession at the date on which this Convention is opened for signature.

ARTICLE XVIII

This Convention shall not affect the rights and obligations of a Contracting Party under the general rules of public international law.

ARTICLE XIX

Any Contracting Party entering into an agreement pursuant to subparagraph (b) of paragraph 3 of Article XI shall furnish without delay to the Director General of the International Atomic Energy Agency for information and dissemination to the other Contracting Parties a copy of such agreement.

The Contracting Parties shall furnish to the Director General for information and dissemination to the other Contracting Parties copies of their respective laws and regulations relating to matters covered by this Convention.

ARTICLE XX

Notwithstanding the termination of the application of this Convention to any Contracting Party, either by termination pursuant to Article XXV or by denunciation pursuant to Article XXVI, the provisions of this Convention shall continue to apply to any nuclear damage caused by a nuclear incident occurring before such termination.

ARTICLE XX A

1. In the event of a dispute between Contracting Parties concerning the interpretation or application of this Convention, the parties to the dispute shall consult with a view to the settlement of the dispute by negotiation or by any other peaceful means of settling disputes acceptable to them.

2. If a dispute of this character referred to in paragraph 1 of this Article cannot be settled within six months from the request for consultation pursuant to paragraph 1 of this Article, it shall, at the request of any party to such dispute, be submitted to arbitration or referred to the International Court of Justice for decision. Where a dispute is submitted to arbitration, if, within six months from the date of the request, the parties to the dispute are unable to agree on the organization of the arbitration, a party may request the President of the International Court of Justice or the Secretary–General of the United Nations to appoint one or more arbitrators. In cases of conflicting requests by the parties to the dispute, the request to the Secretary–General of the United Nations shall have priority.

3. When ratifying, accepting, approving or acceding to this Convention, a State may declare that it does not consider itself bound by either or both of the dispute settlement procedures provided for in paragraph 2 of this Article. The other Contracting Parties shall not be bound by a dispute settlement procedure provided for in paragraph 2 of this Article with respect to a Contracting Party for which such a declaration is in force.

4. A Contracting Party which has made a declaration in accordance with paragraph 3 of this Article may at any time withdraw it by notification to the depositary.

ARTICLE XXVI

(deleted)

ARTICLE XXVIII

This Convention shall be registered by the Director General of the International Atomic Energy Agency in accordance with Article 102 of the Charter of the United Nations.

ARTICLE XXIX

The original of this Convention, of which the English, French, Russian and Spanish texts are equally authentic, shall be deposited with the Director General of the International Atomic Energy Agency, who shall issue certified copies.

IN WITNESS WHEREOF, the undersigned Plenipotentiaries, duly authorized thereto, have signed this Convention.

DONE in Vienna, this twenty-first day of May, one thousand nine hundred and sixty-three.

2.20 CONVENTION ON SUPPLEMENTARY COMPENSATION FOR NUCLEAR DAMAGE.
Adopted in Vienna, 12 September 1997. Not yet in force. *Reprinted*
in **36 ILM 1454 (1997) & 5 Weston & Carlson V.J.14**

The Contracting Parties,

Recognizing the importance of the measures provided in the Vienna Convention
on Civil Liability for Nuclear Damage and the Paris Convention on Third Party
Liability in the Field of Nuclear Energy as well as in national legislation on compensation for nuclear damage consistent with the principles of these Conventions;

Desirous of establishing a worldwide liability regime to supplement and enhance
these measures with a view to increasing the amount of compensation for nuclear
damage;

Recognizing further that such a worldwide liability regime would encourage
regional and global co-operation to promote a higher level of nuclear safety in
accordance with the principles of international partnership and solidarity;

Have Agreed as follows:

CHAPTER I
GENERAL PROVISIONS

Article I
Definitions

For the purposes of this Convention:

(a) "Vienna Convention" means the Vienna Convention on Civil Liability for
Nuclear Damage of 21 May 1963 and any amendment thereto which is in force for a
Contracting Party to this Convention.

(b) "Paris Convention" means the Paris Convention on Third Party Liability in
the Field of Nuclear Energy of 29 July 1960 and any amendment thereto which is in
force for a Contracting Party to this Convention.

(c) "Special Drawing Right", hereinafter referred to as SDR, means the unit of
account defined by the International Monetary Fund and used by it for its own
operations and transactions.

(d) "Nuclear reactor" means any structure containing nuclear fuel in such an
arrangement that a self-sustaining chain process of nuclear fission can occur therein
without an additional source of neutrons.

(e) "Installation State", in relation to a nuclear installation, means the Contracting Party within whose territory that installation is situated or, if it is not situated
within the territory of any State, the Contracting Party by which or under the
authority of which the nuclear installation is operated.

(f) "Nuclear Damage" means:

(i) loss of life or personal injury;

(ii) loss of or damage to property;

and each of the following to the extent determined by the law of the competent
court:

(iii) economic loss arising from loss or damage referred to in sub-paragraph (i) or (ii), insofar as not included in those sub-paragraphs, if incurred by
a person entitled to claim in respect of such loss or damage;

(iv) the costs of measures of reinstatement of impaired environment,
unless such impairment is insignificant, if such measures are actually taken or
to be taken, and insofar as not included in sub-paragraph (ii);

(v) loss of income deriving from an economic interest in any use or enjoyment of the environment, incurred as a result of a significant impairment of that environment, and insofar as not included in sub-paragraph (ii);

(vi) the costs of preventive measures, and further loss or damage caused by such measures;

(vii) any other economic loss, other than any caused by the impairment of the environment, if permitted by the general law on civil liability of the competent court,

in the case of sub-paragraphs (i) to (v) and (vii) above, to the extent that the loss or damage arises out of or results from ionizing radiation emitted by any source of radiation inside a nuclear installation, or emitted from nuclear fuel or radioactive products or waste in, or of nuclear material coming from, originating in, or sent to, a nuclear installation, whether so arising from the radioactive properties of such matter, or from a combination of radioactive properties with toxic, explosive or other hazardous properties of such matter.

(g) "Measures of reinstatement" means any reasonable measures which have been approved by the competent authorities of the State where the measures were taken, and which aim to reinstate or restore damaged or destroyed components of the environment, or to introduce, where reasonable, the equivalent of these components into the environment. The law of the State where the damage is suffered shall determine who is entitled to take such measures.

(h) "Preventive measures" means any reasonable measures taken by any person after a nuclear incident has occurred to prevent or minimize damage referred to in sub-paragraphs (f)(i) to (v) or (vii), subject to any approval of the competent authorities required by the law of the State where the measures were taken.

(i) "Nuclear incident" means any occurrence or series of occurrences having the same origin which causes nuclear damage or, but only with respect to preventive measures, creates a grave and imminent threat of causing such damage.

(j) "Installed nuclear capacity" means for each Contracting Party the total of the number of units given by the formula set out in Article IV.2; and "thermal power" means the maximum thermal power authorized by the competent national authorities.

(k) "Law of the competent court" means the law of the court having jurisdiction under this Convention, including any rules of such law relating to conflict of laws.

(*l*) "Reasonable measures" means measures which are found under the law of the competent court to be appropriate and proportionate, having regard to all the circumstances, for example:

(i) the nature and extent of the damage incurred or, in the case of preventive measures, the nature and extent of the risk of such damage;

(ii) the extent to which, at the time they are taken, such measures are likely to be effective; and

(iii) relevant scientific and technical expertise.

Article II
Purpose and Application

1. The purpose of this Convention is to supplement the system of compensation provided pursuant to national law which:

(a) implements one of the instruments referred to in Article I (a) and (b); or

(b) complies with the provisions of the Annex to this Convention.

2. The system of this Convention shall apply to nuclear damage for which an operator of a nuclear installation used for peaceful purposes situated in the territory of a Contracting Party is liable under either one of the Conventions referred to in Article I or national law mentioned in paragraph 1(b) of this Article.

3. The Annex referred to in paragraph 1(b) shall constitute an integral part of this Convention.

CHAPTER II
COMPENSATION

Article III
Undertaking

1. Compensation in respect of nuclear damage per nuclear incident shall be ensured by the following means:

(a)(i) the Installation State shall ensure the availability of 300 million SDRs or a greater amount that it may have specified to the Depositary at any time prior to the nuclear incident, or a transitional amount pursuant to sub-paragraph (ii);

(ii) a Contracting Party may establish for the maximum of 10 years from the date of the opening for signature of this Convention, a transitional amount of at least 150 million SDRs in respect of a nuclear incident occurring within that period.

(b) beyond the amount made available under sub-paragraph (a), the Contracting Parties shall make available public funds according to the formula specified in Article IV.

2. (a) Compensation for nuclear damage in accordance with paragraph 1(a) shall be distributed equitably without discrimination on the basis of nationality, domicile or residence, provided that the law of the Installation State may, subject to obligations of that State under other conventions on nuclear liability, exclude nuclear damage suffered in a non-Contracting State.

(b) Compensation for nuclear damage in accordance with paragraph 1(b), shall, subject to Articles V and XI.1(b), be distributed equitably without discrimination on the basis of nationality, domicile or residence.

3. If the nuclear damage to be compensated does not require the total amount under paragraph 1(b), the contributions shall be reduced proportionally.

4. The interest and costs awarded by a court in actions for compensation of nuclear damage are payable in addition to the amounts awarded pursuant to paragraphs 1(a) and (b) and shall be proportionate to the actual contributions made pursuant to paragraphs 1(a) and (b), respectively, by the operator liable, the Contracting Party in whose territory the nuclear installation of that operator is situated, and the Contracting Parties together.

Article IV
Calculation of Contributions

1. The formula for contributions according to which the Contracting Parties shall make available the public funds referred to in Article III.1(b) shall be determined as follows:

(a)(i) the amount which shall be the product of the installed nuclear capacity of that Contracting Party multiplied by 300 SDRs per unit of installed capacity; and

(ii) the amount determined by applying the ratio between the United Nations rate of assessment for that Contracting Party as assessed for the year preceding the year in which the nuclear incident occurs, and the total of such rates for all

Contracting Parties to 10% of the sum of the amounts calculated for all Contracting Parties under sub-paragraph (i).

(b) Subject to sub-paragraph (c), the contribution of each Contracting Party shall be the sum of the amounts referred to in sub-paragraphs (a)(i) and (ii), provided that States on the minimum United Nations rate of assessment with no nuclear reactors shall not be required to make contributions.

(c) The maximum contribution which may be charged per nuclear incident to any Contracting Party, other than the Installation State, pursuant to sub-paragraph (b) shall not exceed its specified percentage of the total of contributions of all Contracting Parties determined pursuant to sub-paragraph (b). For a particular Contracting Party, the specified percentage shall be its UN rate of assessment expressed as a percentage plus 8 percentage points. If, at the time an incident occurs, the total installed capacity represented by the Parties to this Convention is at or above a level of 625,000 units, this percentage shall be increased by one percentage point. It shall be increased by one additional percentage point for each increment of 75,000 units by which the capacity exceeds 625,000 units.

2. The formula is for each nuclear reactor situated in the territory of the Contracting Party, 1 unit for each MW of thermal power. The formula shall be calculated on the basis of the thermal power of the nuclear reactors shown at the date of the nuclear incident in the list established and kept up to date in accordance with Article VIII.

3. For the purpose of calculating the contributions, a nuclear reactor shall be taken into account from that date when nuclear fuel elements have been first loaded into the nuclear reactor. A nuclear reactor shall be excluded from the calculation when all fuel elements have been removed permanently from the reactor core and have been stored safely in accordance with approved procedures.

Article V
Geographical Scope

1. The funds provided for under Article III.1(b) shall apply to nuclear damage which is suffered:

(a) in the territory of a Contracting Party; or

(b) in or above maritime areas beyond the territorial sea of a Contracting Party:

(i) on board or by a ship flying the flag of a Contracting Party, or on board or by an aircraft registered in the territory of a Contracting Party, or on or by an artificial island, installation or structure under the jurisdiction of a Contracting Party; or

(ii) by a national of a Contracting Party;

excluding damage suffered in or above the territorial sea of a State not Party to this Convention; or

(c) in or above the exclusive economic zone of a Contracting Party or on the continental shelf of a Contracting Party in connection with the exploitation or the exploration of the natural resources of that exclusive economic zone or continental shelf;

provided that the courts of a Contracting Party have jurisdiction pursuant to Article XIII.

2. Any signatory or acceding State may, at the time of signature of or accession to this Convention or on the deposit of its instrument of ratification, declare that for the purposes of the application of paragraph 1(b)(ii), individuals or certain categories thereof, considered under its law as having their habitual residence in its territory, are assimilated to its own nationals.

3. In this article, the expression "a national of a Contracting Party" shall include a Contracting Party or any of its constituent sub-divisions, or a partnership, or any public or private body whether corporate or not established in the territory of a Contracting Party.

CHAPTER III
ORGANIZATION OF SUPPLEMENTARY FUNDING

Article VI
Notification of Nuclear Damage

Without prejudice to obligations which Contracting Parties may have under other international agreements, the Contracting Party whose courts have jurisdiction shall inform the other Contracting Parties of a nuclear incident as soon as it appears that the damage caused by such incident exceeds, or is likely to exceed, the amount available under Article III.1(a) and that contributions under Article III.1(b) may be required. The Contracting Parties shall without delay make all the necessary arrangements to settle the procedure for their relations in this connection.

Article VII
Call for Funds

1. Following the notification referred to in Article VI, and subject to Article X.3, the Contracting Party whose courts have jurisdiction shall request the other Contracting Parties to make available the public funds required under Article III.1(b) to the extent and when they are actually required and shall have exclusive competence to disburse such funds.

2. Independently of existing or future regulations concerning currency or transfers, Contracting Parties shall authorize the transfer and payment of any contribution provided pursuant to Article III.1(b) without any restriction.

Article VIII
List of Nuclear Installations

1. Each Contracting State shall, at the time when it deposits its instrument of ratification, acceptance, approval or accession, communicate to the Depositary a complete listing of all nuclear installations referred to in Article IV.3. The listing shall contain the necessary particulars for the purpose of the calculation of contributions.

2. Each Contracting State shall promptly communicate to the Depositary all modifications to be made to the list. Where such modifications include the addition of a nuclear installation, the communication must be made at least three months before the expected date when nuclear material will be introduced into the installation.

3. If a Contracting Party is of the opinion that the particulars, or any modification to be made to the list communicated by a Contracting State pursuant to paragraphs 1 and 2, do not comply with the provisions, it may raise objections thereto by addressing them to the Depositary within three months from the date on which it has received notice pursuant to paragraph 5. The Depositary shall forthwith communicate this objection to the State to whose information the objection has been raised. Any unresolved differences shall be dealt with in accordance with the dispute settlement procedure laid down in Article XVI.

4. The Depositary shall maintain, update and annually circulate to all Contracting States the list of nuclear installations established in accordance with this Article. Such list shall consist of all the particulars and modifications referred to in this Article, it being understood that objections submitted under this Article shall have effect retrospective to the date on which they were raised, if they are sustained.

5.   The Depositary shall give notice as soon as possible to each Contracting Party of the communications and objections which it has received pursuant to this Article.

Article IX
Rights of Recourse

1.   Each Contracting Party shall enact legislation in order to enable both the Contracting Party in whose territory the nuclear installation of the operator liable is situated and the other Contracting Parties who have paid contributions referred to in Article III.1(b), to benefit from the operator's right of recourse to the extent that he has such a right under either one of the Conventions referred to in Article I or national legislation mentioned in Article II.1(b) and to the extent that contributions have been made by any of the Contracting Parties.

2.   The legislation of the Contracting Party in whose territory the nuclear installation of the operator liable is situated may provide for the recovery of public funds made available under this Convention from such operator if the damage results from fault on his part.

3.   The Contracting Party whose courts have jurisdiction may exercise the rights of recourse provided for in paragraphs 1 and 2 on behalf of the other Contracting Parties which have contributed.

Article X
Disbursements, Proceedings

1.   The system of disbursements by which the funds required under Article III.1 are to be made available and the system of apportionment thereof shall be that of the Contracting Party whose courts have jurisdiction.

2.   Each Contracting Party shall ensure that persons suffering damage may enforce their rights to compensation without having to bring separate proceedings according to the origin of the funds provided for such compensation and that Contracting Parties may intervene in the proceedings against the operator liable.

3.   No Contracting Party shall be required to make available the public funds referred to in Article III.1(b) if claims for compensation can be satisfied out of the funds referred to in Article III.1(a).

Article XI
Allocation of Funds

The funds provided under Article III.1(b) shall be distributed as follows:

1.   (a) 50% of the funds shall be available to compensate claims for nuclear damage suffered in or outside the Installation State;

(b) 50% of the funds shall be available to compensate claims for nuclear damage suffered outside the territory of the Installation State to the extent that such claims are uncompensated under sub-paragraph (a).

(c) In the event the amount provided pursuant to Article III.1(a) is less than 300 million SDRs:

(i) the amount in paragraph 1(a) shall be reduced by the same percentage as the percentage by which the amount provided pursuant to Article III.1(a) is less than 300 million SDRs; and

(ii) the amount in paragraph 1(b) shall be increased by the amount of the reduction calculated pursuant to sub-paragraph (i).

2.   If a Contracting Party, in accordance with Article III.1(a), has ensured the availability without discrimination of an amount not less than 600 million SDRs, which has been specified to the Depositary prior to the nuclear incident, all funds referred to

in Article III.1(a) and (b) shall, notwithstanding paragraph 1, be made available to compensate nuclear damage suffered in and outside the Installation State.

CHAPTER IV
EXERCISE OF OPTIONS

Article XII

1. Except insofar as this Convention otherwise provides, each Contracting Party may exercise the powers vested in it by virtue of the Vienna Convention or the Paris Convention, and any provisions made thereunder may be invoked against the other Contracting Parties in order that the public funds referred to in Article III.1(b) be made available.

2. Nothing in this Convention shall prevent any Contracting Party from making provisions outside the scope of the Vienna or the Paris Convention and of this Convention, provided that such provision shall not involve any further obligation on the part of the other Contracting Parties, and provided that damage in a Contracting Party having no nuclear installations within its territory shall not be excluded from such further compensation on any grounds of lack of reciprocity.

3. (a) Nothing in this Convention shall prevent Contracting Parties from entering into regional or other agreements with the purpose of implementing their obligations under Article III.1(a) or providing additional funds for the compensation of nuclear damage, provided that this shall not involve any further obligation under this Convention for the other Contracting Parties.

(b) A Contracting Party intending to enter into any such agreement shall notify all other Contracting Parties of its intention. Agreements concluded shall be notified to the Depositary.

CHAPTER V
JURISDICTION AND APPLICABLE LAW

Article XIII
Jurisdiction

1. Except as otherwise provided in this article, jurisdiction over actions concerning nuclear damage from a nuclear incident shall lie only with the courts of the Contracting Party within which the nuclear incident occurs.

2. Where a nuclear incident occurs within the area of the exclusive economic zone of a Contracting Party or, if such a zone has not been established, in an area not exceeding the limits of an exclusive economic zone, were one to be established by that party, jurisdiction over actions concerning nuclear damage from that nuclear incident shall, for the purposes of this Convention, lie only with the courts of that party. The preceding sentence shall apply if that Contracting Party has notified the Depositary of such area prior to the nuclear incident. Nothing in this paragraph shall be interpreted as permitting the exercise of jurisdiction in a manner which is contrary to the international law of the sea, including the United Nations Convention on the Law of the Sea. However, if the exercise of such jurisdiction is inconsistent with the obligations of that Party under Article XI of the Vienna Convention or Article 13 of the Paris Convention in relation to a State not Party to this Convention jurisdiction shall be determined according to those provisions.

3. Where a nuclear incident does not occur within the territory of any Contracting Party or within an area notified pursuant to paragraph 2, or where the place of a nuclear incident cannot be determined with certainty, jurisdiction over actions concerning nuclear damage from the nuclear incident shall lie only with the courts of the Installation State.

4.   Where jurisdiction over actions concerning nuclear damage would lie with the courts of more than one Contracting Party, these Contracting Parties shall determine by agreement which Contracting Party's courts shall have jurisdiction.

5.   A judgment that is no longer subject to ordinary forms of review entered by a court of a Contracting Party having jurisdiction shall be recognized except:

(a) where the judgment was obtained by fraud;

(b) where the party against whom the judgment was pronounced was not given a fair opportunity to present his case; or

(c) where the judgment is contrary to the public policy of the Contracting Party within the territory of which recognition is sought, or is not in accord with fundamental standards of justice.

6.   A judgment which is recognized under paragraph 5 shall, upon being presented for enforcement in accordance with the formalities required by the law of the Contracting Party where enforcement is sought, be enforceable as if it were a judgment of a court of that Contracting Party. The merits of a claim on which the judgment has been given shall not be subject to further proceedings.

7.   Settlements effected in respect of the payment of compensation out of the public funds referred to in Article III.1(b) in accordance with the conditions established by national legislation shall be recognized by the other Contracting Parties.

Article XIV
Applicable Law

1.   Either the Vienna Convention or the Paris Convention or the Annex to this Convention, as appropriate, shall apply to a nuclear incident to the exclusion of the others.

2.   Subject to the provisions of this Convention, the Vienna Convention or the Paris Convention, as appropriate, the applicable law shall be the law of the competent court.

Article XV
Public International Law

This Convention shall not affect the rights and obligations of a Contracting Party under the general rules of public international law.

CHAPTER VI
DISPUTE SETTLEMENT

Article XVI

1.   In the event of a dispute between Contracting Parties concerning the interpretation or application of this Convention, the parties to the dispute shall consult with a view to the settlement of the dispute by negotiation or by any other peaceful means of settling disputes acceptable to them.

2.   If a dispute of this character referred to in paragraph 1 cannot be settled within six months from the request for consultation pursuant to paragraph 1, it shall, at the request of any party to such dispute, be submitted to arbitration or referred to the International Court of Justice for decision. Where a dispute is submitted to arbitration, if, within six months from the date of the request, the parties to the dispute are unable to agree on the organization of the arbitration, a party may request the President of the International Court of Justice or the Secretary–General of the United Nations to appoint one or more arbitrators. In cases of conflicting requests by the parties to the dispute, the request to the Secretary–General of the United Nations shall have priority.

3. When ratifying, accepting, approving or acceding to this Convention, a State may declare that it does not consider itself bound by either or both of the dispute settlement procedures provided for in paragraph 2. The other Contracting Parties shall not be bound by a dispute settlement procedure provided for in paragraph 2 with respect to a Contracting Party for which such a declaration is in force.

4. A Contracting Party which has made a declaration in accordance with paragraph 3 may at any time withdraw it by notification to the Depositary.

ANNEX

A Contracting Party which is not a Party to any of the Conventions mentioned in Article I(a) or (b) of this Convention shall ensure that its national legislation is consistent with the provisions laid down in this Annex insofar as those provisions are not directly applicable within that Contracting Party. A Contracting Party having no nuclear installation on its territory is required to have only that legislation which is necessary to enable such a Party to give effect to its obligations under this Convention.

Article 1
Definitions

1. In addition to the definitions in Article I of this Convention, the following definitions apply for the purposes of this Annex:

(a) "Nuclear Fuel" means any material which is capable of producing energy by a self-sustaining chain process of nuclear fission.

(b) "Nuclear Installation" means:

(i) any nuclear reactor other than one with which a means of sea or air transport is equipped for use as a source of power, whether for propulsion thereof or for any other purpose;

(ii) any factory using nuclear fuel for the production of nuclear material, or any factory for the processing of nuclear material, including any factory for the re-processing of irradiated nuclear fuel; and

(iii) any facility where nuclear material is stored, other than storage incidental to the carriage of such material;

provided that the Installation State may determine that several nuclear installations of one operator which are located at the same site shall be considered as a single nuclear installation.

(c) "Nuclear material" means:

(i) nuclear fuel, other than natural uranium and depleted uranium, capable of producing energy by a self-sustaining chain process of nuclear fission outside a nuclear reactor, either alone or in combination with some other material; and

(ii) radioactive products or waste.

(d) "Operator", in relation to a nuclear installation, means the person designated or recognized by the Installation State as the operator of that installation.

(e) "Radioactive products or waste" means any radioactive material produced in, or any material made radioactive by exposure to the radiation incidental to, the production or utilization of nuclear fuel, but does not include radioisotopes which have reached the final stage of fabrication so as to be usable for any scientific, medical, agricultural, commercial or industrial purpose.

2. An Installation State may, if the small extent of the risks involved so warrants, exclude any nuclear installation or small quantities of nuclear material from the application of this Convention, provided that:

(a) with respect to nuclear installations, criteria for such exclusion have been established by the Board of Governors of the International Atomic Energy Agency and any exclusion by an Installation State satisfies such criteria; and

(b) with respect to small quantities of nuclear material, maximum limits for the exclusion of such quantities have been established by the Board of Governors of the International Atomic Energy Agency and any exclusion by an Installation State is within such established limits.

The criteria for the exclusion of nuclear installations and the maximum limits for the exclusion of small quantities of nuclear material shall be reviewed periodically by the Board of Governors.

Article 2
Conformity of Legislation

1.   The national law of a Contracting Party is deemed to be in conformity with the provisions of Articles 3, 4, 5 and 7 if it contained on 1 January 1995 and continues to contain provisions that:

(a) provide for strict liability in the event of a nuclear incident where there is substantial nuclear damage off the site of the nuclear installation where the incident occurs;

(b) require the indemnification of any person other than the operator liable for nuclear damage to the extent that person is legally liable to provide compensation; and

(c) ensure the availability of at least 1000 million SDRs in respect of a civil nuclear power plant and at least 300 million SDRs in respect of other civil nuclear installations for such indemnification.

2.   If in accordance with paragraph 1, the national law of a Contracting Party is deemed to be in conformity with the provision of Articles 3, 4, 5 and 7, then that Party:

(a) may apply a definition of nuclear damage that covers loss or damage set forth in Article I(f) of this Convention and any other loss or damage to the extent that the loss or damage arises out of or results from the radioactive properties, or a combination of radioactive properties with toxic, explosive or other hazardous properties of nuclear fuel or radioactive products or waste in, or of nuclear material coming from, originating in, or sent to, a nuclear installation; or other ionizing radiation emitted by any source of radiation inside a nuclear installation, provided that such application does not affect the undertaking by that Contracting Party pursuant to Article III of this Convention; and

(b) may apply the definition of nuclear installation in paragraph 3 of this Article to the exclusion of the definition in Article 1.1(b) of this Annex.

3.   For the purpose of paragraph 2 (b) of this Article, "nuclear installation" means:

(a) any civil nuclear reactor other than one with which a means of sea or air transport is equipped for use as a source of power, whether for propulsion thereof or any other purpose; and

(b) any civil facility for processing, reprocessing or storing:

(i) irradiated nuclear fuel; or

(ii) radioactive products or waste that:

(1) result from the reprocessing of irradiated nuclear fuel and contain significant amounts of fission products; or

(2) contain elements that have an atomic number greater than 92 in concentrations greater than 10 nano-curies per gram.

(c) any other civil facility for processing, reprocessing or storing nuclear material unless the Contracting Party determines the small extent of the risks involved with such an installation warrants the exclusion of such a facility from this definition.

4. Where that national law of a Contracting Party which is in compliance with paragraph 1 of this Article does not apply to a nuclear incident which occurs outside the territory of that Contracting Party, but over which the courts of that Contracting Party have jurisdiction pursuant to Article XIII of this Convention, Articles 3 to 11 of the Annex shall apply and prevail over any inconsistent provisions of the applicable national law.

Article 3
Operator Liability

1. The operator of a nuclear installation shall be liable for nuclear damage upon proof that such damage has been caused by a nuclear incident:

(a) in that nuclear installation; or

(b) involving nuclear material coming from or originating in that nuclear installation, and occurring:

(i) before liability with regard to nuclear incidents involving the nuclear material has been assumed, pursuant to the express terms of a contract in writing, by the operator of another nuclear installation;

(ii) in the absence of such express terms, before the operator of another nuclear installation has taken charge of the nuclear material; or

(iii) where the nuclear material is intended to be used in a nuclear reactor with which a means of transport is equipped for use as a source of power, whether for propulsion thereof or for any other purpose, before the person duly authorized to operate such reactor has taken charge of the nuclear material; but

(iv) where the nuclear material has been sent to a person within the territory of a non-Contracting State, before it has been unloaded from the means of transport by which it has arrived in the territory of that non-Contracting State;

(c) involving nuclear material sent to that nuclear installation, and occurring:

(i) after liability with regard to nuclear incidents involving the nuclear material has been assumed by the operator pursuant to the express terms of a contract in writing, from the operator of another nuclear installation;

(ii) in the absence of such express terms, after the operator has taken charge of the nuclear material; or

(iii) after the operator has taken charge of the nuclear material from a person operating a nuclear reactor with which a means of transport is equipped for use as a source of power, whether for propulsion thereof or for any other purpose; but

(iv) where the nuclear material has, with the written consent of the operator, been sent from a person within the territory of a non-Contracting State, only after it has been loaded on the means of transport by which it is to be carried from the territory of that State;

provided that, if nuclear damage is caused by a nuclear incident occurring in a nuclear installation and involving nuclear material stored therein incidentally to the carriage of such material, the provisions of sub-paragraph (a) shall not apply where another operator or person is solely liable pursuant to sub-paragraph (b) or (c).

2.   The Installation State may provide by legislation that, in accordance with such terms as may be specified in that legislation, a carrier of nuclear material or a person handling radioactive waste may, at such carrier or such person's request and with the consent of the operator concerned, be designated or recognized as operator in the place of that operator in respect of such nuclear material or radioactive waste respectively. In this case such carrier or such person shall be considered, for all the purposes of this Convention, as an operator of a nuclear installation situated within the territory of that State.

3.   The liability of the operator for nuclear damage shall be absolute.

4.   Whenever both nuclear damage and damage other than nuclear damage have been caused by a nuclear incident or jointly by a nuclear incident and one or more other occurrences, such other damage shall, to the extent that it is not reasonably separable from the nuclear damage, be deemed to be nuclear damage caused by that nuclear incident. Where, however, damage is caused jointly by a nuclear incident covered by the provisions of this Annex and by an emission of ionizing radiation not covered by it, nothing in this Annex shall limit or otherwise affect the liability, either as regards any person suffering nuclear damage or by way of recourse or contribution, of any person who may be held liable in connection with that emission of ionizing radiation.

5.   (a) No liability shall attach to an operator for nuclear damage caused by a nuclear incident directly due to an act of armed conflict, hostilities, civil war or insurrection.

(b) Except insofar as the law of the Installation State may provide to the contrary, the operator shall not be liable for nuclear damage caused by a nuclear incident caused directly due to a grave natural disaster of an exceptional character.

6.   National law may relieve an operator wholly or partly from the obligation to pay compensation for nuclear damage suffered by a person if the operator proves the nuclear damage resulted wholly or partly from the gross negligence of that person or an act or omission of that person done with the intent to cause damage.

7.   The operator shall not be liable for nuclear damage:

(a) to the nuclear installation itself and any other nuclear installation, including a nuclear installation under construction, on the site where that installation is located; and

(b) to any property on that same site which is used or to be used in connection with any such installation;

(c) unless otherwise provided by national law, to the means of transport upon which the nuclear material involved was at the time of the nuclear incident. If national law provides that the operator is liable for such damage, compensation for that damage shall not have the effect of reducing the liability of the operator in respect of other damage to an amount less than either 150 million SDRs, or any higher amount established by the legislation of a Contracting Party.

8.   Nothing in this Convention shall affect the liability outside this Convention of the operator for nuclear damage for which by virtue of paragraph 7(c) he is not liable under this Convention.

9.   The right to compensation for nuclear damage may be exercised only against the operator liable, provided that national law may permit a direct right of action against any supplier of funds that are made available pursuant to provisions in national law to ensure compensation through the use of funds from sources other than the operator.

10. The operator shall incur no liability for damage caused by a nuclear incident outside the provisions of national law in accordance with this Convention.

Article 4
Liability amounts

1. Subject to Article III.1(a)(ii), the liability of the operator may be limited by the Installation State for any one nuclear incident, either:

(a) to not less than 300 million SDRs; or

(b) to not less then 150 million SDRs provided that in excess of that amount and up to at least 300 million SDRs public funds shall be made available by that State to compensate nuclear damage.

2. Notwithstanding paragraph 1, the Installation State, having regard to the nature of the nuclear installation or the nuclear substances involved and to the likely consequences of an incident originating therefrom, may establish a lower amount of liability of the operator, provided that in no event shall any amount so established be less than 5 million SDRs, and provided that the Installation State ensures that public funds shall be made available up to the amount established pursuant to paragraph 1.

3. The amounts established by the Installation State of the liable operator in accordance with paragraphs 1 and 2, as well as the provisions of any legislation of a Contracting Party pursuant to Article 3.7(c) shall apply wherever the nuclear incident occurs.

Article 5
Financial Security

1. (a) The operator shall be required to have and maintain insurance or other financial security covering his liability for nuclear damage in such amount, of such type and in such terms as the Installation State shall specify. The Installation State shall ensure the payment of claims for compensation for nuclear damage which have been established against the operator by providing the necessary funds to the extent that the yield of insurance or other financial security is inadequate to satisfy such claims, but not in excess of the limit, if any, established pursuant to Article 4. Where the liability of the operator is unlimited, the Installation State may establish a limit of the financial security of the operator liable provided that such limit is not lower than 300 million SDRs. The Installation State shall ensure the payment of claims for compensation for nuclear damage which have been established against the operator to the extent that yield of the financial security is inadequate to satisfy such claims, but not in excess of the amount of the financial security to be provided under this paragraph.

(b) Notwithstanding sub-paragraph (a), the Installation State, having regard to the nature of the nuclear installation or the nuclear substances involved and to the likely consequences of an incident originating therefrom, may establish a lower amount of financial security of the operator, provided that in no event shall any amount so established be less than 5 million SDRs, and provided that the Installation State ensures the payment of claims for compensation for nuclear damage which have been established against the operator by providing necessary funds to the extent that the yield of insurance or other financial security is inadequate to satisfy such claims, and up to the limit provided in sub-paragraph (a).

2. Nothing in paragraph 1 shall require a Contracting Party or any of its constituent sub-divisions to maintain insurance or other financial security to cover their liability as operators.

3. The funds provided by insurance, by other financial security or by the Installation State pursuant to paragraph 1 or Article 4.1(b) shall be exclusively available for compensation due under this Annex.

4. No insurer or other financial guarantor shall suspend or cancel the insurance or other financial security provided pursuant to paragraph 1 without giving notice in writing of at least two months to the competent public authority or, in so far as such insurance or other financial security relates to the carriage of nuclear material, during the period of the carriage in question.

Article 6
Carriage

1. With respect to a nuclear incident during carriage, the maximum amount of liability of the operator shall be governed by the national law of the Installation State.

2. A Contracting Party may subject carriage of nuclear material through its territory to the condition that the amount of liability of the operator be increased to an amount not to exceed the maximum amount of liability of the operator of a nuclear installation situated in its territory.

3. The provisions of paragraph 2 shall not apply to:

(a) carriage by sea where, under international law, there is a right of entry in cases of urgent distress into ports of a Contracting Party or a right of innocent passage through its territory;

(b) carriage by air where, by agreement or under international law, there is a right to fly over or land on the territory of a Contracting Party.

Article 7
Liability of More Than One Operator

1. Where nuclear damage engages the liability of more than one operator, the operators involved shall, in so far as the damage attributable to each operator is not reasonably separable, be jointly and severally liable. The Installation State may limit the amount of public funds made available per incident to the difference, if any, between the amounts hereby established and the amount established pursuant to Article 4.1.

2. Where a nuclear incident occurs in the course of carriage of nuclear material, either in one and the same means of transport, or, in the case of storage incidental to the carriage, in one and the same nuclear installation, and causes nuclear damage which engages the liability of more than one operator, the total liability shall not exceed the highest amount applicable with respect to any one of them pursuant to Article 4.

3. In neither of the cases referred to in paragraphs 1 and 2 shall the liability of any one operator exceed the amount applicable with respect to him pursuant to Article 4.

4. Subject to the provisions of paragraphs 1 to 3, where several nuclear installations of one and the same operator are involved in one nuclear incident, such operator shall be liable in respect of each nuclear installation involved up to the amount applicable with respect to him pursuant to Article 4. The Installation State may limit the amount of public funds made available as provided for in paragraph 1.

Article 8
Compensation Under National Law

1. For purposes of this Convention, the amount of compensation shall be determined without regard to any interest or costs awarded in a proceeding for compensation of nuclear damage.

2. Compensation for damage suffered outside the Installation State shall be provided in a form freely transferable among Contracting Parties.

3. Where provisions of national or public health insurance, social insurance, social security, workmen's compensation or occupational disease compensation systems include compensation for nuclear damage, rights of beneficiaries of such systems and rights of recourse by virtue of such systems shall be determined by the national law of the Contracting Party in which such systems have been established or by the regulations of the intergovernmental organization which has established such systems.

Article 9
Period of Extinction

1. Rights of compensation under this Convention shall be extinguished if an action is not brought within ten years from the date of the nuclear incident. If, however, under the law of the Installation State the liability of the operator is covered by insurance or other financial security or by State funds for a period longer than ten years, the law of the competent court may provide that rights of compensation against the operator shall only be extinguished after a period which may be longer than ten years, but shall not be longer than the period for which his liability is so covered under the law of the Installation State.

2. Where nuclear damage is caused by a nuclear incident involving nuclear material which at the time of the nuclear incident was stolen, lost, jettisoned or abandoned, the period established pursuant to paragraph 1 shall be computed from the date of that nuclear incident, but the period shall in no case, subject to legislation pursuant to paragraph 1, exceed a period of twenty years from the date of the theft, loss, jettison or abandonment.

3. The law of the competent court may establish a period of extinction or prescription of not less than three years from the date on which the person suffering nuclear damage had knowledge or should have had knowledge of the damage and of the operator liable for the damage, provided that the period established pursuant to paragraphs 1 and 2 shall not be exceeded.

4. If the national law of a Contracting Party provides for a period of extinction or prescription greater than ten years from the date of a nuclear incident, it shall contain provisions for the equitable and timely satisfaction of claims for loss of life or personal injury filed within ten years from the date of the nuclear incident.

Article 10
Right of Recourse

National law may provide that the operator shall have a right of recourse only:

(a) if this is expressly provided for by a contract in writing; or

(b) if the nuclear incident results from an act or omission done with intent to cause damage, against the individual who has acted or omitted to act with such intent.

Article 11
Applicable Law

Subject to the provisions of this Convention, the nature, form, extent and equitable distribution of compensation for nuclear damage caused by a nuclear incident shall be governed by the law of the competent court.

E. Outer Space

2.21 **Treaty on Principles Governing the Activities of States in the Exploration and Use of Outer Space, Including the Moon and Other Celestial Bodies.**[e] **Concluded at London, Moscow, and Washington, 27 January 1967. Entered into force, 10 October 1967. 610 UNTS 205;** *reprinted in* **6 ILM 386 (1967) & 5 Weston & Carlson V.E.21**

Article I

The exploration and use of outer space, including the moon and other celestial bodies, shall be carried out for the benefit and in the interests of all countries, irrespective of their degree of economic or scientific development, and shall be the province of all mankind.

Outer space, including the moon and other celestial bodies, shall be free for exploration and use by all States without discrimination of any kind, on a basis of equality and in accordance with international law, and there shall be free access to all areas of celestial bodies.

There shall be freedom of scientific investigation in outer space, including the moon and other celestial bodies, and States shall facilitate and encourage international co-operation in such investigation.

Article II

Outer space, including the moon and other celestial bodies, is not subject to national appropriation by claim of sovereignty, by means of use or occupation, or by any other means.

Article III

States Parties to the Treaty shall carry on activities in the exploration and use of outer space, including the moon and other celestial bodies, in accordance with international law, including the Charter of the United Nations, in the interest of maintaining international peace and security and promoting international co-operation and understanding.

Article IV

States Parties to the Treaty undertake not to place in orbit around the earth any objects carrying nuclear weapons or any other kinds of weapons of mass destruction, instal such weapons on celestial bodies, or station such weapons in outer space in any other manner.

The moon and other celestial bodies shall be used by all States Parties to the Treaty exclusively for peaceful purposes. The establishment of military bases, installations and fortifications, the testing of any type of weapons and the conduct of military manoeuvres on celestial bodies shall be forbidden. The use of military personnel for scientific research or for any other peaceful purposes shall not be prohibited. The use of any equipment or facility necessary for peaceful exploration of the moon and other celestial bodies shall also not be prohibited.

Article V

States Parties to the Treaty shall regard astronauts as envoys of mankind in outer space and shall render to them all possible assistance in the event of accident, distress, or emergency landing on the territory of another State Party or on the high seas. When astronauts make such a landing, they shall be safely and promptly returned to the State of registry of their space vehicle.

---

e. Also known as "the Outer Space Treaty."

In carrying on activities in outer space and on celestial bodies, the astronauts of one State Party shall render all possible assistance to the astronauts of other States Parties.

States Parties to the Treaty shall immediately inform the other States Parties to the Treaty or the Secretary–General of the United Nations of any phenomena they discover in outer space, including the moon and other celestial bodies, which could constitute a danger to the life or health of astronauts.

Article VI

States Parties to the Treaty shall bear international responsibility for national activities in outer space, including the moon and other celestial bodies, whether such activities are carried on by governmental agencies or by non-governmental entities, and for assuring that national activities are carried out in conformity with the provisions set forth in the present Treaty. The activities of non-governmental entities in outer space, including the moon and other celestial bodies, shall require authorization and continuing supervision by the appropriate State Party to the Treaty. When activities are carried on in outer space, including the moon and other celestial bodies, by an international organization, responsibility for compliance with this Treaty shall be borne both by the international organization and by the States Parties to the Treaty participating in such organization.

Article VII

Each State Party to the Treaty that launches or procures the launching of an object into outer space, including the moon and other celestial bodies, and each State Party from whose territory or facility an object is launched, is internationally liable for damage to another State Party to the Treaty or to its natural or juridical persons by such object or its component parts on the Earth, in air space or in outer space, including the moon and other celestial bodies.

Article VIII

A State Party to the Treaty on whose registry an object launched into outer space is carried shall retain jurisdiction and control over such object, and over any personnel thereof, while in outer space or on a celestial body. Ownership of objects launched into outer space, including objects landed or constructed on a celestial body, and of their component parts, is not affected by their presence in outer space or on a celestial body or by their return to the Earth. Such objects or component parts found beyond the limits of the State Party to the Treaty on whose registry they are carried shall be returned to that State Party, which shall, upon request, furnish identifying data prior to their return.

Article IX

In the exploration and use of outer space, including the moon and other celestial bodies, States Parties to the Treaty shall be guided by the principle of co-operation and mutual assistance and shall conduct all their activities in outer space, including the moon and other celestial bodies, with due regard to the corresponding interests of all other States Parties to the Treaty. States Parties to the Treaty shall pursue studies of outer space, including the moon and other celestial bodies, and conduct exploration of them so as to avoid their harmful contamination and also adverse changes in the environment of the Earth resulting from the introduction of extraterrestrial matter and, where necessary, shall adopt appropriate measures for this purpose. If a State Party to the Treaty has reason to believe that an activity or experiment planned by it or its nationals in outer space, including the moon and other celestial bodies, would cause potentially harmful interference with activities of other States Parties in the peaceful exploration and use of outer space, including the moon and other celestial bodies, it shall undertake appropriate international consultations before proceeding with any such activity or experiment. A State Party to the Treaty which has reason to believe that an activity or experiment planned by another State Party in outer space, including the moon and other celestial bodies, would cause potentially harmful interference with activities in the peaceful exploration and use of outer space, including the moon and other celestial bodies, may request consultation concerning the activity or experiment.

Article X

In order to promote international co-operation in the exploration and use of outer space, including the moon and other celestial bodies, in conformity with the purposes of this Treaty, the States Parties to the Treaty shall consider on a basis of equality any requests by other States Parties to the Treaty to be afforded an opportunity to observe the flight of space objects launched by those States.

The nature of such an opportunity for observation and the conditions under which it could be afforded shall be determined by agreement between the States concerned.

Article XI

In order to promote international co-operation in the peaceful exploration and use of outer space, States Parties to the Treaty conducting activities in outer space, including the moon and other celestial bodies, agree to inform the Secretary–General of the United Nations as well as the public and the international scientific community, to the greatest extent feasible and practicable, of the nature, conduct, locations and results of such activities. On receiving the said information, the Secretary–General of the United Nations should be prepared to disseminate it immediately and effectively.

Article XII

All stations, installations, equipment and space vehicles on the moon and other celestial bodies shall be open to representatives of other States Parties to the Treaty on a basis of reciprocity. Such representatives shall give reasonable advance notice of a projected visit, in order that appropriate consultations may be held and that maximum precautions may be taken to assure safety and to avoid interference with normal operations in the facility to be visited.

Article XIII

The provisions of this Treaty shall apply to the activities of States Parties to the Treaty in the exploration and use of outer space, including the moon and other celestial bodies, whether such activities are carried on by a single State Party to the Treaty or jointly with other States, including cases where they are carried on within the framework of international inter-governmental organizations.

Any practical questions arising in connexion with activities carried on by international inter-governmental organizations in the exploration and use of outer space, including the moon and other celestial bodies, shall be resolved by the States Parties to the Treaty either with the appropriate international organization or with one or more States members of that international organization, which are Parties to this Treaty.

Article XIV

1.   This Treaty shall be open to all States for signature. Any State which does not sign this Treaty before its entry into force in accordance with paragraph 3 of this Article may accede to it at any time.

2.   This Treaty shall be subject to ratification by signatory States. Instruments of ratification and instruments of accession shall be deposited with the Governments of the United Kingdom of Great Britain and Northern Ireland, the Union of Soviet

Socialist Republics and the United States of America, which are hereby designated the Depositary Governments.

3. This Treaty shall enter into force upon the deposit of instruments of ratification by five Governments including the Governments designated as Depositary Governments under this Treaty.

4. For States whose instruments of ratification or accession are deposited subsequent to the entry into force of this Treaty, it shall enter into force on the date of the deposit of their instruments of ratification or accession.

5. The Depositary Governments shall promptly inform all signatory and acceding States of the date of each signature, the date of deposit of each instrument of ratification of and accession to this Treaty, the date of its entry into force and other notices.

6. This Treaty shall be registered by the Depositary Governments pursuant to Article 102 of the Charter of the United Nations.

Article XV

Any State Party to the Treaty may propose amendments to this Treaty. Amendments shall enter into force for each State Party to the Treaty accepting the amendments upon their acceptance by a majority of the States Parties to the Treaty and thereafter for each remaining State Party to the Treaty on the date of acceptance by it.

Article XVI

Any State Party to the Treaty may give notice of its withdrawal from the Treaty one year after its entry into force by written notification to the Depositary Governments. Such withdrawal shall take effect one year from the date of receipt of this notification.

Article XVII

This Treaty, of which the English, Russian, French, Spanish and Chinese texts are equally authentic, shall be deposited in the archives of the Depositary Governments. Duly certified copies of this Treaty shall be transmitted by the Depositary Governments to the Governments of the signatory and acceding States.

2.22 CONVENTION ON INTERNATIONAL LIABILITY FOR DAMAGE CAUSED BY SPACE OBJECTS. **Concluded at Washington, London, and Moscow, 29 March 1972. Entered into force, 1 September 1972. 961 UNTS 187, 24 UST 2389, TIAS No 7762;** *reprinted in* **5 Weston & Carlson V.J.4**

Article I. For the purposes of this Convention:

(*a*) The term "damage" means loss of life, personal injury or other impairment of health; or loss of or damage to property of States or of persons, natural or juridical, or property of international intergovernmental organisations;

(*b*) The term "launching" includes attempted launching;

(*c*) The term "launching State" means:

(i) a state which launches or procures the launching of a space object;

(ii) a State from whose territory or facility a space object is launched;

(*d*) The term "space object" includes component parts of a space object as well as its launch vehicle and parts thereof.

Article II. A launching State shall be absolutely liable to pay compensation for damage caused by its space object on the surface of the earth or to aircraft in flight.

Article III. In the event of damage being caused elsewhere than on the surface of the earth to a space object of one launching State or to persons or property on board such a space object by a space object of another launching State, the latter shall be liable only if the damage is due to its fault or the fault of persons for whom it is responsible.

Article IV. 1. In the event of damage being caused elsewhere than on the surface of the earth to a space object of one launching State or to persons or property on board such a space object by a space object of another launching State, and of damage thereby being caused to a third State or to its natural or juridical persons, the first two States shall be jointly and severally liable to the third State, to the extent indicated by the following:

(*a*) If the damage has been caused to the third State on the surface of the earth or to aircraft in flight, their liability to the third State shall be absolute;

(*b*) If the damage has been caused to a space object of the third State or to persons or property on board that space object elsewhere than on the surface of the earth, their liability to the third State shall be based on the fault of either of the first two States or on the fault of persons for whom either is responsible.

2. In all cases of joint and several liability referred to in paragraph 1 of this Article, the burden of compensation for the damage shall be apportioned between the first two States in accordance with the extent to which they were at fault; if the extent of the fault of each of these States cannot be established, the burden of compensation shall be apportioned equally between them. Such apportionment shall be without prejudice to the right of the third State to seek the entire compensation due under this Convention from any or all of the launching States which are jointly and severally liable.

Article V. 1. Whenever two or more States jointly launch a space object, they shall be jointly and severally liable for any damage caused.

2. A launching State which has paid compensation for damage shall have the right to present a claim for indemnification to other participants in the joint launching. The participants in a joint launching may conclude agreements regarding the apportioning among themselves of the financial obligation in respect of which they are jointly and severally liable. Such agreements shall be without prejudice to the right of a State sustaining damage to seek the entire compensation due under this Convention from any or all of the launching States which are jointly and severally liable.

3. A State from whose territory or facility a space object is launched shall be regarded as a participant in a joint launching.

Article VI. 1. Subject to the provisions of paragraph 2 of this Article, exoneration from absolute liability shall be granted to the extent that a launching State establishes that the damage has resulted either wholly or partially from gross negligence or from an act or omission done with intent to cause damage on the part of a claimant State or of natural or juridical persons it represents.

2. No exoneration whatever shall be granted in cases where the damage has resulted from activities conducted by a launching State which are not in conformity with international law including, in particular, the Charter of the United Nations and the Treaty on Principles Governing the Activities of States in the Exploration and Use of Outer Space, including the Moon and Other Celestial Bodies.

Article VII. The provisions of this Convention shall not apply to damage caused by a space object of a launching State to:

(*a*) nationals of that launching State;

(*b*) foreign nationals during such time as they are participating in the operation of that space object from the time of its launching or at any stage thereafter until its descent, or during such time as they are in the immediate vicinity of a planned launching or recovery area as the result of an invitation by that launching State.

Article VIII. 1. A State which suffers damage, or whose natural or juridical persons suffer damage, may present to a launching State a claim for compensation for such damage.

2. If the State of nationality has not presented a claim, another State may, in respect of damage sustained in its territory by any natural or juridical person, present a claim to a launching State.

3. If neither the State of nationality nor the State in whose territory the damage was sustained has presented a claim or notified its intention of presenting a claim, another State may, in respect of damage sustained by its permanent residents, present a claim to a launching State.

Article IX. A claim for compensation for damage shall be presented to a launching State through diplomatic channels. If a State does not maintain diplomatic relations with the launching State concerned, it may request another State to present its claim to that launching State or otherwise represent its interests under this Convention. It may also present its claim through the Secretary–General of the United Nations, provided the claimant State and the launching State are both Members of the United Nations.

Article X. 1. A claim for compensation for damage may be presented to a launching State not later than one year following the date of the occurrence of the damage or the identification of the launching State which is liable.

2. If, however, a State does not know of the occurrence of the damage or has not been able to identify the launching State which is liable, it may present a claim within one year following the date on which it learned of the aforementioned facts; however, this period shall in no event exceed one year following the date on which the State could reasonably be expected to have learned of the facts through the exercise of due diligence.

3. The time-limits specified in paragraphs 1 and 2 of this Article shall apply even if the full extent of the damage may not be known. In this event, however, the claimant State shall be entitled to revise the claim and submit additional documentation after the expiration of such time-limits until one year after the full extent of the damage is known.

Article XI. 1. Presentation of a claim to a launching State for compensation for damage under this Convention shall not require the prior exhaustion of any local remedies which may be available to a claimant State or to natural or juridical persons it represents.

2. Nothing in this Convention shall prevent a State, or natural or juridical persons it might represent, from pursuing a claim in the courts or administrative tribunals or agencies of a launching State. A State shall not, however, be entitled to present a claim under this Convention in respect of the same damage for which a claim is being pursued in the courts or administrative tribunals or agencies of a launching State or under another international agreement which is binding on the States concerned.

Article XII. The compensation which the launching State shall be liable to pay for damage under this Convention shall be determined in accordance with international law and the principles of justice and equity, in order to provide such reparation in respect of the damage as will restore the person, natural or juridical, State or international organisation on whose behalf the claim is presented to the condition which would have existed if the damage had not occurred.

Article XIII. Unless the claimant State and the State from which compensation is due under this Convention agree on another form of compensation, the compensation shall be paid in the currency of the claimant State or, if that State so requests, in the currency of the State from which compensation is due.

Article XIV. If no settlement of a claim is arrived at through diplomatic negotiations as provided for in Article IX, within one year from the date on which the claimant State notifies the launching State that it has submitted the documentation of its claim, the parties concerned shall establish a Claims Commission at the request of either party.

Article XV. 1. The Claims Commission shall be composed of three members: one appointed by the claimant State, one appointed by the launching State and the third member, the Chairman, to be chosen by both parties jointly. Each party shall make its appointment within two months of the request for the establishment of the Claims Commission.

2. If no agreement is reached on the choice of the Chairman within four months of the request for the establishment of the Commission, either party may request the Secretary–General of the United Nations to appoint the Chairman within a further period of two months.

Article XVI. 1. If one of the parties does not make its appointment within the stipulated period, the Chairman shall, at the request of the other party, constitute a single-member Claims Commission.

2. Any vacancy which may arise in the Commission for whatever reason shall be filled by the same procedure adopted for the original appointment.

3. The Commission shall determine its own procedure.

4. The Commission shall determine the place or places where it shall sit and all other administrative matters.

5. Except in the case of decisions and awards by a single-member Commission, all decisions and awards of the Commission shall be by majority vote.

Article XVII. No increase in the membership of the Claims Commission shall take place by reason of two or more claimant States or launching States being joined in any one proceeding before the Commission. The claimant States so joined shall collectively appoint one member of the Commission in the same manner and subject to the same conditions as would be the case for a single claimant State. When two or more launching States are so joined, they shall collectively appoint one member of the

Commission in the same way. If the claimant States or the launching States do not make the appointment within the stipulated period, the Chairman shall constitute a single-member Commission.

Article XVIII. The Claims Commission shall decide the merits of the claim for compensation and determine the amount of compensation payable, if any.

Article XIX. 1. The Claims Commission shall act in accordance with the provisions of Article XII.

2. The decision of the Commission shall be final and binding if the parties have so agreed; otherwise the Commission shall render a final and recommendatory award, which the parties shall consider in good faith. The Commission shall state the reasons for its decision or award.

3. The Commission shall give its decision or award as promptly as possible and no later than one year from the date of its establishment, unless an extension of this period is found necessary by the Commission.

4. The Commission shall make its decision or award public. It shall deliver a certified copy of its decision or award to each of the parties and to the Secretary–General of the United Nations.

Article XX. The expenses in regard to the Claims Commission shall be borne equally by the parties, unless otherwise decided by the Commission.

Article XXI. If the damage caused by a space object presents a large-scale danger to human life or seriously interferes with the living conditions of the population or the functioning of vital centres, the States Parties, and in particular the launching State, shall examine the possibility of rendering appropriate and rapid assistance to the State which has suffered the damage, when it so requests. However, nothing in this Article shall affect the rights or obligations of the States Parties under this Convention.

Article XXII. 1. In this Convention, with the exception of Articles XXIV to XXVII, references to States shall be deemed to apply to any international intergovernmental organisation which conducts space activities if the organisation declares its acceptance of the rights and obligations provided for in this Convention and if a majority of the States members of the organisation are States Parties to this Convention and to the Treaty on Principles Governing the Activities of States in the Exploration and Use of Outer Space, including the Moon and Other Celestial Bodies.

2. States members of any such organisation which are States Parties to this Convention shall take all appropriate steps to ensure that the organisation makes a declaration in accordance with the preceding paragraph.

3. If an international intergovernmental organisation is liable for damage by virtue of the provisions of this Convention, that organisation and those of its members which are States Parties to this Convention shall be jointly and severally liable; provided, however, that:

(*a*) any claim for compensation in respect of such damage shall be first presented to the organisation;

(*b*) only where the organisation has not paid, within a period of six months, any sum agreed or determined to be due as compensation for such damage, may the claimant State invoke the liability of the members which are States Parties to this Convention for the payment of that sum.

4. Any claim, pursuant to the provisions of this Convention, for compensation in respect of damage caused to an organisation which has made a declaration in accordance with paragraph 1 of this Article shall be presented by a State member of the organisation which is a State Party to this Convention.

Article XXIII. 1. The provisions of this Convention shall not affect other international agreements in force in so far as relations between the States Parties to such agreements are concerned.

2. No provision of this Convention shall prevent States from concluding international agreements reaffirming, supplementing or extending its provisions.

Article XXIV. 1. This Convention shall be open to all States for signature. Any State which does not sign this Convention before its entry into force in accordance with paragraph 3 of this Article may accede to it at any time.

2. This Convention shall be subject to ratification by signatory States. Instruments of ratification and instruments of accession shall be deposited with the Governments of the United Kingdom of Great Britain and Northern Ireland, the Union of Soviet Socialist Republics and the United States of America, which are hereby designated the Depositary Governments.

3. This Convention shall enter into force on the deposit of the fifth instrument of ratification.

4. For States whose instruments of ratification or accession are deposited subsequent to the entry into force of this Convention, it shall enter into force on the date of the deposit of their instruments of ratification or accession.

5. The Depositary Governments shall promptly inform all signatory and acceding States of the date of each signature, the date of deposit of each instrument of ratification of and accession to this Convention, the date of its entry into force and other notices.

6. This Convention shall be registered by the Depositary Governments pursuant to Article 102 of the Charter of the United Nations.

Article XXV. Any State Party to this Convention may propose amendments to this Convention. Amendments shall enter into force for each State Party to the Convention accepting the amendments upon their acceptance by a majority of the States Parties to the Convention and thereafter for each remaining State Party on the date of acceptance by it.

Article XXVI. Ten years after the entry into force of this Convention, the question of the review of this Convention shall be included in the provisional agenda of the United Nations General Assembly in order to consider, in the light of past application of the Convention, whether it requires revision. However, at any time after the Convention has been in force for five years, and at the request of one third of the States Parties to the Convention, and with the concurrence of the majority of the States Parties, a conference of the States Parties shall be convened to review this Convention.

Article XXVII. Any State Party to this Convention may give notice of its withdrawal from the Convention one year after its entry into force by written notification to the Depositary Governments. Such withdrawal shall take effect one year from the date of receipt of this notification.

Article XXVIII. This Convention, of which the English, Russian, French, Spanish and Chinese texts are equally authentic, shall be deposited in the archives of the Depositary Governments. Duly certified copies of this Convention shall be transmitted by the Depositary Governments to the Governments of the signatory and acceding States.

2.23 AGREEMENT GOVERNING THE ACTIVITIES OF STATES ON THE MOON AND OTHER CELESTIAL BODIES. **Concluded at New York, 5 December 1979. Entered into force, 11 July 1984. 1363 UNTS 3;** *reprinted in* **18 ILM 1434 (1979) & 5 Weston & Carlson V.E.23**

Article 1

1. The provisions of this Agreement relating to the moon shall also apply to other celestial bodies within the solar system, other than the earth, except in so far as specific legal norms enter into force with respect to any of these celestial bodies.

2. For the purposes of this Agreement reference to the moon shall include orbits around or other trajectories to or around it.

3. This Agreement does not apply to extraterrestrial materials which reach the surface of the earth by natural means.

Article 2

All activities on the moon, including its exploration and use, shall be carried out in accordance with international law, in particular the Charter of the United Nations, and taking into account the Declaration on Principles of International Law concerning Friendly Relations and Co-operation among States in accordance with the Charter of the United Nations, adopted by the General Assembly on 24 October 1970, in the interests of maintaining international peace and security and promoting international co-operation and mutual understanding, and with due regard to the corresponding interests of all other States Parties.

Article 3

1. The moon shall be used by all States Parties exclusively for peaceful purposes.

2. Any threat or use of force or any other hostile act or threat of hostile act on the moon is prohibited. It is likewise prohibited to use the moon in order to commit any such act or to engage in any such threat in relation to the earth, the moon, spacecraft, the personnel of spacecraft or man-made space objects.

3. States Parties shall not place in orbit around or other trajectory to or around the moon objects carrying nuclear weapons or any other kinds of weapons of mass destruction or place or use such weapons on or in the moon.

4. The establishment of military bases, installations and fortifications, the testing of any type of weapons and the conduct of military manoeuvres on the moon shall be forbidden. The use of military personnel for scientific research or for any other peaceful purposes shall not be prohibited. The use of any equipment or facility necessary for peaceful exploration and use of the moon shall also not be prohibited.

Article 4

1. The exploration and use of the moon shall be the province of all mankind and shall be carried out for the benefit and in the interests of all countries, irrespective of their degree of economic or scientific development. Due regard shall be paid to the interests of present and future generations as well as to the need to promote higher standards of living and conditions of economic and social progress and development in accordance with the Charter of the United Nations.

2. States Parties shall be guided by the principle of co-operation and mutual assistance in all their activities concerning the exploration and use of the moon. International co-operation in pursuance of this Agreement should be as wide as possible and may take place on a multilateral basis, on a bilateral basis or through international intergovernmental organizations.

Article 5

1.   States Parties shall inform the Secretary–General of the United Nations as well as the public and the international scientific community, to the greatest extent feasible and practicable, of their activities concerned with the exploration and use of the moon. Information on the time, purposes, locations, orbital parameters and duration shall be given in respect of each mission to the moon as soon as possible after launching, while information on the results of each mission, including scientific results, shall be furnished upon completion of the mission. In the case of a mission lasting more than thirty days, information on conduct of the mission, including any scientific results, shall be given periodically at thirty-day intervals. For missions lasting more than six months, only significant additions to such information need be reported thereafter.

2.   If a State Party becomes aware that another State Party plans to operate simultaneously in the same area of or in the same orbit around or trajectory to or around the moon, it shall promptly inform the other State of the timing of and plans for its own operations.

3.   In carrying out activities under this Agreement, States Parties shall promptly inform the Secretary–General, as well as the public and the international scientific community, of any phenomena they discover in outer space, including the moon, which could endanger human life or health, as well as of any indication of organic life.

Article 6

1.   There shall be freedom of scientific investigation on the moon by all States Parties without discrimination of any kind, on the basis of equality and in accordance with international law.

2.   In carrying out scientific investigations and in furtherance of the provisions of this Agreement, the States Parties shall have the right to collect on and remove from the moon samples of its mineral and other substances. Such samples shall remain at the disposal of those States Parties which caused them to be collected and may be used by them for scientific purposes. States Parties shall have regard to the desirability of making a portion of such samples available to other interested States Parties and the international scientific community for scientific investigation. States Parties may in the course of scientific investigations also use mineral and other substances of the moon in quantities appropriate for the support of their missions.

3.   States Parties agree on the desirability of exchanging scientific and other personnel on expeditions to or installations on the moon to the greatest extent feasible and practicable.

Article 7

1.   In exploring and using the moon, States Parties shall take measures to prevent the disruption of the existing balance of its environment whether by introducing adverse changes in that environment, by its harmful contamination through the introduction of extra-environmental matter or otherwise. States Parties shall also take measures to avoid harmfully affecting the environment of the earth through the introduction of extraterrestrial matter or otherwise.

2.   States Parties shall inform the Secretary–General of the United Nations of the measures being adopted by them in accordance with paragraph 1 of this article and shall also, to the maximum extent feasible, notify him in advance of all placements by them of radio-active materials on the moon and of the purposes of such placements.

3.   States Parties shall report to other States Parties and to the Secretary–General concerning areas of the moon having special scientific interest in order that, without prejudice to the rights of other States Parties, consideration may be given to

the designation of such areas as international scientific preserves for which special protective arrangements are to be agreed upon in consultation with the competent bodies of the United Nations.

Article 8

1. States Parties may pursue their activities in the exploration and use of the moon anywhere on or below its surface, subject to the provisions of this Agreement.

2. For these purposes States Parties may, in particular:

(a) Land their space objects on the moon and launch them from the moon;

(b) Place their personnel, space vehicles, equipment, facilities, stations and installations anywhere on or below the surface of the moon.

Personnel, space vehicles, equipment, facilities, stations and installations may move or be moved freely over or below the surface of the moon.

3. Activities of States Parties in accordance with paragraphs 1 and 2 of this article shall not interfere with the activities of other States Parties on the moon. Where such interference may occur, the States Parties concerned shall undertake consultations in accordance with article 15, paragraphs 2 and 3 of this Agreement.

Article 9

1. States Parties may establish manned and unmanned stations on the moon. A State Party establishing a station shall use only that area which is required for the needs of the station and shall immediately inform the Secretary–General of the United Nations of the location and purposes of that station. Subsequently, at annual intervals that State shall likewise inform the Secretary–General whether the station continues in use and whether its purposes have changed.

2. Stations shall be installed in such a manner that they do not impede the free access to all areas of the moon by personnel, vehicles and equipment of other States Parties conducting activities on the moon in accordance with the provisions of this Agreement or of article I of the Treaty on Principles Governing the Activities of States in the Exploration and Use of Outer Space, including the Moon and Other Celestial Bodies.

Article 10

1. States Parties shall adopt all practicable measures to safeguard the life and health of persons on the moon. For this purpose they shall regard any person on the moon as an astronaut within the meaning of article V of the Treaty on Principles Governing the Activities of States in the Exploration and Use of Outer Space, including the Moon and Other Celestial Bodies and as part of the personnel of a spacecraft within the meaning of the Agreement on the Rescue of Astronauts, the Return of Astronauts and the Return of Objects Launched into Outer Space.

2. States Parties shall offer shelter in their stations, installations, vehicles and other facilities to persons in distress on the moon.

Article 11

1. The moon and its natural resources are the common heritage of mankind, which finds its expression in the provisions of this Agreement and in particular in paragraph 5 of this article.

2. The moon is not subject to national appropriation by any claim of sovereignty, by means of use or occupation, or by any other means.

3. Neither the surface nor the subsurface of the moon, nor any part thereof or natural resources in place, shall become property of any State, international intergov-

ernmental or non-governmental organization, national organization or non-governmental entity or of any natural person. The placement of personnel, space vehicles, equipment, facilities, stations and installations on or below the surface of the moon, including structures connected with its surface or subsurface, shall not create a right of ownership over the surface or the subsurface of the moon or any areas thereof. The foregoing provisions are without prejudice to the international régime referred to in paragraph 5 of this article.

4. States Parties have the right to exploration and use of the moon without discrimination of any kind, on a basis of equality and in accordance with international law and the terms of this Agreement.

5. States Parties to this Agreement hereby undertake to establish an international régime, including appropriate procedures, to govern the exploitation of the natural resources of the moon as such exploitation is about to become feasible. This provision shall be implemented in accordance with article 18 of this Agreement.

6. In order to facilitate the establishment of the international régime referred to in paragraph 5 of this article, States Parties shall inform the Secretary–General of the United Nations as well as the public and the international scientific community, to the greatest extent feasible and practicable, of any natural resources they may discover on the moon.

7. The main purposes of the international régime to be established shall include:

(a) The orderly and safe development of the natural resources of the moon;

(b) The rational management of those resources;

(c) The expansion of opportunities in the use of those resources;

(d) An equitable sharing by all States Parties in the benefits derived from those resources, whereby the interests and needs of the developing countries, as well as the efforts of those countries which have contributed either directly or indirectly to the exploration of the moon, shall be given special consideration.

8. All the activities with respect to the natural resources of the moon shall be carried out in a manner compatible with the purposes specified in paragraph 7 of this article and the provisions of article 6, paragraph 2, of this Agreement.

Article 12

1. States Parties shall retain jurisdiction and control over their personnel, vehicles, equipment, facilities, stations and installations on the moon. The ownership of space vehicles, equipment, facilities, stations and installations shall not be affected by their presence on the moon.

2. Vehicles, installations and equipment or their component parts found in places other than their intended location shall be dealt with in accordance with article 5 of the Agreement on Rescue of Astronauts, the Return of Astronauts and the Return of Objects Launched into Outer Space.

3. In the event of an emergency involving a threat to human life, States Parties may use the equipment, vehicles, installations, facilities or supplies of other States Parties on the moon. Prompt notification of such use shall be made to the Secretary–General of the United Nations or the State Party concerned.

Article 13

A State Party which learns of the crash landing, forced landing or other unintended landing on the moon of a space object, or its component parts, that were not launched by it, shall promptly inform the launching State Party and the Secretary–General of the United Nations.

Article 14

1. States Parties to this Agreement shall bear international responsibility for national activities on the moon, whether such activities are carried on by governmental agencies or by non-governmental entities, and for assuring that national activities are carried out in conformity with the provisions set forth in this Agreement. States Parties shall ensure that non-governmental entities under their jurisdiction shall engage in activities on the moon only under the authority and continuing supervision of the appropriate State Party.

2. States Parties recognize that detailed arrangements concerning liability for damage caused on the moon, in addition to the provisions of the Treaty on Principles Governing the Activities of States in the Exploration and Use of Outer Space, including the Moon and Other Celestial Bodies and the Convention on International Liability for Damage Caused by Space Objects, may become necessary as a result of more extensive activities on the moon. Any such arrangements shall be elaborated in accordance with the procedure provided for in article 18 of this Agreement.

Article 15

1. Each State Party may assure itself that the activities of other States Parties in the exploration and use of the moon are compatible with the provisions of this Agreement. To this end, all space vehicles, equipment, facilities, stations and installations on the moon shall be open to other States Parties. Such States Parties shall give reasonable advance notice of a projected visit, in order that appropriate consultations may be held and that maximum precautions may be taken to assure safety and to avoid interference with normal operations in the facility to be visited. In pursuance of this article, any State Party may act on its own behalf or with the full or partial assistance of any other State Party or through appropriate international procedures within the framework of the United Nations and in accordance with the Charter.

2. A State Party which has reason to believe that another State Party is not fulfilling the obligations incumbent upon it pursuant to this Agreement or that another State Party is interfering with the rights which the former State has under this Agreement may request consultations with that State Party. A State Party receiving such a request shall enter into such consultations without delay. Any other State Party which requests to do so shall be entitled to take part in the consultations. Each State Party participating in such consultations shall seek a mutually acceptable resolution of any controversy and shall bear in mind the rights and interests of all States Parties. The Secretary–General of the United Nations shall be informed of the results of the consultations and shall transmit the information received to all States Parties concerned.

3. If the consultations do not lead to a mutually acceptable settlement which has due regard for the rights and interests of all States Parties, the parties concerned shall take all measures to settle the dispute by other peaceful means of their choice appropriate to the circumstances and the nature of the dispute. If difficulties arise in connexion with the opening of consultations or if consultations do not lead to a mutually acceptable settlement, any State Party may seek the assistance of the Secretary–General, without seeking the consent of any other State Party concerned, in order to resolve the controversy. A State Party which does not maintain diplomatic relations with another State Party concerned shall participate in such consultations, at its choice, either itself or through another State Party or the Secretary–General as intermediary.

Article 16

With the exception of articles 17 to 21, references in this Agreement to States shall be deemed to apply to any international intergovernmental organization which conducts space activities if the organization declares its acceptance of the rights and obligations provided for in this Agreement and if a majority of the States members of the organization are States Parties to this Agreement and to the Treaty on Principles Governing the Activities of States in the Exploration and Use of Outer Space, including the Moon and Other Celestial Bodies. States members of any such organization which are States Parties to this Agreement shall take all appropriate steps to ensure that the organization makes a declaration in accordance with the foregoing.

Article 17

Any State Party to this Agreement may propose amendments to the Agreement. Amendments shall enter into force for each State Party to the Agreement accepting the amendments upon their acceptance by a majority of the States Parties to the Agreement and thereafter for each remaining State Party to the Agreement on the date of acceptance by it.

Article 18

Ten years after the entry into force of this Agreement, the question of the review of the Agreement shall be included in the provisional agenda of the General Assembly of the United Nations in order to consider, in the light of past application of the Agreement, whether it requires revision. However, at any time after the Agreement has been in force for five years, the Secretary–General of the United Nations, as depository, shall, at the request of one third of the States Parties to the Agreement and with the concurrence of the majority of the States Parties, convene a conference of the States Parties to review this Agreement. A review conference shall also consider the question of the implementation of the provisions of article 11, paragraph 5, on the basis of the principle referred to in paragraph 1 of that article and taking into account in particular any relevant technological developments.

Article 19

1.   This Agreement shall be open for signature by all States at United Nations Headquarters in New York.

2.   This Agreement shall be subject to ratification by signatory States. Any State which does not sign this Agreement before its entry into force in accordance with paragraph 3 of this article may accede to it at any time. Instruments of ratification or accession shall be deposited with the Secretary–General of the United Nations.

3.   This Agreement shall enter into force on the thirtieth day following the date of deposit of the fifth instrument of ratification.

4.   For each State depositing its instrument of ratification or accession after the entry into force of this Agreement, it shall enter into force on the thirtieth day following the date of deposit of any such instrument.

5.   The Secretary–General shall promptly inform all signatory and acceding States of the date of each signature, the date of deposit of each instrument of ratification or accession to this Agreement, the date of its entry into force and other notices.

Article 20

Any State Party to this Agreement may give notice of its withdrawal from the Agreement one year after its entry into force by written notification to the Secretary General of the United Nations. Such withdrawal shall take effect one year from the date of receipt of this notification.

PART 3. HYDROSPHERE

A. OCEANS AND SEAS

3.1 CONVENTION ON THE HIGH SEAS.[a] Concluded at Geneva, 29 April 1958. Entered into force, 30 September 1962. 450 UNTS 82, 13 UST 2312, TIAS No 5200; *reprinted in* 5 Weston & Carlson V.F.3

Article 1

The term "high seas" means all parts of the sea that are not included in the territorial sea or in the internal waters of a State.

Article 2

The high seas being open to all nations, no State may validly purport to subject any part of them to its sovereignty. Freedom of the high seas is exercised under the conditions laid down by these articles and by the other rules of international law. It comprises, *inter alia*, both for coastal and non-coastal States:

(1) Freedom of navigation;

(2) Freedom of fishing;

(3) Freedom to lay submarine cables and pipelines;

(4) Freedom to fly over the high seas.

These freedoms, and others which are recognized by the general principles of international law, shall be exercised by all States with reasonable regard to the interests of other States in their exercise of the freedom of the high seas.

Article 3

1. In order to enjoy the freedom of the seas on equal terms with coastal States, States having no sea-coast should have free access to the sea. To this end States situated between the sea and a State having no sea-coast shall by common agreement with the latter, and in conformity with existing international conventions, accord:

(*a*) To the State having no sea-coast, on a basis of reciprocity, free transit through their territory; and

(*b*) To ships flying the flag of that State treatment equal to that accorded to their own ships, or to the ships of any other States, as regards access to seaports and the use of such ports.

2. States situated between the sea and a State having no sea-coast shall settle, by mutual agreement with the latter, and taking into account the rights of the coastal State or State of transit and the special conditions of the State having no sea-coast, all matters relating to freedom of transit and equal treatment in ports, in case such States are not already parties to existing international conventions.

Article 4

Every State, whether coastal or not, has the right to sail ships under its flag on the high seas.

---

a. *See also* Optional Protocol to the 1958 Law of the Sea Conventions Concerning the Compulsory Settlement of Disputes (which provides for reference to the International Court of Justice of disputes arising out of this agreement), concluded 29 April 1958 and entered into force 30 September 1962 (450 UNTS 169).

Article 5

1.   Each State shall fix the conditions for the grant of its nationality to ships, for the registration of ships in its territory, and for the right to fly its flag. Ships have the nationality of the State whose flag they are entitled to fly. There must exist a genuine link between the State and the ship; in particular, the State must effectively exercise its jurisdiction and control in administrative, technical and social matters over ships flying its flag.

2.   Each State shall issue to ships to which it has granted the right to fly its flag documents to that effect.

Article 6

1.   Ships shall sail under the flag of one State only and, save in exceptional cases expressly provided for in international treaties or in these articles, shall be subject to its exclusive jurisdiction on the high seas. A ship may not change its flag during a voyage or while in a port of call, save in the case of a real transfer of ownership or change of registry.

2.   A ship which sails under the flags of two or more States, using them according to convenience, may not claim any of the nationalities in question with respect to any other State, and may be assimilated to a ship without nationality.

Article 7

The provisions of the preceding articles do not prejudice the question of ships employed on the official service of an inter-governmental organization flying the flag of the organization.

Article 8

1.   Warships on the high seas have complete immunity from the jurisdiction of any State other than the flag State.

2.   For the purposes of these articles, the term "warship" means a ship belonging to the naval forces of a State and bearing the external marks distinguishing warships of its nationality, under the command of an officer duly commissioned by the government and whose name appears in the Navy List, and manned by a crew who are under regular naval discipline.

Article 9

Ships owned or operated by a State and used only on government non-commercial service shall, on the high seas, have complete immunity from the jurisdiction of any State other than the flag State.

Article 10

1.   Every State shall take such measures for ships under its flag as are necessary to ensure safety at sea with regard *inter alia* to:

(*a*) The use of signals, the maintenance of communications and the prevention of collisions;

(*b*) The manning of ships and labour conditions for crews taking into account the applicable international labour instruments;

(*c*) The construction, equipment and seaworthiness of ships.

2.   In taking such measures each State is required to conform to generally accepted international standards and to take any steps which may be necessary to ensure their observance.

Article 11

1. In the event of a collision or of any other incident of navigation concerning a ship on the high seas, involving the penal or disciplinary responsibility of the master or of any other person in the service of the ship, no penal or disciplinary proceedings may be instituted against such persons except before the judicial or administrative authorities either of the flag State or of the State of which such person is a national.

2. In disciplinary matters, the State which has issued a master's certificate or a certificate of competence or license shall alone be competent, after due legal process, to pronounce the withdrawal of such certificates, even if the holder is not a national of the State which issued them.

3. No arrest or detention of the ship, even as a measure of investigation, shall be ordered by any authorities other than those of the flag State.

Article 12

1. Every State shall require the master of a ship sailing under its flag, in so far as he can do so without serious danger to the ship, the crew or the passengers,

(*a*) To render assistance to any person found at sea in danger of being lost;

(*b*) To proceed with all possible speed to the rescue of persons in distress if informed of their need of assistance, in so far as such action may reasonably be expected of him;

(*c*) After a collision, to render assistance to the other ship, her crew and her passengers and, where possible, to inform the other ship of the name of his own ship, her port of registry and the nearest port at which she will call.

2. Every coastal State shall promote the establishment and maintenance of an adequate and effective search and rescue service regarding safety on and over the sea and—where circumstances so require—by way of mutual regional arrangements co-operate with neighbouring States for this purpose.

Article 13

Every State shall adopt effective measures to prevent and punish the transport of slaves in ships authorized to fly its flag, and to prevent the unlawful use of its flag for that purpose. Any slave taking refuge on board any ship, whatever its flag, shall *ipso facto* be free.

Article 14

All States shall co-operate to the fullest possible extent in the repression of piracy on the high seas or in any other place outside the jurisdiction of any State.

Article 15

Piracy consists of any of the following acts:

(1) Any illegal acts of violence, detention or any act of depredation, committed for private ends by the crew or the passengers of a private ship or a private aircraft, and directed:

(*a*) On the high seas, against another ship or aircraft, or against persons or property on board such ship or aircraft;

(*b*) Against a ship, aircraft, persons or property in a place outside the jurisdiction of any State;

(2) Any act of voluntary participation in the operation of a ship or of an aircraft with knowledge of facts making it a pirate ship or aircraft;

(3) Any act of inciting or of intentionally facilitating an act described in sub-paragraph 1 or sub-paragraph 2 of this article.

Article 16

The acts of piracy, as defined in article 15, committed by a warship, government ship or government aircraft whose crew has mutinied and taken control of the ship or aircraft are assimilated to acts committed by a private ship.

Article 17

A ship or aircraft is considered a pirate ship or aircraft if it is intended by the persons in dominant control to be used for the purpose of committing one of the acts referred to in article 15. The same applies if the ship or aircraft has been used to commit any such act, so long as it remains under the control of the persons guilty of that act.

Article 18

A ship or aircraft may retain its nationality although it has become a pirate ship or aircraft. The retention or loss of nationality is determined by the law of the State from which such nationality was derived.

Article 19

On the high seas, or in any other place outside the jurisdiction of any State, every State may seize a pirate ship or aircraft, or a ship taken by piracy and under the control of pirates, and arrest the persons and seize the property on board. The courts of the State which carried out the seizure may decide upon the penalties to be imposed, and may also determine the action to be taken with regard to the ships, aircraft or property, subject to the rights of third parties acting in good faith.

Article 20

Where the seizure of a ship or aircraft on suspicion of piracy has been effected without adequate grounds, the State making the seizure shall be liable to the State the nationality of which is possessed by the ship or aircraft, for any loss or damage caused by the seizure.

Article 21

A seizure on account of piracy may only be carried out by warships or military aircraft, or other ships or aircraft on government service authorized to that effect.

Article 22

1. Except where acts of interference derive from powers conferred by treaty, a warship which encounters a foreign merchant ship on the high seas is not justified in boarding her unless there is reasonable ground for suspecting:

(a) That the ship is engaged in piracy; or

(b) That the ship is engaged in the slave trade; or

(c) That though flying a foreign flag or refusing to show its flag, the ship is, in reality, of the same nationality as the warship.

2. In the cases provided for in sub-paragraphs (a), (b) and (c) above, the warship may proceed to verify the ship's right to fly its flag. To this end, it may send a boat under the command of an officer to the suspected ship. If suspicion remains after the documents have been checked, it may proceed to a further examination on board the ship, which must be carried out with all possible consideration.

3. If the suspicions prove to be unfounded, and provided that the ship boarded has not committed any act justifying them, it shall be compensated for any loss or damage that may have been sustained.

Article 23

1. The hot pursuit of a foreign ship may be undertaken when the competent authorities of the coastal State have good reason to believe that the ship has violated the laws and regulations of that State. Such pursuit must be commenced when the foreign ship or one of its boats is within the internal waters or the territorial sea or the contiguous zone of the pursuing State, and may only be continued outside the territorial sea or the contiguous zone if the pursuit has not been interrupted. It is not necessary that, at the time when the foreign ship within the territorial sea or the contiguous zone receives the order to stop, the ship giving the order should likewise be within the territorial sea or the contiguous zone. If the foreign ship is within a contiguous zone, as defined in article 24 of the Convention on the Territorial Sea and the Contiguous Zone, the pursuit may only be undertaken if there has been a violation of the rights for the protection of which the zone was established.

2. The right of hot pursuit ceases as soon as the ship pursued enters the territorial sea of its own country or of a third State.

3. Hot pursuit is not deemed to have begun unless the pursuing ship has satisfied itself by such practicable means as may be available that the ship pursued or one of its boats or other craft working as a team and using the ship pursued as a mother ship are within the limits of the territorial sea, or as the case may be within the contiguous zone. The pursuit may only be commenced after a visual or auditory signal to stop has been given at a distance which enables it to be seen or heard by the foreign ship.

4. The right of hot pursuit may be exercised only by warships or military aircraft, or other ships or aircraft on government service specially authorized to that effect.

5. Where hot pursuit is effected by an aircraft:

(a) The provisions of paragraph 1 to 3 of this article shall apply *mutatis mutandis;*

(b) The aircraft giving the order to stop must itself actively pursue the ship until a ship or aircraft of the coastal State, summoned by the aircraft, arrives to take over the pursuit, unless the aircraft is itself able to arrest the ship. It does not suffice to justify an arrest on the high seas that the ship was merely sighted by the aircraft as an offender or suspected offender, if it was not both ordered to stop and pursued by the aircraft itself or other aircraft or ship which continue the pursuit without interruption.

6. The release of a ship arrested within the jurisdiction of a State and escorted to a port of that State for the purposes of an enquiry before the competent authorities may not be claimed solely on the ground that the ship, in the course of its voyage, was escorted across a portion of the high seas, if the circumstances rendered this necessary.

7. Where a ship has been stopped or arrested on the high seas in circumstances which do not justify the exercise of the right of hot pursuit, it shall be compensated for any loss or damage that may have been thereby sustained.

Article 24

Every State shall draw up regulations to prevent pollution of the seas by the discharge of oil from ships or pipelines or resulting from the exploitation and exploration of the seabed and its subsoil, taking account of existing treaty provisions on the subject.

Article 25

1. Every State shall take measures to prevent pollution of the seas from the dumping of radio-active waste, taking into account any standards and regulations which may be formulated by the competent international organizations.

2. All States shall co-operate with the competent international organizations in taking measures for the prevention of pollution of the seas or air space above, resulting from any activities with radio-active materials or other harmful agents.

Article 26

1. All States shall be entitled to lay submarine cables and pipelines on the bed of the high seas.

2. Subject to its right to take reasonable measures for the exploration of the continental shelf and the exploitation of its natural resources, the coastal State may not impede the laying or maintenance of such cables or pipelines.

3. When laying such cables or pipelines the State in question shall pay due regard to cables or pipelines already in position on the seabed. In particular, possibilities of repairing existing cables or pipelines shall not be prejudiced.

Article 27

Every State shall take the necessary legislative measures to provide that the breaking or injury by a ship flying its flag or by a person subject to its jurisdiction of a submarine cable beneath the high seas done wilfully or through culpable negligence, in such a manner as to be liable to interrupt or obstruct telegraphic or telephonic communications, and similarly the breaking or injury of a submarine pipeline or high-voltage power cable shall be a punishable offence. This provision shall not apply to any break or injury caused by persons who acted merely with the legitimate object of saving their lives or their ships, after having taken all necessary precautions to avoid such break or injury.

Article 28

Every State shall take the necessary legislative measures to provide that, if persons subject to its jurisdiction who are the owners of a cable or pipeline beneath the high seas, in laying or repairing that cable or pipeline, cause a break in or injury to another cable or pipeline, they shall bear the cost of the repairs.

Article 29

Every State shall take the necessary legislative measures to ensure that the owners of ships who can prove that they have sacrificed an anchor, a net or any other fishing gear, in order to avoid injuring a submarine cable or pipeline, shall be indemnified by the owner of the cable or pipeline, provided that the owner of the ship has taken all reasonable precautionary measures beforehand.

Article 30

The provisions of this Convention shall not affect conventions or other international agreements already in force, as between States Parties to them.

Article 31

This Convention shall, until 31 October 1958, be open for signature by all States Members of the United Nations or of any of the specialized agencies, and by any other State invited by the General Assembly of the United Nations to become a Party to the Convention.

Article 32

This Convention is subject to ratification. The instruments of ratification shall be deposited with the Secretary–General of the United Nations.

Article 33

This Convention shall be open for accession by any States belonging to any of the categories mentioned in article 31. The instruments of accession shall be deposited with the Secretary–General of the United Nations.

Article 34

1. This Convention shall come into force on the thirtieth day following the date of deposit of the twenty-second instrument of ratification or accession with the Secretary–General of the United Nations.

2. For each State ratifying or acceding to the Convention after the deposit of the twenty-second instrument of ratification or accession, the Convention shall enter into force on the thirtieth day after deposit by such State of its instrument of ratification or accession.

Article 35

1. After the expiration of a period of five years from the date on which this Convention shall enter into force, a request for the revision of this Convention may be made at any time by any Contracting Party by means of a notification in writing addressed to the Secretary–General of the United Nations.

2. The General Assembly of the United Nations shall decide upon the steps, if any, to be taken in respect of such request.

Article 36

The Secretary–General of the United Nations shall inform all States Members of the United Nations and the other States referred to in article 31:

(*a*) Of signatures to this Convention and of the deposit of instruments of ratification or accession, in accordance with articles 31, 32 and 33;

(*b*) Of the date on which this Convention will come into force, in accordance with article 34;

(*c*) Of requests for revision in accordance with article 35.

Article 37

The original of this Convention, of which the Chinese, English, French, Russian and Spanish texts are equally authentic, shall be deposited with the Secretary–General of the United Nations, who shall send certified copies thereof to all States referred to in article 31.

3.2 Convention on the Continental Shelf.[b] **Concluded at Geneva, 29 April 1958. Entered into force, 10 June 1964. 499 UNTS 311, 15 UST 471, TIAS No 5578;** *reprinted in* **5 Weston & Carlson V.F.4**

Article 1

For the purpose of these articles, the term "continental shelf" is used as referring (a) to the seabed and subsoil of the submarine areas adjacent to the coast but outside the area of the territorial sea, to a depth of 200 metres or, beyond that limit, to where the depth of the superjacent waters admits of the exploitation of the natural resources of the said areas; (b) to the seabed and subsoil of similar submarine areas adjacent to the coasts of islands.

Article 2

1. The coastal State exercises over the continental shelf sovereign rights for the purpose of exploring it and exploiting its natural resources.

2. The rights referred to in paragraph 1 of this article are exclusive in the sense that if the coastal State does not explore the continental shelf or exploit its natural resources, no one may undertake these activities, or make a claim to the continental shelf, without the express consent of the coastal State.

3. The rights of the coastal State over the continental shelf do not depend on occupation, effective or notional, or on any express proclamation.

4. The natural resources referred to in these articles consist of the mineral and other non-living resources of the seabed and subsoil together with living organisms belonging to sedentary species, that is to say, organisms which, at the harvestable stage, either are immobile on or under the seabed or are unable to move except in constant physical contact with the seabed or the subsoil.

Article 3

The rights of the coastal State over the continental shelf do not affect the legal status of the superjacent waters as high seas, or that of the airspace above those waters.

Article 4

Subject to its right to take reasonable measures for the exploration of the continental shelf and the exploitation of its natural resources, the coastal State may not impede the laying or maintenance of submarine cables or pipe lines on the continental shelf.

Article 5

1. The exploration of the continental shelf and the exploitation of its natural resources must not result in any unjustifiable interference with navigation, fishing or the conservation of the living resources of the sea, nor result in any interference with fundamental oceanographic or other scientific research carried out with the intention of open publication.

2. Subject to the provisions of paragraphs 1 and 6 of this article, the coastal State is entitled to construct and maintain or operate on the continental shelf installations and other devices necessary for its exploration and the exploitation of its natural resources, and to establish safety zones around such installations and devices and to take in those zones measures necessary for their protection.

b. *See also* Optional Protocol to the 1958 Law of the Sea Conventions Concerning the Compulsory Settlement of Disputes (which provides for reference to the International Court of Justice of disputes arising out of this agreement), concluded 29 April 1958 and entered into force 30 September 1962 (450 UNTS 169).

3. The safety zones referred to in paragraph 2 of this article may extend to a distance of 500 metres around the installations and other devices which have been erected, measured from each point of their outer edge. Ships of all nationalities must respect these safety zones.

4. Such installations and devices, though under the jurisdiction of the coastal State, do not possess the status of islands. They have no territorial sea of their own, and their presence does not affect the delimitation of the territorial sea of the coastal State.

5. Due notice must be given of the construction of any such installations, and permanent means for giving warning of their presence must be maintained. Any installations which are abandoned or disused must be entirely removed.

6. Neither the installations or devices, nor the safety zones around them, may be established where interference may be caused to the use of recognized sea lanes essential to international navigation.

7. The coastal State is obliged to undertake, in the safety zones, all appropriate measures for the protection of the living resources of the sea from harmful agents.

8. The consent of the coastal State shall be obtained in respect of any research concerning the continental shelf and undertaken there. Nevertheless the coastal State shall not normally withhold its consent if the request is submitted by a qualified institution with a view to purely scientific research into the physical or biological characteristics of the continental shelf, subject to the proviso that the coastal State shall have the right, if it so desires, to participate or to be represented in the research, and that in any event the results shall be published.

Article 6

1. Where the same continental shelf is adjacent to the territories of two or more States whose coasts are opposite each other, the boundary of the continental shelf appertaining to such States shall be determined by agreement between them. In the absence of agreement, and unless another boundary line is justified by special circumstances, the boundary is the median line, every point of which is equidistant from the nearest points of the baselines from which the breadth of the territorial sea of each State is measured.

2. Where the same continental shelf is adjacent to the territories of two adjacent States, the boundary of the continental shelf shall be determined by agreement between them. In the absence of agreement, and unless another boundary line is justified by special circumstances, the boundary shall be determined by application of the principle of equidistance from the nearest points of the baselines from which the breadth of the territorial sea of each State is measured.

3. In delimiting the boundaries of the continental shelf, any lines which are drawn in accordance with the principles set out in paragraphs 1 and 2 of this article should be defined with reference to charts and geographical features as they exist at a particular date, and reference should be made to fixed permanent identifiable points on the land.

Article 7

The provisions of these articles shall not prejudice the right of the coastal State to exploit the subsoil by means of tunnelling irrespective of the depth of water above the subsoil.

Article 8

This Convention shall, until 31 October 1958, be open for signature by all States Members of the United Nations or of any of the specialized agencies, and by any other

State invited by the General Assembly of the United Nations to become a Party to the Convention.

Article 9

This Convention is subject to ratification. The instruments of ratification shall be deposited with the Secretary–General of the United Nations.

Article 10

This Convention shall be open for accession by any States belonging to any of the categories mentioned in article 8. The instruments of accession shall be deposited with the Secretary–General of the United Nations.

Article 11

1. This Convention shall come into force on the thirtieth day following the date of deposit of the twenty-second instrument of ratification or accession with the Secretary–General of the United Nations.

2. For each State ratifying or acceding to the Convention after the deposit of the twenty-second instrument of ratification or accession, the Convention shall enter into force on the thirtieth day after deposit by such State of its instrument of ratification or accession.

Article 12

1. At the time of signature, ratification or accession, any State may make reservations to articles of the Convention other than to articles 1 to 3 inclusive.

2. Any Contracting State making a reservation in accordance with the preceding paragraph may at any time withdraw the reservation by a communication to that effect addressed to the Secretary–General of the United Nations.

Article 13

1. After the expiration of a period of five years from the date on which this Convention shall enter into force, a request for the revision of this Convention may be made at any time by any Contracting Party by means of a notification in writing addressed to the Secretary–General of the United Nations.

2. The General Assembly of the United Nations shall decide upon the steps, if any, to be taken in respect of such request.

Article 14

The Secretary–General of the United Nations shall inform all States Members of the United Nations and the other States referred to in article 8:

(a) Of signatures to this Convention and of the deposit of instruments of ratification or accession, in accordance with articles 8, 9 and 10;

(b) Of the date on which this Convention will come into force, in accordance with article 11;

(c) Of requests for revision in accordance with article 13;

(d) Of reservations to this Convention, in accordance with article 12.

Article 15

The original of this Convention, of which the Chinese, English, French, Russian and Spanish texts are equally authentic, shall be deposited with the Secretary–General of the United Nations, who shall send certified copies thereof to all States referred to in article 8.

3.3 **Convention on the Territorial Sea and Contiguous Zone.**[c] **Concluded at Geneva, 29 April 1958. Entered into force, 10 September 1964. 516 UNTS 205, 15 UST 1606, TIAS No 5639;** *reprinted in* **5 Weston V.F.5**

Part I

TERRITORIAL SEA

Section I. General

Article 1

1. The sovereignty of a State extends, beyond its land territory and its internal waters, to a belt of sea adjacent to its coast, described as the territorial sea.

2. This sovereignty is exercised subject to the provisions of these articles and to other rules of international law.

Article 2

The sovereignty of a coastal State extends to the air space over the territorial sea as well as to its bed and subsoil.

Section II. Limits of the Territorial Sea

Article 3

Except where otherwise provided in these articles, the normal baseline for measuring the breadth of the territorial sea is the low-water line along the coast as marked on large-scale charts officially recognized by the coastal State.

Article 4

1. In localities where the coast line is deeply indented and cut into, or if there is a fringe of islands along the coast in its immediate vicinity, the method of straight baselines joining appropriate points may be employed in drawing the baseline from which the breadth of the territorial sea is measured.

2. The drawing of such baselines must not depart to any appreciable extent from the general direction of the coast, and the sea areas lying within the lines must be sufficiently closely linked to the land domain to be subject to the régime of internal waters.

3. Baselines shall not be drawn to and from low-tide elevations, unless lighthouses or similar installations which are permanently above sea level have been built on them.

4. Where the method of straight baselines is applicable under the provisions of paragraph 1, account may be taken, in determining particular baselines, of economic interests peculiar to the region concerned, the reality and the importance of which are clearly evidenced by a long usage.

5. The system of straight baselines may not be applied by a State in such a manner as to cut off from the high seas the territorial sea of another State.

6. The coastal State must clearly indicate straight baselines on charts, to which due publicity must be given.

---

c. *See also* Optional Protocol to the 1958 Law of the Sea Conventions Concerning the Compulsory Settlement of Disputes (which provides for reference to the International Court of Justice of disputes arising out of this agreement), concluded 29 April 1958 and entered into force 30 September 1962 (450 UNTS 169).

Article 5

1.   Waters on the landward side of the baseline of the territorial sea form part of the internal waters of the State.

2.   Where the establishment of a straight baseline in accordance with article 4 has the effect of enclosing as internal waters areas which previously had been considered as part of the territorial sea or of the high seas, a right of innocent passage, as provided in articles 14 to 23, shall exist in those waters.

Article 6

The outer limit of the territorial sea is the line every point of which is at a distance from the nearest point of the baseline equal to the breadth of the territorial sea.

Article 7

1.   This article relates only to bays the coasts of which belong to a single State.

2.   For the purposes of these articles, a bay is a well-marked indentation whose penetration is in such proportion to the width of its mouth as to contain landlocked waters and constitute more than a mere curvature of the coast. An indentation shall not, however, be regarded as a bay unless its area is as large as, or larger than, that of the semi-circle whose diameter is a line drawn across the mouth of that indentation.

3.   For the purpose of measurement, the area of an indentation is that lying between the low-water mark around the shore of the indentation and a line joining the low-water marks of its natural entrance points. Where, because of the presence of islands, an indentation has more than one mouth, the semi-circle shall be drawn on a line as long as the sum total of the lengths of the lines across the different mouths. Islands within an indentation shall be included as if they were part of the water areas of the indentation.

4.   If the distance between the low-water marks of the natural entrance points of a bay does not exceed twenty-four miles, a closing line may be drawn between these two low-water marks, and the waters enclosed thereby shall be considered as internal waters.

5.   Where the distance between the low-water marks of the natural entrance points of a bay exceeds twenty-four miles, a straight baseline of twenty-four miles shall be drawn within the bay in such a manner as to enclose the maximum area of water that is possible with a line of that length.

6.   The foregoing provisions shall not apply to so-called "historic" bays, or in any case where the straight baseline system provided for in article 4 is applied.

Article 8

For the purpose of delimiting the territorial sea, the outermost permanent harbour works which form an integral part of the harbour system shall be regarded as forming part of the coast.

Article 9

Roadsteads which are normally used for the loading, unloading and anchoring of ships, and which would otherwise be situated wholly or partly outside the outer limit of the territorial sea, are included in the territorial sea. The coastal State must clearly demarcate such roadsteads and indicate them on charts together with their boundaries, to which due publicity must be given.

Article 10

1. An island is a naturally-formed area of land, surrounded by water, which is above water at high-tide.

2. The territorial sea of an island is measured in accordance with the provisions of these articles.

Article 11

1. A low-tide elevation is a naturally-formed area of land which is surrounded by and above water at low-tide but submerged at high-tide. Where a low-tide elevation is situated wholly or partly at a distance not exceeding the breadth of the territorial sea from the mainland or an island, the low-water line on that elevation may be used as the baseline for measuring the breadth of the territorial sea.

2. Where a low-tide elevation is wholly situated at a distance exceeding the breadth of the territorial sea from the mainland or an island, it has no territorial sea of its own.

Article 12

1. Where the coasts of two States are opposite or adjacent to each other, neither of the two States is entitled, failing agreement between them to the contrary, to extend its territorial sea beyond the median line every point of which is equidistant from the nearest points on the baselines from which the breadth of the territorial seas of each of the two States is measured. The provisions of this paragraph shall not apply, however, where it is necessary by reason of historic title or other special circumstances to delimit the territorial seas of the two States in a way which is at variance with this provision.

2. The line of delimitation between the territorial seas of two States lying opposite to each other or adjacent to each other shall be marked on large-scale charts officially recognized by the coastal States.

Article 13

If a river flows directly into the sea, the baseline shall be a straight line across the mouth of the river between points on the low-tide line of its banks.

SECTION III. RIGHT OF INNOCENT PASSAGE

SUB-SECTION A. RULES APPLICABLE TO ALL SHIPS

Article 14

1. Subject to the provisions of these articles, ships of all States, whether coastal or not, shall enjoy the right of innocent passage through the territorial sea.

2. Passage means navigation through the territorial sea for the purpose either of traversing that sea without entering internal waters, or of proceeding to internal waters, or of making for the high seas from internal waters.

3. Passage includes stopping and anchoring, but only in so far as the same are incidental to ordinary navigation or are rendered necessary by *force majeure* or by distress.

4. Passage is innocent so long as it is not prejudicial to the peace, good order or security of the coastal State. Such passage shall take place in conformity with these articles and with other rules of international law.

5. Passage of foreign fishing vessels shall not be considered innocent if they do not observe such laws and regulations as the coastal State may make and publish in order to prevent these vessels from fishing in the territorial sea.

6. Submarines are required to navigate on the surface and to show their flag.

Article 15

1. The coastal State must not hamper innocent passage through the territorial sea.

2. The coastal State is required to give appropriate publicity to any dangers to navigation, of which it has knowledge, within its territorial sea.

Article 16

1. The coastal State may take the necessary steps in its territorial sea to prevent passage which is not innocent.

2. In the case of ships proceeding to internal waters, the coastal State shall also have the right to take the necessary steps to prevent any breach of the conditions to which admission of those ships to those waters is subject.

3. Subject to the provisions of paragraph 4, the coastal State may, without discrimination amongst foreign ships, suspend temporarily in specified areas of its territorial sea the innocent passage of foreign ships if such suspension is essential for the protection of its security. Such suspension shall take effect only after having been duly published.

4. There shall be no suspension of the innocent passage of foreign ships through straits which are used for international navigation between one part of the high seas and another part of the high seas or the territorial sea of a foreign State.

Article 17

Foreign ships exercising the right of innocent passage shall comply with the laws and regulations enacted by the coastal State in conformity with these articles and other rules of international law and, in particular, with such laws and regulations relating to transport and navigation.

SUB–SECTION B. RULES APPLICABLE TO MERCHANT SHIPS

Article 18

1. No charge may be levied upon foreign ships by reason only of their passage through the territorial sea.

2. Charges may be levied upon a foreign ship passing through the territorial sea as payment only for specific services rendered to the ship. These charges shall be levied without discrimination.

Article 19

1. The criminal jurisdiction of the coastal State should not be exercised on board a foreign ship passing through the territorial sea to arrest any person or to conduct any investigation in connexion with any crime committed on board the ship during its passage, save only in the following cases:

(*a*) If the consequences of the crime extend to the coastal State; or

(*b*) If the crime is of a kind to disturb the peace of the country or the good order of the territorial sea; or

(*c*) If the assistance of the local authorities has been requested by the captain of the ship or by the consul of the country whose flag the ship flies; or

(*d*) If it is necessary for the suppression of illicit traffic in narcotic drugs.

2.   The above provisions do not affect the right of the coastal State to take any steps authorized by its laws for the purpose of an arrest or investigation on board a foreign ship passing through the territorial sea after leaving internal waters.

3.   In the cases provided for in paragraphs 1 and 2 of this article, the coastal State shall, if the captain so requests, advise the consular authority of the flag State before taking any steps, and shall facilitate contact between such authority and the ship's crew. In cases of emergency this notification may be communicated while the measures are being taken.

4.   In considering whether or how an arrest should be made, the local authorities shall pay due regard to the interests of navigation.

5.   The coastal State may not take any steps on board a foreign ship passing through the territorial sea to arrest any person or to conduct any investigation in connexion with any crime committed before the ship entered the territorial sea, if the ship, proceeding from a foreign port, is only passing through the territorial sea without entering internal waters.

Article 20

1.   The coastal State should not stop or divert a foreign ship passing through the territorial sea for the purpose of exercising civil jurisdiction in relation to a person on board the ship.

2.   The coastal State may not levy execution against or arrest the ship for the purpose of any civil proceedings, save only in respect of obligations or liabilities assumed or incurred by the ship itself in the course or for the purpose of its voyage through the waters of the coastal State.

3.   The provisions of the previous paragraph are without prejudice to the right of the coastal State, in accordance with its laws, to levy execution against or to arrest, for the purpose of any civil proceedings, a foreign ship lying in the territorial sea, or passing through the territorial sea after leaving internal waters.

SUB–SECTION C.   RULES APPLICABLE TO GOVERNMENT SHIPS OTHER THAN WARSHIPS

Article 21

The rules contained in sub-sections A and B shall also apply to government ships operated for commercial purposes.

Article 22

1.   The rules contained in sub-section A and in article 18 shall apply to government ships operated for non-commercial purposes.

2.   With such exceptions as are contained in the provisions referred to in the preceding paragraph, nothing in these articles affects the immunities which such ships enjoy under these articles or other rules of international law.

SUB–SECTION D.   RULE APPLICABLE TO WARSHIPS

Article 23

If any warship does not comply with the regulations of the coastal State concerning passage through the territorial sea and disregards any request for compliance which is made to it, the coastal State may require the warship to leave the territorial sea.

Part II

CONTIGUOUS ZONE

Article 24

1. In a zone of the high seas contiguous to its territorial sea, the coastal State may exercise the control necessary to:

(*a*) Prevent infringement of its customs, fiscal, immigration or sanitary regulations within its territory or territorial sea;

(*b*) Punish infringement of the above regulations committed within its territory or territorial sea.

2. The contiguous zone may not extend beyond twelve miles from the baseline from which the breadth of the territorial sea is measured.

3. Where the coasts of two States are opposite or adjacent to each other, neither of the two States is entitled, failing agreement between them to the contrary, to extend its contiguous zone beyond the median line every point of which is equidistant from the nearest points on the baselines from which the breadth of the territorial seas of the two States is measured.

Part III

FINAL ARTICLES

Article 25

The provisions of this Convention shall not affect conventions or other international agreements already in force, as between States Parties to them.

Article 26

This Convention shall, until 31 October 1958, be open for signature by all States Members of the United Nations or of any of the specialized agencies, and by any other State invited by the General Assembly of the United Nations to become a Party to the Convention.

Article 27

This Convention is subject to ratification. The instruments of ratification shall be deposited with the Secretary–General of the United Nations.

Article 28

This Convention shall be open for accession by any States belonging to any of the categories mentioned in article 26. The instruments of accession shall be deposited with the Secretary–General of the United Nations.

Article 29

1. This Convention shall come into force on the thirtieth day following the date of deposit of the twenty-second instrument of ratification or accession with the Secretary–General of the United Nations.

2. For each State ratifying or acceding to the Convention after the deposit of the twenty-second instrument of ratification or accession, the Convention shall enter into force on the thirtieth day after deposit by such State of its instrument of ratification or accession.

Article 30

1. After the expiration of a period of five years from the date on which this Convention shall enter into force, a request for the revision of this Convention may be

made at any time by any Contracting Party by means of a notification in writing addressed to the Secretary–General of the United Nations.

2. The General Assembly of the United Nations shall decide upon the steps, if any, to be taken in respect of such request.

Article 31

The Secretary–General of the United Nations shall inform all States Members of the United Nations and the other States referred to in article 26:

(*a*) Of signatures to this Convention and of the deposit of instruments of ratification or accession, in accordance with articles 26, 27 and 28;

(*b*) Of the date on which this Convention will come into force, in accordance with article 29;

(*c*) Of requests for revision in accordance with article 30.

Article 32

The original of this Convention, of which the Chinese, English, French, Russian and Spanish texts are equally authentic, shall be deposited with the Secretary–General of the United Nations, who shall send certified copies thereof to all States referred to in article 26.

3.4 CONVENTION ON THE LIABILITY OF OPERATORS OF NUCLEAR SHIPS. **Concluded at Brussels, 25 May 1962. Not yet in force. IAEA Leg.Ser. No. 4 at 34, 57 AJIL 268 (1963)**

Article I

For the purpose of this Convention:

1. "Nuclear ship" means any ship equipped with a nuclear power plant.

* * *

11. "Warship" means any ship belonging to the naval forces of a State and bearing the external marks distinguishing warships of its nationality, under the command of an officer duly commissioned by the Government of such State and whose name appears in the Navy List, and manned by a crew who are under regular naval discipline.

12. "Applicable national law" means the national law of the court having jurisdiction under the Convention including any rules of such national law relating to conflict of laws.

Article II

1. The operator of a nuclear ship shall be absolutely liable for any nuclear damage upon proof that such damage has been caused by a nuclear incident involving the nuclear fuel of, or radioactive products or waste produced in such ship.

2. Except as otherwise provided in this Convention no person other than the operator shall be liable for such nuclear damage.

* * *

6. Notwithstanding the provisions of paragraph 1 of this Article, the operator shall have a right of recourse:

   a) If the nuclear incident results from a personal act or omission done with intent to cause damage, in which event recourse shall lie against the individual who has acted, or omitted to act, with such intent;

   b) If the nuclear incident occurred as a consequence of any wreck-raising operation, against the person or persons who carried out such operation without the authority of the operator or of the State having licensed the sunken ship or of the State in whose waters the wreck is situated;

   c) If recourse is expressly provided for by contract.

Article III

1. The liability of the operator as regards one nuclear ship shall be limited to 1500 million francs in respect of any one nuclear incident, notwithstanding that the nuclear incident may have resulted from any fault of privity of that operator; such limit shall include neither any interest nor costs awarded by a court in actions for compensation under this Convention.

2. The operator shall be required to maintain insurance, or other financial security covering his liability for nuclear damage, in such amount, of such type and in such terms as the licensing State shall specify. The licensing State shall ensure the payment of claims for compensation for nuclear damage established against the operator by providing the necessary funds up to the limit laid down in paragraph 1 of this Article to the extent that the yield of the insurance or the financial security is inadequate to satisfy such claims.

3. However, nothing in paragraph 2 of this Article shall require any Contracting State or any of its constituent subdivisions, such as States, Republics or Cantons, to

maintain insurance or other financial security to cover their liability as operators of nuclear ships.

4. The franc mentioned in paragraph 1 of this Article is a unit of account constituted by sixty-five and one half milligrams of gold of millesimal fineness nine hundred. The amount awarded may be converted into each national currency in round figures. Conversion into national currencies other than gold shall be effected on the basis of their gold at the date of payment.

* * *

Article VIII

No liability under this Convention shall attach to an operator in respect to nuclear damage caused by a nuclear incident directly due to an act of war, hostilities, civil war or insurrection.

Article IX

The sums provided by insurance, by other financial security or by State indemnification in conformity with paragraph 2 of this Article III shall be exclusively available for compensation due under this Convention.

Article X

1. Any action for compensation shall be brought, at the option of the claimant, either before the courts of the licensing State or before the courts of the Contracting State or States in whose territory nuclear damage has been sustained.

2. If the licensing State has been or might be called upon to ensure the payment of claims for compensation in accordance with paragraph 2 of Article III of this Convention, it may intervene as party in any proceedings brought against the operator.

3. Any immunity from legal processes pursuant to rules of national or international law shall be waived with respect to duties or obligations arising under, or for the purpose of, this Convention. Nothing in this Convention shall make warships or other State-owned or State-operated ships on non-commercial service liable to arrest, attachment or seizure or confer jurisdiction in respect of warships on the courts of any foreign State.

* * *

Article XIII

This Convention applies to nuclear damage caused by a nuclear incident occurring in any part of the world and involving the nuclear fuel of, or radioactive products or waste produced in, a nuclear ship flying the flag of a Contracting State.

* * *

Article XVII

Nothing in this Convention shall affect any right which a Contracting State may have under international law to deny access to its waters and harbours to nuclear ships licensed by another Contracting State, even when it has formally complied with all the provisions of this Convention.

* * *

3.5 INTERNATIONAL CONVENTION RELATING TO INTERVENTION ON THE HIGH SEAS IN CASES OF OIL POLLUTION CASUALTIES (**Without Annex and Protocol**). **Concluded at Brussels, 29 November 1969. Entered into force, 6 May 1975. 970 UNTS 211, 26 UST 765, TIAS No 8068;** *reprinted in* **9 ILM 25 (1986) & 5 Weston & Carlson V.F.7**

Article I. 1. Parties to the present Convention may take such measures on the high seas as may be necessary to prevent, mitigate or eliminate grave and imminent danger to their coastline or related interests from pollution or threat of pollution of the sea by oil, following upon a maritime casualty or acts related to such a casualty, which may reasonably be expected to result in major harmful consequences.

2. However, no measures shall be taken under the present Convention against any warship or other ship owned or operated by a State and used, for the time being, only on government non-commercial service.

Article II. For the purposes of the present Convention:

1. "Maritime casualty" means a collision of ships, stranding or other incident of navigation, or other occurrence on board a ship or external to it resulting in material damage or imminent threat of material damage to a ship or cargo.

2. "Ship" means:

(*a*) any sea-going vessel of any type whatsoever, and

(*b*) any floating craft, with the exception of an installation or device engaged in the exploration and exploitation of the resources of the sea-bed and the ocean floor and the subsoil thereof.

3. "Oil" means crude oil, fuel oil, diesel oil and lubricating oil.

4. "Related interests" means the interests of a coastal State directly affected or threatened by the maritime casualty, such as:

(*a*) maritime coastal, port or estuarine activities, including fisheries activities, constituting an essential means of livelihood of the persons concerned;

(*b*) tourist attractions of the area concerned;

(*c*) the health of the coastal population and the well-being of the area concerned, including conservation of living marine resources and of wildlife.

5. "Organization" means the Inter–Governmental Maritime Consultative Organization.

Article III. When a coastal State is exercising the right to take measures in accordance with Article I, the following provisions shall apply:

(*a*) before taking any measures, a coastal State shall proceed to consultations with other States affected by the maritime casualty, particularly with the flag State or States;

(*b*) the coastal State shall notify without delay the proposed measures to any persons physical or corporate known to the coastal State, or made known to it during the consultations, to have interests which can reasonably be expected to be affected by those measures. The coastal State shall take into account any views they may submit;

(*c*) before any measure is taken, the coastal State may proceed to a consultation with independent experts, whose names shall be chosen from a list maintained by the Organization;

(*d*) in cases of extreme urgency requiring measures to be taken immediately, the coastal State may take measures rendered necessary by the urgency of the situation, without prior notification or consultation or without continuing consultations already begun;

(e) a coastal State shall, before taking such measures and during their course, use its best endeavours to avoid any risk to human life, and to afford persons in distress any assistance of which they may stand in need, and in appropriate cases to facilitate the repatriation of ships' crews, and to raise no obstacle thereto;

(f) measures which have been taken in application of Article I shall be notified without delay to the States and to the known physical or corporate persons concerned, as well as to the Secretary–General of the Organization.

Article IV. 1. Under the supervision of the Organization, there shall be set up and maintained the list of experts contemplated by Article III of the present Convention, and the Organization shall make necessary and appropriate regulations in connexion therewith, including the determination of the required qualifications.

2. Nominations to the list may be made by Member States of the Organization and by Parties to this Convention. The experts shall be paid on the basis of services rendered by the States utilizing those services.

Article V. 1. Measures taken by the coastal State in accordance with Article I shall be proportionate to the damage actual or threatened to it.

2. Such measures shall not go beyond what is reasonably necessary to achieve the end mentioned in Article I and shall cease as soon as that end has been achieved; they shall not unnecessarily interfere with the rights and interests of the flag State, third States and of any persons, physical or corporate, concerned.

3. In considering whether the measures are proportionate to the damage, account shall be taken of:

(a) the extent and probability of imminent damage if those measures are not taken; and

(b) the likelihood of those measures being effective; and

(c) the extent of the damage which may be caused by such measures.

Article VI. Any Party which has taken measures in contravention of the provisions of the present Convention causing damage to others, shall be obliged to pay compensation to the extent of the damage caused by measures which exceed those reasonably necessary to achieve the end mentioned in Article I.

Article VII. Except as specifically provided, nothing in the present Convention shall prejudice any otherwise applicable right, duty, privilege or immunity or deprive any of the Parties or any interested physical or corporate person of any remedy otherwise applicable.

Article VIII. 1. Any controversy between the Parties as to whether measures taken under Article I were in contravention of the provisions of the present Convention, to whether compensation is obliged to be paid under Article VI, and to the amount of such compensation shall, if settlement by negotiation between the Parties involved or between the Party which took the measures and the physical or corporate claimants has not been possible, and if the Parties do not otherwise agree, be submitted upon request of any of the Parties concerned to conciliation or, if conciliation does not succeed, to arbitration, as set out in the Annex to the present Convention.

2. The Party which took the measures shall not be entitled to refuse a request for conciliation or arbitration under provisions of the preceding paragraph solely on the grounds that any remedies under municipal law in its own courts have not been exhausted.

Article IX. 1. The present Convention shall remain open for signature until 31 December 1970 and shall thereafter remain open for accession.

2. States Members of the United Nations or any of the Specialized Agencies or of the International Atomic Energy Agency or Parties to the Statute of the International Court of Justice may become Parties to this Convention by:

    (*a*) signature without reservation as to ratification, acceptance or approval;

    (*b*) signature subject to ratification, acceptance or approval followed by ratification, acceptance or approval; or

    (*c*) accession.

Article X. 1. Ratification, acceptance, approval or accession shall be effected by the deposit of a formal instrument to that effect with the Secretary–General of the Organization.

2. Any instrument of ratification, acceptance, approval or accession deposited after the entry into force of an amendment to the present Convention with respect to all existing Parties or after the completion of all measures required for the entry into force of the amendment with respect to those Parties shall be deemed to apply to the Convention as modified by the amendment.

Article XI. 1. The present Convention shall enter into force on the ninetieth day following the date on which Governments of fifteen States have either signed it without reservation as to ratification, acceptance or approval or have deposited instruments of ratification, acceptance, approval or accession with the Secretary–General of the Organization.

2. For each State which subsequently ratifies, accepts, approves or accedes to it the present Convention shall come into force on the ninetieth day after deposit by such State of the appropriate instrument.

Article XII. 1. The present Convention may be denounced by any Party at any time after the date on which the Convention comes into force for that State.

2. Denunciation shall be effected by the deposit of an instrument with the Secretary–General of the Organization.

3. A denunciation shall take effect one year, or such longer period as may be specified in the instrument of denunciation, after its deposit with the Secretary–General of the Organization.

Article XIII. 1. The United Nations where it is the administering authority for a territory, or any State Party to the present Convention responsible for the international relations of a territory, shall as soon as possible consult with the appropriate authorities of such territories or take such other measures as may be appropriate, in order to extend the present Convention to that territory and may at any time by notification in writing to the Secretary–General of the Organization declare that the present Convention shall extend to such territory.

2. The present Convention shall, from the date of receipt of the notification or from such other date as may be specified in the notification, extend to the territory named therein.

3. The United Nations, or any Party which has made a declaration under paragraph 1 of this Article may at any time after the date on which the Convention has been so extended to any territory declare by notification in writing to the Secretary–General of the Organization that the present Convention shall cease to extend to any such territory named in the notification.

4. The present Convention shall cease to extend to any territory mentioned in such notification one year, or such longer period as may be specified therein, after the date of receipt of the notification by the Secretary–General of the Organization.

Article XIV. 1. A Conference for the purpose of revising or amending the present Convention may be convened by the Organization.

2. The Organization shall convene a Conference of the States Parties to the present Convention for revising or amending the present Convention at the request of not less than one-third of the Parties.

Article XV. 1. The present Convention shall be deposited with the Secretary–General of the Organization.

2. The Secretary–General of the Organization shall:

(*a*) inform all States which have signed or acceded to the Convention of:

(i) each new signature or deposit of instrument together with the date thereof;

(ii) the deposit of any instrument of denunciation of this Convention together with the date of the deposit;

(iii) the extension of the present Convention to any territory under paragraph 1 of Article XIII and of the termination of any such extension under the provisions of paragraph 4 of that Article stating in each case the date on which the present Convention has been or will cease to be so extended;

(*b*) transmit certified true copies of the present Convention to all Signatory States and to all States which accede to the present Convention.

Article XVI. As soon as the present Convention comes into force, the text shall be transmitted by the Secretary–General of the Organization to the Secretariat of the United Nations for registration and publication in accordance with Article 102 of the Charter of the United Nations.

Article XVII. The present Convention is established in a single copy in the English and French languages, both texts being equally authentic. Official translations in the Russian and Spanish languages shall be prepared and deposited with the signed original.

3.6 CONVENTION ON THE PREVENTION OF MARINE POLLUTION BY DUMPING OF WASTES AND OTHER MATTER (**With Annexes and as Amended to 1989 but Without Addendum**).[d] **Concluded at London, Mexico City, Moscow and Washington, 29 December 1972. Entered into force, 30 August 1975. 1046 UNTS 120, 26 UST 2403, TIAS No 8165;** *reprinted in* **11 ILM 1294 (1973); & 5 Weston & Carlson V.I.7**

The Contracting Parties to this Convention,

Recognizing that the marine environment and the living organisms which it supports are of vital importance to humanity, and all people have an interest in assuring that it is so managed that its quality and resources are not impaired;

Recognizing that the capacity of the sea to assimilate wastes and render them harmless, and its ability to regenerate natural resources is not unlimited;

Recognizing that States have, in accordance with the Charter of the United Nations and the principles of international law, the sovereign right to exploit their own resources pursuant to their own environmental policies, and the responsibility to ensure that activities within their jurisdiction or control do not cause damage to the environment of other States or of areas beyond the limits of national jurisdiction;

Recognizing resolution 2749 (XXV) of the General Assembly of the United Nations on the principles governing the sea-bed and the ocean floor and the subsoil thereof, beyond the limits of national jurisdiction;

Noting that marine pollution originates in many sources, such as dumping and discharges through the atmosphere, rivers, estuaries, outfalls and pipelines, and that it is important that States use the best practicable means to prevent such pollution and develop products and processes which will reduce the amount of harmful wastes to be disposed of;

Being convinced that international action to control the pollution of the sea by dumping can and must be taken without delay but that this action should not preclude discussion of measures to control other sources of marine pollution as soon as possible; and

Wishing to improve protection of the marine environment by encouraging States with a common interest in particular geographical areas to enter into appropriate agreements supplementary to this Convention;

Have agreed as follows:

Article I. Contracting Parties shall individually and collectively promote the effective control of all sources of pollution of the marine environment, and pledge themselves especially to take all practicable steps to prevent the pollution of the sea by the dumping of waste and other matter that is liable to create hazards to human health, to harm living resources and marine life, to damage amenities or to interfere with other legitimate uses of the sea.

Article II. Contracting Parties shall, as provided for in the following Articles, take effective measures individually, according to their scientific, technical and economic capabilities, and collectively, to prevent marine pollution caused by dumping and shall harmonize their policies in this regard.

Article III. For the purposes of this Convention:

1.   (*a*) ''Dumping'' means:

(i) any deliberate disposal at sea of wastes or other matter from vessels, aircraft, platforms or other man-made structures at sea;

d.   *See also* Basic Document 3.18, *infra.*

(ii) any deliberate disposal at sea of vessels, aircraft, platforms or other man-made structures at sea.

(b) "Dumping" does not include:

(i) the disposal at sea of wastes or other matter incidental to, or derived from the normal operations of vessels, aircraft, platforms or other man-made structures at sea and their equipment, other than wastes or other matter transported by or to vessels, aircraft, platforms or other man-made structures at sea, operating for the purpose of disposal of such matter or derived from the treatment of such wastes or other matter on such vessels, aircraft, platforms or structures;

(ii) placement of matter for a purpose other than the mere disposal thereof, provided that such placement is not contrary to the aims of this Convention.

(c) The disposal of wastes or other matter directly arising from, or related to the exploration, exploitation and associated off-shore processing of sea-bed mineral resources will not be covered by the provisions of this Convention.

2. "Vessels and aircraft" means waterborne or airborne craft of any type whatsoever. This expression includes air-cushioned craft and floating craft, whether self-propelled or not.

3. "Sea" means all marine waters other than the internal waters of States.

4. "Wastes or other matter" means material and substance of any kind, form or description.

5. "Special permit" means permission granted specifically on application in advance and in accordance with Annex II and Annex III.

6. "General permit" means permission granted in advance and in accordance with Annex III.

7. The "Organisation" means the Organisation designated by the Contracting Parties in accordance with Article XIV(2).

Article IV. 1. In accordance with the provisions of this Convention, Contracting Parties shall prohibit the dumping of any wastes or other matter in whatever form or condition except as otherwise specified below:

(a) the dumping of wastes or other matter listed in Annex I is prohibited;

(b) the dumping of wastes or other matter listed in Annex II requires a prior special permit;

(c) the dumping of all other wastes or matter requires a prior general permit.

2. Any permit shall be issued only after careful consideration of all the factors set forth in Annex III, including prior studies of the characteristics of the dumping site, as set forth in Sections B and C of that Annex.

3. No provision of this Convention is to be interpreted as preventing a Contracting Party from prohibiting, insofar as that Party is concerned, the dumping of wastes or other matter not mentioned in Annex I. That Party shall notify such measures to the Organisation.

Article V. 1. The provisions of Article IV shall not apply when it is necessary to secure the safety of human life or of vessels, aircraft, platforms or other man-made structures at sea in cases of *force majeure* caused by stress of weather, or in any case which constitutes a danger to human life or a real threat to vessels, aircraft, platforms or other man-made structures at sea, if dumping appears to be the only way of averting the threat and if there is every probability that the damage consequent upon such dumping will be less than would otherwise occur. Such dumping shall be so conducted as to minimise the likelihood of damage to human or marine life and shall be reported forthwith to the Organisation.

2. A Contracting Party may issue a special permit as an exception to Article IV(1)(a), in emergencies, posing unacceptable risk relating to human health and admitting no other feasible solution. Before doing so the Party shall consult any other country or countries that are likely to be affected and the Organisation which, after consulting other Parties, and international organisations as appropriate, shall, in accordance with Article XIV promptly recommend to the Party the most appropriate procedures to adopt. The Party shall follow these recommendations to the maximum extent feasible consistent with the time within which action must be taken and with the general obligation to avoid damage to the marine environment and shall inform the Organisation of the action it takes. The Parties pledge themselves to assist one another in such situations.

3. Any Contracting Party may waive its rights under paragraph (2) at the time of, or subsequent to ratification of, or accession to this Convention.

Article VI. 1. Each Contracting Party shall designate an appropriate authority or authorities to:

(a) issue special permits which shall be required prior to, and for, the dumping of matter listed in Annex II and in the circumstances provided for in Article V(2);

(b) issue general permits which shall be required prior to, and for, the dumping of all other matter;

(c) keep records of the nature and quantities of all matter permitted to be dumped and the location, time and method of dumping;

(d) monitor individually, or in collaboration with other Parties and competent international organisations, the condition of the seas for the purposes of this Convention.

2. The appropriate authority or authorities of a Contracting Party shall issue prior special or general permits in accordance with paragraph (1) in respect of matter intended for dumping:

(a) loaded in its territory;

(b) loaded by a vessel or aircraft registered in its territory or flying its flag, when the loading occurs in the territory of a State not party to this Convention.

3. In issuing permits under sub-paragraphs (1)(a) and (b) above, the appropriate authority or authorities shall comply with Annex III, together with such additional criteria, measures and requirements as they may consider relevant.

4. Each Contracting Party, directly or through a Secretariat established under a regional agreement, shall report to the Organisation, and where appropriate to other Parties, the information specified in sub-paragraphs (c) and (d) of paragraph (1) above, and the criteria, measures and requirements it adopts in accordance with paragraph (3) above. The procedure to be followed and the nature of such reports shall be agreed by the Parties in consultation.

Article VII. 1. Each Contracting Party shall apply the measures required to implement the present Convention to all:

(a) vessels and aircraft registered in its territory or flying its flag;

(b) vessels and aircraft loading in its territory or territorial seas matter which is to be dumped;

(c) vessels and aircraft and fixed or floating platforms under its jurisdiction believed to be engaged in dumping.

2. Each Party shall take in its territory appropriate measures to prevent and punish conduct in contravention of the provisions of this Convention.

3. The Parties agree to co-operate in the development of procedures for the effective application of this Convention particularly on the high seas, including procedures for the reporting of vessels and aircraft observed dumping in contravention of the Convention.

4. This Convention shall not apply to those vessels and aircraft entitled to sovereign immunity under international law. However, each Party shall ensure by the adoption of appropriate measures that such vessels and aircraft owned or operated by it act in a manner consistent with the object and purpose of this Convention, and shall inform the Organisation accordingly.

5. Nothing in this convention shall affect the right of each Party to adopt other measures, in accordance with the principles of international law, to prevent dumping at sea.

Article VIII. In order to further the objectives of this Convention, the Contracting Parties with common interests to protect in the marine environment in a given geographical area shall endeavour, taking into account characteristic regional features, to enter into regional agreements consistent with this Convention for the prevention of pollution, especially by dumping. The Contracting Parties to the present Convention shall endeavour to act consistently with the objectives and provisions of such regional agreements, which shall be notified to them by the Organisation. Contracting Parties shall seek to co-operate with the Parties to regional agreements in order to develop harmonized procedures to be followed by Contracting Parties to the different conventions concerned. Special attention shall be given to co-operation in the field of monitoring and scientific research.

Article IX. The Contracting Parties shall promote, through collaboration within the Organisation and other international bodies, support for those Parties which request it for:

(a) the training of scientific and technical personnel;

(b) the supply of necessary equipment and facilities for research and monitoring;

(c) the disposal and treatment of waste and other measures to prevent or mitigate pollution caused by dumping;

preferably within the countries concerned, so furthering the aims and purposes of this Convention.

Article X. In accordance with the principles of international law regarding State responsibility for damage to the environment of other States or to any other area of the environment, caused by dumping of wastes and other matter of all kinds, the Contracting Parties undertake to develop procedures for the assessment of liability and the settlement of disputes regarding dumping.

Article XI. The Contracting Parties shall at their first consultative meeting consider procedures for the settlement of disputes concerning the interpretation and application of this Convention.

Article XII. The Contracting Parties pledge themselves to promote, within the competent specialised agencies and other international bodies, measures to protect the marine environment against pollution caused by:

(a) hydrocarbons, including oil, and their wastes;

(b) other noxious or hazardous matter transported by vessels for purposes other than dumping;

(*c*) wastes generated in the course of operation of vessels, aircraft, platforms and other man-made structures at sea;

(*d*) radio-active pollutants from all sources, including vessels;

(*e*) agents of chemical and biological warfare;

(*f*) wastes or other matter directly arising from, or related to the exploration, exploitation and associated off-shore processing of sea-bed mineral resources.

The Parties will also promote, within the appropriate international organisation, the codification of signals to be used by vessels engaged in dumping.

Article XIII. Nothing in this Convention shall prejudice the codification and development of the law of the sea by the United Nations Conference on the Law of the Sea convened pursuant to Resolution 2750 C(XXV) of the General Assembly of the United Nations nor the present or future claims and legal views of any State concerning the law of the sea and the nature and extent of coastal and flag State jurisdiction. The Contracting Parties agree to consult at a meeting to be convened by the Organisation after the Law of the Sea Conference, and in any case not later than 1976, with a view to defining the nature and extent of the right and the responsibility of a coastal State to apply the Convention in a zone adjacent to its coast.

Article XIV. 1. The Government of the United Kingdom of Great Britain and Northern Ireland as a depositary shall call a meeting of the Contracting Parties not later than three months after the entry into force of this Convention to decide on organisational matters.

2. The Contracting Parties shall designate a competent Organisation existing at the time of that meeting to be responsible for Secretariat duties in relation to this Convention. Any Party to this Convention not being a member of this Organisation shall make an appropriate contribution to the expenses incurred by the Organisation in performing these duties.

3. The Secretariat duties of the Organisation shall include:

(*a*) the convening of consultative meetings of the Contracting Parties not less frequently than once every two years and of special meetings of the Parties at any time on the request of two thirds of the Parties;

(*b*) preparing and assisting, in consultation with the Contracting Parties and appropriate International Organisations, in the development and implementation of procedures referred to in sub-paragraph (4)(*e*) of this Article;

(*c*) considering enquiries by, and information from the Contracting Parties, consulting with them and with the appropriate International Organisations, and providing recommendations to the Parties on questions related to, but not specifically covered by the Convention;

(*d*) conveying to the Parties concerned all notifications received by the Organisation in accordance with Articles IV(3), V(1) and (2), VI(4), XV, XX and XXI.

Prior to the designation of the Organisation these functions shall, as necessary, be performed by the depositary, who for this purpose shall be the Government of the United Kingdom of Great Britain and Northern Ireland.

4. Consultative or special meetings of the Contracting Parties shall keep under continuing review the implementation of this Convention and may, *inter alia:*

(*a*) review and adopt amendments to this Convention and its Annexes in accordance with Article XV;

(*b*) invite the appropriate scientific body or bodies to collaborate with and to advise the Parties or the Organisation on any scientific or technical aspect relevant to this Convention, including particularly the content of the Annexes;

(*c*) receive and consider reports made pursuant to Article VI(4);

(*d*) promote co-operation with and between regional organisations concerned with the prevention of marine pollution;

(*e*) develop or adopt, in consultation with appropriate International Organisations, procedures referred to in Article V(2), including basic criteria for determining exceptional and emergency situations, and procedures for consultative advice and the safe disposal of matter in such circumstances, including the designation of appropriate dumping areas, and recommend accordingly;

(*f*) consider any additional action that may be required.

5. The Contracting Parties at their first consultative meeting shall establish rules of procedure as necessary.

Article XV. 1. (*a*) At meetings of the Contracting Parties called in accordance with Article XIV amendments to this Convention may be adopted by a two-thirds majority of those present. An amendment shall enter into force for the Parties which have accepted it on the sixtieth day after two thirds of the Parties shall have deposited an instrument of acceptance of the amendment with the Organisation. Thereafter the amendment shall enter into force for any other Party 30 days after that Party deposits its instrument of acceptance of the amendment.

(*b*) The Organisation shall inform all Contracting Parties of any request made for a special meeting under Article XIV and of any amendments adopted at meetings of the Parties and of the date on which each such amendment enters into force for each Party.

2. Amendments to the Annexes will be based on scientific or technical considerations. Amendments to the Annexes approved by a two-thirds majority of those present at a meeting called in accordance with Article XIV shall enter into force for each Contracting Party immediately on notification of its acceptance to the Organisation and 100 days after approval by the meeting for all other Parties except for those which before the end of the 100 days make a declaration that they are not able to accept the amendment at that time. Parties should endeavour to signify their acceptance of an amendment to the Organisation as soon as possible after approval at a meeting. A Party may at any time substitute an acceptance for a previous declaration of objection and the amendment previously objected to shall thereupon enter into force for that Party.

3. An acceptance or declaration of objection under this Article shall be made by the deposit of an instrument with the Organisation. The Organisation shall notify all Contracting Parties of the receipt of such instruments.

4. Prior to the designation of the Organisation, the Secretarial functions herein attributed to it shall be performed temporarily by the Government of the United Kingdom of Great Britain and Northern Ireland, as one of the depositaries of this Convention.

Article XVI. This Convention shall be open for signature by any State at London, Mexico City, Moscow and Washington from 29 December 1972 until 31 December 1973.

Article XVII. This Convention shall be subject to ratification. The instruments of ratification shall be deposited with the Governments of Mexico, the Union of Soviet Socialist Republics, the United Kingdom of Great Britain and Northern Ireland, and the United States of America.

Article XVIII. After 31 December 1973, this Convention shall be open for accession by any State. The instruments of accession shall be deposited with the Governments of Mexico, the Union of Soviet Socialist Republics, the United Kingdom of Great Britain and Northern Ireland, and the United States of America.

Article XIX. 1. This Convention shall enter into force on the thirtieth day following the date of deposit of the fifteenth instrument of ratification or accession.

2. For each Contracting Party ratifying or acceding to the Convention after the deposit of the fifteenth instrument of ratification or accession, the Convention shall enter into force on the thirtieth day after deposit by such Party of its instrument of ratification or accession.

Article XX. The depositaries shall inform Contracting Parties:

(*a*) of signatures to this Convention and of the deposit of instruments of ratification, accession or withdrawal, in accordance with Articles XVI, XVII, XVIII and XXI, and

(*b*) of the date on which this Convention will enter into force, in accordance with Article XIX.

Article XXI. Any Contracting Party may withdraw from this Convention by giving six months' notice in writing to a depositary, which shall promptly inform all Parties of such notice.

Article XXII. The original of this Convention of which the English, French, Russian and Spanish texts are equally authentic, shall be deposited with the Governments of Mexico, the Union of Soviet Socialist Republics, the United Kingdom of Great Britain and Northern Ireland and the United States of America who shall send certified copies thereof to all States.

ANNEX I

1. Organohalogen compounds.

2. Mercury and mercury compounds.

3. Cadmium and cadmium compounds.

4. Persistent plastics and other persistent synthetic materials, for example, netting and ropes, which may float or may remain in suspension in the sea in such a manner as to interfere materially with fishing, navigation or other legitimate uses of the sea.

5. Crude oil and its wastes, refined petroleum products, petroleum distillate residues, and any mixtures containing any of these, taken on board for the purpose of dumping.

6. High-level radio-active wastes or other high-level radio-active matter, defined on public health, biological or other grounds, by the competent international body in this field, at present the International Atomic Energy Agency, as unsuitable for dumping at sea.

7. Materials in whatever form (e.g. solids, liquids, semi-liquids, gases or in a living state) produced for biological and chemical warfare.

8. The preceding paragraphs of this Annex do not apply to substances which are rapidly rendered harmless by physical, chemical or biological processes in the sea provided they do not:

(i) make edible marine organisms unpalatable, or

(ii) endanger human health or that of domestic animals.

The consultative procedure provided for under Article XIV should be followed by a Party if there is doubt about the harmlessness of the substances.

9. This Annex does not apply to wastes or other materials (e.g. sewage sludges and dredged spoils) containing the matter referred to in paragraphs 1–5 above as trace contaminants. Such wastes shall be subject to the provisions of Annexes II and III as appropriate.

10. Paragraphs 1 and 5 of this annex do not apply to the disposal of wastes or other matter referred to in these paragraphs by means of incineration at sea. Incineration of such wastes or other matter at sea requires a prior special permit. In the issue of special permits for incineration, the Contracting Parties shall apply the regulations for the control of incineration of wastes and other matter at sea set forth in the addendum to this annex (which shall constitute an integral part of this annex) and take full account of the technical guidelines on the control of incineration of wastes and other matter at sea adopted by the Contracting Parties in consultation.

ANNEX II

The following substances and materials requiring special care are listed for the purposes of Article VI(1)(a).

A. Wastes containing significant amounts of the matters listed below:

arsenic)
lead   )
copper)   and their compounds
zinc   )

organosilicon compounds

cyanides

fluorides

pesticides and their by-products not covered in Annex I.

B. In the issue of permits for the dumping of large quantities of acids and alkalis, consideration shall be given to the possible presence in such wastes of the substances listed in paragraph A and to the following additional substances:

beryllium   )
chromium   )
nickel   )   and their compounds
vanadium   )

C. Containers, scrap metal and other bulky wastes liable to sink to the sea bottom which may present a serious obstacle to fishing or navigation.

D. Radio-active wastes or other radio-active matter not included in Annex I. In the issue of permits for the dumping of this matter, the Contracting Parties should take full account of the recommendations of the competent international body in this field, at present the International Atomic Energy Agency.

E. In the issue of special permits for the incineration of substances and materials listed in this annex, the Contracting Parties shall apply the regulations for the control of incineration of wastes and other matter at sea set forth in the addendum to annex I and take full account of the technical guidelines on the control of incineration of wastes and other matter at sea adopted by the Contracting Parties in consultation, to the extent specified in these regulations and guidelines.

F. Substances which, though of a non-toxic nature, may become harmful due to the quantities in which they are dumped, or which are liable to seriously reduce amenities.

ANNEX III

Provisions to be considered in establishing criteria governing the issue of permits for the dumping of matter at sea, taking into account Article IV(2), include:

A.   Characteristics and composition of the matter

1.   Total amount and average composition of matter dumped (e.g. per year).

2.   Form, e.g. solid, sludge, liquid, or gaseous.

3.   Properties: physical (e.g. solubility and density), chemical and biochemical (e.g. oxygen demand, nutrients) and biological (e.g. presence of viruses, bacteria, yeasts, parasites).

4.   Toxicity.

5.   Persistence: physical, chemical and biological.

6.   Accumulation and biotransformation in biological materials or sediments.

7.   Susceptibility to physical, chemical and biochemical changes and interaction in the aquatic environment with other dissolved organic and inorganic materials.

8.   Probability of production of taints or other changes reducing marketability of resources (fish, shellfish, etc.).

B.   Characteristics of dumping site and method of deposit

1.   Location (e.g. co-ordinates of the dumping area, depth and distance from the coast), location in relation to other areas (e.g. amenity areas, spawning, nursery and fishing areas and exploitable resources).

2.   Rate of disposal per specific period (e.g. quantity per day, per week, per month).

3.   Methods of packaging and containment, if any.

4.   Initial dilution achieved by proposed method of release.

5.   Dispersal characteristics (e.g. effects of currents, tides and wind on horizontal transport and vertical mixing).

6.   Water characteristics (e.g. temperature, pH, salinity, stratification, oxygen indices of pollution—dissolved oxygen (DO), chemical oxygen demand (COD), biochemical oxygen demand (BOD)—nitrogen present in organic and mineral form including ammonia, suspended matter, other nutrients and productivity).

7.   Bottom characteristics (e.g. topography, geochemical and geological characteristics and biological productivity).

8.   Existence and effects of other dumpings which have been made in the dumping area (e.g. heavy metal background reading and organic carbon content).

9.   In issuing a permit for dumping, Contracting Parties should consider whether an adequate scientific basis exists for assessing the consequences of such dumping, as outlined in this Annex, taking into account seasonal variations.

C.   General considerations and conditions

1.   Possible effects on amenities (e.g. presence of floating or stranded material, turbidity, objectionable odour, discolouration and foaming).

2.   Possible effects on marine life, fish and shellfish culture, fish stocks and fisheries, seaweed harvesting and culture.

3.   Possible effects on other uses of the sea (e.g. impairment of water quality for industrial use, underwater corrosion of structures, interference with ship operations from floating materials, interference with fishing or navigation through deposit of waste or solid objects on the sea floor and protection of areas of special importance for scientific or conservation purposes).

4.   The practical availability of alternative land-based methods of treatment, disposal or elimination, or of treatment to render the matter less harmful for dumping at sea.

3.7 MARPOL 73/78: PROTOCOL OF 1978 RELATING TO THE INTERNATIONAL CONVENTION FOR THE PREVENTION OF POLLUTION FROM SHIPS, 1973 (With Convention Text and Excerpts from Annexes I, II & V),[e] concluded at London, 17 February, 1978. Entered into force 2 October 1983. 1341 UNTS 3; *reprinted in* **5 Weston & Carlson V.F.20**

THE PARTIES TO THE PRESENT PROTOCOL,

RECOGNIZING the significant contribution which can be made by the International Convention for the Prevention of Pollution from Ships, 1973, to the protection of the marine environment from pollution from ships,

RECOGNIZING ALSO the need to improve further the prevention and control of marine pollution from ships, particularly oil tankers,

RECOGNIZING FURTHER the need for implementing the Regulations for the Prevention of Pollution by Oil contained in Annex I of that Convention as early and as widely as possible,

ACKNOWLEDGING HOWEVER the need to defer the application of Annex II of that Convention until certain technical problems have been satisfactorily resolved,

CONSIDERING that these objectives may best be achieved by the conclusion of a Protocol Relating to the International Convention for the Prevention of Pollution from Ships, 1973,

HAVE AGREED as follows:

ARTICLE I

General Obligations

1. The Parties to the present Protocol undertake to give effect to the provisions of:

(a) the present Protocol and the Annex hereto which shall constitute an integral part of the present Protocol; and

(b) the International Convention for the Prevention of Pollution from Ships, 1973 (hereinafter referred to as "the Convention"), subject to the modifications and additions set out in the present Protocol.

2. The provisions of the Convention and the present Protocol shall be read and interpreted together as one single instrument.

3. Every reference to the Protocol constitutes at the same time a reference to the Annex hereto.

ARTICLE II

Implementation of Annex II of the Convention

1. Notwithstanding the provisions of Article 14(1) of the Convention, the Parties to the present Protocol agree that they shall not be bound by the provisions of Annex II of the Convention for a period of three years from the date of entry into force of the

---

e. The 1978 Protocol incorporates, with modifications, the provisions of the International Convention for the Prevention of Pollution from Ships, 1973, *signed at London* Nov. 2, 1973, *reprinted in* 12 I.L.M. 1319 (1978). The 1973 Convention never entered into force on its own. Accordingly, as of October 2, 1983, when the 1978 Protocol entered into force, the regime to be applied by the states parties to the 1978 Protocol was the regime contained in the 1973 Convention as modified by the 1978 Protocol. This document therefore reflects the terms of the 1978 Protocol, *and incorporates the 1973 Convention as modified.* Article I of the 1978 Protocol directs that "the provisions of the Convention and the present Protocol shall be read and interpreted together as one single instrument," and the consolidated text of the two instruments has come to be known as MARPOL 73/78. *See* International Maritime Organization, MARPOL 73/78, Consolidated Edition (IMO 1997).

present Protocol or for such longer period as may be decided by a two-thirds majority of the Parties to the present Protocol in the Marine Environment Protection Committee (hereinafter referred to as "the Committee") of the Inter–Governmental Maritime Consultative Organization (hereinafter referred to as "the Organization").

2. During the period specified in paragraph 1 of this Article, the Parties to the present Protocol shall not be under any obligations nor entitled to claim any privileges under the Convention in respect of matters relating to Annex II of the Convention and all reference to Parties in the Convention shall not include the Parties to the present Protocol in so far as matters relating to that Annex are concerned.

ARTICLE III

Communication of Information

The text of Article 11(1)(b) of the Convention is replaced by the following:

"a list of nominated surveyors or recognized organizations which are authorized to act on their behalf in the administration of matters relating to the design, construction, equipment and operation of ships carrying harmful substances in accordance with the provisions of the Regulations for circulation to the Parties for information of their officers. The Administration shall therefore notify the Organization of the specific responsibilities and conditions of the authority delegated to nominated surveyors or recognized organizations."

ARTICLE IV

Signature, Ratification, Acceptance, Approval and Accession

1. The present Protocol shall be open for signature at the Headquarters of the Organization from 1 June 1978 to 31 May 1979 and shall thereafter remain open for accession. States may become Parties to the present Protocol by:

(a) signature without reservation as to ratification, acceptance or approval; or

(b) signature, subject to ratification, acceptance or approval, followed by ratification, acceptance or approval; or

(c) accession.

2. Ratification, acceptance, approval or accession shall be effected by the deposit of an instrument to that effect with the Secretary–General of the Organization.

ARTICLE V

Entry into Force

1. The present Protocol shall enter into force twelve months after the date on which not less than fifteen States, the combined merchant fleets of which constitute not less than fifty per cent of the gross tonnage of the world's merchant shipping, have become Parties to it in accordance with Article IV of the present Protocol.

2. Any instrument of ratification, acceptance, approval or accession deposited after the date on which the present Protocol enters into force shall take effect three months after the date of deposit.

3. After the date on which an amendment to the present Protocol is deemed to have been accepted in accordance with Article 16 of the Convention, any instrument of ratification, acceptance, approval or accession deposited shall apply to the present Protocol as amended.

ARTICLE VI

Amendments

The procedures set out in Article 16 of the Convention in respect of amendments to the Articles, an Annex and an Appendix to an Annex of the Convention shall apply respectively to amendments to the Articles, the Annex and an Appendix to the Annex of the present Protocol.

ARTICLE VII

Denunciation

1. The present Protocol may be denounced by any Party to the present Protocol at any time after the expiry of five years from the date on which the Protocol enters into force for that Party.

2. Denunciation shall be effected by the deposit of an instrument of denunciation with the Secretary–General of the Organization.

3. A denunciation shall take effect twelve months after receipt of the notification by the Secretary–General of the Organization or after the expiry of any other longer period which may be indicated in the notification.

ARTICLE VIII

Depositary

1. The present Protocol shall be deposited with the Secretary–General of the Organization (hereinafter referred to as "the Depositary").

2. The Depositary shall:

(a) inform all States which have signed the present Protocol or acceded thereto of:

(i) each new signature or deposit of an instrument of ratification, acceptance, approval or accession, together with the date thereof;

(ii) the date of entry into force of the present protocol;

(iii) the deposit of any instrument of denunciation of the present Protocol together with the date on which it was received and the date on which the denunciation takes effect;

(iv) any decision made in accordance with Article II(1) of the present Protocol;

(b) transmit certified true copies of the present Protocol to all States which have signed the present Protocol or acceded thereto.

3. As soon as the present Protocol enters into force, a certified true copy thereof shall be transmitted by the Depositary to the Secretariat of the United Nations for registration and publication in accordance with Article 102 of the Charter of the United Nations.

ARTICLE IX

Languages

The present Protocol is established in a single original in the English, French, Russian and Spanish languages, each text being equally authentic. Official translations in the Arabic, German, Italian and Japanese languages shall be prepared and deposited with the signed original.

International Convention for the Prevention of Pollution From Ships, 1973, as amended

ARTICLE 1

General Obligations under the Convention

(1) The Parties to the Convention undertake to give effect to the provisions of the present Convention and those Annexes thereto by which they are bound, in order to

prevent the pollution of the marine environment by the discharge of harmful substances or effluents containing such substances in contravention of the Convention.

(2) Unless expressly provided otherwise, a reference to the present Convention constitutes at the same time a reference to its Protocols and to the Annexes.

ARTICLE 2

Definitions

For the purposes of the present Convention, unless expressly provided otherwise:

(1) "Regulations" means the Regulations contained in the Annexes to the present Convention.

(2) "Harmful substance" means any substance which, if introduced into the sea, is liable to create hazards to human health, to harm living resources and marine life, to damage amenities or to interfere with other legitimate uses of the sea, and includes any substance subject to control by the present Convention.

(3)(a) "Discharge", in relation to harmful substances or effluents containing such substances, means any release howsoever caused from a ship and includes any escape, disposal, spilling, leaking, pumping, emitting or emptying;

(b) "Discharge" does not include:

(i) dumping within the meaning of the Convention on the Prevention of Marine Pollution by Dumping of Wastes and Other Matter, done at London on 13 November 1972; or

(ii) release of harmful substances directly arising from the exploration, exploitation and associated off-shore processing of sea-bed mineral resources; or

(iii) release of harmful substances for purposes of legitimate scientific research into pollution abatement or control.

(4) "Ship" means a vessel of any type whatsoever operating in the marine environment and includes hydrofoil boats, air-cushion vehicles, submersibles, floating craft and fixed or floating platforms.

(5) "Administration" means the Government of the State under whose authority the ship is operating. With respect to a ship entitled to fly a flag of any State, the Administration is the Government of that State. With respect to fixed or floating platforms engaged in exploration and exploitation of the sea-bed and subsoil thereof adjacent to the coast over which the coastal State exercises sovereign rights for the purposes of exploration and exploitation of their natural resources, the Administration is the Government of the coastal State concerned.

(6) "Incident" means an event involving the actual or probable discharge into the sea of a harmful substance, or effluents containing such a substance.

(7) "Organization" means the Inter–Governmental Maritime Consultative Organization.

ARTICLE 3

Application

(1) The present Convention shall apply to:

(a) ships entitled to fly the flag of a Party to the Convention; and

(b) ships not entitled to fly the flag of a Party but which operate under the authority of a Party.

(2) Nothing in the present Article shall be construed as derogating from or extending the sovereign rights of the Parties under international law over the sea-bed and subsoil thereof adjacent to their coasts for the purposes of exploration and exploitation of their natural resources.

(3) The present Convention shall not apply to any warship, naval auxiliary or other ship owned or operated by a State and used, for the time being, only on government non-commercial service. However, each Party shall ensure by the adoption of appropriate measures not impairing the operations or operational capabilities of such ships owned or operated by it, that such ships act in a manner consistent, so far as is reasonable and practicable, with the present Convention.

ARTICLE 4

Violation

(1) Any violation of the requirements of the present Convention shall be prohibited and sanctions shall be established therefor under the law of the Administration of the ship concerned wherever the violation occurs. If the Administration is informed of such a violation and is satisfied that sufficient evidence is available to enable proceedings to be brought in respect of the alleged violation, it shall cause such proceedings to be taken as soon as possible, in accordance with its law.

(2) Any violation of the requirements of the present Convention within the jurisdiction of any Party to the Convention shall be prohibited and sanctions shall be established therefor under the law of that Party. Whenever such a violation occurs, that Party shall either:

(a) cause proceedings to be taken in accordance with its law; or

(b) furnish to the Administration of the ship such information and evidence as may be in its possession that a violation has occurred.

(3) Where information or evidence with respect to any violation of the present Convention by a ship is furnished to the Administration of that ship, the Administration shall promptly inform the Party which has furnished the information or evidence, and the Organization, of the action taken.

(4) The penalties specified under the law of a Party pursuant to the present Article shall be adequate in severity to discourage violations of the present Convention and shall be equally severe irrespective of where the violations occur.

ARTICLE 5

Certificates and Special Rules on Inspection of Ships

(1) Subject to the provisions of paragraph (2) of the present Article a certificate issued under the authority of a Party to the Convention in accordance with the provisions of the Regulations shall be accepted by the other Parties and regarded for all purposes covered by the present Convention as having the same validity as a certificate issued by them.

(2) A ship required to hold a certificate in accordance with the provisions of the Regulations is subject, while in the ports or off-shore terminals under the jurisdiction of a Party, to inspection by officers duly authorized by that Party. Any such inspection shall be limited to verifying that there is on board a valid certificate, unless there are clear grounds for believing that the condition of the ship or its equipment does not correspond substantially with the particulars of that certificate. In that case, or if the ship does not carry a valid certificate, the Party carrying out the inspection shall take such steps as will ensure that the ship shall not sail until it can proceed to sea without presenting an unreasonable threat of harm to the marine environment. That Party

may, however, grant such a ship permission to leave the port or off-shore terminal for the purpose of proceeding to the nearest appropriate repair yard available.

(3) If a Party denies a foreign ship entry to the ports or off-shore terminals under its jurisdiction or takes any action against such a ship for the reason that the ship does not comply with the provisions of the present Convention, the Party shall immediately inform the consul or diplomatic representative of the Party whose flag the ship is entitled to fly, or if this is not possible, the Administration of the ship concerned. Before denying entry or taking such action the Party may request consultation with the Administration of the ship concerned. Information shall also be given to the Administration when a ship does not carry a valid certificate in accordance with the provisions of the Regulations.

(4) With respect to the ships of non-Parties to the Convention, Parties shall apply the requirements of the present Convention as may be necessary to ensure that no more favorable treatment is given to such ships.

ARTICLE 6

Detection of Violations and Enforcement of the Convention

(1) Parties to the Convention shall co-operate in the detection of violations and the enforcement of the provisions of the present Convention, using all appropriate and practicable measures of detection and environmental monitoring, adequate procedures for reporting and accumulation of evidence.

(2) A ship to which the present Convention applies may, in any port or off-shore terminal of a Party, be subject to inspection by officers appointed or authorized by that Party for the purpose of verifying whether the ship has discharged any harmful substances in violation of the provisions of the Regulations. If an inspection indicates a violation of the Convention, a report shall be forwarded to the Administration for any appropriate action.

(3) Any Party shall furnish to the Administration evidence, if any, that the ship has discharged harmful substances or effluents containing such substances in violation of the provisions of the Regulations. If it is practicable to do so, the competent authority of the former Party shall notify the Master of the ship of the alleged violation.

(4) Upon receiving such evidence, the Administration so informed shall investigate the matter, and may request the other party to furnish further or better evidence of the alleged contravention. If the Administration is satisfied that sufficient evidence is available to enable proceedings to be brought in respect of the alleged violation, it shall cause such proceedings to be taken in accordance with its law as soon as possible. The Administration shall promptly inform the Party which has reported the alleged violation, as well as the Organization, of the action taken.

(5) A Party may also inspect a ship to which the present Convention applies when it enters the ports or off-shore terminals under its jurisdiction, if a request for an investigation is received from any Party together with sufficient evidence that the ship has discharged harmful substances or effluents containing such substances in any place. The report of such investigation shall be sent to the Party requesting it and to the Administration so that the appropriate action may be taken under the present Convention.

ARTICLE 7

Undue Delay to Ships

(1) All possible efforts shall be made to avoid a ship being unduly detained or delayed under Articles 4, 5 or 6 of the present Convention.

(2) When a ship is unduly detained or delayed under Articles 4, 5 or 6 of the present Convention, it shall be entitled to compensation for any loss or damage suffered.

ARTICLE 8

Reports on Incidents Involving Harmful Substances

(1) A report of an incident shall be made without delay to the fullest extent possible in accordance with the provisions of Protocol I to the present Convention.

(2) Each Party to the Convention shall:

(a) make all arrangements necessary for an appropriate officer or agency to receive and process all reports on incidents; and

(b) notify the Organization with complete details of such arrangements for circulation to other Parties and Member States of the Organization.

(3) Whenever a Party receives a report under the provisions of the present Article, that Party shall relay the report without delay to:

(a) the Administration of the ship involved; and

(b) any other State which may be affected.

(4) Each Party to the Convention undertakes to issue instructions to its maritime inspection vessels and aircraft and to other appropriate services, to report to its authorities any incident referred to in Protocol I to the present Convention. That Party shall, if it considers it appropriate, report accordingly to the Organization and to any other party concerned.

ARTICLE 9

Other Treaties and Interpretation

(1) Upon its entry into force, the present Convention supersedes the International Convention for the Prevention of Pollution of the Sea by Oil, 1954, as amended, as between Parties to that Convention.

(2) Nothing in the present Convention shall prejudice the codification and development of the law of the sea by the United Nations Conference on the Law of the Sea convened pursuant to Resolution 2750 C(XXV) of the General Assembly of the United Nations nor the present or future claims and legal views of any State concerning the law of the sea and the nature and extent of coastal and flag State jurisdiction.

(3) The term "jurisdiction" in the present Convention shall be construed in the light of international law in force at the time of application or interpretation of the present Convention.

ARTICLE 10

Settlement of Disputes

Any dispute between two or more Parties to the Convention concerning the interpretation or application of the present Convention shall, if settlement by negotiation between the Parties involved has not been possible, and if these Parties do not otherwise agree, be submitted upon request of any of them to arbitration as set out in Protocol II to the present Convention.

ARTICLE 11

Communication of Information

(1) The Parties to the Convention undertake to communicate to the Organization:

(a) the text of laws, orders, decrees and regulations and other instruments which have been promulgated on the various matters within the scope of the present Convention;

(b) a list of nominated surveyors or recognized organizations which are authorized to act on their behalf in the administration of matters relating to the design, construction, equipment and operation of ships carrying harmful substances in accordance with the provisions of the Regulations for circulation to the Parties for information of their officers. The Administration shall therefore notify the Organization of the specific responsibilities and conditions of the authority delegated to nominated surveyors or recognized organizations;

(c) a sufficient number of specimens of their certificates issued under the provisions of the Regulations;

(d) a list of reception facilities including their location, capacity and available facilities and other characteristics;

(e) official reports or summaries of official reports in so far as they show the results of the application of the present Convention; and

(f) an annual statistical report, in a form standardized by the Organization, of penalties actually imposed for infringement of the present Convention.

(2) The Organization shall notify Parties of the receipt of any communications under the present Article and circulate to all Parties any information communicated to it under sub-paragraphs (1)(b) to (f) of the present Article.

ARTICLE 12

Casualties to Ships

(1) Each Administration undertakes to conduct an investigation of any casualty occurring to any of its ships subject to the provisions of the Regulations if such casualty has produced a major deleterious effect upon the marine environment.

(2) Each Party to the Convention undertakes to supply the Organization with information concerning the findings of such investigation, when it judges that such information may assist in determining what changes in the present Convention might be desirable.

ARTICLE 13

Signature, Ratification, Acceptance, Approval and Accession

(1) The present Convention shall remain open for signature at the Headquarters of the Organization from 15 January 1974 until 31 December 1974 and shall thereafter remain open for accession. States may become Parties to the present Convention by:

(a) signature without reservation as to ratification, acceptance or approval; or

(b) signature subject to ratification, acceptance or approval, followed by ratification, acceptance or approval; or

(c) accession.

(2) Ratification, acceptance, approval or accession shall be effected by the deposit of an instrument to that effect with the Secretary–General of the Organization.

(3) The Secretary–General of the Organization shall inform all States which have signed the present Convention or acceded to it of any signature or of the deposit of any new instrument of ratification, acceptance, approval or accession and the date of its deposit.

ARTICLE 14

Optional Annexes

(1) A State may at the time of signing, ratifying, accepting, approving or acceding to the present Convention declare that it does not accept any one or all of Annexes III, IV and V (hereinafter referred to as "Optional Annexes") of the present Convention. Subject to the above, Parties to the Convention shall be bound by any Annex in its entirety.

(2) A State which has declared that it is not bound by an Optional Annex may at any time accept such Annex by depositing with the Organization an instrument of the kind referred to in Article 13(2).

(3) A State which makes a declaration under paragraph (1) of the present Article in respect of an Optional Annex and which has not subsequently accepted that Annex in accordance with paragraph (2) of the present Article shall not be under any obligation nor entitled to claim any privileges under the present Convention in respect of matters related to such Annex and all references to Parties in the present Convention shall not include that State in so far as matters related to such Annex are concerned.

(4) The Organization shall inform the States which have signed or acceded to the present Convention of any declaration under the present Article as well as the receipt of any instrument deposited in accordance with the provisions of paragraph (2) of the present Article.

ARTICLE 15

Entry into Force

(1) The present Convention shall enter into force twelve months after the date on which not less than 15 States, the combined merchant fleets of which constitute not less than fifty per cent of the gross tonnage of the world's merchant shipping, have become parties to it in accordance with Article 13.

(2) An Optional Annex shall enter into force twelve months after the date on which the conditions stipulated in paragraph (1) of the present Article have been satisfied in relation to that Annex.

(3) The Organization shall inform the States which have signed the present Convention or acceded to it of the date on which it enters into force and of the date on which an Optional Annex enters into force in accordance with paragraph (2) of the present Article.

(4) For States which have deposited an instrument of ratification, acceptance, approval or accession in respect of the present Convention or any Optional Annex after the requirements for entry into force thereof have been met but prior to the date of entry into force, the ratification, acceptance, approval or accession shall take effect on the date of entry into force of the Convention or such Annex or three months after the date of deposit of the instrument whichever is the later date.

(5) For States which have deposited an instrument of ratification, acceptance, approval or accession after the date on which the Convention or an Optional Annex entered into force, the Convention or the Optional Annex shall become effective three months after the date of deposit of the instrument.

(6) After the date on which all the conditions required under Article 16 to bring an amendment to the present Convention or an Optional Annex into force have been fulfilled, any instrument of ratification, acceptance, approval or accession deposited shall apply to the Convention or Annex as amended.

ARTICLE 16

Amendments

(1) The present Convention may be amended by any of the procedures specified in the following paragraphs.

(2) Amendments after consideration by the Organization:

(a) any amendment proposed by a Party to the Convention shall be submitted to the Organization and circulated by its Secretary–General to all Members of the Organization and all Parties at least six months prior to its consideration;

(b) any amendment proposed and circulated as above shall be submitted to an appropriate body by the Organization for consideration;

(c) Parties to the Convention, whether or not Members of the Organization, shall be entitled to participate in the proceedings of the appropriate body;

(d) amendments shall be adopted by a two-thirds majority of only the Parties to the Convention present and voting;

(e) if adopted in accordance with sub-paragraph (d) above, amendments shall be communicated by the Secretary–General of the Organization to all the Parties to the Convention for acceptance;

(f) an amendment shall be deemed to have been accepted in the following circumstances:

(i) an amendment to an Article of the Convention shall be deemed to have been accepted on the date on which it is accepted by two-thirds of the Parties, the combined merchant fleets of which constitute not less than fifty per cent of the gross tonnage of the world's merchant fleet;

(ii) an amendment to an Annex to the Convention shall be deemed to have been accepted in accordance with the procedure specified in sub-paragraph (f)(iii) unless the appropriate body, at the time of its adoption, determines that the amendment shall be deemed to have been accepted on the date on which it is accepted by two-thirds of the Parties, the combined merchant fleets of which constitute not less than fifty per cent of the gross tonnage of the world's merchant fleet. Nevertheless, at any time before the entry into force of an amendment to an Annex to the Convention, a Party may notify the Secretary–General of the Organization that its express approval will be necessary before the amendment enters into force for it. The latter shall bring such notification and the date of its receipt to the notice of Parties;

(iii) an amendment to an Appendix to an Annex to the Convention shall be deemed to have been accepted at the end of a period to be determined by the appropriate body at the time of its adoption, which period shall be not less than ten months, unless within that period an objection is communicated to the Organization by not less than one-third of the Parties or by the Parties the combined merchant fleets of which constitute not less than fifty per cent of the gross tonnage of the world's merchant fleet whichever condition is fulfilled;

(iv) an amendment to Protocol I to the Convention shall be subject to the same procedures as for the amendments to the Annexes to the Convention, as provided for in sub-paragraphs (f)(ii) or (f)(iii) above;

(v) an amendment to Protocol II to the Convention shall be subject to the same procedures as for the amendments to an Article of the Convention, as provided for in sub-paragraph (f)(i) above;

(g) the amendment shall enter into force under the following conditions:

(i) in the case of an amendment to an Article of the Convention, to Protocol II, or to Protocol I or to an Annex to the Convention not under the procedure specified in sub-paragraph (f)(iii), the amendment accepted in conformity with the foregoing provisions shall enter into force six months after the date of its acceptance with respect to the Parties which have declared that they have accepted it;

(ii) in the case of an amendment to Protocol I, to an Appendix to an Annex or to an Annex to the Convention under the procedure specified in sub-paragraph (f)(iii), the amendment deemed to have been accepted in accordance with the foregoing conditions shall enter into force six months after its acceptance for all the Parties with the exception of those which, before that date, have made a declaration that they do not accept it or a declaration under subparagraph (f)(ii), that their express approval is necessary.

(3) Amendment by a Conference:

(a) Upon the request of a Party, concurred in by at least one-third of the Parties, the Organization shall convene a Conference of Parties to the Convention to consider amendments to the present Convention.

(b) Every amendment adopted by such a Conference by a two-thirds majority of those present and voting of the Parties shall be communicated by the Secretary–General of the Organization to all Contracting Parties for their acceptance.

(c) Unless the Conference decides otherwise, the amendment shall be deemed to have been accepted and to have entered into force in accordance with the procedures specified for that purpose in paragraph (2)(f) and (g) above.

(4)(a) In the case of an amendment to an Optional Annex, a reference in the present Article to a "Party to the Convention" shall be deemed to mean a reference to a Party bound by that Annex.

(b) Any Party which has declined to accept an amendment to an Annex shall be treated as a non-Party only for the purpose of application of that amendment.

(5) The adoption and entry into force of a new Annex shall be subject to the same procedures as for the adoption and entry into force of an amendment to an Article of the Convention.

(6) Unless expressly provided otherwise, any amendment to the present Convention made under this Article, which relates to the structure of a ship, shall apply only to ships for which the building contract is placed, or in the absence of a building contract, the keel of which is laid, on or after the date on which the amendment comes into force.

(7) Any amendment to a Protocol or to an Annex shall relate to the substance of that Protocol or Annex and shall be consistent with the Articles of the present Convention.

(8) The Secretary–General of the Organization shall inform all Parties of any amendments which enter into force under the present Article, together with the date on which each such amendment enters into force.

(9) Any declaration of acceptance or of objection to an amendment under the present article shall be notified in writing to the Secretary–General of the Organization. The latter shall bring such notification and the date of its receipt to the notice of the Parties to the Convention.

ARTICLE 17

Promotion of Technical Co-operation

The Parties to the Convention shall promote, in consultation with the Organization and other international bodies, with assistance and co-ordination by the Executive

Director of the United Nations Environment Programme, support for those Parties which request technical assistance for:

(a) the training of scientific and technical personnel;

(b) the supply of necessary equipment and facilities for reception and monitoring;

(c) the facilitation of other measures and arrangements to prevent or mitigate pollution of the marine environment by ships; and

(d) the encouragement of research;

preferably within the countries concerned, so furthering the aims and purposes of the present Convention.

ARTICLE 18

Denunciation

(1) The present Convention or any Optional Annex may be denounced by any Parties to the Convention at any time after the expiry of five years from the date on which the Convention or such Annex enters into force for that Party.

(2) Denunciation shall be effected by notification in writing to the Secretary–General of the Organization who shall inform all the other Parties of any such notification received and of the date of its receipt as well as the date on which such denunciation takes effect.

(3) A denunciation shall take effect twelve months after receipt of the notification of denunciation by the Secretary–General of the Organization or after the expiry of any other longer period which may be indicated in the notification.

ARTICLE 19

Deposit and Registration

(1) The present Convention shall be deposited with the Secretary–General of the Organization who shall transmit certified true copies thereof to all States which have signed the present Convention or acceded to it.

(2) As soon as the present Convention enters into force, the text shall be transmitted by the Secretary–General of the Organization to the Secretary–General of the United Nations for registration and publication, in accordance with Article 102 of the Charter of the United Nations.

ARTICLE 20

Languages

The present Convention is established in a single copy in the English, French, Russian and Spanish languages, each text being equally authentic. Official translations in the Arabic, German, Italian and Japanese languages shall be prepared and deposited with the signed original.

Protocol I

Provisions Concerning Reports on Incidents Involving Harmful Substances (in accordance with Article 8 of the Convention)

* * *

Protocol II

Arbitration (in accordance with Article 10 of the Convention)

* * *

Revised Annex I of MARPOL 73/78 (Resolution MEPC.117(52))
Regulations for the Prevention of Pollution by Oil

Regulation 1
Definitions

For the purposes of this Annex:

1. *Oil* means petroleum in any form including crude oil, fuel oil, sludge, oil refuse and refined products (other than those petrochemicals which are subject to the provisions of Annex II of the present Convention) and, without limiting the generality of the foregoing, includes the substances listed in appendix I to this Annex.

2. *Crude oil* means any liquid hydrocarbon mixture occurring naturally in the earth whether or not treated to render it suitable for transportation and includes:

    .1   crude oil from which certain distillate fractions may have been removed; and

    .2   crude oil to which certain distillate fractions may have been added.

* * *

5. *Oil tanker* means a ship constructed or adapted primarily to carry oil in bulk in its cargo spaces and includes combination carriers, any "NLS tanker" as defined in Annex II of the present Convention and any gas carrier as defined in regulation 3.20 of chapter II–1 of SOLAS 74 (as amended), when carrying a cargo or part cargo of oil in bulk.

6. *Crude oil tanker* means an oil tanker engaged in the trade of carrying crude oil.

* * *

11. *Special area* means a sea area where for recognized technical reasons in relation to its oceanographical and ecological condition and to the particular character of its traffic the adoption of special mandatory methods for the prevention of sea pollution by oil is required.

[Descriptions of identified *special areas* are omitted]

* * *

18. *Segregated ballast* means the ballast water introduced into a tank which is completely separated from the cargo oil and oil fuel system and which is permanently allocated to the carriage of ballast or to the carriage of ballast or cargoes other than oil or noxious liquid substances as variously defined in the Annexes of the present Convention.

* * *

28.4 *oil tanker delivered after 1 June 1982* means an oil tanker:

    .1   for which the building contract is placed after 1 June 1979; or

    .2   in the absence of a building contract, the keel of which is laid or which is at a similar stage of construction after 1 January 1980; or

    .3   the delivery of which is after 1 June 1982; or

    .4   which has undergone a major conversion:

.1 for which the contract is placed after 1 June 1979; or

.2 in the absence of a contract, the construction work of which is begun after 1 January 1980; or

.3 which is completed after 1 June 1982.

* * *

28.6 *oil tanker delivered on or after 6 July 1996* means an oil tanker:

.1 for which the building contract is placed on or after 6 July 1993; or

.2 in the absence of a building contract, the keel of which is laid or which is at a similar stage of construction on or after 6 January 1994; or

.3 the delivery of which is on or after 6 July 1996; or

.4 which has undergone a major conversion:

.1 for which the contract is placed on or after 6 July 1993; or

.2 in the absence of a contract, the construction work of which is begun on or after 6 January 1994; or

.3 which is completed on or after 6 July 1996.

* * *

30. *Constructed* means a ship the keel of which is laid or which is at a similar stage of construction.

* * *

Regulation 2
Application

1. Unless expressly provided otherwise, the provisions of this Annex shall apply to all ships.

* * *

Regulation 6
Surveys

1. Every oil tanker of 150 gross tonnage and above, and every other ship of 400 gross tonnage and above shall be subject to the surveys specified below:

.1 an initial survey before the ship is put in service or before the Certificate required under regulation 7 of this Annex is issued for the first time, which shall include a complete survey of its structure, equipment, systems, fittings, arrangements and material in so far as the ship is covered by this Annex. This survey shall be such as to ensure that the structure, equipment, systems, fittings, arrangements and material fully comply with the applicable requirements of this Annex;

.2 a renewal survey at intervals specified by the Administration, but not exceeding 5 years, except where regulation 10.2.2, 10.5, 10.6 or 10.7 of this Annex is applicable. The renewal survey shall be such as to ensure that the structure, equipment, systems, fittings, arrangements and material fully comply with applicable requirements of this Annex;

.3 an intermediate survey within 3 months before or after the second anniversary date or within 3 months before or after the third anniversary date of the Certificate which shall take the place of one of the annual surveys specified in paragraph 1.4 of this regulation. The intermediate survey shall be such as to ensure that the equipment and associated pump and piping systems, including oil discharge monitoring and control systems, crude oil washing systems, oily-water separating equipment and oil filtering systems, fully comply with the applicable requirements of this Annex and are in good working order. Such intermediate surveys shall be endorsed on the Certificate issued under regulation 7 or 8 of this Annex;

.4   an annual survey within 3 months before or after each anniversary date of the Certificate, including a general inspection of the structure, equipment, systems, fittings, arrangements and material referred to in paragraph 1.1 of this regulation to ensure that they have been maintained in accordance with paragraphs 4.1 and 4.2 of this regulation and that they remain satisfactory for the service for which the ship is intended. Such annual surveys shall be endorsed on the Certificate issued under regulation 7 or 8 of this Annex; and

.5   an additional survey either general or partial, according to the circumstances, shall be made after a repair resulting from investigations prescribed in paragraph 4.3 of this regulation, or whenever any important repairs or renewals are made. The survey shall be such as to ensure that the necessary repairs or renewals have been effectively made, that the material and workmanship of such repairs or renewals are in all respects satisfactory and that the ship complies in all respects with the requirements of this Annex.

* * *

3.1   Surveys of ships as regards the enforcement of the provisions of this Annex shall be carried out by officers of the Administration. The Administration may, however, entrust the surveys either to surveyors nominated for the purpose or to organizations recognized by it. Such organizations shall comply with the guidelines adopted by the Organization by resolution A.739(18), as may be amended by the Organization, and the specifications adopted by the Organization by resolution A.789(19), as may be amended by the Organization, provided that such amendments are adopted, brought into force and take effect in accordance with the provisions of article 16 of the present Convention concerning the amendment procedures applicable to this Annex.

3.2   An Administration nominating surveyors or recognizing organizations to conduct surveys as set forth in paragraph 3.1 of this regulation shall, as a minimum, empower any nominated surveyor or recognized organization to:

.1   require repairs to a ship; and

.2   carry out surveys, if requested by the appropriate authorities of a port State.

The Administration shall notify the Organization of the specific responsibilities and conditions of the authority delegated to the nominated surveyors or recognized organizations, for circulation to Parties to the present Convention for the information of their officers.

3.3   When a nominated surveyor or recognized organization determines that the condition of the ship or its equipment does not correspond substantially with the particulars of the Certificate or is such that the ship is not fit to proceed to sea without presenting an unreasonable threat of harm to the marine environment, such surveyor or organization shall immediately ensure that corrective action is taken and shall in due course notify the Administration. If such corrective action is not taken the Certificate shall be withdrawn and the Administration shall be notified immediately; and if the ship is in a port of another Party, the appropriate authorities of the port State shall also be notified immediately. When an officer of the Administration, a nominated surveyor or a recognized organization has notified the appropriate authorities of the port State, the Government of the port State concerned shall give such officer, surveyor or organization any necessary assistance to carry out their obligations under this regulation. When applicable, the Government of the port State concerned shall take such steps as will ensure that the ship shall not sail until it can proceed to sea or leave the port for the purpose of proceeding to the nearest appropriate repair yard available without presenting an unreasonable threat of harm to the marine environment.

3.4 In every case, the Administration concerned shall fully guarantee the completeness and efficiency of the survey and shall undertake to ensure the necessary arrangements to satisfy this obligation.

4.1 The condition of the ship and its equipment shall be maintained to conform with the provisions of the present Convention to ensure that the ship in all respects will remain fit to proceed to sea without presenting an unreasonable threat of harm to the marine environment.

* * *

Regulation 7
Issue or endorsement of certificate

1. An International Oil Pollution Prevention Certificate shall be issued, after an initial or renewal survey in accordance with the provisions of regulation 6 of this Annex, to any oil tanker of 150 gross tonnage and above and any other ships of 400 gross tonnage and above which are engaged in voyages to ports or offshore terminals under the jurisdiction of other Parties to the present Convention.

2. Such certificate shall be issued or endorsed as appropriate either by the Administration or by any persons or organization duly authorized by it. In every case the Administration assumes full responsibility for the certificate.

* * *

Regulation 15
Control of discharge of oil

1. Subject to the provisions of regulation 4 of this annex and paragraphs 2, 3, and 6 of this regulation, any discharge into the sea of oil or oily mixtures from ships shall be prohibited.

A. Discharges outside special areas

2. Any discharge into the sea of oil or oily mixtures from ships of 400 gross tonnage and above shall be prohibited except when all the following conditions are satisfied:

    .1 the ship is proceeding en route;

    .2 the oily mixture is processed through an oil filtering equipment meeting the requirements of regulation 14 of this Annex;

    .3 the oil content of the effluent without dilution does not exceed 15 parts per million;

    .4 the oily mixture does not originate from cargo pump room bilges on oil tankers; and

    .5 the oily mixture, in case of oil tankers, is not mixed with oil cargo residues.

B. Discharges in special areas

3. Any discharge into the sea of oil or oily mixtures from ships of 400 gross tonnage and above shall be prohibited except when all of the following conditions are satisfied:

.1   the ship is proceeding en route;

.2   the oily mixture is processed through an oil filtering equipment meeting the requirements of regulation 14.7 of this Annex;

.3   the oil content of the effluent without dilution does not exceed 15 parts per million;

.4   the oily mixture does not originate from cargo pump room bilges on oil tankers; and

.5   the oily mixture, in case of oil tankers, is not mixed with oil cargo residues.

4.   In respect of the Antarctic area, any discharge into the sea of oil or oily mixtures from any ship shall be prohibited.

5.   Nothing in this regulation shall prohibit a ship on a voyage only part of which is in a special area from discharging outside a special area in accordance with paragraphs 2 of this regulation.

* * *

Regulation 18
Segregated Ballast Tanks

Oil tankers of 20,000 tonnes deadweight and above delivered after 1 June 1982

1.   Every crude oil tanker of 20,000 tonnes deadweight and above and every product carrier of 30,000 tonnes deadweight and above delivered after 1 June 1982, as defined in regulation 1.28.4, shall be provided with segregated ballast tanks and shall comply with paragraphs 2, 3 and 4, or 5 as appropriate, of this regulation.

* * *

Crude oil tankers of 40,000 tonnes deadweight and above delivered on or before 1 June 1982

6.   Subject to the provisions of paragraph 7 of this regulation every crude oil tanker of 40,000 tonnes deadweight and above delivered on or before 1 June 1982, as defined in regulation 1.28.3, shall be provided with segregated ballast tanks and shall comply with the requirements of paragraphs 2 and 3 of this regulation.

* * *

Oil tankers of 70,000 tonnes deadweight and above delivered after 31 December 1979

11.   Oil tankers of 70,000 tonnes deadweight and above delivered after 31 December 1979, as defined in regulation 1.28.2, shall be provided with segregated ballast tanks and shall comply with paragraphs 2, 3 and 4 or paragraph 5 as appropriate of this regulation.

Protective location of segregated ballast

12.   Protective location of segregated ballast spaces.

In every crude oil tanker of 20,000 tonnes deadweight and above and every product carrier of 30,000 tonnes deadweight and above delivered after 1 June 1982, as defined in regulation 1.28.4, except those tankers that meet regulation 19, the segregated ballast tanks required to provide the capacity to comply with the requirements of paragraph 2 of this regulation, which are located within the cargo tank length, shall be arranged in accordance with the requirements of paragraphs 13, 14 and 15 of this regulation to provide a measure of protection against oil outflow in the event of grounding or collision.

* * *

Regulation 19
Double hull and double bottom requirements for oil tankers delivered on or after 6 July 1996

1.   This regulation shall apply to oil tankers of 600 tonnes deadweight and above delivered on or after 6 July 1996, as defined in regulation 1.28.6, as follows:

2.   Every oil tanker of 5,000 tonnes deadweight and above shall:

.1   in lieu of paragraphs 12 to 15 of regulation 18, as applicable, comply with the requirements of paragraph 3 of this regulation unless it is subject to the provisions of paragraphs 4 and 5 of this regulation; and

.2   comply, if applicable, with the requirements of regulation 28.6.

3.   The entire cargo tank length shall be protected by ballast tanks or spaces other than tanks that carry oil as follows:

[description of required design and construction details is omitted]

* * *

Regulation 20
Double hull and double bottom requirements for oil tankers delivered before 6 July 1996

1.   Unless expressly provided otherwise this regulation shall:

.1   apply to oil tankers of 5,000 tonnes deadweight and above, which are delivered before 6 July 1996, as defined in regulation 1.28.5 of this Annex; and

.2   not apply to oil tankers complying with regulation 19 and regulation 28 in respect of paragraph 28.6, which are delivered before 6 July 1996, as defined in regulation 1.28.5 of this Annex; and

.3   not apply to oil tankers covered by subparagraph 1 above which comply with regulation 19.3.1 and 19.3.2 or 19.4 or 19.5 of this Annex, except that the requirement for minimum distances between the cargo tank boundaries and the ship side and bottom plating need not be met in all respects. In that event, the side protection distances shall not be less than those specified in the International Bulk Chemical Code for type 2 cargo tank location and the bottom protection distances at centreline shall comply with regulation 18.15.2 of this Annex.

2.   For the purpose of this regulation:

.1   "Heavy diesel oil" means diesel oil other than those distillates of which more than 50 per cent by volume distils at a temperature not exceeding 340°C when tested by the method acceptable to the Organization.

.2   "Fuel oil" means heavy distillates or residues from crude oil or blends of such materials intended for use as a fuel for the production of heat or power of a quality equivalent to the specification acceptable to the Organization.

3.   For the purpose of this regulation, oil tankers are divided into the following categories:

.1   "Category 1 oil tanker" means an oil tanker of 20,000 tonnes deadweight and above carrying crude oil, fuel oil, heavy diesel oil or lubricating oil as cargo, and of 30,000 tonnes deadweight and above carrying oil other than the above, which does not comply with the requirements for oil tankers delivered after 1 June 1982, as defined in regulation 1.28.4 of this Annex;

.2 "Category 2 oil tanker" means an oil tanker of 20,000 tonnes deadweight and above carrying crude oil, fuel oil, heavy diesel oil or lubricating oil as cargo, and of 30,000 tonnes deadweight and above carrying oil other than the above, which complies with the requirements for oil tankers delivered after 1 June 1982, as defined in regulation 1.28.4 of this Annex; and

.3 "Category 3 oil tanker" means an oil tanker of 5,000 tonnes deadweight and above but less than that specified in subparagraph 1 or 2 of this paragraph.

4. An oil tanker to which this regulation applies shall comply with the requirements of paragraphs 2 to 5, 7 and 8 of regulation 19 and regulation 28 in respect of paragraph 28.6 of this Annex not later than 5 April 2005 or the anniversary of the date of delivery of the ship on the date or in the year specified in the following table:

Category of oil tanker	Date or year
Category 1	5 April 2005 for ships delivered on 5 April 1982 or earlier 2005 for ships delivered after 5 April 1982
Category 2 and Category 3	April 2005 for ships delivered on 5 April 1977 or earlier 2005 for ships delivered after 5 April 1977 but before 1 January 1978 2006 for ships delivered in 1978 and 1979 2007 for ships delivered in 1980 and 1981 2008 for ships delivered in 1982 2009 for ships delivered in 1983 2010 for ships delivered in 1984 or later

5. Notwithstanding the provisions of paragraph 4 of this regulation, in the case of a Category 2 or 3 oil tanker fitted with only double bottoms or double sides not used for the carriage of oil and extending to the entire cargo tank length or double hull spaces which are not used for the carriage of oil and extend to the entire cargo tank length, but which does not fulfil conditions for being exempted from the provisions of paragraph 1.3 of this regulation, the Administration may allow continued operation of such a ship beyond the date specified in paragraph 4 of this regulation, provided that:

.1 the ship was in service on 1 July 2001;

.2 the Administration is satisfied by verification of the official records that the ship complied with the conditions specified above;

.3 the conditions of the ship specified above remain unchanged; and

.4 such continued operation does not go beyond the date on which the ship reaches 25 years after the date of its delivery.

6. A Category 2 or 3 oil tanker of 15 years and over after the date of its delivery shall comply with the Condition Assessment Scheme adopted by the Marine Environment Protection Committee by resolution MEPC.94(46), as amended, provided that such amendments shall be adopted, brought into force and take effect in accordance with the provisions of article 16 of the present Convention relating to amendment procedures applicable to an appendix to an Annex.

7. The Administration may allow continued operation of a Category 2 or 3 oil tanker beyond the date specified in paragraph 4 of this regulation, if satisfactory results of the Condition Assessment Scheme warrant that, in the opinion of the Administration, the ship is fit to continue such operation, provided that the operation shall not go beyond the anniversary of the date of delivery of the ship in 2015 or the date on which the ship reaches 25 years after the date of its delivery, whichever is the earlier date.

8. .1 The Administration of a Party to the present Convention which allows the application of paragraph 5 of this regulation, or allows, suspends, withdraws or declines the application of paragraph 7 of this regulation, to a ship entitled to fly its flag shall forthwith communicate to the Organization for circulation to the Parties to the present Convention particulars thereof, for their information and appropriate action, if any.

.2 A Party to the present Convention shall be entitled to deny entry into the ports or offshore terminals under its jurisdiction of oil tankers operating in accordance with the provisions of:

.1 paragraph 5 of this regulation beyond the anniversary of the date of delivery of the ship in 2015; or

.2 paragraph 7 of this regulation.

In such cases, that Party shall communicate to the Organization for circulation to the Parties to the present Convention particulars thereof for their information.

Regulation 21
Prevention of oil pollution from oil tankers carrying heavy grade oil as cargo

1. This regulation shall:

.1 apply to oil tankers of 600 tonnes deadweight and above carrying heavy grade oil as cargo regardless of the date of delivery; and

.2 not apply to oil tankers covered by subparagraph 1 above which comply with regulations 19.3.1 and 19.3.2 or 19.4 or 19.5 of this Annex, except that the requirement for minimum distances between the cargo tank boundaries and the ship side and bottom plating need not be met in all respects. In that event, the side protection distances shall not be less than those specified in the International Bulk Chemical Code for type 2 cargo tank location and the bottom protection distances at centreline shall comply with regulation 18.15.2 of this Annex.

2. For the purpose of this regulation "heavy grade oil" means any of the following:

.1 crude oils having a density at 15°C higher than 900 kg/m3;

.2 fuel oils having either a density at 15°C higher than 900 kg/m3 or a kinematic viscosity at 50°C higher than 180 mm2/s; or

.3 bitumen, tar and their emulsions.

3. An oil tanker to which this regulation applies shall comply with the provisions of paragraphs 4 to 8 of this regulation in addition to complying with the applicable provisions of regulation 20.

4. Subject to the provisions of paragraphs 5, 6 and 7 of this regulation, an oil tanker to which this regulation applies shall:

.1 if 5,000 tonnes deadweight and above, comply with the requirements of regulation 19 of this Annex not later than 5 April 2005; or

.2 if 600 tonnes deadweight and above but less than 5,000 tonnes deadweight, be fitted with both double bottom tanks or spaces complying with the provisions of regulation 19.6.1 of this Annex, and wing tanks or spaces arranged in accordance with regulation 19.3.1 and complying with the requirement for distance w as referred to in regulation 19.6.2, not later than the anniversary of the date of delivery of the ship in the year 2008.

5. In the case of an oil tanker of 5,000 tonnes deadweight and above, carrying heavy grade oil as cargo fitted with only double bottoms or double sides not used for the carriage of oil and extending to the entire cargo tank length or double hull spaces

which are not used for the carriage of oil and extend to the entire cargo tank length, but which does not fulfil conditions for being exempted from the provisions of paragraph 1.2 of this regulation, the Administration may allow continued operation of such a ship beyond the date specified in paragraph 4 of this regulation, provided that:

.1   the ship was in service on 4 December 2003;

.2   the Administration is satisfied by verification of the official records that the ship complied with the conditions specified above;

.3   the conditions of the ship specified above remain unchanged; and

.4   such continued operation does not go beyond the date on which the ship reaches 25 years after the date of its delivery.

6.   .1 The Administration may allow continued operation of an oil tanker of 5,000 tonnes deadweight and above, carrying crude oil having a density at 15°C higher than 900 kg/m3 but lower than 945 kg/m3, beyond the date specified in paragraph 4.1 of this regulation, if satisfactory results of the Condition Assessment Scheme referred to in regulation 20.6 warrant that, in the opinion of the Administration, the ship is fit to continue such operation, having regard to the size, age, operational area and structural conditions of the ship and provided that the operation shall not go beyond the date on which the ship reaches 25 years after the date of its delivery.

.2   The Administration may allow continued operation of an oil tanker of 600 tonnes deadweight and above but less than 5,000 tonnes deadweight, carrying heavy grade oil as cargo, beyond the date specified in paragraph 4.2 of this regulation, if, in the opinion of the Administration, the ship is fit to continue such operation, having regard to the size, age, operational area and structural conditions of the ship, provided that the operation shall not go beyond the date on which the ship reaches 25 years after the date of its delivery.

7.   The Administration of a Party to the present Convention may exempt an oil tanker of 600 tonnes deadweight and above carrying heavy grade oil as cargo from the provisions of this regulation if the oil tanker:

.1   either is engaged in voyages exclusively within an area under its jurisdiction, or operates as a floating storage unit of heavy grade oil located within an area under its jurisdiction; or

.2   either is engaged in voyages exclusively within an area under the jurisdiction of another Party, or operates as a floating storage unit of heavy grade oil located within an area under the jurisdiction of another Party, provided that the Party within whose jurisdiction the oil tanker will be operating agrees to the operation of the oil tanker within an area under its jurisdiction.

8.   .1 The Administration of a Party to the present Convention which allows, suspends, withdraws or declines the application of paragraph 5, 6 or 7 of this regulation to a ship entitled to fly its flag shall forthwith communicate to the Organization for circulation to the Parties to the present Convention particulars thereof, for their information and appropriate action, if any.

.2   Subject to the provisions of international law, a Party to the present Convention shall be entitled to deny entry of oil tankers operating in accordance with the provisions of paragraph 5 or 6 of this regulation into the ports or offshore terminals under its jurisdiction, or deny ship-to-ship transfer of heavy grade oil in areas under its jurisdiction except when this is necessary for the purpose of securing the safety of a ship or saving life at sea. In such cases, that Party shall communicate to the Organization for circulation to the Parties to the present Convention particulars thereof for their information.

* * *

Regulation 43
Special requirements for the use or carriage of oils in the Antarctic area

1 With the exception of vessels engaged in securing the safety of ships or in a search and rescue operation, the carriage in bulk as cargo or carriage and use as fuel of the following:

.1 crude oils having a density at 15°C higher than 900 kg/m3;

.2 oils, other than crude oils, having a density at 15°C higher than 900 kg/m3 or a kinematic viscosity at 50°C higher than 180 mm2/s; or

.3 bitumen, tar and their emulsions, shall be prohibited in the Antarctic area, as defined in Annex I, regulation 1.11.7.

2 When prior operations have included the carriage or use of oils listed in paragraphs 1.1 to 1.3 of this regulation, the cleaning or flushing of tanks or pipelines is not required.

* * *

Annex II of MARPOL 73/78 (including amendments):
Regulations For the Control of Pollution by Noxious Liquid Substances in Bulk

* * *

Annex III of MARPOL 73/78
Regulations for the Prevention of Pollution by Harmful Substances Carried by Sea in Packaged Form

* * *

Annex IV of MARPOL 73/78
Regulations for the Prevention of Pollution by Sewage From Ships (not yet in force)

* * *

Annex V of MARPOL 73/78
Regulations for the Prevention of Pollution by Garbage From Ships

* * *

Annex VI of MARPOL 73/78
Regulations for the Prevention of Air Pollution from Ships

3.8   United Nations Convention on the Law of the Sea (With Annex V).[f] **Concluded at Montego Bay, 10 December 1982. Entered into force, 16 November 1994. 1833 UNTS 3;** *reprinted in* **21 ILM 1261 (1982) & 5 Weston & Carlson V.F.22**

The States Parties to this Convention,

Prompted by the desire to settle, in a spirit of mutual understanding and co-operation, all issues relating to the law of the sea and aware of the historic significance of this Convention as an important contribution to the maintenance of peace, justice and progress for all peoples of the world,

Noting that developments since the United Nations Conferences on the Law of the Sea held at Geneva in 1958 and 1960 have accentuated the need for a new and generally acceptable Convention on the law of the sea,

Conscious that the problems of ocean space are closely interrelated and need to be considered as a whole,

Recognizing the desirability of establishing through this Convention, with due regard for the sovereignty of all States, a legal order for the seas and oceans which will facilitate international communication, and will promote the peaceful uses of the seas and oceans, the equitable and efficient utilization of their resources, the conservation of their living resources, and the study, protection and preservation of the marine environment,

Bearing in mind that the achievement of these goals will contribute to the realization of a just and equitable international economic order which takes into account the interests and needs of mankind as a whole and, in particular, the special interests and needs of developing countries, whether coastal or land-locked,

Desiring by this Convention to develop the principles embodied in resolution 2749 (XXV) of 17 December 1970 in which the General Assembly of the United Nations solemnly declared *inter alia* that the area of the sea-bed and ocean floor and the subsoil thereof, beyond the limits of national jurisdiction, as well as its resources, are the common heritage of mankind, the exploration and exploitation of which shall be carried out for the benefit of mankind as a whole, irrespective of the geographical location of States,

Believing that the codification and progressive development of the law of the sea achieved in this Convention will contribute to the strengthening of peace, security, co-operation and friendly relations among all nations in conformity with the principles of justice and equal rights and will promote the economic and social advancement of all peoples of the world, in accordance with the Purposes and Principles of the United Nations as set forth in the Charter,

Affirming that matters not regulated by this Convention continue to be governed by the rules and principles of general international law,

Have agreed as follows:

PART I

INTRODUCTION

Article 1

Use of terms and scope

1.   For the purposes of this Convention:

f. This Convention supersedes the 1958 Geneva law of the sea conventions (Basic Documents 4.2, 4.3, 4.4, *supra*, and 6.3, *infra*) upon entry into force for the parties.

(1) "Area" means the sea-bed and ocean floor and subsoil thereof, beyond the limits of national jurisdiction;

(2) "Authority" means the International Sea–Bed Authority;

(3) "activities in the Area" means all activities of exploration for, and exploitation of, the resources of the Area;

(4) "pollution of the marine environment" means the introduction by man, directly or indirectly, of substances or energy into the marine environment, including estuaries, which results or is likely to result in such deleterious effects as harm to living resources and marine life, hazards to human health, hindrance to marine activities, including fishing and other legitimate uses of the sea, impairment of quality for use of sea water and reduction of amenities;

(5)(a) "dumping" means:

(i) any deliberate disposal of wastes or other matter from vessels, aircraft, platforms or other man-made structures at sea;

(ii) any deliberate disposal of vessels, aircraft, platforms or other man-made structures at sea;

(b) "dumping" does not include:

(i) the disposal of wastes or other matter incidental to, or derived from the normal operations of vessels, aircraft, platforms or other man-made structures at sea and their equipment, other than wastes or other matter transported by or to vessels, aircraft, platforms or other man-made structures at sea, operating for the purpose of disposal of such matter or derived from the treatment of such wastes or other matter on such vessels, aircraft, platforms or structures;

(ii) placement of matter for a purpose other than the mere disposal thereof, provided that such placement is not contrary to the aims of this Convention.

2. (1) "States Parties" means States which have consented to be bound by this Convention and for which this Convention is in force.

(2) This Convention applies *mutatis mutandis* to the entities referred to in article 305, paragraph 1(b), (c), (d), (e) and (f), which become Parties to this Convention in accordance with the conditions relevant to each, and to that extent "States Parties" refers to those entities.

PART II

TERRITORIAL SEA AND CONTIGUOUS ZONE

SECTION 1. GENERAL PROVISIONS

Article 2

Legal status of the territorial sea, of the air space over
the territorial sea and of its bed and subsoil

1. The sovereignty of a coastal State extends, beyond its land territory and internal waters and, in the case of an archipelagic State, its archipelagic waters, to an adjacent belt of sea, described as the territorial sea.

2. This sovereignty extends to the air space over the territorial sea as well as to its bed and subsoil.

3. The sovereignty over the territorial sea is exercised subject to this Convention and to other rules of international law.

SECTION 2. LIMITS OF THE TERRITORIAL SEA

Article 3

Breadth of the territorial sea

Every State has the right to establish the breadth of its territorial sea up to a limit not exceeding 12 nautical miles, measured from baselines determined in accordance with this Convention.

Article 4

Outer limit of the territorial sea

The outer limit of the territorial sea is the line every point of which is at a distance from the nearest point of the baseline equal to the breadth of the territorial sea.

Article 5

Normal baseline

Except where otherwise provided in this Convention, the normal baseline for measuring the breadth of the territorial sea is the low-water line along the coast as marked on large-scale charts officially recognized by the coastal State.

Article 6

Reefs

In the case of islands situated on atolls or of islands having fringing reefs, the baseline for measuring the breadth of the territorial sea is the seaward low-water line of the reef, as shown by the appropriate symbol on charts officially recognized by the coastal State.

Article 7

Straight baselines

1. In localities where the coastline is deeply indented and cut into, or if there is a fringe of islands along the coast in its immediate vicinity, the method of straight baselines joining appropriate points may be employed in drawing the baseline from which the breadth of the territorial sea is measured.

2. Where because of the presence of a delta and other natural conditions the coastline is highly unstable, the appropriate points may be selected along the furthest seaward extent of the low-water line and, notwithstanding subsequent regression of the low-water line, the straight baselines shall remain effective until changed by the coastal State in accordance with this Convention.

3. The drawing of straight baselines must not depart to any appreciable extent from the general direction of the coast, and the sea areas lying within the lines must be sufficiently closely linked to the land domain to be subject to the regime of internal waters.

4. Straight baselines shall not be drawn to and from low-tide elevations, unless lighthouses or similar installations which are permanently above sea level have been built on them or except in instances where the drawing of baselines to and from such elevations has received general international recognition.

5. Where the method of straight baselines is applicable under paragraph 1, account may be taken, in determining particular baselines, of economic interests peculiar to the region concerned, the reality and the importance of which are clearly evidenced by long usage.

6. The system of straight baselines may not be applied by a State in such a manner as to cut off the territorial sea of another State from the high seas or an exclusive economic zone.

Article 8

Internal waters

1. Except as provided in Part IV, waters on the landward side of the baseline of the territorial sea form part of the internal waters of the State.

2. Where the establishment of a straight baseline in accordance with the method set forth in article 7 has the effect of enclosing as internal waters areas which had not previously been considered as such, a right of innocent passage as provided in this Convention shall exist in those waters.

Article 9

Mouths of rivers

If a river flows directly into the sea, the baseline shall be a straight line across the mouth of the river between points on the low-water line of its banks.

Article 10

Bays

1. This article relates only to bays the coasts of which belong to a single State.

2. For the purposes of this Convention, a bay is a well-marked indentation whose penetration is in such proportion to the width of its mouth as to contain land-locked waters and constitute more than a mere curvature of the coast. An indentation shall not, however, be regarded as a bay unless its area is as large as, or larger than, that of the semi-circle whose diameter is a line drawn across the mouth of that indentation.

3. For the purpose of measurement, the area of an indentation is that lying between the low-water mark around the shore of the indentation and a line joining the low-water mark of its natural entrance points. Where, because of the presence of islands, an indentation has more than one mouth, the semi-circle shall be drawn on a line as long as the sum total of the lengths of the lines across the different mouths. Islands within an indentation shall be included as if they were part of the water area of the indentation.

4. If the distance between the low-water marks of the natural entrance points of a bay does not exceed 24 nautical miles, a closing line may be drawn between these two low-water marks, and the waters enclosed thereby shall be considered as internal waters.

5. Where the distance between the low-water marks of the natural entrance points of a bay exceeds 24 nautical miles, a straight baseline of 24 nautical miles shall be drawn within the bay in such a manner as to enclose the maximum area of water that is possible with a line of that length.

6. The foregoing provisions do not apply to so-called "historic" bays, or in any case where the system of straight baselines provided for in article 7 is applied.

Article 11

Ports

For the purpose of delimiting the territorial sea, the outermost permanent harbour works which form an integral part of the harbour system are regarded as forming part of the coast. Off-shore installations and artificial islands shall not be considered as permanent harbour works.

Article 12

Roadsteads

Roadsteads which are normally used for the loading, unloading and anchoring of ships, and which would otherwise be situated wholly or partly outside the outer limit of the territorial sea, are included in the territorial sea.

Article 13

Low-tide elevations

1. A low-tide elevation is a naturally formed area of land which is surrounded by and above water at low tide but submerged at high tide. Where a low-tide elevation is situated wholly or partly at a distance not exceeding the breadth of the territorial sea from the mainland or an island, the low-water line on that elevation may be used as the baseline for measuring the breadth of the territorial sea.

2. Where a low-tide elevation is wholly situated at a distance exceeding the breadth of the territorial sea from the mainland or an island, it has no territorial sea of its own.

Article 14

Combination of methods for determining baselines

The coastal State may determine baselines in turn by any of the methods provided for in the foregoing articles to suit different conditions.

Article 15

Delimitation of the territorial sea between States with opposite or adjacent coasts

Where the coasts of two States are opposite or adjacent to each other, neither of the two States is entitled, failing agreement between them to the contrary, to extend its territorial sea beyond the median line every point of which is equidistant from the nearest points on the baselines from which the breadth of the territorial seas of each of the two States is measured. The above provision does not apply, however, where it is necessary by reason of historic title or other special circumstances to delimit the territorial seas of the two States in a way which is at variance therewith.

Article 16

Charts and lists of geographical co-ordinates

1. The baselines for measuring the breadth of the territorial sea determined in accordance with articles 7, 9 and 10, or the limits derived therefrom, and the lines of delimitation drawn in accordance with articles 12 and 15 shall be shown on charts of a scale or scales adequate for ascertaining their position. Alternatively, a list of geographical co-ordinates of points, specifying the geodetic datum, may be substituted.

2. The coastal State shall give due publicity to such charts or lists of geographical co-ordinates and shall deposit a copy of each such chart or list with the Secretary–General of the United Nations.

SECTION 3. INNOCENT PASSAGE IN THE TERRITORIAL SEA
SUBSECTION A. RULES APPLICABLE TO ALL SHIPS

Article 17

Right of innocent passage

Subject to this Convention, ships of all States, whether coastal or land-locked, enjoy the right of innocent passage through the territorial sea.

Article 18

Meaning of passage

1.   Passage means navigation through the territorial sea for the purpose of:

(a) traversing that sea without entering internal waters or calling at a roadstead or port facility outside internal waters; or

(b) proceeding to or from internal waters or a call at such roadstead or port facility.

2.   Passage shall be continuous and expeditious. However, passage includes stopping and anchoring, but only in so far as the same are incidental to ordinary navigation or are rendered necessary by *force majeure* or distress or for the purpose of rendering assistance to persons, ships or aircraft in danger or distress.

Article 19

Meaning of innocent passage

1.   Passage is innocent so long as it is not prejudicial to the peace, good order or security of the coastal State. Such passage shall take place in conformity with this Convention and with other rules of international law.

2.   Passage of a foreign ship shall be considered to be prejudicial to the peace, good order or security of the coastal State if in the territorial sea it engages in any of the following activities:

(a) any threat or use of force against the sovereignty, territorial integrity or political independence of the coastal State, or in any other manner in violation of the principles of international law embodied in the Charter of the United Nations;

(b) any exercise or practice with weapons of any kind;

(c) any act aimed at collecting information to the prejudice of the defence or security of the coastal State;

(d) any act of propaganda aimed at affecting the defence or security of the coastal State;

(e) the launching, landing or taking on board of any aircraft;

(f) the launching, landing or taking on board of any military device;

(g) the loading or unloading of any commodity, currency or person contrary to the customs, fiscal, immigration or sanitary laws and regulations of the coastal State;

(h) any act of wilful and serious pollution contrary to this Convention;

(i) any fishing activities;

(j) the carrying out of research or survey activities;

(k) any act aimed at interfering with any systems of communication or any other facilities or installations of the coastal State;

(*l*) any other activity not having a direct bearing on passage.

Article 20

Submarines and other underwater vehicles

In the territorial sea, submarines and other underwater vehicles are required to navigate on the surface and to show their flag.

Article 21

Laws and regulations of the coastal State relating to innocent passage

1. The coastal State may adopt laws and regulations, in conformity with the provisions of this Convention and other rules of international law, relating to innocent passage through the territorial sea, in respect of all or any of the following:

(a) the safety of navigation and the regulation of maritime traffic;

(b) the protection of navigational aids and facilities and other facilities or installations;

(c) the protection of cables and pipelines;

(d) the conservation of the living resources of the sea;

(e) the prevention of infringement of the fisheries laws and regulations of the coastal State;

(f) the preservation of the environment of the coastal State and the prevention, reduction and control of pollution thereof;

(g) marine scientific research and hydrographic surveys;

(h) the prevention of infringement of the customs, fiscal, immigration or sanitary laws and regulations of the coastal State.

2. Such laws and regulations shall not apply to the design, construction, manning or equipment of foreign ships unless they are giving effect to generally accepted international rules or standards.

3. The coastal State shall give due publicity to all such laws and regulations.

4. Foreign ships exercising the right of innocent passage through the territorial sea shall comply with all such laws and regulations and all generally accepted international regulations relating to the prevention of collisions at sea.

Article 22

Sea lanes and traffic separation schemes in the territorial sea

1. The coastal State may, where necessary, having regard to the safety of navigation, require foreign ships exercising the right of innocent passage through its territorial sea to use such sea lanes and traffic separation schemes as it may designate or prescribe for the regulation of the passage of ships.

2. In particular, tankers, nuclear-powered ships and ships carrying nuclear or other inherently dangerous or noxious substances or materials may be required to confine their passage to such sea lanes.

3. In the designation of sea lanes and the prescription of traffic separation schemes under this article, the coastal State shall take into account:

(a) the recommendations of the competent international organization;

(b) any channels customarily used for international navigation;

(c) the special characteristics of particular ships and channels; and

(d) the density of traffic.

4. The coastal State shall clearly indicate such sea lanes and traffic separation schemes on charts to which due publicity shall be given.

Article 23

Foreign nuclear-powered ships and ships carrying nuclear
or other inherently dangerous or noxious substances

Foreign nuclear-powered ships and ships carrying nuclear or other inherently dangerous or noxious substances shall, when exercising the right of innocent passage through the territorial sea, carry documents and observe special precautionary measures established for such ships by international agreements.

Article 24

Duties of the coastal State

1. The coastal State shall not hamper the innocent passage of foreign ships through the territorial sea except in accordance with this Convention. In particular, in the application of this Convention or of any laws or regulations adopted in conformity with this Convention, the coastal State shall not:

(a) impose requirements on foreign ships which have the practical effect of denying or impairing the right of innocent passage; or

(b) discriminate in form or in fact against the ships of any State or against ships carrying cargoes to, from or on behalf of any State.

2. The coastal State shall give appropriate publicity to any danger to navigation, of which it has knowledge, within its territorial sea.

Article 25

Rights of protection of the coastal State

1. The coastal State may take the necessary steps in its territorial sea to prevent passage which is not innocent.

2. In the case of ships proceeding to internal waters or a call at a port facility outside internal waters, the coastal State also has the right to take the necessary steps to prevent any breach of the conditions to which admission of those ships to internal waters or such a call is subject.

3. The coastal State may, without discrimination in form or in fact among foreign ships, suspend temporarily in specified areas of its territorial sea the innocent passage of foreign ships if such suspension is essential for the protection of its security, including weapons exercises. Such suspension shall take effect only after having been duly published.

Article 26

Charges which may be levied upon foreign ships

1. No charge may be levied upon foreign ships by reason only of their passage through the territorial sea.

2. Charges may be levied upon a foreign ship passing through the territorial sea as payment only for specific services rendered to the ship. These charges shall be levied without discrimination.

SUBSECTION B. RULES APPLICABLE TO MERCHANT SHIPS AND GOVERNMENT SHIPS OPERATED FOR COMMERCIAL PURPOSES

Article 27

Criminal jurisdiction on board a foreign ship

1. The criminal jurisdiction of the coastal State should not be exercised on board a foreign ship passing through the territorial sea to arrest any person or to conduct any investigation in connection with any crime committed on board the ship during its passage, save only in the following cases:

(a) if the consequences of the crime extend to the coastal State;

(b) if the crime is of a kind to disturb the peace of the country or the good order of the territorial sea;

(c) if the assistance of the local authorities has been requested by the master of the ship or by a diplomatic agent or consular officer of the flag State; or

(d) if such measures are necessary for the suppression of illicit traffic in narcotic drugs or psychotropic substances.

2. The above provisions do not affect the right of the coastal State to take any steps authorized by its laws for the purpose of an arrest or investigation on board a foreign ship passing through the territorial sea after leaving internal waters.

3. In the cases provided for in paragraphs 1 and 2, the coastal State shall, if the master so requests, notify a diplomatic agent or consular officer of the flag State before taking any steps, and shall facilitate contact between such agent or officer and the ship's crew. In cases of emergency this notification may be communicated while the measures are being taken.

4. In considering whether or in what manner an arrest should be made, the local authorities shall have due regard to the interests of navigation.

5. Except as provided in Part XII or with respect to violations of laws and regulations adopted in accordance with Part V, the coastal State may not take any steps on board a foreign ship passing through the territorial sea to arrest any person or to conduct any investigation in connection with any crime committed before the ship entered the territorial sea, if the ship, proceeding from a foreign port, is only passing through the territorial sea without entering internal waters.

Article 28

Civil jurisdiction in relation to foreign ships

1. The coastal State should not stop or divert a foreign ship passing through the territorial sea for the purpose of exercising civil jurisdiction in relation to a person on board the ship.

2. The coastal State may not levy execution against or arrest the ship for the purpose of any civil proceedings, save only in respect of obligations or liabilities assumed or incurred by the ship itself in the course or for the purpose of its voyage through the waters of the coastal State.

3. Paragraph 2 is without prejudice to the right of the coastal State, in accordance with its laws, to levy execution against or to arrest, for the purpose of any civil proceedings, a foreign ship lying in the territorial sea, or passing through the territorial sea after leaving internal waters.

SUBSECTION C. RULES APPLICABLE TO WARSHIPS AND OTHER GOVERNMENT SHIPS OPERATED FOR NON–COMMERCIAL PURPOSES

Article 29

Definition of warships

For the purposes of this Convention, "warship" means a ship belonging to the armed forces of a State bearing the external marks distinguishing such ships of its nationality, under the command of an officer duly commissioned by the government of the State and whose name appears in the appropriate service list or its equivalent, and manned by a crew which is under regular armed forces discipline.

Article 30

Non-compliance by warships with the laws and regulations of the coastal State

If any warship does not comply with the laws and regulations of the coastal State concerning passage through the territorial sea and disregards any request for compliance therewith which is made to it, the coastal State may require it to leave the territorial sea immediately.

Article 31

Responsibility of the flag State for damage caused by a warship or other government ship operated for non-commercial purposes

The flag State shall bear international responsibility for any loss or damage to the coastal State resulting from the non-compliance by a warship or other government ship operated for non-commercial purposes with the laws and regulations of the coastal State concerning passage through the territorial sea or with the provisions of this Convention or other rules of international law.

Article 32

Immunities of warships and other government ships operated for non-commercial purposes

With such exceptions as are contained in subsection A and in articles 30 and 31, nothing in this Convention affects the immunities of warships and other government ships operated for non-commercial purposes.

SECTION 4.   CONTIGUOUS ZONE

Article 33

Contiguous zone

1.   In a zone contiguous to its territorial sea, described as the contiguous zone, the coastal State may exercise the control necessary to:

(a) prevent infringement of its customs, fiscal, immigration or sanitary laws and regulations within its territory or territorial sea;

(b) punish infringement of the above laws and regulations committed within its territory or territorial sea.

2.   The contiguous zone may not extend beyond 24 nautical miles from the baselines from which the breadth of the territorial sea is measured.

PART III

STRAITS USED FOR INTERNATIONAL NAVIGATION

SECTION 1.   GENERAL PROVISIONS

Article 34

Legal status of waters forming straits used for international navigation

1.   The régime of passage through straits used for international navigation established in this Part shall not in other respects affect the legal status of the waters forming such straits or the exercise by the States bordering the straits of their sovereignty or jurisdiction over such waters and their air space, bed and subsoil.

2.   The sovereignty or jurisdiction of the States bordering the straits is exercised subject to this Part and to other rules of international law.

Article 35

Scope of this Part

Nothing in this Part affects:

(a) any areas of internal waters within a strait, except where the establishment of a straight baseline in accordance with the method set forth in article 7 has the effect of enclosing as internal waters areas which had not previously been considered as such;

(b) the legal status of the waters beyond the territorial seas of States bordering straits as exclusive economic zones or high seas; or

(c) the legal régime in straits in which passage is regulated in whole or in part by long-standing international conventions in force specifically relating to such straits.

Article 36

High seas routes or routes through exclusive economic zones through straits used for international navigation

This Part does not apply to a strait used for international navigation if there exists through the strait a route through the high seas or through an exclusive economic zone of similar convenience with respect to navigational and hydrographical characteristics; in such routes, the other relevant Parts of this Convention, including the provisions regarding the freedoms of navigation and overflight, apply.

SECTION 2.   TRANSIT PASSAGE

Article 37

Scope of this section

This section applies to straits which are used for international navigation between one part of the high seas or an exclusive economic zone and another part of the high seas or an exclusive economic zone.

Article 38

Right of transit passage

1.   In straits referred to in article 37, all ships and aircraft enjoy the right of transit passage, which shall not be impeded; except that, if the strait is formed by an island of a State bordering the strait and its mainland, transit passage shall not apply if there exists seaward of the island a route through the high seas or through an exclusive economic zone of similar convenience with respect to navigational and hydrographical characteristics.

2.   Transit passage means the exercise in accordance with this Part of the freedom of navigation and overflight solely for the purpose of continuous and expeditious transit of the strait between one part of the high seas or an exclusive economic zone and another part of the high seas or an exclusive economic zone. However, the requirement of continuous and expeditious transit does not preclude passage through the strait for the purpose of entering, leaving or returning from a State bordering the strait, subject to the conditions of entry to that State.

3.   Any activity which is not an exercise of the right of transit passage through a strait remains subject to the other applicable provisions of this Convention.

Article 39

Duties of ships and aircraft during transit passage

1. Ships and aircraft, while exercising the right of transit passage, shall:

    (a) proceed without delay through or over the strait;

    (b) refrain from any threat or use of force against the sovereignty, territorial integrity or political independence of States bordering the strait, or in any other manner in violation of the principles of international law embodied in the Charter of the United Nations;

    (c) refrain from any activities other than those incident to their normal modes of continuous and expeditious transit unless rendered necessary by *force majeure* or by distress;

    (d) comply with other relevant provisions of this Part.

* * *

Article 40

Research and survey activities

During transit passage, foreign ships, including marine scientific research and hydrographic survey ships, may not carry out any research or survey activities without the prior authorization of the States bordering straits.

Article 41

Sea lanes and traffic separation schemes in straits used for international navigation

1. In conformity with this Part, States bordering straits may designate sea lanes and prescribe traffic separation schemes for navigation in straits where necessary to promote the safe passage of ships.

2. Such States may, when circumstances require, and after giving due publicity thereto, substitute other sea lanes or traffic separation schemes for any sea lanes or traffic separation schemes previously designated or prescribed by them.

3. Such sea lanes and traffic separation schemes shall conform to generally accepted international regulations.

4. Before designating or substituting sea lanes or prescribing or substituting traffic separation schemes, States bordering straits shall refer proposals to the competent international organization with a view to their adoption. The organization may adopt only such sea lanes and traffic separation schemes as may be agreed with the States bordering the straits, after which the States may designate, prescribe or substitute them.

5. In respect of a strait where sea lanes or traffic separation schemes through the waters of two or more States bordering the strait are being proposed, the States concerned shall co-operate in formulating proposals in consultation with the competent international organization.

6. States bordering straits shall clearly indicate all sea lanes and traffic separation schemes designated or prescribed by them on charts to which due publicity shall be given.

7. Ships in transit passage shall respect applicable sea lanes and traffic separation schemes established in accordance with this article.

Article 42

Laws and regulations of States bordering straits relating to transit passage

1. Subject to the provisions of this section, States bordering straits may adopt laws and regulations relating to transit passage through straits, in respect of all or any of the following:

(a) the safety of navigation and the regulation of maritime traffic, as provided in article 41;

(b) the prevention, reduction and control of pollution, by giving effect to applicable international regulations regarding the discharge of oil, oily wastes and other noxious substances in the strait;

(c) with respect to fishing vessels, the prevention of fishing, including the stowage of fishing gear;

(d) the loading or unloading of any commodity, currency or person in contravention of the customs, fiscal, immigration or sanitary laws and regulations of States bordering straits.

2. Such laws and regulations shall not discriminate in form or in fact among foreign ships or in their application have the practical effect of denying, hampering or impairing the right of transit passage as defined in this section.

3. States bordering straits shall give due publicity to all such laws and regulations.

4. Foreign ships exercising the right of transit passage shall comply with such laws and regulations.

5. The flag State of a ship or the State of registry of an aircraft entitled to sovereign immunity which acts in a manner contrary to such laws and regulations or other provisions of this Part shall bear international responsibility for any loss or damage which results to States bordering straits.

Article 43

Navigational and safety aids and other improvements and the prevention, reduction and control of pollution

User States and States bordering a strait should by agreement co-operate:

(a) in the establishment and maintenance in a strait of necessary navigational and safety aids or other improvements in aid of international navigation; and

(b) for the prevention, reduction and control of pollution from ships.

Article 44

Duties of States bordering straits

States bordering straits shall not hamper transit passage and shall give appropriate publicity to any danger to navigation or overflight within or over the strait of which they have knowledge. There shall be no suspension of transit passage.

SECTION 3. INNOCENT PASSAGE

Article 45

Innocent passage

1. The régime of innocent passage, in accordance with Part II, section 3, shall apply in straits used for international navigation:

(a) excluded from the application of the régime of transit passage under article 38, paragraph 1; or

(b) between a part of the high seas or an exclusive economic zone and the territorial sea of a foreign State.

2. There shall be no suspension of innocent passage through such straits.

PART IV

ARCHIPELAGIC STATES

Article 46

Use of terms

For the purposes of this Convention:

(a) "archipelagic State" means a State constituted wholly by one or more archipelagos and may include other islands;

(b) "archipelago" means a group of islands, including parts of islands, interconnecting waters and other natural features which are so closely interrelated that such islands, waters and other natural features form an intrinsic geographical, economic and political entity, or which historically have been regarded as such.

Article 47

Archipelagic baselines

1. An archipelagic State may draw straight archipelagic baselines joining the outermost points of the outermost islands and drying reefs of the archipelago provided that within such baselines are included the main islands and an area in which the ratio of the area of the water to the area of the land, including atolls, is between 1 to 1 and 9 to 1.

2. The length of such baselines shall not exceed 100 nautical miles, except that up to 3 per cent of the total number of baselines enclosing any archipelago may exceed that length, up to a maximum length of 125 nautical miles.

3. The drawing of such baselines shall not depart to any appreciable extent from the general configuration of the archipelago.

4. Such baselines shall not be drawn to and from low-tide elevations, unless lighthouses or similar installations which are permanently above sea level have been built on them or where a low-tide elevation is situated wholly or partly at a distance not exceeding the breadth of the territorial sea from the nearest island.

5. The system of such baselines shall not be applied by an archipelagic State in such a manner as to cut off from the high seas or the exclusive economic zone the territorial sea of another State.

6. If a part of the archipelagic waters of an archipelagic State lies between two parts of an immediately adjacent neighbouring State, existing rights and all other legitimate interests which the latter State has traditionally exercised in such waters and all rights stipulated by agreement between those States shall continue and be respected.

* * *

Article 48

Measurement of the breadth of the territorial sea, the contiguous zone, the exclusive economic zone and the continental shelf

The breadth of the territorial sea, the contiguous zone, the exclusive economic zone and the continental shelf shall be measured from archipelagic baselines drawn in accordance with article 47.

Article 49

Legal status of archipelagic waters, of the air space over archipelagic waters and of their bed and subsoil

1. The sovereignty of an archipelagic State extends to the waters enclosed by the archipelagic baselines drawn in accordance with article 47, described as archipelagic waters, regardless of their depth or distance from the coast.

2. This sovereignty extends to the air space over the archipelagic waters, as well as to their bed and subsoil, and the resources contained therein.

* * *

Article 50

Delimitation of internal waters

Within its archipelagic waters, the archipelagic State may draw closing lines for the delimitation of internal waters, in accordance with articles 9, 10 and 11.

Article 51

Existing agreements, traditional fishing rights and existing submarine cables

1. Without prejudice to article 49, an archipelagic State shall respect existing agreements with other States and shall recognize traditional fishing rights and other legitimate activities of the immediately adjacent neighbouring States in certain areas falling within archipelagic waters. The terms and conditions for the exercise of such rights and activities, including the nature, the extent and the areas to which they apply, shall, at the request of any of the States concerned, be regulated by bilateral agreements between them. Such rights shall not be transferred to or shared with third States or their nationals.

2. An archipelagic State shall respect existing submarine cables laid by other States and passing through its waters without making a landfall. An archipelagic State shall permit the maintenance and replacement of such cables upon receiving due notice of their location and the intention to repair or replace them.

Article 52

Right of innocent passage

1. Subject to article 53 and without prejudice to article 50, ships of all States enjoy the right of innocent passage through archipelagic waters, in accordance with Part II, section 3.

2. The archipelagic State may, without discrimination in form or in fact among foreign ships, suspend temporarily in specified areas of its archipelagic waters the innocent passage of foreign ships if such suspension is essential for the protection of its security. Such suspension shall take effect only after having been duly published.

Article 53

Right of archipelagic sea lanes passage

1. An archipelagic State may designate sea lanes and air routes thereabove, suitable for the continuous and expeditious passage of foreign ships and aircraft through or over its archipelagic waters and the adjacent territorial sea.

2. All ships and aircraft enjoy the right of archipelagic sea lanes passage in such sea lanes and air routes.

* * *

6. An archipelagic State which designates sea lanes under this article may also prescribe traffic separation schemes for the safe passage of ships through narrow channels in such sea lanes.

* * *

8. Such sea lanes and traffic separation schemes shall conform to generally accepted international regulations.

Article 54

Duties of ships and aircraft during their passage, research and survey activities, duties of the archipelagic State and laws and regulations of the archipelagic State relating to archipelagic sea lanes passage

Articles 39, 40, 42 and 44 apply *mutatis mutandis* to archipelagic sea lanes passage.

PART V

EXCLUSIVE ECONOMIC ZONE

Article 55

Specific legal régime of the exclusive economic zone

The exclusive economic zone is an area beyond and adjacent to the territorial sea, subject to the specific legal régime established in this Part, under which the rights and jurisdiction of the coastal State and the rights and freedoms of other States are governed by the relevant provisions of this Convention.

Article 56

Rights, jurisdiction and duties of the coastal State in the exclusive economic zone

1. In the exclusive economic zone, the coastal State has:

(a) sovereign rights for the purpose of exploring and exploiting, conserving and managing the natural resources, whether living or non-living, of the waters superjacent to the sea-bed and of the sea-bed and its subsoil, and with regard to other activities for the economic exploitation and exploration of the zone, such as the production of energy from the water, currents and winds;

(b) jurisdiction as provided for in the relevant provisions of this Convention with regard to:

(i) the establishment and use of artificial islands, installations and structures;

(ii) marine scientific research;

(iii) the protection and preservation of the marine environment;

(c) other rights and duties provided for in this Convention.

2. In exercising its rights and performing its duties under this Convention in the exclusive economic zone, the coastal State shall have due regard to the rights and duties of other States and shall act in a manner compatible with the provisions of this Convention.

3. The rights set out in this article with respect to the sea-bed and subsoil shall be exercised in accordance with Part VI.

Article 57

Breadth of the exclusive economic zone

The exclusive economic zone shall not extend beyond 200 nautical miles from the baselines from which the breadth of the territorial sea is measured.

Article 58

Rights and duties of other States in the exclusive economic zone

1. In the exclusive economic zone, all States, whether coastal or land-locked, enjoy, subject to the relevant provisions of this Convention, the freedoms referred to in article 87 of navigation and overflight and of the laying of submarine cables and pipelines, and other internationally lawful uses of the sea related to these freedoms, such as those associated with the operation of ships, aircraft and submarine cables and pipelines, and compatible with the other provisions of this Convention.

2. Articles 88 to 115 and other pertinent rules of international law apply to the exclusive economic zone in so far as they are not incompatible with this Part.

3. In exercising their rights and performing their duties under this Convention in the exclusive economic zone, States shall have due regard to the rights and duties of the coastal State and shall comply with the laws and regulations adopted by the coastal State in accordance with the provisions of this Convention and other rules of international law in so far as they are not incompatible with this Part.

Article 59

Basis for the resolution of conflicts regarding the attribution of rights and jurisdiction in the exclusive economic zone

In cases where this Convention does not attribute rights or jurisdiction to the coastal State or to other States within the exclusive economic zone, and a conflict arises between the interests of the coastal State and any other State or States, the conflict should be resolved on the basis of equity and in the light of all the relevant circumstances, taking into account the respective importance of the interests involved to the parties as well as to the international community as a whole.

Article 60

Artificial islands, installations and structures in the exclusive economic zone

1. In the exclusive economic zone, the coastal State shall have the exclusive right to construct and to authorize and regulate the construction, operation and use of:

    (a) artificial islands;

    (b) installations and structures for the purposes provided for in article 56 and other economic purposes;

    (c) installations and structures which may interfere with the exercise of the rights of the coastal State in the zone.

* * *

Article 61

Conservation of the living resources

1. The coastal State shall determine the allowable catch of the living resources in its exclusive economic zone.

2. The coastal State, taking into account the best scientific evidence available to it, shall ensure through proper conservation and management measures that the maintenance of the living resources in the exclusive economic zone is not endangered

by over-exploitation. As appropriate, the coastal State and competent international organizations, whether subregional, regional or global, shall co-operate to this end.

3. Such measures shall also be designed to maintain or restore populations of harvested species at levels which can produce the maximum sustainable yield, as qualified by relevant environmental and economic factors, including the economic needs of coastal fishing communities and the special requirements of developing States, and taking into account fishing patterns, the interdependence of stocks and any generally recommended international minimum standards, whether subregional, regional or global.

4. In taking such measures the coastal State shall take into consideration the effects on species associated with or dependent upon harvested species with a view to maintaining or restoring populations of such associated or dependent species above levels at which their reproduction may become seriously threatened.

5. Available scientific information, catch and fishing effort statistics, and other data relevant to the conservation of fish stocks shall be contributed and exchanged on a regular basis through competent international organizations, whether subregional, regional or global, where appropriate and with participation by all States concerned, including States whose nationals are allowed to fish in the exclusive economic zone.

Article 62

Utilization of the living resources

1. The coastal State shall promote the objective of optimum utilization of the living resources in the exclusive economic zone without prejudice to article 61.

2. The coastal State shall determine its capacity to harvest the living resources of the exclusive economic zone. Where the coastal State does not have the capacity to harvest the entire allowable catch, it shall, through agreements or other arrangements and pursuant to the terms, conditions, laws and regulations referred to in paragraph 4, give other States access to the surplus of the allowable catch, having particular regard to the provisions of articles 69 and 70, especially in relation to the developing States mentioned therein.

3. In giving access to other States to its exclusive economic zone under this article, the coastal State shall take into account all relevant factors, including, *inter alia,* the significance of the living resources of the area to the economy of the coastal State concerned and its other national interests, the provisions of articles 69 and 70, the requirements of developing States in the subregion or region in harvesting part of the surplus and the need to minimize economic dislocation in States whose nationals have habitually fished in the zone or which have made substantial efforts in research and identification of stocks.

4. Nationals of other States fishing in the exclusive economic zone shall comply with the conservation measures and with the other terms and conditions established in the laws and regulations of the coastal State. These laws and regulations shall be consistent with this Convention. * * *

5. Coastal States shall give due notice of conservation and management laws and regulations.

Article 63

Stocks occurring within the exclusive economic zones of two or more coastal States or both within the exclusive economic zone and in an area beyond and adjacent to it

1. Where the same stock or stocks of associated species occur within the exclusive economic zones of two or more coastal States, these States shall seek, either directly or

through appropriate subregional or regional organizations, to agree upon the measures necessary to co-ordinate and ensure the conservation and development of such stocks without prejudice to the other provisions of this Part.

2.   Where the same stock or stocks of associated species occur both within the exclusive economic zone and in an area beyond and adjacent to the zone, the coastal State and the States fishing for such stocks in the adjacent area shall seek, either directly or through appropriate subregional or regional organizations, to agree upon the measures necessary for the conservation of these stocks in the adjacent area.

Article 64

Highly migratory species

1.   The coastal State and other States whose nationals fish in the region for the highly migratory species listed in Annex I shall co-operate directly or through appropriate international organizations with a view to ensuring conservation and promoting the objective of optimum utilization of such species throughout the region, both within and beyond the exclusive economic zone. In regions for which no appropriate international organization exists, the coastal State and other States whose nationals harvest these species in the region shall co-operate to establish such an organization and participate in its work.

2.   The provisions of paragraph 1 apply in addition to the other provisions of this Part.

Article 65

Marine mammals

Nothing in this Part restricts the right of a coastal State or the competence of an international organization, as appropriate, to prohibit, limit or regulate the exploitation of marine mammals more strictly than provided for in this Part. States shall co-operate with a view to the conservation of marine mammals and in the case of cetaceans shall in particular work through the appropriate international organizations for their conservation, management and study.

Article 66

Anadromous stocks

1.   States in whose rivers anadromous stocks originate shall have the primary interest in and responsibility for such stocks.

* * *

Article 67

Catadromous species

1.   A coastal State in whose waters catadromous species spend the greater part of their life cycle shall have responsibility for the management of these species and shall ensure the ingress and egress of migrating fish.

* * *

Article 68

Sedentary species

This Part does not apply to sedentary species as defined in article 77, paragraph 4.

Article 69

Right of land-locked States

1.   Land-locked States shall have the right to participate, on an equitable basis, in the exploitation of an appropriate part of the surplus of the living resources of the exclusive economic zones of coastal States of the same subregion or region, taking into account the relevant economic and geographical circumstances of all the States concerned and in conformity with the provisions of this article and of articles 61 and 62.

2.   The terms and modalities of such participation shall be established by the States concerned through bilateral, subregional or regional agreements taking into account, *inter alia:*

(a) the need to avoid effects detrimental to fishing communities or fishing industries of the coastal State;

(b) the extent to which the land-locked State, in accordance with the provisions of this article, is participating or is entitled to participate under existing bilateral, subregional or regional agreements in the exploitation of living resources of the exclusive economic zones of other coastal States;

(c) the extent to which other land-locked States and geographically disadvantaged States are participating in the exploitation of the living resources of the exclusive economic zone of the coastal State and the consequent need to avoid a particular burden for any single coastal State or a part of it;

(d) the nutritional needs of the populations of the respective States.

3.   When the harvesting capacity of a coastal State approaches a point which would enable it to harvest the entire allowable catch of the living resources in its exclusive economic zone, the coastal State and other States concerned shall cooperate in the establishment of equitable arrangements on a bilateral, subregional or regional basis to allow for participation of developing land-locked States of the same subregion or region in the exploitation of the living resources of the exclusive economic zones of coastal States of the subregion or region, as may be appropriate in the circumstances and on terms satisfactory to all parties. In the implementation of this provision the factors mentioned in paragraph 2 shall also be taken into account.

4.   Developed land-locked States shall, under the provisions of this article, be entitled to participate in the exploitation of living resources only in the exclusive economic zones of developed coastal States of the same subregion or region having regard to the extent to which the coastal State, in giving access to other States to the living resources of its exclusive economic zone, has taken into account the need to minimize detrimental effects on fishing communities and economic dislocation in States whose nationals have habitually fished in the zone.

5.   The above provisions are without prejudice to arrangements agreed upon in subregions or regions where the coastal States may grant to land-locked States of the same subregion or region equal or preferential rights for the exploitation of the living resources in the exclusive economic zones.

Article 70

Right of geographically disadvantaged States

[This article is in all essential respects identical to Article 69, supra.]

Article 71

Non-applicability of articles 69 and 70

The provisions of articles 69 and 70 do not apply in the case of a coastal State whose economy is overwhelmingly dependent on the exploitation of the living resources of its exclusive economic zone.

Article 72

Restrictions on transfer of rights

* * *

Article 73

Enforcement of laws and regulations of the coastal State

1.   The coastal State may, in the exercise of its sovereign rights to explore, exploit, conserve and manage the living resources in the exclusive economic zone, take such measures, including boarding, inspection, arrest and judicial proceedings, as may be necessary to ensure compliance with the laws and regulations adopted by it in conformity with this Convention.

2.   Arrested vessels and their crews shall be promptly released upon the posting of reasonable bond or other security.

3.   Coastal State penalties for violations of fisheries laws and regulations in the exclusive economic zone may not include imprisonment, in the absence of agreements to the contrary by the States concerned, or any other form of corporal punishment.

4.   In cases of arrest or detention of foreign vessels the coastal State shall promptly notify the flag State, through appropriate channels, of the action taken and of any penalties subsequently imposed.

Article 74

Delimitation of the exclusive economic zone between
States with opposite or adjacent coasts

1.   The delimitation of the exclusive economic zone between States with opposite or adjacent coasts shall be effected by agreement on the basis of international law, as referred to in Article 38 of the Statute of the International Court of Justice, in order to achieve an equitable solution.

2.   If no agreement can be reached within a reasonable period of time, the States concerned shall resort to the procedures provided for in Part XV.

* * *

Article 75

Charts and lists of geographical co-ordinates

* * *

PART VI

CONTINENTAL SHELF

Article 76

Definition of the continental shelf

1.   The continental shelf of a coastal State comprises the sea-bed and subsoil of the submarine areas that extend beyond its territorial sea throughout the natural prolongation of its land territory to the outer edge of the continental margin, or to a distance of 200 nautical miles from the baselines from which the breadth of the territorial sea is measured where the outer edge of the continental margin does not extend up to that distance.

2.   The continental shelf of a coastal State shall not extend beyond the limits provided for in paragraphs 4 to 6.

3. The continental margin comprises the submerged prolongation of the land mass of the coastal State, and consists of the sea-bed and subsoil of the shelf, the slope and the rise. It does not include the deep ocean floor with its oceanic ridges or the subsoil thereof.

4. (a) For the purposes of this Convention, the coastal State shall establish the outer edge of the continental margin wherever the margin extends beyond 200 nautical miles from the baselines from which the breadth of the territorial sea is measured, by either:

(i) a line delineated in accordance with paragraph 7 by reference to the outermost fixed points at each of which the thickness of sedimentary rocks is at least 1 per cent of the shortest distance from such point to the foot of the continental slope; or

(ii) a line delineated in accordance with paragraph 7 by reference to fixed points not more than 60 nautical miles from the foot of the continental slope.

(b) In the absence of evidence to the contrary, the foot of the continental slope shall be determined as the point of maximum change in the gradient at its base.

5. The fixed points comprising the line of the outer limits of the continental shelf on the sea-bed, drawn in accordance with paragraph 4(a)(i) and (ii), either shall not exceed 350 nautical miles from the baselines from which the breadth of the territorial sea is measured or shall not exceed 100 nautical miles from the 2,500 metre isobath, which is a line connecting the depths of 2,500 metres.

6. Notwithstanding the provisions of paragraph 5, on submarine ridges, the outer limit of the continental shelf shall not exceed 350 nautical miles from the baselines from which the breadth of the territorial sea is measured. This paragraph does not apply to submarine elevations that are natural components of the continental margin, such as its plateaux, rises, caps, banks and spurs.

7. The coastal State shall delineate the outer limits of its continental shelf, where that shelf extends beyond 200 nautical miles from the baselines from which the breadth of the territorial sea is measured, by straight lines not exceeding 60 nautical miles in length, connecting fixed points, defined by coordinates of latitude and longitude.

* * *

Article 77

Rights of the coastal State over the continental shelf

1. The coastal State exercises over the continental shelf sovereign rights for the purpose of exploring it and exploiting its natural resources.

2. The rights referred to in paragraph 1 are exclusive in the sense that if the coastal State does not explore the continental shelf or exploit its natural resources, no one may undertake these activities without the express consent of the coastal State.

3. The rights of the coastal State over the continental shelf do not depend on occupation, effective or notional, or on any express proclamation.

4. The natural resources referred to in this Part consist of the mineral and other non-living resources of the seabed and subsoil together with living organisms belonging to sedentary species, that is to say, organisms which, at the harvestable stage, either are immobile on or under the seabed or are unable to move except in constant physical contact with the seabed or the subsoil.

Article 78

Legal status of the superjacent waters and air space
and the rights and freedoms of other States

1. The rights of the coastal State over the continental shelf do not affect the legal status of the superjacent waters or of the air space above those waters.

2. The exercise of the rights of the coastal State over the continental shelf must not infringe or result in any unjustifiable interference with navigation and other rights and freedoms of other States as provided for in this Convention.

Article 79

Submarine cables and pipelines on the continental shelf

1. All States are entitled to lay submarine cables and pipelines on the continental shelf, in accordance with the provisions of this article.

2. Subject to its right to take reasonable measures for the exploration of the continental shelf, the exploitation of its natural resources and the prevention, reduction and control of pollution from pipelines, the coastal State may not impede the laying or maintenance of such cables or pipelines.

3. The delineation of the course for the laying of such pipelines on the continental shelf is subject to the consent of the coastal State.

4. Nothing in this Part affects the right of the coastal State to establish conditions for cables or pipelines entering its territory or territorial sea, or its jurisdiction over cables and pipelines constructed or used in connection with the exploration of its continental shelf or exploitation of its resources or the operations of artificial islands, installations and structures under its jurisdiction.

5. When laying submarine cables or pipelines, States shall have due regard to cables or pipelines already in position. In particular, possibilities of repairing existing cables or pipelines shall not be prejudiced.

Article 80

Artificial islands, installations and structures on the continental shelf

Article 60 applies *mutatis mutandis* to artificial islands, installations and structures on the continental shelf.

Article 81

Drilling on the continental shelf

The coastal State shall have the exclusive right to authorize and regulate drilling on the continental shelf for all purposes.

Article 82

Payments and contributions with respect to the exploitation
of the continental shelf beyond 200 nautical miles

1. The coastal State shall make payments or contributions in kind in respect of the exploitation of the non-living resources of the continental shelf beyond 200 nautical miles from the baselines from which the breadth of the territorial sea is measured.

2. The payments and contributions shall be made annually with respect to all production at a site after the first five years of production at that site. For the sixth year, the rate of payment or contribution shall be 1 per cent of the value or volume of production at the site. The rate shall increase by 1 per cent for each subsequent year

until the twelfth year and shall remain at 7 per cent thereafter. Production does not include resources used in connection with exploitation.

3. A developing State which is a net importer of a mineral resource produced from its continental shelf is exempt from making such payments or contributions in respect of that mineral resource.

4. The payments or contributions shall be made through the Authority, which shall distribute them to States Parties to this Convention, on the basis of equitable sharing criteria, taking into account the interests and needs of developing States, particularly the least developed and the land-locked among them.

Article 83

Delimitation of the continental shelf between States with opposite or adjacent coasts

1. The delimitation of the continental shelf between States with opposite or adjacent coasts shall be effected by agreement on the basis of international law, as referred to in Article 38 of the Statute of the International Court of Justice, in order to achieve an equitable solution.

2. If no agreement can be reached within a reasonable period of time, the States concerned shall resort to the procedures provided for in Part XV.

Article 84

Charts and lists of geographical co-ordinates

* * *

Article 85

Tunnelling

This Part does not prejudice the right of the coastal State to exploit the subsoil by means of tunnelling, irrespective of the depth of water above the subsoil.

PART VII

HIGH SEAS

SECTION 1.   GENERAL PROVISIONS

Article 86

Application of the provisions of this Part

The provisions of this Part apply to all parts of the sea that are not included in the exclusive economic zone, in the territorial sea or in the internal waters of a State, or in the archipelagic waters of an archipelagic State. This article does not entail any abridgement of the freedoms enjoyed by all States in the exclusive economic zone in accordance with article 58.

Article 87

Freedom of the high seas

1. The high seas are open to all States, whether coastal or land-locked. Freedom of the high seas is exercised under the conditions laid down by this Convention and by other rules of international law. It comprises, *inter alia,* both for coastal and land-locked States:

(a) freedom of navigation;

(b) freedom of overflight;

(c) freedom to lay submarine cables and pipelines, subject to Part VI;

(d) freedom to construct artificial islands and other installations permitted under international law, subject to Part VI;

(e) freedom of fishing, subject to the conditions laid down in section 2;

(f) freedom of scientific research, subject to Parts VI and XIII.

2. These freedoms shall be exercised by all States with due regard for the interests of other States in their exercise of the freedom of the high seas, and also with due regard for the rights under this Convention with respect to activities in the Area.

Article 88

Reservation of the high seas for peaceful purposes

The high seas shall be reserved for peaceful purposes.

Article 89

Invalidity of claims of sovereignty over the high seas

No State may validly purport to subject any part of the high seas to its sovereignty.

Article 90

Right of navigation

Every State, whether coastal or land-locked, has the right to sail ships flying its flag on the high seas.

Article 91

Nationality of ships

1. Every State shall fix the conditions for the grant of its nationality to ships, for the registration of ships in its territory, and for the right to fly its flag. Ships have the nationality of the State whose flag they are entitled to fly. There must exist a genuine link between the State and the ship.

2. Every State shall issue to ships to which it has granted the right to fly its flag documents to that effect.

Article 92

Status of ships

1. Ships shall sail under the flag of one State only and, save in exceptional cases expressly provided for in international treaties or in this Convention, shall be subject to its exclusive jurisdiction on the high seas. A ship may not change its flag during a voyage or while in a port of call, save in the case of a real transfer of ownership or change of registry.

2. A ship which sails under the flags of two or more States, using them according to convenience, may not claim any of the nationalities in question with respect to any other State, and may be assimilated to a ship without nationality.

Article 93

Ships flying the flag of the United Nations, its specialized agencies and the International Atomic Energy Agency

The preceding articles do not prejudice the question of ships employed on the official service of the United Nations, its specialized agencies or the International Atomic Energy Agency, flying the flag of the organization.

Article 94

Duties of the flag State

1. Every State shall effectively exercise its jurisdiction and control in administrative, technical and social matters over ships flying its flag.

2. In particular every State shall:

(a) maintain a register of ships containing the names and particulars of ships flying its flag, except those which are excluded from generally accepted international regulations on account of their small size; and

(b) assume jurisdiction under its internal law over each ship flying its flag and its master, officers and crew in respect of administrative, technical and social matters concerning the ship.

3. Every State shall take such measures for ships flying its flag as are necessary to ensure safety at sea with regard, *inter alia,* to:

(a) the construction, equipment and seaworthiness of ships;

(b) the manning of ships, labour conditions and the training of crews, taking into account the applicable international instruments;

(c) the use of signals, the maintenance of communications and the prevention of collisions.

4. Such measures shall include those necessary to ensure:

(a) that each ship, before registration and thereafter at appropriate intervals, is surveyed by a qualified surveyor of ships, and has on board such charts, nautical publications and navigational equipment and instruments as are appropriate for the safe navigation of the ship;

(b) that each ship is in the charge of a master and officers who possess appropriate qualifications, in particular in seamanship, navigation, communications and marine engineering, and that the crew is appropriate in qualification and numbers for the type, size, machinery and equipment of the ship;

(c) that the master, officers and, to the extent appropriate, the crew are fully conversant with and required to observe the applicable international regulations concerning the safety of life at sea, the prevention of collisions, the prevention, reduction and control of marine pollution, and the maintenance of communications by radio.

5. In taking the measures called for in paragraphs 3 and 4 each State is required to conform to generally accepted international regulations, procedures and practices and to take any steps which may be necessary to secure their observance.

6. A State which has clear grounds to believe that proper jurisdiction and control with respect to a ship have not been exercised may report the facts to the flag State. Upon receiving such a report, the flag State shall investigate the matter and, if appropriate, take any action necessary to remedy the situation.

7. Each State shall cause an inquiry to be held by or before a suitably qualified person or persons into every marine casualty or incident of navigation on the high seas involving a ship flying its flag and causing loss of life or serious injury to nationals of another State or serious damage to ships or installations of another State or to the marine environment. The flag State and the other State shall co-operate in the conduct of any inquiry held by that other State into any such marine casualty or incident of navigation.

Article 95

Immunity of warships on the high seas

Warships on the high seas have complete immunity from the jurisdiction of any State other than the flag State.

Article 96

Immunity of ships used only on government non-commercial service

Ships owned or operated by a State and used only on government non-commercial service shall, on the high seas, have complete immunity from the jurisdiction of any State other than the flag State.

Article 97

Penal jurisdiction in matters of collision or in any other incident of navigation

[*See* Basic Document 3.1, Art. 11.]

Article 98

Duty to render assistance

[*See* Basic Document 3.1, Art. 12.]

Article 99

Prohibition of the transport of slaves

[*See* Basic Document 3.1, Art. 13.]

Article 100

Duty to co-operate in the repression of piracy

[*See* Basic Document 3.1, Art. 14.]

Article 101

Definition of piracy

Piracy consists of any of the following acts:

(a) any illegal acts of violence or detention, or any act of depredation, committed for private ends by the crew or the passengers of a private ship or a private aircraft, and directed:

(i) on the high seas, against another ship or aircraft, or against persons or property on board such ship or aircraft;

(ii) against a ship, aircraft, persons or property in a place outside the jurisdiction of any State;

(b) any act of voluntary participation in the operation of a ship or of an aircraft with knowledge of facts making it a pirate ship or aircraft;

(c) any act of inciting or of intentionally facilitating an act described in subparagraph (a) or (b).

Article 102

Piracy by a warship, government ship or government aircraft whose crew has mutinied

* * *

Article 103

Definition of a pirate ship or aircraft

* * *

Article 104

Retention or loss of the nationality of a pirate ship or aircraft

[*See* Basic Document 3.1, Art. 18.]

Article 105

Seizure of a pirate ship or aircraft

[*See* Basic Document 3.1, Art. 19.]

Article 106

Liability for seizure without adequate grounds

[*See* Basic Document 3.1, Art. 20.]

Article 107

Ships and aircraft which are entitled to seize on account of piracy

[*See* Basic Document 3.1, Art. 21.]

Article 108

Illicit traffic in narcotic drugs or psychotropic substances

* * *

Article 109

Unauthorized broadcasting from the high seas

* * *

Article 110

Right of visit

1. Except where acts of interference derive from powers conferred by treaty, a warship which encounters on the high seas a foreign ship, other than a ship entitled to complete immunity in accordance with articles 95 and 96, is not justified in boarding it unless there is reasonable ground for suspecting that:

(a) the ship is engaged in piracy;

(b) the ship is engaged in the slave trade;

(c) the ship is engaged in unauthorized broadcasting and the flag State of the warship has jurisdiction under article 109;

(d) the ship is without nationality; or

(e) though flying a foreign flag or refusing to show its flag, the ship is, in reality, of the same nationality as the warship.

2. In the cases provided for in paragraph 1, the warship may proceed to verify the ship's right to fly its flag. To this end, it may send a boat under the command of an officer to the suspected ship. If suspicion remains after the documents have been checked, it may proceed to a further examination on board the ship, which must be carried out with all possible consideration.

3.   If the suspicions prove to be unfounded, and provided that the ship boarded has not committed any act justifying them, it shall be compensated for any loss or damage that may have been sustained.

4.   These provisions apply *mutatis mutandis* to military aircraft.

5.   These provisions also apply to any other duly authorized ships or aircraft clearly marked and identifiable as being on government service.

Article 111

Right of hot pursuit

1.   The hot pursuit of a foreign ship may be undertaken when the competent authorities of the coastal State have good reason to believe that the ship has violated the laws and regulations of that State. Such pursuit must be commenced when the foreign ship or one of its boats is within the internal waters, the archipelagic waters, the territorial sea or the contiguous zone of the pursuing State, and may only be continued outside the territorial sea or the contiguous zone if the pursuit has not been interrupted. It is not necessary that, at the time when the foreign ship within the territorial sea or the contiguous zone receives the order to stop, the ship giving the order should likewise be within the territorial sea or the contiguous zone. If the foreign ship is within a contiguous zone, as defined in article 33, the pursuit may only be undertaken if there has been a violation of the rights for the protection of which the zone was established.

2.   The right of hot pursuit shall apply *mutatis mutandis* to violations in the exclusive economic zone or on the continental shelf, including safety zones around continental shelf installations, of the laws and regulations of the coastal State applicable in accordance with this Convention to the exclusive economic zone or the continental shelf, including such safety zones.

3.   The right of hot pursuit ceases as soon as the ship pursued enters the territorial sea of its own State or of a third State.

4.   Hot pursuit is not deemed to have begun unless the pursuing ship has satisfied itself by such practicable means as may be available that the ship pursued or one of its boats or other craft working as a team and using the ship pursued as a mother ship is within the limits of the territorial sea, or, as the case may be, within the contiguous zone or the exclusive economic zone or above the continental shelf. The pursuit may only be commenced after a visual or auditory signal to stop has been given at a distance which enables it to be seen or heard by the foreign ship.

5.   The right of hot pursuit may be exercised only by warships or military aircraft, or other ships or aircraft clearly marked and identifiable as being on government service and authorized to that effect.

6.   Where hot pursuit is effected by an aircraft:

(a) the provisions of paragraphs 1 to 4 shall apply *mutatis mutandis;*

(b) the aircraft giving the order to stop must itself actively pursue the ship until a ship or another aircraft of the coastal State, summoned by the aircraft, arrives to take over the pursuit, unless the aircraft is itself able to arrest the ship. It does not suffice to justify an arrest outside the territorial sea that the ship was merely sighted by the aircraft as an offender or suspected offender, if it was not both ordered to stop and pursued by the aircraft itself or other aircraft or ships which continue the pursuit without interruption.

7.   The release of a ship arrested within the jurisdiction of a State and escorted to a port of that State for the purposes of an inquiry before the competent authorities may not be claimed solely on the ground that the ship, in the course of its voyage, was

escorted across a portion of the exclusive economic zone or the high seas, if the circumstances rendered this necessary.

8. Where a ship has been stopped or arrested outside the territorial sea in circumstances which do not justify the exercise of the right of hot pursuit, it shall be compensated for any loss or damage that may have been thereby sustained.

Article 112

Right to lay submarine cables and pipelines

1. All States are entitled to lay submarine cables and pipelines on the bed of the high seas beyond the continental shelf.

2. Article 79, paragraph 5, applies to such cables and pipelines.

Article 113

Breaking or injury of a submarine cable or pipeline

* * *

Article 114

Breaking or injury by owners of a submarine cable or pipeline of another submarine cable or pipeline

* * *

Article 115

Indemnity for loss incurred in avoiding injury to a submarine cable or pipeline

* * *

SECTION 2. CONSERVATION AND MANAGEMENT OF THE LIVING RESOURCES OF THE HIGH SEAS

Article 116

Right to fish on the high seas

All States have the right for their nationals to engage in fishing on the high seas subject to:

(a) their treaty obligations;

(b) the rights and duties as well as the interests of coastal States provided for, *inter alia,* in article 63, paragraph 2, and articles 64 to 67; and

(c) the provisions of this section.

Article 117

Duty of States to adopt with respect to their nationals measures for the conservation of the living resources of the high seas

All States have the duty to take, or to cooperate with other States in taking, such measures for their respective nationals as may be necessary for the conservation of the living resources of the high seas.

Article 118

Co-operation of States in the conservation and management of living resources

States shall co-operate with each other in the conservation and management of living resources in the areas of the high seas. States whose nationals exploit identical living resources, or different living resources in the same area, shall enter into negotiations with a view to taking the measures necessary for the conservation of the living resources concerned. They shall, as appropriate, co-operate to establish subregional or regional fisheries organizations to this end.

Article 119

Conservation of the living resources of the high seas

1. In determining the allowable catch and establishing other conservation measures for the living resources in the high seas, States shall:

(a) take measures which are designed, on the best scientific evidence available to the States concerned, to maintain or restore populations of harvested species at levels which can produce the maximum sustainable yield, as qualified by relevant environmental and economic factors, including the special requirements of developing States, and taking into account fishing patterns, the interdependence of stocks and any generally recommended international minimum standards, whether subregional, regional or global;

(b) take into consideration the effects on species associated with or dependent upon harvested species with a view to maintaining or restoring populations of such associated or dependent species above levels at which their reproduction may become seriously threatened.

2. Available scientific information, catch and fishing effort statistics, and other data relevant to the conservation of fish stocks shall be contributed and exchanged on a regular basis through competent international organizations, whether subregional, regional or global, where appropriate and with participation by all States concerned.

3. States concerned shall ensure that conservation measures and their implementation do not discriminate in form or in fact against the fishermen of any State.

Article 120

Marine mammals

Article 65 also applies to the conservation and management of marine mammals in the high seas.

PART VIII

REGIME OF ISLANDS

Article 121

Régime of islands

1. An island is a naturally formed area of land, surrounded by water, which is above water at high tide.

2. Except as provided for in paragraph 3, the territorial sea, the contiguous zone, the exclusive economic zone and the continental shelf of an island are determined in accordance with the provisions of this Convention applicable to other land territory.

3. Rocks which cannot sustain human habitation or economic life of their own shall have no exclusive economic zone or continental shelf.

PART IX

ENCLOSED OR SEMI–ENCLOSED SEAS

Article 122

Definition

For the purposes of this Convention, "enclosed or semi-enclosed sea" means a gulf, basin or sea surrounded by two or more States and connected to another sea or the ocean by a narrow outlet or consisting entirely or primarily of the territorial seas and exclusive economic zones of two or more coastal States.

Article 123

Co-operation of States bordering enclosed or semi-enclosed seas

States bordering an enclosed or semi-enclosed sea should co-operate with each other in the exercise of their rights and in the performance of their duties under this Convention. * * *

PART X

RIGHT OF ACCESS OF LAND–LOCKED STATES TO AND FROM THE SEA AND FREEDOM OF TRANSIT

Article 124

Use of terms

* * *

Article 125

Right of access to and from the sea and freedom of transit

1. Land-locked States shall have the right of access to and from the sea for the purpose of exercising the rights provided for in this Convention including those relating to the freedom of the high seas and the common heritage of mankind. To this end, land-locked States shall enjoy freedom of transit through the territory of transit States by all means of transport.

* * *

Article 126

Exclusion of application of the most-favoured-nation clause

* * *

Article 127

Customs duties, taxes and other charges

* * *

Article 128

Free zones and other customs facilities

* * *

Article 129

Co-operation in the construction and improvement of means of transport

* * *

Article 130

Measures to avoid or eliminate delays or other difficulties of a technical nature in traffic in transit

* * *

Article 131

Equal treatment in maritime ports

* * *

Article 132

Grant of greater transit facilities

* * *

PART XI

THE AREA

SECTION 1. GENERAL PROVISIONS

Article 133

Use of terms

For the purposes of this Part:

(a) "resources" means all solid, liquid or gaseous mineral resources in situ in the Area at or beneath the sea-bed, including polymetallic nodules;

(b) resources, when recovered from the Area, are referred to as "minerals".

Article 134

Scope of this Part

1. This Part applies to the Area.

2. Activities in the Area shall be governed by the provisions of this Part.

* * *

Article 135

Legal status of the superjacent waters and air space

* * *

SECTION 2. PRINCIPLES GOVERNING THE AREA

Article 136

Common heritage of mankind

The Area and its resources are the common heritage of mankind.

Article 137

Legal status of the Area and its resources

1. No State shall claim or exercise sovereignty or sovereign rights over any part of the Area or its resources, nor shall any State or natural or juridical person appropriate any part thereof. No such claim or exercise of sovereignty or sovereign rights nor such appropriation shall be recognized.

2. All rights in the resources of the Area are vested in mankind as a whole, on whose behalf the Authority shall act. These resources are not subject to alienation. The minerals recovered from the Area, however, may only be alienated in accordance with this Part and the rules, regulations and procedures of the Authority.

3. No State or natural or juridical person shall claim, acquire or exercise rights with respect to the minerals recovered from the Area except in accordance with this Part. Otherwise, no such claim, acquisition or exercise of such rights shall be recognized.

Article 138

General conduct of States in relation to the Area

The general conduct of States in relation to the Area shall be in accordance with the provisions of this Part, the principles embodied in the Charter of the United Nations and other rules of international law in the interests of maintaining peace and security and promoting international co-operation and mutual understanding.

Article 139

Responsibility to ensure compliance and liability for damage

1. States Parties shall have the responsibility to ensure that activities in the Area, whether carried out by States Parties, or state enterprises or natural or juridical persons which possess the nationality of States Parties or are effectively controlled by them or their nationals, shall be carried out in conformity with this Part. The same responsibility applies to international organizations for activities in the Area carried out by such organizations.

* * *

Article 140

Benefit of mankind

1. Activities in the Area shall, as specifically provided for in this Part, be carried out for the benefit of mankind as a whole, irrespective of the geographical location of States, whether coastal or land-locked, and taking into particular consideration the interests and needs of developing States and of peoples who have not attained full independence or other self-governing status recognized by the United Nations in accordance with General Assembly resolution 1514 (XV) and other relevant General Assembly resolutions.

2. The Authority shall provide for the equitable sharing of financial and other economic benefits derived from activities in the Area through any appropriate mechanism, on a non-discriminatory basis, in accordance with article 160, paragraph 2(f)(i).

Article 141

Use of the Area exclusively for peaceful purposes

The Area shall be open to use exclusively for peaceful purposes by all States, whether coastal or land-locked, without discrimination and without prejudice to the other provisions of this Part.

Article 142

Rights and legitimate interests of coastal States

1. Activities in the Area, with respect to resource deposits in the Area which lie across limits of national jurisdiction, shall be conducted with due regard to the rights and legitimate interests of any coastal State across whose jurisdiction such deposits lie.

* * *

Article 143

Marine scientific research

1. Marine scientific research in the Area shall be carried out exclusively for peaceful purposes and for the benefit of mankind as a whole, in accordance with Part XIII.

* * *

Article 144

Transfer of technology

1. The Authority shall take measures in accordance with this Convention:

(a) to acquire technology and scientific knowledge relating to activities in the Area; and

(b) to promote and encourage the transfer to developing States of such technology and scientific knowledge so that all States Parties benefit therefrom.

* * *

Article 145

Protection of the marine environment

Necessary measures shall be taken in accordance with this Convention with respect to activities in the Area to ensure effective protection for the marine environment from harmful effects which may arise from such activities. To this end the Authority shall adopt appropriate rules, regulations and procedures for *inter alia:*

(a) the prevention, reduction and control of pollution and other hazards to the marine environment, including the coastline, and of interference with the ecological balance of the marine environment, particular attention being paid to the need for protection from harmful effects of such activities as drilling, dredging, excavation, disposal of waste, construction and operation or maintenance of installations, pipelines and other devices related to such activities;

(b) the protection and conservation of the natural resources of the Area and the prevention of damage to the flora and fauna of the marine environment.

Article 146

Protection of human life

With respect to activities in the Area, necessary measures shall be taken to ensure effective protection of human life. * * *

Article 147

Accommodation of activities in the Area and in the marine environment

1. Activities in the Area shall be carried out with reasonable regard for other activities in the marine environment.

* * *

Article 148

Participation of developing States in activities in the Area

The effective participation of developing States in activities in the Area shall be promoted as specifically provided for in this Part, having due regard to their special interests and needs, and in particular to the special need of the land-locked and geographically disadvantaged among them to overcome obstacles arising from their disadvantaged location, including remoteness from the Area and difficulty of access to and from it.

Article 149

Archaeological and historical objects

All objects of an archaeological and historical nature found in the Area shall be preserved or disposed of for the benefit of mankind as a whole, particular regard being paid to the preferential rights of the State or country of origin, or the State of cultural origin, or the State of historical and archaeological origin.

SECTION 3. DEVELOPMENT OF RESOURCES OF THE AREA

Article 150

Policies relating to activities in the Area

Activities in the Area shall, as specifically provided for in this Part, be carried out in such a manner as to foster healthy development of the world economy and balanced growth of international trade, and to promote international co-operation for the over-all development of all countries, especially developing States, and with a view to ensuring:

(a) the development of the resources of the Area;

(b) orderly, safe and rational management of the resources of the Area, including the efficient conduct of activities in the Area and, in accordance with sound principles of conservation, the avoidance of unnecessary waste;

(c) the expansion of opportunities for participation in such activities consistent in particular with articles 144 and 148;

(d) participation in revenues by the Authority and the transfer of technology to the Enterprise and developing States as provided for in this Convention;

(e) increased availability of the minerals derived from the Area as needed in conjunction with minerals derived from other sources, to ensure supplies to consumers of such minerals;

(f) the promotion of just and stable prices remunerative to producers and fair to consumers for minerals derived both from the Area and from other sources, and the promotion of long-term equilibrium between supply and demand;

(g) the enhancement of opportunities for all States Parties, irrespective of their social and economic systems or geographical location, to participate in the development of the resources of the Area and the prevention of monopolization of activities in the Area;

(h) the protection of developing countries from adverse effects on their economies or on their export earnings resulting from a reduction in the price of an affected mineral, or in the volume of exports of that mineral, to the extent that such reduction is caused by activities in the Area, as provided in article 151;

(i) the development of the common heritage for the benefit of mankind as a whole; and

(j) conditions of access to markets for the imports of minerals produced from the resources of the Area and for imports of commodities produced from such minerals shall not be more favourable than the most favourable applied to imports from other sources.

Article 151

Production policies

* * *

Article 152

Exercise of powers and functions by the Authority

* * *

Article 153

System of exploration and exploitation

1.   Activities in the Area shall be organized, carried out and controlled by the Authority on behalf of mankind as a whole in accordance with this article as well as other relevant provisions of this Part and the relevant Annexes, and the rules, regulations and procedures of the Authority.

2.   Activities in the Area shall be carried out as prescribed in paragraph 3:

(a) by the Enterprise, and

(b) in association with the Authority by States Parties, or state enterprises or natural or juridical persons which possess the nationality of States Parties or are effectively controlled by them or their nationals, when sponsored by such States, or any group of the foregoing which meets the requirements provided in this Part and in Annex III.

3.   Activities in the Area shall be carried out in accordance with a formal written plan of work drawn up in accordance with Annex III and approved by the Council after review by the Legal and Technical Commission. In the case of activities in the Area carried out as authorized by the Authority by the entities specified in paragraph 2(b), the plan of work shall, in accordance with Annex III, article 3, be in the form of a contract. Such contracts may provide for joint arrangements in accordance with Annex III, article 11.

* * *

Article 154

Periodic review

* * *

Article 155

The Review Conference

* * *

SECTION 4.   THE AUTHORITY

SUBSECTION A.   GENERAL PROVISIONS

Article 156

Establishment of the Authority

1.   There is hereby established the International Sea–Bed Authority, which shall function in accordance with this Part.

2.   All States Parties are ipso facto members of the Authority.

3.   Observers at the Third United Nations Conference on the Law of the Sea who have signed the Final Act and who are not referred to in article 305, paragraph 1(c), (d), (e) or (f), shall have the right to participate in the Authority as observers, in accordance with its rules, regulations and procedures.

4.   The seat of the Authority shall be in Jamaica.

5.   The Authority may establish such regional centres or offices as it deems necessary for the exercise of its functions.

Article 157

Nature and fundamental principles of the Authority

1. The Authority is the organization through which States Parties shall, in accordance with this Part, organize and control activities in the Area, particularly with a view to administering the resources of the Area.

2. The powers and functions of the Authority shall be those expressly conferred upon it by this Convention. The Authority shall have such incidental powers, consistent with this Convention, as are implicit in and necessary for the exercise of those powers and functions with respect to activities in the Area.

3. The Authority is based on the principle of the sovereign equality of all its members.

4. All members of the Authority shall fulfil in good faith the obligations assumed by them in accordance with this Part in order to ensure to all of them the rights and benefits resulting from membership.

Article 158

Organs of the Authority

1. There are hereby established, as the principal organs of the Authority, an Assembly, a Council and a Secretariat.

2. There is hereby established the Enterprise, the organ through which the Authority shall carry out the functions referred to in article 170, paragraph 1.

3. Such subsidiary organs as may be found necessary may be established in accordance with this Part.

4. Each principal organ of the Authority and the Enterprise shall be responsible for exercising those powers and functions which are conferred upon it. In exercising such powers and functions each organ shall avoid taking any action which may derogate from or impede the exercise of specific powers and functions conferred upon another organ.

SUBSECTION B. THE ASSEMBLY

Article 159

Composition, procedure and voting

* * *

Article 160

Powers and functions

1. The Assembly, as the sole organ of the Authority consisting of all the members, shall be considered the supreme organ of the Authority to which the other principal organs shall be accountable as specifically provided for in this Convention. The Assembly shall have the power to establish general policies in conformity with the relevant provisions of this Convention on any question or matter within the competence of the Authority.

* * *

SUBSECTION C. THE COUNCIL

Article 161

Composition, procedure and voting

* * *

Article 162

Powers and functions

1. The Council is the executive organ of the Authority. The Council shall have the power to establish, in conformity with this Convention and the general policies established by the Assembly, the specific policies to be pursued by the Authority on any question or matter within the competence of the Authority.

* * *

Article 163

Organs of the Council

1. There are hereby established the following organs of the Council:

(a) an Economic Planning Commission;

(b) a Legal and Technical Commission.

* * *

Article 164

The Economic Planning Commission

1. Members of the Economic Planning Commission shall have appropriate qualifications such as those relevant to mining, management of mineral resource activities, international trade or international economics. The Council shall endeavour to ensure that the membership of the Commission reflects all appropriate qualifications. The Commission shall include at least two members from developing States whose exports of the categories of minerals to be derived from the Area have a substantial bearing upon their economies.

* * *

Article 165

The Legal and Technical Commission

1. Members of the Legal and Technical Commission shall have appropriate qualifications such as those relevant to exploration for and exploitation and processing of mineral resources, oceanology, protection of the marine environment, or economic or legal matters relating to ocean mining and related fields of expertise. The Council shall endeavour to ensure that the membership of the Commission reflects all appropriate qualifications.

* * *

SUBSECTION D. THE SECRETARIAT

Article 166

The Secretariat

1. The Secretariat of the Authority shall comprise a Secretary–General and such staff as the Authority may require.

2. The Secretary–General shall be elected for four years by the Assembly from among the candidates proposed by the Council and may be re-elected.

3. The Secretary–General shall be the chief administrative officer of the Authority, and shall act in that capacity in all meetings of the Assembly, of the Council and of any subsidiary organ, and shall perform such other administrative functions as are entrusted to the Secretary–General by these organs.

4. The Secretary–General shall make an annual report to the Assembly on the work of the Authority.

Article 167

The staff of the Authority

* * *

Article 168

International character of the Secretariat

1. In the performance of their duties the Secretary–General and the staff shall not seek or receive instructions from any government or from any other source external to the Authority. They shall refrain from any action which might reflect on their position as international officials responsible only to the Authority. * * *

* * *

Article 169

Consultation and co-operation with international and non-governmental organizations

* * *

SUBSECTION E.   THE ENTERPRISE

Article 170

The Enterprise

1. The Enterprise shall be the organ of the Authority which shall carry out activities in the Area directly, pursuant to article 153, paragraph 2(a), as well as the transporting, processing and marketing of minerals recovered from the Area.

2. The Enterprise shall, within the framework of the international legal personality of the Authority, have such legal capacity as is provided for in the Statute set forth in Annex IV. The Enterprise shall act in accordance with this Convention and the rules, regulations and procedures of the Authority, as well as the general policies established by the Assembly, and shall be subject to the directives and control of the Council.

* * *

SUBSECTION F.   FINANCIAL ARRANGEMENTS OF THE AUTHORITY

Article 171

Funds of the Authority

* * *

Article 172

Annual budget of the Authority

* * *

Article 173

Expenses of the Authority

* * *

Article 174

Borrowing power of the Authority

* * *

Article 175

Annual audit

* * *

SUBSECTION G.   LEGAL STATUS, PRIVILEGES AND IMMUNITIES

Article 176

Legal status

The Authority shall have international legal personality and such legal capacity as may be necessary for the exercise of its functions and the fulfilment of its purposes.

Article 177

Privileges and immunities

* * *

Article 178

Immunity from legal process

* * *

Article 179

Immunity from search and any form of seizure

* * *

Article 180

Exemption from restrictions, regulations, controls and moratoria

* * *

Article 181

Archives and official communications of the Authority

* * *

Article 182

Privileges and immunities of certain persons connected with the Authority

* * *

Article 183

Exemption from taxes and customs duties

* * *

SUBSECTION H.   SUSPENSION OF THE EXERCISE
OF RIGHTS AND PRIVILEGES OF MEMBERS

Article 184

Suspension of the exercise of voting rights

A State Party which is in arrears in the payment of its financial contributions to the Authority shall have no vote if the amount of its arrears equals or exceeds the amount of the contribution due from it for the preceding two full years. The Assembly may, nevertheless, permit such a member to vote if it is satisfied that the failure to pay is due to conditions beyond the control of the member.

Article 185

Suspension of exercise of rights and privileges of membership

1.   A State Party which has grossly and persistently violated the provisions of this Part may be suspended from the exercise of the rights and privileges of membership by the Assembly upon the recommendation of the Council.

2.   No action may be taken under paragraph 1 until the Sea–Bed Disputes Chamber has found that a State Party has grossly and persistently violated the provisions of this Part.

SECTION 5.   SETTLEMENT OF DISPUTES AND ADVISORY OPINIONS

Article 186

Sea–Bed Disputes Chamber of the International Tribunal for the Law of the Sea

The establishment of the Sea–Bed Disputes Chamber and the manner in which it shall exercise its jurisdiction shall be governed by the provisions of this section, of Part XV and of Annex VI.

Article 187

Jurisdiction of the Sea–Bed Disputes Chamber

* * *

Article 188

Submission of disputes to a special chamber of the International Tribunal for the Law of the Sea or an ad hoc chamber of the Sea–Bed Disputes Chamber or to binding commercial arbitration

* * *

Article 189

Limitation on jurisdiction with regard to decisions of the Authority

* * *

Article 190

Participation and appearance of sponsoring States Parties in proceedings

* * *

Article 191

Advisory opinions

The Sea–Bed Disputes Chamber shall give advisory opinions at the request of the Assembly or the Council on legal questions arising within the scope of their activities. Such opinions shall be given as a matter of urgency.

PART XII

PROTECTION AND PRESERVATION OF THE MARINE ENVIRONMENT

SECTION 1.   GENERAL PROVISIONS

Article 192

General obligation

States have the obligation to protect and preserve the marine environment.

Article 193

Sovereign right of States to exploit their natural resources

States have the sovereign right to exploit their natural resources pursuant to their environmental policies and in accordance with their duty to protect and preserve the marine environment.

Article 194

Measures to prevent, reduce and control pollution of the marine environment

1.   States shall take, individually or jointly as appropriate, all measures consistent with this Convention that are necessary to prevent, reduce and control pollution of the marine environment from any source, using for this purpose the best practicable means at their disposal and in accordance with their capabilities, and they shall endeavour to harmonize their policies in this connection.

2.   States shall take all measures necessary to ensure that activities under their jurisdiction or control are so conducted as not to cause damage by pollution to other States and their environment, and that pollution arising from incidents or activities under their jurisdiction or control does not spread beyond the areas where they exercise sovereign rights in accordance with this Convention.

3.   The measures taken pursuant to this Part shall deal with all sources of pollution of the marine environment. These measures shall include, *inter alia,* those designed to minimize to the fullest possible extent:

(a) the release of toxic, harmful or noxious substances, especially those which are persistent, from land-based sources, from or through the atmosphere or by dumping;

(b) pollution from vessels, in particular measures for preventing accidents and dealing with emergencies, ensuring the safety of operations at sea, preventing intentional and unintentional discharges, and regulating the design, construction, equipment, operation and manning of vessels;

(c) pollution from installations and devices used in exploration or exploitation of the natural resources of the sea-bed and subsoil, in particular measures for preventing accidents and dealing with emergencies, ensuring the safety of operations at sea, and regulating the design, construction, equipment, operation and manning of such installations or devices;

(d) pollution from other installations and devices operating in the marine environment, in particular measures for preventing accidents and dealing with emergencies, ensuring the safety of operations at sea, and regulating the design, construction, equipment, operation and manning of such installations or devices.

4.   In taking measures to prevent, reduce or control pollution of the marine environment, States shall refrain from unjustifiable interference with activities carried out by other States in the exercise of their rights and in pursuance of their duties in conformity with this Convention.

5. The measures taken in accordance with this Part shall include those necessary to protect and preserve rare or fragile ecosystems as well as the habitat of depleted, threatened or endangered species and other forms of marine life.

Article 195

Duty not to transfer damage or hazards or transform
one type of pollution into another

* * *

Article 196

Use of technologies or introduction of alien or new species

1. States shall take all measures necessary to prevent, reduce and control pollution of the marine environment resulting from the use of technologies under their jurisdiction or control, or the intentional or accidental introduction of species, alien or new, to a particular part of the marine environment, which may cause significant and harmful changes thereto.

2. This article does not affect the application of this Convention regarding the prevention, reduction and control of pollution of the marine environment.

SECTION 2. GLOBAL AND REGIONAL CO–OPERATION

Article 197

Co-operation on a global or regional basis

States shall co-operate on a global basis and, as appropriate, on a regional basis, directly or through competent international organizations, in formulating and elaborating international rules, standards and recommended practices and procedures consistent with this Convention, for the protection and preservation of the marine environment, taking into account characteristic regional features.

Article 198

Notification of imminent or actual damage

When a State becomes aware of cases in which the marine environment is in imminent danger of being damaged or has been damaged by pollution, it shall immediately notify other States it deems likely to be affected by such damage, as well as the competent international organizations.

Article 199

Contingency plans against pollution

In the cases referred to in article 198, States in the area affected, in accordance with their capabilities, and the competent international organizations shall co-operate, to the extent possible, in eliminating the effects of pollution and preventing or minimizing the damage. To this end, States shall jointly develop and promote contingency plans for responding to pollution incidents in the marine environment.

Article 200

Studies, research programmes and exchange of information and data

States shall co-operate, directly or through competent international organizations, for the purpose of promoting studies, undertaking programmes of scientific research and encouraging the exchange of information and data acquired about pollution of the marine environment. They shall endeavour to participate actively in regional and global programmes to acquire knowledge for the assessment of the nature and extent of pollution, exposure to it, and its pathways, risks and remedies.

Article 201

Scientific criteria for regulations

In the light of the information and data acquired pursuant to article 200, States shall co-operate, directly or through competent international organizations, in establishing appropriate scientific criteria for the formulation and elaboration of rules, standards and recommended practices and procedures for the prevention, reduction and control of pollution of the marine environment.

SECTION 3. TECHNICAL ASSISTANCE

Article 202

Scientific and technical assistance to developing States

States shall, directly or through competent international organizations:

(a) promote programmes of scientific, educational, technical and other assistance to developing States for the protection and preservation of the marine environment and the prevention, reduction and control of marine pollution. Such assistance shall include, *inter alia:*

(i) training of their scientific and technical personnel;

(ii) facilitating their participation in relevant international programmes;

(iii) supplying them with necessary equipment and facilities;

(iv) enhancing their capacity to manufacture such equipment;

(v) advice on and developing facilities for research, monitoring, educational and other programmes;

(b) provide appropriate assistance, especially to developing States, for the minimization of the effects of major incidents which may cause serious pollution of the marine environment;

(c) provide appropriate assistance, especially to developing States, concerning the preparation of environmental assessments.

Article 203

Preferential treatment for developing States

Developing States shall, for the purposes of prevention, reduction and control of pollution of the marine environment or minimization of its effects, be granted preference by international organizations in:

(a) the allocation of appropriate funds and technical assistance; and

(b) the utilization of their specialized services.

SECTION 4. MONITORING AND ENVIRONMENTAL ASSESSMENT

Article 204

Monitoring of the risks or effects of pollution

1. States shall, consistent with the rights of other States, endeavour, as far as practicable, directly or through the competent international organizations, to observe, measure, evaluate and analyse, by recognized scientific methods, the risks or effects of pollution of the marine environment.

2. In particular, States shall keep under surveillance the effects of any activities which they permit or in which they engage in order to determine whether these activities are likely to pollute the marine environment.

Article 205

Publication of reports

States shall publish reports of the results obtained pursuant to article 204 or provide such reports at appropriate intervals to the competent international organizations, which should make them available to all States.

Article 206

Assessment of potential effects of activities

When States have reasonable grounds for believing that planned activities under their jurisdiction or control may cause substantial pollution of or significant and harmful changes to the marine environment, they shall, as far as practicable, assess the potential effects of such activities on the marine environment and shall communicate reports of the results of such assessments in the manner provided in article 205.

SECTION 5. INTERNATIONAL RULES AND NATIONAL LEGISLATION TO PREVENT, REDUCE AND CONTROL POLLUTION OF THE MARINE ENVIRONMENT

Article 207

Pollution from land-based sources

1. States shall adopt laws and regulations to prevent, reduce and control pollution of the marine environment from land-based sources, including rivers, estuaries, pipelines and outfall structures, taking into account internationally agreed rules, standards and recommended practices and procedures.

2. States shall take other measures as may be necessary to prevent, reduce and control such pollution.

3. States shall endeavour to harmonize their policies in this connection at the appropriate regional level.

4. States, acting especially through competent international organizations or diplomatic conference, shall endeavour to establish global and regional rules, standards and recommended practices and procedures to prevent, reduce and control pollution of the marine environment from land-based sources, taking into account characteristic regional features, the economic capacity of developing States and their need for economic development. Such rules, standards and recommended practices and procedures shall be re-examined from time to time as necessary.

5. Laws, regulations, measures, rules, standards and recommended practices and procedures referred to in paragraphs 1, 2 and 4 shall include those designed to minimize, to the fullest extent possible, the release of toxic, harmful or noxious substances, especially those which are persistent, into the marine environment.

Article 208

Pollution from sea-bed activities subject to national jurisdiction

[This article is in all essential respects identical to article 207, *supra*.]

Article 209

Pollution from activities in the Area

1. International rules, regulations and procedures shall be established in accordance with Part XI to prevent, reduce and control pollution of the marine environment

from activities in the Area. Such rules, regulations and procedures shall be re-examined from time to time as necessary.

2. Subject to the relevant provisions of this section, States shall adopt laws and regulations to prevent, reduce and control pollution of the marine environment from activities in the Area undertaken by vessels, installations, structures and other devices flying their flag or of their registry or operating under their authority, as the case may be. The requirements of such laws and regulations shall be no less effective than the international rules, regulations and procedures referred to in paragraph 1.

Article 210

Pollution by dumping

1. States shall adopt laws and regulations to prevent, reduce and control pollution of the marine environment by dumping.

2. States shall take other measures as may be necessary to prevent, reduce and control such pollution.

3. Such laws, regulations and measures shall ensure that dumping is not carried out without the permission of the competent authorities of States.

4. States, acting especially through competent international organizations or diplomatic conference, shall endeavour to establish global and regional rules, standards and recommended practices and procedures to prevent, reduce and control such pollution. Such rules, standards and recommended practices and procedures shall be re-examined from time to time as necessary.

5. Dumping within the territorial sea and the exclusive economic zone or onto the continental shelf shall not be carried out without the express prior approval of the coastal State, which has the right to permit, regulate and control such dumping after due consideration of the matter with other States which by reason of their geographical situation may be adversely affected thereby.

6. National laws, regulations and measures shall be no less effective in preventing, reducing and controlling such pollution than the global rules and standards.

Article 211

Pollution from vessels

1. States, acting through the competent international organization or general diplomatic conference, shall establish international rules and standards to prevent, reduce and control pollution of the marine environment from vessels and promote the adoption, in the same manner, wherever appropriate, of routing systems designed to minimize the threat of accidents which might cause pollution of the marine environment, including the coastline, and pollution damage to the related interests of coastal States. Such rules and standards shall, in the same manner, be re-examined from time to time as necessary.

2. States shall adopt laws and regulations for the prevention, reduction and control of pollution of the marine environment from vessels flying their flag or of their registry. Such laws and regulations shall at least have the same effect as that of generally accepted international rules and standards established through the competent international organization or general diplomatic conference.

3. States which establish particular requirements for the prevention, reduction and control of pollution of the marine environment as a condition for the entry of foreign vessels into their ports or internal waters or for a call at their off-shore terminals shall give due publicity to such requirements and shall communicate them to the competent international organization. Whenever such requirements are established in identical form by two or more coastal States in an endeavour to harmonize policy,

the communication shall indicate which States are participating in such co-operative arrangements. Every State shall require the master of a vessel flying its flag or of its registry, when navigating within the territorial sea of a State participating in such co-operative arrangements, to furnish, upon the request of that State, information as to whether it is proceeding to a State of the same region participating in such co-operative arrangements and, if so, to indicate whether it complies with the port entry requirements of that State. This article is without prejudice to the continued exercise by a vessel of its right of innocent passage or to the application of article 25, paragraph 2.

4. Coastal States may, in the exercise of their sovereignty within their territorial sea, adopt laws and regulations for the prevention, reduction and control of marine pollution from foreign vessels, including vessels exercising the right of innocent passage. Such laws and regulations shall, in accordance with Part II, section 3, not hamper innocent passage of foreign vessels.

5. Coastal States, for the purpose of enforcement as provided for in section 6, may in respect of their exclusive economic zones adopt laws and regulations for the prevention, reduction and control of pollution from vessels conforming to and giving effect to generally accepted international rules and standards established through the competent international organization or general diplomatic conference.

6. (a) Where the international rules and standards referred to in paragraph 1 are inadequate to meet special circumstances and coastal States have reasonable grounds for believing that a particular, clearly defined area of their respective exclusive economic zones is an area where the adoption of special mandatory measures for the prevention of pollution from vessels is required for recognized technical reasons in relation to its oceanographical and ecological conditions, as well as its utilization or the protection of its resources and the particular character of its traffic, the coastal States, after appropriate consultations through the competent international organization with any other States concerned, may, for that area, direct a communication to that organization, submitting scientific and technical evidence in support and information on necessary reception facilities. Within 12 months after receiving such a communication, the organization shall determine whether the conditions in that area correspond to the requirements set out above. If the organization so determines, the coastal States may, for that area, adopt laws and regulations for the prevention, reduction and control of pollution from vessels implementing such international rules and standards or navigational practices as are made applicable, through the organization, for special areas. These laws and regulations shall not become applicable to foreign vessels until 15 months after the submission of the communication to the organization.

(b) The coastal States shall publish the limits of any such particular, clearly defined area.

(c) If the coastal States intend to adopt additional laws and regulations for the same area for the prevention, reduction and control of pollution from vessels, they shall, when submitting the aforesaid communication, at the same time notify the organization thereof. Such additional laws and regulations may relate to discharges or navigational practices but shall not require foreign vessels to observe design, construction, manning or equipment standards other than generally accepted international rules and standards; they shall become applicable to foreign vessels 15 months after the submission of the communication to the organization, provided that the organization agrees within 12 months after the submission of the communication.

7. The international rules and standards referred to in this article should include *inter alia* those relating to prompt notification to coastal States, whose coastline or related interests may be affected by incidents, including maritime casualties, which involve discharges or probability of discharges.

Article 212

Pollution from or through the atmosphere

1. States shall adopt laws and regulations to prevent, reduce and control pollution of the marine environment from or through the atmosphere, applicable to the air space under their sovereignty and to vessels flying their flag or vessels or aircraft of their registry, taking into account internationally agreed rules, standards and recommended practices and procedures and the safety of air navigation.

2. States shall take other measures as may be necessary to prevent, reduce and control such pollution.

3. States, acting especially through competent international organizations or diplomatic conference, shall endeavour to establish global and regional rules, standards and recommended practices and procedures to prevent, reduce and control such pollution.

SECTION 6. ENFORCEMENT

Article 213

Enforcement with respect to pollution from land-based sources

States shall enforce their laws and regulations adopted in accordance with article 207 and shall adopt laws and regulations and take other measures necessary to implement applicable international rules and standards established through competent international organizations or diplomatic conference to prevent, reduce and control pollution of the marine environment from land-based sources.

Article 214

Enforcement with respect to pollution from sea-bed activities

States shall enforce their laws and regulations adopted in accordance with article 208 and shall adopt laws and regulations and take other measures necessary to implement applicable international rules and standards established through competent international organizations or diplomatic conference to prevent, reduce and control pollution of the marine environment arising from or in connection with sea-bed activities subject to their jurisdiction and from artificial islands, installations and structures under their jurisdiction, pursuant to articles 60 and 80.

Article 215

Enforcement with respect to pollution from activities in the Area

Enforcement of international rules, regulations and procedures established in accordance with Part XI to prevent, reduce and control pollution of the marine environment from activities in the Area shall be governed by that Part.

Article 216

Enforcement with respect to pollution by dumping

1. Laws and regulations adopted in accordance with this Convention and applicable international rules and standards established through competent international organizations or diplomatic conference for the prevention, reduction and control of pollution of the marine environment by dumping shall be enforced:

(a) by the coastal State with regard to dumping within its territorial sea or its exclusive economic zone or onto its continental shelf;

(b) by the flag State with regard to vessels flying its flag or vessels or aircraft of its registry;

(c) by any State with regard to acts of loading of wastes or other matter occurring within its territory or at its off-shore terminals.

2. No State shall be obliged by virtue of this article to institute proceedings when another State has already instituted proceedings in accordance with this article.

Article 217

Enforcement by flag States

1. States shall ensure compliance by vessels flying their flag or of their registry with applicable international rules and standards, established through the competent international organization or general diplomatic conference, and with their laws and regulations adopted in accordance with this Convention for the prevention, reduction and control of pollution of the marine environment from vessels and shall accordingly adopt laws and regulations and take other measures necessary for their implementation. Flag States shall provide for the effective enforcement of such rules, standards, laws and regulations, irrespective of where a violation occurs.

2. States shall, in particular, take appropriate measures in order to ensure that vessels flying their flag or of their registry are prohibited from sailing, until they can proceed to sea in compliance with the requirements of the international rules and standards referred to in paragraph 1, including requirements in respect of design, construction, equipment and manning of vessels.

3. States shall ensure that vessels flying their flag or of their registry carry on board certificates required by and issued pursuant to international rules and standards referred to in paragraph 1. States shall ensure that vessels flying their flag are periodically inspected in order to verify that such certificates are in conformity with the actual condition of the vessels. These certificates shall be accepted by other States as evidence of the condition of the vessels and shall be regarded as having the same force as certificates issued by them, unless there are clear grounds for believing that the condition of the vessel does not correspond substantially with the particulars of the certificates.

4. If a vessel commits a violation of rules and standards established through the competent international organization or general diplomatic conference, the flag State, without prejudice to articles 218, 220 and 228, shall provide for immediate investigation and where appropriate institute proceedings in respect of the alleged violation irrespective of where the violation occurred or where the pollution caused by such violation has occurred or has been spotted.

5. Flag States conducting an investigation of the violation may request the assistance of any other State whose co-operation could be useful in clarifying the circumstances of the case. States shall endeavour to meet appropriate requests of flag States.

6. States shall, at the written request of any State, investigate any violation alleged to have been committed by vessels flying their flag. If satisfied that sufficient evidence is available to enable proceedings to be brought in respect of the alleged violation, flag States shall without delay institute such proceedings in accordance with their laws.

7. Flag States shall promptly inform the requesting State and the competent international organization of the action taken and its outcome. Such information shall be available to all States.

8. Penalties provided for by the laws and regulations of States for vessels flying their flag shall be adequate in severity to discourage violations wherever they occur.

Article 218

Enforcement by port States

1. When a vessel is voluntarily within a port or at an off-shore terminal of a State, that State may undertake investigations and, where the evidence so warrants, institute proceedings in respect of any discharge from that vessel outside the internal waters, territorial sea or exclusive economic zone of that State in violation of applicable international rules and standards established through the competent international organization or general diplomatic conference.

2. No proceedings pursuant to paragraph 1 shall be instituted in respect of a discharge violation in the internal waters, territorial sea or exclusive economic zone of another State unless requested by that State, the flag State, or a State damaged or threatened by the discharge violation, or unless the violation has caused or is likely to cause pollution in the internal waters, territorial sea or exclusive economic zone of the State instituting the proceedings.

3. When a vessel is voluntarily within a port or at an off-shore terminal of a State, that State shall, as far as practicable, comply with requests from any State for investigation of a discharge violation referred to in paragraph 1, believed to have occurred in, caused, or threatened damage to the internal waters, territorial sea or exclusive economic zone of the requesting State. It shall likewise, as far as practicable, comply with requests from the flag State for investigation of such a violation, irrespective of where the violation occurred.

4. The records of the investigation carried out by a port State pursuant to this article shall be transmitted upon request to the flag State or to the coastal State. Any proceedings instituted by the port State on the basis of such an investigation may, subject to section 7, be suspended at the request of the coastal State when the violation has occurred within its internal waters, territorial sea or exclusive economic zone. The evidence and records of the case, together with any bond or other financial security posted with the authorities of the port State, shall in that event be transmitted to the coastal State. Such transmittal shall preclude the continuation of proceedings in the port State.

Article 219

Measures relating to seaworthiness of vessels to avoid pollution

Subject to section 7, States which, upon request or on their own initiative, have ascertained that a vessel within one of their ports or at one of their off-shore terminals is in violation of applicable international rules and standards relating to seaworthiness of vessels and thereby threatens damage to the marine environment shall, as far as practicable, take administrative measures to prevent the vessel from sailing. Such States may permit the vessel to proceed only to the nearest appropriate repair yard and, upon removal of the causes of the violation, shall permit the vessel to continue immediately.

Article 220

Enforcement by coastal States

1. When a vessel is voluntarily within a port or at an off-shore terminal of a State, that State may, subject to section 7, institute proceedings in respect of any violation of its laws and regulations adopted in accordance with this Convention or applicable international rules and standards for the prevention, reduction and control of pollution from vessels when the violation has occurred within the territorial sea or the exclusive economic zone of that State.

2. Where there are clear grounds for believing that a vessel navigating in the territorial sea of a State has, during its passage therein, violated laws and regulations of that State adopted in accordance with this Convention or applicable international rules and standards for the prevention, reduction and control of pollution from vessels, that State, without prejudice to the application of the relevant provisions of Part II, section 3, may undertake physical inspection of the vessel relating to the violation and may, where the evidence so warrants, institute proceedings, including detention of the vessel, in accordance with its laws, subject to the provisions of section 7.

3. Where there are clear grounds for believing that a vessel navigating in the exclusive economic zone or the territorial sea of a State has, in the exclusive economic zone, committed a violation of applicable international rules and standards for the prevention, reduction and control of pollution from vessels or laws and regulations of that State conforming and giving effect to such rules and standards, that State may require the vessel to give information regarding its identity and port of registry, its last and its next port of call and other relevant information required to establish whether a violation has occurred.

4. States shall adopt laws and regulations and take other measures so that vessels flying their flag comply with requests for information pursuant to paragraph 3.

5. Where there are clear grounds for believing that a vessel navigating in the exclusive economic zone or the territorial sea of a State has, in the exclusive economic zone, committed a violation referred to in paragraph 3 resulting in a substantial discharge causing or threatening significant pollution of the marine environment, that State may undertake physical inspection of the vessel for matters relating to the violation if the vessel has refused to give information or if the information supplied by the vessel is manifestly at variance with the evident factual situation and if the circumstances of the case justify such inspection.

6. Where there is clear objective evidence that a vessel navigating in the exclusive economic zone or the territorial sea of a State has, in the exclusive economic zone, committed a violation referred to in paragraph 3 resulting in a discharge causing major damage or threat of major damage to the coastline or related interests of the coastal State, or to any resources of its territorial sea or exclusive economic zone, that State may, subject to section 7, provided that the evidence so warrants, institute proceedings, including detention of the vessel, in accordance with its laws.

7. Notwithstanding the provisions of paragraph 6, whenever appropriate procedures have been established, either through the competent international organization or as otherwise agreed, whereby compliance with requirements for bonding or other appropriate financial security has been assured, the coastal State if bound by such procedures shall allow the vessel to proceed.

8. The provisions of paragraphs 3, 4, 5, 6 and 7 also apply in respect of national laws and regulations adopted pursuant to article 211, paragraph 6.

Article 221

Measures to avoid pollution arising from maritime casualties

1. Nothing in this Part shall prejudice the right of States, pursuant to international law, both customary and conventional, to take and enforce measures beyond the territorial sea proportionate to the actual or threatened damage to protect their coastline or related interests, including fishing, from pollution or threat of pollution following upon a maritime casualty or acts relating to such a casualty, which may reasonably be expected to result in major harmful consequences.

2. For the purposes of this article, ''maritime casualty'' means a collision of vessels, stranding or other incident of navigation, or other occurrence on board a vessel

or external to it resulting in material damage or imminent threat of material damage to a vessel or cargo.

Article 222

Enforcement with respect to pollution from or through the atmosphere

States shall enforce, within the air space under their sovereignty or with regard to vessels flying their flag or vessels or aircraft of their registry, their laws and regulations adopted in accordance with article 212, paragraph 1, and with other provisions of this Convention and shall adopt laws and regulations and take other measures necessary to implement applicable international rules and standards established through competent international organizations or diplomatic conference to prevent, reduce and control pollution of the marine environment from or through the atmosphere, in conformity with all relevant international rules and standards concerning the safety of air navigation.

SECTION 7. SAFEGUARDS

Article 223

Measures to facilitate proceedings

In proceedings instituted pursuant to this Part, States shall take measures to facilitate the hearing of witnesses and the admission of evidence submitted by authorities of another State, or by the competent international organization, and shall facilitate the attendance at such proceedings of official representatives of the competent international organization, the flag State and any State affected by pollution arising out of any violation. The official representatives attending such proceedings shall have such rights and duties as may be provided under national laws and regulations or international law.

Article 224

Exercise of powers of enforcement

The powers of enforcement against foreign vessels under this Part may only be exercised by officials or by warships, military aircraft, or other ships or aircraft clearly marked and identifiable as being on government service and authorized to that effect.

Article 225

Duty to avoid adverse consequences in the exercise of the powers of enforcement

In the exercise under this Convention of their powers of enforcement against foreign vessels, States shall not endanger the safety of navigation or otherwise create any hazard to a vessel, or bring it to an unsafe port or anchorage, or expose the marine environment to an unreasonable risk.

Article 226

Investigation of foreign vessels

1. (a) States shall not delay a foreign vessel longer than is essential for purposes of the investigations provided for in articles 216, 218 and 220. Any physical inspection of a foreign vessel shall be limited to an examination of such certificates, records or other documents as the vessel is required to carry by generally accepted international rules and standards or of any similar documents which it is carrying; further physical inspection of the vessel may be undertaken only after such an examination and only when:

> (i) there are clear grounds for believing that the condition of the vessel or its equipment does not correspond substantially with the particulars of those documents;

(ii) the contents of such documents are not sufficient to confirm or verify a suspected violation; or

(iii) the vessel is not carrying valid certificates and records.

(b) If the investigation indicates a violation of applicable laws and regulations or international rules and standards for the protection and preservation of the marine environment, release shall be made promptly subject to reasonable procedures such as bonding or other appropriate financial security.

(c) Without prejudice to applicable international rules and standards relating to the seaworthiness of vessels, the release of a vessel may, whenever it would present an unreasonable threat of damage to the marine environment, be refused or made conditional upon proceeding to the nearest appropriate repair yard. Where release has been refused or made conditional, the flag State of the vessel must be promptly notified, and may seek release of the vessel in accordance with Part XV.

2. States shall co-operate to develop procedures for the avoidance of unnecessary physical inspection of vessels at sea.

Article 227

Non-discrimination with respect to foreign vessels

* * *

Article 228

Suspension and restrictions on institution of proceedings

* * *

Article 229

Institution of civil proceedings

Nothing in this Convention affects the institution of civil proceedings in respect of any claim for loss or damage resulting from pollution of the marine environment.

Article 230

Monetary penalties and the observance of recognized rights of the accused

* * *

Article 231

Notification to the flag State and other States concerned

* * *

Article 232

Liability of States arising from enforcement measures

States shall be liable for damage or loss attributable to them arising from measures taken pursuant to section 6 when such measures are unlawful or exceed those reasonably required in the light of available information. States shall provide for recourse in their courts for actions in respect of such damage or loss.

Article 233

Safeguards with respect to straits used for international navigation

* * *

SECTION 8. ICE–COVERED AREAS

Article 234

Ice-covered areas

Coastal States have the right to adopt and enforce non-discriminatory laws and regulations for the prevention, reduction and control of marine pollution from vessels in ice-covered areas within the limits of the exclusive economic zone, where particularly severe climatic conditions and the presence of ice covering such areas for most of the year create obstructions or exceptional hazards to navigation, and pollution of the marine environment could cause major harm to or irreversible disturbance of the ecological balance. Such laws and regulations shall have due regard to navigation and the protection and preservation of the marine environment based on the best available scientific evidence.

SECTION 9. RESPONSIBILITY AND LIABILITY

Article 235

Responsibility and liability

1. States are responsible for the fulfilment of their international obligations concerning the protection and preservation of the marine environment. They shall be liable in accordance with international law.

2. States shall ensure that recourse is available in accordance with their legal systems for prompt and adequate compensation or other relief in respect of damage caused by pollution of the marine environment by natural or juridical persons under their jurisdiction.

3. With the objective of assuring prompt and adequate compensation in respect of all damage caused by pollution of the marine environment, States shall co-operate in the implementation of existing international law and the further development of international law relating to responsibility and liability for the assessment of and compensation for damage and the settlement of related disputes, as well as, where appropriate, development of criteria and procedures for payment of adequate compensation, such as compulsory insurance or compensation funds.

SECTION 10. SOVEREIGN IMMUNITY

Article 236

Sovereign immunity

The provisions of this Convention regarding the protection and preservation of the marine environment do not apply to any warship, naval auxiliary, other vessels or aircraft owned or operated by a State and used, for the time being, only on government non-commercial service. However, each State shall ensure, by the adoption of appropriate measures not impairing operations or operational capabilities of such vessels or aircraft owned or operated by it, that such vessels or aircraft act in a manner consistent, so far as is reasonable and practicable, with this Convention.

SECTION 11. OBLIGATIONS UNDER OTHER CONVENTIONS ON THE PROTECTION AND PRESERVATION OF THE MARINE ENVIRONMENT

Article 237

Obligations under other conventions on the protection and preservation of the marine environment

1. The provisions of this Part are without prejudice to the specific obligations assumed by States under special conventions and agreements concluded previously

which relate to the protection and preservation of the marine environment and to agreements which may be concluded in furtherance of the general principles set forth in this Convention.

2. Specific obligations assumed by States under special conventions, with respect to the protection and preservation of the marine environment, should be carried out in a manner consistent with the general principles and objectives of this Convention.

PART XIII

MARINE SCIENTIFIC RESEARCH

SECTION 1. GENERAL PROVISIONS

Article 238

Right to conduct marine scientific research

All States, irrespective of their geographical location, and competent international organizations have the right to conduct marine scientific research subject to the rights and duties of other States as provided for in this Convention.

Article 239

Right to conduct marine scientific research

States and competent international organizations shall promote and facilitate the development and conduct of marine scientific research in accordance with this Convention.

Article 240

General principles for the conduct of marine scientific research

In the conduct of marine scientific research the following principles shall apply:

(a) marine scientific research shall be conducted exclusively for peaceful purposes;

(b) marine scientific research shall be conducted with appropriate scientific methods and means compatible with this Convention;

(c) marine scientific research shall not unjustifiably interfere with other legitimate uses of the sea compatible with this Convention and shall be duly respected in the course of such uses;

(d) marine scientific research shall be conducted in compliance with all relevant regulations adopted in conformity with this Convention including those for the protection and preservation of the marine environment.

Article 241

Non-recognition of marine scientific research activities as the legal basis for claims

Marine scientific research activities shall not constitute the legal basis for any claim to any part of the marine environment or its resources.

SECTION 2. INTERNATIONAL CO-OPERATION

Article 242

Promotion of international co-operation

* * *

Article 243

Creation of favourable conditions

* * *

Article 244

Publication and dissemination of information and knowledge

* * *

SECTION 3.   CONDUCT AND PROMOTION OF MARINE SCIENTIFIC RESEARCH

Article 245

Marine scientific research in the territorial sea

Coastal States, in the exercise of their sovereignty, have the exclusive right to regulate, authorize and conduct marine scientific research in their territorial sea. Marine scientific research therein shall be conducted only with the express consent of and under the conditions set forth by the coastal State.

Article 246

Marine scientific research in the exclusive economic zone and on the continental shelf

1.   Coastal States, in the exercise of their jurisdiction, have the right to regulate, authorize and conduct marine scientific research in their exclusive economic zone and on their continental shelf in accordance with the relevant provisions of this Convention.

2.   Marine scientific research in the exclusive economic zone and on the continental shelf shall be conducted with the consent of the coastal State.

3.   Coastal States shall, in normal circumstances, grant their consent for marine scientific research projects by other States or competent international organizations in their exclusive economic zone or on their continental shelf to be carried out in accordance with this Convention exclusively for peaceful purposes and in order to increase scientific knowledge of the marine environment for the benefit of all mankind. To this end, coastal States shall establish rules and procedures ensuring that such consent will not be delayed or denied unreasonably.

4.   For the purposes of applying paragraph 3, normal circumstances may exist in spite of the absence of diplomatic relations between the coastal State and the researching State.

5.   Coastal States may however in their discretion withhold their consent to the conduct of a marine scientific research project of another State or competent international organization in the exclusive economic zone or on the continental shelf of the coastal State if that project:

(a) is of direct significance for the exploration and exploitation of natural resources, whether living or non-living; * * *

* * *

Article 247

Marine scientific research projects undertaken by or under the auspices of international organizations

* * *

Article 248

Duty to provide information to the coastal State

States and competent international organizations which intend to undertake marine scientific research in the exclusive economic zone or on the continental shelf of a coastal State shall, not less than six months in advance of the expected starting date of the marine scientific research project, provide that State with a full description of:

(a) the nature and objectives of the project;

(b) the method and means to be used, including name, tonnage, type and class of vessels and a description of scientific equipment;

(c) the precise geographical areas in which the project is to be conducted;

(d) the expected date of first appearance and final departure of the research vessels, or deployment of the equipment and its removal, as appropriate;

(e) the name of the sponsoring institution, its director, and the person in charge of the project; and

(f) the extent to which it is considered that the coastal State should be able to participate or to be represented in the project.

Article 249

Duty to comply with certain conditions

* * *

Article 250

Communications concerning marine scientific research projects

* * *

Article 251

General criteria and guidelines

* * *

Article 252

Implied consent

* * *

Article 253

Suspension or cessation of marine scientific research activities

* * *

Article 254

Rights of neighbouring land-locked and geographically disadvantaged States

* * *

Article 255

Measures to facilitate marine scientific research and assist research vessels

States shall endeavour to adopt reasonable rules, regulations and procedures to promote and facilitate marine scientific research conducted in accordance with this

Convention beyond their territorial sea and, as appropriate, to facilitate, subject to the provisions of their laws and regulations, access to their harbours and promote assistance for marine scientific research vessels which comply with the relevant provisions of this Part.

Article 256

Marine scientific research in the Area

All States, irrespective of their geographical location, and competent international organizations have the right, in conformity with the provisions of Part XI, to conduct marine scientific research in the Area.

Article 257

Marine scientific research in the water column beyond the exclusive economic zone

All States, irrespective of their geographical location, and competent international organizations have the right, in conformity with this Convention, to conduct marine scientific research in the water column beyond the limits of the exclusive economic zone.

SECTION 4. SCIENTIFIC RESEARCH INSTALLATIONS OR EQUIPMENT IN THE MARINE ENVIRONMENT

Article 258

Deployment and use

* * *

Article 259

Legal status

* * *

Article 260

Safety zones

* * *

Article 261

Non-interference with shipping routes

* * *

Article 262

Identification markings and warning signals

* * *

SECTION 5. RESPONSIBILITY AND LIABILITY

Article 263

Responsibility and liability

1. States and competent international organizations shall be responsible for ensuring that marine scientific research, whether undertaken by them or on their behalf, is conducted in accordance with this Convention.

2. States and competent international organizations shall be responsible and liable for the measures they take in contravention of this Convention in respect of marine scientific research conducted by other States, their natural or juridical persons or by competent international organizations, and shall provide compensation for damage resulting from such measures.

3. States and competent international organizations shall be responsible and liable pursuant to article 235 for damage caused by pollution of the marine environment arising out of marine scientific research undertaken by them or on their behalf.

SECTION 6. SETTLEMENT OF DISPUTES AND INTERIM MEASURES

Article 264

Settlement of disputes

Disputes concerning the interpretation or application of the provisions of this Convention with regard to marine scientific research shall be settled in accordance with Part XV, sections 2 and 3.

Article 265

Interim measures

* * *

PART XIV

DEVELOPMENT AND TRANSFER OF MARINE TECHNOLOGY

SECTION 1. GENERAL PROVISIONS

Article 266

Promotion of the development and transfer of marine technology

1. States, directly or through competent international organizations, shall cooperate in accordance with their capabilities to promote actively the development and transfer of marine science and marine technology on fair and reasonable terms and conditions.

* * *

Article 267

Protection of legitimate interests

States, in promoting co-operation pursuant to article 266, shall have due regard for all legitimate interests including, *inter alia,* the rights and duties of holders, suppliers and recipients of marine technology.

Article 268

Basic objectives

* * *

Article 269

Measures to achieve the basic objectives

* * *

SECTION 2. INTERNATIONAL CO–OPERATION

Article 270

Ways and means of international co-operation

* * *

Article 271

Guidelines, criteria and standards

* * *

Article 272

Co-ordination of international programmes

* * *

Article 273

Co-operation with international organizations and the Authority

* * *

Article 274

Objectives of the Authority

* * *

SECTION 3. NATIONAL AND REGIONAL MARINE SCIENTIFIC AND TECHNOLOGICAL CENTRES

Article 275

Establishment of national centres

* * *

Article 276

Establishment of regional centres

* * *

Article 277

Functions of regional centres

* * *

SECTION 4. CO–OPERATION AMONG INTERNATIONAL ORGANIZATIONS

Article 278

Co-operation among international organizations

* * *

PART XV

SETTLEMENT OF DISPUTES

SECTION 1. GENERAL PROVISIONS

Article 279

Obligation to settle disputes by peaceful means

States Parties shall settle any dispute between them concerning the interpretation or application of this Convention by peaceful means in accordance with Article 2, paragraph 3, of the Charter of the United Nations and, to this end, shall seek a solution by the means indicated in Article 33, paragraph 1, of the Charter.

Article 280

Settlement of disputes by any peaceful means chosen by the parties

Nothing in this Part impairs the right of any States Parties to agree at any time to settle a dispute between them concerning the interpretation or application of this Convention by any peaceful means of their own choice.

Article 281

Procedure where no settlement has been reached by the parties

1. If the States Parties which are parties to a dispute concerning the interpretation or application of this Convention have agreed to seek settlement of the dispute by a peaceful means of their own choice, the procedures provided for in this Part apply only where no settlement has been reached by recourse to such means and the agreement between the parties does not exclude any further procedure.

2. If the parties have also agreed on a time-limit, paragraph 1 applies only upon the expiration of that time-limit.

Article 282

Obligations under general, regional or bilateral agreements

If the States Parties which are parties to a dispute concerning the interpretation or application of this Convention have agreed, through a general, regional or bilateral agreement or otherwise, that such dispute shall, at the request of any party to the dispute, be submitted to a procedure that entails a binding decision, that procedure shall apply in lieu of the procedures provided for in this Part, unless the parties to the dispute otherwise agree.

Article 283

Obligation to exchange views

1. When a dispute arises between States Parties concerning the interpretation or application of this Convention, the parties to the dispute shall proceed expeditiously to an exchange of views regarding its settlement by negotiation or other peaceful means.

2. The parties shall also proceed expeditiously to an exchange of views where a procedure for the settlement of such a dispute has been terminated without a settlement or where a settlement has been reached and the circumstances require consultation regarding the manner of implementing the settlement.

Article 284

Conciliation

1. A State Party which is a party to a dispute concerning the interpretation or application of this Convention may invite the other party or parties to submit the dispute to conciliation in accordance with the procedure under Annex V, section 1, or another conciliation procedure.

2. If the invitation is accepted and if the parties agree upon the conciliation procedure to be applied, any party may submit the dispute to that procedure.

3. If the invitation is not accepted or the parties do not agree upon the procedure, the conciliation proceedings shall be deemed to be terminated.

4. Unless the parties otherwise agree, when a dispute has been submitted to conciliation, the proceedings may be terminated only in accordance with the agreed conciliation procedure.

Article 285

Application of this section to disputes submitted pursuant to Part XI

This section applies to any dispute which pursuant to Part XI, section 5, is to be settled in accordance with procedures provided for in this Part. If an entity other than a State Party is a party to such a dispute, this section applies *mutatis mutandis.*

SECTION 2.   COMPULSORY PROCEDURES ENTAILING BINDING DECISIONS

Article 286

Application of procedures under this section

Subject to section 3, any dispute concerning the interpretation or application of this Convention shall, where no settlement has been reached by recourse to section 1, be submitted at the request of any party to the dispute to the court or tribunal having jurisdiction under this section.

Article 287

Choice of procedure

1. When signing, ratifying or acceding to this Convention or at any time thereafter, a State shall be free to choose, by means of a written declaration, one or more of the following means for the settlement of disputes concerning the interpretation or application of this Convention:

(a) the International Tribunal for the Law of the Sea established [in Hamburg, West Germany] in accordance with Annex VI;

(b) the International Court of Justice;

(c) an arbitral tribunal constituted in accordance with Annex VII;

(d) a special arbitral tribunal constituted in accordance with Annex VIII for one or more of the categories of disputes specified therein.

2. A declaration made under paragraph 1 shall not affect or be affected by the obligation of a State Party to accept the jurisdiction of the Sea–Bed Disputes Chamber of the International Tribunal for the Law of the Sea to the extent and in the manner provided for in Part XI, section 5.

3. A State Party, which is a party to a dispute not covered by a declaration in force, shall be deemed to have accepted arbitration in accordance with Annex VII.

4. If the parties to a dispute have accepted the same procedure for the settlement of the dispute, it may be submitted only to that procedure, unless the parties otherwise agree.

5. If the parties to a dispute have not accepted the same procedure for the settlement of the dispute, it may be submitted only to arbitration in accordance with Annex VII, unless the parties otherwise agree.

6. A declaration made under paragraph 1 shall remain in force until three months after notice of revocation has been deposited with the Secretary–General of the United Nations.

7. A new declaration, a notice of revocation or the expiry of a declaration does not in any way affect proceedings pending before a court or tribunal having jurisdiction under this article, unless the parties otherwise agree.

8. Declarations and notices referred to in this article shall be deposited with the Secretary–General of the United Nations, who shall transmit copies thereof to the States Parties.

Article 288

Jurisdiction

1. A court or tribunal referred to in article 287 shall have jurisdiction over any dispute concerning the interpretation or application of this Convention which is submitted to it in accordance with this Part.

2. A court or tribunal referred to in article 287 shall also have jurisdiction over any dispute concerning the interpretation or application of an international agreement related to the purposes of this Convention, which is submitted to it in accordance with the agreement.

3. The Sea–Bed Disputes Chamber of the International Tribunal for the Law of the Sea established in accordance with Annex VI, and any other chamber or arbitral tribunal referred to in Part XI, section 5, shall have jurisdiction in any matter which is submitted to it in accordance therewith.

4. In the event of a dispute as to whether a court or tribunal has jurisdiction, the matter shall be settled by decision of that court or tribunal.

Article 289

Experts

In any dispute involving scientific or technical matters, a court or tribunal exercising jurisdiction under this section may, at the request of a party or *proprio motu,* select in consultation with the parties no fewer than two scientific or technical experts chosen preferably from the relevant list prepared in accordance with Annex VII, article 2, to sit with the court or tribunal but without the right to vote.

Article 290

Provisional measures

1. If a dispute has been duly submitted to a court or tribunal which considers that *prima facie* it has jurisdiction under this Part or Part XI, section 5, the court or tribunal may prescribe any provisional measures which it considers appropriate under the circumstances to preserve the respective rights of the parties to the dispute or to prevent serious harm to the marine environment, pending the final decision.

* * *

6. The parties to the dispute shall comply promptly with any provisional measures prescribed under this article.

Article 291

Access

1. All the dispute settlement procedures specified in this Part shall be open to States Parties.

2. The dispute settlement procedures specified in this Part shall be open to entities other than States Parties only as specifically provided for in this Convention.

Article 292

Prompt release of vessels and crews

1. Where the authorities of a State Party have detained a vessel flying the flag of another State Party and it is alleged that the detaining State has not complied with

the provisions of this Convention for the prompt release of the vessel or its crew upon the posting of a reasonable bond or other financial security, the question of release from detention may be submitted to any court or tribunal agreed upon by the parties or, failing such agreement within 10 days from the time of detention, to a court or tribunal accepted by the detaining State under article 287 or to the International Tribunal for the Law of the Sea, unless the parties otherwise agree.

2. The application for release may be made only by or on behalf of the flag State of the vessel.

3. The court or tribunal shall deal without delay with the application for release and shall deal only with the question of release, without prejudice to the merits of any case before the appropriate domestic forum against the vessel, its owner or its crew. The authorities of the detaining State remain competent to release the vessel or its crew at any time.

4. Upon the posting of the bond or other financial security determined by the court or tribunal, the authorities of the detaining State shall comply promptly with the decision of the court or tribunal concerning the release of the vessel or its crew.

Article 293

Applicable law

1. A court or tribunal having jurisdiction under this section shall apply this Convention and other rules of international law not incompatible with this Convention.

2. Paragraph 1 does not prejudice the power of the court or tribunal having jurisdiction under this section to decide a case *ex aequo et bono,* if the parties so agree.

Article 294

Preliminary proceedings

1. A court or tribunal provided for in article 287 to which an application is made in respect of a dispute referred to in article 297 shall determine at the request of a party, or may determine *proprio motu,* whether the claim constitutes an abuse of legal process or whether *prima facie* it is well founded. If the court or tribunal determines that the claim constitutes an abuse of legal process or is *prima facie* unfounded, it shall take no further action in the case.

* * *

Article 295

Exhaustion of local remedies

Any dispute between States Parties concerning the interpretation or application of this Convention may be submitted to the procedures provided for in this section only after local remedies have been exhausted where this is required by international law.

Article 296

Finality and binding force of decisions

1. Any decision rendered by a court or tribunal having jurisdiction under this section shall be final and shall be complied with by all the parties to the dispute.

2. Any such decision shall have no binding force except between the parties and in respect of that particular dispute.

SECTION 3. LIMITATIONS AND EXCEPTIONS
TO APPLICABILITY OF SECTION 2

Article 297

Limitations on applicability of section 2

1. Disputes concerning the interpretation or application of this Convention with regard to the exercise by a coastal State of its sovereign rights or jurisdiction provided for in this Convention shall be subject to the procedures provided for in section 2 in the following cases:

(a) when it is alleged that a coastal State has acted in contravention of the provisions of this Convention in regard to the freedoms and rights of navigation, overflight or the laying of submarine cables and pipelines, or in regard to other internationally lawful uses of the sea specified in article 58;

(b) when it is alleged that a State in exercising the aforementioned freedoms, rights or uses has acted in contravention of this Convention or of laws or regulations adopted by the coastal State in conformity with this Convention and other rules of international law not incompatible with this Convention; or

(c) when it is alleged that a coastal State has acted in contravention of specified international rules and standards for the protection and preservation of the marine environment which are applicable to the coastal State and which have been established by this Convention or through a competent international organization or diplomatic conference in accordance with this Convention.

2. (a) Disputes concerning the interpretation or application of the provisions of this Convention with regard to marine scientific research shall be settled in accordance with section 2, except that the coastal State shall not be obliged to accept the submission to such settlement of any dispute arising out of:

(i) the exercise by the coastal State of a right or discretion in accordance with article 246; or

(ii) a decision by the coastal State to order suspension or cessation of a research project in accordance with article 253.

(b) A dispute arising from an allegation by the researching State that with respect to a specific project the coastal State is not exercising its rights under articles 246 and 253 in a manner compatible with this Convention shall be submitted, at the request of either party, to conciliation under Annex V, section 2, provided that the conciliation commission shall not call in question the exercise by the coastal State of its discretion to designate specific areas as referred to in article 246, paragraph 6, or of its discretion to withhold consent in accordance with article 246, paragraph 5.

3. (a) Disputes concerning the interpretation or application of the provisions of this Convention with regard to fisheries shall be settled in accordance with section 2, except that the coastal State shall not be obliged to accept the submission to such settlement of any dispute relating to its sovereign rights with respect to the living resources in the exclusive economic zone or their exercise, including its discretionary powers for determining the allowable catch, its harvesting capacity, the allocation of surpluses to other States and the terms and conditions established in its conservation and management laws and regulations.

(b) Where no settlement has been reached by recourse to section 1 of this Part, a dispute shall be submitted to conciliation under Annex V, section 2, at the request of any party to the dispute, when it is alleged that:

(i) a coastal State has manifestly failed to comply with its obligations to ensure through proper conservation and management measures that the maintenance of the living resources in the exclusive economic zone is not seriously endangered;

(ii) a coastal State has arbitrarily refused to determine, at the request of another State, the allowable catch and its capacity to harvest living resources with respect to stocks which that other State is interested in fishing; or

(iii) a coastal State has arbitrarily refused to allocate to any State, under articles 62, 69 and 70 and under the terms and conditions established by the coastal State consistent with this Convention, the whole or part of the surplus it has declared to exist.

(c) In no case shall the conciliation commission substitute its discretion for that of the coastal State.

(d) The report of the conciliation commission shall be communicated to the appropriate international organizations.

(e) In negotiating agreements pursuant to articles 69 and 70, States Parties, unless they otherwise agree, shall include a clause on measures which they shall take in order to minimize the possibility of a disagreement concerning the interpretation or application of the agreement, and on how they should proceed if a disagreement nevertheless arises.

Article 298

Optional exceptions to applicability of section 2

1. When signing, ratifying or acceding to this Convention or at any time thereafter, a State may, without prejudice to the obligations arising under section 1, declare in writing that it does not accept any one or more of the procedures provided for in section 2 with respect to one or more of the following categories of disputes:

(a)(i) disputes concerning the interpretation or application of articles 15, 74 and 83 relating to sea boundary delimitations, or those involving historic bays or titles, provided that a State having made such a declaration shall, when such a dispute arises subsequent to the entry into force of this Convention and where no agreement within a reasonable period of time is reached in negotiations between the parties, at the request of any party to the dispute, accept submission of the matter to conciliation under Annex V, section 2; and provided further that any dispute that necessarily involves the concurrent consideration of any unsettled dispute concerning sovereignty or other rights over continental or insular land territory shall be excluded from such submission;

(ii) after the conciliation commission has presented its report, which shall state the reasons on which it is based, the parties shall negotiate an agreement on the basis of that report; if these negotiations do not result in an agreement, the parties shall, by mutual consent, submit the question to one of the procedures provided for in section 2, unless the parties otherwise agree;

(iii) this subparagraph does not apply to any sea boundary dispute finally settled by an arrangement between the parties, or to any such dispute which is to be settled in accordance with a bilateral or multilateral agreement binding upon those parties;

(b) disputes concerning military activities, including military activities by government vessels and aircraft engaged in non-commercial service, and disputes concerning law enforcement activities in regard to the exercise of sovereign rights or jurisdiction excluded from the jurisdiction of a court or tribunal under article 297, paragraph 2 or 3;

(c) disputes in respect of which the Security Council of the United Nations is exercising the functions assigned to it by the Charter of the United Nations, unless the Security Council decides to remove the matter from its agenda or calls upon the parties to settle it by the means provided for in this Convention.

2. A State Party which has made a declaration under paragraph 1 may at any time withdraw it, or agree to submit a dispute excluded by such declaration to any procedure specified in this Convention.

3. A State Party which has made a declaration under paragraph 1 shall not be entitled to submit any dispute falling within the excepted category of disputes to any procedure in this Convention as against another State Party, without the consent of that party.

4. If one of the States Parties has made a declaration under paragraph 1(a), any other State Party may submit any dispute falling within an excepted category against the declarant party to the procedure specified in such declaration.

5. A new declaration, or the withdrawal of a declaration, does not in any way affect proceedings pending before a court or tribunal in accordance with this article, unless the parties otherwise agree.

6. Declarations and notices of withdrawal of declarations under this article shall be deposited with the Secretary–General of the United Nations, who shall transmit copies thereof to the States Parties.

Article 299

Right of the parties to agree upon a procedure

1. A dispute excluded under article 297 or excepted by a declaration made under article 298 from the dispute settlement procedures provided for in section 2 may be submitted to such procedures only by agreement of the parties to the dispute.

2. Nothing in this section impairs the right of the parties to the dispute to agree to some other procedure for the settlement of such dispute or to reach an amicable settlement.

PART XVI

GENERAL PROVISIONS

Article 300

Good faith and abuse of rights

States Parties shall fulfil in good faith the obligations assumed under this Convention and shall exercise the rights, jurisdiction and freedoms recognized in this Convention in a manner which would not constitute an abuse of right.

Article 301

Peaceful uses of the seas

In exercising their rights and performing their duties under this Convention, States Parties shall refrain from any threat or use of force against the territorial integrity or political independence of any State, or in any other manner inconsistent with the principles of international law embodied in the Charter of the United Nations.

Article 302

Disclosure of information

Without prejudice to the right of a State Party to resort to the procedures for the settlement of disputes provided for in this Convention, nothing in this Convention shall be deemed to require a State Party, in the fulfilment of its obligations under this

Convention, to supply information the disclosure of which is contrary to the essential interests of its security.

Article 303

Archaeological and historical objects found at sea

1. States have the duty to protect objects of an archaeological and historical nature found at sea and shall co-operate for this purpose.

2. In order to control traffic in such objects, the coastal State may, in applying article 33, presume that their removal from the sea-bed in the zone referred to in that article without its approval would result in an infringement within its territory or territorial sea of the laws and regulations referred to in that article.

3. Nothing in this article affects the rights of identifiable owners, the law of salvage or other rules of admiralty, or laws and practices with respect to cultural exchanges.

4. This article is without prejudice to other international agreements and rules of international law regarding the protection of objects of an archaeological and historical nature.

Article 304

Responsibility and liability for damage

The provisions of this Convention regarding responsibility and liability for damage are without prejudice to the application of existing rules and the development of further rules regarding responsibility and liability under international law.

PART XVII

FINAL PROVISIONS

* * *

Article 309

Reservations and exceptions

No reservations or exceptions may be made to this Convention unless expressly permitted by other articles of this Convention.

Article 310

Declarations and statements

Article 309 does not preclude a State, when signing, ratifying or acceding to this Convention, from making declarations or statements, however phrased or named, with a view, *inter alia,* to the harmonization of its laws and regulations with the provisions of this Convention, provided that such declarations or statements do not purport to exclude or to modify the legal effect of the provisions of this Convention in their application to that State.

Article 311

Relation to other conventions and international agreements

1. This Convention shall prevail, as between States Parties, over the Geneva Conventions on the Law of the Sea of 29 April 1958.

2. This Convention shall not alter the rights and obligations of States Parties which arise from other agreements compatible with this Convention and which do not affect the enjoyment by other States Parties of their rights or the performance of their obligations under this Convention.

3. Two or more States Parties may conclude agreements modifying or suspending the operation of provisions of this Convention, applicable solely to the relations between them, provided that such agreements do not relate to a provision derogation from which is incompatible with the effective execution of the object and purpose of this Convention, and provided further that such agreements shall not affect the application of the basic principles embodied herein, and that the provisions of such agreements do not affect the enjoyment by other States Parties of their rights or the performance of their obligations under this Convention.

4. States Parties intending to conclude an agreement referred to in paragraph 3 shall notify the other States Parties through the depositary of this Convention of their intention to conclude the agreement and of the modification or suspension for which it provides.

5. This article does not affect international agreements expressly permitted or preserved by other articles of this Convention.

6. State Parties agree that there shall be no amendments to the basic principle relating to the common heritage of mankind set forth in article 136 and that they shall not be party to any agreement in derogation thereof.

* * *

Article 317

Denunciation

1. A State Party may, by written notification addressed to the Secretary–General of the United Nations, denounce this Convention and may indicate its reasons. Failure to indicate reasons shall not affect the validity of the denunciation. The denunciation shall take effect one year after the date of receipt of the notification, unless the notification specifies a later date.

2. A State shall not be discharged by reason of the denunciation from the financial and contractual obligations which accrued while it was a Party to this Convention, nor shall the denunciation affect any right, obligation or legal situation of that State created through the execution of this Convention prior to its termination for that State.

3. The denunciation shall not in any way affect the duty of any State Party to fulfil any obligation embodied in this Convention to which it would be subject under international law independently of this Convention.

Article 318

Status of Annexes

The Annexes form an integral part of this Convention and, unless expressly provided otherwise, a reference to this Convention or to one of its Parts includes a reference to the Annexes relating thereto.

* * *

ANNEX V. CONCILIATION
SECTION 1. CONCILIATION PROCEDURE PURSUANT TO SECTION 1 OF PART XV

Article 1

Institution of proceedings

If the parties to a dispute have agreed, in accordance with article 284, to submit it to conciliation under this section, any such party may institute the proceedings by written notification addressed to the other party or parties to the dispute.

Article 2

List of conciliators

A list of conciliators shall be drawn up and maintained by the Secretary–General of the United Nations. Every State Party shall be entitled to nominate four conciliators, each of whom shall be a person enjoying the highest reputation for fairness, competence and integrity. The names of the persons so nominated shall constitute the list. If at any time the conciliators nominated by a State Party in the list so constituted shall be fewer than four, that State Party shall be entitled to make further nominations as necessary. The name of a conciliator shall remain on the list until withdrawn by the State Party which made the nomination, provided that such conciliator shall continue to serve on any conciliation commission to which that conciliator has been appointed until the completion of the proceedings before that commission.

Article 3

Constitution of conciliation commission

The conciliation commission shall, unless the parties otherwise agree, be constituted as follows:

(a) Subject to subparagraph (g), the conciliation commission shall consist of five members.

(b) The party instituting the proceedings shall appoint two conciliators to be chosen preferably from the list referred to in article 2 of this Annex, one of whom may be its national, unless the parties otherwise agree. Such appointments shall be included in the notification referred to in article 1 of this Annex.

(c) The other party to the dispute shall appoint two conciliators in the manner set forth in subparagraph (b) within 21 days of receipt of the notification referred to in article 1 of this Annex. If the appointments are not made within that period, the party instituting the proceedings may, within one week of the expiration of that period, either terminate the proceedings by notification addressed to the other party or request the Secretary–General of the United Nations to make the appointments in accordance with subparagraph (e).

(d) Within 30 days after all four conciliators have been appointed, they shall appoint a fifth conciliator chosen from the list referred to in article 2 of this Annex, who shall be chairman. If the appointment is not made within that period, either party may, within one week of the expiration of that period, request the Secretary–General of the United Nations to make the appointment in accordance with subparagraph (e).

(e) Within 30 days of the receipt of a request under subparagraph (c) or (d), the Secretary–General of the United Nations shall make the necessary appointments from the list referred to in article 2 of this Annex in consultation with the parties to the dispute.

(f) Any vacancy shall be filled in the manner prescribed for the initial appointment.

(g) Two or more parties which determine by agreement that they are in the same interest shall appoint two conciliators jointly. Where two or more parties have separate interests or there is a disagreement as to whether they are of the same interest, they shall appoint conciliators separately.

(h) In disputes involving more than two parties having separate interests, or where there is disagreement as to whether they are of the same interest, the parties shall apply subparagraphs (a) to (f) in so far as possible.

Article 4

Procedure

The conciliation commission shall, unless the parties otherwise agree, determine its own procedure. The commission may, with the consent of the parties to the dispute, invite any State Party to submit to it its views orally or in writing. Decisions of the commission regarding procedural matters, the report and recommendations shall be made by a majority vote of its members.

Article 5

Amicable settlement

The commission may draw the attention of the parties to any measures which might facilitate an amicable settlement of the dispute.

Article 6

Functions of the commission

The commission shall hear the parties, examine their claims and objections, and make proposals to the parties with a view to reaching an amicable settlement.

Article 7

Report

1. The commission shall report within 12 months of its constitution. Its report shall record any agreements reached and, failing agreement, its conclusions on all questions of fact or law relevant to the matter in dispute and such recommendations as the commission may deem appropriate for an amicable settlement. The report shall be deposited with the Secretary–General of the United Nations and shall immediately be transmitted by him to the parties to the dispute.

2. The report of the commission, including its conclusions or recommendations, shall not be binding upon the parties.

Article 8

Termination

The conciliation proceedings are terminated when a settlement has been reached, when the parties have accepted or one party has rejected the recommendations of the report by written notification addressed to the Secretary–General of the United Nations, or when a period of three months has expired from the date of transmission of the report to the parties.

Article 9

Fees and expenses

The fees and expenses of the commission shall be borne by the parties to the dispute.

Article 10

Right of parties to modify procedure

The parties to the dispute may by agreement applicable solely to that dispute modify any provision of this Annex.

SECTION 2. COMPULSORY SUBMISSION TO CONCILIATION PROCEDURE PURSUANT TO SECTION 3 OF PART XV

Article 11

Institution of proceedings

1. Any party to a dispute which, in accordance with Part XV, section 3, may be submitted to conciliation under this section, may institute the proceedings by written notification addressed to the other party or parties to the dispute.

2. Any party to the dispute, notified under paragraph 1, shall be obliged to submit to such proceedings.

Article 12

Failure to reply or to submit to conciliation

The failure of a party or parties to the dispute to reply to notification of institution of proceedings or to submit to such proceedings shall not constitute a bar to the proceedings.

Article 13

Competence

A disagreement as to whether a conciliation commission acting under this section has competence shall be decided by the commission.

Article 14

Application of section 1

Articles 2 to 10 of section 1 of this Annex apply subject to this section.

3.9 CONVENTION FOR THE PROTECTION AND DEVELOPMENT OF THE MARINE ENVIRON-
MENT OF THE WIDER CARIBBEAN REGION (CARTAGENA CONVENTION).[g]
**Adopted, 24 Mar 1983. Entered into force, 11 Oct. 1986. 1506 UNTS
157**

The Contracting Parties,

Fully aware of the economic and social value of the marine environment, including
coastal areas, of the wider Caribbean region,

Conscious of their responsibility to protect the marine environment of the wider

Caribbean region for the benefit and enjoyment of present and future generations,

Recognizing the special hydrographic and ecological characteristics of the region
and its vulnerability to pollution,

Recognizing further the threat to the marine environment, its ecological equilibrium, resources and legitimate uses posed by pollution and by the absence of sufficient
integration of an environmental dimension into the development process,

Considering the protection of the ecosystems of the marine environment of the
wider Caribbean region to be one of their principal objectives,

Realizing fully the need for co-operation amongst themselves and with competent
international organizations in order to ensure co-ordinated and comprehensive development without environmental damage,

Recognizing the desirability of securing the wider acceptance of international
marine pollution agreements already in existence,

Noting however, that, in spite of the progress already achieved, these agreements
do not cover all aspects of environmental deterioration and do not entirely meet the
special requirements of the wider Caribbean region,

Have agreed as follows:

Article 1   Convention Area

1.   This Convention shall apply to the wider Caribbean region, hereinafter referred to as "the Convention area" as defined in paragraph 1 of article 2.

2.   Except as may be otherwise provided in any protocol to this Convention, the
Convention area shall not include internal waters of the Contracting Parties.

g.   There are a large number of regional
conventions aimed at protection and conservation of the marine environment. Because of
space limitations, we have included only two
such conventions in this collection: this Convention and the Convention for the Protection
of the Natural Resources and Environment of
the South Pacific (**Basic Document 3.11**).
Other regional conventions include: Kuwait
Regional Convention for Co-operation on the
Protection of the Marine Environment from
Pollution (24 Apr 1978/30 Jun 1979), 1140
UNTS 133; Convention for Co-operation in the
Protection and Development of the Marine and
Coastal Environment of the West and and
Coastal Environment of the West and Conven-
tion for Co-operation in the Protection and
Development of the Marine and Kuwait Re-
Central African Region (23 Mar 1981/5 Aug
1984), *reprinted in* 20 ILM 756; Convention for
the Protection, Management and Development
of the Marine and Coastal Environment of the
Eastern African Region (21 Jun 1985/30 May
1996), 91 RGDIP 1122; Convention on the
Protection of the Marine Environment of the
Baltic Sea Area, (9 Apr 1992/17 Jan 2000),
2099 UNTS 195, *reprinted in* 5 Weston &
Carlson V.F.29; Convention for the Protection
of the Marine Environment of the North–East
Atlantic ("OSPAR Convention") (22 Sep
1992/25 Mar 1998), *reprinted in* 5 Weston &
Carlson V.F.29a; Convention for the Protection
of the Marine Environment and the Coastal
Region of the Mediterranean (10 Jun 1995/9
Jul 2004), *reprinted in* 5 Weston & Carlson
V.F.30a–1; Convention for Cooperation in the
Protection and Sustainable Development of the
Marine and Coastal Environment of the North-
east Pacific (18 Feb 2002/NIF); Framework
Convention for the Protection of the Marine
Environment of the Caspian Sea (4 Nov
2003/12 Aug 2006), *reprinted in* 5 Weston &
Carlson V.F.30e.

Article 2   Definitions

For the purposes of this Convention:

1.   The "Convention area" means the marine environment of the Gulf of Mexico, the Caribbean Sea and the areas of the Atlantic Ocean adjacent thereto, south of 30 deg north latitude and within 200 nautical miles of the Atlantic coasts of the States referred to in article 25 of the Convention.

2.   "Organization" means the institution designated to carry out the functions enumerated in paragraph 1 of article 15.

Article 3   General Provisions

1.   The Contracting Parties shall endeavour to conclude bilateral or multilateral agreements including regional or subregional agreements, for the protection of the marine environment of the Convention area. Such agreements shall be consistent with this Convention and in accordance with international law. Copies of such agreements shall be communicated to the Organization and, through the Organization, to all signatories and Contracting Parties to this Convention.

2.   This Convention and its protocols shall be construed in accordance with international law relating to their subject-matter. Nothing in this Convention or its protocols shall be deemed to affect obligations assumed by the Contracting Parties under agreements previously concluded.

3.   Nothing in this Convention or its protocols shall prejudice the present or future claims or the legal views of any Contracting Party concerning the nature and extent of maritime jurisdiction.

Article 4   General Obligations

1.   The Contracting Parties shall, individually or jointly, take all appropriate measures in conformity with international law and in accordance with this Convention and those of its protocols in force to which they are parties to prevent, reduce and control pollution of the Convention area and to ensure sound environmental management, using for this purpose the best practicable means at their disposal and in accordance with their capabilities.

2.   The Contracting Parties shall, in taking the measures referred to in paragraph 1, ensure that the implementation of those measures does not cause pollution of the marine environment outside the Convention area.

3.   The Contracting Parties shall co-operate in the formulation and adoption of protocols or other agreements to facilitate the effective implementation of this Convention.

4.   The Contracting Parties shall take appropriate measures, in conformity with international law, for the effective discharge of the obligations prescribed in this Convention and its protocols and shall endeavour to harmonize their policies in this regard.

5.   The Contracting Parties shall co-operate with the competent international, regional and subregional organizations for the effective implementation of this Convention and its protocols. They shall assist each other in fulfilling their obligations under this Convention and its protocols.

Article 5   Pollution from Ships

The Contracting Parties shall take all appropriate measures to prevent, reduce and control pollution of the Convention area caused by discharges from ships and, for this purpose, to ensure the effective implementation of the applicable international rules and standards established by the competent international organization.

Article 6   Pollution Caused by Dumping

The Contracting Parties shall take all appropriate measures to prevent, reduce and control pollution of the Convention area caused by dumping of wastes and other matter at sea from ships, aircraft or manmade structures at sea, and to ensure the effective implementation of the applicable international rules and standards.

Article 7   Pollution from Land-based Sources

The Contracting Parties shall take all appropriate measures to prevent, reduce and control pollution of the Convention area caused by coastal disposal or by discharges emanating from rivers, estuaries, coastal establishments, outfall structures, or any other sources on their territories.

Article 8   Pollution from Sea-bed Activities

The Contracting Parties shall take all appropriate measures to prevent, reduce and control pollution of the Convention area resulting directly or indirectly from exploration and exploitation of the sea-bed and its subsoil.

Article 9   Airborne Pollution

The Contracting Parties shall take all appropriate measures to prevent, reduce and control pollution of the Convention area resulting from discharges into the atmosphere from activities under their jurisdiction.

Article 10   Specially Protected Areas

The Contracting Parties shall, individually or jointly, take all appropriate measures to protect and preserve rare or fragile ecosystems, as well as the habitat of depleted, threatened or endangered species, in the Convention area. To this end, the Contracting Parties shall endeavour to establish protected areas. The establishment of such areas shall not affect the rights of other Contracting Parties and third States. In addition, the Contracting Parties shall exchange information concerning the administration and management of such areas.

Article 11   Co-operation in Cases of Emergency

1.   The Contracting Parties shall co-operate in taking all necessary measures to respond to pollution emergencies in the Convention area, whatever the cause of such emergencies, and to control, reduce or eliminate pollution or the threat of pollution resulting therefrom. To this end, the Contracting Parties shall, individually and jointly, develop and promote contingency plans for responding to incidents involving pollution or the threat thereof in the Convention area.

2.   When a Contracting Party becomes aware of cases in which the Convention area is in imminent danger of being polluted or has been polluted, it shall immediately notify other States likely to be affected by such pollution, as well as the competent international organizations. Furthermore, it shall inform, as soon as feasible, such other States and competent international organizations of measures it has taken to minimize or reduce pollution or the threat thereof.

Article 12   Environmental Impact Assessment

1.   As part of their environmental management policies the Contracting Parties undertake to develop technical and other guidelines to assist the planning of their major development projects in such a way as to prevent or minimize harmful impacts on the Convention area.

2.   Each Contracting Party shall assess within its capabilities, or ensure the assessment of, the potential effects of such projects on the marine environment,

particularly in coastal areas, so that appropriate measures may be taken to prevent any substantial pollution of, or significant and harmful changes to, the Convention area.

3. With respect to the assessments referred to in paragraph 2, each Contracting Party shall, with the assistance of the Organization when requested, develop procedures for the dissemination of information and may, where appropriate, invite other Contracting Parties which may be affected to consult with it and to submit comments.

Article 13   Scientific and Technical Co-operation

1. The Contracting Parties undertake to cooperate, directly and, when appropriate, through the competent international and regional organizations, in scientific research, monitoring, and the exchange of data and other scientific information relating to the purposes of this Convention.

2. To this end, the Contracting Parties undertake to develop and co-ordinate their research and monitoring programmes relating to the Convention area and to ensure, in co-operation with the competent international and regional organizations, the necessary links between their research centres and institutes with a view to producing compatible results. With the aim of further protecting the Convention area, the Contracting Parties shall endeavour to participate in international arrangements for pollution research and monitoring.

3. The Contracting Parties undertake to cooperate, directly and, when appropriate, through the competent international and regional organizations, in the provision to other Contracting Parties of technical and other assistance in fields relating to pollution and sound environmental management of the Convention area, taking into account the special needs of the smaller island developing countries and territories.

Article 14   Liability and Compensation

The Contracting Parties shall co-operate with a view to adopting appropriate rules and procedures, which are in conformity with international law, in the field of liability and compensation for damage resulting from pollution of the Convention area.

Article 15   Institutional Arrangements

1. The Contracting Parties designate the United Nations Environment Programme to carry out the following secretariat functions:

a. To prepare and convene the meetings of Contracting Parties and conferences provided for in articles 16, 17 and 18;

b. To transmit the information received in accordance with articles 3, 11 and 22;

c. To perform the functions assigned to it by protocols to this Convention;

d. To consider enquiries by, and information from, the Contracting Parties and to consult with them on questions relating to this Convention, its protocols and annexes thereto;

e. To co-ordinate the implementation of cooperative activities agreed upon by the meetings of Contracting Parties and conferences provided for in articles 16, 17 and 18;

f. To ensure the necessary co-ordination with other international bodies which the Contracting Parties consider competent.

2. Each Contracting Party shall designate an appropriate authority to serve as the channel of communication with the Organization for the purposes of this Convention and its protocols.

Article 16   Meetings of the Contracting Parties

1.   The Contracting Parties shall hold ordinary meetings once every two years and extraordinary meetings at any other time deemed necessary, upon the request of the Organization or at the request of any Contracting Party, provided that such requests are supported by the majority of the Contracting Parties.

2.   It shall be the function of the meetings of the Contracting Parties to keep under review the implementation of this Convention and its protocols and, in particular:

a.   To assess periodically the state of the environment in the Convention area;

b.   To consider the information submitted by the Contracting Parties under article 22;

c.   To adopt, review and amend annexes to this Convention and to its protocols, in accordance with article 19;

d.   To make recommendations regarding the adoption of any additional protocols or any amendments to this Convention or its protocols in accordance with articles 17 and 18;

e.   To establish working groups as required to consider any matters concerning this Convention and its protocols, and annexes thereto;

f.   To consider co-operative activities to be undertaken within the framework of this Convention and its protocols, including their financial and institutional implications, and to adopt decisions relating thereto;

g.   To consider and undertake any other action that may be required for the achievement of the purposes of this Convention and its protocols.

Article 17   Adoption of Protocols

1.   The Contracting Parties, at a conference of plenipotentiaries, may adopt additional protocols to this Convention pursuant to paragraph 3 of article 4.

2.   If so requested by a majority of the Contracting Parties, the Organization shall convene a conference of plenipotentiaries for the purpose of adopting additional protocols to this Convention.

Article 18   Amendment of the Convention and its Protocols

1.   Any Contracting Party may propose amendments to this Convention. Amendments shall be adopted by a conference of plenipotentiaries which shall be convened by the Organization at the request of a majority of the Contracting Parties.

2.   Any Contracting Party to this Convention may propose amendments to any protocol. Such amendments shall be adopted by a conference of plenipotentiaries which shall be convened by the Organization at the request of a majority of the Contracting Parties to the protocol concerned.

3.   The text of any proposed amendment shall be communicated by the Organization to all Contracting Parties at least 90 days before the opening of the conference of plenipotentiaries.

4.   Any amendment to this Convention shall be adopted by a three-fourths majority vote of the Contracting Parties to the Convention which are represented at the conference of plenipotentiaries and shall be submitted by the Depositary for acceptance by all Contracting Parties to the Convention. Amendments to any protocol shall be adopted by a three-fourths majority vote of the Contracting Parties to the protocol which are represented at the conference of plenipotentiaries and shall be submitted by the Depositary for acceptance by all Contracting Parties to the protocol.

5. Instruments of ratification, acceptance or approval of amendments shall be deposited with the Depositary. Amendments adopted in accordance with paragraph 3 shall enter into force between Contracting Parties having accepted such amendments on the thirtieth day following the date of receipt by the Depositary of the instruments of at least three fourths of the Contracting Parties to this Convention or to the protocol concerned, as the case may be. Thereafter the amendments shall enter into force for any other Contracting Party on the thirtieth day after the date on which that Party deposits its instrument.

6. After entry into force of an amendment to this Convention or to a protocol, any new Contracting Party to the Convention or such protocols shall become a Contracting Party to the Convention or protocol as amended.

Article 19   Annexes and Amendments to Annexes

1. Annexes to this Convention or to a protocol shall form an integral part of the Convention or, as the case may be, such protocol.

2. Except as may be otherwise provided in any protocol with respect to its annexes, the following procedure shall apply to the adoption and entry into force of amendments to annexes to this Convention or to annexes to a protocol:

a. Any Contracting Party may propose amendments to annexes to this Convention or to annexes to any protocol at a meeting convened pursuant to article 16;

b. Such amendments shall be adopted by a three-fourths majority vote of the Contracting Parties to the instrument in question present at the meeting referred to in article 16;

c. The Depositary shall without delay communicate the amendments so adopted to all Contracting Parties to the Convention;

d. Any Contracting Party that is unable to accept an amendment to annexes to this Convention or to annexes to any protocol shall so notify the Depositary in writing within 90 days from the date on which the amendment was adopted;

e. The Depositary shall without delay notify all Contracting Parties of notifications received pursuant to the preceding subparagraph;

f. On expiration of the period referred to in subparagraph (d), the amendment to the annex shall become effective for all Contracting Parties to this Convention or to the protocol concerned which have not submitted a notification in accordance with the provisions of that subparagraph;

g. A Contracting Party may at any time substitute an acceptance for a previous declaration of objection, and the amendment shall thereupon enter into force for that Party.

3. The adoption and entry into force of a new annex shall be subject to the same procedure as that for the adoption and entry into force of an amendment to an annex, provided that, if it entails an amendment to the Convention or to one of its protocols, the new annex shall not enter into force until such time as that amendment enters into force.

4. Any amendment to the Annex on Arbitration shall be proposed and adopted, and shall enter into force, in accordance with the procedures set out in article 18.

Article 20   Rules of Procedure and Financial Rules

1. The Contracting Parties shall unanimously adopt rules of procedure for their meetings.

2. The Contracting Parties shall unanimously adopt financial rules, prepared in consultation with the Organization, to determine, in particular, their financial participation under this Convention and under protocols to which they are parties.

Article 21   Special Exercise of the Right to Vote

In their fields of competence, the regional economic integration organizations referred to in article 25 shall exercise their right to vote with a number of votes equal to the number of their member States which are Contracting Parties to this Convention and to one or more protocols. Such organizations shall not exercise their right to vote if the member States concerned exercise theirs, and vice versa.

Article 22   Transmission of Information

The Contracting Parties shall transmit to the Organization information on the measures adopted by them in the implementation of this Convention and of protocols to which they are parties, in such form and at such intervals as the meetings of Contracting Parties may determine.

Article 23   Settlement of Disputes

1. In case of a dispute between Contracting Parties as to the interpretation or application of this Convention or its protocols, they shall seek a settlement of the dispute through negotiation or any other peaceful means of their own choice.

2. If the Contracting Parties concerned cannot settle their dispute through the means mentioned in the preceding paragraph, the dispute shall upon common agreement, except as may be otherwise provided in any protocol to this Convention, be submitted to arbitration under the conditions set out in the Annex on Arbitration. However, failure to reach common agreement on submission of the dispute to arbitration shall not absolve the Contracting Parties from the responsibility of continuing to seek to resolve it by the means referred to in paragraph 1.

3. A Contracting Party may at any time declare that it recognizes as compulsory ipso facto and without special agreement, in relation to any other Contracting Party accepting the same obligation, the application of the arbitration procedure set out in the Annex on Arbitration. Such declaration shall he notified in writing to the Depositary, who shall communicate it to the other Contracting Parties.

Article 24   Relationship Between the Convention and its Protocols

1. No State or regional economic integration organization may become a Contracting Party to this Convention unless it becomes at the same time a Contracting Party to at least one protocol to the Convention. No State or regional economic integration organization may become a Contracting Party to a protocol unless it is, or becomes at the same time, a Contracting Party to the Convention.

2. Decisions concerning any protocol shall be taken only by the Contracting Parties to the protocol concerned.

Article 25   Signature

This Convention and the Protocol concerning Cooperation in Combating Oil Spills in the Wider Caribbean Region shall be open for signature at Cartagena de Indias on 24 March 1983 and at Bogota from 25 March 1983 to 23 March 1984 by States invited to participate in the Conference of Plenipotentiaries on the Protection and Development of the Marine Environment of the Wider Caribbean Region, held at Cartagena de Indias from 21 to 24 March 1983. They shall also be open for signature between the same dates by any regional economic integration organization exercising competence in fields covered by the Convention and that Protocol and having at least one member

State which belongs to the wider Caribbean region, provided that such regional organization has been invited to participate in the Conference of Plenipotentiaries.

Article 26   Ratification, Acceptance and Approval

1.   This Convention and its protocols shall be subject to ratification, acceptance or approval by States. Instruments of ratification, acceptance or approval shall be deposited with the Government of the Republic of Colombia, which will assume the functions of Depositary.

2.   This Convention and its protocols shall also be subject to ratification, acceptance or approval by the organizations referred to in article 25 having at least one member State a party to the Convention. In their instruments of ratification, acceptance or approval, such organizations shall declare the extent of their competence with respect to the matters governed by the Convention and the relevant protocol. Subsequently these organizations shall inform the Depositary of any substantial modification in the extent of their competence.

Article 27   Accession

1.   This Convention and its protocols shall be open for accession by the States and organizations referred to in article 25 as from the day following the date on which the Convention or the protocol concerned is closed for signature.

2.   After entry into force of this Convention and of any protocol, any State or regional economic integration organization not referred to in article 25 may accede to the Convention and to any protocol subject to prior approval by three fourths of the Contracting Parties to the Convention or the protocol concerned, provided that any such regional economic integration organization exercises competence in fields covered by the Convention and the relevant protocol and has at least one member State belonging to the wider Caribbean region, that is a party to the Convention and the relevant protocol.

3.   In their instruments of accession, the organizations referred to in paragraphs 1 and 2 shall declare the extent of their competence with respect to the matters governed by the Convention and the relevant protocol. These organizations shall also inform the Depositary of any substantial modification in the extent of their competence.

4.   Instruments of accession shall be deposited with the Depositary.

Article 28   Entry into Force

1.   This Convention and the Protocol concerning Co-operation in Combating Oil Spills in the Wider Caribbean Region shall enter into force on the thirtieth day following the date of deposit of the ninth instrument of ratification, acceptance or approval of, or accession to, those agreements by the States referred to in article 25.

2.   Any additional protocol to this Convention, except as otherwise provided in such protocol, shall enter into force on the thirtieth day following the date of deposit of the ninth instrument of ratification, acceptance, or approval of such protocol, or of accession thereto.

3.   For the purposes of paragraphs 1 and 2, any instrument deposited by an organization referred to in article 25 shall not be counted as additional to that deposited by any member State of such organization.

4.   Thereafter, this Convention and any protocol shall enter into force with respect to any State or organization referred to in article 25 or article 27 on the thirtieth day following the date of deposit of its instruments of ratification, acceptance, approval or accession.

Article 29   Denunciation

1.   At any time after two years from the date of entry into force of this Convention with respect to a Contracting Party, that Contracting Party may denounce the Convention by giving written notification to the Depositary.

2.   Except as may be otherwise provided in any protocol to this Convention, any Contracting Party may, at any time after two years from the date of entry into force of such protocol with respect to that Contracting Party, denounce the protocol by giving written notification to the Depositary.

3.   Denunciation shall take effect on the ninetieth day after the date on which notification is received by the Depositary.

4.   Any Contracting Party which denounces this Convention shall be considered as also having denounced any protocol to which it was a Contracting Party.

5.   Any Contracting Party which, upon its denunciation of a protocol, is no longer a Contracting Party to any protocol of this Convention, shall be considered as also having denounced the Convention itself.

Article 30   Depositary

1.   The Depositary shall inform the Signatories and the Contracting Parties, as well as the Organization, of:

a.   The signature of this Convention and of its protocols, and the deposit of instruments of ratification, acceptance, approval or accession;

b.   The date on which the Convention or any protocol will come into force for each Contracting Party;

c.   Notification of any denunciation and the date on which it will take effect;

d.   The amendments adopted with respect to the Convention or to any protocol, their acceptance by the Contracting Parties and the date of their entry into force;

e.   All matters relating to new annexes and to the amendment of any annex;

f.   Notifications by regional economic integration organizations of the extent of their competence with respect to matters governed by this Convention and the relevant protocols, and of any modifications thereto.

2.   The original of this Convention and of any protocol shall be deposited with the Depositary, the Government of the Republic of Colombia, which shall send certified copies thereof to the Signatories, the Contracting Parties, and the Organization.

3.   As soon as the Convention and its protocols enter into force, the Depositary shall transmit a certified copy of the instrument concerned to the Secretary–General of the United Nations for registration and publication in accordance with Article 102 of the Charter of the United Nations.

In witness whereof the undersigned, being duly authorized by their respective Governments, have signed this Convention. Done at Cartagena de Indias this twenty-fourth day of March one thousand nine hundred and eighty-three in a single copy in the English, French and Spanish languages, the three texts being equally authentic.

Annex

Arbitration

[omitted]

* * *

3.10 MONTREAL GUIDELINES FOR THE PROTECTION OF THE MARINE ENVIRONMENT AGAINST POLLUTION FROM LAND-BASED SOURCES (**Without Annexes**). **Adopted at Montreal, 24 May 1985. UNEP/GC.13/9/Add.3, UNEP/ GC/DEC/13/1811, UNEP ELPG No.7;** *reprinted in* **5 Weston & Carlson V.F.24**

1. *Definitions*

For the purposes of these guidelines:

(a) "Pollution" means the introduction by man, directly or indirectly, of substances or energy into the marine environment which results or is likely to result in such deleterious effects as harm to living resources and marine ecosystems, hazards to human health, hindrance to marine activities, including fishing and other legitimate uses of the sea, impairment of quality for use of sea water and reduction of amenities;

(b) "Land-based sources" means:

(i) Municipal, industrial or agricultural sources, both fixed and mobile, on land, discharges from which reach the marine environment, in particular:

a. From the coast, including from outfalls discharging directly into the marine environment and through run-off;

b. Through rivers, canals of other watercourses, including underground watercourses; and

c. Via the atmosphere;

(ii) Sources of marine pollution from activities conducted on offshore fixed or mobile facilities within the limits of national jurisdiction, save to the extent that these sources are governed by appropriate international agreements.

(c) "Marine environment" means the maritime area extending, in the case of watercourses, up to the freshwater limit and including inter-tidal zones and salt-water marshes;

(d) "Freshwater limit" means the place in watercourses where, at low tide and in a period of low freshwater flow, there is an appreciable increase in salinity due to the presence of sea water.

2. *Basic obligation*

States have the obligation to protect and preserve the marine environment. In exercising their sovereign right to exploit their natural resources, all States have the duty to prevent, reduce and control pollution of the marine environment.

3. *Discharges affecting other States or areas beyond the limits of national jurisdiction*

States have the duty to ensure that discharges from land-based sources within their territories do not cause pollution to the marine environment of other States or of areas beyond the limits of national jurisdiction.

4. *Adoption of measures against pollution from land-based sources*

(a) States should adopt, individually or jointly, and in accordance with their capabilities, all measures necessary to prevent, reduce and control pollution from land-based sources, including those designed to minimize to the fullest possible extent the release of toxic, harmful or noxious substances; especially those which are persistent, into the marine environment. States should ensure that such measures take into account internationally agreed rules, criteria, standards and recommended practices and procedures.

(b) In taking measures to prevent, reduce and control pollution from land-based sources, States should refrain, in accordance with international law, from unjustifiable interference with activities carried out by other States in the exercise of their sovereign rights and in pursuance of their duties in conformity with internationally agreed rules, criteria, standards and recommended practices and procedures.

5. *Co-operation on a global, regional or bilateral basis*

(a) States should undertake, as appropriate, to establish internationally agreed rules, criteria, standards and recommended practices and procedures to prevent, reduce and control pollution from land-based sources, with a view to co-ordinating their policies in this connection, particularly at the local and regional level. Such rules, criteria, standards and recommended practices and procedures should take into account local ecological, geographical and physical characteristics, the economic capacity of States and their need for sustainable development and environmental protection, and the assimilative capacity of the marine environment, and should be reviewed from time to time as necessary;

(b) States not bordering on the marine environment should co-operate in preventing, reducing and controlling pollution of the marine environment originating or partially originating from releases within their territory into or reaching water basins or watercourses flowing into the marine environment or via the atmosphere. To this end, States concerned should as far as possible, and, as appropriate, in co-operation with competent international organizations, take necessary measures to prevent, reduce and control pollution of the marine environment from land-based sources;

(c) If discharges from a watercourse which flows through the territories of two or more States or forms a boundary between them are likely to cause pollution of the marine environment, the States concerned should co-operate in taking necessary measures to prevent, reduce and control such pollution.

6. *Duty not to transfer or transform pollution from land-based sources*

In taking measures to prevent, reduce and control pollution from land-based sources, States have the duty to act so as not to transfer directly or indirectly, damage or hazards from one area to another or transform such pollution into another type of pollution.

7. *Specially protected areas*

(a) States should, in a manner consistent with international law, take all appropriate measures, such as the establishment of marine sanctuaries and reserves, to protect certain areas to the fullest possible extent from pollution, including that from land-based sources, taking into account the relevant provisions of annex I;

(b) States should, as practicable, undertake to develop, jointly or individually, environmental quality objectives for specially protected areas, conforming with the intended uses, and strive to maintain or ameliorate existing conditions by comprehensive environmental management practices.

8. *Scientific and technical co-operation*

States should co-operate, directly and/or through competent international organizations, in the field of science and technology related to pollution from land-based sources, and exchange data and other scientific information for the purpose of preventing, reducing and controlling such pollution, taking into account national regulations regarding the protection of confidential information. They should, in particular, undertake to develop and co-ordinate to the fullest possible extent their national research programmes and to co-operate in the establishment and implementation of regional and other international research programmes.

9. *Assistance to developing countries*

(a) States should, directly and/or through competent international organizations, promote programmes of assistance to developing countries in the fields of education, environmental and pollution awareness, training, scientific research and transfer of technology and know-how, for the purpose of improving the capacity of the developing countries to prevent, reduce and control pollution from land-based sources and to assess its effects on the marine environment;

(b) Such assistance should include:

(i) Training of scientific and technical personnel;

(ii) Facilitation of the participation of developing countries in relevant international programmes;

(iii) Acquisition, utilization, maintenance and production by those countries of appropriate equipment; and

(iv) Advice on, and development of, facilities for education, training, research, monitoring and other programmes;

(c) States should, directly and/or through competent international organizations, promote programmes of assistance to developing countries for the establishment, as necessary, of infrastructure for the effective implementation of applicable internationally agreed rules, criteria, standards and recommended practices and procedures related to the protection of the marine environment against pollution from land-based sources, including the provision of expert advice on the development of the necessary legal and administrative measures.

10. *Development of a comprehensive environmental management approach*

States should undertake to develop, as far as practicable, a comprehensive environmental management approach to the prevention, reduction and control of pollution from land-based sources, taking into account relevant existing programmes at the bilateral, regional or global level and the provisions of annex I. Such a comprehensive approach should include the identification of desired and attainable water use objectives for the specific marine environments.

11. *Monitoring and data management*

States should endeavour to establish directly or, whenever necessary, through competent international organizations, complementary or joint programmes for monitoring, storage and exchange of data, based, when possible, on compatible procedures and methods, taking into account relevant existing programmes at the bilateral, regional or global level and the provisions of annex III, in order to:

(a) Collect data on natural conditions in the region concerned as regards its physical, biological and chemical characteristics;

(b) Collect data on inputs of substances or energy that cause or potentially cause pollution emanating from land-based sources, including information on the distribution of sources and the quantities introduced to the region concerned;

(c) Assess systematically the levels of pollution along their coasts emanating from land-based sources and the fates and effects of pollution in the region concerned; and

(d) Evaluate the effectiveness of measures in meeting the environmental objectives for specific marine environments.

12. *Environmental assessment*

States should assess the potential effects/impacts, including possible transboundary effects/impacts, of proposed major projects under their jurisdiction or control, particularly in coastal areas, which may cause pollution from land-based sources, so that appropriate measures may be taken to prevent or mitigate such pollution.

13. *Development of control strategies*

(a) States should develop, adopt and implement programmes and measures for the prevention, reduction and control of pollution from land-based sources. They should employ an appropriate control strategy or combination of control strategies, taking into account relevant international or national experience, as described in annex I;

(b) States should, as appropriate, progressively formulate and adopt, in co-operation with competent international organizations, standards based on marine quality or on emissions, as well as recommended practices and procedures, taking into account the provisions of annex I;

(c) Where appropriate, States should undertake to establish priorities for action, based on lists of substances pollution by which should be eliminated and of substances pollution by which should be strictly limited on the basis of their toxicity, persistence, bioaccumulation and other criteria as elaborated in annex II, or in relevant international agreements.

14. *Pollution emergencies arising from land-based sources*

States and, as appropriate, competent international organizations should take all necessary measures for preventing and dealing with marine pollution emergencies from land-based sources, however caused, and for reducing or eliminating damage or the threat of damage therefrom. To this end States should, as appropriate, individually or jointly, develop and promote national and international contingency plans for responding to incidents of pollution from land-based sources and should co-operate with one another and, whenever necessary, through competent international organizations.

15. *Notification, information exchange and consultation*

Whenever releases originating or likely to originate from land-based sources within the territory of a State are likely to cause pollution to the marine environment of one or more other States or of areas beyond the limits of national jurisdiction, that State should immediately notify such other State or States, as well as competent international organizations, and provide them with timely information that will enable them, where necessary, to take appropriate action to prevent, reduce and control such pollution. Furthermore, consultations deemed appropriate by States concerned should be undertaken with a view to preventing, reducing and controlling such pollution.

16. *National laws and procedures*

(a) Each State should adopt and implement national laws and regulations for the protection and preservation of the marine environment against pollution from land-based sources, taking into account internationally agreed rules, criteria, standards and recommended practices and procedures, and take appropriate measures to ensure compliance with such laws and regulations;

(b) Paragraph (a) above is without prejudice to the right of States to take more stringent measures nationally or in co-operation with each other to prevent, reduce and control pollution from land-based sources under their jurisdiction or control;

(c) Each State should, on a reciprocal basis, grant equal access to and non-discriminatory treatment in its courts, tribunals and administrative proceedings to persons in other States who are or may be affected by pollution from land-based sources under its jurisdiction or control.

17. *Liability and compensation for pollution damage emanating from land-based sources*

(a) States should ensure that recourse is available in accordance with their legal systems for prompt and adequate compensation or other relief in respect of damage caused by pollution of the marine environment by natural or juridical persons under their jurisdiction;

(b) To this end, States should formulate and adopt appropriate procedures for the determination of liability for damage resulting from pollution from land-based sources. Such procedures should include measures for addressing damage caused by releases of a significant scale or by the substances referred to in guideline 13(c).

18. *Implementation reports*

States should report, as appropriate, to other States concerned, directly or through competent international organizations, on measures taken, on results achieved and, if the case arises, on difficulties encountered in the implementation of applicable internationally agreed rules, criteria, standards and recommended practices and procedures. To this end, States should designate national authorities as focal points for the reporting of such measures, results and difficulties.

19. *Institutional arrangements*

(a) States should ensure that adequate institutional arrangements are made at the appropriate regional or global level, for the purpose of achieving the objectives of these guidelines, and in particular for promoting the formulation, adoption and application of international rules, criteria, standards and recommended practices and procedures, and for monitoring the condition of the marine environment;

(b) The functions of such institutional arrangements should include:

(i) Periodic assessment of the state of the specific marine environment concerned;

(ii) Formulation and adoption, as appropriate, of a comprehensive environmental management approach consistent with the provisions of guidelines 7 and 10;

(iii) Adoption, review and revision, as necessary, of the lists referred to in guideline 13;

(iv) Development and adoption, as appropriate, of programmes and measures consistent with the provisions of guidelines 10 and 13;

(v) Consideration, where necessary, of the reports and information submitted in accordance with guidelines 15 and 18;

(vi) Recommendation of appropriate measures to be taken for the prevention, reduction and control of pollution from land-based sources, such as assistance to developing countries, the strengthening of regional co-operation mechanisms, consideration of aspects of transboundary pollution, and the difficulties encountered in the implementation of agreed rules; and

(vii) Review of the implementation of relevant internationally agreed rules, criteria, standards and recommended practices and procedures, and of the efficacy of the measures adopted and the advisability of any other measures.

3.11 Convention for the Protection of the Natural Resources and Environ-ment of the South Pacific Region (SREP Convention) (Without Protocols). Concluded at Noumea, 25 November 1986. Entered into force, 22 August 1990. 1990 ATS 31. *Reprinted in* 26 ILM 38 (1987) & 5 Weston & Carlson V.C.6

Article 1

GEOGRAPHICAL COVERAGE

1. This Convention shall apply to the South Pacific Region, hereinafter referred to as "the Convention Area" as defined in paragraph (a) of article 2.

2. Except as may be otherwise provided in any Protocol to this Convention, the Convention Area shall not include internal waters or archipelagic waters of the Parties as defined in accordance with international law.

Article 2

DEFINITIONS

For the purpose of this Convention and its Protocols unless otherwise defined in any such Protocol:

(a) the "Convention Area" shall comprise:

(i) the 200 nautical mile zones established in accordance with interna-tional law off:

American Samoa	Niue
Australia (East Coast and Islands to eastward including Macquarie Island)	Northern Mariana Islands
Cook Islands	Palau
Federated States of Micronesia	Papua New Guinea
Fiji	Pitcairn Islands
French Polynesia	Solomon Islands
Guam	Tokelau
Kiribati	Tonga
Marshall Islands	Tuvalu
Nauru	Vanuatu
New Caledonia and Dependencies	Wallis and Futuna
New Zealand	Western Samoa

(ii) those areas of high seas which are enclosed from all sides by the 200 nautical mile zones referred to in sub-paragraph (i);

(iii) areas of the Pacific Ocean which have been included in the Conven-tion Area pursuant to article 3;

(b) "dumping" means:

— any deliberate disposal at sea of wastes or other matter from vessels, aircraft, platforms or other man-made structures at sea;

— any deliberate disposal at sea of vessels, aircraft, platforms or other man-made structures at sea;

"dumping" does not include:

— the disposal of wastes or other matter incidental to, or derived from the normal operations of vessels, aircraft, platforms or other man-made structures at sea and their equipment, other than wastes or other matter transported by or to vessels, aircraft, platforms or other man-made structures at sea, operating for the purpose of disposal of such matter or derived from the treatment of such wastes or other matter on such vessels, aircraft, platforms or structures;

— placement of matter for a purpose other than the mere disposal thereof, provided that such placement is not contrary to the aims of this Convention;

(c) "wastes or other matter" means material and substances of any kind, form or description;

(d) the following wastes or other matter shall be considered to be non-radioactive: sewage sludge, dredge spoil, fly ash, agricultural wastes, construction materials, vessels, artificial reef building materials and other such materials, provided that they have not been contaminated with radio nuclides of anthropogenic origin (except dispersed global fallout from nuclear weapons testing), nor are potential sources of naturally occurring radio nuclides for commercial purposes, nor have been enriched in natural or artificial radio nuclides;

if there is a question as to whether the material to be dumped should be considered non-radioactive, for the purposes of this Convention, such material shall not be dumped unless the appropriate national authority of the proposed dumper confirms that such dumping would not exceed the individual and collective dose limits of the International Atomic Energy Agency general principles for the exemption of radiation sources and practices from regulatory control. The national authority shall also take into account the relevant recommendations, standards and guidelines developed by the International Atomic Energy Agency;

(e) "vessels" and "aircraft" means waterborne or airborne craft of any type whatsoever. This expression includes air cushioned craft and floating craft, whether self-propelled or not;

(f) "pollution" means the introduction by man, directly or indirectly, of substances or energy into the marine environment (including estuaries) which results or is likely to result in such deleterious effects as harm to living resources and marine life, hazards to human health, hindrance to marine activities, including fishing and other legitimate uses of the sea, impairment of quality for use of sea water and reduction of amenities;

in applying this definition to the Convention obligations, the Parties shall use their best endeavours to comply with the appropriate standards and recommendations established by competent international organisations, including the International Atomic Energy Agency;

(g) "Organisation" means the South Pacific Commission;

(h) "Director" means the Director of the South Pacific Bureau for Economic Co-operation.

Article 3

ADDITION TO THE CONVENTION AREA

Any Party may add areas under its jurisdiction within the Pacific Ocean between the Tropic of Cancer and 60 degrees South latitude and between 130 degrees East longitude and 120 degrees West longitude to the Convention Area. Such addition shall be notified to the Depositary who shall promptly notify the other Parties and the Organisation. Such areas shall be incorporated within the Convention Area ninety days after notification to the Parties by the Depositary, provided there has been no objection to the proposal to add new areas by any Party affected by that proposal. If there is any such objection the Parties concerned will consult with a view to resolving the matter.

Article 4

GENERAL PROVISIONS

1. The Parties shall endeavour to conclude bilateral or multilateral agreements, including regional or sub-regional agreements, for the protection, development and management of the marine and coastal environment of the Convention Area. Such agreements shall be consistent with this Convention and in accordance with international law. Copies of such agreements shall be communicated to the Organisation and through it to all Parties to this Convention.

2. Nothing in this Convention or its Protocols shall be deemed to affect obligations assumed by a Party under agreements previously concluded.

3. Nothing in this Convention and its Protocols shall be construed to prejudice or affect the interpretation and application of any provision or term in the Convention on the Prevention of Marine Pollution by Dumping of Wastes and Other Matter, 1972.

4. This Convention and its Protocols shall be construed in accordance with international law relating to their subject matter.

5. Nothing in this Convention and its Protocols shall prejudice the present or future claims and legal views of any Party concerning the nature and extent of maritime jurisdiction.

6. Nothing in this Convention shall affect the sovereign right of States to exploit, develop and manage their own natural resources pursuant to their own policies, taking into account their duty to protect and preserve the environment. Each Party shall ensure that activities within its jurisdiction or control do not cause damage to the environment of other States or of areas beyond the limits of its national jurisdiction.

Article 5

GENERAL OBLIGATIONS

1. The Parties shall endeavour, either individually or jointly, to take all appropriate measures in conformity with international law and in accordance with this Convention and those Protocols in force to which they are party to prevent, reduce and control pollution of the Convention Area, from any source, and to ensure sound environmental management and development of natural resources, using for this purpose the best practicable means at their disposal, and in accordance with their capabilities. In doing so the Parties shall endeavor to harmonize their policies at the regional level.

2. The Parties shall use their best endeavors to ensure that the implementation of this Convention shall not result in an increase in pollution in the marine environment outside the Convention Area.

3. In addition to the Protocol for the Prevention of Pollution of the South Pacific Region by Dumping and the Protocol Concerning Co-operation in Combating Pollution Emergencies in the South Pacific Region, the Parties shall co-operate in the formulation and adoption of other Protocols prescribing agreed measures, procedures and standards to prevent, reduce and control pollution from all sources or in promoting environmental management in conformity with the objectives of this Convention.

4. The Parties shall, taking into account existing internationally recognized rules, standards, practices and procedures, co-operate with competent global, regional and sub-regional organisations to establish and adopt recommended practices, procedures and measures to prevent, reduce and control pollution from all sources and to promote sustained resource management and to ensure the sound development of

natural resources in conformity with the objectives of this Convention and its Protocols, and to assist each other in fulfilling their obligations under this Convention and its Protocols.

5. The Parties shall endeavor to establish laws and regulations for the effective discharge of the obligations prescribed in this Convention. Such laws and regulations shall be no less effective than international rules, standards and recommended practices and procedures.

Article 6

POLLUTION FROM VESSELS

The Parties shall take all appropriate measures to prevent, reduce and control pollution in the Convention Area caused by discharges from vessels, and to ensure the effective application in the Convention Area of the generally accepted international rules and standards established through the competent international organisation or general diplomatic conference relating to the control of pollution from vessels.

Article 7

POLLUTION FROM LAND–BASED SOURCES

The Parties shall take all appropriate measures to prevent, reduce and control pollution in the Convention Area caused by coastal disposal or by discharges emanating from rivers, estuaries, coastal establishments, outfall structures, or any other sources in their territory.

Article 8

POLLUTION FROM SEA–BED ACTIVITIES

The Parties shall take all appropriate measures to prevent, reduce and control pollution in the Convention Area resulting directly or indirectly from exploration and exploitation of the sea-bed and its subsoil.

Article 9

AIRBORNE POLLUTION

The Parties shall take all appropriate measures to prevent, reduce and control pollution in the Convention Area resulting from discharges into the atmosphere from activities under their jurisdiction.

Article 10

DISPOSAL OF WASTES

1. The Parties shall take all appropriate measures to prevent, reduce and control pollution in the Convention Area caused by dumping from vessels, aircraft, or manmade structures at sea, including the effective application of the relevant internationally recognized rules and procedures relating to the control of dumping of wastes and other matter. The Parties agree to prohibit the dumping of radioactive wastes or other radioactive matter in the Convention area. Without prejudice to whether or not disposal into the seabed and subsoil of wastes or other matter is "dumping", the Parties agree to prohibit the disposal into the seabed and subsoil of the Convention area of radioactive wastes or other radioactive matter.

2. This article shall also apply to the continental shelf of a Party where it extends, in accordance with international law, outward beyond the Convention Area.

Article 11

STORAGE OF TOXIC AND HAZARDOUS WASTES

The Parties shall take all appropriate measures to prevent, reduce and control pollution in the Convention Area resulting from the storage of toxic and hazardous wastes. In particular, the Parties shall prohibit the storage of radioactive wastes or other radioactive matter in the Convention Area.

Article 12

TESTING OF NUCLEAR DEVICES

The Parties shall take all appropriate measures to prevent, reduce and control pollution in the Convention Area which might result from the testing of nuclear devices.

Article 13

MINING AND COASTAL EROSION

The Parties shall take all appropriate measures to prevent, reduce and control environmental damage in the Convention Area, in particular coastal erosion caused by coastal engineering, mining activities, sand removal, land reclamation and dredging.

Article 14

SPECIALLY PROTECTED AREAS AND PROTECTION OF WILD FLORA AND FAUNA

The Parties shall, individually or jointly, take all appropriate measures to protect and preserve rare or fragile ecosystems and depleted, threatened or endangered flora and fauna as well as their habitat in the Convention Area. To this end, the Parties shall, as appropriate, establish protected areas, such as parks and reserves, and prohibit or regulate any activity likely to have adverse effects on the species, ecosystems or biological processes that such areas are designed to protect. The establishment of such areas shall not affect the rights of other Parties or third States under international law. In addition, the Parties shall exchange information concerning the administration and management of such areas.

Article 15

CO-OPERATION IN COMBATING POLLUTION IN CASES OF EMERGENCY

1. The Parties shall co-operate in taking all necessary measures to deal with pollution emergencies in the Convention Area, whatever the cause of such emergencies, and to prevent, reduce and control pollution or the threat of pollution resulting therefrom. To this end, the Parties shall develop and promote individual contingency plans and joint contingency plans for responding to incidents involving pollution or the threat thereof in the Convention Area.

2. When a Party becomes aware of a case in which the Convention Area is in imminent danger of being polluted or has been polluted, it shall immediately notify other countries and territories it deems likely to be affected by such pollution, as well as the Organisation. Furthermore it shall inform, as soon as feasible, such other countries and territories and the Organisation of any measures it has itself taken to reduce or control pollution or the threat thereof.

Article 16

ENVIRONMENTAL IMPACT ASSESSMENT

1. The Parties agree to develop and maintain, with the assistance of competent global, regional and sub-regional organisations as requested, technical guidelines and

legislation giving adequate emphasis to environmental and social factors to facilitate balanced development of their natural resources and planning of their major projects which might affect the marine environment in such a way as to prevent or minimize harmful impacts on the Convention Area.

2. Each Party shall, within its capabilities, assess the potential effects of such projects on the marine environment, so that appropriate measures can be taken to prevent any substantial pollution of, or significant and harmful changes within, the Convention Area.

3. With respect to the assessment referred to in paragraph 2, each Party shall, where appropriate, invite:

(a) public comment according to its national procedures,

(b) other Parties that may be affected to consult with it and submit comments.

The results of these assessments shall be communicated to the Organisation, which shall make them available to interested Parties.

Article 17

SCIENTIFIC AND TECHNICAL CO–OPERATION

1. The Parties shall co-operate, either directly or with the assistance of competent global, regional and sub-regional organisations, in scientific research, environmental monitoring, and the exchange of data and other scientific and technical information related to the purposes of the Convention.

2. In addition, the Parties shall, for the purposes of this Convention, develop and co-ordinate research and monitoring programmes relating to the Convention Area and co-operate, as far as practicable, in the establishment and implementation of regional, sub-regional and international research programmes.

Article 18

TECHNICAL AND OTHER ASSISTANCE

The Parties undertake to co-operate, directly and when appropriate through the competent global, regional and sub-regional organisations, in the provision to other Parties of technical and other assistance in fields relating to pollution and sound environmental management of the Convention Area, taking into account the special needs of the island developing countries and territories.

Article 19

TRANSMISSION OF INFORMATION

The Parties shall transmit to the Organisation information on the measures adopted by them in the implementation of this Convention and of Protocols to which they are Parties, in such form and at such intervals as the Parties may determine.

Article 20

LIABILITY AND COMPENSATION

The Parties shall co-operate in the formulation and adoption of appropriate rules and procedures in conformity with international law in respect of liability and compensation for damage resulting from pollution of the Convention Area.

Article 21

INSTITUTIONAL ARRANGEMENTS

1. The Organisation shall be responsible for carrying out the following secretariat functions:

(a) to prepare and convene the meetings of Parties;

(b) to transmit to the Parties notifications, reports and other information received in accordance with this Convention and its Protocols;

(c) to perform the functions assigned to it by the Protocols to this Convention;

(d) to consider enquiries by, and information from, the Parties and to consult with them on questions relating to this Convention and the Protocols;

(e) to co-ordinate the implementation of co-operative activities agreed upon by the Parties;

(f) to ensure the necessary co-ordination with other competent global, regional and sub-regional bodies;

(g) to enter into such administrative arrangements as may be required for the effective discharge of the secretariat functions;

(h) to perform such other functions as may be assigned to it by the Parties; and

(i) to transmit to the South Pacific Conference and the South Pacific Forum the reports of ordinary and extraordinary meetings of the Parties.

2. Each Party shall designate an appropriate national authority to serve as the channel of communication with the Organisation for the purposes of this Convention.

Article 22

MEETINGS OF THE PARTIES

1. The Parties shall hold ordinary meetings once every two years. Ordinary meetings shall review the implementation of this Convention and its Protocols and, in particular, shall:

(a) assess periodically the state of the environment in the Convention Area;

(b) consider the information submitted by the Parties under article 19;

(c) adopt, review and amend as required annexes to this Convention and to its Protocols, in accordance with the provisions of article 25;

(d) make recommendations regarding the adoption of any Protocols or any amendments to this Convention or its Protocols in accordance with the provisions of articles 23 and 24;

(e) establish working groups as required to consider any matters concerning this Convention and its Protocols;

(f) consider co-operative activities to be undertaken within the framework of this Convention and its Protocols, including their financial and institutional implications and to adopt decisions relating thereto;

(g) consider and undertake any additional action that may be required for the achievement of the purposes of this Convention and its Protocols; and

(h) adopt by consensus financial rules and budget, prepared in consultation with the Organization, to determine, *inter alia,* the financial participation of the Parties under this Convention and those Protocols to which they are party.

2. The Organisation shall convene the first ordinary meeting of the Parties not later than one year after the date on which the Convention enters into force in accordance with article 31.

3. Extraordinary meetings shall be convened at the request of any Party or upon the request of the Organisation, provided that such requests are supported by at least two-thirds of the Parties. It shall be the function of an extraordinary meeting of the

Parties to consider those items proposed in the request for the holding of the extraordinary meeting and any other items agreed to by all the Parties attending the meeting.

4.   The Parties shall adopt by consensus at their first ordinary meeting, rules of procedure for their meetings.

Article 23

ADOPTION OF PROTOCOLS

1.   The Parties may, at a conference of plenipotentiaries, adopt Protocols to this Convention pursuant to paragraph 3 of article 5.

2.   If so requested by a majority of the Parties, the Organisation shall convene a conference of plenipotentiaries for the purpose of adopting Protocols to this Convention.

Article 24

AMENDMENT OF THE CONVENTION AND ITS PROTOCOLS

1.   Any Party may propose amendments to this Convention. Amendments shall be adopted by a conference of plenipotentiaries which shall be convened by the Organisation at the request of two-thirds of the Parties.

2.   Any Party to this Convention may propose amendments to any Protocol. Such amendments shall be adopted by a conference of plenipotentiaries which shall be convened by the Organisation at the request of two-thirds of the Parties to the Protocol concerned.

3.   A proposed amendment to the Convention or any Protocol shall be communicated to the Organisation, which shall promptly transmit such proposal for consideration to all the other Parties.

4.   A conference of plenipotentiaries to consider a proposed amendment to the Convention or any Protocol shall be convened not less than ninety days after the requirements for the convening of the Conference have been met pursuant to paragraphs 1 or 2, as the case may be.

5.   Any amendment to this Convention shall be adopted by a three-fourths majority vote of the Parties to the Convention which are represented at the conference of plenipotentiaries and shall be submitted by the Depositary for acceptance by all Parties to the Convention. Amendments to any Protocol shall be adopted by a three-fourths majority vote of the Parties to the Protocol which are represented at the conference of plenipotentiaries and shall be submitted by the Depositary for acceptance by all Parties to the Protocol.

6.   Instruments of ratification, acceptance or approval of amendments shall be deposited with the Depositary. Amendments shall enter into force between Parties having accepted such amendments on the thirtieth day following the date of receipt by the Depositary of the instruments of at least three-fourths of the Parties to this Convention or to the Protocol concerned, as the case may be. Thereafter the amendments shall enter into force for any other Party on the thirtieth day after the date on which that Party deposits its instrument.

7.   After the entry into force of an amendment to this Convention or to a Protocol, any new Party to the Convention or such protocol shall become a Party to the Convention or Protocol as amended.

Article 25

ANNEXES AND AMENDMENT OF ANNEXES

1.   Annexes to this Convention or to any Protocol shall form an integral part of the Convention or such Protocol respectively.

2. Except as may be otherwise provided in any Protocol with respect to its annexes, the following procedures shall apply to the adoption and entry into force of any amendments to annexes to this Convention or to annexes to any Protocol:

(a) any Party may propose amendments to the annexes to this Convention or annexes to any Protocol;

(b) any proposed amendment shall be notified by the Organisation to the Parties not less than sixty days before the convening of a meeting of the Parties unless this requirement is waived by the meeting;

(c) such amendments shall be adopted at a meeting of the Parties by a three-fourths majority vote of the Parties to the instrument in question;

(d) the Depositary shall without delay communicate the amendments so adopted to all Parties;

(e) any Party that is unable to approve an amendment to the annexes to this Convention or to annexes to any Protocol shall so notify in writing to the Depositary within one hundred days from the date of the communication of the amendment by the Depositary. A Party may at any time substitute an acceptance for a previous declaration of objection, and the amendment shall thereupon enter into force for that Party;

(f) the Depositary shall without delay notify all Parties of any notification received pursuant to the preceding sub-paragraph; and

(g) on expiry of the period referred to in sub-paragraph (e) above, the amendment to the annex shall become effective for all Parties to this Convention or to the Protocol concerned which have not submitted a notification in accordance with the provisions of that sub-paragraph.

3. The adoption and entry into force of a new annex shall be subject to the same procedure as that for the adoption and entry into force of an amendment to an annex as set out in the provisions of paragraph 2, provided that, if any amendment to the Convention or the Protocol concerned is involved, the new annex shall not enter into force until such time as that amendment enters into force.

4. Amendments to the Annex on Arbitration shall be considered to be amendments to this Convention or its Protocols and shall be proposed and adopted in accordance with the procedures set out in article 24.

Article 26

SETTLEMENT OF DISPUTES

1. In case of a dispute between Parties as to the interpretation or application of this Convention or its Protocols, they shall seek a settlement of the dispute through negotiation or any other peaceful means of their own choice. If the Parties concerned cannot reach agreement, they should seek the good offices of, or jointly request mediation by, a third Party.

2. If the Parties concerned cannot settle their dispute through the means mentioned in paragraph 1, the dispute shall, upon common agreement, except as may be otherwise provided in any Protocol to this Convention, be submitted to arbitration under conditions laid down in the Annex on Arbitration to this Convention. However, failure to reach common agreement on submission of the dispute to arbitration shall not absolve the Parties from the responsibility of continuing to seek to resolve it by means referred to in paragraph 1.

3. A Party may at any time declare that it recognizes as compulsory *ipso facto* and without special agreement, in relation to any other Party accepting the same obligation, the application of the arbitration procedure set out in the Annex on

Arbitration. Such declaration shall be notified in writing to the Depositary who shall promptly communicate it to the other Parties.

Article 27

RELATIONSHIP BETWEEN THIS CONVENTION AND ITS PROTOCOLS

1. No State may become a Party to this Convention unless it becomes at the same time a Party to one or more Protocols. No State may become a Party to a Protocol unless it is, or becomes at the same time, a Party to this Convention.

2. Decisions concerning any Protocol pursuant to articles 22, 24 and 25 of this Convention shall be taken only by the Parties to the Protocol concerned.

Article 28

SIGNATURE

This Convention, the Protocol Concerning Co-operation in Combating Pollution Emergencies in the South Pacific Region, and the Protocol for the Prevention of Pollution of the South Pacific Region by Dumping shall be open for signature at the South Pacific Commission Headquarters in Noumea, New Caledonia on 25 November 1986 and at the South Pacific Bureau for Economic Co-operation Headquarters, Suva, Fiji from 26 November 1986 to 25 November 1987 by States which were invited to participate in the Plenipotentiary Meeting of the High Level Conference on the Protection of the Natural Resources and Environment of the South Pacific Region held at Noumea, New Caledonia from 24 November 1986 to 25 November 1986.

Article 29

RATIFICATION, ACCEPTANCE OR APPROVAL

This Convention and any Protocol thereto shall be subject to ratification, acceptance or approval by States referred to in article 28. Instruments of ratification, acceptance or approval shall be deposited with the Director who shall be the Depositary.

Article 30

ACCESSION

1. This Convention and any Protocol thereto shall be open to accession by the States referred to in article 28 as from the day following the date on which the Convention or Protocol concerned was closed for signature.

2. Any State not referred to in paragraph 1 may accede to the Convention and to any Protocol subject to prior approval by three-fourths of the Parties to the Convention or the Protocol concerned.

3. Instruments of accession shall be deposited with the Depositary.

Article 31

ENTRY INTO FORCE

1. This Convention shall enter into force on the thirtieth day following the date of deposit of at least ten instruments of ratification, acceptance, approval or accession.

2. Any Protocol to this Convention, except as otherwise provided in such Protocol, shall enter into force on the thirtieth day following the date of deposit of at least five instruments of ratification, acceptance or approval of such Protocol, or of accession thereto, provided that no Protocol shall enter into force before the Convention. Should the requirements for entry into force of a Protocol be met prior to those for entry into

force of the Convention pursuant to paragraph 1, such Protocol shall enter into force on the same date as the Convention.

3. Thereafter, this Convention and any Protocol shall enter into force with respect to any State referred to in articles 28 or 30 on the thirtieth day following the date of deposit of its instrument of ratification, acceptance, approval or accession.

Article 32

DENUNCIATION

1. At any time after two years from the date of entry into force of this Convention with respect to a Party, that Party may denounce the Convention by giving written notification to the Depositary.

2. Except as may be otherwise provided in any Protocol to this Convention, any Party may, at any time after two years from the date of entry into force of such Protocol with respect to that Party, denounce the Protocol by giving written notification to the Depositary.

3. Denunciation shall take effect ninety days after the date on which notification of denunciation is received by the Depositary.

4. Any Party which denounces this Convention shall be considered as also having denounced any Protocol to which it was a Party.

5. Any Party which, upon its denunciation of a Protocol, is no longer a Party to any Protocol to this Convention, shall be considered as also having denounced this Convention.

Article 33

RESPONSIBILITIES OF THE DEPOSITARY

1. The Depositary shall inform the Parties, as well as the Organisation:

(a) of the signature of this Convention and of any Protocol thereto and of the deposit of instruments of ratification, acceptance, approval, or accession in accordance with articles 29 and 30;

(b) of the date on which the Convention and any Protocol will come into force in accordance with the provisions of article 31;

(c) of notification of denunciation made in accordance with article 32;

(d) of notification of any addition to the Convention Area in accordance with article 3;

(e) of the amendments adopted with respect to the Convention and to any Protocol, their acceptance by the Parties and the date of their entry into force in accordance with the provisions of article 24; and

(f) of the adoption of new annexes and of the amendments of any annex in accordance with article 25.

2. The original of this Convention and of any Protocol thereto shall be deposited with the Depositary who shall send certified copies thereof to the Signatories, the Parties, to the Organisation and to the Secretary–General of the United Nations for registration and publication in accordance with article 102 of the United Nations Charter.

3.12   INTERNATIONAL CONVENTION ON OIL POLLUTION PREPAREDNESS, RESPONSE, AND CO-OPERATION. **Concluded at London, 30 November 1990. Entered into force, 13 May 1995. 1891 UNTS 51.** *Reprinted in* **33 ILM 733 (1991) & 5 Weston & Carlson V.F.28**

Article 1
General provisions

1. Parties undertake, individually or jointly, to take all appropriate measures in accordance with the provisions of this Convention and the Annex thereto to prepare for and respond to an oil pollution incident.

2. The Annex to this Convention shall constitute an integral part of the Convention and a reference to this Convention constitutes at the same time a reference to the Annex.

3. This Convention shall not apply to any warship, naval auxiliary or other ship owned or operated by a State and used, for the time being, only on government non-commercial service. However, each Party shall ensure by the adoption of appropriate measures not impairing the operations or operational capabilities of such ships owned or operated by it, that such ships act in a manner consistent, so far as is reasonable and practicable, with this Convention.

Article 2
Definitions

For the purposes of this Convention:

1. "Oil" means petroleum in any form including crude oil, fuel oil, sludge, oil refuse and refined products.

2. "Oil pollution incident" means an occurrence or series of occurrences having the same origin, which results or may result in a discharge of oil and which poses or may pose a threat to the marine environment, or to the coastline or related interests of one or more States, and which requires emergency action or other immediate response.

3. "Ship" means a vessel of any type whatsoever operating in the marine environment and includes hydrofoil boats, air-cushion vehicles, submersibles, and floating craft of any type.

4. "Offshore unit" means any fixed or floating offshore installation or structure engaged in gas or oil exploration, exploitation or production activities, or loading or unloading of oil.

5. "Sea ports and oil handling facilities" means those facilities which present a risk of an oil pollution incident and includes, inter alia, sea ports, oil terminals, pipelines and other oil handling facilities.

6. "Organization" means the International Maritime Organization.

7. "Secretary–General" means the Secretary–General of the Organization.

Article 3
Oil pollution emergency plans

1. (a) Each Party shall require that ships entitled to fly its flag have on board a shipboard oil pollution emergency plan as required by and in accordance with the provisions adopted by the Organization for this purpose.

(b) A ship required to have on board an oil pollution emergency plan in accordance with subparagraph (a) is subject, while in a port or at an offshore terminal under the jurisdiction of a Party, to inspection by officers duly authorized by that Party, in accordance with the practices provided for in existing international agreements or its national legislation.

2. Each Party shall require that operators of offshore units under its jurisdiction have oil pollution emergency plans, which are co-ordinated with the national system established in accordance with article 6 and approved in accordance with procedures established by the competent national authority.

3. Each Party shall require that authorities or operators in charge of such sea ports and oil handling facilities under its jurisdiction as it deems appropriate have oil pollution emergency plans or similar arrangements which are co-ordinated with the national system established in accordance with article 6 and approved in accordance with procedures established by the competent national authority.

Article 4
Oil pollution reporting procedures

1. Each Party shall:

(a) require masters or other persons having charge of ships flying its flag and persons having charge of offshore units under its jurisdiction to report without delay any event on their ship or offshore unit involving a discharge or probable discharge of oil:

(i) in the case of a ship, to the nearest coastal State;

(ii) in the case of an offshore unit, to the coastal State to whose jurisdiction the unit is subject;

* * *

Article 5
Action on receiving an oil pollution report

1. Whenever a Party receives a report referred to in article 4 or pollution information provided by other sources, it shall:

(a) assess the event to determine whether it is an oil pollution incident;

(b) assess the nature, extent and possible consequences of the oil pollution incident; and

(c) then, without delay, inform all States whose interests are affected or likely to be affected by such oil pollution incident, together with

(i) details of its assessments and any action it has taken, or intends to take, to deal with the incident, and

(ii) further information as appropriate,

until the action taken to respond to the incident has been concluded or until joint action has been decided by such States.

* * *

Article 6
National and regional systems for preparedness and response

1. Each Party shall establish a national system for responding promptly and effectively to oil pollution incidents. This system shall include as a minimum:

(a) the designation of:

(i) the competent national authority or authorities with responsibility for oil pollution preparedness and response;

(ii) the national operational contact point or points, which shall be responsible for the receipt and transmission of oil pollution reports as referred to in article 4; and

(iii) an authority which is entitled to act on behalf of the State to request assistance or to decide to render the assistance requested;

(b) a national contingency plan for preparedness and response which includes the organizational relationship of the various bodies involved, whether public or private, taking into account guidelines developed by the Organization.

2. In addition, each Party, within its capabilities either individually or through bilateral or multilateral co-operation and, as appropriate, in co-operation with the oil and shipping industries, port authorities and other relevant entities, shall establish:

(a) a minimum level of pre-positioned oil spill combating equipment, commensurate with the risk involved, and programmes for its use;

(b) a programme of exercises for oil pollution response organizations and training of relevant personnel;

(c) detailed plans and communication capabilities for responding to an oil pollution incident. Such capabilities should be continuously available; and

(d) a mechanism or arrangement to co-ordinate the response to an oil pollution incident with, if appropriate, the capabilities to mobilize the necessary resources.

3. Each Party shall ensure that current information is provided to the Organization, directly or through the relevant regional organization or arrangements, concerning:

(a) the location, telecommunication data and, if applicable, areas of responsibility of authorities and entities referred to in paragraph (1)(a);

(b) information concerning pollution response equipment and expertise in disciplines related to oil pollution response and marine salvage which may be made available to other States, upon request; and

(c) its national contingency plan.

Article 7
International co-operation in pollution response

1. Parties agree that, subject to their capabilities and the availability of relevant resources, they will co-operate and provide advisory services, technical support and equipment for the purpose of responding to an oil pollution incident, when the severity of such incident so justifies, upon the request of any Party affected or likely to be affected. The financing of the costs for such assistance shall be based on the provisions set out in the Annex to this Convention.

2. A Party which has requested assistance may ask the Organization to assist in identifying sources of provisional financing of the costs referred to in paragraph (1).

3. In accordance with applicable international agreements, each Party shall take necessary legal or administrative measures to facilitate:

(a) the arrival and utilization in and departure from its territory of ships, aircraft and other modes of transport engaged in responding to an oil pollution incident or transporting personnel, cargoes, materials and equipment required to deal with such an incident; and

(b) the expeditious movement into, through, and out of its territory of personnel, cargoes, materials and equipment referred to in subparagraph (a).

Article 8
Research and development

1. Parties agree to co-operate directly or, as appropriate, through the Organization or relevant regional organizations or arrangements in the promotion and exchange of results of research and development programmes relating to the enhance-

ment of the state-of-the-art of oil pollution preparedness and response, including technologies and techniques for surveillance, containment, recovery, dispersion, clean-up and otherwise minimizing or mitigating the effects of oil pollution, and for restoration.

* * *

Article 9
Technical co-operation

* * *

Article 10
Promotion of bilateral and multilateral co-operation in preparedness and response

Parties shall endeavour to conclude bilateral or multilateral agreements for oil pollution preparedness and response. Copies of such agreements shall be communicated to the Organization which should make them available on request to Parties.

Article 11
Relation to other conventions and international agreements

Nothing in this Convention shall be construed as altering the rights or obligations of any Party under any other convention or international agreement.

* * *

Annex
Reimbursement of costs of assistance

1. (a) Unless an agreement concerning the financial arrangements governing actions of Parties to deal with oil pollution incidents has been concluded on a bilateral or multilateral basis prior to the oil pollution incident, Parties shall bear the costs of their respective actions in dealing with pollution in accordance with subparagraph (i) or subparagraph (ii).

(i) If the action was taken by one Party at the express request of another Party, the requesting Party shall reimburse to the assisting Party the cost of its action. The requesting Party may cancel its request at any time, but in that case it shall bear the costs already incurred or committed by the assisting Party.

(ii) If the action was taken by a Party on its own initiative, this Party shall bear the costs of its action.

(b) The principles laid down in subparagraph (a) shall apply unless the Parties concerned otherwise agree in any individual case.

2. Unless otherwise agreed, the costs of action taken by a Party at the request of another Party shall be fairly calculated according to the law and current practice of the assisting Party concerning the reimbursement of such costs.

3. The Party requesting assistance and the assisting Party shall, where appropriate, co-operate in concluding any action in response to a compensation claim. To that end, they shall give due consideration to existing legal regimes. Where the action thus concluded does not permit full compensation for expenses incurred in the assistance operation, the Party requesting assistance may ask the assisting Party to waive reimbursement of the expenses exceeding the sums compensated or to reduce the costs which have been calculated in accordance with paragraph (2). It may also request a postponement of the reimbursement of such costs. In considering such a request, assisting Parties shall give due consideration to the needs of the developing countries.

4. The provisions of this Convention shall not be interpreted as in any way prejudicing the rights of Parties to recover from third parties the costs of actions to deal with pollution or the threat of pollution under other applicable provisions and rules of national and international law. Special attention shall be paid to the 1969 International Convention on Civil Liability for Oil Pollution Damage and the 1971 International Convention on the Establishment of an International Fund for Compensation for Oil Pollution Damage or any subsequent amendment to those Conventions.

3.13 INTERNATIONAL CONVENTION ON CIVIL LIABILITY FOR OIL POLLUTION DAMAGE, 1992.)[h] **Concluded at London, 27 November 1992. Entered into force 30 May 1996. 1956 UNTS 255;** *reprinted in* **5 Weston & Carlson V.J.12**

Article I

For the purposes of this Convention:

1. "Ship" means any sea-going vessel and seaborne craft of any type whatsoever constructed or adapted for the carriage of oil in bulk as cargo, provided that a ship capable of carrying oil and other cargoes shall be regarded as a ship only when it is actually carrying oil in bulk as cargo and during any voyage following such carriage unless it is proved that it has no residues of such carriage of oil in bulk aboard.

2. "Person" means any individual or partnership or any public or private body, whether corporate or not, including a State or any of its constituent subdivisions.

3. "Owner" means the person or persons registered as the owner of the ship or, in the absence of registration, the person or persons owning the ship. However in the case of a ship owned by a State and operated by a company which in that State is registered as the ship's operator, "owner" shall mean such company.

4. "State of the ship's registry" means in relation to registered ships the State of registration of the ship, and in relation to unregistered ships the State whose flag the ship is flying.

5. "Oil" means any persistent hydrocarbon mineral oil such as crude oil, fuel oil, heavy diesel oil and lubricating oil, whether carried on board a ship as cargo or in the bunkers of such a ship.

6. "Pollution damage" means:

(a) loss or damage caused outside the ship by contamination resulting from the escape or discharge of oil from the ship, wherever such escape or discharge may occur, provided that compensation for impairment of the environment other than loss of profit from such impairment shall be limited to costs of reasonable measures of reinstatement actually undertaken or to be undertaken;

(b) the costs of preventive measures and further loss or damage caused by preventive measures.

7. "Preventive measures" means any reasonable measures taken by any person after an incident has occurred to prevent or minimize pollution damage.

8. "Incident" means any occurrence, or series of occurrences having the same origin, which causes pollution damage or creates a grave and imminent threat of causing such damage.

9. "Organization" means the International Maritime Organization.

10. "1969 Liability Convention" means the International Convention on Civil Liability for Oil Pollution Damage, 1969. For States Parties to the Protocol of 1976 to that Convention, the term shall be deemed to include the 1969 Liability Convention as amended by that Protocol.

h. This document reproduces the consolidated text of the International Convention on Civil Liability for Oil Pollution Damage, *concluded at Brussels on* Nov. 29, 1969, 973 U.N.T.S. 3, 9 I.L.M. 45 (1970), as amended by the 1976 and 1992 Protocols to that Convention. The 1992 Protocol provides that the 1969 Liability Convention and the Protocol shall be "read and interpreted together as one single instrument" and that the consolidated text shall be known as the "International Convention on Civil Liability for Oil Pollution Damage, 1992."

Article II

This Convention shall apply exclusively:

(a) to pollution damage caused:

(i) in the territory, including the territorial sea, of a Contracting State, and

(ii) in the exclusive economic zone of a Contracting State, established in accordance with international law, or, if a Contracting State has not established such a zone, in an area beyond and adjacent to the territorial sea of that State determined by that State in accordance with international law and extending not more than 200 nautical miles from the baselines from which the breadth of its territorial sea is measured;

(b) to preventive measures, wherever taken, to prevent or minimize such damage.

Article III

1. Except as provided in paragraphs 2 and 3 of this Article, the owner of a ship at the time of an incident, or, where the incident consists of a series of occurrences, at the time of the first such occurrence, shall be liable for any pollution damage caused by the ship as a result of the incident.

2. No liability for pollution damage shall attach to the owner if he proves that the damage:

(a) resulted from an act of war, hostilities, civil war, insurrection or a natural phenomenon of an exceptional, inevitable and irresistible character, or

(b) was wholly caused by an act or omission done with intent to cause damage by a third party, or

(c) was wholly caused by the negligence or other wrongful act of any Government or other authority responsible for the maintenance of lights or other navigational aids in the exercise of that function.

3. If the owner proves that the pollution damage resulted wholly or partially either from an act or omission done with intent to cause damage by the person who suffered the damage or from the negligence of that person, the owner may be exonerated wholly or partially from his liability to such person.

4. No claim for compensation for pollution damage may be made against the owner otherwise than in accordance with this Convention. Subject to paragraph 5 of this Article, no claim for compensation for pollution damage under this Convention or otherwise may be made against:

(a) the servants or agents of the owner or the members of the crew;

(b) the pilot or any other person who, without being a member of the crew, performs services for the ship;

(c) any charterer (howsoever described, including a bareboat charterer), manager or operator of the ship;

(d) any person performing salvage operations with the consent of the owner or on the instructions of a competent public authority;

(e) any person taking preventive measures;

(f) all servants or agents of persons mentioned in subparagraphs (c), (d) and (e); unless the damage resulted from their personal act or omission, committed with the intent to cause such damage, or recklessly and with knowledge that such damage would probably result.

5. Nothing in this Convention shall prejudice any right of recourse of the owner against third parties.

Article IV

When an incident involving two or more ships occurs and pollution damage results therefrom, the owners of all the ships concerned, unless exonerated under Article III, shall be jointly and severally liable for all such damage which is not reasonably separable.

Article V

1. The owner of a ship shall be entitled to limit his liability under this Convention in respect of any one incident to an aggregate amount calculated as follows:

(a) 3 million units of account for a ship not exceeding 5,000 units of tonnage;

(b) for a ship with a tonnage in excess thereof, for each additional unit of tonnage, 420 units of account in addition to the amount mentioned in subparagraph (a); provided, however, that this aggregate amount shall not in any event exceed 59.7 million units of account.

2. The owner shall not be entitled to limit his liability under this Convention if it is proved that the pollution damage resulted from his personal act or omission, committed with the intent to cause such damage, or recklessly and with knowledge that such damage would probably result.

3. For the purpose of availing himself of the benefit of limitation provided for in paragraph 1 of this Article the owner shall constitute a fund for the total sum representing the limit of his liability with the Court or other competent authority of any one of the Contracting States in which action is brought under Article IX or, if no action is brought, with any Court or other competent authority in any one of the Contracting States in which an action can be brought under Article IX. The fund can be constituted either by depositing the sum or by producing a bank guarantee or other guarantee, acceptable under the legislation of the Contracting State where the fund is constituted, and considered to be adequate by the Court or other competent authority.

4. The fund shall be distributed among the claimants in proportion to the amounts of their established claims.

5. If before the fund is distributed the owner or any of his servants or agents or any person providing him insurance or other financial security has as a result of the incident in question, paid compensation for pollution damage, such person shall, up to the amount he has paid, acquire by subrogation the rights which the person so compensated would have enjoyed under this Convention.

6. The right of subrogation provided for in paragraph 5 of this Article may also be exercised by a person other than those mentioned therein in respect of any amount of compensation for pollution damage which he may have paid but only to the extent that such subrogation is permitted under the applicable national law.

7. Where the owner or any other person establishes that he may be compelled to pay at a later date in whole or in part any such amount of compensation, with regard to which such person would have enjoyed a right of subrogation under paragraph 5 or 6 of this Article, had the compensation been paid before the fund was distributed, the Court or other competent authority of the State where the fund has been constituted may order that a sufficient sum shall be provisionally set aside to enable such person at such later date to enforce his claim against the fund.

8. Claims in respect of expenses reasonably incurred or sacrifices reasonably made by the owner voluntarily to prevent or minimize pollution damage shall rank equally with other claims against the fund.

9. (a) The "unit of account" referred to in paragraph 1 of this Article is the Special Drawing Right as defined by the International Monetary Fund. The amounts mentioned in paragraph 1 shall be converted into national currency on the basis of the value of that currency by reference to the Special Drawing Right on the date of the constitution of the fund referred to in paragraph 3. The value of the national currency, in terms of the Special Drawing Right, of a Contracting State which is a member of the International Monetary Fund shall be calculated in accordance with the method of valuation applied by the International Monetary Fund in effect on the date in question for its operations and transactions. The value of the national currency, in terms of the Special Drawing Right, of a Contracting State which is not a member of the International Monetary Fund shall be calculated in a manner determined by that State.

(b) Nevertheless, a Contracting State which is not a member of the International Monetary Fund and whose law does not permit the application of the provisions of paragraph 9(a) may, at the time of ratification, acceptance, approval of or accession to this Convention or at any time thereafter, declare that the unit of account referred to in paragraph 9(a) shall be equal to 15 gold francs. The gold franc referred to in this paragraph corresponds to sixty-five and a half milligrammes of gold of millesimal fineness nine hundred. The conversion of the gold franc into the national currency shall be made according to the law of the State concerned.

(c) The calculation mentioned in the last sentence of paragraph 9(a) and the conversion mentioned in paragraph 9(b) shall be made in such manner as to express in the national currency of the Contracting State as far as possible the same real value for the amounts in paragraph 1 as would result from the application of the first three sentences of paragraph 9(a). Contracting States shall communicate to the depositary the manner of calculation pursuant to paragraph 9(a), or the result of the conversion in paragraph 9(b) as the case may be, when depositing an instrument of ratification, acceptance, approval of or accession to this Convention and whenever there is a change in either.

10. For the purpose of this Article the ships tonnage shall be the gross tonnage calculated in accordance with the tonnage measurement regulations contained in Annex I of the International Convention on Tonnage Measurement of Ships, 1969.

11. The insurer or other person providing financial security shall be entitled to constitute a fund in accordance with this Article on the same conditions and having the same effect as if it were constituted by the owner. Such a fund may be constituted even if, under the provisions of paragraph 2, the owner is not entitled to limit his liability, but its constitution shall in that case not prejudice the rights of any claimant against the owner.

Article VI

1. Where the owner, after an incident, has constituted a fund in accordance with Article V, and is entitled to limit his liability,

(a) no person having a claim for pollution damage arising out of that incident shall be entitled to exercise any right against any other assets of the owner in respect of such claim;

(b) the Court or other competent authority of any Contracting State shall order the release of any ship or other property belonging to the owner which has been arrested in respect of a claim for pollution damage arising out of that incident, and shall similarly release any bail or other security furnished to avoid such arrest.

2. The foregoing shall, however, only apply if the claimant has access to the Court administering the fund and the fund is actually available in respect or his claim.

Article VII

1. The owner of a ship registered in a Contracting State and carrying more than 2,000 tons of oil in bulk as cargo shall be required to maintain insurance or other financial security, such as the guarantee of a bank or a certificate delivered by an international compensation fund, in the sums fixed by applying the limits of liability prescribed in Article V, paragraph 1 to cover his liability for pollution damage under this Convention.

2. A certificate attesting that insurance or other financial security is in force in accordance with the provisions of this Convention shall be issued to each ship after the appropriate authority of a Contracting State has determined that the requirements of paragraph 1 have been complied with. With respect to a ship registered in a Contracting State such certificate shall be issued or certified by the appropriate authority of the State of the ship's registry; with respect to at ship not registered in a Contracting State it may be issued or certified by the appropriate authority of any Contracting State. This certificate shall be in the form of the annexed model and shall contain the following particulars:

  (a) name of ship and port of registration;

  (b) name and principal place of business of owner;

  (c) type of security;

  (d) name and principal place of business of insurer or other person giving security and, where appropriate, place of business where the insurance or security is established;

  (e) period of validity of certificate which shall not be longer than the period of validity of the insurance or other security.

3. The certificate shall be in the official language or languages of the issuing State. If the language used is neither English nor French, the text shall include a translation into one of these languages.

4. The certificate shall be carried on board the ship and a copy shall be deposited with the authorities who keep the record of the ship's registry or, if the ship is not registered in a Contracting State, with the authorities of the State issuing or certifying the certificate.

5. An insurance or other financial security shall not satisfy the requirements of this Article if it can cease, for reasons other than the expiry of the period of validity of the insurance or security specified in the certificate under paragraph 2 of this Article, before three months have elapsed from the date on which notice of its termination is given to the authorities referred to in paragraph 4 of this Article, unless the certificate has been surrendered to these authorities or a new certificate has been issued within the said period. The foregoing provisions shall similarly apply to any modification which results in the insurance or security no longer satisfying the requirements of this Article.

6. The State of registry shall, subject to the provisions of this Article, determine the conditions of issue and validity of the certificate.

7. Certificates issued or certified under the authority of a Contracting State in accordance with paragraph 2 shall be accepted by other Contracting States for the purposes of this Convention and shall be regarded by other Contracting States as having the same force as certificates issued or certified by them even if issued or certified in respect of a ship not registered in a Contracting State. A Contracting State may at any time request consultation with the issuing or certifying State should it believe that the insurer or guarantor named in the certificate is not financially capable of meeting the obligations imposed by this Convention.

8. Any claim for compensation for pollution damage may be brought directly against the insurer or other person providing financial security for the owner's liability for pollution damage. In such case the defendant may, even if the owner is not entitled to limit his liability according to Article V, paragraph 2, avail himself of the limits of liability prescribed in Article V, paragraph 1. He may further avail himself of the defenses (other than the bankruptcy or winding up of the owner)which the owner himself would have been entitled to invoke. Furthermore, the defendant may avail himself of the defense that the pollution damage resulted from the wilful misconduct of the owner himself, but the defendant shall not avail himself of any other defence which he might have been entitled to invoke in proceedings brought by the owner against him. The defendant shall in any event have the right to require the owner to be joined in the proceedings.

9. Any sums provided by insurance or by other financial security maintained in accordance with paragraph 1 of this Article shall be available exclusively for the satisfaction of claims under this Convention.

10. A Contracting State shall not permit a ship under its flag to which this Article applies to trade unless a certificate has been issued under paragraph 2 or 12 of this Article.

11. Subject to the provisions of this Article, each Contracting State shall ensure, under its national legislation, that insurance or other security to the extent specified in paragraph 1 of this Article is in force in respect of any ship, wherever registered, entering or leaving a port in its territory, or arriving at or leaving an off-shore terminal in its territorial sea, if the ship actually carries more than 2,000 tons of oil in bulk as cargo.

12. If insurance or other financial security is not maintained in respect of a ship owned by a Contracting State, the provisions of this Article relating thereto shall not be applicable to such ship, but the ship shall carry a certificate issued by the appropriate authorities of the State of the ship's registry stating that the ship is owned by that State and that the ship's liability is covered within the limits prescribed by Article V, paragraph 1. Such a certificate shall follow as closely as practicable the model prescribed by paragraph 2 of this Article.

Article VIII

Rights of compensation under this Convention shall be extinguished unless an action is brought thereunder within three years from the date when the damage occurred. However, in no case shall an action be brought after six years from the date of the incident which caused the damage. Where this incident consists of a series of occurrences, the six-years period shall run from the date of the first such occurrence.

Article IX

1. Where an incident has caused pollution damage in the territory, including the territorial sea or an area referred to in Article II, of one or more Contracting States or preventive measures have been taken to prevent or minimize pollution damage in such territory including the territorial sea or area, actions for compensation may only be brought in the Courts of any such Contracting State or States. Reasonable notice of any such action shall be given to the defendant.

2. Each Contracting State shall ensure that its Courts possess the necessary jurisdiction to entertain such actions for compensation.

3. After the fund has been constituted in accordance with Article V the Courts of the State in which the fund is constituted shall be exclusively competent to determine all matters relating to the apportionment and distribution of the fund.

Article X

1. Any judgment given by a Court with jurisdiction in accordance with Article IX which is enforceable in the State of origin where it is no longer subject to ordinary forms of review, shall be recognized in any Contracting State, except:

(a) where the judgment was obtained by fraud; or

(b) where the defendant was not given reasonable notice and a fair opportunity to present his case.

2. A judgment recognized under paragraph 1 of this Article shall be enforceable in each Contracting State as soon as the formalities required in that State have been complied with. The formalities shall not permit the merits of the case to be re-opened.

Article XI

1. The provisions of this Convention shall not apply to warships or other ships owned or operated by a State and used, for the time being, only on government non-commercial service.

2. With respect to ships owned by a Contracting State and used for commercial purposes, each State shall be subject to suit in the jurisdictions set forth in Article IX and shall waive all defences based on its status as a sovereign State.

Article XII

This Convention shall supersede any International Conventions in force or open for signature, ratification or accession at the date on which the Convention is opened for signature, but only to the extent that such Conventions would be in conflict with it; however, nothing in this Article shall affect the obligations of Contracting States to non-Contracting States arising under such International Conventions.

Article XII bis

Transitional provisions

The following transitional provisions shall apply in the case of a State which at the time of an incident is a Party both to this Convention and to the 1969 Liability Convention:

(a) where an incident has caused pollution damage within the scope of this Convention, liability under this Convention shall be deemed to be discharged if, and to the extent that, it also arises under the 1969 Liability Convention;

(b) where an incident has caused pollution damage within the scope of this Convention, and the State is a Party both to this Convention and to the International Convention on the Establishment of an International Fund for Compensation for Oil Pollution Damage, 1971, liability remaining to be discharged after the application of subparagraph (a) of this Article shall arise under this Convention only to the extent that pollution damage remains uncompensated after application of the said 1971 Convention;

(c) in the application of Article III, Paragraph 4, of this Convention the expression "this Convention" shall be interpreted as referring to this Convention or the 1969 Liability Convention, as appropriate;

(d) in the application of Article V, paragraph 3, of this Convention the total sum of the fund to be constituted shall be reduced by the amount by which liability has been deemed to be discharged in accordance with subparagraph (a) of this Article.

Article XII ter

Final clauses

The final clauses of this Convention shall be Articles 12 to 18 of the Protocol of 1992 to amend the 1969 Liability Convention. References in this Convention to Contracting States shall be taken to mean references to the Contracting States of that Protocol.

FINAL CLAUSES

[Articles 12–18 of the 1992 Protocol to Amend the 1969 Liability Convention]

Article 12

Signature, ratification, acceptance, approval and accession

1. This Protocol shall be open for signature at London from 15 January 1993 to 14 January 1994 by all States.

2. Subject to paragraph 4, any State may become a Party to this Protocol by:

   (a) signature subject to ratification, acceptance or approval followed by ratification, acceptance or approval; or

   (b) accession.

3. Ratification, acceptance, approval or accession shall be effected by the deposit of a formal instrument to that effect with the Secretary–General of the Organization.

4. Any Contracting State to the International Convention on the Establishment of an International Fund for Compensation for Oil Pollution Damage, 1971, hereinafter referred to as the 1971 Fund Convention, may ratify, accept, approve or accede to this Protocol only if it ratifies, accepts, approves or accedes to the Protocol of 1992 to amend that Convention at the same time, unless it denounces the 1971 Fund Convention to take effect on the date when this Protocol enters into force for that State.

5. A State which is a Party to this protocol but not a Party to the 1969 Liability Convention shall be bound by the provisions of the 1969 Liability Convention as amended by this Protocol in relation to other States Parties hereto, but shall not be bound by the provisions of the 1969 Liability Convention in relation to States Parties thereto.

6. Any instrument of ratification, acceptance, approval or accession deposited after the entry into force of an amendment to the 1969 Liability Convention as amended by this Protocol shall be deemed to apply to the Convention so amended, as modified by such amendment.

Article 13

Entry into force

1. This Protocol shall enter into force twelve months following the date on which ten States including four States each with not less than one million units of gross tanker tonnage have deposited instruments of ratification, acceptance, approval or accession with the Secretary–General of the Organization.

2. However, any Contracting State to the 1971 Fund Convention may, at the time of the deposit of its instrument of ratification, acceptance, approval or accession in respect of this Protocol, declare that such instrument shall be deemed not to be effective for the purposes of this Article until the end of the six-month period in Article 31 of the Protocol of 1992 to amend the 1971 Fund Convention. A State which is not a Contracting State to the 1971 Fund Convention but which deposits an instrument of ratification, acceptance, approval or accession in respect of the Protocol of 1992 to

amend the 1971 Fund Convention may also make a declaration in accordance with this paragraph at the same time.

3. Any State which has made a declaration in accordance with the preceding paragraph may withdraw it at any time by means of a notification addressed to the Secretary–General of the Organization. Any such withdrawal shall take effect on the date the notification is received, provided that such State shall be deemed to have deposited its instrument of ratification, acceptance, approval or accession in respect of this Protocol on that date.

4. For any State which ratifies, accepts, approves or accedes to it after the conditions in paragraph 1 for entry into force have been met, this Protocol shall enter into force twelve months following the date of deposit by such State of the appropriate instrument.

Article 14
Revision and amendment

1. A Conference for the purpose of revising or amending the 1992 Liability Convention may be convened by the Organization.

2. The Organization shall convene a Conference of Contracting States for the purpose of revising or amending the 1992 Liability Convention at the request of not less than one third of the Contracting States.

Article 15
Amendments of limitation amounts

1. Upon the request of at least one quarter of the Contracting States any proposal to amend the limits of liability laid down in Article V, paragraph 1, of the 1969 Liability Convention as amended by this Protocol shall be circulated by the Secretary–General to all Members of the Organization and to all Contracting States.

2. Any amendment proposed and circulated as above shall be submitted to the Legal Committee of the Organization for consideration at a date at least six months after the date of its circulation.

3. All Contracting States to the 1969 Liability Convention as amended by this Protocol, whether or not Members of the Organization, shall be entitled to participate in the proceeding of the Legal Committee for the consideration and adoption of amendments.

4. Amendments shall be adopted by a two-thirds majority of the Contracting States present and voting in the Legal Committee, expanded as provided for in paragraph 3, on condition that at least one half of the Contracting States shall be present at the time of voting.

5. When acting on a proposal to amend the limits, the Legal Committee shall take into account the experience of incidents and in particular the amount of damage resulting therefrom, changes in the monetary values and the effect of the proposed amendment on the cost of insurance. It shall also take into account the relationship between the limits in Article V, paragraph 1, of the 1969 Liability Convention as amended by this Protocol and those in Article 4, paragraph 4, of the International Convention on the Establishment of an International Fund for Compensation for Oil Pollution Damage, 1992.

6. (a) No amendment of the limits of liability under this Article may be considered before 15 January 1998 nor less than five years from the date of entry into force of a previous amendment under this Article. No amendment under this Article shall be considered before this Protocol has entered into force.

(b) No limit may be increased so as to exceed an amount which corresponds to the limit laid down in the 1969 Liability Convention as amended by this Protocol increased by 6 per cent per year calculated on a compound basis from 15 January 1993.

(c) No limit may be increased so as to exceed an amount which corresponds to the limit laid down in the 1969 Liability Convention as amended by this Protocol multiplied by 3.

7. Any amendment adopted in accordance with paragraph 4 shall be notified by the Organization to all Contracting States. The amendment shall be deemed to have been accepted at the end of a period of eighteen months after the date of notification, unless within that period not less than one quarter of the States that were Contracting States at the time of the adoption of the amendment by the Legal Committee have communicated to the Organization that they do not accept the amendment in which case the amendment is rejected and shall have no effect.

8. An amendment deemed to have been accepted in accordance with paragraph 7 shall enter into force eighteen months after its acceptance.

9. All Contracting States shall be bound by the amendment, unless they denounce this Protocol in accordance with Article 16, paragraphs 1 and 2, at least six months before the amendment enters into force. Such denunciation shall take effect when the amendment enters into force.

10. When an amendment has been adopted by the Legal Committee but the eighteen-month period for its acceptance has not yet expired, a State which becomes a Contracting State during that period shall be bound by the amendment if it enters into force. A State which becomes a Contracting State after that period shall be bound by an amendment which has been accepted in accordance with paragraph 7. In the case referred to in this paragraph, a State becomes bound by an amendment when that amendment enters into force, or when this Protocol enters into force for that State, if later.

Article 16
Denunciation

1. This Protocol may be denounced by any Party at any time after the date on which it enters into force for that Party.

2. Denunciation shall be effected by the deposit of an instrument with the Secretary–General of the Organization.

3. A denunciation shall take effect twelve months, or such longer period as may be specified in the instrument of denunciation, after its deposit with the Secretary–General of the Organization.

4. As between the Parties to this Protocol, denunciation by any of them of the 1969 Liability Convention in accordance with Article XVI thereof shall not be construed in any way as a denunciation of the 1969 Liability Convention as amended by this Protocol.

5. Denunciation of the Protocol of 1992 to amend the 1971 Fund Convention by a State which remains a Party to the 1971 Fund Convention shall be deemed to be a denunciation of this Protocol. Such denunciation shall take effect on the date on which denunciation of the Protocol of 1992 to amend the 1971 Fund Convention takes effect according to Article 34 of that Protocol.

Article 17
Depositary

1. This Protocol and any amendments accepted under Article 15 shall be deposited with the Secretary–General of the Organization.

2. The Secretary–General of the Organization shall:

(a) inform all States which have signed or acceded to this protocol of:

(i) each new signature or deposit of an instrument together with the date thereof;

(ii) each declaration and notification under Article 13 and each declaration and communication under Article 13 and each declaration and communication under Article V, paragraph 9, of the 1992 Liability Convention;

(iii) the date of entry into force of this Protocol;

(iv) any proposal to amend limits of liability which has been made in accordance with Article 15, paragraph 1;

(v) any amendment which has been adopted in accordance with Article 15, paragraph 4;

(vi) any amendment deemed to have been accepted under Article 15, paragraph 7, together with the date on which that amendment shall enter into force in accordance with paragraphs 8 and 9 of that Article;

(vii) the deposit of any instrument of denunciation of this Protocol together with the date of the deposit and the date on which it takes effect;

(viii) any denunciation deemed to have been made under Article 16, paragraph 5;

(ix) any communication called for by any Article of this Protocol;

(b) transmit certified true copies of this Protocol to all Signatory States and to all States which accede to this Protocol.

3. As soon as this Protocol enters into force, the text shall be transmitted by the Secretary–General of the Organization to the Secretariat of the United Nations for registration and publication in accordance with Article 102 of the Charter of the United Nations.

Article 18
Languages

This Protocol is established in a single original in the Arabic, Chinese, English, French, Russian and Spanish languages, each text being equally authentic.

DONE AT LONDON, this twenty-seventh day of November one thousand nine hundred and ninety-two.

IN WITNESS WHEREOF the undersigned, being duly authorized by their respective Governments for that purpose, have signed this Protocol.

ANNEX
CERTIFICATE OF INSURANCE OR OTHER FINANCIAL SECURITY IN RESPECT OF CIVIL LIABILITY FOR OIL POLLUTION DAMAGE

Issued in accordance with the provisions of Article VII of the International Convention on Civil Liability for Oil Pollution Damage, 1992.

Name of ship	Distinctive number or letters	Port of Registry	Name and address of owner

This is to certify that there is in force in respect of the above-named ship a policy of insurance or other financial security satisfying the requirements of Article VII of the International Convention on Civil Liability for Oil Pollution Damage, 1992.

Type of Security ....

Duration of Security ....

Name and Address of the Insurer(s) and/or Guarantor(s)

Name ....

Address ....

This certificate is valid until ....

Issued or certified by the Government of ....

(Full designation of the State)

At .... On ....
                  (Place)   *(Date)*

....
*Signature and Title of issuing or
certifying official*

Explanatory Notes:

1. If desired, the designation of the State may include a reference to the competent public authority of the country where the certificate is issued.

2. If the total amount of security has been furnished by more than one source, the amount of each of them should be indicated.

3. If security is furnished in several forms, these should be enumerated.

4. The entry "Duration of Security" must stipulate the date on which such security takes effect.

3.14 INTERNATIONAL CONVENTION ON THE ESTABLISHMENT OF AN INTERNATIONAL FUND
FOR COMPENSATION FOR OIL POLLUTION DAMAGE, 1992 (Without Annex
and Protocols).[i] Concluded at London, 27 November 1992. Entered
into force, 30 May 1996. 1953 UNTS 330; *reprinted in* 5 Weston &
Carlson V.F.30

* * *

General Provisions

Article 1.   For the purposes of this Convention:

1. "1992 Liability Convention" means the International Convention on Civil
Liability for Oil Pollution Damage, 1992.

1. *bis* "1971 Fund Convention" means the International Convention on the
Establishment of an International fund for Compensation for Oil Pollution Damage,
1971. For States Parties to the Protocol of 1976 to that Convention, the term shall be
deemed to include the 1971 Fund Convention as amended by that Protocol.

2. "Ship", "Person", "Owner", "Oil", "Pollution Damage", "Preventive Measures", "Incident", and "Organization" have the same meaning as in Article I of the
1992 Liability Convention.

3. "Contributing Oil" means crude oil and fuel oil as defined in sub-paragraphs
(*a*) and (*b*) below:

   (*a*) "Crude Oil" means any liquid hydrocarbon mixture occurring naturally in
   the earth whether or not treated to render it suitable for transportation. It also
   includes crude oils from which certain distillate fractions have been removed
   (sometimes referred to as "topped crudes") or to which certain distillate fractions
   have been added (sometimes referred to as "spiked" or "reconstituted" crudes).

   (*b*) "Fuel Oil" means heavy distillates or residues from crude oil or blends of
   such materials intended for use as a fuel for the production of heat or power of a
   quality equivalent to the "American Society for Testing and Materials' Specification for Number Four Fuel Oil (Designation D 396–69)", or heavier.

4. "Unit of account" has the same meaning as in Article V, paragraph 9, of the
1992 Liability Convention.

5. "Ship's tonnage" has the same meaning as in Article V, paragraph 10, of the
1992 Liability Convention.

6. "Ton", in relation to oil, means a metric ton.

7. "Guarantor" means any person providing insurance or other financial security
to cover an owner's liability in pursuance of Article VII, paragraph 1, of the 1992
Liability Convention.

8. "Terminal installation" means any site for the storage of oil in bulk which is
capable of receiving oil from waterborne transportation, including any facility situated
off-shore and linked to such site.

9. Where an incident consists of a series of occurrences, it shall be treated as
having occurred on the date of the first such occurrence.

---

i. This document reproduces the consolidated text of the International Convention on
the Establishment of an International Fund for
Compensation for Oil Pollution Damage (without annex and protocols), *concluded at Brussels,* 1971 U.N.J.Y.B. 103, as amended by the
1976 and 1992 Protocols to that Convention.
The 1992 Protocol provides that the 1971 Fund
Convention and the Protocol shall be "read
and interpreted together as one single instrument" and that the consolidated text shall be
known as the "International Fund for Compensation for Oil Pollution Damage, 1992."

Article 2.   1. An International Fund for compensation for pollution damage, to be named "The International Oil Pollution Compensation Fund 1992" and hereinafter referred to as "the Fund", is hereby established with the following aims:

(a) to provide compensation for pollution damage to the extent that the protection afforded by the 1992 Liability Convention is inadequate;

(b) to give effect to the related purposes set out in this Convention.

2.   The Fund shall in each Contracting State be recognized as a legal person capable under the laws of that State of assuming rights and obligations and of being a party in legal proceedings before the courts of that State. Each Contracting State shall recognize the Director of the Fund (hereinafter referred to as "the Director") as the legal representative of the Fund.

Article 3.   This Convention shall apply exclusively:

(a) to pollution damage caused:

(i) in the territory, including the territorial sea, of a Contracting State, and

(ii) in the exclusive economic zone of a Contracting State, established in accordance with international law, or, if a Contracting State has not established such a zone, in an area beyond and adjacent to the territorial sea of that State determined by that State in accordance with international law baselines from which the breadth of its territorial sea is measured;

(b) to preventive measures, wherever taken, to prevent or minimize such damage.

Compensation

Article 4.   1. For the purpose of fulfilling its function under Article 2, paragraph 1(*a*), the Fund shall pay compensation to any person suffering pollution damage if such person has been unable to obtain full and adequate compensation for the damage under the terms of the 1992 Liability Convention,

(*a*) Because no liability for the damage arises under the 1992 Liability Convention;

(*b*) Because the owner liable for the damage under the 1992 Liability Convention is financially incapable of meeting his obligations in full and any financial security that may be provided under Article VII of that Convention does not cover or is insufficient to satisfy the claims for compensation for the damage; an owner being treated as financially incapable of meeting his obligations and a financial security being treated as insufficient if the person suffering the damage has been unable to obtain full satisfaction of the amount of compensation due under the 1992 Liability Convention after having taken all reasonable steps to pursue the legal remedies available to him;

(*c*) Because the damage exceeds the owner's liability under the 1992 Liability Convention as limited pursuant to Article V, paragraph 1, of that Convention or under the terms of any other international Convention in force or open for signature, ratification or accession at the date of this Convention.

Expenses reasonably incurred or sacrifices reasonably made by the owner voluntarily to prevent or minimize pollution damage shall be treated as pollution damage for the purposes of this Article.

2.   The Fund shall incur no obligation under the preceding paragraph if:

(*a*) It proves that the pollution damage resulted from an act of war, hostilities, civil war or insurrection or was caused by oil which has escaped or been discharged from a warship or other ship owned or operated by a State and used, at the time of the incident, only on Government non-commercial service; or

(b) The claimant cannot prove that the damage resulted from an incident involving one or more ships.

3. If the Fund proves that the pollution damage resulted wholly or partially either from an act or omission done with the intent to cause damage by the person who suffered the damage or from the negligence of that person, the Fund may be exonerated wholly or partially from its obligation to pay compensation to such person. The Fund shall in any event be exonerated to the extent that the shipowner may have been exonerated under Article III, paragraph 3, of the 1992 Liability Convention. However, there shall be no such exoneration of the Fund with regard to preventive measures.

4. (a) Except as otherwise provided in subparagraphs (b) and (c) of this paragraph, the aggregate amount of compensation payable by the Fund under this Article shall in respect of any one incident be limited, so that the total sum of that amount and the amount of compensation actually paid under the 1992 Liability Convention for pollution damage within the scope of application of this Convention as defined in Article 3 shall not exceed 135 million units of account.

(b) Except as otherwise provided in subparagraph (c), the aggregate amount of compensation payable by the Fund under this Article for pollution damage resulting from a natural phenomenon of an exceptional inevitable and irresistible character shall not exceed 135 million units of account.

(c) The maximum amount of compensation referred to in subparagraphs (a) and (b) shall be 200 million units of account with respect to any incident occurring during any period when there are three Parties to this Convention in respect of which the combined relevant quantity of contributing oil received by persons in the territories of such Parties, during the preceding calendar year, equaled or exceeded 600 million tons.

(d) Interest accrued on a fund constituted in accordance with Article V, paragraph 3, of the 1992 Liability Convention, if any, shall not be taken into account for the computation of the maximum compensation payable by the Fund under this Article.

(e) The amounts mentioned in this Article shall be converted into national currency on the basis of the value of that currency by reference to the Special Drawing Right on the date of the decision of the Assembly of the Fund as to the first date of payment of compensation.

5. Where the amount of established claims against the Fund exceeds the aggregate amount of compensation payable under paragraph 4, the amount available shall be distributed in such a manner that the proportion between any established claim and the amount of compensation actually recovered by the claimant under this Convention shall be the same for all claimants.

6. The Assembly of the Fund may decide that, in exceptional cases, compensation in accordance with this Convention can be paid even if the owner of the ship has not constituted a fund in accordance with Article V, paragraph 3, of the 1992 Liability Convention. In such case paragraph 4 (e) of this Article applies accordingly.

7. The Fund shall, at the request of a Contracting State, use its good offices as necessary to assist that State to secure promptly such personnel, material and services as are necessary to enable the State to take measures to prevent or mitigate pollution damage arising from an incident in respect of which the Fund may be called upon to pay compensation under this Convention.

8. The Fund may, on conditions to be laid down in the Internal Regulations, provide credit facilities with a view to the taking of preventive measures against pollution damage arising from a particular incident in respect of which the Fund may be called upon to pay compensation under this Convention.

Article 5. [*deleted*]

Article 6. Rights to compensation under Article 4 shall be extinguished unless an action is brought thereunder or a notification has been made pursuant to Article 7, paragraph 6, within three years from the date when the damage occurred. However, in no case shall an action be brought after six years from the date of the incident which caused the damage.

Article 7. 1. Subject to the subsequent provisions of this Article, any action against the Fund for compensation under Article 4 or indemnification under Article 5 of this Convention shall be brought only before a court competent under Article IX of the 1992 Liability Convention in respect of actions against the owner who is or who would, but for the provisions of Article III, paragraph 2, of that Convention, have been liable for pollution damage caused by the relevant incident.

2. Each Contracting State shall ensure that its courts possess the necessary jurisdiction to entertain such actions against the Fund as are referred to in paragraph 1.

3. Where an action for compensation for pollution damage has been brought before a court competent under Article IX of the 1992 Liability Convention against the owner of a ship or his guarantor, such court shall have exclusive jurisdictional competence over any action against the Fund for compensation or indemnification under the provisions of Article 4 of this Convention in respect of the same damage. However, where an action for compensation for pollution damage under the 1992 Liability Convention has been brought before a court in a State Party to the 1992 Liability Convention but not to this Convention, any action against the Fund under Article 4 of this Convention shall at the option of the claimant be brought either before a court of the State where the Fund has its headquarters or before any court of a State Party to this Convention competent under Article IX of the 1992 Liability Convention.

4. Each Contracting State shall ensure that the Fund shall have the right to intervene as a party to any legal proceedings instituted in accordance with Article IX of the 1992 Liability Convention before a competent court of that State against the owner of a ship or his guarantor.

5. Except as otherwise provided in paragraph 6, the Fund shall not be bound by any judgment or decision in proceedings to which it has not been a party or by any settlement to which it is not a party.

6. Without prejudice to the provisions of paragraph 4, where an action under the 1992 Liability Convention for compensation for pollution damage has been brought against an owner or his guarantor before a competent court in a Contracting State, each party to the proceedings shall be entitled under the national law of that State to notify the Fund of the proceedings. Where such notification has been made in accordance with the formalities required by the law of the court seized and in such time and in such a manner that the Fund has in fact been in a position effectively to intervene as a party to the proceedings, any judgment rendered by the court in such proceedings shall, after it has become final and enforceable in the State where the judgment was given, become binding upon the Fund in the sense that the facts and findings in that judgment may not be disputed by the Fund even if the Fund has not actually intervened in the proceedings.

Article 8. Subject to any decision concerning the distribution referred to in Article 4, paragraph 5, any judgment given against the Fund by a court having jurisdiction in accordance with Article 7, paragraphs 1 and 3, shall, when it has become enforceable in the State of origin and is in that State no longer subject to ordinary forms of review, be recognized and enforceable in each Contracting State on the same conditions as are prescribed in Article X of the 1992 Liability Convention.

Article 9. 1. The Fund shall, in respect of any amount of compensation for pollution damage paid by the Fund in accordance with Article 4, paragraph 1, of this Convention, acquire by subrogation the rights that the person so compensated may enjoy under the 1992 Liability Convention against the owner or his guarantor.

2. Nothing in this Convention shall prejudice any right of recourse or subrogation of the Fund against persons other than those referred to in the preceding paragraph. In any event the right of the Fund to subrogation against such person shall not be less favourable than that of an insurer of the person to whom compensation has been paid.

3. Without prejudice to any other rights of subrogation or recourse against the Fund which may exist, a Contracting State or agency thereof which has paid compensation for pollution damage in accordance with provisions of national law shall acquire by subrogation the rights which the person so compensated would have enjoyed under this Convention.

Contributions

Article 10. 1. Annual contributions to the Fund shall be made in respect of each Contracting State by any person who, in the calendar year referred to in Article 12, paragraph 2(a) or (b), has received in total quantities exceeding 150,000 tons:

(*a*) In the ports or terminal installations in the territory of that State contributing oil carried by sea to such ports or terminal installations; and

(*b*) In any installations situated in the territory of that Contracting State contributing oil which has been carried by sea and discharged in a port or terminal installation of a non-Contracting State, provided that contributing oil shall only be taken into account by virtue of this sub-paragraph on first receipt in a Contracting State after its discharge in that non-Contracting State.

2. (*a*) For the purposes of paragraph 1, where the quantity of contributing oil received in the territory of a Contracting State by any person in a calendar year when aggregated with the quantity of contributing oil received in the same Contracting State in that year by any associated person or persons exceeds 150,000 tons, such person shall pay contributions in respect of the actual quantity received by him notwithstanding that that quantity did not exceed 150,000 tons.

(*b*) "Associated person" means any subsidiary or commonly controlled entity. The question whether a person comes within this definition shall be determined by the national law of the State concerned.

Article 11. [*deleted*]

Article 12. 1. With a view to assessing the amount of annual contributions due, if any, and taking account of the necessity to maintain sufficient liquid funds, the Assembly shall for each calendar year make an estimate in the form of a budget of:

(i) Expenditure

(*a*) Costs and expenses of the administration of the Fund in the relevant year and any deficit from operations in preceding years;

(*b*) Payments to be made by the Fund in the relevant year for the satisfaction of claims against the Fund due under Article 4, including repayment on loans previously taken by the Fund for the satisfaction of such claims, to the extent that the aggregate amount of such claims in respect of any one incident does not exceed four million units of account;

(c) Payments to be made by the Fund in the relevant year for the satisfaction of claims against the Fund due under Article 4, including repayments on loans previously taken by the Fund for the satisfaction of such claims, to the extent that the aggregate amount of such claims in respect of any one incident is in excess of four million units of account;

(ii) Income

(a) Surplus funds from operations in preceding years, including any interest;

(b) annual contributions, if required to balance the budget;

(c) Any other income.

2. The Assembly shall decide the total amount of contributions to be levied. On the basis of that decision, the Director shall, in respect of each Contracting State, calculate for each person referred to in Article 10 the amount of his annual contribution:

(a) In so far as the contribution is for the satisfaction of payments referred to in paragraph 1(i)(a) and (b) on the basis of a fixed sum for each ton of contributing oil received in the relevant State by such persons during the preceding calendar year; and

(b) In so far as the contribution is for the satisfaction of payments referred to in paragraph 1(i)(c) of this article on the basis of a fixed sum for each ton of contributing oil received by such person during the calendar year preceding that in which the incident in question occurred, provided that State was a party to this Convention at the date of the incident.

3. The sums referred to in paragraph 2 above shall be arrived at by dividing the relevant total amount of contributions required by the total amount of contributing oil received in all Contracting States in the relevant year.

4. The annual contribution shall be due on the date to be laid down in the Internal Regulations of the Fund. The Assembly may decide on a different date of payment.

5. The Assembly may decide, under the conditions to be laid down in the Financial Regulations of the Fund, to make transfers between funds received in accordance with article 12.2(a) and funds received in accordance with article 12.2(b).

Article 13. 1. The amount of any contribution due under Article 12 and which is in arrears shall bear interest at a rate which shall be determined in accordance with the Internal Regulations of the Fund, provided that different rates may be fixed for different circumstances.

2. Each Contracting State shall ensure that any obligation to contribute to the Fund arising under this Convention in respect of oil received within the territory of that State is fulfilled and shall take any appropriate measures under its law, including the imposing of such sanctions as it may deem necessary, with a view to the effective execution of any such obligation; provided, however, that such measures shall only be directed against those persons who are under an obligation to contribute to the Fund.

3. Where a person who is liable in accordance with the provisions of Articles 10 and 12 to make contributions to the Fund does not fulfil his obligations in respect of any such contribution or any part thereof and is in arrears, the Director shall take all appropriate action against such person on behalf of the Fund with a view to the recovery of the amount due. However, where the defaulting contributor is manifestly insolvent or the circumstances otherwise so warrant, the Assembly may, upon recommendation of the Director, decide that no action shall be taken or continued against the contributor.

Article 14. 1. Each Contracting State may at the time when it deposits its instrument of ratification or accession or at any time thereafter declare that it assumes itself obligations that are incumbent under this Convention on any person who is liable to contribute to the Fund in accordance with Article 10, paragraph 1, in respect of oil received within the territory of that State. Such declaration shall be made in writing and shall specify which obligations are assumed.

2. Where a declaration under paragraph 1 is made prior to the entry into force of this Convention in accordance with Article 40, it shall be deposited with the Secretary–General of the Organization who shall after the entry into force of the Convention communicate the declaration to the Director.

3. A declaration under paragraph 1 which is made after the entry into force of this Convention shall be deposited with the Director.

4. A declaration made in accordance with this article may be withdrawn by the relevant State giving notice thereof in writing to the Director. Such notification shall take effect three months after the Director's receipt thereof.

5. Any State which is bound by a declaration made under this article shall, in any proceedings brought against it before a competent court in respect of any obligation specified in the declaration, waive any immunity that it would otherwise be entitled to invoke.

Article 15. 1. Each Contracting State shall ensure that any person who receives contributing oil within its territory in such quantities that he is liable to contribute to the Fund appears on a list to be established and kept up to date by the Director in accordance with the subsequent provisions of this article.

2. For the purposes set out in paragraph 1, each Contracting State shall communicate, at a time and in the manner to be prescribed in the Internal Regulations, to the Director the name and address of any person who in respect of that State is liable to contribute to the Fund pursuant to Article 10, as well as data on the relevant quantities of contributing oil received by any such person during the preceding calendar year.

3. For the purposes of ascertaining who are, at any given time, the persons liable to contribute to the Fund in accordance with Article 10, paragraph 1, and of establishing, where applicable, the quantities of oil to be taken into account for any such person when determining the amount of his contribution, the list shall be *prima facie* evidence of the facts stated therein.

4. Where a Contracting State does not fulfill its obligations to submit to the Director the communication referred to in paragraph 2 and this results in a financial loss for the Fund, that Contracting State shall be liable of compensate the Fund for such loss. The Assembly shall, on the recommendation of the Director, decide whether such compensation shall be payable by that Contracting State.

Organization and administration

Article 16. The Fund shall have an Assembly and a Secretariat headed by a Director.

Assembly

Article 17. The Assembly shall consist of all Contracting States to this Convention.

Article 18. The functions of the Assembly shall be:

1. To elect at each regular session its Chairman and two Vice–Chairmen who shall hold office until the next regular session;

2. To determine its own rules of procedure, subject to the provisions of this Convention;

3. To adopt Internal Regulations necessary for the proper functioning of the Fund;

4. To appoint the Director and make provisions for the appointment of such other personnel as may be necessary and determine the terms and conditions of service of the Director and other personnel;

5. To adopt the annual budget and fix the annual contributions;

6. To appoint auditors and approve the accounts of the Fund;

7. To approve settlements of claims against the Fund, to take decisions in respect of the distribution among claimants of the available amount of compensation in accordance with Article 4, paragraph 5, and to determine the terms and conditions according to which provisional payments in respect of claims shall be made with a view to ensuring that victims of pollution damage are compensated as promptly as possible;

8. [*deleted*]

9. To establish any temporary or permanent subsidiary body it may consider to be necessary, to define its terms of reference and to give it the authority needed to perform the functions entrusted to it; when appointing the members of such body, the Assembly shall endeavour to secure an equitable geographical distribution of members and to ensure that the Contracting States, in respect of which the largest quantities of contributing oil are being received, are appropriately represented; the Rules of Procedure of the Assembly may be applied, mutatis mutandis, for the work of such subsidiary body;

10. To determine which non-Contracting States and which inter-governmental and international non-governmental organizations shall be admitted to take part, without voting rights, in meetings of the Assembly, and subsidiary bodies;

11. To give instructions concerning the administration of the Fund to the Director and subsidiary bodies;

12. [*deleted*]

13. To supervise the proper execution of the Convention and of its own decisions;

14. To perform such other functions as are allocated to it under the Convention or are otherwise necessary for the proper operation of the Fund.

Article 19. 1. Regular sessions of the Assembly shall take place once every calendar year upon convocation by the Director.

2. Extraordinary sessions of the Assembly shall be convened by the Director at the request of at least one third of the members of the Assembly and may be convened on the Director's own initiative after consultation with the Chairman of the Assembly. The Director shall give members at least thirty days' notice of such sessions.

Article 20. A majority of the members of the Assembly shall constitute a quorum for its meetings.

Article 21 to 27 [*deleted*]

Secretariat

Article 28. 1. The Secretariat shall comprise the Director and such staff as the administration of the Fund may require.

2. The Director shall be the legal representative of the Fund.

Article 29. 1. The Director shall be the chief administrative officer of the Fund. Subject to the instructions given to him by the Assembly, he shall perform those functions which are assigned to him by this Convention, the Internal Regulations of the Fund and the Assembly.

2. The Director shall in particular:

(*a*) Appoint the personnel required for the administration of the Fund;

(*b*) Take all appropriate measures with a view to the proper administration of the Fund's assets;

(*c*) Collect the contributions due under this Convention while observing in particular the provisions of Article 13, paragraph 3;

(*d*) To the extent necessary to deal with claims against the Fund and carry out the other functions of the Fund, employ the services of legal, financial and other experts;

(*e*) Take all appropriate measures for dealing with claims against the Fund within the limits and on conditions to be laid down in the Internal Regulations, including the final settlement of claims without the prior approval of the Assembly where these Regulations so provide;

(*f*) Prepare and submit to the Assembly the financial statements and budget estimates for each calendar year;

(*g*) Prepare in consultation with the Chairman of the Assembly, and publish a report of the activities of the Fund during the previous calendar year;

(*h*) Prepare, collect and circulate the papers, documents, agenda, minutes and information that may be required for the work of the Assembly and subsidiary bodies.

Article 30. In the performance of their duties the Director and the staff and experts appointed by him shall not seek or receive instructions from any Government or from any authority external to the Fund. They shall refrain from any action which might reflect on their position as international officials. Each Contracting State on its part undertakes to respect the exclusively international character of the responsibilities of the Director and the staff and experts appointed by him, and not to seek to influence them in the discharge of their duties.

Finances

Article 31. 1. Each Contracting State shall bear the salary, travel and other expenses of its own delegation to the Assembly and of its representatives on subsidiary bodies.

2. Any other expenses incurred in the operation of the Fund shall be borne by the Fund.

Voting

Article 32. The following provisions shall apply to voting in the Assembly:

(*a*) Each member shall have one vote;

(*b*) Except as otherwise provided in Article 33, decisions of the Assembly shall be by a majority vote of the members present and voting;

(*c*) Decisions where a three-fourths or a two-thirds majority is required shall be by a three-fourths or two-thirds majority vote, as the case may be, of those present;

(*d*) For the purpose of this article the phrase "members present" means "members present at the meeting at the time of the vote", and the phrase "members present and voting" means "members present and casting an affirmative or negative vote". Members who abstain from voting shall be considered as not voting.

Article 33. The following decisions of the Assembly shall require a two-thirds majority:

(*a*) A decision under Article 13, paragraph 3, not to take or continue action against a contributor;

(*b*) The appointment of the Director under Article 18, paragraph 4;

(*c*) The establishment of subsidiary bodies, under Article 18, paragraph 9, and matters relating to such establishment.

Article 34. 1. The Fund, its assets, income, including contributions, and other property shall enjoy in all Contracting States exemption from all direct taxation.

2. When the Fund makes substantial purchases of movable or immovable property, or has important work carried out which is necessary for the exercise of its official activities and the cost of which includes indirect taxes or sales taxes, the Governments of Member States shall take, whenever possible, appropriate measures for the remission or refund of the amount of such duties and taxes.

3. No exemption shall be accorded in the case of duties, taxes or dues which merely constitute payment for public utility services.

4. The Fund shall enjoy exemption from all customs duties, taxes and other related taxes on articles imported or exported by it or on its behalf for its official use. Articles thus imported shall not be transferred either for consideration or gratis on the territory of the country into which they have been imported except on conditions agreed by the government of that country.

5. Persons contributing to the Fund and victims and owners of ships receiving compensation from the Fund shall be subject to the fiscal legislation of the State where they are taxable, no special exemption or other benefit being conferred on them in this respect.

6. Information relating to individual contributors supplied for the purpose of this Convention shall not be divulged outside the Fund except in so far as it may be strictly necessary to enable the Fund to carry out its functions including the bringing and defending of legal proceedings.

7. Independently of existing or future regulations concerning currency or transfers, Contracting States shall authorize the transfer and payment of any contribution to the Fund and of any compensation paid by the Fund without any restriction.

Transitional Provisions

Article 35. Claims for compensation under Article 4 arising from incidents occurring after the date of entry into force of this Convention may not be brought against the Fund earlier than the one hundred and twentieth day after that date.

Article 36. The Secretary–General of the Organization shall convene the first session of the Assembly. This session shall take place as soon as possible after entry into force of this Convention and, in any case, not more than thirty days after such entry into force.

Article 36 bis. The following transitional provisions shall apply in the period, hereinafter referred to as the transitional period, commencing with the date of entry into force of this Convention and ending with the date on which the denunciations provided for in Article 31 of the 1992 Protocol to amend the 1971 Fund Convention take effect:

(a) In the application of paragraph 1 (a) of Article 2 of this Convention, the reference to the 1992 Liability Convention shall include reference to the International Convention on Civil Liability for Oil Pollution Damage, 1969, either in its original version or as amended by the Protocol thereto of 1976 (referred to in this article as "the 1969 Liability Convention"), and also the 1971 Fund Convention.

(b) Where an incident has caused pollution damage within the scope of this Convention, the Fund shall pay compensation to any person suffering pollution damage only if, and to the extent that, such person has been unable to obtain full and adequate compensation for the damage under the terms of the 1969 Liability Convention, the 1971 Fund Convention and the 1992 Liability Convention, provided that, in respect of pollution damage within the scope of this Convention in respect of a Party to this Convention but not a Party to the 1971 Fund Convention, the Fund shall pay compensation to any person suffering pollution damage only if, and to the extent that, such person would have been unable to obtain full and adequate compensation had that State been party to each of the above-mentioned Conventions.

(c) In the application of Article 4 of this Convention, the amount to be taken into account in determining the aggregate amount of compensation payable by the Fund shall also include the amount of compensation actually paid under the 1969 Liability Convention, if any, and the amount of compensation actually paid or deemed to have been paid under the 1971 Fund Convention.

(d) Paragraph 1 of Article 9 of this Convention shall also apply to the rights enjoyed under the 1969 Liability Convention.

Article 36 ter. 1. Subject to paragraph 4 of this article, the aggregate amount of the annual contributions payable in respect of contributing oil received in a single Contraction State during a calendar year shall not exceed 27.5% of the total amount of annual contributions pursuant to the 1992 Protocol to amend the 1971 Fund Convention, in respect of that calendar year.

2. If the application of the provisions in paragraphs 2 and 3 of Article 12 would result in the aggregate amount of the contributions payable by contributors in a single Contracting State in respect of a given calendar year exceeding 27.5% of the total annual contributions, the contributions payable by all contributors in that State shall be reduced pro rata so that their aggregate contributions equal 27.5% of the total annual contributions to the Fund in respect of that year.

3. If the contributions payable by persons in a given Contracting State shall be reduced pursuant to paragraph 2 of this article, the contributions payable by persons in all other Contracting States shall be increased pro rata so as to ensure that the total amount of contributions payable by all persons liable to contribute to the Fund in respect of the calendar year in question will reach the total amount of contributions decided by the Assembly.

4. The provisions in paragraphs 1 to 3 of this article shall operate until the total quantity of contributing oil received in all Contracting States in a calendar year has reached 750 million tons or until a period of 5 years after the date of entry into force of the said 1992 Protocol has elapsed, whichever occurs earlier.

Article 36 quater. Notwithstanding the provisions of this Convention, the following provisions shall apply to the administration of the Fund during the period in which both the 1971 Fund Convention and this Convention are in force:

(a) The Secretariat of the Fund, established by the 1971 Convention (hereinafter referred to as "the 1971 Fund"), headed by the Director, may also function as the Secretariat and the Director of the Fund.

(b) If, in accordance with subparagraph (a), the Secretariat and the Director of the 1971 Fund also perform the function of Secretariat and Director of the Fund, the Fund shall be represented, in cases of conflict of interests between the 1971 Fund and the Fund, by the Chairman of the Assembly of the Fund.

(c) The Director and the staff and experts appointed by him, performing their duties under this Convention and the 1971 Fund Convention, shall not be regarded as contravening the provisions of Article 30 of this Convention in so far as they discharge their duties in accordance with this article.

(d) The Assembly of the Fund shall endeavour not to take decisions which are incompatible with decisions taken by the Assembly of the 1971 Fund. If differences of opinion with respect to common administrative issues arise, the Assembly of the Fund shall try to reach a consensus with the Assembly of the 1971 Fund, in a spirit of mutual co-operation and with the common aims of both organizations in mind.

(e) The Fund may succeed to the rights, obligations and assets of the 1971 Fund if the Assembly of the 1971 Fund so decides, in accordance with Article 44, paragraph 2, of the 1971 Fund Convention.

(f) The Fund shall reimburse to the 1971 Fund all costs and expenses arising from administrative services performed by the 1971 Fund on behalf of the Fund.

Article 36 quinquies. Final clauses

The final clauses of this Convention shall be Articles 28 to 39 of the Protocol of 1992 to amend the 1971 Fund Convention. References in this Convention to Contracting States shall be taken to mean references to the Contracting States of that Protocol.

FINAL CLAUSES

[Articles 28–39 of the Protocol of 1992 to Amend the 1991 Fund Convention]

Article 28
Signature, ratification, acceptance, approval and accession

1. This Protocol shall be open for signature at London from 15 January 1993 to 14 January 1994 by any State which has signed the 1992 Liability Convention.

2. Subject to paragraph 4, this Protocol shall be ratified, accepted or approved by States which have signed it.

3. Subject to paragraph 4, this Protocol is open for accession by States which did not sign it.

4. This Protocol may be ratified, accepted, approved or acceded to only by States which have ratified, accepted, approved or acceded to the 1992 Liability Convention.

5. Ratification, acceptance, approval or accession shall be effected by the deposit of a formal instrument to that effect with the Secretary–General of the Organization.

6. A State which is a Party to this Protocol but is not a Party to the 1971 Fund Convention shall be bound by the provisions of the 1971 Fund Convention as amended by this Protocol in relation to other Parties hereto, but shall not be bound by the provisions of the 1971 Fund Convention in relation to Parties thereto.

7. Any instrument of ratification, acceptance, approval or accession deposited after the entry into force of an amendment to the 1971 Fund Convention as amended by this Protocol shall be deemed to apply to the Convention so amended, as modified by such amendment.

Article 29
Information on contributing oil

1. Before this Protocol comes into force for a State, that State shall, when depositing an instrument referred to in Article 28, paragraph 5, and annually thereafter at a date to be determined by the Secretary–General of the Organization, communicate to him the name and address of any person who in respect of that State would be liable to contribute to the Fund pursuant to Article 10 of the 1971 Fund Convention as

amended by this Protocol as well as data on the relevant quantities of contributing oil received by any such person in the territory of that State during the preceding calendar year.

2.   During the transitional period, the Director shall, for Parties, communicate annually to the Secretary–General of the Organization data on quantities of contributing oil received by persons liable to contribute to the Fund pursuant to Article 10 of the 1971 Fund Convention as amended by this Protocol.

Article 30
Entry into force

1.   This Protocol shall enter into force twelve months following the date on which the following requirements are fulfilled:

(a)   at least eight States have deposited instruments of ratification, acceptance, approval or accession with the Secretary–General of the Organization; and

(b)   the Secretary–General of the Organization has received information in accordance with Article 29 that those persons who would be liable to contribute pursuant to Article 10 of the 1971 Fund Convention as amended by this Protocol have received during the preceding calendar year a total quantity of at least 450 million tons of contributing oil.

2.   However, this Protocol shall not enter into force before the 1992 Liability Convention has entered into force.

3.   For each State which ratifies, accepts, approves or accedes to this Protocol after the conditions in paragraph 1 for entry into force have been met, the Protocol shall enter into force twelve months following the date of the deposit by such State of the appropriate instrument.

4.   Any State may, at the time of the deposit of its instrument of ratification, acceptance, approval or accession in respect of this Protocol declare that such instrument shall not take effect for the purpose of this article until the end of the six-month period in Article 31.

5.   Any State which has made a declaration in accordance with the preceding paragraph may withdraw it at any time by means of a notification addressed to the Secretary–General of the Organization. Any such withdrawal shall take effect on the date the notification is received, and any State making such a withdrawal shall be deemed to have deposited its instrument of ratification, acceptance, approval or accession in respect of this Protocol on that date.

6.   Any State which has made a declaration under Article 13, paragraph 2, of the Protocol of 1992 to amend the 1969 Liability Convention shall be deemed to have also made a declaration under paragraph 4 of this article. Withdrawal of a declaration under the said Article 13, paragraph 2, shall be deemed to constitute withdrawal also under paragraph 5 of this article.

Article 31
Denunciation of the 1969 and 1971 Conventions

Subject to Article 30, within six months following the date on which the following requirements are fulfilled:

(a)   at least eight States have become Parties to this Protocol or have deposited instruments of ratification, acceptance, approval or accession with the Secretary–General of the Organization, whether or not subject to Article 30, paragraph 4, and

(b)   the Secretary–General of the Organization has received information in accordance with Article 29 that those persons who are or would be liable to contribute pursuant to Article 10 of the 1971 Fund Convention as amended by this Protocol have received during the preceding calendar year a total quantity of at least 750 million tons of contributing oil;

each Party to this Protocol and each State which has deposited an instrument of ratification, acceptance, approval or accession, whether or not subject to Article 30, paragraph 4, shall, if Party thereto, denounce the 1971 Fund Convention and the 1969 Liability Convention with effect twelve months after the expiry of the above-mentioned six-month period.

Article 32
Revision and amendment

1.   A conference for the purpose of revising or amending the 1992 Fund Convention may be convened by the Organization.

2.   The Organization shall convene a Conference of Contracting States for the purpose of revising or amending the 1992 Fund Convention at the request of not less than one third of all Contracting States.

Article 33
Amendment of compensation limits

1.   Upon the request of at least one quarter of the Contracting States, any proposal to amend the limits of amounts of compensation laid down in Article 4, paragraph 4, of the 1971 Fund Convention as amended by this Protocol shall be circulated by the Secretary–General to all Members of the Organization and to all Contracting States.

2.   Any amendment proposed and circulated as above shall be submitted to the legal Committee of the Organization for consideration at a date at least six months after the date of its circulation.

3.   All Contracting States to the 1971 Fund Convention as amended by this Protocol, whether or not Members of the Organization, shall be entitled to participate in the proceedings of the Legal Committee for the consideration and adoption of amendments.

4.   Amendments shall be adopted by a two-thirds majority of the Contracting States present and voting in the Legal Committee, expanded as provided for in paragraph 3, on condition that at least one half of the Contracting States shall be present at the time of voting.

5.   When acting on a proposal to amend the limits, the Legal Committee shall take into account the experience of incidents and in particular the amount of damage resulting therefrom and changes in the monetary values. It shall also take into account the relationship between the limits in Article 4, paragraph 4, of the 1971 Fund Convention as amended by this Protocol and those in Article V, paragraph 1, of the International Convention on Civil Liability for Oil Pollution Damage, 1992.

6.   (a) No amendment of the limits under this article may be considered before 15 January 1998 nor less than five years from the date of entry into force of a previous amendment under this article. No amendment under this article shall be considered before this Protocol has entered into force.

(b) No limit may be increased so as to exceed an amount which corresponds to the limit laid down in the 1971 Fund Convention as amended by this Protocol increased by six per cent per year calculated on a compound basis for 15 January 1993.

(c) No limit may be increased so as to exceed an amount which corresponds to the limit laid down in the 1971 Fund Convention as amended by this Protocol multiplied by three.

7. Any amendment adopted in accordance with paragraph 4 shall be notified by the Organization to all Contracting States. The amendment shall be deemed to have been accepted at the end of a period of eighteen months after the date of notification unless within that period not less than one quarter of the States that were Contracting States at the time of the adoption of the amendment by the Legal Committee have communicated to the Organization that they do not accept the amendment in which case the amendment is rejected and shall have no effect.

8. An amendment deemed to have been accepted in accordance with paragraph 7 shall enter into force eighteen months after its acceptance.

9. All Contracting States shall be bound by the amendment, unless they denounce this Protocol in accordance with Article 34, paragraphs 1 and 2, at least six months before the amendment enters into force. Such denunciation shall take effect when the amendment enters into force.

10. When an amendment has been adopted by the Legal Committee but the eighteen-month period for its acceptance has not yet expired, a State which becomes a Contracting State during that period shall be bound by the amendment if it enters into force. A State which becomes a Contracting State after that period shall be bound by an amendment which has been accepted in accordance with paragraph 7. In the cases referred to in this paragraph, a State becomes bound by an amendment when that amendment enters into force, or when this Protocol enters into force for that State, if later.

Article 34
Denunciation

1. This Protocol may be denounced by any Party at any time after the date on which it enters into force for that Party.

2. Denunciation shall be effected by the deposit of an instrument with the Secretary–General of the Organization.

3. A denunciation shall take effect twelve months, or such longer period as may be specified in the instrument of denunciation, after its deposit with the Secretary–General of the Organization.

4. Denunciation of the 1992 Liability Convention shall be deemed to be a denunciation of this Protocol. Such denunciation shall take effect on the date on which denunciation of the Protocol of 1992 to amend the 1969 Liability Convention takes effect according to Article 16 of that Protocol.

5. Any Contracting State to this Protocol which has not denounced the 1971 Fund Convention and the 1969 Liability Convention as required by Article 31 shall be deemed to have denounced this Protocol with effect twelve months after the expiry of the six-month period mentioned in that article. As from the date on which the denunciations provided for in Article 31 take effect, any Party to this Protocol which deposits an 1969 Liability Convention shall be deemed to have denounced this Protocol with effect from the date on which such instrument takes effect.

6. As between the Parties to this Protocol, denunciation by any of them of the 1971 Fund Convention in accordance with Article 41 thereof shall not be construed in any way as a denunciation of the 1971 Fund Convention as amended by this Protocol.

7. Notwithstanding a denunciation of this Protocol by a Party pursuant to this article, any provisions of this Protocol relating to the obligations to make contributions under Article 10 of the 1971 Fund Convention as amended by this Protocol with

respect to an incident referred to in Article 12, paragraph 2(b), of that amended Convention and occurring before the denunciation takes effect shall continue to apply.

Article 35
Extraordinary sessions of the Assembly

1. Any Contracting State may, within ninety days after the deposit of an instrument of denunciation the result of which it considers will significantly increase the level of contributions for the remaining Contracting States, request the Director to convene an extraordinary session of the Assembly. The Director shall convene the Assembly to meet not later than sixty days after receipt of the request.

2. The Director may convene, on his own initiative, an extraordinary session of the Assembly to meet within sixty days after the deposit of any instrument of denunciation, if he considers that such denunciation will result in a significant increase in the level of contributions of the remaining Contracting States.

3. If the Assembly at an extraordinary session convened in accordance with paragraph 1 or 2 decides that the denunciation will result in a significant increase in the level of contributions for the remaining Contracting States, any such State may, not later than one hundred and twenty days before the date on which the denunciation takes effect, denounce this Protocol with effect from the same date.

Article 36
Termination

1. This Protocol shall cease to be in force on the date when the number of Contracting States falls below three.

2. States which are bound by this Protocol on the day before the date it ceases to be in force shall enable the Fund to exercise its functions as described under Article 37 of this Protocol and shall, for that purpose only, remain bound by this Protocol.

Article 37
Winding up of the Fund

1. If this Protocol ceases to be in force, the Fund shall nevertheless:

(a) meet its obligations in respect of any incident occurring before the Protocol ceased to be in force;

(b) be entitled to exercise its rights to contributions to the extent that these contributions are necessary to meet the obligations under subparagraph (a), including expenses for the administration of the Fund necessary for this purpose.

2. The Assembly shall take all appropriate measures to complete the winding up of the Fund including the distribution in an equitable manner of any remaining assets among those persons who have contributed to the Fund.

3. For the purposes of this article the Fund shall remain a legal person.

Article 38
Depositary

1. This Protocol and any amendments accepted under Article 33 shall be deposited with the Secretary–General of the Organization.

2. The Secretary–General of the Organization shall:

(a) inform all States which have signed or acceded to this Protocol of:

(i) each new signature or deposit of an instrument together with the date thereof,

(ii) each declaration and notification under Article 30 including declarations and withdrawals deemed to have been made in accordance with that Article;

(iii) the date of entry into force of this Protocol;

(iv) the date by which denunciations provided for in Article 31 are required to be made;

(v) any proposal to amend limits of amounts of compensation which has been made in accordance with Article 33, paragraph 1;

(vi) any amendment which has been adopted in accordance with Article 33, paragraph 4;

(vii) any amendment deemed to have been accepted under Article 33, paragraph 7, together with the date on which that amendment shall enter into force in accordance with paragraphs 8 and 9 of that article;

(viii) the deposit of an instrument of denunciation of this Protocol together with the date of the deposit and the date on which it takes effect;

(ix) any denunciation deemed to have been made under Article 34, paragraph 5;

(x) any communication called for by any article in this Protocol;

(b) transmit certified true copies of this Protocol to all Signatory States and to all States which accede to the Protocol.

3.   As soon as this Protocol enters into force, the text shall be transmitted by the Secretary–General of the Organization to the Secretariat of the United Nations for registration and publication in accordance with Article 102 of the Charter of the United Nations.

Article 39
Languages

This protocol is established in a single original in the Arabic, Chinese, English, French, Russian and Spanish languages, each text being equally authentic.

DONE AT LONDON this twenty-seventh day of November one thousand nine hundred and ninety-two.

IN WITNESS WHEREOF the undersigned being duly authorized for that purpose have signed this Protocol.

3.15   1997 SHIPS' ROUTEING AMENDMENT TO THE INTERNATIONAL CONVENTION FOR THE SAFETY OF LIFE AT SEA, 1974. **Concluded at London, 16 May 1995. Entered into force, 1 January 1997. IMO Resolution MSC.46(65)**

Regulation V/8—Routeing

Ships' routeing

(a) Ships' routeing systems contribute to safety of life at sea, safety and efficiency of navigation, and/or protection of the marine environment. Ships' routeing systems are recommended for use by, and may be made mandatory for, all ships, certain categories of ships or ships carrying certain cargoes, when adopted and implemented in accordance with the guidelines and criteria developed by the Organization.

(b) The Organization is recognized as the only international body for developing guidelines, criteria and regulations on an international level for ships' routeing systems. Contracting Governments shall refer proposals for the adoption of ships' routeing systems to the Organization. The Organization will collate and disseminate to Contracting Governments all relevant information with regard to any adopted ships' routeing systems.

(c) This regulation, and its associated guidelines and criteria, does not apply to warships, naval auxiliary or other vessels owned or operated by a Contracting Government and used, for the time being, only on government non-commercial service; however, such ships are encouraged to participate in ships' routeing systems adopted in accordance with this regulation.

(d) The initiation of action for establishing a ships' routeing system is the responsibility of the Government or Governments concerned. In developing such systems for adoption by the Organization, the guidelines and criteria developed by the Organization shall be taken into account.

(e) Ships' routeing systems should be submitted to the Organization for adoption. However, a Government or Governments implementing ships' routeing systems not intended to be submitted to the Organization for adoption or which have not been adopted by the Organization are encouraged to follow, wherever possible, the guidelines and criteria developed by the Organization.

(f) Where two or more Governments have a common interest in a particular area, they should formulate joint proposals for the delineation and use of a routeing system therein on the basis of an agreement between them. Upon receipt of such proposal and before proceeding with the consideration of it for adoption, the Organization shall ensure details of the proposal are disseminated to the Governments which have a common interest in the area, including countries in the vicinity of the proposed ships' routeing system.

(g) Contracting Governments shall adhere to the measures adopted by the Organization concerning ships' routeing. They shall promulgate all information necessary for the safe and effective use of adopted ships' routeing systems. A Government or Governments concerned may monitor traffic in those systems. Contracting Governments will do everything in their power to secure the appropriate use of ships' routeing systems adopted by the Organization.

(h) A ship shall use a mandatory ships' routeing system adopted by the Organization as required for its category or cargo carried and in accordance with the relevant provisions in force unless there are compelling reasons not to use a particular ships' routeing system. Any such reason shall be recorded in the ship's log.

(i) Mandatory ships' routeing systems shall be reviewed by the Contracting Government or Governments concerned in accordance with the guidelines and criteria developed by the Organization.

(j) All adopted ships' routeing systems and actions taken to enforce compliance with those systems shall be consistent with international law, including the relevant provisions of the 1982 United Nations Convention on the Law of the Sea.

(k) Nothing in this regulation nor its associated guidelines and criteria shall prejudice the rights and duties of Governments under international law or the legal regime of international straits.

3.16   GLOBAL PROGRAMME OF ACTION FOR THE PROTECTION OF THE MARINE ENVIRON-
       MENT FROM LAND-BASED ACTIVITIES. **Concluded at Washington, 3 No-
       vember 1995. UNEP(OCA)/LBA/IG.2/7**

I. INTRODUCTION

A. The need for action

1.   The major threats to the health and productivity and biodiversity of the
marine environment result from human activities on land-in coastal areas and further
inland. Most of the pollution load of the oceans, including municipal, industrial and
agricultural wastes and run-off, as well as atmospheric deposition, emanates from such
land-based activities and affects the most productive areas of the marine environment,
including estuaries and near-shore coastal waters. These areas are likewise threatened
by physical alteration of the coastal environment, including destruction of habitats of
vital importance for ecosystem health. Moreover, contaminants which pose risks to
human health and living resources are transported long distances by watercourses,
ocean currents and atmospheric processes.

2.   The bulk of the world's population lives in coastal areas, and there is a
continuing trend towards its concentration in these regions. The health, well-being
and, in some cases, the very survival of coastal populations depend upon the health
and well-being of coastal systems—estuaries and wetlands—as well as their associated
watersheds and drainage basins and near-shore coastal waters. Ultimately, sustainable
patterns of human activity in coastal areas depend upon a healthy marine environment, and vice versa.

B. Aims of the Global Programme of Action

3.   The Global Programme of Action aims at preventing the degradation of the
marine environment from land-based activities by facilitating the realization of the
duty of States to preserve and protect the marine environment. It is designed to assist
States in taking actions individually or jointly within their respective policies, priorities
and resources, which will lead to the prevention, reduction, control and/or elimination
of the degradation of the marine environment, as well as to its recovery from the
impacts of land-based activities. Achievement of the aims of the Programme of Action
will contribute to maintaining and, where appropriate, restoring the productive capacity and biodiversity of the marine environment, ensuring the protection of human
health, as well as promoting the conservation and sustainable use of marine living
resources.

C. Legal and institutional framework

4.   International law, as reflected in the provisions of the United Nations Convention on the Law of the Sea (UNCLOS) and elsewhere, sets forth rights and obligations
of States and provides the international basis upon which to pursue the protection and
sustainable development of the marine and coastal environment and its resources.

5.   In accordance with general international law, while States have the sovereign
right to exploit their natural resources pursuant to their environmental policies, the
enjoyment of such right shall be in accordance with the duty to protect and preserve
the marine environment. This fundamental duty is to protect and preserve the marine
environment from all sources of pollution, including land-based activities. Of particular
significance for the Global Programme of Action are the provisions contained in
articles 207 and 213 of UNCLOS.

6.   Also of particular importance for the Programme of Action is the emphasis, in
parts XII, XIII and XIV of the Convention, dealing, respectively, with protection and
preservation of the marine environment, marine scientific research and the development and transfer of marine technology, on the obligation of States to cooperate in the

development of the marine scientific and technological capacity of developing States and to provide them with scientific and technical assistance.

7. The duty of States to preserve and protect the marine environment has been reflected and elaborated upon in numerous global conventions and regional instruments (e.g. the Convention on the Prevention of Marine Pollution by Dumping of Wastes and Other Matter; Basel Convention on the Control of Transboundary Movements of Hazardous Wastes and their Disposal; Convention on Biological Diversity; United Nations Framework Convention on Climate Change; Regional Seas Conventions; International Convention for the Prevention of Pollution from Ships (MARPOL 73/78), etc.). Innovative new principles and approaches applicable to the prevention of the degradation of the marine environment from land-based activities have been included in a number of such agreements.

8. In 1982, the United Nations Environment Programme (UNEP) took the initiative to develop advice to Governments on addressing impacts on the marine environment from land-based activities. This initiative resulted in the preparation of the Montreal Guidelines for the Protection of the Marine Environment Against Pollution from Land-based Sources in 1985.

9. The duty to protect the marine environment from land-based activities was placed squarely in the context of sustainable development by the United Nations Conference on Environment and Development in 1992. Therein, States agreed it is necessary:

(a) To apply preventive, precautionary, and anticipatory approaches so as to avoid degradation of the marine environment, as well as to reduce the risk of long-term or irreversible adverse effects upon it;

(b) To ensure prior assessment of activities that may have significant adverse impacts upon the marine environment;

(c) To integrate protection of the marine environment into relevant general environmental, social and economic development policies;

(d) To develop economic incentives, where appropriate, to apply clean technologies and other means consistent with the internalization of environmental costs, such as the "polluter pays" principle, so as to avoid degradation of the marine environment;

(e) To improve the living standards of coastal populations, particularly in developing countries, so as to contribute to reducing the degradation of the coastal and marine environment.

10. As set out in paragraph 17.23 of Agenda 21, States agree that provision of additional financial resources, through appropriate international mechanisms, as well as access to cleaner technologies and relevant research, would be necessary to support action by developing countries to implement this commitment.

11. Agenda 21 linked the implementation of those duties with action to implement commitments to integrated management and sustainable development of the marine environment, including coastal areas under national jurisdiction. In this regard, States agreed to implement the provisions of the programme of action adopted at the World Coast Conference in Noordwijk in 1993 and to further develop those provisions in order to make them more operational.

12. Agenda 21 also linked action to combat marine degradation caused by land-based activities to action to address the specific problems of small island developing States. In this regard, States agreed to implement the provisions of the priority areas of the Programme of Action for the Sustainable Development of Small Island Developing States, adopted in Barbados in 1994.

13.   In order to promote, facilitate and finance implementation of Agenda 21 by developing countries, an objective of Agenda 21 is to provide additional financial resources that are both adequate and predictable. Another objective in this context is to promote, facilitate and finance, as appropriate, the access to and the transfer of environmentally sound technologies and corresponding know-how, in particular to developing countries, on favourable terms, including concessional and preferential terms, as mutually agreed, taking into account the need to protect intellectual property rights as well as the special needs of developing countries for the implementation of Agenda 21.

D. The Global Programme of Action

14.   The Programme of Action, therefore, is designed to be a source of conceptual and practical guidance to be drawn upon by national and/or regional authorities in devising and implementing sustained action to prevent, reduce, control and/or eliminate marine degradation from land-based activities. Effective implementation of this Programme of Action is a crucial and essential step forward in the protection of the marine environment and will promote the objectives and goals of sustainable development.

15.   The Global Programme of Action reflects the fact that States face a growing number of commitments flowing from Agenda 21 and related conventions. Its implementation will require new approaches by, and new forms of collaboration among, Governments, organizations and institutions with responsibilities and expertise relevant to marine and coastal areas, at all levels—national, regional and global. These include the promotion of innovative financial mechanisms to generate needed resources.

II. ACTIONS AT THE NATIONAL LEVEL

Basis for Action

16.   Sustainable use of the oceans depends on the maintenance of ecosystem health, public health, food security, and economic and social benefits including cultural values. Many countries depend on sources of income from activities that would be directly threatened by degradation of the marine environment: industries such as fishing and tourism are obvious examples. The subsistence economy of large coastal populations, in particular in the developing countries, is based on marine living resources that would also be threatened by such degradation. Also to be considered are the impacts of such degradation on maritime culture and traditional lifestyles.

17.   Food security is threatened, in particular in developing countries, by the loss of marine living resources that are vital for the adequate provision of food and for combating poverty. Public health considerations from a degraded marine environment manifest themselves through the contamination of seafood, direct contact, such as through bathing, and the use of sea water in desalination and food-processing plants.

Objectives

18.   To develop comprehensive, continuing and adaptive programmes of action within the framework of integrated coastal area management which should include provisions for:

   (a) Identification and assessment of problems;

   (b) Establishment of priorities;

   (c) Setting management objectives for priority problems;

   (d) Identification, evaluation and selection of strategies and measures, including management approaches;

(e) Criteria for evaluating the effectiveness of strategies and programmes;

(f) Programme support elements.

Actions

19.   States should, in accordance with their policies, priorities and resources, develop or review national programmes of action within a few years and take forward action to implement these programmes with the assistance of the international cooperation identified in chapter IV, in particular to developing countries, especially the least developed countries, countries with economies in transition and small island developing States (hereinafter referred to as "countries in need of assistance"). The effective development and implementation of national programmes of action should focus on sustainable, pragmatic and integrated environmental management approaches and processes, such as integrated coastal area management, harmonized, as appropriate, with river basin management and land-use plans.

* * *

III. REGIONAL COOPERATION

Basis for action

29.   Regional and subregional cooperation and arrangements are crucial for successful actions to protect the marine environment from land-based activities. This is particularly so where a number of countries have coasts in the same marine and coastal area, most notably in enclosed or semi-enclosed seas. Such cooperation allows for more accurate identification and assessment of the problems in particular geographic areas and more appropriate establishment of priorities for action in these areas. Such cooperation also strengthens regional and national capacity-building and offers an important avenue for harmonizing and adjusting measures to fit the particular environmental and socio-economic circumstances. It, moreover, supports a more efficient and cost-effective implementation of the programmes of action.

Objectives

30.   To strengthen and, where necessary, create new regional cooperative arrangements and joint actions to support effective action, strategies and programmes for:

(a) Identification and assessment of problems;

(b) Establishment of targets and priorities for action;

(c) Development and implementation of pragmatic and comprehensive management approaches and processes;

(d) Development and implementation of strategies to mitigate and remediate land-based sources of harm to the coastal and marine environment.

Activities

A. Participation in regional and subregional arrangements

31.   States should:

(a) Pursue more active participation, including accession or ratification, as appropriate, in regional seas and other international marine and freshwater agreements, conventions and related arrangements;

(b) Strengthen existing regional conventions and programmes, and their institutional arrangements;

(c) Negotiate as, appropriate, new regional conventions and programmes.

* * *

IV. INTERNATIONAL COOPERATION
Basis for action

36.   Effective international cooperation is important for the successful and cost-effective implementation of the Programme of Action. International cooperation serves a central role in enhancing capacity-building, technology transfer and cooperation, and financial support. Moreover, effective implementation of the Programme of Action requires efficient support from appropriate international agencies. Furthermore, international cooperation is required to ensure regular review of the implementation of the Programme and its further development and adjustment.

37.   At the global level, there is a need for regular reviews of the state of the world marine environment, as well as dialogues, based on reports from relevant regional organizations, on implementation of regional action programmes, including exchange of experiences, the flow of financial resources in support of the implementation, in particular by countries in need of assistance, of national action to prevent and reduce marine degradation caused by land-based activities as well as scientific and technological cooperation and transfer of cleaner technology, in particular, to countries in need of assistance.

Objective

38.   To strengthen existing international cooperation and institutional mechanisms and, where appropriate, to establish new arrangements, in order to support States and regional groups to undertake sustained action to address impacts upon the marine environment from land-based activities. Such actions should be based on the commitments with respect to financial resources contained in chapter 33 of Agenda 21, including paragraph 33.11, and those with respect to transfer of environmentally sound technology, cooperation and capacity-building contained in chapter 34 of Agenda 21, including paragraphs 34.4 and 34.14, as well as the commitments contained in paragraphs 17.23 and 17.48.

Activities

39.   Recommended actions to give effect to these objectives in support of national and regional action to prevent and reduce marine degradation caused by land-based activities fall into four general categories:

(a) Capacity-building;

(b) The mobilization of financial resources;

(c) The international institutional framework;

(d) Additional areas of international cooperation.

* * *

V. RECOMMENDED APPROACHES BY SOURCE CATEGORY

91.   This chapter provides guidance as to the actions that States should consider at national, regional and global levels, in accordance with their national capacities, priorities and available resources, and with the cooperation of the United Nations and other relevant organizations, as appropriate, and with the international cooperation for building capacities and mobilizing resources identified in chapter IV.

92.   In the light of the differences between regions and States and the national priorities referred to in paragraphs 53 and 54 above, each State and each regional

grouping should develop its own programme of action. This may or may not be a separate document but it should include specific targets and a clear timetable showing the dates by which the State or States involved commit themselves at a political level to achieve these targets.

93. In addition, action will be needed on certain matters at the global level, either to address global effects or to facilitate action at the national or regional levels. Specific targets for these matters are set out in this chapter.

A. Sewage

1. Basis for action

94. Recognizing variation in local conditions, domestic waste water improperly discharged to freshwater and coastal environments may present a variety of concerns. These are associated with: (a) pathogens that may result in human health problems through exposure via bathing waters or through contaminated shellfish, (b) suspended solids, (c) significant nutrient inputs, (d) biochemical oxygen demand (BOD), (e) cultural issues such as taboos in some areas, (f) plastics and other marine debris, (g) ecosystem population effects, and (h) heavy metals and other toxic substances, e.g. hydrocarbons, in those cases where industrial sources may have discharged effluent to municipal collection systems.

95. Environmental effects associated with domestic waste-water discharges are generally local with transboundary implications in certain geographic areas. The commonality of sewage-related problems throughout coastal areas of the world is significant. Consequently, domestic waste-water discharges are considered one of the most significant threats to coastal environments worldwide.

2. Objective/proposed target

96. With regard to objectives and targets, paragraph 21.29 of Agenda 21 states:

"Governments, according to their capacities and available resources and with the cooperation of the United Nations and other relevant organizations, as appropriate, should:

"(a) By the year 2000, establish waste treatment and disposal quality criteria, objectives and standards based on the nature and assimilative capacity of the receiving environment;

"(b) By the year 2000, establish sufficient capacity to undertake waste-related pollution impact monitoring and conduct regular surveillance, including epidemiological surveillance, where appropriate;

"(c) By the year 1995, in industrialized countries, and by the year 2005, in developing countries, ensure that at least 50 per cent of all sewage, waste waters and solid wastes are treated or disposed of in conformity with national or international environmental and health quality guidelines;

"(d) By the year 2025, dispose of all sewage, waste waters and solid wastes in conformity with national or international environmental quality guidelines."

* * *

B. Persistent organic pollutants (POPs)

1. Basis for action

100. Persistent organic pollutants (POPs) are a set of organic compounds that: (i) possess toxic characteristics; (ii) are persistent; (iii) are liable to bioaccumulate; (iv) are prone to long-range transport and deposition; and (v) can result in adverse environmental and human health effects at locations near and far from their source.

POPs are typically characterized as having low water solubility and high fat solubility. Most POPs are anthropogenic in origin. Anthropogenic emissions, both point and diffuse, are associated with industrial processes, product use and applications, waste disposal, leaks and spills, and combustion of fuels and waste materials. Once dispersed, clean-up is rarely possible. Because many POPs are relatively volatile, their remobilization and long-distance redistribution through atmospheric pathways often complicates the identification of specific sources.

101.   POPs have long environmental half-lives. Accordingly, successive releases over time result in continued accumulation and the ubiquitous presence of POPs in the global environment.

102.   The primary transport routes into the marine and coastal environment include atmospheric deposition and surface run-off. Regional and global transport is predominately mediated by atmospheric circulation, but also occurs through sediment transport and oceanic circulation. Movement may also occur through a successive migration of short-range movements that result from a sequence of volatilization, deposition, and revolatilization. Due to these transport patterns and chemical characteristics, there is a growing body of evidence demonstrating the systematic migration of these substances to cooler latitudes.

2.   Objective/proposed target

103.   The objective/proposed target is:

(a) To reduce and/or eliminate emissions and discharges of POPs that threaten to accumulate to dangerous levels in the marine and coastal environment;

(b) To give immediate attention to finding and introducing preferable substitutes for chemicals that pose unreasonable and otherwise unmanageable risks to human health and the environment;

(c) To use cleaner production processes, including best available techniques, to reduce and/or eliminate hazardous by-products associated with production, incineration and combustion (e.g. dioxins, furans, hexaclorobenzene, poycyclic aromatic hydrocarbons (PAHs));

(d) To promote best environmental practice for pest control in agriculture and aquaculture.

* * *

C.   Radioactive substances

1.   Basis for action

107.   Radioactive substances (i.e., materials containing radionuclides) have entered and/or are entering the marine and coastal environment, directly or indirectly, as a result of a variety of human activities and practices. These activities include production of energy, reprocessing of spent fuel, military operations, nuclear testing, medical applications and other operations associated with the management and disposal of radioactive wastes and the processing of natural materials by industrial processes. Other activities, such as the transport of radioactive material, pose risks of such releases.

108.   Radioactive materials can present hazards to human health and to the environment. Suspected radioactive contamination of foodstuffs can also have negative effects on marketing of such foodstuffs.

2.   Objective/proposed target

109.   The objective/proposed target is to reduce and/or eliminate emissions and discharges of radioactive substances in order to prevent, reduce and eliminate pollution

of the marine and coastal environment by human-enhanced levels of radioactive substances.

* * *

D. Heavy metals

1. Basis for action

114. Heavy metals are natural constituents of the Earth's crust. Human activities have drastically altered the biochemical and geochemical cycles and balance of some heavy metals. Heavy metals are stable and persistent environmental contaminants since they cannot be degraded or destroyed. Therefore, they tend to accumulate in the soils and sediments. Excessive levels of metals in the marine environment can affect marine biota and pose risk to human consumers of seafood.

115. Metals and their compounds, both inorganic and organic, are released to the environment as a result of a variety of human activities. A wide range of metals and metallic compounds found in the marine environment pose risks to human health through the consumption of seafood where contaminant content and exposure are significant. Many metals are essential to life and only become toxic when exposures to biota become excessive (i.e., exceed some threshold for the introduction of adverse effects). While certain non-essential metals do not have explicit exposure thresholds for the introduction of effects, the nature of biological responses to metal exposure are a direct consequence of exposure and are defined through dose-effect relationships. This differs from the dose-response relationship associated with many synthetic organic contaminants and radionuclides where risk of adverse effects is assumed to be proportional to exposure. Accordingly, it is desirable to minimize such exposures. In contrast, the predominant challenge in the case of heavy metals is one of limiting exposure to levels that do not cause adverse effects.

116. The main anthropogenic sources of heavy metals are various industrial point sources, including present and former mining activities, foundries and smelters, and diffuse sources such as piping, constituents of products, combustion by-products, traffic, etc. Relatively volatile heavy metals and those that become attached to airborne particles can be widely dispersed on very large scales. Heavy metals conveyed in aqueous and sedimentary transport (e.g., river run-off) enter the normal coastal biogeochemical cycle and are largely retained within near-shore and shelf regions.

2. Objective/proposed target

117. The objective/proposed target is to reduce and/or eliminate anthropogenic emissions and discharges in order to prevent, reduce and eliminate pollution caused by heavy metals.

* * *

E. Oils (Hydrocarbons)

1. Basis for action

121. Many oils are liquid and gaseous hydrocarbons of geological origin. While some oils are naturally occurring, a significant proportion of those in the marine and coastal environment have been derived from anthropogenic sources. Most oils from land-based sources are refined petroleum products or their derivatives. Some oils are volatile or easily degraded and disappear rapidly from aquatic systems, but some may persist in the water column or in sediments. Oils may be toxic to aquatic life when ingested or absorbed through skin or gills, interfere with respiratory systems, foul fur and feathers, smother aquatic communities, habitats and bathing beaches, taint seafood and contaminate water supplies.

122. Land-based sources of oils include operational and accidental discharges and emissions from oil exploration, exploitation, refining and storage facilities; urban, industrial and agricultural run-off; transport; and the inappropriate disposal of used lubricating oils. The main pathways to the marine environment include atmospheric dispersion of volatile fractions; storm sewers and sewage treatment works; and rivers. Impacts from land-derived oils will be regional for the more volatile fractions, and local (occasionally regional) for more refractory components.

2. Objective/proposed target

123. The objective is to prevent, reduce and/or eliminate anthropogenic emissions and discharges in order to prevent, reduce and eliminate pollution caused by oil.

* * *

F. Nutrients

1. Basis for action

127. Eutrophication can result from augmentation of nutrient inputs to coastal and marine areas as a consequence of human activities. In general, such eutrophication is usually confined to the vicinity of coastal discharges but, because of both the multiplicity of such discharges and regional atmospheric transport of nutrients, such affected coastal areas can be extensive.

128. The effects of the enhanced mobilization of nutrients are enhanced productivity but these can also result in changes in species diversity, excessive algal growth, dissolved oxygen reductions and associated fish kills and, it is suspected, the increased prevalence or frequency of toxic algal blooms.

2. Objective/proposed target

129. The objective/proposed target is:

(a) To identify, in broad terms, marine areas where nutrient inputs are causing or are likely to cause pollution, directly or indirectly;

(b) To reduce nutrient inputs into the areas identified;

(c) To reduce the number of marine areas where eutrophication is evident;

(d) To protect and, where appropriate, to restore areas of natural denitrification.

* * *

G. Sediment mobilization

1. Basis for action

133. Natural sedimentation and siltation are important in the development and maintenance of numerous coastal habitats. Habitats requiring sediment input include coastal wetlands, lagoons, estuaries and mangroves. Reduction in natural rates of sedimentation can compromise the integrity of these habitats, as can excessive sediment loads, which may bury benthic communities and threaten sensitive habitats such as coral reefs, mangroves, seagrass beds, and rocky substrates.

134. Contaminated sediments, whether they are fresh inputs or dredged, may also lead to pollution, the latter through resuspension or improper disposal.

135. Anthropogenic modifications to sediment mobilization and sedimentation are made by, inter alia, construction activities, forestry operations, agricultural practices, mining practices, hydrological modifications, dredging activities, and coastal erosion. Effects are generally local in nature, but transboundary implications may

occur in some areas where major river systems form a common border and where littoral currents carry inputs across international boundaries.

2. Objective/proposed target

136. The objective/proposed target is to reduce, control and prevent the degradation of the marine environment due to changes in coastal erosion and siltation caused by human activities.

* * *

H. Litter

1. Basis for action

140. Litter threatens marine life through entanglement, suffocation and ingestion and is widely recognized to degrade the visual amenities of marine and coastal areas with negative effects on tourism and general aesthetics. Litter is any persistent manufactured or processed solid material which is discarded, disposed of, or abandoned in the marine and coastal environment, sometimes called marine debris. Litter in the marine environment can also destroy coastal habitats and in some situations interfere with biological production in coastal areas.

141. Litter entering the marine and coastal environment has multiple sources. Sources include poorly managed or illegal waste dumps adjacent to rivers and coastal areas, windblown litter from coastal communities, resin pellets used as industrial feedstocks, and litter that is channelled to the marine and coastal environment through municipal stormwater systems and rivers. Marine litter is also caused by dumping of garbage into the marine and coastal environment by municipal authorities as well as recreational and commercial vessels.

142. While international action has been taken to prevent the discharge of plastics and other persistent wastes from vessels, it has been estimated that approximately 80 per cent of persistent wastes originate from land. Floatable litter is known to travel considerable distances with regional and sometimes broader implications. Resin pellets used as industrial feedstock circulate and deposit on oceanic scales.

143. Uncontrolled burning of litter containing plastics may generate significant quantities of POPs, metals and hydrocarbons which can reach the marine and coastal environment.

2. Objective/proposed target

144. The objective/proposed target is:

(a) To establish controlled and environmentally sound facilities for receiving, collecting, handling and disposing of litter from coastal area communities;

(b) To reduce significantly the amount of litter reaching the marine and coastal environment by the prevention or reduction of the generation of solid waste and improvements in its management, including collection and recycling of litter.a. In this context, paragraph 21.39 of Agenda 21 states:

"The overall objective of this programme is to provide health-protecting environmentally safe waste collection and disposal services to all people. Governments, according to their capacities and available resources and with the cooperation of the United Nations and other relevant organizations, as appropriate, should:

"(a) By the year 2000, have the necessary technical, financial and human resource capacity to provide waste collection services commensurate with needs;

"(b) By the year 2025, provide all urban populations with adequate waste services;

"(c) By the year 2025, ensure that full urban waste service coverage is maintained and sanitation coverage achieved in all rural areas."

* * *

I. Physical alterations and destruction of habitats

1. Basis for action

149. The increase of populations and economic activities in coastal areas is leading to an expansion of construction and alterations to coastal areas and waters. Excavation, oil and gas exploration and exploitation, mining, such as sand and aggregate extraction, the building of ports and marinas and building of coastal defences and other activities linked to urban expansion are giving rise to alterations of coral reefs, shorelands, beachfronts and the seafloor. Important habitats are being destroyed. Wetlands are being transformed into agricultural lands and through coastal development. Tourism, unrestricted and uncontrolled aquaculture, clearance of mangroves and destructive fishing practices, such as the use of dynamite and chemicals, are also causing the physical destruction of important habitats. The introduction of alien species can also have serious effects upon marine ecosystem integrity. Spawning grounds, nurseries and feeding grounds of major living marine resources of crucial importance to world food security are being destroyed. This destruction of habitat exacerbates overharvesting of these living marine resources leading to a growing risk that they are being depleted. This is an increasing threat to the food security of coastal populations, in particular in developing countries.

150. The damming of river systems can result in upstream sedimentation, possible changes in estuarine conditions and interference with fish migration. These adversely affect biological diversity and biological productivity. The practice of saltwinning from saltpan construction in coastal areas can also affect salt concentration levels and biological diversity.

2. Objective/proposed target

151. The objective/proposed target is to:

(a) Safeguard the ecosystem function, maintain the integrity and biological diversity of habitats which are of major socio-economic and ecological interest through integrated management of coastal areas;

(b) Where practicable, restore marine and coastal habitats that have been adversely affected by anthropogenic activities.

* * *

3.17 WASHINGTON DECLARATION ON PROTECTION OF THE MARINE ENVIRONMENT FROM LAND-BASED ACTIVITIES. **Adopted on 1 November 1995. Annex II to the Intergovernmental Conference to Adopt a Global Programme of Action for the Protection of the Marine Environment From Land–Based Activities, UNEP(OCA)/LBA/IG.2/6**

The representatives of Governments and the European Commission participating in the Conference held in Washington from 23 October to 3 November 1995,

Affirming the need and will to protect and preserve the marine environment for present and future generations,

Reaffirming the relevant provisions of chapters 17, 33 and 34 of Agenda 21 and the Rio Declaration on Environment and Development,

Recognizing the interdependence of human populations and the coastal and marine environment, and the growing and serious threat from land-based activities, to both human health and well-being and the integrity of coastal and marine ecosystems and biodiversity,

Further recognizing the importance of integrated coastal area management and the catchment-area-based approach as means of coordinating programmes aimed at preventing marine degradation from land-based activities with economic and social development programmes,

Also recognizing that the alleviation of poverty is an essential factor in addressing the impacts of land-based activities on coastal and marine areas,

Noting that there are major differences among the different regions of the world, and the States which they comprise, in terms of environmental, economic and social conditions and level of development which will lead to different judgments on priorities in addressing problems related to the degradation of the marine environment by land-based activities,

Acknowledging the need to involve major groups in national, regional and international activities to address degradation of the marine environment by land-based activities,

Strongly supporting the processes set forth in decisions 18/31 and 18/32 of 25 May 1995 of the Governing Council of the United Nations Environment Programme for addressing at the global level the priority issues of persistent organic pollutants and adequate treatment of waste water,

Having therefore adopted the Global Programme of Action for the Protection of the Marine Environment from Land-based Activities,

Hereby declare their commitment to protect and preserve the marine environment from the impacts of land-based activities, and

Declare their intention to do so by:

1. Setting as their common goal sustained and effective action to deal with all land-based impacts upon the marine environment, specifically those resulting from sewage, persistent organic pollutants, radioactive substances, heavy metals, oils (hydrocarbons), nutrients, sediment mobilization, litter, and physical alteration and destruction of habitat;

2. Developing or reviewing national action programmes within a few years on the basis of national priorities and strategies;

3. Taking forward action to implement these programmes in accordance with national capacities and priorities;

4. Cooperating to build capacities and mobilize resources for the development and implementation of such programmes, in particular for developing countries,

especially the least developed countries, countries with economies in transition and small island developing States (hereinafter referred to as "countries in need of assistance");

5. Taking immediate preventive and remedial action, wherever possible, using existing knowledge, resources, plans and processes;

6. Promoting access to cleaner technologies, knowledge and expertise to address land-based activities that degrade the marine environment, in particular for countries in need of assistance;

7. Cooperating on a regional basis to coordinate efforts for maximum efficiency and to facilitate action at the national level, including, where appropriate, becoming parties to and strengthening regional cooperative agreements and creating new agreements where necessary;

8. Encouraging cooperative and collaborative action and partnerships, among governmental institutions and organizations, communities, the private sector and non-governmental organizations which have relevant responsibilities and/or experience;

9. Encouraging and/or making available external financing, given that funding from domestic sources and mechanisms for the implementation of the Global Programme of Action by countries in need of assistance may be insufficient;

10. Promoting the full range of available management tools and financing options in implementing national or regional programmes of action, including innovative managerial and financial techniques, while recognizing the differences between countries in need of assistance and developed States;

11. Urging national and international institutions and the private sector, bilateral donors and multilateral funding agencies to accord priority to projects within national and regional programmes to implement the Global Programme of Action and encouraging the Global Environment Facility to support these projects;

12. Calling upon the United Nations Environment Programme, the United Nations Development Programme, the World Bank, the regional development banks, as well as the agencies within the United Nations system to ensure that their programmes support (through, inter alia, financial cooperation, capacity-building and institutional-strengthening mechanisms) the regional structures in place for the protection of the marine environment;

13. According priority to implementation of the Global Programme of Action within the United Nations system, as well as in other global and regional institutions and organizations with responsibilities and capabilities for addressing marine degradation from land-based activities, and specifically:

(a) Securing formal endorsement of those parts of the Global Programme of Action that are relevant to such institutions and organizations and incorporating the relevant provisions into their work programmes;

(b) Establishing a clearing-house mechanism to provide decision makers in all States with direct access to relevant sources of information, practical experience and scientific and technical expertise and to facilitate effective scientific, technical and financial cooperation as well as capacity-building; and

(c) Providing for periodic intergovernmental review of the Global Programme of Action, taking into account regular assessments of the state of the marine environment;

14. Promoting action to deal with the consequences of sea-based activities, such as shipping, offshore activities and ocean dumping, which require national and/or

regional actions on land, including establishing adequate reception and recycling facilities;

15. Giving priority to the treatment and management of waste water and industrial effluents, as part of the overall management of water resources, especially through the installation of environmentally and economically appropriate sewage systems, including studying mechanisms to channel additional resources for this purpose expeditiously to countries in need of assistance;

16. Requesting the Executive Director of the United Nations Environment Programme, in close partnership with the World Health Organization, the United Nations Centre for Human Settlements (Habitat), the United Nations Development Programme and other relevant organizations, to prepare proposals for a plan to address the global nature of the problem of inadequate management and treatment of waste water and its consequences for human health and the environment, and to promote the transfer of appropriate and affordable technology drawn from the best available techniques;

17. Acting to develop, in accordance with the provisions of the Global Programme of Action, a global, legally binding instrument for the reduction and/or elimination of emissions, discharges and, where appropriate, the elimination of the manufacture and use of the persistent organic pollutants identified in decision 18/32 of the Governing Council of the United Nations Environment Programme.

   The nature of the obligations undertaken must be developed recognizing the special circumstances of countries in need of assistance. Particular attention should be devoted to the potential need for the continued use of certain persistent organic pollutants to safeguard human health, sustain food production and to alleviate poverty in the absence of alternatives and the difficulty of acquiring substitutes and transferring of technology for the development and/or production of those substitutes; and

18. Elaborating the steps relating to institutional follow-up, including the clearing-house mechanism, in a resolution of the United Nations General Assembly at its fifty-first session, and in that regard, States should coordinate with the United Nations Environment Programme, as secretariat of the Global Programme of Action, and other relevant agencies within the United Nations system in the development of the resolution and include it on the agenda of the Commission on Sustainable Development at its inter-sessional meeting in February 1996 and its session in April 1996.

3.18 1996 Protocol (on Dumping and Incineration of Wastes and Other Matter at Sea) to the Convention on the Prevention of Marine Pollution by Dumping of Wastes and Other Matter, 1972.[j] **Adopted at London, 7 November 1996. Entered into force, 24 March 2006. IMO Doc LC.2/Circ.380 (1997).** *Reprinted in* **5 Weston & Carlson V.F.30b–1**

Article 1

Definitions

For the purposes of this Protocol:

1. "Convention" means the Convention on the Prevention of Marine Pollution by Dumping of Wastes and Other Matter, 1972, as amended.

2. "Organization" means the International Maritime Organization.

3. "Secretary–General" means the Secretary–General of the Organization.

4. .1 "Dumping" means:

> .1 any deliberate disposal into the sea of wastes or other matter from vessels, aircraft, platforms or other man-made structures at sea;
>
> .2 any deliberate disposal into the sea of vessels, aircraft, platforms or other man-made structures at sea;
>
> .3 any storage of wastes or other matter in the seabed and the subsoil thereof from vessels, aircraft, platforms or other man-made structures at sea; and
>
> .4 any abandonment or toppling at site of platforms or other man-made structures at sea, for the sole purpose of deliberate disposal.

.2 "Dumping" does not include:

> .1 the disposal into the sea of wastes or other matter incidental to, or derived from the normal operations of vessels, aircraft, platforms or other man-made structures at sea and their equipment, other than wastes or other matter transported by or to vessels, aircraft, platforms or other man-made structures at sea, operating for the purpose of disposal of such matter or derived from the treatment of such wastes or other matter on such vessels, aircraft, platforms or other man-made structures;
>
> .2 placement of matter for a purpose other than the mere disposal thereof, provided that such placement is not contrary to the aims of this Protocol; and
>
> .3 notwithstanding paragraph 4.1.4, abandonment in the sea of matter (e.g., cables, pipelines and marine research devices) placed for a purpose other than the mere disposal thereof.

.3 The disposal or storage of wastes or other matter directly arising from, or related to the exploration, exploitation and associated off-shore processing of seabed mineral resources is not covered by the provisions of this Protocol.

5. .1 "Incineration at sea" means the combustion on board a vessel, platform or other man-made structure at sea of wastes or other matter for the purpose of their deliberate disposal by thermal destruction.

> .2 "Incineration at sea" does not include the incineration of wastes or other matter on board a vessel, platform, or other man-made structure at sea if such

---

j. This Protocol supersedes the 1972 Convention on the Prevention of Marine Pollution by Dumping of Wastes and Other Matter (London Dumping Convention) for States that are parties to both. *See* Basic Document 3.6, *supra*.

wastes or other matter were generated during the normal operation of that vessel, platform or other man-made structure at sea.

6. "Vessels and aircraft" means waterborne or airborne craft of any type whatsoever. This expression includes air-cushioned craft and floating craft, whether self-propelled or not.

7. "Sea" means all marine waters other than the internal waters of States, as well as the seabed and the subsoil thereof; it does not include sub-seabed repositories accessed only from land.

8. "Wastes or other matter" means material and substance of any kind, form or description.

9. "Permit" means permission granted in advance and in accordance with relevant measures adopted pursuant to article 4.1.2 or 8.2.

10. "Pollution" means the introduction, directly or indirectly, by human activity, of wastes or other matter into the sea which results or is likely to result in such deleterious effects as harm to living resources and marine ecosystems, hazards to human health, hindrance to marine activities, including fishing and other legitimate uses of the sea, impairment of quality for use of sea water and reduction of amenities.

Article 2
Objectives

Contracting Parties shall individually and collectively protect and preserve the marine environment from all sources of pollution and take effective measures, according to their scientific, technical and economic capabilities, to prevent, reduce and where practicable eliminate pollution caused by dumping or incineration at sea of wastes or other matter. Where appropriate, they shall harmonize their policies in this regard.

Article 3
General obligations

1. In implementing this Protocol, Contracting Parties shall apply a precautionary approach to environmental protection from dumping of wastes or other matter whereby appropriate preventative measures are taken when there is reason to believe that wastes or other matter introduced into the marine environment are likely to cause harm even when there is no conclusive evidence to prove a causal relation between inputs and their effects.

2. Taking into account the approach that the polluter should, in principle, bear the cost of pollution, each Contracting Party shall endeavour to promote practices whereby those it has authorized to engage in dumping or incineration at sea bear the cost of meeting the pollution prevention and control requirements for the authorized activities, having due regard to the public interest.

3. In implementing the provisions of this Protocol, Contracting Parties shall act so as not to transfer, directly or indirectly, damage or likelihood of damage from one part of the environment to another or transform one type of pollution into another.

4. No provision of this Protocol shall be interpreted as preventing Contracting Parties from taking, individually or jointly, more stringent measures in accordance with international law with respect to the prevention, reduction and where practicable elimination of pollution.

Article 4
Dumping of wastes or other matter

1. .1 Contracting Parties shall prohibit the dumping of any wastes or other matter with the exception of those listed in Annex 1.

.2 The dumping of wastes or other matter listed in Annex 1 shall require a permit. Contracting Parties shall adopt administrative or legislative measures to ensure that issuance of permits and permit conditions comply with provisions of Annex 2. Particular attention shall be paid to opportunities to avoid dumping in favour of environmentally preferable alternatives.

2. No provision of this Protocol shall be interpreted as preventing a Contracting Party from prohibiting, insofar as that Contracting Party is concerned, the dumping of wastes or other matter mentioned in Annex 1. That Contracting Party shall notify the Organization of such measures.

Article 5
Incineration at sea

Contracting Parties shall prohibit incineration at sea of wastes or other matter.

Article 6
Export of wastes or other matter

Contracting Parties shall not allow the export of wastes or other matter to other countries for dumping or incineration at sea.

Article 7
Internal waters

1. Notwithstanding any other provision of this Protocol, this Protocol shall relate to internal waters only to the extent provided for in paragraphs 2 and 3.

2. Each Contracting Party shall at its discretion either apply the provisions of this Protocol or adopt other effective permitting and regulatory measures to control the deliberate disposal of wastes or other matter in marine internal waters where such disposal would be "dumping" or "incineration at sea" within the meaning of article 1, if conducted at sea.

3. Each Contracting Party should provide the Organization with information on legislation and institutional mechanisms regarding implementation, compliance and enforcement in marine internal waters. Contracting Parties should also use their best efforts to provide on a voluntary basis summary reports on the type and nature of the materials dumped in marine internal waters.

Article 8
Exceptions

1. The provisions of articles 4.1 and 5 shall not apply when it is necessary to secure the safety of human life or of vessels, aircraft, platforms or other man-made structures at sea in cases of force majeure caused by stress of weather, or in any case which constitutes a danger to human life or a real threat to vessels, aircraft, platforms or other man-made structures at sea, if dumping or incineration at sea appears to be the only way of averting the threat and if there is every probability that the damage consequent upon such dumping or incineration at sea will be less than would otherwise occur. Such dumping or incineration at sea shall be conducted so as to minimize the likelihood of damage to human or marine life and shall be reported forthwith to the Organization.

2. A Contracting Party may issue a permit as an exception to articles 4.1 and 5, in emergencies posing an unacceptable threat to human health, safety, or the marine environment and admitting of no other feasible solution. Before doing so the Contracting Party shall consult any other country or countries that are likely to be affected and the Organization which, after consulting other Contracting Parties, and competent international organizations as appropriate, shall, in accordance with article 18.6 promptly recommend to the Contracting Party the most appropriate procedures to

adopt. The Contracting Party shall follow these recommendations to the maximum extent feasible consistent with the time within which action must be taken and with the general obligation to avoid damage to the marine environment and shall inform the Organization of the action it takes. The Contracting Parties pledge themselves to assist one another in such situations.

3. Any Contracting Party may waive its rights under paragraph 2 at the time of, or subsequent to ratification of, or accession to this Protocol.

Article 9
Issuance of permits and reporting

1. Each Contracting Party shall designate an appropriate authority or authorities to:

.1 issue permits in accordance with this Protocol;

.2 keep records of the nature and quantities of all wastes or other matter for which dumping permits have been issued and where practicable the quantities actually dumped and the location, time and method of dumping; and

.3 monitor individually, or in collaboration with other Contracting Parties and competent international organizations, the condition of the sea for the purposes of this Protocol.

2. The appropriate authority or authorities of a Contracting Party shall issue permits in accordance with this Protocol in respect of wastes or other matter intended for dumping or, as provided for in article 8.2, incineration at sea:

.1 loaded in its territory; and

.2 loaded onto a vessel or aircraft registered in its territory or flying its flag, when the loading occurs in the territory of a State not a Contracting Party to this Protocol.

3. In issuing permits, the appropriate authority or authorities shall comply with the requirements of article 4, together with such additional criteria, measures and requirements as they may consider relevant.

4. Each Contracting Party, directly or through a secretariat established under a regional agreement, shall report to the Organization and where appropriate to other Contracting Parties:

.1 the information specified in paragraphs 1.2 and 1.3;

.2 the administrative and legislative measures taken to implement the provisions of this Protocol, including a summary of enforcement measures; and

.3 the effectiveness of the measures referred to in paragraph 4.2 and any problems encountered in their application.

The information referred to in paragraphs 1.2 and 1.3 shall be submitted on an annual basis. The information referred to in paragraphs 4.2 and 4.3 shall be submitted on a regular basis.

5. Reports submitted under paragraphs 4.2 and 4.3 shall be evaluated by an appropriate subsidiary body as determined by the Meeting of Contracting Parties. This body will report its conclusions to an appropriate Meeting or Special Meeting of Contracting Parties.

Article 10
Application and enforcement

1. Each Contracting Party shall apply the measures required to implement this Protocol to all:

.1   vessels and aircraft registered in its territory or flying its flag;

.2   vessels and aircraft loading in its territory the wastes or other matter which are to be dumped or incinerated at sea; and

.3   vessels, aircraft and platforms or other man-made structures believed to be engaged in dumping or incineration at sea in areas within which it is entitled to exercise jurisdiction in accordance with international law.

2.   Each Contracting Party shall take appropriate measures in accordance with international law to prevent and if necessary punish acts contrary to the provisions of this Protocol.

3.   Contracting Parties agree to co-operate in the development of procedures for the effective application of this Protocol in areas beyond the jurisdiction of any State, including procedures for the reporting of vessels and aircraft observed dumping or incinerating at sea in contravention of this Protocol.

4.   This Protocol shall not apply to those vessels and aircraft entitled to sovereign immunity under international law. However, each Contracting Party shall ensure by the adoption of appropriate measures that such vessels and aircraft owned or operated by it act in a manner consistent with the object and purpose of this Protocol and shall inform the Organization accordingly.

5.   A State may, at the time it expresses its consent to be bound by this Protocol, or at any time thereafter, declare that it shall apply the provisions of this Protocol to its vessels and aircraft referred to in paragraph 4, recognising that only that State may enforce those provisions against such vessels and aircraft.

Article 11
Compliance procedures

1.   No later than two years after the entry into force of this Protocol, the Meeting of Contracting Parties shall establish those procedures and mechanisms necessary to assess and promote compliance with this Protocol. Such procedures and mechanisms shall be developed with a view to allowing for the full and open exchange of information, in a constructive manner.

2.   After full consideration of any information submitted pursuant to this Protocol and any recommendations made through procedures or mechanisms established under paragraph 1, the Meeting of Contracting Parties may offer advice, assistance or co-operation to Contracting Parties and non-Contracting Parties.

Article 12
Regional co-operation

In order to further the objectives of this Protocol, Contracting Parties with common interests to protect the marine environment in a given geographical area shall endeavour, taking into account characteristic regional features, to enhance regional co-operation including the conclusion of regional agreements consistent with this Protocol for the prevention, reduction and where practicable elimination of pollution caused by dumping or incineration at sea of wastes or other matter. Contracting Parties shall seek to co-operate with the parties to regional agreements in order to develop harmonized procedures to be followed by Contracting Parties to the different conventions concerned.

Article 13
Technical co-operation and assistance

1.   Contracting Parties shall, through collaboration within the Organization and in co-ordination with other competent international organizations, promote bilateral and multilateral support for the prevention, reduction and where practicable elimina-

tion of pollution caused by dumping as provided for in this Protocol to those Contracting Parties that request it for:

.1 training of scientific and technical personnel for research, monitoring and enforcement, including as appropriate the supply of necessary equipment and facilities, with a view to strengthening national capabilities;

.2 advice on implementation of this Protocol;

.3 information and technical co-operation relating to waste minimization and clean production processes;

.4 information and technical co-operation relating to the disposal and treatment of waste and other measures to prevent, reduce and where practicable eliminate pollution caused by dumping; and

.5 access to and transfer of environmentally sound technologies and corresponding know-how, in particular to developing countries and countries in transition to market economies, on favourable terms, including on concessional and preferential terms, as mutually agreed, taking into account the need to protect intellectual property rights as well as the special needs of developing countries and countries in transition to market economies.

2. The Organization shall perform the following functions:

.1 forward requests from Contracting Parties for technical co-operation to other Contracting Parties, taking into account such factors as technical capabilities;

.2 co-ordinate requests for assistance with other competent international organizations, as appropriate; and

.3 subject to the availability of adequate resources, assist developing countries and those in transition to market economies, which have declared their intention to become Contracting Parties to this Protocol, to examine the means necessary to achieve full implementation.

Article 14
Scientific and Technical Research

1. Contracting Parties shall take appropriate measures to promote and facilitate scientific and technical research on the prevention, reduction and where practicable elimination of pollution by dumping and other sources of marine pollution relevant to this Protocol. In particular, such research should include observation, measurement, evaluation and analysis of pollution by scientific methods.

2. Contracting Parties shall, to achieve the objectives of this Protocol, promote the availability of relevant information to other Contracting Parties who request it on:

.1 scientific and technical activities and measures undertaken in accordance with this Protocol;

.2 marine scientific and technological programmes and their objectives; and

.3 the impacts observed from the monitoring and assessment conducted pursuant to article 9.1.3.

Article 15
Responsibility and Liability

In accordance with the principles of international law regarding State responsibility for damage to the environment of other States or to any other area of the environment, the Contracting Parties undertake to develop procedures regarding liability arising from the dumping or incineration at sea of wastes or other matter.

Article 16
Settlement of Disputes

1. Any disputes regarding the interpretation or application of this Protocol shall be resolved in the first instance through negotiation, mediation or conciliation, or other peaceful means chosen by parties to the dispute.

2. If no resolution is possible within twelve months after one Contracting Party has notified another that a dispute exists between them, the dispute shall be settled, at the request of a party to the dispute, by means of the Arbitral Procedure set forth in Annex 3, unless the parties to the dispute agree to use one of the procedures listed in paragraph 1 of Article 287 of the 1982 United Nations Convention on the Law of the Sea. The parties to the dispute may so agree, whether or not they are also States Parties to the 1982 United Nations Convention on the Law of the Sea.

3. In the event an agreement to use one of the procedures listed in paragraph 1 of Article 287 of the 1982 United Nations Convention on the Law of the Sea is reached, the provisions set forth in Part XV of that Convention that are related to the chosen procedure would also apply, *mutatis mutandis.*

4 The twelve month period referred to in paragraph 2 may be extended for another twelve months by mutual consent of the parties concerned.

5. Notwithstanding paragraph 2, any State may, at the time it expresses its consent to be bound by this Protocol, notify the Secretary–General that, when it is a party to a dispute about the interpretation or application of article 3.1 or 3.2, its consent will be required before the dispute may be settled by means of the Arbitral Procedure set forth in Annex 3.

Article 17
International Co-operation

Contracting Parties shall promote the objectives of this Protocol within the competent international organizations.

Article 18
Meetings of Contracting Parties

1. Meetings of Contracting Parties or Special Meetings of Contracting Parties shall keep under continuing review the implementation of this Protocol and evaluate its effectiveness with a view to identifying means of strengthening action, where necessary, to prevent, reduce and where practicable eliminate pollution caused by dumping and incineration at sea of wastes or other matter. To these ends, Meetings of Contracting Parties or Special Meetings of Contracting Parties may:

.1 review and adopt amendments to this Protocol in accordance with articles 21 and 22;

.2 establish subsidiary bodies, as required, to consider any matter with a view to facilitating the effective implementation of this Protocol;

.3 invite appropriate expert bodies to advise the Contracting Parties or the Organization on matters relevant to this Protocol;

.4 promote co-operation with competent international organizations concerned with the prevention and control of pollution;

.5 consider the information made available pursuant to article 9.4;

.6 develop or adopt, in consultation with competent international organizations, procedures referred to in article 8.2, including basic criteria for determining exceptional and emergency situations, and procedures for consultative advice and the safe disposal of matter at sea in such circumstances;

.7   consider and adopt resolutions; and

.8   consider any additional action that may be required.

2.   The Contracting Parties at their first Meeting shall establish rules of procedure as necessary.

Article 19
Duties of the Organization

1.   The Organization shall be responsible for Secretariat duties in relation to this Protocol. Any Contracting Party to this Protocol not being a member of this Organization shall make an appropriate contribution to the expenses incurred by the Organization in performing these duties.

2.   Secretariat duties necessary for the administration of this Protocol include:

.1   convening Meetings of Contracting Parties once per year, unless otherwise decided by Contracting Parties, and Special Meetings of Contracting Parties at any time on the request of two-thirds of the Contracting Parties;

.2   providing advice on request on the implementation of this Protocol and on guidance and procedures developed thereunder;

.3   considering enquiries by, and information from Contracting Parties, consulting with them and with the competent international organizations, and providing recommendations to Contracting Parties on questions related to, but not specifically covered by, this Protocol;

.4   preparing and assisting, in consultation with Contracting Parties and the competent international organizations, in the development and implementation of procedures referred to in article 18.6.;

.5   conveying to the Contracting Parties concerned all notifications received by the Organization in accordance with this Protocol; and

.6   preparing, every two years, a budget and a financial account for the administration of this Protocol which shall be distributed to all Contracting Parties.

3.   The Organization shall, subject to the availability of adequate resources, in addition to the requirements set out in article 13.2.3.

.1   collaborate in assessments of the state of the marine environment; and

.2   co-operate with competent international organizations concerned with the prevention and control of pollution.

Article 20
Annexes

Annexes to this Protocol form an integral part of this Protocol.

Article 21
Amendment of the Protocol

1.   Any Contracting Party may propose amendments to the articles of this Protocol. The text of a proposed amendment shall be communicated to Contracting Parties by the Organization at least six months prior to its consideration at a Meeting of Contracting Parties or a Special Meeting of Contracting Parties.

2.   Amendments to the articles of this Protocol shall be adopted by a two-thirds majority vote of the Contracting Parties which are present and voting at the Meeting of Contracting Parties or Special Meeting of Contracting Parties designated for this purpose.

3. An amendment shall enter into force for the Contracting Parties which have accepted it on the sixtieth day after two-thirds of the Contracting Parties shall have deposited an instrument of acceptance of the amendment with the Organization. Thereafter the amendment shall enter into force for any other Contracting Party on the sixtieth day after the date on which that Contracting Party has deposited its instrument of acceptance of the amendment.

4. The Secretary–General shall inform Contracting Parties of any amendments adopted at Meetings of Contracting Parties and of the date on which such amendments enter into force generally and for each Contracting Party.

5. After entry into force of an amendment to this Protocol, any State that becomes a Contracting Party to this Protocol shall become a Contracting Party to this Protocol as amended, unless two-thirds of the Contracting Parties present and voting at the Meeting or Special Meeting of Contracting Parties adopting the amendment agree otherwise.

Article 22
Amendment of the Annexes

1. Any Contracting Party may propose amendments to the Annexes to this Protocol. The text of a proposed amendment shall be communicated to Contracting Parties by the Organization at least six months prior to its consideration by a Meeting of Contracting Parties or Special Meeting of Contracting Parties.

2. Amendments to the Annexes other than Annex 3 will be based on scientific or technical considerations and may take into account legal, social and economic factors as appropriate. Such amendments shall be adopted by a two-thirds majority vote of the Contracting Parties present and voting at a Meeting of Contracting Parties or Special Meeting of Contracting Parties designated for this purpose.

3. The Organization shall without delay communicate to Contracting Parties amendments to the Annexes that have been adopted at a Meeting of Contracting Parties or Special Meeting of Contracting Parties.

4. Except as provided in paragraph 7, amendments to the Annexes shall enter into force for each Contracting Party immediately on notification of its acceptance to the Organization or 100 days after the date of their adoption at a Meeting of Contracting Parties, if that is later, except for those Contracting Parties which before the end of the 100 days make a declaration that they are not able to accept the amendment at that time. A Contracting Party may at any time substitute an acceptance for a previous declaration of objection and the amendment previously objected to shall thereupon enter into force for that Contracting Party.

5. The Secretary–General shall without delay notify Contracting Parties of instruments of acceptance or objection deposited with the Organization.

6. A new Annex or an amendment to an Annex which is related to an amendment to the articles of this Protocol shall not enter into force until such time as the amendment to the articles of this Protocol enters into force.

7. With regard to amendments to Annex 3 concerning the Arbitral Procedure and with regard to the adoption and entry into force of new Annexes the procedures on amendments to the articles of this Protocol shall apply.

Article 23
Relationship Between the Protocol and the Convention

This Protocol will supersede the Convention as between Contracting Parties to this Protocol which are also Parties to the Convention.

Article 24

Signature, Ratification, Acceptance, Approval and Accession

1. This Protocol shall be open for signature by any State at the Headquarters of the Organization from 1 April 1997 to 31 March 1998 and shall thereafter remain open for accession by any State.

2. States may become Contracting Parties to this Protocol by:

.1 signature not subject to ratification, acceptance or approval; or

.2 signature subject to ratification, acceptance or approval, followed by ratification, acceptance or approval; or

.3 accession.

3. Ratification, acceptance, approval or accession shall be effected by the deposit of an instrument to that effect with the Secretary–General.

Article 25

Entry into Force

1. This Protocol shall enter into force on the thirtieth day following the date on which:

.1 at least 26 States have expressed their consent to be bound by this Protocol in accordance with article 24; and

.2 at least 15 Contracting Parties to the Convention are included in the number of States referred to in paragraph 1.1.

2. For each State that has expressed its consent to be bound by this Protocol in accordance with article 24 following the date referred to in paragraph 1, this Protocol shall enter into force on the thirtieth day after the date on which such State expressed its consent.

Article 26

Transitional Period

1. Any State that was not a Contracting Party to the Convention before 31 December 1996 and that expresses its consent to be bound by this Protocol prior to its entry into force or within five years after its entry into force may, at the time it expresses its consent, notify the Secretary–General that, for reasons described in the notification, it will not be able to comply with specific provisions of this Protocol other than those provided in paragraph 2, for a transitional period that shall not exceed that described in paragraph 4.

2. No notification made under paragraph 1 shall affect the obligations of a Contracting Party to this Protocol with respect to incineration at sea or the dumping of radioactive wastes or other radioactive matter.

3. Any Contracting Party to this Protocol that has notified the Secretary–General under paragraph 1 that, for the specified transitional period, it will not be able to comply, in part or in whole, with article 4.1 or article 9 shall nonetheless during that period prohibit the dumping of wastes or other matter for which it has not issued a permit, use its best efforts to adopt administrative or legislative measures to ensure that issuance of permits and permit conditions comply with the provisions of Annex 2, and notify the Secretary–General of any permits issued.

4. Any transitional period specified in a notification made under paragraph 1 shall not extend beyond five years after such notification is submitted.

5. Contracting Parties that have made a notification under paragraph 1 shall submit to the first Meeting of Contracting Parties occurring after deposit of their instrument of ratification, acceptance, approval or accession a programme and timeta-

ble to achieve full compliance with this Protocol, together with any requests for relevant technical co-operation and assistance in accordance with article 13 of this Protocol.

6. Contracting Parties that have made a notification under paragraph 1 shall establish procedures and mechanisms for the transitional period to implement and monitor submitted programmes designed to achieve full compliance with this Protocol. A report on progress toward compliance shall be submitted by such Contracting Parties to each Meeting of Contracting Parties held during their transitional period for appropriate action.

Article 27
Withdrawal

1. Any Contracting Party may withdraw from this Protocol at any time after the expiry of two years from the date on which this Protocol enters into force for that Contracting Party.

2. Withdrawal shall be effected by the deposit of an instrument of withdrawal with the Secretary–General.

3. A withdrawal shall take effect one year after receipt by the Secretary–General of the instrument of withdrawal or such longer period as may be specified in that instrument.

Article 28
Depositary

1. This Protocol shall be deposited with the Secretary–General.

2. In addition to the functions specified in articles 10.5, 16.5, 21.4, 22.5 and 26.5, the Secretary–General shall:

.1 inform all States which have signed this Protocol or acceded thereto of:

.1 each new signature or deposit of an instrument of ratification, acceptance, approval or accession, together with the date thereof;

.2 the date of entry into force of this Protocol; and

.3 the deposit of any instrument of withdrawal from this Protocol together with the date on which it was received and the date on which the withdrawal takes effect.

.2 transmit certified copies of this Protocol to all States which have signed this Protocol or acceded thereto.

3. As soon as this Protocol enters into force, a certified true copy thereof shall be transmitted by the Secretary–General to the Secretariat of the United Nations for registration and publication in accordance with Article 102 of the Charter of the United Nations.

Article 29
Authentic Texts

This Protocol is established in a single original in the Arabic, Chinese, English, French, Russian and Spanish languages, each text being equally authentic.

ANNEX 1
WASTES OR OTHER MATTER THAT MAY BE CONSIDERED FOR DUMPING

1. The following wastes or other matter are those that may be considered for dumping being mindful of the Objectives and General Obligations of this Protocol set out in articles 2 and 3:

.1   dredged material;

.2   sewage sludge;

.3   fish waste, or material resulting from industrial fish processing operations;

.4   vessels and platforms or other man-made structures at sea;

.5   inert, inorganic geological material;

.6   organic material of natural origin; and

.7   bulky items primarily comprising iron, steel, concrete and similarly unharmful materials for which the concern is physical impact, and limited to those circumstances where such wastes are generated at locations, such as small islands with isolated communities, having no practicable access to disposal options other than dumping.

2.   The wastes or other matter listed in paragraphs 1.4 and 1.7 may be considered for dumping, provided that material capable of creating floating debris or otherwise contributing to pollution of the marine environment has been removed to the maximum extent and provided that the material dumped poses no serious obstacle to fishing or navigation.

3.   Notwithstanding the above, materials listed in paragraphs 1.1 to 1.7 containing levels of radioactivity greater than *de minimis* (exempt) concentrations as defined by the IAEA and adopted by Contracting Parties, shall not be considered eligible for dumping; provided further that within 25 years of 20 February 1994, and at each 25 year interval thereafter, Contracting Parties shall complete a scientific study relating to all radioactive wastes and other radioactive matter other than high level wastes or matter, taking into account such other factors as Contracting Parties consider appropriate and shall review the prohibition on dumping of such substances in accordance with the procedures set forth in article 22.

ANNEX 2
ASSESSMENT OF WASTES OR OTHER MATTER THAT MAY BE CONSIDERED FOR DUMPING

* * *

ANNEX 3
ARBITRAL PROCEDURE

* * *

3.19 Protocol Concerning Pollution from Land-Based Sources and Activities to the [Cartagena] Convention for the Protection and Development of the Marine Environment of the Wider Caribbean. Adopted, 6 Oct 1999. Entered into force, 13 Aug 2010. S Treaty Doc 110–1

Article I Definitions

For the purposes of this Protocol:

a. "Convention" means the Convention for the Protection and Development of the Marine Environment of the Wider Caribbean Region (Cartagena de Indias, Colombia, March 1983);

b. "Organisation" means the United Nations Environment Programme as referred to in Article 2(2) of the Convention;

c. "Pollution of the Convention area" means the introduction by humans, directly or indirectly, of substances or energy into the Convention area, which results or is likely to result in such deleterious effects as harm to living resources and marine ecosystems, hazards to human health, hindrance to marine activities, including fishing and other legitimate uses of the sea, impairment of quality for use of sea water and reduction of amenities;

d. "Land-based sources and activities" means those sources and activities causing pollution of the Convention area from coastal disposal or from discharges that emanate from rivers, estuaries, coastal establishments, outfall structures, or other sources on the territory of a Contracting Party, including atmospheric deposition originating from sources located on its territory;

e. "Most Appropriate Technology" means the best of currently available techniques, practices, or methods of operation to prevent, reduce or control pollution of the Convention area that are appropriate to the social, economic, technological, institutional, financial, cultural and environmental conditions of a Contracting Party or Parties; and

f. "Monitoring" means the periodic measurement of environmental quality indicators.

* * *

Article III General Obligations

1. Each Contracting Party shall, in accordance with its laws, the provisions of this Protocol, and international law, take appropriate measures to prevent, reduce and control pollution of the Convention area from land-based sources and activities, using for this purpose the best practicable means at its disposal and in accordance with its capabilities.

2. Each Contracting Party shall develop and implement appropriate plans, programmes and measures. In such plans, programmes and measures, each Contracting Party shall adopt effective means of preventing, reducing or controlling pollution of the Convention area from land-based sources and activities on its territory, including the use of most appropriate technology and management approaches such as integrated coastal area management.

3. Contracting Parties shall, as appropriate, and having due regard to their laws and their individual social, economic and environmental characteristics and the characteristics of a specific area or subregion, jointly develop subregional and regional plans, programmes and measures to prevent, reduce and control pollution of the Convention area from land-based sources and activities.

Article IV Annexes

1. The Contracting Parties shall address the source categories, activities and associated pollutants of concern listed in Annex I to this Protocol through the progressive development and implementation of additional annexes for those source categories, activities, and associated pollutants of concern that are determined by the Contracting Parties as appropriate for regional or sub-regional action. Such annexes shall, as appropriate, include *inter alia*:

    a. effluent and emission limitations and/or management practices based on the factors identified in Annex II to this Protocol; and

    b. timetables for achieving the limits, management practices and measures agreed by the Contracting Parties.

2. In accordance with the provisions of the annexes to which it is party, each Contracting Party shall take measures to prevent, reduce and control pollution of the Convention area from the source categories, activities and pollutants addressed in annexes other than Annexes I and II to this Protocol.

3. The Contracting Parties may also develop such additional annexes as they may deem appropriate, including an annex to address water quality criteria for selected priority pollutants identified in Annex I to this Protocol.

* * *

Article VI Monitoring and Assessment Programmes

1. Each Contracting Party shall formulate and implement monitoring programmes, as appropriate, in accordance with the provisions of this Protocol and relevant national legislation. Such programmes may, *inter alia*:

    a. systematically identify and assess patterns and trends in the environmental quality of the Convention area; and

    b. assess the effectiveness of measures taken to implement the Protocol.

2. Monitoring information shall be made available to the Scientific, Technical and Advisory Committee to facilitate the work of the Committee, as provided in Article XIV.

3. These programmes should avoid duplication of other programmes, particularly of similar regional programmes carried out by competent international organisations.

Article VII Environmental Impact Assessment

1. The Contracting Parties shall develop and adopt guidelines concerning environmental impact assessments, and review and update those guidelines as appropriate.

2. When a Contracting Party has reasonable grounds to believe that a planned land-based activity on its territory, or a planned modification to such an activity, which is subject to its regulatory control in accordance with its laws, is likely to cause substantial pollution of, or significant and harmful changes to, the Convention area, that Contracting Party shall, as far as practicable, review the potential effects of such activity on the Convention area, through means such as an environmental impact assessment.

3. Decisions by the competent government authorities with respect to land-based activities, referred to in paragraph 2 above, should take into account any such review.

4. Each Contracting Party shall, subject to its domestic law and regulations, seek the participation of affected persons in any review process conducted pursuant to

paragraph 2 above, and, where practicable, publish or make available relevant information obtained in this review.

* * *

Article IX   Transboundary Pollution

Where pollution from land-based sources and activities originating from any Contracting Party is likely to affect adversely the coastal or marine environment of one or more of the other Contracting Parties, the Contracting Parties concerned shall use their best efforts to consult at the request of any affected Contracting Party, with a view to resolving the issue.

* * *

ANNEX I
SOURCE CATEGORIES, ACTIVITIES AND ASSOCIATED POLLUTANTS
OF CONCERN

A.   Definitions

For the purposes of subsequent Annexes:

1.   "Point Sources" means sources where the discharges and releases are introduced into the environment from any discernable, confined and discrete conveyance, including but not limited to pipes, channels, ditches, tunnels, conduits or wells from which pollutants are or may be discharged; and

2.   "Non–Point Sources" means sources, other than point sources, from which substances enter the environment as a result of land run-off, precipitation, atmospheric deposition, drainage, seepage or by hydrologic modification.

B.   Priority Source Categories and Activities
Affecting the Convention Area

The Contracting Parties shall take into account the following priority source categories and activities when formulating regional and, as appropriate, sub-regional plans, programmes and measures for the prevention, reduction and control of pollution of the Convention area:

Domestic Sewage

Agricultural Non–Point Sources

Chemical Industries

Extractive Industries and Mining

Food Processing Operations

Manufacture of Liquor and Soft Drinks

Oil Refineries

Pulp and Paper Factories

Sugar Factories and Distilleries

Intensive Animal Rearing Operations

C.   Associated Pollutants of Concern

1.   Primary Pollutants of Concern

The Contracting Parties shall consider, taking into account the recommendations and other work of relevant international organisations, the following list of pollutants of concern, which were identified on the basis of their hazardous or otherwise harmful characteristics, when formulating effluent and emission limitations and management practices for the sources and activities in this Annex:

a. Organohalogen compounds and substances which could result in the formation of these compounds in the marine environment;

b. Organophosphorus compounds and substances which could result in the formation of these compounds in the marine environment;

c. Organotin compounds and substances which could result in the formation of these compounds in the marine environment;

d. Heavy metals and their compounds;

e. Crude petroleum and hydrocarbons;

f. Used lubricating oils;

g. Polycyclic aromatic hydrocarbons;

h. Biocides and their derivatives;

i. Pathogenic micro-organisms;

j. Cyanides and fluorides;

k. Detergents and other non-biodegradable surface tension substances;

l. Nitrogen and phosphorus compounds;

m. Persistent synthetic and other materials, including garbage, that float, flow or remain in suspension or settle to the bottom and affect marine life and hamper the uses of the sea;

n. Compounds with hormone-like effects;

o. Radioactive substances;

p. Sediments; and

q. Any other substance or group of substances with one or more of the characteristics outlined in paragraph 2 below.

2. Characteristics and Other Factors To Be Considered in Evaluating Additional Pollutants of Concern

The Contracting Parties should, taking into account the recommendations and other work of relevant international organisations, consider the following characteristics and factors, where relevant, in evaluating potential pollutants of concern other than those listed in paragraph 1 above:

a. Persistency;

b. Toxicity or other harmful properties (for example, carcinogenic, mutagenic and teratogenic properties);

c. Bio-accumulation;

d. Radioactivity;

e. Potential for causing eutrophication;

f. Impact on, and risks to, health;

g. Potential for migration;

h. Effects at the transboundary level;

i. Risk of undesirable changes in the marine ecosystem, irreversibility or durability of effects;

j. Negative impacts on marine life and the sustainable development of living resources or on other legitimate uses of the seas; and

k. Effects on the taste or smell of marine products intended for human consumption or effects on the smell, colour, transparency or other characteristics of the water in the marine environment.

ANNEX II
FACTORS TO BE USED IN DETERMINING EFFLUENT AND EMISSION SOURCE CONTROLS AND MANAGEMENT FACTORS

A. The Contracting Parties, when developing sub-regional and regional source-specific effluent and emission limitations and management practices pursuant to Article IV of this Protocol, shall evaluate and consider the following factors:

1. Characteristics and Composition of the Waste

    a. Type and size of waste source (for example, industrial process);

    b. Type and form of waste (origin, physical, chemical and biological properties, average composition);

    c. Physical state of waste (solid, liquid, sludge, slurry);

    d. Total quantity (units discharged, for example, per year or per day);

    e. Discharge frequency continuous, intermittent, seasonally variable, etc.);

    f. Concentration with respect to major constituents contained in the wastes emanating from the source or activity; and

    g. Interaction with the receiving environment.

2. Characteristics of the Activity or Source Category

    a. Performance of existing technologies and management practices, including indigenous technologies and management practices;

    b. Age of facilities, as appropriate; and

    c. Existing economic, social and cultural characteristics.

3. Alternative Production, Waste Treatment Technologies or Management Practices

    a. Recycling, recovery and reuse opportunities;

    b. Less hazardous or non-hazardous raw material substitution;

    c. Substitution of cleaner alternative activities or products;

    d. Economic, social and cultural impacts of alternatives, activities or products;

    e. Low-waste or totally clean technologies or processes; and

    f. Alternative disposal activities (for example, land application).

B. Pursuant to Article IV of this Protocol, each Contracting Party shall, at a minimum, apply the effluent and emission source controls and management practices set out in subsequent annexes. A Contracting Party may impose more stringent source controls or management practices. To determine if more stringent limitations are appropriate, a Contracting Party should also take into account characteristics of the discharge site and receiving marine environment, including:

1. Hydrographic, meteorological, geographical and topographical characteristics of the coastal areas;

2. Location and type of the discharge (outfall, canal outlet, gullies, etc.) and its relation to sensitive areas (such as swimming areas, reef systems, sea grass beds, spawning, nursery and fishing areas, shellfish grounds and other areas that are particularly sensitive) and other discharges;

3. Initial dilution achieved at the point of discharge into the receiving marine environment;

4. Dispersion characteristics (due to currents, tides and wind) that may affect the horizontal transport and vertical mixing of the affected waters;

5. Receiving water characteristics with respect to the physical, chemical, biological and ecological conditions in the discharge area; and

6. Capacity of the receiving marine environment to assimilate waste discharges.

C. The Contracting Parties shall keep the source controls and management practices set out in subsequent annexes under review. They shall consider that:

1. If the reduction of inputs resulting from the use of the effluent and emission limitations and management practices established in accordance with this Annex do not lead to environmentally acceptable results, the effluent and emission limitations or management practices may need to be revised; and

2. The appropriate effluent and emission limitations and management practices for a particular source or activity may change with time in light of technological advances, economic and social factors, as well as changes in scientific knowledge and understanding.

ANNEX III   DOMESTIC WASTEWATER

A. Definitions

For the purposes of this Annex:

1. "Domestic wastewater" means all discharges from households, commercial facilities, hotels, septage and any other entity whose discharge includes the following:

    a. Toilet flushing (black water);

    b. Discharges from showers, wash basins, kitchens and laundries (grey water); or

    c. Discharges from small industries, provided their composition and quantity are compatible with treatment in a domestic wastewater system.

    d. Small quantities of industrial waste or processed wastewater may also be found in domestic wastewater. (See Part D—Industrial Pretreatment.)

2. "Class I waters" means waters in the Convention area that, due to inherent or unique environmental characteristics or fragile biological or ecological characteristics or human use, are particularly sensitive to the impacts of domestic wastewater. Class I waters include, but are not limited to:

    a. waters containing coral reefs, seagrass beds, or mangroves;

    b. critical breeding, nursery or forage areas for aquatic and terrestrial life;

    c. areas that provide habitat for species protected under the Protocol Concerning Specially Protected Areas and Wildlife to the Convention (the SPAW Protocol);

    d. protected areas listed in the SPAW Protocol; and

    e. waters used for recreation.

3. "Class II waters" means waters in the Convention area, other than Class I waters, that due to oceanographic, hydrologic, climatic or other factors are less sensitive to the impacts of domestic wastewater and where humans or living resources that are likely to be adversely affected by the discharges are not exposed to such discharges.

4. "Existing domestic wastewater systems" means, with respect to a particular Contracting Party, publicly or privately owned domestic wastewater collection systems,

or collection and treatment systems, that were constructed prior to entry into force of this Annex for such Contracting Party.

5. "New domestic wastewater systems" means, with respect to a particular Contracting Party, publicly or privately owned domestic wastewater collection systems, or collection and treatment systems, that were constructed subsequent to entry into force of this Annex for such Contracting Party, and includes existing domestic wastewater systems which have been subject to substantial modifications after such entry into force.

6. "Household systems" means on-site domestic wastewater disposal systems for homes and small commercial businesses in areas of low population density, or where centralised collection and treatment systems of domestic wastewater are not economically or technologically feasible. Household systems include, but are not limited to, septic tanks and drain fields or mounds, holding tanks, latrines and bio-digesting toilets.

7. "Wastewater collection systems" means any collection or conveyance system designed to collect or channel domestic wastewater from multiple sources.

B. Discharge of Domestic Wastewater

1. Each Contracting Party shall:

a. Consistent with the provisions of this Annex, provide for the regulation of domestic wastewater discharging into, or adversely affecting, the Convention area;

b. To the extent practicable, locate, design and construct domestic wastewater treatment facilities and outfalls such that any adverse effects on, or discharges into, Class I waters, are minimised;

c. Encourage and promote domestic wastewater reuse that minimises or eliminates discharges into, or discharges that adversely affect, the Convention area;

d. Promote the use of cleaner technologies to reduce discharges to a minimum, or to avoid adverse effects within the Convention area; and

e. Develop plans to implement the obligations in this Annex, including, where appropriate, plans for obtaining financial assistance.

2. Each Contracting Party shall be entitled to use whatever technology or approach that it deems appropriate to meet the obligations specified in Part C of this Annex.

C. Effluent Limitations

Each Contracting Party shall ensure that domestic wastewater that discharges into, or adversely affects, the Convention area, is treated by a new or existing domestic wastewater system whose effluent achieves the effluent limitations specified below in paragraphs 1, 2 and 3 of this Part, in accordance with the following timetable:

1. Discharges into Class II Waters

Each Contracting Party shall ensure that domestic wastewater that discharges into, or adversely affects, Class II waters is treated by a new or existing domestic wastewater system whose effluent achieves the following effluent limitations based on a monthly average:

Parameter	Effluent Limit
Total Suspended Solids	150 mg/l*
Biochemical Oxygen Demand (BOD5)	150 mg/l
pH	5–10 pH units

Fats, Oil and Grease	50 mg/l
Floatables	not visible
* Does not include algae from treatment ponds	

Category	Effective Obligation (in years after entry into force for the Contracting Party)	Effluent Sources
1	0	All new domestic wastewater systems
2	10	Existing domestic wastewater systems other than community wastewater systems
3	10*	Communities with 10,000—50,000 inhabitants
4	15	Communities with more than 50,000 inhabitants already possessing wastewater collection systems
5	20	Communities with more than 50,000 inhabitants not possessing wastewater collection systems
6	20	All other communities except those relying exclusively on household systems

* Contracting Parties which decide to give higher priority to categories 4 and 5 may extend their obligations pursuant to category 3 to twenty (20) years (time frame established in category 6).

2. Discharges into Class I Waters

Each Contracting Party shall ensure that domestic wastewater that discharges into, or adversely affects, Class I waters is treated by a new or existing domestic wastewater system whose effluent achieves the following effluent limitations based on a monthly average:

3. All Discharges

a. Each Contracting Party shall take into account the impact that total nitrogen and phosphorus and their compounds may have on the degradation of the Convention area and, to the extent practicable, take appropriate measures to control or reduce the amount of total nitrogen and phosphorus that is discharged into, or may adversely affect, the Convention area.

b. Each Party shall ensure that residual chlorine from domestic wastewater treatment systems is not discharged in concentrations or amounts that would be toxic to marine organisms that reside in or migrate to the Convention area.

D. Industrial Pretreatment

Each Contracting Party shall endeavour, in keeping with its economic capabilities, to develop and implement industrial pretreatment programmes to ensure that industrial discharges into new and existing domestic wastewater treatment systems:

a. do not interfere with, damage or otherwise prevent domestic wastewater collection and treatment systems from meeting the effluent limitations specified in this Annex;

b. do not endanger operations of, or populations in proximity to, collection and treatment systems through exposure to toxic and hazardous substances;

c. do not contaminate sludges or other reusable products from wastewater treatment; and

d. do not contain toxic pollutants in amounts toxic to human health and/or aquatic life.

Parameter	Effluent Limit
Total Suspended Solids	30 mg/l*
Biochemical Oxygen Demand (BOD5)	30 mg/l
pH	5–10 pH units
Fats, Oil and Grease	15 mg/l
Faecal Coliform (Parties may meet effluent limitations either for faecal coliform or for E. coli (freshwater) and enterococci (saline water).)	Faecal Coliform: 200 mpn/100 ml; ora. *E. coli*: 126 organisms/100ml; b. enterococci: 35 organisms/100 ml
Floatables	not visible
* Does not include algae from treatment ponds	

Each Contracting Party shall endeavour to ensure that industrial pretreatment programmes include spill containment and contingency plans.

Each Contracting Party, within the scope of its capabilities, shall promote appropriate industrial wastewater management, such as the use of recirculation and closed loop systems, to eliminate or minimise wastewater discharges to domestic wastewater systems.

E. Household Systems

Each Contracting Party shall strive to, as expeditiously, economically and technologically feasible, in areas without sewage collection, ensure that household systems are constructed, operated and maintained to avoid contamination of surface or ground waters that are likely to adversely affect the Convention area.

For those household systems requiring septage pump out, each Contracting Party shall strive to ensure that the septage is treated through a domestic wastewater system or appropriate land application.

F. Management, Operations and Maintenance

Each Contracting Party shall ensure that new and existing domestic wastewater systems are properly managed and that system managers develop and implement training programmes for wastewater collection and treatment system operators. Managers and operators shall have access to operators' manuals and technical support necessary for proper system operation.

Each Contracting Party shall provide for an evaluation of domestic wastewater systems by competent national authorities to assess compliance with national regulations.

G. Extension Period

1. Any Contracting Party may, at least two years before the effective date of an obligation in categories 2, 3, 4 or 5 of the timetable in Part C above, submit to the Organisation a declaration that, with respect to such category, it is unable to achieve the effluent limitations set forth in paragraphs 1 and 2 of Part C above in accordance with that timetable, provided that such Contracting Party:

a. has developed action plans pursuant to Part B, paragraph 1(e);

b. has achieved the effluent limitations for a subset of the discharges associated with those categories, or a reduction of at least 5 percent of total loading of pollutants associated with those categories; and

c. has taken actions to achieve those effluent limitations, but has been unable to achieve those limitations due to a lack of financial or other capacity.

2. With respect to a Contracting Party that has submitted a declaration pursuant to paragraph 1 above, the effective date of an obligation in the timetable in Part C for categories 2, 3, 4 or 5 of that timetable shall be extended for a period of five years. The five-year period shall be extended for a maximum of one additional five-year period if the Contracting Party submits a new declaration prior to the expiration of the first period, and if it continues to meet the requirements set out in paragraph 1 above.

3. The Contracting Parties recognise that the complete fulfilment* of the obligations contained in this Annex will require the availability and accessibility of financial resources.

ANNEX IV AGRICULTURAL NON–POINT SOURCES OF POLLUTION

A. Definitions

For purposes of this Annex:

1. "Agricultural non-point sources of pollution" means non-point sources of pollution originating from the cultivation of crops and rearing of domesticated animals, excluding intensive animal rearing operations that would otherwise be defined as point sources; and

2. "Best management practices" means economical and achievable structural or non-structural measures designed to prevent, reduce or control the run-off of pollutants into the Convention area.

B. Plans for the Prevention, Reduction and Control of Agricultural Non–Point Sources of Pollution

Each Contracting Party shall, no later than five years after this Annex enters into force for it, formulate policies, plans and legal mechanisms for the prevention, reduction and control of pollution of the Convention area from agricultural non-point sources of pollution that may adversely affect the Convention area. Programmes shall be identified in such policies, plans and legal mechanisms to mitigate pollution of the Convention area from agricultural non-point sources of pollution, in particular, if these sources contain nutrients (nitrogen and phosphorus), pesticides, sediments, pathogens, solid waste or other such pollutants that may adversely affect the Convention area. Plans shall include inter alia the following elements:

1. An evaluation and assessment of agricultural non-point sources of pollution that may adversely affect the Convention area, which may include:

a. an estimation of loadings that may adversely affect the Convention area;

b. an identification of associated environmental impacts and potential risks to human health;

c. the evaluation of the existing administrative framework to manage agricultural non-point sources of pollution;

d. an evaluation of existing best management practices and their effectiveness; and

e. the establishment of monitoring programmes.

---

* In this context, the Spanish word "cumplimiento" that appears in the Spanish text shall have the meaning of the English word "fulfilment" and not "compliance".

2. Education, training and awareness programmes, which may include:

a. the establishment and implementation of programmes for the agricultural sector and the general public to raise awareness of agricultural non-point sources of pollution and their impacts on the marine environment, public health and the economy;

b. the establishment and implementation of programmes at all levels of education on the importance of the marine environment and the impact of pollution from agricultural activities;

c. the establishment and implementation of training programmes for government agencies and the agricultural sector on the implementation of best management practices, including the development of guidance materials for agricultural workers on structural and non-structural best management practices, to prevent, reduce and control agricultural non-point sources of pollution; and

d. the establishment of programmes to facilitate effective technology transfer and information exchange.

3. The development and promotion of economic and non-economic incentive programmes to increase the use of best management practices to prevent, reduce and control pollution of the Convention area from agricultural non-point sources.

4. An assessment and evaluation of legislative and policy measures, including a review of the adequacy of plans, policies and legal mechanisms directed toward the management of agricultural non-point sources and the development of a plan to implement such modifications as may be necessary to achieve best management practices.

C. Reporting

Each Contracting Party shall report on its plans for prevention, reduction and control of pollution of the Convention area from agricultural non-point sources in accordance with Article XII of this Protocol.

3.20 PROTOCOL OF **2003** [SUPPLEMENTARY FUND PROTOCOL] TO THE INTERNATIONAL CONVENTION ON THE ESTABLISHMENT OF AN INTERNATIONAL FUND FOR COMPENSATION FOR OIL POLLUTION DAMAGE, **1992**. Adopted at London, **16 May 2003**. Entered into force, **3 March 2005. Cm 6245**

* * *

Article 2

1. An International Supplementary Fund for compensation for pollution damage, to be named "The International Oil Pollution Compensation Supplementary Fund, 2003" (hereinafter "the Supplementary Fund"), is hereby established.

2. The Supplementary Fund shall in each Contracting State be recognized as a legal person capable under the laws of that State of assuming rights and obligations and of being a party in legal proceedings before the courts of that State. Each Contracting State shall recognize the Director of the Supplementary Fund as the legal representative of the Supplementary Fund.

Article 3

This Protocol shall apply exclusively:

(a) to pollution damage caused:

(i) in the territory, including the territorial sea, of a Contracting State, and

(ii) in the exclusive economic zone of a Contracting State, established in accordance with international law, or, if a Contracting State has not established such a zone, in an area beyond and adjacent to the territorial sea of that State determined by that State in accordance with international law and extending not more than 200 nautical miles from the baselines from which the breadth of its territorial sea is measured;

(b) to preventive measures, wherever taken, to prevent or minimize such damage.

Supplementary Compensation

Article 4

1. The Supplementary Fund shall pay compensation to any person suffering pollution damage if such person has been unable to obtain full and adequate compensation for an established claim for such damage under the terms of the 1992 Fund Convention, because the total damage exceeds, or there is a risk that it will exceed, the applicable limit of compensation laid down in article 4, paragraph 4, of the 1992 Fund Convention in respect of any one incident.

2. (a) The aggregate amount of compensation payable by the Supplementary Fund under this article shall in respect of any one incident be limited, so that the total sum of that amount together with the amount of compensation actually paid under the 1992 Liability Convention **[Basic Document 3.13]** and the 1992 Fund Convention **[Basic Document 3.14]** within the scope of application of this Protocol shall not exceed 750 million units of account.

(b) The amount of 750 million units of account mentioned in paragraph 2(a) shall be converted into national currency on the basis of the value of that currency by reference to the Special Drawing Right on the date determined by the Assembly of the 1992 Fund for conversion of the maximum amount payable under the 1992 Liability and 1992 Fund Conventions.

3. Where the amount of established claims against the Supplementary Fund exceeds the aggregate amount of compensation payable under paragraph 2, the amount available shall be distributed in such a manner that the proportion between any

established claim and the amount of compensation actually recovered by the claimant under this Protocol shall be the same for all claimants.

4. The Supplementary Fund shall pay compensation in respect of established claims as defined in article 1, paragraph 8, and only in respect of such claims.

Article 5

The Supplementary Fund shall pay compensation when the Assembly of the 1992 Fund has considered that the total amount of the established claims exceeds, or there is a risk that the total amount of established claims will exceed the aggregate amount of compensation available under article 4, paragraph 4, of the 1992 Fund Convention **[Basic Document 3.14]** and that as a consequence the Assembly of the 1992 Fund has decided provisionally or finally that payments will only be made for a proportion of any established claim. The Assembly of the Supplementary Fund shall then decide whether and to what extent the Supplementary Fund shall pay the proportion of any established claim not paid under the 1992 Liability Convention and the 1992 Fund Convention.

Article 6

1. Subject to article 15, paragraphs 2 and 3, rights to compensation against the Supplementary Fund shall be extinguished only if they are extinguished against the 1992 Fund under article 6 of the 1992 Fund Convention.

2. A claim made against the 1992 Fund shall be regarded as a claim made by the same claimant against the Supplementary Fund.

Article 7

1. The provisions of article 7, paragraphs 1, 2, 4, 5 and 6, of the 1992 Fund Convention shall apply to actions for compensation brought against the Supplementary Fund in accordance with article 4, paragraph 1, of this Protocol.

2. Where an action for compensation for pollution damage has been brought before a court competent under article IX of the 1992 Liability Convention against the owner of a ship or his guarantor, such court shall have exclusive jurisdictional competence over any action against the Supplementary Fund for compensation under the provisions of article 4 of this Protocol in respect of the same damage. However, where an action for compensation for pollution damage under the 1992 Liability Convention has been brought before a court in a Contracting State to the 1992 Liability Convention but not to this Protocol, any action against the Supplementary Fund under article 4 of this Protocol shall at the option of the claimant be brought either before a court of the State where the Supplementary Fund has its headquarters or before any court of a Contracting State to this Protocol competent under article IX of the 1992 Liability Convention.

3. Notwithstanding paragraph 1, where an action for compensation for pollution damage against the 1992 Fund has been brought before a court in a Contracting State to the 1992 Fund Convention but not to this Protocol, any related action against the Supplementary Fund shall, at the option of the claimant, be brought either before a court of the State where the Supplementary Fund has its headquarters or before any court of a Contracting State competent under paragraph 1.

Article 8

1. Subject to any decision concerning the distribution referred to in article 4, paragraph 3 of this Protocol, any judgment given against the Supplementary Fund by a court having jurisdiction in accordance with article 7 of this Protocol, shall, when it has become enforceable in the State of origin and is in that State no longer subject to ordinary forms of review, be recognized and enforceable in each Contracting State on the same conditions as are prescribed in article X of the 1992 Liability Convention.

2. A Contracting State may apply other rules for the recognition and enforcement of judgments, provided that their effect is to ensure that judgments are recognised and enforced at least to the same extent as under paragraph 1.

Article 9

1. The Supplementary Fund shall, in respect of any amount of compensation for pollution damage paid by the Supplementary Fund in accordance with article 4, paragraph 1, of this Protocol, acquire by subrogation the rights that the person so compensated may enjoy under the 1992 Liability Convention against the owner or his guarantor.

2. The Supplementary Fund shall acquire by subrogation the rights that the person compensated by it may enjoy under the 1992 Fund Convention against the 1992 Fund.

3. Nothing in this Protocol shall prejudice any right of recourse or subrogation of the Supplementary Fund against persons other than those referred to in the preceding paragraphs. In any event the right of the Supplementary Fund to subrogation against such person shall not be less favourable than that of an insurer of the person to whom compensation has been paid.

4. Without prejudice to any other rights of subrogation or recourse against the Supplementary Fund which may exist, a Contracting State or agency thereof which has paid compensation for pollution damage in accordance with provisions of national law shall acquire by subrogation the rights which the person so compensated would have enjoyed under this Protocol.

Contributions

Article 10

1. Annual contributions to the Supplementary Fund shall be made in respect of each Contracting State by any person who, in the calendar year referred to in article 11, paragraph 2(a) or (b), has received in total quantities exceeding 150,000 tons:

(a) in the ports or terminal installations in the territory of that State contributing oil carried by sea to such ports or terminal installations; and

(b) in any installations situated in the territory of that Contracting State contributing oil which has been carried by sea and discharged in a port or terminal installation of a non-Contracting State, provided that contributing oil shall only be taken into account by virtue of this sub-paragraph on first receipt in a Contracting State after its discharge in that non-Contracting State.

2. The provisions of article 10, paragraph 2, of the 1992 Fund Convention shall apply in respect of the obligation to pay contributions to the Supplementary Fund.

* * *

Article 25

Protocols to the 1992 Fund Convention

1. If the limits laid down in the 1992 Fund Convention have been increased by a Protocol thereto, the limit laid down in article 4, paragraph 2(a), may be increased by the same amount by means of the procedure set out in article 24. The provisions of article 24, paragraph 6, shall not apply in such cases.

2. If the procedure referred to in paragraph 1 has been applied, any subsequent amendment of the limit laid down in article 4, paragraph 2, by application of the procedure in article 24 shall, for the purpose of article 24, paragraphs 6(b) and (c), be calculated on the basis of the new limit as increased in accordance with paragraph 1.

* * *

3.21 Guidelines on Places of Refuge for Ships in Need of Assistance. Adopted by the IMO Assembly, 5 December 2003. IMO Doc Res A.949(23)

The Assembly,

* * *

Conscious of the Possibility that ships at sea may find themselves in need of assistance relating to the safety of life and the protection of the marine environment,

* * *

Recognizing Also the need to balance both the prerogative of a ship in need of assistance to seek a place of refuge and the prerogative of a coastal State to protect its coastline,

Recognizing Further that the provision of a common framework to assist coastal States to determine places of refuge for ships in need of assistance and respond effectively to requests for such places of refuge would materially enhance maritime safety and the protection of the marine environment,

* * *

1. *Adopts* the Guidelines on places of refuge for ships in need of assistance, the text of which is set out in the annex to the present resolution;

2. *Invites* Governments to take these Guidelines into account when determining and responding to requests for places of refuge from ships in need of assistance;

* * *

ANNEX
GUIDELINES ON PLACES OF REFUGE FOR SHIPS IN NEED OF ASSISTANCE

1 General

Introduction

Objectives of providing a place of refuge

1.1 Where the safety of life is involved, the provisions of the SAR Convention[k] should be followed. Where a ship is in need of assistance but safety of life is not involved, these guidelines should be followed.

1.2 The issue of "places of refuge" is not a purely theoretical or doctrinal debate but the solution to a practical problem: What to do when a ship finds itself in serious difficulty or in need of assistance without, however, presenting a risk to the safety of life of persons involved. Should the ship be brought into shelter near the coast or into a port or, conversely, should it be taken out to sea?

1.3 When a ship has suffered an incident, the best way of preventing damage or pollution from its progressive deterioration would be to lighten its cargo and bunkers; and to repair the damage. Such an operation is best carried out in a place of refuge.

1.4 However, to bring such a ship into a place of refuge near a coast may endanger the coastal State, both economically and from the environmental point of view, and local authorities and populations may strongly object to the operation.

1.5 While coastal States may be reluctant to accept damaged or disabled ships into their area of responsibility due primarily to the potential for environmental

---

k. International Convention on Maritime Search and Rescue. Adopted at Hamburg, April 27, 1979. Entered into force, June 22, 1985. 1405 UNTS 119.

damage, in fact it is rarely possible to deal satisfactorily and effectively with a marine casualty in open sea conditions.

1.6   In some circumstances, the longer a damaged ship is forced to remain at the mercy of the elements in the open sea, the greater the risk of the vessel's condition deteriorating or the sea, weather or environmental situation changing and thereby becoming a greater potential hazard.

1.7   Therefore, granting access to a place of refuge could involve a political decision which can only be taken on a case-by-case basis with due consideration given to the balance between the advantage for the affected ship and the environment resulting from bringing the ship into a place of refuge and the risk to the environment resulting from that ship being near the coast.

Background

1.8   There are circumstances under which it may be desirable to carry out a cargo transfer operation or other operations to prevent or minimize damage or pollution. For this purpose, it will usually be advantageous to take the ship to a place of refuge.

1.9   Taking such a ship to a place of refuge would also have the advantage of limiting the extent of coastline threatened by damage or pollution, but the specific area chosen may be more severely threatened. Consideration must also be given to the possibility of taking the affected ship to a port or terminal where the transfer or repair work could be done relatively easily. For this reason the decision on the choice and use of a place of refuge will have to be carefully considered.

1.10   The use of places of refuge could encounter local opposition and involve political decisions. The coastal States should recognize that a properly argued technical case, based on a clear description of the state of the casualty, would be of great value in any negotiations which may take place.

1.11   At the international level, the Conventions listed in Appendix 1, as may be amended, constitute, *inter alia*, the legal context within which coastal States and ships act in the envisaged circumstances.

* * *

Definitions

1.18   Ship in need of assistance means a ship in a situation, apart from one requiring rescue of persons on board, that could give rise to loss of the vessel or an environmental or navigational hazard.

1.19   Place of refuge means a place where a ship in need of assistance can take action to enable it to stabilize its condition and reduce the hazards to navigation, and to protect human life and the environment.

* * *

2   GUIDELINES FOR ACTION REQUIRED OF MASTERS AND/OR SALVORS OF SHIPS IN NEED OF A PLACE OF REFUGE

Appraisal of the situation

2.1   The master should, where necessary with the assistance of the company and/or the salvor, identify the reasons for his/her ship's need of assistance. (Refer to paragraph 1 of Appendix 2.)

Identification of hazards and assessment of associated risks

2.2   Having made the appraisal referred to in paragraph 2.1 above, the master, where necessary with the assistance of the company and/or the salvor, should estimate the consequences of the potential casualty, in the following hypothetical situations, taking into account both the casualty assessment factors in their possession and also the cargo and bunkers on board:

- if the ship remains in the same position;

- if the ship continues on its voyage;

- if the ship reaches a place of refuge; or

- if the ship is taken out to sea.

Identification of the required actions

2.3   The master and/or the salvor should identify the assistance they require from the coastal State in order to overcome the inherent danger of the situation. (Refer to paragraph 3 of Appendix 2.)

Contacting the authority of the coastal State

2.4   The master and/or the salvor should make contact with the coastal State in order to transmit to it the particulars referred to in paragraphs 2.1 to 2.3 above....

* * *

3   GUIDELINES FOR ACTIONS EXPECTED OF COASTAL STATES

3.1   Under international law, a coastal State may require the ship's master or company to take appropriate action within a prescribed time limit with a view to halting a threat of danger. In cases of failure or urgency, the coastal State can exercise its authority in taking responsive action appropriate to the threat.

3.2   It is therefore important that coastal States establish procedures to address these issues, even if no established damage and/or pollution has occurred.

3.3   Coastal States should, in particular, establish a Maritime Assistance Service (MAS).[1]

Assessment of places of refuge

Generic assessment and preparatory measures

3.4   It is recommended that coastal States endeavour to establish procedures consistent with these Guidelines by which to receive and act on requests for assistance with a view to authorizing, where appropriate, the use of a suitable place of refuge.

3.5   The maritime authorities (and, where necessary, the port authorities) should, for each place of refuge, make an objective analysis of the advantages and disadvantages of allowing a ship in need of assistance to proceed to a place of refuge, taking into consideration the analysis factors listed in paragraph 2 of Appendix 2.

3.6   The aforementioned analysis, which should take the form of contingency plans, is to be in preparation for the analysis provided for below when an incident occurs.

* * *

Event-specific assessment

Analysis factors

3.9   This analysis should include the following points:

---

1. Unless neighbouring States make the necessary arrangements to establish a joint service.

- seaworthiness of the ship concerned, in particular buoyancy, stability, availability of means of propulsion and power generation, docking ability, etc.;

- nature and condition of cargo, stores, bunkers, in particular hazardous goods;

- distance and estimated transit time to a place of refuge;

- whether the master is still on board;

- the number of other crew and/or salvors and other persons on board and an assessment of human factors, including fatigue;

- the legal authority of the country concerned to require action of the ship in need of assistance;

- whether the ship concerned is insured or not insured;

- if the ship is insured, identification of the insurer, and the limits of liability available;

- agreement by the master and company of the ship to the proposals of the coastal State/salvor to proceed or be brought to a place of refuge;

- provisions of the financial security required;

- commercial salvage contracts already concluded by the master or company of the ship;

- information on the intention of the master and/or salvor;

- designation of a representative of the company at the coastal State concerned;

- risk evaluation factors identified in Appendix 2; and

- any measures already taken.

* * *

3.11   The analysis should include a comparison between the risks involved if the ship remains at sea and the risks that it would pose to the place of refuge and its environment. Such comparison should cover each of the following points:

- safeguarding of human life at sea;

- safety of persons at the place of refuge and its industrial and urban environment (risk of fire or explosion, toxic risk, etc.);

- risk of pollution;

- if the place of refuge is a port, risk of disruption to the port's operation (channels, docks, equipment, other installations);

- evaluation of the consequences if a request for place of refuge is refused, including the possible effect on neighbouring States; and

- due regard should be given, when drawing the analysis, to the preservation of the hull, machinery and cargo of the ship in need of assistance.

After the final analysis has been completed, the maritime authority should ensure that the other authorities concerned are appropriately informed.

Decision-making process for the use of a place of refuge

3.12   When permission to access a place of refuge is requested, there is no obligation for the coastal State to grant it, but the coastal State should weigh all the factors and risks in a balanced manner and give shelter whenever reasonably possible.

* * *

APPENDIX 1

APPLICABLE INTERNATIONAL CONVENTIONS

At the international level, the following Conventions and Protocols are in force and constitute, inter alia, the legal context within which coastal States and ships act in the envisaged circumstances:[2]

- United Nations Convention on the Law of the Sea (UNCLOS), in particular article 221 thereof;

- International Convention relating to Intervention on the High Seas in Cases of Oil Pollution Casualties (the Intervention Convention), 1969, as amended;

- Protocol relating to Intervention on the High Seas in Cases of Pollution by substances other than Oil, 1973;

- International Convention for the Safety of Life at Sea, 1974 (SOLAS 1974), as amended, in particular chapter V thereof;

- International Convention on Salvage, 1989 (the Salvage Convention);

- International Convention on Oil Pollution Preparedness, Response and Co-operation, 1990 (the OPRC Convention);

- International Convention for the Prevention of Pollution from Ships, 1973, as modified by the Protocol of 1978 (MARPOL 73/78);

- International Convention on Maritime Search and Rescue, 1979 (SAR 1979), as amended;

- Convention on the Prevention of Marine Pollution by Dumping of Wastes and Other Matter, 1972;

- Convention Relating to Civil Liability in the Field of Maritime Carriage of Nuclear Material, 1971;

- Convention on Limitation of Liability for Maritime Claims (LLMC), 1976;

- International Convention on Civil Liability for Oil Pollution Damage (CLC), 1969;

- International Convention on Civil Liability for Oil Pollution Damage (CLC), 1992;

- International Convention on the Establishment of an International Fund for Compensation for Oil Pollution Damage (FUND), 1992.

APPENDIX 2

GUIDELINES FOR THE EVALUATION OF RISKS ASSOCIATED WITH THE PROVISION OF PLACES OF REFUGE

When conducting the analysis described in paragraphs 3.4 to 3.8, in addition to the factors described in paragraph 3.9, the following should be considered.

1 Identification of events, such as:

- fire

- explosion

- damage to the ship, including mechanical and/or structural failure

- collision

- pollution

---

2. It is noted that there is at present no international requirement for a State to provide a place of refuge for vessels in need of assistance.

- impaired vessel stability

- grounding.

2   Assessment of risks related to the identified event taking into account:

.1   Environmental and social factors, such as:

- safety of those on board

- threat to public safety . . .

- pollution caused by the ship

- designated environmental areas.

     Are the place of refuge and its approaches located in sensitive areas such as areas of high ecological value which might be affected by possible pollution?

     Is there, on environmental grounds, a better choice of place of refuge close by?

- sensitive habitats and species

- fisheries . . .

- economic/industrial facilities . . .

- amenity resources and tourism

- facilities available . . .

.2   Natural conditions, such as:

- Prevailing winds in the area.

     Is the place of refuge safely guarded against heavy winds and rough seas?

- Tides and tidal currents

- weather and sea conditions . . .

- bathymetry . . .

- seasonal effects including ice

- navigational characteristics . . .

- operational conditions, particularly in the case of a port . . .

* * *

.4   Foreseeable consequences (including in the media) of the different scenarios envisaged with regard to safety of persons and pollution, fire, toxic and explosion risks.

* * *

3.22 REVISED GUIDELINES FOR THE IDENTIFICATION AND DESIGNATION OF PARTICULARLY SENSITIVE SEA AREAS. **Adopted by the IMO Assembly, 1 December 2005. IMO Doc A.982(24) (Annex)**

1 INTRODUCTION

1.1 The Marine Environment Protection Committee (MEPC) of the International Maritime Organization (IMO) began its study of the question of Particularly Sensitive Sea Areas (PSSAs) in response to a resolution of the International Conference on Tanker Safety and Pollution Prevention of 1978. The discussions of this concept from 1986 to 1991 culminated in the adoption of Guidelines for the Designation of Special Areas and the Identification of Particularly Sensitive Sea Areas by Assembly resolution A.720(17) in 1991. In a continuing effort to provide a clearer understanding of the concepts set forth in the Guidelines, the Assembly adopted resolutions A.885(21) and A.927(22). This document is intended to clarify and, where appropriate, strengthen certain aspects and procedures for the identification and designation of PSSAs and the adoption of associated protective measures. It sets forth revised Guidelines for the Identification and Designation of Particularly Sensitive Sea Areas (the Guidelines or PSSA Guidelines).

1.2 A PSSA is an area that needs special protection through action by IMO because of its significance for recognized ecological, socio-economic, or scientific attributes where such attributes may be vulnerable to damage by international shipping activities. At the time of designation of a PSSA, an associated protective measure[3], which meets the requirements of the appropriate legal instrument establishing such measure, must have been approved or adopted by IMO to prevent, reduce, or eliminate the threat or identified vulnerability. Information on each of the PSSAs that has been designated by IMO is available at www.imo.org.

1.3 Many international and regional instruments encourage the protection of areas important for the conservation of biological diversity as well as other areas with high ecological, cultural, historical/archaeological, socio-economic or scientific significance. These instruments further call upon their Parties to protect such vulnerable areas from damage or degradation, including from shipping activities.

1.4 The purpose of these Guidelines is to:

.1 provide guidance to IMO Member Governments in the formulation and submission of applications for designation of PSSAs;

.2 ensure that in the process all interests—those of the coastal State, flag State, and the environmental and shipping communities—are thoroughly considered on the basis of relevant scientific, technical, economic, and environmental information regarding the area at risk of damage from international shipping activities and the associated protective measures to prevent, reduce, or eliminate that risk; and

.3 provide for the assessment of such applications by IMO.

1.5 Identification and designation of any PSSA and the adoption of associated protective measures require consideration of three integral components: the particular attributes of the proposed area, the vulnerability of such an area to damage by international shipping activities, and the availability of associated protective measures within the competence of IMO to prevent, reduce, or eliminate risks from these shipping activities.

---

3. The term "associated protective measure" or "measure" is used both in the singular and plural throughout these Guidelines. It is important to recognize that an identified vulnerability may be addressed by only one or by more than one associated protective measure and that therefore the use of this terminology in the singular or plural should not be taken as any indication to the contrary.

2 INTERNATIONAL SHIPPING ACTIVITIES
AND THE MARINE ENVIRONMENT

2.1   Shipping activity can constitute an environmental hazard to the marine environment in general and consequently even more so to environmentally and/or ecologically sensitive areas. Environmental hazards associated with shipping include:

.1   operational discharges;

.2   accidental or intentional pollution; and

.3   physical damage to marine habitats or organisms.

2.2   Adverse effects and damage may occur to the marine environment and the living resources of the sea as a result of shipping activities. With the increase in global trade, shipping activities are also increasing, thus including greater potential for adverse effects and damage. In the course of routine operations, accidents, and wilful acts of pollution, ships may release a wide variety of substances either directly into the marine environment or indirectly through the atmosphere. Such releases include oil and oily mixtures, noxious liquid substances, sewage, garbage, noxious solid substances, anti-fouling systems, harmful aquatic organisms and pathogens, and even noise. In addition, ships may cause harm to marine organisms and their habitats through physical impact. These impacts may include the smothering of habitats, contamination by anti-fouling systems or other substances through groundings, and ship strikes of marine mammals.

3 PROCESS FOR THE DESIGNATION OF PARTICULARLY
SENSITIVE SEA AREAS

3.1   The IMO is the only international body responsible for designating areas as Particularly Sensitive Sea Areas and adopting associated protective measures. An application to IMO for designation of a PSSA and the adoption of associated protective measures, or an amendment thereto, may be submitted only by a Member Government. Where two or more Governments have a common interest in a particular area, they should formulate a co-ordinated proposal. The proposal should contain integrated measures and procedures for co-operation between the jurisdictions of the proposing Member Governments.

3.2   Member Governments wishing to have IMO designate a PSSA should submit an application to MEPC based on the criteria outlined in section 4, provide information pertaining to the vulnerability of this area to damage from international shipping activities as called for in section 5, and include the proposed associated protective measures as outlined in section 6 to prevent, reduce or eliminate the identified vulnerability. Applications should be submitted in accordance with the procedures set forth in section 7 and the rules adopted by IMO for submission of documents.

3.3   If, in preparing its submission for a PSSA proposal, a Member Government requires technical assistance, that Government is encouraged to request such assistance from IMO.

4 ECOLOGICAL, SOCIO–ECONOMIC, OR SCIENTIFIC
CRITERIA FOR THE IDENTIFICATION OF A
PARTICULARLY SENSITIVE SEA AREA

4.1   The following criteria apply to the identification of PSSAs only with respect to the adoption of measures to protect such areas against damage, or the identified threat of damage, from international shipping activities.

4.2   These criteria do not, therefore, apply to the identification of such areas for the purpose of establishing whether they should be protected from dumping activities, since that is implicitly covered by the London Convention 1972 (the Convention on the

Prevention of Marine Pollution by Dumping of Wastes and Other Matter, 1972) and the 1996 Protocol to that Convention.

4.3 The criteria relate to PSSAs within and beyond the limits of the territorial sea. They can be used by IMO to designate PSSAs beyond the territorial sea with a view to the adoption of international protective measures regarding pollution and other damage caused by ships. They may also be used by national administrations to identify areas within their territorial seas that may have certain attributes reflected in the criteria and be vulnerable to damage by shipping activities.

4.4 In order to be identified as a PSSA, the area should meet at least one of the criteria listed below and information and supporting documentation should be provided to establish that at least one of the criteria exists throughout the entire proposed area, though the same criterion need not be present throughout the entire area. These criteria can be divided into three categories: ecological criteria; social, cultural, and economic criteria; and scientific and educational criteria.

Ecological criteria

4.4.1 Uniqueness or rarity—An area or ecosystem is unique if it is "the only one of its kind".Habitats of rare, threatened, or endangered species that occur only in one area are an example. An area or ecosystem is rare if it only occurs in a few locations or has been seriously depleted across its range. An ecosystem may extend beyond country borders, assuming regional or international significance. Nurseries or certain feeding, breeding, or spawning areas may also be rare or unique.

4.4.2 Critical habitat—A sea area that may be essential for the survival, function, or recovery of fish stocks or rare or endangered marine species, or for the support of large marine ecosystems.

4.4.3 Dependency—An area where ecological processes are highly dependent on biotically structured systems (e.g. coral reefs, kelp forests, mangrove forests, seagrass beds). Such ecosystems often have high diversity, which is dependent on the structuring organisms. Dependency also embraces the migratory routes of fish, reptiles, birds, mammals, and invertebrates.

4.4.4 Representativeness—An area that is an outstanding and illustrative example of specific biodiversity, ecosystems, ecological or physiographic processes, or community or habitat types or other natural characteristics.

4.4.5 Diversity—An area that may have an exceptional variety of species or genetic diversity or includes highly varied ecosystems, habitats, and communities.

4.4.6 Productivity—An area that has a particularly high rate of natural biological production. Such productivity is the net result of biological and physical processes which result in an increase in biomass in areas such as oceanic fronts, upwelling areas and some gyres.

4.4.7 Spawning or breeding grounds—An area that may be a critical spawning or breeding ground or nursery area for marine species which may spend the rest of their life-cycle elsewhere, or is recognized as migratory routes for fish, reptiles, birds, mammals, or invertebrates.

4.4.8 Naturalness—An area that has experienced a relative lack of human-induced disturbance or degradation.

4.4.9 Integrity—An area that is a biologically functional unit, an effective, self-sustaining ecological entity.

4.4.10 Fragility—An area that is highly susceptible to degradation by natural events or by the activities of people. Biotic communities associated with coastal habitats may have a low tolerance to changes in environmental conditions, or they may exist close to the limits of their tolerance (e.g., water temperature, salinity, turbidity or depth). Such communities may suffer natural stresses such as storms or other natural conditions (e.g., circulation patterns) that concentrate harmful substances in water or sediments, low flushing rates, and/or oxygen depletion. Additional stress may be caused by human influences such as pollution and changes in salinity. Thus, an area already subject to stress from natural and/or human factors may be in need of special protection from further stress, including that arising from international shipping activities.

4.4.11 Bio-geographic importance—An area that either contains rare biogeographic qualities or is representative of a biogeographic "type" or types, or contains unique or unusual biological, chemical, physical, or geological features.

Social, cultural and economic criteria

4.4.12 Social or economic dependency—An area where the environmental quality and the use of living marine resources are of particular social or economic importance, including fishing, recreation, tourism, and the livelihoods of people who depend on access to the area.

4.4.13 Human dependency—An area that is of particular importance for the support of traditional subsistence or food production activities or for the protection of the cultural resources of the local human populations.

4.4.14 Cultural heritage—An area that is of particular importance because of the presence of significant historical and archaeological sites. Scientific and educational criteria

4.4.15 Research—An area that has high scientific interest.

4.4.16 Baseline for monitoring studies—An area that provides suitable baseline conditions with regard to biota or environmental characteristics, because it has not had substantial perturbations or has been in such a state for a long period of time such that it is considered to be in a natural or near-natural condition.

4.4.17 Education—An area that offers an exceptional opportunity to demonstrate particular natural phenomena.

4.5 In some cases a PSSA may be identified within a Special Area and vice versa. It should be noted that the criteria with respect to the identification of PSSAs and the criteria for the designation of Special Areas are not mutually exclusive.

5 VULNERABILITY TO IMPACTS FROM INTERNATIONAL SHIPPING

5.1 In addition to meeting at least one of the criteria listed in 4.4, the recognized attributes of the area should be at risk from international shipping activities. This involves consideration of the following factors:

Vessel traffic characteristics

5.1.1 Operational factors—Types of maritime activities (e.g. small fishing boats, small pleasure craft, oil and gas rigs) in the proposed area that by their presence may reduce the safety of navigation.

5.1.2 Vessel types—Types of vessels passing through or adjacent to the area (e.g. high-speed vessels, large tankers, or bulk carriers with small under-keel clearance).

5.1.3 Traffic characteristics—Volume or concentration of traffic, vessel interaction, distance offshore or other dangers to navigation, are such as to involve greater risk of collision or grounding.

5.1.4 Harmful substances carried—Type and quantity of substances on board, whether cargo, fuel or stores, that would be harmful if released into the sea.

Natural factors

5.1.5 Hydrographical—Water depth, bottom and coastline topography, lack of proximate safe anchorages and other factors which call for increased navigational caution.

5.1.6 Meteorological—Prevailing weather, wind strength and direction, atmospheric visibility and other factors which increase the risk of collision and grounding and also the risk of damage to the sea area from discharges.

5.1.7 Oceanographic—Tidal streams, ocean currents, ice, and other factors which increase the risk of collision and grounding and also the risk of damage to the sea area from discharges.

5.2 In proposing an area as a PSSA and in considering the associated protective measures to prevent, reduce, or eliminate the identified vulnerability, other information that might be helpful includes the following:

.1 any evidence that international shipping activities are causing or may cause damage to the attributes of the proposed area, including the significance or risk of the potential damage, the degree of harm that may be expected to cause damage, and whether such damage is reasonably foreseeable, as well as whether damage is of a recurring or cumulative nature;

.2 any history of groundings, collisions, or spills in the area and any consequences of such incidents;

.3 any adverse impacts to the environment outside the proposed PSSA expected to be caused by changes to international shipping activities as a result of PSSA designation;

.4 stresses from other environmental sources; and

.5 any measures already in effect and their actual or anticipated beneficial impact.

6 ASSOCIATED PROTECTIVE MEASURES

6.1 In the context of these Guidelines, associated protective measures for PSSAs are limited to actions that are to be, or have been, approved or adopted by IMO and include the following options:

6.1.1 designation of an area as a Special Area under MARPOL Annexes I, II or V, or a SOx emission control area under MARPOL Annex VI, or application of special discharge restrictions to vessels operating in a PSSA. Procedures and criteria for the designation of Special Areas are contained in the Guidelines for the Designation of Special Areas set forth in annex 1 of Assembly resolution A.927(22). Criteria and procedures for the designation of SOx emission control areas are found in Appendix 3 to MARPOL Annex VI;

6.1.2 adoption of ships' routeing and reporting systems near or in the area, under the International Convention for the Safety of Life at Sea (SOLAS) and in accordance with the General Provisions on Ships' Routeing and the Guidelines and Criteria for Ship Reporting Systems. For example, a PSSA may be designated as an area to be avoided or it may be protected by other ships' routeing or reporting systems; and

6.1.3 development and adoption of other measures aimed at protecting specific sea areas against environmental damage from ships, provided that they have an identified legal basis.

6.2 Consideration should also be given to the potential for the area to be listed on the World Heritage List, declared a Biosphere Reserve, or included on a list of areas of international, regional, or national importance, or if the area is already the subject of such international, regional, or national conservation action or agreements.

6.3   In some circumstances, a proposed PSSA may include within its boundaries a buffer zone, in other words, an area contiguous to the site-specific feature (core area) for which specific protection from shipping is sought. However, the need for such a buffer zone should be justified in terms of how it would directly contribute to the adequate protection of the core area.

7   PROCEDURE FOR THE DESIGNATION OF PARTICULARLY SENSITIVE SEA AREAS AND THE ADOPTION OF ASSOCIATED PROTECTIVE MEASURES

7.1   An application for PSSA designation should contain a proposal for an associated protective measure that the proposing Member Government intends to submit to the appropriate IMO body. If the measure is not already available under an IMO instrument, the proposal should set forth the steps that the proposing Member Government has taken or will take to have the measure approved or adopted by IMO pursuant to an identified legal basis (see paragraph 7.5.2.3).

7.2   Alternatively, if no new associated protective measure is being proposed because IMO measures are already associated with the area to protect it, then the application should identify the threat of damage or damage being caused to the area by international shipping activities and show how the area is already being protected from such identified vulnerability by the associated protective measures. Amendments to existing measures may be introduced to address identified vulnerabilities.

7.3   In the future, additional associated protective measures may also be introduced to address identified vulnerabilities.

7.4   The application should first clearly set forth a summary of the objectives of the proposed PSSA designation, the location of the area, the need for protection, the associated protective measures, and demonstrate how the identified vulnerability will be addressed by existing or proposed associated protective measures. The summary should include the reasons why the associated protective measures are the preferred method for providing protection for the area to be identified as a PSSA.

7.5   Each application should then consist of two parts.

7.5.1   Part I—*Description, significance of the area and vulnerability*

.1   *Description*—a detailed description of the location of the proposed area, along with a nautical chart on which the location of the area and any associated protective measures are clearly marked, should be submitted with the application.

.2   *Significance of the area*—the application should state the significance of the area on the basis of recognized ecological, socio-economic, or scientific attributes and should explicitly refer to the criteria listed above in section 4.

.3   *Vulnerability of the area to damage by international shipping activities*—the application should provide an explanation of the nature and extent of the risks that international shipping activities pose to the environment of the proposed area, noting the factors listed in section 5. The application should describe the particular current or future international shipping activities that are causing or may be expected to cause damage to the proposed area, including the significance of the damage and degree of harm that may result from such activities, either from such activity alone or in combination with other threats.

7.5.2   Part II—*Appropriate associated protective measures and IMO's competence to approve or adopt such measures*

.1   The application should identify the existing and/or proposed associated protective measures and describe how they provide the needed protection from the threats of damage posed by international maritime activities occurring in and around the area. The application should specifically describe how the associated protective measures protect the area from the identified vulnerability.

.2 If the application identifies a new associated protective measure, then the proposing Member Government must append a draft of the proposal which is intended to be submitted to the appropriate Sub–Committee or Committee or, if the measures are not already available in an IMO instrument, information must be provided with regard to its legal basis and/or the steps that the proposing Member Government has taken or will take to establish the legal basis.

.3 The application should identify the legal basis for each measure. The legal bases for such measures are:

(i) any measure that is already available under an existing IMO instrument; or

(ii) any measure that does not yet exist but could become available through amendment of an IMO instrument or adoption of a new IMO instrument. The legal basis for any such measure would only be available after the IMO instrument was amended or adopted, as appropriate; or

(iii) any measure proposed for adoption in the territorial sea[4], or pursuant to Article 211(6) of the United Nations Convention on the Law of the Sea where existing measures or a generally applicable measure (as set forth in subparagraph (ii) above) would not adequately address the particularized need of the proposed area.

.4 These measures may include ships' routeing measures; reporting requirements discharge restrictions; operational criteria; and prohibited activities, and should be specifically tailored to meet the need of the area to prevent, reduce, or eliminate the identified vulnerability of the area from international shipping activities.

.5 The application should clearly specify the category or categories of ships to which the proposed associated protective measures would apply, consistent with the provisions of the United Nations Convention on the Law of the Sea, including those related to vessels entitled to sovereign immunity, and other pertinent instruments.

7.6 The application should indicate the possible impact of any proposed measures on the safety and efficiency of navigation, taking into account the area of the ocean in which the proposed measures are to be implemented. The application should set forth such information as:

.1 consistency with the legal instrument under which the associated protective measure is being proposed;

.2 implications for vessel safety; and

.3 impact on vessel operations, such as existing traffic patterns or usage of the proposed area.

7.7 An application for PSSA designation should address all relevant considerations and criteria in these Guidelines, and should include relevant supporting information for each such item.

7.8 The application should contain a summary of steps taken, if any, by the proposing Member Government to date to protect the proposed area.

7.9 The proposing Member Government should also include in the application the details of action to be taken pursuant to domestic law for the failure of a ship to comply with the requirements of the associated protective measures. Any action taken should be consistent with international law as reflected in the United Nations Convention on the Law of the Sea.

---

4. This provision does not derogate from the rights and duties of coastal States in the territorial sea as provided for in the United Nations Convention on the Law of the Sea.

7.10 The proposing Member Government should submit a separate proposal to the appropriate Sub–Committee or Committee to obtain the approval of any new associated protective measure. Such a proposal must comply with the requirements of the legal instrument relied upon to establish the measure.

8 CRITERIA FOR ASSESSMENT OF APPLICATIONS FOR DESIGNATION OF PARTICULARLY SENSITIVE SEA AREAS AND THE ADOPTION OF ASSOCIATED PROTECTIVE MEASURES

8.1 IMO should consider each application, or amendment thereto, submitted to it by a proposing Member Government on a case-by-case basis to determine whether the area fulfils at least one of the criteria set forth in section 4, the attributes of the area meeting section 4 criteria are vulnerable to damage by international shipping activities as set forth in section 5, and associated protective measures exist or are proposed to prevent, reduce, or eliminate the identified vulnerability.

8.2 In assessing each proposal, IMO should in particular consider:

.1 the full range of protective measures available and determine whether the proposed or existing associated protective measures are appropriate to prevent, reduce, or eliminate the identified vulnerability of the area from international shipping activities;

.2 whether such measures might result in an increased potential for significant adverse effects by international shipping activities on the environment outside the proposed PSSA; and

.3 the linkage between the recognized attributes, the identified vulnerability, the associated protective measure to prevent, reduce, or eliminate that vulnerability, and the overall size of the area, including whether the size is commensurate with that necessary to address the identified need.

8.3 The procedure for considering a PSSA application by IMO is as follows:

.1 the MEPC should bear primary responsibility within IMO for considering PSSA applications and all applications should first be submitted to the MEPC:

.1 the Committee should assess the elements of the proposal against the Guidelines and, as appropriate, should establish a technical group, comprising representatives with appropriate environmental, scientific, maritime, and legal expertise;

.2 the proposing Member Government is encouraged to make a presentation of the proposal, along with nautical charts and other supporting information on the required elements for PSSA designation;

.3 any technical group formed should prepare a brief report to the Committee summarizing their findings and the outcome of its assessment; and

.4 the outcome of the assessment of a PSSA application should be duly reflected in the report of the MEPC;

.2 if appropriate following its assessment, the MEPC should designate the area "in principle" and inform the appropriate Sub–Committee, Committee (which could be the MEPC itself), or the Assembly that is responsible for addressing the particular associated protective measures proposed for the area of the outcome of this assessment;

.3 the appropriate Sub–Committee or Committee which has received a submission by a proposing Member Government for an associated protective measure should review the proposal to determine whether it meets the procedures, criteria, and other requirements of the legal instrument under which the measure is proposed. The Sub–Committee may seek the advice of the MEPC on issues pertinent to the application;

.4   the MEPC should not designate a PSSA until after the associated protective measures are considered and approved by the pertinent Sub–Committee, Committee, or Assembly. If the associated protective measures are not approved by the pertinent IMO body, then the MEPC may reject the PSSA application entirely or request that the proposing Member Government submit new proposals for associated protective measures. A proper record of the proceedings should be included in the report of the MEPC;

.5   for measures that require approval by the Maritime Safety Committee (MSC), the Sub–Committee should forward its recommendation for approval of the associated protective measures to the MSC or, if the Sub–Committee rejects the measures, it should inform the MSC and MEPC and provide a statement of reasons for its decision.

The MSC should consider any such recommendations and, if the measures are to be adopted, it should notify the MEPC of its decision;

.6   if the application is rejected, the MEPC shall notify the proposing Member Government, provide a statement of reasons for its decision and, if appropriate, request the Member Government to submit additional information; and

.7   after approval by the appropriate Sub–Committee, Committee, or, where necessary, the Assembly of the associated protective measures, the MEPC may designate the area as a PSSA.

8.4   IMO should provide a forum for the review and re-evaluation of any associated protective measure adopted, as necessary, taking into account pertinent comments, reports, and observations of the associated protective measures. Member Governments which have ships operating in the area of the designated PSSA are encouraged to bring any concerns with the associated protective measures to IMO so that any necessary adjustments may be made. Member Governments that originally submitted the application for designation with the associated protective measures, should also bring any concerns and proposals for additional measures or modifications to any associated protective measure or the PSSA itself to IMO.

8.5   After the designation of a PSSA and its associated protective measures, IMO should ensure that the effective date of implementation is as soon as possible based on the rules of IMO and consistent with international law.

8.6   IMO should, in assessing applications for designation of PSSAs and their associated protective measures, take into account the technical and financial resources available to developing Member Governments and those with economies in transition.

9   IMPLEMENTATION OF DESIGNATED PSSAs AND THE ASSOCIATED PROTECTIVE MEASURES

9.1   When a PSSA receives final designation, all associated protective measures should be identified on charts in accordance with the symbols and methods of the International Hydrographic Organization (IHO).

9.2   A proposing Member Government should ensure that any associated protective measure is implemented in accordance with international law as reflected in the United Nations Convention on the Law of the Sea.

9.3   Member Governments should take all appropriate steps to ensure that ships flying their flag comply with the associated protective measures adopted to protect the designated PSSA. Those Member Governments which have received information of an alleged violation of an associated protective measure by a ship flying their flag should provide the Government which has reported the offence with the details of any appropriate action taken.

B. FRESHWATER RESOURCES

3.23 TREATY BETWEEN CANADA AND THE UNITED STATES OF AMERICA RELATING TO BOUNDARY WATERS AND QUESTIONS ARISING ALONG THE BOUNDARY BETWEEN THE UNITED STATES AND CANADA.[e] **Concluded at Washington, 11 January 1909. Entered into force, 5 May 1910. 36 Stat 2448, TS No 548**

The United States of America and His Majesty the King of the United Kingdom of Great Britain and Ireland and of the British Dominions beyond the Seas, Emperor of India, being equally desirous to prevent disputes regarding the use of boundary waters and to settle all questions which are now pending between the United States and the Dominion of Canada involving the rights, obligations, or interests of either in relation to the other or to the inhabitants of the other, along their common frontier, and to make provision for the adjustment and settlement of all such questions as may hereafter arise, have resolved to conclude a treaty in furtherance of these ends, and for that purpose have appointed as their respective plenipotentiaries:

The President of the United States of America, Elihu Root, Secretary of State of the United States; and

His Britannic Majesty, the Right Honorable James Bryce, O.M., His Ambassador Extraordinary and Plenipotentiary at Washington;

Who, after having communicated to one another their full powers, found in good and due form, have agreed upon the following articles:

Preliminary Article

For the purposes of this treaty boundary waters are defined as the waters from main shore to main shore of the lakes and rivers and connecting waterways, or the portions thereof, along which the international boundary between the United States and the Dominion of Canada passes, including all bays, arms, and inlets thereof, but not including tributary waters which in their natural channels would flow into such lakes, rivers, and waterways, or waters flowing from such lakes, rivers, and waterways, or the waters of rivers flowing across the boundary.

Article I

The High Contracting Parties agree that the navigation of all navigable boundary waters shall forever continue free and open for the purposes of commerce to the inhabitants and to the ships, vessels, and boats of both countries equally, subject, however, to any laws and regulations of either country, within its own territory, not inconsistent with such privilege of free navigation and applying equally and without discrimination to the inhabitants, ships, vessels, and boats of both countries.

It is further agreed that so long as this treaty shall remain in force, this same right of navigation shall extend to the waters of Lake Michigan and to all canals connecting boundary waters, and now existing or which may hereafter be constructed on either side of the line. Either of the High Contracting Parties may adopt rules and regulations governing the use of such canals within its own territory and may charge tolls for the use thereof, but all such rules and regulations and all tolls charged shall apply alike to the subjects or citizens of the High Contracting Parties and the ships, vessels, and boats of both of the High Contracting Parties, and they shall be placed on terms of equality in the use thereof.

Article II

Each of the High Contracting Parties reserves to itself or to the several State Governments on the one side and the Dominion or Provincial Governments on the other as the case may be, subject to any treaty provisions now existing with respect thereto, the exclusive jurisdiction and control over the use and diversion, whether

---

e. Article 5 terminated by treaty of 27 February 1950.

temporary or permanent, of all waters on its own side of the line which in their natural channels would flow across the boundary or into boundary waters; but it is agreed that any interference with or diversion from their natural channel of such waters on either side of the boundary, resulting in any injury on the other side of the boundary, shall give rise to the same rights and entitle the injured parties to the same legal remedies as if such injury took place in the country where such diversion or interference occurs; but this provision shall not apply to cases already existing or to cases expressly covered by special agreement between the parties hereto.

It is understood, however, that neither of the High Contracting Parties intends by the foregoing provision to surrender any right, which it may have, to object to any interference with or diversions of waters on the other side of the boundary the effect of which would be productive of material injury to the navigation interests on its own side of the boundary.

Article III

It is agreed that, in addition to the uses, obstructions, and diversions heretofore permitted or hereafter provided for by special agreement between the Parties hereto, no further or other uses or obstructions or diversions, whether temporary or permanent, of boundary waters on either side of the line, affecting the natural level or flow of boundary waters on the other side of the line, shall be made except by authority of the United States or the Dominion of Canada within their respective jurisdictions and with the approval, as hereinafter provided, of a joint commission, to be known as the International Joint Commission.

The foregoing provisions are not intended to limit or interfere with the existing rights of the Government of the United States on the one side and the Government of the Dominion of Canada on the other, to undertake and carry on governmental works in boundary waters for the deepening of channels, the construction of breakwaters, the improvement of harbors, and other governmental works for the benefit of commerce and navigation, provided that such works are wholly on its own side of the line and do not materially affect the level or flow of the boundary waters on the other, nor are such provisions intended to interfere with the ordinary use of such waters for domestic and sanitary purposes.

Article IV

The High Contracting Parties agree that, except in cases provided for by special agreement between them, they will not permit the construction or maintenance on their respective sides of the boundary of any remedial or protective works or any dams or other obstructions in waters flowing from boundary waters or in waters at a lower level than the boundary in rivers flowing across the boundary, the effect of which is to raise the natural level of waters on the other side of the boundary unless the construction or maintenance thereof is approved by the aforesaid International Joint Commission.

It is further agreed that the waters herein defined as boundary waters and waters flowing across the boundary shall not be polluted on either side to the injury of health or property on the other.

Article V

The High Contracting Parties agree that it is expedient to limit the diversion of waters from the Niagara River so that the level of Lake Erie and the flow of the stream shall not be appreciably affected. It is the desire of both Parties to accomplish this object with the least possible injury to investments which have already been made in the construction of power plants on the United States side of the river under grants of authority from the State of New York, and on the Canadian side of the river under licenses authorized by the Dominion of Canada and the Province of Ontario.

So long as this treaty shall remain in force, no diversion of the waters of the Niagara River above the Falls from the natural course and stream thereof shall be permitted except for the purposes and to the extent hereinafter provided.

The United States may authorize and permit the diversion within the State of New York of the waters of said river above the Falls of Niagara, for power purposes, not exceeding in the aggregate a daily diversion at the rate of twenty thousand cubic feet of water per second.

The United Kingdom, by the Dominion of Canada, or the Province of Ontario, may authorize and permit the diversion within the Province of Ontario of the waters of said river above the Falls of Niagara, for power purposes, not exceeding in the aggregate a daily diversion at the rate of thirty-six thousand cubic feet of water per second.

The prohibitions of this article shall not apply to the diversion of water for sanitary or domestic purposes, or for the service of canals for the purposes of navigation.

Article VI

The High Contracting Parties agree that the St. Mary and Milk Rivers and their tributaries (in the State of Montana and the Provinces of Alberta and Saskatchewan) are to be treated as one stream for the purposes of irrigation and power, and the waters thereof shall be apportioned equally between the two countries, but in making such equal apportionment more than half may be taken from one river and less than half from the other by either country so as to afford a more beneficial use to each. It is further agreed that in the division of such waters during the irrigation season, between the 1st of April and 31st of October, inclusive, annually, the United States is entitled to a prior appropriation of 500 cubic feet per second of the waters of the Milk River, or so much of such amount as constitutes three-fourths of its natural flow, and that Canada is entitled to a prior appropriation of 500 cubic feet per second of the flow of the St. Mary River, or so much of such amount as constitutes three-fourths of its natural flow.

The channel of the Milk River in Canada may be used at the convenience of the United States for the conveyance, while passing through Canadian territory, of waters diverted from the St. Mary River. The provisions of Article II of this treaty shall apply to any injury resulting to property in Canada from the conveyance of such waters through the Milk River.

The measurement and apportionment of the water to be used by each country shall from time to time be made jointly by the properly constituted reclamation officers of the United States and the properly constituted irrigation officers of His Majesty under the direction of the International Joint Commission.

Article VII

The High Contracting Parties agree to establish and maintain an International Joint Commission of the United States and Canada composed of six commissioners, three on the part of the United States appointed by the President thereof, and three on the part of the United Kingdom appointed by His Majesty on the recommendation of the Governor in Council of the Dominion of Canada.

Article VIII

This International Joint Commission shall have jurisdiction over and shall pass upon all cases involving the use or obstruction or diversion of the waters with respect to which under Articles III and IV of this treaty the approval of this Commission is required, and in passing upon such cases the Commission shall be governed by the following rules or principles which are adopted by the High Contracting Parties for this purpose:

The High Contracting Parties shall have, each on its own side of the boundary, equal and similar rights in the use of the waters hereinbefore defined as boundary waters.

The following order of precedence shall be observed among the various uses enumerated hereinafter for these waters, and no use shall be permitted which tends materially to conflict with or restrain any other use which is given preference over it in this order of precedence:

(1) Uses for domestic and sanitary purposes;

(2) Uses for navigation, including the service of canals for the purposes of navigation;

(3) Uses for power and for irrigation purposes.

The foregoing provisions shall not apply to or disturb any existing uses of boundary waters on either side of the boundary.

The requirement for an equal division may in the discretion of the Commission be suspended in cases of temporary diversions along boundary waters at points where such equal division can not be made advantageously on account of local conditions, and where such diversion does not diminish elsewhere the amount available for use on the other side.

The Commission in its discretion may make its approval in any case conditional upon the construction of remedial or protective works to compensate so far as possible for the particular use or diversion proposed, and in such cases may require that suitable and adequate provision, approved by the Commission, be made for the protection and indemnity against injury of any interests on either side of the boundary.

In cases involving the elevation of the natural level of waters on either side of the line as a result of the construction or maintenance on the other side of remedial or protective works or dams or other obstructions in boundary waters or in waters flowing therefrom or in waters below the boundary in rivers flowing across the boundary, the Commission shall require, as a condition of its approval thereof, that suitable and adequate provision, approved by it, be made for the protection and indemnity of all interests on the other side of the line which may be injured thereby.

The majority of the Commissioners shall have power to render a decision. In case the Commission is evenly divided upon any question or matter presented to it for decision, separate reports shall be made by the Commissioners on each side to their own Government. The High Contracting Parties shall thereupon endeavor to agree upon an adjustment of the question or matter of difference, and if an agreement is reached between them, it shall be reduced to writing in the form of a protocol, and shall be communicated to the Commissioners, who shall take such further proceedings as may be necessary to carry out such agreement.

Article IX

The High Contracting Parties further agree that any other questions or matters of difference arising between them involving the rights, obligations, or interests of either in relation to the other or to the inhabitants of the other along the common frontier between the United States and the Dominion of Canada, shall be referred from time to time to the International Joint Commission for examination and report, whenever either the Government of the United States or the Government of the Dominion of Canada shall request that such questions or matters of difference be so referred.

The International Joint Commission is authorized in each case so referred to examine into and report upon the facts and circumstances of the particular questions and matters referred, together with such conclusions and recommendations as may be appropriate, subject, however, to any restrictions or exceptions which may be imposed with respect thereto by the terms of the reference.

Such reports of the Commission shall not be regarded as decisions of the questions or matters so submitted either on the facts or the law, and shall in no way have the character of an arbitral award.

The Commission shall make a joint report to both Governments in all cases in which all or a majority of the Commissioners agree, and in case of disagreement the minority may make a joint report to both Governments, or separate reports to their respective Governments.

In case the Commission is evenly divided upon any question or matter referred to it for report, separate reports shall be made by the Commissioners on each side to their own Government.

Article X

Any questions or matters of difference arising between the High Contracting Parties involving the rights, obligations, or interests of the United States or of the Dominion of Canada either in relation to each other or to their respective inhabitants, may be referred for decision to the International Joint Commission by the consent of the two Parties, it being understood that on the part of the United States any such action will be by and with the advice and consent of the Senate, and on the part of His Majesty's Government with the consent of the Governor General in Council. In each case so referred, the said Commission is authorized to examine into and report upon the facts and circumstances of the particular questions and matters referred, together with such conclusions and recommendations as may be appropriate, subject, however, to any restrictions or exceptions which may be imposed with respect thereto by the terms of the reference.

A majority of the said Commission shall have power to render a decision or finding upon any of the questions or matters so referred.

If the said Commission is equally divided or otherwise unable to render a decision or finding as to any questions or matters so referred, it shall be the duty of the Commissioners to make a joint report to both Governments, or separate reports to their respective Governments, showing the different conclusions arrived at with regard to the matters or questions so referred, which questions or matters shall thereupon be referred for decision by the High Contracting Parties to an umpire chosen in accordance with the procedure prescribed in the fourth, fifth, and sixth paragraphs of Article XLV of The Hague Convention for the pacific settlement of international disputes, dated October 18, 1907. Such umpire shall have power to render a final decision with respect to those matters and questions so referred on which the Commission failed to agree.

Article XI

A duplicate original of all decisions rendered and joint reports made by the Commission shall be transmitted to and filed with the Secretary of State of the United States and the Governor General of the Dominion of Canada, and to them shall be addressed all communications of the Commission.

Article XII

The International Joint Commission shall meet and organize at Washington promptly after the members thereof are appointed, and when organized the Commission may fix such times and places for its meetings as may be necessary, subject at all times to special call or direction by the two Governments. Each Commissioner, upon the first joint meeting of the Commission after his appointment, shall, before proceeding with the work of the Commission, make and subscribe a solemn declaration in writing that he will faithfully and impartially perform the duties imposed upon him under this treaty, and such declaration shall be entered on the records of the proceedings of the Commission.

The United States and Canadian sections of the Commission may each appoint a secretary, and these shall act as joint secretaries of the Commission at its joint sessions, and the Commission may employ engineers and clerical assistants from time to time as it may deem advisable. The salaries and personal expenses of the Commission and of the secretaries shall be paid by their respective Governments, and all reasonable and necessary joint expenses of the Commission, incurred by it, shall be paid in equal moieties by the High Contracting Parties.

The Commission shall have power to administer oaths to witnesses, and to take evidence on oath whenever deemed necessary in any proceeding, or inquiry, or matter within its jurisdiction under this treaty, and all parties interested therein shall be given convenient opportunity to be heard, and the High Contracting Parties agree to adopt such legislation as may be appropriate and necessary to give the Commission the powers above mentioned on each side of the boundary, and to provide for the issue of subpoenas and for compelling the attendance of witnesses in proceedings before the Commission. The Commission may adopt such rules of procedure as shall be in accordance with justice and equity, and may make such examination in person and through agents or employees as may be deemed advisable.

Article XIII

In all cases where special agreements between the High Contracting Parties hereto are referred to in the foregoing articles, such agreements are understood and intended to include not only direct agreements between the High Contracting Parties, but also any mutual arrangement between the United States and the Dominion of Canada expressed by concurrent or reciprocal legislation on the part of Congress and the Parliament of the Dominion.

Article XIV

The present treaty shall be ratified by the President of the United States of America, by and with the advice and consent of the Senate thereof, and by His Britannic Majesty. The ratifications shall be exchanged at Washington as soon as possible and the treaty shall take effect on the date of the exchange of its ratifications. It shall remain in force for five years, dating from the day of exchange of ratifications, and thereafter until terminated by twelve months' written notice given by either High Contracting Party to the other.

3.24 Helsinki Rules on the Uses of the Waters of International Rivers (Without Comments and Annex).[f] **Adopted by the International Law Association at Helsinki, 20 August 1966. 52 ILA 484 (1967);** *reprinted in* **5 Weston & Carlson V.F.32**

CHAPTER 1

GENERAL

Article I

The general rules of international law as set forth in these chapters are applicable to the use of the waters of an international drainage basin except as may be provided otherwise by convention, agreement or binding custom among the basin States.

* * *

CHAPTER 2

EQUITABLE UTILIZATION OF THE WATERS OF AN INTERNATIONAL DRAINAGE BASIN

Article IV

Each basin State is entitled, within its territory, to a reasonable and equitable share in the beneficial uses of the waters of an international drainage basin.

Article V

(1) What is a reasonable and equitable share within the meaning of Article IV is to be determined in the light of all the relevant factors in each particular case.

(2) Relevant factors which are to be considered include, but are not limited to:

(a) the geography of the basin, including in particular the extent of the drainage area in the territory of each basin State;

(b) the hydrology of the basin, including in particular the contribution of water by each basin State;

(c) the climate affecting the basin;

(d) the past utilization of the waters of the basin, including in particular existing utilization;

(e) the economic and social needs of each basin State;

(f) the population dependent on the waters of the basin in each basin State;

(g) the comparative costs of alternative means of satisfying the economic and social needs of each basin State;

(h) the availability of other resources;

(i) the avoidance of unnecessary waste in the utilization of waters of the basin;

(j) the practicability of compensation to one or more of the co-basin States as a means of adjusting conflicts among uses; and

(k) the degree to which the needs of a basin State may be satisfied, without causing substantial injury to a co-basin State.

(3) The weight to be given to each factor is to be determined by its importance in comparison with that of other relevant factors. In determining what is a reasonable

f. *Superseded by* Basic Document 3.28, *infra.*

and equitable share, all relevant factors are to be considered together and a conclusion reached on the basis of the whole.

* * *

Article X

1. Consistent with the principle of equitable utilization of the waters of an international drainage basin, a State

(a) must prevent any new form of water pollution or any increase in the degree of existing water pollution in an international drainage basin which would cause substantial injury in the territory of a co-basin State, and

(b) should take all reasonable measures to abate existing water pollution in an international drainage basin to such an extent that no substantial damage is caused in the territory of a co-basin State.

2. The rule stated in paragraph 1 of this Article applies to water pollution originating

(a) within a territory of the State, or

(b) outside the territory of the State, if it is caused by the State's conduct.

Article XI

1. In the case of a violation of the rule stated in paragraph 1(a) of Article X of this Chapter, the State responsible shall be required to cease the wrongful conduct and compensate the injured co-basin State for the injury that has been caused to it.

2. In a case falling under the rule stated in paragraph 1(b) of Article X, if a State fails to take reasonable measures, it shall be required promptly to enter into negotiations with the injured State with a view toward reaching a settlement equitable under the circumstances.

* * *

Article XXIX

1. With a view to preventing disputes from arising between basin States as to their legal rights or other interest, it is recommended that each basin State furnish relevant and reasonably available information to the other basin States concerning the waters of a drainage basin within its territory and its use of, and activities with respect to such waters.

2. A State, regardless of its location in a drainage basin, should in particular furnish to any other basin State, the interests of which may be substantially affected, notice of any proposed construction or installation which would alter the regime of the basin in a way which might give rise to a dispute as defined in Article XXVI. The notice should include such essential facts as will permit the recipient to make an assessment of the probable effect of the proposed alteration.

3. A State providing the notice referred to in paragraph 2 of this Article should afford to the recipient a reasonable period of time to make an assessment of the probable effect of the proposed construction or installation and to submit its views thereon to the State furnishing the notice.

4. If a State has failed to give the notice referred to in paragraph 2 of this Article, the alteration by the State in the regime of the drainage basin shall not be given the weight normally accorded to temporal priority in use in the event of a determination of what is a reasonable and equitable share of the waters of the basin.

3.25 SEOUL RULES ON INTERNATIONAL GROUNDWATERS.[g] **Adopted by the International Law Association, 24–30 Aug 1987. Report of the International Law Association on its Sixty–Second Conference, p. 251 (1987)**

Article I—The waters of international aquifers

The waters of an aquifer that is intersected by the boundary between two or more States are international groundwaters if such an aquifer with its waters forms an international basin or part thereof. Those states are basin States within the meaning of the Helsinki Rules **[Basic Document 3.24]** whether or not the aquifer and its waters form surface waters part of a hydraulic system flowing into a common terminus.

Article II—Hydraulic interdependence

1. An aquifer that contributes water to, or receives water from, surface waters of an international basin constitutes part of an international basin for the purposes of the Helsinki Rules **[Basic Document 3.24]**.

2. An aquifer intersected by the boundary between two or more States that does not contribute water to, or receive water from, surface waters of an international drainage basin constitutes an international drainage basin for the purposes of the Helsinki Rules.

3. Basin states, in exercising their rights and performing their duties under international law, shall take into account any interdependence of the groundwater and other waters including any interconnections between aquifers, and any leaching into aquifers caused by activities and areas under their jurisdiction.

Article III—Protection of groundwater

1. Basin states shall prevent or abate the pollution of international groundwaters in accordance with international law applicable to existing, new, increased and highly dangerous pollution. Special consideration shall be given to the long-term effects of the pollution of groundwater.

2. Basin states shall consult and exchange relevant available information and data at the request of any one of them.

(a) for the purpose of preserving the groundwaters of the basin from degradation and protecting form impairment the geologic structure of the aquifers, including recharge areas;

(b) for the purpose of considering joint or parallel quality standards and environmental protection measures applicable to international groundwaters and their aquifers.

3. Basin states shall cooperate, at the request of any one of them, for the purpose of collecting and analyzing additional needed information and data pertinent to the international groundwaters or their aquifers.

Article IV—Groundwater management and surface waters

Basin states should consider the integrated management, including conjunctive use with surface waters, of their international groundwaters at the request of any one of them.

g. *Superseded by* Basic Document 3.28, *infra.*

3.26 Convention on the Protection and Use of Transboundary Watercourses and International Lakes. Concluded at Helsinki, 17 March 1992. Entered into force, 6 October 1996. 1936 UNTS 269. *Reprinted in* 31 ILM 1312 (1992) & 5 Weston & Carlson V.F.36

Article 1—Definitions

For the purposes of this Convention,

1. "Transboundary waters" means any surface or ground waters which mark, cross or are located on boundaries between two or more States; wherever transboundary waters flow directly into the sea, these transboundary waters end at a straight line across their respective mouths between points on the low-water line of their banks;

2. "Transboundary impact" means any significant adverse effect on the environment resulting from a change in the conditions of transboundary waters caused by a human activity, the physical origin of which is situated wholly or in part within an area under the jurisdiction of a Party, within an area under the jurisdiction of another Party. Such effects on the environment include effects on human health and safety, flora, fauna, soil, air, water, climate, landscape and historical monuments or other physical structures or the interaction among these factors; they also include effects on the cultural heritage or socio-economic conditions resulting from alterations to those factors;

3. "Party" means, unless the text otherwise indicates, a Contracting Party to this Convention;

4. "Riparian Parties" means the Parties bordering the same transboundary waters;

* * *

PART I

PROVISIONS RELATING TO ALL PARTIES

Article 2—General Provisions

1. The Parties shall take all appropriate measures to prevent, control and reduce any transboundary impact.

2. The Parties shall, in particular, take all appropriate measures:

(a) To prevent, control and reduce pollution of waters causing or likely to cause transboundary impact;

(b) To ensure that transboundary waters are used with the aim of ecologically sound and rational water management, conservation of water resources and environmental protection;

(c) To ensure that transboundary waters are used in a reasonable and equitable way, taking into particular account their transboundary character, in the case of activities which cause or are likely to cause transboundary impact;

(d) To ensure conservation and, where necessary, restoration of ecosystems.

3. Measures for the prevention, control and reduction of water pollution shall be taken, where possible, at source.

4. These measures shall not directly or indirectly result in a transfer of pollution to other parts of the environment.

5. In taking the measures referred to in paragraphs 1 and 2 of this article, the Parties shall be guided by the following principles:

(a) The precautionary principle, by virtue of which action to avoid the potential transboundary impact of the release of hazardous substances shall not be postponed on the ground that scientific research has not fully proved a causal link between those substances, on the one hand, and the potential transboundary impact, on the other hand;

(b) The polluter-pays principle, by virtue of which costs of pollution prevention, control and reduction measures shall be borne by the polluter;

(c) Water resources shall be managed so that the needs of the present generation are met without compromising the ability of future generations to meet their own needs.

6. The Riparian Parties shall cooperate on the basis of equality and reciprocity, in particular through bilateral and multilateral agreements, in order to develop harmonized policies, programmes and strategies covering the relevant catchment areas, or parts thereof, aimed at the prevention, control and reduction of transboundary impact and aimed at the protection of the environment of transboundary waters or the environment influenced by such waters, including the marine environment.

7. The application of this Convention shall not lead to the deterioration of environmental conditions nor lead to increased transboundary impact.

8. The provisions of this Convention shall not affect the right of Parties individually or jointly to adopt and implement more stringent measures than those set down in this Convention.

* * *

PART II

PROVISIONS RELATING TO RIPARIAN PARTIES

Article 9—Bilateral and Multilateral Cooperation

1. The Riparian Parties shall on the basis of equality and reciprocity enter into bilateral or multilateral agreements or other arrangements, where these do not yet exist, or adapt existing ones, where necessary to eliminate the contradictions with the basic principles of this Convention, in order to define their mutual relations and conduct regarding the prevention, control and reduction of transboundary impact. The Riparian Parties shall specify the catchment area, or part(s) thereof, subject to cooperation. These agreements or arrangements shall embrace relevant issues covered by this Convention, as well as any other issues on which the Riparian Parties may deem it necessary to cooperate.

* * *

Article 10—Consultations

Consultations shall be held between the Riparian Parties on the basis of reciprocity, good faith and good-neighbourliness, at the request of any such Party. Such consultations shall aim at cooperation regarding the issues covered by the provisions of this Convention. Any such consultations shall be conducted through a joint body established under article 9 of this Convention, where one exists.

* * *

3.27 CONVENTION ON THE LAW OF THE NON-NAVIGATIONAL USES OF INTERNATIONAL WATERCOURSES. **Adopted on 21 May 1997. Not yet in force. UN Doc. A/51/869,** *reprinted in* **36 ILM 700 (1997) & 5 Weston & Carlson V.F.37**

PART I.　INTRODUCTION

Article 1

Scope of the present Convention

1.　The present Convention applies to uses of international watercourses and of their waters for purposes other than navigation and to measures of protection, preservation and management related to the uses of those watercourses and their waters.

2.　The uses of international watercourses for navigation is not within the scope of the present Convention except insofar as other uses affect navigation or are affected by navigation.

Article 2

Use of terms

For the purposes of the present Convention:

(a) "Watercourse" means a system of surface waters and groundwaters constituting by virtue of their physical relationship a unitary whole and normally flowing into a common terminus;

(b) "International watercourse" means a watercourse, parts of which are situated in different States;

(c) "Watercourse State" means a State Party to the present Convention in whose territory part of an international watercourse is situated, or a Party that is a regional economic integration organization, in the territory of one or more of whose Member States part of an international watercourse is situated;

(d) "Regional economic integration organization" means an organization constituted by sovereign States of a given region, to which its member States have transferred competence in respect of matters governed by this Convention and which has been duly authorized in accordance with its internal procedures, to sign, ratify, accept, approve or accede to it.

Article 3

Watercourse agreements

1.　In the absence of an agreement to the contrary, nothing in the present Convention shall affect the rights or obligations of a watercourse State arising from agreements in force for it on the date on which it became a party to the present Convention.

2.　Notwithstanding the provisions of paragraph 1, parties to agreements referred to in paragraph 1 may, where necessary, consider harmonizing such agreements with the basic principles of the present Convention.

3.　Watercourse States may enter into one or more agreements, hereinafter referred to as "watercourse agreements", which apply and adjust the provisions of the present Convention to the characteristics and uses of a particular international watercourse or part thereof.

4.　Where a watercourse agreement is concluded between two or more watercourse States, it shall define the waters to which it applies. Such an agreement may be entered into with respect to an entire international watercourse or any part thereof or a particular project, programme or use except insofar as the agreement adversely affects, to a significant extent, the use by one or more other watercourse States of the waters of the watercourse, without their express consent.

5. Where a watercourse State considers that adjustment and application of the provisions of the present Convention is required because of the characteristics and uses of a particular international watercourse, watercourse States shall consult with a view to negotiating in good faith for the purpose of concluding a watercourse agreement or agreements.

6. Where some but not all watercourse States to a particular international watercourse are parties to an agreement, nothing in such agreement shall affect the rights or obligations under the present Convention of watercourse States that are not parties to such an agreement.

Article 4

Parties to watercourse agreements

1. Every watercourse State is entitled to participate in the negotiation of and to become a party to any watercourse agreement that applies to the entire international watercourse, as well as to participate in any relevant consultations.

2. A watercourse State whose use of an international watercourse may be affected to a significant extent by the implementation of a proposed watercourse agreement that applies only to a part of the watercourse or to a particular project, programme or use is entitled to participate in consultations on such an agreement and, where appropriate, in the negotiation thereof in good faith with a view to becoming a party thereto, to the extent that its use is thereby affected.

PART II. GENERAL PRINCIPLES

Article 5

Equitable and reasonable utilization and participation

1. Watercourse States shall in their respective territories utilize an international watercourse in an equitable and reasonable manner. In particular, an international watercourse shall be used and developed by watercourse States with a view to attaining optimal and sustainable utilization thereof and benefits therefrom, taking into account the interests of the watercourse States concerned, consistent with adequate protection of the watercourse.

2. Watercourse States shall participate in the use, development and protection of an international watercourse in an equitable and reasonable manner. Such participation includes both the right to utilize the watercourse and the duty to cooperate in the protection and development thereof, as provided in the present Convention.

Article 6

Factors relevant to equitable and reasonable utilization

1. Utilization of an international watercourse in an equitable and reasonable manner within the meaning of article 5 requires taking into account all relevant factors and circumstances, including:

(a) Geographic, hydrographic, hydrological, climatic, ecological and other factors of a natural character;

(b) The social and economic needs of the watercourse States concerned;

(c) The population dependent on the watercourse in each watercourse State;

(d) The effects of the use or uses of the watercourses in one watercourse State on other watercourse States;

(e) Existing and potential uses of the watercourse;

(f) Conservation, protection, development and economy of use of the water resources of the watercourse and the costs of measures taken to that effect;

(g) The availability of alternatives, of comparable value, to a particular planned or existing use.

2. In the application of article 5 or paragraph 1 of this article, watercourse States concerned shall, when the need arises, enter into consultations in a spirit of cooperation.

3. The weight to be given to each factor is to be determined by its importance in comparison with that of other relevant factors. In determining what is a reasonable and equitable use, all relevant factors are to be considered together and a conclusion reached on the basis of the whole.

Article 7

Obligation not to cause significant harm

1. Watercourse States shall, in utilizing an international watercourse in their territories, take all appropriate measures to prevent the causing of significant harm to other watercourse States.

2. Where significant harm nevertheless is caused to another watercourse State, the States whose use causes such harm shall, in the absence of agreement to such use, take all appropriate measures, having due regard for the provisions of articles 5 and 6, in consultation with the affected State, to eliminate or mitigate such harm and, where appropriate, to discuss the question of compensation.

Article 8

General obligation to cooperate

1. Watercourse States shall cooperate on the basis of sovereign equality, territorial integrity, mutual benefit and good faith in order to attain optimal utilization and adequate protection of an international watercourse.

2. In determining the manner of such cooperation, watercourse States may consider the establishment of joint mechanisms or commissions, as deemed necessary by them, to facilitate cooperation on relevant measures and procedures in the light of experience gained through cooperation in existing joint mechanisms and commissions in various regions.

Article 9

Regular exchange of data and information

1. Pursuant to article 8, watercourse States shall on a regular basis exchange readily available data and information on the condition of the watercourse, in particular that of a hydrological, meteorological, hydrogeological and ecological nature and related to the water quality as well as related forecasts.

2. If a watercourse State is requested by another watercourse State to provide data or information that is not readily available, it shall employ its best efforts to comply with the request but may condition its compliance upon payment by the requesting State of the reasonable costs of collecting and, where appropriate, processing such data or information.

3. Watercourse States shall employ their best efforts to collect and, where appropriate, to process data and information in a manner which facilitates its utilization by the other watercourse States to which it is communicated.

Article 10

Relationship between different kinds of uses

1. In the absence of agreement or custom to the contrary, no use of an international watercourse enjoys inherent priority over other uses.

2. In the event of a conflict between uses of an international watercourse, it shall be resolved with reference to articles 5 to 7, with special regard being given to the requirements of vital human needs.

PART III. PLANNED MEASURES

Article 11

Information concerning planned measures

Watercourse States shall exchange information and consult each other and, if necessary, negotiate on the possible effects of planned measures on the condition of an international watercourse.

Article 12

Notification concerning planned measures with possible adverse effects

Before a watercourse State implements or permits the implementation of planned measures which may have a significant adverse effect upon other watercourse States, it shall provide those States with timely notification thereof. Such notification shall be accompanied by available technical data and information, including the results of any environmental impact assessment, in order to enable the notified States to evaluate the possible effects of the planned measures.

Article 13

Period for reply to notification

Unless otherwise agreed:

(a) A watercourse State providing a notification under article 12 shall allow the notified States a period of six months within which to study and evaluate the possible effects of the planned measures and to communicate the findings to it;

(b) This period shall, at the request of a notified State for which the evaluation of the planned measures poses special difficulty, be extended for a period of six months.

Article 14

Obligations of the notifying State during the period for reply

During the period referred to in article 13, the notifying State:

(a) Shall cooperate with the notified States by providing them, on request, with any additional data and information that is available and necessary for an accurate evaluation; and

(b) Shall not implement or permit the implementation of the planned measures without the consent of the notified States.

Article 15

Reply to notification

The notified States shall communicate their findings to the notifying State as early as possible within the period applicable pursuant to article 13. If a notified State finds that implementation of the planned measures would be inconsistent with the provisions of articles 5 or 7, it shall attach to its finding a documented explanation setting forth the reasons for the finding.

Article 16

Absence of reply to notification

1.   If, within the period applicable pursuant to article 13, the notifying State receives no communication under article 15, it may, subject to its obligations under articles 5 and 7, proceed with the implementation of the planned measures, in accordance with the notification and any other data and information provided to the notified States.

2.   Any claim to compensation by a notified State which has failed to reply within the period applicable pursuant to article 13 may be offset by the costs incurred by the notifying State for action undertaken after the expiration of the time for a reply which would not have been undertaken if the notified State had objected within that period.

Article 17

Consultations and negotiations concerning planned measures

1.   If a communication is made under article 15 that implementation of the planned measures would be inconsistent with the provisions of articles 5 or 7, the notifying State and the State making the communication shall enter into consultations and, if necessary, negotiations with a view to arriving at an equitable resolution of the situation.

2.   The consultations and negotiations shall be conducted on the basis that each State must in good faith pay reasonable regard to the rights and legitimate interests of the other State.

3.   During the course of the consultations and negotiations, the notifying State shall, if so requested by the notified State at the time it makes the communication, refrain from implementing or permitting the implementation of the planned measures for a period of six months unless otherwise agreed.

Article 18

Procedures in the absence of notification

1.   If a watercourse State has reasonable grounds to believe that another watercourse State is planning measures that may have a significant adverse effect upon it, the former State may request the latter to apply the provisions of article 12. The request shall be accompanied by a documented explanation setting forth its grounds.

2.   In the event that the State planning the measures nevertheless finds that it is not under an obligation to provide a notification under article 12, it shall so inform the other State, providing a documented explanation setting forth the reasons for such finding. If this finding does not satisfy the other State, the two States shall, at the request of that other State, promptly enter into consultations and negotiations in the manner indicated in paragraphs 1 and 2 of article 17.

3.   During the course of the consultations and negotiations, the State planning the measures shall, if so requested by the other State at the time it requests the initiation of consultations and negotiations, refrain from implementing or permitting the implementation of those measures for a period of six months unless otherwise agreed.

Article 19

Urgent implementation of planned measures

1.   In the event that the implementation of planned measures is of the utmost urgency in order to protect public health, public safety or other equally important

interests, the State planning the measures may, subject to articles 5 and 7, immediately proceed to implementation, notwithstanding the provisions of article 14 and paragraph 3 of article 17.

2. In such case, a formal declaration of the urgency of the measures shall be communicated without delay to the other watercourse States referred to in article 12 together with the relevant data and information.

3. The State planning the measures shall, at the request of any of the States referred to in paragraph 2, promptly enter into consultations and negotiations with it in the manner indicated in paragraphs 1 and 2 of article 17.

PART IV. PROTECTION, PRESERVATION AND MANAGEMENT

Article 20

Protection and preservation of ecosystems

Watercourse States shall, individually and, where appropriate, jointly, protect and preserve the ecosystems of international watercourses.

Article 21

Prevention, reduction and control of pollution

1. For the purpose of this article, "pollution of an international watercourse" means any detrimental alteration in the composition or quality of the waters of an international watercourse which results directly or indirectly from human conduct.

2. Watercourse States shall, individually and, where appropriate, jointly, prevent, reduce and control the pollution of an international watercourse that may cause significant harm to other watercourse States or to their environment, including harm to human health or safety, to the use of the waters for any beneficial purpose or to the living resources of the watercourse. Watercourse States shall take steps to harmonize their policies in this connection.

3. Watercourse States shall, at the request of any of them, consult with a view to arriving at mutually agreeable measures and methods to prevent, reduce and control pollution of an international watercourse, such as:

(a) Setting joint water quality objectives and criteria;

(b) Establishing techniques and practices to address pollution from point and non-point sources;

(c) Establishing lists of substances the introduction of which into the waters of an international watercourse is to be prohibited, limited, investigated or monitored.

Article 22

Introduction of alien or new species

Watercourse States shall take all measures necessary to prevent the introduction of species, alien or new, into an international watercourse which may have effects detrimental to the ecosystem of the watercourse resulting in significant harm to other watercourse States.

Article 23

Protection and preservation of the marine environment

Watercourse States shall, individually and, where appropriate, in cooperation with other States, take all measures with respect to an international watercourse that are necessary to protect and preserve the marine environment, including estuaries, taking into account generally accepted international rules and standards.

Article 24

Management

1. Watercourse States shall, at the request of any of them, enter into consultations concerning the management of an international watercourse, which may include the establishment of a joint management mechanism.

2. For the purposes of this article, "management" refers, in particular, to:

(a) Planning the sustainable development of an international watercourse and providing for the implementation of any plans adopted; and

(b) Otherwise promoting the rational and optimal utilization, protection and control of the watercourse.

Article 25

Regulation

1. Watercourse States shall cooperate, where appropriate, to respond to needs or opportunities for regulation of the flow of the waters of an international watercourse.

2. Unless otherwise agreed, watercourse States shall participate on an equitable basis in the construction and maintenance or defrayal of the costs of such regulation works as they may have agreed to undertake.

3. For the purposes of this article, "regulation" means the use of hydraulic works or any other continuing measure to alter, vary or otherwise control the flow of the waters of an international watercourse.

Article 26

Installations

1. Watercourse States shall, within their respective territories, employ their best efforts to maintain and protect installations, facilities and other works related to an international watercourse.

2. Watercourse States shall, at the request of any of them which has reasonable grounds to believe that it may suffer significant adverse effects, enter into consultations with regard to:

(a) The safe operation and maintenance of installations, facilities or other works related to an international watercourse; and

(b) The protection of installations, facilities or other works from wilful or negligent acts or the forces of nature.

PART V. HARMFUL CONDITIONS AND EMERGENCY SITUATIONS

Article 27

Prevention and mitigation of harmful conditions

Watercourse States shall, individually and, where appropriate, jointly, take all appropriate measures to prevent or mitigate conditions related to an international watercourse that may be harmful to other watercourse States, whether resulting from natural causes or human conduct, such as flood or ice conditions, water-borne diseases, siltation, erosion, salt-water intrusion, drought or desertification.

Article 28

Emergency situations

1.　For the purposes of this article, "emergency" means a situation that causes, or poses an imminent threat of causing, serious harm to watercourse States or other States and that results suddenly from natural causes, such as floods, the breaking up of ice, landslides or earthquakes, or from human conduct, such as industrial accidents.

2.　A watercourse State shall, without delay and by the most expeditious means available, notify other potentially affected States and competent international organizations of any emergency originating within its territory.

3.　A watercourse State within whose territory an emergency originates shall, in cooperation with potentially affected States and, where appropriate, competent international organizations, immediately take all practicable measures necessitated by the circumstances to prevent, mitigate and eliminate harmful effects of the emergency.

4.　When necessary, watercourse States shall jointly develop contingency plans for responding to emergencies, in cooperation, where appropriate, with other potentially affected States and competent international organizations.

PART VI.　MISCELLANEOUS PROVISIONS

Article 29

International watercourses and installations in time of armed conflict

International watercourses and related installations, facilities and other works shall enjoy the protection accorded by the principles and rules of international law applicable in international and non-international armed conflict and shall not be used in violation of those principles and rules.

Article 30

Indirect procedures

In cases where there are serious obstacles to direct contacts between watercourse States, the States concerned shall fulfil their obligations of cooperation provided for in the present Convention, including exchange of data and information, notification, communication, consultations and negotiations, through any indirect procedure accepted by them.

Article 31

Data and information vital to national defence or security

Nothing in the present Convention obliges a watercourse State to provide data or information vital to its national defence or security. Nevertheless, that State shall cooperate in good faith with the other watercourse States with a view to providing as much information as possible under the circumstances.

Article 32

Non-discrimination

Unless the watercourse States concerned have agreed otherwise for the protection of the interests of persons, natural or juridical, who have suffered or are under a serious threat of suffering significant transboundary harm as a result of activities related to an international watercourse, a watercourse State shall not discriminate on the basis of nationality or residence or place where the injury occurred, in granting to such persons, in accordance with its legal system, access to judicial or other procedures, or a right to claim compensation or other relief in respect of significant harm caused by such activities carried on in its territory.

Article 33

Settlement of disputes

1. In the event of a dispute between two or more Parties concerning the interpretation or application of the present Convention, the Parties concerned shall, in the absence of an applicable agreement between them, seek a settlement of the dispute by peaceful means in accordance with the following provisions.

2. If the Parties concerned cannot reach agreement by negotiation requested by one of them, they may jointly seek the good offices of, or request mediation or conciliation by, a third party, or make use, as appropriate, of any joint watercourse institutions that may have been established by them or agree to submit the dispute to arbitration or to the International Court of Justice.

3. Subject to the operation of paragraph 10, if after six months from the time of the request for negotiations referred to in paragraph 2, the Parties concerned have not been able to settle their dispute through negotiation or any other means referred to in paragraph 2, the dispute shall be submitted, at the request of any of the parties to the dispute, to impartial fact-finding in accordance with paragraphs 4 to 9, unless the Parties otherwise agree.

4. A Fact-finding Commission shall be established, composed of one member nominated by each Party concerned and in addition a member not having the nationality of any of the Parties concerned chosen by the nominated members who shall serve as Chairman.

5. If the members nominated by the Parties are unable to agree on a Chairman within three months of the request for the establishment of the Commission, any Party concerned may request the Secretary–General of the United Nations to appoint the Chairman who shall not have the nationality of any of the parties to the dispute or of any riparian State of the watercourse concerned. If one of the Parties fails to nominate a member within three months of the initial request pursuant to paragraph 3, any other Party concerned may request the Secretary–General of the United Nations to appoint a person who shall not have the nationality of any of the parties to the dispute or of any riparian State of the watercourse concerned. The person so appointed shall constitute a single-member Commission.

6. The Commission shall determine its own procedure.

7. The Parties concerned have the obligation to provide the Commission with such information as it may require and, on request, to permit the Commission to have access to their respective territory and to inspect any facilities, plant, equipment, construction or natural feature relevant for the purpose of its inquiry.

8. The Commission shall adopt its report by a majority vote, unless it is a single-member Commission, and shall submit that report to the Parties concerned setting forth its findings and the reasons therefor and such recommendations as it deems appropriate for an equitable solution of the dispute, which the Parties concerned shall consider in good faith.

9. The expenses of the Commission shall be borne equally by the Parties concerned.

10. When ratifying, accepting, approving or acceding to the present Convention, or at any time thereafter, a Party which is not a regional economic integration organization may declare in a written instrument submitted to the Depositary that, in respect of any dispute not resolved in accordance with paragraph 2, it recognizes as compulsory ipso facto and without special agreement in relation to any Party accepting the same obligation:

(a) Submission of the dispute to the International Court of Justice; and/or

(b) Arbitration by an arbitral tribunal established and operating, unless the parties to the dispute otherwise agreed, in accordance with the procedure laid down in the annex to the present Convention.

A Party which is a regional economic integration organization may make a declaration with like effect in relation to arbitration in accordance with subparagraph (b).

PART VII.   FINAL CLAUSES

Article 34

Signature

The present Convention shall be open for signature by all States and by regional economic integration organizations from ... until ... at United Nations Headquarters in New York.

Article 35

Ratification, acceptance, approval or accession

1.   The present Convention is subject to ratification, acceptance, approval or accession by States and by regional economic integration organizations. The instruments of ratification, acceptance, approval or accession shall be deposited with the Secretary–General of the United Nations.

2.   Any regional economic integration organization which becomes a Party to this Convention without any of its member States being a Party shall be bound by all the obligations under the Convention. In the case of such organizations, one or more of whose member States is a Party to this Convention, the organization and its member States shall decide on their respective responsibilities for the performance of their obligations under the Convention. In such cases, the organization and the member States shall not be entitled to exercise rights under the Convention concurrently.

3.   In their instruments of ratification, acceptance, approval or accession, the regional economic integration organizations shall declare the extent of their competence with respect to the matters governed by the Convention. These organizations shall also inform the Secretary–General of the United Nations of any substantial modification in the extent of their competence.

Article 36

Entry into force

1.   The present Convention shall enter into force on the ninetieth day following the date of deposit of the thirty-fifth instrument of ratification, acceptance, approval or accession with the Secretary–General of the United Nations.

2.   For each State or regional economic integration organization that ratifies, accepts or approves the Convention or accedes thereto after the deposit of the thirty-fifth instrument of ratification, acceptance, approval or accession, the Convention shall enter into force on the ninetieth day after the deposit by such State or regional economic integration organization of its instrument of ratification, acceptance, approval or accession.

3.   For the purposes of paragraphs 1 and 2, any instrument deposited by a regional economic integration organization shall not be counted as additional to those deposited by States.

Article 37

Authentic texts

The original of the present Convention, of which the Arabic, Chinese, English, French, Russian and Spanish texts are equally authentic, shall be deposited with the Secretary–General of the United Nations.

3.28 BERLIN RULES ON WATER RESOURCES (WITHOUT COMMENTS). **Adopted by the International Law Association at Berlin, 21 August 2004. 71 ILA 337.** *Reprinted in* **5 Weston & Carlson V.F.39**

CHAPTER I
SCOPE

Article 1
Scope

1. These Rules express international law applicable to the management of the waters of international drainage basins and applicable to all waters, as appropriate.

2. Nothing in these Rules affects rights or obligations created by treaty or special custom.

Article 2
Implementation of These Rules

1. States shall, where appropriate, enact laws and regulations to accomplish the purposes set forth in these Rules and shall adopt efficient and adequate administrative measures, including management plans, and judicial procedures for the enforcement of these laws and regulations.

2. States shall undertake educational and research programs as necessary to assure the technical capacity necessary for State and communal authorities to fulfill the obligations specified in this Chapter and in other Rules.

Article 3
Definitions

For the purposes of these Articles, these terms have the following meanings:

1. "Aquatic environment" means all surface waters and groundwater, the lands and subsurface geological formations connected to those waters, and the atmosphere related to those waters and lands.

2. "Aquifer" means a subsurface layer or layers of geological strata of sufficient porosity and permeability to allow either a flow of or the withdrawal of usable quantities of groundwater.

3. A "basin State" is a State the territory of which includes any portion of an international drainage basin.

4. "Damage" includes:

   a. loss of life or personal injury;

   b. loss of or injury to property or other economic losses;

   c. environmental harm; and

   d. the costs of reasonable measures to prevent or minimize such loss, injury, or harm.

5. "Drainage basin" means an area determined by the geographic limits of a system of interconnected waters, the surface waters of which normally share a common terminus.

6. "Ecological integrity" means the natural condition of waters and other resources sufficient to assure the biological, chemical, and physical integrity of the aquatic environment.

7. "Environment" includes the waters, land, air, flora, and fauna that exist in a particular region at a particular time.

8. "Environmental harm" includes:

a.   injury to the environment and any other loss or damage caused by such harm; and

b.   the costs of reasonable measures to restore the environment actually undertaken or to be undertaken.

9.   "Flood" means a rising of water to levels that have detrimental effects on or in one or more basin States.

10.   "Flood control" means measures to protect land areas from floods or to minimize damage therefrom.

11.   "Groundwater" means water beneath the surface of the ground located in a saturated zone and in direct contact with the ground or soil.

12.   "Hazardous substances" means substances that are bio-accumulative, carcinogenic, mutagenic, teratogenic, or toxic.

13.   An "international drainage basin" is a drainage basin extending over two or more States.

14.   "Management of waters" and "to manage waters" includes the development, use, protection, allocation, regulation, and control of waters.

15.   "Person" means any natural or juridical person.

16.   "Pollution" means any detrimental change in the composition or quality of waters that results directly or indirectly from human conduct.

17.   "Regional economic integration organization" means an organization constituted by sovereign States of a given region, to which its member States have transferred competence in respect of matters governed by these Rules.

18.   "State" means a sovereign State or a regional economic integration organization.

19.   "Sustainable use" means the integrated management of resources to assure efficient use of and equitable access to waters for the benefit of current and future generations while preserving renewable resources and maintaining non-renewable resources to the maximum extent reasonably possible.

20.   "Vital human needs" means waters used for immediate human survival, including drinking, cooking, and sanitary needs, as well as water needed for the immediate sustenance of a household.

21.   "Waters" means all surface water and groundwater other than marine waters.

CHAPTER II
PRINCIPLES OF INTERNATIONAL LAW GOVERNING THE MANAGEMENT OF ALL WATERS

Article 4
Participation by Persons

States shall take steps to assure that persons likely to be affected are able to participate in the processes whereby decisions are made concerning the management of waters.

Article 5
Conjunctive Management

States shall use their best efforts to manage surface waters, groundwater, and other pertinent waters in a unified and comprehensive manner.

Article 6
Integrated Management

States shall use their best efforts to integrate appropriately the management of waters with the management of other resources.

Article 7
Sustainability

States shall take all appropriate measures to manage waters sustainably.

Article 8
Minimization of Environmental Harm

States shall take all appropriate measures to prevent or minimize environmental harm.

Article 9
Interpretation of These Rules

1. All of these Rules are to be interpreted consistently with the principles of this Chapter.

2. References to States in these Rules encompass States acting individually or jointly and States acting with or through international organizations, as appropriate.

CHAPTER III
INTERNATIONALLY SHARED WATERS

Article 10
Participation by Basin States

1. Basin States have the right to participate in the management of waters of an international drainage basin in an equitable, reasonable, and sustainable manner.

2. Basin States shall define the waters to which an international agreement regarding the management of waters of an international drainage basin applies; such an international agreement may apply to all or part of the waters of an international drainage basin or to a particular project or use, except that a use by one or more basin States shall not cause a significant adverse effect on the rights of or uses in another basin State without the latter State's express consent.

Article 11
Cooperation

Basin States shall cooperate in good faith in the management of waters of an international drainage basin for the mutual benefit of the participating States.

Article 12
Equitable Utilization

1. Basin States shall in their respective territories manage the waters of an international drainage basin in an equitable and reasonable manner having due regard for the obligation not to cause significant harm to other basin States.

2. In particular, basin States shall develop and use the waters of the basin in order to attain the optimal and sustainable use thereof and benefits therefrom, taking into account the interests of other basin States, consistent with adequate protection of the waters.

Article 13
Determining an Equitable and Reasonable Use

1. Equitable and reasonable use within the meaning of Article 12 is to be determined through consideration of all relevant factors in each particular case.

2. Relevant factors to be considered include, but are not limited to:

    a. Geographic, hydrographic, hydrological, hydrogeological, climatic, ecological, and other natural features;

    b. The social and economic needs of the basin States concerned;

    c. The population dependent on the waters of the international drainage basin in each basin State;

    d. The effects of the use or uses of the waters of the international drainage basin in one basin State upon other basin States;

    e. Existing and potential uses of the waters of the international drainage basin;

    f. Conservation, protection, development, and economy of use of the water resources of the international drainage basin and the costs of measures taken to achieve these purposes;

    g. The availability of alternatives, of comparable value, to the particular planned or existing use;

    h. The sustainability of proposed or existing uses; and

    i. The minimization of environmental harm.

3. The weight of each factor is to be determined by its importance in comparison with other relevant factors. In determining what is a reasonable and equitable use, all relevant factors are to be considered together and a conclusion reached on the basis of the whole.

Article 14
Preferences among Uses

1. In determining an equitable and reasonable use, States shall first allocate waters to satisfy vital human needs.

2. No other use or category of uses shall have an inherent preference over any other use or category of uses.

Article 15
Using Allocated Water in Other Basin States

1. Allocation by agreement or otherwise to one basin State does not prevent use by another basin State to the extent that the basin State to which the water is allocated does not in fact use of the water.

2. Use of a water for purposes of this Article includes water necessary to assure ecological flows or otherwise to maintain ecological integrity or to minimize environmental harm.

3. Use of water by a basin State other than the one to which the water is allocated does not preclude the basin State to which the water is allocated from using the water when it chooses to do so.

Article 16
Avoidance of Transboundary Harm

Basin States, in managing the waters of an international drainage basin, shall refrain from and prevent acts or omissions within their territory that cause significant harm to another basin State having due regard for the right of each basin State to make equitable and reasonable use of the waters.

CHAPTER IV
RIGHTS OF PERSONS

Article 17
The Right of Access to Water

1. Every individual has a right of access to sufficient, safe, acceptable, physically accessible, and affordable water to meet that individual's vital human needs.

2. States shall ensure the implementation of the right of access to water on a nondiscriminatory basis.

3. States shall progressively realize the right of access to water by:

a. Refraining from interfering directly or indirectly with the enjoyment of the right;

b. Preventing third parties from interfering with the enjoyment of the right;

c. Taking measures to facilitate individuals access to water, such as defining and enforcing appropriate legal rights of access to and use of water; and

d. Providing water or the means for obtaining water when individuals are unable, through reasons beyond their control, to access water through their own efforts.

4. States shall monitor and review periodically, through a participatory and transparent process, the realization of the right of access to water.

Article 18
Public Participation and Access to Information

1. In the management of waters, States shall assure that persons subject to the State's jurisdiction and likely to be affected by water management decisions are able to participate, directly or indirectly, in processes by which those decisions are made and have a reasonable opportunity to express their views on plans, programs, projects, or activities relating to waters.

2. In order to enable such participation, States shall provide access to information relevant to the management of waters without unreasonable difficulty or unreasonable charges.

3. The information subject to access under this Article includes, without being limited to, impact assessments relating to the management of waters.

4. In providing information consistently with this Article, States need not provide access to information that would compromise:

a. Intellectual property rights, including commercial or industrial secrets;

b. Rights of individual privacy;

c. Criminal investigations or trials;

d. National security; and

e. Information that could endanger ecosystems, historic sites, and other naturally or culturally important objects or locations.

Article 19
Education

States shall undertake education at all levels to promote and encourage understanding of the issues that arise under these Rules.

Article 20
Protection of Particular Communities

States shall take all appropriate steps to protect the rights, interests, and special needs of communities and of indigenous peoples or other particularly vulnerable groups likely to be affected by the management of waters, even while developing the waters for the benefit of the entire State or group of States.

Article 21
Duty to Compensate Displaced by Water Projects or Programs

States shall compensate persons or communities displaced by a water program, project, or activity and shall assure that adequate provisions are made for the preservation of the livelihoods and culture of displaced persons or communities.

CHAPTER V
PROTECTION OF THE AQUATIC ENVIRONMENTS

Article 22
Ecological Integrity

States shall take all appropriate measures to protect the ecological integrity necessary to sustain ecosystems dependent on particular waters.

Article 23
The Precautionary Approach

1.   In implementing obligations under this Chapter, States shall apply the precautionary approach.

2.   States shall take all appropriate measures to prevent, eliminate, reduce, or control harm to the aquatic environment when there is a serious risk of significant adverse effect on or to the sustainable use of waters even without conclusive proof of a causal relation between an act or omission and its expected effects.

Article 24
Ecological Flows

States shall take all appropriate measures to ensure flows adequate to protect the ecological integrity of the waters of a drainage basin, including estuarine waters.

Article 25
Alien Species

States shall take all appropriate measures to prevent the introduction, whether intentionally or otherwise, of alien species into the aquatic environment if the alien species might have a significant adverse effect on an ecosystem dependent on the particular waters.

Article 26
Hazardous Substances

States shall take all appropriate measures to prevent the introduction of hazardous substances into the waters subject to its jurisdiction or control.

Article 27
Pollution

1.   States shall prevent, eliminate, reduce, or control pollution in order to minimize environmental harm.

2. When there is a relevant water quality standard established pursuant to Article 28, States shall take all appropriate measures to assure compliance with that standard.

3. States shall ensure that wastes, pollutants, and hazardous substances are handled, treated, and disposed of using the best available techniques or the best environmental practices, as appropriate to protect the aquatic environment.

Article 28
Establishing Water Quality Standards

1. States shall establish water quality standards sufficient to protect public health and the aquatic environment and to provide water to satisfy needs, in particular for:

     a. Providing drinking water of sufficiently good quality for human health;

     b. Preserving ecosystems;

     c. Providing water for agriculture, including irrigation and animal husbandry; and

     d. Providing for recreational needs with due regard for sanitary and aesthetic requirements.

2. Standards established under this Article shall include, among others:

     a. Specific quality objectives for all waters within a State's jurisdiction or control, taking into account the uses of the particular waters;

     b. Specific quality objectives applicable to a particular basin or part of a basin.

CHAPTER VI
IMPACT ASSESSMENTS

Article 29
The Obligation to Assess Environmental Impacts

1. States shall undertake prior and continuing assessment of the impact of programs, projects, or activities that may have a significant effect on the aquatic environment or the sustainable development of waters.

2. Impacts to be assessed include, among others:

     a. Effects on human health and safety;

     b. Effects on the environment;

     c. Effects on existing or prospective economic activity;

     d. Effects on cultural or socio-economic conditions; and

     e. Effects on the sustainability of the use of waters.

Article 30
Participation in Impact Assessments in Another State

A person who suffers or is under a serious threat of suffering damage from programs, projects, or activities relating to the waters in another State shall be entitled in the other State to the same extent and on the same conditions as a person in that State to participate in an environmental impact assessment procedure.

Article 31
The Impact Assessment Process

Assessment of the impacts of any program, project, or activity shall include, among others:

a.   Assessment of the waters and the environments likely to be affected;

b.   Description of the proposed activity and its likely effects, with particular emphasis on any transboundary effects;

c.   Identification of ecosystems likely to affected, including an assessment of the living and non-living resources of the relevant water basin or basins;

d.   Description of mitigation measures appropriate to minimize environmental harm;

e.   Appraisal of the institutional arrangements and facilities in the relevant drainage basin or basins;

f.   Assessment of the sources and levels of pollutants in the relevant drainage basin or basins, and of their effects on human health, ecological integrity, and amenities;

g.   Identification of human activities that are likely to be affected;

h.   Explanation of predictive methods and underlying assumptions as well as the relevant data used, including identification of gaps in knowledge and uncertainties encountered in compiling the required information, including assessment of the risk of major accidents;

i.   Where appropriate, an outline for monitoring and management programs and plans for post-project analysis;

j.   A statement of the reasonable alternatives, including a non-action alternative; and

k.   An adequate non-technical summary.

CHAPTER VII
EXTREME SITUATIONS

Article 32
Responses to Extreme Conditions

1.   States shall take all appropriate measures to prevent, reduce, eliminate, or control all conditions of waters, whether resulting from human conduct or otherwise, that pose a significant risk:

a.   To human life or health;

b.   Of harm to property; or

c.   Of environmental harm.

2.   States, promptly and using the most expeditious means available, shall notify other potentially affected States and competent international organizations of any harmful condition of waters under this Article that originates within its jurisdiction or control.

3.   States shall develop notification systems and contingency plans for responding to harmful conditions under this Article.

Article 33
Polluting Accidents

1.   States shall take all appropriate measures as quickly as possible to reduce, eliminate, or control pollution resulting from accidental events.

2.   States shall use the most expeditious method available to notify other affected States and competent international organizations of accidents that pose a significant risk of serious pollution to waters within another State's jurisdiction or control, in particular when pollution involves hazardous substances.

3. States shall develop notification systems and contingency plans for responding to accidents under this Article.

Article 34
Floods

1. States shall cooperate in developing and implementing measures for flood control, having due regard to the interests of other States likely to be affected by the flooding.

2. States likely to be affected by flooding shall use the most expeditious method available to communicate among themselves and with international organizations as soon as possible regarding any events likely to create floods or dangerous rises of water levels in their territory, establishing:

    a. An effective system of transmission in order to fulfill this obligation;

    b. Measures to ensure priority to the communication of flood warnings in emergency cases; and

    c. A special system of translation, if necessary, between the basin States.

3. States shall jointly develop contingency plans for responding to foreseeable flood conditions.

4. In addition to contingency plans, cooperation with respect to flood control shall, by agreement between affected States and when appropriate international organizations, include among other matters:

    a. The collection and exchange of relevant data;

    b. The preparation of surveys, investigations, studies, and flood plain maps, and their mutual exchange;

    c. The planning and designing of relevant measures, including flood plain management and flood control works;

    d. The execution, operation, and maintenance of flood control measures;

    e. Flood forecasting and communication of flood warnings;

    f. Developing or strengthening necessary legislation and appropriate institutions for achieving these goals; and

    g. The setting up of a regular information service charged to transmit the height of water levels and the discharge quantities.

5. States shall maintain all flood control measures in good order, and shall ensure the prompt execution of repairs or other emergency measures taken to assure the minimization of damage from flooding.

6. The use of the channel of rivers and lakes for the discharge of excess waters shall be free and not subject to any limitation provided such discharge is not incompatible with the object of flood control and does not adversely affect the rights or interests of other states.

Article 35
Droughts

1. States shall cooperate in the management of waters to prevent, control, or mitigate droughts, having due regard to the interests of other basin States.

2. Cooperation with respect to drought shall, by agreement between affected States and when appropriate with international organizations, include among other matters:

a. An integrated strategy for addressing the physical, biological, and socio-economic aspects of the drought;

b. The definition of criteria that activate the provisions of this Article;

c. An integrated strategy for mitigating the effects of drought and moving towards the sustainable use of waters;

d. The development or strengthening necessary legislation and appropriate institutions for achieving these goals; and

e. The allocation of adequate resources to achieve these goals in accordance with their circumstances and capabilities.

3. States likely to be affected by drought shall promptly communicate among themselves and with competent international organizations whenever the criteria specified pursuant to paragraph 2(b) are met.

4. Nothing in this Article limits the rights of States to protect themselves unilaterally from the effects of droughts so long as the measures taken do not violate obligations under these Rules or otherwise violate the rights of other States.

CHAPTER VIII
GROUNDWATER

Article 36
Application of These Rules to Aquifers

1. The Rules of this Chapter apply to all aquifers, including aquifers that do not contribute water to, or receive water from, surface waters or receive no significant contemporary recharge from any source.

2. States, in managing aquifers, are subject to all Rules expressed in these Articles, taking into account the special characteristics of groundwater.

Article 37
Managing Aquifers Generally

States shall manage groundwater conjunctively with the surface waters of any basin of which it is a part, taking into account any interconnections between aquifers or between and an aquifer and a body of surface water, as well as any impact on aquifers caused by activities within the State's jurisdiction or control.

Article 38
Precautionary Management of Aquifers

States, in accordance with the precautionary approach, shall take early action and develop long-term plans to ensure the sustainable use of groundwater and of the aquifers in which the groundwater is contained.

Article 39
Duty to Acquire Information

In order to comply with this Chapter, States shall take all appropriate steps to acquire the information necessary to manage groundwater and aquifers efficiently and effectively, including:

a. Monitoring groundwater levels, pressures, and quality;

b. Developing aquifer vulnerability maps;

c. Assessing the impacts on groundwater and aquifers of industrial, agricultural, and other activities; and

d. Any other measures appropriate to the circumstances of the aquifer.

Article 40
Sustainability Applied to Groundwater

1.   States shall give effect to the principle of sustainability in managing aquifers, taking into account natural and artificial recharge.

2.   The rule in paragraph 1 does not preclude the withdrawal of groundwater from an aquifer that is receiving no significant contemporary recharge.

Article 41
Protecting Aquifers

1.   States shall take all appropriate measures to prevent, insofar as possible, any pollution of, and the degradation of the hydraulic integrity of, aquifers.

2.   States in fulfilling their obligation to prevent pollution of an aquifer shall take special care to prevent, eliminate, reduce, or control:

   a.   The direct or indirect discharge of pollutants, whether from point or non-point sources;

   b.   The injection of water that is polluted or would otherwise degrade an aquifer;

   c.   Saline water intrusion; or

   d.   Any other source of pollution.

3.   States shall take all appropriate measures to abate the effects of the pollution of aquifers.

4.   States shall integrate aquifers into their programs of general environmental protection, including but not limited to:

   a.   The management of other waters;

   b.   Land use planning and management; and

   c.   Other programs of general environmental protection.

5.   States shall specially protect sites where groundwater is withdrawn from or recharged to an aquifer.

Article 42
Transboundary Aquifers

1.   The Rules applicable to internationally shared waters apply to an aquifer if:

   a.   It is connected to surface waters that are part of an international drainage basin; or

   b.   It is intersected by the boundaries between two or more States even without a connection to surface waters that form an international drainage basin.

2.   Whenever possible and appropriate, basin States sharing an aquifer referred to in paragraph 1 shall manage an aquifer in its entirety.

3.   In managing the waters of an aquifer referred to in paragraph 1, basin States shall consult and exchange information and data at the request of any one of them and shall cooperate in the collection and analyzing additional needed information pertinent to the obligations under these Rules.

4.   Basin States shall cooperate according to the procedures in Chapter XI to set drawdown rates in order to assure the equitable utilization of the waters of an aquifer referred in paragraph 1, having due regard for the obligation not to cause significant harm to other basin States and to the obligation to protect the aquifer.

5.   Basin States sharing an aquifer referred to in paragraph 1 shall cooperate in managing the recharge of the aquifer.

6. Basin States sharing an aquifer referred to in paragraph 1 shall refrain from and prevent acts or omissions within their territory that cause significant harm to another basin State, having due regard to the right of each basin State to make equitable and reasonable use of the waters.

CHAPTER IX
NAVIGATION

Article 43
Freedom of Navigation

1. Subject to the limitations or qualifications in this Chapter, each riparian State is entitled to freedom of navigation on the entire watercourse to which they are riparian on a basis of equality and nondiscrimination.

2. A "riparian State" for purposes of this Chapter is a State traversed by or separated from another State by the navigable portion of a watercourse.

3. A "watercourse" for purposes of this Chapter is a river, lake, or other surface body of water on which navigation is possible from one riparian State to another or from a riparian State to the high seas.

4. A watercourse is "navigable" for purposes of this Chapter if, in its natural or canalized condition, the watercourse is currently used for commercial navigation or is capable of being so used in its natural condition.

5. "Freedom of navigation" for the purposes of this Chapter includes:

   a. Freedom of movement on the entire navigable course of the watercourse;

   b. Freedom to enter ports and to make use of plants and docks; and

   c. Freedom to transport goods and passengers, directly or through transshipment, between the territory of one riparian State and the territory of another riparian State and between the territory of a riparian State and the open sea.

Article 44
Limitations on Freedom of Navigation

1. Absent special arrangements, only vessels of a riparian State are entitled to exercise freedom of navigation.

2. Movement by vessels exercising freedom of navigation shall be continuous and expeditious, and not prejudicial to the peace, good order, or security of the riparian State.

3. Stopping or anchoring is allowed when incidental to ordinary navigation or if necessary because of *force majeure,* distress, or for the rendering of assistance to persons, ships, or aircraft in danger or distress.

4. Riparian States may restrict or prohibit the loading by vessels of a foreign State of goods and passengers in its territory for discharge in such territory.

5. Nondiscriminatory fees may be charged by a riparian State to recover the costs of services provided to vessels exercising freedom of navigation.

Article 45
Regulating Navigation

In order to achieve good order in the navigable portion of a watercourse within its jurisdiction, a riparian State may regulate, limit, or suspend navigation, as appropriate for the purposes of protection of public safety, health, or the environment, over that portion of the watercourse within its jurisdiction, provided the State does not discriminate against the shipping of another riparian State and does not unreasonably interfere with the enjoyment of the rights of freedom of navigation defined in Articles 43 and 44.

Article 46
Maintaining Navigation

Each riparian State is, to the extent of the means available, required to maintain in good order that portion of a navigable watercourse within its jurisdiction.

Article 47
Granting the Right to Navigate to Non–Riparian States

Riparian States, individually or jointly, may grant rights of navigation to non-riparian States on watercourses or other waters within its or their territory.

Article 48
Exclusion of Public Vessels

Freedom of navigation does not apply to the navigation of warships or of a government vessel used for non-commercial purposes except by agreement of the States concerned.

Article 49
Effect of War or Similar Emergencies on Navigation

1. In time of war, other armed conflict, or public emergency constituting a threat to the security of a riparian State, it may take measures derogating from its obligations under this Chapter to the extent strictly required by the exigencies of the situation.

2. No measures taken under this Article are to violate a State's other obligations under international law.

3. Riparian States shall in any case facilitate navigation for humanitarian purposes.

CHAPTER X
PROTECTION OF WATERS AND WATER INSTALLATIONS DURING WAR OR ARMED CONFLICT

Article 50
Rendering Water Unfit for Use

Combatants shall not poison or render otherwise unfit for human consumption water indispensable for the health and survival of the civilian population

Article 51
Targeting Waters or Water Installations

1. Combatants shall not, for military purposes or as reprisals, destroy or divert waters, or destroy water installations, if such actions would cause disproportionate suffering to civilians.

2. In no event shall combatants attack, destroy, remove, or render useless waters and water installations indispensable for the health and survival of the civilian population if such actions may be expected to leave the civilian population with such inadequate water as to cause its death from lack of water or force its movement.

3. In recognition of the vital requirements of any party to a conflict in the defense of its national territory against invasion, a party to the conflict may derogate from the prohibitions contained in paragraphs 1 and 2 within such territories under its own control where required by imperative military necessity.

4. In any event, waters and water installations shall enjoy the protection accorded by the principles and rules of international law applicable in war or armed conflict and shall not be used in violation of those principles and rules.

Article 52
Ecological Targets

Combatants shall not, for military purposes or as reprisals, destroy or divert waters, or destroy water installations, when such acts would cause widespread, long-term, and severe ecological damage prejudicial to the health or survival of the population or if such acts would fundamentally impair the ecological integrity of waters.

Article 53
Dams and Dikes

1. In addition to the other protections provided by these Rules, combatants shall not make dams and dikes the objects of attack, even where these are military objectives, if such an attack may cause the release of dangerous forces and consequent severe losses among the civilian population.

2. This protection ceases if the dam or dike is used for other than its normal function and in regular, significant, and direct support of military operations and such attack is the only feasible way to terminate such use.

Article 54
Occupied Territories

1. An occupying State shall administer water resources in an occupied territory in a way that ensures the sustainable use of the water resources and that minimizes environmental harm.

2. An occupying State shall protect water installations and ensure an adequate water supply to the population of an occupied territory.

Article 55
Effect of War or Armed Conflict on Water Treaties

1. Treaties creating legal regimes for an international watercourse or part thereof are not terminated by war or armed conflict between the parties to the treaty.

2. Such Treaties or parts thereof shall be suspended only where military necessity requires suspension and where suspension does not violate any provision of this Chapter.

CHAPTER XI
INTERNATIONAL COOPERATION AND ADMINISTRATION

Article 56
Exchange of Information

1. Basin States shall regularly provide to other basin States all relevant and available information on the quantity and quality of the waters of a basin or aquifer and on the state of the aquatic environment and the causes for any changes in waters, in an aquifer, or in the aquatic environment, including, but not limited to, a list of all known water withdrawals and sources of pollution.

2. Basin States shall employ their best efforts to collect and, where appropriate, to process data and information in a manner that facilitates its use by other basin States to which it is to be communicated.

3. The exchange of information under this Article shall include all relevant technical information for a program, plan, project, or activity, including the results of any relevant impact assessment.

4. Basin States shall cooperate with other basin States to provide as much information as possible under the circumstances having due regard for the provisions of paragraph 5.

5. States need not provide information that would compromise:

    a. Intellectual property rights, including commercial or industrial secrets;

    b. Rights of individual privacy;

    c. Criminal investigations or trials;

    d. National security; and

    e. Information that could endanger ecosystems, historic sites, and other naturally or culturally important objects or locations.

Article 57
Notification of Programs, Plans Projects, or Activities

1. Basin States shall promptly notify other States or competent international organizations that may be affected significantly by a program, plan, project, or activity.

2. Basin States shall also promptly inform other States or competent international organizations whenever necessary to accomplish obligations set forth in these Rules.

3. A basin State that has reasonable grounds to conclude that a program, project, or activity to be undertaken or already undertaken within another State may involve a significant effect on waters or the aquatic environment within the first State shall so inform the other State, providing documentary support for the conclusion, and request the other State to exchange information under Article 56 and to consult under Article 58.

Article 58
Consultations

1. Basin States shall consult one another and with competent international organizations on actual or potential issues relating to their shared waters or to the aquatic environment in order to reach, by methods of their own choice, a solution consistent with their rights and duties under international law.

2. Basin States that conclude that a program, plan, project, or activity would significantly adversely affect them shall promptly notify the State responsible for the program, plan, project, or activity of those conclusions along with corroborating documentation. Upon receipt of such a claim, the interested States shall promptly consult each other

3. In conducting consultations and negotiations under paragraphs 1 and 2, basin States shall proceed in good faith to give reasonable regard to the rights and legitimate interests of the other basin States involved, and if necessary, to coordinate approaches to the program, plan, project, or activity in order to arrive at an equitable and sustainable resolution of the situation.

4. During consultations, a basin State planning a program, project, or activity shall, if requested the another interested State, refrain from implementing or allowing the implementation of the program, plan, project, or activity for a reasonable period.

5. Consultation shall not be used to delay unreasonably the implementation of programs, plans, projects, or activities that are the subject of the consultation.

Article 59
Failure to Consult

1. If a State subject to a duty to consult pursuant to Article 58 does not enter into consultations or negotiations within a reasonable time, the other interested States may implement a proposed program, plan, project, or activity so long as it is consistent with the State's obligations under these international law.

2. A State's obligation to pay compensation for violations of customary international law to another interested State may be offset by expenses incurred by the obligated State as result of the other State's failure to respond.

Article 60
Requests for Impact Assessments or Other Information

1. A basin State, at the request of another basin State likely to be affected by a program, plan, project, or activity envisaged to occur or occurring within the requested State, shall undertake an impact assessment of the program, plan, project, or activity on an ongoing basis.

2. A basin States, at the request of another basin State likely to be affected by a program, project, or activity envisaged to occur within the requested State, shall provide all relevant information in the requested State's possession or which the requested State can acquire through reasonable efforts, limited as in Article 56(2).

3. A basin State requested by another basin State to provide information or to conduct an impact assessment pursuant to this Article shall employ its best efforts to comply with the request but may condition its compliance upon reciprocal exchanges by the requesting State or upon reimbursement for the reasonable costs of collecting and processing the information.

Article 61
Urgent Implementation of Programs, Plan, Projects, or Activities

1. When implementation of a program, plan, project, or activity is of the utmost importance to the public health, public safety, or similar interests, the basin State considering the program, project, or activity may proceed immediately to implement the program, project, or activity within awaiting the completion of the consultation process, but without violating the other obligations expressed in these Articles.

2. A basin State that undertakes to implement a program, plan, project, or activity pursuant to this Article shall immediately notify other basin States and shall disclose all relevant data and information.

3. Notwithstanding a basin State's decision to implement a program, plan, project, or activity pursuant to this Article, the implementing basin State shall, at the request of another interested basin State, consult and negotiate as provided in Article 58.

Article 62
Harmonization of National Laws and Policies

In enacting national laws pursuant to this Article, basin States shall consult other interested States with a view to harmonizing the laws and policies regarding the equitable use and sustainable development of waters and of the aquatic environment.

Article 63
Protection of Works

1. Basin States shall, within their territories, use their best efforts to maintain and protect installations, facilities, and other works related to the management of waters of an international drainage basin.

2. Basin States shall, at the request of another basin State that has reasonable grounds to conclude that its interests may be significantly adversely affected by an installation, facility, or other work related to waters or the management of waters, enter into consultations regarding:

a. The safe operation and maintenance of the installation, facility, or other work; and

b. The protection of the installation, facility, or other work from intentional or negligent acts or the forces of nature.

Article 64
Establishing Basin Wide or Other Joint Management Arrangements

1. When necessary to ensure the equitable and sustainable use of waters and the prevention of harm, basin States shall establish a basin wide or joint agency or commission with authority to undertake the integrated management of waters of an international drainage basin.

2. When appropriate, basin States shall establish other joint mechanisms for the management of waters.

3. The establishment of a basin wide management mechanism is without prejudice to the creation, existence, or designation of any joint management agency, conciliation commission, or tribunal by the basin States for the resolution of any question or dispute relating to the present or future management of transboundary waters.

Article 65
Minimal Requirements for Joint Management Arrangements

1. A basin wide management mechanism under Article 64 shall have authority over:

a. The coordination and pooling of their scientific and technical research programs;

b. Establishment of harmonized, coordinated, or unified networks for permanent observation and control; and

c. Establishment of joint or harmonized water quality objectives and standards for the whole of or each significant part of a basin.

2. An agreement creating a mechanism under Article 64 shall provide expressly for the mechanism's:

a. Objective and purpose;

b. Nature and composition;

c. Form and duration;

d. Legal status;

e. Area of operation;

f. Functions and powers; and

g. Financial arrangements.

Article 66
Compliance Review

Basin States shall undertake recurring review at regular intervals of the implementation of their commitments under agreements relating to waters, including, when applicable, their implementation of joint management mechanisms, in either event including in the review:

a.   Assessment, on the basis of all information available, of the overall affects of measures relating to the management of waters or of the aquatic environment;

b.   Examination of the obligations of the States involved in a joint management mechanism in light of the objectives for which the mechanism was established and of the evolution of scientific and technological knowledge;

c.   Promotion of appropriate responses by States involved to climate change;

d.   Facilitation of the refinement of methodologies for the effective implementation of the joint management mechanism or other agreements;

e.   Establishment of subsidiary bodies as necessary or proper for the implementation of the joint management mechanism or other agreements;

f.   Mobilization of additional financial resources as necessary and as available for the joint management mechanism or for other agreements;

g.   Arrangement, where appropriate, for the services or cooperation of international organizations, of intergovernmental bodies, and of non-governmental bodies; and

h.   Recommendations regarding any matters necessary or proper for the implementation of the joint management mechanism or other agreements.

Article 67
Sharing Expenses

1.   Expenses for the collection and exchange of relevant information and other joint activities, including the establishment and operation of a basin wide management mechanism, shall be allocated among the basin States based upon:

a.   Receipt of economic benefits;

b.   Receipt of environmental benefits; and

c.   Ability to pay.

2.   Expenses for special works undertaken by agreement in the territory of one State at the request of another State shall be borne by the requesting State, unless otherwise agreed.

CHAPTER XII
STATE RESPONSIBILITY

Article 68
State Responsibility

States are responsible for breaches of international law relating to the management of waters or to the aquatic environment in accordance with the international law of State responsibility.

CHAPTER XIII
LEGAL REMEDIES

Article 69
Access to Courts or Administrative Authorities

1.   A person who suffers or is under a serious threat of suffering damage from the management of water or the aquatic environment in a State shall be entitled to institute proceedings before a competent court or administrative authority of that State in order to obtain an appropriate remedy as specified in Article 70.

2.   Public bodies and non-governmental organizations with a proven interest regarding waters or the aquatic environment in a State shall be entitled, under

appropriate terms and conditions, to institute proceedings or to participate in proceedings instituted by others.

Article 70
Remedies for Damage to Persons

1.   States shall take all appropriate steps to ensure the availability of effective administrative and judicial remedies for persons whose legal rights have been violated and who suffer or are under a serious threat of suffering damage arising from plans, programs, projects, or activities relating to waters or to the aquatic environment subject to the State's jurisdiction or control.

2.   Remedies under this Article shall, as appropriate, provide for:

a.   Determination whether the damaging plan, program, project, or activity should be permitted;

b.   Preventive remedies;

c.   Compensation for damage; and

d.   Any other proper remedy.

Article 71
Remedies for Persons in Other States

1.   In providing access to courts and remedies to persons who suffer or are under a serious threat of suffering damage, States shall not discriminate on the basis of the nationality or residence of the person claiming damage or the place where the damage occurred or may occur.

2.   States shall take all appropriate measures to ensure cooperation between their courts and authorities to ensure that persons who suffer or are under a serious threat of suffering damage resulting from actions in another State relating to the waters of an international drainage basin shall have access to such information as is necessary to enable them to exercise their right to a remedy in a prompt and timely manner.

3.   Public bodies and non-governmental organizations with a proven interest regarding waters or the aquatic environment in States other than the States in which they are established shall be entitled on to institute proceedings or participate in procedures in that other State to the same extent and on the same conditions as public bodies and non-governmental associations established in the other State.

4.   States shall provide, by agreement or otherwise, relative to proceedings involving persons or events in more than one State for:

a.   The jurisdiction of courts or administrative bodies;

b.   The determination of the applicable law; and

c.   The enforcement of judgments.

CHAPTER XIV
SETTLEMENT OF INTERNATIONAL WATER DISPUTES

Article 72
Peaceful Settlement of International Water Disputes

1.   States shall resolve disputes concerning issues within the scope of these Rules through peaceful means.

2.   States involved in the dispute shall consult one another and, when appropriate, competent international organizations, in order to reach, by methods of their own choice, a solution consistent with their rights and duties under international law.

3. Where the facts are in dispute, the States involved in the dispute shall appoint a body to investigate and to determine the disputed facts, the decision of the fact-finding body binding the States only if they have consented to such binding effect.

4. In any procedure to resolve the dispute, the States involved shall invite other States likely to be affected by resolution of the dispute to present their views at an appropriate early stage in the dispute.

5. The means of settlement referred to in this Article are without prejudice to recourse to means of settlement recommended to, or required of, members of regional arrangements or agencies or other international organizations.

Article 73
Arbitration and Litigation

1. If the procedures set forth in Article 72 of these Rules have not succeeded in resolving the dispute, the States or international organizations involved shall agree to submit their dispute to an *ad hoc* or permanent arbitral tribunal, or to a competent international court.

2. Recourse to arbitration or litigation implies an undertaking by the States involved in the dispute to accept any resulting award or judgment as final and binding.

3.29　ILC Draft Articles on the Law of Transboundary Aquifers. Adopted by the International Law Commission, 4 June 2008. Report of the International Law Commission on the Work of its 60th Session, UN GAOR, 63rd Sess, Supp No 10, at 19, UN Doc A/63/10 (2008). *Reprinted in* 5 Weston & Carlson V.F.40

Conscious of the importance for humankind of life supporting groundwater resources in all regions of the world,

Bearing in mind Article 13, paragraph 1 (a), of the Charter of the United Nations, which provides that the General Assembly shall initiate studies and make recommendations for the purpose of encouraging the progressive development of international law and its codification,

Recalling General Assembly resolution 1803 (XVII) of 14 December 1962 on permanent sovereignty over natural resources,

Reaffirming the principles and recommendations adopted by the United Nations Conference on Environment and Development of 1992 in the Rio Declaration on Environment and Development and Agenda 21,

Taking into account increasing demands for freshwater and the need to protect groundwater resources,

Mindful of the particular problems posed by the vulnerability of aquifers to pollution,

Convinced of the need to ensure the development, utilization, conservation, management and protection of groundwater resources in the context of the promotion of the optimal and sustainable development of water resources for present and future generations,

Affirming the importance of international cooperation and good neighbourliness in this field,

Emphasizing the need to take into account the special situation of developing countries,

Recognizing the necessity to promote international cooperation, . . .

PART ONE

INTRODUCTION

Article 1
Scope

The present draft articles apply to:

Utilization of transboundary aquifers or aquifer systems; Other activities that have or are likely to have an impact upon such aquifers or aquifer systems; and Measures for the protection, preservation and management of such aquifers or aquifer systems.

Article 2
Use of terms

For the purposes of the present draft articles:

(a)　"aquifer" means a permeable water-bearing geological formation underlain by a less permeable layer and the water contained in the saturated zone of the formation;

(b)　"aquifer system" means a series of two or more aquifers that are hydraulically connected;

(c) "transboundary aquifer" or "transboundary aquifer system" means respectively, an aquifer or aquifer system, parts of which are situated in different States;

(d) "aquifer State" means a State in whose territory any part of a transboundary aquifer or aquifer system is situated;

(e) "utilization of transboundary aquifers or aquifer systems" includes extraction of water, heat and minerals, and storage and disposal of any substance;

(f) "recharging aquifer" means an aquifer that receives a non-negligible amount of contemporary water recharge;

(g) "recharge zone" means the zone which contributes water to an aquifer, consisting of the catchment area of rainfall water and the area where such water flows to an aquifer by runoff on the ground and infiltration through soil;

(h) "discharge zone" means the zone where water originating from an aquifer flows to its outlets, such as a watercourse, a lake, an oasis, a wetland or an ocean.

PART TWO
GENERAL PRINCIPLES

Article 3
Sovereignty of aquifer States

Each aquifer State has sovereignty over the portion of a transboundary aquifer or aquifer system located within its territory. It shall exercise its sovereignty in accordance with international law and the present draft articles.

Article 4
Equitable and reasonable utilization

Aquifer States shall utilize transboundary aquifers or aquifer systems according to the principle of equitable and reasonable utilization, as follows:

(a) they shall utilize transboundary aquifers or aquifer systems in a manner that is consistent with the equitable and reasonable accrual of benefits therefrom to the aquifer States concerned;

(b) they shall aim at maximizing the long-term benefits derived from the use of water contained therein;

(c) they shall establish individually or jointly a comprehensive utilization plan, taking into account present and future needs of, and alternative water sources for, the aquifer States; and

(d) they shall not utilize a recharging transboundary aquifer or aquifer system at a level that would prevent continuance of its effective functioning.

Article 5
Factors relevant to equitable and reasonable utilization

1. Utilization of a transboundary aquifer or aquifer system in an equitable and reasonable manner within the meaning of draft article 4 requires taking into account all relevant factors, including:

(a) The population dependent on the aquifer or aquifer system in each aquifer State;

(b) The social, economic and other needs, present and future, of the aquifer States concerned;

(c) The natural characteristics of the aquifer or aquifer system;

(d) The contribution to the formation and recharge of the aquifer or aquifer system;

(e) The existing and potential utilization of the aquifer or aquifer system;

(f) The actual and potential effects of the utilization of the aquifer or aquifer system in one aquifer State on other aquifer States concerned;

(g) The availability of alternatives to a particular existing and planned utilization of the aquifer or aquifer system;

(h) The development, protection and conservation of the aquifer or aquifer system and the costs of measures to be taken to that effect;

(i) The role of the aquifer or aquifer system in the related ecosystem.

2. The weight to be given to each factor is to be determined by its importance with regard to a specific transboundary aquifer or aquifer system in comparison with that of other relevant factors. In determining what is equitable and reasonable utilization, all relevant factors are to be considered together and a conclusion reached on the basis of all the factors. However, in weighing different kinds of utilization of a transboundary aquifer or aquifer system, special regard shall be given to vital human needs.

Article 6
Obligation not to cause significant harm

1. Aquifer States shall, in utilizing transboundary aquifers or aquifer systems in their territories, take all appropriate measures to prevent the causing of significant harm to other aquifer States or other States in whose territory a discharge zone is located. Aquifer States shall, in undertaking activities other than utilization of a transboundary aquifer or aquifer system that have, or are likely to have, an impact upon that transboundary aquifer or aquifer system, take all appropriate measures to prevent the causing of significant harm through that aquifer or aquifer system to other aquifer States or other States in whose territory a discharge zone is located.

2. Where significant harm nevertheless is caused to another aquifer State or a State in whose territory a discharge zone is located, the aquifer State whose activities cause such harm shall take, in consultation with the affected State, all appropriate response measures to eliminate or mitigate such harm, having due regard for the provisions of draft articles 4 and 5.

Article 7
General obligation to cooperate

1. Aquifer States shall cooperate on the basis of sovereign equality, territorial integrity, sustainable development, mutual benefit and good faith in order to attain equitable and reasonable utilization and appropriate protection of their transboundary aquifers or aquifer systems.

2. For the purpose of paragraph 1, aquifer States should establish joint mechanisms of cooperation.

Article 8
Regular exchange of data and information

1. Pursuant to draft article 7, aquifer States shall, on a regular basis, exchange readily available data and information on the condition of their transboundary aquifers or aquifer systems, in particular of a geological, hydrogeological, hydrological, meteorological and ecological nature and related to the hydrochemistry of the aquifers or aquifer systems, as well as related forecasts.

2. Where knowledge about the nature and extent of a transboundary aquifer or aquifer system is inadequate, aquifer States concerned shall employ their best efforts to collect and generate more complete data and information relating to such aquifer or

aquifer system, taking into account current practices and standards. They shall take such action individually or jointly and, where appropriate, together with or through international organizations.

3. If an aquifer State is requested by another aquifer State to provide data and information relating to an aquifer or aquifer system that are not readily available, it shall employ its best efforts to comply with the request. The requested State may condition its compliance upon payment by the requesting State of the reasonable costs of collecting and, where appropriate, processing such data or information.

4. Aquifer States shall, where appropriate, employ their best efforts to collect and process data and information in a manner that facilitates their utilization by the other aquifer States to which such data and information are communicated.

Article 9
Bilateral and regional agreements and arrangements

For the purpose of managing a particular transboundary aquifer or aquifer system, aquifer States are encouraged to enter into bilateral or regional agreements or arrangements among themselves. Such agreements or arrangements may be entered into with respect to an entire aquifer or aquifer system or any part thereof or a particular project, programme or utilization except insofar as an agreement or arrangement adversely affects, to a significant extent, the utilization, by one or more other aquifer States of the water in that aquifer or aquifer system, without their express consent.

PART THREE
PROTECTION, PRESERVATION AND MANAGEMENT

Article 10
Protection and preservation of ecosystems

Aquifer States shall take all appropriate measures to protect and preserve ecosystems within, or dependent upon, their transboundary aquifers or aquifer systems, including measures to ensure that the quality and quantity of water retained in an aquifer or aquifer system, as well as that released through its discharge zones, are sufficient to protect and preserve such ecosystems.

Article 11
Recharge and discharge zones

1. Aquifer States shall identify the recharge and discharge zones of transboundary aquifers or aquifer systems that exist within their territory. They shall take appropriate measures to prevent and minimize detrimental impacts on the recharge and discharge processes.

2. All States in whose territory a recharge or discharge zone is located, in whole or in part, and which are not aquifer States with regard to that aquifer or aquifer system, shall cooperate with the aquifer States to protect the aquifer or aquifer system and related ecosystems.

Article 12
Prevention, reduction and control of pollution

Aquifer States shall, individually and, where appropriate, jointly, prevent, reduce and control pollution of their transboundary aquifers or aquifer systems, including through the recharge process, that may cause significant harm to other aquifer States. Aquifer States shall take a precautionary approach in view of uncertainty about the nature and extent of a transboundary aquifer or aquifer system and of its vulnerability to pollution.

Article 13
Monitoring

1. Aquifer States shall monitor their transboundary aquifers or aquifer systems. They shall, wherever possible, carry out these monitoring activities jointly with other aquifer States concerned and, where appropriate, in collaboration with competent international organizations. Where monitoring activities cannot be carried out jointly, the aquifer States shall exchange the monitored data among themselves.

2. Aquifer States shall use agreed or harmonized standards and methodology for monitoring their transboundary aquifers or aquifer systems. They should identify key parameters that they will monitor based on an agreed conceptual model of the aquifers or aquifer systems. These parameters should include parameters on the condition of the aquifer or aquifer system as listed in draft article 8, paragraph 1, and also on the utilization of the aquifers or aquifer systems.

Article 14
Management

Aquifer States shall establish and implement plans for the proper management of their transboundary aquifers or aquifer systems. They shall, at the request of any of them, enter into consultations concerning the management of a transboundary aquifer or aquifer system. A joint management mechanism shall be established, wherever appropriate.

Article 15
Planned activities

1. When a State has reasonable grounds for believing that a particular planned activity in its territory may affect a transboundary aquifer or aquifer system and thereby may have a significant adverse effect upon another State, it shall, as far as practicable, assess the possible effects of such activity.

2. Before a State implements or permits the implementation of planned activities which may affect a transboundary aquifer or aquifer system and thereby may have a significant adverse effect upon another State, it shall provide that State with timely notification thereof. Such notification shall be accompanied by available technical data and information, including any environmental impact assessment, in order to enable the notified State to evaluate the possible effects of the planned activities.

3. If the notifying and the notified States disagree on the possible effect of the planned activities, they shall enter into consultations and, if necessary, negotiations with a view to arriving at an equitable resolution of the situation. They may utilize an independent fact-finding body to make an impartial assessment of the effect of the planned activities.

PART FOUR
MISCELLANEOUS PROVISIONS

Article 16
Technical cooperation with developing States

States shall, directly or through competent international organizations, promote scientific, educational, legal and other cooperation with developing States for the protection and management of transboundary aquifers or aquifer systems, including, *inter alia*:

(a) Strengthening their capacity-building in scientific, technical and legal fields;

(b) Facilitating their participation in relevant international programmes;

(c) Supplying them with necessary equipment and facilities;

(d) Enhancing their capacity to manufacture such equipment;

(e) Providing advice on and developing facilities for research, monitoring, educational and other programmes;

(f) Providing advice on and developing facilities for minimizing the detrimental effects of major activities affecting their transboundary aquifer or aquifer system;

(g) Providing advice in the preparation of environmental impact assessments;

(h) Supporting the exchange of technical knowledge and experience among developing States with a view to strengthening cooperation among them in managing the transboundary aquifer or aquifer system.

Article 17
Emergency situations

1. For the purpose of the present draft article, "emergency" means a situation, resulting suddenly from natural causes or from human conduct, that affects a transboundary aquifer or aquifer system and poses an imminent threat of causing serious harm to aquifer States or other States.

2. The State within whose territory the emergency originates shall:

(a) Without delay and by the most expeditious means available, notify other potentially affected States and competent international organizations of the emergency;

(b) In cooperation with potentially affected States and, where appropriate, competent international organizations, immediately take all practicable measures necessitated by the circumstances to prevent, mitigate and eliminate any harmful effect of the emergency.

3. Where an emergency poses a threat to vital human needs, aquifer States, notwithstanding draft articles 4 and 6, may take measures that are strictly necessary to meet such needs.

4. States shall provide scientific, technical, logistical and other cooperation to other States experiencing an emergency. Cooperation may include coordination of international emergency actions and communications, making available emergency response personnel, emergency response equipment and supplies, scientific and technical expertise and humanitarian assistance.

Article 18
Protection in time of armed conflict

Transboundary aquifers or aquifer systems and related installations, facilities and other works shall enjoy the protection accorded by the principles and rules of international law applicable in international and non-international armed conflict and shall not be used in violation of those principles and rules.

Article 19
Data and information vital to national defence or security

Nothing in the present draft articles obliges a State to provide data or information vital to its national defence or security. Nevertheless, that State shall cooperate in good faith with other States with a view to providing as much information as possible under the circumstances.

Part 4. Lithosphere

A. Chemicals

4.1 FAO International Code of Conduct on the Distribution and Use of Pesticides (as Amended in 1989).[a] Adopted 28 November 1985. 23 FAO Conf Res 10/85; *reprinted in* 5 Weston & Carlson V.H.17

Article 1. Objectives of the Code

1.1 The objectives of this Code are to set forth responsibilities and establish voluntary standards of conduct for all public and private entities engaged in or affecting the distribution and use of pesticides, particularly where there is no or an inadequate national law to regulate pesticides.

1.2 The Code describes the shared responsibility of many segments of society, including governments, individually or in regional groupings, industry, trade and international institutions, to work together so that the benefits to be derived from the necessary and acceptable use of pesticides are achieved without significant adverse effects on people or the environment. To this end, all references in this Code to a government or governments shall be deemed to apply equally to regional groupings of governments for matters falling within their areas of competence.

1.3 The Code addresses the need for a cooperative effort between governments of exporting and importing countries to promote practices which ensure efficient and safe use while minimizing health and environmental concerns due to improper handling or use.

1.4 The entities which are addressed by this Code include international organizations; governments of exporting and importing countries; industry, including manufacturers, trade associations, formulators and distributors; users; and public-sector organizations such as environmental groups, consumer groups and trade unions.

1.5 The standards of conduct set forth by this Code:

1.5.1 encourage responsible and generally accepted trade practices;

1.5.2 assist countries which have not yet established controls designed to regulate the quality and suitability of pesticide products needed in that country and to address the safe handling and use of such products;

1.5.3 promote practices which encourage the safe and efficient use of pesticides, including minimizing adverse effects on humans and the environment and preventing accidental poisoning from improper handling;

1.5.4 ensure that pesticides are used effectively for the improvement of agricultural production and of human, animal and plant health.

1.6 The Code is designed to be used, within the context of national law, as a basis whereby government authorities, pesticide manufacturers, those engaged in trade and any citizens concerned may judge whether their proposed actions and the actions of others constitute acceptable practices.

* * *

a. The voluntary system established by this document has been largely supplanted by mandatory treaty law. *See* Basic Documents 4.4 and 4.5, *infra*. For that reason, only a small portion of this document is reproduced here.

Article 3. Pesticide management

3.1 Governments have the overall responsibility and should take the specific powers to regulate the distribution and use of pesticides in their countries.

3.2 The pesticide industry should adhere to the provisions of this Code as a standard for the manufacture, distribution and advertising of pesticides, particularly in countries lacking appropriate legislation and advisory services.

3.3 Governments of exporting countries should help to the extent possible, directly or through their pesticide industries, to:

3.3.1 provide technical assistance to other countries, especially those with shortages of technical expertise, in the assessment of the relevant data on pesticides, including those provided by industry (see also Article 4);

3.3.2 ensure that good trading practices are followed in the export of pesticides, especially to those countries with no or limited regulatory schemes (see also Articles 8 and 9).

3.4 Manufacturers and traders should observe the following practices in pesticide management, especially in countries without legislation or means of implementing regulations:

3.4.1 supply only pesticides of adequate quality, packaged and labelled as appropriate for each specific market;

3.4.2 pay special attention to formulations, presentation, packaging and labelling in order to reduce hazard to users, to the maximum extent possible consistent with the effective functioning of the pesticide in the particular circumstances in which it is to be used;

3.4.3 provide, with each package of pesticide, information and instructions in a form and language adequate to ensure safe and effective use;

3.4.4 retain an active interest in following their products to the ultimate consumer, keeping track of major uses and the occurrence of any problems arising in the actual use of their products as a basis for determining the need for changes in labelling, directions for use, packaging, formulation or product availability.

3.5 Pesticides whose handling and application require the use of uncomfortable and expensive protective clothing and equipment should be avoided, especially in the case of small scale users in tropical climates.

3.6 National and international organizations, governments, and pesticide industries should take action in coordinated efforts to disseminate educational materials of all types to pesticide users, farmers, farmers' organizations, agricultural workers, unions and other interested parties. Similarly, affected parties should seek and understand educational materials before using pesticides and should follow proper procedures.

3.7 Governments should allocate high priority and adequate resources to the task of effectively managing the availability, distribution and use of pesticides in their countries.

3.8 Concerted efforts should be made by governments and pesticide industries to develop and promote integrated pest management systems and the use of safe, efficient, cost-effective application methods. Public-sector groups and international organizations should actively support such activities.

3.9 International organizations should provide information on specific pesticides and give guidance on methods of analysis through the provision of criteria documents, fact sheets, training sessions, etc.

3.10   It is recognized that the development of resistance of pests to pesticides can be a major problem. Therefore, governments, industry, national institutions, international organizations and public sector groups should collaborate in developing strategies which will prolong the useful life of valuable pesticides and reduce the adverse effects of the development of resistant species.

Article 4.   Testing of Pesticides

4.1   Pesticide manufacturers are expected to:

4.1.1   ensure that each pesticide and pesticide product is adequately and effectively tested by well recognized procedures and test methods so as to fully evaluate its safety, efficacy and fate with regard to the various anticipated conditions in regions or countries of use;

* * *

4.2   Each country should possess or have access to facilities to verify and exercise control over the quality of pesticides offered for sale, to establish the quantity of the active ingredient or ingredients and the suitability of their formulation.

4.3   International organizations and other interested bodies should, within available resources, consider assisting in the establishment of analytical laboratories in pesticide importing countries, either on a country or on a multilateral regional basis; these laboratories should be capable of carrying out product and residue analysis and should have adequate supplies of analytical standards, solvents and reagents.

4.4   Exporting governments and international organizations must play an active role in assisting developing countries in training personnel in the interpretation and evaluation of test data.

4.5   Industry and governments should collaborate in conducting post-registration surveillance or monitoring studies to determine the fate and environmental effect of pesticides under field conditions.

* * *

Article 7.   Availability and Use

7.1   Responsible authorities should give special attention to drafting rules and regulations on the availability of pesticides. These should be compatible with existing levels of training and expertise in handling pesticides on the part of the intended users. The parameters on which such decisions are based vary widely and must be left to the discretion of each government, bearing in mind the situation prevailing in the country.

* * *

7.4   All pesticides made available to the general public should be packaged and labelled in a manner which is consistent with the FAO guidelines on packaging and labelling and with appropriate national regulations.

7.5   Prohibition of the importation, sale and purchase of an extremely toxic product may be desirable if control measures or good marketing practices are insufficient to ensure that the product can be used safely. However, this is a matter for decision in the light of national circumstances.

Article 8.   Distribution and Trade

8.1   Industry should:

8.1.1   test all pesticide products to evaluate safety with regard to human health and the environment prior to marketing, as provided for in Article 4, and ensure that all pesticide products are likewise adequately tested for efficacy and stability and crop tolerance, under procedures that will predict performance under the conditions prevailing in the region where the product is to be used, before they are offered there for sale;

8.1.2   submit the results of all such tests to the local responsible authority for independent evaluation and approval before the products enter trade channels in that country;

8.1.3   take all necessary steps to ensure that pesticides entering international trade conform to relevant FAO, WHO or equivalent specifications for composition and quality (where such specifications have been developed) and to the principles embodied in pertinent FAO guidelines, and in rules and regulations on classification and packaging, marketing, labelling and documentation laid down by international organizations concerned with modes of transport (ICAO, IMO, RID and IATA in particular);

8.1.4   undertake to see that pesticides which are manufactured for export are subject to the same quality requirements and standards as those applied by the manufacturer to comparable domestic products;

8.1.5   ensure that pesticides manufactured or formulated by a subsidiary company meet appropriate quality requirements and standards which should be consistent with the requirements of the host country and of the parent company;

* * *

8.3   Governments of countries importing food and agricultural commodities should recognize good agricultural practices in countries with which they trade and, in accordance with recommendations of the Codex Alimentarius Commission, should establish a legal basis for the acceptance of pesticide residues resulting from such good agricultural practices.

Article 9.   *Information Exchange and Prior Informed Consent*

9.1   The government of any country that takes action to ban or severely restrict the use or handling of a pesticide in order to protect health or the environment should notify FAO as soon a possible of the action it has taken. FAO will notify the designated national authorities in other countries of the action of the notifying government.

9.2   The purpose of notification regarding control action is to give competent authorities in other countries the opportunity to assess the risks associated with the pesticides, and to make timely and informed decisions as to the importation and use of the pesticides concerned, after taking into account local, public health, economic, environmental and administrative conditions. The minimum information to be provided for this purpose should be:

9.2.1   the identity (common name, distinguishing name and chemical name);

9.2.2   a summary of the control action taken and of the reasons for it if the control action bans or restricts certain uses but allows other uses, such information should be included:

9.2.3   an indication of the additional information that is available, and the name and address of the contact point in the country to which a request for further information should be addressed.

Information Exchange Among Countries

9.3   If export of a pesticide banned or severely restricted in the country of export occurs, the country of export should ensure that necessary steps are taken to provide the designated national authority of the country of import with relevant information.

* * *

9.5   Provision of information regarding exports should take place at the time of the first export following the control action, and should recur in the case of any significant development of new information or condition surrounding the control action. It is the intention that the information should be provided prior to export.

9.6 The provision to individual countries of any additional information on the reasons for control actions taken by any country must take into account protection of any proprietary data from unauthorized use.

Prior Informed Consent

9.7 Pesticides that are banned or severely restricted for reasons of health or the environment are subject to the Prior Informed Consent procedure. No pesticide in these categories should be exported to an importing country participating in the PIC procedure contrary to that country's decision made in accordance with the FAO operational procedures for PIC.

* * *

Article 10. Labelling, Packaging, Storage and Disposal

10.1 All pesticide containers should be clearly labelled in accordance with applicable international guidelines, such as the FAO guidelines on good labelling practice.

* * *

4.2 ILO CONVENTION 162 CONCERNING SAFETY IN THE USE OF ASBESTOS. Adopted by the General Conference of the International Labour Organisation, 24 June 1986. Entered into force, 16 June 1989. 1539 UNTS 316

PART I. SCOPE AND DEFINITIONS

Article 1

1. This Convention applies to all activities involving exposure of workers to asbestos in the course of work.

2. A Member ratifying this Convention may, after consultation with the most representative organisations of employers and workers concerned, and on the basis of an assessment of the health hazards involved and the safety measures applied, exclude particular branches of economic activity or particular undertakings from the application of certain provisions of the Convention when it is satisfied that their application to these branches or undertakings is unnecessary.

3. The competent authority, when deciding on the exclusion of particular branches of economic activity or particular undertakings, shall take into account the frequency, duration and level of exposure, as well as the type of work and the conditions at the workplace.

Article 2

For the purpose of this Convention—

(a) the term asbestos means the fibrous form of mineral silicates belonging to rock-forming minerals of the serpentine group, i.e. chrysotile (white asbestos), and of the amphibole group, i.e. actinolite, amosite (brown asbestos, cummingtonite-grunerite), anthophyllite, crocidolite (blue asbestos), tremolite, or any mixture containing one or more of these;

* * *

PART II. GENERAL PRINCIPLES

Article 3

1. National laws or regulations shall prescribe the measures to be taken for the prevention and control of, and protection of workers against, health hazards due to occupational exposure to asbestos.

* * *

Article 5

1. The enforcement of the laws and regulations adopted pursuant to Article 3 of this Convention shall be secured by an adequate and appropriate system of inspection.

2. National laws or regulations shall provide for the necessary measures, including appropriate penalties, to ensure effective enforcement of and compliance with the provisions of this Convention.

Article 6

1. Employers shall be made responsible for compliance with the prescribed measures.

* * *

Article 7

Workers shall be required, within the limits of their responsibility, to comply with prescribed safety and hygiene procedures relating to the prevention and control of, and protection against, health hazards due to occupational exposure to asbestos.

* * *

PART III. PROTECTIVE AND PREVENTIVE MEASURES

Article 9

The national laws or regulations adopted pursuant to Article 3 of this Convention shall provide that exposure to asbestos shall be prevented or controlled by one or more of the following measures:

(a) making work in which exposure to asbestos may occur subject to regulations prescribing adequate engineering controls and work practices, including workplace hygiene;

(b) prescribing special rules and procedures, including authorisation, for the use of asbestos or of certain types of asbestos or products containing asbestos or for certain work processes.

Article 10

Where necessary to protect the health of workers and technically practicable, national laws or regulations shall provide for one or more of the following measures—

(a) replacement of asbestos or of certain types of asbestos or products containing asbestos by other materials or products or the use of alternative technology, scientifically evaluated by the competent authority as harmless or less harmful, whenever this is possible;

(b) total or partial prohibition of the use of asbestos or of certain types of asbestos or products containing asbestos in certain work processes.

* * *

Article 14

Producers and suppliers of asbestos and manufacturers and suppliers of products containing asbestos shall be made responsible for adequate labelling of the container and, where appropriate, the products, in a language and manner easily understood by the workers and the users concerned, as prescribed by the competent authority.

* * *

4.3 UNEP GOVERNING COUNCIL DECISION ON LONDON GUIDELINES FOR THE EXCHANGE OF INFORMATION ON CHEMICALS IN INTERNATIONAL TRADE **(With Annexes II & III and as Amended in 1989).**[b] **Adopted by the UNEP Governing Council at London, 19 June 1987. UNEP/PIC/WG.2/2, at 9, UNEP ELPG No. 10, UNEP/GC/DEC/15/30;** *reprinted in* **5 Weston & Carlson V.I.24**

Introduction to the Guidelines

1. This set of Guidelines is addressed to Governments with a view to assisting them in the process of increasing chemical safety in all countries through the exchange of information on chemicals in international trade. They have been developed on the basis of common elements and principles derived from relevant existing bilateral, regional and global instruments and national regulations, drawing upon experience already gained through their preparation and implementation.

2. The Guidelines are general in nature and are aimed at enhancing the sound management of chemicals through the exchange of scientific, technical, economic and legal information. Special provisions have been included regarding the exchange of information on banned or severely restricted chemicals in international trade, which call for co-operation between exporting and importing countries in the light of their joint responsibility for the protection of human health and the environment at the global level. To this end, all references in these Guidelines to a Government or Governments shall be deemed to apply equally to regional economic integration organizations for matters falling within their areas of competence.

* * *

PART I

GENERAL PROVISIONS

1. Definitions

For the purposes of the Guidelines:

(a) "Chemical" means a chemical substance whether by itself or in a mixture or preparation, whether manufactured or obtained from nature and includes such substances used as industrial chemicals and pesticides;

(b) "Banned chemical" means a chemical which has, for health or environmental reasons, been prohibited for all uses by final governmental regulatory action;

(c) "Severely restricted chemical" means a chemical for which, for health or environmental reasons, virtually all uses have been prohibited nationally by final government regulatory action, but for which certain specific uses remain authorized;

* * *

(g) "Prior informed consent" (PIC) refers to the *principle* that international shipment of a chemical that is banned or severely restricted in order to protect human health or the environment should not proceed without the agreement, where such agreement exists, or contrary to the decision, of the designated national authority in the importing country;

(h) "Prior informed consent procedure" (PIC procedure) means the *procedure* for formally obtaining and disseminating the decisions of importing countries as to whether they wish to receive future shipments of chemicals which have been banned or severely restricted. A specific procedure was established for selecting chemicals for

b. The voluntary guidelines set down in this document have been largely supplanted by mandatory treaty law. *See* Basic Documents 4.4 and 4.5, *infra*. For that reason, only a small portion of this document is reproduced here.

initial implementation of the PIC procedures. These include chemicals which have been previously banned or severely restricted as well as certain pesticide formulations which are acutely toxic. This is explained in annex II.

2. *General Principles*

(a) Both States of export and States of import should protect human health and the environment against potential harm by exchanging information on chemicals in international trade;

(b) In their activities with regard to chemicals, States should act, in so far as is applicable, in accordance with principle 21 of the Declaration of the United Nations Conference on the Human Environment;

(c) States taking measures to regulate chemicals with a view to protecting human, animal or plant life or health, or the environment, should ensure that regulations and standards for this purpose do not create unnecessary obstacles to international trade;

(d) States should ensure that governmental control measures or actions taken with regard to an imported chemical for which information has been received in implementation of the Guidelines are not more restrictive than those applied to the same chemical produced for domestic use or imported from a State other than the one that supplied the information;

(e) States with more advanced systems for the safe management of chemicals should share their experience with those countries in need of improved systems; * * *.

* * *

PART II

NOTIFICATION AND INFORMATION REGARDING BANNED AND SEVERELY RESTRICTED CHEMICALS AND OPERATION OF THE PIC PROCEDURE

6. *Notification of Control Action*

(a) States having taken control action to ban or severely restrict a chemical as defined in these Guidelines should notify IRPTC. IRPTC will disseminate these notifications as provided in these Guidelines;

(b) The purpose of the notification regarding control action is to give competent authorities in other States the opportunity to assess the risks associated with the chemical, and to make timely and informed decisions thereon, taking into account local environmental, public health, economic and administrative conditions, and with regard to existing information on toxicology, safety and regulatory aspects;

(c) The minimum information to be provided for this purpose should be:

(i) The chemical identification/specification of the chemical;

(ii) A summary of the control action taken and of the reasons for it. If the control action bans or restricts certain uses but allows other uses, such information should be included;

(iii) The fact that additional information is available, and the indication of the contact point in the State of export to which a request for further information should be addressed;

(d) To the extent practicable, the designated national authority issuing the notification should provide information concerning alternative measures, such as, for example, integrated pest management procedures, non-chemical alternatives and impact mitigation measures;

(e) Notification of control action should be provided as soon as practicable after the control action is taken. For chemicals banned or severely restricted before the implementation of these Guidelines, an inventory of prior control actions should be provided to IRPTC, unless such information has already been provided and circulated by IRPTC to all designated national authorities.

7.   *Operation of the PIC Procedure*

* * *

7.2   *Identification of Chemicals for Inclusion in the PIC Procedure*

(a) As provided in paragraph 9, IRPTC will notify each participating country of each chemical that is the subject of a notification of a final government control action and that meets the definitions as being banned or severely restricted for environmental or human health reasons for a decision under its conditions of use as to whether that country wishes to permit use and importation of the chemical. . . .

7.3   *Response to Notification of Control Action for Chemicals Identified for Inclusion in the PIC Procedure*

(a) The designated national authority in each participating importing country shall make an initial response to IRPTC within 90 days. A response may take either of two forms:

> (i) A final decision to permit use and importation, to prohibit use and importation or to permit importation only under specified stated conditions;

> (ii) An interim response which may be:

>> a.   A statement that importation is under active review but that final decision has not yet been reached;

>> b.   A request for further information; and/or

>> c.   A request for assistance in evaluating the chemical.

An interim response may also contain a statement permitting importation with or without stated specified conditions or prohibiting importation during the interim period until a final decision is made;

* * *

12.   *Functions of Designated National Authorities*

* * *

(c) *Exports.* It should be the function of designated national authorities, with regard to exports of banned or severely restricted chemicals:

> (i) To ensure the issuance or transmittal of information on exports;

> (ii) To respond to requests for information from other States, especially as regards sources of precautionary information on safe use and handling of the chemicals concerned;

> (iii) To communicate PIC decisions to their export industry;

> (iv) To implement appropriate procedures, within their authority, designed to ensure that exports do not occur contrary to the PIC decisions of participating importing countries;

* * *

4.4 Rotterdam Convention on the Prior Informed Consent Procedure for Certain Hazardous Chemicals and Pesticides in International Trade. **Adopted on 10 September 1998. Entered into force, 24 February 2004. 2244 UNTS 337.** *Reprinted in* **5 Weston & Carlson V.G.5**

The Parties to this Convention,

Aware of the harmful impact on human health and the environment from certain hazardous chemicals and pesticides in international trade,

Recalling the pertinent provisions of the Rio Declaration on Environment and Development and chapter 19 of Agenda 21 on "Environmentally sound management of toxic chemicals, including prevention of illegal international traffic in toxic and dangerous products",

Mindful of the work undertaken by the United Nations Environment Programme (UNEP) and the Food and Agriculture Organization of the United Nations (FAO) in the operation of the voluntary Prior Informed Consent procedure, as set out in the UNEP Amended London Guidelines for the Exchange of Information on Chemicals in International Trade (hereinafter referred to as the "Amended London Guidelines") and the FAO International Code of Conduct on the Distribution and Use of Pesticides (hereinafter referred to as the "International Code of Conduct"),

Taking into account the circumstances and particular requirements of developing countries and countries with economies in transition, in particular the need to strengthen national capabilities and capacities for the management of chemicals, including transfer of technology, providing financial and technical assistance and promoting cooperation among the Parties,

Noting the specific needs of some countries for information on transit movements,

Recognizing that good management practices for chemicals should be promoted in all countries, taking into account, inter alia, the voluntary standards laid down in the International Code of Conduct and the UNEP Code of Ethics on the International Trade in Chemicals,

Desiring to ensure that hazardous chemicals that are exported from their territory are packaged and labelled in a manner that is adequately protective of human health and the environment, consistent with the principles of the Amended London Guidelines and the International Code of Conduct,

Recognizing that trade and environmental policies should be mutually supportive with a view to achieving sustainable development,

Emphasizing that nothing in this Convention shall be interpreted as implying in any way a change in the rights and obligations of a Party under any existing international agreement applying to chemicals in international trade or to environmental protection,

Understanding that the above recital is not intended to create a hierarchy between this Convention and other international agreements,

Determined to protect human health, including the health of consumers and workers, and the environment against potentially harmful impacts from certain hazardous chemicals and pesticides in international trade,

HAVE AGREED AS FOLLOWS:

Article 1
Objective

The objective of this Convention is to promote shared responsibility and cooperative efforts among Parties in the international trade of certain hazardous chemicals in order to protect human health and the environment from potential harm and to contribute to their environmentally sound use, by facilitating information exchange about their characteristics, by providing for a national decision-making process on their import and export and by disseminating these decisions to Parties.

Article 2
Definitions

For the purposes of this Convention:

(a) "Chemical" means a substance whether by itself or in a mixture or preparation and whether manufactured or obtained from nature, but does not include any living organism. It consists of the following categories: pesticide (including severely hazardous pesticide formulations) and industrial;

(b) "Banned chemical" means a chemical all uses of which within one or more categories have been prohibited by final regulatory action, in order to protect human health or the environment. It includes a chemical that has been refused approval for first-time use or has been withdrawn by industry either from the domestic market or from further consideration in the domestic approval process and where there is clear evidence that such action has been taken in order to protect human health or the environment;

(c) "Severely restricted chemical" means a chemical virtually all use of which within one or more categories has been prohibited by final regulatory action in order to protect human health or the environment, but for which certain specific uses remain allowed. It includes a chemical that has, for virtually all use, been refused for approval or been withdrawn by industry either from the domestic market or from further consideration in the domestic approval process, and where there is clear evidence that such action has been taken in order to protect human health or the environment;

(d) "Severely hazardous pesticide formulation" means a chemical formulated for pesticidal use that produces severe health or environmental effects observable within a short period of time after single or multiple exposure, under conditions of use;

(e) "Final regulatory action" means an action taken by a Party, that does not require subsequent regulatory action by that Party, the purpose of which is to ban or severely restrict a chemical;

(f) "Export" and "import" mean, in their respective connotations, the movement of a chemical from one Party to another Party, but exclude mere transit operations;

(g) "Party" means a State or regional economic integration organization that has consented to be bound by this Convention and for which the Convention is in force;

(h) "Regional economic integration organization" means an organization constituted by sovereign States of a given region to which its member States have transferred competence in respect of matters governed by this Convention and which has been duly authorized, in accordance with its internal procedures, to sign, ratify, accept, approve or accede to this Convention;

(i) "Chemical Review Committee" means the subsidiary body referred to in paragraph 6 of Article 18.

Article 3
Scope of the Convention

1. This Convention applies to:

(a) Banned or severely restricted chemicals; and

(b) Severely hazardous pesticide formulations.

2. This Convention does not apply to:

(a) Narcotic drugs and psychotropic substances;

(b) Radioactive materials;

(c) Wastes;

(d) Chemical weapons;

(e) Pharmaceuticals, including human and veterinary drugs;

(f) Chemicals used as food additives;

(g) Food;

(h) Chemicals in quantities not likely to affect human health or the environment provided they are imported:

(i) For the purpose of research or analysis; or

(ii) By an individual for his or her own personal use in quantities reasonable for such use.

Article 4
Designated national authorities

1. Each Party shall designate one or more national authorities that shall be authorized to act on its behalf in the performance of the administrative functions required by this Convention.

2. Each Party shall seek to ensure that such authority or authorities have sufficient resources to perform their tasks effectively.

3. Each Party shall, no later than the date of the entry into force of this Convention for it, notify the name and address of such authority or authorities to the Secretariat. It shall forthwith notify the Secretariat of any changes in the name and address of such authority or authorities.

4. The Secretariat shall forthwith inform the Parties of the notifications it receives under paragraph 3.

Article 5
Procedures for banned or severely restricted chemicals

1. Each Party that has adopted a final regulatory action shall notify the Secretariat in writing of such action. Such notification shall be made as soon as possible, and in any event no later than ninety days after the date on which the final regulatory action has taken effect, and shall contain the information required by Annex I, where available.

2. Each Party shall, at the date of entry into force of this Convention for it, notify the Secretariat in writing of its final regulatory actions in effect at that time, except that each Party that has submitted notifications of final regulatory actions under the Amended London Guidelines or the International Code of Conduct need not resubmit those notifications.

3. The Secretariat shall, as soon as possible, and in any event no later than six months after receipt of a notification under paragraphs 1 and 2, verify whether the notification contains the information required by Annex I. If the notification contains the information required, the Secretariat shall forthwith forward to all Parties a summary of the information received. If the notification does not contain the information required, it shall inform the notifying Party accordingly.

4. The Secretariat shall every six months communicate to the Parties a synopsis of the information received pursuant to paragraphs 1 and 2, including information regarding those notifications which do not contain all the information required by Annex I.

5. When the Secretariat has received at least one notification from each of two Prior Informed Consent regions regarding a particular chemical that it has verified meet the requirements of Annex I, it shall forward them to the Chemical Review Committee. The composition of the Prior Informed Consent regions shall be defined in a decision to be adopted by consensus at the first meeting of the Conference of the Parties.

6. The Chemical Review Committee shall review the information provided in such notifications and, in accordance with the criteria set out in Annex II, recommend to the Conference of the Parties whether the chemical in question should be made subject to the Prior Informed Consent procedure and, accordingly, be listed in Annex III.

Article 6
Procedures for severely hazardous pesticide formulations

1. Any Party that is a developing country or a country with an economy in transition and that is experiencing problems caused by a severely hazardous pesticide formulation under conditions of use in its territory, may propose to the Secretariat the listing of the severely hazardous pesticide formulation in Annex III. In developing a proposal, the Party may draw upon technical expertise from any relevant source. The proposal shall contain the information required by part 1 of Annex IV.

2. The Secretariat shall, as soon as possible, and in any event no later than six months after receipt of a proposal under paragraph 1, verify whether the proposal contains the information required by part 1 of Annex IV. If the proposal contains the information required, the Secretariat shall forthwith forward to all Parties a summary of the information received. If the proposal does not contain the information required, it shall inform the proposing Party accordingly.

3. The Secretariat shall collect the additional information set out in part 2 of Annex IV regarding the proposal forwarded under paragraph 2.

4. When the requirements of paragraphs 2 and 3 above have been fulfilled with regard to a particular severely hazardous pesticide formulation, the Secretariat shall forward the proposal and the related information to the Chemical Review Committee.

5. The Chemical Review Committee shall review the information provided in the proposal and the additional information collected and, in accordance with the criteria set out in part 3 of Annex IV, recommend to the Conference of the Parties whether the severely hazardous pesticide formulation in question should be made subject to the Prior Informed Consent procedure and, accordingly, be listed in Annex III.

Article 7
Listing of chemicals in Annex III

1. For each chemical that the Chemical Review Committee has decided to recommend for listing in Annex III, it shall prepare a draft decision guidance document. The decision guidance document should, at a minimum, be based on the information specified in Annex I, or, as the case may be, Annex IV, and include information on uses of the chemical in a category other than the category for which the final regulatory action applies.

2. The recommendation referred to in paragraph 1 together with the draft decision guidance document shall be forwarded to the Conference of the Parties. The Conference of the Parties shall decide whether the chemical should be made subject to the Prior Informed Consent procedure and, accordingly, list the chemical in Annex III and approve the draft decision guidance document.

3. When a decision to list a chemical in Annex III has been taken and the related decision guidance document has been approved by the Conference of the Parties, the Secretariat shall forthwith communicate this information to all Parties.

Article 8
Chemicals in the voluntary Prior Informed Consent procedure

For any chemical, other than a chemical listed in Annex III, that has been included in the voluntary Prior Informed Consent procedure before the date of the first meeting of the Conference of the Parties, the Conference of the Parties shall decide at that meeting to list the chemical in Annex III, provided that it is satisfied that all the requirements for listing in that Annex have been fulfilled.

Article 9
Removal of chemicals from Annex III

1. If a Party submits to the Secretariat information that was not available at the time of the decision to list a chemical in Annex III and that information indicates that its listing may no longer be justified in accordance with the relevant criteria in Annex II or, as the case may be, Annex IV, the Secretariat shall forward the information to the Chemical Review Committee.

2. The Chemical Review Committee shall review the information it receives under paragraph 1. For each chemical that the Chemical Review Committee decides, in accordance with the relevant criteria in Annex II or, as the case may be, Annex IV, to recommend for removal from Annex III, it shall prepare a revised draft decision guidance document.

3. A recommendation referred to in paragraph 2 shall be forwarded to the Conference of the Parties and be accompanied by a revised draft decision guidance document. The Conference of the Parties shall decide whether the chemical should be removed from Annex III and whether to approve the revised draft decision guidance document.

4. When a decision to remove a chemical from Annex III has been taken and the revised decision guidance document has been approved by the Conference of the Parties, the Secretariat shall forthwith communicate this information to all Parties.

Article 10
Obligations in relation to imports of chemicals listed in Annex III

1. Each Party shall implement appropriate legislative or administrative measures to ensure timely decisions with respect to the import of chemicals listed in Annex III.

2. Each Party shall transmit to the Secretariat, as soon as possible, and in any event no later than nine months after the date of dispatch of the decision guidance document referred to in paragraph 3 of Article 7, a response concerning the future import of the chemical concerned. If a Party modifies this response, it shall forthwith submit the revised response to the Secretariat.

3. The Secretariat shall, at the expiration of the time period in paragraph 2, forthwith address to a Party that has not provided such a response, a written request to do so. Should the Party be unable to provide a response, the Secretariat shall, where appropriate, help it to provide a response within the time period specified in the last sentence of paragraph 2 of Article 11.

4. A response under paragraph 2 shall consist of either:

(a) A final decision, pursuant to legislative or administrative measures:

    (i) To consent to import;

    (ii)   Not to consent to import; or

    (iii) To consent to import only subject to specified conditions; or

(b) An interim response, which may include:

    (i)   An interim decision consenting to import with or without specified conditions, or not consenting to import during the interim period;

    (ii) A statement that a final decision is under active consideration;

    (iii) A request to the Secretariat, or to the Party that notified the final regulatory action, for further information;

    (iv) A request to the Secretariat for assistance in evaluating the chemical.

5.   A response under subparagraphs (a) or (b) of paragraph 4 shall relate to the category or categories specified for the chemical in Annex III.

6.   A final decision should be accompanied by a description of any legislative or administrative measures upon which it is based.

7.   Each Party shall, no later than the date of entry into force of this Convention for it, transmit to the Secretariat responses with respect to each chemical listed in Annex III. A Party that has provided such responses under the Amended London Guidelines or the International Code of Conduct need not resubmit those responses.

8.   Each Party shall make its responses under this Article available to those concerned within its jurisdiction, in accordance with its legislative or administrative measures.

9.   A Party that, pursuant to paragraphs 2 and 4 above and paragraph 2 of Article 11, takes a decision not to consent to import of a chemical or to consent to its import only under specified conditions shall, if it has not already done so, simultaneously prohibit or make subject to the same conditions:

(a) Import of the chemical from any source; and

(b) Domestic production of the chemical for domestic use.

10. Every six months the Secretariat shall inform all Parties of the responses it has received. Such information shall include a description of the legislative or administrative measures on which the decisions have been based, where available. The Secretariat shall, in addition, inform the Parties of any cases of failure to transmit a response.

Article 11
Obligations in relation to exports of chemicals listed in Annex III

1.   Each exporting Party shall:

(a) Implement appropriate legislative or administrative measures to communicate the responses forwarded by the Secretariat in accordance with paragraph 10 of Article 10 to those concerned within its jurisdiction;

(b) Take appropriate legislative or administrative measures to ensure that exporters within its jurisdiction comply with decisions in each response no later than six months after the date on which the Secretariat first informs the Parties of such response in accordance with paragraph 10 of Article 10;

(c) Advise and assist importing Parties, upon request and as appropriate:

(i)   To obtain further information to help them to take action in accordance with paragraph 4 of Article 10 and paragraph 2 (c) below; and

(ii)   To strengthen their capacities and capabilities to manage chemicals safely during their life-cycle.

2.   Each Party shall ensure that a chemical listed in Annex III is not exported from its territory to any importing Party that, in exceptional circumstances, has failed to transmit a response or has transmitted an interim response that does not contain an interim decision, unless:

(a) It is a chemical that, at the time of import, is registered as a chemical in the importing Party; or

(b) It is a chemical for which evidence exists that it has previously been used in, or imported into, the importing Party and in relation to which no regulatory action to prohibit its use has been taken; or

(c) Explicit consent to the import has been sought and received by the exporter through a designated national authority of the importing Party. The importing Party shall respond to such a request within sixty days and shall promptly notify the Secretariat of its decision.

The obligations of exporting Parties under this paragraph shall apply with effect from the expiration of a period of six months from the date on which the Secretariat first informs the Parties, in accordance with paragraph 10 of Article 10, that a Party has failed to transmit a response or has transmitted an interim response that does not contain an interim decision, and shall apply for one year.

Article 12
Export notification

1.   Where a chemical that is banned or severely restricted by a Party is exported from its territory, that Party shall provide an export notification to the importing Party. The export notification shall include the information set out in Annex V.

2.   The export notification shall be provided for that chemical prior to the first export following adoption of the corresponding final regulatory action. Thereafter, the export notification shall be provided before the first export in any calendar year. The requirement to notify before export may be waived by the designated national authority of the importing Party.

3.   An exporting Party shall provide an updated export notification after it has adopted a final regulatory action that results in a major change concerning the ban or severe restriction of that chemical.

4.   The importing Party shall acknowledge receipt of the first export notification received after the adoption of the final regulatory action. If the exporting Party does not receive the acknowledgement within thirty days of the dispatch of the export notification, it shall submit a second notification. The exporting Party shall make reasonable efforts to ensure that the importing Party receives the second notification.

5.   The obligations of a Party set out in paragraph 1 shall cease when:

(a) The chemical has been listed in Annex III;

(b) The importing Party has provided a response for the chemical to the Secretariat in accordance with paragraph 2 of Article 10; and

(c) The Secretariat has distributed the response to the Parties in accordance with paragraph 10 of Article 10.

Article 13
Information to accompany exported chemicals

1. The Conference of the Parties shall encourage the World Customs Organization to assign specific Harmonized System customs codes to the individual chemicals or groups of chemicals listed in Annex III, as appropriate. Each Party shall require that, whenever a code has been assigned to such a chemical, the shipping document for that chemical bears the code when exported.

2. Without prejudice to any requirements of the importing Party, each Party shall require that both chemicals listed in Annex III and chemicals banned or severely restricted in its territory are, when exported, subject to labelling requirements that ensure adequate availability of information with regard to risks and/or hazards to human health or the environment, taking into account relevant international standards.

3. Without prejudice to any requirements of the importing Party, each Party may require that chemicals subject to environmental or health labelling requirements in its territory are, when exported, subject to labelling requirements that ensure adequate availability of information with regard to risks and/or hazards to human health or the environment, taking into account relevant international standards.

4. With respect to the chemicals referred to in paragraph 2 that are to be used for occupational purposes, each exporting Party shall require that a safety data sheet that follows an internationally recognized format, setting out the most up-to-date information available, is sent to each importer.

5. The information on the label and on the safety data sheet should, as far as practicable, be given in one or more of the official languages of the importing Party.

Article 14
Information exchange

1. Each Party shall, as appropriate and in accordance with the objective of this Convention, facilitate:

(a) The exchange of scientific, technical, economic and legal information concerning the chemicals within the scope of this Convention, including toxicological, ecotoxicological and safety information;

(b) The provision of publicly available information on domestic regulatory actions relevant to the objectives of this Convention; and

(c) The provision of information to other Parties, directly or through the Secretariat, on domestic regulatory actions that substantially restrict one or more uses of the chemical, as appropriate.

2. Parties that exchange information pursuant to this Convention shall protect any confidential information as mutually agreed.

3. The following information shall not be regarded as confidential for the purposes of this Convention:

(a) The information referred to in Annexes I and IV, submitted pursuant to Articles 5 and 6 respectively;

(b) The information contained in the safety data sheet referred to in paragraph 4 of Article 13;

(c) The expiry date of the chemical;

(d) Information on precautionary measures, including hazard classification, the nature of the risk and the relevant safety advice; and

(e) The summary results of the toxicological and ecotoxicological tests.

4. The production date of the chemical shall generally not be considered confidential for the purposes of this Convention.

5. Any Party requiring information on transit movements through its territory of chemicals listed in Annex III may report its need to the Secretariat, which shall inform all Parties accordingly.

Article 15
Implementation of the Convention

1. Each Party shall take such measures as may be necessary to establish and strengthen its national infrastructures and institutions for the effective implementation of this Convention. These measures may include, as required, the adoption or amendment of national legislative or administrative measures and may also include:

(a) The establishment of national registers and databases including safety information for chemicals;

(b) The encouragement of initiatives by industry to promote chemical safety; and

(c) The promotion of voluntary agreements, taking into consideration the provisions of Article 16.

2. Each Party shall ensure, to the extent practicable, that the public has appropriate access to information on chemical handling and accident management and on alternatives that are safer for human health or the environment than the chemicals listed in Annex III.

3. The Parties agree to cooperate, directly or, where appropriate, through competent international organizations, in the implementation of this Convention at the subregional, regional and global levels.

4. Nothing in this Convention shall be interpreted as restricting the right of the Parties to take action that is more stringently protective of human health and the environment than that called for in this Convention, provided that such action is consistent with the provisions of this Convention and is in accordance with international law.

Article 16
Technical assistance

The Parties shall, taking into account in particular the needs of developing countries and countries with economies in transition, cooperate in promoting technical assistance for the development of the infrastructure and the capacity necessary to manage chemicals to enable implementation of this Convention. Parties with more advanced programmes for regulating chemicals should provide technical assistance, including training, to other Parties in developing their infrastructure and capacity to manage chemicals throughout their life-cycle.

Article 17
Non–Compliance

The Conference of the Parties shall, as soon as practicable, develop and approve procedures and institutional mechanisms for determining non-compliance with the provisions of this Convention and for treatment of Parties found to be in non-compliance.

Article 18
Conference of the Parties

1. A Conference of the Parties is hereby established.

2. The first meeting of the Conference of the Parties shall be convened by the Executive Director of UNEP and the Director–General of FAO, acting jointly, no later than one year after the entry into force of this Convention. Thereafter, ordinary meetings of the Conference of the Parties shall be held at regular intervals to be determined by the Conference.

3. Extraordinary meetings of the Conference of the Parties shall be held at such other times as may be deemed necessary by the Conference, or at the written request of any Party provided that it is supported by at least one third of the Parties.

4. The Conference of the Parties shall by consensus agree upon and adopt at its first meeting rules of procedure and financial rules for itself and any subsidiary bodies, as well as financial provisions governing the functioning of the Secretariat.

5. The Conference of the Parties shall keep under continuous review and evaluation the implementation of this Convention. It shall perform the functions assigned to it by the Convention and, to this end, shall:

(a) Establish, further to the requirements of paragraph 6 below, such subsidiary bodies as it considers necessary for the implementation of the Convention;

(b) Cooperate, where appropriate, with competent international organizations and intergovernmental and non-governmental bodies; and

(c) Consider and undertake any additional action that may be required for the achievement of the objectives of the Convention.

6. The Conference of the Parties shall, at its first meeting, establish a subsidiary body, to be called the Chemical Review Committee, for the purposes of performing the functions assigned to that Committee by this Convention. In this regard:

(a) The members of the Chemical Review Committee shall be appointed by the Conference of the Parties. Membership of the Committee shall consist of a limited number of government-designated experts in chemicals management. The members of the Committee shall be appointed on the basis of equitable geographical distribution, including ensuring a balance between developed and developing Parties;

(b) The Conference of the Parties shall decide on the terms of reference, organization and operation of the Committee;

(c) The Committee shall make every effort to make its recommendations by consensus. If all efforts at consensus have been exhausted, and no consensus reached, such recommendation shall as a last resort be adopted by a two-thirds majority vote of the members present and voting.

7. The United Nations, its specialized agencies and the International Atomic Energy Agency, as well as any State not Party to this Convention, may be represented at meetings of the Conference of the Parties as observers. Any body or agency, whether national or international, governmental or non-governmental, qualified in matters covered by the Convention, and which has informed the Secretariat of its wish to be represented at a meeting of the Conference of the Parties as an observer may be admitted unless at least one third of the Parties present object. The admission and participation of observers shall be subject to the rules of procedure adopted by the Conference of the Parties.

Article 19
Secretariat

1. A Secretariat is hereby established.

2. The functions of the Secretariat shall be:

(a) To make arrangements for meetings of the Conference of the Parties and its subsidiary bodies and to provide them with services as required;

(b) To facilitate assistance to the Parties, particularly developing Parties and Parties with economies in transition, on request, in the implementation of this Convention;

(c) To ensure the necessary coordination with the secretariats of other relevant international bodies;

(d) To enter, under the overall guidance of the Conference of the Parties, into such administrative and contractual arrangements as may be required for the effective discharge of its functions; and

(e) To perform the other secretariat functions specified in this Convention and such other functions as may be determined by the Conference of the Parties.

3.   The secretariat functions for this Convention shall be performed jointly by the Executive Director of UNEP and the Director–General of FAO, subject to such arrangements as shall be agreed between them and approved by the Conference of the Parties.

4.   The Conference of the Parties may decide, by a three-fourths majority of the Parties present and voting, to entrust the secretariat functions to one or more other competent international organizations, should it find that the Secretariat is not functioning as intended.

Article 20
Settlement of disputes

1.   Parties shall settle any dispute between them concerning the interpretation or application of this Convention through negotiation or other peaceful means of their own choice.

2.   When ratifying, accepting, approving or acceding to this Convention, or at any time thereafter, a Party that is not a regional economic integration organization may declare in a written instrument submitted to the Depositary that, with respect to any dispute concerning the interpretation or application of the Convention, it recognizes one or both of the following means of dispute settlement as compulsory in relation to any Party accepting the same obligation:

(a) Arbitration in accordance with procedures to be adopted by the Conference of the Parties in an annex as soon as practicable; and

(b) Submission of the dispute to the International Court of Justice.

3.   A Party that is a regional economic integration organization may make a declaration with like effect in relation to arbitration in accordance with the procedure referred to in paragraph 2 (a).

4.   A declaration made pursuant to paragraph 2 shall remain in force until it expires in accordance with its terms or until three months after written notice of its revocation has been deposited with the Depositary.

5.   The expiry of a declaration, a notice of revocation or a new declaration shall not in any way affect proceedings pending before an arbitral tribunal or the International Court of Justice unless the parties to the dispute otherwise agree.

6.   If the parties to a dispute have not accepted the same or any procedure pursuant to paragraph 2, and if they have not been able to settle their dispute within twelve months following notification by one party to another that a dispute exists between them, the dispute shall be submitted to a conciliation commission at the request of any party to the dispute. The conciliation commission shall render a report with recommendations. Additional procedures relating to the conciliation commission shall be included in an annex to be adopted by the Conference of the Parties no later than the second meeting of the Conference.

Article 21
Amendments to the Convention

1. Amendments to this Convention may be proposed by any Party.

2. Amendments to this Convention shall be adopted at a meeting of the Conference of the Parties. The text of any proposed amendment shall be communicated to the Parties by the Secretariat at least six months before the meeting at which it is proposed for adoption. The Secretariat shall also communicate the proposed amendment to the signatories to this Convention and, for information, to the Depositary.

3. The Parties shall make every effort to reach agreement on any proposed amendment to this Convention by consensus. If all efforts at consensus have been exhausted, and no agreement reached, the amendment shall as a last resort be adopted by a three-fourths majority vote of the Parties present and voting at the meeting.

4. The amendment shall be communicated by the Depositary to all Parties for ratification, acceptance or approval.

5. Ratification, acceptance or approval of an amendment shall be notified to the Depositary in writing. An amendment adopted in accordance with paragraph 3 shall enter into force for the Parties having accepted it on the ninetieth day after the date of deposit of instruments of ratification, acceptance or approval by at least three fourths of the Parties. Thereafter, the amendment shall enter into force for any other Party on the ninetieth day after the date on which that Party deposits its instrument of ratification, acceptance or approval of the amendment.

Article 22
Adoption and amendment of annexes

1. Annexes to this Convention shall form an integral part thereof and, unless expressly provided otherwise, a reference to this Convention constitutes at the same time a reference to any annexes thereto.

2. Annexes shall be restricted to procedural, scientific, technical or administrative matters.

3. The following procedure shall apply to the proposal, adoption and entry into force of additional annexes to this Convention:

(a) Additional annexes shall be proposed and adopted according to the procedure laid down in paragraphs 1, 2 and 3 of Article 21;

(b) Any Party that is unable to accept an additional annex shall so notify the Depositary, in writing, within one year from the date of communication of the adoption of the additional annex by the Depositary. The Depositary shall without delay notify all Parties of any such notification received. A Party may at any time withdraw a previous notification of non-acceptance in respect of an additional annex and the annex shall thereupon enter into force for that Party subject to subparagraph (c) below; and

(c) On the expiry of one year from the date of the communication by the Depositary of the adoption of an additional annex, the annex shall enter into force for all Parties that have not submitted a notification in accordance with the provisions of subparagraph (b) above.

4. Except in the case of Annex III, the proposal, adoption and entry into force of amendments to annexes to this Convention shall be subject to the same procedures as for the proposal, adoption and entry into force of additional annexes to the Convention.

5. The following procedure shall apply to the proposal, adoption and entry into force of amendments to Annex III:

(a) Amendments to Annex III shall be proposed and adopted according to the procedure laid down in Articles 5 to 9 and paragraph 2 of Article 21;

(b) The Conference of the Parties shall take its decisions on adoption by consensus;

(c) A decision to amend Annex III shall forthwith be communicated to the Parties by the Depositary. The amendment shall enter into force for all Parties on a date to be specified in the decision.

6. If an additional annex or an amendment to an annex is related to an amendment to this Convention, the additional annex or amendment shall not enter into force until such time as the amendment to the Convention enters into force.

Article 23
Voting

1. Each Party to this Convention shall have one vote, except as provided for in paragraph 2 below.

2. A regional economic integration organization, on matters within its competence, shall exercise its right to vote with a number of votes equal to the number of its member States that are Parties to this Convention. Such an organization shall not exercise its right to vote if any of its member States exercises its right to vote, and vice versa.

3. For the purposes of this Convention, "Parties present and voting" means Parties present and casting an affirmative or negative vote.

Article 24
Signature

This Convention shall be open for signature at Rotterdam by all States and regional economic integration organizations on 11 September 1998, and at United Nations Headquarters in New York from 12 September 1998 to 10 September 1999.

Article 25
Ratification, acceptance, approval or accession

1. This Convention shall be subject to ratification, acceptance or approval by States and by regional economic integration organizations. It shall be open for accession by States and by regional economic integration organizations from the day after the date on which the Convention is closed for signature. Instruments of ratification, acceptance, approval or accession shall be deposited with the Depositary.

2. Any regional economic integration organization that becomes a Party to this Convention without any of its member States being a Party shall be bound by all the obligations under the Convention. In the case of such organizations, one or more of whose member States is a Party to this Convention, the organization and its member States shall decide on their respective responsibilities for the performance of their obligations under the Convention. In such cases, the organization and the member States shall not be entitled to exercise rights under the Convention concurrently.

3. In its instrument of ratification, acceptance, approval or accession, a regional economic integration organization shall declare the extent of its competence in respect of the matters governed by this Convention. Any such organization shall also inform the Depositary, who shall in turn inform the Parties, of any relevant modification in the extent of its competence.

Article 26
Entry into force

1. This Convention shall enter into force on the ninetieth day after the date of deposit of the fiftieth instrument of ratification, acceptance, approval or accession.

2. For each State or regional economic integration organization that ratifies, accepts or approves this Convention or accedes thereto after the deposit of the fiftieth instrument of ratification, acceptance, approval or accession, the Convention shall enter into force on the ninetieth day after the date of deposit by such State or regional economic integration organization of its instrument of ratification, acceptance, approval or accession.

3. For the purpose of paragraphs 1 and 2, any instrument deposited by a regional economic integration organization shall not be counted as additional to those deposited by member States of that organization.

Article 27
Reservations

No reservations may be made to this Convention.

Article 28
Withdrawal

1. At any time after three years from the date on which this Convention has entered into force for a Party, that Party may withdraw from the Convention by giving written notification to the Depositary.

2. Any such withdrawal shall take effect upon expiry of one year from the date of receipt by the Depositary of the notification of withdrawal, or on such later date as may be specified in the notification of withdrawal.

Article 29
Depositary

The Secretary–General of the United Nations shall be the Depositary of this Convention.

Article 30
Authentic texts

The original of this Convention, of which the Arabic, Chinese, English, French, Russian and Spanish texts are equally authentic, shall be deposited with the Secretary–General of the United Nations.

Annex I

INFORMATION REQUIREMENTS FOR NOTIFICATIONS MADE PURSUANT TO ARTICLE 5

* * *

Annex II

CRITERIA FOR LISTING BANNED OR SEVERELY RESTRICTED CHEMICALS IN ANNEX III

* * *

Annex III

CHEMICALS SUBJECT TO THE PRIOR INFORMED CONSENT PROCEDURE

Chemical	Relevant CAS number(s)	Category
2,4,5–T	93–76–5	Pesticide
Aldrin	309–00–2	Pesticide
Captafol	2425–06–1	Pesticide
Chlordane	57–74–9	Pesticide
Chlordimeform	6164–98–3	Pesticide
Chlorobenzilate	510–15–6	Pesticide
DDT	50–29–3	Pesticide
Dieldrin	60–57–1	Pesticide
Dinoseb and dinoseb salts	88–85–7	Pesticide
1,2–dibromoethane (EDB)	106–93–4	Pesticide
Fluoroacetamide	640–19–7	Pesticide
HCH (mixed isomers)	608–73–1	Pesticide
Heptachlor	76–44–8	Pesticide
Hexachlorobenzene	118–74–1	Pesticide
Lindane	58–89–9	Pesticide
Mercury compounds, including inorganic mercury compounds, alkyl mercury compounds and alkyloxyalkyl and aryl mercury compounds		Pesticide
Pentachlorophenol	87–86–5	Pesticide
Monocrotophos (Soluble liquid formulations of the substance that exceed 600 g active ingredient/l)	6923–22–4	Severely hazardous pesticide formulation
Methamidophos (Soluble liquid formulations of the substance that exceed 600 g active ingredient/l)	10265–92–6	Severely hazardous pesticide formulation
Phosphamidon (Soluble liquid formulations of the substance that exceed 1000 g active ingredient/l)	13171–21–6 (mixture, (E) & (Z) isomers) 23783–98–4 ((Z)-isomer) 297–99–4 ((E)-isomer)	Severely hazardous pesticide formulation
Methyl-parathion (emulsifiable concentrates (EC) with 19.5%, 40%, 50%, 60% active ingredient and dusts containing 1.5%, 2% and 3% active ingredient)	298–00–0	Severely hazardous pesticide formulation

Chemical	Relevant CAS number(s)	Category
Parathion (all formulations—aerosols, dustable powder (DP), emulsifiable concentrate (EC), granules (GR) and wettable powders (WP)—of this substance are included, except capsule suspensions (CS))	56–38–2	Severely hazardous pesticide formulation
Crocidolite	12001–28–4	Industrial
Polybrominated biphenyls (PBB)	36355–01–8(hexa—) 27858–07–7 (octa—) 13654–09–6 (deca—)	Industrial
Polychlorinated biphenyls (PCB)	1336–36–3	Industrial
Polychlorinated terphenyls (PCT)	61788–33–8	Industrial
Tris (2,3–dibromopropyl) phosphate	126–72–7	Industrial

Annex IV

INFORMATION AND CRITERIA FOR LISTING SEVERELY HAZARDOUS PESTICIDE FORMULATIONS IN ANNEX III

* * *

Annex V

INFORMATION REQUIREMENTS FOR EXPORT NOTIFICATION

1. Export notifications shall contain the following information:

(a) Name and address of the relevant designated national authorities of the exporting Party and the importing Party;

(b) Expected date of export to the importing Party;

(c) Name of the banned or severely restricted chemical and a summary of the information specified in Annex I that is to be provided to the Secretariat in accordance with Article 5. Where more than one such chemical is included in a mixture or preparation, such information shall be provided for each chemical;

(d) A statement indicating, if known, the foreseen category of the chemical and its foreseen use within that category in the importing Party;

(e) Information on precautionary measures to reduce exposure to, and emission of, the chemical;

(f) In the case of a mixture or a preparation, the concentration of the banned or severely restricted chemical or chemicals in question;

(g) Name and the address of the importer;

(h) Any additional information that is readily available to the relevant designated national authority of the exporting Party that would be of assistance to the designated national authority of the importing Party;

2. In addition to the information referred to in paragraph 1, the exporting Party shall provide such further information specified in Annex I as may be requested by the importing Party.

4.5   STOCKHOLM CONVENTION ON PERSISTENT ORGANIC POLLUTANTS. **Adopted at Stockholm, 22 May 2001. Entered into force, 17 May 2004. 2256 UNTS 119;** *reprinted in* **40 ILM 278 (2001) & 5 Weston & Carlson V.I.14c**

The Parties to this Convention,

Recognizing that persistent organic pollutants possess toxic properties, resist degradation, bioaccumulate and are transported, through air, water and migratory species, across international boundaries and deposited far from their place of release, where they accumulate in terrestrial and aquatic ecosystems,

Aware of the health concerns, especially in developing countries, resulting from local exposure to persistent organic pollutants, in particular impacts upon women and, through them, upon future generations,

Acknowledging that the Arctic ecosystems and indigenous communities are particularly at risk because of the biomagnification of persistent organic pollutants and that contamination of their traditional foods is a public health issue,

Conscious of the need for global action on persistent organic pollutants,

Mindful of decision 19/13 C of 7 February 1997 of the Governing Council of the United Nations Environment Programme to initiate international action to protect human health and the environment through measures which will reduce and/or eliminate emissions and discharges of persistent organic pollutants,

Recalling the pertinent provisions of the relevant international environmental conventions, especially the Rotterdam Convention on the Prior Informed Consent Procedure for Certain Hazardous Chemicals and Pesticides in International Trade, and the Basel Convention on the Control of Transboundary Movements of Hazardous Wastes and their Disposal including the regional agreements developed within the framework of its Article 11,

Recalling also the pertinent provisions of the Rio Declaration on Environment and Development and Agenda 21,

Acknowledging that precaution underlies the concerns of all the Parties and is embedded within this Convention,

Recognizing that this Convention and other international agreements in the field of trade and the environment are mutually supportive,

Reaffirming that States have, in accordance with the Charter of the United Nations and the principles of international law, the sovereign right to exploit their own resources pursuant to their own environmental and developmental policies, and the responsibility to ensure that activities within their jurisdiction or control do not cause damage to the environment of other States or of areas beyond the limits of national jurisdiction,

Taking into account the circumstances and particular requirements of developing countries, in particular the least developed among them, and countries with economies in transition, especially the need to strengthen their national capabilities for the management of chemicals, including through the transfer of technology, the provision of financial and technical assistance and the promotion of cooperation among the Parties,

Taking full account of the Programme of Action for the Sustainable Development of Small Island Developing States, adopted in Barbados on 6 May 1994,

Noting the respective capabilities of developed and developing countries, as well as the common but differentiated responsibilities of States as set forth in Principle 7 of the Rio Declaration on Environment and Development,

Recognizing the important contribution that the private sector and non-governmental organizations can make to achieving the reduction and/or elimination of emissions and discharges of persistent organic pollutants,

Underlining the importance of manufacturers of persistent organic pollutants taking responsibility for reducing adverse effects caused by their products and for providing information to users, Governments and the public on the hazardous properties of those chemicals,

Conscious of the need to take measures to prevent adverse effects caused by persistent organic pollutants at all stages of their life cycle,

Reaffirming Principle 16 of the Rio Declaration on Environment and Development which states that national authorities should endeavour to promote the internalization of environmental costs and the use of economic instruments, taking into account the approach that the polluter should, in principle, bear the cost of pollution, with due regard to the public interest and without distorting international trade and investment,

Encouraging Parties not having regulatory and assessment schemes for pesticides and industrial chemicals to develop such schemes,

Recognizing the importance of developing and using environmentally sound alternative processes and chemicals,

Determined to protect human health and the environment from the harmful impacts of persistent organic pollutants,

Have agreed as follows:

Article 1
Objective

Mindful of the precautionary approach as set forth in Principle 15 of the Rio Declaration on Environment and Development, the objective of this Convention is to protect human health and the environment from persistent organic pollutants.

Article 2
Definitions

For the purposes of this Convention:

(a) "Party" means a State or regional economic integration organization that has consented to be bound by this Convention and for which the Convention is in force;

(b) "Regional economic integration organization" means an organization constituted by sovereign States of a given region to which its member States have transferred competence in respect of matters governed by this Convention and which has been duly authorized, in accordance with its internal procedures, to sign, ratify, accept, approve or accede to this Convention;

(c) "Parties present and voting" means Parties present and casting an affirmative or negative vote.

Article 3
Measures to reduce or eliminate releases from intentional production an use

1. Each Party shall:

(a) Prohibit and/or take the legal and administrative measures necessary to eliminate:

    (i) Its production and use of the chemicals listed in Annex A subject to the provisions of that Annex; and

(ii) Its import and export of the chemicals listed in Annex A in accordance with the provisions of paragraph 2; and

(b) Restrict its production and use of the chemicals listed in Annex B in accordance with the provisions of that Annex.

2. Each Party shall take measures to ensure:

(a) That a chemical listed in Annex A or Annex B is imported only:

(i) For the purpose of environmentally sound disposal as set forth in paragraph 1 (d) of Article 6; or

(ii) For a use or purpose which is permitted for that Party under Annex A or Annex B;

(b) That a chemical listed in Annex A for which any production or use specific exemption is in effect or a chemical listed in Annex B for which any production or use specific exemption or acceptable purpose is in effect, taking into account any relevant provisions in existing international prior informed consent instruments, is exported only:

(i) For the purpose of environmentally sound disposal as set forth in paragraph 1 (d) of Article 6;

(ii) To a Party which is permitted to use that chemical under Annex A or Annex B; or

(iii) To a State not Party to this Convention which has provided an annual certification to the exporting Party. Such certification shall specify the intended use of the chemical and include a statement that, with respect to that chemical, the importing State is committed to:

    a. Protect human health and the environment by taking the necessary measures to minimize or prevent releases;

    b. Comply with the provisions of paragraph 1 of Article 6; and

    c. Comply, where appropriate, with the provisions of paragraph 2 of Part II of Annex B.

The certification shall also include any appropriate supporting documentation, such as legislation, regulatory instruments, or administrative or policy guidelines. The exporting Party shall transmit the certification to the Secretariat within sixty days of receipt.

(c) That a chemical listed in Annex A, for which production and use specific exemptions are no longer in effect for any Party, is not exported from it except for the purpose of environmentally sound disposal as set forth in paragraph 1 (d) of Article 6;

(d) For the purposes of this paragraph, the term "State not Party to this Convention" shall include, with respect to a particular chemical, a State or regional economic integration organization that has not agreed to be bound by the Convention with respect to that chemical.

3. Each Party that has one or more regulatory and assessment schemes for new pesticides or new industrial chemicals shall take measures to regulate with the aim of preventing the production and use of new pesticides or new industrial chemicals which, taking into consideration the criteria in paragraph 1 of Annex D, exhibit the characteristics of persistent organic pollutants.

4. Each Party that has one or more regulatory and assessment schemes for pesticides or industrial chemicals shall, where appropriate, take into consideration within these schemes the criteria in paragraph 1 of Annex D when conducting assessments of pesticides or industrial chemicals currently in use.

5. Except as otherwise provided in this Convention, paragraphs 1 and 2 shall not apply to quantities of a chemical to be used for laboratory-scale research or as a reference standard.

6. Any Party that has a specific exemption in accordance with Annex A or a specific exemption or an acceptable purpose in accordance with Annex B shall take appropriate measures to ensure that any production or use under such exemption or purpose is carried out in a manner that prevents or minimizes human exposure and release into the environment. For exempted uses or acceptable purposes that involve intentional release into the environment under conditions of normal use, such release shall be to the minimum extent necessary, taking into account any applicable standards and guidelines.

Article 4
Register of specific exemptions

1. A Register is hereby established for the purpose of identifying the Parties that have specific exemptions listed in Annex A or Annex B. It shall not identify Parties that make use of the provisions in Annex A or Annex B that may be exercised by all Parties. The Register shall be maintained by the Secretariat and shall be available to the public.

2. The Register shall include:

(a) A list of the types of specific exemptions reproduced from Annex A and Annex B;

(b) A list of the Parties that have a specific exemption listed under Annex A or Annex B; and

(c) A list of the expiry dates for each registered specific exemption.

3. Any State may, on becoming a Party, by means of a notification in writing to the Secretariat, register for one or more types of specific exemptions listed in Annex A or Annex B.

4. Unless an earlier date is indicated in the Register by a Party, or an extension is granted pursuant to paragraph 7, all registrations of specific exemptions shall expire five years after the date of entry into force of this Convention with respect to a particular chemical.

5. At its first meeting, the Conference of the Parties shall decide upon its review process for the entries in the Register.

6. Prior to a review of an entry in the Register, the Party concerned shall submit a report to the Secretariat justifying its continuing need for registration of that exemption. The report shall be circulated by the Secretariat to all Parties. The review of a registration shall be carried out on the basis of all available information. Thereupon, the Conference of the Parties may make such recommendations to the Party concerned as it deems appropriate.

7. The Conference of the Parties may, upon request from the Party concerned, decide to extend the expiry date of a specific exemption for a period of up to five years. In making its decision, the Conference of the Parties shall take due account of the special circumstances of the developing country Parties and Parties with economies in transition.

8. A Party may, at any time, withdraw an entry from the Register for a specific exemption upon written notification to the Secretariat. The withdrawal shall take effect on the date specified in the notification.

9. When there are no longer any Parties registered for a particular type of specific exemption, no new registrations may be made with respect to it.

Article 5
Measures to reduce or eliminate releases from unintentional production

Each Party shall at a minimum take the following measures to reduce the total releases derived from anthropogenic sources of each of the chemicals listed in Annex C, with the goal of their continuing minimization and, where feasible, ultimate elimination:

(a) Develop an action plan or, where appropriate, a regional or subregional action plan within two years of the date of entry into force of this Convention for it, and subsequently implement it as part of its implementation plan specified in Article 7, designed to identify, characterize and address the release of the chemicals listed in Annex C and to facilitate implementation of subparagraphs (b) to (e). The action plan shall include the following elements:

(i) An evaluation of current and projected releases, including the development and maintenance of source inventories and release estimates, taking into consideration the source categories identified in Annex C;

(ii) An evaluation of the efficacy of the laws and policies of the Party relating to the management of such releases;

(iii) Strategies to meet the obligations of this paragraph, taking into account the evaluations in (i) and (ii);

(iv) Steps to promote education and training with regard to, and awareness of, those strategies;

(v) A review every five years of those strategies and of their success in meeting the obligations of this paragraph; such reviews shall be included in reports submitted pursuant to Article 15;

(vi) A schedule for implementation of the action plan, including for the strategies and measures identified therein;

(b) Promote the application of available, feasible and practical measures that can expeditiously achieve a realistic and meaningful level of release reduction or source elimination;

(c) Promote the development and, where it deems appropriate, require the use of substitute or modified materials, products and processes to prevent the formation and release of the chemicals listed in Annex C, taking into consideration the general guidance on prevention and release reduction measures in Annex C and guidelines to be adopted by decision of the Conference of the Parties;

(d) Promote and, in accordance with the implementation schedule of its action plan, require the use of best available techniques for new sources within source categories which a Party has identified as warranting such action in its action plan, with a particular initial focus on source categories identified in Part II of Annex C. In any case, the requirement to use best available techniques for new sources in the categories listed in Part II of that Annex shall be phased in as soon as practicable but no later than four years after the entry into force of the Convention for that Party. For the identified categories, Parties shall promote the use of best environmental practices. When applying best available techniques and best environmental practices, Parties should take into consideration the general guidance on prevention and release reduction measures in that Annex and guidelines on best available techniques and best environmental practices to be adopted by decision of the Conference of the Parties;

(e) Promote, in accordance with its action plan, the use of best available techniques and best environmental practices:

(i) For existing sources, within the source categories listed in Part II of Annex C and within source categories such as those in Part III of that Annex; and

(ii) For new sources, within source categories such as those listed in Part III of Annex C which a Party has not addressed under subparagraph (d).

When applying best available techniques and best environmental practices, Parties should take into consideration the general guidance on prevention and release reduction measures in Annex C and guidelines on best available techniques and best environmental practices to be adopted by decision of the Conference of the Parties;

(f) For the purposes of this paragraph and Annex C:

(i) "Best available techniques" means the most effective and advanced stage in the development of activities and their methods of operation which indicate the practical suitability of particular techniques for providing in principle the basis for release limitations designed to prevent and, where that is not practicable, generally to reduce releases of chemicals listed in Part I of Annex C and their impact on the environment as a whole. In this regard:

(ii) "Techniques" includes both the technology used and the way in which the installation is designed, built, maintained, operated and decommissioned;

(iii) "Available" techniques means those techniques that are accessible to the operator and that are developed on a scale that allows implementation in the relevant industrial sector, under economically and technically viable conditions, taking into consideration the costs and advantages; and

(iv) "Best" means most effective in achieving a high general level of protection of the environment as a whole;

(v) "Best environmental practices" means the application of the most appropriate combination of environmental control measures and strategies;

(vi) "New source" means any source of which the construction or substantial modification is commenced at least one year after the date of:

a. Entry into force of this Convention for the Party concerned; or

b. Entry into force for the Party concerned of an amendment to Annex C where the source becomes subject to the provisions of this Convention only by virtue of that amendment.

(g) Release limit values or performance standards may be used by a Party to fulfill its commitments for best available techniques under this paragraph.

Article 6
Measures to reduce or eliminate releases from stockpiles and wastes

1. In order to ensure that stockpiles consisting of or containing chemicals listed either in Annex A or Annex B and wastes, including products and articles upon becoming wastes, consisting of, containing or contaminated with a chemical listed in Annex A, B or C, are managed in a manner protective of human health and the environment, each Party shall:

(a) Develop appropriate strategies for identifying:

(i) Stockpiles consisting of or containing chemicals listed either in Annex A or Annex B; and

(ii) Products and articles in use and wastes consisting of, containing or contaminated with a chemical listed in Annex A, B or C;

(b) Identify, to the extent practicable, stockpiles consisting of or containing chemicals listed either in Annex A or Annex B on the basis of the strategies referred to in subparagraph (a);

(c) Manage stockpiles, as appropriate, in a safe, efficient and environmentally sound manner. Stockpiles of chemicals listed either in Annex A or Annex B, after they are no longer allowed to be used according to any specific exemption specified in Annex A or any specific exemption or acceptable purpose specified in Annex B, except stockpiles which are allowed to be exported according to paragraph 2 of Article 3, shall be deemed to be waste and shall be managed in accordance with subparagraph (d);

(d) Take appropriate measures so that such wastes, including products and articles upon becoming wastes, are:

(i) Handled, collected, transported and stored in an environmentally sound manner;

(ii) Disposed of in such a way that the persistent organic pollutant content is destroyed or irreversibly transformed so that they do not exhibit the characteristics of persistent organic pollutants or otherwise disposed of in an environmentally sound manner when destruction or irreversible transformation does not represent the environmentally preferable option or the persistent organic pollutant content is low, taking into account international rules, standards, and guidelines, including those that may be developed pursuant to paragraph 2, and relevant global and regional regimes governing the management of hazardous wastes;

(iii) Not permitted to be subjected to disposal operations that may lead to recovery, recycling, reclamation, direct reuse or alternative uses of persistent organic pollutants; and

(iv) Not transported across international boundaries without taking into account relevant international rules, standards and guidelines;

(e) Endeavour to develop appropriate strategies for identifying sites contaminated by chemicals listed in Annex A, B or C; if remediation of those sites is undertaken it shall be performed in an environmentally sound manner.

2. The Conference of the Parties shall cooperate closely with the appropriate bodies of the Basel Convention on the Control of Transboundary Movements of Hazardous Wastes and their Disposal to, *inter alia*:

(a) Establish levels of destruction and irreversible transformation necessary to ensure that the characteristics of persistent organic pollutants as specified in paragraph 1 of Annex D are not exhibited;

(b) Determine what they consider to be the methods that constitute environmentally sound disposal referred to above; and

(c) Work to establish, as appropriate, the concentration levels of the chemicals listed in Annexes A, B and C in order to define the low persistent organic pollutant content referred to in paragraph 1 (d) (ii).

Article 7
Implementation plans

1. Each Party shall:

(a) Develop and endeavour to implement a plan for the implementation of its obligations under this Convention;

(b) Transmit its implementation plan to the Conference of the Parties within two years of the date on which this Convention enters into force for it; and

(c) Review and update, as appropriate, its implementation plan on a periodic basis and in a manner to be specified by a decision of the Conference of the Parties.

2. The Parties shall, where appropriate, cooperate directly or through global, regional and subregional organizations, and consult their national stakeholders, including women's groups and groups involved in the health of children, in order to

facilitate the development, implementation and updating of their implementation plans.

3. The Parties shall endeavour to utilize and, where necessary, establish the means to integrate national implementation plans for persistent organic pollutants in their sustainable development strategies where appropriate.

Article 8
Listing of chemicals in Annexes A, B and C

1. A Party may submit a proposal to the Secretariat for listing a chemical in Annexes A, B and/or C. The proposal shall contain the information specified in Annex D. In developing a proposal, a Party may be assisted by other Parties and/or by the Secretariat.

2. The Secretariat shall verify whether the proposal contains the information specified in Annex D. If the Secretariat is satisfied that the proposal contains the information so specified, it shall forward the proposal to the Persistent Organic Pollutants Review Committee.

3. The Committee shall examine the proposal and apply the screening criteria specified in Annex D in a flexible and transparent way, taking all information provided into account in an integrative and balanced manner.

4. If the Committee decides that:

(a) It is satisfied that the screening criteria have been fulfilled, it shall, through the Secretariat, make the proposal and the evaluation of the Committee available to all Parties and observers and invite them to submit the information specified in Annex E; or

(b) It is not satisfied that the screening criteria have been fulfilled, it shall, through the Secretariat, inform all Parties and observers and make the proposal and the evaluation of the Committee available to all Parties and the proposal shall be set aside.

5. Any Party may resubmit a proposal to the Committee that has been set aside by the Committee pursuant to paragraph 4. The resubmission may include any concerns of the Party as well as a justification for additional consideration by the Committee. If, following this procedure, the Committee again sets the proposal aside, the Party may challenge the decision of the Committee and the Conference of the Parties shall consider the matter at its next session. The Conference of the Parties may decide, based on the screening criteria in Annex D and taking into account the evaluation of the Committee and any additional information provided by any Party or observer, that the proposal should proceed.

6. Where the Committee has decided that the screening criteria have been fulfilled, or the Conference of the Parties has decided that the proposal should proceed, the Committee shall further review the proposal, taking into account any relevant additional information received, and shall prepare a draft risk profile in accordance with Annex E. It shall, through the Secretariat, make that draft available to all Parties and observers, collect technical comments from them and, taking those comments into account, complete the risk profile.

7. If, on the basis of the risk profile conducted in accordance with Annex E, the Committee decides:

(a) That the chemical is likely as a result of its long-range environmental transport to lead to significant adverse human health and/or environmental effects such that global action is warranted, the proposal shall proceed. Lack of full scientific certainty shall not prevent the proposal from proceeding. The Committee shall, through the Secretariat, invite information from all Parties and observers relating to the considerations specified in Annex F. It shall then prepare a risk management evaluation that includes an analysis of possible control measures for the chemical in accordance with that Annex; or

(b) That the proposal should not proceed, it shall, through the Secretariat, make the risk profile available to all Parties and observers and set the proposal aside.

8. For any proposal set aside pursuant to paragraph 7 (b), a Party may request the Conference of the Parties to consider instructing the Committee to invite additional information from the proposing Party and other Parties during a period not to exceed one year. After that period and on the basis of any information received, the Committee shall reconsider the proposal pursuant to paragraph 6 with a priority to be decided by the Conference of the Parties. If, following this procedure, the Committee again sets the proposal aside, the Party may challenge the decision of the Committee and the Conference of the Parties shall consider the matter at its next session. The Conference of the Parties may decide, based on the risk profile prepared in accordance with Annex E and taking into account the evaluation of the Committee and any additional information provided by any Party or observer, that the proposal should proceed. If the Conference of the Parties decides that the proposal shall proceed, the Committee shall then prepare the risk management evaluation.

9. The Committee shall, based on the risk profile referred to in paragraph 6 and the risk management evaluation referred to in paragraph 7 (a) or paragraph 8, recommend whether the chemical should be considered by the Conference of the Parties for listing in Annexes A, B and/or C. The Conference of the Parties, taking due account of the recommendations of the Committee, including any scientific uncertainty, shall decide, in a precautionary manner, whether to list the chemical, and specify its related control measures, in Annexes A, B and/or C.

Article 9
Information exchange

1. Each Party shall facilitate or undertake the exchange of information relevant to:

(a) The reduction or elimination of the production, use and release of persistent organic pollutants; and

(b) Alternatives to persistent organic pollutants, including information relating to their risks as well as to their economic and social costs.

2. The Parties shall exchange the information referred to in paragraph 1 directly or through the Secretariat.

3. Each Party shall designate a national focal point for the exchange of such information.

4. The Secretariat shall serve as a clearing-house mechanism for information on persistent organic pollutants, including information provided by Parties, intergovernmental organizations and non-governmental organizations.

5. For the purposes of this Convention, information on health and safety of humans and the environment shall not be regarded as confidential. Parties that exchange other information pursuant to this Convention shall protect any confidential information as mutually agreed.

Article 10
Public information, awareness and education

1. Each Party shall, within its capabilities, promote and facilitate:

(a) Awareness among its policy and decision makers with regard to persistent organic pollutants;

(b) Provision to the public of all available information on persistent organic pollutants, taking into account paragraph 5 of Article 9;

(c) Development and implementation, especially for women, children and the least educated, of educational and public awareness programmes on persistent organic pollutants, as well as on their health and environmental effects and on their alternatives;

(d) Public participation in addressing persistent organic pollutants and their health and environmental effects and in developing adequate responses, including opportunities for providing input at the national level regarding implementation of this Convention;

(e) Training of workers, scientists, educators and technical and managerial personnel;

(f) Development and exchange of educational and public awareness materials at the national and international levels; and

(g) Development and implementation of education and training programmes at the national and international levels.

2. Each Party shall, within its capabilities, ensure that the public has access to the public information referred to in paragraph 1 and that the information is kept up-to-date.

3. Each Party shall, within its capabilities, encourage industry and professional users to promote and facilitate the provision of the information referred to in paragraph 1 at the national level and, as appropriate, subregional, regional and global levels.

4. In providing information on persistent organic pollutants and their alternatives, Parties may use safety data sheets, reports, mass media and other means of communication, and may establish information centres at national and regional levels.

5. Each Party shall give sympathetic consideration to developing mechanisms, such as pollutant release and transfer registers, for the collection and dissemination of information on estimates of the annual quantities of the chemicals listed in Annex A, B or C that are released or disposed of.

Article 11
Research, development and monitoring

1. The Parties shall, within their capabilities, at the national and international levels, encourage and/or undertake appropriate research, development, monitoring and cooperation pertaining to persistent organic pollutants and, where relevant, to their alternatives and to candidate persistent organic pollutants, including on their:

(a) Sources and releases into the environment;

(b) Presence, levels and trends in humans and the environment;

(c) Environmental transport, fate and transformation;

(d) Effects on human health and the environment;

(e) Socio-economic and cultural impacts;

(f) Release reduction and/or elimination; and

(g) Harmonized methodologies for making inventories of generating sources and analytical techniques for the measurement of releases.

2. In undertaking action under paragraph 1, the Parties shall, within their capabilities:

(a) Support and further develop, as appropriate, international programmes, networks and organizations aimed at defining, conducting, assessing and financing research, data collection and monitoring, taking into account the need to minimize duplication of effort;

(b) Support national and international efforts to strengthen national scientific and technical research capabilities, particularly in developing countries and countries with economies in transition, and to promote access to, and the exchange of, data and analyses;

(c) Take into account the concerns and needs, particularly in the field of financial and technical resources, of developing countries and countries with economies in transition and cooperate in improving their capability to participate in the efforts referred to in subparagraphs (a) and (b);

(d) Undertake research work geared towards alleviating the effects of persistent organic pollutants on reproductive health;

(e) Make the results of their research, development and monitoring activities referred to in this paragraph accessible to the public on a timely and regular basis; and

(f) Encourage and/or undertake cooperation with regard to storage and maintenance of information generated from research, development and monitoring.

Article 12
Technical assistance

1. The Parties recognize that rendering of timely and appropriate technical assistance in response to requests from developing country Parties and Parties with economies in transition is essential to the successful implementation of this Convention.

2. The Parties shall cooperate to provide timely and appropriate technical assistance to developing country Parties and Parties with economies in transition, to assist them, taking into account their particular needs, to develop and strengthen their capacity to implement their obligations under this Convention.

3. In this regard, technical assistance to be provided by developed country Parties, and other Parties in accordance with their capabilities, shall include, as appropriate and as mutually agreed, technical assistance for capacity-building relating to implementation of the obligations under this Convention. Further guidance in this regard shall be provided by the Conference of the Parties.

4. The Parties shall establish, as appropriate, arrangements for the purpose of providing technical assistance and promoting the transfer of technology to developing country Parties and Parties with economies in transition relating to the implementation of this Convention. These arrangements shall include regional and subregional centres for capacity-building and transfer of technology to assist developing country Parties and Parties with economies in transition to fulfil their obligations under this Convention. Further guidance in this regard shall be provided by the Conference of the Parties.

5. The Parties shall, in the context of this Article, take full account of the specific needs and special situation of least developed countries and small island developing states in their actions with regard to technical assistance.

Article 13
Financial resources and mechanisms

1. Each Party undertakes to provide, within its capabilities, financial support and incentives in respect of those national activities that are intended to achieve the

objective of this Convention in accordance with its national plans, priorities and programmes.

2. The developed country Parties shall provide new and additional financial resources to enable developing country Parties and Parties with economies in transition to meet the agreed full incremental costs of implementing measures which fulfill their obligations under this Convention as agreed between a recipient Party and an entity participating in the mechanism described in paragraph 6. Other Parties may also on a voluntary basis and in accordance with their capabilities provide such financial resources. Contributions from other sources should also be encouraged. The implementation of these commitments shall take into account the need for adequacy, predictability, the timely flow of funds and the importance of burden sharing among the contributing Parties.

3. Developed country Parties, and other Parties in accordance with their capabilities and in accordance with their national plans, priorities and programmes, may also provide and developing country Parties and Parties with economies in transition avail themselves of financial resources to assist in their implementation of this Convention through other bilateral, regional and multilateral sources or channels.

4. The extent to which the developing country Parties will effectively implement their commitments under this Convention will depend on the effective implementation by developed country Parties of their commitments under this Convention relating to financial resources, technical assistance and technology transfer. The fact that sustainable economic and social development and eradication of poverty are the first and overriding priorities of the developing country Parties will be taken fully into account, giving due consideration to the need for the protection of human health and the environment.

5. The Parties shall take full account of the specific needs and special situation of the least developed countries and the small island developing states in their actions with regard to funding.

6. A mechanism for the provision of adequate and sustainable financial resources to developing country Parties and Parties with economies in transition on a grant or concessional basis to assist in their implementation of the Convention is hereby defined. The mechanism shall function under the authority, as appropriate, and guidance of, and be accountable to the Conference of the Parties for the purposes of this Convention. Its operation shall be entrusted to one or more entities, including existing international entities, as may be decided upon by the Conference of the Parties. The mechanism may also include other entities providing multilateral, regional and bilateral financial and technical assistance. Contributions to the mechanism shall be additional to other financial transfers to developing country Parties and Parties with economies in transition as reflected in, and in accordance with, paragraph 2.

7. Pursuant to the objectives of this Convention and paragraph 6, the Conference of the Parties shall at its first meeting adopt appropriate guidance to be provided to the mechanism and shall agree with the entity or entities participating in the financial mechanism upon arrangements to give effect thereto. The guidance shall address, *inter alia*:

(a) The determination of the policy, strategy and programme priorities, as well as clear and detailed criteria and guidelines regarding eligibility for access to and utilization of financial resources including monitoring and evaluation on a regular basis of such utilization;

(b) The provision by the entity or entities of regular reports to the Conference of the Parties on adequacy and sustainability of funding for activities relevant to the implementation of this Convention;

(c) The promotion of multiple-source funding approaches, mechanisms and arrangements;

(d) The modalities for the determination in a predictable and identifiable manner of the amount of funding necessary and available for the implementation of this Convention, keeping in mind that the phasing out of persistent organic pollutants might require sustained funding, and the conditions under which that amount shall be periodically reviewed; and

(e) The modalities for the provision to interested Parties of assistance with needs assessment, information on available sources of funds and on funding patterns in order to facilitate coordination among them.

8. The Conference of the Parties shall review, not later than its second meeting and thereafter on a regular basis, the effectiveness of the mechanism established under this Article, its ability to address the changing needs of the developing country Parties and Parties with economies in transition, the criteria and guidance referred to in paragraph 7, the level of funding as well as the effectiveness of the performance of the institutional entities entrusted to operate the financial mechanism. It shall, based on such review, take appropriate action, if necessary, to improve the effectiveness of the mechanism, including by means of recommendations and guidance on measures to ensure adequate and sustainable funding to meet the needs of the Parties.

Article 14
Interim financial arrangements

The institutional structure of the Global Environment Facility, operated in accordance with the Instrument for the Establishment of the Restructured Global Environment Facility, shall, on an interim basis, be the principal entity entrusted with the operations of the financial mechanism referred to in Article 13, for the period between the date of entry into force of this Convention and the first meeting of the Conference of the Parties, or until such time as the Conference of the Parties decides which institutional structure will be designated in accordance with Article 1 3. The institutional structure of the Global Environment Facility should fulfill this function through operational measures related specifically to persistent organic pollutants taking into account that new arrangements for this area may be needed.

Article 15
Reporting

1. Each Party shall report to the Conference of the Parties on the measures it has taken to implement the provisions of this Convention and on the effectiveness of such measures in meeting the objectives of the Convention.

2. Each Party shall provide to the Secretariat:

(a) Statistical data on its total quantities of production, import and export of each of the chemicals listed in Annex A and Annex B or a reasonable estimate of such data; and

(b) To the extent practicable, a list of the States from which it has imported each such substance and the States to which it has exported each such substance.

3. Such reporting shall be at periodic intervals and in a format to be decided by the Conference of the Parties at its first meeting.

Article 16
Effectiveness evaluation

1. Commencing four years after the date of entry into force of this Convention, and periodically thereafter at intervals to be decided by the Conference of the Parties, the Conference shall evaluate the effectiveness of this Convention.

2. In order to facilitate such evaluation, the Conference of the Parties shall, at its first meeting, initiate the establishment of arrangements to provide itself with comparable monitoring data on the presence of the chemicals listed in Annexes A, B and C as well as their regional and global environmental transport. These arrangements:

(a) Should be implemented by the Parties on a regional basis when appropriate, in accordance with their technical and financial capabilities, using existing monitoring programmes and mechanisms to the extent possible and promoting harmonization of approaches;

(b) May be supplemented where necessary, taking into account the differences between regions and their capabilities to implement monitoring activities; and

(c) Shall include reports to the Conference of the Parties on the results of the monitoring activities on a regional and global basis at intervals to be specified by the Conference of the Parties.

3. The evaluation described in paragraph 1 shall be conducted on the basis of available scientific, environmental, technical and economic information, including:

(a) Reports and other monitoring information provided pursuant to paragraph 2;

(b) National reports submitted pursuant to Article 15; and

(c) Non-compliance information provided pursuant to the procedures established under Article 17.

Article 17
Non-compliance

The Conference of the Parties shall, as soon as practicable, develop and approve procedures and institutional mechanisms for determining non-compliance with the provisions of this Convention and for the treatment of Parties found to be in non-compliance.

Article 18
Settlement of disputes

1. Parties shall settle any dispute between them concerning the interpretation or application of this Convention through negotiation or other peaceful means of their own choice.

2. When ratifying, accepting, approving or acceding to the Convention, or at any time thereafter, a Party that is not a regional economic integration organization may declare in a written instrument submitted to the depositary that, with respect to any dispute concerning the interpretation or application of the Convention, it recognizes one or both of the following means of dispute settlement as compulsory in relation to any Party accepting the same obligation:

(a) Arbitration in accordance with procedures to be adopted by the Conference of the Parties in an annex as soon as practicable;

(b) Submission of the dispute to the International Court of Justice.

3. A Party that is a regional economic integration organization may make a declaration with like effect in relation to arbitration in accordance with the procedure referred to in paragraph 2 (a).

4. A declaration made pursuant to paragraph 2 or paragraph 3 shall remain in force until it expires in accordance with its terms or until three months after written notice of its revocation has been deposited with the depositary.

5. The expiry of a declaration, a notice of revocation or a new declaration shall not in any way affect proceedings pending before an arbitral tribunal or the International Court of Justice unless the parties to the dispute otherwise agree.

6. If the parties to a dispute have not accepted the same or any procedure pursuant to paragraph 2, and if they have not been able to settle their dispute within twelve months following notification by one party to another that a dispute exists between them, the dispute shall be submitted to a conciliation commission at the request of any party to the dispute. The conciliation commission shall render a report with recommendations. Additional procedures relating to the conciliation commission shall be included in an annex to be adopted by the Conference of the Parties no later than at its second meeting.

Article 19
Conference of the Parties

1. A Conference of the Parties is hereby established.

2. The first meeting of the Conference of the Parties shall be convened by the Executive Director of the United Nations Environment Programme no later than one year after the entry into force of this Convention. Thereafter, ordinary meetings of the Conference of the Parties shall be held at regular intervals to be decided by the Conference.

3. Extraordinary meetings of the Conference of the Parties shall be held at such other times as may be deemed necessary by the Conference, or at the written request of any Party provided that it is supported by at least one third of the Parties.

4. The Conference of the Parties shall by consensus agree upon and adopt at its first meeting rules of procedure and financial rules for itself and any subsidiary bodies, as well as financial provisions governing the functioning of the Secretariat.

5. The Conference of the Parties shall keep under continuous review and evaluation the implementation of this Convention. It shall perform the functions assigned to it by the Convention and, to this end, shall:

(a) Establish, further to the requirements of paragraph 6, such subsidiary bodies as it considers necessary for the implementation of the Convention;

(b) Cooperate, where appropriate, with competent international organizations and intergovernmental and non-governmental bodies; and

(c) Regularly review all information made available to the Parties pursuant to Article 15, including consideration of the effectiveness of paragraph 2 (b) (iii) of Article 3;

(d) Consider and undertake any additional action that may be required for the achievement of the objectives of the Convention.

6. The Conference of the Parties shall, at its first meeting, establish a subsidiary body to be called the Persistent Organic Pollutants Review Committee for the purposes of performing the functions assigned to that Committee by this Convention. In this regard:

(a) The members of the Persistent Organic Pollutants Review Committee shall be appointed by the Conference of the Parties. Membership of the Committee shall consist of government-designated experts in chemical assessment or management. The members of the Committee shall be appointed on the basis of equitable geographical distribution;

(b) The Conference of the Parties shall decide on the terms of reference, organization and operation of the Committee; and

(c) The Committee shall make every effort to adopt its recommendations by consensus. If all efforts at consensus have been exhausted, and no consensus reached, such recommendation shall as a last resort be adopted by a two-thirds majority vote of the members present and voting.

7. The Conference of the Parties shall, at its third meeting, evaluate the continued need for the procedure contained in paragraph 2 (b) of Article 3, including consideration of its effectiveness.

8. The United Nations, its specialized agencies and the International Atomic Energy Agency, as well as any State not Party to this Convention, may be represented at meetings of the Conference of the Parties as observers. Any body or agency, whether national or international, governmental or non-governmental, qualified in matters covered by the Convention, and which has informed the Secretariat of its wish to be represented at a meeting of the Conference of the Parties as an observer may be admitted unless at least one third of the Parties present object. The admission and participation of observers shall be subject to the rules of procedure adopted by the Conference of the Parties.

Article 20
Secretariat

1. A Secretariat is hereby established.

2. The functions of the Secretariat shall be:

(a) To make arrangements for meetings of the Conference of the Parties and its subsidiary bodies and to provide them with services as required;

(b) To facilitate assistance to the Parties, particularly developing country Parties and Parties with economies in transition, on request, in the implementation of this Convention;

(c) To ensure the necessary coordination with the secretariats of other relevant international bodies;

(d) To prepare and make available to the Parties periodic reports based on information received pursuant to Article 15 and other available information;

(e) To enter, under the overall guidance of the Conference of the Parties, into such administrative and contractual arrangements as may be required for the effective discharge of its functions; and

(f) To perform the other secretariat functions specified in this Convention and such other functions as may be determined by the Conference of the Parties.

3. The secretariat functions for this Convention shall be performed by the Executive Director of the United Nations Environment Programme, unless the Conference of the Parties decides, by a three-fourths majority of the Parties present and voting, to entrust the secretariat functions to one or more other international organizations.

Article 21
Amendments to the Convention

1. Amendments to this Convention may be proposed by any Party.

2. Amendments to this Convention shall be adopted at a meeting of the Conference of the Parties. The text of any proposed amendment shall be communicated to the Parties by the Secretariat at least six months before the meeting at which it is proposed for adoption. The Secretariat shall also communicate proposed amendments to the signatories to this Convention and, for information, to the depositary.

3. The Parties shall make every effort to reach agreement on any proposed amendment to this Convention by consensus. If all efforts at consensus have been exhausted, and no agreement reached, the amendment shall as a last resort be adopted by a three-fourths majority vote of the Parties present and voting.

4. The amendment shall be communicated by the depositary to all Parties for ratification, acceptance or approval.

5. Ratification, acceptance or approval of an amendment shall be notified to the depositary in writing. An amendment adopted in accordance with paragraph 3 shall enter into force for the Parties having accepted it on the ninetieth day after the date of deposit of instruments of ratification, acceptance or approval by at least three-fourths of the Parties. Thereafter, the amendment shall enter into force for any other Party on the ninetieth day after the date on which that Party deposits its instrument of ratification, acceptance or approval of the amendment.

Article 22
Adoption and amendment of annexes

1. Annexes to this Convention shall form an integral part thereof and, unless expressly provided otherwise, a reference to this Convention constitutes at the same time a reference to any annexes thereto.

2. Any additional annexes shall be restricted to procedural, scientific, technical or administrative matters.

3. The following procedure shall apply to the proposal, adoption and entry into force of additional annexes to this Convention:

(a) Additional annexes shall be proposed and adopted according to the procedure laid down in paragraphs 1, 2 and 3 of Article 21;

(b) Any Party that is unable to accept an additional annex shall so notify the depositary, in writing, within one year from the date of communication by the depositary of the adoption of the additional annex. The depositary shall without delay notify all Parties of any such notification received. A Party may at any time withdraw a previous notification of non-acceptance in respect of any additional annex, and the annex shall thereupon enter into force for that Party subject to subparagraph (c); and

(c) On the expiry of one year from the date of the communication by the depositary of the adoption of an additional annex, the annex shall enter into force for all Parties that have not submitted a notification in accordance with the provisions of subparagraph (b).

4. The proposal, adoption and entry into force of amendments to Annex A, B or C shall be subject to the same procedures as for the proposal, adoption and entry into force of additional annexes to this Convention, except that an amendment to Annex A, B or C shall not enter into force with respect to any Party that has made a declaration with respect to amendment to those Annexes in accordance with paragraph 4 of Article 25, in which case any such amendment shall enter into force for such a Party on the ninetieth day after the date of deposit with the depositary of its instrument of ratification, acceptance, approval or accession with respect to such amendment.

5. The following procedure shall apply to the proposal, adoption and entry into force of an amendment to Annex D, E or F:

(a) Amendments shall be proposed according to the procedure in paragraphs 1 and 2 of Article 21;

(b) The Parties shall take decisions on an amendment to Annex D, E or F by consensus; and

(c) A decision to amend Annex D, E or F shall forthwith be communicated to the Parties by the depositary. The amendment shall enter into force for all Parties on a date to be specified in the decision.

6. If an additional annex or an amendment to an annex is related to an amendment to this Convention, the additional annex or amendment shall not enter into force until such time as the amendment to the Convention enters into force.

Article 23
Right to vote

1.   Each Party to this Convention shall have one vote, except as provided for in paragraph 2.

2.   A regional economic integration organization, on matters within its competence, shall exercise its right to vote with a number of votes equal to the number of its member States that are Parties to this Convention. Such an organization shall not exercise its right to vote if any of its member States exercises its right to vote, and vice versa.

Article 24
Signature

This Convention shall be open for signature at Stockholm by all States and regional economic integration organizations on 23 May 2001, and at the United Nations Headquarters in New York from 24 May 2001 to 22 May 2002.

Article 25
Ratification, acceptance, approval or accession

1.   This Convention shall be subject to ratification, acceptance or approval by States and by regional economic integration organizations. It shall be open for accession by States and by regional economic integration organizations from the day after the date on which the Convention is closed for signature. Instruments of ratification, acceptance, approval or accession shall be deposited with the depositary.

2.   Any regional economic integration organization that becomes a Party to this Convention without any of its member States being a Party shall be bound by all the obligations under the Convention. In the case of such organizations, one or more of whose member States is a Party to this Convention, the organization and its member States shall decide on their respective responsibilities for the performance of their obligations under the Convention. In such cases, the organization and the member States shall not be entitled to exercise rights under the Convention concurrently.

3.   In its instrument of ratification, acceptance, approval or accession, a regional economic integration organization shall declare the extent of its competence in respect of the matters governed by this Convention. Any such organization shall also inform the depositary, who shall in turn inform the Parties, of any relevant modification in the extent of its competence.

4.   In its instrument of ratification, acceptance, approval or accession, any Party may declare that, with respect to it, any amendment to Annex A, B or C shall enter into force only upon the deposit of its instrument of ratification, acceptance, approval or accession with respect thereto.

Article 26
Entry into force

1.   This Convention shall enter into force on the ninetieth day after the date of deposit of the fiftieth instrument of ratification, acceptance, approval or accession.

2.   For each State or regional economic integration organization that ratifies, accepts or approves this Convention or accedes thereto after the deposit of the fiftieth instrument of ratification, acceptance, approval or accession, the Convention shall enter into force on the ninetieth day after the date of deposit by such State or regional economic integration organization of its instrument of ratification, acceptance, approval or accession.

3. For the purpose of paragraphs 1 and 2, any instrument deposited by a regional economic integration organization shall not be counted as additional to those deposited by member States of that organization.

Article 27
Reservations

No reservations may be made to this Convention.

Article 28
Withdrawal

1. At any time after three years from the date on which this Convention has entered into force for a Party, that Party may withdraw from the Convention by giving written notification to the depositary.

2. Any such withdrawal shall take effect upon the expiry of one year from the date of receipt by the depositary of the notification of withdrawal, or on such later date as may be specified in the notification of withdrawal.

Article 29
Depositary

The Secretary–General of the United Nations shall be the depositary of this Convention.

Article 30
Authentic texts

The original of this Convention, of which the Arabic, Chinese, English, French, Russian and Spanish texts are equally authentic, shall be deposited with the Secretary–General of the United Nations.

IN WITNESS WHEREOF the undersigned, being duly authorized to that effect, have signed this Convention.

Done at Stockholm on this twenty-second day of May, two thousand and one.

ANNEX A
Elimination
PART I

Chemical	Activity	Specific exemption
Aldrin* CAS No: 309–00–2	Production	None
	Use	Local ectoparasiticide Insecticide
Chlordane* CAS No: 57–74–9	Production	As allowed for the Parties listed in the Register
	Use	Local ectoparasiticide Insecticide Termiticide Termiticide in buildings and dams Termiticide in roads Additive in plywood adhesives
Dieldrin* CAS No: 60–57–1	Production	None
	Use	In agricultural operations
Endrin* CAS No: 72–20–8	Production	None
	Use	None

Chemical	Activity	Specific exemption
Heptachlor* CAS No: 76–44–8	Production	None
	Use	Termiticide Termiticide in structures of houses Termiticide (subterranean) Wood treatment In use in underground cable boxes
Hexachlorobenzene CAS No: 118–74–1	Production	As allowed for the Parties listed in the Register
	Use	Intermediate Solvent in pesticide Closed system site limited intermediate
Mirex* CAS No: 2385–85–5	Production	As allowed for the Parties listed in the Register
	Use	Termiticide
Toxaphene* CAS No: 8001–35–2	Production	None
	Use	None
Polychlorinated Biphenyls (PCB)*	Production	None
	Use	Articles in use in accordance with the provisions of Part II of this Annex

Notes:

(i) Except as otherwise specified in this Convention, quantities of a chemical occurring as unintentional trace contaminants in products and articles shall not be considered to be listed in this Annex;

(ii) This note shall not be considered as a production and use specific exemption for purposes of paragraph 2 of Article 3. Quantities of a chemical occurring as constituents of articles manufactured or already in use before or on the date of entry into force of the relevant obligation with respect to that chemical, shall not be considered as listed in this Annex, provided that a Party has notified the Secretariat that a particular type of article remains in use within that Party. The Secretariat shall make such notifications publicly available;

(iii) This note, which does not apply to a chemical that has an asterisk following its name in the Chemical column in Part I of this Annex, shall not be considered as a production and use specific exemption for purposes of paragraph 2 of Article 3. Given that no significant quantities of the chemical are expected to reach humans and the environment during the production and use of a closed-system site-limited intermediate, a Party, upon notification to the Secretariat, may allow the production and use of quantities of a chemical listed in this Annex as a closed-system site-limited intermediate that is chemically transformed in the manufacture of other chemicals that, taking into consideration the criteria in paragraph 1 of Annex D, do not exhibit the characteristics of persistent organic pollutants. This notification shall include information on total production and use of such chemical or a reasonable estimate of such information and information regarding the nature of the closed-system site-limited process including the amount of any non-transformed and unintentional trace contamination of the persistent organic pollutant-starting material in the final product. This procedure applies except as otherwise specified in this Annex. The Secretariat shall make such notifications available to the Conference of the Parties and to the public. Such production or use shall not be considered a production or use specific exemption. Such production and use shall cease after a ten-year period, unless the Party concerned submits a new notification to the Secretariat, in which case the period will be extended for an additional ten years unless the Conference of the Parties, after a review of the production and use decides otherwise. The notification procedure can be repeated;

(iv) All the specific exemptions in this Annex may be exercised by Parties that have registered exemptions in respect of them in accordance with Article 4 with the exception of the use of polychlorinated biphenyls in articles in use in accordance with the provisions of Part II of this Annex, which may be exercised by all Parties.

PART II

Polychlorinated biphenyls

Each Party shall:

(a) With regard to the elimination of the use of polychlorinated biphenyls in equipment (e.g. transformers, capacitors or other receptacles containing liquid stocks) by 2025, subject to review by the Conference of the Parties, take action in accordance with the following priorities:

(i) Make determined efforts to identify, label and remove from use equipment containing greater than 10 per cent polychlorinated biphenyls and volumes greater than 5 litres;

(ii) Make determined efforts to identify, label and remove from use equipment containing greater than 0.05 per cent polychlorinated biphenyls and volumes greater than 5 litres;

(iii) Endeavour to identify and remove from use equipment containing greater than 0.005 percent polychlorinated biphenyls and volumes greater than 0.05 litres;

(b) Consistent with the priorities in subparagraph (a), promote the following measures to reduce exposures and risk to control the use of polychlorinated biphenyls:

(i) Use only in intact and non-leaking equipment and only in areas where the risk from environmental release can be minimised and quickly remedied;

(ii) Not use in equipment in areas associated with the production or processing of food or feed;

(iii) When used in populated areas, including schools and hospitals, all reasonable measures to protect from electrical failure which could result in a fire, and regular inspection of equipment for leaks;

(c) Notwithstanding paragraph 2 of Article 3, ensure that equipment containing polychlorinated biphenyls, as described in subparagraph (a), shall not be exported or imported except for the purpose of environmentally sound waste management;

(d) Except for maintenance and servicing operations, not allow recovery for the purpose of reuse in other equipment of liquids with polychlorinated biphenyls content above 0.005 per cent;

(e) Make determined efforts designed to lead to environmentally sound waste management of liquids containing polychlorinated biphenyls and equipment contaminated with polychlorinated biphenyls having a polychlorinated biphenyls content above 0.005 per cent, in accordance with paragraph 1 of Article 6, as soon as possible but no later than 2028, subject to review by the Conference of the Parties;

(f) In lieu of note (ii) in Part I of this Annex, endeavour to identify other articles containing more than 0.005 per cent polychlorinated biphenyls (e.g. cable-sheaths, cured caulk and painted objects) and manage them in accordance with paragraph 1 of Article 6;

(g) Provide a report every five years on progress in eliminating polychlorinated biphenyls and submit it to the Conference of the Parties pursuant to Article 15;

(h) The reports described in subparagraph (g) shall, as appropriate, be considered by the Conference of the Parties in its reviews relating to polychlorinated biphenyls. The Conference of the Parties shall review progress towards elimination of polychlorinated biphenyls at five year intervals or other period, as appropriate, taking into account such reports.

ANNEX B

Restriction

PART I

Chemical	Activity	Acceptable purpose or specific exemption
DDT (1,1,1–trichloro–2,2–bis (4–chlorophenyl) ethane) CAS No: 50–29–3	Production	Acceptable purpose: Disease vector control use in accor-dance with Part II of this Annex Specific exemption: Intermediate in production of dicofol Intermediate
	Use	Acceptable purpose: Disease vector control in accordance with Part II of this Annex Specific exemption: Production of dicofol Intermediate

Notes:

(i) Except as otherwise specified in this Convention, quantities of a chemical occurring as unintentional trace contaminants in products and articles shall not be considered to be listed in this Annex;

(ii) This note shall not be considered as a production and use acceptable purpose or specific exemption for purposes of paragraph 2 of Article 3. Quantities of a chemical occurring as constituents of articles manufactured or already in use before or on the date of entry into force of the relevant obligation with respect to that chemical, shall not be considered as listed in this Annex, provided that a Party has notified the Secretariat that a particular type of article remains in use within that Party. The Secretariat shall make such notifications publicly available;

(iii) This note shall not be considered as a production and use specific exemption for purposes of paragraph 2 of Article 3. Given that no significant quantities of the chemical are expected to reach humans and the environment during the production and use of a closed-system site-limited intermediate, a Party, upon notification to the Secretariat, may allow the production and use of quantities of a chemical listed in this Annex as a closed-system site-limited intermediate that is chemically trans-formed in the manufacture of other chemicals that, taking into consideration the criteria in paragraph 1 of Annex D, do not exhibit the characteristics of persistent organic pollutants. This notification shall include information on total production and use of such chemical or a reasonable estimate of such information and informa-tion regarding the nature of the closed-system site-limited process including the amount of any non-transformed and unintentional trace contamination of the persistent organic pollutant-starting material in the final product. This procedure applies except as otherwise specified in this Annex. The Secretariat shall make such notifications available to the Conference of the Parties and to the public. Such production or use shall not be considered a production or use specific exemption. Such production and use shall cease after a ten-year period, unless the Party concerned submits a new notification to the Secretariat, in which case the period will be extended for an additional ten years unless the Conference of the Parties, after a review of the production and use decides otherwise. The notification procedure can be repeated;

(iv) All the specific exemptions in this Annex may be exercised by Parties that have registered in respect of them in accordance with Article 4.

PART II
DDT (1,1,1–trichloro–2,2–bis(4–chlorophenyl)ethane)

1. The production and use of DDT shall be eliminated except for Parties that have notified the Secretariat of their intention to produce and/or use it. A DDT Register is hereby established and shall be available to the public. The Secretariat shall maintain the DDT Register.

2. Each Party that produces and/or uses DDT shall restrict such production and/or use for disease vector control in accordance with the World Health Organization recommendations and guidelines on the use of DDT and when locally safe, effective and affordable alternatives are not available to the Party in question.

3. In the event that a Party not listed in the DDT Register determines that it requires DDT for disease vector control, it shall notify the Secretariat as soon as possible in order to have its name added forthwith to the DDT Register. It shall at the same time notify the World Health Organization.

4. Every three years, each Party that uses DDT shall provide to the Secretariat and the World Health Organization information on the amount used, the conditions of such use and its relevance to that Party's disease management strategy, in a format to be decided by the Conference of the Parties in consultation with the World Health Organization.

5. With the goal of reducing and ultimately eliminating the use of DDT, the Conference of the Parties shall encourage:

(a) Each Party using DDT to develop and implement an action plan as part of the implementation plan specified in Article 7. That action plan shall include:

(i) Development of regulatory and other mechanisms to ensure that DDT use is restricted to disease vector control;

(ii) Implementation of suitable alternative products, methods and strategies, including resistance management strategies to ensure the continuing effectiveness of these alternatives;

(iii) Measures to strengthen health care and to reduce the incidence of the disease.

(b) The Parties, within their capabilities, to promote research and development of safe alternative chemical and non-chemical products, methods and strategies for Parties using DDT, relevant to the conditions of those countries and with the goal of decreasing the human and economic burden of disease. Factors to be promoted when considering alternatives or combinations of alternatives shall include the human health risks and environmental implications of such alternatives. Viable alternatives to DDT shall pose less risk to human health and the environment, be suitable for disease control based on conditions in the Parties in question and be supported with monitoring data.

6. Commencing at its first meeting, and at least every three years thereafter, the Conference of the Parties shall, in consultation with the World Health Organization, evaluate the continued need for DDT for disease vector control on the basis of available scientific, technical, environmental and economic information, including:

(a) The production and use of DDT and the conditions set out in paragraph 2;

(b) The availability, suitability and implementation of the alternatives to DDT; and

(c) Progress in strengthening the capacity of countries to transfer safely to reliance on such alternatives.

7. A Party may, at any time, withdraw its name from the DDT Registry upon written notification to the Secretariat. The withdrawal shall take effect on the date specified in the notification.

ANNEX C
Unintentional Production

Part I: Persistent Organic Pollutants Subject to the Requirements of Article 5

This Annex applies to the following persistent organic pollutants when formed and released unintentionally from anthropogenic sources:

Chemical

Polychlorinated dibenzo-p-dioxins and dibenzofurans (PCDD/PCDF)

Hexachlorobenzene (HCB) (CAS No: 118–74–1)

Polychlorinated biphenyls (PCB)

Part II: Source categories

* * *

Part III: Source categories

* * *

Part IV: Definitions

* * *

*Part V: General guidance on best available techniques
and best environmental practices*

* * *

ANNEX D
Information Requirements and Screening Criteria

1. A Party submitting a proposal to list a chemical in Annexes A, B and/or C shall identify the chemical in the manner described in subparagraph (a) and provide the information on the chemical, and its transformation products where relevant, relating to the screening criteria set out in subparagraphs (b) to (e):

* * *

ANNEX E
Information Requirements for the Risk Profile

The purpose of the review is to evaluate whether the chemical is likely, as a result of its long-range environmental transport, to lead to significant adverse human health and/or environmental effects, such that global action is warranted. For this purpose, a risk profile shall be developed that further elaborates on, and evaluates, the information referred to in Annex D and includes, as far as possible, the following types of information:

* * *

ANNEX F
Information on Socio-economic Considerations

An evaluation should be undertaken regarding possible control measures for chemicals under consideration for inclusion in this Convention, encompassing the full range of options, including management and elimination. For this purpose, relevant information should be provided relating to socio-economic considerations associated with possible control measures to enable a decision to be taken by the Conference of the Parties. Such information should reflect due regard for the differing capabilities and conditions among the Parties and should include consideration of the following indicative list of items:

* * *

4.6   DUBAI DECLARATION ON INTERNATIONAL CHEMICALS MANAGEMENT. **Adopted by the International Conference on Chemicals Management, 4–6 February 2006. Available at http://www.saicm.org (accessed Oct. 1, 2011)**

We, the ministers, heads of delegation and representatives of civil society and the private sector, assembled at the International Conference on Chemicals Management in Dubai from 4 to 6 February 2006, declare the following:

1.   The sound management of chemicals is essential if we are to achieve sustainable development, including the eradication of poverty and disease, the improvement of human health and the environment and the elevation and maintenance of the standard of living in countries at all levels of development;

2.   Significant, but insufficient, progress has been made in international chemicals management through the implementation of chapter 19 of Agenda 21 and International Labour Organization Conventions No. 170 on Safety in the Use of Chemicals at Work and No. 174 on the Prevention of Major Industrial Accidents and the Basel Convention on the Control of Transboundary Movements of Hazardous Wastes and Their Disposal, as well as in addressing particularly hazardous chemicals through the recent entry into force of the Rotterdam Convention on the Prior Informed Consent Procedure for Certain Hazardous Chemicals and Pesticides in International Trade and the Stockholm Convention on Persistent Organic Pollutants and the adoption of the Globally Harmonized System for the Classification and Labelling of Chemicals;

3.   The private sector has made considerable efforts to promote chemical safety through voluntary programmes and initiatives such as product stewardship and the chemicals industry's Responsible Care programme;

4.   Non-governmental public health and environmental organizations, trade unions and other civil society organizations have made important contributions to the promotion of chemical safety;

5.   Progress in chemicals management has not, however, been sufficient globally and the environment worldwide continues to suffer from air, water and land contamination, impairing the health and welfare of millions;

6.   The need to take concerted action is accentuated by a wide range of chemical safety concerns at the international level, including a lack of capacity for managing chemicals in developing countries and countries with economies in transition, dependency on pesticides in agriculture, exposure of workers to harmful chemicals and concern about the long-term effects of chemicals on both human health and the environment;

7.   The global production, trade and use of chemicals are increasing, with growth patterns placing an increasing chemicals management burden on developing countries and countries with economies in transition, in particular the least developed among them and small island developing States, and presenting them with special difficulties in meeting this challenge. As a result, fundamental changes are needed in the way that societies manage chemicals;

8.   We are determined to implement the applicable chemicals management agreements to which we are Party, strengthen the coherence and synergies that exist between them and work to address, as appropriate, existing gaps in the framework of international chemicals policy;

9.   We commit ourselves in a spirit of solidarity and partnership to achieving chemical safety and thereby assisting in fighting poverty, protecting vulnerable groups and advancing public health and human security;

10.   We commit ourselves to respecting human rights and fundamental freedoms, understanding and respecting ecosystem integrity and addressing the gap between the

current reality and our ambition to elevate global efforts to achieve the sound management of chemicals;

11. We are unwavering in our commitment to promoting the sound management of chemicals and hazardous wastes throughout their life-cycle, in accordance with Agenda 21 and the Johannesburg Plan of Implementation, in particular paragraph 23. We are convinced that the Strategic Approach to International Chemicals Management constitutes a significant contribution towards the internationally agreed development goals set out in the Millennium Declaration. It builds upon previous international initiatives on chemical safety and promotes the development of a multi- and cross-sectoral and participatory strategic approach;

12. We therefore adopt the Overarching Policy Strategy, which, together with the present declaration, constitutes our firm commitment to the Strategic Approach and its implementation;

13. We recommend the use and further development of the Global Plan of Action, to address current and ever-changing societal needs, as a working tool and guidance document for meeting the commitments to chemicals management expressed in the Rio Declaration on Environment and Development, Agenda 21, the Bahia Declaration on Chemical Safety, the Johannesburg Plan of Implementation, the 2005 World Summit Outcome and this Strategic Approach;

14. We are determined to realize the benefits of chemistry, including green chemistry, for improved standards of living, public health and protection of the environment, and are resolved to continue working together to promote the safe production and use of chemicals;

15. We are committed to strengthening the capacities of all concerned to achieve the sound management of chemicals and hazardous wastes at all levels;

16. We will continue to mobilize national and international financing from public and private sources for the life-cycle management of chemicals;

17. We will work towards closing the gaps and addressing the discrepancies in the capacity to achieve sustainable chemicals management between developed countries on the one hand and developing countries and countries with economies in transition on the other by addressing the special needs of the latter and strengthening their capacities for the sound management of chemicals and the development of safer alternative products and processes, including non-chemical alternatives, through partnerships, technical support and financial assistance;

18. We will work towards effective and efficient governance of chemicals management by means of transparency, public participation and accountability involving all sectors of society, in particular striving for the equal participation of women in chemicals management;

19. We will engage actively in partnerships between Governments, the private sector and civil society, including strengthening participation in the implementation of the Strategic Approach by small and medium-sized enterprises and the informal sector;

20. We stress the responsibility of industry to make available to stakeholders such data and information on health and environmental effects of chemicals as are needed safely to use chemicals and the products made from them;

21. We will facilitate public access to appropriate information and knowledge on chemicals throughout their life cycle, including the risks that they pose to human health and the environment;

22. We will ensure that, when information is made available, confidential commercial and industrial information and knowledge are protected in accordance with national laws or regulations or, in the absence of such laws and regulations, are protected in accordance with international provisions. In making information avail-

able, information on chemicals relating to the health and safety of humans and the environment should not be regarded as confidential;

23. We recognize the need to make special efforts to protect those groups in society that are particularly vulnerable to risks from hazardous chemicals or are highly exposed to them;

24. We are determined to protect children and the unborn child from chemical exposures that impair their future lives;

25. We will endeavour to prevent illegal traffic in toxic, hazardous, banned and severely restricted chemicals and chemical products and wastes;

26. We will promote the sound management of chemicals and hazardous waste as a priority in national, regional and international policy frameworks, including strategies for sustainable development, development assistance and poverty reduction;

27. We will strive to integrate the Strategic Approach into the work programmes of all relevant United Nations organizations, specialized agencies, funds and programmes consistent with their mandates as accorded by their respective governing bodies;

28. We acknowledge that as a new voluntary initiative in the field of international management of chemicals, the Strategic Approach is not a legally binding instrument;

29. We collectively share the view that implementation and taking stock of progress are critical to ensuring success and that, in this regard, a stable and long-term fully participatory and multi-sectoral structure for guidance, review and operational support is essential;

30. We are determined to cooperate fully in an open, inclusive, participatory and transparent manner in the implementation of the Strategic Approach.

B. Hazardous Waste

4.7 OECD Council Decision/Recommendation on Exports of Hazardous Wastes From the OECD Area (With Measures Concerning the Control of Exports of Hazardous Wastes and Appended Definitions). Adopted 5 June 1986. 1986 OECD C(86)64 (Final); *reprinted in* 5 Weston & Carlson V.I.9

The Council

Having regard to Articles 5(*a*) and 5(*b*) of the Convention on the Organisation for Economic Co-operation and Development of 14th December 1960;

Having regard to the Decision and Recommendation of the Council of 1st February 1984 on Transfrontier Movements of Hazardous Waste [C(83)180(Final)] and without prejudice to that Decision and Recommendation;

Having regard to the Resolution of the Council of 20th June, 1985 on International Co-operation Concerning Transfrontier Movements of Hazardous Wastes [C(85)100], by which it has been decided to develop an international system for effective control of transfrontier movements of hazardous wastes, including an international agreement of a legally binding character;

Considering the European Communities Council Directive of 6th December, 1984 on the Supervision and Control within the European Community of the Transfrontier Shipment of Hazardous Waste [84/631/EEC], supplemented by the Decision of the Council of the European Communities of 6th March, 1986;

Considering the work carried out within the United Nations Environment Programme on the environmentally sound management of hazardous wastes;

Considering the particular nature of wastes and the distinction between wastes and products which are traded internationally;

Convinced that the exports of hazardous wastes may, if not properly monitored and controlled, result in serious risks to health and the environment;

On the proposal of the Environment Committee:

I. Decides that Member countries shall:

(*i*) Monitor and control exports of hazardous wastes to a final destination which is outside the OECD area; and for this purpose shall ensure that their competent authorities are empowered to prohibit such exports in appropriate instances;

(*ii*) Apply no less strict controls on transfrontier movements of hazardous wastes involving non-Member countries than they would on movements involving only Member countries;

(*iii*) Prohibit movements of hazardous wastes to a final destination in a non-Member country without the consent of that country and the prior notification to any transit countries of the proposed movements;

(*iv*) Prohibit movements of hazardous wastes to a non-Member country unless the wastes are directed to an adequate disposal facility in that country.

II. Recommends that, to implement this Decision, Member countries should:

(*i*) Seek to conclude bilateral or multilateral agreements with non-Member countries to which frequent exports of hazardous wastes are taking place or are foreseen to take place;

(*ii*) Apply the measures set out below concerning the control of exports of hazardous wastes to a final destination outside the OECD area.

III. Instructs the Environment Committee to take account of the elements of this Decision/Recommendation in developing the draft international agreement referred to in the resolution of the Council of International Co-operation Concerning Transfrontier Movements of Hazardous Wastes [C(85)100].

MEASURES CONCERNING THE CONTROL OF EXPORTS OF HAZARDOUS WASTES

1.   The following measures are designed to facilitate the harmonization of policies concerning transfrontier movements of hazardous wastes to a final destination outside the OECD area. They do not prejudice the implementation of stricter measures which have been or might be adopted at national, regional or world level to reduce the dangers associated with the transport and disposal of hazardous wastes.

2.   These measures should apply in the absence of a bilateral or multilateral agreement concerning transfrontier movements of hazardous wastes between the exporting Member country and the importing non-Member country concerned, and should be taken into account in the negotiation of such an agreement.

3.   Member countries should require, with respect to any export of hazardous wastes to a final destination outside the OECD area, that the measures set out below be taken by the exporter or by the competent authorities of the exporting country.

4.   The exporter should:

(*a*) provide the competent authorities of the importing country (and of any transit countries) with at least the same information that he would provide them if they were Member countries;

(*b*) inform the competent authorities of the importing country of any specific disposal methods legally required or forbidden for such wastes in the exporting country;

(*c*) provide to the competent authorities of the exporting country:

(*i*) the information used by the exporter to assure himself that the proposed disposal operation can be performed in an environmentally sound manner;

(*ii*) certification that the proposed disposal facility may, under the laws and regulations of the importing country, dispose of the kinds of wastes whose export is proposed;

(*iii*) a copy of an undertaking by the operator of the proposed disposal facility that he will dispose of the wastes as foreseen in the disposal contract, and in the facility specified therein;

(*iv*) a copy of the information transmitted to the competent authorities of the importing country to obtain their written consent to the import and disposal of the wastes;

(*v*) a copy of the written consent of the competent authorities of the importing country, and confirmation that the competent authorities of any transit countries have received delivery of notification;

(*d*) demand and receive from the disposer documents confirming that the wastes have been handed over to the disposer and disposed of as foreseen, and put these documents at the disposition of the competent authorities of the exporting country.

5.   Member countries may choose to charge their competent authorities instead of the exporter with some of the tasks listed above.

6.   The competent authorities of the exporting country should:

(*a*) before any final decision is taken, inform the competent authorities of the importing country when they have specific environmental concerns regarding the proposed disposal operation;

(*b*) prohibit the export of the hazardous wastes whenever:

(*i*) they are not satisfied with the information provided under 4(*c*) above;

(*ii*) an objection is made by any country of transit and no appropriate alternative route can be found by the exporter;

(*iii*) the proposed disposal operation is not in conformity with applicable international law;

(*c*) prohibit additional exports of hazardous waste to a given destination when the documents specified in 4(*d*) above were not provided to the exporter by the disposer after a previous export to the same destination;

(*d*) notify the exporter promptly whether or not they object to the proposed transfrontier movement;

(*e*) notify the competent authorities of the importing country if they have prohibited the export of the wastes.

APPENDIX

DEFINITIONS

For the purpose of this Decision/Recommendation:

(*a*) "Waste" means any material considered as waste or legally defined as waste in the country where it is situated or through or to which it is conveyed;

(*b*) "Hazardous waste" means any waste other than radioactive waste considered as hazardous or legally defined as hazardous in the country where it is situated or through or to which it is conveyed, because of the potential risk to man or the environment likely to result from an accident or from improper transport or disposal;

(*c*) "Transfrontier movement of hazardous wastes" means any shipment of wastes from one country to another, where the wastes are considered as being hazardous wastes in at least one of the countries concerned. Hazardous wastes arising from the normal operation of ships, including slopes and residues, shall not be considered a transfrontier movement covered by this Decision/Recommendation;

(*d*) "Exporting country" means any country from which a transfrontier movement of hazardous wastes is initiated or is envisaged;

(*e*) "Importing country" means any country to which a transfrontier movement of hazardous wastes takes place or is envisaged for purpose of disposal (treatment, landfill, storage, dumping or incineration at sea);

(*f*) "Transit country" means any country other than the exporting or importing country across which a transfrontier movement of hazardous waste takes place or is envisaged;

(*g*) "Exporter" means the generator of the wastes or the person in the exporting country who arranges for exporting the wastes at the request and on behalf of the generator;

(*h*) "OECD area" means all land or marine areas under the national jurisdiction of any OECD Member country.

4.8 UNEP GOVERNING COUNCIL DECISION ON CAIRO GUIDELINES AND PRINCIPLES FOR THE ENVIRONMENTALLY SOUND MANAGEMENT OF HAZARDOUS WASTES (Without Annex). Adopted by the UNEP Governing Council at Cairo, 17 June 1987. UNEP/GC/DEC/14/30, UNEP ELPG No. 8; *reprinted in* **5 Weston & Carlson V.I.10**

Introduction

This set of guidelines and principles is addressed to Governments with a view to assisting them in the process of developing policies for the environmentally sound management of hazardous wastes. They have been prepared on the basis of common elements and principles derived from relevant existing bilateral, regional and global agreements and national regulations, drawing upon experience already gained through their preparation and implementation. Special importance is attached to respect for the balance achieved in principle 21 of the Stockholm Declaration on the Human Environment between the rights and duties of States concerning their natural resources and the environment.

These general guidelines cover the management of hazardous wastes from their generation to their final disposal and, in particular, the problem of transfrontier movements of such wastes, which calls for international co-operation between exporting and importing countries in the light of their joint responsibility for the protection of the global environment.

These guidelines are without prejudice to the provisions of particular systems arising from international agreements in the field of hazardous waste management. They have been developed with a view to assisting States in the process of developing appropriate bilateral, regional and multilateral agreements and national legislation for the environmentally sound management of hazardous wastes. The guidelines deal mainly with the administrative aspects of the environmentally sound management of hazardous wastes, and do not claim to give specific guidance on the more technical aspects of dealing with hazardous wastes.

At the present time, waste management differs substantially in different regions of the world, particularly according to their state of economic development. This imbalance necessitates co-operation to improve the management of hazardous wastes in the interest of the environment, especially as regards actual and potential transfrontier movements of such wastes.

Although the guidelines have not been prepared specifically to address the situation of developing countries, they nevertheless provide a framework for effective and environmentally sound hazardous waste management policies in those countries. Implementation of the guidelines should thus help them to avoid serious and costly environmental problems due to mismanagement of hazardous wastes. By implementing the guidelines, countries could incorporate a sound waste management policy into their national economic development policies.

PART 1

GENERAL PROVISIONS

1. Definitions

For the purposes of the present guidelines and principles:

(a) ''Wastes'' means any materials considered as wastes or legally defined as wastes in the State where they are situated or through or to which they are conveyed;

(b) ''Hazardous wastes'' means wastes other than radioactive wastes which, by reason of their chemical reactivity or toxic, explosive, corrosive or other characteristics causing danger or likely to cause danger to health or the environment, whether alone or when coming into contact with other wastes, are legally defined as hazardous in the

State in which they are generated or in which they are disposed of or through which they are transported;

(c) "Management" means the collection, transport (including transfrontier movements), storage (including storage at transfer stations), treatment and disposal of hazardous wastes;

(d) "Transport" means the movement of hazardous wastes from the place at which they are generated until they arrive at an approved site or facility for disposal;

(e) "Disposal" means final disposal;

(f) "Approved site or facility" means a site or facility for the storage, treatment or disposal of hazardous wastes which has been the subject of a prior written authorization or operating permit for this purpose from a competent authority in the State where the site or facility is located.

(g) "Competent authority" means a governmental authority with appropriate qualifications designated or established by a State to be responsible, within such geographical area and with such jurisdiction as the State may think fit, for the planning, organization, authorization and supervision of the management of hazardous wastes;

(h) "Pollution" means the introduction by man, directly or indirectly, of any hazardous wastes into the environment as a result of which there arises any hazard to human health, plant or animal life, harm to living resources or to ecosystems, damage to amenities or interference with other legitimate uses of the environment;

(i) "Contingency" means any accident or other event occurring during the management of hazardous wastes which gives rise to or presents a threat of pollution;

(j) "Territory" means areas over which a State has jurisdiction for the protection of the environment;

(k) "Export" means the movement of hazardous wastes beyond the territory of the State in which they were generated;

(*l*) "State of export" means a State in which hazardous wastes which are the subject of an export are generated;

(m) "State of import" means a State in which hazardous wastes are received for disposal;

(n) "Transit State" means a State, not being the State of export or of import, through the territory of which a movement of hazardous wastes takes place.

2. *General Principles*

(a) States should take such steps as are necessary, whether by legislation or otherwise, to ensure the protection of health and the environment from damage arising from the generation and management of hazardous wastes. To this end, States should, *inter alia,* ensure that transfrontier movements of hazardous wastes are kept to the minimum compatible with the efficient and environmentally sound management of such wastes.

(b) States should take all practicable steps to ensure that the management of hazardous wastes is conducted in accordance with international law applicable in matters of environmental protection.

3. *Non–Discriminatory Control of Hazardous Wastes*

Each State should ensure that, within its jurisdiction, hazardous wastes to be exported are controlled no less stringently than those remaining within its territory.

4. International Cooperation

Without prejudice to the other provisions of these guidelines and principles, States should, in a manner appropriate to their needs and capabilities, initiate and co-operate in:

(a) The achievement and improvement of the environmentally sound management of hazardous wastes;

(b) The development and implementation of new environmentally sound low-waste technologies and the improvement of existing technologies with a view to reducing the generation of hazardous wastes and achieving more effective and efficient methods of ensuring their management in an environmentally sound manner, including the study of the economic, social and environmental effects of the adoption of such new or improved technologies;

(c) Monitoring the effects of the management of hazardous wastes on health and the environment;

(d) Exchanges of information, whether on a bilateral or multilateral basis, with a view to promoting the environmentally sound management of hazardous wastes.

5. Transfer of Technology

States should, in a manner appropriate to their needs and capabilities, whether directly or through the appropriate international organizations, promote actively and in accordance with their legitimate interests the transfer of fair and reasonable conditions of technology related to the environmentally sound management of hazardous wastes. They should also promote the technical capacity of States, especially of developing States, which may need and request technical assistance in this field.

6. Transfer or Transformation of Pollution

States and persons involved in the management of hazardous wastes should recognize that protection of health and the environment is not achieved by the mere transformation of one form of pollution into another, nor by the mere transfer of the effects of pollution from one location to another, but only by the use of the waste treatment option (which may include transformation or transfer) which minimizes the environmental impact.

PART II

GENERATION AND MANAGEMENT OF HAZARDOUS WASTES

7. Preventive Measures

(a) States should take such steps as are appropriate to ensure that the generation of hazardous wastes within their territories is reduced to a minimum.

(b) States should ensure that persons involved in the management of hazardous wastes take such steps as are necessary to prevent pollution arising from such management and, if pollution should occur, to minimize the consequences thereof for health and the environment.

(c) In particular, States should take such steps as are necessary to promote the development and employment of low-waste technologies applicable to activities generating hazardous wastes and the recycling and reuse of hazardous wastes unavoidably produced by such activities.

8. Establishment of Competent Authorities

Each State should designate or establish one or more competent authorities as defined in guideline 1.

PART III

CONTROL OVER DISPOSAL OF HAZARDOUS WASTES

9. Disposal Plans for Hazardous Wastes

(a) States should ensure that each competent authority prepares, in its area of responsibility, in consultation with the other public authorities concerned and with the participation of the public as appropriate, a plan for the management of hazardous wastes describing the arrangements for implementing that plan.

(b) Such plans should be reviewed by the competent authorities to ensure their continuing adequacy in the light of experience in the operation of the plans and of changes in circumstances, including changes in the state of scientific knowledge.

10. Separation of Hazardous Wastes

The competent authorities should ensure that persons concerned in the management of hazardous wastes keep them separate from other wastes where it is necessary to do so for their environmentally sound management.

11. Collection of Hazardous Wastes

States should promote the establishment of a system of collection of hazardous wastes, including those that are generated in small quantities.

12. Duty to Ensure Safe Disposal

States should ensure that persons engaged in activities in the course of which hazardous wastes are generated are required to make appropriate arrangements for the disposal of those wastes in an environmentally sound manner. In particular, they should satisfy themselves as to the capability and reliability of persons and facilities involved in the management of such wastes.

13. Use of Best Practicable Means

States should ensure that persons involved in the management of hazardous wastes employ the best practicable means in all aspects of such management.

14. Approved Sites and Facilities

(a) States should take such steps as are necessary to require that the storage, treatment and disposal of hazardous wastes take place only at approved sites or facilities.

(b) An authorization or operating permit for approved sites or facilities should be granted only if:

(i) An assessment undertaken by or at the request of the competent authority has established that no significant adverse effects on health or the environment are to be expected as a result of such storage, treatment or disposal;

(ii) The competent authority is satisfied as to the suitability of the operator of the facility at which such storage, treatment or disposal is to be carried out, including the technical knowledge and financial means of that operator to carry out the operations in respect of which the authorization or operating permit is sought to be granted and to take the appropriate safety measures in respect thereof.

15. International Listing of Approved Sites and Facilities

For the guidance of their competent authorities and to ensure the optimal use of their disposal facilities in conformity with guideline 2, States should consider the establishment, on a bilateral or multilateral basis, of lists of approved sites and facilities in their respective territories.

16. Transfrontier Effects of Approved Sites and Facilities Pre–Authorization Information

(a) States should ensure that, where it is proposed to grant an authorization or operating permit under guideline 14 in respect of activities which may have significant effects on health or the environment in another State (hereinafter referred to as "the State concerned"), the State concerned is provided in a timely manner by the State entitled to grant the authorization or operating permit (hereinafter referred to as "the authorizing State") with sufficient information, in conformity with the laws and regulations of the latter State, to enable it to evaluate accurately the likely effects of those activities.

(b) The State concerned should respect the confidentiality of the information transmitted to it under paragraph (a) above.

17. Transfrontier Effects Consultation

In the circumstances described in guideline 16, the authorizing State and the State concerned should, prior to the adoption of any decision in the authorizing State as to the granting of the authorization or operating permit, enter into consultations which shall be conducted in good faith. These consultations should take place promptly and should be concluded within a reasonable time.

18. Transfrontier Effects Equal Access and Treatment

In the circumstances described in guideline 16, the authorizing State should accord to the public authorities and nationals of the State concerned the same rights of participation in the administrative and judicial proceedings related to the granting of authorizations or operating permits and in any appeal or review thereof as those which are accorded to its own public authorities and nationals.

PART IV

MONITORING, REMEDIAL ACTION AND RECORD KEEPING

19. Monitoring

(a) States should ensure that the operators of sites or facilities at which hazardous wastes are managed are required, as appropriate, to monitor the effects of those activities on health and the environment and to supply the competent authorities with the results of such monitoring, either periodically or on demand. States should ensure that the protection of abandoned sites or closed facilities against the subsequent unauthorized disposal of hazardous wastes, and the monitoring of such sites or facilities for effects on health and the environment, continue after their abandonment or closure.

(b) States should ensure that the competent authorities have the power to enter upon the sites or facilities mentioned in paragraph (a) above and upon such other premises as may be necessary for the purposes of monitoring the effects upon health and the environment of the activities carried out at those sites or facilities. States should also ensure that the competent authorities have the power to order the cessation, limitation or modification of those activities if it is determined that adverse effects on health and the environment are taking place, or are likely to take place.

(c) States should ensure that appropriate remedial action is taken in cases where monitoring gives indications that management of hazardous wastes has resulted in adverse effects on health or the environment.

(d) States should ensure that persons involved in the management of hazardous wastes keep accurate and precise records, as appropriate, of the relevant information concerning wastes, including the type, quantity, physical and chemical characteristics, origin and location within the site or facility of such wastes.

20. Public Access to Information

States should ensure that competent authorities keep a record of the authorizations or operating permits issued by them under guideline 14, and that the public have access to information concerning the number and types of those authorizations or permits and the conditions attached thereto.

PART V

SAFETY AND CONTINGENCY PLANNING

21. Instruction of Workers

States should ensure that persons employed at sites or facilities at which hazardous wastes are managed receive, on a continuing basis, information on the conditions attached to authorizations or permits, and full and appropriate instruction as to the safety precautions necessary to ensure the protection of health and the environment, including the actions to be taken by them in any contingency.

22. Contingency Plans

States within whose territories hazardous wastes are managed should recognize the need for studies on the risks of sites or facilities, and contingency plans prepared by operators of sites or facilities, or by the competent authorities, as appropriate, and the application of such plans as and when necessary. These plans should take into account any potential adverse effects on health and the environment in other States.

23. Contingency Plans Transfrontier Effects

(a) If a State has reason to believe that a contingency which has arisen within its territory is likely to have significant adverse effects on health and the environment in another State, that State should as soon as practicable supply the other State with the information necessary to enable it to adopt effective counter-measures.

(b) States should provide such assistance as they can reasonably make available to other States in which a contingency has occurred.

PART VI

TRANSPORT OF HAZARDOUS WASTES

24. Transport Rules

States should ensure that the transport of hazardous wastes is conducted in a manner compatible with international conventions and other international instruments governing the transport of hazardous materials or wastes.

25. Transport Documentation

To ensure that hazardous wastes are safely transported for disposal, and to maintain records of the transport and disposal of such wastes, States should establish a system by which all transport of such wastes should be accompanied by a hazardous wastes movement document from the point of generation to the point of disposal. This document should be available to the competent authorities and to all parties involved in the management of such wastes.

26. Notification and Consent Procedure in Respect of Transfrontier Movements of Hazardous Wastes

(a) States should establish a system which ensures that all States involved in a transfrontier movement of hazardous wastes receive full information sufficiently in advance to enable them to assess the proposed movement properly.

(b) A State of export should take such steps as are necessary to ensure that a request from a State of import or transit State for relevant information concerning the transfrontier movement in question elicits a constructive and timely response.

(c) In the absence of bilateral, regional or multilateral arrangements, States should provide that it shall not be lawful for any person to initiate a transfrontier movement of hazardous wastes until the State of import and any transit State have given their consent to that movement.

(d) The consent of the State of import referred to in paragraph (c) above should take the form of an explicit consent, provided always that States may by bilateral or multilateral arrangements adopt a tacit consent procedure.

(e) Any transit State should be notified in a timely manner of a proposed movement, and may object to it within a reasonable time in accordance with its national laws and regulations. The consent of a transit State referred to in paragraph (c) above may also take the form of a tacit consent.

(f) The State of export should not permit a transfrontier movement of hazardous wastes to be initiated unless it is not satisfied that the wastes in question can be managed in an environmentally sound manner, at an approved site or facility and with the consent of the State of import.

(g) In order to facilitate implementation of this guideline, each State should designate an agency which shall be the focal point to which the notifications and inquiries mentioned in the foregoing paragraphs may be addressed.

(h) Nothing in this guideline shall be so construed as to affect the sovereign right of a State to refuse to accept within its territory hazardous wastes originating elsewhere.

27. *States of Export to Readmit Exports*

Where a State of import or transit State, in conformity with its laws and regulations, opposes a transfrontier movement of hazardous wastes into its territory, and where the hazardous wastes which are the subject of the transfrontier movement have already left the State of export, the latter should not object to reimport any of the wastes.

28. *States to Cooperate in the Management of Hazardous Wastes*

States should, in pursuance of guideline 2, enter into bilateral, regional or multilateral agreements for the management of their hazardous wastes in order to ensure the optimal use of their treatment and disposal facilities.

PART VII

LIABILITY AND COMPENSATION

29. *Liability, Insurance and Compensation for Damage Caused by Hazardous Wastes*

States should ensure that provision is made in their national laws and regulations for (a) liability, (b) insurance and (c) compensation and/or other remedies for damage arising from the management of hazardous wastes, and they should take such steps as are necessary to ensure the compatibility and, where appropriate, the harmonization of such laws and regulations.

4.9 OAU COUNCIL OF MINISTERS RESOLUTION ON DUMPING OF NUCLEAR AND INDUSTRIAL WASTE IN AFRICA. Adopted at Addis Ababa, 23 May 1988. *Reprinted in* 28 I.L.M. 567 (1989) & 5 Weston V.I.10a

The Council of Ministers of the Organization of African Unity, meeting in its Forty-eighth Ordinary Session, in Addis Ababa, Ethiopia, from 19 to 23 May 1988,

Aware of the growing practice of dumping nuclear and industrial wastes in African countries by transnational corporations and other enterprises from industrialized countries, which they cannot dispose of within their territories,

Gravely concerned about the growing tendency of some African countries to conclude agreements or arrangements with such corporations and enterprises which facilitate the dumping of nuclear and industrial wastes in their territorial boundaries,

Bearing in mind the harmful effects of radiation from nuclear and other hazardous industrial wastes to human and marine life as well as to the ecosystems on which they depend for their existence:

1. DECLARES that the dumping of nuclear and industrial wastes in Africa is a crime against Africa and the African people;

2. CONDEMNS all transnational corporations and enterprises involved in the introduction, in any form, of nuclear and industrial wastes in Africa; and DEMANDS that they clean up the areas that have already been contaminated by them;

3. CALLS UPON African countries which have concluded or are in the process of concluding agreements or arrangements for dumping nuclear and industrial wastes in their territories to put an end to these transactions;

4. REQUESTS Member States of the OAU to carry out information campaigns among their people about the danger of Nuclear and Industrial Wastes;

5. REQUESTS the Secretary–General of the Organization of African Unity (OAU), in close collaboration with the Director–General of the International Atomic Energy Agency (IAEA), the Executive Secretary of the United Nations Economic Commission for Africa (ECA), the Executive Director of the United Nations Environment Programme (UNEP), and other concerned organizations, to assist African countries to establish appropriate mechanisms for monitoring and control of the movement and disposal of Nuclear and Industrial Wastes in Africa;

6. REQUESTS ALSO the Secretary–General of the Organization of African Unity (OAU) to take appropriate steps to ensure the inscription of The Dumping of Nuclear and Industrial Wastes in Africa as an item on the Agenda of the Forty-third Session of the U.N. General Assembly;

7. REQUESTS FURTHER the Secretary–General of the Organization of African Unity (OAU) to report to the Council of Ministers at its Fiftieth Session, on the implementation of this resolution;

8. CALLS UPON Member States to adhere to the guidelines and principles of Cairo on the dumping of dangerous wastes using ecologically rational methods;

9. INVITES Member States to participate in the Working Group charged with the drafting of the Convention on the Control of the Movement of Dangerous Wastes across Borders.

4.10 Basel Convention on the Control of Transboundary Movements of Hazardous Wastes and Their Disposal (as Amended and With Annexes). Concluded at Basel, 22 March 1989. Entered into force, 5 May 1992. 1673 UNTS 57; *reprinted in* 28 ILM 657 (1989) & 5 Weston & Carlson V.I.11

Preamble

The Parties to this Convention,

Aware of the risk of damage to human health and the environment caused by hazardous wastes and other wastes and the transboundary movement thereof,

Mindful of the growing threat to human health and the environment posed by the increased generation and complexity, and transboundary movement of hazardous wastes and other wastes,

Mindful also that the most effective way of protecting human health and the environment from the dangers posed by such wastes is the reduction of their generation to a minimum in terms of quantity and/or hazard potential,

Convinced that States should take necessary measures to ensure that the management of hazardous wastes and other wastes including their transboundary movement and disposal is consistent with the protection of human health and the environment whatever the place of their disposal,

Noting that States should ensure that the generator should carry out duties with regard to the transport and disposal of hazardous wastes and other wastes in a manner that is consistent with the protection of the environment, whatever the place of disposal.

Fully recognizing that any State has the sovereign right to ban the entry or disposal of foreign hazardous wastes and other wastes in its territory.

Recognizing also the increasing desire for the prohibition of transboundary movements of hazardous wastes and their disposal in other States, especially developing countries,

Recognizing that transboundary movements of hazardous wastes, especially to developing countries, have a high risk of not constituting an environmentally sound management of hazardous wastes as required by this Convention;

Convinced that hazardous wastes and other wastes should, as far as is compatible with environmentally sound and efficient management, be disposed of in the State where they were generated,

Aware also that transboundary movements of such wastes from the State of their generation to any other State should be permitted only when conducted under conditions which do not endanger human health and the environment, and under conditions in conformity with the provisions of this Convention,

Considering that enhanced control of transboundary movement of hazardous wastes and other wastes will act as an incentive for their environmentally sound management and for the reduction of the volume of such transboundary movement,

Convinced that States should take measures for the proper exchange of information on and control of the transboundary movement of hazardous wastes and other wastes from and to those States,

Noting that a number of international and regional agreements have addressed the issue of protection and preservation of the environment with regard to the transit of dangerous goods.

Taking into account the Declaration of the United Nations Conference on the Human Environment (Stockholm, 1972), the Cairo Guidelines and Principles for the

Environmentally Sound Management of Hazardous Wastes adopted by the Governing Council of the United Nations Environment Programme (UNEP) by decision 14/30 of 17 June 1987, the Recommendations of the United Nations Committee of Experts on the Transport of Dangerous Goods (formulated in 1957 and updated biennially), relevant recommendations, declarations, instruments and regulations adopted within the United Nations system and the work and studies done within other international and regional organizations,

Mindful of the spirit, principles, aims and functions of the World Charter for Nature adopted by the General Assembly of the United Nations at its thirty-seventh session (1982) as the rule of ethics in respect of the protection of the human environment and the conservation of natural resources,

Affirming that States are responsible for the fulfilment of their international obligations concerning the protection of human health and protection and preservation of the environment, and are liable in accordance with international law,

Recognizing that in the case of a material breach of the provisions of this Convention or any protocol thereto the relevant international law of treaties shall apply,

Aware of the need to continue the development and implementation of environmentally sound low-waste technologies, recycling options, good house-keeping and management systems with a view to reducing to a minimum the generation of hazardous wastes and other wastes,

Aware also of the growing international concern about the need for stringent control of transboundary movement of hazardous wastes and other wastes, and of the need as far as possible to reduce such movement to a minimum,

Concerned about the problem of illegal transboundary traffic in hazardous wastes and other wastes,

Taking into account also the limited capabilities of the developing countries to manage hazardous wastes and other wastes,

Recognizing the need to promote the transfer of technology for the sound management of hazardous wastes and other wastes produced locally, particularly to the developing countries in accordance with the spirit of the Cairo Guidelines and decision 14/16 of the Governing Council of UNEP on Promotion of the transfer of environmental protection technology,

Recognizing also that hazardous wastes and other wastes should be transported in accordance with relevant international conventions and recommendations,

Convinced also that the transboundary movement of hazardous wastes and other wastes should be permitted only when the transport and the ultimate disposal of such wastes is environmentally sound, and

Determined to protect, by strict control, human health and the environment against the adverse effects which may result from the generation and management of hazardous wastes and other wastes,

HAVE AGREED AS FOLLOWS:

Article 1

Scope of the Convention

1. The following wastes that are subject to transboundary movement shall be "hazardous wastes" for the purposes of this Convention:

(a) Wastes that belong to any category contained in Annex I, unless they do not possess any of the characteristics contained in Annex III; and

(b) Wastes that are not covered under paragraph (a) but are defined as, or are considered to be, hazardous wastes by the domestic legislation of the Party of export, import or transit.

2. Wastes that belong to any category contained in Annex II that are subject to transboundary movement shall be "other wastes" for the purposes of this Convention.

3. Wastes which, as a result of being radioactive, are subject to other international control systems, including international instruments, applying specifically to radioactive materials, are excluded from the scope of this Convention.

4. Wastes which derive from the normal operations of a ship, the discharge of which is covered by another international instrument, are excluded from the scope of this Convention.

Article 2

Definitions

For the purposes of this Convention:

1. "Wastes" are substances or objects which are disposed of or are intended to be disposed of or are required to be disposed of by the provisions of national law;

2. "Management" means the collection, transport and disposal of hazardous wastes or other wastes, including after-care of disposal sites;

3. "Transboundary movement" means any movement of hazardous wastes or other wastes from an area under the national jurisdiction of one State to or through an area under the national jurisdiction of another State or to or through an area not under the national jurisdiction of any State, provided at least two States are involved in the movement;

4. "Disposal" means any operation specified in Annex IV to this Convention;

5. "Approved site or facility" means a site or facility for the disposal of hazardous wastes or other wastes which is authorized or permitted to operate for this purpose by a relevant authority of the State where the site or facility is located;

6. "Competent authority" means one governmental authority designated by a Party to be responsible, within such geographical areas as the Party may think fit, for receiving the notification of a transboundary movement of hazardous wastes or other wastes, and any information related to it, and for responding to such a notification, as provided in Article 6;

7. "Focal point" means the entity of a Party referred to in Article 5 responsible for receiving and submitting information as provided for in Articles 13 and 16;

8. "Environmentally sound management of hazardous wastes or other wastes" means taking all practicable steps to ensure that hazardous wastes or other wastes are managed in a manner which will protect human health and the environment against the adverse effects which may result from such wastes;

9. "Area under the national jurisdiction of a State" means any land, marine area or airspace within which a State exercises administrative and regulatory responsibility in accordance with international law in regard to the protection of human health or the environment;

10. "State of export" means a Party from which a transboundary movement of hazardous wastes or other wastes is planned to be initiated or is initiated;

11. "State of import" means a Party to which a transboundary movement of hazardous wastes or other wastes is planned or takes place for the purpose of disposal therein or for the purpose of loading prior to disposal in an area not under the national jurisdiction of any State;

12. "State of transit" means any State, other than the State of export or import, through which a movement of hazardous wastes or other wastes is planned or takes place;

13. "States concerned" means Parties which are States of export or import, or transit States, whether or not Parties;

14. "Person" means any natural or legal person;

15. "Exporter" means any person under the jurisdiction of the State of export who arranges for hazardous wastes or other wastes to be exported;

16. "Importer" means any person under the jurisdiction of the State of import who arranges for hazardous wastes or other wastes to be imported;

17. "Carrier" means any person who carries out the transport of hazardous wastes or other wastes;

18. "Generator" means any person whose activity produces hazardous wastes or other wastes or, if that person is not known, the person who is in possession and/or control of those wastes;

19. "Disposer" means any person to whom hazardous wastes or other wastes are shipped and who carries out the disposal of such wastes;

20. "Political and/or economic integration organization" means an organization constituted by sovereign States to which its member States have transferred competence in respect of matters governed by this Convention and which has been duly authorized, in accordance with its internal procedures, to sign, ratify, accept, approve, formally confirm or accede to it;

21. "Illegal traffic" means any transboundary movement of hazardous wastes or other wastes as specified in Article 9.

Article 3

National Definitions of Hazardous Wastes

1. Each Party shall, within six months of becoming a Party to this Convention, inform the Secretariat of the Convention of the wastes, other than those listed in Annexes I and II, considered or defined as hazardous under its national legislation and of any requirements concerning transboundary movement procedures applicable to such wastes.

2. Each Party shall subsequently inform the Secretariat of any significant changes to the information it has provided pursuant to paragraph 1.

3. The Secretariat shall forthwith inform all Parties of the information it has received pursuant to paragraphs 1 and 2.

4. Parties shall be responsible for making the information transmitted to them by the Secretariat under paragraph 3 available to their exporters.

Article 4

General Obligations

1. (a) Parties exercising their right to prohibit the import of hazardous wastes or other wastes for disposal shall inform the other Parties of their decision pursuant to Article 13.

(b) Parties shall prohibit or shall not permit the export of hazardous wastes and other wastes to the Parties which have prohibited the import of such wastes, when notified pursuant to subparagraph (a) above.

(c) Parties shall prohibit or shall not permit the export of hazardous wastes and other wastes if the State of import does not consent in writing to the specific import, in the case where that State of import has not prohibited the import of such wastes.

2. Each Party shall take the appropriate measures to:

(a) Ensure that the generation of hazardous wastes and other wastes within it is reduced to a minimum, taking into account social, technological and economic aspects;

(b) Ensure the availability of adequate disposal facilities, for the environmentally sound management of hazardous wastes and other wastes, that shall be located, to the extent possible, within it, whatever the place of their disposal;

(c) Ensure that persons involved in the management of hazardous wastes or other wastes within it take such steps as are necessary to prevent pollution due to hazardous wastes and other wastes arising from such management and, if such pollution occurs, to minimize the consequences thereof for human health and the environment;

(d) Ensure that the transboundary movement of hazardous wastes and other wastes is reduced to the minimum consistent with the environmentally sound and efficient management of such wastes, and is conducted in a manner which will protect human health and the environment against the adverse effects which may result from such movement;

(e) Not allow the export of hazardous wastes or other wastes to a State or group of States belonging to an economic and/or political integration organization that are Parties, particularly developing countries, which have prohibited by their legislation all imports, or if it has reason to believe that the wastes in question will not be managed in an environmentally sound manner, according to criteria to be decided on by the Parties at their first meeting.

(f) Require that information about a proposed transboundary movement of hazardous wastes and other wastes be provided to the States concerned, according to Annex V A, to state clearly the effects of the proposed movement on human health and the environment;

(g) Prevent the import of hazardous wastes and other wastes if it has reason to believe that the wastes in question will not be managed in an environmentally sound manner;

(h) Co-operate in activities with other Parties and interested organizations, directly and through the Secretariat, including the dissemination of information on the transboundary movement of hazardous wastes and other wastes, in order to improve the environmentally sound management of such wastes and to achieve the prevention of illegal traffic;

3. The Parties consider that illegal traffic in hazardous wastes or other wastes is criminal.

4. Each Party shall take appropriate legal, administrative and other measures to implement and enforce the provisions of this Convention, including measures to prevent and punish conduct in contravention of the Convention.

5. A Party shall not permit hazardous wastes or other wastes to be exported to a non-Party or to be imported from a non-Party.

6. The Parties agree not to allow the export of hazardous wastes or other wastes for disposal within the area south of 60 South latitude, whether or not such wastes are subject to transboundary movement.

7. Furthermore, each Party shall:

(a) Prohibit all persons under its national jurisdiction from transporting or disposing of hazardous wastes or other wastes unless such persons are authorized or allowed to perform such types of operations;

(b) Require that hazardous wastes and other wastes that are to be the subject of a transboundary movement be packaged, labelled, and transported in conformity with generally accepted and recognized international rules and standards in the field of packaging, labelling, and transport, and that due account is taken of relevant internationally recognized practices;

(c) Require that hazardous wastes and other wastes be accompanied by a movement document from the point at which a transboundary movement commences to the point of disposal.

8. Each Party shall require that hazardous wastes or other wastes, to be exported, are managed in an environmentally sound manner in the State of import or elsewhere. Technical guidelines for the environmentally sound management of wastes subject to this Convention shall be decided by the Parties at their first meeting.

9. Parties shall take the appropriate measures to ensure that the transboundary movement of hazardous wastes and other wastes only be allowed if:

(a) The State of export does not have the technical capacity and the necessary facilities, capacity or suitable disposal sites in order to dispose of the wastes in question in an environmentally sound and efficient manner; or

(b) The wastes in question are required as a raw material for recycling or recovery industries in the State of import; or

(c) The transboundary movement in question is in accordance with other criteria to be decided by the Parties, provided those criteria do not differ from the objectives of this Convention.

10. The obligation under this Convention of States in which hazardous wastes and other wastes are generated to require that those wastes are managed in an environmentally sound manner may not under any circumstances be transferred to the States of import or transit.

11. Nothing in this Convention shall prevent a Party from imposing additional requirements that are consistent with the provisions of this Convention, and are in accordance with the rules of international law, in order better to protect human health and the environment.

12. Nothing in this Convention shall affect in any way the sovereignty of States over their territorial sea established in accordance with international law, and the sovereign rights and the jurisdiction which States have in their exclusive economic zones and their continental shelves in accordance with international law, and the exercise by ships and aircraft of all States of navigational rights and freedoms as provided for in international law and as reflected in relevant international instruments.

13. Parties shall undertake to review periodically the possibilities for the reduction of the amount and/or the pollution potential of hazardous wastes and other wastes which are exported to other States, in particular to developing countries.

Article 4A

1. Each Party listed in Annex VII shall prohibit all transboundary movements of hazardous wastes which are destined for operations according to Annex IV A, to States not listed in Annex VII.

2. Each Party listed in Annex VII shall phase out by 31 December 1997, and prohibit as of that date, all transboundary movements of hazardous wastes under Article 1(i)(a) of the Convention which are destined for operations according to Annex IV B to States not listed in Annex VII. Such transboundary movement shall not be prohibited unless the wastes in question are characterised as hazardous under the Convention.

Article 5

Designation of Competent Authorities and Focal Point

To facilitate the implementation of this Convention, the Parties shall:

1. Designate or establish one or more competent authorities and one focal point. One competent authority shall be designated to receive the notification in case of a State of transit.

2. Inform the Secretariat, within three months of the date of the entry into force of this Convention for them, which agencies they have designated as their focal point and their competent authorities.

3. Inform the Secretariat, within one month of the date of decision, of any changes regarding the designation made by them under paragraph 2 above.

Article 6

Transboundary Movement between Parties

1. The State of export shall notify, or shall require the generator or exporter to notify, in writing, through the channel of the competent authority of the State of export, the competent authority of the States concerned of any proposed transboundary movement of hazardous wastes or other wastes. Such notification shall contain the declarations and information specified in Annex V A, written in a language acceptable to the State of import. Only one notification needs to be sent to each State concerned.

2. The State of import shall respond to the notifier in writing, consenting to the movement with or without conditions, denying permission for the movement, or requesting additional information. A copy of the final response of the State of import shall be sent to the competent authorities of the States concerned which are Parties.

3. The State of export shall not allow the generator or exporter to commence the transboundary movement until it has received written confirmation that:

(a) The notifier has received the written consent of the State of import; and

(b) The notifier has received from the State of import confirmation of the existence of a contract between the exporter and the disposer specifying environmentally sound management of the wastes in question.

4. Each State of transit which is a Party shall promptly acknowledge to the notifier receipt of the notification. It may subsequently respond to the notifier in writing, within 60 days, consenting to the movement with or without conditions, denying permission for the movement, or requesting additional information. The State of export shall not allow the transboundary movement to commence until it has received the written consent of the State of transit. However, if at any time a Party decides not to require prior written consent, either generally or under specific conditions, for transit transboundary movements of hazardous wastes or other wastes, or modifies its requirements in this respect, it shall forthwith inform the other Parties of its decision pursuant to Article 13. In this latter case, if no response is received by the State of export within 60 days of the receipt of a given notification by the State of transit, the State of export may allow the export to proceed through the State of transit.

5. In the case of a transboundary movement of wastes where the wastes are legally defined as or considered to be hazardous wastes only:

(a) By the State of export, the requirements of paragraph 9 of this Article that apply to the importer or disposer and the State of import shall apply *mutatis mutandis* to the exporter and State of export, respectively:

(b) By the State of import, or by the States of import and transit which are Parties, the requirements of paragraphs 1, 3, 4 and 6 of this Article that apply to the exporter and State of export shall apply *mutatis mutandis* to the importer or disposer and State of import, respectively; or

(c) By any State of transit which is a Party, the provisions of paragraph 4 shall apply to such State.

6. The State of export may, subject to the written consent of the States concerned, allow the generator or the exporter to use a general notification where hazardous wastes or other wastes having the same physical and chemical characteristics are shipped regularly to the same disposer via the same customs office of exit of the State of export via the same customs office of entry of the State of import, and, in the case of transit, via the same customs office of entry and exist of the State or States of transit.

7. The States concerned may make their written consent to the use of the general notification referred to in paragraph 6 subject to the supply of certain information, such as the exact quantities or periodical lists of hazardous wastes or other wastes to be shipped.

8. The general notification and written consent referred to in paragraphs 6 and 7 may cover multiple shipments of hazardous wastes or other wastes during a maximum period of 12 months.

9. The Parties shall require that each person who takes charge of a transboundary movement of hazardous wastes or other wastes sign the movement document either upon delivery or receipt of the wastes in question. They shall also require that the disposer inform both the exporter and the competent authority of the State of export of receipt by the disposer of the wastes in question and, in due course, of the completion of disposal as specified in the notification. If no such information is received within the State of export, the competent authority of the State of export or the exporter shall so notify the State of import.

10. The notification and response required by this Article shall be transmitted to the competent authority of the Parties concerned or to such governmental authority as may be appropriate in the case of non-Parties.

11. Any transboundary movement of hazardous wastes or other wastes shall be covered by insurance, bond or other guarantee as may be required by the State of import or any State of transit which is a Party.

Article 7

Transboundary Movement from a Party through States which are not Parties

Paragraph 2 of Article 6 of the Convention shall apply *mutatis mutandis* to transboundary movement of hazardous wastes or other wastes from a Party through a State or States which are not Parties.

Article 8

Duty to Re-import

When a transboundary movement of hazardous wastes or other wastes to which the consent of the States concerned has been given, subject to the provisions of this Convention, cannot be completed in accordance with the terms of the contract, the State of export shall ensure that the wastes in question are taken back into the State of export, by the exporter, if alternative arrangements cannot be made for their disposal in an environmentally sound manner, within 90 days from the time that the importing State informed the State of export and the Secretariat, or such other period of time as the States concerned agree. To this end, the State of export and any Party of transit shall not oppose, hinder or prevent the return of those wastes to the State of export.

Article 9

Illegal Traffic

1. For the purpose of this Convention, any transboundary movement of hazardous wastes or other wastes:

(a) without notification pursuant to the provisions of this Convention to all States concerned; or

(b) without the consent pursuant to the provisions of this Convention of a State concerned; or

(c) with consent obtained from States concerned through falsification, misrepresentation or fraud; or

(d) that does not conform in a material may with the documents; or

(e) that results in deliberate disposal (e.g. dumping) of hazardous wastes or other wastes in contravention of this Convention and of general principles of international law, shall be deemed to be illegal traffic.

2. In case of a transboundary movement of hazardous wastes or other wastes deemed to be illegal traffic as the result of conduct on the part of the exporter or generator, the State of export shall ensure that the wastes in question are:

(a) taken back by the exporter or the generator or, if necessary, by itself into the State of export, or, if impracticable,

(b) are otherwise disposed of in accordance with the provisions of this Convention, within 30 days from the time the State of export has been informed about the illegal traffic or such other period of time as States concerned may agree. To this end the Parties concerned shall not oppose, hinder or prevent the return of those wastes to the State of export.

3. In the case of a transboundary movement of hazardous wastes or other wastes deemed to be illegal traffic as the result of conduct on the part of the importer or disposer, the State of import shall ensure that the wastes in question are disposed of in an environmentally sound manner by the importer or disposer or, if necessary, by itself within 30 days from the time the illegal traffic has come to the attention of the State of import or such other period of time as the States concerned may agree. To this end, the Parties concerned shall co-operate, as necessary, in the disposal of the wastes in an environmentally sound manner.

4. In cases where the responsibility for the illegal traffic cannot be assigned either to the exporter or generator or to the importer or disposer, the Parties concerned or other Parties, as appropriate, shall ensure, through co-operation, that the wastes in question are disposed of as soon as possible in an environmentally sound manner either in the State of export or the State of import or elsewhere as appropriate.

5. Each Party shall introduce appropriate national/domestic legislation to prevent and punish illegal traffic. The Parties shall co-operate with a view to achieving the objects of this Article.

Article 10

International Co-operation

1. The Parties shall co-operate with each other in order to improve and achieve environmentally sound management of hazardous wastes and other wastes.

2. To this end, the Parties shall:

(a) Upon request, make available information, whether on a bilateral or multilateral basis, with a view to promoting the environmentally sound management of hazardous wastes and other wastes, including harmonization of technical standards and practices for the adequate management of hazardous wastes and other wastes;

(b) Co-operate in monitoring the effects of the management of hazardous wastes on human health and the environment;

(c) Co-operate, subject to their national laws, regulations and policies, in the development and implementation of new environmentally sound low-waste technologies and the improvement of existing technologies with a view to eliminating, as far as practicable, the generation of hazardous wastes and other wastes and achieving more effective and efficient methods of ensuring their management in an environmentally sound manner, including the study of the economic, social and environmental effects of the adoption of such new or improved technologies;

(d) Co-operate actively, subject to their national laws, regulations and policies, in the transfer of technology and management systems related to the environmentally sound management of hazardous wastes and other wastes. They shall also co-operate in developing the technical capacity among Parties, especially those which may need and request technical assistance in this field;

(e) Co-operate in developing appropriate technical guidelines and/or codes of practice.

3. The Parties shall employ appropriate means to co-operate in order to assist developing countries in the implementation of subparagraphs a, b, c and d of paragraph 2 of Article 4.

4. Taking into account the needs of developing countries, co-operation between Parties and the competent international organizations is encouraged to promote, *inter alia,* public awareness, the development of sound management of hazardous wastes and other wastes and the adoption of new low-waste technologies.

Article 11

Bilateral, Multilateral and Regional Agreements

1. Notwithstanding the provisions of Article 4, paragraph 5, Parties may enter into bilateral, multilateral, or regional agreements or arrangements regarding transboundary movement of hazardous wastes or other wastes with Parties or non-Parties provided that such agreements or arrangements do not derogate from the environmentally sound management of hazardous wastes and other wastes as required by this Convention. These agreements or arrangements shall stipulate provisions which are not less environmentally sound than those provided for by this Convention in particular taking into account the interests of developing countries.

2. Parties shall notify the Secretariat of any bilateral, multilateral or regional agreements or arrangements referred to in paragraph 1 and those which they have entered into prior to the entry into force of this Convention for them, for the purpose of controlling transboundary movements of hazardous wastes and other wastes which take place entirely among the Parties to such agreements. The provisions of this Convention shall not affect transboundary movements which take place pursuant of such agreements provided that such agreements are compatible with the environmentally sound management of hazardous wastes and other wastes as required by this Convention.

Article 12

Consultations on Liability

The Parties shall co-operate with a view to adopting, as soon as practicable, a protocol setting out appropriate rules and procedures in the field of liability and compensation for damage resulting from the transboundary movement and disposal of hazardous wastes and other wastes.

Article 13

Transmission of Information

1. The Parties shall, whenever it comes to their knowledge, ensure that, in the case of an accident occurring during the transboundary movement of hazardous wastes or other wastes or their disposal, which are likely to present risks to human health and the environment in other States, those states are immediately informed.

2. The Parties shall inform each other, through the Secretariat, of:

(a) Changes regarding the designation of competent authorities and/or focal points, pursuant to Article 5;

(b) Changes in their national definition of hazardous wastes, pursuant to Article 3; and, as soon as possible,

(c) Decisions made by them not to consent totally or partially to the import of hazardous wastes or other wastes for disposal within the area under their national jurisdiction;

(d) Decisions taken by them to limit or ban the export of hazardous wastes or other wastes;

(e) Any other information required pursuant to paragraph 4 of this Article.

3. The Parties, consistent with national laws and regulations, shall transmit, through the Secretariat, to the Conference of the Parties established under Article 15, before the end of each calendar year, a report on the previous calendar year, containing the following information:

(a) Competent authorities and focal points that have been designated by them pursuant to Article 5;

(b) Information regarding transboundary movements of hazardous wastes or other wastes in which they have been involved, including:

(i) The amount of hazardous wastes and other wastes exported, their category, characteristics, destination, any transit country and disposal method as stated on the response to notification;

(ii) The amount of hazardous wastes and other wastes imported, their category, characteristics, origin, and disposal methods;

(iii) Disposals which did not proceed as intended;

(iv) Efforts to achieve a reduction of the amount of hazardous wastes or other wastes subject to transboundary movement;

(c) Information on the measures adopted by them in implementation of this Convention;

(d) Information on available qualified statistics which have been complied by them on the effects on human health and the environment of the generation, transportation and disposal of hazardous wastes or other wastes;

(e) Information concerning bilateral, multilateral and regional agreements and arrangements entered into pursuant to Article 11 of this Convention;

(f) Information on accidents occurring during the transboundary movement and disposal of hazardous wastes and other wastes and on the measures undertaken to deal with them;

(g) Information on disposal options operated within the area of their national jurisdiction;

(h) Information on measures undertaken for development of technologies for the reduction and/or elimination of production of hazardous wastes and other wastes; and

(i) Such other matters as the Conference of the Parties shall deem relevant.

4. The Parties, consistent with national laws and regulations, shall ensure that copies of each notification concerning any given transboundary movement of hazardous wastes or other wastes, and the response to it, are sent to the Secretariat when a Party considers that its environment may be affected by that transboundary movement has requested that this should be done.

Article 14

Financial Aspects

1. The Parties agree that, according to the specific needs of different regions and subregions, regional or sub-regional centres for training and technology transfers regarding the management of hazardous wastes and other wastes and the minimization of their generation should be established. The Parties shall decide on the establishment of appropriate funding mechanisms of a voluntary nature.

2. The Parties shall consider the establishment of a revolving fund to assist on an interim basis in case of emergency situations to minimize damage from accidents arising from transboundary movement of hazardous wastes and other wastes or during the disposal of those wastes.

Article 15

Conference of the Parties

1. A Conference of the Parties is hereby established. The first meeting of the Conference of the Parties shall be convened by the Executive Director of UNEP not later than one year after the entry into force of this Convention. Thereafter, ordinary meetings of the Conference of the Parties shall be held at regular intervals to be determined by the Conference at its first meeting.

2. Extraordinary meetings of the Conference of the Parties shall be held at such other times as may be deemed necessary by the Conference, or at the written request of any Party, provided that, within six months of the request being communicated to them by the Secretariat, it is supported by at least one third of the Parties.

3. The Conference of the Parties shall by consensus agree upon and adopt rules of procedure for itself and for any subsidiary body it may establish, as well as financial rules to determine in particular the financial participation of the Parties under this Convention.

4. The Parties at their first meeting shall consider any additional measures needed to assist them in fulfilling their responsibilities with respect to the protection and the preservation of the marine environment in the context of this Convention.

5. The Conference of the Parties shall keep under continuous review and evaluation the effective implementation of this Convention, and, in addition, shall:

(a) Promote the harmonization of appropriate policies, strategies and measures for minimizing harm to human health and the environment by hazardous wastes and other wastes;

(b) Consider and adopt, as required, amendments to this Convention and its annexes, taking into consideration, *inter alia,* available scientific, technical, economic and environmental information;

(c) Consider and undertake any additional action that may be required for the achievement of the purposes of this Convention in the light of experience gained in its operation and in the operation of the agreements and arrangements envisaged in Article 11;

(d) Consider and adopt protocols as required; and

(e) Establish such subsidiary bodies as are deemed necessary for the implementation of this Convention.

6. The United Nations, its specialized agencies, as well as any State not party to this Convention, may be represented as observers at meetings of the Conference of the Parties. Any other body or agency, whether national or international, governmental or non-governmental, qualified in fields relating to hazardous wastes or other wastes which has informed the Secretariat of its wish to be represented as an observer at a meeting of the Conference of the Parties, may be admitted unless at least one third of the Parties present object. The admission and participation of observers shall be subject to the rules of procedure adopted by the Conference of the Parties.

7. The Conference of the Parties shall undertake three years after the entry into force of this Convention, and at least every six years thereafter, an evaluation of its effectiveness and, if deemed necessary, to consider the adoption of a complete or partial ban of transboundary movements of hazardous wastes and other wastes in light of the latest scientific, environmental, technical and economic information.

Article 16

Secretariat

1. The functions of the Secretariat shall be:

(a) To arrange for and service meetings provided for in Article 15 and 17;

(b) To prepare and transmit reports based upon information received in accordance with Articles 3, 4, 6, 11 and 13 as well as upon information derived from meetings of subsidiary bodies established upon Article 15 as well as upon, as appropriate, information provided by relevant intergovernmental and nongovernmental entities;

(c) To prepare reports on its activities carried out in implementation of its functions under this Convention and present them to the Conference of the Parties;

(d) To ensure the necessary coordination with relevant international bodies, and in particular to enter into such administrative and contractual arrangements as may be required for the effective discharge of its functions;

(e) To communicate with focal points and competent authorities established by the Parties in accordance with Article 5 of this Convention;

(f) To compile information concerning authorized national sites and facilities of Parties available for the disposal of their hazardous wastes and other wastes and to circulate this information among Parties;

(g) To receive and convey information from and to Parties on:

    sources of technical assistance and training;

    available technical and scientific know-how;

    sources of advice and expertise; and

    availability of resources

with a view to assisting them, upon request, in such areas as:

the handling of the notification system of this Convention;

the management of hazardous wastes and other wastes;

environmentally sound technologies relating to hazardous wastes and other wastes, such as low- and non-waste technology;

the assessment of disposal capabilities and sites;

the monitoring of hazardous wastes and other wastes; and

emergency responses;

(h) To provide Parties, upon request, with information on consultants or consulting firms having the necessary technical competence in the field, which can assist them to examine a notification for a transboundary movement, the concurrence of a shipment of hazardous wastes or other wastes with the relevant notification, and/or the fact that the proposed disposal facilities for hazardous wastes or other wastes are environmentally sound, when they have reason to believe that the wastes in question will not be managed in an environmentally sound manner. Any such examination would not be at the expense of the Secretariat;

(i) To assist Parties upon request in their identification of cases of illegal traffic and to circulate immediately to the Parties concerned any information it has received regarding illegal traffic;

(j) To co-operate with Parties and with relevant and competent international organizations and agencies in the provision of experts and equipment for the purpose of rapid assistance to States in the event of an emergency situation; and

(k) To perform such other functions relevant to the purposes of this Convention as may be determined by the Conference of the Parties.

2. The Secretariat functions will be carried out on an interim basis by UNEP until the completion of the first meeting of the Conference of the Parties held pursuant to Article 15.

3. At its first meeting, the Conference of the Parties shall designate the Secretariat from among those existing competent intergovernmental organizations which have signified their willingness to carry out the Secretariat functions under this Convention. At this meeting, the Conference of the Parties shall also evaluate the implementation by the interim Secretariat of the functions assigned to it, in particular under paragraph 1 above, and decide upon the structures appropriate for those functions.

Article 17

Amendment of the Convention

1. Any Party may propose amendments to this Convention and any Party to a protocol may propose amendments to that protocol. Such amendments shall take due account, *inter alia,* of relevant scientific and technical considerations.

2. Amendments to this Convention shall be adopted at a meeting of the Conference of the Parties. Amendments to any protocol shall be adopted at a meeting of the Parties to the protocol in question. The text of any proposed amendment to this Convention or to any protocol, except as may otherwise be provided in such protocol, shall be communicated to the Parties by the Secretariat at least six months before the meeting at which it is proposed for adoption. The Secretariat shall also communicate proposed amendments to the Signatories to this Convention for information.

3. The Parties shall make every effort to reach agreement on any proposed amendment to this Convention by consensus. If all efforts at consensus have been exhausted, and no agreement reached, the amendment shall as a last resort be adopted

by a three-fourths majority vote of the Parties present and voting at the meeting, and shall be submitted by the Depositary to all Parties for ratification, approval, formal confirmation or acceptance.

4.   The procedure mentioned in paragraph 3 above shall apply to amendments to any protocol, except that a two-thirds majority of the Parties to that protocol present and voting at the meeting shall suffice for their adoption.

5.   Instruments of ratification, approval, formal confirmation or acceptance of amendments shall be deposited with the Depositary. Amendments adopted in accordance with paragraphs 3 or 4 above shall enter into force between Parties having accepted them on the ninetieth day after the receipt by the Depositary of their instrument of ratification, approval, formal confirmation or acceptance by at least three-fourths of the Parties who accepted the amendments to the protocol concerned, except as may otherwise be provided in such protocol. The amendments shall enter into force for any other Party on the ninetieth day after that Party deposits its instrument of ratification, approval, formal confirmation or acceptance of the amendments.

6.   For the purpose of this Article, "Parties present and voting" means Parties present and casting an affirmative or negative vote.

Article 18

Adoption and Amendment of Annexes

1.   The annexes of this Convention or to any protocol shall form an integral part of this Convention or of such protocol, as the case may be and, unless expressly provided otherwise, a reference to this Convention or its protocols constitutes at the same time a reference to any annexes thereto. Such annexes shall be restricted to scientific, technical and administrative matters.

2.   Except as may be otherwise provided in any protocol with respect to its annexes, the following procedure shall apply to the proposal, adoption and entry into force of additional annexes to this Convention or of annexes to a protocol:

(a) Annexes to this Convention and its protocols shall be proposed and adopted according to the procedure laid down in Article 17, paragraphs 2, 3 and 4;

(b) Any Party that is unable to accept an additional annex to this Convention or an annex to any protocol to which it is party shall so notify the Depositary, in writing, within six months from the date of the communication of the adoption by the Depositary. The Depositary shall without delay notify all Parties of any such notification received. A Party may at any time substitute an acceptance for a previous declaration of objection and the annexes shall thereupon enter into force for that Party;

(c) On the expiry of six months from the date of the circulation of the communication by the Depositary, the annex shall become effective for all Parties to this Convention or to any protocol concerned, which have not submitted a notification in accordance with the provision of subparagraph (b) above.

3.   The proposal, adoption and entry into force of amendments to annexes to this Convention or to any protocol shall be subject to the same procedure as for the proposal, adoption and entry into force of annexes to the Convention or annexes to a protocol. Annexes and amendments thereto shall take due account, *inter alia,* of relevant scientific and technical considerations.

4.   If an additional annex or an amendment to an annex involves an amendment to this Convention or to any protocol, the additional annex or amended annex shall not enter into force until such time as the amendment to this Convention or to the protocol enters into force.

Article 19

Verification

Any Party which has reason to believe that another Party is acting or has acted in breach of its obligations under this Convention may inform the Secretariat thereof, and in such an event, shall simultaneously and immediately inform, directly or through the Secretariat, the Party against whom the allegations are made. All relevant information should be submitted by the Secretariat to the Parties.

Article 20

Settlement of Disputes

1. In case of a dispute between Parties as to the interpretation or application of, or compliance with, this Convention or any protocol thereto, they shall seek a settlement of the dispute through negotiation or any other peaceful means of their own choice.

2. If the Parties concerned cannot settle their dispute through the means mentioned in the preceding paragraph, the dispute, if the parties to the dispute agree, shall be submitted to the International Court of Justice or to arbitration under the conditions set out in Annex VI on Arbitration. However, failure to reach common agreement on submission of the dispute to the International Court of Justice or to arbitration shall not absolve the Parties from the responsibility of continuing to seek to resolve it by the means referred to in paragraph 1.

3. When ratifying, accepting, approving, formally confirming or acceding to this Convention, or at any time thereafter, a State or political and/or economic integration organization may declare that it recognizes as compulsory *ipso facto* and without special agreement, in relation to any Party accepting the same obligation:

(a) submission of the dispute to the International Court of Justice; and/or

(b) arbitration in accordance with the procedures set out in Annex VI.

Such declaration shall be notified in writing to the Secretariat which shall communicate it to the Parties.

Article 21

Signature

This Convention shall be open for signature by States, by Namibia, represented by the United Nations Council for Namibia, and by political and/or economic integration organizations, in Basel on 22 March 1989, at the Federal Department of Foreign Affairs of Switzerland in Berne from 23 March 1989 to 30 June 1989 and at United Nations Headquarters in New York from 1 July 1989 to 22 March 1990.

Article 22

Ratification, Acceptance, Formal Confirmation or Approval

1. This Convention shall be subject to ratification, acceptance or approval by States and by Namibia, represented by the United Nations Council for Namibia, and to formal confirmation or approval by political and/or economic integration organizations. Instruments of ratification, acceptance, formal confirmation, or approval shall be deposited with the Depositary.

2. Any organization referred to in paragraph 1 above which becomes a Party to this Convention without any of its member States being a party shall be bound by all the obligations under the Convention. In the case of such organizations, one or more of whose member States is a Party to the Convention, the organization and its member States shall decide on their respective responsibilities for the performance of their

obligations under the Convention. In such cases, the organization and the member States shall not be entitled to exercise rights under the Convention concurrently.

3. In their instruments of formal confirmation or approval, the organizations referred to in paragraph 1 above shall declare the extent of their competence with respect to the matters governed by the Convention. These organizations shall also inform the Depositary, who will inform the Parties of any substantial modification in the extent of their competence.

Article 23

Accession

1. This Convention shall be open for accession by States, by Namibia, represented by the United Nations Council for Namibia, and by political and/or economic integration organizations from the day after the date on which the Convention is closed for signature. The instruments of accession shall be deposited with the Depositary.

2. In their instruments of accession, the organizations referred to in paragraph 1 above shall declare the extent of their competence with respect to the matters governed by the Convention. These organizations shall also inform the Depositary of any substantial modification in the extent of their competence.

3. The provisions of Article 22, paragraph 2, shall apply to political and/or economic integration organizations which accede to this Convention.

Article 24

Right to Vote

1. Except as provided for in paragraph 2 below, each Contracting Party to this Convention shall have one vote.

2. Political and/or economic integration organizations, in matters within their competence, in accordance with Article 22, paragraph 3, and Article 23, paragraph 2, shall exercise their right to vote with a number of votes equal to the number of their member States which are Parties to the Convention or the relevant protocol. Such organizations shall not exercise their right to vote if their member States exercise theirs, and vice versa.

Article 25

Entry into Force

1. This Convention shall enter into force on the ninetieth day after the date of deposit of the twentieth instrument of ratification, acceptance, formal confirmation, approval or accession.

2. For each State or political and/or economic integration organization which ratifies, accepts, approves or formally confirms this Convention or accedes thereto after the date of the deposit of the twentieth instrument of ratification, acceptance, approval, formal confirmation or accession, it shall enter into force on the ninetieth day after the date of deposit by such State or political and/or economic integration organization of its instrument of ratification, acceptance, approval, formal confirmation or accession.

3. For the purposes of paragraphs 1 and 2 above, any instrument deposited by a political and/or economic integration organization shall not be counted as additional to those deposited by member States of such organization.

Article 26

Reservations and Declarations

1. No reservation or exception may be made to this Convention.

2. Paragraph 1 of this Article does not preclude a State or political and/or economic integration organization, when signing, ratifying, accepting, approving, formally confirming or acceding to this Convention, from making declarations or statements, however phrased or named, with a view, *inter alia,* to the harmonization of its laws and regulations with the provisions of this Convention, provided that such declarations or statements do not purport to exclude or to modify the legal effects of the provisions of the Convention in their application to that State.

Article 27

Withdrawal

1. At any time after three years from the date on which this Convention has entered into force for a Party, that Party may withdraw from the Convention by giving written notification to the Depositary.

2. Withdrawal shall be effective one year from receipt of notification by the Depositary, or on such later date as may be specified in the notification.

Article 28

Depositary

The Secretary–General of the United Nations shall be the Depositary of this Convention and of any protocol thereto.

Article 29

Authentic Texts

The original Arabic, Chinese, English, French, Russian and Spanish texts of this Convention are equally authentic.

* * *

ANNEX I

CATEGORIES OF WASTES TO BE CONTROLLED

Waste Streams

     Y1   Clinical wastes from medical care in hospitals, medical centers and clinics

     Y2   Wastes from the production and preparation of pharmaceutical products

     Y3   Waste pharmaceuticals, drugs and medicines

     Y4   Wastes from the production, formulation and use of biocides and phytopharmaceuticals

     Y5   Wastes from the manufacture, formulation and use of wood preserving chemicals

     Y6   Wastes from the production, formulation and use of organic solvents

     Y7   Wastes from heat treatment and tempering operations containing cyanides

     Y8   Waste mineral oils unfit for their originally intended use

     Y9   Waste oils/water, hydrocarbons/water mixtures, emulsions

Y10   Waste substances and articles containing or contaminated with polychlorinated biphenyls (PCBs) and/or polychlorinated terphenyls (PCTs) and/or polybrominated biphenyls (PBBs)

Y11   Waste tarry residues arising from refining, distillation and any pyrolytic treatment

Y12   Wastes from production, formulation and use of inks, dyes, pigments, paints, lacquers, varnish

Y13   Wastes from production, formulation and use of resins, latex, plasticizers, glues/adhesives

Y14   Waste chemical substances arising from research and development or teaching activities which are not identified and/or are new and whose effects on man and/or the environment are not known

Y15   Wastes of an explosive nature not subject to other legislation

Y16   Wastes from production, formulation and use of photographic chemicals and processing materials

Y17   Wastes resulting from surface treatment of metals and plastics

Y18   Residues arising from industrial waste disposal operations

Wastes Having as Constituents:

Y19   Metal carbonyls

Y20   Beryllium; beryllium compounds

Y21   Hexavalent chromium compounds

Y22   Cooper compounds

Y23   Zinc compounds

Y24   Arsenic; arsenic compounds

Y25   Selenium; selenium compounds

Y26   Cadmium; cadmium compounds

Y27   Antimony; antimony compounds

Y28   Tellurium; tellurium compounds

Y29   Mercury; mercury compounds

Y30   Thallium; thallium compounds

Y31   Lead; lead compounds

Y32   Inorganic fluorine compounds excluding calcium fluoride

Y33   Inorganic cyanides

Y34   Acidic solutions or acids in solid form

Y35   Basic solutions or bases in solid form

Y36   Asbestos (dust and fibres)

Y37   Organic phosphorous compounds

Y38   Organic cyanides

Y39   Phenols; phenol compounds including chlorophenols

Y40   Ethers

Y41   Halogenated organic solvents

Y42   Organic solvents excluding halogenated solvents

Y43 Any congenor of polychlorinated dibenzo-furan

Y44 Any congenor of polychlorinated dibenzo-p-dioxin

Y45 Organohalogen compounds other than substances referred to in this Annex (e.g. Y39, Y41, Y42, Y43, Y44).

ANNEX II

CATEGORIES OF WASTES REQUIRING SPECIAL CONSIDERATION

Y46 Wastes collected from households

Y47 Residues arising from the incineration of household wastes

ANNEX III

LIST OF HAZARDOUS CHARACTERISTICS

UN Class[1] Code Characteristics

1 H1 Explosive

An explosive substance or waste is a solid or liquid substance or waste (or mixture of substances or wastes) which is in itself capable by chemical reaction of producing gas at such a temperature and pressure and at such a speed as to cause damage to the surroundings.

3 H3 Flammable liquids

The word "flammable" has the same meaning as "inflammable". Flammable liquids are liquids, or mixtures of liquids, or liquids containing solids in solution or suspension (for example, paints, varnishes, lacquers, etc., but not including substances or wastes otherwise classified on account of their dangerous characteristics) which give off a flammable vapour at temperatures of not more than 60.5C, closed-cup test, or not more than 65.6C, open-cup test. (Since the results of open-cup tests and of closed-cup tests are not strictly comparable and even individual results by the same test are often variable, regulations varying from the above figures to make allowance for such differences would be within the spirit of this definition.)

4.1 H4.1 Flammable solids

Solids, or waste solids, other than those classed as explosives, which under conditions encountered in transport are readily combustible, or may cause or contribute to fire through friction.

4.2 H4.2 Substances or wastes liable to spontaneous combustion

Substances or wastes which are liable to spontaneous heating under normal conditions encountered in transport, or to heating upon contact with air, and being then liable to catch fire.

4.3 H4.3 Substances or wastes which, in contact with water emit flammable gases

Substances or wastes which, by interaction with water, are liable to become spontaneously flammable or to give off flammable gases in dangerous quantities.

5.1 H5.1 Oxidizing

Substances or wastes which, while in themselves not necessarily combustible, may, generally by yielding oxygen cause, or contribute to, the combustion of other materials.

---

1. Corresponds to the hazard classification system included in the United Nations Recommendations on the Transport of Dangerous Goods (ST/SG/AC.10/1Rev.5, United Nations, New York, 1988).

5.2 H5.2 Organic Peroxides

Organic substances or wastes which contain the bivalent-o-o-structure are thermally unstable substances which may undergo exothermic self-accelerating decomposition.

6.1 H6.1 Poisonous (Acute)

Substances or wastes liable either to cause death or serious injury or to harm human health if swallowed or inhaled or by skin contact.

6.2 H6.2 Infectious substances

Substances or wastes containing viable microorganisms or their toxins which are known or suspected to cause disease in animals or humans.

8 H8 Corrosives

Substances or wastes which, by chemical action, will cause severe damage when in contact with living tissue, or, in the case of leakage, will materially damage, or even destroy, other goods or the means of transport; they may also cause other hazards.

9 H10 Liberation of toxic gases in contact with air or water

Substances or wastes which, by interaction with air or water, are liable to give off toxic gases in dangerous quantities.

9 H11 Toxic (Delayed or chronic)

Substances or wastes which, if they are inhaled or ingested or if they penetrate the skin, may involve delayed or chronic effects, including carcinogenicity.

9 H12 Ecotoxic

Substances or wastes which if released present or may present immediate or delayed adverse impacts to the environment by means of bioaccumulation and/or toxic effects upon biotic systems.

9 H13 Capable, by any means, after disposal, of yielding another material, e.g., leachate, which possesses any of the characteristics listed above.

Tests

The potential hazards posed by certain types of wastes are not yet fully documented; tests to define quantitatively these hazards do not exist. Further research is necessary in order to develop means to characterize potential hazards posed to man and/or the environment by these wastes. Standardized tests have been derived with respect to pure substances and materials. Many countries have developed national tests which can be applied to materials listed in Annex I, in order to decide if these materials exhibit any of the characteristics listed in this Annex.

ANNEX IV

DISPOSAL OPERATIONS

A. Operations which do not lead to the Possibility of Resource Recovery, Recycling, Reclamation, Direct re-use or Alternative Users

Section A encompasses all such disposal operations which occur in practice.

D1   Deposit into or onto land, (e.g., landfill, etc.)

D2   Land treatment, (e.g., biodegradation of liquid or sludgy discards in soils, etc.)

D3   Deep injection, (e.g. injection of pumpable discards into wells, salt domes or naturally occurring repositories, etc.)

D4   Surface impoundment, (e.g., placement of liquid or sludge discards into pits, ponds or lagoons, etc.)

D5   Specially engineered landfill, (e.g., placement into lined discrete cells which are capped and isolated from one another and the environment, etc.)

D6   Release into a water body except seas/oceans

D7   Release into seas/oceans including sea-bed insertion

D8   Biological treatment not specified elsewhere in this Annex which results in final compounds or mixtures which are discarded by means of any of the operations in Section A

D9   Physico chemical treatment not specified elsewhere in this Annex which results in final compounds or mixtures which are discarded by means of any of the operations in Section A, (e.g., evaporation, drying, calcination, neutralization, precipitation, etc.)

D10   Incineration on land

D11   Incineration at sea

D12   Permanent storage (e.g., emplacement of containers in a mine, etc.)

D13   Blending or mixing prior to submission to any of the operations in Section A

D14   Repackaging prior to submission to any of the operations in Section A

D15   Storage pending any of the operations in Section A

B.   Operations which may lead to Resource Recovery, Recycling, Reclamation, Direct re-use or Alternative Uses

Section B encompasses all such operations with respect to materials legally defined as or considered to be hazardous waste and which otherwise would have been destined for operations included in Section A

R1   Use as a fuel (other than in direct incineration) or other means to generate energy

R2   Solvent reclamation/regeneration

R3   Recycling/reclamation of organic substances which are not used as solvents

R4   Recycling/reclamation of metals and metal compounds

R5   Recycling/reclamation of other inorganic materials

R6   Regeneration of acids or bases

R7   Recovery of components used for pollution abatement

R8   Recovery of components from catalysts

R9   Used oil-refining or other uses of previously used oil

R10   Land treatment resulting in benefit to agriculture or ecological improvement

R11   Uses of residual materials obtained from any of the operations numbered R1R10

R12   Exchange of wastes for submission to any of the operations numbered R1R11

R13   Accumulation of material intended for any operation in Section B

ANNEX V A

INFORMATION TO BE PROVIDED ON NOTIFICATION

1.   Reason for waste export

2.   Exporter of the waste

3.   Generator(s) of the waste and site of generation

4. Disposer of the waste and actual site of disposal

5. Intended carrier(s) of the waste of their agents, if known

6. Country of export of the waste Competent authority

7. Expected countries of transit Competent authority

8. Country of import of the waste Competent authority

9. General or single notification

10. Projected date(s) of shipment(s) and period of time over which waste is to be exported and proposed itinerary (including point of entry and exit)

11. Means of transport envisaged (road, rail, sea, air, inland waters)

12. Information relating to insurance

13. Designation and physical description of the wastes including Y number and UN number and its composition and information on any special handling requirements including emergency provisions in case of accidents

14. Type of packaging envisaged (e.g. bulk, drummed, tanker)

15. Estimated quantity in weight/volume

16. Process by which the waste is generated

17. For wastes listed in Annex I, classifications from Annex III: hazardous characteristic, H number, and UN class.

18. Method of disposal as per Annex IV

19. Declaration by the generator and exporter that the information is correct

20. Information transmitted (including technical description of the plant) to the exporter or generator from the disposer of the waste upon which the latter has based his assessment that there was no reason to believe that the wastes will not be managed in an environmentally sound manner in accordance with the laws and regulations of the country of import.

21. Information concerning the contract between the exporter and disposer.

ANNEX V B

INFORMATION TO BE PROVIDED ON THE MOVEMENT DOCUMENT

1. Exporter of the waste

2. Generator(s) of the waste and site of generation

3. Disposer of the waste and actual site of disposal

4. Carrier(s) of the waste or his agent(s)

5. Subject of general or single notification

6. The date the transboundary movement started and date(s) and signature on receipt by each person who takes charge of the waste

7. Means of transport (road, rail, inland, waterway, sea, air) including countries of export, transit and import, als point of entry and exit where these have been designated

8. General description of the waste (physical state, proper UN shipping name and class, UN number, Y number and H number as applicable)

9. Information on special handling requirements including emergency provision in case of accidents

10. Type and number of packages

11. Quantity in weight/volume

12. Declaration by the generator or exporter that the information is correct

13. Declaration by the generator or exporter indicating no objection from the component authorities of all States concerned which are Parties

14. Certification by disposer of receipt at designated disposal facility and indication of method of disposal and of the approximate date of disposal

ANNEX VI

ARBITRATION

* * *

4.11 Bamako Convention on the Ban of Import into Africa and the Control of Transboundary Movement and Management of Hazardous Wastes Within Africa (With Annexes). Concluded at Bamako, 29 January 1991. Entered into force, 28 April 1998. 2101 UNTS 177; *reprinted in* 30 ILM 775 (1991) & 5 Weston & Carlson V.I.14

* * *

Article 4

GENERAL OBLIGATIONS

1. Hazardous Waste Import Ban

All Parties shall take appropriate legal, administrative and other measures within the area under their jurisdiction to prohibit the import of all hazardous wastes, for any reason, into Africa from non-Contracting Parties. Such import shall be deemed illegal and a criminal act. All Parties shall:

(a) Forward as soon as possible, all information relating to such illegal hazardous waste import activity to the Secretariat who shall distribute the information to all Contracting Parties;

(b) Co-operate to ensure that no imports of hazardous wastes from a non-Party enter to this Convention. To this end, the Parties shall, at the Conference of the Contracting Parties consider other enforcement mechanisms.

2. Ban on Dumping of Hazardous Wastes at Sea, Internal Waters and Waterways

(a) Parties in conformity with related international conventions and instruments shall, in the exercise of their jurisdiction within their internal waters, territorial seas, exclusive economic zones and continental shelf, adopt legal, administrative and other appropriate measures to control all carriers from non-Parties, and prohibit the dumping at sea of hazardous wastes, including their incineration at sea and their disposal in the seabed and sub-seabed; any dumping of hazardous wastes at sea, including incineration at sea as well as seabed and sub-seabed disposal, by Contracting Parties, whether in internal waters, territorial seas, exclusive economic zones or high seas shall be deemed to be illegal;

(b) Parties shall forward, as soon as possible, all information relating to dumping of hazardous wastes to the Secretariat which shall distribute the information to all Contracting Parties.

3. Waste Generation in Africa

Each Party shall:

(a) Ensure that hazardous waste generators submit to the Secretariat reports regarding the wastes that they generate in order to enable the Secretariat of the Convention to produce a complete hazardous waste audit;

(b) Impose unlimited liability as well as joint and several liability on hazardous waste generators;

(c) Ensure that the generation of hazardous wastes within the area under its jurisdiction is reduced to a minimum taking into account social, technological and economic aspects;

(d) Ensure the availability of adequate treatment and/or disposal facilities, for the environmentally sound management of hazardous wastes which shall be located, to the extent possible, within its jurisdiction;

(e) Ensure that persons involved in the management of hazardous wastes within its jurisdiction take such steps as are necessary to prevent pollution arising from such wastes and, if such pollution occurs, to minimize the consequence thereof for human health and the environment;

The Adoption of Precautionary Measures:

(f) Each Party shall strive to adopt and implement the preventive, precautionary approach to pollution problems which entails, inter-alia, preventing the release into the environment of substances which may cause harm to humans or the environment without waiting for scientific proof regarding such harm. The Parties shall co-operate with each other in taking the appropriate measures to implement the precautionary principle to pollution prevention through the application of clean production methods, rather than the pursuit of a permissible emissions approach based on assimilative capacity assumptions;

(g) In this respect Parties shall promote clean production methods applicable to entire product life cycles including:

> raw material selection, extraction and processing;

> product conceptualisation, design, manufacture and assemblage;

> materials transport during all phases;

> industrial and household usage;

> reintroduction of the product into industrial systems or nature when it no longer serves a useful function;

Clean production shall not include "end-of-pipe" pollution controls such as filters and scrubbers, or chemical, physical or biological treatment. Measures which reduce the volume of waste by incineration or concentration, mask the hazard by dilution, or transfer pollutants from one environmental medium to another, are also excluded.

(h) The issue of the transfer to Africa of polluting technologies shall be kept under systematic review by the Secretariat of the Conference and periodic reports made to the Conference of the Parties.

Obligations in the Transport and Transboundary Movement of Hazardous Wastes from Contracting Parties:

(i) Each Party shall prevent the export of hazardous wastes to States which have prohibited by their legislation or international agreements all such imports, or if it has reason to believe that the wastes in question will not be managed in an environmentally sound manner, according to criteria to be decided on by the Parties at their first meeting;

(j) A Party shall not permit hazardous wastes to be exported to a State which does not have the facilities for disposing of them in an environmentally sound manner;

(k) Each Party shall ensure that hazardous wastes to be exported are managed in an environmentally sound manner in the State of import and of transit. Technical guidelines for the environmentally sound management of wastes subject to this Convention shall be decided by the Parties at their first meeting;

(*l*) The Parties agree not to allow the export of hazardous wastes for disposal within the area South of 60 degrees South Latitude, whether or not such wastes are subject to transboundary movement;

(m) Furthermore, each Party shall:

> (i) prohibit all persons under its national jurisdiction from transporting or disposing of hazardous wastes unless such persons are authorized or allowed to perform such operations;

> (ii) ensure that hazardous wastes that are to be the subject of a transboundary movement are packaged, labelled, and transported in conformity with generally accepted and recognized international rules and standards in the

field of packaging, labelling and transport, and that due account is taken of relevant internationally recognized practices;

(iii) ensure that hazardous wastes be accompanied by a movement document, containing information specified in Annex IV B, from the point at which a transboundary movement commences to the point of disposal;

(n) Parties shall take the appropriate measures to ensure that the transboundary movements of hazardous wastes only are allowed if:

(i) the State of export does not have the technical capacity and the necessary facilities, capacity or suitable disposal sites in order to dispose of the wastes in question in an environmentally sound and efficient manner, or

(ii) the transboundary movement in question is in accordance with other criteria to be decided by the Parties, provided those criteria do not differ from the objectives of this Convention;

(o) Under this Convention, the obligation of States in which hazardous wastes are generated, requiring that those wastes are managed in an environmentally sound manner, may not under any circumstances be transferred to the States of import or transit;

(p) Parties shall undertake to review periodically the possibilities for the reduction of the amount and/or the pollution potential of hazardous wastes which are exported to other States;

(q) Parties exercising their right to prohibit the import of hazardous wastes for disposal shall inform the other Parties of their decision pursuant to Article 13;

(r) Parties shall prohibit or shall not permit the export of hazardous wastes to States which have prohibited the import of such wastes when notified by the Secretariat or any competent authority pursuant to sub-paragraph (q) above;

(s) Parties shall prohibit or shall not permit the export of hazardous wastes if the State of import does not consent in writing to the specific import, in the case where that State of import has not prohibited the import of such wastes;

(t) Parties shall ensure that the transboundary movement of hazardous wastes is reduced to the minimum consistent with the environmentally sound and efficient management of such wastes, and is conducted in a manner which will protect human health and the environment against the adverse effects which may result from such movements;

(u) Parties shall require that information about a proposed transboundary movement of hazardous wastes be provided to the States concerned, according to Annex IV A, and state clearly the potential effects of the proposed movement on human health and the environment.

4. Furthermore

(a) Parties shall undertake to enforce the obligation of this Convention against offenders and infringements according to relevant national laws and/or order to better protect human health and the environment;

(b) Nothing in this Convention shall prevent a Party from imposing additional requirements that are consistent with the provisions of this Convention, and are in accordance with the rules of international law, in order to better protect human health and the environment;

(c) This Convention recognizes the sovereignty of States over their territorial seas, waterways and air space established in accordance with international law, and jurisdiction which States have in their exclusive economic zone and their continental shelves in accordance with international law, and the exercise by ships and aircraft of all

States of navigation rights and freedoms as provided for in international law and as reflected in relevant international instruments.

* * *

Article 6

TRANSBOUNDARY MOVEMENT AND NOTIFICATION PROCEDURES

1. The State of export shall notify, or shall require the generator or exporter to notify, in writing, through the channel of the competent authority of the State of export, the competent authority of the States concerned of any proposed transboundary movement of hazardous wastes. Such notification shall contain the declaration and information specified in Annex IV A, of this Convention, written in a language acceptable to the State of import. Only one notification needs to be sent to each State concerned.

2. The State of import shall respond to the notifier in writing consenting to the movement with or without conditions, denying permission for the movement, or requesting additional information. A copy of the final response of the State of import shall be sent to the competent authorities of the States concerned that are Parties to this Convention.

3. The State of export shall not allow the transboundary movement until it has received:

(a) written consent of the State of import, and

(b) from the State of import written confirmation of the existence of a contract between the exporter and the disposer specifying environmentally sound management of the wastes in question.

4. Each State of transit which is a Party to this Convention shall promptly acknowledge to the notifier receipt of the notification. It may subsequently respond to the notifier in writing within 60 days consenting to the movement with or without conditions, denying permission for the movement, or requesting additional information. The State of export shall not allow the transboundary movement to commence until it has received the written consent of the State of transit.

5. In the case of a transboundary movement of hazardous wastes where the wastes are legally defined as or considered to be hazardous wastes only:

(a) by the State of export, the requirements of paragraph 8 of this Article that apply to the importer or disposer and the State of import shall apply *mutatis mutandis* to the exporter and State of export respectively;

(b) by the State of import or by the States of import and transit which are Parties to this Convention, the requirements of paragraphs 1, 3, 4 and 6 of this Article that apply to the exporter and State of export shall apply *mutatis mutandis* to the importer or disposer and State of import, respectively; or

(c) by any State of transit which is Party to this Convention, the provisions of paragraph 4 shall apply to such State.

6. The State shall use a shipment specific notification even where hazardous wastes having the same physical and chemical characteristics are shipped regularly to the same disposer via the same customs office of entry of the State of import, and in the case of transit via the same customs office of entry and exit of the State or States of transit; specific notification of each and every shipment shall be required and contain the information in Annex IV A of this Convention.

7.   Each Party to this Convention shall limit their points or ports of entry and notify the Secretariat to this effect for distribution to all Contracting Parties. Such points and ports shall be the only ones permitted for the transboundary movement of hazardous wastes.

8.   The Parties to this Convention shall require that each person who takes charge of a transboundary movement of hazardous wastes sign the movement document either upon delivery or receipt of the wastes in question. They shall also require that the disposer inform both the exporter and the competent authority of the State of export of receipt by the disposer of the wastes in question and, in due course, of the completion of disposal as specified in the notification. If no such information is received within the State of export, the competent authority of the State of export or the exporter shall so notify the State of import.

9.   The notification and response by this Article shall be transmitted to the competent authority of the States concerned.

10.   Any transboundary movement of hazardous wastes shall be covered by insurance, bond or other guarantee as may be required by the State of import or any State of transit which is a Party of this Convention.

Article 7

TRANSBOUNDARY MOVEMENT FROM A PARTY THROUGH STATES WHICH ARE NOT PARTIES

Paragraph 2 of Article 6 of the Convention shall apply *mutatis mutandis* to transboundary movements of hazardous wastes from a Party through a State or States which are not Parties.

Article 8

DUTY TO REIMPORT

When a transboundary movement of hazardous wastes to which the consent of the States concerned has been given, subject to the provisions of this Convention, cannot be completed in accordance with the terms of the contract, the State of export shall ensure that the wastes in question are taken back into the State of export, by the exporter, if alternative arrangements cannot be made for their disposal in an environmentally sound manner within a maximum of 90 days from the time that the importing State informed the State of export and the Secretariat. To this end, the State of export and any State of transit shall not oppose, hinder or prevent the return of those wastes to the State of export.

Article 9

ILLEGAL TRAFFIC

1.   For the purpose of this Convention, any transboundary movement of hazardous wastes under the following situations shall be deemed to be illegal traffic:

(a) if carried out without notification, pursuant to the provisions of this Convention, to all States concerned, or

(b) if carried out without the consent, pursuant to the provisions of this Convention, of a State concerned; or

(c) if consent is obtained from States concerned through falsification, misrepresentation or fraud; or

(d) if it does not conform in a material way with the documents; or

(e) if it results in deliberate disposal of hazardous wastes in contravention of this Convention and of general principles of international law.

2. Each State shall introduce appropriate national legislation for imposing criminal penalties on all persons who have planned, carried out, or assisted in such illegal imports. Such penalties shall be sufficiently high to both punish and deter such conduct.

3. In case of a transboundary movement of hazardous wastes deemed to be illegal traffic as the result of conduct on the part of the exporter or generator the State of export shall ensure that the wastes in question are taken back by the exporter or generator or if necessary by itself into the State of export, within 30 days from the time the State of export has been informed about the illegal traffic. To this end the States concerned shall not oppose, hinder or prevent the return of those wastes to the State of export and appropriate legal action shall be taken against the contravenor(s).

4. In the case of a transboundary movement of hazardous wastes deemed to be illegal traffic as the result of conduct on the part of the importer or disposer, the State of import shall ensure that the wastes in question are returned to the exporter by the importer and that legal proceedings according to the provisions of this Convention are taken against the contravenor(s).

* * *

ANNEX I

CATEGORIES OF WASTES WHICH ARE HAZARDOUS WASTES

Waste Streams

Y0   All wastes containing or contaminated by radionuclides, the concentration or properties of which result from human activity.

Y1   Clinical wastes from medical care in hospitals, medical centres and clinics.

Y2   Wastes from the production and preparation of pharmaceutical products.

Y3   Wastes pharmaceuticals, drugs and medicines.

Y4   Wastes from the production, formulation and use of biocides and phytopharmaceuticals.

Y5   Wastes from the manufacture, formulation and use of wood preserving chemicals.

Y6   Wastes from the production, formulation and use of organic solvents.

Y7   Wastes from heat treatment and tempering operations containing cyanides.

Y8   Waste mineral oils unfit for their originally intended use.

Y9   Waste oils/water, hydrocarbons/water mixtures, emulsions.

Y10   Waste substances and articles containing or contaminated with polychlorinated biphenyls (PCBs) and/or polychlorinated terphenyls (PCTs) and/or polybrominated biphenyls (PBBs).

Y11   Waste tarry residues arising from refining, distillation and any pyrolytic treatment.

Y12   Wastes from production, formulation and use of inks, dyes, pigments, paints, lacquers, varnish.

Y13   Wastes from production, formulation and use of resins, latex, plasticizers, glues/adhesives.

Y14   Waste chemical substances arising from research and development or teaching activities which are not identified and/or are new and whose effects on man and/or the environment are not known.

Y15   Wastes of an explosive nature not subject to other legislation.

Y16   Wastes from production, formulation and use of photographic chemicals and processing materials.

Y17   Wastes resulting from surface treatment of metals and plastics.

Y18   Residues arising from industrial waste disposal operations.

Y46   Wastes collected from households, including sewage and sewage sludges.

Y47   Residues arising from the incineration of household wastes.

Wastes having as constituents:

Y19   Metal carbonyls.

Y20   Beryllium; beryllium compounds.

Y21   Hexavalant chromium compounds.

Y22   Copper compounds.

Y23   Zinc compounds.

Y24   Arsenic; arsenic compounds.

Y25   Selenium; selenium compounds.

Y26   Cadmium; cadmium compounds.

Y27   Antimony; antimony compounds.

Y28   Tellurium; tellurium compounds.

Y29   Mercury; mercury compounds.

Y30   Thallium; thallium compounds.

Y31   Lead; lead compounds.

Y32   Inorganic fluorine compounds excluding calcium fluoride.

Y33   Inorganic cyanides.

Y34   Acidic solutions or acids in solid form.

Y35   Basic solutions or bases in solid form.

Y36   Asbestos (dust and fibres).

Y37   Organic phosphorous compounds.

Y38   Organic cyanides.

Y39   Phenols; phenol compounds including chlorophenols.

Y40   Ethers.

Y41   Halogenated organic solvents.

Y42   Organic solvents excluding halogenated solvents.

Y43   Any congenor of polychlorinated dibenzo-furan.

Y44   Any congenor of polychlorinated dibenzo-p-dioxin.

Y45   Organohalogen compounds other than substances referred to in this Annex (e.g., Y39, Y41, Y42, Y43, Y44).

ANNEX II

LIST OF HAZARDOUS CHARACTERISTICS

UN Class[1] Code Characteristics

1 HI Explosive

An explosive substance or waste is a solid or liquid substance or waste (or mixture of substances or wastes) which is in itself capable by chemical reaction or producing gas at such a temperature and pressure and at such a speed as to cause damage to the surroundings.

3 H3 Flammable liquids

The word "flammable" has the same meaning as "inflammable". Flammable liquids are liquids, or mixtures of liquids, or liquids containing solids in solution or suspension (for example paints, varnishes, lacquers, etc., but not including substances or wastes otherwise classified on account of their dangerous characteristics) which give off a flammable vapour at temperatures of not more than 60.5 degrees C, closed up test, or not more than 65.6 degrees C, open-cup test. (Since the results of open-cup tests and of closed-up tests are not strictly comparable and even individual results by the same test are often variable, regulations varying from the above figures to make allowance for such difference would be within the spirit of this definition).

4.1 H4.1 Flammable solids

Solids, or waste solids, other than those classed as explosives, which under conditions encountered in transport are readily combustible, or may cause or contribute to fire through friction.

4.2 H4.2 Substances or wastes liable to spontaneous combustion.

Substances or wastes which are liable to spontaneous heating under normal conditions encountered in transport, or to heating up on contact with air, and being then liable to catch fire.

4.3 H4.3 Substances or wastes which, in contact with water emit flammable gases.

Substances or wastes which, by interaction with water, are liable to become spontaneously flammable or to give off flammable gases in dangerous quantities.

5.1 H5.1 Oxidizing

Substances or wastes which, while in themselves not necessarily combustible, may, generally by yielding oxygen, cause or contribute to the combustion of other materials.

5.2 H5.2 Organic peroxides

Organic substances or wastes which contain the bivalent-O–O-structure are thermally unstable substances which may undergo exothermic self-accelerating decomposition.

6.1 H6.1 Poisonous (Acute)

Substances or wastes liable either to cause death or serious injury or to harm human health if swallowed or inhaled or by skin contact.

6.2 H6.2 Infectious substances.

Substances or wastes containing viable micro organisms or their toxins which are known or suspected to cause disease in animals or humans.

---

1. Corresponds to the hazardous classification system included in the United Nations Recommendations on the Transport of Dangerous Goods (ST/SG/AC.10/1Rev.5, United Nations, New York, 1988).

8   H8   Corrosives

Substances or wastes which, by chemical action, will cause severe damage when in contact with living tissue, or in the case of leakage, will materially damage, or even destroy, other goods or the means of transport; they may also cause other hazards.

9   H10   Liberation of toxic gases in contact with air or water.

Substances or wastes which, by interaction with air or water, are liable to give off toxic gases in dangerous quantities.

9   H11   Toxic (Delayed or chronic)

Substances or wastes which, if they are inhaled or ingested or if they penetrate the skin, may involve delayed or chronic effects, including carcinogenicity.

9   H12   Ecotoxic

Substances or wastes which if released present or may present immediate or delayed adverse impacts to the environment by means of bioaccumulation and/or toxic effects upon biotic systems.

9   H13   Capable, by any means, after disposal, of yielding another material, e.g., leachate, which possesses any of the characteristics listed above.

ANNEX III
DISPOSAL OPERATIONS

D1   Deposit into or onto land, (e.g., landfill, etc.).

D2   Land treatment, (e.g. biodegradation of liquid or sludgy discards in soils, etc.).

D3   Deep injection, (e.g., injection of pumpable discards into wells, salt domes or naturally occurring repositories, etc.).

D4   Surface impoundment, (e.g., placement of liquid into lined discrete cells which are capped and isolated from one another and the environment, etc.).

D5   Specially engineered landfill, (e.g., placement into lined discrete cells which are capped and isolated from one another and the environment, etc.).

D6   Release into a water body except seas/oceans.

D7   Release into seas/oceans including sea-bed insertion.

D8   Biological treatment not specified elsewhere in this Annex which results in final compounds or mixtures which are discarded by means of any of the operations in Annex III.

D9   Physico-chemical treatment not specified elsewhere in the Annex which results in final compounds or mixtures which are discarded by means of any of the operations in Annex III (e.g., evaporation, drying, calcination, neutralisation, precipitation, etc.).

D10   Incineration on land.

D11   Incineration at sea.

D12   Permanent storage, (e.g., emplacement of containers in a mine, etc.).

D13   Blending or mixing prior to submission to any of the operations in Annex III.

D14   Repackaging prior to submission to any of the operations in Annex III.

D15   Storage pending any of the operations in Annex III.

D16   Use of a fuel (other than in direct incineration) or other means to generate energy.

D17   Solvent reclamation/regeneration.

D18   Recycling/reclamation of organic substances which are not used as solvents.

D19   Recycling/reclamation of metals and metal compounds.

D20   Recycling/reclamation of other inorganic materials.

D21   Regeneration of acids and bases.

D22   Recovery of components used for pollution abatement.

D23   Recovery of components from catalysts.

D24   Used oil re-refining or other reuses of previously used oil,

D25   Land treatment resulting in benefit to agriculture or ecological improvement.

D26   Uses of residual materials obtained from any of the operations numbered D1D25.

D27   Exchange of wastes for submission to any of the operations numbered D1D26.

D28   Accumulation of material intended for any operation in Annex III.

ANNEX IV A

INFORMATION TO BE PROVIDED ON NOTIFICATION

* * *

ANNEX IV B

INFORMATION TO BE PROVIDED ON THE MOVEMENT DOCUMENT

* * *

ANNEX V

ARBITRATION

* * *

4.12   Basel Protocol on Liability and Compensation for Damage Resulting From Transboundary Movements of Hazardous Wastes and Their Disposal (With Annexes).[c] Adopted at Basel, 10 December 1999. Not yet in force. UN Doc UNEP/CHW.1/WG/1/9/2.

The Parties to the Protocol,

Having taken into account the relevant provisions of Principle 13 of the 1992 Rio Declaration on Environment and Development, according to which States shall develop international and national legal instruments regarding liability and compensation for the victims of pollution and other environmental damage,

Being Parties to the Basel Convention on the Control of Transboundary Movements of Hazardous Wastes and their Disposal,

Mindful of their obligations under the Convention,

Aware of the risk of damage to human health, property and the environment caused by hazardous wastes and other wastes and the transboundary movement and disposal thereof,

Concerned about the problem of illegal transboundary traffic in hazardous wastes and other wastes,

Committed to Article 12 of the Convention, and emphasizing the need to set out appropriate rules and procedures in the field of liability and compensation for damage resulting from the transboundary movement and disposal of hazardous wastes and other wastes,

Convinced of the need to provide for third party liability and environmental liability in order to ensure that adequate and prompt compensation is available for damage resulting from the transboundary movement and disposal of hazardous wastes and other wastes,

Have agreed as follows:

Article 1
Objective

The objective of the Protocol is to provide for a comprehensive regime for liability and for adequate and prompt compensation for damage resulting from the transboundary movement of hazardous wastes and other wastes and their disposal including illegal traffic in those wastes.

Article 2
Definitions

1.   The definitions of terms contained in the Convention apply to the Protocol, unless expressly provided otherwise in the Protocol.

2.   For the purposes of the Protocol:

(a) ''The Convention'' means the Basel Convention on the Control of Transboundary Movements of Hazardous Wastes and their Disposal;

(b) ''Hazardous wastes and other wastes'' means hazardous wastes and other wastes within the meaning of Article 1 of the Convention;

(c) ''Damage'' means:

(i) Loss of life or personal injury;

(ii) Loss of or damage to property other than property held by the person liable in accordance with the present Protocol;

c.   *See also* Basic Document 4.10, *supra.*

(iii) Loss of income directly deriving from an economic interest in any use of the environment, incurred as a result of impairment of the environment, taking into account savings and costs;

(iv) The costs of measures of reinstatement of the impaired environment, limited to the costs of measures actually taken or to be undertaken; and

(v) The costs of preventive measures, including any loss or damage caused by such measures, to the extent that the damage arises out of or results from hazardous properties of the wastes involved in the transboundary movement and disposal of hazardous wastes and other wastes subject to the Convention;

(d) "Measures of reinstatement" means any reasonable measures aiming to assess, reinstate or restore damaged or destroyed components of the environment. Domestic law may indicate who will be entitled to take such measures;

(e) "Preventive measures" means any reasonable measures taken by any person in response to an incident, to prevent, minimize, or mitigate loss or damage, or to effect environmental clean-up;

(f) "Contracting Party" means a Party to the Protocol;

(g) "Protocol" means the present Protocol;

(h) "Incident" means any occurrence, or series of occurrences having the same origin that causes damage or creates a grave and imminent threat of causing damage;

(i) "Regional economic integration organization" means an organization constituted by sovereign States to which its member States have transferred competence in respect of matters governed by the Protocol and which has been duly authorized, in accordance with its internal procedures, to sign, ratify, accept, approve, formally confirm or accede to it;

(j) "Unit of account" means the Special Drawing Right as defined by the International Monetary Fund.

Article 3
Scope of application

1. The Protocol shall apply to damage due to an incident occurring during a transboundary movement of hazardous wastes and other wastes and their disposal, including illegal traffic, from the point where the wastes are loaded on the means of transport in an area under the national jurisdiction of a State of export. Any Contracting Party may by way of notification to the Depositary exclude the application of the Protocol, in respect of all transboundary movements for which it is the State of export, for such incidents which occur in an area under its national jurisdiction, as regards damage in its area of national jurisdiction. The Secretariat shall inform all Contracting Parties of notifications received in accordance with this Article.

2. The Protocol shall apply:

(a) In relation to movements destined for one of the operations specified in Annex IV to the Convention other than D13, D14, D15, R12 or R13, until the time at which the notification of completion of disposal pursuant to Article 6, paragraph 9, of the Convention has occurred, or, where such notification has not been made, completion of disposal has occurred; and

(b) In relation to movements destined for the operations specified in D13, D14, D15, R12 or R13 of Annex IV to the Convention, until completion of the subsequent disposal operation specified in D1 to D12 and R1 to R11 of Annex IV to the Convention.

3. (a) The Protocol shall apply only to damage suffered in an area under the national jurisdiction of a Contracting Party arising from an incident as referred to in paragraph 1;

(b) When the State of import, but not the State of export, is a Contracting Party, the Protocol shall apply only with respect to damage arising from an incident as referred to in paragraph 1 which takes place after the moment at which the disposer has taken possession of the hazardous wastes and other wastes. When the State of export, but not the State of import, is a Contracting Party, the Protocol shall apply only with respect to damage arising from an incident as referred to in paragraph 1 which takes place prior to the moment at which the disposer takes possession of the hazardous wastes and other wastes. When neither the State of export nor the State of import is a Contracting Party, the Protocol shall not apply;

(c) Notwithstanding subparagraph (a), the Protocol shall also apply to the damages specified in Article 2, subparagraphs 2 (c) (i), (ii) and (v), of the Protocol occurring in areas beyond any national jurisdiction;

(d) Notwithstanding subparagraph (a), the Protocol shall, in relation to rights under the Protocol, also apply to damages suffered in an area under the national jurisdiction of a State of transit which is not a Contracting Party provided that such State appears in Annex A and has acceded to a multilateral or regional agreement concerning transboundary movements of hazardous waste which is in force. Subparagraph (b) will apply mutatis mutandis.

4. Notwithstanding paragraph 1, in case of re-importation under Article 8 or Article 9, subparagraph 2 (a), and Article 9, paragraph 4, of the Convention, the provisions of the Protocol shall apply until the hazardous wastes and other wastes reach the original State of export.

5. Nothing in the Protocol shall affect in any way the sovereignty of States over their territorial seas and their jurisdiction and the right in their respective exclusive economic zones and continental shelves in accordance with international law.

6. Notwithstanding paragraph 1 and subject to paragraph 2 of this Article:

(a) The Protocol shall not apply to damage that has arisen from a transboundary movement of hazardous wastes and other wastes that has commenced before the entry into force of the Protocol for the Contracting Party concerned;

(b) The Protocol shall apply to damage resulting from an incident occurring during a transboundary movement of wastes falling under Article 1, subparagraph 1 (b), of the Convention only if those wastes have been notified in accordance with Article 3 of the Convention by the State of export or import, or both, and the damage arises in an area under the national jurisdiction of a State, including a State of transit, that has defined or considers those wastes as hazardous provided that the requirements of Article 3 of the Convention have been met. In this case strict liability shall be channelled in accordance with Article 4 of the Protocol.

7. (a) The Protocol shall not apply to damage due to an incident occurring during a transboundary movement of hazardous wastes and other wastes and their disposal pursuant to a bilateral, multilateral or regional agreement or arrangement concluded and notified in accordance with Article 11 of the Convention if:

(i) The damage occurred in an area under the national jurisdiction of any of the Parties to the agreement or arrangement;

(ii) There exists a liability and compensation regime, which is in force and is applicable to the damage resulting from such a transboundary movement or disposal provided it fully meets, or exceeds the objective of the Protocol by providing a high level of protection to persons who have suffered damage;

(iii) The Party to the Article 11 agreement or arrangement in which the damage has occurred has previously notified the Depositary of the non-application of the Protocol to any damage occurring in an area under its national jurisdiction due to an incident resulting from movements or disposals referred to in this subparagraph; and

(iv) The Parties to the Article 11 agreement or arrangement have not declared that the Protocol shall be applicable;

(b) In order to promote transparency, a Contracting Party that has notified the Depositary of the non-application of the Protocol shall notify the Secretariat of the applicable liability and compensation regime referred to in subparagraph (a) (ii) and include a description of the regime. The Secretariat shall submit to the Meeting of the Parties, on a regular basis, summary reports on the notifications received;

(c) After a notification pursuant to subparagraph (a) (iii) is made, actions for compensation for damage to which subparagraph (a) (i) applies may not be made under the Protocol.

8. The exclusion set out in paragraph 7 of this Article shall neither affect any of the rights or obligations under the Protocol of a Contracting Party which is not party to the agreement or arrangement mentioned above, nor shall it affect rights of States of transit which are not Contracting Parties.

9. Article 3, paragraph 2, shall not affect the application of Article 16 to all Contracting Parties.

Article 4
Strict liability

1. The person who notifies in accordance with Article 6 of the Convention, shall be liable for damage until the disposer has taken possession of the hazardous wastes and other wastes. Thereafter the disposer shall be liable for damage. If the State of export is the notifier or if no notification has taken place, the exporter shall be liable for damage until the disposer has taken possession of the hazardous wastes and other wastes. With respect to Article 3, subparagraph 6 (b), of the Protocol, Article 6, paragraph 5, of the Convention shall apply <u>mutatis mutandis</u>. Thereafter the disposer shall be liable for damage.

2. Without prejudice to paragraph 1, with respect to wastes under Article 1, subparagraph 1 (b), of the Convention that have been notified as hazardous by the State of import in accordance with Article 3 of the Convention but not by the State of export, the importer shall be liable until the disposer has taken possession of the wastes, if the State of import is the notifier or if no notification has taken place. Thereafter the disposer shall be liable for damage.

3. Should the hazardous wastes and other wastes be re-imported in accordance with Article 8 of the Convention, the person who notified shall be liable for damage from the time the hazardous wastes leave the disposal site, until the wastes are taken into possession by the exporter, if applicable, or by the alternate disposer.

4. Should the hazardous wastes and other wastes be re-imported under Article 9, subparagraph 2 (a), or Article 9, paragraph 4, of the Convention, subject to Article 3 of the Protocol, the person who re-imports shall be held liable for damage until the wastes are taken into possession by the exporter if applicable, or by the alternate disposer.

5. No liability in accordance with this Article shall attach to the person referred to in paragraphs 1 and 2 of this Article, if that person proves that the damage was:

(a) The result of an act of armed conflict, hostilities, civil war or insurrection;

(b) The result of a natural phenomenon of exceptional, inevitable, unforeseeable and irresistible character;

(c) Wholly the result of compliance with a compulsory measure of a public authority of the State where the damage occurred; or

(d) Wholly the result of the wrongful intentional conduct of a third party, including the person who suffered the damage.

6. If two or more persons are liable according to this Article, the claimant shall have the right to seek full compensation for the damage from any or all of the persons liable.

Article 5
Fault-based liability

Without prejudice to Article 4, any person shall be liable for damage caused or contributed to by his lack of compliance with the provisions implementing the Convention or by his wrongful intentional, reckless or negligent acts or omissions. This Article shall not affect the domestic law of the Contracting Parties governing liability of servants and agents.

Article 6
Preventive measures

1. Subject to any requirement of domestic law any person in operational control of hazardous wastes and other wastes at the time of an incident shall take all reasonable measures to mitigate damage arising therefrom.

2. Notwithstanding any other provision in the Protocol, any person in possession and/or control of hazardous wastes and other wastes for the sole purpose of taking preventive measures, provided that this person acted reasonably and in accordance with any domestic law regarding preventive measures, is not thereby subject to liability under the Protocol.

Article 7
Combined cause of the damage

1. Where damage is caused by wastes covered by the Protocol and wastes not covered by the Protocol, a person otherwise liable shall only be liable according to the Protocol in proportion to the contribution made by the wastes covered by the Protocol to the damage.

2. The proportion of the contribution to the damage of the wastes referred to in paragraph 1 shall be determined with regard to the volume and properties of the wastes involved, and the type of damage occurring.

3. In respect of damage where it is not possible to distinguish between the contribution made by wastes covered by the Protocol and wastes not covered by the Protocol, all damage shall be considered to be covered by the Protocol.

Article 8
Right of recourse

1. Any person liable under the Protocol shall be entitled to a right of recourse in accordance with the rules of procedure of the competent court:

(a) Against any other person also liable under the Protocol; and

(b) As expressly provided for in contractual arrangements.

2. Nothing in the Protocol shall prejudice any rights of recourse to which the person liable might be entitled pursuant to the law of the competent court.

Article 9
Contributory fault

Compensation may be reduced or disallowed if the person who suffered the damage, or a person for whom he is responsible under the domestic law, by his own fault, has caused or contributed to the damage having regard to all circumstances.

Article 10
Implementation

1.   The Contracting Parties shall adopt the legislative, regulatory and administrative measures necessary to implement the Protocol.

2.   In order to promote transparency, Contracting Parties shall inform the Secretariat of measures to implement the Protocol, including any limits of liability established pursuant to paragraph 1 of Annex B.

3.   The provisions of the Protocol shall be applied without discrimination based on nationality, domicile or residence.

Article 11
Conflicts with other liability and compensation agreements

Whenever the provisions of the Protocol and the provisions of a bilateral, multilateral or regional agreement apply to liability and compensation for damage caused by an incident arising during the same portion of a transboundary movement, the Protocol shall not apply provided the other agreement is in force for the Party or Parties concerned and had been opened for signature when the Protocol was opened for signature, even if the agreement was amended afterwards.

Article 12
Financial limits

1.   Financial limits for the liability under Article 4 of the Protocol are specified in Annex B to the Protocol. Such limits shall not include any interest or costs awarded by the competent court.

2.   There shall be no financial limit on liability under Article 5.

Article 13
Time limit of liability

1.   Claims for compensation under the Protocol shall not be admissible unless they are brought within ten years from the date of the incident.

2.   Claims for compensation under the Protocol shall not be admissible unless they are brought within five years from the date the claimant knew or ought reasonably to have known of the damage provided that the time limits established pursuant to paragraph 1 of this Article are not exceeded.

3.   Where the incident consists of a series of occurrences having the same origin, time limits established pursuant to this Article shall run from the date of the last of such occurrences. Where the incident consists of a continuous occurrence, such time limits shall run from the end of that continuous occurrence.

Article 14
Insurance and other financial guarantees

1.   The persons liable under Article 4 shall establish and maintain during the period of the time limit of liability, insurance, bonds or other financial guarantees covering their liability under Article 4 of the Protocol for amounts not less than the minimum limits specified in paragraph 2 of Annex B. States may fulfil their obligation under this paragraph by a declaration of self-insurance. Nothing in this paragraph

shall prevent the use of deductibles or co-payments as between the insurer and the insured, but the failure of the insured to pay any deductible or co-payment shall not be a defence against the person who has suffered the damage.

2. With regard to the liability of the notifier, or exporter under Article 4, paragraph 1, or of the importer under Article 4, paragraph 2, insurance, bonds or other financial guarantees referred to in paragraph 1 of this Article shall only be drawn upon in order to provide compensation for damage covered by Article 2 of the Protocol.

3. A document reflecting the coverage of the liability of the notifier or exporter under Article 4, paragraph 1, or of the importer under Article 4, paragraph 2, of the Protocol shall accompany the notification referred to in Article 6 of the Convention. Proof of coverage of the liability of the disposer shall be delivered to the competent authorities of the State of import.

4. Any claim under the Protocol may be asserted directly against any person providing insurance, bonds or other financial guarantees. The insurer or the person providing the financial guarantee shall have the right to require the person liable under Article 4 to be joined in the proceedings. Insurers and persons providing financial guarantees may invoke the defences which the person liable under Article 4 would be entitled to invoke.

5. Notwithstanding paragraph 4, a Contracting Party shall, by notification to the Depositary at the time of signature, ratification, or approval of, or accession to the Protocol, indicate if it does not provide for a right to bring a direct action pursuant to paragraph 4. The Secretariat shall maintain a record of the Contracting Parties who have given notification pursuant to this paragraph.

Article 15
Financial mechanism

1. Where compensation under the Protocol does not cover the costs of damage, additional and supplementary measures aimed at ensuring adequate and prompt compensation may be taken using existing mechanisms.

2. The Meeting of the Parties shall keep under review the need for and possibility of improving existing mechanisms or establishing a new mechanism.

Article 16
State responsibility

The Protocol shall not affect the rights and obligations of the Contracting Parties under the rules of general international law with respect to State responsibility.

PROCEDURES

Article 17
Competent courts

1. Claims for compensation under the Protocol may be brought in the courts of a Contracting Party only where either:

(a) The damage was suffered; or

(b) The incident occurred; or

(c) The defendant has his habitual residence, or has his principal place of business.

2. Each Contracting Party shall ensure that its courts possess the necessary competence to entertain such claims for compensation.

Article 18
Related actions

1. Where related actions are brought in the courts of different Parties, any court other than the court first seized may, while the actions are pending at first instance, stay its proceedings.

2. A court may, on the application of one of the Parties, decline jurisdiction if the law of that court permits the consolidation of related actions and another court has jurisdiction over both actions.

3. For the purpose of this Article, actions are deemed to be related where they are so closely connected that it is expedient to hear and determine them together to avoid the risk of irreconcilable judgements resulting from separate proceedings.

Article 19
Applicable law

All matters of substance or procedure regarding claims before the competent court which are not specifically regulated in the Protocol shall be governed by the law of that court including any rules of such law relating to conflict of laws.

Article 20
Relation between the Protocol and the law of the competent court

1. Subject to paragraph 2, nothing in the Protocol shall be construed as limiting or derogating from any rights of persons who have suffered damage, or as limiting the protection or reinstatement of the environment which may be provided under domestic law.

2. No claims for compensation for damage based on the strict liability of the notifier or the exporter liable under Article 4, paragraph 1, or the importer liable under Article 4, paragraph 2, of the Protocol, shall be made otherwise than in accordance with the Protocol.

Article 21
Mutual recognition and enforcement of judgements

1. Any judgement of a court having jurisdiction in accordance with Article 17 of the Protocol, which is enforceable in the State of origin and is no longer subject to ordinary forms of review, shall be recognized in any Contracting Party as soon as the formalities required in that Party have been completed, except:

(a) Where the judgement was obtained by fraud;

(b) Where the defendant was not given reasonable notice and a fair opportunity to present his case;

(c) Where the judgement is irreconcilable with an earlier judgement validly pronounced in another Contracting Party with regard to the same cause of action and the same parties; or

(d) Where the judgement is contrary to the public policy of the Contracting Party in which its recognition is sought.

2. A judgement recognized under paragraph 1 of this Article shall be enforceable in each Contracting Party as soon as the formalities required in that Party have been completed. The formalities shall not permit the merits of the case to be re-opened.

3. The provisions of paragraphs 1 and 2 of this Article shall not apply between Contracting Parties that are Parties to an agreement or arrangement in force on mutual recognition and enforcement of judgements under which the judgement would be recognizable and enforceable.

Article 22
Relationship of the Protocol with the Basel Convention

Except as otherwise provided in the Protocol, the provisions of the Convention relating to its Protocols shall apply to the Protocol.

Article 23
Amendment of Annex B

1. At its sixth meeting, the Conference of the Parties to the Basel Convention may amend paragraph 2 of Annex B following the procedure set out in Article 18 of the Basel Convention.

2. Such an amendment may be made before the Protocol enters into force.

FINAL CLAUSES
Article 24
Meeting of the Parties

1. A Meeting of the Parties is hereby established. The Secretariat shall convene the first Meeting of the Parties in conjunction with the first meeting of the Conference of the Parties to the Convention after entry into force of the Protocol.

2. Subsequent ordinary Meetings of the Parties shall be held in conjunction with meetings of the Conference of the Parties to the Convention unless the Meeting of the Parties decides otherwise. Extraordinary Meetings of the Parties shall be held at such other times as may be deemed necessary by a Meeting of the Parties, or at the written request of any Contracting Party, provided that within six months of such a request being communicated to them by the Secretariat, it is supported by at least one third of the Contracting Parties.

3. The Contracting Parties, at their first meeting, shall adopt by consensus rules of procedure for their meetings as well as financial rules.

4. The functions of the Meeting of the Parties shall be:

(a) To review the implementation of and compliance with the Protocol;

(b) To provide for reporting and establish guidelines and procedures for such reporting where necessary;

(c) To consider and adopt, where necessary, proposals for amendment of the Protocol or any annexes and for any new annexes; and

(d) To consider and undertake any additional action that may be required for the purposes of the Protocol.

Article 25
Secretariat

1. For the purposes of the Protocol, the Secretariat shall:

(a) Arrange for and service Meetings of the Parties as provided for in Article 24;

(b) Prepare reports, including financial data, on its activities carried out in implementation of its functions under the Protocol and present them to the Meeting of the Parties;

(c) Ensure the necessary coordination with relevant international bodies, and in particular enter into such administrative and contractual arrangements as may be required for the effective discharge of its functions;

(d) Compile information concerning the national laws and administrative provisions of Contracting Parties implementing the Protocol;

(e) Cooperate with Contracting Parties and with relevant and competent international organisations and agencies in the provision of experts and equipment for the purpose of rapid assistance to States in the event of an emergency situation;

(f) Encourage non-Parties to attend the Meetings of the Parties as observers and to act in accordance with the provisions of the Protocol; and

(g) Perform such other functions for the achievement of the purposes of this Protocol as may be assigned to it by the Meetings of the Parties.

2. The secretariat functions shall be carried out by the Secretariat of the Basel Convention.

Article 26
Signature

The Protocol shall be open for signature by States and by regional economic integration organizations Parties to the Basel Convention in Berne at the Federal Department of Foreign Affairs of Switzerland from 6 to 17 March 2000 and at United Nations Headquarters in New York from 1 April 2000 to 10 December 2000.

Article 27
Ratification, acceptance, formal confirmation or approval

1. The Protocol shall be subject to ratification, acceptance or approval by States and to formal confirmation or approval by regional economic integration organizations. Instruments of ratification, acceptance, formal confirmation, or approval shall be deposited with the Depositary.

2. Any organization referred to in paragraph 1 of this Article which becomes a Contracting Party without any of its member States being a Contracting Party shall be bound by all the obligations under the Protocol. In the case of such organizations, one or more of whose member States is a Contracting Party, the organization and its member States shall decide on their respective responsibilities for the performance of their obligations under the Protocol. In such cases, the organization and the member States shall not be entitled to exercise rights under the Protocol concurrently.

3. In their instruments of formal confirmation or approval, the organizations referred to in paragraph 1 of this Article shall declare the extent of their competence with respect to the matters governed by the Protocol. These organizations shall also inform the Depositary, who will inform the Contracting Parties, of any substantial modification in the extent of their competence.

Article 28
Accession

1. The Protocol shall be open for accession by any States and by any regional economic integration organization Party to the Basel Convention which has not signed the Protocol. The instruments of accession shall be deposited with the Depositary.

2. In their instruments of accession, the organizations referred to in paragraph 1 of this Article shall declare the extent of their competence with respect to the matters governed by the Protocol. These organizations shall also inform the Depositary of any substantial modification in the extent of their competence.

3. The provisions of Article 27, paragraph 2, shall apply to regional economic integration organizations which accede to the Protocol.

Article 29
Entry into force

1. The Protocol shall enter into force on the ninetieth day after the date of deposit of the twentieth instrument of ratification, acceptance, formal confirmation, approval or accession.

2. For each State or regional economic integration organization which ratifies, accepts, approves or formally confirms the Protocol or accedes thereto after the date of the deposit of the twentieth instrument of ratification, acceptance, approval, formal confirmation or accession, it shall enter into force on the ninetieth day after the date of deposit by such State or regional economic integration organization of its instrument of ratification, acceptance, approval, formal confirmation or accession.

3. For the purpose of paragraphs 1 and 2 of this Article, any instrument deposited by a regional economic integration organization shall not be counted as additional to those deposited by member States of such organization.

Article 30
Reservations and declarations

1. No reservation or exception may be made to the Protocol. For the purposes of the Protocol, notifications according to Article 3, paragraph 1, Article 3, paragraph 6, or Article 14, paragraph 5, shall not be regarded as reservations or exceptions.

2. Paragraph 1 of this Article does not preclude a State or a regional economic integration organization, when signing, ratifying, accepting, approving, formally confirming or acceding to the Protocol, from making declarations or statements, however phrased or named, with a view, inter alia, to the harmonization of its laws and regulations with the provisions of the Protocol, provided that such declarations or statements do not purport to exclude or to modify the legal effects of the provisions of the Protocol in their application to that State or that organization.

Article 31
Withdrawal

1. At any time after three years from the date on which the Protocol has entered into force for a Contracting Party, that Contracting Party may withdraw from the Protocol by giving written notification to the Depositary.

2. Withdrawal shall be effective one year from receipt of notification by the Depositary, or on such later date as may be specified in the notification.

Article 32
Depositary

The Secretary–General of the United Nations shall be the Depositary of the Protocol.

Article 33
Authentic texts

The original Arabic, Chinese, English, French, Russian and Spanish texts of the Protocol are equally authentic.

ANNEX A
LIST OF STATES OF TRANSIT AS REFERRED TO IN ARTICLE 3, SUBPARA-GRAPH 3 (D)

1. Antigua and Barbuda
2. Bahamas
3. Bahrain
4. Barbados
5. Cape Verde
6. Comoros
7. Cook Islands

8.   Cuba

9.   Cyprus

10.   Dominica

11.   Dominican Republic

12.   Fiji

13.   Grenada

14.   Haiti

15.   Jamaica

16.   Kiribati

17.   Maldives

18.   Malta

19.   Marshall Islands

20.   Mauritius

21.   Micronesia (Federated States of)

22.   Nauru

23.   Netherlands, on behalf of Aruba and the Netherlands Antilles

24.   New Zealand, on behalf of Tokelau

25.   Niue

26.   Palau

27.   Papua New Guinea

28.   Samoa

29.   Sao Tome and Principe

30.   Seychelles

31.   Singapore

32.   Solomon Islands

33.   St. Lucia

34.   St. Kitts and Nevis

35.   St. Vincent and the Grenadines

36.   Tonga

37.   Trinidad and Tobago

38.   Tuvalu

39.   Vanuatu

ANNEX B
FINANCIAL LIMITS

1.   Financial limits for the liability under Article 4 of the Protocol shall be determined by domestic law.

2.   The limits of liability shall:

    (a) For the notifier, exporter or importer, for any one incident, be not less than:

       (i) 1 million units of account for shipments up to and including 5 tonnes;

       (ii) 2 million units of account for shipments exceeding 5 tonnes, up to and including 25 tonnes;

      (iii) 4 million units of account for shipments exceeding 25 tonnes, up to and including 50 tonnes;

      (iv) 6 million units of account for shipments exceeding 50 tonnes, up to and including 1,000 tonnes;

      (v) 10 million units of account for shipments exceeding 1,000 tonnes, up to and including 10,000 tonnes;

      (vi) Plus an additional 1,000 units of account for each additional tonne up to a maximum of 30 million units of account;

  (b) For the disposer, for any one incident, be not less than 2 million units of account for any one incident.

3.   The amounts referred to in paragraph 2 shall be reviewed by the Contracting Parties on a regular basis taking into account, inter alia, the potential risks posed to the environment by the movement of hazardous wastes and other wastes and their disposal, recycling, and the nature, quantity and hazardous properties of the wastes.

4.13 OECD Decision Concerning the Control of Transboundary Movements of Wastes Destined for Recovery Operations (as Amended). Adopted by the OECD Council, 14 June 2001.[d] OECD Doc C(2001)107/FINAL

*The Council, * * ***

CHAPTER I:

I. *Decides* that Member countries shall control transboundary movements of wastes destined for recovery operations within the OECD area in accordance with the provisions set out in Chapter II of this Decision and in the appendices to it.

* * *

CHAPTER II

A. DEFINITIONS

For the purposes of this Decision:

1. *Wastes* are substances or objects, other than radioactive materials covered by other international agreements, which:

    i) are disposed of or are being recovered; or

    ii) are intended to be disposed of or recovered; or

    iii) are required, by the provisions of national law, to be disposed of or recovered.

2. *Hazardous Wastes* are:

    i) Wastes that belong to any category contained in Appendix 1 to this Decision unless they do not possess any of the characteristics contained in Appendix 2 to this Decision; and

    ii) Wastes that are not covered under sub-paragraph 2.(i) but are defined as, or are considered to be, hazardous wastes by the domestic legislation of the Member country of export, import or transit. Member countries shall not be required to enforce laws other than their own.

3. *Disposal* means any of the operations specified in Appendix 5.A to this Decision.

4. *Recovery* means any of the operations specified in Appendix 5.B to this Decision.

* * *

B. GENERAL PROVISIONS

1. Conditions

The following conditions shall apply to transboundary movements of wastes subject to this Decision:

a) The wastes shall be destined for recovery operations within a recovery facility which will recover the wastes in an environmentally sound manner according to national laws, regulations and practices to which the facility is subject.

b) All persons involved in any contracts or arrangements for transboundary movements of wastes destined for recovery operations should have the appropriate legal status, in accordance with domestic legislation and regulations.

---

d. Amended on 28 February 2002, C(2001)107/ADD1; 9 March 2004, C(2004)20; 2 December 2005, C(2005)141; 4 December 2008, C(2008)156.

c) The transboundary movements shall be carried out under the terms of applicable international transport agreements.

d) Any transit of wastes through a non-member country shall be subject to international law and to all applicable national laws and regulations.

2. Control Procedures

A two-tiered system serves to delineate controls to be applied to such transboundary movements of wastes:

a) Green Control Procedure:

Wastes falling under the Green control procedure are those wastes in Appendix 3 to this Decision. This Appendix has two parts:

- Part I contains the wastes in Annex IX of the Basel Convention, some of which are subject to a note for the purposes of this Decision;

- Part II contains additional wastes that OECD Member countries agreed to be subject to the Green control procedure, in accordance with criteria referred to in Appendix 6 to this Decision.

The Green control procedure is described in Section C.

b) Amber Control Procedure:

Wastes falling under the Amber control procedure are those wastes in Appendix 4 to this Decision. This Appendix has two parts:

- Part I contains the wastes in Annexes II and VIII of the Basel Convention, some of which are subject to a note for the purposes of this Decision;

- Part II contains additional wastes that OECD Member countries agreed to be subject to the Amber control procedure, in accordance with criteria referred to in Appendix 6 to this Decision.

The Amber control procedure is described in Section D.

* * *

6. Wastes not Listed in Appendices 3 or 4 to this Decision

Wastes which are destined for recovery operations but have not yet been assigned to Appendices 3 or 4 of this Decision, shall be eligible for transboundary movements pursuant to this Decision subject to the following conditions:

a) Member countries shall identify such wastes and, if appropriate, make applications to the Technical Working Group of the Basel Convention in order to amend the relevant Annexes of the Basel Convention;

b) Pending assignment to a list, such wastes shall be subject to the controls required for the transboundary movements of wastes by the domestic legislation of the countries concerned in order that no country is obliged to enforce laws other than its own;

c) However, if such wastes exhibit a hazardous characteristic listed in Appendix 2 to this Decision as determined by using national procedures[2] and any applicable international agreements, such wastes shall be subject to the Amber control procedure

7. Generator of Mixed or Transformed Waste

If two or more lots of wastes are mixed and/or otherwise subjected to physical or chemical transformation operations, the person who performs these operations shall be deemed to be the generator of the new wastes resulting from these operations.

8. Procedures for Mixtures of Wastes

. . . [A] mixture of wastes, for which no individual entry exists, shall be subject to the following control procedure:

- A mixture of two or more Green wastes shall be subject to the Green control procedure, provided the composition of this mixture does not impair its environmentally sound recovery;

- A mixture of a Green waste and more than a de minimis amount of an Amber waste or a mixture of two or more Amber wastes shall be subject to the Amber control procedure, provided the composition of this mixture does not impair its environmentally sound recovery.

C. GREEN CONTROL PROCEDURE

Transboundary movements of wastes subject to the Green control procedure shall be subject to all existing controls normally applied in commercial transactions.

Regardless of whether or not wastes are included on the list of wastes subject to the Green Control Procedure (Appendix 3), they may not be subject to the Green control procedure if they are contaminated by other materials to an extent which (a) increases the risks associated with the wastes sufficiently to render them appropriate for submission to the amber control procedure, when taking into account the criteria in Appendix 6 to this Decision, or (b) prevents the recovery of the wastes in an environmentally sound manner.

D. AMBER CONTROL PROCEDURE

1. Conditions

(a) Contracts

Transboundary movements of wastes under the Amber control procedure may only occur under the terms of a valid written contract, or chain of contracts, or equivalent arrangements between facilities controlled by the same legal entity, starting with the exporter and terminating at the recovery facility. All persons involved in the contracts, or arrangements shall have appropriate legal status.

The contracts shall:

    i) Clearly identify: the generator of each type of waste, each person who shall have legal control of the wastes and the recovery facility;

    ii) Provide that relevant requirements of this Decision are taken into account and are binding on all parties to the contracts.

    iii) Specify which party to the contract (i) shall assume responsibility for an alternative management of the wastes in compliance with applicable laws and regulations including, if necessary, the return of the wastes in accordance with section D. (3) (a) below and (ii), as the case may be, shall provide the notification for re-export in accordance with section D.(3) (b) below.

* * *

(a) Financial Guarantees

Where applicable, the exporter or the importer shall provide financial guarantees in accordance with national or international law requirements, for alternative recycling, disposal or other means of environmentally sound management of the wastes in cases where arrangements for the transboundary movement and the recovery operations cannot be carried out as foreseen.

* * *

2. Functioning of the Amber Control Procedure:

Procedures are provided under the Amber control procedure for the following two cases:

> Case 1: individual transboundary movements or multiple shipments to a recovery facility;

> Case 2: transboundary movements to pre-consented recovery facilities

Case 1: Individual transboundary movements of wastes or multiple shipments to a recovery facility.

a) Prior to commencement of each transboundary movement of wastes, the exporter shall provide written notification ("single notification") to the competent authorities of the countries concerned. The notification document shall include all of the information listed in Appendix 8....

* * *

d) The competent authorities of the countries concerned shall have thirty (30) days to object, according to their domestic laws, to the proposed transboundary movement of wastes. The thirty (30)–day period for possible objection shall commence upon issuance of the acknowledgement of the competent authority of the country of import.

* * *

f) If no objection has been lodged (tacit consent), the transboundary movement of wastes may commence after this thirty (30)–day period has passed. Tacit consent expires within one (1) calendar year from the end of the thirty (30)–day period.

g) ... The transboundary movement of wastes may commence after all consents are received....

* * *

i) The transboundary movement of wastes may only take place during the period when the consents of all competent authorities (tacit or written consent) are valid.

* * *

m) In cases where essentially similar wastes (e.g. those having essentially similar physical and chemical characteristics) are to be sent periodically to the same recovery facility by the same exporter, the competent authorities of the countries concerned may elect to accept one "general notification" for such multiple shipments for a period of up to one year. Each shipment must be accompanied by its own movement document, which includes the information listed in Appendix 8.B to this Decision.

* * *

Case 2: Transboundary movements of wastes to pre-consented recovery facilities

(a) Competent authorities having jurisdiction over specific recovery facilities in the country of import may decide not to raise objections concerning transboundary movements of certain types of wastes to a specific recovery facility (pre-consented recovery facility). Such decisions can be limited to a specified period of time and can be revoked at any time.

(b) Competent authorities that elect this option shall inform the OECD secretariat of the recovery facility name, address, technologies employed, waste types to which the pre consent applies, and the period covered. The OECD secretariat must also be notified of any revocations.

(c) For all transboundary movements of wastes to such facilities paragraphs (a), (b) and (c) of Case 1 shall apply.

(d) The competent authorities of the countries of export and transit shall have seven (7) working days to object, according to their domestic laws, to the proposed transboundary movement of wastes. . . .

* * *

3.   Duty to Return or Re-export Wastes Subject to the Amber Control Procedure

When a transboundary movement of wastes subject to the Amber control procedure, to which countries concerned have given consent, cannot be completed in accordance with the terms of the contract, for any reason such as illegal shipments, the competent authority of the country of import shall immediately inform the competent authority of the country of export. If alternative arrangements cannot be made to recover these wastes in an environmentally sound manner in the country of import, the following provisions shall apply as the case may be:

(a) Return from a country of import to the country of export:

The competent authority of the country of import shall inform the competent authorities of the countries of export and transit, mentioning in particular the reason for returning the waste. The competent authority of the country of export shall admit the return of those wastes. In addition, the competent authorities of the countries of export and transit shall not oppose or prevent the return of these wastes. The return should take place within ninety (90) days from the time the country of import informs the country of export or such other period of time as the concerned Member countries agree. Any new transit country would require a new notification.

(b) Re-export from a country of import to a country other than the initial country of export:

Re export from a country of import of wastes subject to the Amber control procedure may only occur following notification by an exporter in the country of import to the countries concerned, as well as to the initial country of export. The notification and control procedure shall follow the provisions set out in Case 1 of Section D. (2) with the addition that the provisions concerning the competent authorities of countries concerned shall also apply to the competent authority of the initial country of export.

* * *

APPENDIX 1
CATEGORIES OF WASTES TO BE CONTROLLED
Waste Streams:

* * *

Y10—Waste substances and articles containing or contaminated with polychlorinated biphenyls (PCB's) and/or polychlorinated terphenyls (PCT's) and/or polybrominated biphenyls (PBB's) * * *

Wastes having as Constituents:

* * *

Y20—Beryllium; beryllium compounds * * *

Y26—Cadmium; cadmium compounds * * *

Y29—Mercury; mercury compounds * * *

Y31—Lead; lead compounds

APPENDIX 2
LIST OF HAZARDOUS CHARACTERISTICS

* * *

H6.1:   *Poisonous (Acute).* Substances or wastes liable either to cause death or serious injury or to harm human health if swallowed or inhaled or by skin contact.

* * *

H11:   *Toxic (Delayed or Chronic).* Substances or wastes which, if they are inhaled or ingested or if they penetrate the skin, may involve delayed or chronic effects, including carcinogenicity.

H12:   *Ecotoxic.* Substances or wastes which if released present or may present immediate or delayed adverse impacts to the environment by means of bioaccumulation and/or toxic effects upon biotic systems.

H13:   Capable, by any means, after disposal, of yielding another material, e.g., leachate, which possesses any of the characteristics listed above.

* * *

APPENDIX 3

List of Wastes Subject to the Green control procedure

Regardless of whether or not wastes are included on this list, they may not be subject to the Green control procedure if they are contaminated by other materials to an extent which (a) increases the risks associated with the wastes sufficiently to render them appropriate for submission to the amber control procedure, when taking into account the criteria in Appendix 6, or (b) prevents the recovery of the wastes in an environmentally sound manner.

PART I: Wastes listed in Annex IX of the Basel Convention. . . .

PART II: The following wastes will also be subject to the Green control procedure:

* * *

Other Wastes Containing Metals

GC010   Electrical assemblies consisting only of metals or alloys.

GC020   Electronic scrap (e.g. printed circuit boards, electronic components, wire, etc.) and reclaimed electronic components suitable for base and precious metal recovery.

* * *

APPENDIX 4
List of Wastes Subject To the Amber control procedure

PART I: Wastes listed in Annexes II and VIII of the Basel Convention . . .

* * *

APPENDIX 5A
DISPOSAL OPERATIONS*

Appendix 5.A is meant to encompass all such disposal operations that occur in practice, whether or not they are adequate from the point of view of environmental protection.

* The wording of D1 to D15 in Appendix 5.A is identical to that of Annex IV.A of the Basel Convention.

D1—Deposit into or onto land, (e.g., landfill, etc.) * * *

D6—Release into a water body except seas/oceans * * *

D10—Incineration on land * * *

APPENDIX 5B
RECOVERY OPERATIONS*

Appendix 5.B is meant to encompass all such operations with respect to materials considered to be or legally defined as wastes and which otherwise would have been destined for operations included in Appendix 5.A.

* * *

R4—Recycling/reclamation of metals and metal compounds

R5—Recycling/reclamation of other inorganic materials

* * *

APPENDIX 8
NOTIFICATION AND MOVEMENT DOCUMENTS

A.   Information to be Included in the Notification Document:

1) Serial number or other accepted identifier of notification document.

2) Exporter name, address, telephone, telefax, e-mail and contact person.

3) Recovery facility name, address, telephone, telefax, e-mail and technologies employed.

4) Importer name, address, telephone, telefax, e-mail.

5) Address, telephone, telefax, e-mail of any intended carrier(s) and/or their agents.

6) Country of export and relevant competent authority.

7) Countries of transit and relevant competent authorities.

8) Country of import and relevant competent authority.

9) Single notification or general notification. If general, period of validity requested.

10) Date(s) foreseen for commencement of transboundary movement(s).

11) Means of transport envisaged.

12) Certification that any applicable insurance or other financial guarantee is or shall be in force covering the transboundary movement.

13) Designation of waste type(s) on the appropriate list (Part I or II of Appendix 3 or 4) and their description(s), probable total quantity of each, and any hazardous characteristics.

14) Specification of the recovery operation(s) according to Appendix 5.B to this Decision.

15) Certification of the existence of written contract or chain of contracts or equivalent arrangement as required by this Decision.

16) Certification by the exporter that the information is complete and correct to the best of his knowledge.

---

* The wording of R1 to R13 in Appendix 5.B
is identical to that of Annex IV.B of the Basel
Convention.

B. Information to be Included in the Movement Document:

Include all information at A. above plus:

(a) Date shipment has commenced.

(b) Carrier(s) name, address, telephone, telefax, e-mail.

(c) Type of packaging envisaged.

(d) Any special precautions to be taken by carrier(s).

(e) Declaration by exporter that no objection has been lodged by the competent authorities of all countries concerned. This declaration requires signature of the exporter.

(f) Appropriate signatures for each custody transfer.

4.14 OECD RECOMMENDATION ON THE ENVIRONMENTALLY SOUND MANAGEMENT OF WASTE (AS AMENDED, BUT WITHOUT ANNEXES). Adopted by the OECD Council, 9 June 2004.ᵉ OECD Doc C(2004)100

The Council, * * *

Agreeing that the implementation of environmentally sound and economically efficient management of waste should achieve the following objectives:

1. Sustainable use of natural resources, minimisation of waste and protection of human health and the environment from adverse effects that may result from waste;

2. Fair competition between enterprises throughout the OECD area through the implementation of core "performance elements" (CPEs) by waste management facilities, thus contributing to a level playing field of high environmental standards;

3. Through incentives and measures, diversion of waste streams to the extent possible from facilities operating with low-standards to facilities that manage waste in an environmentally sound and economically efficient manner;

On the proposal of the Environment Policy Committee,

Recommends that Member countries elaborate and implement policies and/or programmes to ensure that waste be managed in an environmentally sound and economically efficient manner. Domestic policies and/or programmes implemented under this Recommendation shall not lead to or create unnecessary obstacles to international trade of waste destined for recovery operations.

For the purpose of this Recommendation, taking into account the size of the enterprise, especially the situation of small and medium size enterprises (SMEs), the type and amount of waste, the nature of the operation and their domestic legislation, Member countries should:

1. Have an adequate regulatory and enforcement infrastructure at an appropriate governmental level, consisting of legal requirements such as authorisations/licences/permits, or standards;

2. Develop and implement practices and instruments that facilitate the efforts of competent authorities to monitor the implementation of the CPEs [Core Performance Elements] listed in Annex I to this Recommendation and control compliance of waste management activities with applicable national and international rules and regulations. In case of non-compliance with existing rules, prompt, adequate and effective actions should be undertaken;

3. Ensure that waste management facilities are operating according to best available techniques while taking into consideration the technical, operational and economic feasibility of doing so, and work towards continually improving environmental performance;

4. Encourage, through appropriate measures, information exchange between producers, waste generators, waste managers and authorities, including participation in sectoral trade or industry association activities addressing these issues, in order to foster waste prevention, optimise recovery operations and minimise quantities as well as potential risk of waste destined for disposal or recovery;

5. Integrate into national policies and/or programmes the core performance elements listed in Annex I to this Recommendation, which constitute the basic requirements to ensure environmentally sound management of waste;

6. Consider incentives and/or relief measures for facilities that fulfil the core performance elements listed in Annex I to this Recommendation;

e. Amended on 16 October 2007, C(2007)97.

7. Implement the technical guidance for environmentally sound management of waste that has been developed by the OECD and, where appropriate, work towards the implementation of other ESM guidance referred to in Annex III to this Recommendation;

8. Move towards internalisation of environmental and human health costs in waste management, taking into account the differences between hazardous and non-hazardous waste;

9. Provide incentives to take part in environmentally sound recycling schemes;

10. Encourage the development and implementation of an environmental liability regime for facilities that carry out risky or potentially risky activities to ensure adequate measures upon definite cessation of activities and to prevent environmental damage;

11. Ensure that the implementation of the core performance elements listed in Annex I to this Recommendation does not discourage recycling in Member countries, recognising, in particular, the flexibility appropriate for each Member country to increase the rates of environmentally sound recovery of low risk waste.

* * *

C. Desertification

4.15 Convention to Combat Desertification in Those Countries Experiencing Serious Drought and/or Desertification, Particularly in Africa. **Adopted on 17 June 1994. Entered into force, 26 December 1996. 1954 UNTS 3;** *reprinted in* **33 ILM 1328 (1994) & 5 Weston V.G.4**

The Parties to this Convention,

Affirming that human beings in affected or threatened areas are at the centre of concerns to combat desertification and mitigate the effects of drought,

Reflecting the urgent concern of the international community, including States and international organizations, about the adverse impacts of desertification and drought,

Aware that arid, semi-arid and dry sub-humid areas together account for a significant proportion of the Earth's land area and are the habitat and source of livelihood for a large segment of its population,

Acknowledging that desertification and drought are problems of global dimension in that they affect all regions of the world and that joint action of the international community is needed to combat desertification and/or mitigate the effects of drought,

Noting the high concentration of developing countries, notably the least developed countries, among those experiencing serious drought and/or desertification, and the particularly tragic consequences of these phenomena in Africa,

Noting also that desertification is caused by complex interactions among physical, biological, political, social, cultural and economic factors,

Considering the impact of trade and relevant aspects of international economic relations on the ability of affected countries to combat desertification adequately,

Conscious that sustainable economic growth, social development and poverty eradication are priorities of affected developing countries, particularly in Africa, and are essential to meeting sustainability objectives,

Mindful that desertification and drought affect sustainable development through their interrelationships with important social problems such as poverty, poor health and nutrition, lack of food security, and those arising from migration, displacement of persons and demographic dynamics,

Appreciating the significance of the past efforts and experience of States and international organizations in combatting desertification and mitigating the effects of drought, particularly in implementing the Plan of Action to Combat Desertification which was adopted at the United Nations Conference on Desertification in 1977,

Realizing that, despite efforts in the past, progress in combatting desertification and mitigating the effects of drought has not met expectations and that a new and more effective approach is needed at all levels within the framework of sustainable development,

Recognizing the validity and relevance of decisions adopted at the United Nations Conference on Environment and Development, particularly of Agenda 21 and its chapter 12, which provide a basis for combatting desertification,

Reaffirming in this light the commitments of developed countries as contained in paragraph 13 of chapter 33 of Agenda 21,

Recalling General Assembly resolution 47/188, particularly the priority in it prescribed for Africa, and all other relevant United Nations resolutions, decisions and programmes on desertification and drought, as well as relevant declarations by African countries and those from other regions,

Reaffirming the Rio Declaration on Environment and Development which states, in its Principle 2, that States have, in accordance with the Charter of the United Nations and the principles of international law, the sovereign right to exploit their own resources pursuant to their own environmental and developmental policies, and the responsibility to ensure that activities within their jurisdiction or control do not cause damage to the environment of other States or of areas beyond the limits of national jurisdiction,

Recognizing that national Governments play a critical role in combating desertification and mitigating the effects of drought and that progress in that respect depends on local implementation of action programmes in affected areas,

Recognizing also the importance and necessity of international cooperation and partnership in combattng desertification and mitigating the effects of drought,

Recognizing the importance of the provision to affected developing countries, particularly in Africa, of effective means, inter alia substantial financial resources, including new and additional funding, and access to technology, without which it will be difficult for them to implement fully their commitments under this Convention,

Expressing concern over the impact of desertification and drought on affected countries in Central Asia and the Transcaucasus,

Stressing the important role played by women in regions affected by desertification and/or drought, particularly in rural areas of developing countries, and the importance of ensuring the full participation of both men and women at all levels in programmes to combat desertification and mitigate the effects of drought,

Emphasizing the special role of non-governmental organizations and other major groups in programmes to combat desertification and mitigate the effects of drought,

Bearing in mind the relationship between desertification and other environmental problems of global dimension facing the international and national communities,

Bearing also in mind the contribution that combating desertification can make to achieving the objectives of the United Nations Framework Convention on Climate Change, the Convention on Biological Diversity and other related environmental conventions,

Believing that strategies to combat desertification and mitigate the effects of drought will be most effective if they are based on sound systematic observation and rigorous scientific knowledge and if they are continuously reevaluated,

Recognizing the urgent need to improve the effectiveness and coordination of international cooperation to facilitate the implementation of national plans and priorities,

Determined to take appropriate action in combating desertification and mitigating the effects of drought for the benefit of present and future generations,

Have agreed as follows:

PART I

INTRODUCTION

Article 1

Use of terms

For the purposes of this Convention:

(a) "desertification" means land degradation in arid, semi-arid and dry sub-humid areas resulting from various factors, including climatic variations and human activities;

(b) "combating desertification" includes activities which are part of the integrated development of land in arid, semi-arid and dry sub-humid areas for sustainable development which are aimed at:

    (i) prevention and/or reduction of land degradation;

    (ii) rehabilitation of partly degraded land; and

    (iii) reclamation of desertified land;

(c) "drought" means the naturally occurring phenomenon that exists when precipitation has been significantly below normal recorded levels, causing serious hydrological imbalances that adversely affect land resource production systems;

(d) "mitigating the effects of drought" means activities related to the prediction of drought and intended to reduce the vulnerability of society and natural systems to drought as it relates to combating desertification;

(e) "land" means the terrestrial bio-productive system that comprises soil, vegetation, other biota, and the ecological and hydrological processes that operate within the system;

(f) "land degradation" means reduction or loss, in arid, semi-arid and dry sub-humid areas, of the biological or economic productivity and complexity of rainfed cropland, irrigated cropland, or range, pasture, forest and woodlands resulting from land uses or from a process or combination of processes, including processes arising from human activities and habitation patterns, such as:

    (i) soil erosion caused by wind and/or water;

    (ii) deterioration of the physical, chemical and biological or economic properties of soil; and

    (iii) long-term loss of natural vegetation;

(g) "arid, semi-arid and dry sub-humid areas" means areas, other than polar and sub-polar regions, in which the ratio of annual precipitation to potential evapotranspiration falls within the range from 0.05 to 0.65;

(h) "affected areas" means arid, semi-arid and/or dry sub-humid areas affected or threatened by desertification;

(i) "affected countries" means countries whose lands include, in whole or in part, affected areas;

(j) "regional economic integration organization" means an organization constituted by sovereign States of a given region which has competence in respect of matters governed by this Convention and has been duly authorized, in accordance with its internal procedures, to sign, ratify, accept, approve or accede to this Convention;

(k) "developed country Parties" means developed country Parties and regional economic integration organizations constituted by developed countries;

Article 2

Objective

1. The objective of this Convention is to combat desertification and mitigate the effects of drought in countries experiencing serious drought and/or desertification, particularly in Africa, through effective action at all levels, supported by international cooperation and partnership arrangements, in the framework of an integrated approach which is consistent with Agenda 21, with a view to contributing to the achievement of sustainable development in affected areas.

2. Achieving this objective will involve long-term integrated strategies that focus simultaneously, in affected areas, on improved productivity of land, and the rehabilita-

tion, conservation and sustainable management of land and water resources, leading to improved living conditions, in particular at the community level.

Article 3

Principles

In order to achieve the objective of this Convention and to implement its provisions, the Parties shall be guided, inter alia, by the following:

(a) the Parties should ensure that decisions on the design and implementation of programmes to combat desertification and/or mitigate the effects of drought are taken with the participation of populations and local communities and that an enabling environment is created at higher levels to facilitate action at national and local levels;

(b) the Parties should, in a spirit of international solidarity and partnership, improve cooperation and coordination at subregional, regional and international levels, and better focus financial, human, organizational and technical resources where they are needed;

(c) the Parties should develop, in a spirit of partnership, cooperation among all levels of government, communities, non-governmental organizations and landholders to establish a better understanding of the nature and value of land and scarce water resources in affected areas and to work towards their sustainable use; and

(d) the Parties should take into full consideration the special needs and circumstances of affected developing country Parties, particularly the least developed among them.

PART II

GENERAL PROVISIONS

Article 4

General obligations

1. The Parties shall implement their obligations under this Convention, individually or jointly, either through existing or prospective bilateral and multilateral arrangements or a combination thereof, as appropriate, emphasizing the need to coordinate efforts and develop a coherent long-term strategy at all levels.

2. In pursuing the objective of this Convention, the Parties shall:

(a) adopt an integrated approach addressing the physical, biological and socio-economic aspects of the processes of desertification and drought;

(b) give due attention, within the relevant international and regional bodies, to the situation of affected developing country Parties with regard to international trade, marketing arrangements and debt with a view to establishing an enabling international economic environment conducive to the promotion of sustainable development;

(c) integrate strategies for poverty eradication into efforts to combat desertification and mitigate the effects of drought;

(d) promote cooperation among affected country Parties in the fields of environmental protection and the conservation of land and water resources, as they relate to desertification and drought;

(e) strengthen subregional, regional and international cooperation;

(f) cooperate within relevant intergovernmental organizations;

(g) determine institutional mechanisms, if appropriate, keeping in mind the need to avoid duplication; and

(h) promote the use of existing bilateral and multilateral financial mechanisms and arrangements that mobilize and channel substantial financial resources to affected developing country Parties in combatting desertification and mitigating the effects of drought.

3. Affected developing country Parties are eligible for assistance in the implementation of the Convention.

Article 5

Obligations of affected country Parties

In addition to their obligations pursuant to Article 4, affected country Parties undertake to:

(a) give due priority to combating desertification and mitigating the effects of drought, and allocate adequate resources in accordance with their circumstances and capabilities;

(b) establish strategies and priorities, within the framework of sustainable development plans and/or policies, to combat desertification and mitigate the effects of drought;

(c) address the underlying causes of desertification and pay special attention to the socio-economic factors contributing to desertification processes;

(d) promote awareness and facilitate the participation of local populations, particularly women and youth, with the support of non-governmental organizations, in efforts to combat desertification and mitigate the effects of drought; and

(e) provide an enabling environment by strengthening, as appropriate, relevant existing legislation and, where they do not exist, enacting new laws and establishing long-term policies and action programmes.

Article 6

Obligations of developed country Parties

In addition to their general obligations pursuant to Article 4, developed country Parties undertake to:

(a) actively support, as agreed, individually or jointly, the efforts of affected developing country Parties, particularly those in Africa, and the least developed countries, to combat desertification and mitigate the effects of drought;

(b) provide substantial financial resources and other forms of support to assist affected developing country Parties, particularly those in Africa, effectively to develop and implement their own long-term plans and strategies to combat desertification and mitigate the effects of drought;

(c) promote the mobilization of new and additional funding pursuant to Article 20, paragraph 2 (b);

(d) encourage the mobilization of funding from the private sector and other non-governmental sources; and

(e) promote and facilitate access by affected country Parties, particularly affected developing country Parties, to appropriate technology, knowledge and know-how.

Article 7

Priority for Africa

In implementing this Convention, the Parties shall give priority to affected African country Parties, in the light of the particular situation prevailing in that region, while not neglecting affected developing country Parties in other regions.

Article 8

Relationship with other conventions

1. The Parties shall encourage the coordination of activities carried out under this Convention and, if they are Parties to them, under other relevant international agreements, particularly the United Nations Framework Convention on Climate Change and the Convention on Biological Diversity, in order to derive maximum benefit from activities under each agreement while avoiding duplication of effort. The Parties shall encourage the conduct of joint programmes, particularly in the fields of research, training, systematic observation and information collection and exchange, to the extent that such activities may contribute to achieving the objectives of the agreements concerned.

2. The provisions of this Convention shall not affect the rights and obligations of any Party deriving from a bilateral, regional or international agreement into which it has entered prior to the entry into force of this Convention for it.

PART III

ACTION PROGRAMMES, SCIENTIFIC AND TECHNICAL COOPERATION AND SUPPORTING MEASURES

Section 1: Action programmes

Article 9

Basic approach

1. In carrying out their obligations pursuant to Article 5, affected developing country Parties and any other affected country Party in the framework of its regional implementation annex or, otherwise, that has notified the Permanent Secretariat in writing of its intention to prepare a national action programme, shall, as appropriate, prepare, make public and implement national action programmes, utilizing and building, to the extent possible, on existing relevant successful plans and programmes, and subregional and regional action programmes, as the central element of the strategy to combat desertification and mitigate the effects of drought. Such programmes shall be updated through a continuing participatory process on the basis of lessons from field action, as well as the results of research. The preparation of national action programmes shall be closely interlinked with other efforts to formulate national policies for sustainable development.

2. In the provision by developed country Parties of different forms of assistance under the terms of Article 6, priority shall be given to supporting, as agreed, national, sub-regional and regional action programmes of affected developing country Parties, particularly those in Africa, either directly or through relevant multilateral organizations or both.

3. The Parties shall encourage organs, funds and programmes of the United Nations system and other relevant intergovernmental organizations, academic institutions, the scientific community and non-governmental organizations in a position to cooperate, in accordance with their mandates and capabilities, to support the elaboration, implementation and follow-up of action programmes.

Article 10

National action programmes

1. The purpose of national action programmes is to identify the factors contributing to desertification and practical measures necessary to combat desertification and mitigate the effects of drought.

2. National action programmes shall specify the respective roles of government, local communities and land users and the resources available and needed. They shall, inter alia:

(a) incorporate long-term strategies to combat desertification and mitigate the effects of drought, emphasize implementation and be integrated with national policies for sustainable development;

(b) allow for modifications to be made in response to changing circumstances and be sufficiently flexible at the local level to cope with different socio-economic, biological and geo-physical conditions;

(c) give particular attention to the implementation of preventive measures for lands that are not yet degraded or which are only slightly degraded;

(d) enhance national climatological, meteorological and hydrological capabilities and the means to provide for drought early warning;

(e) promote policies and strengthen institutional frameworks which develop cooperation and coordination, in a spirit of partnership, between the donor community, governments at all levels, local populations and community groups, and facilitate access by local populations to appropriate information and technology;

(f) provide for effective participation at the local, national and regional levels of non-governmental organizations and local populations, both women and men, particularly resource users, including farmers and pastoralists and their representative organizations, in policy planning, decision-making, and implementation and review of national action programmes; and

(g) require regular review of, and progress reports on, their implementation.

3. National action programmes may include, inter alia, some or all of the following measures to prepare for and mitigate the effects of drought:

(a) establishment and/or strengthening, as appropriate, of early warning systems, including local and national facilities and joint systems at the subregional and regional levels, and mechanisms for assisting environmentally displaced persons;

(b) strengthening of drought preparedness and management, including drought contingency plans at the local, national, subregional and regional levels, which take into consideration seasonal to interannual climate predictions;

(c) establishment and/or strengthening, as appropriate, of food security systems, including storage and marketing facilities, particularly in rural areas;

(d) establishment of alternative livelihood projects that could provide incomes in drought prone areas; and

(e) development of sustainable irrigation programmes for both crops and livestock.

4. Taking into account the circumstances and requirements specific to each affected country Party, national action programmes include, as appropriate, inter alia, measures in some or all of the following priority fields as they relate to combating desertification and mitigating the effects of drought in affected areas and to their populations: promotion of alternative livelihoods and improvement of national economic environments with a view to strengthening programmes aimed at the eradication of poverty and at ensuring food security, demographic dynamics, sustainable management of natural resources, sustainable agricultural practices, development and efficient use of various energy sources, institutional and legal frameworks, strengthening of capabilities for assessment and systematic observation, including hydrological and meteorological services, and capacity building, education and public awareness.

Article 11

Subregional and regional action programmes

Affected country Parties shall consult and cooperate to prepare, as appropriate, in accordance with relevant regional implementation annexes, subregional and/or regional action programmes to harmonize, complement and increase the efficiency of national programmes. The provisions of Article 10 shall apply mutatis mutandis to subregional and regional programmes. Such cooperation may include agreed joint programmes for the sustainable management of transboundary natural resources, scientific and technical cooperation, and strengthening of relevant institutions.

Article 12

International cooperation

Affected country Parties, in collaboration with other Parties and the international community, should cooperate to ensure the promotion of an enabling international environment in the implementation of the Convention. Such cooperation should also cover fields of technology transfer as well as scientific research and development, information collection and dissemination and financial resources.

Article 13

Support for the elaboration and implementation of action programmes

1. Measures to support action programmes pursuant to Article 9 include, inter alia:

(a) financial cooperation to provide predictability for action programmes, allowing for necessary long-term planning;

(b) elaboration and use of cooperation mechanisms which better enable support at the local level, including action through non-governmental organizations, in order to promote the replicability of successful pilot programme activities where relevant;

(c) increased flexibility in project design, funding and implementation in keeping with the experimental, iterative approach indicated for participatory action at the local community level; and

(d) as appropriate, administrative and budgetary procedures that increase the efficiency of cooperation and of support programmes.

2. In providing such support to affected developing country Parties, priority shall be given to African country Parties and to least developed country Parties.

Article 14

Coordination in the elaboration and implementation of action programmes

1. The Parties shall work closely together, directly and through relevant intergovernmental organizations, in the elaboration and implementation of action programmes.

2. The Parties shall develop operational mechanisms, particularly at the national and field levels, to ensure the fullest possible coordination among developed country Parties, developing country Parties and relevant intergovernmental and non-governmental organizations, in order to avoid duplication, harmonize interventions and approaches, and maximize the impact of assistance. In affected developing country Parties, priority will be given to coordinating activities related to international cooperation in order to maximize the efficient use of resources, to ensure responsive assistance, and to facilitate the implementation of national action programmes and priorities under this Convention.

Article 15

Regional implementation annexes

Elements for incorporation in action programmes shall be selected and adapted to the socio-economic, geographical and climatic factors applicable to affected country Parties or regions, as well as to their level of development. Guidelines for the preparation of action programmes and their exact focus and content for particular subregions and regions are set out in the regional implementation annexes.

Section 2: Scientific and technical cooperation

Article 16

Information collection, analysis and exchange

The Parties agree, according to their respective capabilities, to integrate and coordinate the collection, analysis and exchange of relevant short term and long term data and information to ensure systematic observation of land degradation in affected areas and to understand better and assess the processes and effects of drought and desertification. This would help accomplish, inter alia, early warning and advance planning for periods of adverse climatic variation in a form suited for practical application by users at all levels, including especially local populations. To this end, they shall, as appropriate:

(a) facilitate and strengthen the functioning of the global network of institutions and facilities for the collection, analysis and exchange of information, as well as for systematic observation at all levels, which shall, inter alia:

(i) aim to use compatible standards and systems;

(ii) encompass relevant data and stations, including in remote areas;

(iii) use and disseminate modern technology for data collection, transmission and assessment on land degradation; and

(iv) link national, subregional and regional data and information centres more closely with global information sources;

(b) ensure that the collection, analysis and exchange of information address the needs of local communities and those of decision makers, with a view to resolving specific problems, and that local communities are involved in these activities;

(c) support and further develop bilateral and multilateral programmes and projects aimed at defining, conducting, assessing and financing the collection, analysis and exchange of data and information, including, inter alia, integrated sets of physical, biological, social and economic indicators;

(d) make full use of the expertise of competent intergovernmental and non-governmental organizations, particularly to disseminate relevant information and experiences among target groups in different regions;

(e) give full weight to the collection, analysis and exchange of socioeconomic data, and their integration with physical and biological data;

(f) exchange and make fully, openly and promptly available information from all publicly available sources relevant to combating desertification and mitigating the effects of drought; and

(g) subject to their respective national legislation and/or policies, exchange information on local and traditional knowledge, ensuring adequate protection for it and providing appropriate return from the benefits derived from it, on an equitable basis and on mutually agreed terms, to the local populations concerned.

Article 17

Research and development

1. The Parties undertake, according to their respective capabilities, to promote technical and scientific cooperation in the fields of combatting desertification and mitigating the effects of drought through appropriate national, subregional, regional and international institutions. To this end, they shall support research activities that:

(a) contribute to increased knowledge of the processes leading to desertification and drought and the impact of, and distinction between, causal factors, both natural and human, with a view to combatting desertification and mitigating the effects of drought, and achieving improved productivity as well as sustainable use and management of resources;

(b) respond to well defined objectives, address the specific needs of local populations and lead to the identification and implementation of solutions that improve the living standards of people in affected areas;

(c) protect, integrate, enhance and validate traditional and local knowledge, know-how and practices, ensuring, subject to their respective national legislation and/or policies, that the owners of that knowledge will directly benefit on an equitable basis and on mutually agreed terms from any commercial utilization of it or from any technological development derived from that knowledge;

(d) develop and strengthen national, subregional and regional research capabilities in affected developing country Parties, particularly in Africa, including the development of local skills and the strengthening of appropriate capacities, especially in countries with a weak research base, giving particular attention to multidisciplinary and participative socio-economic research;

(e) take into account, where relevant, the relationship between poverty, migration caused by environmental factors, and desertification;

(f) promote the conduct of joint research programmes between national, subregional, regional and international research organizations, in both the public and private sectors, for the development of improved, affordable and accessible technologies for sustainable development through effective participation of local populations and communities; and

(g) enhance the availability of water resources in affected areas, by means of, inter alia, cloud-seeding.

2. Research priorities for particular regions and subregions, reflecting different local conditions, should be included in action programmes. The Conference of the Parties shall review research priorities periodically on the advice of the Committee on Science and Technology.

Article 18

Transfer, acquisition, adaptation and development of technology

1. The Parties undertake, as mutually agreed and in accordance with their respective national legislation and/or policies, to promote, finance and/or facilitate the financing of the transfer, acquisition, adaptation and development of environmentally sound, economically viable and socially acceptable technologies relevant to combatting desertification and/or mitigating the effects of drought, with a view to contributing to the achievement of sustainable development in affected areas. Such cooperation shall be conducted bilaterally or multilaterally, as appropriate, making full use of the expertise of intergovernmental and non-governmental organizations. The Parties shall, in particular:

(a) fully utilize relevant existing national, subregional, regional and international information systems and clearing-houses for the dissemination of information on available technologies, their sources, their environmental risks and the broad terms under which they may be acquired;

(b) facilitate access, in particular by affected developing country Parties, on favourable terms, including on concessional and preferential terms, as mutually agreed, taking into account the need to protect intellectual property rights, to technologies most suitable to practical application for specific needs of local populations, paying special attention to the social, cultural, economic and environmental impact of such technology;

(c) facilitate technology cooperation among affected country Parties through financial assistance or other appropriate means;

(d) extend technology cooperation with affected developing country Parties, including, where relevant, joint ventures, especially to sectors which foster alternative livelihoods; and

(e) take appropriate measures to create domestic market conditions and incentives, fiscal or otherwise, conducive to the development, transfer, acquisition and adaptation of suitable technology, knowledge, know-how and practices, including measures to ensure adequate and effective protection of intellectual property rights.

2. The Parties shall, according to their respective capabilities, and subject to their respective national legislation and/or policies, protect, promote and use in particular relevant traditional and local technology, knowledge, know-how and practices and, to that end, they undertake to:

(a) make inventories of such technology, knowledge, know-how and practices and their potential uses with the participation of local populations, and disseminate such information, where appropriate, in cooperation with relevant intergovernmental and non-governmental organizations;

(b) ensure that such technology, knowledge, know-how and practices are adequately protected and that local populations benefit directly, on an equitable basis and as mutually agreed, from any commercial utilization of them or from any technological development derived therefrom;

(c) encourage and actively support the improvement and dissemination of such technology, knowledge, know-how and practices or of the development of new technology based on them; and

(d) facilitate, as appropriate, the adaptation of such technology, knowledge, know-how and practices to wide use and integrate them with modern technology, as appropriate.

Section 3: Supporting measures

Article 19

Capacity building, education and public awareness

1. The Parties recognize the significance of capacity building—that is to say, institution building, training and development of relevant local and national capacities—in efforts to combat desertification and mitigate the effects of drought. They shall promote, as appropriate, capacity-building:

(a) through the full participation at all levels of local people, particularly at the local level, especially women and youth, with the cooperation of non-governmental and local organizations;

(b) by strengthening training and research capacity at the national level in the field of desertification and drought;

(c) by establishing and/or strengthening support and extension services to disseminate relevant technology methods and techniques more effectively, and by training field agents and members of rural organizations in participatory approaches for the conservation and sustainable use of natural resources;

(d) by fostering the use and dissemination of the knowledge, know-how and practices of local people in technical cooperation programmes, wherever possible;

(e) by adapting, where necessary, relevant environmentally sound technology and traditional methods of agriculture and pastoralism to modern socio-economic conditions;

(f) by providing appropriate training and technology in the use of alternative energy sources, particularly renewable energy resources, aimed particularly at reducing dependence on wood for fuel;

(g) through cooperation, as mutually agreed, to strengthen the capacity of affected developing country Parties to develop and implement programmes in the field of collection, analysis and exchange of information pursuant to Article 16;

(h) through innovative ways of promoting alternative livelihoods, including training in new skills;

(i) by training of decision makers, managers, and personnel who are responsible for the collection and analysis of data for the dissemination and use of early warning information on drought conditions and for food production;

(j) through more effective operation of existing national institutions and legal frameworks and, where necessary, creation of new ones, along with strengthening of strategic planning and management; and

(k) by means of exchange visitor programmes to enhance capacity building in affected country Parties through a long-term, interactive process of learning and study.

2. Affected developing country Parties shall conduct, in cooperation with other Parties and competent intergovernmental and non-governmental organizations, as appropriate, an interdisciplinary review of available capacity and facilities at the local and national levels, and the potential for strengthening them.

3. The Parties shall cooperate with each other and through competent intergovernmental organizations, as well as with non-governmental organizations, in undertaking and supporting public awareness and educational programmes in both affected and, where relevant, unaffected country Parties to promote understanding of the causes and effects of desertification and drought and of the importance of meeting the objective of this Convention. To that end, they shall:

(a) organize awareness campaigns for the general public;

(b) promote, on a permanent basis, access by the public to relevant information, and wide public participation in education and awareness activities;

(c) encourage the establishment of associations that contribute to public awareness;

(d) develop and exchange educational and public awareness material, where possible in local languages, exchange and second experts to train personnel of affected developing country Parties in carrying out relevant education and awareness programmes, and fully utilize relevant educational material available in competent international bodies;

(e) assess educational needs in affected areas, elaborate appropriate school curricula and expand, as needed, educational and adult literacy programmes and opportunities for all, in particular for girls and women, on the identification, conservation and sustainable use and management of the natural resources of affected areas; and

(f) develop interdisciplinary participatory programmes integrating desertification and drought awareness into educational systems and in non-formal, adult, distance and practical educational programmes.

4. The Conference of the Parties shall establish and/or strengthen networks of regional education and training centres to combat desertification and mitigate the effects of drought. These networks shall be coordinated by an institution created or designated for that purpose, in order to train scientific, technical and management personnel and to strengthen existing institutions responsible for education and training in affected country Parties, where appropriate, with a view to harmonizing programmes and to organizing exchanges of experience among them. These networks shall cooperate closely with relevant intergovernmental and non-governmental organizations to avoid duplication of effort.

Article 20

Financial resources

1. Given the central importance of financing to the achievement of the objective of the Convention, the Parties, taking into account their capabilities, shall make every effort to ensure that adequate financial resources are available for programmes to combat desertification and mitigate the effects of drought.

2. In this connection, developed country Parties, while giving priority to affected African country Parties without neglecting affected developing country Parties in other regions, in accordance with Article 7, undertake to:

(a) mobilize substantial financial resources, including grants and concessional loans, in order to support the implementation of programmes to combat desertification and mitigate the effects of drought;

(b) promote the mobilization of adequate, timely and predictable financial resources, including new and additional funding from the Global Environment Facility of the agreed incremental costs of those activities concerning desertification that relate to its four focal areas, in conformity with the relevant provisions of the Instrument establishing the Global Environment Facility;

(c) facilitate through international cooperation the transfer of technology, knowledge and know-how; and

(d) explore, in cooperation with affected developing country Parties, innovative methods and incentives for mobilizing and channeling resources, including those of foundations, non-governmental organizations and other private sector entities, particularly debt swaps and other innovative means which increase financing by reducing the external debt burden of affected developing country Parties, particularly those in Africa.

3. Affected developing country Parties, taking into account their capabilities, undertake to mobilize adequate financial resources for the implementation of their national action programmes.

4. In mobilizing financial resources, the Parties shall seek full use and continued qualitative improvement of all national, bilateral and multilateral funding sources and mechanisms, using consortia, joint programmes and parallel financing, and shall seek to involve private sector funding sources and mechanisms, including those of non-governmental organizations. To this end, the Parties shall fully utilize the operational mechanisms developed pursuant to Article 14.

5. In order to mobilize the financial resources necessary for affected developing country Parties to combat desertification and mitigate the effects of drought, the Parties shall:

(a) rationalize and strengthen the management of resources already allocated for combating desertification and mitigating the effects of drought by using them more effectively and efficiently, assessing their successes and shortcomings, removing hindrances to their effective use and, where necessary, reorienting programmes in light of the integrated long-term approach adopted pursuant to this Convention;

(b) give due priority and attention within the governing bodies of multilateral financial institutions, facilities and funds, including regional development banks and funds, to supporting affected developing country Parties, particularly those in Africa, in activities which advance implementation of the Convention, notably action programmes they undertake in the framework of regional implementation annexes; and

(c) examine ways in which regional and sub-regional cooperation can be strengthened to support efforts undertaken at the national level.

6. Other country Parties are encouraged to provide, on a voluntary basis, knowledge, know-how and techniques related to desertification and/or financial resources to affected developing country Parties.

7. The full implementation by affected developing country Parties, particularly those in Africa, of their obligations under the Convention will be greatly assisted by the fulfilment by developed country Parties of their obligations under the Convention, including in particular those regarding financial resources and transfer of technology. In fulfilling their obligations, developed country Parties should take fully into account that economic and social development and poverty eradication are the first priorities of affected developing country Parties, particularly those in Africa.

Article 21

Financial mechanisms

1. The Conference of the Parties shall promote the availability of financial mechanisms and shall encourage such mechanisms to seek to maximize the availability of funding for affected developing country Parties, particularly those in Africa, to implement the Convention. To this end, the Conference of the Parties shall consider for adoption inter alia approaches and policies that:

(a) facilitate the provision of necessary funding at the national, subregional, regional and global levels for activities pursuant to relevant provisions of the Convention;

(b) promote multiple-source funding approaches, mechanisms and arrangements and their assessment, consistent with Article 20;

(c) provide on a regular basis, to interested Parties and relevant intergovernmental and non-governmental organizations, information on available sources of funds and on funding patterns in order to facilitate coordination among them;

(d) facilitate the establishment, as appropriate, of mechanisms, such as national desertification funds, including those involving the participation of non-governmental organizations, to channel financial resources rapidly and efficiently to the local level in affected developing country Parties; and

(e) strengthen existing funds and financial mechanisms at the sub-regional and regional levels, particularly in Africa, to support more effectively the implementation of the Convention.

2. The Conference of the Parties shall also encourage the provision, through various mechanisms within the United Nations system and through multilateral financial institutions, of support at the national, sub-regional and regional levels to activities that enable developing country Parties to meet their obligations under the Convention.

3. Affected developing country Parties shall utilize, and where necessary, establish and/or strengthen, national coordinating mechanisms, integrated in national development programmes, that would ensure the efficient use of all available financial resources. They shall also utilize participatory processes involving non-governmental organizations, local groups and the private sector, in raising funds, in elaborating as well as implementing programmes and in assuring access to funding by groups at the local level. These actions can be enhanced by improved coordination and flexible programming on the part of those providing assistance.

4. In order to increase the effectiveness and efficiency of existing financial mechanisms, a Global Mechanism to promote actions leading to the mobilization and channeling of substantial financial resources, including for the transfer of technology, on a grant basis, and/or on concessional or other terms, to affected developing country Parties, is hereby established. This Global Mechanism shall function under the authority and guidance of the Conference of the Parties and be accountable to it.

5. The Conference of the Parties shall identify, at its first ordinary session, an organization to house the Global Mechanism. The Conference of the Parties and the organization it has identified shall agree upon modalities for this Global Mechanism to ensure inter alia that such Mechanism:

(a) identifies and draws up an inventory of relevant bilateral and multilateral cooperation programmes that are available to implement the Convention;

(b) provides advice, on request, to Parties on innovative methods of financing and sources of financial assistance and on improving the coordination of cooperation activities at the national level;

(c) provides interested Parties and relevant intergovernmental and non-governmental organizations with information on available sources of funds and on funding patterns in order to facilitate coordination among them; and

(d) reports to the Conference of the Parties, beginning at its second ordinary session, on its activities.

6. The Conference of the Parties shall, at its first session, make appropriate arrangements with the organization it has identified to house the Global Mechanism for the administrative operations of such Mechanism, drawing to the extent possible on existing budgetary and human resources.

7. The Conference of the Parties shall, at its third ordinary session, review the policies, operational modalities and activities of the Global Mechanism accountable to it pursuant to paragraph 4, taking into account the provisions of Article 7. On the basis of this review, it shall consider and take appropriate action.

PART IV

INSTITUTIONS

Article 22

Conference of the Parties

1. A Conference of the Parties is hereby established.

2. The Conference of the Parties is the supreme body of the Convention. It shall make, within its mandate, the decisions necessary to promote its effective implementation. In particular, it shall:

(a) regularly review the implementation of the Convention and the functioning of its institutional arrangements in the light of the experience gained at the national, subregional, regional and international levels and on the basis of the evolution of scientific and technological knowledge;

(b) promote and facilitate the exchange of information on measures adopted by the Parties, and determine the form and timetable for transmitting the information to be submitted pursuant to Article 26, review the reports and make recommendations on them;

(c) establish such subsidiary bodies as are deemed necessary for the implementation of the Convention;

(d) review reports submitted by its subsidiary bodies and provide guidance to them;

(e) agree upon and adopt, by consensus, rules of procedure and financial rules for itself and any subsidiary bodies;

(f) adopt amendments to the Convention pursuant to Articles 30 and 31;

(g) approve a programme and budget for its activities, including those of its subsidiary bodies, and undertake necessary arrangements for their financing;

(h) as appropriate, seek the cooperation of, and utilize the services of and information provided by, competent bodies or agencies, whether national or international, intergovernmental or non-governmental;

(i) promote and strengthen the relationship with other relevant conventions while avoiding duplication of effort; and

(j) exercise such other functions as may be necessary for the achievement of the objective of the Convention.

3. The Conference of the Parties shall, at its first session, adopt its own rules of procedure, by consensus, which shall include decision-making procedures for matters not already covered by decision-making procedures stipulated in the Convention. Such procedures may include specified majorities required for the adoption of particular decisions.

4. The first session of the Conference of the Parties shall be convened by the interim secretariat referred to in Article 35 and shall take place not later than one year after the date of entry into force of the Convention. Unless otherwise decided by the Conference of the Parties, the second, third and fourth ordinary sessions shall be held yearly, and thereafter, ordinary sessions shall be held every two years.

5. Extraordinary sessions of the Conference of the Parties shall be held at such other times as may be decided either by the Conference of the Parties in ordinary session or at the written request of any Party, provided that, within three months of the request being communicated to the Parties by the Permanent Secretariat, it is supported by at least one-third of the Parties.

6. At each ordinary session, the Conference of the Parties shall elect a Bureau. The structure and functions of the Bureau shall be determined in the rules of procedure. In appointing the Bureau, due regard shall be paid to the need to ensure equitable geographical distribution and adequate representation of affected country Parties, particularly those in Africa.

7. The United Nations, its specialized agencies and any State member thereof or observers thereto not Party to the Convention, may be represented at sessions of the Conference of the Parties as observers. Any body or agency, whether national or international, governmental or non-governmental, which is qualified in matters covered by the Convention, and which has informed the Permanent Secretariat of its wish to be represented at a session of the Conference of the Parties as an observer, may be so admitted unless at least one-third of the Parties present object. The admission and participation of observers shall be subject to the rules of procedure adopted by the Conference of the Parties.

8. The Conference of the Parties may request competent national and international organizations which have relevant expertise to provide it with information relevant to Article 16, paragraph (g), Article 17, paragraph 1 (c) and Article 18, paragraph 2(b).

Article 23

Permanent Secretariat

1. A Permanent Secretariat is hereby established.

2. The functions of the Permanent Secretariat shall be:

(a) to make arrangements for sessions of the Conference of the Parties and its subsidiary bodies established under the Convention and to provide them with services as required;

(b) to compile and transmit reports submitted to it;

(c) to facilitate assistance to affected developing country Parties, on request, particularly those in Africa, in the compilation and communication of information required under the Convention;

(d) to coordinate its activities with the secretariats of other relevant international bodies and conventions;

(e) to enter, under the guidance of the Conference of the Parties, into such administrative and contractual arrangements as may be required for the effective discharge of its functions;

(f) to prepare reports on the execution of its functions under this Convention and present them to the Conference of the Parties; and

(g) to perform such other secretariat functions as may be determined by the Conference of the Parties.

3. The Conference of the Parties, at its first session, shall designate a Permanent Secretariat and make arrangements for its functioning.

Article 24

Committee on Science and Technology

1. A Committee on Science and Technology is hereby established as a subsidiary body of the Conference of the Parties to provide it with information and advice on scientific and technological matters relating to combating desertification and mitigating the effects of drought. The Committee shall meet in conjunction with the ordinary sessions of the Conference of the Parties and shall be multidisciplinary and open to the participation of all Parties. It shall be composed of government representatives competent in the relevant fields of expertise. The Conference of the Parties shall decide, at its first session, on the terms of reference of the Committee.

2. The Conference of the Parties shall establish and maintain a roster of independent experts with expertise and experience in the relevant fields. The roster shall be based on nominations received in writing from the Parties, taking into account the need for a multidisciplinary approach and broad geographical representation.

3. The Conference of the Parties may, as necessary, appoint ad hoc panels to provide it, through the Committee, with information and advice on specific issues regarding the state of the art in fields of science and technology relevant to combating desertification and mitigating the effects of drought. These panels shall be composed of experts whose names are taken from the roster, taking into account the need for a multidisciplinary approach and broad geographical representation. These experts shall have scientific backgrounds and field experience and shall be appointed by the Conference of the Parties on the recommendation of the Committee. The Conference of

the Parties shall decide on the terms of reference and the modalities of work of these panels.

Article 25

Networking of institutions, agencies and bodies

1.   The Committee on Science and Technology shall, under the supervision of the Conference of the Parties, make provision for the undertaking of a survey and evaluation of the relevant existing networks, institutions, agencies and bodies willing to become units of a network. Such a network shall support the implementation of the Convention.

2.   On the basis of the results of the survey and evaluation referred to in paragraph 1, the Committee on Science and Technology shall make recommendations to the Conference of the Parties on ways and means to facilitate and strengthen networking of the units at the local, national and other levels, with a view to ensuring that the thematic needs set out in Articles 16 to 19 are addressed.

3.   Taking into account these recommendations, the Conference of the Parties shall:

(a) identify those national, subregional, regional and international units that are most appropriate for networking, and recommend operational procedures, and a time frame, for them; and

(b) identify the units best suited to facilitating and strengthening such networking at all levels.

PART V

PROCEDURES

Article 26

Communication of information

1.   Each Party shall communicate to the Conference of the Parties for consideration at its ordinary sessions, through the Permanent Secretariat, reports on the measures which it has taken for the implementation of the Convention. The Conference of the Parties shall determine the timetable for submission and the format of such reports.

2.   Affected country Parties shall provide a description of the strategies established pursuant to Article 5 and of any relevant information on their implementation.

3.   Affected country Parties which implement action programmes pursuant to Articles 9 to 15 shall provide a detailed description of the programmes and of their implementation.

4.   Any group of affected country Parties may make a joint communication on measures taken at the subregional and/or regional levels in the framework of action programmes.

5.   Developed country Parties shall report on measures taken to assist in the preparation and implementation of action programmes, including information on the financial resources they have provided, or are providing, under the Convention.

6.   Information communicated pursuant to paragraphs 1 to 4 shall be transmitted by the Permanent Secretariat as soon as possible to the Conference of the Parties and to any relevant subsidiary body.

7.   The Conference of the Parties shall facilitate the provision to affected developing countries, particularly those in Africa, on request, of technical and financial support in compiling and communicating information in accordance with this Article,

as well as identifying the technical and financial needs associated with action programmes.

Article 27

Measures to resolve questions on implementation

The Conference of the Parties shall consider and adopt procedures and institutional mechanisms for the resolution of questions that may arise with regard to the implementation of the Convention.

Article 28

Settlement of disputes

1. Parties shall settle any dispute between them concerning the interpretation or application of the Convention through negotiation or other peaceful means of their own choice.

2. When ratifying, accepting, approving, or acceding to the Convention, or at any time thereafter, a Party which is not a regional economic integration organization may declare in a written instrument submitted to the Depositary that, in respect of any dispute concerning the interpretation or application of the Convention, it recognizes one or both of the following means of dispute settlement as compulsory in relation to any Party accepting the same obligation:

(a) arbitration in accordance with a procedure adopted by the Conference of the Parties in an annex as soon as practicable;

(b) submission of the dispute to the International Court of Justice.

3. A Party which is a regional economic integration organization may make a declaration with like effect in relation to arbitration in accordance with the procedure referred to in paragraph 2 (a).

4. A declaration made pursuant to paragraph 2 shall remain in force until it expires in accordance with its terms or until three months after written notice of its revocation has been deposited with the Depositary.

5. The expiry of a declaration, a notice of revocation or a new declaration shall not in any way affect proceedings pending before an arbitral tribunal or the International Court of Justice unless the Parties to the dispute otherwise agree.

6. If the Parties to a dispute have not accepted the same or any procedure pursuant to paragraph 2 and if they have not been able to settle their dispute within twelve months following notification by one Party to another that a dispute exists between them, the dispute shall be submitted to conciliation at the request of any Party to the dispute, in accordance with procedure adopted by the Conference of the Parties in an Annex as soon as practicable.

Article 29

Status of annexes

1. Annexes form an integral part of the Convention and, unless expressly provided otherwise, a reference to the Convention also constitutes a reference to its Annexes.

2. The Parties shall interpret the provisions of the Annexes in a manner that is in conformity with their rights and obligations under the Articles of this Convention.

Article 30

Amendments to the Convention

1. Any Party may propose amendments to the Convention.

2. Amendments to the Convention shall be adopted at an ordinary session of the Conference of the Parties. The text of any proposed amendment shall be communicated to the Parties by the Permanent Secretariat at least six months before the meeting at which it is proposed for adoption. The Permanent Secretariat shall also communicate proposed amendments to the signatories to the Convention.

3. The Parties shall make every effort to reach agreement on any proposed amendment to the Convention by consensus. If all efforts at consensus have been exhausted and no agreement reached, the amendment shall, as a last resort, be adopted by a two-thirds majority vote of the Parties present and voting at the meeting. The adopted amendment shall be communicated by the Permanent Secretariat to the Depositary, who shall circulate it to all Parties for their ratification, acceptance, approval or accession.

4. Instruments of ratification, acceptance, approval or accession in respect of an amendment shall be deposited with the Depositary. An amendment adopted pursuant to paragraph 3 shall enter into force for those Parties having accepted it on the ninetieth day after the date of receipt by the Depositary of an instrument of ratification, acceptance, approval or accession by at least two-thirds of the Parties to the Convention which were Parties at the time of the adoption of the amendment.

5. The amendment shall enter into force for any other Party on the ninetieth day after the date on which that Party deposits with the Depositary its instrument of ratification, acceptance or approval of, or accession to the said amendment.

6. For the purposes of this Article and Article 31, "Parties present and voting" means Parties present and casting an affirmative or negative vote.

Article 31

Adoption and amendment of annexes

1. Any additional annex to the Convention and any amendment to an annex shall be proposed and adopted in accordance with the procedure for amendment of the Convention set forth in Article 30, provided that, in adopting an additional regional implementation annex or amendment to any regional implementation annex, the majority provided for in that Article shall include a two thirds majority vote of the Parties of the region concerned present and voting. The adoption or amendment of an annex shall be communicated by the Depositary to all Parties.

2. An annex, other than an additional regional implementation annex, or an amendment to an annex, other than an amendment to any regional implementation annex, that has been adopted in accordance with paragraph 1, shall enter into force for all Parties to the Convention six months after the date of communication by the Depositary to such Parties of the adoption of such annex or amendment, except for those Parties that have notified the Depositary in writing within that period of their non-acceptance of such annex or amendment. Such annex or amendment shall enter into force for Parties which withdraw their notification of non-acceptance on the ninetieth day after the date on which withdrawal of such notification has been received by the Depositary.

3. An additional regional implementation annex or amendment to any regional implementation annex that has been adopted in accordance with paragraph 1, shall enter into force for all Parties to the Convention six months after the date of the communication by the Depositary to such Parties of the adoption of such annex or amendment, except with respect to:

(a) any Party that has notified the Depositary in writing, within such six month period, of its non-acceptance of that additional regional implementation annex or of the amendment to the regional implementation annex, in which case such annex or amendment shall enter into force for Parties which withdraw their notification of non-acceptance on the ninetieth day after the date on which withdrawal of such notification has been received by the Depositary; and

(b) any Party that has made a declaration with respect to additional regional implementation annexes or amendments to regional implementation annexes in accordance with Article 34, paragraph 4, in which case any such annex or amendment shall enter into force for such a Party on the ninetieth day after the date of deposit with the Depositary of its instrument of ratification, acceptance, approval or accession with respect to such annex or amendment.

4. If the adoption of an annex or an amendment to an annex involves an amendment to the Convention, that annex or amendment to an annex shall not enter into force until such time as the amendment to the Convention enters into force.

Article 32

Right to vote

1. Except as provided for in paragraph 2, each Party to the Convention shall have one vote.

2. Regional economic integration organizations, in matters within their competence, shall exercise their right to vote with a number of votes equal to the number of their member States that are Parties to the Convention. Such an organization shall not exercise its right to vote if any of its member States exercises its right, and vice versa.

PART VI

FINAL PROVISIONS

Article 33

Signature

This Convention shall be opened for signature at Paris, on 14 October, 1994, by States Members of the United Nations or any of its specialized agencies or that are Parties to the Statute of the International Court of Justice and by regional economic integration organizations. It shall remain open for signature, thereafter, at the United Nations Headquarters in New York until 26 December, 1996.

Article 34

Ratification, acceptance, approval and accession

1. The Convention shall be subject to ratification, acceptance, approval or accession by States and by regional economic integration organizations. It shall be open for accession from the day after the date on which the Convention is closed for signature. Instruments of ratification, acceptance, approval or accession shall be deposited with the Depositary.

2. Any regional economic integration organization which becomes a Party to the Convention without any of its member States being a Party to the Convention shall be bound by all the obligations under the Convention. Where one or more member States of such an organization are also Party to the Convention, the organization and its member States shall decide on their respective responsibilities for the performance of their obligations under the Convention. In such cases, the organization and the member States shall not be entitled to exercise rights under the Convention concurrently.

3. In their instruments of ratification, acceptance, approval or accession, regional economic integration organizations shall declare the extent of their competence with respect to the matters governed by the Convention. They shall also promptly inform

the Depositary, who shall in turn inform the Parties, of any substantial modification in the extent of their competence.

4. In its instrument of ratification, acceptance, approval or accession, any Party may declare that, with respect to it, any additional regional implementation annex or any amendment to any regional implementation annex shall enter into force only upon the deposit of its instrument of ratification, acceptance, approval or accession with respect thereto.

Article 35

Interim arrangements

The secretariat functions referred to in Article 23 will be carried out on an interim basis by the secretariat established by the General Assembly of the United Nations in its resolution 47/188 of 22 December 1992, until the completion of the first session of the Conference of the Parties.

Article 36

Entry into force

1. The Convention shall enter into force on the ninetieth day after the date of deposit of the fiftieth instrument of ratification, acceptance, approval or accession.

2. For each State or regional economic integration organization ratifying, accepting, approving or acceding to the Convention after the deposit of the fiftieth instrument of ratification, acceptance, approval or accession, the Convention shall enter into force on the ninetieth day after the date of deposit by such State or regional economic integration organization of its instrument of ratification, acceptance, approval or accession.

3. For the purposes of paragraphs 1 and 2, any instrument deposited by a regional economic integration organization shall not be counted as additional to those deposited by States members of the organization.

Article 37

Reservations

No reservations may be made to this Convention.

Article 38

Withdrawal

1. At any time after three years from the date on which the Convention has entered into force for a Party, that Party may withdraw from the Convention by giving written notification to the Depositary.

2. Any such withdrawal shall take effect upon expiry of one year from the date of receipt by the Depositary of the notification of withdrawal, or on such later date as may be specified in the notification of withdrawal.

Article 39

Depositary

The Secretary–General of the United Nations shall be the Depositary of the Convention.

Article 40

Authentic texts

The original of the present Convention, of which the Arabic, Chinese, English, French, Russian and Spanish texts are equally authentic, shall be deposited with the Secretary–General of the United Nations.

IN WITNESS WHEREOF the undersigned, being duly authorized to that effect, have signed the present Convention.

DONE AT Paris, this 17th day of June one thousand nine hundred and ninety-four.

ANNEX I

REGIONAL IMPLEMENTATION ANNEX FOR AFRICA

Article 1

Scope

This Annex applies to Africa, in relation to each Party and in conformity with the Convention, in particular its Article 7, for the purpose of combating desertification and/or mitigating the effects of drought in its arid, semi-arid and dry sub-humid areas.

Article 2

Purpose

The purpose of this Annex, at the national, subregional and regional levels in Africa and in the light of its particular conditions, is to:

(a) identify measures and arrangements, including the nature and processes of assistance provided by developed country Parties, in accordance with the relevant provisions of the Convention;

(b) provide for the efficient and practical implementation of the Convention to address conditions specific to Africa; and

(c) promote processes and activities relating to combating desertification and/or mitigating the effects of drought within the arid, semi-arid and dry sub-humid areas of Africa.

Article 3

Particular conditions of the African region

In carrying out their obligations under the Convention, the Parties shall, in the implementation of this Annex, adopt a basic approach that takes into consideration the following particular conditions of Africa:

(a) the high proportion of arid, semi-arid and dry sub-humid areas;

(b) the substantial number of countries and populations adversely affected by desertification and by the frequent recurrence of severe drought;

(c) the large number of affected countries that are landlocked;

(d) the widespread poverty prevalent in most affected countries, the large number of least developed countries among them, and their need for significant amounts of external assistance, in the form of grants and loans on concessional terms, to pursue their development objectives;

(e) the difficult socio-economic conditions, exacerbated by deteriorating and fluctuating terms of trade, external indebtedness and political instability, which induce internal, regional and international migrations;

(f) the heavy reliance of populations on natural resources for subsistence which, compounded by the effects of demographic trends and factors, a weak technological base and unsustainable production practices, contributes to serious resource degradation;

(g) the insufficient institutional and legal frameworks, the weak infrastructural base and the insufficient scientific, technical and educational capacity, leading to substantial capacity building requirements; and

(h) the central role of actions to combat desertification and/or mitigate the effects of drought in the national development priorities of affected African countries.

Article 4

Commitments and obligations of African country Parties

1. In accordance with their respective capabilities, African country Parties undertake to:

(a) adopt the combating of desertification and/or the mitigation of the effects of drought as a central strategy in their efforts to eradicate poverty;

(b) promote regional cooperation and integration, in a spirit of solidarity and partnership based on mutual interest, in programmes and activities to combat desertification and/or mitigate the effects of drought;

(c) rationalize and strengthen existing institutions concerned with desertification and drought and involve other existing institutions, as appropriate, in order to make them more effective and to ensure more efficient use of resources;

(d) promote the exchange of information on appropriate technology, knowledge, know-how and practices between and among them; and

(e) develop contingency plans for mitigating the effects of drought in areas degraded by desertification and/or drought.

2. Pursuant to the general and specific obligations set out in Articles 4 and 5 of the Convention, affected African country Parties shall aim to:

(a) make appropriate financial allocations from their national budgets consistent with national conditions and capabilities and reflecting the new priority Africa has accorded to the phenomenon of desertification and/or drought;

(b) sustain and strengthen reforms currently in progress toward greater decentralization and resource tenure as well as reinforce participation of local populations and communities; and

(c) identify and mobilize new and additional national financial resources, and expand, as a matter of priority, existing national capabilities and facilities to mobilize domestic financial resources.

Article 5

Commitments and obligations of developed country Parties

1. In fulfilling their obligations pursuant to Articles 4, 6 and 7 of the Convention, developed country Parties shall give priority to affected African country Parties and, in this context, shall:

(a) assist them to combat desertification and/or mitigate the effects of drought by, inter alia, providing and/or facilitating access to financial and/or other resources, and promoting, financing and/or facilitating the financing of the transfer, adaptation and access to appropriate environmental technologies and know-how, as mutually agreed and in accordance with national policies, taking into account their adoption of poverty eradication as a central strategy;

(b) continue to allocate significant resources and/or increase resources to combat desertification and/or mitigate the effects of drought; and

(c) assist them in strengthening capacities to enable them to improve their institutional frameworks, as well as their scientific and technical capabilities, information collection and analysis, and research and development for the purpose of combating desertification and/or mitigating the effects of drought.

2. Other country Parties may provide, on a voluntary basis, technology, knowledge and know-how relating to desertification and/or financial resources, to affected African country Parties. The transfer of such knowledge, know-how and techniques is facilitated by international cooperation.

Article 6

Strategic planning framework for sustainable development

1. National action programmes shall be a central and integral part of a broader process of formulating national policies for the sustainable development of affected African country Parties.

2. A consultative and participatory process involving appropriate levels of government, local populations, communities and non-governmental organizations shall be undertaken to provide guidance on a strategy with flexible planning to allow maximum participation from local populations and communities. As appropriate, bilateral and multilateral assistance agencies may be involved in this process at the request of an affected African country Party.

Article 7

Timetable for preparation of action programmes

Pending entry into force of this Convention, the African country Parties, in cooperation with other members of the international community, as appropriate, shall, to the extent possible, provisionally apply those provisions of the Convention relating to the preparation of national, subregional and regional action programmes.

Article 8

Content of national action programmes

1. Consistent with Article 10 of the Convention, the overall strategy of national action programmes shall emphasize integrated local development programmes for affected areas, based on participatory mechanisms and on integration of strategies for poverty eradication into efforts to combat desertification and mitigate the effects of drought. The programmes shall aim at strengthening the capacity of local authorities and ensuring the active involvement of local populations, communities and groups, with emphasis on education and training, mobilization of non-governmental organizations with proven expertise and strengthening of decentralized governmental structures.

2. National action programmes shall, as appropriate, include the following general features:

(a) the use, in developing and implementing national action programmes, of past experiences in combatting desertification and/or mitigating the effects of drought, taking into account social, economic and ecological conditions;

(b) the identification of factors contributing to desertification and/or drought and the resources and capacities available and required, and the setting up of appropriate policies and institutional and other responses and measures necessary to combat those phenomena and/or mitigate their effects; and

(c) the increase in participation of local populations and communities, including women, farmers and pastoralists, and delegation to them of more responsibility for management.

3. National action programmes shall also, as appropriate, include the following:

(a) measures to improve the economic environment with a view to eradicating poverty:

(i) increasing incomes and employment opportunities, especially for the poorest members of the community, by:

— developing markets for farm and livestock products;

— creating financial instruments suited to local needs;

— encouraging diversification in agriculture and the setting-up of agricultural enterprises; and

—developing economic activities of a paraagricultural or non-agricultural type;

(ii) improving the long-term prospects of rural economies by the creation of:

— incentives for productive investment and access to the means of production; and

— price and tax policies and commercial practices that promote growth;

(iii) defining and applying population and migration policies to reduce population pressure on land; and

(iv) promoting the use of drought resistant crops and the application of integrated dry-land farming systems for food security purposes;

(b) measures to conserve natural resources:

(i) ensuring integrated and sustainable management of natural resources, including:

— agricultural land and pastoral land;

— vegetation cover and wildlife;

— forests;

— water resources; and

— biological diversity;

(ii) training with regard to, and strengthening, public awareness and environmental education campaigns and disseminating knowledge of techniques relating to the sustainable management of natural resources; and

(iii) ensuring the development and efficient use of diverse energy sources, the promotion of alternative sources of energy, particularly solar energy, wind energy and biogas, and specific arrangements for the transfer, acquisition and adaptation of relevant technology to alleviate the pressure on fragile natural resources;

(c) measures to improve institutional organization:

(i) defining the roles and responsibilities of central government and local authorities within the framework of a land use planning policy;

(ii) encouraging a policy of active decentralization, devolving responsibility for management and decision-making to local authorities, and encouraging initiatives and the assumption of responsibility by local communities and the establishment of local structures; and

(iii) adjusting, as appropriate, the institutional and regulatory framework of natural resource management to provide security of land tenure for local populations;

(d) measures to improve knowledge of desertification:

(i) promoting research and the collection, processing and exchange of information on the scientific, technical and socio-economic aspects of desertification;

(ii) improving national capabilities in research and in the collection, processing, exchange and analysis of information so as to increase understanding and to translate the results of the analysis into operational terms; and

(iii) encouraging the medium and long term study of:

— socio-economic and cultural trends in affected areas;

— qualitative and quantitative trends in natural resources; and

— the interaction between climate and desertification; and

(e) measures to monitor and assess the effects of drought:

(i) developing strategies to evaluate the impacts of natural climate variability on regional drought and desertification and/or to utilize predictions of climate variability on seasonal to interannual time scales in efforts to mitigate the effects of drought;

(ii) improving early warning and response capacity, efficiently managing emergency relief and food aid, and improving food stocking and distribution systems, cattle protection schemes and public works and alternative livelihoods for drought prone areas; and

(iii) monitoring and assessing ecological degradation to provide reliable and timely information on the process and dynamics of resource degradation in order to facilitate better policy formulations and responses.

Article 9

Preparation of national action programmes and implementation and evaluation indicators

Each affected African country Party shall designate an appropriate national coordinating body to function as a catalyst in the preparation, implementation and evaluation of its national action programme. This coordinating body shall, in the light of Article 3 and as appropriate:

(a) undertake an identification and review of actions, beginning with a locally driven consultation process, involving local populations and communities and with the cooperation of local administrative authorities, developed country Parties and intergovernmental and non-governmental organizations, on the basis of initial consultations of those concerned at the national level;

(b) identify and analyze the constraints, needs and gaps affecting development and sustainable land use and recommend practical measures to avoid duplication by making full use of relevant ongoing efforts and promote implementation of results;

(c) facilitate, design and formulate project activities based on interactive, flexible approaches in order to ensure active participation of the population in affected areas, to minimize the negative impact of such activities, and to identify and prioritize requirements for financial assistance and technical cooperation;

(d) establish pertinent, quantifiable and readily verifiable indicators to ensure the assessment and evaluation of national action programmes, which encompass actions in the short, medium and long terms, and of the implementation of such programmes; and

(e) prepare progress reports on the implementation of the national action programmes.

Article 10

Organizational framework of subregional action programmes

1. Pursuant to Article 4 of the Convention, African country Parties shall cooperate in the preparation and implementation of subregional action programmes for

central, eastern, northern, southern and western Africa and, in that regard, may delegate the following responsibilities to relevant subregional intergovernmental organizations:

(a) acting as focal points for preparatory activities and coordinating the implementation of the subregional action programmes;

(b) assisting in the preparation and implementation of national action programmes;

(c) facilitating the exchange of information, experience and know-how as well as providing advice on the review of national legislation; and

(d) any other responsibilities relating to the implementation of subregional action programmes.

2. Specialized subregional institutions may provide support, upon request, and/or be entrusted with the responsibility to coordinate activities in their respective fields of competence.

Article 11

Content and preparation of subregional action programmes

Subregional action programmes shall focus on issues that are better addressed at the subregional level. They shall establish, where necessary, mechanisms for the management of shared natural resources. Such mechanisms shall effectively handle transboundary problems associated with desertification and/or drought and shall provide support for the harmonious implementation of national action programmes. Priority areas for subregional action programmes shall, as appropriate, focus on:

(a) joint programmes for the sustainable management of transboundary natural resources through bilateral and multilateral mechanisms, as appropriate;

(b) coordination of programmes to develop alternative energy sources;

(c) cooperation in the management and control of pests as well as of plant and animal diseases;

(d) capacity building, education and public awareness activities that are better carried out or supported at the subregional level;

(e) scientific and technical cooperation, particularly in the climatological, meteorological and hydrological fields, including networking for data collection and assessment, information sharing and project monitoring, and coordination and prioritization of research and development activities;

(f) early warning systems and joint planning for mitigating the effects of drought, including measures to address the problems resulting from environmentally induced migrations;

(g) exploration of ways of sharing experiences, particularly regarding participation of local populations and communities, and creation of an enabling environment for improved land use management and for use of appropriate technologies;

(h) strengthening of the capacity of subregional organizations to coordinate and provide technical services, as well as establishment, reorientation and strengthening of subregional centres and institutions; and

(i) development of policies in fields, such as trade, which have impact upon affected areas and populations, including policies for the coordination of regional marketing regimes and for common infrastructure.

Article 12

Organizational framework of the regional action programme

1. Pursuant to Article 11 of the Convention, African country Parties shall jointly determine the procedures for preparing and implementing the regional action programme.

2. The Parties may provide appropriate support to relevant African regional institutions and organizations to enable them to assist African country Parties to fulfil their responsibilities under the Convention.

Article 13

Content of the regional action programme

The regional action programme includes measures relating to combating desertification and/or mitigating the effects of drought in the following priority areas, as appropriate:

(a) development of regional cooperation and coordination of sub-regional action programmes for building regional consensus on key policy areas, including through regular consultations of sub-regional organizations;

(b) promotion of capacity building in activities which are better implemented at the regional level;

(c) the seeking of solutions with the international community to global economic and social issues that have an impact on affected areas taking into account Article 4, paragraph 2 (b) of the Convention;

(d) promotion among the affected country Parties of Africa and its subregions, as well as with other affected regions, of exchange of information and appropriate techniques, technical know-how and relevant experience;

(e) promotion of scientific and technological cooperation particularly in the fields of climatology, meteorology, hydrology, water resource development and alternative energy sources;

(f) coordination of sub-regional and regional research activities and identification of regional priorities for research and development;

(g) coordination of networks for systematic observation and assessment and information exchange, as well as their integration into world wide networks; and

(h) coordination of and reinforcement of sub-regional and regional early warning systems and drought contingency plans.

Article 14

Financial resources

1. Pursuant to Article 20 of the Convention and Article 4, paragraph 2, affected African country Parties shall endeavour to provide a macroeconomic framework conducive to the mobilization of financial resources and shall develop policies and establish procedures to channel resources more effectively to local development programmes, including through non-governmental organizations, as appropriate.

2. Pursuant to Article 21, paragraphs 4 and 5 of the Convention, the Parties agree to establish an inventory of sources of funding at the national, subregional, regional and international levels to ensure the rational use of existing resources and to identify gaps in resource allocation, to facilitate implementation of the action programmes. The inventory shall be regularly reviewed and up-dated.

3. Consistent with Article 7 of the Convention, the developed country Parties shall continue to allocate significant resources and/or increased resources and other

forms of assistance to affected African country Parties on the basis of partnership agreements and arrangements referred to in Article 18, giving, inter alia, due attention to matters related to debt, international trade and marketing arrangements in accordance with Article 4, paragraph 2 (b) of the Convention.

Article 15

Financial Mechanisms

1. Consistent with Article 7 of the Convention and considering the particular situation prevailing in this region, the Parties shall pay special attention to the implementation in Africa of the provisions of Article 21, paragraph 1 (d) and (e) of the Convention, notably by:

(a) facilitating the establishment of mechanisms, such as national desertification funds, to channel financial resources to the local level; and

(b) strengthening existing funds and financial mechanisms at the subregional and regional levels.

2. Consistent with Articles 20 and 21 of the Convention, the Parties which are also members of the governing bodies of relevant regional and subregional financial institutions, including the African Development Bank and the African Development Fund, shall promote efforts to give due priority and attention to the activities of those institutions that advance the implementation of this Annex.

3. The Parties shall streamline, to the extent possible, procedures for channeling funds to affected African country Parties.

Article 16

Technical assistance and cooperation

The Parties undertake, in accordance with their respective capabilities, to rationalize technical assistance to, and cooperation with, African country Parties with a view to increasing project and programme effectiveness by, inter alia:

(a) limiting the costs of support measures and backstopping, especially overhead costs, so that, in any case, such costs shall only represent an appropriately low percentage of the total cost of the project so as to maximize project efficiency;

(b) giving preference to the utilization of competent national experts or, where necessary, competent experts from within the subregion and/or region, in project design, preparation and implementation, and to the building of local expertise where it does not exist; and

(c) effectively managing and coordinating, as well as efficiently utilizing, technical assistance to be provided.

Article 17

Transfer, acquisition, adaptation and access to environmentally sound technology

In implementing Article 18 of the Convention relating to transfer, acquisition, adaptation and development of technology, the Parties undertake to give priority to African country Parties and, as necessary, to develop with them new models of partnership and cooperation with a view to strengthening capacity building in the fields of scientific research and development and information collection and dissemination to enable them to implement their strategies to combat desertification and mitigate the effects of drought.

Article 18

Coordination and partnership agreements

1. African country Parties shall coordinate the preparation, negotiation and implementation of national, subregional and regional action programmes. They may involve, as appropriate, other Parties and relevant intergovernmental and non-governmental organizations in this process.

2. The objectives of such coordination shall be to ensure that financial and technical cooperation is consistent with the Convention and to provide the necessary continuity in the use and administration of resources.

3. African country Parties shall organize consultative processes at the national, subregional and regional levels. These consultative processes may:

(a) serve as a forum to negotiate and conclude partnership agreements based on national, subregional and regional action programmes; and

(b) specify the contribution of African country Parties and other members of the consultative groups to the programmes and identify priorities and agreements on implementation and evaluation indicators, as well as funding arrangements for implementation.

4. The Permanent Secretariat may, at the request of African country Parties, pursuant to Article 23 of the Convention, facilitate the convocation of such consultative processes by:

(a) providing advice on the organization of effective consultative arrangements, drawing on experiences from other such arrangements;

(b) providing information to relevant bilateral and multilateral agencies concerning consultative meetings or processes, and encouraging their active involvement; and

(c) providing other information that may be relevant in establishing or improving consultative arrangements.

5. The subregional and regional coordinating bodies shall, inter alia:

(a) recommend appropriate adjustments to partnership agreements;

(b) monitor, assess and report on the implementation of the agreed subregional and regional programmes; and

(c) aim to ensure efficient communication and cooperation among African country Parties.

6. Participation in the consultative groups shall, as appropriate, be open to Governments, interested groups and donors, relevant organs, funds and programmes of the United Nations system, relevant subregional and regional organizations, and representatives of relevant non-governmental organizations. Participants of each consultative group shall determine the modalities of its management and operation.

7. Pursuant to Article 14 of the Convention, developed country Parties are encouraged to develop, on their own initiative, an informal process of consultation and coordination among themselves, at the country, subregional and regional levels, and, at the request of an affected African country Party or of an appropriate subregional or regional organization, to participate in a national, subregional or regional consultative process that would evaluate and respond to assistance needs in order to facilitate implementation.

Article 19

Follow-up arrangements

Follow-up of this annex shall be carried out by African country Parties in accordance with the Convention as follows:

(a) at the national level, by a mechanism the composition of which should be determined by each affected African country Party and which shall include representatives of local communities and shall function under the supervision of the national coordinating body referred to in Article 9;

(b) at the subregional level, by a multidisciplinary scientific and technical consultative committee, the composition and modalities of operation of which shall be determined by the African country Parties of the subregion concerned; and

(c) at the regional level, by mechanisms defined in accordance with the relevant provisions of the Treaty establishing the African Economic Community, and by an African Scientific and Technical Advisory Committee.

* * *

PART 5. BIOSPHERE

A. GENERAL BIODIVERSITY PROTECTION

5.1 CONVENTION ON NATURE PROTECTION AND WILDLIFE PRESERVATION IN THE WESTERN HEMISPHERE (Without Annex). Concluded at Washington, 12 October 1940. Entered into force, 1 May 1942. 161 UNTS 193, 56 Stat 1354, TS No 981; *reprinted in* 5A Weston & Carlson V.H.1

Preamble

The Governments of the American Republics, wishing to protect and preserve in their natural habitat representatives of all species and genera of their native flora and fauna, including migratory birds, in sufficient numbers and over areas extensive enough to assure them from becoming extinct through any agency within man's control; and

Wishing to protect and preserve scenery of extraordinary beauty, unusual and striking geologic formations, regions and natural objects of aesthetic, historic or scientific value, and areas characterized by primitive conditions in those cases covered by this Convention; and

Wishing to conclude a convention on the protection of nature and the preservation of flora and fauna to effectuate the foregoing purposes, have agreed upon the following Articles:

Article I
Description of terms used in the wording of this Convention

1. The expression NATIONAL PARKS shall denote:

Areas established for the protection and preservation of superlative scenery, flora and fauna of national significance which the general public may enjoy and from which it may benefit when placed under public control.

2. The expression NATIONAL RESERVES shall denote:

Regions established for conservation and utilization of natural resources under government control, on which protection of animal and plant life will be afforded in so far as this may be consistent with the primary purpose of such reserves.

3. The expression NATURE MONUMENTS shall denote:

Regions, objects, or living species of flora or fauna of aesthetic, historic or scientific interest to which strict protection is given. The purpose of nature monuments is the protection of a specific object, or a species of flora or fauna, and setting aside an area, an object, or a single species, as an inviolate nature monument, except for duly authorized scientific investigations or government inspection.

4. The expression STRICT WILDERNESS RESERVES shall denote:

A region under public control characterized by primitive conditions of flora, fauna, transportation and habitation wherein there is no provision for the passage of motorized transportation and all commercial developments are included.

5. The expression MIGRATORY BIRDS shall denote:

Birds of those species, all or some of whose individual members, may in any season cross any of the boundaries between the American countries. Some of the species of the following families are examples of birds characterized as migratory: Charadriidae, Scolopacidae, Caprimulgidae, Hirundinidae.

Article II

1. The Contracting Governments will explore at once the possibility of establishing in their territories national parks, national reserves, nature monuments, and strict wilderness reserves as defined in the preceding article. In cases where such establishment is feasible, the creation thereof shall be begun as soon as possible after the effective date of the present Convention.

2. If in any country the establishment of national parks, national reserves, nature monuments, or strict wilderness reserves is found to be impractical at present, suitable areas, objects or living species of fauna or flora, as the case may be, shall be selected as early as possible to be transformed into national parks, national reserves, nature monuments or strict wilderness reserves as soon as, in the opinion of the authorities concerned, circumstances will permit.

3. The Contracting Governments shall notify the Pan American Union of the establishment of any national parks, national reserves, nature monuments, or strict wilderness reserves, and of the legislation, including the methods of administrative control, adopted in connection therewith.

Article III

The Contracting Governments agree that the boundaries of national parks shall not be altered, or any portion thereof be capable of alienation, except by the competent legislative authority. The resources of these reserves shall not be subject to exploitation for commercial profit.

The Contracting Governments agree to prohibit hunting, killing and capturing of members of the fauna and destruction or collection of representatives of the flora in national parks except by or under the direction or control of the park authorities, or for duly authorized scientific investigations.

The Contracting Governments further agree to provide facilities for public recreation and education in national parks consistent with the purposes of this Convention.

Article IV

The Contracting Governments agree to maintain the strict wilderness reserves inviolate, as far as practicable, except for duly authorized scientific investigations or government inspection, or such uses as are consistent with the purposes for which the area was established.

Article V

1. The Contracting Governments agree to adopt, or to propose such adoption to their respective appropriate law-making bodies, suitable laws and regulations for the protection and preservation of flora and fauna within their national boundaries, but not included in the national parks, national reserves, nature monuments, or strict wilderness reserves referred to in Article II hereof. Such regulations shall contain proper provisions for the taking of specimens of flora and fauna for scientific study and investigation by properly accredited individuals and agencies.

2. The Contracting Governments agree to adopt, or to recommend that their respective legislatures adopt, laws which will assure the protection and preservation of the natural scenery, striking geological formations, and regions and natural objects of aesthetic interest or historic or scientific value.

Article VI

The Contracting Governments agree to cooperate among themselves in promoting the objectives of the present Convention. To this end they will lend proper assistance, consistent with national laws, to scientists of the American Republics engaged in research and field study; they may, when circumstances warrant, enter into agreements with one another or with scientific institutions of the Americas in order to increase the effectiveness of this collaboration; and they shall make available to all the American Republics equally through publication or otherwise the scientific knowledge resulting from such cooperative effort.

Article VII

The Contracting Governments shall adopt appropriate measures for the protection of migratory birds of economic or aesthetic value or to prevent the threatened extinction of any given species. Adequate measures shall be adopted which will permit, in so far as the respective governments may see fit, a rational utilization of migratory birds for the purpose of sports as well as for food, commerce, and industry, and for scientific study and investigation.

Article VIII

The protection of the species mentioned in the Annex to the present Convention is declared to be of special urgency and importance. Species included therein shall be protected as completely as possible, and their hunting, killing, capturing, or taking, shall be allowed only with the permission of the appropriate government authorities in the country. Such permission shall be granted only under special circumstances, in order to further scientific purposes, or when essential for the administration of the area in which the animal or plant is found.

Article IX

Each Contracting Government shall take the necessary measures to control and regulate the importation, exportation and transit of protected fauna or flora or any part thereof by the following means:

1. The issuing of certificates authorizing the exportation or transit of protected species of flora or fauna, or parts thereof.

2. The prohibition of the importation of any species of fauna or flora or any part thereof protected by the country of origin unless accompanied by a certificate of lawful exportation as provided for in Paragraph 1 of this Article.

Article X

1. The terms of this convention shall in no way be interpreted as replacing international agreements previously entered into by one or more of the High Contracting Powers.

2. The Pan American Union shall notify the Contracting Parties of any information relevant to the purposes of the present Convention communicated to it by any national museums or by any organizations, national or international, established within their jurisdiction and interested in the purposes of the Convention.

Article XI

1. The original of the present Convention in Spanish, English, Portuguese and French shall be deposited with the Pan American Union and opened for signature by the American Governments on October 12, 1940.

2. The present Convention shall remain open for signature by the American Governments. The instruments of ratification shall be deposited with the Pan Ameri-

can Union, which shall notify their receipt and the dates thereof, and the terms of any accompanying declarations or reservations, to all participating Governments.

3. The present Convention shall come into force three months after the deposit of not less than five ratifications with the Pan American Union.

4. Any ratification received after the date of the entry into force of the Convention, shall take effect three months after the date of its deposit with the Pan American Union.

Article XII

1. Any Contracting Government may at any time denounce the present Convention by a notification in writing addressed to the Pan American Union. Such denunciation shall take effect one year after the date of the receipt of the notification by the Pan American Union, provided, however, that no denunciation shall take effect until the expiration of five years from the date of the entry into force of this Convention.

2. If, as the result of simultaneous or successive denunciations, the number of Contracting Governments is reduced to less than three, the Convention shall cease to be in force from the date on which the last of such denunciations takes effect in accordance with the provisions of the preceding Paragraph.

3. The Pan American Union shall notify all of the American Governments of any denunciations and the date on which they take effect.

4. Should the Convention cease to be in force under the provisions of Paragraph 2 of this article, the Pan American Union shall notify all of the American Governments, indicating the date on which this will become effective.

IN WITNESS WHEREOF, the undersigned Plenipotentiaries, having deposited their full powers found to be in due and proper form, sign this Convention at the Pan American Union, Washington, D.C., on behalf of their respective Governments and affix thereto their seals on the dates appearing opposite their signatures.

* * *

5.2   AFRICAN CONVENTION ON THE CONSERVATION OF NATURE AND NATURAL RESOURCES (Without List of Protected Species).[a] **Concluded at Algiers, 15 September 1968. Entered into force, 16 June 1969. 1001 UNTS 3;** *reprinted in* **5A Weston & Carlson V.H.7**

PREAMBLE

We, the Heads of State and Government of Independent African States,

Fully conscious that soil, water, flora and faunal resources constitute a capital of vital importance to mankind;

Confirming, as we accepted upon declaring our adherence to the Charter of the Organization of African Unity, that we know that it is our duty "to harness the natural and human resources of our continent for the total advancement of our peoples in spheres of human endeavour";

Fully conscious of the ever-growing importance of natural resources from an economic, nutritional, scientific, educational, cultural and aesthetic point of view;

Conscious of the dangers which threaten some of these irreplaceable assets;

Accepting that the utilization of the natural resources must aim at satisfying the needs of man according to the carrying capacity of the environment;

Desirous of undertaking individual and joint action for the conservation, utilization and development of these assets by establishing and maintaining their rational utilization for the present and future welfare of mankind;

Convinced that one of the most appropriate means of achieving this end is to bring into force a convention;

Have agreed as follows:

Article I

The Contracting States hereby establish an African Convention on the Conservation of nature and natural resources.

Article II. FUNDAMENTAL PRINCIPLE

The Contracting States shall undertake to adopt the measures necessary to ensure conservation, utilization and development of soil, water, flora and faunal resources in accordance with scientific principles and with due regard to the best interests of the people.

Article III. DEFINITIONS

For purposes of the present Convention, the meaning of the following expressions shall be as defined below:

1. "Natural Resources" means renewable resources; that is soil, water, flora and fauna.

2. "Specimen" means an individual example of a species of wild animal or wild plant or part of a wild plant.

3. "Trophy" means any dead animal specimen or part thereof whether included in a manufactured or processed object or otherwise dealt with, unless it has lost its original identity; also nests, eggs and eggshells.

4. "Conservation area" means any protected natural resource area, whether it be a strict natural reserve, a national park or a special reserve;

a. A Revised African Convention on the Conservation of Nature and Natural Resources was adopted on July 11, 2003. The Revised Convention is not yet in force. *See* 5 Weston & Carlson V.C.16.

(a) "strict nature reserve" means an area:

(1) under State control and the boundaries of which may not be altered nor any portion alienated except by the competent legislative authority,

(2) throughout which any form of hunting or fishing, any undertaking connected with forestry, agriculture or mining, any grazing, any excavation or prospecting, drilling, levelling of the ground or construction, any work tending to alter the configuration of the soil or the character of the vegetation, any water pollution and, generally, any act likely to harm or disturb the fauna or flora, including introduction of zoological or botanical species, whether indigenous or imported, wild or domesticated, are strictly forbidden,

(3) where it shall be forbidden to reside, enter, traverse or camp, and where it shall be forbidden to fly over at low altitude, without a special written permit from the competent authority, and in which scientific investigations (including removal of animals and plants in order to maintain an ecosystem) may only be undertaken by permission of the competent authority;

(b) "national park" means an area:

(1) under State control and the boundaries of which may not be altered or any portion alienated except by the competent legislative authority,

(2) exclusively set aside for the propagation, protection, conservation and management of vegetation and wild animals as well as for the protection of sites, landscapes or geological formations of particular scientific or aesthetic value, for the benefit and enjoyment of the general public, and

(3) in which the killing, hunting and capture of animals and the destruction or collection of plants are prohibited except for scientific and management purposes and on the condition that such measures are taken under the direction or control of the competent authority,

(4) covering any aquatic environment to which all of the provisions of section (b)(13) above are applicable.

The activities prohibited in strict nature reserve under the provisions of section (a)(2) of paragraph 4 of this article are equally prohibited in national parks except in so far as they are necessary to enable the park authorities to implement the provisions of section (2) of this paragraph, by applying, for example, appropriate management practices, and to enable the public to visit these parks; however, sport fishing may be practiced with the authorization and under the control of the competent authority.

(c) "special reserve" means other protected areas such as:

(1) "game reserve" which shall denote an area

(a) set aside for the conservation, management and propagation of wild animal life and the protection and management of its habitat,

(b) within which the hunting, killing or capture of fauna shall be prohibited except by or under the direction or control of the reserve authorities,

(c) where settlement and other human activities shall be controlled or prohibited;

(2) "partial reserve" or "sanctuary" which shall denote an area

(a) set aside to protect characteristic wildlife and especially bird communities, or to protect particularly threatened animal or plant species and especially those listed in the Annex to this Convention, together with the biotopes essential for their survival,

(b) in which all other interests and activities shall be subordinated to this end;

(3) "soil", "water" or "forest" reserve shall denote areas set aside to protect such resources.

Article IV. SOIL

The Contracting States shall take effective measures for conservation and improvement of the soil and shall in particular combat erosion and misuse of the soil. To this end:

(a) they shall establish land-use plans based on scientific investigations (ecological, pedological, economic, and sociological) and, in particular, classification of land-use capability;

(b) they shall, when implementing agricultural practices and agrarian reforms,

> (1) improve soil-conservation and introduce improved farming methods, which ensure long-term productivity of the land,

> (2) control erosion caused by various forms of land-use which may lead to loss of vegetation cover.

Article V. WATER

1. The Contracting States shall establish policies for conservation, utilization and development of underground and surface water, and shall endeavour to guarantee for their populations a sufficient and continuous supply of suitable water, taking appropriate measures with due regard to

> (1) the study of water cycles and the investigation of each catchment area,

> (2) the co-ordination and planning of water resources development projects,

> (3) the administration and control of all water utilization, and

> (4) prevention and control of water pollution.

2. Where surface or underground water resources are shared by two or more of the Contracting States, the latter shall act in consultation, and if the need arises, set up inter-State Commissions to study and resolve problems arising from the joint use of these resources, and for the joint development and conservation thereof.

Article VI. FLORA

1. The Contracting States shall take all necessary measures for the protection of flora and to ensure its best utilization and development. To this end the Contracting States shall:

(a) adopt scientifically-based conservation, utilization and management plans of forests and rangeland, taking into account the social and economic needs of the States concerned, the importance of the vegetation cover for the maintenance of the water balance of an area, the productivity of soils and the habitat requirements of the fauna;

(b) observe section (a) above by paying particular attention to controlling bush fires, forest exploitation, land clearing for cultivation, and over-grazing by domestic and wild animals;

(c) set aside areas for forest reserves and carry out afforestation programmes where necessary;

(d) limitation of forest grazing to season and intensities that will not prevent forest regeneration; and

(e) establish botanical gardens to perpetuate plant species of particular interest.

2. The Contracting States also shall undertake the conservation of plant species or communities, which are threatened and/or of special scientific or aesthetic value by ensuring that they are included in conservation areas.

Article VII. FAUNAL RESOURCES

1. The Contracting States shall ensure conservation, wise use and development of faunal resources and their environment, within the framework of land-use planning and of economic and social development. Management shall be carried out in accordance with plans based on scientific principles, and to that end the Contracting States shall:

(a) manage wildlife populations inside designated areas according to the objectives of such areas and also manage exploitable wildlife populations outside such areas for an optimum sustained yield, compatible with and complementary to other land uses; and

(b) manage aquatic environments, whether in fresh, brackish or coastal water, with a view to minimize deleterious effects of any water and land use practice which might adversely affect aquatic habitats.

2. The Contracting States shall adopt adequate legislation on hunting, capture and fishing, under which:

(a) the issue of permits is properly regulated;

(b) unauthorized methods are prohibited;

(c) the following methods of hunting, capture and fishing are prohibited:

(1) any methods liable to cause a mass destruction of wild animals,

(2) the use of drugs, poisons, poisoned weapons or poisoned baits,

(3) the use of explosives,

(4) the following methods of hunting and capture are particularly prohibited:

1 the use of mechanically propelled vehicles,

2 the use of fire,

3 the use of fire arms capable of firing more than one round at each pull of the trigger,

4 hunting or capture at night,

5 the use of missiles containing detonators;

(d) the following methods of hunting or capture are as far as possible prohibited:

(1) the use of nets and stockades,

(2) the use of concealed traps, pits, snares, set-gun traps, deadfalls, and hunting from a blind or hide;

(e) with a view to as rational use as possible of game meat the abandonment by hunters of carcasses of animals, which represent a food resource, is prohibited.

Capture of animals with the aid of drugs or mechanically-propelled vehicles, or hunting or capture by night if carried out by, or under the control of, the competent authority shall nevertheless be exempted from the prohibitions under (c) above.

Article VIII. PROTECTED SPECIES

1. The Contracting States recognize that it is important and urgent to accord a special protection to those animal and plant species that are threatened with extinction, or which may become so, and to the habitat necessary to their survival. Where such a species is represented only in the territory of one Contracting State, that State

has a particular responsibility for its protection. These species which are, or may be listed, according to the degree of protection that shall be given to them are placed in Class A or B of the annex to this Convention, and shall be protected by Contracting States as follows:

(1) species in Class A shall be totally protected throughout the entire territory of the Contracting States; the hunting, killing, capture or collection of specimens shall be permitted only on the authorization in each case of the highest competent authority and only if required in the national interest or for scientific purposes; and

(2) species in Class B shall be totally protected, but may be hunted, killed, captured or collected under special authorization granted by the competent authority.

2. The competent authority of each Contracting State shall examine the necessity of applying the provisions of this article to species not listed in the annex, in order to conserve the indigenous flora and fauna of their respective countries. Such additional species shall be placed in Class A or B by the State concerned, according to its specific requirements.

Article IX. TRAFFIC IN SPECIMENS AND TROPHIES

1. In the case of animal species to which Article VIII does not apply the Contracting States shall:

(*a*) regulate trade in and transport of specimens and trophies;

(*b*) control the application of these regulations in such a way as to prevent trade in specimens and trophies which have been illegally captured or killed or obtained.

2. In the case of plant and animal species to which Article VIII, paragraph (1), applies, the Contracting States shall:

(*a*) take all measures similar to those in paragraph (1);

(*b*) make the export of such specimens and trophies subject to an authorization:

(1) additional to that required for their capture, killing or collection by Article VIII

(2) which indicates their destination,

(3) which shall not be given unless the specimens or trophies have been obtained legally,

(4) which shall be examined prior to exportation;

(5) which shall be on a standard form, as may be arranged under Article XVI;

(*c*) make the import and transit of such specimens and trophies subject to the presentation of the authorization required under section (*b*) above, with due provision for the confiscation of specimens and trophies exported illegally, without prejudice to the application of other penalties.

Article X. CONSERVATION AREAS

1. The Contracting States shall maintain and extend where appropriate, within their territory and where applicable in their territorial waters, the conservation areas existing at the time of entry into force of the present Convention and, preferably within the framework of land-use planning programmes, assess the necessity of establishing additional conservation areas in order to:

(1) protect those ecosystems which are most representative of and particularly those which are in any respect peculiar to their territories;

(2) ensure conservation of all species and more particularly of those listed or may be listed in the annex to this Convention;

2. The Contracting States shall establish where necessary, around the borders of conservation areas, zones within which the competent authorities shall control activities detrimental to the protected natural resources.

Article XI. Customary Rights

The Contracting States shall take all necessary legislative measures to reconcile customary rights with the provisions of this Convention.

Article XII. Research

The Contracting States shall encourage and promote research in conservation, utilization and management of natural resources and shall pay particular attention to ecological and sociological factors.

Article XIII. Conservation Education

1. (a) The Contracting States shall ensure that their peoples appreciate their close dependence on natural resources and that they understand the need, and rules for, the rational utilization of these resources.

(b) For this purpose they shall ensure that the principles indicated in paragraph (1):

> (1) are included in educational programmes at all levels,

> (2) form the object of information campaigns capable of acquainting the public with, and winning it over to, the idea of conservation.

2. In order to put into effect paragraph (1) above, the Contracting States shall make maximum use of the educational value of conservation areas.

Article XIV. Development Plans

1. The Contracting States shall ensure that conservation and management of natural resources are treated as an integral part of national and/or regional development plans.

2. In the formulation of all development plans, full consideration shall be given to ecological, as well as to economic and social factors.

3. Where any development plan is likely to affect the natural resources of another State, the latter shall be consulted.

Article XV. Organization of National Conservation Services

Each Contracting State shall establish, if it has not already done so, a single agency empowered to deal with all matters covered by this Convention, but, where this is not possible a co-ordinating machinery shall be established for this purpose.

Article XVI. Inter-state Co-operation

1. The Contracting States shall co-operate:

(a) whenever such co-operation is necessary to give effect to the provisions of this Convention, and

(b) whenever any national measure is likely to affect the natural resources of any other State.

2. The Contracting States shall supply the Organization of African Unity with:

(a) the text of laws, decrees, regulations and instructions in force in their territories, which are intended to ensure the implementation of this Convention,

(b) reports on the results achieved in applying the provisions of this Convention, and

(c) all the information necessary for the complete documentation of matters dealt with by this Convention if requested.

3. If so requested by Contracting States, the Organization of African Unity shall organize any meeting which may be necessary to dispose of any matters covered by this Convention. Requests for such meetings must be made by at least three of the Contracting States and be approved by two thirds of the States which it is proposed should participate in such meetings.

4. Any expenditure arising from this Convention, which devolves upon the Organization of African Unity shall be included in its regular budget, unless shared by the Contracting States or otherwise defrayed.

Article XVII.   PROVISION FOR EXCEPTIONS

1. The provisions of this Convention shall not affect the responsibilities of Contracting States concerning:

    (1) the paramount interest of the State,

    (2) "force majeure",

    (3) defence of human life.

2. The provisions of this Convention shall not prevent Contracting States:

    (1) in time of famine,

    (2) for the protection of public health,

    (3) in defence of property,

to enact measures contrary to the provisions of the Convention, provided their application is precisely defined in respect of aim, time and place.

Article XVIII.   SETTLEMENT OF DISPUTES

Any dispute between the Contracting States relating to the interpretation or application of this Convention, which cannot be settled by negotiation, shall at the request of any party be submitted to the Commission of Mediation, Conciliation and Arbitration of the Organization of African Unity.

Article XIX.   SIGNATURE AND RATIFICATION

1. This Convention shall be open for signature immediately after being approved by the Assembly of Heads of State and Government of the Organization of African Unity.

2. This Convention shall be ratified by each of the Contracting States. The instruments of ratification shall be deposited with the Administrative Secretary–General of the Organization of African Unity.

Article XX.   RESERVATIONS

1. At the time of signature, ratification or accession, any State may declare its acceptance of this Convention in part only, provided that such reservation may not apply to the provisions of Articles IIXI.

2. Reservations made in conformity with the preceding paragraph shall be deposited together with the instruments of ratification or accession.

3. Any Contracting State which has formulated a reservation in conformity with the preceding paragraph may at any time withdraw it by notifying the Administrative Secretary–General of the Organization of African Unity.

Article XXI. ENTRY INTO FORCE

1. This Convention shall come into force on the thirtieth day following the date of deposit of the fourth instrument of ratification or accession with the Administrative Secretary–General of the Organization of African Unity, who shall inform participating States accordingly.

2. In the case of a State ratifying or acceding to the Convention after the depositing of the fourth instrument of ratification or accession, the Convention shall come into force on the thirtieth day after the deposit by such State of its instrument of ratification or accession.

3. The London Convention of 1933 or any other Convention on the conservation of flora and fauna in their natural state shall cease to have effect in States in which this Convention has come into force.

Article XXII. ACCESSION

1. After the date of approval specified in Article XIX, paragraph (1), this Convention shall be open to accession by any independent and sovereign African State.

2. The instruments of accession shall be deposited with the Administrative Secretary–General of the Organization of African Unity.

Article XXIII. DENUNCIATION

1. Any Contracting State may denounce this Convention by notification in writing addressed to the Administrative Secretary–General of the Organization of African Unity.

2. Such denunciation shall take effect, for such a State, one year after the date of receipt of its notification by the Administrative Secretary–General of the Organization of African Unity.

3. No denunciation shall, however, be made before the expiry of a period of five years from the date at which for the State concerned this Convention comes into force.

Article XXIV. REVISION

1. After the expiry of a period of five years from the date of entry into force of this Convention, any Contracting State may at any time make a request for the revision of part or the whole of this Convention by notification in writing addressed to the Administrative Secretary–General of the Organization of African Unity.

2. In the event of such a request the appropriate organ of the Organization of African Unity shall deal with the matter in accordance with the provision of sections 3 and 4 of Article XVI of this Convention.

3. (i) At the request of one or more Contracting States and notwithstanding the provisions of paragraphs (1) and (2) of this Article, the annex to this Convention may be revised or added to by the appropriate organ of the Organization of African Unity.

(ii) Such revision or addition shall come into force three months after the approval by the appropriate organ of the Organization of African Unity.

Article XXV. FINAL PROVISIONS

The original of this Convention of which both the English and the French texts are authentic, shall be deposited with the Administrative Secretary–General of the Organization of African Unity.

LIST OF PROTECTED SPECIES

* * *

5.3 CONVENTION ON WETLANDS OF INTERNATIONAL IMPORTANCE ESPECIALLY AS WATER-FOWL HABITAT (AS AMENDED).[b] **Concluded at Ramsar, 2 February 1971. Entered into force, 21 December 1975. 996 UNTS 245;** *reprinted in* **11 ILM 969 (1972) & 5A Weston & Carlson V.F.33**

The Contracting Parties

Recognizing the interdependence of Man and his environment;

Considering the fundamental ecological functions of wetlands as regulators of water regimes and as habitats supporting a characteristic flora and fauna, especially waterfowl;

Being Convinced that wetlands constitute a resource of great economic, cultural, scientific, and recreational value, the loss of which would be irreparable;

Desiring to stem the progressive encroachment on and loss of wetlands now and in the future;

Recognizing that waterfowl in their seasonal migrations may transcend frontiers and so should be regarded as an international resource;

Being Confident that the conservation of wetlands and their flora and fauna can be ensured by combining far-sighted national policies with co-ordinated international action;

Have agreed as follows:

Article 1

1. For the purpose of this Convention wetlands are areas of marsh, fen, peatland or water, whether natural or artificial, permanent or temporary, with water that is static or flowing, fresh, brackish or salt, including areas of marine water the depth of which at low tide does not exceed six metres.

2. For the purpose of this Convention waterfowl are birds ecologically dependent on wetlands.

Article 2

1. Each Contracting Party shall designate suitable wetlands within its territory for inclusion in a List of Wetlands of International Importance, hereinafter referred to as "the List" which is maintained by the bureau established under Article 8. The boundaries of each wetland shall be precisely described and also delimited on a map and they may incorporate riparian and coastal zones adjacent to the wetlands, and islands or bodies of marine water deeper than six metres at low tide lying within the wetlands, especially where these have importance as waterfowl habitat.

2. Wetlands should be selected for the List on account of their international significance in terms of ecology, botany, zoology, limnology or hydrology. In the first instance wetlands of international importance to waterfowl at any season should be included.

3. The inclusion of a wetland in the List does not prejudice the exclusive sovereign rights of the Contracting Party in whose territory the wetland is situated.

4. Each Contracting Party shall designate at least one wetland to be included in the List when signing this Convention or when depositing its instrument of ratification or accession, as provided in Article 9.

b. This Convention was amended by the Paris Protocol, concluded 3 December 1982 and entered into force 1 October 1986 (22 ILM 698), and by the Regina Amendments to Arti-cles 6 and 7, adopted 28 May 1987, and entered into force on 1 May 1994 (1990 Misc 6, Cm 983).

5.   Any Contracting Party shall have the right to add to the List further wetlands situated within its territory, to extend the boundaries of those wetlands already included by it in the List, or, because of its urgent national interests, to delete or restrict the boundaries of wetlands already included by it in the List and shall, at the earliest possible time, inform the organization or government responsible for the continuing bureau duties specified in Article 8 of any such changes.

6.   Each Contracting Party shall consider its international responsibilities for the conservation, management and wise use of migratory stocks of waterfowl, both when designating entries for the List and when exercising its right to change entries in the List relating to wetlands within its territory.

Article 3

1.   The Contracting Parties shall formulate and implement their planning so as to promote the conservation of the wetlands included in the List, and as far as possible the wise use of wetlands in their territory.

2.   Each Contracting Party shall arrange to be informed at the earliest possible time if the ecological character of any wetland in its territory and included in the List has changed, is changing or is likely to change as the result of technological developments, pollution or other human interference. Information on such changes shall be passed without delay to the organization or government responsible for the continuing bureau duties specified in Article 8.

Article 4

1.   Each Contracting Party shall promote the conservation of wetlands and waterfowl by establishing nature reserves on wetlands, whether they are included in the List or not, and provide adequately for their wardening.

2.   Where a Contracting Party in its urgent national interest, deletes or restricts the boundaries of a wetland included in the List, it should as far as possible compensate for any loss of wetland resources, and in particular it should create additional nature reserves for waterfowl and for the protection, either in the same area or elsewhere, of an adequate portion of the original habitat.

3.   The Contracting Parties shall encourage research and the exchange of data and publications regarding wetlands and their flora and fauna.

4.   The Contracting Parties shall endeavour through management to increase waterfowl populations on appropriate wetlands.

5.   The Contracting Parties shall promote the training of personnel competent in the fields of wetland research, management and wardening.

Article 5

1.   The Contracting Parties shall consult with each other about implementing obligations arising from the Convention especially in the case of a wetland extending over the territories of more than one Contracting Party or where a water system is shared by Contracting Parties. They shall at the same time endeavour to coordinate and support present and future policies and regulations concerning the conservation of wetlands and their flora and fauna.

Article 6

1.   There shall be established a Conference of the Contracting Parties to review and promote the implementation of this Convention. The Bureau referred to in Article 8, paragraph 1, shall convene ordinary meetings of the Conference of the Contracting Parties at intervals of not more than three years, unless the Conference decides otherwise, and extraordinary meetings at the written requests of at least one third of

the Contracting Parties. Each ordinary meeting of the Conference of the Contracting Parties shall determine the time and venue of the next ordinary meeting.

2. The Conference of the Contracting Parties shall be competent:

a) to discuss the implementation of this Convention;

b) to discuss additions to and changes in the List;

c) to consider information regarding changes in the ecological character of wetlands included in the List provided in accordance with paragraph 2 of Article 3;

d) to make general or specific recommendations to the Contracting Parties regarding the conservation, management and wise use of wetlands and their flora and fauna;

e) to request relevant international bodies to prepare reports and statistics on matters which are essentially international in character affecting wetlands;

f) to adopt other recommendations, or resolutions, to promote the functioning of this Convention.

3. The Contracting Parties shall ensure that those responsible at all levels for wetlands management shall be informed of, and take into consideration, recommendations of such Conferences concerning the conservation, management and wise use of wetlands and their flora and fauna.

4. The Conference of the Contracting Parties shall adopt rules of procedure for each of its meetings.

5. The Conference of the Contracting Parties shall establish and keep under review the financial regulations of this Convention. At each of its ordinary meetings, it shall adopt the budget for the next financial period by a two-third majority of Contracting Parties present and voting.

6. Each Contracting Party shall contribute to the budget according to a scale of contributions adopted by unanimity of the Contracting Parties present and voting at a meeting of the ordinary Conference of the Contracting Parties.

Article 7

1. The representatives of the Contracting Parties at such Conferences should include persons who are experts on wetlands or waterfowl by reason of knowledge and experience gained in scientific, administrative or other appropriate capacities.

2. Each of the Contracting Parties represented at a Conference shall have one vote, recommendations, resolutions and decisions being adopted by a simple majority of the Contracting Parties present and voting, unless otherwise provided for in this Convention.

Article 8

1. The International Union for Conservation of Nature and Natural Resources shall perform the continuing bureau duties under this Convention until such time as another organization or government is appointed by a majority of two-thirds of all Contracting Parties.

2. The continuing bureau duties shall be, inter alia:

a) to assist in the convening and organizing of Conferences specified in Article 6;

b) to maintain the List of Wetlands of International Importance and to be informed by the Contracting Parties of any additions, extensions, deletions or restrictions concerning wetlands included in the List provided in accordance with paragraph 5 of Article 2;

c) to be informed by the Contracting Parties of any changes in the ecological character of wetlands included in the List provided in accordance with paragraph 2 of Article 3;

d) to forward notification of any alterations to the List, or changes in character of wetlands included therein, to all Contracting Parties and to arrange for these matters to be discussed at the next Conference;

e) to make known to the Contracting Party concerned, the recommendations of the Conferences in respect of such alterations to the List or of changes in the character of wetlands included therein.

Article 9

1. This Convention shall remain open for signature indefinitely.

2. Any member of the United Nations or of one of the Specialized Agencies or of the International Atomic Energy Agency or Party to the Statute of the International Court of Justice may become a Party to this Convention by:

(a) signature without reservation as to ratification;

(b) signature subject to ratification followed by ratification;

(c) accession.

3. Ratification or accession shall be effected by the deposit of an instrument of ratification or accession with the Director–General of the United Nations Educational, Scientific and Cultural Organization (hereinafter referred to as "the Depositary").

Article 10

1. This Convention shall enter into force four months after seven States have become Parties to this Convention in accordance with paragraph 2 of Article 9.

2. Thereafter this Convention shall enter into force for each Contracting Party four months after the day of its signature without reservation as to ratification, or its deposit of an instrument of ratification or accession.

Article 10 bis

1. This Convention may be amended at a meeting of the Contracting Parties convened for that purpose in accordance with this article.

2. Proposals for amendment may be made by any Contracting Party.

3. The text of any proposed amendment and the reasons for it shall be communicated to the organization or government performing the continuing bureau duties under the Convention (hereinafter referred to as "the Bureau") and shall promptly be communicated by the Bureau to all Contracting Parties. Any comments on the text by the Contracting Parties shall be communicated to the Bureau within three months of the date on which the amendments were communicated to the Contracting Parties by the Bureau. The Bureau shall, immediately after the last day for submission of comments, communicate to the Contracting Parties all comments submitted by that day.

4. A meeting of Contracting Parties to consider an amendment communicated in accordance with paragraph 3 shall be convened by the Bureau upon the written request of one third of the Contracting Parties. The Bureau shall consult the Parties concerning the time and venue of the meeting.

5. Amendments shall be adopted by a two-thirds majority of the Contracting Parties present and voting.

6. An amendment adopted shall enter into force for the Contracting Parties which have accepted it on the first day of the fourth month following the date on

which two thirds of the Contracting Parties have deposited an instrument of acceptance with the Depositary. For each Contracting Party which deposits an instrument of acceptance after the date on which two thirds of the Contracting Parties have deposited an instrument of acceptance, the amendment shall enter into force on the first day of the fourth month following the date of the deposit of its instrument of acceptance.

Article 11

1. This Convention shall continue in force for an indefinite period.

2. Any Contracting Party may denounce this Convention after a period of five years from the date on which it entered into force for that party by giving written notice thereof to the Depositary. Denunciation shall take effect four months after the day on which notice thereof is received by the Depositary.

Article 12

1. The Depositary shall inform all States that have signed and acceded to this Convention as soon as possible of:

(a) signatures to the Convention;

(b) deposits of instruments of ratification of this Convention;

(c) deposits of instruments of accession to this Convention;

(d) the date of entry into force of this Convention;

(e) notifications of denunciation of this Convention.

2. When this Convention has entered into force, the Depositary shall have it registered with the Secretariat of the United Nations in accordance with Article 102 of the Charter.

IN WITNESS WHEREOF, the undersigned, being duly authorized to that effect, have signed this Convention.

DONE at Ramsar this 2nd day of February 1971, in a single original in the English, French, German and Russian languages, all texts being equally authentic* which shall be deposited with the Depositary which shall send true copies thereof to all Contracting Parties.

5.4 Convention on International Trade in Endangered Species of Wild Fauna and Flora (Cites) (With Appendices and as Amended). Concluded at Washington, 3 March 1973. Entered into force, 1 July 1975. 993 UNTS 243, 27 UST 1087, TIAS No 8249, *reprinted in* 12 ILM 1085 (1973) & 5A Weston & Carlson V.H.10

The Contracting States,

RECOGNIZING that wild fauna and flora in their many beautiful and varied forms are an irreplaceable part of the natural systems of the earth which must be protected for this and the generations to come;

CONSCIOUS of the ever-growing value of wild fauna and flora from aesthetic, scientific, cultural, recreational and economic points of view;

RECOGNIZING that peoples and States are and should be the best protectors of their own wild fauna and flora;

RECOGNIZING, in addition, that international cooperation is essential for the protection of certain species of wild fauna and flora against over-exploitation through international trade;

CONVINCED of the urgency of taking appropriate measures to this end;

HAVE AGREED as follows:

Article I
Definitions

For the purpose of the present Convention, unless the context otherwise requires:

(a) "Species" means any species, sub-species, or geographically separate population thereof;

(b) "Specimen" means:

(i) any animal or plant, whether alive or dead;

(ii) in the case of an animal: for species included in Appendices I and II, any readily recognizable part or derivative thereof; and for species included in Appendix III, any readily recognizable part or derivative thereof specified in Appendix III in relation to the species; and

(iii) in the case of a plant: for species included in Appendix I, any readily recognizable part or derivative thereof; and for species included in Appendices II and III, any readily recognizable part or derivative thereof specified in Appendices II and III in relation to the species;

(c) "Trade" means export, re-export, import and introduction from the sea;

(d) "Re-export" means export of any specimen that has previously been imported;

(e) "Introduction from the sea" means transportation into a State of specimens of any species which were taken in the marine environment not under the jurisdiction of any State;

(f) "Scientific Authority" means a national scientific authority designated in accordance with Article IX;

(g) "Management Authority" means a national management authority designated in accordance with Article IX;

(h) "Party" means a State for which the present Convention has entered into force.

Article II
Fundamental Principles

1. Appendix I shall include all species threatened with extinction which are or may be affected by trade. Trade in specimens of these species must be subject to particularly strict regulation in order not to endanger further their survival and must only be authorized in exceptional circumstances.

2. Appendix II shall include:

(a) all species which although not necessarily now threatened with extinction may become so unless trade in specimens of such species is subject to strict regulation in order to avoid utilization incompatible with their survival; and

(b) other species which must be subject to regulation in order that trade in specimens of certain species referred to in sub-paragraph (a) of this paragraph may be brought under effective control.

3. Appendix III shall include all species which any Party identifies as being subject to regulation within its jurisdiction for the purpose of preventing or restricting exploitation, and as needing the cooperation of other parties in the control of trade.

4. The Parties shall not allow trade in specimens of species included in Appendices I, II and III except in accordance with the provisions of the present Convention.

Article III
Regulation of Trade in Specimens of Species included in Appendix I

1. All trade in specimens of species included in Appendix I shall be in accordance with the provisions of this Article.

2. The export of any specimen of a species included in Appendix I shall require the prior grant and presentation of an export permit. An export permit shall only be granted when the following conditions have been met:

(a) a Scientific Authority of the State of export has advised that such export will not be detrimental to the survival of that species;

(b) a Management Authority of the State of export is satisfied that the specimen was not obtained in contravention of the laws of that State for the protection of fauna and flora;

(c) a Management Authority of the State of export is satisfied that any living specimen will be so prepared and shipped as to minimize the risk of injury, damage to health or cruel treatment; and

(d) a Management Authority of the State of export is satisfied that an import permit has been granted for the specimen.

3. The import of any specimen of a species included in Appendix I shall require the prior grant and presentation of an import permit and either an export permit or a re-export certificate. An import permit shall only be granted when the following conditions have been met:

(a) a Scientific Authority of the State of import has advised that the import will be for purposes which are not detrimental to the survival of the species involved;

(b) a Scientific Authority of the State of import is satisfied that the proposed recipient of a living specimen is suitably equipped to house and care for it; and

(c) a Management Authority of the State of import is satisfied that the specimen is not to be used for primarily commercial purposes.

4. The re-export of any specimen of a species included in Appendix I shall require the prior grant and presentation of a re-export certificate. A re-export certificate shall only be granted when the following conditions have been met:

(a) a Management Authority of the State of re-export is satisfied that the specimen was imported into that State in accordance with the provisions of the present Convention;

(b) a Management Authority of the State of re-export is satisfied that any living specimen will be so prepared and shipped as to minimize the risk of injury, damage to health or cruel treatment; and

(c) a Management Authority of the State of re-export is satisfied that an import permit has been granted for any living specimen.

5. The introduction from the sea of any specimen of a species included in Appendix I shall require the prior grant of a certificate from a Management Authority of the State of introduction. A certificate shall only be granted when the following conditions have been met:

(a) a Scientific Authority of the State of introduction advises that the introduction will not be detrimental to the survival of the species involved;

(b) a Management Authority of the State of introduction is satisfied that the proposed recipient of a living specimen is suitably equipped to house and care for it; and

(c) a Management Authority of the State of introduction is satisfied that the specimen is not to be used for primarily commercial purposes.

Article IV
Regulation of Trade in Specimens of Species included in Appendix II

1. All trade in specimens of species included in Appendix II shall be in accordance with the provisions of this Article.

2. The export of any specimen of a species included in Appendix II shall require the prior grant and presentation of an export permit. An export permit shall only be granted when the following conditions have been met:

(a) a Scientific Authority of the State of export has advised that such export will not be detrimental to the survival of that species;

(b) a Management Authority of the State of export is satisfied that the specimen was not obtained in contravention of the laws of that State for the protection of fauna and flora; and

(c) a Management Authority of the State of export is satisfied that any living specimen will be so prepared and shipped as to minimize the risk of injury, damage to health or cruel treatment.

3. A Scientific Authority in each Party shall monitor both the export permits granted by that State for specimens of species included in Appendix II and the actual exports of such specimens. Whenever a Scientific Authority determines that the export of specimens of any such species should be limited in order to maintain that species throughout its range at a level consistent with its role in the ecosystems in which it occurs and well above the level at which that species might become eligible for inclusion in Appendix I, the Scientific Authority shall advise the appropriate Management Authority of suitable measures to be taken to limit the grant of export permits for specimens of that species.

4. The import of any specimen of a species included in Appendix II shall require the prior presentation of either an export permit or a re-export certificate.

5. The re-export of any specimen of a species included in Appendix II shall require the prior grant and presentation of a re-export certificate. A re-export certificate shall only be granted when the following conditions have been met:

(a) a Management Authority of the State of re-export is satisfied that the specimen was imported into that State in accordance with the provisions of the present Convention; and

(b) a Management Authority of the State of re-export is satisfied that any living specimen will be so prepared and shipped as to minimize the risk of injury, damage to health or cruel treatment.

6. The introduction from the sea of any specimen of a species included in Appendix II shall require the prior grant of a certificate from a Management Authority of the State of introduction. A certificate shall only be granted when the following conditions have been met:

(a) a Scientific Authority of the State of introduction advises that the introduction will not be detrimental to the survival of the species involved; and

(b) a Management Authority of the State of introduction is satisfied that any living specimen will be so handled as to minimize the risk of injury, damage to health or cruel treatment.

7. Certificates referred to in paragraph 6 of this Article may be granted on the advice of a Scientific Authority, in consultation with other national scientific authorities or, when appropriate, international scientific authorities, in respect of periods not exceeding one year for total numbers of specimens to be introduced in such periods.

Article V
Regulation of Trade in Specimens of Species included in Appendix III

1. All trade in specimens of species included in Appendix III shall be in accordance with the provisions of this Article.

2. The export of any specimen of a species included in Appendix III from any State which has included that species in Appendix III shall require the prior grant and presentation of an export permit. An export permit shall only be granted when the following conditions have been met:

(a) a Management Authority of the State of export is satisfied that the specimen was not obtained in contravention of the laws of that State for the protection of fauna and flora; and

(b) a Management Authority of the State of export is satisfied that any living specimen will be so prepared and shipped as to minimize the risk of injury, damage to health or cruel treatment.

3. The import of any specimen of a species included in Appendix III shall require, except in circumstances to which paragraph 4 of this Article applies, the prior presentation of a certificate of origin and, where the import is from a State which has included that species in Appendix III, an export permit.

4. In the case of re-export, a certificate granted by the Management Authority of the State of re-export that the specimen was processed in that State or is being re-exported shall be accepted by the State of import as evidence that the provisions of the present Convention have been complied with in respect of the specimen concerned.

Article VI
Permits and Certificates

1. Permits and certificates granted under the provisions of Articles III, IV, and V shall be in accordance with the provisions of this Article.

2. An export permit shall contain the information specified in the model set forth in Appendix IV, and may only be used for export within a period of six months from the date on which it was granted.

3. Each permit or certificate shall contain the title of the present Convention, the name and any identifying stamp of the Management Authority granting it and a control number assigned by the Management Authority.

4. Any copies of a permit or certificate issued by a Management Authority shall be clearly marked as copies only and no such copy may be used in place of the original, except to the extent endorsed thereon.

5. A separate permit or certificate shall be required for each consignment of specimens.

6. A Management Authority of the State of import of any specimen shall cancel and retain the export permit or re-export certificate and any corresponding import permit presented in respect of the import of that specimen.

7. Where appropriate and feasible a Management Authority may affix a mark upon any specimen to assist in identifying the specimen. For these purposes "mark" means any indelible imprint, lead seal or other suitable means of identifying a specimen, designed in such a way as to render its imitation by unauthorized persons as difficult as possible.

Article VII
Exemptions and Other Special Provisions Relating to Trade

1. The provisions of Articles III, IV and V shall not apply to the transit or transshipment of specimens through or in the territory of a Party while the specimens remain in Customs control.

2. Where a Management Authority of the State of export or re-export is satisfied that a specimen was acquired before the provisions of the present Convention applied to that specimen, the provisions of Articles III, IV and V shall not apply to that specimen where the Management Authority issues a certificate to that effect.

3. The provisions of Articles III, IV and V shall not apply to specimens that are personal or household effects. This exemption shall not apply where:

(a) in the case of specimens of a species included in Appendix I, they were acquired by the owner outside his State of usual residence, and are being imported into that State; or

(b) in the case of specimens of species included in Appendix II:

(i) they were acquired by the owner outside his State of usual residence and in a State where removal from the wild occurred;

(ii) they are being imported into the owner's State of usual residence; and

(iii) the State where removal from the wild occurred requires the prior grant of export permits before any export of such specimens;

unless a Management Authority is satisfied that the specimens were acquired before the provisions of the present Convention applied to such specimens.

4. Specimens of an animal species included in Appendix I bred in captivity for commercial purposes, or of a plant species included in Appendix I artificially propagated for commercial purposes, shall be deemed to be specimens of species included in Appendix II.

5. Where a Management Authority of the State of export is satisfied that any specimen of an animal species was bred in captivity or any specimen of a plant species was artificially propagated, or is a part of such an animal or plant or was derived therefrom, a certificate by that Management Authority to that effect shall be accepted in lieu of any of the permits or certificates required under the provisions of Articles III, IV or V.

6. The provisions of Articles III, IV and V shall not apply to the non-commercial loan, donation or exchange between scientists or scientific institutions registered by a Management Authority of their State, of herbarium specimens, other preserved, dried or embedded museum specimens, and live plant material which carry a label issued or approved by a Management Authority.

7. A Management Authority of any State may waive the requirements of Articles III, IV and V and allow the movement without permits or certificates of specimens which form part of a travelling zoo, circus, menagerie, plant exhibition or other travelling exhibition provided that:

(a) the exporter or importer registers full details of such specimens with that Management Authority;

(b) the specimens are in either of the categories specified in paragraphs 2 or 5 of this Article; and

(c) the Management Authority is satisfied that any living specimen will be so transported and cared for as to minimize the risk of injury, damage to health or cruel treatment.

Article VIII
Measures to be Taken by the Parties

1. The Parties shall take appropriate measures to enforce the provisions of the present Convention and to prohibit trade in specimens in violation thereof. These shall include measures:

(a) to penalize trade in, or possession of, such specimens, or both; and

(b) to provide for the confiscation or return to the State of export of such specimens.

2. In addition to the measures taken under paragraph 1 of this Article a Party may, when it deems it necessary, provide for any method of internal reimbursement for expenses incurred as a result of the confiscation of a specimen traded in violation of the measures taken in the application of the provisions of the present Convention.

3. As far as possible, the Parties shall ensure that specimens shall pass through any formalities required for trade with a minimum of delay. To facilitate such passage, a Party may designate ports of exit and ports of entry at which specimens must be presented for clearance. The Parties shall ensure further that all living specimens, during any period of transit, holding or shipment, are properly cared for so as to minimize the risk of injury, damage to health or cruel treatment.

4. Where a living specimen is confiscated as a result of measures referred to in paragraph 1 of this Article:

(a) the specimen shall be entrusted to a Management Authority of the State of confiscation;

(b) the Management Authority shall, after consultation with the State of export, return the specimen to that State at the expense of that State, or to a rescue centre or such other place as the Management Authority deems appropriate and consistent with the purposes of the present Convention; and

(c) the Management Authority may obtain the advice of a Scientific Authority, or may, whenever it considers it desirable, consult the Secretariat in order to facilitate the decision under sub-paragraph (b) of this paragraph, including the choice of a rescue centre or other place.

5. A rescue centre as referred to in paragraph 4 of this Article means an institution designated by a Management Authority to look after the welfare of living specimens, particularly those that have been confiscated.

6. Each Party shall maintain records of trade in specimens of species included in Appendices I, II and III which shall cover:

(a) the names and addresses of exporters and importers; and

(b) the number and type of permits and certificates granted; the States with which such trade occurred; the numbers or quantities and types of specimens, names of species as included in Appendices I, II and III and, where applicable, the size and sex of the specimens in question.

7. Each Party shall prepare periodic reports on its implementation of the present Convention and shall transmit to the Secretariat:

(a) an annual report containing a summary of the information specified in sub-paragraph (b) of paragraph 6 of this Article; and

(b) a biennial report on legislative, regulatory and administrative measures taken to enforce the provisions of the present Convention.

8. The information referred to in paragraph 7 of this Article shall be available to the public where this is not inconsistent with the law of the Party concerned.

Article IX
Management and Scientific Authorities

1. Each Party shall designate for the purposes of the present Convention:

(a) one or more Management Authorities competent to grant permits or certificates on behalf of that Party; and

(b) one or more Scientific Authorities.

2. A State depositing an instrument of ratification, acceptance, approval or accession shall at that time inform the Depositary Government of the name and address of the Management Authority authorized to communicate with other Parties and with the Secretariat.

3. Any changes in the designations or authorizations under the provisions of this Article shall be communicated by the Party concerned to the Secretariat for transmission to all other Parties.

4. Any Management Authority referred to in paragraph 2 of this Article shall if so requested by the Secretariat or the Management Authority of another Party, communicate to it impression of stamps, seals or other devices used to authenticate permits or certificates.

Article X
Trade with States not Party to the Convention

Where export or re-export is to, or import is from, a State not a Party to the present Convention, comparable documentation issued by the competent authorities in that State which substantially conforms with the requirements of the present Convention for permits and certificates may be accepted in lieu thereof by any Party.

Article XI
Conference of the Parties

1. The Secretariat shall call a meeting of the Conference of the Parties not later than two years after the entry into force of the present Convention.

2. Thereafter the Secretariat shall convene regular meetings at least once every two years, unless the Conference decides otherwise, and extraordinary meetings at any time on the written request of at least one-third of the Parties.

3. At meetings, whether regular or extraordinary, the Parties shall review the implementation of the present Convention and may:

(a) make such provision as may be necessary to enable the Secretariat to carry out its duties *and adopt financial provisions*;[c]

(b) consider and adopt amendments to Appendices I and II in accordance with Article XV;

(c) review the progress made towards the restoration and conservation of the species included in Appendices I, II and III;

(d) receive and consider any reports presented by the Secretariat or by any Party; and

(e) where appropriate, make recommendations for improving the effectiveness of the present Convention.

4. At each regular meeting, the Parties may determine the time and venue of the next regular meeting to be held in accordance with the provisions of paragraph 2 of this Article.

5. At any meeting, the Parties may determine and adopt rules of procedure for the meeting.

6. The United Nations, its Specialized Agencies and the International Atomic Energy Agency, as well as any State not a Party to the present Convention, may be represented at meetings of the Conference by observers, who shall have the right to participate but not to vote.

7. Any body or agency technically qualified in protection, conservation or management of wild fauna and flora, in the following categories, which has informed the Secretariat of its desire to be represented at meetings of the Conference by observers, shall be admitted unless at least one-third of the Parties present object:

(a) international agencies or bodies, either governmental or non-governmental, and national governmental agencies and bodies; and

(b) national non-governmental agencies or bodies which have been approved for this purpose by the State in which they are located. Once admitted, these observers shall have the right to participate but not to vote.

Article XII
The Secretariat

1. Upon entry into force of the present Convention, a Secretariat shall be provided by the Executive Director of the United Nations Environment Programme. To the extent and in the manner he considers appropriate, he may be assisted by suitable inter-governmental or non-governmental international or national agencies and bodies technically qualified in protection, conservation and management of wild fauna and flora.

2. The functions of the Secretariat shall be:

(a) to arrange for and service meetings of the Parties;

(b) to perform the functions entrusted to it under the provisions of Articles XV and XVI of the present Convention;

(c) to undertake scientific and technical studies in accordance with programmes authorized by the Conference of the parties as will contribute to the implementation of the present Convention, including studies concerning standards for appropriate preparation and shipment of living specimens and the means of identifying specimens;

---

c. The italicized language was added by the Bonn Amendment, which was adopted on June 22, 1979 and entered into force on April 13, 1987. 141 of the 175 members of CITES are parties to the Bonn Amendment.

(d) to study the reports of Parties and to request from Parties such further information with respect thereto as it deems necessary to ensure implementation of the present Convention;

(e) to invite the attention of the Parties to any matter pertaining to the aims of the present Convention;

(f) to publish periodically and distribute to the Parties current editions of Appendices I, II and III together with any information which will facilitate identification of specimens of species included in those Appendices;

(g) to prepare annual reports to the Parties on its work and on the implementation of the present Convention and such other reports as meetings of the Parties may request;

(h) to make recommendations for the implementation of the aims and provisions of the present Convention, including the exchange of information of a scientific or technical nature;

(i) to perform any other function as may be entrusted to it by the Parties.

Article XIII
International Measures

1. When the Secretariat in the light of information received is satisfied that any species included in Appendices I or II is being affected adversely by trade in specimens of that species or that the provisions of the present Convention are not being effectively implemented, it shall communicate such information to the authorized Management Authority of the Party or Parties concerned.

2. When any Party receives a communication as indicated in paragraph 1 of this Article, it shall, as soon as possible, inform the Secretariat of any relevant facts insofar as its laws permit and, where appropriate, propose remedial action. Where the Party considers that an inquiry is desirable, such inquiry may be carried out by one or more persons expressly authorized by the Party.

3. The information provided by the Party or resulting from any inquiry as specified in paragraph 2 of this Article shall be reviewed by the next Conference of the Parties which may make whatever recommendations it deems appropriate.

Article XIV
Effect on Domestic Legislation and International Conventions

1. The provisions of the present Convention shall in no way affect the right of Parties to adopt:

(a) stricter domestic measures regarding the conditions for trade, taking, possession or transport of specimens of species included in Appendices I, II and III, or the complete prohibition thereof; or

(b) domestic measures restricting or prohibiting trade, taking, possession, or transport of species not included in Appendices I, II or III.

2. The provisions of the present Convention shall in no way affect the provisions of any domestic measures or the obligations of Parties deriving from any treaty, convention, or international agreement relating to other aspects of trade, taking, possession, or transport of specimens which is in force or subsequently may enter into force for any Party including any measure pertaining to the Customs, public health, veterinary or plant quarantine fields.

3. The provisions of the present Convention shall in no way affect the provisions of, or the obligations deriving from, any treaty, convention or international agreement concluded or which may be concluded between States creating a union or regional trade agreement establishing or maintaining a common external customs control and

removing customs control between the parties thereto insofar as they relate to trade among the States members of that union or agreement.

4. A State Party to the present Convention, which is also a Party to any other treaty, convention or international agreement which is in force at the time of the coming into force of the present Convention and under the provisions of which protection is afforded to marine species included in Appendix II, shall be relieved of the obligations imposed on it under the provisions of the present Convention with respect to trade in specimens of species included in Appendix II that are taken by ships registered in that State and in accordance with the provisions of such other treaty, convention or international agreement.

5. Notwithstanding the provisions of Articles III, IV and V, any export of a specimen taken in accordance with paragraph 4 of this Article shall only require a certificate from a Management Authority of the State of introduction to the effect that the specimen was taken in accordance with the provisions of the other treaty, convention or international agreement in question.

6. Nothing in the present Convention shall prejudice the codification and development of the law of the sea by the United Nations Conference on the Law of the Sea convened pursuant to Resolution 2750 C(XXV) of the General Assembly of the United Nations nor the present or future claims and legal views of any State concerning the law of the sea and the nature and extent of coastal and flag State jurisdiction.

Article XV
Amendments to Appendices I and II

1. The following provisions shall apply in relation to amendments to Appendices I and II at meetings of the Conference of the Parties:

(a) Any Party may propose an amendment to Appendix I or II for consideration at the next meeting. The text of the proposed amendment shall be communicated to the Secretariat at least 150 days before the meeting. The Secretariat shall consult the other Parties and interested bodies on the amendment in accordance with the provisions of sub-paragraphs (b) and (c) of paragraph 2 of this Article and shall communicate the response to all Parties not later than 30 days before the meeting.

(b) Amendments shall be adopted by a two-thirds majority of Parties present and voting. For these purposes "Parties present and voting" means Parties present and casting an affirmative or negative vote. Parties abstaining from voting shall not be counted among the two-thirds required for adopting an amendment.

(c) Amendments adopted at a meeting shall enter into force 90 days after that meeting for all Parties except those which make a reservation in accordance with paragraph 3 of this Article.

2. The following provisions shall apply in relation to amendments to Appendices I and II between meetings of the Conference of the Parties:

(a) Any Party may propose an amendment to Appendix I or II for consideration between meetings by the postal procedures set forth in this paragraph.

(b) For marine species, the Secretariat shall, upon receiving the text of the proposed amendment, immediately communicate it to the Parties. It shall also consult inter-governmental bodies having a function in relation to those species especially with a view to obtaining scientific data these bodies may be able to provide and to ensuring co-ordination with any conservation measures enforced by such bodies. The Secretariat shall communicate the views expressed and data provided by these bodies and its own findings and recommendations to the Parties as soon as possible.

(c) For species other than marine species, the Secretariat shall, upon receiving the text of the proposed amendment, immediately communicate it to the Parties, and, as soon as possible thereafter, its own recommendations.

(d) Any Party may, within 60 days of the date on which the Secretariat communicated its recommendations to the Parties under sub-paragraphs (b) or (c) of this paragraph, transmit to the Secretariat any comments on the proposed amendment together with any relevant scientific data and information.

(e) The Secretariat shall communicate the replies received together with its own recommendations to the Parties as soon as possible.

(f) If no objection to the proposed amendment is received by the Secretariat within 30 days of the date the replies and recommendations were communicated under the provisions of sub-paragraph (e) of this paragraph, the amendment shall enter into force 90 days later for all Parties except those which make a reservation in accordance with paragraph 3 of this Article.

(g) If an objection by any Party is received by the Secretariat, the proposed amendment shall be submitted to a postal vote in accordance with the provisions of sub-paragraphs (h), (i) and (j) of this paragraph.

(h) The Secretariat shall notify the Parties that notification of objection has been received.

(i) Unless the Secretariat receives the votes for, against or in abstention from at least one-half of the Parties within 60 days of the date of notification under sub-paragraph (h) of this paragraph, the proposed amendment shall be referred to the next meeting of the Conference for further consideration.

(j) Provided that votes are received from one-half of the Parties, the amendment shall be adopted by a two-thirds majority of Parties casting an affirmative or negative vote.

(k) The Secretariat shall notify all Parties of the result of the vote.

(l) If the proposed amendment is adopted it shall enter into force 90 days after the date of the notification by the Secretariat of its acceptance for all Parties except those which make a reservation in accordance with paragraph 3 of this Article.

3.   During the period of 90 days provided for by sub-paragraph (c) of paragraph 1 or sub-paragraph (l) of paragraph 2 of this Article any Party may by notification in writing to the Depositary Government make a reservation with respect to the amendment. Until such reservation is withdrawn the Party shall be treated as a State not a Party to the present Convention with respect to trade in the species concerned.

Article XVI
Appendix III and Amendments thereto

1.   Any Party may at any time submit to the Secretariat a list of species which it identifies as being subject to regulation within its jurisdiction for the purpose mentioned in paragraph 3 of Article II. Appendix III shall include the names of the Parties submitting the species for inclusion therein, the scientific names of the species so submitted, and any parts or derivatives of the animals or plants concerned that are specified in relation to the species for the purposes of sub-paragraph (b) of Article I.

2.   Each list submitted under the provisions of paragraph 1 of this Article shall be communicated to the Parties by the Secretariat as soon as possible after receiving it. The list shall take effect as part of Appendix III 90 days after the date of such communication. At any time after the communication of such list, any Party may by notification in writing to the Depositary Government enter a reservation with respect to any species or any parts or derivatives, and until such reservation is withdrawn, the

State shall be treated as a State not a Party to the present Convention with respect to trade in the species or part or derivative concerned.

3.   A Party which has submitted a species for inclusion in Appendix III may withdraw it at any time by notification to the Secretariat which shall communicate the withdrawal to all Parties. The withdrawal shall take effect 30 days after the date of such communication.

4.   Any Party submitting a list under the provisions of paragraph 1 of this Article shall submit to the Secretariat a copy of all domestic laws and regulations applicable to the protection of such species, together with any interpretations which the Party may deem appropriate or the Secretariat may request. The Party shall, for as long as the species in question is included in Appendix III, submit any amendments of such laws and regulations or any new interpretations as they are adopted.

Article XVII
Amendment of the Convention

1.   An extraordinary meeting of the Conference of the Parties shall be convened by the Secretariat on the written request of at least one-third of the Parties to consider and adopt amendments to the present Convention. Such amendments shall be adopted by a two-thirds majority of Parties present and voting. For these purposes "Parties present and voting" means Parties present and casting an affirmative or negative vote. Parties abstaining from voting shall not be counted among the two-thirds required for adopting an amendment.

2.   The text of any proposed amendment shall be communicated by the Secretariat to all Parties at least 90 days before the meeting.

3.   An amendment shall enter into force for the Parties which have accepted it 60 days after two-thirds of the Parties have deposited an instrument of acceptance of the amendment with the Depositary Government. Thereafter, the amendment shall enter into force for any other Party 60 days after that Party deposits its instrument of acceptance of the amendment.

Article XVIII
Resolution of Disputes

1.   Any dispute which may arise between two or more Parties with respect to the interpretation or application of the provisions of the present Convention shall be subject to negotiation between the Parties involved in the dispute.

2.   If the dispute cannot be resolved in accordance with paragraph 1 of this Article, the Parties may, by mutual consent, submit the dispute to arbitration, in particular that of the Permanent Court of Arbitration at The Hague, and the Parties submitting the dispute shall be bound by the arbitral decision.

Article XIX
Signature

The present Convention shall be open for signature at Washington until 30th April 1973 and thereafter at Berne until 31st December 1974.

Article XX
Ratification, Acceptance, Approval

The present Convention shall be subject to ratification, acceptance or approval. Instruments of ratification, acceptance or approval shall be deposited with the Government of the Swiss Confederation which shall be the Depositary Government.

Article XXI
Accession

The present Convention shall be open indefinitely for accession. Instruments of accession shall be deposited with the Depositary Government.[d]

Article XXII
Entry into Force

1. The present Convention shall enter into force 90 days after the date of deposit of the tenth instrument of ratification, acceptance, approval or accession, with the Depositary Government.

2. For each State which ratifies, accepts or approves the present Convention or accedes thereto after the deposit of the tenth instrument of ratification, acceptance, approval or accession, the present Convention shall enter into force 90 days after the deposit by such State of its instrument of ratification, acceptance, approval or accession.

Article XXIII
Reservations

1. The provisions of the present Convention shall not be subject to general reservations. Specific reservations may be entered in accordance with the provisions of this Article and Articles XV and XVI.

2. Any State may, on depositing its instrument of ratification, acceptance, approval or accession, enter a specific reservation with regard to:

(a) any species included in Appendix I, II or III; or

(b) any parts or derivatives specified in relation to a species included in Appendix III.

3. Until a Party withdraws its reservation entered under the provisions of this Article, it shall be treated as a State not a Party to the present Convention with respect to trade in the particular species or parts or derivatives specified in such reservation.

d. An amendment to the Convention adopted in Gaborone, but not yet in force, further adds to Article XXI, after the words "Depositary Government," the following 5 paragraphs:

1. This Convention shall be open for accession by regional economic integration organizations constituted by sovereign States which have competence in respect of the negotiation, conclusion and implementation of international agreements in matters transferred to them by their Member States and covered by this Convention.

2. In their instruments of accession, such organizations shall declare the extent of their competence with respect to the matters governed by the Convention. These organizations shall also inform the Depositary Government of any substantial modification in the extent of their competence. Notifications by regional economic integration organizations concerning their competence with respect to matters governed by this Convention and modifications thereto shall be distributed to the Parties by the Depositary Government.

3. In matters within their competence, such regional economic organizations shall exercise the rights and fulfill the obligations which this Convention attributes to their Member States, which are Parties to the Convention. In such cases the Member States of the organization shall not be entitled to exercise such rights individually.

4. In the fields of their competence, regional economic integration organizations shall exercise their right to vote with a number of votes equal to the number of their Member States which are Parties to the Convention. Such organizations shall not exercise their right to vote if their Member States exercise theirs, and vice versa.

5. Any reference to "Party" in the sense used in Article 1(h) of this Convention to "State"/ "States" or to "State Party"/"States Parties" to the Convention shall be construed as including a reference to any regional economic organization having competence in respect of the negotiation, conclusion and application of international agreements in matters covered by this Convention.

Article XXIV
Denunciation

Any Party may denounce the present Convention by written notification to the Depositary Government at any time. The denunciation shall take effect twelve months after the Depositary Government has received the notification.

Article XXV
Depositary

1. The original of the present Convention, in the Chinese, English, French, Russian and Spanish languages, each version being equally authentic, shall be deposited with the Depositary Government, which shall transmit certified copies thereof to all States that have signed it or deposited instruments of accession to it.

2. The Depositary Government shall inform all signatory and acceding States and the Secretariat of signatures, deposit of instruments of ratification, acceptance, approval or accession, entry into force of the present Convention, amendments thereto, entry and withdrawal of reservations and notifications of denunciation.

3. As soon as the present Convention enters into force, a certified copy thereof shall be transmitted by the Depositary Government to the Secretariat of the United Nations for registration and publication in accordance with Article 102 of the Charter of the United Nations.

Appendices I, II and III[e]

Interpretation

1. Species included in these Appendices are referred to:

   a) by the name of the species; or

   b) as being all of the species included in a higher taxon or designated part thereof.

2. The abbreviation "spp." is used to denote all species of a higher taxon.

3. Other references to taxa higher than species are for the purposes of information or classification only. The common names included after the scientific names of families are for reference only. They are intended to indicate the species within the family concerned that are included in the Appendices. In most cases this is not all of the species within the family.

4. The following abbreviations are used for plant taxa below the level of species:

   a) "ssp." is used to denote subspecies; and

   b) "var(s)." is used to denote variety (varieties).

5. As none of the species or higher taxa of FLORA included in Appendix I is annotated to the effect that its hybrids shall be treated in accordance with the provisions of Article III of the Convention, this means that artificially propagated hybrids produced from one or more of these species or taxa may be traded with a certificate of artificial propagation, and that seeds and pollen (including pollinia), cut flowers, seedling or tissue cultures obtained in vitro, in solid or liquid media, transported in sterile containers of these hybrids are not subject to the provisions of the Convention.

6. The names of the countries in parentheses placed against the names of species in Appendix III are those of the Parties submitting these species for inclusion in this Appendix.

e. Only those portions of the CITES appendices relating to whales (cetaceans) and elephants are reproduced here. Complete copies of the appendices are available from the CITES secretariat at www.cites.org (accessed on Oct. 2, 2011).

7. When a species is included in one of the Appendices, all parts and derivatives of the species are also included in the same Appendix unless the species is annotated to indicate that only specific parts and derivatives are included. The symbol #followed by a number placed against the name of a species or higher taxon included in Appendix II or III refers to a footnote that indicates the parts or derivatives of plants that are designated as 'specimens' subject to the provisions of the Convention in accordance with Article I, paragraph (b), subparagraph (iii).

Appendices (excerpts)

I	II	III
CETACEA Dolphins, porpoises, whales		
	CETACEA spp. (Except the species included in Appendix I....)	
Balaenidae Bowhead whale, right whales		
Balaena mysticetus *Eubalaena* spp.		
Balaenopteridae Humpback whale, rorquals		
Balaenoptera acutorostrata (Except the population of West Greenland, which is included in Appendix II) *Balaenoptera bonaerensis* *Balaenoptera borealis* *Balaenoptera edini* *Balaenoptera musculus* *Balaenoptera physalus* *Megaptera novaeangliae*		
Delphinidae Dolphins		
Orcaella brevirostris *Orcaella heinsohni* Sotalia spp. *Sousa* spp.		
Eschrichtiidae Grey whale		
Eschrichtius robustus		
Iniidae River dolphins		
Lipotes vexillifer		
Neobalaenidae Pygmy right whale		
Caperea marginata		
Phocoenidae Porpoises		
Neophocaena phocaenoides *Phocoena sinus*		
Physeteridae Sperm whales		
Physeter macrocephalus		
Platanistidae River dolphins		
Platanista spp.		
Ziphiidae Beaked whales, bottle-nosed whales		
Berardius spp. *Hyperoodon* spp.		
PROBOSCIDEA		
Elephantidae Elephants		

Elephas maximus *Loxodonta africana* (Except the populations of Botswana, Namibia, South Africa and Zimbabwe, which are included in Appendix II)	*Loxodonta africana*[5] (Only the populations of Botswana, Namibia, South Africa and Zimbabwe; all other populations are included in Appendix I)	

[5]   Populations of Botswana, Namibia, South Africa and Zimbabwe (listed in Appendix II)
    For the exclusive purpose of allowing:
    a)   trade in hunting trophies for non-commercial purposes;
    b)   trade in live animals to appropriate and acceptable destinations, as defined in Resolution Conf. 11.20, for Botswana and Zimbabwe and for in situ conservation programmes for Namibia and South Africa;
    c)   trade in hides;
    d)   trade in hair;
    e)   trade in leather goods for commercial or non-commercial purposes for Botswana, Namibia and South Africa and for non-commercial purposes for Zimbabwe;
    f)   trade in individually marked and certified ekipas incorporated in finished jewellery for non-commercial purposes for Namibia and ivory carvings for non-commercial purposes for Zimbabwe;
    g)   trade in registered raw ivory (for Botswana, Namibia, South Africa and Zimbabwe, whole tusks and pieces) subject to the following:
        i)   only registered government-owned stocks, originating in the State (excluding seized ivory and ivory of unknown origin);
        ii)   only to trading partners that have been verified by the Secretariat, in consultation with the Standing Committee, to have sufficient national legislation and domestic trade controls to ensure that the imported ivory will not be re-exported and will be managed in accordance with all requirements of Resolution Conf. 10.10 (Rev. CoP14) concerning domestic manufacturing and trade;
        iii)   not before the Secretariat has verified the prospective importing countries and the registered government-owned stocks;
        iv)   raw ivory pursuant to the conditional sale of registered government-owned ivory stocks agreed at CoP12, which are 20,000 kg (Botswana), 10,000 kg (Namibia) and 30,000 kg (South Africa);
        v)   in addition to the quantities agreed at CoP12, government-owned ivory from Botswana, Namibia, South Africa and Zimbabwe registered by 31 January 2007 and verified by the Secretariat may be traded and despatched, with the ivory in paragraph g) iv) above, in a single sale per destination under strict supervision of the Secretariat;
        vi)   the proceeds of the trade are used exclusively for elephant conservation and community conservation and development programmes within or adjacent to the elephant range; and
        vii)   the additional quantities specified in paragraph g) v) above shall be traded only after the Standing Committee has agreed that the above conditions have been met; and
    h)   no further proposals to allow trade in elephant ivory from populations already in Appendix II shall be submitted to the Conference of the Parties for the period from CoP14 and ending nine years from the date of the single sale of ivory that is to take place in accordance with provisions in paragraphs g) i), g) ii), g) iii), g) vi) and g) vii). In addition such further proposals shall be dealt with in accordance with Decisions 14.77 and 14.78 (Rev. CoP15).
    On a proposal from the Secretariat, the Standing Committee can decide to cause this trade to cease partially or completely in the event of non-compliance by exporting or importing countries, or in the case of proven detrimental impacts of the trade on other elephant populations.
    All other specimens shall be deemed to be specimens of species included in Appendix I and the trade in them shall be regulated accordingly.

5.5 ENDANGERED SPECIES ACT OF 1973 (as Amended). 16 U.S.C. 1531, 1537 & 1537A

§ 1531. Congressional findings and declaration of purposes and policy

(a) Findings

The Congress finds and declares that–

(1) various species of fish, wildlife, and plants in the United States have been rendered extinct as a consequence of economic growth and development untempered by adequate concern and conservation;

(2) other species of fish, wildlife, and plants have been so depleted in numbers that they are in danger of or threatened with extinction;

(3) these species of fish, wildlife, and plants are of esthetic, ecological, educational, historical, recreational, and scientific value to the Nation and its people;

(4) the United States has pledged itself as a sovereign state in the international community to conserve to the extent practicable the various species of fish or wildlife and plants facing extinction, pursuant to—

(A) migratory bird treaties with Canada and Mexico;

(B) the Migratory and Endangered Bird Treaty with Japan;

(C) the Convention on Nature Protection and Wildlife Preservation in the Western Hemisphere;

(D) the International Convention for the Northwest Atlantic Fisheries;

(E) the International Convention for the High Seas Fisheries of the North Pacific Ocean;

(F) the Convention on International Trade in Endangered Species of Wild Fauna and Flora; and

(G) other international agreements; and

(5) encouraging the States and other interested parties, through Federal financial assistance and a system of incentives, to develop and maintain conservation programs which meet national and international standards is a key to meeting the Nation's international commitments and to better safeguarding, for the benefit of all citizens, the Nation's heritage in fish, wildlife, and plants.

(b) Purposes

The purposes of this chapter are to provide a means whereby the ecosystems upon which endangered species and threatened species depend may be conserved, to provide a program for the conservation of such endangered species and threatened species, and to take such steps as may be appropriate to achieve the purposes of the treaties and conventions set forth in subsection (a) of this section.

(c) Policy

(1) It is further declared to be the policy of Congress that all Federal departments and agencies shall seek to conserve endangered species and threatened species and shall utilize their authorities in furtherance of the purposes of this chapter.

(2) It is further declared to be the policy of Congress that Federal agencies shall cooperate with State and local agencies to resolve water resource issues in concert with conservation of endangered species.

(Pub.L. 93–205, § 2, Dec. 28, 1973, 87 Stat. 884; Pub.L. 96–159, § 1, Dec. 28, 1979, 93 Stat. 1225; Pub.L. 97–304, § 9(a), Oct. 13, 1982, 96 Stat. 1426; Pub.L. 100–478, Title I, § 1013(a), Oct. 7, 1988, 102 Stat. 2315; Pub.L. 112–28, Aug. 12, 2011.)

§ 1537. International cooperation

(a) Financial assistance

As a demonstration of the commitment of the United States to the worldwide protection of endangered species and threatened species, the President may, subject to the provisions of section 1306 of Title 31, use foreign currencies accruing to the United States Government under the Food for Peace Act [7 U.S.C.A. § 1691 et seq.] or any other law to provide to any foreign country (with its consent) assistance in the development and management of programs in that country which the Secretary determines to be necessary or useful for the conservation of any endangered species or threatened species listed by the Secretary pursuant to section 1533 of this title. The President shall provide assistance (which includes, but is not limited to, the acquisition, by lease or otherwise, of lands, waters, or interests therein) to foreign countries under this section under such terms and conditions as he deems appropriate. Whenever foreign currencies are available for the provision of assistance under this section, such currencies shall be used in preference to funds appropriated under the authority of section 1542 of this title.

(b) Encouragement of foreign programs

In order to carry out further the provisions of this chapter, the Secretary, through the Secretary of State, shall encourage—

(1) foreign countries to provide for the conservation of fish or wildlife and plants including endangered species and threatened species listed pursuant to section 1533 of this title;

(2) the entering into of bilateral or multilateral agreements with foreign countries to provide for such conservation; and

(3) foreign persons who directly or indirectly take fish or wildlife or plants in foreign countries or on the high seas for importation into the United States for commercial or other purposes to develop and carry out with such assistance as he may provide, conservation practices designed to enhance such fish or wildlife or plants and their habitat.

(c) Personnel

After consultation with the Secretary of State, the Secretary may—

(1) assign or otherwise make available any officer or employee of his department for the purpose of cooperating with foreign countries and international organizations in developing personnel resources and programs which promote the conservation of fish or wildlife or plants; and

(2) conduct or provide financial assistance for the educational training of foreign personnel, in this country or abroad, in fish, wildlife, or plant management, research and law enforcement and to render professional assistance abroad in such matters.

(d) Investigations

After consultation with the Secretary of State and the Secretary of the Treasury, as appropriate, the Secretary may conduct or cause to be conducted such law enforcement investigations and research abroad as he deems necessary to carry out the purposes of this chapter.

(Pub.L. 93–205, § 8, Dec. 28, 1973, 87 Stat. 892; Pub.L. 96–159, § 5, Dec. 28, 1979, 93 Stat. 1228; Pub.L. 110–246, Title III, § 3001(b)(1)(A), (b)(2)(N), June 18, 2008, 122 Stat. 1820; Pub.L. 112–28, Aug. 12, 2011.)

§ 1537a.   Convention implementation

(a) Management Authority and Scientific Authority

The Secretary of the Interior (hereinafter in this section referred to as the "Secretary") is designated as the Management Authority and the Scientific Authority for purposes of the Convention and the respective functions of each such Authority shall be carried out through the United States Fish and Wildlife Service.

(b) Management Authority functions

The Secretary shall do all things necessary and appropriate to carry out the functions of the Management Authority under the Convention.

(c) Scientific Authority functions; determinations

(1) The Secretary shall do all things necessary and appropriate to carry out the functions of the Scientific Authority under the Convention.

(2) The Secretary shall base the determinations and advice given by him under Article IV of the Convention with respect to wildlife upon the best available biological information derived from professionally accepted wildlife management practices; but is not required to make, or require any State to make, estimates of population size in making such determinations or giving such advice.

(d) Reservations by the United States under Convention

If the United States votes against including any species in Appendix I or II of the Convention and does not enter a reservation pursuant to paragraph (3) of Article XV of the Convention with respect to that species, the Secretary of State, before the 90th day after the last day on which such a reservation could be entered, shall submit to the Committee on Merchant Marine and Fisheries of the House of Representatives, and to the Committee on the Environment and Public Works of the Senate, a written report setting forth the reasons why such a reservation was not entered.

(e) Wildlife Preservation in Western Hemisphere

(1) The Secretary of the Interior (hereinafter in this subsection referred to as the "Secretary"), in cooperation with the Secretary of State, shall act on behalf of, and represent, the United States in all regards as required by the Convention on Nature Protection and Wildlife Preservation in the Western Hemisphere (56 Stat. 1354, T.S. 982, hereinafter in this subsection referred to as the "Western Convention"). In the discharge of these responsibilities, the Secretary and the Secretary of State shall consult with the Secretary of Agriculture, the Secretary of Commerce, and the heads of other agencies with respect to matters relating to or affecting their areas of responsibility.

(2) The Secretary and the Secretary of State shall, in cooperation with the contracting parties to the Western Convention and, to the extent feasible and appropriate, with the participation of State agencies, take such steps as are necessary to implement the Western Convention. Such steps shall include, but not be limited to—

(A) cooperation with contracting parties and international organizations for the purpose of developing personnel resources and programs that will facilitate implementation of the Western Convention;

(B) identification of those species of birds that migrate between the United States and other contracting parties, and the habitats upon which those species depend, and the implementation of cooperative measures to ensure that such species will not become endangered or threatened; and

(C) identification of measures that are necessary and appropriate to implement those provisions of the Western Convention which address the protection of wild plants.

(3) No later than September 30, 1985, the Secretary and the Secretary of State shall submit a report to Congress describing those steps taken in accordance with the requirements of this subsection and identifying the principal remaining actions yet necessary for comprehensive and effective implementation of the Western Convention.

(4) The provisions of this subsection shall not be construed as affecting the authority, jurisdiction, or responsibility of the several States to manage, control, or regulate resident fish or wildlife under State law or regulations.

(Pub.L. 93–205, § 8A, as added Pub.L. 96–159, § 6(a) (1), Dec. 28, 1979, 93 Stat. 1228, and amended Pub.L. 97–304, § 5, Oct. 13, 1982, 96 Stat. 1421; Pub.L. 112–28, Aug. 12, 2011.)

5.6 CONVENTION ON THE CONSERVATION OF MIGRATORY SPECIES OF WILD ANIMALS **(Without Appendices) (as Amended 1985, 1988). Signed at Bonn, 23 June 1979. Entered into force, 1 November 1983. 1651 UNTS 333;** *reprinted in* **19 ILM 15 (1980) & 5A Weston & Carlson V.H.11**

The Contracting Parties,

RECOGNIZING that wild animals in their innumerable forms are an irreplaceable part of the earth's natural system which must be conserved for the good of mankind;

AWARE that each generation of man holds the resources of the earth for future generations and has an obligation to ensure that this legacy is conserved and, where utilized, is used wisely;

CONSCIOUS of the ever-growing value of wild animals from environmental, ecological, genetic, scientific, aesthetic, recreational, cultural, educational, social and economic points of view;

CONCERNED particularly with those species of wild animals that migrate across or outside national jurisdictional boundaries;

RECOGNIZING that the States are and must be the protectors of the migratory species of wild animals that live within or pass through their national jurisdictional boundaries;

CONVINCED that conservation and effective management of migratory species of wild animals require the concerted action of all States within the national jurisdictional boundaries of which such species spend any part of their life cycle;

RECALLING Recommendation 32 of the Action Plan adopted by the United Nations Conference on the Human Environment (Stockholm, 1972) and noted with satisfaction at the Twenty-seventh Session of the General Assembly of the United Nations,

HAVE AGREED as follows:

Article I
Interpretation

1. For the purpose of this Convention:

a) "Migratory species" means the entire population or any geographically separate part of the population of any species or lower taxon of wild animals, a significant proportion of whose members cyclically and predictably cross one or more national jurisdictional boundaries;

b) "Conservation status of a migratory species" means the sum of the influences acting on the migratory species that may affect its long-term distribution and abundance;

c) "Conservation status" will be taken as "favourable" when:

(1) population dynamics data indicate that the migratory species is maintaining itself on a long-term basis as a viable component of its ecosystems;

(2) the range of the migratory species is neither currently being reduced, nor is likely to be reduced, on a long-term basis;

(3) there is, and will be in the foreseeable future sufficient habitat to maintain the population of the migratory species on a long-term basis; and

(4) the distribution and abundance of the migratory species approach historic coverage and levels to the extent that potentially suitable ecosystems exist and to the extent consistent with wise wildlife management;

d) "Conservation status" will be taken as "unfavourable" if any of the conditions set out in sub-paragraph (c) of this paragraph is not met;

e) "Endangered" in relation to a particular migratory species means that the migratory species is in danger of extinction throughout all or a significant portion of its range;

f) "Range" means all the areas of land or water that a migratory species inhabits, stays in temporarily, crosses or overflies at any time on its normal migration route;

g) "Habitat" means any area in the range of a migratory species which contains suitable living conditions for that species;

h) "Range State" in relation to a particular migratory species means any State (and where appropriate any other Party referred to under subparagraph (k) of this paragraph) that exercises jurisdiction over any part of the range of that migratory species, or a State, flag vessels of which are engaged outside national jurisdictional limits in taking that migratory species;

i) "Taking" means taking, hunting, fishing capturing, harassing, deliberate killing, or attempting to engage in any such conduct;

j) "Agreement" means an international agreement relating to the conservation of one or more migratory species as provided for in Articles IV and V of this Convention; and

k) "Party" means a State or any regional economic integration organization constituted by sovereign States which has competence in respect of the negotiation, conclusion and application of international Agreements in matters covered by this Convention for which this Convention is in force.

2. In matters within their competence, the regional economic integration organizations which are Parties to this Convention shall in their own name exercise the rights and fulfil the responsibilities which this Convention attributes to their member States. In such cases the member States of these organizations shall not be entitled to exercise such rights individually.

3. Where this Convention provides for a decision to be taken by either a two-thirds majority or a unanimous decision of "the Parties present and voting" this shall mean "the Parties present and casting an affirmative or negative vote". Those abstaining from voting shall not be counted amongst "the Parties present and voting" in determining the majority.

Article II
Fundamental principles

1. The Parties acknowledge the importance of migratory species being conserved and of Range States agreeing to take action to this end whenever possible and appropriate, paying special attention to migratory species the conservation status of which is unfavourable, and taking individually or in co-operation appropriate and necessary steps to conserve such species and their habitat.

2. The Parties acknowledge the need to take action to avoid any migratory species becoming endangered.

3. In particular, the Parties:

a) should promote, co-operate in and support research relating to migratory species;

b) shall endeavour to provide immediate protection for migratory species included in Appendix I; and

c) shall endeavour to conclude Agreements covering the conservation and management of migratory species included in Appendix II.

Article III

Endangered migratory species: Appendix I

1. Appendix I shall list migratory species which are endangered.

2. A migratory species may be listed in Appendix I provided that reliable evidence, including the best scientific evidence available, indicates that the species is endangered.

3. A migratory species may be removed from Appendix I when the Conference of the Parties determines that:

a) reliable evidence, including the best scientific evidence available, indicates that the species is no longer endangered, and

b) the species is not likely to become endangered again because of loss of protection due to its removal from Appendix I.

4. Parties that are Range States of a migratory species listed in Appendix I shall endeavour:

a) to conserve and, where feasible and appropriate, restore those habitats of the species which are of importance in removing the species from danger of extinction;

b) to prevent, remove, compensate for or minimize, as appropriate, the adverse effects of activities or obstacles that seriously impede or prevent the migration of the species; and

c) to the extent feasible and appropriate, to prevent, reduce or control factors that are endangering or are likely to further endanger the species, including strictly controlling the introduction of, or controlling or eliminating, already introduced exotic species.

5. Parties that are Range States of a migratory species listed in Appendix I shall prohibit the taking of animals belonging to such species. Exceptions may be made to this prohibition only if:

a) the taking is for scientific purposes;

b) the taking is for the purpose of enhancing the propagation or survival of the affected species;

c) the taking is to accommodate the needs of traditional subsistence users of such species; or

d) extraordinary circumstances so require; provided that such exceptions are precise as to content and limited in space and time. Such taking should not operate to the disadvantage of the species.

6. The Conferences of the Parties may recommend to the Parties that are Range States of a migratory species listed in Appendix I that they take further measures considered appropriate to benefit the species.

7. The Parties shall as soon as possible inform the Secretariat of any exceptions made pursuant to paragraph 5 of this Article.

Article IV

Migratory species to be the subject of agreements: Appendix II

1. Appendix II shall list migratory species which have an unfavourable conservation status and which require international agreements for their conservation and management, as well as those which have a conservation status which would significantly benefit from the international cooperation that could be achieved by an international agreement.

2. If the circumstances so warrant, a migratory species may be listed both in Appendix I and Appendix II.

3. Parties that are Range States of migratory species listed in Appendix II shall endeavour to conclude Agreements where these should benefit the species and should give priority to those species in an unfavourable conservation status.

4. Parties are encouraged to take action with a view to concluding agreements for any population or any geographically separate part of the population of any species or lower taxon of wild animals, members of which periodically cross one or more national jurisdiction boundaries.

5. The Secretariat shall be provided with a copy of each Agreement concluded pursuant to the provisions of this Article.

Article V
Guidelines for agreements

1. The object of each Agreement shall be to restore the migratory species concerned to a favourable conservation status or to maintain it in such a status. Each Agreement should deal with those aspects of the conservation and management of the migratory species concerned which serve to achieve that object.

2. Each Agreement should cover the whole of the range of the migratory species concerned and should be open to accession by all Range States of that species, whether or not they are Parties to this Convention.

3. An Agreement should, wherever possible, deal with more than one migratory species.

4. Each Agreement should:

a) identify the migratory species covered;

b) describe the range and migration route of the migratory species;

c) provide for each Party to designate its national authority concerned with the implementation of the Agreement,

d) establish, if necessary, appropriate machinery to assist in carrying out the aims of the Agreement, to monitor its effectiveness, and to prepare reports for the Conference of the Parties;

e) provide for procedures for the settlement of disputes between Parties to the Agreement; and

f) at a minimum, prohibit, in relation to a migratory species of the Order Cetacea, any taking that is not permitted for that migratory species under any other multilateral Agreement and provide for accession to the Agreement by States that are not Range States of that migratory species.

5. Where appropriate and feasible, each Agreement should provide for but not be limited to:

a) periodic review of the conservation status of the migratory species concerned and the identification of the factors which may be harmful to that status;

b) co-ordinated conservation and management plans;

c) research into the ecology and population dynamics of the migratory species concerned, with special regard to migration;

d) the exchange of information on the migratory species concerned, special regard being paid to the exchange of the results of research and of relevant statistics;

e) conservation and, where required and feasible, restoration of the habitats of importance in maintaining a favourable conservation status, and protection of such habitats from disturbances, including strict control of the introduction of, or control of already introduced, exotic species detrimental to the migratory species;

f) maintenance of a network of suitable habitats appropriately disposed in relation to the migration routes;

g) where it appears desirable, the provision of new habitats favourable to the migratory species or reintroduction of the migratory species into favourable habitats;

h) elimination of, to the maximum extent possible, or compensation for activities and obstacles which hinder or impede migration;

i) prevention, reduction or control of the release into the habitat of the migratory species of substances harmful to that migratory species;

j) measures based on sound ecological principles to control and manage the taking of the migratory species;

k) procedures for co-ordinating action to suppress illegal taking;

l) exchange of information on substantial threats to the migratory species;

m) emergency procedures whereby conservation action would be considerably and rapidly strengthened when the conservation status of the migratory species is seriously affected; and

n) making the general public aware of the contents and aims of the Agreement.

Article VI
Range states

1. A list of the Range States of migratory species listed in Appendices I and II shall be kept up to date by the Secretariat using information it has received from the Parties.

2. The Parties shall keep the Secretariat informed in regard to which of the migratory species listed in Appendices I and II they consider themselves to be Range States, including provision of information on their flag vessels engaged outside national jurisdictional limits in taking the migratory species concerned and, where possible, future plans in respect of such taking.

3. The Parties which are Range States for migratory species listed in Appendix I or Appendix II should inform the Conference of the Parties through the Secretariat, at least six months prior to each ordinary meeting of the Conference, on measures that they are taking to implement the provisions of this Convention for these species.

Article VII
The conference of the parties

1. The Conference of the Parties shall be the decision-making organ of this Convention.

2. The Secretariat shall call a meeting of the Conference of the Parties not later than two years after the entry into force of this Convention.

3. Thereafter the Secretariat shall convene ordinary meetings of the Conference of the Parties at intervals of not more than three years, unless the Conference decides otherwise, and extraordinary meetings at any time on the written request of at least one-third of the Parties.

4. The Conference of the Parties shall establish and keep under review the financial regulations of this Convention. The Conference of the Parties shall, at each of its ordinary meetings, adopt the budget for the next financial period. Each Party shall contribute to this budget according to a scale to be agreed upon by the Conference. Financial regulations, including the provisions on the budget and the scale of contributions as well as their modifications, shall be adopted by unanimous vote of the Parties present and voting.

5. At each of its meetings the Conference of the Parties shall review the implementation of this Convention and may in particular:

a) review and assess the conservation status of migratory species;

b) review the progress made towards the conservation of migratory species, especially those listed in Appendices I and II;

c) make such provision and provide such guidance as may be necessary to enable the Scientific Council and the Secretariat to carry out their duties;

d) receive and consider any reports presented by the Scientific Council, the Secretariat, any Party or any standing body established pursuant to an Agreement;

e) make recommendations to the Parties for improving the conservation status of migratory species and review the progress being made under Agreements;

f) in those cases where an Agreement has not been concluded, make recommendations for the convening of meetings of the Parties that are Range States of a migratory species or group of migratory species to discuss measures to improve the conservation status of the species;

g) make recommendations to the Parties for improving the effectiveness of this Convention; and

h) decide on any additional measure that should be taken to implement the objectives of this Convention.

6. Each meeting of the Conference of the Parties should determine the time and venue of the next meeting.

7. Any meeting of the Conference of the Parties shall determine and adopt rules of procedure for that meeting. Decisions at a meeting of the Conference of the Parties shall require a two-thirds majority of the Parties present and voting, except where otherwise provided for by this Convention.

8. The United Nations, its Specialized Agencies, the International Atomic Energy Agency, as well as any State not a party to this Convention and, for each Agreement, the body designated by the parties to that Agreement, may be represented by observers at meetings of the Conference of the Parties.

9. Any agency or body technically qualified in protection, conservation and management of migratory species, in the following categories, which has informed the Secretariat of its desire to be represented at meetings of the Conference of the Parties by observers, shall be admitted unless at least one-third of the Parties present object:

a) international agencies or bodies, either governmental or non-governmental, and national governmental agencies and bodies; and

b) national non-governmental agencies or bodies which have been approved for this purpose by the State in which they are located.

Once admitted, these observers shall have the right to participate but not to vote.

Article VIII
The scientific council

1. At its first meeting, the Conference of the Parties shall establish a Scientific Council to provide advice on scientific matters.

2. Any Party may appoint a qualified expert as a member of the Scientific Council. In addition, the Scientific Council shall include as members qualified experts selected and appointed by the Conference of the Parties; the number of these experts, the criteria for their selection and the terms of their appointments shall be as determined by the Conference of the Parties.

3. The Scientific Council shall meet at the request of the Secretariat as required by the Conference of the Parties.

4. Subject to the approval of the Conference of the Parties, the Scientific Council shall establish its own rules of procedure.

5. The Conference of the Parties shall determine the functions of the Scientific Council, which may include:

a) providing scientific advice to the Conference of the Parties, to the Secretariat, and, if approved by the Conference of the Parties, to any body set up under this Convention or an Agreement or to any Party;

b) recommending research and the co-ordination of research on migratory species, evaluating the results of such research in order to ascertain the conservation status of migratory species and reporting to the Conference of the Parties on such status and measures for its improvement;

c) making recommendations to the Conference of the Parties as to the migratory species to be included in Appendices I and II, together with an indication of the range of such migratory species;

d) making recommendations to the Conference of the Parties as to specific conservation and management measures to be included in Agreements on migratory species; and

e) recommending to the Conference of the Parties solutions to problems relating to the scientific aspects of the implementation of this Convention, in particular with regard to the habitats of migratory species.

Article IX
The secretariat

1. For the purposes of this Convention a Secretariat shall be established.

2. Upon entry into force of this Convention, the Secretariat is provided by the Executive Director of the United Nations Environment Programme. To the extent and in the manner he considers appropriate, he may be assisted by suitable intergovernmental or non-governmental, international or national agencies and bodies technically qualified in protection, conservation and management of wild animals.

3. If the United Nations Environment Programme is no longer able to provide the Secretariat, the Conference of the Parties shall make alternative arrangements for the Secretariat.

4. The functions of the Secretariat shall be:

a) to arrange for and service meetings: (i) of the Conference of the Parties, and (ii) of the Scientific Council;

b) to maintain liaison with and promote liaison between the Parties, the standing bodies set up under Agreements and other international organizations concerned with migratory species;

c) to obtain from any appropriate source reports and other information which will further the objectives and implementation of this Convention and to arrange for the appropriate dissemination of such information;

d) to invite the attention of the Conference of the Parties to any matter pertaining to the objectives of this Convention;

e) to prepare for the Conference of the Parties reports on the work of the Secretariat and on the implementation of this Convention;

f) to maintain and publish a list of Range States of all migratory species included in Appendices I and II;

g) to promote, under the direction of the Conference of the Parties, the conclusion of Agreements,

h) to maintain and make available to the Parties a list of Agreements and, if so required by the Conference of the Parties, to provide any information on such Agreements;

i) to maintain and publish a list of the recommendations made by the Conference of the Parties pursuant to sub-paragraphs (e), (f) and (g) of paragraph 5 of Article VII or of decisions made pursuant to sub-paragraph (h) of that paragraph;

j) to provide for the general public information concerning this Convention and its objectives; and

k) to perform any other function entrusted to it under this Convention or by the Conference of the Parties.

Article X
Amendment of the convention

1. This Convention may be amended at any ordinary or extraordinary meeting of the Conference of the Parties.

2. Proposals for amendment may be made by any Party.

3. The text of any proposed amendment and the reasons for it shall be communicated to the Secretary at least one hundred and fifty days before the meeting at which it is to be considered and shall promptly be communicated by the Secretary to all Parties. Any comments on the text by the Parties shall be communicated to the Secretariat not less than sixty days before the meeting begins. The Secretariat shall, immediately after the last day for submission of comments, communicate to the Parties all comments submitted by that day.

4. Amendments shall be adopted by a two-thirds majority of Parties present and voting.

5. An amendment adopted shall enter into force for all Parties which have accepted it on the first day of the third month following the date on which two-thirds of the Parties have deposited an instrument of acceptance with the Depositary. For each Party which deposits an instrument of acceptance after the date on which two-thirds of the Parties have deposited an instrument of acceptance, the amendment shall enter into force for that Party on the first day of the third month following the deposit of its instrument of acceptance.

Article XI
Amendment of the appendices

1. Appendices I and II may be amended at any ordinary or extraordinary meeting of the Conference of the Parties.

2. Proposals for amendment may be made by any Party.

3. The text of any proposed amendment and the reasons for it, based on the best scientific evidence available, shall be communicated to the Secretariat at least one hundred and fifty days before the meeting and shall promptly be communicated by the Secretariat to all Parties. Any comments on the text by the Parties shall be communicated to the Secretariat not less than sixty days before the meeting begins. The Secretariat shall, immediately after the last day for submission of comments, communicate to the Parties all comments submitted by that day.

4. Amendments shall be adopted by a two-thirds majority of Parties present and voting.

5. An amendment to the Appendices shall enter into force for all Parties ninety days after the meeting of the Conference of the Parties at which it was adopted, except for those Parties which make a reservation in accordance with paragraph 6 of this Article.

6. During the period of ninety days provided for in paragraph 5 of this Article, any Party may by notification in writing to the Depositary make a reservation with respect to the amendment. A reservation to an amendment may be withdrawn by written notification to the Depositary and thereupon the amendment shall enter into force for that Party ninety days after the reservation is withdrawn.

Article XII
Effect on international conventions and other legislation

1. Nothing in this Convention shall prejudice the codification and development of the law of the sea by the United Nations Conference on the Law of the Sea convened pursuant to Resolution 2750 C (XXV) of the General Assembly of the United Nations nor the present or future claims and legal views of any State concerning the law of the sea and the nature and extent of coastal and flag State jurisdiction.

2. The provisions of this Convention shall in no way affect the rights or obligations of any Party deriving from any existing treaty, convention or Agreement.

3. The provisions of this Convention shall in no way affect the right of Parties to adopt stricter domestic measures concerning the conservation of migratory species listed in Appendices I and II or to adopt domestic measures concerning the conservation of species not listed in Appendices I and II.

Article XIII
Settlement of disputes

1. Any dispute which may arise between two or more Parties with respect to the interpretation or application of the provisions of this Convention shall be subject to negotiation between the Parties involved in the dispute.

2. If the dispute cannot be resolved in accordance with paragraph 1 of this Article, the Parties may, by mutual consent, submit the dispute to arbitration, in particular that of the Permanent Court of Arbitration at The Hague, and the Parties submitting the dispute shall be bound by the arbitral decision.

Article XIV
Reservations

1. The provisions of this Convention shall not be subject to general reservations. Specific reservations may be entered in accordance with the provisions of this Article and Article XI.

2. Any State or regional economic integration organization may, on depositing its instrument of ratification, acceptance, approval or accession, enter a specific reservation with regard to the presence on either Appendix I or Appendix II or both, of any migratory species and shall then not be regarded as a Party in regard to the subject of that reservation until ninety days after the Depositary has transmitted to the Parties notification that such reservation has been withdrawn.

Article XV
Signature

This Convention shall be open for signature at Bonn for all States and any regional economic integration organization until the twenty-second day of June, 1980.

Article XVI
Ratification, acceptance, approval

This Convention shall be subject to ratification, acceptance or approval. Instruments of ratification, acceptance or approval shall be deposited with the Government of the Federal Republic of Germany, which shall be the Depositary.

Article XVII
Accession

After the twenty-second day of June 1980 this Convention shall be open for accession by all non-signatory States and any regional economic integration organization. Instruments of accession shall be deposited with the Depositary.

Article XVIII
Entry into force

1. This Convention shall enter into force on the first day of the third month following the date of deposit of the fifteenth instrument of ratification, acceptance, approval or accession with the Depositary.

2. For each State or each regional economic integration organization which ratifies, accepts or approves this Convention or accedes thereto after the deposit of the fifteenth instrument of ratification, acceptance, approval or accession, this Convention shall enter into force on the first day of the third month following the deposit by such State or such organization of its instrument of ratification, acceptance, approval or accession.

Article XIX
Denunciation

Any Party may denounce this Convention by written notification to the Depositary at any time. The denunciation shall take effect twelve months after the Depositary has received the notification.

Article XX
Depositary

1. The original of this Convention, in the English, French, German, Russian and Spanish languages, each version being equally authentic, shall be deposited with the Depositary. The Depositary shall transmit certified copies of each of these versions to all States and all regional economic integration organizations that have signed the Convention or deposited instruments of accession to it.

2. The Depositary shall, after consultation with the Governments concerned, prepare official versions of the text of this Convention in the Arabic and Chinese languages.

3. The Depositary shall inform all signatory and acceding States and all signatory and acceding regional economic integration organizations and the Secretariat of signatures, deposit of instruments of ratification, acceptance, approval or accession, entry into force of this Convention, amendments thereto, specific reservations and notifications of denunciation.

4. As soon as this Convention enters into force, a certified copy thereof shall be transmitted by the Depositary to the Secretariat of the United Nations for registration and publication in accordance with Article 102 of the Charter of the United Nations. In witness whereof the undersigned, being duly authorized to that effect, have signed this Convention.

Done at Bonn on 23 June 1979.

5.7 CONVENTION ON BIOLOGICAL DIVERSITY (With Annexes). Concluded at Rio de Janeiro, 5 June 1992. Entered into force, 29 December 1993. 1760 UNTS 79; *reprinted in* 31 ILM 818 (1992) & 5A Weston & Carlson V.H.22

Preamble

The Contracting Parties,

Conscious of the intrinsic value of biological diversity and of the ecological, genetic, social, economic, scientific, educational, cultural, recreational and aesthetic values of biological diversity and its components,

Conscious also of the importance of biological diversity for evolution and for maintaining life sustaining systems of the biosphere,

Affirming that the conservation of biological diversity is a common concern of humankind,

Reaffirming that States have sovereign rights over their own biological resources,

Reaffirming also that States are responsible for conserving their biological diversity and for using their biological resources in a sustainable manner,

Concerned that biological diversity is being significantly reduced by certain human activities,

Aware of the general lack of information and knowledge regarding biological diversity and of the urgent need to develop scientific, technical and institutional capacities to provide the basic understanding upon which to plan and implement appropriate measures,

Noting that it is vital to anticipate, prevent and attack the causes of significant reduction or loss of biological diversity at source,

Noting also that where there is a threat of significant reduction or loss of biological diversity, lack of full scientific certainty should not be used as a reason for postponing measures to avoid or minimize such a threat,

Noting further that the fundamental requirement for the conservation of biological diversity is the *in-situ* conservation of ecosystems and natural habitats and the maintenance and recovery of viable populations of species in their natural surroundings,

Noting further that *ex-situ* measures, preferably in the country of origin, also have an important role to play,

Recognizing the close and traditional dependence of many indigenous and local communities embodying traditional lifestyles on biological resources, and the desirability of sharing equitably benefits arising from the use of traditional knowledge, innovations and practices relevant to the conservation of biological diversity and the sustainable use of its components,

Recognizing also the vital role that women play in the conservation and sustainable use of biological diversity and affirming the need for the full participation of women at all levels of policy-making and implementation for biological diversity conservation,

Stressing the importance of, and the need to promote, international, regional and global cooperation among States and intergovernmental organizations and the non-governmental sector for the conservation of biological diversity and the sustainable use of its components,

Acknowledging that the provision of new and additional financial resources and appropriate access to relevant technologies can be expected to make a substantial difference in the world's ability to address the loss of biological diversity,

Acknowledging further that special provision is required to meet the needs of developing countries, including the provision of new and additional financial resources and appropriate access to relevant technologies,

Noting in this regard the special conditions of the least developed countries and small island States,

Acknowledging that substantial investments are required to conserve biological diversity and that there is the expectation of a broad range of environmental, economic and social benefits from those investments,

Recognizing that economic and social development and poverty eradication are the first and overriding priorities of developing countries,

Aware that conservation and sustainable use of biological diversity is of critical importance for meeting the food, health and other needs of the growing world population, for which purpose access to and sharing of both genetic resources and technologies are essential,

Noting that, ultimately, the conservation and sustainable use of biological diversity will strengthen friendly relations among States and contribute to peace for humankind,

Desiring to enhance and complement existing international arrangements for the conservation of biological diversity and sustainable use of its components, and

Determined to conserve and sustainably use biological diversity for the benefit of present and future generations.

Have agreed as follows:

Article 1. Objectives

The objectives of this Convention, to be pursued in accordance with its relevant provisions, are the conservation of biological diversity, the sustainable use of its components and the fair and equitable sharing of the benefits arising out of the utilization of genetic resources, including by appropriate access to genetic resources and by appropriate transfer of relevant technologies, taking into account all rights over those resources and to technologies, and by appropriate funding.

Article 2. Use of Terms

For the purposes of this Convention:

"Biological diversity" means the variability among living organisms from all sources including, *inter alia,* terrestrial, marine and other aquatic ecosystems and the ecological complexes of which they are part; this includes diversity within species, between species and of ecosystems.

"Biological resources" includes genetic resources, organisms or parts thereof, populations, or any other biotic component of ecosystems with actual or potential use or value for humanity.

"Biotechnology" means any technological application that uses biological systems, living organisms, or derivatives thereof, to make or modify products or processes for specific use.

"Country of origin of genetic resources" means the country which possesses those genetic resources in *in-situ* conditions.

"Country providing genetic resources" means the country supplying genetic resources collected from *in-situ* sources, including populations of both wild and domesticated species, or taken from *ex-situ* sources, which may or may not have originated in that country.

"Domesticated or cultivated species" means species in which the evolutionary process has been influenced by humans to meet their needs.

"Ecosystem" means a dynamic complex of plant, animal and micro-organism communities and their non-living environment interacting as a functional unit.

"Ex-situ conservation" means the conservation of components of biological diversity outside their natural habitats.

"Genetic material" means any material of plant, animal, microbial or other origin containing functional units of heredity.

"Genetic resources" means genetic material of actual or potential value.

"Habitat" means the place or type of site where an organism or population naturally occurs.

"In-situ conditions" means conditions where genetic resources exist within ecosystems and natural habitats, and, in the case of domesticated or cultivated species, in the surroundings where they have developed their distinctive properties.

"In-situ conservation" means the conservation of ecosystems and natural habitats and the maintenance and recovery of viable populations of species in their natural surroundings and, in the case of domesticated or cultivated species, in the surroundings where they have developed their distinctive properties.

"Protected area" means a geographically defined area which is designated or regulated and managed to achieve specific conservation objectives.

"Regional economic integration organization" means an organization constituted by sovereign States of a given region, to which its member States have transferred competence in respect of matters governed by this Convention and which has been duly authorized, in accordance with its internal procedures, to sign, ratify, accept, approve or accede to it.

"Sustainable use" means the use of components of biological diversity in a way and at a rate that does not lead to the long-term decline of biological diversity, thereby maintaining its potential to meet the needs and aspirations of present and future generations.

"Technology" includes biotechnology.

Article 3. Principle

States have, in accordance with the Charter of the United Nations and the principles of international law, the sovereign right to exploit their own resources pursuant to their own environmental policies, and the responsibility to ensure that activities within their jurisdiction or control do not cause damage to the environment of other States or of areas beyond the limits of national jurisdiction.

Article 4. Jurisdictional Scope

Subject to the rights of other States, and except as otherwise expressly provided in this Convention, the provisions of this Convention apply, in relation to each Contracting Party:

(a) In the case of components of biological diversity, in areas within the limits of its national jurisdiction; and

(b) In the case of processes and activities, regardless of where their effects occur, carried out under its jurisdiction or control, within the area of its national jurisdiction or beyond the limits of national jurisdiction.

Article 5. Cooperation

Each Contracting Party shall, as far as possible and as appropriate, cooperate with other Contracting Parties, directly or, where appropriate, through competent international organizations, in respect of areas beyond national jurisdiction and on other matters of mutual interest, for the conservation and sustainable use of biological diversity.

Article 6. General Measures for Conservation and Sustainable Use

Each Contracting Party shall, in accordance with its particular conditions and capabilities:

(a) Develop national strategies, plans or programmes for the conservation and sustainable use of biological diversity or adapt for this purpose existing strategies, plans or programmes which shall reflect, inter alia, the measures set out in this Convention relevant to the Contracting Party concerned; and

(b) Integrate, as far as possible and as appropriate, the conservation and sustainable use of biological diversity into relevant sectoral or cross-sectoral plans, programmes and policies.

Article 7. Identification and Monitoring

Each Contracting Party shall, as far as possible and as appropriate, in particular for the purposes of Articles 8 to 10:

(a) Identify components of biological diversity important for its conservation and sustainable use having regard to the indicative list of categories set down in Annex I;

(b) Monitor, through sampling and other techniques, the components of biological diversity identified pursuant to subparagraph (a) above, paying particular attention to those requiring urgent conservation measures and those which offer the greatest potential for sustainable use;

(c) Identify processes and categories of activities which have or are likely to have significant adverse impacts on the conservation and sustainable use of biological diversity, and monitor their effects through sampling and other techniques; and

(d) Maintain and organize, by any mechanism data, derived from identification and monitoring activities pursuant to subparagraphs (a), (b) and (c) above.

Article 8. In-situ Conservation

Each Contracting Party shall, as far as possible and as appropriate:

(a) Establish a system of protected areas or areas where special measures need to be taken to conserve biological diversity;

(b) Develop, where necessary, guidelines for the selection, establishment and management of protected areas or areas where special measures need to be taken to conserve biological diversity;

(c) Regulate or manage biological resources important for the conservation of biological diversity whether within or outside protected areas, with a view to ensuring their conservation and sustainable use;

(d) Promote the protection of ecosystems, natural habitats and the maintenance of viable populations of species in natural surroundings;

(e) Promote environmentally sound and sustainable development in areas adjacent to protected areas with a view to furthering protection of these areas;

(f) Rehabilitate and restore degraded ecosystems and promote the recovery of threatened species, *inter alia,* through the development and implementation of plans or other management strategies;

(g) Establish or maintain means to regulate, manage or control the risks associated with the use and release of living modified organisms resulting from biotechnology which are likely to have adverse environmental impacts that could affect the conservation and sustainable use of biological diversity, taking also into account the risks to human health;

(h) Prevent the introduction of, control or eradicate those alien species which threaten ecosystems, habitats or species;

(i) Endeavour to provide the conditions needed for compatibility between present uses and the conservation of biological diversity and the sustainable use of its components;

(j) Subject to its national legislation, respect, preserve and maintain knowledge, innovations and practices of indigenous and local communities embodying traditional lifestyles relevant for the conservation and sustainable use of biological diversity and promote their wider application with the approval and involvement of the holders of such knowledge, innovations and practices and encourage the equitable sharing of the benefits arising from the utilization of such knowledge, innovations and practices;

(k) Develop or maintain necessary legislation and/or other regulatory provisions for the protection of threatened species and populations;

(*l*) Where a significant adverse effect on biological diversity has been determined pursuant to Article 7, regulate or manage the relevant processes and categories of activities; and

(m) Cooperate in providing financial and other support for *in-situ* conservation outlined in subparagraphs (a) to (*l*) above, particularly to developing countries.

Article 9.   Ex-situ Conservation

Each Contracting Party shall, as far as possible and as appropriate, and predominantly for the purpose of complementing *in-situ* measures:

(a) Adopt measures for the *ex-situ* conservation of components of biological diversity, preferably in the country of origin of such components;

(b) Establish and maintain facilities for *ex-situ* conservation of and research on plants, animals and micro-organisms, preferably in the country of origin of genetic resources;

(c) Adopt measures for the recovery and rehabilitation of threatened species and for their reintroduction into their natural habitats under appropriate conditions;

(d) Regulate and manage collection of biological resources from natural habitats for *ex-situ* conservation purposes so as not to threaten ecosystems and *in-situ* populations of species, except where special temporary *ex-situ* measures are required under subparagraph (c) above; and

(e) Cooperate in providing financial and other support for *ex-situ* conservation outlined in subparagraphs (a) to (d) above and in the establishment and maintenance of *ex-situ* conservation facilities in developing countries.

Article 10.   Sustainable Use of Components of Biological Diversity

Each Contracting Party shall, as far as possible and as appropriate:

(a) Integrate consideration of the conservation and sustainable use of biological resources into national decision-making;

(b) Adopt measures relating to the use of biological resources to avoid or minimize adverse impacts on biological diversity;

(c) Protect and encourage customary use of biological resources in accordance with traditional cultural practices that are compatible with conservation or sustainable use requirements;

(d) Support local populations to develop and implement remedial action in degraded areas where biological diversity has been reduced; and

(e) Encourage cooperation between its governmental authorities and its private sector in developing methods for sustainable use of biological resources.

Article 11. Incentive Measures

Each Contracting Party shall, as far as possible and as appropriate, adopt economically and socially sound measures that act as incentives for the conservation and sustainable use of components of biological diversity.

Article 12. Research and Training

The Contracting Parties, taking into account the special needs of developing countries, shall:

(a) Establish and maintain programmes for scientific and technical education and training in measures for the identification, conservation and sustainable use of biological diversity and its components and provide support for such education and training for the specific needs of developing countries;

(b) Promote and encourage research which contributes to the conservation and sustainable use of biological diversity, particularly in developing countries, *inter alia,* in accordance with decisions of the Conference of the Parties taken in consequence of recommendations of the Subsidiary Body on Scientific, Technical and Technological Advice; and

(c) In keeping with the provisions of Articles 16, 18 and 20, promote and cooperate in the use of scientific advances in biological diversity research in developing methods for conservation and sustainable use of biological resources.

Article 13. Public Education and Awareness

The Contracting Parties shall:

(a) Promote and encourage understanding of the importance of, and the measures required for, the conservation of biological diversity, as well as its propagation through media, and the inclusion of these topics in educational programmes; and

(b) Cooperate, as appropriate, with other States and international organizations in developing educational and public awareness programmes, with respect to conservation and sustainable use of biological diversity.

Article 14. Impact Assessment and Minimizing Adverse Impacts

1. Each Contracting Party, as far as possible and as appropriate, shall:

(a) Introduce appropriate procedures requiring environmental impact assessment of its proposed projects that are likely to have significant adverse effects on biological diversity with a view to avoiding or minimizing such effects and, where appropriate, allow for public participation in such procedures;

(b) Introduce appropriate arrangements to ensure that the environmental consequences of its programmes and policies that are likely to have significant adverse impacts on biological diversity are duly taken into account;

(c) Promote, on the basis of reciprocity, notification, exchange of information and consultation on activities under their jurisdiction or control which are likely to significantly affect adversely the biological diversity of other States or areas beyond the limits of national jurisdiction, by encouraging the conclusion of bilateral, regional or multilateral arrangements, as appropriate;

(d) In the case of imminent or grave danger or damage, originating under its jurisdiction or control, to biological diversity within the area under jurisdiction of other States or in areas beyond the limits of national jurisdiction, notify immediately the potentially affected States of such danger or damage, as well as initiate action to prevent or minimize such danger or damage; and

(e) Promote national arrangements for emergency responses to activities or events, whether caused naturally or otherwise, which present a grave and imminent danger to biological diversity and encourage international cooperation to supplement such national efforts and, where appropriate and agreed by the States or regional economic integration organizations concerned, to establish joint contingency plans.

2. The Conference of the Parties shall examine, on the basis of studies to be carried out, the issue of liability and redress, including restoration and compensation, for damage to biological diversity, except where such liability is a purely internal matter.

Article 15.   Access to Genetic Resources

1. Recognizing the sovereign rights of States over their natural resources, the authority to determine access to genetic resources rests with the national governments and is subject to national legislation.

2. Each Contracting Party shall endeavour to create conditions to facilitate access to genetic resources for environmentally sound uses by other Contracting Parties and not to impose restrictions that run counter to the objectives of this Convention.

3. For the purpose of this Convention, the genetic resources being provided by a Contracting Party, as referred to in this Article and Articles 16 and 19, are only those that are provided by Contracting Parties that are countries of origin of such resources or by the Parties that have acquired the genetic resources in accordance with this Convention.

4. Access, where granted, shall be on mutually agreed terms and subject to the provisions of this Article.

5. Access to genetic resources shall be subject to prior informed consent of the Contracting Party providing such resources, unless otherwise determined by that Party.

6. Each Contracting Party shall endeavour to develop and carry out scientific research based on genetic resources provided by other Contracting Parties with the full participation of, and where possible in, such Contracting Parties.

7. Each Contracting Party shall take legislative, administrative or policy measures, as appropriate, and in accordance with Articles 16 and 19 and, where necessary, through the financial mechanism established by Articles 20 and 21 with the aim of sharing in a fair and equitable way the results of research and development and the benefits arising from the commercial and other utilization of genetic resources with the Contracting Party providing such resources. Such sharing shall be upon mutually agreed terms.

Article 16.   Access to and Transfer of Technology

1. Each Contracting Party, recognizing that technology includes biotechnology, and that both access to and transfer of technology among Contracting Parties are essential elements for the attainment of the objectives of this Convention, undertakes subject to the provisions of this Article to provide and/or facilitate access for and

transfer to other Contracting Parties of technologies that are relevant to the conservation and sustainable use of biological diversity or make use of genetic resources and do not cause significant damage to the environment.

2. Access to and transfer of technology referred to in paragraph 1 above to developing countries shall be provided and/or facilitated under fair and most favourable terms, including on concessional and preferential terms where mutually agreed, and, where necessary, in accordance with the financial mechanism established by Articles 20 and 21. In the case of technology subject to patents and other intellectual property rights, such access and transfer shall be provided on terms which recognize and are consistent with the adequate and effective protection of intellectual property rights. The application of this paragraph shall be consistent with paragraphs 3, 4 and 5 below.

3. Each Contracting Party shall take legislative, administrative or policy measures, as appropriate, with the aim that Contracting Parties, in particular those that are developing countries, which provide genetic resources are provided access to and transfer of technology which makes use of those resources, on mutually agreed terms, including technology protected by patents and other intellectual property rights, where necessary, through the provisions of Articles 20 and 21 and in accordance with international law and consistent with paragraphs 4 and 5 below.

4. Each Contracting Party shall take legislative, administrative or policy measures, as appropriate, with the aim that the private sector facilitates access to, joint development and transfer of technology referred to in paragraph 1 above for the benefit of both governmental institutions and the private sector of developing countries and in this regard shall abide by the obligations included in paragraphs 1, 2 and 3 above.

5. The Contracting Parties, recognizing that patents and other intellectual property rights may have an influence on the implementation of this Convention, shall cooperate in this regard subject to national legislation and international law in order to ensure that such rights are supportive of and do not run counter to its objectives.

Article 17.   Exchange of Information

1. The Contracting Parties shall facilitate the exchange of information, from all publicly available sources, relevant to the conservation and sustainable use of biological diversity, taking into account the special needs of developing countries.

2. Such exchange of information shall include exchange of results of technical, scientific and socio-economic research, as well as information on training and surveying programmes, specialized knowledge, indigenous and traditional knowledge as such and in combination with the technologies referred to in Article 16, paragraph 1. It shall also, where feasible, include repatriation of information.

Article 18.   Technical and Scientific Cooperation

1. The Contracting Parties shall promote international technical and scientific cooperation in the field of conservation and sustainable use of biological diversity, where necessary, through the appropriate international and national institutions.

2. Each Contracting Party shall promote technical and scientific cooperation with other Contracting Parties, in particular developing countries, in implementing this Convention, inter alia, through the development and implementation of national policies. In promoting such cooperation, special attention should be given to the development and strengthening of national capabilities, by means of human resources development and institution building.

3. The Conference of the Parties, at its first meeting, shall determine how to establish a clearing-house mechanism to promote and facilitate technical and scientific cooperation.

4. The Contracting Parties shall, in accordance with national legislation and policies, encourage and develop methods of cooperation for the development and use of technologies, including indigenous and traditional technologies, in pursuance of the objectives of this Convention. For this purpose, the Contracting Parties shall also promote cooperation in the training of personnel and exchange of experts.

5. The Contracting Parties shall, subject to mutual agreement, promote the establishment of joint research programmes and joint ventures for the development of technologies relevant to the objectives of this Convention.

Article 19. *Handling of Biotechnology and Distribution of its Benefits*

1. Each Contracting Party shall take legislative, administrative or policy measures, as appropriate, to provide for the effective participation in biotechnological research activities by those Contracting Parties, especially developing countries, which provide the genetic resources for such research, and where feasible in such Contracting Parties.

2. Each Contracting Party shall take all practicable measures to promote and advance priority access on a fair and equitable basis by Contracting Parties, especially developing countries, to the results and benefits arising from biotechnologies based upon genetic resources provided by those Contracting Parties. Such access shall be on mutually agreed terms.

3. The Parties shall consider the need for and modalities of a protocol setting out appropriate procedures, including, in particular, advance informed agreement, in the field of the safe transfer, handling and use of any living modified organism resulting from biotechnology that may have adverse effect on the conservation and sustainable use of biological diversity.

4. Each Contracting Party shall, directly or by requiring any natural or legal person under its jurisdiction providing the organisms referred to in paragraph 3 above, provide any available information about the use and safety regulations required by that Contracting Party in handling such organisms, as well as any available information on the potential adverse impact of the specific organisms concerned to the Contracting Party into which those organisms are to be introduced.

Article 20. *Financial Resources*

1. Each Contracting Party undertakes to provide, in accordance with its capabilities, financial support and incentives in respect of those national activities which are intended to achieve the objectives of this Convention, in accordance with its national plans, priorities and programmes.

2. The developed country Parties shall provide new and additional financial resources to enable developing country Parties to meet the agreed full incremental costs to them of implementing measures which fulfil the obligations of this Convention and to benefit from its provisions and which costs are agreed between a developing country Party and the institutional structure referred to in Article 21, in accordance with policy, strategy, programme priorities and eligibility criteria and an indicative list of incremental costs established by the Conference of the Parties. Other Parties, including countries undergoing the process of transition to a market economy, may voluntarily assume the obligations of the developed country Parties. For the purpose of this Article, the Conference of the Parties, shall at its first meeting establish a list of developed country Parties and other Parties which voluntarily assume the obligations of the developed country Parties. The Conference of the Parties shall periodically

review and if necessary amend the list. Contributions from other countries and sources on a voluntary basis would also be encouraged. The implementation of these commitments shall take into account the need for adequacy, predictability and timely flow of funds and the importance of burden-sharing among the contributing Parties included in the list.

3.   The developed country Parties may also provide, and developing country Parties avail themselves of, financial resources related to the implementation of this Convention through bilateral, regional and other multilateral channels.

4.   The extent to which developing country Parties will effectively implement their commitments under this Convention will depend on the effective implementation by developed country Parties of their commitments under this Convention related to financial resources and transfer of technology and will take fully into account the fact that economic and social development and eradication of poverty are the first and overriding priorities of the developing country Parties.

5.   The Parties shall take full account of the specific needs and special situation of least developed countries in their actions with regard to funding and transfer of technology.

6.   The Contracting Parties shall also take into consideration the special conditions resulting from the dependence on, distribution and location of, biological diversity within developing country Parties, in particular small island States.

7.   Consideration shall also be given to the special situation of developing countries, including those that are most environmentally vulnerable, such as those with arid and semi-arid zones, coastal and mountainous areas.

Article 21.   Financial Mechanism

1.   There shall be a mechanism for the provision of financial resources to developing country Parties for purposes of this Convention on a grant or concessional basis the essential elements of which are described in this Article. The mechanism shall function under the authority and guidance of, and be accountable to, the Conference of the Parties for purposes of this Convention. The operations of the mechanism shall be carried out by such institutional structure as may be decided upon by the Conference of the Parties at its first meeting. For purposes of this Convention, the Conference of the Parties shall determine the policy, strategy, programme priorities and eligibility criteria relating to the access to and utilization of such resources. The contributions shall be such as to take into account the need for predictability, adequacy and timely flow of funds referred to in Article 20 in accordance with the amount of resources needed to be decided periodically by the Conference of the Parties and the importance of burden-sharing among the contributing Parties included in the list referred to in Article 20, paragraph 2. Voluntary contributions may also be made by the developed country Parties and by other countries and sources. The mechanism shall operate within a democratic and transparent system of governance.

2.   Pursuant to the objectives of this Convention, the Conference of the Parties shall at its first meeting determine the policy, strategy and programme priorities, as well as detailed criteria and guidelines for eligibility for access to and utilization of the financial resources including monitoring and evaluation on a regular basis of such utilization. The Conference of the Parties shall decide on the arrangements to give effect to paragraph 1 above after consultation with the institutional structure entrusted with the operation of the financial mechanism.

3.   The Conference of the Parties shall review the effectiveness of the mechanism established under this Article, including the criteria and guidelines referred to in paragraph 2 above, not less than two years after the entry into force of this

Convention and thereafter on a regular basis. Based on such review, it shall take appropriate action to improve the effectiveness of the mechanism if necessary.

4. The Contracting Parties shall consider strengthening existing financial institutions to provide financial resources for the conservation and sustainable use of biological diversity.

Article 22. Relationship with Other International Conventions

1. The provisions of this Convention shall not affect the rights and obligations of any Contracting Party deriving from any existing international agreement, except where the exercise of those rights and obligations would cause a serious damage or threat to biological diversity.

2. Contracting Parties shall implement this Convention with respect to the marine environment consistently with the rights and obligations of States under the law of the sea.

Article 23. Conference of the Parties

1. A Conference of the Parties is hereby established. The first meeting of the Conference of the Parties shall be convened by the Executive Director of the United Nations Environment Programme not later than one year after the entry into force of this Convention. Thereafter, ordinary meetings of the Conference of the Parties shall be held at regular intervals to be determined by the Conference at its first meeting.

2. Extraordinary meetings of the Conference of the Parties shall be held at such other times as may be deemed necessary by the Conference, or at the written request of any Party, provided that, within six months of the request being communicated to them by the Secretariat, it is supported by at least one third of the Parties.

3. The Conference of the Parties shall by consensus agree upon and adopt rules of procedure for itself and for any subsidiary body it may establish, as well as financial rules governing the funding of the Secretariat. At each ordinary meeting, it shall adopt a budget for the financial period until the next ordinary meeting.

4. The Conference of the Parties shall keep under review the implementation of this Convention, and, for this purpose, shall:

(a) Establish the form and the intervals for transmitting the information to be submitted in accordance with Article 26 and consider such information as well as reports submitted by any subsidiary body;

(b) Review scientific, technical and technological advice on biological diversity provided in accordance with Article 25;

(c) Consider and adopt, as required, protocols in accordance with Article 28;

(d) Consider and adopt, as required, in accordance with Articles 29 and 30, amendments to this Convention and its annexes;

(e) Consider amendments to any protocol, as well as to any annexes thereto, and, if so decided, recommend their adoption to the Parties to the protocol concerned;

(f) Consider and adopt, as required, in accordance with Article 30, additional annexes to this Convention;

(g) Establish such subsidiary bodies, particularly to provide scientific and technical advice, as are deemed necessary for the implementation of this Convention;

(h) Contact, through the Secretariat, the executive bodies of conventions dealing with matters covered by this Convention with a view to establishing appropriate forms of cooperation with them; and

(i) Consider and undertake any additional action that may be required for the achievement of the purposes of this Convention in the light of experience gained in its operation.

5. The United Nations, its specialized agencies and the International Atomic Energy Agency, as well as any State not Party to this Convention, may be represented as observers at meetings of the Conference of the Parties. Any other body or agency, whether governmental or nongovernmental, qualified in fields relating to conservation and sustainable use of biological diversity, which has informed the Secretariat of its wish to be represented as an observer at a meeting of the Conference of the Parties, may be admitted unless at least one third of the Parties present object. The admission and participation of observers shall be subject to the rules of procedure adopted by the Conference of the Parties.

Article 24. Secretariat

1. A secretariat is hereby established. Its functions shall be:

(a) To arrange for and service meetings of the Conference of the Parties provided for in Article 23;

(b) To perform the functions assigned to it by any protocol;

(c) To prepare reports on the execution of its functions under this Convention and present them to the Conference of the Parties;

(d) To coordinate with other relevant international bodies and, in particular to enter into such administrative and contractual arrangements as may be required for the effective discharge of its functions; and

(e) To perform such other functions as may be determined by the Conference of the Parties.

2. At its first ordinary meeting, the Conference of the Parties shall designate the secretariat from amongst those existing competent international organizations which have signified their willingness to carry out the secretariat functions under this Convention.

Article 25. Subsidiary Body on Scientific, Technical and Technological Advice

1. A subsidiary body for the provision of scientific, technical and technological advice is hereby established to provide the Conference of the Parties and, as appropriate, its other subsidiary bodies with timely advice relating to the implementation of this Convention. This body shall be open to participation by all Parties and shall be multidisciplinary. It shall comprise government representatives competent in the relevant field of expertise. It shall report regularly to the Conference of the Parties on all aspects of its work.

2. Under the authority of and in accordance with guidelines laid down by the Conference of the Parties, and upon its request, this body shall:

(a) Provide scientific and technical assessments of the status of biological diversity;

(b) Prepare scientific and technical assessments of the effects of types of measures taken in accordance with the provisions of this Convention;

(c) Identify innovative, efficient and state-of-the-art technologies and know-how relating to the conservation and sustainable use of biological diversity and advise on the ways and means of promoting development and/or transferring such technologies;

(d) Provide advice on scientific programmes and international cooperation in research and development related to conservation and sustainable use of biological diversity; and

(e) Respond to scientific, technical, technological and methodological questions that the Conference of the Parties and its subsidiary bodies may put to the body.

3. The functions, terms of reference, organization and operation of this body may be further elaborated by the Conference of the Parties.

Article 26.   Reports

Each Contracting Party shall, at intervals to be determined by the Conference of the Parties, present to the Conference of the Parties, reports on measures which it has taken for the implementation of the provisions of this Convention and their effectiveness in meeting the objectives of this Convention.

Article 27.   Settlement of Disputes

1. In the event of a dispute between Contracting Parties concerning the interpretation or application of this Convention, the parties concerned shall seek solution by negotiation.

2. If the parties concerned cannot reach agreement by negotiation, they may jointly seek the good offices of, or request mediation by, a third party.

3. When ratifying, accepting, approving or acceding to this Convention, or at any time thereafter, a State or regional economic integration organization may declare in writing to the Depositary that for a dispute not resolved in accordance with paragraph 1 or paragraph 2 above, it accepts one or both of the following means of dispute settlement as compulsory:

(a) Arbitration in accordance with the procedure laid down in Part 1 of Annex II;

(b) Submission of the dispute to the International Court of Justice.

4. If the parties to the dispute have not, in accordance with paragraph 3 above, accepted the same or any procedure, the dispute shall be submitted to conciliation in accordance with Part 2 of Annex II unless the parties otherwise agree.

5. The provisions of this Article shall apply with respect to any protocol except as otherwise provided in the protocol concerned.

Article 28.   Adoption of Protocols

1. The Contracting Parties shall cooperate in the formulation and adoption of protocols to this Convention.

2. Protocols shall be adopted at a meeting of the Conference of the Parties.

3. The text of any proposed protocol shall be communicated to the Contracting Parties by the Secretariat at least six months before such a meeting.

Article 29.   Amendment of the Convention or Protocols

1. Amendments to this Convention may be proposed by any Contracting Party. Amendments to any protocol may be proposed by any Party to that protocol.

2. Amendments to this Convention shall be adopted at a meeting of the Conference of the Parties. Amendments to any protocol shall be adopted at a meeting of the Parties to the Protocol in question. The text of any proposed amendment to this Convention or to any protocol, except as may otherwise be provided in such protocol, shall be communicated to the Parties to the instrument in question by the Secretariat at least six months before the meeting at which it is proposed for adoption. The Secretariat shall also communicate proposed amendments to the signatories to this Convention for information.

3. The Parties shall make every effort to reach agreement on any proposed amendment to this Convention or to any protocol by consensus. If all efforts at

consensus have been exhausted, and no agreement reached, the amendment shall as a last resort be adopted by a two-thirds majority vote of the Parties to the instrument in question present and voting at the meeting, and shall be submitted by the Depositary to all Parties for ratification, acceptance or approval.

4. Ratification, acceptance or approval of amendments shall be notified to the Depositary in writing. Amendments adopted in accordance with paragraph 3 above shall enter into force among Parties having accepted them on the ninetieth day after the deposit of instruments of ratification, acceptance or approval by at least two thirds of the Contracting Parties to this Convention or of the Parties to the protocol concerned, except as may otherwise be provided in such protocol. Thereafter the amendments shall enter into force for any other Party on the ninetieth day after that Party deposits its instrument of ratification, acceptance or approval of the amendments.

5. For the purposes of this Article, "Parties present and voting" means Parties present and casting an affirmative or negative vote.

Article 30. Adoption and Amendment of Annexes

1. The annexes to this Convention or to any protocol shall form an integral part of the Convention or of such protocol, as the case may be, and, unless expressly provided otherwise, a reference to this Convention or its protocols constitutes at the same time a reference to any annexes thereto. Such annexes shall be restricted to procedural, scientific, technical and administrative matters.

2. Except as may be otherwise provided in any protocol with respect to its annexes, the following procedure shall apply to the proposal, adoption and entry into force of additional annexes to this Convention or of annexes to any protocol:

(a) Annexes to this Convention or to any protocol shall be proposed and adopted according to the procedure laid down in Article 29;

(b) Any Party that is unable to approve an additional annex to this Convention or an annex to any protocol to which it is Party shall so notify the Depositary, in writing, within one year from the date of the communication of the adoption by the Depositary. The Depositary shall without delay notify all Parties of any such notification received. A Party may at any time withdraw a previous declaration of objection and the annexes shall thereupon enter into force for that Party subject to subparagraph (c) below;

(c) On the expiry of one year from the date of the communication of the adoption by the Depositary, the annex shall enter into force for all Parties to this Convention or to any protocol concerned which have not submitted a notification in accordance with the provisions of subparagraph (b) above.

3. The proposal, adoption and entry into force of amendments to annexes to this Convention or to any protocol shall be subject to the same procedure as for the proposal, adoption and entry into force of annexes to the Convention or annexes to any protocol.

4. If an additional annex or an amendment to an annex is related to an amendment to this Convention or to any protocol, the additional annex or amendment shall not enter into force until such time as the amendment to the Convention or to the protocol concerned enters into force.

Article 31. Right to Vote

1. Except as provided for in paragraph 2 below, each Contracting Party to this Convention or to any protocol shall have one vote.

2. Regional economic integration organizations, in matters within their competence, shall exercise their right to vote with a number of votes equal to the number of

their member States which are Contracting Parties to this Convention or the relevant protocol. Such organizations shall not exercise their right to vote if their member States exercise theirs, and vice versa.

Article 32.   Relationship between this Convention and Its Protocols

1.   A State or a regional economic integration organization may not become a Party to a protocol unless it is, or becomes at the same time, a Contracting Party to this Convention.

2.   Decisions under any protocol shall be taken only by the Parties to the protocol concerned. Any Contracting Party that has not ratified, accepted or approved a protocol may participate as an observer in any meeting of the parties to that protocol.

Article 33.   Signature

This Convention shall be open for signature at Rio de Janeiro by all States and any regional economic integration organization from 5 June 1992 until 14 June 1992, and at the United Nations Headquarters in New York from 15 June 1992 to 4 June 1993.

Article 34.   Ratification, Acceptance or Approval

1.   This Convention and any protocol shall be subject to ratification, acceptance or approval by States and by regional economic integration organizations. Instruments of ratification, acceptance or approval shall be deposited with the Depositary.

2.   Any organization referred to in paragraph 1 above which becomes a Contracting Party to this Convention or any protocol without any of its member States being a Contracting Party shall be bound by all the obligations under the Convention or the protocol, as the case may be. In the case of such organizations, one or more of whose member States is a Contracting Party to this Convention or relevant protocol, the organization and its member States shall decide on their respective responsibilities for the performance of their obligations under the Convention or protocol, as the case may be. In such cases, the organization and the member States shall not be entitled to exercise rights under the Convention or relevant protocol concurrently.

3.   In their instruments of ratification, acceptance or approval, the organizations referred to in paragraph 1 above shall declare the extent of their competence with respect to the matters governed by the Convention or the relevant protocol. These organizations shall also inform the Depositary of any relevant modification in the extent of their competence.

Article 35.   Accession

1.   This Convention and any protocol shall be open for accession by States and by regional economic integration organizations from the date on which the Convention or the protocol concerned is closed for signature. The instruments of accession shall be deposited with the Depositary.

2.   In their instruments of accession, the organizations referred to in paragraph 1 above shall declare the extent of their competence with respect to the matters governed by the Convention or the relevant protocol. These organizations shall also inform the Depositary of any relevant modification in the extent of their competence.

3.   The provisions of Article 34, paragraph 2, shall apply to regional economic integration organizations which accede to this Convention or any protocol.

Article 36.   Entry Into Force

1.   This Convention shall enter into force on the ninetieth day after the date of deposit of the thirtieth instrument of ratification, acceptance, approval or accession.

2. Any protocol shall enter into force on the ninetieth day after the date of deposit of the number of instruments of ratification, acceptance, approval or accession, specified in that protocol, has been deposited.

3. For each Contracting Party which ratifies, accepts or approves this Convention or accedes thereto after the deposit of the thirtieth instrument of ratification, acceptance, approval or accession, it shall enter into force on the ninetieth day after the date of deposit by such Contracting Party of its instrument of ratification, acceptance, approval or accession.

4. Any protocol, except as otherwise provided in such protocol, shall enter into force for a Contracting Party that ratifies, accepts or approves that protocol or accedes thereto after its entry into force pursuant to paragraph 2 above, on the ninetieth day after the date on which that Contracting Party deposits its instrument of ratification, acceptance, approval or accession, or on the date on which this Convention enters into force for that Contracting Party, whichever shall be the later.

5. For the purposes of paragraphs 1 and 2 above, any instrument deposited by a regional economic integration organization shall not be counted as additional to those deposited by member States of such organization.

Article 37. *Reservations*

No reservations may be made to this Convention.

Article 38. *Withdrawals*

1. At any time after two years from the date on which this Convention has entered into force for a Contracting Party, that Contracting Party may withdraw from the Convention by giving written notification to the Depositary.

2. Any such withdrawal shall take place upon expiry of one year after the date of its receipt by the Depositary, or on such later date as may be specified in the notification of the withdrawal.

3. Any Contracting Party which withdraws from this Convention shall be considered as also having withdrawn from any protocol to which it is party.

Article 39. *Financial Interim Arrangements*

Provided that it has been fully restructured in accordance with the requirements of Article 21, the Global Environment Facility of the United Nations Development Programme, the United Nations Environment Programme and the International Bank for Reconstruction and Development shall be the institutional structure referred to in Article 21 on an interim basis, for the period between the entry into force of this Convention and the first meeting of the Conference of the Parties or until the Conference of the Parties decides which institutional structure will be designated in accordance with Article 21.

Article 40. *Secretariat Interim Arrangements*

The secretariat to be provided by the Executive Director of the United Nations Environment Programme shall be the secretariat referred to in Article 24, paragraph 2, on an interim basis for the period between the entry into force of this Convention and the first meeting of the Conference of the Parties.

Article 41. *Depositary*

The Secretary–General of the United Nations shall assume the functions of Depositary of this Convention and any protocols.

Article 42. Authentic Texts

The original of this Convention, of which the Arabic, Chinese, English, French, Russian and Spanish texts are equally authentic, shall be deposited with the Secretary–General of the United Nations.

ANNEX I
IDENTIFICATION AND MONITORING

1. Ecosystems and habitats: containing high diversity, large numbers of endemic or threatened species, or wilderness; required by migratory species; of social, economic, cultural or scientific importance; or, which are representative, unique or associated with key evolutionary or other biological processes;

2. Species and communities which are: threatened; wild relatives of domesticated or cultivated species; of medicinal, agricultural or other economic value; or social, scientific or cultural importance; or importance for research into the conservation and sustainable use of biological diversity, such as indicator species; and

3. Described genomes and genes of social, scientific or economic importance.

* * *

5.8 CARTAGENA PROTOCOL ON BIOSAFETY TO THE CONVENTION ON BIOLOGICAL DIVERSITY (WITH ANNEXES).[f] **Adopted at Montreal, 29 January 2000. Entered into force, 11 September 2003. 2226 UNTS 208;** *reprinted in* **5A Weston & Carlson V.H.26**

The Parties to this Protocol,

Being Parties to the Convention on Biological Diversity, hereinafter referred to as "the Convention",

Recalling Article 19, paragraphs 3 and 4, and Articles 8 (g) and 17 of the Convention,

Recalling also decision II/5 of 17 November 1995 of the Conference of the Parties to the Convention to develop a Protocol on biosafety, specifically focusing on transboundary movement of any living modified organism resulting from modern biotechnology that may have adverse effect on the conservation and sustainable use of biological diversity, setting out for consideration, in particular, appropriate procedures for advance informed agreement,

Reaffirming the precautionary approach contained in Principle 15 of the Rio Declaration on Environment and Development,

Aware of the rapid expansion of modern biotechnology and the growing public concern over its potential adverse effects on biological diversity, taking also into account risks to human health,

Recognizing that modern biotechnology has great potential for human well-being if developed and used with adequate safety measures for the environment and human health,

Recognizing also the crucial importance to humankind of centres of origin and centres of genetic diversity,

Taking into account the limited capabilities of many countries, particularly developing countries, to cope with the nature and scale of known and potential risks associated with living modified organisms,

Recognizing that trade and environment agreements should be mutually supportive with a view to achieving sustainable development,

Emphasizing that this Protocol shall not be interpreted as implying a change in the rights and obligations of a Party under any existing international agreements,

Understanding that the above recital is not intended to subordinate this Protocol to other international agreements,

Have agreed as follows:

Article 1

Objective

In accordance with the precautionary approach contained in Principle 15 of the Rio Declaration on Environment and Development, the objective of this Protocol is to contribute to ensuring an adequate level of protection in the field of the safe transfer, handling and use of living modified organisms resulting from modern biotechnology that may have adverse effects on the conservation and sustainable use of biological diversity, taking also into account risks to human health, and specifically focusing on transboundary movements.

---

f. *See also* Basic Document V.H.22, *supra*.

Article 2
General Provisions

1.   Each Party shall take necessary and appropriate legal, administrative and other measures to implement its obligations under this Protocol.

2.   The Parties shall ensure that the development, handling, transport, use, transfer and release of any living modified organisms are undertaken in a manner that prevents or reduces the risks to biological diversity, taking also into account risks to human health.

3.   Nothing in this Protocol shall affect in any way the sovereignty of States over their territorial sea established in accordance with international law, and the sovereign rights and the jurisdiction which States have in their exclusive economic zones and their continental shelves in accordance with international law, and the exercise by ships and aircraft of all States of navigational rights and freedoms as provided for in international law and as reflected in relevant international instruments.

4.   Nothing in this Protocol shall be interpreted as restricting the right of a Party to take action that is more protective of the conservation and sustainable use of biological diversity than that called for in this Protocol, provided that such action is consistent with the objective and the provisions of this Protocol and is in accordance with that Party's other obligations under international law.

5.   The Parties are encouraged to take into account, as appropriate, available expertise, instruments and work undertaken in international forums with competence in the area of risks to human health.

Article 3
Use of Terms

For the purposes of this Protocol:

(a) "Conference of the Parties" means the Conference of the Parties to the Convention;

(b) "Contained use" means any operation, undertaken within a facility, installation or other physical structure, which involves living modified organisms that are controlled by specific measures that effectively limit their contact with, and their impact on, the external environment;

(c) "Export" means intentional transboundary movement from one Party to another Party;

(d) "Exporter" means any legal or natural person, under the jurisdiction of the Party of export, who arranges for a living modified organism to be exported;

(e) "Import" means intentional transboundary movement into one Party from another Party;

(f) "Importer" means any legal or natural person, under the jurisdiction of the Party of import, who arranges for a living modified organism to be imported;

(g) "Living modified organism" means any living organism that possesses a novel combination of genetic material obtained through the use of modern biotechnology;

(h) "Living organism" means any biological entity capable of transferring or replicating genetic material, including sterile organisms, viruses and viroids;

(i) "Modern biotechnology" means the application of:

a.   In vitro nucleic acid techniques, including recombinant deoxyribonucleic acid (DNA) and direct injection of nucleic acid into cells or organelles, or

b. Fusion of cells beyond the taxonomic family, that overcome natural physiological reproductive or recombination barriers and that are not techniques used in traditional breeding and selection;

(j) "Regional economic integration organization" means an organization constituted by sovereign States of a given region, to which its member States have transferred competence in respect of matters governed by this Protocol and which has been duly authorized, in accordance with its internal procedures, to sign, ratify, accept, approve or accede to it;

(k) "Transboundary movement" means the movement of a living modified organism from one Party to another Party, save that for the purposes of Articles 17 and 24 transboundary movement extends to movement between Parties and non-Parties.

Article 4
Scope

This Protocol shall apply to the transboundary movement, transit, handling and use of all living modified organisms that may have adverse effects on the conservation and sustainable use of biological diversity, taking also into account risks to human health.

Article 5
Pharmaceuticals

Notwithstanding Article 4 and without prejudice to any right of a Party to subject all living modified organisms to risk assessment prior to the making of decisions on import, this Protocol shall not apply to the transboundary movement of living modified organisms which are pharmaceuticals for humans that are addressed by other relevant international agreements or organisations.

Article 6
Transit and Contained Use

1. Notwithstanding Article 4 and without prejudice to any right of a Party of transit to regulate the transport of living modified organisms through its territory and make available to the Biosafety Clearing–House, any decision of that Party, subject to Article 2, paragraph 3, regarding the transit through its territory of a specific living modified organism, the provisions of this Protocol with respect to the advance informed agreement procedure shall not apply to living modified organisms in transit.

2. Notwithstanding Article 4 and without prejudice to any right of a Party to subject all living modified organisms to risk assessment prior to decisions on import and to set standards for contained use within its jurisdiction, the provisions of this Protocol with respect to the advance informed agreement procedure shall not apply to the transboundary movement of living modified organisms destined for contained use undertaken in accordance with the standards of the Party of import.

Article 7
Application of the Advance Informed Agreement Procedure

1. Subject to Articles 5 and 6, the advance informed agreement procedure in Articles 8 to 10 and 12 shall apply prior to the first intentional transboundary movement of living modified organisms for intentional introduction into the environment of the Party of import.

2. "Intentional introduction into the environment" in paragraph 1 above, does not refer to living modified organisms intended for direct use as food or feed, or for processing.

3. Article 11 shall apply prior to the first transboundary movement of living modified organisms intended for direct use as food or feed, or for processing.

4. The advance informed agreement procedure shall not apply to the intentional transboundary movement of living modified organisms identified in a decision of the Conference of the Parties serving as the meeting of the Parties to this Protocol as being not likely to have adverse effects on the conservation and sustainable use of biological diversity, taking also into account risks to human health.

Article 8
Notification

1. The Party of export shall notify, or require the exporter to ensure notification to, in writing, the competent national authority of the Party of import prior to the intentional transboundary movement of a living modified organism that falls within the scope of Article 7, paragraph 1. The notification shall contain, at a minimum, the information specified in Annex I.

2. The Party of export shall ensure that there is a legal requirement for the accuracy of information provided by the exporter.

Article 9
Acknowledgement of Receipt of Notification

1. The Party of import shall acknowledge receipt of the notification, in writing, to the notifier within ninety days of its receipt.

2. The acknowledgement shall state:

(a) The date of receipt of the notification;

(b) Whether the notification, prima facie, contains the information referred to in Article 8;

(c) Whether to proceed according to the domestic regulatory framework of the Party of import or according to the procedure specified in Article 10.

3. The domestic regulatory framework referred to in paragraph 2 (c) above, shall be consistent with this Protocol.

4. A failure by the Party of import to acknowledge receipt of a notification shall not imply its consent to an intentional transboundary movement.

Article 10
Decision Procedure

1. Decisions taken by the Party of import shall be in accordance with Article 15.

2. The Party of import shall, within the period of time referred to in Article 9, inform the notifier, in writing, whether the intentional transboundary movement may proceed:

(a) Only after the Party of import has given its written consent; or

(b) After no less than ninety days without a subsequent written consent.

3. Within two hundred and seventy days of the date of receipt of notification, the Party of import shall communicate, in writing, to the notifier and to the Biosafety Clearing–House the decision referred to in paragraph 2 (a) above:

(a) Approving the import, with or without conditions, including how the decision will apply to subsequent imports of the same living modified organism;

(b) Prohibiting the import;

(c) Requesting additional relevant information in accordance with its domestic regulatory framework or Annex I; in calculating the time within which the Party of import is to respond, the number of days it has to wait for additional relevant information shall not be taken into account; or

(d) Informing the notifier that the period specified in this paragraph is extended by a defined period of time.

4. Except in a case in which consent is unconditional, a decision under paragraph 3 above, shall set out the reasons on which it is based.

5. A failure by the Party of import to communicate its decision within two hundred and seventy days of the date of receipt of the notification shall not imply its consent to an intentional transboundary movement.

6. Lack of scientific certainty due to insufficient relevant scientific information and knowledge regarding the extent of the potential adverse effects of a living modified organism on the conservation and sustainable use of biological diversity in the Party of import, taking also into account risks to human health, shall not prevent that Party from taking a decision, as appropriate, with regard to the import of the living modified organism in question as referred to in paragraph 3 above, in order to avoid or minimize such potential adverse effects.

7. The Conference of the Parties serving as the meeting of the Parties shall, at its first meeting, decide upon appropriate procedures and mechanisms to facilitate decision-making by Parties of import.

Article 11
Procedure for Living Modified Organisms Intended for Direct Use as Food or Feed, or for Processing

1. A Party that makes a final decision regarding domestic use, including placing on the market, of a living modified organism that may be subject to transboundary movement for direct use as food or feed, or for processing shall, within fifteen days of making that decision, inform the Parties through the Biosafety Clearing–House. This information shall contain, at a minimum, the information specified in Annex II. The Party shall provide a copy of the information, in writing, to the national focal point of each Party that informs the Secretariat in advance that it does not have access to the Biosafety Clearing–House. This provision shall not apply to decisions regarding field trials.

2. The Party making a decision under paragraph 1 above, shall ensure that there is a legal requirement for the accuracy of information provided by the applicant.

3. Any Party may request additional information from the authority identified in paragraph (b) of Annex II.

4. A Party may take a decision on the import of living modified organisms intended for direct use as food or feed, or for processing, under its domestic regulatory framework that is consistent with the objective of this Protocol.

5. Each Party shall make available to the Biosafety Clearing–House copies of any national laws, regulations and guidelines applicable to the import of living modified organisms intended for direct use as food or feed, or for processing, if available.

6. A developing country Party or a Party with an economy in transition may, in the absence of the domestic regulatory framework referred to in paragraph 4 above, and in exercise of its domestic jurisdiction, declare through the Biosafety Clearing–House that its decision prior to the first import of a living modified organism intended for direct use as food or feed, or for processing, on which information has been provided under paragraph 1 above, will be taken according to the following:

(a) A risk assessment undertaken in accordance with Article 15; and

(b) A decision made within a predictable timeframe, not exceeding two hundred and seventy days.

7. Failure by a Party to communicate its decision according to paragraph 6 above, shall not imply its consent or refusal to the import of a living modified organism intended for direct use as food or feed, or for processing, unless otherwise specified by the Party.

8. Lack of scientific certainty due to insufficient relevant scientific information and knowledge regarding the extent of the potential adverse effects of a living modified organism on the conservation and sustainable use of biological diversity in the Party of import, taking also into account risks to human health, shall not prevent that Party from taking a decision, as appropriate, with regard to the import of that living modified organism intended for direct use as food or feed, or for processing, in order to avoid or minimize such potential adverse effects.

9. A Party may indicate its needs for financial and technical assistance and capacity-building with respect to living modified organisms intended for direct use as food or feed, or for processing. Parties shall cooperate to meet these needs in accordance with Articles 22 and 28.

Article 12
Review of Decisions

1. A Party of import may, at any time, in light of new scientific information on potential adverse effects on the conservation and sustainable use of biological diversity, taking also into account the risks to human health, review and change a decision regarding an intentional transboundary movement. In such case, the Party shall, within thirty days, inform any notifier that has previously notified movements of the living modified organism referred to in such decision, as well as the Biosafety Clearing–House, and shall set out the reasons for its decision.

2. A Party of export or a notifier may request the Party of import to review a decision it has made in respect of it under Article 10 where the Party of export or the notifier considers that:

(a) A change in circumstances has occurred that may influence the outcome of the risk assessment upon which the decision was based; or

(b) Additional relevant scientific or technical information has become available.

3. The Party of import shall respond in writing to such a request within ninety days and set out the reasons for its decision.

4. The Party of import may, at its discretion, require a risk assessment for subsequent imports.

Article 13
Simplified Procedure

1. A Party of import may, provided that adequate measures are applied to ensure the safe intentional transboundary movement of living modified organisms in accordance with the objective of this Protocol, specify in advance to the Biosafety Clearing–House:

(a) Cases in which intentional transboundary movement to it may take place at the same time as the movement is notified to the Party of import; and

(b) Imports of living modified organisms to it to be exempted from the advance informed agreement procedure.

Notifications under subparagraph (a) above, may apply to subsequent similar movements to the same Party.

2. The information relating to an intentional transboundary movement that is to be provided in the notifications referred to in paragraph 1 (a) above, shall be the information specified in Annex I.

Article 14
Bilateral, Regional and Multilateral Agreements and Arrangements

1. Parties may enter into bilateral, regional and multilateral agreements and arrangements regarding intentional transboundary movements of living modified organisms, consistent with the objective of this Protocol and provided that such agreements and arrangements do not result in a lower level of protection than that provided for by the Protocol.

2. The Parties shall inform each other, through the Biosafety Clearing–House, of any such bilateral, regional and multilateral agreements and arrangements that they have entered into before or after the date of entry into force of this Protocol.

3. The provisions of this Protocol shall not affect intentional transboundary movements that take place pursuant to such agreements and arrangements as between the parties to those agreements or arrangements.

4. Any Party may determine that its domestic regulations shall apply with respect to specific imports to it and shall notify the Biosafety Clearing–House of its decision.

Article 15
Risk Assessment

1. Risk assessments undertaken pursuant to this Protocol shall be carried out in a scientifically sound manner, in accordance with Annex III and taking into account recognized risk assessment techniques. Such risk assessments shall be based, at a minimum, on information provided in accordance with Article 8 and other available scientific evidence in order to identify and evaluate the possible adverse effects of living modified organisms on the conservation and sustainable use of biological diversity, taking also into account risks to human health.

2. The Party of import shall ensure that risk assessments are carried out for decisions taken under Article 10. It may require the exporter to carry out the risk assessment.

3. The cost of risk assessment shall be borne by the notifier if the Party of import so requires.

Article 16
Risk Management

1. The Parties shall, taking into account Article 8 (g) of the Convention, establish and maintain appropriate mechanisms, measures and strategies to regulate, manage and control risks identified in the risk assessment provisions of this Protocol associated with the use, handling and transboundary movement of living modified organisms.

2. Measures based on risk assessment shall be imposed to the extent necessary to prevent adverse effects of the living modified organism on the conservation and sustainable use of biological diversity, taking also into account risks to human health, within the territory of the Party of import.

3. Each Party shall take appropriate measures to prevent unintentional transboundary movements of living modified organisms, including such measures as requiring a risk assessment to be carried out prior to the first release of a living modified organism.

4. Without prejudice to paragraph 2 above, each Party shall endeavour to ensure that any living modified organism, whether imported or locally developed, has undergone an appropriate period of observation that is commensurate with its life-cycle or generation time before it is put to its intended use.

5. Parties shall cooperate with a view to:

(a) Identifying living modified organisms or specific traits of living modified organisms that may have adverse effects on the conservation and sustainable use of biological diversity, taking also into account risks to human health; and

(b) Taking appropriate measures regarding the treatment of such living modified organisms or specific traits.

Article 17
Unintentional Transboundary Movements and Emergency Measures

1. Each Party shall take appropriate measures to notify affected or potentially affected States, the Biosafety Clearing–House and, where appropriate, relevant international organizations, when it knows of an occurrence under its jurisdiction resulting in a release that leads, or may lead, to an unintentional transboundary movement of a living modified organism that is likely to have significant adverse effects on the conservation and sustainable use of biological diversity, taking also into account risks to human health in such States. The notification shall be provided as soon as the Party knows of the above situation.

2. Each Party shall, no later than the date of entry into force of this Protocol for it, make available to the Biosafety Clearing–House the relevant details setting out its point of contact for the purposes of receiving notifications under this Article.

3. Any notification arising from paragraph 1 above, should include:

(a) Available relevant information on the estimated quantities and relevant characteristics and/or traits of the living modified organism;

(b) Information on the circumstances and estimated date of the release, and on the use of the living modified organism in the originating Party;

(c) Any available information about the possible adverse effects on the conservation and sustainable use of biological diversity, taking also into account risks to human health, as well as available information about possible risk management measures;

(d) Any other relevant information; and

(e) A point of contact for further information.

4. In order to minimize any significant adverse effects on the conservation and sustainable use of biological diversity, taking also into account risks to human health, each Party, under whose jurisdiction the release of the living modified organism referred to in paragraph 1 above, occurs, shall immediately consult the affected or potentially affected States to enable them to determine appropriate responses and initiate necessary action, including emergency measures.

Article 18
Handling, Transport, Packaging and Identification

1. In order to avoid adverse effects on the conservation and sustainable use of biological diversity, taking also into account risks to human health, each Party shall take necessary measures to require that living modified organisms that are subject to intentional transboundary movement within the scope of this Protocol are handled, packaged and transported under conditions of safety, taking into consideration relevant international rules and standards.

2. Each Party shall take measures to require that documentation accompanying:

(a) Living modified organisms that are intended for direct use as food or feed, or for processing, clearly identifies that they "may contain" living modified organisms and are not intended for intentional introduction into the environment, as well as a contact point for further information. The Conference of the Parties serving as the meeting of the Parties to this Protocol shall take a decision on the detailed requirements for this purpose, including specification of their identity and any unique identification, no later than two years after the date of entry into force of this Protocol;

(b) Living modified organisms that are destined for contained use clearly identifies them as living modified organisms; and specifies any requirements for the safe handling, storage, transport and use, the contact point for further information, including the name and address of the individual and institution to whom the living modified organisms are consigned; and

(c) Living modified organisms that are intended for intentional introduction into the environment of the Party of import and any other living modified organisms within the scope of the Protocol, clearly identifies them as living modified organisms; specifies the identity and relevant traits and/or characteristics, any requirements for the safe handling, storage, transport and use, the contact point for further information and, as appropriate, the name and address of the importer and exporter; and contains a declaration that the movement is in conformity with the requirements of this Protocol applicable to the exporter.

3.   The Conference of the Parties serving as the meeting of the Parties to this Protocol shall consider the need for and modalities of developing standards with regard to identification, handling, packaging and transport practices, in consultation with other relevant international bodies.

Article 19
Competent National Authorities and National Focal Points

1.   Each Party shall designate one national focal point to be responsible on its behalf for liaison with the Secretariat. Each Party shall also designate one or more competent national authorities, which shall be responsible for performing the administrative functions required by this Protocol and which shall be authorized to act on its behalf with respect to those functions. A Party may designate a single entity to fulfil the functions of both focal point and competent national authority.

2.   Each Party shall, no later than the date of entry into force of this Protocol for it, notify the Secretariat of the names and addresses of its focal point and its competent national authority or authorities. Where a Party designates more than one competent national authority, it shall convey to the Secretariat, with its notification thereof, relevant information on the respective responsibilities of those authorities. Where applicable, such information shall, at a minimum, specify which competent authority is responsible for which type of living modified organism. Each Party shall forthwith notify the Secretariat of any changes in the designation of its national focal point or in the name and address or responsibilities of its competent national authority or authorities.

3.   The Secretariat shall forthwith inform the Parties of the notifications it receives under paragraph 2 above, and shall also make such information available through the Biosafety Clearing–House.

Article 20
Information Sharing and the Biosafety Clearing-house

1.   A Biosafety Clearing–House is hereby established as part of the clearing-house mechanism under Article 18, paragraph 3, of the Convention, in order to:

(a) Facilitate the exchange of scientific, technical, environmental and legal information on, and experience with, living modified organisms; and

(b) Assist Parties to implement the Protocol, taking into account the special needs of developing country Parties, in particular the least developed and small island developing States among them, and countries with economies in transition as well as countries that are centres of origin and centres of genetic diversity.

2. The Biosafety Clearing–House shall serve as a means through which information is made available for the purposes of paragraph 1 above. It shall provide access to information made available by the Parties relevant to the implementation of the Protocol. It shall also provide access, where possible, to other international biosafety information exchange mechanisms.

3. Without prejudice to the protection of confidential information, each Party shall make available to the Biosafety Clearing–House any information required to be made available to the Biosafety Clearing–House under this Protocol, and:

(a) Any existing laws, regulations and guidelines for implementation of the Protocol, as well as information required by the Parties for the advance informed agreement procedure;

(b) Any bilateral, regional and multilateral agreements and arrangements;

(c) Summaries of its risk assessments or environmental reviews of living modified organisms generated by its regulatory process, and carried out in accordance with Article 15, including, where appropriate, relevant information regarding products thereof, namely, processed materials that are of living modified organism origin, containing detectable novel combinations of replicable genetic material obtained through the use of modern biotechnology;

(d) Its final decisions regarding the importation or release of living modified organisms; and

(e) Reports submitted by it pursuant to Article 33, including those on implementation of the advance informed agreement procedure.

4. The modalities of the operation of the Biosafety Clearing–House, including reports on its activities, shall be considered and decided upon by the Conference of the Parties serving as the meeting of the Parties to this Protocol at its first meeting, and kept under review thereafter.

Article 21
Confidential Information

1. The Party of import shall permit the notifier to identify information submitted under the procedures of this Protocol or required by the Party of import as part of the advance informed agreement procedure of the Protocol that is to be treated as confidential. Justification shall be given in such cases upon request.

2. The Party of import shall consult the notifier if it decides that information identified by the notifier as confidential does not qualify for such treatment and shall, prior to any disclosure, inform the notifier of its decision, providing reasons on request, as well as an opportunity for consultation and for an internal review of the decision prior to disclosure.

3. Each Party shall protect confidential information received under this Protocol, including any confidential information received in the context of the advance informed agreement procedure of the Protocol. Each Party shall ensure that it has procedures to protect such information and shall protect the confidentiality of such information in a manner no less favourable than its treatment of confidential information in connection with domestically produced living modified organisms.

4. The Party of import shall not use such information for a commercial purpose, except with the written consent of the notifier.

5. If a notifier withdraws or has withdrawn a notification, the Party of import shall respect the confidentiality of commercial and industrial information, including research and development information as well as information on which the Party and the notifier disagree as to its confidentiality.

6.   Without prejudice to paragraph 5 above, the following information shall not be considered confidential:

(a) The name and address of the notifier;

(b) A general description of the living modified organism or organisms;

(c) A summary of the risk assessment of the effects on the conservation and sustainable use of biological diversity, taking also into account risks to human health; and

(d) Any methods and plans for emergency response.

Article 22
Capacity-building

1.   The Parties shall cooperate in the development and/or strengthening of human resources and institutional capacities in biosafety, including biotechnology to the extent that it is required for biosafety, for the purpose of the effective implementation of this Protocol, in developing country Parties, in particular the least developed and small island developing States among them, and in Parties with economies in transition, including through existing global, regional, subregional and national institutions and organizations and, as appropriate, through facilitating private sector involvement.

2.   For the purposes of implementing paragraph 1 above, in relation to cooperation, the needs of developing country Parties, in particular the least developed and small island developing States among them, for financial resources and access to and transfer of technology and know-how in accordance with the relevant provisions of the Convention, shall be taken fully into account for capacity-building in biosafety. Cooperation in capacity-building shall, subject to the different situation, capabilities and requirements of each Party, include scientific and technical training in the proper and safe management of biotechnology, and in the use of risk assessment and risk management for biosafety, and the enhancement of technological and institutional capacities in biosafety. The needs of Parties with economies in transition shall also be taken fully into account for such capacity-building in biosafety.

Article 23
Public Awareness and Participation

1.   The Parties shall:

(a) Promote and facilitate public awareness, education and participation concerning the safe transfer, handling and use of living modified organisms in relation to the conservation and sustainable use of biological diversity, taking also into account risks to human health. In doing so, the Parties shall cooperate, as appropriate, with other States and international bodies;

(b) Endeavour to ensure that public awareness and education encompass access to information on living modified organisms identified in accordance with this Protocol that may be imported.

2.   The Parties shall, in accordance with their respective laws and regulations, consult the public in the decision-making process regarding living modified organisms and shall make the results of such decisions available to the public, while respecting confidential information in accordance with Article 21.

3.   Each Party shall endeavour to inform its public about the means of public access to the Biosafety Clearing–House.

Article 24
Non-parties

1. Transboundary movements of living modified organisms between Parties and non-Parties shall be consistent with the objective of this Protocol. The Parties may enter into bilateral, regional and multilateral agreements and arrangements with non-Parties regarding such transboundary movements.

2. The Parties shall encourage non-Parties to adhere to this Protocol and to contribute appropriate information to the Biosafety Clearing–House on living modified organisms released in, or moved into or out of, areas within their national jurisdictions.

Article 25
Illegal Transboundary Movements

1. Each Party shall adopt appropriate domestic measures aimed at preventing and, if appropriate, penalizing transboundary movements of living modified organisms carried out in contravention of its domestic measures to implement this Protocol. Such movements shall be deemed illegal transboundary movements.

2. In the case of an illegal transboundary movement, the affected Party may request the Party of origin to dispose, at its own expense, of the living modified organism in question by repatriation or destruction, as appropriate.

3. Each Party shall make available to the Biosafety Clearing–House information concerning cases of illegal transboundary movements pertaining to it.

Article 26
Socio-economic Considerations

1. The Parties, in reaching a decision on import under this Protocol or under its domestic measures implementing the Protocol, may take into account, consistent with their international obligations, socio-economic considerations arising from the impact of living modified organisms on the conservation and sustainable use of biological diversity, especially with regard to the value of biological diversity to indigenous and local communities.

2. The Parties are encouraged to cooperate on research and information exchange on any socio-economic impacts of living modified organisms, especially on indigenous and local communities.

Article 27
Liability and Redress

The Conference of the Parties serving as the meeting of the Parties to this Protocol shall, at its first meeting, adopt a process with respect to the appropriate elaboration of international rules and procedures in the field of liability and redress for damage resulting from transboundary movements of living modified organisms, analysing and taking due account of the ongoing processes in international law on these matters, and shall endeavour to complete this process within four years.

Article 28
Financial Mechanism and Resources

1. In considering financial resources for the implementation of this Protocol, the Parties shall take into account the provisions of Article 20 of the Convention.

2. The financial mechanism established in Article 21 of the Convention shall, through the institutional structure entrusted with its operation, be the financial mechanism for this Protocol.

3. Regarding the capacity-building referred to in Article 22 of this Protocol, the Conference of the Parties serving as the meeting of the Parties to this Protocol, in providing guidance with respect to the financial mechanism referred to in paragraph 2 above, for consideration by the Conference of the Parties, shall take into account the need for financial resources by developing country Parties, in particular the least developed and the small island developing States among them.

4. In the context of paragraph 1 above, the Parties shall also take into account the needs of the developing country Parties, in particular the least developed and the small island developing States among them, and of the Parties with economies in transition, in their efforts to identify and implement their capacity-building requirements for the purposes of the implementation of this Protocol.

5. The guidance to the financial mechanism of the Convention in relevant decisions of the Conference of the Parties, including those agreed before the adoption of this Protocol, shall apply, mutatis mutandis, to the provisions of this Article.

6. The developed country Parties may also provide, and the developing country Parties and the Parties with economies in transition avail themselves of, financial and technological resources for the implementation of the provisions of this Protocol through bilateral, regional and multilateral channels.

Article 29
Conference of the Parties Serving as the Meeting of the Parties to this Protocol

1. The Conference of the Parties shall serve as the meeting of the Parties to this Protocol.

2. Parties to the Convention that are not Parties to this Protocol may participate as observers in the proceedings of any meeting of the Conference of the Parties serving as the meeting of the Parties to this Protocol. When the Conference of the Parties serves as the meeting of the Parties to this Protocol, decisions under this Protocol shall be taken only by those that are Parties to it.

3. When the Conference of the Parties serves as the meeting of the Parties to this Protocol, any member of the bureau of the Conference of the Parties representing a Party to the Convention but, at that time, not a Party to this Protocol, shall be substituted by a member to be elected by and from among the Parties to this Protocol.

4. The Conference of the Parties serving as the meeting of the Parties to this Protocol shall keep under regular review the implementation of this Protocol and shall make, within its mandate, the decisions necessary to promote its effective implementation. It shall perform the functions assigned to it by this Protocol and shall:

(a) Make recommendations on any matters necessary for the implementation of this Protocol;

(b) Establish such subsidiary bodies as are deemed necessary for the implementation of this Protocol;

(c) Seek and utilize, where appropriate, the services and cooperation of, and information provided by, competent international organizations and intergovernmental and non-governmental bodies;

(d) Establish the form and the intervals for transmitting the information to be submitted in accordance with Article 33 of this Protocol and consider such information as well as reports submitted by any subsidiary body;

(e) Consider and adopt, as required, amendments to this Protocol and its annexes, as well as any additional annexes to this Protocol, that are deemed necessary for the implementation of this Protocol; and

(f) Exercise such other functions as may be required for the implementation of this Protocol.

5. The rules of procedure of the Conference of the Parties and financial rules of the Convention shall be applied, _mutatis mutandis_, under this Protocol, except as may be otherwise decided by consensus by the Conference of the Parties serving as the meeting of the Parties to this Protocol.

6. The first meeting of the Conference of the Parties serving as the meeting of the Parties to this Protocol shall be convened by the Secretariat in conjunction with the first meeting of the Conference of the Parties that is scheduled after the date of the entry into force of this Protocol. Subsequent ordinary meetings of the Conference of the Parties serving as the meeting of the Parties to this Protocol shall be held in conjunction with ordinary meetings of the Conference of the Parties, unless otherwise decided by the Conference of the Parties serving as the meeting of the Parties to this Protocol.

7. Extraordinary meetings of the Conference of the Parties serving as the meeting of the Parties to this Protocol shall be held at such other times as may be deemed necessary by the Conference of the Parties serving as the meeting of the Parties to this Protocol, or at the written request of any Party, provided that, within six months of the request being communicated to the Parties by the Secretariat, it is supported by at least one third of the Parties.

8. The United Nations, its specialized agencies and the International Atomic Energy Agency, as well as any State member thereof or observers thereto not party to the Convention, may be represented as observers at meetings of the Conference of the Parties serving as the meeting of the Parties to this Protocol. Any body or agency, whether national or international, governmental or non-governmental, that is qualified in matters covered by this Protocol and that has informed the Secretariat of its wish to be represented at a meeting of the Conference of the Parties serving as a meeting of the Parties to this Protocol as an observer, may be so admitted, unless at least one third of the Parties present object. Except as otherwise provided in this Article, the admission and participation of observers shall be subject to the rules of procedure, as referred to in paragraph 5 above.

Article 30
Subsidiary Bodies

1. Any subsidiary body established by or under the Convention may, upon a decision by the Conference of the Parties serving as the meeting of the Parties to this Protocol, serve the Protocol, in which case the meeting of the Parties shall specify which functions that body shall exercise.

2. Parties to the Convention that are not Parties to this Protocol may participate as observers in the proceedings of any meeting of any such subsidiary bodies. When a subsidiary body of the Convention serves as a subsidiary body to this Protocol, decisions under the Protocol shall be taken only by the Parties to the Protocol.

3. When a subsidiary body of the Convention exercises its functions with regard to matters concerning this Protocol, any member of the bureau of that subsidiary body representing a Party to the Convention but, at that time, not a Party to the Protocol, shall be substituted by a member to be elected by and from among the Parties to the Protocol.

Article 31
Secretariat

1. The Secretariat established by Article 24 of the Convention shall serve as the secretariat to this Protocol.

2. Article 24, paragraph 1, of the Convention on the functions of the Secretariat shall apply, _mutatis mutandis_, to this Protocol.

3. To the extent that they are distinct, the costs of the secretariat services for this Protocol shall be met by the Parties hereto. The Conference of the Parties serving as the meeting of the Parties to this Protocol shall, at its first meeting, decide on the necessary budgetary arrangements to this end.

Article 32
Relationship with the Convention

Except as otherwise provided in this Protocol, the provisions of the Convention relating to its protocols shall apply to this Protocol.

Article 33
Monitoring and Reporting

Each Party shall monitor the implementation of its obligations under this Protocol, and shall, at intervals to be determined by the Conference of the Parties serving as the meeting of the Parties to this Protocol, report to the Conference of the Parties serving as the meeting of the Parties to this Protocol on measures that it has taken to implement the Protocol.

Article 34
Compliance

The Conference of the Parties serving as the meeting of the Parties to this Protocol shall, at its first meeting, consider and approve cooperative procedures and institutional mechanisms to promote compliance with the provisions of this Protocol and to address cases of non-compliance. These procedures and mechanisms shall include provisions to offer advice or assistance, where appropriate. They shall be separate from, and without prejudice to, the dispute settlement procedures and mechanisms established by Article 27 of the Convention.

Article 35
Assessment and Review

The Conference of the Parties serving as the meeting of the Parties to this Protocol shall undertake, five years after the entry into force of this Protocol and at least every five years thereafter, an evaluation of the effectiveness of the Protocol, including an assessment of its procedures and annexes.

Article 36
Signature

This Protocol shall be open for signature at the United Nations Office at Nairobi by States and regional economic integration organizations from 15 to 26 May 2000, and at United Nations Headquarters in New York from 5 June 2000 to 4 June 2001.

Article 37
Entry into Force

1. This Protocol shall enter into force on the ninetieth day after the date of deposit of the fiftieth instrument of ratification, acceptance, approval or accession by States or regional economic integration organizations that are Parties to the Convention.

2. This Protocol shall enter into force for a State or regional economic integration organization that ratifies, accepts or approves this Protocol or accedes thereto after its entry into force pursuant to paragraph 1 above, on the ninetieth day after the date on which that State or regional economic integration organization deposits its instrument of ratification, acceptance, approval or accession, or on the date on which

the Convention enters into force for that State or regional economic integration organization, whichever shall be the later.

3. For the purposes of paragraphs 1 and 2 above, any instrument deposited by a regional economic integration organization shall not be counted as additional to those deposited by member States of such organization.

Article 38
Reservations

No reservations may be made to this Protocol.

Article 39
Withdrawal

1. At any time after two years from the date on which this Protocol has entered into force for a Party, that Party may withdraw from the Protocol by giving written notification to the Depositary.

2. Any such withdrawal shall take place upon expiry of one year after the date of its receipt by the Depositary, or on such later date as may be specified in the notification of the withdrawal.

Article 40
Authentic Texts

The original of this Protocol, of which the Arabic, Chinese, English, French, Russian and Spanish texts are equally authentic, shall be deposited with the Secretary–General of the United Nations.

Annex I

INFORMATION REQUIRED IN NOTIFICATIONS
UNDER ARTICLES 8, 10 AND 13

(a) Name, address and contact details of the exporter.

(b) Name, address and contact details of the importer.

(c) Name and identity of the living modified organism, as well as the domestic classification, if any, of the biosafety level of the living modified organism in the State of export.

(d) Intended date or dates of the transboundary movement, if known.

(e) Taxonomic status, common name, point of collection or acquisition, and characteristics of recipient organism or parental organisms related to biosafety.

(f) Centres of origin and centres of genetic diversity, if known, of the recipient organism and/or the parental organisms and a description of the habitats where the organisms may persist or proliferate.

(g) Taxonomic status, common name, point of collection or acquisition, and characteristics of the donor organism or organisms related to biosafety.

(h) Description of the nucleic acid or the modification introduced, the technique used, and the resulting characteristics of the living modified organism.

(i) Intended use of the living modified organism or products thereof, namely, processed materials that are of living modified organism origin, containing detectable novel combinations of replicable genetic material obtained through the use of modern biotechnology.

(j) Quantity or volume of the living modified organism to be transferred.

(k) A previous and existing risk assessment report consistent with Annex III.

(l) Suggested methods for the safe handling, storage, transport and use, including packaging, labelling, documentation, disposal and contingency procedures, where appropriate.

(m) Regulatory status of the living modified organism within the State of export (for example, whether it is prohibited in the State of export, whether there are other restrictions, or whether it has been approved for general release) and, if the living modified organism is banned in the State of export, the reason or reasons for the ban.

(n) Result and purpose of any notification by the exporter to other States regarding the living modified organism to be transferred.

(o) A declaration that the above-mentioned information is factually correct.

Annex II

INFORMATION REQUIRED CONCERNING LIVING MODIFIED ORGANISMS INTENDED FOR DIRECT USE AS FOOD OR FEED, OR FOR PROCESSING UNDER ARTICLE 11

(a) The name and contact details of the applicant for a decision for domestic use.

(b) The name and contact details of the authority responsible for the decision.

(c) Name and identity of the living modified organism.

(d) Description of the gene modification, the technique used, and the resulting characteristics of the living modified organism.

(e) Any unique identification of the living modified organism.

(f) Taxonomic status, common name, point of collection or acquisition, and characteristics of recipient organism or parental organisms related to biosafety.

(g) Centres of origin and centres of genetic diversity, if known, of the recipient organism and/or the parental organisms and a description of the habitats where the organisms may persist or proliferate.

(h) Taxonomic status, common name, point of collection or acquisition, and characteristics of the donor organism or organisms related to biosafety.

(i) Approved uses of the living modified organism.

(j) A risk assessment report consistent with Annex III.

(k) Suggested methods for the safe handling, storage, transport and use, including packaging, labelling, documentation, disposal and contingency procedures, where appropriate.

Annex III

RISK ASSESSMENT UNDER ARTICLE 15

Objective

1. The objective of risk assessment, under this Protocol, is to identify and evaluate the potential adverse effects of living modified organisms on the conservation and sustainable use of biological diversity in the likely potential receiving environment, taking also into account risks to human health.

Use of risk assessment

2. Risk assessment is, <u>inter alia</u>, used by competent authorities to make informed decisions regarding living modified organisms.

General principles

3. Risk assessment should be carried out in a scientifically sound and transparent manner, and can take into account expert advice of, and guidelines developed by, relevant international organizations.

4. Lack of scientific knowledge or scientific consensus should not necessarily be interpreted as indicating a particular level of risk, an absence of risk, or an acceptable risk.

5. Risks associated with living modified organisms or products thereof, namely, processed materials that are of living modified organism origin, containing detectable novel combinations of replicable genetic material obtained through the use of modern biotechnology, should be considered in the context of the risks posed by the non-modified recipients or parental organisms in the likely potential receiving environment.

6. Risk assessment should be carried out on a case-by-case basis. The required information may vary in nature and level of detail from case to case, depending on the living modified organism concerned, its intended use and the likely potential receiving environment.

Methodology

7. The process of risk assessment may on the one hand give rise to a need for further information about specific subjects, which may be identified and requested during the assessment process, while on the other hand information on other subjects may not be relevant in some instances.

8. To fulfil its objective, risk assessment entails, as appropriate, the following steps:

(a) An identification of any novel genotypic and phenotypic characteristics associated with the living modified organism that may have adverse effects on biological diversity in the likely potential receiving environment, taking also into account risks to human health;

(b) An evaluation of the likelihood of these adverse effects being realized, taking into account the level and kind of exposure of the likely potential receiving environment to the living modified organism;

(c) An evaluation of the consequences should these adverse effects be realized;

(d) An estimation of the overall risk posed by the living modified organism based on the evaluation of the likelihood and consequences of the identified adverse effects being realized;

(e) A recommendation as to whether or not the risks are acceptable or manageable, including, where necessary, identification of strategies to manage these risks; and

(f) Where there is uncertainty regarding the level of risk, it may be addressed by requesting further information on the specific issues of concern or by implementing appropriate risk management strategies and/or monitoring the living modified organism in the receiving environment.

Points to consider

9. Depending on the case, risk assessment takes into account the relevant technical and scientific details regarding the characteristics of the following subjects:

(a) Recipient organism or parental organisms. The biological characteristics of the recipient organism or parental organisms, including information on taxonomic status, common name, origin, centres of origin and centres of genetic diversity, if known, and a description of the habitat where the organisms may persist or proliferate;

(b) <u>Donor organism or organisms</u>. Taxonomic status and common name, source, and the relevant biological characteristics of the donor organisms;

(c) <u>Vector</u>. Characteristics of the vector, including its identity, if any, and its source or origin, and its host range;

(d) <u>Insert or inserts and/or characteristics of modification</u>. Genetic characteristics of the inserted nucleic acid and the function it specifies, and/or characteristics of the modification introduced;

(e) <u>Living modified organism</u>. Identity of the living modified organism, and the differences between the biological characteristics of the living modified organism and those of the recipient organism or parental organisms;

(f) <u>Detection and identification of the living modified organism</u>. Suggested detection and identification methods and their specificity, sensitivity and reliability;

(g) <u>Information relating to the intended use</u>. Information relating to the intended use of the living modified organism, including new or changed use compared to the recipient organism or parental organisms; and

(h) <u>Receiving environment</u>. Information on the location, geographical, climatic and ecological characteristics, including relevant information on biological diversity and centres of origin of the likely potential receiving environment.

5.9 Non-legally Binding Statement on All Types of Forests.[g] **Adopted by the UN General Assembly, 17 Dec 2007. GA Res 62/98 (Annex), UN GAOR, 62nd Sess., Suppl. No. 49 at 219, UN Doc A/RES/62/98 (Annex) (2008),** *reprinted in* **5A Weston & Carlson V.H.29**

Member States,

Recognizing that forests and trees outside forests provide multiple economic, social and environmental benefits, and emphasizing that sustainable forest management contributes significantly to sustainable development and poverty eradication,

Recalling the Non-legally Binding Authoritative Statement of Principles for a Global Consensus on Management, Conservation and Sustainable Development of All Types of Forests (Forest Principles); chapter 11 of Agenda 21; the proposals for action of the Intergovernmental Panel on Forests/Intergovernmental Forum on Forests; resolutions and decisions of the United Nations Forum on Forests; the Johannesburg Declaration on Sustainable Development and the Plan of Implementation of the World Summit on Sustainable Development; the Monterrey Consensus of the International Conference on Financing for Development; the internationally agreed development goals, including the Millennium Development Goals; the 2005 World Summit Outcome; and existing international legally binding instruments relevant to forests,

Welcoming the accomplishments of the international arrangement on forests since its inception by the Economic and Social Council in its resolution 2000/35 of 18 October 2000, and recalling the decision of the Council, in its resolution 2006/49 of 28 July 2006, to strengthen the international arrangement on forests,

Reaffirming their commitment to the Rio Declaration on Environment and Development, including that States have, in accordance with the Charter of the United Nations and the principles of international law, the sovereign right to exploit their own resources pursuant to their own environmental and developmental policies and the responsibility to ensure that activities within their jurisdiction or control do not cause damage to the environment of other States or of areas beyond the limits of national jurisdiction, and to the common but differentiated responsibilities of countries, as set out in Principle 7 of the Rio Declaration,

Recognizing that sustainable forest management, as a dynamic and evolving concept, is intended to maintain and enhance the economic, social and environmental value of all types of forests, for the benefit of present and future generations,

Expressing their concern about continued deforestation and forest degradation, as well as the slow rate of afforestation and forest cover recovery and reforestation, and the resulting adverse impact on economies, the environment, including biological diversity, and the livelihoods of at least a billion people and their cultural heritage, and emphasizing the need for more effective implementation of sustainable forest management at all levels to address these critical challenges,

Recognizing the impact of climate change on forests and sustainable forest management, as well as the contribution of forests to addressing climate change,

Reaffirming the special needs and requirements of countries with fragile forest ecosystems, including those of low-forest-cover countries,

Stressing the need to strengthen political commitment and collective efforts at all levels, to include forests in national and international development agendas, to enhance national policy coordination and international cooperation and to promote

g. *See also* Nonlegally Binding Authoritative Statement of Principles for a Global Consensus on the Management, Conservation and Sustainable Development of All Types of Forests. Adopted by the UN Conference on Environment and Development at Rio de Janeiro, 13 June 1992. U.N. Doc. A/CONF. 151/26 (Vol. III) (1992); reprinted in 31 I.L.M. 881 (1992) & 5A Weston & Carlson V.H.23.

intersectoral coordination at all levels for the effective implementation of sustainable management of all types of forests,

Emphasizing that effective implementation of sustainable forest management is critically dependent upon adequate resources, including financing, capacity development and the transfer of environmentally sound technologies, and recognizing in particular the need to mobilize increased financial resources, including from innovative sources, for developing countries, including least developed countries, landlocked developing countries and small island developing States, as well as countries with economies in transition,

Also emphasizing that implementation of sustainable forest management is also critically dependent upon good governance at all levels,

Noting that the provisions of this instrument do not prejudice the rights and obligations of Member States under international law,

Have committed themselves as follows:

I. Purpose

1.   The purpose of this instrument is:

(a) To strengthen political commitment and action at all levels to implement effectively sustainable management of all types of forests and to achieve the shared global objectives on forests;

(b) To enhance the contribution of forests to the achievement of the internationally agreed development goals, including the Millennium Development Goals, in particular with respect to poverty eradication and environmental sustainability;

(c) To provide a framework for national action and international cooperation.

II. Principles

2.   Member States should respect the following principles, which build upon the Rio Declaration on Environment and Development and the Rio Forest Principles:

(a) The instrument is voluntary and non-legally binding;

(b) Each State is responsible for the sustainable management of its forests and for the enforcement of its forest-related laws;

(c) Major groups as identified in Agenda 21, local communities, forest owners and other relevant stakeholders contribute to achieving sustainable forest management and should be involved in a transparent and participatory way in forest decision-making processes that affect them, as well as in implementing sustainable forest management, in accordance with national legislation;

(d) Achieving sustainable forest management, in particular in developing countries as well as in countries with economies in transition, depends on significantly increased, new and additional financial resources from all sources;

(e) Achieving sustainable forest management also depends on good governance at all levels;

(f) International cooperation, including financial support, technology transfer, capacity-building and education, plays a crucial catalytic role in supporting the efforts of all countries, particularly developing countries as well as countries with economies in transition, to achieve sustainable forest management.

III. Scope

3.   The present instrument applies to all types of forests.

4.   Sustainable forest management, as a dynamic and evolving concept, aims to maintain and enhance the economic, social and environmental values of all types of forests, for the benefit of present and future generations.

IV.   Global objectives on forests

5.   Member States reaffirm the following shared global objectives on forests and their commitment to work globally, regionally and nationally to achieve progress towards their achievement by 2015:

Global objective 1

Reverse the loss of forest cover worldwide through sustainable forest management, including protection, restoration, afforestation and reforestation, and increase efforts to prevent forest degradation;

Global objective 2

Enhance forest-based economic, social and environmental benefits, including by improving the livelihoods of forest-dependent people;

Global objective 3

Increase significantly the area of protected forests worldwide and other areas of sustainably managed forests, as well as the proportion of forest products from sustainably managed forests;

Global objective 4

Reverse the decline in official development assistance for sustainable forest management and mobilize significantly increased, new and additional financial resources from all sources for the implementation of sustainable forest management.

V.   National policies and measures

6.   To achieve the purpose of the present instrument, and taking into account national policies, priorities, conditions and available resources, Member States should:

(a) Develop, implement, publish and, as necessary, update national forest programmes or other strategies for sustainable forest management which identify actions needed and contain measures, policies or specific goals, taking into account the relevant proposals for action of the Intergovernmental Panel on Forests/Intergovernmental Forum on Forests and resolutions of the United Nations Forum on Forests;

(b) Consider the seven thematic elements of sustainable forest management,[1] which are drawn from the criteria identified by existing criteria and indicators processes, as a reference framework for sustainable forest management and, in this context, identify, as appropriate, specific environmental and other forest-related aspects within those elements for consideration as criteria and indicators for sustainable forest management;

(c) Promote the use of management tools to assess the impact on the environment of projects that may significantly affect forests, and promote good environmental practices for such projects;

(d) Develop and implement policies that encourage the sustainable management of forests to provide a wide range of goods and services and that also contribute to poverty reduction and the development of rural communities;

(e) Promote efficient production and processing of forest products, with a view, inter alia, to reducing waste and enhancing recycling;

(f) Support the protection and use of traditional forest-related knowledge and practices in sustainable forest management with the approval and involvement of the holders of such knowledge, and promote fair and equitable sharing of benefits from

---

1.   The elements are (i) extent of forest resources; (ii) forest biological diversity; (iii) forest health and vitality; (iv) productive functions of forest resources; (v) protective functions of forest resources; (vi) socio-economic functions of forests; and (vii) legal, policy and institutional framework.

their utilization, in accordance with national legislation and relevant international agreements;

(g) Further develop and implement criteria and indicators for sustainable forest management that are consistent with national priorities and conditions;

(h) Create enabling environments to encourage private-sector investment, as well as investment by and involvement of local and indigenous communities, other forest users and forest owners and other relevant stakeholders, in sustainable forest management, through a framework of policies, incentives and regulations;

(i) Develop financing strategies that outline the short-, medium- and long-term financial planning for achieving sustainable forest management, taking into account domestic, private-sector and foreign funding sources;

(j) Encourage recognition of the range of values derived from goods and services provided by all types of forests and trees outside forests, as well as ways to reflect such values in the marketplace, consistent with relevant national legislation and policies;

(k) Identify and implement measures to enhance cooperation and cross-sectoral policy and programme coordination among sectors affecting and affected by forest policies and management, with a view to integrating the forest sector into national decision-making processes and promoting sustainable forest management, including by addressing the underlying causes of deforestation and forest degradation, and by promoting forest conservation;

(*l*) Integrate national forest programmes, or other strategies for sustainable forest management, as referred to in paragraph 6 (*a*) above, into national strategies for sustainable development, relevant national action plans and poverty-reduction strategies;

(m) Establish or strengthen partnerships, including public-private partnerships, and joint programmes with stakeholders to advance the implementation of sustainable forest management;

(n) Review and, as needed, improve forest-related legislation, strengthen forest law enforcement and promote good governance at all levels in order to support sustainable forest management, to create an enabling environment for forest investment and to combat and eradicate illegal practices, in accordance with national legislation, in the forest and other related sectors;

(o) Analyse the causes of, and address solutions to, threats to forest health and vitality from natural disasters and human activities, including threats from fire, pollution, pests, disease and invasive alien species;

(p) Create, develop or expand, and maintain networks of protected forest areas, taking into account the importance of conserving representative forests, by means of a range of conservation mechanisms, applied within and outside protected forest areas;

(q) Assess the conditions and management effectiveness of existing protected forest areas with a view to identifying improvements needed;

(r) Strengthen the contribution of science and research in advancing sustainable forest management by incorporating scientific expertise into forest policies and programmes;

(s) Promote the development and application of scientific and technological innovations, including those that can be used by forest owners and local and indigenous communities to advance sustainable forest management;

(t) Promote and strengthen public understanding of the importance of and the benefits provided by forests and sustainable forest management, including through public awareness programmes and education;

(u) Promote and encourage access to formal and informal education, extension and training programmes on the implementation of sustainable forest management;

(v) Support education, training and extension programmes involving local and indigenous communities, forest workers and forest owners, in order to develop resource management approaches that will reduce the pressure on forests, particularly fragile ecosystems;

(w) Promote active and effective participation by major groups, local communities, forest owners and other relevant stakeholders in the development, implementation and assessment of forest-related national policies, measures and programmes;

(x) Encourage the private sector, civil society organizations and forest owners to develop, promote and implement in a transparent manner voluntary instruments, such as voluntary certification systems or other appropriate mechanisms, to develop and promote forest products from sustainably managed forests harvested in accordance with domestic legislation, and to improve market transparency;

(y) Enhance access by households, small-scale forest owners, forest-dependent local and indigenous communities, living in and outside forest areas, to forest resources and relevant markets in order to support livelihoods and income diversification from forest management, consistent with sustainable forest management.

VI. International cooperation and means of implementation

7. To achieve the purpose of the present instrument, Member States should:

(a) Make concerted efforts to secure a sustained high-level political commitment to strengthen the means of implementation of sustainable forest management, including financial resources, to provide support, in particular for developing countries and countries with economies in transition, as well as to mobilize and provide significantly increased, new and additional financial resources from private, public, domestic and international sources to and within developing countries, as well as countries with economies in transition;

(b) Reverse the decline in official development assistance for sustainable forest management and mobilize significantly increased, new and additional financial resources from all sources for the implementation of sustainable forest management;

(c) Take action to raise the priority of sustainable forest management in national development plans and other plans, including poverty-reduction strategies, in order to facilitate increased allocation of official development assistance and financial resources from other sources for sustainable forest management;

(d) Develop and establish positive incentives, in particular for developing countries as well as countries with economies in transition, to reduce the loss of forests, to promote reforestation, afforestation and rehabilitation of degraded forests, to implement sustainable forest management and to increase the area of protected forests;

(e) Support the efforts of countries, particularly developing countries as well as countries with economies in transition, to develop and implement economically, socially and environmentally sound measures that act as incentives for the sustainable management of forests;

(f) Strengthen the capacity of countries, in particular developing countries, to significantly increase the production of forest products from sustainably managed forests;

(g) Enhance bilateral, regional and international cooperation with a view to promoting international trade in forest products from sustainably managed forests harvested according to domestic legislation;

(h) Enhance bilateral, regional and international cooperation to address illicit international trafficking in forest products through the promotion of forest law enforcement and good governance at all levels;

(i) Strengthen, through enhanced bilateral, regional and international cooperation, the capacity of countries to combat effectively illicit international trafficking in forest products, including timber, wildlife and other forest biological resources;

(j) Strengthen the capacity of countries to address forest-related illegal practices, including wildlife poaching, in accordance with domestic legislation, through enhanced public awareness, education, institutional capacity-building, technological transfer and technical cooperation, law enforcement and information networks;

(k) Enhance and facilitate access to and transfer of appropriate, environmentally sound and innovative technologies and corresponding know-how relevant to sustainable forest management and to efficient value-added processing of forest products, in particular to developing countries, for the benefit of local and indigenous communities;

(*l*) Strengthen mechanisms that enhance sharing among countries and the use of best practices in sustainable forest management, including through freeware-based information and communications technology;

(m) Strengthen national and local capacity in keeping with their conditions for the development and adaptation of forest-related technologies, including technologies for the use of fuelwood;

(n) Promote international technical and scientific cooperation, including South–South cooperation and triangular cooperation, in the field of sustainable forest management, through the appropriate international, regional and national institutions and processes;

(*o*) Enhance the research and scientific forest-related capacities of developing countries and countries with economies in transition, particularly the capacity of research organizations to generate and have access to forest-related data and information, and promote and support integrated and interdisciplinary research on forest-related issues, and disseminate research results;

(p) Strengthen forestry research and development in all regions, particularly in developing countries and countries with economies in transition, through relevant organizations, institutions and centres of excellence, as well as through global, regional and subregional networks;

(q) Strengthen cooperation and partnerships at the regional and subregional levels to promote sustainable forest management;

(r) As members of the governing bodies of the organizations that form the Collaborative Partnership on Forests, help ensure that the forest-related priorities and programmes of members of the Partnership are integrated and mutually supportive, consistent with their mandates, taking into account relevant policy recommendations of the United Nations Forum on Forests;

(s) Support the efforts of the Collaborative Partnership on Forests to develop and implement joint initiatives.

VII. Monitoring, assessment and reporting

8. Member States should monitor and assess progress towards achieving the purpose of the present instrument.

9. Member States should submit, on a voluntary basis, taking into account the availability of resources and the requirements and conditions for the preparation of reports for other bodies or instruments, national progress reports as part of their regular reporting to the Forum.

VIII. Working modalities

10. The Forum should address, within the context of its multi-year programme of work, the implementation of the present instrument.

5.10 NAGOYA-KUALA LUMPUR SUPPLEMENTARY PROTOCOL ON LIABILITY AND REDRESS TO THE CARTAGENA PROTOCOL ON BIOSAFETY. **Adopted at Nagoya, 15 October 2010. Not yet in force. UN Doc UNEP/CBD/BS/COP–MOP/ 5/17**

The Parties to this Supplementary Protocol,

Being Parties to the Cartagena Protocol on Biosafety to the Convention on Biological

Diversity, hereinafter referred to as "the Protocol",

Taking into account Principle 13 of the Rio Declaration on Environment and Development,

Reaffirming the precautionary approach contained in Principle 15 of the Rio Declaration on Environment and Development,

Recognizing the need to provide for appropriate response measures where there is damage or sufficient likelihood of damage, consistent with the Protocol,

Recalling Article 27 of the Protocol,

Have agreed as follows:

Article 1   Objective

The objective of this Supplementary Protocol is to contribute to the conservation and sustainable use of biological diversity, taking also into account risks to human health, by providing international rules and procedures in the field of liability and redress relating to living modified organisms.

Article 2   Use of Terms

1.   The terms used in Article 2 of the Convention on Biological Diversity, hereinafter referred to as "the Convention", and Article 3 of the Protocol shall apply to this Supplementary Protocol.

2.   In addition, for the purposes of this Supplementary Protocol:

(a) "Conference of the Parties serving as the meeting of the Parties to the Protocol" means the Conference of the Parties to the Convention serving as the meeting of the Parties to the Protocol;

(b) "Damage" means an adverse effect on the conservation and sustainable use of biological diversity, taking also into account risks to human health, that:

(i) Is measurable or otherwise observable taking into account, wherever available, scientifically-established baselines recognized by a competent authority that takes into account any other human induced variation and natural variation; and

(ii) Is significant as set out in paragraph 3 below;

(c) "Operator" means any person in direct or indirect control of the living modified organism which could, as appropriate and as determined by domestic law, include, *inter alia*, the permit holder, person who placed the living modified organism on the market, developer, producer, notifier, exporter, importer, carrier or supplier;

(d) "Response measures" means reasonable actions to:

(i) Prevent, minimize, contain, mitigate, or otherwise avoid damage, as appropriate;

(ii) Restore biological diversity through actions to be undertaken in the following order of preference:

a. Restoration of biological diversity to the condition that existed before the damage occurred, or its nearest equivalent; and where the competent authority determines this is not possible;

b. Restoration by, inter alia, replacing the loss of biological diversity with other components of biological diversity for the same, or for another type of use either at the same or, as appropriate, at an alternative location.

3. A "significant" adverse effect is to be determined on the basis of factors, such as:

(a) The long-term or permanent change, to be understood as change that will not be redressed through natural recovery within a reasonable period of time;

(b) The extent of the qualitative or quantitative changes that adversely affect the components of biological diversity;

(c) The reduction of the ability of components of biological diversity to provide goods and services;

(d) The extent of any adverse effects on human health in the context of the Protocol.

Article 3   Scope

1. This Supplementary Protocol applies to damage resulting from living modified organisms which find their origin in a transboundary movement. The living modified organisms referred to are those:

(a) Intended for direct use as food or feed, or for processing;

(b) Destined for contained use;

(c) Intended for intentional introduction into the environment.

2. With respect to intentional transboundary movements, this Supplementary Protocol applies to damage resulting from any authorized use of the living modified organisms referred to in paragraph 1 above.

3. This Supplementary Protocol also applies to damage resulting from unintentional transboundary movements as referred to in Article 17 of the Protocol as well as damage resulting from illegal transboundary movements as referred to in Article 25 of the Protocol.

4. This Supplementary Protocol applies to damage resulting from a transboundary movement of living modified organisms that started after the entry into force of this Supplementary Protocol for the Party into whose jurisdiction the transboundary movement was made.

5. This Supplementary Protocol applies to damage that occurred in areas within the limits of the national jurisdiction of Parties.

6. Parties may use criteria set out in their domestic law to address damage that occurs within the limits of their national jurisdiction.

7. Domestic law implementing this Supplementary Protocol shall also apply to damage resulting from transboundary movements of living modified organisms from non-Parties.

Article 4   Causation

A causal link shall be established between the damage and the living modified organism in question in accordance with domestic law.

Article 5   Response Measures

1.   Parties shall require the appropriate operator or operators, in the event of damage, subject to any requirements of the competent authority, to:

(a) Immediately inform the competent authority;

(b) Evaluate the damage; and

(c) Take appropriate response measures.

2.   The competent authority shall:

(a) Identify the operator which has caused the damage;

(b) Evaluate the damage; and

(c) Determine which response measures should be taken by the operator.

3.   Where relevant information, including available scientific information or information available in the Biosafety Clearing–House, indicates that there is a sufficient likelihood that damage will result if timely response measures are not taken, the operator shall be required to take appropriate response measures so as to avoid such damage.

4.   The competent authority may implement appropriate response measures, including, in particular, when the operator has failed to do so.

5.   The competent authority has the right to recover from the operator the costs and expenses of, and incidental to, the evaluation of the damage and the implementation of any such appropriate response measures. Parties may provide, in their domestic law, for other situations in which the operator may not be required to bear the costs and expenses.

6.   Decisions of the competent authority requiring the operator to take response measures should be reasoned. Such decisions should be notified to the operator. Domestic law shall provide for remedies, including the opportunity for administrative or judicial review of such decisions. The competent authority shall, in accordance with domestic law, also inform the operator of the available remedies. Recourse to such remedies shall not impede the competent authority from taking response measures in appropriate circumstances, unless otherwise provided by domestic law.

7.   In implementing this Article and with a view to defining the specific response measures to be required or taken by the competent authority, Parties may, as appropriate, assess whether response measures are already addressed by their domestic law on civil liability.

8.   Response measures shall be implemented in accordance with domestic law.

Article 6   Exemptions

1.   Parties may provide, in their domestic law, for the following exemptions:

(a) Act of God or *force majeure*; and

(b) Act of war or civil unrest.

2.   Parties may provide, in their domestic law, for any other exemptions or mitigations as they may deem fit.

Article 7   Time Limits

Parties may provide, in their domestic law, for:

(a) Relative and/or absolute time limits including for actions related to response measures; and

(b) The commencement of the period to which a time limit applies.

Article 8   Financial Limits

Parties may provide, in their domestic law, for financial limits for the recovery of costs and expenses related to response measures.

Article 9   Right of Recourse

This Supplementary Protocol shall not limit or restrict any right of recourse or indemnity that an operator may have against any other person.

Article 10   Financial Security

1.   Parties retain the right to provide, in their domestic law, for financial security.

2.   Parties shall exercise the right referred to in paragraph 1 above in a manner consistent with their rights and obligations under international law, taking into account the final three preambular paragraphs of the Protocol.

3.   The first meeting of the Conference of the Parties serving as the meeting of the Parties to the Protocol after the entry into force of the Supplementary Protocol shall request the Secretariat to undertake a comprehensive study which shall address, *inter alia*:

(a) The modalities of financial security mechanisms;

(b) An assessment of the environmental, economic and social impacts of such mechanisms, in particular on developing countries; and

(c) An identification of the appropriate entities to provide financial security.

Article 11   Responsibility of States for Internationally Wrongful Acts

This Supplementary Protocol shall not affect the rights and obligations of States under the rules of general international law with respect to the responsibility of States for internationally wrongful acts.

Article 12   Implementation and Relation to Civil Liability

1.   Parties shall provide, in their domestic law, for rules and procedures that address damage. To implement this obligation, Parties shall provide for response measures in accordance with this Supplementary Protocol and may, as appropriate:

(a) Apply their existing domestic law, including, where applicable, general rules and procedures on civil liability;

(b) Apply or develop civil liability rules and procedures specifically for this purpose; or

(c) Apply or develop a combination of both.

2.   Parties shall, with the aim of providing adequate rules and procedures in their domestic law on civil liability for material or personal damage associated with the damage as defined in Article 2, paragraph 2 (b):

(a) Continue to apply their existing general law on civil liability;

(b) Develop and apply or continue to apply civil liability law specifically for that purpose; or

(c) Develop and apply or continue to apply a combination of both.

3.   When developing civil liability law as referred to in subparagraphs (b) or (c) of paragraphs 1 or 2 above, Parties shall, as appropriate, address, *inter alia*, the following elements:

(a) Damage;

(b) Standard of liability, including strict or fault-based liability;

(c) Channelling of liability, where appropriate;

(d) Right to bring claims.

Article 13   Assessment and Review

The Conference of the Parties serving as the meeting of the Parties to the Protocol shall undertake a review of the effectiveness of this Supplementary Protocol five years after its entry into force and every five years thereafter, provided information requiring such a review has been made available by Parties. The review shall be undertaken in the context of the assessment and review of the Protocol as specified in Article 35 of the Protocol, unless otherwise decided by the Parties to this Supplementary Protocol. The first review shall include a review of the effectiveness of Articles 10 and 12.

Article 14   Conference of the Parties Serving as the Meeting of The Parties to the Protocol

1.   Subject to paragraph 2 of Article 32 of the Convention, the Conference of the Parties serving as the meeting of the Parties to the Protocol shall serve as the meeting of the Parties to this Supplementary Protocol.

2.   The Conference of the Parties serving as the meeting of the Parties to the Protocol shall keep under regular review the implementation of this Supplementary Protocol and shall make, within its mandate, the decisions necessary to promote its effective implementation. It shall perform the functions assigned to it by this Supplementary Protocol and, *mutatis mutandis*, the functions assigned to it by paragraphs 4 (a) and (f) of Article 29 of the Protocol.

Article 15   Secretariat

The Secretariat established by Article 24 of the Convention shall serve as the secretariat to this Supplementary Protocol.

Article 16   Relationship with the Convention and the Protocol

1.   This Supplementary Protocol shall supplement the Protocol and shall neither modify nor amend the Protocol.

2.   This Supplementary Protocol shall not affect the rights and obligations of the Parties to this Supplementary Protocol under the Convention and the Protocol.

3.   Except as other wise provided in this Supplementary Protocol, the provisions of the Convention and the Protocol shall apply, mutatis mutandis, to this Supplementary Protocol.

4.   Without prejudice to paragraph 3 above, this Supplementary Protocol shall not affect the rights and obligations of a Party under international law.

Article 17   Signature

This Supplementary Protocol shall be open for signature by Parties to the Protocol at the United Nations Headquarters in New York from 7 March 2011 to 6 March 2012.

Article 18   Entry into Force

1.   This Supplementary Protocol shall enter into force on the ninetieth day after the date of deposit of the fortieth instrument of ratification, acceptance, approval or accession by States or regional economic integration organizations that are Parties to the Protocol.

2.   This Supplementary Protocol shall enter into force for a State or regional economic integration organization that ratifies, accepts or approves it or accedes thereto after the deposit of the fortieth instrument as referred to in paragraph 1 above,

on the ninetieth day after the date on which that State or regional economic integration organization deposits its instrument of ratification, acceptance, approval, or accession, or on the date on which the Protocol enters into force for that State or regional economic integration organization, whichever shall be the later.

3. For the purposes of paragraphs 1 and 2 above, any instrument deposited by a regional economic integration organization shall not be counted as additional to those deposited by member States of such organization.

Article 19   Reservations

No reservations may be made to this Supplementary Protocol.

Article 20   Withdrawal

1. At any time after two years from the date on which this Supplementary Protocol has entered into force for a Party, that Party may withdraw from this Supplementary Protocol by giving written notification to the Depositary.

2. Any such withdrawal shall take place upon expiry of one year after the date of its receipt by the Depositary, or on such later date as may be specified in the notification of the withdrawal.

3. Any Party which withdraws from the Protocol in accordance with Article 39 of the Protocol shall be considered as also having withdrawn from this Supplementary Protocol.

Article 21   Authentic Texts

The original of this Supplementary Protocol, of which the Arabic, Chinese, English, French, Russian and Spanish texts are equally authentic, shall be deposited with the Secretary–General of the United Nations.

IN WITNESS WHEREOF the undersigned, being duly authorized to that effect, have signed this Supplementary Protocol.

DONE at Nagoya on this fifteenth day of October two thousand and ten.

5.11 NAGOYA PROTOCOL ON ACCESS TO GENETIC RESOURCES AND THE FAIR AND EQUITABLE SHARING OF BENEFITS ARISING FROM THEIR UTILIZATION TO THE CONVENTION ON BIOLOGICAL DIVERSITY, **Adopted at Nagoya (Japan), 29 October 2010. Not yet in force. Report of the Tenth Meeting of the Conference of the Parties to the Convention on Biological Diversity, UN Doc UNEP/CBD/COP/10/27 (Annex I) at 87 (2011)**

The Parties to this Protocol,

Being Parties to the Convention on Biological Diversity, hereinafter referred to as "the Convention",

Recalling that the fair and equitable sharing of benefits arising from the utilization of genetic resources is one of three core objectives of the Convention, and recognizing that this Protocol pursues the implementation of this objective within the Convention,

Reaffirming the sovereign rights of States over their natural resources and according to the provisions of the Convention,

Recalling further Article 15 of the Convention,

Recognizing the important contribution to sustainable development made by technology transfer and cooperation to build research and innovation capacities for adding value to genetic resources in developing countries, in accordance with Articles 16 and 19 of the Convention,

Recognizing that public awareness of the economic value of ecosystems and biodiversity and the fair and equitable sharing of this economic value with the custodians of biodiversity are key incentives for the conservation of biological diversity and the sustainable use of its components,

Acknowledging the potential role of access and benefit-sharing to contribute to the conservation and sustainable use of biological diversity, poverty eradication and environmental sustainability and thereby contributing to achieving the Millennium Development Goals,

Acknowledging the linkage between access to genetic resources and the fair and equitable sharing of benefits arising from the utilization of such resources,

Recognizing the importance of providing legal certainty with respect to access to genetic resources and the fair and equitable sharing of benefits arising from their utilization,

Further recognizing the importance of promoting equity and fairness in negotiation of mutually agreed terms between providers and users of genetic resources,

Recognizing also the vital role that women play in access and benefit-sharing and affirming the need for the full participation of women at all levels of policy-making and implementation for biodiversity conservation,

Determined to further support the effective implementation of the access and benefit-sharing provisions of the Convention,

Recognizing that an innovative solution is required to address the fair and equitable sharing of benefits derived from the utilization of genetic resources and traditional knowledge associated with genetic resources that occur in transboundary situations or for which it is not possible to grant or obtain prior informed consent,

Recognizing the importance of genetic resources to food security, public health, biodiversity conservation, and the mitigation of and adaptation to climate change,

Recognizing the special nature of agricultural biodiversity, its distinctive features and problems needing distinctive solutions,

Recognizing the interdependence of all countries with regard to genetic resources for food and agriculture as well as their special nature and importance for achieving food security worldwide and for sustainable development of agriculture in the context of poverty alleviation and climate change and acknowledging the fundamental role of the International Treaty on Plant Genetic Resources for Food and Agriculture and the FAO Commission on Genetic Resources for Food and Agriculture in this regard,

Mindful of the International Health Regulations (2005) of the World Health Organization and the importance of ensuring access to human pathogens for public health preparedness and response purposes,

Acknowledging ongoing work in other international forums relating to access and benefit-sharing,

Recalling the Multilateral System of Access and Benefit-sharing established under the International Treaty on Plant Genetic Resources for Food and Agriculture developed in harmony with the Convention,

Recognizing that international instruments related to access and benefit-sharing should be mutually supportive with a view to achieving the objectives of the Convention,

Recalling the relevance of Article 8(j) of the Convention as it relates to traditional knowledge associated with genetic resources and the fair and equitable sharing of benefits arising from the utilization of such knowledge,

Noting the interrelationship between genetic resources and traditional knowledge, their inseparable nature for indigenous and local communities, the importance of the traditional knowledge for the conservation of biological diversity and the sustainable use of its components, and for the sustainable livelihoods of these communities,

Recognizing the diversity of circumstances in which traditional knowledge associated with genetic resources is held or owned by indigenous and local communities,

Mindful that it is the right of indigenous and local communities to identify the rightful holders of their traditional knowledge associated with genetic resources, within their communities,

Further recognizing the unique circumstances where traditional knowledge associated with genetic resources is held in countries, which may be oral, documented or in other forms, reflecting a rich cultural heritage relevant for conservation and sustainable use of biological diversity,

Noting the United Nations Declaration on the Rights of Indigenous Peoples, and

Affirming that nothing in this Protocol shall be construed as diminishing or extinguishing the existing rights of indigenous and local communities,

Have agreed as follows:

Article 1—Objective

The objective of this Protocol is the fair and equitable sharing of the benefits arising from the utilization of genetic resources, including by appropriate access to genetic resources and by appropriate transfer of relevant technologies, taking into account all rights over those resources and to technologies, and by appropriate funding, thereby contributing to the conservation of biological diversity and the sustainable use of its components.

Article 2—Use of Terms

The terms defined in Article 2 of the Convention shall apply to this Protocol. In addition, for the purposes of this Protocol:

(a) "Conference of the Parties" means the Conference of the Parties to the Convention;

(b) "Convention" means the Convention on Biological Diversity;

(c) "Utilization of genetic resources" means to conduct research and development on the genetic and/or biochemical composition of genetic resources, including through the application of biotechnology as defined in Article 2 of the Convention;

(d) "Biotechnology" as defined in Article 2 of the Convention means any technological application that uses biological systems, living organisms, or derivatives thereof, to make or modify products or processes for specific use;

(e) "Derivative" means a naturally occurring biochemical compound resulting from the genetic expression or metabolism of biological or genetic resources, even if it does not contain functional units of heredity.

Article 3—Scope

This Protocol shall apply to genetic resources within the scope of Article 15 of the Convention and to the benefits arising from the utilization of such resources. This Protocol shall also apply to traditional knowledge associated with genetic resources within the scope of the Convention and to the benefits arising from the utilization of such knowledge.

Article 4—Relationship with International Agreements and Instruments

1. The provisions of this Protocol shall not affect the rights and obligations of any Party deriving from any existing international agreement, except where the exercise of those rights and obligations would cause a serious damage or threat to biological diversity. This paragraph is not intended to create a hierarchy between this Protocol and other international instruments.

2. Nothing in this Protocol shall prevent the Parties from developing and implementing other relevant international agreements, including other specialized access and benefit-sharing agreements, provided that they are supportive of and do not run counter to the objectives of the Convention and this Protocol.

3. This Protocol shall be implemented in a mutually supportive manner with other international instruments relevant to this Protocol. Due regard should be paid to useful and relevant ongoing work or practices under such international instruments and relevant international organizations, provided that they are supportive of and do not run counter to the objectives of the Convention and this Protocol.

4. This Protocol is the instrument for the implementation of the access and benefit-sharing provisions of the Convention. Where a specialized international access and benefit-sharing instrument applies that is consistent with, and does not run counter to the objectives of the Convention and this Protocol, this Protocol does not apply for the Party or Parties to the specialized instrument in respect of the specific genetic resource covered by and for the purpose of the specialized instrument.

Article 5—Fair and Equitable Benefit-sharing

1. In accordance with Article 15, paragraphs 3 and 7 of the Convention, benefits arising from the utilization of genetic resources as well as subsequent applications and commercialization shall be shared in a fair and equitable way with the Party providing such resources that is the country of origin of such resources or a Party that has acquired the genetic resources in accordance with the Convention. Such sharing shall be upon mutually agreed terms.

2. Each Party shall take legislative, administrative or policy measures, as appropriate, with the aim of ensuring that benefits arising from the utilization of genetic

resources that are held by indigenous and local communities, in accordance with domestic legislation regarding the established rights of these indigenous and local communities over these genetic resources, are shared in a fair and equitable way with the communities concerned, based on mutually agreed terms.

3. To implement paragraph 1 above, each Party shall take legislative, administrative or policy measures, as appropriate.

4. Benefits may include monetary and non-monetary benefits, including but not limited to those listed in the Annex.

5. Each Party shall take legislative, administrative or policy measures, as appropriate, in order that the benefits arising from the utilization of traditional knowledge associated with genetic resources are shared in a fair and equitable way with indigenous and local communities holding such knowledge. Such sharing shall be upon mutually agreed terms.

Article 6—Access to Genetic Resources

1. In the exercise of sovereign rights over natural resources, and subject to domestic access and benefit-sharing legislation or regulatory requirements, access to genetic resources for their utilization shall be subject to the prior informed consent of the Party providing such resources that is the country of origin of such resources or a Party that has acquired the genetic resources in accordance with the Convention, unless otherwise determined by that Party.

2. In accordance with domestic law, each Party shall take measures, as appropriate, with the aim of ensuring that the prior informed consent or approval and involvement of indigenous and local communities is obtained for access to genetic resources where they have the established right to grant access to such resources.

3. Pursuant to paragraph 1 above, each Party requiring prior informed consent shall take the necessary legislative, administrative or policy measures, as appropriate, to:

(a) Provide for legal certainty, clarity and transparency of their domestic access and benefit-sharing legislation or regulatory requirements;

(b) Provide for fair and non-arbitrary rules and procedures on accessing genetic resources;

(c) Provide information on how to apply for prior informed consent;

(d) Provide for a clear and transparent written decision by a competent national authority, in a cost-effective manner and within a reasonable period of time;

(e) Provide for the issuance at the time of access of a permit or its equivalent as evidence of the decision to grant prior informed consent and of the establishment of mutually agreed terms, and notify the Access and Benefit-sharing Clearing–House accordingly;

(f) Where applicable, and subject to domestic legislation, set out criteria and/or processes for obtaining prior informed consent or approval and involvement of indigenous and local communities for access to genetic resources; and

(g) Establish clear rules and procedures for requiring and establishing mutually agreed terms. Such terms shall be set out in writing and may include, *inter alia*:

(i) A dispute settlement clause;

(ii) Terms on benefit-sharing, including in relation to intellectual property rights;

(iii) Terms on subsequent third-party use, if any; and

(iv) Terms on changes of intent, where applicable.

Article 7—Access to Traditional Knowledge Associated with Genetic Resources

In accordance with domestic law, each Party shall take measures, as appropriate, with the aim of ensuring that traditional knowledge associated with genetic resources that is held by indigenous and local communities is accessed with the prior and informed consent or approval and involvement of these indigenous and local communities, and that mutually agreed terms have been established.

Article 8—Special Considerations

In the development and implementation of its access and benefit-sharing legislation or regulatory requirements, each Party shall:

(a) Create conditions to promote and encourage research which contributes to the conservation and sustainable use of biological diversity, particularly in developing countries, including through simplified measures on access for non-commercial research purposes, taking into account the need to address a change of intent for such research;

(b) Pay due regard to cases of present or imminent emergencies that threaten or damage human, animal or plant health, as determined nationally or internationally. Parties may take into consideration the need for expeditious access to genetic resources and expeditious fair and equitable sharing of benefits arising out of the use of such genetic resources, including access to affordable treatments by those in need, especially in developing countries;

(c) Consider the importance of genetic resources for food and agriculture and their special role for food security.

Article 9—Contribution to Conservation and Sustainable Use

The Parties shall encourage users and providers to direct benefits arising from the utilization of genetic resources towards the conservation of biological diversity and the sustainable use of its components.

Article 10—Global Multilateral Benefit-sharing Mechanism

Parties shall consider the need for and modalities of a global multilateral benefit-sharing mechanism to address the fair and equitable sharing of benefits derived from the utilization of genetic resources and traditional knowledge associated with genetic resources that occur in transboundary situations or for which it is not possible to grant or obtain prior informed consent. The benefits shared by users of genetic resources and traditional knowledge associated with genetic resources through this mechanism shall be used to support the conservation of biological diversity and the sustainable use of its components globally.

Article 11—Transboundary Cooperation

1. In instances where the same genetic resources are found *in situ* within the territory of more than one Party, those Parties shall endeavour to cooperate, as appropriate, with the involvement of indigenous and local communities concerned, where applicable, with a view to implementing this Protocol.

2. Where the same traditional knowledge associated with genetic resources is shared by one or more indigenous and local communities in several Parties, those Parties shall endeavour to cooperate, as appropriate, with the involvement of the indigenous and local communities concerned, with a view to implementing the objective of this Protocol.

Article 12—Traditional Knowledge Associated with Genetic Resources

1. In implementing their obligations under this Protocol, Parties shall in accordance with domestic law take into consideration indigenous and local communities' customary laws, community protocols and procedures, as applicable, with respect to traditional knowledge associated with genetic resources.

2. Parties, with the effective participation of the indigenous and local communities concerned, shall establish mechanisms to inform potential users of traditional knowledge associated with genetic resources about their obligations, including measures as made available through the Access and Benefit-sharing Clearing–House for access to and fair and equitable sharing of benefits arising from the utilization of such knowledge.

3. Parties shall endeavour to support, as appropriate, the development by indigenous and local communities, including women within these communities, of:

(a) Community protocols in relation to access to traditional knowledge associated with genetic resources and the fair and equitable sharing of benefits arising out of the utilization of such knowledge;

(b) Minimum requirements for mutually agreed terms to secure the fair and equitable sharing of benefits arising from the utilization of traditional knowledge associated with genetic resources; and

(c) Model contractual clauses for benefit-sharing arising from the utilization of traditional knowledge associated with genetic resources.

4. Parties, in their implementation of this Protocol, shall, as far as possible, not restrict the customary use and exchange of genetic resources and associated traditional knowledge within and amongst indigenous and local communities in accordance with the objectives of the Convention.

Article 13—National Focal Points and Competent National Authorities

1. Each Party shall designate a national focal point on access and benefit-sharing. The national focal point shall make information available as follows:

(a) For applicants seeking access to genetic resources, information on procedures for obtaining prior informed consent and establishing mutually agreed terms, including benefit-sharing;

(b) For applicants seeking access to traditional knowledge associated with genetic resources, where possible, information on procedures for obtaining prior informed consent or approval and involvement, as appropriate, of indigenous and local communities and establishing mutually agreed terms including benefit-sharing; and

(c) Information on competent national authorities, relevant indigenous and local communities and relevant stakeholders.

The national focal point shall be responsible for liaison with the Secretariat.

2. Each Party shall designate one or more competent national authorities on access and benefit-sharing. Competent national authorities shall, in accordance with applicable national legislative, administrative or policy measures, be responsible for granting access or, as applicable, issuing written evidence that access requirements have been met and be responsible for advising on applicable procedures and requirements for obtaining prior informed consent and entering into mutually agreed terms.

3. A Party may designate a single entity to fulfil the functions of both focal point and competent national authority.

4. Each Party shall, no later than the date of entry into force of this Protocol for it, notify the Secretariat of the contact information of its national focal point and its competent national authority or authorities. Where a Party designates more than one

competent national authority, it shall convey to the Secretariat, with its notification thereof, relevant information on the respective responsibilities of those authorities. Where applicable, such information shall, at a minimum, specify which competent authority is responsible for the genetic resources sought. Each Party shall forthwith notify the Secretariat of any changes in the designation of its national focal point or in the contact information or responsibilities of its competent national authority or authorities.

5. The Secretariat shall make information received pursuant to paragraph 4 above available through the Access and Benefit-sharing Clearing–House.

Article 14—The Access and Benefit-sharing Clearing-house and Information–Sharing

1. An Access and Benefit-sharing Clearing–House is hereby established as part of the clearing-house mechanism under Article 18, paragraph 3, of the Convention. It shall serve as a means for sharing of information related to access and benefit-sharing. In particular, it shall provide access to information made available by each Party relevant to the implementation of this Protocol.

2. Without prejudice to the protection of confidential information, each Party shall make available to the Access and Benefit-sharing Clearing–House any information required by this Protocol, as well as information required pursuant to the decisions taken by the Conference of the Parties serving as the meeting of the Parties to this Protocol. The information shall include:

(a) Legislative, administrative and policy measures on access and benefit-sharing;

(b) Information on the national focal point and competent national authority or authorities; and

(c) Permits or their equivalent issued at the time of access as evidence of the decision to grant prior informed consent and of the establishment of mutually agreed terms.

3. Additional information, if available and as appropriate, may include:

(a) Relevant competent authorities of indigenous and local communities, and information as so decided;

(b) Model contractual clauses;

(c) Methods and tools developed to monitor genetic resources; and

(d) Codes of conduct and best practices.

4. The modalities of the operation of the Access and Benefit-sharing Clearing-House, including reports on its activities, shall be considered and decided upon by the Conference of the Parties serving as the meeting of the Parties to this Protocol at its first meeting, and kept under review thereafter.

Article 15—Compliance with Domestic Legislation or Regulatory
Requirements on Access and Benefit-sharing

1. Each Party shall take appropriate, effective and proportionate legislative, administrative or policy measures to provide that genetic resources utilized within its jurisdiction have been accessed in accordance with prior informed consent and that mutually agreed terms have been established, as required by the domestic access and benefit-sharing legislation or regulatory requirements of the other Party.

2. Parties shall take appropriate, effective and proportionate measures to address situations of non-compliance with measures adopted in accordance with paragraph 1 above.

3. Parties shall, as far as possible and as appropriate, cooperate in cases of alleged violation of domestic access and benefit-sharing legislation or regulatory requirements referred to in paragraph 1 above.

Article 16—Compliance with Domestic Legislation or Regulatory Requirements on Access and Benefit–Sharing for Traditional Knowledge Associated with Genetic Resources

1. Each Party shall take appropriate, effective and proportionate legislative, administrative or policy measures, as appropriate, to provide that traditional knowledge associated with genetic resources utilized within their jurisdiction has been accessed in accordance with prior informed consent or approval and involvement of indigenous and local communities and that mutually agreed terms have been established, as required by domestic access and benefit-sharing legislation or regulatory requirements of the other Party where such indigenous and local communities are located.

2. Each Party shall take appropriate, effective and proportionate measures to address situations of non-compliance with measures adopted in accordance with paragraph 1 above.

3. Parties shall, as far as possible and as appropriate, cooperate in cases of alleged violation of domestic access and benefit-sharing legislation or regulatory requirements referred to in paragraph 1 above.

Article 17—Monitoring the Utilization of Genetic Resources

1. To support compliance, each Party shall take measures, as appropriate, to monitor and to enhance transparency about the utilization of genetic resources. Such measures shall include:

(a) The designation of one or more checkpoints, as follows:

(i) Designated checkpoints would collect or receive, as appropriate, relevant information related to prior informed consent, to the source of the genetic resource, to the establishment of mutually agreed terms, and/or to the utilization of genetic resources, as appropriate;

(ii) Each Party shall, as appropriate and depending on the particular characteristics of a designated checkpoint, require users of genetic resources to provide the information specified in the above paragraph at a designated checkpoint. Each Party shall take appropriate, effective and proportionate measures to address situations of non-compliance;

(iii) Such information, including from internationally recognized certificates of compliance where they are available, will, without prejudice to the protection of confidential information, be provided to relevant national authorities, to the Party providing prior informed consent and to the Access and Benefit-sharing Clearing–House, as appropriate;

(iv) Checkpoints must be effective and should have functions relevant to implementation of this subparagraph (a). They should be relevant to the utilization of genetic resources, or to the collection of relevant information at, *inter alia,* any stage of research, development, innovation, pre-commercialization or commercialization.

(b) Encouraging users and providers of genetic resources to include provisions in mutually agreed terms to share information on the implementation of such terms, including through reporting requirements; and

(c) Encouraging the use of cost-effective communication tools and systems.

2. A permit or its equivalent issued in accordance with Article 6, paragraph 3 (e) and made available to the Access and Benefit-sharing Clearing–House, shall constitute an internationally recognized certificate of compliance.

3. An internationally recognized certificate of compliance shall serve as evidence that the genetic resource which it covers has been accessed in accordance with prior informed consent and that mutually agreed terms have been established, as required by the domestic access and benefit-sharing legislation or regulatory requirements of the Party providing prior informed consent.

4. The internationally recognized certificate of compliance shall contain the following minimum information when it is not confidential:

(a) Issuing authority;

(b) Date of issuance;

(c) The provider;

(d) Unique identifier of the certificate;

(e) The person or entity to whom prior informed consent was granted;

(f) Subject-matter or genetic resources covered by the certificate;

(g) Confirmation that mutually agreed terms were established;

(h) Confirmation that prior informed consent was obtained; and

(i) Commercial and/or non-commercial use.

Article 18—Compliance with Mutually Agreed Terms

1. In the implementation of Article 6, paragraph 3 (g) (i) and Article 7, each Party shall encourage providers and users of genetic resources and/or traditional knowledge associated with genetic resources to include provisions in mutually agreed terms to cover, where appropriate, dispute resolution including:

(a) The jurisdiction to which they will subject any dispute resolution processes;

(b) The applicable law; and/or

(c) Options for alternative dispute resolution, such as mediation or arbitration.

2. Each Party shall ensure that an opportunity to seek recourse is available under their legal systems, consistent with applicable jurisdictional requirements, in cases of disputes arising from mutually agreed terms.

3. Each Party shall take effective measures, as appropriate, regarding:

(a) Access to justice; and

(b) The utilization of mechanisms regarding mutual recognition and enforcement of foreign judgments and arbitral awards.

4. The effectiveness of this article shall be reviewed by the Conference of the Parties serving as the meeting of the Parties to this Protocol in accordance with Article 31 of this Protocol.

Article 19—Model Contractual Clauses

1. Each Party shall encourage, as appropriate, the development, update and use of sectoral and cross-sectoral model contractual clauses for mutually agreed terms.

2. The Conference of the Parties serving as the meeting of the Parties to this Protocol shall periodically take stock of the use of sectoral and cross-sectoral model contractual clauses.

Article 20—Codes of Conduct, Guidelines and Best Practices And/or Standards

1. Each Party shall encourage, as appropriate, the development, update and use of voluntary codes of conduct, guidelines and best practices and/or standards in relation to access and benefit-sharing.

2. The Conference of the Parties serving as the meeting of the Parties to this Protocol shall periodically take stock of the use of voluntary codes of conduct, guidelines and best practices and/or standards and consider the adoption of specific codes of conduct, guidelines and best practices and/or standards.

Article 21—Awareness–Raising

Each Party shall take measures to raise awareness of the importance of genetic resources and traditional knowledge associated with genetic resources, and related access and benefit-sharing issues. Such measures may include, *inter alia*:

(a) Promotion of this Protocol, including its objective;

(b) Organization of meetings of indigenous and local communities and relevant stakeholders;

(c) Establishment and maintenance of a help desk for indigenous and local communities and relevant stakeholders;

(d) Information dissemination through a national clearing-house;

(e) Promotion of voluntary codes of conduct, guidelines and best practices and/or standards in consultation with indigenous and local communities and relevant stake-holders;

(f) Promotion of, as appropriate, domestic, regional and international exchanges of experience;

(g) Education and training of users and providers of genetic resources and traditional knowledge associated with genetic resources about their access and benefit-sharing obligations;

(h) Involvement of indigenous and local communities and relevant stakeholders in the implementation of this Protocol; and

(i) Awareness-raising of community protocols and procedures of indigenous and local communities.

Article 22—Capacity

1. The Parties shall cooperate in the capacity-building, capacity development and strengthening of human resources and institutional capacities to effectively implement this Protocol in developing country Parties, in particular the least developed countries and small island developing States among them, and Parties with economies in transition, including through existing global, regional, subregional and national institutions and organizations. In this context, Parties should facilitate the involvement of indigenous and local communities and relevant stakeholders, including non-governmental organizations and the private sector.

2. The need of developing country Parties, in particular the least developed countries and small island developing States among them, and Parties with economies in transition for financial resources in accordance with the relevant provisions of the Convention shall be taken fully into account for capacity-building and development to implement this Protocol.

3. As a basis for appropriate measures in relation to the implementation of this Protocol, developing country Parties, in particular the least developed countries and small island developing States among them, and Parties with economies in transition should identify their national capacity needs and priorities through national capacity

self-assessments. In doing so, such Parties should support the capacity needs and priorities of indigenous and local communities and relevant stakeholders, as identified by them, emphasizing the capacity needs and priorities of women.

4. In support of the implementation of this Protocol, capacity-building and development may address, inter alia, the following key areas:

(a) Capacity to implement, and to comply with the obligations of, this Protocol;

(b) Capacity to negotiate mutually agreed terms;

(c) Capacity to develop, implement and enforce domestic legislative, administrative or policy measures on access and benefit-sharing; and

(d) Capacity of countries to develop their endogenous research capabilities to add value to their own genetic resources.

5. Measures in accordance with paragraphs 1 to 4 above may include, inter alia:

(a) Legal and institutional development;

(b) Promotion of equity and fairness in negotiations, such as training to negotiate mutually agreed terms;

(c) The monitoring and enforcement of compliance;

(d) Employment of best available communication tools and Internet-based systems for access and benefit-sharing activities;

(e) Development and use of valuation methods;

(f) Bioprospecting, associated research and taxonomic studies;

(g) Technology transfer, and infrastructure and technical capacity to make such technology transfer sustainable;

(h) Enhancement of the contribution of access and benefit-sharing activities to the conservation of biological diversity and the sustainable use of its components;

(i) Special measures to increase the capacity of relevant stakeholders in relation to access and benefit-sharing; and

(j) Special measures to increase the capacity of indigenous and local communities with emphasis on enhancing the capacity of women within those communities in relation to access to genetic resources and/or traditional knowledge associated with genetic resources.

6. Information on capacity-building and development initiatives at national, regional and international levels, undertaken in accordance with paragraphs 1 to 5 above, should be provided to the Access and Benefit-sharing Clearing–House with a view to promoting synergy and coordination on capacity-building and development for access and benefit-sharing.

Article 23—Technology Transfer, Collaboration and Cooperation

In accordance with Articles 15, 16, 18 and 19 of the Convention, the Parties shall collaborate and cooperate in technical and scientific research and development programmes, including biotechnological research activities, as a means to achieve the objective of this Protocol. The Parties undertake to promote and encourage access to technology by, and transfer of technology to, developing country Parties, in particular the least developed countries and small island developing States among them, and Parties with economies in transition, in order to enable the development and strengthening of a sound and viable technological and scientific base for the attainment of the objectives of the Convention and this Protocol. Where possible and appropriate such collaborative activities shall take place in and with a Party or the Parties providing genetic resources that is the country or are the countries of origin of such resources or a Party or Parties that have acquired the genetic resources in accordance with the Convention.

Article 24—Non–Parties

The Parties shall encourage non-Parties to adhere to this Protocol and to contribute appropriate information to the Access and Benefit-sharing Clearing–House.

Article 25—Financial Mechanism and Resources

1. In considering financial resources for the implementation of this Protocol, the Parties shall take into account the provisions of Article 20 of the Convention.

2. The financial mechanism of the Convention shall be the financial mechanism for this Protocol.

3. Regarding the capacity-building and development referred to in Article 22 of this Protocol, the Conference of the Parties serving as the meeting of the Parties to this Protocol, in providing guidance with respect to the financial mechanism referred to in paragraph 2 above, for consideration by the Conference of the Parties, shall take into account the need of developing country Parties, in particular the least developed countries and small island developing States among them, and of Parties with economies in transition, for financial resources, as well as the capacity needs and priorities of indigenous and local communities, including women within these communities.

4. In the context of paragraph 1 above, the Parties shall also take into account the needs of the developing country Parties, in particular the least developed countries and small island developing States among them, and of the Parties with economies in transition, in their efforts to identify and implement their capacity-building and development requirements for the purposes of the implementation of this Protocol.

5. The guidance to the financial mechanism of the Convention in relevant decisions of the Conference of the Parties, including those agreed before the adoption of this Protocol, shall apply, *mutatis mutandis*, to the provisions of this Article.

6. The developed country Parties may also provide, and the developing country Parties and the Parties with economies in transition avail themselves of, financial and other resources for the implementation of the provisions of this Protocol through bilateral, regional and multilateral channels.

Article 26—Conference of the Parties Serving as the Meeting of the Parties to this Protocol

1. The Conference of the Parties shall serve as the meeting of the Parties to this Protocol.

2. Parties to the Convention that are not Parties to this Protocol may participate as observers in the proceedings of any meeting of the Conference of the Parties serving as the meeting of the Parties to this Protocol. When the Conference of the Parties serves as the meeting of the Parties to this Protocol, decisions under this Protocol shall be taken only by those that are Parties to it.

3. When the Conference of the Parties serves as the meeting of the Parties to this Protocol, any member of the Bureau of the Conference of the Parties representing a Party to the Convention but, at that time, not a Party to this Protocol, shall be substituted by a member to be elected by and from among the Parties to this Protocol.

4. The Conference of the Parties serving as the meeting of the Parties to this Protocol shall keep under regular review the implementation of this Protocol and shall make, within its mandate, the decisions necessary to promote its effective implementation. It shall perform the functions assigned to it by this Protocol and shall:

(a) Make recommendations on any matters necessary for the implementation of this Protocol;

(b) Establish such subsidiary bodies as are deemed necessary for the implementation of this Protocol;

(c) Seek and utilize, where appropriate, the services and cooperation of, and information provided by, competent international organizations and intergovernmental and non-governmental bodies;

(d) Establish the form and the intervals for transmitting the information to be submitted in accordance with Article 29 of this Protocol and consider such information as well as reports submitted by any subsidiary body;

(e) Consider and adopt, as required, amendments to this Protocol and its Annex, as well as any additional annexes to this Protocol, that are deemed necessary for the implementation of this Protocol; and

(f) Exercise such other functions as may be required for the implementation of this Protocol.

5. The rules of procedure of the Conference of the Parties and financial rules of the Convention shall be applied, mutatis mutandis, under this Protocol, except as may be otherwise decided by consensus by the Conference of the Parties serving as the meeting of the Parties to this Protocol.

6. The first meeting of the Conference of the Parties serving as the meeting of the Parties to this Protocol shall be convened by the Secretariat and held concurrently with the first meeting of the Conference of the Parties that is scheduled after the date of the entry into force of this Protocol. Subsequent ordinary meetings of the Conference of the Parties serving as the meeting of the Parties to this Protocol shall be held concurrently with ordinary meetings of the Conference of the Parties, unless otherwise decided by the Conference of the Parties serving as the meeting of the Parties to this Protocol.

7. Extraordinary meetings of the Conference of the Parties serving as the meeting of the Parties to this Protocol shall be held at such other times as may be deemed necessary by the Conference of the Parties serving as the meeting of the Parties to this Protocol, or at the written request of any Party, provided that, within six months of the request being communicated to the Parties by the Secretariat, it is supported by at least one third of the Parties.

8. The United Nations, its specialized agencies and the International Atomic Energy Agency, as well as any State member thereof or observers thereto not party to the Convention, may be represented as observers at meetings of the Conference of the Parties serving as the meeting of the Parties to this Protocol. Any body or agency, whether national or international, governmental or non-governmental, that is qualified in matters covered by this Protocol and that has informed the Secretariat of its wish to be represented at a meeting of the Conference of the Parties serving as a meeting of the Parties to this Protocol as an observer, may be so admitted, unless at least one third of the Parties present object. Except as otherwise provided in this Article, the admission and participation of observers shall be subject to the rules of procedure, as referred to in paragraph 5 above.

Article 27—Subsidiary Bodies

1. Any subsidiary body established by or under the Convention may serve this Protocol, including upon a decision of the Conference of the Parties serving as the meeting of the Parties to this Protocol. Any such decision shall specify the tasks to be undertaken.

2.   Parties to the Convention that are not Parties to this Protocol may participate as observers in the proceedings of any meeting of any such subsidiary bodies. When a subsidiary body of the Convention serves as a subsidiary body to this Protocol, decisions under this Protocol shall be taken only by Parties to this Protocol.

3.   When a subsidiary body of the Convention exercises its functions with regard to matters concerning this Protocol, any member of the bureau of that subsidiary body representing a Party to the Convention but, at that time, not a Party to this Protocol, shall be substituted by a member to be elected by and from among the Parties to this Protocol.

Article 28—Secretariat

1.   The Secretariat established by Article 24 of the Convention shall serve as the secretariat to this Protocol.

2.   Article 24, paragraph 1, of the Convention on the functions of the Secretariat shall apply, *mutatis mutandis*, to this Protocol.

3.   To the extent that they are distinct, the costs of the secretariat services for this Protocol shall be met by the Parties hereto. The Conference of the Parties serving as the meeting of the Parties to this Protocol shall, at its first meeting, decide on the necessary budgetary arrangements to this end.

Article 29—Monitoring and Reporting

Each Party shall monitor the implementation of its obligations under this Protocol, and shall, at intervals and in the format to be determined by the Conference of the Parties serving as the meeting of the Parties to this Protocol, report to the Conference of the Parties serving as the meeting of the Parties to this Protocol on measures that it has taken to implement this Protocol.

Article 30—Procedures and Mechanisms to Promote Compliance with this Protocol

The Conference of the Parties serving as the meeting of the Parties to this Protocol shall, at its first meeting, consider and approve cooperative procedures and institutional mechanisms to promote compliance with the provisions of this Protocol and to address cases of non-compliance. These procedures and mechanisms shall include provisions to offer advice or assistance, where appropriate. They shall be separate from, and without prejudice to, the dispute settlement procedures and mechanisms under Article 27 of the Convention.

Article 31—Assessment and Review

The Conference of the Parties serving as the meeting of the Parties to this Protocol shall undertake, four years after the entry into force of this Protocol and thereafter at intervals determined by the Conference of the Parties serving as the meeting of the Parties to this Protocol, an evaluation of the effectiveness of this Protocol.

Article 32—Signature

This Protocol shall be open for signature by Parties to the Convention at the United Nations Headquarters in New York, from 2 February 2011 to 1 February 2012.

Article 33—Entry into Force

1.   This Protocol shall enter into force on the ninetieth day after the date of deposit of the fiftieth instrument of ratification, acceptance, approval or accession by States or regional economic integration organizations that are Parties to the Convention.

2. This Protocol shall enter into force for a State or regional economic integration organization that ratifies, accepts or approves this Protocol or accedes thereto after the deposit of the fiftieth instrument as referred to in paragraph 1 above, on the ninetieth day after the date on which that State or regional economic integration organization deposits its instrument of ratification, acceptance, approval or accession, or on the date on which the Convention enters into force for that State or regional economic integration organization, whichever shall be the later.

3. For the purposes of paragraphs 1 and 2 above, any instrument deposited by a regional economic integration organization shall not be counted as additional to those deposited by member States of such organization.

Article 34—Reservations

No reservations may be made to this Protocol.

Article 35—Withdrawal

1. At any time after two years from the date on which this Protocol has entered into force for a Party, that Party may withdraw from this Protocol by giving written notification to the Depositary.

2. Any such withdrawal shall take place upon expiry of one year after the date of its receipt by the Depositary, or on such later date as may be specified in the notification of the withdrawal.

Article 36—Authentic Texts

The original of this Protocol, of which the Arabic, Chinese, English, French, Russian and Spanish texts are equally authentic, shall be deposited with the Secretary–General of the United Nations.

Annex
MONETARY AND NON–MONETARY BENEFITS

1. Monetary benefits may include, but not be limited to:

(a) Access fees/fee per sample collected or otherwise acquired;

(b) Up-front payments;

(c) Milestone payments;

(d) Payment of royalties;

(e) Licence fees in case of commercialization;

(f) Special fees to be paid to trust funds supporting conservation and sustainable use of biodiversity;

(g) Salaries and preferential terms where mutually agreed;

(h) Research funding;

(i) Joint ventures;

(j) Joint ownership of relevant intellectual property rights.

2. Non-monetary benefits may include, but not be limited to:

(a) Sharing of research and development results;

(b) Collaboration, cooperation and contribution in scientific research and development programmes, particularly biotechnological research activities, where possible in the Party providing genetic resources;

(c) Participation in product development;

(d) Collaboration, cooperation and contribution in education and training;

(e) Admittance to ex situ facilities of genetic resources and to databases;

(f) Transfer to the provider of the genetic resources of knowledge and technology under fair and most favourable terms, including on concessional and preferential terms where agreed, in particular, knowledge and technology that make use of genetic resources, including biotechnology, or that are relevant to the conservation and sustainable utilization of biological diversity;

(g) Strengthening capacities for technology transfer;

(h) Institutional capacity-building;

(i) Human and material resources to strengthen the capacities for the administration and enforcement of access regulations;

(j) Training related to genetic resources with the full participation of countries providing genetic resources, and where possible, in such countries;

(k) Access to scientific information relevant to conservation and sustainable use of biological diversity, including biological inventories and taxonomic studies;

(*l*) Contributions to the local economy;

(m) Research directed towards priority needs, such as health and food security, taking into account domestic uses of genetic resources in the Party providing genetic resources;

(n) Institutional and professional relationships that can arise from an access and benefit-sharing agreement and subsequent collaborative activities;

(*o*) Food and livelihood security benefits;

(p) Social recognition;

(q) Joint ownership of relevant intellectual property rights.

B. Fishing

5.12 Convention on Fishing and Conservation of the Living Resources of the High Seas.[h] **Concluded at Geneva, 29 April 1958. Entered into force, 20 March 1966. 559 UNTS 285, 17 UST 138, TIAS No 5969[i];** *reprinted in* **5A Weston & Carlson V.H.5**

Article 1

1. All States have the right for their nationals to engage in fishing on the high seas, subject (*a*) to their treaty obligations, (*b*) to the interests and rights of coastal States as provided for in this Convention, and (*c*) to the provisions contained in the following articles concerning conservation of the living resources of the high seas.

2. All States have the duty to adopt, or to co-operate with other States in adopting, such measures for their respective nationals as may be necessary for the conservation of the living resources of the high seas.

Article 2

As employed in this Convention, the expression "conservation of the living resources of the high seas" means the aggregate of the measures rendering possible the optimum sustainable yield from those resources so as to secure a maximum supply to food and other marine products. Conservation programmes should be formulated with a view to securing in the first place a supply of food for human consumption.

Article 3

A State whose nationals are engaged in fishing any stock or stocks of fish or other living marine resources in any area of the high seas where the nationals of other States are not thus engaged shall adopt, for its own nationals, measures in that area when necessary for the purpose of the conservation of the living resources affected.

Article 4

1. If the nationals of two or more States are engaged in fishing the same stock or stocks of fish or other living marine resources in any area or areas of the high seas, these States shall, at the request of any of them, enter into negotiations with a view to prescribing by agreement for their nationals the necessary measures for the conservation of the living resources affected.

2. If the States concerned do not reach agreement within twelve months, any of the parties may initiate the procedure contemplated by article 9.

Article 5

1. If, subsequent to the adoption of the measures referred to in articles 3 and 4, nationals of other States engage in fishing the same stock or stocks of fish or other living marine resources in any area or areas of the high seas, the other States shall apply the measures, which shall not be discriminatory in form or in fact, to their own nationals not later than seven months after the date on which the measures shall have been notified to the Director–General of the Food and Agriculture Organization of the United Nations. The Director–General shall notify such measures to any State which so requests and, in any case, to any State specified by the State initiating the measure.

h. *See also* Basic Documents 3.1, 3.2 and 3.3, *supra.*

i. *See also* Optional Protocol to the 1958 Law of the Sea Conventions Concerning the Compulsory Settlement of Disputes (which provides for reference to the International Court of Justice of disputes arising out of this agreement), concluded 29 April 1958 and entered into force 30 September 1962 (450 UNTS 169).

2. If these other States do not accept the measures so adopted and if no agreement can be reached within twelve months, any of the interested parties may initiate the procedure contemplated by article 9. Subject to paragraph 2 of article 10, the measures adopted shall remain obligatory pending the decision of the special commission.

Article 6

1. A coastal State has a special interest in the maintenance of the productivity of the living resources in any area of the high seas adjacent to its territorial sea.

2. A coastal State is entitled to take part on an equal footing in any system of research and regulation for purposes of conservation of the living resources of the high seas in that area, even though its nationals do not carry on fishing there.

3. A state whose nationals are engaged in fishing in any area of the high seas adjacent to the territorial sea of a State shall, at the request of that coastal State, enter into negotiations with a view to prescribing by agreement the measures necessary for the conservation of the living resources of the high seas in that area.

4. A State whose nationals are engaged in fishing in any area of the high seas adjacent to the territorial sea of a coastal State shall not enforce conservation measures in that area which are opposed to those which have been adopted by the coastal State, but may enter into negotiations with the coastal State with a view to prescribing by agreement the measures necessary for the conservation of the living resources of the high seas in that area.

5. If the States concerned do not reach agreement with respect to conservation measures within twelve months, any of the parties may initiate the procedure contemplated by article 9.

Article 7

1. Having regard to the provisions of paragraph 1 of article 6, any coastal State may, with a view to the maintenance of the productivity of the living resources of the sea, adopt unilateral measures of conservation appropriate to any stock of fish or other marine resources in any area of the high seas adjacent to its territorial sea, provided that negotiations to that effect with the other States concerned have not led to an agreement within six months.

2. The measures which the coastal State adopts under the previous paragraph shall be valid as to other States only if the following requirements are fulfilled:

(*a*) That there is a need for urgent application of conservation measures in the light of the existing knowledge of the fishery;

(*b*) That the measures adopted are based on appropriate scientific findings;

(*c*) That such measures do not discriminate in form or in fact against foreign fishermen.

3. These measures shall remain in force pending the settlement, in accordance with the relevant provisions of this Convention, of any disagreement as to their validity.

4. If the measures are not accepted by the other States concerned, any of the parties may initiate the procedure contemplated by article 9. Subject to paragraph 2 of article 10, the measures adopted shall remain obligatory pending the decision of the special commission.

5. The principles of geographical demarcation as defined in article 12 of the Convention on the Territorial Sea and the Contiguous Zone shall be adopted when coasts of different States are involved.

Article 8

1. Any State which, even if its nationals are not engaged in fishing in an area of the high seas not adjacent to its coast, has a special interest in the conservation of the living resources of the high seas in that area, may request the State or States whose nationals are engaged in fishing there to take the necessary measures of conservation under articles 3 and 4 respectively, at the same time mentioning the scientific reasons which in its opinion make such measures necessary, and indicating its special interest.

2. If no agreement is reached within twelve months, such State may initiate the procedure contemplated by article 9.

Article 9

1. Any dispute which may arise between States under articles 4, 5, 6, 7 and 8 shall, at the request of any of the parties, be submitted for settlement to a special commission of five members, unless the parties agree to seek a solution by another method of peaceful settlement, as provided for in Article 33 of the Charter of the United Nations.

2. The members of the commission, one of whom shall be designated as chairman, shall be named by agreement between the States in dispute within three months of the request for settlement in accordance with the provisions of this article. Failing agreement they shall, upon the request of any State party, be named by the Secretary-General of the United Nations, within a further three-month period, in consultation with the States in dispute and with the President of the International Court of Justice and the Director-General of the Food and Agriculture Organization of the United Nations, from amongst well-qualified persons being nationals of States not involved in the dispute and specializing in legal, administrative or scientific questions relating to fisheries, depending upon the nature of the dispute to be settled. Any vacancy arising after the original appointment shall be filled in the same manner as provided for the initial selection.

3. Any State party to proceedings under these articles shall have the right to name one of its nationals to the special commission, with the right to participate fully in the proceedings on the same footing as a member of the commission, but without the right to vote or to take part in the writing of the commission's decision.

4. The commission shall determine its own procedure, assuring each party to the proceedings a full opportunity to be heard and to present its case. It shall also determine how the costs and expenses shall be divided between the parties to the dispute, failing agreement by the parties on this matter.

5. The special commission shall render its decision within a period of five months from the time it is appointed unless it decides, in case of necessity, to extend the time limit for a period not exceeding three months.

6. The special commission shall, in reaching its decisions, adhere to these articles and to any special agreements between the disputing parties regarding settlement of the dispute.

7. Decisions of the commission shall be by majority vote.

Article 10

1. The special commission shall, in disputes arising under article 7, apply the criteria listed in paragraph 2 of that article. In disputes under articles 4, 5, 6 and 8, the commission shall apply the following criteria, according to the issues involved in the dispute:

(*a*) Common to the determination of disputes arising under articles 4, 5 and 6 are the requirements:

(i) That scientific findings demonstrate the necessity of conservation measures;

(ii) That the specific measures are based on scientific findings and are practicable; and

(iii) That the measures do not discriminate, in form or in fact, against fishermen of other States;

(b) Applicable to the determination of disputes arising under article 8 is the requirement that scientific findings demonstrate the necessity for conservation measures, or that the conservation programme is adequate, as the case may be.

2. The special commission may decide that pending its award the measures in dispute shall not be applied, provided that, in the case of disputes under article 7, the measures shall only be suspended when it is apparent to the commission on the basis of *prima facie* evidence that the need for the urgent application of such measures does not exist.

Article 11

The decisions of the special commission shall be binding on the States concerned and the provisions of paragraph 2 of Article 94 of the Charter of the United Nations shall be applicable to those decisions. If the decisions are accompanied by any recommendations, they shall receive the greatest possible consideration.

Article 12

1. If the factual basis of the award of the special commission is altered by substantial changes in the conditions of the stock or stocks of fish or other living marine resources or in methods of fishing, any of the States concerned may request the other States to enter into negotiations with a view to prescribing by agreement the necessary modifications in the measures of conservation.

2. If no agreement is reached within a reasonable period of time, any of the States concerned may again resort to the procedure contemplated by article 9 provided that at least two years have elapsed from the original award.

Article 13

1. The regulation of fisheries conducted by means of equipment embedded in the floor of the sea in areas of the high seas adjacent to the territorial sea of a State may be undertaken by that State where such fisheries have long been maintained and conducted by its nationals, provided that non-nationals are permitted to participate in such activities on an equal footing with nationals except in areas where such fisheries have by long usage been exclusively enjoyed by such nationals. Such regulations will not, however, affect the general status of the areas as high seas.

2. In this article, the expression "fisheries conducted by means of equipment embedded in the floor of the sea" means those fisheries using gear with supporting members embedded in the sea floor, constructed on a site and left there to operate permanently or, if removed, restored each season on the same site.

Article 14

In articles 1, 3, 4, 5, 6 and 8, the term "nationals" means fishing boats or craft of any size having the nationality of the State concerned, according to the law of that State, irrespective of the nationality of the members of their crews.

Article 15

This Convention shall, until 31 October 1958, be open for signature by all States Members of the United Nations or of any of the specialized agencies, and by any other

State invited by the General Assembly of the United Nations to become a Party to the Convention.

Article 16

This Convention is subject to ratification. The instruments of ratification shall be deposited with the Secretary–General of the United Nations.

Article 17

This Convention shall be open for accession by any States belonging to any of the categories mentioned in article 15. The instruments of accession shall be deposited with the Secretary–General of the United Nations.

Article 18

1. This Convention shall come into force on the thirtieth day following the date of deposit of the twenty-second instrument of ratification or accession with the Secretary–General of the United Nations.

2. For each State ratifying or acceding to the Convention after the deposit of the twenty-second instrument of ratification or accession, the Convention shall enter into force on the thirtieth day after deposit by such State of its instrument of ratification or accession.

Article 19

1. At the time of signature, ratification or accession, any State may make reservations to articles of the Convention other than to articles 6, 7, 9, 10, 11 and 12.

2. Any contracting State making a reservation in accordance with the preceding paragraph may at any time withdraw the reservation by a communication to that effect addressed to the Secretary–General of the United Nations.

Article 20

1. After the expiration of a period of five years from the date on which this Convention shall enter into force, a request for the revision of this Convention may be made at any time by any contracting party by means of a notification in writing addressed to the Secretary–General of the United Nations.

2. The General Assembly of the United Nations shall decide upon the steps, if any, to be taken in respect of such request.

Article 21

The Secretary–General of the United Nations shall inform all States Members of the United Nations and the other States referred to in article 15:

(*a*) Of signatures to this Convention and of the deposit of instruments of ratification or accession, in accordance with articles 15, 16 and 17;

(*b*) Of the date on which this Convention will come into force, in accordance with article 18;

(*c*) Of requests for revision in accordance with article 20;

(*d*) Of reservations to this Convention, in accordance with article 19.

Article 22

The original of this Convention, of which the Chinese, English, French, Russian and Spanish texts are equally authentic, shall be deposited with the Secretary–General of the United Nations, who shall send certified copies thereof to all States referred to in article 15.

5.13 **CONVENTION FOR THE PROHIBITION OF FISHING WITH LONG DRIFTNETS IN THE SOUTH PACIFIC (Without Protocols). Concluded at Wellington, 23 November 1989. Entered into force, 17 May 1991. 1899 UNTS 3; *reprinted in* 29 ILM 1454 (1990) & 5A Weston & Carlson V.H.18**

The Parties to this Convention,

RECOGNISING the importance of marine living resources to the people of the South Pacific region;

PROFOUNDLY CONCERNED at the damage now being done by pelagic drift-net fishing to the albacore tuna resource and to the environment and economy of the South Pacific region;

CONCERNED ALSO for the navigational threat posed by drift-net fishing;

NOTING that the increasing fishing capacity induced by large scale drift-net fishing threatens the fish stocks in the South Pacific;

MINDFUL OF the relevant rules of international law, including the provisions of the United Nations Convention on the Law of the Sea, done at Montego Bay on 10 December 1982, in particular Parts V, VII and XVI;

RECALLING the Declaration of the South Pacific Forum at Tarawa, 11 July 1989, that a Convention should be adopted to ban the use of drift nets in the South Pacific region;

RECALLING ALSO the Resolution of the 29th South Pacific Conference at Guam, which called for an immediate ban on the practice of drift-net fishing in the South Pacific Commission region;

HAVE AGREED as follows:

Article 1

DEFINITIONS

For the purpose of this Convention and its Protocols:

(a) The "Convention Area",

(i) Subject to subparagraph (ii) of this paragraph, shall be the area lying within 10 degrees North latitude and 50 degrees South latitude and 130 degrees East longitude and 120 degrees West longitude, and shall also include all waters under the fisheries jurisdiction of any Party to this Convention;

(ii) In the case of a State or Territory which is Party to the Convention by virtue of paragraph 1(b) or 1(c) of article 10, it shall include only waters under the fisheries jurisdiction of that Party, adjacent to the Territory referred to in paragraph 1(b) or 1(c) of article 10.

(b) "drift net" means a gillnet or other net or a combination of nets which is more than 2.5 kilometres in length the purpose of which is to enmesh, entrap or entangle fish by drifting on the surface of or in the water;

(c) "drift net fishing activities" means:

(i) catching, taking or harvesting fish with the use of a drift net;

(ii) attempting to catch, take or harvest fish with the use of a drift net;

(iii) engaging in any other activity which can reasonably be expected to result in the catching, taking or harvesting of fish with the use of a drift net, including searching for and locating fish to be taken by that method;

(iv) any operations at sea in support of, or in preparation for, any activity described in this paragraph, including operations of placing, searching for or recovering fish aggregating devices or associated electronic equipment such as radio beacons;

(v) aircraft use, relating to the activities described in this paragraph, except for flights in emergencies involving the health or safety of crew members or the safety of a vessel; or

(vi) transporting, transshipping and processing any drift-net catch, and cooperation in the provision of food, fuel and other supplies for vessels equipped for or engaged in drift-net fishing.

(d) the "FFA" means the South Pacific Forum Fisheries Agency; and

(e) "fishing vessel" means any vessel or boat equipped for or engaged in searching for, catching, processing or transporting fish or other marine organisms.

Article 2

MEASURES REGARDING NATIONALS AND VESSELS

Each Party undertakes to prohibit its nationals and vessels documented under its laws from engaging in drift-net fishing activities within the Convention Area.

Article 3

MEASURES AGAINST DRIFTNET FISHING ACTIVITIES

1. Each Party undertakes:

(a) not to assist or encourage the use of driftnets within the Convention Area; and

(b) to take measures consistent with international law to restrict drift-net fishing activities within the Convention Area, including but not limited to:

(i) prohibiting the use of driftnets within areas under its fisheries jurisdiction; and

(ii) prohibiting the transshipment of drift-net catches within areas under its jurisdiction.

2. Each Party may also take measures consistent with international law to:

(a) prohibit the landing of drift-net catches within its territory;

(b) prohibit the processing of drift-net catches in facilities under its jurisdiction;

(c) prohibit the importation of any fish or fish product, whether processed or not, which was caught using a driftnet;

(d) restrict port access and port servicing facilities for drift-net fishing vessels; and

(e) prohibit the possession of drift nets on board any fishing vessel within areas under its fisheries jurisdiction.

3. Nothing in this Convention shall prevent a Party from taking measures against drift-net fishing activities which are stricter than those required by the Convention.

Article 4

ENFORCEMENT

1. Each Party shall take appropriate measures to ensure the application of the provisions of this Convention.

2. The Parties undertake to collaborate to facilitate surveillance and enforcement of measures taken by Parties pursuant to this Convention.

3. The Parties undertake measures leading to the withdrawal of good standing on the Regional Register of Foreign Fishing Vessels maintained by the FFA against any vessel engaging in drift-net fishing activities.

Article 5

CONSULTATION WITH NONPARTIES

1. The Parties shall seek to consult with any State which is eligible to become a Party to this Convention on any matter relating to drift-net fishing activities which appear to affect adversely the conservation of marine living resources within the Convention Area or the implementation of the Convention and its protocols.

2. The Parties shall seek to reach agreement with any State referred to in paragraph 1 of this article, concerning the prohibitions established pursuant to articles 2 and 3.

Article 6

INSTITUTIONAL ARRANGEMENTS

1. The FFA shall be responsible for carrying out the following functions:

(a) the collection, preparation and dissemination of information on drift-net fishing activities within the Convention Area;

(b) the facilitation of scientific analyses on the effects of drift-net fishing activities within the Convention Area, including consultations with appropriate regional and international organizations; and

(c) the preparation and transmission to the Parties of the annual report on any drift-net fishing activities within the Convention Area and the measures taken to implement this Convention or its Protocols.

2. Each Party shall expeditiously convey to the FFA:

(a) information on the measures adopted by it pursuant to the implementation of the Convention; and

(b) information on, and scientific analyses on the effects of, drift-net fishing activities relevant to the Convention Area.

3. All Parties, including States or Territories not members of the FFA, and the FFA shall cooperate to promote the effective implementation of this article.

Article 7

REVIEW AND CONSULTATION AMONG PARTIES

1. Without prejudice to the conduct of consultations among Parties by other means, the FFA, at the request of three Parties, shall convene meetings of the Parties to review the implementation of this Convention and its Protocols.

2. Parties to the Protocols shall be invited to any such meeting and to participate in a manner to be determined by the Parties to the Convention.

Article 8

CONSERVATION AND MANAGEMENT MEASURES

Parties to this Convention shall co-operate with each other and with appropriate distant water fishing nations and other entities or organizations in the development of conservation and management measures for South Pacific albacore tuna within the Convention Area.

Article 9

PROTOCOLS

This Convention may be supplemented by Protocols or associated instruments to further its objectives.

Article 10

SIGNATURE, RATIFICATION AND ACCESSION

1.   This Convention shall be open for signature by:

(a) any member of the FFA; and

(b) any State in respect of any Territory situated within the Convention Area for which it is internationally responsible; or

(c) any Territory situated within the Convention Area which has been authorized to sign the Convention and to assume rights and obligations under it by the Government of the State which is internationally responsible for it.

2.   This Convention is subject to ratification by members of the FFA and the other States and Territories referred to in paragraph 1 of this article. The instruments of ratification shall be deposited with the Government of New Zealand which shall be the depositary.

3.   This Convention shall remain open for accession by the members of the FFA and the other States and Territories referred to in paragraph 1 of this article. The instruments of accession shall be deposited with the Depositary.

Article 11

RESERVATIONS

This Convention shall not be subject to reservations.

Article 12

AMENDMENTS

1.   Any Party may propose amendments to this Convention.

2.   Amendments shall be adopted by consensus among the Parties.

3.   Any amendments adopted shall be submitted by the Depositary to all Parties for ratification, approval or acceptance.

4.   An amendment shall enter into force thirty days after receipt by the Depositary of instruments of ratification, approval or acceptance from all Parties.

Article 13

ENTRY INTO FORCE

1.   This Convention shall enter into force on the date of deposit of the fourth instrument of ratification or accession.

2.   For any member of the FFA or a State or Territory which ratifies or accedes to this Convention after the date of deposit of the fourth instrument of ratification or accession, the Convention shall enter into force on the date of deposit of its instruments of ratification or accession.

Article 14

CERTIFICATION AND REGISTRATION

1.   The original of this Convention and its Protocols shall be deposited with the Depositary, which shall transmit certified copies to all States and Territories eligible to become Party to Convention and to all States eligible to become Party to a Protocol to the Convention.

2.   The Depositary shall register this Convention and its Protocols in accordance with Article 102 of the Charter of the United Nations.

5.14 RESOLUTION ON LARGE-SCALE PELAGIC DRIFTNET FISHING AND ITS IMPACT ON THE LIVING MARINE RESOURCES OF THE WORLD'S OCEANS AND SEAS. Adopted by the UN General Assembly, 22 December 1989. UN Doc A/RES/44/225; *reprinted in* 29 ILM 1555 (1990) & 5A Weston and Carlson V.H.19

The General Assembly,

Noting that many countries are disturbed by the increase in the use of large-scale pelagic driftnets, which can reach or exceed 30 miles (48 kilometres) in total length, to catch living marine resources on the high seas of the world's oceans and seas,

Mindful that large-scale pelagic driftnet fishing, a method of fishing with a net or a combination of nets intended to be held in a more or less vertical position by floats and weights, the purpose of which is to enmesh fish by drifting on the surface of or in the water, can be a highly indiscriminate and wasteful fishing method that is widely considered to threaten the effective conservation of living marine resources, such as highly migratory and anadromous species of fish, birds and marine mammals,

Drawing attention to the fact that the present resolution does not address the question of small-scale driftnet fishing traditionally conducted in coastal waters, especially by developing countries, which provides an important contribution to their subsistence and economic development,

Expressing concern that, in addition to targeted species of fish, non-targeted fish, marine mammals, seabirds and other living marine resources of the world's oceans and seas can become entangled in large-scale pelagic driftnets, either in those in active use or in those that are lost or discarded, and as a result of such entanglement are often either injured or killed,

Recognizing that more than one thousand fishing vessels use large-scale pelagic driftnets in the Pacific, Atlantic and Indian Oceans and in other areas of the high seas,

Recognizing also that any regulatory measure to be taken for the conservation and management of living marine resources should take account of the best available scientific data and analysis,

Recalling the relevant principles elaborated in the United Nations Convention on the Law of the Sea,

Affirming that, in accordance with the relevant articles of the Convention, all members of the international community have a duty to co-operate globally and regionally in the conservation and management of living resources on the high seas, and a duty to take, or to co-operate with others in taking, such measures for their nationals as may be necessary for the conservation of those resources,

Recalling that, in accordance with the relevant articles of the Convention, it is the responsibility of all members of the international community to ensure the conservation and management of living marine resources and the protection and preservation of the living marine environment within their exclusive economic zones,

Noting the serious concern, particularly among coastal States and States with fishing interests, that the overexploitation of living marine resources of the high seas adjacent to the exclusive economic zones of coastal States is likely to have an adverse impact on the same resources within such zones, and noting also, in this regard, the responsibility for co-operation in accordance with the relevant articles of the Convention,

Noting further that the countries of the South Pacific Forum and the South Pacific Commission, in recognition of the importance of living marine resources to the people of the South Pacific region, have called for a cessation of such fishing in the South Pacific and the implementation of effective management programmes,

Taking note of the adoption of the Tarawa Declaration on this subject by the Twentieth South Pacific Forum at Tarawa, Kiribati, on 11 July 1989 and the adoption by South Pacific States and territories of the Convention on the Prohibition of Driftnet Fishing in the South Pacific, at Wellington on 24 November 1989,

Noting that some members of the international community have entered into co-operative enforcement and monitoring programmes for the immediate evaluation of the impact of large-scale pelagic driftnet fishing,

Recognizing that some members of the international community have taken steps to reduce their driftnet operations in some regions in response to regional concerns,

1. *Calls upon* all members of the international community, particularly those with fishing interests, to strengthen their co-operation in the conservation and management of living marine resources;

2. *Calls upon* all those involved in large-scale pelagic driftnet fishing to co-operate fully with the international community, and especially with coastal States and the relevant international and regional organizations, in the enhanced collection and sharing of statistically sound scientific data in order to continue to assess the impact of such fishing methods and to secure conservation of the world's living marine resources;

3. *Recommends* that all interested members of the international community, particularly within regional organizations, continue to consider and, by 30 June 1991, review the best available scientific data on the impact of large-scale pelagic driftnet fishing and agree upon further co-operative regulation and monitoring measures, as needed;

4. *Also recommends* that all members of the international community, bearing in mind the special role of regional organizations and regional and bilateral co-operation in the conservation and management of living marine resources as reflected in the relevant articles of the United Nations Convention on the Law of the Sea, agree to the following measures:

(a) Moratoria should be imposed on all large-scale pelagic driftnet fishing by 30 June 1992, with the understanding that such a measure will not be imposed in a region or, if implemented, can be lifted, should effective conservation and management measures be taken based upon statistically sound analysis to be jointly made by concerned parties of the international community with an interest in the fishery resources of the region, to prevent unacceptable impact of such fishing practices on that region and to ensure the conservation of the living marine resources of that region;

(b) Immediate action should be taken to reduce progressively large-scale pelagic driftnet fishing activities in the South Pacific region with a view to the cessation of such activities by 1 July 1991, as an interim measure, until appropriate conservation and management arrangements for South Pacific albacore tuna resources are entered into by the parties concerned;

(c) Further expansion of large-scale pelagic driftnet fishing on the high seas of the North Pacific and all the other high seas outside the Pacific Ocean should cease immediately, with the understanding that this measure will be reviewed subject to the conditions in paragraph 4(a) of the present resolution;

5. *Encourages* those coastal countries which have exclusive economic zones adjacent to the high seas to take appropriate measures and to co-operate in the collection and submission of scientific information on driftnet fishing in their own exclusive economic zones, taking into account the measures taken for the conservation of living marine resources of the high seas;

6. *Requests* specialized agencies, particularly the Food and Agriculture Organization of the United Nations, and other appropriate organs, organizations and programmes of the United Nations system, as well as the various regional and subregional fisheries organizations, urgently to study large-scale pelagic driftnet fishing and its impact on living marine resources and to report their views to the Secretary–General;

7. *Requests* the Secretary–General to bring the present resolution to the attention of all members of the international community, intergovernmental organizations, non-governmental organizations in consultative status with the Economic and Social Council, and well-established scientific institutions with expertise in relation to living marine resources;

8. *Requests* the Secretary–General to submit to the General Assembly at its forty-fifth session a report on the implementation of the present resolution.

5.15 RESOLUTION 46/215 ON LARGE-SCALE PELAGIC DRIFTNET FISHING AND ITS IMPACT ON THE LIVING MARINE RESOURCES OF THE WORLD'S OCEANS AND SEAS. **Adopted by the UN General Assembly, 20 December 1991. UN Doc A/RES/46/215; *reprinted in* 30 ILM 241 (1991) & 5A Weston and Carlson V.H.21**

The General Assembly,

Recalling its resolutions 44/225 and 45/197, concerning large-scale pelagic drift-net fishing and its impact on the living marine resources of the world's oceans and seas, including enclosed and semi-enclosed seas, which took into account the concerns of the developing countries and were adopted by consensus on 22 December 1989 and 21 December 1990, respectively,

Also recalling, in particular, that the General Assembly recommended that all members of the international community agree to certain measures specified in the operative paragraphs of resolution 44/225,

Further recalling the relevant principles elaborated in the United Nations Convention on the Law of the Sea, which are referred to in the seventh to tenth preambular paragraphs of resolution 44/225,

Expressing deep concern about reports of expansion of large-scale pelagic drift-net fishing activities on the high seas in contravention of resolutions 44/225 and 45/197, including attempts to expand large-scale pelagic drift-net fishing in the high seas areas of the Indian Ocean,

Commending the unilateral, regional and international efforts that have been undertaken by members of the international community and international organizations to implement and support the objectives of resolutions 44/225 and 45/197,

Noting that at the Twenty-second South Pacific Forum, held at Palikir on 29 and 30 July 1991, the heads of Government reaffirmed their opposition to large-scale pelagic drift-net fishing, and in this regard, *inter alia,* welcomed the entry into force on 17 May 1991 of the Convention for the Prohibition of Fishing with Long Drift-nets in the South Pacific,

Recalling the Castries Declaration, in which the Authority of the Organization of Eastern Caribbean States resolved to establish a regional regime for the regulation and management of the pelagic resources in the Lesser Antilles region that would outlaw the use of drift-nets and called upon other States in the region to cooperate in this regard,

Welcoming the actions taken that have resulted in the cessation of all large-scale pelagic drift-net fishing activities in the South Pacific in advance of the date stipulated in paragraph 4(*b*) of resolution 44/225 for the termination of such activities,

Also welcoming the decision of other members of the international community to cease large-scale pelagic drift-net fishing on the high seas,

Commending the efforts of many members of the international community to compile data on large-scale pelagic drift-net fishing and to submit their findings to the Secretary–General,

Noting the contributions to the report of the Secretary–General made by some members of the international community and by intergovernmental and non-governmental organizations,

Noting also the significant concerns expressed by members of the international community and competent regional fisheries bodies regarding the impact of large-scale pelagic drift-net fishing on the marine environment,

Noting further that, in accordance with paragraph 3 of resolution 44/225, some members of the international community have reviewed the best available scientific data on the impact of large-scale pelagic drift-net fishing and have failed to conclude that this practice has no adverse impact which threatens the conservation and sustainable management of living marine resources,

Noting that the grounds for concerns expressed about the unacceptable impact of large-scale pelagic drift-net fishing in resolutions 44/225 and 45/197 have been confirmed and that evidence has not demonstrated that the impact can be fully prevented,

Recognizing that a moratorium on large-scale pelagic drift-net fishing is required, notwithstanding that it will have adverse socio-economic effects on the communities involved in high seas pelagic drift-net fishing operations,

1. *Recalls* its resolutions 44/225 and 45/197;

2. *Commends* the efforts jointly to collect statistically sound data regarding large-scale pelagic drift-net fishing in the North Pacific Ocean, which were reviewed at the meeting of scientists held at Sidney, Canada, in June 1991, and presented at the symposium on the high seas drift-net fisheries in the North Pacific Ocean, held at Tokyo in November 1991 under the auspices of the International North Pacific Fisheries Commission;

3. *Calls upon* all members of the international community to implement resolutions 44/225 and 45/197 by, *inter alia,* taking the following actions:

(*a*) Beginning on 1 January 1992, reduce fishing effort in existing large-scale pelagic high seas drift-net fisheries by, *inter alia,* reducing the number of vessels involved, the length of the nets and the area of operation, so as to achieve, by 30 June 1992, a 50 per cent reduction in fishing effort;

(*b*) Continue to ensure that the areas of operation of large-scale pelagic high seas drift-net fishing are not expanded and, beginning on 1 January 1992, are further reduced in accordance with paragraph 3(*a*) of the present resolution;

(*c*) Ensure that a global moratorium on all large-scale pelagic drift-net fishing is fully implemented on the high seas of the world's oceans and seas, including enclosed seas and semi-enclosed seas, by 31 December 1992;

4. *Reaffirms* the importance it attaches to compliance with the present resolution and encourages all members of the international community to take measures, individually and collectively, to prevent large-scale pelagic drift-net fishing operations on the high seas of the world's oceans and seas, including enclosed seas and semi-enclosed seas;

5. *Requests* the Secretary–General to bring the present resolution to the attention of all members of the international community, intergovernmental and non-governmental organizations and well-established scientific institutions with expertise in relation to living marine resources;

6. *Requests* the members and organizations referred to above to submit to the Secretary–General information concerning activities or conduct inconsistent with the terms of the present resolution;

7. *Also requests* the Secretary–General to submit to the General Assembly at its forty-seventh session a report on the implementation of the present resolution.

5.16 AGREEMENT TO PROMOTE COMPLIANCE WITH INTERNATIONAL CONSERVATION AND MANAGEMENT MEASURES BY FISHING VESSELS ON THE HIGH SEAS. **Adopted by the Twenty-seventh Session of the Food and Agriculture Organization of the United Nations Conference, 24 November 1993. Entered into force, 24 April 2003. 2221 UNTS 91;** *reprinted in* **33 ILM 968 (1994)**

Preamble

The Parties to this Agreement,

Recognizing that all States have the right for their nationals to engage in fishing on the high seas, subject to the relevant rules of international law, as reflected in the United Nations Convention on the Law of the Sea,

Further recognizing that, under international law as reflected in the United Nations Convention on the Law of the Sea, all States have the duty to take, or to cooperate with other States in taking, such measures for their respective nationals as may be necessary for the conservation of the living resources of the high seas,

Acknowledging the right and interest of all States to develop their fishing sectors in accordance with their national policies, and the need to promote cooperation with developing countries to enhance their capabilities to fulfil their obligations under this Agreement,

Recalling that Agenda 21, adopted by the United Nations Conference on Environment and Development, calls upon States to take effective action, consistent with international law, to deter reflagging of vessels by their nationals as a means of avoiding compliance with applicable conservation and management rules for fishing activities on the high seas,

Further recalling that the Declaration of Cancun, adopted by the International Conference on Responsible Fishing, also calls on States to take action in this respect,

Bearing in mind that under Agenda 21, States commit themselves to the conservation and sustainable use of marine living resources on the high seas,

Calling upon States which do not participate in global, regional or subregional fisheries organizations or arrangements to join or, as appropriate, to enter into understandings with such organizations or with parties to such organizations or arrangements with a view to achieving compliance with international conservation and management measures,

Conscious of the duties of every State to exercise effectively its jurisdiction and control over vessels flying its flag, including fishing vessels and vessels engaged in the transhipment of fish,

Mindful that the practice of flagging or reflagging fishing vessels as a means of avoiding compliance with international conservation and management measures for living marine resources, and the failure of flag States to fulfil their responsibilities with respect to fishing vessels entitled to fly their flag, are among the factors that seriously undermine the effectiveness of such measures,

Realizing that the objective of this Agreement can be achieved through specifying flag States' responsibility in respect of fishing vessels entitled to fly their flags and operating on the high seas, including the authorization by the flag State of such operations, as well as through strengthened international cooperation and increased transparency through the exchange of information on high seas fishing,

Noting that this Agreement will form an integral part of the International Code of Conduct for Responsible Fishing called for in the Declaration of Cancun,

Desiring to conclude an international agreement within the framework of the Food and Agriculture Organization of the United Nations, hereinafter referred to as FAO, under Article XIV of the FAO Constitution,

Have agreed as follows:

Article I
Definitions

For the purposes of this Agreement:

(a) "fishing vessel" means any vessel used or intended for use for the purposes of the commercial exploitation of living marine resources, including mother ships and any other vessels directly engaged in such fishing operations;

(b) "international conservation and management measures" means measures to conserve or manage one or more species of living marine resources that are adopted and applied in accordance with the relevant rules of international law as reflected in the 1982 United Nations Convention on the Law of the Sea. Such measures may be adopted either by global, regional or subregional fisheries organizations, subject to the rights and obligations of their members, or by treaties or other international agreements;

(c) "length" means

(i) for any fishing vessel built after 18 July 1982, 96 percent of the total length on a waterline at 85 percent of the least moulded depth measured from the top of the keel, or the length from the foreside of the stem to the axis of the rudder stock on that waterline, if that be greater. In ships designed with a rake of keel the waterline on which this length is measured shall be parallel to the designed waterline;

(ii) for any fishing vessel built before 18 July 1982, registered length as entered on the national register or other record of vessels;

(d) "record of fishing vessels" means a record of fishing vessels in which are recorded pertinent details of the fishing vessel. It may constitute a separate record for fishing vessels or form part of a general record of vessels;

(e) "regional economic integration organization" means a regional economic integration organization to which its member States have transferred competence over matters covered by this Agreement, including the authority to make decisions binding on its member States in respect of those matters;

(f) "vessels entitled to fly its flag" and "vessels entitled to fly the flag of a State", includes vessels entitled to fly the flag of a member State of a regional economic integration organization.

Article II
Application

1. Subject to the following paragraphs of this Article, this Agreement shall apply to all fishing vessels that are used or intended for fishing on the high seas.

2. A Party may exempt fishing vessels of less than 24 metres in length entitled to fly its flag from the application of this Agreement unless the Party determines that such an exemption would undermine the object and purpose of this Agreement, provided that such exemptions:

(a) shall not be granted in respect of fishing vessels operating in fishing regions referred to in paragraph 3 below, other than fishing vessels that are entitled to fly the flag of a coastal State of that fishing region; and

(b) shall not apply to the obligations undertaken by a Party under paragraph 1 of Article III, or paragraph 7 of Article VI of this Agreement.

3. Without prejudice to the provisions of paragraph 2 above, in any fishing region where bordering coastal States have not yet declared exclusive economic zones, or equivalent zones of national jurisdiction over fisheries, such coastal States as are Parties to this Agreement may agree, either directly or through appropriate regional fisheries organizations, to establish a minimum length of fishing vessels below which this Agreement shall not apply in respect of fishing vessels flying the flag of any such coastal State and operating exclusively in such fishing region.

Article III
Flag state responsibility

1. (a) Each Party shall take such measures as may be necessary to ensure that fishing vessels entitled to fly its flag do not engage in any activity that undermines the effectiveness of international conservation and management measures.

(b) In the event that a Party has, pursuant to paragraph 2 of Article II, granted an exemption for fishing vessels of less than 24 metres in length entitled to fly its flag from the application of other provisions of this Agreement, such Party shall nevertheless take effective measures in respect of any such fishing vessel that undermines the effectiveness of international conservation and management measures. These measures shall be such as to ensure that the fishing vessel ceases to engage in activities that undermine the effectiveness of the international conservation and management measures.

2. In particular, no Party shall allow any fishing vessel entitled to fly its flag to be used for fishing on the high seas unless it has been authorized to be so used by the appropriate authority or authorities of that Party. A fishing vessel so authorized shall fish in accordance with the conditions of the authorization.

3. No Party shall authorize any fishing vessel entitled to fly its flag to be used for fishing on the high seas unless the Party is satisfied that it is able, taking into account the links that exist between it and the fishing vessel concerned, to exercise effectively its responsibilities under this Agreement in respect of that fishing vessel.

4. Where a fishing vessel that has been authorized to be used for fishing on the high seas by a Party ceases to be entitled to fly the flag of that Party, the authorization to fish on the high seas shall be deemed to have been cancelled.

5. (a) No Party shall authorize any fishing vessel previously registered in the territory of another Party that has undermined the effectiveness of international conservation and management measures to be used for fishing on the high seas, unless it is satisfied that

(i) any period of suspension by another Party of an authorization for such fishing vessel to be used for fishing on the high seas has expired; and

(ii) no authorization for such fishing vessel to be used for fishing on the high seas has been withdrawn by another Party within the last three years.

(b) The provisions of subparagraph (a) above shall also apply in respect of fishing vessels previously registered in the territory of a State which is not a Party to this Agreement, provided that sufficient information is available to the Party concerned on the circumstances in which the authorization to fish was suspended or withdrawn.

(c) The provisions of subparagraphs (a) and (b) shall not apply where the ownership of the fishing vessel has subsequently changed, and the new owner has provided sufficient evidence demonstrating that the previous owner or operator has no further legal, beneficial or financial interest in, or control of, the fishing vessel.

(d) Notwithstanding the provisions of subparagraphs (a) and (b) above, a Party may authorize a fishing vessel, to which those subparagraphs would otherwise apply, to be used for fishing on the high seas, where the Party concerned, after having taken into account all relevant facts, including the circumstances in which the fishing authorization has been withdrawn by the other Party or State, has determined that to grant an authorization to use the vessel for fishing on the high seas would not undermine the object and purpose of this Agreement.

6. Each Party shall ensure that all fishing vessels entitled to fly its flag that it has entered in the record maintained under Article IV are marked in such a way that they can be readily identified in accordance with generally accepted standards, such as the FAO Standard Specifications for the Marking and Identification of Fishing Vessels.

7. Each Party shall ensure that each fishing vessel entitled to fly its flag shall provide it with such information on its operations as may be necessary to enable the Party to fulfil its obligations under this Agreement, including in particular information pertaining to the area of its fishing operations and to its catches and landings.

8. Each Party shall take enforcement measures in respect of fishing vessels entitled to fly its flag which act in contravention of the provisions of this Agreement, including, where appropriate, making the contravention of such provisions an offence under national legislation. Sanctions applicable in respect of such contraventions shall be of sufficient gravity as to be effective in securing compliance with the requirements of this Agreement and to deprive offenders of the benefits accruing from their illegal activities. Such sanctions shall, for serious offences, include refusal, suspension or withdrawal of the authorization to fish on the high seas.

Article IV
Records of fishing vessels

Each Party shall, for the purposes of this Agreement, maintain a record of fishing vessels entitled to fly its flag and authorized to be used for fishing on the high seas, and shall take such measures as may be necessary to ensure that all such fishing vessels are entered in that record.

Article V
International cooperation

1. The Parties shall cooperate as appropriate in the implementation of this Agreement, and shall, in particular, exchange information, including evidentiary material, relating to activities of fishing vessels in order to assist the flag State in identifying those fishing vessels flying its flag reported to have engaged in activities undermining international conservation and management measures, so as to fulfil its obligations under Article III.

2. When a fishing vessel is voluntarily in the port of a Party other than its flag State, that Party, where it has reasonable grounds for believing that the fishing vessel has been used for an activity that undermines the effectiveness of international conservation and management measures, shall promptly notify the flag State accordingly. Parties may make arrangements regarding the undertaking by port States of such investigatory measures as may be considered necessary to establish whether the fishing vessel has indeed been used contrary to the provisions of this Agreement.

3. The Parties shall, when and as appropriate, enter into cooperative agreements or arrangements of mutual assistance on a global, regional, subregional or bilateral basis so as to promote the achievement of the objectives of this Agreement.

Article VI
Exchange of information

1. Each Party shall make readily available to FAO the following information with respect to each fishing vessel entered in the record required to be maintained under Article IV:

(a) name of fishing vessel, registration number, previous names (if known), and port of registry;

(b) previous flag (if any);

(c) International Radio Call Sign (if any);

(d) name and address of owner or owners;

(e) where and when built;

(f) type of vessel;

(g) length.

2. Each Party shall, to the extent practicable, make available to FAO the following additional information with respect to each fishing vessel entered in the record required to be maintained under Article IV:

(a) name and address of operator (manager) or operators (managers) (if any);

(b) type of fishing method or methods;

(c) moulded depth;

(d) beam;

(e) gross register tonnage;

(f) power of main engine or engines.

3. Each Party shall promptly notify to FAO any modifications to the information listed in paragraphs 1 and 2 of this Article.

4. FAO shall circulate periodically the information provided under paragraphs 1, 2, and 3 of this Article to all Parties, and, on request, individually to any Party. FAO shall also, subject to any restrictions imposed by the Party concerned regarding the distribution of information, provide such information on request individually to any global, regional or subregional fisheries organization.

5. Each Party shall also promptly inform FAO of-

(a) any additions to the record;

(b) any deletions from the record by reason of—

    (i) the voluntary relinquishment or non-renewal of the fishing authorization by the fishing vessel owner or operator;

    (ii) the withdrawal of the fishing authorization issued in respect of the fishing vessel under paragraph 8 of Article III;

    (iii) the fact that the fishing vessel concerned is no longer entitled to fly its flag;

    (iv) the scrapping, decommissioning or loss of the fishing vessel concerned; or

    (v) any other reason.

6. Where information is given to FAO under paragraph 5 (b) above, the Party concerned shall specify which of the reasons listed in that paragraph is applicable.

7. Each Party shall inform FAO of

(a) any exemption it has granted under paragraph 2 of Article II, the number and type of fishing vessel involved and the geographical areas in which such fishing vessels operate; and

(b) any agreement reached under paragraph 3 of Article II.

8. (a) Each Party shall report promptly to FAO all relevant information regarding any activities of fishing vessels flying its flag that undermine the effectiveness of international conservation and management measures, including the identity of the

fishing vessel or vessels involved and measures imposed by the Party in respect of such activities. Reports on measures imposed by a Party may be subject to such limitations as may be required by national legislation with respect to confidentiality, including, in particular, confidentiality regarding measures that are not yet final.

(b) Each Party, where it has reasonable grounds to believe that a fishing vessel not entitled to fly its flag has engaged in any activity that undermines the effectiveness of international conservation and management measures, shall draw this to the attention of the flag State concerned and may, as appropriate, draw it to the attention of FAO. It shall provide the flag State with full supporting evidence and may provide FAO with a summary of such evidence. FAO shall not circulate such information until such time as the flag State has had an opportunity to comment on the allegation and evidence submitted, or to object as the case may be.

9. Each Party shall inform FAO of any cases where the Party, pursuant to paragraph 5 (d) of Article III, has granted an authorization notwithstanding the provisions of paragraph 5 (a) or 5 (b) of Article III. The information shall include pertinent data permitting the identification of the fishing vessel and the owner or operator and, as appropriate, any other information relevant to the Party's decision.

10. FAO shall circulate promptly the information provided under paragraphs 5, 6, 7, 8 and 9 of this Article to all Parties, and, on request, individually to any Party. FAO shall also, subject to any restrictions imposed by the Party concerned regarding the distribution of information, provide such information promptly on request individually to any global, regional or subregional fisheries organization.

11. The Parties shall exchange information relating to the implementation of this Agreement, including through FAO and other appropriate global, regional and subregional fisheries organizations.

Article VII
Cooperation with developing countries

The Parties shall cooperate, at a global, regional, subregional or bilateral level, and, as appropriate, with the support of FAO and other international or regional organizations, to provide assistance, including technical assistance, to Parties that are developing countries in order to assist them in fulfilling their obligations under this Agreement.

Article VIII
Non-parties

1. The Parties shall encourage any State not party to this Agreement to accept this Agreement and shall encourage any non-Party to adopt laws and regulations consistent with the provisions of this Agreement.

2. The Parties shall cooperate in a manner consistent with this Agreement and with international law to the end that fishing vessels entitled to fly the flags of non-Parties do not engage in activities that undermine the effectiveness of international conservation and management measures.

3. The Parties shall exchange information amongst themselves, either directly or through FAO, with respect to activities of fishing vessels flying the flags of non-Parties that undermine the effectiveness of international conservation and management measures.

Article IX
Settlement of disputes

1. Any Party may seek consultations with any other Party or Parties on any dispute with regard to the interpretation or application of the provisions of this Agreement with a view to reaching a mutually satisfactory solution as soon as possible.

2. In the event that the dispute is not resolved through these consultations within a reasonable period of time, the Parties in question shall consult among themselves as soon as possible with a view to having the dispute settled by negotiation, inquiry, mediation, conciliation, arbitration, judicial settlement or other peaceful means of their own choice.

3. Any dispute of this character not so resolved shall, with the consent of all Parties to the dispute, be referred for settlement to the International Court of Justice, to the International Tribunal for the Law of the Sea upon entry into force of the 1982 United Nations Convention on the Law of the Sea or to arbitration. In the case of failure to reach agreement on referral to the International Court of Justice, to the International Tribunal for the Law of the Sea or to arbitration, the Parties shall continue to consult and cooperate with a view to reaching settlement of the dispute in accordance with the rules of international law relating to the conservation of living marine resources.

Article X
Acceptance

1. This Agreement shall be open to acceptance by any Member or Associate Member of FAO, and to any non-member State that is a member of the United Nations, or of any of the specialized agencies of the United Nations or of the International Atomic Energy Agency.

2. Acceptance of this Agreement shall be effected by the deposit of an instrument of acceptance with the Director–General of FAO, hereinafter referred to as the Director–General.

3. The Director–General shall inform all Parties, all Members and Associate Members of FAO and the Secretary–General of the United Nations of all instruments of acceptance received.

4. When a regional economic integration organization becomes a Party to this Agreement, such regional economic integration organization shall, in accordance with the provisions of Article II.7 of the FAO Constitution, as appropriate, notify such modifications or clarifications to its declaration of competence submitted under Article II.5 of the FAO Constitution as may be necessary in light of its acceptance of this Agreement. Any Party to this Agreement may, at any time, request a regional economic integration organization that is a Party to this Agreement to provide information as to which, as between the regional economic integration organization and its Member States, is responsible for the implementation of any particular matter covered by this Agreement. The regional economic integration organization shall provide this information within a reasonable time.

Article XI
Entry into force

1. This Agreement shall enter into force as from the date of receipt by the Director–General of the twenty-fifth instrument of acceptance.

2. For the purpose of this Article, an instrument deposited by a regional economic integration organization shall not be counted as additional to those deposited by member States of such an organization.

Article XII
Reservations

Acceptance of this Agreement may be made subject to reservations which shall become effective only upon unanimous acceptance by all Parties to this Agreement. The Director–General shall notify forthwith all Parties of any reservation. Parties not having replied within three months from the date of the notification shall be deemed to have accepted the reservation. Failing such acceptance, the State or regional economic integration organization making the reservation shall not become a Party to this Agreement.

Article XIII
Amendments

1. Any proposal by a Party for the amendment of this Agreement shall be communicated to the Director–General.

2. Any proposed amendment of this Agreement received by the Director–General from a Party shall be presented to a regular or special session of the Conference for approval and, if the amendment involves important technical changes or imposes additional obligations on the Parties, it shall be considered by an advisory committee of specialists convened by FAO prior to the Conference.

3. Notice of any proposed amendment of this Agreement shall be transmitted to the Parties by the Director–General not later than the time when the agenda of the session of the Conference at which the matter is to be considered is dispatched.

4. Any such proposed amendment of this Agreement shall require the approval of the Conference and shall come into force as from the thirtieth day after acceptance by two-thirds of the Parties. Amendments involving new obligations for Parties, however, shall come into force in respect of each Party only on acceptance by it and as from the thirtieth day after such acceptance. Any amendment shall be deemed to involve new obligations for Parties unless the Conference, in approving the amendment, decides otherwise by consensus.

5. The instruments of acceptance of amendments involving new obligations shall be deposited with the Director–General, who shall inform all Parties of the receipt of acceptance and the entry into force of amendments.

6. For the purpose of this Article, an instrument deposited by a regional economic integration organization shall not be counted as additional to those deposited by member States of such an organization.

Article XIV
Withdrawal

Any Party may withdraw from this Agreement at any time after the expiry of two years from the date upon which the Agreement entered into force with respect to that Party, by giving written notice of such withdrawal to the Director–General who shall immediately inform all the Parties and the Members and Associate Members of FAO of such withdrawal. Withdrawal shall become effective at the end of the calendar year following that in which the notice of withdrawal has been received by the Director–General.

Article XV
Duties of the depositary

The Director–General shall be the Depositary of this Agreement. The Depositary shall:

(a) send certified copies of this Agreement to each Member and Associate Member of FAO and to such non-member States as may become party to this Agreement;

(b) arrange for the registration of this Agreement, upon its entry into force, with the Secretariat of the United Nations in accordance with Article 102 of the Charter of the United Nations;

(c) inform each Member and Associate Member of FAO and any non-member States as may become Party to this Agreement of:

(i) instruments of acceptance deposited in accordance with Article X;

(ii) the date of entry into force of this Agreement in accordance with Article XI;

(iii) proposals for and the entry into force of amendments to this Agreement in accordance with Article XIII;

(iv) withdrawals from this Agreement pursuant to Article XIV.

5.17   Agreement for the Implementation of the Provisions of the United Nations Convention of the Law of the Sea of 10 December 1982 Relating to the Conservation and Management of Straddling Fish Stocks and Highly Migratory Fish Stocks. **Adopted by the U.N. Conference on Straddling Fish Stocks and Highly Migratory Fish Stocks, 4 August 1995. Opened for signatures, 4 December 1995. Entered into force, 11 December 2001. 2167 UNTS 3;** *reprinted in* **34 ILM 1542 (1995) & 5A Weston & Carlson V.H.24**

The States Parties to this Agreement,

Recalling the relevant provisions of the United Nations Convention on the Law of the Sea of 10 December 1982,

Determined to ensure the long-term conservation and sustainable use of straddling fish stocks and highly migratory fish stocks,

Resolved to improve cooperation between States to that end,

Calling for more effective enforcement by flag States, port States and coastal States of the conservation and management measures adopted for such stocks,

Seeking to address in particular the problems identified in chapter 17, programme area C, of Agenda 21 adopted by the United Nations Conference on Environment and Development, namely, that the management of high seas fisheries is inadequate in many areas and that some resources are overutilized, and noting that there are problems of unregulated fishing, over-capitalization, excessive fleet size, vessel reflagging to escape controls, insufficiently selective gear, unreliable databases and lack of sufficient cooperation between States,

Committing themselves to responsible fisheries,

Conscious of the need to avoid adverse impacts on the marine environment, preserve biodiversity, maintain the integrity of marine ecosystems and minimize the risk of long-term or irreversible effects of fishing operations,

Recognizing the need for specific assistance, including financial, scientific and technological assistance, in order that developing States can participate effectively in the conservation, management and sustainable use of straddling fish stocks and highly migratory fish stocks,

Convinced that an agreement for the implementation of the relevant provisions of the Convention would best serve these purposes and contribute to the maintenance of international peace and security,

Affirming that matters not regulated by the Convention or by this Agreement continue to be governed by the rules and principles of general international law,

Have agreed as follows:

PART I
GENERAL PROVISIONS

Article 1
Use of terms and scope

1.   For the purposes of this Agreement:

(a) "Convention" means the United Nations Convention on the Law of the Sea of 10 December 1982;

(b) "conservation and management measures" means measures to conserve and manage one or more species of living marine resources that are adopted and applied consistent with the relevant rules of international law as reflected in the Convention and this Agreement;

(c) "fish" includes molluscs and crustaceans except those belonging to sedentary species as defined in article 77 of the Convention; and

(d) "arrangement" means a cooperative mechanism established in accordance with the Convention and this Agreement by two or more States for the purpose, inter alia, of establishing conservation and management measures in a subregion or region for one or more straddling fish stocks or highly migratory fish stocks.

2. (a) "States Parties" means States which have consented to be bound by this Agreement and for which the Agreement is in force.

(b) This Agreement applies mutatis mutandis:

(i) to any entity referred to in article 305, paragraph 1 (c), (d) and (e), of the Convention and

(ii) subject to article 47, to any entity referred to as an "international organization" in Annex IX, article 1, of the Convention which becomes a Party to this Agreement, and to that extent "States Parties" refers to those entities.

3. This Agreement applies mutatis mutandis to other fishing entities whose vessels fish on the high seas.

Article 2
Objective

The objective of this Agreement is to ensure the long-term conservation and sustainable use of straddling fish stocks and highly migratory fish stocks through effective implementation of the relevant provisions of the Convention.

Article 3
Application

1. Unless otherwise provided, this Agreement applies to the conservation and management of straddling fish stocks and highly migratory fish stocks beyond areas under national jurisdiction, except that articles 6 and 7 apply also to the conservation and management of such stocks within areas under national jurisdiction, subject to the different legal regimes that apply within areas under national jurisdiction and in areas beyond national jurisdiction as provided for in the Convention.

2. In the exercise of its sovereign rights for the purpose of exploring and exploiting, conserving and managing straddling fish stocks and highly migratory fish stocks within areas under national jurisdiction, the coastal State shall apply mutatis mutandis the general principles enumerated in article 5.

3. States shall give due consideration to the respective capacities of developing States to apply articles 5, 6 and 7 within areas under national jurisdiction and their need for assistance as provided for in this Agreement. To this end, Part VII applies mutatis mutandis in respect of areas under national jurisdiction.

Article 4
Relationship between this Agreement and the Convention

Nothing in this Agreement shall prejudice the rights, jurisdiction and duties of States under the Convention. This Agreement shall be interpreted and applied in the context of and in a manner consistent with the Convention.

PART II
CONSERVATION AND MANAGEMENT OF STRADDLING FISH STOCKS AND HIGHLY MIGRATORY FISH STOCKS

Article 5
General principles

In order to conserve and manage straddling fish stocks and highly migratory fish stocks, coastal States and States fishing on the high seas shall, in giving effect to their duty to cooperate in accordance with the Convention:

(a) adopt measures to ensure long-term sustainability of straddling fish stocks and highly migratory fish stocks and promote the objective of their optimum utilization;

(b) ensure that such measures are based on the best scientific evidence available and are designed to maintain or restore stocks at levels capable of producing maximum sustainable yield, as qualified by relevant environmental and economic factors, including the special requirements of developing States, and taking into account fishing patterns, the interdependence of stocks and any generally recommended international minimum standards, whether subregional, regional or global;

(c) apply the precautionary approach in accordance with article 6;

(d) assess the impacts of fishing, other human activities and environmental factors on target stocks and species belonging to the same ecosystem or associated with or dependent upon the target stocks;

(e) adopt, where necessary, conservation and management measures for species belonging to the same ecosystem or associated with or dependent upon the target stocks, with a view to maintaining or restoring populations of such species above levels at which their reproduction may become seriously threatened;

(f) minimize pollution, waste, discards, catch by lost or abandoned gear, catch of non-target species, both fish and non-fish species (hereinafter referred to as non-target species) and impacts on associated or dependent species, in particular endangered species, through measures including, to the extent practicable, the development and use of selective, environmentally safe and cost-effective fishing gear and techniques;

(g) protect biodiversity in the marine environment;

(h) take measures to prevent or eliminate overfishing and excess fishing capacity and to ensure that levels of fishing effort do not exceed those commensurate with the sustainable use of fishery resources;

(i) take into account the interests of artisanal and subsistence fishers;

(j) collect and share, in a timely manner, complete and accurate data concerning fishing activities on, inter alia, vessel position, catch of target and non-target species and fishing effort, as set out in Annex I, as well as information from national and international research programmes;

(k) promote and conduct scientific research and develop appropriate technologies in support of fishery conservation and management; and

(*l*) implement and enforce conservation and management measures through effective monitoring, control and surveillance.

Article 6
Application of the precautionary approach

1. States shall apply the precautionary approach widely to conservation, management and exploitation of straddling fish stocks and highly migratory fish stocks in order to protect the living marine resources and preserve the marine environment.

2. States shall be more cautious when information is uncertain, unreliable or inadequate. The absence of adequate scientific information shall not be used as a reason for postponing or failing to take conservation and management measures.

3. In implementing the precautionary approach, States shall:

(a) improve decision-making for fishery resource conservation and management by obtaining and sharing the best scientific information available and implementing improved techniques for dealing with risk and uncertainty;

(b) apply the guidelines set out in Annex II and determine, on the basis of the best scientific information available, stock-specific reference points and the action to be taken if they are exceeded;

(c) take into account, inter alia, uncertainties relating to the size and productivity of the stocks, reference points, stock condition in relation to such reference points, levels and distribution of fishing mortality and the impact of fishing activities on non-target and associated or dependent species, as well as existing and predicted oceanic, environmental and socio-economic conditions; and

(d) develop data collection and research programmes to assess the impact of fishing on non-target and associated or dependent species and their environment, and adopt plans which are necessary to ensure the conservation of such species and to protect habitats of special concern.

4. States shall take measures to ensure that, when reference points are approached, they will not be exceeded. In the event that they are exceeded, States shall, without delay, take the action determined under paragraph 3 (b) to restore the stocks.

5. Where the status of target stocks or non-target or associated or dependent species is of concern, States shall subject such stocks and species to enhanced monitoring in order to review their status and the efficacy of conservation and management measures. They shall revise those measures regularly in the light of new information.

6. For new or exploratory fisheries, States shall adopt as soon as possible cautious conservation and management measures, including, inter alia, catch limit and effort limit. Such measures shall remain in force until there are sufficient data to allow assessment of the impact of the fisheries on the long-term sustainability of the stocks, whereupon conservation and management measures based on that assessment shall be implemented. The latter measures shall, if appropriate, allow for the gradual development of the fisheries.

7. If a natural phenomenon has a significant adverse impact on the status of straddling fish stocks or highly migratory fish stocks, States shall adopt conservation and management measures on an emergency basis to ensure that fishing activity does not exacerbate such adverse impact. States shall also adopt such measures on an emergency basis where fishing activity presents a serious threat to the sustainability of such stocks. Measures taken on an emergency basis shall be temporary and shall be based on the best scientific evidence available.

Article 7
Compatibility of conservation and management measures

1. Without prejudice to the sovereign rights of coastal States for the purpose of exploring and exploiting, conserving and managing the living marine resources within areas under national jurisdiction as provided for in the Convention, and the right of all States for their nationals to engage in fishing on the high seas in accordance with the Convention:

(a) with respect to straddling fish stocks, the relevant coastal States and the States whose nationals fish for such stocks in the adjacent high seas area shall seek, either directly or through the appropriate mechanisms for cooperation provided for in Part III, to agree upon the measures necessary for the conservation of these stocks in the adjacent high seas area;

(b) with respect to highly migratory fish stocks, the relevant coastal States and other States whose nationals fish for such stocks in the region shall cooperate, either directly or through the appropriate mechanisms for cooperation provided for in Part III, with a view to ensuring conservation and promoting the objective of optimum utilization of such stocks throughout the region, both within and beyond the areas under national jurisdiction.

2. Conservation and management measures established for the high seas and those adopted for areas under national jurisdiction shall be compatible in order to ensure conservation and management of the straddling fish stocks and highly migratory fish stocks in their entirety. To this end, coastal States and States fishing on the high seas have a duty to cooperate for the purpose of achieving compatible measures in respect of such stocks. In determining compatible conservation and management measures, States shall:

(a) take into account the conservation and management measures adopted and applied in accordance with article 61 of the Convention in respect of the same stocks by coastal States within areas under national jurisdiction and ensure that measures established in respect of such stocks for the high seas do not undermine the effectiveness of such measures;

(b) take into account previously agreed measures established and applied for the high seas in accordance with the Convention in respect of the same stocks by relevant coastal States and States fishing on the high seas;

(c) take into account previously agreed measures established and applied in accordance with the Convention in respect of the same stocks by a subregional or regional fisheries management organization or arrangement;

(d) take into account the biological unity and other biological characteristics of the stocks and the relationships between the distribution of the stocks, the fisheries and the geographical particularities of the region concerned, including the extent to which the stocks occur and are fished in areas under national jurisdiction;

(e) take into account the respective dependence of the coastal States and the States fishing on the high seas on the stocks concerned; and

(f) ensure that such measures do not result in harmful impact on the living marine resources as a whole.

3. In giving effect to their duty to cooperate, States shall make every effort to agree on compatible conservation and management measures within a reasonable period of time.

4. If no agreement can be reached within a reasonable period of time, any of the States concerned may invoke the procedures for the settlement of disputes provided for in Part VIII.

5. Pending agreement on compatible conservation and management measures, the States concerned, in a spirit of understanding and cooperation, shall make every effort to enter into provisional arrangements of a practical nature. In the event that they are unable to agree on such arrangements, any of the States concerned may, for the purpose of obtaining provisional measures, submit the dispute to a court or tribunal in accordance with the procedures for the settlement of disputes provided for in Part VIII.

6. Provisional arrangements or measures entered into or prescribed pursuant to paragraph 5 shall take into account the provisions of this Part, shall have due regard to the rights and obligations of all States concerned, shall not jeopardize or hamper the reaching of final agreement on compatible conservation and management measures and shall be without prejudice to the final outcome of any dispute settlement procedure.

7. Coastal States shall regularly inform States fishing on the high seas in the subregion or region, either directly or through appropriate subregional or regional fisheries management organizations or arrangements, or through other appropriate

means, of the measures they have adopted for straddling fish stocks and highly migratory fish stocks within areas under their national jurisdiction.

8. States fishing on the high seas shall regularly inform other interested States, either directly or through appropriate subregional or regional fisheries management organizations or arrangements, or through other appropriate means, of the measures they have adopted for regulating the activities of vessels flying their flag which fish for such stocks on the high seas.

PART III
MECHANISMS FOR INTERNATIONAL COOPERATION CONCERNING STRADDLING FISH STOCKS AND HIGHLY MIGRATORY FISH STOCKS

Article 8
Cooperation for conservation and management

1. Coastal States and States fishing on the high seas shall, in accordance with the Convention, pursue cooperation in relation to straddling fish stocks and highly migratory fish stocks either directly or through appropriate subregional or regional fisheries management organizations or arrangements, taking into account the specific characteristics of the subregion or region, to ensure effective conservation and management of such stocks.

2. States shall enter into consultations in good faith and without delay, particularly where there is evidence that the straddling fish stocks and highly migratory fish stocks concerned may be under threat of over-exploitation or where a new fishery is being developed for such stocks. To this end, consultations may be initiated at the request of any interested State with a view to establishing appropriate arrangements to ensure conservation and management of the stocks. Pending agreement on such arrangements, States shall observe the provisions of this Agreement and shall act in good faith and with due regard to the rights, interests and duties of other States.

3. Where a subregional or regional fisheries management organization or arrangement has the competence to establish conservation and management measures for particular straddling fish stocks or highly migratory fish stocks, States fishing for the stocks on the high seas and relevant coastal States shall give effect to their duty to cooperate by becoming members of such organization or participants in such arrangement, or by agreeing to apply the conservation and management measures established by such organization or arrangement. States having a real interest in the fisheries concerned may become members of such organization or participants in such arrangement. The terms for participation in such organization or arrangement shall not preclude such States from membership or participation; nor shall they be applied in a manner which discriminates against any State or group of States having a real interest in the fisheries concerned.

4. Only those States which are members of such an organization or participants in such an arrangement, or which agree to apply the conservation and management measures established by such organization or arrangement, shall have access to the fishery resources to which those measures apply.

5. Where there is no subregional or regional fisheries management organization or arrangement to establish conservation and management measures for a particular straddling fish stock or highly migratory fish stock, relevant coastal States and States fishing on the high seas for such stock in the subregion or region shall cooperate to establish such an organization or enter into other appropriate arrangements to ensure conservation and management of such stock and shall participate in the work of the organization or arrangement.

6. Any State intending to propose that action be taken by an intergovernmental organization having competence with respect to living resources should, where such

action would have a significant effect on conservation and management measures already established by a competent subregional or regional fisheries management organization or arrangement, consult through that organization or arrangement with its members or participants. To the extent practicable, such consultation should take place prior to the submission of the proposal to the intergovernmental organization.

Article 9
Subregional and regional fisheries management organizations and arrangements

1. In establishing subregional or regional fisheries management organizations or in entering into subregional or regional fisheries management arrangements for straddling fish stocks and highly migratory fish stocks, States shall agree, inter alia, on:

(a) the stocks to which conservation and management measures apply, taking into account the biological characteristics of the stocks concerned and the nature of the fisheries involved;

(b) the area of application, taking into account article 7, paragraph 1, and the characteristics of the subregion or region, including socio-economic, geographical and environmental factors;

(c) the relationship between the work of the new organization or arrangement and the role, objectives and operations of any relevant existing fisheries management organizations or arrangements; and

(d) the mechanisms by which the organization or arrangement will obtain scientific advice and review the status of the stocks, including, where appropriate, the establishment of a scientific advisory body.

2. States cooperating in the formation of a subregional or regional fisheries management organization or arrangement shall inform other States which they are aware have a real interest in the work of the proposed organization or arrangement of such cooperation.

Article 10
Functions of subregional and regional fisheries management organizations and arrangements

In fulfilling their obligation to cooperate through subregional or regional fisheries management organizations or arrangements, States shall:

(a) agree on and comply with conservation and management measures to ensure the long-term sustainability of straddling fish stocks and highly migratory fish stocks;

(b) agree, as appropriate, on participatory rights such as allocations of allowable catch or levels of fishing effort;

(c) adopt and apply any generally recommended international minimum standards for the responsible conduct of fishing operations;

(d) obtain and evaluate scientific advice, review the status of the stocks and assess the impact of fishing on non-target and associated or dependent species;

(e) agree on standards for collection, reporting, verification and exchange of data on fisheries for the stocks;

(f) compile and disseminate accurate and complete statistical data, as described in Annex I, to ensure that the best scientific evidence is available, while maintaining confidentiality where appropriate;

(g) promote and conduct scientific assessments of the stocks and relevant research and disseminate the results thereof;

(h) establish appropriate cooperative mechanisms for effective monitoring, control, surveillance and enforcement;

(i) agree on means by which the fishing interests of new members of the organization or new participants in the arrangement will be accommodated;

(j) agree on decision-making procedures which facilitate the adoption of conservation and management measures in a timely and effective manner;

(k) promote the peaceful settlement of disputes in accordance with Part VIII;

(*l*) ensure the full cooperation of their relevant national agencies and industries in implementing the recommendations and decisions of the organization or arrangement; and

(m) give due publicity to the conservation and management measures established by the organization or arrangement.

Article 11
New members or participants

In determining the nature and extent of participatory rights for new members of a subregional or regional fisheries management organization, or for new participants in a subregional or regional fisheries management arrangement, States shall take into account, inter alia:

(a) the status of the straddling fish stocks and highly migratory fish stocks and the existing level of fishing effort in the fishery;

(b) the respective interests, fishing patterns and fishing practices of new and existing members or participants;

(c) the respective contributions of new and existing members or participants to conservation and management of the stocks, to the collection and provision of accurate data and to the conduct of scientific research on the stocks;

(d) the needs of coastal fishing communities which are dependent mainly on fishing for the stocks;

(e) the needs of coastal States whose economies are overwhelmingly dependent on the exploitation of living marine resources; and

(f) the interests of developing States from the subregion or region in whose areas of national jurisdiction the stocks also occur.

Article 12
Transparency in activities of subregional and regional fisheries management organizations and arrangements

1. States shall provide for transparency in the decision-making process and other activities of subregional and regional fisheries management organizations and arrangements.

2. Representatives from other intergovernmental organizations and representatives from non-governmental organizations concerned with straddling fish stocks and highly migratory fish stocks shall be afforded the opportunity to take part in meetings of subregional and regional fisheries management organizations and arrangements as observers or otherwise, as appropriate, in accordance with the procedures of the organization or arrangement concerned. Such procedures shall not be unduly restrictive in this respect. Such intergovernmental organizations and non-governmental organizations shall have timely access to the records and reports of such organizations and arrangements, subject to the procedural rules on access to them.

Article 13
Strengthening of existing organizations and arrangements

States shall cooperate to strengthen existing subregional and regional fisheries management organizations and arrangements in order to improve their effectiveness in establishing and implementing conservation and management measures for straddling fish stocks and highly migratory fish stocks.

Article 14
Collection and provision of information and cooperation in scientific research

1. States shall ensure that fishing vessels flying their flag provide such information as may be necessary in order to fulfil their obligations under this Agreement. To this end, States shall in accordance with Annex I:

(a) collect and exchange scientific, technical and statistical data with respect to fisheries for straddling fish stocks and highly migratory fish stocks;

(b) ensure that data are collected in sufficient detail to facilitate effective stock assessment and are provided in a timely manner to fulfil the requirements of subregional or regional fisheries management organizations or arrangements; and

(c) take appropriate measures to verify the accuracy of such data.

2. States shall cooperate, either directly or through subregional or regional fisheries management organizations or arrangements:

(a) to agree on the specification of data and the format in which they are to be provided to such organizations or arrangements, taking into account the nature of the stocks and the fisheries for those stocks; and

(b) to develop and share analytical techniques and stock assessment methodologies to improve measures for the conservation and management of straddling fish stocks and highly migratory fish stocks.

3. Consistent with Part XIII of the Convention, States shall cooperate, either directly or through competent international organizations, to strengthen scientific research capacity in the field of fisheries and promote scientific research related to the conservation and management of straddling fish stocks and highly migratory fish stocks for the benefit of all. To this end, a State or the competent international organization conducting such research beyond areas under national jurisdiction shall actively promote the publication and dissemination to any interested States of the results of that research and information relating to its objectives and methods and, to the extent practicable, shall facilitate the participation of scientists from those States in such research.

Article 15
Enclosed and semi-enclosed seas

In implementing this Agreement in an enclosed or semi-enclosed sea, States shall take into account the natural characteristics of that sea and shall also act in a manner consistent with Part IX of the Convention and other relevant provisions thereof.

Article 16
*Areas of high seas surrounded entirely by an area under the national
jurisdiction of a single State*

1. States fishing for straddling fish stocks and highly migratory fish stocks in an area of the high seas surrounded entirely by an area under the national jurisdiction of a single State and the latter State shall cooperate to establish conservation and management measures in respect of those stocks in the high seas area. Having regard to the natural characteristics of the area, States shall pay special attention to the

establishment of compatible conservation and management measures for such stocks pursuant to article 7. Measures taken in respect of the high seas shall take into account the rights, duties and interests of the coastal State under the Convention, shall be based on the best scientific evidence available and shall also take into account any conservation and management measures adopted and applied in respect of the same stocks in accordance with article 61 of the Convention by the coastal State in the area under national jurisdiction. States shall also agree on measures for monitoring, control, surveillance and enforcement to ensure compliance with the conservation and management measures in respect of the high seas.

2. Pursuant to article 8, States shall act in good faith and make every effort to agree without delay on conservation and management measures to be applied in the carrying out of fishing operations in the area referred to in paragraph 1. If, within a reasonable period of time, the fishing States concerned and the coastal State are unable to agree on such measures, they shall, having regard to paragraph 1, apply article 7, paragraphs 4, 5 and 6, relating to provisional arrangements or measures. Pending the establishment of such provisional arrangements or measures, the States concerned shall take measures in respect of vessels flying their flag in order that they do not engage in fisheries which could undermine the stocks concerned.

PART IV
NON–MEMBERS AND NON–PARTICIPANTS

Article 17

Non-members of organizations and non-participants in arrangements

1. A State which is not a member of a subregional or regional fisheries management organization or is not a participant in a subregional or regional fisheries management arrangement, and which does not otherwise agree to apply the conservation and management measures established by such organization or arrangement, is not discharged from the obligation to cooperate, in accordance with the Convention and this Agreement, in the conservation and management of the relevant straddling fish stocks and highly migratory fish stocks.

2. Such State shall not authorize vessels flying its flag to engage in fishing operations for the straddling fish stocks or highly migratory fish stocks which are subject to the conservation and management measures established by such organization or arrangement.

3. States which are members of a subregional or regional fisheries management organization or participants in a subregional or regional fisheries management arrangement shall, individually or jointly, request the fishing entities referred to in article 1, paragraph 3, which have fishing vessels in the relevant area to cooperate fully with such organization or arrangement in implementing the conservation and management measures it has established, with a view to having such measures applied de facto as extensively as possible to fishing activities in the relevant area. Such fishing entities shall enjoy benefits from participation in the fishery commensurate with their commitment to comply with conservation and management measures in respect of the stocks.

4. States which are members of such organization or participants in such arrangement shall exchange information with respect to the activities of fishing vessels flying the flags of States which are neither members of the organization nor participants in the arrangement and which are engaged in fishing operations for the relevant stocks. They shall take measures consistent with this Agreement and international law to deter activities of such vessels which undermine the effectiveness of subregional or regional conservation and management measures.

PART V
DUTIES OF THE FLAG STATE

Article 18
Duties of the flag State

1. A State whose vessels fish on the high seas shall take such measures as may be necessary to ensure that vessels flying its flag comply with subregional and regional conservation and management measures and that such vessels do not engage in any activity which undermines the effectiveness of such measures.

2. A State shall authorize the use of vessels flying its flag for fishing on the high seas only where it is able to exercise effectively its responsibilities in respect of such vessels under the Convention and this Agreement.

3. Measures to be taken by a State in respect of vessels flying its flag shall include:

(a) control of such vessels on the high seas by means of fishing licences, authorizations or permits, in accordance with any applicable procedures agreed at the subregional, regional or global level;

(b) establishment of regulations:

(i) to apply terms and conditions to the licence, authorization or permit sufficient to fulfil any subregional, regional or global obligations of the flag State;

(ii) to prohibit fishing on the high seas by vessels which are not duly licensed or authorized to fish, or fishing on the high seas by vessels otherwise than in accordance with the terms and conditions of a licence, authorization or permit;

(iii) to require vessels fishing on the high seas to carry the licence, authorization or permit on board at all times and to produce it on demand for inspection by a duly authorized person; and

(iv) to ensure that vessels flying its flag do not conduct unauthorized fishing within areas under the national jurisdiction of other States;

(c) establishment of a national record of fishing vessels authorized to fish on the high seas and provision of access to the information contained in that record on request by directly interested States, taking into account any national laws of the flag State regarding the release of such information;

(d) requirements for marking of fishing vessels and fishing gear for identification in accordance with uniform and internationally recognizable vessel and gear marking systems, such as the Food and Agriculture Organization of the United Nations Standard Specifications for the Marking and Identification of Fishing Vessels;

(e) requirements for recording and timely reporting of vessel position, catch of target and non-target species, fishing effort and other relevant fisheries data in accordance with subregional, regional and global standards for collection of such data;

(f) requirements for verifying the catch of target and non-target species through such means as observer programmes, inspection schemes, unloading reports, supervision of transshipment and monitoring of landed catches and market statistics;

(g) monitoring, control and surveillance of such vessels, their fishing operations and related activities through, inter alia:

(i) the implementation of national inspection schemes and subregional and regional schemes for cooperation in enforcement pursuant to articles 21 and 22, including requirements for such vessels to permit access by duly authorized inspectors from other States;

(ii) the implementation of national observer programmes and subregional and regional observer programmes in which the flag State is a participant, including requirements for such vessels to permit access by observers from other States to carry out the functions agreed under the programmes; and

(iii) the development and implementation of vessel monitoring systems, including, as appropriate, satellite transmitter systems, in accordance with any national programmes and those which have been subregionally, regionally or globally agreed among the States concerned;

(h) regulation of transshipment on the high seas to ensure that the effectiveness of conservation and management measures is not undermined; and

(i) regulation of fishing activities to ensure compliance with subregional, regional or global measures, including those aimed at minimizing catches of non-target species.

4. Where there is a subregionally, regionally or globally agreed system of monitoring, control and surveillance in effect, States shall ensure that the measures they impose on vessels flying their flag are compatible with that system.

PART VI
COMPLIANCE AND ENFORCEMENT

Article 19

Compliance and enforcement by the flag State

1. A State shall ensure compliance by vessels flying its flag with subregional and regional conservation and management measures for straddling fish stocks and highly migratory fish stocks. To this end, that State shall:

(a) enforce such measures irrespective of where violations occur;

(b) investigate immediately and fully any alleged violation of subregional or regional conservation and management measures, which may include the physical inspection of the vessels concerned, and report promptly to the State alleging the violation and the relevant subregional or regional organization or arrangement on the progress and outcome of the investigation;

(c) require any vessel flying its flag to give information to the investigating authority regarding vessel position, catches, fishing gear, fishing operations and related activities in the area of an alleged violation;

(d) if satisfied that sufficient evidence is available in respect of an alleged violation, refer the case to its authorities with a view to instituting proceedings, without delay, in accordance with its laws and, where appropriate, detain the vessel concerned; and

(e) ensure that, where it has been established, in accordance with its laws, a vessel has been involved in the commission of a serious violation of such measures, the vessel does not engage in fishing operations on the high seas until such time as all outstanding sanctions imposed by the flag State in respect of the violation have been complied with.

2. All investigations and judicial proceedings shall be carried out expeditiously. Sanctions applicable in respect of violations shall be adequate in severity to be effective in securing compliance and to discourage violations wherever they occur and shall deprive offenders of the benefits accruing from their illegal activities. Measures applicable in respect of masters and other officers of fishing vessels shall include provisions which may permit, inter alia, refusal, withdrawal or suspension of authorizations to serve as masters or officers on such vessels.

Article 20

International cooperation in enforcement

1. States shall cooperate, either directly or through subregional or regional fisheries management organizations or arrangements, to ensure compliance with and

enforcement of subregional and regional conservation and management measures for straddling fish stocks and highly migratory fish stocks.

2. A flag State conducting an investigation of an alleged violation of conservation and management measures for straddling fish stocks or highly migratory fish stocks may request the assistance of any other State whose cooperation may be useful in the conduct of that investigation. All States shall endeavour to meet reasonable requests made by a flag State in connection with such investigations.

3. A flag State may undertake such investigations directly, in cooperation with other interested States or through the relevant subregional or regional fisheries management organization or arrangement. Information on the progress and outcome of the investigations shall be provided to all States having an interest in, or affected by, the alleged violation.

4. States shall assist each other in identifying vessels reported to have engaged in activities undermining the effectiveness of subregional, regional or global conservation and management measures.

5. States shall, to the extent permitted by national laws and regulations, establish arrangements for making available to prosecuting authorities in other States evidence relating to alleged violations of such measures.

6. Where there are reasonable grounds for believing that a vessel on the high seas has been engaged in unauthorized fishing within an area under the jurisdiction of a coastal State, the flag State of that vessel, at the request of the coastal State concerned, shall immediately and fully investigate the matter. The flag State shall cooperate with the coastal State in taking appropriate enforcement action in such cases and may authorize the relevant authorities of the coastal State to board and inspect the vessel on the high seas. This paragraph is without prejudice to article 111 of the Convention.

7. States Parties which are members of a subregional or regional fisheries management organization or participants in a subregional or regional fisheries management arrangement may take action in accordance with international law, including through recourse to subregional or regional procedures established for this purpose, to deter vessels which have engaged in activities that undermine the effectiveness of or otherwise violate the conservation and management measures established by that organization or arrangement from fishing on the high seas in the subregion or region until such time as appropriate action is taken by the flag State.

Article 21
Subregional and regional cooperation in enforcement

1. In any high seas area covered by a subregional or regional fisheries management organization or arrangement, a State Party which is a member of such organization or a participant in such arrangement may, through its duly authorized inspectors, board and inspect, in accordance with paragraph 2, fishing vessels flying the flag of another State Party to this Agreement, whether or not such State Party is also a member of the organization or a participant in the arrangement, for the purpose of ensuring compliance with conservation and management measures for straddling fish stocks and highly migratory fish stocks established by that organization or arrangement.

2. States shall establish, through subregional or regional fisheries management organizations or arrangements, procedures for boarding and inspection pursuant to paragraph 1, as well as procedures to implement other provisions of this article. Such procedures shall be consistent with this article and the basic procedures set out in article 22 and shall not discriminate against non-members of the organization or non-participants in the arrangement. Boarding and inspection as well as any subsequent

enforcement action shall be conducted in accordance with such procedures. States shall give due publicity to procedures established pursuant to this paragraph.

3. If, within two years of the adoption of this Agreement, any organization or arrangement has not established such procedures, boarding and inspection pursuant to paragraph 1, as well as any subsequent enforcement action, shall, pending the establishment of such procedures, be conducted in accordance with this article and the basic procedures set out in article 22.

4. Prior to taking action under this article, inspecting States shall, either directly or through the relevant subregional or regional fisheries management organization or arrangement, inform all States whose vessels fish on the high seas in the subregion or region of the form of identification issued to their duly authorized inspectors. The vessels used for boarding and inspection shall be clearly marked and identifiable as being on government service. At the time of becoming a Party to this Agreement, a State shall designate an appropriate authority to receive notifications pursuant to this article and shall give due publicity of such designation through the relevant subregional or regional fisheries management organization or arrangement.

5. Where, following boarding and inspection, there are clear grounds for believing that a vessel has engaged in any activity contrary to the conservation and management measures referred to in paragraph 1, the inspecting State shall, where appropriate, secure evidence and shall promptly notify the flag State of the alleged violation.

6. The flag State shall respond to the notification referred to in paragraph 5 within three working days of its receipt, or such other period as may be prescribed in procedures established in accordance with paragraph 2, and shall either:

(a) fulfil, without delay, its obligations under article 19 to investigate and, if evidence so warrants, take enforcement action with respect to the vessel, in which case it shall promptly inform the inspecting State of the results of the investigation and of any enforcement action taken; or

(b) authorize the inspecting State to investigate.

7. Where the flag State authorizes the inspecting State to investigate an alleged violation, the inspecting State shall, without delay, communicate the results of that investigation to the flag State. The flag State shall, if evidence so warrants, fulfil its obligations to take enforcement action with respect to the vessel. Alternatively, the flag State may authorize the inspecting State to take such enforcement action as the flag State may specify with respect to the vessel, consistent with the rights and obligations of the flag State under this Agreement.

8. Where, following boarding and inspection, there are clear grounds for believing that a vessel has committed a serious violation, and the flag State has either failed to respond or failed to take action as required under paragraphs 6 or 7, the inspectors may remain on board and secure evidence and may require the master to assist in further investigation including, where appropriate, by bringing the vessel without delay to the nearest appropriate port, or to such other port as may be specified in procedures established in accordance with paragraph 2. The inspecting State shall immediately inform the flag State of the name of the port to which the vessel is to proceed. The inspecting State and the flag State and, as appropriate, the port State shall take all necessary steps to ensure the well-being of the crew regardless of their nationality.

9. The inspecting State shall inform the flag State and the relevant organization or the participants in the relevant arrangement of the results of any further investigation.

10. The inspecting State shall require its inspectors to observe generally accepted international regulations, procedures and practices relating to the safety of the vessel

and the crew, minimize interference with fishing operations and, to the extent practicable, avoid action which would adversely affect the quality of the catch on board. The inspecting State shall ensure that boarding and inspection is not conducted in a manner that would constitute harassment of any fishing vessel.

11. For the purposes of this article, a serious violation means:

(a) fishing without a valid licence, authorization or permit issued by the flag State in accordance with article 18, paragraph 3 (a);

(b) failing to maintain accurate records of catch and catch-related data, as required by the relevant subregional or regional fisheries management organization or arrangement, or serious misreporting of catch, contrary to the catch reporting requirements of such organization or arrangement;

(c) fishing in a closed area, fishing during a closed season or fishing without, or after attainment of, a quota established by the relevant subregional or regional fisheries management organization or arrangement;

(d) directed fishing for a stock which is subject to a moratorium or for which fishing is prohibited;

(e) using prohibited fishing gear;

(f) falsifying or concealing the markings, identity or registration of a fishing vessel;

(g) concealing, tampering with or disposing of evidence relating to an investigation;

(h) multiple violations which together constitute a serious disregard of conservation and management measures; or

(i) such other violations as may be specified in procedures established by the relevant subregional or regional fisheries management organization or arrangement.

12. Notwithstanding the other provisions of this article, the flag State may, at any time, take action to fulfil its obligations under article 19 with respect to an alleged violation. Where the vessel is under the direction of the inspecting State, the inspecting State shall, at the request of the flag State, release the vessel to the flag State along with full information on the progress and outcome of its investigation.

13. This article is without prejudice to the right of the flag State to take any measures, including proceedings to impose penalties, according to its laws.

14. This article applies mutatis mutandis to boarding and inspection by a State Party which is a member of a subregional or regional fisheries management organization or a participant in a subregional or regional fisheries management arrangement and which has clear grounds for believing that a fishing vessel flying the flag of another State Party has engaged in any activity contrary to relevant conservation and management measures referred to in paragraph 1 in the high seas area covered by such organization or arrangement, and such vessel has subsequently, during the same fishing trip, entered into an area under the national jurisdiction of the inspecting State.

15. Where a subregional or regional fisheries management organization or arrangement has established an alternative mechanism which effectively discharges the obligation under this Agreement of its members or participants to ensure compliance with the conservation and management measures established by the organization or arrangement, members of such organization or participants in such arrangement may agree to limit the application of paragraph 1 as between themselves in respect of the conservation and management measures which have been established in the relevant high seas area.

16. Action taken by States other than the flag State in respect of vessels having engaged in activities contrary to subregional or regional conservation and management measures shall be proportionate to the seriousness of the violation.

17. Where there are reasonable grounds for suspecting that a fishing vessel on the high seas is without nationality, a State may board and inspect the vessel. Where evidence so warrants, the State may take such action as may be appropriate in accordance with international law.

18. States shall be liable for damage or loss attributable to them arising from action taken pursuant to this article when such action is unlawful or exceeds that reasonably required in the light of available information to implement the provisions of this article.

Article 22
Basic procedures for boarding and inspection pursuant to article 21

1. The inspecting State shall ensure that its duly authorized inspectors:

(a) present credentials to the master of the vessel and produce a copy of the text of the relevant conservation and management measures or rules and regulations in force in the high seas area in question pursuant to those measures;

(b) initiate notice to the flag State at the time of the boarding and inspection;

(c) do not interfere with the master's ability to communicate with the authorities of the flag State during the boarding and inspection;

(d) provide a copy of a report on the boarding and inspection to the master and to the authorities of the flag State, noting therein any objection or statement which the master wishes to have included in the report;

(e) promptly leave the vessel following completion of the inspection if they find no evidence of a serious violation; and

(f) avoid the use of force except when and to the degree necessary to ensure the safety of the inspectors and where the inspectors are obstructed in the execution of their duties. The degree of force used shall not exceed that reasonably required in the circumstances.

2. The duly authorized inspectors of an inspecting State shall have the authority to inspect the vessel, its licence, gear, equipment, records, facilities, fish and fish products and any relevant documents necessary to verify compliance with the relevant conservation and management measures.

3. The flag State shall ensure that vessel masters:

(a) accept and facilitate prompt and safe boarding by the inspectors;

(b) cooperate with and assist in the inspection of the vessel conducted pursuant to these procedures;

(c) do not obstruct, intimidate or interfere with the inspectors in the performance of their duties;

(d) allow the inspectors to communicate with the authorities of the flag State and the inspecting State during the boarding and inspection;

(e) provide reasonable facilities, including, where appropriate, food and accommodation, to the inspectors; and

(f) facilitate safe disembarkation by the inspectors.

4. In the event that the master of a vessel refuses to accept boarding and inspection in accordance with this article and article 21, the flag State shall, except in circumstances where, in accordance with generally accepted international regulations, procedures and practices relating to safety at sea, it is necessary to delay the boarding

and inspection, direct the master of the vessel to submit immediately to boarding and inspection and, if the master does not comply with such direction, shall suspend the vessel's authorization to fish and order the vessel to return immediately to port. The flag State shall advise the inspecting State of the action it has taken when the circumstances referred to in this paragraph arise.

Article 23
Measures taken by a port State

1. A port State has the right and the duty to take measures, in accordance with international law, to promote the effectiveness of subregional, regional and global conservation and management measures. When taking such measures a port State shall not discriminate in form or in fact against the vessels of any State.

2. A port State may, inter alia, inspect documents, fishing gear and catch on board fishing vessels, when such vessels are voluntarily in its ports or at its offshore terminals.

3. States may adopt regulations empowering the relevant national authorities to prohibit landings and transshipments where it has been established that the catch has been taken in a manner which undermines the effectiveness of subregional, regional or global conservation and management measures on the high seas.

4. Nothing in this article affects the exercise by States of their sovereignty over ports in their territory in accordance with international law.

PART VII
REQUIREMENTS OF DEVELOPING STATES

Article 24
Recognition of the special requirements of developing States

1. States shall give full recognition to the special requirements of developing States in relation to conservation and management of straddling fish stocks and highly migratory fish stocks and development of fisheries for such stocks. To this end, States shall, either directly or through the United Nations Development Programme, the Food and Agriculture Organization of the United Nations and other specialized agencies, the Global Environment Facility, the Commission on Sustainable Development and other appropriate international and regional organizations and bodies, provide assistance to developing States.

2. In giving effect to the duty to cooperate in the establishment of conservation and management measures for straddling fish stocks and highly migratory fish stocks, States shall take into account the special requirements of developing States, in particular:

(a) the vulnerability of developing States which are dependent on the exploitation of living marine resources, including for meeting the nutritional requirements of their populations or parts thereof;

(b) the need to avoid adverse impacts on, and ensure access to fisheries by, subsistence, small-scale and artisanal fishers and women fishworkers, as well as indigenous people in developing States, particularly small island developing States; and

(c) the need to ensure that such measures do not result in transferring, directly or indirectly, a disproportionate burden of conservation action onto developing States.

Article 25
Forms of cooperation with developing States

1. States shall cooperate, either directly or through subregional, regional or global organizations:

(a) to enhance the ability of developing States, in particular the least-developed among them and small island developing States, to conserve and manage straddling fish stocks and highly migratory fish stocks and to develop their own fisheries for such stocks;

(b) to assist developing States, in particular the least-developed among them and small island developing States, to enable them to participate in high seas fisheries for such stocks, including facilitating access to such fisheries subject to articles 5 and 11; and

(c) to facilitate the participation of developing States in subregional and regional fisheries management organizations and arrangements.

2. Cooperation with developing States for the purposes set out in this article shall include the provision of financial assistance, assistance relating to human resources development, technical assistance, transfer of technology, including through joint venture arrangements, and advisory and consultative services.

3. Such assistance shall, inter alia, be directed specifically towards:

(a) improved conservation and management of straddling fish stocks and highly migratory fish stocks through collection, reporting, verification, exchange and analysis of fisheries data and related information;

(b) stock assessment and scientific research; and

(c) monitoring, control, surveillance, compliance and enforcement, including training and capacity-building at the local level, development and funding of national and regional observer programmes and access to technology and equipment.

Article 26
Special assistance in the implementation of this Agreement

1. States shall cooperate to establish special funds to assist developing States in the implementation of this Agreement, including assisting developing States to meet the costs involved in any proceedings for the settlement of disputes to which they may be parties.

2. States and international organizations should assist developing States in establishing new subregional or regional fisheries management organizations or arrangements, or in strengthening existing organizations or arrangements, for the conservation and management of straddling fish stocks and highly migratory fish stocks.

PART VIII
PEACEFUL SETTLEMENT OF DISPUTES

Article 27
Obligation to settle disputes by peaceful means

States have the obligation to settle their disputes by negotiation, inquiry, mediation, conciliation, arbitration, judicial settlement, resort to regional agencies or arrangements, or other peaceful means of their own choice.

Article 28
Prevention of disputes

States shall cooperate in order to prevent disputes. To this end, States shall agree on efficient and expeditious decision-making procedures within subregional and regional fisheries management organizations and arrangements and shall strengthen existing decision-making procedures as necessary.

Article 29
Disputes of a technical nature

Where a dispute concerns a matter of a technical nature, the States concerned may refer the dispute to an ad hoc expert panel established by them. The panel shall confer with the States concerned and shall endeavour to resolve the dispute expeditiously, without recourse to binding procedures for the settlement of disputes.

Article 30
Procedures for the settlement of disputes

1.   The provisions relating to the settlement of disputes set out in Part XV of the Convention apply mutatis mutandis to any dispute between States Parties to this Agreement concerning the interpretation or application of this Agreement, whether or not they are also Parties to the Convention.

2.   The provisions relating to the settlement of disputes set out in Part XV of the Convention apply mutatis mutandis to any dispute between States Parties to this Agreement concerning the interpretation or application of a subregional, regional or global fisheries agreement relating to straddling fish stocks or highly migratory fish stocks to which they are parties, including any dispute concerning the conservation and management of such stocks, whether or not they are also Parties to the Convention.

3.   Any procedure accepted by a State Party to this Agreement and the Convention pursuant to article 287 of the Convention shall apply to the settlement of disputes under this Part, unless that State Party, when signing, ratifying or acceding to this Agreement, or at any time thereafter, has accepted another procedure pursuant to article 287 for the settlement of disputes under this Part.

4.   A State Party to this Agreement which is not a Party to the Convention, when signing, ratifying or acceding to this Agreement, or at any time thereafter, shall be free to choose, by means of a written declaration, one or more of the means set out in article 287, paragraph 1, of the Convention for the settlement of disputes under this Part. Article 287 shall apply to such a declaration, as well as to any dispute to which such State is a party which is not covered by a declaration in force. For the purposes of conciliation and arbitration in accordance with Annexes V, VII and VIII to the Convention, such State shall be entitled to nominate conciliators, arbitrators and experts to be included in the lists referred to in Annex V, article 2, Annex VII, article 2, and Annex VIII, article 2, for the settlement of disputes under this Part.

5.   Any court or tribunal to which a dispute has been submitted under this Part shall apply the relevant provisions of the Convention, of this Agreement and of any relevant subregional, regional or global fisheries agreement, as well as generally accepted standards for the conservation and management of living marine resources and other rules of international law not incompatible with the Convention, with a view to ensuring the conservation of the straddling fish stocks and highly migratory fish stocks concerned.

Article 31
Provisional measures

1.   Pending the settlement of a dispute in accordance with this Part, the parties to the dispute shall make every effort to enter into provisional arrangements of a practical nature.

2.   Without prejudice to article 290 of the Convention, the court or tribunal to which the dispute has been submitted under this Part may prescribe any provisional measures which it considers appropriate under the circumstances to preserve the respective rights of the parties to the dispute or to prevent damage to the stocks in

question, as well as in the circumstances referred to in article 7, paragraph 5, and article 16, paragraph 2.

3. A State Party to this Agreement which is not a Party to the Convention may declare that, notwithstanding article 290, paragraph 5, of the Convention, the International Tribunal for the Law of the Sea shall not be entitled to prescribe, modify or revoke provisional measures without the agreement of such State.

Article 32

Limitations on applicability of procedures for the settlement of disputes

Article 297, paragraph 3, of the Convention applies also to this Agreement.

PART IX

NON–PARTIES TO THIS AGREEMENT

Article 33

Non-parties to this agreement

1. States Parties shall encourage non-parties to this Agreement to become parties thereto and to adopt laws and regulations consistent with its provisions.

2. States Parties shall take measures consistent with this Agreement and international law to deter the activities of vessels flying the flag of non-parties which undermine the effective implementation of this Agreement.

PART X

GOOD FAITH AND ABUSE OF RIGHTS

Article 34

Good faith and abuse of rights

States Parties shall fulfil in good faith the obligations assumed under this Agreement and shall exercise the rights recognized in this Agreement in a manner which would not constitute an abuse of right.

Part XI

RESPONSIBILITY AND LIABILITY

Article 35

Responsibility and liability

States Parties are liable in accordance with international law for damage or loss attributable to them in regard to this Agreement.

PART XII

REVIEW CONFERENCE

Article 36

Review conference

1. Four years after the date of entry into force of this Agreement, the Secretary–General of the United Nations shall convene a conference with a view to assessing the effectiveness of this Agreement in securing the conservation and management of straddling fish stocks and highly migratory fish stocks. The Secretary–General shall invite to the conference all States Parties and those States and entities which are entitled to become parties to this Agreement as well as those intergovernmental and non-governmental organizations entitled to participate as observers.

2. The conference shall review and assess the adequacy of the provisions of this Agreement and, if necessary, propose means of strengthening the substance and methods of implementation of those provisions in order better to address any continu-

ing problems in the conservation and management of straddling fish stocks and highly migratory fish stocks.

PART XIII
FINAL PROVISIONS

Article 37
Signature

This Agreement shall be open for signature by all States and the other entities referred to in article 1, paragraph 2(b), and shall remain open for signature at United Nations Headquarters for twelve months from the fourth of December 1995.

Article 38
Ratification

This Agreement is subject to ratification by States and the other entities referred to in article 1, paragraph 2(b). The instruments of ratification shall be deposited with the Secretary–General of the United Nations.

Article 39
Accession

This Agreement shall remain open for accession by States and the other entities referred to in article 1, paragraph 2(b). The instruments of accession shall be deposited with the Secretary–General of the United Nations.

Article 40
Entry into force

1. This Agreement shall enter into force 30 days after the date of deposit of the thirtieth instrument of ratification or accession.

2. For each State or entity which ratifies the Agreement or accedes thereto after the deposit of the thirtieth instrument of ratification or accession, this Agreement shall enter into force on the thirtieth day following the deposit of its instrument of ratification or accession.

Article 41
Provisional application

1. This Agreement shall be applied provisionally by a State or entity which consents to its provisional application by so notifying the depositary in writing. Such provisional application shall become effective from the date of receipt of the notification.

2. Provisional application by a State or entity shall terminate upon the entry into force of this Agreement for that State or entity or upon notification by that State or entity to the depositary in writing of its intention to terminate provisional application.

Article 42
Reservations and exceptions

No reservations or exceptions may be made to this Agreement.

Article 43
Declarations and statements

Article 42 does not preclude a State or entity, when signing, ratifying or acceding to this Agreement, from making declarations or statements, however phrased or named, with a view, inter alia, to the harmonization of its laws and regulations with the provisions of this Agreement, provided that such declarations or statements do not purport to exclude or to modify the legal effect of the provisions of this Agreement in their application to that State or entity.

Article 44
Relation to other agreements

1. This Agreement shall not alter the rights and obligations of States Parties which arise from other agreements compatible with this Agreement and which do not affect the enjoyment by other States Parties of their rights or the performance of their obligations under this Agreement.

2. Two or more States Parties may conclude agreements modifying or suspending the operation of provisions of this Agreement, applicable solely to the relations between them, provided that such agreements do not relate to a provision derogation from which is incompatible with the effective execution of the object and purpose of this Agreement, and provided further that such agreements shall not affect the application of the basic principles embodied herein, and that the provisions of such agreements do not affect the enjoyment by other States Parties of their rights or the performance of their obligations under this Agreement.

3. States Parties intending to conclude an agreement referred to in paragraph 2 shall notify the other States Parties through the depositary of this Agreement of their intention to conclude the agreement and of the modification or suspension for which it provides.

Article 45
Amendment

1. A State Party may, by written communication addressed to the Secretary-General of the United Nations, propose amendments to this Agreement and request the convening of a conference to consider such proposed amendments. The Secretary–General shall circulate such communication to all States Parties. If, within six months from the date of the circulation of the communication, not less than one half of the States Parties reply favourably to the request, the Secretary–General shall convene the conference.

2. The decision-making procedure applicable at the amendment conference convened pursuant to paragraph 1 shall be the same as that applicable at the United Nations Conference on Straddling Fish Stocks and Highly Migratory Fish Stocks, unless otherwise decided by the conference. The conference should make every effort to reach agreement on any amendments by way of consensus and there should be no voting on them until all efforts at consensus have been exhausted.

3. Once adopted, amendments to this Agreement shall be open for signature by States Parties for twelve months from the date of adoption at United Nations Headquarters, unless otherwise provided in the amendment itself.

4. Articles 38, 39, 47 and 50 apply to all amendments to this Agreement.

5. Amendments to this Agreement shall enter into force for the States Parties ratifying or acceding to them on the thirtieth day following the deposit of instruments of ratification or accession by two thirds of the States Parties. Thereafter, for each State Party ratifying or acceding to an amendment after the deposit of the required number of such instruments, the amendment shall enter into force on the thirtieth day following the deposit of its instrument of ratification or accession.

6. An amendment may provide that a smaller or a larger number of ratifications or accessions shall be required for its entry into force than are required by this article.

7. A State which becomes a Party to this Agreement after the entry into force of amendments in accordance with paragraph 5 shall, failing an expression of a different intention by that State:

(a) be considered as a Party to this Agreement as so amended; and

(b) be considered as a Party to the unamended Agreement in relation to any State Party not bound by the amendment.

Article 46
Denunciation

1. A State Party may, by written notification addressed to the Secretary-General of the United Nations, denounce this Agreement and may indicate its reasons. Failure to indicate reasons shall not affect the validity of the denunciation. The denunciation shall take effect one year after the date of receipt of the notification, unless the notification specifies a later date.

2. The denunciation shall not in any way affect the duty of any State Party to fulfil any obligation embodied in this Agreement to which it would be subject under international law independently of this Agreement.

Article 47
Participation by international organizations

1. In cases where an international organization referred to in Annex IX, article 1, of the Convention does not have competence over all the matters governed by this Agreement, Annex IX to the Convention shall apply mutatis mutandis to participation by such international organization in this Agreement, except that the following provisions of that Annex shall not apply:

(a) article 2, first sentence; and

(b) article 3, paragraph 1.

2. In cases where an international organization referred to in Annex IX, article 1, of the Convention has competence over all the matters governed by this Agreement, the following provisions shall apply to participation by such international organization in this Agreement:

(a) at the time of signature or accession, such international organization shall make a declaration stating:

(i) that it has competence over all the matters governed by this Agreement;

(ii) that, for this reason, its member States shall not become States Parties, except in respect of their territories for which the international organization has no responsibility; and

(iii) that it accepts the rights and obligations of States under this Agreement;

(b) participation of such an international organization shall in no case confer any rights under this Agreement on member States of the international organization;

(c) in the event of a conflict between the obligations of an international organization under this Agreement and its obligations under the agreement establishing the international organization or any acts relating to it, the obligations under this Agreement shall prevail.

Article 48
Annexes

1. The Annexes form an integral part of this Agreement and, unless expressly provided otherwise, a reference to this Agreement or to one of its Parts includes a reference to the Annexes relating thereto.

2. The Annexes may be revised from time to time by States Parties. Such revisions shall be based on scientific and technical considerations. Notwithstanding the provisions of article 45, if a revision to an Annex is adopted by consensus at a meeting

of States Parties, it shall be incorporated in this Agreement and shall take effect from the date of its adoption or from such other date as may be specified in the revision. If a revision to an Annex is not adopted by consensus at such a meeting, the amendment procedures set out in article 45 shall apply.

Article 49
Depositary

The Secretary–General of the United Nations shall be the depositary of this Agreement and any amendments or revisions thereto.

Article 50
Authentic texts

The Arabic, Chinese, English, French, Russian and Spanish texts of this Agreement are equally authentic.

IN WITNESS WHEREOF, the undersigned Plenipotentiaries, being duly authorized thereto, have signed this Agreement.

OPENED FOR SIGNATURE at New York, this fourth day of December, one thousand nine hundred and ninety-five, in a single original, in the Arabic, Chinese, English, French, Russian and Spanish languages.

ANNEX I
STANDARD REQUIREMENTS FOR THE COLLECTION AND SHARING OF DATA

Article 1
General principles

1. The timely collection, compilation and analysis of data are fundamental to the effective conservation and management of straddling fish stocks and highly migratory fish stocks. To this end, data from fisheries for these stocks on the high seas and those in areas under national jurisdiction are required and should be collected and compiled in such a way as to enable statistically meaningful analysis for the purposes of fishery resource conservation and management. These data include catch and fishing effort statistics and other fishery-related information, such as vessel-related and other data for standardizing fishing effort. Data collected should also include information on non-target and associated or dependent species. All data should be verified to ensure accuracy. Confidentiality of non-aggregated data shall be maintained. The dissemination of such data shall be subject to the terms on which they have been provided.

2. Assistance, including training as well as financial and technical assistance, shall be provided to developing States in order to build capacity in the field of conservation and management of living marine resources. Assistance should focus on enhancing capacity to implement data collection and verification, observer programmes, data analysis and research projects supporting stock assessments. The fullest possible involvement of developing State scientists and managers in conservation and management of straddling fish stocks and highly migratory fish stocks should be promoted.

Article 2
Principles of data collection, compilation and exchange

The following general principles should be considered in defining the parameters for collection, compilation and exchange of data from fishing operations for straddling fish stocks and highly migratory fish stocks:

(a) States should ensure that data are collected from vessels flying their flag on fishing activities according to the operational characteristics of each fishing method (e.g., each individual tow for trawl, each set for long-line and purse-seine, each school fished for pole-and-line and each day fished for troll) and in sufficient detail to facilitate effective stock assessment;

(b) States should ensure that fishery data are verified through an appropriate system;

(c) States should compile fishery-related and other supporting scientific data and provide them in an agreed format and in a timely manner to the relevant subregional or regional fisheries management organization or arrangement where one exists. Otherwise, States should cooperate to exchange data either directly or through such other cooperative mechanisms as may be agreed among them;

(d) States should agree, within the framework of subregional or regional fisheries management organizations or arrangements, or otherwise, on the specification of data and the format in which they are to be provided, in accordance with this Annex and taking into account the nature of the stocks and the fisheries for those stocks in the region. Such organizations or arrangements should request non-members or non-participants to provide data concerning relevant fishing activities by vessels flying their flag;

(e) such organizations or arrangements shall compile data and make them available in a timely manner and in an agreed format to all interested States under the terms and conditions established by the organizations or arrangements; and

(f) scientists of the flag State and from the relevant subregional or regional fisheries management organization or arrangement should analyse the data separately or jointly, as appropriate.

Article 3
Basic fishery data

1. States shall collect and make available to the relevant subregional or regional fisheries management organization or arrangement the following types of data in sufficient detail to facilitate effective stock assessment in accordance with agreed procedures:

(a) time series of catch and effort statistics by fishery and fleet;

(b) total catch in number, nominal weight or both by species (both target and non-target) as is appropriate to each fishery. [Nominal weight is defined by the Food and Agriculture Organization of the United Nations as the live-weight equivalent of the landings];

(c) discard statistics, including estimates where necessary, reported as number or nominal weight by species, as is appropriate to each fishery;

(d) effort statistics appropriate to each fishing method; and

(e) fishing location, date and time fished and other statistics on fishing operations as appropriate.

2. States shall also collect where appropriate and provide to the relevant subregional or regional fisheries management organization or arrangement information to support stock assessment, including:

(a) composition of the catch according to length, weight and sex;

(b) other biological information supporting stock assessments, such as information on age, growth, recruitment, distribution and stock identity; and

(c) other relevant research, including surveys of abundance, biomass surveys, hydro-acoustic surveys, research on environmental factors affecting stock abundance, and oceanographic and ecological studies.

Article 4
Vessel data and information

1.   States should collect the following types of vessel-related data for standardizing fleet composition and vessel fishing power and for converting between different measures of effort in the analysis of catch and effort data:

(a) vessel identification, flag and port of registry;

(b) vessel type;

(c) vessel specifications (e.g., material of construction, date built, registered length, gross registered tonnage, power of main engines, hold capacity and catch storage methods); and

(d) fishing gear description (e.g., types, gear specifications and quantity).

2.   The flag State will collect the following information:

(a) navigation and position fixing aids;

(b) communication equipment and international radio call sign; and

(c) crew size.

Article 5
Reporting

A State shall ensure that vessels flying its flag send to its national fisheries administration and, where agreed, to the relevant subregional or regional fisheries management organization or arrangement, logbook data on catch and effort, including data on fishing operations on the high seas, at sufficiently frequent intervals to meet national requirements and regional and international obligations. Such data shall be transmitted, where necessary, by radio, telex, facsimile or satellite transmission or by other means.

Article 6
Data verification

States or, as appropriate, subregional or regional fisheries management organizations or arrangements should establish mechanisms for verifying fishery data, such as:

(a) position verification through vessel monitoring systems;

(b) scientific observer programmes to monitor catch, effort, catch composition (target and non-target) and other details of fishing operations;

(c) vessel trip, landing and transshipment reports; and

(d) port sampling.

Article 7
Data exchange

1.   Data collected by flag States must be shared with other flag States and relevant coastal States through appropriate subregional or regional fisheries management organizations or arrangements. Such organizations or arrangements shall compile data and make them available in a timely manner and in an agreed format to all interested States under the terms and conditions established by the organizations or arrangements, while maintaining confidentiality of non-aggregated data, and should, to the extent feasible, develop database systems which provide efficient access to data.

2.   At the global level, collection and dissemination of data should be effected through the Food and Agriculture Organization of the United Nations. Where a subregional or regional fisheries management organization or arrangement does not

exist, that organization may also do the same at the subregional or regional level by arrangement with the States concerned.

ANNEX II
GUIDELINES FOR THE APPLICATION OF PRECAUTIONARY REFERENCE POINTS IN CONSERVATION AND MANAGEMENT OF STRADDLING FISH STOCKS AND HIGHLY MIGRATORY FISH STOCKS

1. A precautionary reference point is an estimated value derived through an agreed scientific procedure, which corresponds to the state of the resource and of the fishery, and which can be used as a guide for fisheries management.

2. Two types of precautionary reference points should be used: conservation, or limit, reference points and management, or target, reference points. Limit reference points set boundaries which are intended to constrain harvesting within safe biological limits within which the stocks can produce maximum sustainable yield. Target reference points are intended to meet management objectives.

3. Precautionary reference points should be stock-specific to account, inter alia, for the reproductive capacity, the resilience of each stock and the characteristics of fisheries exploiting the stock, as well as other sources of mortality and major sources of uncertainty.

4. Management strategies shall seek to maintain or restore populations of harvested stocks, and where necessary associated or dependent species, at levels consistent with previously agreed precautionary reference points. Such reference points shall be used to trigger pre-agreed conservation and management action. Management strategies shall include measures which can be implemented when precautionary reference points are approached.

5. Fishery management strategies shall ensure that the risk of exceeding limit reference points is very low. If a stock falls below a limit reference point or is at risk of falling below such a reference point, conservation and management action should be initiated to facilitate stock recovery. Fishery management strategies shall ensure that target reference points are not exceeded on average.

6. When information for determining reference points for a fishery is poor or absent, provisional reference points shall be set. Provisional reference points may be established by analogy to similar and better-known stocks. In such situations, the fishery shall be subject to enhanced monitoring so as to enable revision of provisional reference points as improved information becomes available.

7. The fishing mortality rate which generates maximum sustainable yield should be regarded as a minimum standard for limit reference points. For stocks which are not overfished, fishery management strategies shall ensure that fishing mortality does not exceed that which corresponds to maximum sustainable yield, and that the biomass does not fall below a predefined threshold. For overfished stocks, the biomass which would produce maximum sustainable yield can serve as a rebuilding target.

5.18 CODE OF CONDUCT FOR RESPONSIBLE FISHERIES. **Adopted by the Twenty-eighth Session of the Food and Agriculture Organization of the United Nations, 31 October 1995.**

* * *

INTRODUCTION

Fisheries, including aquaculture, provide a vital source of food, employment, recreation, trade and economic well being for people throughout the world, both for present and future generations and should therefore be conducted in a responsible manner. This Code sets out principles and international standards of behaviour for responsible practices with a view to ensuring the effective conservation, management and development of living aquatic resources, with due respect for the ecosystem and biodiversity. The Code recognizes the nutritional, economic, social, environmental and cultural importance of fisheries, and the interests of all those concerned with the fishery sector. The Code takes into account the biological characteristics of the resources and their environment and the interests of consumers and other users. States and all those involved in fisheries are encouraged to apply the Code and give effect to it.

1—NATURE AND SCOPE OF THE CODE

1.1 This Code is voluntary. However, certain parts of it are based on relevant rules of international law, including those reflected in the United Nations Convention on the Law of the Sea of 10 December 1982. The Code also contains provisions that may be or have already been given binding effect by means of other obligatory legal instruments amongst the Parties, such as the Agreement to Promote Compliance with International Conservation and Management Measures by Fishing Vessels on the High Seas, 1993, which, according to FAO Conference resolution 15/93, paragraph 3, forms an integral part of the Code.

1.2 The Code is global in scope, and is directed toward members and non-members of FAO, fishing entities, subregional, regional and global organizations, whether governmental or non-governmental, and all persons concerned with the conservation of fishery resources and management and development of fisheries, such as fishers, those engaged in processing and marketing of fish and fishery products and other users of the aquatic environment in relation to fisheries.

* * *

2—OBJECTIVES OF THE CODE

The objectives of the Code are to:

1. establish principles, in accordance with the relevant rules of international law, for responsible fishing and fisheries activities, taking into account all their relevant biological, technological, economic, social, environmental and commercial aspects;

2. establish principles and criteria for the elaboration and implementation of national policies for responsible conservation of fisheries resources and fisheries management and development;

* * *

10. provide standards of conduct for all persons involved in the fisheries sector.

3—RELATIONSHIP WITH OTHER INTERNATIONAL INSTRUMENTS

3.1 The Code is to be interpreted and applied in conformity with the relevant rules of international law, as reflected in the United Nations Convention on the Law of the Sea, 1982. Nothing in this Code prejudices the rights, jurisdiction and duties of States under international law as reflected in the Convention.

3.2   The Code is also to be interpreted and applied:

a.   in a manner consistent with the relevant provisions of the Agreement for the Implementation of the Provisions of the United Nations Convention on the Law of the Sea of 10 December 1982 Relating to the Conservation and Management of Straddling Fish Stocks and Highly Migratory Fish Stocks;

b.   in accordance with other applicable rules of international law, including the respective obligations of States pursuant to international agreements to which they are party; and

c.   in the light of the 1992 Declaration of Cancun, the 1992 Rio Declaration on Environment and Development, and Agenda 21 adopted by the United Nations Conference on Environment and Development (UNCED), in particular Chapter 17 of Agenda 21, and other relevant declarations and international instruments.

4—IMPLEMENTATION, MONITORING AND UPDATING

4.1   All members and non-members of FAO, fishing entities and relevant subregional, regional and global organizations, whether governmental or non-governmental, and all persons concerned with the conservation, management and utilization of fisheries resources and trade in fish and fishery products should collaborate in the fulfilment and implementation of the objectives and principles contained in this Code.

* * *

6—GENERAL PRINCIPLES

6.1   States and users of living aquatic resources should conserve aquatic ecosystems. The right to fish carries with it the obligation to do so in a responsible manner so as to ensure effective conservation and management of the living aquatic resources.

6.2   Fisheries management should promote the maintenance of the quality, diversity and availability of fishery resources in sufficient quantities for present and future generations in the context of food security, poverty alleviation and sustainable development. Management measures should not only ensure the conservation of target species but also of species belonging to the same ecosystem or associated with or dependent upon the target species.

6.3   States should prevent overfishing and excess fishing capacity and should implement management measures to ensure that fishing effort is commensurate with the productive capacity of the fishery resources and their sustainable utilization. States should take measures to rehabilitate populations as far as possible and when appropriate.

6.4   Conservation and management decisions for fisheries should be based on the best scientific evidence available, also taking into account traditional knowledge of the resources and their habitat, as well as relevant environmental, economic and social factors. States should assign priority to undertake research and data collection in order to improve scientific and technical knowledge of fisheries including their interaction with the ecosystem. In recognizing the transboundary nature of many aquatic ecosystems, States should encourage bilateral and multilateral cooperation in research, as appropriate.

6.5   States and subregional and regional fisheries management organizations should apply a precautionary approach widely to conservation, management and exploitation of living aquatic resources in order to protect them and preserve the aquatic environment, taking account of the best scientific evidence available. The absence of adequate scientific information should not be used as a reason for postponing or failing to take measures to conserve target species, associated or dependent species and non-target species and their environment.

6.6   Selective and environmentally safe fishing gear and practices should be further developed and applied, to the extent practicable, in order to maintain biodiversity and to conserve the population structure and aquatic ecosystems and protect fish quality. Where proper selective and environmentally safe fishing gear and practices exist, they should be recognized and accorded a priority in establishing conservation and management measures for fisheries. States and users of aquatic ecosystems should minimize waste, catch of non-target species, both fish and non-fish species, and impacts on associated or dependent species.

* * *

6.10   Within their respective competences and in accordance with international law, including within the framework of subregional or regional fisheries conservation and management organizations or arrangements, States should ensure compliance with and enforcement of conservation and management measures and establish effective mechanisms, as appropriate, to monitor and control the activities of fishing vessels and fishing support vessels.

6.11   States authorizing fishing and fishing support vessels to fly their flags should exercise effective control over those vessels so as to ensure the proper application of this Code. They should ensure that the activities of such vessels do not undermine the effectiveness of conservation and management measures taken in accordance with international law and adopted at the national, subregional, regional or global levels. States should also ensure that vessels flying their flags fulfil their obligations concerning the collection and provision of data relating to their fishing activities.

6.12   States should, within their respective competences and in accordance with international law, cooperate at subregional, regional and global levels through fisheries management organizations, other international agreements or other arrangements to promote conservation and management, ensure responsible fishing and ensure effective conservation and protection of living aquatic resources throughout their range of distribution, taking into account the need for compatible measures in areas within and beyond national jurisdiction.

* * *

7—FISHERIES MANAGEMENT

7.1   General

7.1.1   States and all those engaged in fisheries management should, through an appropriate policy, legal and institutional framework, adopt measures for the long-term conservation and sustainable use of fisheries resources. Conservation and management measures, whether at local, national, subregional or regional levels, should be based on the best scientific evidence available and be designed to ensure the long-term sustainability of fishery resources at levels which promote the objective of their optimum utilization and maintain their availability for present and future generations; short term considerations should not compromise these objectives.

* * *

7.1.3   For transboundary fish stocks, straddling fish stocks, highly migratory fish stocks and high seas fish stocks, where these are exploited by two or more States, the States concerned, including the relevant coastal States in the case of straddling and highly migratory stocks, should cooperate to ensure effective conservation and management of the resources. This should be achieved, where appropriate, through the establishment of a bilateral, subregional or regional fisheries organization or arrangement.

7.1.4 A subregional or regional fisheries management organization or arrangement should include representatives of States in whose jurisdictions the resources occur, as well as representatives from States which have a real interest in the fisheries on the resources outside national jurisdictions. Where a subregional or regional fisheries management organization or arrangement exists and has the competence to establish conservation and management measures, those States should cooperate by becoming a member of such organization or a participant in such arrangement, and actively participate in its work.

7.1.5 A State which is not a member of a subregional or regional fisheries management organization or is not a participant in a subregional or regional fisheries management arrangement should nevertheless cooperate, in accordance with relevant international agreements and international law, in the conservation and management of the relevant fisheries resources by giving effect to any conservation and management measures adopted by such organization or arrangement.

* * *

7.1.7 States should establish, within their respective competences and capacities, effective mechanisms for fisheries monitoring, surveillance, control and enforcement to ensure compliance with their conservation and management measures, as well as those adopted by subregional or regional organizations or arrangements.

* * *

7.2 Management objectives

7.2.1 Recognizing that long-term sustainable use of fisheries resources is the overriding objective of conservation and management, States and subregional or regional fisheries management organizations and arrangements should, inter alia, adopt appropriate measures, based on the best scientific evidence available, which are designed to maintain or restore stocks at levels capable of producing maximum sustainable yield, as qualified by relevant environmental and economic factors, including the special requirements of developing countries.

7.2.2 Such measures should provide inter alia that:

a. excess fishing capacity is avoided and exploitation of the stocks remains economically viable;

b. the economic conditions under which fishing industries operate promote responsible fisheries;

c. the interests of fishers, including those engaged in subsistence, small-scale and artisanal fisheries, are taken into account;

d. biodiversity of aquatic habitats and ecosystems is conserved and endangered species are protected;

e. depleted stocks are allowed to recover or, where appropriate, are actively restored;

f. adverse environmental impacts on the resources from human activities are assessed and, where appropriate, corrected; and

g. pollution, waste, discards, catch by lost or abandoned gear, catch of non-target species, both fish and non-fish species, and impacts on associated or dependent species are minimized, through measures including, to the extent practicable, the development and use of selective, environmentally safe and cost-effective fishing gear and techniques.

7.2.3   States should assess the impacts of environmental factors on target stocks and species belonging to the same ecosystem or associated with or dependent upon the target stocks, and assess the relationship among the populations in the ecosystem.

* * *

7.5   *Precautionary approach*

7.5.1   States should apply the precautionary approach widely to conservation, management and exploitation of living aquatic resources in order to protect them and preserve the aquatic environment. The absence of adequate scientific information should not be used as a reason for postponing or failing to take conservation and management measures.

7.5.2   In implementing the precautionary approach, States should take into account, inter alia, uncertainties relating to the size and productivity of the stocks, reference points, stock condition in relation to such reference points, levels and distribution of fishing mortality and the impact of fishing activities, including discards, on non-target and associated or dependent species, as well as environmental and socio-economic conditions.

7.5.3   States and subregional or regional fisheries management organizations and arrangements should, on the basis of the best scientific evidence available, inter alia, determine:

a.   stock specific target reference points, and, at the same time, the action to be taken if they are exceeded; and

b.   stock-specific limit reference points, and, at the same time, the action to be taken if they are exceeded; when a limit reference point is approached, measures should be taken to ensure that it will not be exceeded.

7.5.4   In the case of new or exploratory fisheries, States should adopt as soon as possible cautious conservation and management measures, including, inter alia, catch limits and effort limits. Such measures should remain in force until there are sufficient data to allow assessment of the impact of the fisheries on the long-term sustainability of the stocks, whereupon conservation and management measures based on that assessment should be implemented. The latter measures should, if appropriate, allow for the gradual development of the fisheries.

7.5.5   If a natural phenomenon has a significant adverse impact on the status of living aquatic resources, States should adopt conservation and management measures on an emergency basis to ensure that fishing activity does not exacerbate such adverse impact. States should also adopt such measures on an emergency basis where fishing activity presents a serious threat to the sustainability of such resources. Measures taken on an emergency basis should be temporary and should be based on the best scientific evidence available.

7.6   *Management measures*

7.6.1   States should ensure that the level of fishing permitted is commensurate with the state of fisheries resources.

7.6.2   States should adopt measures to ensure that no vessel be allowed to fish unless so authorized, in a manner consistent with international law for the high seas or in conformity with national legislation within areas of national jurisdiction.

7.6.3   Where excess fishing capacity exists, mechanisms should be established to reduce capacity to levels commensurate with the sustainable use of fisheries resources so as to ensure that fishers operate under economic conditions that promote responsible fisheries. Such mechanisms should include monitoring the capacity of fishing fleets.

7.6.4   The performance of all existing fishing gear, methods and practices should be examined and measures taken to ensure that fishing gear, methods and practices which are not consistent with responsible fishing are phased out and replaced with more acceptable alternatives. In this process, particular attention should be given to the impact of such measures on fishing communities, including their ability to exploit the resource.

7.6.5 States and fisheries management organizations and arrangements should regulate fishing in such a way as to avoid the risk of conflict among fishers using different vessels, gear and fishing methods.

7.6.6 When deciding on the use, conservation and management of fisheries resources, due recognition should be given, as appropriate, in accordance with national laws and regulations, to the traditional practices, needs and interests of indigenous people and local fishing communities which are highly dependent on fishery resources for their livelihood.

7.6.7 In the evaluation of alternative conservation and management measures, their cost-effectiveness and social impact should be considered.

7.6.8 The efficacy of conservation and management measures and their possible interactions should be kept under continuous review. Such measures should, as appropriate, be revised or abolished in the light of new information.

7.6.9 States should take appropriate measures to minimize waste, discards, catch by lost or abandoned gear, catch of non-target species, both fish and non-fish species, and negative impacts on associated or dependent species, in particular endangered species. Where appropriate, such measures may include technical measures related to fish size, mesh size or gear, discards, closed seasons and areas and zones reserved for selected fisheries, particularly artisanal fisheries. Such measures should be applied, where appropriate, to protect juveniles and spawners. States and subregional or regional fisheries management organizations and arrangements should promote, to the extent practicable, the development and use of selective, environmentally safe and cost effective gear and techniques.

7.6.10 States and subregional and regional fisheries management organizations and arrangements, in the framework of their respective competences, should introduce measures for depleted resources and those resources threatened with depletion that facilitate the sustained recovery of such stocks. They should make every effort to ensure that resources and habitats critical to the well-being of such resources which have been adversely affected by fishing or other human activities are restored.

* * *

8—Fishing Operations

8.1 Duties of all States

8.1.1 States should ensure that only fishing operations allowed by them are conducted within waters under their jurisdiction and that these operations are carried out in a responsible manner.

* * *

8.1.4 States should, in accordance with international law, within the framework of subregional or regional fisheries management organizations or arrangements, cooperate to establish systems for monitoring, control, surveillance and enforcement of applicable measures with respect to fishing operations and related activities in waters outside their national jurisdiction.

* * *

8.2 Flag State duties

* * *

8.2.2 Flag States should ensure that no fishing vessels entitled to fly their flag fish on the high seas or in waters under the jurisdiction of other States unless such vessels have been issued with a Certificate of Registry and have been authorized to fish by the competent authorities. Such vessels should carry on board the Certificate of Registry and their authorization to fish.

* * *

8.2.7 Flag States should take enforcement measures in respect of fishing vessels entitled to fly their flag which have been found by them to have contravened applicable conservation and management measures, including, where appropriate, making the contravention of such measures an offence under national legislation. Sanctions applicable in respect of violations should be adequate in severity to be effective in securing compliance and to discourage violations wherever they occur and should deprive offenders of the benefits accruing from their illegal activities. Such sanctions may, for serious violations, include provisions for the refusal, withdrawal or suspension of the authorization to fish.

* * *

8.5 Fishing gear selectivity

8.5.1 States should require that fishing gear, methods and practices, to the extent practicable, are sufficiently selective so as to minimize waste, discards, catch of non-target species, both fish and non-fish species, and impacts on associated or dependent species and that the intent of related regulations is not circumvented by technical devices. In this regard, fishers should cooperate in the development of selective fishing gear and methods. States should ensure that information on new developments and requirements is made available to all fishers.

8.5.2 In order to improve selectivity, States should, when drawing up their laws and regulations, take into account the range of selective fishing gear, methods and strategies available to the industry.

8.5.3 States and relevant institutions should collaborate in developing standard methodologies for research into fishing gear selectivity, fishing methods and strategies.

8.5.4 International cooperation should be encouraged with respect to research programmes for fishing gear selectivity, and fishing methods and strategies, dissemination of the results of such research programmes and the transfer of technology.

* * *

11—POST-HARVEST PRACTICES AND TRADE

* * *

11.2 Responsible international trade

11.2.1 The provisions of this Code should be interpreted and applied in accordance with the principles, rights and obligations established in the World Trade Organization (WTO) Agreement.

11.2.2 International trade in fish and fishery products should not compromise the sustainable development of fisheries and responsible utilization of living aquatic resources.

11.2.3 States should ensure that measures affecting international trade in fish and fishery products are transparent, based, when applicable, on scientific evidence, and are in accordance with internationally agreed rules.

11.2.4 Fish trade measures adopted by States to protect human or animal life or health, the interests of consumers or the environment, should not be discriminatory and should be in accordance with internationally agreed trade rules, in particular the principles, rights and obligations established in the Agreement on the Application of Sanitary and Phytosanitary Measures and the Agreement on Technical Barriers to Trade of the WTO.

* * *

11.2.8   States should not link access to markets to the purchase of specific technology or sale of other products.

11.2.9   States should cooperate in complying with relevant international agreements regulating trade in endangered species.

11.2.10   States should develop international agreements for trade in live specimens where there is a risk of environmental damage in importing or exporting States.

11.2.11   States should cooperate to promote adherence to, and effective implementation of relevant international standards for trade in fish and fishery products and living aquatic resource conservation.

11.2.12   States should not undermine conservation measures for living aquatic resources in order to gain trade or investment benefits.

11.2.13   States should cooperate to develop internationally acceptable rules or standards for trade in fish and fishery products in accordance with the principles, rights, and obligations established in the WTO Agreement.

11.2.14   States should cooperate with each other and actively participate in relevant regional and multilateral fora, such as the WTO, in order to ensure equitable, non-discriminatory trade in fish and fishery products as well as wide adherence to multilaterally agreed fishery conservation measures.

11.2.15   States, aid agencies, multilateral development banks and other relevant international organizations should ensure that their policies and practices related to the promotion of international fish trade and export production do not result in environmental degradation or adversely impact the nutritional rights and needs of people for whom fish is critical to their health and well being and for whom other comparable sources of food are not readily available or affordable.

* * *

C. WHALING

5.19 INTERNATIONAL CONVENTION FOR THE REGULATION OF WHALING (**Without Schedule but as Amended by 1956 Protocol). Concluded at Washington, 2 December 1946. Entered into force, 10 November 1948. 161 UNTS 72, TIAS No. 1849; 338 UNTS 366, 10 UST 952, TIAS No 4228;** *reprinted in* **5A Weston & Carlson V.H.2**

The Governments whose duly authorized representatives have subscribed hereto,

Recognizing the interest of the nations of the world in safeguarding for future generations the great natural resources represented by the whale stocks;

Considering that the history of whaling has seen overfishing of one area after another and of one species of whale after another to such a degree that it is essential to protect all species of whales from further overfishing;

Recognizing that the whale stocks are susceptible of natural increases if whaling is properly regulated, and that increases in the size of whale stocks will permit increases in the numbers of whales which may be captured without endangering these natural resources;

Recognizing that it is in the common interest to achieve the optimum level of whale stocks as rapidly as possible without causing wide-spread economic and nutritional distress;

Recognizing that in the course of achieving these objectives, whaling operations should be confined to those species best able to sustain exploitation in order to give an interval for recovery to certain species of whales now depleted in numbers;

Desiring to establish a system of international regulation for the whale fisheries to ensure proper and effective conservation and development of whale stocks on the basis of the principles embodied in the provisions of the International Agreement for the Regulation of Whaling signed in London on June 8, 1937 and the protocols to that Agreement signed in London on June 24, 1938 and November 26, 1945; and

Having decided to conclude a convention to provide for the proper conservation of whale stocks and thus make possible the orderly development of the whaling industry;

Have agreed as follows:

Article I

1. This Convention includes the Schedule attached thereto which forms an integral part thereof. All references to "Convention" shall be understood as including the said Schedule either in its present terms or as amended in accordance with the provisions of Article V.

2. This Convention applies to factory ships, land stations, and whale catchers under the jurisdiction of the Contracting Governments, and to all waters in which whaling is prosecuted by such factory ships, land stations, and whale catchers.

Article II

As used in this Convention

1. "factory ship" means a ship in which or on which whales are treated whether wholly or in part;

2. "land station" means a factory on the land at which whales are treated whether wholly or in part;

3. "whale catcher" means a helicopter, or other aircraft, or a ship, used for the purpose of hunting, taking, killing, towing, holding on to, or scouting for whales;

4. "Contracting Government" means any Government which has deposited an instrument of ratification or has given notice of adherence to this Convention.

Article III

1. The Contracting Governments agree to establish an International Whaling Commission, hereinafter referred to as the Commission, to be composed of one member of each Contracting Government. Each member shall have one vote and may be accompanied by one or more experts and advisers.

2. The Commission shall elect from its own members a Chairman and Vice Chairman and shall determine its own Rules of Procedure. Decisions of the Commission shall be taken by a simple majority of those members voting except that a three-fourths majority of those members voting shall be required for action in pursuance of Article V. The Rules of Procedure may provide for decisions otherwise than at meetings of the Commission.

3. The Commission may appoint its own Secretary and staff.

4. The Commission may set up, from among its own members and experts or advisers, such committees as it considers desirable to perform such functions as it may authorize.

5. The expenses of each member of the Commission and of his experts and advisers shall be determined and paid by his own Government.

6. Recognizing that specialized agencies related to the United Nations will be concerned with the conservation and development of whale fisheries and the products arising therefrom and desiring to avoid duplication of functions, the Contracting Governments will consult among themselves within two years after the coming into force of this Convention to decide whether the Commission shall be brought within the framework of a specialized agency related to the United Nations.

7. In the meantime the Government of the United Kingdom of Great Britain and Northern Ireland shall arrange, in consultation with the other Contracting Governments, to convene the first meeting of the Commission, and shall initiate the consultation referred to in paragraph 6 above.

8. Subsequent meetings of the Commission shall be convened as the Commission may determine.

Article IV

1. The Commission may either in collaboration with or through independent agencies of the Contracting Governments or other public or private agencies, establishments, or organizations, or independently

(a) encourage, recommend, or if necessary, organize studies and investigations relating to whales and whaling;

(b) collect and analyze statistical information concerning the current condition and trend of the whale stocks and the effects of whaling activities thereon;

(c) study, appraise, and disseminate information concerning methods of maintaining and increasing the populations of whale stocks.

2. The Commission shall arrange for the publication of reports of its activities, and it may publish independently or in collaboration with the International Bureau for Whaling Statistics at Sandefjord in Norway and other organizations and agencies such reports as it deems appropriate, as well as statistical, scientific, and other pertinent information relating to whales and whaling.

Article V

1. The Commission may amend from time to time the provisions of the Schedule by adopting regulations with respect to the conservation and utilization of whale resources, fixing (a) protected and unprotected species; (b) open and closed seasons; (c) open and closed waters, including the designation of sanctuary areas; (d) size limits for each species; (e) time, methods, and intensity of whaling (including the maximum catch of whales to be taken in any one season); (f) types and specifications of gear and apparatus and appliances which may be used; (g) methods of measurement; (h) catch returns and other statistical and biological records; and (i) methods of inspection.

2. These amendments of the Schedule (a) shall be such as are necessary to carry out the objectives and purposes of this Convention and to provide for the conservation, development, and optimum utilization of the whale resources; (b) shall be based on scientific findings; (c) shall not involve restrictions on the number or nationality of factory ships or land stations, nor allocate specific quotas to any factory ship or land station or to any group of factory ships or land stations; and (d) shall take into consideration the interests of the consumers of whale products and the whaling industry.

3. Each of such amendments shall become effective with respect to the Contracting Governments ninety days following notification of the amendment by the Commission to each of the Contracting Governments, except that (a) if any Government presents to the Commission objection to any amendment prior to the expiration of this ninety-day period, the amendment shall not become effective with respect to any of the Governments for an additional ninety days; (b) thereupon, any other Contracting Government may present objection to the amendment at any time prior to the expiration of the additional ninety-day period, or before the expiration of thirty days from the date of receipt of the last objection received during such additional ninety-day period, whichever date shall be the later; and (c) thereafter, the amendment shall become effective with respect to all Contracting Governments which have not presented objection but shall not become effective with respect to any Government which has so objected until such date as the objection is withdrawn. The Commission shall notify each Contracting Government immediately upon receipt of each objection and withdrawal and each Contracting Government shall acknowledge receipt of all notification of amendments, objections, and withdrawals.

4. No amendments shall become effective before July 1, 1949.

Article VI

The Commission may from time to time make recommendations to any or all Contracting Governments on any matters which relate to whales or whaling and to the objectives and purposes of this Convention.

Article VII

The Contracting Governments shall ensure prompt transmission to the International Bureau for Whaling Statistics at Sandefjord in Norway, or to such other body as the Commission may designate, of notifications and statistical and other information required by this Convention in such form and manner as may be prescribed by the Commission.

Article VIII

1. Notwithstanding anything contained in this Convention, any Contracting Government may grant to any of its nationals a special permit authorizing that national to kill, take, and treat whales for purposes of scientific research subject to such restrictions as to number and subject to such other conditions as the Contracting Government thinks fit, and the killing, taking, and treating of whales in accordance

with the provisions of this Article shall be exempt from the operation of this Convention. Each Contracting Government shall report at once to the Commission all such authorizations which it has granted. Each Contracting Government may at any time revoke any such special permit which it has granted.

2. Any whales taken under these special permits shall so far as practicable be processed and the proceeds shall be dealt with in accordance with directions issued by the Government by which the permit was granted.

3. Each Contracting Government shall transmit to such body as may be designated by the Commission, in so far as practicable, and at intervals of not more than one year, scientific information available to that Government with respect to whales and whaling, including the results of research conducted pursuant to paragraph 1 of this Article and to Article IV.

4. Recognizing that continuous collection and analysis of biological data in connection with the operations of factory ships and land stations are indispensable to sound and constructive management of the whale fisheries, the Contracting Governments will take all practicable measures to obtain such data.

Article IX

1. Each Contracting Government shall take appropriate measures to ensure the application of the provisions of this Convention and the punishment of infractions against the said provisions in operations carried out by persons or by vessels under its jurisdiction.

2. No bonus or other remuneration calculated with relation to the results of their work shall be paid to the gunners and crews of whale catchers in respect of any whales the taking of which is forbidden by this Convention.

3. Prosecution for infractions against or contraventions of this Convention shall be instituted by the Government having jurisdiction over the offense.

4. Each Contracting Government shall transmit to the Commission full details of each infraction of the provisions of this Convention by persons or vessels under the jurisdiction of that Government as reported by its inspectors. This information shall include a statement of measures taken for dealing with the infraction and of penalties imposed.

Article X

1. This Convention shall be ratified and the instruments of ratification shall be deposited with the Government of the United States of America.

2. Any Government which has not signed this Convention may adhere thereto after it enters into force by a notification in writing to the Government of the United States of America.

3. The Government of the United States of America shall inform all other signatory Governments and all adhering Governments of all ratifications deposited and adherences received.

4. This Convention shall, when instruments of ratification have been deposited by at least six signatory Governments, which shall include the Governments of the Netherlands, Norway, the Union of Soviet Socialist Republics, the United Kingdom of Great Britain and Northern Ireland, and the United States of America, enter into force with respect to those Governments and shall enter into force with respect to each Government which subsequently ratifies or adheres on the date of the deposit of its instrument of ratification or the receipt of its notification of adherence.

5. The provisions of the Schedule shall not apply prior to July 1, 1948. Amendments to the Schedule adopted pursuant to Article V shall not apply prior to July 1, 1949.

Article XI

Any Contracting Government may withdraw from this Convention on June thirtieth of any year by giving notice on or before January first of the same year to the depositary Government, which upon receipt of such a notice shall at once communicate it to the other Contracting Governments. Any other Contracting Government may, in like manner, within one month of the receipt of a copy of such notice from the depositary Government, give notice of withdrawal, so that the Convention shall cease to be in force on June thirtieth of the same year with respect to the Government giving notice of withdrawal.

This Convention shall bear the date on which it is opened for signature and shall remain open for signature for a period of fourteen days thereafter.

SCHEDULE

(As amended by the Commission in June 2010 at the 62nd Annual Meeting at Agadir, Morocco)

* * *

III. CAPTURE

* * *

7. (a) In accordance with Article V(1)(c) of the Convention, commercial whaling, whether by pelagic operations or from land stations, is prohibited in a region designated as the Indian Ocean Sanctuary. This comprises the waters of the Northern Hemisphere from the coast of Africa to 100°E, including the Red and Arabian Seas and the Gulf of Oman; and the waters of the Southern Hemisphere in the sector from 20°E to 130°E, with the Southern boundary set at 55°S. This prohibition applies irrespective of such catch limits for baleen or toothed whales as may from time to time be determined by the Commission. This prohibition shall be reviewed by the Commission at its Annual Meeting in 2002.[1]

(b) In accordance with Article V(1)(c) of the Convention, commercial whaling, whether by pelagic operations or from land stations, is prohibited in a region designated as the Southern Ocean Sanctuary. This Sanctuary comprises the waters of the Southern Hemisphere southwards of the following line: starting from 40 degrees S, 50 degrees W; thence due east to 20 degrees E; thence due south to 55 degrees S; thence due east to 130 degrees E; thence due north to 40 degrees S; thence due east to 130 degrees W; thence due south to 60 degrees S; thence due east to 50 degrees W; thence due north to the point of beginning. This prohibition applies irrespective of the conservation status of baleen and toothed whale stocks in this Sanctuary, as may from time to time be determined by the Commission. However, this prohibition shall be reviewed ten years after its initial adoption and at succeeding ten year intervals, and could be revised at such times by the Commission. Nothing in this sub-paragraph is intended to prejudice the special legal and political status of Antarctica.[2,3]

* * *

1. At its 54th Annual Meeting in 2002, the Commission agreed to continue this prohibition but did not discuss whether or not it should set a time when it should be reviewed again.

2. The Government of Japan lodged an objection within the prescribed period to paragraph 7(b) to the extent that it applies to the Antarctic minke whale stocks. The Government of the Russian Federation also lodged an

10. All stocks of whales shall be classified in one of three categories according to the advice of the Scientific Committee as follows:

(a) A Sustained Management Stock (SMS) is a stock which is not more than 10 per cent of Maximum Sustainable Yield (hereinafter referred to as MSY) stock level below MSY stock level, and not more than 20 per cent above that level; MSY being determined on the basis of the number of whales. When a stock has remained at a stable level for a considerable period under a regime of approximately constant catches, it shall be classified as a Sustained Management Stock in the absence of any positive evidence that it should be otherwise classified. Commercial whaling shall be permitted on Sustained Management Stocks according to the advice of the Scientific Committee. These stocks are listed in Tables 1, 2 and 3 of this Schedule. For stocks at or above the MSY stock level, the permitted catch shall not exceed 90 per cent of the MSY. For stocks between the MSY stock level and 10 per cent below that level, the permitted catch shall not exceed the number of whales obtained by taking 90 per cent of the MSY and reducing that number by 10 per cent for every 1 per cent by which the stock falls short of the MSY stock level.

(b) An Initial Management Stock (IMS) is a stock more than 20 per cent of MSY stock level above MSY stock level. Commercial whaling shall be permitted on Initial Management Stocks according to the advice of the Scientific Committee as to measures necessary to bring the stocks to the MSY stock level and then optimum level in an efficient manner and without risk of reducing them below this level. The permitted catch for such stocks will not be more than 90 per cent of MSY as far as this is known, or, where it will be more appropriate, catching effort shall be limited to that which will take 90 per cent of MSY in a stock at MSY stock level.

In the absence of any positive evidence that a continuing higher percentage will not reduce the stock below the MSY stock level no more than 5 per cent of the estimated initial exploitable stock shall be taken in any one year. Exploitation should not commence until an estimate of stock size has been obtained which is satisfactory in the view of the Scientific Committee. Stocks classified as Initial Management Stock are listed in Tables 1, 2 and 3 of this Schedule.

(c) A Protection Stock (PS) is a stock which is below 10 per cent of MSY stock level below MSY stock level. There shall be no commercial whaling on Protection Stocks. Stocks so classified are listed in Tables 1, 2 and 3 of this Schedule.

(d) Notwithstanding the other provisions of paragraph 10 there shall be a moratorium on the taking, killing or treating of whales, except minke whales, by factory ships or whale catchers attached to factory ships. This moratorium applies to sperm whales, killer whales and baleen whales, except minke whales.

(e) Notwithstanding the other provisions of paragraph 10, catch limits for the killing for commercial purposes of whales from all stocks for the 1986 coastal and the 1985/86 pelagic seasons and thereafter shall be zero. This provision will be kept under review, based upon the best scientific advice, and by 1990 at the latest the Commission will undertake a comprehensive assessment of the effects of this decision on whale

objection to paragraph 7(b) within the prescribed period but withdrew it on 26 October 1994. For all Contracting Governments except Japan paragraph 7(b) came into force on 6 December 1994.

3. Paragraph 7(b) contains a provision for review of the Southern Ocean Sanctuary "ten years after its initial adoption". Paragraph 7(b) was adopted at the 46th (1994) Annual Meeting. Therefore, the first review is due in 2004.

stocks and consider modification of this provision and the establishment of other catch limits.[4,5,6]

4. The Governments of Japan, Norway, Peru and the Union of Soviet Socialist Republics lodged objection to paragraph 10(e) within the prescribed period. For all other Contracting Governments this paragraph came into force on 3 February 1983. Peru withdrew its objection on 22 July 1983. The Government of Japan withdrew its objections with effect from 1 May 1987 with respect to commercial pelagic whaling; from 1 October 1987 with respect to commercial coastal whaling for minke and Bryde's whales; and from 1 April 1988 with respect to commercial coastal sperm whaling. The objections of Norway and the Russian Federation not having been withdrawn, the paragraph is not binding upon these Governments.

5. Iceland's instrument of adherence to the International Convention for the Regulation of Whaling and the Protocol to the Convention deposited on 10 October 2002 states that Iceland 'adheres to the aforesaid Convention and Protocol with a reservation with respect to paragraph 10(e) of the Schedule attached to the Convention'. The instrument further states the following:

'Notwithstanding this, the Government of Iceland will not authorise whaling for commercial purposes by Icelandic vessels before 2006 and, thereafter, will not authorise such whaling while progress is being made in negotiations within the IWC on the RMS. This does not apply, however, in case of the so-called moratorium on whaling for commercial purposes, contained in paragraph 10(e) of the Schedule not being lifted within a reasonable time after the completion of the RMS. Under no circumstances will whaling for commercial purposes be authorised without a sound scientific basis and an effective management and enforcement scheme.'

6. The Governments of Argentina, Australia, Brazil, Chile, Finland, France, Germany, Italy, Mexico, Monaco, the Netherlands, New Zealand, Peru, San Marino, Spain, Sweden, UK and the USA have lodged objections to Iceland's reservation to paragraph 10(e).

5.20   International Whaling Commission, Rules of Procedure. **Available from the International Whaling Commission at http://www.iwcoffice. org/_documents/commission/rules2010.pdf (accessed September 6, 2011)**

A.   Representation

1.   A Government party to the International Convention for the Regulation of Whaling, 1946 (hereafter referred to as the Convention) shall have the right to appoint one Commissioner and shall furnish the Secretary of the Commission with the name of its Commissioner and his/her designation and notify the Secretary promptly of any changes in the appointment. The Secretary shall inform other Commissioners of such appointment.

B.   Meetings

1.   The Commission shall hold a regular Annual Meeting in such place as the Commission may determine.

* * *

C.   Observers

1.   (a) Any Government not a party to the Convention or any intergovernmental organisation may be represented at meetings of the Commission by an observer or observers, if such non-party government or intergovernmental organisation has previously attended any meeting of the Commission, or if it submits its request in writing to the Commission 60 days prior to the start of the meeting, or if the Commission issues an invitation to attend.

(b) Any non-governmental organisation which expresses an interest in matters covered by the Convention, may be accredited as an observer. Requests for accreditation must be submitted in writing to the Commission 60 days prior to the start of the meeting and the Commission may issue an invitation with respect to such request. Such submissions shall include the standard application form for non-governmental organisations which will be provided by the Secretariat. These applications shall remain available for review by Contracting Governments.

Once a non-governmental organisation has been accredited through the application process above, it will remain accredited until the Commission decides otherwise.

* * *

2.   Observers accredited in accordance with Rule C.1.(a) and (b) are admitted to all meetings of the Commission and the Technical Committee, and to any meetings of subsidiary groups of the Commission and the Technical Committee, except the Commissioners-only meetings and the meetings of the Finance and Administration Committee.

* * *

E.   Decision-making

The Commission shall make every effort to reach its decisions by consensus. If all efforts to reach consensus have been exhausted and no agreement reached, the following Rules of Procedure shall apply:

1.   Each Commissioner shall have the right to vote at Plenary Meetings of the Commission and in his/her absence his/her deputy or alternate shall have such right. Experts and advisers may address Plenary Meetings of the Commission but shall not be entitled to vote. They may vote at the meetings of any committee to which they

have been appointed, provided that when such vote is taken, representatives of any Contracting Government shall only exercise one vote.

2. (a) The right to vote of representatives of any Contracting Government shall be suspended automatically when the annual payment of a Contracting Government including any interest due has not been received by the Commission. . . .

(b) The Commissioner of a new Contracting Government shall not exercise the right to vote either at meetings or by postal or other means: (i) until 30 days after the date of adherence, although they may participate fully in discussions of the Commission; and (ii) unless the Commission has received the Government's financial contribution or part contribution for the year prescribed in Financial Regulation E.3.

3. (a) Where a vote is taken on any matter before the Commission, a simple majority of those casting an affirmative or negative vote shall be decisive, except that a three-fourths majority of those casting an affirmative or negative vote shall be required for action in pursuance of Article V of the Convention.

(b) Action in pursuance of Article V shall contain the text of the regulations proposed to amend the Schedule. A proposal that does not contain such regulatory text does not constitute an amendment to the Schedule and therefore requires only a simple majority vote. A proposal that does not contain such regulatory text to revise the Schedule but would commit the Commission to amend the Schedule in the future can neither be put to a vote nor adopted.

(c) At meetings of committees appointed by the Commission, a simple majority of those casting an affirmative or negative vote shall also be decisive. The committee shall report to the Commission if the decision has been arrived at as a result of the vote.

(d) Votes shall be taken by show of hands, or by roll call, as in the opinion of the Chair, appears to be most suitable. The election of the Chair, Vice–Chair, the appointment of the Secretary of the Commission, and the selection of IWC Annual Meeting venues shall, upon request by a Commissioner, all proceed by secret ballot.

4. Between meetings of the Commission or in the case of emergency, a vote of the Commissioners may be taken by post, or other means of communication in which case the necessary simple, or where required three-fourths majority, shall be of the total number of Contracting Governments whose right to vote has not been suspended under paragraph 2.

F. Chair

1. The Chair of the Commission shall be elected from time to time from among the Commissioners and shall take office at the conclusion of the Annual Meeting at which he/she is elected. The Chair shall serve for a period of three years and shall not be eligible for re-election as Chair until a further period of three years has elapsed. The Chair shall, however, remain in office until a successor is elected.

2. The duties of the Chair shall be:

(a) to preside at all meetings of the Commission;

(b) to decide all questions of order raised at meetings of the Commission, subject to the right of any Commissioner to appeal against any ruling of the Chair.

(c) to call for votes and to announce the result of the vote to the Commission;

(d) to develop, with appropriate consultation, draft agenda for meetings of the Commission.

* * *

H. Secretary

1. The Commission shall appoint a Secretary and shall designate staff positions to be filled through appointments made by the Secretary. The Commission shall fix the terms of employment, rate of remuneration including tax assessment and superannuation and travelling expenses for the members of the Secretariat.

2. The Secretary is the executive officer of the Commission. . . .

* * *

J. Schedule amendments, recommendations under Article VI *and Resolutions*

1. No item of business which involves amendment of the Schedule to the Convention, recommendations under Article VI of the Convention, or Resolutions of the Commission, shall be the subject of decisive action by the Commission unless the full draft text has been circulated to the Commissioners at least 60 days in advance of the meeting at which the matter is to be discussed.

2. Notwithstanding the advance notice requirements for draft Resolutions in Rule J.1, at the recommendation of the Chair in consultation with the Advisory Committee, the Commission may decide to consider urgent draft Resolutions which arise after the 60 day deadline where there have been important developments that warrant action in the Commission. The full draft text of any such Resolution must be circulated to all Commissioners prior to the opening of the meeting at which the draft Resolution is to be considered.

3. Notwithstanding Rules J.1 and J.2, the Commission may adopt Resolutions on any matter that may arise during a meeting only when consensus is achieved.

* * *

M. Committees

1. The Commission shall establish a Scientific Committee, a Technical Committee and a Finance and Administration Committee. Commissioners shall notify their desire to be represented on the Scientific, Technical and Finance and Administration Committees 28 days prior to the meetings, and shall designate the approximate size of their delegations.

2. The Chair may constitute such ad hoc committees as may be necessary from time to time, with similar arrangements for notification of the numbers of participants as in paragraph 1 above where appropriate. Each committee shall elect its Chair. The Secretary shall furnish appropriate secretarial services to each committee.

3. Sub-committees and working groups may be designated by the Commission to consider technical issues as appropriate, and each will report to the Technical Committee or the plenary session of the Commission as the Commission may decide.

4. The Scientific Committee shall review the current scientific and statistical information with respect to whales and whaling, shall review current scientific research programmes of Governments, other international organisations or of private organisations, shall review the scientific permits and scientific programmes for which Contracting Governments plan to issue scientific permits, shall consider such additional matters as may be referred to it by the Commission or by the Chair of the Commission, and shall submit reports and recommendations to the Commission.

5. The preliminary report of the Scientific Committee should be completed and available to all Commissioners by the opening date of the Annual Commission Meeting.

6. The Secretary shall be an *ex officio* member of the Scientific Committee without vote.

7. The Technical Committee shall, as directed by the Commission or the Chair of the Commission, prepare reports and make recommendations on:

(a) Management principles, categories, criteria and definitions, taking into account the recommendations of the Scientific Committee, as a means of helping the Commission to deal with management issues as they arise;

(b) technical and practical options for implementation of conservation measures based on Scientific Committee advice;

(c) the implementation of decisions taken by the Commission through resolutions and through Schedule provisions;

(d) Commission agenda items assigned to it;

(e) any other matters.

* * *

R. Amendment of Rules

1. These Rules of Procedure and the Rules of Debate may be amended from time to time by a simple majority of the Commissioners voting, but the full draft text of any proposed amendment shall be circulated to the Commissioners at least 60 days in advance of the meeting at which the matter is to be discussed.

* * *

RULES OF DEBATE

A. Right to Speak

1. The Chair shall call upon speakers in the order in which they signify their desire to speak.

2. A Commissioner or Observer may speak only if called upon by the Chair, who may call a speaker to order if his/her remarks are not relevant to the subject under discussion.

3. A speaker shall not be interrupted except on a point of order. He/she may, however, with the permission of the Chair, give way during his/her speech to allow any other Commissioner to request elucidation on a particular point in that speech.

4. The Chair of a committee or working group may be accorded precedence for the purpose of explaining the conclusion arrived at by his/her committee or group.

B. Submission of Motions

1. Proposals and amendments shall normally be introduced in writing in the working language of the meeting and shall be submitted to the Secretariat which shall circulate copies to all delegations in the session. As a general rule, no proposal shall be discussed at any plenary session unless copies of it have been circulated to all delegations normally no later than 6pm, or earlier if so determined by the Chair in consultation with the Commissioners, on the day preceding the plenary session. The presiding officer may, however, permit the discussion and consideration of amendments, or motions, as to procedure, even though such amendments, or motions have not been circulated previously.

C. Procedural Motions

1. During the discussion of any matter, a Commissioner may rise to a point of order, and the point of order shall be immediately decided by the Chair in accordance with these Rules of Procedure. A Commissioner may appeal against any ruling of the Chair. The appeal shall be immediately put to the vote and the question voted upon

shall be stated as: Shall the decision of the Chair be overturned? The Chair's ruling shall stand unless a majority of the Commissioners present and voting otherwise decide. A Commissioner rising to a point of order may not speak on the substance of the matter under discussion.

* * *

3. Notwithstanding anything in these Rules, the Chair may suspend the meeting for a brief period at any time in order to allow informal discussions aimed at reaching consensus consistent with Rule E of the Rules of Procedure.

D. Arrangements for Debate

1. The Commission may, in a proposal by the Chair or by a Commissioner, limit the time to be allowed to each speaker and the number of times the members of a delegation may speak on any question. When the debate is subject to such limits, and a speaker has spoken for his allotted time, the Chair shall call him/her to order without delay.

* * *

4. A Commissioner may at any time move the closure of the debate on the particular subject or question under discussion, whether or not any other Commissioner has signified the wish to speak. Permission to speak on the motion for the closure of the debate shall be accorded only to two Commissioners wishing to speak against the motion, after which the motion shall immediately be put to the vote. The Chair may limit the time to be allowed to speakers under this rule.

E. Procedure for Voting on Motions and Amendments

1. A Commissioner may move that parts of a proposal or of an amendment shall be voted on separately. . . .

2. When the amendment is moved to a proposal, the amendment shall be voted on first. . . .

* * *

PART 6. POLAR REGIONS

A. ANTARCTIC

6.1 ANTARCTIC TREATY.[a] **Concluded at Washington, 1 December 1959. Entered into force, 23 June 1961. 402 UNTS 71, 12 UST 794;** *reprinted in* **19 ILM 860 (1980) & 5 Weston & Carlson V.D.1**

The Governments of Argentina, Australia, Belgium, Chile, the French Republic, Japan, New Zealand, Norway, the Union of South Africa, the Union of Soviet Socialist Republics, the United Kingdom of Great Britain and Northern Ireland, and the United States of America,

Recognizing that it is in the interest of all mankind that Antarctica shall continue forever to be used exclusively for peaceful purposes and shall not become the scene or object of international discord;

Acknowledging the substantial contributions to scientific knowledge resulting from international cooperation in scientific investigation in Antarctica;

Convinced that the establishment of a firm foundation for the continuation and development of such cooperation on the basis of freedom of scientific investigation in Antarctica as applied during the International Geophysical Year accords with the interests of science and the progress of all mankind;

Convinced also that a treaty ensuring the use of Antarctica for peaceful purposes only and the continuance of international harmony in Antarctica will further the purposes and principles embodied in the Charter of the United Nations;

Have agreed as follows:

Article I

1. Antarctica shall be used for peaceful purposes only. There shall be prohibited, *inter alia,* any measures of a military nature, such as the establishment of military bases and fortifications, the carrying out of military maneuvers, as well as the testing of any type of weapons.

2. The present Treaty shall not prevent the use of military personnel or equipment for scientific research or for any other peaceful purpose.

Article II

Freedom of scientific investigation in Antarctica and cooperation toward that end, as applied during the International Geophysical Year, shall continue, subject to the provisions of the present Treaty.

Article III

1. In order to promote international cooperation in scientific investigation in Antarctica, as provided for in Article II of the present Treaty, the Contracting Parties agree that, to the greatest extent feasible and practicable:

(*a*) information regarding plans for scientific programs in Antarctica shall be exchanged to permit maximum economy and efficiency of operations;

a. *See also* Basic Document 6.9, *infra.*

(*b*) scientific personnel shall be exchanged in Antarctica between expeditions and stations;

(*c*) scientific observations and results from Antarctica shall be exchanged and made freely available.

2. In implementing this Article, every encouragement shall be given to the establishment of cooperative working relations with those Specialized Agencies of the United Nations and other international organizations having a scientific or technical interest in Antarctica.

Article IV

1. Nothing contained in the present Treaty shall be interpreted as:

(*a*) a renunciation by any Contracting Party of previously asserted rights of or claims to territorial sovereignty in Antarctica;

(*b*) a renunciation or diminution by any Contracting Party of any basis of claim to territorial sovereignty in Antarctica which it may have whether as a result of its activities or those of its nationals in Antarctica, or otherwise;

(*c*) prejudicing the position of any Contracting Party as regards its recognition or non-recognition of any other State's right of or claim or basis of claim to territorial sovereignty in Antarctica.

2. No acts or activities taking place while the present Treaty is in force shall constitute a basis for asserting, supporting or denying a claim to territorial sovereignty in Antarctica or create any rights of sovereignty in Antarctica. No new claim, or enlargement of an existing claim, to territorial sovereignty in Antarctica shall be asserted while the present Treaty is in force.

Article V

1. Any nuclear explosions in Antarctica and the disposal there of radioactive waste material shall be prohibited.

2. In the event of the conclusion of international agreements concerning the use of nuclear energy, including nuclear explosions and the disposal of radioactive waste material, to which all of the Contracting Parties whose representatives are entitled to participate in the meetings provided for under Article IX are parties, the rules established under such agreements shall apply in Antarctica.

Article VI

The provisions of the present Treaty shall apply to the area south of 60E South Latitude, including all ice shelves, but nothing in the present Treaty shall prejudice or in any way affect the rights, or the exercise of the rights, of any State under international law with regard to the high seas within that area.

Article VII

1. In order to promote the objectives and ensure the observance of the provisions of the present Treaty, each Contracting Party whose representatives are entitled to participate in the meetings referred to in Article IX of the Treaty shall have the right to designate observers to carry out any inspection provided for by the present Article. Observers shall be nationals of the Contracting Parties which designate them. The names of observers shall be communicated to every other Contracting Party having the right to designate observers, and like notice shall be given of the termination of their appointment.

2. Each observer designated in accordance with the provisions of paragraph 1 of this Article shall have complete freedom of access at any time to any or all areas of Antarctica.

3. All areas of Antarctica, including all stations, installations and equipment within those areas, and all ships and aircraft at points of discharging or embarking cargoes or personnel in Antarctica, shall be open at all times to inspection by any observers designated in accordance with paragraph 1 of this Article.

4. Aerial observation may be carried out at any time over any or all areas of Antarctica by any of the Contracting Parties having the right to designate observers.

5. Each Contracting Party shall, at the time when the present Treaty enters into force for it, inform the other Contracting Parties, and thereafter shall give them notice in advance, of

(*a*) all expeditions to and within Antarctica, on the part of its ships or nationals, and all expeditions to Antarctica organized in or proceeding from its territory;

(*b*) all stations in Antarctica occupied by its nationals; and

(*c*) any military personnel or equipment intended to be introduced by it into Antarctica subject to the conditions prescribed in paragraph 2 of Article I of the present Treaty.

Article VIII

1. In order to facilitate the exercise of their functions under the present Treaty, and without prejudice to the respective positions of the Contracting Parties relating to jurisdiction over all other persons in Antarctica, observers designated under paragraph 1 of Article VII and scientific personnel exchanged under subparagraph 1(*b*) of Article III of the Treaty, and members of the staffs accompanying any such persons, shall be subject only to the jurisdiction of the Contracting Party of which they are nationals in respect of all acts or omissions occurring while they are in Antarctica for the purpose of exercising their functions.

2. Without prejudice to the provisions of paragraph 1 of this Article, and pending the adoption of measures in pursuance of subparagraph 1(*e*) of Article IX, the Contracting Parties concerned in any case of dispute with regard to the exercise of jurisdiction in Antarctica shall immediately consult together with a view to reaching a mutually acceptable solution.

Article IX

1. Representatives of the Contracting Parties named in the preamble to the present Treaty shall meet at the City of Canberra within two months after the date of entry into force of the Treaty, and thereafter at suitable intervals and places, for the purpose of exchanging information, consulting together on matters of common interest pertaining to Antarctica, and formulating and considering, and recommending to their Governments, measures in furtherance of the principles and objectives of the Treaty, including measures regarding:

(*a*) use of Antarctica for peaceful purposes only;

(*b*) facilitation of scientific research in Antarctica;

(*c*) facilitation of international scientific cooperation in Antarctica;

(*d*) facilitation of the exercise of the rights of inspection provided for in Article VII of the Treaty;

(*e*) questions relating to the exercise of jurisdiction in Antarctica;

(*f*) preservation and conservation of living resources in Antarctica.

2. Each Contracting Party which has become a party to the present Treaty by accession under Article XIII shall be entitled to appoint representatives to participate in the meetings referred to in paragraph 1 of the present Article, during such time as that Contracting Party demonstrates its interest in Antarctica by conducting substantial scientific research activity there, such as the establishment of a scientific station or the despatch of a scientific expedition.

3. Reports from the observers referred to in Article VII of the present Treaty shall be transmitted to the representatives of the Contracting Parties participating in the meetings referred to in paragraph 1 of the present Article.

4. The measures referred to in paragraph 1 of this Article shall become effective when approved by all the Contracting Parties whose representatives were entitled to participate in the meetings held to consider those measures.

5. Any or all of the rights established in the present Treaty may be exercised as from the date of entry into force of the Treaty whether or not any measures facilitating the exercise of such rights have been proposed, considered or approved as provided in this Article.

Article X

Each of the Contracting Parties undertakes to exert appropriate efforts, consistent with the Charter of the United Nations, to the end that no one engages in any activity in Antarctica contrary to the principles or purposes of the present Treaty.

Article XI

1. If any dispute arises between two or more of the Contracting Parties concerning the interpretation or application of the present Treaty, those Contracting Parties shall consult among themselves with a view to having the dispute resolved by negotiation, inquiry, mediation, conciliation, arbitration, judicial settlement or other peaceful means of their own choice.

2. Any dispute of this character not so resolved shall, with the consent, in each case, of all parties to the dispute, be referred to the International Court of Justice for settlement; but failure to reach agreement on reference to the International Court shall not absolve parties to the dispute from the responsibility of continuing to seek to resolve it by any of the various peaceful means referred to in paragraph 1 of this Article.

Article XII

1. (*a*) The present Treaty may be modified or amended at any time by unanimous agreement of the Contracting Parties whose representatives are entitled to participate in the meetings provided for under Article IX. Any such modification or amendment shall enter into force when the depositary Government has received notice from all such Contracting Parties that they have ratified it.

    (*b*) Such modification or amendment shall thereafter enter into force as to any other Contracting Party when notice of ratification by it has been received by the depositary Government. Any such Contracting Party from which no notice of ratification is received within a period of two years from the date of entry into force of the modification or amendment in accordance with the provisions of subparagraph 1 (*a*) of this Article shall be deemed to have withdrawn from the present Treaty on the date of the expiration of such period.

2. (*a*) If after the expiration of thirty years from the date of entry into force of the present Treaty, any of the Contracting Parties whose representatives are entitled to participate in the meetings provided for under Article IX so requests by a communi-

cation addressed to the depositary Government, a Conference of all the Contracting Parties shall be held as soon as practicable to review the operation of the Treaty.

(b) Any modification or amendment to the present Treaty which is approved at such a Conference by a majority of the Contracting Parties there represented, including a majority of those whose representatives are entitled to participate in the meetings provided for under Article IX, shall be communicated by the depositary Government to all the Contracting Parties immediately after the termination of the Conference and shall enter into force in accordance with the provisions of paragraph 1 of the present Article.

(c) If any such modification or amendment has not entered into force in accordance with the provisions of subparagraph 1 (a) of this Article within a period of two years after the date of its communication to all the Contracting Parties, any Contracting Party may at any time after the expiration of that period give notice to the depositary Government of its withdrawal from the present Treaty; and such withdrawal shall take effect two years after the receipt of the notice by the depositary Government.

Article XIII

1. The present Treaty shall be subject to ratification by the signatory States. It shall be open for accession by any State which is a Member of the United Nations, or by any other State which may be invited to accede to the Treaty with the consent of all the Contracting Parties whose representatives are entitled to participate in the meetings provided for under Article IX of the Treaty.

2. Ratification of or accession to the present Treaty shall be effected by each State in accordance with its constitutional processes.

3. Instruments of ratification and instruments of accession shall be deposited with the Government of the United States of America, hereby designated as the depositary Government.

4. The depositary Government shall inform all signatory and acceding States of the date of each deposit of an instrument of ratification or accession, and the date of entry into force of the Treaty and of any modification or amendment thereto.

5. Upon the deposit of instruments of ratification by all the signatory States, the present Treaty shall enter into force for those States and for States which have deposited instruments of accession. Thereafter the Treaty shall enter into force for any acceding State upon the deposit of its instrument of accession.

6. The present Treaty shall be registered by the depositary Government pursuant to Article 102 of the Charter of the United Nations.

Article XIV

The present Treaty, done in the English, French, Russian and Spanish languages, each version being equally authentic, shall be deposited in the archives of the Government of the United States of America, which shall transmit duly certified copies thereof to the Governments of the signatory and acceding States.

**6.2 CERTAIN RECOMMENDATIONS OF THIRD ANTARCTIC TREATY CONSULTATIVE MEETING,
      ANNEX: AGREED MEASURES FOR THE CONSERVATION OF ANTARCTIC FAUNA AND
      FLORA. Concluded at Brussels, 13 June 1964. 17 UST 992, TIAS No
      6058; *reprinted in* 5 Weston & Carlson V.D.2**

The Representatives, taking into consideration Article IX of the Antarctic Treaty, and recalling Recommendation I–VIII of the First Consultative Meeting and Recommendation II–II of the Second Consultative Meeting, recommend to their Governments that they approve as soon as possible and implement without delay the annexed "Agreed Measures for the Conservation of Antarctic Fauna and Flora".

Preamble

The Governments participating in the Third Consultative Meeting under Article IX of the Antarctic Treaty,

Desiring to implement the principles and purposes of the Antarctic Treaty;

Recognising the scientific importance of the study of Antarctic fauna and flora, their adaptation to their rigorous environment, and their interrelationship with that environment;

Considering the unique nature of these fauna and flora, their circumpolar range, and particularly their defencelessness and susceptibility to extermination;

Desiring by further international collaboration within the framework of the Antarctic Treaty to promote and achieve the objectives of protection, scientific study, and rational use of these fauna and flora; and

Having particular regard to the conservation principles developed by the Scientific Committee on Antarctic Research (SCAR) of the International Council of Scientific Unions;

Hereby consider the Treaty Area as a Special Conservation Area and have agreed on the following measures:

Article I

1. These Agreed Measures shall apply to the same area to which the Antarctic Treaty is applicable (hereinafter referred to as the Treaty Area) namely the area south of 60E South Latitude, including all ice shelves.

However, nothing in these Agreed Measures shall prejudice or in any way affect the rights, or the exercise of the rights, of any State under international law with regard to the high seas within the Treaty Area, or restrict the implementation of the provisions of the Antarctic Treaty with respect to inspection.

2. The Annexes to these Agreed Measures shall form an integral part thereof, and all references to the Agreed Measures shall be considered to include the Annexes.

Article II

For the purposes of these Agreed Measures:

a) "Native mammal" means any member, at any stage of its life cycle, of any species belonging to the Class Mammalia indigenous to the Antarctic or occurring there through natural agencies of dispersal, excepting whales;

b) "native bird" means any member, at any stage of its life cycle (including eggs), of any species of the Class Aves indigenous to the Antarctic or occurring there through natural agencies of dispersal;

c) "native plant" means any kind of vegetation at any stage of its life cycle (including seeds), indigenous to the Antarctic or occurring there through natural agencies of dispersal;

d) "appropriate authority" means any person authorised by a Participating Government to issue permits under these Agreed Measures;

e) "permit" means a formal permission in writing issued by an appropriate authority;

f) "participating government" means any Government for which these Agreed Measures have become effective in accordance with Article XIII of these Agreed Measures.

Article III

Each Participating Government shall take appropriate action to carry out these Agreed Measures.

Article IV

The Participating Governments shall prepare and circulate to members of expeditions and stations information to ensure understanding and observance of the provisions of these Agreed Measures, setting forth in particular prohibited activities, and providing lists of specially protected species and specially protected areas.

Article V

The provisions of these Agreed Measures shall not apply in cases of extreme emergency involving possible loss of human life or involving the safety of ships or aircraft.

Article VI

1. Each Participating Government shall prohibit within the Treaty Area the killing, wounding, capturing or molesting of any native mammal or native bird, or any attempt at any such act, except in accordance with a permit.

2. Such permits shall be drawn in terms as specific as possible and issued only for the following purposes:

a) to provide indispensable food for men or dogs in the Treaty Area in limited quantities, and in conformity with the purposes and principles of these Agreed Measures;

b) to provide specimens for scientific study or scientific information;

c) to provide specimens for museums, zoological gardens, or other educational or cultural institutions or uses.

3. Permits for Specially Protected Areas shall be issued only in accordance with the provisions of Article VIII.

4. Participating Governments shall limit the issue of such permits so as to ensure as far as possible that:

a) no more native mammals or birds are killed or taken in any year than can normally be replaced by natural reproduction in the following breeding season;

b) the variety of species and the balance of the natural ecological systems existing within the Treaty Area are maintained.

5. The species of native mammals and birds listed in Annex A of these Measures shall be designated "Specially Protected Species", and shall be accorded special protection by Participating Governments.

6. A Participating Government shall not authorise an appropriate authority to issue a permit with respect to a Specially Protected Species except in accordance with paragraph 7 of this Article.

7. A permit may be issued under this Article with respect to a Specially Protected Species, provided that:

a) it is issued for a compelling scientific purpose, and;

b) the actions permitted thereunder will not jeopardise the existing natural ecological system or the survival of that species.

Article VII

1. Each Participating Government shall take appropriate measures to minimize harmful interference within the Treaty Area with the normal living conditions of any native mammal or bird, or any attempt at such harmful interference, except as permitted under Article VI.

2. The following acts and activities shall be considered as harmful interference:

a) allowing dogs to run free;

b) flying helicopters or other aircraft in a manner which would unnecessarily disturb bird and seal concentrations, or landing close to such concentrations (e.g. within 200 metres);

c) driving vehicles unnecessarily close to concentrations of birds and seals (e.g. within 200 metres);

d) use of explosives close to concentrations of birds and seals;

e) discharge of firearms close to bird and seal concentrations (e.g. within 300 metres);

f) any disturbance of bird and seal colonies during the breeding period by persistent attention from persons on foot.

However, the above activities, with the exception of those mentioned in a) and e) may be permitted to the minimum extent necessary for the establishment, supply and operation of stations.

3. Each Participating Government shall take all reasonable steps towards the alleviation of pollution of the waters adjacent to the coast and ice shelves.

Article VIII

1. The areas of outstanding scientific interest listed in Annex B shall be designated "Specially Protected Areas" and shall be accorded special protection by the Participating Governments in order to preserve their unique natural ecological system.

2. In addition to the prohibitions and measures of protection dealt with in other Articles of these Agreed Measures, the Participating Governments shall in Specially Protected Areas further prohibit:

a) the collection of any native plant, except in accordance with a permit;

b) the driving of any vehicle.

3. A permit issued under Article VI shall not have effect within a Specially Protected Area except in accordance with paragraph 4 of the present Article.

4. A permit shall have effect within a Specially Protected Area provided that:

a) it was issued for a compelling scientific purpose which cannot be served elsewhere; and

b) the actions permitted thereunder will not jeopardise the natural ecological system existing in that Area.

Article IX

1. Each Participating Government shall prohibit the bringing into the Treaty Area of any species of animal or plant not indigenous to that Area, except in accordance with a permit.

2. Permits under paragraph 1 of this Article shall be drawn in terms as specific as possible and shall be issued to allow the importation only of the animals and plants listed in Annex C. When any such animal or plant might cause harmful interference with the natural system if left unsupervised within the Treaty Area, such permits shall require that it be kept under controlled conditions and, after it has served its purpose, it shall be removed from the Treaty Area or destroyed.

3. Nothing in paragraphs 1 and 2 of this Article shall apply to the importation of food into the Treaty Area so long as animals and plants used for this purpose are kept under controlled conditions.

4. Each Participating Government undertakes to ensure that all reasonable precautions shall be taken to prevent the accidental introduction of parasites and diseases into the Treaty Area. In particular, the precautions listed in Annex D shall be taken.

Article X

Each Participating Government undertakes to exert appropriate efforts, consistent with the Charter of the United Nations, to the end that no one engages in any activity in the Treaty Area contrary to the principles or purposes of these Agreed Measures.

Article XI

Each Participating Government whose expeditions use ships sailing under flags of nationalities other than its own shall, as far as feasible, arrange with the owners of such ships that the crews of these ships observe these Agreed Measures.

Article XII

1. The Participating Governments may make such arrangements as may be necessary for the discussion of such matters as:

a) the collection and exchange of records (including records of permits) and statistics concerning the numbers of each species of native mammal and bird killed or captured annually in the Treaty Area;

b) the obtaining and exchange of information as to the status of native mammals and birds in the Treaty Area, and the extent to which any species needs protection;

c) the number of native mammals or birds which should be permitted to be harvested for food, scientific study, or other uses in the various regions;

d) the establishment of a common form in which this information shall be submitted by Participating Governments in accordance with paragraph 2 of this Article.

2. Each Participating Government shall inform the other Governments in writing before the end of November of each year of the steps taken and information collected in the preceding period of July 1st to June 30th relating to the implementation of these Agreed Measures. Governments exchanging information under paragraph 5 of Article VII of the Antarctic Treaty may at the same time transmit the information relating to the implementation of these Agreed Measures.

Article XIII

1. After the receipt by the Government designated in Recommendation I–XIV (5) of notification of approval by all Governments whose representatives are entitled to participate in meetings provided for under Article IX of the Antarctic Treaty, these Agreed Measures shall become effective for those Governments.

2. Thereafter any other Contracting Party to the Antarctic Treaty may, in consonance with the purposes of Recommendation III–VII, accept these Agreed Measures by notifying the designated Government of its intention to apply the Agreed Measures and to be bound by them. The Agreed Measures shall become effective with regard to such Governments on the date of receipt of such notification.

3. The designated Government shall inform the Governments referred to in paragraph 1 of this Article of each notification of approval, the effective date of these Agreed Measures and of each notification of acceptance. The designated Government shall also inform any Government which has accepted these Agreed Measures of each subsequent notification of acceptance.

Article XIV

1. These Agreed Measures may be amended at any time by unanimous agreement of the Governments whose Representatives are entitled to participate in meetings under Article IX of the Antarctic Treaty.

2. The Annexes, in particular, may be amended as necessary through diplomatic channels.

3. An amendment proposed through diplomatic channels shall be submitted in writing to the designated Government which shall communicate it to the Governments referred to in paragraph 1. of the present Article for approval; at the same time, it shall be communicated to the other Participating Governments.

4. Any amendment shall become effective on the date on which notifications of approval have been received by the designated Government from all of the Governments referred to in paragraph 1. of this article.

5. The designated Government shall notify those same Governments of the date of receipt of each approval communicated to it and the date on which the amendment will become effective for them.

6. Such amendment shall become effective on that same date for all other Participating Governments, except those which before the expiry of two months after that date notify the designated Government that they do not accept it.

ANNEXES TO THESE AGREED MEASURES

Annex A

Specially protected species

* * *

Annex B

Specially protected areas

Annex C

Importation of animals and plants

The following animals and plants may be imported into the Treaty Area in accordance with permits issued under Article IX (2) of these Agreed Measures:

    a) sledge dogs;

    b) domestic animals and plants;

c) laboratory animals and plants.

Annex D

Precautions to prevent accidental introduction of parasites and diseases into the Treaty Area

The following precautions shall be taken:

1. <u>Dogs</u>: All dogs imported into the Treaty Area shall be inoculated against the following diseases:

a) distemper;

b) contagious canine hepatitis;

c) rabies

d) leptospirosis (*L. canicola* and *L. icterohaemorrhagicae*).

Each dog shall be inoculated at least two months before the time of its arrival in the Treaty Area.

2. <u>Poultry</u>: Notwithstanding the provisions of Article IX (3) of these Agreed Measures, no living poultry shall be brought into the Treaty Area after July 1st 1966.

6.3 CONVENTION FOR THE CONSERVATION OF ANTARCTIC SEALS (With Annex). Concluded at London, 1 June 1972. Entered into force, 11 March 1978. 1080 UNTS 175; 29 UST 441, TIAS No 8826; *reprinted in* 11 ILM 251 (1972) & 5 Weston & Carlson V.D.3

The Contracting Parties,

Recalling the Agreed Measures for the Conservation of Antarctic Fauna and Flora, adopted under the Antarctic Treaty signed at Washington on 1 December 1959;

Recognizing the general concern about the vulnerability of Antarctic seals to commercial exploitation and the consequent need for effective conservation measures;

Recognizing that the stocks of Antarctic seals are an important living resource in the marine environment which requires an international agreement for its effective conservation;

Recognizing that this resource should not be depleted by over-exploitation, and hence that any harvesting should be regulated so as not to exceed the levels of the optimum sustainable yield;

Recognizing that in order to improve scientific knowledge and so place exploitation on a rational basis, every effort should be made both to encourage biological and other research on Antarctic seal populations and to gain information from such research and from the statistics of future sealing operations, so that further suitable regulations may be formulated;

Noting that the Scientific Committee on Antarctic Research of the International Council of Scientific Unions (SCAR) is willing to carry out the tasks requested of it in this Convention;

Desiring to promote and achieve the objectives of protection, scientific study and rational use of Antarctic seals, and to maintain a satisfactory balance within the ecological system,

Have agreed as follows:

Article 1
Scope

1.   This Convention applies to the seas south of 60E South Latitude, in respect of which the Contracting Parties affirm the provisions of Article IV of the Antarctic Treaty.

2.   This Convention may be applicable to any or all of the following species:

Southern elephant seal *Mirounga leonina,*

Leopard seal *Hydrurga leptonyx,*

Weddell seal *Leptonychotes weddelli,*

Crabeater seal *Lobodon carcinophagus,*

Ross seal *Ommatophoca rossi,*

Southern fur seals *Arctocephalus* sp.

3.   The Annex to this Convention forms an integral part thereof.

Article 2
Implementation

1.   The Contracting Parties agree that the species of seals enumerated in Article 1 shall not be killed or captured within the Convention area by their nationals or vessels under their respective flags except in accordance with the provisions of this Convention.

2. Each Contracting Party shall adopt for its nationals and for vessels under its flag such laws, regulations and other measures, including a permit system as appropriate, as may be necessary to implement this Convention.

Article 3
Annexed Measures

1. This Convention includes an Annex specifying measures which the Contracting Parties hereby adopt. Contracting Parties may from time to time in the future adopt other measures with respect to the conservation, scientific study and rational and humane use of seal resources, prescribing *inter alia:*

(a) permissible catch;

(b) protected and unprotected species;

(c) open and closed seasons;

(d) open and closed areas, including the designation of reserves;

(e) the designation of special areas where there shall be no disturbance of seals;

(f) limits relating to sex, size, or age for each species;

(g) restrictions relating to time of day and duration, limitations of effort and methods of sealing;

(h) types and specifications of gear and apparatus and appliances which may be used;

(i) catch returns and other statistical and biological records;

(j) procedures for facilitating the review and assessment of scientific information;

(k) other regulatory measures including an effective system of inspection.

2. The measures adopted under paragraph 1 of this Article shall be based upon the best scientific and technical evidence available.

3. The Annex may from time to time be amended in accordance with the procedures provided for in Article 9.

Article 4
Special Permits

1. Notwithstanding the provisions of this Convention, any Contracting Party may issue permits to kill or capture seals in limited quantities and in conformity with the objectives and principles of this Convention for the following purposes:

(a) to provide indispensable food for men or dogs;

(b) to provide for scientific research; or

(c) to provide specimens for museums, educational or cultural institutions.

2. Each Contracting Party shall, as soon as possible, inform the other Contracting Parties and SCAR of the purpose and content of all permits issued under paragraph 1 of this Article and subsequently of the numbers of seals killed or captured under these permits.

Article 5
Exchange of Information and Scientific Advice

1. Each Contracting Party shall provide to the other Contracting Parties and to SCAR the information specified in the Annex within the period indicated therein.

2. Each Contracting Party shall also provide to the other Contracting Parties and to SCAR before 31 October each year information on any steps it has taken in accordance with Article 2 of this Convention during the preceding period 1 July to 30 June.

3. Contracting Parties which have no information to report under the two preceding paragraphs shall indicate this formally before 31 October each year.

4. SCAR is invited:

(a) to assess information received pursuant to this Article; encourage exchange of scientific data and information among the Contracting Parties; recommend programmes for scientific research; recommend statistical and biological data to be collected by sealing expeditions within the Convention area; and suggest amendments to the Annex; and

(b) to report on the basis of the statistical, biological and other evidence available when the harvest of any species of seal in the Convention area is having a significantly harmful effect on the total stocks of such species or on the ecological system in any particular locality.

5. SCAR is invited to notify the Depositary which shall report to the Contracting Parties when SCAR estimates in any sealing season that the permissible catch limits for any species are likely to be exceeded and, in that case, to provide an estimate of the date upon which the permissible catch limits will be reached. Each Contracting Party shall then take appropriate measures to prevent its nationals and vessels under its flag from killing or capturing seals of that species after the estimated date until the Contracting Parties decide otherwise.

6. SCAR may if necessary seek the technical assistance of the Food and Agriculture Organization of the United Nations in making its assessments.

7. Notwithstanding the provisions of paragraph 1 of Article 1 the Contracting Parties shall, in accordance with their internal law, report to each other and to SCAR, for consideration statistics relating to the Antarctic seals listed in paragraph 2 of Article 1 which have been killed or captured by their nationals and vessels under their respective flags in the area of floating sea ice north of 60E South Latitude.

Article 6
Consultations Between Contracting Parties

1. At any time after commercial sealing has begun a Contracting Party may propose through the Depositary that a meeting of Contracting Parties be convened with a view to:

(a) establishing by a two-third majority of the Contracting Parties, including the concurring votes of all States signatory to this Convention present at the meeting, an effective system of control, including inspection, over the implementation of the provisions of this Convention;

(b) establishing a commission to perform such functions under this Convention as the Contracting Parties may deem necessary; or

(c) considering other proposals, including:

(i) the provision of independent scientific advice;

(ii) the establishment, by a two-thirds majority, of a scientific advisory committee which may be assigned some or all of the functions requested of SCAR under this Convention, if commercial sealing reaches significant proportions;

(iii) the carrying out of scientific programmes with the participation of the Contracting Parties; and

(iv) the provision of further regulatory measures, including moratoria.

2. If one-third of the Contracting Parties indicate agreement the Depositary shall convene such a meeting, as soon as possible.

3. A meeting shall be held at the request of any Contracting Party, if SCAR reports that the harvest of any species of Antarctic seal in the area to which this Convention applies is having a significantly harmful effect on the total stocks or the ecological system in any particular locality.

Article 7
Review of Operations

The Contracting Parties shall meet within five years after the entry into force of this Convention and at least every five years thereafter to review the operation of the Convention.

Article 8
Amendments to the Convention

1. This Convention may be amended at any time. The text of any amendment proposed by a Contracting Party shall be submitted to the Depositary, which shall transmit it to all the Contracting Parties.

2. If one third of the Contracting Parties request a meeting to discuss the proposed amendment the Depositary shall call such a meeting.

3. An amendment shall enter into force when the Depositary has received instruments of ratification or acceptance thereof from all the Contracting Parties.

Article 9
Amendments to the Annex

1. Any Contracting Party may propose amendments to the Annex to this Convention. The text of any such proposed amendment shall be submitted to the Depositary which shall transmit it to all Contracting Parties.

2. Each such proposed amendment shall become effective for all Contracting Parties six months after the date appearing on the notification from the Depositary to the Contracting Parties, if within 120 days of the notification date, no objection has been received and two-thirds of the Contracting Parties have notified the Depositary in writing of their approval.

3. If an objection is received from any Contracting Party within 120 days of the notification date, the matter shall be considered by the Contracting Parties at their next meeting. If unanimity on the matter is not reached at the meeting, the Contracting Parties shall notify the Depositary within 120 days from the date of closure of the meeting of their approval or rejection of the original amendment or of any new amendment proposed by the meeting. If, by the end of this period, two-thirds of the Contracting Parties have approved such amendment, it shall become effective six months from the date of the closure of the meeting for those Contracting Parties which have by then notified their approval.

4. Any Contracting Party which has objected to a proposed amendment may at any time withdraw that objection, and the proposed amendment shall become effective with respect to such Party immediately if the amendment is already in effect, or at such time as it becomes effective under the terms of this Article.

5. The Depositary shall notify each Contracting Party immediately upon receipt of each approval or objection, of each withdrawal of objection, and of the entry into force of any amendment.

6. Any State which becomes a party to this Convention after an amendment to the Annex has entered into force shall be bound by the Annex as so amended. Any State which becomes a Party to this Convention during the period when a proposed amendment is pending may approve or object to such an amendment within the time limits applicable to other Contracting Parties.

Article 10
Signature

This Convention shall be open for signature at London from 1 June to 31 December 1972 by States participating in the Conference on the Conservation of Antarctic Seals held at London from 3 to 11 February 1972.

Article 11
Ratification

This Convention is subject to ratification or acceptance. Instruments of ratification or acceptance shall be deposited with the Government of the United Kingdom of Great Britain and Northern Ireland, hereby designated as the Depositary.

Article 12
Accession

The Convention shall be open for accession by any State which may be invited to accede to this Convention with the consent of all the Contracting Parties.

Article 13
Entry into Force

1. This Convention shall enter into force on the thirtieth day following the date of deposit of the seventh instrument of ratification or acceptance.

2. Thereafter this Convention shall enter into force for each ratifying, accepting or acceding State on the thirtieth day after deposit by such State of its instrument of ratification, acceptance or accession.

Article 14
Withdrawal

Any Contracting Party may withdraw from this Convention on 30 June of any year by giving notice on or before 1 January of the same year to the Depositary which upon receipt of such a notice shall at once communicate it to the other Contracting Parties. Any other Contracting Party may, in like manner, within one month of the receipt of a copy of such a notice from the Depositary, give notice of withdrawal, so that the Convention shall cease to be in force on 30 June of the same year with respect to the Contracting Party giving such notice.

Article 15
Notification by the Depositary

The Depositary shall notify all signatory and acceding States of the following:

(a) signatures of this Convention, the deposit of instruments of ratification, acceptance or accession and notices of withdrawal;

(b) the date of entry into force of this Convention and of any amendments to it or its Annex.

Article 16
Certified Copies and Registration

1. This Convention, done in the English, French, Russian and Spanish languages, each version being equally authentic, shall be deposited in the archives of the

Government of the United Kingdom of Great Britain and Northern Ireland, which shall transmit duly certified copies thereof to all signatory and acceding States.

2. This Convention shall be registered by the Depositary pursuant to Article 102 of the Charter of the United Nations.

ANNEX

1. *Permissible Catch*

The Contracting Parties shall in any one year, which shall run from 1 July to 30 June inclusive, restrict the total number of seals of each species killed or captured to the numbers specified below. These numbers are subject to review in the light of scientific assessments.

(a) in the case of Crabeater seals *Lobodon carcinophague* 175,000

(b) in the case of Leopard seals *Hydrurga leptonyx* 12,000

(c) in the case of Weddell seals *Leptonychotes weddelli,* 5,000

2. *Protected Species*

(a) It is forbidden to kill or capture Ross seals *Ommatophoca rossi,* Southern elephant seals *Mirounga leonina,* or fur seals of the genus *Arctocephalus.*

(b) In order to protect the adult breeding stock during the period when it is most concentrated and vulnerable, it is forbidden to kill or capture any Weddell seal *Leptonychotes weddelli* one year old or older between 1 September and 31 January inclusive.

3. *Closed Season and Sealing Season*

The period between 1 March and 31 August inclusive is a Closed Season, during which the killing or capturing of seals is forbidden. The period 1 September to the last day in February constitutes a Sealing Season.

4. *Sealing Zones*

Each of the sealing zones listed in this paragraph shall be closed in numerical sequence to all sealing operations for the seal species listed in paragraph 1 of this Annex for the period 1 September to the last day of February inclusive. Such closures shall begin with the same zone as is closed under paragraph 2 of Annex B to Annex 1 of the Report of the Fifth Antarctic Treaty Consultative Meeting at the moment the Convention enters into force. Upon the expiration of each closed period, the affected zone shall reopen.

Zone 1—between 60E and 120E West Longitude

Zone 2—between 0E and 60E West Longitude, together with that part of the Weddell Sea lying westward of 60E West Longitude

Zone 3—between 0E and 70E East Longitude

Zone 4—between 70E and 130E East Longitude

Zone 5—between 130E East Longitude and 170E West Longitude

Zone 6—between 120E and 170E West Longitude.

5. *Seal Reserves*

It is forbidden to kill or capture seals in the following reserves, which are seal breeding areas or the site of long-term scientific research:

(a) The area around the South Orkmov Islands between 60E 20N and 60E 56N South Latitude and 44E 05N and 46E 25N West Longitude.

(b) The area of the southwestern Ross Sea south of 76E South Latitude and west of 170E East Longitude.

(c) The area of Edisto Inlet south and west of a line drawn between Cape Hallet at 72E 19N South Latitude, 170E 18N East Longitude, and Helm Point, at 72E 11N South Latitude, 72E 11N South Latitude, 170E 00N East Longitude.

6. *Exchange of Information*

(a) Contracting Parties shall provide before 31 October each year to other Contracting Parties and to SCAR a summary of statistical information on all seals killed or captured by their respective flags in the Convention areas, in respect of the preceding period 1 July to 30 June. This information shall include by zones and months:

(i) The gross and nett [sic] tonnage, brake horse-power, number of crew, and number of days' operation of vessels under the flag of the Contracting Party:

(ii) The number of adult individuals and pups of each species taken. When specifically requested, this information shall be provided in respect of each ship, together with its daily position at noon each operating day and the catch on that day.

(b) When an industry has started, reports of the number of seals of each species killed or captured in each zone shall be made to SCAR in the form and at the intervals (not shorter than once a week) requested by that body.

(c) Contracting Parties shall provide to SCAR biological information concerning in particular

(i) Sex

(ii) Reproductive condition

(iii) Age

SCAR may request additional information or material with the approval of the Contracting Parties.

(d) Contracting Parties shall provide to other Contracting Parties and to SCAR at least 30 days in advance of departure from their home ports, information on proposed sealing expenditures.

7. *Sealing Methods*

(a) SCAR is invited to report on methods of sealing and to make recommendations with a view to ensuring that the killing or capturing of seals is quick, painless and efficient. Contracting Parties, as appropriate, shall adopt rules for their nationals and vessels under their respective flags engaged in the killing and capturing of seals, giving due consideration to the views of SCAR.

(b) In the light of the available scientific and technical data, Contracting Parties agree to take appropriate steps to ensure that their nationals and vessels under their respective flags refrain from killing, or capturing seals in the water, except in limited quantities to provide for scientific research in conformity with the objectives and principles of this Convention. Such research shall include studies as to the effectiveness of methods of sealing from the viewpoint of the management and humane and rational utilization of the Antarctic seal resources for conservation purposes. The undertaking and the results of any such scientific research programme shall be communicated to SCAR and the Depositary which shall transmit them to the Contracting Parties.

6.4 CONVENTION ON THE CONSERVATION OF ANTARCTIC MARINE LIVING RESOURCES (CCAMLR) (Without Annex). Concluded at Canberra, 20 May 1980. Entered into force, 7 April 1982. 1329 UNTS 47; *reprinted in* 19 ILM 841 (1980) & 5 Weston & Carlson V.D.4

THE CONTRACTING PARTIES,

RECOGNIZING the importance of safeguarding the environment and protecting the integrity of the ecosystem of the seas surrounding Antarctica;

NOTING the concentration of marine living resources found in Antarctic waters and the increased interest in the possibilities offered by the utilization of these resources as a source of protein;

CONSCIOUS of the urgency of ensuring the conservation of Antarctic marine living resources;

CONSIDERING that it is essential to increase knowledge of the Antarctic marine ecosystem and its components so as to be able to base decisions on harvesting on sound scientific information;

BELIEVING that the conservation of Antarctic marine living resources calls for international cooperation with due regard for the provisions of the Antarctic Treaty and with the active involvement of all States engaged in research or harvesting activities in Antarctic waters;

RECOGNIZING the prime responsibilities of the Antarctic Treaty Consultative Parties for the protection and preservation of the Antarctic environment and, in particular, their responsibilities under Article IX, paragraph 1(f) of the Antarctic Treaty in respect of the preservation and conservation of living resources in Antarctica;

RECALLING the action already taken by the Antarctic Treaty Consultative Parties including, in particular, the agreed measures for the conservation of Antarctic fauna and flora, as well as the provisions of the Convention for the conservation of Antarctic seals;

BEARING in mind the concern regarding the conservation of Antarctic marine living resources expressed by the consultative parties at the ninth consultative meeting of the Antarctic Treaty and the importance of the provisions of recommendations IX–2 which led to the establishment of the present convention;

BELIEVING that it is in the interest of all mankind to preserve the waters surrounding the Antarctic continent for peaceful purposes only and to prevent their becoming the scene or object of international discord;

RECOGNIZING, in the light of the foregoing, that it is desirable to establish suitable machinery for recommending, promoting, deciding upon and coordinating the measures and scientific studies needed to ensure the conservation of Antarctic marine living organisms,

HAVE AGREED AS FOLLOWS:

Article I

1. This Convention applies to the Antarctic marine living resources of the area south of 60E South latitude and to the Antarctic marine living resources of the area between that latitude and the Antarctic Convergence which form part of the Antarctic marine ecosystem.

2. Antarctic marine living resources means the populations of fin fish, molluscs, crustaceans and all other species of living organisms, including birds, found south of the Antarctic Convergence.

3. The Antarctic marine ecosystem means the complex of relationships of Antarctic marine living resources with each other and with their physical environment.

4. The Antarctic Convergence shall be deemed to be a line joining the following points along parallels of latitude and meridians of longitude:

> 50ES, 0E; 50ES, 30EE; 45ES, 30EE; 45ES, 80EE; 55ES, 80EE; 55ES, 150EE; 60ES, 150EE; 60ES, 50EW; 50ES, 50EW; 50ES, 0E.

Article II

1. The objective of this Convention is the Conservation of Antarctic marine living resources.

2. For the purposes of this Convention, the term "conservation" includes rational use.

3. Any harvesting and associated activities in the area to which this Convention applies shall be conducted in accordance with the provisions of this Convention and with the following principles of conservation:

(*a*) prevention of decrease in the size of any harvested population to levels below those which ensure its stable recruitment. For this purpose its size should not be allowed to fall below a level close to that which ensures the greatest net annual increment;

(*b*) maintenance of the ecological relationships between harvested, dependent and related populations of Antarctic marine living resources and the restoration of depleted populations to the levels defined in sub-paragraph (a) above;

and

(*c*) prevention of changes or minimization of the risk of changes in the marine ecosystem which are not potentially reversible over two or three decades, taking into account the state of available knowledge of the direct and indirect impact of harvesting, the effect of the introduction of alien species, the effects of associated activities on the marine ecosystem and of the effects of environmental changes, with the aim of making possible the sustained conservation of Antarctic marine living resources.

Article III

The Contracting Parties, whether or not they are Parties to the Antarctic Treaty, agree that they will not engage in any activities in the Antarctic Treaty area contrary to the principles and purposes of that Treaty and that, in their relations with each other, they are bound by the obligations contained in Articles I and V of the Antarctic Treaty.

Article IV

1. With respect to the Antarctic Treaty area, all Contracting Parties, whether or not they are Parties to the Antarctic Treaty, are bound by Articles IV and VI of the Antarctic Treaty in their relations with each other.

2. Nothing in this Convention and no acts or activities taking place while the present Convention is in force shall:

(*a*) constitute a basis for asserting, supporting or denying a claim to territorial sovereignty in the Antarctic Treaty area or create any rights of sovereignty in the Antarctic Treaty area;

(*b*) be interpreted as a renunciation or diminution by any Contracting Party of, or as prejudicing, any right or claim or basis of claim to exercise coastal state jurisdiction under international law within the area to which this Convention applies;

(*c*) be interpreted as prejudicing the position of any Contracting Party as regards its recognition or non-recognition of any such right, claim or basis of claim;

(*d*) affect the provision of Article IV, paragraph 2, of the Antarctic Treaty that no new claim, or enlargement of an existing claim, to territorial sovereignty in Antarctica shall be asserted while the Antarctic Treaty is in force.

Article V

1. The Contracting Parties which are not Parties to the Antarctic Treaty acknowledge the special obligations and responsibilities of the Antarctic Treaty Consultative Parties for the protection and preservation of the environment of the Antarctic Treaty area.

2. The Contracting Parties which are not Parties to the Antarctic Treaty agree that, in their activities in the Antarctic Treaty area, they will observe as and when appropriate the Agreed Measures for the Conservation of Antarctic Fauna and Flora and such other measures as have been recommended by the Antarctic Treaty Consultative Parties in fulfilment of their responsibility for the protection of the Antarctic environment from all forms of harmful human interference.

3. For the purposes of this Convention, "Antarctic Treaty Consultative Parties" means the Contracting Parties to the Antarctic Treaty whose Representatives participate in meetings under Article IX of the Antarctic Treaty.

Article VI

Nothing in this Convention shall derogate from the rights and obligations of Contracting Parties under the International Convention for the Regulation of Whaling and the Convention for the Conservation of Antarctic Seals.

Article VII

1. The Contracting Parties hereby establish and agree to maintain the Commission for the Conservation of Antarctic Marine Living Resources (hereinafter referred to as "the Commission").

2. Membership in the Commission shall be as follows:

(*a*) each Contracting Party which participated in the meeting at which this Convention was adopted shall be a Member of the Commission;

(*b*) each State Party which has acceded to this Convention pursuant to Article XXIX shall be entitled to be a Member of the Commission during such time as that acceding party is engaged in research or harvesting activities in relation to the marine living resources to which this Convention applies;

(*c*) each regional economic integration organization which has acceded to this Convention pursuant to Article XXIX shall be entitled to be a Member of the Commission during such time as its States members are so entitled;

(*d*) a Contracting Party seeking to participate in the work of the Commission pursuant to sub-paragraphs (b) and (c) above shall notify the Depositary of the basis upon which it seeks to become a Member of the Commission and of its willingness to accept conservation measures in force. The Depositary shall communicate to each Member of the Commission such notification and accompanying information. Within two months of receipt of such communication from the Depositary, any Member of the Commission may request that a special meeting of the Commission be held to consider the matter. Upon receipt of such request, the Depositary shall call such a meeting. If there is no request for a meeting, the Contracting Party submitting the notification shall be deemed to have satisfied the requirements for Commission Membership.

3. Each Member of the Commission shall be represented by one representative who may be accompanied by alternate representatives and advisers.

Article VIII

The Commission shall have legal personality and shall enjoy in the territory of each of the States Parties such legal capacity as may be necessary to perform its function and achieve the purposes of this Convention. The privileges and immunities to be enjoyed by the Commission and its staff in the territory of a State Party shall be determined by agreement between the Commission and the State Party concerned.

Article IX

1. The function of the Commission shall be to give effect to the objective and principles set out in Article II of this Convention. To this end, it shall:

(*a*) facilitate research into and comprehensive studies of Antarctic marine living resources and of the Antarctic marine ecosystem;

(*b*) compile data on the status of and changes in population of Antarctic marine living resources and on factors affecting the distribution, abundance and productivity of harvested species and dependent or related species or populations;

(*c*) ensure the acquisition of catch and effort statistics on harvested populations;

(*d*) analyse, disseminate and publish the information referred to in subparagraphs (b) and (c) above and the reports of the Scientific Committee;

(*e*) identify conservation needs and analyse the effectiveness of conservation measures;

(*f*) formulate, adopt and revise conservation measures on the basis of the best scientific evidence available, subject to the provisions of paragraph 5 of this Article;

(*g*) implement the system of observation and inspection established under Article XXIV of this Convention;

(*h*) carry out such other activities as are necessary to fulfil the objective of this Convention.

2. The conservation measures referred to in paragraph 1(f) above include the following:

(*a*) the designation of the quantity of any species which may be harvested in the area to which this Convention applies;

(*b*) the designation of regions and sub-regions based on the distribution of populations of Antarctic marine living resources;

(*c*) the designation of the quantity which may be harvested from the populations of regions and sub-regions;

(*d*) the designation of protected species;

(*e*) the designation of the size, age and, as appropriate, sex of species which may be harvested;

(*f*) the designation of open and closed seasons for harvesting;

(*g*) the designation of the opening and closing of areas, regions or sub-regions for purposes of scientific study or conservation, including special areas for protection and scientific study;

(*h*) regulation of the effort employed and methods of harvesting, including fishing gear, with a view, inter alia, to avoiding undue concentration of harvesting in any region or sub-region;

(*i*) the taking of such other conservation measures as the Commission considers necessary for the fulfilment of the objective of this Convention, including measures concerning the effects of harvesting and associated activities on components of the marine ecosystem other than the harvested populations.

3. The Commission shall publish and maintain a record of all conservation measures in force.

4. In exercising its functions under paragraph 1 above, the Commission shall take full account of the recommendations and advice of the Scientific Committee.

5. The Commission shall take full account of any relevant measures or regulations established or recommended by the Consultative Meetings pursuant to Article IX of the Antarctic Treaty or by existing fisheries commissions responsible for species which may enter the area to which this Convention applies, in order that there shall be no inconsistency between the rights and obligations of a Contracting Party under such regulations or measures and conservation measures which may be adopted by the Commission.

6. Conservation measures adopted by the Commission in accordance with this Convention shall be implemented by Members of the Commission in the following manner:

(*a*) the Commission shall notify conservation measures to all Members of the Commission;

(*b*) conservation measures shall become binding upon all Members of the Commission 180 days after such notification, except as provided in subparagraphs (c) and (d) below;

(*c*) if a Member of the Commission, within ninety days following the notification specified in sub-paragraph (a), notifies the Commission that it is unable to accept the conservation measure, in whole or in part, the measure shall not, to the extent stated, be binding upon that Member of the Commission;

(*d*) in the event that any Member of the Commission invokes the procedure set forth in sub-paragraph (c) above, the Commission shall meet at the request of any Member of the Commission to review the conservation measure. At the time of such meeting and within thirty days following the meeting, any Member of the Commission shall have the right to declare that it is no longer able to accept the conservation measure, in which case the Member shall no longer be bound by such measure.

Article X

1. The Commission shall draw the attention of any State which is not a Party to this Convention to any activity undertaken by its nationals or vessels which, in the opinion of the Commission, affects the implementation of the objective of this Convention.

2. The Commission shall draw the attention of all Contracting Parties to any activity which, in the opinion of the Commission, affects the implementation by a Contracting Party of the objective of this Convention or the compliance by that Contracting Party with its obligations under this Convention.

Article XI

The Commission shall seek to cooperate with Contracting Parties which may exercise jurisdiction in marine areas adjacent to the area to which this Convention applies in respect of the conservation of any stock or stocks of associated species which occur both within those areas and the area to which this Convention applies, with a view to harmonizing the conservation measures adopted in respect of such stocks.

Article XII

1. Decisions of the Commission on matters of substance shall be taken by consensus. The question of whether a matter is one of substance shall be treated as a matter of substance.

2. Decisions on matters other than those referred to in paragraph 1 above shall be taken by a simple majority of the Members of the Commission present and voting.

3. In Commission consideration of any item requiring a decision, it shall be made clear whether a regional economic integration organization will participate in the taking of the decision and, if so, whether any of its member States will also participate. The number of Contracting Parties so participating shall not exceed the number of member States of the regional economic integration organization which are Members of the Commission.

4. In the taking of decisions pursuant to this Article, a regional economic integration organization shall have only one vote.

Article XIII

1. The headquarters of the Commission shall be established at Hobart, Tasmania, Australia.

2. The Commission shall hold a regular annual meeting. Other meetings shall also be held at the request of one-third of its members and as otherwise provided in this Convention. The first meeting of the Commission shall be held within three months of the entry into force of this Convention, provided that among the Contracting Parties there are at least two States conducting harvesting activities within the area to which this Convention applies. The first meeting shall, in any event, be held within one year of the entry into force of this Convention. The Depositary shall consult with the signatory States regarding the first Commission meeting, taking into account that a broad representation of such States is necessary for the effective operation of the Commission.

3. The Depositary shall convene the first meeting of the Commission at the headquarters of the Commission. Thereafter, meetings of the Commission shall be held at its headquarters, unless it decides otherwise.

4. The Commission shall elect from among its members a Chairman and Vice–Chairman, each of whom shall serve for a term of two years and shall be eligible for re-election for one additional term. The first Chairman shall, however, be elected for an initial term of three years. The Chairman and Vice–Chairman shall not be representatives of the same Contracting Party.

5. The Commission shall adopt and amend as necessary the rules of procedure for the conduct of its meetings, except with respect to the matters dealt with in Article XII of this Convention.

6. The Commission may establish such subsidiary bodies as are necessary for the performance of its functions.

Article XIV

1. The Contracting Parties hereby establish the Scientific Committee for the Conservation of Antarctic Marine Living Resources (hereinafter referred to as "the Scientific Committee") which shall be a consultative body to the Commission. The Scientific Committee shall normally meet at the headquarters of the Commission unless the Scientific Committee decides otherwise.

2. Each Member of the Commission shall be a member of the Scientific Committee and shall appoint a representative with suitable scientific qualifications who may be accompanied by other experts and advisers.

3.   The Scientific Committee may seek the advice of other scientists and experts as may be required on an ad hoc basis.

Article XV

1.   The Scientific Committee shall provide a forum for consultation and cooperation concerning the collection, study and exchange of information with respect to the marine living resources to which this Convention applies. It shall encourage and promote cooperation in the field of scientific research in order to extend knowledge of the marine living resources of the Antarctic marine ecosystem.

2.   The Scientific Committee shall conduct such activities as the Commission may direct in pursuance of the objective of this Convention and shall:

(*a*) establish criteria and methods to be used for determinations concerning the conservation measures referred to in Article IX of this Convention;

(*b*) regularly assess the status and trends of the populations of Antarctic marine living resources;

(*c*) analyse data concerning the direct and indirect effects of harvesting on the populations of Antarctic marine living resources;

(*d*) assess the effects of proposed changes in the methods or levels of harvesting and proposed conservation measures;

(*e*) transmit assessments, analyses, reports and recommendations to the Commission as requested or on its own initiative regarding measures and research to implement the objective of this Convention;

(*f*) formulate proposals for the conduct of international and national programs of research into Antarctic marine living resources.

3.   In carrying out its functions, the Scientific Committee shall have regard to the work of other relevant technical and scientific organizations and to the scientific activities conducted within the framework of the Antarctic Treaty.

Article XVI

1.   The first meeting of the Scientific Committee shall be held within three months of the first meeting of the Commission. The Scientific Committee shall meet thereafter as often as may be necessary to fulfil its functions.

2.   The Scientific Committee shall adopt and amend as necessary its rules of procedure. The rules and any amendments thereto shall be approved by the Commission. The rules shall include procedures for the presentation of minority reports.

3.   The Scientific Committee may establish, with the approval of the Commission, such subsidiary bodies as are necessary for the performance of its functions.

Article XVII

1.   The Commission shall appoint an Executive Secretary to serve the Commission and Scientific Committee according to such procedures and on such terms and conditions as the Commission may determine. His term of office shall be for four years and he shall be eligible for reappointment.

2.   The Commission shall authorize such staff establishment for the Secretariat as may be necessary and the Executive Secretary shall appoint, direct and supervise such staff according to such rules and procedures and on such terms and conditions as the Commission may determine.

3.   The Executive Secretary and Secretariat shall perform the functions entrusted to them by the Commission.

Article XVIII

The official languages of the Commission and of the Scientific Committee shall be English, French, Russian and Spanish.

Article XIX

1. At each annual meeting, the Commission shall adopt by consensus its budget and the budget of the Scientific Committee.

2. A draft budget for the Commission and the Scientific Committee and any subsidiary bodies shall be prepared by the Executive Secretary and submitted to the Members of the Commission at least sixty days before the annual meeting of the Commission.

3. Each Member of the Commission shall contribute to the budget. Until the expiration of five years after the entry into force of this Convention, the contribution of each Member of the Commission shall be equal. Thereafter the contribution shall be determined in accordance with two criteria: the amount harvested and an equal sharing among all Members of the Commission. The Commission shall determine by consensus the proportion in which these two criteria shall apply.

4. The financial activities of the Commission and Scientific Committee shall be conducted in accordance with financial regulations adopted by the Commission and shall be subject to an annual audit by external auditors selected by the Commission.

5. Each Member of the Commission shall meet its own expenses arising from attendance at meetings of the Commission and of the Scientific Committee.

6. A Member of the Commission that fails to pay its contributions for two consecutive years shall not, during the period of its default, have the right to participate in the taking of decisions in the Commission.

Article XX

1. The Members of the Commission shall, to the greatest extent possible, provide annually to the Commission and to the Scientific Committee such statistical, biological and other data and information as the Commission and Scientific Committee may require in the exercise of their functions.

2. The Members of the Commission shall provide, in the manner and at such intervals as may be prescribed, information about their harvesting activities, including fishing areas and vessels, so as to enable reliable catch and effort statistics to be compiled.

3. The Members of the Commission shall provide to the Commission at such intervals as may be prescribed information on steps taken to implement the conservation measures adopted by the Commission.

4. The Members of the Commission agree that in any of their harvesting activities, advantage shall be taken of opportunities to collect data needed to assess the impact of harvesting.

Article XXI

1. Each Contracting Party shall take appropriate measures within its competence to ensure compliance with the provisions of this Convention and with conservation measures adopted by the Commission to which the Party is bound in accordance with Article IX of this Convention.

2. Each Contracting Party shall transmit to the Commission information on measures taken pursuant to paragraph 1 above, including the imposition of sanctions for any violation.

Article XXII

1. Each Contracting Party undertakes to exert appropriate efforts, consistent with the Charter of the United Nations, to the end that no one engages in any activity contrary to the objective of this Convention.

2. Each Contracting Party shall notify the Commission of any such activity which comes to its attention.

Article XXIII

1. The Commission and the Scientific Committee shall co-operate with the Antarctic Treaty Consultative Parties on matters falling within the competence of the latter.

2. The Commission and the Scientific Committee shall co-operate, as appropriate, with the Food and Agriculture Organization of the United Nations and with other Specialised Agencies.

3. The Commission and the Scientific Committee shall seek to develop co-operative working relationships, as appropriate, with inter-governmental and non-governmental organizations which could contribute to their work, including the Scientific Committee on Antarctic Research, the Scientific Committee on Oceanic Research and the International Whaling Commission.

4. The Commission may enter into agreements with the organizations referred to in this Article and with other organizations as may be appropriate. The Commission and the Scientific Committee may invite such organizations to send observers to their meetings and to meetings of their subsidiary bodies.

Article XXIV

1. In order to promote the objective and ensure observance of the provisions of this Convention, the Contracting Parties agree that a system of observation and inspection shall be established.

2. The system of observation and inspection shall be elaborated by the Commission on the basis of the following principles:

(a) Contracting Parties shall cooperate with each other to ensure the effective implementation of the system of observation and inspection, taking account of the existing international practice. This system shall include, inter alia, procedures for boarding and inspection by observers and inspectors designated by the Members of the Commission and procedures for flag state prosecution and sanctions on the basis of evidence resulting from such boarding and inspections. A report of such prosecutions and sanctions imposed shall be included in the information referred to in Article XXI of this Convention;

(b) in order to verify compliance with measures adopted under this Convention, observation and inspection shall be carried out on board vessels engaged in scientific research or harvesting of marine living resources in the area to which this Convention applies, through observers and inspectors designated by the Members of the Commission and operating under terms and conditions to be established by the Commission;

(c) designated observers and inspectors shall remain subject to the jurisdiction of the Contracting Party of which they are nationals. They shall report to the Member of the Commission by which they have been designated which in turn shall report to the Commission.

3. Pending the establishment of the system of observation and inspection, the Members of the Commission shall seek to establish interim arrangements to designate observers and inspectors and such designated observers and inspectors shall be

entitled to carry out inspections in accordance with the principles set out in paragraph 2 above.

Article XXV

1. If any dispute arises between two or more of the Contracting Parties concerning the interpretation or application of this Convention, those Contracting Parties shall consult among themselves with a view to having the dispute resolved by negotiation, inquiry, mediation, conciliation, arbitration, judicial settlement or other peaceful means of their own choice.

2. Any dispute of this character not so resolved shall, with the consent in each case of all Parties to the dispute, be referred for settlement to the International Court of Justice or to arbitration; but failure to reach agreement on reference to the International Court or to arbitration shall not absolve Parties to the dispute from the responsibility of continuing to seek to resolve it by any of the various peaceful means referred to in paragraph 1 above.

3. In cases where the dispute is referred to arbitration, the arbitral tribunal shall be constituted as provided in the Annex to this Convention.

Article XXVI

1. This Convention shall be open for signature at Canberra from 1 August to 31 December 1980 by the States participating in the Conference on the Conservation of Antarctic Marine Living Resources held at Canberra from 7 to 20 May 1980.

2. The States which so sign will be the original signatory States of the Convention.

Article XXVII

1. This Convention is subject to ratification, acceptance or approval by signatory States.

2. Instruments of ratification, acceptance or approval shall be deposited with the Government of Australia, hereby designated as the Depositary.

Article XXVIII

1. This Convention shall enter into force on the thirtieth day following the date of deposit of the eighth instrument of ratification, acceptance or approval by States referred to in paragraph 1 of Article XXVI of this Convention.

2. With respect to each State or regional economic integration organization which subsequent to the date of entry into force of this Convention deposits an instrument of ratification, acceptance, approval or accession, the Convention shall enter into force on the thirtieth day following such deposit.

Article XXIX

1. This Convention shall be open for accession by any State interested in research or harvesting activities in relation to the marine living resources to which this Convention applies.

2. This Convention shall be open for accession by regional economic integration organizations constituted by sovereign States which include among their members one or more States Members of the Commission and to which the States members of the organization have transferred, in whole or in part, competences with regard to the matters covered by this Convention. The accession of such regional economic integration organizations shall be the subject of consultations among Members of the Commission.

Article XXX

1.   This Convention may be amended at any time.

2.   If one-third of the Members of the Commission request a meeting to discuss a proposed amendment the Depositary shall call such a meeting.

3.   An amendment shall enter into force when the Depositary has received instruments of ratification, acceptance or approval thereof from all the Members of the Commission.

4.   Such amendment shall thereafter enter into force as to any other Contracting Party when notice of ratification, acceptance or approval by it has been received by the Depositary. Any such Contracting Party from which no such notice has been received within a period of one year from the date of entry into force of the amendment in accordance with paragraph 3 above shall be deemed to have withdrawn from this Convention.

Article XXXI

1.   Any Contracting Party may withdraw from this Convention on 30 June of any year, by giving written notice not later than 1 January of the same year to the Depositary, which, upon receipt of such a notice, shall communicate it forthwith to the other Contracting Parties.

2.   Any other Contracting Party may, within sixty days of the receipt of a copy of such a notice from the Depositary, give written notice of withdrawal to the Depositary in which case the Convention shall cease to be in force on 30 June of the same year with respect to the Contracting Party giving such notice.

3.   Withdrawal from this Convention by any Member of the Commission shall not affect its financial obligations under this Convention.

Article XXXII

The Depositary shall notify all Contracting Parties of the following:

(a) signatures of this Convention and the deposit of instruments of ratification, acceptance, approval or accession;

(b) the date of entry into force of this Convention and of any amendment thereto.

Article XXXIII

1.   This Convention, of which the English, French, Russian and Spanish texts are equally authentic, shall be deposited with the Government of Australia which shall transmit duly certified copies thereof to all signatory and acceding Parties.

2.   This Convention shall be registered by the Depositary pursuant to Article 102 of the Charter of the United Nations.

6.5 RESOLUTION ON THE QUESTION OF ANTARCTICA. **Adopted by the UN General Assembly, 15 December 1983. GA Res 38/77, UN GAOR, 38th Sess, Supp No 47, at 69, UN Doc A/38/69 (1983)**

The General Assembly,

Having considered the item entitled "Question of Antarctica",

Conscious of the increasing international awareness of and interest in Antarctica,

Bearing in mind the Antarctic Treaty and the significance of the system it has developed,

Taking into account the debate on this item at its thirty-eighth session,

Convinced of the advantages of a better knowledge of Antarctica,

Affirming the conviction that, in the interest of all mankind, Antarctica should continue forever to be used exclusively for peaceful purposes and that it should not become the scene or object of international discord,

Recalling the relevant paragraphs of the Economic Declaration adopted by the Seventh Conference of Heads of State or Government of the Non–Aligned Countries, held at New Delhi from 7 to 12 March 1983,

1. *Requests* the Secretary–General to prepare a comprehensive, factual and objective study on all aspects of Antarctica, taking fully into account the Antarctica Treaty system and other relevant factors;

2. *Also requests* the Secretary–General to seek the views of all Member States in the preparation of the study;

3. *Requests* those States conducting scientific research in Antarctica, other interested States, the relevant specialized agencies, organs, organizations and bodies of the United Nations system and relevant international organizations having scientific or technical information on Antarctica to lend the Secretary–General whatever assistance he may request for the purpose of carrying out the study;

4. *Requests* the Secretary–General to report to the General Assembly at its thirty-ninth session;

5. *Decides* to include in the provisional agenda of its thirty-ninth session the item entitled "Question of Antarctica".

6.6 RESOLUTION ON THE QUESTION OF ANTARCTICA. **Adopted by the UN General Assembly, 17 December 1984. GA Res 39/152, UN GAOR, 39th Sess, Supp No 51, at 94, UN Doc A/39/51 (1984)**

The General Assembly,

Recalling its resolution 38/77 of 15 December 1983,

Having considered the item entitled "Question of Antarctica",

Taking note of the study on the question of Antarctica,

Conscious of the increasing international awareness of and interest in Antarctica,

Bearing in mind the Antarctic Treaty and the significance of the system it has developed,

Taking into account the debate on this item at its thirty-ninth session,

Convinced of the advantages of a better knowledge of Antarctica,

Affirming the conviction that, in the interest of all mankind, Antarctica should continue forever to be used exclusively for peaceful purposes and that it should not become the scene or object of international discord,

Recalling the relevant paragraphs of the Economic Declaration adopted at the Seventh Conference of Heads of State or Government of Non–Aligned Countries, held at New Delhi from 7 to 12 March 1983,

1. *Expresses its appreciation* to the Secretary–General for the study on the question of Antarctica;

2. *Decides* to include in the provisional agenda of its fortieth session the item entitled "Question of Antarctica".

6.7 Convention on the Regulation of Antarctic Mineral Resource Activities (CRAMRA) (Without Annex for Arbitral Tribunal).[b] Concluded at Wellington, 2 June 1988. Not yet in force. Doc AMR/SCM/88/78; *reprinted in* 27 ILM 859 (1988) & 5 Weston & Carlson V.D.5

CHAPTER I: GENERAL PROVISIONS

Article 1
Definitions

For the purposes of this Convention:

1. "Antarctic Treaty" means the Antarctic Treaty done at Washington on 1 December 1959.

2. "Antarctic Treaty Consultative Parties" means the Contracting Parties to the Antarctic Treaty entitled to appoint representatives to participate in the meetings referred to in Article IX of that Treaty.

3. "Antarctic Treaty area" means the area to which the provisions of the Antarctic Treaty apply in accordance with Article VI of that Treaty.

4. "Convention for the Conservation of Antarctic Seals" means the Convention done at London on 1 June 1972.

5. "Convention on the Conservation of Antarctic Marine Living Resources" means the Convention done at Canberra on 20 May 1980.

6. "Mineral resources" means all non-living natural non-renewable resources, including fossil fuels, metallic and non-metallic minerals.

7. "Antarctic mineral resource activities" means prospecting, exploration or development, but does not include scientific research activities within the meaning of Article III of the Antarctic Treaty.

8. "Prospecting" means activities, including logistic support, aimed at identifying areas of mineral resource potential for possible exploration and development, including geological, geochemical and geophysical investigations and field observations, the use of remote sensing techniques and collection of surface, seafloor and sub-ice samples. Such activities do not include dredging and excavations, except for the purpose of obtaining small-scale samples, or drilling, except shallow drilling into rock and sediment to depths not exceeding 25 metres, or such other depth as the Commission may determine for particular circumstances.

9. "Exploration" means activities, including logistic support, aimed at identifying and evaluating specific mineral resource occurrences or deposits, including exploratory drilling, dredging and other surface or subsurface excavations required to determine the nature and size of mineral resource deposits and the feasibility of their development, but excluding pilot projects or commercial production.

10. "Development" means activities, including logistic support, which take place following exploration and are aimed at or associated with exploitation of specific mineral resource deposits, including pilot projects, processing, storage and transport activities.

11. "Operator" means:

(*a*) a Party; or

(*b*) an agency or instrumentality of a Party; or

(*c*) a juridical person established under the law of a Party or;

(*d*) a joint venture consisting exclusively of any combination of any of the foregoing,

b. Effectively superseded by Basic Document 6.9. Entry into force is not expected.

which is undertaking Antarctic mineral resource activities and for which there is a Sponsoring State.

12. "Sponsoring State" means the Party with which an Operator has a substantial and genuine link, through being:

(a) in the case of a Party, that Party;

(b) in the case of an agency or instrumentality of a Party, that Party;

(c) in the case of a juridical person other than an agency or instrumentality of a Party, the Party:

(i) under whose law that juridical person is established and to whose law it is subject, without prejudice to any other law which might be applicable, and

(ii) in whose territory the management of that juridical person is located, and

(iii) to whose effective control that juridical person is subject;

(d) in the case of a joint venture not constituting a juridical person:

(i) where the managing member of the joint venture is a Party or an agency or instrumentality of a Party, that Party; or

(ii) in any other cases, where in relation to a Party the managing member of the joint venture satisfies the requirements of subparagraph (c) above, that Party.

13. "Managing member of the joint venture" means that member which the participating members in the joint venture have by agreement designated as having responsibility for central management of the joint venture, including the functions of organising and supervising the activities to be undertaken, and controlling the financial resources involved.

14. "Effective control" means the ability of the Sponsoring State to ensure the availability of substantial resources of the Operator for purposes connected with the implementation of this Convention, through the location of such resources in the territory of the Sponsoring State or otherwise.

15. "Damage to the Antarctic environment or dependent or associated ecosystems" means any impact on the living or non-living components of that environment or those ecosystems, including harm to atmospheric, marine or terrestrial life, beyond that which is negligible or which has been assessed and judged to be acceptable pursuant to this Convention.

16. "Commission" means the Antarctic Mineral Resources Commission established pursuant to Article 18.

17. "Regulatory Committee" means an Antarctic Mineral Resources Regulatory Committee established pursuant to Article 39.

18. "Advisory Committee" means the Scientific, Technical and Environmental Advisory Committee established pursuant to Article 13.

19. "Special Meeting of Parties" means the Meeting referred to in Article 28.

20. "Arbitral Tribunal" means an Arbitral Tribunal constituted as provided for in the Annex, which forms an integral part of this Convention.

Article 2
Objectives and General Principles

1. This Convention is an integral part of the Antarctic Treaty system, comprising the Antarctic Treaty, the measures in effect under that Treaty, and its associated

separate legal instruments, the prime purpose of which is to ensure that Antarctica shall continue forever to be used exclusively for peaceful purposes and shall not become the scene or object of international discord. The Parties provide through this Convention, the principles it establishes, the rules it prescribes, the institutions it creates and the decisions adopted pursuant to it, a means for:

(*a*) assessing the possible impact on the environment of Antarctic mineral resource activities;

(*b*) determining whether Antarctic mineral resource activities are acceptable;

(*c*) governing the conduct of such Antarctic mineral resource activities as may be found acceptable; and

(*d*) ensuring that any Antarctic mineral resource activities are undertaken in strict conformity with this Convention.

2. In implementing this Convention, the Parties shall ensure that Antarctic mineral resource activities, should they occur, take place in a manner consistent with all the components of the Antarctic Treaty system and the obligations flowing therefrom.

3. In relation to Antarctic mineral resource activities, should they occur, the Parties acknowledge the special responsibility of the Antarctic Treaty Consultative Parties for the protection of the environment and the need to:

(*a*) protect the Antarctic environment and dependent and associated ecosystems;

(*b*) respect Antarctica's significance for, and influence on, the global environment;

(*c*) respect other legitimate uses of Antarctica;

(*d*) respect Antarctica's scientific value and aesthetic and wilderness qualities;

(*e*) ensure the safety of operations in Antarctica;

(*f*) promote opportunities for fair and effective participation of all Parties; and

(*g*) take into account the interests of the international community as a whole.

Article 3
Prohibition of Antarctic Mineral Resource Activities Outside This Convention

No Antarctic mineral resource activities shall be conducted except in accordance with this Convention and measures in effect pursuant to it and, in the case of exploration or development, with a Management Scheme approved pursuant to Article 48 or 54.

Article 4
Principles Concerning Judgments on Antarctic Mineral Resource Activities

1. Decisions about Antarctic mineral resource activities shall be based upon information adequate to enable informed judgments to be made about their possible impacts and no such activities shall take place unless this information is available for decisions relevant to those activities.

2. No Antarctic mineral resource activity shall take place until it is judged, based upon assessment of its possible impacts on the Antarctic environment and on dependent and on associated ecosystems, that the activity in question would not cause:

(*a*) significant adverse effects on air and water quality;

(*b*) significant changes in atmospheric, terrestrial or marine environments;

(*c*) significant change in the distribution, abundance or productivity of populations of species of fauna or flora;

(*d*) further jeopardy to endangered or threatened species or populations of such species; or

(*e*) degradation of, or substantial risk to, areas of special biological, scientific, historic, aesthetic or wilderness significance.

3. No Antarctic mineral resource activity shall take place until it is judged, based upon assessment of its possible impacts, that the activity in question would not cause significant adverse effects on global or regional climate or weather patterns.

4. No Antarctic mineral resource activity shall take place until it is judged that:

(*a*) technology and procedures are available to provide for safe operations and compliance with paragraphs 2 and 3 above;

(*b*) there exists the capacity to monitor key environmental parameters and ecosystem components so as to identify any adverse effects of such activity and to provide for the modification of operating procedures as may be necessary in the light of the results of monitoring or increased knowledge of the Antarctic environment or dependent or associated ecosystems; and

(*c*) there exists the capacity to respond effectively to accidents, particularly those with potential environmental effects.

5. The judgments referred to in paragraphs 2, 3 and 4 above shall take into account the cumulative impacts of possible Antarctic mineral resource activities both by themselves and in combination with other such activities and other uses of Antarctica.

Article 5
Area of Application

1. This Convention shall, subject to paragraphs 2, 3 and 4 below, apply to the Antarctic Treaty area.

2. Without prejudice to the responsibilities of the Antarctic Treaty Consultative Parties under the Antarctic Treaty and measures pursuant to it, the Parties agree that this Convention shall regulate Antarctic mineral resource activities which take place on the continent of Antarctica and all Antarctic islands, including all ice shelves, south of 60E south latitude and in the seabed and subsoil of adjacent offshore areas up to the deep seabed.

3. For the purposes of this Convention "deep seabed" means the seabed and subsoil beyond the geographic extent of the continental shelf as the term continental shelf is defined in accordance with international law.

4. Nothing in this Article shall be construed as limiting the application of other Articles of this Convention in so far as they relate to possible impacts outside the area referred to in paragraphs 1 and 2 above, including impacts on dependent or on associated ecosystems.

Article 6
Cooperation and International Participation

In the implementation of this Convention cooperation within its framework shall be promoted and encouragement given to international participation in Antarctic mineral resource activities by interested Parties which are Antarctic Treaty Consultative Parties and by other interested Parties, in particular, developing countries in either category. Such participation may be realised through the Parties themselves and their Operators.

Article 7
Compliance with This Convention

1. Each Party shall take appropriate measures within its competence to ensure compliance with this Convention and any measures in effect pursuant to it.

2. If a Party is prevented by the exercise of jurisdiction by another Party from ensuring compliance in accordance with paragraph 1 above, it shall not, to the extent that it is so prevented, bear responsibility for that failure to ensure compliance.

3. If any jurisdictional dispute related to compliance with this Convention or any measure in effect pursuant to it arises between two or more Parties, the Parties concerned shall immediately consult together with a view to reaching a mutually acceptable solution.

4. Each Party shall notify the Executive Secretary, for circulation to all other Parties, of the measures taken pursuant to paragraph 1 above.

5. Each Party shall exert appropriate efforts, consistent with the Charter of the United Nations, to the end that no one engages in any Antarctic mineral resource activities contrary to the objectives and principles of this Convention.

6. Each Party may, whenever it deems it necessary, draw the attention of the Commission to any activity which in its opinion affects the implementation of the objectives and principles of this Convention.

7. The Commission shall draw the attention of all Parties to any activity which, in the opinion of the Commission, affects the implementation of the objectives and principles of this Convention or the compliance by any Party with its obligations under this Convention and any measures in effect pursuant to it.

8. The Commission shall draw the attention of any State which is not a Party to this Convention to any activity undertaken by that State, its agencies or instrumentalities, natural or juridical persons, ships, aircraft or other means of transportation which, in the opinion of the Commission, affects the implementation of the objectives and principles of this Convention. The Commission shall inform all Parties accordingly.

9. Nothing in this Article shall affect the operation of Article 12(7) of this Convention or Article VIII of the Antarctic Treaty.

Article 8
Response Action and Liability

1. An Operator undertaking any Antarctic mineral resource activity shall take necessary and timely response action, including prevention, containment, clean up and removal measures, if the activity results in or threatens to result in damage to the Antarctic environment or dependent or associated ecosystems. The Operator, through its Sponsoring State, shall notify the Executive Secretary, for circulation to the relevant institutions of this Convention and to all Parties, of action taken pursuant to this paragraph.

2. An Operator shall be strictly liable for:

(*a*) damage to the Antarctic environment or dependent or associated ecosystems arising from its Antarctic mineral resource activities, including payment in the event that there has been no restoration to the *status quo ante;*

(*b*) loss of or impairment to an established use, as referred to in Article 15, or loss of or impairment to an established use of dependent or associated ecosystems, arising directly out of damage described in subparagraph (a) above;

(*c*) loss of or damage to property of a third party or loss of life or personal injury of a third party arising directly out of damage described in subparagraph (a) above; and

(*d*) reimbursement of reasonable costs by whomsoever incurred relating to necessary response action, including prevention, containment, clean up and removal measures, and action taken to restore the *status quo ante* where Antarctic mineral resource activities undertaken by that Operator result in or threaten to result in damage to the Antarctic environment or dependent or associated ecosystems.

3. (*a*) Damage of the kind referred to in paragraph 2 above which would not have occurred or continued if the Sponsoring State had carried out its obligations under this Convention with respect to its Operator shall, in accordance with international law, entail liability of that Sponsoring State. Such liability shall be limited to that portion of liability not satisfied by the Operator or otherwise.

(*b*) Nothing in subparagraph (a) above shall affect the application of the rules of international law applicable in the event that damage not referred to in that subparagraph would not have occurred or continued if the Sponsoring State had carried out its obligations under this Convention with respect to its Operator.

4. An Operator shall not be liable pursuant to paragraph 2 above if it proves that the damage has been caused directly by, and to the extent that it has been caused directly by:

(*a*) an event constituting in the circumstances of Antarctica a natural disaster of an exceptional character which could not reasonably have been foreseen; or

(*b*) armed conflict, should it occur notwithstanding the Antarctic Treaty, or an act of terrorism directed against the activities of the Operator, against which no reasonable precautionary measures could have been effective.

5. Liability of an Operator for any loss of life, personal injury or loss of or damage to property other than that governed by this Article shall be regulated by applicable law and procedures.

6. If an Operator proves that damage has been caused totally or in part by an intentional or grossly negligent act or omission of the party seeking redress, that Operator may be relieved totally or in part from its obligation to pay compensation in respect of the damage suffered by such party.

7. (*a*) Further rules and procedures in respect of the provisions on liability set out in this Article shall be elaborated through a separate Protocol which shall be adopted by consensus by the members of the Commission and shall enter into force according to the procedure provided for in Article 62 for the entry into force of this Convention.

(*b*) Such rules and procedures shall be designed to enhance the protection of the Antarctic environment and dependent and associated ecosystems.

(*c*) Such rules and procedures:

(i) may contain provisions for appropriate limits on liability, where such limits can be justified:

(ii) without prejudice to Article 57, shall prescribe means and mechanisms such as a claims tribunal or other fora by which claims against Operators pursuant to this Article may be assessed and adjudicated:

(iii) shall ensure that a means is provided to assist with immediate response action, and to satisfy liability under paragraph 2 above in the event, *inter alia,* that an Operator liable is financially incapable of meeting its obligation in full that it exceeds any relevant limits of liability, that there is a defence to liability or that the loss or damage is of undetermined origin.

Unless it is determined during the elaboration of the Protocol that there are other effective means of meeting these objectives, the Protocol shall establish a Fund or Funds and make provision in respect of such Fund or Funds, *inter alia,* for the following:

—financing by Operators or on industry wide bases;

—ensuring the permanent liquidity and mandatory supplementation thereof in the event of insufficiency;

—reimbursement of costs of response action, by whomsoever incurred.

8.   Nothing in paragraphs 4, 6 and 7 above or in the Protocol adopted pursuant to paragraph 7 shall affect in any way the provisions of paragraph 1 above.

9.   No application for an exploration or development permit shall be made until the Protocol provided for in paragraph 7 above is in force for the Party lodging such application.

10.   Each Party, pending the entry into force for it of the Protocol provided for in paragraph 7 above, shall ensure, consistently with Article 7 and in accordance with its legal system, that recourse is available in its national courts for adjudicating liability claims pursuant to paragraphs 2, 4 and 6 above against Operators which are engaged in prospecting. Such recourse shall include the adjudication of claims against any Operator it has sponsored. Each Party shall also ensure, in accordance with its legal system, that the Commission has the right to appear as a party in its national courts to pursue relevant liability claims under paragraph 2(a) above.

11.   Nothing in this Article or in the Protocol provided for in paragraph 7 above shall be construed so as to:

(*a*) preclude the application of existing rules on liability, and the development in accordance with international law of further such rules, which may have application to either States or Operators; or

(*b*) affect the right of an Operator incurring liability pursuant to this Article to seek redress from another party which caused or contributed to the damage in question.

12.   When compensation has been paid other than under this Convention liability under this Convention shall be offset by the amount of such payment.

Article 9
Protection of Legal Positions under the Antarctic Treaty

Nothing in this Convention and no acts or activities taking place while this Convention is in force shall:

(*a*) constitute a basis for asserting, supporting or denying a claim to territorial sovereignty in the Antarctic Treaty area or create any rights of sovereignty in the Antarctic Treaty area;

(*b*) be interpreted as a renunciation or diminution by any Party of, or as prejudicing, any right or claim or basis of claim to territorial sovereignty in Antarctica or to exercise coastal state jurisdiction under international law;

(*c*) be interpreted as prejudicing the position of any Party as regards its recognition or non-recognition of any such right, claim or basis of claim; or (*d*) affect the provision of Article IV(2) of the Antarctic Treaty that no new claim, or enlargement of an existing claim, to territorial sovereignty in Antarctica shall be asserted while the Antarctic Treaty is in force.

Article 10
Consistency with the Other Components of the Antarctic Treaty System

1.   Each Party shall ensure that Antarctic mineral resource activities take place in a manner consistent with the components of the Antarctic Treaty system, including the Antarctic Treaty, the Convention for the Conservation of Antarctic Seals and the Convention on the Conservation of Antarctic Marine Living Resources and the measures in effect pursuant to those instruments.

2.   The Commission shall consult and cooperate with the Antarctic Treaty Consultative Parties, the Contracting Parties to the Convention for the Conservation of Antarctic Seals, and the Commission for the Conservation of Antarctic Marine Living Resources with a view to ensuring the achievement of the objectives and principles of this Convention and avoiding any interference with the achievement of the objectives and principles of the Antarctic Treaty, the Convention for the Conservation of Antarctic Seals or the Convention on the Conservation of Antarctic Marine Living Resources, or inconsistency between the measures in effect pursuant to those instruments and measures in effect pursuant to this Convention.

Article 11
Inspection under the Antarctic Treaty

All stations, installations and equipment, in the Antarctic Treaty area, relating to Antarctic mineral resource activities, as well as ships and aircraft supporting such activities at points of discharging or embarking cargoes or personnel at such stations and installations, shall be open at all times to inspection by observers designated under Article VII of the Antarctic Treaty for the purposes of that Treaty.

Article 12
Inspection under This Convention

1.   In order to promote the objectives and principles and to ensure the observance of this Convention and measures in effect pursuant to it, all stations, installations and equipment relating to Antarctic mineral resource activities in the area in which these activities are regulated by this Convention, as well as ships and aircraft supporting such activities at points of discharging or embarking cargoes or personnel anywhere in that area shall be open at all times to inspection by:

(*a*) observers designated by any member of the Commission who shall be nationals of that member; and

(*b*) observers designated by the Commission or relevant Regulatory Committees.

2.   Aerial inspection may be carried out at any time over the area in which Antarctic mineral resource activities are regulated by this Convention.

3.   The Commission shall maintain an up-to-date list of observers designated pursuant to paragraph 1(a) and (b) above.

4.   Reports from the observers shall be transmitted to the Commission and to any Regulatory Committee having competence in the area where the inspection has been carried out.

5.   Observers shall avoid interference with the safe and normal operations of stations, installations and equipment visited and shall respect measures adopted by the Commission to protect confidentiality of data and information.

6. Inspections undertaken pursuant to paragraph 1(a) and (b) above shall be compatible and reinforce each other and shall not impose an undue burden on the operation of stations, installations and equipment visited.

7. In order to facilitate the exercise of their functions under this Convention, and without prejudice to the respective positions of the Parties relating to jurisdiction over all other persons in the area in which Antarctic mineral resource activities are regulated by this Convention, observers designated under this Article shall be subject only to the jurisdiction of the Party of which they are nationals in respect of all acts or omissions occurring while they are in that area for the purpose of exercising their functions.

8. No exploration or development shall take place in an area identified pursuant to Article 41 until effective provision has been made for inspection in that area.

Article 13
Protected Areas

1. Antarctic mineral resource activities shall be prohibited in any area designated as a Specially Protected Area or a Site of Special Scientific Interest under Article IX(1) of the Antarctic Treaty. Such activities shall also be prohibited in any other area designated as a protected area in accordance with Article IX(1) of the Antarctic Treaty, except to the extent that the relevant measure provides otherwise pending any designation becoming effective in accordance with Article IX(4) of the Antarctic Treaty, no Antarctic mineral resource activities shall take place in any such area which would prejudice the purpose for which it was designated.

2. The Commission shall also prohibit or restrict Antarctic mineral resource activities in any area which, for historic, ecological, environmental, scientific or other reasons, it has designated as a protected area.

3. In exercising its powers under paragraph 2 above or under Article 41 the Commission shall consider whether to restrict or prohibit Antarctic mineral resource activities in any area, in addition to those referred to in paragraph 1 above, protected or set aside pursuant to provisions of other components of the Antarctic Treaty system, to ensure the purposes which they are designated.

4. In relation to any area in which Antarctic mineral resource activities are prohibited or restricted in accordance with paragraph 1, 2 or 3 above, the Commission shall consider whether, for the purposes of Article 4(2)(e), it would be prudent, additionally, to prohibit or restrict Antarctic mineral resource activities in adjacent areas for the purpose of creating a buffer zone.

5. The Commission shall give effect to Article 10(2) in acting pursuant to paragraphs 2, 3 and 4 above.

6. The Commission shall, where appropriate, bring any decisions it takes pursuant to this Article to the attention of the Antarctic Treaty Consultative Parties, the Contracting Parties to the Convention for the Conservation of Antarctic Seals, the Commission for the Conservation of Antarctic Marine Living Resources and the Scientific Committee on Antarctic Research.

Article 14
Non–Discrimination

In the implementation of this Convention there shall be no discrimination against any Party or its Operators.

Article 15
Respect for Other Uses of Antarctica

1. Decisions about Antarctic mineral resource activities shall take into account the need to respect other established uses of Antarctica, including:

(*a*) the operation of stations and their associated installations, support facilities and equipment in Antarctica;

(*b*) scientific investigation in Antarctic and cooperation therein;

(*c*) the conservation, including national use, of Antarctic marine living resources;

(*d*) tourism;

(*e*) the preservation of historic monuments; and

(*f*) navigation and aviation, that are consistent with the Antarctic Treaty system.

2. Antarctic mineral resource activities shall be conducted so as to respect any uses of Antarctica as referred to in paragraph 1 above.

Article 16
Availability and Confidentiality of Data and Information

Data and information obtained from Antarctic mineral resource activities shall, to the greatest extent practicable and feasible, be made freely available, provided that:

(*a*) as regards data and information of commercial value deriving from prospecting, they may be retained by the Operator in accordance with Article 37;

(*b*) as regards data and information deriving from exploration or development, the Commission shall adopt measures relating, as appropriate, to their release and to ensure the confidentiality of data and information of commercial value.

Article 17
Notifications and Provisional Exercise of Functions of the Executive Secretary

1. Where in this Convention there is a reference to the provision of information, a notification or a report to any institution provided for in this Convention and that institution has not been established, the information, notification or report shall be provided to the Executive Secretary who shall circulate it as required.

2. Where in this Convention a function is assigned to the Executive Secretary and no Executive Secretary has been appointed under Article 33, that function shall be performed by the Depositary.

CHAPTER II: INSTITUTIONS
Article 18
Commission

1. There is hereby established the Antarctic Mineral Resources Commission.

2. Membership of the Commission shall be as follows:

(*a*) each Party which was an Antarctic Treaty Consultative Party on the date when this Convention was opened for signature; and

(*b*) each other Party during such time as it is actively engaged in substantial scientific, technical or environmental research in the area to which this Convention applies directly relevant to decisions about Antarctic mineral resource activities, particularly the assessments and judgments called for in Article 4; and

(*c*) each other Party sponsoring Antarctic mineral resource exploration or development during such time as the relevant Management Scheme is in force.

3. A Party seeking to participate in the work of the Commission pursuant to subparagraph (b) or (c) above shall notify the Depositary of the basis upon which it

seeks to become a member of the Commission. In the case of a Party which is not an Antarctic Treaty Consultative Party, such notification shall include a declaration of intent to abide by recommendations pursuant to Article IX(1) of the Antarctic Treaty. The Depositary shall communicate to each member of the Commission such notification and accompanying information.

4. The Commission shall consider the notification at its next meeting. In the event that a Party referred to in paragraph 2(b) above submitting a notification pursuant to paragraph 3 above is an Antarctic Treaty Consultative Party, it shall be deemed to have satisfied the requirements for Commission membership unless more than one-third of the members of the Commission object at the meeting at which such notification is considered. Any other Party submitting a notification shall be deemed to have satisfied the requirements for Commission membership if no member of the Commission objects at the meeting at which such notification is considered.

5. Each member of the Commission shall be represented by one representative who may be accompanied by alternate representatives and advisers.

6. Observer status in the Commission shall be open to any Party and to any Contracting Party to the Antarctic Treaty which is not a Party to this Convention.

Article 19
Commission Meetings

1. (*a*) The first meeting of the Commission, held for the purpose of taking organizational, financial and other decisions necessary for the effective functioning of this Convention and its institutions, shall be convened within six months of the entry into force of this Convention.

(*b*) After the Commission has held the meeting or meetings necessary to take the decisions referred to in subparagraph (a) above, the Commission shall not hold further meetings except in accordance with paragraph 2 or 3 below.

2. Meetings of the Commission shall be held within two months of:

(*a*) receipt of a notification pursuant to Article 39;

(*b*) a request by at least six members of the Commission; or

(*c*) a request by a member of a Regulatory Committee in accordance with Article 49(1).

3. The Commission may establish a regular schedule of meetings if it determines that it is necessary for the effective functioning of this Convention.

4. Unless the Commission decides otherwise, its meetings shall be convened by the Executive Secretary

5. Each member of the Commission shall be represented by one representative who may be accompanied by alternate representatives and advisers.

6. Observer status in the Commission shall be open to any Party and to any Contracting Party to the Antarctic Treaty which is not a Party to this Convention.

Article 20
Commission Procedure

1. The Commission shall elect from among its members a Chairman and two Vice–Chairmen, each of whom shall be a representative of a different Party.

2. (*a*) Until such time as the Commission has established a regular schedule of meetings in accordance with Article 19(3), the Chairman and Vice–Chairmen shall be elected to serve for a period of two years, provided that if no meeting is held during that period they shall continue to serve until the conclusion of the first meeting held thereafter.

(*b*) When a regular schedule of meetings has been established, the Chairman and Vice–Chairmen shall be elected to serve for a period of two years.

3. The Commission shall adopt its rules of procedure. Such rules may include provisions concerning the number of terms of office which the Chairman and Vice–Chairmen may serve and for the rotation of such offices.

4. The Commission may establish such subsidiary bodies as are necessary for the performance of its functions.

5. The Commission may decide to establish a permanent headquarters which shall be in New Zealand.

6. The Commission shall have legal personality and shall enjoy in the territory of each Party such legal capacity as may be necessary to perform its functions and achieve the objectives of this Convention.

7. The privileges and immunities to be enjoyed by the Commission, the Secretariat and representatives attending meetings in the territory of a Party shall be determined by agreement between the Commission and the Party concerned.

Article 21
Functions of the Commission

1. The functions of the Commission shall be:

(*a*) to facilitate and promote the collection and exchange of scientific, technical and other information and research projects necessary to predict, detect and assess the possible environmental impact of Antarctic mineral resource activities, including the monitoring of key environmental parameters and ecosystem components;

(*b*) to designate areas in which Antarctic mineral resource activities shall be prohibited or restricted in accordance with Article 13, and to perform the related functions assigned to it in that Article;

(*c*) to adopt measures for the protection of the Antarctic environment and dependent and associated ecosystems and for the promotion of safe and effective exploration and development techniques and, as it may deem appropriate, to make available a handbook of such measures;

(*d*) to determine, in accordance with Article 41, whether or not to identify an area for possible exploration and development, and to perform the related functions assigned to it in Article 42;

(*e*) to adopt measures relating to prospecting applicable to all relevant Operators:

(i) to determine for particular circumstances maximum drilling depths in accordance with Article 1(8);

(ii) to restrict or prohibit prospecting consistently with Articles 13, 37 and 38;

(*f*) to ensure the effective application of Articles 12(4), 37(7) and (8), 38(2) and 39(2), which require the submission to the Commission of information, notifications and reports;

(*g*) to give advance public notice of matters upon which it is requesting the advice of the Advisory Committee;

(*h*) to adopt measures relating to the availability and confidentiality of data and information, including measures pursuant to Article 16;

(*i*) to elaborate the principle of non-discrimination set forth in Article 14;

(*j*) to adopt measures with respect to maximum block sizes;

(*k*) to perform the functions assigned to it in Article 29;

(*l*) to review action by Regulatory Committees in accordance with Article 49;

(*m*) to adopt measures in accordance with Articles 6 and 41(1)(d) related to the promotion of cooperation and to participation in Antarctic mineral resource activities;

(*n*) to adopt general measures pursuant to Article 51(6);

(*o*) to take decisions on budgetary matters and adopt financial regulations in accordance with Article 35;

(*p*) to adopt measures regarding fees payable in connection with notifications submitted pursuant to Articles 37 and 39 and applications lodged pursuant to Articles 44 and 53, the purpose of which fees shall be to cover the administrative costs of handling such notifications and applications;

(*q*) to adopt measures regarding levies payable by Operators engaged in exploration and development, the principal purpose of which levies shall be to cover the costs of the institutions of this Convention;

(*r*) to determine in accordance with Article 35(7) the disposition of revenues, if any, accruing to the Commission which are surplus to the requirements for financing the budget pursuant to Article 35;

(*s*) to perform the functions assigned to it in Article 7(7) and (8);

(*t*) to perform the functions relating to inspection assigned to it in Article 12;

(*u*) to consider monitoring reports received pursuant to Article 52;

(*v*) to perform the functions relating to dispute settlement assigned to it in Article 59;

(*w*) to perform the functions relating to consultation and cooperation assigned to it in Article 10(2) and 34;

(*x*) to keep under review the conduct of Antarctic mineral resource activities with a view to safeguarding the protection of the Antarctic environment in the interest of all mankind; and

(*y*) to perform such other functions as are provided for elsewhere in this Convention.

2. In performing its functions the Commission shall seek and take full account of the views of the Advisory Committee provided in accordance with Article 26.

3. Each measure adopted by the Commission shall specify the date on which it comes into effect.

4. The Commission shall, subject to Article 16 and measures in effect pursuant to it and paragraph 1(h) above, ensure that a publicly available record of its meetings and decisions and of information, notifications and reports submitted to it is maintained.

Article 22
Decision Making in the Commission

1. The Commission shall take decisions on matters of substance by a three-quarters majority of the members present and voting. When a question arises as to whether a matter is one of substance or not, that matter shall be treated as one of substance unless otherwise decided by a three-quarters majority of the members present and voting.

2. Notwithstanding paragraph 1 above, consensus shall be required for the following:

(*a*) the adoption of the budget and decisions on budgetary and related matters pursuant to Article 22(1)(p), (q) and (r) and Article 35(1), (2), (3), (4) and (5);

(*b*) decisions taken pursuant to Article 21(1)(i);

(*c*) decisions taken pursuant to Article 41(2).

3. Decisions on matters of procedure shall be taken by a simple majority of the members present and voting.

4. Nothing in this Article shall be interpreted as preventing the Commission, in taking decisions on matters of substance, from endeavouring to reach a consensus.

5. For the purposes of this Article, consensus means the absence of a formal objection. If, with respect to any decision covered by paragraph 2(c) above, the Chairman of the Commission determines that there would be such an objection he shall consult the members of the Commission. If, as a result of these consultations, the Chairman determines that an objection would remain, he shall convene those members most directly interested for the purpose of seeking to reconcile the differences and producing a generally acceptable proposal.

Article 23
Advisory Committee

1. There is hereby established the Scientific, Technical and Environmental Advisory Committee.

2. Membership of the Advisory Committee shall be open to all Parties.

3. Each member of the advisory Committee shall be represented by one representative with suitable scientific, technical or environmental competence who may be accompanied by alternate representatives and by experts and advisers.

4. Observer status in the Advisory Committee shall be open to any Contracting Party to the Antarctic Treaty or to the Convention on the Conservation of Antarctic Marine Living Resources which is not a Party to this Convention.

Article 24
Advisory Committee Meetings

1. Unless the Commission decides otherwise, the Advisory Committee shall be convened for its first meeting within six months of the first meeting of the Commission. It shall meet thereafter as necessary to fulfill its functions on the basis of a schedule established by the Commission.

2. Meetings of the Advisory Committee, in addition to those scheduled pursuant to paragraph 1 above, shall be convened at the request of at least six members of the Commission or pursuant to Article 40(1).

3. Unless the Commission decides otherwise, the meetings of the Advisory Committee shall be convened by the Executive Secretary.

Article 25
Advisory Committee Procedure

1. The Advisory Committee shall elect from among its members a Chairman and two Vice–Chairmen, each of whom shall be a representative of a different Party.

2. (*a*) Until such time as the Commission has established a schedule of meetings in accordance with Article 24(1), the Chairman and Vice–Chairmen shall be elected to serve for a period of two years, provided that if no meeting is held during that period they shall continue to serve until the conclusion of the first meeting held thereafter.

(*b*) When a schedule of meetings has been established, the Chairman and Vice–Chairmen shall be elected to serve for a period of two years.

3. The Advisory Committee shall give advance public notice of its meetings and of matters to be considered at each meeting so as to permit the receipt and consideration of views on such matters from international organizations having an interest in them. For this purpose the Advisory Committee may, subject to review by the Commission, establish procedures for the transmission of relevant information to these organizations.

4. The Advisory Committee shall, by a two-thirds majority of the members present and voting, adopt its rules of procedure. Such rules may include provisions concerning the number of terms of office which the Chairman and Vice–Chairmen may serve and for the rotation of such offices. The rules of procedure and any amendments thereto shall be subject to approval by the Commission.

5. The Advisory Committee may establish such subcommittees, subject to budgetary approval, as may be necessary for the performance of its functions.

Article 26
Functions of the Advisory Committee

1. The Advisory Committee shall advise the Commission and Regulatory Committees, as required by this Convention, or as requested by them, on the scientific, technical and environmental aspects of Antarctic mineral resources activities. It shall provide a forum for consultation and cooperation concerning the collection, exchange and evaluation of information related to the scientific, technical and environmental aspects of Antarctic mineral resource activities.

2. It shall provide advice to:

(*a*) the Commission relating to its functions under Articles 21(1)(a) to (f), (u) and 35(7)(a) (in matters relating to scientific research) as well as on the implementation of Article 4; and

(*b*) Regulatory Committees with respect to:

(i) the implementation of Article 4;

(ii) scientific, technical and environmental aspects of Articles 43(3) and (5), 45, 47, 51, 52 and 54;

(iii) data to be collected and reported in accordance with Articles 47 and 52; and

(iv) the scientific, technical and environmental implications of reports and reported data provided in accordance with Articles 47 and 53.

3. It shall provide advice to the Commission and to Regulatory Committees on:

(*a*) criteria in respect of the judgments required under Article 4(2) and (3) for the purposes of Article 4(1);

(*b*) types of data and information required to carry out its functions, and how they should be collected reported and archived;

(*c*) scientific research which would contribute to the base of data and information required in subparagraph (b) above;

(*d*) effective procedures and systems for data and information analysis, evaluation, presentation and dissemination to facilitate the judgments referred to in Article 4; and

(*e*) possibilities for scientific, technical and environmental cooperation amongst interested Parties which are developing countries and other Parties.

4. The Advisory Committee, in providing advice on decisions to be taken in accordance with Articles 41, 43, 45 and 54 shall, in each case, undertake a comprehensive environmental and technical assessment of the proposed actions. Such assess-

ments shall be based on all information, and any amplifications thereof, available to the Advisory Committee, including the information provided pursuant to Articles 39(2)(e), 44(2)(b)(iii) and 53(2)(b). The assessments of the Advisory Committee shall, in each case, address the nature and scope of the decisions to be taken and shall include consideration, as appropriate, of, *inter alia:*

(*a*) the adequacy of existing information to enable informed judgments to be made;

(*b*) the nature, extent, duration and intensity of likely direct environmental impacts resulting from the proposed activity;

(*c*) possible indirect impacts;

(*d*) means and alternatives by which such direct or indirect impacts might be reduced, including environmental consequences of the alternative of not proceeding;

(*e*) cumulative impacts of the proposed activity in the light of existing or planned activities;

(*f*) capacity to respond effectively to accidents with potential environmental effects;

(*g*) the environmental significance of unavoidable impacts; and

(*h*) the probabilities of accidents and their environmental consequences.

5. In preparing its advice the Advisory Committee may seek information and advice from other scientists and experts or scientific organizations as may be required on an *ad hoc* basis.

6. The Advisory Committee shall, with a view to promoting international participation in Antarctic mineral resource activities as provided for in Article 6, provide advice concerning the availability to interested developing country Parties and other Parties, of the information referred to in paragraph 3 above, of training programmes related to scientific, technical and environmental matters bearing on Antarctic mineral resource activities, and of opportunities for cooperation among Parties in these programmes.

Article 27
Reporting by the Advisory Committee

The Advisory Committee shall present a report on each of its meetings to the Commission and to any relevant Regulatory Committee. The report shall cover all matters considered at the meeting and shall reflect the conclusions reached and all the views expressed by members of the Advisory Committee. The report shall be circulated by the Executive Secretary to all Parties, and to observers attending the meeting, and shall thereupon be made publicly available.

Article 28
Special Meeting of Parties

1. A Special Meeting of Parties shall, as required, be convened in accordance with Article 40(2) and shall have the functions, in relation to the identification of an area for possible exploration and development, specified in Article 40(3).

2. Membership of a Special Meeting of Parties shall be open to all Parties, each of which shall be represented by one representative who may be accompanied by alternate representative who may be accompanied by alternate representatives and advisers.

3. Observer status at a Special Meeting of Parties shall be open to any Contracting Party to the Antarctic Treaty which is not a Party to this Convention.

4. Each Special Meeting of Parties shall elect from among its members a Chairman and Vice–Chairman, each of whom shall serve for the duration of that meeting. The Chairman and Vice–Chairman shall not be representatives of the same Party.

5. The Special Meeting of Parties shall, by a two-thirds majority of the members present and voting, adopt its rules of procedure. Until such time as this has been done the Special Meeting of Parties shall apply provisional rules of procedure drawn up by the Commission.

6. Unless the Commission decides otherwise, a Special Meeting of Parties shall be convened by the Executive Secretary and shall be held at the same venue as the meeting of the Commission convened to consider the identification of an area for possible exploration and development.

Article 29
Regulatory Committees

1. An Antarctic Mineral Resources Regulatory Committee shall be established for each area identified by the Commission pursuant to Article 41.

* * *

CHAPTER III: PROSPECTING

Article 37
Prospecting

1. Prospecting shall not confer upon any Operator any right to Antarctic mineral resources.

2. Prospecting shall at all times be conducted in compliance with this Convention and with measures in effect pursuant to this Convention, but shall not require authorization by the institutions of this Convention.

* * *

7. The Sponsoring State shall notify the Commission at least nine months in advance of the commencement of planned prospecting. . . .

* * *

Article 38
Consideration of Prospecting by the Commission

1. If a member of the Commission considers that a notification submitted in accordance with Article 37(7) or (8), or ongoing prospecting, causes concern as to consistency with this Convention or measures in effect pursuant thereto, that member may request the Sponsoring State to provide a clarification. If that member considers that an adequate response is not forthcoming from the Sponsoring State within a reasonable time, the member may request that the Commission be convened in accordance with Article 19(2)(b) to consider the question and take appropriate action.

2. If measures applicable to all relevant Operators are adopted by the Commission following a request made in accordance with paragraph 1 above, Sponsoring States that have submitted notifications in accordance with Article 37(7) or (8), and Sponsoring States whose Operators are conducting prospecting, shall ensure that the plans and activities of their Operators are modified to the extent necessary to conform with those measures within such time limit as the Commission may prescribe, and shall notify the Commission accordingly.

CHAPTER IV: EXPLORATION

Article 39
Requests for Identification of an Area for Possible Exploration and Development

1. Any Party may submit to the Executive Secretary a notification requesting that the Commission identify an area for possible exploration and development of a particular mineral resource or resources.

* * *

Article 41
Action by the Commission

1. The Commission shall, as soon as possible after receipt of the report of the Special Meeting of Parties, consider whether or not it will identify an area as requested. Taking full account of the views and giving special weight to the conclusions of the Special Meeting of Parties, and taking full account of the views and the conclusions of the Advisory Committee, the Commission shall determine whether such identification would be consistent with this Convention. For this purpose:

(a) the Commission shall ensure that an area to be identified shall be such that, taking into account all factors relevant to such identification, including the physical, geological, environmental and other characteristics of such area, it forms a coherent unit for the purposes of resource management. The Commission shall thus consider whether an area to be identified should include all or part of that which was requested in the notification and, subject to the necessary assessments having been made, adjacent areas not covered by that notification;

(b) the Commission shall consider whether there are, within an area requested or to be identified, any areas in which exploration and development are or should be prohibited or restricted in accordance with Article 13;

(c) the Commission shall specify the mineral resource or resources for which the area would be identified;

(d) the Commission shall give effect to Article 6, by elaborating opportunities for joint ventures or different forms of participation, up to a defined level, including procedures for offering such participation, in possible exploration and development, within the area, by interested Parties which are Antarctic Treaty Consultative Parties and by other interested Parties, in particular, developing countries in either category;

(e) the Commission shall prescribe any additional associated conditions necessary to ensure that an area to be identified is consistent with other provisions of this Convention and may prescribe general guidelines relating to the operational requirements for exploration and development in an area to be identified including measures establishing maximum block sizes and advice concerning related support activities; and

(f) the Commission shall give effect to the requirement in Article 59 to establish additional procedures for the settlement of disputes.

2. After it has completed its consideration in accordance with paragraph 1 above, the Commission shall identify an area for possible exploration and development if there is a consensus of Commission members that such identification is consistent with this Convention.

* * *

Article 44
Application for an Exploration Permit

1. Following completion of the work undertaken pursuant to Article 43, any Party, on behalf of an Operator for which it is the Sponsoring State, may lodge with the Regulatory Committee an application for an exploration permit within the periods established by the Regulatory Committee pursuant to Article 43(2)(c).

* * *

Article 45
Examination of Applications

1. The Regulatory Committee shall meet as soon as possible after an application has been lodged pursuant to Article 44, for the purpose of elaborating a Management Scheme. . . .

* * *

Article 47
Scope of the Management Scheme

The Management Scheme shall prescribe the specific terms and conditions for exploration and development of the mineral resource or resources concerned within the relevant block. . . .

* * *

CHAPTER V: DEVELOPMENT

Article 53
Application for a Development Permit

1. At any time during the period in which an approved Management Scheme and exploration permit are in force for an Operator, the Sponsoring State may, on behalf of that Operator, lodge with the Regulatory Committee an application for a development permit.

2. An application shall be accompanied by the fees established by the Regulatory Committee in accordance with Article 43(2)(b) and shall contain:

(*a*) an updated description of the planned development identifying any modifications proposed to the approved Management Scheme and any additional measures to be taken, consequent upon such modifications, to ensure consistency with this Convention, including any measures in effect pursuant thereto and the general requirements referred to in Article 43(3);

(*b*) a detailed assessment of the environmental and other impacts of the planned development, taking into account Articles 15 and 26(4);

(*c*) a recertification by the Sponsoring State of the technical competence and financial capacity of the Operator and that the Operator has a substantial and genuine link with it as defined in Article 1(12);

(*d*) a recertification by the Sponsoring State of the capacity of the Operator to comply with the general requirements referred to in Article 43(3);

(*e*) updated information in relation to all other matters specified in Article 44(2); and

(*f*) such further information as may be required by the Regulatory Committee or in measures adopted by the Commission.

Article 54
Examination of Applications and Issue of Development Permits

1. The Regulatory Committee shall meet as soon as possible after an application has been lodged pursuant to Article 53.

2. The Regulatory Committee shall determine whether the application contains sufficient or adequate information pursuant to Article 53(2). In performing this function it may at any time seek further information from the Sponsoring State consistent with Article 53(2).

3. The Regulatory Committee shall consider whether:

(a) the application reveals modifications to the planned development previously envisaged;

(b) the planned development would cause previously unforeseen impacts on the Antarctic environment or dependent or associated ecosystems, either as a result of any modifications referred to in subparagraph (a) above or in the light of increased knowledge.

4. The Regulatory Committee shall consider any modifications to the Management Scheme necessary in the light of paragraph 3 above to ensure that the development activities proposed would be undertaken consistently with this Convention as well as measures in effect pursuant thereto and the general requirements referred to in Article 43(3). However, the financial obligations specified in the approved Management Scheme may not be revised without the consent of the Sponsoring State, unless provided for in the Management Scheme itself.

5. If the Regulatory Committee in accordance with Article 32 approves modifications under paragraph 4 above, or if it does not consider that such modifications are necessary, the Regulatory Committee shall issue without delay a development permit.

6. In performing its functions under this Article, the Regulatory Committee shall seek and take full account of the views of the Advisory Committee. To that end the Regulatory Committee shall refer to the Advisory Committee all parts of the application which are necessary for it to provide advice pursuant to Article 26, together with any other relevant information.

CHAPTER VI: DISPUTES SETTLEMENT

Article 55
Disputes Between Two or More Parties

Articles 56, 57 and 58 apply to disputes between two or more Parties.

Article 56
Choice of Procedure

1. Each Party, when signing, ratifying, accepting, approving or acceding to this Convention, or at any time thereafter, may choose, by written declaration, one or both of the following means for the settlement of disputes concerning the interpretation or application of this Convention:

(a) the International Court of Justice;

(b) the Arbitral Tribunal.

2. A declaration made under paragraph 1 above shall not affect the operation of Article 57(1), (3), (4) and (5).

3. A Party that has not made a declaration under paragraph 1 above or in respect of which a declaration is no longer in force shall be deemed to have accepted the competence of the Arbitral Tribunal.

4. If the parties to a dispute have accepted the same means for the settlement of a dispute, the dispute may be submitted only to that procedure, unless the parties otherwise agree.

5. If the parties to a dispute have not accepted the same means for the settlement of a dispute, or if they have both accepted both means, the dispute may be submitted only to the Arbitral Tribunal, unless the parties otherwise agree.

6. A declaration made under paragraph 1 above shall remain in force until it expires in accordance with its terms or until 3 months after written notice of revocation has been deposited with the Depositary.

7. A new declaration, a notice of revocation or the expiry of a declaration shall not in any way affect proceedings pending before the International Court of Justice or the Arbitral Tribunal, unless the parties to the dispute otherwise agree.

8. Declarations and notices referred to in this Article shall be deposited with the Depositary who shall transmit copies thereof to all Parties.

[*Provisions on dispute settlement and final clauses omitted because of space limitations.*]

* * *

6.8 RESOLUTION ON THE QUESTION OF ANTARCTICA. **Adopted by the UN General Assembly, 15 December 1989. GA Res 44/124, UN GAOR, 44th Sess, Supp No 49, at 91, UN Doc A/44/49 (1989)**

A

The General Assembly,

Recalling its resolution 43/83 B of 7 December 1988,

Having considered the item entitled "Question of Antarctica",

Noting with regret that the racist *apartheid* régime of South Africa, which has been suspended from participation in the General Assembly of the United Nations, has continued to participate in the meetings of the Antarctic Treaty Consultative Parties,

Recalling the resolution adopted by the Council of Ministers of the Organization of African Unity at its fiftieth ordinary session, held at Addis Ababa from 17 to 22 July 1989,

Recalling also the final document on Antarctica adopted by the Ninth Conference of Heads of State or Government of Non–Aligned Countries, held at Belgrade from 4 to 7 September 1989,

Recalling further that the Antarctic Treaty is, by its terms, intended to further the purposes and principles embodied in the Charter of the United Nations,

Noting that the policy of *apartheid* practised by the racist minority régime of South Africa, which has been universally condemned, constitutes a threat to regional and international peace and security,

1. *Views with concern* the continuing participation of the *apartheid* régime of South Africa in the meetings of the Antarctic Treaty Consultative Parties;

2. *Appeals once again* to the Antarctic Treaty Consultative Parties to take urgent measures to exclude the racist *apartheid* régime of South Africa from participation in the meetings of the Consultative Parties at the earliest possible date;

3. *Invites* the States parties to the Antarctic Treaty to inform the Secretary–General of the actions taken regarding the provisions of the present resolution;

4. *Requests* the Secretary–General to submit a report in this regard to the General Assembly at its forty-fifth session;

5. *Decides* to include in the provisional agenda of its forty-fifth session the item entitled "Question of Antarctica".

B

The General Assembly,

Having considered the item entitled "Question of Antarctica",

Recalling its resolutions 38/77 of 15 December 1983, 39/152 of 17 December 1984, 40/156 A and B of 16 December 1985, 41/88 A and B of 4 December 1986, 42/46 A and B of 30 November 1987 and 43/83 A and B of 7 December 1988,

Recalling also the relevant paragraphs of the Political Declaration adopted by the Eighth Conference of Heads of State or Government of Non–Aligned Countries, held at Harare from 1 to 6 September 1986, and the resolution on Antarctica adopted by the Council of Ministers of the Organization of African Unity at its forty-second ordinary session, held at Addis Ababa from 10 to 17 July 1985, as well as the relevant paragraphs of the decision of the Council of Ministers of the League of Arab States meeting at Tunis on 17 and 18 September 1986 and resolution 25/5–P(IS) adopted by the Fifth Islamic Summit Conference of the Organization of the Islamic Conference, held at Kuwait from 26 to 29 January 1987, the final document on Antarctica adopted by the Ninth Conference of Heads of State or Government of Non–Aligned Countries, held at Belgrade from 4 to 7 September 1989 and the communiqué issued by Commonwealth Heads of Government at Kuala Lumpur on 24 October 1989,

Taking into account the debates on this item held since its thirty-eighth session,

Welcoming the increasing awareness of and interest in Antarctica shown by the international community,

Convinced of the advantages to the whole of mankind of a better knowledge of Antarctica,

Affirming its conviction that, in the interest of all mankind, Antarctica should continue forever to be used exclusively for peaceful purposes and that it should not become the scene or object of international discord,

Reaffirming the principle that the international community is entitled to information covering all aspects of Antarctica and that the United Nations should be made the repository for all such information in accordance with General Assembly resolutions 41/88 A, 42/46 B and 43/83 A,

Conscious of the particular significance of Antarctica to the international community in terms, *inter alia,* of international peace and security, environment, its effects on global climatic conditions, economy and scientific research,

Conscious also of the interrelationship between Antarctica and the physical, chemical and biological processes that regulate the total Earth system,

Reaffirming that the management and use of Antarctica should be conducted in accordance with the purposes and principles of the Charter of the United Nations and in the interest of maintaining international peace and security and of promoting international co-operation for the benefit of mankind as a whole,

Affirming the necessity of ensuring, in the interest of all mankind, comprehensive environmental protection and conservation of the Antarctic environment and its dependent and associated ecosystems through negotiations with the full participation of all members of the international community,

Conscious of the environmental degradation that prospecting and mining in and around Antarctica would pose to the Antarctic and global environment and ecosystems,

Convinced of the need to prevent or minimize any impact of human activity resulting from the large number of scientific stations and expeditions in Antarctica on the environment and its dependent and associated ecosystems,

Taking into account all aspects pertaining to all areas covered by the Antarctic Treaty system,

Taking note with appreciation of the reports of the Secretary–General on the question of Antarctica,

1. *Expresses its regret* that, despite the numerous resolutions in which it has called upon the Antarctic Treaty Consultative Parties to invite the Secretary–General or his representative to their meetings, including their consultative meetings, the Secretary–General was not invited to the Preparatory Meeting of the XVth Antarctic Treaty Consultative Meeting or to the XVth Consultative Meeting, held in Paris from 9 to 13 May and from 9 to 20 October 1989, respectively;

2. *Reiterates its call* upon the Antarctic Treaty Consultative Parties to invite the Secretary–General or his representative to all meetings of the Treaty parties, including their consultative meetings;

3. *Requests* the Secretary–General to submit a report on his evaluations thereon to the General Assembly at its forty-fifth session;

4. *Expresses the conviction* that, in view of the significant impact that Antarctica exerts on the global environment and ecosystems, any régime to be established for the

protection and conservation of the Antarctic environment and its dependent and associated ecosystems, in order to be for the benefit of mankind as a whole and in order to gain the universal acceptability necessary to ensure full compliance and enforcement, must be negotiated with the full participation of all members of the international community;

5.   *Urges* all members of the international community to support all efforts to ban prospecting and mining in and around Antarctica and to ensure that all activities are carried out exclusively for the purpose of peaceful scientific investigation and that all such activities ensure the maintenance of international peace and security in Antarctica and the protection of its environment and are for the benefit of all mankind;

6.   *Expresses its conviction* that the establishment, through negotiations with the full participation of all members of the international community, of Antarctica as a nature reserve or a world park would ensure the protection and conservation of its environment and its dependent and associated ecosystems for the benefit of all mankind;

7.   *Also expresses its conviction,* in view of the large number of scientific stations and expeditions, that international scientific research should be enhanced through the establishment of international stations devoted to scientific investigations of global significance, regulated by stringent environmental safeguards, so as to avoid or minimize any adverse impact of human activities on the Antarctic environment and its dependent and associated ecosystems;

8.   *Urges* all States Members of the United Nations to co-operate with the Secretary–General and to continue consultations on all aspects relating to Antarctica;

9.   *Decides* to include in the provisional agenda of its forty-fifth session the item entitled "Question of Antarctica".

6.9   Protocol on Environmental Protection to the Antarctic Treaty (With Annexes I, III & VI Only).[c] Concluded at Madrid, 4 October 1991. Entered into force, 14 January 1998.[d] XI ATSCM/2; *reprinted in* 30 ILM 1461 (1991) & 5 Weston & Carlson V.D.6

PREAMBLE

The States Parties to this Protocol to the Antarctic Treaty, hereinafter referred to as the Parties,

Convinced of the need to enhance the protection of the Antarctic environment and dependent and associated ecosystems;

Convinced of the need to strengthen the Antarctic Treaty system so as to ensure that Antarctica shall continue forever to be used exclusively for peaceful purposes and shall not become the scene or object of international discord;

Bearing in mind the special legal and political status of Antarctica and the special responsibility of the Antarctic Treaty Consultative Parties to ensure that all activities in Antarctica are consistent with the purposes and principles of the Antarctic Treaty;

Recalling the designation of Antarctica as a Special Conservation Area and other measures adopted under the Antarctic Treaty system to protect the Antarctic environment and dependent and associated ecosystems;

Acknowledging further the unique opportunities Antarctica offers for scientific monitoring of and research on processes of global as well as regional importance;

Reaffirming the conservation principles of the Convention on the Conservation of Antarctic Marine Living Resources;

Convinced that the development of a comprehensive regime for the protection of the Antarctic environment and dependent and associated ecosystems is in the interest of mankind as a whole;

Desiring to supplement the Antarctic Treaty to this end;

Have agreed as follows:

ARTICLE 1
DEFINITIONS

For the purposes of this Protocol:

(a) "The Antarctic Treaty" means the Antarctic Treaty done at Washington on 1 December 1959;

(b) "Antarctic Treaty area" means the area to which the provisions of the Antarctic Treaty apply in accordance with Article VI of that Treaty;

(c) "Antarctic Treaty Consultative Meetings" means the meetings referred to in Article IX of the Antarctic Treaty;

(d) "Antarctic Treaty Consultative Parties" means the Contracting Parties to the Antarctic Treaty entitled to appoint representatives to participate in the meetings referred to in Article IX of that Treaty;

(e) "Antarctic Treaty system" means the Antarctic Treaty, the measures in effect under that Treaty, its associated separate international instruments in force and the measures in effect under those instruments;

c. *See also* Basic Document 6.1, *supra.*

d. The Protocol and Annexes I–IV were effective on 14 January 1998. Annex V was adopted on 18 October 1991 and went into force on 24 May 2002. Annex VI was adopted on 17 June 2005 and is not in force at this writing.

(f) "Arbitral Tribunal" means the Arbitral Tribunal established in accordance with the Schedule to this Protocol, which forms an integral part thereof;

(g) "Committee" means the Committee for Environmental Protection established in accordance with Article 11.

ARTICLE 2
OBJECTIVE AND DESIGNATION

The Parties commit themselves to the comprehensive protection of the Antarctic environment and dependent and associated ecosystems and hereby designate Antarctica as a natural reserve, devoted to peace and science.

ARTICLE 3
ENVIRONMENTAL PRINCIPLES

1. The protection of the Antarctic environment and dependent and associated ecosystems and the intrinsic value of Antarctica, including its wilderness and aesthetic values and its value as an area for the conduct of scientific research, in particular research essential to understanding the global environment, shall be fundamental considerations in the planning and conduct of all activities in the Antarctic Treaty area.

2. To this end:

(a) activities in the Antarctic Treaty area shall be planned and conducted so as to limit adverse impacts on the Antarctic environment and dependent and associated ecosystems;

(b) activities in the Antarctic Treaty area shall be planned and conducted so as to avoid:

(i) adverse effects on climate or weather patterns;

(ii) significant adverse effects on air or water quality;

(iii) significant changes in the atmospheric, terrestrial (including aquatic), glacial or marine environments;

(iv) detrimental changes in the distribution, abundance or productivity of species or populations of species of fauna and flora;

(v) further jeopardy to endangered or threatened species or populations of such species; or

(vi) degradation of, or substantial risk to, areas of biological, scientific, historic, aesthetic or wilderness significance;

(c) activities in the Antarctic Treaty area shall be planned and conducted on the basis of information sufficient to allow prior assessments of, and informed judgments about, their possible impacts on the Antarctic environment and dependent and associated ecosystems and on the value of Antarctica for the conduct of scientific research; such judgments shall take full account of:

(i) the scope of the activity, including its area, duration and intensity;

(ii) the cumulative impacts of the activity, both by itself and in combination with other activities in the Antarctic Treaty area;

(iii) whether the activity will detrimentally affect any other activity in the Antarctic Treaty area;

(iv) whether technology and procedures are available to provide for environmentally safe operations;

(v) whether there exists the capacity to monitor key environmental parameters and ecosystem components so as to identify and provide early warning of any adverse effects of the activity and to provide for such modification of operating procedures as may be necessary in the light of the results of monitoring or increased knowledge of the Antarctic environment and dependent and associated ecosystems; and

(vi) whether there exists the capacity to respond promptly and effectively to accidents, particularly those with potential environmental effects;

(d) regular and effective monitoring shall take place to allow assessment of the impacts of ongoing activities, including the verification of predicted impacts;

(e) regular and effective monitoring shall take place to facilitate early detection of the possible unforeseen effects of activities carried on both within and outside the Antarctic Treaty area on the Antarctic environment and dependent and associated ecosystems.

3. Activities shall be planned and conducted in the Antarctic Treaty area so as to accord priority to scientific research and to preserve the value of Antarctica as an area for the conduct of such research, including research essential to understanding the global environment.

4. Activities undertaken in the Antarctic Treaty area pursuant to scientific research programmes, tourism and all other governmental and non-governmental activities in the Antarctic Treaty area for which advance notice is required in accordance with Article VII(5) of the Antarctic Treaty, including associated logistic support activities, shall:

(a) take place in a manner consistent with the principles in this Article; and

(b) be modified, suspended or cancelled if they result in or threaten to result in impacts upon the Antarctic environment or dependent or associated ecosystems inconsistent with those principles.

ARTICLE 4
RELATIONSHIP WITH THE OTHER COMPONENTS OF THE ANTARCTIC TREATY SYSTEM

1. This Protocol shall supplement the Antarctic Treaty and shall neither modify nor amend that Treaty.

2. Nothing in this Protocol shall derogate from the rights and obligations of the Parties to this Protocol under the other international instruments in force within the Antarctic Treaty system.

ARTICLE 5
CONSISTENCY WITH THE OTHER COMPONENTS OF THE ANTARCTIC TREATY SYSTEM

The Parties shall consult and co-operate with the Contracting Parties to the other international instruments in force within the Antarctic Treaty system and their respective institutions with a view to ensuring the achievement of the objectives and principles of this Protocol and avoiding any interference with the achievement of the objectives and principles of those instruments or any inconsistency between the implementation of those instruments and of this Protocol.

ARTICLE 6
CO–OPERATION

1. The Parties shall co-operate in the planning and conduct of activities in the Antarctic Treaty area. To this end, each Party shall endeavour to:

(a) promote co-operative programmes of scientific, technical and educational value, concerning the protection of the Antarctic environment and dependent and associated ecosystems;

(b) provide appropriate assistance to other Parties in the preparation of environmental impact assessments;

(c) provide to other Parties upon request information relevant to any potential environmental risk and assistance to minimize the effects of accidents which may damage the Antarctic environment or dependent and associated ecosystems;

(d) consult with other Parties with regard to the choice of sites for prospective stations and other facilities so as to avoid the cumulative impacts caused by their excessive concentration in any location;

(e) where appropriate, undertake joint expeditions and share the use of stations and other facilities; and

(f) carry out such steps as may be agreed upon at Antarctic Treaty Consultative Meetings.

2. Each Party undertakes, to the extent possible, to share information that may be helpful to other Parties in planning and conducting their activities in the Antarctic Treaty area, with a view to the protection of the Antarctic environment and dependent and associated ecosystems.

3. The Parties shall co-operate with those Parties which may exercise jurisdiction in areas adjacent to the Antarctic Treaty area with a view to ensuring that activities in the Antarctic Treaty area do not have adverse environmental impacts on those areas.

ARTICLE 7
PROHIBITION OF MINERAL RESOURCE ACTIVITIES

Any activity relating to mineral resources, other than scientific research, shall be prohibited.

ARTICLE 8
ENVIRONMENTAL IMPACT ASSESSMENT

1. Proposed activities referred to in paragraph 2 below shall be subject to the procedures set out in Annex I for prior assessment of the impacts of those activities on the Antarctic environment or on dependent or associated ecosystems according to whether those activities are identified as having:

(a) less than a minor or transitory impact;

(b) a minor or transitory impact; or

(c) more than a minor or transitory impact.

2. Each Party shall ensure that the assessment procedures set out in Annex I are applied in the planning processes leading to decisions about any activities undertaken in the Antarctic Treaty area pursuant to scientific research programmes, tourism and all other governmental and non-governmental activities in the Antarctic Treaty area for which advance notice is required under Article VII(5) of the Antarctic Treaty, including associated logistic support activities.

3. The assessment procedures set out in Annex I shall apply to any change in an activity whether the change arises from an increase or decrease in the intensity of an existing activity, from the addition of an activity, the decommissioning of a facility, or otherwise.

4. Where activities are planned jointly by more than one Party, the Parties involved shall nominate one of their number to coordinate the implementation of the environmental impact assessment procedures set out in Annex I.

ARTICLE 9
ANNEXES

1. The Annexes to this Protocol shall form an integral part thereof.

2. Annexes, additional to Annexes I–IV, may be adopted and become effective in accordance with Article IX of the Antarctic Treaty.

3. Amendments and modifications to Annexes may be adopted and become effective in accordance with Article IX of the Antarctic Treaty, provided that any Annex may itself make provision for amendments and modifications to become effective on an accelerated basis.

4. Annexes and any amendments and modifications thereto which have become effective in accordance with paragraphs 2 and 3 above shall, unless an Annex itself provides otherwise in respect of the entry into effect of any amendment or modification thereto, become effective for a Contracting Party to the Antarctic Treaty which is not an Antarctic Treaty Consultative Party, or which was not an Antarctic Treaty Consultative Party at the time of the adoption, when notice of approval of that Contracting Party has been received by the Depositary.

5. Annexes shall, except to the extent that an Annex provides otherwise, be subject to the procedures for dispute settlement set out in Articles 18 to 20.

ARTICLE 10
ANTARCTIC TREATY CONSULTATIVE MEETINGS

1. Antarctic Treaty Consultative Meetings shall, drawing upon the best scientific and technical advice available:

(a) define, in accordance with the provisions of this Protocol, the general policy for the comprehensive protection of the Antarctic environment and dependent and associated ecosystems; and

(b) adopt measures under Article IX of the Antarctic Treaty for the implementation of this Protocol.

2. Antarctic Treaty Consultative Meetings shall review the work of the Committee and shall draw fully upon its advice and recommendations in carrying out the tasks referred to in paragraph 1 above, as well as upon the advice of the Scientific Committee on Antarctic Research.

ARTICLE 11
COMMITTEE FOR ENVIRONMENTAL PROTECTION

1. There is hereby established the Committee for Environmental Protection.

2. Each Party shall be entitled to be a member of the Committee and to appoint a representative who may be accompanied by experts and advisers.

3. Observer status in the Committee shall be open to any Contracting Party to the Antarctic Treaty which is not a Party to this Protocol.

4. The Committee shall invite the President of the Scientific Committee on Antarctic Research and the Chairman of the Scientific Committee for the Conservation of Antarctic Marine Living Resources to participate as observers at its sessions. The Committee may also, with the approval of the Antarctic Treaty Consultative Meeting, invite such other relevant scientific, environmental and technical organisations which can contribute to its work to participate as observers at its sessions.

5. The Committee shall present a report on each of its sessions to the Antarctic Treaty Consultative Meeting. The report shall cover all matters considered at the session and shall reflect the views expressed. The report shall be circulated to the

Parties and to observers attending the session, and shall thereupon be made publicly available.

6. The Committee shall adopt its rules of procedure which shall be subject to approval by the Antarctic Treaty Consultative Meeting.

ARTICLE 12
FUNCTIONS OF THE COMMITTEE

1. The functions of the Committee shall be to provide advice and formulate recommendations to the Parties in connection with the implementation of this Protocol, including the operation of its Annexes, for consideration at Antarctic Treaty Consultative Meetings, and to perform such other functions as may be referred to it by the Antarctic Treaty Consultative Meetings. In particular, it shall provide advice on:

(a) the effectiveness of measures taken pursuant to this Protocol;

(b) the need to update, strengthen or otherwise improve such measures;

(c) the need for additional measures, including the need for additional Annexes, where appropriate;

(d) the application and implementation of the environmental impact assessment procedures set out in Article 8 and Annex I;

(e) means of minimising or mitigating environmental impacts of activities in the Antarctic Treaty area;

(f) procedures for situations requiring urgent action, including response action in environmental emergencies;

(g) the operation and further elaboration of the Antarctic Protected Area system;

(h) inspection procedures, including formats for inspection reports and checklists for the conduct of inspections;

(i) the collection, archiving, exchange and evaluation of information related to environmental protection;

(j) the state of the Antarctic environment; and

(k) the need for scientific research, including environmental monitoring, related to the implementation of this Protocol.

2. In carrying out its functions, the Committee shall, as appropriate, consult with the Scientific Committee on Antarctic Research, the Scientific Committee for the Conservation of Antarctic Marine Living Resources and other relevant scientific, environmental and technical organizations.

ARTICLE 13
COMPLIANCE WITH THIS PROTOCOL

1. Each Party shall take appropriate measures within its competence, including the adoption of laws and regulations, administrative actions and enforcement measures, to ensure compliance with this Protocol.

2. Each Party shall exert appropriate efforts, consistent with the Charter of the United Nations, to the end that no one engages in any activity contrary to this Protocol.

3. Each Party shall notify all other Parties of the measures it takes pursuant to paragraphs 1 and 2 above.

4. Each Party shall draw the attention of all other Parties to any activity which in its opinion affects the implementation of the objectives and principles of this Protocol.

5. The Antarctic Treaty Consultative Meetings shall draw the attention of any State which is not a Party to this Protocol to any activity undertaken by that State, its agencies, instrumentalities, natural or juridical persons, ships, aircraft or other means of transport which affects the implementation of the objectives and principles of this Protocol.

ARTICLE 14
INSPECTION

1. In order to promote the protection of the Antarctic environment and dependent and associated ecosystems, and to ensure compliance with this Protocol, the Antarctic Treaty Consultative Parties shall arrange, individually or collectively, for inspections by observers to be made in accordance with Article VII of the Antarctic Treaty.

2. Observers are:

(a) observers designated by any Antarctic Treaty Consultative Party who shall be nationals of that Party; and

(b) any observers designated at Antarctic Treaty Consultative Meetings to carry out inspections under procedures to be established by an Antarctic Treaty Consultative Meeting.

3. Parties shall co-operate fully with observers undertaking inspections, and shall ensure that during inspections, observers are given access to all parts of stations, installations, equipment, ships and aircraft open to inspection under Article VII(3) of the Antarctic Treaty, as well as to all records maintained thereon which are called for pursuant to this Protocol.

4. Reports of inspections shall be sent to the Parties whose stations, installations, equipment, ships or aircraft are covered by the reports. After those Parties have been given the opportunity to comment, the reports and any comments thereon shall be circulated to all the Parties and to the Committee, considered at the next Antarctic Treaty Consultative Meeting, and thereafter made publicly available.

ARTICLE 15
EMERGENCY RESPONSE ACTION

1. In order to respond to environmental emergencies in the Antarctic Treaty area, each Party agrees to:

(a) provide for prompt and effective response action to such emergencies which might arise in the performance of scientific research programmes, tourism and all other governmental and nongovernmental activities in the Antarctic Treaty area for which advance notice is required under Article VII(5) of the Antarctic Treaty, including associated logistic support activities; and

(b) establish contingency plans for response to incidents with potential adverse effects on the Antarctic environment or dependent and associated ecosystems.

2. To this end, the Parties shall:

(a) co-operate in the formulation and implementation of such contingency plans; and

(b) establish procedures for immediate notification of, and co-operative response to, environmental emergencies.

3. In the implementation of this Article, the Parties shall draw upon the advice of the appropriate international organisations.

ARTICLE 16
LIABILITY

Consistent with the objectives of this Protocol for the comprehensive protection of the Antarctic environment and dependent and associated ecosystems, the Parties undertake to elaborate rules and procedures relating to liability for damage arising from activities taking place in the Antarctic Treaty area and covered by this Protocol. Those rules and procedures shall be included in one or more Annexes to be adopted in accordance with Article 9(2).

ARTICLE 17
ANNUAL REPORT BY PARTIES

1. Each Party shall report annually on the steps taken to implement this Protocol. Such reports shall include notifications made in accordance with Article 13(3), contingency plans established in accordance with Article 15 and any other notifications and information called for pursuant to this Protocol for which there is no other provision concerning the circulation and exchange of information.

2. Reports made in accordance with paragraph 1 above shall be circulated to all Parties and to the Committee, considered at the next Antarctic Treaty Consultative Meeting, and made publicly available.

ARTICLE 18
DISPUTE SETTLEMENT

If a dispute arises concerning the interpretation or application of this Protocol, the parties to the dispute shall, at the request of any one of them, consult among themselves as soon as possible with a view to having the dispute resolved by negotiation, inquiry, mediation, conciliation, arbitration, judicial settlement or other peaceful means to which the parties to the dispute agree.

ARTICLE 19
CHOICE OF DISPUTE SETTLEMENT PROCEDURE

1. Each Party, when signing, ratifying, accepting, approving or acceding to this Protocol, or at any time thereafter, may choose, by written declaration, one or both of the following means for the settlement of disputes concerning the interpretation or application of Articles 7, 8 and 15 and, except to the extent that an Annex provides otherwise, the provisions of any Annex and, insofar as it relates to these Articles and provisions, Article 13:

(a) the International Court of Justice;

(b) the Arbitral Tribunal.

2. A declaration made under paragraph 1 above shall not affect the operation of Article 18 and Article 20(2).

3. A Party which has not made a declaration under paragraph 1 above or in respect of which a declaration is no longer in force shall be deemed to have accepted the competence of the Arbitral Tribunal.

4. If the parties to a dispute have accepted the same means for the settlement of a dispute, the dispute may be submitted only to that procedure, unless the parties otherwise agree.

5. If the parties to a dispute have not accepted the same means for the settlement of a dispute, or if they have both accepted both means, the dispute may be submitted only to the Arbitral Tribunal, unless the parties otherwise agree.

6. A declaration made under paragraph 1 above shall remain in force until it expires in accordance with its terms or until three months after written notice of revocation has been deposited with the Depositary.

7. A new declaration, a notice of revocation or the expiry of a declaration shall not in any way affect proceedings pending before the International Court of Justice or the Arbitral Tribunal, unless the parties to the dispute otherwise agree.

8. Declarations and notices referred to in this Article shall be deposited with the Depositary who shall transmit copies thereof to all Parties.

ARTICLE 20
DISPUTE SETTLEMENT PROCEDURE

1. If the parties to a dispute concerning the interpretation or application of Articles 7, 8 or 15 or, except to the extent that an Annex provides otherwise, the provisions of any Annex or, insofar as it relates to these Articles and provisions, Article 13, have not agreed on a means for resolving it within 12 months of the request for consultation pursuant to Article 18, the dispute shall be referred, at the request of any party to the dispute, for settlement in accordance with the procedure determined by Article 19(4) and (5).

2. The Arbitral Tribunal shall not be competent to decide or rule upon any matter within the scope of Article IV of the Antarctic Treaty. In addition, nothing in this Protocol shall be interpreted as conferring competence or jurisdiction on the International Court of Justice or any other tribunal established for the purpose of settling disputes between Parties to decide or otherwise rule upon any matter within the scope of Article IV of the Antarctic Treaty.

ARTICLE 21
SIGNATURE

This Protocol shall be open for signature at Madrid on the 4th of October 1991 and thereafter at Washington until the 3rd of October 1992 by any State which is a Contracting Party to the Antarctic Treaty.

ARTICLE 22
RATIFICATION, ACCEPTANCE, APPROVAL OR ACCESSION

1. This Protocol is subject to ratification, acceptance or approval by signatory States.

2. After the 3rd of October 1992 this Protocol shall be open for accession by any State which is a Contracting Party to the Antarctic Treaty.

3. Instruments of ratification, acceptance, approval or accession shall be deposited with the Government of the United States of America, hereby designated as the Depositary.

4. After the date on which this Protocol has entered into force, the Antarctic Treaty Consultative Parties shall not act upon a notification regarding the entitlement of a Contracting Party to the Antarctic Treaty to appoint representatives to participate in Antarctic Treaty Consultative Meetings in accordance with Article IX(2) of the Antarctic Treaty unless that Contracting Party has first ratified, accepted, approved or acceded to this Protocol.

ARTICLE 23
ENTRY INTO FORCE

1. This Protocol shall enter into force on the thirtieth day following the date of deposit of instruments of ratification, acceptance, approval or accession by all States

which are Antarctic Treaty Consultative Parties at the date on which this Protocol is adopted.

2. For each Contracting Party to the Antarctic Treaty which, subsequent to the date of entry into force of this Protocol, deposits an instrument of ratification, acceptance, approval or accession, this Protocol shall enter into force on the thirtieth day following such deposit.

ARTICLE 24
RESERVATIONS

Reservations to this Protocol shall not be permitted.

ARTICLE 25
MODIFICATION OR AMENDMENT

1. Without prejudice to the provisions of Article 9, this Protocol may be modified or amended at any time in accordance with the procedures set forth in Article XII(1)(a) and (b) of the Antarctic Treaty.

2. If, after the expiration of 50 years from the date of entry into force of this Protocol, any of the Antarctic Treaty Consultative Parties so requests by a communication addressed to the Depositary, a conference shall be held as soon as practicable to review the operation of this Protocol.

3. A modification or amendment proposed at any Review Conference called pursuant to paragraph 2 above shall be adopted by a majority of the Parties, including 3/4 of the States which are Antarctic Treaty Consultative Parties at the time of adoption of this Protocol.

4. A modification or amendment adopted pursuant to paragraph 3 above shall enter into force upon ratification, acceptance, approval or accession by 3/4 of the Antarctic Treaty Consultative Parties, including ratification, acceptance, approval or accession by all States which are Antarctic Treaty Consultative Parties at the time of adoption of this Protocol.

5. (a) With respect to Article 7, the prohibition on Antarctic mineral resource activities contained therein shall continue unless there is in force a binding legal regime on Antarctic mineral resource activities that includes an agreed means for determining whether, and, if so, under which conditions, any such activities would be acceptable. This regime shall fully safeguard the interests of all States referred to in Article IV of the Antarctic Treaty and apply the principles thereof. Therefore, if a modification or amendment to Article 7 is proposed at a Review Conference referred to in paragraph 2 above, it shall include such a binding legal regime.

(b) If any such modification or amendment has not entered into force within 3 years of the date of its adoption, any Party may at any time thereafter notify the Depositary of its withdrawal from this Protocol, and such withdrawal shall take effect 2 years after receipt of the notification by the Depositary.

ARTICLE 26
NOTIFICATIONS BY THE DEPOSITARY

The Depositary shall notify all Contracting Parties to the Antarctic Treaty of the following:

(a) signatures of this Protocol and the deposit of instruments of ratification, acceptance, approval or accession;

(b) the date of entry into force of this Protocol and any additional Annex thereto;

(c) the date of entry into force of any amendment or modification to this Protocol;

(d) the deposit of declarations and notices pursuant to Article 19; and

(e) any notification received pursuant to Article 25(5)(b)

ARTICLE 27
AUTHENTIC TEXTS AND REGISTRATION WITH THE UNITED NATIONS

1. This Protocol, done in the English, French, Russian and Spanish languages, each version being equally authentic, shall be deposited in the archives of the Government of the United States of America, which shall transmit duly certified copies thereof to all Contracting Parties to the Antarctic Treaty.

2. This Protocol shall be registered by the Depositary pursuant to Article 102 of the Charter of the United Nations.

* * *

Annex I

ENVIRONMENTAL IMPACT ASSESSMENT

ARTICLE 1
Preliminary Stage

1. The environmental impacts of proposed activities referred to in Article 8 of the Protocol shall, before their commencement, be considered in accordance with appropriate national procedures.

2. If an activity is determined as having less than a minor or transitory impact, the activity may proceed forthwith.

ARTICLE 2
Initial Environmental Evaluation

1. Unless it has been determined that an activity will have less than a minor or transitory impact, or unless a Comprehensive Environmental Evaluation is being prepared in accordance with Article 3, an Initial Environmental Evaluation shall be prepared. It shall contain sufficient detail to assess whether a proposed activity may have more than a minor or transitory impact and shall include:

(a) a description of the proposed activity, including its purpose, location, duration, and intensity; and

(b) consideration of alternatives to the proposed activity and any impacts that the activity may have, including consideration of cumulative impacts in the light of existing and known planned activities.

2. If an Initial Environmental Evaluation indicates that a proposed activity is likely to have no more than a minor or transitory impact, the activity may proceed, provided that appropriate procedures, which may include monitoring, are put in place to assess and verify the impact of the activity.

ARTICLE 3
Comprehensive Environmental Evaluation

1. If an Initial Environmental Evaluation indicates or if it is otherwise determined that a proposed activity is likely to have more than a minor or transitory impact, a Comprehensive Environmental Evaluation shall be prepared.

2. A Comprehensive Environmental Evaluation shall include:

(a) a description of the proposed activity including its purpose, location, duration and intensity, and possible alternatives to the activity, including the alternatives of not proceeding, and the consequences of those alternatives;

(b) a description of the initial environmental reference state with which predicted changes are to be compared and a prediction of the future environmental reference state in the absence of the proposed activity;

(c) a description of the methods and data used to forecast the impacts of the proposed activity;

(d) estimation of the nature, extent, duration, and intensity of the likely direct impacts of the proposed activity;

(e) consideration of possible indirect or second order impacts of the proposed activity;

(f) consideration of cumulative impacts of the proposed activity in the light of existing activities and other known planned activities;

(g) identification of measures, including monitoring programmes, that could be taken to minimise or mitigate impacts of the proposed activity and to detect unforeseen impacts and that could provide early warning of any adverse effects of the activity as well as to deal promptly and effectively with accidents;

(h) identification of unavoidable impacts of the proposed activity;

(i) consideration of the effects of the proposed activity on the conduct of scientific research and on other existing uses and values;

(j) an identification of gaps in knowledge and uncertainties encountered in compiling the information required under this paragraph;

(k) a non-technical summary of the information provided under this paragraph; and

(*l*) the name and address of the person or organization which prepared the Comprehensive Environmental Evaluation and the address to which comments thereon should be directed.

3. The draft Comprehensive Environmental Evaluation shall be made publicly available and shall be circulated to all Parties, which shall also make it publicly available, for comment. A period of 90 days shall be allowed for the receipt of comments.

4. The draft Comprehensive Environmental Evaluation shall be forwarded to the Committee at the same time as it is circulated to the Parties, and at least 120 days before the next Antarctic Treaty Consultative Meeting, for consideration as appropriate.

5. No final decision shall be taken to proceed with the proposed activity in the Antarctic Treaty area unless there has been an opportunity for consideration of the draft Comprehensive Environmental Evaluation by the Antarctic Treaty Consultative Meeting on the advice of the Committee, provided that no decision to proceed with a proposed activity shall be delayed through the operation of this paragraph for longer than 15 months from the date of circulation of the draft Comprehensive Environmental Evaluation.

6. A final Comprehensive Environmental Evaluation shall address and shall include or summarise comments received on the draft Comprehensive Environmental Evaluation. The final Comprehensive Environmental Evaluation, notice of any decisions relating thereto, and any evaluation of the significance of the predicted impacts in relation to the advantages of the proposed activity, shall be circulated to all Parties, which shall also make them publicly available, at least 60 days before the commencement of the proposed activity in the Antarctic Treaty area.

ARTICLE 4
Decisions to Be Based on Comprehensive Environmental Evaluations

Any decision on whether a proposed activity, to which Article 3 applies, should proceed, and, if so, whether in its original or in a modified form, shall be based on the Comprehensive Environmental Evaluation as well as other relevant considerations.

ARTICLE 5
Monitoring

1. Procedures shall be put in place, including appropriate monitoring of key environmental indicators, to assess and verify the impact of any activity that proceeds following the completion of a Comprehensive Environmental Evaluation.

2. The procedures referred to in paragraph 1 above and in Article 2(2) shall be designed to provide a regular and verifiable record of the impacts of the activity in order, *inter alia,* to:

(a) enable assessments to be made of the extent to which such impacts are consistent with the Protocol; and

(b) provide information useful for minimising or mitigating impacts, and, where appropriate, information on the need for suspension, cancellation or modification of the activity.

ARTICLE 6
Circulation of Information

1. The following information shall be circulated to the Parties, forwarded to the Committee and made publicly available:

(a) a description of the procedures referred to in Article 1;

(b) an annual list of any Initial Environmental Evaluations prepared in accordance with Article 2 and any decisions taken in consequence thereof;

(c) significant information obtained, and any action taken in consequence thereof, from procedures put in place in accordance with Articles 2(2) and 5; and

(d) information referred to in Article 3(6).

2. Any Initial Environmental Evaluation prepared in accordance with Article 2 shall be made available on request.

ARTICLE 7
Cases of Emergency

1. This Annex shall not apply in cases of emergency relating to the safety of human life or of ships, aircraft, or equipment and facilities of high value, or the protection of the environment, which require an activity to be undertaken without completion of the procedures set out in this Annex.

2. Notice of activities undertaken in cases of emergency, which would otherwise have required preparation of a Comprehensive Environmental Evaluation, shall be circulated immediately to all Parties and to the Committee and a full explanation of the activities carried out shall be provided within 90 days of those activities.

ARTICLE 8
Amendment or Modification

1. This Annex may be amended or modified by a measure adopted in accordance with Article IX(1) of the Antarctic Treaty. Unless the measure specifies otherwise, the amendment or modification shall be deemed to have been approved, and shall become effective, one year after the close of the Antarctic Treaty Consultative Meeting at

which it was adopted, unless one or more of the Antarctic Treaty Consultative Parties notifies the Depositary, within that period, that it wishes an extension of that period or that it is unable to approve the measure.

2. Any amendment or modification of this Annex which becomes effective in accordance with paragraph 1 above shall thereafter become effective as to any other Party when notice of approval by it has been received by the Depositary.

* * *

Annex III

WASTE DISPOSAL AND WASTE MANAGEMENT

ARTICLE 1
General Obligations

1. This Annex shall apply to activities undertaken in the Antarctic Treaty area pursuant to scientific research programmes, tourism and all other governmental and non-governmental activities in the Antarctic Treaty area for which advance notice is required under Article VII (5) of the Antarctic Treaty, including associated logistic support activities.

2. The amount of wastes produced or disposed of in the Antarctic Treaty area shall be reduced as far as practicable so as to minimise impact on the Antarctic environment and to minimise interference with the natural values of Antarctica, with scientific research and with other uses of Antarctica which are consistent with the Antarctic Treaty.

3. Waste storage, disposal and removal from the Antarctic Treaty area, as well as recycling and source reduction, shall be essential considerations in the planning and conduct of activities in the Antarctic Treaty area.

4. Wastes removed from the Antarctic Treaty area shall, to the maximum extent practicable, be returned to the country from which the activities generating the waste were organized or to any other country in which arrangements have been made for the disposal of such wastes in accordance with relevant international agreements.

5. Past and present waste disposal sites on land and abandoned work sites of Antarctic activities shall be cleaned up by the generator of such wastes and the user of such sites. This obligation shall not be interpreted as requiring:

(a) the removal of any structure designated as a historic site or monument; or

(b) the removal of any structure or waste material in circumstances where the removal by any practical option would result in greater adverse environmental impact than leaving the structure or waste material in its existing location.

ARTICLE 2
Waste Disposal by Removal From the Antarctic Treaty Area

1. The following wastes, if generated after entry into force of this Annex, shall be removed from the Antarctic Treaty area by the generator of such wastes:

(a) radio-active materials;

(b) electrical batteries;

(c) fuel, both liquid and solid;

(d) wastes containing harmful levels of heavy metals or acutely toxic or harmful persistent compounds;

(e) poly-vinyl chloride (PVC), polyurethane foam, polystyrene foam, rubber and lubricating oils, treated timbers and other products which contain additives that could produce harmful emissions if incinerated;

(f) all other plastic wastes, except low density polyethylene containers (such as bags for storing wastes), provided that such containers shall be incinerated in accordance with Article 3(1);

(g) fuel drums; and

(h) other solid, non-combustible wastes;

provided that the obligation to remove drums and solid non-combustible wastes contained in subparagraphs (g) and (h) above shall not apply in circumstances where the removal of such wastes by any practical option would result in greater adverse environmental impact than leaving them in their existing locations.

2. Liquid wastes which are not covered by paragraph 1 above and sewage and domestic liquid wastes, shall, to the maximum extent practicable, be removed from the Antarctic Treaty area by the generator of such wastes.

3. The following wastes shall be removed from the Antarctic Treaty area by the generator of such wastes, unless incinerated, autoclaved or otherwise treated to be made sterile:

(a) residues of carcasses of imported animals;

(b) laboratory culture of micro-organisms and plant pathogens; and

(c) introduced avian products.

ARTICLE 3

Waste Disposal by Incineration

1. Subject to paragraph 2 below, combustible wastes, other than those referred to in Article 2(1), which are not removed from the Antarctic Treaty area shall be burnt in incinerators which to the maximum extent practicable reduce harmful emissions. Any emissions standards and equipment guidelines which may be recommended by, inter alia, the Committee and the Scientific Committee on Antarctic Research shall be taken into account. The solid residue of such incineration shall be removed from the Antarctic Treaty area.

2. All open burning of wastes shall be phased out as soon as practicable, but no later than the end of the 1998/1999 season. Pending the completion of such phase-out, when it is necessary to dispose of wastes by open burning, allowance shall be made for the wind direction and speed and the type of wastes to be burnt to limit particulate deposition and to avoid such deposition over areas of special biological, scientific, historic, aesthetic or wilderness significance including, in particular, areas accorded protection under the Antarctic Treaty.

ARTICLE 4

Other Waste Disposal on Land

1. Wastes not removed or disposed of in accordance with Articles 2 and 3 shall not be disposed of onto ice-free areas or into fresh water systems.

2. Sewage, domestic liquid wastes and other liquid wastes not removed from the Antarctic Treaty area in accordance with Article 2, shall, to the maximum extent practicable, not be disposed of onto sea ice, ice shelves or the grounded ice-sheet, provided that such wastes which are generated by stations located inland on ice shelves or on the grounded ice-sheet may be disposed of in deep ice pits where such disposal is the only practicable option. Such pits shall not be located on known ice-flow lines which terminate at ice-free areas or in areas of high ablation.

3. Wastes generated at field camps shall, to the maximum extent practicable, be removed by the generator of such wastes to supporting stations or ships for disposal in accordance with this Annex.

ARTICLE 5
Disposal of Waste in the Sea

1. Sewage and domestic liquid wastes may be discharged directly into the sea, taking into account the assimilative capacity of the receiving marine environment and provided that:

(a) such discharge is located, wherever practicable, where conditions exist for initial dilution and rapid dispersal; and

(b) large quantities of such wastes (generated in a station where the average weekly occupancy over the austral summer is approximately 30 individuals or more) shall be treated at least by maceration.

2. The by-product of sewage treatment by the Rotary Biological Contactor process or similar processes may be disposed of into the sea provided that such disposal does not adversely affect the local environment, and provided also that any such disposal at sea shall be in accordance with Annex IV to the Protocol.

ARTICLE 6
Storage of Waste

All wastes to be removed from the Antarctic Treaty area, or otherwise disposed of, shall be stored in such a way as to prevent their dispersal into the environment.

ARTICLE 7
Prohibited Products

No polychlorinated biphenyls (PCBs), non-sterile soil, polystyrene beads, chips or similar forms of packaging, or pesticides (other than those required for scientific, medical or hygiene purposes) shall be introduced onto land or ice shelves or into water in the Antarctic Treaty area.

ARTICLE 8
Waste Management Planning

1. Each Party which itself conducts activities in the Antarctic Treaty area shall, in respect of those activities, establish a waste disposal classification system as a basis for recording wastes and to facilitate studies aimed at evaluating the environmental impacts of scientific activity and associated logistic support. To that end, wastes produced shall be classified as:

(a) sewage and domestic liquid wastes (Group 1);

(b) other liquid wastes and chemicals, including fuels and lubricants (Group 2);

(c) solids to be combusted (Group 3);

(d) other solid wastes (Group 4); and

(e) radioactive material (Group 5).

2. In order to reduce further the impact of waste on the Antarctic environment, each such Party shall prepare and annually review and update its waste management plans (including waste reduction, storage and disposal), specifying for each fixed site, for field camps generally, and for each ship (other than small boats that are part of the operations of fixed sites or of ships and taking into account existing management plans for ships):

(a) programmes for cleaning up existing waste disposal sites and abandoned work sites;

(b) current and planned waste management arrangements, including final disposal;

(c) current and planned arrangements for analysing the environmental effects of waste and waste management; and

(d) other efforts to minimise any environmental effects of wastes and waste management.

3. Each such Party shall, as far as is practicable, also prepare an inventory of locations of past activities (such as traverses, fuel depots, field bases, crashed aircraft) before the information is lost, so that such locations can be taken into account in planning future scientific programmes (such as snow chemistry, pollutants in lichens or ice core drilling).

ARTICLE 9
Circulation and Review of Waste Management Plans

1. The waste management plans prepared in accordance with Article 8, reports on their implementation, and the inventories referred to in Article 8(3), shall be included in the annual exchanges of information in accordance with Articles III and VII of the Antarctic Treaty and related Recommendations under Article IX of the Antarctic Treaty.

2. Each Party shall send copies of its waste management plans, and reports on their implementation and review, to the Committee.

3. The Committee may review waste management plans and reports thereon and may offer comments, including suggestions for minimising impacts and modifications and improvement to the plans, for the consideration of the Parties.

4. The Parties may exchange information and provide advice on, inter alia, available low waste technologies, reconversion of existing installations, special requirements for effluents, and appropriate disposal and discharge methods.

ARTICLE 10
Management Practices

Each Party shall:

(a) designate a waste management official to develop and monitor waste management plans; in the field, this responsibility shall be delegated to an appropriate person at each site;

(b) ensure that members of its expeditions receive training designed to limit the impact of its operations on the Antarctic environment and to inform them of requirements of this Annex; and

(c) discourage the use of poly-vinyl chloride (PVC) products and ensure that its expeditions to the Antarctic Treaty area are advised of any PVC products they may introduce into that area in order that these products may be removed subsequently in accordance with this Annex.

ARTICLE 11
Review

This Annex shall be subject to regular review in order to ensure that it is updated to reflect improvement in waste disposal technology and procedures and to ensure thereby maximum protection of the Antarctic environment.

ARTICLE 12
Cases of Emergency

1. This Annex shall not apply in cases of emergency relating to the safety of human life or of ships, aircraft or equipment and facilities of high value or the protection of the environment.

2. Notice of activities undertaken in cases of emergency shall be circulated immediately to all Parties and to the Committee.

ARTICLE 13
Amendment or Modification

1. This Annex may be amended or modified by a measure adopted in accordance with Article IX(1) of the Antarctic Treaty. Unless the measure specifies otherwise, the amendment or modification shall be deemed to have been approved, and shall become effective, one year after the close of the Antarctic Treaty Consultative Meeting at which it was adopted, unless one or more of the Antarctic Treaty Consultative Parties notifies the Depositary, within that time period, that it wishes an extension of that period or that it is unable to approve the amendment.

2. Any amendment or modification of this Annex which becomes effective in accordance with paragraph 1 above shall thereafter become effective as to any other Party when notice of approval by it has been received by the Depositary.

* * *

Annex VI
LIABILITY ARISING FROM ENVIRONMENTAL EMERGENCIES

Article 1
Scope

This Annex shall apply to environmental emergencies in the Antarctic Treaty area which relate to scientific research programmes, tourism and all other governmental and non-governmental activities in the Antarctic Treaty area for which advance notice is required under Article VII(5) of the Antarctic Treaty, including associated logistic support activities. Measures and plans for preventing and responding to such emergencies are also included in this Annex. It shall apply to all tourist vessels that enter the Antarctic Treaty area. It shall also apply to environmental emergencies in the Antarctic Treaty area which relate to other vessels and activities as may be decided in accordance with Article 13.

Article 2
Definitions

For the purposes of this Annex:

(a) *"Decision"* means a Decision adopted pursuant to the Rules of Procedure of Antarctic Treaty Consultative Meetings and referred to in Decision 1 (1995) of the XIXth Antarctic Treaty Consultative Meeting;

(b) *"Environmental emergency"* means any accidental event that has occurred, having taken place after the entry into force of this Annex, and that results in, or imminently threatens to result in, any significant and harmful impact on the Antarctic environment;

(c) *"Operator"* means any natural or juridical person, whether governmental or non-governmental, which organises activities to be carried out in the Antarctic Treaty area. An operator does not include a natural person who is an employee, contractor, subcontractor, or agent of, or who is in the service of, a natural or juridical person, whether governmental or non-governmental, which organises activities to be carried out in the Antarctic Treaty area, and does not include a juridical person that is a contractor or subcontractor acting on behalf of a State operator;

(d) *"Operator of the Party"* means an operator that organises, in that Party's territory, activities to be carried out in the Antarctic Treaty area, and:

(i) those activities are subject to authorisation by that Party for the Antarctic Treaty area; or

(ii) in the case of a Party which does not formally authorise activities for the Antarctic Treaty area, those activities are subject to a comparable regulatory process by that Party.

The terms "its operator", "Party of the operator", and "Party of that operator" shall be interpreted in accordance with this definition;

(e) *"Reasonable"*, as applied to preventative measures and response action, means measures or actions which are appropriate, practicable, proportionate and based on the availability of objective criteria and information, including:

(i) risks to the Antarctic environment, and the rate of its natural recovery;

(ii) risks to human life and safety; and

(iii) technological and economic feasibility;

(f) *"Response action"* means reasonable measures taken after an environmental emergency has occurred to avoid, minimise or contain the impact of that environmental emergency, which to that end may include clean-up in appropriate circumstances, and includes determining the extent of that emergency and its impact;

(g) *"The Parties"* means the States for which this Annex has become effective in accordance with Article 9 of the Protocol.

Article 3
Preventative Measures

1. Each Party shall require its operators to undertake reasonable preventative measures that are designed to reduce the risk of environmental emergencies and their potential adverse impact.

2. Preventative measures may include:

(a) specialised structures or equipment incorporated into the design and construction of facilities and means of transportation;

(b) specialised procedures incorporated into the operation or maintenance of facilities and means of transportation; and

(c) specialised training of personnel.

Article 4
Contingency Plans

1. Each Party shall require its operators to:

(a) establish contingency plans for responses to incidents with potential adverse impacts on the Antarctic environment or dependent and associated ecosystems; and

(b) co-operate in the formulation and implementation of such contingency plans.

2. Contingency plans shall include, when appropriate, the following components:

(a) procedures for conducting an assessment of the nature of the incident;

(b) notification procedures;

(c) identification and mobilisation of resources;

(d) response plans;

(e) training;

(f) record keeping; and

(g) demobilisation.

3. Each Party shall establish and implement procedures for immediate notification of, and co-operative responses to, environmental emergencies, and shall promote the use of notification procedures and co-operative response procedures by its operators that cause environmental emergencies.

Article 5
Response Action

1. Each Party shall require each of its operators to take prompt and effective response action to environmental emergencies arising from the activities of that operator.

2. In the event that an operator does not take prompt and effective response action, the Party of that operator and other Parties are encouraged to take such action, including through their agents and operators specifically authorised by them to take such action on their behalf.

3. (a) Other Parties wishing to take response action to an environmental emergency pursuant to paragraph 2 above shall notify their intention to the Party of the operator and the Secretariat of the Antarctic Treaty beforehand with a view to the Party of the operator taking response action itself, except where a threat of significant and harmful impact to the Antarctic environment is imminent and it would be reasonable in all the circumstances to take immediate response action, in which case they shall notify the Party of the operator and the Secretariat of the Antarctic Treaty as soon as possible.

(b) Such other Parties shall not take response action to an environmental emergency pursuant to paragraph 2 above, unless a threat of significant and harmful impact to the Antarctic environment is imminent and it would be reasonable in all the circumstances to take immediate response action, or the Party of the operator has failed within a reasonable time to notify the Secretariat of the Antarctic Treaty that it will take the response action itself, or where that response action has not been taken within a reasonable time after such notification.

(c) In the case that the Party of the operator takes response action itself, but is willing to be assisted by another Party or Parties, the Party of the operator shall coordinate the response action.

4. However, where it is unclear which, if any, Party is the Party of the operator or it appears that there may be more than one such Party, any Party taking response action shall make best endeavours to consult as appropriate and shall, where practicable, notify the Secretariat of the Antarctic Treaty of the circumstances.

5. Parties taking response action shall consult and coordinate their action with all other Parties taking response action, carrying out activities in the vicinity of the environmental emergency, or otherwise impacted by the environmental emergency, and shall, where practicable, take into account all relevant expert guidance which has been provided by permanent observer delegations to the Antarctic Treaty Consultative Meeting, by other organisations, or by other relevant experts.

Article 6
Liability

1. An operator that fails to take prompt and effective response action to environmental emergencies arising from its activities shall be liable to pay the costs of response action taken by Parties pursuant to Article 5(2) to such Parties.

2. (a) When a State operator should have taken prompt and effective response action but did not, and no response action was taken by any Party, the State operator shall be liable to pay the costs of the response action which should have been undertaken, into the fund referred to in Article 12.

(b) When a non-State operator should have taken prompt and effective response action but did not, and no response action was taken by any Party, the non-State operator shall be liable to pay an amount of money that reflects as much as possible the costs of the response action that should have been taken. Such money is to be paid directly to the fund referred to in Article 12, to the Party of that operator or to the Party that enforces the mechanism referred to in Article 7(3). A Party receiving such money shall make best efforts to make a contribution to the fund referred to in Article 12 which at least equals the money received from the operator.

3. Liability shall be strict.

4. When an environmental emergency arises from the activities of two or more operators, they shall be jointly and severally liable, except that an operator which establishes that only part of the environmental emergency results from its activities shall be liable in respect of that part only.

5. Notwithstanding that a Party is liable under this Article for its failure to provide for prompt and effective response action to environmental emergencies caused by its warships, naval auxiliaries, or other ships or aircraft owned or operated by it and used, for the time being, only on government non-commercial service, nothing in this Annex is intended to affect the sovereign immunity under international law of such warships, naval auxiliaries, or other ships or aircraft.

Article 7
Actions

1. Only a Party that has taken response action pursuant to Article 5(2) may bring an action against a non-State operator for liability pursuant to Article 6(1) and such action may be brought in the courts of not more than one Party where the operator is incorporated or has its principal place of business or his or her habitual place of residence. However, should the operator not be incorporated in a Party or have its principal place of business or his or her habitual place of residence in a Party, the action may be brought in the courts of the Party of the operator within the meaning of Article 2(d). Such actions for compensation shall be brought within three years of the commencement of the response action or within three years of the date on which the Party bringing the action knew or ought reasonably to have known the identity of the operator, whichever is later. In no event shall an action against a non-State operator be commenced later than 15 years after the commencement of the response action.

2. Each Party shall ensure that its courts possess the necessary jurisdiction to entertain actions under paragraph 1 above.

3. Each Party shall ensure that there is a mechanism in place under its domestic law for the enforcement of Article 6(2)(b) with respect to any of its non-State operators within the meaning of Article 2(d), as well as where possible with respect to any non-State operator that is incorporated or has its principal place of business or his or her habitual place of residence in that Party. Each Party shall inform all other Parties of this mechanism in accordance with Article 13(3) of the Protocol. Where there are multiple Parties that are capable of enforcing Article 6(2)(b) against any given non-State operator under this paragraph, such Parties should consult amongst themselves as to which Party should take enforcement action. The mechanism referred to in this paragraph shall not be invoked later than 15 years after the date the Party seeking to invoke the mechanism became aware of the environmental emergency.

4. The liability of a Party as a State operator under Article 6(1) shall be resolved only in accordance with any enquiry procedure which may be established by the Parties, the provisions of Articles 18, 19 and 20 of the Protocol and, as applicable, the Schedule to the Protocol on Arbitration.

5. (a) The liability of a Party as a State operator under Article 6(2)(a) shall be resolved only by the Antarctic Treaty Consultative Meeting and, should the question remain unresolved, only in accordance with any enquiry procedure which may be established by the Parties, the provisions of Articles 18, 19 and 20 of the Protocol and, as applicable, the Schedule to the Protocol on Arbitration.

(b) The costs of the response action which should have been undertaken and was not, to be paid by a State operator into the fund referred to in Article 12, shall be approved by means of a Decision. The Antarctic Treaty Consultative Meeting should seek the advice of the Committee on Environmental Protection as appropriate.

6. Under this Annex, the provisions of Articles 19(4), 19(5), and 20(1) of the Protocol, and, as applicable, the Schedule to the Protocol on Arbitration, are only applicable to liability of a Party as a State operator for compensation for response action that has been undertaken to an environmental emergency or for payment into the fund.

Article 8
Exemptions from Liability

1. An operator shall not be liable pursuant to Article 6 if it proves that the environmental emergency was caused by:

(a) an act or omission necessary to protect human life or safety;

(b) an event constituting in the circumstances of Antarctica a natural disaster of an exceptional character, which could not have been reasonably foreseen, either generally or in the particular case, provided all reasonable preventative measures have been taken that are designed to reduce the risk of environmental emergencies and their potential adverse impact;

(c) an act of terrorism; or

(d) an act of belligerency against the activities of the operator.

2. A Party, or its agents or operators specifically authorised by it to take such action on its behalf, shall not be liable for an environmental emergency resulting from response action taken by it pursuant to Article 5(2) to the extent that such response action was reasonable in all the circumstances.

Article 9
Limits of Liability

1. The maximum amount for which each operator may be liable under Article 6(1) or Article 6(2), in respect of each environmental emergency, shall be as follows:

(a) for an environmental emergency arising from an event involving a ship:

(i) one million SDR for a ship with a tonnage not exceeding 2,000 tons;

(ii) for a ship with a tonnage in excess thereof, the following amount in addition to that referred to in (i) above:

- for each ton from 2,001 to 30,000 tons, 400 SDR;

- for each ton from 30,001 to 70,000 tons, 300 SDR; and

- for each ton in excess of 70,000 tons, 200 SDR;

(b) for an environmental emergency arising from an event which does not involve a ship, three million SDR.

2. (a) Notwithstanding paragraph 1(a) above, this Annex shall not affect:

(i) the liability or right to limit liability under any applicable international limitation of liability treaty; or

(ii) the application of a reservation made under any such treaty to exclude the application of the limits therein for certain claims;provided that the applicable limits are at least as high as the following: for a ship with a tonnage not exceeding 2,000 tons, one million SDR; and for a ship with a tonnage in excess thereof, in addition, for a ship with a tonnage between 2,001 and 30,000 tons, 400 SDR for each ton; for a ship with a tonnage from 30,001 to 70,000 tons, 300 SDR for each ton; and for each ton in excess of 70,000 tons, 200 SDR for each ton.

(b) Nothing in subparagraph (a) above shall affect either the limits of liability set out in paragraph 1(a) above that apply to a Party as a State operator, or the rights and obligations of Parties that are not parties to any such treaty as mentioned above, or the application of Article 7(1) and Article 7(2).

3. Liability shall not be limited if it is proved that the environmental emergency resulted from an act or omission of the operator, committed with the intent to cause such emergency, or recklessly and with knowledge that such emergency would probably result.

4. The Antarctic Treaty Consultative Meeting shall review the limits in paragraphs 1(a) and 1(b) above every three years, or sooner at the request of any Party. Any amendments to these limits, which shall be determined after consultation amongst the Parties and on the basis of advice including scientific and technical advice, shall be made under the procedure set out in Article 13(2).

5. For the purpose of this Article:

(a) "ship" means a vessel of any type whatsoever operating in the marine environment and includes hydrofoil boats, air-cushion vehicles, submersibles, floating craft and fixed or floating platforms;

(b) "SDR" means the Special Drawing Rights as defined by the International Monetary Fund;

(c) a ship's tonnage shall be the gross tonnage calculated in accordance with the tonnage measurement rules contained in Annex I of the International Convention on Tonnage Measurement of Ships, 1969.

Article 10
State Liability

A Party shall not be liable for the failure of an operator, other than its State operators, to take response action to the extent that that Party took appropriate measures within its competence, including the adoption of laws and regulations, administrative actions and enforcement measures, to ensure compliance with this Annex.

Article 11
Insurance and Other Financial Security

1. Each Party shall require its operators to maintain adequate insurance or other financial security, such as the guarantee of a bank or similar financial institution, to cover liability under Article 6(1) up to the applicable limits set out in Article 9(1) and Article 9(2).

2. Each Party may require its operators to maintain adequate insurance or other financial security, such as the guarantee of a bank or similar financial institution, to cover liability under Article 6(2) up to the applicable limits set out in Article 9(1) and Article 9(2).

3. Notwithstanding paragraphs 1 and 2 above, a Party may maintain self-insurance in respect of its State operators, including those carrying out activities in the furtherance of scientific research.

Article 12
The Fund

1. The Secretariat of the Antarctic Treaty shall maintain and administer a fund, in accordance with Decisions including terms of reference to be adopted by the Parties, to provide, inter alia, for the reimbursement of the reasonable and justified costs incurred by a Party or Parties in taking response action pursuant to Article 5(2).

2. Any Party or Parties may make a proposal to the Antarctic Treaty Consultative Meeting for reimbursement to be paid from the fund. Such a proposal may be approved by the Antarctic Treaty Consultative Meeting, in which case it shall be approved by way of a Decision. The Antarctic Treaty Consultative Meeting may seek the advice of the Committee of Environmental Protection on such a proposal, as appropriate.

3. Special circumstances and criteria, such as: the fact that the responsible operator was an operator of the Party seeking reimbursement; the identity of the responsible operator remaining unknown or not subject to the provisions of this Annex; the unforeseen failure of the relevant insurance company or financial institution; or an exemption in Article 8 applying, shall be duly taken into account by the Antarctic Treaty Consultative Meeting under paragraph 2 above.

4. Any State or person may make voluntary contributions to the fund.

Article 13
Amendment or Modification

1. This Annex may be amended or modified by a Measure adopted in accordance with Article IX(1) of the Antarctic Treaty.

2. In the case of a Measure pursuant to Article 9(4), and in any other case unless the Measure in question specifies otherwise, the amendment or modification shall be deemed to have been approved, and shall become effective, one year after the close of the Antarctic Treaty Consultative Meeting at which it was adopted, unless one or more Antarctic Treaty Consultative Parties notifies the Depositary, within that time period, that it wishes any extension of that period or that it is unable to approve the Measure.

3. Any amendment or modification of this Annex which becomes effective in accordance with paragraph 1 or 2 above shall thereafter become effective as to any other Party when notice of approval by it has been received by the Depositary.

B. ARCTIC

6.10 ARCTIC ENVIRONMENTAL PROTECTION STRATEGY (AEPS). **Adopted by the eight Arctic countries, 14 June 1991.** *Reprinted in* **30 I.L.M. 1624 (1991)**

PREFACE

In September 1989, on the initiative of the government of Finland, officials from the eight Arctic countries met in Rovaniemi, Finland to discuss cooperative measures to protect the Arctic environment. They agreed to work towards a meeting of circumpolar Ministers responsible for Arctic environmental issues. The September 1989 meeting was followed by preparatory meetings in Yellowknife, Canada in April 1990; Kiruna, Sweden in January 1991; and, Rovaniemi, Finland in June 1991.

In addition to the numerous technical and scientific reports prepared under this initiative, the Arctic Environmental Protection Strategy was developed. This Strategy represents the culmination of the cooperative efforts of the eight Arctic countries:

Canada

Denmark

Finland

Iceland

Norway

Sweden

Union of Soviet Socialist Republics

United States of America.

The eight Arctic countries were assisted in the preparation of the Strategy by the following observers:

Inuit Circumpolar Conference

Nordic Saami Council

USSR Association of Small Peoples of the North

Federal Republic of Germany

Poland

United Kingdom

United Nations Economic Commission for Europe

United Nations Environment Program

International Arctic Science Committee

1. INTRODUCTION

There is a growing national and international appreciation of the importance of Arctic ecosystems and an increasing knowledge of global pollution and resulting environmental threats. The Arctic is highly sensitive to pollution and much of its human population and culture is directly dependent on the health of the region's ecosystems. Limited sunlight, ice cover that inhibits energy penetration, low mean and extreme temperatures, low species diversity and biological productivity and long-lived organisms with high lipid levels all contribute to the sensitivity of the Arctic ecosystem and cause it to be easily damaged. This vulnerability of the Arctic to pollution requires that action be taken now, or degradation may become irreversible.

The governments of the Arctic countries have become increasingly aware of the need for, and their responsibility to combat these threats to the Arctic ecosystem. On the initiative of Finland, the eight Arctic countries of USSR, USA, Sweden, Norway, Iceland, Finland, Denmark and Canada have met to prepare a strategy to protect the Arctic environment. The Arctic countries realize that the pollution problems of today do not respect national boundaries and that no state alone will be able to act effectively against environmental threats to the Arctic. They have also been moved by the international call for action expressed by the World Commission on Environment and Development as well as the concerns of the indigenous peoples living in the Arctic region. The Arctic countries with the participation of Arctic indigenous peoples have prepared this environmental protection Strategy. The Strategy builds on the initiatives already taken nationally and by indigenous peoples to protect the Arctic environment.

It is recognized that this Strategy, and its implementation, must incorporate the knowledge and culture of indigenous peoples. It is understood that the cultures and the continued existence of the indigenous peoples have been built on the sound stewardship of nature and its resources.

The use of natural resources is an important activity of Arctic nations. Therefore, this Strategy should allow for sustainable economic development in the north so that such development does not have unacceptable ecological or cultural impacts. The Strategy must also rely on the best scientific and technological advice that countries are able to produce and share.

Arctic ecosystems are influenced and in some cases threatened by factors occurring also outside the Arctic. In turn, the Arctic also exerts an important influence on the global environment. The implementation of an Arctic Environmental Protection Strategy will therefore benefit both the Arctic countries and the world at large. The Strategy is also designed to guide development in a way that will safeguard the Arctic environment for future generations and in a manner that is compatible with nature.

The Arctic countries are committed to international cooperation to ensure the protection of the Arctic environment and its sustainable and equitable development, while protecting the cultures of indigenous peoples.

Only through careful stewardship by Arctic countries and Arctic peoples can environmental damage and degradation be prevented. These are the challenges which must be taken up in order to secure our common future.

The Strategy is comprised of a number of component parts, beginning with a statement of objectives. These objectives establish the broad direction in which the eight-Arctic countries are intending to move. The objectives are accompanied by statements of principle which are designed to guide the actions of Arctic countries individually and collectively, as they move toward achievement of the objectives. The Strategy also describes the problems and priorities which the eight Arctic countries agree need to be addressed at this time.

Tools, whether legal, scientific or administrative, are also reviewed in order to define appropriate mechanisms for implementation of the Strategy. This is particularly relevant to that section of the Strategy which defines the specific actions that the eight countries will undertake jointly or individually to deal with priority issues and pollution problems. The implementation of the Strategy will be carried out through national legislation and in accordance with international law, including customary international law as reflected in the 1982 United Nations Convention on the Law of the Sea.

Finally, the Strategy outlines plans for future cooperation towards the implementation of the Strategy.

2. OBJECTIVES AND PRINCIPLES

2.1 Objectives

The objectives of the Arctic Environmental Protection Strategy are:

i) To protect the Arctic ecosystem including humans;

ii) To provide for the protection, enhancement and restoration of environmental quality and the sustainable utilization of natural resources, including their use by local populations and indigenous peoples in the Arctic;

iii) To recognize and, to the extent possible, seek to accommodate the traditional and cultural needs, values and practices of the indigenous peoples as determined by themselves, related to the protection of the Arctic environment;

iv) To review regularly the state of the Arctic environment;

v) To identify, reduce, and, as a final goal, eliminate pollution.

2.2 Principles:

The Arctic Environmental Protection Strategy and its implementation by the eight Arctic countries will be guided by the following principles:

i) Management, planning and development activities shall provide for the conservation, sustainable utilization and protection of Arctic ecosystems and natural resources for the benefit and enjoyment of present and future generations, including indigenous peoples;

ii) Use and management of natural resources shall be based on an approach which considers the value and interdependent nature of ecosystem components;

iii) Management, planning and development activities which may significantly affect the Arctic ecosystems shall:

> a) be based on informed assessments of their possible impacts on the Arctic environment, including cumulative impacts;

> b) provide for the maintenance of the regions's ecological systems and biodiversity;

> c) respect the Arctic's significance for and influence on the global climate;

> d) be compatible with the sustainable utilization of Arctic ecosystems;

> e) take into account the results of scientific investigations and the traditional knowledge of indigenous peoples;

vi) Information and knowledge concerning Arctic ecosystems and resource use will be developed and shared to support planning and should precede, accompany and follow development activities;

vii) Consideration of the health, social, economic and cultural needs and values of indigenous peoples shall be incorporated into management, planning and development activities;

viii) Development of a network of protected areas shall be encouraged and promoted with due regard for the needs of indigenous peoples;

ix) International cooperation to protect the Arctic environment shall be supported and promoted.

x) Mutual cooperation in fulfilling national and international responsibilities in the Arctic consistent with this Strategy, including the use, transfer and/or trade, of the most effective and appropriate technology to protect the environment, shall be promoted and developed.

3. PROBLEMS AND PRIORITIES

* * *

3.1   Persistent Organic Contaminants . . .

3.2   Oil Pollution . . .

3.3   Heavy Metals . . .

3.4   Noise

The waters of the Arctic region are a unique noise environment mainly due to the presence of ice. The ambient noise is strongly influenced by the dynamic processes of ice formation, melt, deformation and movement. This situation is different from ice free waters. In periods where ice cracking and wind noise are absent, areas covered by shore-fast ice are among the quietest underwater environments.

Human activities create noise types and levels, which may disturb marine mammals, or mask the "natural" sounds of importance to those mammals. Some types of noise may affect fish as well as marine mammals. There are a number of serious gaps in our knowledge of the effects of underwater noise on marine mammals, including the inability to assess the effect of repeated noise exposure on stocks.

There is considerable evidence that most types of disturbance do not cause mortality. However, some noisy activities, including low level overflights by aircraft, near seals and walrus at haul out sites can cause mortality through stampedes or abandonment.

Many marine mammals seem able to adapt to or at least tolerate many types of disturbances or increased noise levels. However the scarcity of direct evidence of serious consequences from disturbances does not necessarily mean that marine mammals are not stressed or affected in some other way. Noise from human activities may cause short-term or long-term behavioral reactions and temporary displacement of various marine mammals. The biological significance of most of these reactions is unknown.

Moving sound sources, notably boats and aircraft, seem to be more disturbing than stationary sources, e.g. dredges and drillships. The effects on fish and wildlife of cumulative exposure to noise are largely unknown.

3.5   Radioactivity . . .

3.6   Acidification . . .

4.   INTERNATIONAL MECHANISMS FOR THE PROTECTION OF THE ARCTIC ENVIRONMENT

* * *

4.4   Noise

Existing legal instruments do not address the effects of noise on the Arctic ecosystem. There may be a need for Arctic countries to agree on the adoption of procedures to ensure that in the planning and conduct of activities in the Arctic, measures are taken to facilitate the adequate monitoring of the potential disturbance from noise including the verification of predicted effects and the identification of any unforeseen effects. Such evaluations should ensure that environmental protection measures are given due consideration.

* * *

5.   ACTIONS

* * *

5.4 Noise

i) The effects of noise associated with Arctic marine and terrestrial projects should be evaluated as part of the project planning and approval processes, and if significant adverse noise effects on the specific components of Arctic ecosystems are predicted, then measures should be implemented to avoid or mitigate the impact.

ii) Efforts should be made to improve the knowledge on marine mammal auditory function, communication and behavior and the current noise exposure assessment techniques. For specific project evaluations, site-specific data should be addressed before and during the evaluation. This includes determining how much exposure migrating stocks are encountering throughout the year.

* * *

6. ARCTIC MONITORING AND ASSESSMENT PROGRAM

The eight Arctic countries recognize that the Arctic region represents one of the relatively pristine areas on earth. It is therefore of great importance to preserve and to protect the Arctic.

Measurements in the Arctic indicate that pollutants originating from anthropogenic activities in the mid-latitudes are transported to the Arctic by atmospheric processes, ocean currents and rivers, and that pollutants are deposited and accumulated in the Arctic environment and its ecosystems.

Exploitation of natural resources, and concomitant urban and industrial expansion within the Arctic region, also contribute to the degradation of the Arctic environment and affect the living conditions for the people of the region.

Distinguishing human-induced changes from changes caused by natural phenomena in the Arctic will require monitoring of selected key indicators of the Arctic Environment. Therefore, the eight Arctic countries have agreed to promote development of an Arctic Monitoring and Assessment Program (AMAP) in order to understand and document these changes and so that the monitoring results may be used to anticipate adverse biological, chemical and physical changes to the ecosystem and to prevent, minimize and mitigate these adverse effects.

The primary objective of the AMAP is the measurement of the levels of anthropogenic pollutants and the assessment of their effects in relevant component parts of the Arctic environment. The assessments should be presented in status reports to relevant fora as a basis for necessary steps to be taken to reduce the pollution.

Two of the most significant threats to the present Arctic environment may come from climate change, induced by global warming, and the effects of stratospheric ozone depletion. Programs to detect and determine the causes and effects of climate change and ozone depletion are to a large extent being developed by other international groupings and in other fora.

It is important for AMAP to be aware of these programs and to develop links with them from an Arctic perspective in order to encourage and facilitate an Arctic component in climate programs. Data obtained for assessing climate change will provide important inputs to the AMAP dataset. In turn, AMAP data will be relevant to climate change programs in the Arctic.

The pollution data available from the Arctic region are with a few exceptions based on research programs performed within limited subject areas by national programs and not supported by bilateral or international cooperation. There is an urgent need for cooperation among local and regional efforts and global programs in order to obtain better documentation on the environmental situation in the Arctic especially with regard to long-range air and marine pollution.

From the outset, the AMAP should as far as possible be based on existing programs. The program should be initiated in a step by step fashion as indicated in the proposal for the AMAP.

* * *

7. PROTECTION OF THE ARCTIC MARINE ENVIRONMENT

The eight Arctic Countries recognize their particular interests and responsibilities as neighbouring countries in the Arctic, and emphasize the need to take preventive measures directly or through competent international organizations, consistent in particular with the 1982 United Nations Convention on the Law of the Sea regarding marine pollution in the Arctic, irrespective of origin.

* * *

8. EMERGENCY PREVENTION, PREPAREDNESS AND RESPONSE

At the same time as the Arctic is exhibiting signs of serious contamination from pollutants carried via long range transport from mid latitudes, there has been an increase in development activities and shipping within the Arctic. These activities can have serious environmental consequences in the Arctic as a result of accidents leading, inter alia, to spills and discharges of oil and other harmful substances. The vulnerability of the Arctic ecosystem to these sudden intrusions will be variable. Some limited mapping of areas sensitive to oil spills has been conducted but more remains to be done. The relative hazard/risk associated with different activities is also not well documented, nor is the geographic distribution of high risk activities.

* * *

8.1 Actions

The Arctic countries agree to the following framework for taking early cooperative action on emergency prevention, preparedness and response in the Arctic. They will take steps to review existing bilateral and multilateral arrangements in order to evaluate the adequacy of the geographical coverage of the Arctic regions by cooperative agreements. They will also take steps to convene a meeting of experts to consider and recommend the necessary system of cooperation. . . .

9. CONSERVATION OF ARCTIC FLORA AND FAUNA

The health of Arctic flora and fauna is a key concern of the Arctic countries. These flora and fauna assume special significance in this region since they are an essential factor helping to define the culture and survival of the people living there. Although isolated geographically from the industrialized temperate regions of the globe, it has now been amply demonstrated that this has not excluded Arctic flora and fauna from the negative consequences of human activities in mid latitudes. The impacts on the Arctic have escalated over the past several decades and both scientific and traditional knowledge have been pointing to the danger signals. Many of these concerns are enumerated in the six Arctic state of the Environment reports. They confirm that Arctic flora, fauna and their habitats are being threatened by large scale economic development projects; long range transport of pollutants; and degradation of habitats.

The problems facing Arctic flora, fauna and habitats are not confined to any one country but are circumpolar in nature. Furthermore, because of the uniqueness of Arctic ecosystems, strategies to deal with these problems will differ from those of other regions.

Several multilateral and bilateral agreements which pertain to the conservation of Arctic flora and fauna and their habitats are currently in existence. Most however, have been designed to be universally applicable to, or to apply to, a wider geographical area than the Arctic. Only the Agreement on Conservation of Polar Bears and some individual provisions in other agreements provide a specific Arctic focus.

The eight Arctic countries should therefore seek to create a distinct forum for scientists, indigenous peoples and conservation managers engaged in Arctic flora, fauna and habitat related activities to exchange data and information on issues such as shared species and habitats and to collaborate, as appropriate, for more effective research, sustainable utilization and conservation.

9.1 Actions

The eight Arctic countries are mindful of the need to conserve Arctic flora and fauna and their habitats in their natural diversity, and protect these resources from the pollution threats described in this Arctic Environmental Protection Strategy. They recognize the special relationship and importance of Arctic flora and fauna and their habitats to indigenous peoples. The countries also recognize the benefits to be gained from sharing scientific and management information, traditional knowledge, and other data with respect to Arctic flora and fauna and their habitats. With due regard to existing international cooperation, and in an effort to improve research and information aimed at protecting these resources and their habitats from pollution and environmental degradation, they have reached the following understanding:

* * *

iv) The eight Arctic countries will each seek to develop more effective laws, regulations and practices for the conservation of Arctic flora and fauna, their diversity, and their habitats in close cooperation with Arctic indigenous peoples;

* * *

6.11 NUUK DECLARATION ON ENVIRONMENT AND DEVELOPMENT IN THE ARCTIC. **Adopted by the Ministers of the Arctic Counties, at Nuuk, Greenland, 16 September 1993. 1993 WL 645202**

We, the Ministers of the Arctic Countries,

Recognizing the special role and responsibilities of the Arctic Countries with respect to the protection of the Arctic environment,

Acknowledging that the Arctic environment consists of ecosystems with unique features and resources which are especially slow to recover from the impact of human activities, and as such, require special protective measures,

Further acknowledging that the indigenous peoples who have been permanent residents of the Arctic for millenia, are at risk from environmental degradation,

Determined individually and jointly, to conserve and protect the Arctic environment for the benefit of present and future generations, as well as for the global environment,

Noting that in order to achieve sustainable development, environmental protection shall constitute an integral part of the development process and cannot be considered in isolation from it,

Recognizing the importance of applying the results of the United Nations Conference on Environment and Development to the Arctic region,

Welcoming the efforts of the eight Arctic Countries to implement, through the Arctic Environmental Protection Strategy, relevant provisions of the Rio Declaration, Agenda 21 and the Forest Principles, efforts which include the Arctic Monitoring and Assessment Program (AMAP), and the Working Groups on the Conservation of Arctic Flora and Fauna (CAFF), Emergency Prevention, Preparedness and Response, and the Protection of the Arctic Marine Environment,

Affirming Principle 2 of the Rio Declaration on Environment and Development which affirms that States have, in accordance with the Charter of the United Nations and the principles of international law, the sovereign right to exploit their own resources pursuant to their own environmental and developmental policies, and the responsibility to ensure that activities within their jurisdiction or control do not cause damage to the environment of other States or of areas beyond the limits of national jurisdiction,

Further affirming Principle 22 of the Rio Declaration, which states that: "indigenous people and their communities.... have a vital role in environmental management and development because of their knowledge and traditional practices. States should recognize and duly support their identity, culture and interests and enable their effective participation in the achievement of sustainable development."

hereby make the following Declaration.

1. We reaffirm our commitment to the protection of the Arctic Environment as a priority and to the implementation of the Arctic Environmental Protection Strategy.

2. We adopt the report of the Second Ministerial Conference of the Arctic Environmental Protection Strategy, and endorse its provisions to implement the Strategy, in particular:

- seeking resources to enable each country to fully participate in the program activities under the Arctic Environmental Protection Strategy;

- endeavouring to support, through these resources, joint projects in order to ensure that each country is able to participate in the activities of the Arctic Monitoring and Assessment Program (AMAP), including the completion of national implementation plans and the comprehensive assessment of results;

- establishing a working group to assess the need for further action or instruments to prevent pollution of the Arctic marine environment and to evaluate the need for action in appropriate international fora to obtain international recognition of the particularly sensitive character of the ice-covered sea areas of the Arctic;

- reaffirming the commitment to sustainable development, including the sustainable use of renewable resources by indigenous peoples, and to that end agreeing to establish a Task Force for this purpose.

- underlining the necessity of a notification system and improved cooperation for mutual aid in case of accidents in the Arctic area:

- reaffirming that management, planning and development activities shall provide for the conservation, sustainable use and protection of Arctic flora and fauna for the benefit and enjoyment of present and future generations, including local populations and indigenous peoples.

3.   We will cooperate to conserve, protect and, as appropriate, restore the ecosystems of the Arctic. We will in particular cooperate to strengthen the knowledge base and to develop information and monitoring systems for the Arctic region.

4.   We recognize that effective domestic environmental legislation is a prerequisite to the protection of the environment. As Ministers we shall promote legislation required for the protection of the Arctic environment.

5.   We support the achievements of the United Nations Conference on Environment and Development, and state our beliefs that the Principles of the Rio Declaration on Environment and Development have particular relevance with respect to sustainable development in the Arctic.

6.   We believe that decisions relating to Arctic activities must be made in a transparent fashion and therefore undertake to facilitate, through national rules and legislation, appropriate access to information concerning such decisions, to participation in such decisions and to judicial and administrative proceedings.

7.   We recognize the special role of the indigenous peoples in environmental management and development in the Arctic, and of the significance of their knowledge and traditional practices, and will promote their effective participation in the achievement of sustainable development in the Arctic.

8.   We believe that development in the Arctic must incorporate the application of precautionary approaches to development with environmental implications, including prior assessment and systematic observation of the impacts of such development. Therefore we shall maintain, as appropriate, or put into place as quickly as possible, an internationally transparent domestic process for the environmental impact assessment of proposed activities that are likely to have a significant adverse impact on the Arctic environment and are subject to decisions by competent national authorities. To this end we support the implementation of the provisions of the Convention on Environmental Impact Assessment in a Transboundary Context.

9.   We underline the importance of prior and timely notification and consultation regarding activities that may have significant adverse transboundary environmental effects, including preparedness for natural disasters and other emergencies that are likely to produce sudden harmful effects on the Arctic environment or its peoples.

10.   We recognize the need for effective application of existing legal instruments relevant to protection of the Arctic environment, and will cooperate in the future development of such instruments, as needed. We support the early ratification of the United Nations Conventions on Biological Diversity and Climate Change.

11.   We undertake to consider the development of regional instruments concerned with the protection of the Arctic environment.

6.12 AGREEMENT BETWEEN THE GOVERNMENT OF THE UNITED STATES OF AMERICA AND THE GOVERNMENT OF THE RUSSIAN FEDERATION ON COOPERATION IN THE PREVENTION OF POLLUTION OF THE ENVIRONMENT IN THE ARCTIC. **Signed at Moscow, 16 December 1994. Entered into force, 16 December 1994. State Dept No 95–28, 1994 WL 761204 (Treaty)**

The Government of the United States of America and the Government of the Russian Federation (hereinafter referred to as the Parties),

Recognizing the sensitivity of the Arctic environment and our mutual commitment to protect the Arctic environment and to promote the social and economic interests of local, especially indigenous populations, including their traditional way of life;

Concerned over the potential threats posed by contaminants in the Arctic region to the health of the indigenous and local populations of the region as well as to its flora and fauna;

Convinced that cooperation and sharing of experience between the Parties will contribute to understanding and effective response to any such threat both on a national basis and within broader international efforts to protect the Arctic environment;

Desiring to build upon the results of the American–Russian Summit held in Vancouver, April 3–4, 1993;

Noting the particular importance of relevant provisions of Part XII of the United Nations Convention on the Law of the Sea of 1982; the provisions of the Convention on the Prevention of Marine Pollution by Dumping of Wastes and Other Matter of 1972; and the provisions of the Arctic Environmental Protection Strategy of 1991;

Have agreed as follows:

Article 1

The Parties shall cooperate in the prevention, reduction and control of pollution in the Arctic marine and terrestrial environment resulting from the accidental or intentional introduction of contaminants into that environment.

To this end the Parties shall cooperate in research, monitoring, assessment and other activities, bilaterally and in the appropriate multilateral fora.

Article 2

1. The Parties shall cooperate in the conduct of scientific research, monitoring, and assessment activities to determine the potential impacts of contaminants in the Arctic environment, including, inter alia:

    1) the pathways by which such contaminants reach and are dispersed within the Arctic environment;

    2) the effects of such contaminants, including rates of bio-accumulation, upon Arctic flora and fauna, including fish populations; and

    3) the effects of such contaminants upon human health in the Arctic environment, especially upon local and indigenous populations.

2. The Parties further shall cooperate in the monitoring and assessment of levels of hazardous contamination in the Arctic environment, including, inter alia:

    1) exchange of data and information on the effects of disposal and release of such contaminants introduced directly or indirectly into the Arctic environment;

    2) determination of the level, chemical composition, and patterns of such contamination caused by releases from sites at which materials have been stored, processed or disposed; and

3) determination of the amount, concentrations and dynamics of transport of such contaminants introduced into the marine zone, including through rivers and other watercourses, natural or artificial, and via ice transport and ice rafted sediment.

3. The Parties shall consult with regard to technical solutions for the elimination of radioactive and other types of contamination impacts.

4. The Parties shall cooperate in the conduct of joint scientific research to predict ecological impacts of the existing disposals of radioactive waste and consult with regard to technical solutions for the elimination of disposals in places where ecological safety is not insured.

5. Cooperation between the Parties in scientific research and monitoring referred to in this Article shall take place bilaterally, and within the appropriate international, including regional, mechanisms, in particular the Arctic Monitoring and Assessment Program of the Arctic Environmental Protection Strategy of 1991 and the International Arctic Seas Assessment Program of 1993 the International Atomic Energy Agency.

Article 3

1. Each Party shall facilitate joint activities under Article 2 in areas that are under its jurisdiction in accordance with international law and that are or are believed to be contaminated, under such reasonable conditions as it may establish.

2. The Parties shall ensure that the data and information resulting from such research and monitoring are exchanged and made freely available on a reciprocal basis.

Article 4

The Parties shall promote the development of specific measures to give effect to this Agreement, including:

1) programs for the exchange of scientists, students and experts;

2) organization of seminars and meetings of experts;

3) organization of joint research activities, including marine scientific research cruises;

4) development of Geographic Information Systems, data bases and inventories on Arctic environmental data;

5) cooperation in emergency preparedness exercises and prompt exchange of information concerning major accidental releases of contaminants into the Arctic environment; and

6) exchange of information on technologies and assessment methodologies applicable within the framework of this Agreement and on relevant environmental protection legislation and regulations.

Article 5

Activities under this Agreement, including specific projects and programs, shall be carried out by responsible agencies of each Party in accordance with the Agreement Between the Government of the Union of Soviet Socialist Republics and the Government of the United States on Cooperation in Ocean Studies of 1990 and the Agreement between the Government of the United States and the Government of the Russian Federation on Cooperation in the Field of Protection of the Environment and National Resources of 1994 and under the overall coordination of the United States–Russian Commission on Economic and Technological Cooperation or under any other coordinating body as may be agreed by the Parties.

Article 6

1. All activities undertaken pursuant to this Agreement shall be conducted in accordance with the applicable laws, regulations, and procedures in both countries and shall be subject to the availability of funds and personnel.

2. Scientific and technological information resulting from cooperation under this Agreement, other than information which is not disclosed for national security, commercial or industrial reasons, shall be made freely available, unless otherwise agreed.

3. Issues of intellectual property created or furnished in the course of joint activities under this Agreement shall be governed by Annex II of the Agreement between the Government of the United States of America and the Government of the Russian Federation on Science and Technology Cooperation, signed at Moscow December 16, 1993.

Article 7

The Parties shall resolve by consultation any differences as to the interpretation or application of this Agreement.

Article 8

1. This Agreement shall enter into force upon signature and remain in force for a period of five years, and may be extended for additional five year periods upon written agreement of the Parties.

2. Either Party may terminate this Agreement by so notifying the other Party in writing. Such termination shall be effective six months from such written notification.

6.13 DECLARATION ON THE ESTABLISHMENT OF THE ARCTIC COUNCIL. **Signed at Ottawa, 19 September 1996.** *Reprinted in* **35 ILM 1382 & 1 Weston & Carlson I.B.1a**

The representatives of the Governments of Canada, Denmark, Finland, Iceland, Norway, the Russian Federation, Sweden and the United States of America (hereinafter referred to as the Arctic States) meeting in Ottawa;

Affirming our commitment to the well-being of the inhabitants of the Arctic, including recognition of the special relationship and unique contributions to the Arctic of indigenous people and their communities;

Affirming our commitment to sustainable development in the Arctic region, including economic and social development, improved health conditions and cultural well-being;

Affirming concurrently our commitment to the protection of the Arctic environment, including the health of Arctic ecosystems, maintenance of biodiversity in the Arctic region and conservation and sustainable use of natural resources;

Recognizing the contributions of the Arctic Environmental Protection Strategy to these commitments;

Recognizing the traditional knowledge of the indigenous people of the Arctic and their communities and taking note of its importance and that of Arctic science and research to the collective understanding of the circumpolar Arctic;

Desiring further to provide a means for promoting cooperative activities to address Arctic issues requiring circumpolar cooperation, and to ensure full consultation with and the full involvement of indigenous people and their communities and other inhabitants of the Arctic in such activities;

Recognizing the valuable contribution and support of the Inuit Circumpolar Conference, Saami Council, and the Association of the Indigenous Minorities of the North, Siberia, and the Far East of the Russian Federation in the development of the Arctic Council;

Desiring to provide for regular intergovernmental consideration of and consultation on Arctic issues.

Hereby declare:

1. The Arctic Council is established as a high level forum to:

(a) provide a means for promoting cooperation, coordination and interaction among the Arctic States, with the involvement of the Arctic indigenous communities and other Arctic inhabitants on common Arctic issues,[1] in particular issues of sustainable development and environmental protection in the Arctic.

(b) oversee and coordinate the programs established under the AEPS on the Arctic Monitoring and Assessment Program (AMAP); Conservation of Arctic Flora and Fauna (CAFF); Protection of the Arctic Marine Environment (PAME); and Emergency Prevention, Preparedness and Response (EPPR).

(c) adopt terms of reference for, and oversee and coordinate a sustainable development program.

(d) disseminate information, encourage education and promote interest in Arctic-related issues.

2. Members of the Arctic Council are: Canada, Denmark, Finland, Iceland, Norway, the Russian Federation, Sweden and the United States of America (the Arctic States).

---

1. The Arctic Council should not deal with matters related to military security.

The Inuit Circumpolar Conference, the Saami Council and the Association of Indigenous Minorities of the North, Siberia and the Far East of the Russian Federation are Permanent Participants in the Arctic Council. Permanent participation equally is open to other Arctic organizations of indigenous peoples[2] with majority Arctic indigenous constituency, representing:

(a) a single indigenous people resident in more than one Arctic State; or

(b) more than one Arctic indigenous people resident in a single Arctic state.

The determination that such an organization has met this criterion is to be made by decision of the Council. The number of Permanent Participants should at any time be less than the number of members.

The category of Permanent Participation is created to provide for active participation and full consultation with the Arctic indigenous representatives within the Arctic Council.

3. Observer status in the Arctic Council is open to:

(a) non-Arctic states;

(b) inter-governmental and inter-parliamentary organizations, global and regional; and

(c) non-governmental organizations that the Council determines can contribute to its work.

4. The Council should normally meet on a biennial basis, with meetings of senior officials taking place more frequently, to provide for liaison and co-ordination. Each Arctic State should designate a focal point on matters related to the Arctic Council.

5. Responsibility for hosting meetings of the Arctic Council, including provision of secretariat support functions, should rotate sequentially among the Arctic States.

6. The Arctic Council, as its first order of business, should adopt rules of procedure for its meetings and those of its working groups.

7. Decisions of the Arctic Council are to be by consensus of the Members.

8. The Indigenous Peoples' Secretariat established under AEPS is to continue under the framework of the Arctic Council.

9. The Arctic Council should regularly review the priorities and financing of its programs and associated structures.

* * *

10. FURTHER COOPERATION

Continuity and further cooperation are essential for increasing the protection of the Arctic environment. In order to ensure this continuity and cooperation, the eight Arctic countries agree to hold regular Meetings on the Arctic Environment.

* * *

2. The use of the term "peoples" in this Declaration shall not be construed as having any implications as regard the rights which law.may attach to the term under international al

6.14 The Ilulissat Declaration on the Arctic Ocean. Adopted at the Arctic
      Ocean Conference in Ilulissat, Greenland, 28 May 2008. Available
      from the Arctic Council Secretariat at <www.arctic-council.org>.
      Reprinted in 5 Weston & Carlson V.F.30h

The Arctic Ocean stands at the threshold of significant changes. Climate change
and the melting of ice have a potential impact on vulnerable ecosystems, the livelihoods of local inhabitants and indigenous communities, and the potential exploitation
of natural resources.

By virtue of their sovereignty, sovereign rights and jurisdiction in large areas of
the Arctic Ocean the five coastal states are in a unique position to address these
possibilities and challenges. In this regard, we recall that an extensive international
legal framework applies to the Arctic Ocean as discussed between our representatives
at the meeting in Oslo on 15 and 16 October 2007 at the level of senior officials.
Notably, the law of the sea provides for important rights and obligations concerning
the delineation of the outer limits of the continental shelf, the protection of the marine
environment, including ice-covered areas, freedom of navigation, marine scientific
research, and other uses of the sea. We remain committed to this legal framework and
to the orderly settlement of any possible overlapping claims.

This framework provides a solid foundation for responsible management by the
five coastal States and other users of this Ocean through national implementation and
application of relevant provisions. We therefore see no need to develop a new
comprehensive international legal regime to govern the Arctic Ocean. We will keep
abreast of the developments in the Arctic Ocean and continue to implement appropriate measures.

The Arctic Ocean is a unique ecosystem, which the five coastal states have a
stewardship role in protecting. Experience has shown how shipping disasters and
subsequent pollution of the marine environment may cause irreversible disturbance of
the ecological balance and major harm to the livelihoods of local inhabitants and
indigenous communities. We will take steps in accordance with international law both
nationally and in cooperation among the five states and other interested parties to
ensure the protection and preservation of the fragile marine environment of the Arctic
Ocean. In this regard we intend to work together including through the International
Maritime Organization to strengthen existing measures and develop new measures to
improve the safety of maritime navigation and prevent or reduce the risk of ship-based
pollution in the Arctic Ocean.

The increased use of Arctic waters for tourism, shipping, research and resource
development also increases the risk of accidents and therefore the need to further
strengthen search and rescue capabilities and capacity around the Arctic Ocean to
ensure an appropriate response from states to any accident. Cooperation, including on
the sharing of information, is a prerequisite for addressing these challenges. We will
work to promote safety of life at sea in the Arctic Ocean, including through bilateral
and multilateral arrangements between or among relevant states.

The five coastal states currently cooperate closely in the Arctic Ocean with each
other and with other interested parties. This cooperation includes the collection of
scientific data concerning the continental shelf, the protection of the marine environment and other scientific research. We will work to strengthen this cooperation, which
is based on mutual trust and transparency, inter alia, through timely exchange of data
and analyses.

The Arctic Council and other international fora, including the Barents Euro–
Arctic Council, have already taken important steps on specific issues, for example with
regard to safety of navigation, search and rescue, environmental monitoring and
disaster response and scientific cooperation, which are relevant also to the Arctic
Ocean. The five coastal states of the Arctic Ocean will continue to contribute actively
to the work of the Arctic Council and other relevant international fora.

PART 7. MISCELLANEOUS

A. ECONOMIC TRADE/DEVELOPMENT

7.1 GENERAL AGREEMENT ON TARIFFS AND TRADE (GATT) 1947 (Without Annexes, Protocols and Schedules But as Revised to 1994). Concluded at Geneva, 30 October 1947. Currently in effect as part of GATT 1994.[a] 55 UNTS 187, TIAS No 1700; *reprinted in* **4 Weston & Carlson IV.C.1: Arts. I:1, III:1–4, IX:1, XI:1 and XX**

ARTICLE I

General Most–Favoured–Nation Treatment

1. With respect to customs duties and charges of any kind imposed on or in connection with importation or exportation or imposed on the international transfer of payments for imports or exports, and with respect to the method of levying such duties and charges, and with respect to all rules and formalities in connection with importation and exportation, and with respect to all matters referred to in paragraphs 2 and 4 of Article III, any advantage, favour, privilege or immunity granted by any contracting party to any product originating in or destined for any other country shall be accorded immediately and unconditionally to the like product originating in or destined for the territories of all other contracting parties.

* * *

ARTICLE III

National Treatment on Internal Taxation and Regulation

1. The contracting parties recognize that internal taxes and other internal charges, and laws, regulations and requirements affecting the internal sale, offering for sale, purchase, transportation, distribution or use of products, and internal quantitative regulations requiring the mixture processing or use of products in specified amounts or proportions, should not be applied to imported or domestic products so as to afford protection to domestic production.

2. The products of the territory of any contracting party imported into the territory of any other contracting party shall not be subject, directly or indirectly, to internal taxes or other internal charges of any kind in excess of those applied, directly or indirectly, to like domestic products. Moreover, no contracting party shall otherwise apply internal taxes or other internal charges to imported or domestic products in a manner contrary to the principles set forth in paragraph 1.

3. With respect to any existing internal tax which is inconsistent with the provisions of paragraph 2, but which is specifically authorized under a trade agreement, in force on April 10, 1947, in which the import duty on the taxed product is bound against increase, the contracting party imposing the tax shall be free to postpone the application of the provisions of paragraph 2 to such tax until such time as it can obtain release from the obligations of such trade agreement in order to permit

---

a. This document reproduces portions of the text of the original GATT 1947, as revised through 1 January 1994. GATT 1947 has been superceded and replaced by GATT 1994, which is part of Annex 1A of the Agreement Establishing the World Trade Organization (*see* Basic Document 7.7). Because GATT 1994 incorporates GATT 1947 by reference, we have reproduced relevant sections of GATT 1947 in this Documents Supplement.

the increase of such duty to the extent necessary to compensate for the elimination of the protective element of the tax.

4. The products of the territory of any contracting party imported into the territory of any other contracting party shall be accorded treatment no less favourable than that accorded to like products of national origin in respect of all laws, regulations and requirements affecting their internal sale, offering for sale, purchase, transportation, distribution or use. The provisions of this paragraph shall not prevent the applications of differential internal transportation charges which are based exclusively on the economic operation of the means of transport and not on the nationality of the product.

* * *

ARTICLE IX

Marks of Origin

1. Each contracting party shall accord to the products of the territories of their contracting parties treatment with regard to marking requirements no less favourable than the treatment accorded to like products of any third country.

* * *

ARTICLE XI

General Elimination of Quantitative Restrictions

1. No prohibitions or restrictions other than duties, taxes or other charges, whether made effective through quotas, import or export licences or other measures, shall be instituted or maintained by any contracting party on the importation of any product of the territory of any other contracting party or on the exportation or sale for export of any product destined for the territory of any other contracting party.

* * *

ARTICLE XX

General Exceptions

Subject to the requirement that such measures are not applied in a manner which would constitute a means of arbitrary or unjustifiable discrimination between countries where the same conditions prevail, or a disguised restriction on international trade, nothing in this Agreement shall be construed to prevent the adoption or enforcement by any contracting party of measures:

(a) necessary to protect public morals;

(b) necessary to protect human, animal or plant life or health;

(c) relating to the importation or exportation of gold or silver;

(d) necessary to secure compliance with laws or regulations which are not inconsistent with the provisions of this Agreement, including those relating to customs enforcement, the enforcement of monopolies operated under paragraph 4 of Article II and Article XVII, the protection of patents, trade marks and copyrights, and the prevention of deceptive practices;

(e) relating to the products of prison labour;

(f) imposed for the protection of national treasures of artistic, historic or archaeological value;

(g) relating to the conservation of exhaustible natural resources if such measures are made effective in conjunction with restrictions on domestic production or consumption;

(h) undertaken in pursuance of obligations under any intergovernmental commodity agreement which conforms to criteria submitted to the contracting parties and not disapproved by them or which is itself so submitted and not so disapproved;

(i) involving restrictions on exports of domestic materials necessary to ensure essential quantities of such materials to a domestic processing industry during periods when the domestic price of such materials is held below the world price as part of a governmental stabilization plan; *Provided* that such restrictions shall not operate to increase the exports of or the protection afforded to such domestic industry, and shall not depart from the provisions of this Agreement relating to nondiscrimination;

(j) essential to the acquisition or distribution of products in general or local short supply; *Provided* that any such measures shall be consistent with the principle that all contracting parties are entitled to an equitable share of the international supply of such products, and that any such measures which are inconsistent with the other provisions of this Agreement shall be discontinued as soon as the conditions giving rise to them have ceased to exist. The contracting parties shall review the need for this sub-paragraph not later than 30 June 1960.

7.2   Declaration on the Establishment of a New International Economic Order. Adopted by the U.N. General Assembly, 1 May 1974. GA Res 3201 (S–VI), UN GAOR, 6th Special Sess, Supp No 1, at 3, UN Doc A/9559 (1974); *reprinted in* 13 ILM 715 (1974) & 4 Weston & Carlson IV.F.3

We, the Members of the United Nations,

* * *

Solemnly proclaim our united determination to work urgently for the Establishment of a New International Economic Order based on equity, sovereign equality, interdependence, common interest and cooperation among all States, irrespective of their economic and social systems which shall correct inequalities and redress existing injustices, make it possible to eliminate the widening gap between the developed and the developing countries and ensure steadily accelerating economic and social development and peace and justice for present and future generations, and, to that end, declare:

1. ... The developing countries, which constitute 70 per cent of the world's population, account for only 30 per cent of the world's income. It has proved impossible to achieve an even and balanced development of the international community under the existing international economic order. The gap between the developed and the developing countries continues to widen in a system which was established at a time when most of the developing countries did not even exist as independent States and which perpetuates inequality.

* * *

3. ... International co-operation for development is the shared goal and common duty of all countries. Thus the political, economic and social well-being of present and future generations depends more than ever on co-operation between all the members of the international community on the basis of sovereign equality and the removal of the disequilibrium that exists between them.

4. The new international economic order should be founded on full respect for the following principles:

a. Sovereign equality of States, self-determination of all peoples, inadmissibility of the acquisition of territories by force, territorial integrity and non-interference in the internal affairs of other States;

b. The broadest co-operation of all the States members of the international community, based on equity, whereby the prevailing disparities in the world may be banished and prosperity secured for all;

c. Full and effective participation on the basis of equality of all countries in the solving of world economic problems in the common interest of all countries, bearing in mind the necessity to ensure the accelerated development of all the developing countries, while devoting particular attention to the adoption of special measures in favour of the least developed land-locked and island developing countries as well as those developing countries most seriously affected by economic crises and natural calamities, without losing sight of the interests of other developing countries;

d. The right of every country to adopt the economic and social system that it deems the most appropriate for its own development and not to be subjected to discrimination of any kind as a result;

e. Full permanent sovereignty of every State over its natural resources and all economic activities. In order to safeguard these resources, each State is entitled to exercise effective control over them and their exploitation with means suitable to its own situation, including the right to nationalization or transfer of ownership to its nationals, this right being an expression of the full permanent sovereignty of the State.

No State may be subjected to economic, political or any other type of coercion to prevent the free and full exercise of this inalienable right;

f. The right of all States, territories and peoples under foreign occupation, alien and colonial domination or apartheid to restitution and full compensation for the exploitation arid depletion of, and damages to, the natural resources and all other resources of those States, territories and peoples;

* * *

n. Preferential and non-reciprocal treatment for developing countries, wherever feasible, in all fields of international economic co-operation whenever possible;

o. Securing favourable conditions for the transfer of financial resources to developing countries.

p. Giving to the developing countries access to the achievements of modern science and technology, and promoting the transfer of technology and the creation of indigenous technology for the benefit of the developing countries in forms and in accordance with procedures which are suited to their economies;

q. The need for all States to put an end to the waste of natural resources, including food products;

* * *

7.3 Charter of Economic Rights and Duties of States. **Adopted by the U.N. General Assembly, 12 December 1974. G.A. Res. 3281, U.N. GAOR, 29th Sess., Supp. No. 31, at 50, UN Doc. A/9631 (1975);** *reprinted in* **14 I.L.M. 251 (1975) & 4 Weston IV.F.5:** *Arts. 3, 30*

Article 3. In the exploitation of natural resources shared by two or more countries, each State must co-operate on the basis of a system of information and prior consultations in order to achieve optimum use of such resources without causing damage to the legitimate interest of others.

* * *

Article 30. The protection, preservation and enhancement of the environment for the present and future generations is the responsibility of all States. All States shall endeavour to establish their own environmental and developmental policies in conformity with such responsibility. The environmental policies of all States shall enhance and not adversely affect the present and future development potential of developing countries. All States have the responsibility to ensure that activities within their jurisdiction or control do not cause damage to the environment of other States or of areas beyond the limits of national jurisdiction. All States should co-operate in evolving international norms and regulations in the field of the environment.

7.4 NORTH AMERICAN FREE TRADE AGREEMENT (NAFTA). **Concluded on 17 December 1992. Entered into force, 1 January 1994.** *Reprinted in* **32 ILM 289 & 605 (1993) & 4 Weston & Carlson IV.C.7:** *Arts. 101, 104, 1102–1105, 1110, 1116*

Article 101: Establishment of the Free Trade Area

The Parties to this Agreement, consistent with Article XXIV of the General Agreement on Tariffs and Trade, hereby establish a free trade area.

* * *

Article 104: Relation to Environmental and Conservation Agreements

1. In the event of any inconsistency between this Agreement and the specific trade obligations set out in:

a) the Convention on International Trade in Endangered Species of Wild Fauna and Flora, done at Washington, March 3, 1973, as amended June 22, 1979,

b) the Montreal Protocol on Substances that Deplete the Ozone Layer, done at Montreal, September 16, 1987, as amended June 29, 1990,

c) the Basel Convention on the Control of Transboundary Movements of Hazardous Wastes and Their Disposal, done at Basel, March 22, 1989, on its entry into force for Canada, Mexico and the United States, or

d) the agreements set out in Annex 104.1,

such obligations shall prevail to the extent of the inconsistency, provided that where a Party has a choice among equally effective and reasonably available means of complying with such obligations, the Party chooses the alternative that is the least inconsistent with the other provisions of this Agreement.

2. The Parties may agree in writing to modify Annex 104.1 to include any amendment to an agreement referred to in paragraph 1, and any other environmental or conservation agreement.

* * *

CHAPTER ELEVEN: INVESTMENT

SECTION A—INVESTMENT

Article 1102: National Treatment

1. Each Party shall accord to investors of another Party treatment no less favorable than that it accords, in like circumstances, to its own investors with respect to the establishment, acquisition, expansion, management, conduct, operation, and sale or other disposition of investments.

2. Each Party shall accord to investments of investors of another Party treatment no less favorable than that it accords, in like circumstances, to investments of its own investors with respect to the establishment, acquisition, expansion, management, conduct, operation, and sale or other disposition of investments.

* * *

Article 1103: Most–Favored–Nation Treatment

1. Each Party shall accord to investors of another Party treatment no less favorable than that it accords, in like circumstances, to investors of any other Party or of a non-Party with respect to the establishment, acquisition, expansion, management, conduct, operation, and sale or other disposition of investments.

2. Each Party shall accord to investments of investors of another Party treatment no less favorable than that it accords, in like circumstances, to investments of investors of any other Party or of a non-Party with respect to the establishment, acquisition, expansion, management, conduct, operation, and sale or other disposition of investments.

Article 1104: Standard of Treatment

Each Party shall accord to investors of another Party and to investments of investors of another Party the better of the treatment required by Articles 1102 and 1103.

Article 1105: Minimum Standard of Treatment

1. Each Party shall accord to investments of investors of another Party treatment in accordance with international law, including fair and equitable treatment and full protection and security.

2. Without prejudice to paragraph 1 and notwithstanding Article 1108(7)(b), each Party shall accord to investors of another Party, and to investments of investors of another Party, non-discriminatory treatment with respect to measures it adopts or maintains relating to losses suffered by investments in its territory owing to armed conflict or civil strife.

3. Paragraph 2 does not apply to existing measures relating to subsidies or grants that would be inconsistent with Article 1102 but for Article 1108(7)(b).

* * *

Article 1110: Expropriation and Compensation

1. No Party may directly or indirectly nationalize or expropriate an investment of an investor of another Party in its territory or take a measure tantamount to nationalization or expropriation of such an investment ("expropriation"), except:

(a) for a public purpose;

(b) on a non-discriminatory basis;

(c) in accordance with due process of law and Article 1105(1); and

(d) on payment of compensation in accordance with paragraphs 2 through 6.

* * *

SECTION B: SETTLEMENT OF DISPUTES BETWEEN A PARTY AND AN INVESTOR OF ANOTHER PARTY

* * *

Article 1116: Claim by an Investor of a Party on Its Own Behalf

1. An investor of a Party may submit to arbitration under this Section a claim that another Party has breached an obligation under:

(a) Section A. . . .

* * *

7.5 NORTH AMERICAN AGREEMENT ON ENVIRONMENTAL COOPERATION (With Annexes). **Concluded at Mexico City, Washington and Ottawa, 8, 9, 12 & 14 September 1993. Entered into force, 1 January 1994. *Reprinted in* 32 ILM 1480 (1993)**

PREAMBLE

The Government of the United States of America, the Government of Canada and the Government of the United Mexican States:

CONVINCED of the importance of the conservation, protection and enhancement of the environment in their territories and the essential role of cooperation in these areas in achieving sustainable development for the well-being of present and future generations;

REAFFIRMING the sovereign right of States to exploit their own resources pursuant to their own environmental and development policies and their responsibility to ensure that activities within their jurisdiction or control do not cause damage to the environment of other States or of areas beyond the limits of national jurisdiction;

RECOGNIZING the interrelationship of their environments;

ACKNOWLEDGING the growing economic and social links between them, including the North American Free Trade Agreement (NAFTA);

RECONFIRMING the importance of the environmental goals and objectives of the NAFTA, including enhanced levels of environmental protection;

EMPHASIZING the importance of public participation in conserving, protecting and enhancing the environment;

NOTING the existence of differences in their respective natural endowments, climatic and geographical conditions, and economic, technological and infrastructural capabilities;

REAFFIRMING the Stockholm Declaration on the Human Environment of 1972 and the Rio Declaration on Environment and Development of 1992;

RECALLING their tradition of environmental cooperation and expressing their desire to support and build on international environmental agreements and existing policies and laws, in order to promote cooperation between them; and

CONVINCED of the benefits to be derived from a framework, including a Commission, to facilitate effective cooperation on the conservation, protection and enhancement of the environment in their territories;

HAVE AGREED AS FOLLOWS:

PART ONE

OBJECTIVES

Article 1: Objectives

The objectives of this Agreement are to:

(a) foster the protection and improvement of the environment in the territories of the Parties for the well-being of present and future generations;

(b) promote sustainable development based on cooperation and mutually supportive environmental and economic policies;

(c) increase cooperation between the Parties to better conserve, protect, and enhance the environment, including wild flora and fauna;

(d) support the environmental goals and objectives of the NAFTA;

(e) avoid creating trade distortions or new trade barriers;

(f) strengthen cooperation on the development and improvement of environmental laws, regulations, procedures, policies and practices;

(g) enhance compliance with, and enforcement of, environmental laws and regulations;

(h) promote transparency and public participation in the development of environmental laws, regulations and policies;

(i) promote economically efficient and effective environmental measures; and

(j) promote pollution prevention policies and practices.

PART TWO

OBLIGATIONS

Article 2: General Commitments

1. Each Party shall, with respect to its territory:

(a) periodically prepare and make publicly available reports on the state of the environment;

(b) develop and review environmental emergency preparedness measures;

(c) promote education in environmental matters, including environmental law;

(d) further scientific research and technology development in respect of environmental matters;

(e) assess, as appropriate, environmental impacts; and

(f) promote the use of economic instruments for the efficient achievement of environmental goals.

2. Each Party shall consider implementing in its law any recommendation developed by the Council under Article 10(5)(b).

3. Each Party shall consider prohibiting the export to the territories of the other Parties of a pesticide or toxic substance whose use is prohibited within the Party's territory. When a Party adopts a measure prohibiting or severely restricting the use of a pesticide or toxic substance in its territory, it shall notify the other Parties of the measure, either directly or through an appropriate international organization.

Article 3: Levels of Protection

Recognizing the right of each Party to establish its own levels of domestic environmental protection and environmental development policies and priorities, and to adopt or modify accordingly its environmental laws and regulations, each Party shall ensure that its laws and regulations provide for high levels of environmental protection and shall strive to continue to improve those laws and regulations.

Article 4: Publication

1. Each Party shall ensure that its laws, regulations, procedures and administrative rulings of general application respecting any matter covered by this Agreement are promptly published or otherwise made available in such a manner as to enable interested persons and Parties to become acquainted with them.

2. To the extent possible, each Party shall:

(a) publish in advance any such measure that it proposes to adopt; and

(b) provide interested persons and Parties a reasonable opportunity to comment on such proposed measures.

Article 5: Government Enforcement Action

1. With the aim of achieving high levels of environmental protection and compliance with its environmental laws and regulations, each Party shall effectively enforce its environmental laws and regulations through appropriate governmental action, subject to Article 37, such as:

(a) appointing and training inspectors;

(b) monitoring compliance and investigating suspected violations, including through on-site inspections;

(c) seeking assurances of voluntary compliance and compliance agreements;

(d) publicly releasing non-compliance information;

(e) issuing bulletins or other periodic statements on enforcement procedures;

(f) promoting environmental audits;

(g) requiring record keeping and reporting;

(h) providing or encouraging mediation and arbitration services;

(i) using licenses, permits or authorizations;

(j) initiating, in a timely manner, judicial, quasi-judicial or administrative proceedings to seek appropriate sanctions or remedies for violations of its environmental laws and regulations;

(k) providing for search, seizure or detention; or

(*l*) issuing administrative orders, including orders of a preventative, curative or emergency nature.

2. Each Party shall ensure that judicial, quasi-judicial or administrative enforcement proceedings are available under its law to sanction or remedy violations of its environmental laws and regulations.

3. Sanctions and remedies provided for a violation of a Party's environmental laws and regulations shall, as appropriate:

(a) take into consideration the nature and gravity of the violation, any economic benefit derived from the violation by the violator, the economic condition of the violator, and other relevant factors; and

(b) include compliance agreements, fines, imprisonment, injunctions, the closure of facilities, and the cost of containing or cleaning up pollution.

Article 6: Private Access to Remedies

1. Each Party shall ensure that interested persons may request the Party's competent authorities to investigate alleged violations of its environmental laws and regulations and shall give such requests due consideration in accordance with law.

2. Each Party shall ensure that persons with a legally recognized interest under its law in a particular matter have appropriate access to administrative, quasi-judicial or judicial proceedings for the enforcement of the Party's environmental laws and regulations.

3. Private access to remedies shall include rights, in accordance with the Party's law, such as:

(a) to sue another person under that Party's jurisdiction for damages;

(b) to seek sanctions or remedies such as monetary penalties, emergency closures or orders to mitigate the consequences of violations of its environmental laws and regulations;

(c) to request the competent authorities to take appropriate action to enforce that Party's environmental laws and regulations in order to protect the environment or to avoid environmental harm; or

(d) to seek injunctions where a person suffers, or may suffer, loss, damage or injury as a result of conduct by another person under that Party's jurisdiction contrary to that Party's environmental laws and regulations or from tortious conduct.

Article 7: Procedural Guarantees

1. Each Party shall ensure that its administrative, quasi-judicial and judicial proceedings referred to in Articles 5(2) and 6(2) are fair, open and equitable, and to this end shall provide that such proceedings:

(a) comply with due process of law;

(b) are open to the public, except where the administration of justice otherwise requires;

(c) entitle the parties to the proceedings to support or defend their respective positions and to present information or evidence; and

(d) are not unnecessarily complicated and do not entail unreasonable charges or time limits or unwarranted delays.

2. Each Party shall provide that final decisions on the merits of the case in such proceedings are:

(a) in writing and preferably state the reasons on which the decisions are based;

(b) made available without undue delay to the parties to the proceedings and, consistent with its law, to the public; and

(c) based on information or evidence in respect of which the parties were offered the opportunity to be heard.

3. Each Party shall provide, as appropriate, that parties to such proceedings have the right, in accordance with its law, to seek review and, where warranted, correction of final decisions issued in such proceedings.

4. Each Party shall ensure that tribunals that conduct or review such proceedings are impartial and independent and do not have any substantial interest in the outcome of the matter.

PART THREE

COMMISSION FOR ENVIRONMENTAL COOPERATION

Article 8: The Commission

1. The Parties hereby establish the Commission for Environmental Cooperation.

2. The Commission shall comprise a Council, a Secretariat and a Joint Public Advisory Committee.

Section A: The Council

Article 9: Council Structure and Procedures

1. The Council shall comprise cabinet-level or equivalent representatives of the Parties, or their designees.

2. The Council shall establish its rules and procedures.

3. The Council shall convene:

(a) at least once a year in regular session; and

(b) in special session at the request of any Party.

Regular sessions shall be chaired successively by each Party.

4. The Council shall hold public meetings in the course of all regular sessions. Other meetings held in the course of regular or special sessions shall be public where the Council so decides.

5. The Council may:

(a) establish, and assign responsibilities to, ad hoc or standing committees, working groups or expert groups;

(b) seek the advice of non-governmental organizations or persons, including independent experts; and

(c) take such other action in the exercise of its functions as the Parties may agree.

6. All decisions and recommendations of the Council shall be taken by consensus, except as the Council may otherwise decide or as otherwise provided in this Agreement.

7. All decisions and recommendations of the Council shall be made public, except as the Council may otherwise decide or as otherwise provided in this Agreement.

Article 10: Council Functions

1. The Council shall be the governing body of the Commission and shall:

(a) serve as a forum for the discussion of environmental matters within the scope of this Agreement;

(b) oversee the implementation and develop recommendations on the further elaboration of this Agreement and, to this end, the Council shall, within four years after the date of entry into force of this Agreement, review its operation and effectiveness in the light of experience;

(c) oversee the Secretariat;

(d) address questions and differences that may arise between the Parties regarding the interpretation or application of this Agreement;

(e) approve the annual program and budget of the Commission; and

(f) promote and facilitate cooperation between the Parties with respect to environmental matters.

2. The Council may consider, and develop recommendations regarding:

(a) comparability of techniques and methodologies for data gathering and analysis, data management and electronic data communications on matters covered by this Agreement;

(b) pollution prevention techniques and strategies;

(c) approaches and common indicators for reporting on the state of the environment;

(d) the use of economic instruments for the pursuit of domestic and internationally agreed environmental objectives;

(e) scientific research and technology development in respect of environmental matters;

(f) promotion of public awareness regarding the environment;

(g) transboundary and border environmental issues, such as the long-range transport of air and marine pollutants;

(h) exotic species that may be harmful;

(i) the conservation and protection of wild flora and fauna and their habitat, and specially protected natural areas;

(j) the protection of endangered and threatened species;

(k) environmental emergency preparedness and response activities;

(*l*) environmental matters as they relate to economic development;

(m) the environmental implications of goods throughout their life cycles;

(n) human resource training and development in the environmental field;

(o) the exchange of environmental scientists and officials;

(p) approaches to environmental compliance and enforcement;

(q) ecologically sensitive national accounts;

(r) eco-labelling; and

(s) other matters as it may decide.

3. The Council shall strengthen cooperation on the development and continuing improvement of environmental laws and regulations, including by:

(a) promoting the exchange of information on criteria and methodologies used in establishing domestic environmental standards; and

(b) without reducing levels of environmental protection, establishing a process for developing recommendations on greater compatibility of environmental technical regulations, standards and conformity assessment procedures in a manner consistent with the NAFTA.

4. The Council shall encourage:

(a) effective enforcement by each Party of its environmental laws and regulations;

(b) compliance with those laws and regulations; and

(c) technical cooperation between the Parties.

5. The Council shall promote and, as appropriate, develop recommendations regarding:

(a) public access to information concerning the environment that is held by public authorities of each Party, including information on hazardous materials and activities in its communities, and opportunity to participate in decision-making processes related to such public access; and

(b) appropriate limits for specific pollutants, taking into account differences in ecosystems.

6. The Council shall cooperate with the NAFTA Free Trade Commission to achieve the environmental goals and objectives of the NAFTA by:

(a) acting as a point of inquiry and receipt for comments from non-governmental organizations and persons concerning those goals and objectives;

(b) providing assistance in consultations under Article 1114 of the NAFTA where a Party considers that another Party is waiving or derogating from, or offering to waive or otherwise derogate from, an environmental measure as an encouragement to establish, acquire, expand or retain an investment of an investor, with a view to avoiding any such encouragement;

(c) contributing to the prevention or resolution of environment-related trade disputes by:

(i) seeking to avoid disputes between the Parties,

(ii) making recommendations to the Free Trade Commission with respect to the avoidance of such disputes, and

(iii) identifying experts able to provide information or technical advice to NAFTA committees, working groups and other NAFTA bodies;

(d) considering on an ongoing basis the environmental effects of the NAFTA; and

(e) otherwise assisting the Free Trade Commission in environment-related matters.

7. Recognizing the significant bilateral nature of many transboundary environmental issues, the Council shall, with a view to agreement between the Parties pursuant to this Article within three years on obligations, consider and develop recommendations with respect to:

(a) assessing the environmental impact of proposed projects subject to decisions by a competent government authority and likely to cause significant adverse transboundary effects, including a full evaluation of comments provided by other Parties and persons of other Parties;

(b) notification, provision of relevant information and consultation between Parties with respect to such projects; and

(c) mitigation of the potential adverse effects of such projects.

8. The Council shall encourage the establishment by each Party of appropriate administrative procedures pursuant to its environmental laws to permit another Party to seek the reduction, elimination or mitigation of transboundary pollution on a reciprocal basis.

9. The Council shall consider and, as appropriate, develop recommendations on the provision by a Party, on a reciprocal basis, of access to and rights and remedies before its courts and administrative agencies for persons in another Party's territory who have suffered or are likely to suffer damage or injury caused by pollution originating in its territory as if the damage or injury were suffered in its territory.

Section B: The Secretariat

Article 11: Secretariat Structure and Procedures

1. The Secretariat shall be headed by an Executive Director, who shall be chosen by the Council for a three-year term, which may be renewed by the Council for one additional three-year term. The position of Executive Director shall rotate consecutively between nationals of each Party. The Council may remove the Executive Director solely for cause.

2. The Executive Director shall appoint and supervise the staff of the Secretariat, regulate their powers and duties and fix their remuneration in accordance with general standards to be established by the Council. The general standards shall provide that:

(a) staff shall be appointed and retained, and their conditions of employment shall be determined, strictly on the basis of efficiency, competence and integrity;

(b) in appointing staff, the Executive Director shall take into account lists of candidates prepared by the Parties and by the Joint Public Advisory Committee;

(c) due regard shall be paid to the importance of recruiting an equitable proportion of the professional staff from among the nationals of each Party; and

(d) the Executive Director shall inform the Council of all appointments.

3. The Council may decide, by a two-thirds vote, to reject any appointment that does not meet the general standards. Any such decision shall be made and held in confidence.

4. In the performance of their duties, the Executive Director and the staff shall not seek or receive instructions from any government or any other authority external to the Council. Each Party shall respect the international character of the responsibilities of the Executive Director and the staff and shall not seek to influence them in the discharge of their responsibilities.

5. The Secretariat shall provide technical, administrative and operational support to the Council and to committees and groups established by the Council, and such other support as the Council may direct.

6. The Executive Director shall submit for the approval of the Council the annual program and budget of the Commission, including provision for proposed cooperative activities and for the Secretariat to respond to contingencies.

7. The Secretariat shall, as appropriate, provide the Parties and the public information on where they may receive technical advice and expertise with respect to environmental matters.

8. The Secretariat shall safeguard:

(a) from disclosure information it receives that could identify a non-governmental organization or person making a submission if the person or organization so requests or the Secretariat otherwise considers it appropriate; and

(b) from public disclosure any information it receives from any non-governmental organization or person where the information is designated by that non-governmental organization or person as confidential or proprietary.

Article 12: Annual Report of the Commission

1. The Secretariat shall prepare an annual report of the Commission in accordance with instructions from the Council. The Secretariat shall submit a draft of the report for review by the Council. The final report shall be released publicly.

2. The report shall cover:

(a) activities and expenses of the Commission during the previous year;

(b) the approved program and budget of the Commission for the subsequent year;

(c) the actions taken by each Party in connection with its obligations under this Agreement, including data on the Party's environmental enforcement activities;

(d) relevant views and information submitted by non-governmental organizations and persons, including summary data regarding submissions, and any other relevant information the Council deems appropriate;

(e) recommendations made on any matter within the scope of this Agreement; and

(f) any other matter that the Council instructs the Secretariat to include.

3. The report shall periodically address the state of the environment in the territories of the Parties.

Article 13: Secretariat Reports

1. The Secretariat may prepare a report for the Council on any matter within the scope of the annual program. Should the Secretariat wish to prepare a report on any other environmental matter related to the cooperative functions of this Agreement, it shall notify the Council and may proceed unless, within 30 days of such notification, the Council objects by a two-thirds vote to the preparation of the report. Such other environmental matters shall not include issues related to whether a Party has failed to enforce its environmental laws and regulations. Where the Secretariat does not have specific expertise in the matter under review, it shall obtain the assistance of one or more independent experts of recognized experience in the matter to assist in the preparation of the report.

2. In preparing such a report, the Secretariat may draw upon any relevant technical, scientific or other information, including information:

(a) that is publicly available;

(b) submitted by interested non-governmental organizations and persons;

(c) submitted by the Joint Public Advisory Committee;

(d) furnished by a Party;

(e) gathered through public consultations, such as conferences, seminars and symposia; or

(f) developed by the Secretariat, or by independent experts engaged pursuant to paragraph 1.

3. The Secretariat shall submit its report to the Council, which shall make it publicly available, normally within 60 days following its submission, unless the Council otherwise decides.

Article 14: Submissions on Enforcement Matters

1. The Secretariat may consider a submission from any non-governmental organization or person asserting that a Party is failing to effectively enforce its environmental law, if the Secretariat finds that the submission:

(a) is in writing in a language designated by that Party in a notification to the Secretariat;

(b) clearly identifies the person or organization making the submission;

(c) provides sufficient information to allow the Secretariat to review the submission, including any documentary evidence on which the submission may be based;

(d) appears to be aimed at promoting enforcement rather than at harassing industry;

(e) indicates that the matter has been communicated in writing to the relevant authorities of the Party and indicates the Party's response, if any; and

(f) is filed by a person or organization residing or established in the territory of a Party.

2. Where the Secretariat determines that a submission meets the criteria set out in paragraph 1, the Secretariat shall determine whether the submission merits requesting a response from the Party. In deciding whether to request a response, the Secretariat shall be guided by whether:

(a) the submission alleges harm to the person or organization making the submission;

(b) the submission, alone or in combination with other submissions, raises matters whose further study in this process would advance the goals of this Agreement;

(c) private remedies available under the Party's law have been pursued; and

(d) the submission is drawn exclusively from mass media reports.

Where the Secretariat makes such a request, it shall forward to the Party a copy of the submission and any supporting information provided with the submission.

3. The Party shall advise the Secretariat within 30 days or, in exceptional circumstances and on notification to the Secretariat, within 60 days of delivery of the request:

(a) whether the matter is the subject of a pending judicial or administrative proceeding, in which case the Secretariat shall proceed no further; and

(b) of any other information that the Party wishes to submit, such as

i) whether the matter was previously the subject of a judicial or administrative proceeding, and

ii) whether private remedies in connection with the matter are available to the person or organization making the submission and whether they have been pursued.

Article 15: Factual Record

1. If the Secretariat considers that the submission, in the light of any response provided by the Party, warrants developing a factual record, the Secretariat shall so inform the Council and provide its reasons.

2. The Secretariat shall prepare a factual record if the Council, by a two-thirds vote, instructs it to do so.

3. The preparation of a factual record by the Secretariat pursuant to this Article shall be without prejudice to any further steps that may be taken with respect to any submission.

4. In preparing a factual record, the Secretariat shall consider any information furnished by a Party and may consider any relevant technical, scientific or other information:

(a) that is publicly available;

(b) submitted by interested non-governmental organizations or persons;

(c) submitted by the Joint Public Advisory Committee; or

(d) developed by the Secretariat or by independent experts.

5. The Secretariat shall submit a draft factual record to the Council. Any Party may provide comments on the accuracy of the draft within 45 days thereafter.

6. The Secretariat shall incorporate, as appropriate, any such comments in the final factual record and submit it to the Council.

7. The Council may, by a two-thirds vote, make the final factual record publicly available, normally within 60 days following its submission.

Section C: Advisory Committees

Article 16: Joint Public Advisory Committee

1. The Joint Public Advisory Committee shall comprise 15 members, unless the Council otherwise decides. Each Party or, if the Party so decides, its National Advisory Committee convened under Article 17, shall appoint an equal number of members.

* * *

5. The Joint Public Advisory Committee may provide relevant technical, scientific or other information to the Secretariat, including for purposes of developing a factual record under Article 15. The Secretariat shall forward to the Council copies of any such information.

* * *

PART FOUR

COOPERATION AND PROVISION OF INFORMATION

Article 20: Cooperation

1. The Parties shall at all times endeavor to agree on the interpretation and application of this Agreement, and shall make every attempt through cooperation and consultations to resolve any matter that might affect its operation.

2. To the maximum extent possible, each Party shall notify any other Party with an interest in the matter of any proposed or actual environmental measure that the

Party considers might materially affect the operation of this Agreement or otherwise substantially affect that other Party's interests under this Agreement.

3. On request of any other Party, a Party shall promptly provide information and respond to questions pertaining to any such actual or proposed environmental measure, whether or not that other Party has been previously notified of that measure.

4. Any Party may notify any other Party of, and provide to that Party, any credible information regarding possible violations of its environmental law, specific and sufficient to allow the other Party to inquire into the matter. The notified Party shall take appropriate steps in accordance with its law to so inquire and to respond to the other Party.

Article 21: Provision of Information

1. On request of the Council or the Secretariat, each Party shall, in accordance with its law, provide such information as the Council or the Secretariat may require, including:

(a) promptly making available any information in its possession required for the preparation of a report or factual record, including compliance and enforcement data; and

(b) taking all reasonable steps to make available any other such information requested.

2. If a Party considers that a request for information from the Secretariat is excessive or otherwise unduly burdensome, it may so notify the Council. The Secretariat shall revise the scope of its request to comply with any limitations established by the Council by a two-thirds vote.

3. If a Party does not make available information requested by the Secretariat, as may be limited pursuant to paragraph 2, it shall promptly advise the Secretariat of its reasons in writing.

PART FIVE

CONSULTATION AND RESOLUTION OF DISPUTES

Article 22: Consultations

1. Any Party may request in writing consultations with any other Party regarding whether there has been a persistent pattern of failure by that other Party to effectively enforce its environmental law.

* * *

Article 23: Initiation of Procedures

1. If the consulting Parties fail to resolve the matter pursuant to Article 22 within 60 days of delivery of a request for consultations, or such other period as the consulting Parties may agree, any such Party may request in writing a special session of the Council.

* * *

4. The Council may:

(a) call on such technical advisers or create such working groups or expert groups as it deems necessary.

(b) have recourse to good offices, conciliation, mediation or such other dispute resolution procedures, or

(c) make recommendations.

as may assist the consulting Parties to reach a mutually satisfactory resolution of the dispute. Any such recommendations shall be made public if the Council, by a two-thirds vote, so decides.

* * *

Article 24: Request for an Arbitral Panel

1. If the matter has not been resolved within 60 days after the Council has convened pursuant to Article 23, the Council shall, on the written request of any consulting Party and by a two-thirds vote, convene an arbitral panel to consider the matter where the alleged persistent pattern of failure by the Party complained against to effectively enforce its environmental law relates to a situation involving workplaces, firms, companies or sectors that produce goods or provide services:

(a) traded between the territories of the Parties; or

(b) that compete, in the territory of the Party complained against, with goods or services produced or provided by persons of another Party.

* * *

7.6 MARRAKESH MINISTERIAL DECISION ON TRADE AND ENVIRONMENT. Adopted by the Trade Negotiations Committee of the Uruguay Round of Multilateral Trade Negotiations, at Marrakesh on 14 April 1994. MTN/TNC/W/141; *reprinted in* 33 ILM 1267 (1994)

Ministers, meeting on the occasion of signing the Final Act embodying the results of the Uruguay Round of Multilateral Trade Negotiations at Marrakesh on 15 April 1994,

Recalling the preamble of the Agreement establishing the World Trade Organization (WTO), which states that members' "relations in the field of trade and economic endeavour should be conducted with a view to raising standards of living, ensuring full employment and a large and steadily growing volume of real income and effective demand, and expanding the production of and trade in goods and services, while allowing for the optimal use of the world's resources in accordance with the objective of sustainable development, seeking both to protect and preserve the environment and to enhance the means for doing so in a manner consistent with their respective needs and concerns at different levels of economic development,"

Noting:

—the Rio Declaration on Environment and Development, Agenda 21, and its follow-up in GATT, as reflected in the statement of the Chairman of the Council of Representatives to the CONTRACTING PARTIES at their 48th Session in December 1992, as well as the work of the Group on Environmental Measures and International Trade, the Committee on Trade and Development, and the Council of Representatives;

—the work programme envisaged in the Decision on Trade in Services and the Environment; and

—the relevant provisions of the Agreement on Trade–Related Aspects of Intellectual Property Rights,

Considering that there should not be, nor need be, any policy contradiction between upholding and safeguarding an open, non-discriminatory and equitable multilateral trading system on the one hand, and acting for the protection of the environment, and the promotion of sustainable development on the other,

Desiring to coordinate the policies in the field of trade and environment, and this without exceeding the competence of the multilateral trading system, which is limited to trade policies and those trade-related aspects of environmental policies which may result in significant trade effects for its members,

Decide:

—to direct the first meeting of the General Council of the WTO to establish a Committee on Trade and Environment open to all members of the WTO to report to the first biennial meeting of the Ministerial Conference after the entry into force of the WTO when the work and terms of reference of the Committee will be reviewed, in the light of recommendations of the Committee,

—that the TNC Decision of 15 December 1993 which reads, in part, as follows:

"(a) to identify the relationship between trade measures and environmental measures, in order to promote sustainable development;

(b) to make appropriate recommendations on whether any modifications of the provisions of the multilateral trading system are required, compatible with the open, equitable and non-discriminatory nature of the system, as regards, in particular:

—the need for rules to enhance positive interaction between trade and environmental measures, for the promotion of sustainable development, with special consideration to the needs of developing countries, in particular those of the least developed among them; and

—the avoidance of protectionist trade measures, and the adherence to effective multilateral disciplines to ensure responsiveness of the multilateral trading system to environmental objectives set forth in Agenda 21 and the Rio Declaration, in particular Principle 12; and

—surveillance of trade measures used for environmental purposes, of trade-related aspects of environmental measures which have significant trade effects, and of effective implementation of the multilateral disciplines governing those measures;''

constitutes, along with the preambular language above, the terms of reference of the Committee on Trade and Environment,

—that, within these terms of reference, and with the aim of making international trade and environmental policies mutually supportive, the Committee will initially address the following matters, in relation to which any relevant issue may be raised:

—the relationship between the provisions of the multilateral trading system and trade measures for environmental purposes, including those pursuant to multilateral environmental agreements;

—the relationship between environmental policies relevant to trade and environmental measures with significant trade effects and the provisions of the multilateral trading system;

—the relationship between the provisions of the multilateral trading system and:

(a) charges and taxes for environmental purposes

(b) requirements for environmental purposes relating to products, including standards and technical regulations, packaging, labelling and recycling;

—the provisions of the multilateral trading system with respect to the transparency of trade measures used for environmental purposes and environmental measures and requirements which have significant trade effects;

—the relationship between the dispute settlement mechanisms in the multilateral trading system and those found in multilateral environmental agreements;

—the effect of environmental measures on market access, especially in relation to developing countries, in particular to the least developed among them, and environmental benefits of removing trade restrictions and distortions;

—the issue of exports of domestically prohibited goods,

—that the Committee on Trade and Environment will consider the work programme envisaged in the Decision on Trade in Services and the Environment and the relevant provisions of the Agreement on Trade–Related Aspects of Intellectual Property Rights as an integral part of its work, within the above terms of reference,

—that, pending the first meeting of the General Council of the WTO, the work of the Committee on Trade and Environment should be carried out by a Sub-Committee of the Preparatory Committee of the World Trade Organization (PCWTO), open to all members of the PCWTO,

—to invite the Sub–Committee of the Preparatory Committee, and the Committee on Trade and Environment when it is established, to provide input to the relevant bodies in respect of appropriate arrangements for relations with intergovernmental and non-governmental organizations referred to in Article V of the WTO.

7.7 AGREEMENT ESTABLISHING THE WORLD TRADE ORGANIZATION. **Adopted on 15 April 1994. Entered into force, 1 January 1995. 1867 UNTS 3;** *reprinted in* **33 ILM 1125 (1994) & 4 Weston IV.C.2a:** *Preamble, Articles II, III: 3, IV:2,3*

The *Parties* to this Agreement,

Recognizing that their relations in the field of trade and economic endeavour should be conducted with a view to raising standards of living, ensuring full employment and a large and steadily growing volume of real income and effective demand, and expanding the production of and trade in goods and services, while allowing for the optimal use of the world's resources in accordance with the objective of sustainable development, seeking both to protect and preserve the environment and to enhance the means for doing so in a manner consistent with their respective needs and concerns at different levels of economic development,

Recognizing further that there is need for positive efforts designed to ensure that developing countries, and especially the least developed among them, secure a share in the growth in international trade commensurate with the needs of their economic development,

Being desirous of contributing to these objectives by entering into reciprocal and mutually advantageous arrangements directed to the substantial reduction of tariffs and other barriers to trade and to the elimination of discriminatory treatment in international trade relations,

Resolved, therefore, to develop an integrated, more viable and durable multilateral trading system encompassing the General Agreement on Tariffs and Trade, the results of past trade liberalization efforts, and all of the results of the Uruguay Round of Multilateral Trade Negotiations,

Determined to preserve the basic principles and to further the objectives underlying this multilateral trading system,

Agree as follows:

* * *

Article II

Scope of the WTO

1. The WTO shall provide the common institutional framework for the conduct of trade relations among its Members in matters related to the agreements and associated legal instruments included in the Annexes to this Agreement.

2. The agreements and associated legal instruments included in Annexes 1, 2 and 3 (hereinafter referred to as "Multilateral Trade Agreements") are integral parts of this Agreement, binding on all Members.

3. The agreements and associated legal instruments included in Annex 4 (hereinafter referred to as "Plurilateral Trade Agreements") are also part of this Agreement for those Members that have accepted them, and are binding on those Members. The Plurilateral Trade Agreements do not create either obligations or rights for Members that have not accepted them.

4. The General Agreement on Tariffs and Trade 1994 as specified in Annex 1A (hereinafter referred to as "GATT 1994") is legally distinct from the General Agreement on Tariffs and Trade, dated 30 October 1947, annexed to the Final Act Adopted at the Conclusion of the Second Session of the Preparatory Committee of the United Nations Conference on Trade and Employment, as subsequently rectified, amended or modified (hereinafter referred to as "GATT 1947").

Article III

Functions of the WTO

* * *

3. The WTO shall administer the Understanding on Rules and Procedures Governing the Settlement of Disputes (hereinafter referred to as the "Dispute Settlement Understanding" or "DSU") in Annex 2 to this Agreement.

* * *

Article IV

Structure of the WTO

* * *

2. There shall be a General Council composed of representatives of all the Members, which shall meet as appropriate. In the intervals between meetings of the Ministerial Conference, its functions shall be conducted by the General Council. The General Council shall also carry out the functions assigned to it by this Agreement. The General Council shall establish its rules of procedure and approve the rules of procedure for the Committees provided for in paragraph 7.

3. The General Council shall convene as appropriate to discharge the responsibilities of the Dispute Settlement Body provided for in the Dispute Settlement Understanding. The Dispute Settlement Body may have its own chairman and shall establish such rules of procedure as it deems necessary for the fulfilment of those responsibilities.

* * *

7.8 AGREEMENT ON TECHNICAL BARRIERS TO TRADE. **Concluded at Marrakesh, 15 April 1994. Entered into force, 1 January 1995. 1868 UNTS 120;** *reprinted in* **33 ILM 81 (1994)**

Article 1

General Provisions

1.1 General terms for standardization and procedures for assessment of conformity shall normally have the meaning given to them by definitions adopted within the United Nations system and by international standardizing bodies taking into account their context and in the light of the object and purpose of this Agreement.

1.2 However, for the purposes of this Agreement the meaning of the terms given in Annex 1 applies.

1.3 All products, including industrial and agricultural products, shall be subject to the provisions of this Agreement.

1.4 Purchasing specifications prepared by governmental bodies for production or consumption requirements of governmental bodies are not subject to the provisions of this Agreement but are addressed in the Agreement on Government Procurement, according to its coverage.

1.5 The provisions of this Agreement do not apply to sanitary and phytosanitary measures as defined in Annex A of the Agreement on the Application of Sanitary and Phytosanitary Measures.

1.6 All references in this Agreement to technical regulations, standards and conformity assessment procedures shall be construed to include any amendments thereto and any additions to the rules or the product coverage thereof, except amendments and additions of an insignificant nature.

TECHNICAL REGULATIONS AND STANDARDS

Article 2

Preparation, Adoption and Application of Technical Regulations by Central Government Bodies

With respect to their central government bodies:

2.1 Members shall ensure that in respect of technical regulations, products imported from the territory of any Member shall be accorded treatment no less favourable than that accorded to like products of national origin and to like products originating in any other country.

2.2 Members shall ensure that technical regulations are not prepared, adopted or applied with a view to or with the effect of creating unnecessary obstacles to international trade. For this purpose, technical regulations shall not be more trade-restrictive than necessary to fulfil a legitimate objective, taking account of the risks non-fulfilment would create. Such legitimate objectives are, inter alia: national security requirements; the prevention of deceptive practices; protection of human health or safety, animal or plant life or health, or the environment. In assessing such risks, relevant elements of consideration are, inter alia: available scientific and technical information, related processing technology or intended end-uses of products.

2.3 Technical regulations shall not be maintained if the circumstances or objectives giving rise to their adoption no longer exist or if the changed circumstances or objectives can be addressed in a less trade-restrictive manner.

2.4 Where technical regulations are required and relevant international standards exist or their completion is imminent, Members shall use them, or the relevant parts of them, as a basis for their technical regulations except when such international standards or relevant parts would be an ineffective or inappropriate means for the fulfilment of the legitimate objectives pursued, for instance because of fundamental climatic or geographical factors or fundamental technological problems.

2.5 A Member preparing, adopting or applying a technical regulation which may have a significant effect on trade of other Members shall, upon the request of another Member, explain the justification for that technical regulation in terms of the provisions of paragraphs 2 to 4. Whenever a technical regulation is prepared, adopted or applied for one of the legitimate objectives explicitly mentioned in paragraph 2, and is in accordance with relevant international standards, it shall be rebuttably presumed not to create an unnecessary obstacle to international trade.

2.6 With a view to harmonizing technical regulations on as wide a basis as possible, Members shall play a full part, within the limits of their resources, in the preparation by appropriate international standardizing bodies of international standards for products for which they either have adopted, or expect to adopt, technical regulations.

2.7 Members shall give positive consideration to accepting as equivalent technical regulations of other Members, even if these regulations differ from their own, provided they are satisfied that these regulations adequately fulfil the objectives of their own regulations.

2.8 Wherever appropriate, Members shall specify technical regulations based on product requirements in terms of performance rather than design or descriptive characteristics.

2.9 Whenever a relevant international standard does not exist or the technical content of a proposed technical regulation is not in accordance with the technical content of relevant international standards, and if the technical regulation may have a significant effect on trade of other Members, Members shall:

> 2.9.1 publish a notice in a publication at an early appropriate stage, in such a manner as to enable interested parties in other Members to become acquainted with it, that they propose to introduce a particular technical regulation;

> 2.9.2 notify other Members through the Secretariat of the products to be covered by the proposed technical regulation, together with a brief indication of its objective and rationale. Such notifications shall take place at an early appropriate stage, when amendments can still be introduced and comments taken into account;

> 2.9.3 upon request, provide to other Members particulars or copies of the proposed technical regulation and, whenever possible, identify the parts which in substance deviate from relevant international standards;

> 2.9.4 without discrimination, allow reasonable time for other Members to make comments in writing, discuss these comments upon request, and take these written comments and the results of these discussions into account.

2.10 Subject to the provisions in the lead-in to paragraph 9, where urgent problems of safety, health, environmental protection or national security arise or threaten to arise for a Member, that Member may omit such of the steps enumerated in paragraph 9 as it finds necessary, provided that the Member, upon adoption of a technical regulation, shall:

> 2.10.1 notify immediately other Members through the Secretariat of the particular technical regulation and the products covered, with a brief indication of the objective and the rationale of the technical regulation, including the nature of the urgent problems;

> 2.10.2 upon request, provide other Members with copies of the technical regulation;

2.10.3 without discrimination, allow other Members to present their comments in writing, discuss these comments upon request, and take these written comments and the results of these discussions into account.

2.11 Members shall ensure that all technical regulations which have been adopted are published promptly or otherwise made available in such a manner as to enable interested parties in other Members to become acquainted with them.

2.12 Except in those urgent circumstances referred to in paragraph 10, Members shall allow a reasonable interval between the publication of technical regulations and their entry into force in order to allow time for producers in exporting Members, and particularly in developing country Members, to adapt their products or methods of production to the requirements of the importing Member.

* * *

Article 12

Special and Differential Treatment of Developing Country Members

12.1 Members shall provide differential and more favourable treatment to developing country Members to this Agreement, through the following provisions as well as through the relevant provisions of other Articles of this Agreement.

12.2 Members shall give particular attention to the provisions of this Agreement concerning developing country Members' rights and obligations and shall take into account the special development, financial and trade needs of developing country Members in the implementation of this Agreement, both nationally and in the operation of this Agreement's institutional arrangements.

12.3 Members shall, in the preparation and application of technical regulations, standards and conformity assessment procedures, take account of the special development, financial and trade needs of developing country Members, with a view to ensuring that such technical regulations, standards and conformity assessment procedures do not create unnecessary obstacles to exports from developing country Members.

12.4 Members recognize that, although international standards, guides or recommendations may exist, in their particular technological and socio-economic conditions, developing country Members adopt certain technical regulations, standards or conformity assessment procedures aimed at preserving indigenous technology and production methods and processes compatible with their development needs. Members therefore recognize that developing country Members should not be expected to use international standards as a basis for their technical regulations or standards, including test methods, which are not appropriate to their development, financial and trade needs.

12.5 Members shall take such reasonable measures as may be available to them to ensure that international standardizing bodies and international systems for conformity assessment are organized and operated in a way which facilitates active and representative participation of relevant bodies in all Members, taking into account the special problems of developing country Members.

12.6 Members shall take such reasonable measures as may be available to them to ensure that international standardizing bodies, upon request of developing country Members, examine the possibility of, and, if practicable, prepare international standards concerning products of special interest to developing country Members.

12.7 Members shall, in accordance with the provisions of Article 11, provide technical assistance to developing country Members to ensure that the preparation and application of technical regulations, standards and conformity assessment procedures do not create unnecessary obstacles to the expansion and diversification of exports from developing country Members. In determining the terms and conditions of the technical assistance, account shall be taken of the stage of development of the requesting Members and in particular of the least-developed country Members.

12.8 It is recognized that developing country Members may face special problems, including institutional and infrastructural problems, in the field of preparation and application of technical regulations, standards and conformity assessment procedures. It is further recognized that the special development and trade needs of developing country Members, as well as their stage of technological development, may hinder their ability to discharge fully their obligations under this Agreement. Members, therefore, shall take this fact fully into account. Accordingly, with a view to ensuring that developing country Members are able to comply with this Agreement, the Committee on Technical Barriers to Trade provided for in Article 13 (referred to in this Agreement as the "Committee") is enabled to grant, upon request, specified, time-limited exceptions in whole or in part from obligations under this Agreement. When considering such requests the Committee shall take into account the special problems, in the field of preparation and application of technical regulations, standards and conformity assessment procedures, and the special development and trade needs of the developing country Member, as well as its stage of technological development, which may hinder its ability to discharge fully its obligations under this Agreement. The Committee shall, in particular, take into account the special problems of the least-developed country Members.

12.9 During consultations, developed country Members shall bear in mind the special difficulties experienced by developing country Members in formulating and implementing standards and technical regulations and conformity assessment procedures, and in their desire to assist developing country Members with their efforts in this direction, developed country Members shall take account of the special needs of the former in regard to financing, trade and development.

12.10 The Committee shall examine periodically the special and differential treatment, as laid down in this Agreement, granted to developing country Members on national and international levels.

* * *

Article 14

Consultation and Dispute Settlement

14.1 Consultations and the settlement of disputes with respect to any matter affecting the operation of this Agreement shall take place under the auspices of the Dispute Settlement Body and shall follow, mutatis mutandis, the provisions of Articles XXII and XXIII of GATT 1994, as elaborated and applied by the Dispute Settlement Understanding.

* * *

ANNEX 1

TERMS AND THEIR DEFINITIONS FOR THE PURPOSE OF THIS AGREEMENT

The terms presented in the sixth edition of the ISO/IEC Guide 2: 1991, General Terms and Their Definitions Concerning Standardization and Related Activities, shall, when used in this Agreement, have the same meaning as given in the definitions in the said Guide taking into account that services are excluded from the coverage of this Agreement.

For the purpose of this Agreement, however, the following definitions shall apply:

1. Technical regulation

Document which lays down product characteristics or their related processes and production methods, including the applicable administrative provisions, with which compliance is mandatory. It may also include or deal exclusively with terminology, symbols, packaging, marking or labelling requirements as they apply to a product, process or production method.

* * *

2. Standard

Document approved by a recognized body, that provides, for common and repeated use, rules, guidelines or characteristics for products or related processes and production methods, with which compliance is not mandatory. It may also include or deal exclusively with terminology, symbols, packaging, marking or labelling requirements as they apply to a product, process or production method.

Explanatory note

The terms as defined in ISO/IEC Guide 2 cover products, processes and services. This Agreement deals only with technical regulations, standards and conformity assessment procedures related to products or processes and production methods. Standards as defined by ISO/IEC Guide 2 may be mandatory or voluntary. For the purpose of this Agreement standards are defined as voluntary and technical regulations as mandatory documents. Standards prepared by the international standardization community are based on consensus. This Agreement covers also documents that are not based on consensus.

3. Conformity assessment procedures

Any procedure used, directly or indirectly, to determine that relevant requirements in technical regulations or standards are fulfilled.

* * *

6. Central government body

Central government, its ministries and departments or any body subject to the control of the central government in respect of the activity in question.

Explanatory note:

In the case of the European Communities the provisions governing central government bodies apply. However, regional bodies or conformity assessment systems may be established within the European Communities, and in such cases would be subject to the provisions of this Agreement on regional bodies or conformity assessment systems.

* * *

7.9   WTO Agreement on the Application of Sanitary and Phytosanitary Measures. **Concluded at Marrakesh, 15 April 1994. Entered into force, 1 January 1995. 1867 UNTS 493**

Article 1—General Provisions

1.   This Agreement applies to all sanitary and phytosanitary measures which may, directly or indirectly, affect international trade. Such measures shall be developed and applied in accordance with the provisions of this Agreement.

2.   For the purposes of this Agreement, the definitions provided in Annex A shall apply.

3.   The annexes are an integral part of this Agreement.

4.   Nothing in this Agreement shall affect the rights of Members under the Agreement on Technical Barriers to Trade with respect to measures not within the scope of this Agreement.

Article 2—Basic Rights and Obligations

1.   Members have the right to take sanitary and phytosanitary measures necessary for the protection of human, animal or plant life or health, provided that such measures are not inconsistent with the provisions of this Agreement.

2.   Members shall ensure that any sanitary or phytosanitary measure is applied only to the extent necessary to protect human, animal or plant life or health, is based on scientific principles and is not maintained without sufficient scientific evidence, except as provided for in paragraph 7 of Article 5.

3.   Members shall ensure that their sanitary and phytosanitary measures do not arbitrarily or unjustifiably discriminate between Members where identical or similar conditions prevail, including between their own territory and that of other Members. Sanitary and phytosanitary measures shall not be applied in a manner which would constitute a disguised restriction on international trade.

4.   Sanitary or phytosanitary measures which conform to the relevant provisions of this Agreement shall be presumed to be in accordance with the obligations of the Members under the provisions of GATT 1994 which relate to the use of sanitary or phytosanitary measures, in particular the provisions of Article XX(b).

Article 3—Harmonization

1.   To harmonize sanitary and phytosanitary measures on as wide a basis as possible, Members shall base their sanitary or phytosanitary measures on international standards, guidelines or recommendations, where they exist, except as otherwise provided for in this Agreement, and in particular in paragraph 3.

2.   Sanitary or phytosanitary measures which conform to international standards, guidelines or recommendations shall be deemed to be necessary to protect human, animal or plant life or health, and presumed to be consistent with the relevant provisions of this Agreement and of GATT 1994.

3.   Members may introduce or maintain sanitary or phytosanitary measures which result in a higher level of sanitary or phytosanitary protection than would be achieved by measures based on the relevant international standards, guidelines or recommendations, if there is a scientific justification, or as a consequence of the level of sanitary or phytosanitary protection a Member determines to be appropriate in accordance with the relevant provisions of paragraphs 1 through 8 of Article 5.[1]

---

1. For the purposes of paragraph 3 of Article 3, there is a scientific justification if, on the basis of an examination and evaluation of available scientific information in conformity with the relevant provisions of this Agreement, a Member determines that the relevant

Notwithstanding the above, all measures which result in a level of sanitary or phytosanitary protection different from that which would be achieved by measures based on international standards, guidelines or recommendations shall not be inconsistent with any other provision of this Agreement.

4. Members shall play a full part, within the limits of their resources, in the relevant international organizations and their subsidiary bodies, in particular the Codex Alimentarius Commission, the International Office of Epizootics, and the international and regional organizations operating within the framework of the International Plant Protection Convention, to promote within these organizations the development and periodic review of standards, guidelines and recommendations with respect to all aspects of sanitary and phytosanitary measures.

5. The Committee on Sanitary and Phytosanitary Measures provided for in paragraphs 1 and 4 of Article 12 (referred to in this Agreement as the "Committee") shall develop a procedure to monitor the process of international harmonization and coordinate efforts in this regard with the relevant international organizations.

Article 4—Equivalence

1. Members shall accept the sanitary or phytosanitary measures of other Members as equivalent, even if these measures differ from their own or from those used by other Members trading in the same product, if the exporting Member objectively demonstrates to the importing Member that its measures achieve the importing Member's appropriate level of sanitary or phytosanitary protection. For this purpose, reasonable access shall be given, upon request, to the importing Member for inspection, testing and other relevant procedures.

2. Members shall, upon request, enter into consultations with the aim of achieving bilateral and multilateral agreements on recognition of the equivalence of specified sanitary or phytosanitary measures.

Article 5—Assessment of Risk and Determination of the Appropriate Level of Sanitary or Phytosanitary Protection

1. Members shall ensure that their sanitary or phytosanitary measures are based on an assessment, as appropriate to the circumstances, of the risks to human, animal or plant life or health, taking into account risk assessment techniques developed by the relevant international organizations.

2. In the assessment of risks, Members shall take into account available scientific evidence; relevant processes and production methods; relevant inspection, sampling and testing methods; prevalence of specific diseases or pests; existence of pest- or disease-free areas; relevant ecological and environmental conditions; and quarantine or other treatment.

3. In assessing the risk to animal or plant life or health and determining the measure to be applied for achieving the appropriate level of sanitary or phytosanitary protection from such risk, Members shall take into account as relevant economic factors: the potential damage in terms of loss of production or sales in the event of the entry, establishment or spread of a pest or disease; the costs of control or eradication in the territory of the importing Member; and the relative cost-effectiveness of alternative approaches to limiting risks.

4. Members should, when determining the appropriate level of sanitary or phytosanitary protection, take into account the objective of minimizing negative trade effects.

international standards, guidelines or recommendations are not sufficient to achieve its appropriate level of sanitary or phytosanitary protection.

5. With the objective of achieving consistency in the application of the concept of appropriate level of sanitary or phytosanitary protection against risks to human life or health, or to animal and plant life or health, each Member shall avoid arbitrary or unjustifiable distinctions in the levels it considers to be appropriate in different situations, if such distinctions result in discrimination or a disguised restriction on international trade. Members shall cooperate in the Committee, in accordance with paragraphs 1, 2 and 3 of Article 12, to develop guidelines to further the practical implementation of this provision. In developing the guidelines, the Committee shall take into account all relevant factors, including the exceptional character of human health risks to which people voluntarily expose themselves.

6. Without prejudice to paragraph 2 of Article 3, when establishing or maintaining sanitary or phytosanitary measures to achieve the appropriate level of sanitary or phytosanitary protection, Members shall ensure that such measures are not more trade-restrictive than required to achieve their appropriate level of sanitary or phytosanitary protection, taking into account technical and economic feasibility.[2]

7. In cases where relevant scientific evidence is insufficient, a Member may provisionally adopt sanitary or phytosanitary measures on the basis of available pertinent information, including that from the relevant international organizations as well as from sanitary or phytosanitary measures applied by other Members. In such circumstances, Members shall seek to obtain the additional information necessary for a more objective assessment of risk and review the sanitary or phytosanitary measure accordingly within a reasonable period of time.

8. When a Member has reason to believe that a specific sanitary or phytosanitary measure introduced or maintained by another Member is constraining, or has the potential to constrain, its exports and the measure is not based on the relevant international standards, guidelines or recommendations, or such standards, guidelines or recommendations do not exist, an explanation of the reasons for such sanitary or phytosanitary measure may be requested and shall be provided by the Member maintaining the measure.

* * *

Article 10—Special and Differential Treatment

1. In the preparation and application of sanitary or phytosanitary measures, Members shall take account of the special needs of developing country Members, and in particular of the least-developed country Members.

2. Where the appropriate level of sanitary or phytosanitary protection allows scope for the phased introduction of new sanitary or phytosanitary measures, longer time-frames for compliance should be accorded on products of interest to developing country Members so as to maintain opportunities for their exports.

3. With a view to ensuring that developing country Members are able to comply with the provisions of this Agreement, the Committee is enabled to grant to such countries, upon request, specified, time-limited exceptions in whole or in part from obligations under this Agreement, taking into account their financial, trade and development needs.

4. Members should encourage and facilitate the active participation of developing country Members in the relevant international organizations.

---

2. For purposes of paragraph 6 of Article 5, a measure is not more trade-restrictive than required unless there is another measure, reasonably available taking into account technical and economic feasibility, that achieves the appropriate level of sanitary or phytosanitary protection and is significantly less restrictive to trade.

Article 11—Consultations and Dispute Settlement

1. The provisions of Articles XXII and XXIII of GATT 1994 as elaborated and applied by the Dispute Settlement Understanding shall apply to consultations and the settlement of disputes under this Agreement, except as otherwise specifically provided herein.

2. In a dispute under this Agreement involving scientific or technical issues, a panel should seek advice from experts chosen by the panel in consultation with the parties to the dispute. To this end, the panel may, when it deems it appropriate, establish an advisory technical experts group, or consult the relevant international organizations, at the request of either party to the dispute or on its own initiative.

3. Nothing in this Agreement shall impair the rights of Members under other international agreements, including the right to resort to the good offices or dispute settlement mechanisms of other international organizations or established under any international agreement.

* * *

ANNEX A

DEFINITIONS[3]

1. Sanitary or phytosanitary measure—Any measure applied:

(a) to protect animal or plant life or health within the territory of the Member from risks arising from the entry, establishment or spread of pests, diseases, disease-carrying organisms or disease-causing organisms;

(b) to protect human or animal life or health within the territory of the Member from risks arising from additives, contaminants, toxins or disease-causing organisms in foods, beverages or feedstuffs;

(c) to protect human life or health within the territory of the Member from risks arising from diseases carried by animals, plants or products thereof, or from the entry, establishment or spread of pests; or

(d) to prevent or limit other damage within the territory of the Member from the entry, establishment or spread of pests.

Sanitary or phytosanitary measures include all relevant laws, decrees, regulations, requirements and procedures including, inter alia, end product criteria; processes and production methods; testing, inspection, certification and approval procedures; quarantine treatments including relevant requirements associated with the transport of animals or plants, or with the materials necessary for their survival during transport; provisions on relevant statistical methods, sampling procedures and methods of risk assessment; and packaging and labelling requirements directly related to food safety.

2. Harmonization—The establishment, recognition and application of common sanitary and phytosanitary measures by different Members.

3. International standards, guidelines and recommendations

(a) for food safety, the standards, guidelines and recommendations established by the Codex Alimentarius Commission relating to food additives, veterinary drug and pesticide residues, contaminants, methods of analysis and sampling, and codes and guidelines of hygienic practice;

(b) for animal health and zoonoses, the standards, guidelines and recommendations developed under the auspices of the International Office of Epizootics;

---

3. For the purpose of these definitions, "animal" includes fish and wild fauna; "plant" includes forests and wild flora; "pests" include weeds; and "contaminants" include pesticide and veterinary drug residues and extraneous matter.

(c) for plant health, the international standards, guidelines and recommendations developed under the auspices of the Secretariat of the International Plant Protection Convention in cooperation with regional organizations operating within the framework of the International Plant Protection Convention; and

(d) for matters not covered by the above organizations, appropriate standards, guidelines and recommendations promulgated by other relevant international organizations open for membership to all Members, as identified by the Committee.

4. Risk assessment—The evaluation of the likelihood of entry, establishment or spread of a pest or disease within the territory of an importing Member according to the sanitary or phytosanitary measures which might be applied, and of the associated potential biological and economic consequences; or the evaluation of the potential for adverse effects on human or animal health arising from the presence of additives, contaminants, toxins or disease-causing organisms in food, beverages or feedstuffs.

5. Appropriate level of sanitary or phytosanitary protection—The level of protection deemed appropriate by the Member establishing a sanitary or phytosanitary measure to protect human, animal or plant life or health within its territory.

NOTE: Many Members otherwise refer to this concept as the "acceptable level of risk".

* * *

7.10 UNDERSTANDING ON RULES AND PROCEDURES GOVERNING THE SETTLEMENT OF DISPUTES. **Concluded at Marrakesh, 15 April 1994. Entered into force 1 January 1995. Marrakesh Agreement Establishing the World Trade Organization, Annex 2;** *reprinted in* **33 ILM 1226 (1994) & 4 Weston & Carlson IV.C.3**

* * *

Article 2

Administration

1. The Dispute Settlement Body is hereby established to administer these rules and procedures and, except as otherwise provided in a covered agreement, the consultation and dispute settlement provisions of the covered agreements. Accordingly, the DSB shall have the authority to establish panels, adopt panel and Appellate Body reports, maintain surveillance of implementation of rulings and recommendations, and authorize suspension of concessions and other obligations under the covered agreements. With respect to disputes arising under a covered agreement which is a Plurilateral Trade Agreement, the term "Member" as used herein shall refer only to those Members that are parties to the relevant Plurilateral Trade Agreement. Where the DSB administers the dispute settlement provisions of a Plurilateral Trade Agreement, only those Members that are parties to that Agreement may participate in decisions or actions taken by the DSB with respect to that dispute.

* * *

Article 11

Function of Panels

The function of panels is to assist the DSB in discharging its responsibilities under this Understanding and the covered agreements. Accordingly, a panel should make an objective assessment of the matter before it, including an objective assessment of the facts of the case and the applicability of and conformity with the relevant covered agreements, and make such other findings as will assist the DSB in making the recommendations or in giving the rulings provided for in the covered agreements. Panels should consult regularly with the parties to the dispute and give them adequate opportunity to develop a mutually satisfactory solution.

* * *

Article 16

Adoption of Panel Reports

* * *

4. Within 60 days after the date of circulation of a panel report to the Members, the report shall be adopted at a DSB meeting[1] unless a party to the dispute formally notifies the DSB of its decision to appeal or the DSB decides by consensus not to adopt the report. If a party has notified its decision to appeal, the report by the panel shall not be considered for adoption by the DSB until after completion of the appeal. This adoption procedure is without prejudice to the right of Members to express their views on a panel report.

---

1. If a meeting of the DSB is not scheduled within this period at a time that enables the requirements of paragraphs 1 and 4 of Article 16 to be met, a meeting of the DSB shall be held for this purpose.

Article 17

Appellate Review

Standing Appellate Body

1. A standing Appellate Body shall be established by the DSB. The Appellate Body shall hear appeals from panel cases. It shall be composed of seven persons, three of whom shall serve on any one case. Persons serving on the Appellate Body shall serve in rotation. Such rotation shall be determined in the working procedures of the Appellate Body.

* * *

Adoption of Appellate Body Reports

14. An Appellate Body report shall be adopted by the DSB and unconditionally accepted by the parties to the dispute unless the DSB decides by consensus not to adopt the Appellate Body report within 30 days following its circulation to the Members. This adoption procedure is without prejudice to the right of Members to express their views on an Appellate Body report.

* * *

Article 21

Surveillance of Implementation of Recommendations and Rulings

1. Prompt compliance with recommendations or rulings of the DSB is essential in order to ensure effective resolution of disputes to the benefit of all Members.

* * *

B.   Human Rights/Social Justice

7.11   U.S. Alien Tort Statute, 28 U.S.C. § 1350, 1 Stat. 73 (1789)

The district courts shall have original jurisdiction of any civil action by an alien for a tort only, committed in violation of the law of nations or a treaty of the United States.

7.12   ＡＭＥＲＩＣＡＮ ＤＥＣＬＡＲＡＴＩＯＮ ＯＦ ＴＨＥ ＲＩＧＨＴＳ ＡＮＤ ＤＵＴＩＥＳ ＯＦ ＭＡＮ, O.A.S. ＲＥＳ. XXX, **adopted by the Ninth International Conference of American States (1948),** *reprinted in* **Basic Documents Pertaining to Human Rights in the Inter–American System, OEA/Ser.L.V/II.82 doc.6 rev.1 at 17 (1992):** *Preamble & Arts I, V–IX, XI, XIII, XXIII*

Preamble

All men are born free and equal, in dignity and in rights, and, being endowed by nature with reason and conscience, they should conduct themselves as brothers one to another.

The fulfillment of duty by each individual is a prerequisite to the rights of all. Rights and duties are interrelated in every social and political activity of man. While rights exalt individual liberty, duties express the dignity of that liberty.

Duties of a juridical nature presuppose others of a moral nature which support them in principle and constitute their basis.

Inasmuch as spiritual development is the supreme end of human existence and the highest expression thereof, it is the duty of man to serve that end with all his strength and resources.

Since culture is the highest social and historical expression of that spiritual development, it is the duty of man to preserve, practice and foster culture by every means within his power.

And, since moral conduct constitutes the noblest flowering of culture, it is the duty of every man always to hold it in high respect.

Chapter 1. Rights

Right to life, liberty and personal security.

Article I. Every human being has the right to life, liberty and the security of his person.

* * *

Right to protection of honor, personal reputation, and private and family life.

Article V. Every person has the right to the protection of the law against abusive attacks upon his honor, his reputation, and his private and family life.

Right to a family and to protection thereof.

Article VI. Every person has the right to establish a family, the basic element of society, and to receive protection therefor.

Right to protection for mothers and children.

Article VII. All women, during pregnancy and the nursing period, and all children have the right to special protection, care and aid.

Right to residence and movement.

Article VIII. Every person has the right to fix his residence within the territory of the state of which he is a national, to move about freely within such territory, and not to leave it except by his own will.

Right to inviolability of the home.

Article IX. Every person has the right to the inviolability of his home.

* * *

Right to the preservation of health and to well-being.

Article XI. Every person has the right to the preservation of his health through sanitary and social measures relating to food, clothing, housing and medical care, to the extent permitted by public and community resources.

* * *

Right to the benefits of culture.

Article XIII. Every person has the right to take part in the cultural life of the community, to enjoy the arts, and to participate in the benefits that result from intellectual progress, especially scientific discoveries.

He likewise has the right to the protection of his moral and material interests as regards his inventions or any literary, scientific or artistic works of which he is the author.

* * *

Right to property.

Article XXIII. Every person has a right to own such private property as meets the essential needs of decent living and helps to maintain the dignity of the individual and of the home.

* * *

7.13 Convention on the Prevention and Punishment of the Crime of Genocide. **Concluded at New York, 9 December 1948. Entered into force, 12 January 1951. 78 UNTS 277;** *reprinted in* **3 Weston & Carlson III.J.2:** *Arts. II–IV*

Article II. In the present Convention, genocide means any of the following acts committed with intent to destroy, in whole or in part, a national, ethnical, racial or religious group, as such:

(a) Killing members of the group;

(b) Causing serious bodily or mental harm to members of the group;

(c) Deliberately inflicting on the group conditions of life calculated to bring about its physical destruction in whole or in part;

(d) Imposing measures intended to prevent births within the group;

(e) Forcibly transferring children of the group to another group.

Article III. The following acts shall be punishable:

(a) Genocide;

(b) Conspiracy to commit genocide;

(c) Direct and public incitement to commit genocide;

(d) Attempt to commit genocide;

(e) Complicity in genocide.

Article IV. Persons committing genocide or any of the other acts enumerated in Article III shall be punished, whether they are constitutionally responsible rulers, public officials or private individuals.

7.14 UNIVERSAL DECLARATION OF HUMAN RIGHTS. Adopted by the U.N. General Assembly, 10 December 1948. GA Res 217A, UN GAOR, 3rd Sess, Pt I, Resolutions, at 71, UN Doc A/810; *reprinted in* 3 Weston & Carlson III.A.1

PREAMBLE

Whereas recognition of the inherent dignity and of the equal and inalienable rights of all members of the human family is the foundation of freedom, justice and peace in the world,

Whereas disregard and contempt for human rights have resulted in barbarous acts which have outraged the conscience of mankind, and the advent of a world in which human beings shall enjoy freedom of speech and belief and freedom from fear and want has been proclaimed as the highest aspiration of the common people,

Whereas it is essential, if man is not to be compelled to have recourse, as a last resort, to rebellion against tyranny and oppression, that human rights should be protected by the rule of law,

Whereas it is essential to promote the development of friendly relations between nations,

Whereas the peoples of the United Nations have in the Charter reaffirmed their faith in fundamental human rights, in the dignity and worth of the human person and in the equal rights of men and women and have determined to promote social progress and better standards of life in larger freedom,

Whereas Member States have pledged themselves to achieve, in co-operation with the United Nations, the promotion of universal respect for and observance of human rights and fundamental freedoms,

Whereas a common understanding of these rights and freedoms is of the greatest importance for the full realization of this pledge,

Now, therefore,

The General Assembly

Proclaims this Universal Declaration of Human Rights as a common standard of achievement for all peoples and all nations, to the end that every individual and every organ of society, keeping this Declaration constantly in mind, shall strive by teaching and education to promote respect for these rights and freedoms and by progressive measures, national and international, to secure their universal and effective recognition and observance, both among the peoples of Member States themselves and among the peoples of territories under their jurisdiction.

Article 1. All human beings are born free and equal in dignity and rights. They are endowed with reason and conscience and should act towards one another in a spirit of brotherhood.

Article 2. Everyone is entitled to all the rights and freedoms set forth in this Declaration, without distinction of any kind, such as race, colour, sex, language, religion, political or other opinion, national or social origin, property, birth or other status.

Furthermore, no distinction shall be made on the basis of the political, jurisdictional or international status of the country or territory to which a person belongs, whether it be independent, trust, non-self-governing or under any other limitation of sovereignty.

Article 3. Everyone has the right to life, liberty and the security of person.

Article 4. No one shall be held in slavery or servitude; slavery and the slave trade shall be prohibited in all their forms.

Article 5. No one shall be subjected to torture or to cruel, inhuman or degrading treatment or punishment.

Article 6. Everyone has the right to recognition everywhere as a person before the law.

Article 7. All are equal before the law and are entitled without any discrimination to equal protection of the law. All are entitled to equal protection against any discrimination in violation of this Declaration and against any incitement to such discrimination.

Article 8. Everyone has the right to an effective remedy by the competent national tribunals for acts violating the fundamental rights granted him by the constitution or by law.

Article 9. No one shall be subjected to arbitrary arrest, detention or exile.

Article 10. Everyone is entitled in full equality to a fair and public hearing by an independent and impartial tribunal, in the determination of his rights and obligations and of any criminal charge against him.

Article 11. (1) Everyone charged with a penal offence has the right to be presumed innocent until proved guilty according to law in a public trial at which he has had all the guarantees necessary for his defence.

    (2) No one shall be held guilty of any penal offence on account of any act or omission which did not constitute a penal offence, under national or international law, at the time when it was committed. Nor shall a heavier penalty be imposed than the one that was applicable at the time the penal offence was committed.

Article 12. No one shall be subjected to arbitrary interference with his privacy, family, home or correspondence, nor to attacks upon his honour and reputation. Everyone has the right to the protection of the law against such interference or attacks.

Article 13. (1) Everyone has the right to freedom of movement and residence within the borders of each State.

    (2) Everyone has the right to leave any country, including his own, and to return to his country.

Article 14. (1) Everyone has the right to seek and to enjoy in other countries asylum from persecution.

    (2) This right may not be invoked in the case of prosecutions genuinely arising from nonpolitical crimes or from acts contrary to the purposes and principles of the United Nations.

Article 15. (1) Everyone has the right to a nationality.

    (2) No one shall be arbitrarily deprived of his nationality nor denied the right to change his nationality.

Article 16. (1) Men and women of full age, without any limitation due to race, nationality or religion, have the right to marry and to found a family. They are entitled to equal rights as to marriage, during marriage and at its dissolution.

    (2) Marriage shall be entered into only with the free and full consent of the intending spouses.

    (3) The family is the natural and fundamental group unit of society and is entitled to protection by society and the State.

Article 17. (1) Everyone has the right to own property alone as well as in association with others.

    (2) No one shall be arbitrarily deprived of his property.

Article 18. Everyone has the right to freedom of thought, conscience and religion; this right includes freedom to change his religion or belief, and freedom, either alone or in community with others and in public or private, to manifest his religion or belief in teaching, practice, worship and observance.

Article 19. Everyone has the right to freedom of opinion and expression; this right includes freedom to hold opinions without interference and to seek, receive and impart information and ideas through any media and regardless of frontiers.

Article 20. (1) Everyone has the right to freedom of peaceful assembly and association.

(2) No one may be compelled to belong to an association.

Article 21. (1) Everyone has the right to take part in the government of his country, directly or through freely chosen representatives.

(2) Everyone has the right of equal access to public service in his country.

(3) The will of the people shall be the basis of the authority of government; this will shall be expressed in periodic and genuine elections which shall be by universal and equal suffrage and shall be held by secret vote or by equivalent free voting procedures.

Article 22. Everyone, as a member of society, has the right to social security and is entitled to realization, through national effort and international co-operation and in accordance with the organization and resources of each State, of the economic, social and cultural rights indispensable for his dignity and the free development of his personality.

Article 23. (1) Everyone has the right to work, to free choice of employment, to just and favourable conditions of work and to protection against unemployment.

(2) Everyone, without any discrimination, has the right to equal pay for equal work.

(3) Everyone who works has the right to just and favourable remuneration ensuring for himself and his family an existence worthy of human dignity, and supplemented, if necessary, by other means of social protection.

(4) Everyone has the right to form and to join trade unions for the protection of his interests.

Article 24. Everyone has the right to rest and leisure, including reasonable limitation of working hours and periodic holidays with pay.

Article 25. (1) Everyone has the right to a standard of living adequate for the health and well-being of himself and of his family, including food, clothing, housing and medical care and necessary social services, and the right to security in the event of unemployment, sickness, disability, widowhood, old age or other lack of livelihood in circumstances beyond his control.

(2) Motherhood and childhood are entitled to special care and assistance. All children, whether born in or out of wedlock, shall enjoy the same social protection.

Article 26. (1) Everyone has the right to education. Education shall be free, at least in the elementary and fundamental stages. Elementary education shall be compulsory. Technical and professional education shall be made generally available and higher education shall be equally accessible to all on the basis of merit.

(2) Education shall be directed to the full development of the human personality and to the strengthening of respect for human rights and fundamental freedoms. It shall promote understanding, tolerance and friendship among all nations, racial or religious groups, and shall further the activities of the United Nations for the maintenance of peace.

(3) Parents have a prior right to choose the kind of education that shall be given to their children.

Article 27. (1) Everyone has the right freely to participate in the cultural life of the community, to enjoy the arts and to share in scientific advancement and its benefits.

(2) Everyone has the right to the protection of the moral and material interests resulting from any scientific, literary or artistic production of which he is the author.

Article 28. Everyone is entitled to a social and international order in which the rights and freedoms set forth in this Declaration can be fully realized.

Article 29. (1) Everyone has duties to the community in which alone the free and full development of his personality is possible.

(2) In the exercise of his rights and freedoms, everyone shall be subject only to such limitations as are determined by law solely for the purpose of securing due recognition and respect for the rights and freedoms of others and of meeting the just requirements of morality, public order and the general welfare in a democratic society.

(3) These rights and freedoms may in no case be exercised contrary to the purposes and principles of the United Nations.

Article 30. Nothing in this Declaration may be interpreted as implying for any State, group or person any right to engage in any activity or to perform any act aimed at the destruction of any of the rights and freedoms set forth herein.

7.15   UNESCO DECLARATION ON THE PRINCIPLES OF INTERNATIONAL CULTURAL CO-OPERATION. Adopted on 4 November 1966. *Reprinted in* United Nations, Human Rights: A Compilation of International Instruments 409 (1988)

The General Conference of the United Nations Educational, Scientific and Cultural Organization, met in Paris for its fourteenth session, this fourth day of November 1966, being the twentieth anniversary of the foundation of the Organization,

Recalling that the Constitution of the Organization declares that "since wars begin in the minds of men, it is in the minds of men that the defences of peace must be constructed" and that the peace must be founded, if it is not to fail, upon the intellectual and moral solidarity of mankind,

Recalling that the Constitution also states that the wide diffusion of culture and the education of humanity for justice and liberty and peace are indispensable to the dignity of man and constitute a sacred duty which all the nations must fulfil in a spirit of mutual assistance and concern,

Considering that the Organization's Member States, believing in the pursuit of truth and the free exchange of ideas and knowledge, have agreed and determined to develop and to increase the means of communication between their peoples,

Considering that, despite the technical advances which facilitate the development and dissemination of knowledge and ideas, ignorance of the way of life and customs of peoples still presents an obstacle to friendship among the nations, to peaceful co-operation and to the progress of mankind,

Taking account of the Universal Declaration of Human Rights, the Declaration of the Rights of the Child, the Declaration on the Granting of Independence to Colonial Countries and Peoples, the United Nations Declaration on the Elimination of All Forms of Racial Discrimination, the Declaration on the Promotion among Youth of the Ideals of Peace, Mutual Respect and Understanding between Peoples, and the Declaration on the Inadmissibility of Intervention in the Domestic Affairs of States and the Protection of their Independence and Sovereignty, proclaimed successively by the General Assembly of the United Nations,

Convinced by the experience of the Organization's first twenty years that, if international cultural co-operation is to be strengthened, its principles require to be affirmed,

Proclaims this Declaration of the principles of international cultural co-operation, to the end that governments, authorities, organizations, associations and institutions responsible for cultural activities may constantly be guided by these principles; and for the purpose, as set out in the Constitution of the Organization, of advancing, through the educational, scientific and cultural relations of the peoples of the world, the objectives of peace and welfare that are defined in the Charter of the United Nations:

Article 1

1.   Each culture has a dignity and value which must be respected and preserved.

2.   Every people has the right and the duty to develop its culture.

3.   In their rich variety and diversity, and in the reciprocal influences they exert on one another, all cultures form part of the common heritage belonging to all mankind.

Article II

Nations shall endeavour to develop the various branches of culture side by side and, as far as possible, simultaneously, so as to establish a harmonious balance between technical progress and the intellectual and moral advancement of mankind.

Article III

International cultural co-operation shall cover all aspects of intellectual and creative activities relating to education, science and culture.

Article IV

The aims of international cultural co-operation in its various forms, bilateral or multilateral, regional or universal, shall be:

1. To spread knowledge, to stimulate talent and to enrich cultures;

2. To develop peaceful relations and friendship among the peoples and bring about a better understanding of each other's way of life;

3. To contribute to the application of the principles set out in the United Nations Declarations that are recalled in the Preamble to this Declaration;

4. To enable everyone to have access to knowledge, to enjoy the arts and literature of all peoples, to share in advances made in science in all parts of the world and in the resulting benefits, and to contribute to the enrichment of cultural life;

5. To raise the level of the spiritual and material life of man in all parts of the world.

Article V

Cultural co-operation is a right and a duty for all peoples and all nations, which should share with one another their knowledge and skills.

Article VI

International co-operation, while promoting the enrichment of all cultures through its beneficent action, shall respect the distinctive character of each.

Article VII

1. Broad dissemination of ideas and knowledge, based on the freest exchange and discussion, is essential to creative activity, the pursuit of truth and the development of the personality.

2. In cultural co-operation, stress shall be laid on ideas and values conducive to the creation of a climate of friendship and peace. Any mark of hostility in attitudes and in expression of opinion shall be avoided. Every effort shall be made, in presenting and disseminating information, to ensure its authenticity.

Article VIII

Cultural co-operation shall be carried on for the mutual benefit of all the nations practising it. Exchanges to which it gives rise shall be arranged in a spirit of broad reciprocity.

Article IX

Cultural co-operation shall contribute to the establishment of stable, long-term relations between peoples, which should be subjected as little as possible to the strains which may arise in international life.

Article X

Cultural co-operation shall be specially concerned with the moral and intellectual education of young people in a spirit of friendship, international understanding and peace and shall foster awareness among States of the need to stimulate talent and promote the training of the rising generations in the most varied sectors.

Article XI

1. In their cultural relations, States shall bear in mind the principles of the United Nations. In seeking to achieve international co-operation, they shall respect the sovereign equality of States and shall refrain from intervention in matters which are essentially within the domestic jurisdiction of any State.

2. The principles of this Declaration shall be applied with due regard for human rights and fundamental freedoms.

7.16 INTERNATIONAL COVENANT ON ECONOMIC, SOCIAL AND CULTURAL RIGHTS. Concluded at **New York, 16 December 1966. Entered into force, 3 January 1976. 993 UNTS 3;** *reprinted in* **3 Weston & Carlson III.A.2:** *Arts. 1, 2, 10, 15, 25*

* * *

Article 1. (1) All peoples have the right of self-determination. By virtue of that right they freely determine their political status and freely pursue their economic, social and cultural development.

(2) All peoples may, for their own ends, freely dispose of their natural wealth and resources without prejudice to any obligations arising out of international economic co-operation, based upon the principle of mutual benefit, and international law. In no case may a people be deprived of its own means of subsistence.

(3) The States Parties to the present Covenant, including those having responsibility for the administration of Non–Self–Governing and Trust Territories, shall promote the realization of the right of self-determination, and shall respect that right, in conformity with the provisions of the Charter of the United Nations.

* * *

Article 2. (1) Each State Party to the present Covenant undertakes to take steps, individually and through international assistance and co-operation, especially economic and technical, to the maximum of its available resources, with a view to achieving progressively the full realization of the rights recognized in the present Covenant by all appropriate means, including particularly the adoption of legislative measures.

(2) The States Parties to the present Covenant undertake to guarantee that the rights enunciated in the present Covenant will be exercised without discrimination of any kind as to race, colour, sex, language, religion, political or other opinion, national or social origin, property, birth or other status.

(3) Developing countries, with due regard to human rights and their national economy, may determine to what extent they would guarantee the economic rights recognized in the present Covenant to non-nationals.

* * *

Article 10. The States Parties to the present Covenant recognize that:

(1) The widest possible protection and assistance should be accorded to the family, which is the natural and fundamental group unit of society, particularly for its establishment and while it is responsible for the care and education of dependent children. Marriage must be entered into with the free consent of the intending spouses.

(2) Special protection should be accorded to mothers during a reasonable period before and after childbirth. During such period working mothers should be accorded paid leave or leave with adequate social security benefits.

(3) Special measures of protection and assistance should be taken on behalf of all children and young persons without any discrimination for reasons of parentage or other conditions. Children and young persons should be protected from economic and social exploitation. Their employment in work harmful to their morals or health or dangerous to life or likely to hamper their normal development should be punishable by law. States should also set age limits below which the paid employment of child labour should be prohibited and punishable by law.

* * *

Article 15. (1) The States Parties to the present Covenant recognize the right of everyone:

(a) To take part in cultural life;

(b) To enjoy the benefits of scientific progress and its applications;

(c) To benefit from the protection of the moral and material interests resulting from any scientific, literary or artistic production of which he is the author.

(2) The steps to be taken by the States Parties to the present Covenant to achieve the full realization of this right shall include those necessary for the conservation, the development and the diffusion of science and culture.

(3) The States Parties to the present Covenant undertake to respect the freedom indispensable for scientific research and creative activity.

(4) The States Parties to the present Covenant recognize the benefits to be derived from the encouragement and development of international contacts and co-operation in the scientific and cultural fields.

* * *

Article 25. Nothing in the present Covenant shall be interpreted as impairing the inherent right of all peoples to enjoy and utilize fully and freely their natural wealth and resources.

7.17 INTERNATIONAL COVENANT ON CIVIL AND POLITICAL RIGHTS. **Concluded at New York, 16 December 1966. Entered into force, 23 March 1976. 999 UNTS 171;** *reprinted in* **3 Weston & Carlson III.A.3:** *Arts. 1, 2, 6, 14, 23, 24, 27, 47*

* * *

Article 1. (1) All peoples have the right of self-determination. By virtue of that right they freely determine their political status and freely pursue their economic, social and cultural development.

(2) All peoples may, for their own ends, freely dispose of their natural wealth and resources without prejudice to any obligations arising out of international economic co-operation, based upon the principle of mutual benefit, and international law. In no case may a people be deprived of its own means of subsistence.

(3) The States Parties to the present Covenant, including those having responsibility for the administration of Non–Self–Governing and Trust Territories, shall promote the realization of the right of self-determination, and shall respect that right, in conformity with the provisions of the Charter of the United Nations.

* * *

Article 2. (1) Each State Party to the present Covenant undertakes to respect and to ensure to all individuals within its territory and subject to its jurisdiction the rights recognized in the present Covenant, without distinction of any kind, such as race, colour, sex, language, religion, political or other opinion, national or social origin, property, birth or other status.

(2) Where not already provided for by existing legislative or other measures, each State Party to the present Covenant undertakes to take the necessary steps, in accordance with its constitutional processes and with the provisions of the present Covenant, to adopt such legislative or other measures as may be necessary to give effect to the rights recognized in the present Covenant.

(3) Each State Party to the present Covenant undertakes:

(a) To ensure that any person whose rights or freedoms as herein recognized are violated shall have an effective remedy, notwithstanding that the violation has been committed by persons acting in an official capacity;

(b) To ensure that any person claiming such a remedy shall have his right thereto determined by competent judicial, administrative or legislative authorities, or by any other competent authority provided for by the legal system of the State, and to develop the possibilities of judicial remedy;

(c) To ensure that the competent authorities shall enforce such remedies when granted.

* * *

Article 6. (1) Every human being has the inherent right to life. This right shall be protected by law. No one shall be arbitrarily deprived of his life.

(2) In countries which have not abolished the death penalty, sentence of death may be imposed only for the most serious crimes in accordance with the law in force at the time of the commission of the crime and not contrary to the provisions of the present Covenant and to the Convention on the Prevention and Punishment of the Crime of Genocide. This penalty can only be carried out pursuant to a final judgment rendered by a competent court.

(3) When deprivation of life constitutes the crime of genocide, it is understood that nothing in this article shall authorize any State Party to the present Covenant to derogate in any way from any obligation assumed under the provi-

sions of the Convention on the Prevention and Punishment of the Crime of Genocide.

(4) Anyone sentenced to death shall have the right to seek pardon or commutation of the sentence. Amnesty, pardon or commutation of the sentence of death may be granted in all cases.

(5) Sentence of death shall not be imposed for crimes committed by persons below eighteen years of age and shall not be carried out on pregnant women.

(6) Nothing in this article shall be invoked to delay or to prevent the abolition of capital punishment by any State Party to the present Covenant.

* * *

Article 14. (1) All persons shall be equal before the courts and tribunals. In the determination of any criminal charge against him, or of his rights and obligations in a suit at law, everyone shall be entitled to a fair and public hearing by a competent, independent and impartial tribunal established by law. The Press and the public may be excluded from all or part of a trial for reasons of morals, public order (*ordre public*) or national security in a democratic society, or when the interest of the private lives of the parties so requires, or to the extent strictly necessary in the opinion of the court in special circumstances where publicity would prejudice the interests of justice; but any judgment rendered in a criminal case or in a suit at law shall be made public except where the interest of juvenile persons otherwise requires or the proceedings concern matrimonial disputes or the guardianship of children.

(2) Everyone charged with a criminal offence shall have the right to be presumed innocent until proved guilty according to law.

(3) In the determination of any criminal charge against him, everyone shall be entitled to the following minimum guarantees, in full equality:

(a) To be informed promptly and in detail in a language which he understands of the nature and cause of the charge against him;

(b) To have adequate time and facilities for the preparation of his defence and to communicate with counsel of his own choosing;

(c) To be tried without undue delay;

(d) To be tried in his presence, and to defend himself in person or through legal assistance of his own choosing; to be informed, if he does not have legal assistance, of this right; and to have legal assistance assigned to him, in any case where the interests of justice so require, and without payment by him in any such case if he does not have sufficient means to pay for it;

(e) To examine, or have examined, the witnesses against him and to obtain the attendance and examination of witnesses on his behalf under the same conditions as witnesses against him;

(f) To have the free assistance of an interpreter if he cannot understand or speak the language used in court;

(g) Not to be compelled to testify against himself or to confess guilt.

(4) In the case of juvenile persons, the procedure shall be such as will take account of their age and the desirability of promoting their rehabilitation.

(5) Everyone convicted of a crime shall have the right to his conviction and sentence being reviewed by a higher tribunal according to law.

(6) When a person has by a final decision been convicted of a criminal offense and when subsequently his conviction has been reversed or he has been pardoned on the ground that a new or newly discovered fact shows conclusively that there has been a miscarriage of justice, the person who has suffered punishment as a result of such

conviction shall be compensated according to law, unless it is proved that the non-disclosure of the unknown fact in time is wholly or partly attributable to him.

(7) No one shall be liable to be tried or punished again for an offence for which he has already been finally convicted or acquitted in accordance with the law and penal procedure of each country.

* * *

Article 23. (1) The family is the natural and fundamental group unit of society and is entitled to protection by society and the State.

(2) The right of men and women of marriageable age to marry and to found a family shall be recognized.

(3) No marriage shall be entered into without the free and full consent of the intending spouses.

(4) States Parties to the present Covenant shall take appropriate steps to ensure equality of rights and responsibilities of spouses as to marriage, during marriage and at its dissolution. In the case of dissolution, provision shall be made for the necessary protection of any children.

Article 24. (1) Every child shall have, without any discrimination as to race, colour, sex, language, religion, national or social origin, property or birth, the right to such measures of protection as are required by his status as a minor, on the part of his family, society and the State.

(2) Every child shall be registered immediately after birth and shall have a name.

(3) Every child has the right to acquire a nationality.

* * *

Article 27. In those States in which ethnic, religious or linguistic minorities exist, persons belonging to such minorities shall not be denied the right, in community with the other members of their group, to enjoy their own culture, to profess and practise their own religion, or to use their own language.

* * *

Article 47. Nothing in the present Covenant shall be interpreted as impairing the inherent right of all peoples to enjoy and utilize fully and freely their natural wealth and resources.

7.18 FINAL ACT OF THE UNITED NATIONS INTERNATIONAL CONFERENCE ON HUMAN RIGHTS. Concluded at Teheran, 13 May 1968. *Reprinted in* United Nations, Human Rights: A Compilation of International Instruments 43 (1988) & 3 Weston & Carlson III.U.1

The International Conference on Human Rights,

Having met at Teheran from April 22 to May 13, 1968 to review the progress made in the twenty years since the adoption of the Universal Declaration of Human Rights and to formulate a programme for the future,

Having considered the problems relating to the activities of the United Nations for the promotion and encouragement of respect for human rights and fundamental freedoms,

Bearing in mind the resolutions adopted by the Conference,

Noting that the observance of the International Year for Human Rights takes place at a time when the world is undergoing a process of unprecedented change,

Having regard to the new opportunities made available by the rapid progress of science and technology,

Believing that, in an age when conflict and violence prevail in many parts of the world, the fact of human interdependence and the need for human solidarity are more evident than ever before,

Recognizing that peace is the universal aspiration of mankind and that peace and justice are indispensable to the full realization of human rights and fundamental freedoms,

Solemnly proclaims that:

1. It is imperative that the members of the international community fulfil their solemn obligations to promote and encourage respect for human rights and fundamental freedoms for all without distinctions of any kind such as race, colour, sex, language, religion, political or other opinions;

2. The Universal Declaration of Human Rights states a common understanding of the peoples of the world concerning the inalienable and inviolable rights of all members of the human family and constitutes an obligation for the members of the international community;

3. The International Covenant on Civil and Political Rights, the International Covenant on Economic, Social and Cultural Rights, the Declaration on the Granting of Independence to Colonial Countries and Peoples, the International Convention on the Elimination of All Forms of Racial Discrimination as well as other conventions and declarations in the field of human rights adopted under the auspices of the United Nations, the specialized agencies and the regional intergovernmental organizations, have created new standards and obligations to which States should conform;

4. Since the adoption of the Universal Declaration of Human Rights the United Nations has made substantial progress in defining standards for the enjoyment and protection of human rights and fundamental freedoms. During this period many important international instruments were adopted but much remains to be done in regard to the implementation of those rights and freedoms;

5. The primary aim of the United Nations in the sphere of human rights is the achievement by each individual of the maximum freedom and dignity. For the realization of this objective, the laws of every country should grant each individual, irrespective of race, language, religion or political belief, freedom of expression, of information, of conscience and of religion, as well as the right to participate in the political, economic, cultural and social life of his country;

6. States should reaffirm their determination effectively to enforce the principles enshrined in the Charter of the United Nations and in other international instruments that concern human rights and fundamental freedoms;

7. Gross denials of human rights under the repugnant policy of *apartheid* is a matter of the gravest concern to the international community. This policy of *apartheid,* condemned as a crime against humanity, continues seriously to disturb international peace and security. It is therefore imperative for the international community to use every possible means to eradicate this evil. The struggle against *apartheid* is recognized as legitimate;

8. The peoples of the world must be made fully aware of the evils of racial discrimination and must join in combating them. The implementation of this principle of non-discrimination, embodied in the Charter of the United Nations, the Universal Declaration of Human Rights, and other international instruments in the field of human rights, constitutes a most urgent task of mankind at the international as well as at the national level. All ideologies based on racial superiority and intolerance must be condemned and resisted;

9. Eight years after the General Assembly's Declaration on the Granting of Independence to Colonial Countries and Peoples the problems of colonialism continue to preoccupy the international community. It is a matter of urgency that all Member States should co-operate with the appropriate organs of the United Nations so that effective measures can be taken to ensure that the Declaration is fully implemented;

10. Massive denials of human rights, arising out of aggression or any armed conflict with their tragic consequences, and resulting in untold human misery, engender reactions which could engulf the world in ever growing hostilities. It is the obligation of the international community to co-operate in eradicating such scourges;

11. Gross denials of human rights arising from discrimination on grounds of race, religion, belief or expressions of opinion outrage the conscience of mankind and endanger the foundations of freedom, justice and peace in the world;

12. The widening gap between the economically developed and developing countries impedes the realization of human rights in the international community. The failure of the Development Decade to reach its modest objectives makes it all the more imperative for every nation, according to its capacities, to make the maximum possible effort to close this gap;

13. Since human rights and fundamental freedoms are indivisible, the full realization of civil and political rights without the enjoyment of economic, social and cultural rights is impossible. The achievement of lasting progress in the implementation of human rights is dependent upon sound and effective national and international policies of economic and social development;

14. The existence of over seven hundred million illiterates throughout the world is an enormous obstacle to all efforts at realizing the aims and purposes of the Charter of the United Nations and the provisions of the Universal Declaration of Human Rights. International action aimed at eradicating illiteracy from the face of the earth and promoting education at all levels requires urgent attention;

15. The discrimination of which women are still victims in various regions of the world must be eliminated. An inferior status for women is contrary to the Charter of the United Nations as well as the provisions of the Universal Declaration of Human Rights. The full implementation of the Declaration on the Elimination of Discrimination against Women is a necessity for the progress of mankind;

16.   The protection of the family and of the child remains the concern of the international community. Parents have a basic human right to determine freely and responsibly the number and the spacing of their children;

17.   The aspirations of the younger generation for a better world, in which human rights and fundamental freedoms are fully implemented, must be given the highest encouragement. It is imperative that youth participate in shaping the future of mankind;

18.   While recent scientific discoveries and technological advances have opened vast prospects for economic, social and cultural progress, such developments may nevertheless endanger the rights and freedoms of individuals and will require continuing attention;

19.   Disarmament would release immense human and material resources now devoted to military purposes. These resources should be used for the promotion of human rights and fundamental freedoms. General and complete disarmament is one of the highest aspirations of all peoples;

Therefore,

The International Conference on Human Rights,

1.   *Affirming* its faith in the principles of the Universal Declaration of Human Rights and other international instruments in this field,

2.   *Urges* all peoples and governments to dedicate themselves to the principles enshrined in the Universal Declaration of Human Rights and to redouble their efforts to provide for all human beings a life consonant with freedom and dignity and conducive to physical, mental, social and spiritual welfare.

7.19 AMERICAN CONVENTION ON HUMAN RIGHTS. **Concluded at San José, 22 November 1969. Entered into force, 18 July 1978. OASTS No 36, OAS Off Rec O.E.A./Ser. L/V/II.23 doc. 21 rev. 6 (1979);** *reprinted in* **9 ILM 673 (1970) & 3 Weston & Carlson III.B.24:** *Arts. 1, 4, 16, 21, 27*

* * *

Article 1. Obligation to Respect Rights

1. The States Parties to this Convention undertake to respect the rights and freedoms recognized herein and to ensure to all persons subject to their jurisdiction the free and full exercise of those rights and freedoms, without any discrimination for reasons of race, color, sex, language, religion, political or other opinion, national or social origin, economic status, birth, or any other social condition.

2. For the purposes of this Convention, "person" means every human being.

* * *

Article 4. Right to Life

1. Every person has the right to have his life respected. This right shall be protected by law and, in general, from the moment of conception. No one shall be arbitrarily deprived of his life.

2. In countries that have not abolished the death penalty, it may be imposed only for the most serious crimes and pursuant to a final judgment rendered by a competent court and in accordance with a law establishing such punishment, enacted prior to the commission of the crime. The application of such punishment shall not be extended to crimes to which it does not presently apply.

3. The death penalty shall not be reestablished in states that have abolished it.

4. In no case shall capital punishment be inflicted for political offenses or related common crimes.

5. Capital punishment shall not be imposed upon persons who, at the time the crime was committed, were under 18 years of age or over 70 years of age; nor shall it be applied to pregnant women.

6. Every person condemned to death shall have the right to apply for amnesty, pardon, or commutation of sentence, which may be granted in all cases. Capital punishment shall not be imposed while such a petition is a pending decision by the competent authority.

* * *

Article 16. Freedom of Association

1. Everyone has the right to associate freely for ideological, religious, political, economic, labor, social, cultural, sports, or other purposes.

2. The exercise of this right shall be subject only to such restrictions established by law as may be necessary in a democratic society, in the interest of national security, public safety or public order, or to protect public health or morals or the rights and freedoms of others.

3. The provisions of this article do not bar the imposition of legal restrictions, including even deprivation of the exercise of the right of association, on members of the armed forces and the police.

* * *

Article 21. Right to Property

1. Everyone has the right to the use and enjoyment of his property. The law may subordinate such use and enjoyment to the interest of society.

2. No one shall be deprived of his property except upon payment of just compensation, for reasons of public utility or social interest, and in the cases and according to the forms established by law.

3. Usury and any other form of exploitation of man by man shall be prohibited by law.

* * *

Article 27. Suspension of Guarantees

1. In time of war, public danger, or other emergency that threatens the independence or security of a State Party, it may take measures derogating from its obligations under the present Convention to the extent and for the period of time strictly required by the exigencies of the situation, provided that such measures are not inconsistent with its other obligations under international law and do not involve discrimination on the ground of race, color, sex, language, religion, or social origin.

2. The foregoing provision does not authorize any suspension of the following articles: Article 3 (Right to Juridical Personality), Article 4 (Right to Life), Article 5 (Right to Humane Treatment), Article 6 (Freedom from Slavery), Article 9 (Freedom from Ex Post Facto Laws), Article 12 (Freedom of Conscience and Religion), Article 17 (Rights of the Family), Article 18 (Right to a Name), Article 19 (Rights of the Child), Article 20 (Right to Nationality), and Article 23 (Right to Participate in Government), or of the judicial guarantees essential for the protection of such rights.

3. Any State Party availing itself of the right of suspension shall immediately inform the other States Parties, through the Secretary General of the Organization of American States, of the provisions the application of which it has suspended, the reasons that gave rise to the suspension, and the date set for the termination of such suspension.

* * *

7.20 DECLARATION ON SOCIAL PROGRESS AND DEVELOPMENT. **Adopted by the U.N. General Assembly, 11 December 1969. GA Res 2542, UN GAOR, 24th Sess, Supp No 30, at 49, UN Doc A/7630 (1970);** *reprinted in* **3 Weston & Carlson III.R.1:** *Arts. 1–5, 8–9, 11(b), 12(b), 13(c), 22(a–c), 23(d–e)*

PART I

Principles

Article 1

All peoples and all human beings, without distinction as to race, colour, sex, language, religion, nationality, ethnic origin, family or social status, or political or other conviction, shall have the right to live in dignity and freedom and to enjoy the fruits of social progress and should, on their part, contribute to it.

Article 2

Social progress and development shall be founded on respect for the dignity and value of the human person and shall ensure the promotion of human rights and social justice, which requires:

(*a*) The immediate and final elimination of all forms of inequality, exploitation of peoples and individuals, colonialism and racism, including nazism and *apartheid,* and all other policies and ideologies opposed to the purposes and principles of the United Nations;

(*b*) The recognition and effective implementation of civil and political rights as well as of economic, social and cultural rights without any discrimination.

Article 3

The following are considered primary conditions of social progress and development:

(*a*) National independence based on the right of peoples to self-determination;

(*b*) The principle of non-interference in the internal affairs of States;

(*c*) Respect for the sovereignty and territorial integrity of States;

(*d*) Permanent sovereignty of each nation over its natural wealth and resources;

(*e*) The right and responsibility of each State and, as far as they are concerned, each nation and people to determine freely its own objectives of social development, to set its own priorities and to decide in conformity with the principles of the Charter of the United Nations the means and methods of their achievement without any external interference;

(*f*) Peaceful coexistence, peace, friendly relations and co-operation among States irrespective of differences in their social, economic or political systems.

Article 4

The family as a basic unit of society and the natural environment for the growth and well-being of all its members, particularly children and youth, should be assisted and protected so that it may fully assume its responsibilities within the community. Parents have the exclusive right to determine freely and responsibly the number and spacing of their children.

Article 5

Social progress and development require the full utilization of human resources, including, in particular:

(a) The encouragement of creative initiative under conditions of enlightened public opinion;

(b) The dissemination of national and international information for the purpose of making individuals aware of changes occurring in society as a whole;

(c) The active participation of all elements of society, individually or through associations, in defining and in achieving the common goals of development with full respect for the fundamental freedoms embodied in the Universal Declaration of Human Rights;

(d) The assurance to disadvantaged or marginal sectors of the population of equal opportunities for social and economic advancement in order to achieve an effectively integrated society.

* * *

Article 8

Each Government has the primary role and ultimate responsibility of ensuring the social progress and well-being of its people, of planning social development measures as part of comprehensive development plans, of encouraging and co-ordinating or integrating all national efforts towards this end and of introducing necessary changes in the social structure. In planning social development measures, the diversity of the needs of developing and developed areas, and of urban and rural areas, within each country, shall be taken into due account.

Article 9

Social progress and development are the common concerns of the international community, which shall supplement, by concerted international action, national efforts to raise the living standards of peoples.

Social progress and economic growth require recognition of the common interest of all nations in the exploration, conservation, use and exploitation, exclusively for peaceful purposes and in the interests of all mankind, of those areas of the environment such as outer space and the sea-bed and ocean floor and the subsoil thereof, beyond the limits of national jurisdiction, in accordance with the purposes and principles of the Charter of the United Nations.

PART II

Objectives

* * *

Social progress and development shall aim equally at the progressive attainment of the following main goals:

Article 11

* * *

(b) The protection of the rights of the mother and child; concern for the upbringing and health of children; the provision of measures to safeguard the health and welfare of women and particularly of working mothers during pregnancy and the infancy of their children, as well as of mothers whose earnings are the sole source of livelihood for the family; the granting to women of pregnancy and maternity leave and allowances without loss of employment or wages;

* * *

Article 12

* * *

(*b*) The elimination of all forms of discrimination and exploitation and all other practices and ideologies contrary to the purposes and principles of the Charter of the United Nations;

* * *

Social progress and development shall finally aim at the attainment of the following main goals:

Article 13

* * *

(*c*) The protection and improvement of the human environment.

* * *

Article 22

(*a*) The development and co-ordination of policies and measures designed to strengthen the essential functions of the family as a basic unit of society;

(*b*) The formulation and establishment, as needed, of programmes in the field of population, within the framework of national demographic policies and as part of the welfare medical services, including education, training of personnel and the provision to families of the knowledge and means necessary to enable them to exercise their right to determine freely and responsibly the number and spacing of their children;

(*c*) The establishment of appropriate child-care facilities in the interest of children and working parents.

The achievement of the objectives of social progress and development finally requires the implementation of the following means and methods:

Article 23

* * *

(*d*) The provision to the developing countries of technical, financial and material assistance and of favourable conditions to facilitate the direct exploitation of their national resources and natural wealth by those countries with a view to enabling the peoples of those countries to benefit fully from their national resources;

(*e*) The expansion of international trade based on principles of equality and non-discrimination, the rectification of the position of developing countries in international trade by equitable terms of trade, a general non-reciprocal and non-discriminatory system of preferences for the exports of developing countries to the developed countries, the establishment and implementation of general and comprehensive commodity agreements, and the financing of reasonable buffer stocks by international institutions.

* * *

7.21 CONVENTION FOR THE PROTECTION OF THE WORLD CULTURAL AND NATURAL HERITAGE. **Concluded at Paris, 16 November 1972. Entered into force, 17 December 1975. 1037 UNTS 151, 27 UST 37;** *reprinted in* **11 ILM 1358 (1972) & 5 Weston & Carlson V.B.4:** *Article 1-7, 13, 19, 22*

The General Conference of the United Nations Educational, Scientific and Cultural Organization meeting in Paris from 17 October to 21 November 1972, at its seventeenth session,

Noting that the cultural heritage and the natural heritage are increasingly threatened with destruction not only by the traditional causes of decay, but also by changing social and economic conditions which aggravate the situation with even more formidable phenomena of damage or destruction,

Considering that deterioration or disappearance of any item of the cultural or natural heritage constitutes a harmful impoverishment of the heritage of all the nations of the world,

* * *

Considering that parts of the cultural or natural heritage are of outstanding interest and therefore need to be preserved as part of the world heritage of mankind as a whole,

Considering that, in view of the magnitude and gravity of the new dangers threatening them, it is incumbent on the international community as a whole to participate in the protection of the cultural and natural heritage of outstanding universal value, by the granting of collective assistance which, although not taking the place of action by the State concerned, will serve as an effective complement thereto,

* * *

Adopts this sixteenth day of November 1972 this Convention.

I. DEFINITIONS OF THE CULTURAL AND THE NATURAL HERITAGE

Article 1

For the purposes of this Convention, the following shall be considered as "cultural heritage":

monuments: architectural works, works of monumental sculpture and painting, elements or structures of an archaeological nature, inscriptions, cave dwellings and combinations of features, which are of outstanding universal value from the point of view of history, art or science;

groups of buildings: groups of separate or connected buildings which, because of their architecture, their homogeneity or their place in the landscape, are of outstanding universal value from the point of view of history, art or science;

sites: works of man or the combined works of nature and of man, and areas including archaeological sites which are of outstanding universal value from the historical, aesthetic, ethnological or anthropological points of view.

Article 2

For the purposes of this Convention, the following shall be considered as "natural heritage":

natural features consisting of physical and biological formations or groups of such formations, which are of outstanding universal value from the aesthetic or scientific point of view;

geological and physiographical natural sites or precisely delineated natural areas of outstanding universal value from the point of view of science, conservation or natural beauty.

Article 3

It is for each State Party to this Convention to identify and delineate the different properties situated on its territory mentioned in Article 1 and 2 above.

II. NATIONAL PROTECTION AND INTERNATIONAL PROTECTION OF THE CULTURAL AND NATURAL HERITAGE

Article 4

Each State Party to this Convention recognizes that the duty of ensuring the identification, protection, conservation, presentation and transmission to future generations of the cultural and natural heritage referred to in Articles 1 and 2 and situated on its territory, belongs primarily to that State. It will do all it can to this end, to the utmost of its own resources and, where appropriate, with any international assistance and co-operation, in particular, financial, artistic, scientific and technical, which it may be able to obtain.

Article 5

To ensure that effective and active measures are taken for the protection, conservation and presentation of the cultural and natural heritage situated on its territory, each State Party to this Convention shall endeavour, in so far as possible, and as appropriate for each country:

(a) to adopt a general policy which aims to give the cultural and natural heritage a function in the life of the community and to integrate the protection of that heritage into comprehensive planning programmes;

(b) to set up within its territories, where such services do not exist, one or more services for the protection, conservation and presentation of the cultural and natural heritage with an appropriate staff and possessing the means to discharge their functions;

(c) to develop scientific and technical studies and research and to work out such operating methods as will make the State capable of counteracting the dangers that threaten its cultural or natural heritage;

(d) to take the appropriate legal, scientific, technical, administrative and financial measures necessary for the identification, protection, conservation, presentation and rehabilitation of this heritage; and

(e) to foster the establishment or development of national or regional centres for training in the protection, conservation and presentation of the cultural and natural heritage and to encourage scientific research in this field.

Article 6

1. Whilst fully respecting the sovereignty of the States on whose territory the cultural and natural heritage mentioned in Articles 1 and 2 is situated, and without prejudice to property rights provided by national legislation, the States Parties to this Convention recognize that such heritage constitutes a world heritage for whose protection it is the duty of the international community as a whole to co-operate.

2. The States Parties undertake, in accordance with the provisions of this Convention, to give their help in the identification, protection, conservation and preservation of the cultural and natural heritage referred to in paragraphs 2 and 4 of Article 11 if the States on whose territory it is situated so request.

3. Each State Party to this Convention undertakes not to take any deliberate measures which might damage directly or indirectly the cultural and natural heritage referred to in Articles 1 and 2 situated on the territory of other States Parties to this Convention.

Article 7

For the purpose of this Convention, international protection of the world cultural and natural heritage shall be understood to mean the establishment of a system of international co-operation and assistance designed to support States Parties to the Convention in their efforts to conserve and identify that heritage.

* * *

Article 13

1. The World Heritage Committee shall receive and study requests for international assistance formulated by States Parties to this Convention with respect to property forming part of the cultural or natural heritage, situated in their territories, and included or potentially suitable for inclusion in the lists referred to in paragraphs 2 and 4 of Article 11. The purpose of such requests may be to secure the protection, conservation, presentation or rehabilitation of such property.

2. Requests for international assistance under paragraph 1 of this article may also be concerned with identification of cultural or natural property defined in Articles 1 and 2, when preliminary investigations have shown that further inquiries would be justified.

3. The Committee shall decide on the action to be taken with regard to these requests, determine where appropriate, the nature and extent of its assistance, and authorize the conclusion, on its behalf, of the necessary arrangements with the government concerned.

4. The Committee shall determine an order of priorities for its operations. It shall in so doing bear in mind the respective importance for the world cultural and natural heritage of the property requiring protection, the need to give international assistance to the property most representative of a natural environment or of the genius and the history of the peoples of the world, the urgency of the work to be done, the resources available to the States on whose territory the threatened property is situated and in particular the extent to which they are able to safeguard such property by their own means.

* * *

V. CONDITIONS AND ARRANGEMENTS FOR INTERNATIONAL ASSISTANCE

Article 19

Any State Party to this Convention may request international assistance for property forming part of the cultural or natural heritage of outstanding universal value situated within its territory. It shall submit with its request such information and documentation provided for in Article 21 as it has in its possession and as will enable the Committee to come to a decision.

* * *

Article 22

Assistance granted by the World Heritage Committee may take the following forms:

(a) studies concerning the artistic, scientific and technical problems raised by the protection, conservation, presentation and rehabilitation of the cultural and natural heritage, as defined in paragraphs 2 and 4 of Article 11 of this Convention;

(b) provision of experts, technicians and skilled labour to ensure that the approved work is correctly carried out;

(c) training of staff and specialists at all levels in the field of identification, protection, conservation, presentation and rehabilitation of the cultural and natural heritage;

(d) supply of equipment which the State concerned does not possess or is not in a position to acquire;

(e) low-interest or interest-free loans which might be repayable on a long-term basis;

(f) the granting, in exceptional cases and for special reasons, of non-repayable subsidies.

7.22   CONVENTION ON THE ELIMINATION OF ALL FORMS OF DISCRIMINATION AGAINST WOMEN. **Concluded at New York, 18 December 1979. Entered into force, 3 September 1981. 1249 UNTS 13;** *reprinted in* **19 ILM 33 (1980) & 3 Weston & Carlson III.C.12:** *Art. 12*

Article 12. (1) States Parties shall take all appropriate measures to eliminate discrimination against women in the field of health care in order to ensure, on a basis of equality of men and women, access to health care services, including those related to family planning.

(2) Notwithstanding the provisions of paragraph 1 above, States Parties shall ensure to women appropriate services in connexion with pregnancy, confinement and the post-natal period, granting free services where necessary, as well as adequate nutrition during pregnancy and lactation.

7.23 DECLARATION ON THE RIGHT TO DEVELOPMENT. **Adopted by the U.N. General Assembly, 4 December 1986. GA Res 41/128 (Annex), UN GAOR, 41st Sess, Supp No 53, at 186, UN Doc A/41/53 (1987);** *reprinted in* **3 Weston & Carlson III.R.2**

The General Assembly,

Bearing in mind the purposes and principles of the Charter of the United Nations relating to the achievement of international co-operation in solving international problems of an economic, social, cultural or humanitarian nature, and in promoting and encouraging respect for human rights and fundamental freedoms for all without distinction as to race, sex, language or religion,

Recognizing that development is a comprehensive economic, social, cultural and political process, which aims at the constant improvement of the well-being of the entire population and of all individuals on the basis of their active, free and meaningful participation in development and in the fair distribution of benefits resulting there-from,

Considering that under the provisions of the Universal Declaration of Human Rights everyone is entitled to a social and international order in which the rights and freedoms set forth in that Declaration can be fully realized,

Recalling the provisions of the International Covenant on Economic, Social and Cultural Rights and the International Covenant on Civil and Political Rights,

Recalling further the relevant agreements, conventions, resolutions, recommendations and other instruments of the United Nations and its specialized agencies concerning the integral development of the human being, economic and social progress and development of all peoples, including those instruments concerning decolonization, the prevention of discrimination, respect for, and observance of, human rights and fundamental freedoms, the maintenance of international peace and security and the further promotion of friendly relations and co-operation among States in accordance with the Charter,

Recalling the right of peoples to self-determination, by virtue of which they have the right freely to determine their political status and to pursue their economic, social and cultural development,

Recalling further the right of peoples to exercise, subject to relevant provisions of both International Covenants on Human Rights, their full and complete sovereignty over all their natural wealth and resources,

Mindful of the obligation of States under the Charter to promote universal respect for and observance of human rights and fundamental freedoms for all without distinction of any kind such as race, colour, sex, language, religion, political or other opinion, national or social origin, property, birth or other status,

Considering that the elimination of the massive and flagrant violations of the human rights of the peoples and individuals affected by situations such as those resulting from colonialism, neo-colonialism, *apartheid,* all forms of racism and racial discrimination, foreign domination and occupation, aggression and threats against national sovereignty, national unity and territorial integrity and threats of war would contribute to the establishment of circumstances propitious to the development of a great part of mankind,

Concerned at the existence of serious obstacles to development, as well as to the complete fulfilment of human beings and of peoples, constituted, *inter alia,* by the denial of civil, political, economic, social and cultural rights, and considering that all human rights and fundamental freedoms are indivisible and interdependent and that, in order to promote development, equal attention and urgent consideration should be given to the implementation, promotion and protection of civil, political, economic, social and cultural rights and that, accordingly, the promotion of, respect for, and enjoyment of certain human rights and fundamental freedoms cannot justify the denial of other human rights and fundamental freedoms,

Considering that international peace and security are essential elements for the realization of the right to development,

Reaffirming that there is a close relationship between disarmament and development and that progress in the field of disarmament would considerably promote progress in the field of development and that resources released through disarmament measures should be devoted to the economic and social development and well-being of all peoples and, in particular, those of the developing countries,

Recognizing that the human person is the central subject of the development process and that development policy should therefore make the human being the main participant and beneficiary of development,

Recognizing that the creation of conditions favourable to the development of peoples and individuals is the primary responsibility of their States,

Aware that efforts to promote and protect human rights at the international level should be accompanied by efforts to establish a new international economic order,

Confirming that the right to development is an inalienable human right and that equality of opportunity for development is a prerogative both of nations and of individuals who make up nations,

Proclaims the following Declaration on the right to development:

ARTICLE 1

1. The right to development is an inalienable human right by virtue of which every human person and all peoples are entitled to participate in, contribute to, and enjoy economic, social, cultural and political development, in which all human rights and fundamental freedoms can be fully realized.

2. The human right to development also implies the full realization of the right of peoples to self-determination, which includes, subject to relevant provisions of both International Covenants on Human Rights, the exercise of their inalienable right to full sovereignty over all their natural wealth and resources.

ARTICLE 2

1. The human person is the central subject of development and should be the active participant and beneficiary of the right to development.

2. All human beings have a responsibility for development, individually and collectively, taking into account the need for full respect of their human rights and fundamental freedoms as well as their duties to the community, which alone can ensure the free and complete fulfilment of the human being, and they should therefore promote and protect an appropriate political, social and economic order for development.

3. States have the right and the duty to formulate appropriate national development policies that aim at the constant improvement of the well-being of the entire population and of all individuals, on the basis of their active, free and meaningful participation in development and in the fair distribution of the benefits resulting therefrom.

ARTICLE 3

1. States have the primary responsibility for the creation of national and international conditions favourable to the realization of the right to development.

2. The realization of the right to development requires full respect for the principles of international law concerning friendly relations and co-operation among States in accordance with the Charter of the United Nations.

3. States have the duty to co-operate with each other in ensuring development and eliminating obstacles to development. States should fulfil their rights and duties in such a manner as to promote a new international economic order based on sovereign equality, interdependence, mutual interest and co-operation among all States, as well as to encourage the observance and realization of human rights.

ARTICLE 4

1. States have the duty to take steps, individually and collectively, to formulate international development policies with a view to facilitating the full realization of the right to development.

2. Sustained action is required to promote more rapid development of developing countries. As a complement to the efforts of developing countries effective international co-operation is essential in providing these countries with appropriate means and facilities to foster their comprehensive development.

ARTICLE 5

States shall take resolute steps to eliminate the massive and flagrant violations of the human rights of peoples and human beings affected by situations such as those resulting from *apartheid*, all forms of racism and racial discrimination, colonialism, foreign domination and occupation, aggression, foreign interference and threats against national sovereignty, national unity and territorial integrity, threats of war and refusal to recognize the fundamental right of peoples to self-determination.

ARTICLE 6

1. All States should co-operate with a view to promoting, encouraging and strengthening universal respect for and observance of all human rights and fundamental freedoms for all without any distinction as to race, sex, language and religion.

2. All human rights and fundamental freedoms are indivisible and interdependent, equal attention and urgent consideration should be given to the implementation, promotion and protection of civil, political, economic, social and cultural rights.

3. States should take steps to eliminate obstacles to development resulting from failure to observe civil and political rights as well as economic, social and cultural rights.

ARTICLE 7

All States should promote the establishment, maintenance and strengthening of international peace and security and, to that end, should do their utmost to achieve general and complete disarmament under effective international control as well as to ensure that the resources released by effective disarmament measures are used for comprehensive development, in particular that of the developing countries.

ARTICLE 8

1. States should undertake, at the national level, all necessary measures for the realization of the right to development and shall ensure, *inter alia*, equality of opportunity for all in their access to basic resources, education, health services, food, housing, employment and the fair distribution of income. Effective measures should be undertaken to ensure that women have an active role in the development process. Appropriate economic and social reforms should be made with a view to eradicating all social injustices.

2. States should encourage popular participation in all spheres as an important factor in development and in the full realization of all human rights.

ARTICLE 9

1. All the aspects of the right to development set forth in this Declaration are indivisible and interdependent and each of them should be considered in the context of the whole.

2. Nothing in this Declaration shall be construed as being contrary to the purposes and principles of the United Nations, or as implying that any State, group or person has a right to engage in any activity or to perform any act aimed at the violation of the rights set forth in the Universal Declaration of Human Rights and in the International Covenants on Human Rights.

ARTICLE 10

Steps should be taken to ensure the full exercise and progressive enhancement of the right to development, including the formulation, adoption and implementation of policy, legislative and other measures at the national and international levels.

7.24 International Labour Organization Convention (No. 169) Concerning Indigenous and Tribal Peoples in Independent Countries. Concluded at Geneva, 27 June 1989. Entered into force, 5 September 1991. 1650 UNTS 383; *reprinted in* 28 ILM 1382 (1989) & 3 Weston & Carlson III.F.2: *Arts.* 1–7, 13–16, 23, & 32

Part I. General Policy

Article 1

1.   This Convention applies to:

(a) tribal peoples in independent countries whose social, cultural and economic conditions distinguish them from other sections of the national community, and whose status is regulated wholly or partially by their own customs or traditions or by special laws or regulations;

(b) peoples in independent countries who are regarded as indigenous on account of their descent from the populations which inhabited the country, or a geographical region to which the country belongs, at the time of conquest or colonisation or the establishment of present state boundaries and who, irrespective of their legal status, retain some or all of their own social, economic, cultural and political institutions.

2.   Self-identification as indigenous or tribal shall be regarded as a fundamental criterion for determining the groups to which the provisions of this Convention apply.

3.   The use of the term "peoples" in this Convention shall not be construed as having any implications as regards the rights which may attach to the term under international law.

Article 2

1.   Governments shall have the responsibility for developing, with the participation of the peoples concerned, co-ordinated and systematic action to protect the rights of these peoples and to guarantee respect for their integrity.

2.   Such action shall include measures for:

(a) ensuring that members of these peoples benefit on an equal footing from the rights and opportunities which national laws and regulations grant to other members of the population;

(b) promoting the full realisation of the social, economic and cultural rights of these peoples with respect for their social and cultural identity, their customs and traditions and their institutions;

(c) assisting the members of the peoples concerned to eliminate socio-economic gaps that may exist between indigenous and other members of the national community, in a manner compatible with their aspirations and ways of life.

Article 3

1.   Indigenous and tribal peoples shall enjoy the full measure of human rights and fundamental freedoms without hindrance or discrimination. The provisions of the Convention shall be applied without discrimination to male and female members of these peoples.

2.   No form of force or coercion shall be used in violation of the human rights and fundamental freedoms of the peoples concerned, including the rights contained in this Convention.

Article 4

1.   Special measures shall be adopted as appropriate for safeguarding the persons, institutions, property, labour, cultures and environment of the peoples concerned.

2. Such special measures shall not be contrary to the freely-expressed wishes of the peoples concerned.

3. Enjoyment of the general rights of citizenship, without discrimination, shall not be prejudiced in any way by such special measures.

Article 5

In applying the provisions of this Convention:

(a) the social, cultural, religious and spiritual values and practices of these peoples shall be recognised and protected, and due account shall be taken of the nature of the problems which face them both as groups and as individuals;

(b) the integrity of the values, practices and institutions of these peoples shall be respected;

(c) policies aimed at mitigating the difficulties experienced by these peoples in facing new conditions of life and work shall be adopted, with the participation and co-operation of the peoples affected.

Article 6

1. In applying the provisions of this Convention, governments shall:

(a) consult the peoples concerned, through appropriate procedures and in particular through their representative institutions, whenever consideration is being given to legislative or administrative measures which may affect them directly;

(b) establish means by which these peoples can freely participate, to at least the same extent as other sectors of the population, at all levels of decision-making in elective institutions and administrative and other bodies responsible for policies and programmes which concern them;

(c) establish means for the full development of these peoples' own institutions and initiatives, and in appropriate cases provide the resources necessary for this purpose.

2. The consultations carried out in application of this Convention shall be undertaken, in good faith and in a form appropriate to the circumstances, with the objective of achieving agreement or consent to the proposed measures.

Article 7

1. The peoples concerned shall have the right to decide their own priorities for the process of development as it affects their lives, beliefs, institutions and spiritual well-being and the lands they occupy or otherwise use, and to exercise control, to the extent possible, over their own economic, social and cultural development. In addition, they shall participate in the formulation, implementation and evaluation of plans and programmes for national and regional development which may affect them directly.

2. The improvement of the conditions of life and work and levels of health and education of the peoples concerned, with their participation and co-operation, shall be a matter of priority in plans for the overall economic development of areas they inhabit. Special projects for development of the areas in question shall also be so designed as to promote such improvement.

3. Governments shall ensure that, whenever appropriate, studies are carried out, in co-operation with the peoples concerned, to assess the social, spiritual, cultural and environmental impact on them of planned development activities. The results of these studies shall be considered as fundamental criteria for the implementation of these activities.

4. Governments shall take measures, in co-operation with the peoples concerned, to protect and preserve the environment of the territories they inhabit.

* * *

Part II. Land

Article 13

1. In applying the provisions of this Part of the Convention governments shall respect the special importance for the cultures and spiritual values of the peoples concerned of their relationship with the lands or territories, or both as applicable, which they occupy or otherwise use, and in particular the collective aspects of this relationship.

2. The use of the term "lands" in Articles 15 and 16 shall include the concept of territories, which covers the total environment of the areas which the peoples concerned occupy or otherwise use.

Article 14

1. The rights of ownership and possession of the peoples concerned over the lands which they traditionally occupy shall be recognised. In addition, measures shall be taken in appropriate cases to safeguard the right of the peoples concerned to use lands not exclusively occupied by them, but to which they have traditionally had access for their subsistence and traditional activities. Particular attention shall be paid to the situation of nomadic peoples and shifting cultivators in this respect.

2. Governments shall take steps as necessary to identify the lands which the peoples concerned traditionally occupy, and to guarantee effective protection of their rights of ownership and possession.

3. Adequate procedures shall be established within the national legal system to resolve land claims by the peoples concerned.

Article 15

1. The rights of the peoples concerned to the natural resources pertaining to their lands shall be specially safeguarded. These rights include the right of these peoples to participate in the use, management and conservation of these resources.

2. In cases in which the State retains the ownership of mineral or sub-surface resources or rights to other resources pertaining to lands, governments shall establish or maintain procedures through which they shall consult these peoples, with a view to ascertaining whether and to what degree their interests would be prejudiced, before undertaking or permitting any programmes for the exploration or exploitation of such resources pertaining to their lands. The peoples concerned shall wherever possible participate in the benefits of such activities, and shall receive fair compensation for any damages which they may sustain as a result of such activities.

Article 16

1. Subject to the following paragraphs of this Article, the peoples concerned shall not be removed from the lands which they occupy.

2. Where the relocation of these peoples is considered necessary as an exceptional measure, such relocation shall take place only with their free and informed consent. Where their consent cannot be obtained, such relocation shall take place only following appropriate procedures established by national laws and regulations, including public inquiries where appropriate, which provide the opportunity for effective representation of the peoples concerned.

3. Whenever possible, these peoples shall have the right to return to their traditional lands, as soon as the grounds for relocation cease to exist.

4. When such return is not possible, as determined by agreement or, in the absence of such agreement, through appropriate procedures, these peoples shall be provided in all possible cases with lands of quality and legal status at least equal to that of the lands previously occupied by them, suitable to provide for their present needs and future development. Where the peoples concerned express a preference for compensation in money or in kind, they shall be so compensated under appropriate guarantees.

5. Persons thus relocated shall be fully compensated for any resulting loss or injury.

* * *

Article 23

1. Handicrafts, rural and community-based industries, and subsistence economy and traditional activities of the peoples concerned, such as hunting, fishing, trapping and gathering, shall be recognised as important factors in the maintenance of their cultures and in their economic self-reliance and development. Governments shall, with the participation of these people and whenever appropriate, ensure that these activities are strengthened and promoted.

2. Upon the request of the peoples concerned, appropriate technical and financial assistance shall be provided wherever possible, taking into account the traditional technologies and cultural characteristics of these peoples, as well as the importance of sustainable and equitable development.

* * *

Part VII. Contacts and Co-operation Across Borders

Article 32

Governments shall take appropriate measures, including by means of international agreements, to facilitate contacts and co-operation between indigenous and tribal peoples across borders, including activities in the economic, social, cultural, spiritual and environmental fields.

7.25 CONVENTION ON THE RIGHTS OF THE CHILD. **Concluded at New York, 20 November 1989. Entered into force, 2 September 1990. 1577 UNTS 3;** *reprinted in* **28 ILM 1448 (1989) & 3 Weston & Carlson III.D.3: Art. 2**

Article 2

1.   States Parties shall respect and ensure the rights set forth in the present Convention to each child within their jurisdiction without discrimination of any kind, irrespective of the child's or his or her parent's or legal guardian's race, colour, sex, language, religion, political or other opinion, national, ethnic or social origin, property, disability, birth or other status.

2.   States Parties shall take all appropriate measures to ensure that the child is protected against all forms of discrimination or punishment on the basis of the status, activities, expressed opinions, or beliefs of the child's parents, legal guardians, or family members.

7.26 UNITED NATIONS GENERAL ASSEMBLY DECLARATION ON THE RIGHTS OF INDIGE-
NOUS PEOPLES. **Adopted, 13 September 2007. GA Res 61/295, UN
GAOR, 61st Sess, 106/107th mtg, UN Doc A/61/L.67 (2007);** *reprinted
in* **46 ILM 1013 (2007) & 3 Weston & Carlson III.F.6:** *Articles 1, 3, 7–
12, 18–20, 24–29, 31–32, 39–40*

Article 1

Indigenous peoples have the right to the full enjoyment, as a collective or as
individuals, of all human rights and fundamental freedoms as recognized in the
Charter of the United Nations, the Universal Declaration of Human Rights and
international human rights law.

* * *

Article 3

Indigenous peoples have the right to self-determination. By virtue of that right
they freely determine their political status and freely pursue their economic, social and
cultural development.

* * *

Article 7

1. Indigenous individuals have the rights to life, physical and mental integrity,
liberty and security of person.

2. Indigenous peoples have the collective right to live in freedom, peace and
security as distinct peoples and shall not be subjected to any act of genocide or any
other act of violence, including forcibly removing children of the group to another
group.

Article 8

1. Indigenous peoples and individuals have the right not to be subjected to forced
assimilation or destruction of their culture.

2. States shall provide effective mechanisms for prevention of, and redress for:

(a) Any action which has the aim or effect of depriving them of their integrity as
distinct peoples, or of their cultural values or ethnic identities;

(b) Any action which has the aim or effect of dispossessing them of their lands,
territories or resources;

(c) Any form of forced population transfer which has the aim or effect of violating
or undermining any of their rights;

(d) Any form of forced assimilation or integration;

(e) Any form of propaganda designed to promote or incite racial or ethnic
discrimination directed against them.

Article 9

Indigenous peoples and individuals have the right to belong to an indigenous
community or nation, in accordance with the traditions and customs of the community
or nation concerned. No discrimination of any kind may arise from the exercise of such
a right.

Article 10

Indigenous peoples shall not be forcibly removed from their lands or territories.
No relocation shall take place without the free, prior and informed consent of the

indigenous peoples concerned and after agreement on just and fair compensation and, where possible, with the option of return.

Article 11

1. Indigenous peoples have the right to practise and revitalize their cultural traditions and customs. This includes the right to maintain, protect and develop the past, present and future manifestations of their cultures, such as archaeological and historical sites, artefacts, designs, ceremonies, technologies and visual and performing arts and literature.

2. States shall provide redress through effective mechanisms, which may include restitution, developed in conjunction with indigenous peoples, with respect to their cultural, intellectual, religious and spiritual property taken without their free, prior and informed consent or in violation of their laws, traditions and customs.

Article 12

1. Indigenous peoples have the right to manifest, practise, develop and teach their spiritual and religious traditions, customs and ceremonies; the right to maintain, protect, and have access in privacy to their religious and cultural sites; the right to the use and control of their ceremonial objects; and the right to the repatriation of their human remains.

2. States shall seek to enable the access and/or repatriation of ceremonial objects and human remains in their possession through fair, transparent and effective mechanisms developed in conjunction with indigenous peoples concerned.

* * *

Article 18

Indigenous peoples have the right to participate in decision-making in matters which would affect their rights, through representatives chosen by themselves in accordance with their own procedures, as well as to maintain and develop their own indigenous decision-making institutions.

Article 19

States shall consult and cooperate in good faith with the indigenous peoples concerned through their own representative institutions in order to obtain their free, prior and informed consent before adopting and implementing legislative or administrative measures that may affect them.

Article 20

1. Indigenous peoples have the right to maintain and develop their political, economic and social systems or institutions, to be secure in the enjoyment of their own means of subsistence and development, and to engage freely in all their traditional and other economic activities.

2. Indigenous peoples deprived of their means of subsistence and development are entitled to just and fair redress.

* * *

Article 24

1. Indigenous peoples have the right to their traditional medicines and to maintain their health practices, including the conservation of their vital medicinal plants, animals and minerals. . . .

2. * * *

Article 25

Indigenous peoples have the right to maintain and strengthen their distinctive spiritual relationship with their traditionally owned or otherwise occupied and used lands, territories, waters and coastal seas and other resources and to uphold their responsibilities to future generations in this regard.

Article 26

1.   Indigenous peoples have the right to the lands, territories and resources which they have traditionally owned, occupied or otherwise used or acquired.

2.   Indigenous peoples have the right to own, use, develop and control the lands, territories and resources that they possess by reason of traditional ownership or other traditional occupation or use, as well as those which they have otherwise acquired.

3.   States shall give legal recognition and protection to these lands, territories and resources. Such recognition shall be conducted with due respect to the customs, traditions and land tenure systems of the indigenous peoples concerned.

Article 27

States shall establish and implement, in conjunction with indigenous peoples concerned, a fair, independent, impartial, open and transparent process, giving due recognition to indigenous peoples' laws, traditions, customs and land tenure systems, to recognize and adjudicate the rights of indigenous peoples pertaining to their lands, territories and resources, including those which were traditionally owned or otherwise occupied or used. Indigenous peoples shall have the right to participate in this process.

Article 28

1.   Indigenous peoples have the right to redress, by means that can include restitution or, when this is not possible, just, fair and equitable compensation, for the lands, territories and resources which they have traditionally owned or otherwise occupied or used, and which have been confiscated, taken, occupied, used or damaged without their free, prior and informed consent.

2.   Unless otherwise freely agreed upon by the peoples concerned, compensation shall take the form of lands, territories and resources equal in quality, size and legal status or of monetary compensation or other appropriate redress.

Article 29

1.   Indigenous peoples have the right to the conservation and protection of the environment and the productive capacity of their lands or territories and resources. States shall establish and implement assistance programmes for indigenous peoples for such conservation and protection, without discrimination.

2.   States shall take effective measures to ensure that no storage or disposal of hazardous materials shall take place in the lands or territories of indigenous peoples without their free, prior and informed consent.

3.   States shall also take effective measures to ensure, as needed, that programmes for monitoring, maintaining and restoring the health of indigenous peoples, as developed and implemented by the peoples affected by such materials, are duly implemented.

* * *

Article 31

1.   Indigenous peoples have the right to maintain, control, protect and develop their cultural heritage, traditional knowledge and traditional cultural expressions, as

well as the manifestations of their sciences, technologies and cultures, including human and genetic resources, seeds, medicines, knowledge of the properties of fauna and flora, oral traditions, literatures, designs, sports and traditional games and visual and performing arts. They also have the right to maintain, control, protect and develop their intellectual property over such cultural heritage, traditional knowledge, and traditional cultural expressions.

2.   In conjunction with indigenous peoples, States shall take effective measures to recognize and protect the exercise of these rights.

Article 32

1.   Indigenous peoples have the right to determine and develop priorities and strategies for the development or use of their lands or territories and other resources.

2.   States shall consult and cooperate in good faith with the indigenous peoples concerned through their own representative institutions in order to obtain their free and informed consent prior to the approval of any project affecting their lands or territories and other resources, particularly in connection with the development, utilization or exploitation of mineral, water or other resources.

3.   States shall provide effective mechanisms for just and fair redress for any such activities, and appropriate measures shall be taken to mitigate adverse environmental, economic, social, cultural or spiritual impact.

* * *

Article 39

Indigenous peoples have the right to have access to financial and technical assistance from States and through international cooperation, for the enjoyment of the rights contained in this Declaration.

Article 40

Indigenous peoples have the right to access to and prompt decision through just and fair procedures for the resolution of conflicts and disputes with States or other parties, as well as to effective remedies for all infringements of their individual and collective rights. Such a decision shall give due consideration to the customs, traditions, rules and legal systems of the indigenous peoples concerned and international human rights.

* * *

C. War/Peace

7.27 Convention (No. IV) Respecting the Laws and Customs of War on Land, With Annex of Regulations.[b] **Concluded at The Hague, 18 October 1907. Entered into force, 26 January 1910. 36 Stat 2277, TS No 539;** *reprinted in* **2 Weston & Carlson II.B.1**

* * *

Article 1

The Contracting Powers shall issue instructions to their armed land forces which shall be in conformity with the Regulations respecting the Laws and Customs of War on Land, annexed to the present Convention.

Article 2

The provisions contained in the Regulations referred to in Article 1, as well as in the present Convention, do not apply except between Contracting Powers, and then only if all the belligerents are parties to the Convention.

Article 3

A belligerent party which violates the provisions of the said Regulations shall, if the case demands, be liable to pay compensation. It shall be responsible for all acts committed by persons forming part of its armed forces.

Article 4

The present Convention, duly ratified, shall as between the Contracting Powers, be substituted for the Convention of the 29th July, 1899, respecting the Laws and Customs of War on Land.

The Convention of 1899 remains in force as between the Powers which signed it, and which do not also ratify the present Convention.

Article 5

The present Convention shall be ratified as soon as possible.

The ratifications shall be deposited at The Hague.

The first deposit of ratifications shall be recorded in a procès-verbal signed by the Representatives of the Powers which take part therein and by the Netherlands Minister for Foreign Affairs.

The subsequent deposits of ratifications shall be made by means of a written notification, addressed to the Netherlands Government and accompanied by the instrument of ratification.

A duly certified copy of the procès-verbal relative to the first deposit of ratifications, of the notifications mentioned in the preceding paragraph, as well as of the instruments of ratifications, shall be immediately sent by the Netherlands Government, through the diplomatic channel, to the Powers invited to the Second Peace

---

b. The Preamble to this Convention (No. IV) which contains the famous "De Martens clause," after its author Feodor de Martens, the principal Russian delegate to the First and Second Hague Peace Conferences of 1899 and 1907 has been omitted. The "De Martens Clause" provides:

Until a more complete code of the laws of war has been issued, the High Contracting Parties deem it expedient to declare that, in cases not included in the Regulations adopted by them, the inhabitants and the belligerents remain under the protection and the rule of the principles of the law of nations, as they result from the usages established among civilized peoples, from the laws of humanity, and from the dictates of the public conscience.

Conference, as well as to the other Powers which have adhered to the Convention. In the cases contemplated in the preceding paragraph the said Government shall at the same time inform them of the date on which it received the notification.

Article 6

Non–Signatory Powers may adhere to the present Convention.

The Power which desires to adhere notifies in writing its intention to the Netherlands Government, forwarding to it the act of adhesion, which shall be deposited in the archives of the said Government.

This Government shall at once transmit to all the other Powers a duly certified copy of the notification as well as the act of adhesion, mentioning the date on which it received the notification.

Article 7

The present Convention shall come into force, in the case of the Powers which were a party to the first deposit of ratifications, sixty days after the date of the procès-verbal of this deposit, and, in the case of the Powers which ratify subsequently or which adhere, sixty days after the notification of their ratification or of their adhesion has been received by the Netherlands Government.

Article 8

In the event of one of the Contracting Powers wishing to denounce the present Convention, the denunciation shall be notified in writing to the Netherlands Government, which shall at once communicate a duly certified copy of the notification to all the other Powers, informing them of the date on which it was received.

The denunciation shall only have effect in regard to the notifying Power, and one year after the notification has reached the Netherlands Government.

Article 9

A register kept by the Netherlands Ministry for Foreign Affairs shall give the date of the deposit of ratifications made in virtue of Article 5, paragraphs 3 and 4, as well as the date on which the notifications of adhesion (Article 6, paragraph 2) or of denunciation (Article 8, paragraph 1) were received.

Each Contracting Power is entitled to have access to this register and to be supplied with duly certified extracts.

ANNEX TO THE CONVENTION

Regulations Respecting the Laws and Customs of War on Land

SECTION 1. ON BELLIGERENTS

CHAPTER I. *The Qualifications of Belligerents*

Article 1

The laws, rights, and duties of war apply not only to armies, but also to militia and volunteer corps fulfilling the following conditions:

> 1. To be commanded by a person responsible for his subordinates;
>
> 2. To have a fixed distinctive emblem recognizable at a distance;
>
> 3. To carry arms openly; and
>
> 4. To conduct their operations in accordance with the laws and customs of war.

In countries where militia or volunteer corps constitute the army, or form part of it, they are included under the denomination "army".

* * *

SECTION II. HOSTILITIES

CHAPTER I. *Means of Injuring the Enemy, Sieges, and Bombardments*

Article 22

The right of belligerents to adopt means of injuring the enemy is not unlimited.

Article 23

In addition to the prohibitions provided by special Conventions, it is especially forbidden:

(a) To employ poison or poisoned weapons;

(b) To kill or wound treacherously individuals belonging to the hostile nation or army;

(c) To kill or wound an enemy who, having laid down his arms, or having no longer means of defence, has surrendered at discretion;

(d) To declare that no quarter will be given;

(e) To employ arms, projectiles, or material calculated to cause unnecessary suffering;

(f) To make improper use of a flag of truce, of the national flag, or of the military insignia and uniform of the enemy, as well as the distinctive badges of the Geneva Convention;

(g) To destroy or seize the enemy's property, unless such destruction or seizure be imperatively demanded by the necessities of war;

(h) To declare abolished, suspended, or inadmissible in a Court of law the rights and actions of the nationals of the hostile party.

A belligerent is likewise forbidden to compel the nationals of the hostile party to take part in the operations of war directed against their own country, even if they were in the belligerent's service before the commencement of the war.

Article 24

Ruses of war and the employment of measures necessary for obtaining information about the enemy and the country are considered permissible.

Article 25

The attack or bombardment, by whatever means, of towns, villages, dwellings, or buildings which are undefended is prohibited.

Article 26

The officer in command of an attacking force must, before commencing a bombardment, except in cases of assault, do all in his power to warn the authorities.

Article 27

In sieges and bombardments all necessary steps must be taken to spare, as far as possible, buildings dedicated to religion, art, science, or charitable purposes, historic monuments, hospitals, and places where the sick and wounded are collected, provided they are not being used at the time for military purposes.

It is the duty of the besieged to indicate the presence of such buildings or places by distinctive and visible signs, which shall be notified to the enemy beforehand.

Article 28

The pillage of a town or place, even when taken by assault, is prohibited.

* * *

7.28 GENEVA CONVENTION (NO. IV) RELATIVE TO THE PROTECTION OF CIVILIAN PERSONS IN TIME OF WARS (Without Annexes).[c] Concluded at Geneva, 12 August 1949. Entered into force, 21 October 1950. 75 UNTS 287, 6 TS No 3114, TIAS No 3362; *reprinted in* 2 Weston & Carlson II.B.14: *Arts. 2, 53, 146, 147, 158*

* * *

Article 2

In addition to the provisions which shall be implemented in peacetime, the present Convention shall apply to all cases of declared war or of any other armed conflict which may arise between two or more of the High Contracting Parties, even if the state of war is not recognized by one of them.

The Convention shall also apply to all cases of partial or total occupation of the territory of a High Contracting Party, even if the said occupation meets with no armed resistance.

Although one of the Powers in conflict may not be a party to the present Convention, the Powers who are parties thereto shall remain bound by it in their mutual relations. They shall furthermore be bound by the Convention in relation to the said Power, if the latter accepts and applies the provisions thereof.

* * *

Article 53

Any destruction by the Occupying Power of real or personal property belonging individually or collectively to private persons, or to the State, or to other public authorities, or to social or cooperative organizations, is prohibited, except where such destruction is rendered absolutely necessary by military operations.

* * *

Article 146

The High Contracting Parties undertake to enact any legislation necessary to provide effective penal sanctions for persons committing, or ordering to be committed, any of the grave breaches of the present Convention defined in the following Article.

Each High Contracting Party shall be under the obligation to search for persons alleged to have committed, or to have ordered to be committed, such grave breaches, and shall bring such persons, regardless of their nationality, before its own courts. It may also, if it prefers, and in accordance with the provisions of its own legislation, hand such persons over for trial to another High Contracting Party concerned, provided such High Contracting Party has made out a prima facie case.

Each High Contracting Party shall take measures necessary for the suppression of all acts contrary to the provisions of the present Convention other than the grave breaches defined in the following Article.

In all circumstances, the accused persons shall benefit by safeguards of proper trial and defence, which shall not be less favourable than those provided by Article 105 and those following of the Geneva Convention relative to the Treatment of Prisoners of War of August 12, 1949.

c. *See also* Basic Document 7.33, *infra*

Article 147

Grave breaches to which the preceding Article relates shall be those involving any of the following acts, if committed against persons or property protected by the present Convention: wilful killing, torture or inhuman treatment, including biological experiments, wilfully causing great suffering or serious injury to body or health, unlawful deportation or transfer or unlawful confinement of a protected person, compelling a protected person to serve in the forces of a hostile Power, or wilfully depriving a protected person of the right of fair and regular trial prescribed in the present Convention, taking of hostages and extensive destruction and appropriation of property, not justified by military necessity and carried out unlawfully and wantonly.

* * *

Article 158

Each of the High Contracting Parties shall be at liberty to denounce the present Convention.

The denunciation shall be notified in writing to the Swiss Federal Council, which shall transmit it to the Governments of all the High Contracting Parties.

The denunciation shall take effect one year after the notification thereof has been made to the Swiss Federal Council. However, a denunciation of which notification has been made at a time when the denouncing Power is involved in a conflict shall not take effect until peace has been concluded, and until after operations connected with the release, repatriation and re-establishment of the person protected by the present Convention have been terminated.

The denunciation shall have effect only in respect of the denouncing Power. It shall in no way impair the obligations which the Parties to the conflict shall remain bound to fulfil by virtue of the principles of the law of nations, as they result from the usages established among civilized peoples, from the laws of humanity and the dictates of the public conscience.

7.29 PRINCIPLES OF INTERNATIONAL LAW RECOGNIZED IN THE CHARTER OF THE NUREM-
BERG TRIBUNAL AND IN THE JUDGMENT OF THE TRIBUNAL.[d] **Adopted by the
U.N. International Law Commission, 2 August 1950. 2 YBILC 374
(1950);** *reprinted in* **2 Weston & Carlson II.E.4**

PRINCIPLE I

*Any person who commits an act which constitutes a crime under international law is
responsible therefor and liable to punishment.*

98.   This principle is based on the first paragraph of article 6 of the Charter of the
Nuremberg Tribunal which established the competence of the Tribunal to try and
punish persons who, acting in the interests of the European Axis countries, whether as
individuals or as members of organizations, committed any of the crimes defined in
sub-paragraphs (a), (b) and (c) of article 6. The text of the Charter declared punishable
only persons "acting in the interests of the European Axis countries" but, as a matter
of course, Principle I is now formulated in general terms.

99.   The general rule underlying Principle I is that international law may impose
duties on individuals directly without any interposition of internal law. The findings of
the Tribunal were very definite on the question whether rules of international law may
apply to individuals. "That international law imposes duties and liabilities upon
individuals as well as upon States", said the judgment of the Tribunal, "has long been
recognized". It added: "Crimes against international law are committed by men, not
by abstract entities, and only by punishing individuals who commit such crimes can
the provision of international law be enforced."

PRINCIPLE II

*The fact that internal law does not impose a penalty for an act which constitutes a
crime under international law does not relieve the person who committed the act from
responsibility under international law.*

100.   This principle is a corollary to Principle I. Once it is admitted that
individuals are responsible for crimes under international law, it is obvious that they
are not relieved from their international responsibility by the fact that their acts are
not held to be crimes under the law of any particular country.

101.   The Charter of the Nurnberg Tribunal referred, in express terms, to this
relation between international and national responsibility only with respect to crimes
against humanity. Sub-paragraph (c) of article 6 of the Charter defined as crimes
against humanity certain acts "whether or not [committed] in violation of the domestic
law of the country where perpetrated". The Commission has formulated Principle II in
general terms.

102.   The principle that a person who has committed an international crime is
responsible therefore and liable to punishment under international law, independently
of the provisions of internal law, implies what is commonly called the "supremacy" of
international law over national law. The Tribunal considered that international law
can bind individuals even if national law does not direct them to observe the rules of
international law, as shown by the following statement of the judgment: " * * * the
very essence of the Charter is that individuals have international duties which
transcend the national obligations of obedience imposed by the individual State".

PRINCIPLE III

*The fact that a person who committed an act which constitutes a crime under
international law acted as Head of State or responsible Government official does not
relieve him from responsibility under international law.*

d.   *See also* Affirmation of the Principles of
International Law Recognized by the Charter
of the Nuremberg Tribunal, GA Res. 95, 1st
Sess., Supp. for 23 Oct.–15 Dec. 1946, at 188,
UN Doc. A/236 (1946).

103.   This principle is based on article 7 of the Charter of the Nurnberg Tribunal. According to the Charter and the judgment, the act that an individual acted as Head of State or responsible government official did not relieve him from international responsibility. "The principle of international law which, under certain circumstances, protects the representatives of a State", said the Tribunal, "cannot be applied to acts which are condemned as criminal by international law. The authors of these acts cannot shelter themselves behind their official position in order to be freed from punishment. . . ." The same idea was also expressed in the following passage of the findings: "He who violates the laws of war cannot obtain immunity while acting in pursuance of the authority of the State if the State in authorizing action moves outside its competence under international law."

104.   The last phrase of article 7 of the Charter, "or mitigating punishment", has not been retained in the formulation of Principle III. The Commission considers that the question of mitigating punishment is a matter for the competent court to decide.

PRINCIPLE IV

The fact that a person acted pursuant to order of his Government or of a superior does not relieve him from responsibility under international law, provided a moral choice was in fact possible to him.

105.   This text is based on the principle contained in article 88 of the Charter of the Nurnberg Tribunal as interpreted in the judgment. The idea expressed in Principle IV is that superior orders are not a defence provided a moral choice was possible to the accused. In conformity with this conception, the Tribunal rejected the argument of the defence that there could not be any responsibility since most of the defendants acted under the orders of Hitler. The Tribunal declared: "The provisions of this article [article 8] are in conformity with the law of all nations. That a soldier was ordered to kill or torture in violation of the international law of war has never been recognized as a defence to such acts of brutality, though, as the Charter here provides, the order may be urged in mitigation of the punishment. The true test, which is found in varying degrees in the criminal law of most nations, is not the existence of the order but whether moral choice was in fact possible."

106.   The last phrase of article 88 of the Charter "but may be considered in mitigation of punishment, if the Tribunal determines that justice so requires", has not been retained for the reason stated under Principle III, in paragraph 104 above.

PRINCIPLE V

Any person charged with a crime under international law has the right to a fair trial on the facts and law.

107.   The principle that a defendant charged with a crime under international law must have the right to a fair trial was expressly recognized and carefully developed by the Charter of the Nurnberg Tribunal. The Charter contained a chapter entitled: "Fair Trial for Defendants," which for the purpose of ensuring such fair trial provided the following procedure:

"a   The indictment shall include full particulars specifying in details the charges against the defendants. A copy of the indictment and of all the documents lodged with the indictment, translated into a language which he understands, shall be furnished to the defendant at a reasonable time before the trial.

"b   During any preliminary examination or trial of a defendant he shall have the right to give any explanation relevant to the charges made against him.

"c   A preliminary examination of a defendant and his trial shall be conducted in, or translated into, a language which the defendant understands.

"d A defendant shall have the right to conduct his own defence before the Tribunal or to have the assistance of counsel.

"e A defendant shall have the right through himself or through his counsel to present evidence at the trial in support of his defence, and to cross-examine any witness called by the prosecution."

108. The right to a fair trial was also referred to in the judgment itself. The Tribunal said in this respect: "With regard to the constitution of the Court all that the defendants are entitled to ask is to receive a fair trial on the facts and law."

109. In the view of the Commission, the expression "fair trial" should be understood in the light of the above-quoted provisions of the Charter of the Nurnberg Tribunal.

PRINCIPLE VI

The crimes hereinafter set out are punishable as crimes under international law:

(a) *Crimes against peace:*

(i) *Planning, preparation, initiation or waging of a war of aggression or a war in violation of international treaties, agreements or assurances;*

(ii) *Participation in a common plan or conspiracy for the accomplishment of any of the acts mentioned under (i).*

110. Both categories of crimes are characterized by the fact that they are connected with "war of aggression or war in violation of international treaties, agreements or assurances".

111. The Tribunal made a general statement to the effect that its Charter was "the expression of international law existing at the time to its creation". It, in particular, refuted the argument of the defence that aggressive war was not an international crime. For this refutation the Tribunal relied primarily on the General Treaty for the Renunciation of War of 27 August 1928 (Kellogg–Briand Pact) which in 1939 was in force between sixty-three States. "The nations who signed the Pact or adhered to it unconditionally", said the Tribunal, "condemned recourse to war for the future as an instrument of policy, and expressly renounced it. After the signing of the Pact, any nation resorting to war as an instrument of national policy breaks the Pact. In the opinion of the Tribunal, the solemn renunciation of war as an instrument of national policy necessarily involves the proposition that such a war is illegal in international law; and that those who planned and waged such a war, with its inevitable and terrible consequences, are committing a crime in so doing. War for the solution of international controversies undertaken as an instrument of national policy certainly includes a war of aggression, and such a war is therefore outlawed by the Pact".

112. In support of its interpretation of the Kellogg–Briand Pact, the Tribunal cited some other international instruments which condemned war of aggression as an international crime. The draft of a Treaty of Mutual Assistance sponsored by the League of Nations in 1923 declared, in its article 1, "that aggressive war is an international crime". The Preamble to the League of Nations Protocol for the Pacific Settlement of International disputes (Geneva Protocol), of 1924, "recognizing the solidarity of the members of the International Community", stated that "a war of aggression constitutes a violation of this solidarity, and is an international crime", and that the contracting parties were "desirous of facilitating the complete application of the system provided in the Covenant of the League of Nations for the pacific settlement of disputes between the States and of ensuring the repression of international crimes". The declaration concerning wars of aggression adopted on 24 September 1927 by the Assembly of the League of Nations declared, in its preamble, that war was an "international crime". The resolution unanimously adopted on 18 February

1928 by twenty-one American Republics at the Sixth (Havana) International Conference of American States, provided that "war of aggression constitutes an international crime against the human species".

113. The Charter of the Nurnberg Tribunal did not contain any definition of "war of aggression", nor was there any such definition in the judgment of the Tribunal. It was by reviewing the historical events before and during the war that it found that certain of the defendants planned and waged aggressive wars against twelve nations and were therefore guilty of a series of crimes.

114. According to the Tribunal, this made it unnecessary to discuss the subject in further detail, or to consider at any length the extent to which these aggressive wars were also "wars in violation of international treaties, agreements, or assurances".

115. The term "assurances" is understood by the Commission as including any pledge or guarantee of peace given by a State, even unilaterally.

116. The terms "planning" and "preparation" of a war of aggression were considered by the Tribunal as comprising all the stages in the bringing about of a war of aggression from the planning to the actual initiation of the war. In view of that, the Tribunal did not make any clear distinction between planning and preparation. As stated in the judgment, "planning and preparation are essential to the making of war".

117. The meaning of the expression "waging of a war of aggression" was discussed in the Commission during the consideration of the definition of "crimes against peace". Some members of the Commission feared that everyone in uniform who fought in a war of aggression might be charged with the "waging" of such a war. The Commission understands the expression to refer only to high ranking military personnel and high State officials, and believes that this was also the view of the Tribunal.

118. A legal notion of the Charter to which the defence objected was the one concerning "conspiracy". The Tribunal recognized that "conspiracy is not defined in the Charter". However, it stated the meaning of the term, though only in a restricted way. "But in the opinion of the Tribunal", it was said in the judgment, "the conspiracy must be clearly outlined in its criminal purpose. It must not be too far removed from the time of decision and of action. The planning, to be criminal, must not rest merely on the declarations of a party programme such as are found in the twenty-five points of the Nazi Party, announced in 1920, or the political affirmations expressed in *Mein Kampf* in later years. The Tribunal must examine whether a concrete plan to wage war existed, and determine the participants in that concrete plan".

(b) *War crimes:*

> *Violations of the laws or customs of war which include, but are not limited to, murder, ill-treatment or deportation to slave-labour or for any other purpose of civilian population of or in occupied territory, murder or ill-treatment of prisoners of war, of persons on the seas, killing of hostages, plunder of public or private property, wanton destruction of cities, towns, or villages, or devastation not justified by military necessity.*

119. The Tribunal emphasized that before the last war the crimes defined by article 6(b) of its Charter were already recognized as crimes under international law. The Tribunal stated that such crimes were covered by specific provisions of the Regulations annexed to The Hague Convention of 1907 respecting the Laws and Customs of War on Land and of the Geneva Convention of 1929 on the Treatment of Prisoners of War. After enumerating the said provisions, the Tribunal stated: "That violation of these provisions constituted crimes for which the guilty individuals were punishable is too well settled to admit or argument."

(c) *Crimes against humanity:*

Murder, extermination, enslavement, deportation and other inhuman acts done against any civilian population, or persecutions on political, racial or religious grounds, when such acts are done or such persecutions are carried on in execution of or in connexion with any crime against peace or any war crime.

120. Article 6(c) of the Charter of the Nurnberg Tribunal distinguished two categories of punishable acts, to wit: first, murder, extermination, enslavement, deportation and other inhuman acts committed against any civilian population, before or during the war, and second, persecution on political, racial or religious grounds. Acts within these categories, according to the Charter, constituted international crimes only when committed "in execution of or in connexion with any crimes within the jurisdiction of the Tribunal". The crimes referred to as falling, within the jurisdiction of the Tribunal were crimes against peace and war crimes.

121. Though it found that "political opponents were murdered in Germany before the war, and that many of them were kept in concentration camps in circumstances of great horror and cruelty", that "the policy of persecution, repression and murder of civilians in Germany before the war of 1939, who were likely to be hostile to the Government, was most ruthlessly carried out", and that "the persecution of Jews during the same period is established beyond all doubt", the Tribunal considered that it had not been satisfactorily proved that before the outbreak of war these acts had been committed in execution of, or in connexion with, any crime within the jurisdiction of the Tribunal. For this reason the Tribunal declared itself unable to "make a general declaration that the acts before 1939 were crimes against humanity within the meaning of the Charter".

122. The Tribunal did not, however, thereby exclude the possibility that crimes against humanity might be committed also before a war.

123. In its definition of crimes against humanity the Commission has omitted the phrase "before or during the war" contained in article 6(c) of the Charter of the Nurnberg Tribunal because this phrase referred to a particular war, the war of 1939. The omission of the phrase does not mean that the Commission considers that crimes against humanity can be committed only during a War. On the contrary, the Commission is of the opinion that such crimes may take place also before a war in connexion with crimes against peace.

124. In accordance with article 6(c) of the Charter, the above formulation characterizes as crimes against humanity murder, extermination, enslavement, etc., committed against "any" civilian population. This means that these acts may be crimes against humanity even if they are committed by the perpetrator against his own population.

PRINCIPLE VII

Complicity in the commission of a crime against peace, a war crime, or a crime against humanity as set forth in Principle VI is a crime under international law.

125. The only provision in the Charter of the Nurnberg Tribunal regarding responsibility for complicity was that of the last paragraph of article 6 which reads as follows: "Leaders, organizers, instigators and accomplices participating in the formulation or execution of a common plan or conspiracy to commit any of the foregoing crimes are responsible for all acts performed by any persons in execution of such a plan."

126. The Tribunal, commenting on this provision in connexion with its discussion of count one of the indictment, which charged certain defendants with conspiracy to commit aggressive war, war crimes and crimes against humanity, said that, in its opinion, the provision did not "add a new and separate crime to those already listed". In the view of the Tribunal, the provision was designed to "establish the responsibility

of persons participating in a common plan" to prepare, initiate and wage aggressive war. Interpreted literally, this statement would seem to imply that the complicity rule did not apply to crimes perpetrated by individual action.

127. On the other hand, the Tribunal convicted several of the defendants of war crimes and crimes against humanity because they gave orders resulting in atrocious and criminal acts which they did not commit themselves. In practice, therefore, the Tribunal seems to have applied general principles of criminal law regarding complicity. This view is corroborated by expressions used by the Tribunal in assessing the guilt of particular defendants.

7.30 DRAFT ARTICLES ON THE DRAFT CODE OF CRIMES AGAINST THE PEACE AND SECURITY OF MANKIND (as revised through 1991). First adopted by the UN International Law Commission, 4 December 1954. GA Res 46/405, UN GAOR, 46th Sess, Supp No 10, at 198, UN Doc A/46/405 (1991); *reprinted in* 30 ILM 1554 (1991) & 2 Weston & Carlson II.E.5

PART I

CHAPTER 1. DEFINITION AND CHARACTERIZATION

Article 1

Definition

The crimes [under international law] defined in this Code constitute crimes against the peace and security of mankind.

Article 2

Characterization

The characterization of an act or omission as a crime against the peace and security of mankind is independent of internal law. The fact that an act or omission is or is not punishable under internal law does not affect this characterization.

CHAPTER 2. GENERAL PRINCIPLES

Article 3

Responsibility and punishment

1.   An individual who commits a crime against the peace and security of mankind is responsible therefore and is liable to punishment.

2.   An individual who aids, abets or provides the means for the commission of a crime against the peace and security of mankind or conspires in or directly incites the commission of such a crime is responsible therefore and is liable to punishment.

3.   An individual who commits an act constituting an attempt to commit a crime against the peace and security of mankind [as set out in articles * * *] is responsible therefore and is liable to punishment. Attempt means any commencement of execution of a crime that failed or was halted only because of circumstances independent of the perpetrator's intention.

Article 4

Motives

Responsibility for a crime against the peace and security of mankind is not affected by any motives invoked by the accused which are not covered by the definition of the crime.

Article 5

Responsibility of States

Prosecution of an individual for a crime against the peace and security of mankind does not relieve a State of any responsibility under international law for an act or omission attributable to it.

Article 6

Obligation to try or extradite

1.   A State in whose territory an individual alleged to have committed a crime against the peace and security of mankind is present shall either try or extradite him.

2. If extradition is requested by several States, special consideration shall be given to the request of the State in whose territory the crime was committed.

3. The provisions of paragraphs 1 and 2 do not prejudge the establishment and the jurisdiction of an international criminal court.

Article 7

Non-applicability of statutory limitations

No statutory limitation shall apply to crimes against the peace and security of mankind.

Article 8

Judicial guarantees

An individual charged with a crime against the peace and security of mankind shall be entitled without discrimination to the minimum guarantees due to all human beings with regard to the law and the facts. In particular, he shall have the right to be presumed innocent until proved guilty and have the rights:

(a) in the determination of any charge against him, to have a fair and public hearing by a competent, independent and impartial tribunal duly established by law or by treaty;

(b) to be informed promptly and in detail in a language which he understands of the nature and cause of the charge against him;

(c) to have adequate time and facilities for the preparation of his defence and to communicate with counsel of his own choosing;

(d) to be tried without undue delay;

(e) to be tried in his presence, and to defend himself in person or through legal assistance of his own choosing; to be informed, if he does not have legal assistance, of this right; and to have legal assistance assigned to him and without payment by him in any such case if he does not have sufficient means to pay for it;

(f) to examine, or have examined, the witnesses against him and to obtain the attendance and examination of witnesses on his behalf under the same conditions as witnesses against him;

(g) to have the free assistance of an interpreter if he cannot understand or speak the language used in court;

(h) not to be compelled to testify against himself or to confess guilt.

Article 9

Non bis in idem

1. No one shall be tried or punished for a crime under this Code for which he has already been finally convicted or acquitted by an international criminal court.

2. Subject to paragraphs 3, 4 and 5, no one shall be tried or punished for a crime under this Code in respect of an act for which he has already been finally convicted or acquitted by a national court, provided that, if a punishment was imposed, it has been enforced or is in the process of being.

3. Notwithstanding the provisions of paragraph 2, an individual may be tried and punished by an international criminal court or by a national court for a crime under this Code if the act which was the subject of a trial and judgement as an ordinary crime corresponds to one of the crimes characterized in this Code.

4. Notwithstanding the provisions of paragraph 2, an individual may be tried and punished by a national court of another State for a crime under the Code:

(a) if the act which was the subject of the previous judgement took place in the territory of that State; or

(b) if that State has been the main victim of the crime.

5. In the case of a subsequent conviction under this Code, the court, in passing sentence, shall deduct any penalty imposed and implemented as a result of a previous conviction for the same act.

Article 10

Non-retroactivity

1. No one shall be convicted under this Code for acts committed before its entry into force.

2. Nothing in this article shall preclude the trial and punishment of anyone for any act which, at the time when it was committed, was criminal in accordance with international law or domestic law applicable in conformity with international law.

Article 11

Order of a Government or a superior

The fact that an individual charged with a crime against the peace and security of mankind acted pursuant to an order of a Government or a superior does not relieve him of criminal responsibility if, in the circumstances at the time, it was possible for him not to comply with that order.

Article 12

Responsibility of the superior

The fact that a crime against the peace and security of mankind was committed by a subordinate does not relieve his superiors of criminal responsibility, if they knew or had information enabling them to conclude, in the circumstances at the time, that the subordinate was committing or was going to commit such a crime and if they did not take all feasible measures within their power to prevent or repress the crime.

Article 13

Official position and responsibility

The official position of an individual who commits a crime against the peace and security of mankind, and particularly the fact that he acts as head of State or Government, does not relieve him of criminal responsibility.

Article 14

Defences and extenuating circumstances

1. The competent court shall determine the admissibility of defences under the general principles of law, in the light of the character of each crime.

2. In passing sentence, the court shall, where appropriate, take into account extenuating circumstances.

PART II

CRIMES AGAINST THE PEACE AND SECURITY OF MANKIND

Article 15

Aggression

1. An individual who as leader or organizer plans, commits, or orders the commission of an act of aggression shall, on conviction thereof, be sentenced [to * * *].

2. Aggression is the use of armed force by a State against the sovereignty, territorial integrity or political independence of another State, or in any other manner inconsistent with the Charter of the United Nations.

3. The first use of armed force by a State in contravention of the Charter shall constitute prima facie evidence of an act of aggression, although the Security Council may, in conformity with the Charter, conclude that a determination that an act of aggression has been committed would not be justified in the light of other relevant circumstances, including the fact that the acts concerned or their consequences are not of sufficient gravity.

4. Any of the following acts, regardless of a declaration of war, constitutes an act of aggression, due regard being paid to paragraphs 2 and 3:

(a) the invasion or attack by the armed forces of a State of the territory of another State, or any military occupation, however temporary, resulting from such invasion or attack, or any annexation by the use of force of the territory of another State or part thereof;

(b) bombardment by the armed forces of a State against the territory of another State or the use of any weapons by a State against the territory of another State;

(c) the blockade of the port or coasts of a State by the armed forces of another State;

(d) an attack by the armed forces of a State on the land, sea or air forces, or marine and air fleets of another State;

(e) the use of armed forces of one State which are within the territory of another State with the agreement of the receiving State, in contravention of the conditions provided for in the agreement, or any extension of their presence in such territory beyond the termination of the agreement;

(f) the action of a State in allowing its territory, which it has placed at the disposal of another State, to be used by that other State for perpetrating an act of aggression against a third State;

(g) the sending by or on behalf of a State of armed bands, groups, irregulars or mercenaries, which carry out acts of armed force against another State of such gravity as to amount to the acts listed above, or its substantial involvement therein;

(h) any other acts determination by the Security Council as constituting acts of aggression under the provisions of the Charter;

[5. Any determination by the Security Council as to the existence of an act of aggression is binding on national courts.]

6. Nothing in this article shall be interpreted as in any way enlarging or diminishing the scope of the Charter of the United Nations including its provisions concerning cases in which the use of force is lawful.

7. Nothing in this article could in any way prejudice the right to self-determination, freedom and independence, as derived from the Charter, of peoples forcibly deprived of that right and referred to in the Declaration on Principles of International Law concerning Friendly Relations and Cooperation among States in accordance with the Charter of the United Nations, particularly peoples under colonial and racist regimes or other forms of alien domination, nor the right of these peoples to struggle to that end and to seek and receive support, in accordance with the principles of the Charter and in conformity with the above-mentioned Declaration.

Article 16

Threat of aggression

1. An individual who as leader or organizer commits or orders the commission of a threat of aggression shall, on conviction thereof, be sentenced [to * * *].

2. Threat of aggression consists of declarations, communications, demonstrations of force or any other measures which would give good reason to the Government of a State to believe that aggression is being seriously contemplated against that State.

Article 17

Intervention

1. An individual who as leader or organizer commits or orders the commission of an act of intervention in the internal or external affairs of a State shall, on conviction thereof, be sentenced [to * * *].

2. Intervention in the internal or external affairs of a State consists of fomenting [armed] subversive or terrorist activities or by organizing, assisting or financing such activities, or supplying arms for the purpose of such activities, thereby [seriously] undermining the free exercise by that State of its sovereign rights.

3. Nothing in this article shall in any way prejudice the right of peoples to self-determination as enshrined in the Charter of the United Nations.

Article 18

Colonial domination and other forms of alien domination

An individual who as leader or organizer establishes or maintains by force or orders the establishment or maintenance by force of colonial domination or any other form of alien domination contrary to the right of peoples to self-determination as enshrined in the Charter of the United Nations, shall, on conviction thereof, be sentenced [to * * *].

Article 19

Genocide

1. An individual who commits or orders the commission of an act of genocide shall, on conviction thereof, be sentenced [to * * *].

2. Genocide means any of the following acts committed with intent to destroy, in whole or in part, a national, ethnic, racial or religious group as such:

(a) killing members of the group;

(b) causing serious bodily or mental harm to members of the group;

(c) deliberately inflicting on the group conditions of life calculated to bring about its physical destruction in whole or in part;

(d) imposing measures intended to prevent births within the group.

Article 20

Apartheid

1. An individual who as leader or organizer commits or orders the commission of the crime of apartheid shall, on conviction thereof, be sentenced [to * * *].

2. Apartheid consists of any of the following acts based on policies and practices of racial segregation and discrimination committed for the purpose of establishing or maintaining domination by one racial group over any other racial group and systematically oppressing it:

(a) denial to a member or members of a racial group of the right to life and liberty of person;

(b) deliberate imposition on a racial group of living conditions calculated to cause its physical destruction in whole or in part;

(c) any legislative measures and other measures calculated to prevent a racial group from participating in the political, social, economic and cultural life of the country and the deliberate creation of conditions preventing the full development of such a group;

(d) any measures, including legislative measures, designated to divide the population along racial lines, in particular by the creation of separate reserves and ghettos for the members of a racial group, the prohibition of marriages among members of various racial groups or the expropriation of landed property belonging to a racial group or to members thereof;

(e) exploitation of the labour of the members of a racial group, in particular by submitting them to forced labour;

(f) persecution of organizations and persons, by depriving them of fundamental rights and freedoms, because they oppose apartheid.

Article 21

Systematic or mass violations of human rights

An individual who commits or orders the commission of any of the following violations of human rights:

- murder

- torture

- establishing or maintaining over persons a status of slavery, servitude or forced labour

- persecution on social, political, racial, religious or cultural grounds in a systematic manner or on a mass scale; or

- deportation or forcible transfer of population shall, on conviction thereof, be sentenced [to * * *].

Article 22

Exceptionally serious war crimes

1. An individual who commits or orders the commission of an exceptionally serious war crime shall, on conviction thereof, be sentenced [to * * *].

2. For the purposes of this Code, an exceptionally serious war crime is an exceptionally serious violation of principles and rules of international law applicable in armed conflict consisting of any of the following acts:

(a) acts of inhumanity, cruelty or barbarity directed against the life, dignity or physical or mental integrity of persons[, in particular wilful killing, torture, mutilation, biological experiments, taking of hostages, compelling a protected person to serve in the forces of a hostile Power, unjustifiable delay in the repatriation of prisoners of war after the cessation of active hostilities, deportation or transfer of the civilian population and collective punishment];

(b) establishment of settlers in an occupied territory and changes to the demographic composition of an occupied territory;

(c) use of unlawful weapons;

(d) employing methods or means of warfare which are intended or may be expected to cause widespread, long-term and severe damage to the natural environment;

(e) large-scale destruction of civilian property;

(f) wilful attacks on property of exceptional religious, historical or cultural value.

Article 23

Recruitment, use, financing and training of mercenaries

1. An individual who as an agent or representative of a State commits or orders the commission of any of the following acts:

- recruitment, use, financing or training of mercenaries for activities directed against another State or for the purpose of opposing the legitimate exercise of the inalienable right of peoples to self-determination as recognized under international law

shall, on conviction thereof, be sentenced [to * * *].

2. A mercenary is any individual who:

(a) is specially recruited locally or abroad in order to fight in an armed conflict;

(b) is motivated to take part in the hostilities essentially by the desire for private gain and, in fact, is promised, by or on behalf of a party to the conflict, material compensation substantially in excess of that promised or paid to combatants of similar rank and functions in the armed forces of that party;

(c) is neither a national or a party to the conflict nor a resident of territory controlled by a party to the conflict;

(d) is not a member of the armed forces of a party to the conflict; and

(e) has not been sent by a State which is not a party to the conflict on official duty as a member of its armed forces.

3. A mercenary is also any individual who, in any other situation:

(a) is specially recruited locally or abroad for the purpose of participating in a concerted act of violence aimed at:

(i) overthrowing a Government or otherwise undermining the constitution order of a State; or

(ii) undermining the territorial integrity of a State;

(b) is motivated to take part therein essentially by the desire for significant private gain and is prompted by the promise or payment of material compensation;

(c) is neither a national nor a resident of the State against which such an act is directed;

(d) has not been sent by a State on official duty; and

(e) is not a member of the armed forces of the State is whose territory the act is undertaken.

Article 24

International terrorism

An individual who as an agent or representative of a State commits or orders the commission of any of the following acts:

- undertaking, organizing, assisting, financing, encouraging or tolerating act against another State directed at persons or property and of such a nature as to create a state of terror in the minds of public figures, groups of persons or the general public

shall, on conviction thereof, be sentenced [to * * *].

Article 25

Illicit traffic in narcotic drugs

1. An individual who commits or orders the commission of any of the following acts:

- undertaking, organizing, facilitating, financing or encouraging illicit traffic in narcotic drugs on a large scale, whether within the confines of a State or in a transboundary context

shall, on conviction thereof, be sentenced [to * * *].

2. For the purposes of paragraph 1, facilitating or encouraging illicit traffic in narcotic drugs includes the acquisition, holding, conversion or transfer of property by an individual who knows that such property is derived from the crime described in this article in order to conceal or disguise the illicit origin of the property.

3. Illicit traffic in narcotic drugs means any production, manufacture, extraction, preparation, offering, offering for sale, distribution, sale, delivery on any terms whatsoever, brokerage, dispatch, dispatch in transit, transport, importation or exportation of any narcotic drug or any psychotropic substance contrary to international law.

Article 26

Wilful and severe damage to the environment

An individual who wilfully causes or orders the causing of widespread, long-term and severe damage to the natural environment shall, on conviction thereof, be sentenced [to * * *].

7.31 TREATY ON THE NON-PROLIFERATION OF NUCLEAR WEAPONS. **Concluded at London, Moscow, and Washington, 1 July 1968. Entered into force, 5 March 1970. 729 UNTS 161, 21 TS 483, TIAS No 6839;** *reprinted in* **7 ILM 809 (1968) & 2 Weston & Carlson II.C.17:** *Arts. III, VI*

Article III

1. Each non-nuclear-weapon State Party to the Treaty undertakes to accept safeguards, as set forth in an agreement to be negotiated and concluded with the International Atomic Energy Agency in accordance with the Statute of the International Atomic Energy Agency and the Agency's safeguards system, for the exclusive purpose of verification of the fulfilment of its obligations assumed under this Treaty with a view to preventing diversion of nuclear energy from peaceful uses to nuclear weapons or other nuclear explosive devices. Procedures for the safeguards required by this Article shall be followed with respect to source or special fissionable material whether it is being produced, processed or used in any principal nuclear facility or is outside any such facility. The safeguards required by this Article shall be applied on all source or special fissionable material in all peaceful nuclear activities within the territory of such State, under its jurisdiction, or carried out under its control anywhere.

2. Each State Party to the Treaty undertakes not to provide: (a) source or special fissionable material, or (b) equipment or material especially designed or prepared for the processing, use or production of special fissionable material, to any non-nuclear-weapon State for peaceful purposes, unless the source or special fissionable material shall be subject to the safeguards required by this Article.

3. The safeguards required by this Article shall be implemented in a manner designed to comply with Article IV of this Treaty, and to avoid hampering the economic or technological development of the Parties or international co-operation in the field of peaceful nuclear activities, including the international exchange of nuclear material and equipment for the processing, use or production of nuclear material for peaceful purposes in accordance with the provisions of this Article and the principle of safeguarding set forth in the Preamble of the Treaty.

4. Non-nuclear-weapon States Party to the Treaty shall conclude agreements with the International Atomic Energy Agency to meet the requirements of this Article either individually or together with other States in accordance with the Statute of the International Atomic Energy Agency. Negotiation of such agreements shall commence within 180 days from the original entry into force of this Treaty. For States depositing their instruments of ratification or accession after the 180–day period, negotiation of such agreements shall commence not later than the date of such deposit. Such agreements shall enter into force not later than eighteen months after the date of initiation of negotiations.

* * *

Article VI

Each of the Parties to the Treaty undertakes to pursue negotiations in good faith on effective measures relating to cessation of the nuclear arms race at an early date and to nuclear disarmament, and on a treaty on general and complete disarmament under strict and effective international control.

7.32 Convention on the Prohibition of Military or Any Other Hostile Use of Environmental Modification Techniques (ENMOD) (Without Annex). Adopted by the U.N. General Assembly, 10 December 1976. Entered into force, 5 October 1978. 1108 UNTS 151, 31 TS 333, TIAS No 9614; *reprinted in* 16 ILM 88 (1977) & 2 Weston & Carlson II.B.19

The States Parties to this Convention,

Guided by the interest of consolidating peace, and wishing to contribute to the cause of halting the arms race, and of bringing about general and complete disarmament under strict and effective international control, and of saving mankind from the danger of using new means of warfare,

Determined to continue negotiations with a view to achieving effective progress towards further measures in the field of disarmament,

Recognizing that scientific and technical advances may open new possibilities with respect to modification of the environment,

Recalling the Declaration of the United Nations Conference on the Human Environment, adopted at Stockholm on 16 June 1972,

Realizing that the use of environmental modification techniques for peaceful purposes could improve the interrelationship of man and nature and contribute to the preservation and improvement of the environment for the benefit of present and future generations,

Recognizing, however, that military or any other hostile use of such techniques could have effects extremely harmful to human welfare,

Desiring to prohibit effectively military or any other hostile use of environmental modification techniques in order to eliminate the dangers to mankind from such use, and affirming their willingness to work towards the achievement of this objective,

Desiring also to contribute to the strengthening of trust among nations and to the further improvement of the international situation in accordance with the purposes and principles of the Charter of the United Nations,

Have agreed on the following:

Article I

1. Each State Party to this Convention undertakes not to engage in military or any other hostile use of environmental modification techniques having widespread, long-lasting or severe effects as the means of destruction, damage or injury to any other State Party.

2. Each State Party to this Convention undertakes not to assist, encourage or induce any State, group of States or international organization to engage in activities contrary to the provisions of paragraph 1 of this article.

Article II

As used in article I, the term "environmental modification techniques" refers to any technique for changing—through the deliberate manipulation of natural processes—the dynamics, composition or structure of the earth, including its biota, lithosphere, hydrosphere and atmosphere, or of outer space.

Article III

1. The provisions of this Convention shall not hinder the use of environmental modification techniques for peaceful purposes and shall be without prejudice to the generally recognized principles and applicable rules of international law concerning such use.

2. The States Parties to this Convention undertake to facilitate, and have the right to participate in, the fullest possible exchange of scientific and technological information on the use of environmental modification techniques for peaceful purposes. States Parties in a position to do so shall contribute, alone or together with other States or international organizations, to international economic and scientific co-operation in the preservation, improvement and peaceful utilization of the environment, with due consideration for the needs of the developing areas of the world.

Article IV

Each State Party to this Convention undertakes to take any measures it considers necessary in accordance with its constitutional processes to prohibit and prevent any activity in violation of the provisions of the Convention anywhere under its jurisdiction or control.

Article V

1. The States Parties to this Convention undertake to consult one another and to co-operate in solving any problems which may arise in relation to the objectives of, or in the application of the provisions of, the Convention. Consultation and co-operation pursuant to this article may also be undertaken through appropriate international procedures within the framework of the United Nations and in accordance with its Charter. These international procedures may include the services of appropriate international organizations, as well as of a Consultative Committee of Experts as provided for in paragraph 2 of this article.

2. For the purposes set forth in paragraph 1 of this article, the Depositary shall, within one month of the receipt of a request from any State Party to this Convention, convene a Consultative Committee of Experts. Any State Party may appoint an expert to this Committee whose functions and rules of procedure are set out in the annex, which constitutes an integral part of the Convention. The committee shall transmit to the Depositary a summary of its findings of fact, incorporating all views and information presented to the Committee during its proceedings. The Depositary shall distribute the summary to all States Parties.

3. Any State Party to this Convention which has reasons to believe that any other State Party is acting in breach of obligations deriving from the provisions of the Convention may lodge a complaint with the Security Council of the United Nations. Such a complaint should include all relevant information as well as all possible evidence supporting its validity.

4. Each State Party to this Convention undertakes to co-operate in carrying out any investigation which the Security Council may initiate, in accordance with the provisions of the Charter of the United Nations, on the basis of the complaint received by the Council. The Security Council shall inform the States Parties of the results of the investigation.

5. Each State Party to this Convention undertakes to provide or support assistance, in accordance with the provisions of the Charter of the United Nations, to any State Party which so requests, if the Security Council decides that such Party has been harmed or is likely to be harmed as a result of violation of the Convention.

Article VI

1. Any State Party may propose amendments to this Convention. The text of any proposed amendment shall be submitted to the Depositary, who shall promptly circulate it to all States Parties.

2. An amendment shall enter into force for all States Parties which have accepted it, upon the deposit with the Depositary of instruments of acceptance by a

majority of States Parties. Thereafter it shall enter into force for any remaining State Party on the date of deposit of its instrument of acceptance.

Article VII

This Convention shall be of unlimited duration.

Article VIII

1. Five years after the entry into force of this Convention, a conference of the States Parties to the Convention shall be convened by the Depositary at Geneva. The conference shall review the operation of the Convention with a view to ensuring that its purposes and provisions are being realized, and shall in particular examine the effectiveness of the provisions of article I, paragraph 1, in eliminating the dangers of military or any other hostile use of environmental modification techniques.

2. At intervals of not less than five years thereafter, a majority of the States Parties to this Convention may obtain, by submitting a proposal to this effect to the Depositary, the convening of a conference with the same objectives.

3. If no review conference has been convened pursuant to paragraph 2 of this article within ten years following the conclusion of a previous review conference, the Depositary shall solicit the views of all States Parties to this Convention on the holding of such a conference. If one third or ten of the States Parties, whichever number is less, respond affirmatively, the Depositary shall take immediate steps to convene the conference.

Article IX

1. This Convention shall be open to all States for signature. Any State which does not sign the Convention before its entry into force in accordance with paragraph 3 of this article may accede to it at any time.

2. This Convention shall be subject to ratification by signatory States. Instruments of ratification and of accession shall be deposited with the Secretary–General of the United Nations.

3. This Convention shall enter into force upon the deposit with the Depositary of instruments of ratification by twenty Governments in accordance with paragraph 2 of this article.

4. For those States whose instruments of ratification or accession are deposited after the entry into force of this Convention, it shall enter into force on the date of the deposit of their instruments of ratification or accession.

5. The Depositary shall promptly inform all signatory and acceding States of the date of each signature, the date of deposit of each instrument of ratification or accession and the date of the entry into force of this Convention and of any amendments thereto, as well as of the receipt of other notices.

6. This Convention shall be registered by the Depositary in accordance with Article 102 of the Charter of the United Nations.

Article X

This Convention, of which the Arabic, Chinese, English, French, Russian and Spanish texts are equally authentic, shall be deposited with the Secretary–General of the United Nations who shall send certified copies thereof to the Governments of the signatory and acceding States.

7.33 Protocol Additional (No. I) to the Geneva Conventions of August 12, 1949, and Relating to the Protection of Victims of International Armed Conflicts.[e] Concluded at Geneva, 8 June 1977. Entered into force, 7 December 1978. 1125 UNTS 3; *reprinted in* 16 ILM 1391 (1977) & 2 Weston & Carlson II.B.20: *Arts. 1, 35, 36, 51, 54–58, 85*

Article 1—General principles and scope of application

1. The High Contracting Parties undertake to respect and to ensure respect for this Protocol in all circumstances.

2. In cases not covered by this Protocol or by other internation agreements, civilians and combatants remain under the protection and authority of the principles of international law derived from established custom, from the principles of humanity and from dictates of public conscience.

3. This Protocol, which supplements the Geneva Conventions of 12 August 1949 for the protection of war victims, shall apply in the situations referred to in Article 2 common to those Conventions.

4. The situations referred to in the preceding paragraph include armed conflicts in which peoples are fighting against colonial domination and alien occupation and against racist regimes in the exercise of their right of self-determination, as enshrined in the Charter of the United Nations and Declaration of Principles of International Law concerning Friendly Relations and Co-operation among States in accordance with the Charter of the United Nations.

* * *

Article 35—Basic rules

1. In any armed conflict, the right of the Parties to the conflict to choose methods or means of warfare is not unlimited.

2. It is prohibited to employ weapons, projectiles and material and methods of warfare of a nature to cause superfluous injury or unnecessary suffering.

3. It is prohibited to employ methods or means of warfare which are intended, or may be expected, to cause widespread, long-term and severe damage to the natural environment.

Article 36—New weapons

In the study, development, acquisition or adoption of a new weapon, means or method of warfare, a High Contracting Party is under an obligation to determine whether its employment would, in some or all circumstances, be prohibited by this Protocol or by any other rule of international law applicable to the High Contracting Party.

* * *

Article 51—Protection of the civilian population

1. The civilian population and individual civilians shall enjoy general protection against dangers arising from military operations. To give effect to this protection, the following rules, which are additional to other applicable rules of international law, shall be observed in all circumstances.

2. The civilian population as such, as well as individual civilians, shall not be the object of attack. Acts or threats of violence the primary purpose of which is to spread terror among the civilian population are prohibited.

e. *See Basic* Document 7.28, *supra*.

3. Civilians shall enjoy the protection afforded by this section, unless and for such time as they take a direct part in hostilities.

4. Indiscriminate attacks are prohibited. Indiscriminate attacks are:

(a) those which are not directed at a specific military objective;

(b) those which employ a method or means of combat which cannot be directed at a specific military objective; or

(c) those which employ a method or means of combat the effects of which cannot be limited as required by this Protocol;

and consequently, in each such case, are of a nature to strike military objectives and civilians or civilian objects without distinction.

5. Among others, the following types of attacks are to be considered as indiscriminate:

(a) an attack by bombardment by any methods or means which treats as a single military objective a number of clearly separated and distinct military objectives located in a city, town, village or other area containing a similar concentration of civilians or civilian objects; and

(b) an attack which may be expected to cause incidental loss of civilian life, injury to civilians, damage to civilian objects, or a combination thereof, which would be excessive in relation to the concrete and direct military advantage anticipated.

6. Attacks against the civilian population or civilians by way of reprisals are prohibited.

7. The presence or movements of the civilian population or individual civilians shall not be used to render certain points or areas immune from military operations, in particular in attempts to shield military objectives from attacks or to shield, favour or impede military operations. The Parties to the conflict shall not direct the movement of the civilian population or individual civilians in order to attempt to shield military objectives from attacks or to shield military operations.

8. Any violation of these prohibitions shall not release the Parties to the conflict from their legal obligations with respect to the civilian population and civilians, including the obligation to take the precautionary measures provided for in Article 57.

* * *

Article 54—Protection of objects indispensable to the survival of the civilian population

1. Starvation of civilians as a method of warfare is prohibited.

2. It is prohibited to attack, destroy, remove or render useless objects indispensable to the survival of the civilian population, such as food-stuffs, agricultural areas for the production of food-stuffs, crops, livestock, drinking water installations and supplies and irrigation works, for the specific purpose of denying them for their sustenance value to the civilian population or to the adverse Party, whatever the motive, whether in order to starve out civilians, to cause them to move away, or for any other motive.

3. The prohibitions in paragraph 2 shall not apply to such of the objects covered by it as are used by an adverse Party:

(a) as sustenance solely for the members of its armed forces; or

(b) if not as sustenance, then in direct support of military action, provided, however, that in no event shall actions against these objects be taken which may be expected to leave the civilian population with such inadequate food or water as to cause its starvation or force its movement.

4. These objects shall not be made the object of reprisals.

5. In recognition of the vital requirements of any Party to the conflict in the deference of its national territory against invasion, derogation from the prohibitions contained in paragraph 2 may be made by a Party to the conflict within such territory under its own control where required by imperative military necessity.

Article 55—Protection of the natural environment

1. Care shall be taken in warfare to protect the natural environment against widespread, long-term and severe damage. This protection includes a prohibition of the use of methods or means of warfare which are intended or may be expected to cause such damage to the natural environment and thereby to prejudice the health or survival of the population.

2. Attacks against the natural environment by way of reprisals are prohibited.

Article 56—Protection of works and installations containing dangerous forces

1. Works or installations containing dangerous forces, namely dams, dykes and nuclear electrical generating stations, shall not be made the object of attack, even where these objects are military objectives, if such attack may cause the release of dangerous forces and consequent severe losses among the civilian population. Other military objectives located at or in the vicinity of these works or installations shall not be made the object of attack if such attack may cause the release of dangerous forces from the works or installations and consequent severe losses among the civilian population.

2. The special protection against attack provided by paragraph 1 shall cease:

(a) for a dam or a dyke only if it is used for other than its normal function and in regular, significant and direct support of military operations and if such attack is the only feasible way to terminate such support;

(b) for a nuclear electrical generating station only if it provides electric power in regular, significant and direct support of military operations and if such attack is the only feasible way to terminate such support;

(c) for other military objectives located at or in the vicinity of these works or installations only if they are used in regular, significant and direct support of military operations and if such attack is the only feasible way to terminate such support.

3. In all cases, the civilian population and individual civilians shall remain entitled to all the protection accorded them by international law, including the protection of the precautionary measures provided for in Article 57. If the protection ceases and any of the works, installations or military objectives mentioned in paragraph 1 is attacked, all practical precautions shall be taken to avoid the release of dangerous forces.

4. It is prohibited to make any of the works, installations or military objectives mentioned in paragraph 1 the object of reprisals.

5. The Parties to the conflict shall endeavour to avoid locating any military objectives in the vicinity of the works or installations mentioned in paragraph 1. Nevertheless, installations erected for the sole purpose of defending the protected works or installations from attack are permissible and shall not themselves be made the object of attack, provided that they are not used in hostilities except for defensive actions necessary to respond to attacks against the protected works or installations and that their armament is limited to weapons capable only of repelling hostile action against the protected works or installations.

6. The High Contracting Parties and the Parties to the conflict are urged to conclude further agreements among themselves to provide additional protection for objects containing dangerous forces.

7. In order to facilitate the identification of the objects protected by this article, the Parties to the conflict may mark them with a special sign consisting of a group of three bright orange circles placed on the same axis, as specified in Article 16 of Annex I to this Protocol. The absence of such marking in no way relieves any Party to the conflict of its obligations under this Article.

CHAPTER IV

PRECAUTIONARY MEASURES

Article 57—Precautions in attack

1. In the conduct of military operations, constant care shall be taken to spare the civilian population, civilians and civilian objects.

2. With respect to attacks, the following precautions shall be taken:

(a) those who plan or decide upon an attack shall:

(i) do everything feasible to verify that the objectives to be attacked are neither civilians nor civilian objects and are not subject to special protection but are military objectives within the meaning of paragraph 2 of Article 52 and that it is not prohibited by the provisions of this Protocol to attack them;

(ii) take all feasible precautions in the choice of means and methods of attack with a view to avoiding, and in any event to minimizing, incidental loss of civilian life, injury to civilians and damage to civilian objects;

(iii) refrain from deciding to launch any attack which may be expected to cause incidental loss of civilian life, injury to civilians, damage to civilian objects, or a combination thereof, which would be excessive in relation to the concrete and direct military advantage anticipated.

(b) an attack shall be cancelled or suspended if it becomes apparent that the objective is not a military one or is subject to special protection or that the attack may be expected to cause incidental loss of civilian life, injury to civilians, damage to civilian objects, or a combination thereof, which would be excessive in relation to the concrete and direct military advantage anticipated;

(c) effective advance warning shall be given of attacks which may affect the civilian population, unless circumstances do not permit.

3. When a choice is possible between several military objectives for obtaining a similar military advantage; the objective to be selected shall be that the attack on which may be expected to cause the least danger to civilian lives and to civilian objects.

4. In the conduct of military operations at sea or in the air, each Party to the conflict shall, in conformity with its rights and duties under the rules of international law applicable in armed conflict, take all reasonable precautions to avoid losses of civilian lives and damage to civilian objects.

5. No provision of this article may be constructed as authorizing any attacks against the civilian population, civilians or civilian objects.

Article 58—Precautions against the effects of attacks

The Parties to the conflict shall, to the maximum extent feasible:

(a) without prejudice to Article 49 of the Fourth Convention, endeavour to remove the civilian population, individual civilians and civilian objects under their control from the vicinity of military objectives;

(b) avoid locating military objectives within or near densely populated areas;

(c) take the other necessary precautions to protect the civilian population, individual civilians and civilian objects under their control against the dangers resulting from military operations.

* * *

Article 85—Repression of breaches of this protocol

1. The provisions of the Conventions relating to the repression of breaches and grave breaches, supplemented by this Section, shall apply to the repression of breaches and grave breaches of this Protocol.

2. Acts described as grave breaches in the Conventions are grave breaches of this Protocol if committed against persons in the power of an adverse Party protected by Articles 44, 45 and 73 of this Protocol, or against the wounded, sick and shipwrecked of the adverse Party who are protected by this Protocol, or against those medical or religious personnel, medical units or medical transports which are under the control of the adverse Party and are protected by this Protocol.

3. In addition to the grave breaches defined in Article 11, the following acts shall be regarded as grave breaches of this Protocol, when committed wilfully, in violation of the relevant provisions of this Protocol, and causing death or serious injury to body or health:

(a) making the civilian population or individual civilians the object of attack;

(b) launching an indiscriminate attack affecting the civilian population or civilian objects in the knowledge that such attack will cause excessive loss of life, injury to civilians or damage to civilian objects, as defined in Article 57, paragraph 2(a)(iii);

(c) launching an attack against works or installations containing dangerous forces in the knowledge that such attack will cause excessive loss of life, injury to civilians or damage to civilian objects, as defined in Article 57, paragraph 2(a)(iii);

(d) making non-defended localities and demilitarized zones the object of attack;

(e) making a person the object of attack in the knowledge that he is *hors de combat;*

(f) the perfidious use, in violation of Article 37, of the distinctive emblem of the red cross, red crescent or red lion and sun or of other protective signs recognized by the Conventions or this Protocol.

4. In addition to the grave breaches defined in the preceding paragraphs and in the Conventions, the following shall be regarded as grave breaches of this Protocol, when committed wilfully and in violation of the Conventions or the Protocol.

(a) the transfer by the occupying Power of parts of its own civilian populations into the territory it occupies, or the deportation or transfer of all or parts of the population of the occupied territory within or outside this territory, in violation of Article 49 of the Fourth Convention;

(b) unjustifiable delay in the repatriation of prisoners of war or civilians;

(c) practices of *apartheid* and other inhuman and degrading practices involving outrages upon personal dignity, based on racial discrimination.

(d) making the clearly-recognized historic monuments, works of art or places of worship which constitute the cultural or spiritual heritage of peoples and to which special protection has been given by special arrangement, for example, within the framework of a competent international organization, the object of attack, causing as a result extensive destruction thereof, where there is no evidence of the violation by the adverse Party of Article 53, subparagraph (b), and when such historic monuments, works of art and places of worship are not located in the immediate proximity of military objectives;

(e) depriving a person protected by the Conventions or referred to in paragraph 2 of this Article of the rights of fair and regular trial.

5. Without prejudice to the application of the Conventions and of this Protocol, grave breaches of these instruments shall be regarded as war crimes.

7.34 SOUTH PACIFIC NUCLEAR FREE ZONE TREATY. Adopted by the South Pacific Forum on 6 August 1985. Entered into force, 11 Dec 1986. 1445 UNTS 177. *Reprinted in* 2 Weston & Carlson II.C.29.

The Parties to this Treaty,

United in their commitment to a world at peace;

* * *

Determined to ensure, so far as lies within their power, that the bounty and beauty of the land and sea in their region shall remain the heritage of their peoples and their descendants in perpetuity to be enjoyed by all in peace;

* * *

Determined to keep the region free of environmental pollution by radioactive wastes and other radioactive matter;

* * *

Have agreed as follows:

Article 1
Usage of Terms

For the purposes of this Treaty and its Protocols:

(a) "South Pacific Nuclear Free Zone" means the areas described in Annex 1 as illustrated by the map attached to that Annex;

(b) "territory" means internal waters, territorial sea and archipelagic waters, the seabed and subsoil beneath, the land territory and the airspace above them;

(c) "nuclear explosive device" means any nuclear weapon or other explosive device capable of releasing nuclear energy, irrespective of the purpose for which it could be used. The term includes such a weapon or device in unassembled and partly assembled forms, but does not include the means of transport or delivery of such a weapon or device if separable from and not an indivisible part of it;

(d) "stationing" means emplantation, emplacement, transportation on land or inland waters, stockpiling, storage, installation and deployment.

* * *

Article 3
Renunciation of Nuclear Explosive Devices

Each Party undertakes:

(a) not to manufacture or otherwise acquire, possess or have control over any nuclear explosive device by any means anywhere inside or outside the South Pacific Nuclear Free Zone;

(b) not to seek or receive any assistance in the manufacture or acquisition of any nuclear explosive device;

(c) not to take any action to assist or encourage the manufacture or acquisition of any nuclear explosive device by any State.

Article 5
Prevention of Stationing of Nuclear Explosive Devices

1. Each Party undertakes to prevent in its territory the stationing of any nuclear explosive device.

2. Each Party in the exercise of its sovereign rights remains free to decide for itself whether to allow visits by foreign ships and aircraft to its ports and airfields, transit of its airspace by foreign aircraft, and navigation by foreign ships in its territorial sea or archipelagic waters in a manner not covered by the rights of innocent passage, archipelagic sea lane passage or transit passage of straits.

Article 6
Prevention of Testing of Nuclear Explosive Devices

Each Party undertakes:

(a) to prevent in its territory the testing of any nuclear explosive device;

(b) not to take any action to assist or encourage the testing of any nuclear explosive device by any State.

* * *

ANNEX 1
SOUTH PACIFIC NUCLEAR FREE ZONE

A. The area bounded by a line:

(1) commencing at the point of intersection of the Equator by the maritime boundary between Indonesia and Papua New Guinea;

(2) running thence northerly along that maritime boundary to its intersection by the outer limit of the exclusive economic zone of Papua New Guinea;

(3) thence generally north-easterly, easterly and south-easterly along that outer limit to its intersection by the Equator;

(4) thence east along the Equator to its intersection by the meridian of Longitude 163 degrees East;

(5) thence north along that meridian to its intersection by the parallel of Latitude 3 degrees North;

(6) thence east along that parallel to its intersection by the meridian of Longitude 171 degrees East;

(7) thence north along that meridian to its intersection by the parallel of Latitude 4 degrees North;

(8) thence east along that parallel to its intersection by the meridian of Longitude 180 degrees East;

(9) thence south along that meridian to its intersection by the Equator;

(10) thence east along the Equator to its intersection by the meridian of Longitude 165 degrees West;

(11) thence north along that meridian to its intersection by the parallel of Latitude 5 degrees 30 minutes North;

(12) thence east along that parallel to its intersection by the meridian of Longitude 154 degrees West;

(13) thence south along that meridian to its intersection by the Equator;

(14) thence east along the Equator to its intersection by the meridian of Longitude 115 degrees West;

(15) thence south along that meridian to its intersection by the parallel of Latitude 60 degrees South;

(16) thence west along that parallel to its intersection by the meridian of Longitude 115 degrees East;

(17) thence north along that meridian to its southernmost intersection by the outer limit of the territorial sea of Australia;

(18) thence generally northerly and easterly along the outer limit of the territorial sea of Australia to its intersection by the meridian of Longitude 136 degrees 45 minutes East;

(19) thence north-easterly along the geodesic to the point of Latitude 10 degrees 50 minutes South, Longitude 139 degrees 12 minutes East;

(20) thence north-easterly along the maritime boundary between Indonesia and Papua New Guinea to where it joins the land border between those two countries;

(21) thence generally northerly along that land border to where it joins the maritime boundary between Indonesia and Papua New Guinea, on the northern coastline of Papua New Guinea; and

(22) thence generally northerly along that boundary to the point of commencement.

B. The areas within the outer limits of the territorial seas of all Australian islands lying westward of the area described in paragraph A and north of Latitude 60 degrees South, provided that any such areas shall cease to be part of the South Pacific Nuclear Free Zone upon receipt by the depositary of written notice from the Government of Australia stating that the areas have become subject to another treaty having an object and purpose substantially the same as that of this Treaty.

(illustrative map not included)

7.35 UNITED NATIONS SECURITY COUNCIL RESOLUTION 687 (CONCERNING THE RESTO-
RATION OF PEACE AND SECURITY IN IRAQ AND KUWAIT). **Adopted at the
2981st mtg., 3 April 1991. UN Doc S/RES/687 (1991);** *reprinted in* **30
ILM 846 (1991) & 2 Weston & Carlson II.D.25**

The Security Council.

Recalling its resolutions 660 (1990) of 2 August 1990, 661 (1990) of 6 August 1990,
662 (1990) of 9 August 1990, 664 (1990) of 18 August 1990, 665 (1990) of 25 August
1990, 666 (1990) of 13 September 1990, 667 (1990) of 16 September 1990, 669 (1990)
of 24 September 1990, 670 (1990) of 25 September 1990, 674 (1990) of 29 October
1990, 677 (1990) of 28 November 1990, 678 (1990) of 29 November 1990 and 686
(1991) of 2 March 1991,

Welcoming the restoration to Kuwait of its sovereignty, independence and territorial integrity and the return of its legitimate Government,

Affirming the commitment of all Member States to the sovereignty, territorial
integrity and political independence of Kuwait and Iraq, and noting the intention
expressed by the Member States cooperating with Kuwait under paragraph 2 of
resolution 678 (1990) to bring their military presence in Iraq to an end as soon as
possible consistent with paragraph 8 of resolution 686 (1991),

Reaffirming the need to be assured to Iraq's peaceful intentions in the light of its
unlawful invasion and occupation of Kuwait,

Taking note of the letter sent by the Minister for Foreign Affairs of Iraq on 27
February 1991 and those sent pursuant to resolution 686 (1991),

Noting that Iraq and Kuwait, as independent sovereign States, signed at Baghdad
on 4 October 1963 "Agreed Minutes Between the State of Kuwait and the Republic of
Iraq Regarding the Restoration of Friendly Relations, Recognition and Related Matters", thereby recognizing formally the boundary between Iraq and Kuwait and the
allocation of islands, which were registered with the United Nations in accordance
with Article 102 of the Charter of the United Nations and in which Iraq recognized the
independence and complete sovereignty of the State of Kuwait within its borders as
specified and accepted in the letter of the Prime Minister of Iraq dated 21 July 1932,
and as accepted by the Ruler of Kuwait in his letter dated 10 August 1932,

Conscious of the need for demarcation of the said boundary,

Conscious also of the statements by Iraq threatening to use weapons in violation
of its obligations under the Geneva Protocol for the Prohibition of the Use of War of
Asphyxiating, Poisonous or Other Gases, and of Bacteriological Methods of Warfare,
signed at Geneva on 17 June 1925, and of its prior use of chemical weapons and
affirming that grave consequences would follow any further use by Iraq of such
weapons,

Recalling that Iraq has subscribed to the Declaration adopted by all States
participating in the Conference of States Parties to the 1925 Geneva Protocol and
Other Interested States, held in Paris from 7 to 11 January 1989, establishing the
objective of universal elimination of chemical and biological weapons,

Recalling also that Iraq has signed the Convention on the Prohibition of the
Development, Production and Stockpiling of Bacteriological (Biological) and Toxin
Weapons and on Their Destruction, of 10 April 1972,

Noting the importance of Iraq ratifying this Convention,

Noting moreover the importance of all States adhering to this Convention and
encouraging its forthcoming Review Conference to reinforce the authority, efficiency
and universal scope of the convention,

Stressing the importance of an early conclusion by the Conference on Disarmament of its work on a Convention on the Universal Prohibition of Chemical Weapons and of universal adherence thereto,

Aware of the use by Iraq of ballistic missiles in unprovoked attacks and therefore of the need to take specific measures in regard to such missiles located in Iraq,

Concerned by the reports in the hands of Member States that Iraq has attempted to acquire materials for a nuclear-weapons programme contrary to its obligations under the Treaty on the Non–Proliferation of Nuclear Weapons of 1 July 1968,

Recalling the objective of the establishment of a nuclear-weapons-free zone in the region of the Middle East,

Conscious of the threat that all weapons of mass destruction pose to peace and security in the area and of the need to work towards the establishment in the Middle East of a zone free of such weapons,

Conscious also of the objective of achieving balanced and comprehensive control of armaments in the region,

Conscious further of the importance of achieving the objectives noted above using all available means, including a dialogue among the States of the region,

Noting that resolution 686 (1991) marked the lifting of the measures imposed by resolution 661 (1990) in so far as they applied to Kuwait,

Noting that despite the progress being made in fulfilling the obligations of resolution 686 (1991), many Kuwait and third country nations are still not accounted for and property remains unreturned,

Recalling the International Convention against the Taking of Hostages, opened for signature at New York on 18 December 1979, which categorizes all acts of taking hostages as manifestations of international terrorism,

Deploring threats made by Iraq during the recent conflict to make use of terrorism against targets outside Iraq and the taking of hostages by Iraq,

Taking note with grave concern of the reports of the Secretary–General of 20 March 1991 and 28 March 1991, and conscious of the necessity to meet urgently the humanitarian needs in Kuwait and Iraq,

Bearing in mind its objective of restoring international peace and security in the area as set out in recent resolutions of the Security Council,

Conscious of the need to take the following measures acting under Chapter VII of the Charter,

1. *Affirms* all thirteen resolutions noted above, except as expressly changed below to achieve the goals of this resolution, including a formal cease-fire;

A

2. *Demands* that Iraq and Kuwait respect the inviolability of the international boundary and the allocation of islands set out in the "Agreed Minutes Between the State of Kuwait and the Republic of Iraq Regarding the Restoration of Friendly Relations, Recognition and Related Matters", signed by them in the exercise of their sovereignty at Baghdad on 4 October 1963 and registered with the United Nations and published by the United Nations in document 7063, United Nations, Treaty Series, 1964;

3. *Calls upon* the Secretary–General to lend his assistance to make arrangements with Iraq and Kuwait to demarcate the boundary between Iraq and Kuwait, drawing on appropriate material, including the map transmitted by Security Council document S/22412 and to report back to the Security Council within one month;

4. *Decides* to guarantee the inviolability of the above-mentioned international boundary and to take as appropriate all necessary measures to that end in accordance with the Charter of the United Nations;

B

5. *Requests* the Secretary–General, after consulting with Iraq and Kuwait, to submit within three days to the Security Council for its approval a plan for the immediate deployment of a United Nations observer unit to monitor the Khor Abdullah and a demilitarized zone, which is hereby established, extending ten kilometres into Iraq and five kilometres into Kuwait from the boundary referred to in the "Agreed Minutes Between the State of Kuwait and the Republic of Iraq Regarding the Restoration of Friendly Relations, Recognition and Related Matters" of 4 October 1963; to deter violations of the boundary through its presence in and surveillance of the demilitarized zone; to observe any hostile or potentially hostile action mounted from the territory of one State to the other; and for the Secretary–General to report regularly to the Security Council on the operations of the unit, and immediately if there are serious violations of the zone or potential threats to peace;

6. *Notes* that as soon as the Secretary–General notifies the Security Council of the completion of the deployment of the United Nations observer unit, the conditions will be established for the Member States cooperating with Kuwait in accordance with resolution 678 (1990) to bring their military presence in Iraq to an end consistent with resolution 686 (1991);

C

7. *Invites* Iraq to reaffirm unconditionally its obligations under the Geneva Protocol for the Prohibition of the Use in War of Asphyxiating, Poisonous or Other Gases, and of Bacteriological Methods of Warfare, signed at Geneva on 17 June 1925, and to ratify the Convention on the Prohibition of the Development, Production and Stockpiling of Bacteriological (Biological) and Toxin Weapons and on Their Destruction, of 10 April 1972;

8. *Decides* that Iraq shall unconditionally accept the destruction, removal, or rendering harmless, under international supervision, of:

(a) All chemical and biological weapons and all stocks of agents and all related subsystems and components and all research, development, support and manufacturing facilities;

(b) All ballistic missiles with range greater than 150 kilometres and related major parts, and repair and production facilities;

9. *Decides,* for the implementation of paragraph 8 above, the following:

(a) Iraq shall submit to the Secretary–General, within fifteen days of the adoption of the present resolution, a declaration of the locations, amounts and types of all items specified in paragraph 8 and agree to urgent, on-site inspection as specified below;

(b) The Secretary–General, in consultation with the appropriate Governments and, where appropriate, with the Director–General of the World Health Organization, within forty-five days of the passage of the present resolution, shall develop, and submit to the Council for approval, a plan calling for the completion of the following acts within forty-five days of such approval:

(i) The forming of a Special Commission, which shall carry out immediate on-site inspection of Iraq's biological, chemical and missile capabilities, based on Iraq's declarations and the designation of any additional locations by the Special Commission itself;

(ii) The yielding by Iraq of possession to the Special Commission for destruction, removal or rendering harmless, taking into account the requirements of public safety, of all items specified under paragraph 8(a) above, including items at the additional locations designated by the Special Commission under paragraph 9(b)(i) above and the destruction by Iraq, under the supervision of the Special Commission, of all its missile capabilities, including launchers, as specified under paragraph 8(b) above;

(iii) The provision by the Special Commission of the assistance and cooperation to the Director–General of the International Atomic Energy Agency required in paragraphs 12 and 13 below;

10. *Decides* that Iraq shall unconditionally undertake not to use, develop, construct or acquire any of the items specified in paragraphs 8 and 9 above and requests the Secretary–General, in consultation with the Special Commission, to develop a plan for the future ongoing monitoring and verification of Iraq's compliance with this paragraph, to be submitted to the Security Council for approval within one hundred and twenty days of the passage of this resolution;

11. *Invites* Iraq to reaffirm unconditionally its obligations under the Treaty on the Non–Proliferation of Nuclear Weapons of 1 July 1968;

12. *Decides* that Iraq shall unconditionally agree not to acquire or develop nuclear weapons or nuclear-weapons-usable material or any subsystems or components or any research, development, support or manufacturing facilities related to the above; to submit to the Secretary–General and the Director–General of the International Atomic Energy Agency within fifteen days of the adoption of the present resolution a declaration of the locations, amounts, and types of all items specified above; to place all of its nuclear-weapons-usable materials under the exclusive control, for custody and removal, of the International Atomic Energy Agency, with the assistance and cooperation of the Special Commission as provided for in the plan of the Secretary–General discussed in paragraph 9(b) above; to accept, in accordance with the arrangements provided for in paragraph 13 below, urgent on-site inspection and the destruction, removal or rendering harmless as appropriate of all items specified above; and to accept the plan discussed in paragraph 13 below for the future ongoing monitoring and verification of its compliance with these undertakings;

13. *Requests* the Director–General of the International Atomic Energy Agency, through the Secretary–General, with the assistance and cooperation of the Special Commission as provided for in the plan of the Secretary–General in paragraph 9(b) above, to carry out immediate on-site inspection of Iraq's nuclear capabilities based on Iraq's declarations and the designation of any additional locations by the Special Commission; to develop a plan for submission to the Security Council within forty-five days calling for the destruction, removal, or rendering harmless as appropriate of all items listed in paragraph 12 above; to carry out the plan within forty-five days following approval by the Security Council; and to develop a plan, taking into account the rights and obligations of Iraq under the Treaty on the Non–Proliferation of Nuclear Weapons of 1 July 1968, for the future ongoing monitoring and verification of Iraq's compliance with paragraph 12 above, including an inventory of all nuclear material in Iraq subject to the Agency's verification and inspections to confirm that Agency safeguards cover all relevant nuclear activities in Iraq, to be submitted to the Security Council for approval within one hundred and twenty days of the passage of the present resolution;

14. *Takes note* that the actions to be taken by Iraq in paragraphs 8, 9, 10, 11, 12 and 13 of the present resolution represent steps towards the goal of establishing in the Middle East a zone free from weapons of mass destruction and all missiles for their delivery and the objective of a global ban on chemical weapons;

D

15. *Requests* the Secretary–General to report to the Security Council on the steps taken to facilitate the return of all Kuwait property seized by Iraq, including a list of any property that Kuwait claims has not been returned or which has not been returned intact;

E

16. *Reaffirms* that Iraq, without prejudice to the debts and obligations of Iraq arising prior to 2 August 1990, which will be addressed through the normal mechanisms, is liable under international law for any direct loss, damage, including environmental damage and the depletion of natural resources, or injury to foreign Governments, nationals and corporations, as a result of Iraq's unlawful invasion and occupation of Kuwait;

17. *Decides* that all Iraqi statements made since 2 August 1990 repudiating its foreign debt are null and void, and demands that Iraq adhere scrupulously to all of its obligations concerning servicing and repayment of its foreign debt;

18. *Decides* also to create a fund to pay compensation for claims that fall within paragraph 16 above and to establish a Commission that will administer the fund;

19. *Directs* the Secretary–General to develop and present to the Security Council for decision, no later than thirty days following the adoption of the present resolution, recommendations for the fund to meet the requirement for the payment of claims established in accordance with paragraph 18 above and for a programme to implement the decisions in paragraphs 16, 17 and 18 above, including: administration of the fund; mechanisms for determining the appropriate level of Iraq's contribution to the fund based on a percentage of the value of the exports of petroleum and petroleum products from Iraq not to exceed a figure to be suggested to the Council by the Secretary–General, taking into account the requirements of the people of Iraq, Iraq's payment capacity as assessed in conjunction with the international financial institutions taking into consideration external debt service, and the needs of the Iraqi economy; arrangements for ensuring that payments are made to the fund; the process by which funds will be allocated and claims paid; appropriate procedures for evaluating losses, listing claims and verifying their validity and resolving disputed claims in respect of Iraq's liability as specified in paragraph 16 above; and the composition of the Commission designated above;

F

20. *Decides,* effective immediately, that the prohibition against the sale or supply to Iraq of commodities or products, other than medicine and health supplies, and prohibitions against financial transactions related thereto contained in resolution 661 (1990) shall not apply to foodstuffs notified to the Security Council Committee established by resolution 661 (1990) concerning the situations between Iraq and Kuwait or, with the approval of that Committee, under the simplified and accelerated "no-objection" procedure, to materials and supplies for essential civilian needs as identified in the report of the Secretary–General dated essential civilian needs as identified in the report of the Secretary–General dated 20 March 1991, and in any further findings of humanitarian need by the Committee;

21. *Decides* that the Security Council shall review the provisions of paragraph 20 above every sixty days in the light of the policies and practices of the Government of Iraq, including the implementation of all relevant resolutions of the Security Council, for the purpose of determining whether to reduce or lift the prohibitions referred to therein;

22. *Decides* that upon the approval by the Security Council of the programme called for in paragraph 19 above and upon Council agreement that Iraq has completed all actions contemplated in paragraphs 8, 9, 10, 11, 12 and 13 above, the prohibitions against the import of commodities and products originating in Iraq and the prohibitions against financial transactions related thereto contained in resolution 661 (1990) shall have no further force or effect;

23. *Decides* that, pending action by the Security Council under paragraph 22 above, the Security Council Committee established by resolution 661 (1990) shall be empowered to approve, when required to assure adequate financial resources on the part of Iraq to carry out the activities under paragraph 20 above, exceptions to the prohibition against the import of commodities and products originating in Iraq;

24. *Decides* that, in accordance with resolution 661 (1990) and subsequent related resolutions and until a further decision is taken by the Security Council, all States shall continue to prevent the sale or supply, or the promotion or facilitation of such sale or supply, to Iraq by their nationals, or from their territories or using their flag vessels or aircraft, of:

   (a) Arms and related *materiel* of all types, specifically including the sale or transfer through other means of all forms of conventional military equipment, including for paramilitary forces, and spare parts and components and their means of production, for such equipment;

   (b) Items specified and defined in paragraphs 8 and 12 above not otherwise covered above;

   (c) Technology under licensing or other transfer arrangements used in the production, utilization or stockpiling of items specified in subparagraphs (a) and (b) above;

   (d) Personnel or materials for training or technical support services relating to the design, development, manufacture, use, maintenance or support of items specified in subparagraphs (a) and (b) above;

25. *Calls upon* all States and international organizations to act strictly in accordance with paragraph 24 above, notwithstanding the existence of any contracts, agreements, licences or any other arrangements;

26. *Requests* the Secretary–General, in consultation with appropriate Governments, to develop within sixty days, for the approval of the Security Council, guidelines to facilitate full international implementation of paragraphs 24 and 25 above and paragraph 27 below, and to make them available to all States and to establish procedure for updating these guidelines periodically;

27. *Calls upon* all states to maintain such national controls and procedures and to take such other actions consistent with the guidelines to be established by the Security Council under paragraph 26 above as may be necessary to ensure compliance with the terms of paragraph 24 above, and calls upon international organizations to take all appropriate steps to assist in ensuring such full compliance;

28. *Agrees* to review its decisions in paragraphs 22, 23, 24 and 25 above, except for the items specified and defined in paragraphs 8 and 12 above, on a regular basis and in any case one hundred and twenty days following passage of the present resolution, taking into account Iraq's compliance with the resolution and general progress towards the control of armaments in the region;

29. *Decides* that all States, including Iraq, shall take the necessary measures to ensure that no claim shall lie at the instance of the Government of Iraq, or of any person or body in Iraq, or of any person claiming through or for the benefit of any such person or body, in connection with any contract or other transaction where its

performance was affected by reason of the measures taken by the Security Council in resolution 661 (1990) and related resolutions;

G

30. *Decides* that, in furtherance of its commitment to facilitate the repatriation of all Kuwaiti and third country national, Iraq shall extend all necessary cooperation to the International Committee of the Red Cross, providing lists of such persons, facilitating the access of the International Committee of the Red Cross to all such persons wherever located or detained and facilitating the search by the International Committee of the Red Cross for those Kuwaiti and third country nationals still unaccounted for;

31. *Invites* the International Committee of the Red Cross to keep the Secretary–General apprised as appropriate of all activities undertaken in connection with facilitating the repatriation or return of all Kuwaiti and third country nationals or their remains present in Iraq on or after 2 August 1990;

H

32. *Requires* Iraq to inform the Security Council that it will not commit or support any act of international terrorism or allow any organization directed towards commission of such acts to operate within its territory and to condemn unequivocally and renounce all acts, methods and practices of terrorism;

I

33. *Declares* that, upon official notification by Iraq to the Secretary–General and to the Security Council of its acceptance of the provisions above, a formal cease-fire is effective between Iraq and Kuwait and the Member States cooperating with Kuwait in accordance with resolution 678 (1990);

34. *Decides* to remain seized of the matter and to take such further steps as may be required for the implementation of the present resolution and to secure peace and security in the area.

7.36 INTERNATIONAL CONVENTION FOR THE SUPPRESSION OF ACTS OF NUCLEAR TERROR-ISM. **Adopted at New York, 13 April 2005. Entered into force, 7 July 2007. 2445 UNTS 89:** *Articles 1–4, 9–11, 14–16, 23*

Article 1

For the purposes of this Convention:

1. "Radioactive material" means nuclear material and other radioactive substances which contain nuclides which undergo spontaneous disintegration (a process accompanied by emission of one or more types of ionizing radiation, such as alpha-, beta-, neutron particles and gamma rays) and which may, owing to their radiological or fissile properties, cause death, serious bodily injury or substantial damage to property or to the environment.

* * *

3. "Nuclear facility" means:

(*a*) Any nuclear reactor, including reactors installed on vessels, vehicles, aircraft or space objects for use as an energy source in order to propel such vessels, vehicles, aircraft or space objects or for any other purpose;

(*b*) Any plant or conveyance being used for the production, storage, processing or transport of radioactive material.

* * *

5. "State or government facility" includes any permanent or temporary facility or conveyance that is used or occupied by representatives of a State, members of a Government, the legislature or the judiciary or by officials or employees of a State or any other public authority or entity or by employees or officials of an intergovernmental organization in connection with their official duties.

6. "Military forces of a State" means the armed forces of a State which are organized, trained and equipped under its internal law for the primary purpose of national defence or security and persons acting in support of those armed forces who are under their formal command, control and responsibility.

Article 2

1. Any person commits an offence within the meaning of this Convention if that person unlawfully and intentionally:

* * *

(*b*) Uses in any way radioactive material or a device, or uses or damages a nuclear facility in a manner which releases or risks the release of radioactive material:

(i) With the intent to cause death or serious bodily injury; or

(ii) With the intent to cause substantial damage to property or to the environment; or

(iii) With the intent to compel a natural or legal person, an international organization or a State to do or refrain from doing an act.

* * *

4. Any person also commits an offence if that person:

(*a*) Participates as an accomplice in an offence as set forth in paragraph 1, 2 or 3 of the present article; or

(*b*) Organizes or directs others to commit an offence as set forth in paragraph 1, 2 or 3 of the present article; or

(c) In any other way contributes to the commission of one or more offences as set forth in paragraph 1, 2 or 3 of the present article by a group of persons acting with a common purpose; such contribution shall be intentional and either be made with the aim of furthering the general criminal activity or purpose of the group or be made in the knowledge of the intention of the group to commit the offence or offences concerned.

Article 3

This Convention shall not apply where the offence is committed within a single State, the alleged offender and the victims are nationals of that State, the alleged offender is found in the territory of that State and no other State has a basis under article 9, paragraph 1 or 2, to exercise jurisdiction, except that the provisions of articles 7, 12, 14, 15, 16 and 17 shall, as appropriate, apply in those cases.

Article 4

1. Nothing in this Convention shall affect other rights, obligations and responsibilities of States and individuals under international law, in particular the purposes and principles of the Charter of the United Nations and international humanitarian law.

2. The activities of armed forces during an armed conflict, as those terms are understood under international humanitarian law, which are governed by that law are not governed by this Convention, and the activities undertaken by military forces of a State in the exercise of their official duties, inasmuch as they are governed by other rules of international law, are not governed by this Convention.

3. The provisions of paragraph 2 of the present article shall not be interpreted as condoning or making lawful otherwise unlawful acts, or precluding prosecution under other laws.

4. This Convention does not address, nor can it be interpreted as addressing, in any way, the issue of the legality of the use or threat of use of nuclear weapons by States.

* * *

Article 9

1. Each State Party shall take such measures as may be necessary to establish its jurisdiction over the offences set forth in article 2 when:

(a) The offence is committed in the territory of that State; or

(b) The offence is committed on board a vessel flying the flag of that State or an aircraft which is registered under the laws of that State at the time the offence is committed; or

(c) The offence is committed by a national of that State.

2. A State Party may also establish its jurisdiction over any such offence when:

(a) The offence is committed against a national of that State; or

(b) The offence is committed against a State or government facility of that State abroad, including an embassy or other diplomatic or consular premises of that State; or

(c) The offence is committed by a stateless person who has his or her habitual residence in the territory of that State; or

(d) The offence is committed in an attempt to compel that State to do or abstain from doing any act; or (*e*) The offence is committed on board an aircraft which is operated by the Government of that State.

* * *

Article 10

1. Upon receiving information that an offence set forth in article 2 has been committed or is being committed in the territory of a State Party or that a person who has committed or who is alleged to have committed such an offence may be present in its territory, the State Party concerned shall take such measures as may be necessary under its national law to investigate the facts contained in the information.

2. Upon being satisfied that the circumstances so warrant, the State Party in whose territory the offender or alleged offender is present shall take the appropriate measures under its national law so as to ensure that person's presence for the purpose of prosecution or extradition.

* * *

6. When a State Party, pursuant to the present article, has taken a person into custody, it shall immediately notify, directly or through the Secretary–General of the United Nations, the State s Parties which have established jurisdiction in accordance with article 9, paragraphs 1 and 2, and, if it considers it advisable, any other interested States Parties, of the fact that that person is in custody and of the circumstances which warrant that person's detention. The State which makes the investigation contemplated in paragraph 1 of the present article shall promptly inform the said States Parties of its findings and shall indicate whether it intends to exercise jurisdiction.

Article 11

1. The State Party in the territory of which the alleged offender is present shall, in cases to which article 9 applies, if it does not extradite that person, be obliged, without exception whatsoever and whether or not the offence was committed in its territory, to submit the case without undue delay to its competent authorities for the purpose of prosecution, through proceedings in accordance with the laws of that State. Those authorities shall take their decision in the same manner as in the case of any other of fence of a grave nature under the law of that State.

2. Whenever a State Party is permitted under its national law to extradite or otherwise surrender one of its nationals only upon the condition that the person will be returned to that State to serve the sentence imposed as a result of the trial or proceeding for which the extradition or surrender of the person was sought, and this State and the State seeking the extradition of the person agree with this option and other terms they may deem appropriate, such a conditional extradition or surrender shall be sufficient to discharge the obligation set forth in paragraph 1 of the present article.

* * *

Article 14

1. States Parties shall afford one another the greatest measure of assistance in connection with investigations or criminal or extradition proceedings brought in respect of the offences set forth in article 2, including assistance in obtaining evidence at their disposal necessary for the proceedings.

2. States Parties shall carry out their obligations under paragraph 1 of the present article in conformity with any treaties or other arrangements on mutual legal assistance that may exist between them. In the absence of such treaties or arrange-

ments, States Parties shall afford one another assistance in accordance with their national law.

Article 15

None of the offences set forth in article 2 shall be regarded, for the purposes of extradition or mutual legal assistance, as a political offence or as an offence connected with a political offence or as an offence inspired by political motives. Accordingly, a request for extradition or for mutual legal assistance based on such an offence may not be refused on the sole ground that it concerns a political offence or an offence connected with a political offence or an offence inspired by political motives.

Article 16

Nothing in this Convention shall be interpreted as imposing an obligation to extradite or to afford mutual legal assistance if the requested State Party has substantial grounds for believing that the request for extradition for offences set forth in article 2 or for mutual legal assistance with respect to such offences has been made for the purpose of prosecuting or punishing a person on account of that person's race, religion, nationality, ethnic origin or political opinion or that compliance with the request would cause prejudice to that person's position for any of these reasons.

* * *

Article 23

1. Any dispute between two or more States Parties concerning the interpretation or application of this Convention which cannot be settled through negotiation within a reasonable time shall, at the request of one of them, be submitted to arbitration. If, within six months of the date of the request for arbitration, the parties are unable to agree on the organization of the arbitration, any one of those parties may refer the dispute to the International Court of Justice, by application, in conformity with the Statute of the Court.

2. Each State may, at the time of signature, ratification, acceptance or approval of this Convent ion or accession thereto, declare that it does not consider itself bound by paragraph 1 of the present article. The other States Parties shall not be bound by paragraph 1 with respect to any State Party which has made such a reservation.

3. Any State which has made a reservation in accordance with paragraph 2 of the present article may at any time withdraw that reservation by notification to the Secretary–General of the United Nations.

Part 8. Arbitral/Judicial Decisions

8.1 Bering Sea Fur Seals Arbitration (GB v. US). 1 Moore's Int'l Arb. Awards 755 (1893)

[*Eds.*—After acquiring the Alaska territory by purchase from Russia in 1867, the United States adopted legislation aimed at protecting populations of fur-bearing animals, including fur-seals, from over-exploitation. Acting pursuant to this legislation, the U.S. seized several British vessels that were engaged in the hunting and killing of seals on the high seas, at least 60 miles from the nearest U.S.-owned land. The seals being hunted by the British vessels were known to make their home on the Pribolof Islands, within US territory, and the evidence suggested that pelagic sealing by the British and others was decimating the seal herd.

Britain protested the seizures and, after a long period of negotiation, the two countries agreed to submit the dispute to arbitration.

Five specific questions were submitted for arbitration. The following excerpts concern the fifth and final question: whether the United States had "any right, and, if so, what right, of protection or property in the fur-seals frequenting the islands of the United States in Behring Sea when such seals are found outside the ordinary 3–mile limit?"]

Excerpts from the Written Argument of the United States[a]

The controversy to be determined arises between two different nations, and it has been submitted to the judgment of a tribunal composed, in part, of the citizens of several other nations. It is immediately obvious that it must be adjudged upon principles and rules which both nations and all the Arbitrators alike acknowledge; that is to say, those which are dictated by that *general standard of justice* upon which civilized nations are agreed; and this is *international law*. Just as, in municipal societies, municipal law, aside from legislative enactments, is to be found in the general standard of justice which is acknowledged by the members of each particular state, so, in the larger society of nations, international law is to be found in the general standard of justice acknowledged by the members of that society....

* * *

Some writers have been inclined to question the propriety of designating as law that body of principles and rules which it is asserted are binding upon nations, for the reason that there is no common superior power which may be appealed to for their enforcement. But this is a superficial view.... The public opinion of the civilized world is a power to which all nations are forced to submit. No nation can afford to take up arms in defence of an assertion which is pronounced by that opinion to be erroneous....

* * *

[A]lthough the actual practice and usages of nations are the best evidence of what is agreed upon as the law of nations, it is not the only evidence. These prove what nations have *in fact* agreed to as binding law. But, in the absence of evidence to the contrary, nations are to be *presumed* to agree upon what natural and universal justice dictates. It is upon the basis of this presumption that municipal law is from time to time developed and enlarged by the decisions of judicial tribunals and jurists which make up the unwritten municipal jurisprudence. Sovereign states are presumed to

---

a. IX Fur Seal Arbitration 2–8 (Washington: Government Printing Office 1895).

have sanctioned as law the general principles of justice, and this constitutes the authority of municipal tribunals to declare the law in cases where legislation is silent.... So also in international law, if a case arises for which the practice and usages of nations have furnished no rule, an international tribunal like the present is not to infer that no rule exists. The consent of nations is to be presumed in favor of the dictates of natural justice, and that source never fails to supply a rule....

* * *

The [United States position] is that the United States have, by reason of the nature and habits of the seals and their ownership of the breeding grounds to which the herds resort ... a property interest in those herds as well while they are in the high seas its upon the land.

* * *

The position taken on the part of Great Britain is [that the seals] do not belong to any nation or to any men; that they are *res communes*, or, *res nullius*; in other words, that they are *not the subject* of property, and are consequently open to pursuit and capture on the high seas by the citizens of any nation. This position is based upon the assertion that they belong to the class of wild animals, animals, *feræ naturæ*, and that these are not the subject of ownership....

* * *

Inasmuch as the present controversy upon this point is one between nations, ... [t]he rule of decision must be found in international law.... But the question whether a particular thing is the subject of property, as between nations, is substantially the same as the question whether the same thing is property as between individuals in a particular nation. Now, it so happens that ... the municipal jurisprudence of all nations, proceeding upon the law of nature, is everywhere in substantial accord upon the question what things are the subject of property. That jurisprudence, therefore, so far as it is consentaneous, may be invoked in this controversy, as directly evidencing the law of nature, and, therefore, of nations.

* * *

[T]he *essential facts* which, according to [the] doctrines [of municipal law], render animals commonly designated as wild, the subjects of property not only while in the actual custody of their masters but also when temporarily absent therefrom, are that the *care and industry of man* acting upon a *natural disposition* of the animals to *return* to a place of wonted resort, secures their *voluntary* and *habitual return to his custody* and *power,* so as to enable him to *deal with them in a similar manner,* and to obtain from them *similar benefits,* as in the case of *domestic* animals. They are thus for all the purposes of *property* assimilated to domestic animals. It is the *nature and habits* of the animal, which enable man, by the practice of *art, care, and industry,* to bring about these *useful results* that constitute the foundation upon which the law makes its award of property, and extends to this product of human industry the protection of owner- ship. This species of property is well described as property *per industriam.*

The Alaskan fur-seals are a typical instance for the application of this doctrine. They are by the imperious and unchangeable instincts of their nature impelled to return from their wanderings to the *same place;* they are defenseless against man, and in returning to the same place voluntarily subject themselves to his power, and enable him to treat them in the same way and to obtain from them the same benefits as maybe had in the case of domestic animals. They thus become the subjects of ordinary husbandry as much as sheep or any other cattle. All that is needed to secure this return, is the exercise of care and industry on the part of the human owner of the place of resort. He must *abstain* from billing or repelling them when they seek to return to it, and must invite and cherish such return. He must defend them against all enemies by land or sea. And in making his selections for slaughter, he must disturb them as little as possible and take *males* only. All these conditions are perfectly supplied by the United States, and their title is thus fully substantiated.

* * *

[The United States then proceeded to argue that the fundamental principles supporting the institution of private property justified a conclusion of U.S. ownership in this situation. In particular, the U.S. argued that the institution of private property served to preserve social "order and peace" by satisfying the "desire of human nature for exclusive ownership" and that property ownership encouraged the "progress and advancement" of society by encouraging individual effort through the reward of ownership of what is produced. But, said the U.S., these principles make clear that ownership is only for social purposes and property is ultimately held in trust for all—that fact—that property is an institution created by the law of nature to serve social purposes—was especially salient in supporting its claim to the ownership of the seals.]

* * *

But what is the extent of the dominion which is thus given by the law of nature to the owner of property? This question has much importance in the present discussion and deserves deliberate consideration.

* * *

First. No possessor of property, whether an individual man, or a nation, has an absolute title to it. His title is coupled with a trust for the benefit of mankind.

Second. The title is further limited. The things themselves are not given him, but only the *usufruct* or *increase*. He is but the custodian of the stock, or principal thing, holding it in trust for the present and future generations of man.

The first of these propositions is stated almost in the language employed by one of the highest authorities on the law of nature and nations. Says Puffendorf, "God gave the world, not to this, nor to that man, but to the human race in general." The bounties of nature are gifts not so much to those whose situation enables them to gather them, but to those who need them for *use*. And Locke, "God gave the world to men in common." If it be asked how this gift in common can be reconciled with the exclusive possession which the institution of property gives to particular nations and particular men, the answer is by the instrumentality of commerce which springs into existence with the beginnings of civilization as a part of the order of nature. . . . Every bounty of nature, however it may be gathered by this, or that man, will eventually find its way, through the instrumentality of commerce, to those who want it for its inherent qualities. . . . But for commerce, and the exchanges effected by it, the greatest part of the wealth of the world would be wasted, or unimproved. . . .

[I]t follows that, by the law of nature, every nation, so far as it possesses the fruits of the earth in a measure more than sufficient to satisfy its own needs, is, in the truest sense, a *trustee* of the surplus for the benefit of those in other parts of the world who need them, and are willing to give in exchange for them the products of their own labor; and the truth of this conclusion and of the views from which it is drawn will be found fully confirmed by a glance at the approved usages of nations. . . . [C]ommerce is obligatory upon all nations; . . . no nation is permitted to seclude itself from the rest of mankind and interdict all commerce with foreign nations. Temporary prohibition of commerce for special reasons of necessity are, indeed, allowed; but they must not be made permanent.

. . . The instances in history are rare in which nations have exhibited unwillingness to engage in commercial intercourse; but they . . . have sometimes actually occurred. Such a refusal is generally believed to have been the real, though it was not the avowed, cause of the war waged by Great Britain against China in 1840.

For the purposes of further illustration, ... [l]et it be supposed that some particular region from which alone a commodity deemed necessary by man everywhere, such as Peruvian bark, could be procured, was within the exclusive dominion of a particular power, and that it should absolutely prohibit the exportation of the commodity; could there be any well-founded doubt that other nations would be justified, under the law of nature, in compelling that nation by arms to permit free commerce in such commodity?

And this trust, of which we are speaking, is not limited to that surplus of a nation's production which is not needed for its own wants, but extends to its means and capabilities for production. No nation has, by the law of nature, a right to destroy its sources and means of production or leave them unimproved. None has the right to convert any portion of the earth into a waste or desolation, or to permit any part which may be made fruitful to remain a waste. To destroy the source from which any human blessing flows is not merely an error, it is a *crime*. And the wrong is not limited by the boundaries of nations, but is inflicted upon those to whom the blessing would be useful wherever they may dwell. And those to whom the wrong is done have the right to redress it.

Let the case of the article of India rubber be ... taken for an illustration, and let it be supposed that the nation which held the fields from which the world obtained its chief supply should destroy its plantations and refuse to continue the cultivation, can it be doubted that other nations would, by the law of nature, be justified in taking possession by force of the territory of the recreant Power and establishing over it a governmental authority which would assure a continuance of the cultivation? And what would this be but a removal of the unfaithful trustee, and the appointment of one who would perform the trust?

It is, indeed, upon this ground, and this ground alone, that the conquest by civilized nations of countries occupied by savages has been, or can be, defended. The great nations of Europe took possession by force and divided among themselves the great continents of North and South America. Great Britain has incorporated into her extensive empire vast territories in India, and Australia by force, and against the will of their original inhabitants. She is now, with France and Germany as rivals, endeavoring to establish and extend her dominion in the savage regions of Africa. The United States, from time to time, expel the native tribes of Indians from their homes to make room for their own people. These acts of the most civilized, and Christian nations are inexcusable robberies, unless they can be defended, under the law of nature, by the argument that these uncivilized countries were the gifts of nature to man, and that their inhabitants refused, or were unable, to perform that great trust, imposed upon all nations, to make the capabilities of the countries which they hold subservient to the needs of man. And this argument is a sufficient defense, not indeed for the thousand excesses which have stained these conquests, but for the conquests themselves.

The second proposition above advanced, namely, that the title which nature bestows upon man to her gifts is of the *usufruct* only, is, indeed, but a corollary from that which has just been discussed, or rather a part of it, for in saying that the gift is not to this nation or that, but to mankind, all generations, future as well as present, are intended. The earth was designed as the permanent abode of man through ceaseless generations. Each generation, as it appears upon the scene, is entitled only to use the fair inheritance. It is against the law of nature that any waste should be committed to the disadvantage of the succeeding tenants. . . .

The obligation not to invade the stock of the provision made by nature for the support of human life is in an especial manner imposed upon *civilized* societies; for the danger proceeds almost wholly from them. It is commerce, the fruit of civilization, and which at the same time extends and advances it, that subjects the production of each part of the globe to the demands of every other part, and thus threatens, unless the tendency is counteracted by efficient husbandry, to encroach upon the sources of supply.... [W]ith the advance of civilization, the increase in population, and the multiplication of wants, a peril of overconsumption arises, and along with it a development of that prudential wisdom which seeks to avert the danger.

The great and principal instrumentality designed to counteract this threatening tendency is the institution of *private individual property,* which, by holding out to every man the promise that he shall have the exclusive possession and enjoyment of any increase in the products of nature which he may effect by his care, labor, and abstinence, brings into play the powerful motive of self-interest, stimulates the exertion in every direction of all his faculties, both of mind and body, and thus leads to a prodigiously increased production of the fruits of the earth.

* * *

The inquiry which has thus been prosecuted into the grounds and reasons upon which the institution of property stands fully substantiates, it is believed, the main proposition with which it began, namely, *that where any useful animals so far subject themselves to the control of particular anew as to enable them exclusively to cultivate such animals and obtain the annual increase for the supply of human wants, and at the sane time to preserve the stock, they have a property interest in them.* And this conclusion, deducible from the broad and general doctrines of the law of nature, is confirmed by the actual fact as exhibited in the usages and laws of all civilized states. Wherever a useful animal exhibits in its nature and habits this quality, it must be denominated and treated as the subject of property and as well between nations as between individual men....

In the added light thrown by this inquiry into the foundations of the institution of property the case of the fur-seal can be no longer open to doubt, if it ever was. It is a typical instance. Polygamous in its nature, compelled to breed upon the land, and confined to that element for half the year, gentle and confiding in disposition, nearly defenceless against attack, it seems almost to implore the protection of man, and to offer to him as a reward that superfluity of increase which is not needed for the continuance of the race. Its own habits go very far to effect a separation of this superfluity, leaving little to be done by man to make it complete. The selections for slaughter are easily made without disturbance or injury to the herd. The return of the herd to the same spot to submit to renewed drafts is assured by the most imperious instincts and necessities of the animal's nature. During the entire period of all absences the *animus revertendi* is ever present. The conditions are, as observed by the eminent naturalist, Prof. Huxley, *ideal.* All that is needed to make the full extent of the blessing to mankind available is the exercise on the one hand of care, self-denial, and industry on the part of man at the breeding places, and, on the other, exemption from the destructive pursuit at sea. The first requisite is supplied. A rich reward is offered for, and will certainly assure, the exercise of art and industry upon the land. All that is demanded from the from the law is that exemption from destructive pursuit on the sea which the award of a property interest will insure.

* * *

Excerpts from the Arbitral Award

... We, the said Baron de Courcel, Lord Hannen, Sir John Thompson, Marquis Visconti Venosta and Mr. Gregers Gram, being a majority of the said arbitrators, do decide and determine that the United States has not any right of protection or property in the fur-seals frequenting the islands of the United States in Behring Sea, when such seals are found outside the ordinary three-mile limit.

Excerpt From Comments of Alphonse de Courcel, President of the Tribunal

We have felt obliged to maintain intact the fundamental principles of that august law of nations, which extends itself like the vault of heaven above all countries, and which borrows the laws of nature herself to protect the peoples of the earth, one against another, by inculcating in them the dictates of mutual goodwill.

Excerpt From Comments of Senator Morgan

[Justice Harlan] and I [the arbitrators appointed by the United States] concurred in the view that the treaty [for arbitration of this case] presented [the question of the right of the U.S. to protect the seals] in its broadest aspect [including the question of the equity of the situation]. Our honorable colleagues, however, did not so construe the scope of the duty prescribed to the Tribunal by the treaty. They considered that these questions of the right of property and protection in respect to the fur-seals were to be decided upon the existing state of the law, and, finding no existing precedent in the international law, they did not feel warranted in creating one.

As the rights claimed by the United States could only be supported by international law, in their estimation, and inasmuch as that law is silent on the subject, they felt that under the treaty they could find no legal foundation for the rights claimed that extended beyond the limits of the territorial jurisdiction of the United States.

Excerpts From Separate Opinion of Mr. Justice Harlan

The only possible objection that can be urged against the claim of ownership of these fur seal animals by the United States is the general rule that animals *ferae naturae* are not subject to individual ownership. But ... an exception to this rule ... is everywhere recognized, which admits of individual ownership of useful wild animals, the supply of which is limited, and which, by reason of their nature and habits, and the control or power which man may acquire over them, are susceptible of ownership, that is, are capable of exclusive appropriation. All of these conditions are fulfilled in the case of the Pribilof fur seals. It is not denied that they are useful animals, or that the supply is limited. The experience of the past proves that the race can be easily exterminated if man is allowed to hunt and slaughter them wherever they may be found, on the land or in the high seas. It is equally beyond dispute that they may be exclusively appropriated, because they come, at stated periods, to the islands of the United States, where they remain under such control that the increase can be obtained for the benefit of the world without any injurious diminution of the stock.

The reason why the doctrines to which I have adverted have been taught more directly and fully in municipal jurisprudence [than in international law] is that questions of property more frequently arise between individuals.... [But] where the same grounds and reasons exist for the recognition of property, as between nations, that are found in ... municipal law, [the writers on international law] have conceded national ownership. Illustrations of this rule are the cases of pearl and other oyster beds, coral reefs, etc., situated on the sea outside of territorial waters, in some instances thirty or more miles. These gifts of nature are exhaustible, and would be soon exhausted if treated as *res nullius*, and left open to the indiscriminate enjoyment of the people of all nations. They cannot well be enjoyed unless they are under particular control, so that the product may be taken at the right season and in limited amounts. In other words, they require that sort of care, restraint, and self-denial which is induced only by a recognition of property in those who bestow such care, and practice such restraint and self-denial.

* * *

That the United States, by its ownership of Pribilof Islands, is in a condition to reap the benefit of these animals, and preserve the race, and that no other nation, by any action it may alone take, can accomplish these beneficial results, and that the preservation of the race does not admit of their being taken at any other place than at their breeding grounds, are conclusive reasons why the law should recognize its claim of property.

* * *

If the claim of the United States to own these fur seals rests, in law, upon a sound foundation, the next inquiry is whether it may protect is property? There can be but one answer to this question.... No one questions its right to afford protection ... while the seals are on its islands, and while they are within territorial waters. That right—if the United States *owns* the seals—is not lost while they are temporarily absent in the high seas....

[Do British citizens have a right to hunt these animals on the high seas, free of interference from the United States?] [N]o individual can be said to have a *right*, under international law, to *exterminate a race* of valuable animals, for the sake simply of the temporary profit realized from such practices....

* * *

[T]he mind instantly recoils from the suggestion that [the destruction of these animals, for temporary gain, by methods that are inhuman and barbarous, and which will surely result in the speedy extermination of the entire race is] in the exercise of a *right* protected by the law of nations, and must be submitted to by the United States....

* * *

With entire truth, therefore, it may be said that the extermination of this race of animals by the destructive methods of pelagic sealing, involving necessarily the killing in vast numbers of female seals heavy with young or nursing their pups, or impregnated, is a crime against the law of nature, and consequently without any sanction whatever in the law of nations. That law, indeed, recognizes the freedom of the seas for the peoples of all nations, and no nations have stood more firmly by that doctrine or are more interested in its enforcement than Great Britain and the United States. But I have not found in any treatise upon international law, or in the judgment of any court, a hint even that this doctrine confers upon individuals or associations a *right* to employ methods for the taking of useful animals found in the high seas which will exterminate the race, when all know ... that such animals may be readily taken at their breeding grounds, and not elsewhere, by methods that regularly give their increase for man's use without at all impairing or diminishing the stock. One method results in the extermination of the race, whereby the object of its creation is entirely defeated; the other results in its preservation, whereby that object is secured. It is inconceivable that the law of nations gives or recognizes the right to employ the former....

8.2 NORTH ATLANTIC COAST FISHERIES CASE (GB v. US). 11 UNRIAA 173 (Perm. Ct. of Arb. 1910)

[*Eds.*—In a 1783 Treaty of Peace between Great Britain and the United States, Britain agreed to allow US inhabitants to continue to fish in the coastal fisheries of Newfoundland, Labrador, and other parts of the North Atlantic coast of Canada. Following the War of 1812 (which Britain viewed as abrogating the 1783 Treaty of Peace), the United States and Great Britain addressed the question of US fishing rights off the Canadian coast in a new Treaty of Commerce concluded 20 October 1818. For more than 80 years, the precise meaning of the 1818 Treaty was disputed by the parties, and the scope of US fishing rights in British Canadian waters was contested. In 1905, the dispute intensified after Newfoundland adopted severely restrictive fisheries legislation. The US and Great Britain submitted their dispute to arbitration in January 1909. The Arbitral Tribunal issued its award on 7 September 1910.

A central question in the arbitration was whether the fishing rights granted to the US by the 1818 Treaty of Commerce were subject to regulation by the territorial sovereign (or its political subunits) or whether the grant of fishing rights to the US was an abrogation of British sovereignty sufficient to preclude Great Britain (or Newfoundland) from imposing fishing restrictions on US fishermen without the consent of the United States.]

Excerpts from the Award of the Arbitrators

[By] Article I of the Convention signed at London on the 20th day of October, 1818, between Great Britain and the United States, it was agreed as follows:

[T]he Inhabitants of the . . . United States shall have forever, in common with the Subjects of His Britannic Majesty, the Liberty to take Fish of every kind on [limited portions of] the Southern Coast of Newfoundland . . ., on [limited portions of] the Western and Northern Coast of Newfoundland, . . . and . . . on [limited portions of] the Southern Coast of Labrador. . . .

* * *

It is contended on the part of the United States that the exercise of such liberty [as is granted by Article I of the 1818 Convention] is not subject to limitations or restraints by Great Britain, Canada, or Newfoundland in the form of municipal laws, ordinances, or regulations . . . unless [the] appropriateness, necessity, reasonableness, and fairness [of such regulations] [is] determined by the United States and Great Britain by common accord and the United States concurs in [the] enforcement [of such regulations].

* * *

The Treaty of 1818 contains no explicit disposition in regard to the right of regulation, reasonable or otherwise; it neither reserves that right in express terms, nor refers to it in any way. It is therefore incumbent on this Tribunal to answer the [questions in this case] by interpreting the general terms of Article I of the Treaty, and more especially the words 'the inhabitants of the United States shall have, for ever, in common with the subjects of His Britannic Majesty, the liberty to take fish of every kind'. [Our] interpretation must be conformable to the general import of the instrument, the general intention of the parties to it, the subject matter of the contract, the expressions actually used and the evidence submitted.

* * *

[T]he right to regulate the liberties conferred by the Treaty of 1818 is an attribute of sovereignty, and as such must be held to reside in the territorial sovereign, unless the contrary be provided[.] [O]ne of the essential elements of sovereignty is that it is to be exercised within territorial limits, and that, failing proof to the contrary, the territory is co-terminous with the Sovereignty[.] [I]t follows that the burden of [proving] that the right to regulate does not reside independently in Great Britain, the territorial Sovereign[,] must fall on the United States. And for the purpose of sustaining this burden, the United States have put forward the [contention that] . . . :

> the liberties of fishery granted to the United States constitute an International servitude in their favour over the territory of Great Britain, thereby involving a derogation from the sovereignty of Great Britain, the servient State, and that therefore Great Britain is deprived, by reason of the grant, of its independent right to regulate the fishery.

The Tribunal is unable to agree with this contention. . . .

[T]he doctrine of international servitude in the sense which is now sought to be attributed to it originated in the peculiar and now obsolete conditions prevailing in the Holy Roman Empire of which the *domini terrae* were not fully sovereigns; they holding territory under the Roman Empire, subject at least theoretically, and in some respects also practically, to the Courts of that Empire; their right being, moreover, rather of a civil than of a public nature, partaking more of the character of *dominium* than of *imperium*, and therefore certainly not a complete sovereignty. . . . [I]n contradistinction to this quasi-sovereignty with its incoherent attributes acquired at various times, by various means, and not impaired in its character by being incomplete in any one respect or by being limited in favour of another territory and its possessor, the modern State, and particularly Great Britain, has never admitted partition of sovereignty, owing to the constitution of a modern State requiring essential sovereignty and independence . . . [.]

Because this doctrine [of international servitude is] but little suited to the principle of sovereignty which prevails in States under a system of constitutional government such as Great Britain and the United States, and to the present international relations of Sovereign States, [it] has found little, if any, support from modern publicists. It could therefore in the general interest of the Community of Nations, and of the Parties to this Treaty, be affirmed by this Tribunal only on the express evidence of an International contract[.]

[E]ven if these liberties of fishery constituted an International servitude, the servitude would derogate from the sovereignty of the servient State only in so far as the exercise of the rights of sovereignty by the servient State would be contrary to the exercise of the servitude right by the dominant State. . . . [I]t is evident that, though every regulation of the fishery is to some extent a limitation, as it puts limits to the exercise of the fishery at will, yet such regulations as are reasonable and made for the purpose of securing and preserving the fishery and its exercise for the common benefit, are clearly to be distinguished from those restrictions and 'molestations', the annulment of which was the purpose of the American demands . . . in 1782, and such regulations consequently cannot be held to be inconsistent with a servitude . . . [.]

* * *

[Because] the recognition of a concurrent right of consent to the United States would affect the independence of Great Britain, which would become dependent on the Government of the United States for the exercise of its sovereign right of regulation, and, considering that such a co-dominium would be contrary to the constitution of both sovereign States[,] the burden of proof is imposed on the United States to show that the independence of Great Britain was thus impaired by international contract in 1818 and that a co-dominium was created.

For the purpose of such proof it is contended by the United States:

> . . . That a concurrent right to co-operate in the making and enforcement of regulations is the only possible and proper security to their inhabitants for the

enjoyment of their liberties of fishery, and that such a right must be held to be implied in the grant of those liberties by the Treaty under interpretation.

The Tribunal is unable to accede to this claim. . . .

[E]very State has to execute the obligations incurred by Treaty *bona fide*, and is urged thereto by the ordinary sanctions of International Law in regard to observance of Treaty obligations. Such sanctions are, for instance, appeal to public opinion, publication of correspondence, censure by Parliamentary vote, demand for arbitration with the odium attendant on a refusal to arbitrate, rupture of relations, reprisal, etc. But no reason has been shown why this Treaty, in this respect, should be considered as different from every other Treaty under which the right of a State to regulate the action of foreigners admitted by it on its territory is recognized[.]

* * *

[I]f the consent of the United States were requisite for the fishery a general veto would be accorded them, the full exercise of which would be socially subversive and would lead to the consequence of an unregulatable fishery . . . [.]

In any event, Great Britain, as the local sovereign, has the duty of preserving and protecting the fisheries. In so far as it is necessary for that purpose, Great Britain is not only entitled, but obliged, to provide for the protection and preservation of the fisheries; always remembering that the exercise of this right of legislation is limited by the obligation to execute the Treaty in good faith. This has been admitted by counsel and recognized by Great Britain in limiting the right of regulation to that of reasonable regulation. The inherent defect of this limitation of reasonableness, without any sanction except in diplomatic remonstrance, has been supplied by the submission to arbitral award as to existing regulations in accordance with Arts. II and III of the Special Agreement, and as to further regulation by the obligation to submit their reasonableness to an arbitral test in accordance with Art. IV of the Agreement.

* * *

[T]he right to make reasonable regulations, not inconsistent with the obligations of the Treaty, which is all that is claimed by Great Britain, for a fishery which both Parties admit requires regulation for its preservation, is not a restriction of or an invasion of the liberty granted to the inhabitants of the United States. This grant does not contain words to justify the assumption that the sovereignty of Great Britain upon its own territory was in any way affected; nor can words be found in the Treaty transferring any part of that sovereignty to the United States. Great Britain assumed only duties with regard to the exercise of its sovereignty. The sovereignty of Great Britain over the coastal waters and territory of Newfoundland remains after the Treaty as unimpaired as it was before. But from the Treaty results an obligatory relation whereby the right of Great Britain to exercise its right of sovereignty by making regulations is limited to such regulations as are made in good faith, and are not in violation of the Treaty . . . [.]

* * *

Now therefore this Tribunal decides and awards as follows:

The right of Great Britain to make regulations without the consent of the United States, as to the exercise of the liberty to take fish referred to in Article I of the Treaty of October 20th, 1818, in the form of municipal laws, ordinances or rules of Great Britain, Canada or Newfoundland is inherent to the sovereignty of Great Britain.

The exercise of that right by Great Britain is, however, limited by the said Treaty in respect of the said liberties therein granted to the inhabitants of the United States in that such regulations must be made bona fide and must not be in violation of the said Treaty.

Regulations which are (1) appropriate or necessary for the protection and preservation of such fisheries, or (2) desirable or necessary on grounds of public order and morals without unnecessarily interfering with the fishery itself; and in both cases equitable and fair as between local and American fishermen, and not so framed as to give unfairly an advantage to the former over the latter class, are not inconsistent with the obligation to execute the Treaty in good faith, and are therefore reasonable and not in violation of the Treaty.

* * *

8.3   TRAIL SMELTER ARBITRATION (US v. Can). 3 UNRIAA 1905 (1941)

[*Eds.*—This case resulted from sulphur dioxide (SO$_2$) fumes emitted into the atmosphere by a smelter plant owned by a Canadian corporation (the Consolidated Mining and Smelting Company of Canada, Limited), located on the Columbia River at Trail, British Columbia, seven miles from the State of Washington. The Trail smelter plant was alleged to have caused environmental damage in Washington.

The dispute was referred to a special Arbitral Tribunal composed of one American chosen by the United States, one Canadian chosen by Canada, and a Belgian chosen by the United States and Canada jointly. The Convention establishing the Tribunal called for the application of the "law and practice followed in dealing with cognate questions in the United States of America as well as international law and practice," and it directed the Tribunal to "give consideration to the desire of the high contracting parties to reach a solution just to all parties concerned." 3 UNRIAA 1905, 1908 (1938). In a prior decision, the Tribunal had determined that the air pollution created by the smelter had caused damage in the State of Washington over a 12-year period, from 1925 to 1937. In the decision excerpted here, reported on March 11, 1941, the Tribunal held Canada responsible and directed both injunctive relief and payment of an indemnity.]

Excerpts from the Award of the Arbitrators

In 1896, a smelter was started under American auspices near the locality known as Trail, B.C. In 1906, the Consolidated Mining and Smelting Company of Canada, Limited, obtained a charter of incorporation from the Canadian authorities, and that company acquired the smelter plant at Trail as it then existed. Since that time, the Canadian company, without interruption, has operated the Smelter, and from time to time has greatly added to the plant until it has become one of the best and largest equipped smelting plants on the American continent. In 1925 and 1927, two stacks of the plant were erected to 409 feet in height and the Smelter greatly increased its daily smelting of zinc and lead ores. This increased production resulted in more sulphur dioxide fumes and higher concentrations being emitted into the air. In 1916, about 5,000 tons of sulphur per month were emitted; in 1924, about 4,700 tons; in 1926, about 9,000 tons—an amount which rose near to 10,000 tons per month in 1930. In other words, about 300–500 tons of sulphur were being emitted daily in 1930. (It is to be noted that one ton of sulphur is substantially the equivalent of two tons of sulphur dioxide or SO$_2$.)

From 1925, at least, to 1937, damage occurred in the State of Washington, resulting from the sulphur dioxide emitted from the Trail Smelter as stated in the previous decision [of 16 April 1938].

* * *

[142]. The first problem which arises is whether the question should be answered on the basis of the law followed in the United States or on the basis of international law. The Tribunal, however, finds that this problem need not be solved here as the law followed in the United States in dealing with the quasi-sovereign rights of the States of the Union, in the matter of air pollution, whilst more definite, is in conformity with the general rules of international law.

[143]. Particularly in reaching its conclusions as regards this question as well as the next, the Tribunal has given consideration to the desire of the high contracting parties "to reach a solution just to all parties concerned".

[144]. As Professor Eagleton puts in (*Responsibility of States in International Law,* 1928, p. 80): "A State owes at all times a duty to protect other States against injurious acts by individuals from within its jurisdiction." A great number of such general pronouncements by leading authorities concerning the duty of a State to

respect other States and their territory have been presented to the Tribunal. These and many others have been carefully examined. International decisions, in various matters, from the Alabama case onward, and also earlier ones, are based on the same general principle, and, indeed, this principle, as such, has not been questioned by Canada. But the real difficulty often arises rather when it comes to determine what, *pro subjecta materie,* is deemed to constitute an injurious act.

[145]. A case concerning, as the present one does, territorial relations, decided by the Federal Court of Switzerland between the Cantons of Soleure and Argovia, may serve to illustrate the relativity of the rule. Soleure brought a suit against her sister State to enjoin use of a shooting establishment which endangered her territory. The court, in granting the injunction, said: "this right (sovereignty) excludes . . . not only the usurpation and exercise of sovereign rights (of another State) . . . but also an actual encroachment which might prejudice the natural use of the territory and the free movement of its inhabitants." . . . [Argovia made certain improvements of its shooting ranges to limit the threat to Soleure's territory, but] [t]hese . . . were considered as insufficient protection by Soleure. [The Federal Court, however,] permitted [the resumption of shooting] after completion of the . . . improvements. . . . "The demand of the Government of Soleure", said the court, "that all endangerment be absolutely abolished apparently goes too far." The court found that all risk whatever had not been eliminated, . . . [but] that there was a federal duty for the communes to provide facilities for military target practice and that "no more precautions may be demanded for shooting ranges near the boundaries of two Cantons than are required from shooting ranges in the interior of a Canton". . . .

[146]. No case of air pollution dealt with by an international tribunal has been brought to the attention of the Tribunal nor does the Tribunal know of any such case. The nearest analogy is that of water pollution. But, here also, no decision of an international tribunal has been cited or has been found.

[147]. There are, however, as regards both air pollution and water pollution, certain decisions of the Supreme Court of the United States which may legitimately be taken as a guide in this field of international law, for it is reasonable to follow by analogy, in international cases, precedents established by that court in dealing with controversies between States of the Union or with other controversies concerning the quasi-sovereign rights of such States, where no contrary rule prevails in international law and no reason for rejecting such precedents can be adduced from the limitations of sovereignty inherent in the Constitution of the United States.

[148]. In the suit of the *State of Missouri v. the State of Illinois* (200 U.S. 496, 521) concerning the pollution, within the boundaries of Illinois, of the Illinois River, an affluent of the Mississippi flowing into the latter where it forms the boundary between that State and Missouri, an injunction was refused. "Before this court ought to intervene", said the court, "the case should be of serious magnitude, clearly and fully proved, and the principle to be applied should be one which the court is prepared deliberately to maintain against all considerations on the other side. (See *Kansas v. Colorado,* 185 U.S. 125.)" The court found that the practice complained of was general along the shores of the Mississippi River at that time, that it was followed by Missouri itself and that thus a standard was set up by the defendant which the claimant was entitled to invoke.

* * *

[150]. In the more recent suit of the State of New York against the State of New Jersey (256 U.S. 296, 309), concerning the pollution of New York Bay, the injunction was also refused for lack of proof, some experts believing that the plans which were in dispute would result in the presence of "offensive odors and unsightly deposits", other equally reliable experts testifying that they were confidently of the opinion that the waters would be sufficiently purified. The court, referring to *Missouri v. Illinois,* said:

" . . . the burden upon the State of New York of sustaining the allegations of its bill is much greater than that imposed upon a complainant in an ordinary suit between private parties. Before this court can be moved to exercise its extraordinary power under the Constitution to control the conduct of one State at the suit of another, the threatened invasion of rights must be of serious magnitude and it must be established by clear and convincing evidence."

[151]. What the Supreme Court says there of its power under the Constitution equally applies to the extraordinary power granted this Tribunal under the Convention. What is true between States of the Union is, at least, equally true concerning the relations between the United States and the Dominion of Canada.

[152]. In another recent case concerning water pollution (283 U.S. 473), the complainant was successful. The City of New York was enjoined, at the request of the State of New Jersey, to desist, within a reasonable time limit, from the practice of disposing of sewage by dumping it into the sea, a practice which was injurious to the coastal waters of New Jersey in the vicinity of her bathing resorts.

[153]. In the matter of air pollution itself, the leading decisions are those of the Supreme Court in the *State of Georgia v. Tennessee Copper Company and Ducktown Sulphur, Copper and Iron Company, Limited.* Although dealing with a suit against private companies, the decisions were on questions cognate to those here at issue. Georgia stated that it had in vain sought relief from the State of Tennessee, on whose territory the smelters were located, and the court defined the nature of the suit by saying: "This is a suit by a State for an injury to it in its capacity of quasi-sovereign. In that capacity, the State has an interest independent of and behind the titles of its citizens, in all the earth and air within its domain."

[154]. On the question whether an injunction should be granted or not, the court said (206 U.S. 230):

It [the state] has the last word as to whether its mountains shall be stripped of their forests and its inhabitants shall breathe pure air * * *. It is not lightly to be presumed to give up quasi-sovereign rights . . . , [and] it may insist that an infraction of them shall be stopped. . . . Without excluding the considerations that equity always takes into account [in an action for an injunction], it is a fair and reasonable demand on the part of a sovereign that the air over its territory should not be polluted on a great scale by sulphurous acid gas, that the forests on its mountains, be they better or worse, and whatever domestic destruction they may have suffered, should not be further destroyed or threatened by the act of persons beyond its control, that the crops and orchards on its hills should not be endangered from the same source. . . . Whether Georgia, by insisting upon this claim, is doing more harm than good to her own citizens, is for her to determine. The possible disaster to those outside the State must be accepted as a consequence of her standing upon her extreme rights.

[155]. Later on, however, when the court actually framed an injunction, in the case of the *Ducktown Company* (237 U.S. 474, 477) (an agreement on the basis of an annual compensation was reached with the most important of the two smelters, the Tennessee Copper Company), they did not go beyond a decree "adequate to diminish materially the present probability of damage to its (Georgia's) citizens".

[156]. Great progress in the control of fumes has been made by science in the last few years and this progress should be taken into account.

[157]. The Tribunal, therefore, finds that the above decisions, taken as a whole, constitute an adequate basis for its conclusions, namely, that, under the principles of international law, as well as of the law of the United States, no State has the right to use or permit the use of its territory in such a manner as to cause injury by fumes in

or to the territory of another or the properties or persons therein, when the case is of serious consequence and the injury is established by clear and convincing evidence.

[158].   The decisions of the Supreme Court of the United States which are the basis of these conclusions are decisions in equity and a solution inspired by them, together with the régime hereinafter prescribed, will, in the opinion of the Tribunal, be "just to all parties concerned", as long, at least, as the present conditions in the Columbia River Valley continue to prevail.

[159].   Considering the circumstances of the case, the Tribunal holds that the Dominion of Canada is responsible in international law for the conduct of the Trail Smelter. Apart from the undertakings in the Convention, it is, therefore, the duty of the Government of the Dominion of Canada to see to it that this conduct should be in conformity with the obligation of the Dominion under international law as herein determined.

[160].   The Tribunal, therefore, answers Question No. 2 as follows: (2) So long as the present conditions in the Columbia River Valley prevail, the Trail Smelter shall be required to refrain from causing any damage through fumes in the State of Washington; the damage herein referred to and its extent being such as would be recoverable under the decisions of the courts of the United States in suits between private individuals. The indemnity for such damage should be fixed in such manner as the Governments, acting under Article XI of the Convention, should agree upon.

8.4 CORFU CHANNEL CASE (U.K. v. Alb.), 1949 I.C.J. 4

[*Eds.* On May 15, 1946, British warships passing through the Corfu Channel, in Albanian territorial waters, were fired upon by Albanian coastal batteries; and on October 22, 1946, two British warships passing through that Channel struck mines, which caused damage to the vessels and loss of lives among the crews. On November 1213, 1946, without Albanian consent, units of the Royal British Navy swept for mines that part of the Corfu Channel that was situated in Albanian waters. The United Kingdom raised the issue in the Security Council, which recommended that the two Parties refer the matter to the International Court of Justice. When the case first came up for hearing, Albania unsuccessfully raised a Preliminary Objection to the Court's jurisdiction (1948 I.C.J. 4, 15). At the hearing on the merits, pursuant to a Special Agreement between the State parties, the Court had to consider the following two questions:

"(1) Is Albania responsible under international law for the explosions which occurred on the 22nd October 1946 in Albanian waters and for the damage and loss of human life which resulted from them and is there any duty to pay compensation?"

"(2) Has the United Kingdom under international law violated the sovereignty of the Albanian People's Republic by reason of the acts of the Royal Navy in Albanian waters on the 22nd October and on the 12th and 13th November 1946 and is there any duty to give satisfaction?"

On April 9, 1949, by 11 votes to 5, the Court held that Albania was responsible for the explosions and the ensuing damage, and, unanimously, that the United Kingdom had violated Albanian sovereignty in November. In so holding, the Court reasoned as follows:]

Excerpts from Judgment of the International Court of Justice

[16]. By the first part of the Special Agreement, the following question is submitted to the Court:

"(1) Is Albania responsible under international law for the explosions which occurred on the 22nd October 1946 in Albanian waters and for the damage and loss of human life which resulted from them and is there any duty to pay compensation?"

[17]. On October 22nd, 1946, a squadron of British warships, the cruisers *Mauritius* and *Leander* and the destroyers *Saumarez* and *Volage,* left the port of Corfu and proceeded northward through a channel previously swept for mines in the North Corfu Strait. The cruiser *Mauritius* was leading, followed by the destroyer *Saumarez;* at a certain distance thereafter came the cruiser *Leander* followed by the destroyer *Volage.* Outside the Bay of Saranda, *Saumarez* struck a mine and was heavily damaged. *Volage* was ordered to give her assistance and to take her in tow. Whilst towing the damaged ship, *Volage* struck a mine and was much damaged. Nevertheless, she succeeded in towing the other ship back to Corfu.

[18]. Three weeks later, on November 13th, the North Corfu Channel was swept by British minesweepers and twenty-two moored mines were cut. Two mines were taken to Malta for expert examination. During the minesweeping operation it was thought that the mines were of the German GR type, but it was subsequently established that they were of the German GY type.

* * *

[28]. The Court consequently finds that the following facts are established. The two ships were mined in Albanian territorial waters in a previously swept and check-swept channel just at the place where a newly laid minefield consisting of moored contact German GY mines was discovered three weeks later. The damage sustained by

the ships was inconsistent with damage which could have been caused by floating mines, magnetic ground mines, magnetic moored mines, or German GR mines, but its nature and extent were such as would be caused by mines of the type found in the minefield. In such circumstances the Court arrives at the conclusion that the explosions were due to mines belonging to that minefield.

[29]. Such are the facts upon which the Court must, in order to reply to the first question of the Special Agreement, give judgment as to Albania's responsibility for the explosions on October 22nd, 1946, and for the damage and loss of human life which resulted, and for the compensation, if any, due in respect of such damage and loss.

[30]. To begin with, the foundation for Albania's responsibility, as alleged by the United Kingdom, must be considered. On this subject, the main position of the United Kingdom is to be found in its submission No. 2: that the minefield which caused the explosions was laid between May 15th, 1946, and October 22nd, 1946, by or with the connivance or knowledge of the Albanian Government.

[31]. The Court considered first the various grounds for responsibility alleged in this submission.

[32]. In fact, although the United Kingdom Government never abandoned its contention that Albania herself laid the mines, very little attempt was made by the Government to demonstrate this point. In the written Reply, the United Kingdom Government takes note of the Albanian Government's formal statement that it did not lay the mines, and was not in a position to do so, as Albania possessed no navy; and that, on the whole Albanian littoral, the Albanian authorities only had a few launches and motor boats. In the light of these statements, the Albanian Government was called upon, in the Reply, to disclose the circumstances in which two Yugoslav war vessels, the *Mljet* and the *Meljine,* carrying contact mines of the GY type, sailed southward from the port of Sibenik on or about October 18th, and proceeded to the Corfu Channel. The United Kingdom Government, having thus indicated the argument upon which it was thenceforth to concentrate, stated that it proposed to show that the said warships, with the knowledge and connivance of the Albanian Government, laid mines in the Corfu Channel just before October 22nd, 1946. The facts were presented in the same light and in the same language in the oral reply by Counsel for the United Kingdom Government at the sittings on January 17th and 18th, 1949.

[33]. Although the suggestion that the minefield was laid by Albania was repeated in the United Kingdom statement in Court on January 18th, 1949, and in the final submissions read in Court on the same day, this suggestion was in fact hardly put forward at that time except *pro memoria,* and no evidence in support was furnished.

[34]. In these circumstances, the Court need pay no further attention to this matter.

[35]. The Court now comes to the second alternative argument of the United Kingdom Government, namely, that the minefield was laid with the connivance of the Albanian Government. According to this argument, the minelaying operation was carried out by two Yugoslav warships at a date prior to October 22nd, but very near that date. This would imply collusion between the Albanian and the Yugoslav Governments, consisting either of a request by the Albanian Government to the Yugoslav Government for assistance, or of acquiescence by the Albanian authorities in the laying of the mines.

* * *

[42]. In the light of the information now available to the Court, the authors of the minelaying remain unknown. In any case, the task of the Court, as defined by the Special Agreement, is to decide whether Albania is responsible, under international law, for the explosions which occurred on October 22nd, 1946, and to give judgment as to the compensation, if any.

[43]. Finally, the United Kingdom Government put forward the argument that, whoever the authors of the minelaying were, it could not have been done without the Albanian Government's knowledge.

[44]. It is clear that knowledge of the minelaying cannot be imputed to the Albanian Government by reason merely of the fact that a minefield discovered in Albanian territorial waters caused the explosions of which the British warships were the victims. It is true, as international practice shows, that a State on whose territory or in whose waters an act contrary to international law has occurred, may be called upon to give an explanation. It is also true that that State cannot evade such a request by limiting itself to a reply that it is ignorant of the circumstances of the act and of its authors. The State may, up to a certain point, be bound to supply particulars of the use made by it of the means of information and inquiry at its disposal. But it cannot be concluded from the mere fact of the control exercised by a State over its territory and waters that that State necessarily knew, or ought to have known, of any unlawful act perpetrated therein, nor yet that it necessarily knew, or should have known, the authors. This fact, by itself and apart from other circumstances, neither involves *prima facie* responsibility nor shifts the burden of proof.

[45]. On the other hand, the fact of this exclusive territorial control exercised by a State within its frontiers has a bearing upon the methods of proof available to establish the knowledge of that State as to such events. By reason of this exclusive control, the other State, the victim of a breach of international law, is often unable to furnish direct proof of facts giving rise to responsibility. Such a State should be allowed a more liberal recourse to inferences of fact and circumstantial evidence. This indirect evidence is admitted in all systems of law, and its use is recognized by international decisions. It must be regarded as of special weight when it is based on a series of facts linked together and leading logically to a single conclusion.

[46]. The Court must examine therefore whether it has been established by means of indirect evidence that Albania has knowledge of minelaying in her territorial waters independently of any connivance on her part in this operation. The proof may be drawn from inferences of fact, provided that they leave *no room* for reasonable doubt. The elements of fact on which these inferences can be based may differ from those which are relevant to the question of connivance.

[47]. In the present case, two series of facts, which corroborate one another, have to be considered: the first relates to Albania's attitude before and after the disaster of October 22nd, 1946; the other concerns the feasibility of observing minelaying from the Albanian coast.

[48]. 1. It is clearly established that the Albanian Government constantly kept a close watch over the waters of the North Corfu Channel, at any rate after May 1946.... This vigilance sometimes went so far as to involve the use of force....

* * *

[53]. Another indication of the Albanian Government's knowledge consists in the fact that that Government did not notify the presence of mines in its waters, at the moment when it must have known this, at the latest after the sweep on November 13th, and further, whereas the Greek Government immediately appointed a Commission to inquire into the events of October 22nd, the Albanian Government took no decision of such a nature, nor did it proceed to the judicial investigation incumbent, in such a case, on the territorial sovereign.

[54]. This attitude does not seem reconcilable with the alleged ignorance of the Albanian authorities that the minefield had been laid in Albanian territorial waters. It could be explained if the Albanian Government, while knowing of the minelaying, desired the circumstances of the operation to remain secret.

[55]. 2. As regards the possibility of observing minelaying from the Albanian coast, the Court regards the following facts, relating to the technical conditions of a secret minelaying and to the Albanian surveillance, as particularly important.

[56]. The Bay of Saranda and the channel used by shipping through the Strait are, from their geographical configuration, easily watched; the entrance of the bay is dominated by heights offering excellent observation points, both over the bay and over the Strait; whilst the channel throughout is close to the Albanian coast. The laying of a minefield in these waters could hardly fail to have been observed by the Albanian coastal defences.

[57]. On this subject, it must first be said that the minelaying operation itself must have required a certain time. The method adopted required, according to the Experts of the Court, the methodical and well thought-out laying of two rows of mines that had clearly a combined offensive and defensive purpose: offensive, to prevent the passage, through the Channel, of vessels drawing ten feet of water or more; defensive, to prevent vessels of the same draught from entering the Bay of Saranda. The report of the Experts reckons the time that the minelayers would have been in the waters, between Cape Kiephali and St. George's Monastery, at between two and two and a half hours. This is sufficient time to attract the attention of the observation posts, placed, as the Albanian Government stated, at Cape Kiephali and St. George's Monastery.

* * *

[62]. The Court cannot fail to give great weight to the opinion of the Experts who examined the locality in a manner giving every guarantee of correct and impartial information. Apart from the existence of a look-out post at Cape Denta, which has not been proved, the Court, basing itself on the declarations of the Albanian Government that look-out posts were stationed at Cape Kiephali and St. George's Monastery, refers to the following conclusions in the Experts' Report: (1) that in the case of minelaying from the North towards the South, the minelayers would have been seen from Cape Kiephali; (2) in the case of minelaying from the South, the minelayers would have been seen from Cape Kiephali and St. George's Monastery.

[63]. From all the facts and observations mentioned above, the Court draws the conclusion that the laying of the minefield which caused the explosions on October 22nd, 1946, could not have been accomplished without the knowledge of the Albanian Government.

[64]. The obligations resulting for Albania from this knowledge are not disputed between the Parties. Counsel for the Albanian Government expressly recognized that [*translation*] "if Albania had been informed of the operation before the incidents of October 22nd, and in time to warn the British vessels and shipping in general of the existence of mines in the Corfu Channel, her responsibility would be involved * * *.".

[65]. The obligations incumbent upon the Albanian authorities consisted in notifying, for the benefit of shipping in general, the existence of a minefield in Albanian territorial waters and in warning the approaching British warships of the imminent danger to which the minefield exposed them. Such obligations are based, not on the Hague Convention of 1907, No. VIII, which is applicable in time of war, but on certain general and well-recognized principles, namely: elementary considerations of humanity, even more exacting in peace than in war; the principle of the freedom of maritime communication; and every State's obligation not to allow knowingly its territory to be used for acts contrary to the rights of other States.

[66]. In fact, Albania neither notified the existence of the minefield, nor warned the British warships of the danger they were approaching.

[67]. But Albania's obligation to notify shipping of the existence of mines in her waters depends on her having obtained knowledge of that fact in sufficient time before October 22nd; and the duty of the Albanian coastal authorities to warn the British

ships depends on the time that elapsed between the moment that these ships were reported and the moment of the first explosion.

[68]. On this subject, the Court makes the following observations. As has already been stated, the Parties agree that the mines were recently laid. It must be concluded that the minelaying, whatever may have been its exact date, was done at a time when there was a close Albanian surveillance over the Strait. If it be supposed that it took place at the last possible moment, i.e., in the night of October 21st–22nd, the only conclusion to be drawn would be that a general notification to the shipping of all States before the time of the explosions would have been difficult, perhaps even impossible. But this would certainly not have prevented the Albanian authorities from taking, as they should have done, all necessary steps immediately to warn ships near the danger zone, more especially those that were approaching that zone. When on October 22nd about 13.00 hours the British warships were reported by the look-out post at St. George's Monastery to the Commander of the Coastal Defences as approaching Cape Long, it was perfectly possible for the Albanian authorities to use the interval of almost two hours that elapsed before the explosion affecting *Saumarez* (14.53 hours or 14.55 hours) to warn the vessels of the danger into which they were running.

[69]. In fact, nothing was attempted by the Albanian authorities to prevent the disaster. These grave omissions involve the international responsibility of Albania.

[70]. The Court therefore reaches the conclusion that Albania is responsible under international law for the explosions which occurred on October 22nd, 1946, in Albanian waters, and for the damage and loss of human life which resulted from them, and that there is a duty upon Albania to pay compensation to the United Kingdom.

* * *

[84]. In the second part of the Special Agreement, the following question is submitted to the Court:

"(2). Has the United Kingdom under international law violated the sovereignty of the Albanian People's Republic by reason of the acts of the Royal Navy in Albanian waters on the 22nd October and on the 12th and 13th November 1946 and is there any duty to give satisfaction?"

[85]. The Court will first consider whether the sovereignty of Albania was violated by reason of the acts of the British Navy in Albanian waters on October 22nd, 1946.

* * *

[91]. It is, in the opinion of the Court, generally recognized and in accordance with international custom that States in time of peace have a right to send their warships through straits used for international navigation between two parts of the high seas without the previous authorization of a coastal State, provided that the passage is *innocent*. Unless otherwise prescribed in an international convention, there is no right for a coastal State to prohibit such passage through straits in time of peace.

[92]. The Albanian Government does not dispute that the North Corfu Channel is a strait in the geographical sense; but it denies that this Channel belongs to the class of international highways through which a right of passage exists, on the grounds that it is only of secondary importance and not even a necessary route between two parts of the high seas, and that it is used almost exclusively for local traffic to and from the ports of Corfu and Saranda.

* * *

[94]. One fact of particular importance is that the North Corfu Channel constitutes a frontier between Albania and Greece, that a part of it is wholly within the

territorial waters of these States, and that the Strait is of special importance to Greece by reason of the traffic to and from the port of Corfu.

[95]. Having regard to these various considerations, the Court has arrived at the conclusion that the North Corfu Channel should be considered as belonging to the class of international highways through which passage cannot be prohibited by a coastal State in time of peace.

[96]. On the other hand, it is a fact that the two coastal States did not maintain normal relations, that Greece had made territorial claims precisely with regard to a part of Albanian territory bordering on the Channel, that Greece had declared that she considered herself technically in a state of war with Albania, and that Albania, invoking the danger of Greek incursions, had considered it necessary to take certain measures of vigilance in this region. The Court is of opinion that Albania, in view of these exceptional circumstances, would have been justified in issuing regulations in respect of the passage of warships through the Strait, but not in prohibiting such passage or in subjecting it to the requirement of special authorization.

[97]. For these reasons the Court is unable to accept the Albanian contention that the Government of the United Kingdom has violated Albanian sovereignty by sending the warships through the Strait without having obtained the previous authorization of the Albanian Government.

[98]. In these circumstances, it is unnecessary to consider the more general question, much debated by the Parties, whether States under international law have a right to send warships in time of peace through territorial waters not included in a strait.

* * *

[101]. It remains, therefore, to consider whether the *manner* in which the passage was carried out was consistent with the principle of innocent passage and to examine the various contentions of the Albanian Government in so far as they appear to be relevant.

* * *

[108]. Having examined the various contentions of the Albanian Government in so far as they appear to be relevant, the Court has arrived at the conclusion that the United Kingdom did not violate the sovereignty of Albania by reason of the acts of the British Navy in Albanian waters on October 22nd, 1946.

[109]. In addition to the passage of the United Kingdom warships on October 22nd, 1946, the second question in the Special Agreement relates to the acts of the Royal Navy in Albanian waters on November 12th and 13th, 1946. This is the minesweeping operation called "Operation Retail" by the Parties during the proceedings. This name will be used in the present Judgment.

* * *

[112]. The United Kingdom Government does not dispute that "Operation Retail" was carried out against the clearly expressed wish of the Albanian Government. It recognizes that the operation had not the consent of the international mine clearance organizations, that it could not be justified as the exercise of a right of innocent passage, and lastly that, in principle, international law does not allow a State to assemble a large number of warships in the territorial waters of another State and to carry out minesweeping in those waters. The United Kingdom Government states that the operation was one of extreme urgency, and that it considered itself entitled to carry it out without anybody's consent.

* * *

[118].　The Court cannot accept such a line of defence. The Court can only regard the alleged right of intervention as the manifestation of a policy of force, such as has, in the past, given rise to most serious abuses and such as cannot, whatever be the present defects in international organization, find a place in international law. Intervention is perhaps still less admissible in the particular form it would take here; for, from the nature of things, it would be reserved for the most powerful States, and might easily lead to perverting the administration of international justice itself.

8.5 LAKE LANOUX ARBITRATION **(Spain v. Fr.), 12 UNRIAA 281 (1957)**

[*Eds.*—Lake Lanoux is located in France on the southern slope of the Pyrenees mountains. The lake is fed by streams located entirely in French territory. The Font–Vive stream flows out of Lake Lanoux and is one of the headwaters of the River Carol. The river Carol, in turn, flows through French territory for about 25 kilometres before entering Spain.

The Lake Lanoux Arbitration concerned a dispute between France and Spain over a plan by France to divert the waters of Lake Lanoux toward the River Ariège. The French and Spanish first began discussing French plans for diversion of the lake's waters in 1917. They negotiated over the plans intermittently for the next 35 years. During the course of these negotiations, France modified its plans on several occasions in response to Spanish concerns. France finally concluded to divert the waters of Lake Lanoux toward the River Ariège for the purpose feeding a hydroelectric power plant. As a result of the diversion, Lake Lanoux waters would no longer flow into the Font–Vive stream and thence into the River Carol. However, to ensure that the River Carol continued to receive a volume of water equal to the volume it had previously received from Lake Lanoux, France proposed to build a tunnel to carry waters of the River Ariège to the River Carol in a quantity sufficient to replace the waters lost from Lake Lanoux.

Spain objected to this plan, and the Arbitration ensued. A central issue in the arbitration was whether France's actions were in violation of the three Treaties of Bayonne, which had fixed the Franco–Spanish border in the 1860s, and the Additional Act of May 26, 1866 to those Treaties, which added regulations applicable to the frontier region, including regulations relating to the control and enjoyment of waters of common use between the two countries.

Spain pointed out that France's plan for the diversion (and subsequent replacement) of the Lake Lanoux waters that normally flowed into the River Carol "would produce a modification of the physical features of the hydrographic basic of the Carol, because it would radically alter its structure from its source onwards by the effect of the total removal of the volume of water which now flows along its natural course." The restoration of the water with water "of differing provenance" would effectively mean that France had appropriated to itself all the waters that naturally formed the river basin. Since those waters are "common [to France and Spain] by nature," Spain claimed that France could not appropriate them unilaterally, even if it restored the lost waters with replacement water from another source. In other words, Spain said, the "system of community" established by its treaties with France meant that the works at Lake Lanoux could not proceed without its agreement. In addition to its treaty claims, Spain argued that a review of general international river law—as revealed in the treaty practice of states, in the decisions of federal courts in various countries, and in the writings of publicists—demonstrated that a significant change in an international watercourse could not be made without agreement among the co-riparians.

The Arbitral Tribunal rejected all of Spain's claims, for the reasons expressed in the following excerpts.]

Excerpts from the Opinion of the Tribunal

1. The public works envisaged in the French scheme are wholly situate in France; the most important part if not the whole of the effects of such works will be felt in French territory; they would concern waters which Article 8 of the Additional Act submits to French territorial sovereignty:

> Article 8. All standing and flowing waters, whether they are in the private or public domain, are subject to the sovereignty of the State in which they are

located, and therefore to that State's legislation, except for the modifications agreed upon between the two Governments.

* * *

This text itself imposes a reservation on the principle of territorial sovereignty ("except for the modifications agreed upon between the two Governments"); some provisions of the Treaty and of the Additional Act of 1866 contain the most important of these modifications; there may be others. It has been contended before the Tribunal that these modifications should be strictly construed because they are in derogation of sovereignty. The Tribunal could not recognize such an absolute rule of construction. Territorial sovereignty plays the part of a presumption. It must bend before all international obligations, whatever their origin, but only before such obligations.

The question is therefore to determine the obligations of the French Government in this case.

* * *

[The Tribunal then began by considering whether the French plan for diversion and restitution of the waters was generally consistent with the treaties between the two countries. It concluded that the plan did not inherently violate the treaties.]

4. The Additional Act of May 26, 1866, includes a section headed "Control and enjoyment of waters of common user between the two countries." [Articles 9 and 10 of this Act clearly authorize France to erect works for the use of the waters of a shared watercourse, so long as it does not impair the rights of Spanish users of the watercourse.]

* * *

6. [Because France will replace all diverted waters with an equivalent volume of water from the River Ariege,] none of the guaranteed users will suffer in his enjoyment of the waters . . .; at the lowest water level, the volume of the surplus waters of the Carol, at the boundary, will at no time suffer a diminution; it may even, by virtue of the minimum guarantee given by France, benefit by an increase in volume assured by the [diversion of the] waters of the Ariege [into the Carol]. . . .

* * *

[Spain has not claimed] that the works would bring about an ultimate pollution of the waters of the Carol or that the returned waters would have a chemical composition or a temperature or some other characteristic which could injure Spanish interests. . . .

[Nor has Spain claimed] that, by their technical character, the works envisaged by the French project could not . . . ensure the restitution of a volume of water corresponding to the natural contribution of the Lanoux to the Carol. . . .

7. [Instead], [t]he Spanish Government . . . [alleges] that the French scheme modifies the natural conditions of the hydrographic basin of Lake Lanoux by diverting its waters into the Ariège and thus making the restoration of the waters of the Carol physically dependent on human will, which would involve the *de facto* preponderance of one Party in place of the equality of the two Parties as provided by the Treaty of Bayonne of May 26, 1866, and by the Additional Act of the same date.

. . . [Spain] invokes Article 12 of the Additional Act:

> Article 12. The downstream lands are obliged to receive from the higher lands of the neighbouring country the waters which flow naturally therefrom together with what they carry, without the hand of man having contributed thereto. There may be constructed neither a dam, nor any obstacle capable of harming the upper riparian owners, to whom it is likewise forbidden to do

anything which might increase the burdens attached to the servitude of the downstream lands.

According to the Spanish Government, [Article 12 establishes] the conception that neither of the Parties may, without the consent of the other, modify the natural flow of the waters. . . .

8. . . . The Tribunal does not overlook the reality [that], from the point of view of physical geography, . . . each river basin . . . constitutes . . . 'a unit'. But this observation does not authorize the absolute consequences that the Spanish argument would draw from it. The unity of a basin is sanctioned at the juridical level only to the extent that it corresponds to human realities. The water which by nature constitutes a fungible item may be the object of a restitution which does not change its qualities in regard to human needs. A diversion with restitution, such as that envisaged by the French project, does not change a state of affairs organized for the working of the requirements of social life.

The state of modern technology leads to more and more frequent justifications of the fact that waters used for the production of electric energy should not be returned to their natural course. Water is taken higher and higher up and it is carried ever farther, and in so doing it is sometimes diverted to another river basin, in the same State or in another country within the same federation, or even in a third State. Within federations, the judicial decisions have recognized the validity of this last practice *(Wyoming v. Colorado* * * * [259 U.S. 419]) and the instances cited by Dr. J. E. Berber, *Die Rechtsqgellen des internationalen Wassernutzungrechts, p.* 180, and by M. Sauser–Hall, 'L'Utilisation industrielle des fleuves internationaux', [in] *Recueil des Cours de l'Académie de Droit international de la Haye,* 1953, vol. 83, p. 544; for Switzerland, [see] *Recueil des Arrêts du Tribunal Fédéral,* vol. 78, Part I, pp. 14 *et seq.).*

The Tribunal therefore is of opinion that the diversion with restitution as envisaged in the French scheme and proposals is not contrary to the Treaty and to the Additional Act of 1866.

* * *

[The Tribunal then shifted its consideration to the question whether France was required to reach agreement with Spain before taking any actions affecting the shared watercourse.]

11. . . . To admit that jurisdiction in a certain field can no longer be exercised except on the condition of, or by way of, an agreement between two States, is to place an essential restriction on the sovereignty of a State, and such restriction could only be admitted if there were clear and convincing evidence. Without doubt, international practice does reveal some special cases in which this hypothesis has become reality; thus, sometimes two States exercise conjointly jurisdiction over certain territories (joint ownership, *co-imperixm,* or *condominium);* likewise, in certain international arrangements, the representatives of States exercise conjointly a certain jurisdiction in the name of those States or in the name of organizations. But these cases are exceptional, and international judicial decisions are slow to recognize their existence, especially when they impair the territorial sovereignty of a State, as would be the case in the present matter.

* * *

13. The Spanish Government endeavoured to establish [that] current positive international law [requires agreement of all co-riparians before modification of a watercourse is permitted]. Certain principles [relied on by Spain] . . . are . . ., [in fact], of no interest for the problem now under examination. Thus, [the] principle which prohibits the upstream State from altering the waters of a river in such a fashion as

seriously to prejudice the downstream State [has] no application to the present case because ... the French scheme will not alter the waters of the Carol. In fact, States are today perfectly conscious of the importance of the conflicting interests brought into play by the industrial use of international rivers, and of the necessity to reconcile them by mutual concessions. The only way to arrive at such compromises of interests is to conclude agreements on an increasingly comprehensive basis. International practice reflects the conviction that States ought to strive to conclude such agreements: there would thus appear to be an obligation to accept in good faith all communications and contracts which could, by a broad comparison of interests and by reciprocal good will, provide States with the best conditions for concluding agreements....

But ... [a] rule that States may utilize the hydraulic power of international watercourses only on condition of a *prior* agreement between the interested States cannot be established as a custom, even less as a general principle of law. The history of the formulation of the multilateral Convention signed at Geneva on December 9, 1923, relative to the Development of Hydraulic Power Affecting More than One State, is very characteristic in this connection.... [T]he Convention, in its final form, provides (Article I) that

> "[The present Convention] in no way alters the freedom of each State, within the framework of international law, to carry out on its territory all operations for the development of hydraulic power which it desires";

there is provided only an obligation upon the interested signatory States to join in a common study of a development programme; the execution of this programme is obligatory only for those States which have formally subscribed to it.

Customary international law ... does not [support interpreting] ... the Treaty and of the Additional Act of 1866 [to require] prior agreement; even less does it permit us to conclude that there exists a general principle of law or a custom to this effect.

* * *

23. In the present case, the Spanish Government reproaches the French Government for not having based the development scheme for the waters of Lake Lanoux on a foundation of absolute equality.... [Spain complains] ... that the French Government has imposed its scheme unilaterally without associating the Spanish Government with it in a common search for an acceptable solution. [Spain also alleges] that the French scheme does not maintain a just balance between French interests and Spanish interests. The French scheme, in the Spanish view, would serve perfectly French interests, especially those related to the production of electric energy, but would not take into sufficient consideration Spanish interests in connection with irrigation. According to the Spanish Government, the French Government refused to take into consideration schemes which, in the opinion of the Spanish Government, would have involved a very small sacrifice of French interests and great advantages for the Spanish rural economy....

On a theoretical basis the Spanish argument is unacceptable to the Tribunal, for Spain tends to put rights and simple interests on the same plane.

* * *

France is entitled to exercise her rights; she cannot ignore Spanish interests.

Spain is entitled to demand that her rights be respected and that her interests be taken into consideration.

As a matter of form, the upstream State has, procedurally, a right of initiative; it is not obliged to associate the downstream State in the elaboration of its schemes. If, in the course of discussions, the downstream State submits schemes to it, the upstream State must examine them, but it has the right to give preference to the solution contained in its own scheme provided that it takes into consideration in a reasonable manner the interests of the State.

24.   In the case of Lake Lanoux, France has maintained to the end the solution which consists in diverting the waters of the Carol to the Ariege with full restitution. By making this choice France is only making use of a right; the development works of Lake Lanoux are on French territory, the financing of and responsibility for the enterprise fall upon France, and France alone is the judge of works of public utility which are to be executed on her own territory. . . .

On her side, Spain cannot invoke a right to insist on a development of Lake Lanoux based on the needs of Spanish agriculture. In effect, if France were to renounce all of the works envisaged on her territory, Spain could not demand that other works in conformity with her wishes should be carried out. Therefore, she can only urge her interests in order to obtain, within the framework of the scheme decided upon by France, terms which reasonably safeguard them.

It remains to be established whether this requirement had been fulfilled.

In whatever fashion one regards the course of dealings covering the period 1917–1954, it is beyond doubt that the French position became very flexible and even transformed. From a promise of compensation but without restoration of diverted water, it passed to a partial restoration; then * * * to complete restoration.

* * *

When one examines the question of whether France, either in the course of the dealings or in her proposals, has taken Spanish interests into sufficient consideration, it must be stressed how closely linked together are the obligation to take into consideration, in the course of negotiations, adverse interests and the obligation to give a reasonable place to these interests in the solution finally adopted. A State which has conducted negotiations with understanding and good faith in accordance with Article 11 of the Additional Act is not relieved from giving a reasonable place to adverse interests in the solution it adopts simply because the conversations have been interrupted even though owing to the intransigence of its partner. Conversely, in determining the manner in which a scheme has taken into consideration the interests involved, the way in which negotiations have developed, the total number of the interests which have been presented, the price which each Party was ready to pay to have those interests safeguarded, are all essential factors in establishing, with regard to the obligations set out in Article II of the Additional Act, the merits of that scheme.

Having regard to all the circumstances of the case, set out above, the Tribunal is of opinion that the French scheme complies with the obligations of Article 11 of the Additional Act [to ensure that the interests of both sides are safeguarded].

8.6   NUCLEAR TESTS CASES (N.Z. v. Fr.),[b] 1974 ICJ 253

[*Eds.*—In 1973, Australia and New Zealand instituted proceedings before the International Court of Justice challenging the legality of French atmospheric nuclear tests in the South Pacific at France's Mururoa atoll. France denied the Court's competence and refused to appear. In the decision from which the following excerpts are taken, six judges of the ICJ decided that a number of public statements made by France had rendered the case "moot" and that no decision on the merits of the legal issues was necessary. Three other judges concurred in the dismissal of the case, but on the ground that France's atmospheric nuclear tests so clearly did not violate international law that it was unnecessary to consider the legal merits of the case. Six judges dissented, arguing that there were important issues concerning the legality of atmospheric nuclear testing and that the Court should address those issues.]

Excerpts from the Judgment of the Court (N.Z. v. Fr.)

* * *

17. Prior to the filing of the Application instituting proceedings in this case, the French Government had carried out atmospheric tests of nuclear devices at its Centre d'expérimentations du Pacifique in the territory of French Polynesia, in the years 1966, 1967, 1968, 1970, 1971 and 1972.... The French Government has created "Prohibited Zones" for aircraft and "Dangerous Zones" for aircraft and shipping, in order to exclude aircraft and shipping from the area of the tests centre; these "zones" have been put into effect during the period of testing in each year in which tests have been carried out.

18. As the United Nations Scientific Committee on the Effects of Atomic Radiation has recorded in its successive reports to the General Assembly, the testing of nuclear devices in the atmosphere has entailed the release into the atmosphere and the consequent dissipation, in varying degrees throughout the world, of measurable quantities of radio-active matter. It is asserted by New Zealand [and Australia] that the French atmospheric tests have caused some fall-out of this kind to be deposited, *inter alia,* on New Zealand [and Australian] territory; France has maintained, in particular, that the radio-active matter produced by its tests has been so infinitesimal that it may be regarded as negligible and that any fall-out on New Zealand [or Australian] territory has never involved any danger to the health of the population of New Zealand [or Australia]. * * *

* * *

20. Recently a number of authoritative statements have been made on behalf of the French Government concerning its intentions as to future nuclear testing in the South Pacific region....

* * *

35. ... The first statement is contained in the communiqué issued by the Office of the President of the French Republic on 8 June 1974, shortly before the commencement of the 1974 series of French nuclear tests:

> "The Decree reintroducing the security measures in the South Pacific nuclear test zone has been published in the Official Journal of 8 June 1974.

> The Office of the President of the Republic takes this opportunity of stating that in view of the stage reached in carrying out the French nuclear defence

---

b. The court's judgment in the case of Australia v. France, identical in all essential respects, is omitted due to space limitations.   Excerpts from some of the concurring and dissenting opinions are drawn from that case, however.

programme France will be in a position to pass on to the stage of underground explosions as soon as the series of tests planned for this summer is completed."

36.   The second is contained in a Note of 10 June 1974 from the French Embassy in Wellington to the New Zealand Ministry of Foreign Affairs:

"It should ... be pointed out that the decision taken by the Office of the President of the French Republic to have the opening of the nuclear test series preceded by a press communiqué represents a departure from the practice of previous years. This procedure has been chosen in view of the fact that a new element has intervened in the development of the programme for perfecting the French deterrent force. This new element is as follows: France, at the point which has been reached in the execution of its programme of defence by nuclear means, will be in a position to move to the stage of underground firings as soon as the test series planned for this summer is completed.

Thus the atmospheric tests which will be carried out shortly will, in the normal course of events, be the last of this type.

The French authorities express the hope that the New Zealand Government will find this information of some interest and will wish to take it into consideration."

* * *

38.   The third French statement is contained in a reply made on 1 July 1974 by the President of the [French] Republic to [a letter from] the New Zealand Prime Minister ...:

"In present circumstances, it is at least gratifying for me to note the positive reaction in your letter to the announcement in the communiqué of 8 June 1974 that we are going over to underground tests. There is in this a new element whose importance will not, I trust, escape the New Zealand Government."

* * *

40.   The next statement to be considered ... will be that made on 25 July at a press conference given by the President of the Republic, when he said:

" * * * on this question of nuclear tests, you know that the Prime Minister had publicly expressed himself in the National Assembly in his speech introducing the Government's programme. He had indicated that French nuclear testing would continue. I had myself made it clear that this round of atmospheric tests would be the last, and so the members of the Government were completely informed of our intentions in this respect * * * "

41.   On 16 August 1974, in the course of an interview on French television, the Minister of Defence said that the French Government had done its best to ensure that the 1974 nuclear tests would be the last atmospheric tests.

42.   On 25 September 1974, the French Minister for Foreign Affairs, addressing the United Nations General Assembly, said:

"We have now reached a stage in our nuclear technology that makes it possible for us to continue our programme by underground testing, and we have taken steps to do so as early as next year."

43.   On 11 October 1974, the Minister of Defence held a press conference during which he stated twice, in almost identical terms, that there would not be any atmospheric tests in 1975 and that France was ready to proceed to underground tests. When the comment was made that he had not added "in the normal course of events", he agreed that he had not. This latter point is relevant in view of the Note of 10 June 1974 from the French Embassy in Wellington to the Ministry of Foreign Affairs of New

Zealand (paragraph 36 above), to the effect that the atmospheric tests contemplated "will, in the normal course of events, be the last of this type". The Minister also mentioned that, whether or not other governments had been officially advised of the decision, they could become aware of it through the press and by reading the communiqués issued by the Office of the President of the Republic.

44. In view of the foregoing, the Court finds that the communiqué issued on 8 June 1974 (paragraph 35 above), the French Embassy's Note of 10 June 1974 (paragraph 36 above) and the President's letter of 1 July 1974 (paragraph 38) conveyed to New Zealand the announcement that France, following the conclusion of the 1974 series of tests, would cease the conduct of atmospheric nuclear tests. Special attention is drawn to the hope expressed in the Note of 10 June 1974 "that the New Zealand Government will find this information of some interest and will wish to take it into consideration", and the reference in that Note and in the letter of 1 July 1974 to "a new element" whose importance is urged upon the New Zealand Government. The Court must consider in particular the President's statement of 25 July 1974 (paragraph 40 above) followed by the Defence Minister's statement of 11 October 1974 (paragraph 43). These reveal that the official statements made on behalf of France concerning future nuclear testing are not subject to whatever proviso, if any, was implied by the expression "in the normal course of events *[normalement]*".

* * *

46. It is well recognized that declarations made by way of unilateral acts, concerning legal or factual situations, may have the effect of creating legal obligations. Declarations of this kind may be, and often are, very specific. When it is the intention of the State making the declaration that it should become bound according to its terms, that intention confers on the declaration the character of a legal undertaking, the State being thenceforth legally required to follow a course of conduct consistent with the declaration. An undertaking of this kind, if given publicly, and with an intent to be bound, even though not made within the context of international negotiations, is binding. In these circumstances, nothing in the nature of a *quid pro quo,* nor any subsequent acceptance of the declaration, nor even any reply or reaction from other States, is required for the declaration to take effect, since such a requirement would be inconsistent with the strictly unilateral nature of the juridical act by which the pronouncement by the State was made.

47. Of course, not all unilateral acts imply obligation; but a State may choose to take up a certain position in relation to a particular matter with the intention of being bound the intention is to be ascertained by interpretation of the act. When States make statements by which their freedom of action is to be limited, a restrictive interpretation is called for.

48. With regard to the question of form, it should be observed that this is not a domain in which international law imposes any special or strict requirements. Whether a statement is made orally or in writing makes no essential difference, for such statements made in particular circumstances may create commitments in international law, which does not require that they should be couched in written form. Thus the question of form is not decisive. As the Court said in its Judgment on the preliminary objections in the case concerning the *Temple of Preah Vihear:*

"Where * * * as is generally the case in international law, which places the principal emphasis on the intention of the parties, the law prescribes no particular form, parties are free to choose what form they please provided their intention clearly results from it." (*I.C.J. Reports 1961,* p. 31.)

The Court further stated in the same case: " * * * the sole relevant question is whether the language employed in any given declaration does reveal a clear intention * * * " (*ibid.,* p. 32).

49.   One of the basic principles governing the creation and performance of legal obligations, whatever their source, is the principle of good faith. Trust and confidence are inherent in international co-operation, in particular in an age when this co-operation in many fields is becoming increasingly essential. Just as the very rule of *pacta sunt servanda* in the law of treaties is based on good faith, so also is the binding character of an international obligation assumed by unilateral declaration. Thus interested States may take cognizance of unilateral declarations and place confidence in them, and are entitled to require that the obligation thus created be respected.

* * *

51.   Of the statements by the French Government now before the Court, the most essential are clearly those made by the President of the Republic. There can be no doubt, in view of his functions, that his public communications or statements, oral or written, as Head of State, are in international relations acts of the French State. His statements, and those of members of the French Government acting under his authority, up to the last statement made by the Minister of Defence (of 11 October 1974), constitute a whole. Thus, in whatever form these statements were expressed, they must be held to constitute an engagement of the State, having regard to their intention and to the circumstances in which they were made.

52.   The unilateral statements of the French authorities were made outside the Court, publicly and *erga omnes,* even if some of them were communicated to the Government of New Zealand. As was observed above, to have legal effect, there was no need for these statements to be addressed to a particular State, nor was acceptance by any other State required. The general nature and characteristics of these statements are decisive for the evaluation of the legal implications, and it is to the interpretation of the statements that the Court must now proceed. . . .

53.   In announcing that the 1974 series of atmospheric tests would be the last, the French Government conveyed to the world at large, including the Applicant, its intention effectively to terminate these tests. It was bound to assume that other States might take note of these statements and rely on their being effective. The validity of these statements and their legal consequences must be considered within the general framework of the security of international intercourse, and the confidence and trust which are so essential in the relations among States. It is from the actual substance of these statements and from the circumstances attending their making, that the legal implications of the unilateral act must be deduced. The objects of these statements are clear and they were addressed to the international community as a whole, and the Court holds that they constitute an undertaking possessing legal effect. The Court considers that the President of the Republic, in deciding upon the effective cessation of atmospheric tests, gave an undertaking to the international community to which his words were addressed. It is true that the French Government has consistently maintained that its nuclear experiments do not contravene any subsisting provision of international law, nor did France recognize that it was bound by any rule of international law to terminate its tests, but this does not affect the legal consequences of the statements examined above. The Court finds that the unilateral undertaking resulting from these statements cannot be interpreted as having been made in implicit reliance on an arbitrary power of reconsideration. The Court finds further that the French Government has undertaken an obligation the precise nature and limits of which must be understood in accordance with the actual terms in which they have been publicly expressed.

* * *

55.   Thus the Court faces a situation in which the objective of the Applicant has in effect been accomplished, inasmuch as the Court finds that France has undertaken the obligation to hold no further nuclear tests in the atmosphere in the South Pacific.

[The Judgment of the Court was, accordingly, for termination of the action with no decision on the merits of the legal issues raised by Australia and New Zealand.]

Excerpts from Separate Opinion of Judge Gros (Austl. v. Fr.)

[*Eds.*— Judge Gros supported the Court's Judgment because it "puts an end to the action" brought by the Australia and New Zealand. He argued, however, that the action should be terminated because the French nuclear tests did not violate international law.]

6. [Beginning in 1953 and continuing until 1973, the Government of] Australia has associated itself with various atmospheric explosions above or in the vicinity of its own territory, and ... by its conduct it has expressed an unequivocal view [that such tests are lawful.]

7. The first atmospheric nuclear explosion effected by the United Kingdom occurred on 3 October 1952 in the Montebello Islands, which are situated near the north-west coast of Australia. It was the Australian Minister of Defence who announced that the test had been successful, and the Prime Minister of Australia described it as "one further proof of the very important fact that scientific development in the British Commonwealth is at an extremely high level".... The Prime Minister of the United Kingdom sent a message of congratulation to the Prime Minister of Australia. The Navy and Air Force and other Australian government departments were associated with the preparation and execution of the test; three safety-zones were forbidden for overflight and navigation, on pain of imprisonment and fines. [Further tests followed with the full participation of Australia and New Zealand.]

* * *

8. Active participation in repeated atmospheric tests over several years in itself constitutes admission that such tests were in accordance with the rules of international law....

* * *

13. ... The Applicant has disqualified itself by its conduct and may not submit a claim based on a double standard of conduct and of law. What was good for Australia along with the United Kingdom and the United States cannot be unlawful for other States....

* * *

Excerpts from Separate Opinion of Judge Pétren

[*Eds.*—Judge Pétren also voted for the judgment of the Court, agreeing that the claims of Australia and New Zealand were "without object." However, he rejected the claim that the French declarations were binding and argued, as did Judge Gros, that the French atmospheric tests were lawful.]

[W]hat is first and foremost necessary is to ask oneself whether atmospheric tests of nuclear weapons are, generally speaking, governed by norms of international law, or whether they belong to a highly political domain where the international norms of legality or illegality are still at the gestation stage....

* * *

... Since the Second World War, certain States have conducted atmospheric nuclear tests for the purpose of enabling them to pass from the atomic to the thermonuclear stage in the field of armaments. The conduct of these States proves that their Governments have not been of the opinion that customary international law forbade atmospheric nuclear tests. What is more, the Treaty of 1963 whereby the first three States to have acquired nuclear weapons mutually banned themselves from carrying out further atmospheric tests can be denounced. By the provision [permitting denunciation,] the signatories of the Treaty showed that they were still of the opinion that customary international law did not prohibit atmospheric nuclear tests.

To ascertain whether a customary rule [prohibiting atmospheric nuclear tests] might have [now] come into being, it would appear ... important to learn what attitude is taken up by States which have not yet carried out the tests necessary for reaching the nuclear stage. For such States the prohibition of atmospheric nuclear tests could signify the division of the international community into two groups: States possessing nuclear weapons and States not possessing them. If a State which does not possess nuclear arms refrains from carrying out the atmospheric tests which would enable it to acquire them and if that abstention is motivated not by political or economic considerations but by a conviction that such tests are prohibited by customary international law, the attitude of that State would constitute an element in the formation of such a custom. But where can one find proof that a sufficient number of States, economically and technically capable of manufacturing nuclear weapons, refrain from carrying out atmospheric nuclear tests because they consider that customary international law forbids them to do so? The example recently given by China when it exploded a very powerful bomb in the atmosphere is sufficient to demolish the contention that there exists at present a rule of customary international law prohibiting atmospheric nuclear tests. It would be unrealistic to close one's eyes to the attitude, in that respect, of the State with the largest population in the world.

To complete this brief outline, one may ask what has been the attitude of the numerous States on whose territory radio-active fall-out from the atmospheric tests of the nuclear Powers has been deposited and continues to be desposited. Have they, generally speaking, protested to these Powers, pointing out that their tests were in breach of customary international law? I do not observe that such has been the case. The resolutions passed in the General Assembly of the United Nations cannot be regarded as equivalent to legal protests made by one State to another and concerning concrete instances. They indicate the existence of a strong current of opinion in favour of proscribing atmospheric nuclear tests. That is a political task of the highest urgency, but it is one which remains to be accomplished. Thus the claim submitted to the Court by Australia belongs to the political domain and is situated outside the framework of international law as it exists today.

* * *

Excerpts from Joint Dissenting Opinion of Judges Onyeama, Dillard, Jiménez de Aréchaga and Sir Humphrey Waldock

[*Eds.*—The dissenters rejected both the Court's conclusion that France's unilateral statements were legally binding and the concurring Judges' view that the dispute was political and not legal. The dissenters argued that there was a sufficient legal basis for the complaints of Australia and New Zealand to justify a hearing and judgment on the merits.]

110. ... A dispute is political, and therefore non-justiciable, where the claim is demonstrably rested on other than legal considerations, e.g., on political, economic or military considerations.... In the present case, however, the Applicant invokes legal rights and does not merely pursue its political interest; it expressly asks the Court to determine and apply what it contends are existing rules of international law. In short, it asks for the settlement of the dispute "on the basis of respect for law", which is the very hall-mark of a request for judicial, not political settlement of an international dispute....

* * *

112.   Nor is our conclusion in any way affected by the suggestion that in the present case the Court, in order to give effect to Australia's claims, would have to modify rather than apply the existing law. Quite apart from the fact that the Applicant explicitly asks the Court to apply the existing law, it does not seem to us that the Court is here called upon to do anything other than exercise its normal function of deciding the dispute by applying the law in accordance with the express directions given to the Court in Article 38 of the Statute. We fully recognize that, as was emphasized by the Court recently in the *Fisheries Jurisdiction* cases, "the Court, as a court of law, cannot render judgment *sub specie legis ferendae*, or anticipate the law before the legislator has laid it down" (*I.C.J. Reports 1974*, at pp. 23–24 and 192). . . . [However, in] the present case, the Court is asked to perform its perfectly normal function of assessing the various elements of State practice and legal opinion adduced by the Applicant as indicating the development of a rule of customary law [and determining whether] . . . the alleged rule [has] indeed acquired the character of *lex lata*.

113.   . . . [I]n alleging violations of its territorial sovereignty and of rights derived from the principle of the freedom of the high seas, the Applicant also rests its case on long-established—indeed elemental—rights. . . .

114.   These observations also apply to the suggestion that the Applicant is in no position to claim the existence of a rule of customary international law operative against France inasmuch as the Applicant did not object to, and even actively assisted in, the conduct of atmospheric nuclear tests in the Pacific Ocean region prior to 1963. Clearly this is a matter involving the whole concept of the evolutionary character of customary international law upon which the Court should not pronounce in these preliminary proceedings. The very basis of the Applicant's legal position, as presented to the Court, is that in connection with and after the tests in question there developed a growing awareness of the dangers of nuclear fall-out and a climate of public opinion strongly opposed to atmospheric tests; and that the conclusion of the Moscow Test Ban Treaty in 1963 led to the development of a rule of customary law prohibiting such tests. The Applicant has also drawn attention to its own constant opposition to atmospheric tests from 1963 onwards. Consequently, although the earlier conduct of the Applicant is no doubt one of the elements which would have had to be taken into account by the Court, it would have been upon the evidence of State practice as a whole that the Court would have had to make its determination of the existence or non-existence of the alleged rule. In short, however relevant, this point appears to us to belong essentially to the legal merits of the case, and not to be one appropriate for determination in the present preliminary proceedings.

* * *

117.   Finally, we turn to the question of Australia's legal interest in respect of the claims which she advances. With regard to the right said to be inherent in Australia's territorial sovereignty, we think that she is justified in considering that her legal interest in the defence of that right is self-evident. Whether or not she can succeed in persuading the Court that the particular right which she claims falls within the scope of the principle of territorial sovereignty. she clearly has a legal interest to litigate that issue in defence of her territorial sovereignty. With regard to the right to be free from atmospheric tests, said to be possessed by Australia in common with other States, the question of "legal interest" again appears to us to be part of the general legal merits of the case. If the materials adduced by Australia were to convince the Court of the existence of a general rule of international law, prohibiting atmospheric nuclear tests, the Court would at the same time have to determine what is the precise character and content of that rule and, in particular, whether it confers a right on every State individually to prosecute a claim to secure respect for the rule. In short, the question of "legal interest" cannot be separated from the substantive legal issue of the existence

and scope of the alleged rule of customary international law. Although we recognize that the existence of a so-called *actio popularis* in international law is a matter of controversy, the observations of this Court in the *Barcelona Traction, Light and Power Company, Limited* case suffice to show that the question is one that may be considered as capable of rational legal argument and a proper subject of litigation before this Court.

* * *

Excerpts from the Dissenting Opinion of Judge De Castro

[*Eds.*—Judge de Castro's dissent provides a clear statement of the view (held by many of the judges) that the French statements were not binding.]

3. ... For a promise to be legally binding on a State, it is necessary that the authorities from which it emanates should be competent ... to bind the State (a question of internal constitutional law and international law) and that they should manifest the intention and will to bind the State (a question of interpretation). One has therefore to ask whether the French authorities which made the statements had the power, and were willing, to place the French State under obligation to renounce all possibility of resuming atmospheric nuclear tests, even in the event that such tests should again prove necessary for the sake of national defence....

The identification of the necessary conditions to render a promise ... legally binding has always been a problem in municipal law and, since Grotius at least, in international law also. When an obligation arises whereby a person is bound to act, or refrain from acting, in such and such a way, this results in a restraint upon his freedom ... in favour of another ...; for that reason ... the law generally requires that there should be a *quid pro quo* from the beneficiary to the promiser. Hence—and this should not be forgotten—any promise ... can be withdrawn at any time before its regular acceptance by the person to whom it is made....

4. ... Do those statements of the French authorities with which the Judgment is concerned mean anything other than the notification to the French people—or the world at large—of the nuclear-test policy which the Government will be following in the immediate future? Do those statements contain a genuine promise never, in any circumstances, to carry out any more nuclear tests in the atmosphere? Can those statements be said to embody the French Government's firm intention to bind itself to carry out no more nuclear tests in the atmosphere? Do these same statements possess a legal force such as to debar the French State from changing its mind and following some other policy in the domain of nuclear tests, such as to place it vis-a-vis other States under an obligation to carry out no more nuclear tests in the atmosphere?

To these questions one may reply that the French Government has made up its mind to cease atmospheric nuclear testing from now on, and has informed the public of its intention to do so. But I do not feel that it is possible to go farther. I see no indication warranting a presumption that France wished to bring into being an international obligation, possessing the same binding force as a treaty—and vis-á-vis whom, the whole world?

Excerpts from Dissenting Opinion of Judge Sir Garfield Barwick

* * * [T]he various bases of illegality which the Applicant has put before the Court in support of its present Application ... can be ... listed as follows:

(1) unlawfulness in the modification of the physical conditions of the Australian territory and environment;

(2) unlawfulness in the pollution of the Australian atmosphere and of the resources of its adjacent seas;

* * *

(4) breach of legal norms concerning atmospheric testing of nuclear weapons.

* * *

[T]here is a radical distinction to be made between the claim[] that violation of territorial and decisional sovereignty by the intrusion and deposition of radio-active nuclides . . . is unlawful according to international law, and the claim that the testing of nuclear weapons has become unlawful according to the customary international law. . . .

In the first instance, it is the intrusion of the ionized particles of matter into the air, sea and land of Australia which is said to be in breach of its rights sustained by international law. It is not fundamentally significant in this claim that the atomic explosions from which the ionized particles have come into the Australian environment were explosions for the purpose of developing nuclear weapons, though in fact that is what happened.

But in the second instance the customary law is claimed now to include a prohibition on the testing of nuclear weapons. The particular purpose of the detonations by France is thus of the essence of the suggested prohibition. . . .

* * *

. . . It is the infraction of territorial sovereignty by the intrusion and deposition of nuclides which is the major basis of the claim [of Australia].

* * *

It is not disputed in the case that the deposition of radio-active particles of matter (nuclides) on Australian territory and their intrusion into the Australian environment of sea and air occurs in a short space of time after a nuclear explosion takes place in the French Pacific territory of Mururoa, due to the inherent nature and consequences of such explosions and the prevailing movements of air in the southern hemisphere. Thus it may be taken that that deposition and intrusion is caused, and that it is known that it will be caused, by those explosions.

* * *

[Australia's] claim is that the deposition and intrusion of the nuclides is an infringement of its right to territorial and, as it says, decisional sovereignty. It is part of this claim that the mere deposition and intrusion of this particular and potentially harmful physical matter is a breach of Australia's undoubted sovereign right to territorial integrity, a right clearly protected by international law.

France . . . asserts that the right to territorial integrity in relevant respects is only a right not to be subjected to actual and demonstrable damage by matter intruded into its territory and environment. . . . Put another way, it is claimed that France's right to do as she will on her own territory in exercise of her own sovereign rights is only qualified by the obligation not thereby to cause injury to another State; that means, as I understand the French point of view, not to do actual damage presently provable to the Australian territory or environment of air and sea. In such a formulation it would seem that France claims that although the nuclides were inherently dangerous, their deposition and intrusion into the Australian territory and environment did not relevantly cause damage to Australia or people within its territory. Damage in that view would not have been caused unless some presently demonstrable injury had been caused to land or persons by the nuclear fall-out.

* * *

Thus France and Australia are, in my opinion, in difference as to what is the relevant international law regulating their rights and obligations in relation to the consequences on Australian territory or in its environment of nuclear explosions taking place on French territory. To borrow an expression from municipal law, one, but not the only, aspect of the dispute is whether actual and demonstrable damage is of the "gist" of the right to territorial integrity or is the intrusion of radio-active nuclides into the environment *per se* a breach of that right.

In resolving the question whether damage is of the essence of the right to territorial integrity in relation to the intrusion of physical matter into territory, there may arise what is a large question as to the classification of substances which may not be introduced with impunity by one State on to and into the territory and environment of another. Is there a possible limitation or qualification of the right to territorial and environmental integrity which springs from the nature of the activity which generates the substance which is deposited or intruded into the State's territory and environment? There are doubtless uses of territory by a State which are of such a nature that the consequences for another State and its territory and environment of such a use must be accepted by that other State. It may very well be that a line is to be drawn between depositions and intrusions which are lawful and must be borne and those which are unlawful; on the other hand it may be that because of the unique nature of nuclides and the internationally unnecessary and internationally unprofitable activity which gives rise to their dissemination, no more need be decided than the question whether the intrusion of such nuclides so derived is unlawful.

It is important, in my opinion, to bear in mind throughout that we are here dealing with the emission and deposit of radio-active substances which are in themselves inherently dangerous. There may be differences of opinion as to how dangerous they may prove to be, but no dissent from the view that they are intrinsically harmful and that their harmful effect is neither capable of being prevented nor, indeed, capable of being ascertained with any degree of certainty. I mention these possibilities merely as indicating the scope of the legal considerations which the dispute of the Parties in relation to territorial sovereignty evokes.

* * *

The claim in relation to the testing of nuclear weapons in the atmosphere stands on a quite different footing from the foregoing. It is a claim that Australia's rights are infringed by the testing of nuclear weapons by France in the atmosphere of the South Pacific....

* * *

It is said that there has been such a progression of general opinion amongst the nations, evidenced in treaty, resolution and expression of international opinion, that the stage has been reached where the prohibition of the testing of nuclear weapons is now part of the customary international law.

It cannot be doubted that that customary law is subject to growth and to accretion as international opinion changes and hardens into law. It should not be doubted that the Court is called upon to play its part in the discernment of that growth and in the authoritative declaration that in point of law that growth has taken place to the requisite extent and that the stretch of customary law has been attained. The Court will, of course, confine itself to declaring what the law has already become, and in doing so will not be altering the law or deciding what the law ought to be, as distinct from declaring what it is.

I think it must be considered that it is legally possible that at some stage the testing of nuclear weapons could become, or could have become, prohibited by the customary international law. Treaties, resolutions, expressions of opinion and international practice, may all combine to produce the evidence of that customary law. The time when such a law emerges will not necessarily be deferred until all nations have acceded to a test ban treaty, or until opinion of the nations is universally held in the same sense. Customary law amongst the nations does not, in my opinion, depend on universal acceptance. Conventional law limited to the parties to the convention may become in appropriate circumstances customary law. On the other hand, it may be that even a widely accepted test ban treaty does not create or evidence a state of customary international law in which the testing of nuclear weapons is unlawful, and that resolutions of the United Nations and other expressions of international opinion, however frequent, numerous and emphatic, are insufficient to warrant the view that customary law now embraces a prohibition on the testing of nuclear weapons.

* * *

The difficulties in the way of establishing such a change in the customary international law are fairly obvious, and they are very considerable, but, as I have indicated earlier, it is not the validity of the claim that is in question at this stage. The question is whether a dispute as to the law exists. However much the mind may be impressed by the difficulties in the way of accepting the view that customary international law has reached the point of including a prohibition against the testing of nuclear weapons, it cannot, in my opinion, be said that such a claim is absurd or frivolous, or *ex facie* so untenable that it could be denied that the claim and its rejection have given rise to a dispute as to legal rights. . . .

There remains, however, another and a difficult question, namely whether Australia has an interest to maintain an application for a declaration that the customary law has reached the point of including a prohibition against the testing of nuclear weapons.

In expressing its claim, it is noticeable that the Applicant speaks of its right as being a right along with all other States. It does not claim an individual right exclusive to itself. In its Memorial, it puts the obligation not to test nuclear weapons as owed by each State to every other State in the international community; thus it is claimed that each State can be held to have a legal interest in the maintenance of a prohibition against the testing of nuclear weapons. The Applicant, in support of this conclusion, relies upon the *obiter dictum* in the *Barcelona Traction, Light and Power Company, Limited* case (*Belgium v. Spain, supra, I.C.J. Reports 1970*, at p. 32):

> "When a State admits into its territory foreign investments or foreign nationals, whether natural or juristic persons, it is bound to extend to them the protection of the law and assumes obligations concerning the treatment to be afforded them. These obligations, however, are neither absolute nor unqualified. In particular, an essential distinction should be drawn between the obligations of a State towards the international community as a whole, and those arising vis-à-vis another State in the field of diplomatic protection. By their very nature the former are the concern of all States. In view of the importance of the rights involved, all States can be held to have a legal interest in their protection: they are obligations *erga omnes*.
>
> Such obligations derive, for example, in contemporary international law, from the outlawing of acts of aggression, and of genocide, as also from the principles and rules concerning the basic rights of the human person, including protection from slavery and racial discrimination. Some of the corresponding rights of protection have entered into the body of general international law (*Reservations to the Convention on the Prevention and Punishment of the Crime of Genocide, Advisory Opinion, I.C.J. Reports 1951*, p. 23); others are conferred by international instruments of a universal or quasiuniversal character."

The Applicant says that the prohibition it claims now to exist in the customary international law against the testing of nuclear weapons is of the same kind as the instances of laws concerning the basic rights of the human person as are given in paragraph 34 of the Court's Judgment in the *Barcelona Traction, Light and Power Company, Limited* case, and that therefore the obligation to observe the prohibition is *erga omnes*. The Applicant says that in consequence the right to observance of the prohibition is a right of each State corresponding to the duty of each State to observe the prohibition, a duty which the Applicant claims is owed by each State to each and every other State.

If this submission were accepted, the Applicant would, in my opinion, have the requisite legal interest, the *locus standi* to maintain this basis of its claim. The right it claims in its dispute with France would be its right: the obligation it claims France to be under, namely an obligation to refrain from the atmospheric testing of nuclear weapons, would be an obligation owed to Australia. . . .

* * *

There is a further aspect of the possession of the requisite legal interest to maintain this basis of the Applicant's claim which has to be considered. The Applicant claims to have been specially affected by the breach of the prohibition against atmospheric testing of nuclear weapons. Conformably with its other bases of claim the Applicant says that there has been deleterious fall-out on to and into its land and environment from what it claims to be the unlawful atmospheric testing of nuclear weapons. It may well be that when the facts are fully examined, this basis of a legal interest to maintain the Application in relation to the testing of nuclear weapons may be made out, both in point of fact and in point of law, but again the matter is not, in my opinion, a question of an exclusively preliminary nature.

8.7   CASE CONCERNING THE GABCÍKOVO-NAGYMAROS PROJECT (Hung v. Slovk),[c] 1997 ICJ 7

[*Eds.*—The Danube River is the second longest river in Europe. It originates in the Black Forest Mountains of Germany, and flows east to the Black Sea, passing through nine countries (Germany, Austria, Slovakia, Hungary, Croatia, Serbia, Bulgaria, Romania, and Ukraine) on the way. The river is navigable for most of its course, and three national capitals (Vienna, Budapest, and Belgrade) are built on its banks. The Danube has been used for commercial transportation for centuries. It is also used by several nations for hydroelectric power generation, for agricultural irrigation, and as a dump for industrial and other wastes. Both accidental and intentional pollution have caused grave harm to the Danube's ecosystem and sometimes rendered its waters unfit for drinking or irrigation.

In 1977, the Hungarian People's Republic and the Czechoslovak People's Republic, signed a treaty "aimed at the production of hydroelectricity, the improvement of navigation on the relevant section of the Danube, and the protection of the areas along the banks against flooding." The treaty called for the construction of two hydroelectric power plants, one at Gabcíkovo, in Czechoslovakia, and one at Nagymaros, in Hungary. A system of locks and dams was to be constructed to support each power plant.

The dam that was to support the Gabcíkovo power plant (in Czechoslovakia) was to be build at Dunakiliti, in Hungary, with a resulting reservoir stretching upstream into Czechoslovakia. Water was to be diverted from the Danube (and the reservoir) via a bypass canal (in Czechoslovak territory). The Gabcíkovo power plant and the Gabcíkovo System of Locks (for navigation of boats and barges) were to be constructed on the bypass, and the water was to be returned to the old bed of the Danube downstream. The Nagymaros portion of the project (including locks and a hydroelectric power plant) was to be built downstream of the Gabcíkovo/Dunakiliti works, entirely in Hungarian territory.

The parties regarded the Gabcíkovo/Nagymaros Project as "a single and indivisible operational system of works." They agreed to participate equally in the cost of the works and in sharing the power created by the hydroelectric plants. They also "undertook to ensure that the quality of water in the Danube" would not be impaired by the Project, and "that compliance with the obligations for the protection of nature arising in connection with the construction and operation of the System of Locks would be observed."

Work on the Project started in 1978. In 1983, work was slowed by mutual agreement, and the date for putting the power plants into operation was postponed. In February 1989, however, the parties agreed to accelerate the project. But that plan was undermined by an emerging concern for the environment (and worries about the adverse environmental consequences of development projects) that swept Eastern Europe during this time.]

Excerpts from the Judgment of the Court

32.   In the wake of the profound political and economic changes which occurred . . . in central Europe [around 1989 and thereafter], the Gabcíkovo–Nagymaros Project was the object, in Czechoslovakia and more particularly in Hungary, of increasing apprehension, both within a section of public opinion and in some scientific circles. The uncertainties not only about the economic viability of the Project, but also, and more so, as to the guarantees it offered for preservation of the environment, engendered a climate of growing concern and opposition with regard to the Project.

---

c. Additional excerpts from this case are included in Chapter 2 of the main text of *International Environmental Law and World*   *Order: A Problem–Oriented Coursebook* (3rd ed. 2011).

33.   It was against this background that, on 13 May 1989, the Government of Hungary adopted a resolution to suspend works at Nagymaros, and ordered [studies of the environmental, economic, and legal impact of halting or altering the entire Project.] . . .

34.   At a meeting held [between representatives of the Parties] . . . on 8 and 9 June 1989, Hungary gave Czechoslovakia a number of assurances concerning the continuation of works in the Gabcíkovo sector, and the signed Protocol which records that meeting contains the following passage:

> The Hungarian Government Commissioner and the Hungarian Plenipotentiary stated, that the Hungarian side will complete construction of the Gabcíkovo Project in the agreed time and in accordance with the project plans. Directives have already been given to continue works suspended in the area due to misunderstanding.

[However, Hungary reiterated its intention to cease work on the Nagymaros portion of the Project due to the lack of "adequate knowledge of the consequences of environmental risks" associated with the original plan. Following the recommendations of the Hungarian Academy of Sciences, Hungary indicated that it intended to conduct "further thorough and time consuming studies" to determine whether the "adverse impacts will ensue for certain," and to make its final decision on continuation of the Project only after completion of those studies. . . .

In late July, Hungary announced that in addition to suspending work at Nagymaros, it was also suspending work on the closure of the riverbed at Dunakiliti, an essential step in completion of the Gabcíkovo portion of the Project.]

37.   In the ensuing period, negotiations were conducted at various levels between the two States, but proved fruitless. Finally, by a letter dated 4 October 1989, the Hungarian Prime Minister formally proposed to Czechoslovakia that the Nagymaros sector of the Project be abandoned and that an agreement be concluded with a view to reducing the ecological risks associated with the Gabcíkovo sector of the Project. He proposed that that agreement should be concluded before 30 July 1990. . . .

38.   During winter 1989–1990, the political situation in Czechoslovakia and Hungary alike was transformed, and the new Governments were confronted with many new problems.

In spring 1990, the new Hungarian Government, in presenting its National Renewal Programme, announced that the whole of the Gabcíkovo–Nagymaros Project was a "mistake" and that it would initiate negotiations as soon as possible with the Czechoslovak Government "on remedying and sharing the damages". On 20 December 1990, the Hungarian Government adopted a resolution for the opening of negotiations with Czechoslovakia on the termination of the Treaty by mutual consent and the conclusion of an agreement addressing the consequences of the termination. On 15 February 1991, the Hungarian Plenipotentiary transmitted a draft agreement along those lines to his Czechoslovak counterpart.

On the same day, the Czechoslovak President declared that the Gabcíkovo–Nagymaros Project constituted a "totalitarian, gigomaniac monument which is against nature", while emphasizing that "the problem [was] that [the Gabcíkovo power plant] [had] already been built". For his part, the Czechoslovak Minister of the Environment stated, in a speech given to Hungarian parliamentary committees on 11 September 1991, that "the G/N Project [was] an old, obsolete one", but that, if there were "many reasons to change, modify the treaty . . . it [was] not acceptable to cancel the treaty . . . and negotiate later on".

During the ensuing period, Hungary refrained from completing the work for which it was still responsible at Dunakiliti. . . .

On 7 April 1993, Hungary and Slovakia (now a newly independent state) agreed to submit their differences over the Gabcíkovo–Nagymaros Project to [this Court] for decision. . . .

40.   Throughout the proceedings, Hungary contended that . . . it never suspended the application of the 1977 Treaty itself. To justify its conduct, it relied essentially on a "state of ecological necessity."

* * *

According to Hungary, the principal ecological dangers which would have been caused by this system were as follows. [As a result of implementation of the original plan for Gabcíkovo/Dunakiliti], . . . the groundwater level would have fallen in most of the Szigetköz. Furthermore, the groundwater would then no longer have been supplied by the Danube—which, on the contrary, would have acted as a drain—but by the reservoir of stagnant water at Dunakiliti and the side-arms which would have become silted up. In the long term, the quality of water would have been seriously impaired. As for the surface water, risks of eutrophication would have arisen, particularly in the reservoir; instead of the old Danube there would have been a river choked with sand, where only a relative trickle of water would have flowed. The network of arms would have been for the most part cut off from the principal bed. The fluvial fauna and flora, like those in the alluvial plains, would have been condemned to extinction.

As for Nagymaros, Hungary argued that, if that dam had been built, the bed of the Danube upstream would have silted up and, consequently, the quality of the water collected in the bank-filtered wells would have deteriorated in this sector. What is more, the operation of the Gabcíkovo power plant in peak mode would have occasioned significant daily variations in the water level in the reservoir upstream, which would have constituted a threat to aquatic habitats in particular. Furthermore, the construction and operation of the Nagymaros dam would have caused the erosion of the riverbed downstream, along Szentendre Island. The water level of the river would therefore have fallen in this section and the yield of the bank-filtered wells providing two-thirds of the water supply of the city of Budapest would have appreciably diminished. The filter layer would also have shrunk or perhaps even disappeared, and fine sediments would have been deposited in certain pockets in the river. For this twofold reason, the quality of the infiltrating water would have been severely jeopardized.

From all these predictions, in support of which it quoted a variety of scientific studies, Hungary concluded that a "state of ecological necessity" did indeed exist in 1989.

* * *

44.   . . . Slovakia denied that there had been any kind of "ecological state of necessity" in this case either in 1989 or subsequently. It invoked the authority of various scientific studies when it claimed that Hungary had given an exaggeratedly pessimistic description of the situation. Slovakia did not, of course, deny that ecological problems could have arisen. However, it asserted that they could to a large extent have been remedied. . . .

50.   In the present case, the Parties are in agreement in considering that the existence of a state of necessity must be evaluated in the light of the criteria laid down by the International Law Commission in Article 33 of the Draft Articles on the International Responsibility of States that it adopted on first reading. That provision is worded as follows:

Article 33.   State of necessity

1.   A state of necessity may not be invoked by a State as a ground for precluding the wrongfulness of an act of that State not in conformity with an international obligation of the State unless:

(a) the act was the only means of safeguarding an essential interest of the State against a grave and imminent peril; and

(b) the act did not seriously impair an essential interest of the State towards which the obligation existed.

2.   In any case, a state of necessity may not be invoked by a State as a ground for precluding wrongfulness:

(a) if the international obligation with which the act of the State is not in conformity arises out of a peremptory norm of general international law; or

(b) if the international obligation with which the act of the State is not in conformity is laid down by a treaty which, explicitly or implicitly, excludes the possibility of invoking the state of necessity with respect to that obligation; or

(c) if the State in question has contributed to the occurrence of the state of necessity.

In its Commentary, the Commission defined the "state of necessity" as being

the situation of a State whose sole means of safeguarding an essential interest threatened by a grave and imminent peril is to adopt conduct not in conformity with what is required of it by an international obligation to another State *(ibid.*, para. 1).

It concluded that "the notion of state of necessity is . . . deeply rooted in general legal thinking."

51.   The Court considers, first of all, that the state of necessity is a ground recognized by customary international law for precluding the wrongfulness of an act not in conformity with an international obligation. It observes moreover that such ground for precluding wrongfulness can only be accepted on an exceptional basis. . . .

52.   In the present case, the following basic conditions set forth in Draft Article 33 are relevant: it must have been occasioned by an "essential interest" of the State which is the author of the act conflicting with one of its international obligations; that interest must have been threatened by a "grave and imminent peril"; the act being challenged must have been the "only means" of safeguarding that interest; that act must not have "seriously impair[ed] an essential interest" of the State towards which the obligation existed; and the State which is the author of that act must not have "contributed to the occurrence of the state of necessity". Those conditions reflect customary international law.

The Court will now endeavour to ascertain whether those conditions had been met at the time of the suspension and abandonment, by Hungary, of the works that it was to carry out in accordance with the 1977 Treaty.

53.   The Court has no difficulty in acknowledging that the concerns expressed by Hungary for its natural environment in the region affected by the Gabcíkovo–Nagymaros Project related to an "essential interest" of that State, within the meaning given to that expression in Article 33 of the Draft of the International Law Commission.

The Commission, in its Commentary, indicated that one should not, in that context, reduce an "essential interest" to a matter only of the "existence" of the State, and that the whole question was, ultimately, to be judged in the light of the particular case (see *Yearbook of the International Law Commission*, 1980, Vol. II, Part 2, p. 49, para. 32); at the same time, it included among the situations that could occasion a state of necessity, "a grave danger to . . . the ecological preservation of all or some of [the] territory [of a State];" and specified, with reference to State practice, that "it is primarily in the last two decades that safeguarding the ecological balance has come to be considered an 'essential interest' of all States."

The Court recalls that it has recently had occasion to stress, in the following terms, the great significance that it attaches to respect for the environment, not only for States but also for the whole of mankind:

the environment is not an abstraction but represents the living space, the quality of life and the very health of human beings, including generations unborn. The existence of the general obligation of States to ensure that activities within their jurisdiction and control respect the environment of other States or of areas beyond national control is now part of the corpus of international law relating to the environment. (*Legality of the Threat or Use of Nuclear Weapons, Advisory Opinion, I.C.J. Reports 1996*, pp. 241–242, para. 29.)

54. The verification of the existence, in 1989, of the "peril" invoked by Hungary, of its "grave and imminent" nature, as well as of the absence of any "means" to respond to it, other than the measures taken by Hungary to suspend and abandon the works, are all complex processes.

As the Court has already indicated (see paragraphs 33 *et seq.* above), Hungary on several occasions expressed, in 1989, its "uncertainties" as to the ecological impact of putting in place the Gabčíkovo–Nagymaros barrage system, which is why it asked insistently for new scientific studies to be carried out.

The Court considers, however, that, serious though these uncertainties might have been they could not, alone, establish the objective existence of a "peril" in the sense of a component element of a state of necessity. The word "peril" certainly evokes the idea of "risk"; that is precisely what distinguishes "peril" from material damage. But a state of necessity could not exist without a "peril" duly established at the relevant point in time; the mere apprehension of a possible "peril" could not suffice in that respect. It could moreover hardly be otherwise, when the "peril" constituting the state of necessity has at the same time to be "grave" and "imminent". "Imminence" is synonymous with "immediacy" or "proximity" and goes far beyond the concept of "possibility". As the International Law Commission emphasized in its commentary, the "extremely grave and imminent" peril must "have been a threat to the interest at the actual time." That does not exclude, in the view of the Court, that a "peril" appearing in the long term might be held to be "imminent" as soon as it is established, at the relevant point in time, that the realization of that peril, however far off it might be, is not thereby any less certain and inevitable.

The Hungarian argument on the state of necessity could not convince the Court unless it was at least proven that a real, "grave" and "imminent" "peril" existed in 1989 and that the measures taken by Hungary were the only possible response to it.

* * *

55. ... Hungary maintained that, if the works at Nagymaros had been carried out as planned, the environment—and in particular the drinking water resources—in the area would have been exposed to serious dangers on account of problems linked to the upstream reservoir on the one hand and, on the other, the risks of erosion of the riverbed downstream.

The Court notes that the dangers ascribed to the upstream reservoir were mostly of a long-term nature and, above all, that they remained uncertain.... [A]ny dangers associated with the putting into service of the Nagymaros portion of the Project would have been closely linked to the extent to which it was operated in peak mode and to the modalities of such operation. [The final rules for operation of the power plant had not been decided.] It follows that, even if it could have been established—which, in the Court's appreciation of the evidence before it, was not the case—that the reservoir would ultimately have constituted a "grave peril" for the environment in the area, one would be bound to conclude that the peril was not "imminent" at the time at which Hungary suspended and then abandoned the works relating to the dam.

With regard to the lowering of the riverbed downstream of the Nagymaros dam, the danger could have appeared at once more serious and more pressing, in so far as it was the supply of drinking water to the city of Budapest which would have been affected. The Court would however point out that the bed of the Danube in the vicinity of Szentendre had already been deepened prior to 1980 in order to extract building materials, and that the river had from that time attained, in that sector, the depth required by the 1977 Treaty. The peril invoked by Hungary had thus already materialized to a large extent for a number of years, so that it could not, in 1989, represent a peril arising entirely out of the project. The Court would stress, however, that, even supposing, as Hungary maintained, that the construction and operation of the dam would have created serious risks, Hungary had means available to it, other than the suspension and abandonment of the works, of responding to that situation. It could for example have proceeded regularly to discharge gravel into the river downstream of the dam. It could likewise, if necessary, have supplied Budapest with drinking water by processing the river water in an appropriate manner. The two Parties expressly recognized that that possibility remained open even though—and this is not determinative of the state of necessity—the purification of the river water, like the other measures envisaged, clearly would have been a more costly technique.

56.   The Court now comes to the Gabcíkovo sector. It will recall that Hungary's concerns in this sector related on the one hand to the quality of the surface water in the Dunakiliti reservoir, with its effects on the quality of the groundwater in the region, and on the other hand, more generally, to the level, movement and quality of both the surface water and the groundwater in the whole of the Szigetköz, with their effects on the fauna and flora in the alluvial plain of the Danube (see paragraph 40 above).

Whether in relation to the Dunakiliti site or to the whole of the Szigetköz, the Court finds here again, that the peril claimed by Hungary was to be considered in the long term, and, more importantly, remained uncertain. As Hungary itself acknowledges, the damage that it apprehended had primarily to be the result of some relatively slow natural processes, the effects of which could not easily be assessed.

* * * The report dated 23 June 1989 by the *ad hoc* Committee of the Hungarian Academy of Sciences, which was also referred to in paragraph 35 of the present Judgment, does not express any awareness of an authenticated peril—even in the form of a definite peril, whose realization would have been inevitable in the long term * * *.

The Court also notes that, in these proceedings, Hungary acknowledged that, as a general rule, the quality of the Danube waters had improved over the past 20 years, even if those waters remained subject to hypertrophic conditions.

However "grave" it might have been, it would accordingly have been difficult, in the light of what is said above, to see the alleged peril as sufficiently certain and therefore "imminent" in 1989.

The Court moreover considers that Hungary could, in this context also, have resorted to other means in order to respond to the dangers that it apprehended. In particular, within the framework of the original Project, Hungary seemed to be in a position to control at least partially the distribution of the water between the bypass canal, the old bed of the Danube and the side-arms. It should not be overlooked that the Dunakiliti dam was located in Hungarian territory and that Hungary could construct the works needed to regulate flows along the old bed of the Danube and the side-arms.

* * *

57.   The Court concludes from the foregoing that, with respect to both Nagymaros and Gabcíkovo, the perils invoked by Hungary, without prejudging their possible gravity, were not sufficiently established in 1989, nor were they "imminent"; and that

Hungary had available to it at that time means of responding to these perceived perils other than the suspension and abandonment of works with which it had been entrusted. What is more, negotiations were under way which might have led to a review of the Project and the extension of some of its time-limits, without there being need to abandon it. . . .

Moreover, the Court notes that Hungary decided to conclude the 1977 Treaty . . . [and that] Hungary was . . . presumably aware of the situation as then known, [including the existence of environmental risks], when it assumed its obligations under the Treaty. . . . Hungary contended before the Court that [earlier environmental] studies had been inadequate and that the state of knowledge at that time was not such as to make possible a complete evaluation of the ecological implications of the Gabcíkovo–Nagymaros Project. It is nonetheless the case that although the principal object of the 1977 Treaty was the construction of a System of Locks for the production of electricity, improvement of navigation on the Danube and protection against flooding, the need to ensure the protection of the environment had not escaped the parties, as can be seen from Articles 15, 19 and 20 of the Treaty.

What is more, the Court cannot fail to note the positions taken by Hungary after the entry into force of the 1977 Treaty. In 1983, Hungary asked that the works under the Treaty should go forward more slowly, for reasons that were essentially economic but also, subsidiarily, related to ecological concerns. In 1989, when, according to Hungary itself, the state of scientific knowledge had undergone a significant development, it asked for the works to be speeded up, and then decided, three months later, to suspend them and subsequently to abandon them. . . .

The Court infers from all these elements that, in the present case, even if it had been established that there was, in 1989, a state of necessity linked to the performance of the 1977 Treaty, Hungary would not have been permitted to rely upon that state of necessity in order to justify its failure to comply with its treaty obligations, as it had helped, by act or omission to bring it about.

* * *

59. In the light of the conclusions reached above, the Court * * * finds that Hungary was not entitled to suspend and subsequently abandon, in 1989, the works on the Nagymaros Project and on the part of the Gabcíkovo Project for which the 1977 Treaty and related instruments attributed responsibility to it.

* * *

104. Hungary further argued that it was entitled to invoke a number of events which, cumulatively, would have constituted a fundamental change of circumstances [justifying its failure to perform the treaty]. In this respect it specified profound changes of a political nature, the Project's diminishing economic viability, the progress of environmental knowledge and the development of new norms and prescriptions of international environmental law * * *.

The Court recalls that, in the *Fisheries Jurisdiction* case (*I.C.J. Reports 1973*, p. 63, para. 36), it stated that,

Article 62 of the Vienna Convention on the Law of Treaties, . . . may in many respects be considered as a codification of existing customary law on the subject of the termination of a treaty relationship on account of change of circumstances.

The prevailing political situation was certainly relevant for the conclusion of the 1977 Treaty. But the Court will recall that the Treaty provided for a joint investment programme for the production of energy, the control of floods and the improvement of navigation on the Danube. In the Court's view, the prevalent political conditions were thus not so closely linked to the object and purpose of the Treaty that they constituted an essential basis of the consent of the parties and, in changing, radically altered the extent of the obligations still to be performed. The same holds good for the economic system in force at the time of the conclusion of the 1977 Treaty. Besides, even though the estimated profitability of the Project might have appeared less in 1992 than in 1977, it does not appear from the record before the Court that it was bound to diminish to such an extent that the treaty obligations of the parties would have been radically transformed as a result.

The Court does not consider that new developments in the state of environmental knowledge and of environmental law can be said to have been completely unforeseen. What is more, the formulation of Articles 15, 19 and 20, designed to accommodate change, made it possible for the parties to take account of such developments and to apply them when implementing those treaty provisions.

[Thus, the] changed circumstances advanced by Hungary are, in the Court's view, not of such a nature, either individually or collectively, that their effect would radically transform the extent of the obligations still to be performed in order to accomplish the Project. A fundamental change of circumstances must have been unforeseen; the existence of the circumstances at the time of the Treaty's conclusion must have constituted an essential basis of the consent of the parties to be bound by the Treaty. The negative and conditional wording of Article 62 of the Vienna Convention on the Law of Treaties is a clear indication moreover that the stability of treaty relations requires that the plea of fundamental change of circumstances be applied only in exceptional cases.

* * *

111. Finally, the Court will address Hungary's claim that it was entitled to terminate the 1977 Treaty because new requirements of international law for the protection of the environment precluded performance of the Treaty.

112. Neither of the Parties contended that new peremptory norms of environmental law had emerged since the conclusion of the 1977 Treaty, and the Court will consequently not be required to examine the scope of Article 64 of the Vienna Convention on the Law of Treaties. On the other hand, the Court wishes to point out that newly developed norms of environmental law are relevant for the implementation of the Treaty and that the parties could, by agreement, incorporate them through the application of Articles 15, 19 and 20 of the Treaty. These articles do not contain specific obligations of performance but require the parties, in carrying out their obligations to ensure that the quality of water in the Danube is not impaired and that nature is protected, to take new environmental norms into consideration when agreeing upon the means to be specified in the Joint Contractual Plan.

By inserting these evolving provisions in the Treaty, the parties recognized the potential necessity to adapt the Project. Consequently, the Treaty is not static, and is open to adapt to emerging norms of international law. By means of Articles 15 and 19, new environmental norms can be incorporated in the Joint Contractual Plan.

The responsibility to do this was a joint responsibility. The obligations contained in Articles 15, 19 and 20 are, by definition, general and have to be transformed into specific obligations of performance through a process of consultation and negotiation. Their implementation thus requires a mutual willingness to discuss in good faith actual and potential environmental risks. * * *

The awareness of the vulnerability of the environment and the recognition that environmental risks have to be assessed on a continuous basis have become much stronger in the years since the Treaty's conclusion. These new concerns have enhanced the relevance of Articles 15, 19 and 20.

113. The Court recognizes that both Parties agree on the need to take environmental concerns seriously and to take the required precautionary measures, but they fundamentally disagree on the consequences this has for the joint Project. In such a

case, third-party involvement may be helpful and instrumental in finding a solution, provided each of the Parties is flexible in its position.

114. Finally, Hungary maintained that by their conduct both parties had repudiated the Treaty and that a bilateral treaty repudiated by both parties cannot survive. The Court is of the view, however, that although it has found that both Hungary and Czechoslovakia failed to comply with their obligations under the 1977 Treaty, this reciprocal wrongful conduct did not bring the Treaty to an end nor justify its termination. The Court would set a precedent with disturbing implications for treaty relations and the integrity of the rule *pacta sunt servanda* if it were to conclude that a treaty in force between States, which the parties have implemented in considerable measure and at great cost over a period of years, might be unilaterally set aside on grounds of reciprocal non-compliance. It would be otherwise, of course, if the parties decided to terminate the Treaty by mutual consent. But in this case, while Hungary purported to terminate the Treaty, Czechoslovakia consistently resisted this act and declared it to be without legal effect.

115. In light of the conclusions it has reached above, the Court ... finds that the notification of termination by Hungary ... did not have the legal effect of terminating the 1977 Treaty and related instruments.

* * *

139. The Court is of the opinion that the Parties are under a legal obligation, during the negotiations [that must now be held], to consider, within the context of the 1977 Treaty, in what way the multiple objectives of the Treaty can best be served, keeping in mind that all of them should be fulfilled.

140. It is clear that the Project's impact upon, and its implications for, the environment are of necessity a key issue. The numerous scientific reports which have been presented to the Court by the Parties—even if their conclusions are often contradictory—provide abundant evidence that this impact and these implications are considerable.

In order to evaluate the environmental risks, current standards must be taken into consideration. This is not only allowed by the wording of Articles 15 and 19, but even prescribed, to the extent that these articles impose a continuing—and thus necessarily evolving—obligation on the parties to maintain the quality of the water of the Danube and to protect nature.

The Court is mindful that, in the field of environmental protection, vigilance and prevention are required on account of the often irreversible character of damage to the environment and of the limitations inherent in the very mechanism of reparation of this type of damage.

Throughout the ages, mankind has, for economic and other reasons, constantly interfered with nature. In the past, this was often done without consideration of the effects upon the environment. Owing to new scientific insights and to a growing awareness of the risks for mankind—for present and future generations—of pursuit of such interventions at an unconsidered and unabated pace, new norms and standards have been developed, set forth in a great number of instruments during the last two decades. Such new norms have to be taken into consideration, and such new standards given proper weight, not only when States contemplate new activities but also when continuing with activities begun in the past. This need to reconcile economic development with protection of the environment is aptly expressed in the concept of sustainable development.

For the purposes of the present case, this means that the Parties together should look afresh at the effects on the environment of the operation of the Gabcíkovo power plant. In particular they must find a satisfactory solution for the volume of water to be released into the old bed of the Danube and into the side-arms on both sides of the river.

141. It is not for the Court to determine what shall be the final result of these negotiations to be conducted by the Parties. It is for the Parties themselves to find an agreed solution that takes account of the objectives of the Treaty, which must be pursued in a joint and integrated way, as well as the norms of international environmental law and the principles of the law of international watercourses. The Court will recall in this context that, as it said in the *North Sea Continental Shelf* cases:

> [the Parties] are under an obligation so to conduct themselves that the negotiations are meaningful, which will not be the case when either of them insists upon its own position without contemplating any modification of it (*I.C.J. Reports 1969*, p. 47, para. 85).

142. What is required in the present case by the rule *pacta sunt servanda*, as reflected in Article 26 of the Vienna Convention of 1969 on the Law of Treaties, is that the Parties find an agreed solution within the co-operative context of the Treaty. . . .

8.8 EC MEASURES CONCERNING MEAT AND MEAT PRODUCTS (HORMONES), WTO Doc. WT/DS26/AB/R (WTO Appellate Body Report, Jan. 16, 1998)

[*Eds.*—In 1996, the United States and Canada filed complaints with the WTO against the European Community's ban on imports of meat and meat products derived from cattle to which certain natural and synthetic hormones had been administered. The hormones in question are generally administered to promote growth, and the European ban was prompted by public fear of potential adverse health effects from consuming meat from hormone-treated cattle. The ban was also supported by European farmers, who faced severe competition from imported beef and beef products.]

Excerpts from the Appellate Body Report

172.   Under Article 3.3 of the *SPS Agreement*, a Member may decide to set for itself a level of protection different from that implicit in the international standard, and to implement or embody that level of protection in a measure not "based on" the international standard. The Member's appropriate level of protection may be higher than that implied in the international standard. The right of a Member to determine its own appropriate level of sanitary protection is an important right. . . .

* * *

173.   The right of a Member to define its appropriate level of protection is not, however, an absolute or unqualified right. Article 3.3 also makes this clear:

Members may introduce or maintain sanitary or phytosanitary measures which result in a higher level of sanitary or phytosanitary protection than would be achieved by measures based on the relevant international standards, guidelines or recommendations, if there is a scientific justification, or as a consequence of the level of sanitary or phytosanitary protection a Member determines to be appropriate in accordance with the relevant provisions of paragraphs 1 through 8 of Article 5. . . .

* * *

206.   Most, if not all, of the scientific studies referred to by the European Communities, in respect of the five hormones involved here, concluded that their use for growth promotion purposes is "safe'" if the hormones are administered in accordance with the requirements of good veterinary practice. Where the condition of observance of good veterinary practice (which is much the same condition attached to the standards, guidelines and recommendations of Codex with respect to the use of the five hormones for growth promotion) is not followed, the logical inference is that the use of such hormones for growth promotion purposes may or may not be "safe." The SPS Agreement requires assessment of the potential for adverse effects on human health arising from the presence of contaminants and toxins in food. We consider that the object and purpose of the SPS Agreement justify the examination and evaluation of all such risks for human health whatever their precise and immediate origin may be. We do not mean to suggest that risks arising from potential abuse in the administration of controlled substances and from control problems need to be, or should be, evaluated by risk assessors in each and every case. When and if risks of these types do in fact arise, risk assessors may examine and evaluate them. . . .

207.   The question that arises, therefore, is whether the European Communities did, in fact, submit a risk assessment demonstrating and evaluating the existence and level of risk arising in the present case from abusive use of hormones and the difficulties of control of the administration of hormones for growth promotion purposes, within the United States and Canada as exporting countries, and at the frontiers of the European Communities as an importing country. Here, we must agree with the finding of the Panel that the European Communities in fact restricted itself to pointing out the condition of administration of hormones "in accordance with good practice" "without further providing an assessment of the potential adverse effects

related to non compliance with such practice." The record of the panel proceedings shows that the risk arising from abusive use of hormones for growth promotion combined with control problems for the hormones at issue, may have been examined on two occasions in a scientific manner. The first occasion may have occurred at the proceedings before the Committee of Inquiry into the Problem of Quality in the Meat Sector established by the European Parliament, the results of which constituted the basis of the Pimenta Report of 1989. However, none of the original studies and evidence put before the Committee of Inquiry was submitted to the Panel. The second occasion could have been the 1995 EC Scientific Conference on Growth Promotion in Meat Production. One of the three workshops of this Conference examined specifically the problems of "detection and control." However, only one of the studies presented to the workshop discussed systematically some of the problems arising from the combination of potential abuse and problems of control of hormones and other substances. The study presented a theoretical framework for the systematic analysis of such problems, but did not itself investigate and evaluate the actual problems that have arisen at the borders of the European Communities or within the United States, Canada and other countries exporting meat and meat products to the European Communities. At best, this study may represent the beginning of an assessment of such risks.

208. In the absence of any other relevant documentation, we find that the European Communities did not actually proceed to an assessment, within the meaning of Articles 5.1 and 5.2, of the risks arising from the failure of observance of good veterinary practice combined with problems of control of the use of hormones for growth promotion purposes. The absence of such a risk assessment, when considered in conjunction with the conclusion actually reached by most, if not all, of the scientific studies relating to the other aspects of risk noted earlier, leads us to the conclusion that no risk assessment that reasonably supports or warrants the import prohibition embodied in the EC Directives was furnished to the Panel. We affirm, therefore, the ultimate conclusion of the Panel that the EC import prohibition is not based on a risk assessment within the meaning of Articles 5.1 and 5.2 of the SPS Agreement and is, therefore, inconsistent with the requirements of Article 5.1.

209. Since we have concluded above that an SPS measure, to be consistent with Article 3.3, has to comply with, inter alia, the requirements contained in Article 5.1, it follows that the EC measures at issue, by failing to comply with Article 5.1, are also inconsistent with Article 3.3 of the SPS Agreement.

8.9 UNITED STATES-IMPORT PROHIBITION OF CERTAIN SHRIMP AND SHRIMP PRODUCTS, **WTO Doc. WT/DS58/AB/R (WTO Appellate Body Report, 12 October 1998)**

[*Eds.*—The United States required domestic shrimp trawlers to equip their nets with turtle excluder devices (TEDs) to prevent the nets from entrapping sea turtles and drowning them. The United States also banned importation of shrimp from other states unless those states had similar requirements in place for their shrimp trawlers. *See* Public Law 101–162, section 609 (1990); *Earth Island Institute, et al.v. Christopher, et al.*, 913 F.Supp. 559 (U.S. C.I.T. 1995). India, Malaysia, Pakistan and Thailand filed a complaint alleging that the shrimp import restrictions violated GATT rules. The United States conceded a probable violation of GATT Article XI, but declined to discuss arguments that its law also violated Articles I and III of GATT. *See* WTO Panel Report, *United States–Import Prohibition of Certain Shrimp and Shrimp Products*, paragraph 3.143, WT/DS58/R (15 May 1998)(reporting position of U.S.) Instead, it argued that its actions were justified under GATT Article XX.]

Excerpts from the Appellate Body Report

113. Article XX of the GATT 1994 reads, in its relevant parts:

Article XX

General Exceptions

Subject to the requirement that such measures are not applied in a manner which would constitute a means of arbitrary or unjustifiable discrimination between countries where the same conditions prevail, or a disguised restriction on international trade, nothing in this Agreement shall be construed to prevent the adoption or enforcement by any Member of measures:

. . .

(*b*) necessary to protect human, animal or plant life or health;

. . .

(*g*) relating to the conservation of exhaustible natural resources if such measures are made effective in conjunction with restrictions on domestic production or consumption;

[*Eds.*—Following the analytical framework developed by the Appellate Body, a party invoking Article XX must first show that a trade measure is "provisionally justified" under one of the exceptions listed in the Article. If the measure is provisionally justified, it will be upheld unless it is applied in a way that violates the terms of the introductory paragraph of Article XX.]

114. [The meaning of GATT **(Basic Document 7.1)** must be ascertained by applying the "customary rules of interpretation of public international law."] As we have emphasized numerous times, these rules call for an examination of the ordinary meaning of the words of a treaty, read in their context, and in the light of the object and purpose of the treaty involved. A treaty interpreter must begin with, and focus upon, the text of the particular provision to be interpreted. It is in the words constituting that provision, read in their context, that the object and purpose of the states parties to the treaty must first be sought. Where the meaning imparted by the text itself is equivocal or inconclusive, or where confirmation of the correctness of the reading of the text itself is desired, light from the object and purpose of the treaty as a whole may usefully be sought.

* * *

B. Article XX(g): Provisional Justification of Section 609

125.   In claiming justification for its measure, the United States primarily invokes Article XX(g). Justification under Article XX(b) is claimed only in the alternative; that is, the United States suggests that we should look at Article XX(b) only if we find that Section 609 does not fall within the ambit of Article XX(g). We proceed, therefore, to the first tier of the analysis of Section 609 and to our consideration of whether it may be characterized as provisionally justified under the terms of Article XX(g).

* * *

1.   "Exhaustible Natural Resources"

127.   We begin with the threshold question of whether Section 609 is a measure concerned with the conservation of "exhaustible natural resources" within the meaning of Article XX(g). . . . India, Pakistan and Thailand contended that a "reasonable interpretation" of the term "exhaustible" is that the term refers to "finite resources such as minerals, rather than biological or renewable resources." In their view, such finite resources were exhaustible "because there was a limited supply which could and would be depleted unit for unit as the resources were consumed." Moreover, they argued, if "all" natural resources were considered to be exhaustible, the term "exhaustible" would become superfluous. They also referred to the drafting history of Article XX(g), and, in particular, to the mention of minerals, such as manganese, in the context of arguments made by some delegations that "export restrictions" should be permitted for the preservation of scarce natural resources. For its part, Malaysia added that sea turtles, being living creatures, could only be considered under Article XX(b), since Article XX(g) was meant for "nonliving exhaustible natural resources." It followed, according to Malaysia, that the United States cannot invoke both the Article XX(b) and the Article XX(g) exceptions simultaneously.

128.   We are not convinced by these arguments. Textually, Article XX(g) is *not* limited to the conservation of "mineral" or "non-living" natural resources. The complainants' principal argument is rooted in the notion that "living" natural resources are "renewable" and therefore cannot be "exhaustible" natural resources. We do not believe that "exhaustible" natural resources and "renewable" natural resources are mutually exclusive. One lesson that modern biological sciences teach us is that living species, though in principle, capable of reproduction and, in that sense, "renewable' " are in certain circumstances indeed susceptible of depletion, exhaustion and extinction, frequently because of human activities. Living resources are just as "finite" as petroleum, iron ore and other non-living resources.

129.   The words of Article XX(g), "exhaustible natural resources' " were actually crafted more than 50 years ago. They must be read by a treaty interpreter in the light of contemporary concerns of the community of nations about the protection and conservation of the environment. . . . The preamble of the WTO Agreement—which informs not only the GATT 1994 **[Basic Document 7.1]**, but also the other covered agreements—explicitly acknowledges "the objective of *sustainable development*":

> The *Parties* to this Agreement,
>
> *Recognizing* that their relations in the field of trade and economic endeavour should be conducted *with a view to raising standards of living, ensuring full employment and a large and steadily growing volume of real income and effective demand*, and *expanding the production of and trade in goods and services*, while allowing for the optimal use of the world's resources in accordance with the *objective of sustainable development, seeking both to protect and preserve the environment and to enhance the means for doing so* in a manner consistent with their respective needs and concerns at different levels of economic development, . . . (emphasis added).

130.   From the perspective embodied in the preamble of the *WTO Agreement* [**Basic Document 7.7**], we note that the generic term "natural resources" in Article XX(g) is not "static" in its content or reference but is rather "by definition, evolutionary." It is, therefore, pertinent to note that modern international conventions and declarations make frequent references to natural resources as embracing both living and non-living resources. For instance, the 1982 United Nations Convention on the Law of the Sea ("UNCLOS") [**Basic Document 3.8**], in [Article 56, 61 and 62] repeatedly refers ... to "living resources" in specifying rights and duties of states in their exclusive economic zones. The Convention on Biological Diversity [**Basic Document 5.7**] uses the concept of "biological resources." Agenda 21 [**Basic Document 1.28**] speaks most broadly of "natural resources" and goes into detailed statements about "marine living resources." ...

131.   Given the recent acknowledgement by the international community of the importance of concerted bilateral or multilateral action to protect living natural resources, and recalling the explicit recognition by WTO Members of the objective of sustainable development in the preamble of the *WTO Agreement*, we believe it is too late in the day to suppose that Article XX(g) of the GATT 1994 may be read as referring only to the conservation of exhaustible mineral or other non-living natural resources. Moreover, two adopted GATT 1947 panel reports previously found fish to be an "exhaustible natural resource" within the meaning of Article XX(g). We hold that, in line with the principle of effectiveness in treaty interpretation, measures to conserve exhaustible natural resources, whether *living* or *non-living*, may fall within Article XX(g).

132.   We turn next to the issue of whether the living natural resources sought to be conserved by the measure are "exhaustible" under Article XX(g). That this element is present in respect of the five species of sea turtles here involved appears to be conceded by all the participants and third participants in this case. The exhaustibility of sea turtles would in fact have been very difficult to controvert since all of the seven recognized species of sea turtles are today listed in Appendix 1 of the Convention on International Trade in Endangered Species of Wild Fauna and Flora ("CITES") [**Basic Document 5.4**]. The list in Appendix 1 includes "all species *threatened with extinction* which are or may be affected by trade" (emphasis added).

133.   Finally, we observe that sea turtles are highly migratory animals, passing in and out of waters subject to the rights of jurisdiction of various coastal states and the high seas. In the Panel Report, the Panel said:

> ... Information brought to the attention of the Panel, including documented statements from the experts, tends to *confirm the fact that sea turtles, in certain circumstances of their lives, migrate through the waters of several countries and the high sea.* ... (emphasis added)

The sea turtle species here at stake, i.e., covered by Section 609, are all known to occur in waters over which the United States exercises jurisdiction. Of course, it is not claimed that *all* populations of these species migrate to, or traverse, at one time or another, waters subject to United States jurisdiction. Neither the appellant nor any of the appellees claims any rights of exclusive ownership over the sea turtles, at least not while they are swimming freely in their natural habitat—the oceans. We do not pass upon the question of whether there is an implied jurisdictional limitation in Article XX(g), and if so, the nature or extent of that limitation. We note only that in the specific circumstances of the case before us, there is a sufficient nexus between the migratory and endangered marine populations involved and the United States for purposes of Article XX(g).

134.   For all the foregoing reasons, we find that the sea turtles here involved constitute "exhaustible natural resources" for purposes of Article XX(g) of the GATT 1994.

2. "Relating to the Conservation of [Exhaustible Natural Resources]"

135.   Article XX(g) requires that the measure sought to be justified be one which "relat[es] to" the conservation of exhaustible natural resources. In making this determination, the treaty interpreter essentially looks into the relationship between the measure at stake and the legitimate policy of conserving exhaustible natural resources. It is well to bear in mind that the policy of protecting and conserving the endangered sea turtles here involved is shared by all participants and third participants in this appeal, indeed, by the vast majority of the nations of the world. None of the parties to this dispute question the genuineness of the commitment of the others to that policy.

* * *

137.   In the present case, we must examine the relationship between the general structure and design of the measure here at stake, Section 609, and the policy goal it purports to serve, that is, the conservation of sea turtles.

138.   Section 609(b)(1) imposes an import ban on shrimp that have been harvested with commercial fishing technology which may adversely affect sea turtles. This provision is designed to influence countries to adopt national regulatory programs requiring the use of TEDs by their shrimp fishermen. In this connection, it is important to note that the general structure and design of Section 609 *cum* implementing guidelines is fairly narrowly focused. There are two basic exemptions from the import ban, both of which relate clearly and directly to the policy goal of conserving sea turtles. First, Section 609, as elaborated in the 1996 Guidelines, excludes from the import ban shrimp harvested "under conditions that do not adversely affect sea turtles." Thus, the measure, by its terms, excludes from the import ban: aquaculture shrimp; shrimp species (such as *pandalid* shrimp) harvested in water areas where sea turtles do not normally occur; and shrimp harvested exclusively by artisanal methods, even from non-certified countries. The harvesting of such shrimp clearly does not affect sea turtles. Second, under Section 609(b)(2), the measure exempts from the import ban shrimp caught in waters subject to the jurisdiction of certified countries.

139.   There are two types of certification for countries under Section 609(b)(2). First, under Section 609(b)(2)(C), a country may be certified as having a fishing environment that does not pose a threat of incidental taking of sea turtles in the course of commercial shrimp trawl harvesting. There is no risk, or only a negligible risk, that sea turtles will be harmed by shrimp trawling in such an environment.

140.   The second type of certification is provided by Section 609(b)(2)(A) and (B). Under these provisions, as further elaborated in the 1996 Guidelines, a country wishing to export shrimp to the United States is required to adopt a regulatory program that is comparable to that of the United States program and to have a rate of incidental take of sea turtles that is comparable to the average rate of United States' vessels. This is, essentially, a requirement that a country adopt a regulatory program requiring the use of TEDs by commercial shrimp trawling vessels in areas where there is a likelihood of intercepting sea turtles. This requirement is, in our view, directly connected with the policy of conservation of sea turtles. It is undisputed among the participants, and recognized by the experts consulted by the Panel, that the harvesting of shrimp by commercial shrimp trawling vessels with mechanical retrieval devices in waters where shrimp and sea turtles coincide is a significant cause of sea turtle mortality. Moreover, the Panel did "not question . . . the fact generally acknowledged by the experts that TEDs, when properly installed and adapted to the local area, would be an effective tool for the preservation of sea turtles."

141.   In its general design and structure, therefore, Section 609 is not a simple, blanket prohibition of the importation of shrimp imposed without regard to the consequences (or lack thereof) of the mode of harvesting employed upon the incidental

capture and mortality of sea turtles. Focusing on the design of the measure here at stake, it appears to us that Section 609, *cum* implementing guidelines, is not disproportionately wide in its scope and reach in relation to the policy objective of protection and conservation of sea turtle species. The means are, in principle, reasonably related to the ends. The means and ends relationship between Section 609 and the legitimate policy of conserving an exhaustible, and, in fact, endangered species, is observably a close and real one. . . .

142. In our view, therefore, Section 609 is a measure "relating to" the conservation of an exhaustible natural resource within the meaning of Article XX(g) of the GATT 1994.

* * *

3. "If Such Measures are Made Effective in conjunction with Restrictions on Domestic Production or Consumption"

* * *

144. . . . [Regulations issued pursuant to the Endangered Species Act] require United States shrimp trawlers to use approved TEDs "in areas and at times when there is a likelihood of intercepting sea turtles' " with certain limited exceptions. . . .

145. Accordingly, we hold that Section 609 is a measure made effective in conjunction with the restrictions on domestic harvesting of shrimp, as required by Article XX(g).

B. *The Introductory Clauses of Article XX: Characterizing Section 609 under the Chapeau's Standards*

* * *

147. Although provisionally justified under Article XX(g), Section 609, if it is ultimately to be justified as an exception under Article XX, must also satisfy the requirements of the introductory clauses—the "chapeau"—of Article XX, that is,

Article XX
General Exceptions

Subject to the requirement that such measures are *not applied in a manner which would constitute a means of arbitrary or unjustifiable discrimination between countries where the same conditions prevail,* or *a disguised restriction on international trade,* nothing in this Agreement shall be construed to prevent the adoption or enforcement by any Member of measures: (emphasis added)

We turn, hence, to the task of appraising Section 609, and specifically the manner in which it is applied under the chapeau of Article XX; that is, to the second part of the two-tier analysis required under Article XX.

* * *

156. . . . . [T]he chapeau of Article XX . . . embodies the recognition on the part of WTO Members of the need to maintain a balance of rights and obligations between the right of a Member to invoke one or another of the exceptions of Article XX, specified in paragraphs (a) to (j), on the one hand, and the substantive rights of the other Members under the GATT 1994, on the other hand. Exercise by one Member of its right to invoke an exception, such as Article XX(g), if abused or misused, will, to that extent, erode or render naught the substantive treaty rights in, for example, Article XI:1, of other Members. Similarly, because the GATT 1994 itself makes available the exceptions of Article XX, in recognition of the legitimate nature of the

policies and interests there embodied, the right to invoke one of those exceptions is not to be rendered illusory. . . .

* * *

159.   The task of interpreting and applying the chapeau is, hence, essentially the delicate one of locating and marking out a line of equilibrium between the right of a Member to invoke an exception under Article XX and the rights of the other Members under varying substantive provisions (e.g., Article XI) of the GATT 1994, so that neither of the competing rights will cancel out the other and thereby distort and nullify or impair the balance of rights and obligations constructed by the Members themselves in that Agreement. The location of the line of equilibrium, as expressed in the chapeau, is not fixed and unchanging; the line moves as the kind and the shape of the measures at stake vary and as the facts making up specific cases differ.

160.   With these general considerations in mind, we address now the issue of whether the *application* of the United States measure, although the measure itself falls within the terms of Article XX(g), nevertheless constitutes "a means of arbitrary or unjustifiable discrimination between countries where the same conditions prevail" or "a disguised restriction on international trade." . . .

2.   "Unjustifiable Discrimination"

* * *

163.   The actual *application* of the [U.S. import restriction], through the implementation of the 1996 Guidelines and the regulatory practice of administrators, *requires* other WTO Members to adopt a regulatory program that is not merely *comparable*, but rather *essentially the same*, as that applied to the United States shrimp trawl vessels. Thus, the effect of the application of Section 609 is to establish a rigid and unbending standard by which United States officials determine whether or not countries will be certified, thus granting or refusing other countries the right to export shrimp to the United States. Other specific policies and measures that an exporting country may have adopted for the protection and conservation of sea turtles are not taken into account, in practice, by the administrators making the comparability determination.

164.   We understand that the United States also applies a uniform standard throughout its territory, regardless of the particular conditions existing in certain parts of the country. The United States requires the use of approved TEDs at all times by domestic, commercial shrimp trawl vessels operating in waters where there is any likelihood that they may interact with sea turtles, regardless of the actual incidence of sea turtles in those waters, the species of those sea turtles, or other differences or disparities that may exist in different parts of the United States. It may be quite acceptable for a government, in adopting and implementing a domestic policy, to adopt a single standard applicable to all its citizens throughout that country. However, it is not acceptable, in international trade relations, for one WTO Member to use an economic embargo to *require* other Members to adopt essentially the same comprehensive regulatory program, to achieve a certain policy goal, as that in force within that Member's territory, *without* taking into consideration different conditions which may occur in the territories of those other Members.

165.   Furthermore, when this dispute was before the Panel and before us, the United States did not permit imports of shrimp harvested by commercial shrimp trawl vessels using TEDs comparable in effectiveness to those required in the United States if those shrimp originated in waters of countries not certified under Section 609. In other words, *shrimp caught using methods identical to those employed in the United States* have been excluded from the United States market solely because they have been caught in waters of *countries that have not been certified by the United States*. The

resulting situation is difficult to reconcile with the declared policy objective of protecting and conserving sea turtles. This suggests to us that this measure, in its application, is more concerned with effectively influencing WTO Members to adopt essentially the same comprehensive regulatory regime as that applied by the United States to its domestic shrimp trawlers, even though many of those Members may be differently situated. We believe that discrimination results not only when countries in which the same conditions prevail are differently treated, but also when the application of the measure at issue does not allow for any inquiry into the appropriateness of the regulatory program for the conditions prevailing in those exporting countries.

166.   Another aspect of the application of Section 609 that bears heavily in any appraisal of justifiable or unjustifiable discrimination is the failure of the United States to engage the appellees, as well as other Members exporting shrimp to the United States, in serious, across-the-board negotiations with the objective of concluding bilateral or multilateral agreements for the protection and conservation of sea turtles, before enforcing the import prohibition against the shrimp exports of those other Members. . . .

167.   *A propos* this failure to have prior consistent recourse to diplomacy as an instrument of environmental protection policy, which produces discriminatory impacts on countries exporting shrimp to the United States with which no international agreements are reached or even seriously attempted, a number of points must be made. First, the Congress of the United States expressly recognized the importance of securing international agreements for the protection and conservation of the sea turtle species in enacting this law. . . .

168.   Second, the protection and conservation of highly migratory species of sea turtles, that is, the very policy objective of the measure, demands concerted and cooperative efforts on the part of the many countries whose waters are traversed in the course of recurrent sea turtle migrations. The need for, and the appropriateness of, such efforts have been recognized in the WTO itself as well as in a significant number of other international instruments and declarations. As stated earlier, the Decision on Trade and Environment, which provided for the establishment of the CTE and set out its terms of reference, refers to both the Rio Declaration on Environment and Development and Agenda 21. Of particular relevance is Principle 12 of the Rio Declaration on Environment and Development, which states, in part:

> Unilateral actions to deal with environmental challenges outside the jurisdiction of the importing country should be avoided. *Environmental measures addressing transboundary or global environmental problems should, as far as possible, be based on international consensus.* (emphasis added)

In almost identical language, paragraph 2.22(i) of Agenda 21 provides:

> Governments should encourage GATT, UNCTAD and other relevant international and regional economic institutions to examine, in accordance with their respective mandates and competences, the following propositions and principles: . . .
>
> > (i) Avoid unilateral action to deal with environmental challenges outside the jurisdiction of the importing country. *Environmental measures addressing transborder problems should, as far as possible, be based on an international consensus.* (emphasis added)

Moreover, we note that Article 5 of the Convention on Biological Diversity states:

> . . . each contracting party shall, as far as possible and as appropriate, cooperate with other contracting parties directly or, where appropriate, through competent international organizations, in respect of areas beyond

national jurisdiction and on other matters of mutual interest, for the conservation and sustainable use of biological diversity.

* * *

169.   Third, the United States did negotiate and conclude one regional international agreement for the protection and conservation of sea turtles: The Inter–American Convention. . . .

* * *

171.   The Inter–American Convention thus provides convincing demonstration that an alternative course of action was reasonably open to the United States for securing the legitimate policy goal of its measure, a course of action other than the unilateral and non-consensual procedures of the import prohibition under Section 609. It is relevant to observe that an import prohibition is, ordinarily, the heaviest "weapon" in a Member's armoury of trade measures. The record does not, however, show that serious efforts were made by the United States to negotiate similar agreements with any other country or group of countries before (and, as far as the record shows, after) Section 609 was enforced on a world-wide basis on 1 May 1996. Finally, the record also does not show that the appellant, the United States, attempted to have recourse to such international mechanisms as exist to achieve cooperative efforts to protect and conserve sea turtles before imposing the import ban.

172.   Clearly, the United States negotiated seriously with some, but not with other Members (including the appellees), that export shrimp to the United States. The effect is plainly discriminatory and, in our view, unjustifiable. The unjustifiable nature of this discrimination emerges clearly when we consider the cumulative effects of the failure of the United States to pursue negotiations for establishing consensual means of protection and conservation of the living marine resources here involved, notwithstanding the explicit statutory direction in Section 609 itself to initiate negotiations as soon as possible for the development of bilateral and multilateral agreements. The principal consequence of this failure may be seen in the resulting unilateralism evident in the application of Section 609. As we have emphasized earlier, the policies relating to the necessity for use of particular kinds of TEDs in various maritime areas, and the operating details of these policies, are all shaped by the Department of State, without the participation of the exporting Members. The system and processes of certification are established and administered by the United States agencies alone. The decision-making involved in the grant, denial or withdrawal of certification to the exporting Members, is, accordingly, also unilateral. The unilateral character of the application of Section 609 heightens the disruptive and discriminatory influence of the import prohibition and underscores its unjustifiability.

* * *

8.10 SOUTHERN BLUEFIN TUNA CASES (NZ v. Japan; Aust. v. Japan) (Provisional Measures), ITLOS Cases Nos. 3 & 4 (Int'l Trib. L. Sea, 27 August 1999)

[*Eds.*—In July 1999, New Zealand brought a claim against Japan alleging that Japan had failed to comply with its obligation to cooperate in the conservation of southern bluefin tuna by, *inter alia*, undertaking unilateral experimental fishing for the species in 1998 and 1999. New Zealand alleged violations of Articles 64 and 116 to 119 of the United Nations Convention on the Law of the Sea. It requested establishment of an arbitral tribunal, and procedures for creation of the tribunal were begun.

New Zealand also asked the International Tribunal for the Law of the Sea (a judicial body, not an arbitral body) to order provisional measures of protection for the southern bluefin tuna, pending the establishment and decision of the arbitral tribunal. Japan argued that there was no urgent threat to southern bluefin tuna stocks sufficient to justify the taking of provisional action.

The UNCLOS Tribunal sided with New Zealand.]

Excerpts from the Order of the Tribunal

67. *Considering* that, in accordance with article 290 of the Convention, the Tribunal may prescribe provisional measures to preserve the respective rights of the parties to the dispute or to prevent serious harm to the marine environment;

* * *

71. *Considering* that there is no disagreement between the parties that the stock of southern bluefin tuna is severely depleted and is at its historically lowest levels and that this is a cause for serious biological concern;

72. *Considering* that Australia and New Zealand contend that, by unilaterally implementing an experimental fishing programme, Japan has failed to comply with its obligations under articles 64 and 118 of the Convention, which require the parties to cooperate in the conservation and management of the southern bluefin tuna stock, and that the actions of Japan have resulted in a threat to the stock;

73. *Considering* that Japan contends that the scientific evidence available shows that the implementation of its experimental fishing programme will cause no further threat to the southern bluefin tuna stock and that the experimental fishing programme remains necessary to reach a more reliable assessment of the potential of the stock to recover;

74. *Considering* that Australia and New Zealand maintain that the scientific evidence available shows that the amount of southern bluefin tuna taken under the experimental fishing programme could endanger the existence of the stock;

* * *

77. *Considering* that, in the view of the Tribunal, the parties should in the circumstances act with prudence and caution to ensure that effective conservation measures are taken to prevent serious harm to the stock of southern bluefin tuna;

78. *Considering* that the parties should intensify their efforts to cooperate with other participants in the fishery for southern bluefin tuna with a view to ensuring conservation and promoting the objective of optimum utilization of the stock;

79. *Considering* that there is scientific uncertainty regarding measures to be taken to conserve the stock of southern bluefin tuna and that there is no agreement among the parties as to whether the conservation measures taken so far have led to the improvement in the stock of southern bluefin tuna;

80. *Considering* that, although the Tribunal cannot conclusively assess the scientific evidence presented by the parties, it finds that measures should be taken as a matter of urgency to preserve the rights of the parties and to avert further deterioration of the southern bluefin tuna stock;

* * *

90. *For these reasons*, the Tribunal *prescribes*, pending a decision of the arbitral tribunal, the following measures:

* * *

... Australia, Japan and New Zealand shall ensure, unless they agree otherwise, that their annual catches do not exceed the annual national allocations at the levels last agreed by the parties ... ;

... Australia, Japan and New Zealand shall each refrain from conducting an experimental fishing programme involving the taking of a catch of southern bluefin tuna, except with the agreement of the other parties or unless the experimental catch is counted against its annual national allocation ... ;

... Australia, Japan and New Zealand should resume negotiations without delay with a view to reaching agreement on measures for the conservation and management of southern bluefin tuna; ...

Excerpts from Separate Opinion by Judge Laing

1. ... [T]his an "historic proceeding". Three outstanding global citizens are before this Tribunal in a case involving regional cooperation in which significant natural and economic resources are involved. The case presents the issue of how scientific uncertainty can be handled in a judicial context. It involves questions relating to the interpretation of the 1982 United Nations Convention on the Law of the Sea (UNCLOS) and its interaction with cognate conventions. Above all, in this case the Tribunal makes decisions of fundamental importance to the institution of provisional measures and potentially of critical relevance to an aspect of international environmental law.

* * *

12. ... The Applicants based their Requests for provisional measures on articles 64, 116–119 and 300 of UNCLOS; the 1993 Convention, the parties' practice thereunder, "as well as their obligations under general international law, in particular the precautionary principle".... They argued that the principle must be applied by States in taking decisions about actions which entail threats of serious or irreversible damage to the environment, where there is scientific uncertainty about the effect of such actions. The principle requires caution and vigilance in decision-making in the face of such uncertainty.

13. The Tribunal's Order does not refer to the "precautionary principle". Instead, ... it chronicles the opposing views of the Applicants and Respondent about the condition of the stock [and the Order] recites that "the parties should in the circumstances act with 'prudence and caution' to ensure that effective conservation measures are taken to prevent serious harm to the stock". [The Order] further notes the scientific disagreement about appropriate measures to conserve the stock and the non-agreement of the parties about whether the measures actually taken have led to improvement[,] [and it] states the Tribunal's conclusion [that] article 290–type of measures [are needed] despite the Tribunal's inability conclusively to assess the scientific evidence. In my view, these statements are pregnant with meaning. In order to clarify and critique what I understand that the Tribunal has stated, I must first explore the background of the so-called precautionary principle of international environmental relations and law.

Background on Environmental Precaution

14.   The notion of environmental precaution largely stems from diplomatic practice and treaty-making in the spheres, originally, of international marine pollution and, now, of biodiversity, climate change, pollution generally and, broadly, the environment. Its main thesis is that, in the face of serious risk to or grounds (as appropriately qualified) for concern about the environment, scientific uncertainty or the absence of complete proof should not stand in the way of positive action to minimize risks or take actions of a conservatory, preventative or curative nature. In addition to scientific uncertainty, the most frequently articulated conditions or circumstances are concerns of an intergenerational nature and forensic or proof difficulties, generally in the context of rapid change and perceived high risks. The thrust of the notion is vesting a broad dispensation to policy makers, seeking to provide guidance to administrative and other decision-makers and shifting the burden of proof to the State in control of the territory from which the harm might emanate or to the responsible actor. The notion has been rapidly adopted in most recent instruments and policy documents on the protection and preservation of the environment.

15.   Even as questioning of the acceptability of the precautionary notion diminishes, challenges increase regarding such specifics as: the wide potential ambit of its coverage; the clarity of operational criteria; the monetary costs of environmental regulation; possible public health risks associated with the very remedies improvised to avoid risk; diversity and vagueness of articulations of the notion; uncertainties about attendant obligations, and the imprecision and subjectivity of such a value-laden notion. Nevertheless, the notion has been "broadly accepted for international action, even if the consequence of its application in a given situation remains open to interpretation" (A. D'Amato and K. Engel, *International Environmental Law Anthology* (1996), p. 22).

16.   However, it is not possible, on the basis of the materials available and arguments presented on this application for provisional measures, to determine whether, as the Applicants contend, customary international law recognizes a precautionary principle.[6]

Precaution in Marine Living Resource Management

17.   However, it cannot be denied that UNCLOS adopts a precautionary *approach*. This may be gleaned, *inter alia,* from preambular paragraph 4, identifying as an aspect of the "legal order for the seas and oceans" "the conservation of their living resources * * * ". Several provisions ... of the Convention ... identify conservation as a crucial value.... Article 116 ... has been stated to point to the precautionary "principle" of fisheries management, while article 119 has been said to reflect a precautionary "approach" "when scientific data is not available or is inadequate to enable comprehensive decision-making" (Virginia Commentary, Vol. IV, pp. 288, 310). Most of these are the very provisions before this Tribunal today. Strikingly, also, article 290, paragraph 1's reference to serious harm to the marine environment as a basis for provisional measures also underscores the salience of the approach.

* * *

19.   ... [T]he Tribunal has [evidently] adopted the precautionary approach for the purposes of [determining whether to impose] provisional measures in such a case as the present. In my view, adopting an *approach*, rather than a principle, appropriately imports a certain degree of flexibility and tends, though not dispositively, to

---

6. It might be noted that treaties and formal instruments use different language of obligation; the notion is stated variously (as a principle, approach, concept, measures, action); no authoritative judicial decision unequivocally supports the notion; doctrine is indecisive, and domestic juridical materials are uncertain or evolving.

underscore reticence about making premature pronouncements about desirable normative structures.

* * *

21. ... [I]n my view, while the Tribunal has drawn its conclusions and based its prescriptions in the face of scientific uncertainty, it has not, *per se,* engaged in an explicit reversal of the burden of proof.... The cautiousness of the Tribunal's Order thus becomes apparent. This is commendable, since this entire area is fraught with difficulty.

* * *

Excerpts from Separate Opinion by Judge Tullio Treves

1. I concur with the Order of the Tribunal. The reasons set out in it in support of the urgency of the measures prescribed require, however, a few developments and clarifications.

2. The requirement of urgency is part of the very nature of provisional measures....

* * *

8. The urgency needed in the present case does not, in my opinion, concern the danger of a collapse of the [southern bluefin tuna] stock in the months which will elapse between the reading of the Order and the time when the arbitral tribunal will be in a position to prescribe provisional measures. This event, in light of scientific evidence, is uncertain and unlikely. The urgency concerns the stopping of a trend towards such collapse. The measures prescribed by the Tribunal aim at stopping the deterioration in the southern bluefin tuna stock. Each step in such deterioration can be seen as "serious harm" because of its cumulative effect towards the collapse of the stock. There is no controversy that such deterioration has been going on for years. However, as there is scientific uncertainty as to whether the situation of the stock has recently improved, the Tribunal must assess the urgency of the prescription of its measures in the light of prudence and caution. This approach, which may be called precautionary, is hinted at in the Order, in particular in paragraph 77. However, that paragraph refers it to the future conduct of the parties. While, of course, a precautionary approach by the parties in their future conduct is necessary, such precautionary approach, in my opinion, is necessary also in the assessment by the Tribunal of the urgency of the measures it might take. In the present case, it would seem to me that the requirement of urgency is satisfied only in the light of such precautionary approach. I regret that this is not stated explicitly in the Order.

9. I fully understand the reluctance of the Tribunal in taking a position as to whether the precautionary approach is a binding principle of customary international law. Other courts and tribunals, recently confronted with this question, have avoided to give an answer. In my opinion, in order to resort to the precautionary approach for assessing the urgency of the measures to be prescribed in the present case, it is not necessary to hold the view that this approach is dictated by a rule of customary international law. The precautionary approach can be seen as a logical consequence of the need to ensure that, when the arbitral tribunal decides on the merits, the factual situation has not changed. In other words, a precautionary approach seems to me inherent in the very notion of provisional measures. It is not by chance that in some languages the very concept of "caution" can be found in the terms used to designate provisional measures: for instance, in Italian, *misure cautelari,* in Portuguese, *medidas cautelares*, in Spanish, *medidas cautelares* or *medidas precautorias.*

8.11 *European Communities–Measures Affecting Asbestos and Asbestos-Containing Products*, **WTO Doc WT/DS135/AB/R (WTO Appellate Body Report, 12 March 2001)**

[*Eds.*—France banned the manufacture, sale and import of "all varieties of asbestos fibres" and of "any product containing asbestos fibres." It permitted limited and temporary exceptions for certain materials or products containing asbestos fibres when no substitute for those fibres was available that would pose a lesser risk to workers and would meet the safety requirements for the product in question.

Canada filed a complaint with the WTO, claiming that the French decree was inconsistent with the EC's obligations under Articles III and XI of the GATT 1994 **(Basic Document 7.1)** and was not justified under Article XX. Canada complained, in particular, that the decree unfairly discriminated against cement products made with asbestos fibres (as opposed to cement products made with other types of fibres).]

Excerpts from the Appellate Body Report

C. Examining the "Likeness" of Products under Article III:4 of the GATT 1994

110. We turn to consideration of how a treaty interpreter should proceed in determining whether products are "like" under Article III:4. As in Article III:2, in this determination, "[n]o one approach . . . will be appropriate for all cases." Rather, an assessment utilizing "an unavoidable element of individual, discretionary judgement" has to be made on a case-by-case basis. The Report of the Working Party on *Border Tax Adjustments* outlined an approach for analyzing "likeness" that has been followed and developed since by several panels and the Appellate Body. This approach has, in the main, consisted of employing four general criteria in analyzing "likeness": (i) the properties, nature and quality of the products; (ii) the end-uses of the products; (iii) consumers' tastes and habits—more comprehensively termed consumers' perceptions and behaviour—in respect of the products; and (iv) the tariff classification of the products. We note that these four criteria comprise four categories of "characteristics" that the products involved might share: (i) the physical properties of the products; (ii) the extent to which the products are capable of serving the same or similar end-uses; (iii) the extent to which consumers perceive and treat the products as alternative means of performing particular functions in order to satisfy a particular want or demand; and (iv) the international classification of the products for tariff purposes.

* * *

113. The European Communities argues that the inquiry into the physical properties of products must include a consideration of the risks posed by the product to human health. In examining the physical properties of the product at issue in this dispute, the Panel found that "it was not appropriate to apply the 'risk' criterion proposed by the EC." . . . [A]s we have said, in examining the "likeness" of products, panels must evaluate *all* of the relevant evidence. We are very much of the view that evidence relating to the health risks associated with a product may be pertinent in an examination of "likeness" under Article III:4 of the GATT 1994. We do not, however, consider that the evidence relating to the health risks associated with chrysotile asbestos fibres need be examined under a *separate* criterion, because we believe that this evidence can be evaluated under the existing criteria of physical properties, and of consumers' tastes and habits, to which we will come below.

114. Panels must examine fully the physical properties of products. In particular, panels must examine those physical properties of products that are likely to influence the competitive relationship between products in the marketplace. In the case of chrysotile asbestos fibres, their molecular structure, chemical composition, and fibrillation capacity are important because the microscopic particles and filaments of chrysotile asbestos fibres are carcinogenic in humans, following inhalation. . . .

This carcinogenicity, or toxicity, constitutes, as we see it, a defining aspect of the physical properties of chrysotile asbestos fibres. The evidence indicates that PCG fibres, in contrast, do not share these properties, at least to the same extent. We do not see how this highly significant physical difference *cannot* be a consideration in examining the physical properties of a product as part of a determination of "likeness" under Article III:4 of the GATT 1994.

* * *

116. We, therefore, find that the Panel erred, in paragraph 8.132 of the Panel Report, in excluding the health risks associated with chrysotile asbestos fibres from its examination of the physical properties of that product.

* * *

3. Cement-based products containing chrysotile and PCG fibres

* * *

128. As the Panel said, the primary physical difference between cement-based products containing chrysotile asbestos fibres and cement-based products containing PCG fibres lies in the particular fibre incorporated into the product. This difference is important because, as we have said in our examination of fibres, we believe that the health risks associated with a product may be relevant to the inquiry into the physical properties of a product when making a determination of "likeness" under Article III:4 of the GATT 1994. This is also true for cement-based products containing the different fibres. In examining the *physical properties* of the two sets of cement-based products, it cannot be ignored that one set of products contains a fibre known to be highly carcinogenic, while the other does not.... We, therefore, reverse the Panel's finding, in paragraph 8.149 of the Panel Report, that these health risks are not relevant in examining the "likeness" of the cement-based products.

* * *

VII. Article XX(b) of the GATT 1994 and Article 11 of the DSU

155. Under Article XX(b) of the GATT 1994, the Panel examined ... whether the measure at issue is "necessary to protect human ... life or health." ...

* * *

168. As to Canada's third argument, relating to the level of protection, we note that it is undisputed that WTO Members have the right to determine the level of protection of health that they consider appropriate in a given situation. France has determined, and the Panel accepted, that the chosen level of health protection by France is a "halt" to the spread of *asbestos*-related health risks. By prohibiting all forms of amphibole asbestos, and by severely restricting the use of chrysotile asbestos, the measure at issue is clearly designed and apt to achieve that level of health protection. Our conclusion is not altered by the fact that PCG fibres might pose a risk to health. The scientific evidence before the Panel indicated that the risk posed by the PCG fibres is, in any case, *less* than the risk posed by chrysotile asbestos fibres, although that evidence did *not* indicate that the risk posed by PCG fibres is non-existent. Accordingly, it seems to us perfectly legitimate for a Member to seek to halt the spread of a highly risky product while allowing the use of a less risky product in its place. In short, we do not agree with Canada's third argument.

169. In its fourth argument, Canada asserts that the Panel erred in finding that "controlled use" is not a reasonably available alternative to the Decree. This last argument is based on Canada's assertion that ... an alternative measure is only excluded as a "reasonably available" alternative if implementation of that measure is "impossible." ...

170. Looking at this issue now, we believe that, in determining whether a suggested alternative measure is "reasonably available' " several factors must be taken into account, besides the difficulty of implementation. In *Thailand–Restrictions on Importation of and Internal Taxes on Cigarettes*, the panel made the following observations on the applicable standard for evaluating whether a measure is "necessary" under Article XX(b):

> The import restrictions imposed by Thailand could be considered to be "necessary" in terms of Article XX(b) only if there were no alternative measure consistent with the General Agreement, or less inconsistent with it, which Thailand could *reasonably be expected to employ to achieve its health policy objectives*. (emphasis added)

171. In our Report in *Korea–Beef*, we addressed the issue of "necessity" under Article XX(d) of the GATT 1994. In that appeal, we found that the panel was correct in following the standard set forth by the panel in *United States–Section 337 of the Tariff Act of 1930*:

> It was clear to the Panel that a contracting party cannot justify a measure inconsistent with another GATT provision as "necessary" in terms of Article XX(d) if an alternative measure which it could reasonably be expected to employ and which is not inconsistent with other GATT provisions is available to it. By the same token, in cases where a measure consistent with other GATT provisions is not reasonably available, a contracting party is bound to use, among the measures reasonably available to it, that which entails the least degree of inconsistency with other GATT provisions.

172. We indicated in *Korea–Beef* that one aspect of the "weighing and balancing process . . . comprehended in the determination of whether a WTO-consistent alternative measure" is reasonably available is the extent to which the alternative measure "contributes to the realization of the end pursued." In addition, we observed, in that case, that "[t]he more vital or important [the] common interests or values" pursued, the easier it would be to accept as "necessary" measures designed to achieve those ends. In this case, the objective pursued by the measure is the preservation of human life and health through the elimination, or reduction, of the well-known, and life-threatening, health risks posed by asbestos fibres. The value pursued is both vital and important in the highest degree. The remaining question, then, is whether there is an alternative measure that would achieve the same end and that is less restrictive of trade than a prohibition.

173. Canada asserts that "controlled use" represents a "reasonably available" measure that would serve the same end. The issue is, thus, whether France could reasonably be expected to employ "controlled use" practices to achieve its chosen level of health protection—a halt in the spread of asbestos-related health risks.

174. In our view, France could not reasonably be expected to employ *any* alternative measure if that measure would involve a continuation of the very risk that the Decree seeks to "halt." Such an alternative measure would, in effect, prevent France from achieving its chosen level of health protection. On the basis of the scientific evidence before it, the Panel found that, in general, the efficacy of "controlled use" remains to be demonstrated. Moreover, even in cases where "controlled use" practices are applied "with greater certainty' " the scientific evidence suggests that the level of exposure can, in some circumstances, still be high enough for there to be a "significant residual risk of developing asbestos-related diseases." The Panel found too that the efficacy of "controlled use" is particularly doubtful for the building industry and for DIY enthusiasts, which are the most important users of cement-based products containing chrysotile asbestos. Given these factual findings by the Panel, we believe that "controlled use" would not allow France to achieve its chosen level of health protection by halting the spread of asbestos-related health risks. "Controlled use" would, thus, not be an alternative measure that would achieve the end sought by France.

8.12   THE MOX PLANT CASE (Ire v. UK)(Provisional Measures), ITLOS Case No. 10 (Int'l Trib. Law of the Sea, 3 December 2001)

[*Eds.*—In the 1950s, the United Kingdom began reprocessing nuclear waste fuel at a site in northwest England originally called Windscale and now known as Sellafield. The processing operations result in intentional and accidental radioactive discharges from the facility into marine waters, and Ireland had become concerned about the impact of these discharges on the Irish Sea as early as 1957.

In October 2001, the United Kingdom authorized British Nuclear Fuels (BNFL) to begin operating a plant for the manufacture of mixed oxide (MOX) fuel from uranium and plutonium oxides at the Sellafield site. In response, Ireland instituted arbitral proceedings under the UN Convention on the Law of the Sea alleging that operation of the MOX plant would result in an increased level of radioactive discharges into the marine environment from the MOX plant itself and from other parts of the Sellafield facility that supplied material to the MOX plant.

Ireland also claimed some of the radioactive materials used as raw materials in the plant would come from outside the UK, and that the MOX fuel produced by the plant would be exported to nuclear reactors outside the UK. The transportation of these hazardous materials, said Ireland, would potentially occur on ships traveling through the Irish Sea and in close proximity to Ireland, thus posing a further risk of injury to the marine environment and to the territory of Ireland.

Ireland further claimed that the United Kingdom had failed to provide it with adequate information about the potential risks to the marine environment arising from operation of the MOX plant.

According to Ireland, the United Kingdom's authorization of the MOX plant thus violated a variety of obligations, both substantive and procedural, relating to protection of the marine environment. While the parties were awaiting the establishment of an arbitral tribunal, Ireland asked the International Tribunal for the Law of the Sea to adopt various provisional measures, including requirements that the United Kingdom prevent the operation of the MOX plant and take any necessary steps to ensure that no radioactive substances moved into or out of waters over which the UK has sovereignty. The Tribunal refused to grant the provisional measures requested by Ireland, but it fashioned some of its own.]

Excerpts from the Order of the Tribunal

81. *Considering* that, in the circumstances of this case, the Tribunal does not find that the urgency of the situation requires the prescription of the provisional measures requested by Ireland, in the short period before the constitution of the Annex VII arbitral tribunal;

82. *Considering,* however, that the duty to cooperation is a fundamental principle in the prevention of pollution of the marine environment under Part XII of the [United Nations Convention on the Law of the Sea] and general international law . . . ;

* * *

84. *Considering* that, in the view of the Tribunal, prudence and caution require that Ireland and the United Kingdom cooperate in exchanging information concerning risks or effects of the operation of the MOX plant and in devising ways to deal with them, as appropriate;

* * *

89. *For these reasons,* THE TRIBUNAL, . . . Unanimously, *prescribes,* pending a decision by the Annex VII arbitral tribunal, the following provisional measure . . . :

Ireland and the United Kingdom shall cooperate and shall, for this purpose, enter into consultations forthwith in order to:

> (a) exchange further information with regard to possible consequences for the Irish Sea arising out of the commissioning of the MOX plant;
>
> (b) monitor risks or the effects of the operation of the MOX plant for the Irish Sea;
>
> (c) devise, as appropriate, measures to prevent pollution of the marine environment which might result from the operation of the MOX plant.

Joint Declaration of Judges Caminos, Yamamoto, Park, Akl, Marsit, Eiriksson and Jesus

The dispute between Ireland and the United Kingdom as it appears before the Tribunal is characterized by an almost total lack of agreement on the scientific evidence with respect to the possible consequences of the operation of the MOX plant on the marine environment of the Irish Sea.

* * *

[There has been an] almost complete lack of cooperation between the Governments of Ireland and the United Kingdom with respect to the environmental impact of the planned operations....

The Tribunal has identified the duty to cooperate as a fundamental principle in the regime of the prevention of pollution of the marine environment under Part XII of the Convention and general international law. Against the background of that duty, we regard the most effective measure that the Tribunal could have adopted was to require the parties to cooperate forthwith. It is not, we trust, an idle hope that the results of the consultations prescribed will include a common understanding of the scientific evidence and a common appreciation of the measures which must be taken with respect to the plant to prevent harm to the marine environment.

Excerpt from Separate Opinion of Judge Mensah

In the present case, all that was required of the Tribunal was to consider whether any rights of Ireland or the United Kingdom or any threat of serious harm to the marine environment needed protection in the period prior to the composition of the Annex VII arbitral tribunal. On that point, I agree with the conclusion that the evidence before the Tribunal does not suffice to show either that irreversible prejudice might occur to any rights of Ireland or that serious harm to the marine environment might occur, solely as a result of the commissioning of the MOX plant, *in the period between now and the constitution of the Annex VII arbitral tribunal.* In coming to this conclusion I have taken into account the information that the constitution of the Annex VII arbitral tribunal is expected to be completed before the beginning of the spring of 2002, as well as the commitment made by the United Kingdom that there will be no maritime transport of radioactive material before the summer of 2002 (paragraphs 78 and 79 of the Order).

* * *

... [I]t is not reasonable to believe that any pollution of Ireland's marine environment might occur in the period between the issue of the Order of this Tribunal and the constitution of the Annex VII arbitral tribunal, sometime before the spring of 2002.

With regard to the "procedural rights" (cooperation and consultation) which Ireland claims have been violated by the United Kingdom, I agree with the Tribunal that some at least of these are "rights" that may "be appropriate for protection" by provisional measures under article 290 of the Convention (paragraph 82 of the Order).

However, I do not find that any irreparable prejudice to Ireland has occurred or might occur before the constitution of the arbitral tribunal. In my view none of the violations of the procedural rights arising from the duty to cooperate or to consult or to undertake appropriate environmental assessments are "irreversible" in the sense that they cannot effectively be enforced against the United Kingdom by decision of the Annex VII arbitral tribunal, if the arbitral tribunal were to conclude that any such violations have in fact occurred. . . .

Separate Opinion of Judge Anderson

* * *

In its principal submission, the Applicant sought the equivalent of an injunction restraining pendente lite the Respondent from allowing the MOX plant to commence operations and production on 20 December 2001—a request which the Tribunal clearly did not accept. It is common ground that the plant is situated on the territory of the United Kingdom and thus under the sovereignty of the United Kingdom. In the terms of the draft articles on Prevention of Transboundary Harm from Hazardous Activities recently adopted by the International Law Commission, the plant will conduct "activities not prohibited by international law." In the terms of the Convention on the Law of the Sea, the plant falls to be considered in the context of article 193, which reads:

States have the sovereign right to exploit their natural resources pursuant to their environmental policies and in accordance with their duty to protect and preserve the marine environment.

The operation of the plant involves a dry process, but, as an indirect result of normal cleaning work, it is expected to result in the introduction of some very small amounts of liquid and gaseous substances and energy into the marine environment of the Irish Sea by two pathways: first, via an outfall structure . . . and secondly via the atmosphere. . . .

The question before the Tribunal was whether there would be irreparable harm to any of the rights claimed by the Applicant under articles 123, 192 to 194, 197, 206, 207, 211, 212 and 213 [of UNCLOS]. . . . These rights were categorised, in broad terms, as the right to ensure that the Irish Sea will not be subject to additional radioactive pollution; procedural rights to have the Respondent prepare proper environmental impact statements; and the right to cooperation and coordination over the protection of the Irish Sea as a semi-enclosed sea. As regards the first category, in view of the small scale of the introductions from the MOX plant and its distance of over 100 miles from Ireland, it is not clear to me that there will be irreparable prejudice to any rights of the Applicant or "serious harm to the marine environment" for the purposes of article 290, paragraph 5, especially recalling the short period of time before the constitution of the arbitral tribunal. Turning to the second category, in view of the existence not only of a national environmental impact statement and a study prepared for the EC Commission, but also the positive formal opinion issued by the EC Commission after a review by independent experts (on which both parties relied, albeit in different ways), it is not clear to me that any procedural rights claimed by the Applicant suffered irreparable prejudice.

As regards the third category, cooperation and consultation, in regard to which the Applicant relied upon article 123, I would add the following. . . .

* * *

[A]rticle 123 . . . can be viewed in many ways as a particular application to the law of the sea of the general duty of States to cooperate, as laid down in Article 2 of the Charter of the UN. . . . Article 123 was cast in weak terms ("should"/"shall endeavour") in order to safeguard the worldwide application of the Convention's provisions and its unified character. Article 123 provides a choice: States bordering a semi-enclosed sea are to endeavour to coordinate their actions in certain matters (in simple terms, fisheries management, environmental protection and marine scientific research) either "directly or through an appropriate regional organization". In other words, article 123 does not require cooperation to be at the bilateral level so long as there is cooperation through an appropriate regional body.... In the case of the Irish Sea, the management of living resources is coordinated by means of the common fisheries policy of the EC; environmental protection, including the monitoring of the level of nuclear radiation, is coordinated through Euratom, the EC and OSPAR; and research into the scientific qualities of the waters and the status of the living resources is coordinated through the International Council for the Exploration of the Sea, as well as through EC programmes. In my opinion, since the appropriate bodies do exist in regard to the Irish Sea and there is extensive, if not full, coordination through such bodies and since, moreover, there clearly have been some bilateral contacts between the parties at ministerial level in regard to the Irish Sea, there is little to be examined in the Applicant's claims under article 123 [and it was inappropriate for the Tribunal to order further cooperation as a provisional measure].

Excerpts From Separate Opinion of Judge Wolfrum

I concur fully with paragraph 89 as well as with the reasoning of the Order in general. The following observations are meant to add to the reasoning or to emphasise certain elements therein.

* * *

It is still a matter of discussion whether the precautionary principle or the precautionary approach in international environmental law has become part of customary international law. The Tribunal did not speak of the precautionary principle or approach in its Order in the Southern Bluefin Tuna Cases. Note should be taken of the fact, though, that the precautionary principle is part of the OSPAR Convention.

This principle or approach applied in international environmental law reflects the necessity of making environment-related decisions in the face of scientific uncertainty about the potential future harm of a particular activity. There is no general agreement as to the consequences which flow from the implementation of this principle other than the fact that the burden of proof concerning the possible impact of a given activity is reversed. A State interested in undertaking or continuing a particular activity has to prove that such activities will not result in any harm, rather than the other side having to prove that it will result in harm.

Nevertheless, Ireland could not, for several reasons, rely on the precautionary principle or approach in this case, even it were to be accepted that it is part of customary international law. If the Tribunal had prescribed provisional measures for the preservation of the marine environment under the jurisdiction of Ireland, it could have done so only after a summary assessment of the radioactivity of the Irish Sea, the potential impact the MOX plant might have and whether such impact prejudiced the rights of Ireland. This, however, is an issue to be dealt with under the merits by the Annex VII arbitral tribunal.... [P]rovisional measures should not anticipate a judgment on the merits.... [This] limitation cannot be overruled by invoking the precautionary principle[, otherwise] ... the granting of provisional measures becomes automatic when an applicant argues with some plausibility that its rights may be prejudiced or that there was serious risk to the marine environment....

Ireland cannot rely on the reasoning of the Order in the Southern Bluefin Tuna Cases. The situation there was quite different. The parties had agreed that the tuna stock was at its "... historically lowest levels ...". The Tribunal only stated that the parties should "... act with prudence and caution ..." to ensure that effective conservation measures are taken to prevent serious harm. Here the Tribunal was in fact being asked to qualify the possible introduction of radioactivity as "deleterious", without being able to assess evidence about the situation prevailing in the Irish Sea. In my view there was, under the present circumstances, no room for applying the precautionary principle to the prescription of provisional measures for the preservation of the substantive rights of Ireland or the protection of the marine environment.

* * *

I fully endorse, however, paragraphs 82 to 84 of the Order, considering that the obligation to cooperate is the overriding principle of international environmental law, in particular when the interests of neighbouring States are at stake. The duty to cooperate denotes an important shift in the general orientation of the international legal order. It balances the principle of sovereignty of States and thus ensures that community interests are taken into account vis-à-vis individualistic State interests. It is a matter of prudence and caution as well as in keeping with the overriding nature of the obligation to co-operate that the parties should engage therein as prescribed in paragraph 89 of the Order.

Separate Opinion of Judge *Ad Hoc* Székely

1. I disagreed with the decision of the Tribunal not to grant the provisional measures requested by Ireland. . . .

* * *

10. In paragraph 5 of Part 1 of its Request for provisional measures (p. 4), Ireland advanced the key concept that the MOX plant "will further intensify nuclear activities in the coast of the Irish Sea", an argument shared, for instance, by Norway, while expressing its regret at the decision to authorize the plant (see paragraph 13 of the Request, p. 8). Ireland consistently reiterated this concept in the hearings.

11. This argument, in turn, necessarily brought to the forefront of the case the lamentable record of the past performance of the Sellafield complex, plagued as it has been by several accidents . . . , or the documented lack of a "proper safety culture" alluded to in the Report of the United Kingdom Nuclear Installations Inspectorate . . . , a matter which was equally disregarded by the Tribunal, even when it was an important indicator of the risks involved not only in the potential commissioning and operation of the new integrated plant, but also in not granting the requested provisional measures.

* * *

13. A mere reading of the surprisingly empty and superficial 1993 Environmental Impact Statement is sufficient to fully support the Irish allegations [that the British Government has not properly considered the environmental consequences of its actions], in the sense that the Statement is totally inadequate by any standard.

14. This . . . alone should have been sufficient for the Tribunal to take a positive stand on the requested provisional measures, since the environmental impact assessment is a central tool of the international law of prevention.

15. Regrettably, the Tribunal failed to realize and accept that the 1993 Statement contains exclusively the unilateral assertions of, precisely, the proponent of the projected plant; that such assertions (invariably limited to simply alleging that there would be no environmental impacts whatsoever) failed to be backed by the most elementary appropriate scientific or technical support; that none of those assertions had been independently validated (since BNFL is a public limited company whose shares are all held by the United Kingdom Secretary of State for Trade and Industry and by the Treasury Solicitor); that the EIS was totally partial and incomplete in all respects (since it did not include a specific assessment of impacts on the marine environment, of impacts resulting from discharges or from the transport and international movements of radioactive materials, that is, the very activities that were the

subject of the requested provisional measures); and, above all, that since no potential impacts were admitted or identified in the Statement, neither it, nor the authorization to go ahead with the plant, included any measures to prevent, mitigate, reduce or control any potential environmental impacts....

16. [S]uch dramatic failures ... meant that the United Kingdom did not comply with its obligations under article 206 of the Law of the Sea Convention, compliance to which Ireland had a specific substantial right (in addition to the fact that, by failing to provide Ireland with all the necessary reports and documentation surrounding the EIS, the United Kingdom equally failed to comply with its obligations under articles 204 and 205).

17. Consequently, the United Kingdom did not comply either with its obligations of prevention under articles 102, 103, 194 and 207 of the Convention, compliance, again, to which Ireland was entitled as a substantial, and not merely correlative, procedural right.... [T]he above contraventions would involve irreparable prejudice to Ireland's rights if the plant were to be commissioned without a previous adequate environmental impact assessment.

18. As surprising as the above is the conclusion reached by the Tribunal, without any basis in law or in science, to give the United Kingdom, and not Ireland, the benefit of the doubt about the risk of harm alleged by Ireland. The Tribunal in the end acted on the United Kingdom allegation "that the risk of pollution, if any, from the operation of the MOX plant would be infinitesimally small" (paragraph 72 of the Order's Considerata), even when the United Kingdom did not adduce any sort of evidence to substantiate and support such a radical allegation.

19. The Tribunal did the same regarding the allegations of the United Kingdom in the sense that "the commissioning of the MOX plant on or around 20 December 2001 [would] not, even arguably, cause serious harm to the marine environment or irreparable prejudice to the rights of Ireland" (see paragraph 73), that "neither the commissioning of the MOX plant nor the introduction of plutonium into the system [was] irreversible" (see paragraph 74), and that "the manufacture of MOX fuel present[ed] negligible security risks" (see paragraph 76).

20. On what legal or scientific basis the Tribunal chose to accept such unilateral and unproven allegations is nowhere to be found in the Order and, consequently, the Tribunal failed to comply with article 30, paragraph 1, of its Statute, which mandates that a judgement "shall state the reasons on which it is based", and with article 125, paragraph 1(i), of its Rules, which provides that a judgment shall contain "the reasons of law on which it is based".

* * *

22. In any case, since the Tribunal was not provided with legal and scientific support for the allegations of the United Kingdom and, since it was obviously not impressed by the evidence provided by Ireland to support its own allegations, it should have been responsive, in the face of such uncertainty, to the Irish demands regarding the application of the precautionary principle.... It is regrettable that it did not do so, since had it done so this would have led to the granting of the provisional measure requested by Ireland regarding the suspension of the commissioning of the plant.

8.13 DISPUTE CONCERNING ACCESS TO INFORMATION UNDER ARTICLE 9 OF THE OSPAR CONVENTION (Ire v. UK), 23 UNRIAA 59 (Decision of the Arbitral Tribunal, 2 July 2003)

Excerpts From the Opinion of the Tribunal

1. This matter concerns a dispute between Ireland as claimant and the United Kingdom of Great Britain and Northern Ireland ("the United Kingdom") as respondent, determined by a Tribunal constituted pursuant to the 1992 Convention for the Protection of the Marine Environment of the North–East Atlantic ("the OSPAR Convention"). The issue concerns access to information as defined by the OSPAR Convention. Ireland has requested access to information redacted from reports prepared as part of the approval process for the commissioning of a Mixed Oxide Plant ("the MOX Plant") in the United Kingdom, based on Ireland's understanding of Article 9 of the OSPAR Convention.[g] The United Kingdom has declined to provide the information requested based on its understanding of the OSPAR Convention.

* * *

6. Article 9 provides [that the Contracting Parties "shall ensure that their competent authorities are required to make available ... to any natural or legal person, in response to any reasonable request, ... any available information ... on the state of the maritime area" and "on activities or measures adversely affecting or likely to affect it." Article 9(3) permits the Parties "in accordance with their national legal systems ... to provide for a request for such information to be refused where it affects" certain matters requiring confidentiality, including "commercial and industrial confidentiality."]

* * *

15. British Nuclear Fuels, plc ("BNFL"), a public limited company wholly owned by the United Kingdom, owns and operates a licensed nuclear enterprise at Sellafield in Cumbria. In 1993, BNFL applied to the local authority for permission to build a MOX Plant to process spent nuclear fuels by retrieving and blending separated plutonium oxide and uranium oxide into pellets to be reused as fuel in nuclear reactors. BNFL prepared and submitted Environmental Statements to the relevant

---

g. Article 9 of the OSPAR Convention reads in full, as follows:

ARTICLE 9

ACCESS TO INFORMATION

1. The Contracting Parties shall ensure that their competent authorities are required to make available the information described in paragraph 2 of this Article to any natural or legal person, in response to any reasonable request, without that person's having to prove an interest, without unreasonable charges, as soon as possible and at the latest within two months.

2. The information referred to in paragraph 1 of this Article is any available information in written, visual, aural or data-base form on the state of the maritime area, on activities or measures adversely affecting or likely to affect it and on activities or measures introduced in accordance with the Convention.

3. The provisions of this Article shall not affect the right of Contracting Parties, in accordance with their national legal systems and applicable international regulations, to provide for a request for such information to be refused where it affects:

(a) the confidentiality of the proceedings of public authorities, international relations and national defence;

(b) public security;

(c) matters which are, or have been, sub judice, or under enquiry (including disciplinary enquiries), or which are the subject of preliminary investigation proceedings;

(d) commercial and industrial confidentiality, including intellectual property;

(e) the confidentiality of personal data and/or files;

(f) material supplied by a third party without that party being under a legal obligation to do so;

(g) material, the disclosure of which would make it more likely that the environment to which such material related would be damaged.

4. The reasons for a refusal to provide the information requested must be given.

authorities, as required by United Kingdom law. Relevant consents to build the Plant were given in 1994, and construction was completed in 1996.

* * *

18. [Before the MOX Plant could be commissioned and put into operation, the United Kingdom had to fulfil a number of] international legal obligations with respect to the environmental consequences of commissioning [the Plant]. . . . [In particular], the domestic agency approving the Plant was required to ensure whatever environmental detriments it might cause were economically justified. . . .

* * *

20. Accordingly, over a period of eight weeks in 1997, the United Kingdom Environment Agency ("the Agency") held a public consultation on the economic justification of the MOX Plant at Sellafield. This initial public consultation emerged as the first of five such consultations.

* * *

25. In preparation for the second consultation, the Agency asked BNFL to provide additional information in the form of a business case that could be independently examined. It invited prominent financial consultants to tender for the work and selected the PA Consulting Group, London ("PA") to carry out a detailed assessment. As the Agency's Explanatory Memorandum under the Radioactive Substances Act explained, in addition, "PA was requested to identify if there were areas of the economic case that were not commercially sensitive which could be published in the public domain."

26. PA submitted the full version of its report ("the PA Report") to BNFL and, pursuant to the Agency's request, then considered what data should be redacted. After consulting with BNFL about redactions, PA made recommendations, which were reviewed and finally determined by the Agency, and reflected in a public version of the PA Report released in December 1997 ("the 1997 PA Report"). PA gave a detailed explanation of the basis for redactions from its full report on "commercial confidentiality" grounds under section 4(2) of the United Kingdom's Environmental Information Regulations (1992) ("the 1992 Regulations"). . . .

* * *

[The Agency then held several additional rounds of public consultation. The consultation process was interrupted when BNFL "discovered that fuel pellet diameter readings at the MOX demonstration facility had been falsified." When the consultation process recommenced, Ireland argued that it was impossible for it and others to accurately assess the economic justification for the MOX Plant given "the absence of critical information relating to primary economic factors" in the materials that had been released.

BNFL prepared a new document "setting out the economic justification for the MOX Plant" and that document, as well as public comments on the plant, were evaluated by a consulting firm in the so-called ADL Report. The ADL Report was released to the public with redations of "that information whose publication would cause unreasonable damage to BNFL's commercial operations or to the economic case for the MOX plant." Ireland demand a release of an unredacted copy of the ADL Report.]

* * *

43. The United Kingdom refused to disclose [either the full PA Report or the full ADL Report], contending . . . that:

First, Article 9 of the OSPAR Convention does not establish a direct right to receive information. Rather it requires Contracting Parties to establish a domestic framework for the disclosure of information. This the United Kingdom has done. . . .

Second, . . . the information [sought by Ireland] is insufficiently proximate to the state of the maritime area or to measures or activities affecting or likely to affect it. It is not information within the scope of Article 9(2) of the Convention. . . .

Third, in the event that the United Kingdom is wrong on this point, Article 9(3)(d) of the Convention affirms the right of the Contracting Parties, in accordance with their national legal systems and applicable international regulations, to provide for a request for information to be refused on grounds of commercial confidentiality. The United Kingdom has legislated to this effect. Its refusal to disclose the particular information requested by Ireland is consistent with both national law and applicable international regulations.

* * *

123. The [first] issue [is] whether . . . the obligation of a Contracting Party under Article 9(1) is completely discharged by putting in place an appropriate domestic regulatory framework so that disputes about specific applications of the obligations under Article 9 are to be exclusively determined within the municipal law of the Contracting Party. Should this be the case, the appropriate forum for Ireland with respect to its claims that information to which it was entitled under the OSPAR Convention was improperly withheld will be found in the United Kingdom municipal system.

* * *

133. In the context of the language used within Article 9, it . . . appear[s] plain to the Tribunal is that the obligation expressed in Article 9(1) by the requirement that a Contracting Party "shall ensure" the stipulated result is a reflection of a deliberate rather than a lax choice of vocabulary. It illustrates the application of a chosen (and strong) level of expression, deftly applied by the drafters to the particular and, to them, important subject matter of disclosure of information to any persons, whether nationals or not, who request it. . . .

134. On that approach, the Tribunal finds that the obligation is to be construed as expressed at the mandatory end of the scale. The applied requirement of Article 9(1) is read by the Tribunal as imposing an obligation upon the United Kingdom, as a Contracting Party, to ensure something, namely that its competent authorities "are required to make available the information described in paragraph 2 . . . to any natural legal person, in response to any reasonable request."

* * *

137. For these reasons in this aspect it appears to the Tribunal that Article 9(1) is advisedly pitched at a level that imposes an obligation of result rather than merely to provide access to a domestic regime which is directed at obtaining the required result.

* * *

144. The proposed reading of Article 9(1) also is consistent with contemporary principles of state responsibility. A State is internationally responsible for the acts of its organs. On conventional principles, a State covenanting with other States to put in place a domestic framework and review mechanisms remains responsible to those other States for the adequacy of this framework and the conduct of its competent

authorities who, in the exercise of their executive functions, engage the domestic system.

* * *

146.   It follows as an ordinary matter of obligation between States, that even where international law assigns competence to a national system, there is no exclusion of responsibility of a State for the inadequacy of such a national system or the failure of its competent authorities to act in a way prescribed by an international obligation or implementing legislation. Adopting a contrary approach would lead to the deferral of responsibility by States and the frustration of the international legal system.

* * *

161.   ... In its Memorial, Ireland identified ... 14 categories [of redacted information, including] information relating to: (A) Estimated annual production capacity of the MOX facility; (B) Time taken to reach this capacity; (C) Sales volumes; (D) Probability of achieving higher sales volumes; (E) Probability of being able to win contracts for recycling fuel in 'significant quantities'; (F) Estimated sales demand; (G) Percentage of plutonium already on site; (H) Maximum throughput figures; (I) Life span of the MOX facility; (J) Number of employees; (K) Price of MOX fuel; (L) Whether, and to what extent, there are firm contracts to purchase MOX from Sellafield; (M) Arrangements for transport of plutonium to, and MOX from, Sellafield; (N) Likely number of such transports.

... The [next] issue before the Tribunal is whether the redacted portions of the PA and ADL Reports, viewed as categories, constitute "information" within the meaning of Article 9(2). The Tribunal distinguishes here between the categories of redaction and the *content* of those categories. A determination under Article 9(3)(d) would require a detailed examination of the content of the various categories of redaction [to determine whether the redacted information was 'confidential' commercial information]. A determination under Article 9(2) requires only an examination of the categories of redaction, in order to determine whether they fall within the definition of "information" in Article 9(2).

162.   As will be recalled, Article 9(2) provides:

The information referred to in paragraph 1 of this Article is any available information in written, visual, aural or data-base form on the state of the maritime area, on activities or measures adversely affecting or likely to affect it and on activities or measures introduced in accordance with the Convention.

163.   Article 9(2), whose chapeau is "Access to Information," establishes the scope of information to which, subject to specific enumerated rights of refusal in Article 9(3), the obligation in Article 9(1) relates. The scope of the information in the provision is not environmental, in general, but, in keeping with the focus of the OSPAR Convention, "the state of the maritime area." It is manifest to the Tribunal that none of the above 14 categories in Ireland's list can plausibly be characterized as "information * * * on the state of the maritime area." The Tribunal could, thus, rest its decision on the fact that none of the material in the 14 categories falls within the definition of "information" in Article 9(2).

* * *

168.   Article 1 does not define "information" but it is clear that it is a broad and inclusive reference with respect to the state of the maritime area. The point of emphasis, however, is that it is "information" about the state of the maritime area. The three categories of "information ... on the state of the maritime area" in Article 9(2) are: (i) "any available information" on "the state of the maritime area," (ii) "any available information" on "activities or measures adversely affecting or likely to affect

... the maritime area," [and] (iii) "any available information" on "activities or measures introduced in accordance with the Convention."

* * *

179.   In the opinion of the Tribunal, Ireland has failed to demonstrate that the 14 categories of redacted items in the PA and ADL Reports, insofar as they may be taken to be activities or measures with respect to the commissioning and operation of a MOX Plant at Sellafield, are "information ... on the state of the maritime area" or, even if they were, are likely adversely to affect the maritime area.

The Claims by Ireland are dismissed.

Excerpts From Dissenting Opinion of Gavan Griffith QC

* * *

37.   ... [T]he majority in paragraph 163 asserts as a *"manifest"* conclusion that none of the 14 categories of information identified by them in the Majority Opinion may *"plausibly be characterized"* as *"information ... on the state of the maritime area"*....

38.   To my mind, ... it is the majority's error that here becomes manifest by reason of its misstatement of the terms of Article 9(2). As a matter of unambiguous grammatical construction, the expression of the second category of information [in Article 9(2)] is incapable of being confined to *"information ... on the state of the maritime area"* in the same terms as the first category of information.... [N]o part of the definition of the second or third categories of information [in Article 9(2) requires that the information falling within those categories must be] *"on the state of the maritime area"*. For this reason the majority's conclusion (in para. 163) that it could have rested *"its decision on the fact that none of the material in the 14 categories falls within the definition of 'information' "* cannot be sustained by the text of Article 9(2).

* * *

93.   The defining issue for the Tribunal's consideration is whether a link exists between the harmful activity and the information contained in the PA and ADL Reports.

* * *

96.   Plainly, the PA and ADL Reports are a cause (or, more correctly, one of the causes) necessary for a harmful activity to occur, in the sense that ... had the Reports not been provided, the harmful activity would not be authorised or occur.

* * *

98.   The United Kingdom does not contest its obligation to justify the operation of the MOX Plant by a process that *"requires a consideration of whether the benefits of the practice outweigh the detriments"*. It also agreed with Ireland that the PA and ADL Report processes were carried out *"within the context of the justification exercise under Euratom Directive 96/29 (replacing Directives 80/836 and 84/467)"*.

99.   Ireland contended that the obligation to justify requires an identification of the economic costs and benefits of the MOX Plant operation, and that, because of the omission of the economic data from the public domain versions of the PA and ADL Reports, Ireland is unable to assess whether potential negative environmental consequences of the MOX Plant operations are justified from the economic standpoint.

* * *

106.   The intention and purpose of the United Kingdom to treat economic data as having direct relevance to the environment is discerned from the contents of the

DEFRA Decision ("the Decision") on the justification of the MOX Plant, adopted on 3 October 2001, and, in particular, from the circumstances that—

— the essence of the obligation of justification is described by the Decision as: *"the requirement of justification is based on the internationally accepted principle of radiological protection that no practice involving exposure to radiation should be adopted unless it produces sufficient benefits to the exposed individuals or to society in general to offset radiation and any other detriment it may cause"*;

— the Decision states that *"the application of the justification test requires the consideration of environmental, safety, economic, social and other benefits and disbenefits"*; . . . and

— paragraphs 56–70 of the Decision extensively analyse environmental detriments that may be caused by the manufacture of MOX fuel as well as safety and security concerns associated with the Plant's operation. These detriments are further balanced against economic and other benefits in paragraphs 71–81. This balance, of environmental concerns *vis-à-vis* future profits, is based primarily on the calculations produced by ADL in its Report.

107.   I demur to the contention of the United Kingdom that each of the PA and ADL Reports has nothing to do with the state of the maritime area embraced by the Convention. This is because each was commissioned by the United Kingdom Government in the framework of the mandated justification exercise considering whether economic benefits offset environmental harm. This balancing process was acknowledged in the United Kingdom's Counter–Memorial as requiring *"a consideration of whether the benefits of the practice outweigh the [environmental] detriments"*.

108.   The significance of the environmental factors during the economic analysis is further confirmed by the explicit language of the ADL Report—

[the Plant] cannot operate without passing a test of justification: *the benefits of a practice involving ionising radiation need to outweigh any environmental or other detriments.*

109.   The economic data collected and presented in the PA and ADL Reports was an integral and necessary part of the required process to determine whether the pollution of the marine environment might be legitimised under the nuclear regimes. It was this data that was deployed by the decision-makers, (at the executive level of Ministers of State) in the justification exercise for the commissioning of the MOX Plant.

110.   At this point, the interdependence between economic data and environmental impacts becomes evident. It is inherent in the justification test that economic analyses may be determinative of whether future environmental harm is legitimate and whether the activity that is likely adversely to affect the maritime area should be authorised. Without economic data the exercise of justification becomes meaningless, as the second integral part of the entire test (namely the economic, social, and any other benefits in justification) will be missing.

111.   It is the economic analyses that provide the balancing factor to the scales of assessment in a justification process calibrated by the EURATOM Regulations to favour the environment. In the terms of physics, the moment tilting the balance against approval can only be offset by a larger moment arising from the justification exercise. That was the inherent function of the Reports. As information so directly integral to the process of assessment, such information must be characterised as bearing a most direct relevance to the state of the marine environment of the North–East Atlantic. To my mind, it would be futile for the exercise, and also confound the purpose of the justification regime, to qualify by unexpressed limitations the broad definition of information under Article 9(2) (as has the majority) to enable access only

to the purely environmental side of the balance and to exclude the information taken into account on the other side of the scale.

* * *

I am of the opinion that the whole of the PA and ADL Reports, including the redacted items, is information within Article 9(1) and (2) and that on such finding being made the dispute called for further hearing and consideration of the contention by the United Kingdom that Article 9(3)(d) justified the redactions made to these Reports.

8.14 IRON RHINE RAILWAY ARBITRATION (**Belg v. Neth), 27 UNRIAA 127 (Decision of the Arbitral Tribunal, 24 May 2005)**

[*Eds.*—The "Iron Rhine" is a railway linking the port of Antwerp, Belgium, to the Rhine basin in Germany, via the Netherlands provinces of Noord–Brabant and Limburg. The Iron Rhine was used continuously from 1879 until World War I. Commercial traffic was halted during World War I, but resumed (albeit at a lower level of intensity) after the war. The railway was destroyed during World War II, but rebuilt afterwards. For many years the line was used only lightly, and through traffic between Belgium and Germany ceased completely in 1991. During the 1990s, the Netherlands designated a number of nature reserves in the provinces through which the Iron Rhine runs, some of which include parts of the route of the railway.

In 1998, the Prime Minister of Belgium initiated formal discussions with the Netherlands about reactivation of the Iron Rhine. As a result of these discussions, the two governments adopted, in March 2000, a Memorandum of Understanding that called for environmental impact studies of the proposed reactivation and established a timetable for phasing in renewed use of the line.

The environmental impact studies were completed in 2001, but the parties were unable to agree on the conditions that should be imposed on the use of the line and on the allocation of costs necessary for making the line suitable for long-term reactivation. In particular, they disagreed over the meaning of Article XII of an 1839 treaty pursuant to which the original railway had been built. Article XII provides (as translated by the Tribunal):

> In the case that in Belgium a new [rail]road would have been built ..., which would lead to the Maas facing the Dutch canton of Sittard, then Belgium would be at liberty to ask Holland, which in that hypothesis would not refuse it, that the said road ... be extended ... entirely at the cost and expense of Belgium, through the canton of Sittard, up to the borders of Germany. This road or canal ... would be constructed ... by engineers and workers ... who would execute the agreed works at the expense of Belgium, all without any burden to Holland, and without prejudice to the exclusive rights of sovereignty over the territory which would be crossed by the road or canal in question.

Two main points were in dispute. First, whether the Netherlands's treaty obligation to permit construction and operation of the railway limited its sovereign right to impose " 'highly expensive' environmental protection measures" as a condition of allowing the line to be reactivated. Second, whether Belgium's obligation to bear the "cost and expense" of any "agreed works" on the line included an obligation to pay for environmental protection measures required by the Netherlands.]

Excerpts from the Award of the Tribunal

45. Belgium and the Netherlands are both parties to the Vienna Convention on the Law of Treaties of 23 May 1969 ("Vienna Convention") (United Nations Treaty Series ("U.N.T.S."), Vol. 1155, p. 331). It is precisely because some terms in that Convention reflected customary law, and some were new, that Article 4 provided generally for nonretroactivity of the Convention, but "without prejudice to the application of any rules set forth in the present Convention to which treaties would be subject under international law independently of the Convention." It is now well established that the provisions on interpretation of treaties contained in Articles 31 and 32 of the Convention reflect preexisting customary international law, and thus may be (unless there are particular indications to the contrary) applied to treaties concluded before the entering into force of the Vienna Convention in 1980....

* * *

50. The Netherlands has placed emphasis on the fact that a right of transit by one country across the territory of another can only arise as a matter of specific agreement [and is a limitation on sovereignty that must be] ... construed restrictively. ...

* * *

53. ... The principle of restrictive interpretation, whereby treaties are to be interpreted in favour of state sovereignty in case of doubt, is not in fact mentioned in the provisions of the Vienna Convention. The object and purpose of a treaty, taken together with the intentions of the parties, are the prevailing elements for interpretation. Indeed, it has also been noted in the literature that a too rigorous application of the principle of restrictive interpretation might be inconsistent with the primary purpose of the treaty. ... Restrictive interpretation thus has particularly little role to play in certain categories of treaties—such as, for example, human rights treaties. Indeed, some authors note that the principle has not been relied upon in any recent jurisprudence of international courts and tribunals and that its contemporary relevance is to be doubted. ...

54. The Award in the *Lac Lanoux Arbitration* ... remains to this day a very useful guide to the present type of inevitable tension between rights on one's own territory given under a treaty, and reservations as to sovereignty. ... As the *Lac Lanoux* tribunal held, ... "Territorial sovereignty plays the part of a presumption. It must bend before all international obligations, whatever their origin, but only before such obligations." The *Lac Lanoux* tribunal observed that in the application of this observation "the question is therefore to determine the obligations of the French Government in this case. ..." ...

55. In precisely that same way, the sovereignty reserved to the Netherlands under Article XII of the 1839 Treaty of Separation cannot be understood save by first determining Belgium's rights, and the Netherlands' obligations in relation thereto. This is to be done not by invocation of the principle of restrictive interpretation, but rather by examining—using the normal rules of interpretation identified in Articles 31 and 32 of the Vienna Convention—exactly what rights have been afforded to Belgium. All else falls within the Netherlands' sovereignty. ...

* * *

58. ... Article 31, paragraph 3, subparagraph (c) of the Vienna Convention on the Law of Treaties makes reference to "any relevant rules of international law applicable in the relations between the parties." For this reason[,] ... the Tribunal has examined any provisions of European law that might be considered of possible relevance in this case. ... Provisions of general international law are also applicable to the relations between the Parties, and thus should be taken into account in interpreting Article XII of the 1839 Treaty of Separation. ... Further, international environmental law has relevance to the relations between the Parties. There is considerable debate as to what, within the field of environmental law, constitutes "rules" or "principles"; what is "soft law"; and which environmental treaty law or principles have contributed to the development of customary international law. Without entering further into those controversies, the Tribunal notes that in all of these categories "environment" is broadly referred to as including air, water, land, flora and fauna, natural ecosystems and sites, human health and safety, and climate. The emerging principles, whatever their current status, make reference to conservation, management, notions of prevention and of sustainable development, and protection for future generations.

59. Since the Stockholm Conference on the Environment in 1972 there has been a marked development of international law relating to the protection of the environment. Today, both international and EC law require the integration of appropriate

environmental measures in the design and implementation of economic development activities. Principle 4 of the Rio Declaration on Environment and Development, adopted in 1992 (31 I.L.M. p. 874, at p. 877), which reflects this trend, provides that "environmental protection shall constitute an integral part of the development process and cannot be considered in isolation from it." Importantly, these emerging principles now integrate environmental protection into the development process. Environmental law and the law on development stand not as alternatives but as mutually reinforcing, integral concepts, which require that where development may cause significant harm to the environment there is a duty to prevent, or at least mitigate, such harm (*see* paragraph 222). This duty, in the opinion of the Tribunal, has now become a principle of general international law. This principle applies not only in autonomous activities but also in activities undertaken in implementation of specific treaties between the Parties. The Tribunal would recall the observation of the International Court of Justice in the *Gabčíkovo–Nagymaros* case that "[t]his need to reconcile economic development with protection of the environment is aptly expressed in the concept of sustainable development" (*Gabčíkovo–Nagymaros (Hungary/Slovakia), Judgment, I.C.J. Reports 1997*, p. 7 at p. 78, para. 140). And in that context the Court further clarified that "new norms have to be taken into consideration, and ... new standards given proper weight, not only when States contemplate new activities but also when continuing with activities begun in the past" (*Ibid.*). In the view of the Tribunal this dictum applies equally to the Iron Rhine railway.

* * *

61.   The Tribunal now turns to the application of the principles of interpretation to the relevant treaty provisions.

* * *

70.   The dispute that arises is as to ... whether the costs and expenses to be incurred by Belgium [for the upgrading and restoration of the line] should include the costs and expenses [of] the environmental protection measures required by Netherlands law. Belgium denies ... a duty [to pay such costs], on the ground that these measures are not measures necessitated by the physical extension of the line—they are measures unilaterally undertaken by the Netherlands in the exercise of its sovereignty. Belgium further claims that it should have been consulted before the various areas were declared protected nature reserves.... Further, Belgium asserts that the proposed measures for noise protection, in particular tunnelling, are not the least costly available to mitigate any environmental harm.

71.   The Netherlands asserts that it has the sovereign right to assess the appropriate means to protect the environment to EC and its own domestic standards; that it has sought to identify objectively, through expert reports, those means; and that the measures would not otherwise have been necessary save for Belgium's request for a restoration and significant upgrading of the capacity of the Iron Rhine railway.

72.   There is merit in both arguments. The Tribunal finds it necessary, in order to answer this matter, first to ascertain whether the project is one which would attract the cost allocation provisions of Article XII, and second, if so, to see if the costs and expenses of the measures envisaged by the Netherlands are integral to the extension of the Iron Rhine line.

* * *

79.   ... [The intertemporal rule with respect to treaty interpretation provides that] regard should be had in interpreting Article XII to juridical facts as they stood in 1839. In particular, it is certainly the case that, in 1839, it was envisaged that the costs for any extension of a new road or canal that Belgium might ask for would be limited and relatively modest. The great advances that were later to be made in electrification,

track design and specification, freight stock, and so forth—and the concomitant costs—could not have been foreseen by the Parties. At the same time, . . . the Tribunal [does not need] to be oblivious either to later facts that bear on the effective application of the treaty, nor indeed to all later legal developments. It has long been established that the understanding of conceptual or generic terms in a treaty may be seen as "an essentially relative question; it depends upon the development of international relations". . . . Some terms are "not static, but were by definition evolutionary. . . ." Where a term can be classified as generic "the presumption necessarily arises that its meaning was intended to follow the evolution of the law and to correspond with the meaning attached to the expression by the law in force at any given time". . . .

80. In the present case it is not a conceptual or generic term that is in issue, but rather new technical developments relating to the operation and capacity of the railway. But here, too, it seems that an evolutive interpretation, which would ensure an application of the treaty that would be effective in terms of its object and purpose, will be preferred to a strict application of the intertemporal rule. Thus in the *Gabčíkovo–Nagymaros* case, the International Court was prepared to accept, in interpreting a treaty that predated certain recent norms of environmental law, that "the Treaty is not static, and is open to adapt to emerging norms of international law." . . .

81. Finally, the Tribunal notes a general support among the leading writers today for evolutive interpretation of treaties. . . . Rudolf Bernhardt explains it thus: "The object and purpose of a treaty plays . . . a central role in treaty interpretation. This reference to object and purpose can be understood as entry into a certain dynamism. If it is the purpose of a treaty to create longer lasting and solid relations between the parties . . . , it is hardly compatible with this purpose to eliminate new developments in the process of treaty interpretation" (42 *German Yearbook of International Law* (1999) at pp. 16–17).

* * *

87. As for the injunction in Article 31, paragraph 1 of the Vienna Convention that a term be read "in context" for its correct interpretation, the Tribunal notes that the relevant context of the phrase "without prejudice to the exclusive rights of sovereignty" is its location in a paragraph which also includes rights given to Belgium. The Netherlands has necessarily already derogated from its territorial sovereignty in allowing a railway to be built, at the request of another state, over its territory. The sovereignty reserved is over the territory over which the track runs. The Netherlands has forfeited no more sovereignty than that which is necessary for the track to be built and to operate to allow a commercial connection from Belgium to Germany across Limburg. It thus retains the police power throughout that area, the power to establish health and safety standards for work being done on the track, and the power to establish environmental standards in that area.

* * *

160. . . . [A]s a consequence of the reservation of sovereignty in Article XII of the 1839 Treaty of Separation, the Netherlands may exercise its rights of sovereignty in relation to the territory over which the Iron Rhine railway passes, unless this would conflict with the treaty rights granted to Belgium, or rights that Belgium may hold under general international law, or constraints imposed by EC law.

* * *

162. In the view of Belgium, the limitations flowing from Article XII entail that the Netherlands is under the obligation to exercise its legislative and decision-making power in good faith and in a reasonable manner and so as not to deprive Belgium's transit right of its substance or to render the exercise of the right unreasonably

difficult (BR, p. 69, para. 70). The Netherlands does not contest these limitations, but contends that its actions fully comply with these requirements.

* * *

168. Various Netherlands acts and decrees apply to the reactivation of the Iron Rhine railway. Of particular importance are those dealing with technical and safety issues, such as the technical specifications for the track and railroad crossings, and those dealing with environmental issues (land-use planning, health and soil protection, and nature preservation).... The dispute between the Parties about the consequences of the implementation of Netherlands legislation focuses in particular on the environmental legislation. The legislation considered most relevant by the Parties in their pleadings includes the following. [Tribunal then discusses the Noise Abatement Act, the Railway Noise Abatement Decree, the Flora and Fauna Act, the Environmental management Act, the Environmental Impact Assessment Decree, the Netherlands National Park Policies and provincial environmental regulations, all of which have some impact on the proposed railway alteration and extension and all of which would require extensive and expensive measures to limit the environmental impact of the railway, including noise.]

* * *

202. With respect to the measures envisaged by the Netherlands discussed above, Belgium argues that the Netherlands is under an obligation to apply its legislation in the way least unfavourable for Belgium; in not doing so the Netherlands would be acting contrary to the principles of reasonableness and good faith. Belgium regards some of the measures envisaged as an unnecessary interference with its transit right. They would constitute a breach by the Netherlands of its obligations towards Belgium....

203. The Netherlands argues that it treats the reactivation of the Iron Rhine railway in the same way as other railways in the Netherlands. It accepts Belgium's right to reactivation, but it sees no reason why the Iron Rhine railway should be treated more favourably than regular Netherlands railways. In requiring the envisaged measures for the reactivation, the Netherlands claims that it is acting reasonably and in good faith. Its actions do not constitute an abuse of right, and are not arbitrary or discriminatory. In fact, it asserts that its legislative requirements are applied in the most favourable way for Belgium....

204. In the view of the Tribunal, the obligations of the Netherlands under Article XII of the 1839 Treaty of Separation do not require it to apply its national legislation and policy with respect to the reactivation of the Iron Rhine railway in a more favourable way than with respect to other railways in the Netherlands, unless such non-discriminatory application would amount to a denial of Belgium's transit right or render the exercise of that right unreasonably difficult.

205. The Tribunal concludes that the measures as such as presently envisaged by the Netherlands cannot be regarded as amounting to a denial of Belgium's transit right or render the exercise of the right unreasonably difficult....

* * *

219. ... [A]lthough Article XII was directed towards the construction of ... the Iron Rhine, the right of transit there provided for also covers the reactivation of the track and its use through time. The specific financial provisions of Article XII were formulated in respect of the construction of a new road, canal or track. The real questions, so far as allocation of costs is concerned, are the following: what elements of Article XII relating to costs are applicable to a reactivation that is not a construction of a new railway but is nonetheless within the ambit of Article XII? And what other elements within Article XII, interpreted in accordance with the legal principles

explained ... above, may illuminate the allocation of costs for the reactivation that Belgium seeks and is entitled to?

220. The Tribunal finds itself in the presence of three points of departure for its analysis of these questions. The first is that, in matters other than those specifically provided for in relation to the construction of a new line, the Netherlands retains its rights of sovereignty. The second is that a major adaptation and modernisation of an existing railway must today include necessary environmental protection measures as an integral component of such a project. It has been shown in paragraphs 58 and 59 that rules of international law on protection of the environment are applicable law between the Parties in the interpretation of the conventional regime for the Iron Rhine railway. As a third point, the Tribunal will remain mindful that the financial burdens associated with the reactivation must not fall in such a way as effectively to prevent or render unreasonably difficult the exercise of Belgium's right of transit under Article XII of the 1839 Treaty of Separation. These elements, taken together, suggest that the costs are not to be borne solely by Belgium as if it were "a new road"; but neither are they to be borne solely by the Netherlands. The financial obligations of the Parties must therefore be subjected to careful balancing. Such balancing requires a variety of factors to be taken into account. ...

221. The Tribunal considers that Belgium is in principle entitled to exercise its right of transit in a way which corresponds to its current economic needs. At the same time, the concern of the Netherlands for its environment and the impact thereon of the intended, much more intensive, use of the railway line is to be viewed as legitimate. Such exercise of Belgium's right of transit and the Netherlands' legitimate environmental concerns are to be, as far as possible, reconciled. The Tribunal notes that such a reconciliation of rights echoes the balancing of interests reflected in Article XII of the 1839 Treaty of Separation. ... [T]he object and purpose of the Treaty suggests an interpretation that would include within the ambit of the balance [struck in Article XII] new needs and developments relating to operation and capacity. ... As the Tribunal has already observed above ..., economic development is to be reconciled with the protection of the environment, and, in so doing, new norms have to be taken into consideration, including when activities begun in the past are now expanded and upgraded.

222. The use of the Iron Rhine railway started some 120 years ago and it is now envisaged and requested by Belgium at a substantially increased and intensified level. Such new use is susceptible of having an adverse impact on the environment and causing harm to it. Today, in international environmental law, a growing emphasis is being put on the duty of prevention. Much of international environmental law has been formulated by reference to the impact that activities in one territory may have on the territory of another. The International Court of Justice expressed the view that "[t]he existence of the general obligation of States to ensure that activities within their jurisdiction and control respect the environment of other States or of areas beyond national control is now part of the corpus of international law relating to the environment." ...

223. Applying the principles of international environmental law, the Tribunal observes that it is faced, in the instant case, not with a situation of a transboundary effect of the economic activity in the territory of one state on the territory of another state, but with the effect of the exercise of a treaty-guaranteed right of one state in the territory of another state and a possible impact of such exercise on the territory of the latter state. The Tribunal is of the view that, by analogy, where a state exercises a right under international law within the territory of another state, considerations of environmental protection also apply. The exercise of Belgium's right of transit, as it has formulated its request, thus may well necessitate measures by the Netherlands to protect the environment to which Belgium will have to contribute as an integral element of its request. The reactivation of the Iron Rhine railway cannot be viewed in

isolation from the environmental protection measures necessitated by the intended use of the railway line. These measures are to be fully integrated into the project and its costs.

* * *

226. The Belgian obligation to fund the environmental element of the overall costs of the reactivation is integral to its exercise of its right of transit. . . .

* * *

234. . . . The Tribunal is aware that the major cost factor . . . in relation to the whole project of the reactivation of the Iron Rhine is attributable to the envisaged tunnel in the Meinweg. . . . The construction of such a tunnel is envisaged in light of the fact that the track lies in the Meinweg area designated as a national park by the Netherlands Minister of Agriculture, Nature Management and Fisheries on 1 June 1995 and as a "Silent Area" by the Province of Limburg. When the Netherlands took that decision it already knew that the historic route crossed that area and that Belgium, despite not exercising since 1991 its right of transit, had reserved its right to the use of the line in the future. The Tribunal is of the view that the Netherlands' decision to declare the Meinweg a national park in an area over which Belgium was entitled under treaty to a right of transit, though a permitted act of Netherlands' sovereignty, cannot remain without financial consequence for the Netherlands. On the other hand, the Belgian Government reserved its right only in abstract terms, and did not specify the parameters of its future use of the line before the decisions of the Netherlands were taken. The construction of the tunnel is required not only in view of the intensive use envisaged by Belgium, . . . but also arises out of the Netherlands' decision to establish a national park in the area which was already crossed by the historic route. The Tribunal considers that both Parties contributed to the occurrence of the situation which now requires much more costly measures. The Tribunal is therefore of the view that the costs for the tunnel in the Meinweg are to be apportioned equally between the Parties.

8.15 CASE CONCERNING PULP MILLS ON THE RIVER URUGUAY (**Argentina v. Uruguay**) (**Merits**), **2010 ICJ** ___

[*Eds*. Argentine brought an action complaining that Uruguay's construction of two pulp mills on the River Uruguay, which forms the border between the two countries, had been authorized and conducted in violation of an agreement between the two countries concerning use of the River (the "1975 Statute") and would, or had, caused damage to the quality of the river's waters, ecological damage, and pollution.]

I. LEGAL FRAMEWORK AND FACTS OF THE CASE

25. The dispute before the Court has arisen in connection with the planned construction authorized by Uruguay of one pulp mill and the construction and commissioning of another, also authorized by Uruguay, on the River Uruguay....

26. The boundary between Argentina and Uruguay in the River Uruguay is defined by the bilateral Treaty entered into for that purpose at Montevideo on 7 April 1961 ... Article 7 [of the Treaty] provides for the establishment by the parties of a "régime for the use of the river" covering various subjects, including the conservation of living resources and the prevention of water pollution of the river....

27. The "régime for the use of the river" contemplated in Article 7 of the 1961 Treaty was established through the 1975 Statute.... Article 1 of the 1975 Statute states that the parties adopted it "in order to establish the joint machinery necessary for the optimum and rational utilization of the River Uruguay, in strict observance of the rights and obligations arising from treaties and other international agreements in force for each of the parties." ... The 1975 Statute sets up the Administrative Commission of the River Uruguay (hereinafter "CARU"....)

* * *

65. ... In interpreting the terms of the 1975 Statute, the Court will have recourse to the customary rules on treaty interpretation as reflected in Article 31 of the Vienna Convention. Accordingly the 1975 Statute is to be "interpreted in good faith in accordance with the ordinary meaning to be given to the terms of the [Statute] in their context and in light of its object and purpose". That interpretation will also take into account, together with the context, "any relevant rules of international law applicable in the relations between the parties."

* * *

III. THE ALLEGED BREACH OF PROCEDURAL OBLIGATIONS

* * *

81. ... [Articles 7–12 of the Statute impose] procedural obligations of informing, notifying and negotiating [under the auspices of CARU].... These obligations are all the more vital when a shared resource is at issue, as in the case of the River Uruguay, which can only be protected through close and continuous co-operation between the riparian States.

* * *

90. Since CARU serves as a framework for consultation between the parties, particularly in the case of the planned works contemplated in Article 7, first paragraph, of the 1975 Statute, neither of them may depart from that framework unilaterally, as they see fit, and put other channels of communication in its place. By creating CARU and investing it with all the resources necessary for its operation, the parties have sought to provide the best possible guarantees of stability, continuity and

effectiveness for their desire to co-operate in ensuring "the optimum and rational utilization of the River Uruguay".

* * *

101. The Court points out that the principle of prevention, as a customary rule, has its origins in the due diligence that is required of a State in its territory. It is "every State's obligation not to allow knowingly its territory to be used for acts contrary to the rights of other States" (Corfu Channel (United Kingdom v. Albania), Merits, Judgment, I.C.J. Reports 1949, p. 22). A State is thus obliged to use all the means at its disposal in order to avoid activities which take place in its territory, or in any area under its jurisdiction, causing significant damage to the environment of another State. This Court has established that this obligation "is now part of the corpus of international law relating to the environment" (Legality of the Threat or Use of Nuclear Weapons, Advisory Opinion, I.C.J. Reports 1996 (I), p. 242, para. 29).

102. In the view of the Court, the obligation to inform CARU allows for the initiation of co-operation between the Parties which is necessary in order to fulfil the obligation of prevention. . . .

* * *

105. The Court considers that the State planning activities referred to in Article 7 of the Statute is required to inform CARU as soon as it is in possession of a plan which is sufficiently developed to enable CARU to make the preliminary assessment (required by paragraph 1 of that provision) of whether the proposed works might cause significant damage to the other party. . . . [T]he duty to inform CARU will become applicable at the stage when the relevant authority has had the project referred to it with the aim of obtaining initial environmental authorization and before the granting of that authorization.

106. The Court observes that, in the present case, Uruguay did not transmit to CARU the information required by Article 7, first paragraph, in respect of the CMB (ENCE) and Orion (Botnia) mills, despite the requests made to it by the Commission to that effect on several occasions. . . .

* * *

111. Consequently, the Court concludes . . . that Uruguay, by not informing CARU of the planned works before the issuing of the initial environmental authorizations for each of the mills and for the port terminal adjacent to the Orion (Botnia) mill, has failed to comply with the obligation imposed on it by Article 7, first paragraph, of the 1975 Statute.

* * *

113. In the opinion of the Court, the obligation to notify is intended to create the conditions for successful co-operation between the parties, enabling them to assess the plan's impact on the river on the basis of the fullest possible information and, if necessary, to negotiate the adjustments needed to avoid the potential damage that it might cause.

* * *

117. . . . Uruguay maintains that it [conducted assessments in accordance with its domestic legislation and it] was not required to transmit the environmental impact assessments to Argentina before issuing the initial environmental authorizations to the companies, these authorizations having been adopted on the basis of its legislation on the subject.

* * *

119. The Court notes that the environmental impact assessments which are necessary to reach a decision on any plan that is liable to cause significant transboundary harm to another State must be notified by the party concerned to the other party, through CARU, pursuant to Article 7, second and third paragraphs, of the 1975 Statute. This notification is intended to enable the notified party to participate in the process of ensuring that the assessment is complete, so that it can then consider the plan and its effects with a full knowledge of the facts (Article 8 of the 1975 Statute).

120. The Court observes that this notification must take place before the State concerned decides on the environmental viability of the plan, taking due account of the environmental impact assessment submitted to it.

121. In the present case, the Court observes that the notification to Argentina of the environmental impact assessments for the CMB (ENCE) and Orion (Botnia) mills did not take place through CARU, and that Uruguay only transmitted those assessments to Argentina after having issued the initial environmental authorizations for the two mills in question.... Uruguay ought not, prior to notification, to have issued the initial environmental authorizations and the authorizations for construction on the basis of the environmental impact assessments submitted to DINAMA. Indeed by doing so, Uruguay gave priority to its own legislation over its procedural obligations under the 1975 Statute and disregarded the well-established customary rule reflected in Article 27 of the Vienna Convention on the Law of Treaties, according to which "[a] party may not invoke the provisions of its internal law as justification for its failure to perform a treaty".

122. The Court concludes from the above that Uruguay failed to comply with its obligation to notify the plans to Argentina through CARU under Article 7, second and third paragraphs, of the 1975 Statute.

* * *

139. ... The Court is aware that the negotiation provided for in Article 12 of the 1975 Statute forms part of the overall procedure laid down in Articles 7 to 12, which is structured in such a way that the parties, in association with CARU, are able, at the end of the process, to fulfil their obligation to prevent any significant transboundary harm which might be caused by potentially harmful activities planned by either one of them.

* * *

144. Consequently, in the opinion of the Court, as long as the procedural mechanism for co-operation between the parties to prevent significant damage to one of them is taking its course, the State initiating the planned activity is obliged not to authorize such work and, a fortiori, not to carry it out.

* * *

147. In the view of the Court, there would be no point to the co-operation mechanism provided for by Articles 7 to 12 of the 1975 Statute if the party initiating the planned activity were to authorize or implement it without waiting for that mechanism to be brought to a conclusion. Indeed, if that were the case, the negotiations between the parties would no longer have any purpose.

* * *

149. The Court concludes from the above ... that by authorizing the construction of the mills and the port terminal at Fray Bentos before the expiration of the period of negotiation, Uruguay failed to comply with the obligation to negotiate laid

down by Article 12 of the Statute. Consequently, Uruguay disregarded the whole of the co-operation mechanism provided for in Articles 7 to 12 of the 1975 Statute.

* * *

IV. SUBSTANTIVE OBLIGATIONS

* * *

4. The obligation to prevent pollution and preserve the aquatic environment (Article 41)

190.   Article 41 provides that:

Without prejudice to the functions assigned to the Commission in this respect, the parties undertake:

> (a) to protect and preserve the aquatic environment and, in particular, to prevent its pollution, by prescribing appropriate rules and [adopting appropriate] measures in accordance with applicable international agreements and in keeping, where relevant, with the guidelines and recommendations of international technical bodies;
>
> (b) not to reduce in their respective legal systems:
>
> 1.   the technical requirements in force for preventing water pollution, and
>
> 2.   the severity of the penalties established for violations;
>
> (c) to inform one another of any rules which they plan to prescribe with regard to water pollution in order to establish equivalent rules in their respective legal systems.

191.   Argentina claims that by allowing the discharge of additional nutrients into a river that is eutrophic and suffers from reverse flow and stagnation, Uruguay violated the obligation to prevent pollution, as it failed to prescribe appropriate measures in relation to the Orion (Botnia) mill, and failed to meet applicable international environmental agreements, including the Biodiversity Convention **[Basic Document 5.7]** and the Ramsar Convention **[Basic Document 5.3]**. It maintains that the 1975 Statute prohibits any pollution which is prejudicial to the protection and preservation of the aquatic environment or which alters the ecological balance of the river. Argentina further argues that the obligation to prevent pollution of the river is an obligation of result and extends not only to protecting the aquatic environment proper, but also to any reasonable and legitimate use of the river, including tourism and other recreational uses.

192.   Uruguay contends that the obligation laid down in Article 41 (a) of the 1975 Statute to "prevent . . . pollution" does not involve a prohibition on all discharges into the river. It is only those that exceed the standards jointly agreed by the Parties within CARU in accordance with their international obligations, and that therefore have harmful effects, which can be characterized as "pollution" under Article 40 of the 1975 Statute. Uruguay also maintains that Article 41 creates an obligation of conduct, and not of result, but that it actually matters little since Uruguay has complied with its duty to prevent pollution by requiring the plant to meet best available technology ("BAT") standards.

193.   Before turning to the analysis of Article 41, the Court recalls that:

"The existence of the general obligation of States to ensure that activities within their jurisdiction and control respect the environment of other States or of areas beyond national control is now part of the corpus of international law relating to the environment." (Legality of the Threat or Use of Nuclear Weapons, Advisory Opinion, I.C.J. Reports 1996 (I), pp. 241–242, para. 29.)

* * *

195.   In view of the central role of this provision in the dispute between the Parties in the present case and their profound differences as to its interpretation and application, the Court will make a few remarks of a general character on the normative content of Article 41 before addressing the specific arguments of the Parties. First, in the view of the Court, Article 41 makes a clear distinction between regulatory functions entrusted to CARU under the 1975 Statute, which are dealt with in Article 56 of the Statute, and the obligation it imposes on the Parties to adopt rules and measures individually to "protect and preserve the aquatic environment and, in particular, to prevent its pollution". Thus, the obligation assumed by the Parties under Article 41, which is distinct from those under Articles 36 and 56 of the 1975 Statute, is to adopt appropriate rules and measures within the framework of their respective domestic legal systems to protect and preserve the aquatic environment and to prevent pollution. This conclusion is supported by the wording of paragraphs (b) and (c) of Article 41, which refer to the need not to reduce the technical requirements and severity of the penalties already in force in the respective legislation of the Parties as well as the need to inform each other of the rules to be promulgated so as to establish equivalent rules in their legal systems.

196.   Secondly, it is the opinion of the Court that a simple reading of the text of Article 41 indicates that it is the rules and measures that are to be prescribed by the Parties in their respective legal systems which must be "in accordance with applicable international agreements" and "in keeping, where relevant, with the guidelines and recommendations of international technical bodies".

197.   Thirdly, the obligation to "preserve the aquatic environment, and in particular to prevent pollution by prescribing appropriate rules and measures" is an obligation to act with due diligence in respect of all activities which take place under the jurisdiction and control of each party. It is an obligation which entails not only the adoption of appropriate rules and measures, but also a certain level of vigilance in their enforcement and the exercise of administrative control applicable to public and private operators, such as the monitoring of activities undertaken by such operators, to safeguard the rights of the other party. The responsibility of a party to the 1975 Statute would therefore be engaged if it was shown that it had failed to act diligently and thus take all appropriate measures to enforce its relevant regulations on a public or private operator under its jurisdiction. The obligation of due diligence under Article 41 (a) in the adoption and enforcement of appropriate rules and measures is further reinforced by the requirement that such rules and measures must be "in accordance with applicable international agreements" and "in keeping, where relevant, with the guidelines and recommendations of international technical bodies". This requirement has the advantage of ensuring that the rules and measures adopted by the parties both have to conform to applicable international agreements and to take account of internationally agreed technical standards.

198.   Finally, the scope of the obligation to prevent pollution must be determined in light of the definition of pollution given in Article 40 of the 1975 Statute. Article 40 provides that: "For the purposes of this Statute, pollution shall mean the direct or indirect introduction by man into the aquatic environment of substances or energy which have harmful effects." The term "harmful effects" is defined in the CARU Digest as:

"any alteration of the water quality that prevents or hinders any legitimate use of the water, that causes deleterious effects or harm to living resources, risks to human health, or a threat to water activities including fishing or reduction of recreational activities" (Title I, Chapter I, Section. 2, Article 1 (c) of the Digest (E3)).

* * *

204. It is the opinion of the Court that in order for the Parties properly to comply with their obligations under Article 41 (a) and (b) of the 1975 Statute, they must, for the purposes of protecting and preserving the aquatic environment with respect to activities which may be liable to cause transboundary harm, carry out an environmental impact assessment. As the Court has observed in the case concerning the Dispute Regarding Navigational and Related Rights,

> there are situations in which the parties' intent upon conclusion of the treaty was, or may be presumed to have been, to give the terms used—or some of them—a meaning or content capable of evolving, not one fixed once and for all, so as to make allowance for, among other things, developments in international law (Dispute Regarding Navigational and Related Rights (Costa Rica v. Nicaragua), Judgment of 13 July 2009, para. 64).

In this sense, the obligation to protect and preserve, under Article 41 (a) of the Statute, has to be interpreted in accordance with a practice, which in recent years has gained so much acceptance among States that it may now be considered a requirement under general international law to undertake an environmental impact assessment where there is a risk that the proposed industrial activity may have a significant adverse impact in a transboundary context, in particular, on a shared resource. Moreover, due diligence, and the duty of vigilance and prevention which it implies, would not be considered to have been exercised, if a party planning works liable to affect the régime of the river or the quality of its waters did not undertake an environmental impact assessment on the potential effects of such works.

205. The Court observes that neither the 1975 Statute nor general international law specify the scope and content of an environmental impact assessment. . . . [T]he UNEP Goals and Principles [of Environmental Impact Assessment] is not binding on the Parties, but, as guidelines issued by an international technical body, has to be taken into account by each Party in accordance with Article 41 (a) in adopting measures within its domestic regulatory framework. Moreover, this instrument provides only that the "environmental effects in an EIA should be assessed with a degree of detail commensurate with their likely environmental significance" (Principle 5) without giving any indication of minimum core components of the assessment. Consequently, it is the view of the Court that it is for each State to determine in its domestic legislation or in the authorization process for the project, the specific content of the environmental impact assessment required in each case, having regard to the nature and magnitude of the proposed development and its likely adverse impact on the environment as well as to the need to exercise due diligence in conducting such an assessment. The Court also considers that an environmental impact assessment must be conducted prior to the implementation of a project. Moreover, once operations have started and, where necessary, throughout the life of the project, continuous monitoring of its effects on the environment shall be undertaken.

* * *

265. [After reviewing in depth Argentina's claims that Uruguay had failed to conduct an adequate environmental impact assessment and that the projects would cause unacceptable pollution and ecological damage, the Court concluded:] . . . [T]here is no conclusive evidence in the record to show that Uruguay has not acted with the requisite degree of due diligence or that the discharges of effluent from the Orion (Botnia) mill have had deleterious effects or caused harm to living resources or to the quality of the water or the ecological balance of the river since it started its operations

in November 2007. Consequently, on the basis of the evidence submitted to it, the Court concludes that Uruguay has not breached its obligations under Article 41.

* * *

267. Having concluded that Uruguay breached its procedural obligations under the 1975 Statute (see paragraphs 111, 122, 131, 149, 157 and 158 above), it is for the Court to draw the conclusions following from these internationally wrongful acts giving rise to Uruguay's international responsibility and to determine what that responsibility entails.

* * *

269. The Court considers that its finding of wrongful conduct by Uruguay in respect of its procedural obligations per se constitutes a measure of satisfaction for Argentina. As Uruguay's breaches of the procedural obligations occurred in the past and have come to an end, there is no cause to order their cessation.

* * *

273. The Court recalls that customary international law provides for restitution as one form of reparation for injury, restitution being the re-establishment of the situation which existed before occurrence of the wrongful act. The Court further recalls that, where restitution is materially impossible or involves a burden out of all proportion to the benefit deriving from it, reparation takes the form of compensation or satisfaction, or even both. . . .

274. Like other forms of reparation, restitution must be appropriate to the injury suffered, taking into account the nature of the wrongful act having caused it. As the Court has made clear,

> [w]hat constitutes 'reparation in an adequate form' clearly varies depending upon the concrete circumstances surrounding each case and the precise nature and scope of the injury, since the question has to be examined from the viewpoint of what is the 'reparation in an adequate form' that corresponds to the injury (Avena and Other Mexican Nationals (Mexico v. United States of America), Judgment, I.C.J. Reports 2004 (I), p. 59, para. 119).

275. . . . [C]onstruction of [the Orion (Botnia) mill] that mill began before negotiations had come to an end, in breach of the procedural obligations laid down in the 1975 Statute. [However], . . . the operation of the Orion (Botnia) mill has not resulted in the breach of substantive obligations laid down in the 1975 Statute. . . . As Uruguay was not barred from proceeding with the construction and operation of the Orion (Botnia) mill after the expiration of the period for negotiation and as it breached no substantive obligation under the 1975 Statute, ordering the dismantling of the mill would not, in the view of the Court, constitute an appropriate remedy for the breach of procedural obligations.

276. As Uruguay has not breached substantive obligations arising under the 1975 Statute, the Court is likewise unable, for the same reasons, to uphold Argentina's claim in respect of compensation for alleged injuries suffered in various economic sectors, specifically tourism and agriculture.

* * *

282. For these reasons, the Court . . . finds that the Eastern Republic of Uruguay has breached its procedural obligations under Articles 7 to 12 of the 1975 Statute of the River Uruguay and that the declaration by the Court of this breach constitutes appropriate satisfaction. . . .

STATUS OF BASIC DOCUMENTS IN INTERNATIONAL ENVIRONMENTAL LAW AND WORLD ORDER (CURRENT TO 1 JAN 2011 UNLESS OTHERWISE INDICATED)

*For the texts of reservations, declarations, and statements of understanding, and objections qualifying the ratification of, or accession or succession to, the multilateral treaties listed herein, see **United Nations Multilateral Treaties Deposited with the Secretary General**, available at http://treaties.un.org (accessed October 21, 2011).*

1. CONSTITUTIVE/ORGANIC

A. General

1.1 CONSTITUTION OF THE UNITED STATES OF AMERICA
Concluded: 17 Sep 1787
Entered into force: 21 Jun 1788 (pursuant to Article VII)

1.2 CHARTER OF THE UNITED NATIONS
Concluded: 26 Jun 45
Entered into force: 24 Oct 45
Parties: 192
Original members: 51
Argentina (24 Sep 45), Australia (1 Nov 45), Belarus (Byelorussian SSR) (24 Oct 45), Belgium (27 Dec 45), Bolivia (14 Nov 45), Brazil (21 Sep 45), Canada (9 Nov 45), Chile (11 Oct 45), China* (28 Sep 45), Colombia (5 Nov 45), Costa Rica (2 Nov 45), Cuba (15 Oct 45), Czechoslovakia (19 Oct 45), Denmark (9 Oct 45), Dominican Republic (4 Sep 45), Ecuador (21 Dec 45), Egypt (22 Oct 45), El Salvador (26 Sep 45), Ethiopia (13 Nov 45), France (31 Aug 45), Greece (25 Oct 45), Guatemala (21 Nov 45), Haiti (27 Sep 45), Honduras (17 Dec 45), India (30 Oct 45), Iran (16 Oct 45), Iraq (21 Dec 45), Lebanon (17 Oct 45), Liberia (15 Oct 45), Luxembourg (2 Nov 45), Mexico (7 Nov 45), Netherlands (10 Dec 45), New Zealand (10 Sep 45), Nicaragua (6 Sep 45), Norway (27 Nov 45), Panama (13 Nov 45), Paraguay (12 Oct 45), Peru (31 Oct 45), Philippines (11 Oct 45), Poland (24 Oct 45), Russia (USSR) (24 Oct 45), Saudi Arabia (18 Oct 45), South Africa (7 Nov 45), Syria (19 Oct 45), Turkey (28 Sep 45), Ukraine (Ukrainian SSR) (24 Oct 45), United Kingdom (20 Oct 45), United States (8 Aug 45), Uruguay (18 Dec 45), Venezuela (15 Nov 45), Yugoslavia (19 Oct 45)

> * China was originally represented in the UN by the Government of the Republic of China (R.O.C.) on Taiwan until 25 October 1971. Since then, China has been represented by the Government of the People's Republic of China. The R.O.C. is not a member of the UN and has no representation.

Non-signatories admitted under Article 4: 143
Afghanistan (9 Nov 46), Albania (14 Dec 55), Algeria (8 Oct 62), Andorra (28 Jul 93), Angola (1 Dec 76), Antigua/Barbuda (11 Nov 81), Armenia (2 Mar 92), Austria (14 Dec 55), Azerbaijan (2 Mar 92), Bahamas (18 Sep 73), Bahrain (21 Sep 71), Bangladesh (17 Sep 74), Barbados (9 Dec 66), Belize (25 Sep 81), Benin (20 Sep 60), Bhutan (21 Sep 71), Bosnia–Herzegovina (22 May 92), Botswana (17 Oct 66), Brunei (21 Sep 84), Bulgaria (14 Dec 55), Burkina Faso (20 Sep 60),

Burundi (18 Sep 62), Cambodia (14 Dec 55), Cameroon (20 Sep 60), Cape Verde (16 Sep 75), Central African Republic (20 Sep 60), Chad (20 Sep 60), Comoros (12 Nov 75), Congo (Brazzaville) (20 Sep 60), Congo (Kinshasa) (20 Sep 60), Côte d'Ivoire (20 Sep 60), Croatia (22 May 92), Cyprus (20 Sep 60), Czech Republic (19 Jan 93),*** Djibouti (20 Sep 77), Dominica (18 Dec 78), Equatorial Guinea (12 Nov 68), Eritrea (28 May 93), Estonia (17 Sep 91), Fiji (13 Oct 70), Finland (14 Dec 55), Gabon (20 Sep 60), Gambia (21 Sep 65), Georgia (31 Jul 92), Germany (18 Sep 73), Ghana (8 Mar 57), Grenada (17 Sep 74), Guinea (12 Dec 58), Guinea–Bissau (17 Sep 74), Guyana (20 Sep 66), Hungary (14 Dec 55), Iceland (9 Nov 46), Indonesia (28 Sep 50), Ireland (14 Dec 55), Israel (11 May 49), Italy (14 Dec 55), Jamaica (18 Sep 62), Japan (18 Dec 56), Jordan (14 Dec 55), Kazakhstan (2 Mar 92), Kenya (16 Dec 63), Kiribati (14 Sep 99), Korea (North) (17 Sep 91), Korea (South) (17 Sep 91), Kuwait (14 May 63), Kyrgyzstan (2 Mar 92), Laos (14 Dec 55), Latvia (17 Sep 91), Lesotho (17 Oct 66), Libya (14 Dec 55), Liechtenstein (18 Sep 90), Lithuania (17 Sep 91), Macedonia (8 Apr 93), Madagascar (20 Sep 60), Malawi (1 Dec 64), Malaysia (17 Sep 57), Maldives (21 Sep 65), Mali (28 Sep 60), Malta (1 Dec 64), Marshall Islands (17 Sep 91), Mauritania (27 Oct 61), Mauritius (24 Apr 68), Micronesia (17 Sep 91), Moldova (2 Mar 92), Monaco (28 May 93), Mongolia (27 Oct 61), Montenegro (19 Jul 2006), Morocco (12 Nov 56), Mozambique (16 Sep 75), Myanmar (Burma) (19 Apr 48), Namibia (23 Apr 90), Nauru (14 Sep 99), Nepal (14 Dec 55), Niger (20 Sep 60), Nigeria (7 Oct 60), Oman (7 Oct 71), Pakistan (30 Sep 47), Palau (15 Dec 94), Papua New Guinea (10 Oct 75), Portugal (14 Dec 55), Qatar (21 Sep 71), Romania (14 Dec 55), Rwanda (18 Sep 62), Samoa (15 Dec 76), San Marino (2 Mar 92), São Tomé/Principe (16 Sep 75), Senegal (28 Sep 60), Serbia (1 Nov 2000),**** Seychelles (21 Sep 76), Sierra Leone (27 Sep 61), Singapore (21 Sep 65), Slovakia (19 Jan 93),*** Slovenia (22 May 92), Solomon Islands (19 Sep 78), Somalia (20 Sep 60), Spain (14 Dec 55), Sri Lanka (14 Dec 55), St Kitts/Nevis (23 Sep 83), St Lucia (18 Sep 79), St Vincent/Grenadines (16 Sep 80), Sudan (12 Nov 56), Suriname (4 Dec 75), Swaziland (24 Sep 68), Sweden (9 Nov 46), Switzerland (10 Sep 2002), Tajikistan (2 Mar 92), Tanzania (14 Dec 61),Thailand (15 Dec 46), Timor–Leste (27 Sep 2002), Togo (20 Sep 60), Tonga (14 Sep 99), Trinidad/Tobago (18 Sep 62), Tunisia (12 Nov 56), Turkmenistan (2 Mar 92), Tuvalu (5 Sep 2000), Uganda (25 Oct 62), United Arab Emirates (9 Dec 71), Uzbekistan (2 Mar 92), Vanuatu (15 Sep 81), Vietnam (20 Sep 77), Yemen (30 Sep 47), Zambia (1 Dec 64), Zimbabwe (25 Aug 80)

* Only 49 of the original 51 member states are counted in this grand total. Czechoslovakia and Yugoslavia are not counted because, via succession and name change, they were replaced by the Czech Republic and by Serbia and Montenegro, respectively. For further details, see infra the footnotes immediately following.

* * China is an original member of the UN, the Charter having been signed and ratified on its behalf on, respectively, 26 Jun 45 and 28 Sep 45 by the Government of the Republic of China, which continued to represent China in the UN until 25 Oct 71.

* * * Czechoslovakia was an original member of the UN until its dissolution on 31 Dec 92, the Charter having been signed and ratified on its behalf on, respectively, 26 Jun 45 and 19 Oct 45.

* * * * Formerly "Yugoslavia," until the country was officially renamed "Serbia and Montenegro" on 3 Feb 2003. On 3 Jun 2006, the National Assembly of the Republic of Montenegro adopted a Declaration of Independence, and on 28 Jun 2006, Montenegro was admitted to the membership of the United Nations. Throughout all volumes of this publication, "Serbia" replaces "Yugoslavia" for all treaty actions performed by the former Yugoslavia, an original member of the UN when it ratified the UN Charter on 19 Oct 1945. The name "Yugoslavia" is hereinafter retained for all non-treaty instruments (e.g., UN declarations and resolutions) performed by the former Yugoslavia before 3 Feb 2003. The name "Montenegro" is used for all treaties actually signed or ratified under that name and all non-treaty instruments adopted after 3 Jun 2006 when Montenegro declared its independence from Serbia.

1.3 STATUTE OF THE INTERNATIONAL COURT OF JUSTICE
Concluded: 26 Jun 45
Entered into force: 24 Oct 45

> *Note:* The Statute is part of the UN Charter (Basic Document I.2, *supra*). All members of the UN are parties to the Statute. Non-members may become parties to the Statute on conditions set in each case by the General Assembly on the recommendation of the Security Council. (Charter Article 93)

Non-members who are parties to the Statute: 1
Nauru (29 Jan 88)

1.4 STATUTE OF THE INTERNATIONAL ATOMIC ENERGY AGENCY (IAEA)
Concluded: 26 Oct 56
Entered into force: 29 Jul 57
IAEA Members: 151

Afghanistan (31 May 57), Albania (23 Aug 57), Algeria (24 Dec 63), Angola (9 Nov 99), Argentina (3 Oct 57), Armenia (27 Sep 93), Australia (29 Jul 57), Austria (10 May 57), Azerbaijan (30 May 2001), Bahrain (23 Jun 2009), Bangladesh (27 Sep 72), Belarus (8 Apr 57), Belgium (29 Apr 58), Belize (31 Mar 2006), Benin (26 May 99), Bolivia (15 Mar 63), Bosnia–Herzegovina (19 Sep 95), Botswana (20 Mar 2002), Brazil (29 Jul 57), Bulgaria (17 Aug 57), Burkina Faso (14 Sep 98), Burundi (24 Jun 2009), Cambodia (23 Nov 2009**), Cameroon (13 Jul 64), Canada (29 Jul 57), Central African Republic (5 Jan 2001), Chad (2 Nov 2005), Chile (19 Sep 60), China (1 Jan 84), Colombia (30 Sep 60), Congo (Brazzaville) (15 Jul 2009), Congo (Kinshasa) (10 Oct 61), Costa Rica (25 Mar 65), Côte d'Ivoire (19 Nov 63), Croatia (12 Feb 93), Cuba (1 Oct 57), Cyprus (7 Jun 65), Czech Republic (27 Sep 93), Denmark (16 Jul 57), Dominican Republic (11 Jul 57), Ecuador (3 Mar 58), Egypt (4 Sep 57), El Salvador (22 Nov 57), Eritrea (20 Dec 2002), Estonia (31 Jan 92), Ethiopia (30 Sep 57), Finland (7 Jan 58), France (29 Jul 57), Gabon (21 Jan 64), Georgia (23 Feb 96), Germany (1 Oct 57), Ghana (28 Sep 60), Greece (30 Sep 57), Guatemala (29 Mar 57), Haiti (7 Oct 57), Honduras (24 Feb 2003), Hungary (8 Aug 57), Iceland (6 Aug 57), India (16 Jul 57), Indonesia (7 Aug 57), Iran (16 Sep 58), Iraq (4 Mar 59), Ireland (6 Jan 70), Israel (12 Jul 57), Italy (30 Sep 57), Jamaica (29 Dec 65), Japan (16 Jul 57), Jordan (18 Apr 66), Kazakhstan (14 Feb 94), Kenya (12 Jul 65), Korea (South) (8 Aug 57), Kuwait (1 Dec 64), Kyrgyzstan (10 Sep 2003), Latvia (10 Apr 97), Lebanon (29 Jun 61), Lesotho (13 Jul 2009), Liberia (5 Oct 62), Libya (9 Sep 63), Liechtenstein (13 Dec 68), Lithuania (18 Nov 93), Luxembourg (29 Jan 58), Macedonia (25 Feb 94), Madagascar (22 Mar 65), Malawi (2 Oct 2006), Malaysia (15 Jan 69), Mali (10 Aug 61), Malta (29 Sep 97), Marshall Islands (26 Jan 94), Mauritania (23 Nov 2004), Mauritius (31 Dec 74), Mexico (7 Apr 58), Moldova (24 Sep 97), Monaco (19 Sep 57), Mongolia (20 Sep 73), Montenegro (13 Oct 2006), Morocco (17 Sep 57), Mozambique (18 Sep 2006), Myanmar (Burma) (18 Oct 57), Namibia (17 Feb 83), Nepal (8 Jul 2008), Netherlands (30 Jul 57), New Zealand (13 Sep 57), Nicaragua (25 Mar 77*), Niger (27 Mar 69), Nigeria (25 Mar 64), Norway (10 Jun 57), Oman (5 Feb 2009), Pakistan (2 May 57), Palau (2 Mar 2007), Panama (2 Mar 66), Paraguay (30 Sep 57), Peru (30 Sep 57),

Philippines (2 Sep 58), Poland (31 Jul 57), Portugal (12 Jul 57), Qatar (27 Feb 76), Romania (12 Apr 57), Saudi Arabia (13 Dec 62), Senegal (1 Nov 60), Serbia (4 Feb 2003), Seychelles (22 Apr 2003), Sierra Leone (4 Jun 67), Singaporè (5 Jan 67), Slovakia (27 Sep 93), Slovenia (21 Sep 92), South Africa (6 Jun 57), Spain (26 Aug 57), Sri Lanka (22 Aug 57), Sudan (17 Jul 58), Sweden (19 Jun 57), Switzerland (5 Apr 57), Syria (6 Jun 63), Tajikistan (10 Sep 2001), Tanzania (6 Jan 76), Thailand (15 Oct 57), Tunisia (14 Oct 57), Turkey (19 Jul 57), Uganda (30 Aug 67), Ukraine (31 Jul 57), United Arab Emirates (15 Jan 76), United Kingdom (29 Jul 57), United States (29 Jul 57), Uruguay (22 Jan 63), USSR (Russia) (8 Apr 57), Uzbekistan (26 Jan 94), Vatican City (20 Aug 57), Venezuela (19 Aug 57), Vietnam (24 Sep 57), Yemen (14 Oct 94), Zambia (8 Jan 69), Zimbabwe (1 Aug 86)
Withdrawals: 1
Korea (North) (13 Jun 94)

Note: Dates are dates of the deposit of legal instruments.

1.5   **EUROPEAN UNION: CONSOLIDATED VERSION OF THE TREATY ESTABLISHING THE EUROPEAN ECONOMIC COMMUNITY**
Concluded: 25 Mar 57 (Rome), 7 Feb 92 (Maastricht), 2 Oct 97 (Amsterdam), 26 Feb 2001 (Nice), 13 Dec 2007 (Lisbon)
Entered into force: 1 Jan 58 (Rome), 1 Nov 93 (Maastricht), 1 May 99 (Amsterdam), 1 Feb 2003 (Nice), 1 Dec 2009 (Lisbon)
Parties: 27 (dates are for ratification of the Treaty of Lisbon)
Parties: 27
Austria (13 May 2008), Belgium (15 Oct 2008), Bulgaria (28 Apr 2008),Cyprus (26 Aug 2008), Czech Republic (3 Nov 2008), Denmark (29 May 2008), Estonia (23 Sep 2008), Finland (30 Sep 2008), France (14 Feb 2008), Germany (25 Sep 2009), Greece (12 Aug 2008), Hungary (2 Jun 2008), Ireland (23 Oct 2008), Italy (8 Aug 2008), Latvia (16 Jun 2008), Lithuania (26 Aug 2008), Luxembourg (21 Jul 2008), Malta (6 Feb 2008), Netherlands (12 Sep 2008), Poland (13 Oct 2009), Portugal (17 Jun 2008), Romania (11 Mar 2008), Slovakia (24 Jun 2008), Slovenia (24 Apr 2008), Spain (8 Oct 2008), Sweden (10 Dec 2008), United Kingdom (16 Jul 2008)

1.6   **VIENNA CONVENTION ON THE LAW OF TREATIES**
Concluded: 23 May 69
Entered into force: 27 Jan 80
Total Parties: 111
Signed but not ratified: 15
Afghanistan (23 May 69), Bolivia (23 May 69), Cambodia (23 May 69), Côte d'Ivoire (23 Jul 69), El Salvador (16 Feb 70), Ethiopia (30 Apr 70), Ghana (23 May 69), Iran (23 May 69), Kenya (23 May 69), Madagascar (23 May 69), Nepal (23 May 69),Pakistan (29 Apr 70), Trinidad/Tobago (23 May 69), United States (24 Apr 70), Zambia (23 May 69)
Ratified/acceded/accepted without qualification: 76
Albania (27 Jun 2001), Andorra (5 Apr 2004), Australia (13 Jun 74), Austria (30 Apr 79), Barbados (24 Jun 71), Bosnia–Herzegovina (1 Sep 93), Burkina Faso (25 May 2006), Cameroon (23 Oct 91), Central African Republic (10 Dec 71), Congo (Brazzaville) (12 Apr 82), Congo (Kinshasa) (25 Jul 77), Croatia (12 Oct 92), Cyprus (28 Dec 76), Czech Republic* (22 Feb 93),Dominican Republic (1 Apr 2010), Egypt (11 Feb 82), Estonia (21 Oct 91), Gabon (5 Nov 2004), Georgia (8 Jun 95), Greece (30 Oct 74), Guinea (16 Sep 2005), Guyana (15 Sep 2005), Haiti (25 Aug 80), Honduras (20 Sep 79), Hungary (19 Jun 87), Ireland (7 Aug 2006), Italy (25 Jul 74), Jamaica (28 Jul 70), Japan (2 Jul 81), Kazakhstan (5 Jan 94),

Kiribati (15 Sep 2005), Korea (South) (27 Apr 77), Kyrgyzstan (11 May 99), Laos (31 Mar 98), Latvia (4 May 93), Lesotho (3 Mar 72), Liberia (29 Aug 85), Libya (22 Dec 2008), Liechtenstein (8 Feb 90), Lithuania (15 Jan 92), Luxembourg (23 May 2003), Macedonia (8 Jul 99), Malawi (23 Aug 83), Malaysia (27 Jul 94), Maldives (14 Sep 2005), Mali (31 Aug 98), Mauritius (18 Jan 73), Mexico (25 Sep 74), Moldova (26 Jan 93), Montenegro (23 Oct 2006), Mozambique (8 May 2001), Myanmar (Burma) (16 Sep 98), Nauru (5 May 78), Niger (27 Oct 71), Nigeria (31 Jul 69), Panama (28 Jul 80), Paraguay (3 Feb 72), Philippines (15 Nov 72), Poland (2 Jul 90), Rwanda (3 Jan 80), Senegal (11 Apr 86), Serbia (12 Mar 2001), Slovakia (28 May 93),* Slovenia (6 Jul 92), Solomon Islands (9 Aug 89), Spain (16 May 72), Sudan (18 Apr 90), Suriname (31 Jan 91), St Vincent/Grenadines (27 Apr 99), Sweden (4 Feb 75), Switzerland (7 May 90), Tajikistan (6 May 96), Togo (28 Dec 79), Turkmenistan (4 Jan 96), Uruguay (5 Mar 82), Uzbekistan (12 Jul 95), Vatican City (25 Feb 77)

Ratified/acceded/accepted with qualification: 34

Algeria (8 Nov 88), Argentina (5 Dec 72), Armenia (17 May 2005), Belarus (1 May 86), Belgium (1 Sep 92), Brazil (25 Sep 2009), Bulgaria (21 Apr 87), Canada (14 Oct 70), Chile (9 Apr 81), China (3 Sep 97), Colombia (10 Apr 85), Costa Rica (22 Nov 96), Cuba (9 Sep 98), Denmark (1 Jun 76), Ecuador (11 Feb 2005), Finland (19 Aug 77), Germany (21 Jul 87), Guatemala (12 May 1969), Kuwait (11 Nov 75), Mongolia (16 May 88), Morocco (26 Sep 72), Netherlands (9 Apr 85), New Zealand (4 Aug 71), Oman (18 Oct 90), Peru (14 Sep 2000), Portugal (6 Feb 2004), Saudi Arabia (14 Apr 2003), Syria (2 Oct 70), Tanzania (12 Apr 76), Tunisia (23 Jun 71), Ukraine (14 May 86), United Kingdom (25 Jun 71), USSR (Russia) (29 Apr 86), Vietnam (10 Oct 2001)

    * Succeeding Czechoslovakia (29 Jul 87).

1.8   DECLARATION ON PRINCIPLES OF INTERNATIONAL LAW CONCERNING FRIENDLY RELATIONS AND CO-OPERATION AMONG STATES IN ACCORDANCE WITH THE CHARTER OF THE UNITED NATIONS

Adopted without recorded vote: 24 Oct 70

1.9   ARTICLES ON THE RESPONSIBILITY OF STATES FOR INTERNATIONALLY WRONGFUL ACTS

Adopted by the International Law Commission: 3 Aug 2001
Taken note of by the UN General Assembly: 12 Dec 2001

1.10   GUIDING PRINCIPLES APPLICABLE TO UNILATERAL DECLARATIONS OF STATES CAPABLE OF CREATING LEGAL OBLIGATIONS

Adopted by the International Law Commission: 4 Aug 2006

B. *Environmental*

1.11   UNGA RESOLUTION 1803 ON PERMANENT SOVEREIGNTY OVER NATURAL RESOURCES

Adopted: 14 Dec 62
For: 87

Afghanistan, Algeria, Argentina, Australia, Austria, Belgium, Benin, Bolivia, Brazil, Burkina Faso, Burundi, Cambodia, Cameroon, Canada, Central African Republic, Chad, Chile, China, Colombia, Congo (Leopoldville), Costa Rica, Côte d'Ivoire, Cyprus, Dominican Republic, El Salvador, Ethiopia, Finland, Greece, Guatemala, Guinea, Haiti, Honduras, Iceland, India, Indonesia, Iran, Iraq, Ireland, Israel, Italy, Jamaica, Japan, Jordan, Lebanon, Liberia, Libya, Luxem-

bourg, Madagascar, Malaysia, Mali, Mauritania, Mexico, Morocco, Netherlands, New Zealand, Nicaragua, Niger, Nigeria, Norway, Pakistan, Panama, Paraguay, Peru, Philippines, Rwanda, Saudi Arabia, Senegal, Sierra Leone, Spain, Sri Lanka, Sweden, Syria, Tanzania, Thailand, Togo, Trinidad and Tobago, Tunisia, Turkey, Uganda, United Arab Emirates, United Kingdom, United States, Uruguay, Venezuela, Yemen, Yugoslavia
Against: 2
France, South Africa
Abstain: 12
Belarus (Byelorussian SSR), Bulgaria, Cuba, Czechoslovakia, Ghana, Hungary, Mongolia, Myanmar, Poland, Romania, Ukraine (Ukrainian SSR), Union of Soviet Socialist Republics

1.12 STOCKHOLM DECLARATION OF THE UNITED NATIONS CONFERENCE ON THE HUMAN ENVIRONMENT
Adopted: 16 Jun 72
For: 103*
Against: 0
Abstain: 12

* Adopted with no roll call vote recorded

1.13 UNGA RESOLUTION 2997 ON THE INSTITUTIONAL AND FINANCIAL ARRANGEMENT FOR INTERNATIONAL ENVIRONMENT COOPERATION [ESTABLISHING THE UNITED NATIONS ENVIRONMENT PROGRAMME (UNEP)]
Adopted: 15 Dec 72
For: 116*
Against: 0
Abstain: 10

* Adopted with no roll call vote recorded

1.14 UNGA RESOLUTION 3129 ON CO-OPERATION IN THE FIELD OF THE ENVIRONMENT CONCERNING NATURAL RESOURCES SHARED BY TWO OR MORE STATES
Adopted: 13 Dec 73
For: 77
Algeria, Argentina, Australia, Bahrain, Botswana, Burundi, Cameroon, Canada, Central African Republic, Chad, Congo, Cyprus, Dahomey, Egypt, El Salvador, Fiji, Gabon, Gambia, Ghana, Greece, Guatemala, Guinea, Indonesia, Iran, Iraq, Ireland, Jamaica, Jordan, Kenya, Kuwait, Laos, Lesotho, Liberia, Libya, Madagascar, Malawi, Malaysia, Mali, Mauritania, Mexico, Morocco, Nepal, Netherlands, New Zealand, Niger, Nigeria, Norway, Oman, Pakistan, Peru, Qatar, Romania, Rwanda, Saudi Arabia, Senegal, Sierra Leone, Singapore, Somalia, Sri Lanka, Sudan, Swaziland, Syria, Thailand, Togo, Tunisia, Uganda, United Arab Emirates, Upper Volta, Yemen, Yemen (Democratic), Yugoslavia, Zaire, Zambia
Against: 5
Bolivia, Brazil, Nicaragua, Paraguay, Portugal
Abstain: 43
Afghanistan, Austria, Barbados, Belgium, Bhutan, Bulgaria, Burma, Belarus (Byelorussian SSR), Chile, China, Colombia, Côte d'Ivoire, Costa Rica, Czechoslovakia, Denmark, Ecuador, Ethiopia, Finland, France, Germany (East), Germany (West), Guyana, Hungary, Iceland, India, Israel, Italy, Japan, Lebanon, Luxembourg, Mongolia, Poland, Russia (USSR), South Africa, Spain, Sweden, Trinidad and Tobago, Turkey, Ukraine (Ukrainian SSR), United Kingdom, United States, Uruguay, Venezuela

1.15 UNGA RESOLUTION 3171 ON PERMANENT SOVEREIGNTY OVER NATURAL RE-
SOURCES
Adopted: 17 Dec 73
For: 108
Afghanistan, Albania, Algeria, Argentina, Australia, Austria, Bahrain, Barbados,
Belarus (Byelorussian SSR), Benin, Bhutan, Bolivia, Botswana, Brazil, Bulgaria,
Burundi, Cambodia, Cameroon, Canada, Chad, Chile, China, Congo, Costa Rica,
Côte d'Ivoire, Cuba, Cyprus, Czechoslovakia, Dominican Republic, Ecuador,
Egypt, El Salvador, Equatorial Guinea, Ethiopia, Fiji, Finland, Gabon, Germany
(East), Ghana, Guatemala, Guinea, Guyana, Haiti, Honduras, Hungary, Iceland,
India, Indonesia, Iran, Iraq, Jamaica, Jordan, Kenya, Kuwait, Lebanon, Lesotho,
Liberia, Libya, Madagascar, Malawi, Malaysia, Mali, Malta, Mexico, Mongolia,
Morocco, Myanmar, Nepal, New Zealand, Niger, Nigeria, Oman, Pakistan,
Panama, Paraguay, Peru, Philippines, Poland, Qatar, Romania, Russia (USSR),
Rwanda, Saudi Arabia, Senegal, Sierra Leone, Singapore, Somalia, Spain, Sri
Lanka, Sudan, Sweden, Syria, Tanzania, Thailand, Togo, Trinidad and Tobago,
Tunisia, Turkey, Uganda, Ukraine (Ukrainian SSR), United Arab Emirates,
Uruguay, Venezuela, Yemen, Yemen (Democratic), Yugoslavia, Zaire, Zambia
Against: 1
United Kingdom
Abstain: 16
Belgium, Denmark, France, German Federal Republic, Greece, Ireland, Israel,
Italy, Japan, Luxembourg, Netherlands, Nicaragua, Norway, Portugal, South
Africa, United States

1.16 FINAL ACT OF THE CONFERENCE ON SECURITY AND CO-OPERATION IN EUROPE
Adopted: 1 Aug 75
Conferees: 35
Austria, Belgium, Bulgaria, Canada, Cyprus, Czechoslovakia, Denmark, Finland,
France, German Democratic Republic, German Federal Republic, Greece, Holy
See, Hungary, Iceland, Ireland, Italy, Liechtenstein, Luxembourg, Malta, Mona-
co, Netherlands, Norway, Poland, Portugal, Romania, Russia (USSR), San
Marino, Spain, Sweden, Switzerland, Turkey, United Kingdom, United States,
Yugoslavia
Signed: 35
Austria, Belgium, Bulgaria, Canada, Cyprus, Czechoslovakia, Denmark, Finland,
France, German Democratic Republic, German Federal Republic, Greece, Holy
See, Hungary, Iceland, Ireland, Italy, Liechtenstein, Luxembourg, Malta, Mona-
co, Netherlands, Norway, Poland, Portugal, Romania, Russia (USSR), San
Marino, Spain, Sweden, Switzerland, Turkey, United Kingdom, United States,
Yugoslavia

1.17 DRAFT PRINCIPLES OF CONDUCT IN THE FIELD OF THE ENVIRONMENT FOR GUIDANCE
OF STATES IN THE CONSERVATION AND HARMONIOUS UTILIZATION OF NATURAL
RESOURCES SHARED BY TWO OR MORE STATES
Approved by UNEP Governing Council: 19 May 78

1.18 UNGA RESOLUTION 35/48 ON HISTORICAL RESPONSIBILITY OF STATES FOR THE
PRESERVATION OF NATURE FOR PRESENT AND FUTURE GENERATIONS
Adopted: 30 Oct 80
For: 68*

Against: 0
Abstain: 47

> * Adopted with no roll call vote recorded

1.19 ILA Rules on International Law Applicable to Transfrontier Pollution
Adopted: 4 Sep 82

1.20 World Charter for Nature
Adopted: 28 Oct 82
For: 111
Afghanistan, Angola, Australia, Austria, Bahrain, Bangladesh, Barbados, Belarus (Byelorussian SSR), Belgium, Benin, Bulgaria, Burkina Faso, Burundi, Cambodia, Canada, Cape Verde, Central African Republic, Chad, China, Cameroon, Comoros, Congo, Costa Rica, Cuba, Cyprus, Czechoslovakia, Denmark, Djibouti, Egypt, El Salvador, Equatorial Guinea, Ethiopia, Finland, France, Gabon, Gambia, Germany (East), Germany (West), Greece, Guinea, Guinea–Bissau, Honduras, Hungary, Iceland, India, Indonesia, Iran, Iraq, Ireland, Italy, Côte d'Ivoire, Jamaica, Japan, Kenya, Kuwait, Lao People's Democratic Republic, Libya, Luxembourg, Madagascar, Malawi, Malaysia, Maldives, Mali, Malta, Mauitania, Mongolia, Morocco, Mozambique, Nepal, Netherlands, New Zealand, Nicaragua, Niger, Nigeria, Norway, Oman, Pakistan, Papua New Guinea, Poland, Portugal, Qatar, Romania, Russia (USSR), Rwanda, Samoa, São Tomé and Príncipe, Saudi Arabia, Senegal, Seychelles, Singapore, Solomon Islands, Somalia, Spain, Sri Lanka, Sudan, Swaziland, Sweden, Tanzania, Thailand, Togo, Tunisia, Turkey, Uganda, Ukraine (Ukrainian SSR), United Arab Emirates, United Kingdom, Uruguay, Yemen, Yugoslavia, Zaire, Zambia
Against: 1
United States
Abstain: 18
Algeria, Argentina, Bolivia, Brazil, Chile, Colombia, Dominican Republic, Ecuador, Ghana, Guyana, Lebanon, Mexico, Paraguay, Peru, Philippines, Suriname, Trinidad and Tobago, Venezuela

1.21 Experts Group on Environmental Law of the World Commission on Environment and Development, Legal Principles for Environmental Protection and Sustainable Development
Adopted: 18–20 Jun 86

1.22 Restatement (Third) of the Foreign Relations Law of the United States (§§ 601–604)
Adopted: 14 May 87

1.23 Declaration of the Hague
Adopted: 11 Mar 89
Conferees: 24
Australia, Brazil, Canada, Côte d'Ivoire, Egypt, France, Germany (West), Hungary, India, Indonesia, Italy, Japan, Jordan, Kenya, Malta, Norway, New Zealand, Netherlands, Senegal, Spain, Sweden, Tunisia, Venezuela, Zimbabwe

1.24 Langkawi Commonwealth Heads of Government Declaration on Environment
Unanimously adopted by the Heads of the Commonwealth States (49 at the time): 21 Oct 89

1.25 UNGA R<small>ESOLUTION</small> 45/94 <small>ON THE</small> N<small>EED TO</small> E<small>NSURE A</small> H<small>EALTHY</small> E<small>NVIRONMENT</small>
<small>FOR THE</small> W<small>ELL</small>-B<small>EING OF</small> I<small>NDIVIDUALS</small>
Adopted without vote: 14 Dec 90

1.26 C<small>ONVENTION ON</small> E<small>NVIRONMENTAL</small> I<small>MPACT</small> A<small>SSESSMENT IN A</small> T<small>RANSBOUNDARY</small>
C<small>ONTEXT</small>
Concluded: 25 Feb 91
Entered into force: 10 Sep 97
Total Parties: 45
Signed but not ratified: 3
Iceland (26 Feb 91), United States (26 Feb 91), Russia (6 Jun 91)
Ratified/acceded/accepted without qualification: 42
Albania (4 Oct 91), Armenia (21 Feb 97), Austria (27 Jul 94), Azerbaijan (25
Mar 99), Belarus (10 Nov 2005), Belgium (2 Jul 99), Bosnia/Herzegovina (14 Dec
2009), Bulgaria (12 May 95), Croatia (8 Jul 96), Cyprus (2 Jul 2000), Czech
Republic (26 Feb 2001), Denmark (14 Mar 97), European Community (24 Jun
97), Estonia (25 Apr 2001), Finland (10 Aug 95), Germany (8 Aug 2002), Greece
(24 Feb 98), Hungary (11 Jul 97), Ireland (25 Jul 2002), Italy (19 Jan 95),
Kazakhstan (11 Jan 2001), Kyrgyzstan (1 May 2001), Latvia (31 Aug 98),
Liechtenstein (9 Jul 98), Lithuania (11 Jan 2001), Luxembourg (29 Aug 95),
Macedonia (31 Aug 99), Malta (20 Oct 2010), Moldova (4 Jan 94), Montenegro (9
Jul 2009), Netherlands (28 Feb 95), Norway (23 Jun 93), Poland (12 Jun 97),
Portugal (6 Apr 2000), Romania (29 Mar 2001), Serbia (18 Dec 2007), Slovakia
(19 Nov 99), Slovenia (5 Aug 98), Spain (10 Sep 92), Sweden (24 Jan 92),
Switzerland (16 Sep 96), Ukraine (20 Jul 99), United Kingdom (10 Oct 97)
Ratified/acceded/accepted with qualification: 2
Canada (13 May 98), France (15 Jun 2001)

1.27 R<small>IO</small> D<small>ECLARATION ON</small> E<small>NVIRONMENT AND</small> D<small>EVELOPMENT</small>
*Adopted by consensus by the UN Conference on Environment and Devel-
opment:* 13 Jun 92

1.28 A<small>GENDA</small> **21**
Approved by the UN Conference on Environment and Development: 13
Jun 92

1.29 UNGA R<small>ESOLUTION ON</small> I<small>NSTITUTIONAL</small> A<small>RRANGEMENT TO</small> F<small>OLLOW</small> U<small>P THE</small> U<small>NITED</small>
N<small>ATIONS</small> C<small>ONFERENCE ON</small> E<small>NVIRONMENT AND</small> D<small>EVELOPMENT</small>
Adopted without recorded vote: 22 Dec 92

1.30 I<small>NSTRUMENT FOR THE</small> E<small>STABLISHMENT OF THE</small> R<small>ESTRUCTURED</small> G<small>LOBAL</small> E<small>NVIRON-</small>
<small>MENT</small> F<small>ACILITY</small> **(GEF)**
Concluded: 16 Mar 94
Adopted by the Implementing Agencies of the GEF: 13 May 94 (UNDP), 24
May 94 (IBRD), and 18 Jun 94 (UNEP)

1.31 N<small>AIROBI</small> D<small>ECLARATION AND</small> G<small>OVERNING</small> C<small>OUNCIL</small> D<small>ECISION ON THE</small> R<small>OLE</small>, M<small>AN-</small>
<small>DATE AND</small> G<small>OVERNANCE OF THE</small> U<small>NITED</small> N<small>ATIONS</small> E<small>NVIRONMENT</small> P<small>ROGRAMME</small>
Adopted by the UNEP Governing Council: 7 Feb 97

1.32   INSTITUTE OF INTERNATIONAL LAW RESOLUTION ON RESPONSIBILITY AND LIABILITY UNDER INTERNATIONAL LAW FOR ENVIRONMENTAL DAMAGE
Adopted: 4 Sep 97

1.33   CONVENTION ON ACCESS TO INFORMATION, PUBLIC PARTICIPATION IN DECISION-MAKING AND ACCESS TO JUSTICE IN ENVIRONMENTAL MATTERS (AARHUS CONVENTION)
Concluded: 25 Jun 98
Entered into force: 30 Oct 2001
Total Parties: 44
Signed but not ratified: 5 (all dates of signature are 25 Jun 98)
Iceland, Ireland, Liechtenstein, Monaco, Switzerland
Ratified/acceded/accepted without qualification: 40
Albania (27 Jun 2001), Armenia (1 Aug 2001), Austria (17 Jan 2005), Azerbaijan (23 Mar 2000), Belarus (9 Mar 2000), Belgium (21 Jan 2003), Bosnia/Herzegovina (1 Oct 2008), Bulgaria (17 Dec 2003), Croatia (27 Mat 2007), Cyprus (19 Sep 2003), Czech Republic (6 Jul 2004), Estonia (2 Aug 2001), European Community (17 Feb 2005), Finland (1 Sep 2004), Georgia (11 Apr 2000), Germany (15 Jan 2007), Greece (27 Jan 2006), Hungary (3 Jul 2001), Italy (13 Jun 2001), Kazakhstan (11 Jan 2001), Kyrgyzstan (1 May 2001), Latvia (14 Jun 2002), Lithuania (28 Jan 2002), Luxembourg (25 Oct 2005), Macedonia (22 Jul 99), Malta (23 Apr 2002), Moldova (9 Aug 99), Montenegro (2 Nov 2009), Netherlands (29 Dec 2004), Norway (2 May 2003), Poland (15 Feb 2002), Portugal (9 Jun 2003), Romania (11 Jul 2000), Serbia (31 Jul 2009), Slovakia (5 Dec 2005), Slovenia (29 Jul 2004), Spain (29 Dec 2004), Tajikistan (17 Jul 2001), Turkmenistan (25 Jun 99), Ukraine (18 Nov 99), United Kingdom (23 Feb 2005)
Ratified/acceded/accepted with qualification: 3
Denmark (29 Sep 2000), France (8 Jul 2002), Sweden (20 May 2005)

1.34   THE EARTH CHARTER
Adopted at the Hague by the Earth Charter Commission: 29 Jun 2000

1.35   UNITED NATIONS MILLENNIUM DECLARATION
Adopted without vote: 8 Sep 2000

1.36   DRAFT PREAMBLE AND ARTICLES ON PREVENTION OF TRANSBOUNDARY HARM FROM HAZARDOUS ACTIVITIES
Adopted by the International Law Commission: 11 May 2001

1.37   JOHANNESBURG DECLARATION ON SUSTAINABLE DEVELOPMENT
Adopted by the Conferees at the World Summit on Sustainable Development: 4 Sep 2002

1.38   JOHANNESBURG PLAN OF IMPLEMENTATION
Approved by the World Summit on Sustainable Development: 4 Sep 2002

1.39   PROTOCOL ON STRATEGIC ENVIRONMENTAL ASSESSMENT
Adopted: 21 May 2003
Entered into force: 11 Jul 2010
Signed but not ratified: 15 (all dates 21 May 2003 unless otherwise indicated)
Belgium, Bosnia/Herzegovina, Cyprus, Denmark, France, Georgia, Greece, Ireland, Italy, Latvia, Macedonia, Moldova, Portugal, Ukraine, United Kingdom
Ratified/acceded/accepted without qualification: 23

Albania (2 Dec 2005), Armenia (24 Jan 2011), Austria (23 Mar 2010), Bulgaria (25 Jan 2007), Croatia (6 Oct 2009), Czech Republic (19 Jul 2005), Estonia (12 Apr 2010), European Community (12 Nov 2008), Finland (18 Apr 2005), Germany (22 Feb 2007), Hungary (26 Nov 2010), Lithuania (22 Mar 2011), Luxembourg (2 Jul 2008), Montenegro (2 Nov 2009), Netherlands (8 Dec 2009), Norway (11 Oct 2007), Poland (21 Jun 2011), Romania (8 Mar 2010), Serbia (8 Jul 2010), Slovakia (29 May 2008), Slovenia (23 Apr 2010), Spain (24 Sep 2009), Sweden (30 Mar 2006)

1.40 **PROTOCOL ON POLLUTANT RELEASE AND TRANSFER REGISTERS**
Adopted: 21 May 2003
Entered into force: 8 Oct 2009
Signed but not ratified: 13 (all dates 21 May 2003 unless otherwise indicated)
Armenia, Bosnia/Herzegovina, Cyprus, Georgia, Greece, Ireland, Italy, Moldova, Montenegro (23 Oct 2006), Poland, Serbia, Tajikistan, Ukraine
Ratified/acceded/accepted without qualification: 27
Albania (16 Jun 2009), Austria (23 Mar 2010), Belgium (12 Mar 2009), Bulgaria (15 Jan 2010), Croatia (14 Jul 2008), Czech Republic (12 Aug 2009), Denmark (13 Oct 2008), Estonia (15 Aug 2007), European Community (21 Feb 2006), Finland (21 Apr 2009), France (10 Jul 2009), Germany (28 Aug 2007), Hungary (13 Jul 2009), Latvia (24 Apr 2008), Lithuania (5 Mar 2009), Luxembourg (7 Feb 2006), Macedonia (2 Nov 2010), Netherlands (11 Feb 2008), Norway (27 Jun 2008), Portugal (8 Oct 2009), Romania (26 Aug 2009), Slovakia (1 Apr 2008), Slovenia (23 April 2010), Spain (24 Sep 2009), Sweden (15 Oct 2008), Switzerland (27 Apr 2007), United Kingdom (31 Jul 2009)

1.41 **WORLD BANK OPERATIONAL POLICIES 4.00, 4.01, AND 4.10**
Adopted by the World Bank: March 2005

1.42 **DRAFT PRINCIPLES ON THE ALLOCATION OF LOSS IN THE CASE OF TRANSBOUNDARY HARM ARISING OUT OF HAZARDOUS ACTIVITIES**
Adopted by the International Law Commission: 8 Aug 2006

1.43 **DRAFT UN GENERAL ASSEMBLY DECLARATION ON THE ECOLOGICAL RIGHTS AND RESPONSIBILITIES OF PRESENT AND FUTURE GENERATIONS**
Adopted as Recommendation No. 13 of the Climate Legacy Initiative: 2009

2. ATMOSPHERE/SPACE

A. Air Pollution

2.1 **CONVENTION ON LONG-RANGE TRANSBOUNDARY AIR POLLUTION (LRTAP)**
Concluded: 13 Nov 79
Entered into force: 16 Mar 83
Total parties: 51
Signed but not ratified: 2
San Marino (14 Nov 79), Vatican City (14 Nov 79)
Ratified/accepted/approved without qualification: 50
Albania (2 Dec 2005), Armenia (21 Feb 97), Austria (16 Dec 82), Azerbaijan (3 Jul 2002), Belarus (14 May 80), Belgium (15 Jul 82), Bosnia–Herzegovina (1 Sep 93), Bulgaria (9 Jun 81), Canada (15 Dec 81), Croatia (21 Sep 92), Cyprus (20 Nov 91), Czech Republic (30 Sep 93), Denmark (18 Jun 82), Estonia (7 Mar 2000), European Community (15 Jul 82), Finland (15 Apr 81), France (3 Nov 81), Georgia (11 Feb 99), Germany (15 Jul 82), Greece (30 Aug 83), Hungary (22

Sep 80), Iceland (5 May 83), Ireland (15 Jul 82), Italy (15 Jul 82), Kazakhstan (11 Jan 2001), Kyrgyzstan (25 May 2000), Latvia (15 Jul 94), Liechtenstein (22 Nov 83), Lithuania (25 Jan 94), Luxembourg (15 Jul 82), Macedonia (30 Dec 97), Malta (14 Mar 97), Moldova (9 Jun 95), Monaco (27 Aug 99), Montenegro (23 Oct 2006), Netherlands (15 Jul 82), Norway (13 Feb 81), Poland (19 Jul 85), Portugal (29 Sep 80), Serbia (12 Mar 2001), Slovakia (28 May 93), Slovenia (6 Jul 92), Spain (15 Jun 82), Sweden (12 Feb 81), Switzerland (6 May 83), Turkey (18 Apr 83), Ukraine (5 Jun 80), United Kingdom (15 Jul 82), United States (30 Nov 81), USSR (Russia) (22 May 80)
Ratified/accepted/approved with qualification: 1
Romania (27 Feb 91)

2.2 **MEMORANDUM OF INTENT BETWEEN CANADA AND THE UNITED STATES CONCERNING TRANSBOUNDARY AIR POLLUTION**
Concluded: 5 Aug 80
Entered into force: 5 Aug 80

2.3 **MEXICO–UNITED STATES AGREEMENT TO CO-OPERATE IN THE SOLUTION OF ENVIRONMENTAL PROBLEMS IN THE BORDER AREA**
Concluded: 14 Aug 83
Entered into force: 16 Feb 84

2.4 **CONVENTION ON THE TRANSBOUNDARY EFFECTS OF INDUSTRIAL ACCIDENTS**
Concluded: 17 Mar 92
Entered into force: 19 Apr 2000
Total Parties: 40
Signed but not ratified: 2
Canada (18 Mar 92), United States (18 Mar 92)
Ratified/acceded/accepted without qualification: 36
Albania (5 Jan 94), Armenia (21 Feb 97), Austria (4 Aug 99), Azerbaijan (16 Jun 2004), Belarus (25 Jun 2003), Belgium (6 Apr 2006), Bulgaria (12 May 95), Croatia (20 Jan 2000), Cyprus (31 Aug 2005), Czech Republic (12 Jun 2000), Denmark (28 Mar 2001), Estonia (17 May 2000), Finland (13 Sep 99), France (3 Oct 2003), Germany (9 Sep 98), Greece (24 Feb 98), Hungary (2 Jun 94), Italy (2 Jul 2002), Kazakhstan (11 Jan 2001), Latvia (29 Jun 2004), Lithuania (12 Nov 2000), Luxembourg (8 Aug 94), Macedonia (2 Mar 2010), Moldova (4 Jan 94), Monaco (28 Aug 2001), Montenegro (19 May 2009), Norway (1 Apr 93), Poland (8 Sep 2003), Portugal (2 Nov 2006), Romania (22 May 2003), Russia (1 Feb 94), Serbia (31 Jul 2009), Slovakia (9 Sep 2003), Slovenia (13 May 2002), Spain (16 May 97), Sweden (22 Sep 99), Switzerland (21 May 99), United Kingdom (5 Aug 2002)
Ratified/accepted/approved with qualification: 2
European Communities (24 Apr 98), Netherlands (6 Nov 2006)

2.5 **PROTOCOL TO THE 1979 CONVENTION ON LONG-RANGE TRANSBOUNDARY AIR POLLUTION TO ABATE ACIDIFICATION, EUTROPHICATION AND GROUND-LEVEL OZONE**
Adopted: 30 Nov 99
Entered into force: 17 May 2005
Signed but not ratified: 9
Armenia (1 Dec 99), Austria (1 Dec 99), Canada (1 Dec 99), Greece (1 Mar 2000), Ireland (1 Dec 99), Italy (1 Dec 99), Liechtenstein (1 Dec 99), Poland (30 May 2000), Moldova (23 May 2000)
Ratified/acceded/accepted without qualification: 26
Belgium (13 Sep 2007), Bulgaria (5 Jul 2005), Croatia (07 Oct 2008), Cyprus (11

Apr 2007), Czech Republic (12 Aug 2004), Denmark (11 Jun 2002), European Community (23 Jun 2003), Finland (23 Dec 2003), France (10 Apr 2007), Germany (21 Oct 2004), Hungary (13 Nov 2006), Latvia (25 May 2004), Lithuania (2 Sep 2004), Luxemburg (7 Aug 2001), Macedonia (1 Nov 2010), Netherlands (5 Feb 2004), Norway (30 Jan 2002), Portugal (16 Feb 2005), Romania (5 Sep 2003), Slovakia (28 Apr 2005), Slovenia (4 May 2004), Spain (28 Jan 2005), Sweden (28 Mar 2002), Switzerland (14 Sep 2005), United Kingdom (8 Dec 2005), United States (22 Nov 2004)

2.6 DIRECTIVE 2001/81/EC ON NATIONAL EMISSION CEILINGS FOR CERTAIN ATMOSPHERIC POLLUTANTS
Adopted by the European Parliament and the Council of the European Union: 23 October 2001
Entered into force: 27 November 2001
Total parties: 27

> *Note:* All members of the European Union are bound by this Directive. For a list of EU members, see Basic Document 1.5 in this Status Appendix.

2.7 DIRECTIVE 2008/50/EC OF 21 MAY 2008 ON AMBIENT AIR QUALITY AND CLEANER AIR FOR EUROPE.
Adopted by the European Parliament and the Council of the European Union: 21 May 2008
Entered into force: 11 June 2008
Total parties: 27

> *Note:* All members of the European Union are bound by this Directive. For a list of EU members, see Basic Document 1.5 in this Status Appendix.

B. *Climate Change*

2.8 UNITED NATIONS FRAMEWORK CONVENTION ON CLIMATE CHANGE
Concluded: 9 May 92
Entered into force: 21 Mar 94
Total parties: 195
Ratified/acceded/accepted without qualification: 192
Afghanistan (19 Sep 2002), Albania (3 Oct 94), Algeria (9 Jun 93), Andorra (2 Mar 2011), Angola (17 May 2000), Antigua/Barbuda (2 Feb 93), Argentina (11 Mar 94), Armenia (14 May 93), Australia (30 Dec 92), Austria (28 Feb 94), Azerbaijan (16 May 95), Bahamas (29 Mar 94), Bahrain (28 Dec 94), Bangladesh (15 Apr 94), Barbados (23 Mar 94), Belarus (11 May 2000), Belgium (16 Jan 96), Belize (31 Oct 94), Benin (30 Jun 94), Bhutan (25 Aug 95), Bolivia (3 Oct 94), Bosnia–Herzegovina (7 Sep 2000), Botswana (27 Jan 94), Brazil (28 Feb 94), Brunei (7 Aug 2007), Burkina Faso (2 Sep 93), Burundi (6 Jan 97), Cambodia (18 Dec 95), Cameroon (19 Oct 94), Canada (4 Dec 92), Cape Verde (29 Mar 95), Central African Republic (10 Mar 95), Chad (7 Jun 94), Chile (22 Dec 94), China (5 Jan 93), Colombia (22 Mar 95), Comoros (31 Oct 94), Congo (Brazzaville) (14 Oct 96), Congo (Kinshasa) (9 Jan 95), Cook Islands (20 Apr 93), Costa Rica (26 Aug 94), Côte d'Ivoire (29 Nov 94), Croatia (8 Apr 96), Cyprus (15 Oct 97), Czech Republic (7 Oct 93), Denmark (21 Dec 93), Djibouti (27 Aug 95), Dominica (21 Jun 93), Dominican Republic (7 Oct 98), Ecuador (23 Feb 93), Egypt (5 Dec 94), El Salvador (4 Dec 95), Equatorial Guinea (16 Aug 2000), Eritrea (24 Apr 95), Estonia (27 Jul 94), Ethiopia (5 Apr 94), European Community (21 Dec 93), Fiji (25 Feb 93), Finland (3 May 94), France (25 Mar 94), Gabon (21 Jan 98), Gambia (10 Jun 94), Georgia (29 Jul 94), Germany (9 Dec 93), Ghana (6 Sep 95), Greece (4 Aug 94), Grenada (11 Aug 94), Guatemala (15 Dec 95), Guinea (7 May 93), Guinea–Bissau (27 Oct 95), Guyana (29 Aug 94), Haiti (25 Sep 96),

Honduras (19 Oct 95), Iceland (16 Jun 93), India (1 Nov 93), Indonesia (23 Aug 94), Iran (18 Jul 96), Iraq (28 Jul 2009), Ireland (20 Apr 94), Israel (4 Jun 96), Italy (15 Apr 94), Jamaica (6 Jan 95), Japan (28 May 93), Jordan (12 Nov 93), Kazakhstan (17 May 95), Kenya (30 Aug 94), Kiribati (7 Feb 95), Korea (North) (5 Dec 94), Korea (South) (14 Dec 93), Kuwait (28 Dec 94), Kyrgyzstan (25 May 2000), Laos (4 Jan 95), Latvia (23 Mar 95), Lebanon (15 Dec 94), Lesotho (7 Feb 95), Liberia (5 Nov 2002), Libya (14 Jun 99), Liechtenstein (22 Jun 94), Lithuania (24 Mar 95), Luxembourg (9 May 94), Macedonia (28 Jan 98), Madagascar (2 Jun 99), Malawi (21 Apr 94), Malaysia (13 Jul 94), Maldives (9 Nov 92), Mali (28 Dec 94), Malta (17 Mar 94), Marshall Islands (8 Oct 92), Mauritania (20 Jan 94), Mauritius (4 Sep 92), Mexico (11 Mar 93), Micronesia (18 Nov 93), Moldova (9 Jun 95), Monaco (20 Nov 92), Mongolia (30 Sep 93), Morocco (28 Dec 95), Montenegro (23 Oct 2006), Mozambique (25 Aug 95), Myanmar (Burma) (25 Nov 94), Namibia (16 May 95), Nauru (11 Nov 93), Nepal (2 May 94), Netherlands (20 Dec 93), New Zealand (16 Sep 93), Nicaragua (31 Oct 95), Niger (25 Jul 95), Nigeria (29 Aug 94), Niue (28 Feb 96), Norway (9 Jul 93), Oman (8 Feb 95), Pakistan (1 Jun 94), Palau (10 Dec 99), Panama (23 May 95), Papua New Guinea (16 Mar 93), Paraguay (24 Feb 94), Peru (7 Jun 93), Philippines (2 Aug 94), Poland (28 Jul 94), Portugal (21 Dec 93), Qatar (18 Apr 96), Romania (8 Jun 94), Russia (28 Dec 94), Rwanda (18 Aug 98), Samoa (29 Nov 94), San Marino (28 Oct 94), São Tomé/Príncipe (29 Sep 99), Saudi Arabia (28 Dec 94), Senegal (17 Oct 94), Serbia (3 Sep 97), Seychelles (22 Sep 92), Sierra Leone (22 Jun 95), Singapore (29 May 97), Slovakia (25 Aug 94), Slovenia (1 Dec 95), South Africa (29 May 97), Spain (21 Dec 93), Solomon Islands (28 Dec 94), Somalia (11 Sep 2009), Sri Lanka (23 Nov 93), St Kitts/Nevis (7 Jan 3), St Lucia (14 Jun 93), St Vincent/Grenadines (2 Dec 96), Sudan (19 Nov 93), Suriname (14 Oct 97), Swaziland (7 Oct 96), Sweden (23 Jun 93), Switzerland (10 Dec 93), Syria (4 Jan 96), Tajikistan (7 Jan 98), Tanzania (17 Apr 96), Thailand (28 Dec 94), Timor Leste (10 Oct 2006), Togo (8 Mar 95), Tonga (20 Jul 98), Trinidad/Tobago (24 Jun 94), Tunisia (15 Jul 93),Turkey (24 Feb 2004), Turkmenistan (5 Jun 95), Tuvalu (26 Oct 93), Uganda (8 Sep 93), Ukraine (13 May 97), United Arab Emirates (29 Dec 95), United Kingdom (8 Dec 93), United States (15 Oct 92), Uruguay (18 Aug 94), Uzbekistan (20 Jun 93), Vanuatu (25 Mar 93), Venezuela (28 Dec 94), Vietnam (16 Nov 94), Yemen (21 Feb 96), Zambia (28 May 93), Zimbabwe (3 Nov 92)

Ratified/acceded/accepted with qualification: 3
Bulgaria (12 May 95), Cuba (5 Jan 94), Hungary (24 Feb 94)

2.9 **KYOTO PROTOCOL TO THE UNITED NATIONS FRAMEWORK CONVENTION ON CLIMATE CHANGE**
Adopted: 11 Dec 97
Entered into force: 16 Feb 2005
Total Parties: 192
Signed but not ratified: 1
United States of America (12 Nov 98)
Ratified/acceded/accepted without qualification: 189
Albania (1 Apr 2005), Algeria (16 Feb 2005), Angola (8 May 2007), Antigua/Barbuda (3 Nov 98), Argentina (28 Sep 2001), Armenia (25 Apr 2003), Australia (12 Dec 2007), Austria (31 May 2002), Azerbaijan (28 Sep 2000), Bahamas (9 Apr 99), Bahrain (31 Jan 2006), Bangladesh (22 Oct 2001), Barbados (7 Aug 2000), Belarus (26 Aug 2005), Belgium (31 May 2002), Belize (26 Sep 2003), Benin (25 Feb 2002), Bhutan (26 Aug 2002), Bolivia (30 Nov 99), Bosnia/ Herzegovina (16 Apr 2007), Botswana (8 Aug 2003), Brazil (23 Aug 2002), Brunei (20 Aug 2009), Bulgaria (15 Aug 2002), Burkina Faso (31 Mar 2005), Burundi (18 Oct 2001), Cambodia (22 Aug 2002), Cameroon (28 Aug 2002), Canada (17 Dec 2002), Cape

Verde (10 Feb 2006), Central African Republic (18 Mar 2008), Chad (18 Aug 2009), Chile (26 Aug 2002), China (30 Aug 2002), Colombia (30 Nov 2001), Comoros (10 Apr 2008), Congo (Brazzaville) (12 Feb 2007), Congo (Kinshasa) (23 Mar 2005), Cook Islands (27 Aug 2001), Costa Rica (9 Aug 2002), Côte d'Ivoire (23 Apr 2007), Croatia (30 May 2007), Cuba (30 Apr 2002), Cyprus (16 Jul 99), Czech Republic (15 Nov 2001), Djibouti (12 Mar 2002), Dominica (25 Jan 2005), Dominican Republic (12 Feb 2002), Ecuador (13 Jan 2000), Egypt (12 Jan 2005), El Salvador (30 Nov 98), Equatorial Guinea (16 Aug 2000), Eritrea (28 Jul 2005), Estonia (14 Oct 2002), Ethiopia (14 Apr 2005), European Community (31 May 2002), Fiji (17 Sep 98), Finland (31 May 2002), Gabon (12 Dec 2006), Gambia (1 Jun 2001), Georgia (16 Jun 99), Germany (31 May 2002), Ghana (30 May 2003), Greece (31 May 2002), Grenada (6 Aug 2002), Guatemala (5 Oct 99), Guinea (7 Sep 2000), Guinea–Bissau (18 Nov 2005), Guyana (5 Aug 2003), Haiti (6 Jul 2005), Honduras (19 Jul 2000), Hungary (21 Aug 2002), Iceland (23 May 2002), India (26 Aug 2002), Indonesia (2 Dec 2004), Iran (22 Aug 2005), Iraq (28 Jul 2009), Ireland (31 May 2002), Israel (15 Mar 2004), Italy (31 May 2002), Jamaica (28 Jun 99), Japan (4 Jun 2002), Jordan (17 Jan 2003), Kazakhstan (19 Jun 2009), Kenya (25 Feb 2005), Kiribati (7 Sep 2000), Korea (North) (27 Apr 2005), Korea (South) (8 Nov 2002), Kuwait (11 Mar 2005), Kyrgyzstan (13 May 2003), Laos (6 Feb 2003), Latvia (5 Jul 2002), Lebanon (13 Nov 2006), Lesotho (6 Sep 2000), Liberia (5 Nov 2002), Libya (24 Aug 2006), Liechtenstein (3 Dec 2004), Lithuania (3 Jan 2003), Luxembourg (31 May 2002), Macedonia (18 Nov 2004), Madagascar (24 Sep 2003), Malawi (26 Oct 2001), Malaysia (4 Sep 2002), Maldives (30 Dec 98), Mali (28 Mar 2002), Malta (11 Nov 2001), Marshall Islands (11 Aug 2003), Mauritania (22 Jul 2005), Mauritius (9 May 2001), Mexico (7 Sep 2000), Micronesia (21 Jun 99), Moldova (22 Apr 2003), Mongolia (15 Dec 99), Monaco (27 Feb 2006), Montenegro (4 Jun 2007), Morocco (25 Jan 2002), Mozambique (18 Jan 2005), Myanmar (13 Aug 2003), Namibia (4 Sep 2003), Nauru (16 Aug 2001), Nepal (16 Sep 2005), Netherlands (31 May 2002), Nicaragua (18 Nov 99), Nigeria (10 Dec 2004), Niger (30 Sep 2004), Niue (6 May 99), Norway (30 May 2002), Oman (19 Jan 2005), Pakistan (11 Jan 2005), Palau (10 Dec 99), Panama (5 Mar 99), Papua New Guinea (28 Mar 2002), Paraguay (27 Aug 99), Peru (12 Sep 2002), Philippines (20 Nov 2003), Poland (13 Dec 2002), Portugal (31 May 2002), Qatar (11 Jan 2005), Romania (19 Mar 2001), Rwanda (22 Jul 2004), Russia (18 Nov 2004), St Lucia (20 Aug 2003), St Vincent/Grenadines (31 Dec 2004), Samoa (27 Nov 2000), San Marino (28 April 2010), Sao Tome/Principe (25 Apr 08), Saudi Arabia (31 Jan 2005), Senegal (20 Jul 2001), Serbia (19 Oct 2007), Seychelles (22 Jul 2002), Sierra Leone (10 Nov 2006), Singapore (12 Apr 2006), Slovakia (31 May 2002), Slovenia (2 Aug 2002), Solomon Islands (13 Mar 2003), Somalia (26 July 2010), South Africa (31 Jul 2002), Spain (31 May 2002), Sri Lanka (3 Sep 2002), St Kitts/Nevis (08 Apr 2008), Sudan (2 Nov 2004), Suriname (25 Sep 2006), Swaziland (13 Jan 2006), Sweden (31 May 2002), Switzerland (9 Jul 2003), Syria (27 Jan 2006), Tajikistan (05 Jan 2009), Tanzania (26 Aug 2002), Thailand (28 Aug 2002), Timor–Leste (14 Jan 2008), Togo (2 Jul 2004), Tonga (14 Jan 2008), Trinidad/Tobago (28 Jan 99), Tunisia (22 Jan 2003), Turkey (28 May 2009), Turkmenistan (11 Jan 99), Tuvalu (16 Nov 98), Uganda (25 Mar 2002), Ukraine (12 Apr 2004), United Arab Emirates (26 Jan 2005), United Kingdom (31 May 2002), Uruguay (5 Feb 2001), Uzbekistan (12 Oct 99), Vanuatu (17 Jul 2001), Venezuela (18 Feb 2005), Vietnam (25 Sep 2002), Yemen (15 Sep 2004), Zambia (7 Jul 2006), Zimbabwe (30 Jun 2009)

Ratified/acceded/accepted with qualification: 3

Denmark (31 May 2002), France (31 May 2002), New Zealand (19 Dec 2002)

2.10 MALÉ DECLARATION ON THE HUMAN DIMENSION OF GLOBAL CLIMATE CHANGE
      Adopted by the Conference of the Alliance of Small Island States: 14
      November 2007

2.11 COPENHAGEN ACCORD
      Adopted: 18 December 2009
      Total Parties: 141
      States agreeing to the Accord at Copenhagen: 114
      Albania, Algeria, Armenia, Australia, Austria, Bahamas, Bangladesh, Belarus,
      Belgium, Benin, Bhutan, Bosnia and Herzegovina, Botswana, Brazil, Bulgaria,
      Burkina Faso, Cambodia, Canada, Central African Republic, Chile, China,
      Colombia, Congo, Costa Rica, Côte d'Ivoire, Croatia, Cyprus, Czech Republic,
      Democratic Republic of Congo, Denmark, Djibouti, Eritrea, Estonia, Ethiopia,
      European Union, Fiji, Finland, France, Gabon, Georgia, Germany, Ghana,
      Greece, Guatemala, Guinea, Guyana, Hungary, Iceland, India, Indonesia, Ire-
      land, Israel, Italy, Japan, Jordan, Kazakhstan, Kiribati, Lao People's Democratic
      Republic, Latvia, Lesotho, Liechtenstein, Lithuania, Luxemburg, Madagascar,
      Malawi, Maldives, Mali, Malta, Marshall Islands, Mauritania, Mexico, Monaco,
      Mongolia, Montenegro, Morocco, Namibia, Nepal, Netherlands, New Zealand,
      Norway, Palau, Panama, Papua New Guinea, Peru, Poland, Portugal, Republic
      of Korea, Republic of Moldova, Romania, Russian Federation, Rwanda, Samoa,
      San Marino, Senegal, Serbia, Sierra Leone, Singapore, Slovakia, Slovenia, South
      Africa, Spain, Sweden, Swaziland, Switzerland, The Former Yugoslav Republic
      of Macedonia, Tonga, Trinidad and Tobago, Tunisia, United Arab Emirates,
      United Kingdom of Great Britain and Northern Ireland, United Republic of
      Tanzania, United States of America, Uruguay, Zambia
      States expressing agreement to the Accord subsequent to Copenhagen:
      27
      Afghanistan, Angola, Antigua and Barbuda, Barbados, Belize, Brunei Darussa-
      lam, Burundi, Cameroon, Cape Verde, Chad, Comores, Gambia, Guinea–Bissau,
      Honduras, Jamaica, Kenya, Liberia, Mauritius, Mozambique, Nigeria, Saint
      Lucia, Tajikistan, Timor–Leste, Togo, Uganda, Ukraine, Viet Nam

C. Ozone Depletion

2.12 VIENNA CONVENTION FOR THE PROTECTION OF THE OZONE LAYER
      Concluded: 22 Mar 85
      Entered into force: 22 Sep 88
      Ratified/acceded/accepted without qualification: 196
      Afghanistan (17 Jul 2004), Albania (8 Oct 99), Algeria (20 Oct 92), Andorra (26
      Jan 2009), Angola (17 May 2000), Antigua/Barbuda (3 Dec 92), Argentina (18
      Jan 90), Armenia (1 Oct 99), Australia (16 Sep 87), Austria (19 Aug 87),
      Azerbaijan (12 Jun 96), Bahamas (1 Apr 93), Bahrain (27 Apr 90), Bangladesh
      (2 Aug 90), Barbados (16 Oct 92), Belarus (20 Jun 86), Belgium (17 Oct 88),
      Belize (6 Jun 97), Benin (1 Jul 93), Bhutan (23 Aug 2004), Bolivia (3 Oct 94),
      Bosnia–Herzegovina (1 Sep 93), Botswana (4 Dec 91), Brazil (19 Mar 90), Brunei
      (26 Jul 90), Bulgaria (20 Nov 90), Burkina Faso (30 Mar 89), Burundi (6 Jan
      97), Cambodia (27 Jun 2001), Cameroon (30 Aug 89), Canada (4 Jun 86), Cape
      Verde (31 Jul 2001), Central African Republic (29 Mar 93), Chad (18 May 89),
      Chile (6 Mar 90), China (11 Sep 89), Colombia (16 Jul 90), Comoros (31 Oct 94),
      Congo (Brazzaville) (16 Nov 94), Congo (Kinshasa) (30 Oct 94), Cook Islands (22
      Dec 2003), Costa Rica (30 Jul 91), Côte d'Ivoire (5 Apr 93), Croatia (21 Sep 92),
      Cuba (14 Jul 92), Cyprus (28 May 92), Czech Republic (1 Jan 93), Denmark (29
      Sep 88), Djibouti (30 Jul 99), Dominica (31 Mar 93), Dominican Republic (18
      May 93), Ecuador (10 Apr 90), Egypt (9 May 88), El Salvador (2 Oct 92),
      Equatorial Guinea (17 Aug 88), Eritrea (10 Mar 2005), Estonia (17 Oct 96),

Ethiopia (11 Oct 94), European Community (17 Oct 88), Fiji (23 Oct 89), Finland (26 Sep 86), France (4 Dec 87), Gabon (9 Feb 94), Gambia (25 Jul 90), Georgia (21 Mar 96), Germany (30 Sep 88), Ghana (24 Jul 89), Greece (29 Dec 88), Grenada (31 Mar 93), Guatemala (11 Sep 87), Guinea (25 Jun 92), Guinea Bissau (12 Nov 2002), Guyana (12 Aug 93), Haiti (29 Mar 2000), Honduras (14 Oct 93), Hungary (4 May 88), Iceland (29 Aug 89), India (18 Mar 91), Indonesia (26 Jun 92), Iran (3 Oct 90), Iraq (25 Jun 2008), Ireland (15 Sep 88), Israel (30 Jun 92), Italy (19 Sep 88), Jamaica (31 Mar 93), Japan (30 Sep 88), Jordan (31 May 89), Kazakhstan (26 Aug 98), Kenya (9 Nov 88), Kiribati (7 Jan 93), Korea (North (24 Jan 95), Korea (South) (27 Feb 92), Kuwait (23 Nov 92), Kyrgyzstan (31 May 2000), Laos (21 Aug 98), Latvia (28 Apr 95), Lebanon (30 Mar 93), Lesotho (25 Mar 94), Liberia (15 Jan 96), Libya (11 Jul 90), Liechtenstein (8 Feb 89), Lithuania (18 Jan 95), Luxembourg (17 Oct 88), Macedonia (10 Mar 94), Madagascar (7 Nov 96), Malawi (9 Jan 91), Malaysia (29 Aug 89), Maldives (26 Apr 88), Mali (28 Oct 94), Malta (15 Sep 88), Marshall Islands (11 Mar 93), Mauritania (26 May 94), Mauritius (18 Aug 92), Mexico (14 Sep 87), Micronesia (3 Aug 94), Moldova (24 Oct 96), Monaco (12 Mar 93), Mongolia (7 Mar 96), Montenegro (23 Oct 2006), Morocco (28 Dec 95), Mozambique (9 Sep 94), Myanmar (Burma) (24 Nov 93), Namibia (20 Sep 93), Nauru (12 Nov 2001), Nepal (6 Jul 94), Netherlands (28 Sep 88), New Zealand (2 Jun 87), Nicaragua (5 Mar 93), Niger (9 Oct 92), Nigeria (31 Oct 88), Niue (22 Dec 2003), Norway (23 Sep 86), Oman (20 Jun 99), Pakistan (18 Dec 92), Palau (29 May 2001), Panama (13 Feb 89), Papua New Guinea (27 Oct 92), Paraguay (3 Dec 92), Peru(7 Apr 89), Philippines (17 Jul 91), Poland (13 Jul 90), Portugal (17 Oct 88), Qatar (22 Jan 96), Romania (27 Jan 93), Rwanda (11 Oct 2001), Samoa (21 Dec 92), San Marino (23 Apr 2009), São Tomé/Principe (19 Nov 2001), Saudi Arabia (1 Mar 93), Senegal (19 Mar 93), Serbia (16 Apr 90), Seychelles (6 Jan 93), Sierra Leone (29 Aug 2001), Singapore (5 Jan 89), Slovakia (1 Jan 93), Slovenia (6 Jul 92), Solomon Islands (17 Jun 93), Somalia (1 Aug 2001), South Africa (15 Jan 90), Spain (25 Jul 88), Sri Lanka (15 Dec 89), St Kitts/Nevis (10 Aug 92), St Lucia (28 Jul 93), St Vincent/Grenadines (2 Dec 96), Sudan (29 Jan 93), Suriname (14 Oct 97), Swaziland (10 Nov 92), Sweden (26 Nov 86) Switzerland (17 Dec 87), Syria (12 Dec 89), Tajikistan (6 May 96), Tanzania (7 Apr 93), Thailand (7 Jul 89), Timore–Leste (16 Sep 2009), Togo (25 Feb 91), Tonga (29 Jul 98), Trinidad/Tobago (28 Aug 89), Tunisia (25 Sep 89), Turkey (20 Sep 91), Turkmenistan (18 Nov 93), Tuvalu (15 Jul 93), Uganda (24 Jun 88), Ukraine (18 Jun 86), United Arab Emirates (22 Dec 89), United Kingdom (15 May 87), United States (27 Aug 86), Uruguay (27 Feb 89), USSR (Russia) (18 Jun 86), Uzbekistan (18 May 93), Vanuatu (21 Nov 94), Venezuela (1 Sep 88), Vatican City (5 May 2008), Vietnam (26 Jan 94), Yemen (21 Feb 96), Zambia (24 Jan 90), Zimbabwe (3 Nov 92)

2.13   MONTREAL PROTOCOL ON SUBSTANCES THAT DEPLETE THE OZONE LAYER (AS AMENDED)

Concluded: 16 Sep 87

Entered into force: 1 Jan 89

Total parties: 196

Ratified/acceded/accepted without qualification: 196

Afghanistan (17 Jun 2004), Albania (8 Oct 99), Algeria (20 Oct 92), Andorra (26 Jan 2009), Angola (17 May 2000), Antigua/Barbuda (3 Dec 92), Argentina (18 Sep 90), Armenia (1 Oct 99), Australia (19 May 89), Austria (3 May 89), Azerbaijan (12 Jun 96)), Bahamas (4 May 93), Bahrain (27 Apr 90), Bangladesh (2 Aug 90), Barbados (16 Oct 92), Belarus (31 Oct 88), Belgium (30 Dec 88), Belize (9 Jan 98), Benin (1 Jul 93), Bhutan (23 Aug 2004), Bolivia (3 Oct 94), Bosnia–Herzegovina (6 Mar 92), Botswana (4 Dec 91), Brazil (19 Mar 90),

Brunei (27 May 93), Bulgaria (20 Nov 90), Burkina Faso (20 Jul 89), Burundi (6 Jan 97), Cambodia (27 Jun 2001), Cameroon (30 Aug 89), Canada (30 Jun 88), Cape Verde (31 Jul 2001), Central African Republic (29 Mar 93), Chad (7 Jun 94), Chile (26 Mar 90), China (14 Jun 91) Colombia (6 Dec 93), Comoros (31 Oct 94), Congo (Brazzaville) (16 Nov 94), Congo (Kinshasa) (30 Nov 94), Cook Islands (22 Dec 2003), Costa Rica (30 Jul 91), Côte d'Ivoire (5 Apr 93), Croatia (8 Oct 91), Cuba (14 Jul 92), Cyprus (28 May 92), Czech Republic (30 Sep 93), Denmark (16 Dec 88), Djibouti (30 Jul 99), Dominica (31 Mar 93), Dominican Republic (18 May 93), Ecuador (30 Apr 90), Egypt (2 Aug 88), El Salvador (2 Oct 92), Equatorial Guinea (6 Sep 2006), Eritrea (10 Mar 2005), Estonia (17 Oct 96), Ethiopia (11 Oct 94), Fiji (23 Oct 89), European Community (16 Dec 88), Finland (23 Dec 88), France (28 Dec 88), Gabon (9 Feb 94), Gambia (25 Jul 90), Georgia (21 Mar 96), Germany (16 Dec 88), Ghana (24 Jul 89), Greece (29 Dec 88), Grenada (31 Mar 93), Guatemala (7 Nov 89), Guinea (25 Jun 92), Guinea Bissau (12 Nov 2002), Guyana (12 Aug 93), Haiti (29 Mar 2000), Honduras (14 Oct 93), Hungary (20 Apr 89), Iceland (29 Aug 89), India (19 Jun 92), Indonesia (26 Jun 92), Iran (3 Oct 90), Iraq 25 Jun 2008), Ireland (16 Dec 88), Israel (30 Jun 92), Italy (16 Dec 88), Jamaica (31 Mar 93), Japan (30 Sep 88), Jordan (31 May 89), Kazakhstan (26 Aug 98), Kenya (9 Nov 88), Kiribati (7 Jan 93), Korea (North) (24 Jan 95), Korea (South) (27 Feb 92), Kuwait (23 Nov 92), Kyrgyzstan (31 May 2000), Laos (21 Aug 98), Latvia (28 Apr 95), Lebanon (31 Mar 93), Lesotho (25 Mar 94), Liberia (15 Jan 96), Libya (11 Jul 90), Liechtenstein (8 Feb 89), Lithuania (18 Jan 95), Luxembourg (17 Oct 88), Macedonia (10 Mar 94), Madagascar (7 Nov 96), Malawi (9 Jan 91), Malaysia (29 Aug 89), Maldives (16 May 89), Mali (28 Oct 94), Malta (29 Dec 88), Marshall Islands (11 Mar 93), Mauritania (26 May 94), Mauritius (18 Aug 92), Mexico (31 Mar 88), Micronesia (6 Sep 95), Moldova (24 Oct 96), Monaco (12 Mar 93), Mongolia (7 Mar 96), Montenegro (23 Oct 2006), Morocco (28 Dec 95), Mozambique (9 Sep 94), Myanmar (Burma) (24 Nov 93), Namibia (20 Sep 93), Nauru (12 Nov 2001), Nepal (6 Jul 94), Netherlands (16 Dec 88), New Zealand (21 Jul 88), Nicaragua (5 Mar 93), Niger (9 Oct 92), Nigeria (31 Oct 88), Niue (22 Dec 2003), Norway (24 Jun 88), Oman (30 Jun 99), Pakistan (18 Dec 92), Palau (29 May 2001), Panama (3 Mar 89), Papua New Guinea (27 Oct 92), Paraguay (3 Dec 92), Peru (31 Mar 93), Philippines (17 Jul 91), Poland (13 Jul 90), Portugal (17 Oct 88), Qatar (22 Jan 96), Romania (27 Jan 93), Rwanda (11 Oct 2001), Samoa (21 Dec 92), San Marino (23 Apr 2009), São Tomé/Principe (19 Nov 2001), Saudi Arabia (1 Mar 93), Senegal (6 May 93), Serbia (3 Jan 91), Seychelles (6 Jan 93), Sierra Leone (29 Aug 2001), Singapore (5 Jan 89), Slovakia (28 May 93), Slovenia (6 Jul 92), Solomon Islands (17 Jun 93), Somalia (1 Aug 2001), South Africa (15 Jan 90), Spain (16 Dec 88), Sri Lanka (15 Dec 89), St Kitts/Nevis (10 Aug 92), St Lucia (28 Jul 93), St Vincent/Grenadines (2 Dec 96), Sudan (29 Jan 93), Suriname (14 Oct 97), Swaziland (10 Nov 92), Sweden (29 Jun 88), Switzerland (28 Dec 88), Syria (12 Dec 89), Tajikistan (7 Jan 98), Tanzania (16 Apr 93), Thailand (7 Jul 89), Timor–Leste (16 Sep 2009), Togo (25 Feb 91), Tonga (29 Jul 98), Trinidad/Tobago (28 Aug 89), Tunisia (25 Sep 89), Turkey (20 Sep 91), Turkmenistan (18 Nov 93), Tuvalu (15 Jul 93), Uganda(15 Sep 88), Ukraine (20 Sep 88), United Arab Emirates (22 Dec 89), United Kingdom (16 Dec 88), United States (21 Apr 88), Uruguay (8 Jan 1), USSR (Russia) (10 Nov 88), Uzbekistan (18 May 93), Vanuatu (21 Nov 94), Vatican City (5 May 2008), Venezuela (6 Feb 89), Vietnam (26 Jan 94), Yemen (21 Feb 96), Zambia (24 Jan 90), Zimbabwe (3 Nov 92)

London Amendment entered into force: 10 Aug 92
Ratifying London Amendment: 196
Copenhagen Amendment entered into force: 14 Jun 94
Ratifying Copenhagen Amendment: 194

Montreal Amendment entered into force: 10 Nov 1999
Ratifying Montreal Amendment: 185
Beijing Amendment entered into force: 25 Feb 2002
Ratifying Beijing Amendment: 171

D. Nuclear

2.14 CONVENTION ON THIRD PARTY LIABILITY IN THE FIELD OF NUCLEAR ENERGY
Concluded: 29 Jul 60
Entered into force: 1 Apr 68
Signed but not ratified: 2
Austria (29 Jul 60), Luxembourg (29 Jul 60)
Ratified/accepted/approved (qualifications undetermined): 15
Belgium (3 Aug 66), Denmark (4 Sep 74), Finland (16 Jun 72), France (9 Mar 66), Germany (30 Sep 75), Greece (12 May 70), Italy (17 Sep 75), Netherlands (28 Dec 79), Norway (2 Jul 73), Portugal (29 Sep 77), Slovenia (16 Oct 2001), Spain (31 Oct 61), Sweden (1 Apr 68), Turkey (10 Oct 61), United Kingdom (23 Feb 66)
Ratified/accepted/approved with qualification: 1
Switzerland (9 Mar 2009)*

> * Switzerland's ratification applies to the Convention as amended by the 1964, 1982, and 2004 Protocols thereto. Because the 2004 Protocol has not yet entered into force, Switzerland is not yet a party to the Convention.

2.15 CONVENTION SUPPLEMENTARY TO THE **1960** CONVENTION ON THIRD PARTY LIABILITY IN THE FIELD OF NUCLEAR ENERGY
Concluded: 31 Jan 63
Entered into force: 4 Dec 74
Signed but not ratified: 2
Austria (31 Jan 63), Luxembourg (31 Jan 63)
Ratified/accepted/approved (qualifications undetermined): 12
Belgium (20 Aug 85), Denmark (4 Sep 74), Finland (14 Jan 77), France (30 Mar 66), Germany (1 Oct 75), Italy (3 Feb 76), Netherlands (28 Sep 79), Norway (9 Jul 73), Slovenia (5 Jun 2003), Spain (27 Jul 66), Sweden (3 Apr 68), United Kingdom (24 Mar 66)
Ratified/accepted/approved with qualification: 1
Switzerland (11 Mar 2009)*

> * Switzerland's ratification applies to the Supplementary Convention as amended by the 1964, 1982, and 2004 Protocols thereto. Because the 2004 Protocol has not yet entered into force, Switzerland is not yet a party to the Supplementary Convention.

2.16 IAEA CONVENTION ON EARLY NOTIFICATION OF A NUCLEAR ACCIDENT
Concluded: 26 Sep 86
Entered into force: 27 Oct 86
Total parties: 112*
Signed but not ratified: 11
Afghanistan (26 Sep 86), Congo (Kinshasa) (30 Sep 86), Côte d'Ivoire (26 Sep 86), Korea (North) (26 Sep 86), Niger (26 Sep 86), Paraguay (2 Oct 86), Sierra Leone (25 Mar 87), Sudan (26 Sep 86), Syria (2 Jul 87), Vatican City (26 Sep 86), Zimbabwe (26 Sep 86)
Ratified/acceded/accepted without qualification: 70
Algeria (15 Jan 2004), Angola (22 Dec 2004), Armenia (24 Aug 93), Albania (30 Sep 2003), Australia (22 Sep 87), Austria (18 Feb 88), Bangladesh (7 Jan 88),

Belgium (4 Jan 99), Bosnia Herzegovina (30 Jun 98), Brazil (4 Dec 90), Bulgaria (24 Feb 88), Cameroon (17 Jan 2006),Canada (18 Jan 90), Chile (15 Nov 2005), Colombia (28 Mar 2003), Costa Rica (16 Sep 91), Croatia (29 Sep 92), Cyprus (4 Jan 89), Czech Republic (24 Mar 93), Denmark (26 Sep 86), Dominican Republic (29 Apr 2010), Estonia (9 May 94), Finland (11 Dec 86), Gabon (19 Feb 2008), Georgia (06 Oct 2010), Greece (6 Jun 91), Guatemala (8 Aug 88), Hungary (10 Mar 87), Iceland (27 Sep 89), Ireland (13 Sep 91), Japan (9 Jun 87), Jordan (11 Dec 87), Kazakhstan (10 Mar 2010), Korea (South) (8 Jun 90), Kuwait (13 May 2003), Latvia (28 Dec 92), Lebanon (17 Apr 97), Libya (13 Aug 2009), Liechtenstein (19 Apr 94), Lithuania (16 Nov 94), Luxembourg (26 Sep 2000), Macedonia (20 Sep 96), Mali (1 Oct 2007), Mauritania (19 Sep 2011), Mexico (10 May 88), Moldova (7 May 98), Mongolia (11 Jun 87), Montenegro (21 Mar 2007), Morocco (7 Oct 93), Mozambique (30 Oct 2009), New Zealand (11 Mar 87), Nigeria (10 Aug 90), Norway (26 Sep 86), Panama (1 Apr 99), Philippines (5 May 97), Poland (24 Mar 88), Portugal (30 Apr 93), Qatar (4 Nov 2005), Senegal (24 Dec 2008), Serbia (5 Feb 2002), Singapore (15 Dec 97), Slovakia (10 Feb 93), Slovenia (7 Jul 92), St Vincent/Grenadines (18 Sept 2001), Sweden (27 Feb 87), Switzerland (31 May 88), Tajikistan (1 Sep 2011), Tanzania (27 Jan 2005), Tunisia (24 Feb 89), Uruguay (21 Dec 89)

Ratified/acceded/accepted with qualification: 42*

Argentina (17 Jan 90), Bahrain (5 May 2011), Belarus (26 Jan 87), Bolivia (22 Aug 2003), China (10 Sep 87), Cuba (8 Jan 91), Egypt (6 Jul 88), El Salvador (26 Jan 2005), EURATOM (14 Nov 2006), FAO (19 Oct 90), France (6 Mar 89), Germany (14 Sep 89), India (28 Jan 88), Indonesia (12 Nov 93), Iran (9 Oct 2000), Iraq (21 Jul 88), Israel (25 May 89), Italy (8 Feb 90), Malaysia (1 Sep 87), Mauritius (17 Aug 92), Monaco (19 Jul 89), Myanmar (18 Dec 97), Netherlands (23 Sep 91), Nicaragua (11 Nov 93), Oman (9 Jul 2009), Pakistan (11 Sep 89), Peru (17 Jul 95), Romania (12 Jun 90), Russia (23 Dec 86 & 26 Dec 91), Saudi Arabia (3 Nov 89), South Africa (10 Aug 87), Spain (13 Sep 89), Sri Lanka (11 Jan 91), Thailand (21 Mar 89), Turkey (3 Jan 91), Ukraine (26 Jan 87), United Arab Emirates (2 Oct 87), United Kingdom (9 Feb 90), United States (19 Sep 88), Vietnam (29 Sep 87), WHO (10 Aug 98), WMO (17 Apr 90)

* Includes four non-state parties.

2.17 IAEA CONVENTION ON ASSISTANCE IN THE CASE OF A NUCLEAR ACCIDENT OR RADIOLOGICAL EMERGENCY

Concluded: 26 Sep 86
Entered into force: 26 Feb 87
Total parties: 107*
Signed but not ratified: 11

Afghanistan (26 Sep 86), Congo (Kinshasa) (30 Sep 86), Côte d'Ivoire (26 Sep 86), Korea (North) (29 Sep 86), Niger (26 Sep 86), Paraguay (2 Oct 86), Sierra Leone (25 Mar 87), Sudan (26 Sep 86), Syria (2 Jul 87), Vatican City (26 Sep 86), Zimbabwe (26 Sep 86)

Ratified/accepted/approved without qualification: 57

Albania (30 Apr 2003), Algeria (15 Jan 2004), Armenia (24 Aug 93), Bangladesh (7 Jan 88), Belgium (4 Jan 99), Bosnia Herzegovina (30 Jun 98), Brazil (4 Dec 90), Bulgaria (24 Feb 88), Cameroon (17 Jan 2006), Chile (22 Sep 2004), Colombia (23 Jun 2005), Costa Rica (16 Sep 91), Croatia (29 Sep 92), Cyprus (4 Jan 89), Czech Republic (24 Mar 93), Estonia (9 May 94), Gabon (19 Feb 2008), Greece (6 Jun 91), Guatemala (8 Aug 88), Hungary (10 Mar 87), Iceland (27 Jan 2006), Ireland (13 Sep 91), Jordan (11 Dec 87), Kazakhstan (10 March 2010), Kuwait (13 May 2003), Latvia (28 Dec 92), Lebanon (17 Apr 97), Libya (27 Jun 90), Liechtenstein (19 Apr 94), Lithuania (21 Sep 2000), Luxembourg (26 Sep

2000), Macedonia (20 Sep 96), Mali (1 Oct 2007), Mauritania (19 Sep 2011), Mexico (10 May 88), Moldova (7 May 98), Mongolia (11 Jun 87), Montenegro (21 Mar 2007), Morocco (7 Oct 93), Mozambique (30 Oct 2009), Nigeria (10 Aug 90), Norway (26 Sep 86), Panama (1 Apr 99), Philippines (5 May 97), Poland (24 Mar 88), Portugal (23 Oct 2003), Qatar (4 Nov 2005), Senegal (24 Dec 2008), Serbia (5 Feb 2002), Singapore (15 Dec 97), Slovakia (10 Feb 93), Slovenia (7 Jul 92), St Vincent/Grenadines (18 Sep 2001), Switzerland (31 May 88), Tanzania (27 Jan 2005), Tunisia (24 Feb 89), Uruguay (21 Dec 89)

Ratified/accepted/approved with qualification: 50*
Argentina (17 Jan 90), Australia (22 Sep 87), Austria (21 Nov 89), Belarus (26 Jan 87), Bolivia (22 Aug 2003), Canada (12 Aug 2002), China (10 Sep 87), Cuba (8 Jan 91), Denmark (26 Sep 2008), Egypt (17 Oct 88), El Salvador (28 Jul 2005), EURATOM (14 Nov 2006), FAO (19 Oct 90), Finland (27 Nov 90), France (6 Mar 89), Germany (14 Sep 89), India (28 Jan 88), Indonesia (12 Nov 93), Iran (9 Oct 2000), Iraq (21 Jul 88), Israel (25 May 89), Italy (25 Oct 90), Japan (9 Jun 87), Korea (South) (8 Jun 90), Malaysia (1 Sep 87), Mauritius 917 Aug 92), Monaco (19 Jul 89), Netherlands (23 Sep 91), New Zealand (11 Mar 87), Nicaragua (11 Nov 93), Oman (9 Jul 2009), Pakistan (11 Sep 89), Peru (17 Jul 95), Romania (12 Jun 90), Russia (23 Dec 86 & 26 Dec 91), Saudi Arabia (3 Nov 89), South Africa (10 Aug 87), Spain (13 Sep 89), Sri Lanka (11 Jan 91), Sweden (24 Jun 92), Thailand (21 Mar 89), Turkey (3 Jan 91), Ukraine (26 Jan 87), United Arab Emirates (2 Oct 87), United Kingdom (9 Feb 90), United States (19 Sep 88), Vietnam (29 Sep 87), WHO (10 Aug 88), WMO (17 Apr 90)

* Includes four non-state parties.

2.18 IAEA Convention on Nuclear Safety
Concluded: 17 Jun 94
Entered into force: 24 Oct 96
Total parties: 74*
Signed but not ratified: 10
Algeria (20 Sep 94), Cuba (20 Sep 94), Egypt (20 Sep 94), Israel (22 Sep 94), Monaco (16 Sep 96), Morocco (1 Dec 94), Nicaragua (23 Sep 94), Philippines (14 Oct 94), Sudan (20 Sep 94), Syria (23 Sep 94),

Ratified/acceded/accepted without qualification: 71
Albania (29 Jun 2011), Argentina (17 Apr 97, Armenia (21 Sep 98), Australia (24 Dec 96), Austria (26 Aug 97), Bahrain (11 Nov 2010), Bangladesh (21 Sep 95), Belarus (29 Oct 98), Belgium (13 Jan 97), Brazil (4 Mar 97), Bosnia and Herzegovina (21 Jun 2010), Bulgaria (8 Nov 95), Canada (12 Dec 95), Chile (20 Dec 96), China (9 Apr 96), Croatia (18 Apr 96), Czech Republic (18 Sep 95), Cyprus (17 Mar 99), Estonia (3 Feb 2006), Finland (22 Jan 96), France (13 Sep 95), Germany (20 Jan 97), Ghana (01 Jun 2011), Greece (20 Jun 97), Hungary (18 Mar 96), Iceland (4 Jun 2008), India (31 Mar 2005), Indonesia (12 Apr 2002), Ireland (11 Jul 96), Italy (15 Apr 98), Japan (12 May 95), Jordan (12 Jun 2009), Kazakhstan (10 Mar 2010), Korea (South) (19 Sep 95), Kuwait (11 May 2006), Latvia (25 Oct 96), Lebanon (5 Jun 96), Libya (13 Aug 2009), Lithuania (12 Jun 96), Luxembourg(7 Apr 97), Macedonia (15 Mar 2006), Mali (13 May 96), Malta (15 Nov 2007), Mexico 26 Jul 96), Moldova (7 May 98), Netherlands (15 Oct 96), Nigeria (4 Apr 2007), Norway (29 Sep 94), Pakistan (30 Sep 97), Peru (1 Jul 97), Poland (14 Jun 95), Portugal (20 May 98), Romania (1 Jun 95), Russia (12 Jul 96), Saudi Arabia (18 Mar 2010), Senegal (24 Dec 2008), Singapore (15 Dec 97), Slovakia (7 Mar 95), Slovenia (20 Nov 96), South Africa (24 Dec 96), Spain (4 Jul 95), Sweden (11 Sep 95), Switzerland (12Sep 96), Sri Lanka (11 Aug 99), Tunisia (21 April 2010), Turkey (8 Mar 95), United Arab Emirates (31 Jul 2009), United Kingdom (17 Jan 96), United States (11 Apr 99),

Uruguay (3 Sep 2003), Vietnam (16 Apr 2010)
Ratified/acceded/accepted with qualification: 3*
Denmark (13 Nov 98), EURATOM (31 Jan 2000), Ukraine (8 Apr 98)

  * Includes one non-state party.

2.19   1997 VIENNA CONVENTION ON CIVIL LIABILITY FOR NUCLEAR DAMAGE

The 1997 Vienna Convention is the combined text of the 1963 Vienna Convention on Civil Liability for Nuclear Damage and the 1997 Protocol to Amend that Convention. The status information provided below is for both the 1997 Vienna Convention and the original 1963 Convention.

1997 Vienna Convention on Civil Liability for Nuclear Damage:

Concluded: 12 Sep 97
Entered into force: 4 Oct 2003
Total Parties: 9
Signed but not ratified: 9
Czech Republic (18 Jun 98), Hungary (29 Sep 97), Indonesia (6 Oct 97), Italy (26 Jan 98), Lebanon (30 Sep 97), Lithuania (30 Sep 97), Peru (4 Jun 98), Philippines (10 Mar 98), Ukraine (29 Sep 97)
Ratified/accepted/approved without qualification: 8
Argentina (14 Nov 2000), Belarus (4 Jul 2003), Khazakhstan (29 Mar 2011), Latvia (5 Dec 2001), Montenegro (4 Mar 2011), Morocco (6 Jul 99), Poland (21 Sep 2010), Romania (29 Dec 98)
Ratified/accepted/approved with qualification: 1
Saudi Arabia (17 Mar 2011)

1963 Vienna Convention on Civil Liability for Nuclear Damage

Concluded: 21 May 63
Entered into force: 12 Nov 77
Total parties: 38
Signed but not ratified: 5
Colombia (21 May 63), Israel (19 Aug 97), Morocco (30 Nov 84), Spain (6 Sep 63), United Kingdom (11 Nov 64)
Ratified/accepted/approved without qualification: 37
Argentina (25 Apr 67), Armenia (24 Aug 93), Belarus (9 Feb 98), Bolivia (10 Apr 68), Bosnia–Herzegovina (30 Jun 98), Brazil (26 Mar 93), Bulgaria (24 Aug 94), Cameroon (6 Mar 64), Croatia (29 Sep 92), Cuba (25 Oct 65), Czech Republic (24 Mar 94), Egypt (5 Nov 65), Estonia (9 Mar 94), Hungary (28 Jul 89), Kazakhstan (29 Mar 2011), Latvia (15 Mar 95), Lebanon (17 Apr 97), Lithuania (15 Sep 92), Macedonia (8 Apr 94), Mexico (25 Apr 89), Moldova (7 May 98), Montenegro (21 Mar 2007), Niger (24 Jul 79), Nigeria (4 Apr 2007), Peru (26 Aug 80), Philippines (15 Nov 65), Poland (23 Jan 90), Romania (29 Dec 92), Russia (13 May 2005), Saudi Arabia (17 Mar 2011), Senegal (24 Dec 2008), Serbia (5 Feb 2002), Slovakia (7 Mar 95), St Vincent/Grenadines (18 Sep 2001), Trinidad/Tobago (31 Jan 66), Ukraine (20 Sep 96), Uruguay (13 Apr 99)
Ratified/accepted/approved with qualification: 1
Chile (23 Nov 89)
Termination of application: 1
Slovenia (12 Nov 2002)

2.20   CONVENTION ON SUPPLEMENTARY COMPENSATION FOR NUCLEAR DAMAGE
Concluded: 12 Sep 97
Not in force as of 20 September 2011
Signed but not ratified: 13

Argentina (19 Dec 97), Australia (1 Oct 97), Czech Republic (18 Jun 98), Indonesia (6 Oct 97), Italy (26 Jan 98), Lebanon (30 Sep 97), Lithuania (30 Sep 97), Morocco (29 Sep 97), Peru (4 Jun 98), Phillipines (10 Mar 98), Romania (30 Sep 97), Ukraine (29 Sep 97), United States (29 Sep 97)
Ratified without qualification: 3
Argentina (14 Nov 2000), Morocco (6 Jul 1999), Romania (2 Mar 1999)
Ratified with qualification: 1
United States (21 May 2008)

E. Outer Space

2.21 TREATY ON PRINCIPLES GOVERNING THE ACTIVITIES OF STATES IN THE EXPLORATION AND USE OF OUTER SPACE, INCLUDING THE MOON AND OTHER CELESTIAL BODIES
Concluded: 27 Jan 67
Entered into force: 10 Oct 67
Signed but not ratified: 26
Bolivia (27 Jan 67), Botswana (27 Jan 67), Burundi (27 Jan 67), Cameroon (27 Jan 67), Central African Republic (27 Jan 67), Colombia (27 Jan 67), Congo (Kinshasa) (27 Jan 67), Ethiopia (27 Jan 67), Gambia (2 Jun 67), Ghana (3 Mar 67), Guyana (3 Feb 67), Haiti (27 Jan 67), Honduras (27 Jan 67), Iran (27 Jan 67), Jordan (2 Feb 67), Lesotho (27 Jan 67), Macedonia (27 Jan 67), Malaysia (21 Feb 67), Nicaragua (13 Feb 67), Panama (27 Jan 67), Philippines (27 Jan 67), Rwanda (27 Jan 67), Serbia & Montenegro (27 Jan 67), Somalia (2 Feb 67), Trinidad/Tobago (24 Jul 67), Vatican City (5 Apr 67)
Ratified/acceded/accepted without qualifications: 100
Afghanistan (17 Mar 88), Algeria (27 Jan 92), Antigua/Barbuda (26 Jan 89), Argentina (26 Mar 69), Australia (10 Oct 67), Austria (26 Feb 68), Bahamas (11 Aug 76), Bangladesh (14 Jan 86), Barbados (12 Sep 68), Belarus (31 Oct 67), Belgium (31 Mar 73), Benin (2 Jul 86), Brazil (5 Mar 69), Bulgaria (19 Apr 67), Burkina Faso (18 Jun 68), Canada (10 Oct 67), Chile (8 Oct 81), China (12 Jan 84), Cuba (3 Jun 77), Cyprus (5 Jul 72), Czech Republic (29 Sep 93), Denmark (10 Oct 67), Dominican Republic (21 Nov 68), Ecuador (7 Mar 69), Egypt (10 Oct 67), El Salvador (15 Jan 69), Equatorial Guinea (16 Jan 89), Fiji (14 Aug 72), Finland (12 Jul 67), France (5 Aug 70), Germany (10 Feb 71), Greece (19 Jan 71), Guinea–Bissau (20 Aug 76), Hungary (26 Jun 67), Iceland (5 Feb 68), India (18 Jan 82), Indonesia (25 Jun 2002), Iraq (23 Sep 69), Ireland (19 Jul 68), Israel (1 Mar 77), Italy (4 May 72), Jamaica (10 Aug 70), Japan (10 Oct 67), Kazakhstan (11 Jun 98), Kenya (19 Jan 84), Korea (North) (3 May 2009), Korea (North) (3 May 2009), Korea (South) (13 Oct 67), Kuwait (20 Jun 72), Laos (15 Jan 73), Lebanon (31 Mar 69), Libya (3 Jul 68), Luxembourg (17 Jan 2006), Madagascar (22 Aug 68), Mali (11 Jun 68), Mauritius (21 Apr 69), Mexico (31 Jan 68), Mongolia (10 Oct 67), Morocco (21 Dec 67), Myanmar (Burma)(18 Mar 70), Nepal (10 Oct 67), Netherlands (31 May 68), New Zealand (10 Oct 69), Niger (17 Apr 67), Nigeria (14 Nov 67), Norway (1 Jul 69), Pakistan (8 Apr 68), Papua New Guinea (27 Oct 80), Peru (1 Mar 79), Poland (30 Jan 68), Portugal (29 May 96), Romania (9 Apr 68), San Marino (3 Feb 69), Saudi Arabia (17 Dec 76), Seychelles (5 Jan 78), Sierra Leone (25 Oct 67), Singapore (10 Sep 76), Slovakia (17 May 93), South Africa (8 Oct 68), Spain (27 Nov 68), Sri Lanka (18 Nov 86), St Vincent/Grenadines (13 May 99), Sweden (11 Oct 67), Switzerland (18 Dec 69), Syria (19 Nov 68),Thailand (5 Sep 68), Togo (26 Jun 89), Tonga (7 Jul 71), Tunisia (28 Mar 68), Turkey (27 Mar 68), Uganda (24 Apr 68), Ukraine (31 Oct 67), United Arab Emirates (4 Oct 2000), United Kingdom (10 Oct 67), United States (10 Oct 67), Uruguay (31 Aug 70), USSR (Russia) (10 Oct 67), Venezuela (3 Mar 70), Vietnam (20 Jun 80), Yemen (1 Jun 79), Zambia (28 Aug 73)

Note: Only one date of signature or deposit is given for a State, although that State may have signed or deposited at different times in different cities or with different depositaries. We have preferred dates of signature in London or deposit with the United Kingdom when those dates are known. If there has been no deposit with the United Kingdom, we give the deposit date with the United States or the USSR (Russia).

2.22 CONVENTION ON THE INTERNATIONAL LIABILITY FOR DAMAGE CAUSED BY SPACE OBJECTS
Concluded: 29 Mar 72
Entry into force: 1 Sep 72
Total parties: 90
Signed but not ratified: 23
Burundi (29 Mar 72), Cambodia (29 Mar 72), Central African Republic (27 Apr 72), Colombia (29 Mar 72), Congo (Kinshasa) (29 Mar 72), Costa Rica (29 Mar 72), Egypt (6 Jun 72), El Salvador (29 Mar 72), Gambia (8 Aug 72), Ghana (29 Mar 72), Guatemala (29 Mar 72), Haiti (29 Mar 72), Honduras (29 Mar 72), Iceland (29 Mar 72), Jordan (6 Jun 72), Nepal (29 Mar 72), Nicaragua (11 Apr 72), Oman (23 Jun 72), Philippines (22 Aug 72), Rwanda (29 Mar 72), Sierra Leone (14 Jul 72), South Africa (29 Mar 72), Tanzania (31 May 72)
Ratified/accepted/approved without qualification: 87
Algeria (17 Oct 2006), Antigua/Barbuda (26 Jan 89), Argentina (14 Nov 86), Australia (20 Feb 75), Austria (10 Jan 80), Belarus (27 Dec 73), Belgium (13 Aug 76), Benin (25 Apr 75), Bosnia–Herzegovina (22 Jul 94), Botswana (11 Mar 74), Brazil (9 Mar 73), Bulgaria (16 May 72), Canada (20 Feb 75), Chile (1 Dec 76), Cuba (25 Nov 82), Cyprus (15 May 73), Czech Republic (29 Sep 93), Denmark (1 Apr 77), Dominican Republic (23 Feb 1973), Ecuador (17 Aug 72), European Space Agency (23 Sep 76), EUMETSAT (29 Sep 2005), EUTELSAT (30 Nov 87), Fiji (4 Apr 73), Finland (1 Feb 77), France (31 Dec 75), Gabon (5 Feb 82), Germany (18 Dec 75), Greece (4 May 77), Hungary (27 Dec 72), India (9 Jul 79), Indonesia (18 Jun 96), Iran (21 Feb 74), Iraq (4 Oct 72), Ireland (29 Jun 72), Israel (23 Jun 77), Italy (22 Feb 83), Japan (20 Jun 83), Kazakhstan (11 Jun 1998), Kenya (25 Sep 75), Laos (25 Apr 73), Lebanon (29 Mar 1972), Liechtenstein (9 Jan 80), Luxembourg (18 Oct 83), Macedonia (20 Oct 1975), Mali (9 Jun 72), Malta (13 Jan 78), Mexico (8 Apr 74), Mongolia (14 Sep 72), Montenegro (date as yet undetermined), Morocco (15 Mar 83), Netherlands (17 Feb 81), New Zealand (30 Oct 74), Niger (1 Sep 72), Nigeria (21 Dec 2005), Norway (3 Apr 95), Pakistan (10 Apr 73), Panama (5 Jun 74), Papua New Guinea (27 Oct 80), Peru (6 Nov 2002), Poland (25 Jan 73), Qatar (11 Jan 74), Romania (18 Mar 80), Saudi Arabia (17 Dec 76), Senegal (26 Mar 75), Serbia (20 Oct 75), Seychelles (5 Jan 78), Singapore (19 Aug 75), Slovakia (1 Jan 1993), Slovenia (27 May 92), Spain (2 Jan 80), Sri Lanka (3 May 73), St Vincent/Grenadines (13 May 99), Sweden (15 Jun 76), Switzerland (22 Jan 74), Syria (6 Feb 80), Togo (26 Apr 76), Trinidad/Tobago (8 Feb 80), Tunisia (6 Jun 73), Turkey (15 Feb 2007), Ukraine (16 Oct 73), United Arab Emirates (4 Oct 2000), United Kingdom (9 Oct 73), United States (9 Oct 73), Uruguay (7 Jan 77), USSR (Russia) (9 Oct 73), Venezuela (1 Aug 78), Zambia (28 Aug 73)
Ratified/accepted/approved with qualification: 3
China (20 Dec 88), Korea (South) (14 Jan 80), Kuwait (30 Oct 72)

2.23 AGREEMENT GOVERNING THE ACTIVITIES OF STATES ON THE MOON AND OTHER CELESTIAL BODIES
Concluded: 5 Dec 79
Entered into force: 11 Jul 84

Signed but not ratified: 4

France (29 Jan 80), Guatemala (20 Nov 80), India (18 Jan 82), Romania (17 Apr 80)

Ratified/acceded/accepted without qualification: 13

Australia (7 Jul 86), Austria (11 Jun 84), Belgium (29 Jun 2004), Chile (12 Nov 81), Kazakhstan (11 Jan 2001), Lebanon (12 Apr 2006), Mexico (11 Oct 91), Morocco (21 Jan 93), Netherlands (17 Feb 83), Pakistan (27 Feb 86), Peru (23 Nov 2005), Philippines (26 May 81), Uruguay (9 Nov 81)

3. HYDROSPHERE

A. *Oceans and Seas*

3.1 CONVENTION ON THE HIGH SEAS

Concluded: 29 Apr 58

Entered into force: 30 Sep 62

Total parties: 63

Signed but not ratified: 19

Argentina (29 Apr 58), Bolivia (17 Oct 58), Canada (29 Apr 58), Colombia (29 Apr 58), Cuba (29 Apr 58), France (30 Oct 58), Ghana (29 Apr 58), Iceland (29 Apr 58), Iran (28 May 58), Ireland (2 Oct 58), Lebanon (29 May 58), Liberia (27 May 58), New Zealand (29 Oct 58), Pakistan (31 Oct 58), Panama (2 May 58), Sri Lanka (30 Oct 58), Tunisia (30 Oct 58), Uruguay (29 Apr 58), Vatican City (30 Apr 58)

Ratified/acceded/accepted without qualification: 51

Afghanistan (28 Apr 59), Australia (14 May 63), Austria (10 Jan 74), Belgium (6 Jan 72), Bosnia–Herzegovina (1 Sep 93), Burkina Faso (4 Oct 65), Cambodia (18 Mar 60), Central African Republic (15 Oct 62), Costa Rica (16 Feb 72), Croatia (3 Aug 92), Cyprus (23 May 88), Denmark (26 Sep 68), Dominican Republic (11 Aug 64), Fiji (25 Mar 71),Finland (16 Feb 65), Germany (26 Jul 73), Guatemala (27 Nov 61), Haiti (29 Mar 60), Israel (6 Sep 61), Italy (17 Dec 64), Jamaica (8 Oct 65), Japan (10 Jun 68), Kenya (20 Jun 69), Latvia (12 Nov 92), Lesotho (23 Oct 73), Madagascar (31 Jul 62), Malawi (3 Nov 65), Malaysia (21 Dec 60), Mauritius (5 Oct 70), Montenegro (23 Oct 2006), Mongolia (15 Oct 76), Nepal (28 Dec 62), Netherlands (18 Feb 66), Nigeria (26 Jun 61), Portugal (8 Jan 63), Senegal (25 Apr 61), Serbia (12 Mar 2001), Sierra Leone (13 Mar 62), Slovenia (6 Jul 92), Solomon Islands (3 Sep 81), South Africa (9 Apr 63), Spain (25 Feb 71), Swaziland (16 Oct 70), Switzerland (18 May 66), Thailand (2 Jul 68), Tonga (29 Jun 71), Trinidad/Tobago (11 Apr 66), Uganda (14 Sep 64), United Kingdom (14 Mar 60), United States (12 Apr 61), Venezuela (15 Aug 61)

Ratified/acceded/accepted with qualification: 12

Albania (7 Dec 64), Belarus (27 Feb 61), Bulgaria (31 Aug 62), Czech Republic (22 Feb 93), Hungary (6 Dec 61), Indonesia (10 Aug 61), Mexico (2 Aug 66), Poland (29 Jun 62), Romania (12 Dec 61), Slovakia (28 May 93), Ukraine (12 Jan 61), USSR (Russia) (22 Nov 60)

3.2 CONVENTION ON THE CONTINENTAL SHELF

Concluded: 29 Apr 58

Entered into force: 10 Jun 64

Total parties: 58

Signed but not ratified: 21

Afghanistan (30 Oct 58), Argentina (29 Apr 58), Bolivia (17 Oct 58), Chile (31 Oct 58), Cuba (29 Apr 58), Ecuador (31 Oct 58), Germany (30 Oct 58), Ghana (29 Apr 58), Iceland (29 Apr 58), Indonesia (8 May 58), Iran (28 May 58), Ireland (2 Oct 58), Lebanon (29 May 58), Liberia (27 May 58), Nepal (29 Apr 58), Pakistan (31 Oct 58), Panama (2 May 58), Peru (31 Oct 58), Sri Lanka (30 Oct

58), Tunisia (30 Oct 58), Uruguay (29 Apr 58)

Ratified/acceded/accepted without qualification: 52

Albania (17 Feb 64), Australia (14 May 63), Belarus (27 Feb 61), Bosnia–
Herzegovina (12 Jan 94), Bulgaria (31 Aug 62), Cambodia (18 Mar 60), Colombia
(8 Jan 62), Costa Rica (16 Feb 72), Croatia (3 Aug 92), Cyprus (11 Apr 74),
Czech Republic (22 Feb 93), Denmark (12 Jun 63), Dominican Republic (11 Aug
64), Fiji (25 Mar 71), Finland (16 Feb 65), Guatemala (27 Nov 61), Haiti (29 Mar
60), Israel (6 Sep 61), Jamaica (8 Oct 65), Kenya (20 Jun 69), Latvia (2 Dec 92),
Lesotho (23 Oct 73), Madagascar (31 Jul 62), Malawi (3 Nov 65), Malaysia (21
Dec 60), Malta (19 May 66), Mauritius (5 Oct 70), Mexico (2 Aug 66), Montenegro (23 Oct 2006), Netherlands (18 Feb 66), New Zealand (18 Jan 65), Nigeria (28
Apr 71), Norway (9 Sep 71), Poland (29 Jun 62), Portugal (8 Jan 63), Romania
(12 Dec 61), Senegal (25 Apr 61), Sierra Leone (25 Nov 66), Slovakia (28 May
93), Solomon Islands (3 Sep 81), South Africa (9 Apr 63), Swaziland (16 Oct 70),
Sweden (1 Jun 66), Switzerland (18 May 66), Thailand (2 Jul 68), Tonga (29 Jun
71), Trinidad/Tobago (11 Jul 68), Uganda (14 Sep 64), Ukraine (12 Jan 61),
United Kingdom (11 May 64), United States (12 Apr 61), USSR (Russia) (22 Nov
60)

Ratified/acceded/accepted with qualification: 6

Canada (6 Feb 70), France (14 Jun 65), Greece (6 Nov 72), Serbia (12 Mar 2001),
Spain (25 Feb 71), Venezuela (15 Aug 61)

Denunciation: 1

Senegal (30 Mar 76)

> * Denunciation objected by United Kingdom. Senegal still listed as a party by
> depositary.

3.3   **CONVENTION ON THE TERRITORIAL SEA AND CONTIGUOUS ZONE**

Concluded: 29 Apr 58

Entered into force: 10 Sep 64

Total parties: 52

Signed but not ratified: 22

Afghanistan (30 Oct 58), Argentina (29 Apr 58), Austria (27 Oct 58), Bolivia (17
Oct 58), Canada (29 Apr 58), Colombia (29 Apr 58), Costa Rica (29 Apr 58),
Cuba (29 Apr 58), Ghana (29 Apr 58), Guatemala (29 Apr 58), Iceland (29 Apr
58), Iran (28 May 58), Ireland (2 Oct 58), Liberia (27 May 58), Nepal (29 Apr
58), New Zealand (29 Oct 58), Pakistan (31 Oct 58), Panama (2 May 58), Sri
Lanka (30 Oct 58), Tunisia (30 Oct 58), Uruguay (29 Apr 58), Vatican City (30
Apr 58)

Ratified/acceded/accepted without qualification: 40

Australia (14 May 63), Belgium (6 Jan 72), Bosnia–Herzegovina (1 Sep 93),
Cambodia (18 Mar 60), Croatia (3 Aug 92), Denmark (26 Sep 68), Dominican
Republic (11 Aug 64), Fiji (25 Mar 71), Finland (16 Feb 65), Haiti (29 Mar 60),
Israel (6 Sep 61), Jamaica(8 Oct 65), Japan (10 Jun 68), Kenya (20 Jun 69),
Latvia (17 Nov 92), Lithuania (31 Jan 92), Lesotho (23 Oct 73), Madagascar (31
Jul 62), Malawi (3 Nov 65), Malaysia (21 Dec 60), Malta (19 May 66), Mauritius
(5 Oct 70), Montenegro (23 Oct 2006), Netherlands (18 Feb 66), Nigeria (26 Jun
61), Portugal (8 Jan 63), Senegal (25 Apr 61), Serbia (12 Mar 2001), Sierra
Leone (13 Mar 62), Slovenia (6 Jul 92), South Africa (9 Apr 63), Spain (25 Feb
71), Swaziland (16 Oct 70), Switzerland (18 May 66), Thailand (2 Jul 68), Tonga
(29 Jun 71), Trinidad/Tobago (11 Apr 66), Uganda (14 Sep 64), United Kingdom
(14 Mar 60), United States (12 Apr 61)

Ratified/acceded/accepted with qualification: 12

Belarus (27 Feb 61), Bulgaria (31 Aug 62), Czech Republic (22 Feb 93), Hungary
(6 Dec 61), Italy (17 Dec 64), Mexico (2 Aug 66), Romania (12 Dec 61), Slovakia

(28 May 93), Solomon Islands (3 Sep 81), Ukraine (12 Jan 61), USSR (Russia) (22 Nov 60), Venezuela (15 Aug 61)
Denunciation: 1
Senegal (9 Jul 71)

Note: Denunciation objected by United Kingdom. Senegal still listed as a party by depositary.

3.4 CONVENTION ON THE LIABILITY OF OPERATORS OF NUCLEAR SHIPS
Concluded: 25 May 62
Not in force
Signed but not ratified: 14
Belgium (25 May 62), China (25 May 62), Gernmany (25 Oct 74), India (25 May 62), Indonesia (25 May 62), Ireland (25 May 62), Liberia (25 May 62), Malaysia (25 May 62), Monaco (25 May 62), Monaco (25 May 62), Panama (25 May 62), Philippines (25 May 62), Republic of Kora (25 May 62), United Arab Emirates (25 May 62), Yugoslavia (25 May 62)
Ratified/accepted/approved without qualification: 5
Lebanon (3 Jun 75), Madagascar (13 Jul 65), Portugal (31 Jun 68), Syria (1 Aug 74), Zaire (17 Jul 67)
Ratified/accepted/approved with qualification: 2
Netherlands (30 Mar 74), Suriname (20 Mar 74)

3.5 INTERNATIONAL CONVENTION RELATING TO INTERVENTION ON THE HIGH SEAS IN CASES OF OIL POLLUTION CASUALTIES
Concluded: 29 Nov 69
Entered into force: 6 May 75
Total parties: 86
Signed but not ratified: 5
Greece (14 Apr 70), Guatemala (29 Nov 69), Korea (South) (29 Nov 69), Madagascar (29 Nov 69), Romania (30 Dec 70)
Ratified/accepted/approved without qualification: 81
Angola (4 Oct 2001), Barbados (6 May 94), Bahamas (22 Jul 76), Bangladesh (6 Nov 81), Belgium (21 Oct 71), Benin (11 Nov 85), Brazil (18 Jan 2008), Cameroon (14 May 84), Chile (28 Feb 95), China (23 Feb 90), Côte d'Ivoire (8 Jan 88), Croatia (8 Oct 91), Denmark (18 Dec 70), Djibouti (1 Mar 90), Dominican Republic (5 Feb 75), Ecuador (23 Dec 76), Egypt (3 Feb 89), Equatorial Guinea (24 Apr 96), Estonia (16 May 2008), Fiji (15 Aug 72), Finland (6 Sep 76), France (10 May 72), Gabon (21 Jan 82), Germany (7 May 75), Ghana (20 Apr 78), Georgia (25 Aug 95), Guyana (10 Dec 97), Iceland (17 Jul 80), India (16 Jun 2000), Iran (23 Oct 97), Ireland (21 Aug 80), Italy (27 Feb 79), Jamaica (13 Mar 91), Japan (6 Apr 71), Kuwait (2 Apr 81), Latvia (4 Oct 2001), Lebanon (5 Jun 75), Liberia (25 Sep 72), Marshall Islands (16 Oct 95), Mauritania (24 Nov 97), Mauritius (17 Dec 2002), Mexico (8 Apr 76), Monaco (24 Feb 75), Montenegro (3 Jun 2006), Morocco (11 Apr 74), Namibia (24 Feb 2004), Netherlands (19 Sep 75), New Zealand (26 Mar 75), Nicaragua (15 Nov 94), Nigeria (12 Mar 2004), Norway (12 Jul 72), Oman (24 Jan 85), Pakistan (13 Jan 95), Panama (7 Jan 76), Papua New Guinea (12 Mar 80), Poland (1 Jun 76), Portugal (15 Feb 80), Qatar (2 Jun 88), Senegal (27 Mar 72), Serbia (3 Jun 2006), Slovenia (25 Jun 91), South Africa (1 Jul 86), Spain (8 Nov 73), Sri Lanka (12 Apr 83), St Kitts/Nevis (7 Oct 2004), St Lucia (20 May 2004), St Vincent/Grenadines (12 May 99), Suriname (25 Nov 75), Sweden (8 Feb 73), Switzerland (15 Dec 87), Syria (6 Feb 75), Tanzania (16 May 2006), Tonga (1 Feb 96), Trinidad/Tobago (06 May 2000), Tunisia (4 May 76), Ukraine (17 Dec 93), United Arab Emirates (15 Dec 83), United Kingdom (12 Jan 71), United

States (21 Feb 74), Vanuatu (14 Sep 92), Yemen (6 Mar 79)
Ratified/accepted/approved with qualification: 5
Argentina (21 Apr 1987), Australia (7 Nov 83), Bulgaria (2 Nov 83), Cuba (5 May 76), USSR (Russia) (30 Dec 74)

3.6   CONVENTION ON THE PREVENTION OF MARINE POLLUTION BY DUMPING OF WASTES AND OTHER MATTER
Concluded: 29 Dec 72
Entered into force: 30 Aug 75
Superseded by Basic Document 3.18 for states that are party to both
Signed but not ratified: 14
Cambodia (2 Jan 73), Chad (29 Dec 72), Colombia (29 Dec 72), Kuwait (1 Mar 73), Lebanon (29 Dec 72), Lesotho (8 Jan 73), Liberia (29 Dec 72), Nepal (29 Dec 72), Senegal (29 Dec 72), Somalia (16 Apr 73), Taiwan (29 Dec 72), Togo (21 Nov 73), Uruguay (29 Dec 72), Venezuela (30 May 73)
Ratified/accepted/approved without qualification: 87
Afghanistan (2 Apr 75), Antigua/Barbuda (6 Jan 89), Argentina (11 Sep 79), Australia (21 Aug 85), Azerbaijan (1 Jul 97), Barbados (4 May 94), Belarus (29 Jan 76), Belgium (12 Jun 85), Benin (28 Apr 2011), Bolivia (10 Jun 99), Brazil (26 Jul 82), Bulgaria (25 Jan 2006), Canada (13 Nov 75), Cape Verde (26 May 77), Chile (4 Aug 77), China (5 Nov 85), Congo (Kinshasa) (16 Sep 75), Costa Rica (16 Jun 86), Côte d'Ivoire (9 Oct 87), Croatia (8 Oct 91), Cuba (1 Dec 75), Cyprus (7 Jun 90), Denmark (23 Oct 74), Dominican Republic (7 Dec 73), Egypt (30 Jun 92), Equatorial Guinea (21 Jan 2004), Finland (3 May 79), France (3 Feb 77), Gabon (5 Feb 82), Germany (8 Nov 77), Greece (10 Aug 81), Guatemala (14 Jul 75), Haiti (28 Aug 75), Honduras (2 May 80), Hungary (5 Feb 76), Iceland (24 May 73), Iran (20 Jan 97), Ireland (17 Feb 82), Italy (30 Apr 84), Jamaica (22 Mar 91), Japan (15 Oct 80), Jordan (11 Nov 74), Kenya (7 Jan 76), Kiribati (12 Jul 79), Korea (South) (21 Dec 93), Libya (22 Nov 76), Luxembourg (21 Feb 91), Malta (28 Dec 89), Mexico (7 Apr 75), Monaco (16 May 77), Montenegro (3 Jun 2006), Morocco (18 Feb 77), Nauru (26 Jul 82), Netherlands (2 Dec 77), New Zealand (30 Apr 75), Nigeria (19 Mar 76), Norway (4 Apr 74), Oman (13 Mar 84), Pakistan (9 Mar 95), Panama (31 Jul 75), Papua New Guinea (10 Mar 80), Peru (7 May 2003), Philippines (10 Aug 73), Poland (23 Jan 79), Portugal (14 Apr 78), Serbia (3 Jun 2006), Seychelles (29 Oct 84), Sierra Leone (12 Mar 2008), Slovenia (25 Jun 91), Solomon Islands (7 Jul 78), South Africa (7 Aug 78), Spain (31 Jul 74), St Lucia (23 Aug 85), St Vincent/Grenadines (24 Oct 2001), Suriname (21 Oct 80), Sweden (21 Feb 74), Switzerland (31 Jul 79), Syria (6 May 2009), Tanzania (28 Jul 2008), Tonga (8 Nov 95), Tunisia (13 Apr 76), Ukraine (5 Feb 76), United Arab Emirates (9 Aug 74), United Kingdom (17 Nov 75), United States (29 Apr 74), USSR (Russia) (30 Dec 75), Vanuatu (22 Sep 92)

3.7   MARPOL 73/78: PROTOCOL OF 1978 RELATING TO THE INTERNATIONAL CONVENTION FOR THE PREVENTION OF POLLUTION FROM SHIPS, 1973
Concluded: 2 Nov 73 (Convention); 17 Feb 78 (Protocol)
Entered into force: Protocol and Annex I (2 Oct 83), Annex II (6 Apr 87), Annex III (1 Jul 92), Annex IV (27 Sep 2003), Annex V (31 Dec 88), 1997 Amending Protocol and Annex VI (19 May 2005)
Total parties: 151
Protocol ratified/acceded/accepted without qualification: 137*
Albania (9 Jan 2007), Angola (4 Oct 2001), Antigua/Barbuda (29 Jan 88), Australia (14 Oct 87), Austria (27 May 88), Azerbaijan (16 Jul 2004), Bahamas (7 Jun 83), Bahrain (27 Apr 2007), Bangladesh (18 Dec 2002), Barbados (6 May

94), Belarus (7 Jan 94), Belgium (6 Mar 84), Belize (26 May 95), Benin (11 Feb 2000), Bolivia (4 Jun 99), Brunei (23 Oct 86), Cambodia (28 Nov 94), Cameroon (18 Sep 2009), Cape Verde (4 Jul 2003), Chile (10 Oct 94), China (1 Jul 83), Colombia (27 Jul 81), Comoros (22 Nov 2000), Congo (Brazzaville) (7 Sep 2004), Cook Islands (12 Mar 2007), Côte d'Ivoire (5 Oct 87), Croatia (8 Oct 91), Cuba (21 Dec 92), Cyprus (22 Jun 89), Czech Republic (1 Jan 93), Djibouti (1 Mar 90), Dominica (21 Jun 2000), Dominican Republic (24 Jun 99), Ecuador (18 May 90), Egypt (7 Aug 86), El Salvador (24 Sep 2008), Equatorial Guinea (24 Apr 96), Estonia (16 Dec 91), Finland (20 Sep 83), Gabon (26 Apr 83), Gambia (1 Nov 91), Georgia (8 Nov 94), Germany (21 Jan 82), Ghana (3 Jun 91), Greece (23 Sep 82), Guatemala (3 Nov 97), Guinea (2 Oct 2002), Guyana (10 Dec 97), Honduras (21 Aug 2001), Hungary (14 Jan 85), Iceland (25 Jun 85), India (24 Sep 86), Iran (25 Oct 2002), Ireland (6 Jan 95), Israel (31 Aug 83), Italy (1 Oct 82), Jamaica (13 Mar 91), Jordan (2 Jun 2006), Kazakhstan (7 Mar 94), Kenya (15 Dec 92), Kiribati (5 Feb 2007), Korea (North) (1 May 85), Korea (South) (23 Jul 84), Kuwait (7 Aug 2007), Latvia (20 May 92), Lebanon (18 Jul 83), Liberia (28 Oct 80), Libya (28 Apr 2005), Lithuania (4 Dec 91), Luxembourg (14 Feb 91), Madagascar (30 Nov 2005), Malawi (17 Dec 2001), Malaysia (31 Jan 97), Maldives (20 May 2005), Malta (21 Jun 91), Marshall Islands (26 Apr 88), Mauritania (24 Nov 97), Mauritius (6 Apr 95), Mexico (23 Apr 92), Moldova (11 Jan 2006), Monaco (20 Aug 92), Mongolia (15 Oct 2003), Montenegro (3 Jun 2006), Morocco (12 Oct 93), Mozambique (9 Feb 2006), Myanmar (Burma) (4 May 88), Namibia (18 Dec 2002), Netherlands (30 Jun 83), New Zealand (25 Sep 98), Nicaragua (1 Feb 2001), Nigeria (24 May 2002), Norway (15 Jul 80), Pakistan (22 Nov 94), Palau (29 Sep 2011), Panama (20 Feb 85), Papua New Guinea (25 Oct 93), Peru (25 Apr 80), Philippines (15 Jun 2001), Poland (1 Apr 86), Portugal (22 Oct 87), Qatar (8 Mar 2006), Romania (15 Apr 93), Russia (3 Nov 83), Samoa (7 Feb 2002), São Tomé/Príncipe (29 Oct 98), Saudi Arabia (23 May 2005), Senegal (16 Jan 97), Serbia (3 Jun 2006), Seychelles (28 Nov 90), Singapore (1 Nov 90), Sierra Leone (26 Jul 2001), Slovakia (1 Jan 93), Slovenia (25 Jun 91), South Africa (28 Nov 84), Spain (6 Jul 84), Sri Lanka (24 Jun 97), St Kitts/Nevis (24 Dec 97), St Lucia (12 Jul 2000), St Vincent/Grenadines (28 Oct 83), Solomon Islands (30 Jun 2004), Suriname (4 No 88), Sweden (9 Jun 80), Switzerland (15 Dec 87),Tanzania (23 Jul 2008), Thailand (2 Nov 2007), Togo (9 Feb 90), Tonga (1 Feb 96), Trinidad/Tobago (6 Mar 2000), Tunisia (10 Oct 80), Turkey (10 Oct 90), Turkmenistan (4 Feb 2009), Tuvalu (22 Aug 85), United Arab Emirates (15 Jan 2007), Uruguay (30 Apr 79), Vanuatu (13 Apr 89), Venezuela (29 Jul 94), Vietnam (29 May 91)

Protocol ratified/acceded/accepted with qualifications: 14
Algeria (31 Jan 89), Argentina (31 Aug 93), Brazil (29 Jan 88), Bulgaria (12 Dec 84), Canada (16 Nov 92), Denmark (27 Nov 80), France (25 Sep 81), Indonesia (21 Oct 86), Japan (9 Jun 83), Oman (13 Mar 84), Syria (9 Nov 88), Ukraine (25 Oct 93), United Kingdom (22 May 80), United States (12 Aug 80)

Optional Annex III ratified/acceded/accepted: 135
Optional Annex IV ratified/acceded/accepted: 129
Optional Annex V ratified/acceded/accepted: 143
1997 Amending Protocol (adding Annex VI) ratified/acceded/accepted without qualification: 67

* Parties to the protocol are required to accept annexes I and II.

3.8 UNITED NATIONS CONVENTION ON THE LAW OF THE SEA
Concluded: 10 Dec 82
Entered into force: 16 Nov 94
Total parties: 162

Signed but not ratified: 16

Afghanistan (18 Mar 83), Bhutan (10 Dec 82), Burundi (10 Dec 82), Cambodia (1 Jul 83), Central African Republic (4 Dec 84), Colombia (10 Dec 82), El Salvador (5 Dec 84), Ethiopia (10 Dec 82), Iran (10 Dec 82), Korea (North) (10 Dec 82), Libya (3 Dec 84), Liechtenstein (30 Nov 84), Niger(10 Dec 82), Rwanda (10 Dec 82), Swaziland (18 Jan 84), United Arab Emirates (10 Dec 82)

Ratified/acceded/accepted without qualification: 126

Albania (23 Jun 2003), Angola (5 Dec 90), Antigua/Barbuda (2 Feb 89), Armenia (9 Dec 2002), Australia (5 Oct 94), Austria (14 Jul 95), Bahamas (29 Jul 83), Bahrain (30 May 85), Barbados (12 Oct 93), Belarus (30 Aug 2006), Belgium (13 Nov 98), Belize (13 Aug 83), Benin (16 Oct 97), Bolivia (28 Apr 95), Bosnia–Herzegovina (12 Jan 94), Botswana (2 May 90), Brunei (5 Nov 96), Bulgaria (15 May 96), Burkina Faso (25 Jan 2005), Cameroon (19 Nov 85), Canada (7 Nov 2003), Chad (14 Aug 2009), Comoros (21 Jun 94), Congo (Brazzaville) (9 Jul 2008), Congo (Kinshasa) (17 Feb 89), Cook Islands (15 Feb 95), Costa Rica (21 Sep 92), Côte d'Ivoire (26 Mar 84), Croatia (5 Apr 95), Cuba (15 Aug 84), Cyprus (12 Dec 88), Czech Republic (21 Jun 96), Denmark (16 Nov 2004), Djibouti (8 Oct 91), Dominica (24 Oct 91), Dominican Republic (10 Jul 2009), Estonia (26 Aug 2005), European Community (1 Apr 98), Fiji (10 Dec 82), Gabon (11 Mar 98), Gambia (22 May 84), Georgia (21 Mar 96), Germany (14 Oct 94), Ghana (7 Jun 83), Grenada (25 Apr 91), Guinea (6 Sep 85), Guinea–Bissau (25 Aug 86), Guyana (16 Nov 93), Haiti (31 Jul 96), Honduras (5 Oct 93), Hungary (5 Feb 2002), Indonesia (3 Feb 86), Iraq (30 Jul 85), Ireland (21 Jun 96), Jamaica (21 Mar 83), Japan (20 Jun 96), Jordan (27 Nov 95), Kenya (2 Mar 89), Kiribati (24 Feb 2003), Korea (South) (29 Jan 96), Kuwait (2 May 86), Laos (5 Jun 98), Latvia (23 Dec 2004), Lebanon (5 Jan 95), Lesotho (31 May 2007), Liberia (25 Sep 2008), Lithuania (12 Nov 2003), Luxembourg (5 Oct 2000), Macedonia (19 Aug 94), Madagascar (22 Aug 2001), Malawi (28 Sep 2011), Maldives (7 Sep 2000), Mali (16 Jul 85), Marshall Islands (9 Aug 91), Mauritania (17 Jul 96), Mauritius (4 Nov 94), Mexico (18 Mar 83), Micronesia (29 Apr 91), Moldova (6 Feb 2007), Monaco (20 Mar 96), Mongolia (13 Aug 96), Montenegro (23 Oct 2006), Morocco (31 May 2007), Mozambique (13 Mar 97), Myanmar (Burma) (21 May 96), Namibia (18 Apr 83), Nauru (23 Jan 96), Nepal (2 Nov 98), Netherlands (28 Jun 96), New Zealand (19 Jul 96), Nicaragua (3 May 2000), Nigeria (14 Aug 86), Niue (11 Oct 2006), Norway (24 Jun 96), Palau (30 Sep 96), Papua New Guinea (14 Jan 97), Paraguay (26 Sep 86), Poland (13 Nov 98), Samoa (14 Aug 95), Senegal (25 Oct 84), Seychelles (16 Sep 91), Sierra Leone (12 Dec 94), Singapore (17 Nov 94), Slovakia (8 May 96)), Solomon Islands (23 Jun 97), Somalia (24 Jul 89), South Africa (23 Dec 97), Sri Lanka (19 Jul 94), St Kitts/Nevis (7 Jan 93), St Lucia (27 Mar 85), St Vincent/Grenadines (1 Oct 93), Sudan (23 Jan 85), Suriname (9 Jul 98), Switzerland (1 May 2009), Thailand (15 May 2010), Tanzania (30 Sep 85), Togo (16 Apr 85), Tonga (2 Aug 95), Trinidad/Tobago (25 Apr 86), Tuvalu (9 Dec 2002), Uganda (9 Nov 90), United Kingdom (25 Jul 97), Vanuatu (10 Aug 99), Vietnam (25 Jul 94), Zambia (7 Mar 83), Zimbabwe (24 Feb 93)

Ratified/acceded/accepted with qualification: 36

Algeria (11 Jun 96), Argentina (1 Dec 95), Bangladesh (27 Jun 2001), Brazil (22 Dec 88), Cape Verde (10 Aug 87), Chile (25 Aug 97), China (7 Jun 96), Egypt (26 Aug 83), Equatorial Guinea (21 Jul 97), Finland (21 Jun 96), France (11 Apr 96), Greece (21 Jul 95), Guatemala (11 Feb 97), Iceland (21 Jun 85), India (29 Jun 95), Italy (13 Jan 95), Malaysia (14 Oct 96), Malta (20 May 93), Oman (17 Aug 89), Pakistan (26 Feb 97), Panama (1 Jul 96), Philippines (8 May 84), Portugal (3 Nov 97), Qatar (9 Dec 2002), Romania (17 Dec 96), Russia (12 Mar 97), São Tomé/Príncipe (3 Nov 87), Saudi Arabia (24 Apr 96), Serbia (12 Mar 2001), Slovenia (16 Jun 95), Spain (15 Jan 97), Sweden (25 Jun 96), Tunisia (24 Apr 85), Ukraine (26 Jul 99), Uruguay (10 Dec 92), Yemen (21 Jul 87)

3.9 CONVENTION FOR THE PROTECTION AND DEVELOPMENT OF THE MARINE ENVIRON-
MENT OF THE WIDER CARIBBEAN REGION (CARTAGENA CONVENTION)
Concluded: 24 Mar 1983
Entered into force: 11 Oct. 1986
Signed but not ratified: 3
Honduras (24 Mar 83), Nicaragua (24 Mar 83), EEC (24 Mar 83)
Ratified/acceded/accepted/approved: 22
Antigua & Barbuda (11 Sep 86), Barbados (28 May 85), Belize (22 Sep 99),
Colombia (3 Mar 88), Costa Rica (1 Aug 91), Cuba (15 Sep 88), Dominica (5 Oct
90), Dominican Republic (24 Nov 98), France (13 Nov 85), Grenada (17 Aug 87),
Guatemala (18 Dec 89), Jamaica (1 Apr 87), Mexico (11 Apr 85), Netherlands (16
Apr 84), Panama (7 Nov 87), St. Kitts & Nevis (15 Jun 99), Saint Lucia (30 Nov
84), St. Vincent & the Grenadines (11 Jul 90), Trinidad & Tobago (24 Jan 86),
United Kingdom (28 Feb 86), United States (31 Oct 84), Venezuela (18 Dec 86)

3.10 MONTREAL GUIDELINES FOR THE PROTECTION OF THE MARINE ENVIRONMENT
AGAINST POLLUTION FROM LAND-BASED SOURCES
Adopted: 24 May 85

3.11 CONVENTION FOR THE PROTECTION OF THE NATURAL RESOURCES AND ENVIRON-
MENT OF THE SOUTH PACIFIC REGION
Concluded: 25 Nov 86
Entered into force: 22 Aug 90
Total parties: 12
Signed but not ratified: 3
Palau (25 Nov 86), Tuvalu (14 Aug 87), United Kingdom (16 Jul 87)
Ratified/accepted/approved without qualification: 10
Australia (19 Jul 89), Cook Islands (9 Sep 87), Fiji (18 Sep 89), Marshall Islands
(4 May 87), Micronesia (29 Nov 88), Nauru (28 Aug 95), New Zealand (3 May
90), Papua New Guinea (15 Sep 89), Samoa (23 Jul 90), Solomon Islands (10
Aug 89)
Ratified/accepted/approved with qualification: 2 (as of at least 1 Mar 97)
France (17 Jul 90), United States (10 Jun 91)

3.12 INTERNATIONAL CONVENTION ON OIL POLLUTION PREPAREDNESS, RESPONSE, AND
CO-OPERATION
Concluded: 30 November 1990
Entered into force: 13 May 1995
Total parties: 103
Signed but not ratified: 4
Côte d'Ivoire (30 Nov 90), Gambia (30 Nov 91), Ghana (30 Nov 90), Philippines
(30 Nov 90)
Ratified/acceded/accepted without qualification: 101
Albania (2 Jan 2008), Algeria (8 Mar 2005), Angola (4 Oct 2001), Antigua/Barbu-
da (5 Apr 99), Argentina (13 Jul 94), Australia (6 Jul 92), Azerbaijan (16 Jul
2004), Bahamas (4 Oct 2001), Bangladesh (23 Jul 2004), Benin (5 Feb 2010),
Brazil (21 Jul 98), Bulgaria (5 Apr 2001), Cameroon (18 Sep 2009), Canada (7
Mar 94), Cape Verde (4 Jul 2003), Chile (15 Oct 97), China (30 Mar 98),
Comoros (5 Jan 2000), Congo (Brazzaville) (7 Sep 2004), Croatia (12 Jan 98),
Cuba (10 Apr 2008), Djibouti (19 Jan 98), Dominica (31 Aug 2001), Ecuador (29
Jan 2002), Egypt (29 Jun 92), El Salvador (9 Oct 95), Estonia (16 May 2008),
Finland (21 Jul 93), France (6 Nov 92), Gabon (12 Apr 2005), Georgia (20 Feb

96), Germany (15 Feb 95), Ghana (2 Jun 2010), Greece (7 Mar 95), Guinea (2 Oct 2002), Guyana (10 Mar 98), Iceland (21 Jun 93), India (11 Nov 97), Iran (25 Feb 98), Ireland (26 Apr 2001), Israel (24 Mar 99), Italy (2 Mar 99), Jamaica (8 Sep 2000), Japan (17 Oct 95), Jordan (14 Apr 2004), Kenya (21 Jul 99), Korea (South) (9 Nov 99), Latvia (30 Nov 2001), Lebanon (30 Mar 2005), Liberia (5 Oct 95), Lithuania (23 Dec 2002), Libya (18 Jun 2004), Madagascar (20 May 2002), Malaysia (30 Jul 97), Malta (21 Jan 2003), Marshall Islands (16 Oct 95), Mauritania (22 Nov 99), Mauritius (2 Dec 99), Mexico (13 May 95), Monaco (19 Oct 99), Morocco (29 Apr 2003), Mozambique (9 Nov 2005), Namibia (18 Jun 2007), Netherlands (1 Dec 94), New Zealand (2 Jul 99), Nigeria (25 May 93), Norway (8 Mar 94), Oman (26 Jun 2008), Pakistan (21 Jul 93), Palau (29 Sep 2011), Peru (24 Apr 2002), Poland (12 Jun 2003), Portugal (27 Feb 2006), Qatar (8 May 2007), Romania (17 Nov 2000), Russia (18 Sep 2009), Samoa (18 May 2004), Saudi Arabia (30 July 2009), Senegal (24 Mar 94), Seychelles (26 Jun 92), Sierra Leone (10 Mar 2008), Singapore (10 Mar 99), Slovenia (31 May 2001), South Africa (4 Jul 2008), Spain (12 Jan 94), St Kitts/Nevis (7 Oct 2004), St Lucia (20 May 2004), Sweden (30 Mar 92), Switzerland (4 Jul 96), Syria (14 Mar 2003), Tanzania (16 May 2006), Thailand (20 Apr 2000), Tonga (1 Feb 96), Trinidad/Tobago (6 Mar 2000), Tunisia (23 Oct 95), Turkey (1 Jul 2004), United Kingdom (16 Sep 97), United States (27 Mar 92), Uruguay (27 Sep 94), Vanuatu (18 Feb 99), Venezuela (12 Dec 94)
Ratified/acceded/accepted with qualification: 2
Colombia (11 Jun 2008), Denmark (22 Oct 96)

3.13 **INTERNATIONAL CONVENTION ON CIVIL LIABILITY FOR OIL POLLUTION DAMAGE, 1992**
The 1992 Oil Pollution Damage Liability Convention is an updated version of the 1969 International Convention on Civil Liability for Oil Pollution Damage, revised and renamed by a 1992 Protocol. The status information covers both the 1969 Convention and the 1992 Convention.

1969 Convention:

> ***Concluded:*** 29 Nov 69
> ***Entered into force:*** 19 Jun 75
> ***Total parties to 1969 Civil Liability Convention:*** 38

1992 Convention:

> ***Concluded:*** 27 Nov 92
> ***Entered into force:*** 30 May 96
> ***Total parties to 1992 Civil Liability Convention:*** 126
> ***Ratified/accepted/approved without qualification:*** 124
> Albania (30 Jun 2005), Algeria (11 Jun 98), Angola (4 Oct 2001), Antigua/Barbuda (14 Jun 2000), Argentina (13 Oct 2000), Australia (9 Oct 1995), Bahamas (1 Apr 97), Azerbaijan (16 Jul 2004), Bahrain (3 May 96), Barbados (7 Jul 98), Belgium (6 Oct 98), Belize (27 Nov 98), Benin (5 Feb 2010), Brunei (2 Jan 2002), Bulgaria (28 Nov 2003), Cambodia (8 Jun 2001), Cameroon (15 Oct 2001), Canada (29 May 98), Cape Verde (4 Jul 2003), Chile (29 May 2002), China (5 Jan 99), Colombia (19 Nov 2001), Comoros (5 Jan 2000), Congo (7 Aug 2002), Cook Islands (12 Mar 2007), Croatia (12 Jan 98), Cyprus (12 May 97), Denmark (30 May 95), Djibouti (8 Jan 2001), Dominica (31 Aug 2001), Dominican Republic (24 Jun 99), Ecuador (11 Dec 2007), Egypt (21 Apr 95), El Salvador (31 Jan 2002), Estonia (6 Jul 2004), Fiji (30 Nov 99), Finland (24 Nov 95), France (29 Sep 94), Gabon (31 May 2002), Georgia (18 Apr 2000), Germany (29 Sep 94), Ghana (3 Feb 2003), Greece (9 Oct 95), Grenada (7 Jan 98), Guinea (2 Oct 2002), Hungary (30 Mar 2007), Iceland (13 Nov 98), India

(15 Nov 99), Indonesia (18 Mar 99), Iran (24 Oct 2007), Ireland (15 May 97), Israel (21 Oct 2004), Italy (16 Sep 99), Jamaica (6 Jun 97), Japan (24 Aug 94), Kenya (2 Feb 2000), Kiribati (5 Feb 2007), Korea (South) (7 Mar 97), Kuwait (16 Apr 2004), Latvia (9 Mar 98), Lebanon (30 Mar 2005), Liberia (5 Oct 95), Lithuania (27 Jun 2000), Luxembourg (21 Nov 2005), Madagascar (21 May 2002), Malaysia (9 Jun 2004), Maldives (20 May 2005), Malta (6 Jan 2000), Marshall Islands (16 Oct 95), Mauritius (6 Dec 99), Mexico (30 May 94), Moldova (11 Oct 2005), Monaco (8 Nov 96), Mongolia (8 Aug 2008), Morocco (22 Aug 2000), Mozambique (26 Apr 2002), Namibia (19 Nov 2002), Netherlands (15 Nov 96), Nigeria (24 May 2002), Norway (3 Apr 95), Oman (8 Jul 94), Pakistan (2 Mar 2005), Palau (29 Sep 2011), Panama (18 Mar 99), Papua New Guinea (23 Jan 2001), Peru (1 Sep 2005), Philippines (7 Jul 97), Poland (21 Dec 99), Portugal (13 Nov 2001), Qatar (20 Nov 2001), Romania (27 Nov 2000), Russia (20 Mar 2000), Samoa (1 Feb 2002), Saudi Arabia (23 May 2005), Senegal (2 Aug 2011), Serbia (25 May 2011), Seychelles (23 Jul 99), Sierra Leone (4 Jun 2001), Singapore (18 Sep 97), Slovenia (19 Jul 2000), Solomon Islands (30 Jun 2004), South Africa (1 Sep 2004), Spain (6 Jul 95), Sri Lanka (22 Jan 99), St Kitts/Nevis (7 Oct 2004), St Lucia (20 May 2004), St Vincent/Grenadines (9 Oct 2001), Sweden (25 May 95), Switzerland (4 Jul 96), Syria (22 Feb 2005), Tanzania (18 Dec 2002), Tonga (10 Dec 99), Trinidad/Tobago (6 Mar 2000), Tunisia (29 Jan 97), Turkmenistan (21 Sep 2009), Tuvalu (30 Jun 2004), Ukraine (29 Nov 2007), United Arab Emirates (19 Nov 97), United Kingdom (29 Sep 94), Uruguay (9 Jul 97), Vanuatu (18 Feb 99), Venezuela (22 Jul 98), Vietnam (17 Jun 2003)

Ratified/accepted/approved with qualification: 2

New Zealand (25 Jun 98), Turkey (17 Aug 2001)

Associate members: 3

Faroe Islands, Hong Kong, Macau

3.14   INTERNATIONAL CONVENTION ON THE ESTABLISHMENT OF AN INTERNATIONAL FUND FOR COMPENSATION FOR OIL POLLUTION DAMAGE, 1992

The 1992 Fund Convention is an updated version of the 1971 International Convention on the Establishment of an International Fund for Compensation for Oil Pollution Damage, as revised and renamed by a 1992 Protocol. The status information provided below covers both the 1971 Convention and the 1992 Convention.

1971 Convention:

Concluded: 18 Dec 71

Entered into force: 16 Oct 78

Total parties to 1971 Fund Convention: 14

1992 Convention:

Concluded: 27 Nov 92

Entered into force: 30 May 96

Total parties to 1992 Fund Convention: 108

Ratified/acceded/accepted without qualifications: 104

Albania (30 Jun 2005), Algeria (11 Jun 98), Angola (4 Oct 2001), Antigua/Barbuda (14 Jun 2000), Argentina (13 Oct 2000), Australia (9 Oct 95), Bahamas (1 Apr 97), Bahrain (3 May 96), Barbados (7 Jul 98), Belgium (6 Oct 98), Belize (27 Nov 98), Benin (5 Feb 2010), Brunei (31 Jan 2002), Bulgaria (18 Nov 2005), Cambodia (8 Jun 2001), Cameroon (15 Oct 2001), Canada (29 May 98), Cape Verde (4 Jul 2003), Colombia (19 Nov 2001), Comoros (5 Jan 2000), Congo (7 Aug 2002), Cook Islands (12 Mar 2007), Croatia (12 Jan 98), Cyprus (12 May 97), Denmark (30 May 95), Djibouti (8 Jan 2001), Dominica (31 Aug

2001), Dominican Republic (24 Jun 99), Ecuador (11 Dec 2007), Estonia (6 Aug 2004), Fiji (30 Nov 99), Finland (24 Nov 95), France (29 Sep 94), Gabon (31 May 2002), Georgia (18 Apr 2000), Germany (29 Sep 94), Ghana (3 Feb 2003), Greece (9 Oct 95), Grenada (7 Jan 98), Guinea (2 Oct 2002), Hungary (30 Mar 2007), Iceland (13 Nov 98), India (21 Jun 2000), Iran (5 Nov 2008), Ireland (15 May 97), Israel (21 Oct 2004), Italy (16 Sep 99), Jamaica (24 Jun 97), Japan (24 Aug 94), Kenya (2 Feb 2000), Kiribati (5 Feb 2007), Korea (South) (7 Mar 97), Latvia (6 Apr 98), Liberia (5 Oct 95), Lithuania (27 Jun 2000), Luxembourg (21 Nov 2005), Madagascar (21 May 2002), Malaysia (9 Jun 2004), Maldives (20 May 2005), Malta (6 Jan 2000), Marshall Islands (16 Oct 95), Mauritius (6 Dec 99), Mexico (13 May 94), Monaco (8 Nov 96), Morocco (22 Aug 2000), Mozambique (26 Apr 2002), Namibia (18 Dec 2002), Netherlands (15 Nov 97), Nigeria (24 May 2002), Norway (3 Apr 95), Oman (8 Jul 94), Palau (29 Sep 2011), Panama (18 Mar 99), Papua New Guinea (23 Jan 2001), Philippines (7 Jul 97), Poland (21 Dec 99), Portugal (13 Nov 2001), Qatar (20 Nov 2001), Russia (20 Mar 2000), Samoa (1 Feb 2002), Senegal (2 Aug 2011), Serbia (15 May 2011), Seychelles (23 Jul 99), Sierra Leone (4 Jun 2001), Singapore (31 Dec 97), Slovenia (19 Jul 2000), South Africa (1 Oct 2004), Spain (6 Jul 95), Sri Lanka (22 Jan 99), St Kitts/Nevis (2 Mar 2005), St Lucia (20 May 2004), St Vincent/Grenadines (9 Oct 2001), Sweden (25 May 95), Switzerland (10 Oct 2005), Tanzania (19 Nov 2002), Tonga (10 Dec 99), Trinidad/Tobago (6 Mar 2000), Tunisia (29 Jan 97), Tuvalu (30 Jun 2004), United Arab Emirates (19 Nov 97), United Kingdom (29 Sep 94), Uruguay (9 Jul 97), Vanuatu (18 Feb 99), Venezuela (22 Jul 98)

Ratified/acceded/accepted with qualification: 4

China (5 Jan 99), New Zealand (25 Jun 98), Syria (24 Apr 2009), Turkey (17 Aug 2001)

3.15   1997 SHIPS' ROUTEING AMENDMENT TO THE INTERNATIONAL CONVENTION FOR THE SAFETY OF LIFE AT SEA (SOLAS)

Adopted: 16 May 95
Entered into force: 1 Jan 97
Parties to SOLAS: 161

Albania (7 Jun 2004), Algeria (3 Nov 83), Angola (3 Oct 91), Antigua and Barbuda (9 Feb 87), Argentina (5 December 1979), Australia (17 Aug 83), Austria (27 May 88), Azerbaijan (1 Jul 97), Bahamas (16 Feb 79), Bahrain (21 Oct 85), Bangladesh (6 Nov 81), Barbados (1 Sep 82), Belarus (7 Jan 94), Belgium (24 Sep 79), Belize (2 Apr 91), Benin (1 Nov 85), Bolivia (4 Jun 99), Brazil (22 May 80), Brunei Darussalam (23 Oct 86), Bulgaria (2 Nov 83), Cambodia (28 Nov 94), Cameroon (14 May 84), Canada (8 May 78), Cape Verde (28 Apr 77), Chile (28 Mar 80), China (7 Jan 80), Colombia (31 Oct 80), Comoros (22 Nov 2000), Congo (Brazzaville) (10 Sep 85), Congo (Kinshasa) (17 Dec 2004), Cook Islands (30 Jun 2003), Costa Rica (6 Jun 2011), Cote D'Ivoire (5 Oct 87), Croatia (8 Oct 91), Cuba (19 Jun 92), Cyprus (11 Oct 85), Czech Republic (1 Jan 93), Dominica (21 Jun 2000), Denmark (8 Mar 78), Djibouti (1 Mar 84), Dominican Republic (10 Apr 80), Ecuador (28 May 82), Egypt (4 Sep 81), Equatorial Guinea (24 Apr 96), Eritrea (22 Apr 96), Estonia (16 Dec 91), Ethiopia (18 Jul 85), Fiji (4 Mar 83), Finland (21 Nov 80), France (1 Nov 74), Gabon (21 Apr 82), Gambia (1 Nov 91), Georgia (19 Apr 94), Germany (26 Mar 79), Ghana (19 May 83), Greece (12 May 80), Grenada (28 Jun 2004), Guatemala (22 Oct 82), Guinea (19 Apr 81), Guyana (10 Dec 97), Haiti (6 Apr 89), Honduras (24 Sep 85), Hungary (9 Jan 80), Iceland (6 Jul 83), India (16 Jun 76), Indonesia (17 Feb 81), Iran (17 Oct 94), Iraq (14 Dec 90), Ireland (29 Nov 83), Israel (15 May 79), Italy (11 Jun 80), Jamaica (14 Oct 83), Japan (15 May 80), Jordan (7 Aug 85) Kazakhstan (7 Mar 94), Korea (North) (1 Aug 85), Korea

(South) (31 Dec 80), Kenya (21 Jul 99), Kiribati (5 Feb 2007), Kuwait (29 Jun 79), Latvia (20 May 92), Lebanon (29 Nov 83), Liberia (14 Nov 77), Libya (2 Jul 81), Lithuania (4 Dec 91), Luxembourg (14 Feb 91), Madagascar (7 Jun 96), Malawi (9 Mar 93), Malaysia (19 Oct 83), Maldives (14 Jan 81), Malta (8 Aug 86), Marshall Islands (26 Apr 88), Mauritania (24 Nov 97), Mauritius (1 Feb 88), Mexico (28 Nov 77), Moldova (11 Oct 2005), Monaco (1 Nov 74), Mongolia (26 Jun 2002), Montenegro (3 Jun 2006), Morocco (28 Jun 90), Mozambique (23 Dec 96), Myanmar (11 Nov 87), Namibia (27 Nov 2000), Netherlands (10 Jul 78),New Zealand (23 May 90),Nicaragua (17 Dec 2004), Nigeria (7 May 81), Norway (15 Feb 77)), Oman (25 Apr 85), Pakistan (10 Apr 85), Palau (29 Sep 2011), Panama (9 Mar 78), Papua New Guinea (12 Nov 80), Paraguay (15 Jun 2004), Peru (4 Dec 79), Philippines (15 Dec 81), Poland (15 Mar 84), Portugal (7 Nov 83), Qatar (22 Dec 80), Romania (24 May 79), Russia (9 Jan 80), St. Kitts & Nevis (11 Jun 2004), Saint Lucia (20 May 2004), Saint Vincent and the Grenadines (28 Oct 83), Samoa (14 Mar 97), São Tomé & Principe (29 Oct 98), Saudi Arabia (24 Apr 85), Senegal (6 Jan 97), Serbia (3 Jun 2006), Seychelles (10 May 88), Sierra Leone (13 Aug 93), Singapore (16 Mar 81), Slovakia (1 Jan 93), Slovenia (25 Jun 91), Solomon Islands (30 Jun 2004), South Africa (23 May 80), Spain (5 Sep 78), Sri Lanka (30 Aug 83), Sudan (15 May 90), Suriname (4 Nov 88), Sweden (7 Jul 78), Switzerland (1 Oct 81), Syria (20 Jul 2001), Tanzania (28 Mar 2001), Thailand (18 Dec 84), Togo (19 Jul 89), Tonga (12 Apr 77), Trinidad and Tobago (15 Feb 79), Tunisia (6 Aug 80), Turkey (31 Jul 80), Turkmenistan (4 Feb 2009), Tuvalu (22 Aug 85), Ukraine (1 Nov 74), United Arab Emirates (15 Dec 83), United Kingdom (7 Oct 77), United States (7 Sep 78), Uruguay (30 Apr 79), Vanuatu (28 Jul 82), Venezuela (1 Nov 74), Viet Nam (18 Dec 90), Yemen (6 Mar 79)

3.16 GLOBAL PROGRAMME OF ACTION FOR THE PROTECTION OF THE MARINE ENVIRON-MENT FROM LAND-BASED ACTIVITIES
Adopted by consensus: 3 Nov 95
Conferees: 110
Antigua and Barbuda, Argentina, Australia, Bahrain, Bangladesh, Belarus, Belgium, Belize, Benin, Bhutan, Botswana, Brazi, Bulgaria, Burkina Faso, Burundi, Cambodia, Cameroon, Canada, Chad, Chile, China, Colombia, Comoros, Congo, Costa Rica, Cote D'ivoire, Croatia, Cuba, Denmark, Dominica, Ecuador, Egypt, Estonia, Ethiopia, Finland, France, Gambia, Georgia, Germany, Ghana, Greece, Honduras, Iceland, India, Indonesia, Israel, Italy, Jamaica, Japan, Jordan, Kazakstan, Kenya, Kiribati, Kuwait, Malawi, Malaysia, Maldives, Malta, Marshall Islands, Mauritius, Mexico, Micronesia (Federated States of), Monaco, Mozambique, Nauru, Netherlands, New Zealand, Nicaragua, Niger, Nigeria, Norway, Pakistan, Peru, Philippines, Poland, Republic of Korea, Romania, Russian Federation, Rwanda, Saint Lucia, Samoa, Sao Tome and Principe, Saudi Arabia, Senegal, Seychelles, Sierra Leone, Slovenia, South Africa, Spain, Sri Lanka, Sweden, Switzerland, Thailand, Togo, Tunisia, Turkey, Turkmenistan, Uganda, United Kingdom of Great Britain and Northern Ireland, United Republic of Tanzania, United States of America, Uruguay, Vanuatu, Venezuela, Yemen, Zaire, Zambia, Zimbabwe

3.17 WASHINGTON DECLARATION ON PROTECTION OF THE MARINE ENVIRONMENT FROM LAND-BASED ACTIVITIES
Adopted by consensus: 1 Nov 95
Conferees: See Basic Document 3.16, *supra*

3.18 1996 PROTOCOL (ON DUMPING AND INCINERATION OF WASTES AND OTHER MATTER AT SEA) TO THE 1972 LONDON CONVENTION ON THE PREVENTION OF MARINE POLLUTION BY DUMPING OF WASTES AND OTHER MATTER
Adopted: 7 Nov 1996
Entered into force: 24 Mar 2006
Supersedes Basic Document 3.6 for States that are parties to both.
Total Parties: 41
Ratified/acceded/accepted without qualification: 37
Angola (4 Oct 2001), Australia (4 Dec 2000), Barbados (25 Jul 2006), Belgium (13 Feb 2006), Bulgaria (25 Jan 2006), Canada (15 May 2000), Chile (26 Sep 2011), Egypt (26 May 2004), France (7 Jan 2004), Georgia (18 Apr 2000), Germany (16 Oct 98), Ghana (2 Jun 2010), Iceland (21 May 2003), Ireland (26 Apr 2001), Italy (13 Oct 2006), Japan (2 Oct 2007), Kenya (14 Jan 2008), Luxembourg (21 Nov 2005), Marshall Islands (9 May 2008), Mexico (22 Feb 2006), Netherlands (24 Sep 2008), Nigeria (1 Oct 2010), Norway (16 Dec 99), St Kitts/Nevis (7 Oct 2004), Saudi Arabia (2 Feb 2006), Sierra Leone (10 Mar 2008), Slovenia (3 Mar 2006), South Africa (23 Dec 98), Spain (24 Mar 99), Suriname (11 Feb 2007), Sweden (16 Oct 2000), Switzerland (8 Sep 2000), Tonga (18 Sep 2003), Trinidad/Tobago (6 Mar 2000), United Kingdom (15 Dec 98), Vanuatu (18 Feb 99), Yemen (24 Jan 2011)
Ratified/acceded/accepted with qualification: 4
Denmark (17 Apr 97), China (29 Sep 2006), Korea (South) (22 Jan 2009), New Zealand (30 Jul 2001)

3.19 PROTOCOL CONCERNING POLLUTION FROM LAND-BASED SOURCES AND ACTIVITIES TO THE [CARTAGENA] CONVENTION FOR THE PROTECTION AND DEVELOPMENT OF THE MARINE ENVIRONMENT OF THE WIDER CARIBBEAN
Adopted: 6 Oct 1999
Entered into force: 13 Aug 2010
Signed but not ratified: 4
Colombia (2 Oct 2000), Costa Rica (6 Oct 99), Dominican Republic (3 Aug 2000), Netherlands (6 Oct 99)
Ratified/acceded/accepted/approved: 6
Belize (4 Jan 2008), France (4 May 2007), Panama (9 Jul 2003), Saint Lucia (30 Jan 2008), Trinidad & Tobago (28 Mar 2003), United States (13 Feb 2009)

3.20 PROTOCOL OF 2003 [SUPPLEMENTARY FUND PROTOCOL] TO THE INTERNATIONAL CONVENTION ON THE ESTABLISHMENT OF AN INTERNATIONAL FUND FOR COMPENSATION FOR OIL POLLUTION DAMAGE, 1992
Adopted: 16 May 2003
Entered into force: 3 March 2005
Ratified/acceded/accepted without qualification: 27
Australia (13 July 2009), Barbados (6 December 2005), Belgium (4 November 2005), Canada (2 October 2009), Croatia (17 February 2006), Denmark (24 February 2004), Estonia (14 October 2008), Finland (27 May 2004), France (29 June 2004), Germany (24 November 2004), Greece (23 October 2006), Hungary (30 March 2007), Ireland (signature) 5 July 2004), Italy (20 October 2005), Japan (13 July 2004), Latvia (18 April 2006), Lithuania (22 November 2005), Morocco (4 November 2009), Netherlands (16 June 2005), Norway (31 March 2004), Poland (9 December 2008), Portugal (15 February 2005), Republic of Korea ((6 May 2010), Slovenia (3 March 2006), Spain (3 December 2004), Sweden (5 May 2005), United Kingdom (8 June 2006)

3.21 GUIDELINES ON PLACES OF REFUGE FOR SHIPS IN NEED OF ASSISTANCE
Adopted by the IMO Assembly: 5 December 2003

3.22 REVISED GUIDELINES FOR THE IDENTIFICATION AND DESIGNATION OF PARTICULARLY
SENSITIVE SEA AREAS
Adopted by the IMO Assembly: 1 December 2005

B. Freshwater Resources

3.23 TREATY BETWEEN CANADA AND THE UNITED STATES RELATING TO BOUNDARY
WATERS AND QUESTIONS ARISING ALONG THE BOUNDARY BETWEEN THE UNITED
STATES AND CANADA
Concluded: 11 Jan 09
Entered into force: 5 May 10

3.24 HELSINKI RULES ON THE USES OF THE WATERS OF INTERNATIONAL RIVERS
Adopted by the International Law Association: 20 August 66
Superseded by Basic Document 3.28, infra

3.25 SEOUL RULES ON INTERNATIONAL GROUNDWATERS.
Adopted by the International Law Association: 24–30 Aug 87
Superseded by Basic Document 3.28, infra

3.26 CONVENTION ON THE PROTECTION AND USE OF TRANSBOUNDARY WATERCOURSES
AND INTERNATIONAL LAKES
Concluded: 17 Mar 92
Entered into force: 6 Oct 96
Total parties: 38
Signed but not ratified: 1
United Kingdom (18 Mar 92)
Ratified/acceded/accepted without qualification: 35
Albania (5 Jan 94), Austria (25 Jul 96), Azerbaijan (3 Aug 2000), Belarus (28
May 2003), Belgium (8 Nov 2000), Bosnia & Herzegovina (3 Dec 2009), Bulgaria
(28 Oct 2003),Croatia (8 Jul 96), Czech Republic (12 Jun 2000), Estonia (16 Jun
95), European Community (14 Sep 95), Finland (21 Feb 96), France (30 Jun 98),
Greece (6 Sep 96), Hungary (2 Sep 94), Italy (23 May 96), Kazakhstan (11 Jan
2001), Latvia (10 Dec 96), Liechtenstein (19 Nov 97), Lithuania (28 Apr 2000),
Luxembourg (7 Jun 94), Moldova (4 Jan 94), Netherlands (14 Mar 95), Norway
(1 Apr 93), Poland (15 Mar 2000), Portugal (9 Dec 94), Romania (31 May 95),
Russia (2 Nov 93), Serbia (27 Aug 2010), Slovakia (7 Jul 99), Slovenia (13 Apr
99), Sweden (5 Aug 93), Switzerland (23 May 95), Ukraine (8 Oct 99), Uzbekis-
tan (4 Sep 2007)
Ratified/acceded/accepted with qualification: 3
Denmark (28 May 97), Germany (30 Jan 95), Spain (16 Feb 2000)

3.27 UNITED NATIONS CONVENTION ON THE LAW OF THE NON-NAVIGATIONAL USES OF
INTERNATIONAL WATERCOURSES
Concluded: 21 May 97
Not yet in force
Signed but not ratified: 5
Côte d'Ivoire (25 Sep 98), Luxembourg (14 Oct 97), Paraguay (25 Aug 98),
Venezuela (22 Sep 97), Yemen (17 May 2000)
Ratified/accepted/approved without qualification: 24
Burkina Faso (22 Mar 2011), Finland (23 Jan 98), France (24 Feb 2011),

Germany (15 Jan 2007), Greece (2 Dec 2010), Guinea-Bissau (19 May 2010), Hungary (26 Jan 2000), Iraq (9 Jul 2001), Jordan (22 Jun 99), Lebanon (25 May 99), Libya (14 Jun 2005), Morocco (13 Apr 2011), Namibia (29 Aug 2001), Netherlands (9 Jan 2001), Nigeria (27 Sep 2010), Norway (30 Sep 98), Portugal (22 Jun 2005), Qatar (28 Feb 2002), South Africa (26 Oct 98), Space (24 Sep 2009), Sweden (15 Jun 2000), Syria (2 Apr 98), Tunisia (22 Apr 2009) Uzbekistan (4 Sep 2007)

3.28 BERLIN RULES ON WATER RESOURCES
Adopted by the International Law Association at Berlin: 21 Aug 2004
Supersedes Basic Documents 3.24 & 3.25, supra

3.29 DRAFT ARTICLES ON THE LAW OF TRANSBOUNDARY AQUIFERS
Adopted by the International Law Commission: 4 Jun 2008

4. LITHOSPHERE

A. Chemicals

4.1 FAO INTERNATIONAL CODE OF CONDUCT ON THE DISTRIBUTION AND USE OF PESTICIDES
Adopted: 28 Nov 85

4.2 ILO CONVENTION 162 CONCERNING SAFETY IN THE USE OF ASBESTOS
Adopted: 24 June 1986.
Entered into force: 16 June 1989
1539 UNTS 316

4.3 UNEP GOVERNING COUNCIL DECISION ON LONDON GUIDELINES FOR THE EXCHANGE OF INFORMATION ON CHEMICALS IN INTERNATIONAL TRADE
Adopted: 19 Jun 87

4.4 ROTTERDAM CONVENTION ON THE PRIOR INFORMED CONSENT PROCEDURE FOR CERTAIN HAZARDOUS CHEMICALS AND PESTICIDES IN INTERNATIONAL TRADE
Concluded: 10 Sep 98
Entered into force: 24 Feb 2004
Total parties: 144
Signed but not ratified: 10
Angola (11 Sep 98), Barbados (11 Sep 98), Indonesia (11 Sep 98), Israel (20 May 99), Seychelles (11 Sep 98), St Lucia (25 Jan 99), Tajikistan (28 Sep 98), Tunisia (11 Sep 98), Turkey (11 Sep 98), United States (11 Sep 98)
Ratified/accepted/approved without qualification: 136
Albania (9 Aug 2010), Antigua and Barbuda (23 Aug 2010), Argentina (11 Jun 2004), Armenia (26 Nov 2003), Australia (20 May 2004), Austria (27 Aug 2002), Belgium (23 Oct 2002), Belize (20 Apr 2005), Benin (5 Jan 2004), Bolivia (18 Dec 2003), Bosnia/Herzegovina (19 Mar 2007), Botswana (5 Feb 2008), Brazil (16 Jun 2004), Bulgaria (25 Jul 2000), Burkina Faso (11 Nov 2002), Burundi (23 Sep 2004), Cameroon (20 May 2002), Canada (26 Aug 2002), Cape Verde (1 Mar 2006), Chad (10 Mar 2004), Chile (20 Jan 2005), China (22 Mar 2005), Colombia (3 Dec 2008), Congo (Brazzaville)(13 Jul 2006), Congo (Kinshasa) (23 Mar 2005), Cook Islands (29 Jun 2004), Costa Rica (13 Aug 2009), Côte d'Ivoire (20 Jan 2004), Croatia (16 Nov 2007), Cuba (22 Feb 2008), Cyprus (17 Dec 2004), Czech Republic (12 Jun 2000), Djibouti (10 Nov 2004), Dominica (30 Dec 2005), Dominican Republic (24 Mar 2006), Ecuador (4 May 2004), El Salvador (8 Sep 99), Equatorial Guinea (7 Feb 2003), Eritrea (10 Mar 2005), Estonia (13 Jun

2006), Ethiopia (9 Jan 2003), European Community (20 Dec 2002), Finland (4 Jun 2004), France (17 Feb 2004), Gabon (18 Dec 2003), Gambia (26 Feb 2002), Georgia (27 Feb 2007), Germany (11 Jan 2001), Ghana (30 May 2003), Greece (23 Dec 2003), Guatemala (19 Apr 2010), Guinea (7 Sep 2000), Guinea–Bissau (12 Jun 2008), Guyana (25 Jun 2007), Honduras (26 Sep 2011), Hungary (31 Oct 2000), India (24 May 2005), Iran (26 Aug 2004), Ireland (10 Jun 2005), Italy (27 Aug 2002), Jamaica (20 Aug 2002),Japan (15 Jun 2004), Jordan (22 July 2002), Kazakhstan (1 Nov 2007), Kenya (3 Feb 2005), Korea (North) (6 Feb 2004), Korea (South) (11 Aug 2003), Kuwait (12 May 2006), Kyrgyzstan (25 May 2000), Laos (21 Sep 2010), Latvia (23 Apr 2003), Lebanon (13 Nov 2006), Lesotho (30 May 2008), Liberia (22 Sep 2004), Libya (9 Jul 2002), Liechtenstein (18 Jun 2004), Lithuania (17 Mar 2004), Luxembourg (28 Aug 2002), Macedonia (12 Aug 2010), Madagascar (22 Sep 2004), Malawi (27 Feb 2009), Malaysia (4 Sep 2002), Maldives (17 Oct 2006), Mali (5 Jun 2003), Marshall Islands (27 Jan 2003), Mauritania (22 Jul 2005), Mauritius (5 Aug 2005), Mexico (4 May 2005), Moldova (27 Jan 2005), Mongolia (8 Mar 2001), Morocco (25 Apr 2011), Mozambique (15 Apr 2010), Namibia (24 Jun 2005), Nepal (9 Feb 2007), Netherlands (20 Apr 2000), Nicaragua (19 Sep 2008), Niger (16 Feb 2006), Nigeria (28 Jun 2001), Norway (25 Oct 2001), Oman (31 Jan 2000), Pakistan (14 Jul 2005), Panama (18 Aug 2000), Paraguay (18 Aug 2003), Peru (14 Sep 2005), Philippines (13 Jul 2006), Poland (14 Sep 2005), Portugal (16 Feb 2005), Qatar (10 Dec 2004), Romania (2 Sep 2003), Russia (28 Apr 2011), Rwanda (7 Jan 2004), Samoa (30 May 2002), Saudi Arabia (7 Sep 2000), Senegal (20 Jul 2001), Serbia (31 Jul 2009), Singapore (24 May 2005), Slovakia (26 Jan 2007), Slovenia (17 Nov 99), Somalia (26 July 2010), South Africa (4 Sep 2002), Spain (2 Mar 2004), Sri Lanka (19 Jan 2006), St. Vincent and the Grenadines (29 Oct 2010), Sudan (17 Feb 2005), Suriname (30 May 2000), Sweden (10 Oct 2003), Switzerland (10 Jan 2002), Syria (24 Sep 2003), Tanzania (26 Aug 2002), Thailand (19 Feb 2002), Tonga (31 Mar 2010), Togo (23 Jun 2004), Trinidad & Tobago (16 Dec 2009), Uganda (18 Aug 2008), Ukraine (6 Dec 2002), United Arab Emirates (10 Sep 2002), United Kingdom (17 Jun 2004),Uruguay (4 Mar 2003), Venezuela (19 Apr 2005), Vietnam (7 May 2007), Yemen (4 Feb 2006), Zambia (28 Jan 2011)

Ratified/acceded/accepted with qualification: 2
Denmark (15 Jan 2004), New Zealand (23 Sep 2003)

4.5   Stockholm Convention on Persistent Organic Pollutants
Adopted: 22 May 2001
Entered into force: 17 May 2004
Total Parties: 176
Signed but not ratified: 9 (All dates 23 May 2001 unless otherwise indicated)
Brunei (21 May 2002), Haiti, Israel (30 Jul 2001), Italy, Malaysia (16 May 2002), Malta, Saudi Arabia (14 Mar 2002), United States, Zimbabwe
Ratified/acceded/accepted without qualification: 173
Albania (4 Oct 2004), Algeria (22 Sep 2006), Angola (23 Oct 2006), Antigua/Barbuda (10 Sep 2003), Argentina (25 Jan 2005), Armenia (26 Nov 2003), Australia (20 May 2004), Austria (27 Aug 2002), Azerbaijan (13 Jan 2004), Bahamas (3 Oct 2005), Bahrain (31 Jan 2006), Bangladesh (12 Mar 2007), Barbados (7 Jun 2004), Belarus (3 Feb 2004), Belgium (25 May 2006), Belize (25 Jan 2010), Benin (5 Jan 2004), Bolivia (3 Jun 2003), Botswana (28 Oct 2002), Bosnia/Herzegovina (30 Mar 2010), Brazil (16 Jun 2004), Bulgaria (20 Dec 2004), Burkina Faso (31 Dec 2004), Burundi (2 Aug 2005), Cambodia (25 Aug 2006), Cameroon (19 May 2009), Canada (23 May 2001), Cape Verde (1 Mar 2006), Central African Republic (12 Feb 2008), Chad (10 Mar 2004), Chile (20 Jan 2005), China (13 Aug 2004), Colombia (22 Oct 2008), Comoros (23 Feb 2007), Congo (Brazzaville) (12

Feb 2007), Congo (Kinshasa) (23 Mar 2005), Cook Islands (29 Jun 2004), Costa Rica (6 Feb 2007), Côte d'Ivoire (20 Jan 2004), Croatia (30 Jan 2007), Cuba (21 Dec 2007), Cyprus (7 Mar 2005), Czech Republic (6 Aug 2002), Djibouti (11 Mar 2004), Dominica (8 Aug 2003), Dominican Republic (4 May 2007), Ecuador (7 Jun 2004), Egypt (2 May 2003), Eritrea (10 Mar 2005), Estonia (7 Nov 2008), Ethiopia (9 Jan 2003), European Community (16 Nov 2004), Fiji (20 Jun 2001), Finland (3 Sep 2002), France (17 Feb 2004), Gabon (7 May 2007), Gambia (28 Apr 2006), Georgia(4 Oct 2006), Germany (25 Apr 2002), Ghana (30 May 2003), Greece(3 May 2006), Guatemala (30 Jul 2008), Guinea (11 Dec 2007), Guinea–Bissau (6 Aug 2008), Guyana (12 Sep 2007), Honduras (23 May 2005), Hungary (14 Mar 2008), Iceland (29 May 2002), India (13 Jan 2006), Indonesia (28 Sep 2009), Iran (6 Feb 2006), Ireland (3 Aug 2010), Jamaica (1 Jun 2007), Japan (30 Aug 2002), Jordan (8 Nov 2004), Kazakhstan (9 Nov 2007), Kenya (24 Sep 2004), Kiribati (7 Sep 2004), Korea (North) (26 Aug 2002), Korea (South) (25 Jan 2007), Kuwait (12 Jun 2006), Kyrgyzstan (12 Dec 2006), Laos (28 Jun 2006), Latvia (28 Oct 2004),Lebanon (3 Jan 2003), Lesotho (23 Jan 2002), Liberia (23 May 2002), Libya (14 Jun 2005), Liechtenstein (3 Dec 2004), Lithuania (5 Dec 2006), Luxembourg (7 Feb 2003), Macedonia (27 May 2004), Madagascar (18 Nov 2005), Malawi (27 Feb 2009), Maldives (17 Oct 2006), Mali (5 Sep 2003), Marshall Islands (27 Jan 2003), Mauritania (22 Jul 2005), Mauritius (13 Jul 2004), Mexico (10 Feb 2003), Micronesia (15 Jul 2005), Moldova (7 Apr 2004), Monaco (20 Oct 2004), Mongolia (30 Apr 2004), Montenegro (31 Mar 2011), Morocco (15 Jun 2004), Mozambique (31 Oct 2005), Myanmar (19 Apr 2004), Namibia (24 Jun 2005), Nauru (9 May 2002), Nepal (6 Mar 2007), Netherlands (28 Jan 2002), Nicaragua (1 Dec 2005), Niger (12 Apr 2006), Nigeria (24 May 2004), Niue (2 Sep 2005), Norway (11 Jul 2002), Oman (19 Jan 2005), Pakistan (17 Apr 2008), Palau (8 Sep 2011), Panama (5 Mar 2003), Papua New Guinea (7 Oct 2003), Paraguay (1 Apr 2004), Peru (14 Sep 2005), Philippines (27 Feb 2004), Poland (23 Oct 2008), Portugal (15 Jul 2004), Qatar (10 Dec 2004), Romania (28 Oct 2004), Russia (17 Aug 2011), Rwanda (5 Jun 2002), Samoa (4 Feb 2002), São Tomé/Principe (12 Apr 2006), Senegal (8 Oct 2003), Serbia (31 Jul 2009), Seychelles (3 Jun 2008), Sierra Leone (26 Sep 2003), Singapore (24 May 2005), Slovakia (5 Aug 2002), Slovenia (4 May 2004), Solomon Islands (28 Jul 2004), Somalia (26 Jul 2010), South Africa (4 Sep 2002), Spain (28 May 2004), Sri Lanka (22 Dec 2005), St Kitts/Nevis (21 May 2004), St Lucia (4 Oct 2002), St Vincent/Grenadines (15 Sep 2005), Sudan (29 Aug 2006), Suriname (20 Sep 2011), Swaziland (13 Jan 2006), Sweden (8 May 2002), Switzerland (30 Jul 2003), Syria (5 Aug 2005), Tajikistan (8 Feb 2007), Tanzania (30 Apr 2004), Thailand (31 Jan 2005), Togo (22 Jul 2004), Tonga (23 Oct 2009), Trinidad/Tobago (13 Dec 2002), Tunisia (17 Jun 2004), Turkey (14 Oct 2009), Tuvalu (19 Jan 2004), Uganda (20 Jul 2004), Ukraine (25 Sep 2007), United Arab Emirates (11 Jul 2002), United Kingdom (17 Jan 2005), Uruguay (9 Feb 2004), Vanuatu (16 Sep 2005), Venezuela (19 Apr 2005), Vietnam (22 Jul 2002), Yemen (9 Jan 2004), Zambia (7 Jul 2006)

Ratified/Acceded/Accepted/Approved with qualification: 3

Denmark (17 Dec 2003), New Zealand (24 Sep 2004), El Salvador (27 May 2008)

4.6   **D**UBAI **D**ECLARATION ON **I**NTERNATIONAL **C**HEMICALS **M**ANAGEMENT
Adopted by the International Conference on Chemicals Management: 4–6 February 2006

B. Hazardous Wastes

4.7   **OECD C**OUNCIL **D**ECISION/**R**ECOMMENDATION ON **E**XPORTS OF **H**AZARDOUS **W**ASTES FROM THE **OECD A**REA
Adopted: 5 Jun 86

4.8 UNEP GOVERNING COUNCIL DECISION ON CAIRO GUIDELINES AND PRINCIPLES FOR THE ENVIRONMENTALLY SOUND MANAGEMENT OF HAZARDOUS WASTES
Adopted: 17 Jun 87

4.9 OAU COUNCIL OF MINISTERS RESOLUTION ON DUMPING OF NUCLEAR AND INDUSTRIAL WASTE IN AFRICA
Adopted: 23 May 88

4.10 BASEL CONVENTION ON THE CONTROL OF TRANSBOUNDARY MOVEMENTS OF HAZARDOUS WASTES AND THEIR DISPOSAL
Concluded: 22 Mar 89
Entered into force: 5 May 92
Total parties: 178
Signed but not ratified: 3 (as of at least 4 Jun 98)
Afghanistan (22 Mar 89), Haiti (22 Mar 89), United States (22 Mar 90)
Ratified/accepted/approved without qualification: 168
Albania (29 Jun 99), Algeria (15 Sep 98), Andorra (23 Jul 99), Antigua/Barbuda (5 Apr 93), Argentina (27 Jun 91), Armenia (1 Oct 99), Australia (5 Feb 92), Austria (12 Jan 93), Azerbaijan (1 Jun 2002), Bahamas (12 Aug 92), Bahrain (15 Oct 92), Bangladesh (1 Apr 93), Barbados (24 Aug 95), Belarus (10 Dec 99), Belgium (1 Nov 93), Belize (23 May 97), Benin (4 Dec 97), Bhutan (26 Aug 2002), Bolivia (15 Nov 96), Bosnia/Herzegovina (16 Mar 2001), Botswana (20 May 98), Brazil (1 Oct 92), Brunei (17 Dec 2002), Bulgaria (16 Feb 96), Burkina Faso (4 Nov 99), Burundi (6 Jan 97), Cambodia (2 Mar 2001), Cameroon (9 Feb 2001), Canada (28 Aug 92), Cape Verde (2 Jul 99), Central African Republic (24 Feb 2006), Chad (10 Mar 2004), Chile (11 Aug 92), China (17 Dec 91), Colombia (31 Dec 96), Comoros (31 Oct 94), Congo (Brazzaville) (20 Apr 2007), Congo (Kinshasa) (6 Oct 94), Cook Islands (29 Jun 2004), Costa Rica (7 Mar 95), Côte d'Ivoire (1 Dec 94), Croatia (9 May 94), Cuba (3 Oct 94),Cyprus (17 Sep 92), Czech Republic (30 Sep 93), Djibouti (31 May 2002), Dominica (5 May 98), Dominican Republic (10 Jul 2000), Egypt (8 Jan 93), El Salvador (13 Dec 91), Equatorial Guinea (7 Feb 2003), Eritrea (10 Mar 2005), Estonia (21 Jul 92), Ethiopia (12 Apr 2000), European Community (7 Feb 94), Finland (19 Nov 91), France (7 Jan 91), Gabon (6 Jun 2008), Gambia (15 Dec 97), Georgia (20 May 99), Ghana (30 May 2003), Greece (4 Aug 94), Guatemala (15 May 95), Guinea (26 Apr 95), Guinea–Bissau (9 Feb 2005), Guyana (4 Apr 2001), Honduras (27 Mar 96), Hungary (21 May 90), Iceland (28 Jun 95), India (24 Jun 92), Iran (5 Jan 93), Iraq (2 May 2011), Ireland (7 Feb 94), Israel (14 Dec 94), Jamaica (23 Jan 2003), Jordan (22 Jun 89), Kazakhstan (3 Jun 2003), Kenya (1 Jun 2000), Kiribati (7 Sep 2000), Korea (North)(10 Jul 2008), Korea (South) (28 Feb 94), Kuwait (11 Oct 93), Kyrgyzstan (13 Aug 96), Laos (21 Sep 2010), Latvia (14 Apr 92), Lebanon (21 Dec 94), Lesotho (31 May 2000), Liberia (22 Sep 2004), Libya (12 Jul 2001), Liechtenstein (27 Jan 92), Lithuania (22 Apr 99), Luxembourg (7 Feb 94), Macedonia (16 Jul 97), Madagascar (2 Jun 99), Malawi (21 Apr 94), Malaysia (8 Oct 93), Maldives (28 Apr 92), Mali (5 Dec 2000), Malta (19 Jun 2000), Marshall Islands (27 Jan 2003), Mauritania (16 Aug 96), Mauritius (24 Nov 92), Mexico (22 Feb 91), Micronesia (6 Sep 95), Moldova (2 Jul 98), Monaco (31 Aug 92), Mongolia (15 Apr 97), Montenegro (22 Nov 2006), Morocco (28 Dec 95), Mozambique (13 Mar 97), Namibia (15 May 95), Nauru (12 Nov 2001), Nepal (15 Oct 96), Netherlands (16 Apr 93), New Zealand (20 Dec 94), Nicaragua (3 Jun 97), Niger (17 Jun 98), Nigeria (13 Mar 91), Norway (2 Jul 90), Oman (8 Feb 95), Pakistan (26 Jul 94), Palau (8 Sep 2011), Panama (22 Feb 91),

Papua New Guinea (1 Sep 95), Paraguay (28 Sep 95), Peru (23 Nov 93), Philippines (21 Oct 93), Poland (20 Mar 92), Portugal (26 Jan 94), Qatar (9 Aug 95), Russia (31 Jan 95), Rwanda (7 Jan 2004), Samoa (22 Mar 2002), Saudi Arabia (7 Mar 90), Senegal (10 Nov 92), Serbia (18 Apr 2000), Seychelles (11 May 93), Slovakia (28 May 93), Slovenia (7 Oct 93), Somalia (26 Jul 2010), South Africa (5 May 94), Spain (7 Feb 94), Sri Lanka (28 Aug 92), St Kitts/Nevis (7 Sep 94), St Lucia (9 Dec 93), St Vincent/Grenadines (2 Dec 96), Sudan (9 Jan 2006), Suriname (20 Sep 2011), Swaziland (8 Aug 2005), Sweden (2 Aug 91), Switzerland (31 Jan 90), Syria (22 Jan 92), Tanzania (7 Apr 93), Thailand (24 Nov 97), Togo (2 Jul 2004), Tonga (26 Mar 2010), Trinidad/Tobago (18 Feb 94), Tunisia (11 Oct 95), Turkey (22 Jun 94), Turkmenistan (25 Sep 96), Uganda (11 Mar 99), Ukraine (8 Oct 99), United Arab Emirates (17 Nov 92), Uruguay (20 Dec 91), Uzbekistan (7 Feb 96), Venezuela (3 Mar 98), Vietnam (13 Mar 95), Yemen (21 Feb 96), Zambia (15 Nov 94)

***Ratified/accepted/approved with qualification:* 9**

Denmark (6 Feb 94), Ecuador (23 Feb 93), Germany (21 Apr 95), Indonesia (20 Sep 93), Italy (7 Feb 94), Japan (17 Sep 93), Romania (27 Feb 91), Singapore (2 Jan 96), United Kingdom (7 Feb 94)

4.11 BAMAKO CONVENTION ON THE BAN OF IMPORT INTO AFRICA AND THE CONTROL OF TRANSBOUNDARY MOVEMENT AND MANAGEMENT OF HAZARDOUS WASTES WITHIN AFRICA

Concluded: 30 Jan 91

Entered into force: 22 Apr 98

Signed but not ratified: 18

Angola (2 Feb 2010), Central African Republic (30 Jan 91), Chad (27 Jan 92), Djibouti (20 Dec 91), Ghana (2 Jul 2004), Guinea (30 Jan 91), Guinea Bissau (1 Mar 91), Kenya (17 Dec 2003), Lesotho (1 Jun 91), Liberia (16 Dec 2003), Madagascar (17 Mar 2004), Nigeria (22 Dec 2008), Rwanda (26 Aug 91), São Tomé/Principe (1 Feb 2010), Sierra Leone (9 Dec 2003), Somalia (1 Jun 91), Swaziland (29 Jun 92), Zambia (3 Aug 2005)

Ratified/accepted/approved without qualification: 24

Benin (21 Jan 98), Burkina Faso (10 Jun 2009), Burundi (17 Jul 2006), Cameroon (21 Dec 1995), Comoros (16 Apr 2004), Congo (Brazzaville)(25 June 97), Congo (Kinshasa) (13 Apr 95), Côte d'Ivoire (16 Sep 94), Egypt (23 Jun 2004), Ethiopia (28 Aug 2003), Gabon (18 May 2007), Gambia (8 Sep 2000), Libya (28 Jan 93), Mali (21 Feb 96), Mauritius (26 Nov 92), Mozambique (29 Mar 99), Niger (12 Dec 96), Senegal (29 Mar 94), Sudan (11 Nov 93), Tanzania (5 Apr 93), Togo (23 Aug 96), Tunisia (14 May 92), Uganda (27 May 99), Zimbabwe (3 Aug 92)

4.12 BASEL PROTOCOL ON LIABILITY AND COMPENSATION FOR DAMAGE RESULTING FROM TRANSBOUNDARY MOVEMENTS OF HAZARDOUS WASTES AND THEIR DISPOSAL (WITH ANNEXES)

Adopted: 10 December 1999

Not yet in force

Signed but not ratified: 12

Chile (8 Dec 2000), Costa Rica (27 Apr 2000), Denmark (5 Dec 2000), Finland (8 Dec 2000), France (8 Dec 2000), Hungary (5 Dec 2000), Luxembourg (28 Aug 2000), Macedonia (3 Apr 2000), Monaco (17 Mar 2000), Sweden (1 Dec 2000), Switzerland (9 Mar 2000), United Kingdom (7 Dec 2000)

Ratified/acceded/accepted without qualification: 10

Botswana (17 Jun 2004), Colombia (22 Jul 2008), Congo (Brazzaville) (20 Apr 2007), Congo (Kinshasa) (23 Mar 2005), Ethiopia (8 Oct 2003), Ghana (9 Jun

2005), Liberia (16 Sep 2005), Syria (5 Oct 2004), Togo (2 Jul 2004), Yemen (25 Aug 2009)

4.13 OECD DECISION CONCERNING THE CONTROL OF TRANSBOUNDARY MOVEMENTS OF WASTES DESTINED FOR RECOVERY OPERATIONS (AS AMENDED)
Adopted by the OECD Council: 14 June 2001

4.14 OECD RECOMMENDATION ON THE ENVIRONMENTALLY SOUND MANAGEMENT OF WASTE (AS AMENDED, BUT WITHOUT ANNEXES)
Adopted by the OECD Council: 9 June 2004

C. Desertification

4.15 UNITED NATIONS CONVENTION TO COMBAT DESERTIFICATION IN THOSE COUNTRIES EXPERIENCING SERIOUS DROUGHT AND/OR DESERTIFICATION, PARTICULARLY IN AFRICA
Adopted: 17 Jun 94
Entered into force: 26 Dec 96
Total parties: 194
*Ratified/accepted/approved without qualification:*191
Afghanistan (1 Nov 95), Albania (27 Apr 2000), Algeria (22 May 96), Andorra (15 Jul 2002), Angola (30 Jun 97), Antigua/Barbuda (6 Jun 97), Argentina (6 Jan 97), Armenia (2 Jul 97), Australia (15 May 2000), Austria (2 Jun 97), Azerbaijan (10 Aug 98), Bahamas (10 Nov 2000), Bahrain (14 Jul 97), Bangladesh (26 Jan 96), Barbados (14 May 97), Belarus (29 Aug 2001), Belgium (30 Jun 97), Belize (23 Jul 98), Benin (29 Aug 96), Bhutan (20 Aug 2003), Bolivia (1 Aug 96), Bosnia/Herzegovina (26 Aug 2002), Botswana (11 Sep 96), Brazil (25 Jun 97), Brunei (4 Dec 2002), Bulgaria (21 Feb 2001), Burkina Faso (26 Jan 96), Burundi (6 Jan 97), Cambodia (18 Aug 97), Cameroon (29 May 97), Canada (1 Dec 95), Cape Verde (8 May 95), Central African Republic (5 Sep 96), Chad (27 Sep 96), Chile (11 Nov 97), China (18 Feb 97), Colombia (8 Jun 99), Comoros (3 Mar 98), Congo (Brazzaville) (12 Jul 99), Congo (Kinshasa) (12 Sep 97), Cook Islands (21 Aug 98), Costa Rica (5 Jan 98), Côte d'Ivoire (4 Mar 97), Croatia (6 Oct 2000), Cuba (13 Mar 97), Cyprus (29 Mar 2000), Czech Republic (25 Jan 2000), Denmark (22 Dec 95), Djibouti (12 Jun 97), Dominica (8 Dec 97), Dominican Republic (26 Jun 97), Ecuador (6 Sep 95), Egypt (7 Jul 95), El Salvador (27 Jun 97), Equatorial Guinea (27 Jun 97), Eritrea (14 Aug 96), Ethiopia (27 Jun 97), European Community (26 Mar 98), Fiji (26 Aug 98), Finland (20 Sep 95), France (12 Jun 97), Gabon (6 Sep 96), Gambia (11 Jun 96), Georgia (23 Jul 99), Germany (10 Jul 96), Ghana (27 Dec 96), Greece (5 May 97), Grenada (28 May 97), Guatemala (10 Sep 98), Guinea (23 Jun 97), Guinea–Bissau (27 Oct 95), Guyana (26 Jun 97), Haiti (25 Sep 96), Honduras (25 Jun 97), Iceland (3 Jun 97), India (17 Dec 96), Indonesia (31 Aug 98), Iran (29 Apr 97), Iraq (28 May 2010), Ireland (31 Jul 97), Israel (26 Mar 96), Italy (23 Jun 97), Jamaica (12 Nov 97), Japan (11 Sep 98), Jordan (21 Oct 96), Kazakhstan (9 Jul 97), Kenya (24 Jun 97), Kiribati (8 Sep 98), Korea (North) (29 Dec 2003), Korea (South) (17 Aug 99), Kyrgyzstan (19 Sep 97), Laos (20 Sep 96), Latvia (21 Aug 2002), Lebanon (16 May 96), Lesotho (12 Sep 95), Liberia (2 Mar 98), Libya (22 Jul 96), Liechtenstein (29 Dec 99), Lithuania (25 Jul 2003), Luxembourg (4 Feb 97), Macedonia (6 Mar 2002), Madagascar (25 Jun 97), Malawi (13 Jun 96), Malaysia (25 Jun 97), Maldives (3 Sep 2002), Mali (31 Oct 95), Malta (30 Jun 98), Marshall Islands (2 Jun 98), Mauritania (7 Aug 96), Mauritius (23 Jan 96), Mexico (3 Apr 95), Micronesia (25 Mar 96), Moldova (10 Mar 99), Monaco (5 Mar 99), Mongolia (3 Sep 96), Montenegro (4 Jun 2007), Morocco (7 Nov 96), Mozambique (13 Mar 97), Myanmar (Burma) (2 Jan 97), Namibia (16 May 97),

Nauru (22 Sep 98), Nepal (15 Oct 96), Netherlands (27 Jun 95), Nicaragua (17 Feb 98), Niger (19 Jan 96), Nigeria (8 Jul 97), Niue (14 Aug 98), Norway (30 Aug 96), Oman (23 Jul 96), Pakistan (24 Feb 97), Palau (15 Jun 99), Panama (4 Apr 96), Papua New Guinea (6 Dec 2000), Paraguay (15 Jan 97), Peru (9 Nov 95), Philippines (10 Feb 2000), Poland (14 Nov 2001), Portugal (1 Apr 96), Qatar (15 Mar 99), Romania (19 Aug 98), Russia (29 May 2003), Rwanda (22 Oct 98), Samoa (21 Aug 98), San Marino (23 Jul 99), São Tomé/Príncipe (8 Jul 98), Saudi Arabia (25 Jun 97), Senegal (26 Jul 95), Serbia (18 Dec 2007), Seychelles (26 Jun 97), Sierra Leone (25 Sep 97), Singapore (26 Apr 99), Slovakia (7 Jan 2002), Slovenia (28 Jun 2001), Solomon Islands (16 Apr 99), Somalia (24 Jul 2002), South Africa (30 Sep 97), Spain (30 Jan 96), Sri Lanka (9 Dec 98), St Kitts/Nevis (30 Jan 97), St Lucia (2 Jul 97), St Vincent/Grenadines (16 Mar 98), Sudan (24 Nov 95), Suriname (1 Jun 2000), Swaziland (7 Oct 96), Sweden (12 Dec 95), Switzerland (19 Jan 96), Syria (10 Jun 97), Tajikistan (16 Jul 97), Tanzania (19 Jun 97), Thailand (7 Mar 2001), Timor–Leste (20 Aug 2003), Togo (4 Oct 95), Tonga (25 Sep 98), Trinidad/Tobago (8 Jun 2000), Tunisia (11 Oct 95), Turkey (31 Mar 98), Turkmenistan (18 Sep 96), Tuvalu (14 Sep 98), Uganda (25 Jun 97), Ukraine (27 Aug 2002), United Arab Emirates (21 Oct 98), United Kingdom (18 Oct 96), Uruguay (17 Feb 99), Uzbekistan (31 Oct 95), Vanuatu (10 Aug 99), Venezuela (29 Jun 98),Vietnam (25 Aug 98), Yemen (14 Jan 97), Zambia (19 Sep 96), Zimbabwe (23 Sep 97)

***Ratified/accepted/approved with qualification:* 3**
Kuwait (27 Jun 97), New Zealand (7 Sep 2000), United States (17 Nov 2000)

5. BIOSPHERE

A. *General Biodiversity Protection*

5.1   CONVENTION ON NATURE PROTECTION AND WILDLIFE PRESERVATION IN THE WESTERN HEMISPHERE
Concluded: 12 Oct 40
Entered into force: 1 May 42
Signed but not ratified: 3
Bolivia (12 Oct 40), Colombia (17 Jan 41), Cuba (12 Oct 40)
Ratified/accepted/approved without qualification: 18
Brazil (26 Aug 65), Chile (4 Dec 67), Costa Rica (12 Jan 67), Dominican Republic (3 Mar 42), Ecuador (20 Oct 44), El Salvador (2 Dec 41), Guatemala (14 Aug 41), Haiti (31 Jan 42), Mexico (27 Mar 42), Nicaragua (22 May 46), Panama (16 Mar 72), Paraguay (30 Jan 81), Peru (22 Sep 46), Suriname (30 Apr 85), Trindad/Tobago (24 Apr 69), United States (28 Apr 41), Uruguay (9 Apr 70), Venezuela (3 Nov 41)
Ratified/accepted/approved with qualification: 1
Argentina (27 Jun 46)

5.2   AFRICAN CONVENTION ON THE CONSERVATION OF NATURE AND NATURAL RE-SOURCES
Concluded: 15 Sep 68
Entered into force: 16 Jun 69
Signed but not ratified: 15
Benin (15 Sep 68), Botswana (15 Sep 68), Burundi (15 Sep 68), Chad (15 Sep 68), Comoros (15 Sep 68), Ethiopia (15 Sep 68), Gambia (15 Sep 68), Guinea (15 Sep 68), Lesotho (15 Sep 68), Libya (15 Sep 68), Mauritania (15 Sep 68), Mauritius (15 Sep 68), Sierra Leone (15 Sep 68), Somalia (15 Sep 68)
Ratified/accepted/approved without qualification: 30
Algeria (24 May 83), Burkina Faso (29 Aug 69), Cameroon (29 Sep 78), Central African Republic (16 Mar 70), Comoros (16 Apr 2004), Congo (Brazzaville) (29

Apr 81), Congo (Kinshasa) (14 Oct 76), Côte d'Ivoire (15 Jan 69), Djibouti (17 Apr 78), Egypt (16 Apr 72), Gabon (18 Nov 88), Ghana (17 May 69), Kenya (12 May 69), Liberia (22 Nov 78), Madagascar (23 Sep 71), Malawi (12 Mar 73), Mali (20 Jun 74), Mozambique (1 Apr 81), Niger (27 Jan 70), Nigeria (7 May 74), Rwanda (4 Feb 80), Senegal (24 Feb 72), Seychelles (14 Oct 77), Sudan (30 Oct 73), Swaziland (7 Apr 69), Tanzania (15 Nov 74), Togo (20 Nov 79), Tunisia (4 Feb 77), Uganda (30 Nov 77), Zambia (1 May 72)

5.3 CONVENTION ON WETLANDS OF INTERNATIONAL IMPORTANCE ESPECIALLY AS WATER-FOWL HABITAT
Concluded: 2 Feb 71
Entered into force: 21 Dec 75
Ratified/acceded/accepted without qualification: 159
Albania (31 Oct 95), Algeria** (4 Nov 83), Antigua/Barbuda (2 Jun 2005), Argentina* (4 May 92), Armenia (6 Jul 93), Australia* (8 May 74), Austria* (16 Dec 82), Azerbaijan (21 May 2001), Bahamas (7 Feb 97), Bahrain (27 Oct 97), Bangladesh (21 May 92), Barbados (12 Dec 2005), Belarus (10 Sep 99), Belgium** (4 Mar 86), Belize (22 Apr 98), Benin (24 Jan 2000), Bolivia (27 Jun 90), Bosnia/Herzegovina (1 Mar 92), Botswana (9 Dec 96), Brazil (24 May 93), Bulgaria* (24 Sep 75), Burkina Faso (27 Jun 90), Burundi (5 Jun 2002), Cambodia (23 Jun 99), Cameroon (20 Mar 2006), Canada* (15 Jan 81), Cape Verde (18 Jul 2005), Central African Republic* (5 Dec 2005), Chad (13 Jun 90), Chile (27 Jul 81), China (31 Mar 92), Colombia (18 Jan 98), Comoros (9 Feb 95), Congo (Brazzaville) (18 Jun 98), Congo (Kinshasa) (18 Jan 96), Côte d'Ivoire (27 Feb 96), Costa Rica (27 Dec 91), Croatia (2 Nov 92), Cuba (12 Apr 2001), Cyprus (11 Jul 2001), Czech Republic (26 Mar 93), Denmark (2 Sep 77), Djibouti (22 Dec 2002), Dominican Republic (15 May 2002), Ecuador (7 Sep 90), Egypt (9 Sep 88), El Salvador (22 Jan 99), Equatorial Guinea (2 Jun 2003), Estonia (29 Mar 94), Fiji (11 Feb 2006), Finland* (28 May 74), France (1 Oct 86), Gabon (30 Dec 86), Gambia (16 Sep 96), Georgia (7 Feb 97), Germany* (26 Feb 76), Ghana (22 Feb 88), Greece (21 Aug 75), Guatemala (26 Jun 90), Guinea (18 Nov 92), Guinea–Bissau (14 May 90), Honduras (23 Jun 93), Hungary* (11 Apr 79), Iceland (2 Dec 77), India (1 Oct 81), Indonesia (8 Apr 92), Iran (23 Jun 75), Iraq* (17 Oct 2007), Ireland* (15 Nov 84), Israel (12 Nov 96), Italy (14 Dec 76), Jamaica (7 Oct 97), Japan* (17 Jun 80), Jordan (10 Jan 77), Kenya (5 Jun 90), Kazakhstan (2 Jan 2007), Korea (South) (28 Mar 97), Kyrgyzstan (12 Dec 2002), Latvia (25 Jul 95), Lebanon (16 Apr 99), Lesotho* (1 Jul 2004), Liberia (2 Jul 2003), Libya (5 Apr 2000), Liechtenstein* (6 Aug 91), Lithuania (20 Aug 93), Luxembourg (15 Apr 98), Macedonia (4 Apr 95), Madagascar (25 Sep 98), Malawi (14 Nov 96), Malaysia (10 Nov 94), Mali (25 May 87), Malta (30 Sep 88), Marshall Islands (13 Jul 2004), Mauritania (22 Oct 82), Mauritius (30 May 2001), Mexico (4 Jul 86), Moldova (20 Jun 2000), Monaco (20 Aug 97), Mongolia (8 Dec 97), Montenegro*** (26 Apr 2007), Morocco (20 Jun 80), Mozambique* (3 Aug 2004), Myanmar* (17 Nov 2004), Namibia (23 Aug 95), Nepal (17 Dec 87), Netherlands* (23 May 80), New Zealand (13 Aug 76), Nicaragua (30 Jul 97), Niger (30 Apr 87), Nigeria (2 Oct 2000), Norway* (9 Jul 74), Pakistan* (23 Jul 76), Panama (26 Nov 90), Palau (18 Oct 2002), Papua New Guinea (16 Mar 93), Paraguay (7 Jun 95), Peru (30 Mar 92), Philippines (8 Jul 94), Poland (22 Nov 77), Portugal (24 Nov 80), Romania (21 May 91), Rwanda (1 Dec 2005), Samoa* (6 Oct 2004), Sao Tome/Principe (21 Aug 2006), Senegal (11 Jul 77), Serbia (27 Apr 1992), Seychelles* (22 Nov 2004), Sierra Leone (13 Dec 99), Slovakia (31 Mar 93), Slovenia (28 Oct 92), South Africa (12 Mar 75), Spain (4 May 82), Sri Lanka (15 Jun 90), St Lucia (19 Feb 2002), Sudan (7 Jan 2005), Suriname** (22 Jul 85), Sweden* (5 Dec 74), Switzerland* (16 Jan 76), Syria (5 Mar 98), Tajikistan (18 Jul 2001), Tanzania (13 Apr 2000), Thailand (13 May 98), Togo (4 Jul 95),

Trinidad/Tobago (21 Dec 92), Tunisia (24 Nov 80), Turkey (13 Jul 94), Turkmenistan (03 Mar 2009), Uganda (4 Mar 88), Ukraine (16 Jan 97), United Arab Emirates* (29 Aug 2007), United Kingdom* (5 Jan 76), United States (18 Dec 86), Uruguay** (22 May 84), USSR (Russia)* (11 Oct 76), Uzbekistan (8 Oct 2001), Venezuela (23 Nov 88), Vietnam (20 Sep 88), Yemen (8 Oct 2007), Zambia (28 Aug 91)

* Indicates acceptance of amendments to articles 6 and 7 of the Convention adopted by the Extraordinary Conference of States Parties on 28 May 1987.

* * Indicates acceptance of the 1971 Convention only.

* * * Succession

5.4   **INTERNATIONAL CONVENTION ON INTERNATIONAL TRADE IN ENDANGERED SPECIES OF WILD FAUNA AND FLORA (CITES)**
Concluded: 3 Mar 73
Entered into force: 1 Jul 75
Total parties: 175
Ratified/accepted/approved without qualification: 161
Afghanistan (30 Oct 85), Albania (27 Jun 2003), Algeria (23 Nov 83), Antigua/Barbuda (8 Jul 97), Argentina (8 Jan 81), Armenia (23 October 2008), Australia (29 Jul 76), Austria (27 Jan 82), Azerbaijan (23 Nov 98), Bahamas (20 Jun 79), Bangladesh (20 Nov 81), Barbados (9 Dec 92), Belarus (10 Aug 95), Belgium (3 Oct 83), Belize (19 Aug 86), Benin (28 Feb 84), Bhutan (15 Aug 2002), Bolivia (6 Jul 79), Bosnia/Herzegovina (21 Jan 2009), Botswana (14 Nov 77), Brazil (6 Aug 75), Brunei (4 May 90), Bulgaria (16 Jan 91), Burkina Faso (13 Oct 89), Burundi (8 Aug 88), Cambodia (4 Jul 97), Cameroon (5 Jun 81), Canada (10 Apr 75), Cape Verde (10 Aug 2005), Central African Republic (27 Aug 80), Chad (2 Feb 89), Chile (14 Feb 75), China (8 Jan 81), Colombia (31 Aug 81), Comoros (23 Nov 94), Congo (Brazzaville) (31 Jan 83), Congo (Kinshasa) (20 Jul 76), Costa Rica (30 Jun 75), Côte d'Ivoire (21 Nov 94), Croatia (14 Mar 2000), Cyprus (18 Oct 74), Czech Republic (14 Apr 93), Denmark (26 Jul 77), Djibouti (7 Feb 92), Dominica (4 Aug 95), Dominican Republic (17 Dec 86), Ecuador (11 Feb 75), Egypt (4 Jan 78), El Salvador (30 Apr 87), Equatorial Guinea (10 Mar 92), Eritrea (24 Oct 94), Estonia (22 Jul 92), Ethiopia (5 Apr 89), Fiji (30 Sep 97), Finland (10 May 76), France (11 May 78), Gabon (13 Feb 89), Gambia (26 Aug 77), Georgia (13 Sep 96), Germany (22 Mar 76), Ghana (14 Nov 75), Greece (8 Oct 92), Grenada (30 Aug 99), Guatemala (7 Nov 79), Guinea (21 Sep 81), Guinea–Bissau (16 May 90), Guyana (27 May 77), Honduras (15 Mar 85), Hungary (29 May 85), India (20 Jul 76), Indonesia (28 Dec 78), Iran (3 Aug 76), Ireland (8 Jan 2002), Israel (18 Dec 79), Italy (2 Oct 79), Jamaica (23 Apr 97), Jordan (14 Dec 78), Kazakhstan (20 Jan 2000), Kenya (13 Dec 78), Korea (South) (9 Jul 73), Kuwait (12 Aug 2002), Kyrgyzstan (4 Jun 2007), Laos (1 Mar 2004), Latvia (11 Feb 97), Lesotho (1 Oct 2003), Liberia (11 Mar 81), Libya (28 Jan 2003), Lithuania (10 Dec 2001), Luxembourg (13 Dec 83), Madagascar (20 Aug 75), Malaysia (20 Oct 77), Mali (18 Jul 94), Malta (17 Apr 89), Mauritania (13 Mar 98), Mauritius (28 Apr 75), Mexico (2 Jul 91), Moldova (29 Mar 2001), Monaco (19 Apr 78), Mongolia (5 Jan 96), Montenegro (26 mar 2007), Morocco (16 Oct 75), Mozambique (25 Mar 81), Myanmar (13 Jun 97), Nepal (18 Jun 75), Netherlands (19 Apr 84), New Zealand (10 May 89), Nicaragua (6 Aug 77), Niger (8 Sep 75), Nigeria (9 May 74), Oman (19 Mar 2008), Pakistan (20 Apr 76), Panama (17 Aug 78), Papua New Guinea (12 Dec 75), Paraguay (15 Nov 76), Peru (27 Jun 75), Poland (12 Dec 89), Portugal (11 Feb 80), Qatar (8 May 2001), Romania (18 Aug 94), Russia (13 Jan 92), Rwanda (20 Oct 80), Samoa (9 Nov 2004), San Marino (22 Jul 2005), São Tomé/Principe (9 Aug 2001), Senegal (5 Aug 77), Serbia (27 Feb 2002), Seychelles (8 Feb 77),

Sierra Leone (28 Oct 94), Singapore (30 Nov 86), Slovakia (2 Mar 93), Slovenia (24 Jan 2000), Solomon Islands (26 Mar 2007), Somalia (2 Dec 85), South Africa (15 Jul 75), Spain (30 May 86), Sri Lanka (4 May 82), St Kitts/Nevis (14 Feb 94), St Lucia (15 Dec 82), Sudan (26 Nov 82), Swaziland (26 Feb 97), Sweden (20 Aug 74), Syria (30 Apr 2003), Tanzania (29 Nov 79), Thailand (21 Jan 83), Togo (23 Oct 78), Trinidad/Tobago (19 Jan 84), Tunisia (10 Jul 74), Turkey (23 Sep 96), Uganda (18 Jul 91), Ukraine (30 Dec 99), United Arab Emirates (8 Feb 90), United Kingdom (2 Aug 76), United States (14 Jan 74), Uruguay (2 Apr 75), Uzbekistan (10 Jul 97), Vanuatu (17 Jul 89), Venezuela (24 Oct 77), Vietnam (20 Jan 94), Yemen (5 May 97), Zambia (24 Nov 80), Zimbabwe (19 May 81)
Ratified/accepted/approved with reservation relating to Appendix I: 14 Cuba (20 Apr 90), Iceland (3 Jan 2000), Japan (6 Aug 80), Liechtenstein (30 Nov 79), Macedonia (4 Jul 2000), Malawi (5 Feb 82), Namibia (18 Dec 90), Norway (27 Jul 76), Palau (16 Apr 2004), Philippines (18 Aug 81), Saudi Arabia (12 Mar 96), St Vincent/Grenadines (30 Nov 88), Suriname (17 Nov 80), Switzerland (9 Jul 74)

5.5   **ENDANGERED SPECIES ACT OF 1973, AS AMENDED**
Enacted: 28 Dec 73 (amended 1979, 1982, 1988, 2011)

5.6   **CONVENTION ON THE CONSERVATION OF MIGRATORY SPECIES OF WILD ANIMALS**
Concluded: 23 Jun 79
Entered into force: 1 Nov 83
Total parties: 116
Signed but not ratified: 2
Central African Republic (23 Jun 79), Jamaica (20 Jun 80)
Ratified/acceded/accepted without qualification: 110
Albania (1 Sep 2001*), Algeria (1 Dec 2005*), Angola (1 Dec 2006*), Antigua & Barbuda (1 Oct 2007*), Armenia (1 Mar 2011*), Australia (1 Jul 86), Austria (1 Jul 2005*), Bangladesh (1 Dec 2005*), Belarus (1 Sep 2003*), Belgium (11 Jul 90), Benin (14 Jan 86), Bulgaria (1 Nov 99*), Burkina Faso (9 Oct 89), Burundi (I Jul 2011*), Cameroon (7 Sep 81), Cape Verde (1 May 2006), Chad (1 Sep 97*), Chile (15 Sep 81), Congo (Brazzaville) (1 Jan 2000*), Congo (Kinshasa) (22 Jun 90), Cook Islands (2 May 2006), Costa Rica (1 Aug 2007*), Côte d'Ivoire (1 Jul 2003*), Croatia (1 Oct 2000*), Cuba (1 Feb 2008*), Cyprus (1 Nov 2001*), Czech Republic (8 Feb 94), Djibouti (1 Nov 2004), Ecuador (1 Feb 2004), Egypt (11 Feb 82), Equatorial Guinea (8 Jan 2010), Eritrea (1 Feb 2005*), Estonia (1 Oct 2008*), Ethiopia (1 Jan 2010), European Community (1 Aug 83), Finland (3 Oct 88), France (7 Jan 90), Gabon (01 Aug 2008*), Gambia (1 Aug 2001*), Georgia (1 Jun 2000*), Germany (31 Jul 84), Ghana (19 Jan 88), Greece (1 Oct 99*), Guinea (1 Aug 93*), Guinea–Bissau (19 Jun 95), Honduras (1 Apr 2007*), Hungary (12 Jul 83), India (4 May 82), Iran (1 Feb 2008*), Ireland (5 Aug 83), Israel (17 May 83), Italy (26 Aug 83), Jordan (1 Mar 2001*), Kazakhstan (1 May 2006), Kenya (1 May 99*), Latvia (1 Jul 99*), Liberia (1 Dec 2004*), Libya (1 Sep 2002*), Liechtenstein (1 Nov 97*), Lithuania (1 Feb 2002*), Luxembourg (30 Nov 82), Macedonia (1 Nov 99*), Madagascar (1 Jan 2007*), Mali (28 Jul 87), Malta (1 Jun 2001*), Mauritania (1 Jul 98*), Mauritius (1 Jun 2004*), Moldova (1 Apr 2001*), Monaco (23 Mar 87), Mongolia (1 Nov 99*), Montenegro (1 Mar 2009*), Morocco (12 Aug 93), Mozambique (1 Aug 2009), Netherlands (5 Jun 81), Niger (3 Jul 80), Nigeria (15 Oct 86), Pakistan (22 Sep 87), Palau (1 Feb 2008*), Panama (20 Feb 89), Paraguay (1 Jan 99*), Peru (1 Jun 97*), Philippines (1 Feb 94*), Poland (1 Feb 96), Portugal (21 Jan 81), Romania (1 Jul 98*), Rwanda (1 Jan 2005*), Samoa (1 Nov 2005*), São Tomé/Principe (1 Dec 2001*), Saudi Arabia (17 Dec 90), Senegal (18 Mar 88), Serbia (1 March 2008*),

Seychelles (1 Aug 2005*), Slovakia (1 Mar 95*), Slovenia (1 Feb 99*), Somalia (11 Nov 85), South Africa (27 Sep 91), Spain (12 Feb 85), Sri Lanka (6 Jun 90), Sweden (9 Jun 83), Switzerland (1 Jul 95), Syria (1 Jun 2003*), Tajikistan (1 Feb 2001*), Tanzania (1 Jul 99*), Togo (1 Feb 96), Tunisia (27 May 87), Uganda (1 Aug 2000*), Ukraine (1 Nov 99*), United Kingdom (23 Jul 85), Uruguay (1 Feb 90), Uzbekistan (1 Sep 98*), Yemen (1 Dec 2006*)

Ratified/acceded/accepted with qualification: 6

Argentina (1 Jan 92*), Bolivia (1 Mar 2003*), Denmark (5 Aug 82), France (23 Apr 90), New Zealand (1 Oct 2000*), Norway (30 May 85)

* Date of entry into force for this state.

5.7   CONVENTION ON BIOLOGICAL DIVERSITY
Concluded: 5 Jun 92
Entered into force: 29 Dec 93
Total parties: 193
Signed but not ratified: 1
United States (4 Jun 93)
Ratified/accepted/approved without qualification: 191
Afghanistan (19 Sep 2002), Albania (5 Jan 94), Algeria (14 Aug 95), Angola (1 Apr 98), Antigua/Barbuda (9 Mar 93), Argentina (22 Nov 94), Armenia (14 May 93), Australia (18 Jun 93), Austria (18 Aug 94), Azerbaijan (3 Aug 2000), Bahamas (2 Sep 93), Bahrain (30 Aug 96), Bangladesh (3 May 94), Barbados (10 Dec 93), Belarus (8 Sep 93), Belgium (22 Nov 96), Belize (30 Dec 93), Benin (30 Jun 94), Bhutan (25 Aug 95), Bolivia (3 Oct 94), Bosnia/Herzegovina (26 Aug 2002), Botswana (12 Oct 95), Brazil (28 Feb 94), Brunei (28 Apr 2008), Bulgaria (17 Apr 96), Burkina Faso (2 Sep 93), Burundi (15 Apr 97), Cambodia (9 Feb 95), Cameroon (19 Oct 94), Canada (4 Dec 92), Cape Verde (29 Mar 95), Central African Republic (15 Mar 95), Chad (7 Jun 94), China (5 Jan 93), Colombia (28 Nov 94), Comoros (29 Sep 94), Congo (Brazzaville) (1 Aug 96), Congo (Kinshasa) (3 Dec 94), Cook Islands (20 Apr 93), Costa Rica (26 Aug 94), Côte d'Ivoire (29 Nov 94), Croatia (7 Oct 96), Cuba (8 Mar 94), Cyprus (10 Jul 96), Czech Republic (3 Dec 93), Denmark (21 Dec 93), Djibouti (1 Sep 94), Dominica (6 Apr 94), Dominican Republic (25 Nov 96), Ecuador (23 Feb 93), Egypt (2 Jun 94), El Salvador (8 Sep 94), Equatorial Guinea (6 Dec 94), Eritrea (21 Mar 96), Estonia (27 Jul 94), Ethiopia (5 Apr 94), European Community (21 Dec 93), Fiji (25 Feb 93), Finland (27 Jul 94), France (1 Jul 94), Gabon (14 Mar 97), Gambia (10 Jun 94), Georgia (2 Jun 94), Germany (21 Dec 93), Ghana (29 Aug 94), Greece (4 Aug 94), Grenada (11 Aug 94), Guatemala (10 Jul 95), Guinea (7 May 93), Guinea–Bissau (27 Oct 95), Guyana (29 Aug 94), Haiti (25 Sep 96), Honduras (31 Jul 95), Hungary (24 Feb 94), Iceland (12 Sep 94), India (18 Feb 94), Indonesia (23 Aug 94), Iran (6 Aug 96), Iraq (28 Jul 2009), Ireland (22 Mar 96), Israel (7 Aug 95), Italy (15 Apr 94), Jamaica (6 Jan 95), Japan (28 May 93), Jordan (12 Nov 93), Kazakhstan (6 Sep 94), Kenya (26 Jul 94, Kiribati (16 Aug 94), Korea (North) (26 Oct 94), Korea (South) (3 Oct 94), Kuwait (2 Aug 2002), Kyrgyzstan (6 Aug 96), Laos (20 Sep 96), Latvia (14 Dec 95), Lebanon (15 Dec 94), Lesotho (10 Jan 95), Liberia (8 Nov 2000), Libya (12 Jul 2001), Liechtenstein (19 Nov 97), Lithuania (1 Feb 96), Luxembourg (9 May 94), Macedonia (2 Dec 97), Madagascar (4 Mar 96), Malawi (2 Feb 94), Malaysia (24 Jun 94), Maldives (9 Nov 92), Mali (29 Mar 95), Malta (29 Dec 2000), Marshall Islands (8 Oct 92), Mauritania (16 Aug 96), Mauritius (4 Sep 92), Mexico (11 Mar 93), Micronesia (20 Jun 94), Monaco (20 Nov 92), Mongolia (30 Sep 93), Moldova (20 Oct 95), Montenegro (23 Oct 2006), Morocco (21 Aug 95), Mozambique (25 Aug 95), Myanmar (Burma) (25 Nov 94), Namibia (16 May 97), Nauru (11 Nov 93), Nepal (23 Nov 93), Netherlands (12 Jun 94), New Zealand (16 Sep 93),

Nicaragua (20 Nov 95), Niger (25 Jul 95), Nigeria (29 Aug 94), Niue (28 Feb 96), Norway (9 Jul 93), Oman (8 Feb 95), Pakistan (26 Jul 94), Palau (6 Jan 99), Panama (17 Jan 95), Papua New Guinea (16 Mar 93), Paraguay (24 Feb 94), Peru (7 Jun 93), Philippines (8 Oct 93), Poland (18 Jan 96), Portugal (21 Dec 93), Qatar (21 Aug 96), Romania (17 Aug 94), Russia (5 Apr 95), Rwanda (29 May 96), Samoa (9 Feb 94), San Marino (28 Oct 94), São Tomé/Principe (29 Sep 99), Saudi Arabia (3 Oct 2001), Senegal (17 Oct 94), Serbia (1 Mar 2002), Seychelles (22 Sep 92), Sierra Leone (12 Dec 94), Singapore (21 Dec 95), Slovakia (25 Aug 94), Slovenia (9 Jul 96), Solomon Islands (3 Oct 95), Somalia (11 Sep 2009), South Africa (2 Nov 95), Spain (21 Dec 93), Sri Lanka (23 Mar 94), St Kitts/Nevis (7 Jan 93), St Lucia (28 Jul 93), St Vincent/Grenadines (3 Jun 96), Suriname (12 Jan 96), Swaziland (9 Nov 94), Sweden (16 Dec 93), Switzerland (21 Nov 94), Syria (4 Jan 96), Tajikistan (29 Oct 97), Tanzania (8 Mar 96), Thailand (31 Oct 2003), Timor Leste (10 Oct 2006), Togo (4 Oct 95), Tonga (19 May 98), Trinidad/Tobago (1 Aug 96), Tunisia (15 Jul 93), Turkey (14 Feb 97), Turkmenistan (18 Sep 96), Tuvalu (20 Dec 2002), Uganda (8 Sep 93), Ukraine (7 Feb 95), United Arab Emirates (10 Feb 2000), United Kingdom (3 Jun 94), Uruguay (5 Nov 93), Uzbekistan (19 Jul 95), Vanuatu (25 Mar 93), Venezuela (13 Sep 94), Vietnam (16 Nov 94), Yemen (21 Feb 96), Zambia (28 May 93), Zimbabwe (11 Nov 94)

Ratified/accepted/approved with qualification: 2

Chile (9 Sep 94), Sudan (30 Oct 95)

5.8 CARTAGENA PROTOCOL ON BIOSAFETY TO THE CONVENTION ON BIOLOGICAL DIVERSITY (WITH ANNEXES)

Adopted: 29 Jan 2000

Entered into force: 11 Sep 2003

Total parties: 161

Signed but not ratified: 10 (all dates 24 May 2000, except as indicated) Argentina, Canada (19 Apr 2001), Chile, Cook Islands (21 May 2001), Haiti, Iceland (1 Jun 2001), Jamaica (4 Jun 2001), Monaco, Nepal (2 Mar 2001), Uruguay (1 Jun 2001)

Ratified/acceded/accepted without qualification: 158

Albania (8 Feb 2005), Algeria (5 Aug 2004), Angola (27 Feb 2009), Antigua/Barbuda (10 Sep 2003), Armenia (30 Apr 2004), Austria (27 Aug 2002), Azerbaijan (1 Apr 2005), Bahamas (15 Jan 2004), Bangladesh (5 Feb 2004), Barbados (6 Sept 2002), Belarus (26 Aug 2002), Belgium (15 Apr 2004), Belize (12 Feb 2004), Benin (2 Mar 2005), Bhutan (26 Aug 2002), Bolivia (22 Apr 2002), Bosnia & Herzegovina (1 Oct 2009), Botswana (11 Jun 2002), Brazil (24 Nov 2003), Bulgaria (13 Oct 2000), Burkina Faso (4 Aug 2003), Burundi (2 Oct 2008), Cambodia (17 Sep 2003), Cameroon (20 Feb 2003), Cape Verde (1 Nov 2005), Central African Republic (18 Nov 2008), Chad (1 Nov 2006), Colombia (20 May 2003), Comoros (25 Mar 2009), Congo (Brazzaville) (13 Jul 2006), Congo (Kinshasa) (23 Mar 2005), Costa Rica (6 Feb 2007), Croatia (29 Aug 2002), Cuba (17 Sep 2002), Cyprus (5 Dec 2003), Czech Republic (8 Oct 2001), Djibouti (8 Apr 2002), Dominica (13 Jul 2004), Dominican Republic (20 Jun 2006), Ecuador (30 Jan 2003), Egypt (23 Dec 2003), El Salvador (26 Sep 2003), Eritrea (10 Mar 2005), Estonia (24 Mar 2004), Ethiopia (9 Oct 2003), European Community (27 Aug 2002), Fiji (5 Jun 2001), Finland (9 Jul 2004), France (7 Apr 2003), Gabon (2 May 2007), Gambia (9 Jun 2004), Georgia (4 Nov 2008), Germany (20 Nov 2003), Ghana (30 May 2003), Greece (21 May 2004), Grenada (5 Feb 2004), Guatemala (28 Oct 2004), Guinea (11 Dec 2007), Guinea Bissau (19 May 2010), Guyana (18 Mar 2008), Honduras (18 Nov 2008), Hungary (13 Jan 2004), India (17 Jan 2003), Indonesia (3 Dec 2004), Iran (20 Nov 2003), Ireland (14 Nov 2003), Italy (24 Mar 2004), Japan (21 Nov 2003), Jordan (11 Nov 2003),

Kazakhstan (8 Sep 2008), Kenya (24 Jan 2002), Kiribati (20 Apr 2004), Korea (North) (29 Jul 2003), Korea (South) (3 Oct 2007), Kyrgyzstan (5 Oct 2005), Laos (3 Aug 2004), Latvia (13 Feb 2004), Lesotho (20 Sep 2001), Liberia (15 Feb 2002), Libya (14 Jun 2005), Lithuania (7 Nov 2003), Luxembourg (28 Aug 2002), Madagascar (24 Nov 2003), Macedonia (14 Jun 2005), Malawi (27 Feb 2009), Malaysia (3 Sep 2003), Maldives (3 Sep 2002), Mali (28 Aug 2002), Malta (5 Jan 2007), Marshall Islands (27 Jan 2003), Mauritania (22 Jul 2005), Mauritius (11 Apr 2002), Mexico (27 Aug 2002), Moldova (4 Mar 2003), Mongolia (22 Jul 2003), Montenegro (23 Oct 2006), Morocco (25 Apr 2011), Mozambique (21 Oct 2002), Myanmar (13 Feb 2008), Namibia (10 Feb 2005), Nauru (12 Nov 2001), Netherlands (8 Jan 2002), Nicaragua (28 Aug 2002), Niger (30 Sep 2004), Nigeria (15 Jul 2003), Niue (8 Jul 2002), Norway (10 May 2001), Oman (11 Apr 2003), Pakistan (2 Mar 2009), Palau (13 Jun 2003), Panama (1 May 2002), Paraguay (10 Mar 2004), Papua New Guinea (14 Oct 2005), Peru (14 Apr 2004), Philippines (5 Oct 2006), Poland (10 Dec 2003), Portugal (30 Sep 2004), Qatar (14 Mar 2007), Romania (30 Jun 2003), Rwanda (22 Jul 2004), Samoa (30 May 2002), Saudi Arabia (9 Aug 2007), Senegal (8 Oct 2003), Serbia (8 Feb 2006), Seychelles (13 May 2004), Slovakia (24 Nov 2003), Slovenia (20 Nov 2002), Solomon Islands (28 Jul 2004), Somalia (26 Jul 2010), South Africa (14 Aug 2003), Spain(16 Jan 2002), Sri Lanka (28 Apr 2004), St Kitts/Nevis (23 May 2001), St Lucia (16 Jun 2005), St Vincent/Grenadines (27 Aug 2003), Swaziland (13 Jan 2006), Sudan (13 Jun 2005), Suriname (27 Mar 2008), Sweden (8 Aug 2002), Switzerland (26 Mar 2002), Syria (1 Apr 2004), Tajikistan (12 Feb 2004), Tanzania (24 Apr 2003), Thailand (10 Oct 2005), Togo (2 Jul 2004), Tonga (18 Sep 2003), Trinidad/Tobago (5 Oct 2000), Tunisia (22 Jan 2003), Turkey (24 Oct 2003), Turkmenistan (21 Aug 2008), Uganda (30 Nov 2001), Ukraine (6 Dec 2002), United Kingdom (19 Nov 2003), Venezuela (13 May 2002), Vietnam (21 Jan 2004), Yemen (1 Dec 2005), Zambia (27 Apr 2004), Zimbabwe (25 Feb 2005)
Ratified/acceded/accepted with qualification: 3
China (8 Jun 2005), Denmark (27 Aug 2002), New Zealand (24 Feb 2005)

5.9   Non-Legally Binding Statement on All Types of Forests
Adopted: 17 Dec 2007

5.10   Nagoya-Kuala Lumpur Supplementary Protocol on Liability and Redress to the Cartagena Protocol on Biosafety
Adopted: 15 October 2010
Not yet in force
Signed but not ratified: 35
Antigua and Barbuda (9 Aug 2011), Austria (11 May 2011), Belgium (20 Sep 2011), Bulgaria (11 May 2011), Cape Verde (26 Sep 2011), Colombia (7 Mar 2011), Czech Republic (11 May 2011), Denmark (7 Mar 2011), European Union (11 May 2011), Finland (11 May 2011), France (11 May 2011), Germany (20 Sep 2011), Hungary (11 May 2011), India (11 Oct 2011), Ireland (11 May 2011), Italy (14 Jun 2011), Latvia (11 May 2011), Lithuania (11 May 2011), Luxembourg (11 May 2011), Madagascar (22 Sep 2011), Mauritania (18 May 2011), Montenegro (11 May 2011), Mozambique (26 Sep 2011), Netherlands (7 Mar 2011), Panama (3 May 2011), Peru (4 May 2011), Poland (20 Sep 2011), Portugal (20 Sep 2011), Romania (11 May 2011), Slovenia (11 May 2011), Spain (21 Jul 2011), Sweden (7 Mar 2011), Switzerland (11 May 2011), Togo (27 Sep 2011), Tunisia (11 May 2011)

5.11   Nagoya Protocol on Access to Genetic Resources and the Fair and Equitable Sharing of Benefits Arising from Their Utilization to the

CONVENTION ON BIOLOGICAL DIVERSITY
Adopted: 29 October 2010
Not yet in force
Signed but not ratified: 65
Algeria (2 Feb 2011), Antigua and Barbuda (28 Jul 2011), Austria (23 Jun 2011), Bangladesh (6 Sep 2011), Belgium (20 Sep 2011), Bhutan (20 Sep 2011), Brazil (2 Feb 2011), Bulgaria (23 Jun 2011), Burkina Faso (20 Sep 2011), Cape Verde (26 Sep 2011), Central African Republic (6 Apr 2011), Colombia (2 Feb 2011), Congo (23 Sep 2011), Costa Rica (6 Jul 2011), Czech Republic (23 Jun 2011), Congo (Kinshasa) (21 Sep 2011), Denmark (23 Jun 2011), Djibouti (19 Oct 2011), Dominican Republic (20 Sep 2011), Ecuador (1 Apr 2011), European Union (23 Jun 2011), Finland (23 Jun 2011), France (20 Sep 2011), Gabon (13 May 2011), Germany (23 Jun 2011), Ghana (20 May 2011), Greece (20 Sep 2011), Grenada (22 Sep 2011), Guatemala (11 May 2011), Hungary (23 Jun 2011), India (11 May 2011), Indonesia (11 May 2011), Italy (23 Jun 2011), Japan (11 May 2011), Luxembourg (23 Jun 2011), Madagascar (22 Sep 2011), Mali (19 Apr 2011), Mauritania (18 May 2011), Mexico (24 Feb 2011), Mozambique (26 Sep 2011), Netherlands (23 Jun 2011), Niger (26 Sep 2011), Norway (11 May 2011), Palau (20 Sep 2011), Panama (3 May 2011), Peru (4 May 2011), Poland (20 Sep 2011), Portugal (20 Sep 2011), Republic of Korea (20 Sep 2011), Romania (20 Sep 2011), Rwanda (28 Feb 2011), Serbia (20 Sep 2011), Seychelles (15 Apr 2011), Slovenia (27 Sep 2011), South Africa (11 May 2011), Spain (21 Jul 2011), Sudan (21 Apr 2011), Sweden (23 Jun 2011), Switzerland (11 May 2011), Tajikistan (20 Sep 2011), Togo (27 Sep 2011), Tunisia (11 May 2011), United Kingdom (23 Jun 2011), Uruguay (19 Jul 2011), Yemen (2 Feb 2011)

B. Fishing

5.12 CONVENTION ON FISHING AND CONSERVATION OF LIVING RESOURCES OF THE HIGH SEAS
Concluded: 29 Apr 58
Entered into force: 20 Mar 66
Total parties: 38
Signed but not ratified: 21
Afghanistan (30 Oct 58), Argentina (29 Apr 58), Bolivia (17 Oct 58), Canada (29 Apr 58), Costa Rica (29 Apr 58), Cuba (29 Apr 58), Ghana (29 Apr 58), Iceland (29 Apr 58), Indonesia (8 May 58), Iran (28 May 58), Ireland (2 Oct 58), Israel (29 Apr 58), Lebanon (29 May 58), Liberia (27 May 58), Nepal (29 Apr 58), New Zealand (29 Oct 58), Pakistan (31 Oct 58), Panama (2 May 58), Sri Lanka (30 Oct 58), Tunisia (30 Oct 58), Uruguay (29 Apr 58)
Ratified/acceded/accepted without qualification: 37
Australia (14 May 63), Belgium (6 Jan 72), Bosnia–Herzegovina (12 Jan 94), Burkina Faso (4 Oct 65), Cambodia (18 Mar 60), Colombia (3 Jan 63), Dominican Republic (11 Aug 64), Fiji (25 Mar 71), Finland (16 Feb 65), France (18 Sep 70), Haiti (29 Mar 60), Jamaica (16 Apr 64), Kenya (20 Jun 69), Lesotho (23 Oct 73), Madagascar (31 Jul 62), Malawi (3 Nov 65), Malaysia (21 Dec 60), Mauritius (5 Oct 70), Mexico (2 Aug 66), Montenegro (23 Oct 2006), Netherlands (18 Feb 66), Nigeria (26 Jun 61), Portugal (8 Jan 63), Senegal (25 Apr 61), Serbia (12 Mar 2001) Sierra Leone (13 Mar 62), Spain (25 Feb 71), Solomon Islands (3 Sep 81), South Africa (9 Apr 63), Switzerland (18 May 66), Thailand (2 Jul 68), Tonga (29 Jun 71), Trinidad/Tobago (11 Apr 66), Uganda (14 Sep 64), United Kingdom (14 Mar 60), United States (12 Apr 61),Venezuela (10 Jul 63)
Ratified/acceded/accepted with qualification: 1
Denmark (26 Sep 68)

5.13 CONVENTION FOR THE PROHIBITION OF FISHING WITH LONG DRIFTNETS IN THE SOUTH PACIFIC
Concluded: 24 Nov 89
Entered into force: 17 May 91
Signed but not ratified: 4
France (30 Apr 90), Marshall Islands (29 Nov 89), Tuvalu (13 Feb 90), Vanuatu (13 Feb 90)
Ratified/accepted/approved without qualification: 13
Australia (6 Jul 92), Cook Islands (24 Jan 90), Fiji (18 Jan 94), Kiribati (10 Jan 92), Micronesia (20 Dec 90), Nauru (14 Oct 92), New Zealand (17 May 91), Niue (9 Jun 97), Palau (21 Jan 99), Samoa (9 Sep 96), Solomon Islands (19 Jan 98), Tokelau (17 May 91), United States (28 Feb 92)

5.14 **UNGA** RESOLUTION **44/225** ON LARGE-SCALE PELAGIC DRIFTNET FISHING AND ITS IMPACT ON THE LIVING MARINE RESOURCES OF THE WORLD'S OCEANS AND SEAS
Adopted unanimously: 22 Dec 89

5.15 **UNGA** RESOLUTION **46/215** ON LARGE-SCALE PELAGIC DRIFTNET FISHING AND ITS IMPACT ON THE LIVING MARINE RESOURCES OF THE WORLD'S OCEANS AND SEAS
Adopted without recorded vote: 20 Dec 91

5.16 AGREEMENT TO PROMOTE COMPLIANCE WITH INTERNATIONAL CONSERVATION AND MANAGEMENT MEASURES BY FISHING VESSELS ON THE HIGH SEAS
Adopted: 24 Nov 93
Entered into force: 24 Apr 2003
Ratified/accepted/approved without qualifications: 39
Albania (8 Nov 2005), Angola (7 Mar 2006), Argentina (24 Jun 1996), Australia (19 Aug 2004), Barbados (26 Oct 2000), Belize (19 Jul 2005), Benin (4 Jan 1999), Brazil (2 Mar 2009), Canada (20 May 1994), Cape Verde (27 Jan 2006), Chile (23 Jan 2004), Cook Islands (30 Oct 2006), Cyprus (19 Jul 2000), Egypt (14 Aug 2001), European Union (6 Aug 1996), Georgia (7 Sep 1994), Ghana (12 May 2003), Japan (20 Jun 2000), Korea (South) (24 Apr 2003), Madagascar (26 Oct 1994), Mauritius (27 Mar 2003), Mexico (11 Mar 1999), Morocco (30 Jan 2001), Mozambique (9 Jan 2009), Myanmar (8 Sep 1994), Namibia (7 Aug 1998), New Zealand (14 July 2005), Norway (28 Dec 1994), Oman (1st July 2008), Peru (23 Feb 2001), St. Kitts & Nevis (24 Jun 1994), St. Lucia 23 Oct 2002), Senegal (8 Sep 2009), Seychelles (7 Apr 2000), Sweden (25 Oct 1994), Syria (13 Nov 2002), Tanzania (17 Feb 1999), United States of America (19 Dec 1995), Uruguay (11 Nov 1999)

5.17 AGREEMENT FOR THE IMPLEMENTATION OF THE PROVISIONS OF THE UNITED NATIONS CONVENTION ON THE LAW OF THE SEA OF **10 DECEMBER 1982**, RELATING TO THE CONSERVATION AND MANAGEMENT OF STRADDLING FISH STOCKS AND HIGHLY MIGRATORY FISH STOCKS
Concluded: 4 Aug 95
Entered into force: 11 Dec 2001
Signed but not ratified: 16
Argentina (4 Dec 95), Bangladesh (4 Dec 95), Burkina Faso (15 Oct 96), China (6 Nov 96), Côte d'Ivoire (24 Jan 96), Egypt (5 Dec 95), Gabon (7 Oct 96), Guinea–Bissau (4 Dec 95), Israel (4 Dec 95), Jamaica (4 Dec 95), Mauritania (21 Dec 95), Morocco (4 Dec 95), Pakistan (15 Feb 96), Philippines (30 Aug 96), Uganda (10 Oct 96), Vanuatu (23 Jul 96)
Ratified/acceded/accepted without qualification: 78
Australia (23 Dec 99), Austria (19 Dec 2003), Bahamas (16 Jan 97), Barbados (22 Sep 2000), Belgium (19 Dec 2003), Belize (14 Jul 2005), Brazil (8 Mar 2000),

Bulgaria (13 Dec 2006), Canada (3 Aug 99), Cook Islands (1 Apr 99), Costa Rica (18 Jun 2001), Cyprus (25 Sep 2002), Czech Republic (19 Mar 2007), Denmark (19 Dec 2003), Estonia (7 Aug 2006), European Community (19 Dec 2003), Fiji (12 Dec 96), Finland (19 Dec 2003), France (19 Dec 2003), Germany (19 Dec 2003), Greece (19 Dec 2003), Guinea (16 Sep 2005), Hungary (16 May 2008), Iceland (14 Feb 97), India (19 Aug 2003), Indonesia (28 Sep 2009), Iran (17 Apr 98), Ireland (19 Dec 2003), Italy (19 Dec 2003), Japan (7 Aug 2006), Kenya (13 Jul 2004), Kiribati (15 Sep 2005), Korea (South) (1 Feb 2008), Latvia (5 Feb 2007), Liberia (16 Sep 2005), Lithuania (1 Mar 2007), Luxembourg (19 Dec 2003), Maldives (30 Dec 98), Malta (11 Nov 2001), Marshall Islands (19 Mar 2003), Mauritius (25 Mar 97), Micronesia (23 May 97), Monaco (9 Jun 99), Mozambique (10 Dec 2008), Namibia (8 Apr 98), Nauru (10 Jan 97), Netherlands (19 Dec 2003), New Zealand (18 Apr 2001), Nigeria (2 Nov 2009), Niue (11 Oct 2006), Norway (30 Dec 96), Oman (14 May 2008), Palau (26 Mar 2008), Panama (16 Dec 2008), Papua New Guinea (4 Jun 99), Poland (14 Mar 2006), Portugal (19 Dec 2003), Romania (16 Jul 2007), Russia (4 Aug 97), Samoa (25 Oct 96), Senegal (30 Jan 97), Seychelles (20 Mar 98), Slovakia (6 Nov 2008), Slovenia (15 Jun 2006), Solomon Islands (13 Feb 97), South Africa (14 Aug 2003), Spain (19 Dec 2003), Sri Lanka (24 Oct 96), St Lucia (9 Aug 96), St. Vincent and the Grenadines (29 Oct 2010), Sweden (19 Dec 2003), Tonga (31 Jul 96), Trinidad/Tobago (13 Sep 2006), Tuvalu (2 Feb 2009), Ukraine (27 Feb 2003), United Kingdom (10 Dec 2001), United States (21 Aug 96), Uruguay (10 Sep 99)

5.18 **FAO CODE OF CONDUCT FOR RESPONSIBLE FISHERIES**
Adopted: 31 Oct 95

C. Whaling

5.19 **INTERNATIONAL CONVENTION FOR THE REGULATION OF WHALING**
Concluded: 2 Dec 46
Entered into force: 10 Nov 48
Total parties: 89
Ratified/acceded/accepted without qualification: 86
Antigua/Barbuda (21 Jul 82), Argentina (18 May 60), Australia (1 Dec 47), Austria (20 May 1994), Belgium (15 Jul 2004), Belize (17 Jun 2003), Benin (26 Apr 2002), Brazil (4 Jan 74), Bulgaria (10 Aug 2009), Cambodia (1 Jun 2006), Cameroon (14 Jun 2005), China (24 Sep 80), Colombia (22 Mar 2011), Congo (Brazzaville) (29 May 2008), Costa Rica (24 Jul 1981), Côte d'Ivoire (8 Jul 2004), Croatia (10 Jan 2007), Cyprus (26 Feb 2007), Czech Republic (26 Jan 2005), Denmark (23 May 50), Dominica (18 Jun 92), Dominican Republic (30 Jul 2009), Ecuador (10 May 2007), Eritrea (10 Oct 2007), Estonia (07 Jan 2009), Finland (23 Feb 83), France (3 Dec 48), Gabon (8 May 2002), Gambia (17 May 2005), Germany (2 Jul 82), Ghana (17 Jul 2009), Greece (16 May 2007), Grenada (7 Apr 93), Guatemala (16 May 2006), Guinea–Bissau (29 May 2007), Hungary (1 May 2004), Iceland (10 Oct 2002), India (9 Mar 81), Ireland (2 Jan 85), Israel (7 Jun 2006), Italy (12 Feb 1998), Japan (21 Apr 1951), Kenya (2 Dec 81), Kiribati (28 Dec 2004), Korea (South) (29 Dec 78), Laos (22 May 2007), Lithuania (25 Nov 2008), Luxembourg (10 Jun 2005), Mali (17 Aug 2004), Marshall Islands (1 Jun 2006), Mauritania (23 Dec 2003), Mexico (30 Jun 49), Monaco (15 Mar 82), Mongolia (16 May 2002), Morocco (12 Feb 2001), Nauru (15 Jun 2005), Netherlands (14 Jun 77), New Zealand (15 Jun 76), Nicaragua (5 Jun 2003), Norway (23 Sep 60), Oman (15 Jul 80), Palau (8 May 2002), Panama (12 Jun 2001), Poland (17 Apr 2009), Portugal (14 May 2002), Romania (09 Apr 2008), San Marino (16 Apr 2002), Senegal (15 Jul 82), Slovakia (22 Mar 2005), Slovenia (20 Sep 2006), Solomon Islands (10 May 93), South Africa (5 May 48), Spain (6 Jul 79), Suriname (15 Jul 2004), St Kitts/Nevis (24 Jun 92), St Lucia (29 Jun 81), St

Vincent/Grenadines (22 Jul 81), Sweden (15 Jun 79),Switzerland (29 May 80), Tanzania (23 Jun 2008), Togo (15 Jun 2005), Tuvalu (30 Jun 2004), United Kingdom (17 Jun 47), United States (18 Jul 47), Uruguay* (27 Sep 2007), USSR (Russia) (11 Sep 48), Venezuela (11 Jul 91)
Ratified/acceded/accepted with qualification: 3
Chile (6 Jul 79), Peru (18 Jun 79), Iceland (10 Oct 2002)
Denunciations: 7
Canada (30 Jun 82), Egypt (30 Jun 89), Jamaica (30 Jun 84), Mauritius (30 Jun 88), Philippines (30 Jun 88), Seychelles (30 Jun 1995), Venezuela (30 Jun 1999)

5.20 INTERNATIONAL WHALING COMMISSION, RULES OF PROCEDURE
Adopted with most recent amendments: 24 June 2010

6. POLAR REGIONS

A. Antarctic

6.1 ANTARCTIC TREATY
Concluded: 1 Dec 59
Entered into force: 23 Jun 61
Total parties: 48
Argentina (23 Jun 61)*, Australia (23 Jun 61)*, Austria (25 Aug 87), Belarus (27 Dec 2006), Belgium (26 Jun 60)*, Brazil (16 May 75)*, Bulgaria (11 Sep 78)*, Canada (4 May 88), Chile (23 Jun 61)*, China (8 Jun 83)*, Colombia (31 Jan 89), Cuba (16 Aug 84), Czech Republic (1 Jan 93), Denmark (20 May 65), Ecuador (15 Sep 87)*, Estonia (17 May 2001), Finland (15 May 84)*, France (16 Sep 60)*, Germany (5 Feb 79)*, Greece (8 Jan 87), Guatemala (31 Jul 91), Hungary (27 Jan 84), India (19 Aug 83)*, Italy (18 Mar 81)*, Japan (4 Aug 60)*, Korea (North) (21 Jan 87), Korea (South) (28 Nov 86)*, Monaco (31 May 2008), Netherlands (30 Mar 67)*, New Zealand (1 Nov 60)*, Norway (24 Aug 60)*, Papua New Guinea (16 Mar 81), Peru (10 Apr 81)*, Poland (8 Jun 61)*, Portugal (29 Jan 2010), Romania (15 Sep 71), Russia (2 Nov 60)*, Slovakia (1 Jan 93), South Africa (21 Jun 60)*, Spain (31 Mar 82)*, Sweden (25 Apr 84)*, Switzerland (15 Nov 90), Turkey (24 Jan 96), Ukraine (28 Oct 92)*, United Kingdom (31 May 60)*, United States (18 Aug 60)*, Uruguay (11 Jan 80)* Venezuela (24 Mar 99)

* Consultative parties: 28.

6.2 CERTAIN RECOMMENDATIONS OF THIRD ANTARCTIC TREATY CONSULTATIVE MEETING, ANNEX: AGREED MEASURES FOR THE CONSERVATION OF ANTARCTIC FAUNA AND FLORA
Adopted: 13 Jun 64
Entered into force: 1 Nov 1982
Approved: 22
Argentina (3 Sep 65), Australia (1 Sep 80), Belgium (25 Jan 78), Brazil (27 Oct 88), Chile (23 Nov 70), China (11 Dec 85), France (20 Sep 72), Germany (23 Aug 88), India (7 Mar 88), Italy (22 Apr 87), Japan (1 Nov 82), Korea (South) (10 May 95), Netherlands (10 Oct 2003), New Zealand (23 Dec 71), Norway (1 Dec 65), Poland (11 Jul 77), South Africa (5 Oct 64), Spain (8 Apr 88), United Kingdom (10 Sep 68), United States (31 Jul 79), Uruguay (10 Oct 89), USSR (Russia) (20 Feb 65)
Termination of application of measures: 1 July 2011

Note: By Decision 1 at ATCM XXXIV, the treaty parties determined that the Agreed Measures on Fauna and Flora were no longer current and therefore required "no further action by the Parties." The Agreed Measures have been effectively superseded by the Protocol on Environmental Protection to the Antarctic Treaty, Basic Document 6.9, *infra*, and its annexes.

6.3   CONVENTION FOR THE CONSERVATION OF ANTARCTIC SEALS
Concluded: 11 Feb 72
Entered into force: 11 Mar 78
Signed but not ratified: 1 (as of at least 1 Mar 97)
New Zealand (9 Jun 72)
Ratified/acceded/accepted without qualification: 16
Argentina (7 Mar 78), Australia (1 Jul 87), Belgium (9 Feb 78), Brazil (11 Feb 91), Canada (4 Oct 90), Chile (7 Feb 80), France (19 Feb 75), Germany (30 Sep 87), Italy (2 Apr 92), Japan (28 Aug 80), Norway (10 Dec 73), Poland (15 Aug 80), South Africa (15 Aug 72), United Kingdom (10 Sep 74), United States (19 Jan 77), USSR (Russia) (8 Feb 78)

6.4   CONVENTION ON THE CONSERVATION OF ANTARCTIC MARINE LIVING RESOURCES (CCAMLR)
Concluded: 20 May 80
Entered into force: 7 Apr 82
Total Parties: 34
Ratified/accepted/approved without qualification: 32
Australia (6 May 81), Belgium (22 Feb 84), Brazil (28 Jan 86), Bulgaria (1 Sep 92), Canada (1 Jul 88), Chile (22 Jul 81), China (19 Sep 2006), Cook Islands (20 Oct 2005), European Community (21 Apr 82), Finland (6 Sep 89), Germany (23 Apr 82), Greece (12 Feb 87), India (17 Jun 85), Italy (29 Mar 89), Japan (26 May 81), Korea (South) (29 Mar 85), Mauritius (2 Oct 2004), Namibia (29 Jun 2000), Netherlands (23 Feb 90), New Zealand (8 Mar 82), Norway (6 Dec 83), Peru (23 Jun 89), Poland (28 Mar 84), South Africa (23 Jul 81), Spain (9 Apr 84), Sweden (6 Jun 84), Ukraine (22 Apr 94), United Kingdom (31 Aug 81), United States (18 Feb 82), Uruguay (22 Mar 85), USSR (Russia) (26 May 81), Vanuatu (20 Jun 2001)
Ratified/accepted/approved with qualification: 2 (as of at least 1 Mar 97)
Argentina (28 May 82), France (16 Sep 82)

6.5   UNGA RESOLUTION 38/77 ON THE QUESTION OF ANTARCTICA
Adopted without recorded vote: 15 Dec 83

6.6   UNGA RESOLUTION 39/152 ON THE QUESTION OF ANTARCTICA
Adopted without recorded vote: 17 Dec 84

6.7   CONVENTION ON THE REGULATION OF ANTARCTIC MINERAL RESOURCE ACTIVITIES (CRAMRA)
Concluded: 2 Jun 88
Not in force. Effectively superseded by Basic Document 6.9, infra.
Signed but not ratified: 19
Argentina (17 Mar 89), Brazil (25 Nov 88), Chile (17 Mar 89), China (28 Jun 89), Czechoslovakia (24 Feb 1989), Denmark (25 Feb 89), Finland (25 Nov 88), Germany (22 Nov 1989), Japan (22 Nov 89), Korea (South) (25 Nov 88), New Zealand (25 Nov 88), Norway (25 Nov 88), Poland (25 Feb 89), South Africa (25 Nov 88), Sweden (25 Nov 88), United Kingdom (22 Mar 89), United States (30 Nov 88), Uruguay (25 Nov 88), USSR (Russia) (25 Nov 88)

6.8 UNGA RESOLUTION 44/124 ON THE QUESTION OF ANTARCTICA
Adopted: 15 Dec 89
For Part A: 114
Afghanistan, Albania, Algeria, Angola, Antigua and Barbuda, Argentina, Bahamas, Bahrain, Bangladesh, Barbados, Benin, Bhutan, Bolivia, Brazil, Brunei Darussalam, Burkina Faso, Burundi, Cameroon, Cape Verde, Central African Republic, Chad, China, Colombia, Congo, Costa Rica, Côte d'Ivoire, Cuba, Cyprus, Democratic Kampuchea, Democratic Yemen, Djibouti, Dominica, Dominican Republic, Ecuador, Egypt, El Salvador, Ethiopia, Fiji, Gabon, Gambia, Ghana, Grenada, Guatemala, Guinea, Guinea–Bissau, Guyana, Haiti, Honduras, India, Indonesia, Iran, Iraq, Jamaica, Jordan, Kenya, Kuwait, Lao People's Democratic Republic, Lebanon, Lesotho, Liberia, Libya, Madagascar, Malawi, Malaysia, Maldives, Mali, Mauritania, Mexico, Mongolia, Morocco, Mozambique, Myanmar, Nepal, Nicaragua, Niger, Nigeria, Oman, Pakistan, Panama, Peru, Philippines, Qatar, Romania, Rwanda, Saint Kitts and Nevis, Saint Lucia, Saint Vincent and the Grenadines, São Tomé and Príncipe, Saudi Arabia, Senegal, Seychelles, Sierra Leone, Singapore, Solomon Islands, Somalia, Sri Lanka, Sudan, Suriname, Syria, Thailand, Togo, Trinidad and Tobago, Tunisia, Uganda, United Arab Emirates, Tanzania, Vanuatu, Venezuela, Viet Nam, Yemen, Yugoslavia, Zaire, Zambia, Zimbabwe
Against Part A: 0
Abstain Part A: 6
Ireland, Luxembourg, Malta, Mauritius, Portugal, Swaziland
For Part B: 100
Albania, Algeria, Angola, Antigua and Barbuda, Bahamas, Bahrain, Bangladesh, Barbados, Benin, Bhutan, Bolivia, Botswana, Brunei Darussalam, Burkina Faso, Burundi, Cameroon, Cape Verde, Central African Republic, Chad, Congo, Costa Rica, Côte d'Ivoire, Cyprus, Democratic Kampuchea, Djibouti, Dominica, Dominican Republic, Egypt, El Salvador, Ethiopia, Gabon, Gambia, Ghana, Grenada, Guatemala, Guinea, Guinea–Bissau, Guyana, Haiti, Honduras, Indonesia, Iran, Iraq, Jamaica, Jordan, Kenya, Kuwait, Lebanon, Lesotho, Liberia, Libya, Madagascar, Malawi, Malaysia, Maldives, Mali, Mauritiania, Mexico, Morocco, Mozambique, Myanmar, Nepal, Niger, Nigeria, Oman, Pakistan, Panama, Philippines, Qatar, Romania, Rwanda, Saint Kitts and Nevis, Saint Lucia, Saint Vincent and the Grenadines, São Tomé and Príncipe, Saudi Arabia, Senegal, Seychelles, Sierra Leone, Singapore, Solomon Islands, Somalia, Sri Lanka, Sudan, Suriname, Syria, Thailand, Togo, Trinidad and Tobago, Tunisia, Uganda, United Arab Emirates, Tanzania, Vanuatu, Venezuela, Yemen, Yugoslavia, Zaire, Zambia, Zimbabwe
Against Part B: 0
Abstain Part B: 9
China, Fiji, Ireland, Luxembourg, Malta, Mauritius, Portugal, Swaziland, Turkey

6.9 PROTOCOL ON ENVIRONMENTAL PROTECTION TO THE ANTARCTIC TREATY
Concluded: 4 Oct 91
Entered into force: 14 Jan 98 (Protocol and Annexes I–IV); Annex V was adopted on 18 Oct 1991 and entered into force on 24 May 2002; Annex VI was adopted on 17 Jun 2005 and is not yet in force.
Signed but not ratified: 7
Austria (4 Oct 91), Colombia (4 Oct 91), Denmark (2 July 92), Hungary (4 Oct 91), Korea (North) (4 Oct 91), Slovakia (1 Jan 93), Switzerland (4 Oct 91)
Ratified/acceded/accepted: 34
Argentina (28 Oct 93), Australia (6 Apr 94), Belarus (15 Aug 2008), Belgium (26 Apr 96), Brazil (15 Aug 95), Bulgaria (21 Apr 98), Canada (13 Dec 2003), Chile

(11 Jan 95), China (2 Aug 94), Czech Republic (25 Aug 2004), Ecuador (4 Jan 93), Finland (1 Nov 96), France (5 Feb 93), Germany (25 Nov 94), Greece (23 May 95), India (26 Apr 96), Italy (31 Mar 95), Japan (15 Dec 97), Korea (South) (2 Jan 96), Monaco (31 Jul 2009), Netherlands (14 Apr 94), New Zealand (22 Dec 94), Norway (16 Jun 93), Peru (8 Mar 93), Poland (1 Nov 95), Romania (3 Feb 2003), Russia (6 Aug 97), South Africa (3 Aug 95), Spain (1 Jul 92), Sweden (30 Mar 94), Ukraine (25 May 2001), United Kingdom (25 Apr 95), United States (17 Apr 97), Uruguay (11 Jan 95)

Annex V approved: 28

Argentina (4 Aug 95), Australia (7 Jun 95), Belgium (23 Oct 2000), Brazil (20 May 98), Bulgaria (5 May 99), Chile (25 Mar 98), China (26 Jan 95), Ecuador (15 Nov 2001), Finland (2 Apr 97), France (26 Apr 95), Germany (1 Sep 98), India (24 May 2002), Italy (11 Feb 98), Japan (17 Dec 97), Korea (South) (5 Jun 96), Netherlands (18 Mar 98), New Zealand (21 Oct 92), Norway (13 Oct 93), Peru (17 Mar 99), Poland (20 Sep 95), Romania (5 Mar 2003), Russia (19 Jun 2001), South Africa (14 Jun 95), Spain (18 Feb 2000), Sweden (7 Apr 94), United Kingdom (21 May 96), United States (6 May 98), Uruguay (15 May 95)

Annex VI approved: 5

Finland (14 Dec 2010), Peru (10 Jul 2007), Poland (15 Jan 2009), Spain (17 Dec 2008), Sweden (8 Jun 2006)

B. Arctic

6.10 Arctic Environmental Protection Strategy (AEPS)
Adopted: 14 Jun 91
Conferees: 8
Canada, Denmark, Finland, Iceland, Norway, Sweden, Union of Soviet Socialist Republics, United States of America

6.11 Nuuk Declaration on Environment and Development in the Arctic
Adopted by the Ministers of the Arctic Countries: 16 Sep 93
Conferees: 8
Canada, Denmark, Finland, Iceland, Norway, the Russian Federation, Sweden, United States of America

6.12 Agreement between the United States of America and the Russian Federation on Cooperation in the Prevention of Pollution of the Environment in the Arctic
Concluded: 16 Dec 94
Entered into force: 16 Dec 94

6.13 Declaration on the Establishment of the Arctic Council
Adopted unanimously and signed by representatives of the Arctic States: 19 Sep 96
Signatories: 8
Canada, Denmark, Finland, Iceland, Norway, the Russian Federation, Sweden, United States of America

6.14 The Ilulissat Declaration on the Arctic Ocean
Adopted at the Arctic Ocean Conference in Ilulissat (Greenland): 28 May 2008
Conferees: 5
Canada, Denmark, Norway, Russia, United States

7. MISCELLANEOUS

A. *Economic Trade/Development*

7.1 GENERAL AGREEMENT ON TARIFFS AND TRADE (GATT) 1947
Concluded: 30 Oct 47
Entered into force: 1 Jan 48 (through Protocol of Provisional Application)
Terminated: 31 Dec 95
Currently in effect as part of GATT 1994. See Basic Document 7.7, *infra* for status information.

Following the entry into force of the Agreement Establishing the World Trade Organization, the parties to GATT 1947 withdrew from that agreement. However, the provisions of GATT 1947 have continued to remain in effect as part of GATT 1994, a "legally distinct" agreement which nevertheless incorporates GATT 1947 by reference. GATT 1994 is part of Annex 1A to the WTO Agreement (Basic Document 7.7) and is binding on all countries party to that Agreement. Status information on the WTO Agreement is provided below.

7.2 DECLARATION ON THE ESTABLISHMENT OF A NEW INTERNATIONAL ECONOMIC ORDER
Adopted without recorded vote: 1 May 74

7.3 CHARTER OF ECONOMIC RIGHTS AND DUTIES OF STATES
Adopted: 12 Dec 74
For: 120
Afghanistan, Albania, Algeria, Argentina, Australia, Bahamas, Bahrain, Bangladesh, Barbados, Benin, Bhutan, Bolivia, Botswana, Brazil, Bulgaria, Burkina Faso, Burma, Burundi, Byelorussian SSR (Belarus), Cambodia, Cameroon, Central African Republic, Chad, Chile, China, Colombia, Congo, Côte d'Ivoire, Costa Rica, Cuba, Cyprus, Czechoslovakia, Dominican Republic, Ecuador, Egypt, El Salvador, Equatorial Guinea, Ethiopia, Fiji, Finland, Gabon, Gambia, German Democratic Republic, Ghana, Greece, Grenada, Guatemala, Guinea, Guinea–Bissau, Guyana, Haiti, Honduras, Hungary, Iceland, India, Indonesia, Iran, Iraq, Jamaica, Jordan, Kenya, Kuwait, Laos, Lebanon, Lesotho, Liberia, Libya, Madagascar, Malawi, Malaysia, Mali, Malta, Mauritania, Mauritius, Mozambique, Mexico, Mongolia, Morocco, Nepal, New Zealand, Nicaragua, Niger, Nigeria, Oman, Pakistan, Panama, Paraguay, Peru, Philippines, Poland, Portugal, Qatar, Romania, Rwanda, Saudi Arabia, Senegal, Sierra Leone, Singapore, Somalia, Sri Lanka, Sudan, Swaziland, Sweden, Syria, Tanzania, Thailand, Togo, Trinidad/Tobago, Tunisia, Turkey, Uganda, Ukrainian SSR, United Arab Emirates, Uruguay, USSR, Venezuela, Yemen, Yugoslavia, Zaire, Zambia
Against: 7
Belgium, Denmark, Germany, Luxembourg, Norway, United Kingdom, United States
Abstaining: 10
Austria, Canada, France, Ireland, Israel, Italy, Japan, Netherlands, Norway, Spain

7.4 NORTH AMERICAN FREE TRADE AGREEMENT (NAFTA)
Concluded: 8 Dec 92/17 Dec 92 (Washington), 11 Dec 92/17 Dec 92 (Ottawa), 14 Dec 92/17 Dec 92 (Mexico City)
Entered into force: 1 Jan 94
Parties: 3
Canada, Mexico, United States

7.5 NORTH AMERICAN AGREEMENT ON ENVIRONMENTAL COOPERATION
Concluded: 8, 9, 12 & 14 Sep 93

Entered into force: 1 Jan 94
Ratified/accepted/approved without qualification: 3
Canada (12 & 14 Sep 93), Mexico (8 & 14 Sep 93), United States of America (9 & 14 Sep 93)

7.6   MARRAKESH MINISTERIAL DECISION ON TRADE AND ENVIRONMENT
Adopted: 14 Apr 94
Conferees: 125
The Decision was adopted by the Trade Negotiations Committee of the Uruguay Round of Multilateral Trade Negotiations, meeting at the ministerial level on the occasion of the signing of the Final Act that concluded the Uruguay Round and adopted the Agreement Establishing the World Trade Organization. For status information on the WTO Agreement, see Basic Document 7.7, infra.

7.7   AGREEMENT ESTABLISHING THE WORLD TRADE ORGANIZATION
Concluded: 15 Apr 94
Entered into force: 1 January 1995
Members: 153
Albania (8 Sep 2000), Angola (1 Dec 96), Antigua/Barbuda (1 Jan 95), Argentina (1 Jan 95), Armenia (5 Feb 2003), Australia (1 Jan 95), Austria (1 Jan 95), Bahrain (1 Jan 95), Bangladesh 1 Jan 95), Barbados (1 Jan 95), Belgium (1 Jan 95), Belize (1 Jan 95), Benin (22 Feb 96), Bolivia (13 Sep 95), Botswana (31 May 95), Brazil (1 Jan 95), Brunei (1 Jan 95), Bulgaria (1 Dec 96), Burkina Faso (3 Jun 95), Burundi (23 Jul 95), Cambodia (13 Oct 2004), Cameroon (13 Dec 95), Canada (1 Jan 95), Cape Verde (23 Jul 2008), Central African Republic (31 May 95), Chad (19 Oct 96), Chile (1 Jan 95), China (11 Dec 2001), Colombia (30 Apr 95), Congo (Brazzaville) (27 Mar 97), Congo (Kinshasa) (1 Jan 97), Costa Rica (1 Jan 95), Côte d'Ivoire (1 Jan 95), Croatia (30 Nov 2000), Cuba (20 Apr 95), Cyprus (30 Jul 95), Czech Republic (1 Jan 95), Denmark (1 Jan 95), Djibouti (31 May 95), Dominica (1 Jan 95), Dominican Republic (9 Mar 95), Ecuador (21 Jan 96), Egypt (30 Jun 95), El Salvador (7 May 95), Estonia (13 Nov 99), European Communities (1 Jan 95), Fiji (14 Jan 96), Finland (1 Jan 95), France (1 Jan 95), Gabon (1 Jan 95), Gambia (23 Oct 96), Georgia (14 Jun 2000), Germany (1 Jan 95), Ghana (1 Jan 95), Greece (1 Jan 95), Grenada (22 Feb 96), Guatemala (21 Jul 95), Guinea (25 Oct 95), Guinea Bissau (31 May 95), Guyana (1 Jan 95), Haiti (30 Jan 96), Honduras (1 Jan 95), Hong Kong (China) (1 Jan 95), Hungary (1 Jan 95), Iceland (1 Jan 95), India (1 Jan 95), Indonesia (1 Jan 95), Ireland (1 Jan 95), Israel (21 Apr 95), Italy (1 Jan 95), Jamaica (9 Mar 95), Japan (1 Jan 95), Jordan (11 Apr 00), Kenya (1 Jan 95), Korea (South) (1 Jan 95), Kuwait (1 Jan 95), Kyrgyzstan (20 Nov 98), Latvia (10 Feb 99), Lesotho (31 May 95), Liechtenstein (1 Sep 95), Lithuania (31 May 2001), Luxembourg (1 Jan 95), Macau (1 Jan 95), Macedonia (4 Apr 2003), Madagascar (17 Nov 95), Malawi (31 May 95), Malaysia (1 Jan 95), Maldives (31 May 95), Mali (31 May 95), Malta (1 Jan 95), Mauritania (31 May 95), Mauritius (1 Jan 95), Mexico (1 Jan 95), Moldova (26 Jul 2001), Mongolia (29 Jan 97), Morocco (1 Jan 95), Mozambique (26 Aug 95), Myanmar (Burma) (1 Jan 95), Namibia (1 Jan 95), Nepal (23 Apr 2004), Netherlands/Netherlands Antilles (1 Jan 95), New Zealand (1 Jan 95), Nicaragua (3 Sep 95), Niger (13 Dec 96), Nigeria (1 Jan 95), Norway (1 Jan 95), Oman (9 Nov 2000), Pakistan (1 Jan 95), Panama (6 Sep 97), Papua New Guinea (9 Jun 96), Paraguay (1 Jan 95), Peru (1 Jan 95), Philippines (1 Jan 95), Poland (1 Jul 95), Portugal (1 Jan 95), Qatar (13 Jan 96), Romania (1 Jan 95), Rwanda (22 May 96), Saudi Arabia (11 Dec 2005), Senegal (1 Jan 95), Sierra Leone (23 Jul 95), Singapore (1 Jan 95), Slovakia (1 Jan 95), Slovenia (30 Jul 95), Solomon Islands (26 Jul 96), South Africa (1 Jan 95), Spain (1 Jan 95), Sri

Lanka (1 Jan 95), St Kitts/Nevis (21 Feb 96), St Lucia (1 Jan 95), St Vincent/Grenadines (1 Jan 95), Suriname (1 Jan 95), Swaziland (1 Jan 95), Sweden (1 Jan 95), Switzerland (1 Jul 95), Taiwan (1 Jan 2002), Tanzania (1 Jan 95), Thailand (1 Jan 95), Togo (31 May 95), Tonga (27 Jul 2007), Trinidad/Tobago (1 Mar 95), Tunisia (29 Mar 95), Turkey (26 Mar 95), Uganda (1 Jan 95), Ukraine (16 May 2008), United Arab Emirates (10 Apr 96), United Kingdom (1 Jan 95), United States (1 Jan 95), Uruguay (1 Jan 95), Venezuela (1 Jan 95), Vietnam (11 Jan 2007), Zambia (1 Jan 95), Zimbabwe (3 Mar 95)

7.8 AGREEMENT ON TECHNICAL BARRIERS TO TRADE
Concluded: 15 Apr 94
Entered into force: 1 Jan 95
The Agreement on Technical Barriers to Trade is part of Annex 1A to the WTO Agreement and is binding on all parties to that Agreement. For status information, see Basic Document 7.7, supra.

7.9 AGREEMENT ON THE APPLICATION OF SANITARY AND PHYTOSANITARY MEASURES
Concluded: 15 Apr 94
Entered into force: 1 Jan 95
The Agreement on the Application of Sanitary and Phytosanitary Measures is part of Annex 1A to the WTO Agreement and is binding on all parties to that Agreement. For status information, see Basic Document 7.7, supra.

7.10 UNDERSTANDING ON RULES AND PROCEDURES GOVERNING THE SETTLEMENT OF DISPUTES
Concluded: 15 Apr 94
Entered into force: 1 Jan 95
The Dispute Settlement Understanding is Annex 2 to the WTO Agreement and is binding on all parties to that Agreement. For status information, see Basic Document 7.7, supra.

B. Human Rights/Social Justice

7.11 UNITED STATES ALIEN TORT STATUTE
Adopted: 1789

7.12 AMERICAN DECLARATION OF THE RIGHTS AND DUTIES OF MAN
Adopted by the Ninth International Conference of American States: 30 Mar—2 May 48
Signed: 21
Argentina, Bolivia, Brazil, Chile, Colombia, Costa Rica, Cuba, Dominican Republic, Ecuador, El Salvador, Guatemala, Haiti, Honduras, Mexico, Nicaragua, Panama, Paraguay, Peru, United States, Uruguay, Venezuela

7.13 CONVENTION ON THE PREVENTION AND PUNISHMENT OF THE CRIME OF GENOCIDE
Concluded: 9 Dec 48
Entered into force: 12 Jan 51
Total parties: 141 (as of 23 Mar 2011)
Signed but not ratified: 1 (as of 23 Mar 2011)
Dominican Republic (11 Dec 48)
Ratified/acceded/accepted without qualification: 111 (as of 23 Mar 2011)
Afghanistan (22 Mar 56), Andorra (22 Sep 2006), Antigua/Barbuda (25 Oct 88), Armenia (23 Jun 93), Australia (8 Jul 49), Austria (19 Mar 58), Azerbaijan (16 Aug 96), Bahamas (5 Aug 75), Barbados (14 Jan 80), Belgium (5 Sep 51), Belize

(10 Mar 98), Bolivia (14 Jun 2005), Bosnia–Herzegovina (29 Dec 92), Brazil (15 Apr 52), Burkina Faso (14 Sep 65), Burundi (6 Jan 97), Cambodia (14 Oct 50), Canada (3 Sep 52), Chile (3 Jun 53), Colombia (27 Oct 59), Comoros (27 Sep 2004), Congo (Kinshasa) (31 May 62), Costa Rica (14 Oct 50), Côte d'Ivoire (18 Dec 95), Croatia (12 Oct 92), Cuba (4 Mar 53), Cyprus (29 Mar 82), Czech Republic (22 Feb 93), Denmark (15 Jun 51), Ecuador (21 Dec 49), Egypt (8 Feb 52), El Salvador (28 Sep 50), Estonia (21 Oct 91), Ethiopia (1 Jul 49), Fiji (11 Jan 73), Finland (18 Dec 59), France (14 Oct 50), Gabon (21 Jan 83), Gambia (29 Dec 78), Georgia (11 Oct 93), Germany (24 Nov 54), Ghana (24 Dec 58), Greece (8 Dec 54), Guatemala (13 Jan 50), Guinea (7 Sep 2000), Haiti (14 Oct 50), Honduras (5 Mar 52), Iceland (29 Aug 49), Iran (14 Aug 56), Iraq (20 Jan 59), Ireland (22 Jun 76), Israel (9 Mar 50), Italy (4 Jun 52), Jamaica (23 Sep 68), Jordan (3 Apr 50), Kazakhstan (26 Aug 98), Korea (North) (31 Jan 89), Korea (South) (14 Oct 50), Kuwait (7 Mar 95), Kyrgyzstan (5 Sep 97), Laos (8 Dec 50), Latvia (14 Apr 92), Lebanon (17 Dec 53), Lesotho (29 Nov 74), Liberia (9 Jun 50), Libya (16 May 89), Liechtenstein (24 Mar 94), Lithuania (1 Feb 96), Luxembourg (7 Oct 81), Macedonia (18 Jan 94), Maldives (24 Apr 84), Mali (16 Jul 79), Mexico (22 Jul 52), Moldova (26 Jan 93), Monaco (30 Mar 50), Mozambique (18 Apr 83), Namibia (28 Nov 94), Nepal (17 Jan 69), Netherlands (20 Jun 66), New Zealand (28 Dec 78), Nicaragua (29 Jan 52), Nigeria (27 Jul 2009), Norway (22 Jul 49), Pakistan (12 Oct 57), Panama (11 Jan 50), Papua New Guinea (27 Jan 82), Paraguay (3 Oct 2001), Peru (24 Feb 60), Saudi Arabia (13 Jul 50), Senegal (4 Aug 83), Seychelles (5 May 92), Slovakia (28 May 93), Slovenia (6 Jul 92), South Africa (10 Dec 98), Sri Lanka (12 Oct 50), St Vincent/Grenadines (9 Nov 81), Sudan (13 Oct 2003), Sweden (27 May 52), Switzerland (7 Sep 2000), Syria (25 Jun 55), Tanzania (5 Apr 84), Togo (24 May 84), Tonga (16 Feb 72), Trinidad/Tobago (13 Dec 2002), Tunisia (29 Nov 56), Turkey (31 Jul 50), Uganda (14 Nov 95), United Kingdom (30 Jan 70), Uruguay (11 Jul 67), Uzbekistan (9 Sep 99), Zimbabwe (13 May 91)

Ratified/acceded/accepted with qualification: 30 (as of 23 Mar 2011)
Albania (12 May 55), Algeria (31 Oct 63), Argentina (5 Jun 56), Bahrain (27 Mar 90), Bangladesh (5 Oct 98), Belarus (11 Aug 54), Bulgaria (21 Jul 50), China (18 Apr 83), Hungary (7 Jan 52), India (27 Aug 59), Malaysia (20 Dec 94), Mongolia (5 Jan 67), Montenegro (23 Oct 2006), Morocco (24 Jan 58), Myanmar (Burma) (14 Mar 56), Philippines (7 Jul 50), Poland (14 Nov 50), Portugal (9 Feb 99), Romania (2 Nov 50), Rwanda (16 Apr 75), Serbia (12 Mar 2001), Singapore (18 Aug 95), Spain (13 Sep 68), Ukraine (15 Nov 54), United Arab Emirates (11 Nov 2005), United States (25 Nov 88), USSR (Russia) (3 May 54), Venezuela (12 Jul 60), Vietnam (9 Jun 81), Yemen (9 Feb 87)

7.14 **U**NIVERSAL **D**ECLARATION OF **H**UMAN **R**IGHTS
Adopted: 10 Dec 48
For: 48
Afghanistan, Argentina, Australia, Belgium, Bolivia, Brazil, Canada, Chile, China, Colombia, Costa Rica, Cuba, Denmark, Dominican Republic, Ecuador, Egypt, El Salvador, Ethiopia, France, Greece, Guatemala, Haiti, Iceland, India, Iran, Iraq, Lebanon, Liberia, Luxembourg, Mexico, Myanmar, Netherlands, New Zealand, Nicaragua, Norway, Pakistan, Panama, Paraguay, Peru, Philippines, Siam (Thailand), Sweden, Syria, Turkey, United Kingdom, United States, Uruguay, Venezuela
Against: 0
Abstain: 8
Belarus (Byelorussian SSR), Czechoslovakia, Poland, Russia (USSR), Saudi Arabia, South Africa, Ukraine (Ukrainian SSR), Yugoslavia

7.15 **UNESCO** Declaration on the Principles of International Cultural Co-operation
      Adopted: 4 Nov 66

7.16 International Covenant on Economic, Social and Cultural Rights
      Concluded: 16 Dec 66
      Entered into force: 3 Jan 76
      Total parties: 160 (as of 16 Mar 2011)
      Signed but not ratified: 6 (as of 16 Mar2011)
      Belize (6 Sep 2000), Comoros (25 Sep 2008), Cuba (28 Feb 2008), São Tomé/Principe (31 Oct 95), South Africa (3 Oct 94), United States (5 Oct 77)
      Ratified/acceded/accepted without qualification: 115 (as of 16 Mar 2011)
      Albania (4 Oct 91), Angola (10 Jan 92), Argentina (8 Aug 86), Armenia (13 Sep 93), Australia (10 Dec 75), Austria (10 Sep 78), Azerbaijan (13 Aug 92), Belarus (12 Nov 73), Benin (12 Mar 92), Bolivia (12 Aug 82), Bosnia–Herzegovina (1 Sep 93), Brazil (24 Jan 92), Burkina Faso (4 Jan 99), Burundi (9 May 90), Cambodia (26 May 92), Cameroon (27 Jun 84), Canada (19 May 76), Cape Verde (6 Aug 93), Central African Republic (8 May 81), Chad (9 Jun 95), Chile (10 Feb 72), Colombia (29 Oct 69), Congo (Brazzaville) (5 Oct 83), Congo (Kinshasa) (1 Nov 76), Costa Rica (29 Nov 68), Côte d'Ivoire (26 Mar 92), Croatia (12 Oct 92), Cyprus (2 Apr 69), Djibouti (5 Nov 2002), Dominica (17 Jun 93), Dominican Republic (4 Jan 78), Ecuador (6 Mar 69), El Salvador (30 Nov 79), Equatorial Guinea (25 Sep 87), Eritrea (17 Apr 2001), Estonia (21 Oct 91), Ethiopia (11 Jun 93), Finland (19 Aug 75), Gabon (21 Jan 83), Gambia (29 Dec 78), Georgia (3 May 94), Germany (17 Dec 73), Ghana (7 Sep 2000), Greece (16 May 85), Grenada (6 Sep 91), Guatemala (19 May 88), Guinea–Bissau (2 Jul 92), Guyana (15 Feb 77), Honduras (17 Feb 81), Iceland (22 Aug 79), Iran (24 Jun 75), Israel (3 Oct 91), Italy (15 Sep 78), Jamaica (3 Oct 75), Jordan (28 May 75), Kazakhstan (24 Jan 2006), Korea (North) (14 Sep 81), Korea (South) (10 Apr 90), Kyrgyzstan (7 Oct 94), Laos (13 Feb 2007), Latvia (14 Apr 92), Lebanon (3 Nov 72), Lesotho (9 Sep 92), Liberia (22 Sep 2004), Liechtenstein (10 Dec 98), Lithuania (20 Nov 91), Luxembourg (18 Aug 83), Macedonia (18 Jan 94), Malawi (22 Dec 93), Maldives (19 Sep 2006), Mali (16 Jul 74), Mauritania (17 Nov 2004), Mauritius (12 Dec 73), Moldova (26 Jan 93), Montenegro (23 Oct 2006), Morocco (3 May 79), Namibia (28 Nov 94), Nepal (14 May 91), Nicaragua (12 Mar 80), Niger (7 Mar 86), Nigeria (29 Jul 93), Pakistan (17 Apr 2008), Panama (8 Mar 77), Papua New Guinea (21 Jul 2008) Paraguay (10 Jun 92), Peru (28 Apr 78), Philippines (7 Jun 74), Poland (18 Mar 77), Portugal (31 Jul 78), St Vincent/Grenadines (9 Nov 81), San Marino (18 Oct 85), Senegal (13 Feb 78), Serbia (12 Mar 2001), Seychelles (5 May 92), Sierra Leone (23 Aug 96), Slovenia (6 Jul 92), Solomon Islands (17 Mar 82), Somalia (24 Jan 90), Spain (27 Apr 77), Sri Lanka (11 Jun 80), Sudan (18 Mar 86), Suriname (28 Dec 76), Swaziland (26 Mar 2004), Switzerland (18 Jun 92), Tajikistan (4 Jan 99), Tanzania (11 Jun 76), Timor–Leste (16 Apr 2003), Togo (24 May 84), Tunisia (18 Mar 69), Turkmenistan (1 May 97), Uganda (21 Jan 87), Uruguay (1 Apr 70), Uzbekistan (28 Sep 95), Venezuela (10 May 78), Zimbabwe (13 May 91)
      Ratified/acceded/accepted with qualification: 45 (as of 16 Mar 2011)
      Afghanistan (24 Jan 83), Algeria (12 Sep 89), Bahamas (4 Dec 2008), Bahrain (27 Sep 2007), Bangladesh (5 Oct 98), Barbados (5 Jan 73), Belgium (21 Apr 83), Bulgaria (21 Sep 70), China (27 Mar 2001), Czech Republic (22 Feb 93), Denmark (6 Jan 72), Egypt (14 Jan 82), France (4 Nov 80), Guinea (24 Jan 78), Hungary (17 Jan 74), India (10 Apr 79), Indonesia (23 Feb 2006), Iraq (25 Jan 71), Ireland (8 Dec 89), Japan (21 Jun 79), Kenya (1 May 72), Kuwait (21 May 96), Libya (15 May 70), Madagascar (22 Sep 71), Malta (13 Sep 90), Mexico (23 Mar 81), Monaco (28 Aug 97), Mongolia (18 Nov 74), Netherlands (11 Dec 78),

New Zealand (28 Dec 78), Norway (13 Sep 72), Romania (9 Dec 74), Rwanda (16 Apr 75), Slovakia (28 May 93), Sweden (6 Dec 71), Syria (21 Apr 69), Thailand (5 Sep 99), Trinidad/Tobago (8 Dec 78), Turkey (23 Sep 2003), Ukraine (12 Nov 73), United Kingdom (20 May76), USSR Russia (16 Oct 73), Vietnam (24 Sep 82), Yemen (9 Feb 87), Zambia (10 Apr 84)

7.17 **INTERNATIONAL COVENANT ON CIVIL AND POLITICAL RIGHTS**
Concluded: 16 Dec 66
Entered into force: 23 Mar 76
Total parties: 167 (as of 16 Mar 2011)
Signed but not ratified: 5 (as of 16 Mar 2011)
China (5 Oct 98), Comoros (25 Sep), Cuba (28 Feb 2008), Nauru (12 Nov 2001), São Tomé/Principe (31 Oct 95)
Ratified/acceded/accepted without qualification: 106 (as of 16 Mar 2011)
Albania (4 Oct 91), Andorra (22 Sep 2006), Angola (10 Jan 92), Armenia (23 Jun 93), Azerbaijan (13 Aug 92), Belarus (12 Nov 73), Benin (12 Mar 92), Bolivia (12 Aug 82), Bosnia–Herzegovina (1 Sep 93), Brazil (24 Jan 92), Burkina Faso (4 Jan 99), Burundi (9 May 90), Cambodia (26 May 92), Cameroon (27 Jun 84), Canada (19 May 76), Cape Verde (6 Aug 93), Central African Republic (8 May 81), Chad (9 Jun 95), Chile (10 Feb 72), Colombia (29 Oct 69), Congo (Kinshasa) (1 Nov 76), Costa Rica (29 Nov 68), Côte d'Ivoire (26 Mar 92), Croatia (12 Oct 92), Cyprus (2 Apr 69), Djibouti (5 Nov 2002), Dominica (17 Jun 93), Dominican Republic (4 Jan 78), Ecuador (6 Mar 69), El Salvador (30 Nov 79), Equatorial Guinea (25 Sep 87), Eritrea (22 Jan 2002), Estonia (21 Oct 91), Ethiopia (11 Jun 93), Gabon (21 Jan 83), Georgia (3 May 94), Ghana (7 Sep 2000), Greece (5 May 97), Grenada (6 Sep 91), Guatemala (5 May 92), Guinea–Bissau (1 Nov 2010), Haiti (6 Feb 91), Honduras (25 Aug 97), Iran (24 Jun 75), Jamaica (3 Oct 75), Jordan (28 May 75), Kazakhstan (24 Jan 2006), Kenya (1 May 72), Korea (North) (14 Sep 81), Kyrgyzstan (7 Oct 94), Laos (25 Sep 2009), Latvia (14 Apr 92), Lebanon (3 Nov 72), Lesotho (9 Sep 92), Liberia (22 Sep 2004), Lithuania (20 Nov 91), Macedonia (18 Jan 94), Madagascar (21 Jun 71), Malawi (22 Dec 93), Mali (16 Jul 74), Mauritius (12 Dec 73), Moldova (26 Jan 93), Montenegro (23 Oct 2006), Morocco (3 May 79), Mozambique (21 Jul 93), Namibia (28 Nov 94), Nepal (14 May 91), Nicaragua (12 Mar 80), Niger (7 Mar 86), Nigeria (29 Jul 93), Panama (8 Mar 77), Papua New Guinea (21 Jul 2008), Paraguay (10 Jun 92), Peru (28 Apr 78), Philippines (23 Oct 86), Poland (18 Mar 77), Portugal (15 Jun 78), Rwanda (16 Apr 75), St Vincent/Grenadines (9 Nov 81), Samoa (15 Feb 2008), San Marino (18 Oct 85), Senegal (13 Feb 78), Serbia (12 Mar 2001), Seychelles (5 May 92), Sierra Leone (23 Aug 96), Slovenia (6 Jul 92), Somalia (24 Jan 90), South Africa (10 Dec 98), Spain (27 Apr 77), Sri Lanka (11 Jun 80), Sudan (18 Mar 86), Suriname (28 Dec 76), Swaziland (26 Mar 2004), Tajikistan (4 Jan 99), Tanzania (11 Jun 76), Timor–Leste (18 Sep 2003), Togo (24 May 84), Tunisia (18 Mar 69), Turkmenistan (1 May 97), Uganda (21 Jun 95), Uruguay (1 Apr 70), Uzbekistan (28 Sep 95), Vanuatu (21 Nov 2008), Zambia (10 Apr 84), Zimbabwe (13 May 91)
Ratified/acceded/accepted with qualification: 61 (as of 16 Mar 2011)
Afghanistan (24 Jan 83), Algeria (12 Sep 89), Argentina (8 Aug 86), Australia (13 Aug 80), Austria (10 Sep 78), Bahamas (23 Dec 2008), Bahrain (20 Sep 2006), Bangladesh (6 Sep 2000), Barbados (5 Jan 73), Belgium (21 Apr 83), Belize (10 Jun 96), Botswana (8 Sep 2000), Bulgaria (21 Sep 70), Congo (Brazzaville) (5 Oct 83), Czech Republic (22 Feb 93), Denmark (6 Jan 72), Egypt (14 Jan 82), Finland (19 Aug 75), France (4 Nov 80), Gambia (22 Mar 79), Germany (17 Dec 73), Guinea (24 Jan 78), Guyana (15 Feb 77), Hungary (17 Jan 74), Iceland (22 Aug 79), India (10 Apr 79), Indonesia (23 Feb 2006), Iraq (25 Jan 71), Ireland (8 Dec 89), Israel (3 Oct 91), Italy (15 Sep 78), Japan (21

Jun 79), Korea (South) (10 Apr 90), Kuwait (21 May 96), Libya (15 May 70), Liechtenstein (10 Dec 98), Luxembourg (18 Aug 83), Maldives (19 Sep 2006), Malta (13 Sep 90), Mauritania (17 Nov 2004), Mexico (23 Mar 81), Monaco (28 Aug 97), Mongolia (18 Nov 74), Netherlands (11 Dec 78), New Zealand (28 Dec 78), Norway (13 Sep 72), Pakistan (23 Jun 2010), Romania (9 Dec 74), Slovakia (28 May 93), Sweden (6 Dec 71), Switzerland (18 Jun 92), Syria (21 Apr 69), Thailand (29 Oct 96), Trinidad/Tobago (21 Dec 78), Turkey (23 Sep 2003), Ukraine (12 Nov 73), United Kingdom (20 May 76), United States (8 Jun 92), USSR (Russia) (16 Oct 73), Venezuela (10 May 78), Vietnam (24 Sep 82), Yemen (9 Feb 87)

7.18 FINAL ACT OF THE UNITED NATIONS INTERNATIONAL CONFERENCE ON HUMAN RIGHTS AT TEHERAN
Adopted: 13 May 68

7.19 AMERICAN CONVENTION ON HUMAN RIGHTS
Concluded: 22 Nov 69
Entered into force: 18 Jul 78
Total parties: 24 (as of 18 Mar 2011)
Signed but not ratified: 1 (as of 18 Mar 2011)
United States (1 Jun 77)
Ratified/acceded/accepted without qualification: 10 (as of 18 Mar 2011)
Bolivia* (19 Jul 79), Costa Rica* (8 Apr 70), Grenada (18 Jul 78), Haiti* (27 Sep 77), Honduras* (8 Sep 77), Jamaica* (7 Aug 78), Panama* (22 Jun 78), Paraguay* (24 Aug 89), Peru* (28 Jul 78), Suriname* (12 Nov 87)
Ratified/acceded/accepted with qualification: 14 (as of 18 Mar 2011)
Argentina* (5 Sep 84), Barbados (27 Nov 82), Brazil* (25 Sep 92), Chile* (21 Aug 90), Colombia* (31 Jul 73), Dominica (11 Jun 93), Dominican Republic (19 Apr 78), Ecuador* (28 Dec 77), El Salvador* (23 Jun 78), Guatemala* (25 May 78), Mexico* (24 Mar 81), Nicaragua* (25 Sep 79), Uruguay* (19 Apr 85), Venezuela* (9 Aug 77)
Denunciation: 1 (as of 18 Mar 2011)
Trinidad/Tobago (26 May 98)

7.20 DECLARATION ON SOCIAL PROGRESS AND DEVELOPMENT
Adopted: 11 Dec 69
For: 119*
Against: 0
Abstain: 2

  * Adopted with no roll call vote recorded

7.21 CONVENTION FOR THE PROTECTION OF THE WORLD CULTURAL AND NATURAL HERITAGE
Adopted unanimously by the UNESCO General Conference: 16 Nov 72
Entered into force: 17 Dec 75
Total Parties: 188 (as of 4 Oct 2011)
Ratified/acceded/accepted/approved without qualification: 177
Afghanistan (20 Mar 79), Albania (10 Jul 89), Algeria (24 Jun 74), Angola (7 Nov 91), Antigua/Barbuda (1 Nov 83), Argentina (23 Aug 78), Armenia (5 Sep 93), Andorra (3 Jan 97), Australia (22 Aug 74), Austria (18 Dec 92), Azerbaijan (16 Dec 93), Bahrain (28 May 91), Bangladesh (3 Aug 83), Barbados (24 Apr 2002), Belarus (12 Oct 88), Belgium (24 Jul 96), Belize (6 Nov 90), Benin (14 Jun 82), Bhutan (22 Oct 2001), Bolivia(4 Oct 76), Bosnia–Herzegovina (12 Jul

93), Botswana (23 Nov 98), Brunei Darussalam (12 Aug 2011), Burkina Faso (2 Apr 87), Burundi (19 May 82), Cambodia (28 Nov 91), Cameroon (7 Dec 82), Canada (23 Jul 76), Central African Republic (22 Dec 80), Chad (23 Jun 99), Chile (20 Feb 80), China (12 Dec 85), Colombia (24 May 83), Comoros (27 Sep 00), Congo (Brazzaville) (10 Dec 87), Congo (Kinshasa) (23 Sep 74), Cook Islands (16 Jan 2009), Costa Rica (23 Aug 77), Côte d'Ivoire (9 Jan 81), Croatia (6 Jul 92), Cuba (24 Mar 81), Cyprus (14 Aug 75), Czech Republic (26 Mar 93), Djibouti (30 Aug 2007), Dominica (4 Apr 95), Dominican Republic (12 Feb 85), Ecuador (16 Jun 75), Egypt (7 Feb 74), El Salvador (8 Oct 91), Equatorial Guinea (10 Mar 2011), Equatorial Guinea (10 Mar 2010), Eritrea (24 Oct 2001), Estonia (27 Oct 95), Ethiopia (6 Jul 77), Fiji (21 Nov 90), Finland (4 Mar 87), Gabon (30 Dec 86), Gambia (1 Jul 87), Georgia (4 Nov 92), Ghana (4 Jul 75), Greece (17 Jul 81), Grenada (13 Aug 98), Guatemala (16 Jan 79), Guinea (18 Mar 79), Guinea–Bissau (28 Jan 2006), Guyana (20 Jun 77), Haiti (18 Jan 80), Honduras (8 Jun 79), Hungary (15 Jul 85), Iceland (19 Dec 95), India (14 Nov 77), Indonesia(6 Jul 89), Iran (26 Feb 75), Iraq (5 Mar 74), Ireland (16 Sep 91), Israel (6 Oct 99), Italy (23 Jun 78), Jamaica (14 Jun 83), Japan (30 Jun 92), Jordan (5 May 75), Kazakhstan (29 Apr 94), Kenya (5 Jun 91), Kiribati (12 May 2000), Korea (North) (21 Jul 98), Korea (South) (14 Sep 88), Kuwait (6 Jun 2002), Kyrgyzstan (3 Jul 95), Laos (20 Mar 87), Latvia (10 Jan 95), Lebanon (3 Feb 83), Lesotho (25 Nov 2003), Liberia (28 Mar 2002), Libya (13 Oct 78), Lithuania (31 Mar 92), Luxembourg (28 Sep 83), Macedonia (30 Apr 97), Madagascar (19 Jul 83), Malawi (5 Jan 82), Malaysia (7 Dec 88), Maldives (22 May 86), Mali (5 Apr 77), Malta (14 Nov 78), Marshall Islands (24 Apr 2002), Mauritania (2 Mar 81), Mauritius (19 Sep 95), Mexico (23 Feb 84), Micronesia (22 Jul 2002), Monaco (7 Nov 78), Mongolia (2 Feb 90), Montenegro (3 Jun 2006), Morocco (28 Oct 75), Mozambique (27 Oct 82), Myanmar (Burma) (29 Apr 94), Namibia (6 Apr 2000), Nepal (20 Jun 78), Netherlands (26 Aug 92), New Zealand (22 Nov 84), Nicaragua (17 Dec 79), Niue (23 Jan 2001), Niger (23 Dec 74), Nigeria (23 Oct 74), Pakistan (23 Jul 76), Palau (11 Jun 2002), Panama (3 Mar 78), Papua New Guinea (28 Jul 97), Paraguay (27 Apr 88), Peru (24 Feb 82), Philippines (19 Sep 85), Poland (29 Jun 76), Portugal (30 Sep 80), Qatar (12 Sep 84), Romania (16 May 90), Rwanda (28 Dec 2000), Samoa (28 Aug 2001), San Marino (18 Oct 91), Sao Tome/Principe (25 Jul 2006), Saudi Arabia (7 Aug 78), Senegal (13 Feb 76), Serbia/ (11 Sep 2001), Seychelles (9 Apr 80), Sierra Leone (7 Jan 2005), Slovakia (31 Mar 93), Slovenia (5 Nov 92), Solomon Islands (10 Jun 92), Spain (4 May 82), Sri Lanka (6 Jun 80), St Kitts/Nevis (10 Jul 86), St Lucia (14 Oct 91), St Vincent/Grenadines (3 Feb 2003), Sudan (6 Jun 74), Suriname (23 Oct 97), Swaziland (30 Nov 2005), Sweden (22 Jan 85), Switzerland (17 Sep 75), Syria (13 Aug 75), Tajikistan (28 Aug 92), Tanzania (2 Aug 77), Thailand (17 Sep 87), Togo (15 Apr 98), Tonga (3 Jun 2004), Trinidad/Tobago (16 Feb 2005), Tunisia (10 Mar 75), Turkey (16 Mar 83), Turkmenistan (30 Sep 94), Uganda (20 Nov 87), Ukraine (12 Oct 88), United Arab Emirates (11 May 2001), United Kingdom (29 May 84), Uruguay (9 Mar 89), USSR (Russia) (12 Oct 88), Uzbekistan (31 Jan 93), Vanuatu (13 Jun 2002), Venezuela (30 Oct 90), Vietnam (19 Oct 87), Yemen (7 Oct 80), Zambia (4 Jun 84), Zimbabwe (16 Aug 82)

Ratified/acceded/accepted/approved with qualification: 12

Brazil (1 Sep 77), Bulgaria (7 Mar 74), Cape Verde (28 Apr 88), Denmark (25 Jul 79), France (27 Jun 75), Germany (23 Aug 76), Moldova (23 Sep 2002), Norway (12 May 77), Oman (6 Oct 81), South Africa (10 Jul 97), United States (7 Dec 73), Vatican City (7 Oct 82)

7.22 CONVENTION ON THE ELIMINATION OF ALL FORMS OF DISCRIMINATION AGAINST WOMEN

Concluded: 18 Dec 79
Entered into force: 3 Sep 81
Total parties: 186 (as of 18 Mar 2011)
Signed but not ratified: 1 (as of 18 Mar 2011)
United States (17 Jul 80)
Ratified/acceded/accepted without qualification: 122 (as of 18 Mar 2011)
Afghanistan (5 Mar 2003), Albania (11 May 94), Andorra (15 Jan 97), Angola
(17 Sep 86), Antigua/Barbuda (1 Aug 89), Armenia (13 Sep 93), Azerbaijan (10
Jul 95), Barbados (16 Oct 80), Belarus (4 Feb 81), Belgium (10 Jul 85), Belize
(16 May 90), Benin (12 Mar 92), Bhutan (31 Aug 81), Bolivia (8 Jun 90), Bosnia–
Herzegovina (1 Sep 93), Botswana (13 Aug 96), Bulgaria (8 Feb 82), Burkina
Faso (14 Oct 87), Burundi (8 Jan 92), Cambodia (15 Oct 92), Cameroon (23 Aug
94), Canada (10 Dec 81), Cape Verde (5 Dec 80), Central African Republic (21
Jun 91), Chad (9 Jun 95), Colombia (19 Jan 82), Comoros (31 Oct 94), Congo
(Brazzaville) (26 Jul 82), Congo (Kinshasa) (17 Oct 86), Costa Rica (4 Apr 86),
Côte d'Ivoire (18 Dec 95), Croatia (9 Sep 92), Cyprus (23 Jul 85), Czech Republic
(22 Feb 93), Denmark (21 Apr 83), Djibouti (2 Dec 98), Dominica (15 Sep 80),
Dominican Republic (2 Sep 82), Ecuador (9 Nov 81), Equatorial Guinea (23 Oct
84), Eritrea (5 Sep 95), Estonia (21 Oct 91), Fiji (28 Aug 95), Finland (4 Sep 86),
Gabon (21 Jan 83), Gambia (16 Apr 93), Georgia (26 Oct 94), Ghana (2 Jan 86),
Greece (7 Jun 83), Grenada (30 Aug 90), Guatemala (12 Aug 82), Guinea (9 Aug
82), Guinea–Bissau (23 Aug 85), Guyana (17 Jul 80), Haiti (20 Jul 81),
Honduras (3 Mar 83), Hungary (22 Dec 80), Iceland (18 Jun 85), Japan (25 Jun
85), Kazakhstan (26 Aug 98), Kenya (9 Mar 84), Kiribati (17 Mar 2004),
Kyrgyzstan (10 Feb 97), Laos (14 Aug 81), Latvia (14 Apr 92), Liberia (17 Jul
84), Lithuania (18 Jan 94), Macedonia (18 Jan 94), Madagascar (17 Mar 89),
Malawi (12 Mar 87), Mali (10 Sep 85), Marshall Islands (2 Mar 2006), Moldova
(1 Jul 94), Mongolia (20 Jul 81), Montenegro (23 Oct 2006), Mozambique (21
Apr 97), Namibia (23 Nov 92), Nepal (22 Apr 91), Nicaragua (27 Oct 81),
Nigeria (13 Jun 85), Norway (21 May 81), Panama (29 Oct 81), Papua New
Guinea (12 Jan 95), Paraguay (6 Apr 87), Peru (13 Sep 82), Philippines (5 Aug
81), Poland (30 Jul 80), Portugal (30 Jul 80), Romania (7 Jan 82), Rwanda (2
Mar 81), Samoa (25 Sep 92), San Marino (10 Dec 2003), São Tomé/Principe (3
Jun 2003), Senegal (5 Feb 85), Serbia (26 Feb 82), Seychelles (5 May 92), Sierra
Leone (11 Nov 88), Slovakia (28 May 93), Slovenia (6 Jul 92), Solomon Islands
(6 May 2002), South Mica (15 Dec 95), Sri Lanka (5 Oct 81), St Kitts/Nevis (25
Apr 85), St Lucia (8 Oct 82), St Vincent/Grenadines (4 Aug 81), Suriname (1
Mar 93), Swaziland (26 Mar 2004), Sweden (2 Jul 80), Tajikistan (26 Oct 93),
Tanzania (20 Aug 85), Timor–Leste (16 Apr 2003), Togo (26 Sep 83), Turkmen-
istan (1 May 97), Tuvalu (6 Oct 99), Uganda (22 Jul 85), Ukraine (12 Mar 81),
Uruguay (9 Oct 81), USSR (Russia) (23 Jan 81), Uzbekistan (19 Jul 95),
Vanuatu (8 Sep 95), Zambia (21 Jun 85), Zimbabwe (13 May 91)
Ratified/acceded/accepted with qualification: 64 (as of 18 Mar 2011)
Algeria (22 May 96), Argentina (15 Jul 85), Australia (28 Jul 83), Austria (31
Mar 82), Bahamas (6 Oct 93), Bahrain (18 Jul 2002), Bangladesh (6 Nov 84),
Brazil (1 Feb 84), Brunei (24 May 2006), Chile (7 Dec 89), China (4 Nov 80),
Cook Islands (11 Aug 2006), Cuba (17 Jul 80), Egypt (18 Sep 81), El Salvador
(19 Aug 81), Ethiopia (10 Sep 81), France (14 Dec 83), Germany (10 Jul 85),
India (9 Jul 93), Indonesia (13 Sep 84), Iraq (13 Aug 86), Ireland (23 Dec 85),
Israel (3 Oct 91), Italy (10 Jun 85), Jamaica (19 Oct 84), Jordan (1 Jul 92),
Korea (North) (27 Feb 2001), Korea (South) (27 Dec 84), Kuwait (2 Sep 94),
Lebanon (16 Apr 97), Lesotho (22 Aug 95), Libya (16 May 89), Liechtenstein (2
Dec 95), Luxembourg (2 Feb 89), Malaysia (5 Jul 95), Maldives (1 Jul 93), Malta
(8 Mar 91), Mauritania (10 May 2001), Mauritius (9 Jul 84), Mexico (23 Mar 81),
Micronesia (1 Sep 2004), Monaco (18 Mar 2005), Morocco (21 Jun 93), Myanmar

(Burma) (22 Jul 97), Netherlands (23 Jul 91), New Zealand (10 Jan 85), Niger (8 Oct 99), Oman (7 Feb 2006), Qatar (29 Apr 2009), Pakistan (12 Mar 96), Saudi Arabia (7 Sep 2000), Singapore (5 Oct 95), Spain (5 Jan 84), Switzerland (27 Mar 97), Syria (23 Mar 2003), Thailand (9 Aug 85), Trinidad/Tobago (12 Jan 90), Tunisia (20 Dec 85), Turkey (20 Dec 85), United Arab Emirates (6 Oct 2004), United Kingdom (7 Apr 86), Venezuela (2 May 83), Vietnam (17 Feb 82), Yemen (30 May 84)

7.23 DECLARATION ON THE RIGHT TO DEVELOPMENT
Adopted: 4 Dec 86
For: 146
Afghanistan, Algeria, Angola, Antigua and Barbuda, Argentina, Australia, Austria, Bahamas, Bahrain, Bangladesh, Barbados, Belarus (Byelorussian SSR), Belgium, Belize, Benin, Bhutan, Bolivia, Botswana, Brazil, Brunei, Bulgaria, Burkina Faso, Burundi, Cambodia, Cameroon, Canada, Cape Verde, Central African Republic, Chad, Chile, China, Colombia, Comoros, Congo, Costa Rica, Côte d'Ivoire, Cuba, Cyprus, Czechoslovakia, Djibouti, Dominican Republic, Ecuador, Egypt, El Salvador, Equatorial Guinea, Ethiopia, Fiji, France, Gabon, Gambia, German Democratic Republic, Ghana, Greece, Grenada, Guatemala, Guinea, Guinea–Bissau, Guyana, Haiti, Honduras, Hungary, India, Indonesia, Iran, Iraq, Ireland, Italy, Jamaica, Jordan, Kenya, Kuwait, Lao People's Democratic Republic, Lebanon, Lesotho, Liberia, Libya, Luxembourg, Madagascar, Malawi, Malaysia, Maldives, Mali, Mauritania, Mauritius, Mexico, Mongolia, Morocco, Mozambique, Myanmar, Nepal, Netherlands, New Zealand, Nicaragua, Niger, Nigeria, Norway, Oman, Pakistan, Panama, Papua New Guinea, Paraguay, Peru, Philippines, Poland, Portugal, Qatar, Romania, Russia (USSR), Rwanda, Samoa, São Tomé and Príncipe, Saudi Arabia, Senegal, Seychelles, Sierra Leone, Singapore, Solomon Islands, Somalia, Spain, Sri Lanka, St. Kitts and Nevis, St. Lucia, St. Vincent and the Grenadines, Sudan, Suriname, Swaziland, Syria, Tanzania, Thailand, Togo, Trinidad and Tobago, Tunisia, Turkey, Uganda, Ukraine (Ukrainian SSR), United Arab Emirates, Uruguay, Vanuatu, Venezuela, Vietnam, Yemen, Yemen (Democratic), Yugoslavia, Zaire, Zambia, Zimbabwe
Against: 1
United States
Abstain: 8
Denmark, Finland, Germany (West), Iceland, Israel, Japan, Sweden, United Kingdom

7.24 INTERNATIONAL LABOR ORGANIZATION CONVENTION (NO. 169) CONCERNING INDIGENOUS AND TRIBAL PEOPLES IN INDEPENDENT COUNTRIES
Concluded: 27 Jun 89
Entered into force: 5 Sep 91
Ratified/acceded/accepted without qualification: 22 (as of 17 Mar 2011)
Argentina (3 Jul 2000), Bolivia (11 Dec 91), Brazil (25 Jul 2002), Central African Republic (30 Aug 2010), Chile (15 Sep 2008), Colombia (7 Aug 91), Costa Rica (2 Apr 93), Denmark (22 Feb 96), Dominica (25 Jun 2002), Ecuador (15 May 98), Fiji (3 Mar 98), Guatemala (5 Jun 96), Honduras (28 Mar 95), Mexico (5 Sep 90), Nepal (14 Sep 2007), Netherlands (2 Feb 98), Nicaragua (25 Aug 2010), Norway (19 Jun 90), Paraguay (10 Aug 93), Peru (2 Feb 94), Spain (15 Feb 2007), Venezuela (22 May 2002)

7.25 CONVENTION ON THE RIGHTS OF THE CHILD
Concluded: 20 Nov 89

Entered into force: 2 Sep 90
Total parties: 193 (as of 18 Mar 2011)
Signed but not ratified: 2 (as of 18 Mar 2011)
Somalia (9 May 2002), United States (16 Feb 95)
Ratified/acceded/accepted without qualification: 125 (as of 18 Mar 2011)
Albania (27 Feb 92), Angola (5 Dec 90), Antigua/Barbuda (5 Oct 93), Armenia (23 Jun 93), Azerbaijan (13 Aug 92), Bahrain (13 Feb 92), Barbados (9 Oct 90), Belarus (1 Oct 90), Belize (2 May 90), Benin (3 Aug 90), Bhutan (1 Aug 90), Bolivia (26 Jun 90), Brazil (24 Sep 90), Bulgaria (3 Jun 91), Burkina Faso (31 Aug 90), Burundi (19 Oct 90), Cambodia (15 Oct 92), Cameroon (11 Jan 93), Cape Verde (4 Jun 92), Central African Republic (23 Apr 92), Chad (2 Oct 90), Chile (13 Aug 90), Comoros (22 Jun 93), Congo (Brazzaville) (14 Oct 93), Congo (Kinshasa) (27 Sep 90), Costa Rica (21 Aug 90), Côte d'Ivoire (4 Feb 91), Cyprus (7 Feb 91), Dominica (13 Mar 91), Dominican Republic (11 Jun 91), Egypt (6 Jul 90), El Salvador (10 Jul 90), Equatorial Guinea (15 Jul 92), Eritrea (3 Aug 94), Estonia (21 Oct 91), Ethiopia (14 May 91), Fiji (13 Aug 93), Finland (20 Jun 91), Gabon (9 Feb 94), Gambia (8 Aug 90), Georgia (2 Jun 94), Ghana (5 Feb 90), Greece (11 May 93), Grenada (5 Nov 90), Guinea (13 Jul 90), Guinea–Bissau (20 Aug 90), Guyana (14 Jan 91), Haiti (8 Jun 95), Honduras (10 Aug 90), Hungary (7 Oct 91), Israel (3 Oct 91), Italy (5 Sep 91), Jamaica (14 May 91), Kazakhstan (12 Aug 94), Kenya (30 Jul 90), Korea (North) (21 Sep 90), Kyrgyzstan (7 Oct 94), Laos (8 May 91), Latvia (14 Apr 92), Lebanon (14 May 91), Lesotho (10 Mar 92), Liberia (4 Jun 93), Libya (15 Apr 93), Lithuania (31 Jan 92), Macedonia (2 Dec 93), Madagascar (19 Mar 91), Malawi (2 Jan 91), Malta (30 Sep 90), Marshall Islands (4 Oct 93), Mexico (21 Sep 90), Micronesia (5 May 93), Moldova (26 Jan 93), Mongolia (5 Jul 90), Montenegro (23 Oct 2006), Mozambique (26 Apr 94), Namibia (30 Sep 90), Nauru (27 Jul 94), Nepal (14 Sep 90), Nicaragua (5 Oct 90), Niger (30 Sep 90), Nigeria (19 Apr 91), Niue (20 Dec 95), Norway (8 Jan 91), Palau (4 Aug 95), Panama (12 Dec 90), Papua New Guinea (2 Mar 93), Paraguay (25 Sep 90), Peru (4 Sep 90), Philippines (21 Aug 90), Portugal (21 Sep 90), Romania (28 Sep 90), Rwanda (24 Jan 91), San Marino (25 Nov 91), São Tomé/Principe (14 May 91), Senegal (31 Jul 90), Serbia (12 Mar 2001), Seychelles (7 Sep 90), Sierra Leone (18 Jun 90), Slovenia (6 Jul 92), Solomon Islands (10 Apr 95), South Africa (16 Jun 95), Sri Lanka (12 Jul 91), St Kitts/Nevis (24 Jul 90), St Lucia (16 Jun 93), St Vincent/Grenadines (26 Oct 93), Sudan (3 Aug 90), Suriname (1 Mar 93), Sweden (29 Jun 90), Tajikistan (26 Oct 93), Tanzania (10 Jun 91), Timor–Leste (16 Apr 2003), Togo (1 Aug 90), Tonga (6 Nov 95), Trinidad/Tobago (5 Dec 91), Turkmenistan (20 Sep 93), Tuvalu (22 Sep 95), Uganda (17 Aug 90), Ukraine (28 Aug 91), USSR (Russia (16 Aug 90), Uzbekistan (29 Jun 94), Vanuatu (7 Jul 93), Vietnam (28 Feb 90), Yemen (1 May 91), Zambia (6 Dec 91), Zimbabwe (11 Sep 90)
Ratified/acceded/accepted with qualification: 68 (as of 18 Mar 2011)
Afghanistan (28 Mar 94), Algeria (16 Apr 93), Andorra (2 Jan 96), Argentina (4 Dec 90), Australia (17 Dec 90), Austria (6 Aug 92), Bahamas (20 Feb 91), Bangladesh (3 Aug 90), Belgium (16 Dec 91), Bosnia–Herzegovina (1 Sep 93), Botswana (14 Mar 95), Brunei (27 Dec 95), Canada (13 Dec 91), China (2 Mar 92), Colombia (28 Jan 91), Cook Islands (6 Jun 97), Croatia (12 Oct 92), Cuba (21 Aug 91), Czech Republic (22 Feb 93), Denmark (19 Jul 91), Djibouti (6 Dec 90), Ecuador (23 Mar 90), France (7 Aug 90), Germany (6 Mar 92), Guatemala (6 Jun 90), Iceland (28 Oct 92), India (11 Dec 92), Indonesia (5 Sep 90), Iran (13 Jul 94), Iraq (15 Jun 94), Ireland (28 Sep 92), Japan (22 Apr 94), Jordan (24 May 91), Kiribati (11 Dec 95), Korea (South) (20 Nov 90), Kuwait (21 Oct 91), Liechtenstein (22 Dec 95), Luxembourg (7 Mar 94), Malaysia (17 Feb 95), Maldives (11 Feb 91), Mali (20 Sep 90), Mauritania (16 May 91), Mauritius (26 Jul 90), Monaco (21 Jun 93), Morocco (21 Jun 93), Myanmar (Burma) (15 Jul

91), Netherlands (6 Feb 95), New Zealand (6 Apr 93), Oman (9 Dec 96), Pakistan (12 Nov 90), Poland (7 Jun 91), Qatar (3 Apr 95), Samoa (29 Nov 94), Saudi Arabia (26 Jan 96), Singapore (5 Oct 95), Slovakia (28 May 93), Spain (6 Dec 90), Swaziland (7 Sep 95), Switzerland (24 Feb 97), Syria (15 Jul 93), Thailand (27 Mar 92), Tunisia (30 Jan 92), Turkey (4 Apr 95), United Arab Emirates (3 Jan 97), United Kingdom (16 Dec 91), Uruguay (20 Nov 90), Vatican City (20 Apr 90), Venezuela (13 Sep 90)

7.26   United Nations Declaration on the Rights of Indigenous Peoples
Adopted: 13 Sep 2007
For: 143
Afghanistan, Albania, Algeria, Andorra, Angola, Antigua and Barbuda, Argentina, Armenia, Austria, Bahamas, Bahrain, Barbados, Belarus, Belgium, Belize, Benin, Bolivia, Bosnia and Herzegovina, Botswana, Brazil, Brunei Darussalam, Bulgaria, Burkina Faso, Cambodia, Cameroon, Cape Verde, Central African Republic, Chile, China, Comoros, Congo, Costa Rica, Croatia, Cuba, Cyprus, Czech Republic, Democratic People's Republic of Korea, Democratic Republic of the Congo, Denmark, Djibouti, Dominica, Dominican Republic, Ecuador, Egypt, El Salvador, Estonia, Finland, France, Gabon, Germany, Ghana, Greece, Guatemala, Guinea, Guyana, Haiti, Honduras, Hungary, Iceland, India, Indonesia, Iran, Iraq, Ireland, Italy, Jamaica, Japan, Jordan, Kazakhstan, Kuwait, Lao People's Democratic Republic, Latvia, Lebanon, Lesotho, Liberia, Libya, Liechtenstein, Lithuania, Luxembourg, Madagascar, Malawi, Malaysia, Maldives, Mali, Malta, Mauritius, Mexico, Micronesia (Federated States of), Moldova, Monaco, Mongolia, Mozambique, Myanmar, Namibia, Nepal, Netherlands, Nicaragua, Niger, Norway, Oman, Pakistan, Panama, Paraguay, Peru, Philippines, Poland, Portugal, Qatar, Republic of Korea, Saint Lucia, Saint Vincent and the Grenadines, San Marino, Saudi Arabia, Senegal, Serbia, Sierra Leone, Singapore, Slovakia, Slovenia, South Africa, Spain, Sri Lanka, Sudan, Suriname, Swaziland, Sweden, Switzerland, Syria, Thailand, The former Yugoslav Republic of Macedonia, Timor–Leste, Trinidad and Tobago, Tunisia, Turkey, United Arab Emirates, United Kingdom, United Republic of Tanzania, Uruguay, Venezuela, Viet Nam, Yemen, Zambia, Zimbabwe
Against: 4
Australia, Canada, New Zealand, United States
Abstain: 11
Azerbaijan, Bangladesh, Bhutan, Burundi, Colombia, Georgia, Kenya, Nigeria, Russia, Samoa, Ukraine

C. War/Peace

7.27   Convention (No. IV) Respecting the Laws and Customs of War on Land, With Annex of Regulations
Concluded: 18 Oct 07
Entered into force: 26 Jan 10
Total Parties: 35 (as of 23 Feb 2011)
Signed but not ratified: 15 (as of 23 Feb 2011)
Argentina (18 Oct 07), Bulgaria (18 Oct 07), Chile (18 Oct 07), Colombia (18 Oct 07), Ecuador (18 Oct 07), Greece (18 Oct 07), Italy (18 Oct 07), Montenegro (18 Oct 07), Paraguay (18 Oct 07), Persia (Iran) (18 Oct 07), Peru (18 *Oct 07), Serbia (18 Oct 07), Turkey (18 Oct 07), Uruguay (18 Oct 07), Venezuela (18 Oct 07)*
Ratified/acceded/accepted without qualification: 31 (as of 23 Feb 2011)
Belarus (4 Jun 62), Belgium (8 Aug 10), Bolivia (27 Nov 09), Brazil (5 Jan 14), China (10 May 17), Cuba (22 Feb 12), Denmark (27 Nov 09), Dominican Republic (16 May 58), El Salvador (27 Nov 09), Ethiopia (5 Aug 35), Fiji (2 Apr

73), Finland (30 Dec 18), France (7 Oct 10), Guatemala (15 May 11), Haiti (2 Feb 10), Liberia (4 Feb 14), Luxembourg (5 Sep 12), Mexico (27 Nov 09), Netherlands (27 Nov 09), Nicaragua (16 Dec 09), Norway (19 Sep 10), Panama (11 Sep 11), Poland (9 May 25), Portugal (13 Apr 11), Romania (1 Mar 12), Siam (Thailand) (12 Mar 10), South Africa (10 Mar 78), Sweden (27 Oct 09), Switzerland (12 May 10), United Kingdom (27 Nov 09), United States (27 Nov 09)

Ratified/acceded/accepted with qualification: 4 (as of 23 Feb 2011)
Austria–Hungary (27 Nov 09), Germany (27 Nov 09), Japan (13 Dec 11), Russia (27 Nov 09)

7.28 **GENEVA CONVENTION (NO. IV) RELATIVE TO THE PROTECTION OF CIVILIAN PERSONS IN TIME OF WAR%**
Concluded: 12 Aug 49
Entered into force: 21 Oct 50
Total Parties: 194 (as of 31 Mar 2011)
Ratified/acceded/accepted without qualification: 171 (as of 31 Mar 2011)
Afghanistan (26 Sep 56), Algeria (20 Jun 60), Andorra (17 Sep 93), Antigua/Barbuda (6 Oct 86), Argentina (18 Sep 56), Armenia (7 Jun 93), Austria (27 Aug 53), Azerbaijan (1 Jun 93), Bahamas (11 Jul 75), Bahrain (30 Nov 71), Belarus (3 Aug 54), Belgium (3 Sep 52), Belize (29 Jun 84), Benin (14 Dec 61), Bhutan (10 Jan 91), Bolivia (10 Dec 76), Bosnia–Herzegovina (31 Dec 92), Botswana (29 Mar 68), Brazil (29 Jun 57), Brunei (14 Oct 91), Bulgaria (22 Jul 54), Burkina Faso (7 Nov 61), Burundi (27 Dec 71), Cambodia (8 Dec 58), Cameroon (16 Sep 63), Canada (14 May 65), Cape Verde (11 Jun 84), Central African Republic (1 Aug 66), Chad (5 Aug 70), Chile (12 Oct 50), Colombia (8 Nov 61), Comoros (21 Nov 85), Congo (Brazzaville) (4 Feb 67), Congo (Kinshasa) (24 Feb 61), Cook Islands (11 Jan 2001), Costa Rica (15 Oct 69), Côte d'Ivoire (28 Dec 61), Croatia (11 May 92), Cuba (15 Apr 54), Cyprus (23 May 62), Czech Republic (5 Feb 93), Denmark (27 Jun 51), Djibouti (3 Jun 78), Dominica (28 Sep 81), Dominican Republic (22 Jan 58), Ecuador (11 Aug 54), Egypt (10 Nov 52), El Salvador (17 Jun 53), Equatorial Guinea (24 Jul 86), Eritrea (14 Aug 2000), Estonia (18 Jan 93), Ethiopia (2 Oct 69), Fiji (9 Aug 71), Finland (22 Feb 55), France (28 Jun 51), Gabon (26 Feb 65), Gambia (20 Oct 66), Georgia (14 Sep 93), Ghana (2 Aug 58), Greece (5 Jun 56), Grenada (13 Apr 81), Guatemala (14 May 52), Guinea (11 Jul 84), Guyana (22 Jul 68), Haiti (11 Apr 57), Honduras (31 Dec 65), Hungary (12 Apr 89), Iceland (10 Aug 65), India (9 Nov 50), Indonesia (30 Sep 58), Iraq (14 Feb 56), Ireland (27 Sep 62), Italy (17 Dec 51), Jamaica (17 Jul 64), Japan (21 Apr 53), Jordan (29 May 51), Kazakhstan (5 May 92), Kenya (20 Sep 66), Kiribati (5 Jan 89), Kyrgyzstan (18 Sep 92), Laos (29 Oct 56), Latvia (24 Dec 91), Lebanon (10 Apr 51), Lesotho (20 May 68), Liberia (29 Mar 54), Libya (22 May 56), Liechtenstein (21 Sep 50), Lithuania (3 Oct 96), Luxembourg (1 Jul 53), Madagascar (18 Jul 63), Malawi (5 Jan 68), Malaysia (24 Aug 62), Maldives (18 Jun 91), Mali (24 May 65), Malta (22 Aug 68), Marshall Islands (1 Jun 2004), Mauritania (30 Oct 62), Mauritius (18 Aug 70), Mexico (29 Oct 52), Micronesia (19 Sep 95), Moldova (24 May 93), Monaco (5 Jul 50), Mongolia (20 Feb 58), Montenegro (2 Aug 2006), Morocco (26 Jul 56), Mozambique (14 Mar 83), Myanmar (Burma) (25 Aug 92), Namibia* (22 Aug 91), Nauru (27 Jun 2006), Nepal (7 Feb 64), Netherlands (3 Aug 54), New Zealand (2 May 59), Nicaragua (17 Dec 53), Niger (21 Apr 64), Nigeria (20 Jun 61), Norway (3 Aug 51), Oman (31 Jan 74), Palau (25 Jun 96), Panama (10 Feb 56), Papua New Guinea (26 May 76), Paraguay (23 Oct 61), Peru (15 Feb 56), Philippines (6 Mar 52), Poland (26 Nov 54), Qatar (15 Oct 75), Romania (1 Jun 54), Rwanda (5 Mar 64), Samoa (23 Aug 84), San Marino (29 Aug 53), São Tomé/Principe (21 May 76), Saudi Arabia (18 May 63), Senegal (18 May 63), Serbia (16 Oct 2001),

Seychelles (8 Nov 84), Sierra Leone (10 Jun 65), Singapore (27 Apr 73), Slovakia (2 Apr 93), Slovenia (26 Mar 92), Solomon Islands (6 Jul 81), Somalia (12 Jul 62), South Africa (31 Mar 52), Spain (4 Aug 52), Sri Lanka (28 Feb 59), St Kitts/Nevis (14 Feb 86), St Lucia (18 Sep 81), St Vincent/Grenadines (1 Apr 81), Sudan (23 Sep 57), Swaziland (28 Jun 73), Sweden (28 Dec 53), Switzerland (31 Mar 50), Syria (2 Nov 53), Tajikistan (13 Jan 93), Tanzania (12 Dec 62), Thailand (29 Dec 54), Timor–Leste (8 May 2003), Togo (6 Jan 62), Tonga (13 Apr 78), Trinidad/Tobago (24 Sep 63), Tunisia (4 May 57), Turkey (10 Feb 54), Turkmenistan (10 Apr 92), Tuvalu (19 Feb 81), Uganda (18 May 64), Ukraine (3 Aug 54), United Arab Emirates (10 May 72), Uzbekistan (8 Oct 93), Vanuatu (27 Oct 82), Vatican City (22 Feb 51), Venezuela (13 Feb 56), Zambia (19 Oct 66), Zimbabwe (7 Mar 83)

Ratified/acceded/accepted with qualification: 23 (as of 31 Mar 2011)
Albania (27 May 57), Angola (20 Sep 84), Australia (14 Oct 58), Bangladesh (4 Apr 72), Barbados (10 Sep 68), China (28 Dec 56), Germany (3 Sep 54), Guinea–Bissau (20 Feb 74), Iran (20 Feb 57), Israel (12 Aug 49), Korea (North) (27 Aug 57), Korea (South) (16 Aug 66), Kuwait (2 Sep 67), Macedonia (1 Sep 93), Pakistan (12 Jun 51), Portugal (14 Mar 61), Suriname (13 Oct 76), United Kingdom (23 Sep 57), United States (2 Aug 55), Uruguay (5 Mar 69), USSR (Russia) (10 May 54), Vietnam (28 Jun 57), Yemen (16 Jul 70)

* The acceptance by Namibia was by the UN Council for Namibia.

7.29 PRINCIPLES OF INTERNATIONAL LAW RECOGNIZED IN THE CHARTER OF THE NUREMBERG TRIBUNAL AND IN THE JUDGMENT OF THE TRIBUNAL
Adopted: 2 Aug 50

7.30 DRAFT ARTICLES ON THE DRAFT CODE OF CRIMES AGAINST THE PEACE AND SECURITY OF MANKIND (AS REVISED THROUGH **1991**)
First adopted: 4 Dec 54

7.31 TREATY ON THE NON-PROLIFERATION OF NUCLEAR WEAPONS
Concluded: 1 Jul 68
Entered into force: 5 Mar 70
Total Parties: 190 (as of 8 Feb 2011)*
Ratified/acceded/accepted without qualification: 174 (as of 8 Feb 2011)*
Afghanistan** (4 Feb 70/5 Feb 70), Albania*** (12 Sep 90/14 Sep 90/28 Sep 90), Algeria (12 Jan 95), Andorra (7 Jun 96/25 Jun 96/2 Jul 96), Angola (14 Oct 96), Antigua/Barbuda (17 Jun 85), Armenia (21 Jun 93/15 Jul 93), Austria** (27 Jun 69), Azerbaijan (22 Sep 92), Bahamas (11 Aug 76/13 Aug 76/30 Aug 76), Bangladesh** (31 Aug 79/27 Sep 79), Barbados (21 Feb 80), Belarus (9 Feb 93/22 Jul 93/23 Jul 93), Belgium** (2 May 75/4 May 75), Belize (9 Aug 85), Benin (31 Oct 72), Bhutan** (23 May 85), Bolivia (26 May 70), Bosnia–Herzegovina (15 Aug 94), Botswana (28 Apr 69), Brazil (18 Sep 98), Brunei** (26 Mar 85), Bulgaria** (5 Sep 69/18 Sep 69/3 Nov 69), Burkina Faso (3 Mar 70), Burundi (19 Mar 71), Cambodia (2 Jun 72), Cameroon (8 Jan 69), Canada** (8 Jan 69), Cape Verde (24 Oct 79), Central African Republic (25 Oct 70), Chad (10 Mar 71/11 Mar 71/23 Mar 71), Chile (25 May 95), Colombia*** (8 Apr 86/29 Apr 86/30 Apr 86), Comoros (4 Oct 95), Congo (Brazzaville) (23 Oct 78), Congo (Kinshasa) (4 Aug 70), Costa Rica** (3 Mar 70), Côte d'Ivoire** (6 Mar 73), Croatia (29 Jun 92), Cuba (4 Nov 2002), Cyprus** (10 Feb 70/15 Feb 70/5 Mar 70), Czech Republic**** (1 Jan 93/5 April 93/9 Apr 93), Denmark** (3 Jan 69), Djibouti (16 Oct 96), Dominica (10 Aug 84), Dominican Republic** (24 Jul 71), Ecuador** (7 Mar 69), El Salvador** (11 Jul 72), Equatorial Guinea (1 Nov 84), Eritrea (16 Mar 95), Estonia (7 Jan 92/31 Jan 92), Ethiopia** (5 Feb 70/5 Mar

70), Fiji** (21 Jul 72/14 Aug 72/29 Aug 72), Finland** (5 Feb 69), France (2 Aug 92/3 Aug 92), Gabon (19 Feb 74), Gambia** (12 May 75), Georgia (7 Mar 94), Ghana** (4 May 70/5 May 70/11 May 70), Greece** (11 Mar 70), Grenada (2 Sep 75/3 Dec 75), Guatemala** (22 Sep 70), Guinea (29 Apr 85), Guinea–Bissau (20 Aug 76), Guyana (19 Oct 93), Haiti (2 Jun 70), Honduras** (16 May 73), Hungary** (27 May 69), Iceland** (18 Jul 69), Iran** (2 Feb 70/10 Feb 70/5 Mar 70), Iraq** (29 Oct 69), Ireland** (1 Jul 68/2 Jul 68/4 Jul 68), Jamaica** (5 Mar 70), Jordan** (11 Feb 70), Kazakhstan (14 Feb 94/20 Mar 94/21 Mar 94), Kenya (11 Jun 70), Kiribati** (18 Apr 85), Korea (North) (12 Dec 85), Korea (South) (23 Apr 75), Kyrgyzstan (5 Jul 94), Laos (20 Feb 70/5 Mar 70), Latvia (31 Jan 92), Lebanon** (15 Jul 70/20 Nov 70), Lesotho** (20 May 70), Liberia (5 Mar 70), Libya** (26 May 75), Liechtenstein** (20 Apr 78), Lithuania (23 Sep 91), Luxembourg** (2 May 75/4 May 75), Macedonia (30 Mar 95/12 Apr 95), Madagascar** (8 Oct 70), Malawi** (18 Feb 86/19 Feb 86/4 Mar 86), Malaysia** (5 Mar 70), Maldive Islands** (7 Apr 70), Mali (10 Feb 70/5 Mar 70), Malta** (6 Feb 70), Marshall Islands (30 Jan 95), Mauritania (26 Oct 93), Mauritius** (8 Apr 69/14 Apr 69/25 Apr 69), Micronesia (14 Apr 95), Moldova (11 Oct 94), Monaco (13 Mar 95), Mongolia** (14 May 69), Montenegro (3 Jun 2006), Morocco** (27 Nov 70/30 Nov 70/16 Dec 70), Mozambique (4 Sep 90/12 Sep 90/20 Sep 90), Myanmar (Burma) (2 Dec 92), Namibia (2 Oct 92/7 Oct 92/9 Oct 92), Nauru** (7 Jun 82), Nepal** (5 Jan 70/9 Jan 70/3 Feb 70), Netherlands** (2 May 75), New Zealand** (10 Sep 69), Nicaragua** (6 Mar 73), Niger (9 Oct 92), Nigeria** (27 Sep 68/7 Oct 68/14 Oct 68), Norway** (5 Feb 69), Oman (23 Jan 97), Palau (14 Apr 95), Panama (13 Jan 77), Papua New Guinea** (13 Jan 82/25 Jan 82/16 Feb 82), Paraguay** (4 Feb 70/5 Mar 70), Peru** (3 Mar 70), Philippines** (5 Oct 72/16 Oct 72/20 Oct 72), Poland** (12 Jun 69), Portugal** (15 Dec 77), Qatar (3 Apr 89/10 May 89/13 Jun 89), Romania** (4 Feb 70), Rwanda (20 May 75), Samoa** (17 Mar 75/18 Mar 75/26 Mar 75), San Marino (10 Aug 70/20 Aug 70/31 Aug 70), São Tomé/Principe (20 Jul 83), Saudi Arabia (3 Oct 88), Senegal** (17 Dec 70/22 Dec 70/15 Jan 71), Serbia (4 Mar 70/5 Mar 70), Seychelles (12 Mar 85/14 Mar 85/8 Apr 85), (Thailand)** (7 Dec 72), Sierra Leone (26 Feb 75), Singapore** (10 Mar 76), Slovakia**** (1 Jan 93/17 Apr 93/31 May 93), Slovenia (7 Apr 92/20 Aug 92), Solomon Islands (17 Jun 81), Somalia (5 Mar 70/12 Nov 70), South Africa** (10 Jul 91), Spain** (5 Nov 87), Sri Lanka** (5 Mar 79), St Lucia** (28 Dec 79), Sudan** (31 Oct 73/22 Nov 73/10 Dec 73), Suriname** (30 Jun 76), Swaziland** (11 Dec 69/16 Dec 69/12 Jan 70), Sweden** (9 Jan 70), Tajikistan (17 Jan 94), Tanzania (31 May 91/7 Jun 91/18 Jun 91), Thailand** (7 Dec 72), Timor–Leste (5 May 2003), Togo (26 Feb 70), Tonga (7 Jul 71/15 Jul 71/24 Aug 71), Trinidad/Tobago (30 Oct 86), Tunisia** (26 Feb 70), Turkey** (17 Apr 80), Turkmenistan (29 Sep 94), Tuvalu** (19 Jan 79), Uganda (20 Oct 82), Ukraine (5 Dec 94), United Arab Emirates (26 Sep 95), United Kingdom (29 Nov 68), United States (5 Mar 70), Uruguay** (31 Aug 70), USSR (Russia) (5 Mar 70), Uzbekistan** (7 May 92), Vanuatu (24 Aug 95), Venezuela** (25 Sep 75/26 Sep 75/3 Oct 75), Vietnam** (14 Jun 82), Yemen (1 Jun 79/14 May 86), Zambia (15 May 91/22 May 91/5 Jul 91), Zimbabwe (26 Sep 91/4 Oct 91)

Ratified/acceded/accepted with qualification: 16 (as of 8 Feb 2011)
Argentina (10 Feb 95/17 Feb 95), Australia** (23 Jan 73), Bahrain (3 Nov 88), China (PRC) (9 Mar 92/12 Mar 92/17 Mar 92), Egypt** (26 Feb 81), Germany** (2 May 75), Indonesia (12 Jul 79), Italy** (2 May 75/4 May 75), Japan (8 Jun 76), Kuwait (17 Nov 89), Mexico** (21 Jan 69), St Kitts/Nevis***** (6 Nov 84), St Vincent/Grenadines (6 Nov 84), Switzerland** (9 Mar 77), Syria (24 Sep 69), Vatican City** (25 Feb 71)

Note: Dates are dates of deposit of instrument of ratification in London, Moscow, and/or Washington from earliest to latest where more than one.

* Taiwan, whose authorities have expressed adherence to the treaty since 27 Jan 70, is not included in the official totals recorded here because of the international recognition of the People's Republic of China as the sole legal government of China. However, the United States at least regards Taiwan as bound by the NPT's provisions.

* * Has NPT safeguard agreement that has entered into force as of 31 Oct 92.

* * * Non–NPT, full-scope safeguards agreement in force.

* * * * Succeeding Czechoslovakia (1 Jul 68).

* * * * * The United States considers St Kitts/Nevis as "bound by the obligations in the treaty" on the basis of a general declaration of succession deposited with the UN Secretary–General.

7.32 CONVENTION ON THE PROHIBITION OF MILITARY OR ANY OTHER HOSTILE USE OF ENVIRONMENTAL MODIFICATION TECHNIQUES (ENMOD)
Concluded: 10 Dec 76
Entered into force: 5 Oct 78
Total Parties: 74 (as of 4 Mar 2011)
Signed but not ratified: 16 (as of 4 Mar 2011)
Bolivia (18 May 77), Congo (Kinshasa) (28 Feb 78), Ethiopia (18 May 77), Iceland (18 May 77), Iran (18 May 77), Iraq (15 Aug 77), Lebanon (18 May 77), Liberia (18 May 77), Luxembourg (18 May 77), Morocco (18 May 77), Portugal (18 May 77), Sierra Leone (12 Apr 78), Syria (4 Aug 77), Turkey (18 May 77), Uganda (18 May 77), Vatican City (27 May 77)
Ratified/acceded/accepted without qualification: 65 (as of 4 Mar 2011)
Afghanistan (22 Oct 85), Algeria (19 Dec 91), Antigua/Barbuda (25 Oct 88), Armenia (15 May 2002), Australia (7 Sep 84), Bangladesh (3 Oct 79), Belarus (7 Jun 78), Belgium (12 Jul 82), Benin (30 Jun 86), Brazil (12 Oct 84), Bulgaria (31 May 78), Canada (11 Jun 81), Cape Verde (3 Oct 79), Chile (26 Apr 94), Costa Rica (7 Feb 96), Cuba (10 Apr 78), Cyprus (12 Apr 78), Czech Republic (22 Feb 93), Denmark (19 Apr 78), Dominica (9 Nov 92), Egypt (1 Apr 82), Finland (12 May 78), Germany (24 May 83), Ghana (22 Jun 78), Greece (23 Aug 83), Honduras (16 Aug 2010), Hungary (19 Apr 78), India (15 Dec 78), Ireland (16 Dec 82), Italy (27 Nov 81), Japan (9 Jun 82), Kazakhstan (25 Apr 2005), Korea (North) (8 Nov 84), Laos (5 Oct 78), Lithuania (16 Apr 2002), Malawi (5 Oct 78), Mauritius (9 Dec 92), Mongolia (19 May 78), Nicaragua (6 Sep 2007), Niger (17 Feb 93), Norway (15 Feb 79), Pakistan (27 Feb 86), Panama (13 May 2003), Papua New Guinea (28 Oct 80), Poland (8 Jun 78), Romania (6 May 83), São Tomé/Principe (5 Oct 79), Slovakia (28 May 93), Slovenia (20 Apr 2005), Solomon Islands (19 Jun 81), Spain (19 Jul 78), Sri Lanka (25 Apr 78), St Lucia (27 May 93), St Vincent/Grenadines (27 Oct 79), Sweden (27 Apr 84), Tajikistan (12 Oct 99), Tunisia (11 May 78), Ukraine (13 Jun 78), United Kingdom (16 May 78), United States (17 Jan 80), Uruguay (16 Sep 93), USSR (Russia) (30 May 78), Uzbekistan (26 May 93), Vietnam (26 Aug 80), Yemen (20 Jul 77)
Ratified/acceded/accepted with qualification: 9 (as of 4 Mar 2011)
Argentina (20 Mar 87), Austria (17 Jan 90), China (8 Jun 2005), Guatemala (21 Mar 88), Korea (South) (2 Dec 86), Kuwait (2 Jan 80), Netherlands (15 Apr 83), New Zealand (7 Sep 84), Switzerland (5 Aug 88)

7.33 PROTOCOL ADDITIONAL (NO. I) TO THE GENEVA CONVENTIONS OF AUGUST 12, 1949, AND RELATING TO THE PROTECTION OF VICTIMS OF INTERNATIONAL ARMED

Conflicts
Concluded: 8 Jun 77
Entered into force: 7 Dec 78
Total Parties: 169 (as of 24 Feb 2011)
Signed but not ratified: 4 (as of 24 Feb 2011)
Iran (12 Dec 77), Morocco (12 Dec 77), Pakistan (12 Dec 77), United States (12 Dec 77)

Ratified/acceded/accepted without qualification: 131 (as of 24 Feb 2011)
Afghanistan (10 Nov 2009), Albania (16 Jul 93), Antigua/Barbuda (6 Oct 86), Armenia (7 Jun 93), Bahamas (10 Apr 80), Bahrain (30 Oct 86), Bangladesh (8 Sep 80), Barbados (19 Feb 90), Belarus (23 Oct 89), Belize (29 Jun 84), Benin (28 May 86), Bolivia (8 Dec 83), Bosnia–Herzegovina (31 Dec 92), Botswana (23 May 79), Brazil (5 May 92), Brunei (14 Oct 91), Bulgaria (26 Sep 89), Burkina Faso (20 Oct 87), Burundi (10 Jun 93), Cambodia (14 Jan 98), Cameroon (16 Mar 84), Cape Verde (16 Mar 95), Central African Republic (17 Jul 84), Chad (17 Jan 97), Chile (24 Apr 91), Colombia (1 Sep 93), Comoros (21 Nov 85), Congo (Brazzaville) (10 Nov 83), Congo (Kinshasa) (3 Jun 82), Cook Islands (7 May 2002), Costa Rica (15 Dec 83), Côte d'Ivoire (20 Sep 89), Cuba (25 Nov 82), Cyprus (1 Jun 79), Czech Republic (5 Feb 93), Djibouti (8 Apr 91), Dominica (25 Apr 96), Dominican Republic (26 May 94), Ecuador (10 Apr 79), El Salvador (23 Nov 78), Equatorial Guinea (24 Jul 86), Estonia (18 Jan 93), Ethiopia (8 Apr 94), Fiji (30 Jul 2008), Gabon (8 Apr 80), Gambia (12 Jan 89), Georgia (14 Sep 93), Ghana (28 Feb 78), Grenada (23 Sep 98), Guatemala (19 Oct 87), Guinea (11 Jul 84), Guinea–Bissau (21 Oct 86), Guyana (18 Jan 88), Haiti (20 Dec 2006), Honduras (16 Feb 95), Hungary (12 Apr 89), Jamaica (29 Jul 86), Jordan (1 May 79), Kazakhstan (5 May 92), Kenya (23 Feb 99), Korea (North) (9 Mar 88), Kuwait (17 Jan 85), Kyrgyzstan (18 Sep 92), Laos (18 Nov 80), Latvia (24 Dec 91), Lebanon (23 Jul 97), Lesotho (20 May 94), Liberia (30 Jun 88), Libya (7 Jun 78), Lithuania (13 Jul 2000), Luxembourg (29 Aug 89), Madagascar (8 May 92), Malawi (7 Oct 91), Maldives (3 Sep 91), Mali (8 Feb 89), Mauritania (14 Mar 80), Mexico (10 Mar 83), Micronesia (19 Sep 95), Moldova (24 May 93), Monaco (7 Jan 2000), Montenegro (2 Aug 2006), Mozambique (14 Mar 83), Namibia (17 Jun 94), Nauru (27 Jun 2006), Nicaragua (19 Jul 99), Niger (8 Jun 79), Nigeria (10 Oct 88), Norway (14 Dec 81), Palau (25 Jun 96), Panama (18 Sep 95), Paraguay (30 Nov 90), Peru (14 Jul 89), Poland (23 Oct 91), Romania (21 Jun 90), Rwanda (19 Nov 84), Samoa (23 Aug 84), San Marino (5 Apr 94), São Tomé/Principe (5 Jul 96), Senegal (7 May 85), Serbia (16 Oct 2001), Seychelles (8 Nov 84), Sierra Leone (21 Oct 86), Slovakia (2 Apr 93), Slovenia (26 Mar 92), Solomon Islands (19 Sep 88), South Africa (21 Nov 95), St Kitts/Nevis (14 Feb 86), St Lucia (7 Oct 82), St Vincent/Grenadines (8 Apr 83), Sudan (7 Mar 2006), Suriname (16 Dec 85), Swaziland (2 Nov 95), Switzerland (17 Feb 82), Tajikistan (13 Jan 93), Tanzania (15 Feb 83), Timor–Leste (12 Apr 2005), Togo (21 Jun 84), Tonga (20 Jan 2003), Trinidad/Tobago (20 Jul 2001), Tunisia (9 Aug 79), Turkmenistan (10 Apr 92), Uganda (13 Mar 91), Ukraine (25 Jan 90), Uruguay (13 Dec 85), Uzbekistan (8 Oct 93), Vanuatu (28 Feb 85), Venezuela (23 Jul 98), Vietnam (19 Oct 81), Yemen (17 Apr 90), Zambia (4 May 95), Zimbabwe (19 Oct 92)

Ratified/acceded/accepted with qualification: **38** (as of 224 Feb 2011)
Algeria (16 Aug 89), Angola (20 Sep 84), Argentina (26 Nov 86), Australia (21 Jun 91), Austria (13 Aug 82), Belgium (20 May 86), Canada (20 Nov 90), China (14 Sep 83), Croatia (11 May 92), Denmark (17 Jun 82), Egypt (9 Oct 92), Finland (7 Aug 80), France (11 Apr 2001), Germany (14 Feb 91), Greece (31 Mar 89), Iceland (10 Apr 87), Ireland (19 May 99), Italy (27 Feb 86), Japan (31 Aug 2004), Korea (South) (15 Jan 82), Liechtenstein (10 Aug 89), Macedonia (1 Sep 93), Malta (17 Apr 89), Mauritius (22 Mar 82), Mongolia (6 Dec 95), Netherlands

(26 Jun 87), New Zealand (8 Feb 88), Oman (29 Mar 84), Portugal (27 May 92), Qatar (5 Apr 88), Saudi Arabia (21 Aug 87), Spain (21 Apr 89), Sweden (31 Aug 79), Syria (14 Nov 83), United Arab Emirates (9 Mar 83), United Kingdom (28 Jan 98), USSR (Russia) (29 Sep 89), Vatican City (21 Nov 85)

7.34 SOUTH PACIFIC NUCLEAR FREE ZONE TREATY (TREATY OF RAROTONGA)
Concluded: 6 Aug 85
Entered into force: 11 Dec 86
Total Parties: 13 (as of 20 Feb 2011)
Ratified/acceded/accepted without qualification: 13 (as of 20 Feb 2011)
Australia (11 Dec 86), Cook Islands (28 Oct 85), Fiji (4 Oct 85), Kiribati (28 Oct 86), Nauru (13 Apr 87), New Zealand (13 Nov 86), Niue (12 May 86), Papua New Guinea (15 Sep 89), Samoa (20 Oct 86), Solomon Islands (27 Jan 89), Tonga (18 Dec 2000), Tuvalu (16 Jan 86), Vanuatu (9 Feb 96)

7.35 UNSC RESOLUTION 687 (CONCERNING THE RESTORATION OF PEACE AND SECURITY IN IRAQ AND KUWAIT)
Adopted: 3 Apr 91
For: 12
Austria, Belgium, China, Côte d'Ivoire, France, India, Romania, Russia (USSR), United Kingdom, United States, Zaire, Zimbabwe
Against: 1
Cuba
Abstain: 2
Ecuador, Yemen

7.36 CONVENTION FOR THE SUPPRESSION OF ACTS OF NUCLEAR TERRORISM
Concluded: 13 Apr 2005
Entered into force: 7 July 2007
Total Parties: 76 (as of 13 Mar 2011)
Signed but not ratified: 61 (as of 13 Mar 2011)
Afghanistan (29 Dec 2005), Albania (23 Nov 2005), Andorra (11 May 2006), Argentina (14 Sep 2005), Australia (14 Sep 2005), Benin (15 Sep 2005), Bosnia/Herzegovina (7 Dec 2005), Bulgaria (14 Sep 2005), Burkina Faso (21 Sep 2005), Cambodia (7 Dec 2006), Canada (14 Sep 2005), Colombia (1 Nov 2006), Costa Rica (15 Sep 2005), Djibouti (14 Jun 2006), Ecuador (15 Sep 2005), Egypt (20 Sep 2005), Estonia (14 Sep 2005), France (14 Sep 2005), Ghana (6 Nov 2006), Greece (15 Sep 2005), Guatemala (20 Sep 2005), Guinea (16 Sep 2005), Guyana (15 Sep 2005), Iceland (16 Sep 2005), Ireland (15 Sep 2005), Israel (27 Dec 2006), Italy (14 Sep 2005), Jamaica (5 Dec 2006), Jordan (16 Nov 2005), Korea (South) (16 Sep 2005), Kuwait (16 Sep 2005), Liberia (16 Sep 2005), Madagascar (15 Sep 2005), Malaysia (16 Sep 2005), Malta (15 Sep 2005), Mauritius (14 Sep 2005), Monaco (14 Sep 2005), Montenegro (23 Oct 2006), Mozambique (1 May 2006), New Zealand (14 Sep 2005), Norway (16 Sep 2005), Palau (15 Sep 2005), Philippines (15 Sep 2005), Portugal (21 Sep 2005), Qatar (16 Feb 2006), Rwanda (6 Mar 2006), São Tomé/Principe (19 Dec 2005), Senegal (21 Sep 2005), Seychelles (7 Oct 2005), Sierra Leone (14 Sep 2005), Singapore (1 Dec 2006), Swaziland (15 Sep 2005), Sweden (14 Sep 2005), Syria (14 Sep 2005), Tajikistan (14 Sep 2005), Thailand (14 Sep 2005), Timor–Leste (16 Sep 2005), Togo (15 Sep 2005), Turkey (14 Sep 2005), United States (14 Sep 2005), Uruguay (16 Sep 2005)
Ratified acceded/accepted without qualification: 64 (as of 13 Mar 2011)
Antigua/Barbuda (1 Dec 2009), Armenia (22 Sep 2010), Austria (14 Sep 2006), Bangladesh (7 Jun 2007), Belarus (17 Mar 2007), Brazil (25 Sep 2009), Burundi

(24 Sep 2008), Central African Republic (19 Feb 2008), Chile (27 Sep 2010), China (8 Nov 2010), Comoros (12 Mar 2007), Congo (Kinshasa) (23 Sep 2010), Croatia (30 May 2007), Cyprus (28 Jan 2008), Czech Republic (25 Jul 2006), Denmark (20 Mar 2007), Dominican Republic (11 Jun 2008), El Salvador (27 Nov 2006), Fiji (15 May 2008), Finland (13 Jan 2009), Gabon (1 Oct 2007), Germany (8 Feb 2008), Guinea–Bissau (6 Aug 2008), Hungary (12 Apr 2007), Japan (3 Aug 2007), Kazakhstan (31 Jul 2008), Kenya (13 Apr 2006), Kiribati (26 Sep 2008), Kyrgyzstan (2 Oct 2007), Latvia (25 Jul 2006), Lebanon (13 Nov 2006), Lesotho (22 Sep 2010), Libya (22 Dec 2008), Liechtenstein (25 Sep 2009), Lithuania (19 Jul 2007), Luxembourg (2 Oct 2008), Malawi (7 Oct 2009). Mali (5 Nov 2009), Mauritania (28 Apr 2008), Mexico (27 Jun 2006), Mongolia (6 Oct 2006), Nauru (24 Aug 2010), Netherlands (30 Jun 2010), Nicaragua (25 Feb 2009), Niger (2 Jul 2008), Panama (21 Jun 2007), Paraguay (29 Jan 2009), Peru (29 May 2009), Poland (8 Apr 2010), Romania (24 Jan 2007), Serbia (26 Sep 2006), Slovakia (23 Mar 2006), Slovenia (17 Dec 2009), Solomon Islands (24 Sep 2009), South Africa (9 May 2007), Spain (22 Feb 2007), Sri Lanka (27 Sep 2007), Switzerland (15 Oct 2008), Macedonia (19 Mar 2007), Tunisia (28 Sep 2010), Turkmenistan (28 Mar 2008), Ukraine (25 Sep 2007), United Kingdom (24 Sep 2009), Uzbekistan (29 Apr 2008)

Ratified acceded/accepted with qualification: 12 (as of 13 Mar 2011) Azerbaijan (28 Jan 2009), Bahrain (4 May 2010), Belgium (2 Oct 2009), Cuba (17 Jun 2009), Georgia (23 Apr 2010), India (1 Dec 2006), Moldova (18 Apr 2008), Morocco (31 Mar 2010), Russia (29 Jan 2007), Saudi Arabia (7 Dec 2007), St Vincent/Grenadines (8 Jul 2010), United Arab Emirates (10 Jan 2008)

†